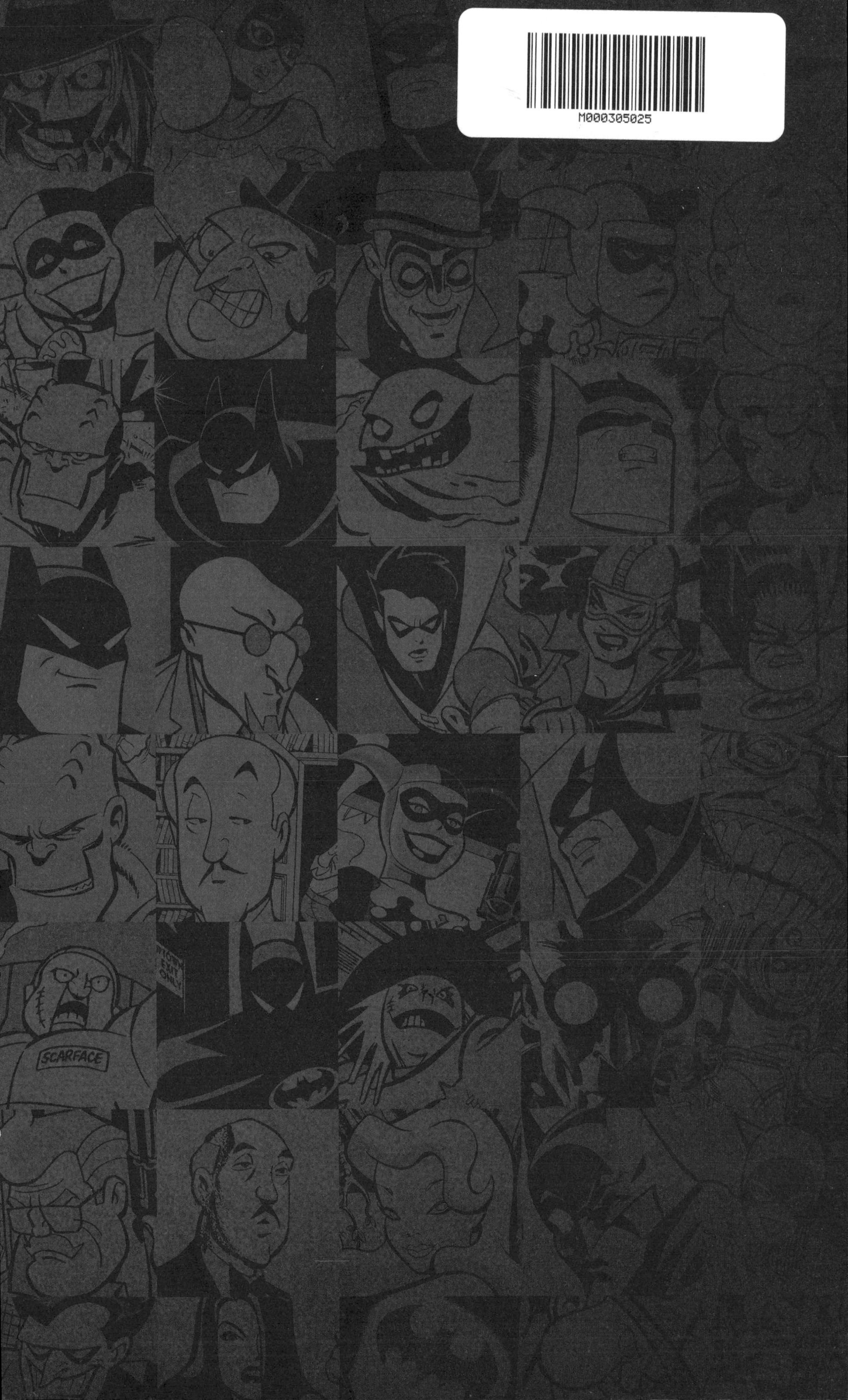
SCARFACE

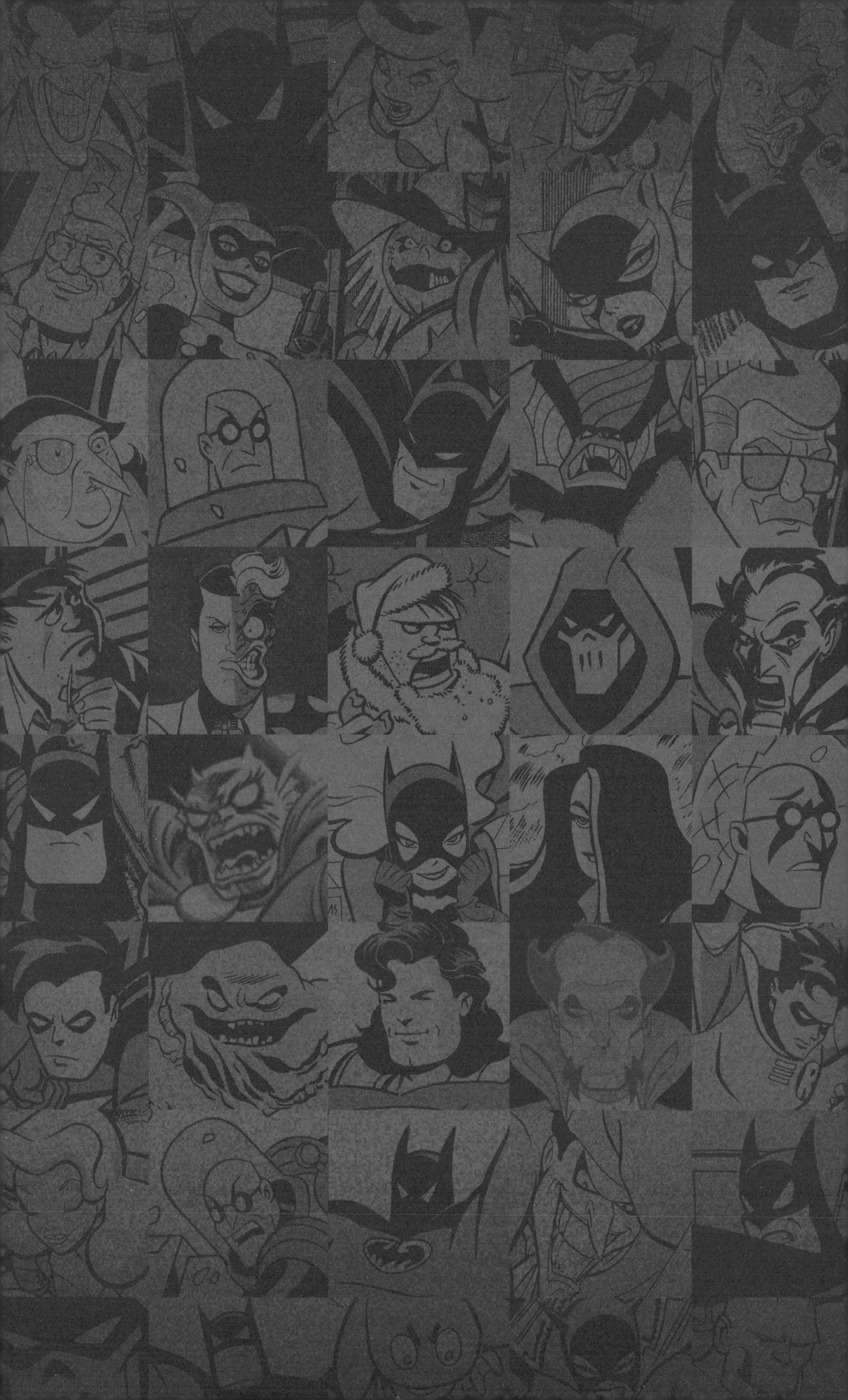

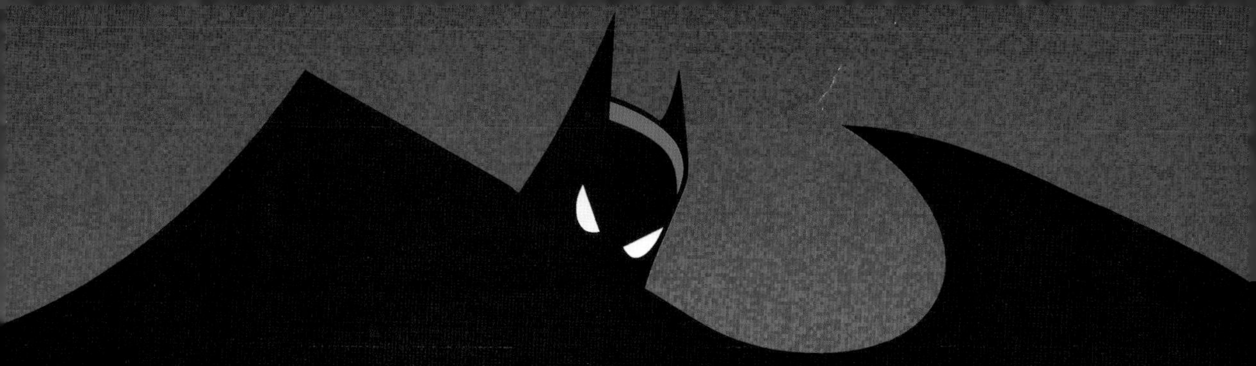

THE BATMAN ADVENTURES
OMNIBUS

KELLEY PUCKETT · PAUL DINI · BRUCE TIMM · TY TEMPLETON · MARTIN PASKO
MICHAEL REAVES · ALAN GRANT · DAN RASPLER · GLEN MURAKAMI · RONNIE DEL CARMEN
WRITERS

MIKE PAROBECK · BRUCE TIMM · TY TEMPLETON · BRAD RADER · DEV MADAN
GLEN MURAKAMI · DAN RIBA · RICK BURCHETT · MATT WAGNER · DAN DeCARLO
KLAUS JANSON · JOHN BYRNE · RONNIE DEL CARMEN · KEVIN ALTIERI
PENCILLERS

RICK BURCHETT · BRUCE TIMM · GLEN MURAKAMI · DAN RIBA
KLAUS JANSON · RONNIE DEL CARMEN · BUTCH LUKIC
INKERS

RICK TAYLOR · GLEN MURAKAMI · BRUCE TIMM · RONNIE DEL CARMEN
COLORISTS

TIM HARKINS · RICHARD STARKINGS AND COMICRAFT · TODD KLEIN
LETTERERS

BRUCE TIMM AND JOHN CALMETTE
COLLECTION COVER ARTISTS

BATMAN CREATED BY BOB KANE WITH BILL FINGER
SUPERMAN CREATED BY JERRY SIEGEL AND JOE SHUSTER
BY SPECIAL ARRANGEMENT WITH THE JERRY SIEGEL FAMILY

SCOTT PETERSON MARK CHIARELLO Editors – Original Series
DARREN VINCENZO Associate Editor – Original Series
REZA LOKMAN Editor – Collected Edition
STEVE COOK Design Director – Books
DAMIAN RYLAND Publication Design
SUZANNAH ROWNTREE Publication Production

MARIE JAVINS VP – Editor-in-Chief

JIM LEE President, Publisher & Chief Creative Officer
ANNE DePIES Senior VP & General Manager
LARRY BERRY VP – Brand Design & Creative Services
DON FALLETTI VP – Manufacturing & Production
LAWRENCE GANEM VP – Editorial Programming & Talent Strategy
ALISON GILL Senior VP – Manufacturing & Operations
NICK J. NAPOLITANO VP – Publishing & Business Operations
NANCY SPEARS VP – Sales & Marketing

THE BATMAN ADVENTURES OMNIBUS

DC Comics, 4000 Warner Blvd., Bldg. 700, 2nd Floor, Burbank, CA 91522
Printed by Transcontinental Interglobe, Beauceville, QC, Canada. 7/21/23. First Printing.
ISBN: 978-1-77952-119-4

Library of Congress Cataloging-in-Publication Data is available.

PEFC Certified
This product is from sustainably managed forests and controlled sources
PEFC
PEFC/01-31-106
www.pefc.org

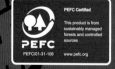

All covers illustrated by MIKE PAROBECK and RICK BURCHETT unless otherwise noted.

INTRODUCTION

He was a dark and stormy knight. It was the early nineties, and Batman, the character that started the "grim and gritty" movement with *Batman: The Dark Knight Returns*, was a victim of his own success. Ever grimmer and grittier was the order of the day, and Batman soon found it hard to keep up with homicidal superheroes like Wolverine and the Punisher. Batman doesn't kill, and wasn't about to start, but the readers were voting with their wallets and everything else was fair game. I myself joined DC editorial just as they were wrapping up the infamous "Robin gets killed with a crowbar" storyline. How's *that* for gritty!

Into this unfortunate environment walked Paul Dini and Bruce Timm with a cold blast of genius called *Batman: The Animated Series*. Gone was the overwrought, hyper-violent soap opera of the comics world, replaced with simple, powerful, self-contained stories. Hard jaws, clean lines, chiaroscuro, and art deco filled the screen instead of the crosshatching and dubious anatomy of the then-dominant Image style. The show was supposed to be for children, but those were adult

DC editors next to me cheering and clapping in the screening room after an advance look at the now-famous *BTAS* intro sequence.

Walking back from the screening to the offices afterward, it hit me—I liked their Batman better than ours! Not the stories—we were working with great writers at the top of their game—but the character. Their Batman, freed from the trappings of modern comics, was more iconic, more elemental, more Batman. How lucky, I thought, are those writers... getting to work with that Batman...

...which brings us to the collection you hold in your hands! *The Batman Adventures* premiered in 1992 as a monthly "companion" to the TV series. But instead of doing adaptations, we were set free (thanks, Scott!) to create our own stories in the style of the show. Luckily for you, the reader, there is plenty of story in these pages not written by me, including Paul and Bruce's Eisner Award-winning "Mad Love." But as I'm responsible for most of the original series as well as

the *Mask of the Phantasm* adaptation (every writer's dream—sanctioned plagiarism!), I hope you'll indulge me as I reminisce.

The Batman Adventures was my first comics series, and to be let loose in this archetypal, almost Jungian playground of iconic characters…it's hard for me to put in words just how much fun it was. Fortunately, I didn't put it in words—I put it in the stories you're about to read! It's pretty obvious, looking over those issues, just how much everyone involved—writers, artists, letterers (we had the best sound effects in all of comics, hands down)—loved what we were doing. Our friends on the "real" Batman books were always mired in continuity, crossovers, the latest *en vogue* art style, etc. But we were off in our own little world, entertaining each other with our stories and art, marveling at our good fortune.

I have to take a moment here to talk about Mike Parobeck, who left us far, far too young. Simply put, Mike's art was the heart and soul of the series. I was fortunate enough to work with many extremely talented artists over the years, both here and elsewhere, but nothing in my creative life compares to the collaboration we enjoyed. I'm the only person in the world who can say that for three years, Mike

Parobeck drew my dreams. Wherever you are, Mike, thank you.

The late, great Denny O'Neil once told me the secret to writing superheroes: "Old wine in a new bottle." The trick, he said, is that the readers don't actually know what they want. They think they want new heroes, new villains, everything new, but they really don't. They want the old wine, but in a new bottle. Batman readers want the same Batman, the "real" Batman, but in new tales, new adventures. They want the Batman they remember, in stories they don't.

It's my sincere hope that you enjoy this shiny new bottle we made, so long ago.

KELLEY PUCKETT

April 2023

KELLEY PUCKETT has been writing comics for far too long, by general consensus. He has worked on such series as *The Batman Adventures*, *Batgirl*, *Batman: Black & White*, *Kinetic*, and *Supergirl* for DC Comics.

FOREWORD

It wasn't supposed to be so good.

Look, don't get me wrong. Of *course* it was supposed to be good. I was going to hire good creators to adapt episodes of *Batman: The Animated Series* and do so in a timely manner—and considering how late a start we got on the miniseries, time was very much of the essence. But the readers were absolutely going to get their money's worth.

...But...

Let me back up a bit. When DC Comics VP of editorial/legendary artist Dick Giordano, Batman group editor/legendary writer Denny O'Neil, and I (decidedly non-legendary Batman assistant editor) were shown an advance screening of the first *Batman: The Animated Series* episode, it was immediately agreed that we'd produce a miniseries to tie in. Denny's plate was more than full at the time, so I was handed the job, despite only having been in editorial for a few months.

I don't know whose idea it was to create original stories rather than adapt episodes. But once I'd decided that was the direction I wanted to take, I knew there was one person who'd be perfect for writing at least the first few issues.

Kelley Puckett had been my predecessor as assistant editor on the Batman line of comic books before going freelance. I'd read his stuff and it was already obvious that his writing was extraordinary. What's more, he and Denny had traveled out to Burbank to talk to the creators of the series early on. Kelley had seen the designs, he'd read the scripts, and he knew the series about as well as anyone not actually in Burbank.

I knew I wanted each issue to be standalone—it was the era of huge crossovers, some of which I was very much involved in and loved—but decided there should be something that tied the first three together, and Kelley knew exactly how to do that.

So the questions of writer and story were taken care of. But who to get to draw it? There were lots of good candidates...until I heard about Ty Templeton.

I couldn't believe my luck. Ty the Guy had been one of my favorite artists since I saw his first issue of *Justice League America*. Usually he was in the snowy tundra

somewhere above Buffalo, but it turned out he was actually in the next office at the exact moment I was asking if there was any chance he'd be interested and available.

I quickly sprinted the 10 feet next door and confiscated his passport. My dazzling wit and larceny skills persuaded him to come aboard for the first three issues. In addition to his amazing abilities as a penciller, Ty was and is a top-notch writer, inker, colorist, and letterer. On top of that, he's a professional actor and remarkable musician. It's frankly unfair that so much talent should be contained in one human being. But since I was the beneficiary, I didn't complain. Especially since there was virtually no reference for the show available for Ty. So, in those pre-internet days, he scoured every magazine he could for any tiny glimpse of show previews and somehow extrapolated from there. Insanity.

Artist extraordinaire Rick Burchett—the secret weapon of the entire run—was brought on to ink Ty's pencils, and Rick Taylor threatened to do bodily harm if not allowed to color, matching the dramatic palette and hard cuts of the series flawlessly. The bouncy lettering of Tim Harkins rounded out the team perfectly.

Ty had to leave after the first three issues due to prior commitments. Fortunately, I had Martin Pasko—an established comic book pro and one of the writers of the animated series—and Brad Rader, an artist on the show, in the wings. Scheduling meant Marty was only able to write one issue before Kelley came back.

The original plan was for us just to do a six-issue miniseries. But before the first issue was even printed, then-publisher Paul Levitz saw some of the pages. Leafing through them, he commented upon how great they looked and said we should probably just make it an ongoing.

I was delighted! But I'd only planned for six issues. I was pretty sure I could keep Kelley and Rick and Rick and Tim on...but who was going to pencil it?

Which is when I learned that Mike Parobeck was available.

It was the early nineties, a time when more lines on a character meant better. Mike's style, with its decidedly minimalist approach, was not the hot thing at the time. And yet one glance was all it took to see that he was something else. This guy was The Real Thing. He could *draw*.

What's more, his storytelling was insane: crystal clear and yet imaginative and exciting. He was fast, turning out two pages a day. And he was reliable, never, ever missing a deadline—in fact, it was a challenge keeping up with him. That's one reason we started giving away two original pieces of art per month—it was Mike's idea as a way of trying to boost sales...and keep busy.

Mike hit the ground running on the first issue and then somehow got even better from there. He and Kelley clicked from the first, and he and Rick Burchett had already worked together and formed the perfect team. Check out the third page of issue #23: Kelley had written something like "Batman throws his batarang, which hits the fleeing bad guy," and Mike transformed it into *that*. Then Rick Burchett added his trademark broken speed lines and vibrating-face effect and indicated where the shading should go, and the end result is magnificent.

An interesting thing happened once Kelley and Mike and Rick started working together. We noticed that less was more, so pages started getting pared down and opened up. From somewhere around #8 (their second issue) on, I made Kelley stick to a maximum of four panels—and sometimes even fewer—and in doing so, we found the emotional impact was greater. The same with Kelley's dialogue: he's one of the very best in the business, and even as his panel descriptions often got more and more detailed, he was putting fewer and sparser balloons on the page. The effect was for the comic to feel faster, lighter, almost as though the figures were animated.

We started to focus even more on the tone of the book. We'd go back and forth between issues that featured an established villain and issues featuring new ones, or between funnier, lighter stories and ones that skewed darker. But we always made sure the stories would be accessible to even the youngest of readers. And in doing so, we found ourselves appealing to older, more erudite readers as well, who were able to appreciate the phenomenal level of craft and passion the creators were bringing, and would understand the cultural references slipped in. My model was the great Chuck Jones, who directed Bugs Bunny cartoons that could make you laugh when you were five years old...and laugh even harder when you saw them for the 20th time decades hence.

I remember the day issue #13—the Talia issue—came out, when I got a call from one of the most popular and

respected writer/artists in the entire industry, winner of multiple Eisner Awards for his very sophisticated creator-owned stuff. "There will not be a better comic book published this year, by anyone," he said.

Everyone working on the book was having fun, and conversations tended to quickly devolve into an embarrassing mutual admiration society, despite what the team's cameos in #16 would indicate. But after a while, schedules finally began to catch up to us, and other writers and pencillers joined the fray, including the redoubtable Rick Burchett taking over pencilling duties for several issues.

And when, after nearly three years, the animated series went in a new direction, Kelley and Mike decided to move on to other things. It seemed like a good time to wrap things up, and we did so with our second and final three-parter, by Kelley, Mike, Rick, and the return of Ty the Guy, bringing things full circle.

Back when we were finishing up the first issue, we were still in need of a title. There were many suggestions, most from me, none especially good. Which is when Denny O'Neil proved, yet again, why he was Denny O'Neil. "*The Batman Adventures*," he proclaimed, and there was a collective sigh of "Oh, of course." What, exactly, did it mean, and why did it apply to this book? That was never entirely clear, and yet it didn't matter; it was different, it was memorable, and it fit perfectly.

So much so that from then on, to this day, whenever a comic book company wanted to create a new comic book that was aimed at younger readers, they added the word *adventures* to the end: *X-Men Adventures*, *Spider-Man Adventures*, *WildC.A.T.s Adventures*, *Star Wars Adventures*. Everyone knew what that meant.

Often imitated, never surpassed: *The Batman Adventures*.

SCOTT PETERSON

April 2023

SCOTT PETERSON got his start in comics at DC, where he edited their flagship title *Detective Comics* as well as *Batman: Black & White*, *Green Arrow*, and *Nightwing*. Scott also edited *The Batman Adventures*, the first series in the influential "Adventures" subgenre. He later went on to write a four-year run on *Batman: Gotham Adventures*, *Truckus Maximus*, and *Batman: Kings of Fear*. Scott lives in the Pacific Northwest with his magnificent wife, children's author Melissa Wiley, and their children.

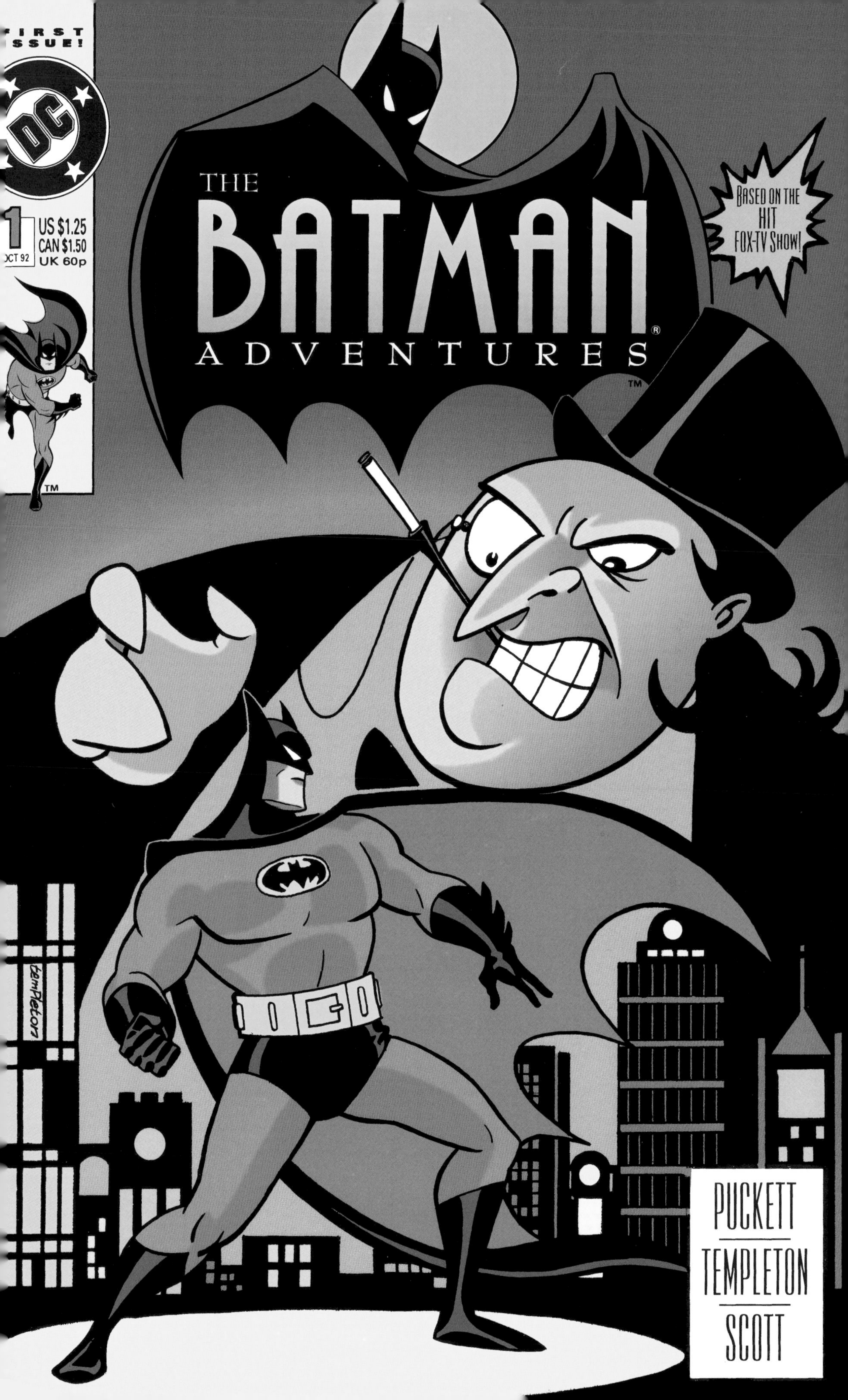
FIRST ISSUE!
DC
1
US $1.25
CAN $1.50
UK 60p
OCT 92
THE BATMAN ADVENTURES
BASED ON THE HIT FOX-TV SHOW!
Templeton
PUCKETT
TEMPLETON
SCOTT

PENGUIN'S BIG SCORE

ACT ONE: CHARM SCHOOL DROPOUT!

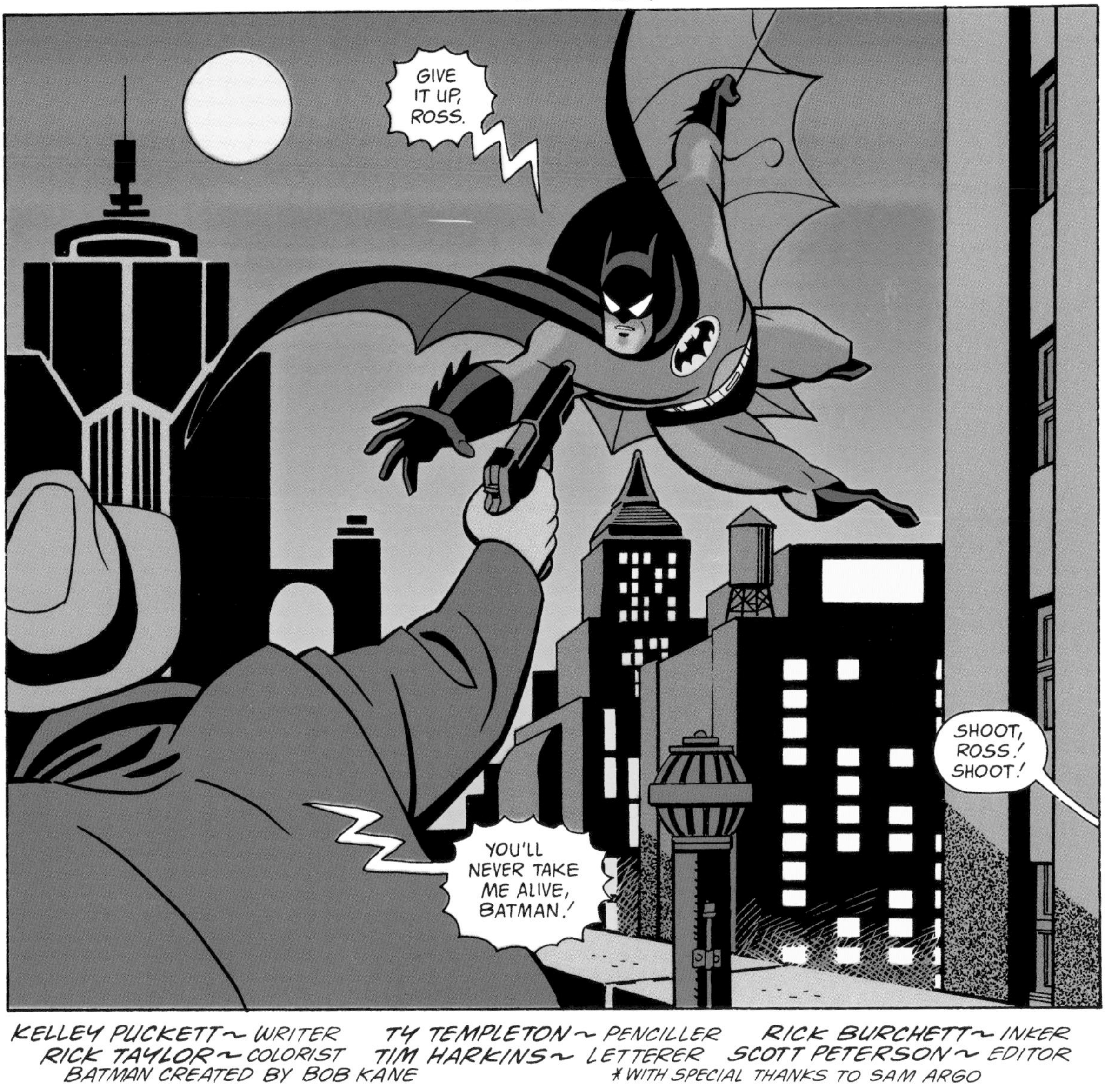
GIVE IT UP, ROSS.
YOU'LL NEVER TAKE ME ALIVE, BATMAN!
SHOOT, ROSS! SHOOT!

KELLEY PUCKETT ~ WRITER TY TEMPLETON ~ PENCILLER RICK BURCHETT ~ INKER
RICK TAYLOR ~ COLORIST TIM HARKINS ~ LETTERER SCOTT PETERSON ~ EDITOR
BATMAN CREATED BY BOB KANE *WITH SPECIAL THANKS TO SAM ARGO

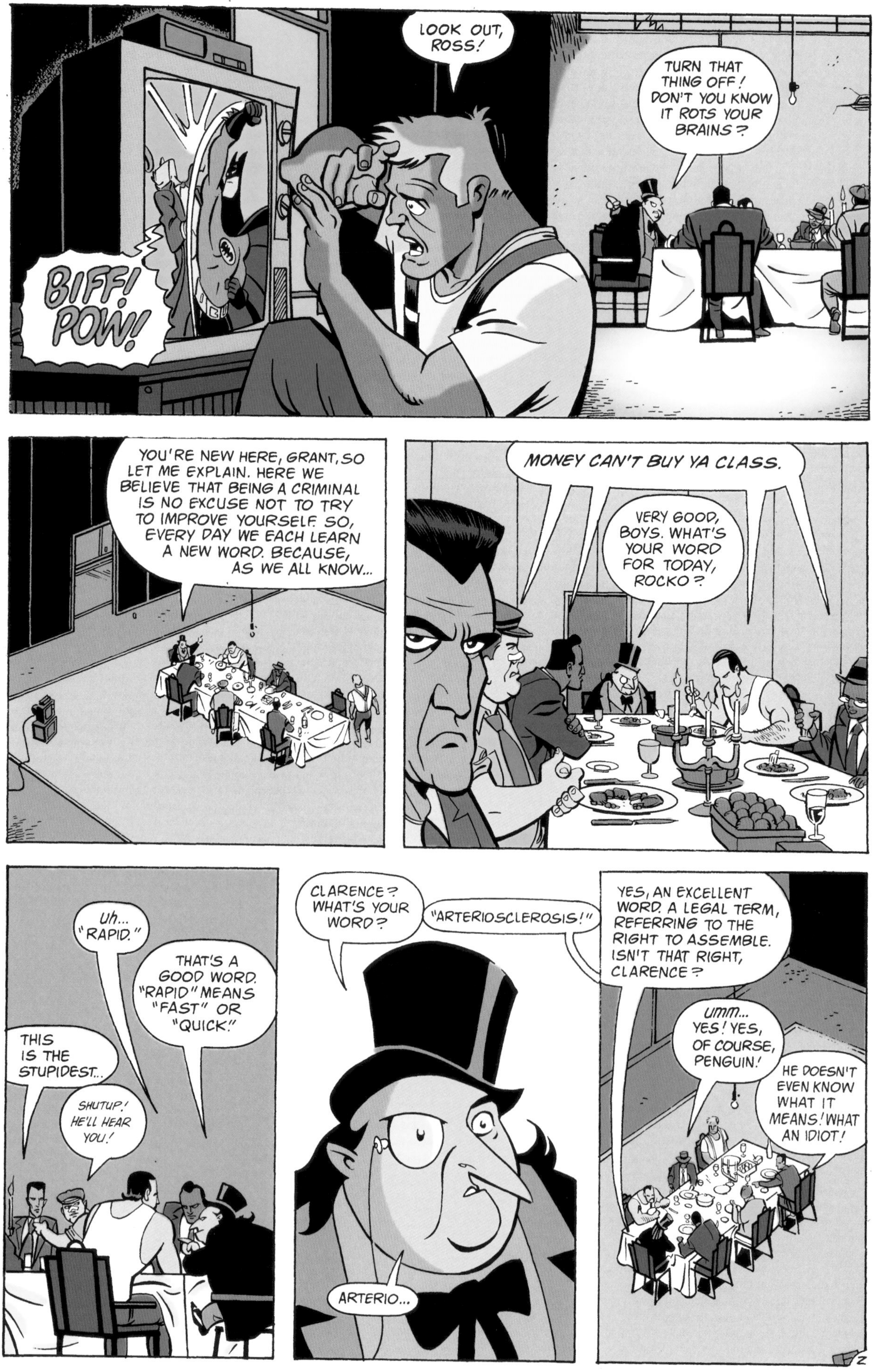
LOOK OUT, ROSS!
BIFF! POW!
TURN THAT THING OFF! DON'T YOU KNOW IT ROTS YOUR BRAINS?
YOU'RE NEW HERE, GRANT, SO LET ME EXPLAIN. HERE WE BELIEVE THAT BEING A CRIMINAL IS NO EXCUSE NOT TO TRY TO IMPROVE YOURSELF. SO, EVERY DAY WE EACH LEARN A NEW WORD. BECAUSE, AS WE ALL KNOW...
MONEY CAN'T BUY YA CLASS.
VERY GOOD, BOYS. WHAT'S YOUR WORD FOR TODAY, ROCKO?
Uh... "RAPID."
THAT'S A GOOD WORD. "RAPID" MEANS "FAST" OR "QUICK."
THIS IS THE STUPIDEST...
SHUTUP! HE'LL HEAR YOU!
CLARENCE? WHAT'S YOUR WORD?
"ARTERIOSCLEROSIS!"
ARTERIO...
YES, AN EXCELLENT WORD. A LEGAL TERM, REFERRING TO THE RIGHT TO ASSEMBLE. ISN'T THAT RIGHT, CLARENCE?
Umm... YES! YES, OF COURSE, PENGUIN!
HE DOESN'T EVEN KNOW WHAT IT MEANS! WHAT AN IDIOT!

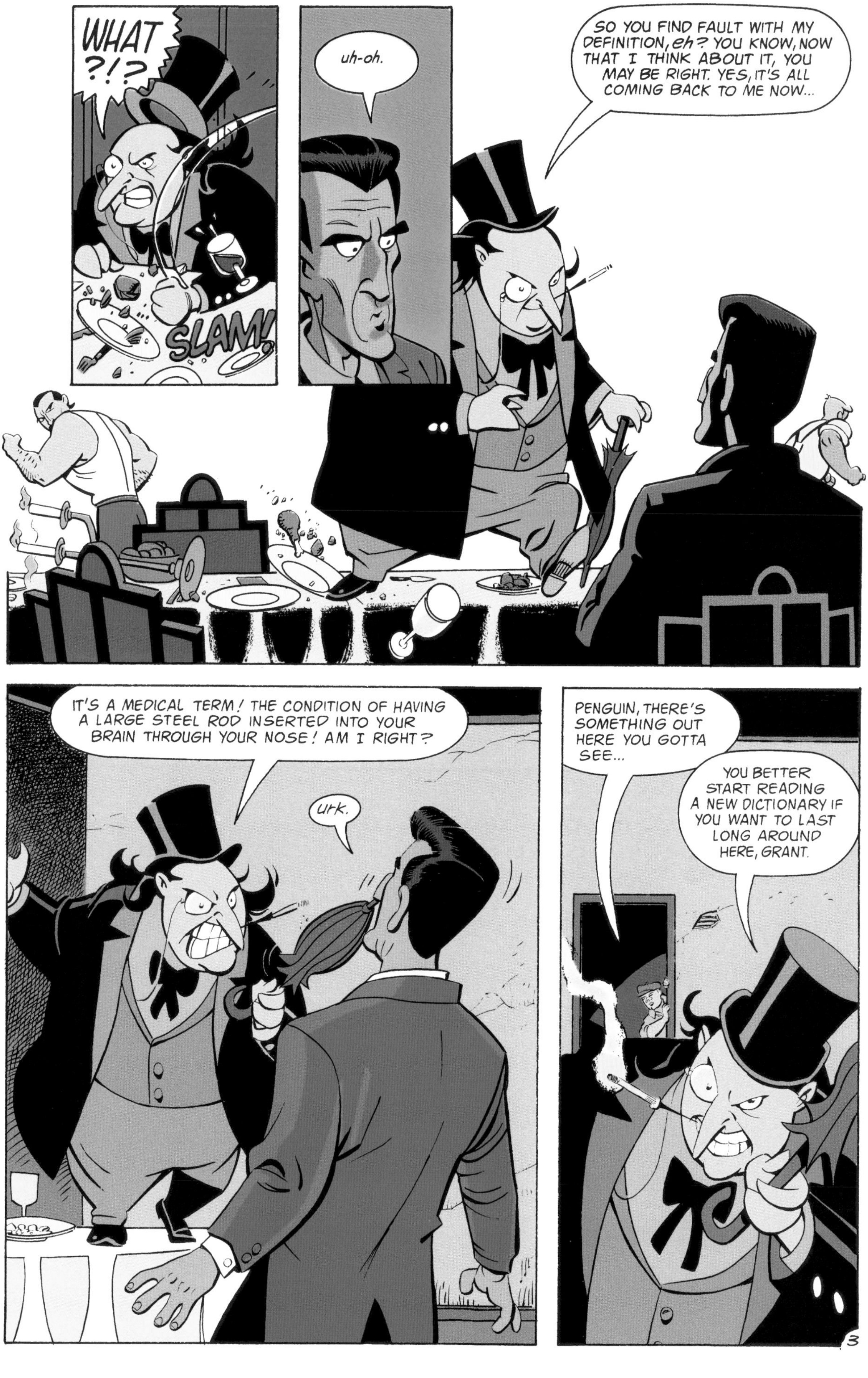
WHAT ?!?
SLAM!
uh-oh.
SO YOU FIND FAULT WITH MY DEFINITION, eh? YOU KNOW, NOW THAT I THINK ABOUT IT, YOU MAY BE RIGHT. YES, IT'S ALL COMING BACK TO ME NOW...
IT'S A MEDICAL TERM! THE CONDITION OF HAVING A LARGE STEEL ROD INSERTED INTO YOUR BRAIN THROUGH YOUR NOSE! AM I RIGHT?
urk.
PENGUIN, THERE'S SOMETHING OUT HERE YOU GOTTA SEE...
YOU BETTER START READING A NEW DICTIONARY IF YOU WANT TO LAST LONG AROUND HERE, GRANT.
3

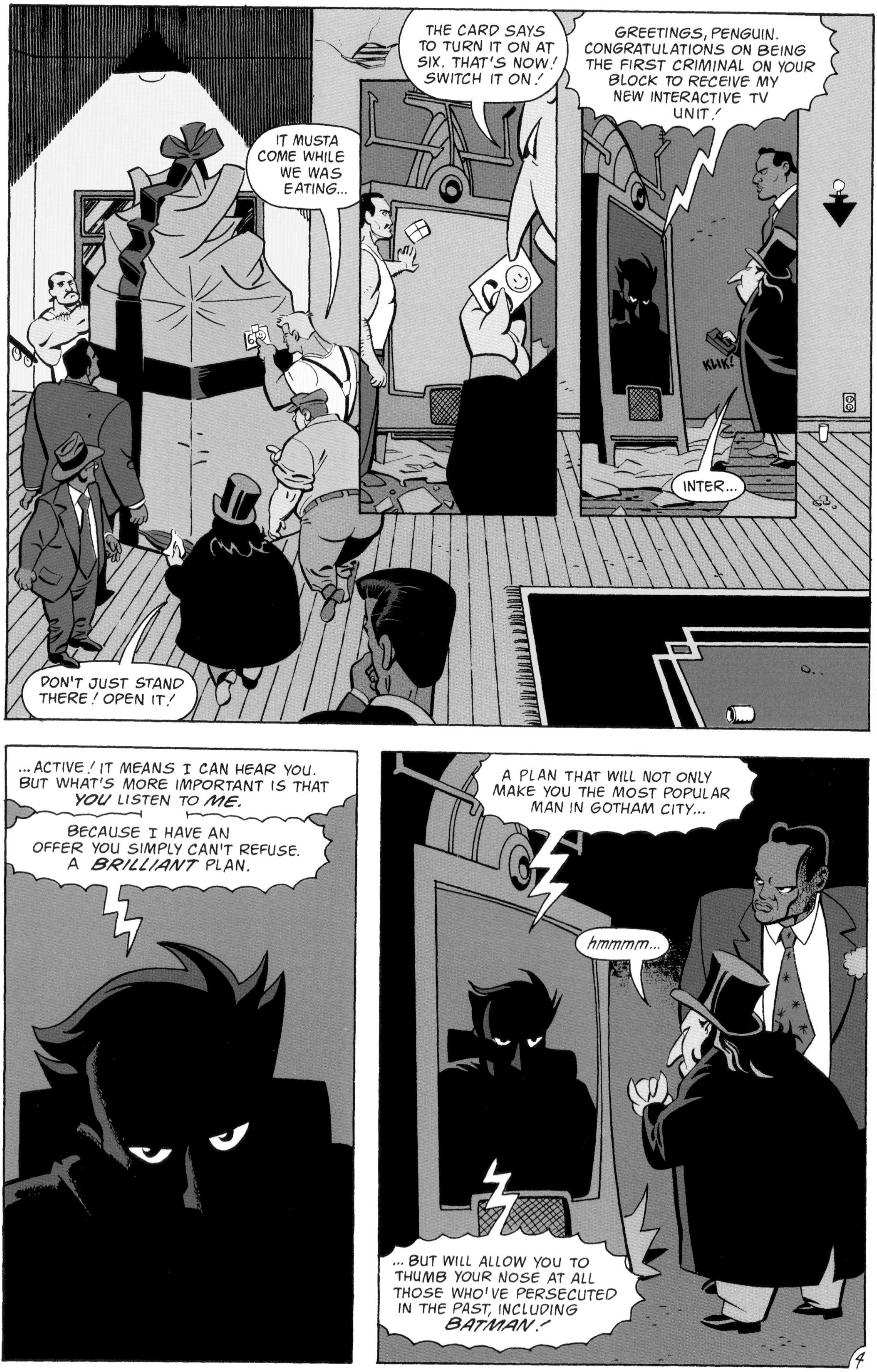
DON'T JUST STAND THERE! OPEN IT!
IT MUSTA COME WHILE WE WAS EATING...
THE CARD SAYS TO TURN IT ON AT SIX. THAT'S NOW! SWITCH IT ON!
KLIK!
GREETINGS, PENGUIN. CONGRATULATIONS ON BEING THE FIRST CRIMINAL ON YOUR BLOCK TO RECEIVE MY NEW INTERACTIVE TV UNIT!
INTER...
...ACTIVE! IT MEANS I CAN HEAR YOU. BUT WHAT'S MORE IMPORTANT IS THAT YOU LISTEN TO ME.
BECAUSE I HAVE AN OFFER YOU SIMPLY CAN'T REFUSE. A BRILLIANT PLAN.
A PLAN THAT WILL NOT ONLY MAKE YOU THE MOST POPULAR MAN IN GOTHAM CITY...
hmmmm...
...BUT WILL ALLOW YOU TO THUMB YOUR NOSE AT ALL THOSE WHO'VE PERSECUTED IN THE PAST, INCLUDING BATMAN!
4

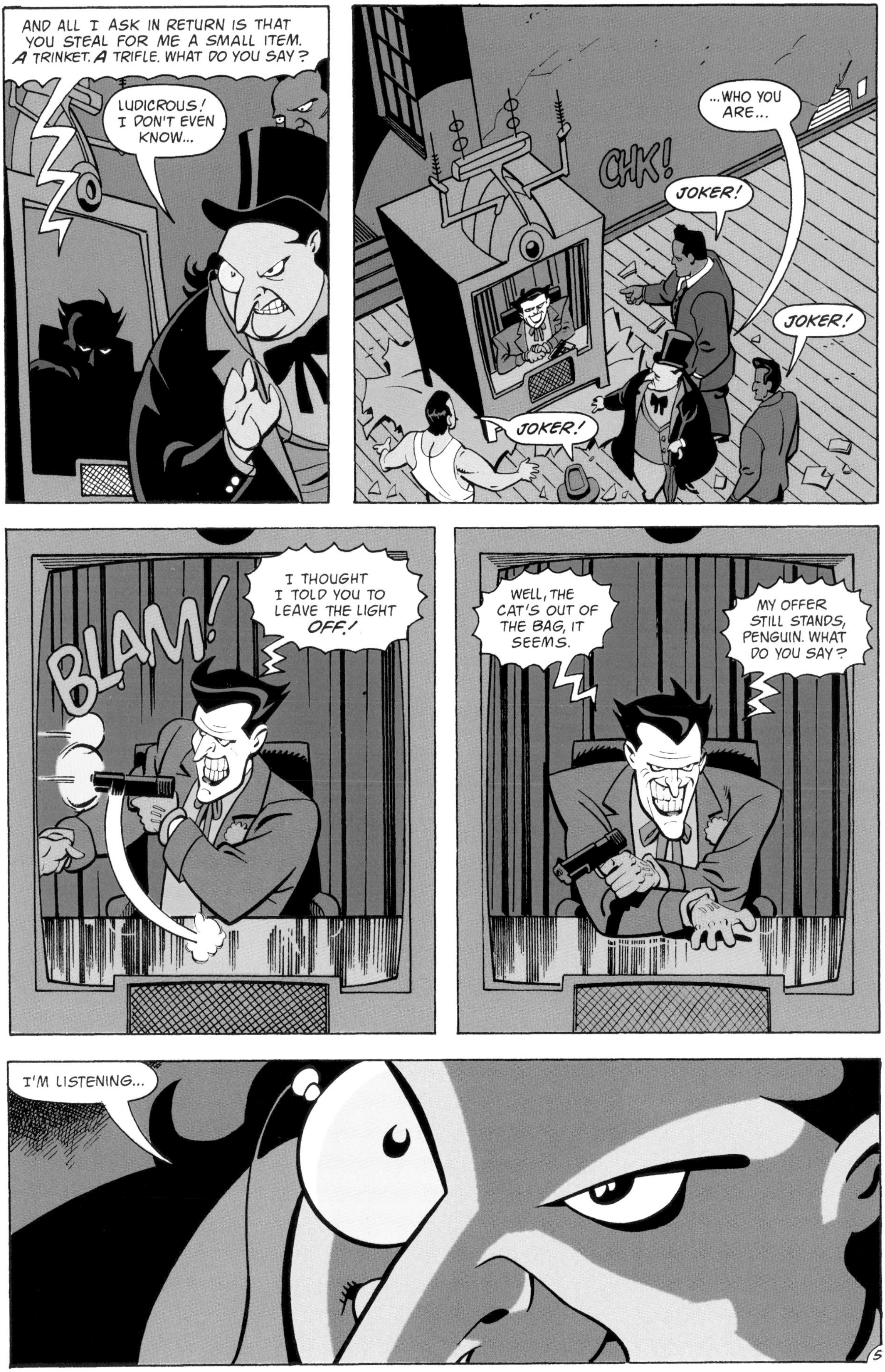
AND ALL I ASK IN RETURN IS THAT YOU STEAL FOR ME A SMALL ITEM. A TRINKET. A TRIFLE. WHAT DO YOU SAY?
LUDICROUS! I DON'T EVEN KNOW...
CHK!
...WHO YOU ARE...
JOKER!
JOKER!
JOKER!
BLAM!
I THOUGHT I TOLD YOU TO LEAVE THE LIGHT OFF!
WELL, THE CAT'S OUT OF THE BAG, IT SEEMS.
MY OFFER STILL STANDS, PENGUIN. WHAT DO YOU SAY?
I'M LISTENING...
5

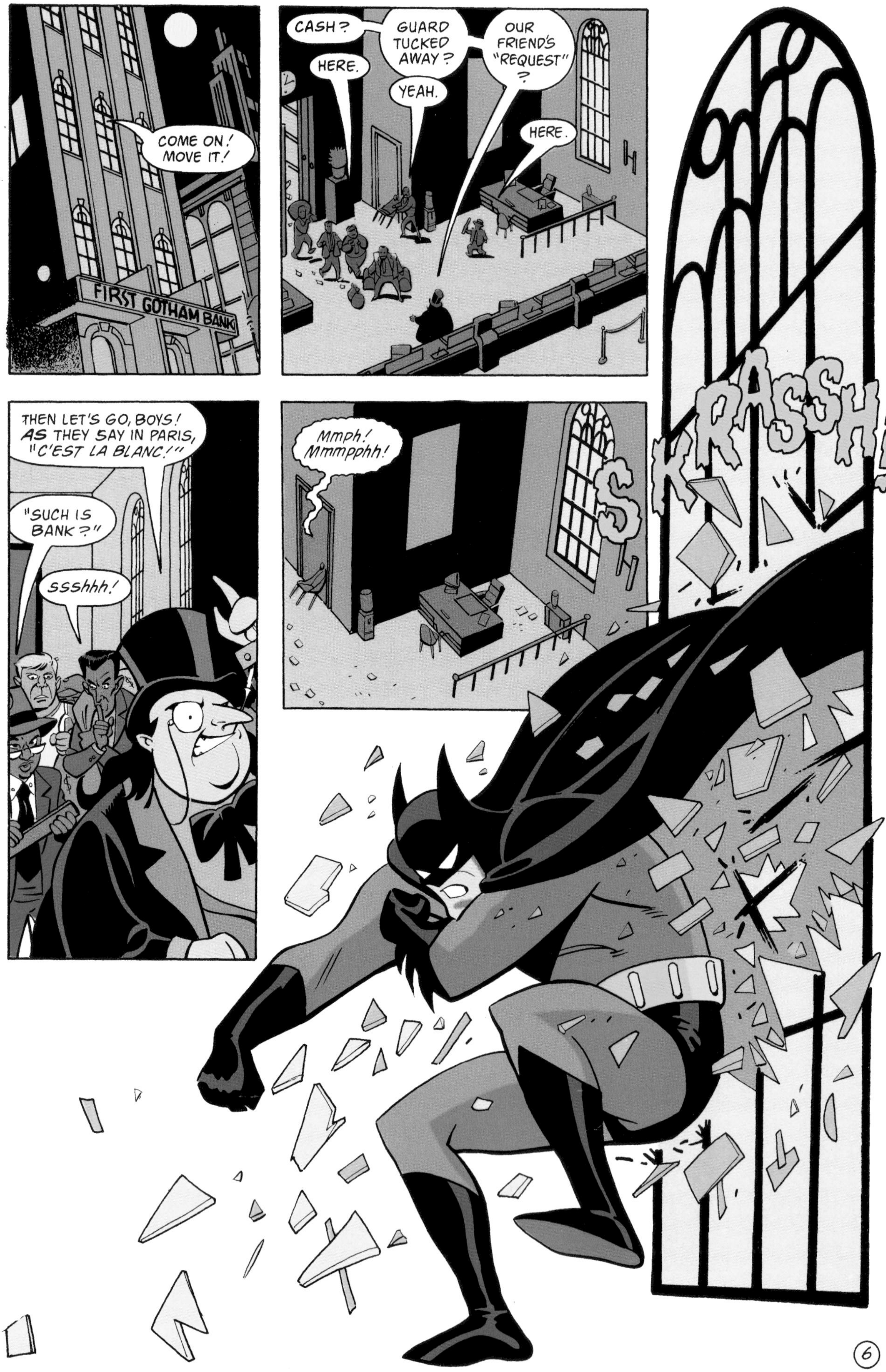
COME ON! MOVE IT!
FIRST GOTHAM BANK
CASH?
HERE.
GUARD TUCKED AWAY?
YEAH.
OUR FRIEND'S "REQUEST"?
HERE.
THEN LET'S GO, BOYS! AS THEY SAY IN PARIS, "C'EST LA BLANC!"
"SUCH IS BANK?"
SSSHHH!
Mmph! Mmmpphh!
SKRASSH!
6

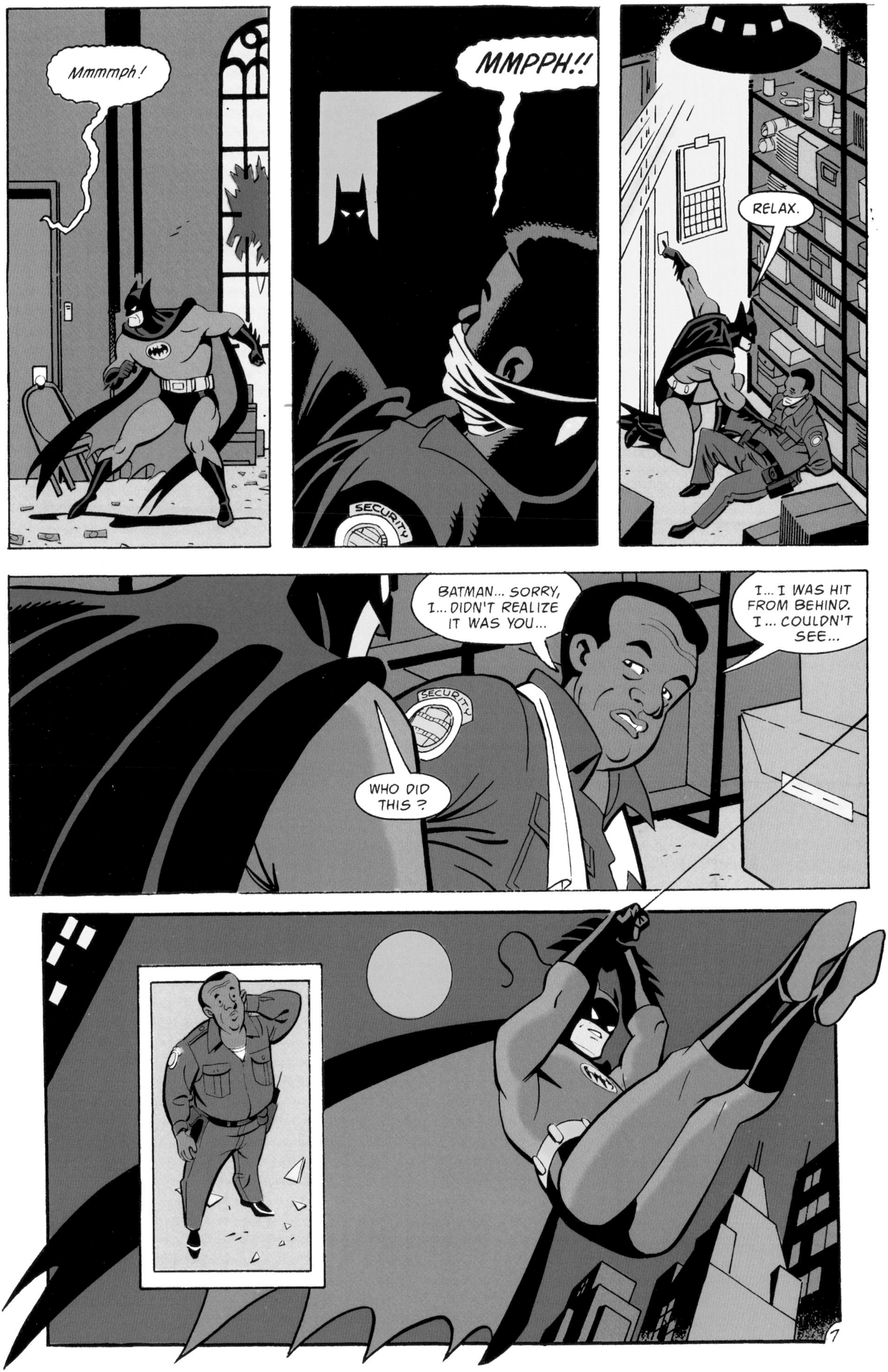
Mmmmph!
MMPPH!!
SECURITY
RELAX.
BATMAN... SORRY, I... DIDN'T REALIZE IT WAS YOU...
I... I WAS HIT FROM BEHIND. I... COULDN'T SEE...
SECURITY
WHO DID THIS ?
7

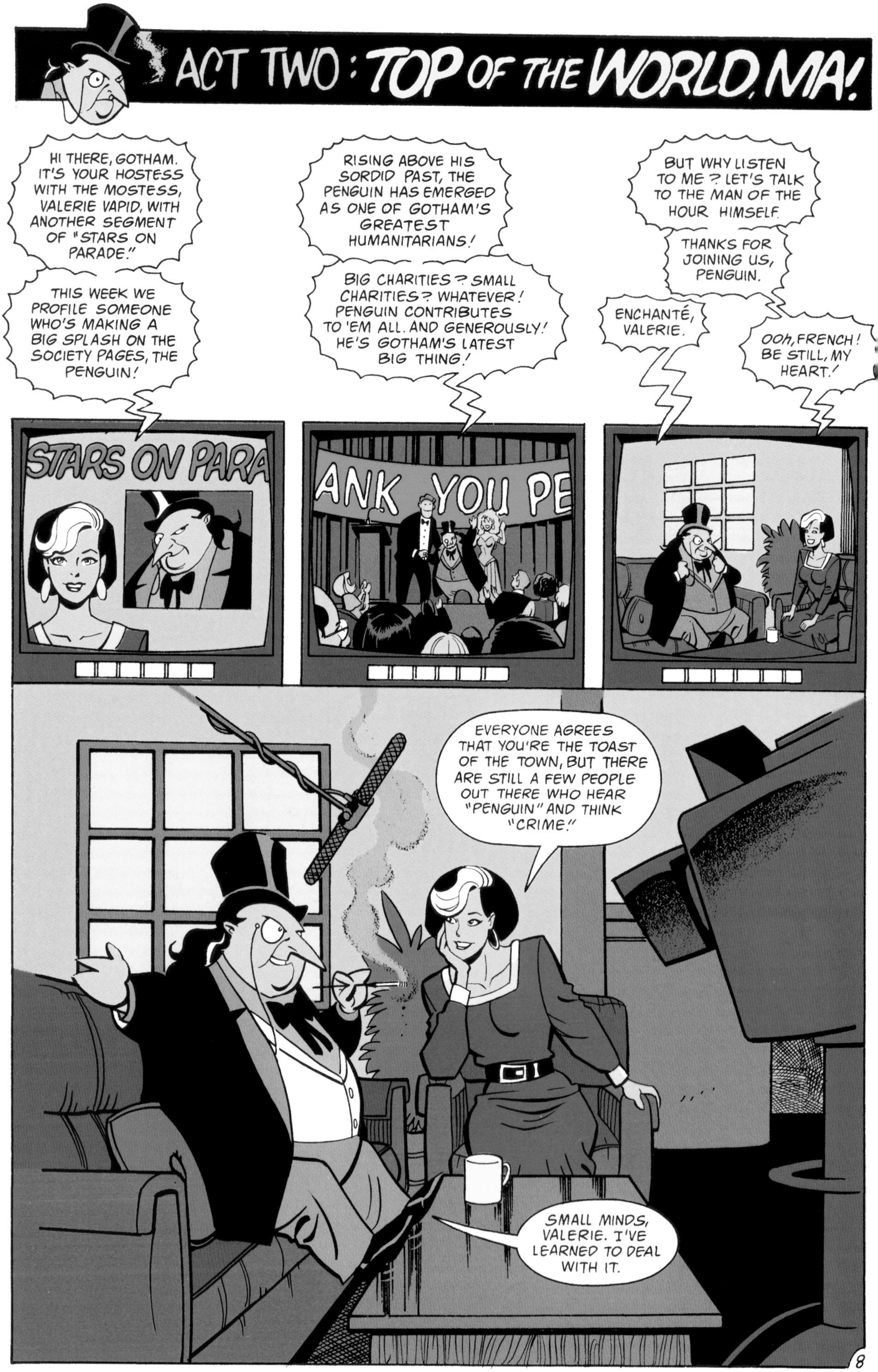
ACT TWO: TOP OF THE WORLD, MA!
HI THERE, GOTHAM. IT'S YOUR HOSTESS WITH THE MOSTESS, VALERIE VAPID, WITH ANOTHER SEGMENT OF "STARS ON PARADE."
THIS WEEK WE PROFILE SOMEONE WHO'S MAKING A BIG SPLASH ON THE SOCIETY PAGES, THE PENGUIN!
STARS ON PARA
RISING ABOVE HIS SORDID PAST, THE PENGUIN HAS EMERGED AS ONE OF GOTHAM'S GREATEST HUMANITARIANS!
BIG CHARITIES? SMALL CHARITIES? WHATEVER! PENGUIN CONTRIBUTES TO 'EM ALL. AND GENEROUSLY! HE'S GOTHAM'S LATEST BIG THING!
ANK YOU PE
BUT WHY LISTEN TO ME? LET'S TALK TO THE MAN OF THE HOUR HIMSELF.
THANKS FOR JOINING US, PENGUIN.
ENCHANTÉ, VALERIE.
Ooh, FRENCH! BE STILL, MY HEART!
EVERYONE AGREES THAT YOU'RE THE TOAST OF THE TOWN, BUT THERE ARE STILL A FEW PEOPLE OUT THERE WHO HEAR "PENGUIN" AND THINK "CRIME."
SMALL MINDS, VALERIE. I'VE LEARNED TO DEAL WITH IT.
8

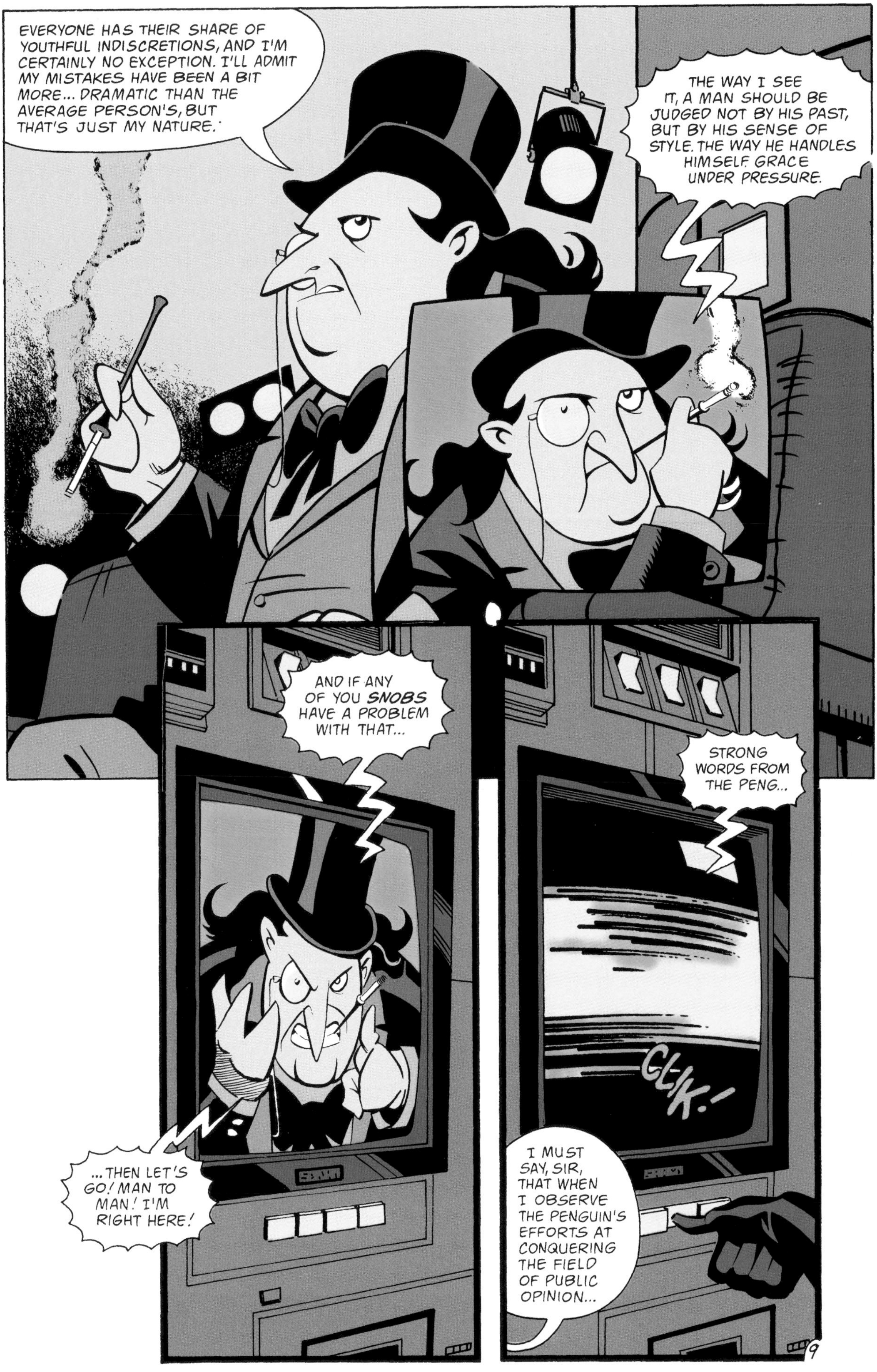
EVERYONE HAS THEIR SHARE OF YOUTHFUL INDISCRETIONS, AND I'M CERTAINLY NO EXCEPTION. I'LL ADMIT MY MISTAKES HAVE BEEN A BIT MORE... DRAMATIC THAN THE AVERAGE PERSON'S, BUT THAT'S JUST MY NATURE.
THE WAY I SEE IT, A MAN SHOULD BE JUDGED NOT BY HIS PAST, BUT BY HIS SENSE OF STYLE. THE WAY HE HANDLES HIMSELF. GRACE UNDER PRESSURE.
AND IF ANY OF YOU SNOBS HAVE A PROBLEM WITH THAT...
...THEN LET'S GO! MAN TO MAN! I'M RIGHT HERE!
STRONG WORDS FROM THE PENG...
CLIK!
I MUST SAY, SIR, THAT WHEN I OBSERVE THE PENGUIN'S EFFORTS AT CONQUERING THE FIELD OF PUBLIC OPINION...
9

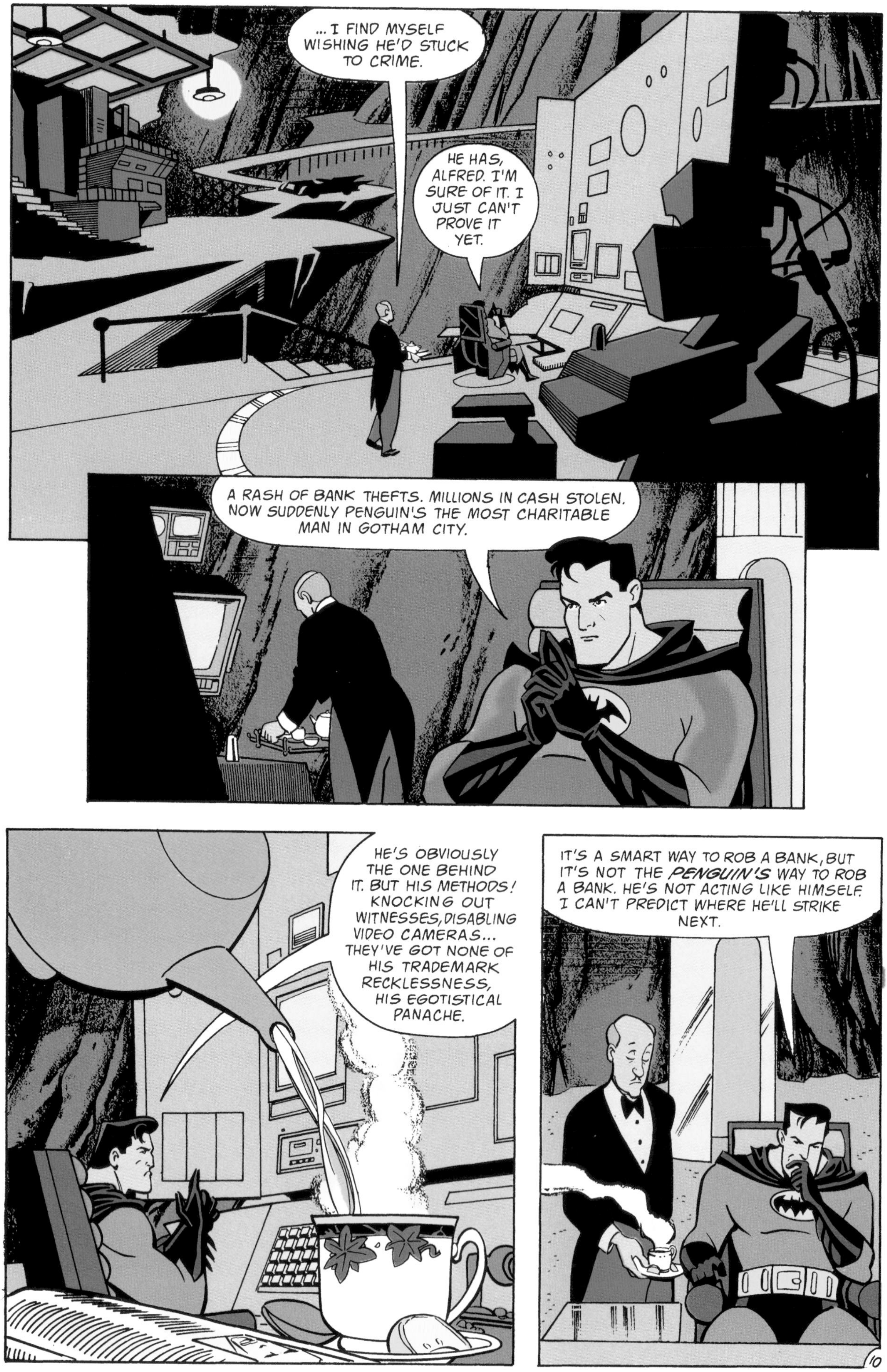
...I FIND MYSELF WISHING HE'D STUCK TO CRIME.
HE HAS, ALFRED. I'M SURE OF IT. I JUST CAN'T PROVE IT YET.
A RASH OF BANK THEFTS. MILLIONS IN CASH STOLEN. NOW SUDDENLY PENGUIN'S THE MOST CHARITABLE MAN IN GOTHAM CITY.
HE'S OBVIOUSLY THE ONE BEHIND IT. BUT HIS METHODS! KNOCKING OUT WITNESSES, DISABLING VIDEO CAMERAS... THEY'VE GOT NONE OF HIS TRADEMARK RECKLESSNESS, HIS EGOTISTICAL PANACHE.
IT'S A SMART WAY TO ROB A BANK, BUT IT'S NOT THE *PENGUIN'S* WAY TO ROB A BANK. HE'S NOT ACTING LIKE HIMSELF. I CAN'T PREDICT WHERE HE'LL STRIKE NEXT.
10

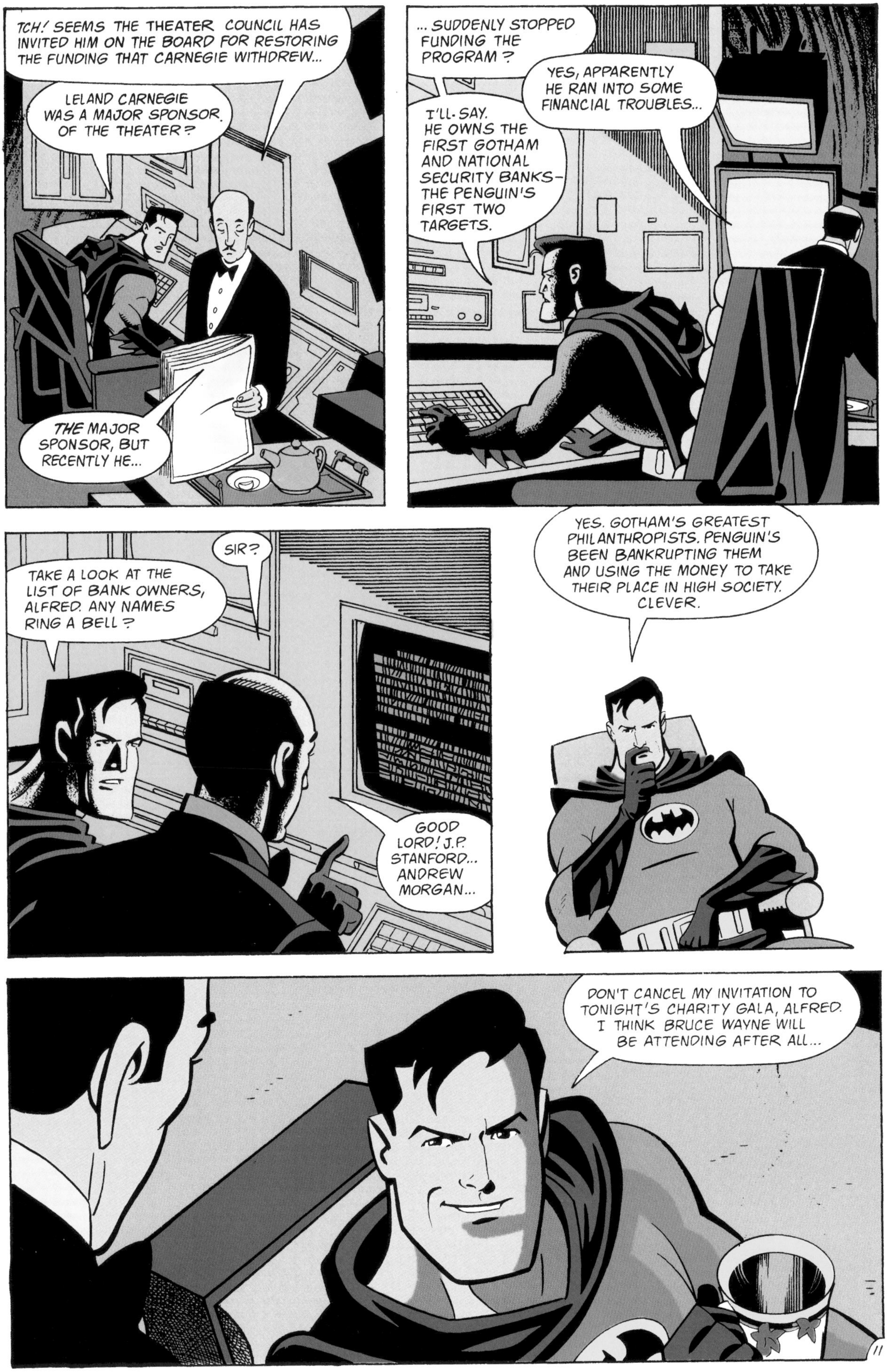
TCH! SEEMS THE THEATER COUNCIL HAS INVITED HIM ON THE BOARD FOR RESTORING THE FUNDING THAT CARNEGIE WITHDREW...
LELAND CARNEGIE WAS A MAJOR SPONSOR OF THE THEATER?
THE MAJOR SPONSOR, BUT RECENTLY HE...
... SUDDENLY STOPPED FUNDING THE PROGRAM?
YES, APPARENTLY HE RAN INTO SOME FINANCIAL TROUBLES...
I'LL SAY. HE OWNS THE FIRST GOTHAM AND NATIONAL SECURITY BANKS-- THE PENGUIN'S FIRST TWO TARGETS.
TAKE A LOOK AT THE LIST OF BANK OWNERS, ALFRED. ANY NAMES RING A BELL?
SIR?
GOOD LORD! J.P. STANFORD... ANDREW MORGAN...
YES. GOTHAM'S GREATEST PHILANTHROPISTS. PENGUIN'S BEEN BANKRUPTING THEM AND USING THE MONEY TO TAKE THEIR PLACE IN HIGH SOCIETY. CLEVER.
DON'T CANCEL MY INVITATION TO TONIGHT'S CHARITY GALA, ALFRED. I THINK BRUCE WAYNE WILL BE ATTENDING AFTER ALL...
11

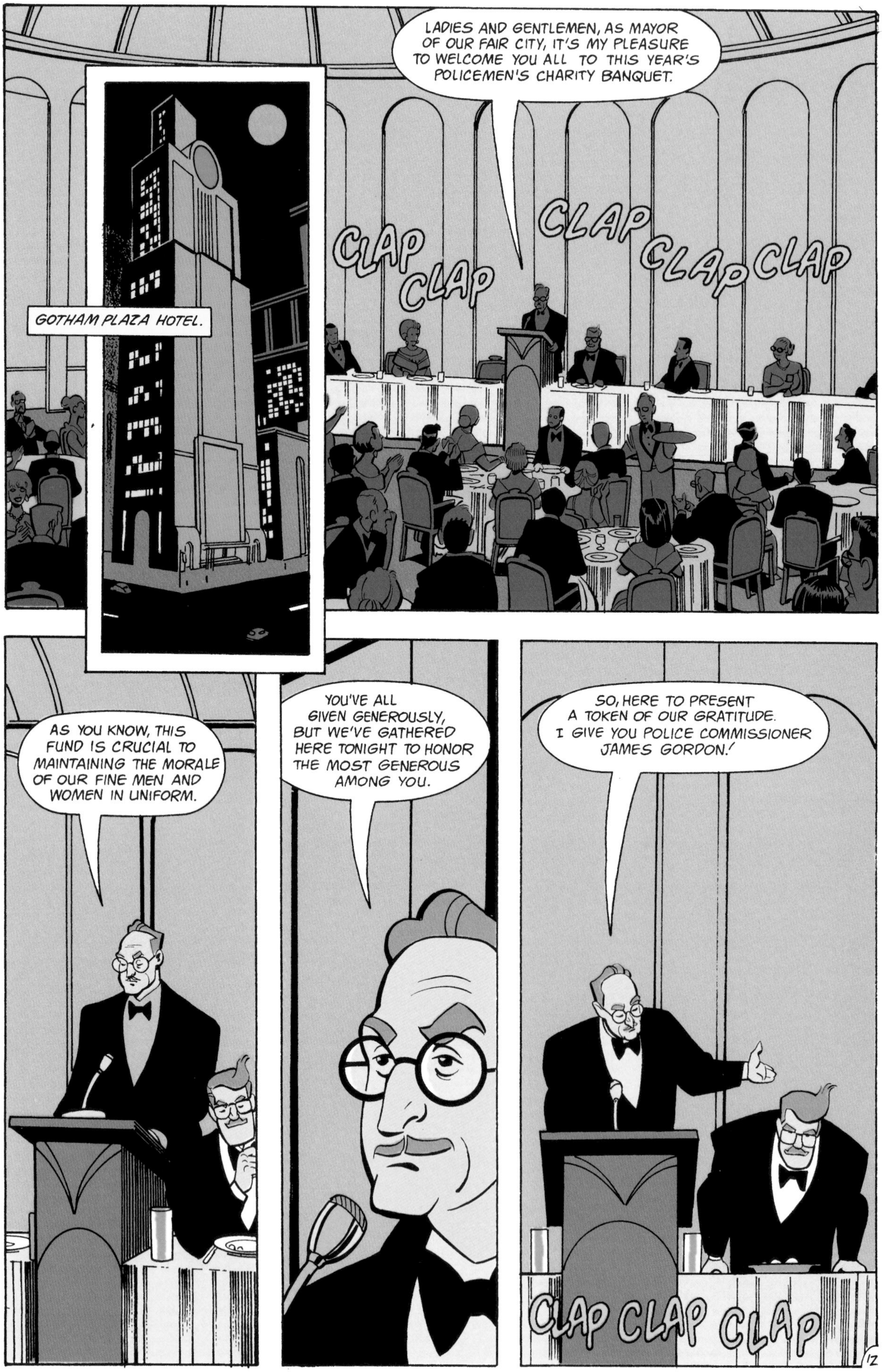
GOTHAM PLAZA HOTEL.
LADIES AND GENTLEMEN, AS MAYOR OF OUR FAIR CITY, IT'S MY PLEASURE TO WELCOME YOU ALL TO THIS YEAR'S POLICEMEN'S CHARITY BANQUET.
CLAP CLAP
CLAP CLAP CLAP
AS YOU KNOW, THIS FUND IS CRUCIAL TO MAINTAINING THE MORALE OF OUR FINE MEN AND WOMEN IN UNIFORM.
YOU'VE ALL GIVEN GENEROUSLY, BUT WE'VE GATHERED HERE TONIGHT TO HONOR THE MOST GENEROUS AMONG YOU.
SO, HERE TO PRESENT A TOKEN OF OUR GRATITUDE, I GIVE YOU POLICE COMMISSIONER JAMES GORDON!
CLAP CLAP CLAP

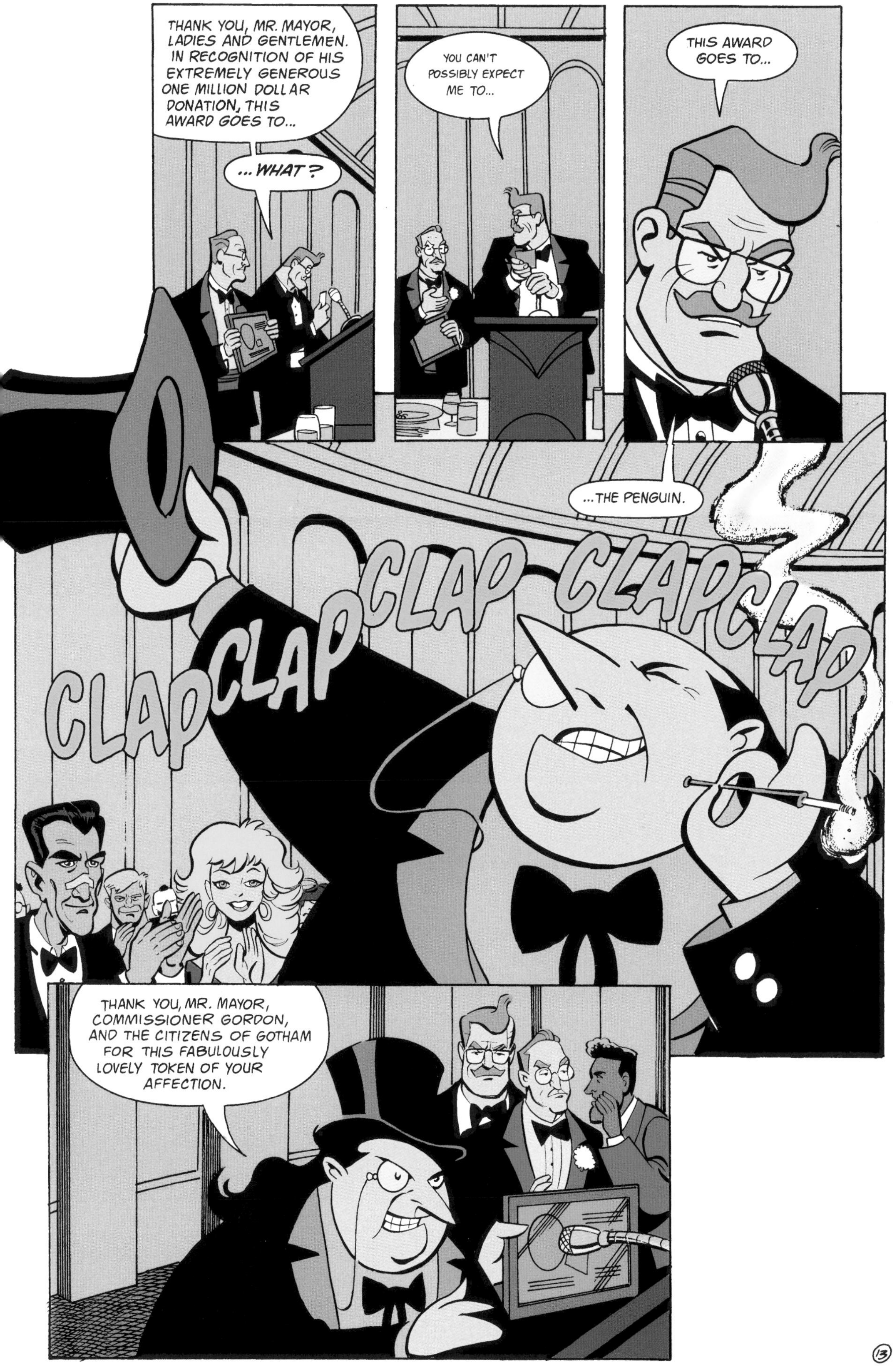
THANK YOU, MR. MAYOR, LADIES AND GENTLEMEN. IN RECOGNITION OF HIS EXTREMELY GENEROUS ONE MILLION DOLLAR DONATION, THIS AWARD GOES TO...
...WHAT?
YOU CAN'T POSSIBLY EXPECT ME TO...
THIS AWARD GOES TO...
...THE PENGUIN.
CLAP CLAP CLAP CLAP CLAP CLAP
THANK YOU, MR. MAYOR, COMMISSIONER GORDON, AND THE CITIZENS OF GOTHAM FOR THIS FABULOUSLY LOVELY TOKEN OF YOUR AFFECTION.
13

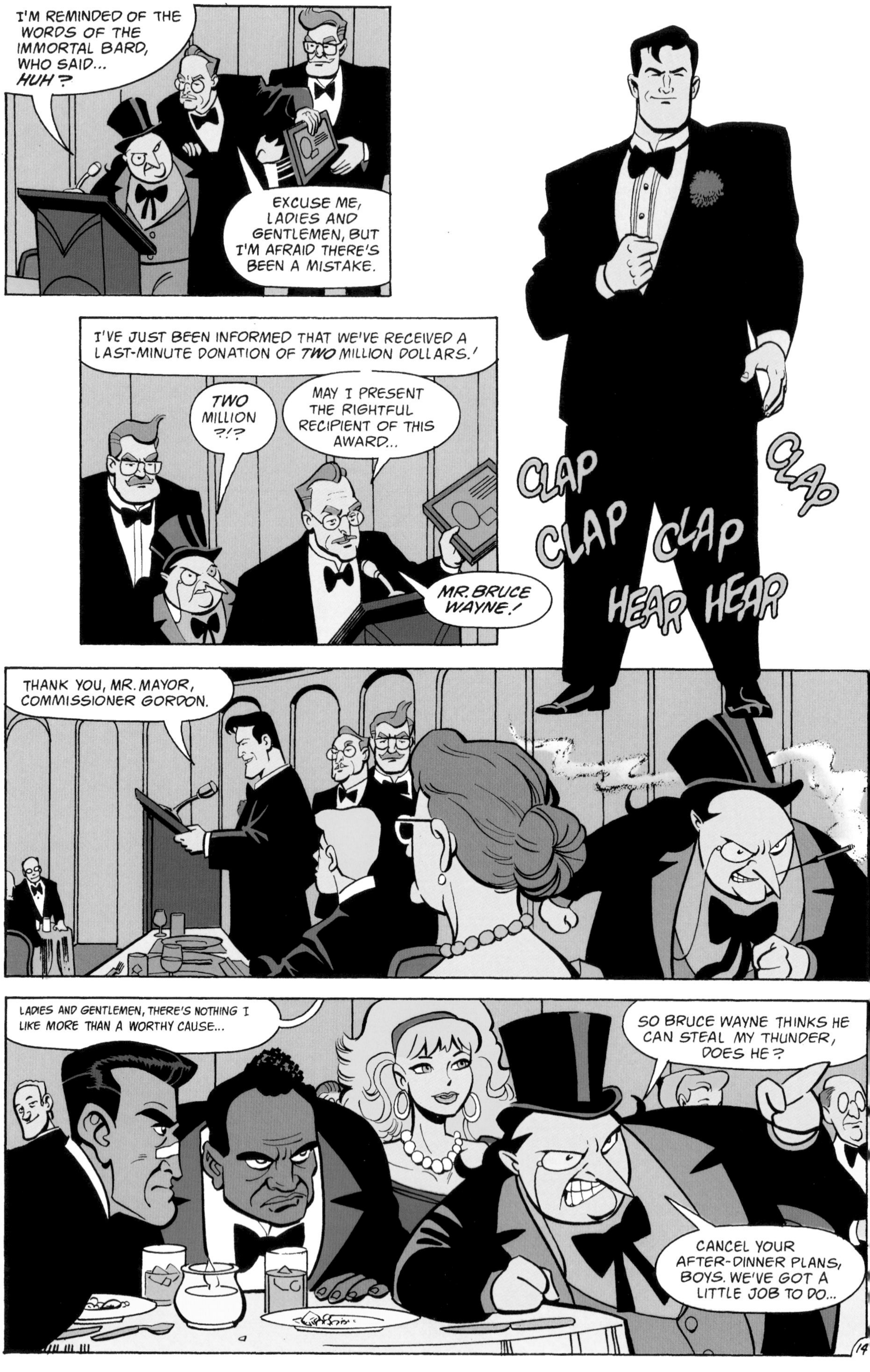

I'M REMINDED OF THE WORDS OF THE IMMORTAL BARD, WHO SAID... HUH?
EXCUSE ME, LADIES AND GENTLEMEN, BUT I'M AFRAID THERE'S BEEN A MISTAKE.
I'VE JUST BEEN INFORMED THAT WE'VE RECEIVED A LAST-MINUTE DONATION OF TWO MILLION DOLLARS.!
TWO MILLION ?!?
MAY I PRESENT THE RIGHTFUL RECIPIENT OF THIS AWARD...
MR. BRUCE WAYNE!
CLAP
CLAP
CLAP
CLAP
HEAR HEAR
THANK YOU, MR. MAYOR, COMMISSIONER GORDON.
LADIES AND GENTLEMEN, THERE'S NOTHING I LIKE MORE THAN A WORTHY CAUSE...
SO BRUCE WAYNE THINKS HE CAN STEAL MY THUNDER, DOES HE?
CANCEL YOUR AFTER-DINNER PLANS, BOYS. WE'VE GOT A LITTLE JOB TO DO...
14

ACT THREE: POWER OF THE PRESS!

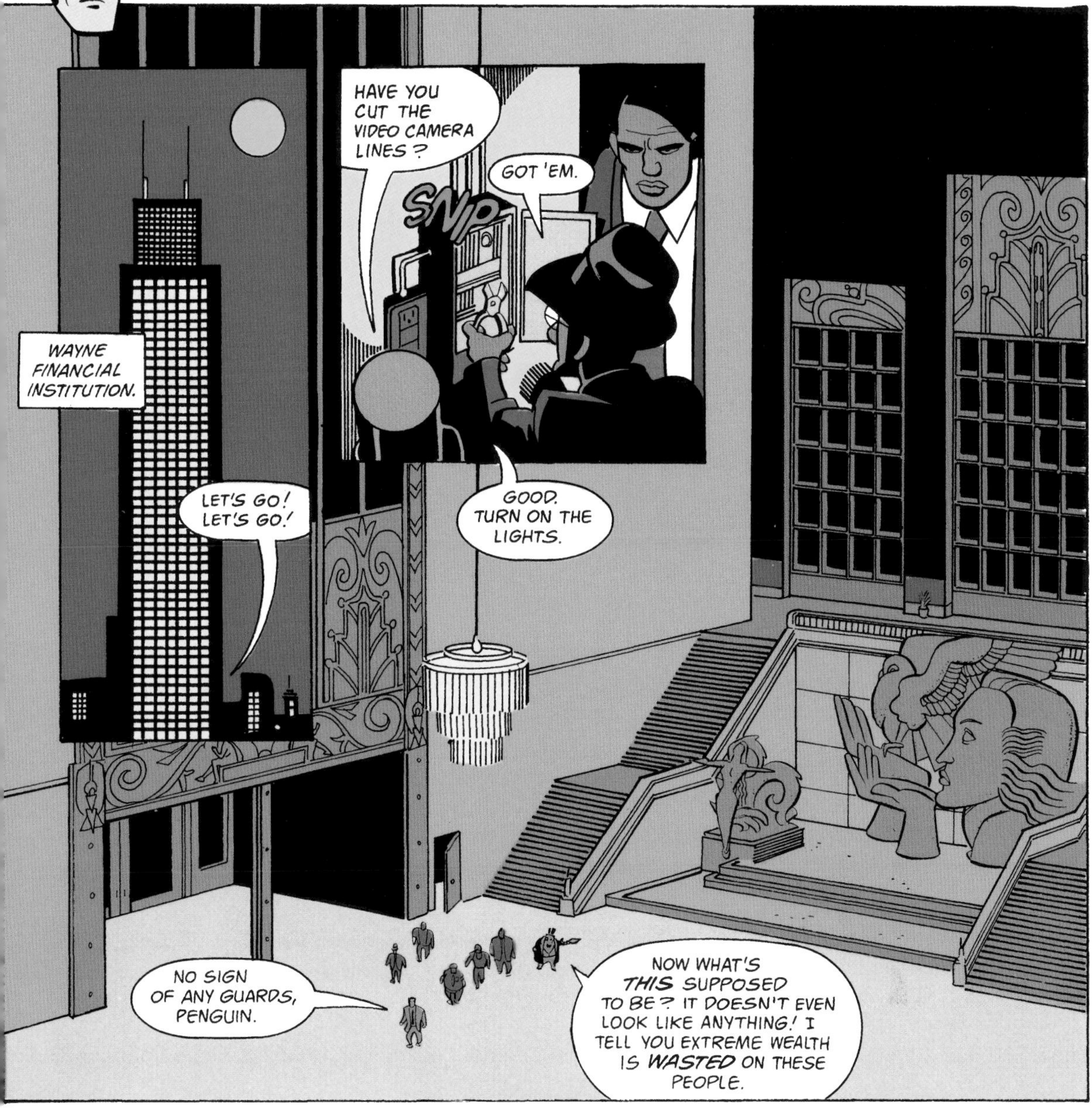
WAYNE FINANCIAL INSTITUTION.
HAVE YOU CUT THE VIDEO CAMERA LINES?
GOT 'EM.
SNIP
GOOD. TURN ON THE LIGHTS.
LET'S GO! LET'S GO!
NO SIGN OF ANY GUARDS, PENGUIN.
NOW WHAT'S THIS SUPPOSED TO BE? IT DOESN'T EVEN LOOK LIKE ANYTHING! I TELL YOU EXTREME WEALTH IS WASTED ON THESE PEOPLE.

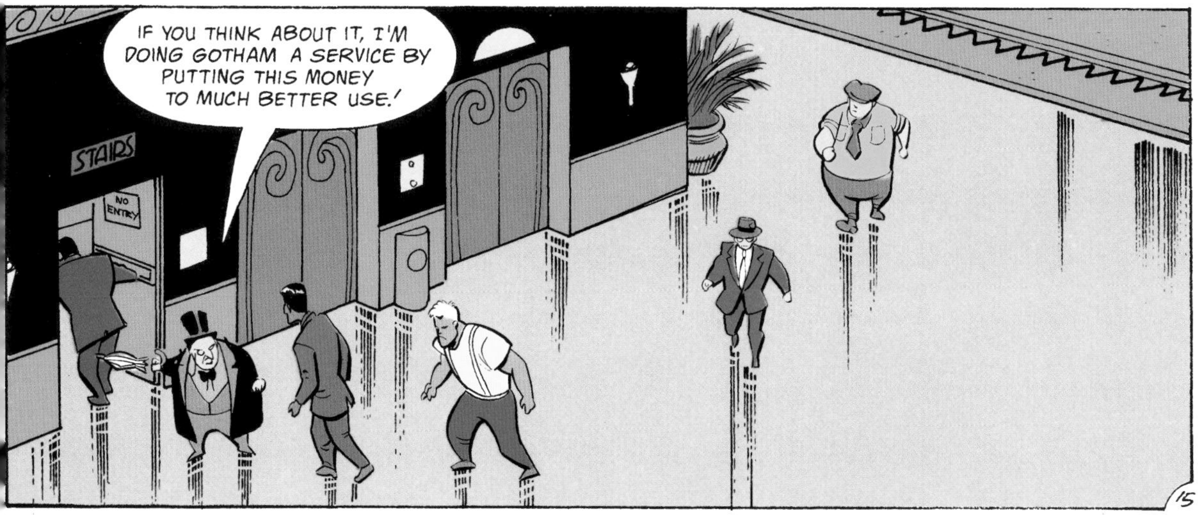
IF YOU THINK ABOUT IT, I'M DOING GOTHAM A SERVICE BY PUTTING THIS MONEY TO MUCH BETTER USE!
STAIRS
NO ENTRY
15

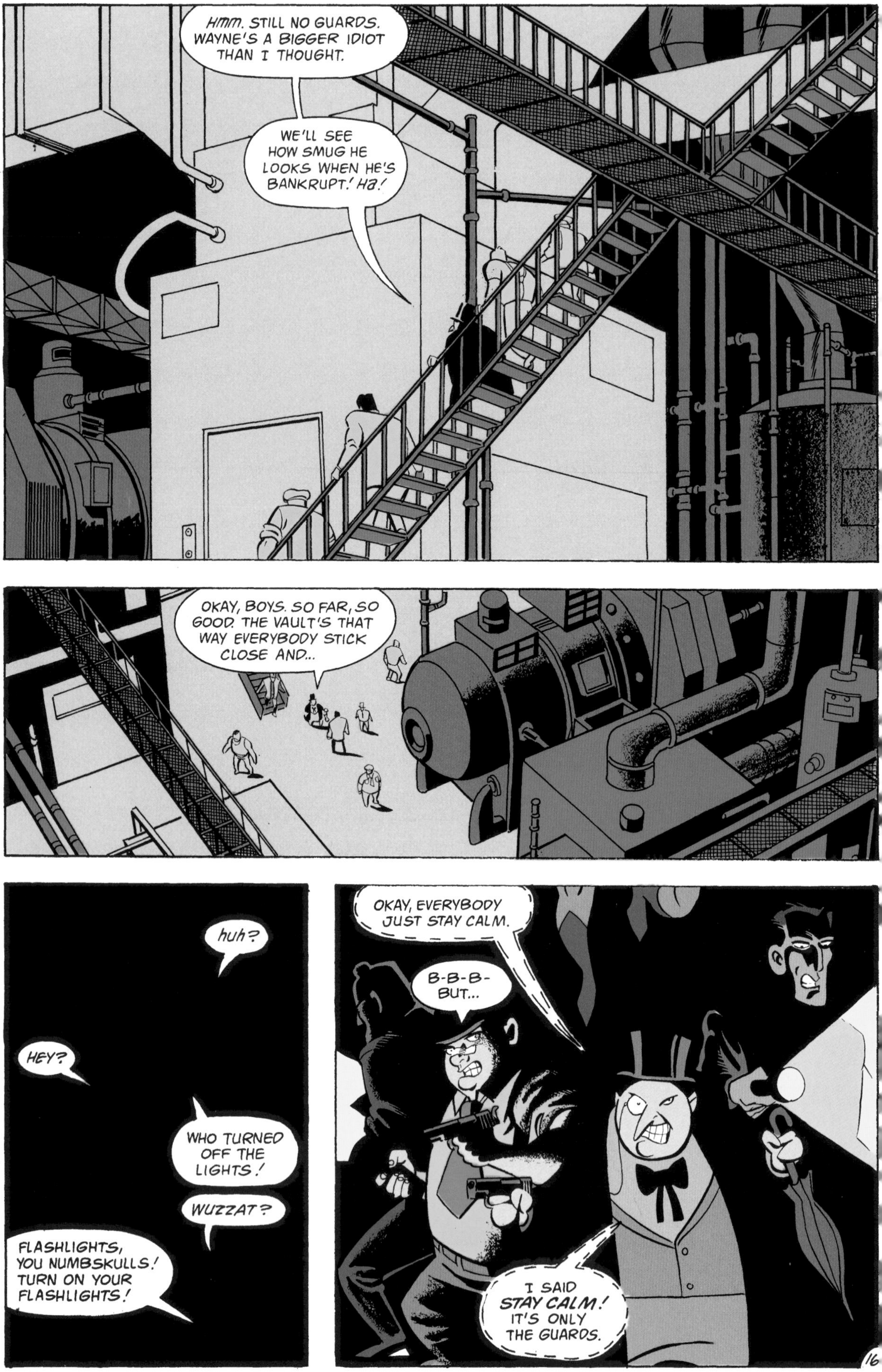
HMM. STILL NO GUARDS. WAYNE'S A BIGGER IDIOT THAN I THOUGHT.
WE'LL SEE HOW SMUG HE LOOKS WHEN HE'S BANKRUPT! HA!
OKAY, BOYS. SO FAR, SO GOOD. THE VAULT'S THAT WAY. EVERYBODY STICK CLOSE AND...
huh?
HEY?
WHO TURNED OFF THE LIGHTS!
WUZZAT?
FLASHLIGHTS, YOU NUMBSKULLS! TURN ON YOUR FLASHLIGHTS!
OKAY, EVERYBODY JUST STAY CALM.
B-B-B-BUT...
I SAID STAY CALM! IT'S ONLY THE GUARDS.
16

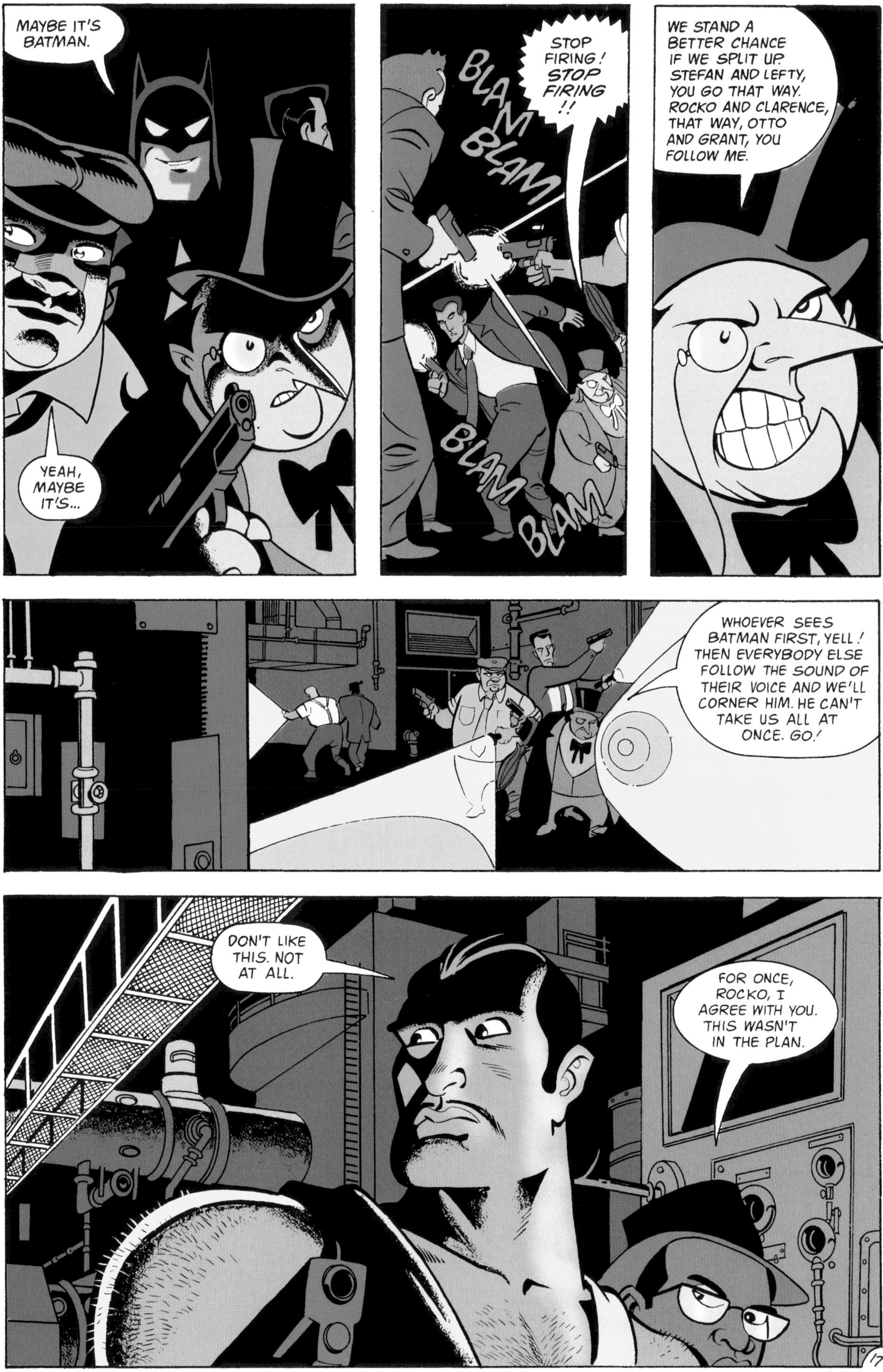
MAYBE IT'S BATMAN.
YEAH, MAYBE IT'S...
BLAM BLAM BLAM
STOP FIRING! STOP FIRING!!
BLAM BLAM
WE STAND A BETTER CHANCE IF WE SPLIT UP. STEFAN AND LEFTY, YOU GO THAT WAY. ROCKO AND CLARENCE, THAT WAY, OTTO AND GRANT, YOU FOLLOW ME.
WHOEVER SEES BATMAN FIRST, YELL! THEN EVERYBODY ELSE FOLLOW THE SOUND OF THEIR VOICE AND WE'LL CORNER HIM. HE CAN'T TAKE US ALL AT ONCE. GO!
DON'T LIKE THIS. NOT AT ALL.
FOR ONCE, ROCKO, I AGREE WITH YOU. THIS WASN'T IN THE PLAN.
17

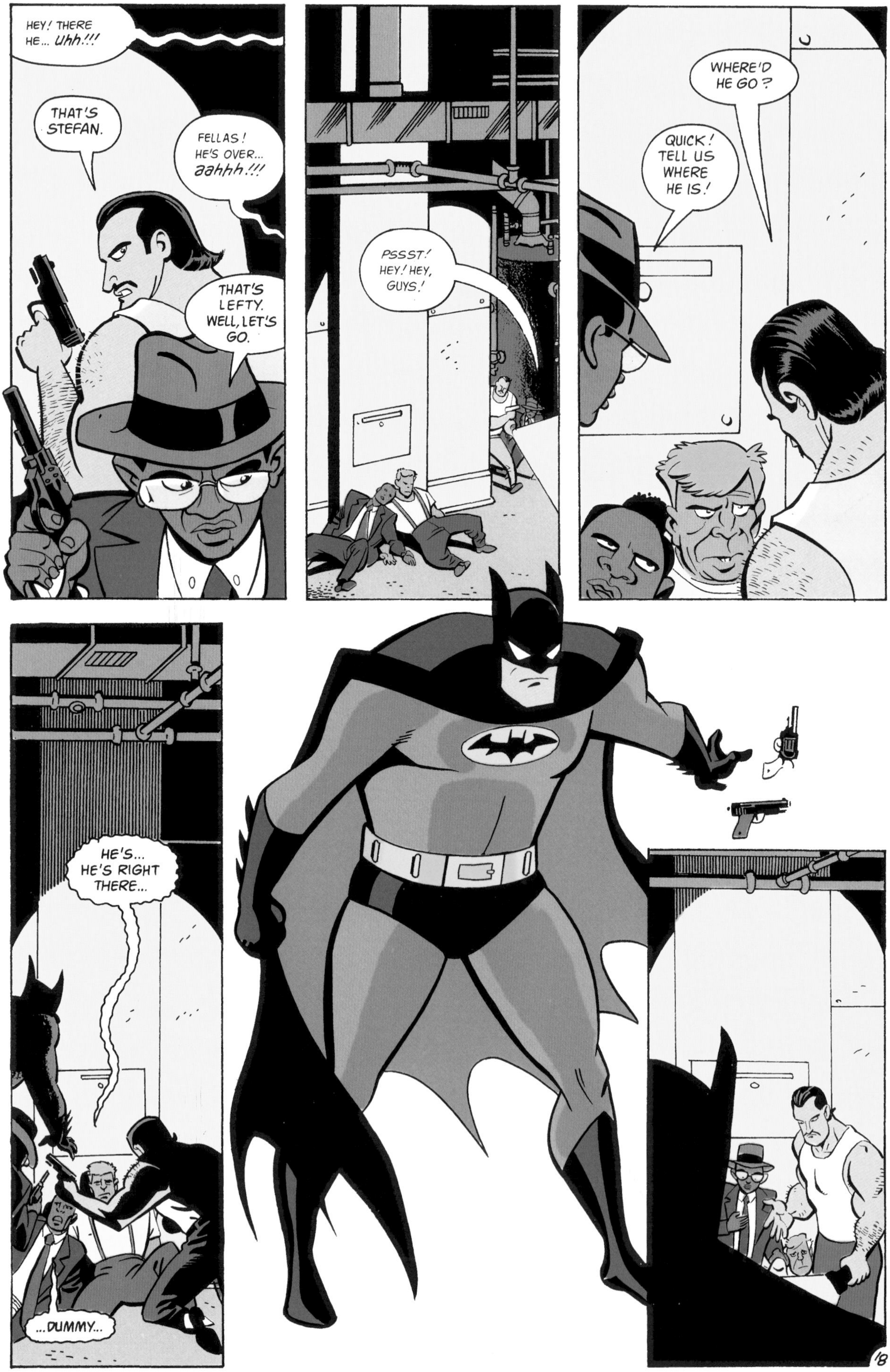
HEY! THERE HE... Uhh!!!
THAT'S STEFAN.
FELLAS! HE'S OVER... aahhh!!!
THAT'S LEFTY. WELL, LET'S GO.
PSSST! HEY! HEY, GUYS!
WHERE'D HE GO?
QUICK! TELL US WHERE HE IS!
HE'S... HE'S RIGHT THERE...
...DUMMY...
18

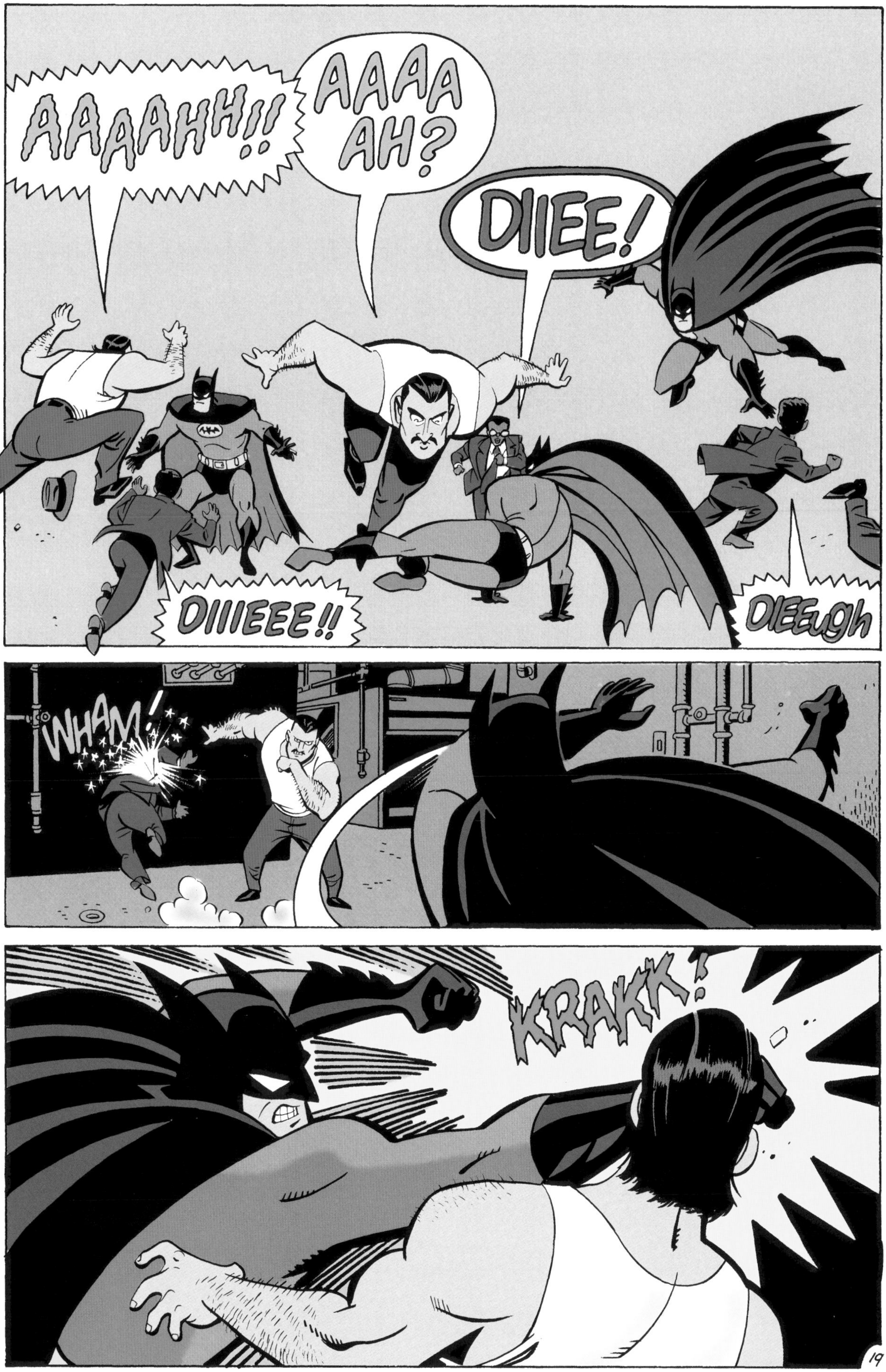
AAAAHH!!
AAAA AH?
DIIEE!
DIIIEEE!!
DIEEugh
WHAM!
KRAKK!
19

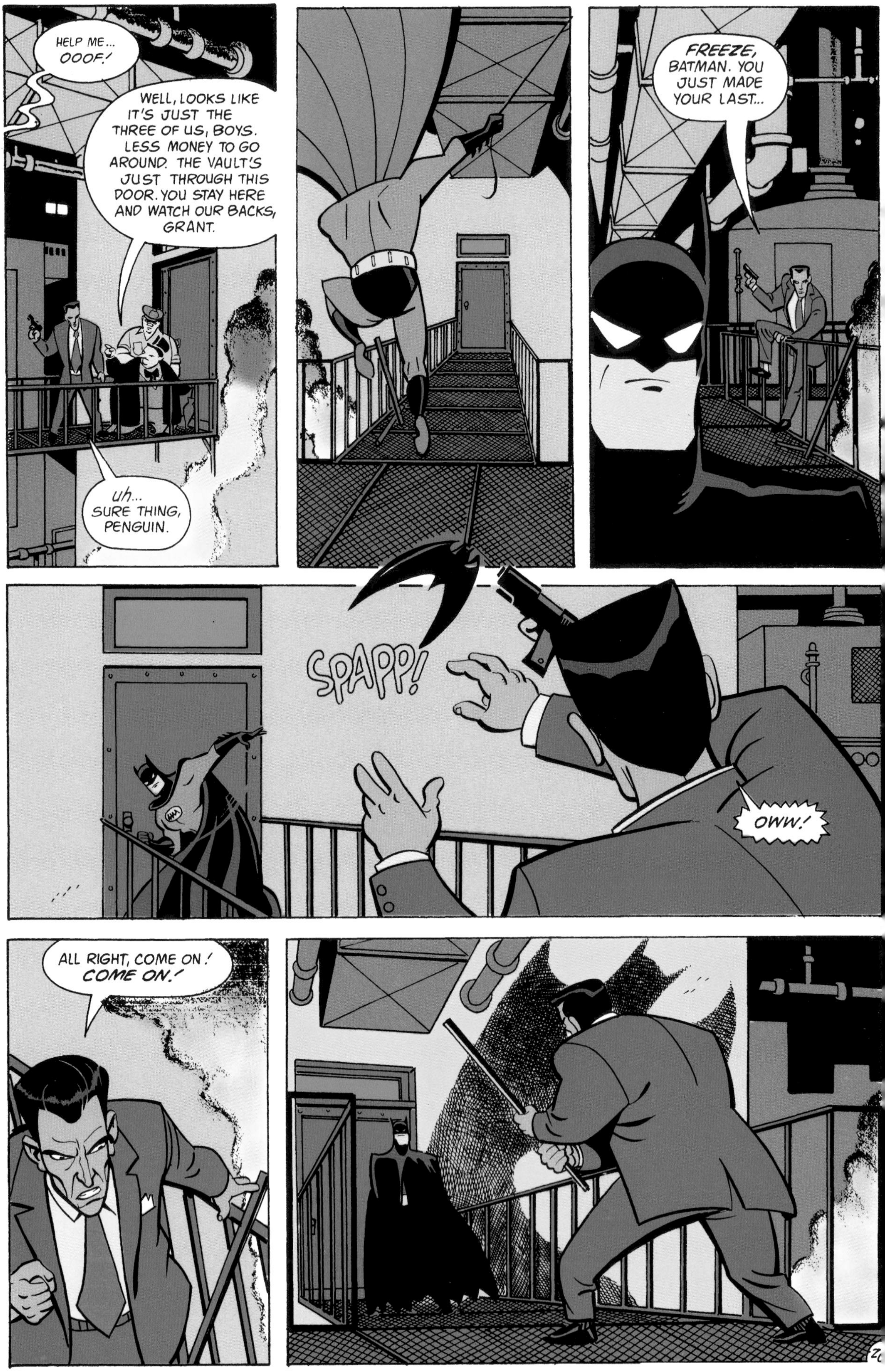
HELP ME... OOOF!
WELL, LOOKS LIKE IT'S JUST THE THREE OF US, BOYS. LESS MONEY TO GO AROUND. THE VAULT'S JUST THROUGH THIS DOOR. YOU STAY HERE AND WATCH OUR BACKS, GRANT.
uh... SURE THING, PENGUIN.
FREEZE, BATMAN. YOU JUST MADE YOUR LAST...
SPAPP!
OWW!
ALL RIGHT, COME ON! COME ON!

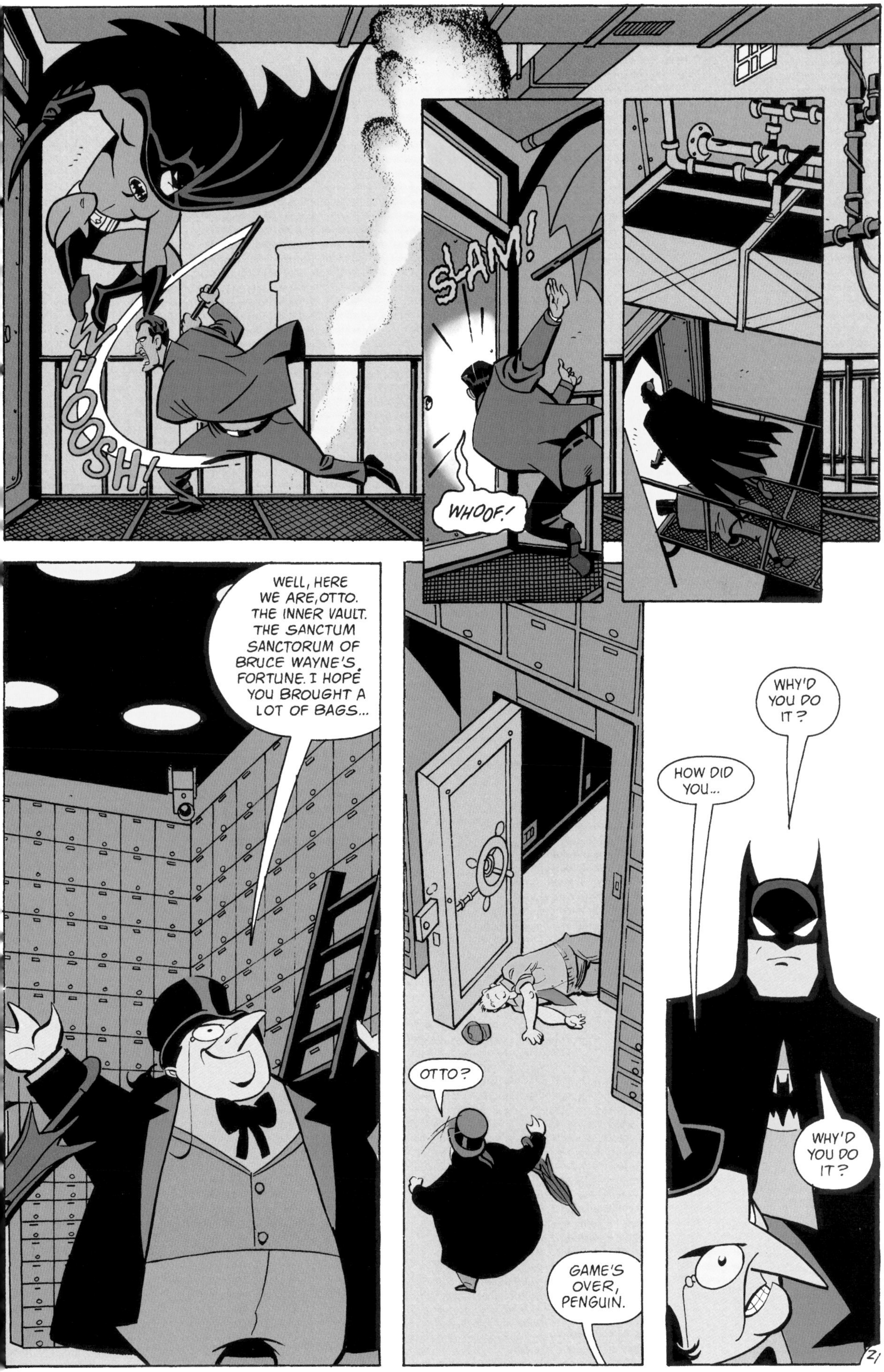
WHOOSH!
SLAM!
WHOOF!
WELL, HERE WE ARE, OTTO. THE INNER VAULT. THE SANCTUM SANCTORUM OF BRUCE WAYNE'S FORTUNE. I HOPE YOU BROUGHT A LOT OF BAGS...
OTTO?
GAME'S OVER, PENGUIN.
HOW DID YOU...
WHY'D YOU DO IT?
WHY'D YOU DO IT?
21

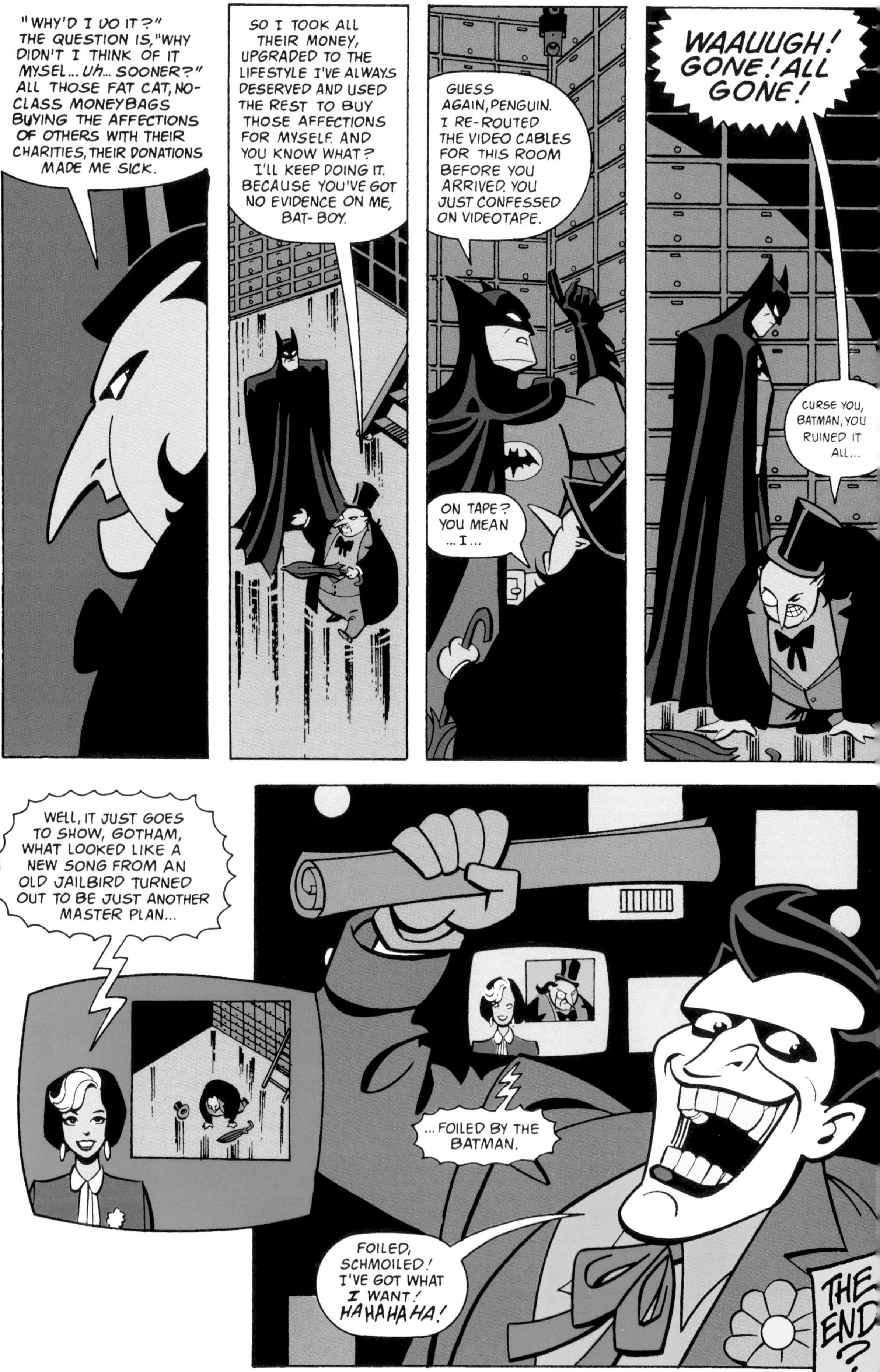
"WHY'D I DO IT?" THE QUESTION IS, "WHY DIDN'T I THINK OF IT MYSEL... Uh... SOONER?" ALL THOSE FAT CAT, NO-CLASS MONEYBAGS BUYING THE AFFECTIONS OF OTHERS WITH THEIR CHARITIES, THEIR DONATIONS MADE ME SICK.
SO I TOOK ALL THEIR MONEY, UPGRADED TO THE LIFESTYLE I'VE ALWAYS DESERVED AND USED THE REST TO BUY THOSE AFFECTIONS FOR MYSELF. AND YOU KNOW WHAT? I'LL KEEP DOING IT. BECAUSE YOU'VE GOT NO EVIDENCE ON ME, BAT-BOY.
GUESS AGAIN, PENGUIN. I RE-ROUTED THE VIDEO CABLES FOR THIS ROOM BEFORE YOU ARRIVED. YOU JUST CONFESSED ON VIDEOTAPE.
ON TAPE? YOU MEAN ...I...
WAAUUGH! GONE! ALL GONE!
CURSE YOU, BATMAN, YOU RUINED IT ALL...
WELL, IT JUST GOES TO SHOW, GOTHAM, WHAT LOOKED LIKE A NEW SONG FROM AN OLD JAILBIRD TURNED OUT TO BE JUST ANOTHER MASTER PLAN...
...FOILED BY THE BATMAN.
FOILED, SCHMOILED! I'VE GOT WHAT I WANT! HAHAHAHA!
THE END?

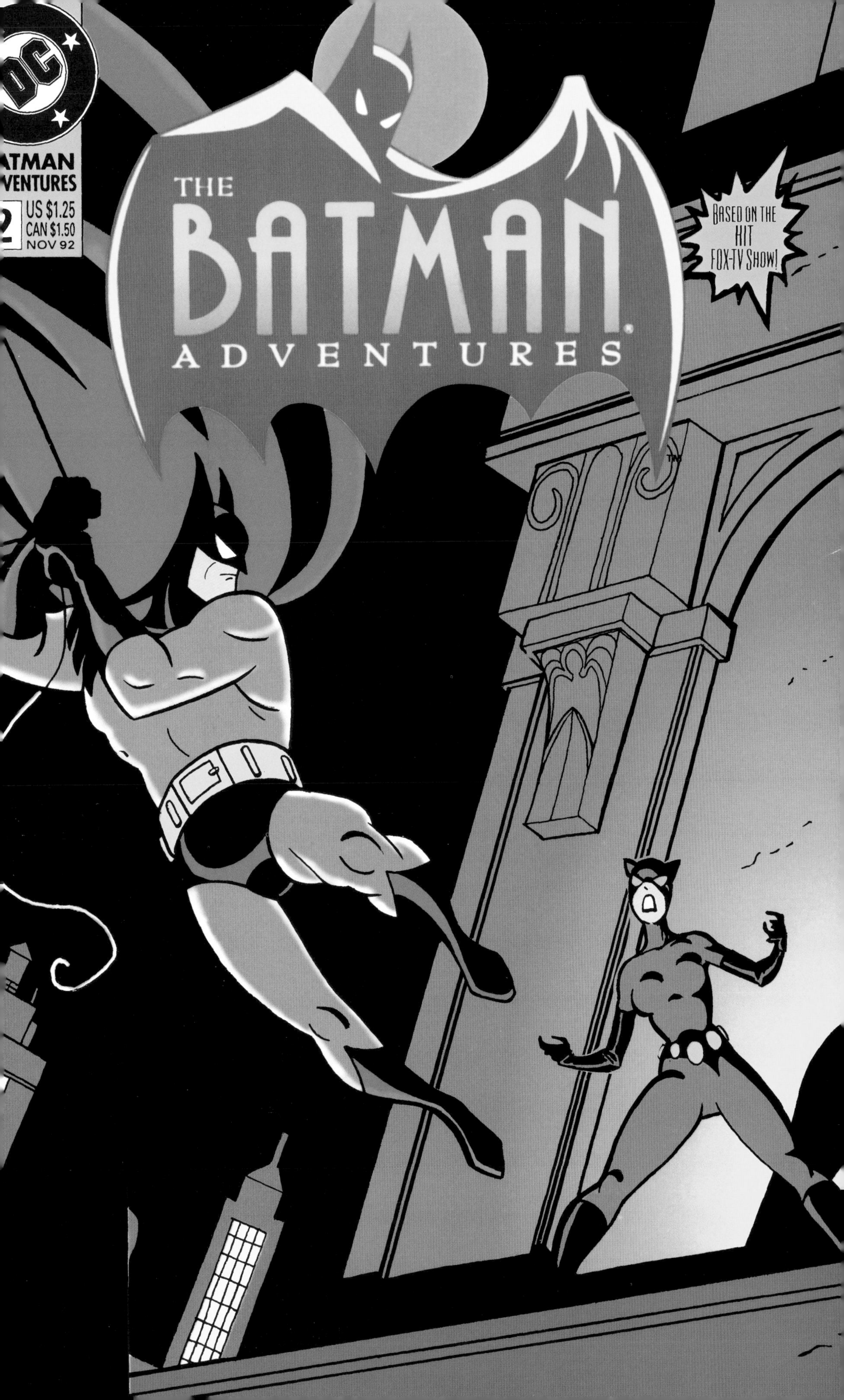
DC
BATMAN ADVENTURES
2
US $1.25
CAN $1.50
NOV 92
THE BATMAN ADVENTURES
TM
BASED ON THE HIT FOX-TV SHOW!

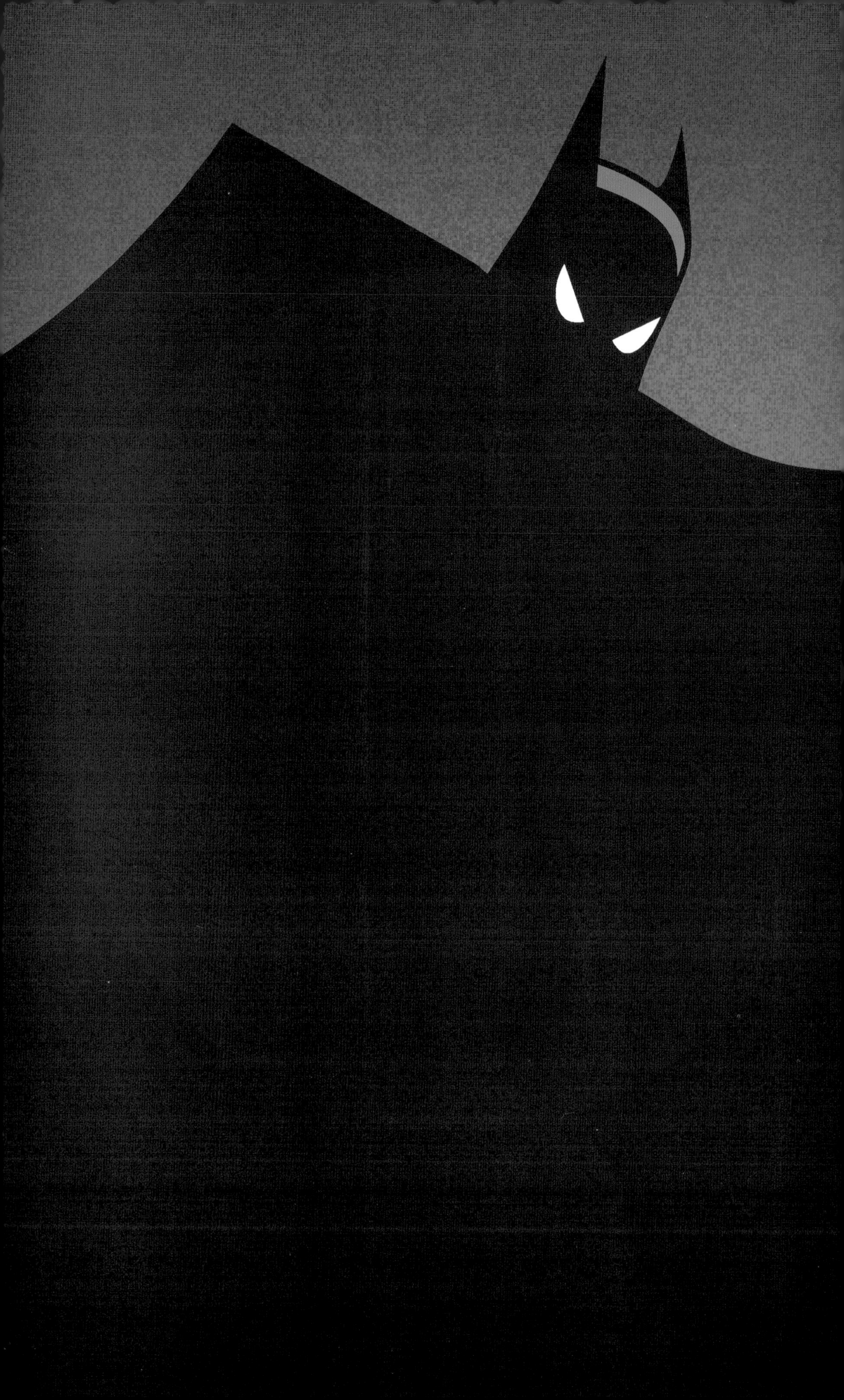

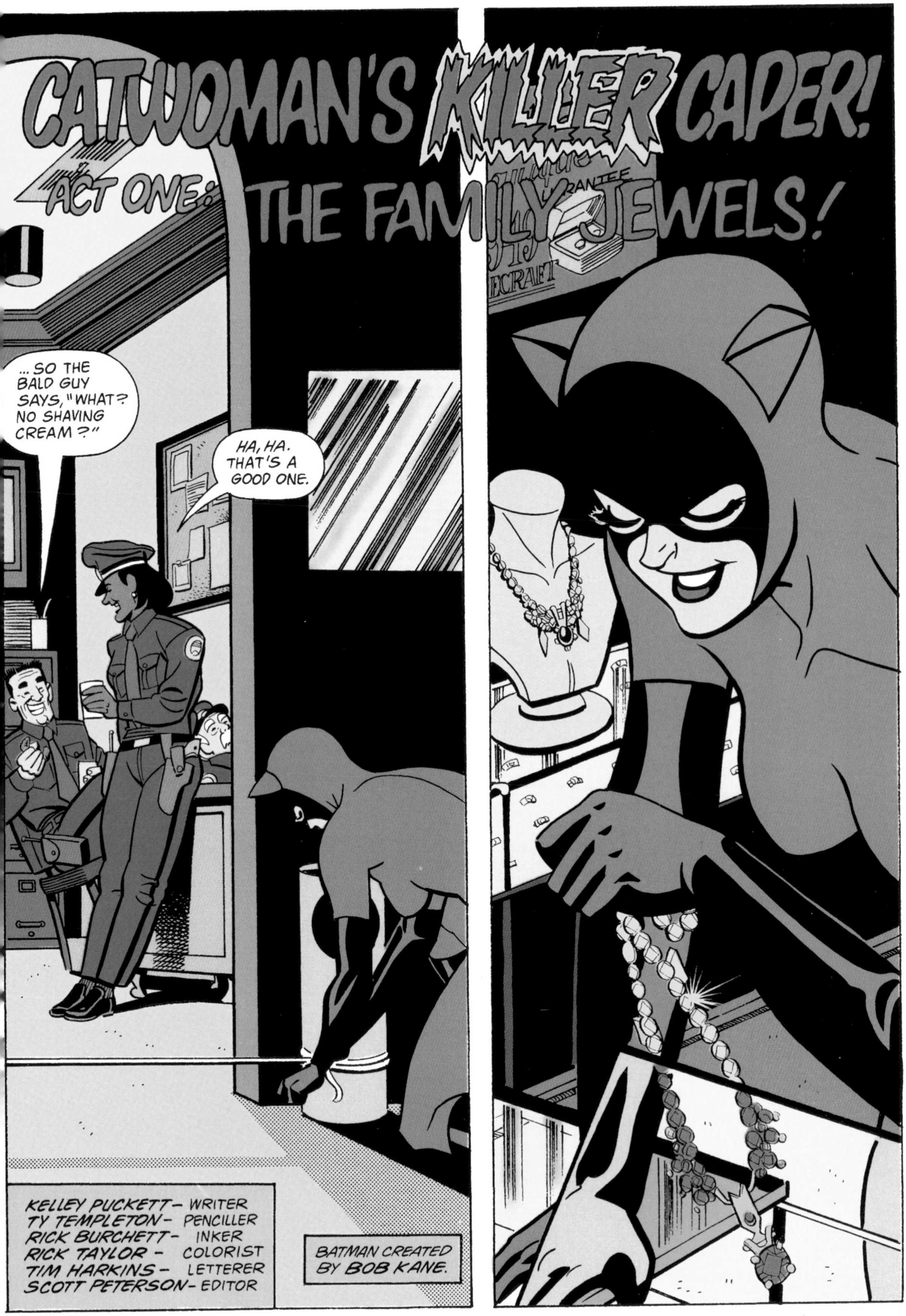
CATWOMAN'S KILLER CAPER!
ACT ONE: THE FAMILY JEWELS!
... SO THE BALD GUY SAYS, "WHAT? NO SHAVING CREAM?"
HA, HA. THAT'S A GOOD ONE.
KELLEY PUCKETT- WRITER
TY TEMPLETON- PENCILLER
RICK BURCHETT- INKER
RICK TAYLOR - COLORIST
TIM HARKINS- LETTERER
SCOTT PETERSON- EDITOR
BATMAN CREATED BY BOB KANE.

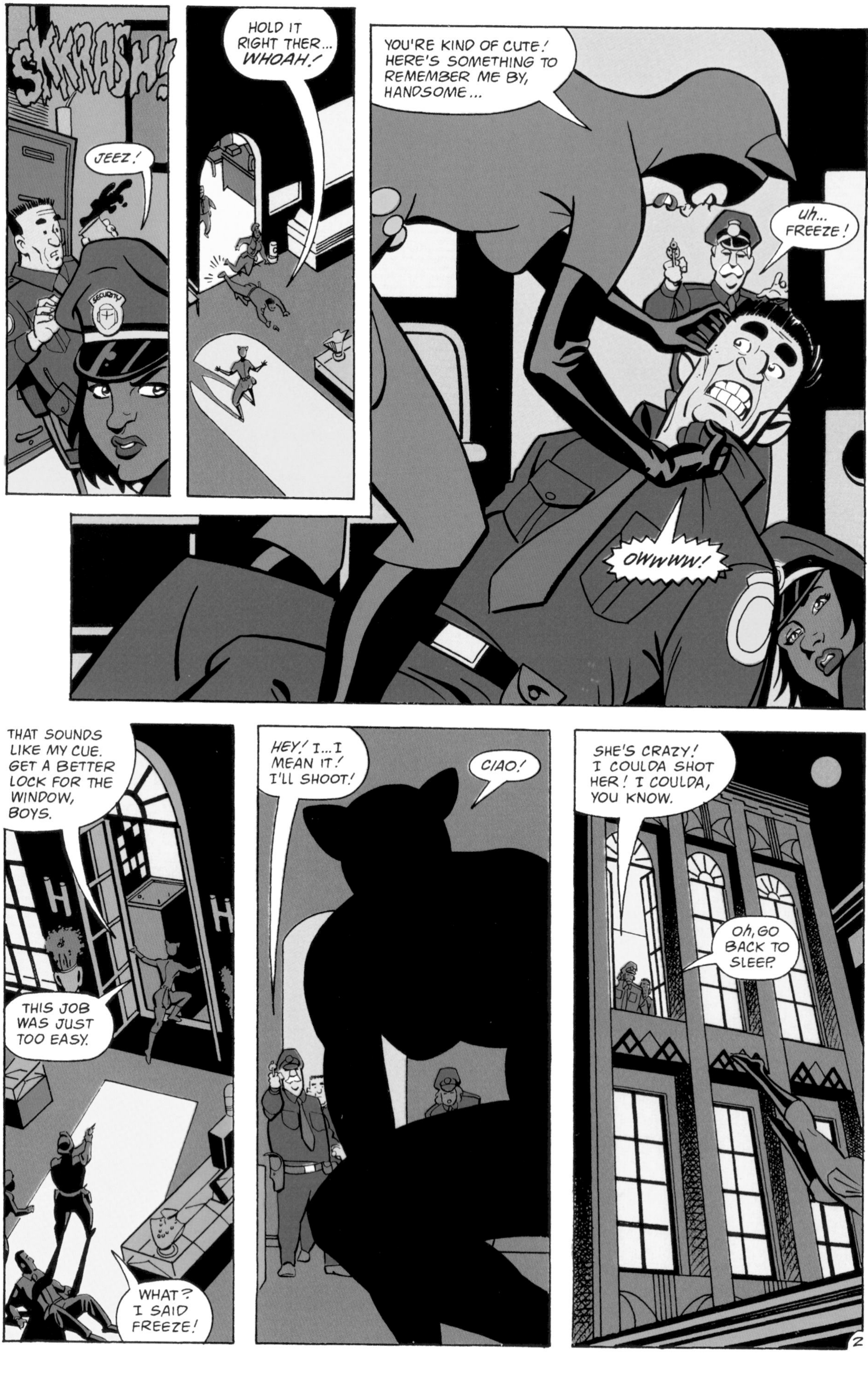
SKKRASH!
JEEZ!
HOLD IT RIGHT THER... WHOAH!
YOU'RE KIND OF CUTE! HERE'S SOMETHING TO REMEMBER ME BY, HANDSOME...
uh... FREEZE!
OWWWW!
THAT SOUNDS LIKE MY CUE. GET A BETTER LOCK FOR THE WINDOW, BOYS.
THIS JOB WAS JUST TOO EASY.
WHAT? I SAID FREEZE!
HEY! I...I MEAN IT! I'LL SHOOT!
CIAO!
SHE'S CRAZY! I COULDA SHOT HER! I COULDA, YOU KNOW.
Oh, GO BACK TO SLEEP.
2

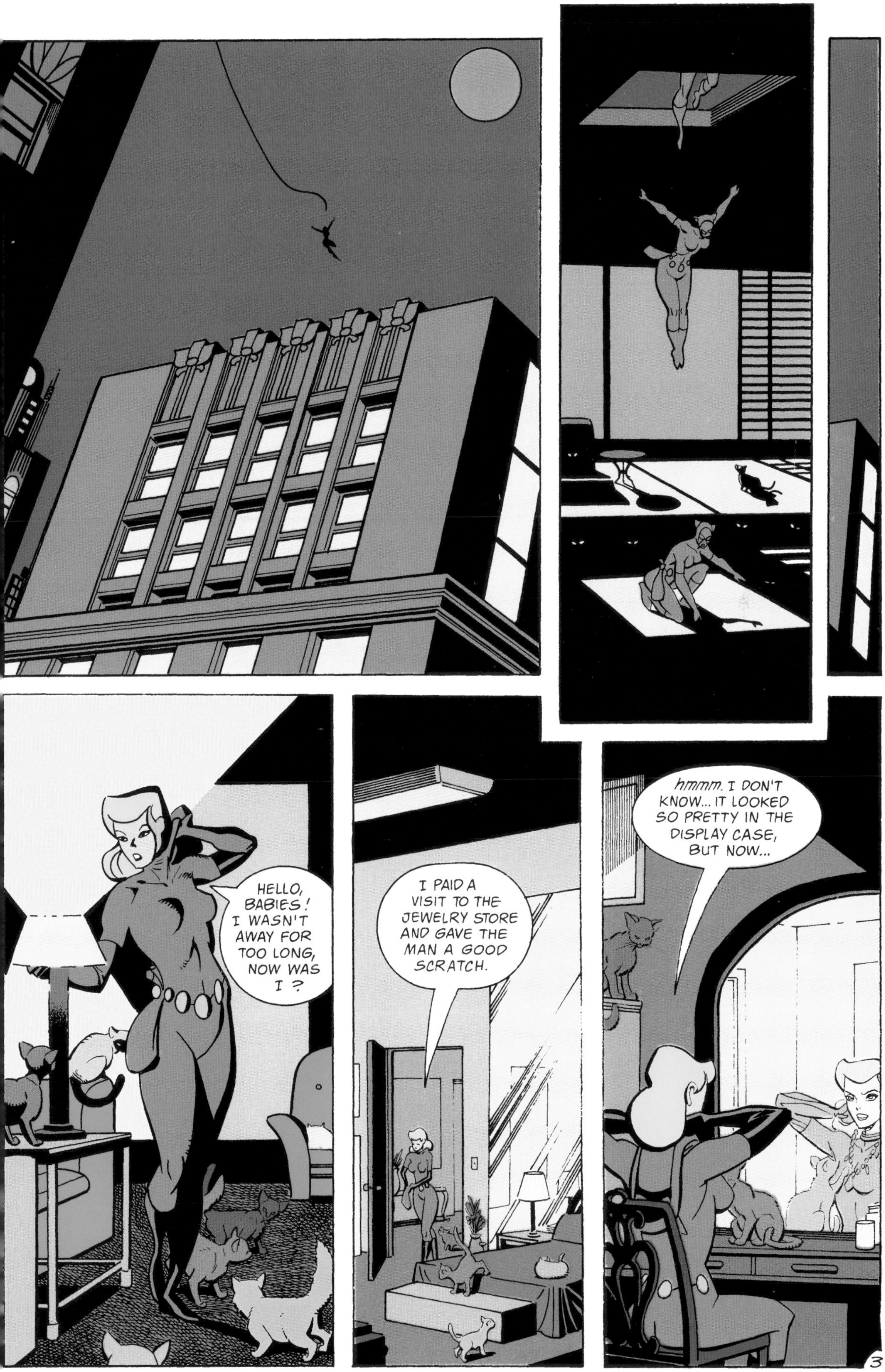
HELLO, BABIES! I WASN'T AWAY FOR TOO LONG, NOW WAS I?
I PAID A VISIT TO THE JEWELRY STORE AND GAVE THE MAN A GOOD SCRATCH.
hmmm. I DON'T KNOW... IT LOOKED SO PRETTY IN THE DISPLAY CASE, BUT NOW...
3

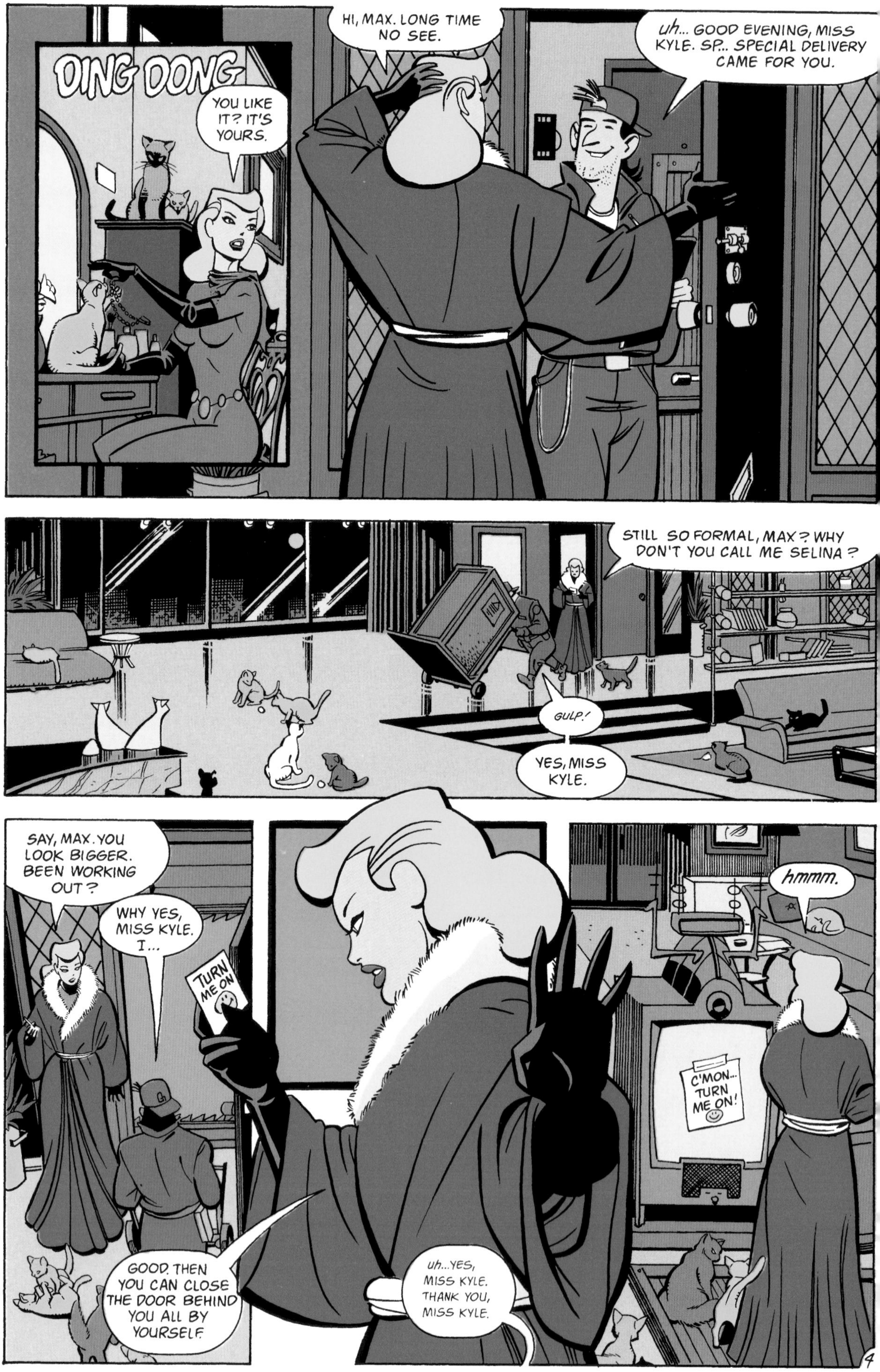
DING DONG
YOU LIKE IT? IT'S YOURS.
HI, MAX. LONG TIME NO SEE.
uh... GOOD EVENING, MISS KYLE. SP... SPECIAL DELIVERY CAME FOR YOU.
STILL SO FORMAL, MAX? WHY DON'T YOU CALL ME SELINA?
GULP!
YES, MISS KYLE.
SAY, MAX. YOU LOOK BIGGER. BEEN WORKING OUT?
WHY YES, MISS KYLE. I...
TURN ME ON
hmmm.
C'MON... TURN ME ON!
GOOD. THEN YOU CAN CLOSE THE DOOR BEHIND YOU ALL BY YOURSELF.
uh...YES, MISS KYLE. THANK YOU, MISS KYLE.
4

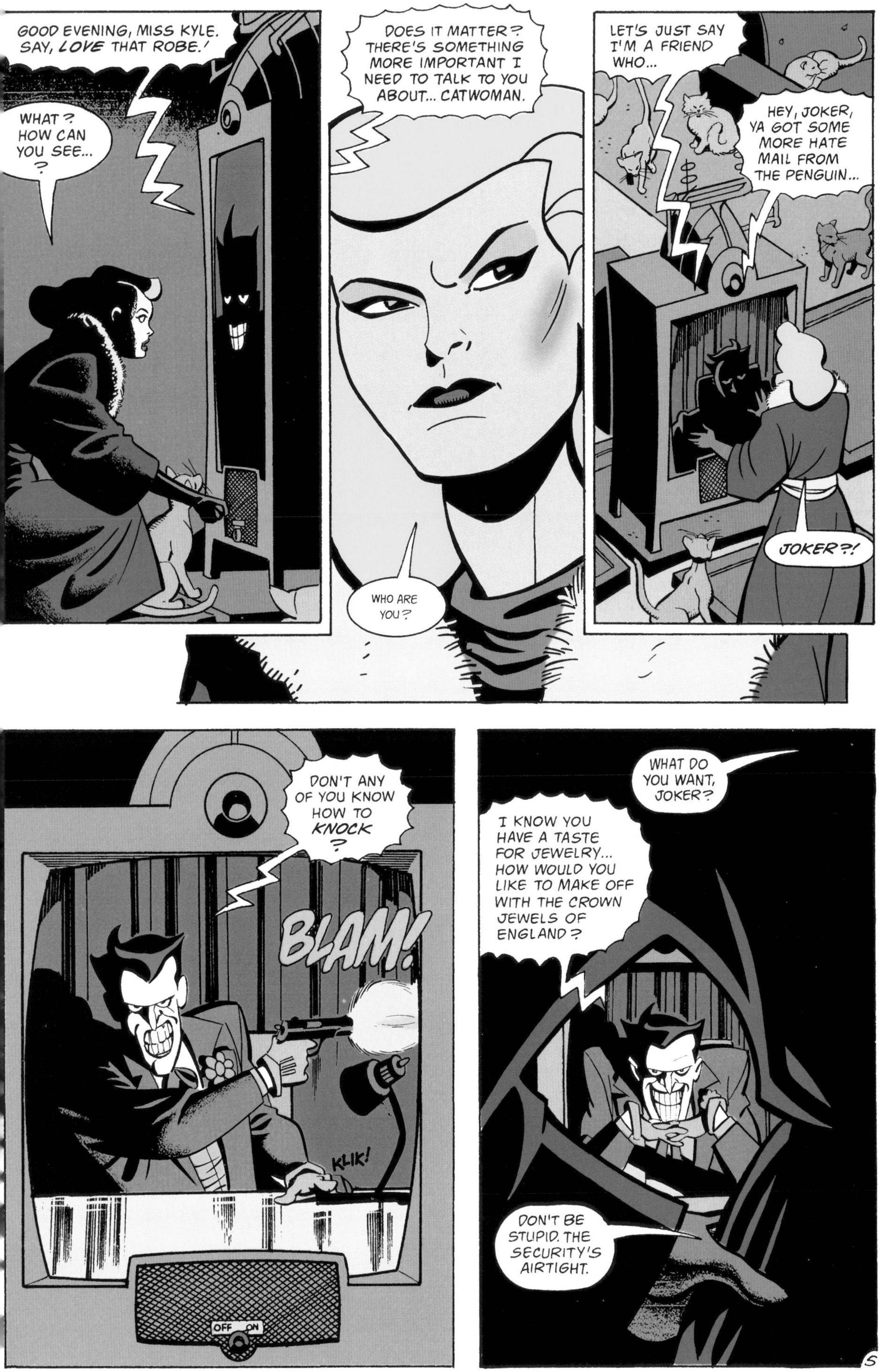

GOOD EVENING, MISS KYLE. SAY, LOVE THAT ROBE.!
WHAT? HOW CAN YOU SEE...?
DOES IT MATTER? THERE'S SOMETHING MORE IMPORTANT I NEED TO TALK TO YOU ABOUT... CATWOMAN.
WHO ARE YOU?
LET'S JUST SAY I'M A FRIEND WHO...
HEY, JOKER, YA GOT SOME MORE HATE MAIL FROM THE PENGUIN...
JOKER?!
DON'T ANY OF YOU KNOW HOW TO KNOCK?
BLAM!
KLIK!
OFF ON
WHAT DO YOU WANT, JOKER?
I KNOW YOU HAVE A TASTE FOR JEWELRY... HOW WOULD YOU LIKE TO MAKE OFF WITH THE CROWN JEWELS OF ENGLAND?
DON'T BE STUPID. THE SECURITY'S AIRTIGHT.

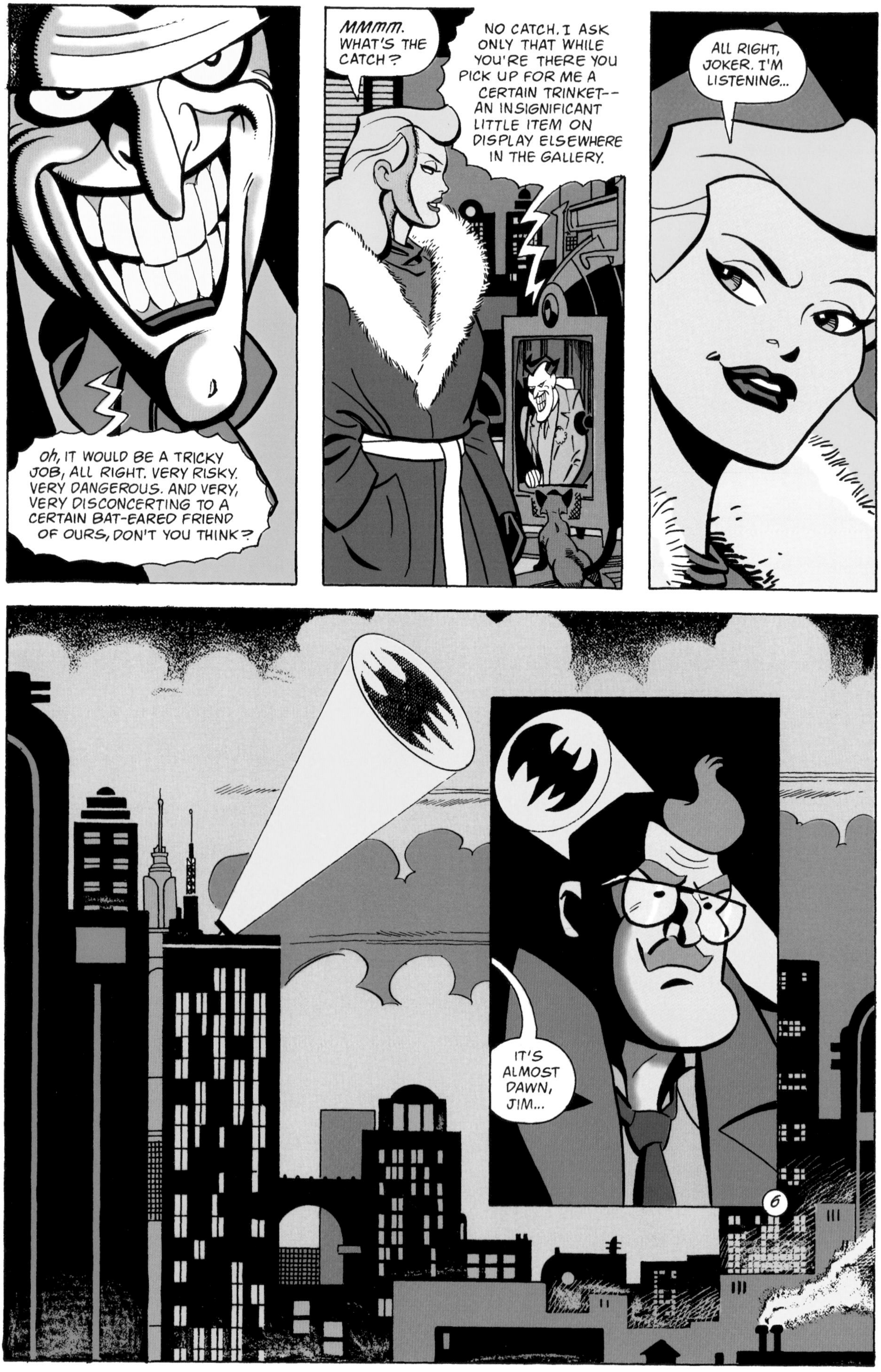
oh, IT WOULD BE A TRICKY JOB, ALL RIGHT. VERY RISKY. VERY DANGEROUS. AND VERY, VERY DISCONCERTING TO A CERTAIN BAT-EARED FRIEND OF OURS, DON'T YOU THINK?
MMMM. WHAT'S THE CATCH?
NO CATCH. I ASK ONLY THAT WHILE YOU'RE THERE YOU PICK UP FOR ME A CERTAIN TRINKET-- AN INSIGNIFICANT LITTLE ITEM ON DISPLAY ELSEWHERE IN THE GALLERY.
ALL RIGHT, JOKER. I'M LISTENING...
IT'S ALMOST DAWN, JIM...
6

...YOU KNOW I DON'T LIKE TO BE OUT THIS LATE.

THIS COULDN'T WAIT.

RECOGNIZE THESE?

THE CROWN JEWELS OF GREAT BRITAIN. THEY'RE ON DISPLAY AT THE TOWER OF LONDON.

NOT ANYMORE. THEY WERE STOLEN LAST NIGHT. THE THIEF KNOCKED OUT TWO GUARDS AND FOILED A *VERY* HIGH-TECH SECURITY SYSTEM. THE GUARDS SAW NOTHING, BUT THE THIEF LEFT A CALLING CARD.

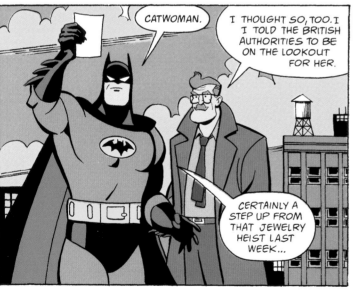

CATWOMAN.

I THOUGHT SO, TOO. I TOLD THE BRITISH AUTHORITIES TO BE ON THE LOOKOUT FOR HER.

CERTAINLY A STEP UP FROM THAT JEWELRY HEIST LAST WEEK...

I ALSO TOLD THEM YOU'D PROBABLY BE IN LONDON BEFORE I HAD A CHANCE TO TURN YOU OVER TO THEM FOR QUESTIONING.

THANKS, JIM. YOU KEEP STICKING YOUR NECK OUT FOR ME.

YOU KEEP MAKING IT WORTH MY WHILE.

7

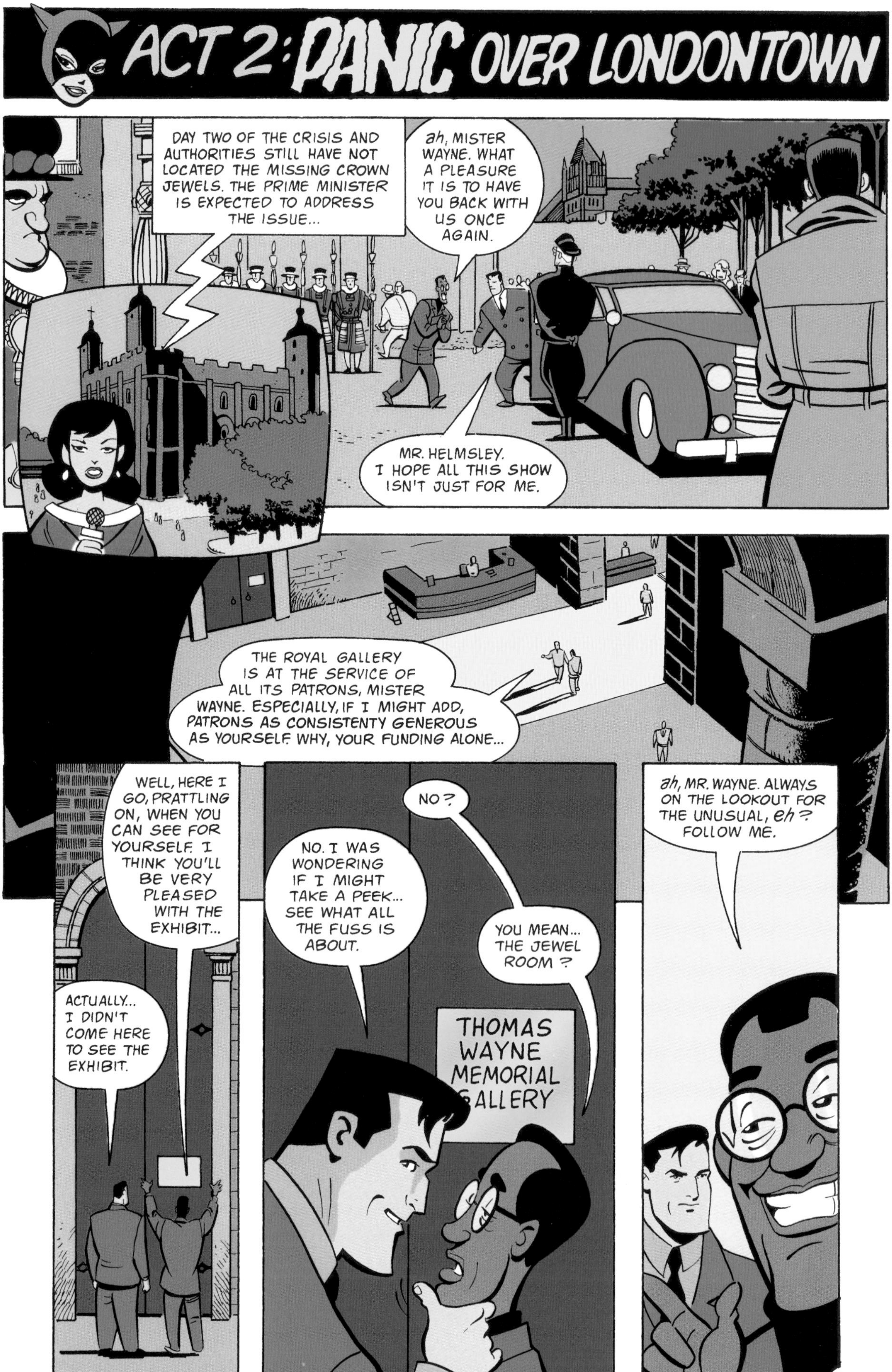

ACT 2: PANIC OVER LONDONTOWN
DAY TWO OF THE CRISIS AND AUTHORITIES STILL HAVE NOT LOCATED THE MISSING CROWN JEWELS. THE PRIME MINISTER IS EXPECTED TO ADDRESS THE ISSUE...
ah, MISTER WAYNE. WHAT A PLEASURE IT IS TO HAVE YOU BACK WITH US ONCE AGAIN.
MR. HELMSLEY. I HOPE ALL THIS SHOW ISN'T JUST FOR ME.
THE ROYAL GALLERY IS AT THE SERVICE OF ALL ITS PATRONS, MISTER WAYNE. ESPECIALLY, IF I MIGHT ADD, PATRONS AS CONSISTENTY GENEROUS AS YOURSELF. WHY, YOUR FUNDING ALONE...
WELL, HERE I GO, PRATTLING ON, WHEN YOU CAN SEE FOR YOURSELF. I THINK YOU'LL BE VERY PLEASED WITH THE EXHIBIT...
ACTUALLY... I DIDN'T COME HERE TO SEE THE EXHIBIT.
NO?
NO. I WAS WONDERING IF I MIGHT TAKE A PEEK... SEE WHAT ALL THE FUSS IS ABOUT.
YOU MEAN... THE JEWEL ROOM?
THOMAS WAYNE MEMORIAL GALLERY
ah, MR. WAYNE. ALWAYS ON THE LOOKOUT FOR THE UNUSUAL, eh? FOLLOW ME.
8

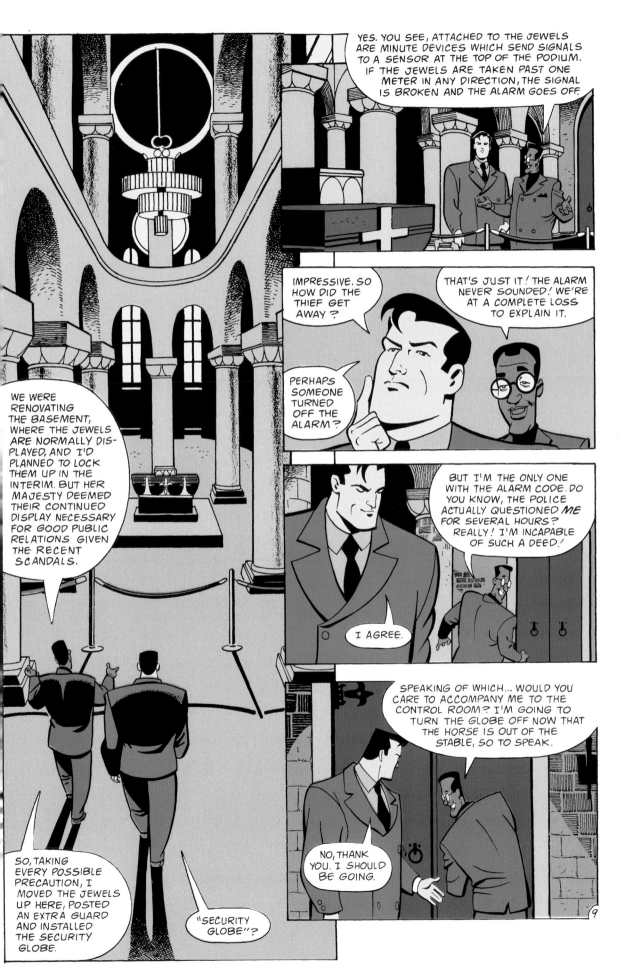

YES. YOU SEE, ATTACHED TO THE JEWELS ARE MINUTE DEVICES WHICH SEND SIGNALS TO A SENSOR AT THE TOP OF THE PODIUM. IF THE JEWELS ARE TAKEN PAST ONE METER IN ANY DIRECTION, THE SIGNAL IS BROKEN AND THE ALARM GOES OFF.

IMPRESSIVE. SO HOW DID THE THIEF GET AWAY?

THAT'S JUST IT! THE ALARM NEVER SOUNDED! WE'RE AT A COMPLETE LOSS TO EXPLAIN IT.

PERHAPS SOMEONE TURNED OFF THE ALARM?

WE WERE RENOVATING THE BASEMENT, WHERE THE JEWELS ARE NORMALLY DISPLAYED, AND I'D PLANNED TO LOCK THEM UP IN THE INTERIM. BUT HER MAJESTY DEEMED THEIR CONTINUED DISPLAY NECESSARY FOR GOOD PUBLIC RELATIONS GIVEN THE RECENT SCANDALS.

BUT I'M THE ONLY ONE WITH THE ALARM CODE. DO YOU KNOW, THE POLICE ACTUALLY QUESTIONED ME FOR SEVERAL HOURS? REALLY! I'M INCAPABLE OF SUCH A DEED!

I AGREE.

SPEAKING OF WHICH... WOULD YOU CARE TO ACCOMPANY ME TO THE CONTROL ROOM? I'M GOING TO TURN THE GLOBE OFF NOW THAT THE HORSE IS OUT OF THE STABLE, SO TO SPEAK.

NO, THANK YOU. I SHOULD BE GOING.

SO, TAKING EVERY POSSIBLE PRECAUTION, I MOVED THE JEWELS UP HERE, POSTED AN EXTRA GUARD AND INSTALLED THE SECURITY GLOBE.

"SECURITY GLOBE"?

9

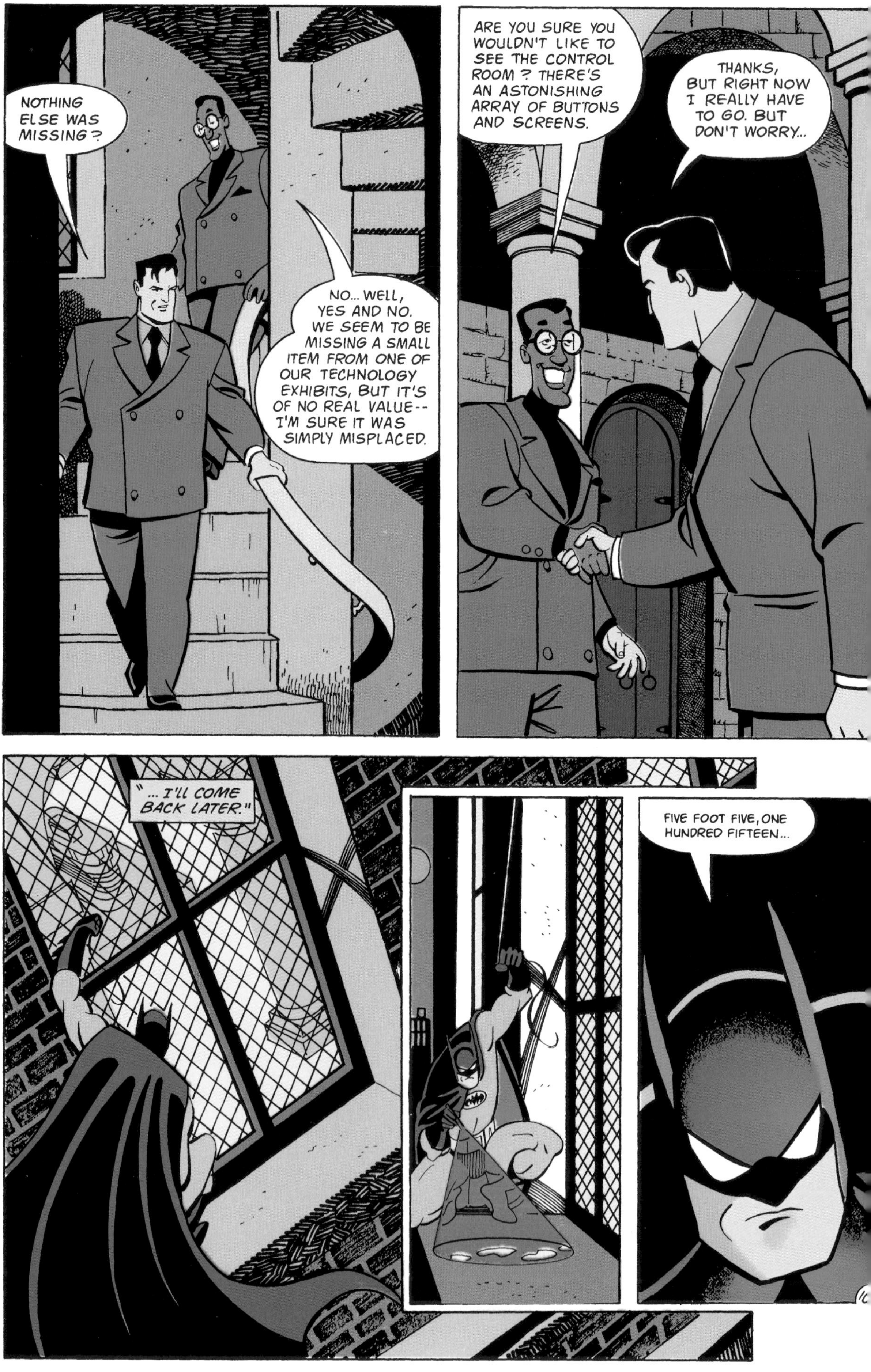
NOTHING ELSE WAS MISSING?
NO... WELL, YES AND NO. WE SEEM TO BE MISSING A SMALL ITEM FROM ONE OF OUR TECHNOLOGY EXHIBITS, BUT IT'S OF NO REAL VALUE-- I'M SURE IT WAS SIMPLY MISPLACED.
ARE YOU SURE YOU WOULDN'T LIKE TO SEE THE CONTROL ROOM? THERE'S AN ASTONISHING ARRAY OF BUTTONS AND SCREENS.
THANKS, BUT RIGHT NOW I REALLY HAVE TO GO. BUT DON'T WORRY...
"...I'LL COME BACK LATER."
FIVE FOOT FIVE, ONE HUNDRED FIFTEEN...

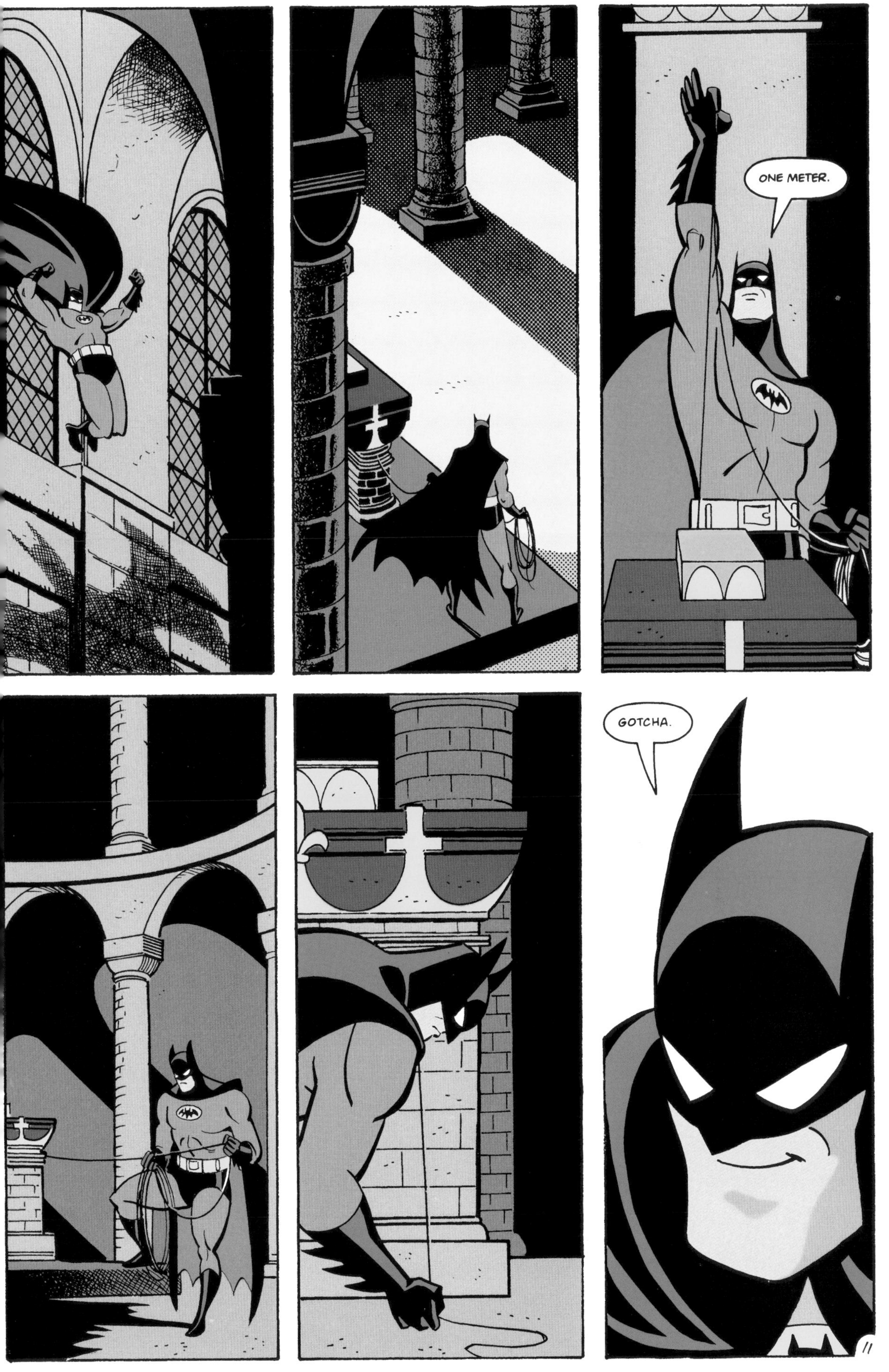
ONE METER.
GOTCHA.
11

LONDON REGENCY.

... AUTHORITIES REFUSED TO SPECULATE ON WHAT HE MIGHT HAVE BEEN DOING THERE.

A MEMORIAL SERVICE FOR THE AMBASSADOR WILL BE HELD ON THURSDAY NEXT.

COME ON! GET TO THE *REAL* NEWS!

THIS SHOULD KEEP JOKER HAPPY.

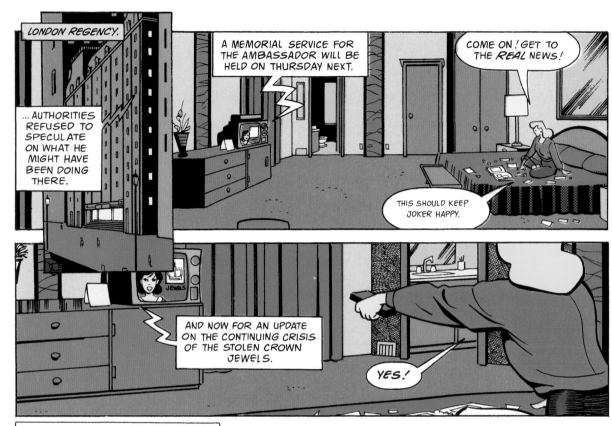

AND NOW FOR AN UPDATE ON THE CONTINUING CRISIS OF THE STOLEN CROWN JEWELS.

YES!

WE'VE EXAMINED THE EVIDENCE IN CONSIDERABLE DETAIL AND CAN NOW SAY WITH ALMOST ABSOLUTE CERTAINTY THAT THE CROWN JEWELS HAVE IN FACT BEEN STOLEN.

WE NOW BEGIN THE LONG AND DIFFICULT PROCESS OF DETERMINING THE IDENTITY OF THE PERSON OR PERSONS RESPONSIBLE FOR THE THEFT.

REC

HA! IDIOTS!

MORE ON THIS STORY AS IT DEVELOPS. WE GO NOW TO THE EAST END, WHERE REPORTER TAYLOR MACDONALD HAS A STORY OF A DARING ESCAPE FROM NORWICH COURTHOUSE.

THEY HAVEN'T GOT A CLUE...

12

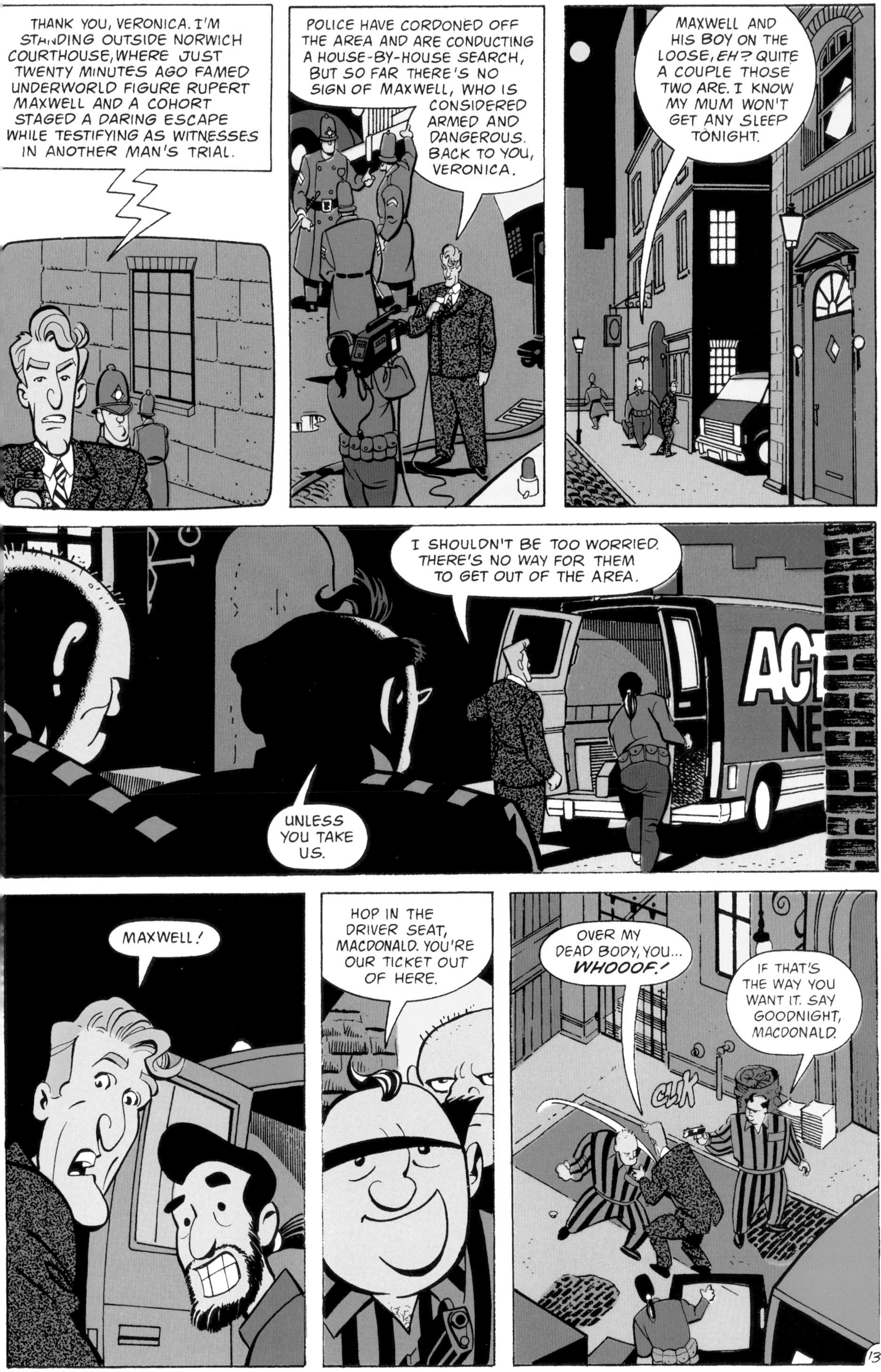
THANK YOU, VERONICA. I'M STANDING OUTSIDE NORWICH COURTHOUSE, WHERE JUST TWENTY MINUTES AGO FAMED UNDERWORLD FIGURE RUPERT MAXWELL AND A COHORT STAGED A DARING ESCAPE WHILE TESTIFYING AS WITNESSES IN ANOTHER MAN'S TRIAL.
POLICE HAVE CORDONED OFF THE AREA AND ARE CONDUCTING A HOUSE-BY-HOUSE SEARCH, BUT SO FAR THERE'S NO SIGN OF MAXWELL, WHO IS CONSIDERED ARMED AND DANGEROUS. BACK TO YOU, VERONICA.
MAXWELL AND HIS BOY ON THE LOOSE, *EH?* QUITE A COUPLE THOSE TWO ARE. I KNOW MY MUM WON'T GET ANY SLEEP TONIGHT.
I SHOULDN'T BE TOO WORRIED. THERE'S NO WAY FOR THEM TO GET OUT OF THE AREA.
UNLESS YOU TAKE US.
ACT NE
MAXWELL!
HOP IN THE DRIVER SEAT, MACDONALD. YOU'RE OUR TICKET OUT OF HERE.
OVER MY DEAD BODY, YOU... **WHOOOF!**
IF THAT'S THE WAY YOU WANT IT. SAY GOODNIGHT, MACDONALD.
CLIK
13

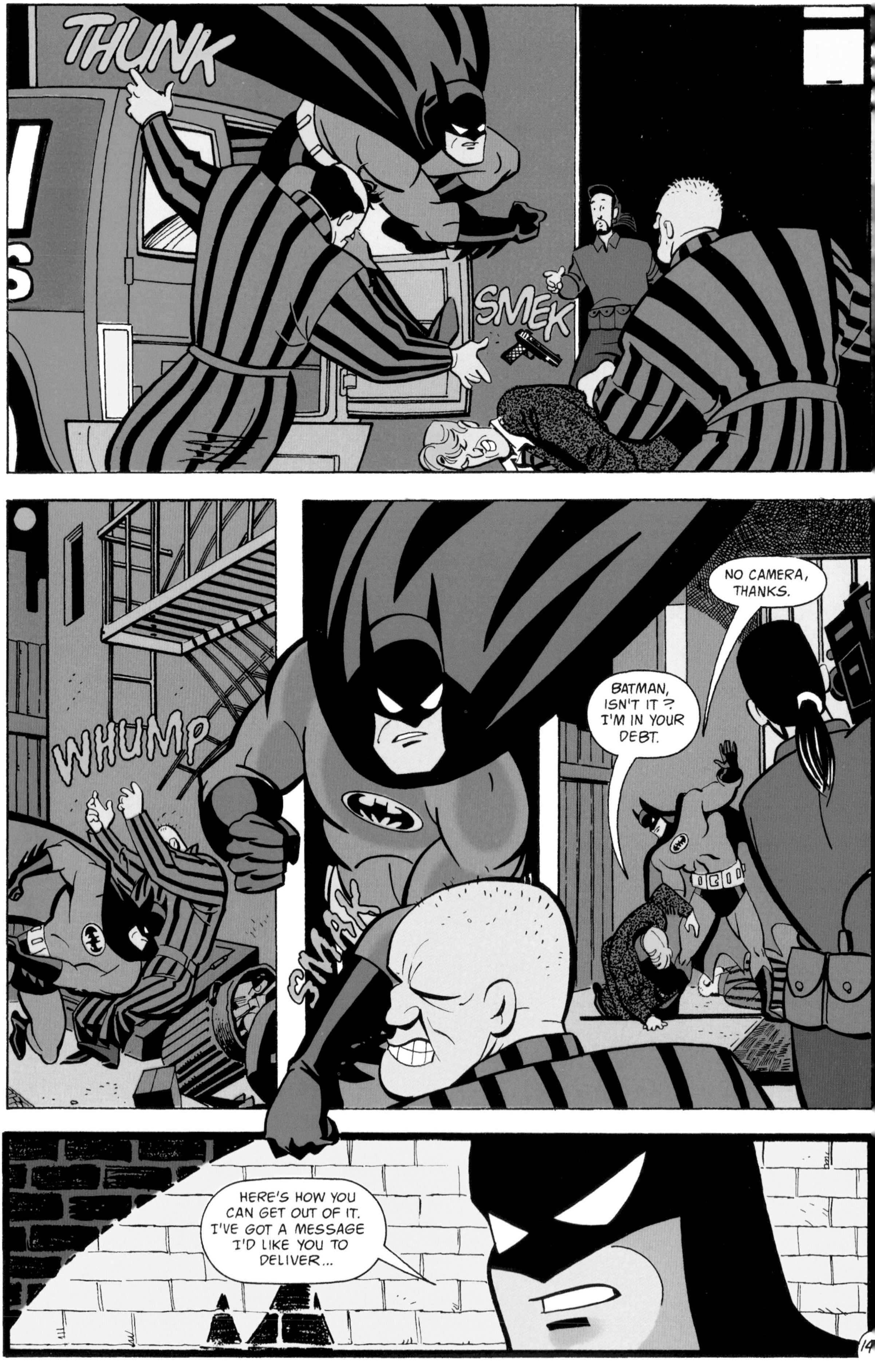
THUNK
SMEK
WHUMP
SMAK
NO CAMERA, THANKS.
BATMAN, ISN'T IT? I'M IN YOUR DEBT.
HERE'S HOW YOU CAN GET OUT OF IT. I'VE GOT A MESSAGE I'D LIKE YOU TO DELIVER...
14

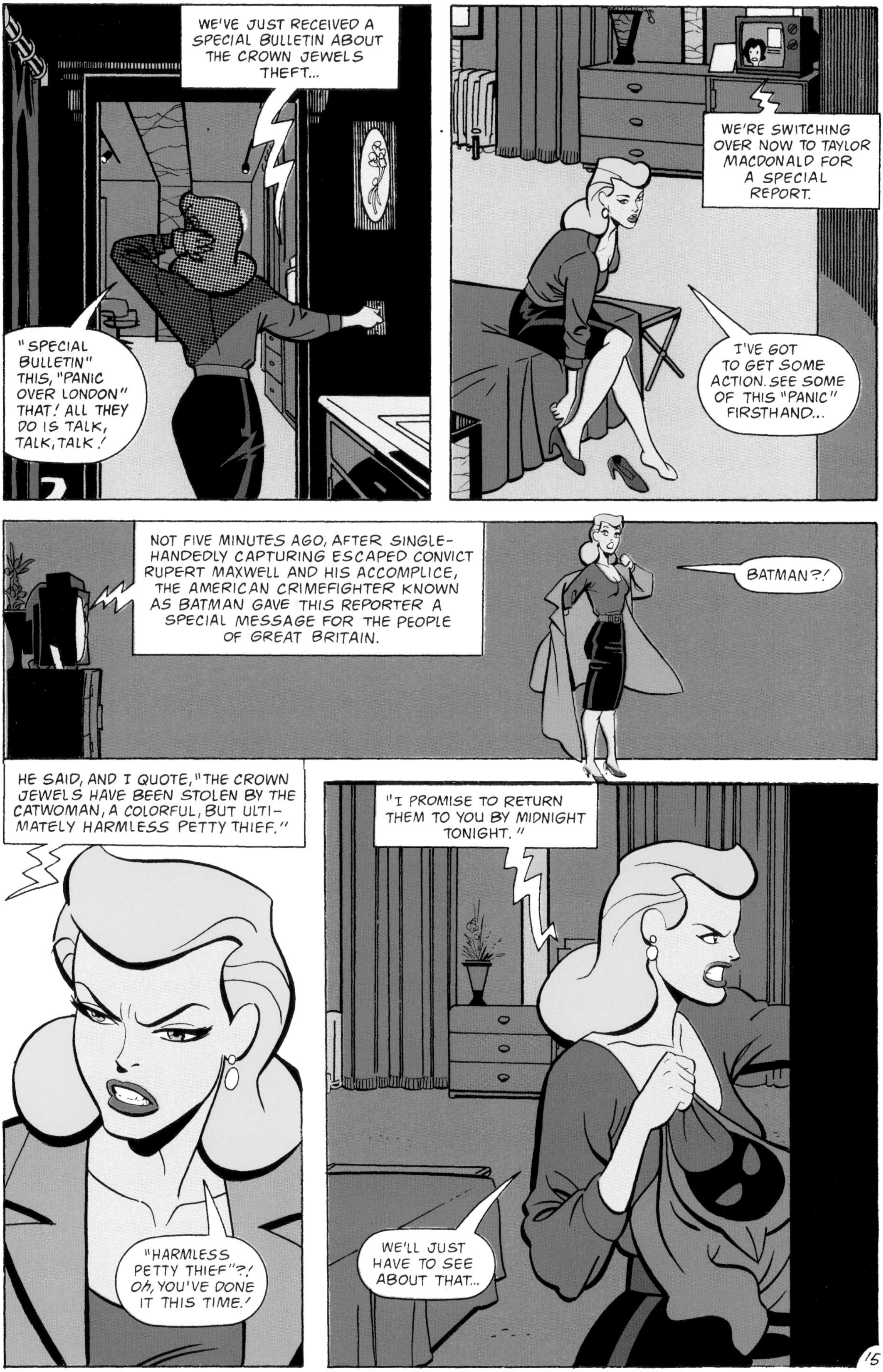

WE'VE JUST RECEIVED A SPECIAL BULLETIN ABOUT THE CROWN JEWELS THEFT...
"SPECIAL BULLETIN" THIS, "PANIC OVER LONDON" THAT! ALL THEY DO IS TALK, TALK, TALK!
WE'RE SWITCHING OVER NOW TO TAYLOR MACDONALD FOR A SPECIAL REPORT.
I'VE GOT TO GET SOME ACTION. SEE SOME OF THIS "PANIC" FIRSTHAND...
NOT FIVE MINUTES AGO, AFTER SINGLE-HANDEDLY CAPTURING ESCAPED CONVICT RUPERT MAXWELL AND HIS ACCOMPLICE, THE AMERICAN CRIMEFIGHTER KNOWN AS BATMAN GAVE THIS REPORTER A SPECIAL MESSAGE FOR THE PEOPLE OF GREAT BRITAIN.
BATMAN?!
HE SAID, AND I QUOTE, "THE CROWN JEWELS HAVE BEEN STOLEN BY THE CATWOMAN, A COLORFUL, BUT ULTIMATELY HARMLESS PETTY THIEF."
"HARMLESS PETTY THIEF"?! Oh, YOU'VE DONE IT THIS TIME!
"I PROMISE TO RETURN THEM TO YOU BY MIDNIGHT TONIGHT."
WE'LL JUST HAVE TO SEE ABOUT THAT...
15

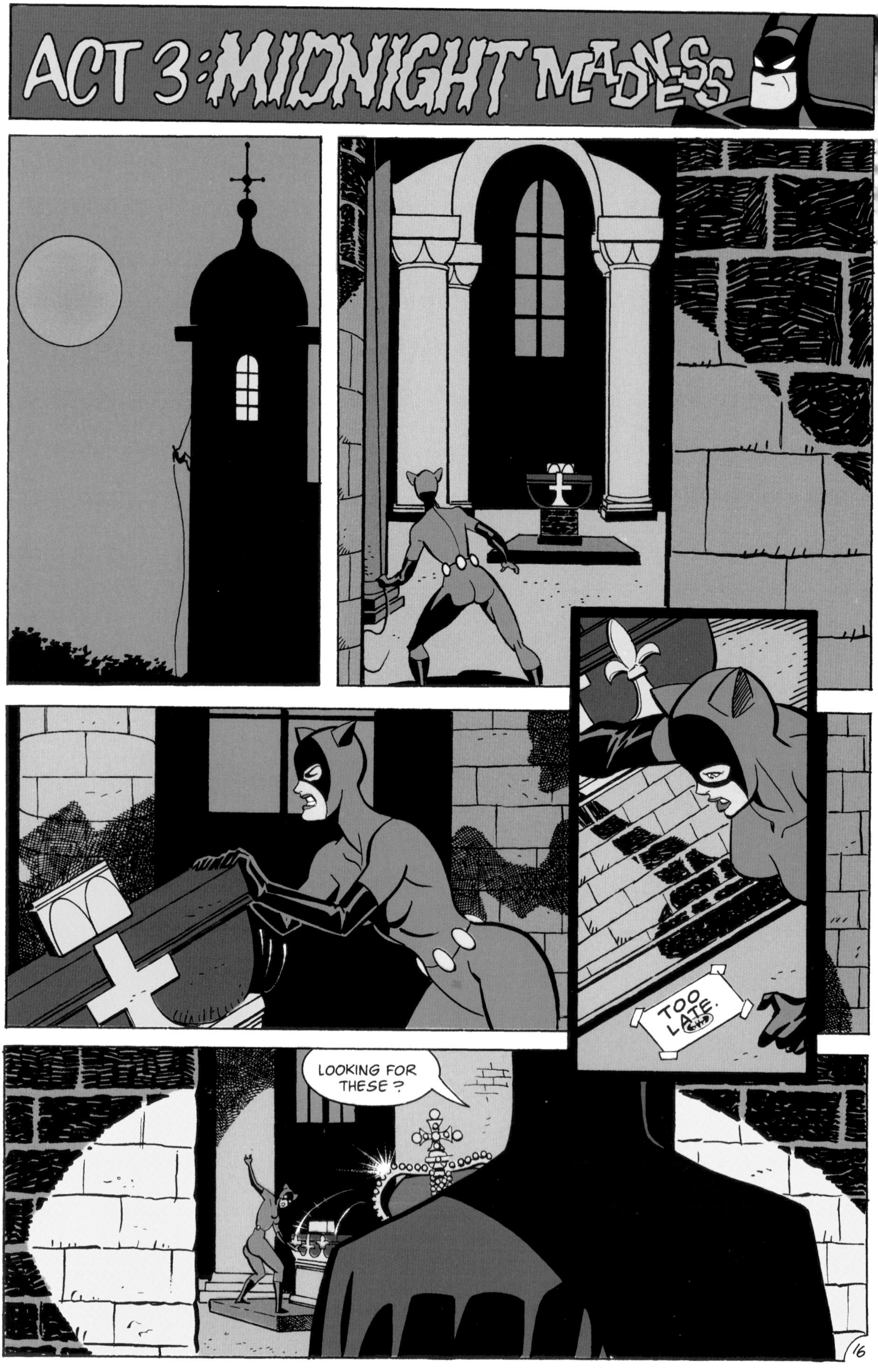
ACT 3: MIDNIGHT MADNESS
TOO LATE.
LOOKING FOR THESE?
16

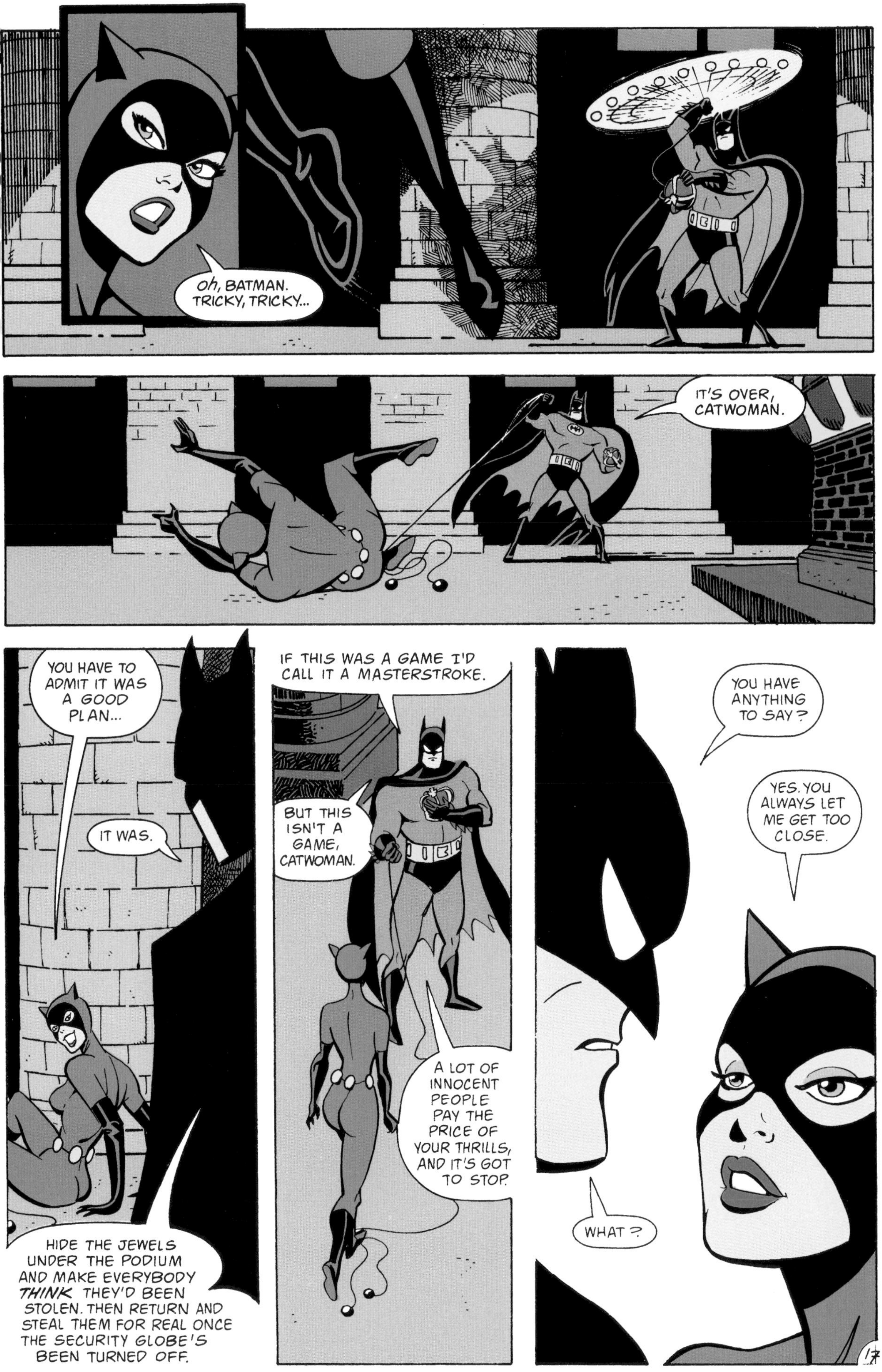

oh, BATMAN. TRICKY, TRICKY...
IT'S OVER, CATWOMAN.
YOU HAVE TO ADMIT IT WAS A GOOD PLAN...
IT WAS.
HIDE THE JEWELS UNDER THE PODIUM AND MAKE EVERYBODY THINK THEY'D BEEN STOLEN. THEN RETURN AND STEAL THEM FOR REAL ONCE THE SECURITY GLOBE'S BEEN TURNED OFF.
IF THIS WAS A GAME I'D CALL IT A MASTERSTROKE.
BUT THIS ISN'T A GAME, CATWOMAN.
A LOT OF INNOCENT PEOPLE PAY THE PRICE OF YOUR THRILLS, AND IT'S GOT TO STOP.
YOU HAVE ANYTHING TO SAY?
YES. YOU ALWAYS LET ME GET TOO CLOSE.
WHAT?
17

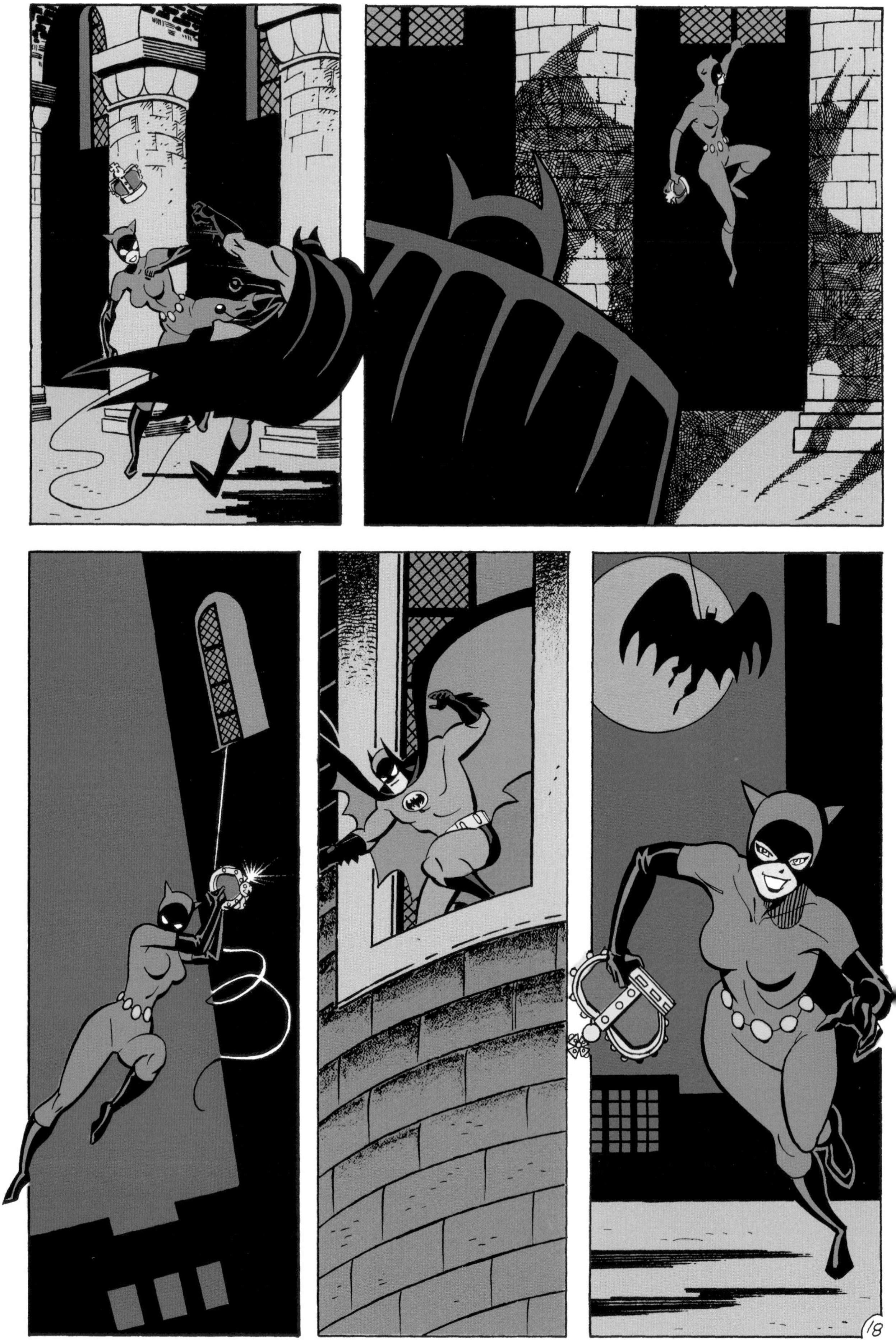
18

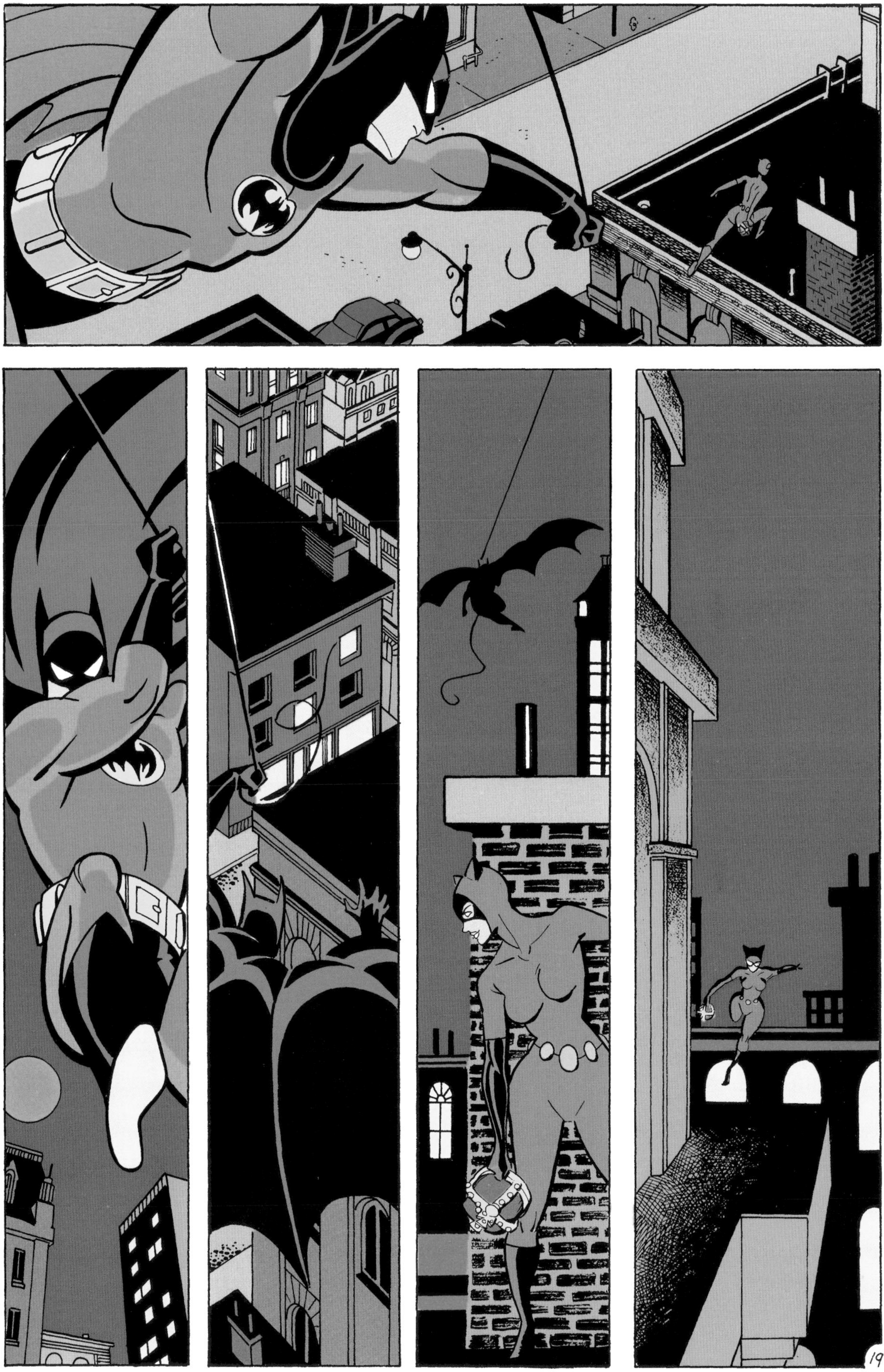
19

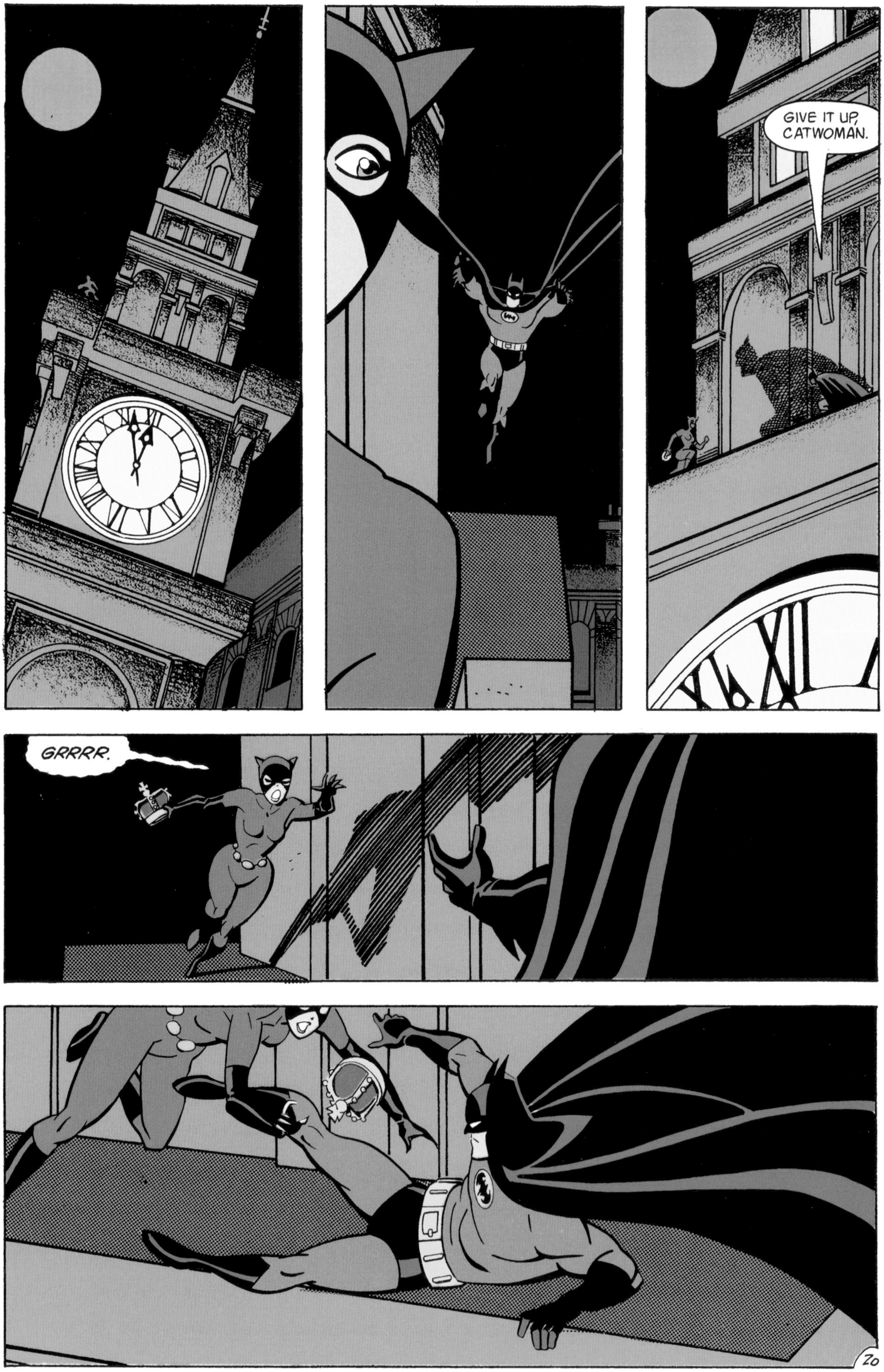

GIVE IT UP, CATWOMAN.
GRRRR.
20

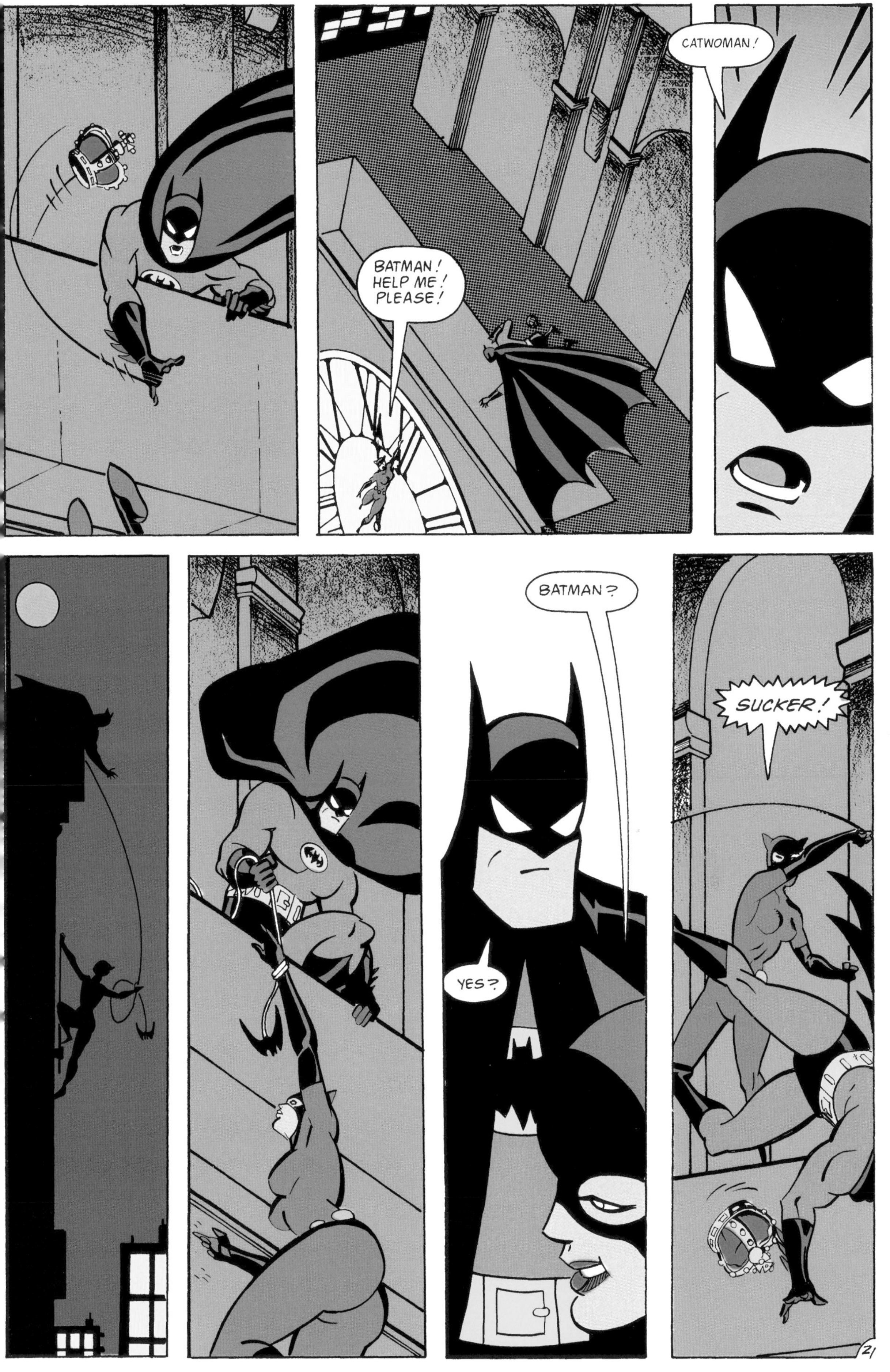
CATWOMAN!
BATMAN! HELP ME! PLEASE!
BATMAN?
YES?
SUCKER!
21

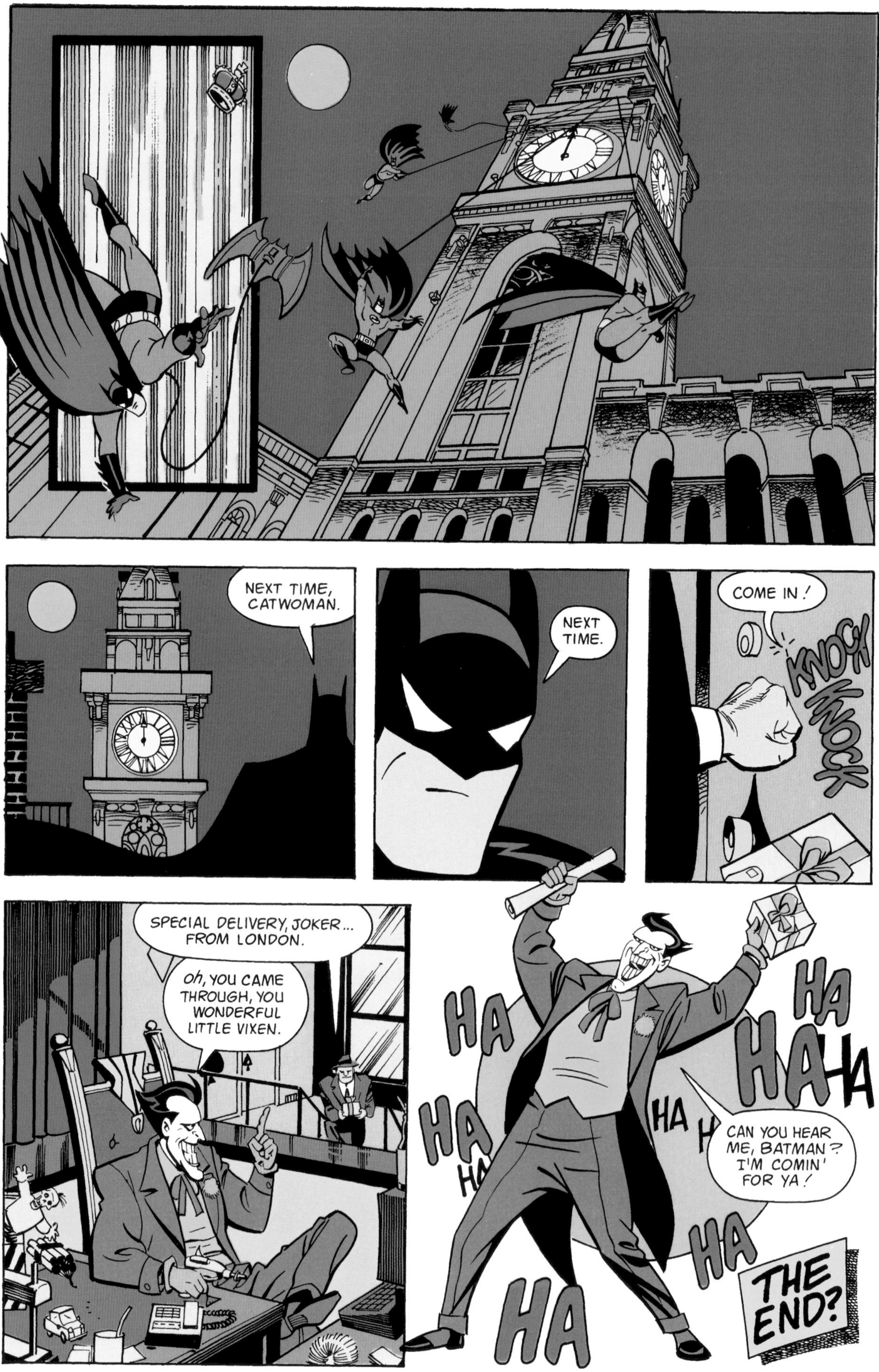
NEXT TIME, CATWOMAN.
NEXT TIME.
COME IN!
KNOCK KNOCK
SPECIAL DELIVERY, JOKER... FROM LONDON.
Oh, YOU CAME THROUGH, YOU WONDERFUL LITTLE VIXEN.
HA HA HA HA HA HA HA HA HA HA
CAN YOU HEAR ME, BATMAN? I'M COMIN' FOR YA!
THE END?

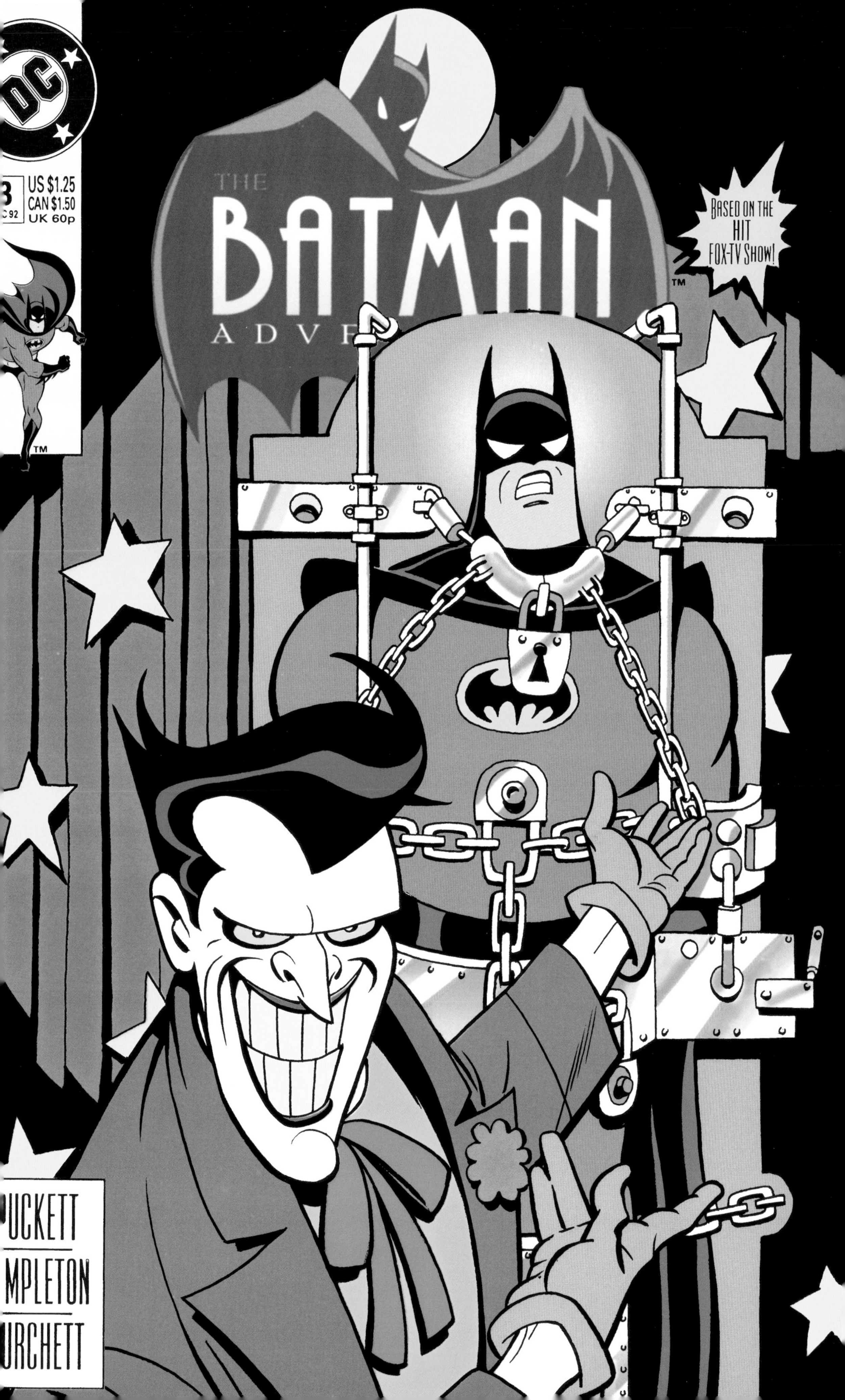
US $1.25
CAN $1.50
UK 60p
THE
BATMAN
ADV
BASED ON THE HIT FOX-TV SHOW!
UCKETT
MPLETON
URCHETT

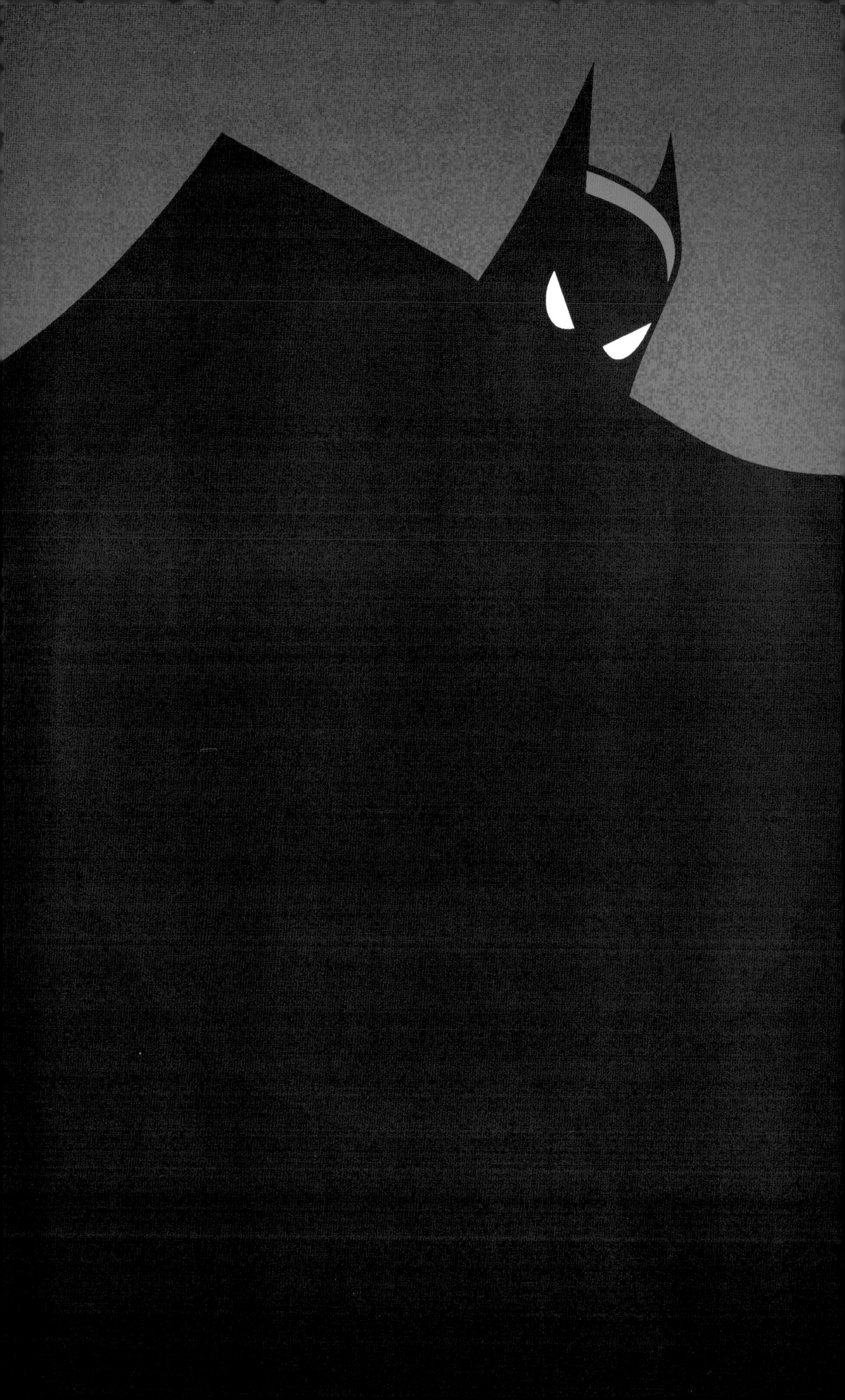

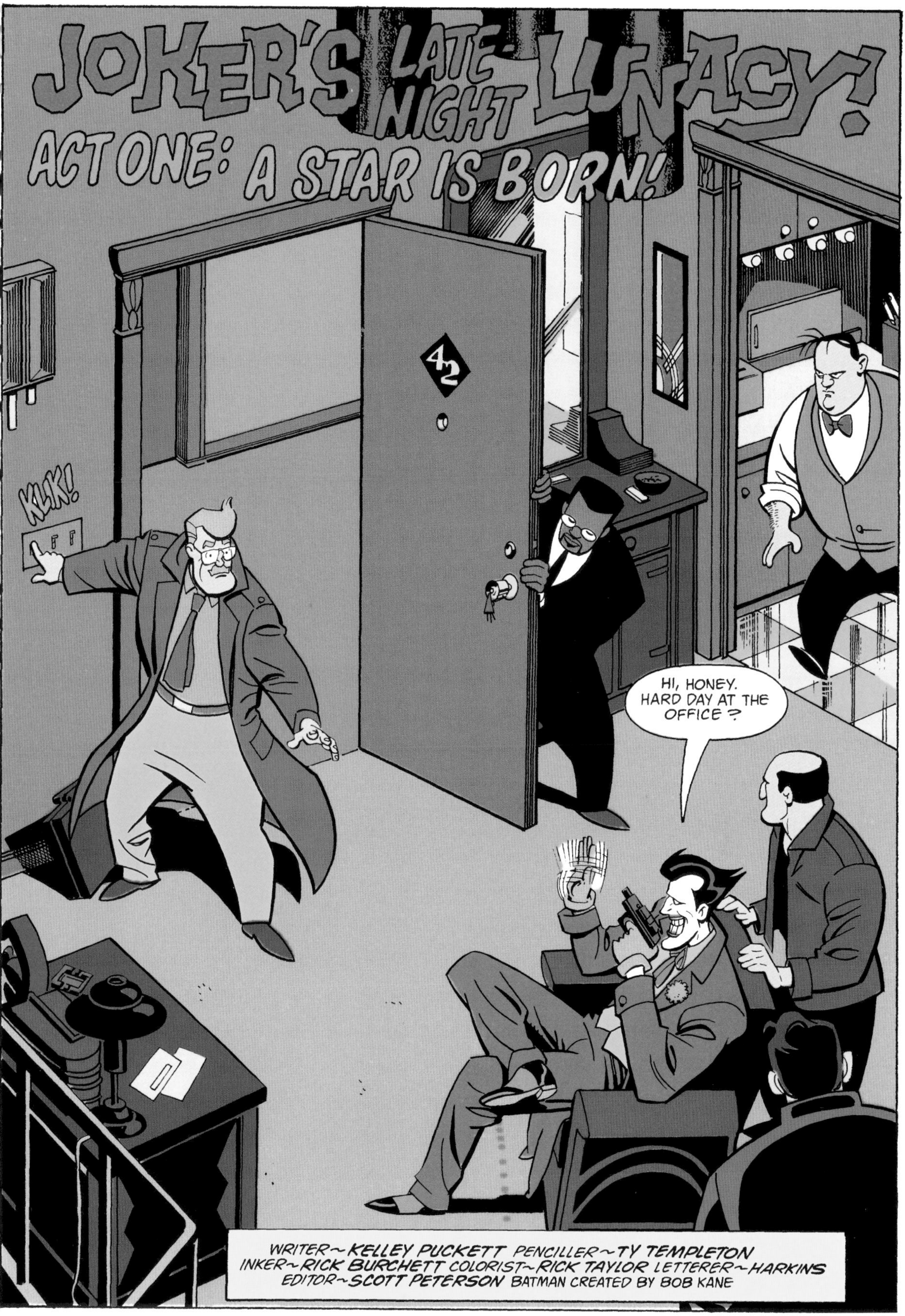
JOKER'S LATE-NIGHT LUNACY!
ACT ONE: A STAR IS BORN!
KLIK!
42
HI, HONEY. HARD DAY AT THE OFFICE?
WRITER~KELLEY PUCKETT PENCILLER~TY TEMPLETON
INKER~RICK BURCHETT COLORIST~RICK TAYLOR LETTERER~HARKINS
EDITOR~SCOTT PETERSON BATMAN CREATED BY BOB KANE

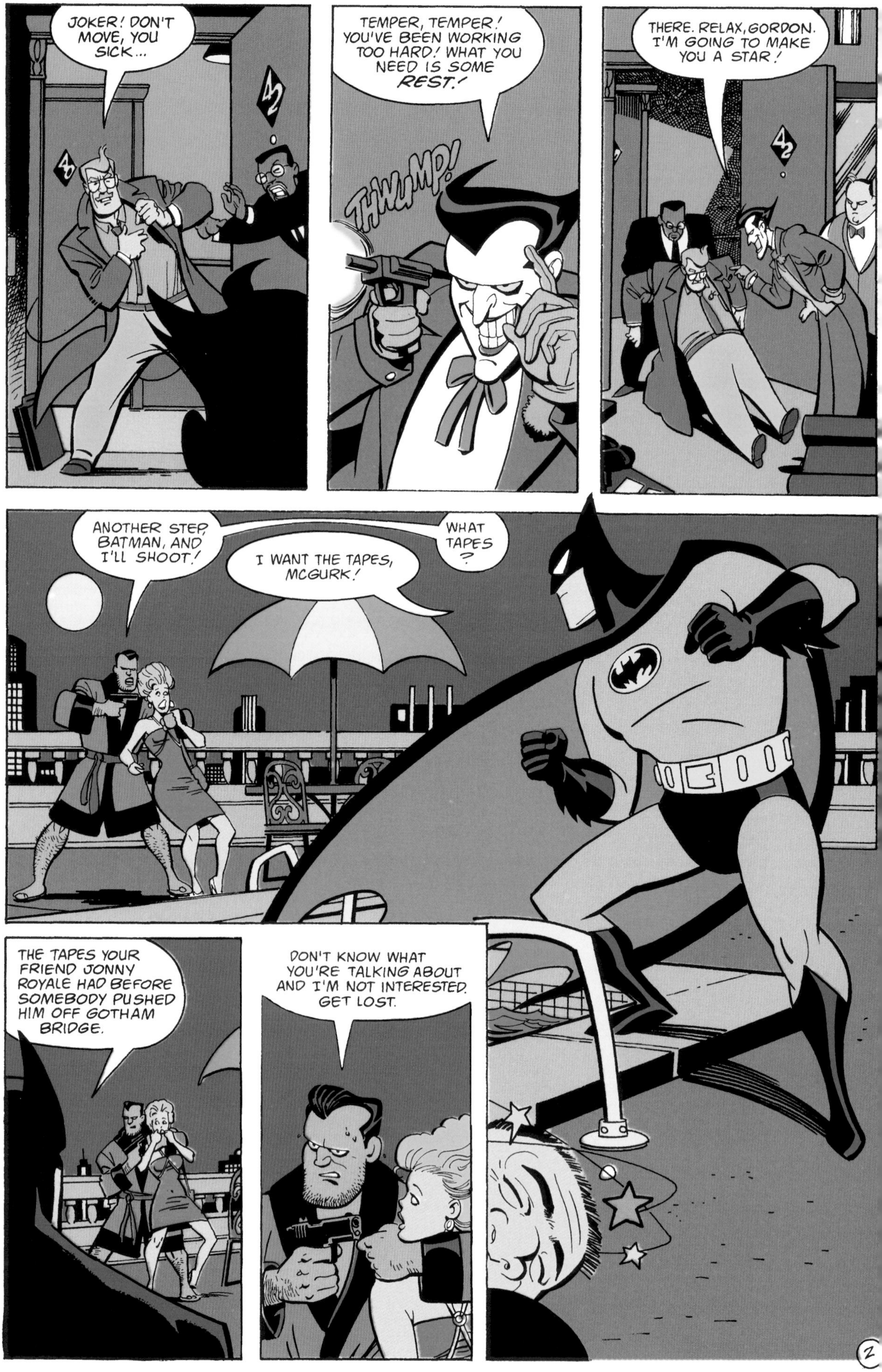

JOKER! DON'T MOVE, YOU SICK...
TEMPER, TEMPER! YOU'VE BEEN WORKING TOO HARD! WHAT YOU NEED IS SOME REST!
THWUMP!
THERE. RELAX, GORDON. I'M GOING TO MAKE YOU A STAR!
ANOTHER STEP, BATMAN, AND I'LL SHOOT!
I WANT THE TAPES, MCGURK!
WHAT TAPES?
THE TAPES YOUR FRIEND JONNY ROYALE HAD BEFORE SOMEBODY PUSHED HIM OFF GOTHAM BRIDGE.
DON'T KNOW WHAT YOU'RE TALKING ABOUT AND I'M NOT INTERESTED. GET LOST.
2

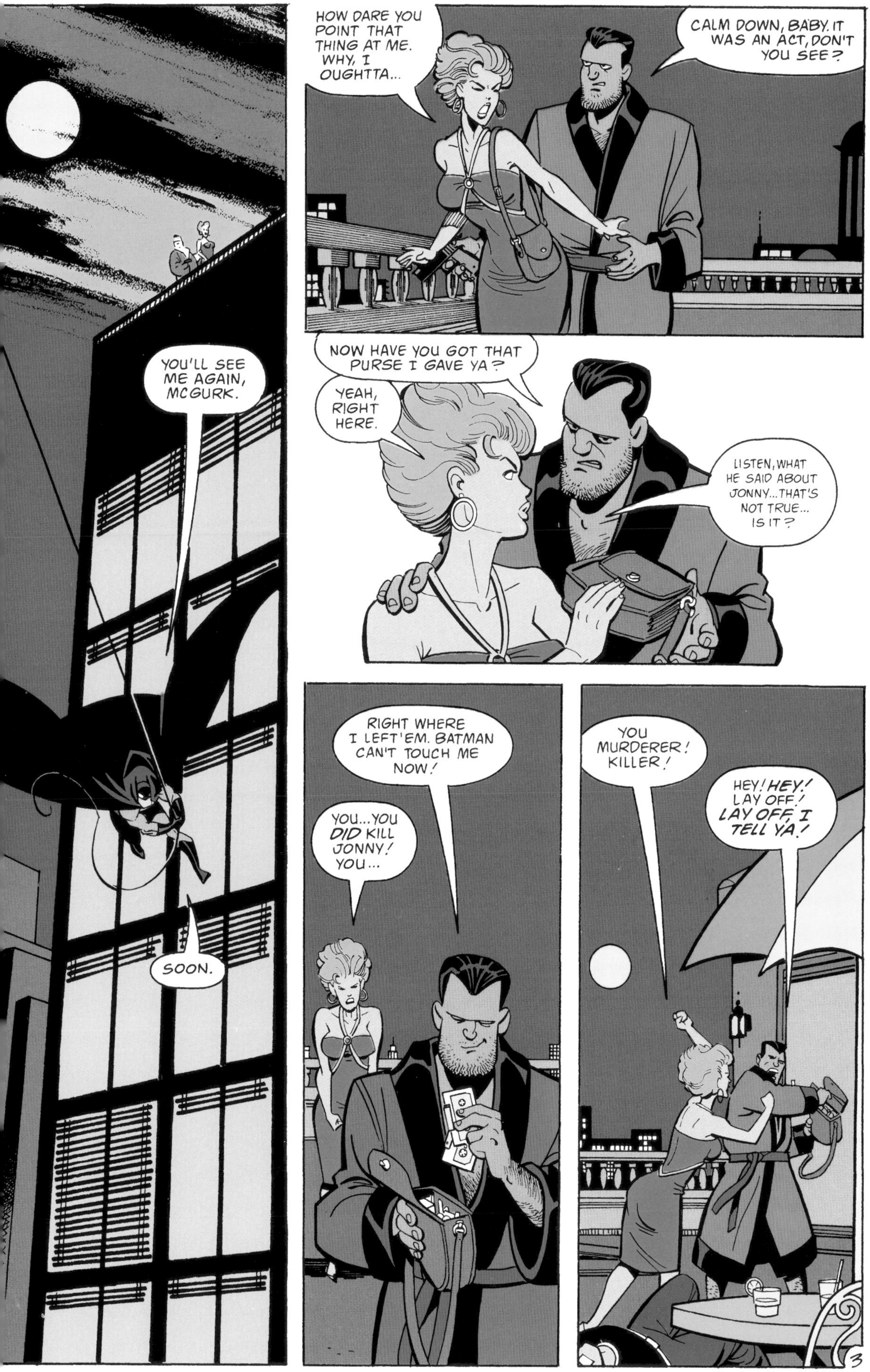
YOU'LL SEE ME AGAIN, MCGURK.
SOON.
HOW DARE YOU POINT THAT THING AT ME. WHY, I OUGHTTA...
CALM DOWN, BABY. IT WAS AN ACT, DON'T YOU SEE?
NOW HAVE YOU GOT THAT PURSE I GAVE YA?
YEAH, RIGHT HERE.
LISTEN, WHAT HE SAID ABOUT JONNY...THAT'S NOT TRUE... IS IT?
RIGHT WHERE I LEFT'EM. BATMAN CAN'T TOUCH ME NOW!
YOU...YOU DID KILL JONNY! YOU...
YOU MURDERER! KILLER!
HEY! HEY! LAY OFF! LAY OFF, I TELL YA!
3

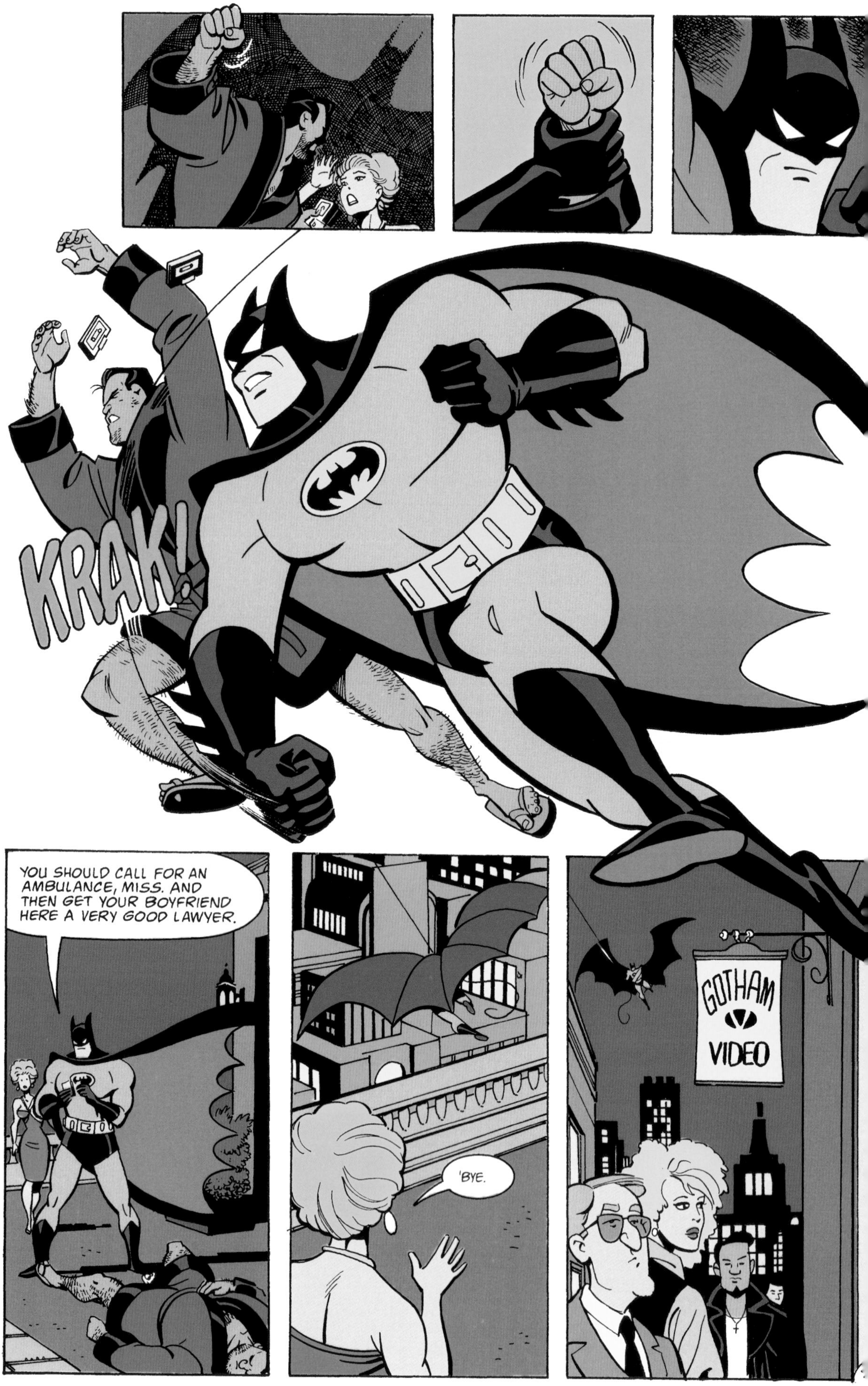
KRAK!
YOU SHOULD CALL FOR AN AMBULANCE, MISS. AND THEN GET YOUR BOYFRIEND HERE A VERY GOOD LAWYER.
'BYE.
GOTHAM
VIDEO

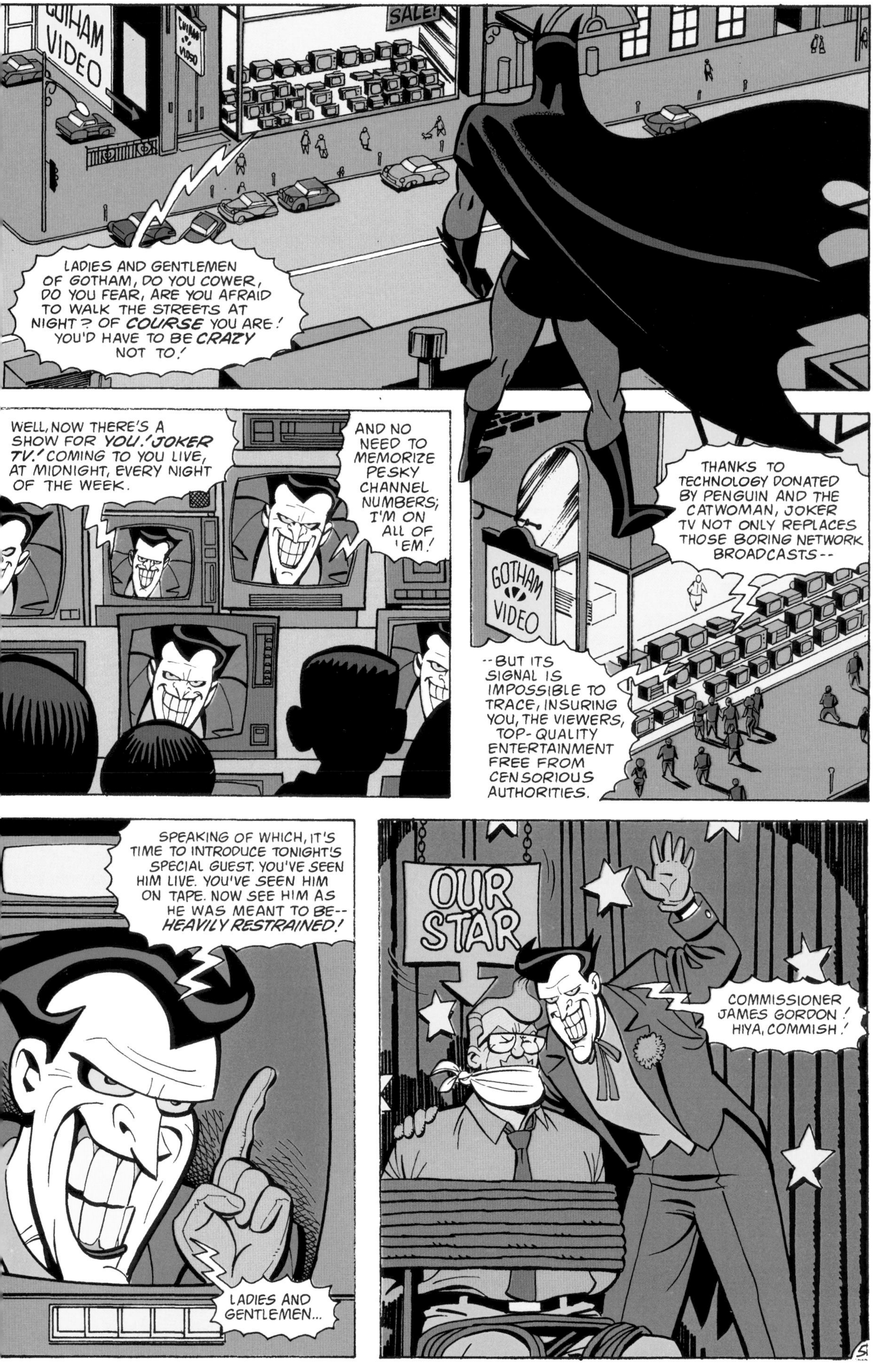
GOTHAM VIDEO
SALE!
LADIES AND GENTLEMEN OF GOTHAM, DO YOU COWER, DO YOU FEAR, ARE YOU AFRAID TO WALK THE STREETS AT NIGHT? OF COURSE YOU ARE! YOU'D HAVE TO BE CRAZY NOT TO!
WELL, NOW THERE'S A SHOW FOR YOU! 'JOKER TV!' COMING TO YOU LIVE, AT MIDNIGHT, EVERY NIGHT OF THE WEEK.
AND NO NEED TO MEMORIZE PESKY CHANNEL NUMBERS; I'M ON ALL OF 'EM!
THANKS TO TECHNOLOGY DONATED BY PENGUIN AND THE CATWOMAN, JOKER TV NOT ONLY REPLACES THOSE BORING NETWORK BROADCASTS--
GOTHAM VIDEO
--BUT ITS SIGNAL IS IMPOSSIBLE TO TRACE, INSURING YOU, THE VIEWERS, TOP-QUALITY ENTERTAINMENT FREE FROM CENSORIOUS AUTHORITIES.
SPEAKING OF WHICH, IT'S TIME TO INTRODUCE TONIGHT'S SPECIAL GUEST. YOU'VE SEEN HIM LIVE. YOU'VE SEEN HIM ON TAPE. NOW SEE HIM AS HE WAS MEANT TO BE-- HEAVILY RESTRAINED!
LADIES AND GENTLEMEN...
OUR STAR
COMMISSIONER JAMES GORDON! HIYA, COMMISH!

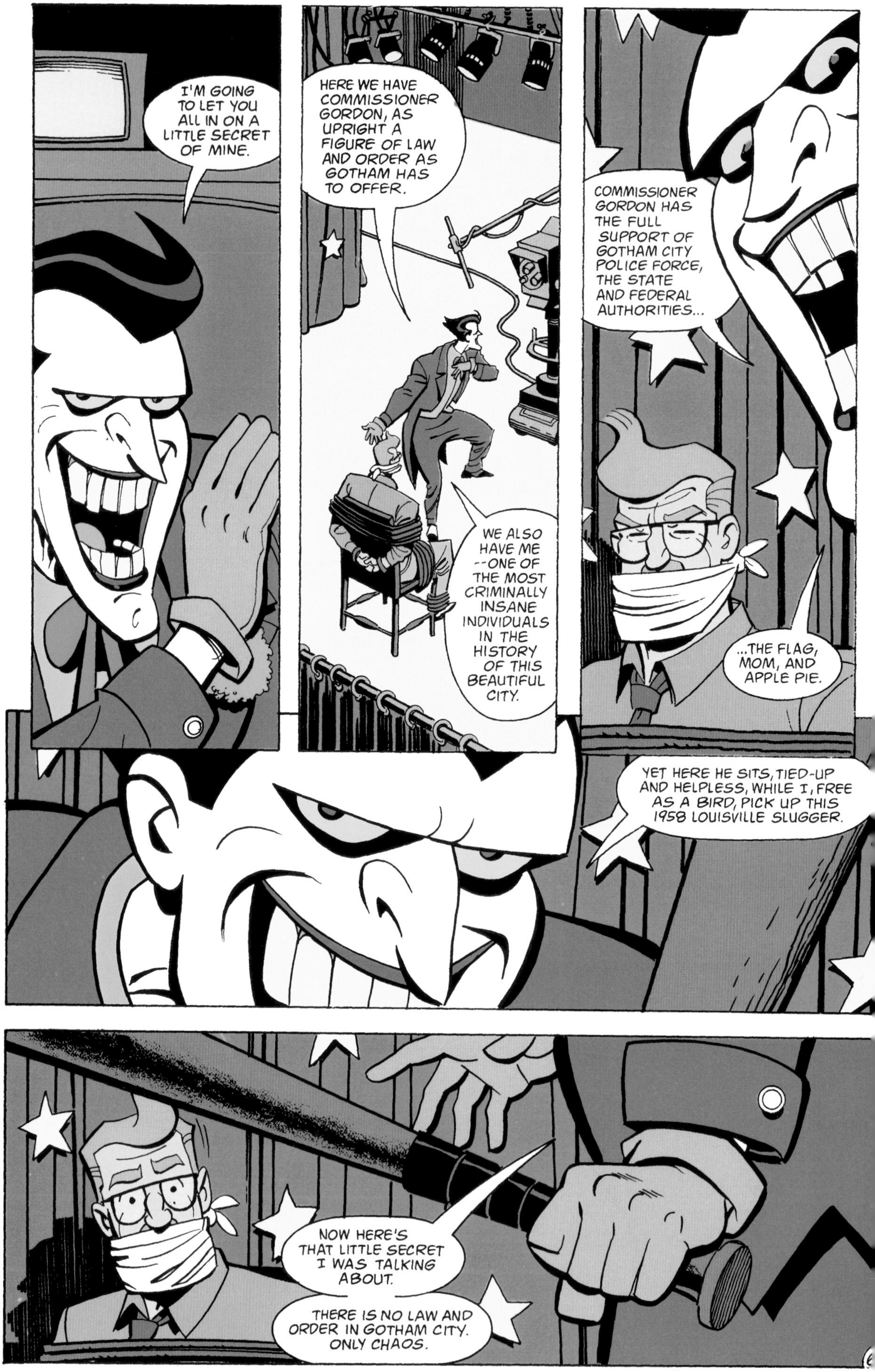
I'M GOING TO LET YOU ALL IN ON A LITTLE SECRET OF MINE.
HERE WE HAVE COMMISSIONER GORDON, AS UPRIGHT A FIGURE OF LAW AND ORDER AS GOTHAM HAS TO OFFER.
WE ALSO HAVE ME --ONE OF THE MOST CRIMINALLY INSANE INDIVIDUALS IN THE HISTORY OF THIS BEAUTIFUL CITY.
COMMISSIONER GORDON HAS THE FULL SUPPORT OF GOTHAM CITY POLICE FORCE, THE STATE AND FEDERAL AUTHORITIES...
...THE FLAG, MOM, AND APPLE PIE.
YET HERE HE SITS, TIED-UP AND HELPLESS, WHILE I, FREE AS A BIRD, PICK UP THIS 1958 LOUISVILLE SLUGGER.
NOW HERE'S THAT LITTLE SECRET I WAS TALKING ABOUT.
THERE IS NO LAW AND ORDER IN GOTHAM CITY. ONLY CHAOS.

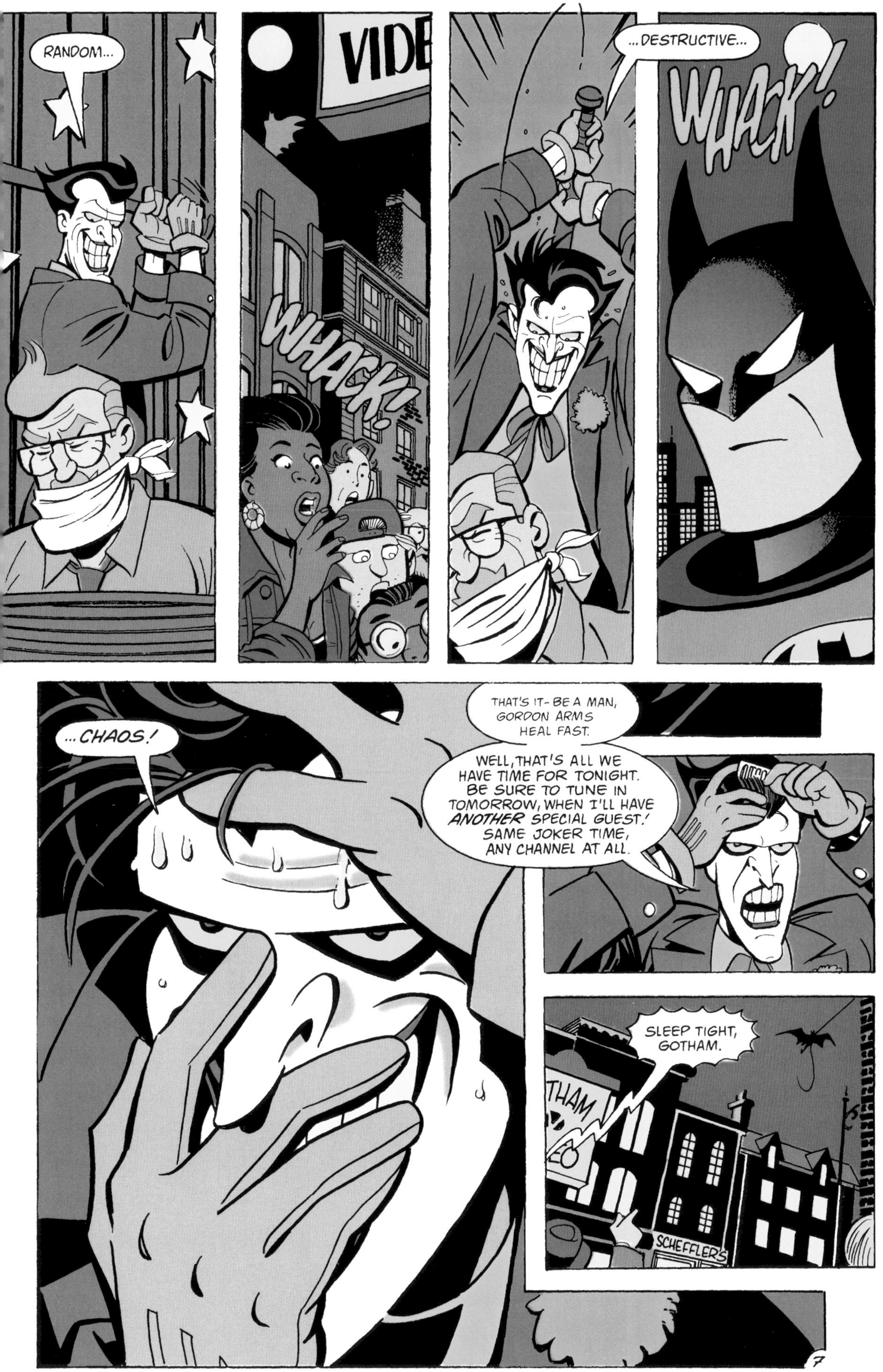
RANDOM...
VIDE
WHACK!
...DESTRUCTIVE...
WHACK!
...CHAOS!
THAT'S IT- BE A MAN, GORDON ARMS HEAL FAST.
WELL, THAT'S ALL WE HAVE TIME FOR TONIGHT. BE SURE TO TUNE IN TOMORROW, WHEN I'LL HAVE ANOTHER SPECIAL GUEST! SAME JOKER TIME, ANY CHANNEL AT ALL.
SLEEP TIGHT, GOTHAM.
SCHEFFLER'S
7

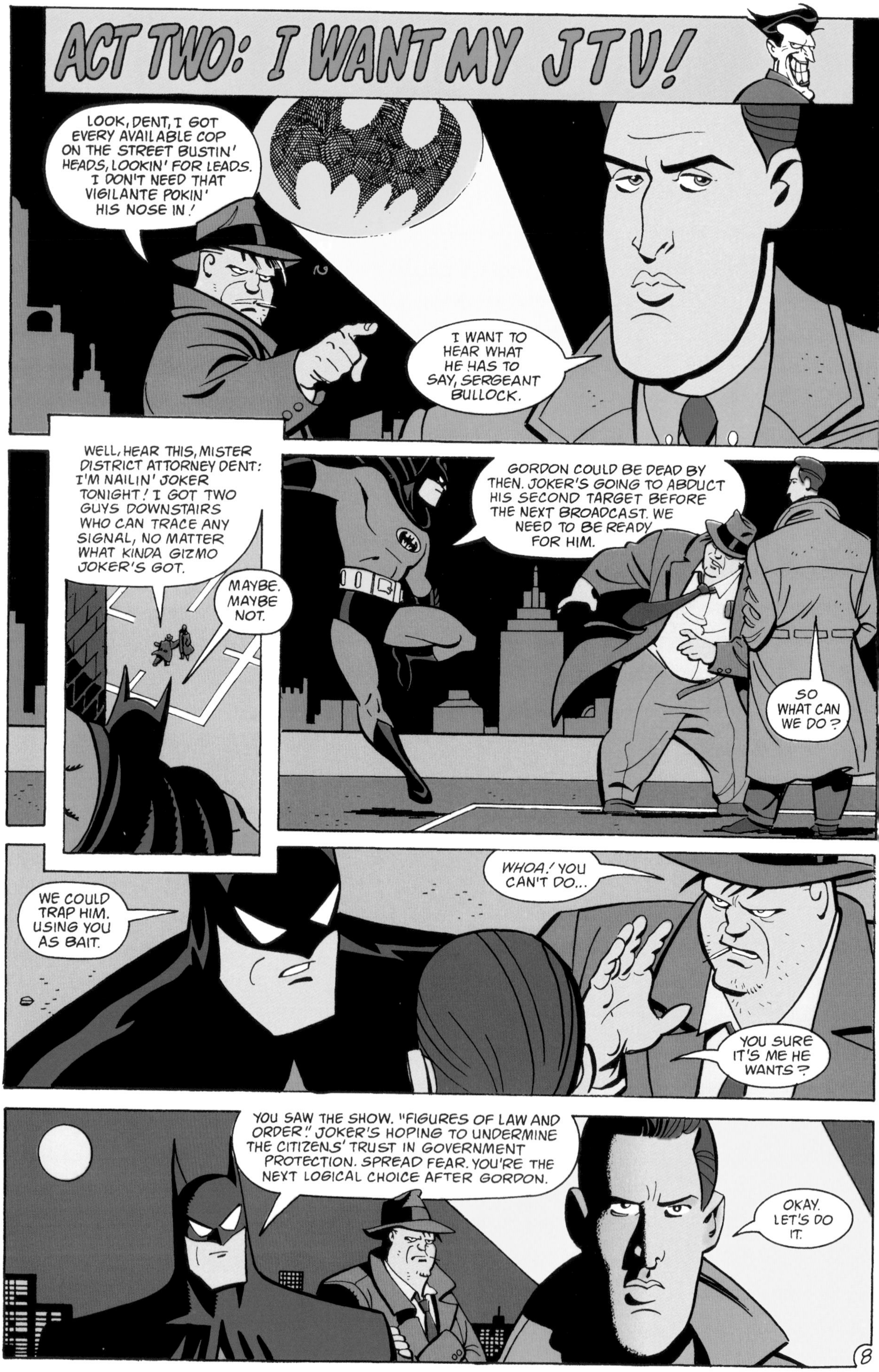
ACT TWO: I WANT MY JTV!
LOOK, DENT, I GOT EVERY AVAILABLE COP ON THE STREET BUSTIN' HEADS, LOOKIN' FOR LEADS. I DON'T NEED THAT VIGILANTE POKIN' HIS NOSE IN!
I WANT TO HEAR WHAT HE HAS TO SAY, SERGEANT BULLOCK.
WELL, HEAR THIS, MISTER DISTRICT ATTORNEY DENT: I'M NAILIN' JOKER TONIGHT! I GOT TWO GUYS DOWNSTAIRS WHO CAN TRACE ANY SIGNAL, NO MATTER WHAT KINDA GIZMO JOKER'S GOT.
MAYBE. MAYBE NOT.
GORDON COULD BE DEAD BY THEN. JOKER'S GOING TO ABDUCT HIS SECOND TARGET BEFORE THE NEXT BROADCAST. WE NEED TO BE READY FOR HIM.
SO WHAT CAN WE DO?
WE COULD TRAP HIM. USING YOU AS BAIT.
WHOA! YOU CAN'T DO...
YOU SURE IT'S ME HE WANTS?
YOU SAW THE SHOW. "FIGURES OF LAW AND ORDER." JOKER'S HOPING TO UNDERMINE THE CITIZENS' TRUST IN GOVERNMENT PROTECTION. SPREAD FEAR. YOU'RE THE NEXT LOGICAL CHOICE AFTER GORDON.
OKAY. LET'S DO IT.
8

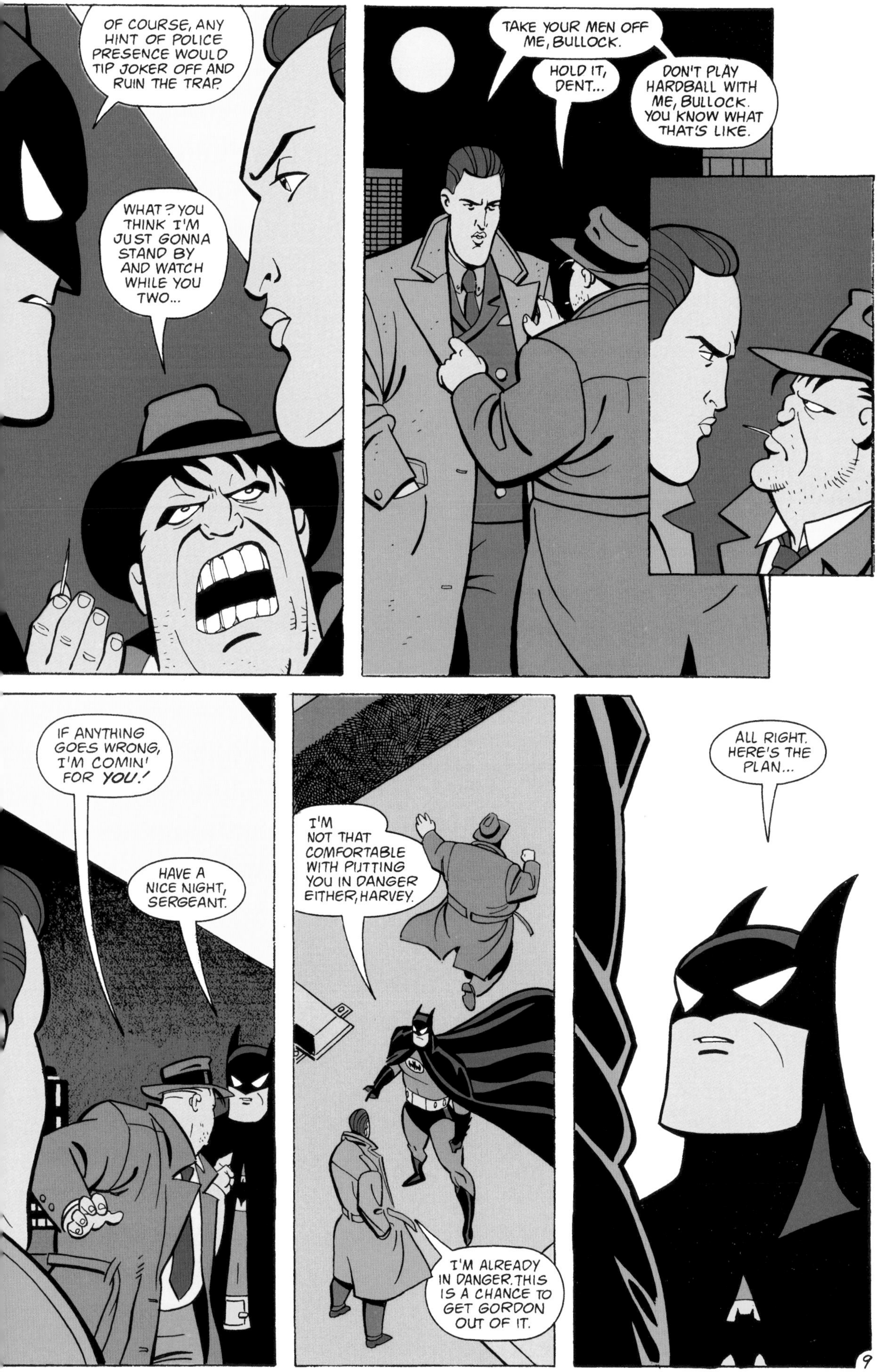
OF COURSE, ANY HINT OF POLICE PRESENCE WOULD TIP JOKER OFF AND RUIN THE TRAP.
WHAT? YOU THINK I'M JUST GONNA STAND BY AND WATCH WHILE YOU TWO...
TAKE YOUR MEN OFF ME, BULLOCK.
HOLD IT, DENT...
DON'T PLAY HARDBALL WITH ME, BULLOCK. YOU KNOW WHAT THAT'S LIKE.
IF ANYTHING GOES WRONG, I'M COMIN' FOR YOU!
HAVE A NICE NIGHT, SERGEANT.
I'M NOT THAT COMFORTABLE WITH PUTTING YOU IN DANGER EITHER, HARVEY.
I'M ALREADY IN DANGER. THIS IS A CHANCE TO GET GORDON OUT OF IT.
ALL RIGHT. HERE'S THE PLAN...
9

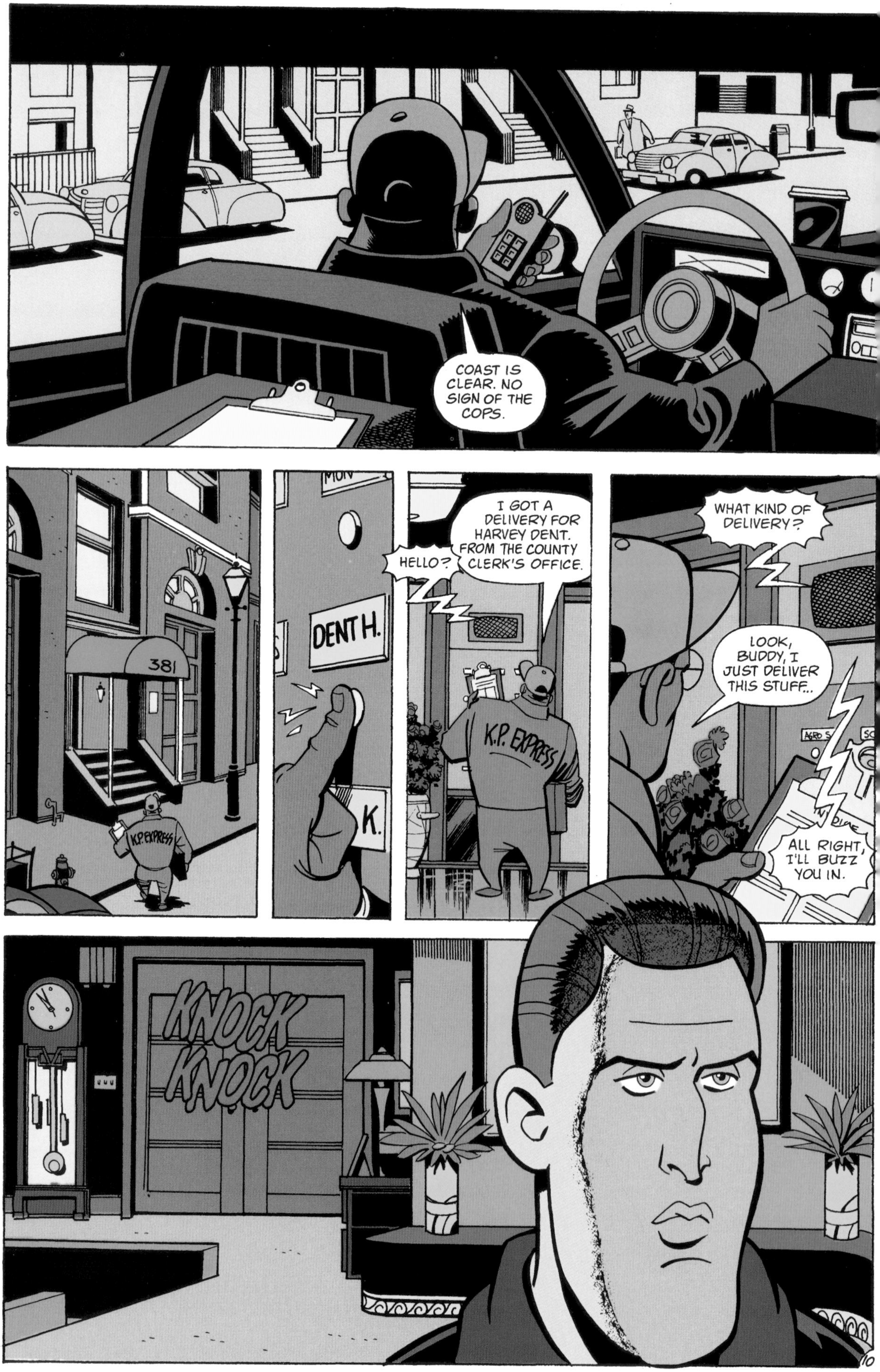
COAST IS CLEAR. NO SIGN OF THE COPS.
381
DENT H.
K.
HELLO?
I GOT A DELIVERY FOR HARVEY DENT. FROM THE COUNTY CLERK'S OFFICE.
K.P. EXPRESS
WHAT KIND OF DELIVERY?
LOOK, BUDDY, I JUST DELIVER THIS STUFF...
ALL RIGHT, I'LL BUZZ YOU IN.
KNOCK KNOCK
10

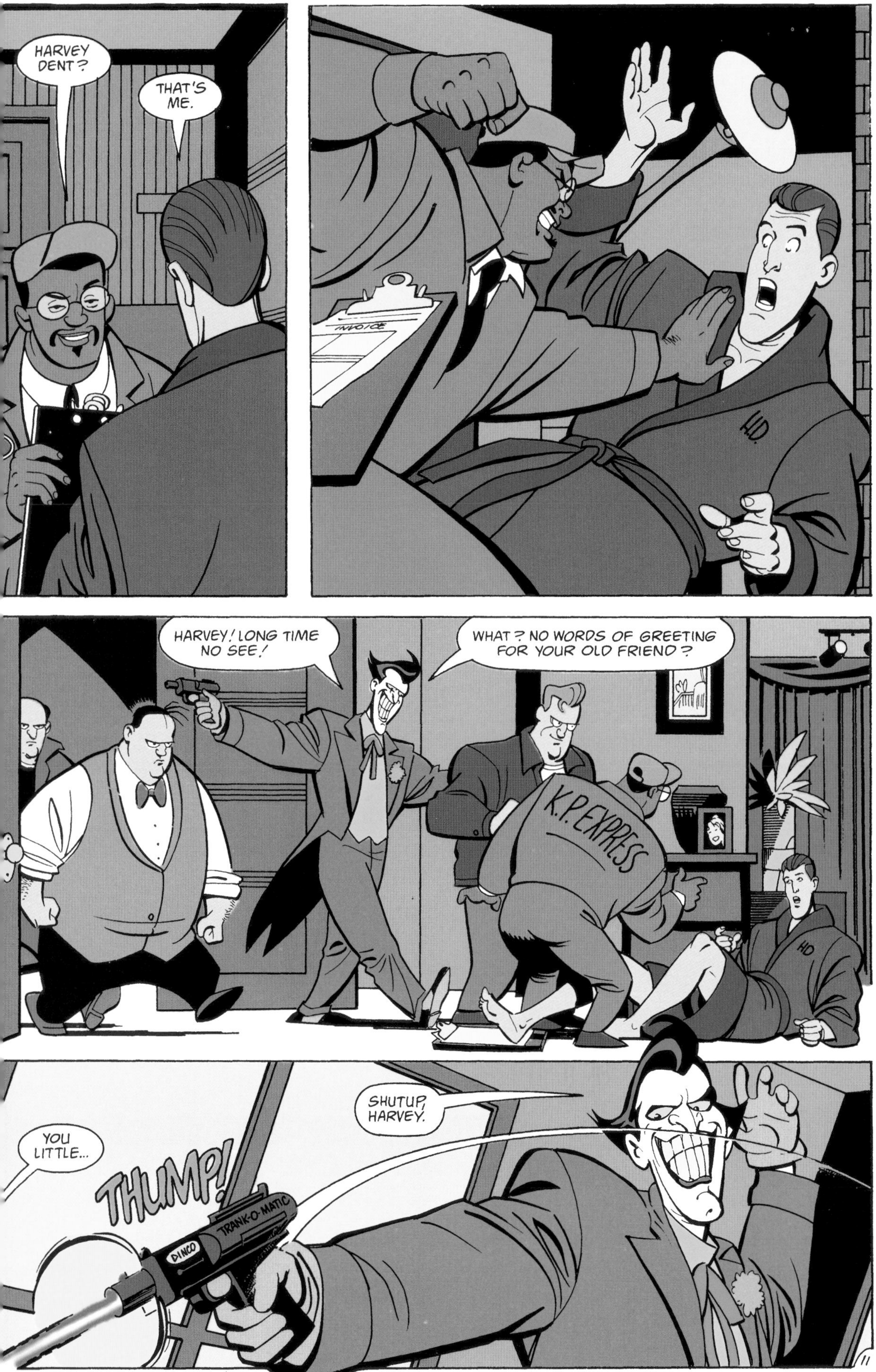
HARVEY DENT?
THAT'S ME.
INVOICE
HD
HARVEY! LONG TIME NO SEE!
WHAT? NO WORDS OF GREETING FOR YOUR OLD FRIEND?
K.P. EXPRESS
HD
YOU LITTLE...
SHUTUP, HARVEY.
THUMP!
TRANK-O-MATIC
DINCO
11

THIS IS WAY, WAY, *WAY* TOO EASY. BATMAN'S CLOSE BY. I CAN SMELL HIM.

MOVE OUT CAREFULLY AND WATCH YOUR BACKS.

LET'S GO.

DON'T DAWDLE!

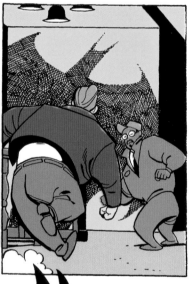

CHOK!

12

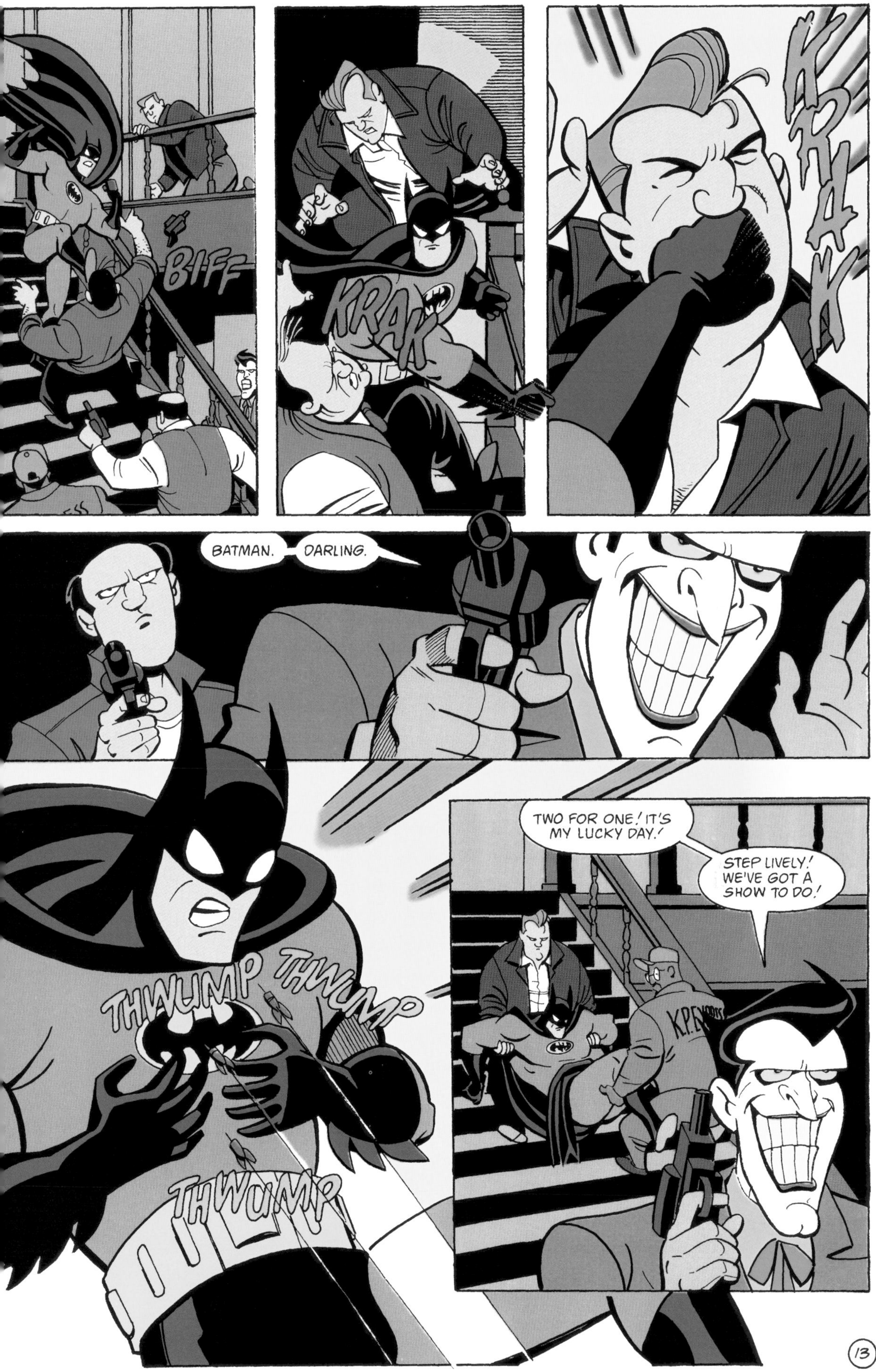
BIFF
KRAK
KRAK
BATMAN.
DARLING.
THWUMP THWUMP
THWUMP
TWO FOR ONE! IT'S MY LUCKY DAY!
STEP LIVELY! WE'VE GOT A SHOW TO DO!
13

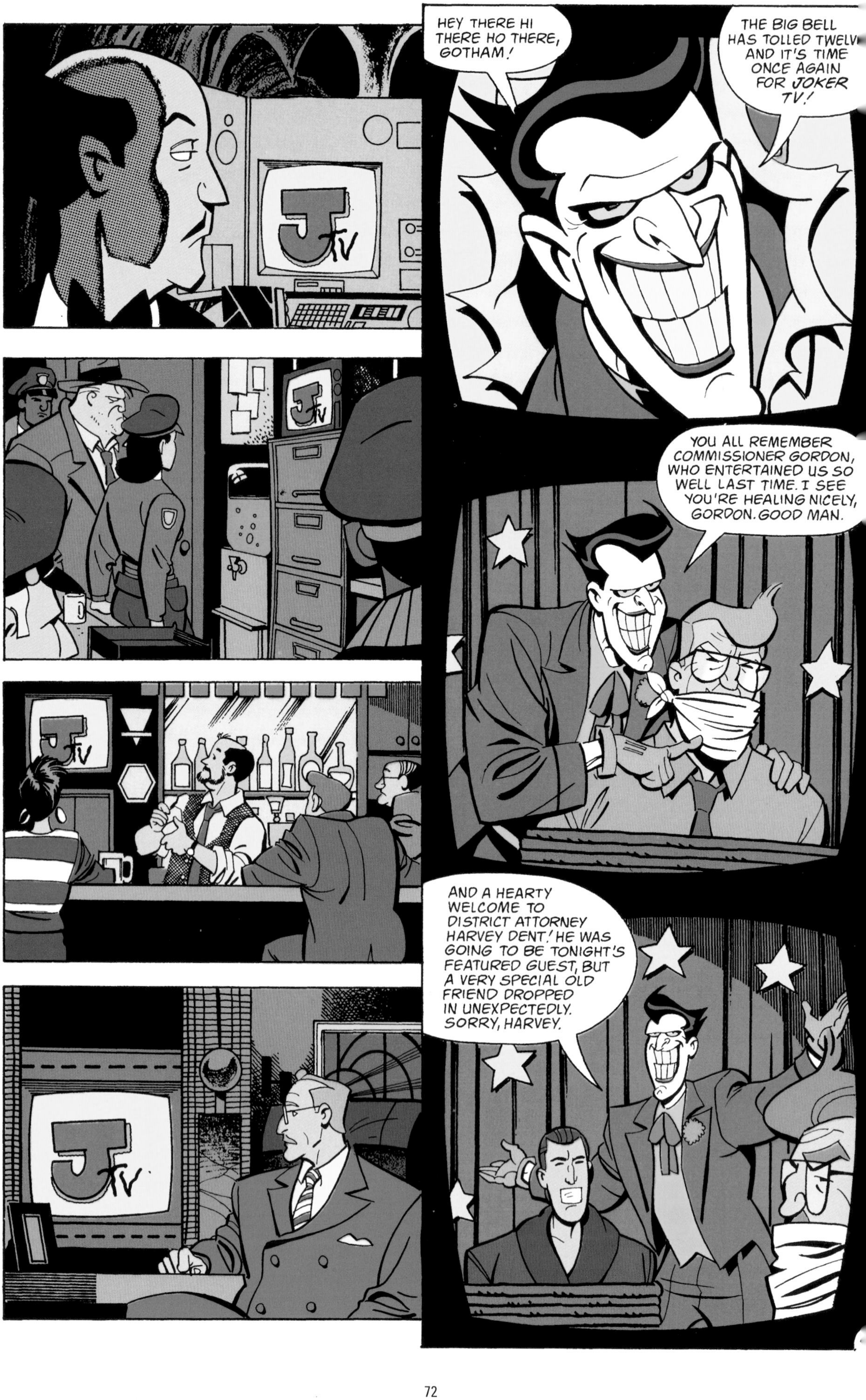

J TV
HEY THERE HI THERE HO THERE, GOTHAM!
THE BIG BELL HAS TOLLED TWELVE AND IT'S TIME ONCE AGAIN FOR JOKER TV!
YOU ALL REMEMBER COMMISSIONER GORDON, WHO ENTERTAINED US SO WELL LAST TIME. I SEE YOU'RE HEALING NICELY, GORDON. GOOD MAN.
AND A HEARTY WELCOME TO DISTRICT ATTORNEY HARVEY DENT! HE WAS GOING TO BE TONIGHT'S FEATURED GUEST, BUT A VERY SPECIAL OLD FRIEND DROPPED IN UNEXPECTEDLY. SORRY, HARVEY.

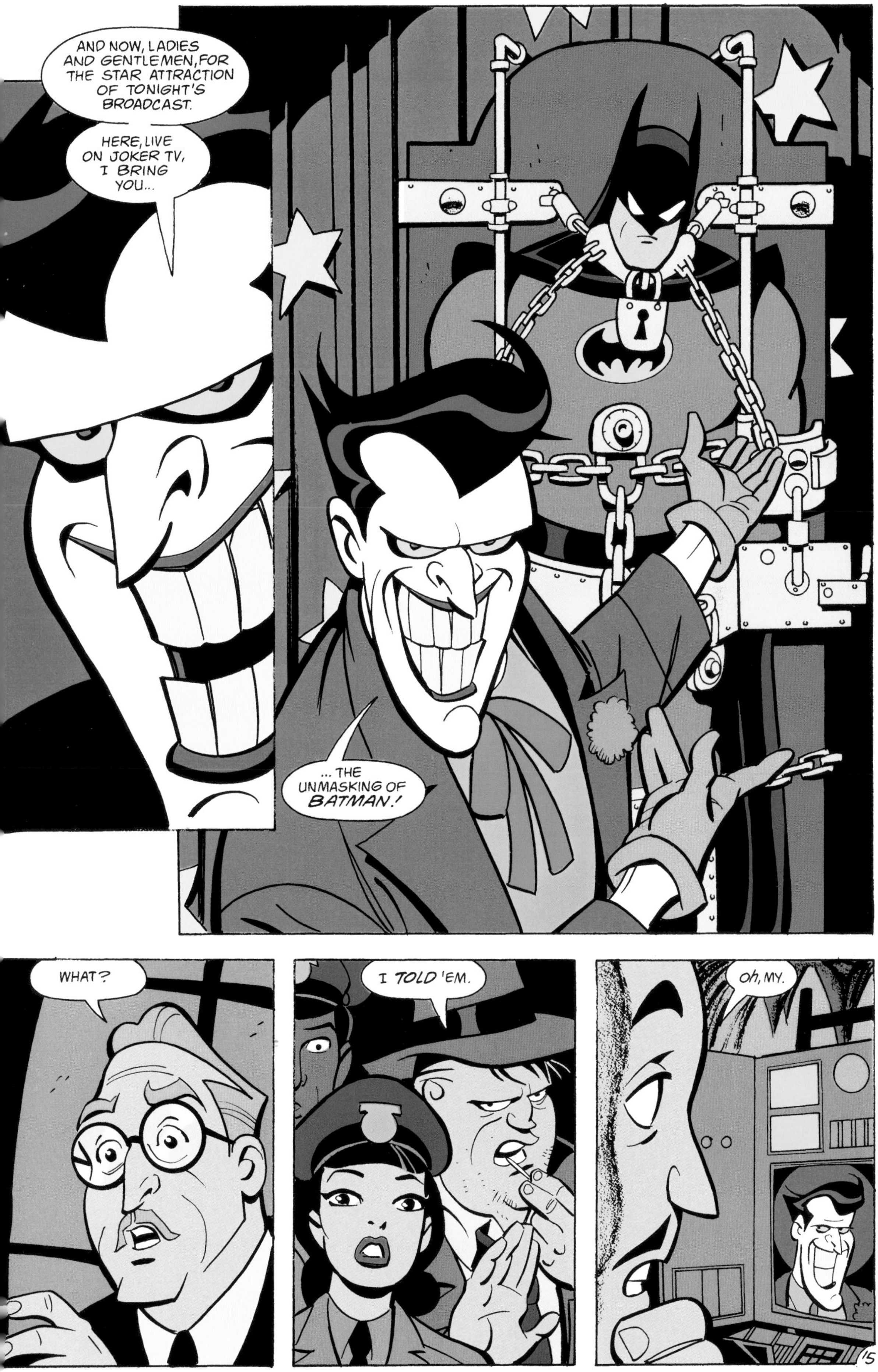
AND NOW, LADIES AND GENTLEMEN, FOR THE STAR ATTRACTION OF TONIGHT'S BROADCAST.
HERE, LIVE ON JOKER TV, I BRING YOU...
... THE UNMASKING OF BATMAN!
WHAT?
I TOLD 'EM.
oh, MY.
15

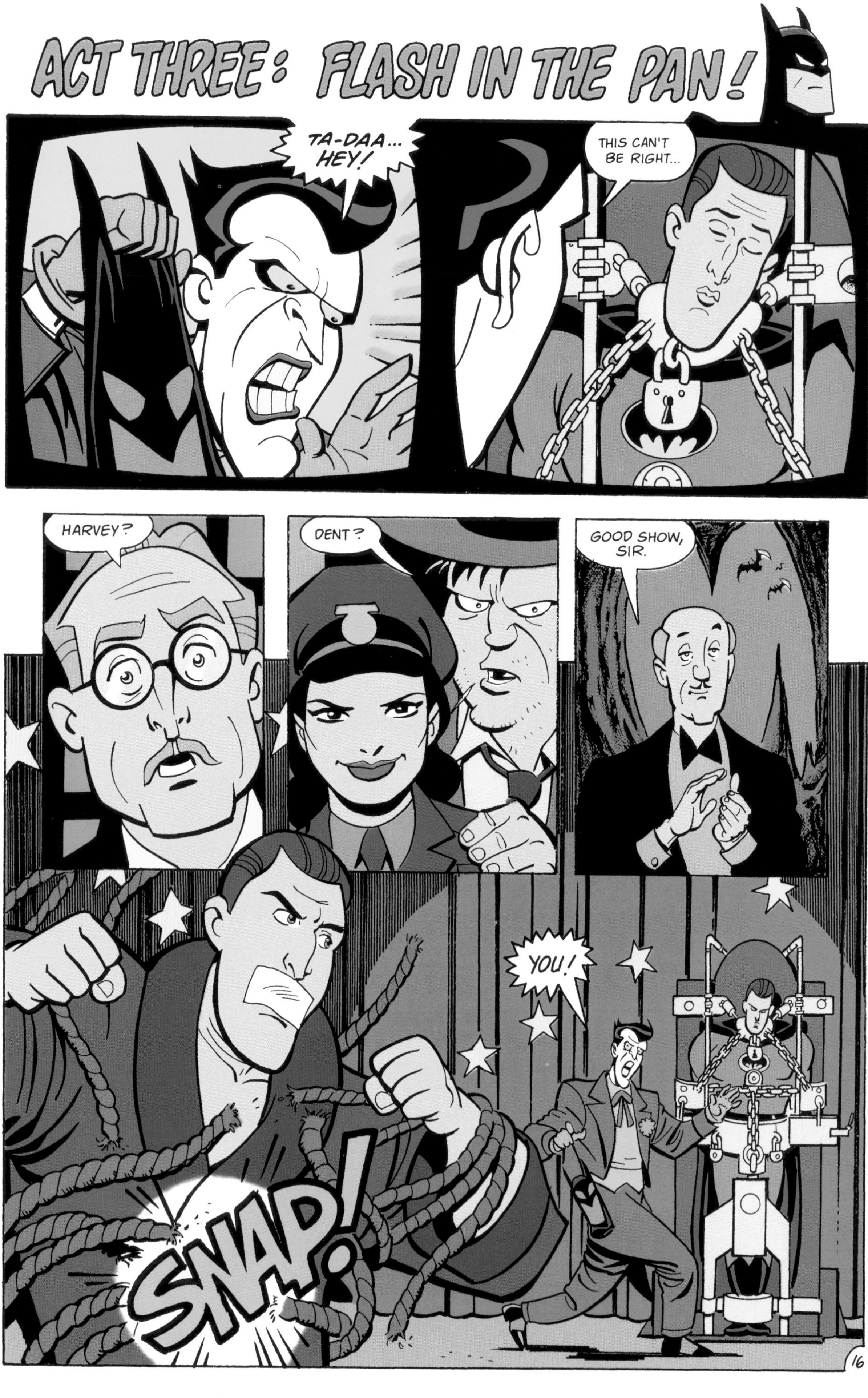
ACT THREE: FLASH IN THE PAN!
TA-DAA... HEY!
THIS CAN'T BE RIGHT...
HARVEY?
DENT?
GOOD SHOW, SIR.
YOU!
SNAP!
16

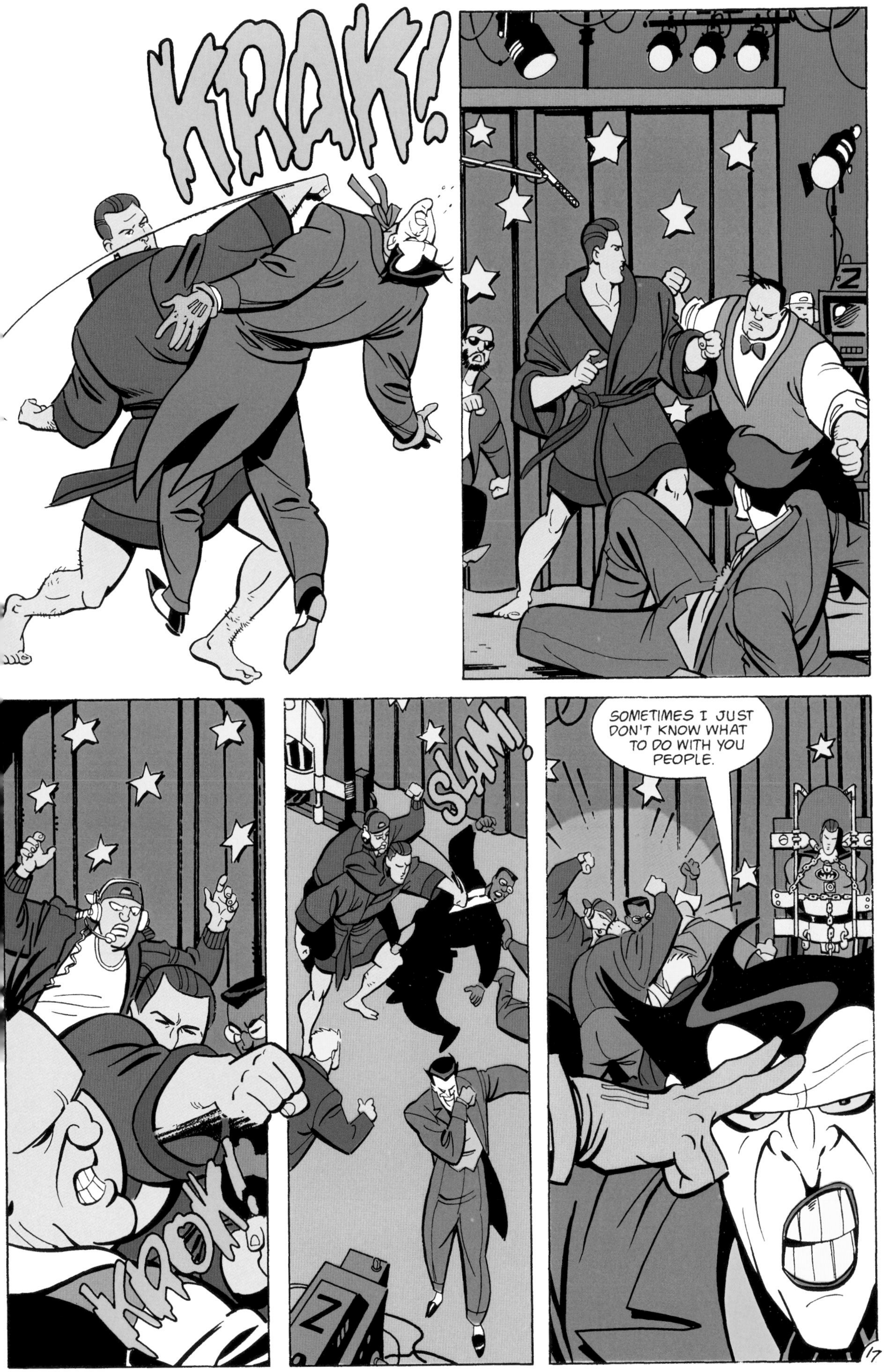
KRAK!
SLAM!
SOMETIMES I JUST DON'T KNOW WHAT TO DO WITH YOU PEOPLE.

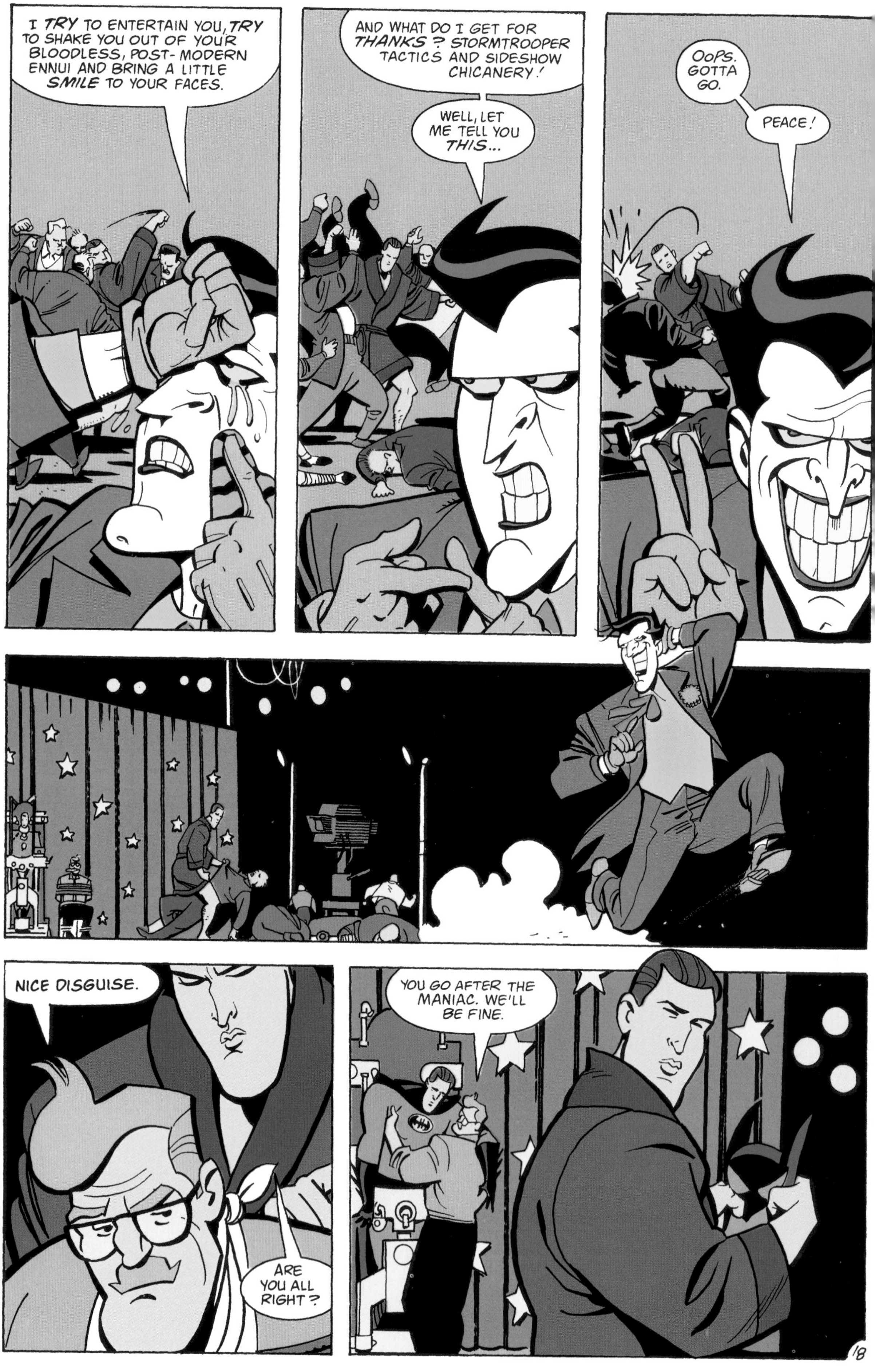
I TRY TO ENTERTAIN YOU, TRY TO SHAKE YOU OUT OF YOUR BLOODLESS, POST-MODERN ENNUI AND BRING A LITTLE SMILE TO YOUR FACES.
AND WHAT DO I GET FOR THANKS? STORMTROOPER TACTICS AND SIDESHOW CHICANERY!
WELL, LET ME TELL YOU THIS...
OOPS. GOTTA GO.
PEACE!
NICE DISGUISE.
ARE YOU ALL RIGHT?
YOU GO AFTER THE MANIAC. WE'LL BE FINE.
18

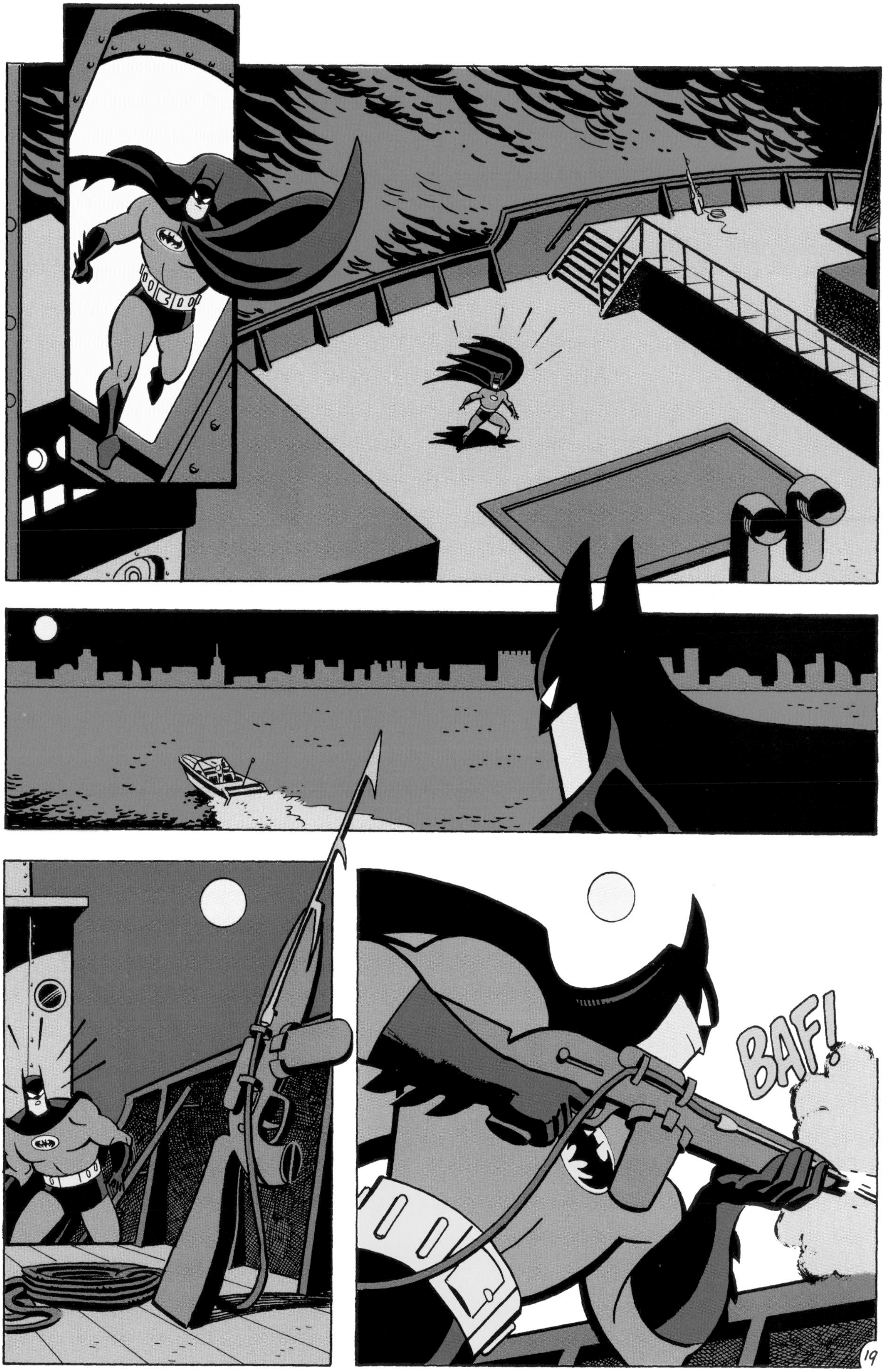
BAF!
19

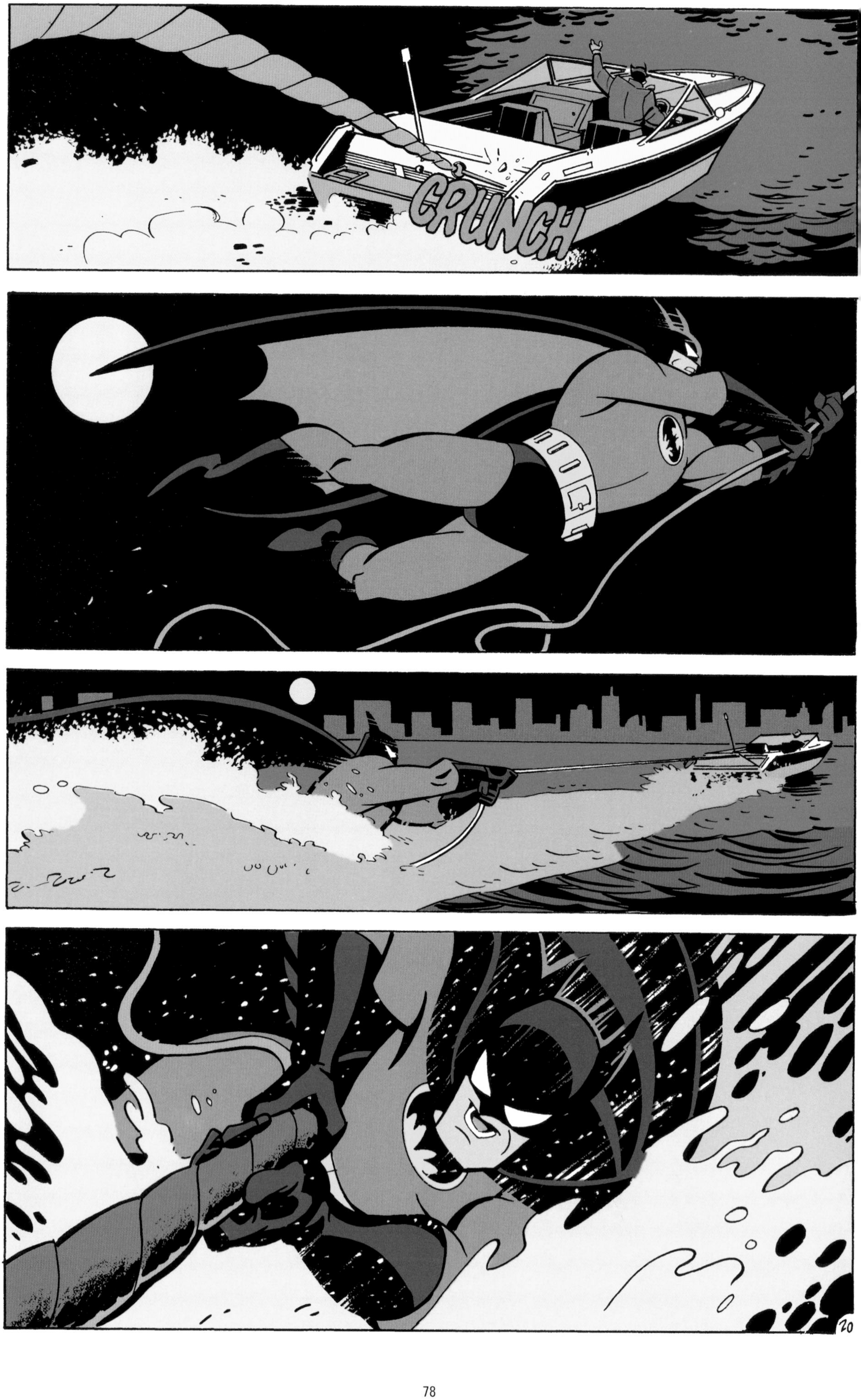
CRUNCH
20

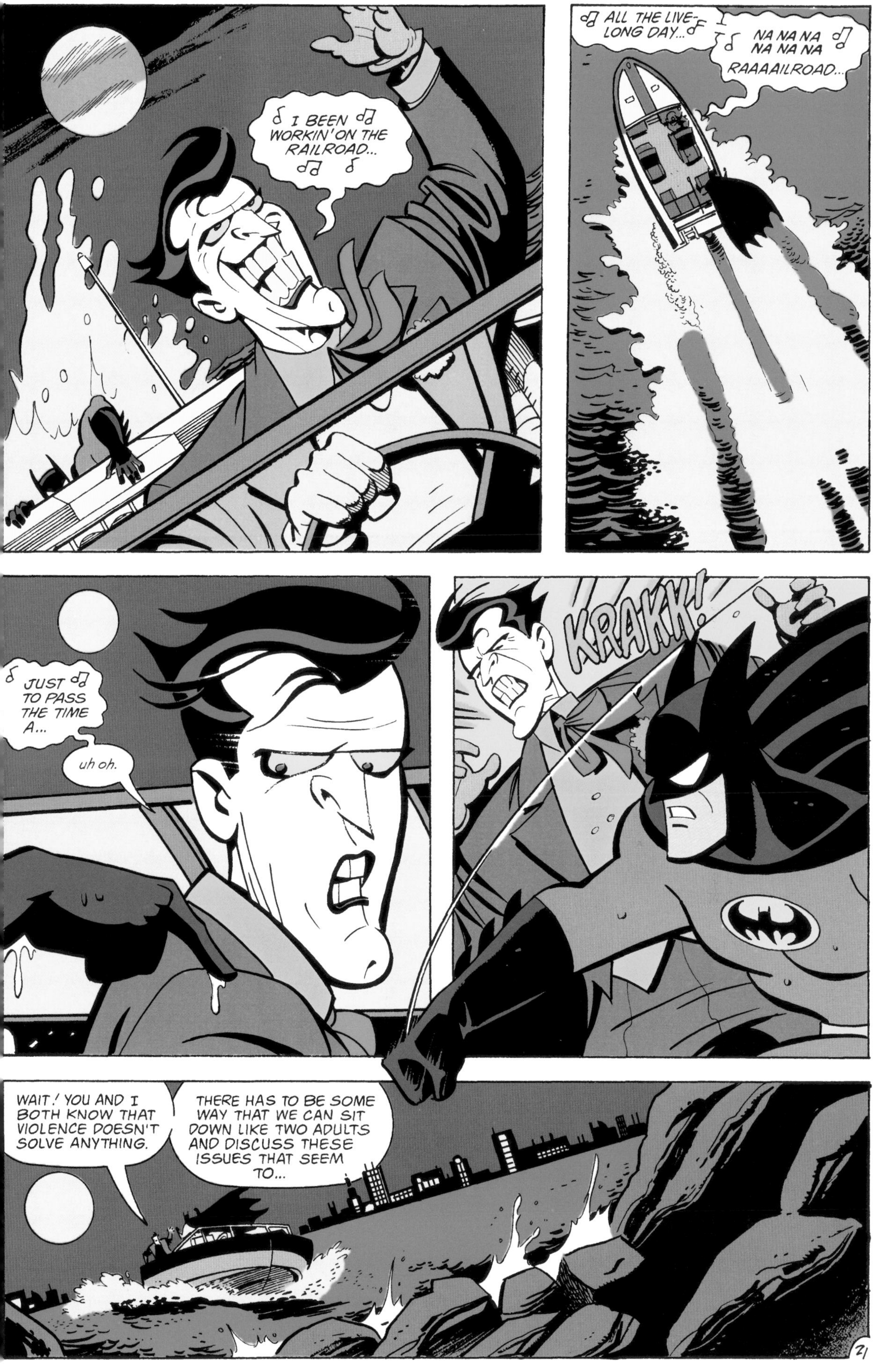
I BEEN WORKIN' ON THE RAILROAD...
ALL THE LIVE-LONG DAY...
NA NA NA NA NA NA RAAAAILROAD...
JUST TO PASS THE TIME A...
uh oh.
KRAKK!
WAIT! YOU AND I BOTH KNOW THAT VIOLENCE DOESN'T SOLVE ANYTHING.
THERE HAS TO BE SOME WAY THAT WE CAN SIT DOWN LIKE TWO ADULTS AND DISCUSS THESE ISSUES THAT SEEM TO...
21

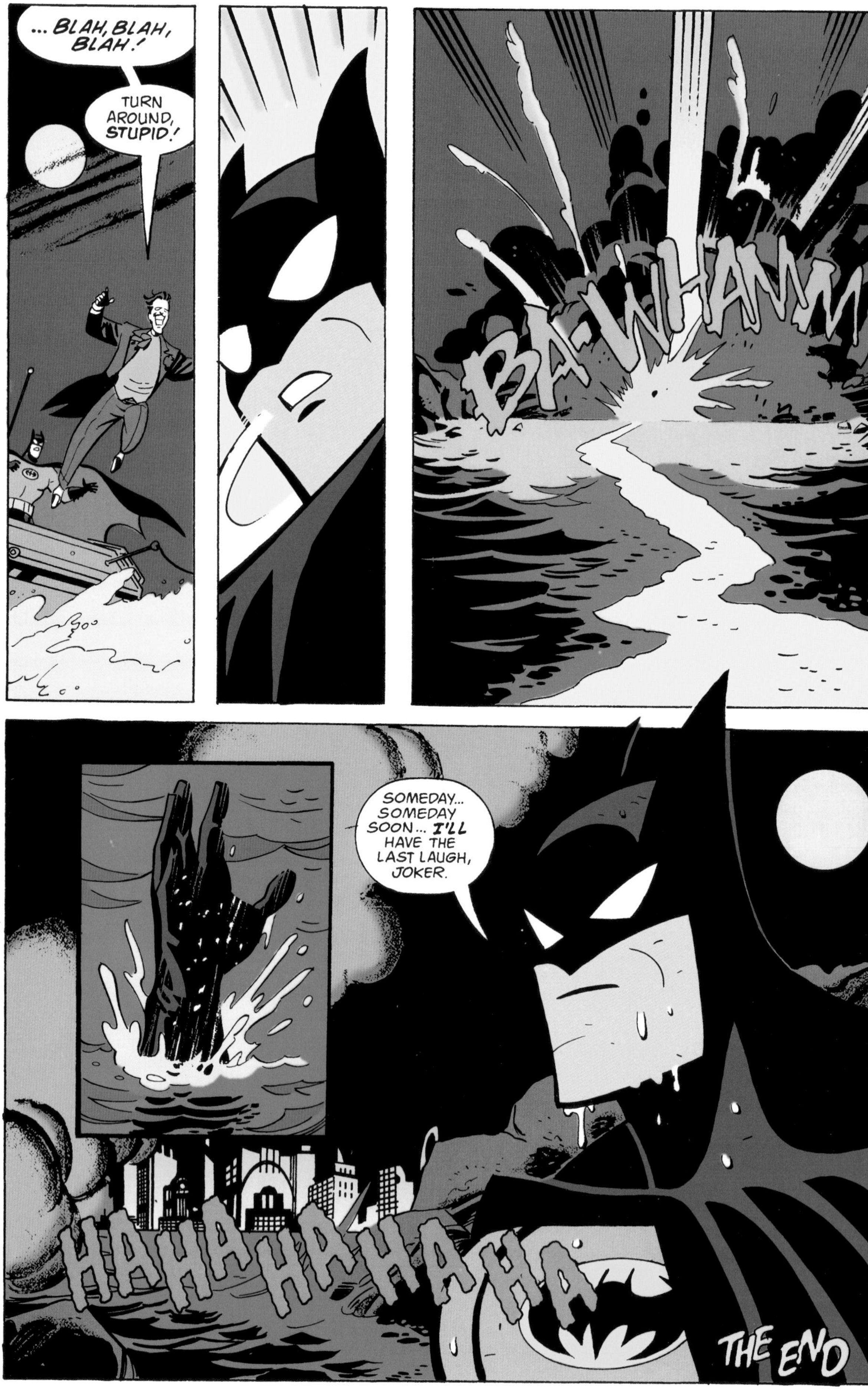
... BLAH, BLAH, BLAH!
TURN AROUND, STUPID!
BA-WHAMM
SOMEDAY... SOMEDAY SOON... I'LL HAVE THE LAST LAUGH, JOKER.
HA HA HA HA HA HA HA
THE END

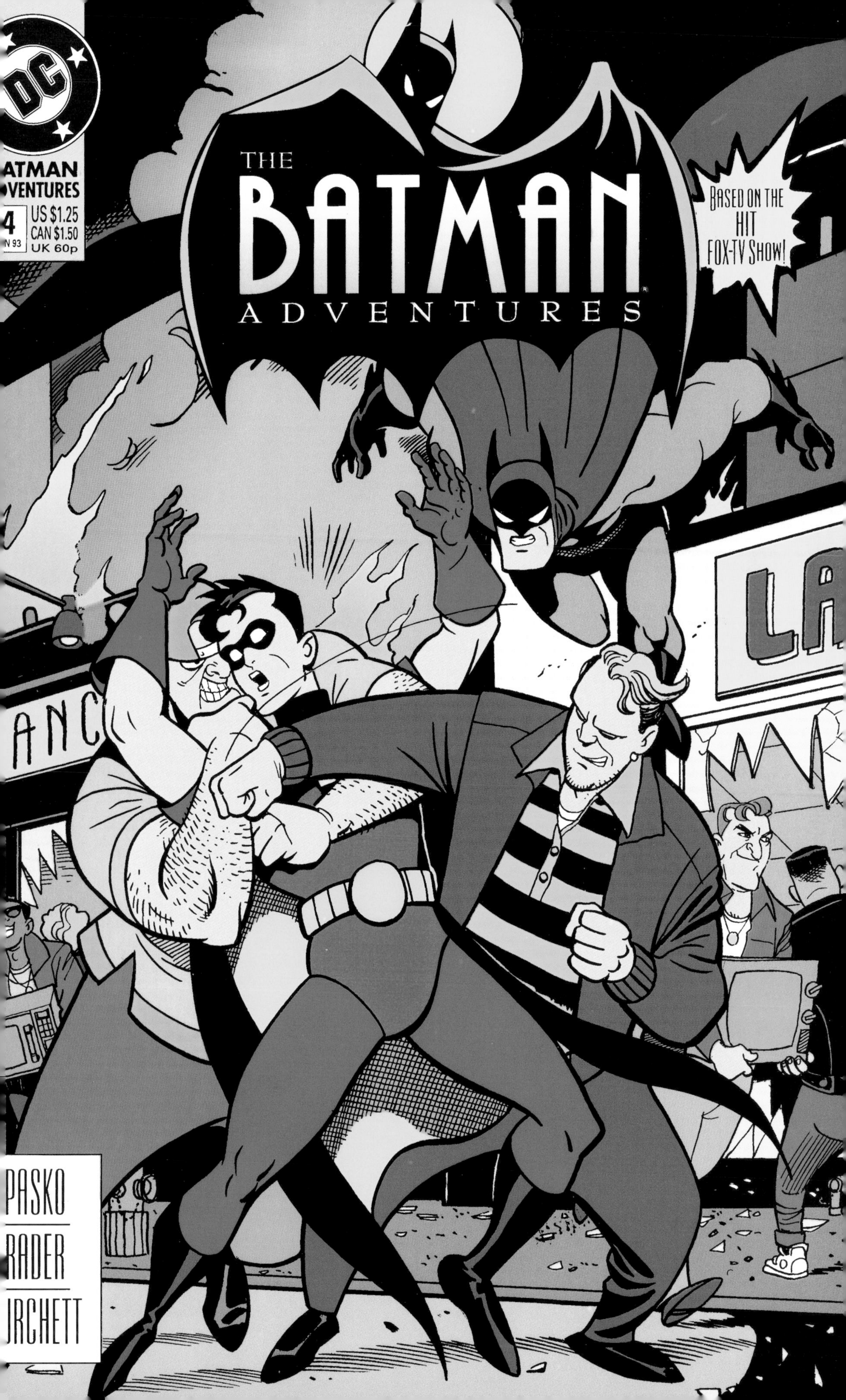
ATMAN
VENTURES
4
N 93
US $1.25
CAN $1.50
UK 60p
THE
BATMAN
ADVENTURES
BASED ON THE HIT FOX-TV SHOW!
ANC
LA
PASKO
RADER
JRCHETT

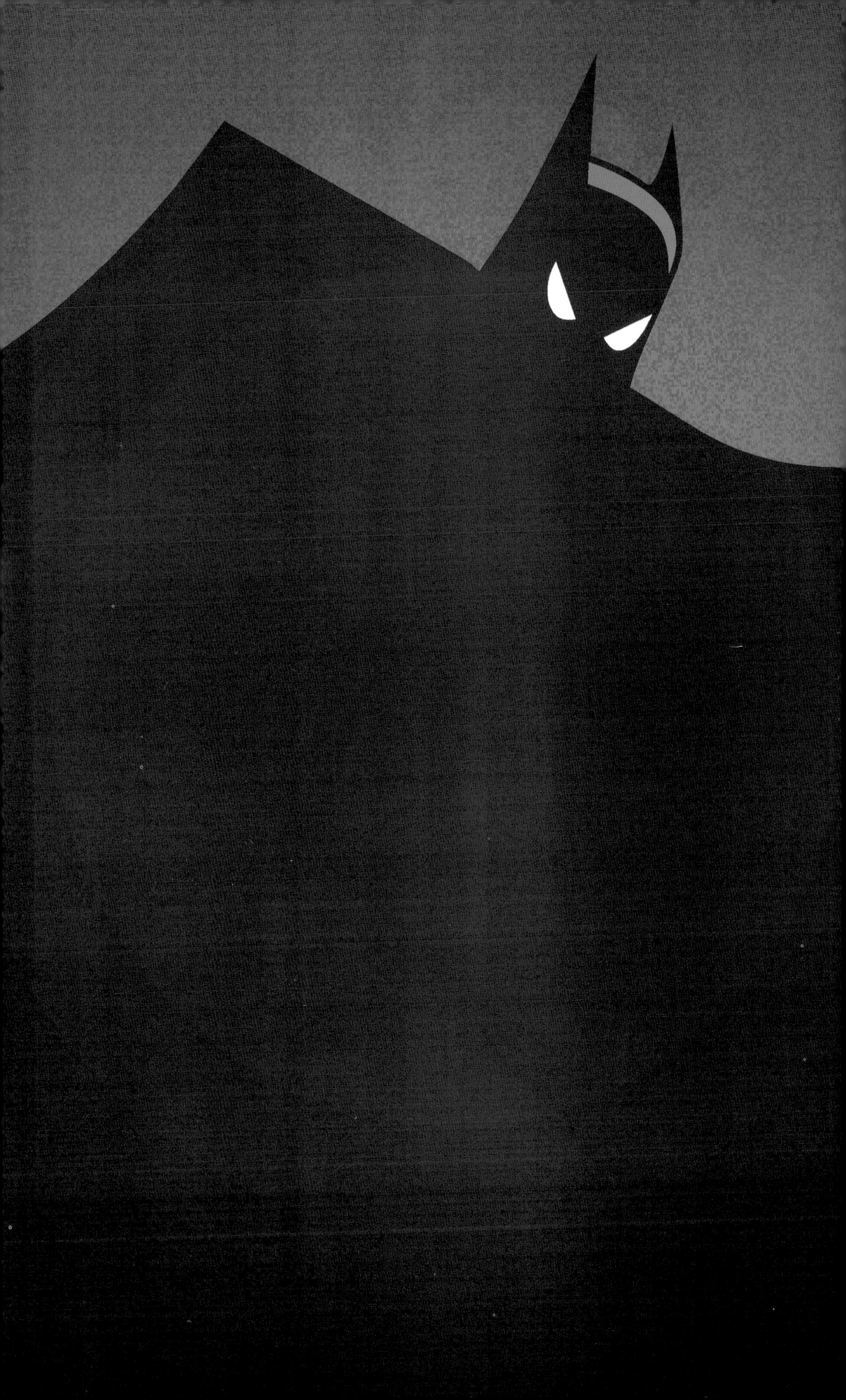

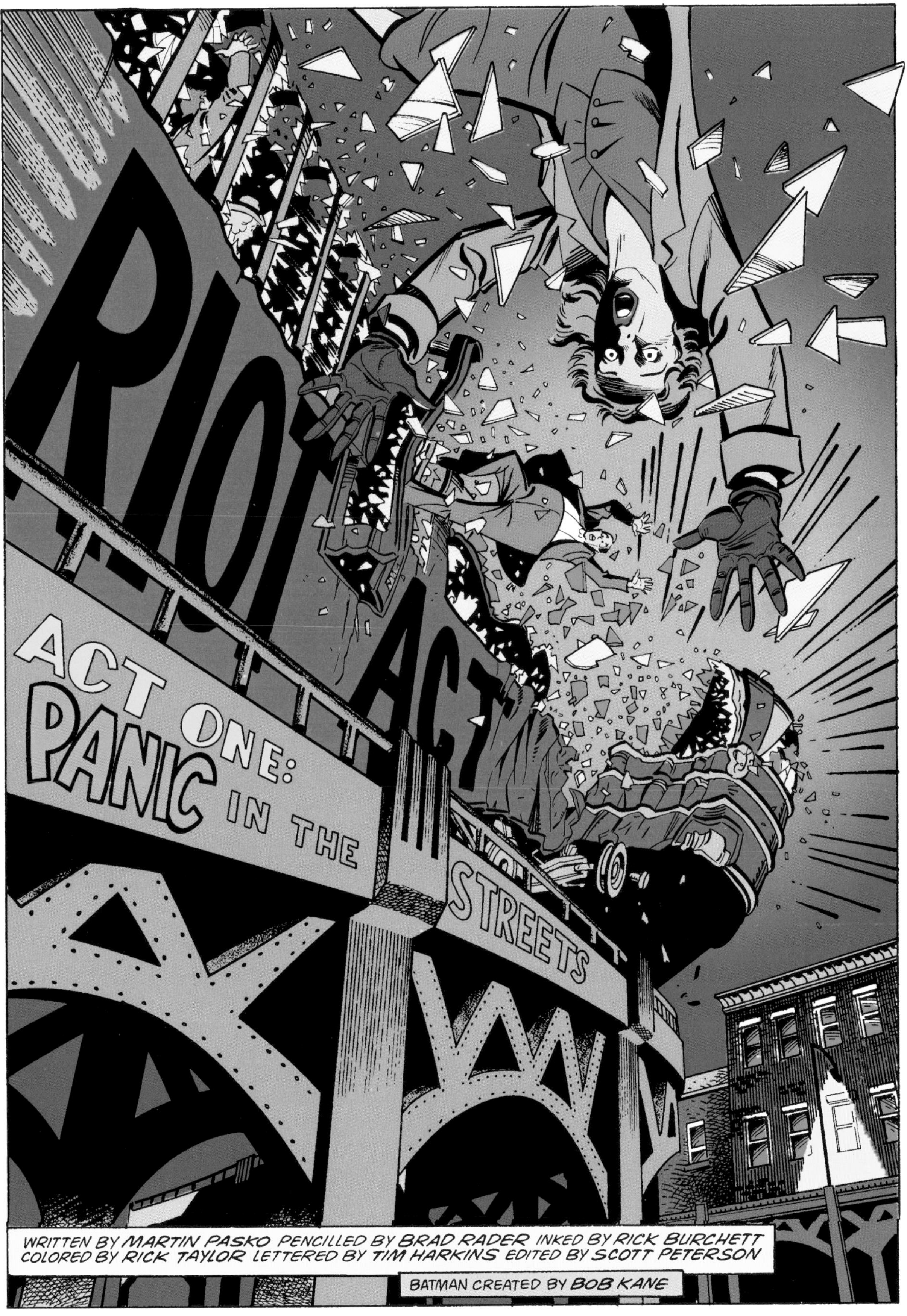
RIOT ACT
ACT ONE: PANIC IN THE STREETS
WRITTEN BY MARTIN PASKO PENCILLED BY BRAD RADER INKED BY RICK BURCHETT
COLORED BY RICK TAYLOR LETTERED BY TIM HARKINS EDITED BY SCOTT PETERSON
BATMAN CREATED BY BOB KANE

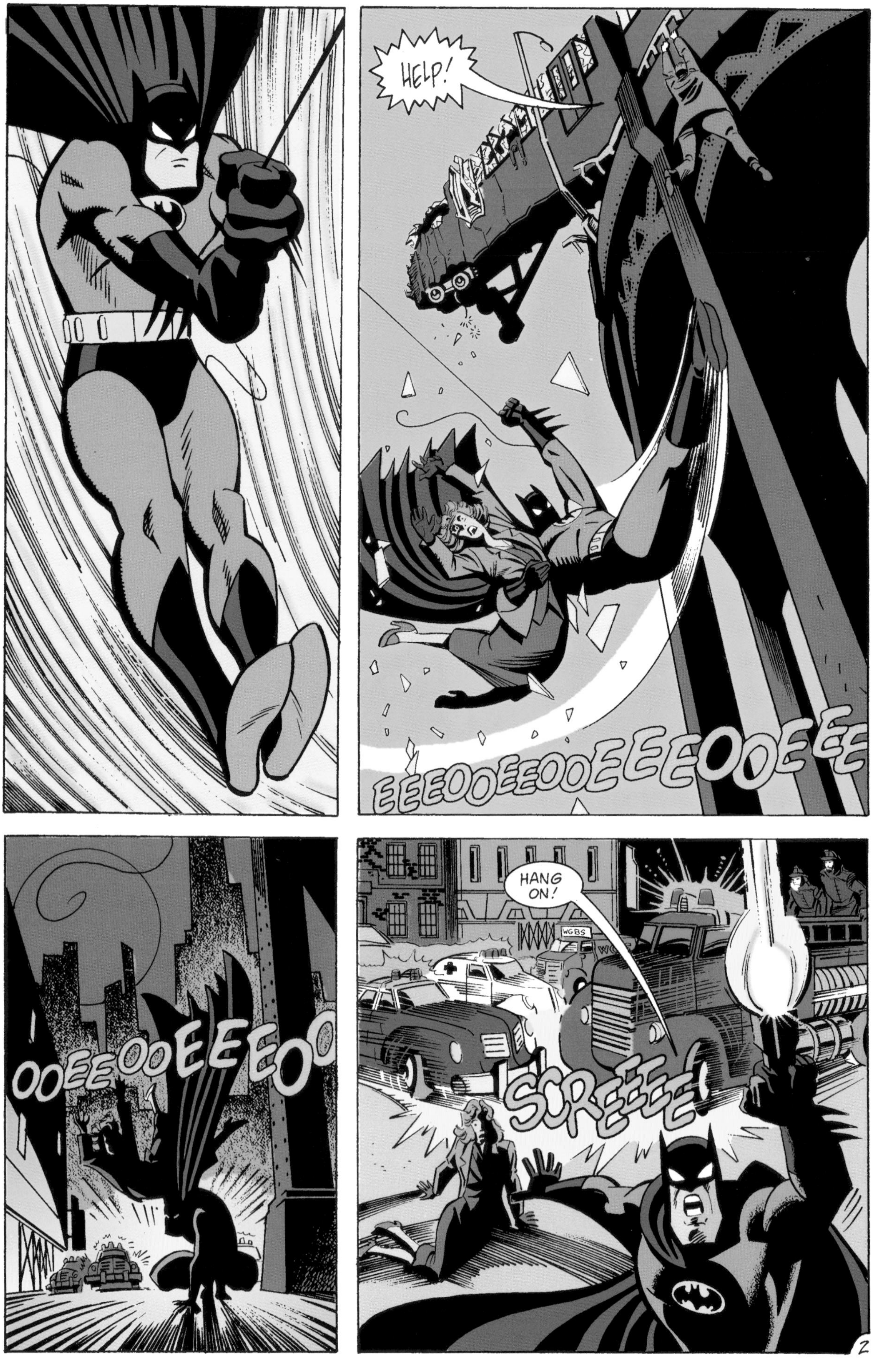
HELP!
EEEOOEEEOOEEEOOEEE
OOEEOOEEEOO
HANG ON!
WGBS
SCREEEEE
2

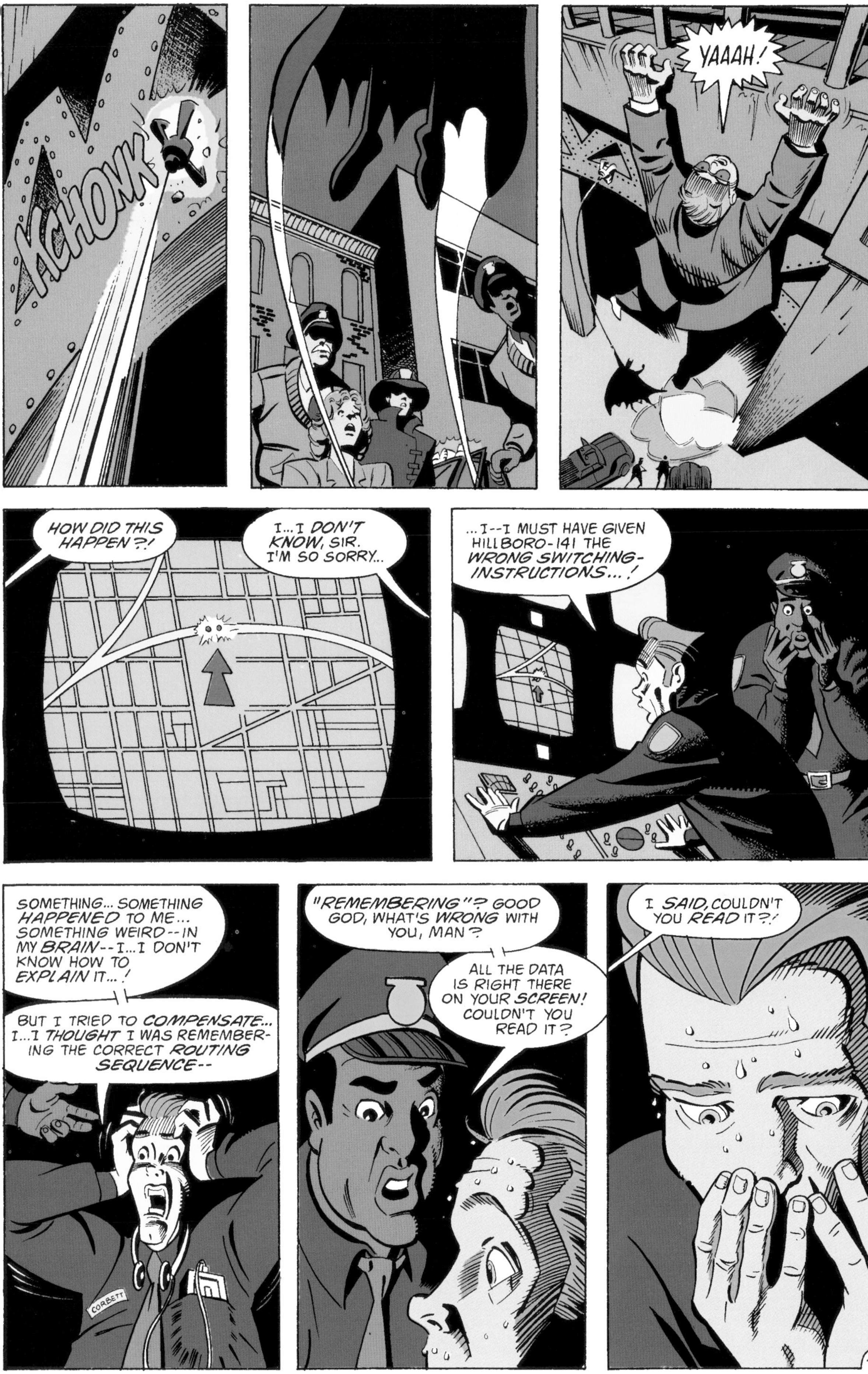
KCHONK
YAAAH!
HOW DID THIS HAPPEN?!
I...I DON'T KNOW, SIR. I'M SO SORRY...
...I--I MUST HAVE GIVEN HILLBORO-141 THE WRONG SWITCHING-INSTRUCTIONS...!
SOMETHING... SOMETHING HAPPENED TO ME... SOMETHING WEIRD--IN MY BRAIN--I...I DON'T KNOW HOW TO EXPLAIN IT...!
BUT I TRIED TO COMPENSATE... I...I THOUGHT I WAS REMEMBERING THE CORRECT ROUTING SEQUENCE--
CORBETT
"REMEMBERING"? GOOD GOD, WHAT'S WRONG WITH YOU, MAN?
ALL THE DATA IS RIGHT THERE ON YOUR SCREEN! COULDN'T YOU READ IT?
I SAID, COULDN'T YOU READ IT?!
3

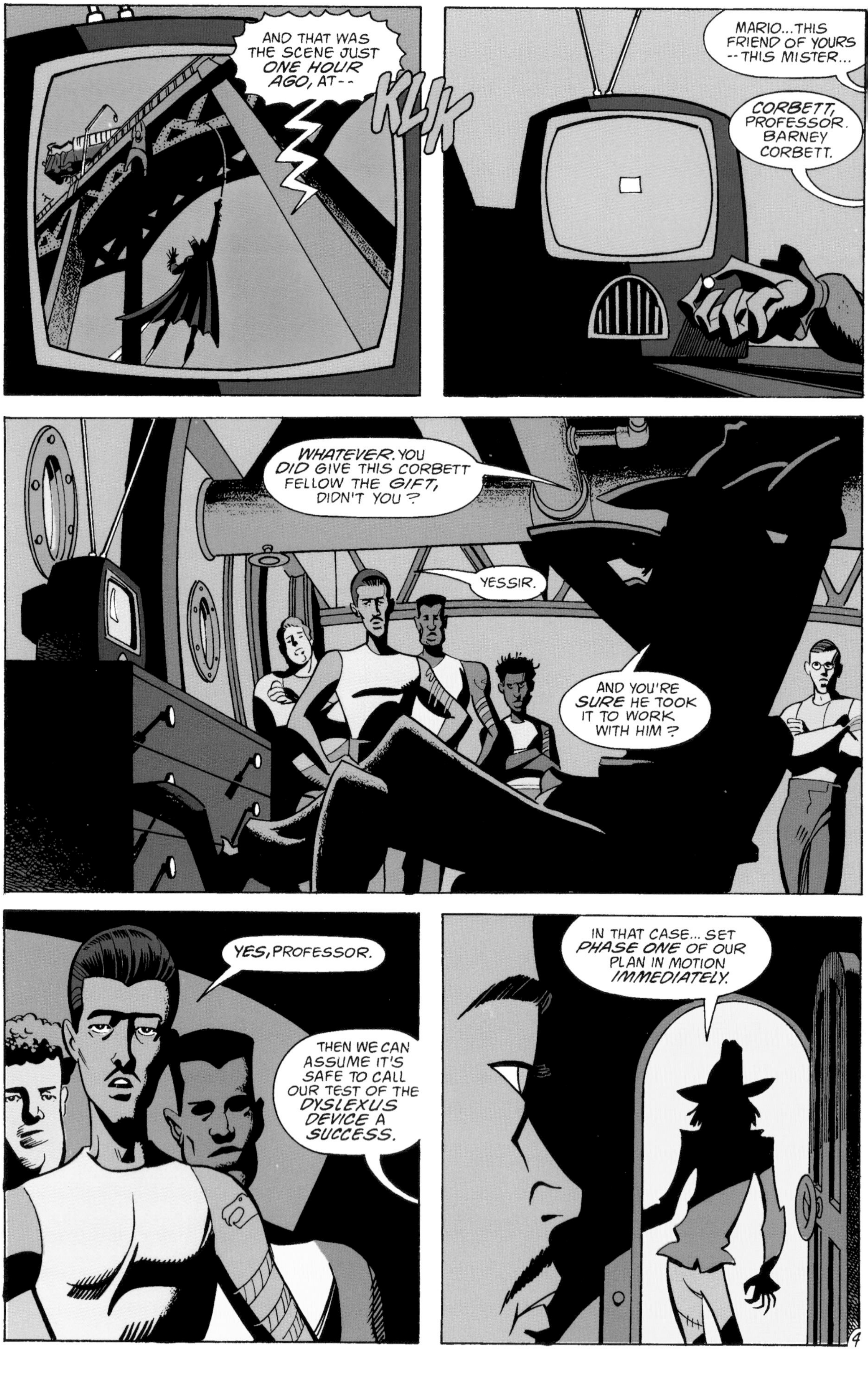
AND THAT WAS THE SCENE JUST ONE HOUR AGO, AT--
KLIK
MARIO... THIS FRIEND OF YOURS --THIS MISTER...
CORBETT, PROFESSOR. BARNEY CORBETT.
WHATEVER. YOU DID GIVE THIS CORBETT FELLOW THE GIFT, DIDN'T YOU?
YESSIR.
AND YOU'RE SURE HE TOOK IT TO WORK WITH HIM?
YES, PROFESSOR.
THEN WE CAN ASSUME IT'S SAFE TO CALL OUR TEST OF THE DYSLEXUS DEVICE A SUCCESS.
IN THAT CASE... SET PHASE ONE OF OUR PLAN IN MOTION IMMEDIATELY.
4

THIS IS *SUMMER GLEESON* REPORTING LIVE--

--FROM THE CORNER OF SCHIFF AND MOLDOFF IN *DOWNTOWN GOTHAM*--

-- IN THE MIDST OF THE WORST CASE OF *GRIDLOCK* IN RECENT MEMORY--

--CAUSED *NOT* BY THE USUAL RUSH-HOUR TRAFFIC--

--BUT BY THOUSANDS OF DISORIENTED MOTORISTS AND PEDESTRIANS WHO SEEM TO BE *LOST*--

-- AND BY *ACCIDENTS* CAUSED BY DRIVERS WHO ARE *DISOBEYING* POSTED DIRECTIONS OR SWERVING TO AVOID PEOPLE MILLING ABOUT AIMLESSLY--

NOW SHOWING
COOL KILL

"-- BECAUSE THE *STREET SIGNS* HAVE BECOME *MEANINGLESS* TO THEM!"

YOU GOT IT, *TOO?*

YEAH! ONE MINUTE I WAS READIN' THE PAPER--AN' THE NEXT, I COULDN'T MAKE OUT *NOTHIN'!*

APPARENTLY--INCREDIBLE AS IT MAY SEEM--HUNDREDS UPON THOUSANDS OF GOTHAMITES ARE SUDDENLY AND INEXPLICABLY *LOSING THE ABILITY TO READ!*

I--I CAN'T *REMEMBER...!* I KNOW I *USED* TO KNOW HOW...

FIRST BANK OF GOTHAM

5

...BUT I *CAN'T* ANY-MORE! IT'S LIKE A PART OF MY BRAIN *BURNED OUT* OR SUMPIN'...!

BUSINESS ALL OVER THE CITY, AS WELL AS *PUBLIC TRANSPORTATION* AND MANY *OTHER* MUNICIPAL SERVICES HAVE BEEN THROWN INTO DISARRAY--

-- AND SOME MAY BE FORCED TO *SHUT DOWN* ALTOGETHER UNTIL THE CAUSE OF THIS BIZARRE PHENOMENON IS DISCOVERED AND ITS EFFECTS *REVERSED.*

NOW BACK TO DIRK BRICKER IN THE *WGBS* NEWSROOM. DIRK...?

THANK YOU, SUMMER. WE'LL CONTINUE WITH OUR ONGOING COVERAGE OF THE STRANGE *CRISIS* GRIPPING GOTHAM IN JUST A MOMENT.

BUT RIGHT NOW, THESE OTHER HEADLINES AT THE TOP OF THE NEWS: MAYOR HILL HAS...

...CALLED A PRESS CONFERENCE...

CALLED A PRESS CONFER-ENC TO ANNOUNCE THE FORMATION OF A COALITION THAT WILL

...TO... TO...

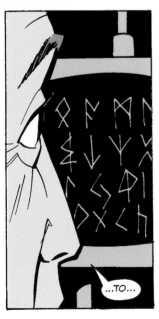

...TO...

PLEASE STAND BY

MY WORD...!

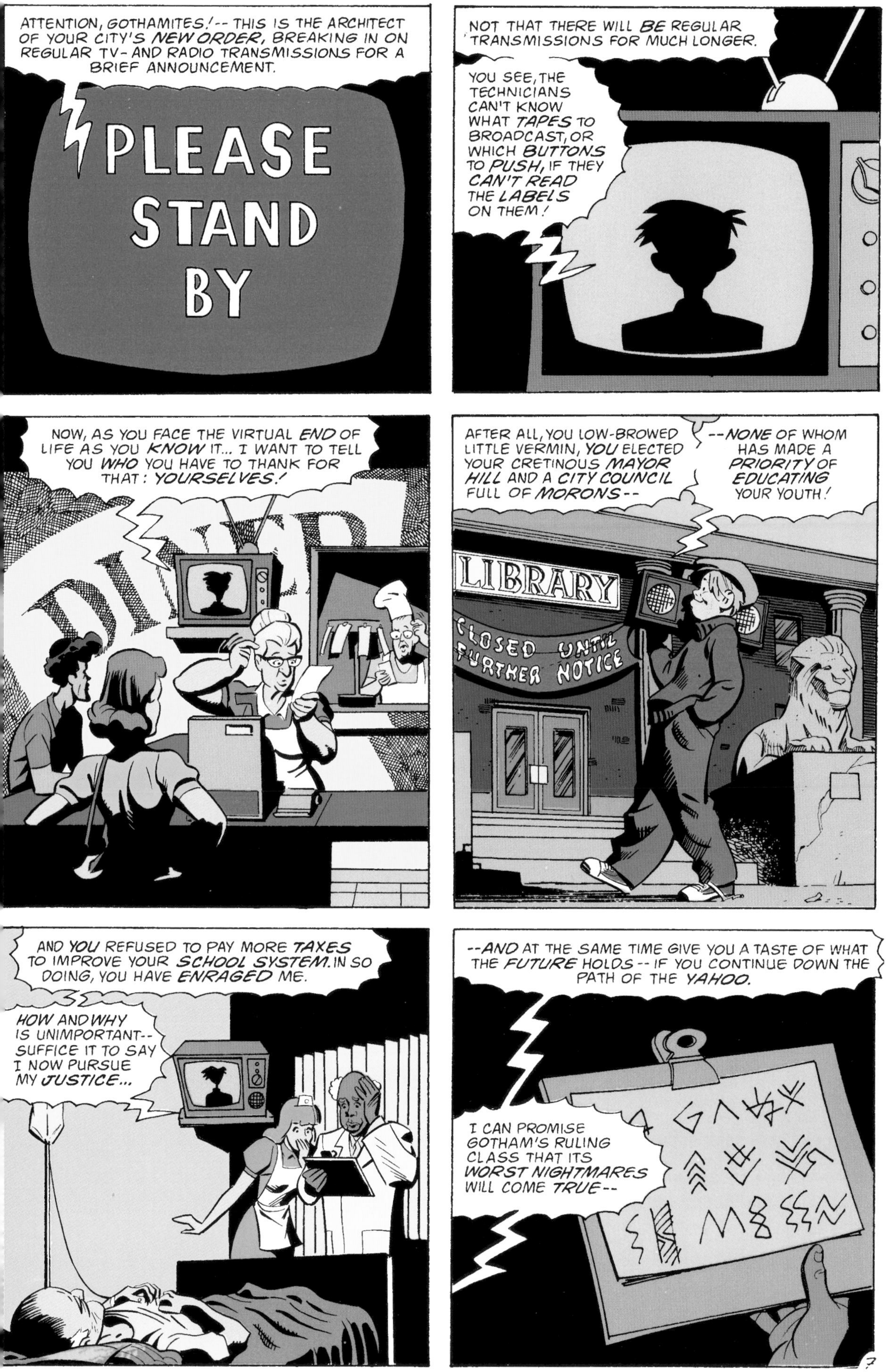
ATTENTION, GOTHAMITES!-- THIS IS THE ARCHITECT OF YOUR CITY'S NEW ORDER, BREAKING IN ON REGULAR TV- AND RADIO TRANSMISSIONS FOR A BRIEF ANNOUNCEMENT.
PLEASE STAND BY
NOT THAT THERE WILL BE REGULAR TRANSMISSIONS FOR MUCH LONGER.
YOU SEE, THE TECHNICIANS CAN'T KNOW WHAT TAPES TO BROADCAST, OR WHICH BUTTONS TO PUSH, IF THEY CAN'T READ THE LABELS ON THEM!
NOW, AS YOU FACE THE VIRTUAL END OF LIFE AS YOU KNOW IT... I WANT TO TELL YOU WHO YOU HAVE TO THANK FOR THAT: YOURSELVES!
AFTER ALL, YOU LOW-BROWED LITTLE VERMIN, YOU ELECTED YOUR CRETINOUS MAYOR HILL AND A CITY COUNCIL FULL OF MORONS--
--NONE OF WHOM HAS MADE A PRIORITY OF EDUCATING YOUR YOUTH!
LIBRARY
CLOSED UNTIL FURTHER NOTICE
AND YOU REFUSED TO PAY MORE TAXES TO IMPROVE YOUR SCHOOL SYSTEM. IN SO DOING, YOU HAVE ENRAGED ME.
HOW AND WHY IS UNIMPORTANT-- SUFFICE IT TO SAY I NOW PURSUE MY JUSTICE...
--AND AT THE SAME TIME GIVE YOU A TASTE OF WHAT THE FUTURE HOLDS -- IF YOU CONTINUE DOWN THE PATH OF THE YAHOO.
I CAN PROMISE GOTHAM'S RULING CLASS THAT ITS WORST NIGHTMARES WILL COME TRUE--
7

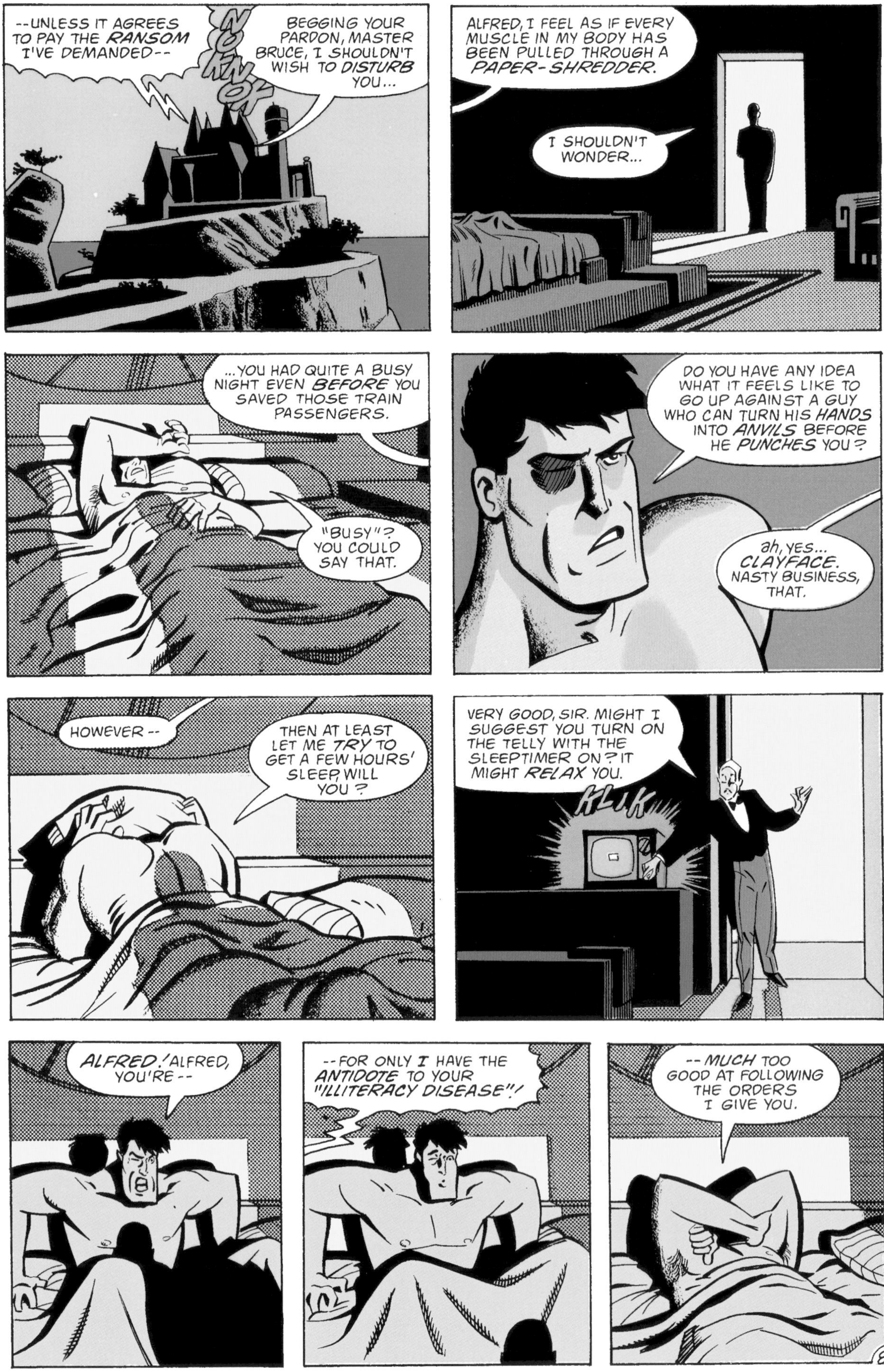
--UNLESS IT AGREES TO PAY THE RANSOM I'VE DEMANDED--
NOK NOK
BEGGING YOUR PARDON, MASTER BRUCE, I SHOULDN'T WISH TO DISTURB YOU...
ALFRED, I FEEL AS IF EVERY MUSCLE IN MY BODY HAS BEEN PULLED THROUGH A PAPER-SHREDDER.
I SHOULDN'T WONDER...
...YOU HAD QUITE A BUSY NIGHT EVEN BEFORE YOU SAVED THOSE TRAIN PASSENGERS.
"BUSY"? YOU COULD SAY THAT.
DO YOU HAVE ANY IDEA WHAT IT FEELS LIKE TO GO UP AGAINST A GUY WHO CAN TURN HIS HANDS INTO ANVILS BEFORE HE PUNCHES YOU?
ah, YES... CLAYFACE. NASTY BUSINESS, THAT.
HOWEVER--
THEN AT LEAST LET ME TRY TO GET A FEW HOURS' SLEEP, WILL YOU?
VERY GOOD, SIR. MIGHT I SUGGEST YOU TURN ON THE TELLY WITH THE SLEEPTIMER ON? IT MIGHT RELAX YOU.
KLIK
ALFRED! ALFRED, YOU'RE--
--FOR ONLY I HAVE THE ANTIDOTE TO YOUR "ILLITERACY DISEASE"!
--MUCH TOO GOOD AT FOLLOWING THE ORDERS I GIVE YOU.
8

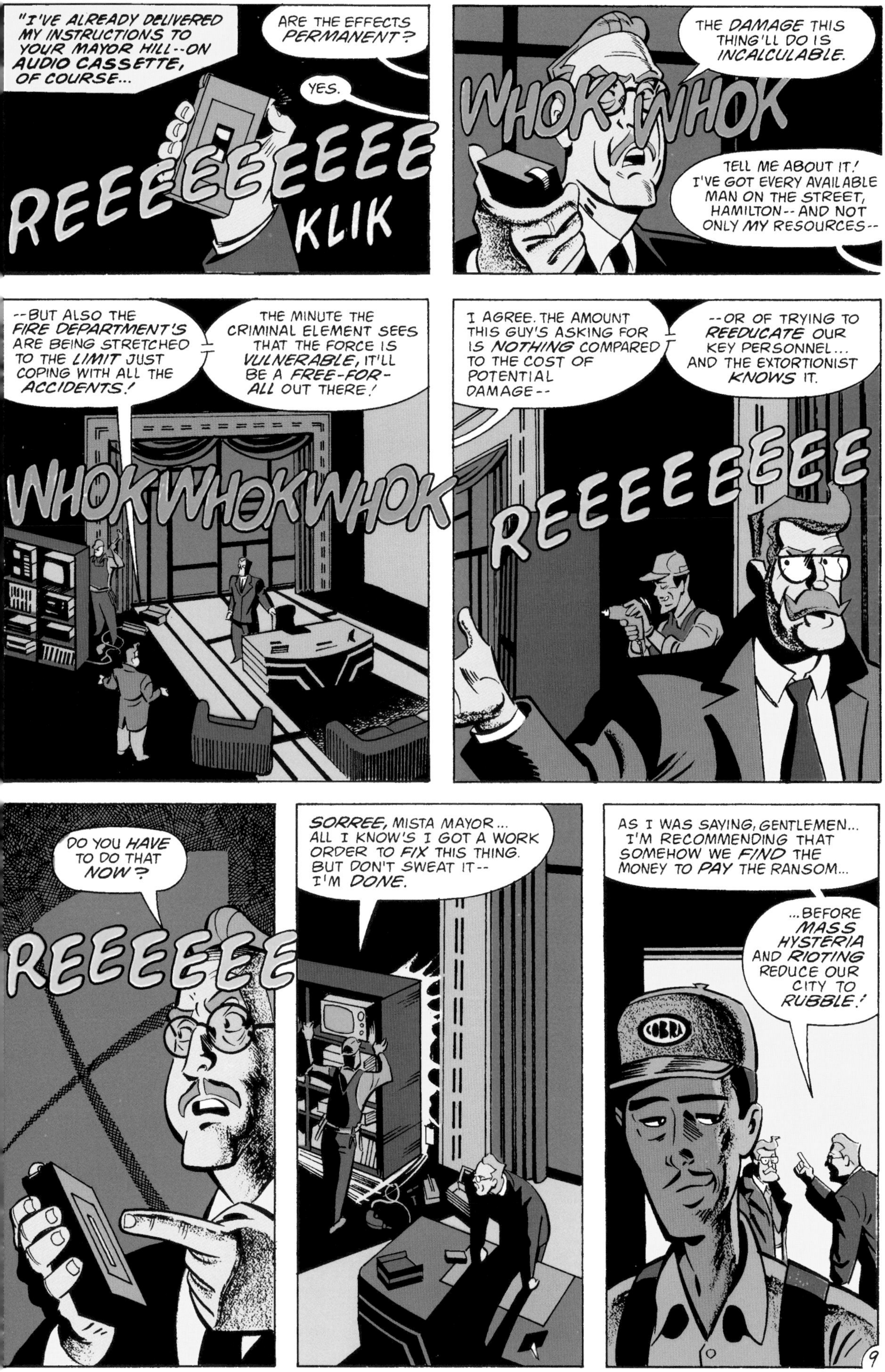

"I'VE ALREADY DELIVERED MY INSTRUCTIONS TO YOUR MAYOR HILL--ON AUDIO CASSETTE, OF COURSE...
ARE THE EFFECTS PERMANENT?
YES.
REEEEEEEEEE
KLIK
THE DAMAGE THIS THING'LL DO IS INCALCULABLE.
WHOK WHOK
TELL ME ABOUT IT! I'VE GOT EVERY AVAILABLE MAN ON THE STREET, HAMILTON--AND NOT ONLY MY RESOURCES--
--BUT ALSO THE FIRE DEPARTMENT'S ARE BEING STRETCHED TO THE LIMIT JUST COPING WITH ALL THE ACCIDENTS!
THE MINUTE THE CRIMINAL ELEMENT SEES THAT THE FORCE IS VULNERABLE, IT'LL BE A FREE-FOR-ALL OUT THERE!
WHOKWHOKWHOK
I AGREE. THE AMOUNT THIS GUY'S ASKING FOR IS NOTHING COMPARED TO THE COST OF POTENTIAL DAMAGE--
--OR OF TRYING TO REEDUCATE OUR KEY PERSONNEL... AND THE EXTORTIONIST KNOWS IT.
REEEEEEEEE
DO YOU HAVE TO DO THAT NOW?
REEEEEEE
SORREE, MISTA MAYOR... ALL I KNOW'S I GOT A WORK ORDER TO FIX THIS THING. BUT DON'T SWEAT IT-- I'M DONE.
AS I WAS SAYING, GENTLEMEN... I'M RECOMMENDING THAT SOMEHOW WE FIND THE MONEY TO PAY THE RANSOM...
...BEFORE MASS HYSTERIA AND RIOTING REDUCE OUR CITY TO RUBBLE!
COBRA
9

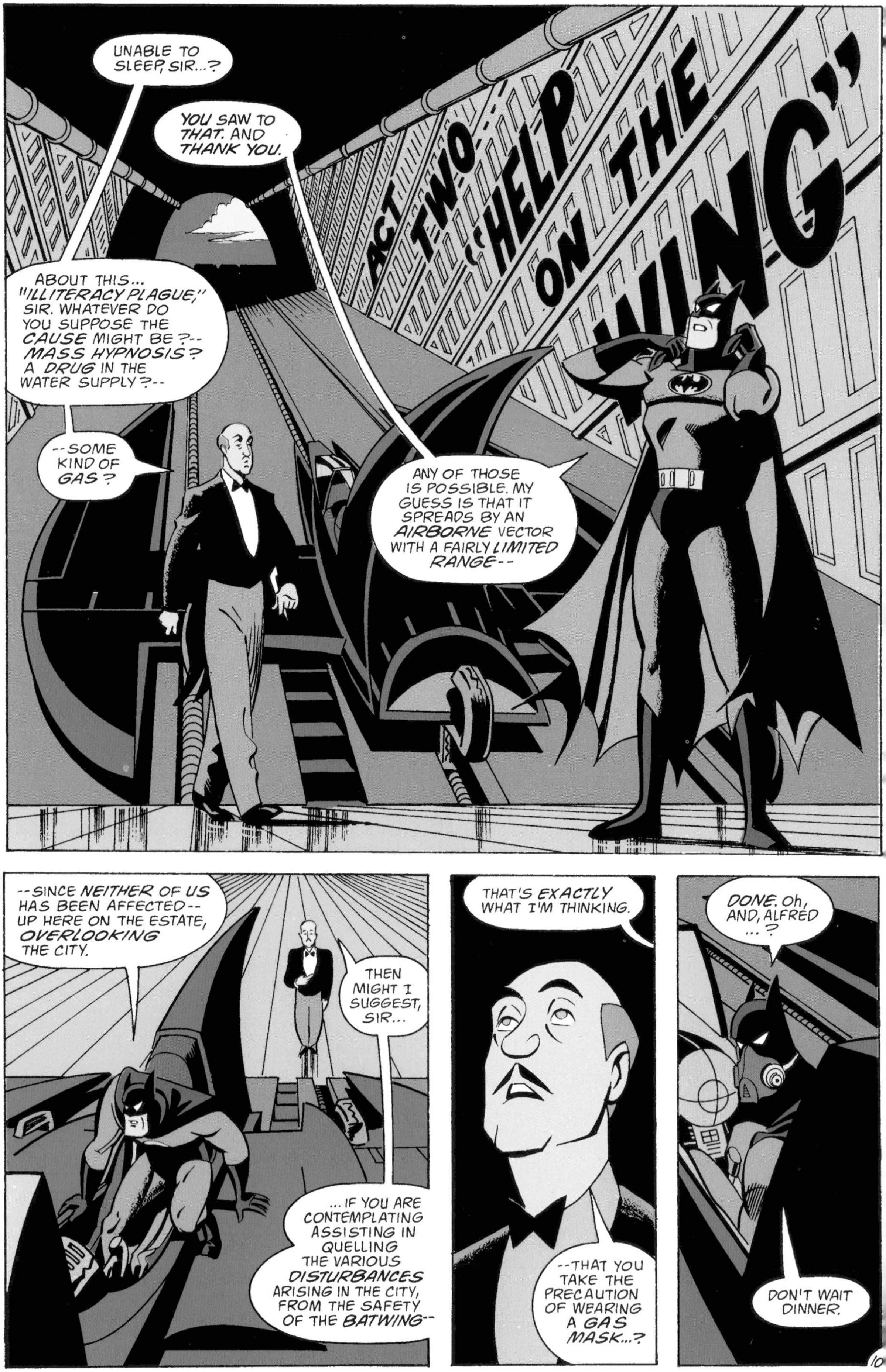
UNABLE TO SLEEP, SIR...?
YOU SAW TO THAT. AND THANK YOU.
ACT TWO "HELP ON THE WING"
ABOUT THIS... "ILLITERACY PLAGUE," SIR. WHATEVER DO YOU SUPPOSE THE CAUSE MIGHT BE?-- MASS HYPNOSIS? A DRUG IN THE WATER SUPPLY?--
--SOME KIND OF GAS?
ANY OF THOSE IS POSSIBLE. MY GUESS IS THAT IT SPREADS BY AN AIRBORNE VECTOR WITH A FAIRLY LIMITED RANGE--
--SINCE NEITHER OF US HAS BEEN AFFECTED-- UP HERE ON THE ESTATE, OVERLOOKING THE CITY.
THEN MIGHT I SUGGEST, SIR...
...IF YOU ARE CONTEMPLATING ASSISTING IN QUELLING THE VARIOUS DISTURBANCES ARISING IN THE CITY, FROM THE SAFETY OF THE BATWING--
THAT'S EXACTLY WHAT I'M THINKING.
--THAT YOU TAKE THE PRECAUTION OF WEARING A GAS MASK...?
DONE. Oh, AND, ALFRED ...?
DON'T WAIT DINNER.
10

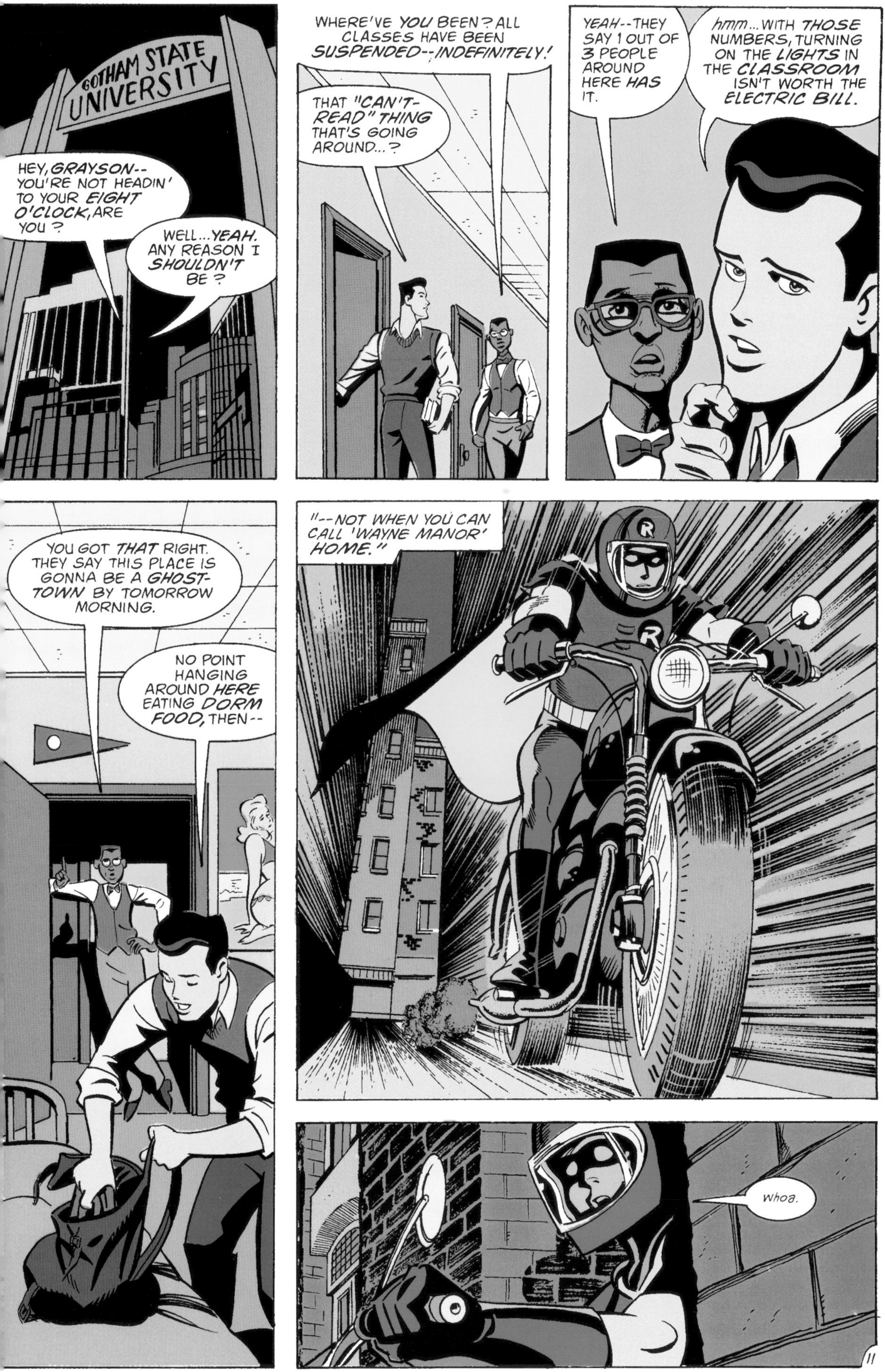
GOTHAM STATE UNIVERSITY
HEY, GRAYSON-- YOU'RE NOT HEADIN' TO YOUR EIGHT O'CLOCK, ARE YOU?
WELL... YEAH. ANY REASON I SHOULDN'T BE?
WHERE'VE YOU BEEN? ALL CLASSES HAVE BEEN SUSPENDED--INDEFINITELY!
THAT "CAN'T-READ" THING THAT'S GOING AROUND...?
YEAH--THEY SAY 1 OUT OF 3 PEOPLE AROUND HERE HAS IT.
hmm... WITH THOSE NUMBERS, TURNING ON THE LIGHTS IN THE CLASSROOM ISN'T WORTH THE ELECTRIC BILL.
YOU GOT THAT RIGHT. THEY SAY THIS PLACE IS GONNA BE A GHOST-TOWN BY TOMORROW MORNING.
NO POINT HANGING AROUND HERE EATING DORM FOOD, THEN--
"--NOT WHEN YOU CAN CALL 'WAYNE MANOR' HOME."
Whoa.
11

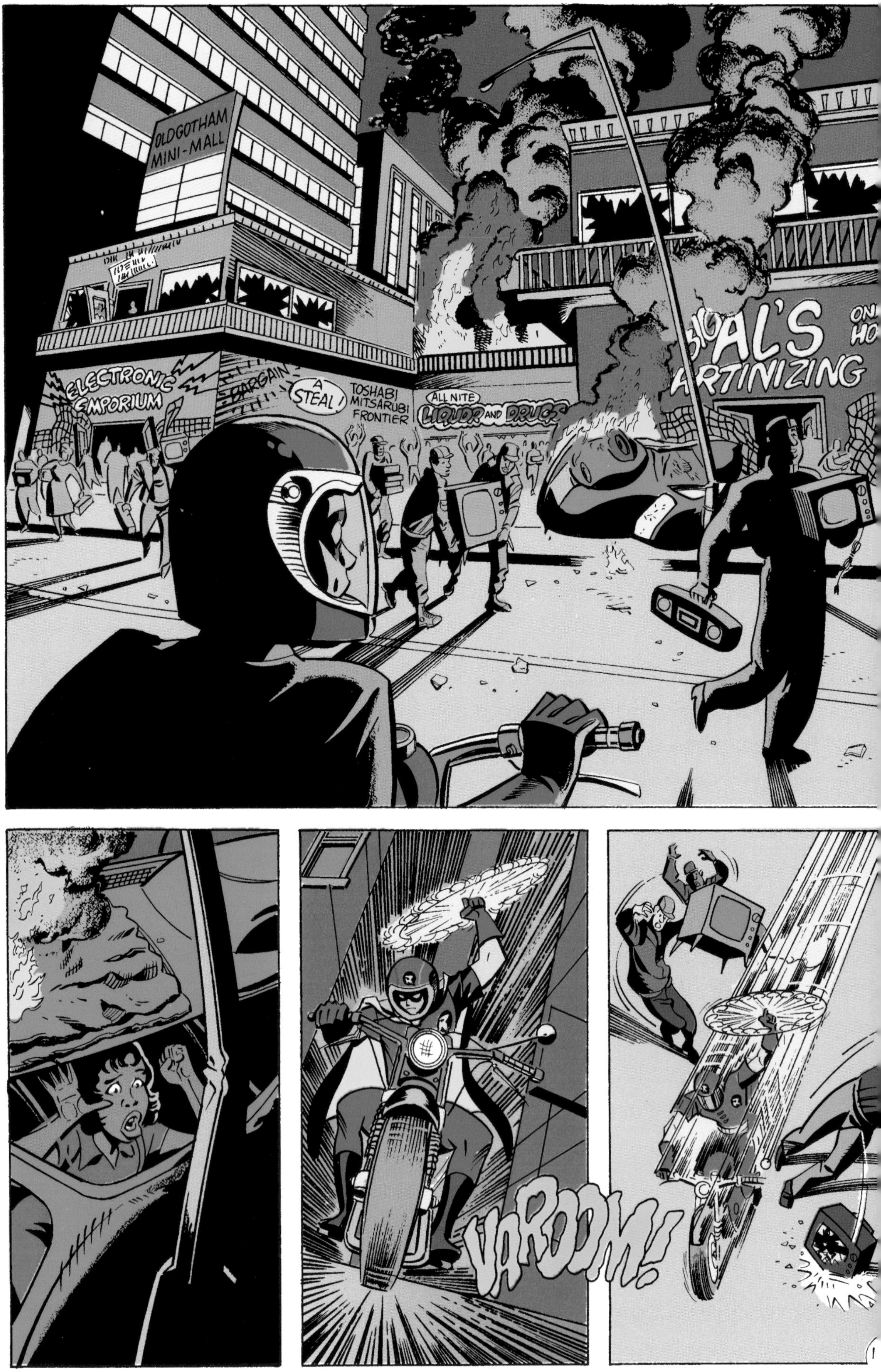
OLDGOTHAM
MINI-MALL
ELECTRONIC
EMPORIUM
BARGAIN
A STEAL!
TOSHABI
MITSARUBI
FRONTIER
ALL NITE
LIQUOR AND DRUGS
BIG AL'S
ARTINIZING
VAROOM!

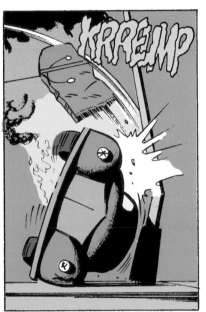

"THE WORST FEARS OF LAW ENFORCEMENT OFFICIALS ARE BEING REALIZED AT THIS HOUR--

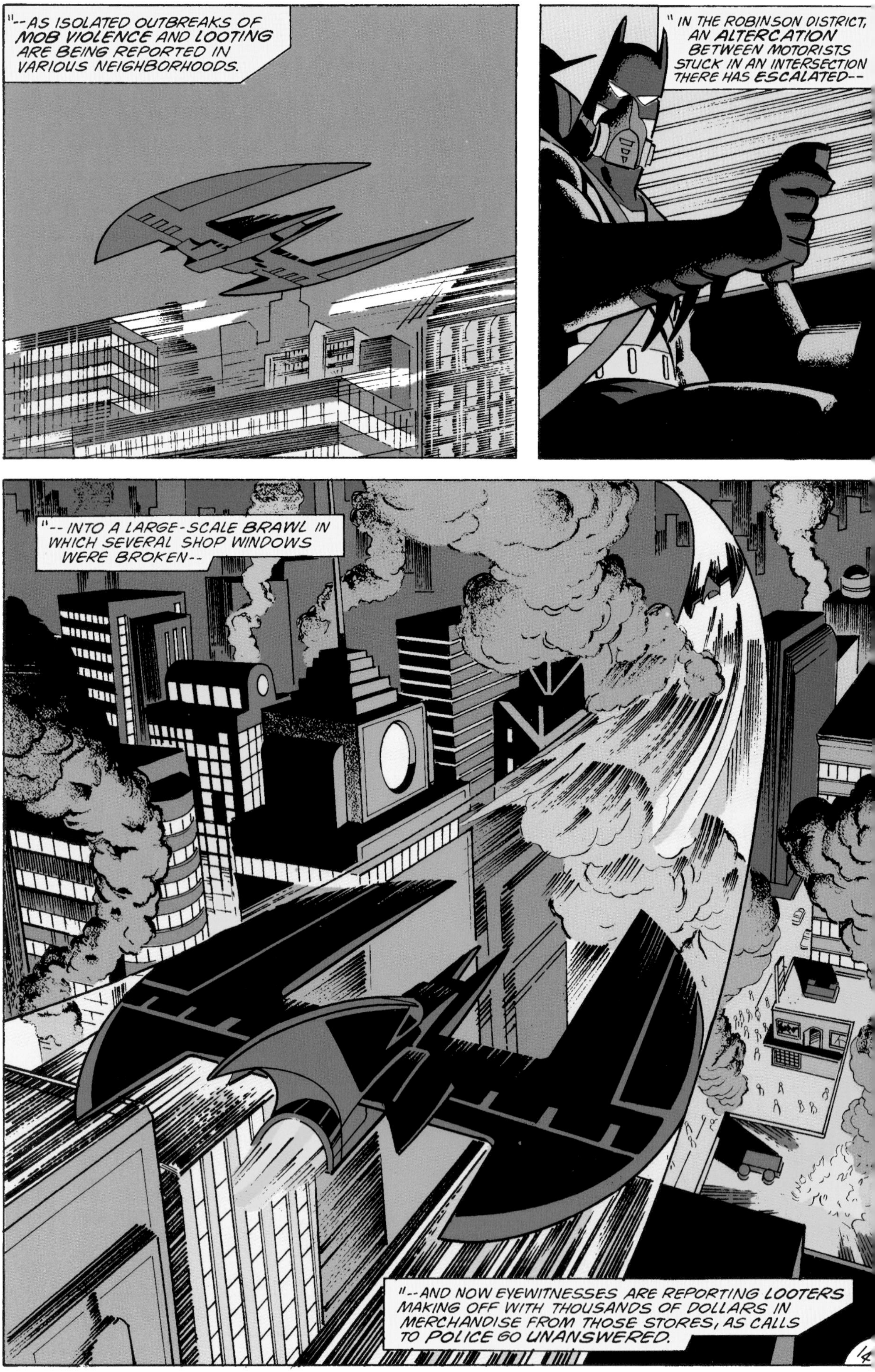
"--AS ISOLATED OUTBREAKS OF MOB VIOLENCE AND LOOTING ARE BEING REPORTED IN VARIOUS NEIGHBORHOODS.
" IN THE ROBINSON DISTRICT, AN ALTERCATION BETWEEN MOTORISTS STUCK IN AN INTERSECTION THERE HAS ESCALATED--
"--INTO A LARGE-SCALE BRAWL IN WHICH SEVERAL SHOP WINDOWS WERE BROKEN--
"--AND NOW EYEWITNESSES ARE REPORTING LOOTERS MAKING OFF WITH THOUSANDS OF DOLLARS IN MERCHANDISE FROM THOSE STORES, AS CALLS TO POLICE GO UNANSWERED.
14

"SPOKESPERSONS FOR BOTH THE POLICE AND FIRE DEPARTMENTS--

"--CONFIRM A RECORD NUMBER OF CALLS FOR ASSISTANCE--

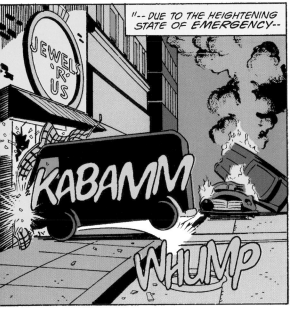

"-- DUE TO THE HEIGHTENING STATE OF EMERGENCY--

KABAMM

WHUMP

"-- BUT DENY THAT THE DEMANDS FOR HELP--

"--EXCEED THE NUMBER OF PERSONNEL AVAILABLE TO RESPOND!"

uh...

...uh...

15

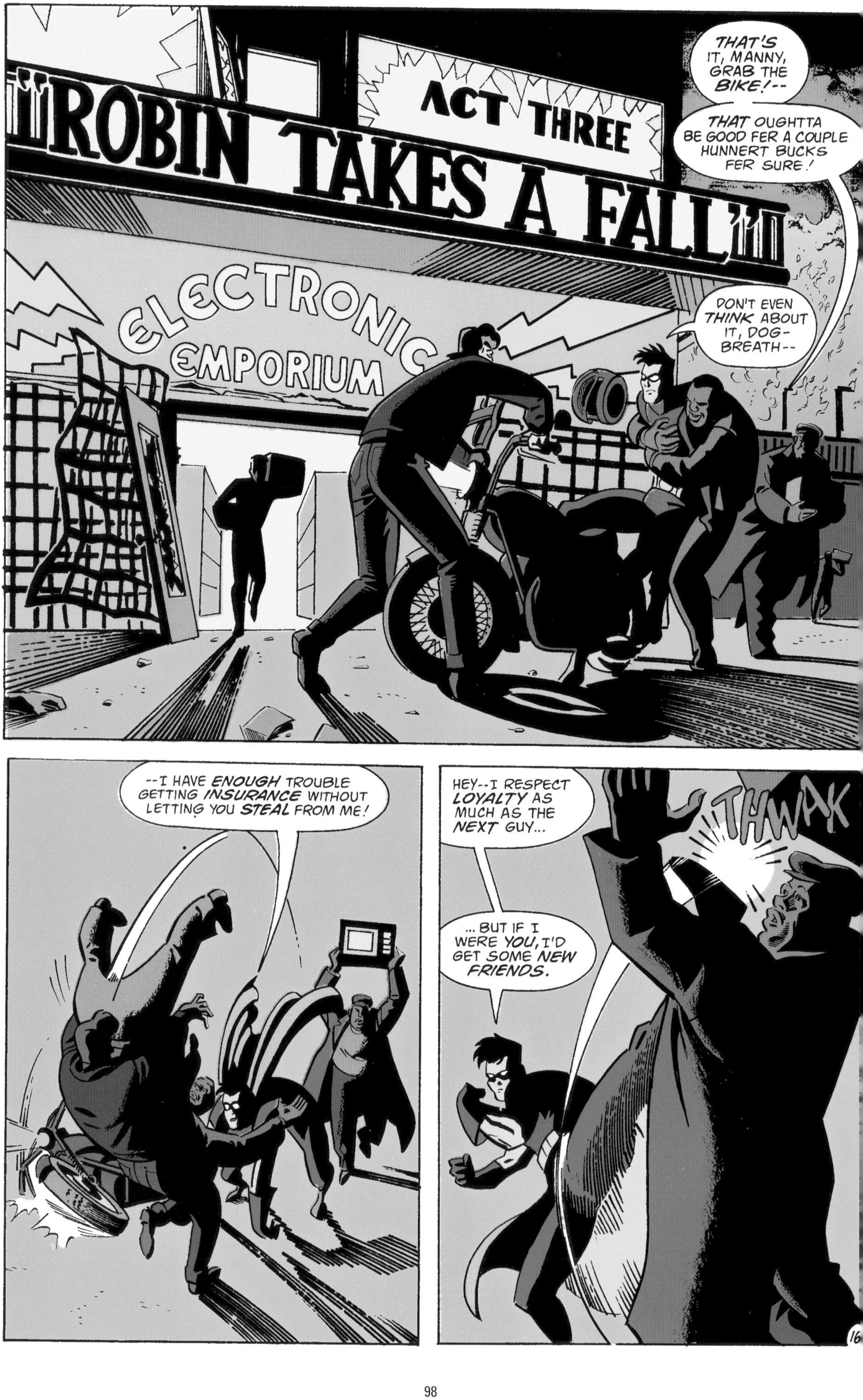
ACT THREE
"ROBIN TAKES A FALL"
ELECTRONIC EMPORIUM
THAT'S IT, MANNY, GRAB THE BIKE!--
THAT OUGHTTA BE GOOD FER A COUPLE HUNNERT BUCKS FER SURE!
DON'T EVEN THINK ABOUT IT, DOG-BREATH--
--I HAVE ENOUGH TROUBLE GETTING INSURANCE WITHOUT LETTING YOU STEAL FROM ME!
HEY--I RESPECT LOYALTY AS MUCH AS THE NEXT GUY...
...BUT IF I WERE YOU, I'D GET SOME NEW FRIENDS.
THWAK
16

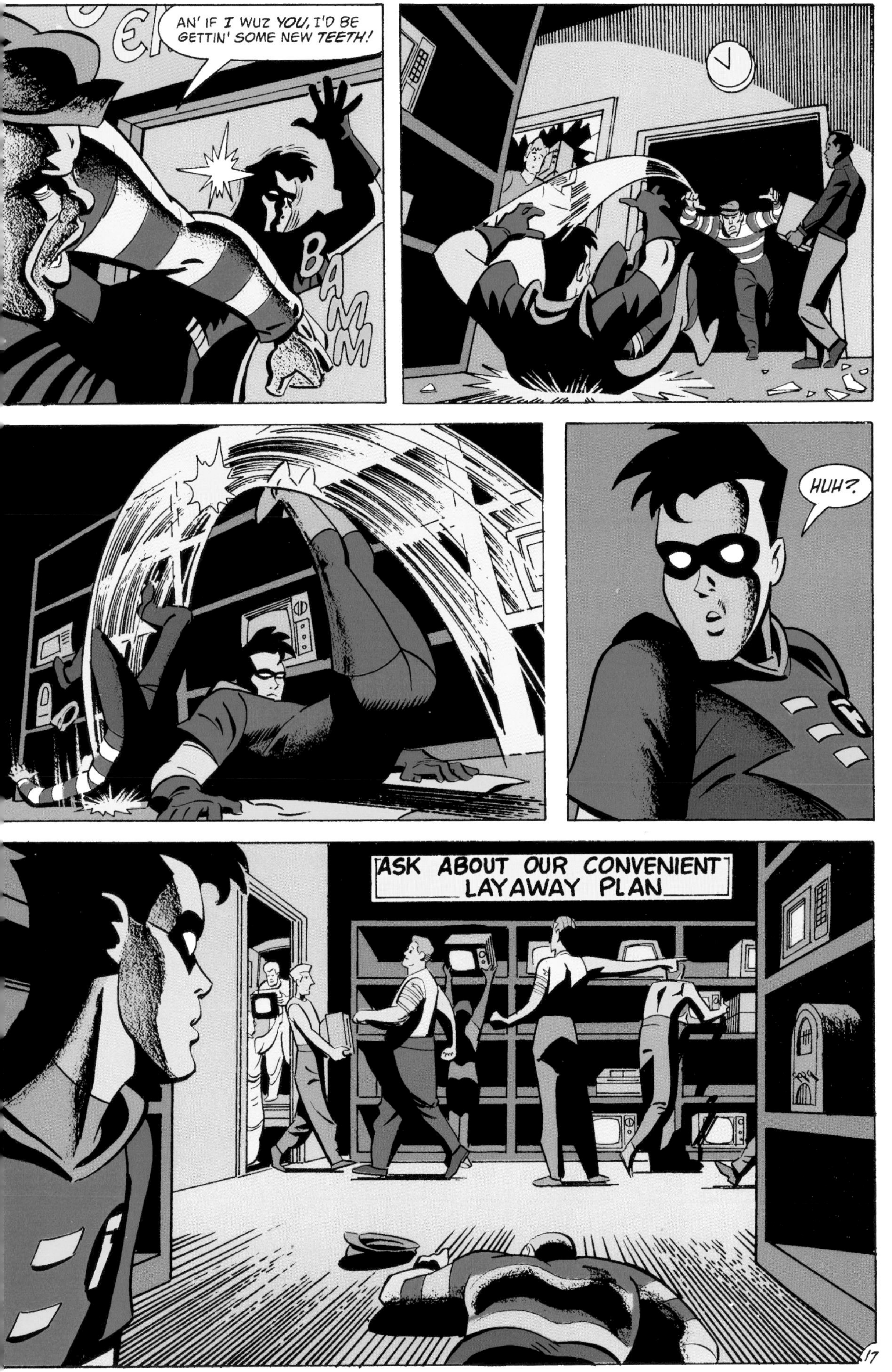

AN' IF I WUZ YOU, I'D BE GETTIN' SOME NEW TEETH!
BAMM
HUH?
ASK ABOUT OUR CONVENIENT LAYAWAY PLAN
17

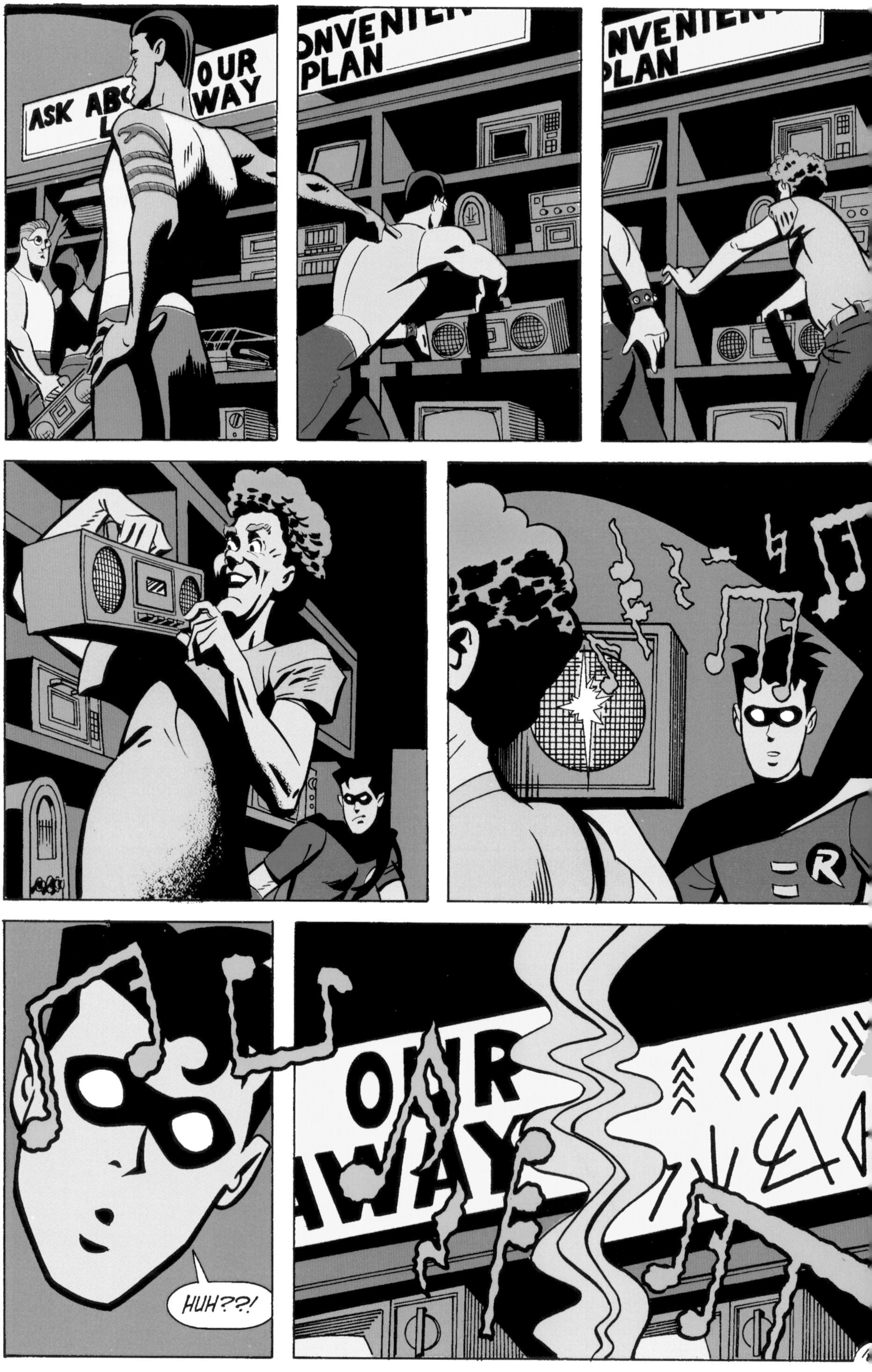
ASK ABO
OUR
WAY
ONVENIEN
PLAN
NVENIEN
PLAN
HUH??!
OUR
AWAY

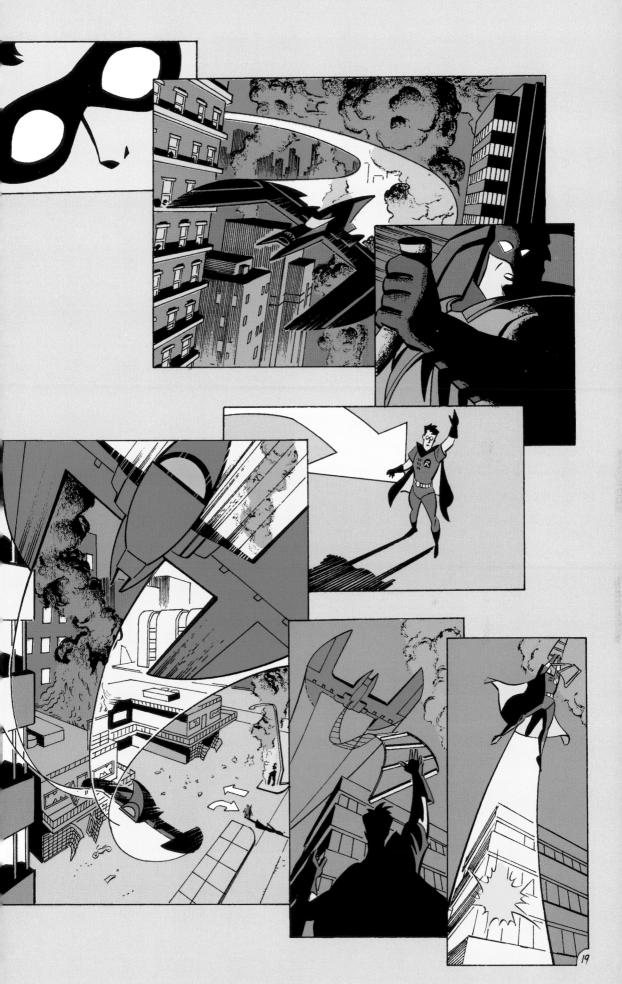

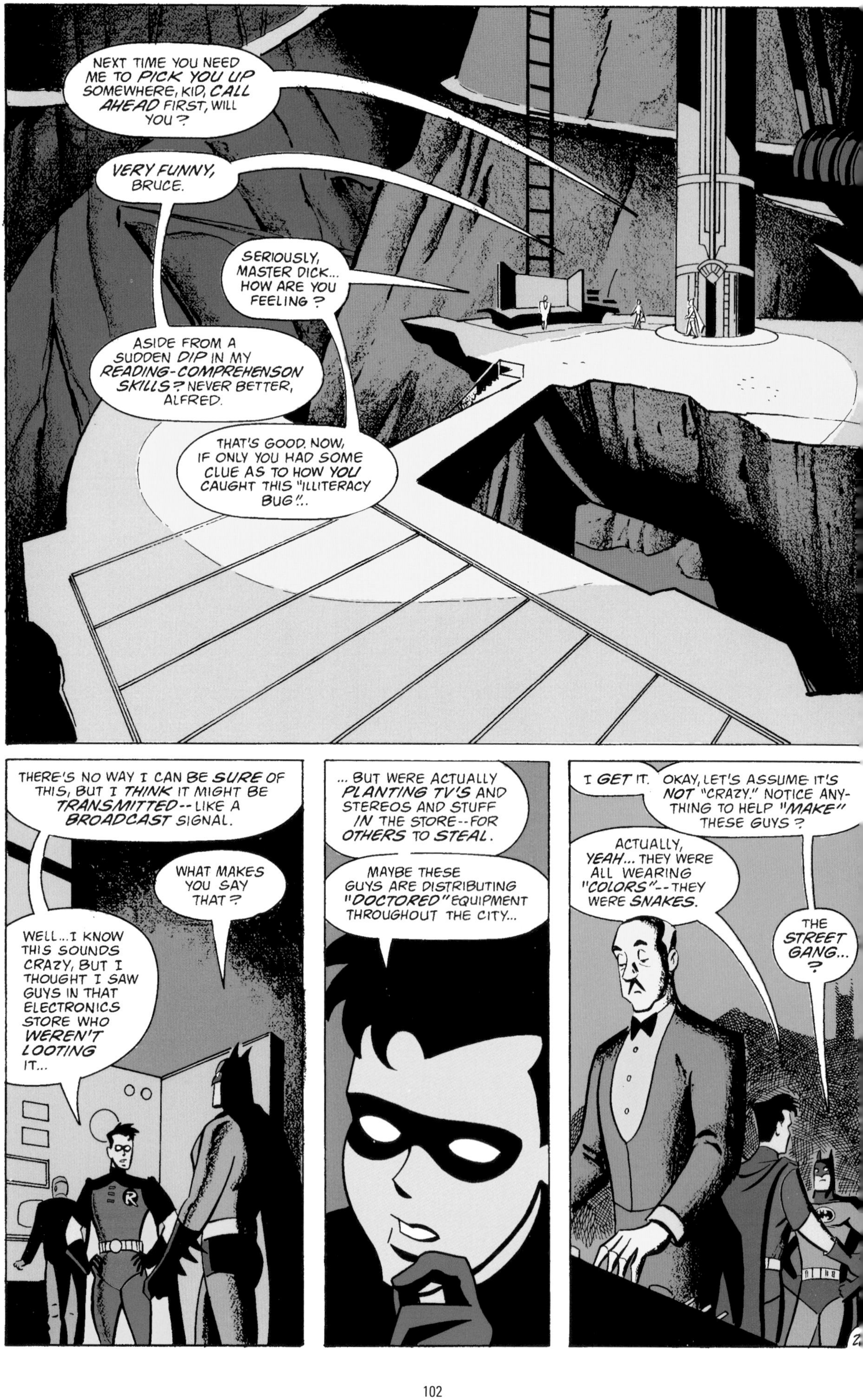
NEXT TIME YOU NEED ME TO PICK YOU UP SOMEWHERE, KID, CALL AHEAD FIRST, WILL YOU?
VERY FUNNY, BRUCE.
SERIOUSLY, MASTER DICK... HOW ARE YOU FEELING?
ASIDE FROM A SUDDEN DIP IN MY READING-COMPREHENSON SKILLS? NEVER BETTER, ALFRED.
THAT'S GOOD. NOW, IF ONLY YOU HAD SOME CLUE AS TO HOW YOU CAUGHT THIS "ILLITERACY BUG"!..
THERE'S NO WAY I CAN BE SURE OF THIS, BUT I THINK IT MIGHT BE TRANSMITTED--LIKE A BROADCAST SIGNAL.
WHAT MAKES YOU SAY THAT?
WELL...I KNOW THIS SOUNDS CRAZY, BUT I THOUGHT I SAW GUYS IN THAT ELECTRONICS STORE WHO WEREN'T LOOTING IT...
...BUT WERE ACTUALLY PLANTING TV'S AND STEREOS AND STUFF IN THE STORE--FOR OTHERS TO STEAL.
MAYBE THESE GUYS ARE DISTRIBUTING "DOCTORED" EQUIPMENT THROUGHOUT THE CITY...
I GET IT.
OKAY, LET'S ASSUME IT'S NOT "CRAZY." NOTICE ANYTHING TO HELP "MAKE" THESE GUYS?
ACTUALLY, YEAH... THEY WERE ALL WEARING "COLORS"--THEY WERE SNAKES.
THE STREET GANG...?

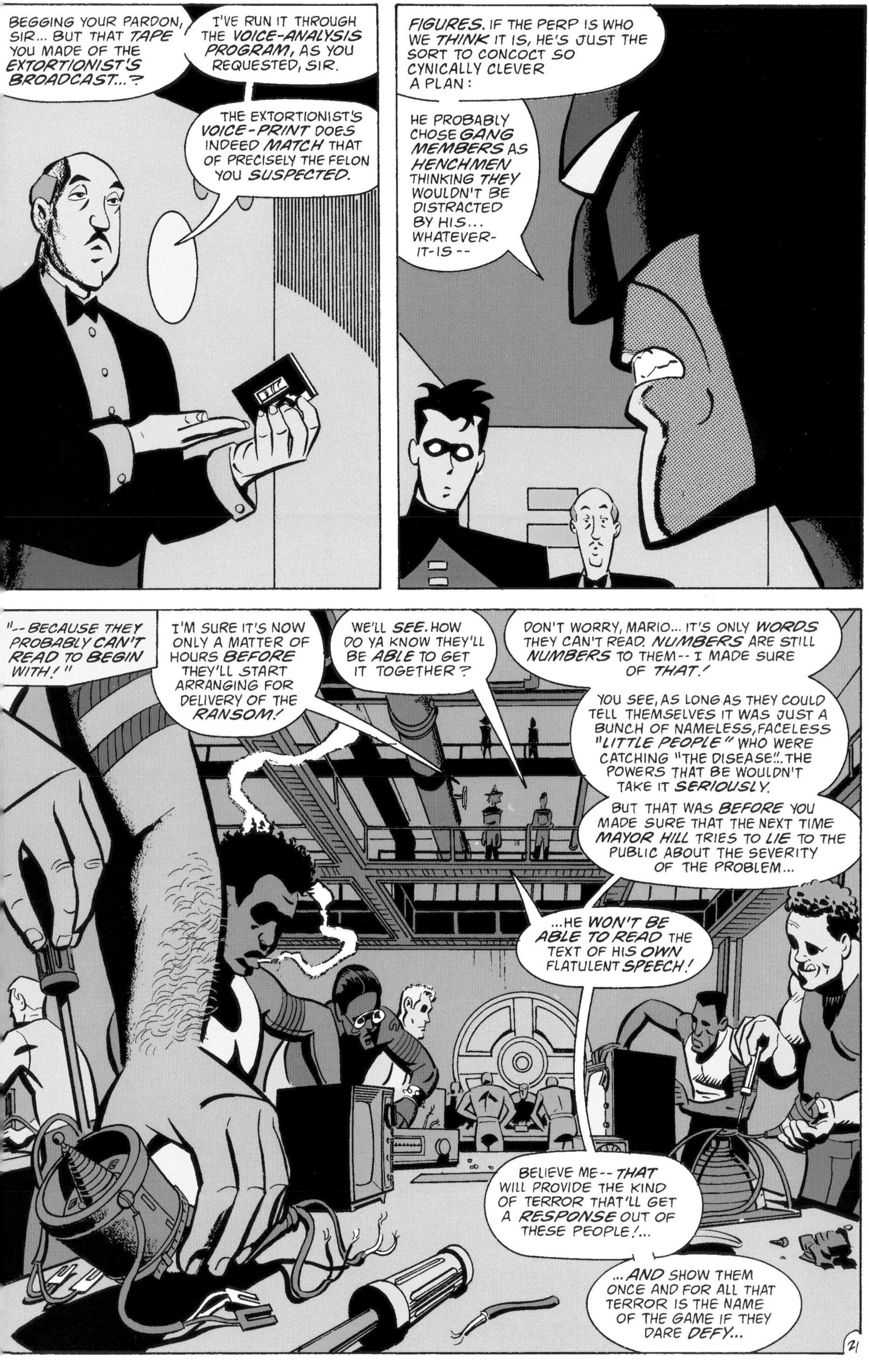
BEGGING YOUR PARDON, SIR... BUT THAT TAPE YOU MADE OF THE EXTORTIONIST'S BROADCAST...?
I'VE RUN IT THROUGH THE VOICE-ANALYSIS PROGRAM, AS YOU REQUESTED, SIR.
THE EXTORTIONIST'S VOICE-PRINT DOES INDEED MATCH THAT OF PRECISELY THE FELON YOU SUSPECTED.
FIGURES. IF THE PERP IS WHO WE THINK IT IS, HE'S JUST THE SORT TO CONCOCT SO CYNICALLY CLEVER A PLAN:
HE PROBABLY CHOSE GANG MEMBERS AS HENCHMEN THINKING THEY WOULDN'T BE DISTRACTED BY HIS... WHATEVER-IT-IS --
"-- BECAUSE THEY PROBABLY CAN'T READ TO BEGIN WITH!"
I'M SURE IT'S NOW ONLY A MATTER OF HOURS BEFORE THEY'LL START ARRANGING FOR DELIVERY OF THE RANSOM!
WE'LL SEE. HOW DO YA KNOW THEY'LL BE ABLE TO GET IT TOGETHER?
DON'T WORRY, MARIO... IT'S ONLY WORDS THEY CAN'T READ. NUMBERS ARE STILL NUMBERS TO THEM -- I MADE SURE OF THAT.'
YOU SEE, AS LONG AS THEY COULD TELL THEMSELVES IT WAS JUST A BUNCH OF NAMELESS, FACELESS "LITTLE PEOPLE" WHO WERE CATCHING "THE DISEASE"... THE POWERS THAT BE WOULDN'T TAKE IT SERIOUSLY.
BUT THAT WAS BEFORE YOU MADE SURE THAT THE NEXT TIME MAYOR HILL TRIES TO LIE TO THE PUBLIC ABOUT THE SEVERITY OF THE PROBLEM...
...HE WON'T BE ABLE TO READ THE TEXT OF HIS OWN FLATULENT SPEECH!
BELIEVE ME -- THAT WILL PROVIDE THE KIND OF TERROR THAT'LL GET A RESPONSE OUT OF THESE PEOPLE!...
...AND SHOW THEM ONCE AND FOR ALL THAT TERROR IS THE NAME OF THE GAME IF THEY DARE DEFY...
21

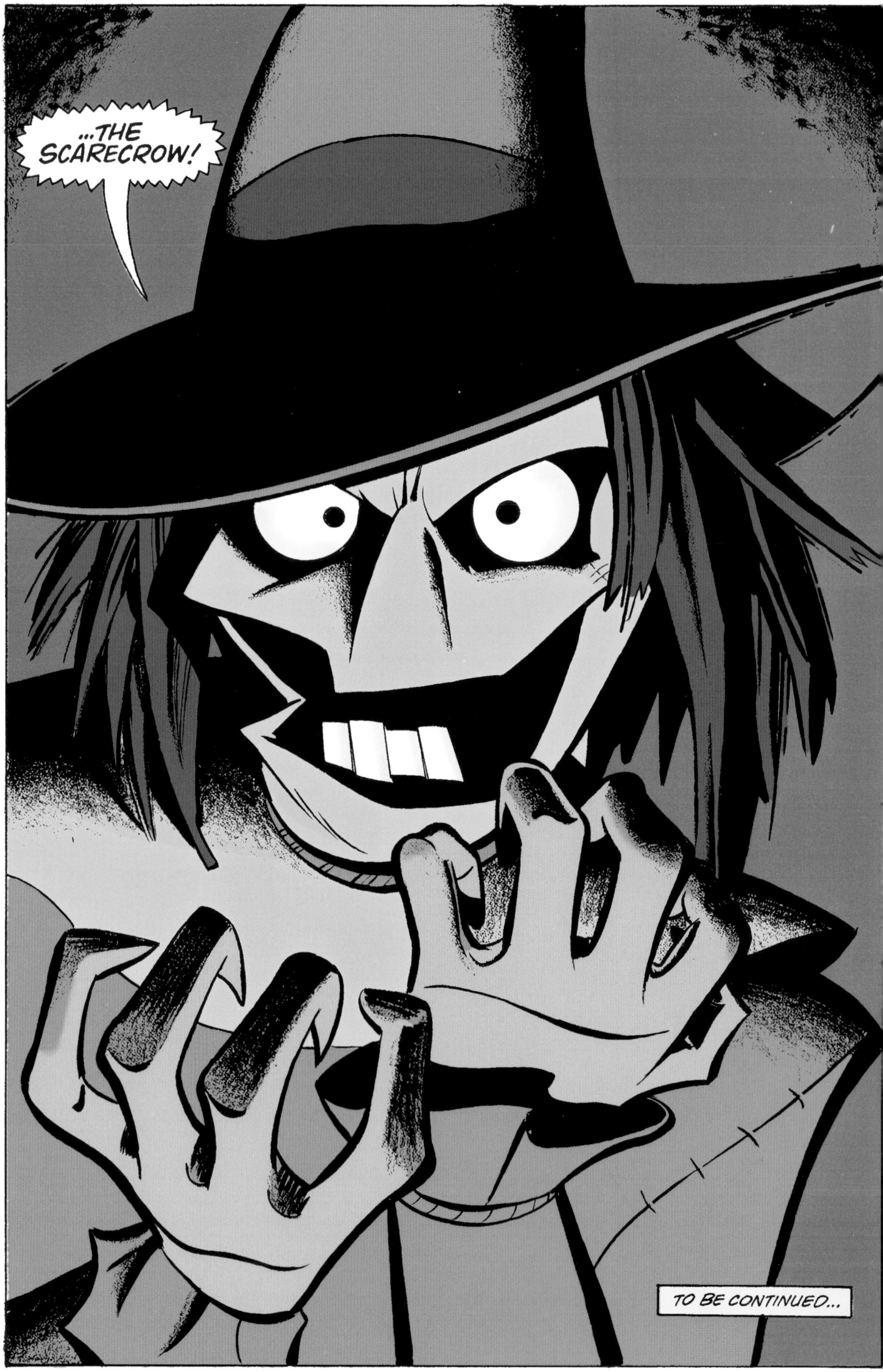
...THE SCARECROW!
TO BE CONTINUED...

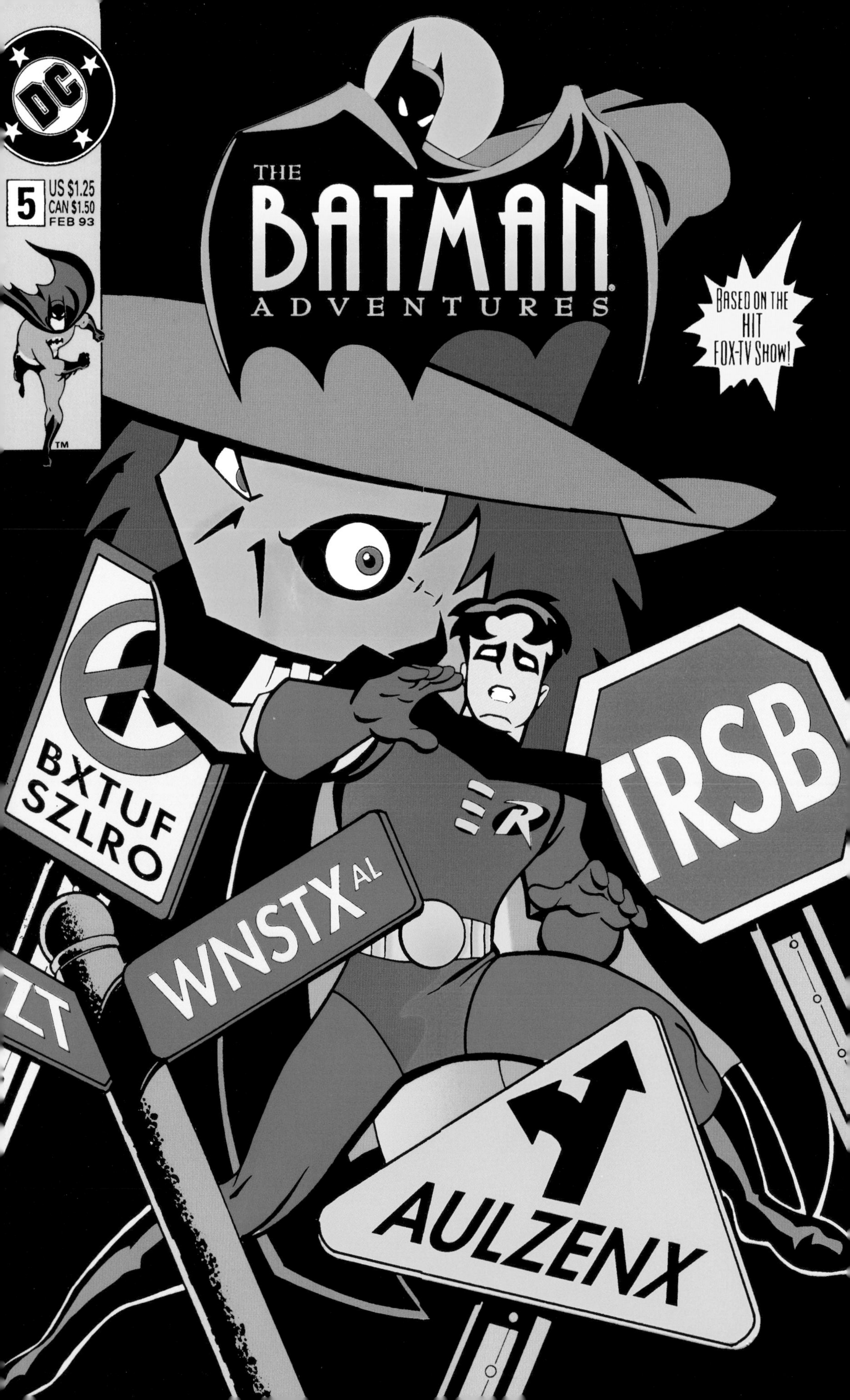

DC
5
US $1.25
CAN $1.50
FEB 93
THE
BATMAN
ADVENTURES
BASED ON THE HIT FOX-TV SHOW!
BXTUF SZLRO
TRSB
WNSTX AL
ZT
AULZENX

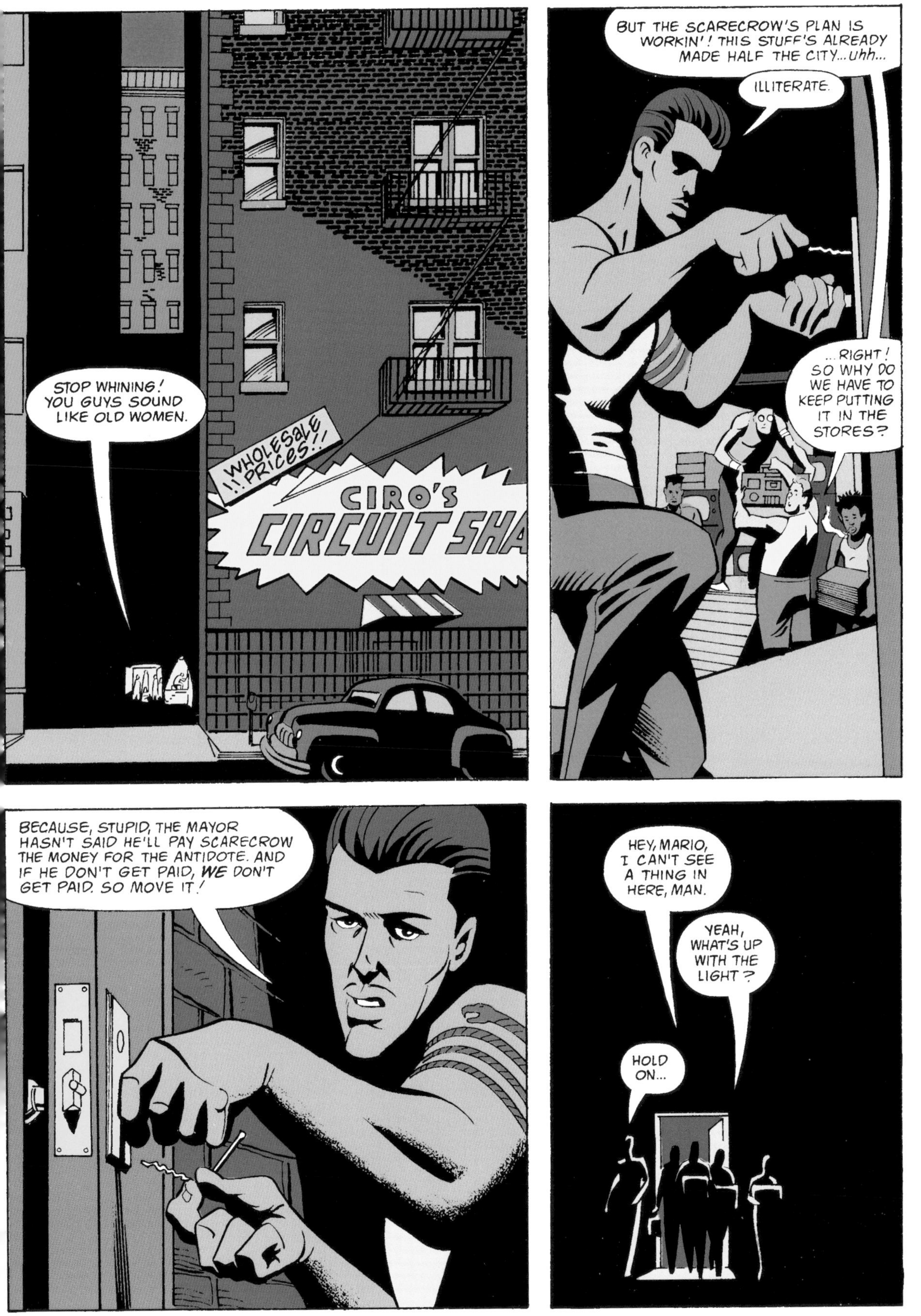

STOP WHINING! YOU GUYS SOUND LIKE OLD WOMEN.
!! WHOLESALE PRICES!!
CIRO'S CIRCUIT SHA
BUT THE SCARECROW'S PLAN IS WORKIN'! THIS STUFF'S ALREADY MADE HALF THE CITY...uhh...
ILLITERATE.
...RIGHT! SO WHY DO WE HAVE TO KEEP PUTTING IT IN THE STORES?
BECAUSE, STUPID, THE MAYOR HASN'T SAID HE'LL PAY SCARECROW THE MONEY FOR THE ANTIDOTE. AND IF HE DON'T GET PAID, WE DON'T GET PAID. SO MOVE IT!
HEY, MARIO, I CAN'T SEE A THING IN HERE, MAN.
YEAH, WHAT'S UP WITH THE LIGHT?
HOLD ON...

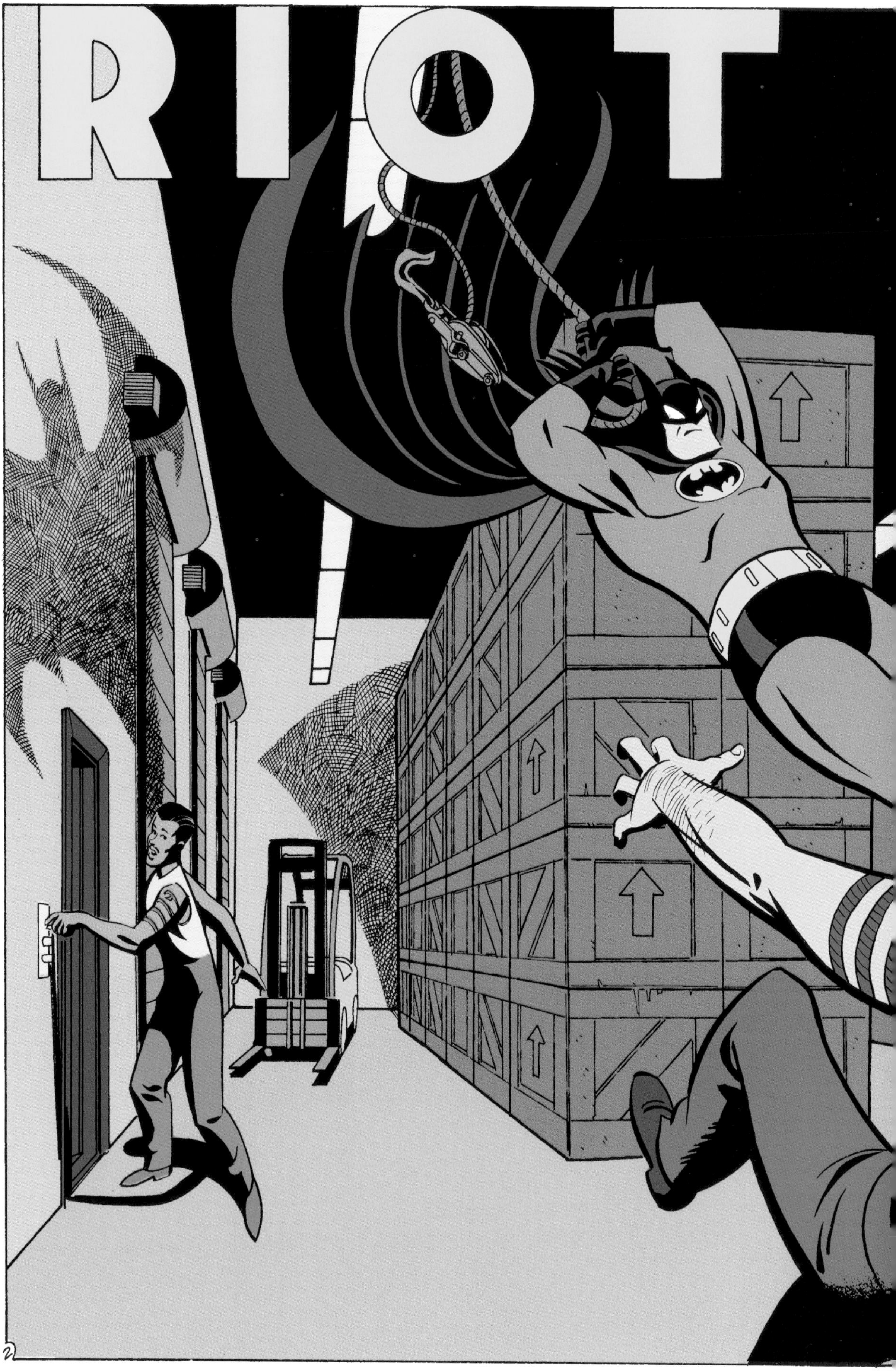
RIOT

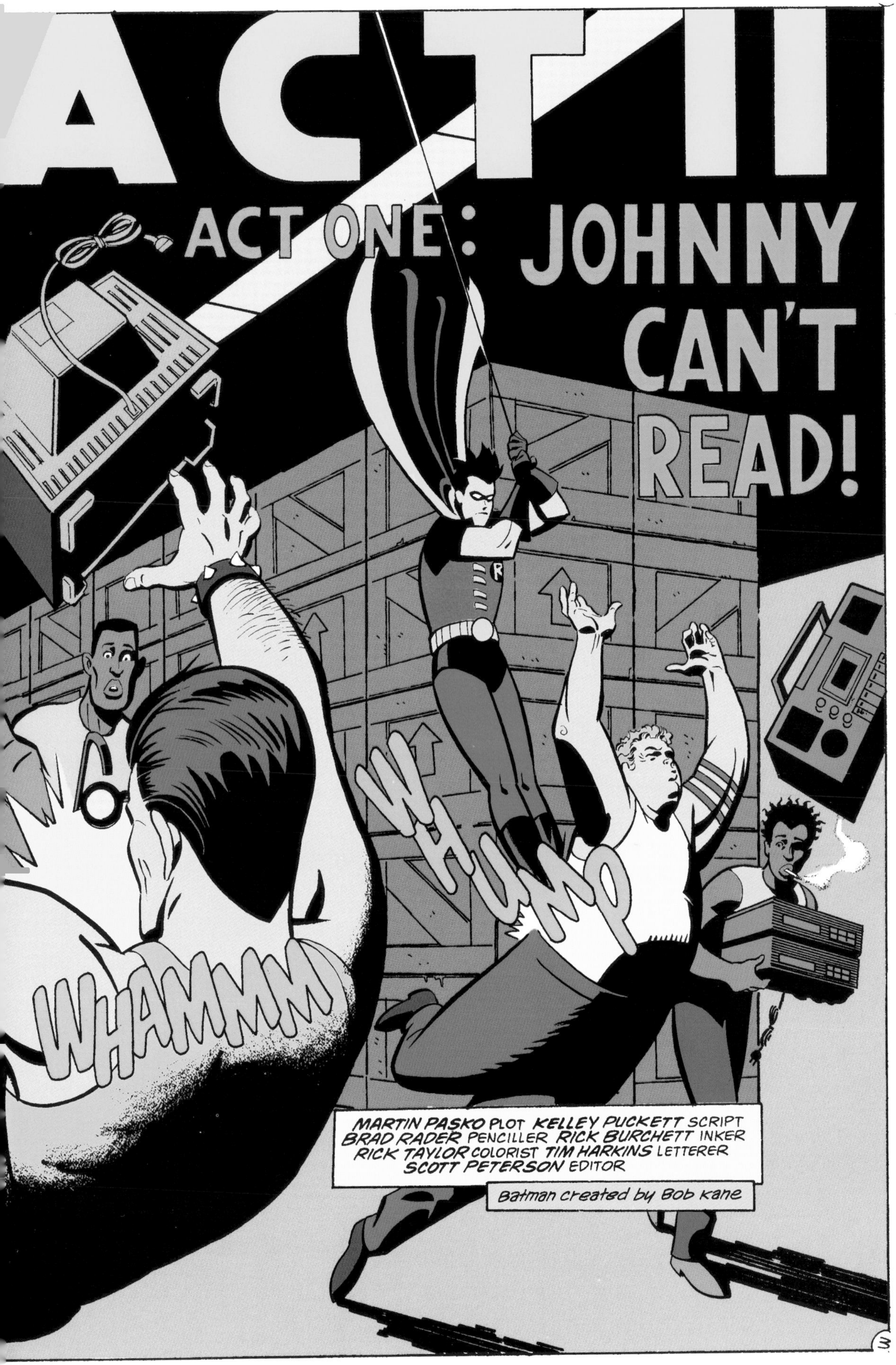
ACT II
ACT ONE: JOHNNY CAN'T READ!
WHAMMM
WHUMP
MARTIN PASKO PLOT KELLEY PUCKETT SCRIPT
BRAD RADER PENCILLER RICK BURCHETT INKER
RICK TAYLOR COLORIST TIM HARKINS LETTERER
SCOTT PETERSON EDITOR
Batman created by Bob Kane
3

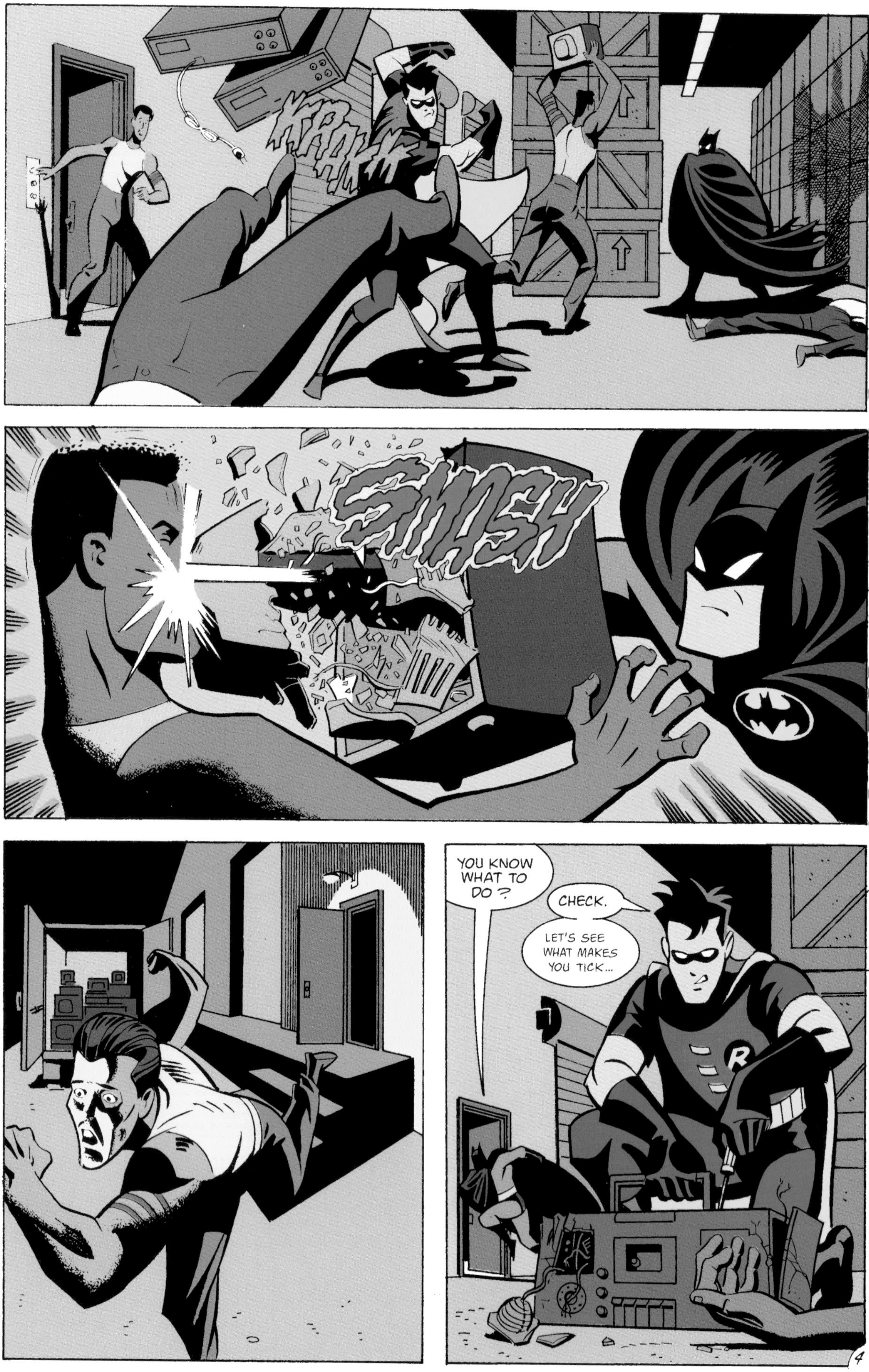
KRAKK
SMASH
YOU KNOW WHAT TO DO?
CHECK.
LET'S SEE WHAT MAKES YOU TICK...
4

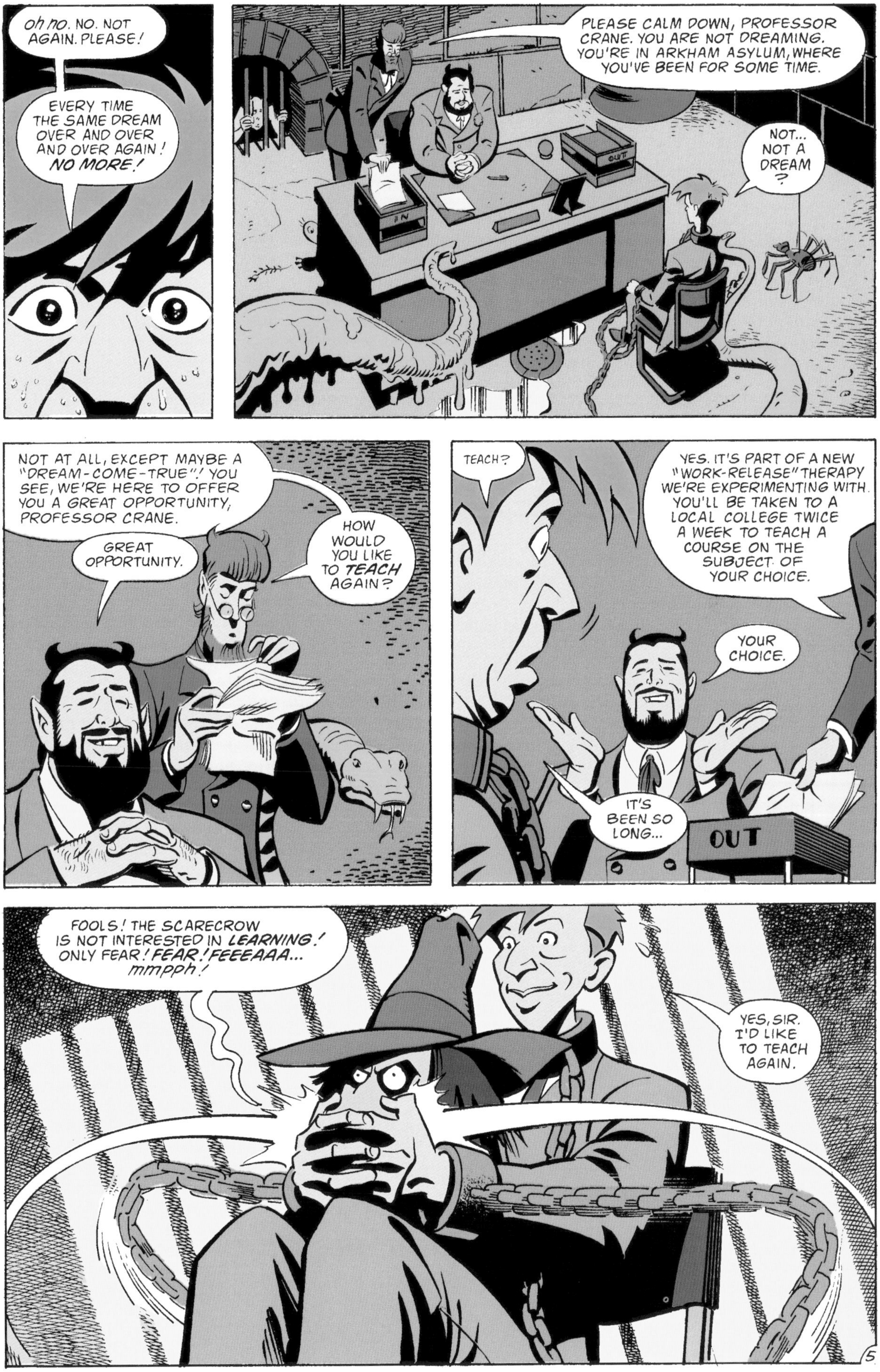
oh no. NO. NOT AGAIN. PLEASE!
EVERY TIME THE SAME DREAM OVER AND OVER AND OVER AGAIN! NO MORE!
PLEASE CALM DOWN, PROFESSOR CRANE. YOU ARE NOT DREAMING. YOU'RE IN ARKHAM ASYLUM, WHERE YOU'VE BEEN FOR SOME TIME.
NOT... NOT A DREAM?
IN
OUT
NOT AT ALL, EXCEPT MAYBE A "DREAM-COME-TRUE"! YOU SEE, WE'RE HERE TO OFFER YOU A GREAT OPPORTUNITY, PROFESSOR CRANE.
GREAT OPPORTUNITY.
HOW WOULD YOU LIKE TO TEACH AGAIN?
TEACH?
YES. IT'S PART OF A NEW "WORK-RELEASE" THERAPY WE'RE EXPERIMENTING WITH. YOU'LL BE TAKEN TO A LOCAL COLLEGE TWICE A WEEK TO TEACH A COURSE ON THE SUBJECT OF YOUR CHOICE.
YOUR CHOICE.
IT'S BEEN SO LONG...
OUT
FOOLS! THE SCARECROW IS NOT INTERESTED IN LEARNING! ONLY FEAR! FEAR! FEEEAAA... mmpph!
YES, SIR. I'D LIKE TO TEACH AGAIN.
5

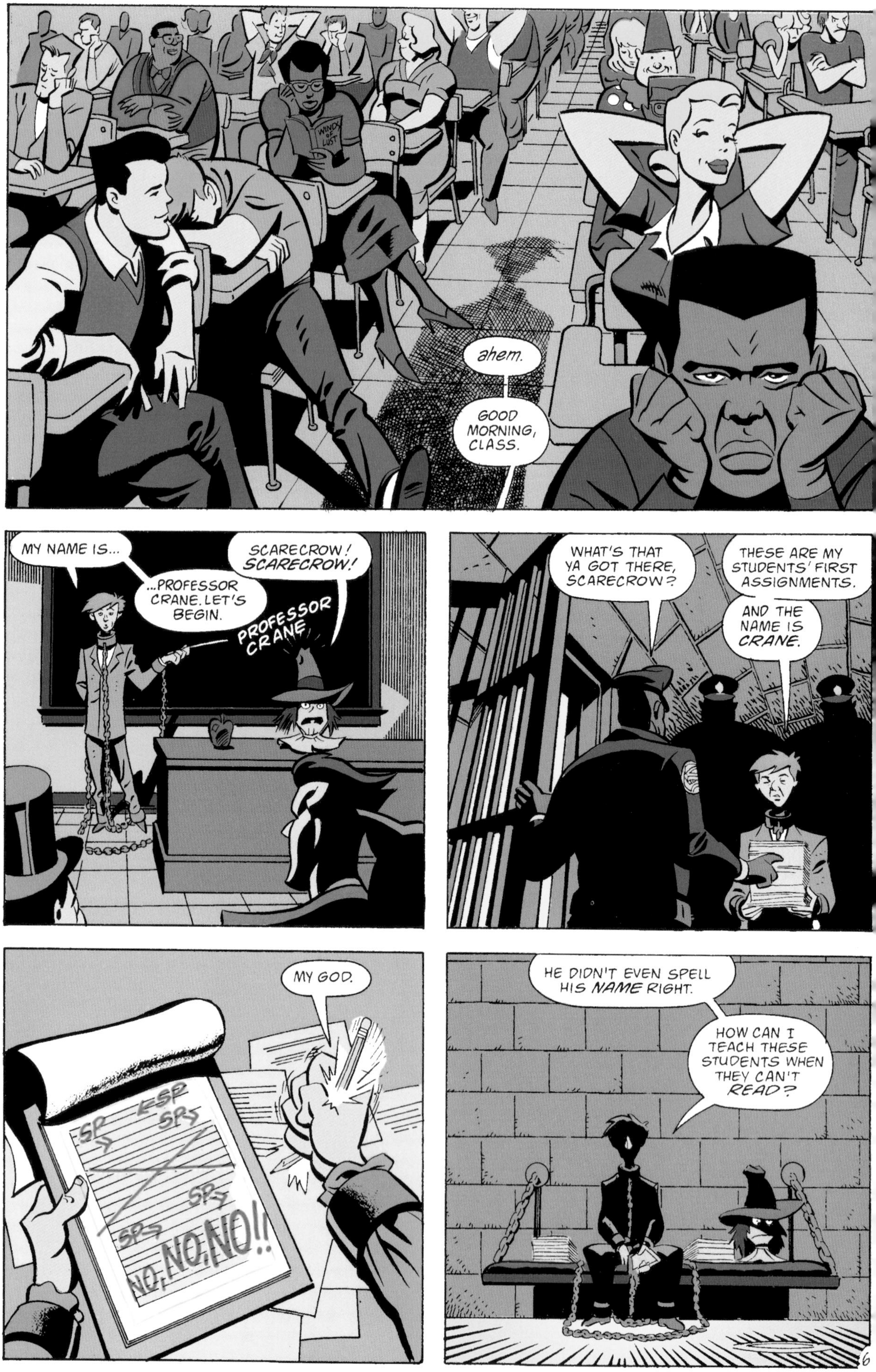
WINDS OF LUST
ahem.
GOOD MORNING, CLASS.
MY NAME IS...
...PROFESSOR CRANE. LET'S BEGIN.
SCARECROW! SCARECROW!
PROFESSOR CRANE
WHAT'S THAT YA GOT THERE, SCARECROW?
THESE ARE MY STUDENTS' FIRST ASSIGNMENTS.
AND THE NAME IS CRANE.
MY GOD.
SP
SP
SP
SP
SP
NO, NO, NO!!
HE DIDN'T EVEN SPELL HIS NAME RIGHT.
HOW CAN I TEACH THESE STUDENTS WHEN THEY CAN'T READ?
6

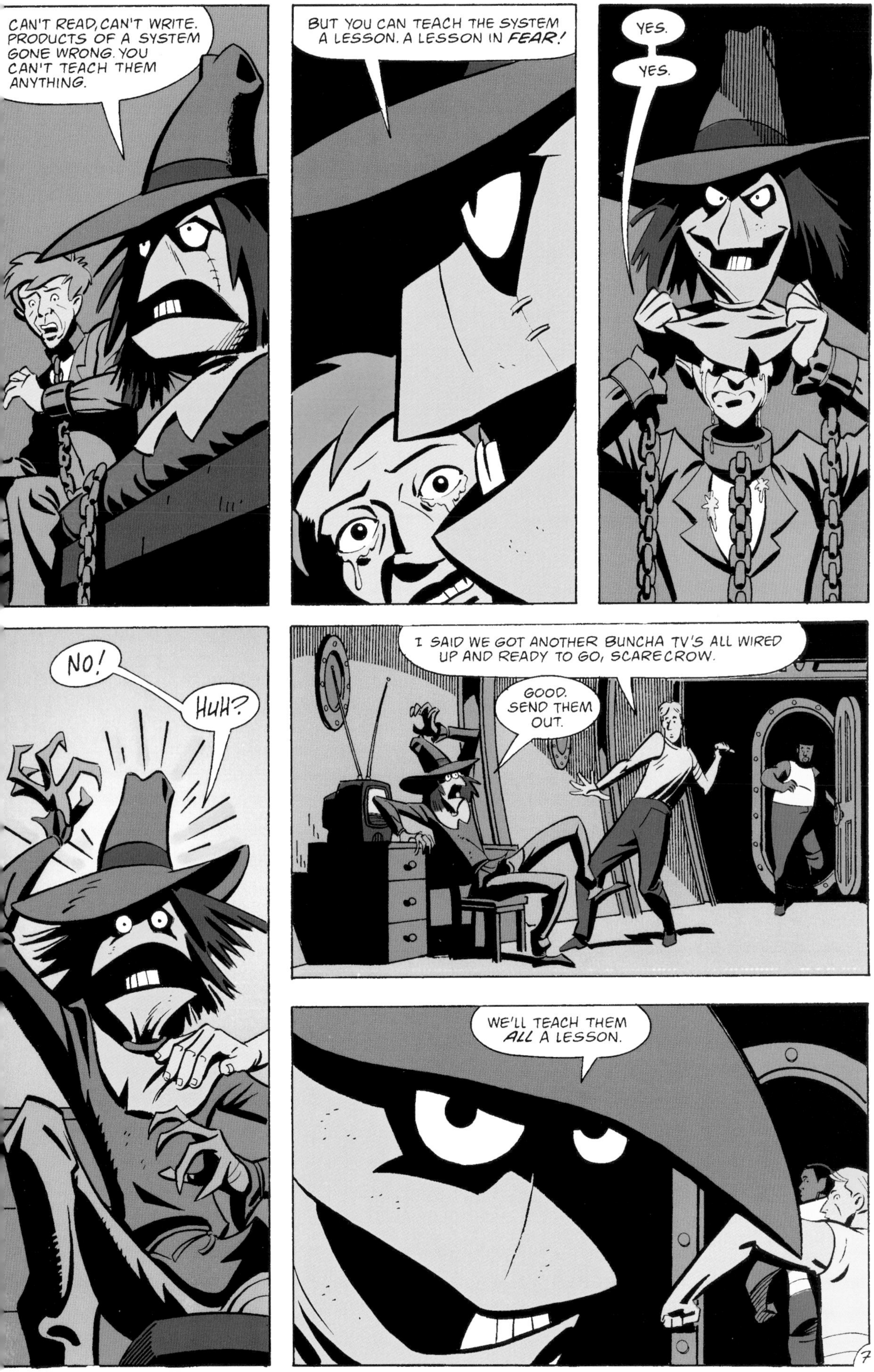
CAN'T READ, CAN'T WRITE. PRODUCTS OF A SYSTEM GONE WRONG. YOU CAN'T TEACH THEM ANYTHING.
BUT YOU CAN TEACH THE SYSTEM A LESSON. A LESSON IN FEAR!
YES.
YES.
NO!
HUH?
I SAID WE GOT ANOTHER BUNCHA TV'S ALL WIRED UP AND READY TO GO, SCARECROW.
GOOD. SEND THEM OUT.
WE'LL TEACH THEM ALL A LESSON.
7

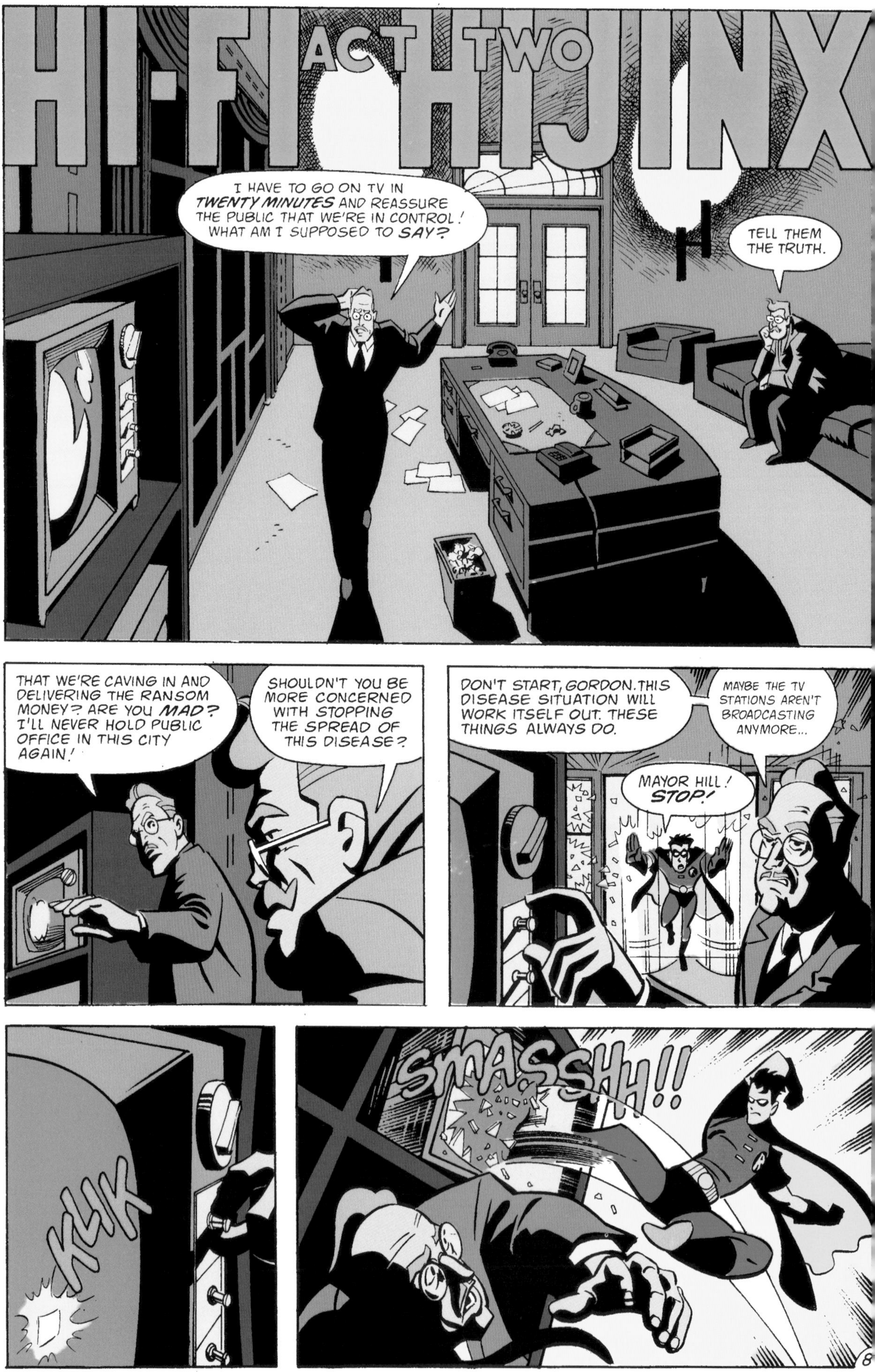
HI-FI HIJINX
ACT TWO
I HAVE TO GO ON TV IN TWENTY MINUTES AND REASSURE THE PUBLIC THAT WE'RE IN CONTROL! WHAT AM I SUPPOSED TO SAY?
TELL THEM THE TRUTH.
THAT WE'RE CAVING IN AND DELIVERING THE RANSOM MONEY? ARE YOU MAD? I'LL NEVER HOLD PUBLIC OFFICE IN THIS CITY AGAIN!
SHOULDN'T YOU BE MORE CONCERNED WITH STOPPING THE SPREAD OF THIS DISEASE?
DON'T START, GORDON. THIS DISEASE SITUATION WILL WORK ITSELF OUT. THESE THINGS ALWAYS DO.
MAYBE THE TV STATIONS AREN'T BROADCASTING ANYMORE...
MAYOR HILL! STOP!
KLIK
SMASSHH!!
8

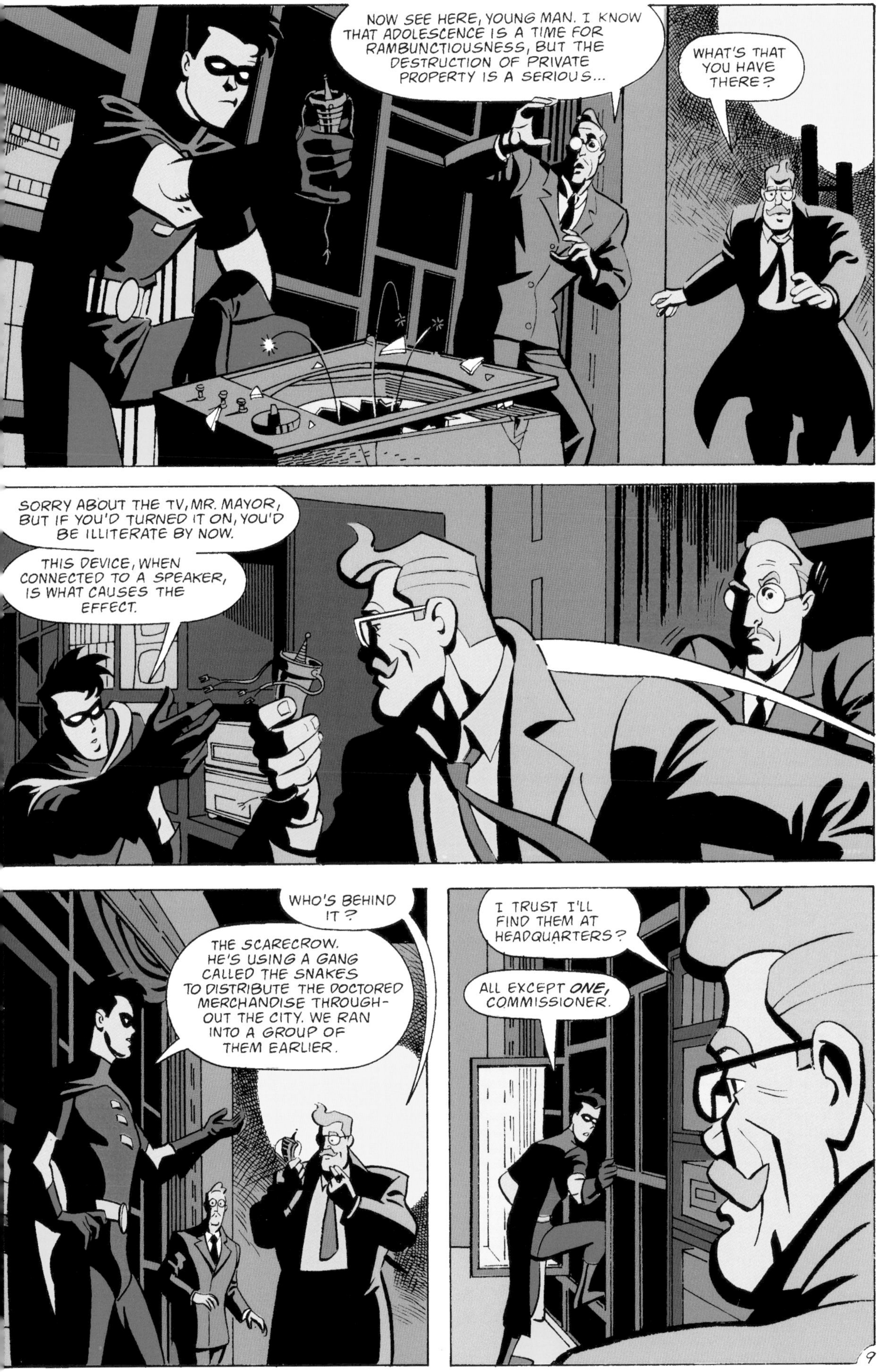
NOW SEE HERE, YOUNG MAN. I KNOW THAT ADOLESCENCE IS A TIME FOR RAMBUNCTIOUSNESS, BUT THE DESTRUCTION OF PRIVATE PROPERTY IS A SERIOUS...
WHAT'S THAT YOU HAVE THERE?
SORRY ABOUT THE TV, MR. MAYOR, BUT IF YOU'D TURNED IT ON, YOU'D BE ILLITERATE BY NOW.
THIS DEVICE, WHEN CONNECTED TO A SPEAKER, IS WHAT CAUSES THE EFFECT.
WHO'S BEHIND IT?
THE SCARECROW. HE'S USING A GANG CALLED THE SNAKES TO DISTRIBUTE THE DOCTORED MERCHANDISE THROUGH-OUT THE CITY. WE RAN INTO A GROUP OF THEM EARLIER.
I TRUST I'LL FIND THEM AT HEADQUARTERS?
ALL EXCEPT *ONE*, COMMISSIONER.
9

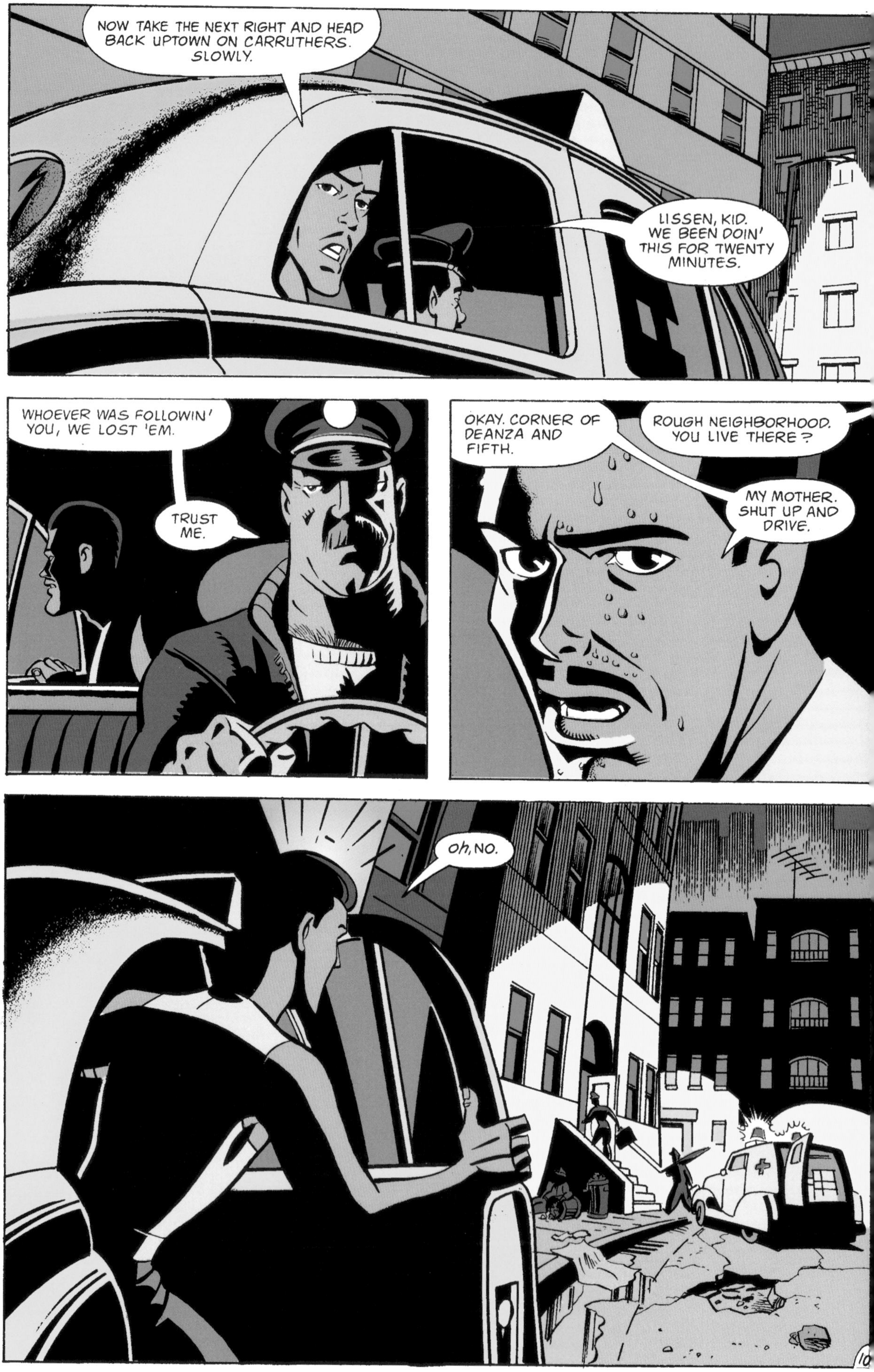
NOW TAKE THE NEXT RIGHT AND HEAD BACK UPTOWN ON CARRUTHERS. SLOWLY.
LISSEN, KID. WE BEEN DOIN' THIS FOR TWENTY MINUTES.
WHOEVER WAS FOLLOWIN' YOU, WE LOST 'EM.
TRUST ME.
OKAY. CORNER OF DEANZA AND FIFTH.
ROUGH NEIGHBORHOOD. YOU LIVE THERE?
MY MOTHER. SHUT UP AND DRIVE.
oh, NO.
10

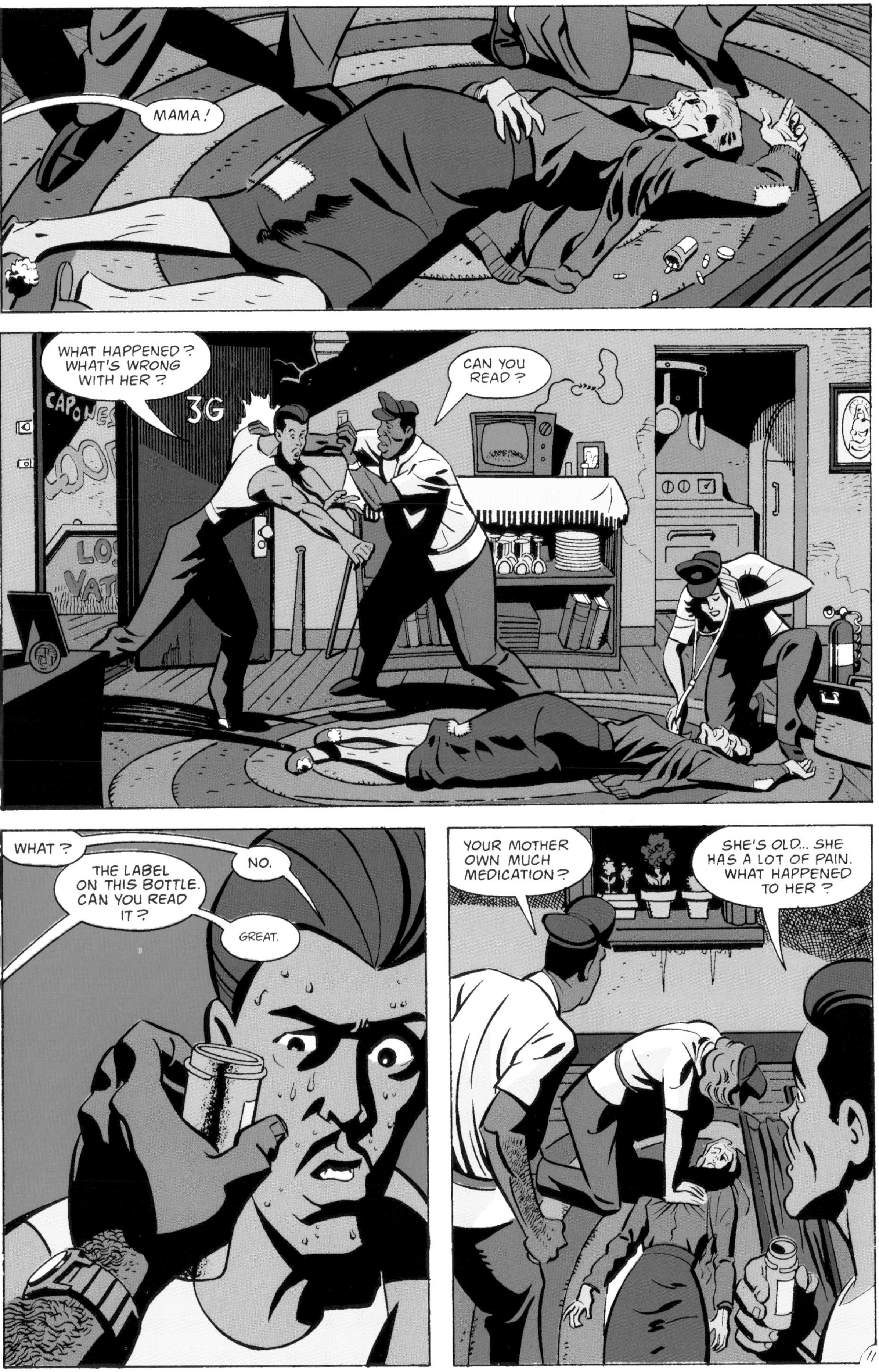
MAMA!
WHAT HAPPENED? WHAT'S WRONG WITH HER?
CAN YOU READ?
3G
WHAT?
NO.
THE LABEL ON THIS BOTTLE. CAN YOU READ IT?
GREAT.
YOUR MOTHER OWN MUCH MEDICATION?
SHE'S OLD... SHE HAS A LOT OF PAIN. WHAT HAPPENED TO HER?

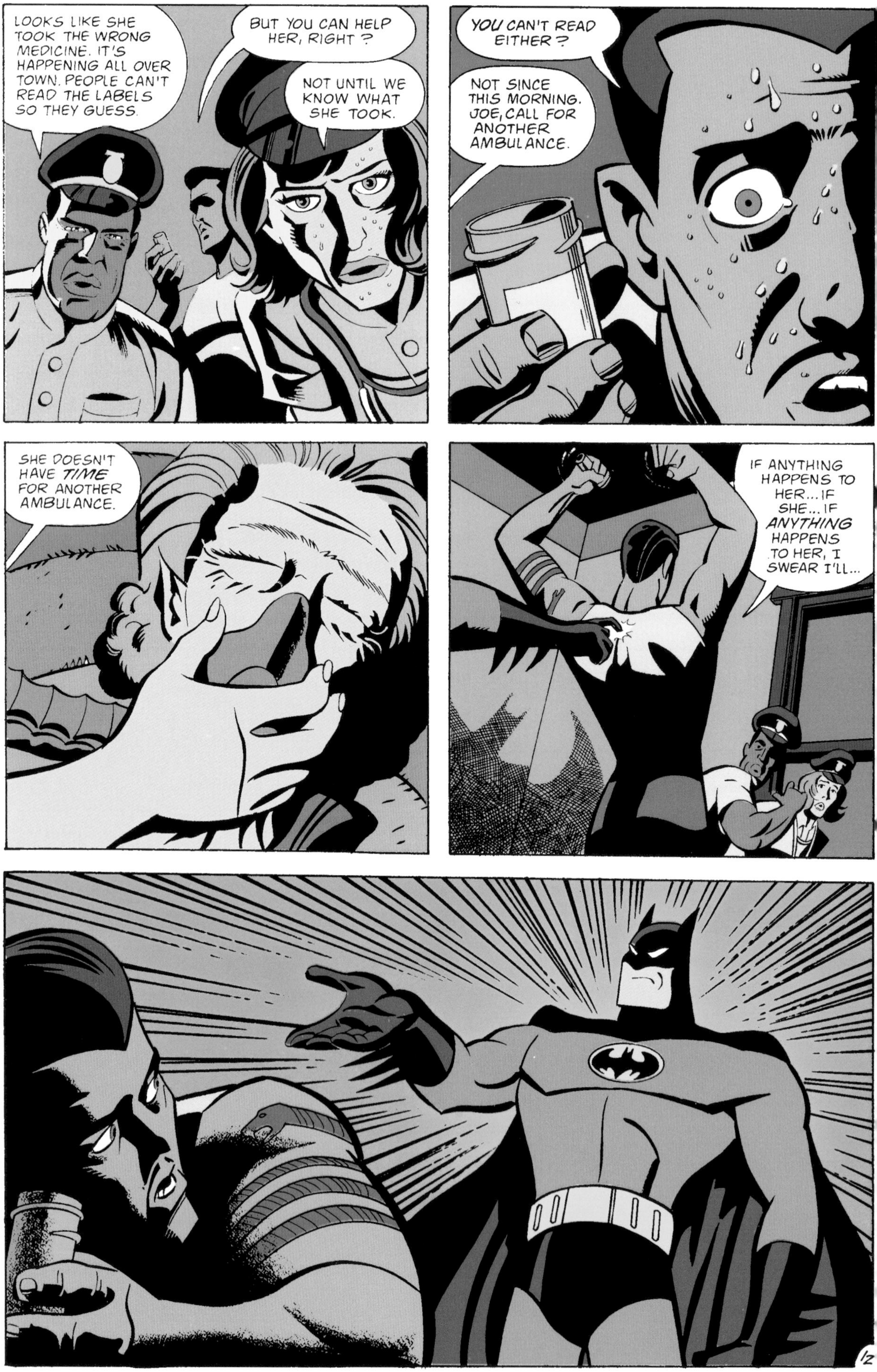
LOOKS LIKE SHE TOOK THE WRONG MEDICINE. IT'S HAPPENING ALL OVER TOWN. PEOPLE CAN'T READ THE LABELS SO THEY GUESS.
BUT YOU CAN HELP HER, RIGHT?
NOT UNTIL WE KNOW WHAT SHE TOOK.
YOU CAN'T READ EITHER?
NOT SINCE THIS MORNING. JOE, CALL FOR ANOTHER AMBULANCE.
SHE DOESN'T HAVE TIME FOR ANOTHER AMBULANCE.
IF ANYTHING HAPPENS TO HER... IF SHE... IF ANYTHING HAPPENS TO HER, I SWEAR I'LL...
12

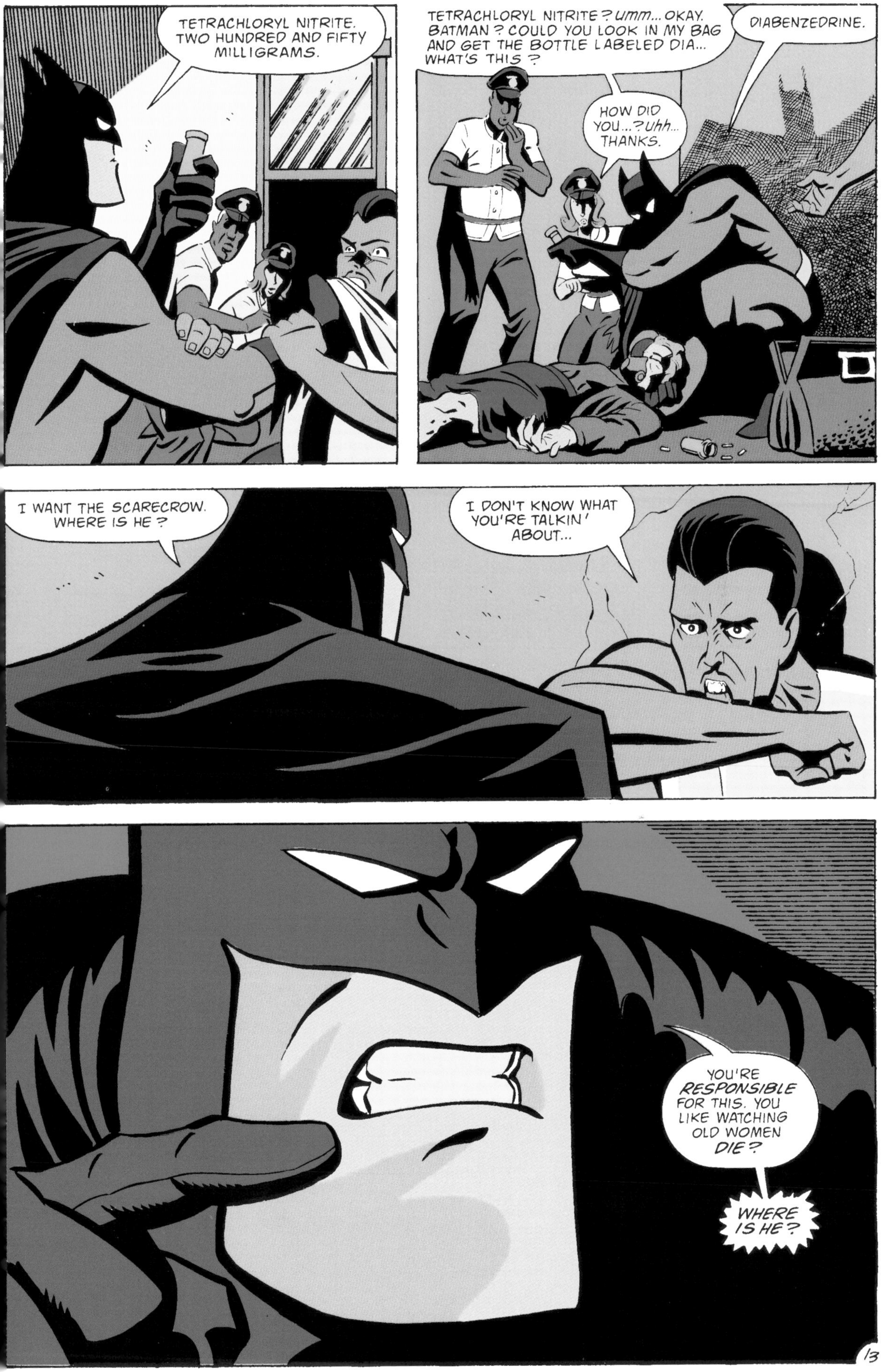
TETRACHLORYL NITRITE. TWO HUNDRED AND FIFTY MILLIGRAMS.
TETRACHLORYL NITRITE? UMM... OKAY. BATMAN? COULD YOU LOOK IN MY BAG AND GET THE BOTTLE LABELED DIA... WHAT'S THIS?
DIABENZEDRINE.
HOW DID YOU...? UHH... THANKS.
I WANT THE SCARECROW. WHERE IS HE?
I DON'T KNOW WHAT YOU'RE TALKIN' ABOUT...
YOU'RE RESPONSIBLE FOR THIS. YOU LIKE WATCHING OLD WOMEN DIE?
WHERE IS HE?
13

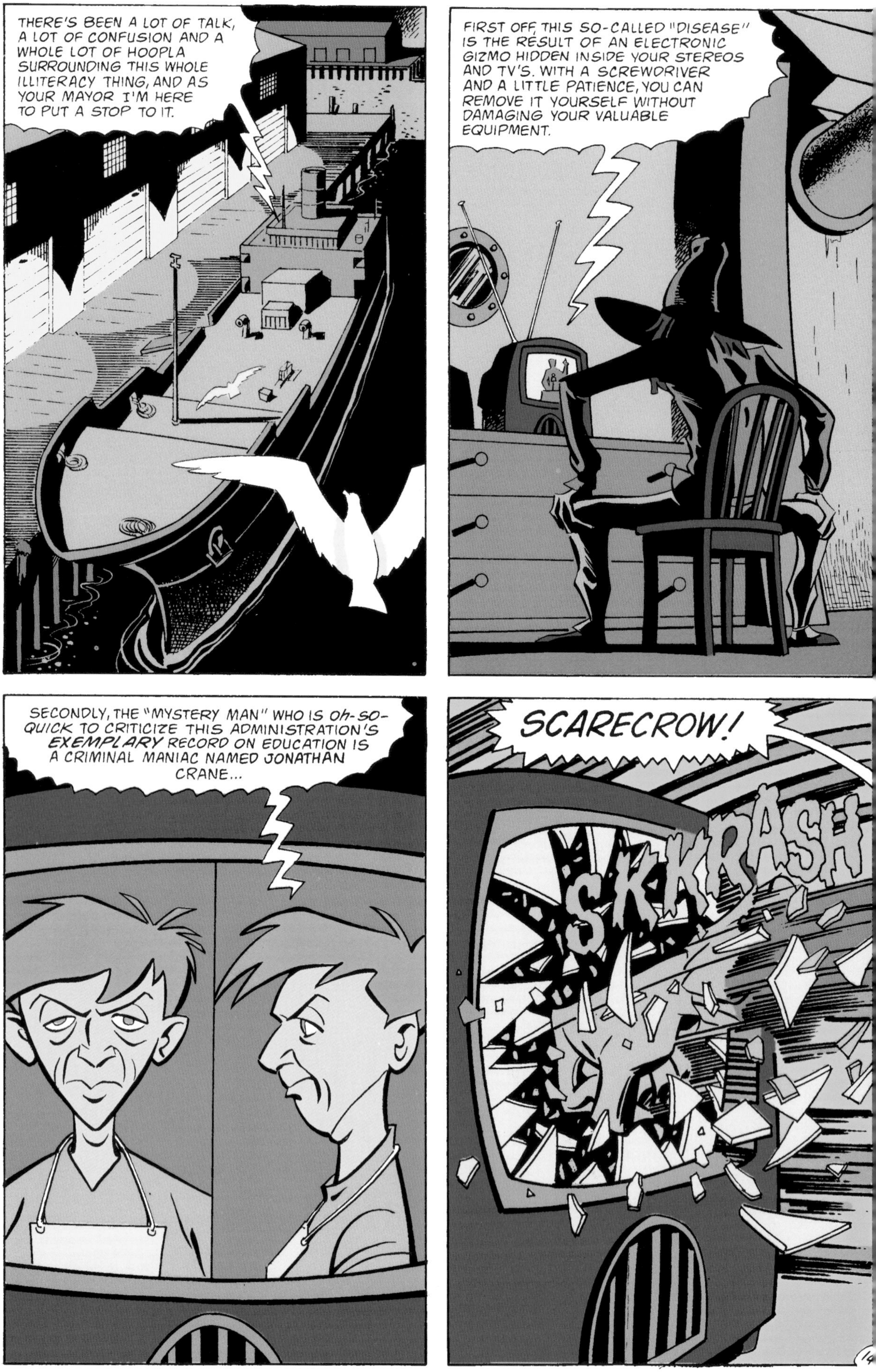
THERE'S BEEN A LOT OF TALK, A LOT OF CONFUSION AND A WHOLE LOT OF HOOPLA SURROUNDING THIS WHOLE ILLITERACY THING, AND AS YOUR MAYOR I'M HERE TO PUT A STOP TO IT.
FIRST OFF, THIS SO-CALLED "DISEASE" IS THE RESULT OF AN ELECTRONIC GIZMO HIDDEN INSIDE YOUR STEREOS AND TV'S. WITH A SCREWDRIVER AND A LITTLE PATIENCE, YOU CAN REMOVE IT YOURSELF WITHOUT DAMAGING YOUR VALUABLE EQUIPMENT.
SECONDLY, THE "MYSTERY MAN" WHO IS *oh-so-quick* TO CRITICIZE THIS ADMINISTRATION'S *EXEMPLARY* RECORD ON EDUCATION IS A CRIMINAL MANIAC NAMED JONATHAN CRANE...
SCARECROW!
SKKRASH

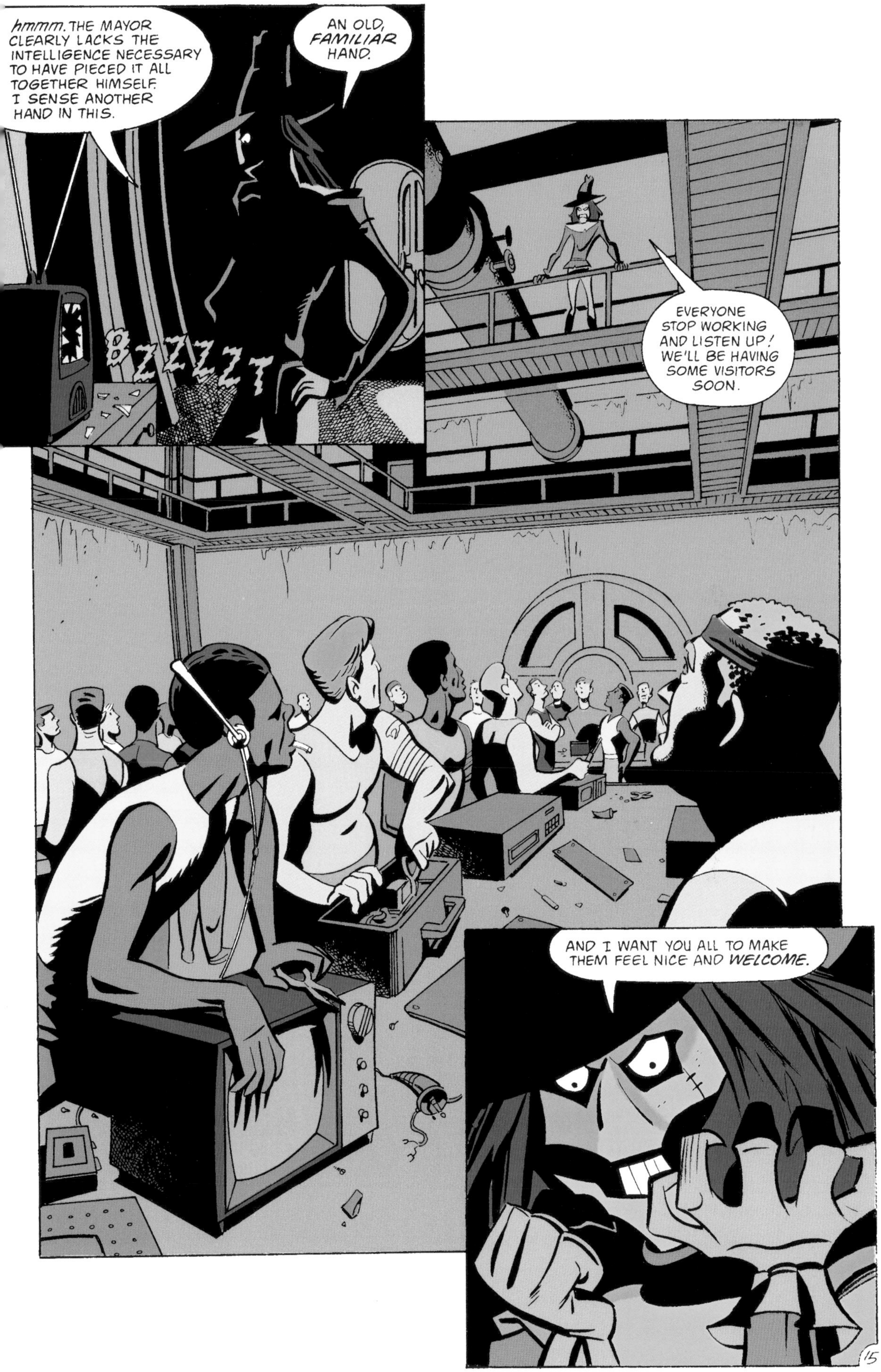
hmmm. THE MAYOR CLEARLY LACKS THE INTELLIGENCE NECESSARY TO HAVE PIECED IT ALL TOGETHER HIMSELF. I SENSE ANOTHER HAND IN THIS.
AN OLD, FAMILIAR HAND.
BZZZZZT
EVERYONE STOP WORKING AND LISTEN UP! WE'LL BE HAVING SOME VISITORS SOON.
AND I WANT YOU ALL TO MAKE THEM FEEL NICE AND WELCOME.
15

ACT THREE

THOSE WHO CANT DO!

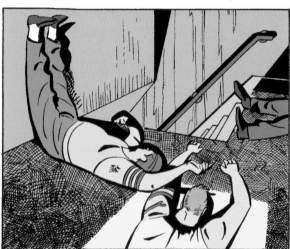

SO FAR, SO GOOD...

I DIDN'T START THIS FIGHT, BATMAN...

16

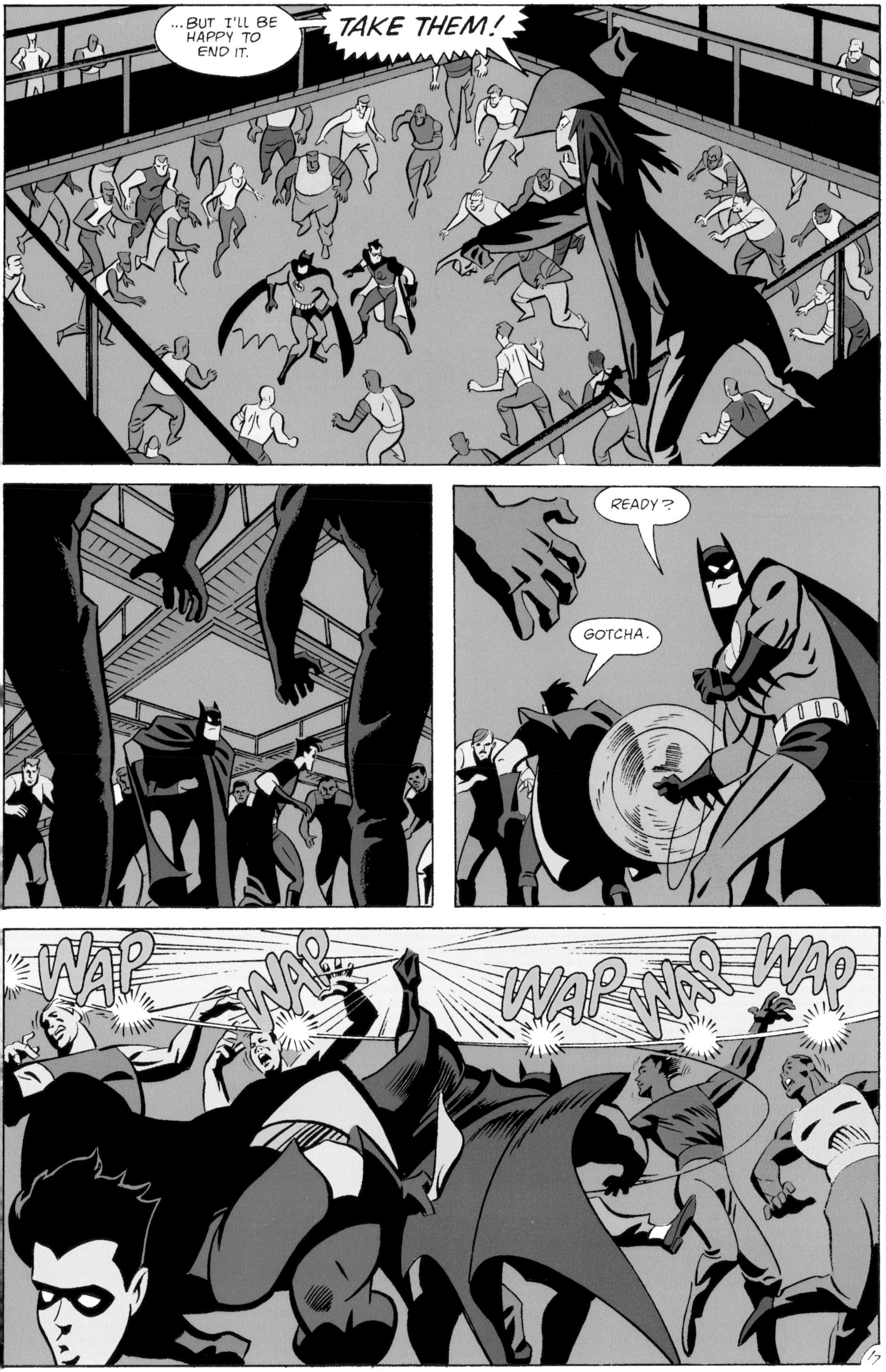

...BUT I'LL BE HAPPY TO END IT.
TAKE THEM!
READY?
GOTCHA.
WAP
WAP
WAP
WAP
WAP
17

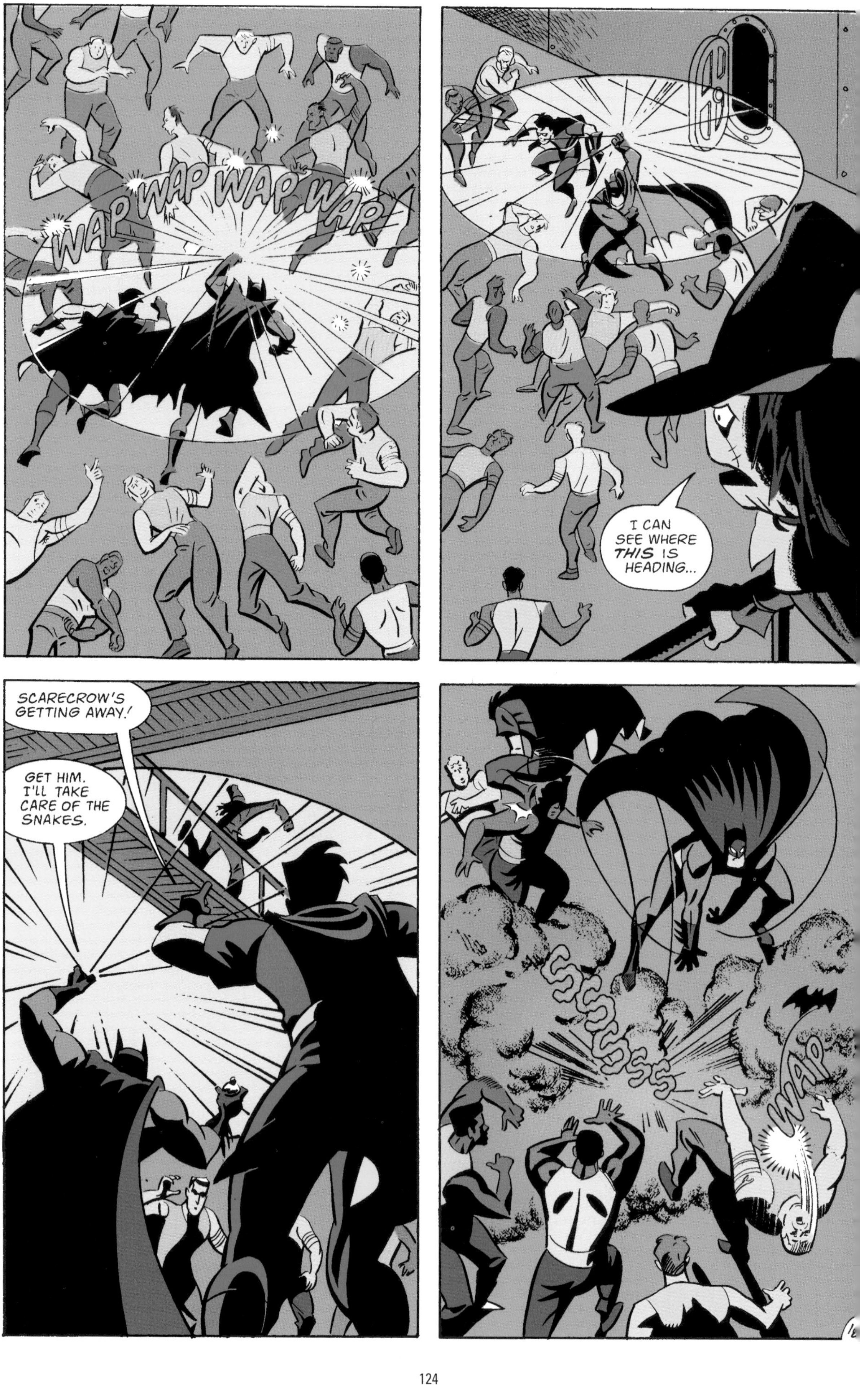
WAP WAP WAP WAP WAP
I CAN SEE WHERE THIS IS HEADING...
SCARECROW'S GETTING AWAY!
GET HIM. I'LL TAKE CARE OF THE SNAKES.
SSSSSSS
WAP

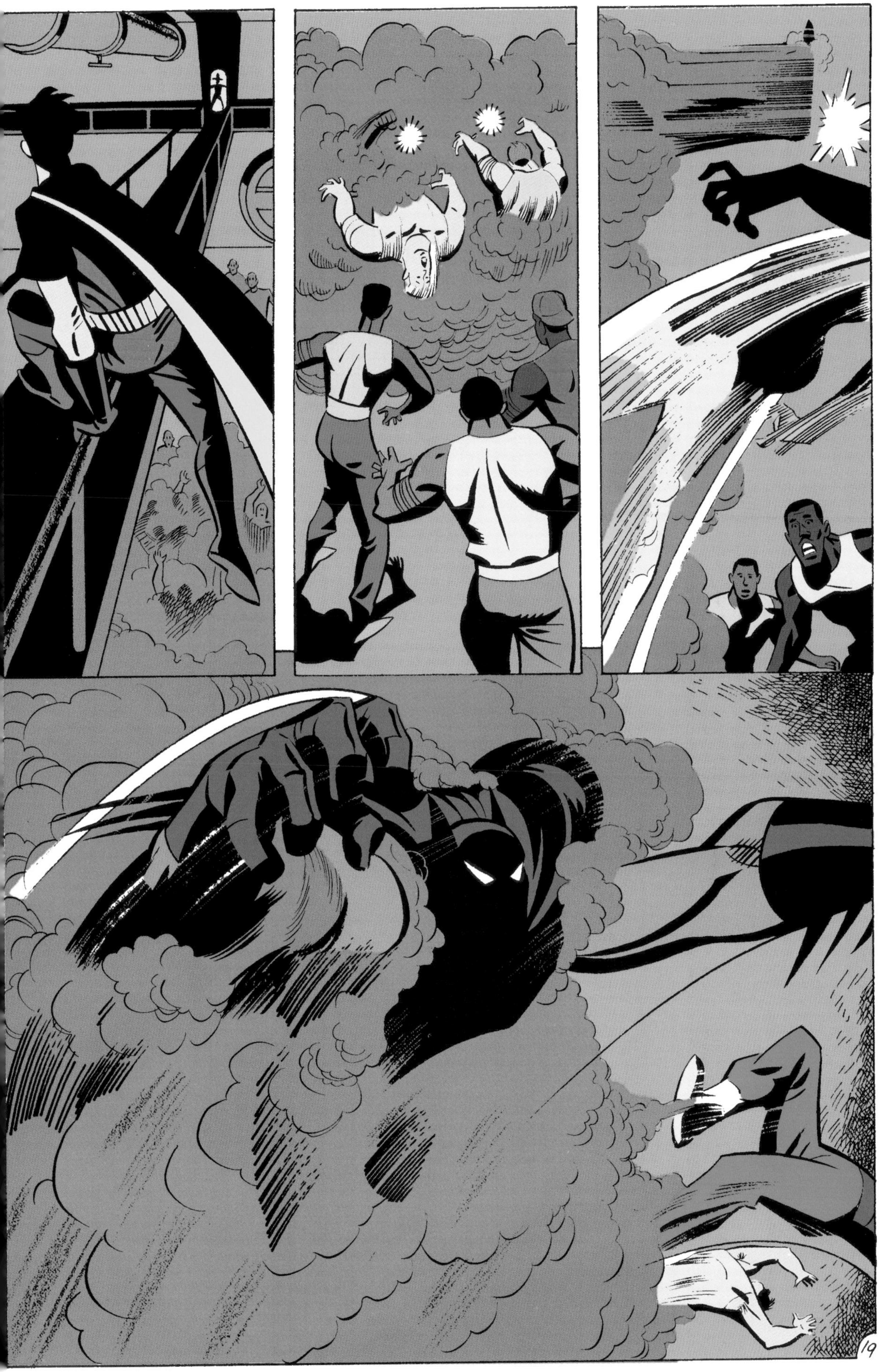
19

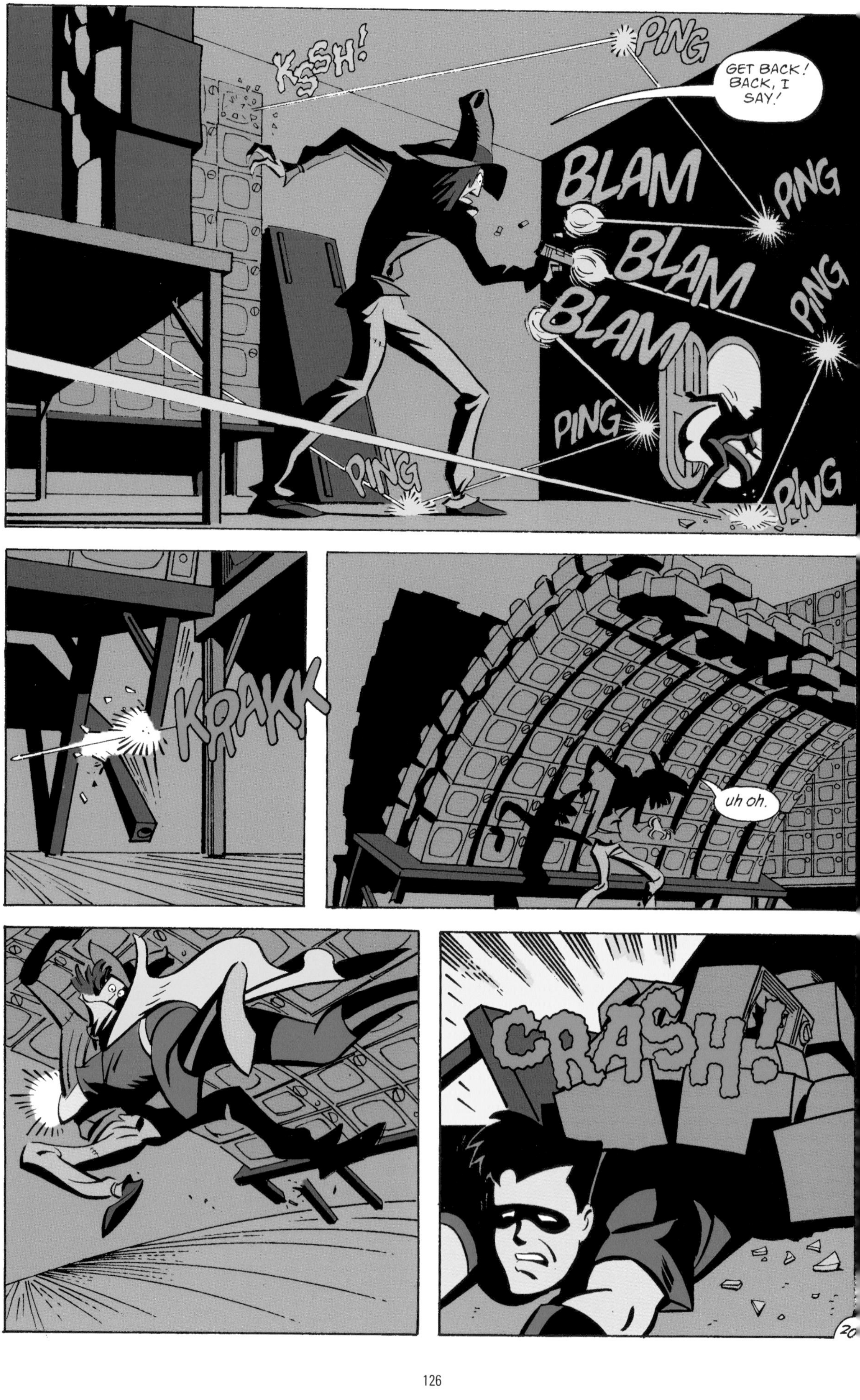
KSSH!
PING
GET BACK! BACK, I SAY!
BLAM
PING
BLAM
PING
BLAM
PING
PING
PING
KRAKK
uh oh.
CRASH!

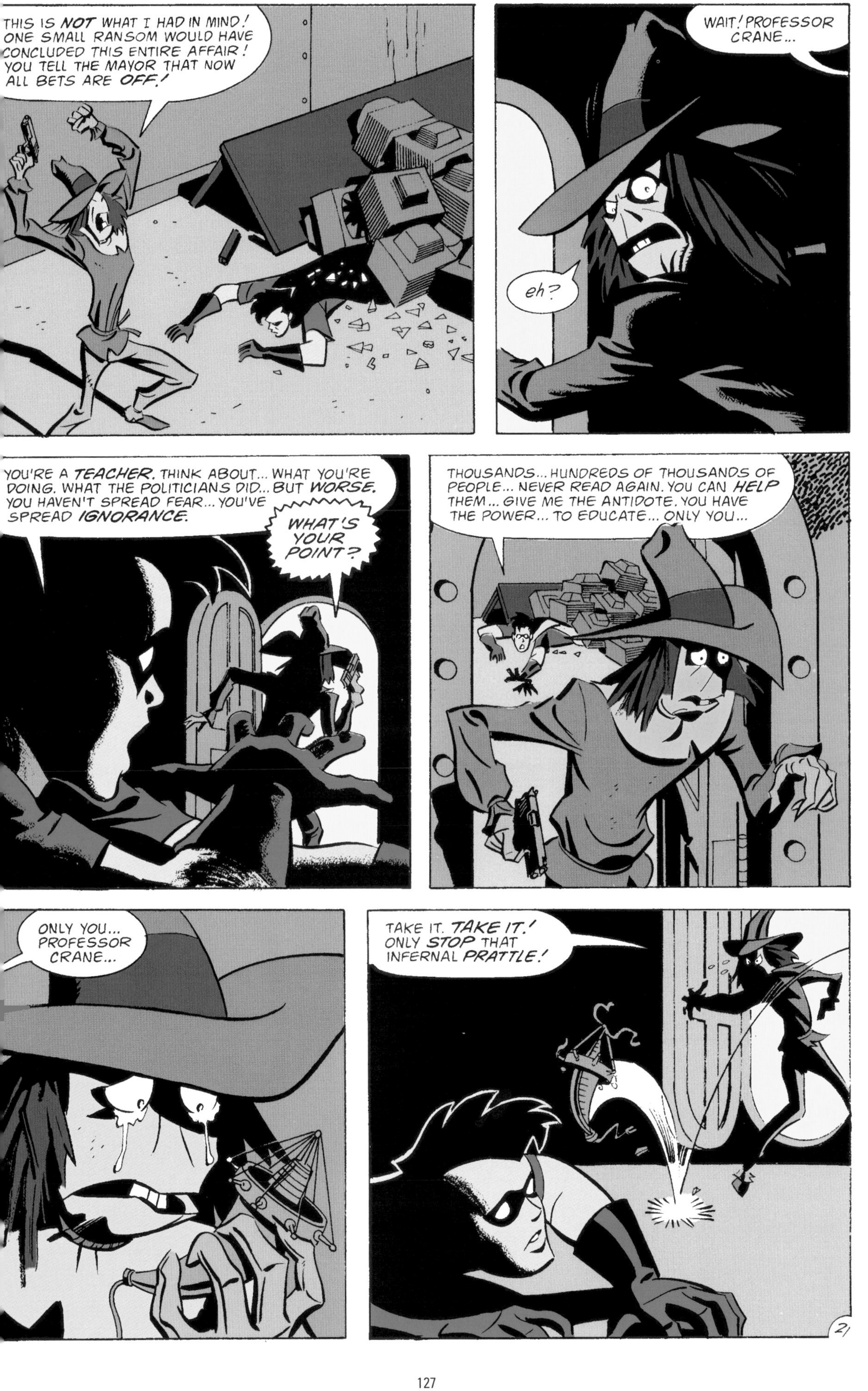
THIS IS NOT WHAT I HAD IN MIND! ONE SMALL RANSOM WOULD HAVE CONCLUDED THIS ENTIRE AFFAIR! YOU TELL THE MAYOR THAT NOW ALL BETS ARE OFF!
WAIT! PROFESSOR CRANE...
eh?
YOU'RE A TEACHER. THINK ABOUT... WHAT YOU'RE DOING. WHAT THE POLITICIANS DID... BUT WORSE. YOU HAVEN'T SPREAD FEAR... YOU'VE SPREAD IGNORANCE.
WHAT'S YOUR POINT?
THOUSANDS... HUNDREDS OF THOUSANDS OF PEOPLE... NEVER READ AGAIN. YOU CAN HELP THEM... GIVE ME THE ANTIDOTE. YOU HAVE THE POWER... TO EDUCATE... ONLY YOU...
ONLY YOU... PROFESSOR CRANE...
TAKE IT. TAKE IT! ONLY STOP THAT INFERNAL PRATTLE!
21

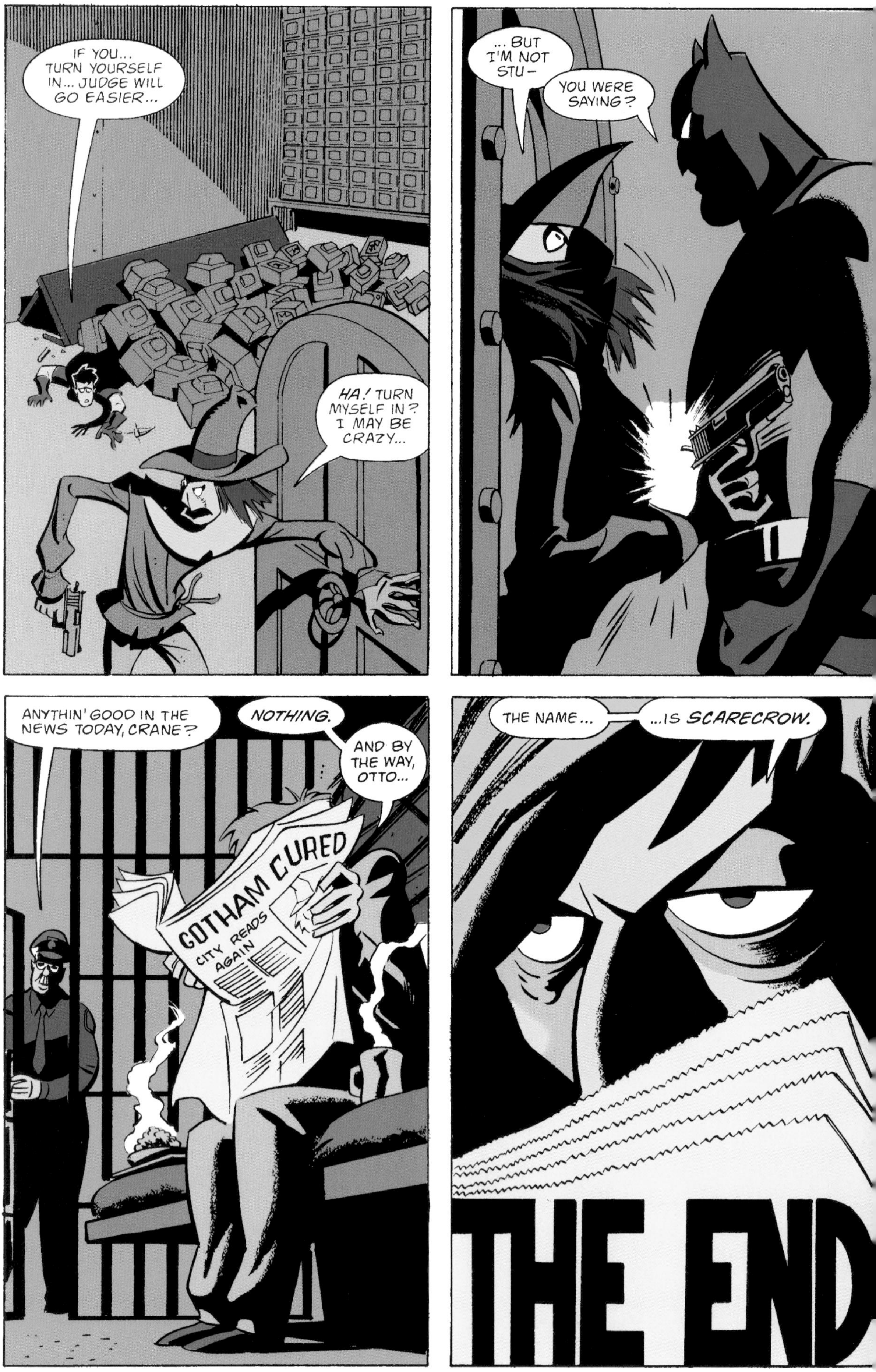
IF YOU... TURN YOURSELF IN... JUDGE WILL GO EASIER...
HA! TURN MYSELF IN? I MAY BE CRAZY...
... BUT I'M NOT STU–
YOU WERE SAYING?
ANYTHIN' GOOD IN THE NEWS TODAY, CRANE?
NOTHING.
AND BY THE WAY, OTTO...
GOTHAM CURED
CITY READS AGAIN
THE NAME...
...IS SCARECROW.
THE END

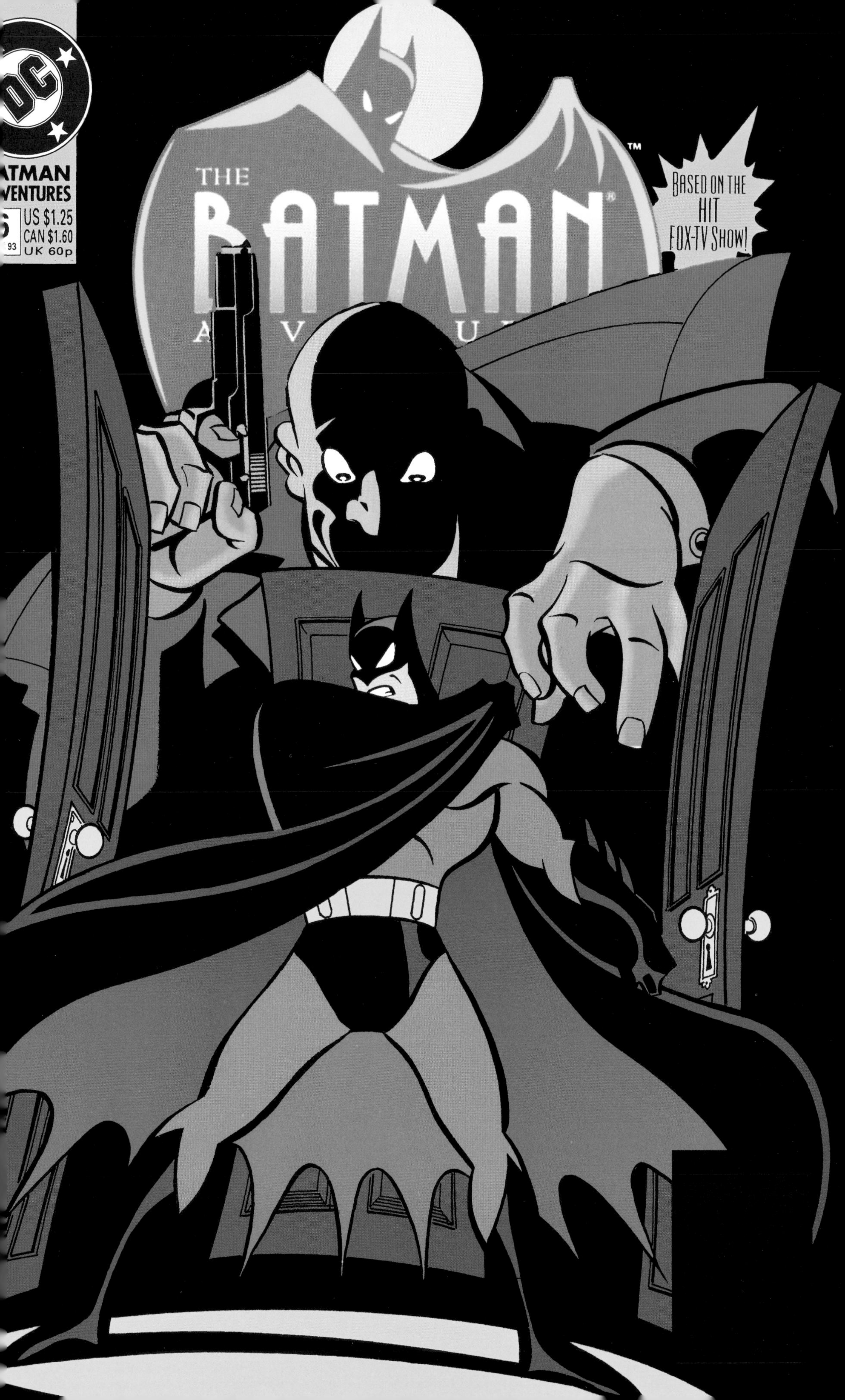

ATMAN
VENTURES
US $1.25
CAN $1.60
UK 60p
THE
BATMAN
BASED ON THE
HIT
FOX-TV SHOW!

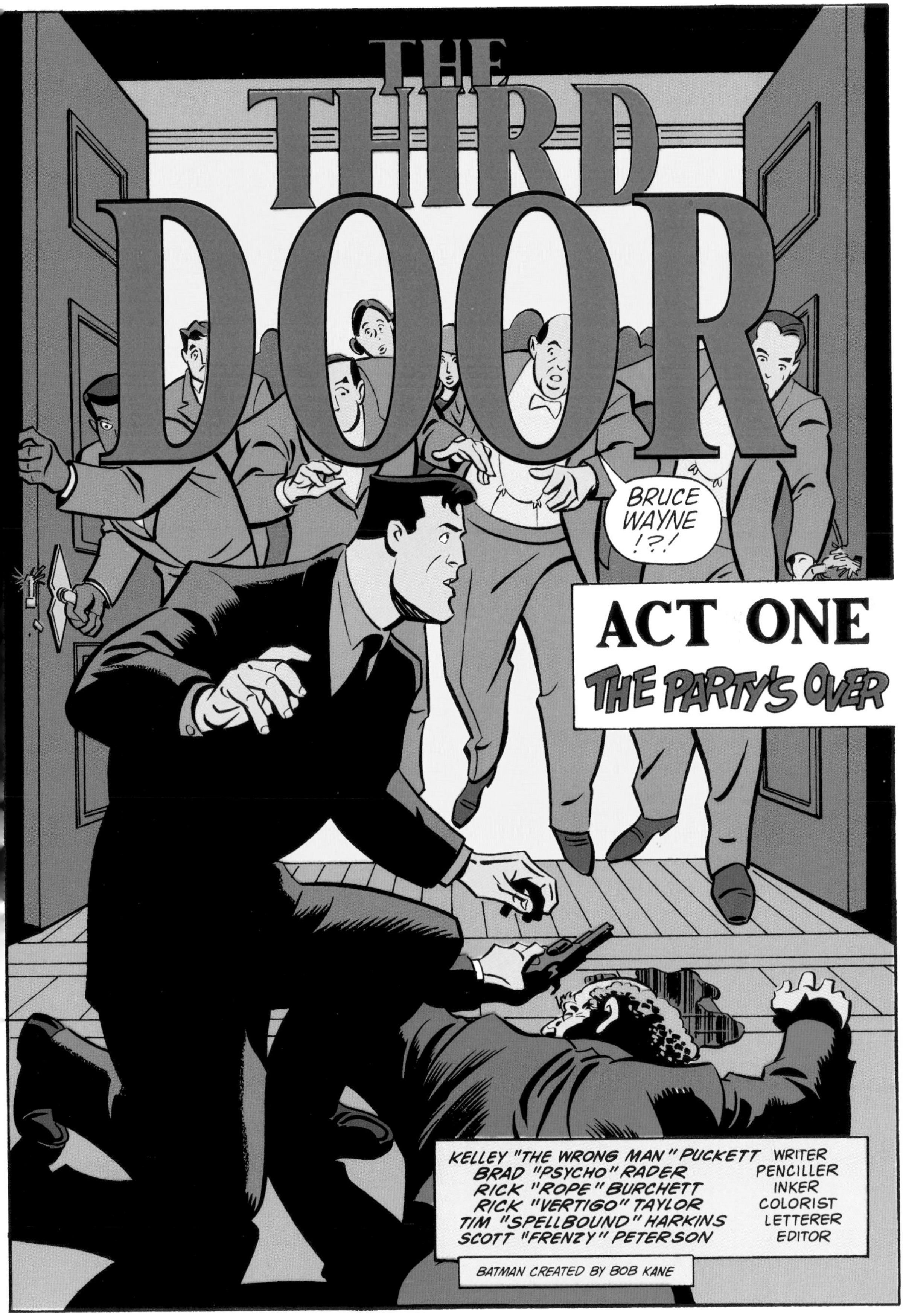
THE THIRD DOOR
BRUCE WAYNE !?!
ACT ONE
THE PARTY'S OVER
KELLEY "THE WRONG MAN" PUCKETT WRITER
BRAD "PSYCHO" RADER PENCILLER
RICK "ROPE" BURCHETT INKER
RICK "VERTIGO" TAYLOR COLORIST
TIM "SPELLBOUND" HARKINS LETTERER
SCOTT "FRENZY" PETERSON EDITOR
BATMAN CREATED BY BOB KANE

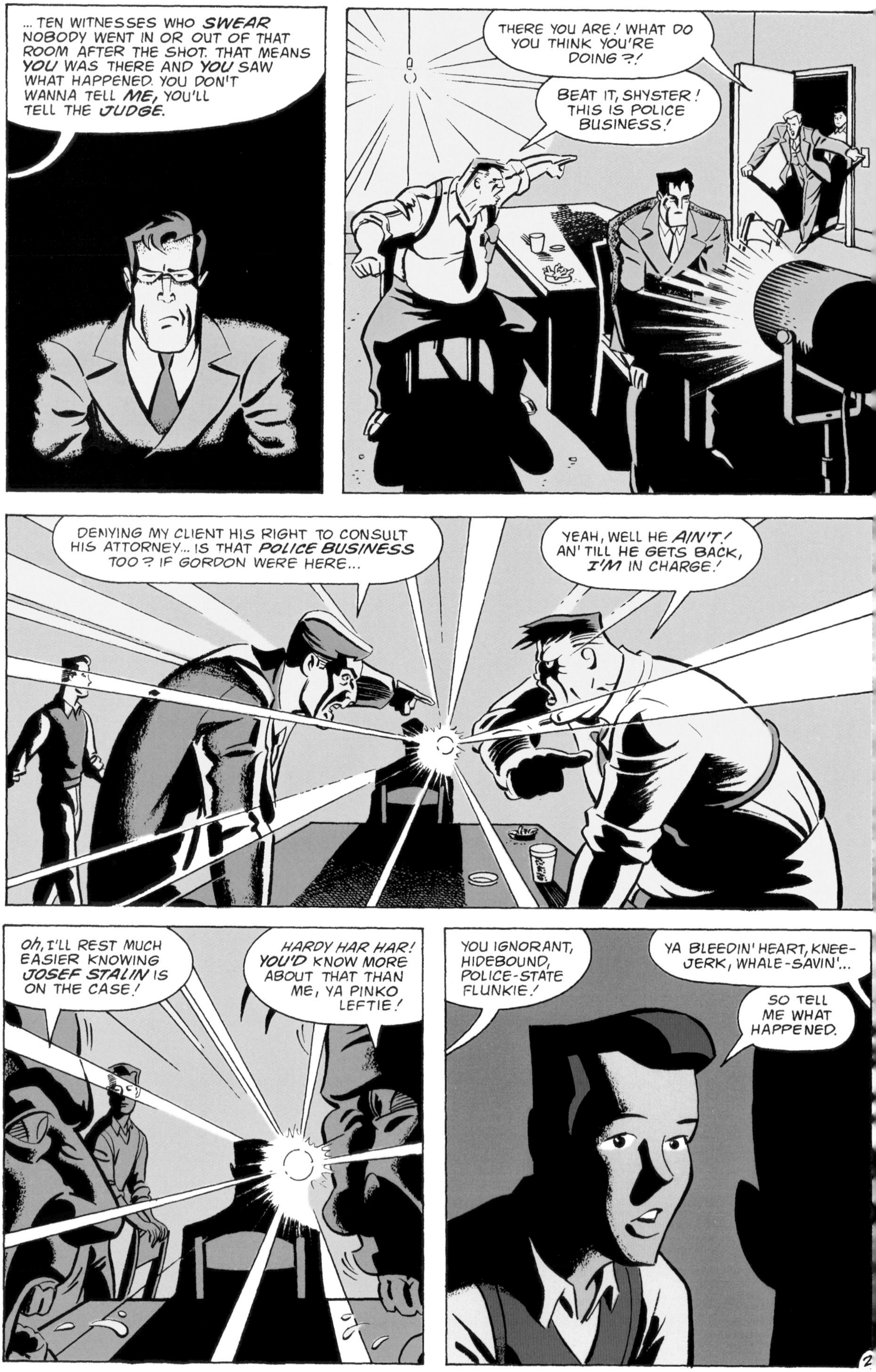
... TEN WITNESSES WHO SWEAR NOBODY WENT IN OR OUT OF THAT ROOM AFTER THE SHOT. THAT MEANS YOU WAS THERE AND YOU SAW WHAT HAPPENED. YOU DON'T WANNA TELL ME, YOU'LL TELL THE JUDGE.
THERE YOU ARE! WHAT DO YOU THINK YOU'RE DOING?!
BEAT IT, SHYSTER! THIS IS POLICE BUSINESS!
DENYING MY CLIENT HIS RIGHT TO CONSULT HIS ATTORNEY... IS THAT POLICE BUSINESS TOO? IF GORDON WERE HERE...
YEAH, WELL HE AIN'T! AN' TILL HE GETS BACK, I'M IN CHARGE!
OH, I'LL REST MUCH EASIER KNOWING JOSEF STALIN IS ON THE CASE!
HARDY HAR HAR! YOU'D KNOW MORE ABOUT THAT THAN ME, YA PINKO LEFTIE!
YOU IGNORANT, HIDEBOUND, POLICE-STATE FLUNKIE!
YA BLEEDIN' HEART, KNEE-JERK, WHALE-SAVIN'...
SO TELL ME WHAT HAPPENED.

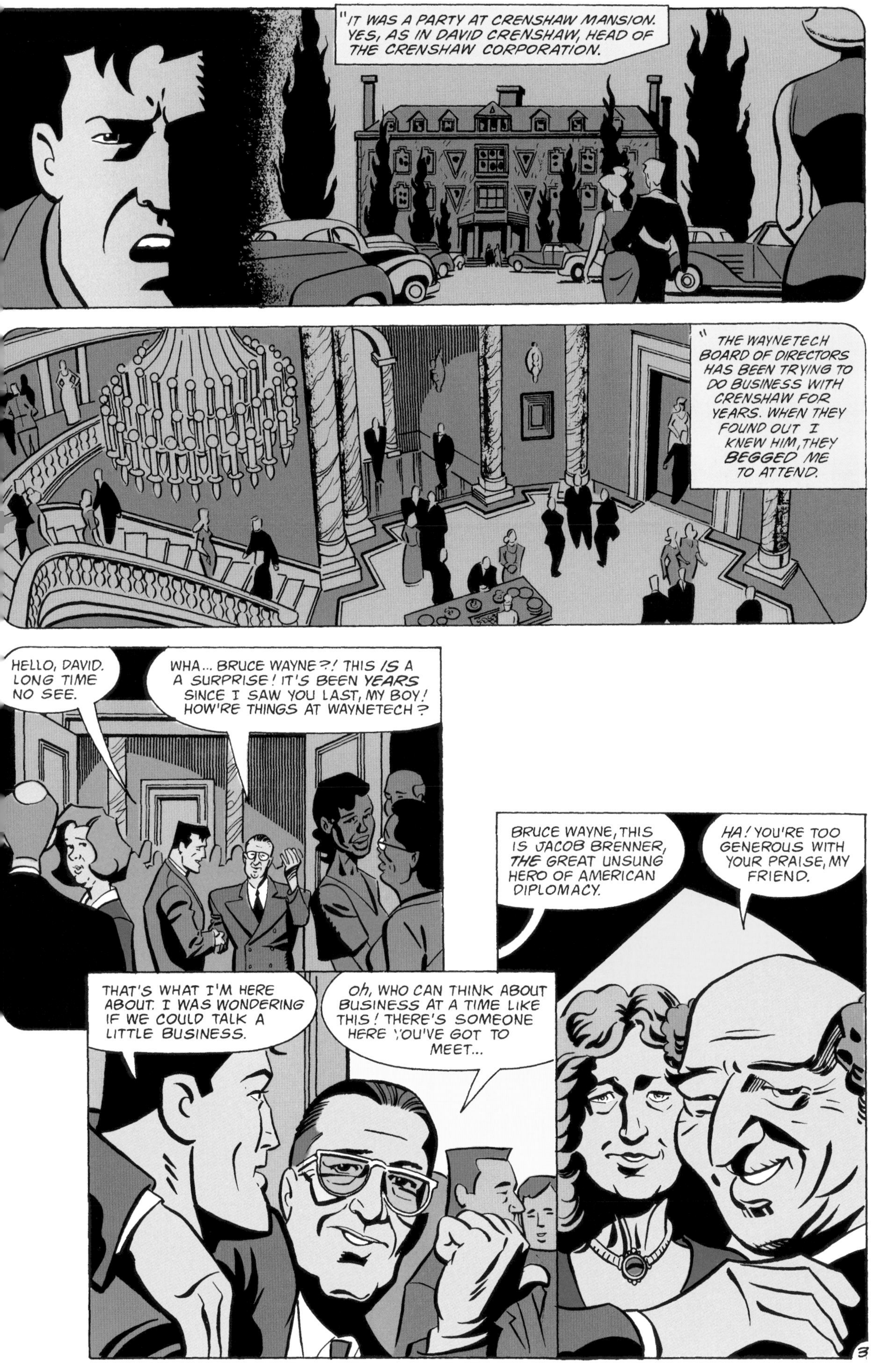
"IT WAS A PARTY AT CRENSHAW MANSION. YES, AS IN DAVID CRENSHAW, HEAD OF THE CRENSHAW CORPORATION.
"THE WAYNETECH BOARD OF DIRECTORS HAS BEEN TRYING TO DO BUSINESS WITH CRENSHAW FOR YEARS. WHEN THEY FOUND OUT I KNEW HIM, THEY BEGGED ME TO ATTEND.
HELLO, DAVID. LONG TIME NO SEE.
WHA... BRUCE WAYNE?! THIS IS A A SURPRISE! IT'S BEEN YEARS SINCE I SAW YOU LAST, MY BOY! HOW'RE THINGS AT WAYNETECH?
THAT'S WHAT I'M HERE ABOUT. I WAS WONDERING IF WE COULD TALK A LITTLE BUSINESS.
OH, WHO CAN THINK ABOUT BUSINESS AT A TIME LIKE THIS! THERE'S SOMEONE HERE YOU'VE GOT TO MEET...
BRUCE WAYNE, THIS IS JACOB BRENNER, THE GREAT UNSUNG HERO OF AMERICAN DIPLOMACY.
HA! YOU'RE TOO GENEROUS WITH YOUR PRAISE, MY FRIEND.
3

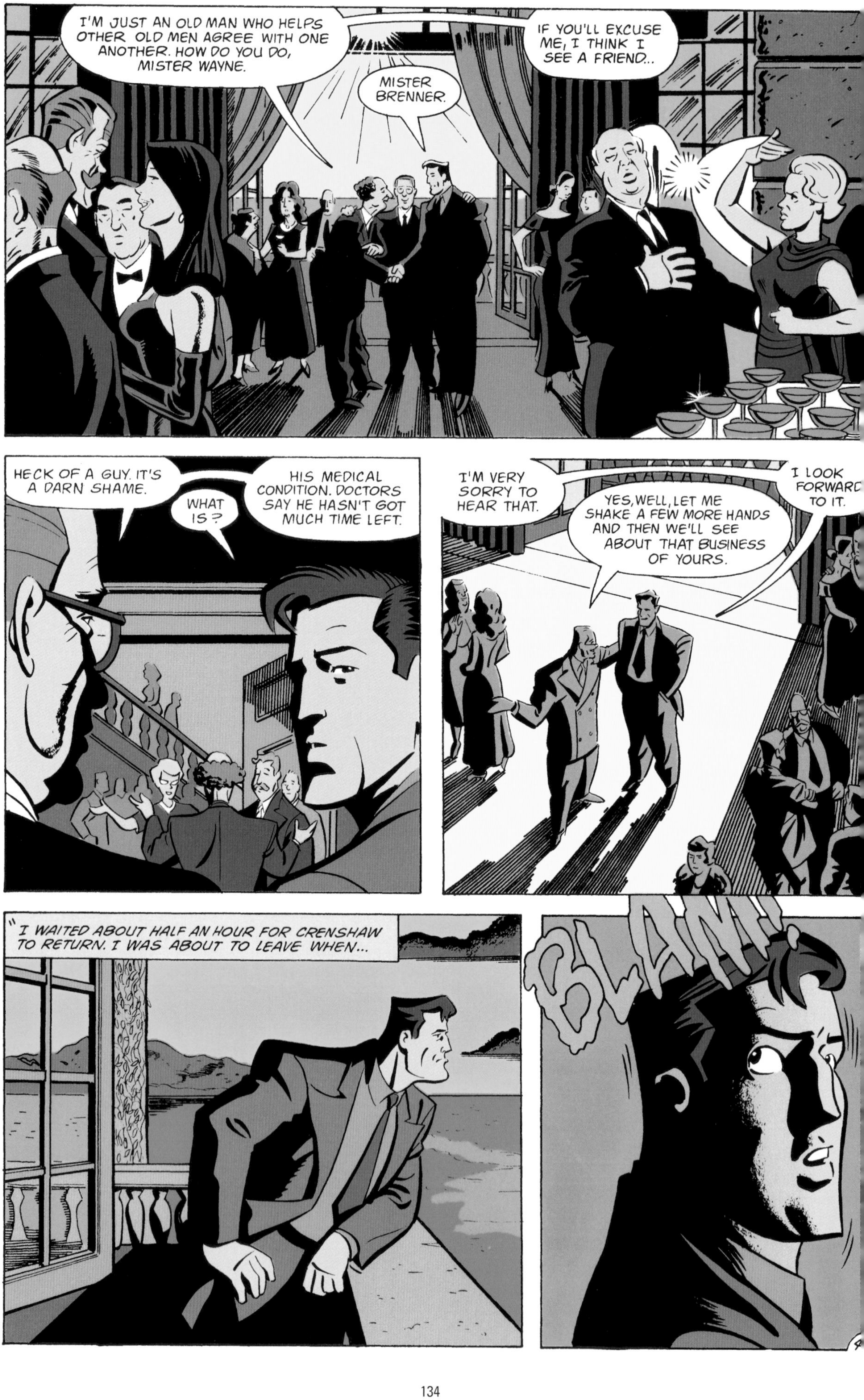

I'M JUST AN OLD MAN WHO HELPS OTHER OLD MEN AGREE WITH ONE ANOTHER. HOW DO YOU DO, MISTER WAYNE.
MISTER BRENNER.
IF YOU'LL EXCUSE ME, I THINK I SEE A FRIEND...
HECK OF A GUY. IT'S A DARN SHAME.
WHAT IS?
HIS MEDICAL CONDITION. DOCTORS SAY HE HASN'T GOT MUCH TIME LEFT.
I'M VERY SORRY TO HEAR THAT.
YES, WELL, LET ME SHAKE A FEW MORE HANDS AND THEN WE'LL SEE ABOUT THAT BUSINESS OF YOURS.
I LOOK FORWARD TO IT.
"I WAITED ABOUT HALF AN HOUR FOR CRENSHAW TO RETURN. I WAS ABOUT TO LEAVE WHEN...

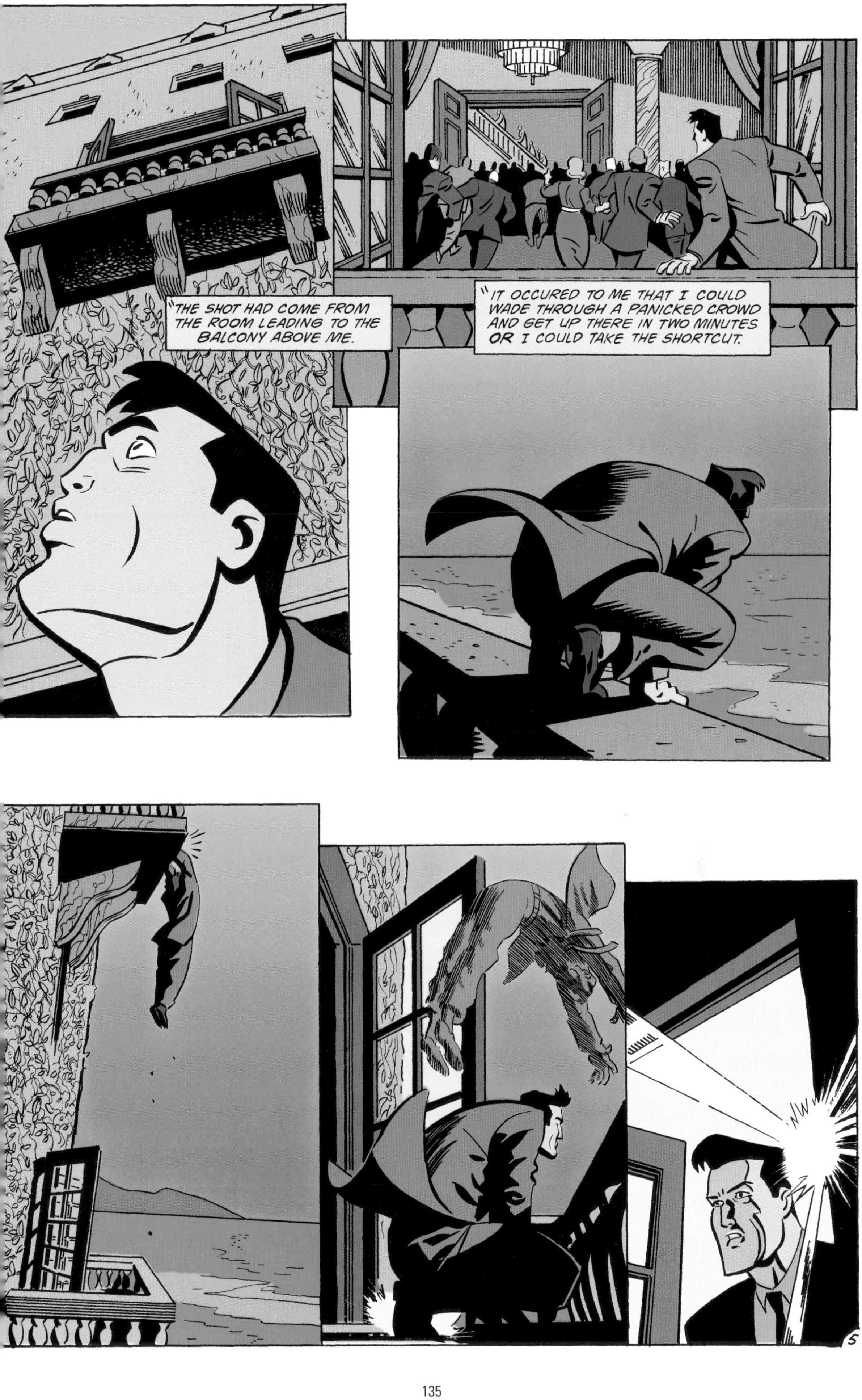
"THE SHOT HAD COME FROM THE ROOM LEADING TO THE BALCONY ABOVE ME.
"IT OCCURED TO ME THAT I COULD WADE THROUGH A PANICKED CROWD AND GET UP THERE IN TWO MINUTES OR I COULD TAKE THE SHORTCUT.

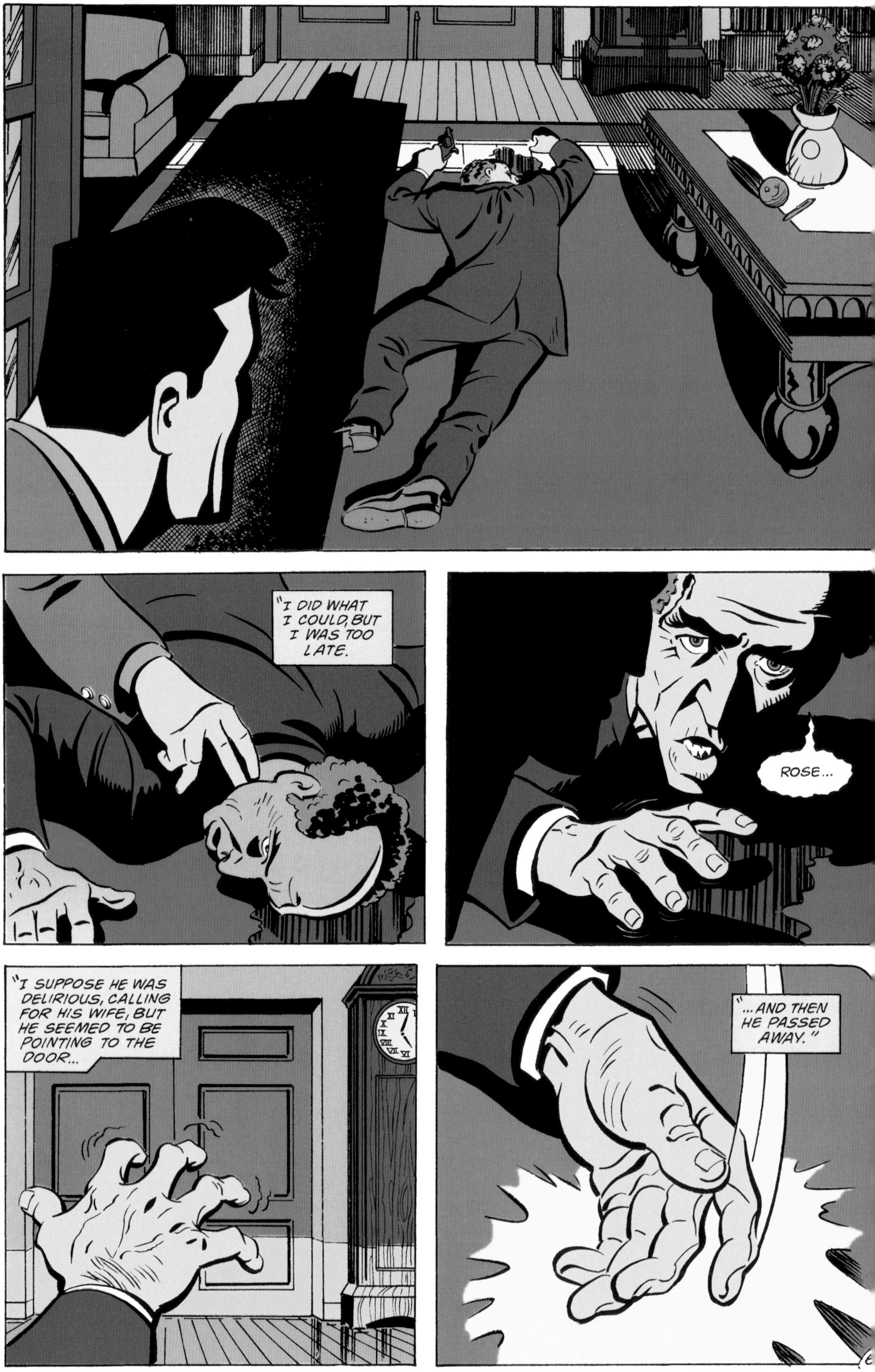
"I DID WHAT I COULD, BUT I WAS TOO LATE.
ROSE...
"I SUPPOSE HE WAS DELIRIOUS, CALLING FOR HIS WIFE, BUT HE SEEMED TO BE POINTING TO THE DOOR...
"...AND THEN HE PASSED AWAY."

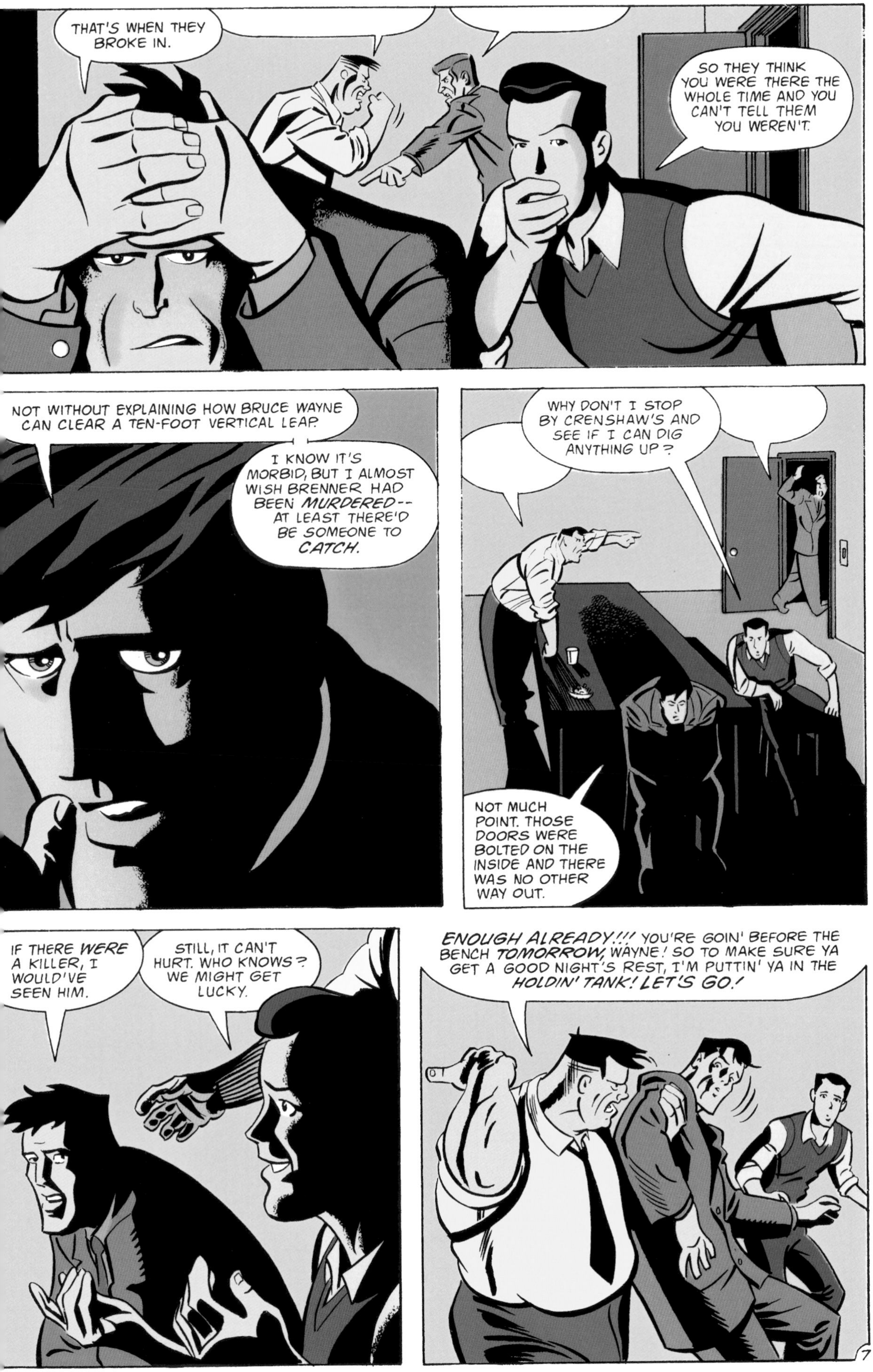
THAT'S WHEN THEY BROKE IN.
SO THEY THINK YOU WERE THERE THE WHOLE TIME AND YOU CAN'T TELL THEM YOU WEREN'T.
NOT WITHOUT EXPLAINING HOW BRUCE WAYNE CAN CLEAR A TEN-FOOT VERTICAL LEAP.
I KNOW IT'S MORBID, BUT I ALMOST WISH BRENNER HAD BEEN MURDERED-- AT LEAST THERE'D BE SOMEONE TO CATCH.
WHY DON'T I STOP BY CRENSHAW'S AND SEE IF I CAN DIG ANYTHING UP?
NOT MUCH POINT. THOSE DOORS WERE BOLTED ON THE INSIDE AND THERE WAS NO OTHER WAY OUT.
IF THERE WERE A KILLER, I WOULD'VE SEEN HIM.
STILL, IT CAN'T HURT. WHO KNOWS? WE MIGHT GET LUCKY.
ENOUGH ALREADY!!! YOU'RE GOIN' BEFORE THE BENCH TOMORROW, WAYNE! SO TO MAKE SURE YA GET A GOOD NIGHT'S REST, I'M PUTTIN' YA IN THE HOLDIN' TANK! LET'S GO!
7

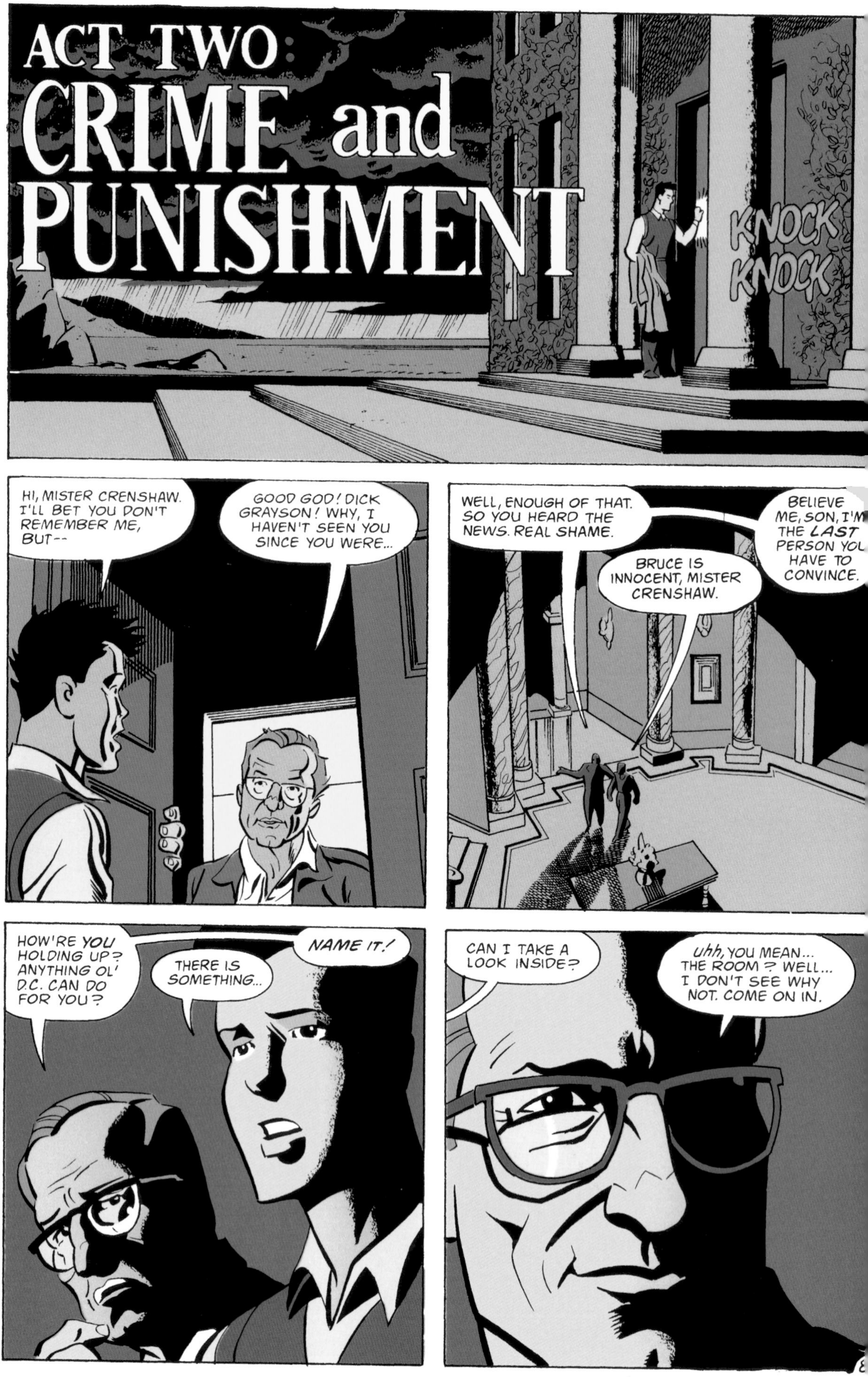
ACT TWO:
CRIME and PUNISHMENT
KNOCK KNOCK
HI, MISTER CRENSHAW. I'LL BET YOU DON'T REMEMBER ME, BUT--
GOOD GOD! DICK GRAYSON! WHY, I HAVEN'T SEEN YOU SINCE YOU WERE...
WELL, ENOUGH OF THAT. SO YOU HEARD THE NEWS. REAL SHAME.
BRUCE IS INNOCENT, MISTER CRENSHAW.
BELIEVE ME, SON, I'M THE LAST PERSON YOU HAVE TO CONVINCE.
HOW'RE YOU HOLDING UP? ANYTHING OL' D.C. CAN DO FOR YOU?
THERE IS SOMETHING...
NAME IT!
CAN I TAKE A LOOK INSIDE?
uhh, YOU MEAN... THE ROOM? WELL... I DON'T SEE WHY NOT. COME ON IN.

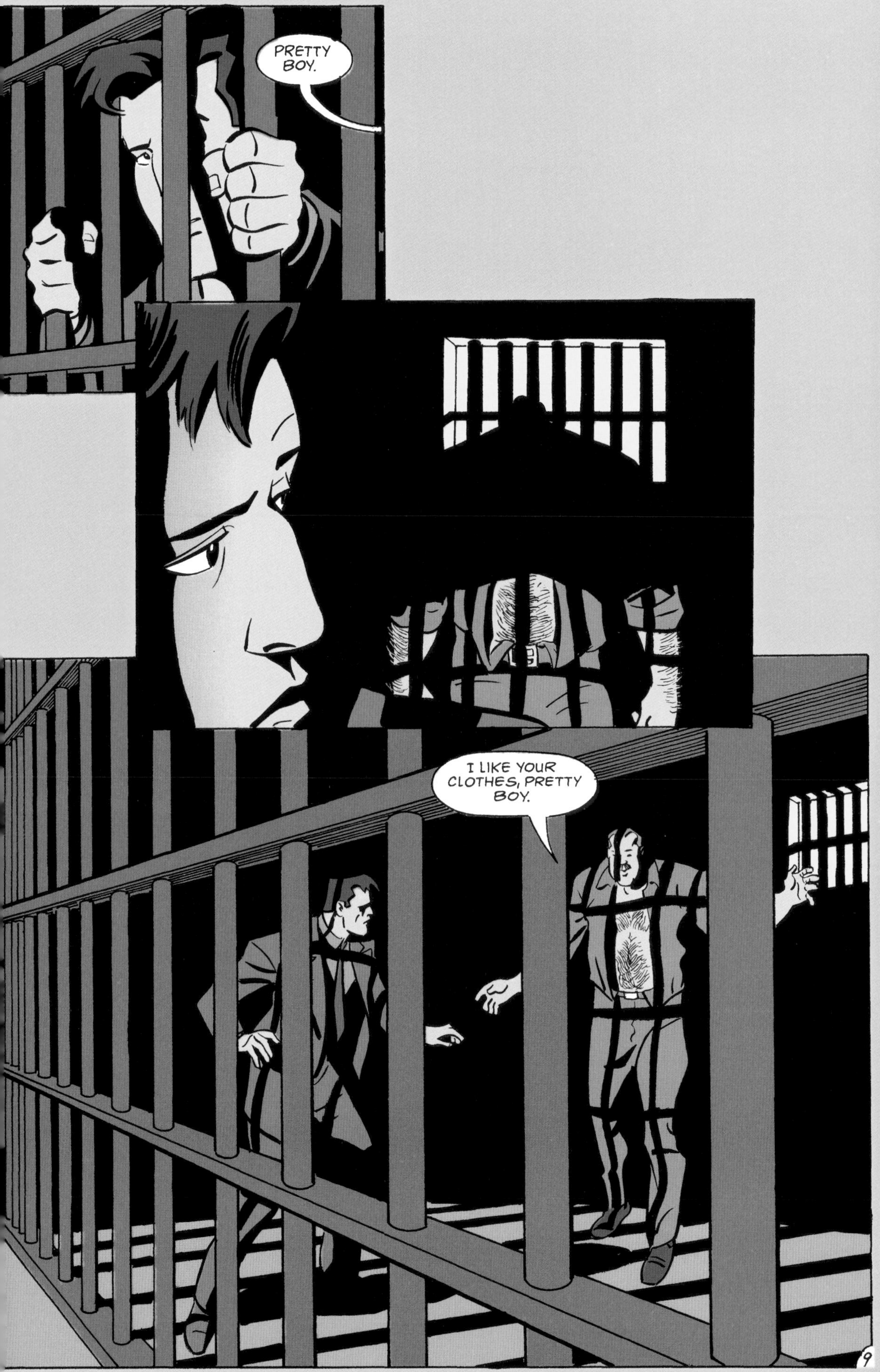
PRETTY BOY.
I LIKE YOUR CLOTHES, PRETTY BOY.
9

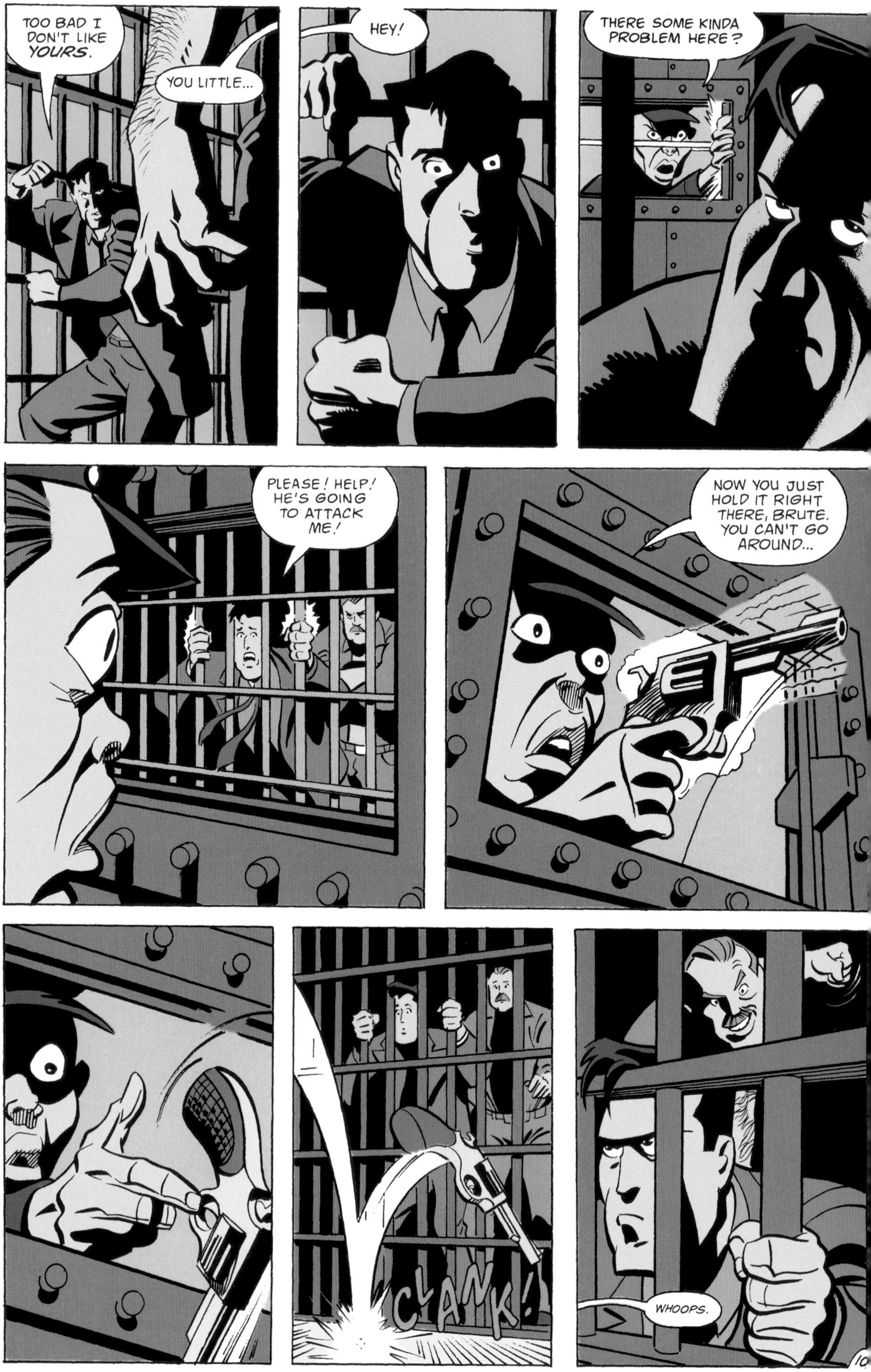

TOO BAD I DON'T LIKE YOURS.
YOU LITTLE...
HEY!
THERE SOME KINDA PROBLEM HERE?
PLEASE! HELP! HE'S GOING TO ATTACK ME!
NOW YOU JUST HOLD IT RIGHT THERE, BRUTE. YOU CAN'T GO AROUND...
CLANK!
WHOOPS.
10

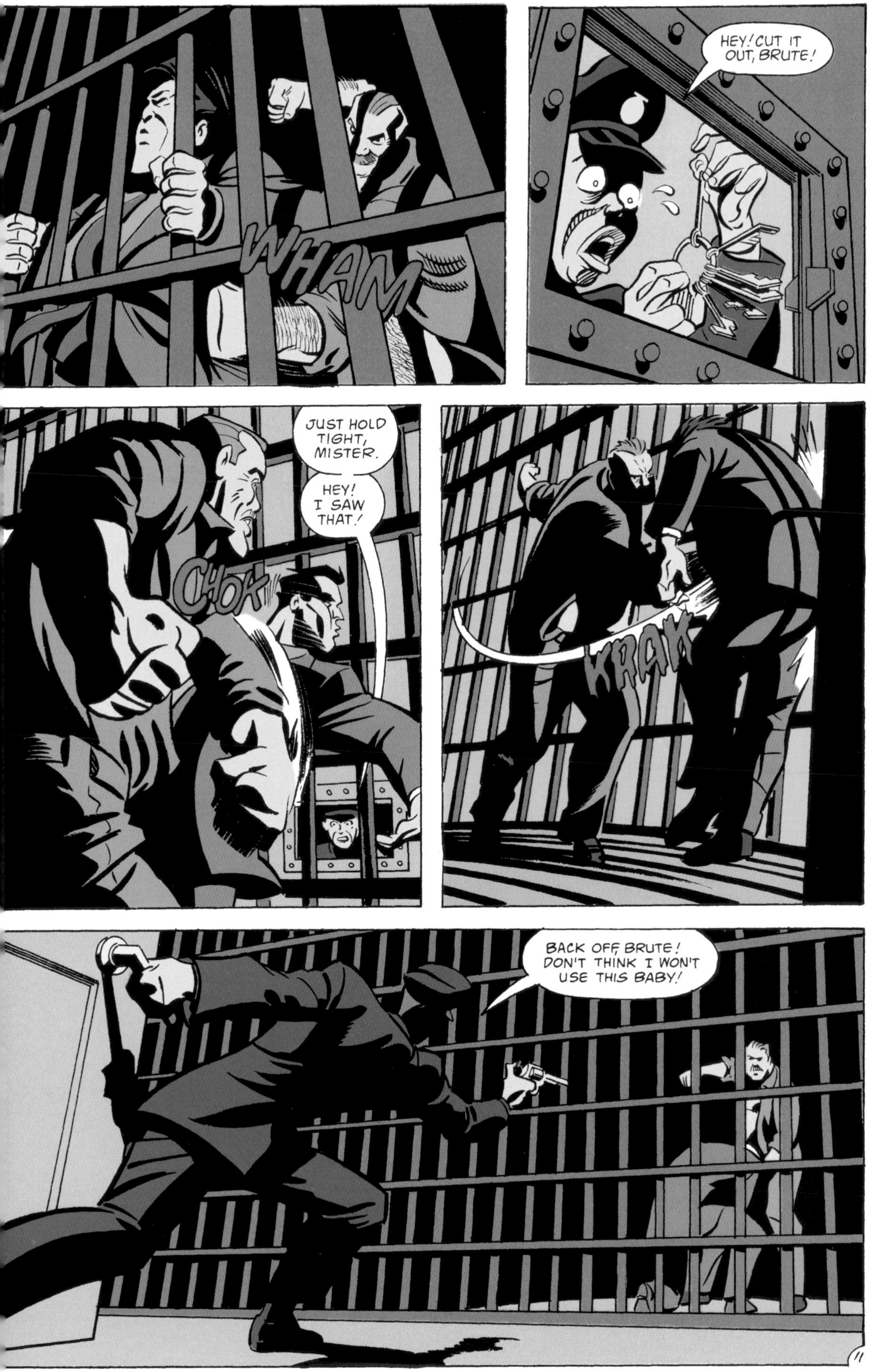

WHAM
HEY! CUT IT OUT, BRUTE!
JUST HOLD TIGHT, MISTER.
HEY! I SAW THAT!
CHOK
KRAK
BACK OFF, BRUTE! DON'T THINK I WON'T USE THIS BABY!
11

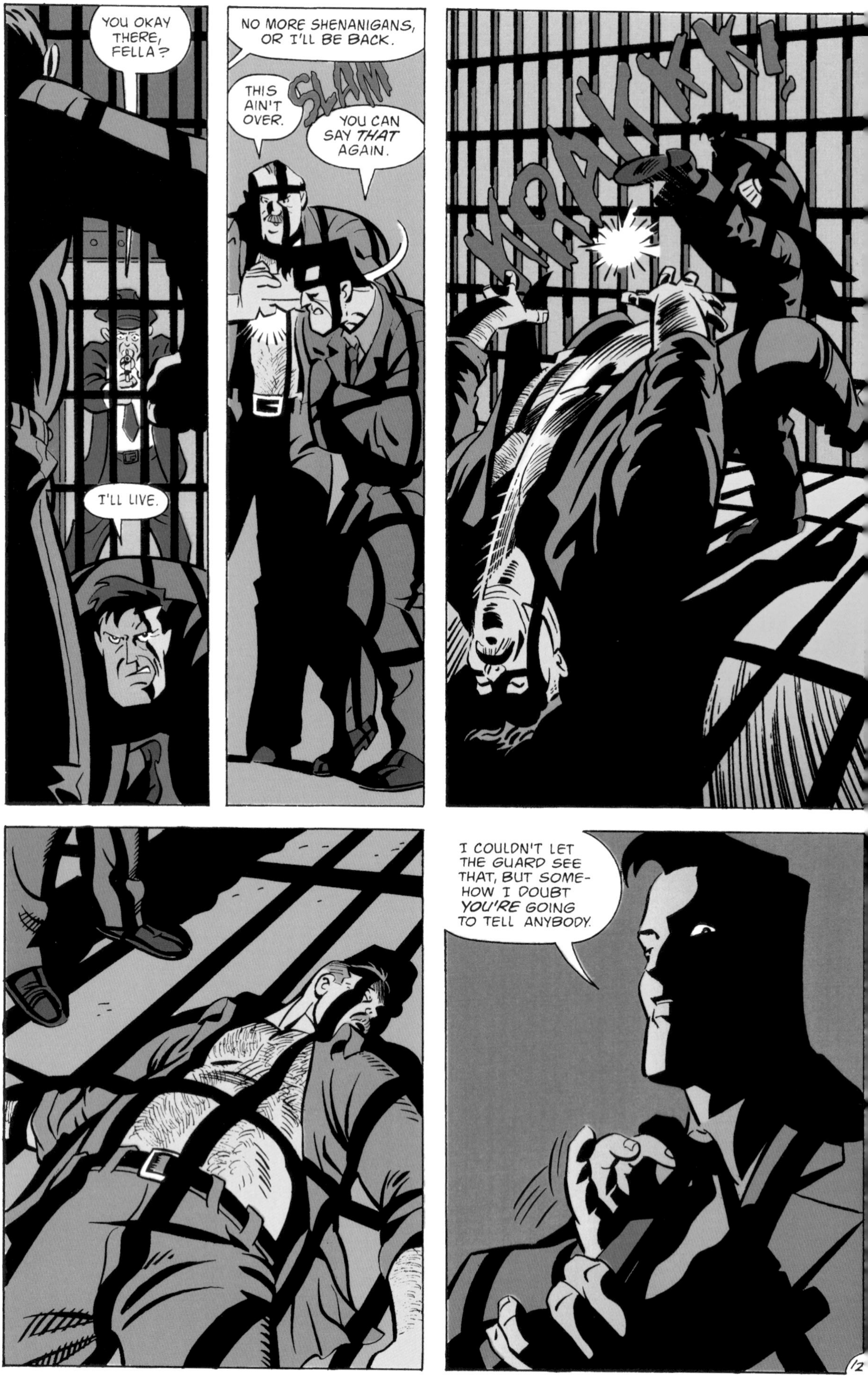
YOU OKAY THERE, FELLA?
I'LL LIVE.
NO MORE SHENANIGANS, OR I'LL BE BACK.
THIS AIN'T OVER.
SLAM
YOU CAN SAY *THAT* AGAIN.
KRAKKK!
I COULDN'T LET THE GUARD SEE THAT, BUT SOMEHOW I DOUBT *YOU'RE* GOING TO TELL ANYBODY.
12

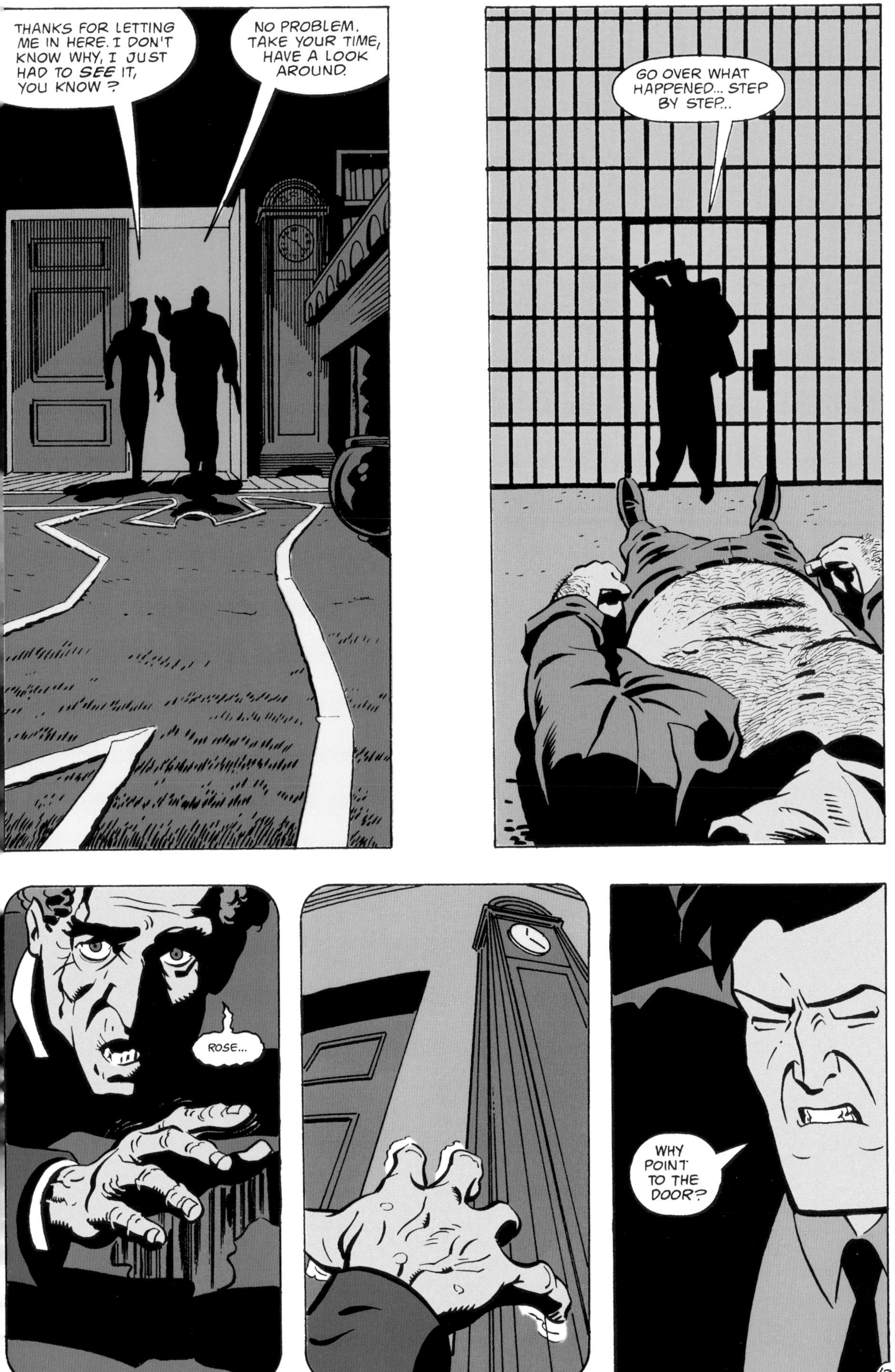
THANKS FOR LETTING ME IN HERE. I DON'T KNOW WHY, I JUST HAD TO SEE IT, YOU KNOW?
NO PROBLEM. TAKE YOUR TIME, HAVE A LOOK AROUND.
GO OVER WHAT HAPPENED... STEP BY STEP...
ROSE...
WHY POINT TO THE DOOR?
13

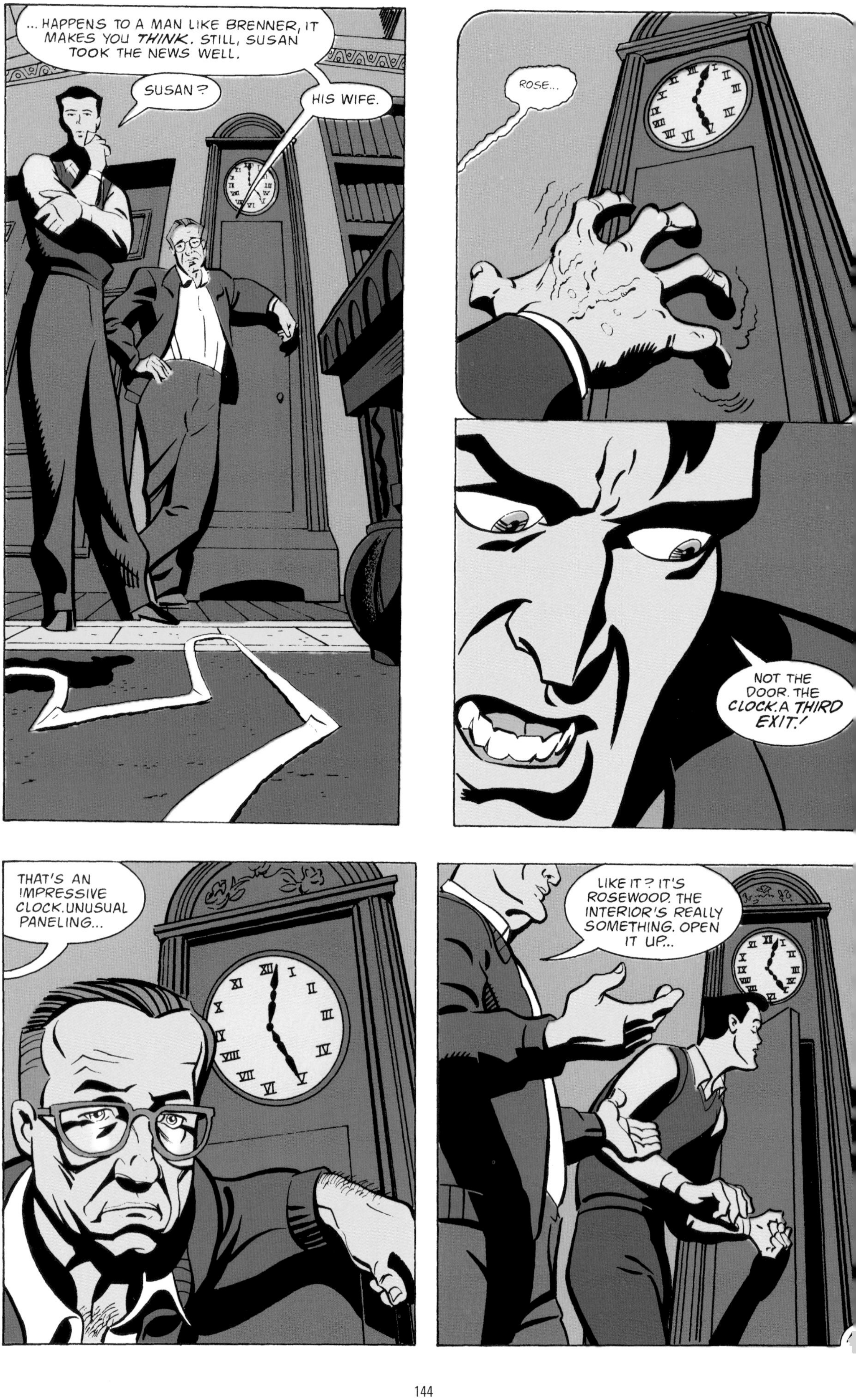

... HAPPENS TO A MAN LIKE BRENNER, IT MAKES YOU THINK. STILL, SUSAN TOOK THE NEWS WELL.
SUSAN?
HIS WIFE.
ROSE...
NOT THE DOOR. THE CLOCK. A THIRD EXIT!
THAT'S AN IMPRESSIVE CLOCK. UNUSUAL PANELING...
LIKE IT? IT'S ROSEWOOD. THE INTERIOR'S REALLY SOMETHING. OPEN IT UP..

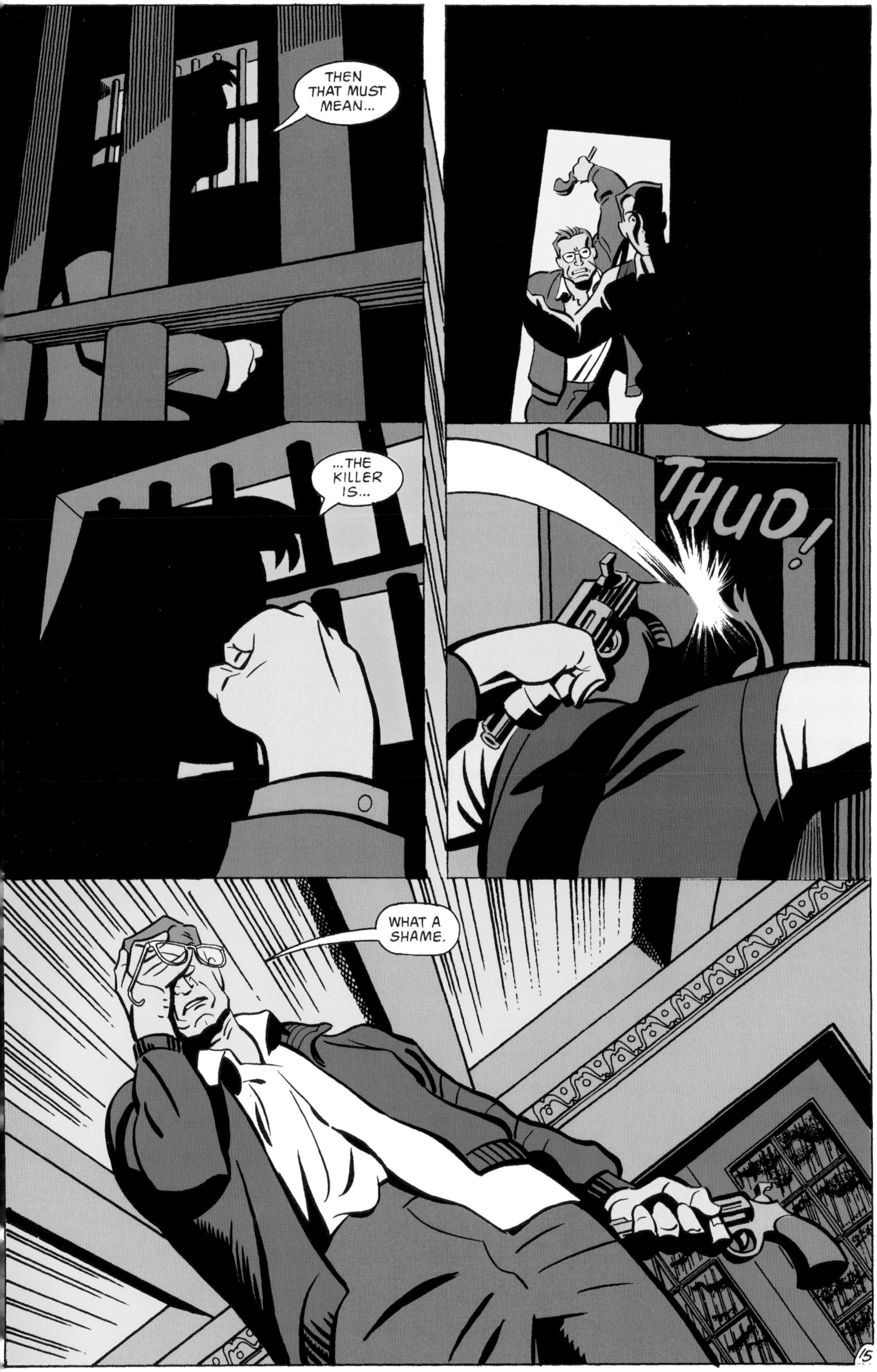
THEN THAT MUST MEAN...
...THE KILLER IS...
THUD!
WHAT A SHAME.
15

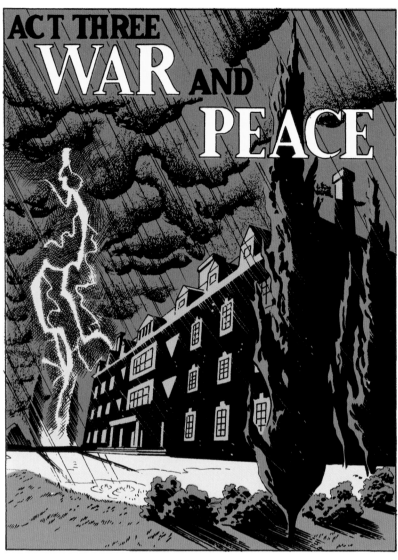

ACT THREE
WAR AND PEACE

HAVE TO STAY *CALM.* THE DRIVER WILL BE HERE *SOON.*

I'LL FLY SOUTH, RELAX, REVIEW MY OPTIONS. GET RID OF THE... *LIABILITY* ALONG THE WAY. WHAT'S NEEDED NOW IS *PATIENCE.*

WHAT'S TAKING HIM SO LONG?!?

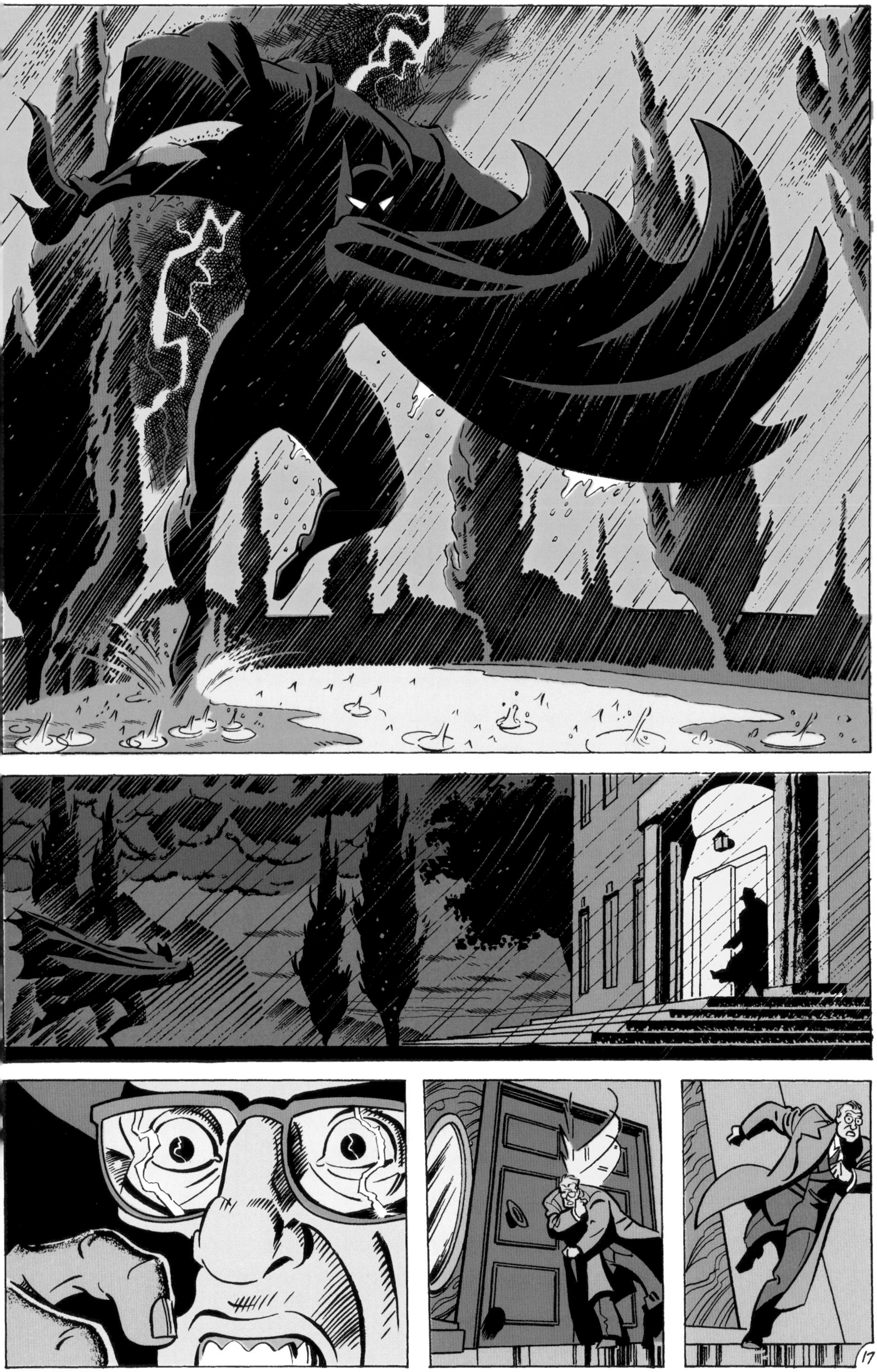
17

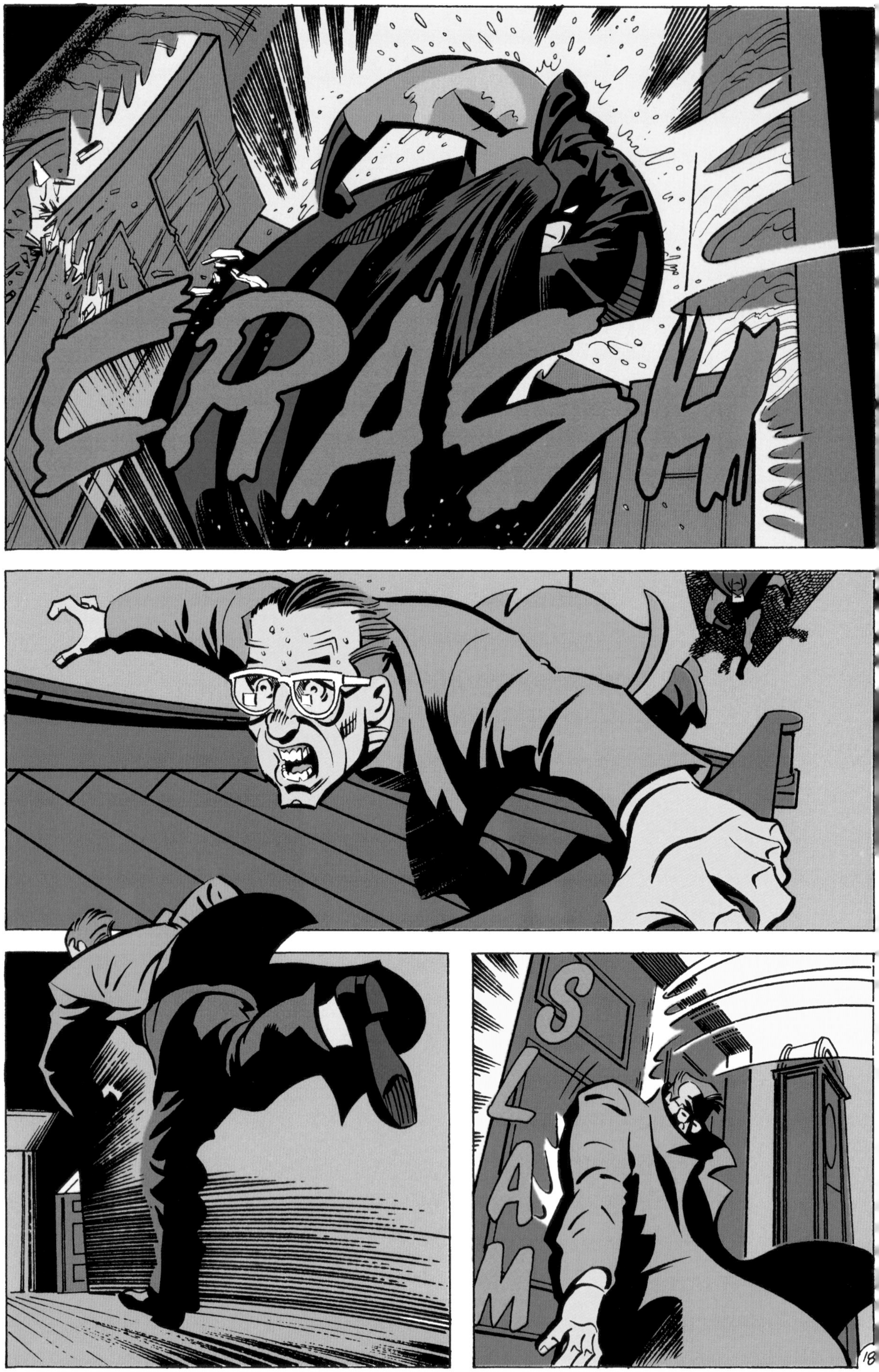
CRASH
SLAM
18

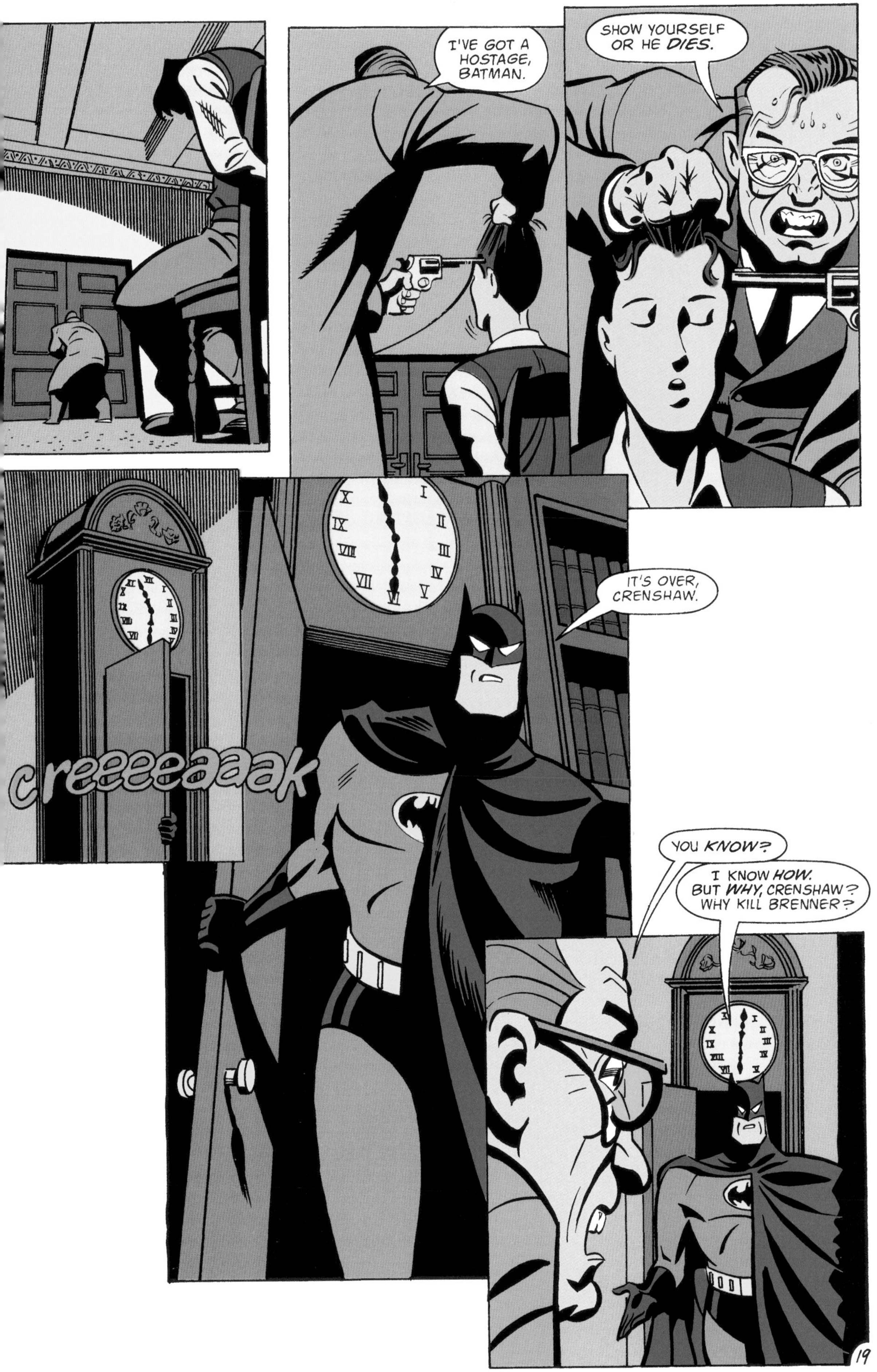
I'VE GOT A HOSTAGE, BATMAN.
SHOW YOURSELF OR HE DIES.
creeeeaaak
IT'S OVER, CRENSHAW.
YOU KNOW?
I KNOW HOW. BUT WHY, CRENSHAW? WHY KILL BRENNER?
19

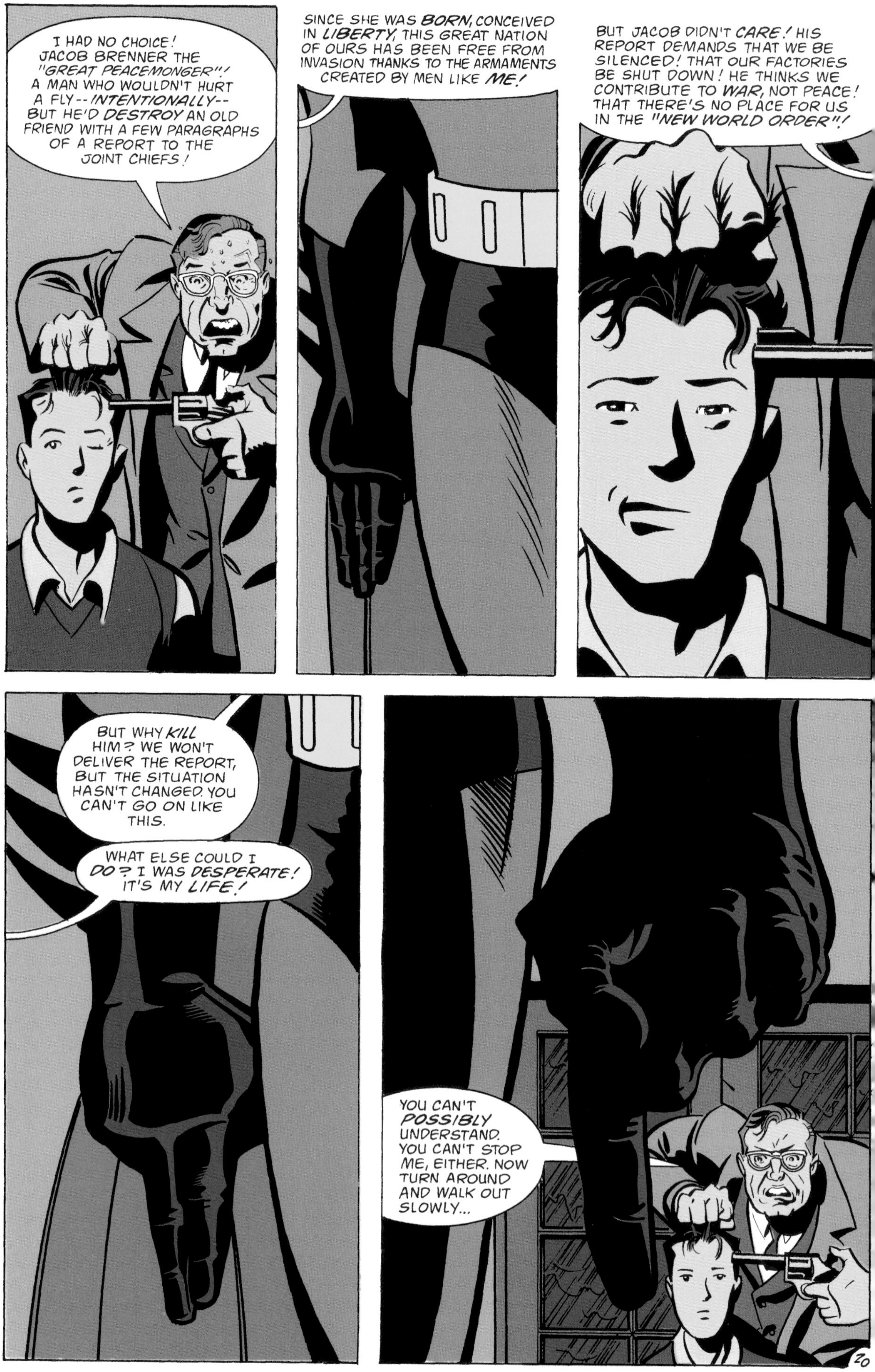
I HAD NO CHOICE! JACOB BRENNER THE "GREAT PEACEMONGER"! A MAN WHO WOULDN'T HURT A FLY--INTENTIONALLY-- BUT HE'D DESTROY AN OLD FRIEND WITH A FEW PARAGRAPHS OF A REPORT TO THE JOINT CHIEFS!
SINCE SHE WAS BORN, CONCEIVED IN LIBERTY, THIS GREAT NATION OF OURS HAS BEEN FREE FROM INVASION THANKS TO THE ARMAMENTS CREATED BY MEN LIKE ME!
BUT JACOB DIDN'T CARE! HIS REPORT DEMANDS THAT WE BE SILENCED! THAT OUR FACTORIES BE SHUT DOWN! HE THINKS WE CONTRIBUTE TO WAR, NOT PEACE! THAT THERE'S NO PLACE FOR US IN THE "NEW WORLD ORDER"!
BUT WHY KILL HIM? WE WON'T DELIVER THE REPORT, BUT THE SITUATION HASN'T CHANGED. YOU CAN'T GO ON LIKE THIS.
WHAT ELSE COULD I DO? I WAS DESPERATE! IT'S MY LIFE!
YOU CAN'T POSSIBLY UNDERSTAND. YOU CAN'T STOP ME, EITHER. NOW TURN AROUND AND WALK OUT SLOWLY...
20

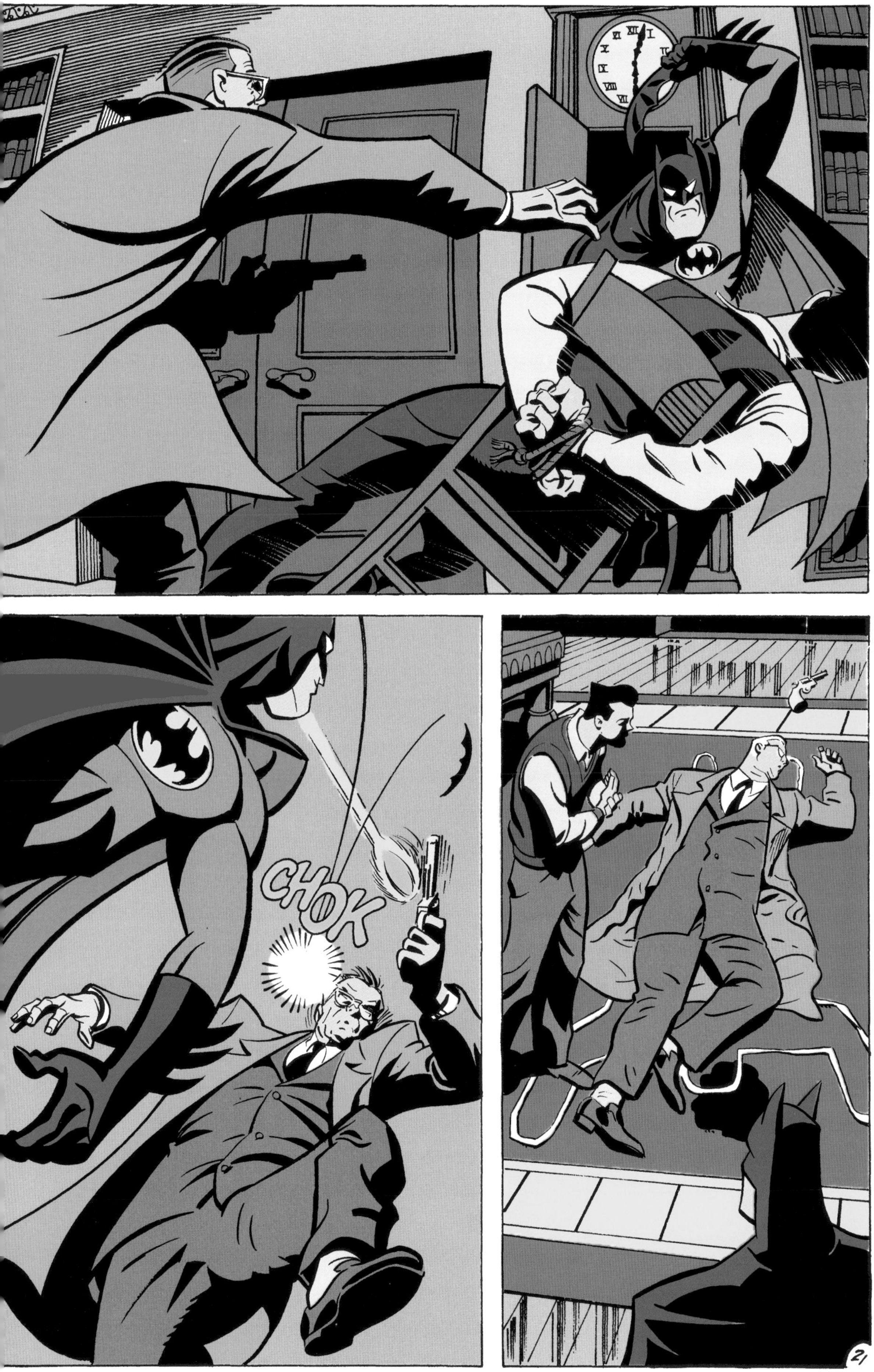
CHOK
21

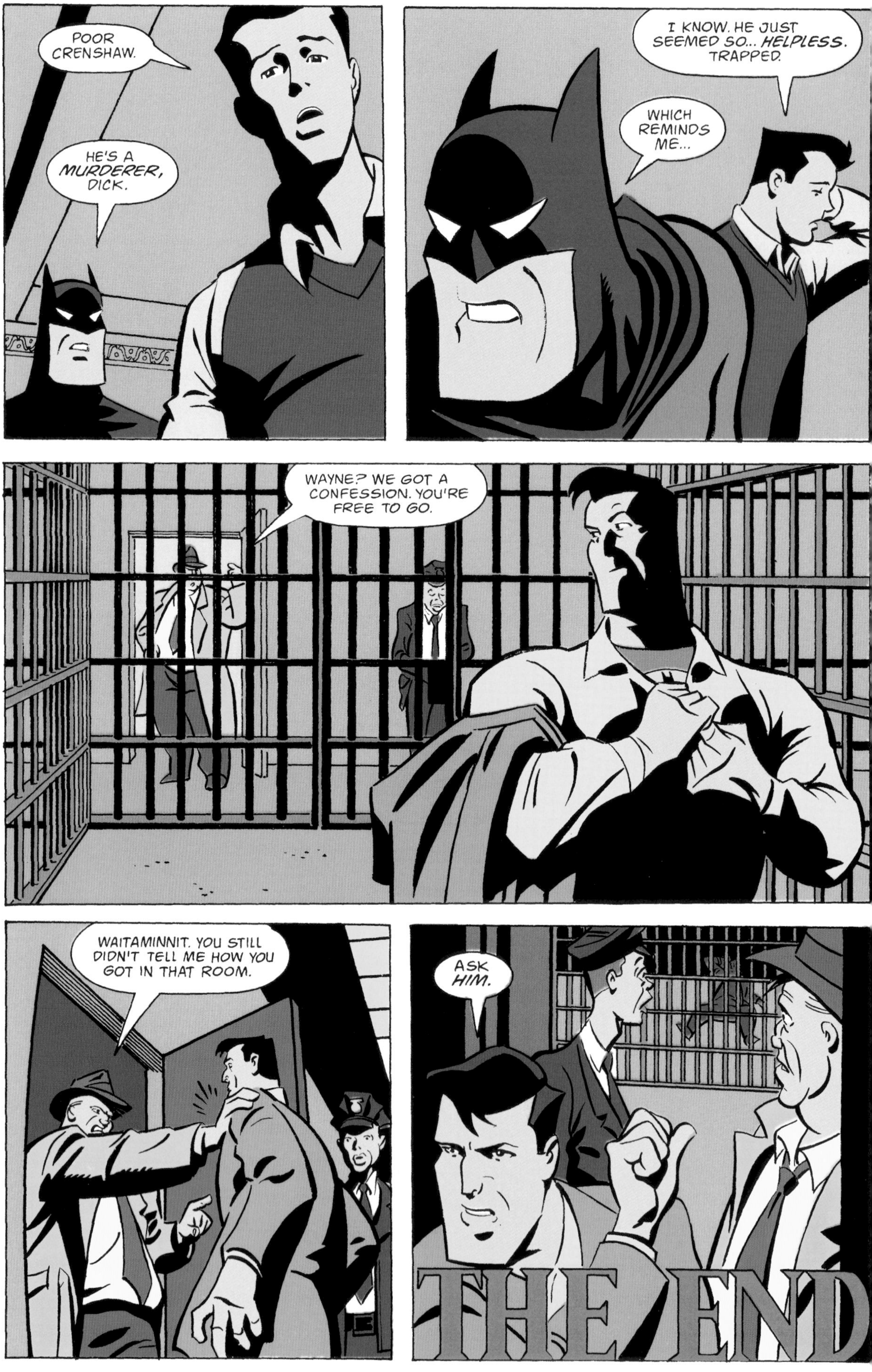

POOR CRENSHAW.
HE'S A MURDERER, DICK.
I KNOW. HE JUST SEEMED SO... HELPLESS. TRAPPED.
WHICH REMINDS ME...
WAYNE? WE GOT A CONFESSION. YOU'RE FREE TO GO.
WAITAMINNIT. YOU STILL DIDN'T TELL ME HOW YOU GOT IN THAT ROOM.
ASK HIM.
THE END

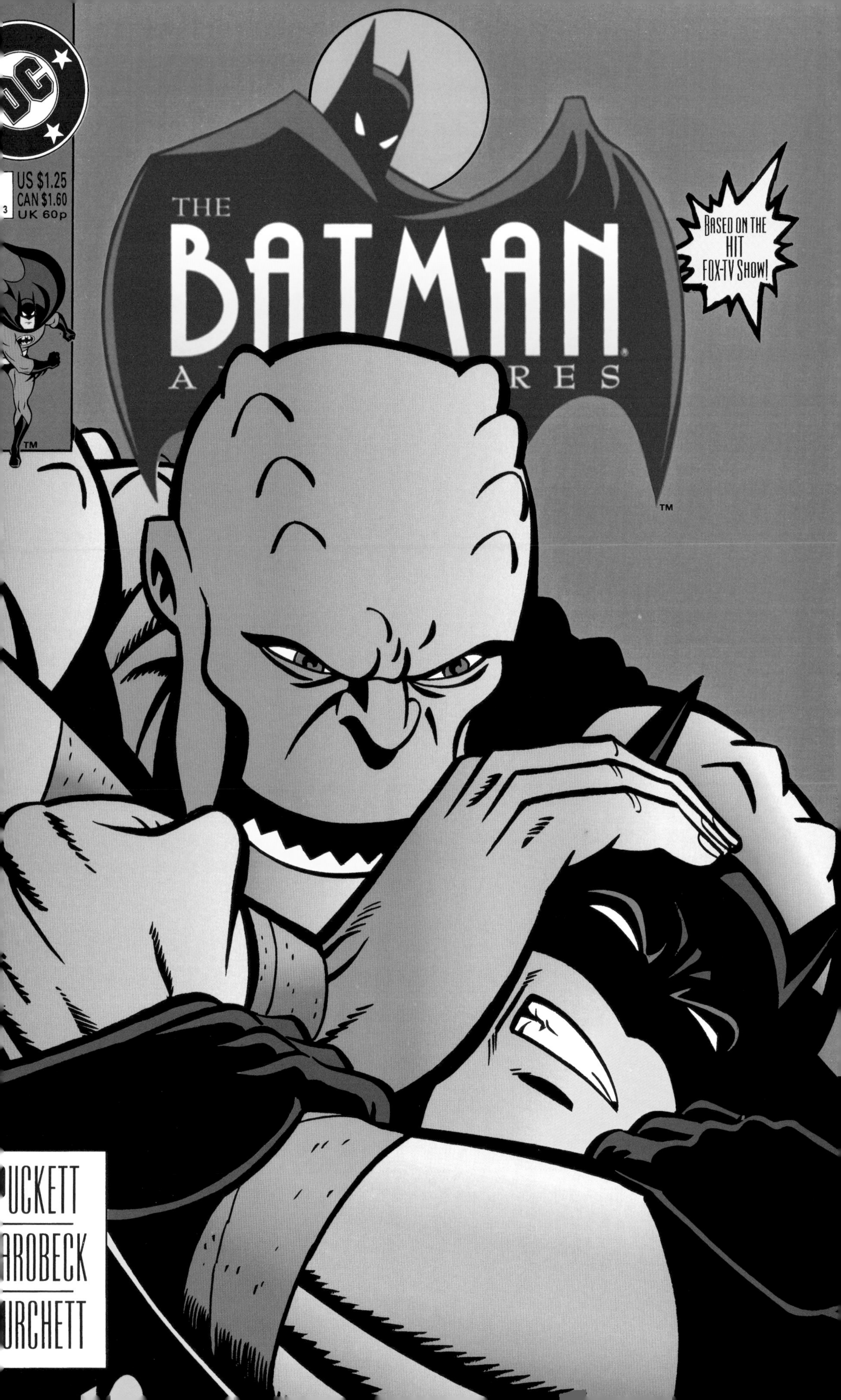

US $1.25
CAN $1.60
UK 60p
THE
BATMAN
RES
BASED ON THE HIT FOX-TV SHOW!
UCKETT
AROBECK
URCHETT

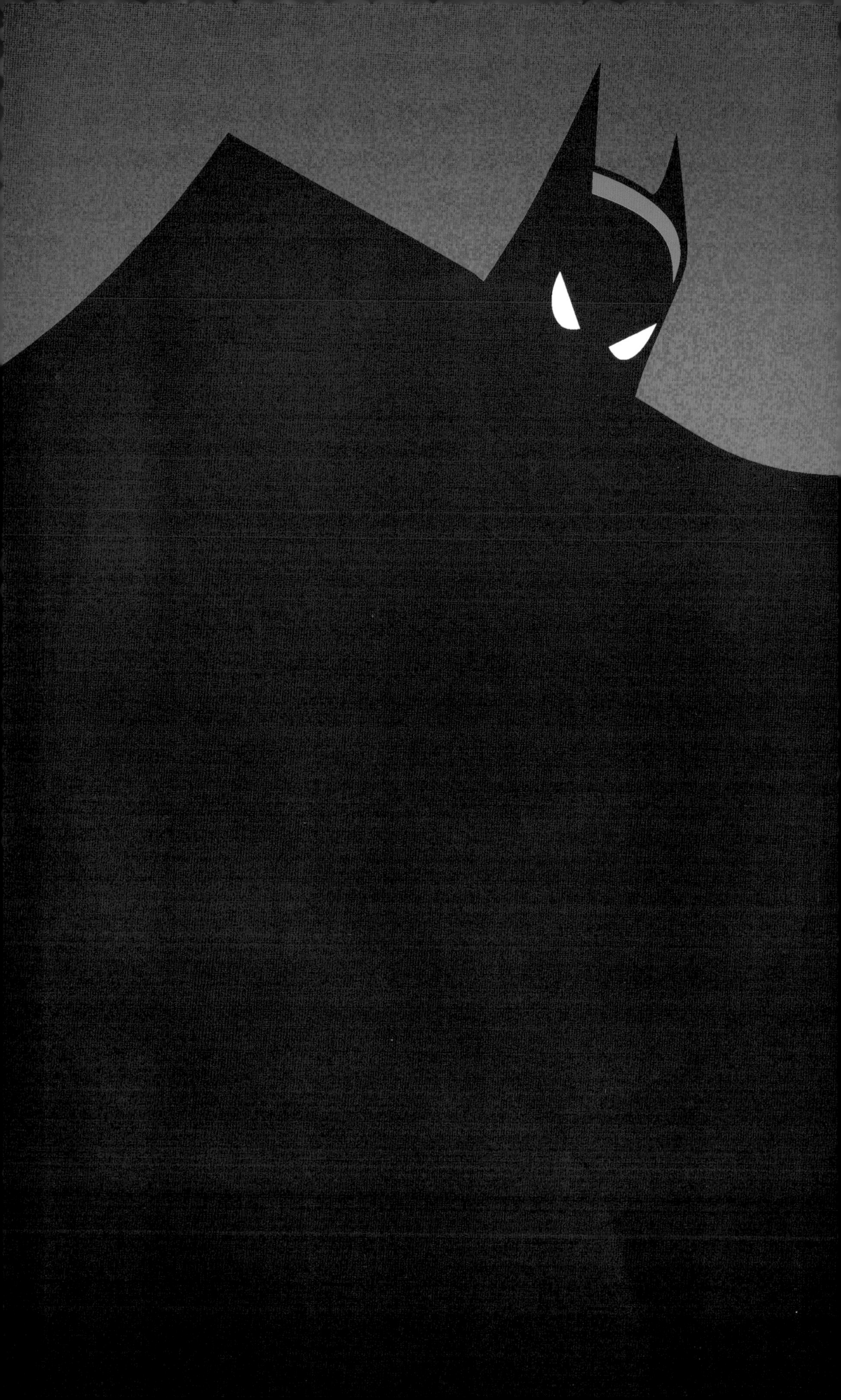

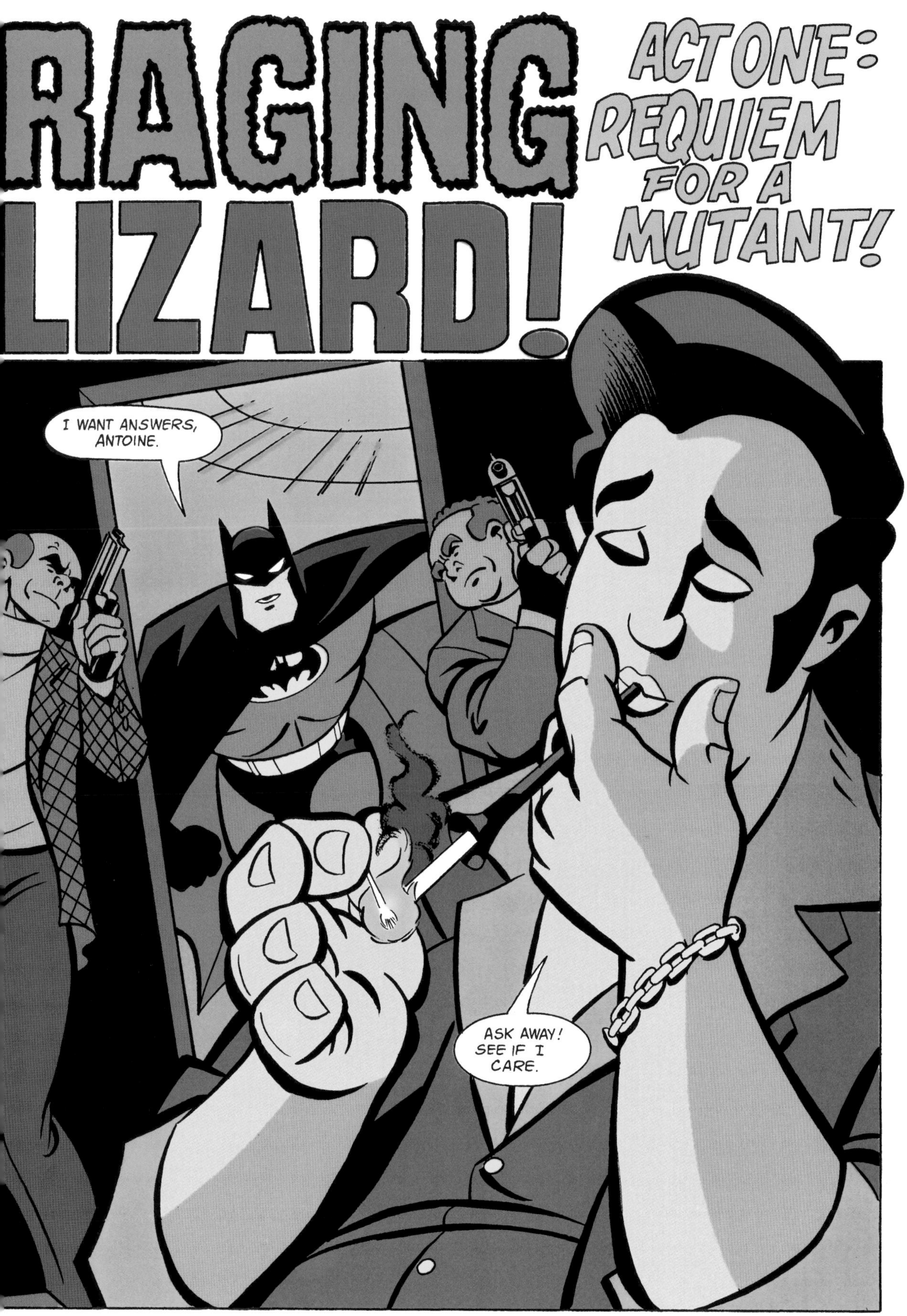

RAGING LIZARD!
ACT ONE: REQUIEM FOR A MUTANT!
I WANT ANSWERS, ANTOINE.
ASK AWAY! SEE IF I CARE.

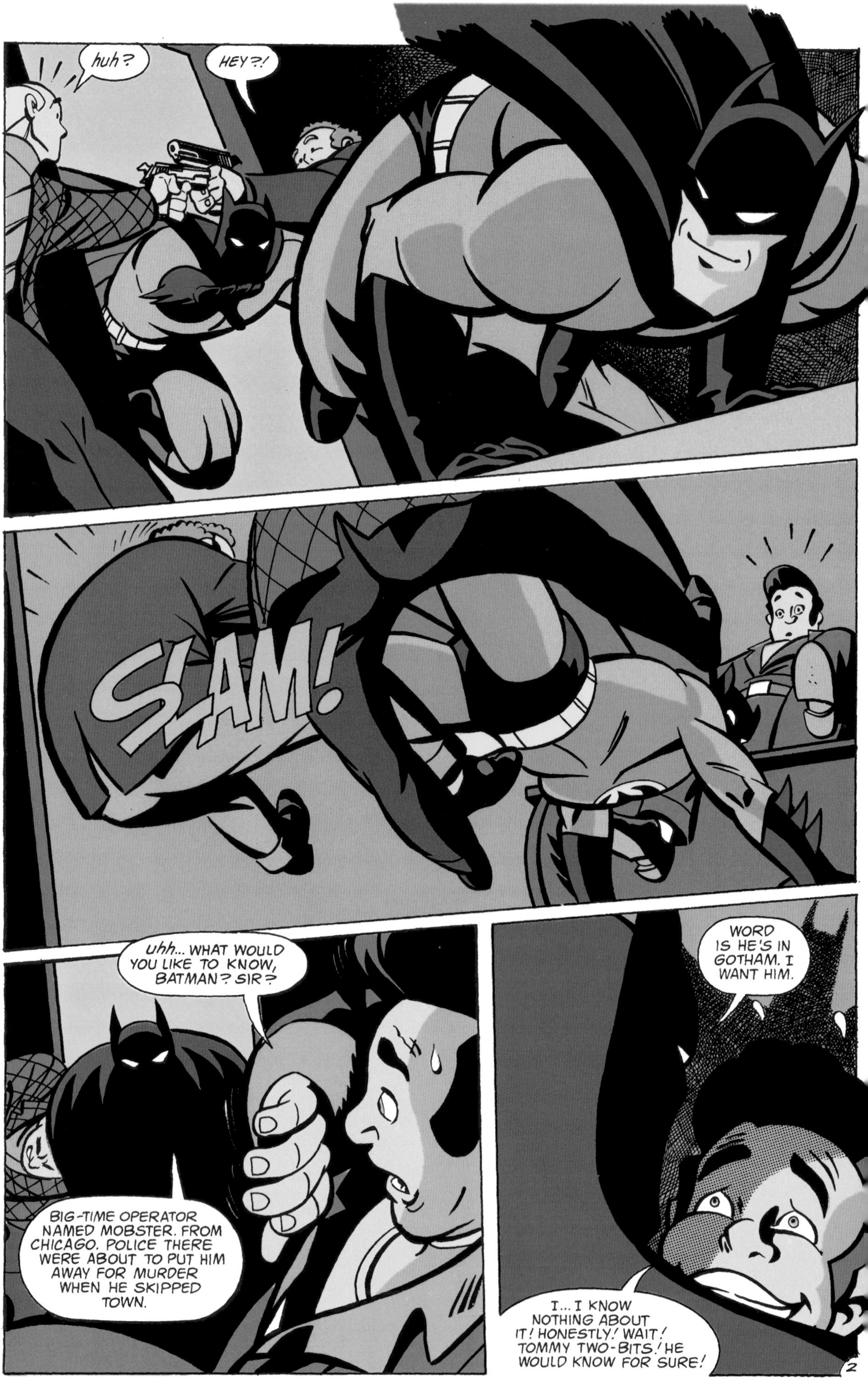
huh?
HEY?!
SLAM!
uhh... WHAT WOULD YOU LIKE TO KNOW, BATMAN? SIR?
BIG-TIME OPERATOR NAMED MOBSTER. FROM CHICAGO. POLICE THERE WERE ABOUT TO PUT HIM AWAY FOR MURDER WHEN HE SKIPPED TOWN.
WORD IS HE'S IN GOTHAM. I WANT HIM.
I... I KNOW NOTHING ABOUT IT! HONESTLY! WAIT! TOMMY TWO-BITS! HE WOULD KNOW FOR SURE!
2

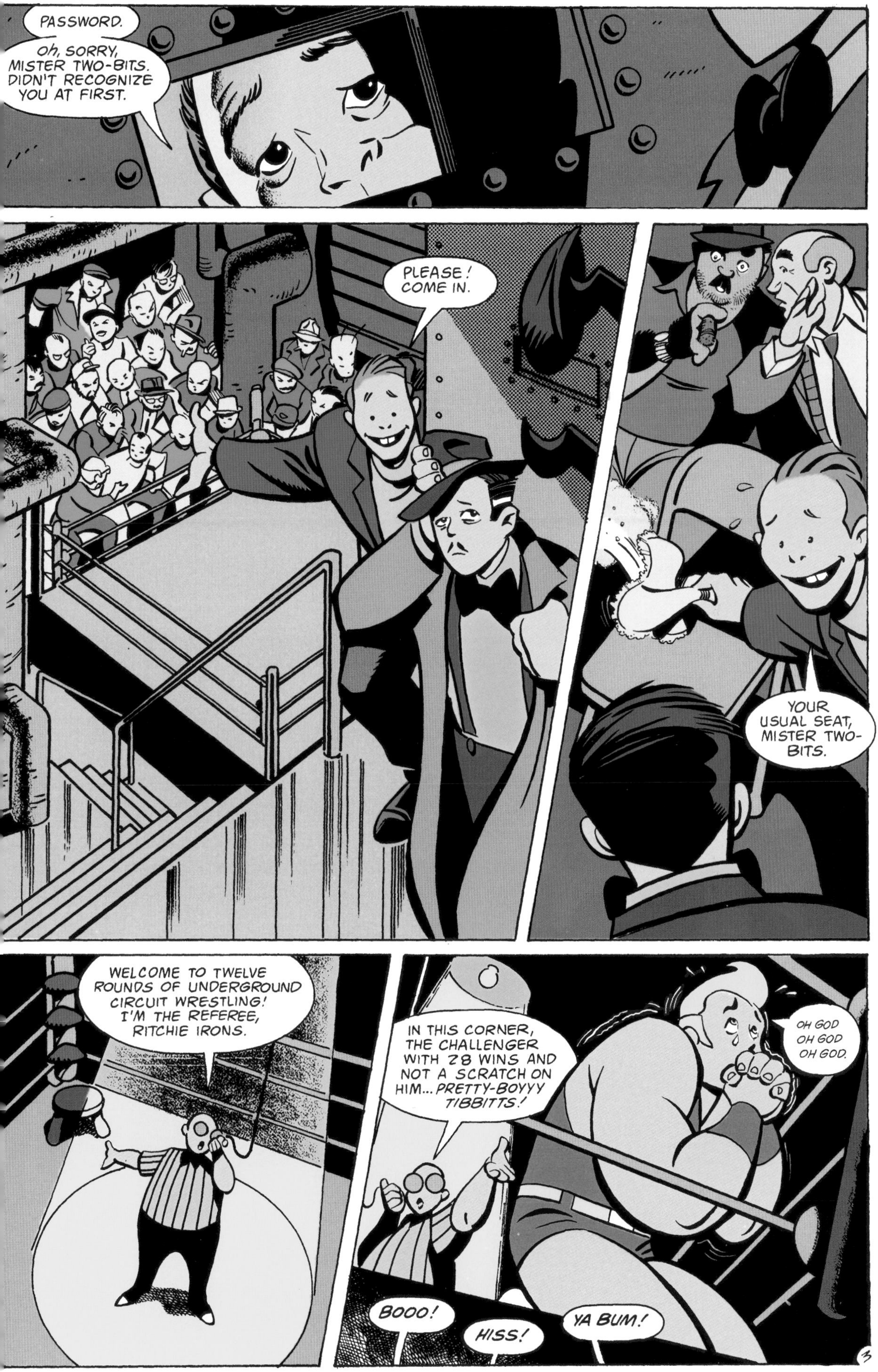

PASSWORD.
Oh, SORRY, MISTER TWO-BITS. DIDN'T RECOGNIZE YOU AT FIRST.
PLEASE! COME IN.
YOUR USUAL SEAT, MISTER TWO-BITS.
WELCOME TO TWELVE ROUNDS OF UNDERGROUND CIRCUIT WRESTLING! I'M THE REFEREE, RITCHIE IRONS.
IN THIS CORNER, THE CHALLENGER WITH 28 WINS AND NOT A SCRATCH ON HIM... PRETTY-BOYYY TIBBITTS!
OH GOD OH GOD OH GOD.
BOOO!
HISS!
YA BUM!
3

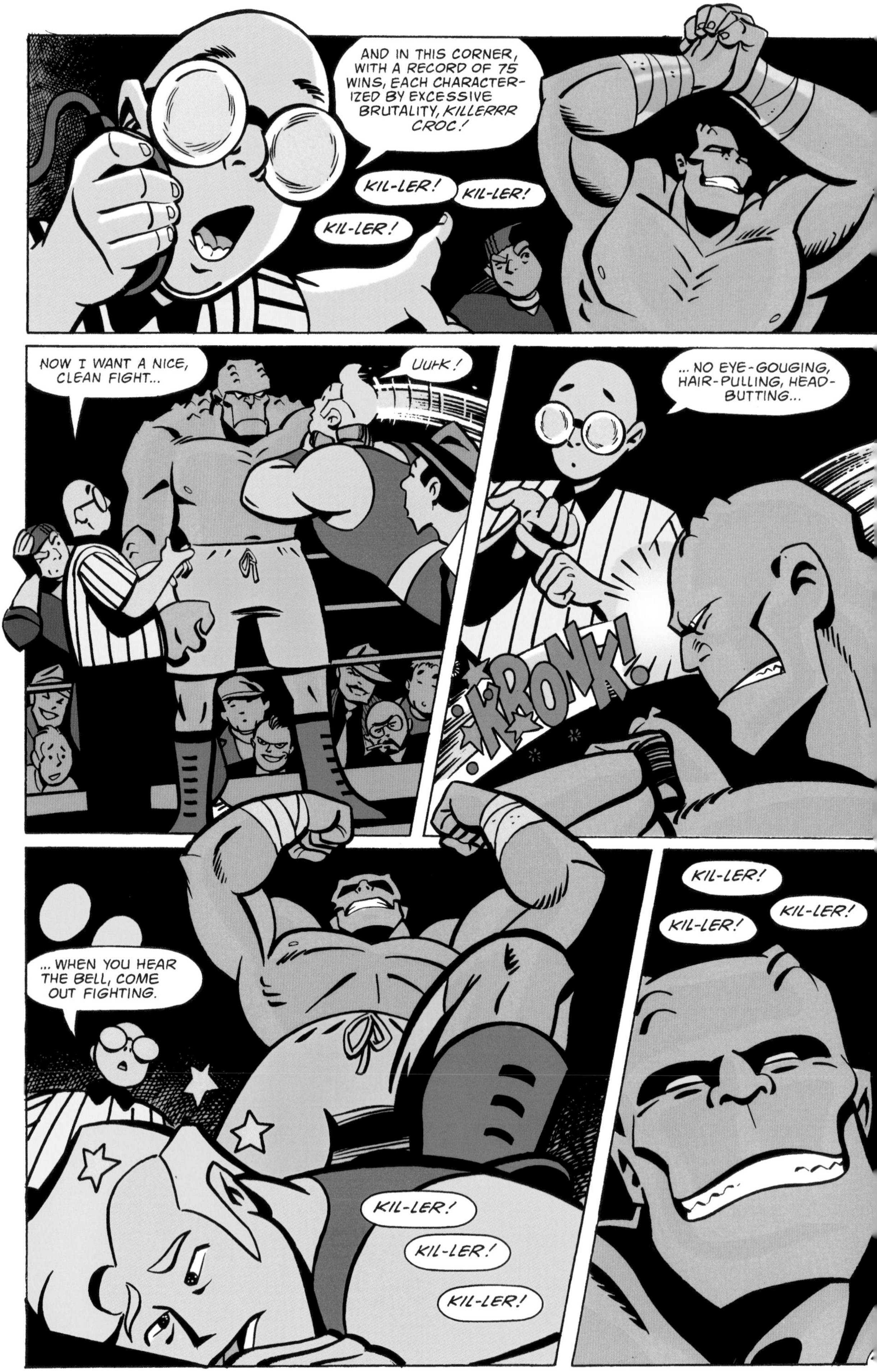

AND IN THIS CORNER, WITH A RECORD OF 75 WINS, EACH CHARACTERIZED BY EXCESSIVE BRUTALITY, KILLERRR CROC!
KIL-LER!
KIL-LER!
KIL-LER!
NOW I WANT A NICE, CLEAN FIGHT...
UUFK!
...NO EYE-GOUGING, HAIR-PULLING, HEAD-BUTTING...
KRONK!
...WHEN YOU HEAR THE BELL, COME OUT FIGHTING.
KIL-LER!
KIL-LER!
KIL-LER!
KIL-LER!
KIL-LER!
KIL-LER!

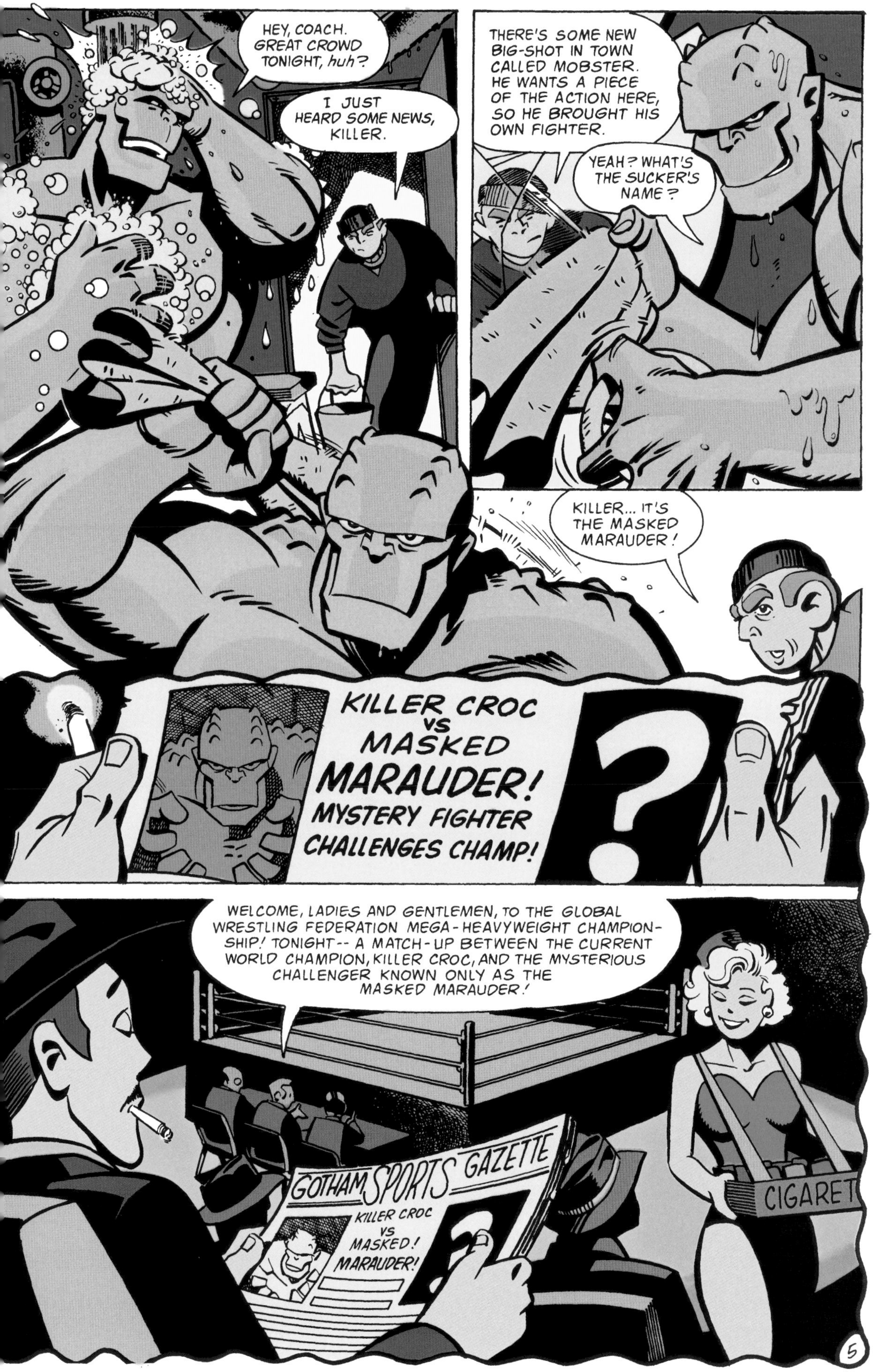
HEY, COACH. GREAT CROWD TONIGHT, huh?
I JUST HEARD SOME NEWS, KILLER.
THERE'S SOME NEW BIG-SHOT IN TOWN CALLED MOBSTER. HE WANTS A PIECE OF THE ACTION HERE, SO HE BROUGHT HIS OWN FIGHTER.
YEAH? WHAT'S THE SUCKER'S NAME?
KILLER... IT'S THE MASKED MARAUDER!
KILLER CROC VS MASKED MARAUDER! MYSTERY FIGHTER CHALLENGES CHAMP!
?
WELCOME, LADIES AND GENTLEMEN, TO THE GLOBAL WRESTLING FEDERATION MEGA-HEAVYWEIGHT CHAMPIONSHIP! TONIGHT-- A MATCH-UP BETWEEN THE CURRENT WORLD CHAMPION, KILLER CROC, AND THE MYSTERIOUS CHALLENGER KNOWN ONLY AS THE MASKED MARAUDER!
GOTHAM SPORTS GAZETTE
KILLER CROC VS MASKED! MARAUDER!
CIGARET
5

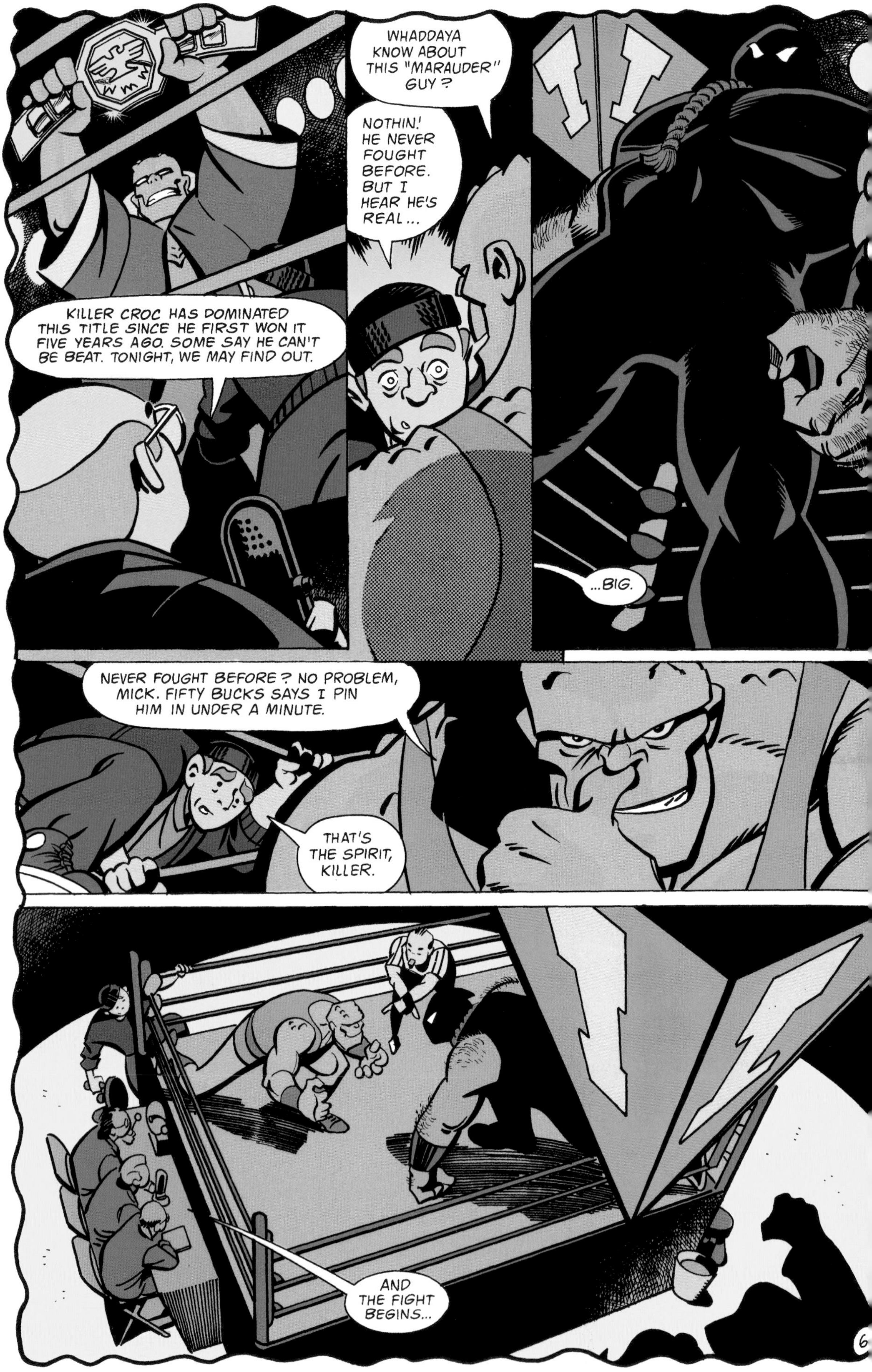
KILLER CROC HAS DOMINATED THIS TITLE SINCE HE FIRST WON IT FIVE YEARS AGO. SOME SAY HE CAN'T BE BEAT. TONIGHT, WE MAY FIND OUT.
WHADDAYA KNOW ABOUT THIS "MARAUDER" GUY?
NOTHIN'! HE NEVER FOUGHT BEFORE. BUT I HEAR HE'S REAL...
...BIG.
NEVER FOUGHT BEFORE? NO PROBLEM, MICK. FIFTY BUCKS SAYS I PIN HIM IN UNDER A MINUTE.
THAT'S THE SPIRIT, KILLER.
AND THE FIGHT BEGINS...
6

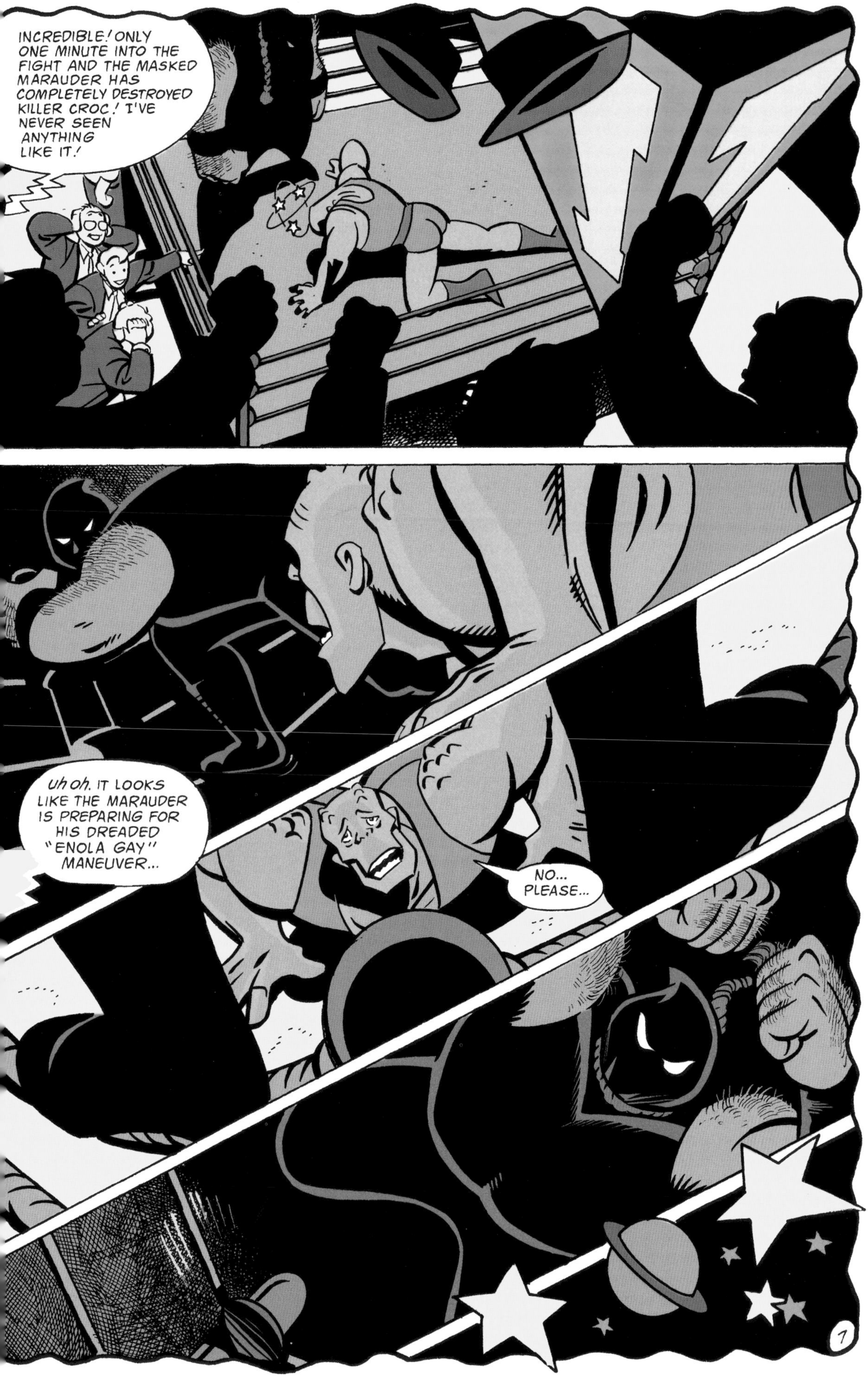
INCREDIBLE! ONLY ONE MINUTE INTO THE FIGHT AND THE MASKED MARAUDER HAS COMPLETELY DESTROYED KILLER CROC! I'VE NEVER SEEN ANYTHING LIKE IT!
uh oh. IT LOOKS LIKE THE MARAUDER IS PREPARING FOR HIS DREADED "ENOLA GAY" MANEUVER...
NO... PLEASE...
7

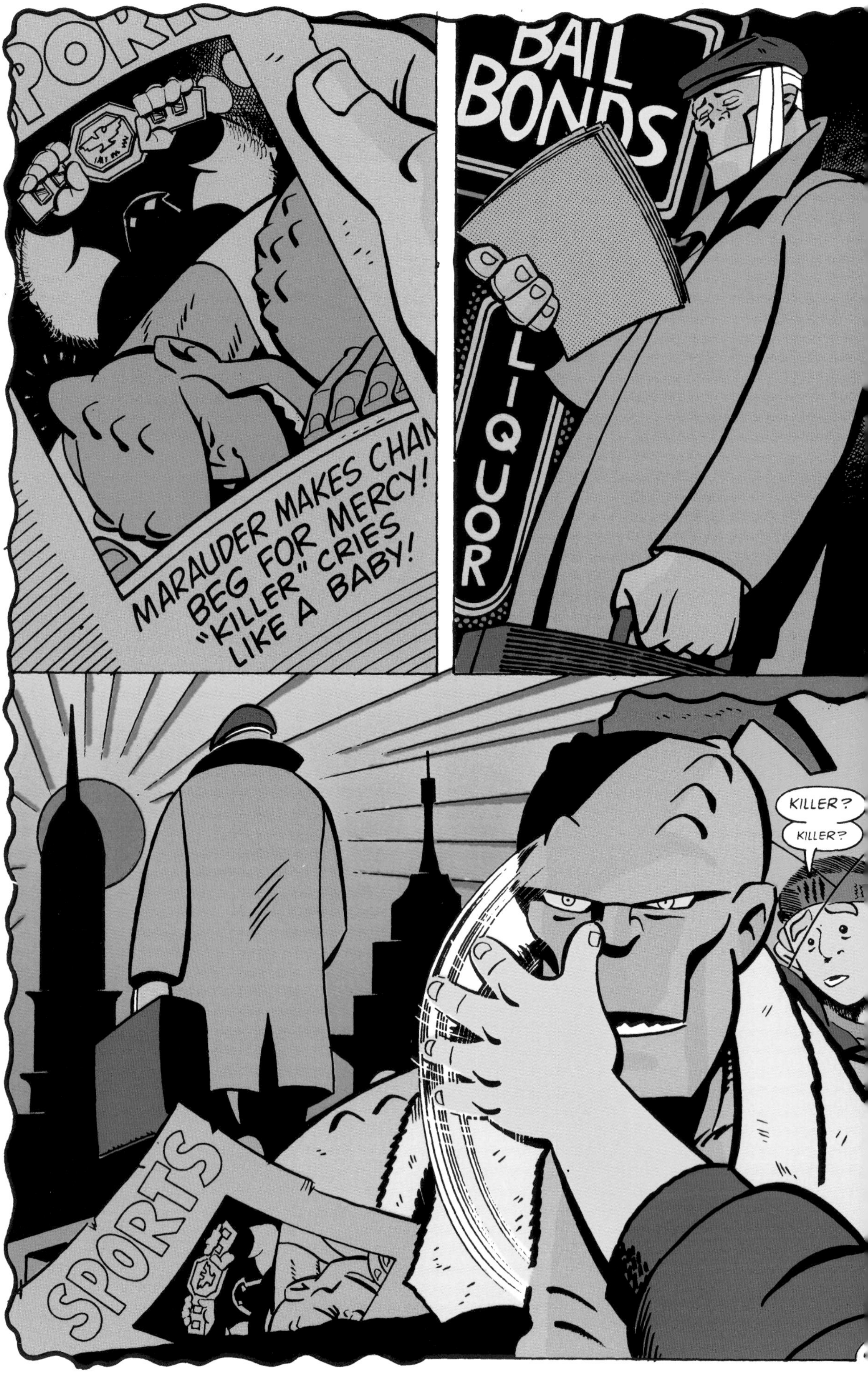
MARAUDER MAKES CHAM
BEG FOR MERCY!
"KILLER" CRIES
LIKE A BABY!
BAIL
BONDS
LIQUOR
KILLER?
KILLER?
SPORTS

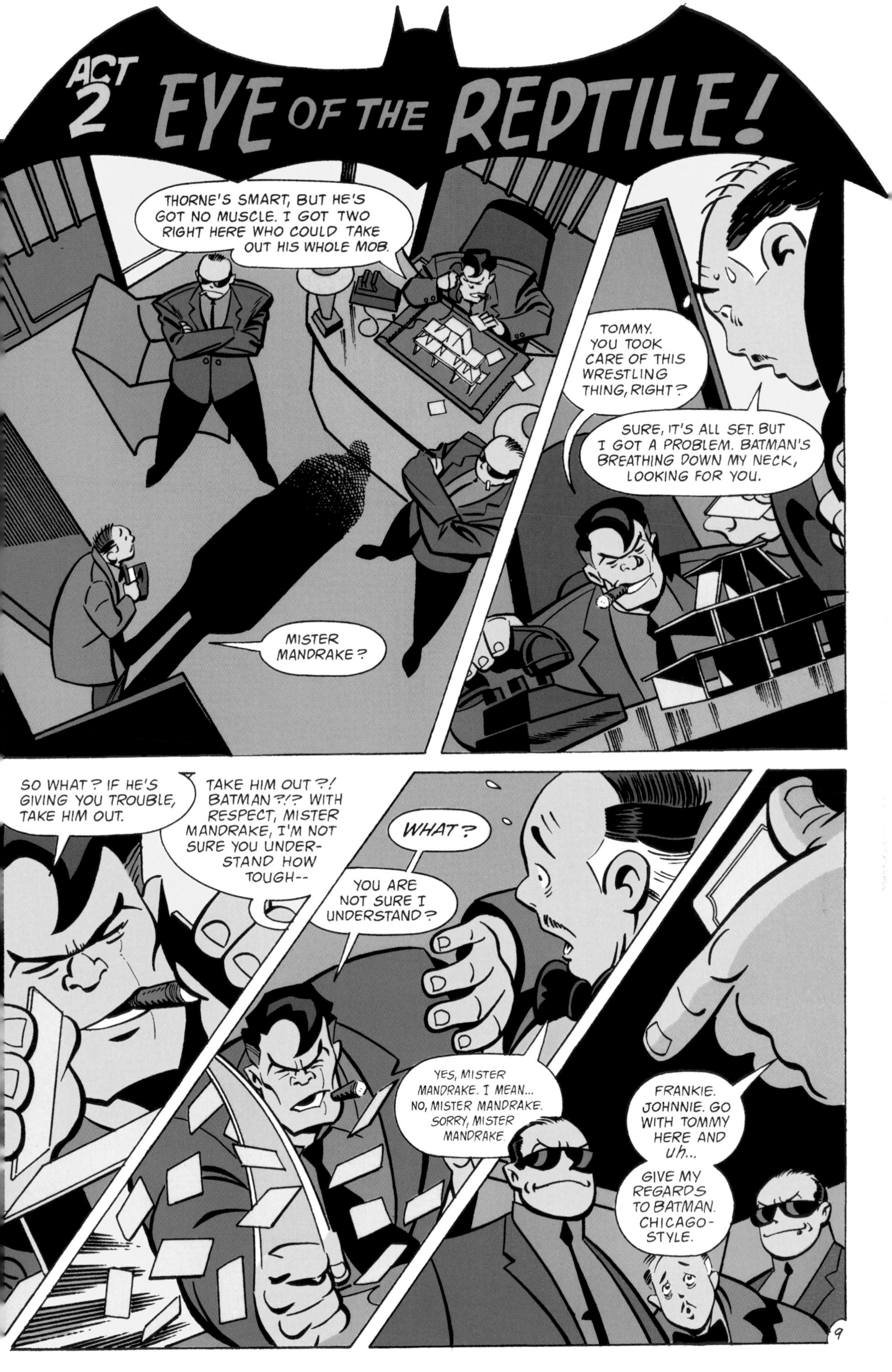
ACT 2
EYE OF THE REPTILE!
THORNE'S SMART, BUT HE'S GOT NO MUSCLE. I GOT TWO RIGHT HERE WHO COULD TAKE OUT HIS WHOLE MOB.
MISTER MANDRAKE?
TOMMY. YOU TOOK CARE OF THIS WRESTLING THING, RIGHT?
SURE, IT'S ALL SET. BUT I GOT A PROBLEM. BATMAN'S BREATHING DOWN MY NECK, LOOKING FOR YOU.
SO WHAT? IF HE'S GIVING YOU TROUBLE, TAKE HIM OUT.
TAKE HIM OUT?! BATMAN?!? WITH RESPECT, MISTER MANDRAKE, I'M NOT SURE YOU UNDERSTAND HOW TOUGH--
WHAT?
YOU ARE NOT SURE I UNDERSTAND?
YES, MISTER MANDRAKE. I MEAN... NO, MISTER MANDRAKE. SORRY, MISTER MANDRAKE.
FRANKIE. JOHNNIE. GO WITH TOMMY HERE AND uh...
GIVE MY REGARDS TO BATMAN. CHICAGO-STYLE.
9

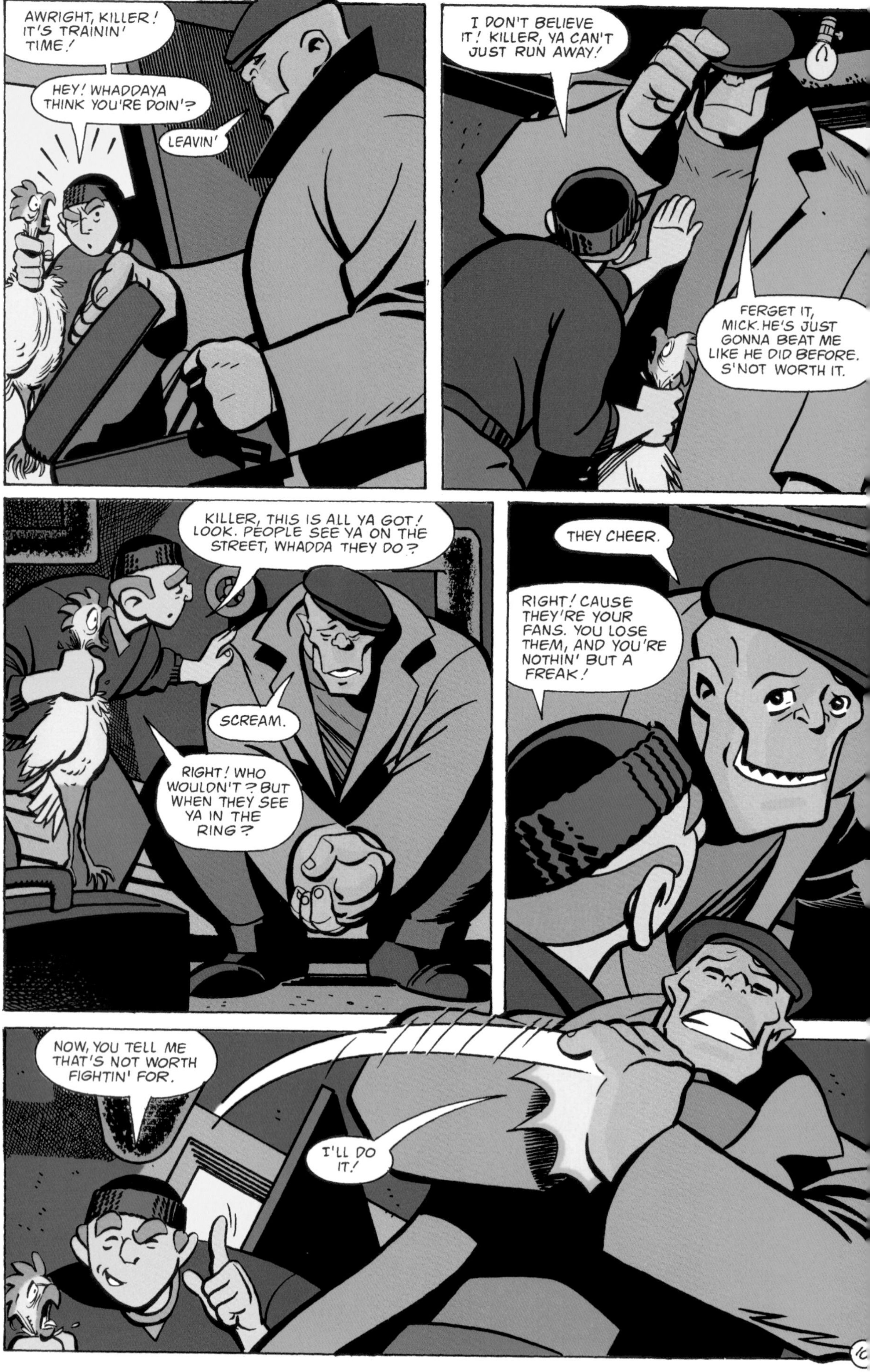
AWRIGHT, KILLER! IT'S TRAININ' TIME!
HEY! WHADDAYA THINK YOU'RE DOIN'?
LEAVIN'
I DON'T BELIEVE IT! KILLER, YA CAN'T JUST RUN AWAY!
FERGET IT, MICK. HE'S JUST GONNA BEAT ME LIKE HE DID BEFORE. S'NOT WORTH IT.
KILLER, THIS IS ALL YA GOT! LOOK. PEOPLE SEE YA ON THE STREET, WHADDA THEY DO?
SCREAM.
RIGHT! WHO WOULDN'T? BUT WHEN THEY SEE YA IN THE RING?
THEY CHEER.
RIGHT! CAUSE THEY'RE YOUR FANS. YOU LOSE THEM, AND YOU'RE NOTHIN' BUT A FREAK!
NOW, YOU TELL ME THAT'S NOT WORTH FIGHTIN' FOR.
I'LL DO IT!

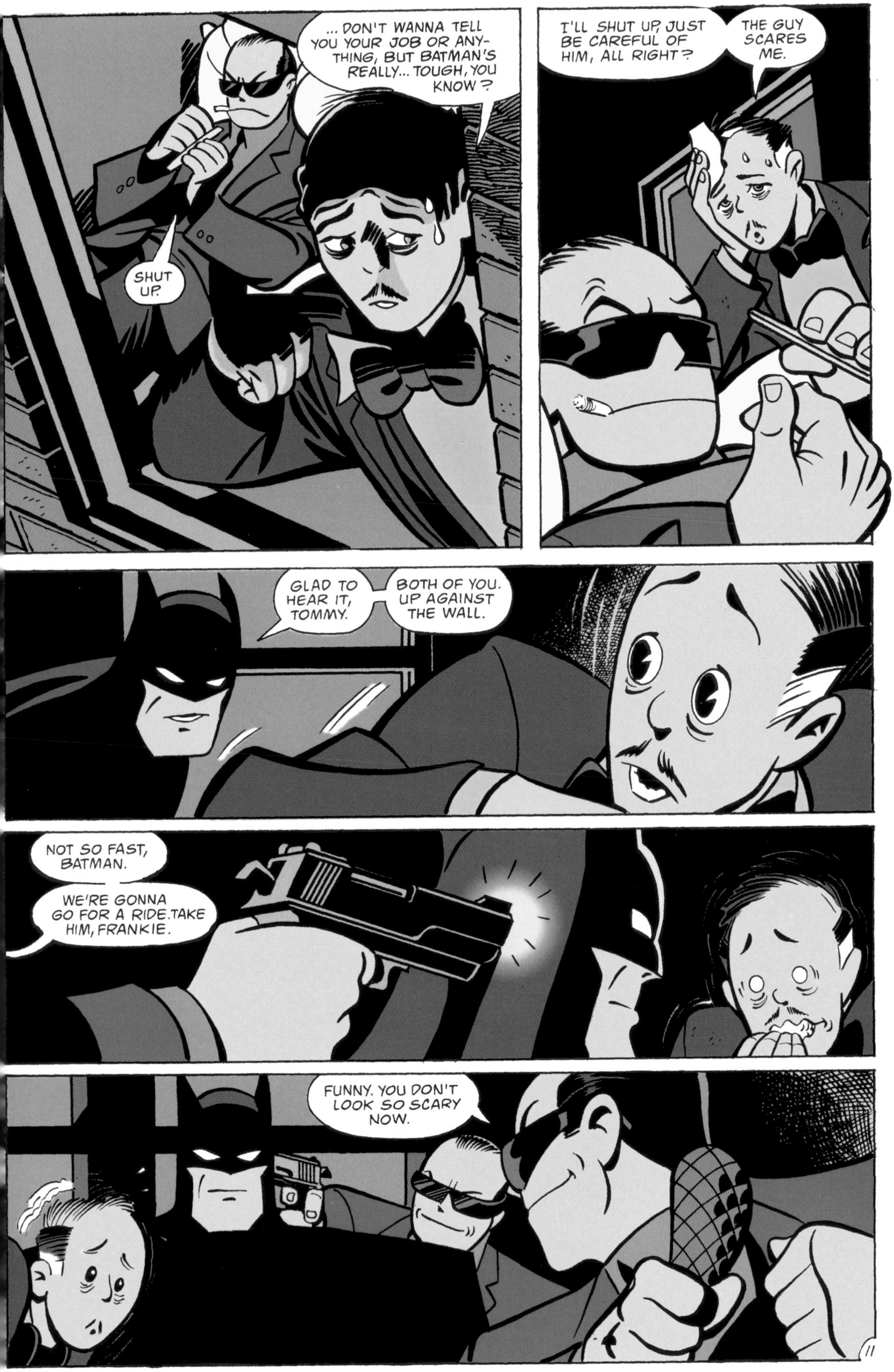
... DON'T WANNA TELL YOU YOUR JOB OR ANYTHING, BUT BATMAN'S REALLY... TOUGH, YOU KNOW?
SHUT UP.
I'LL SHUT UP, JUST BE CAREFUL OF HIM, ALL RIGHT?
THE GUY SCARES ME.
GLAD TO HEAR IT, TOMMY.
BOTH OF YOU. UP AGAINST THE WALL.
NOT SO FAST, BATMAN.
WE'RE GONNA GO FOR A RIDE. TAKE HIM, FRANKIE.
FUNNY. YOU DON'T LOOK SO SCARY NOW.
11

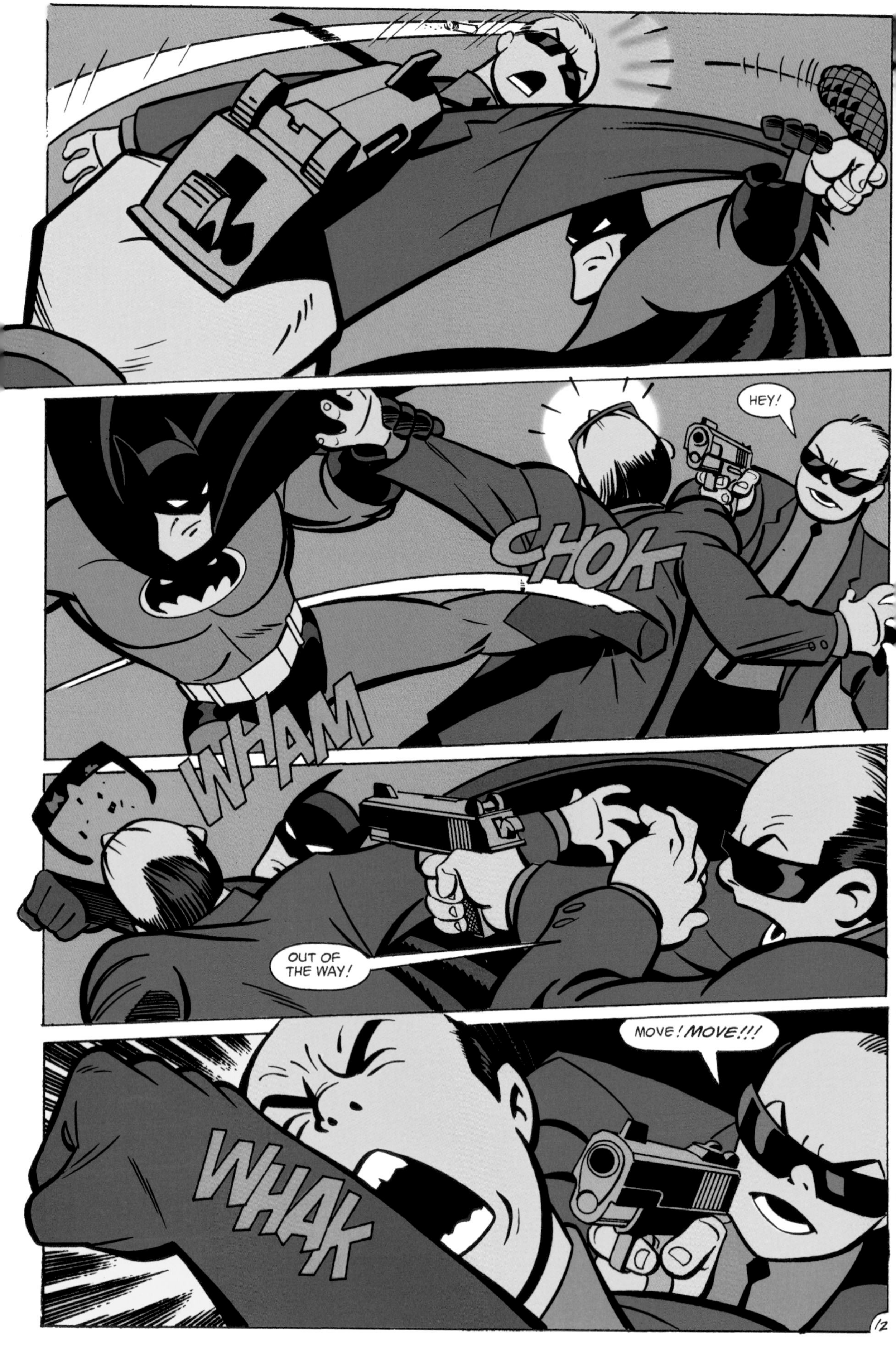
HEY!
CHOK
WHAM
OUT OF THE WAY!
MOVE! MOVE!!!
WHAK
12

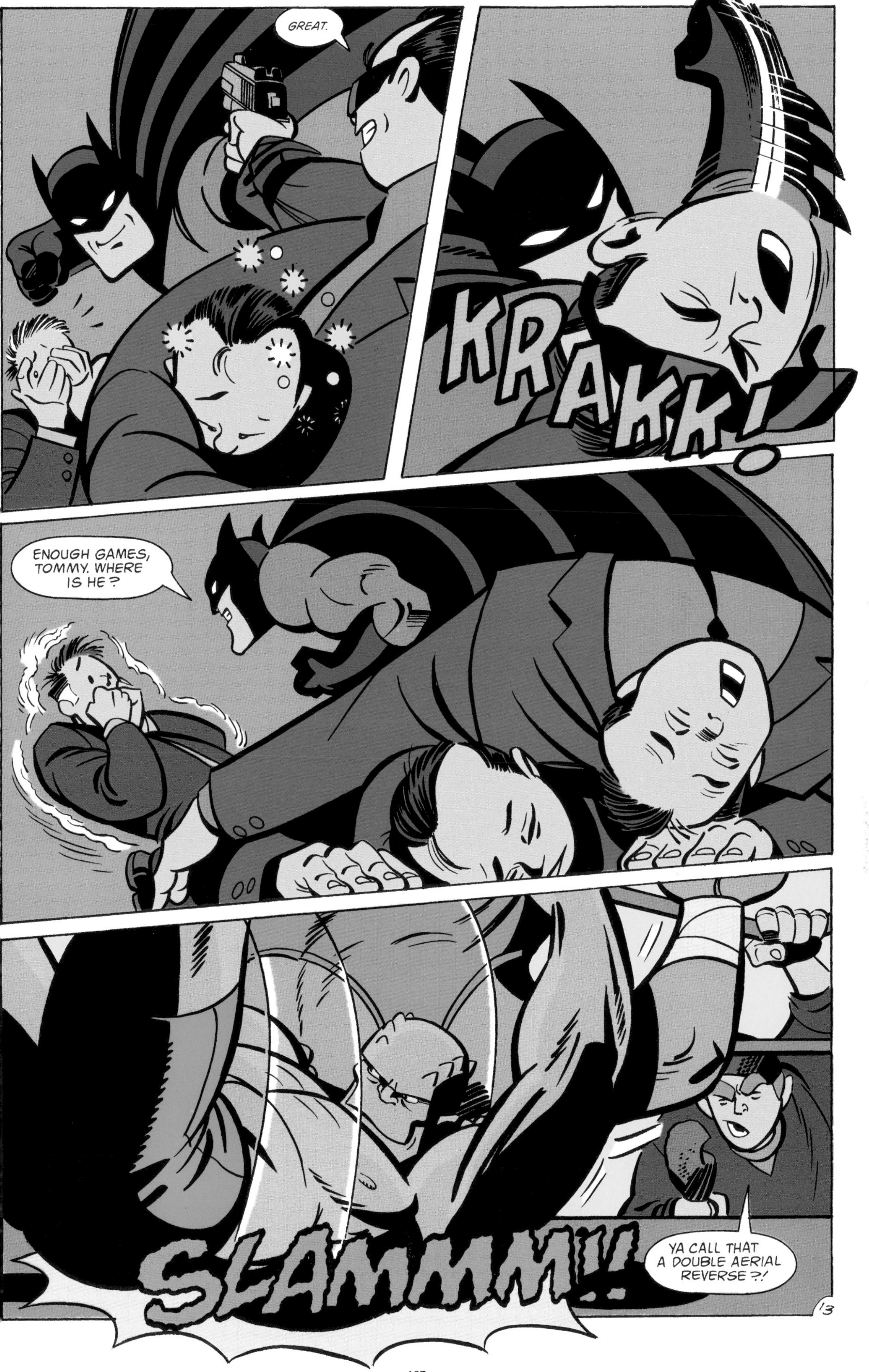
GREAT.
KRAKK!
ENOUGH GAMES, TOMMY. WHERE IS HE?
SLAMMM!!
YA CALL THAT A DOUBLE AERIAL REVERSE?!
13

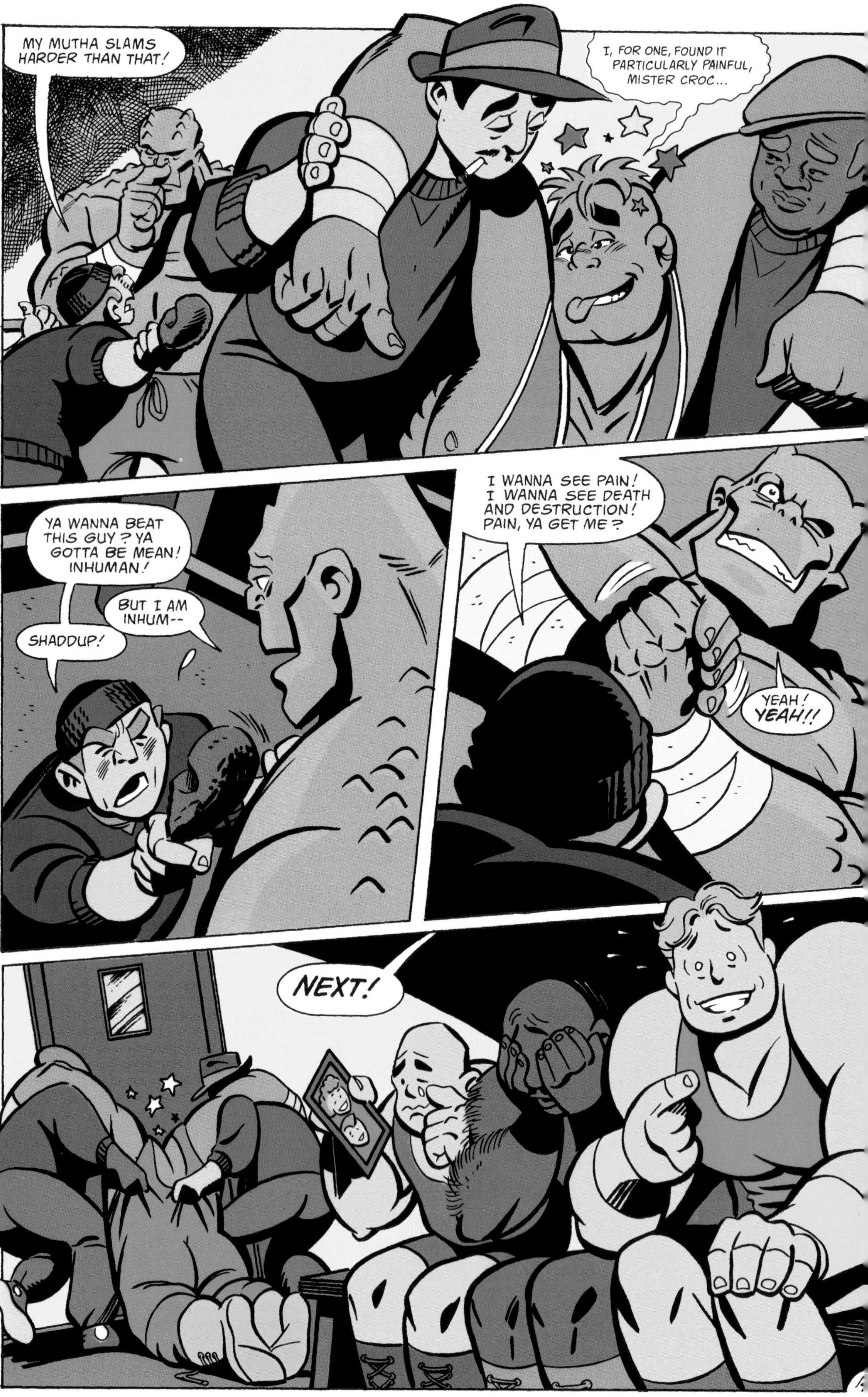
MY MUTHA SLAMS HARDER THAN THAT!
I, FOR ONE, FOUND IT PARTICULARLY PAINFUL, MISTER CROC...
YA WANNA BEAT THIS GUY? YA GOTTA BE MEAN! INHUMAN!
BUT I AM INHUM--
SHADDUP!
I WANNA SEE PAIN! I WANNA SEE DEATH AND DESTRUCTION! PAIN, YA GET ME?
YEAH! YEAH!!
NEXT!

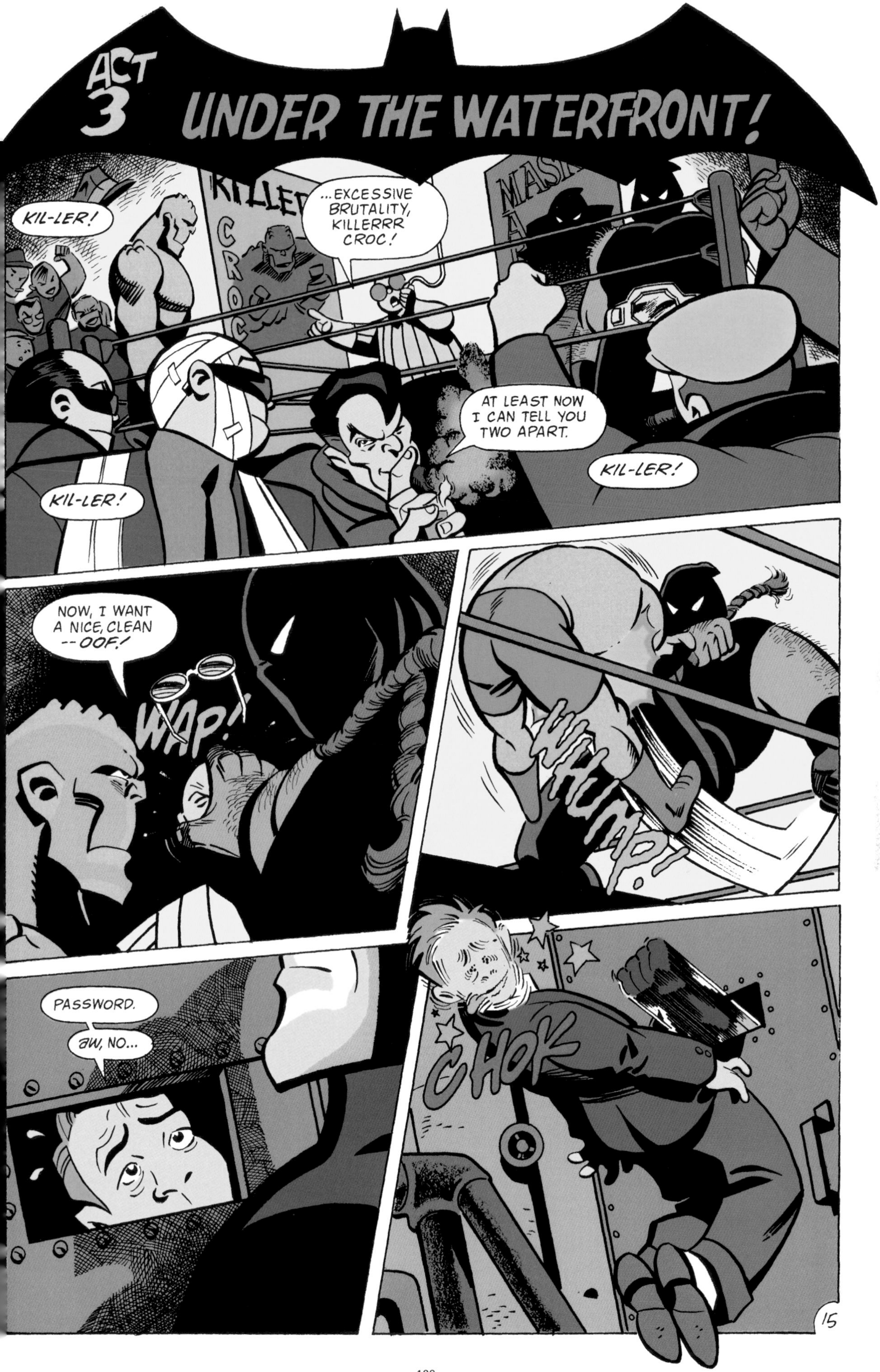
ACT 3 UNDER THE WATERFRONT!
KILLER CROC
KIL-LER!
...EXCESSIVE BRUTALITY, KILLERRR CROC!
AT LEAST NOW I CAN TELL YOU TWO APART.
KIL-LER!
KIL-LER!
NOW, I WANT A NICE, CLEAN --OOF!
WAP!
WHUMP!
PASSWORD.
aw, NO...
CHOK
15

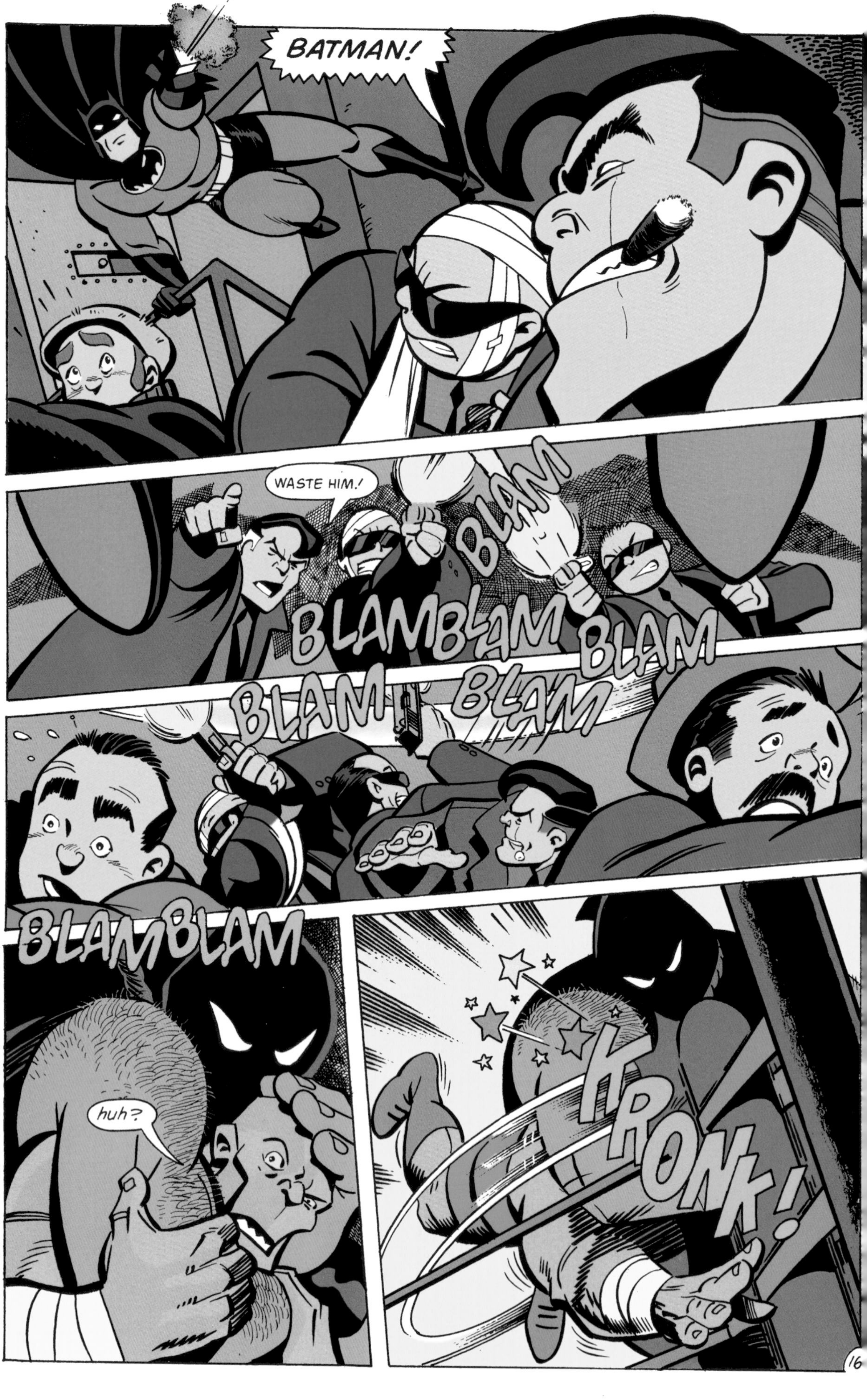
BATMAN!
WASTE HIM!
BLAM BLAM
BLAMBLAM
BLAM
BLAM
BLAM BLAM
BLAMBLAM
huh?
KRONK!
16

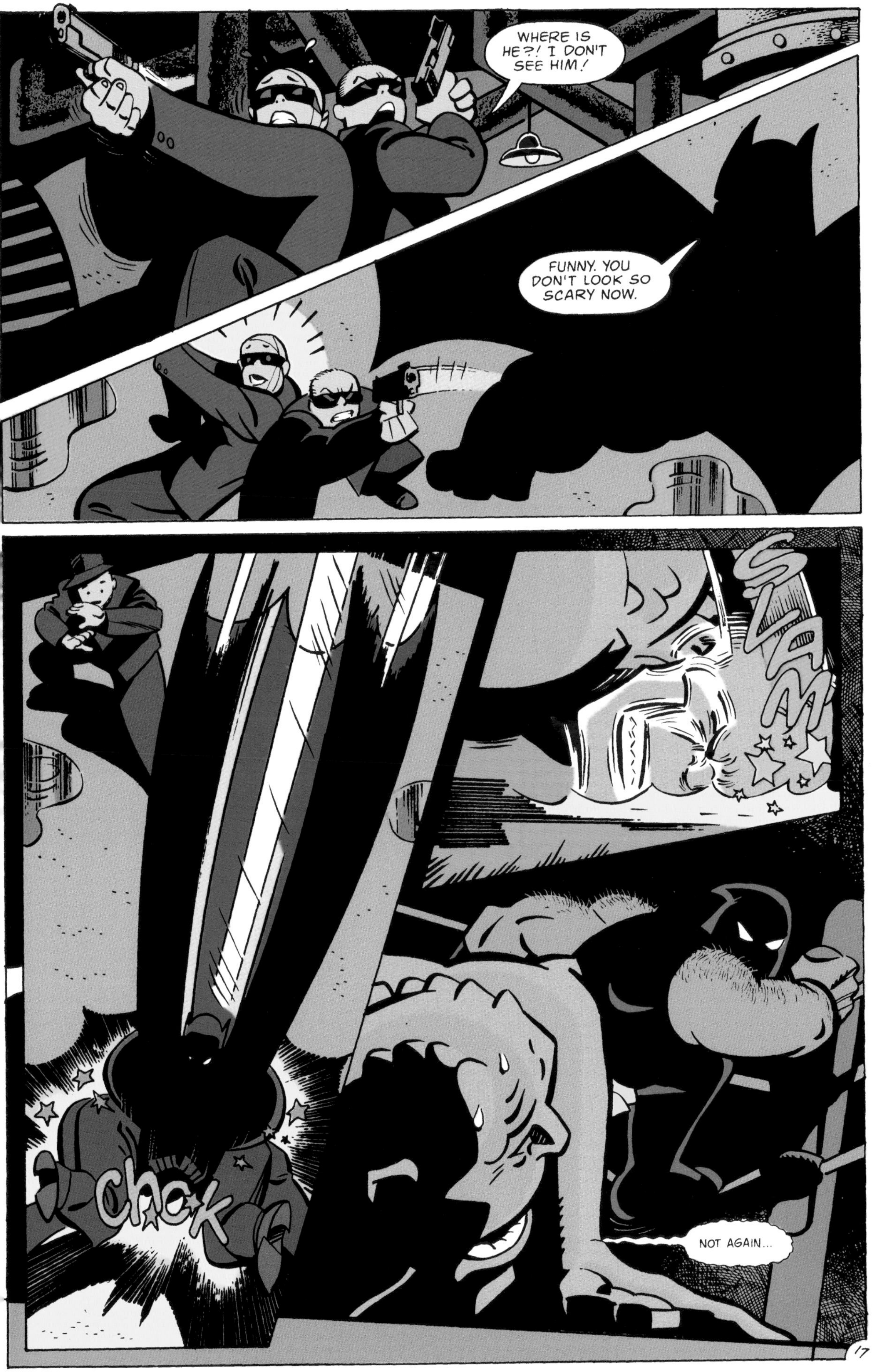
WHERE IS HE?! I DON'T SEE HIM!
FUNNY. YOU DON'T LOOK SO SCARY NOW.
SLAM
CHOK
NOT AGAIN...
17

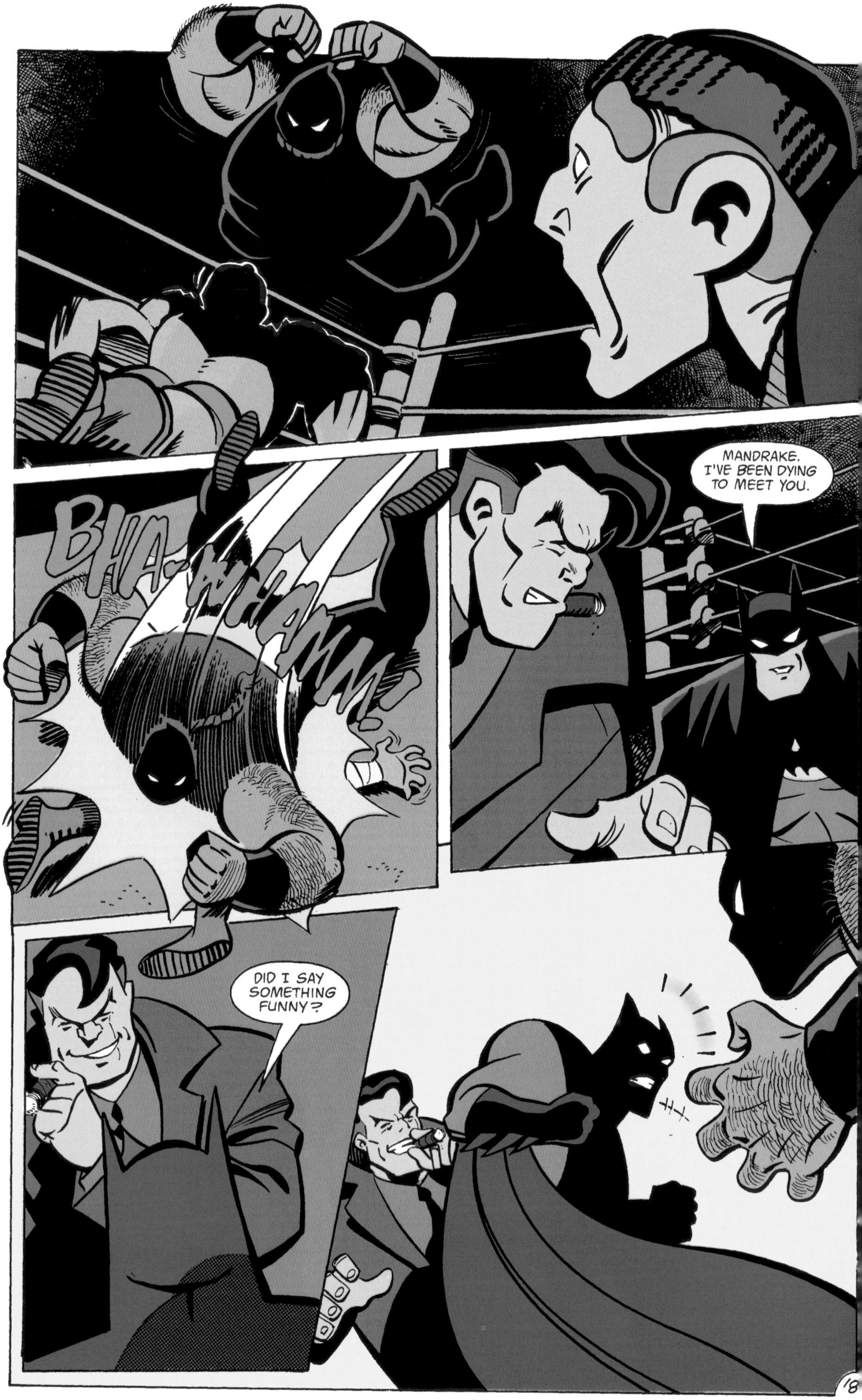
BHA-WHAMM!
MANDRAKE. I'VE BEEN DYING TO MEET YOU.
DID I SAY SOMETHING FUNNY?
18

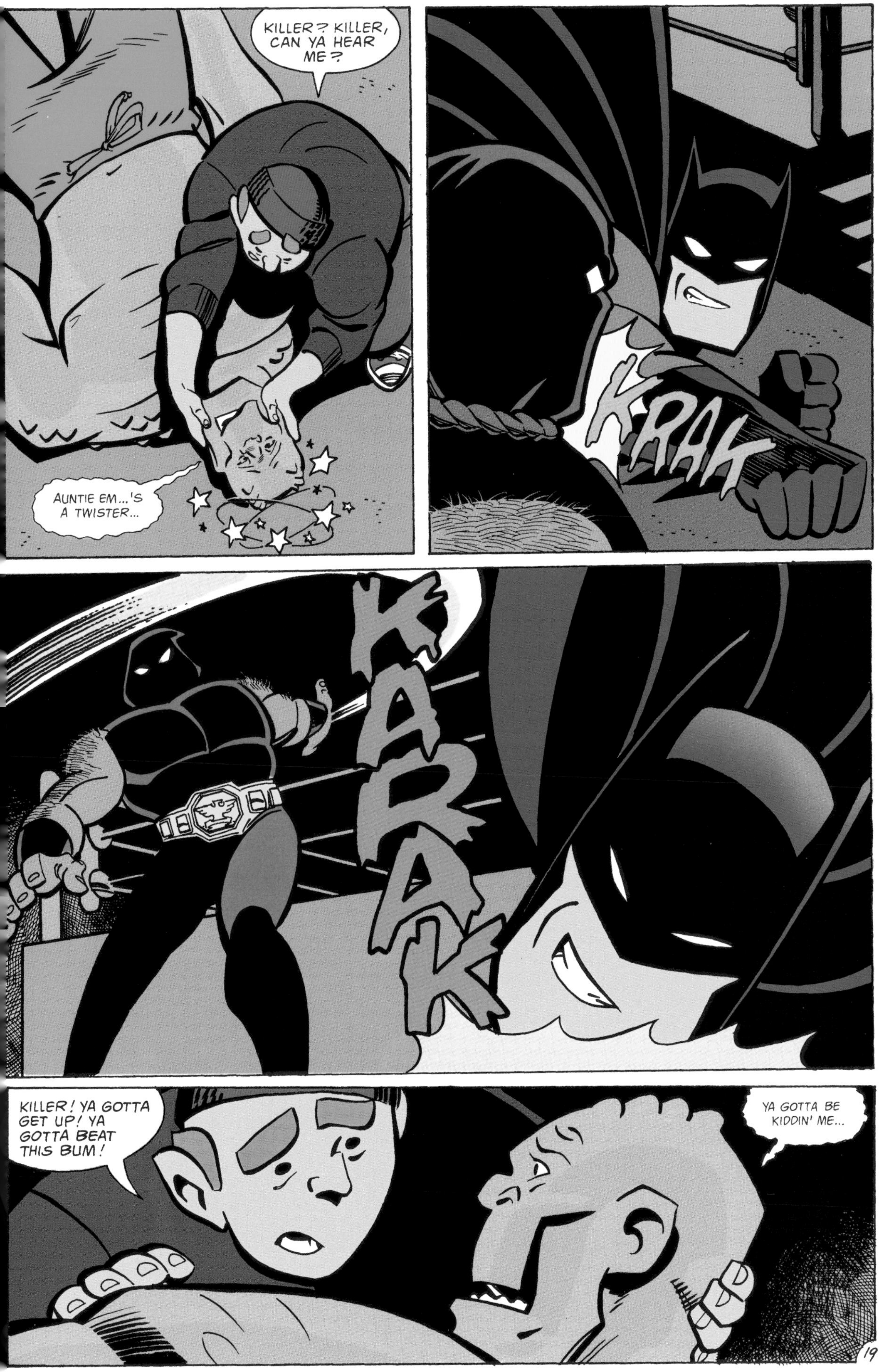
KILLER? KILLER, CAN YA HEAR ME?
AUNTIE EM...'S A TWISTER...
KRAK
KARAK
KILLER! YA GOTTA GET UP! YA GOTTA BEAT THIS BUM!
YA GOTTA BE KIDDIN' ME...
19

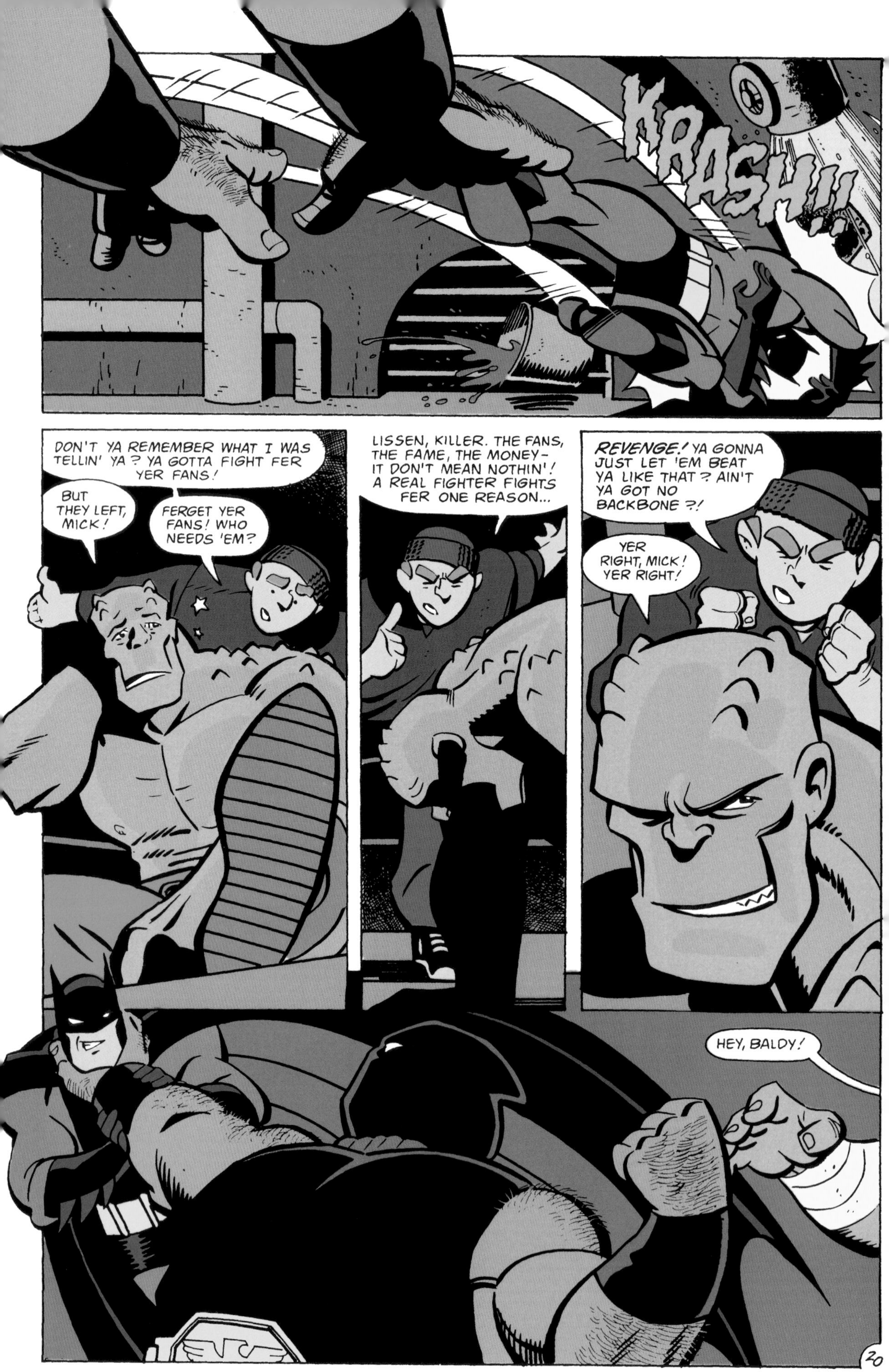
KRASH!!
DON'T YA REMEMBER WHAT I WAS TELLIN' YA? YA GOTTA FIGHT FER YER FANS!
BUT THEY LEFT, MICK!
FERGET YER FANS! WHO NEEDS 'EM?
LISSEN, KILLER. THE FANS, THE FAME, THE MONEY- IT DON'T MEAN NOTHIN'! A REAL FIGHTER FIGHTS FER ONE REASON...
REVENGE! YA GONNA JUST LET 'EM BEAT YA LIKE THAT? AIN'T YA GOT NO BACKBONE?!
YER RIGHT, MICK! YER RIGHT!
HEY, BALDY!
20

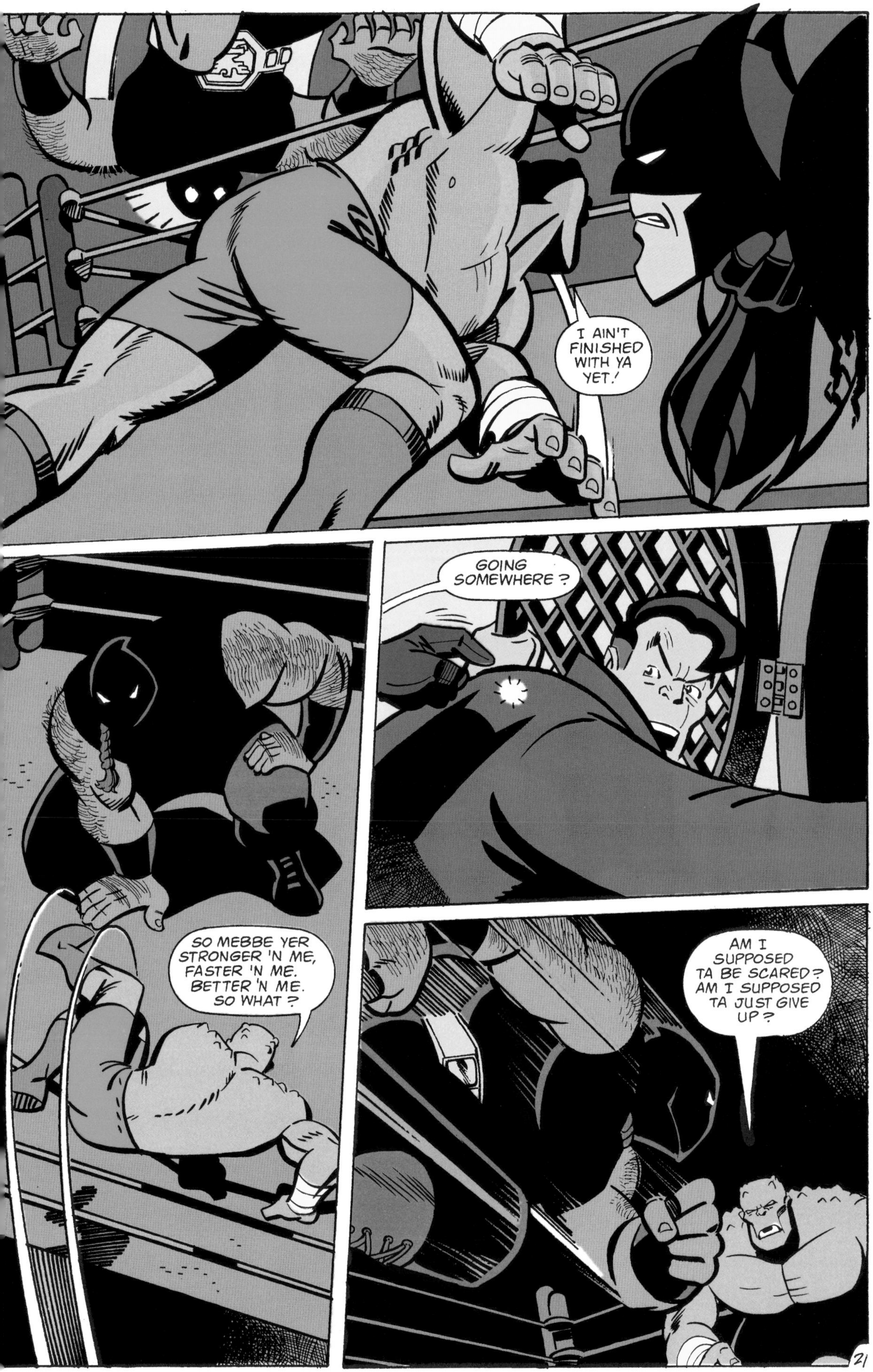
I AIN'T FINISHED WITH YA YET!
GOING SOMEWHERE?
SO MEBBE YER STRONGER 'N ME, FASTER 'N ME. BETTER 'N ME. SO WHAT?
AM I SUPPOSED TA BE SCARED? AM I SUPPOSED TA JUST GIVE UP?
21

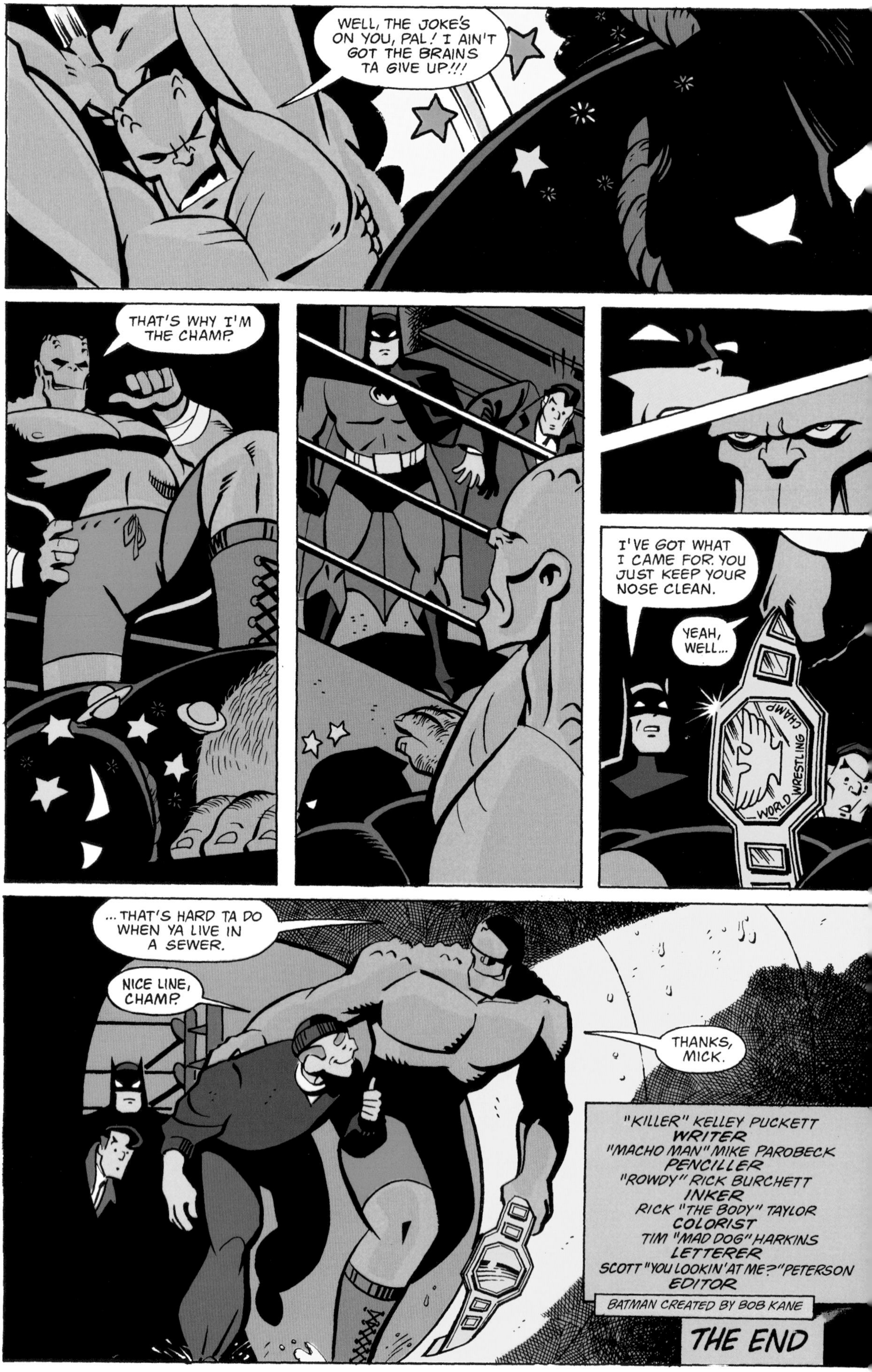
WELL, THE JOKE'S ON YOU, PAL! I AIN'T GOT THE BRAINS TA GIVE UP!!!
THAT'S WHY I'M THE CHAMP.
I'VE GOT WHAT I CAME FOR. YOU JUST KEEP YOUR NOSE CLEAN.
YEAH, WELL...
WORLD WRESTLING CHAMP
...THAT'S HARD TA DO WHEN YA LIVE IN A SEWER.
NICE LINE, CHAMP.
THANKS, MICK.
"KILLER" KELLEY PUCKETT WRITER
"MACHO MAN" MIKE PAROBECK PENCILLER
"ROWDY" RICK BURCHETT INKER
RICK "THE BODY" TAYLOR COLORIST
TIM "MAD DOG" HARKINS LETTERER
SCOTT "YOU LOOKIN' AT ME?" PETERSON EDITOR
BATMAN CREATED BY BOB KANE
THE END

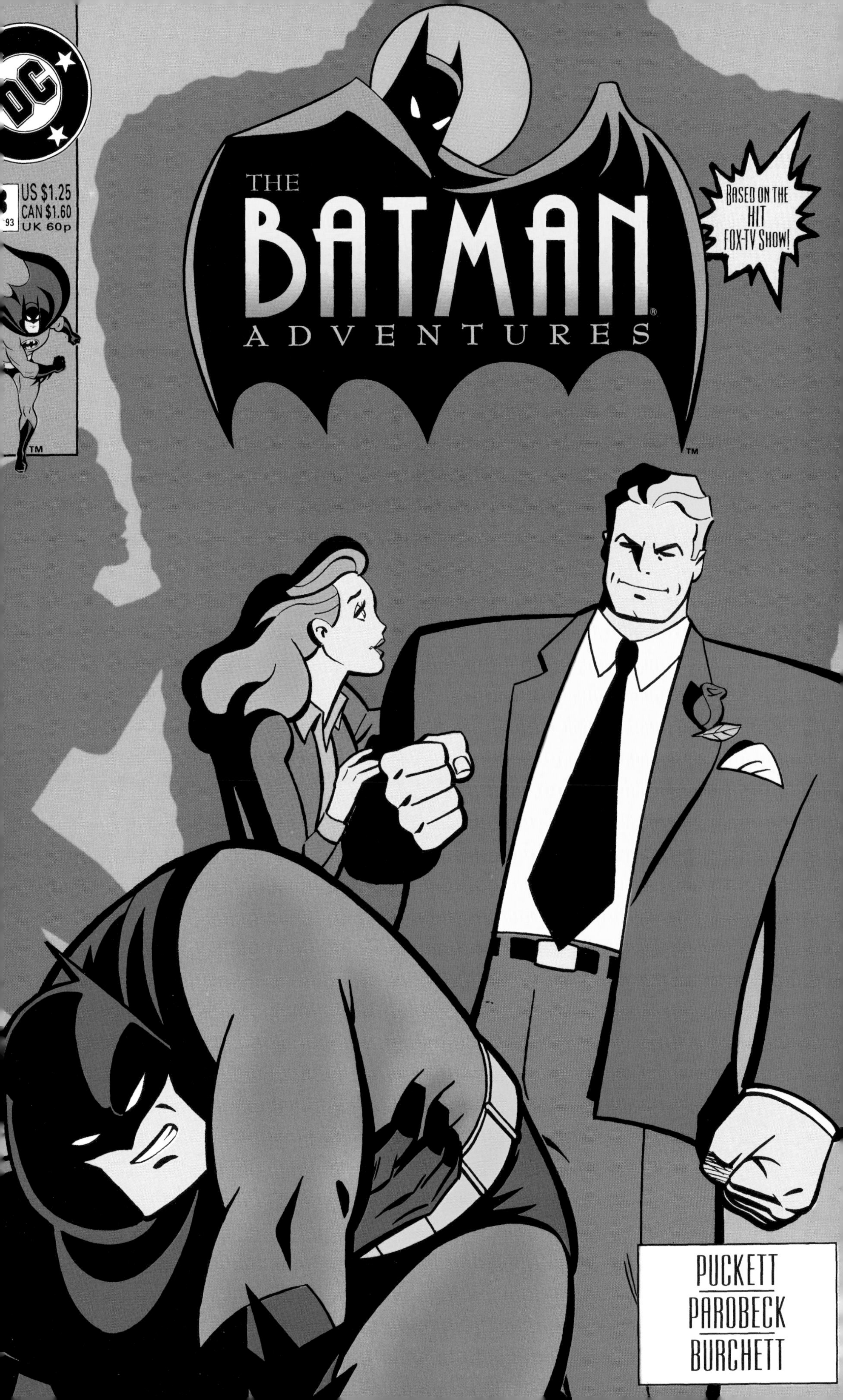
DC
US $1.25
CAN $1.60
UK 60p
THE
BATMAN
ADVENTURES
BASED ON THE HIT FOX-TV SHOW!
PUCKETT
PAROBECK
BURCHETT

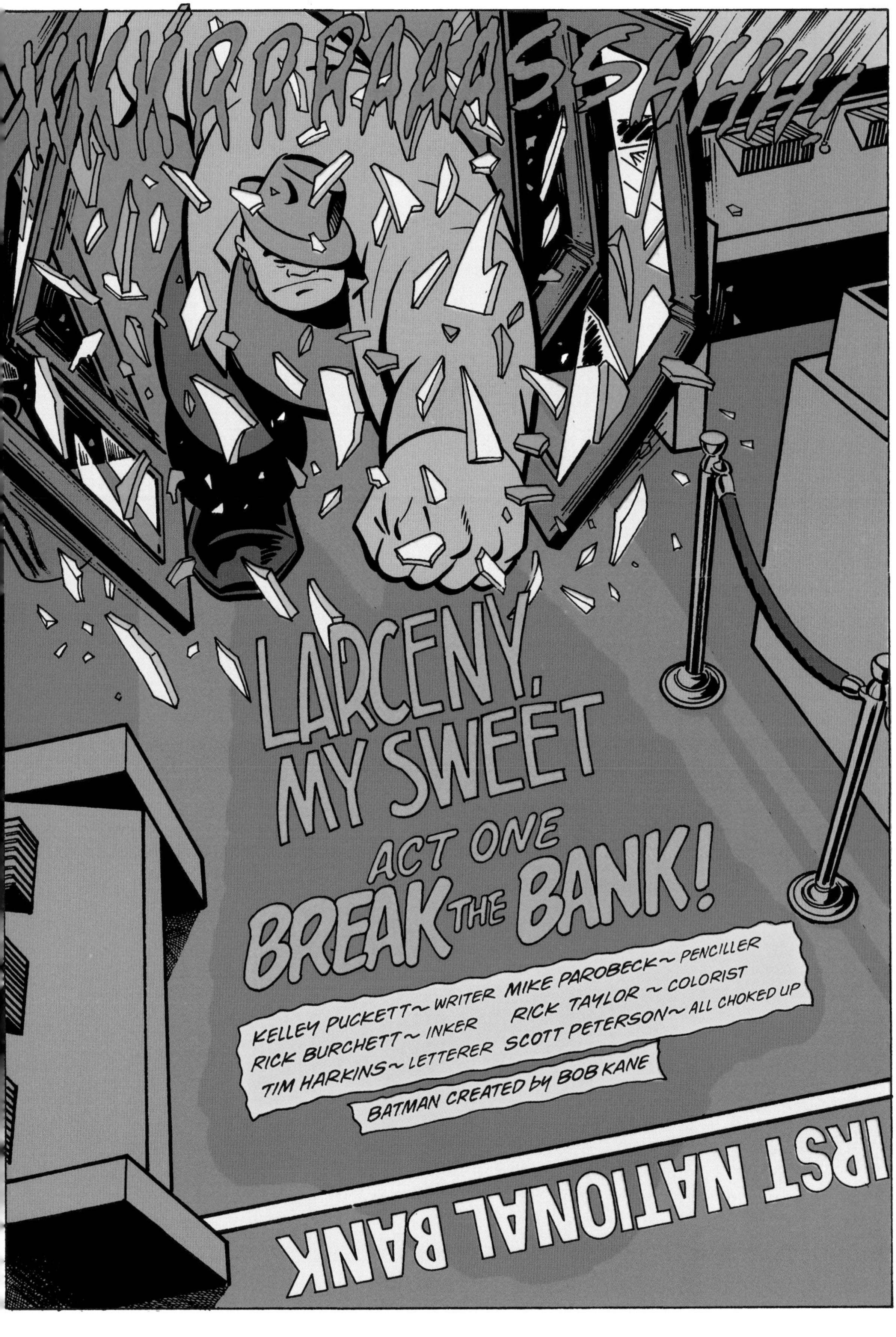
KKKRRRAAASSHHH!
LARCENY, MY SWEET
ACT ONE
BREAK THE BANK!
KELLEY PUCKETT ~ WRITER MIKE PAROBECK ~ PENCILLER
RICK BURCHETT ~ INKER RICK TAYLOR ~ COLORIST
TIM HARKINS ~ LETTERER SCOTT PETERSON ~ ALL CHOKED UP
BATMAN CREATED BY BOB KANE
IRST NATIONAL BANK

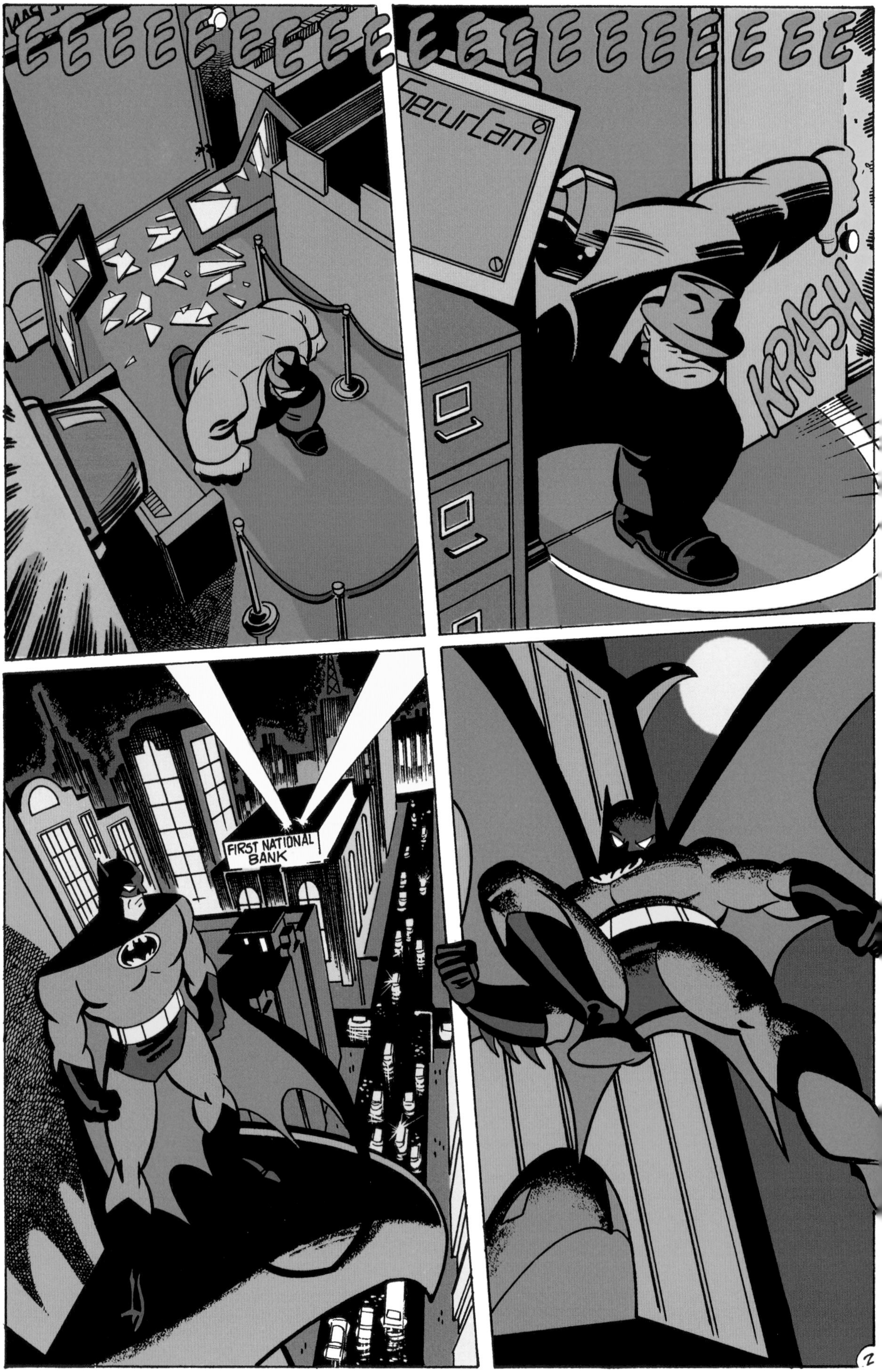
EEEEEEEEEEEEEEEEEEEEEE
SecurCam
KRASH
FIRST NATIONAL BANK

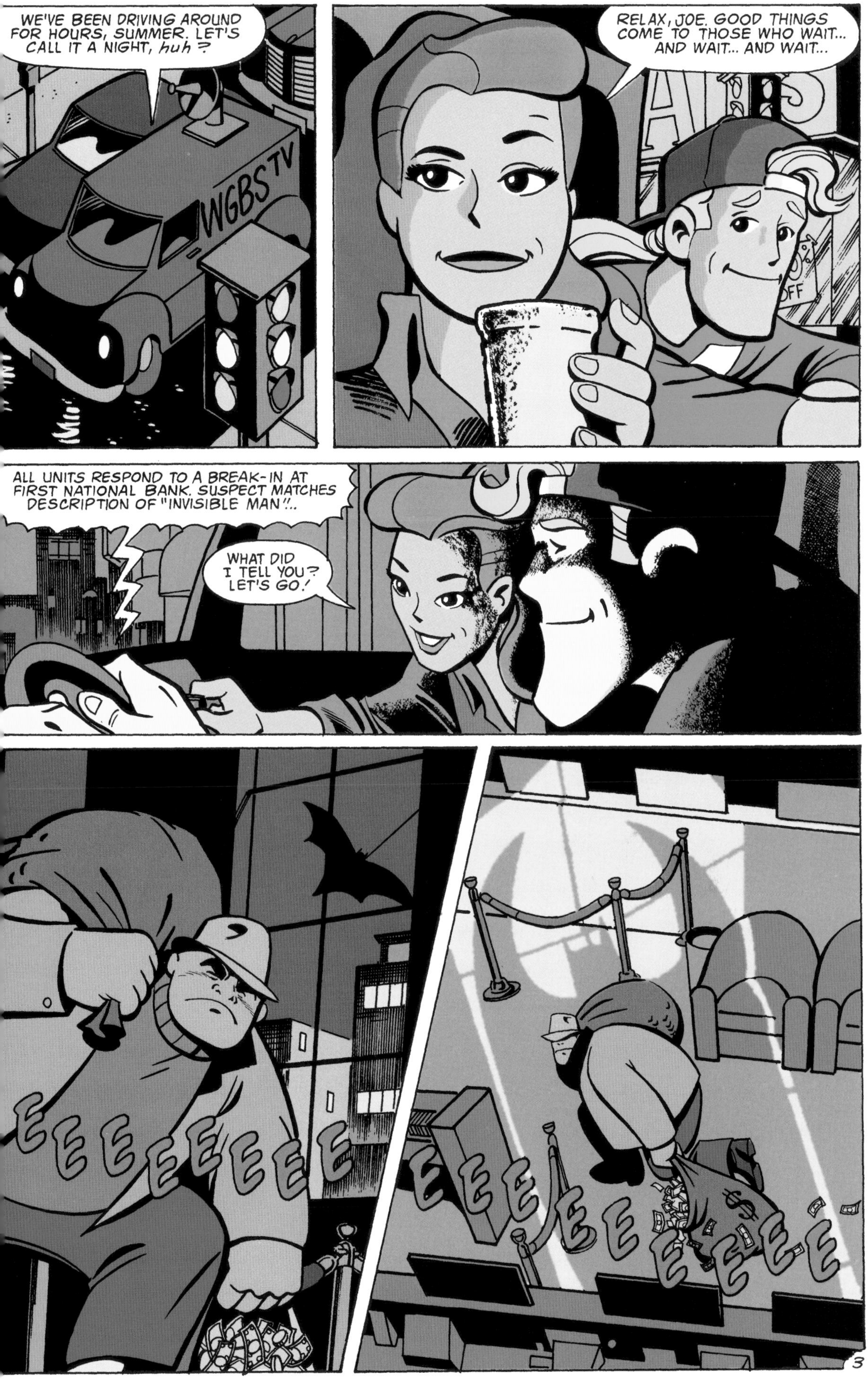
WE'VE BEEN DRIVING AROUND FOR HOURS, SUMMER. LET'S CALL IT A NIGHT, huh?
WGBS TV
RELAX, JOE. GOOD THINGS COME TO THOSE WHO WAIT... AND WAIT... AND WAIT...
ALL UNITS RESPOND TO A BREAK-IN AT FIRST NATIONAL BANK. SUSPECT MATCHES DESCRIPTION OF "INVISIBLE MAN"..
WHAT DID I TELL YOU? LET'S GO!
EEEEEEEEE
EEEEEEEEEE
3

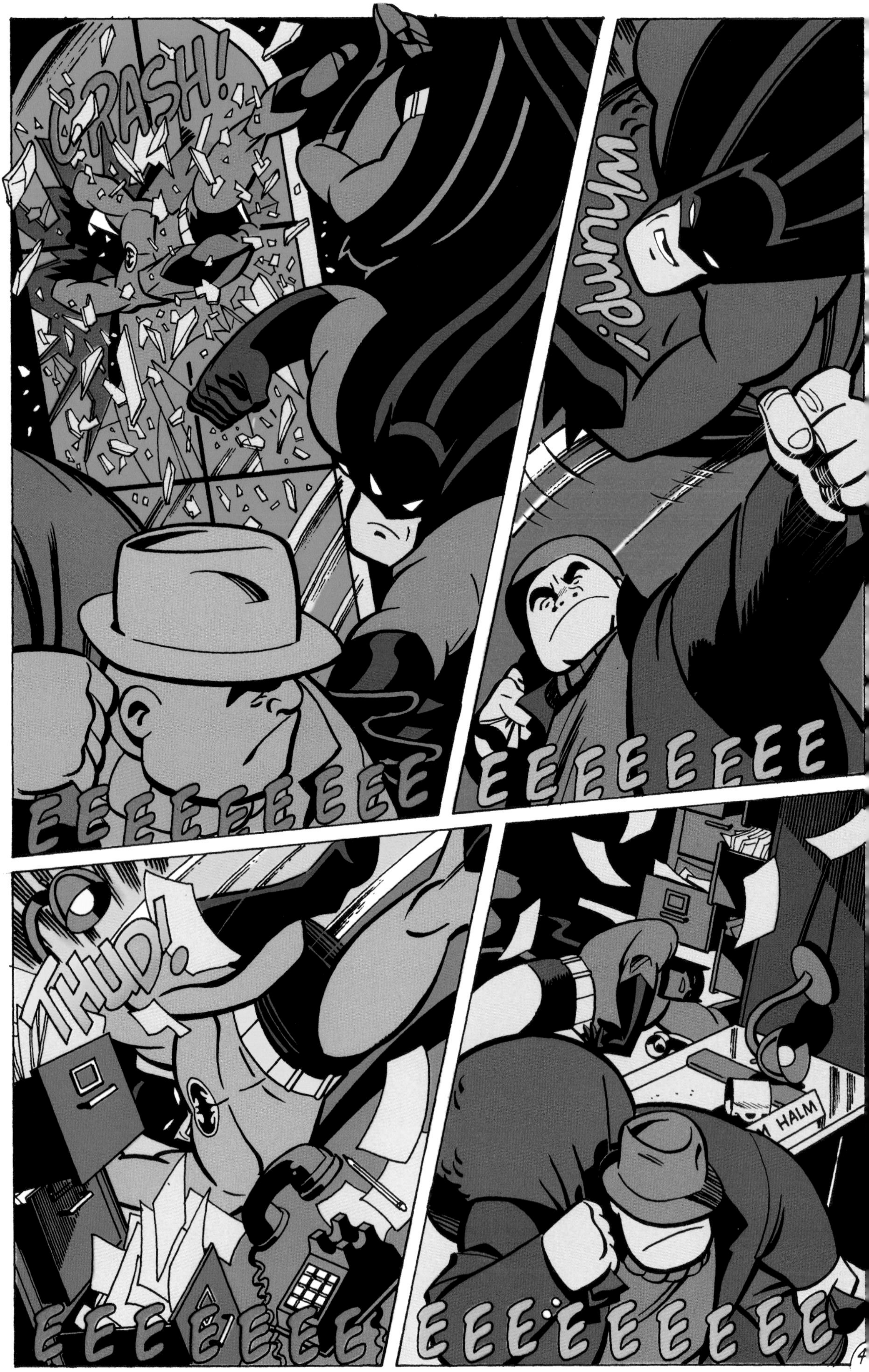
CRASH!
EEEEEEEEE
Whump!
EEEEEEEE
THUD!
EEEEEEEE
HALM
EEEEEEEEEE

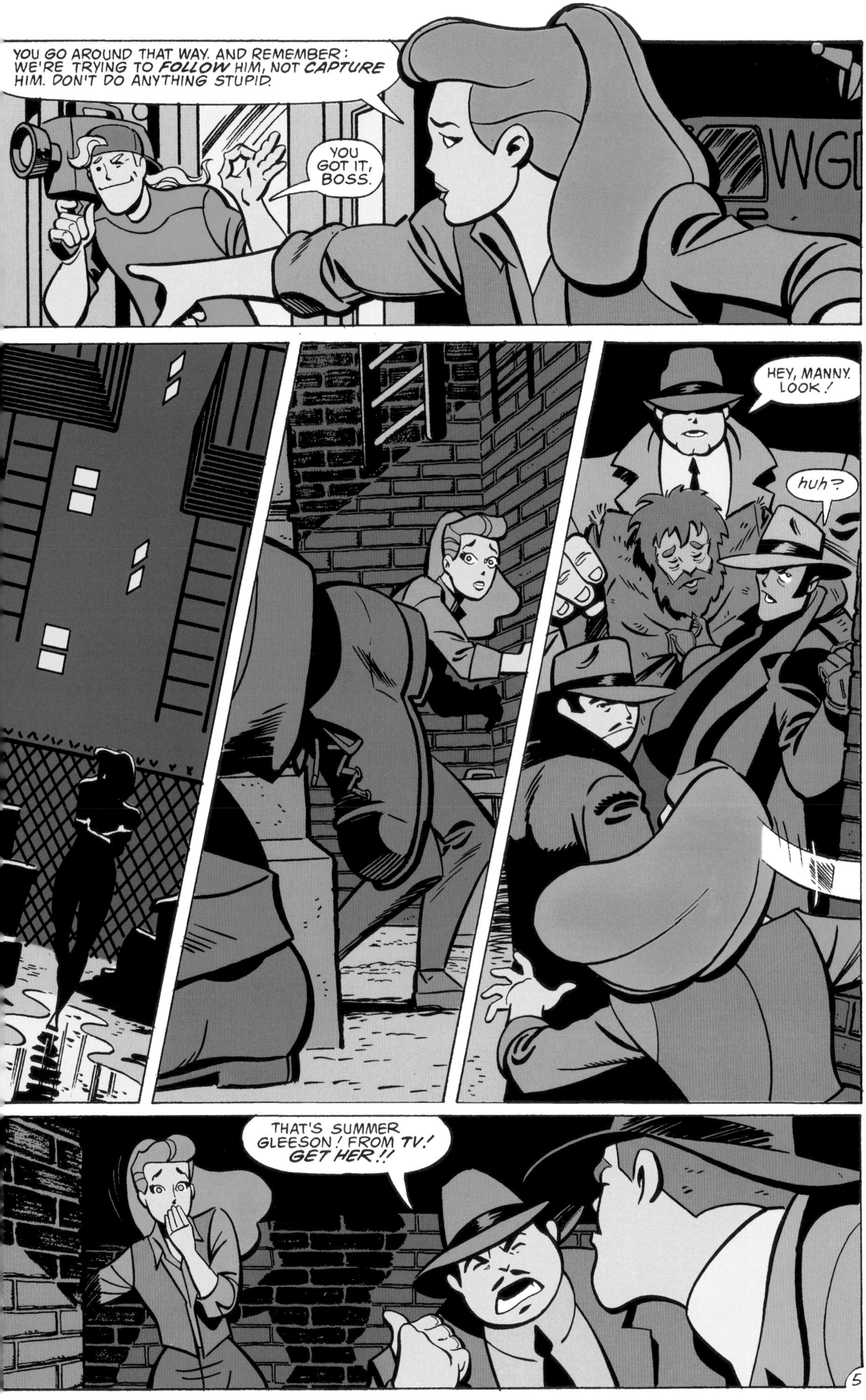
YOU GO AROUND THAT WAY. AND REMEMBER: WE'RE TRYING TO FOLLOW HIM, NOT CAPTURE HIM. DON'T DO ANYTHING STUPID.
YOU GOT IT, BOSS.
WGB
HEY, MANNY. LOOK!
huh?
THAT'S SUMMER GLEESON! FROM TV! GET HER!!
5

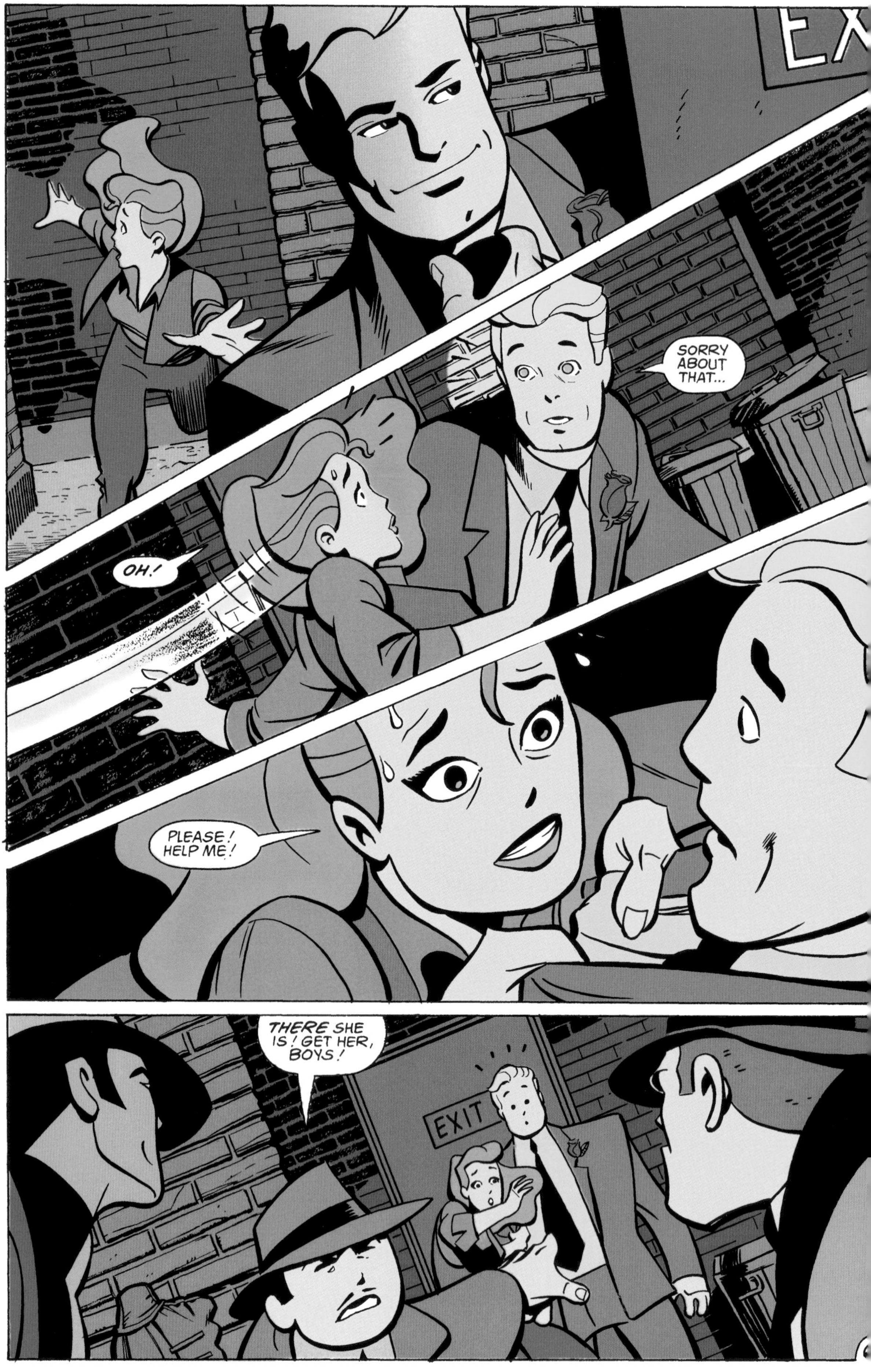

SORRY ABOUT THAT...
OH!
PLEASE! HELP ME!
THERE SHE IS! GET HER, BOYS!
EXIT

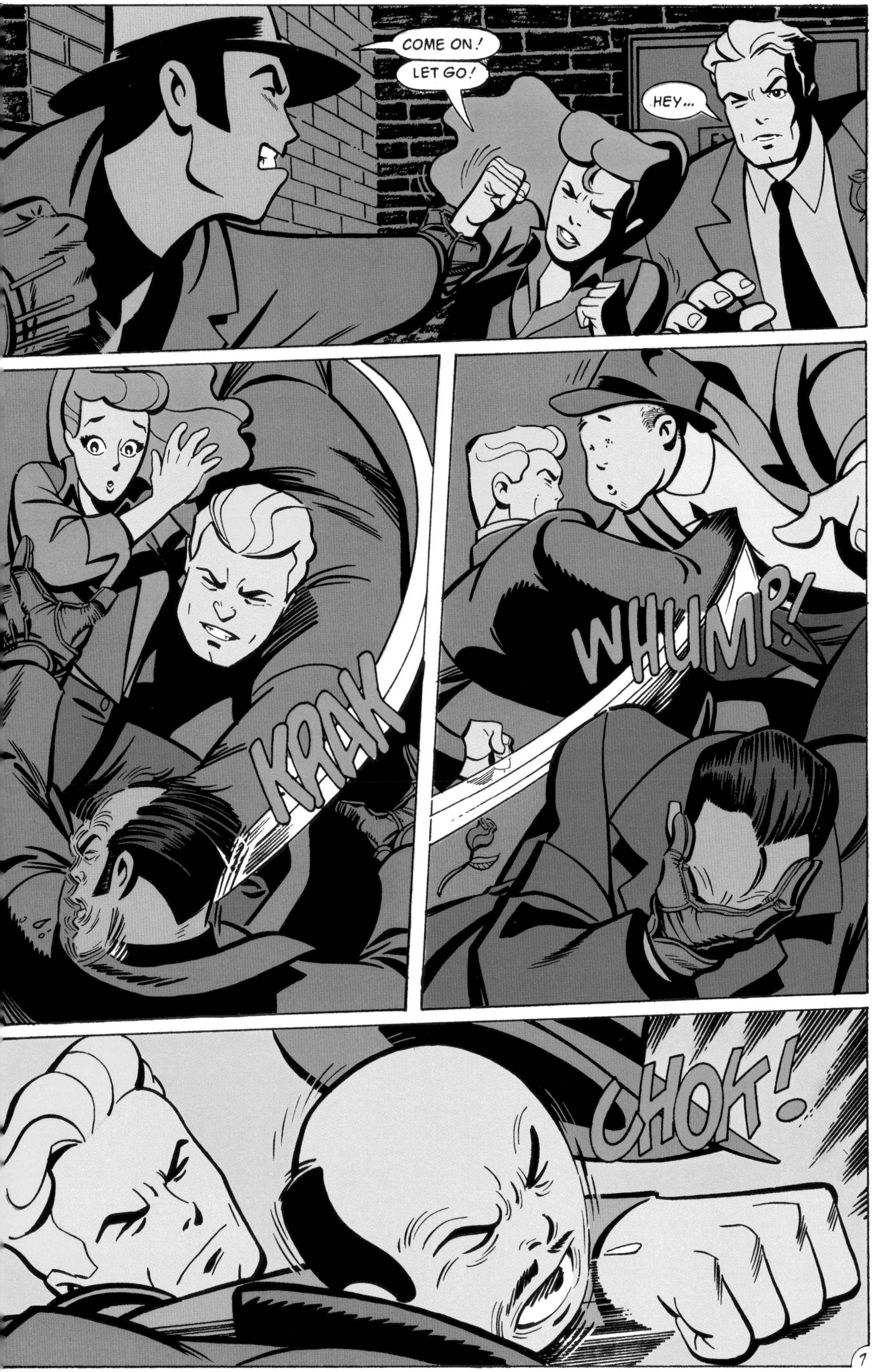

COME ON!
LET GO!
HEY...
KRAK
WHUMP!
CHOK!
7

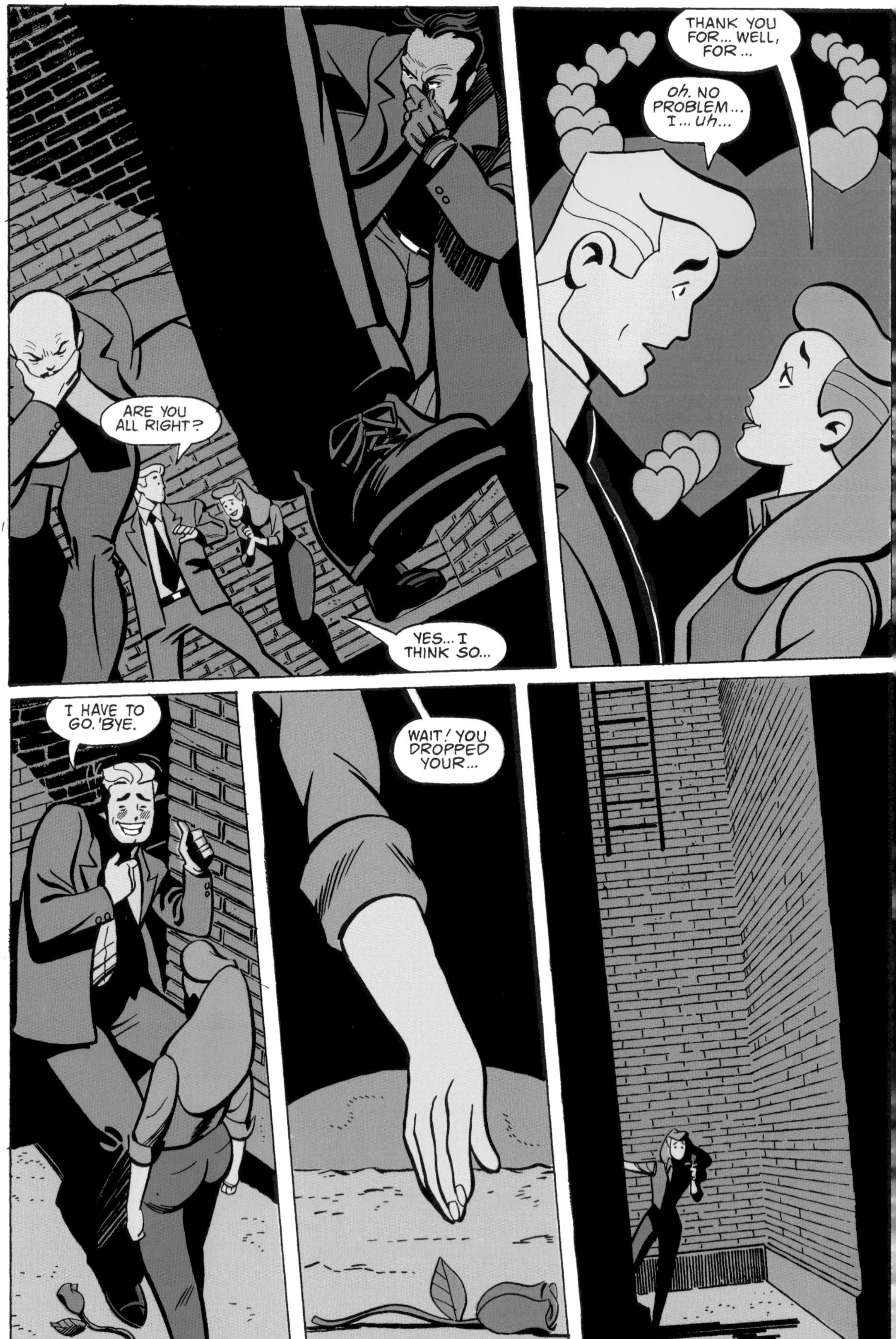
ARE YOU ALL RIGHT?
YES... I THINK SO...
THANK YOU FOR... WELL, FOR...
oh. NO PROBLEM... I... uh...
I HAVE TO GO. 'BYE.
WAIT! YOU DROPPED YOUR...
8

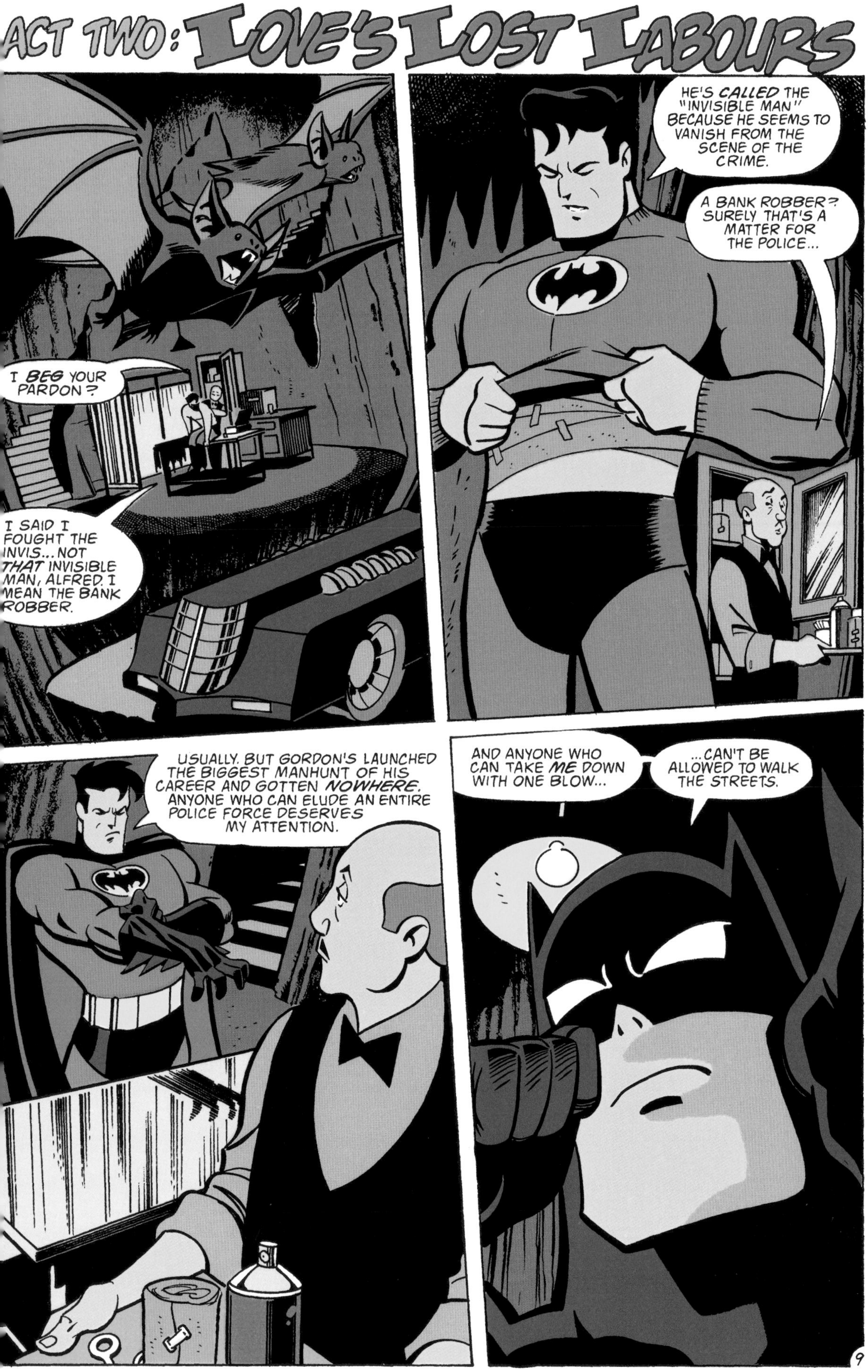
ACT TWO: LOVE'S LOST LABOURS
I BEG YOUR PARDON?
I SAID I FOUGHT THE INVIS... NOT THAT INVISIBLE MAN, ALFRED. I MEAN THE BANK ROBBER.
HE'S CALLED THE "INVISIBLE MAN" BECAUSE HE SEEMS TO VANISH FROM THE SCENE OF THE CRIME.
A BANK ROBBER? SURELY THAT'S A MATTER FOR THE POLICE...
USUALLY. BUT GORDON'S LAUNCHED THE BIGGEST MANHUNT OF HIS CAREER AND GOTTEN NOWHERE. ANYONE WHO CAN ELUDE AN ENTIRE POLICE FORCE DESERVES MY ATTENTION.
AND ANYONE WHO CAN TAKE ME DOWN WITH ONE BLOW...
...CAN'T BE ALLOWED TO WALK THE STREETS.
9

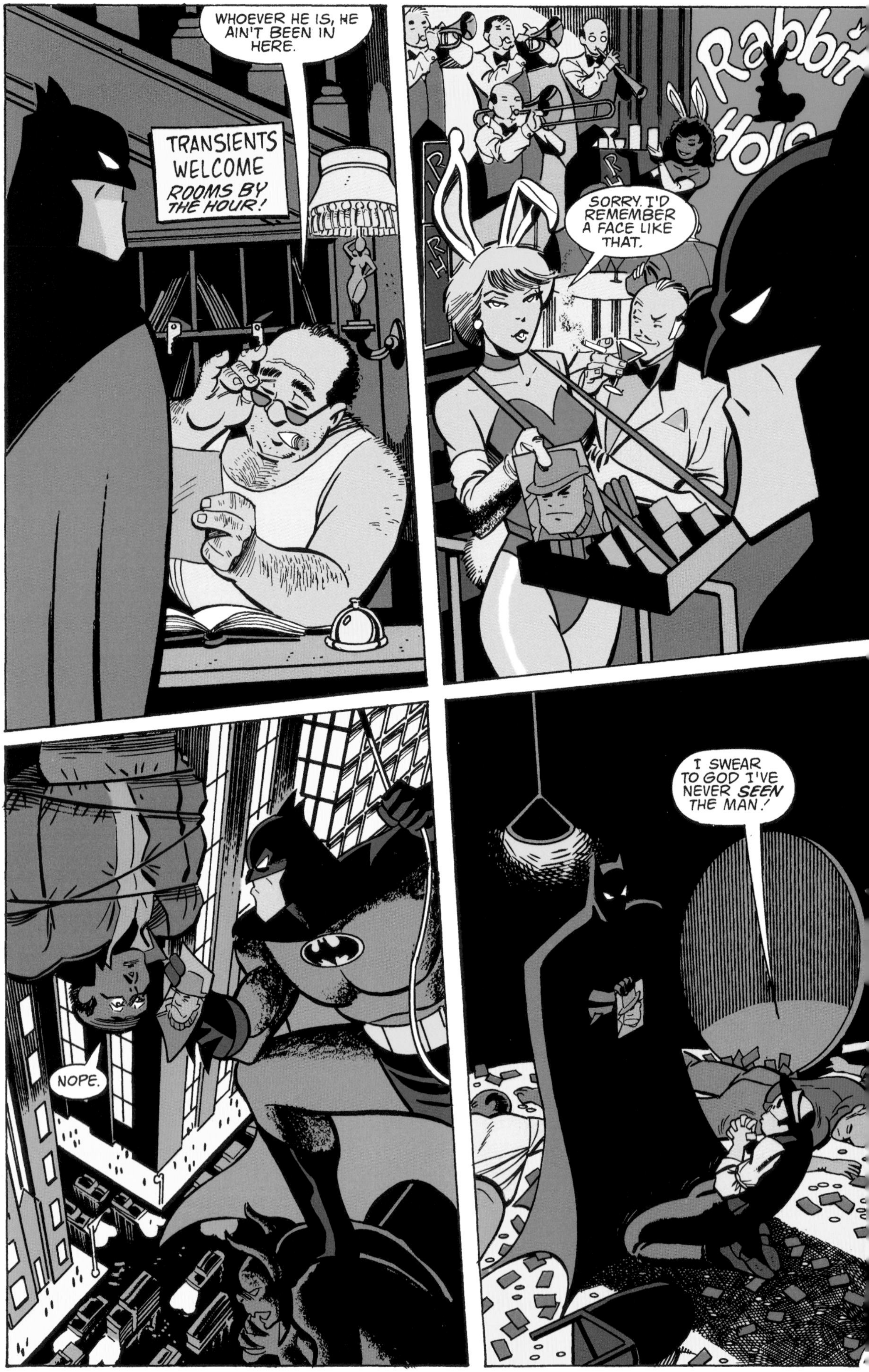

WHOEVER HE IS, HE AIN'T BEEN IN HERE.
TRANSIENTS WELCOME ROOMS BY THE HOUR!
Rabbit Hole
SORRY. I'D REMEMBER A FACE LIKE THAT.
NOPE.
I SWEAR TO GOD I'VE NEVER SEEN THE MAN!

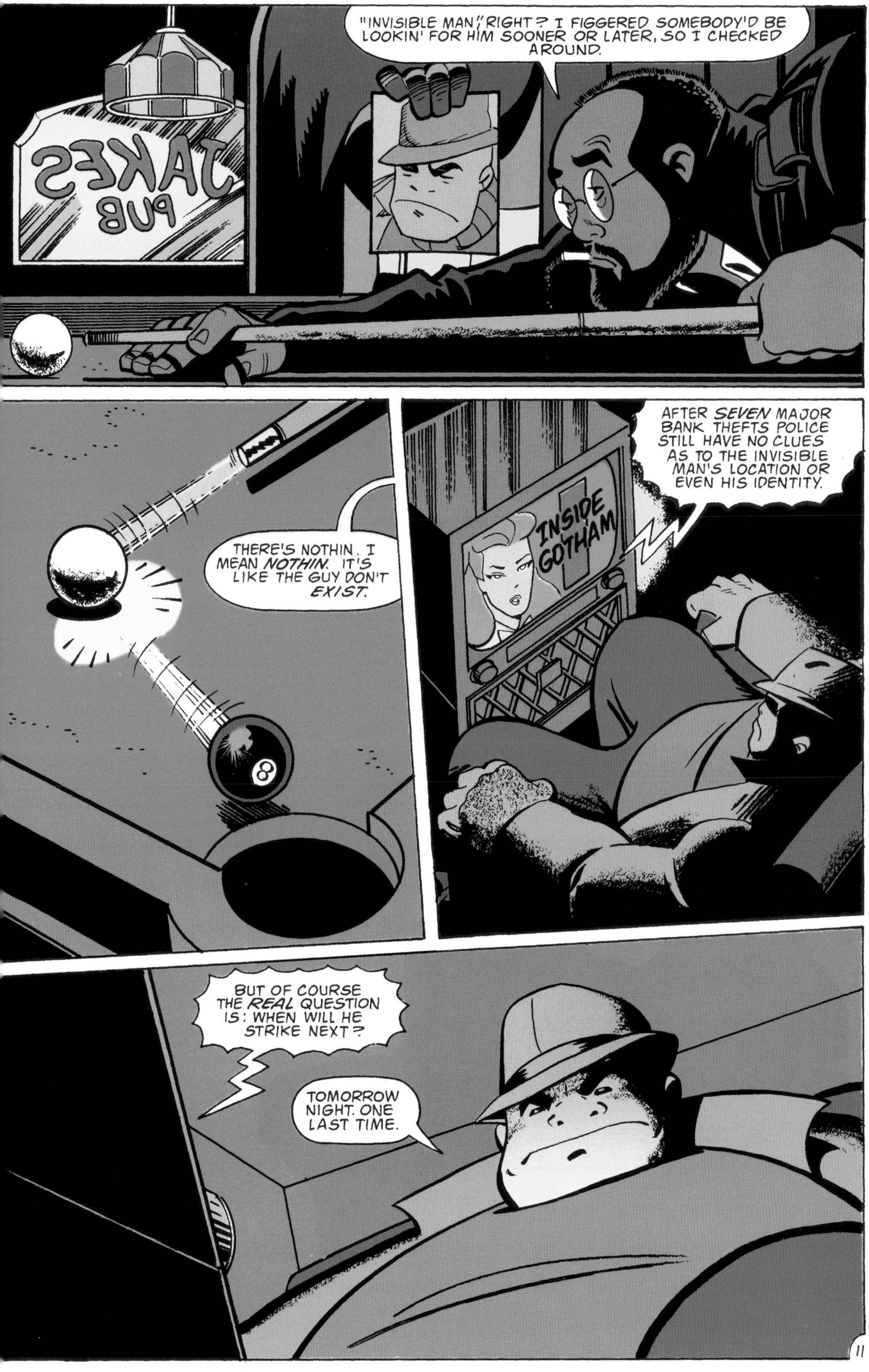
"INVISIBLE MAN," RIGHT? I FIGGERED SOMEBODY'D BE LOOKIN' FOR HIM SOONER OR LATER, SO I CHECKED AROUND.
JAKES PUB
THERE'S NOTHIN. I MEAN *NOTHIN.* IT'S LIKE THE GUY DON'T *EXIST.*
AFTER *SEVEN* MAJOR BANK THEFTS POLICE STILL HAVE NO CLUES AS TO THE INVISIBLE MAN'S LOCATION OR EVEN HIS IDENTITY.
INSIDE GOTHAM
BUT OF COURSE THE *REAL* QUESTION IS: WHEN WILL HE STRIKE NEXT?
TOMORROW NIGHT. ONE LAST TIME.
11

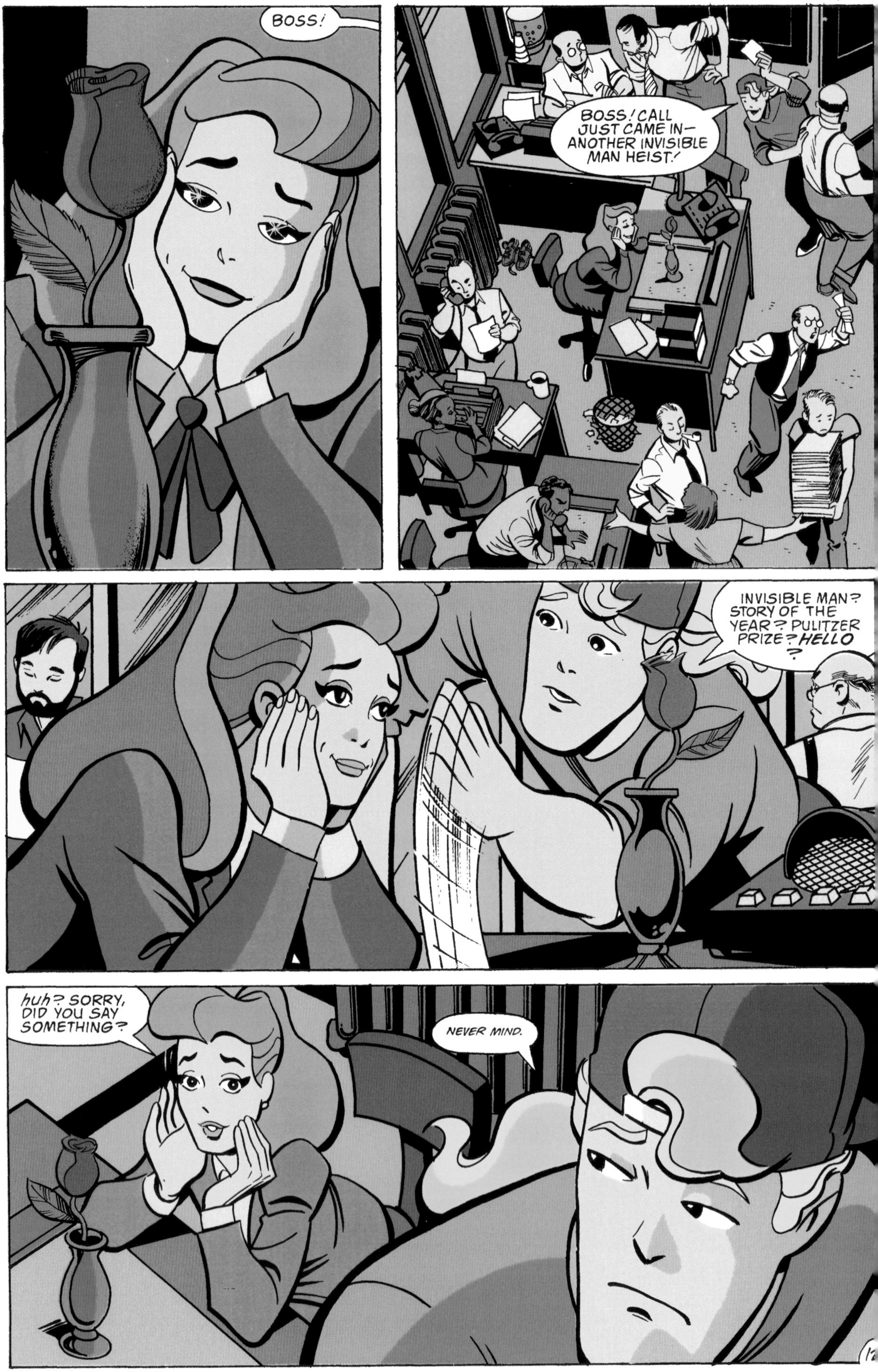
BOSS!
BOSS! CALL JUST CAME IN— ANOTHER INVISIBLE MAN HEIST!
INVISIBLE MAN? STORY OF THE YEAR? PULITZER PRIZE? HELLO?
huh? SORRY, DID YOU SAY SOMETHING?
NEVER MIND.

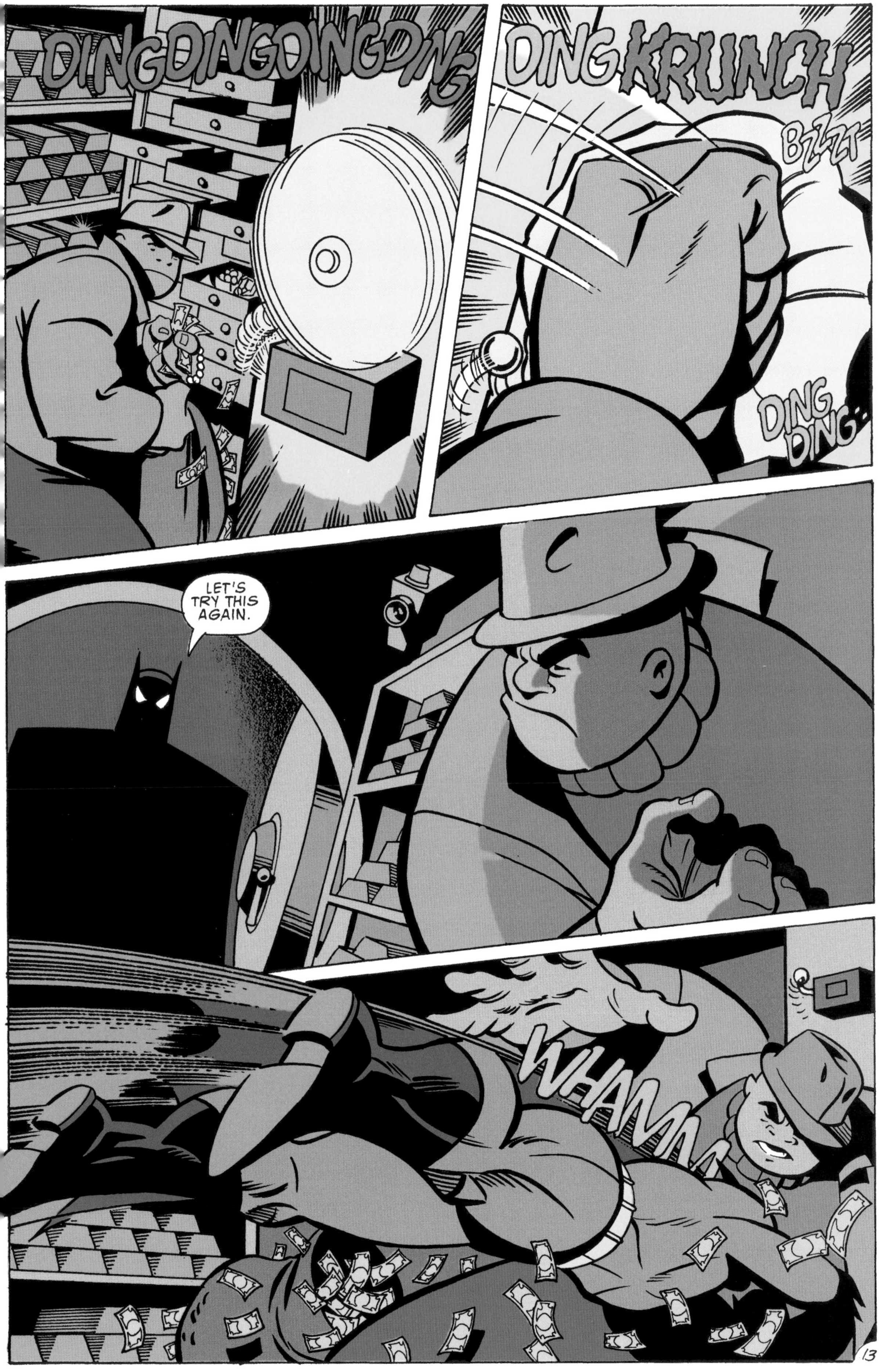
DINGDINGDINGDINGDING
DING KRUNCH
BZZZT
DING DING
LET'S TRY THIS AGAIN.
WHAMM
13

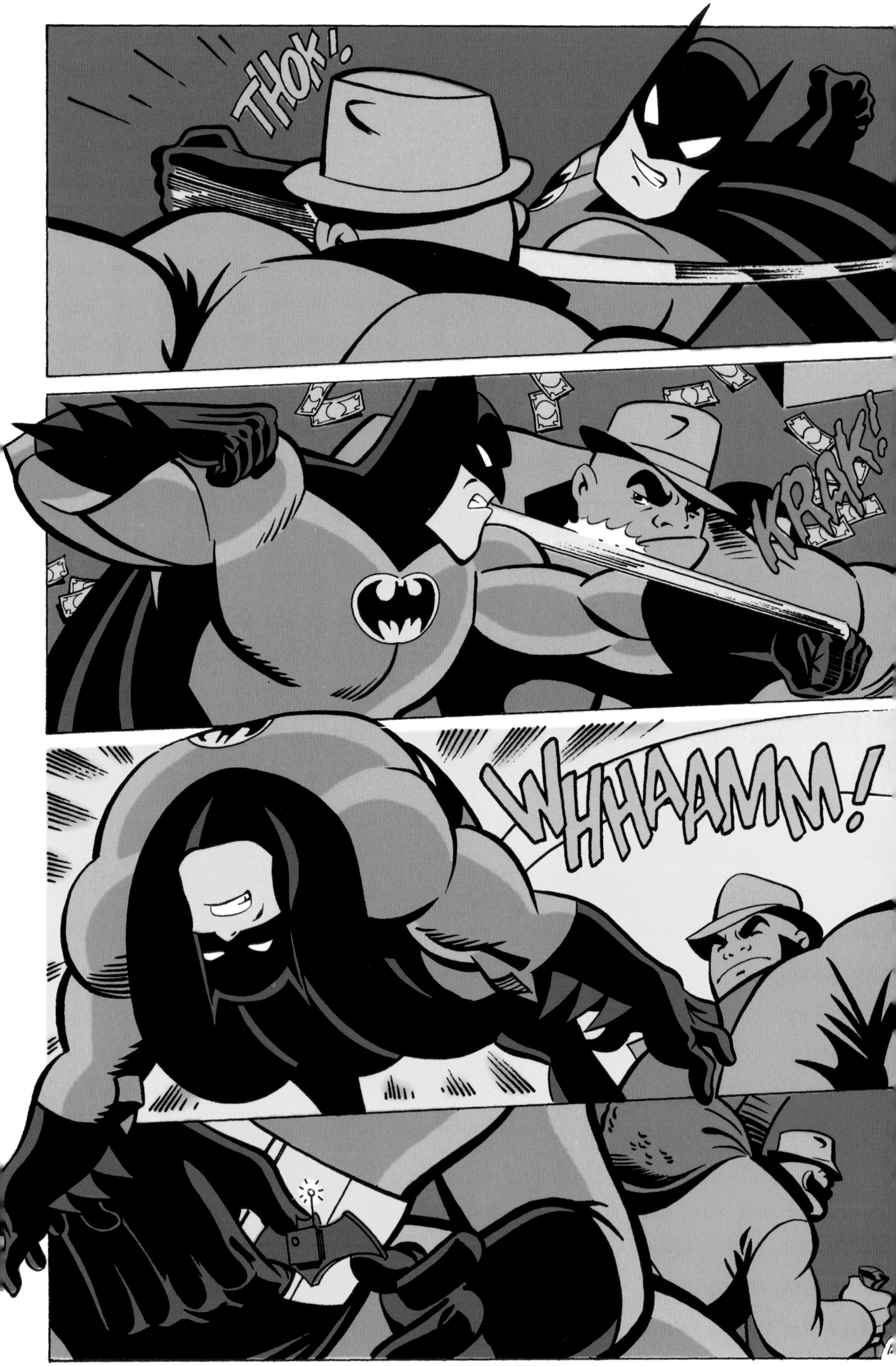
THOK!
KRAK!
WHHAAMM!

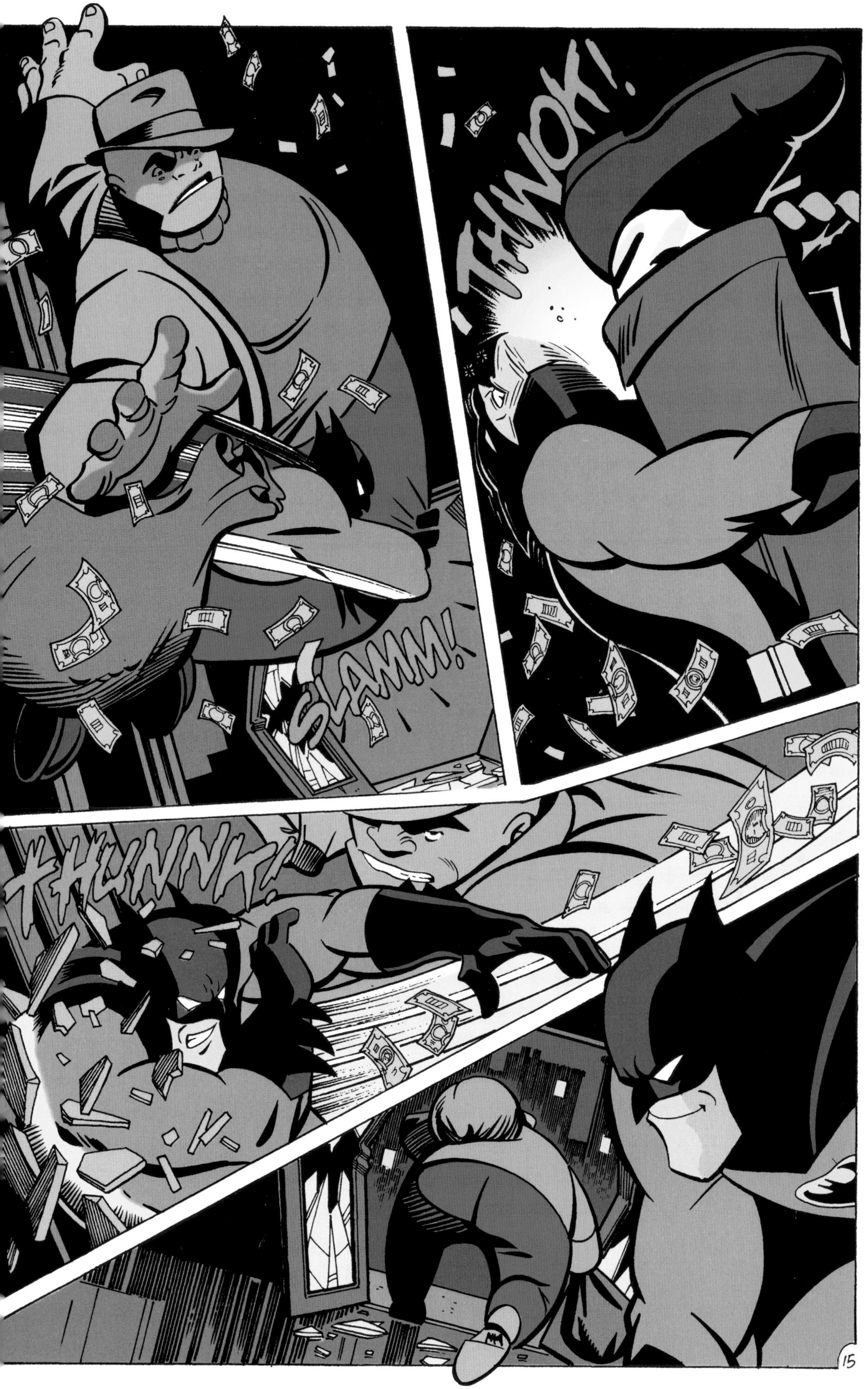
SLAMM!
THWOK!
THUNNK!
15

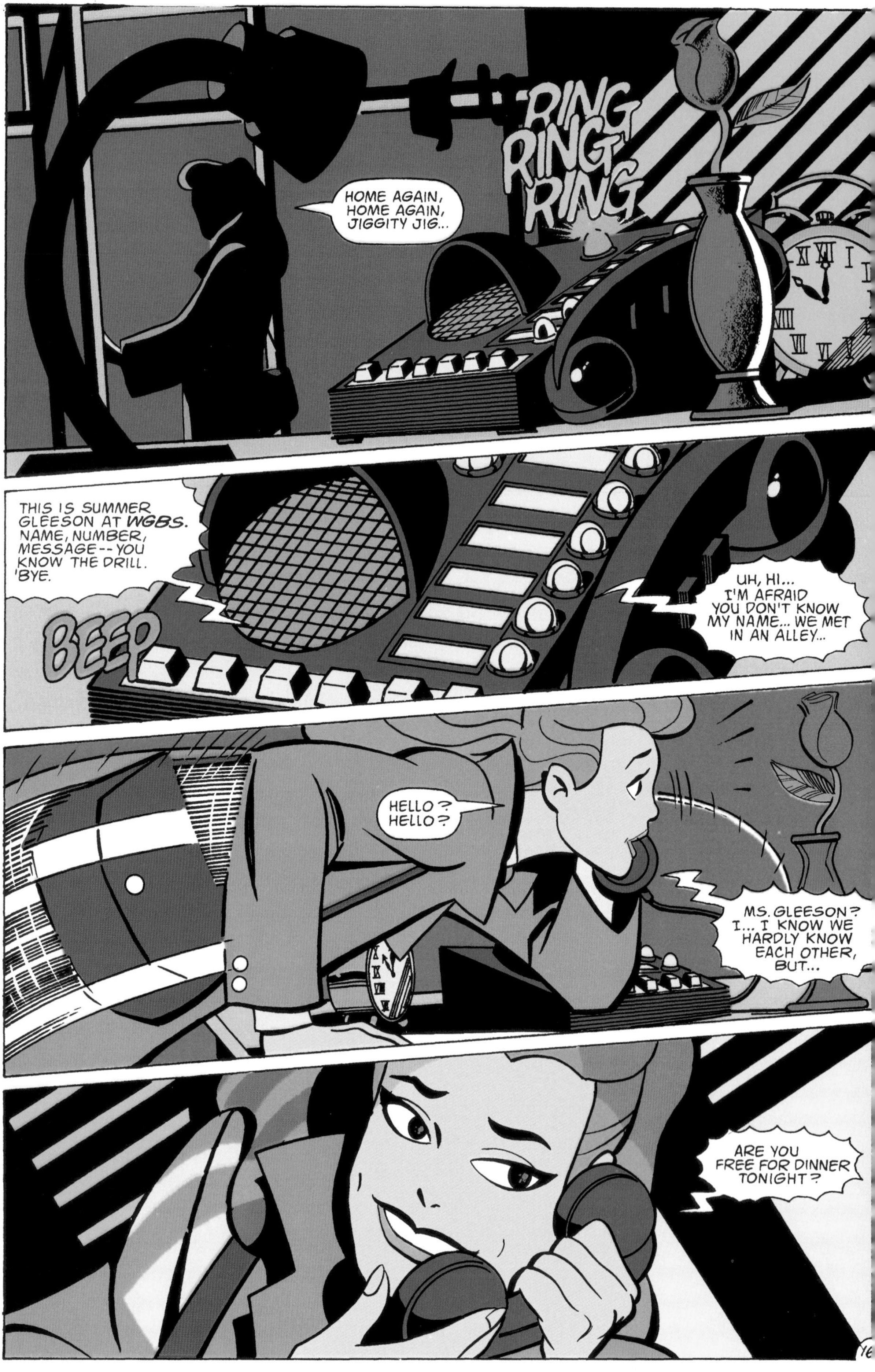
RING
RING
RING
HOME AGAIN, HOME AGAIN, JIGGITY JIG...
THIS IS SUMMER GLEESON AT WGBS. NAME, NUMBER, MESSAGE--YOU KNOW THE DRILL. 'BYE.
BEEP
UH, HI... I'M AFRAID YOU DON'T KNOW MY NAME... WE MET IN AN ALLEY...
HELLO? HELLO?
MS. GLEESON? I... I KNOW WE HARDLY KNOW EACH OTHER, BUT...
ARE YOU FREE FOR DINNER TONIGHT?
16

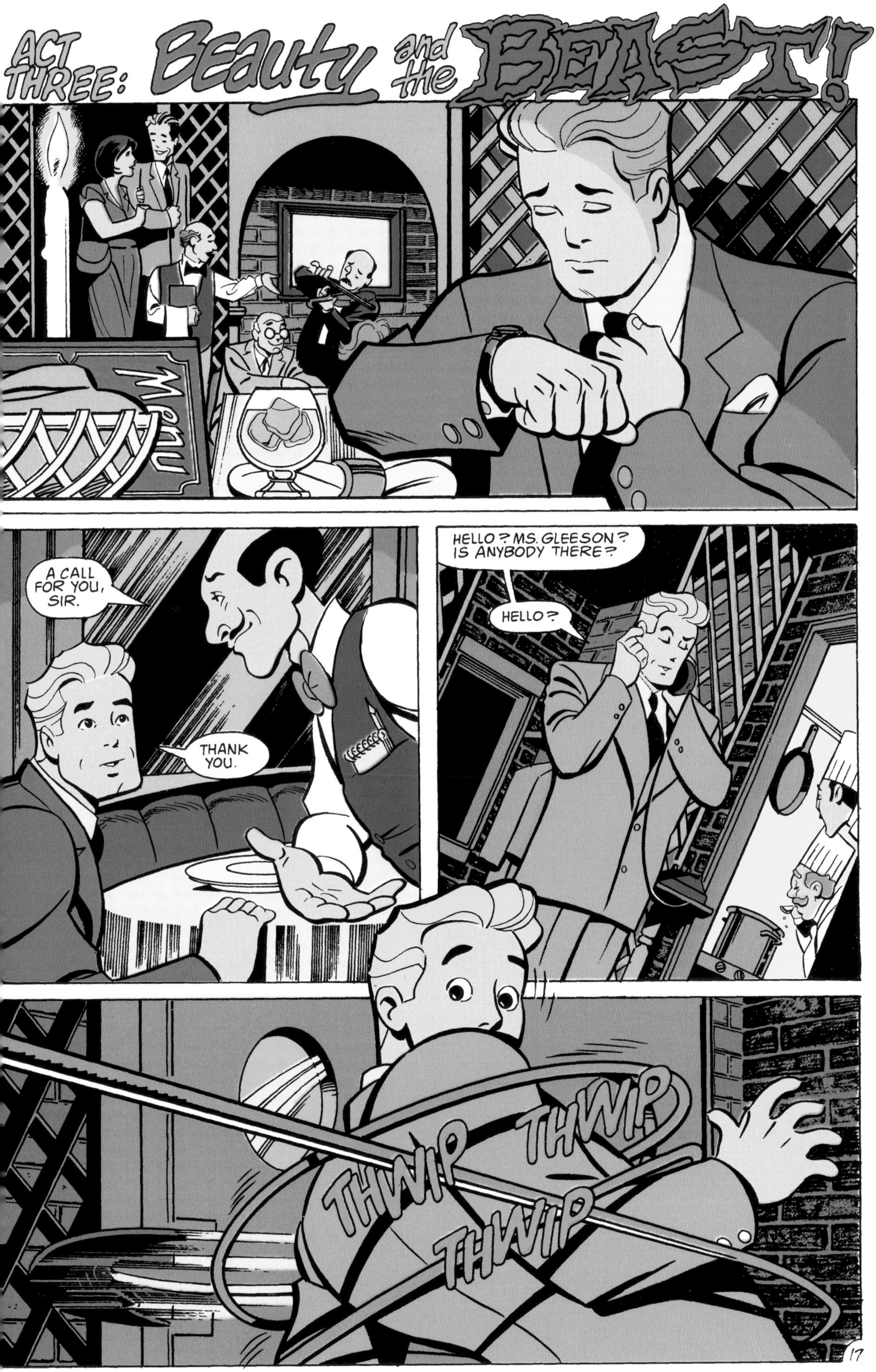
ACT THREE: BEAUTY and the BEAST!
Menu
A CALL FOR YOU, SIR.
THANK YOU.
HELLO? MS. GLEESON? IS ANYBODY THERE?
HELLO?
THWIP THWIP THWIP THWIP
17

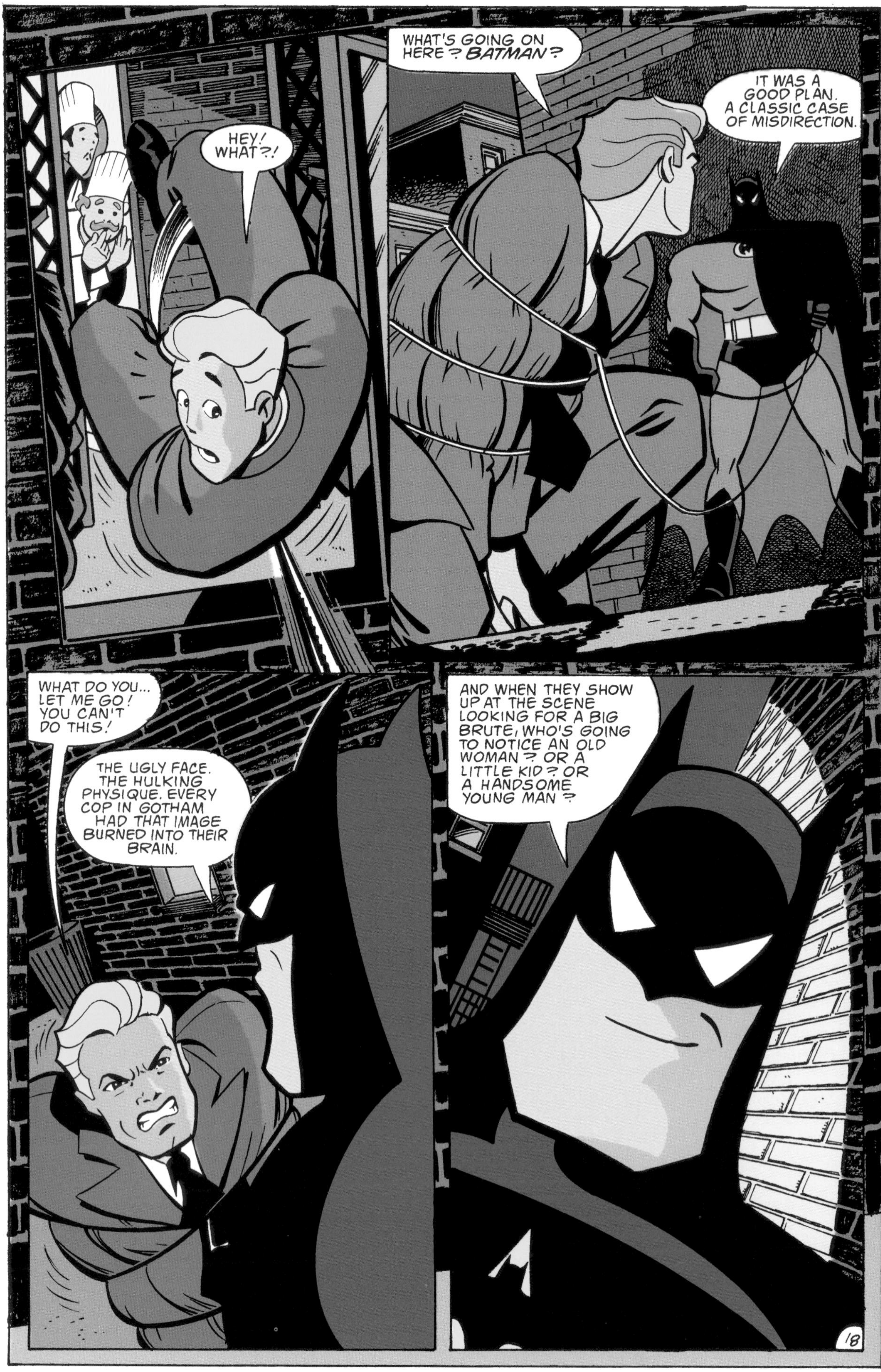
HEY! WHAT?!
WHAT'S GOING ON HERE? BATMAN?
IT WAS A GOOD PLAN. A CLASSIC CASE OF MISDIRECTION.
WHAT DO YOU... LET ME GO! YOU CAN'T DO THIS!
THE UGLY FACE. THE HULKING PHYSIQUE. EVERY COP IN GOTHAM HAD THAT IMAGE BURNED INTO THEIR BRAIN.
AND WHEN THEY SHOW UP AT THE SCENE LOOKING FOR A BIG BRUTE, WHO'S GOING TO NOTICE AN OLD WOMAN? OR A LITTLE KID? OR A HANDSOME YOUNG MAN?
18

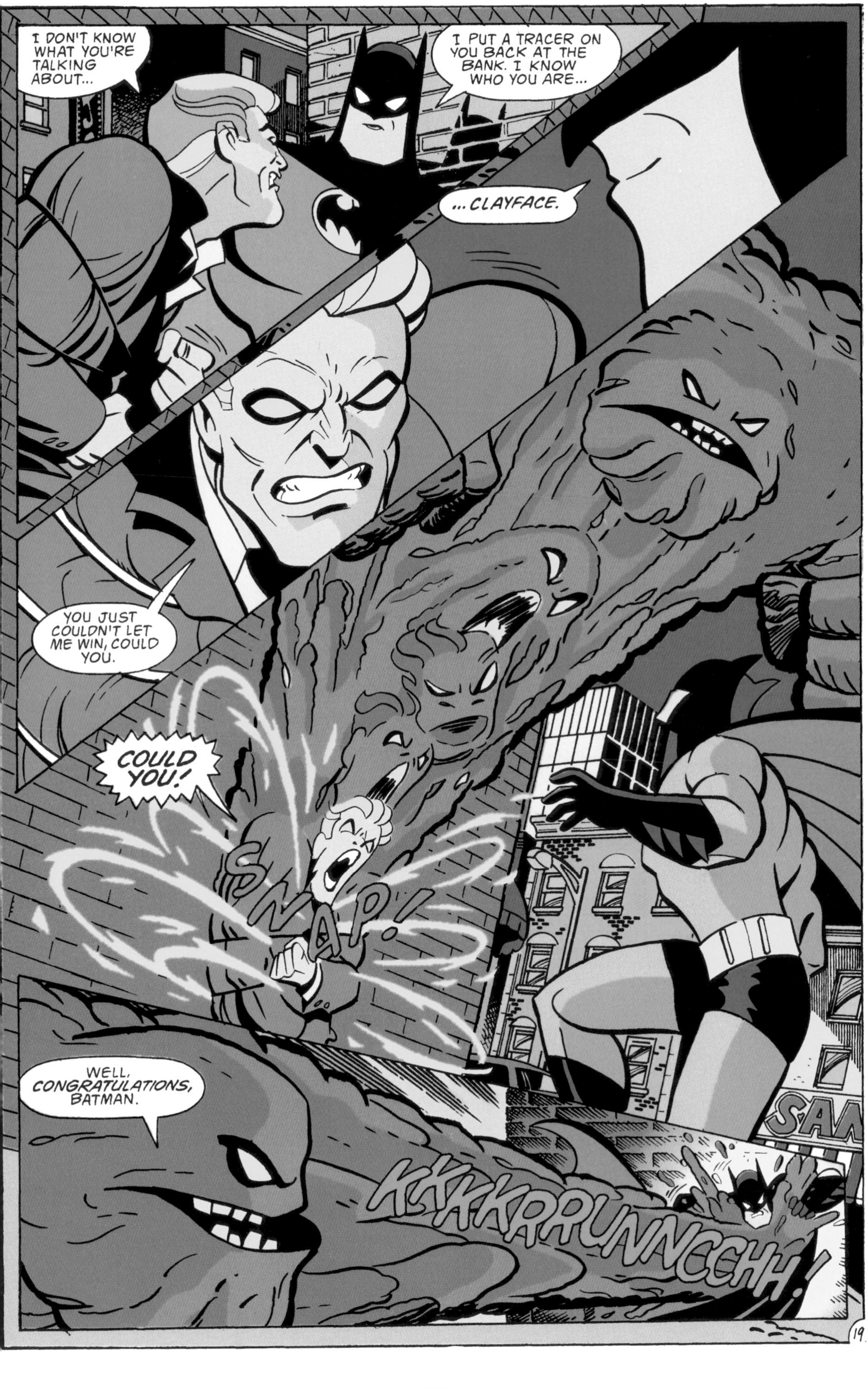
I DON'T KNOW WHAT YOU'RE TALKING ABOUT...
I PUT A TRACER ON YOU BACK AT THE BANK. I KNOW WHO YOU ARE...
...CLAYFACE.
YOU JUST COULDN'T LET ME WIN, COULD YOU.
COULD YOU!
SNAP!
WELL, CONGRATULATIONS, BATMAN.
KKKKRRUNNCCHH!
19

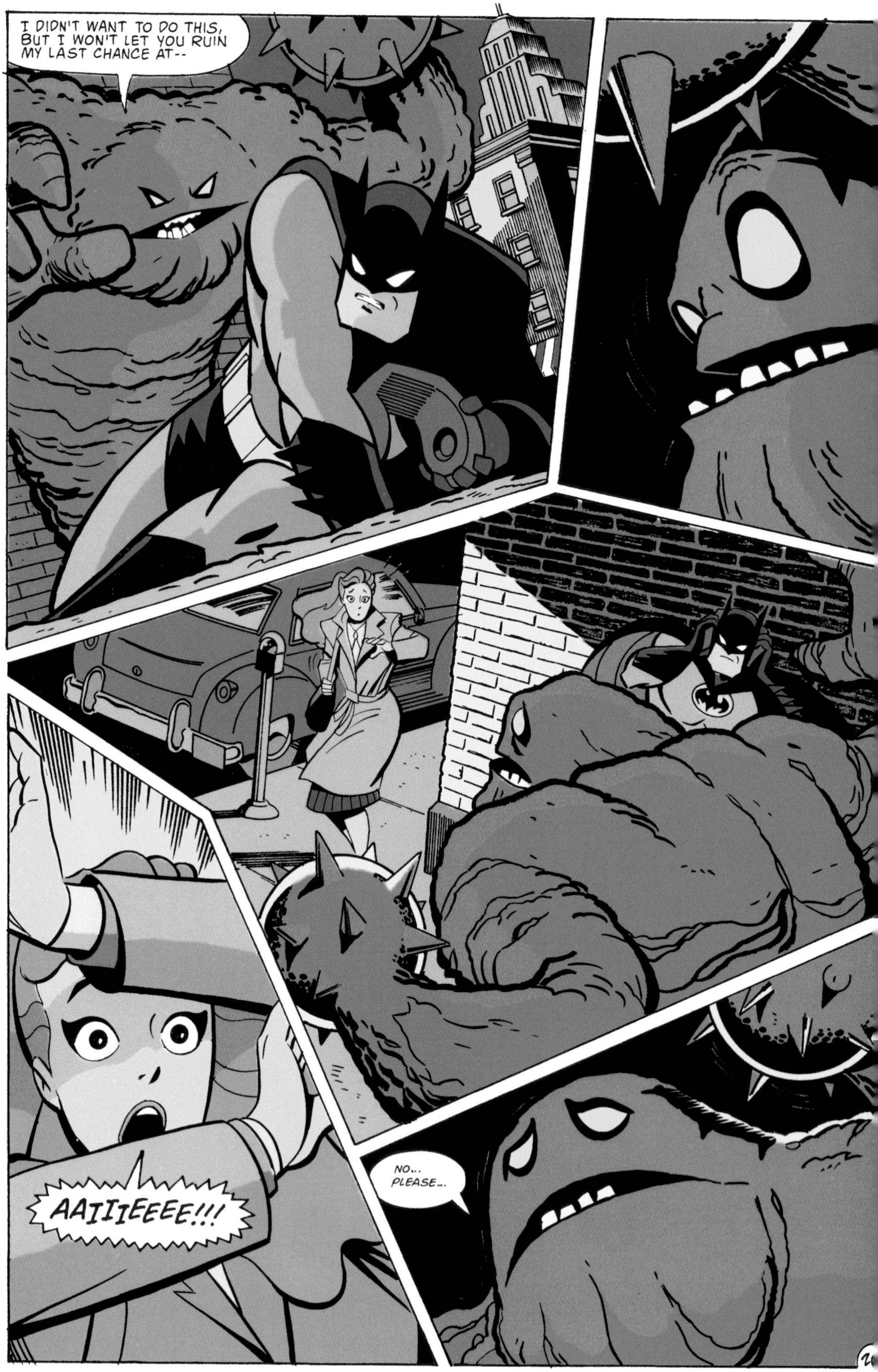
I DIDN'T WANT TO DO THIS, BUT I WON'T LET YOU RUIN MY LAST CHANCE AT--
AAIIIEEEE!!!
NO.. PLEASE..

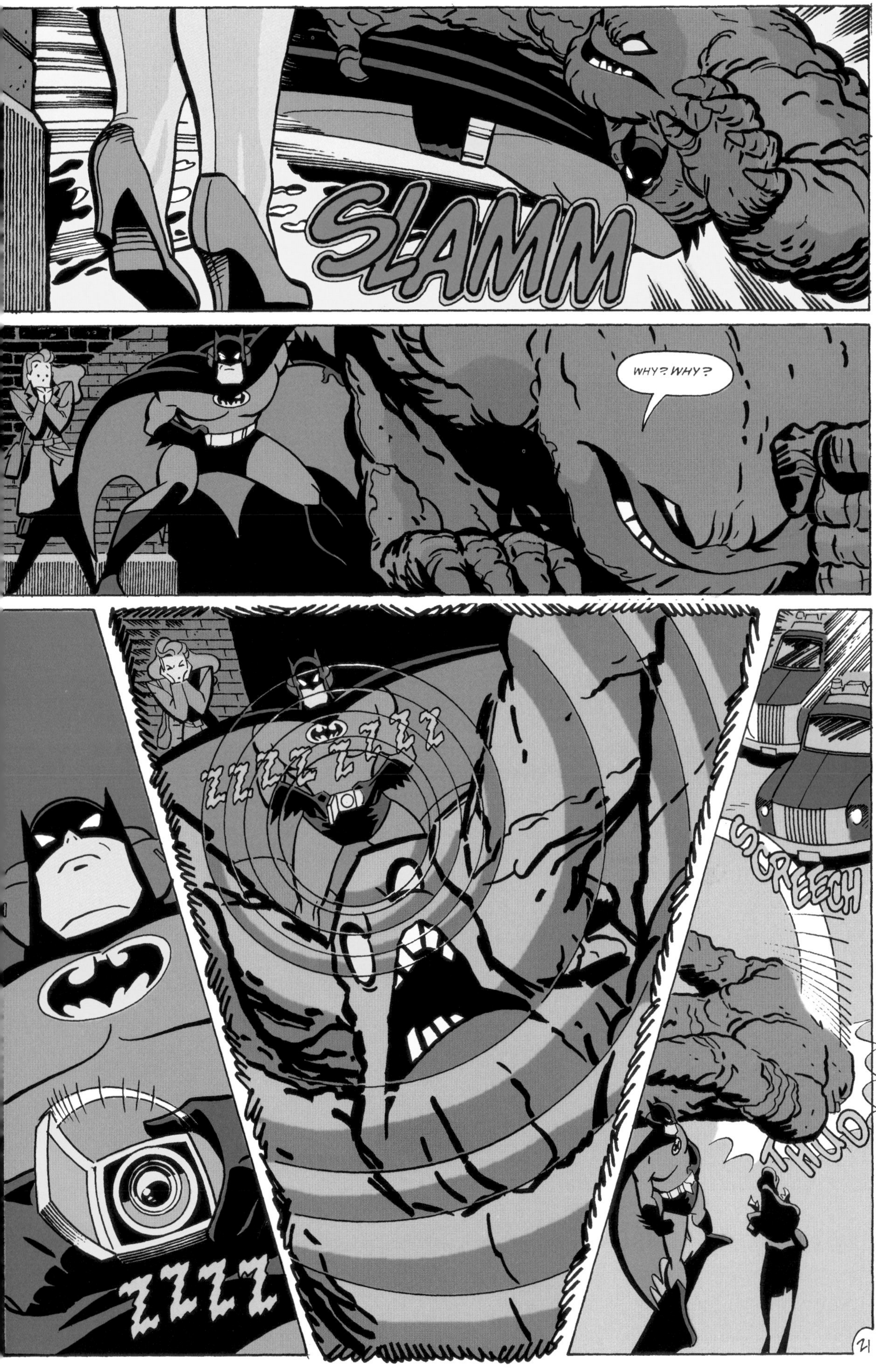
SLAMM
WHY? WHY?
ZZZZ
ZZZZZZZZZ
SCREECH
THUD
21

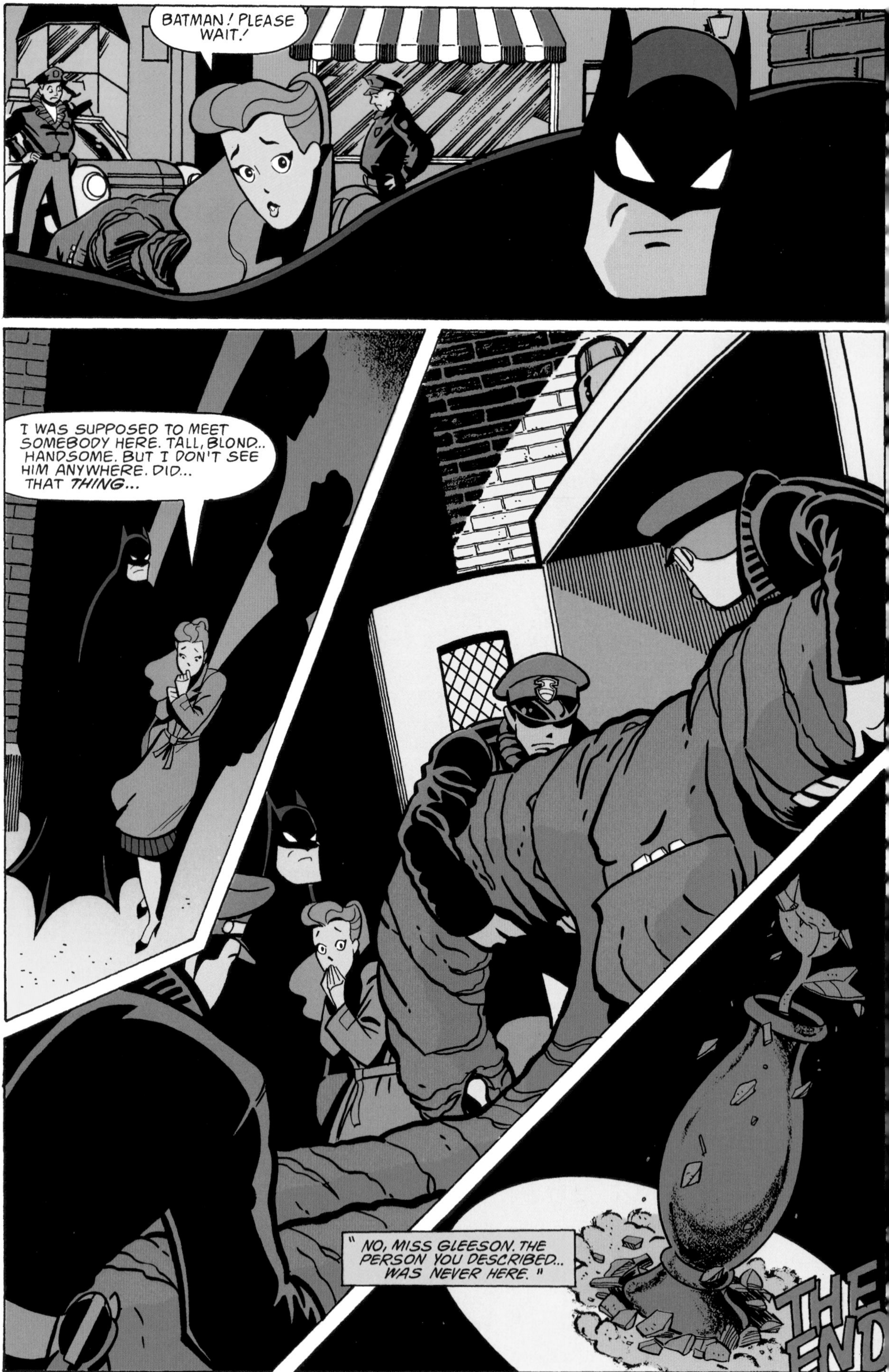
BATMAN! PLEASE WAIT!
I WAS SUPPOSED TO MEET SOMEBODY HERE. TALL, BLOND.. HANDSOME. BUT I DON'T SEE HIM ANYWHERE. DID... THAT THING...
" NO, MISS GLEESON. THE PERSON YOU DESCRIBED... WAS NEVER HERE. "
THE END

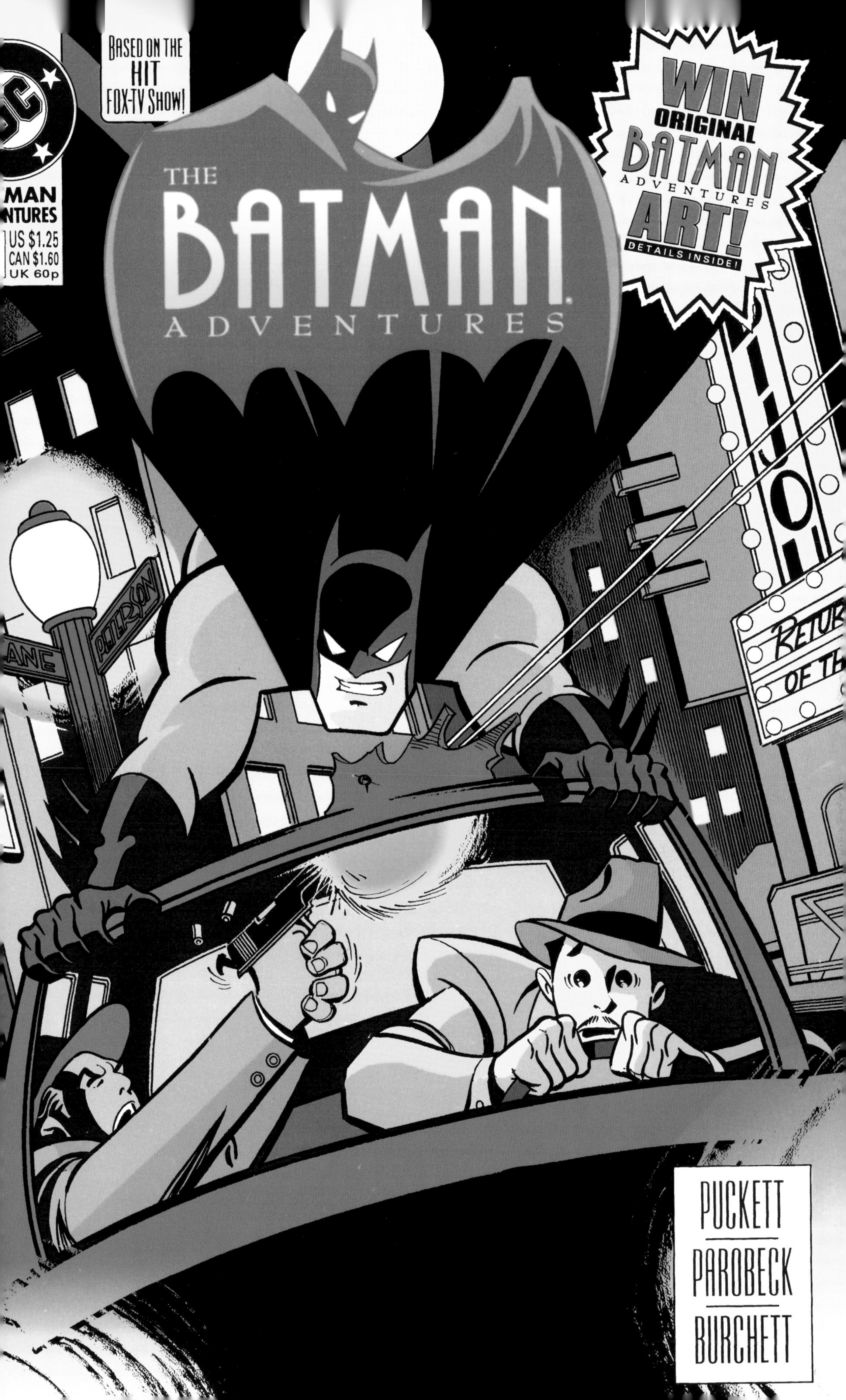
BASED ON THE HIT FOX-TV SHOW!
MAN
NTURES
US $1.25
CAN $1.60
UK 60p
THE BATMAN ADVENTURES
WIN ORIGINAL BATMAN ADVENTURES ART!
DETAILS INSIDE!
PETERSON
ANE
RETUR
OF TH
PUCKETT
PAROBECK
BURCHETT

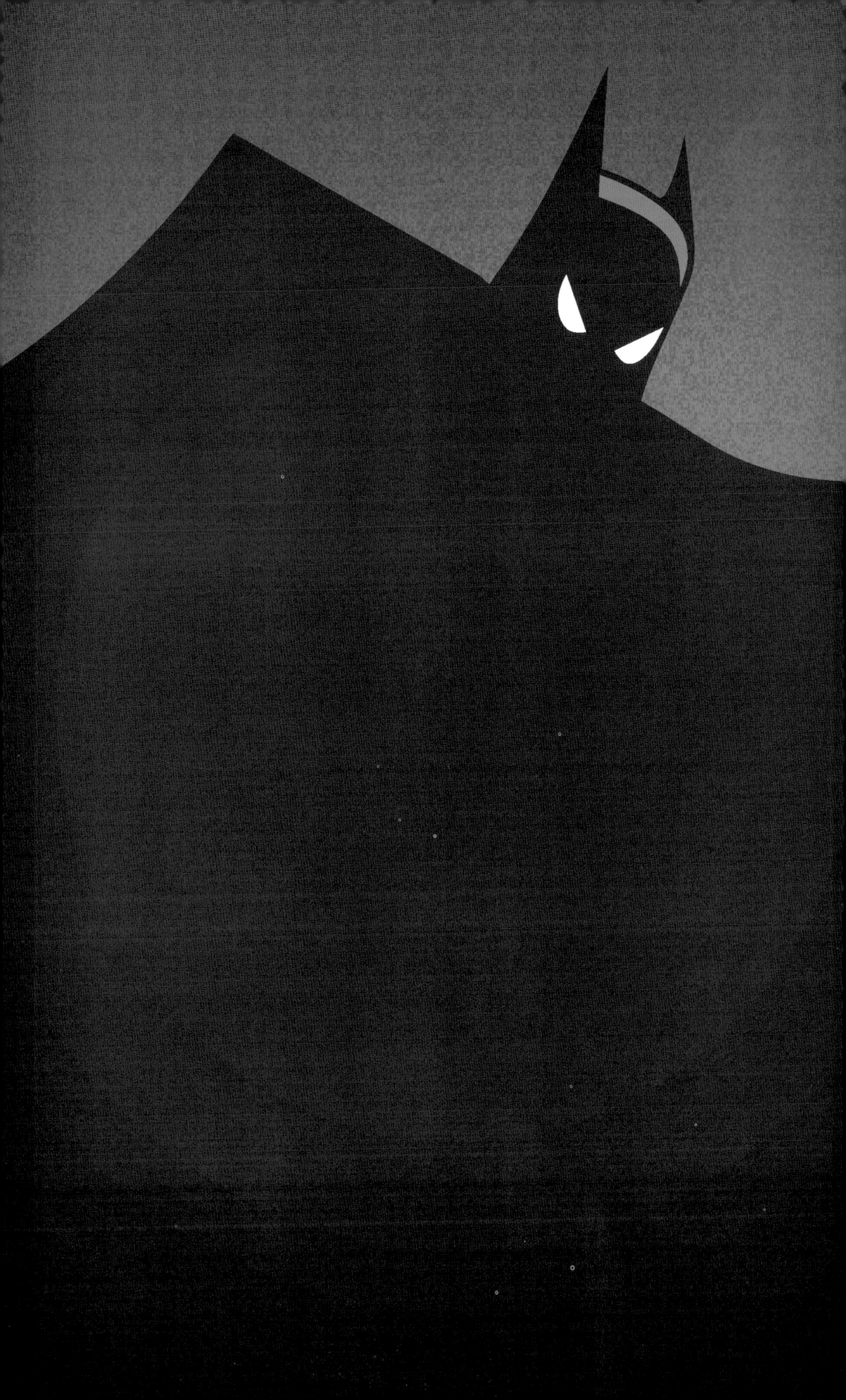

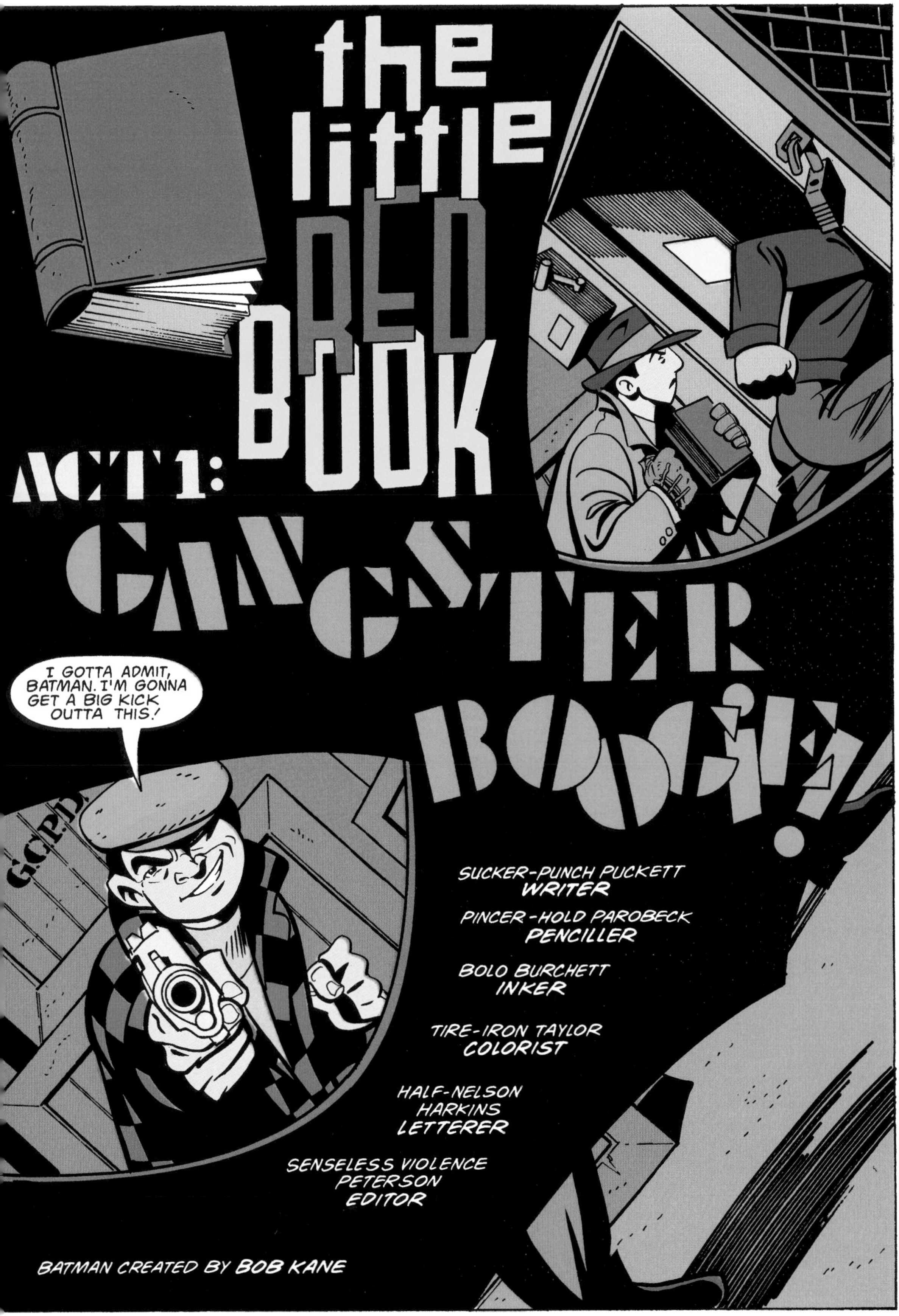
the little RED BOOK
ACT 1: GANGSTER BOOGIE!
I GOTTA ADMIT, BATMAN. I'M GONNA GET A BIG KICK OUTTA THIS!
G.C.P.D.
SUCKER-PUNCH PUCKETT WRITER
PINCER-HOLD PAROBECK PENCILLER
BOLO BURCHETT INKER
TIRE-IRON TAYLOR COLORIST
HALF-NELSON HARKINS LETTERER
SENSELESS VIOLENCE PETERSON EDITOR
BATMAN CREATED BY BOB KANE

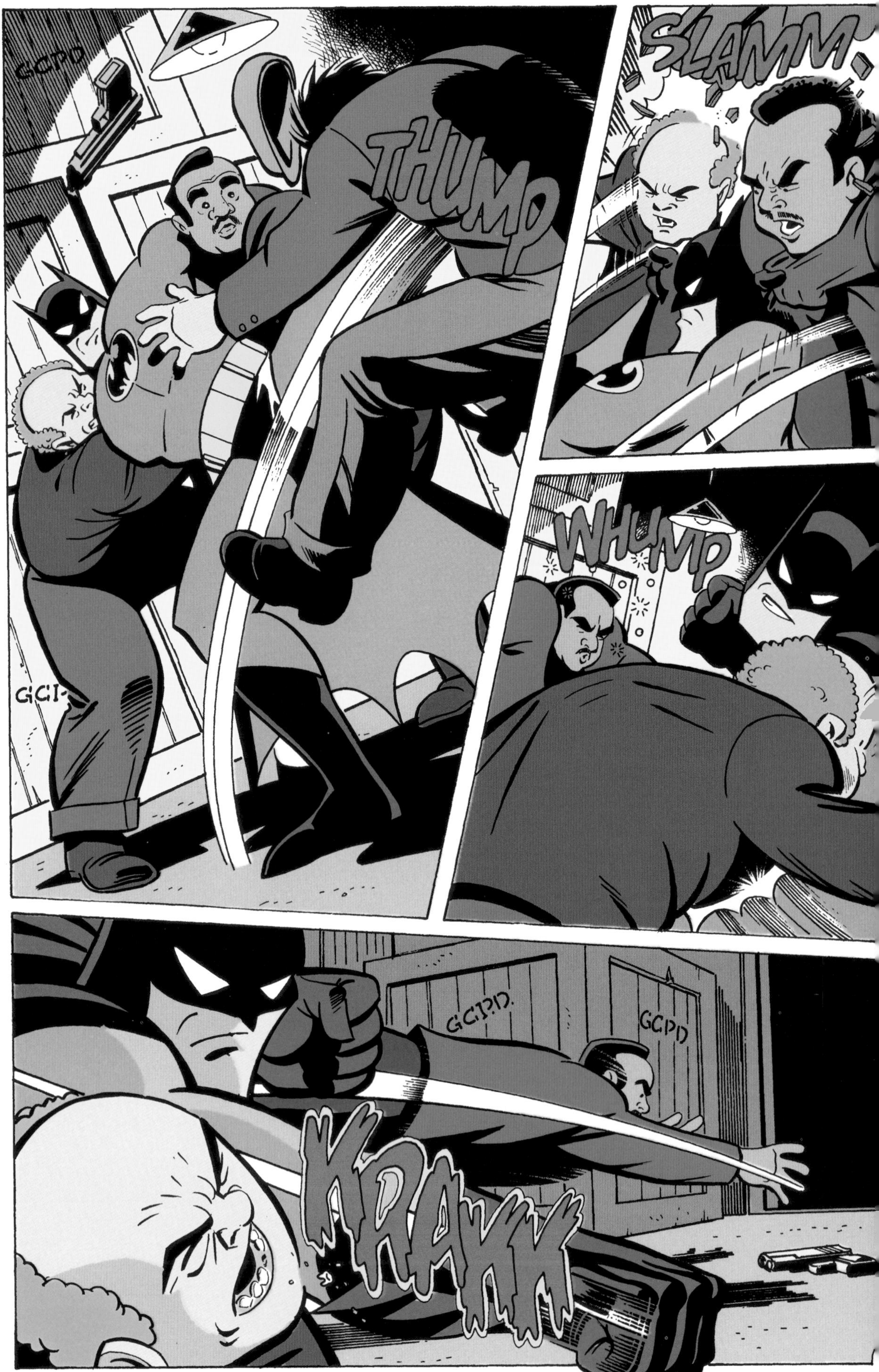
GCPD
THUMP
GCI-
SLAMM
WHUMP
GCPD.
GCPD
KRAKK

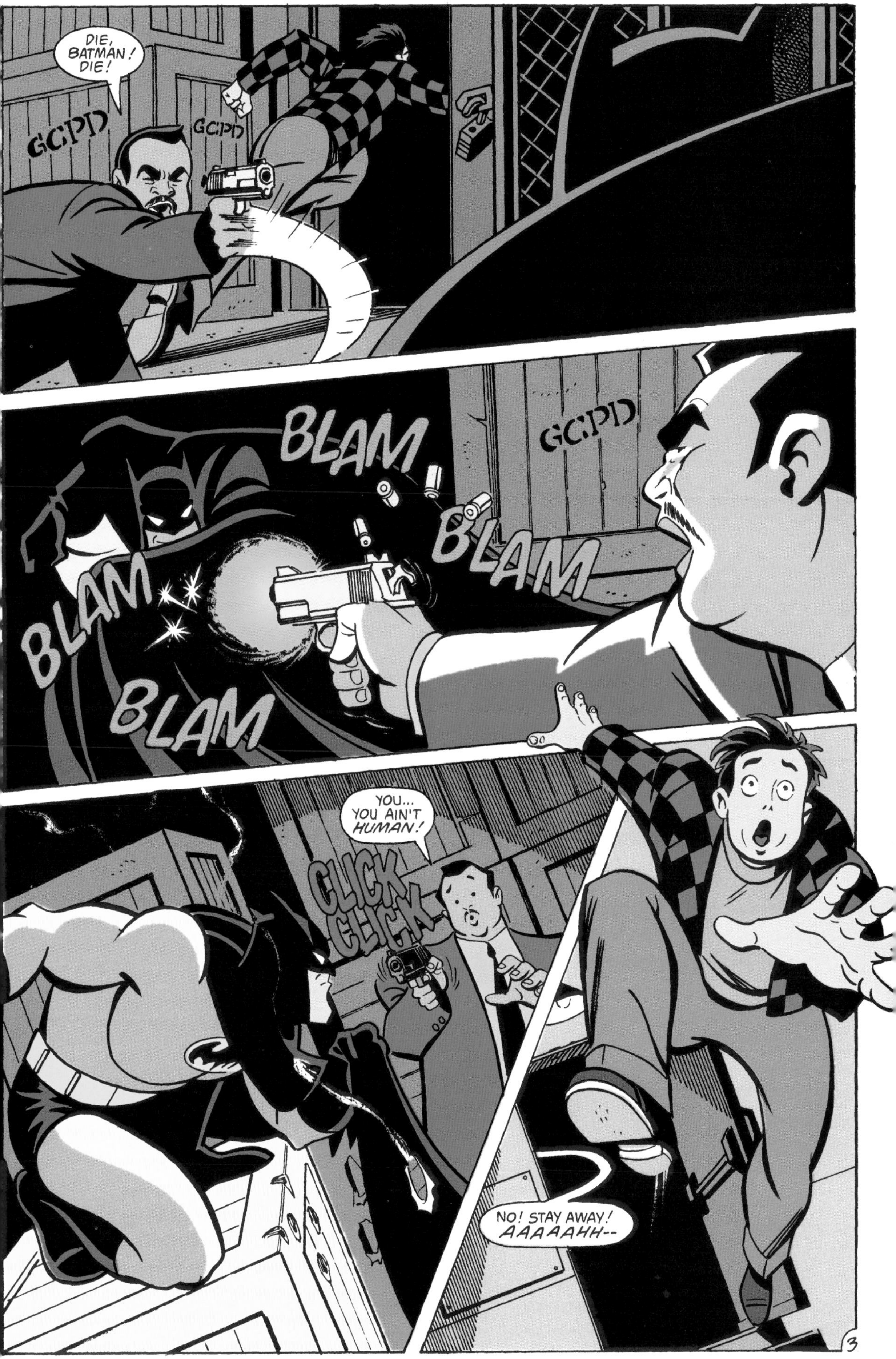
DIE, BATMAN! DIE!
GCPD
GCPD
BLAM
BLAM
BLAM
BLAM
GCPD
YOU... YOU AIN'T HUMAN!
CLICK CLICK
NO! STAY AWAY! AAAAAHH--
3

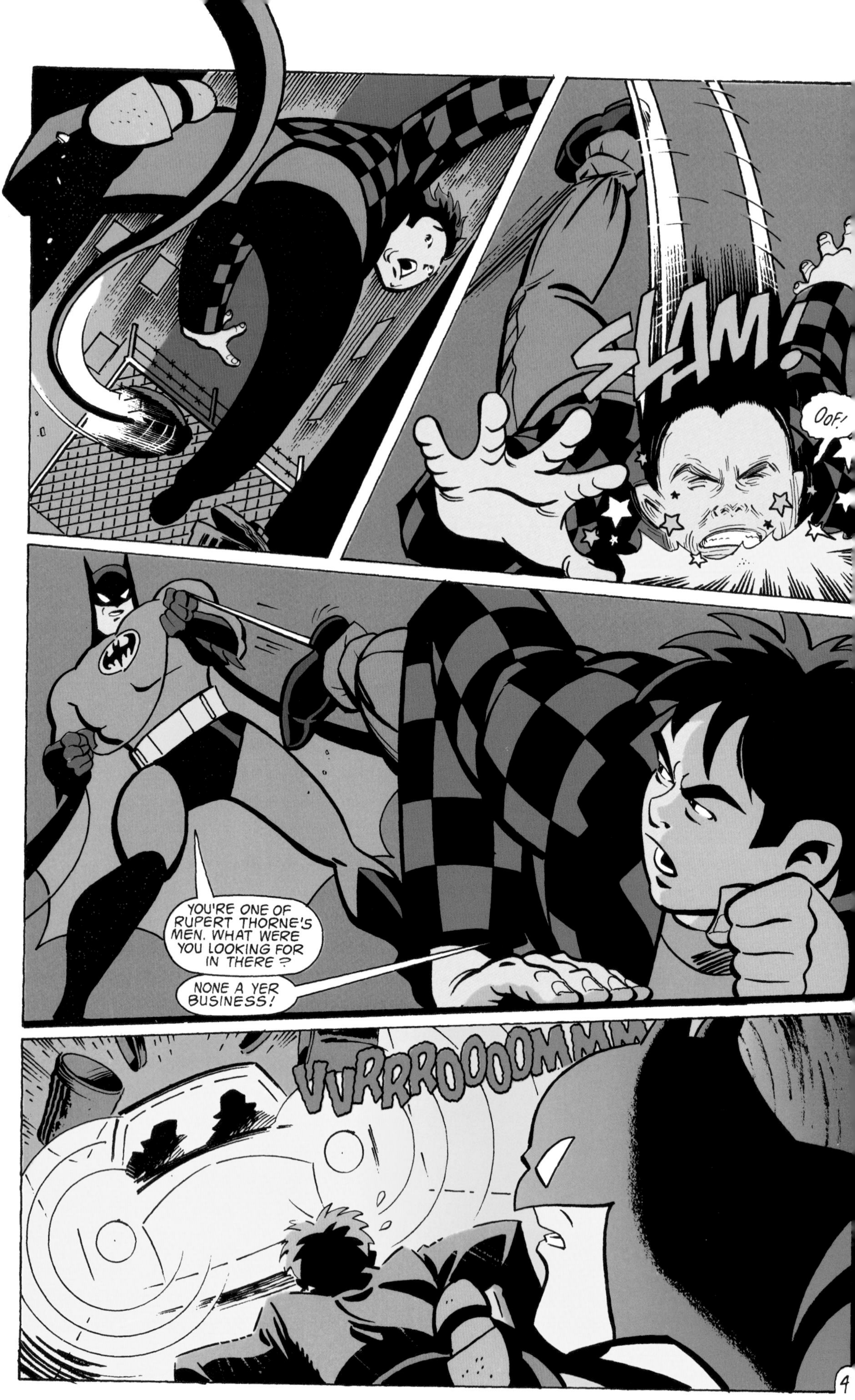
SLAM!
OOF!
YOU'RE ONE OF RUPERT THORNE'S MEN. WHAT WERE YOU LOOKING FOR IN THERE?
NONE A YER BUSINESS!
VVRRROOOOOMMMM
4

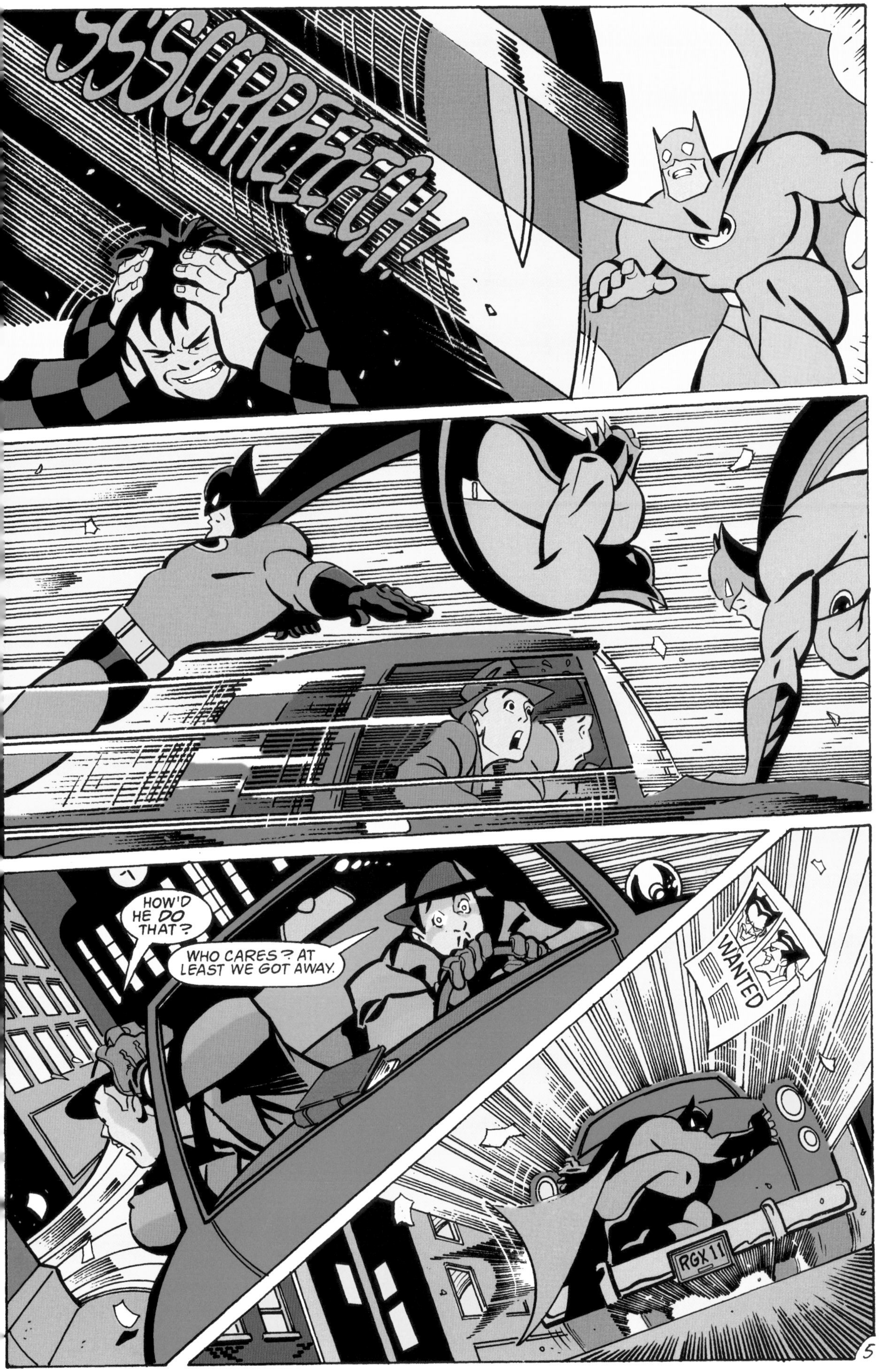
SSSCRREEEECH!
HOW'D HE DO THAT?
WHO CARES? AT LEAST WE GOT AWAY.
WANTED
RGX 11
5

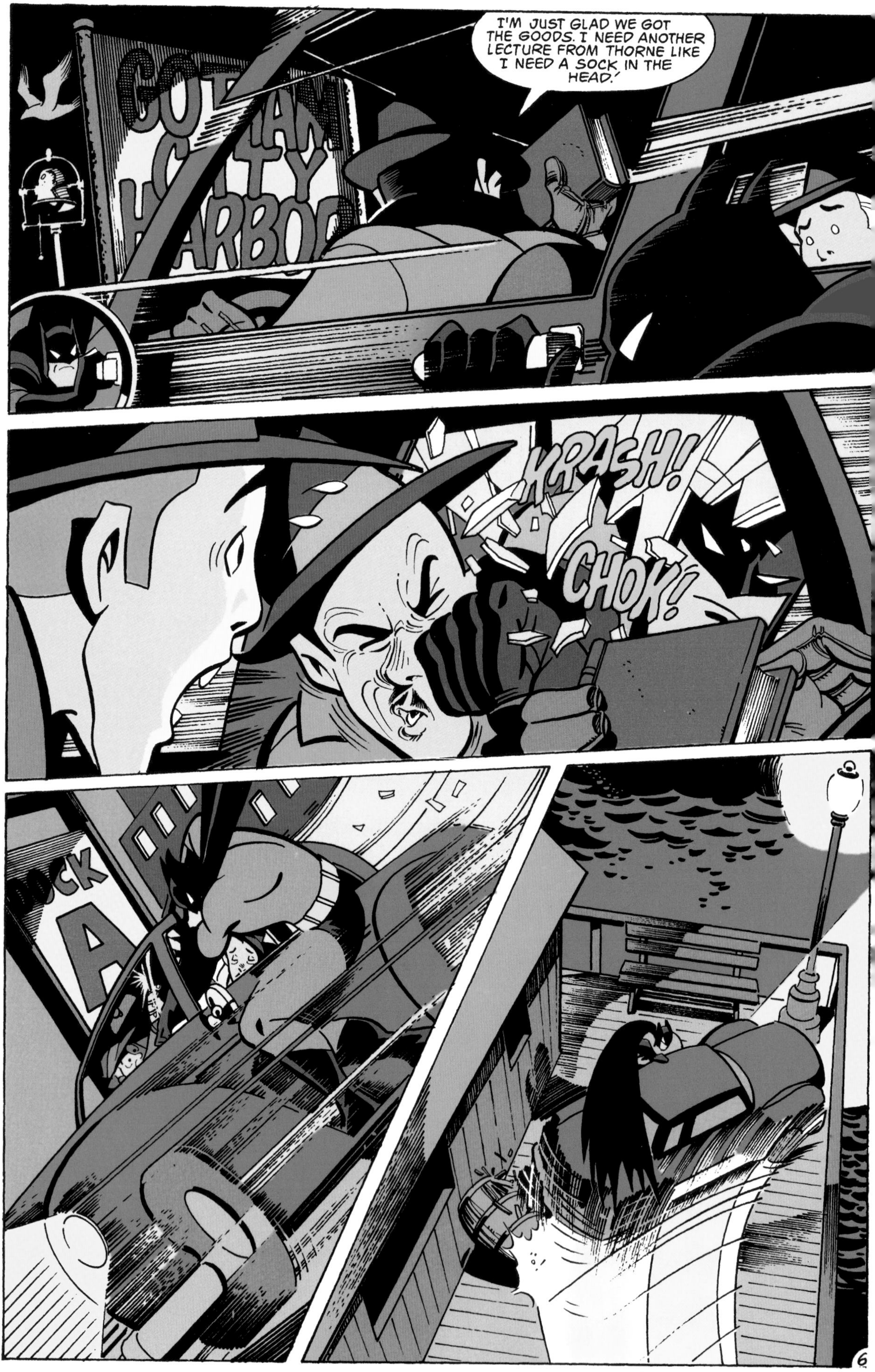

GOTHAM CITY HARBOR
I'M JUST GLAD WE GOT THE GOODS. I NEED ANOTHER LECTURE FROM THORNE LIKE I NEED A SOCK IN THE HEAD.'
KRASH!
CHOK!
DOCK A

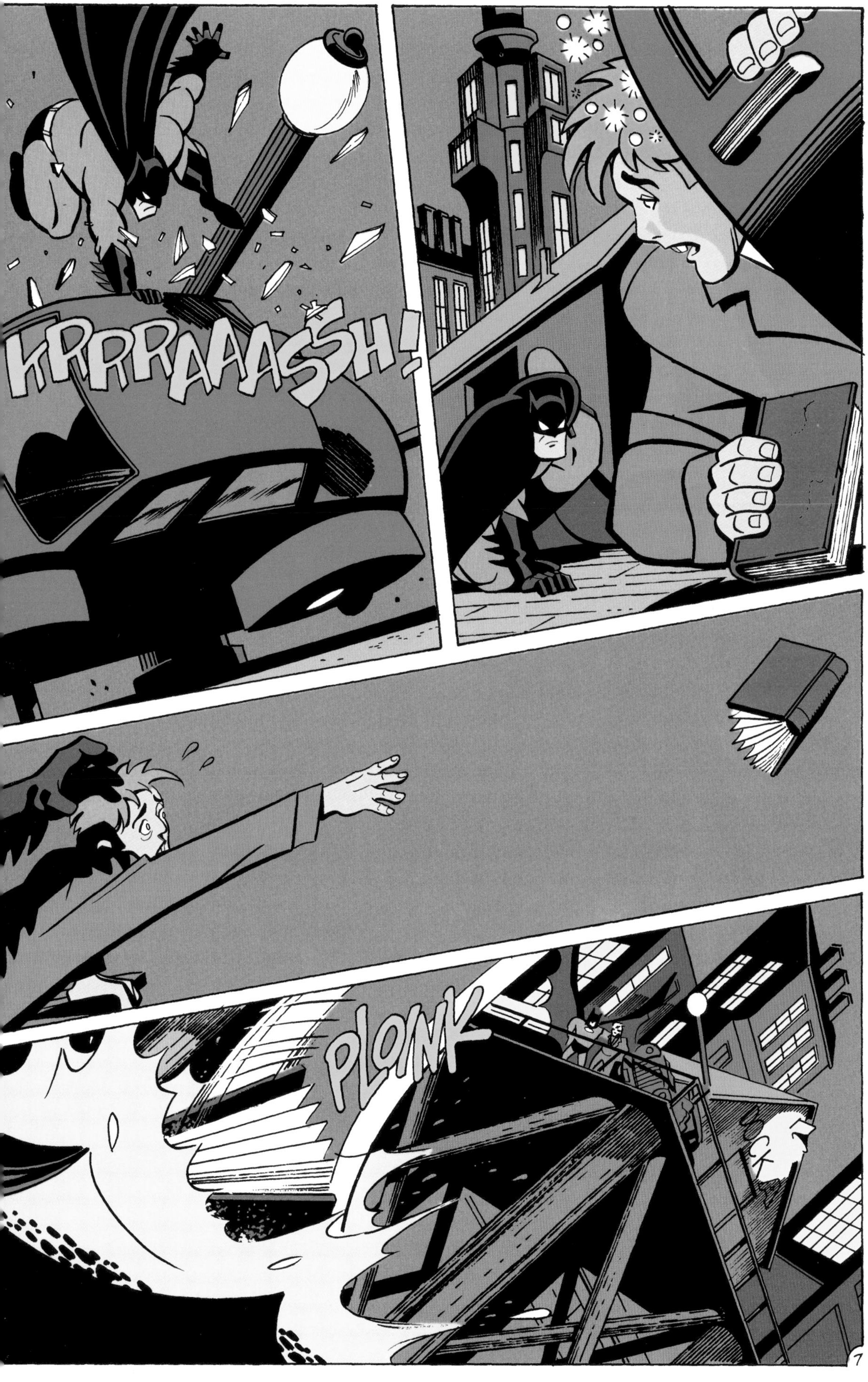
KRRRAAASSH!
PLONK
7

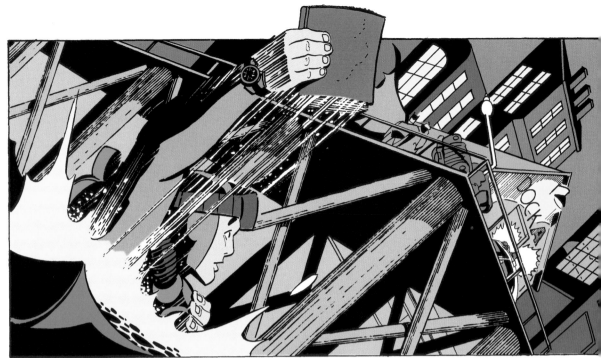

MUSH. NAMES, DATES, ACCOUNT NUMBERS... OUR BEST EVIDENCE AGAINST THORNE IN *YEARS*, AND NOW...

IT'S NOT *FAIR*. I WAS GOING TO *BREAK* THORNE WITH THIS BOOK. WITH *THIS BOOK*, DENT WAS GOING TO WALK INTO COUR TOMORROW AND PUT THORNE *AWAY*.

JIM...

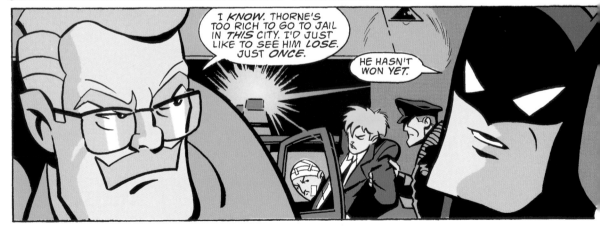

I *KNOW*. THORNE'S TOO RICH TO GO TO JAIL IN *THIS* CITY. I'D JUST LIKE TO SEE HIM *LOSE*. JUST *ONCE*.

HE HASN'T WON *YET*.

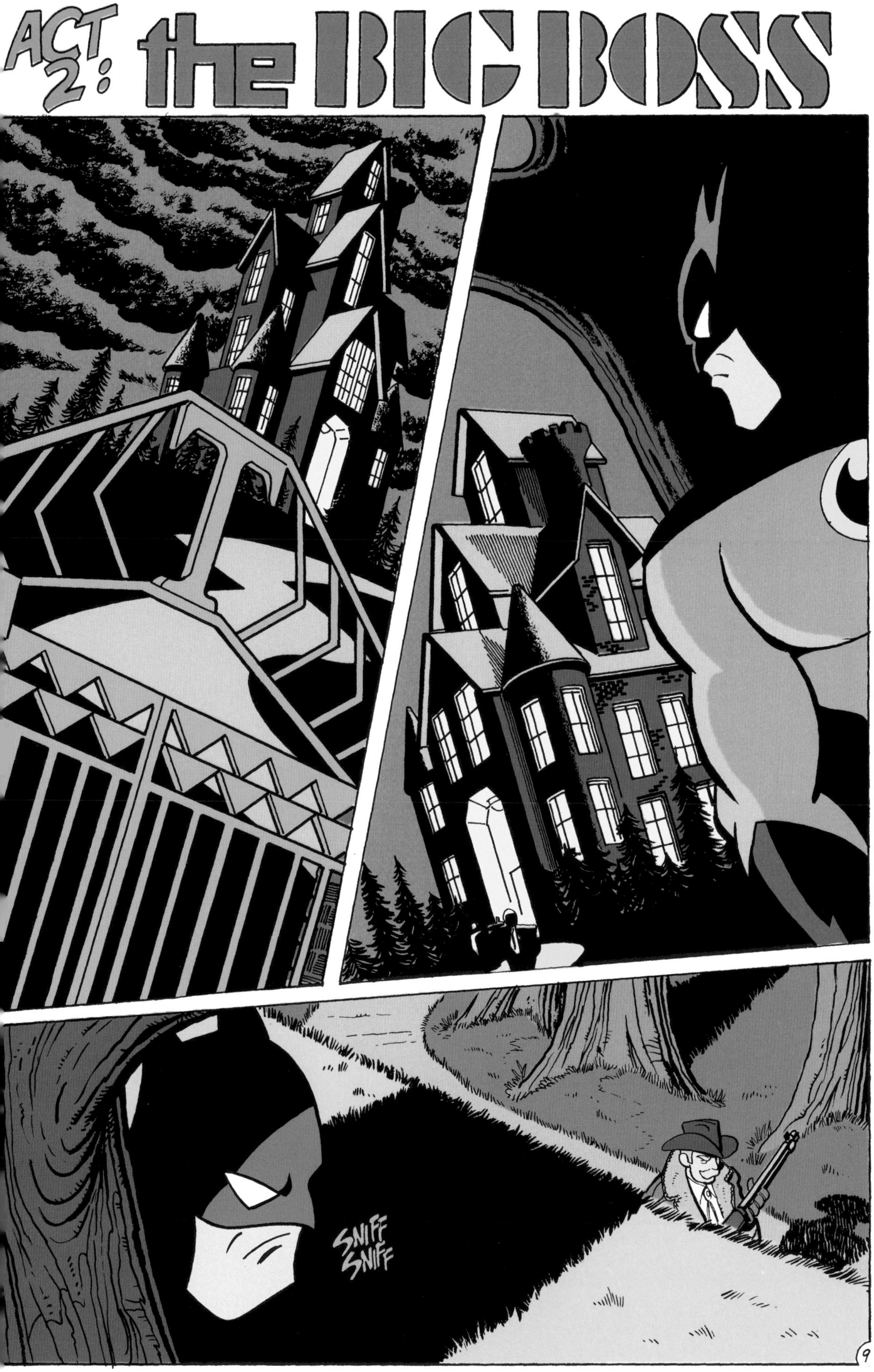
ACT 2: the BIG BOSS
SNIFF SNIFF
9

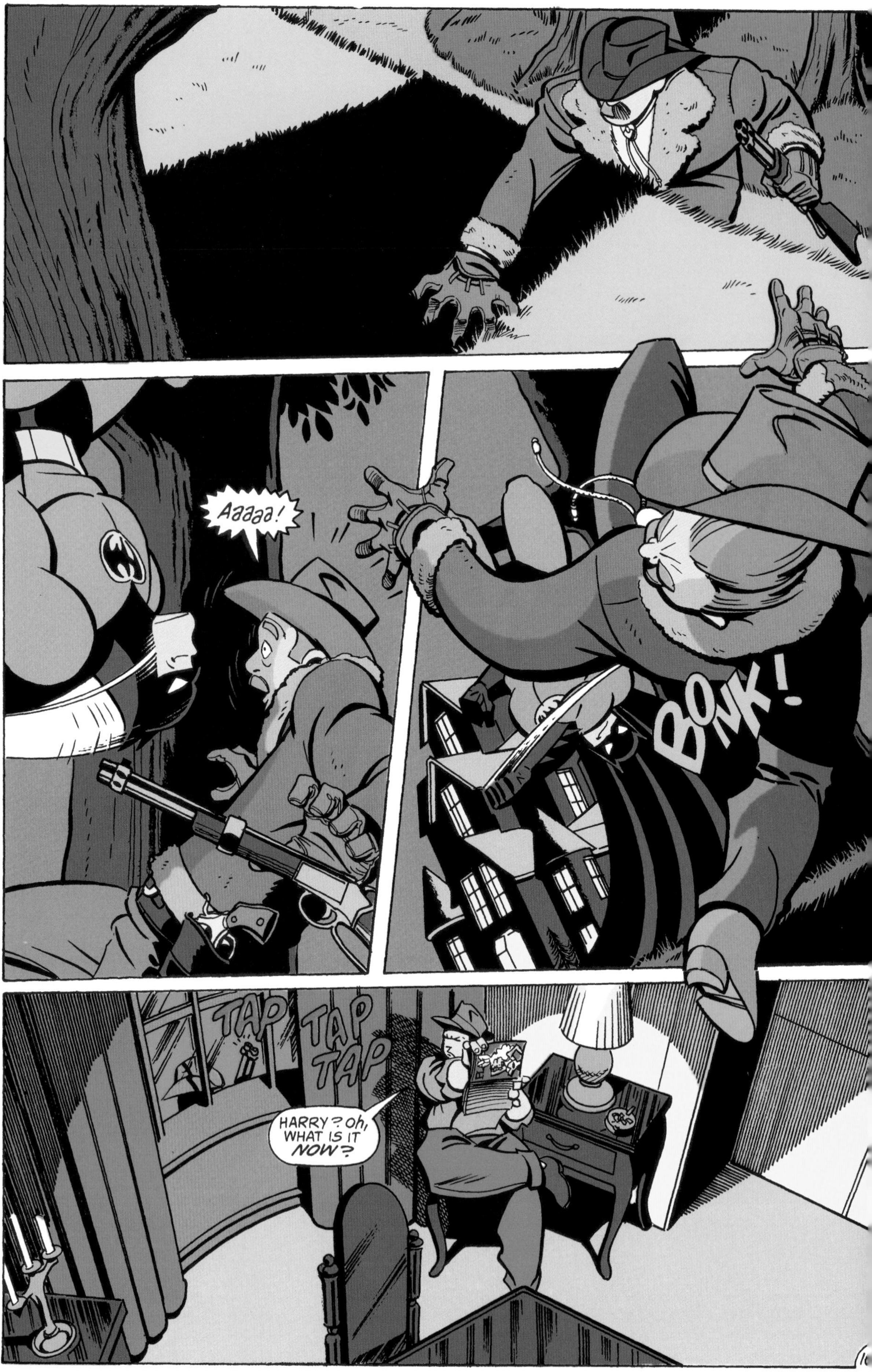
Aaaaa!
BONK!
TAP
TAP TAP
HARRY? oh, WHAT IS IT NOW?

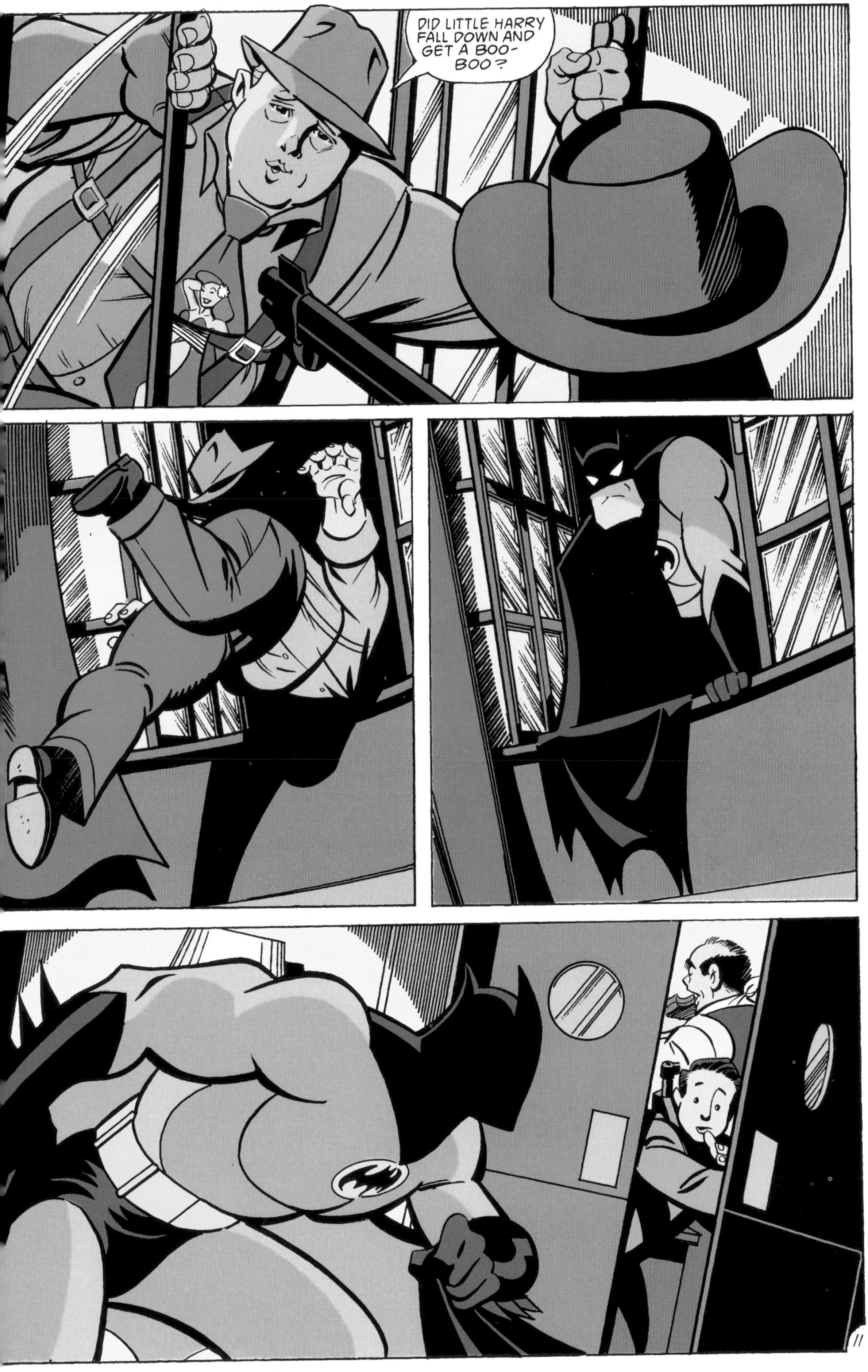
DID LITTLE HARRY FALL DOWN AND GET A BOO-BOO?
11

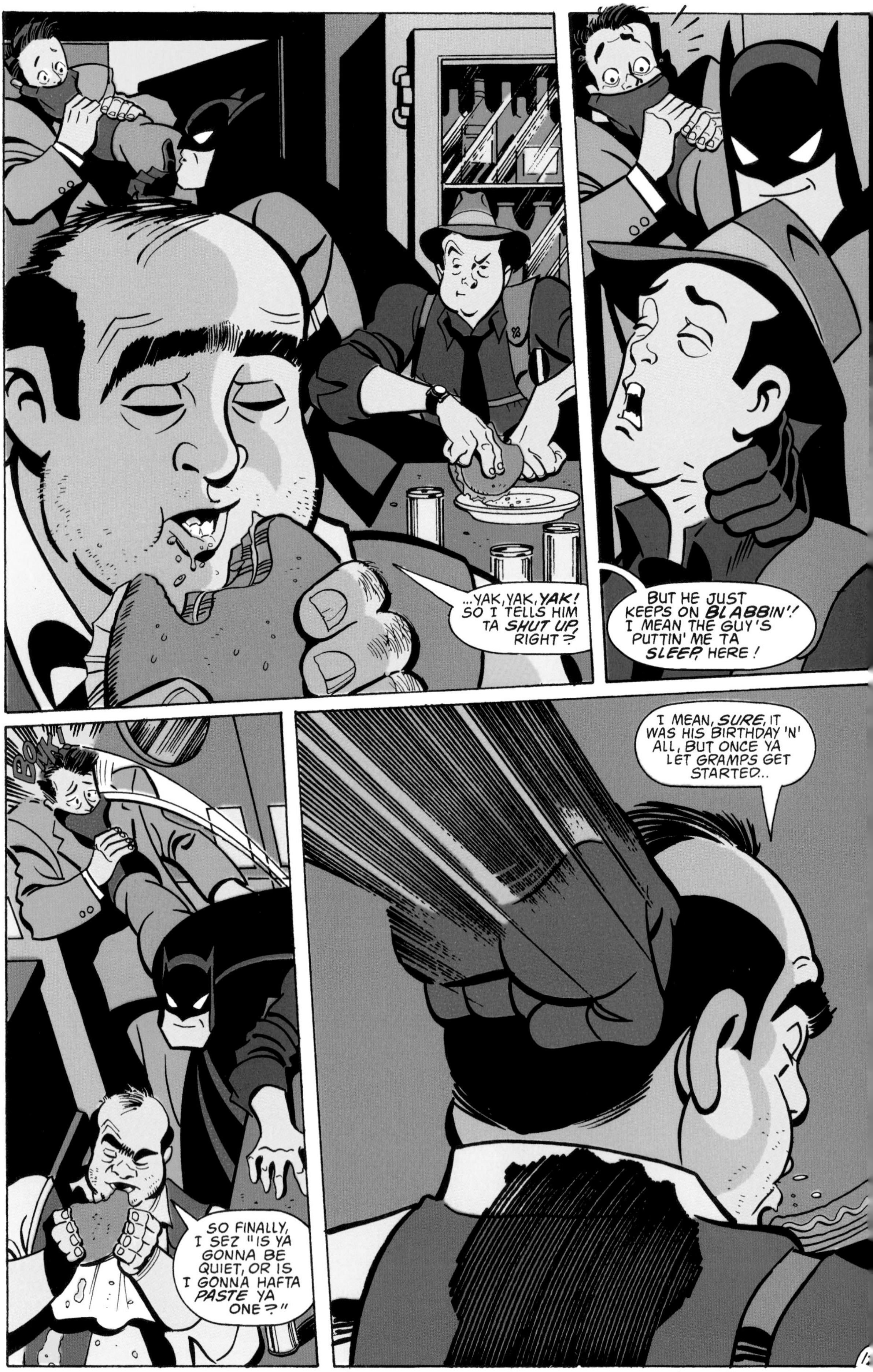
...YAK, YAK, YAK! SO I TELLS HIM TA SHUT UP, RIGHT?
BUT HE JUST KEEPS ON BLABBIN'! I MEAN THE GUY'S PUTTIN' ME TA SLEEP, HERE!
BOK!
SO FINALLY, I SEZ "IS YA GONNA BE QUIET, OR IS I GONNA HAFTA PASTE YA ONE?"
I MEAN, SURE, IT WAS HIS BIRTHDAY 'N' ALL, BUT ONCE YA LET GRAMPS GET STARTED...

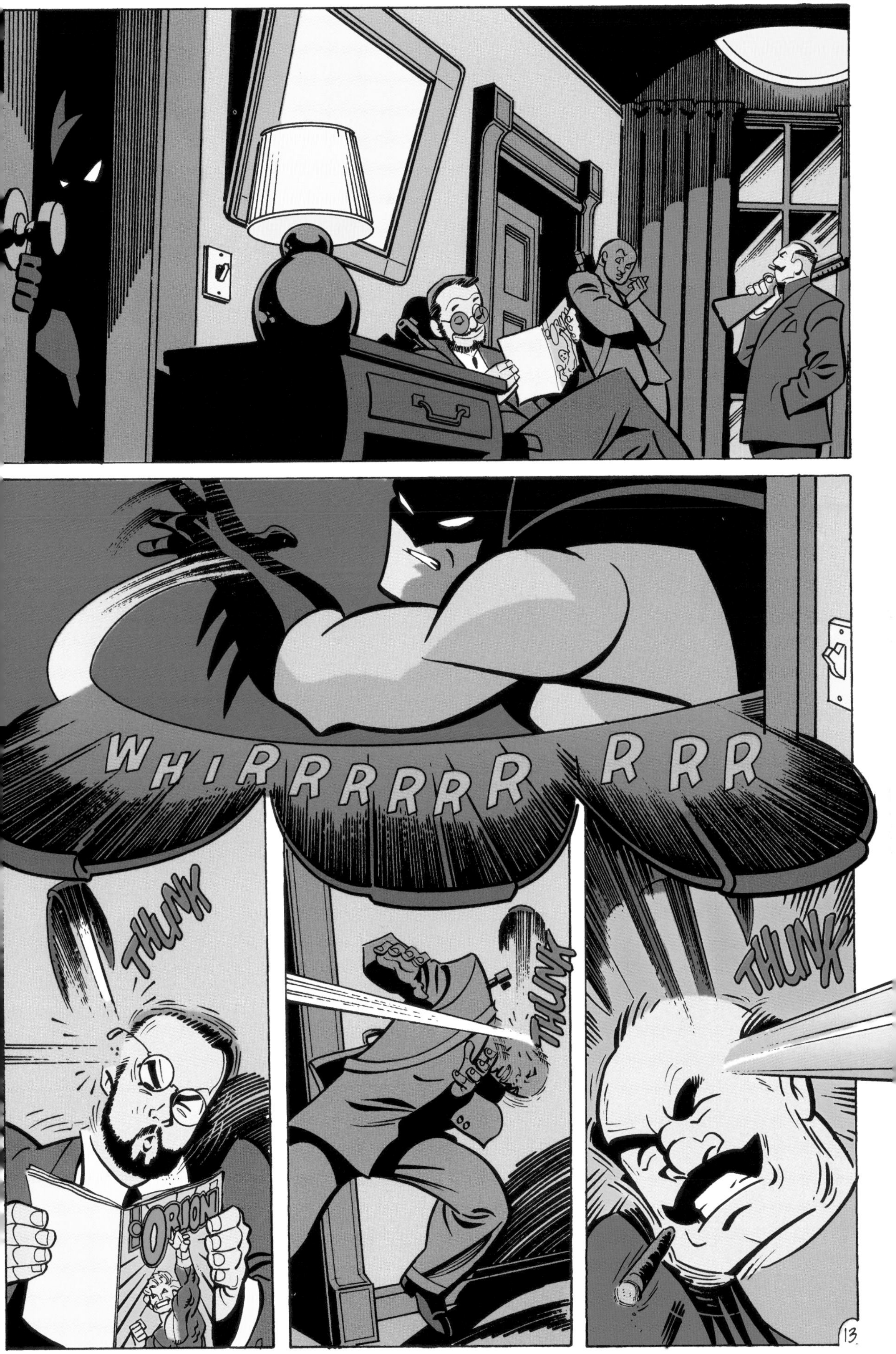
WHIRRRRRR RRR
THUNK
THUNK
THUNK
ORION
13

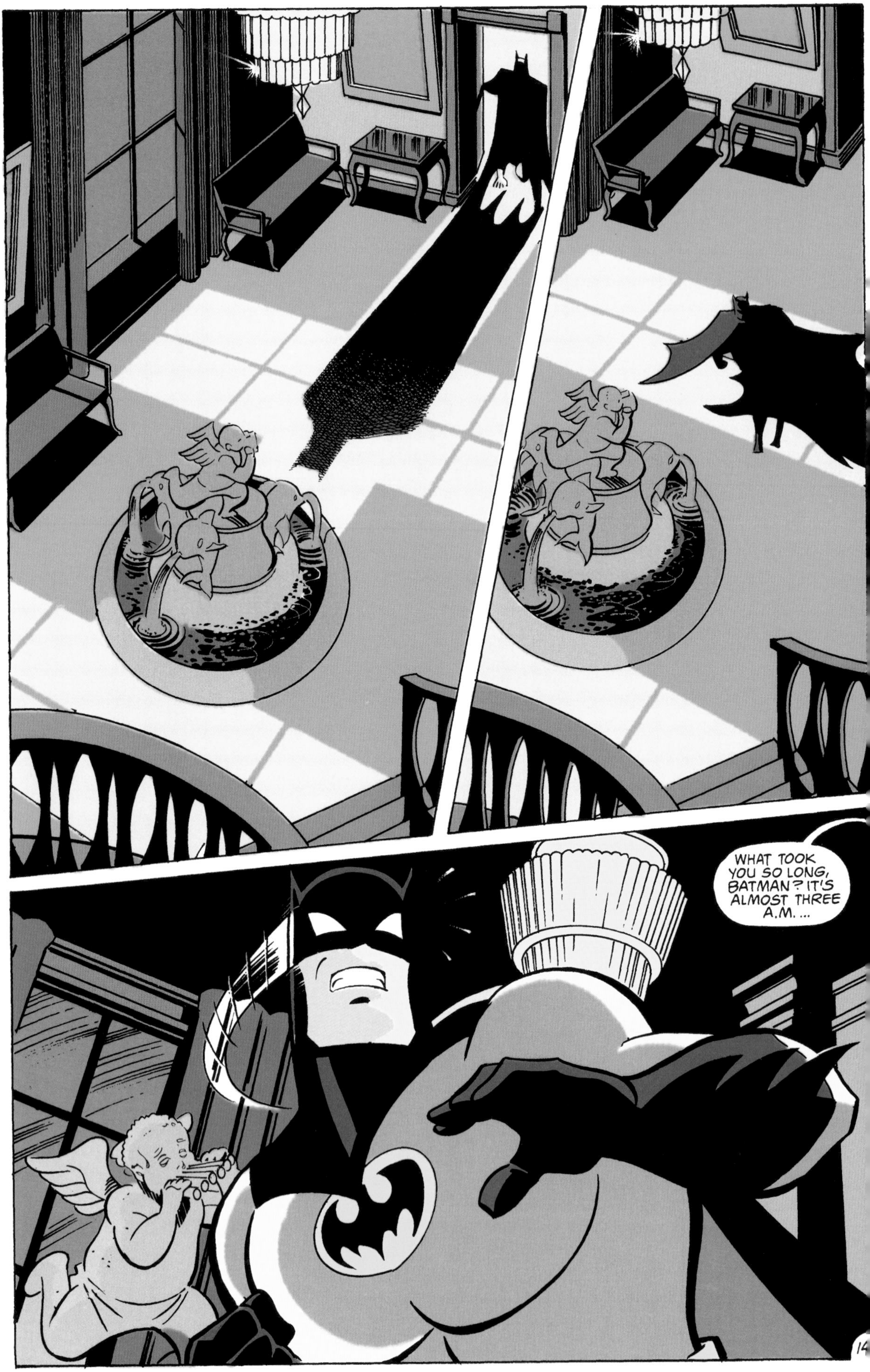
WHAT TOOK YOU SO LONG, BATMAN? IT'S ALMOST THREE A.M. ...
14

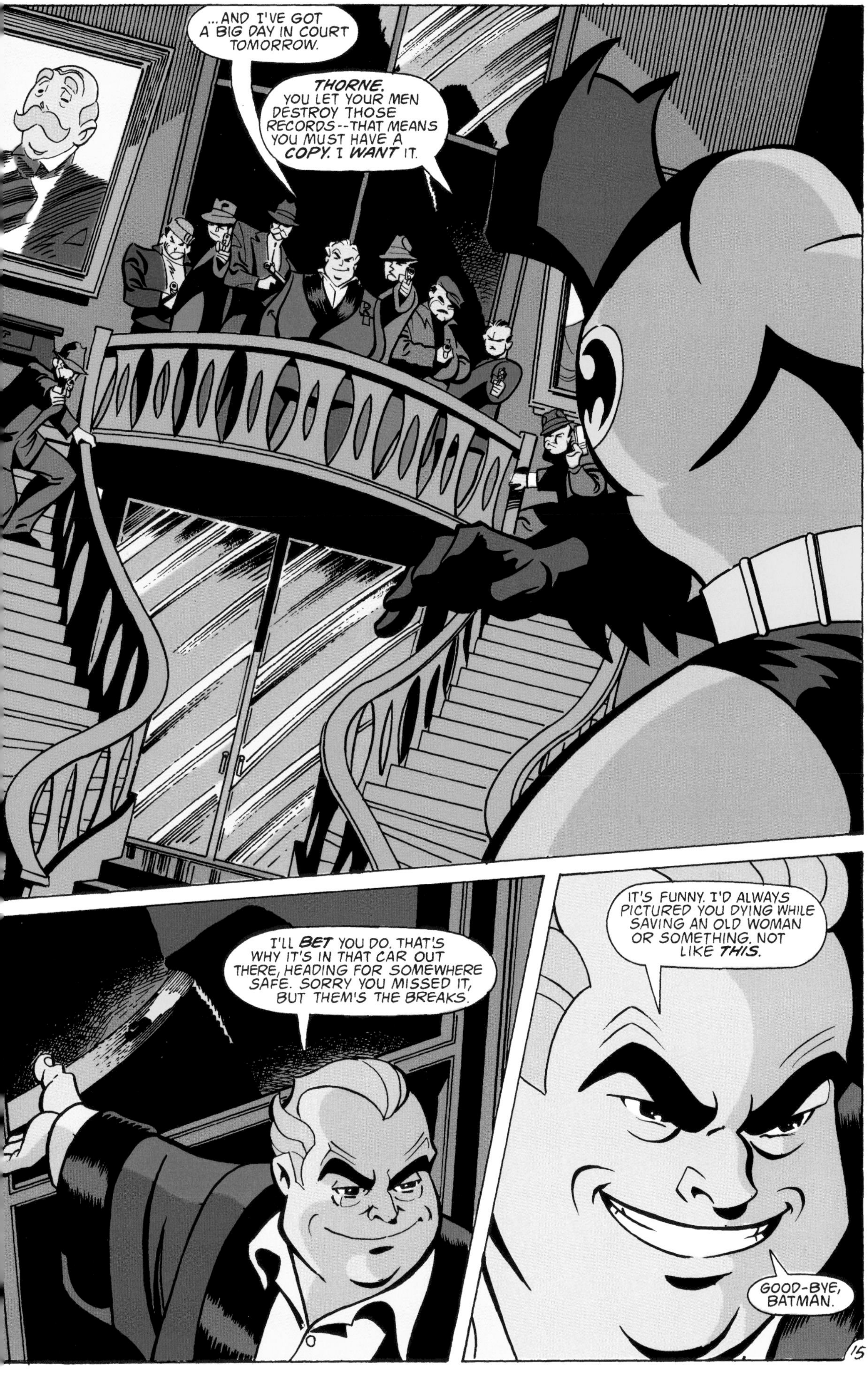

...AND I'VE GOT A BIG DAY IN COURT TOMORROW.
THORNE. YOU LET YOUR MEN DESTROY THOSE RECORDS--THAT MEANS YOU MUST HAVE A COPY. I WANT IT.
I'LL BET YOU DO. THAT'S WHY IT'S IN THAT CAR OUT THERE, HEADING FOR SOMEWHERE SAFE. SORRY YOU MISSED IT, BUT THEM'S THE BREAKS.
IT'S FUNNY. I'D ALWAYS PICTURED YOU DYING WHILE SAVING AN OLD WOMAN OR SOMETHING. NOT LIKE THIS.
GOOD-BYE, BATMAN.
15

ACT 3: RUPERT'S RECKONING!

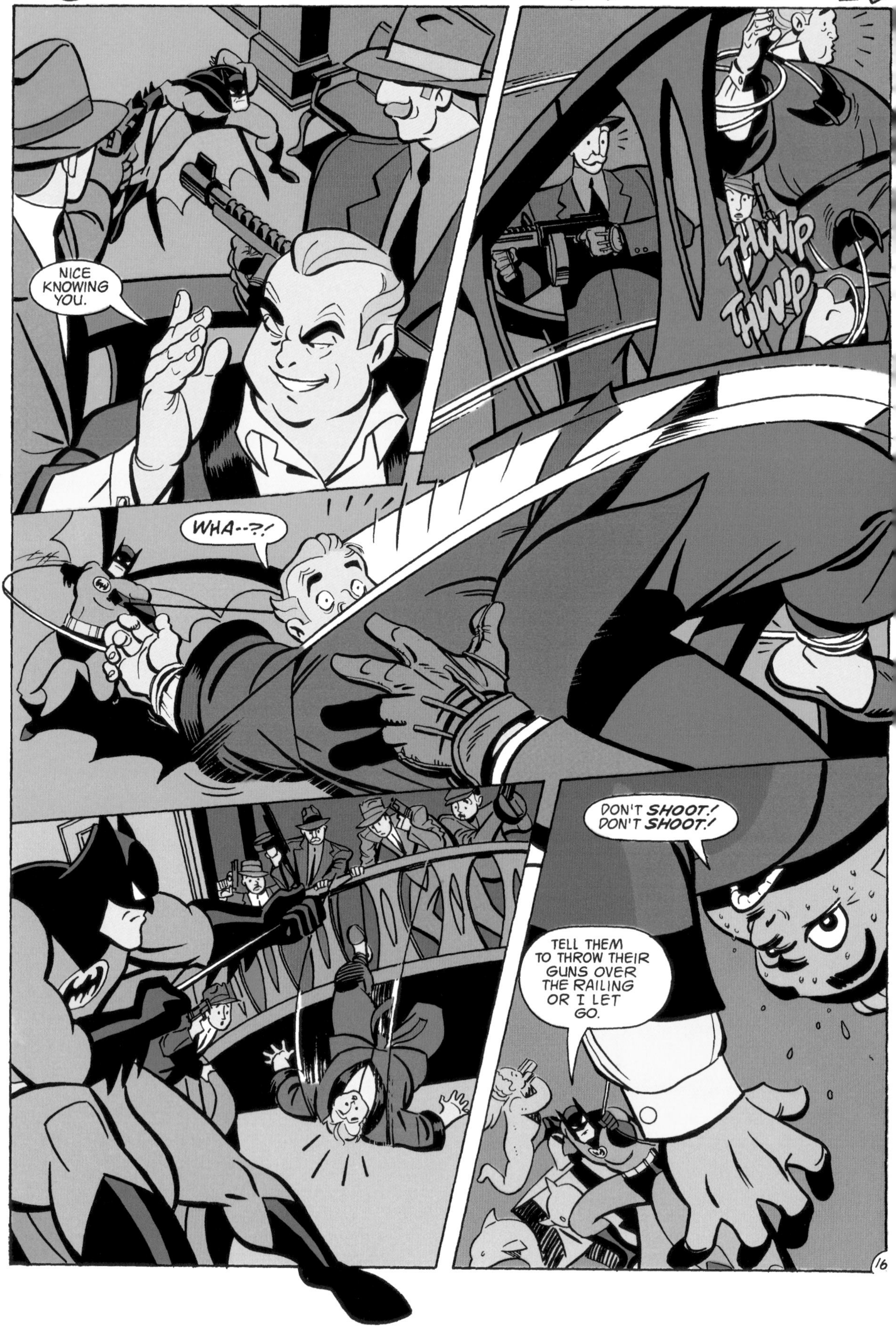

NICE KNOWING YOU.
THWIP
THWIP
WHA--?!
DON'T SHOOT! DON'T SHOOT!
TELL THEM TO THROW THEIR GUNS OVER THE RAILING OR I LET GO.
16

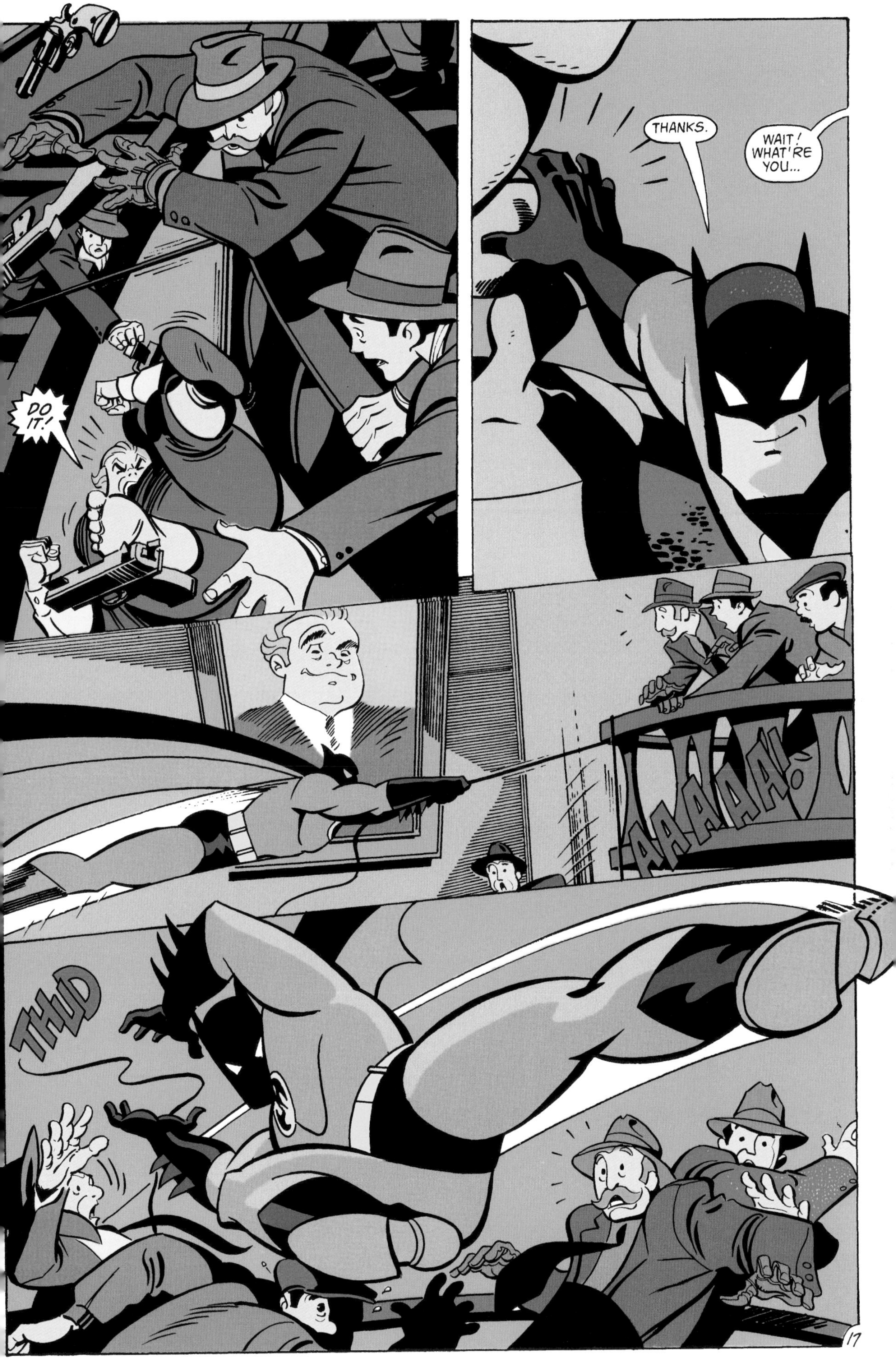
DO IT!
THANKS.
WAIT! WHAT'RE YOU...
AAAAAA!
THUD
17

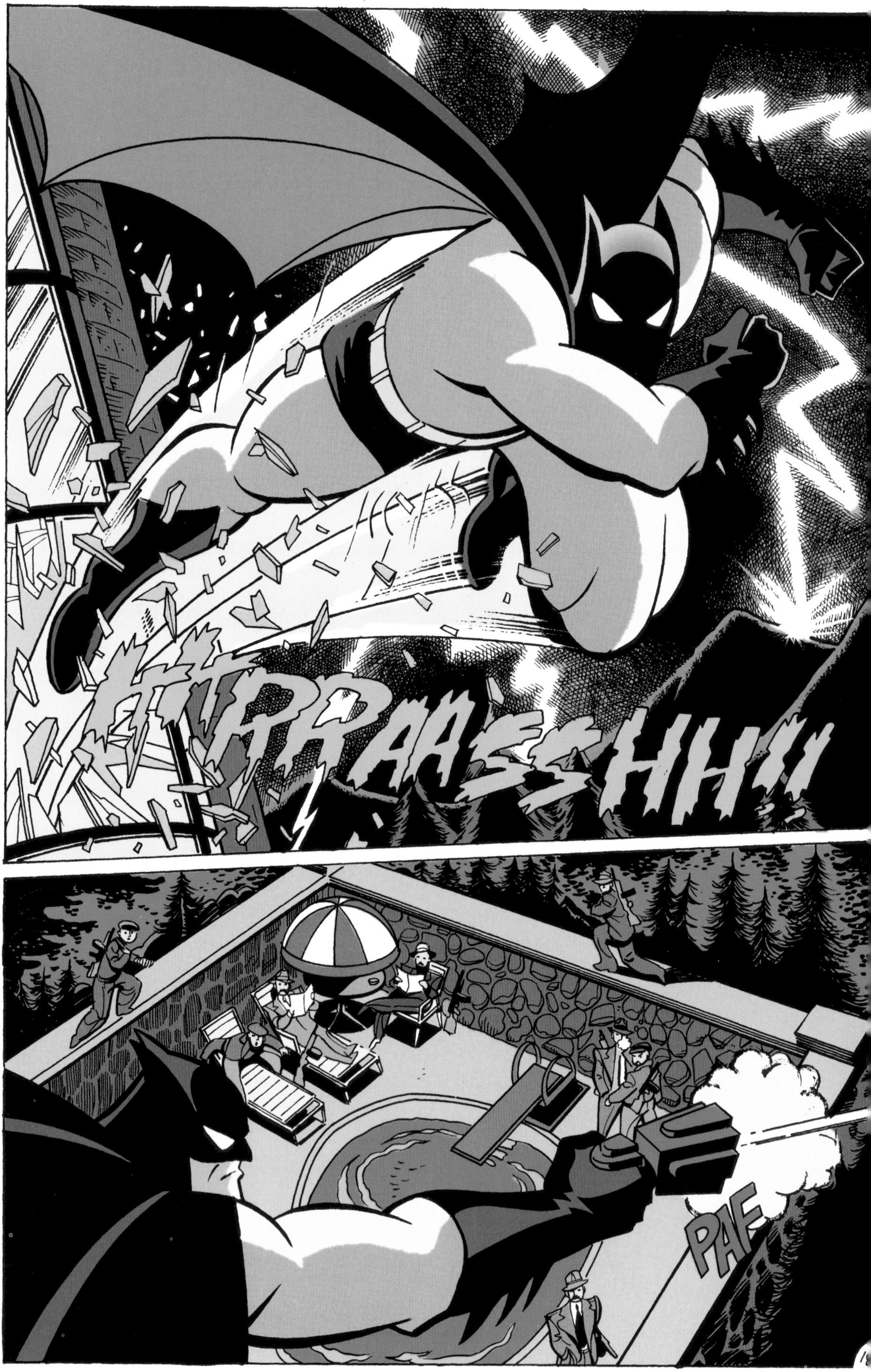
KRRAASSHH!!
PAF

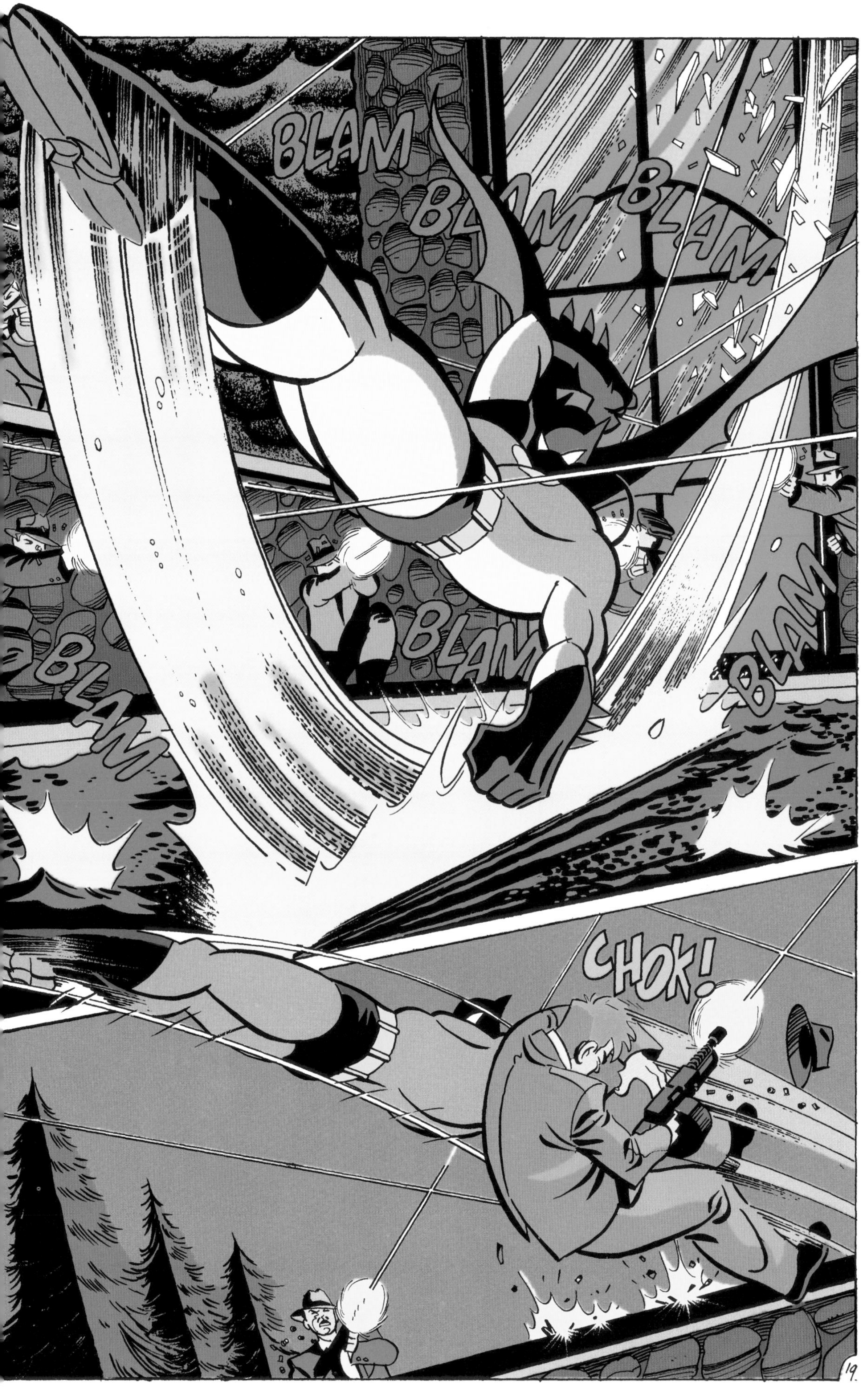
BLAM
BLAM
BLAM
BLAM
BLAM
BLAM
CHOK!
19

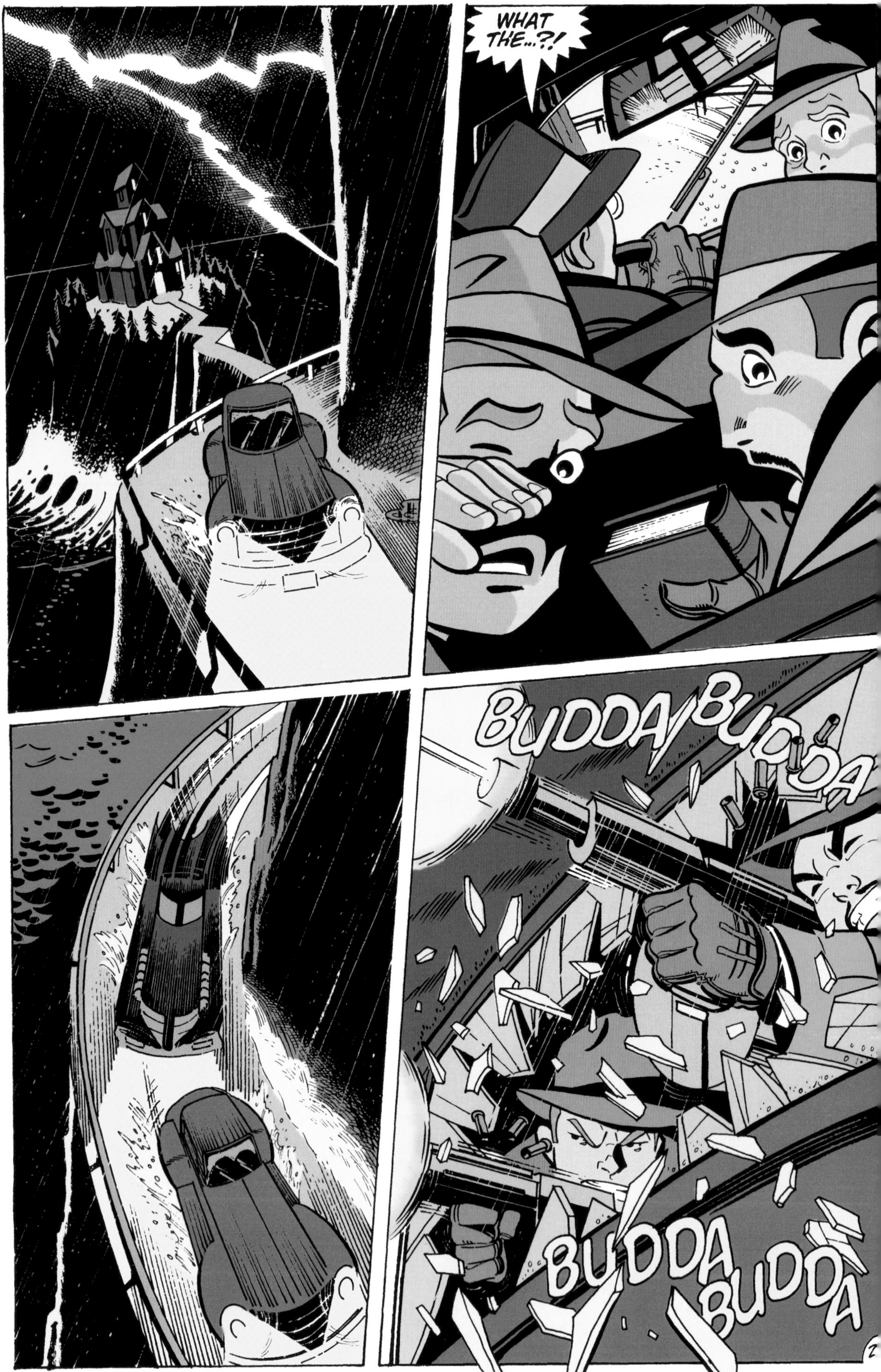
WHAT THE...?!
BUDDA BUDDA
BUDDA BUDDA

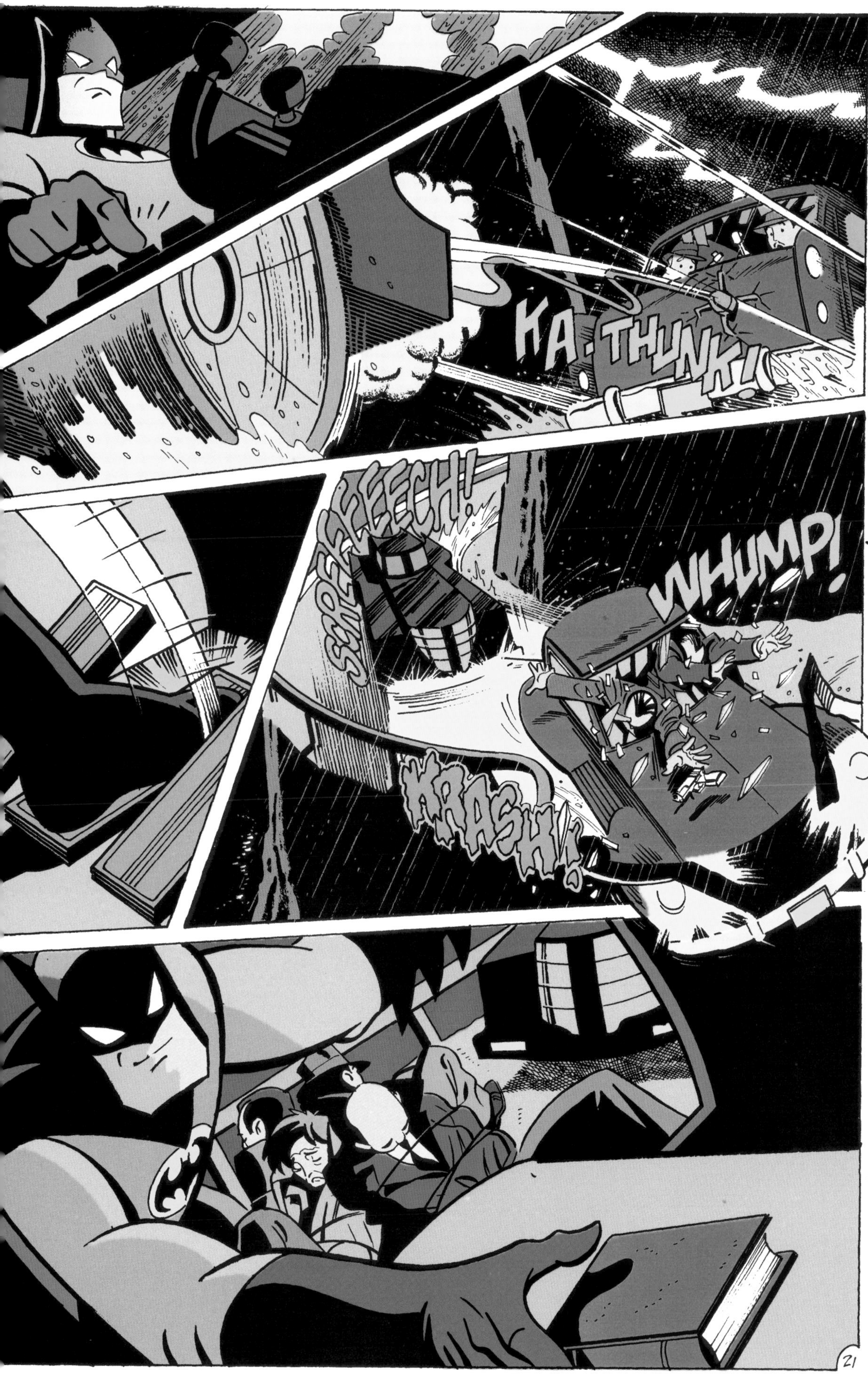
KA-THUNK!
SCREEEEECH!
WHUMP!
KRASH!!
21

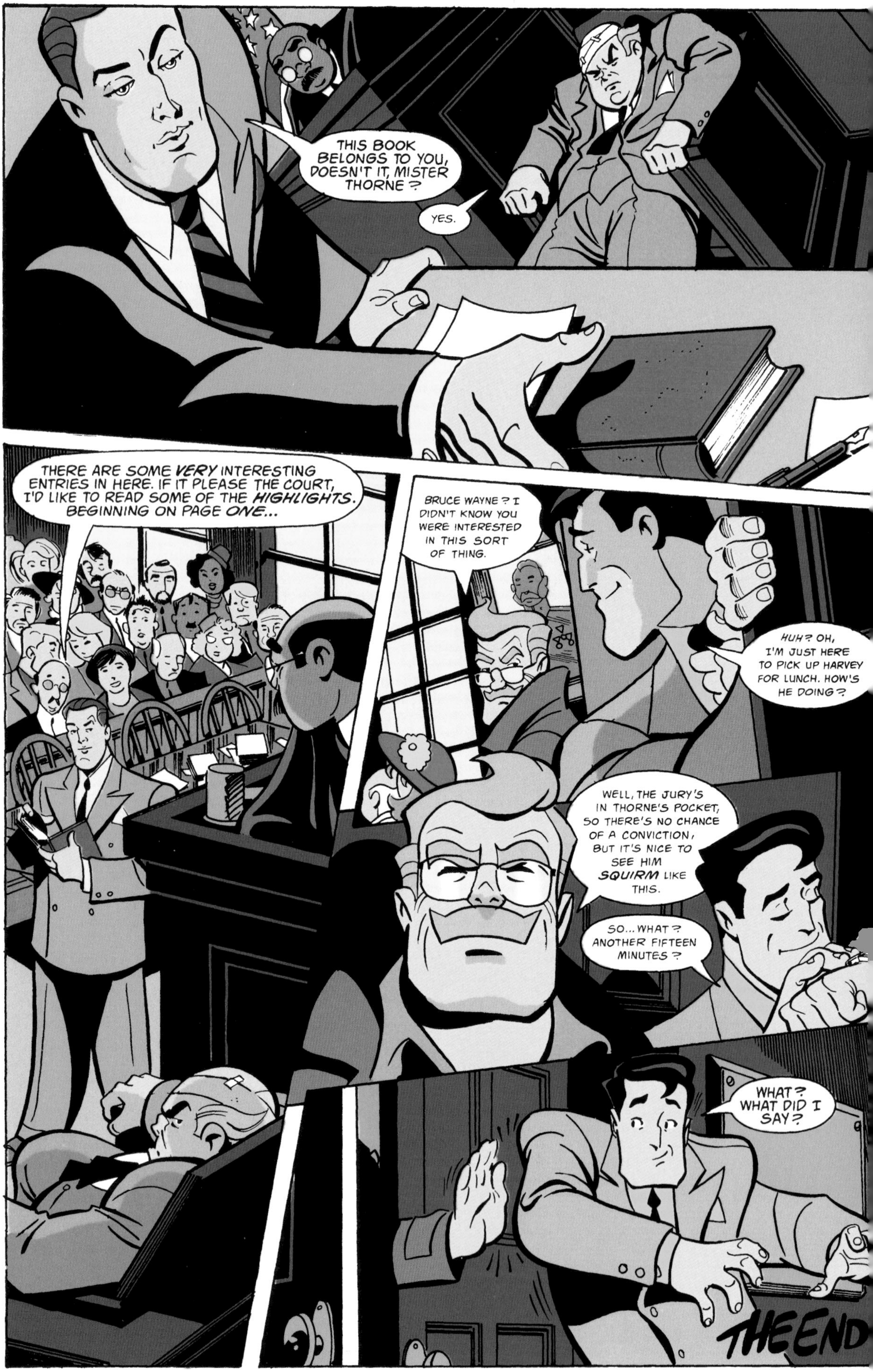
THIS BOOK BELONGS TO YOU, DOESN'T IT, MISTER THORNE?
YES.
THERE ARE SOME VERY INTERESTING ENTRIES IN HERE. IF IT PLEASE THE COURT, I'D LIKE TO READ SOME OF THE HIGHLIGHTS. BEGINNING ON PAGE ONE...
BRUCE WAYNE? I DIDN'T KNOW YOU WERE INTERESTED IN THIS SORT OF THING.
HUH? OH, I'M JUST HERE TO PICK UP HARVEY FOR LUNCH. HOW'S HE DOING?
WELL, THE JURY'S IN THORNE'S POCKET, SO THERE'S NO CHANCE OF A CONVICTION, BUT IT'S NICE TO SEE HIM SQUIRM LIKE THIS.
SO... WHAT? ANOTHER FIFTEEN MINUTES?
WHAT? WHAT DID I SAY?
THE END

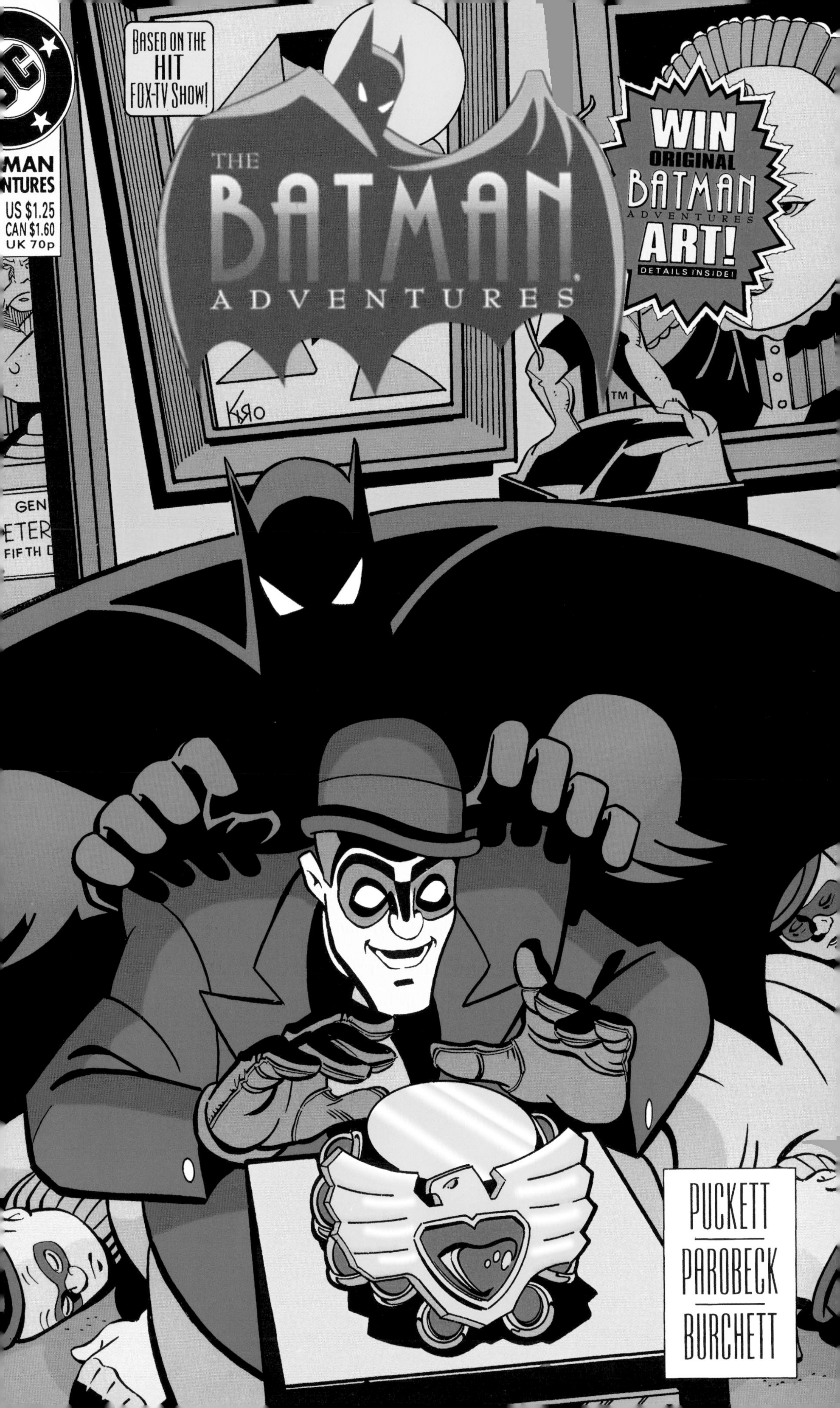

DC
MAN
NTURES
US $1.25
CAN $1.60
UK 70p
BASED ON THE HIT FOX-TV SHOW!
THE BATMAN ADVENTURES
WIN ORIGINAL BATMAN ADVENTURES ART!
DETAILS INSIDE!
GEN
ETER
FIFTH D
PUCKETT
PAROBECK
BURCHETT

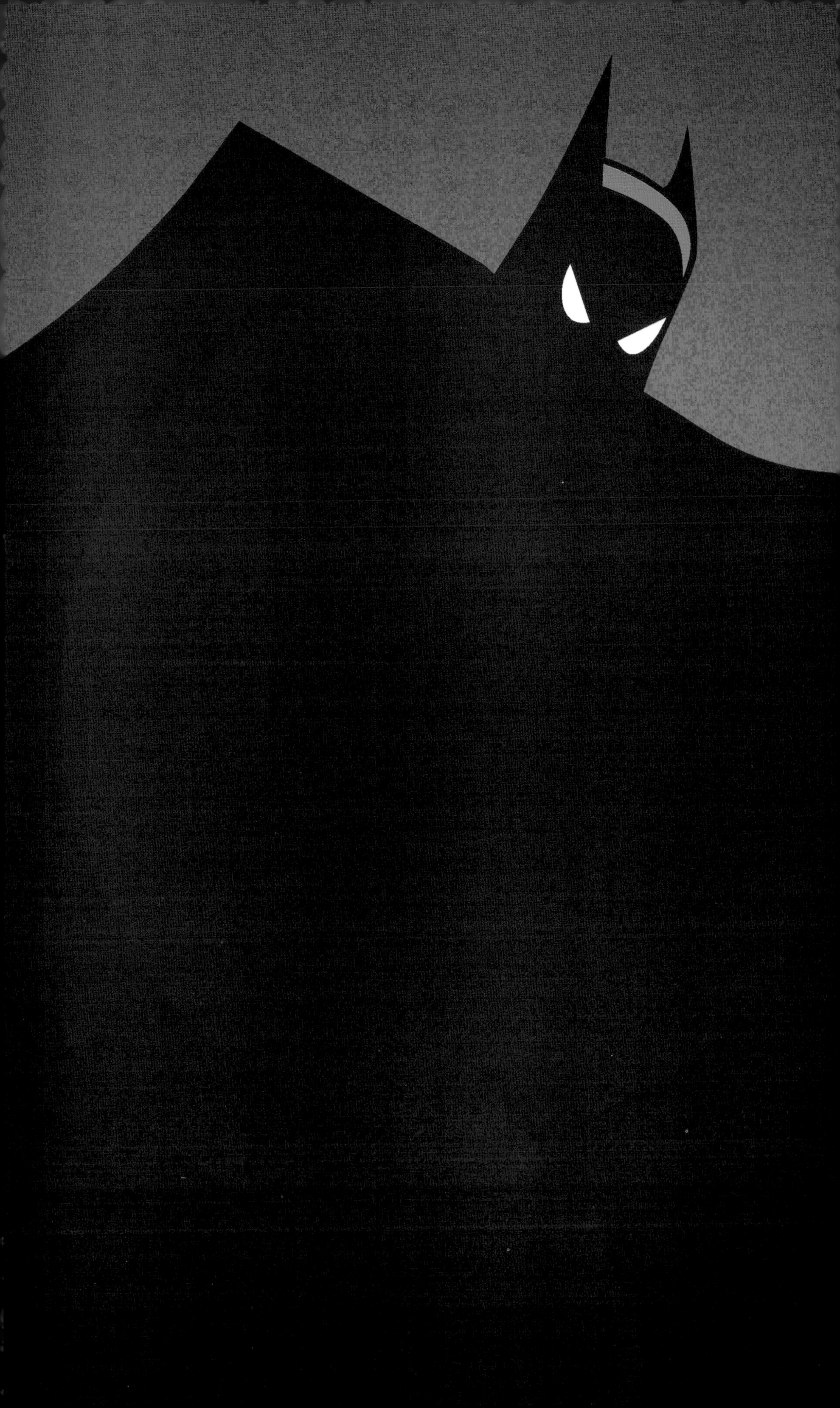

THE LAST RIDDLER STORY

ACT 1: NYGMA'S NADIR!

KELLEY PUCKETT	WRITER
MIKE PAROBECK	PENCILLER
RICK BURCHETT	INKER
RICK TAYLOR	COLORIST
TIM HARKINS	LETTERER
SCOTT PETERSON	EDITOR

BATMAN CREATED BY BOB KANE

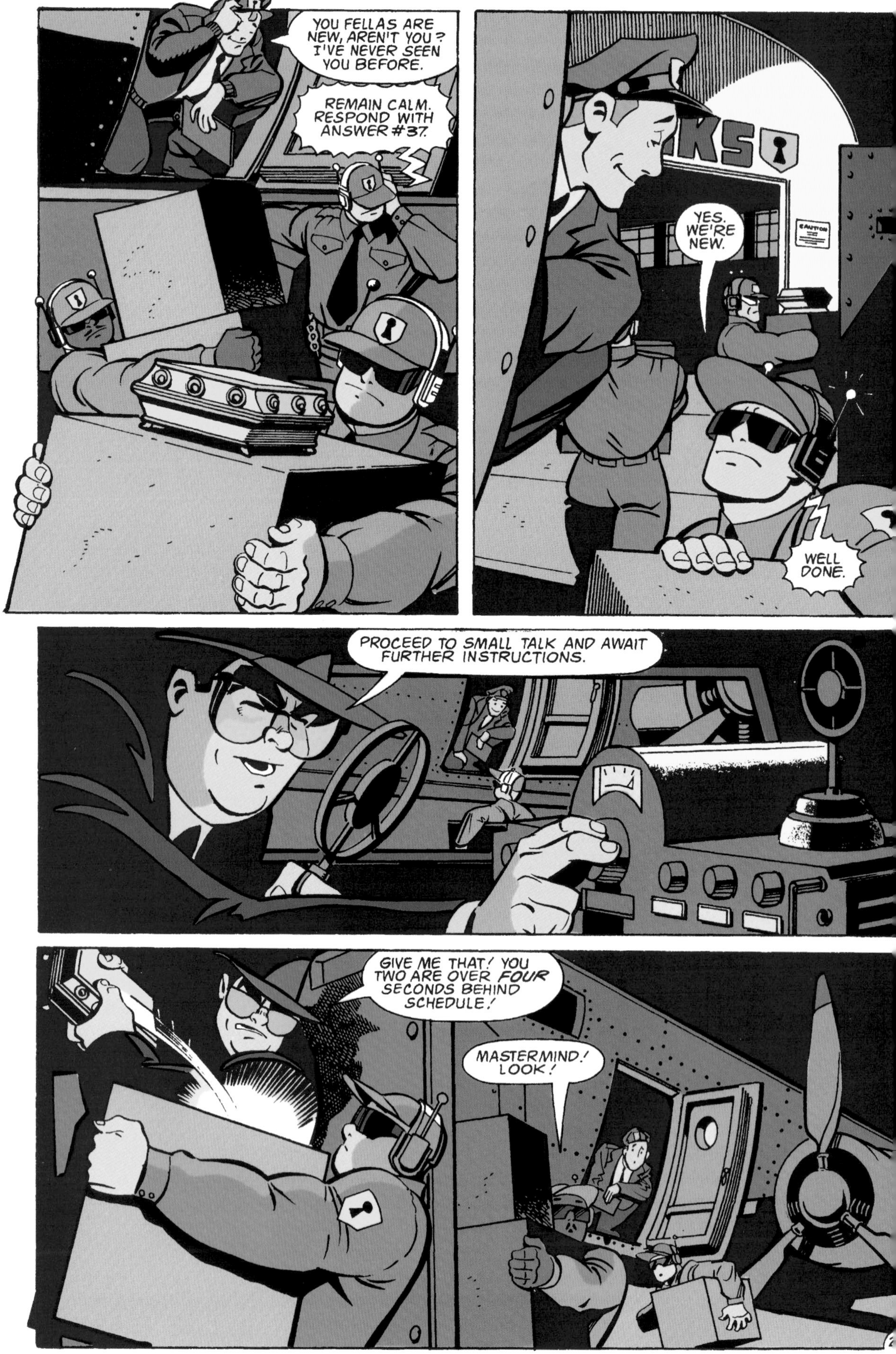
YOU FELLAS ARE NEW, AREN'T YOU? I'VE NEVER SEEN YOU BEFORE.
REMAIN CALM. RESPOND WITH ANSWER #37.
YES. WE'RE NEW.
WELL DONE.
PROCEED TO SMALL TALK AND AWAIT FURTHER INSTRUCTIONS.
GIVE ME THAT! YOU TWO ARE OVER *FOUR* SECONDS BEHIND SCHEDULE!
MASTERMIND! LOOK!

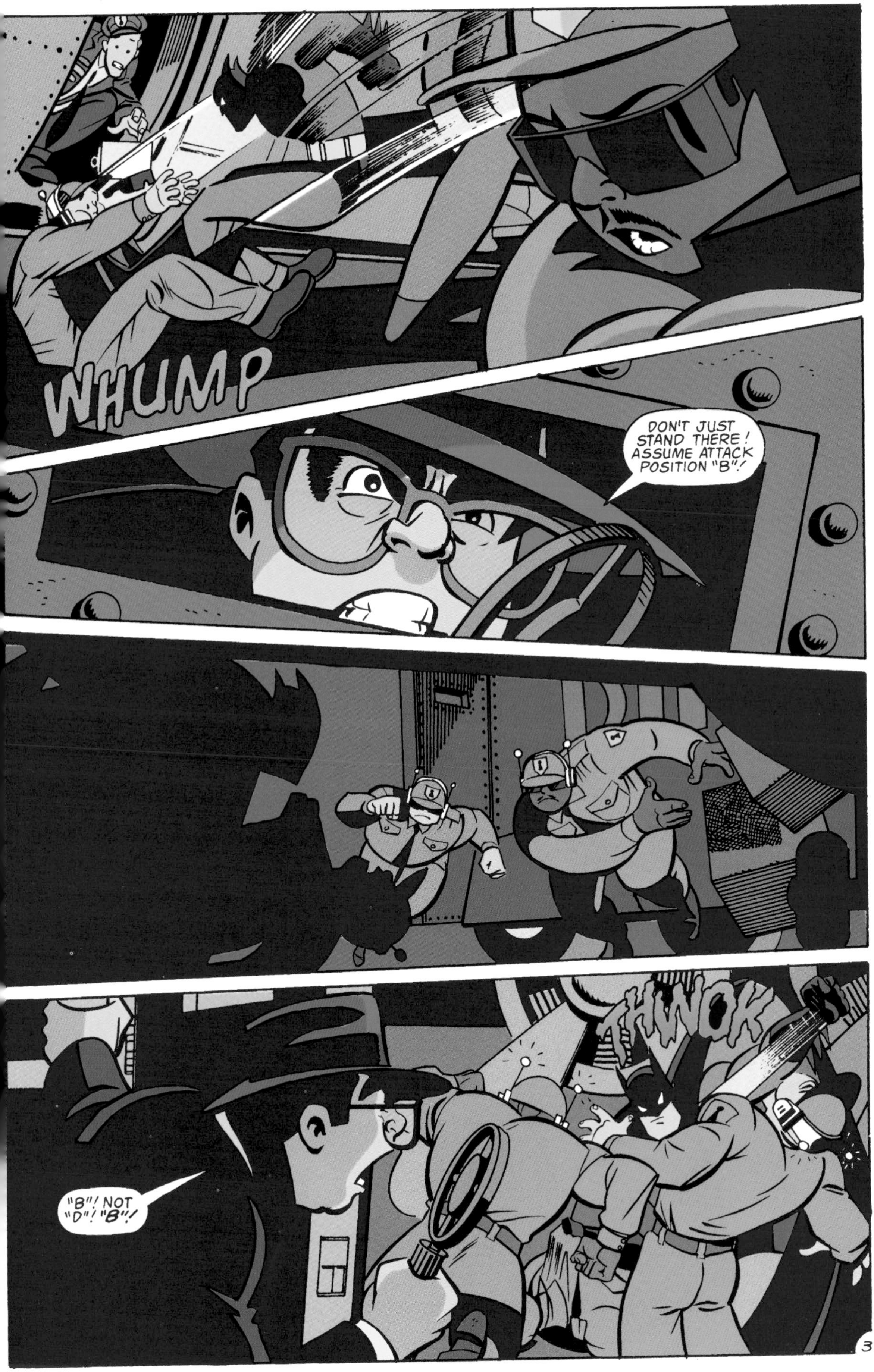

WHUMP
DON'T JUST STAND THERE! ASSUME ATTACK POSITION "B"!
THWOK
"B"! NOT "D"! "B"!
3

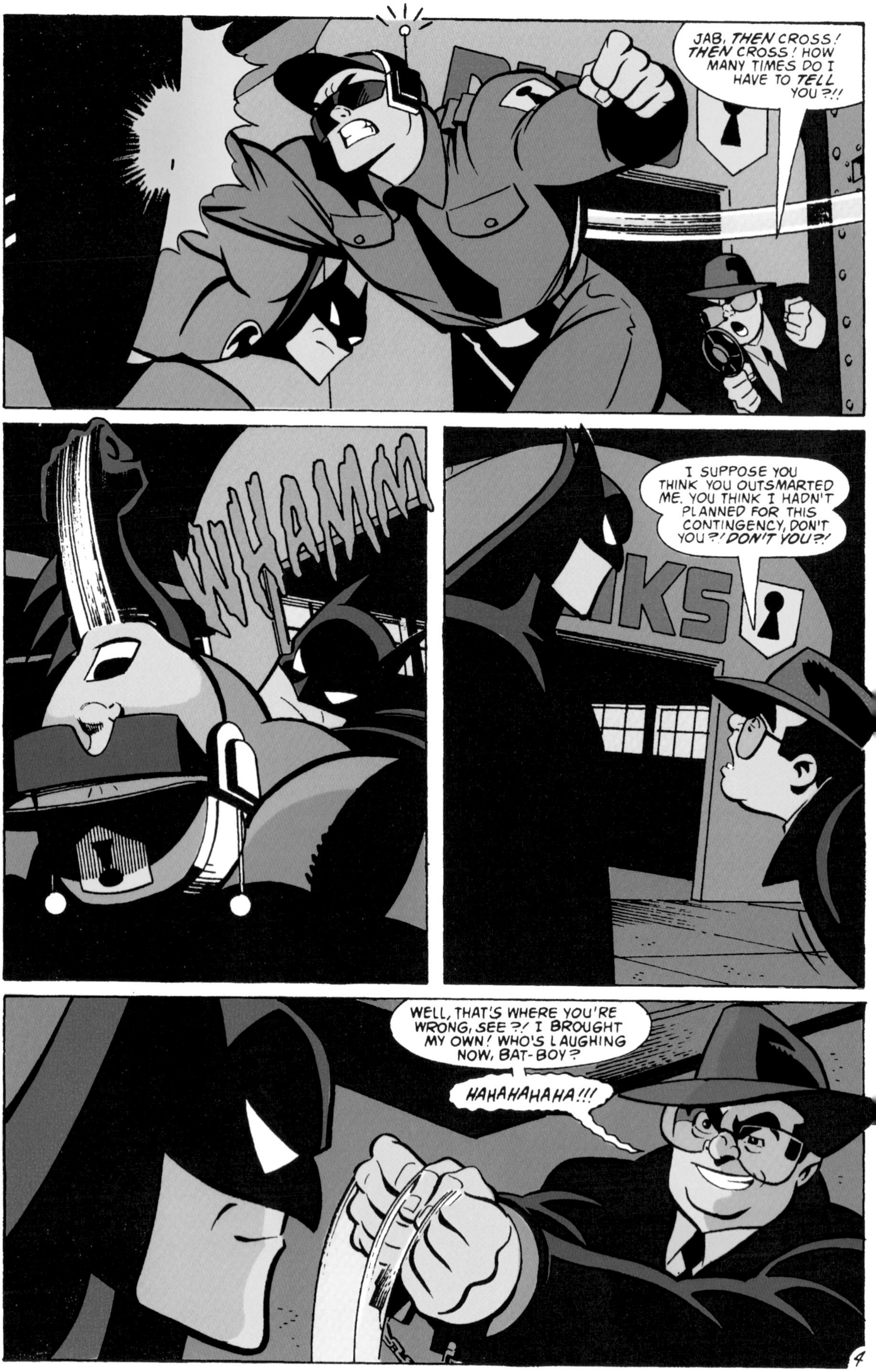

JAB, THEN CROSS! THEN CROSS! HOW MANY TIMES DO I HAVE TO TELL YOU?!!
WHAMM
I SUPPOSE YOU THINK YOU OUTSMARTED ME. YOU THINK I HADN'T PLANNED FOR THIS CONTINGENCY, DON'T YOU?! DON'T YOU?!
WELL, THAT'S WHERE YOU'RE WRONG, SEE?! I BROUGHT MY OWN! WHO'S LAUGHING NOW, BAT-BOY?
HAHAHAHAHA!!!
4

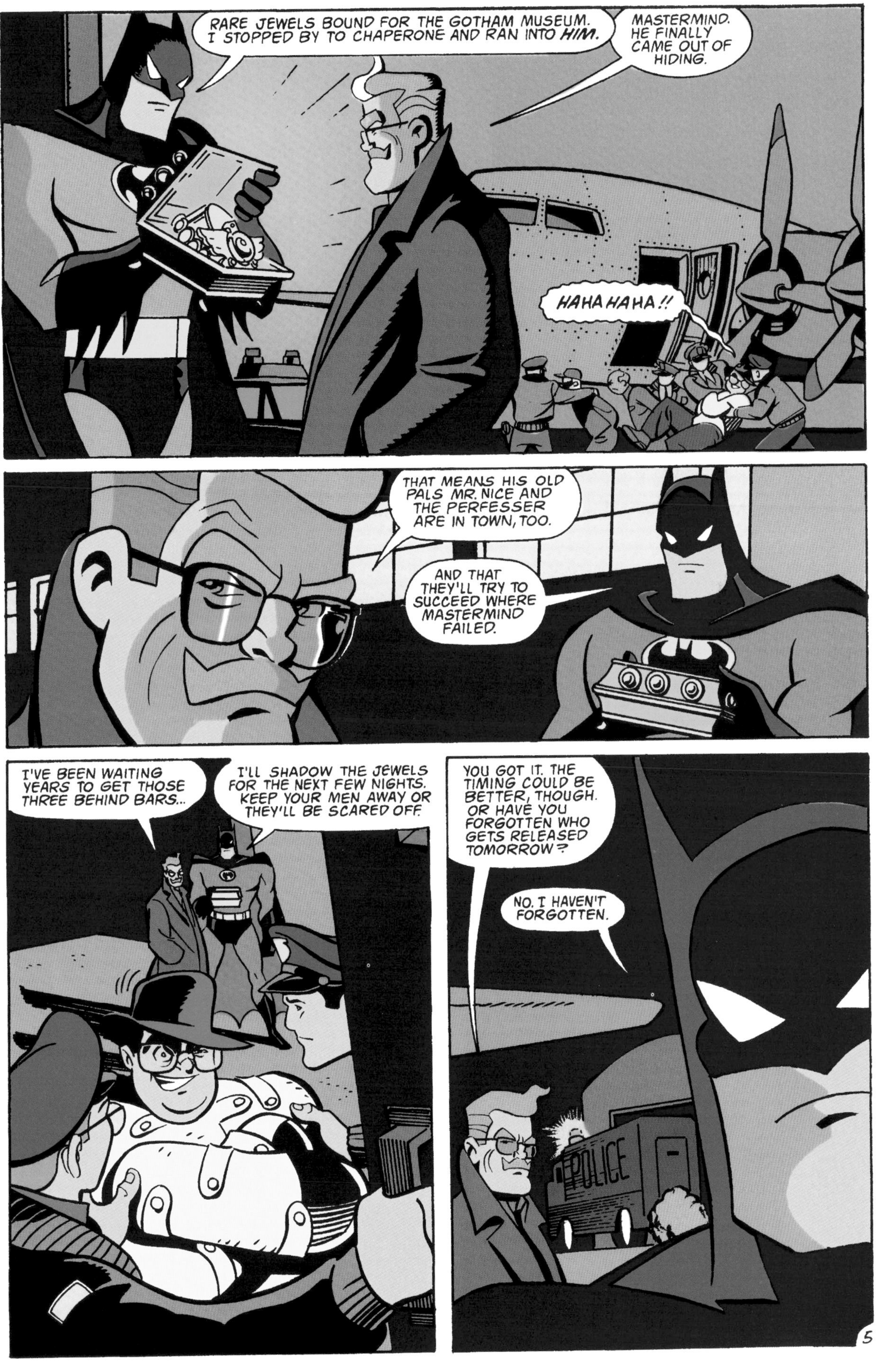
RARE JEWELS BOUND FOR THE GOTHAM MUSEUM. I STOPPED BY TO CHAPERONE AND RAN INTO *HIM.*
MASTERMIND. HE FINALLY CAME OUT OF HIDING.
HAHA HAHA!!
THAT MEANS HIS OLD PALS MR. NICE AND THE PERFESSER ARE IN TOWN, TOO.
AND THAT THEY'LL TRY TO SUCCEED WHERE MASTERMIND FAILED.
I'VE BEEN WAITING YEARS TO GET THOSE THREE BEHIND BARS...
I'LL SHADOW THE JEWELS FOR THE NEXT FEW NIGHTS. KEEP YOUR MEN AWAY OR THEY'LL BE SCARED OFF.
YOU GOT IT. THE TIMING COULD BE BETTER, THOUGH. OR HAVE YOU FORGOTTEN WHO GETS RELEASED TOMORROW?
NO, I HAVEN'T FORGOTTEN.
POLICE
5

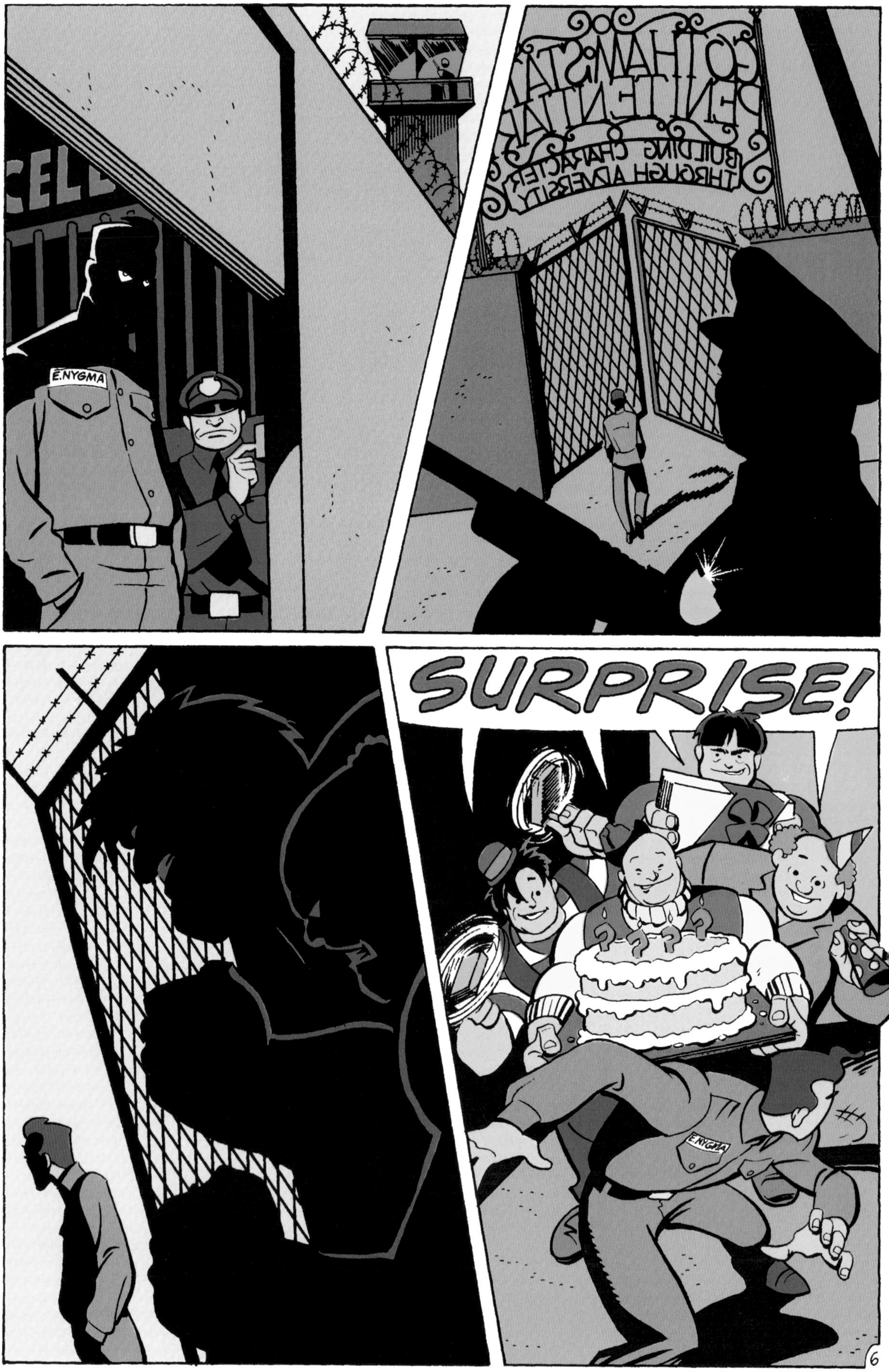
E.NYGMA
SURPRISE!
E.NYGMA
6

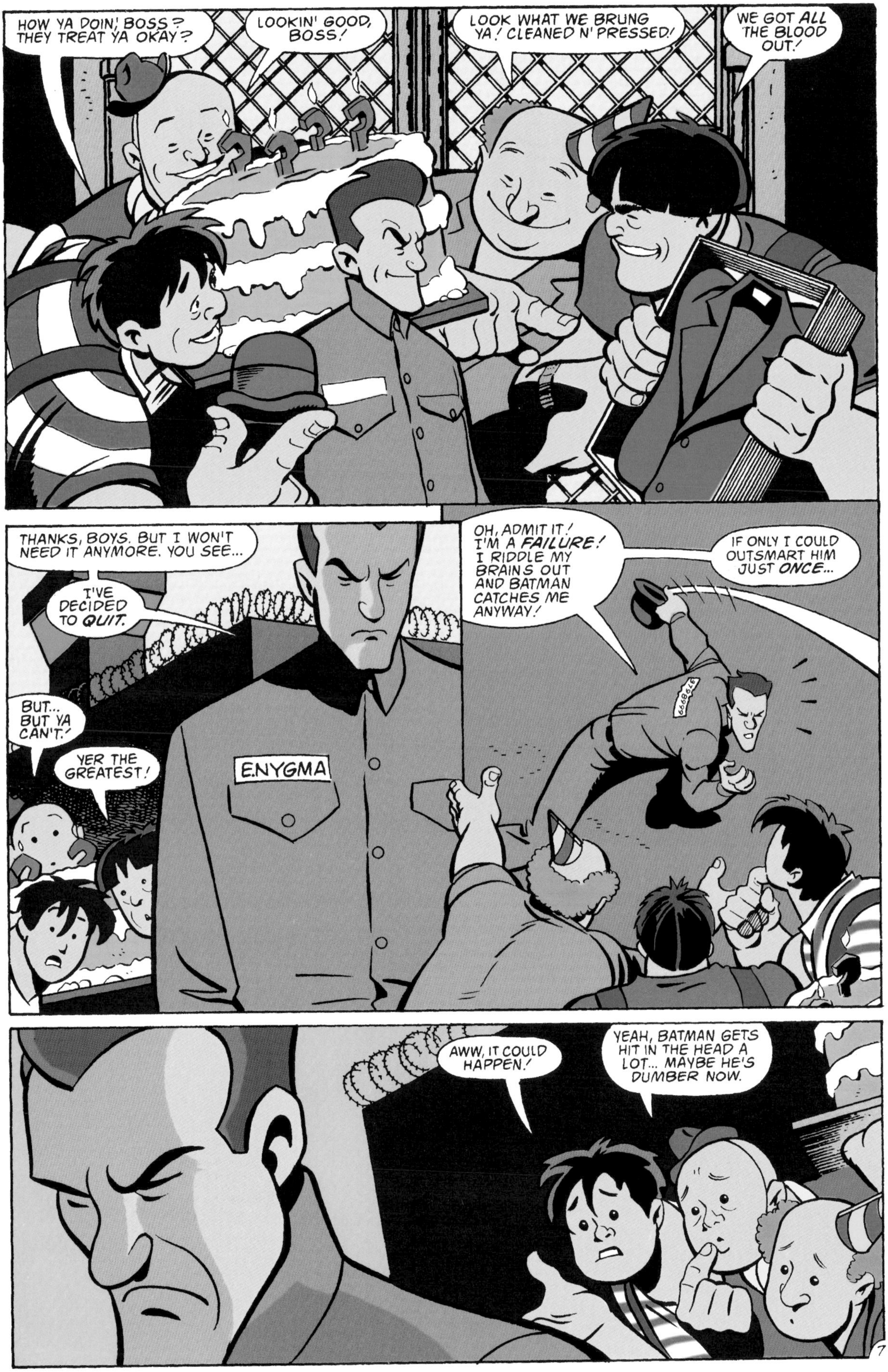

HOW YA DOIN', BOSS? THEY TREAT YA OKAY?
LOOKIN' GOOD, BOSS!
LOOK WHAT WE BRUNG YA! CLEANED N' PRESSED!
WE GOT ALL THE BLOOD OUT!
THANKS, BOYS. BUT I WON'T NEED IT ANYMORE. YOU SEE...
I'VE DECIDED TO QUIT.
BUT... BUT YA CAN'T!
YER THE GREATEST!
ENYGMA
OH, ADMIT IT! I'M A FAILURE! I RIDDLE MY BRAINS OUT AND BATMAN CATCHES ME ANYWAY!
IF ONLY I COULD OUTSMART HIM JUST ONCE...
AWW, IT COULD HAPPEN!
YEAH, BATMAN GETS HIT IN THE HEAD A LOT... MAYBE HE'S DUMBER NOW.
7

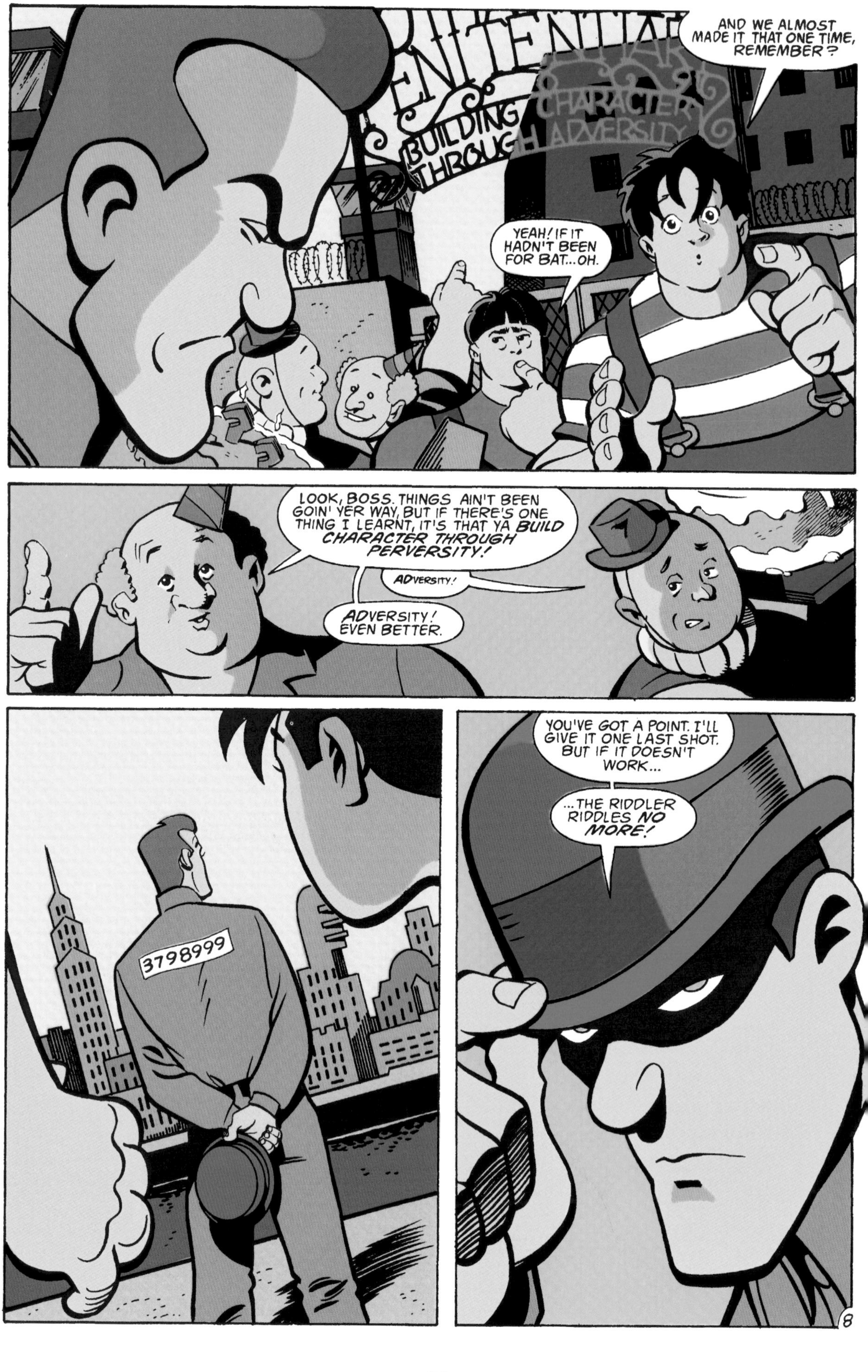

BUILDING CHARACTER THROUGH ADVERSITY
AND WE ALMOST MADE IT THAT ONE TIME, REMEMBER?
YEAH! IF IT HADN'T BEEN FOR BAT...OH.
LOOK, BOSS. THINGS AIN'T BEEN GOIN' YER WAY, BUT IF THERE'S ONE THING I LEARNT, IT'S THAT YA BUILD CHARACTER THROUGH PERVERSITY!
ADVERSITY!
ADVERSITY! EVEN BETTER.
3798999
YOU'VE GOT A POINT. I'LL GIVE IT ONE LAST SHOT. BUT IF IT DOESN'T WORK...
...THE RIDDLER RIDDLES NO MORE!
8

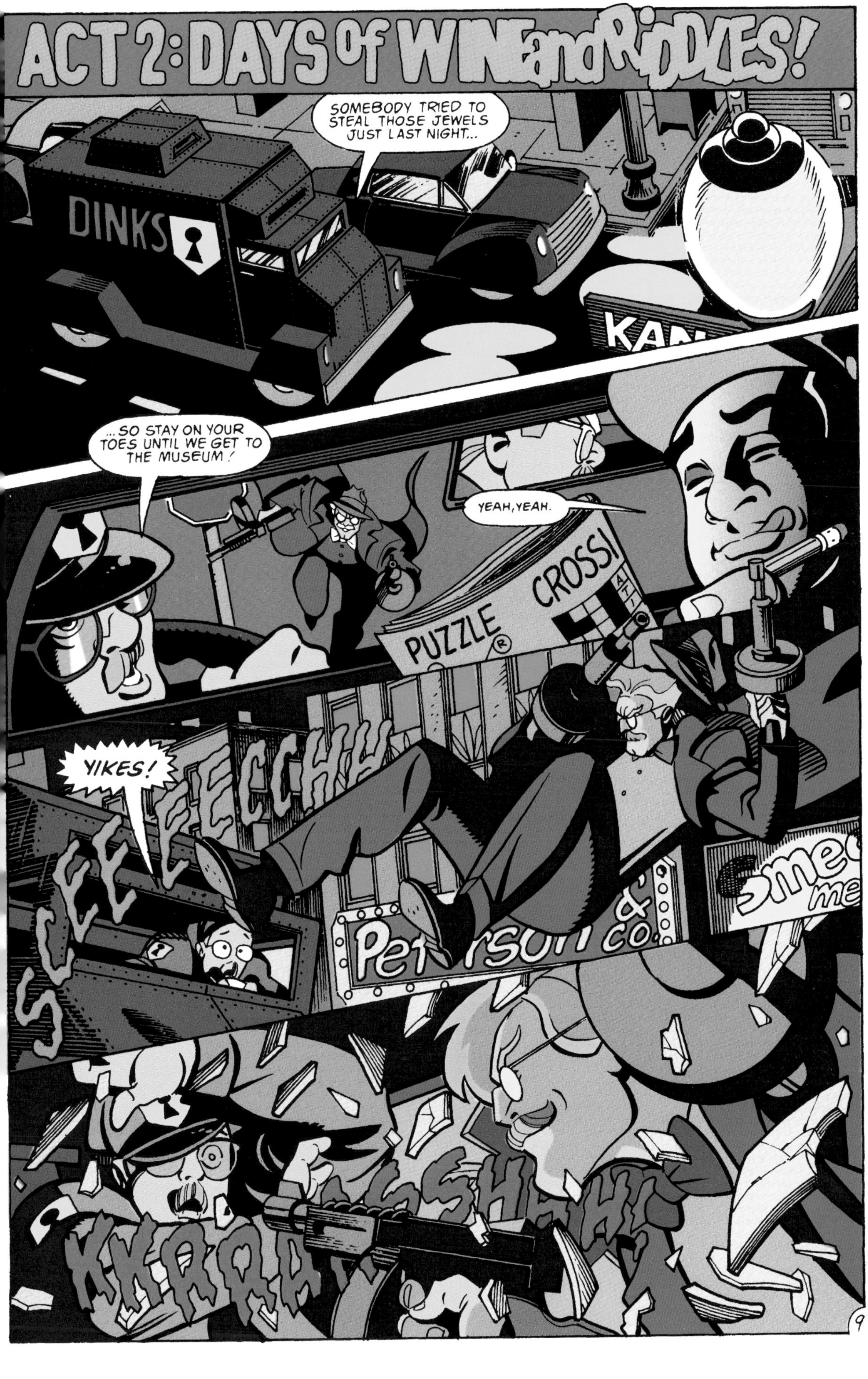
ACT 2: DAYS of WINE and RIDDLES!
SOMEBODY TRIED TO STEAL THOSE JEWELS JUST LAST NIGHT...
DINKS
KAN
...SO STAY ON YOUR TOES UNTIL WE GET TO THE MUSEUM!
YEAH, YEAH.
PUZZLE CROSS
YIKES!
SKREEECCHH
Peterson & co.
KKRAASSHH
9

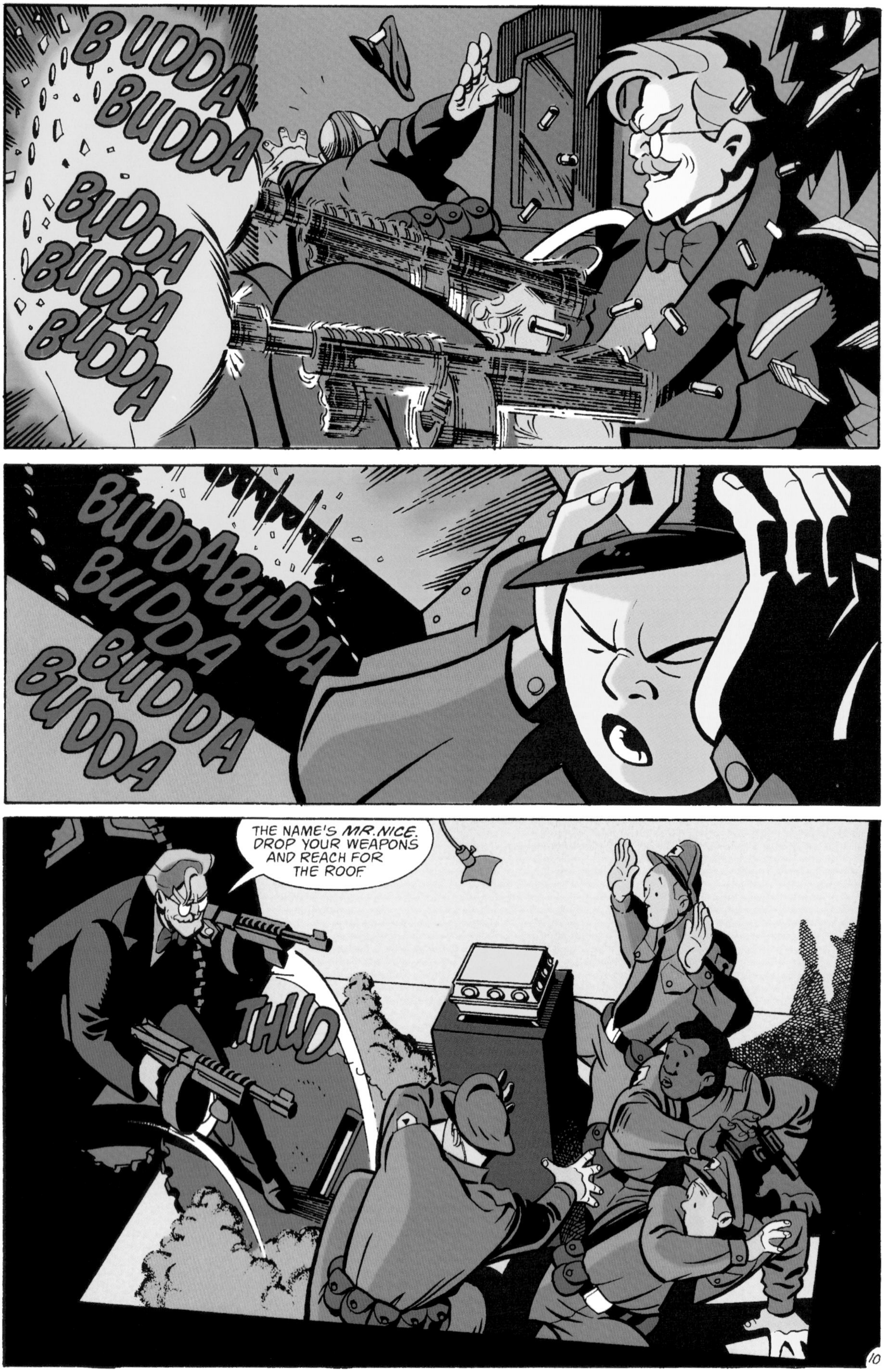
BUDDA
BUDDA
BUDDA
BUDDA
BUDDA
BUDDABUDDA
BUDDA
BUDDA
BUDDA
BUDDA
THE NAME'S MR. NICE. DROP YOUR WEAPONS AND REACH FOR THE ROOF.
THUD
10

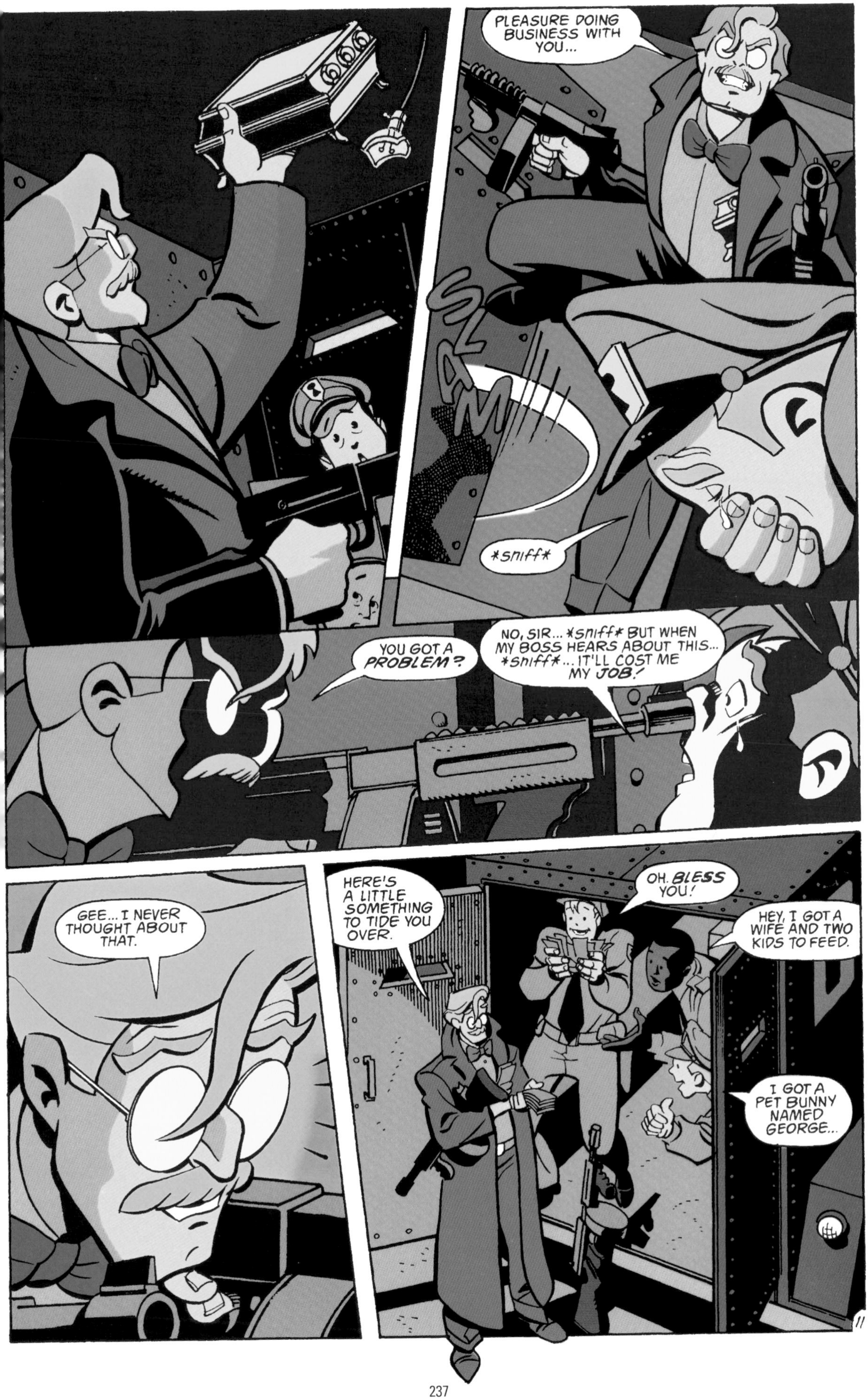
PLEASURE DOING BUSINESS WITH YOU...
SLAM
sniff
YOU GOT A PROBLEM?
NO, SIR... *sniff* BUT WHEN MY BOSS HEARS ABOUT THIS... *sniff*... IT'LL COST ME MY JOB!
GEE... I NEVER THOUGHT ABOUT THAT.
HERE'S A LITTLE SOMETHING TO TIDE YOU OVER.
OH. BLESS YOU!
HEY, I GOT A WIFE AND TWO KIDS TO FEED.
I GOT A PET BUNNY NAMED GEORGE...
11

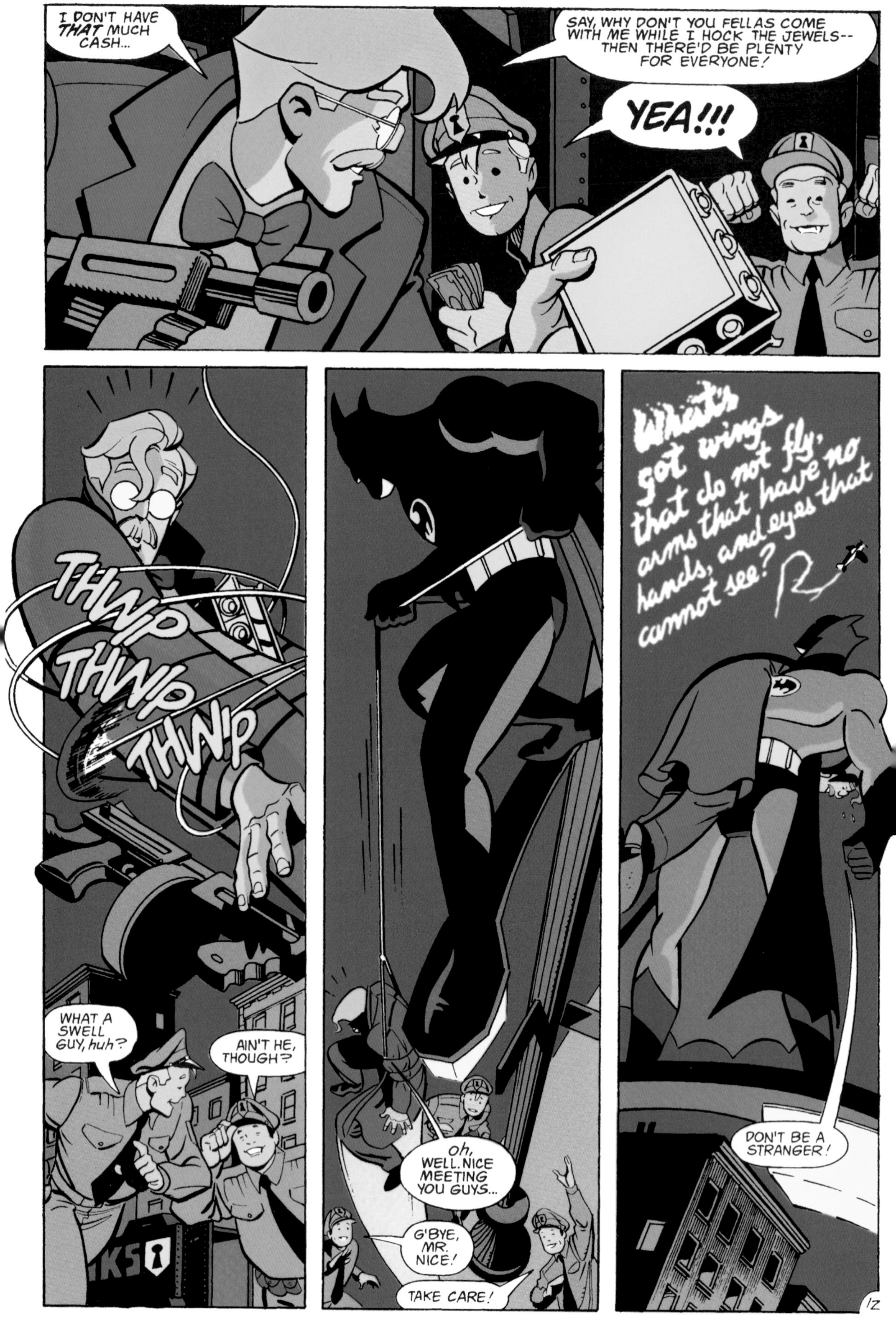
I DON'T HAVE THAT MUCH CASH...
SAY, WHY DON'T YOU FELLAS COME WITH ME WHILE I HOCK THE JEWELS-- THEN THERE'D BE PLENTY FOR EVERYONE!
YEA!!!
THWIP THWIP THWIP
WHAT A SWELL GUY, huh?
AIN'T HE, THOUGH?
oh, WELL. NICE MEETING YOU GUYS...
G'BYE, MR. NICE!
TAKE CARE!
What's got wings that do not fly, arms that have no hands, and eyes that cannot see? R
DON'T BE A STRANGER!
12

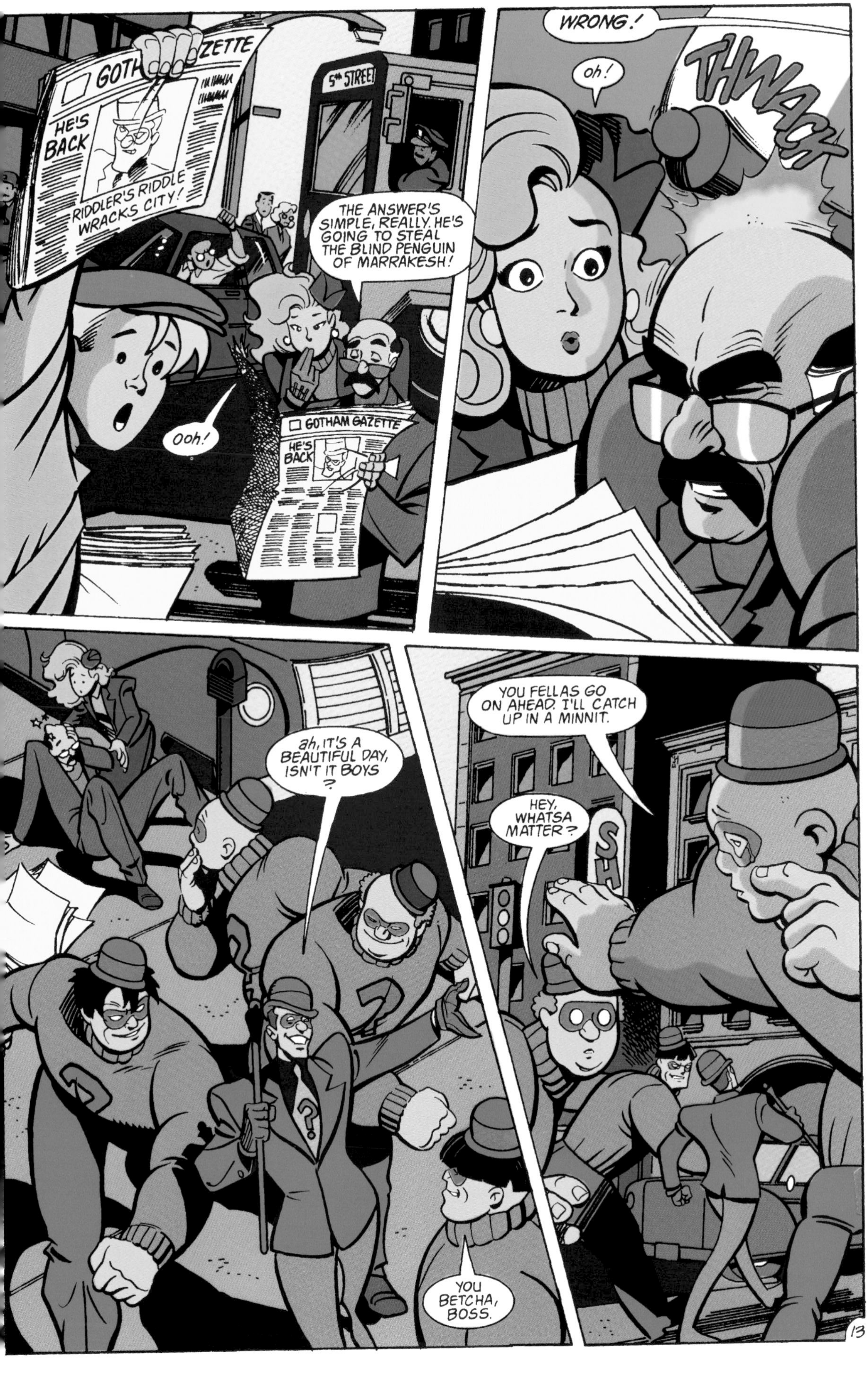
GOTHAM GAZETTE
HE'S BACK
RIDDLER'S RIDDLE WRACKS CITY!
5th STREET
THE ANSWER'S SIMPLE, REALLY. HE'S GOING TO STEAL THE BLIND PENGUIN OF MARRAKESH!
Ooh!
GOTHAM GAZETTE
HE'S BACK
WRONG!
oh!
THWACK
ah, IT'S A BEAUTIFUL DAY, ISN'T IT BOYS?
YOU BETCHA, BOSS.
YOU FELLAS GO ON AHEAD. I'LL CATCH UP IN A MINNIT.
HEY, WHATSA MATTER?
13

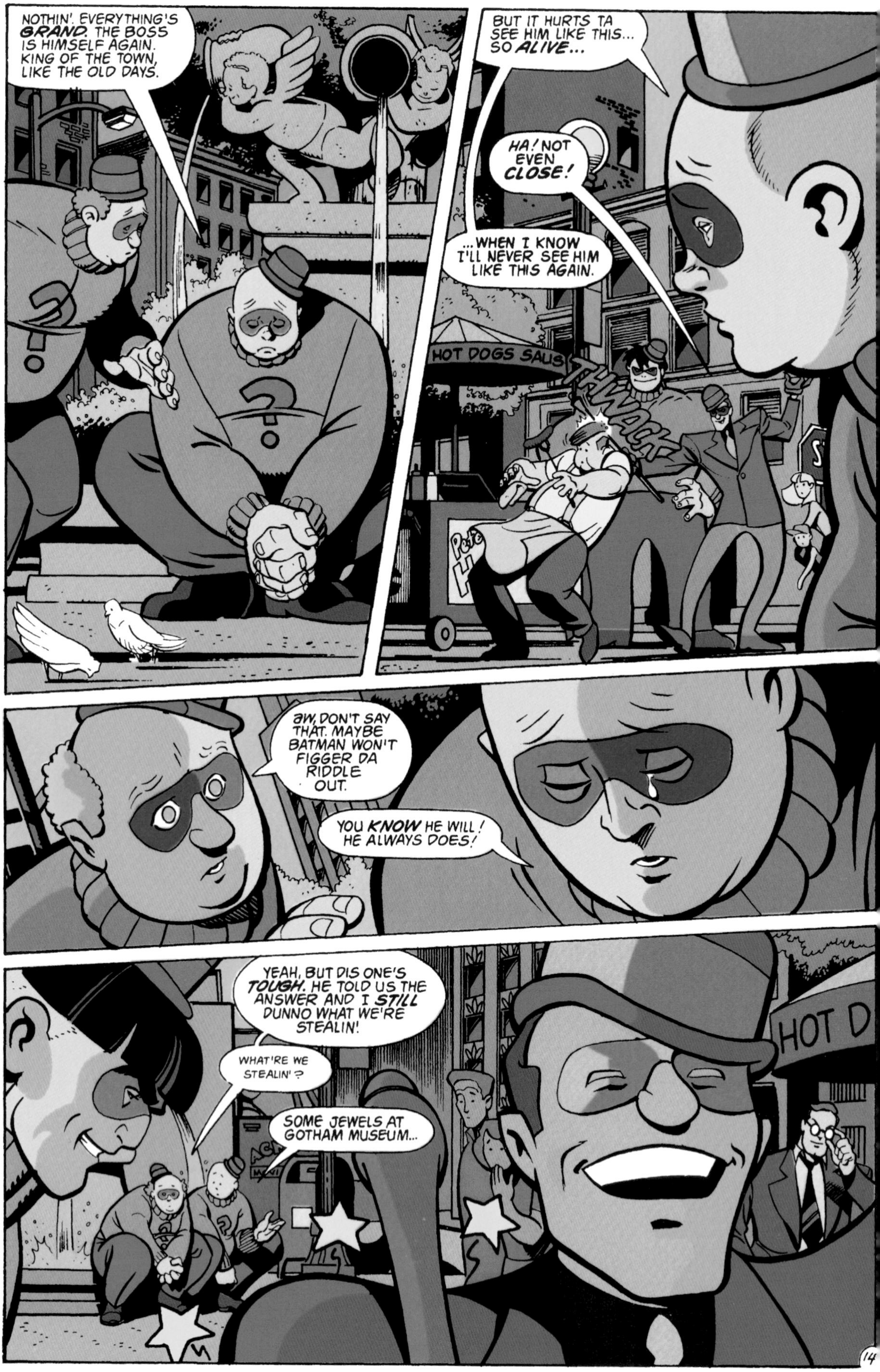
NOTHIN'. EVERYTHING'S GRAND. THE BOSS IS HIMSELF AGAIN. KING OF THE TOWN, LIKE THE OLD DAYS.
BUT IT HURTS TA SEE HIM LIKE THIS... SO ALIVE...
HA! NOT EVEN CLOSE!
...WHEN I KNOW I'LL NEVER SEE HIM LIKE THIS AGAIN.
HOT DOGS SAUS
THWACK
AW, DON'T SAY THAT. MAYBE BATMAN WON'T FIGGER DA RIDDLE OUT.
YOU KNOW HE WILL! HE ALWAYS DOES!
YEAH, BUT DIS ONE'S TOUGH. HE TOLD US THE ANSWER AND I STILL DUNNO WHAT WE'RE STEALIN'.
WHAT'RE WE STEALIN'?
SOME JEWELS AT GOTHAM MUSEUM...
HOT D
14

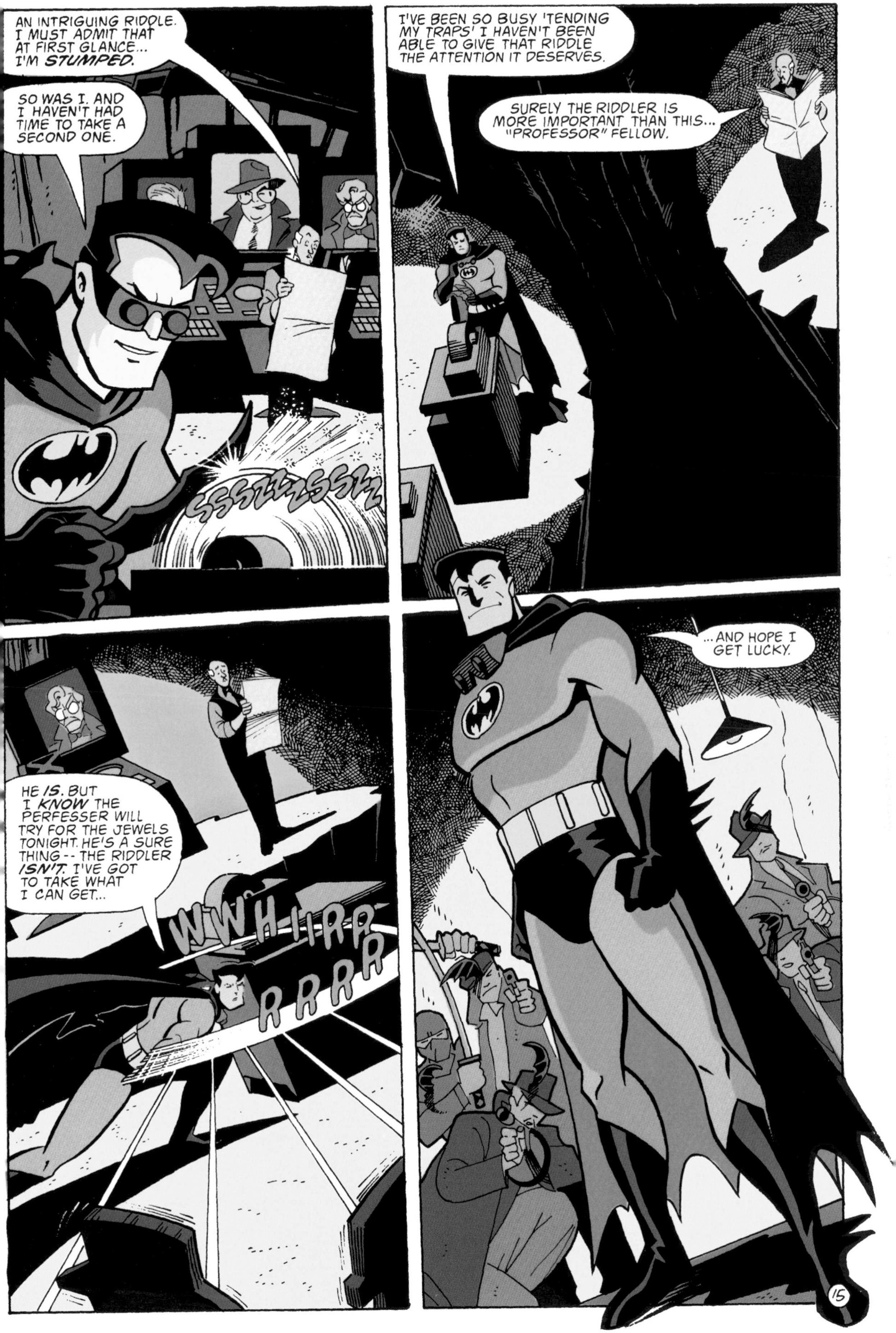
AN INTRIGUING RIDDLE. I MUST ADMIT THAT AT FIRST GLANCE... I'M STUMPED.
SO WAS I. AND I HAVEN'T HAD TIME TO TAKE A SECOND ONE.
SSSZZZZSSSZZ
I'VE BEEN SO BUSY 'TENDING MY TRAPS' I HAVEN'T BEEN ABLE TO GIVE THAT RIDDLE THE ATTENTION IT DESERVES.
SURELY THE RIDDLER IS MORE IMPORTANT THAN THIS... "PROFESSOR" FELLOW.
HE IS. BUT I KNOW THE PERFESSER WILL TRY FOR THE JEWELS TONIGHT. HE'S A SURE THING -- THE RIDDLER ISN'T. I'VE GOT TO TAKE WHAT I CAN GET...
WWHIIRRRRRRR
...AND HOPE I GET LUCKY.
15

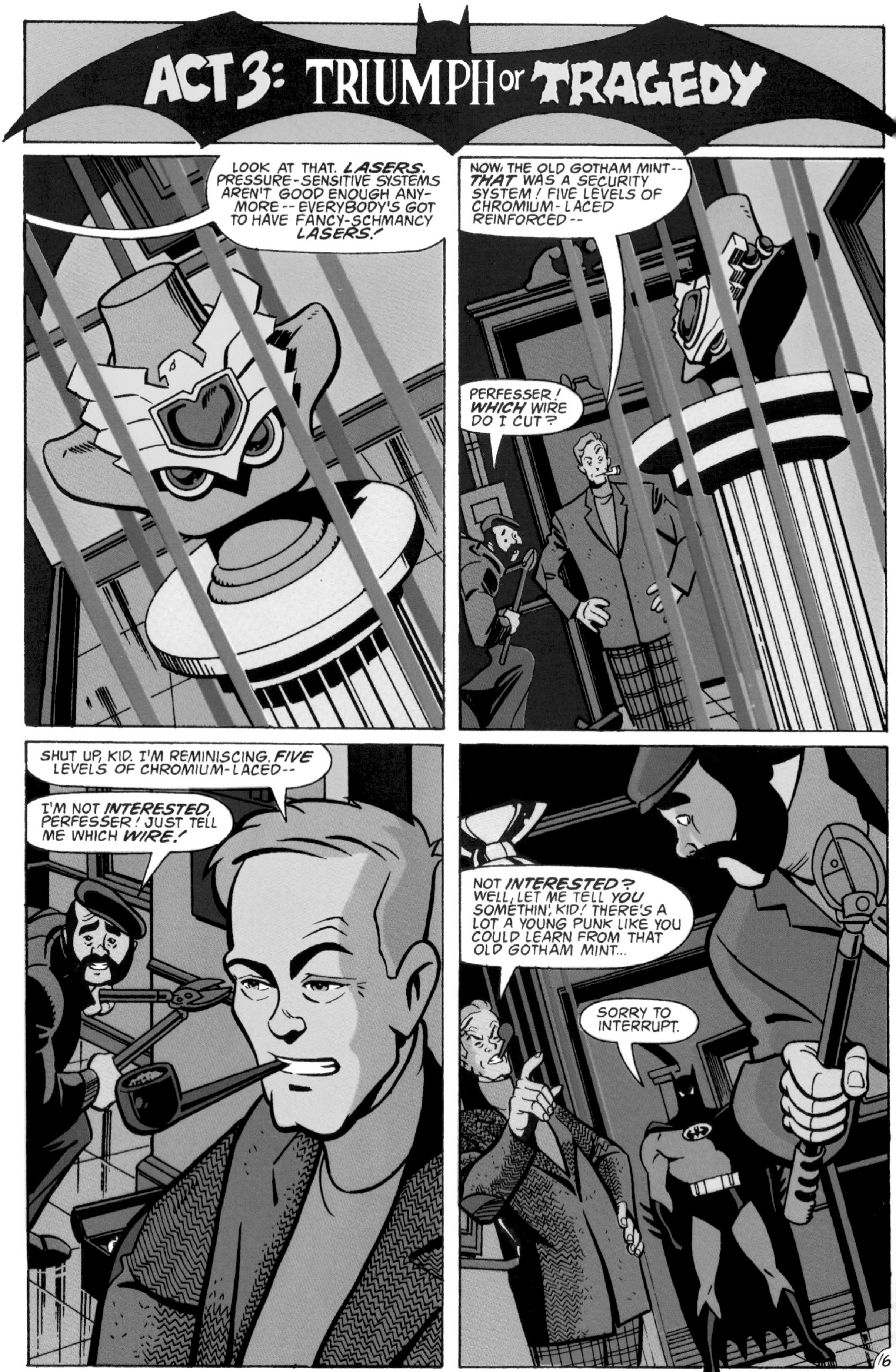

ACT 3: TRIUMPH or TRAGEDY
LOOK AT THAT. LASERS. PRESSURE-SENSITIVE SYSTEMS AREN'T GOOD ENOUGH ANY-MORE -- EVERYBODY'S GOT TO HAVE FANCY-SCHMANCY LASERS!
NOW, THE OLD GOTHAM MINT -- THAT WAS A SECURITY SYSTEM! FIVE LEVELS OF CHROMIUM-LACED REINFORCED --
PERFESSER! WHICH WIRE DO I CUT?
SHUT UP, KID. I'M REMINISCING. FIVE LEVELS OF CHROMIUM-LACED --
I'M NOT INTERESTED, PERFESSER! JUST TELL ME WHICH WIRE!
NOT INTERESTED? WELL, LET ME TELL YOU SOMETHIN', KID! THERE'S A LOT A YOUNG PUNK LIKE YOU COULD LEARN FROM THAT OLD GOTHAM MINT...
SORRY TO INTERRUPT.
16

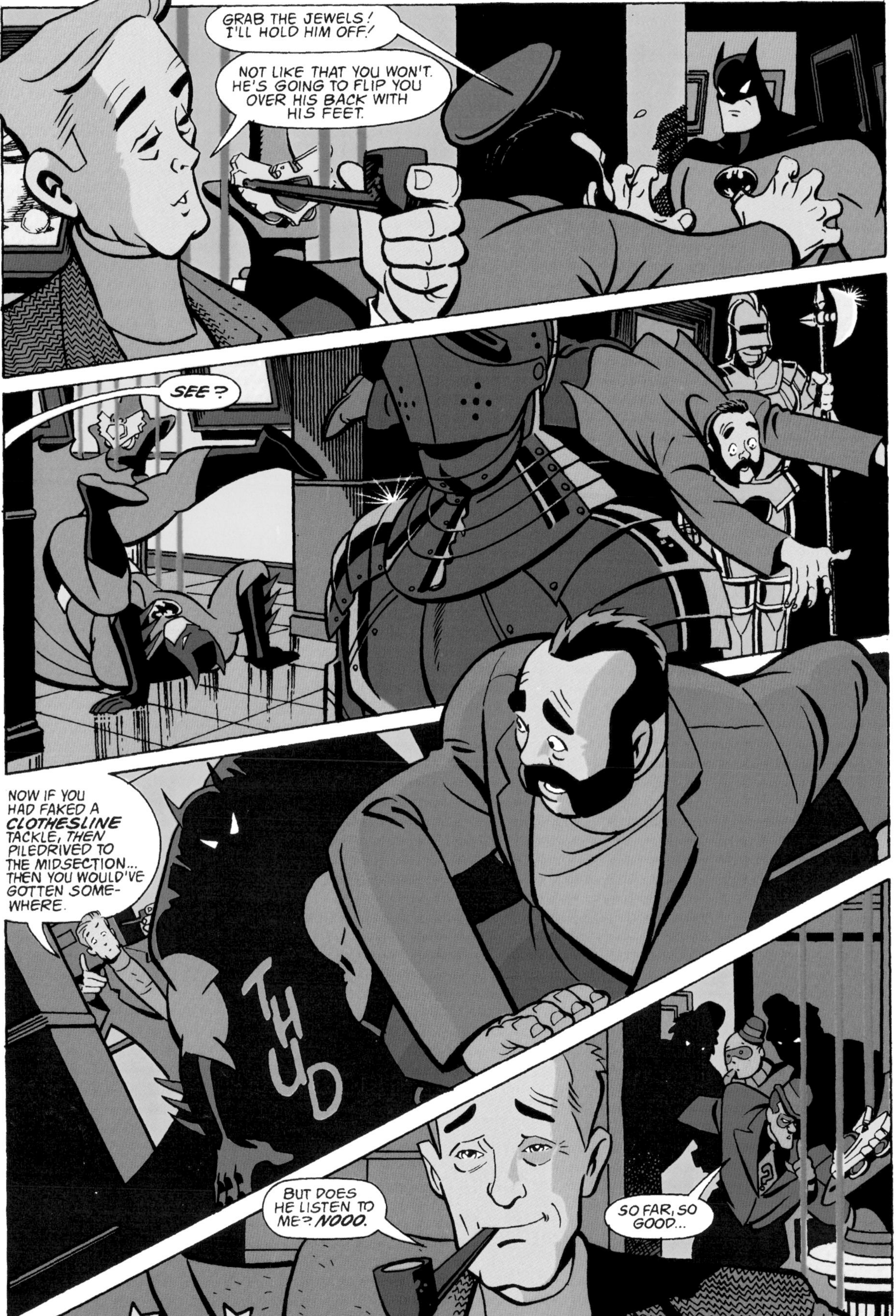
GRAB THE JEWELS! I'LL HOLD HIM OFF!
NOT LIKE THAT YOU WON'T. HE'S GOING TO FLIP YOU OVER HIS BACK WITH HIS FEET.
SEE?
NOW IF YOU HAD FAKED A CLOTHESLINE TACKLE, THEN PILEDRIVED TO THE MIDSECTION... THEN YOU WOULD'VE GOTTEN SOME-WHERE.
THUD
BUT DOES HE LISTEN TO ME? NOOO.
SO FAR, SO GOOD...
17

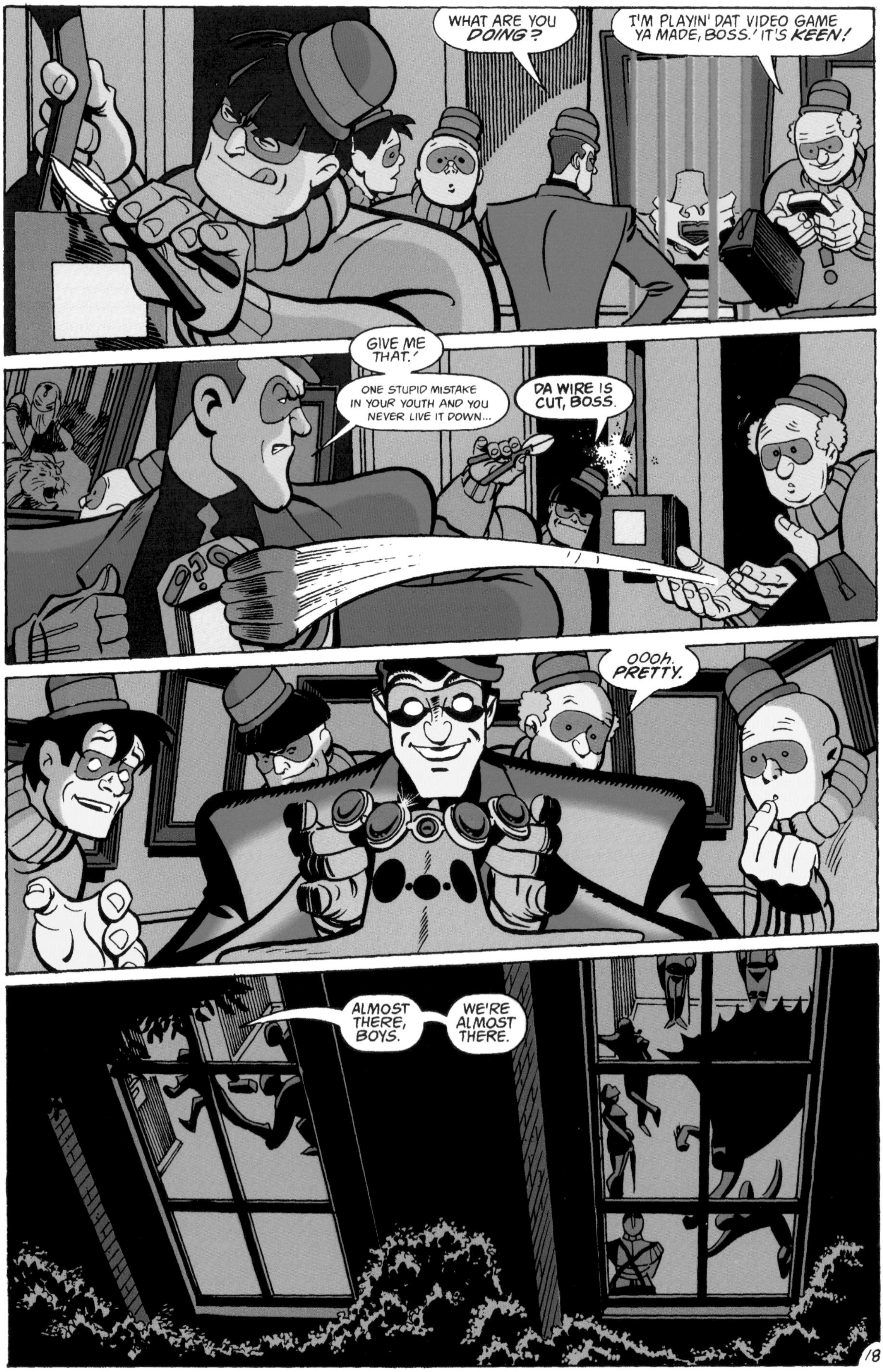
WHAT ARE YOU DOING?
I'M PLAYIN' DAT VIDEO GAME YA MADE, BOSS.' IT'S KEEN!
GIVE ME THAT.'
ONE STUPID MISTAKE IN YOUR YOUTH AND YOU NEVER LIVE IT DOWN...
DA WIRE IS CUT, BOSS.
oooh. PRETTY.
ALMOST THERE, BOYS.
WE'RE ALMOST THERE.
18

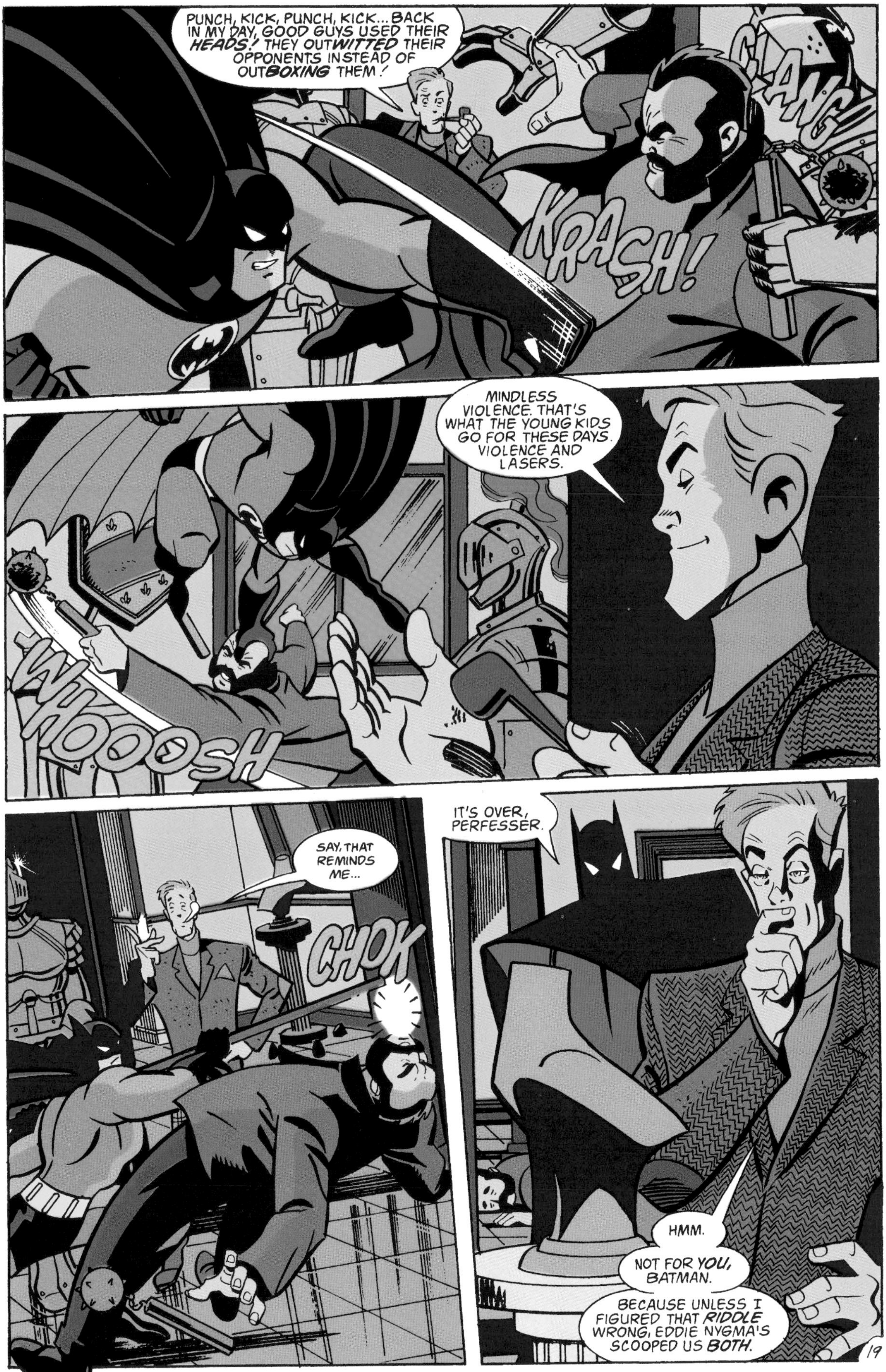

PUNCH, KICK, PUNCH, KICK... BACK IN MY DAY, GOOD GUYS USED THEIR HEADS! THEY OUTWITTED THEIR OPPONENTS INSTEAD OF OUTBOXING THEM!
CLANG
KRASH!
MINDLESS VIOLENCE. THAT'S WHAT THE YOUNG KIDS GO FOR THESE DAYS. VIOLENCE AND LASERS.
WHOOOSH
SAY, THAT REMINDS ME...
CHOK
IT'S OVER, PERFESSER.
HMM.
NOT FOR YOU, BATMAN.
BECAUSE UNLESS I FIGURED THAT RIDDLE WRONG, EDDIE NYGMA'S SCOOPED US BOTH.
19

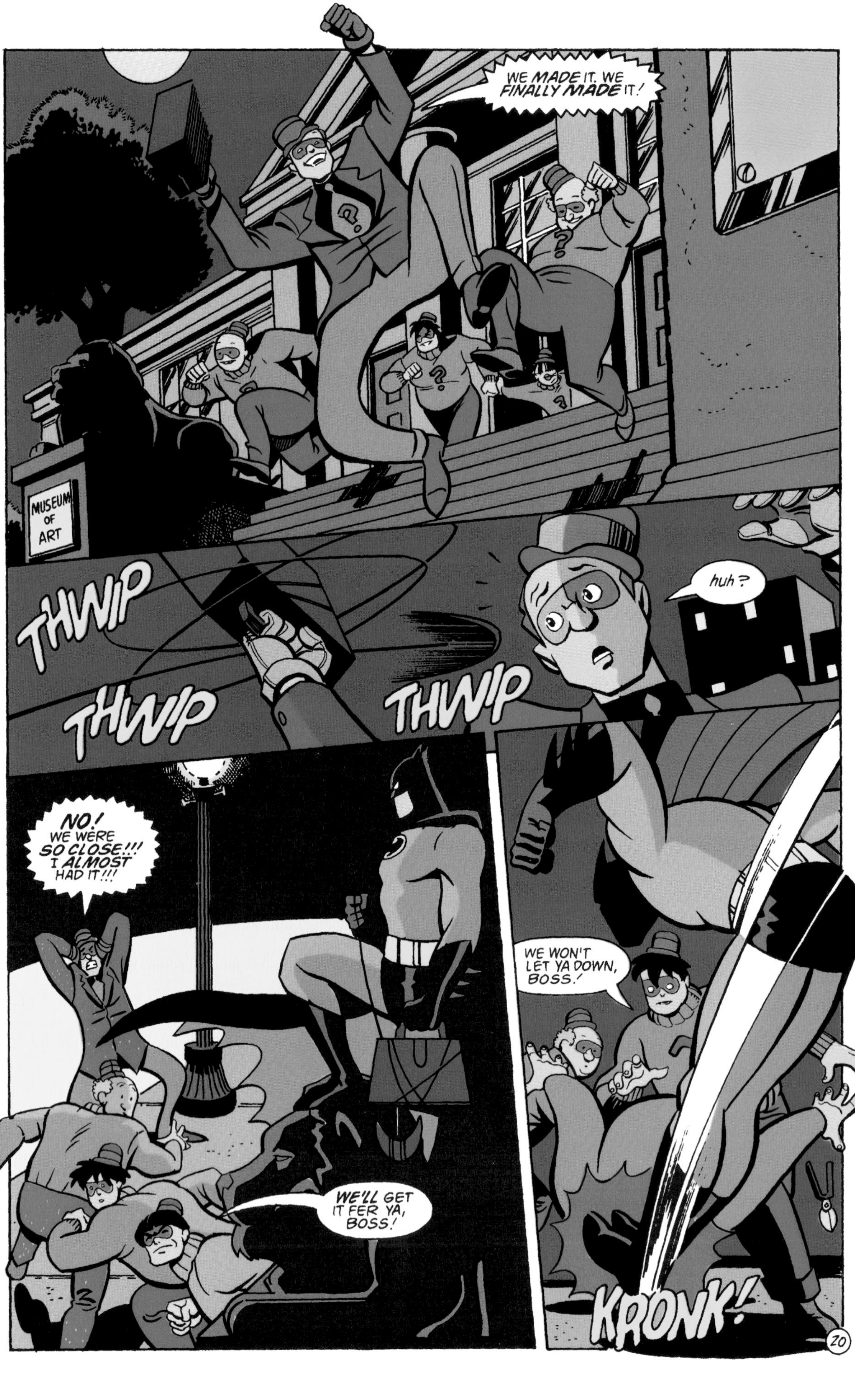
WE MADE IT. WE FINALLY MADE IT!
MUSEUM OF ART
THWIP
THWIP
THWIP
huh?
NO! WE WERE SO CLOSE!!! I ALMOST HAD IT!!!
WE'LL GET IT FER YA, BOSS!
WE WON'T LET YA DOWN, BOSS!
KRONK!
20

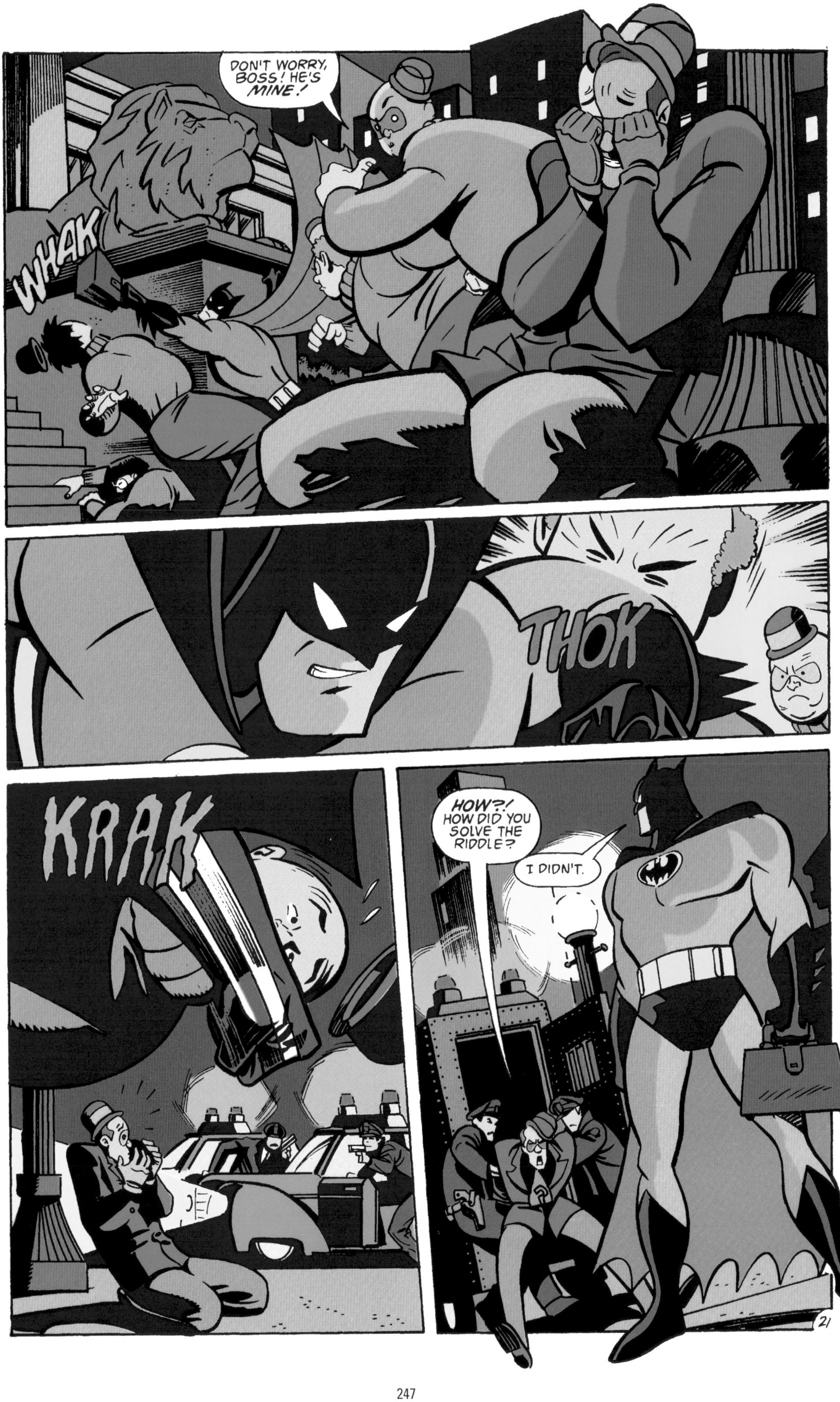
DON'T WORRY, BOSS! HE'S MINE!
WHAK
THOK
KRAK
HOW?! HOW DID YOU SOLVE THE RIDDLE?
I DIDN'T.
21

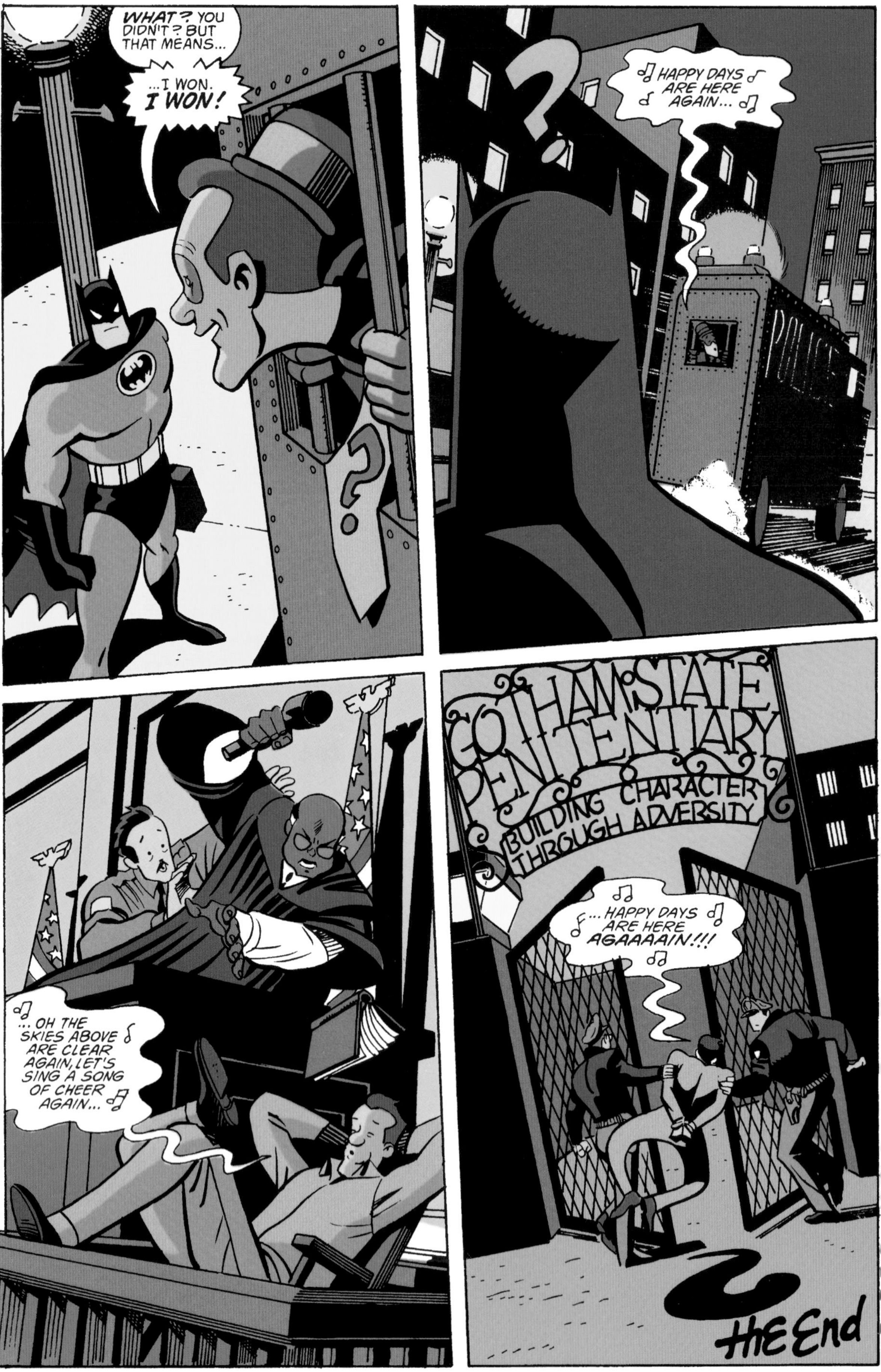
WHAT? YOU DIDN'T? BUT THAT MEANS...
...I WON. I WON!
♫ HAPPY DAYS ♪ ARE HERE ♪ AGAIN... ♫
POLICE
♫ ...OH THE SKIES ABOVE ♪ ARE CLEAR AGAIN, LET'S SING A SONG OF CHEER AGAIN... ♫
GOTHAM STATE PENITENTIARY
BUILDING CHARACTER THROUGH ADVERSITY
♫ ♪ ...HAPPY DAYS ♫ ARE HERE AGAAAAIN!!! ♫
THE End

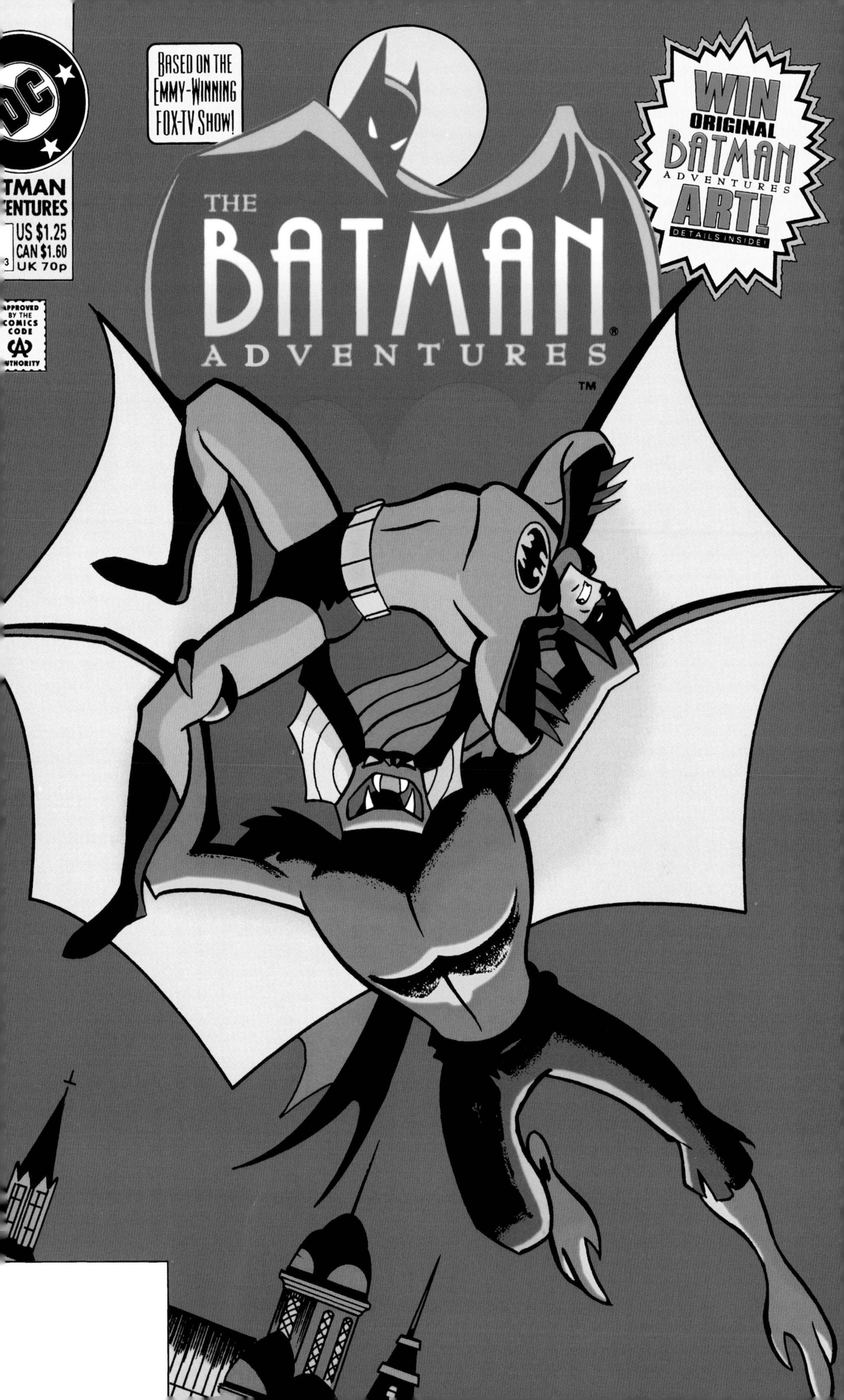

BASED ON THE EMMY-WINNING FOX-TV SHOW!
THE BATMAN ADVENTURES
TM
WIN ORIGINAL BATMAN ADVENTURES ART!
DETAILS INSIDE!
US $1.25
CAN $1.60
UK 70p
APPROVED BY THE COMICS CODE AUTHORITY

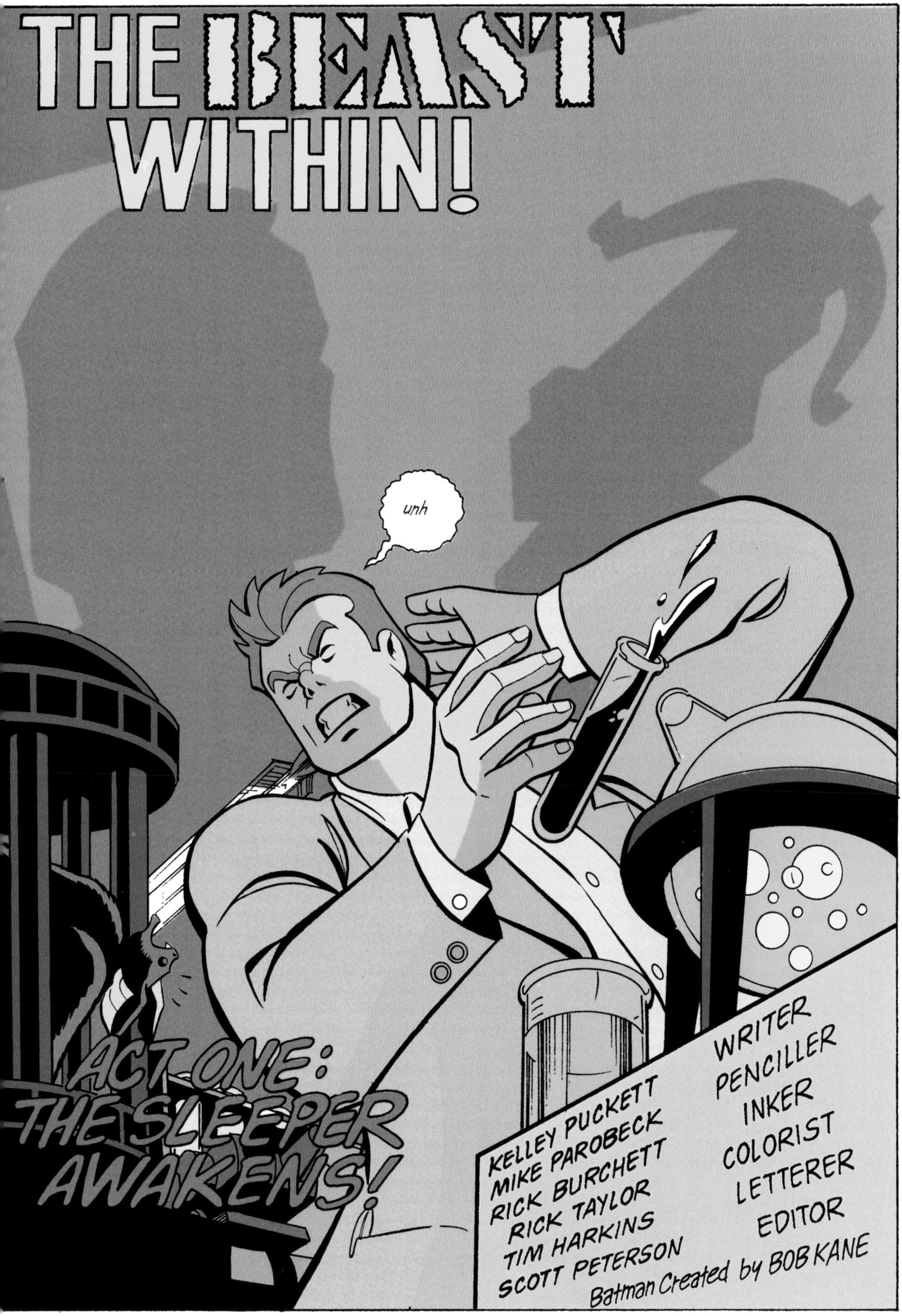

THE BEAST WITHIN!
unh
ACT ONE: THE SLEEPER AWAKENS!
KELLEY PUCKETT WRITER
MIKE PAROBECK PENCILLER
RICK BURCHETT INKER
RICK TAYLOR COLORIST
TIM HARKINS LETTERER
SCOTT PETERSON EDITOR
Batman Created by BOB KANE

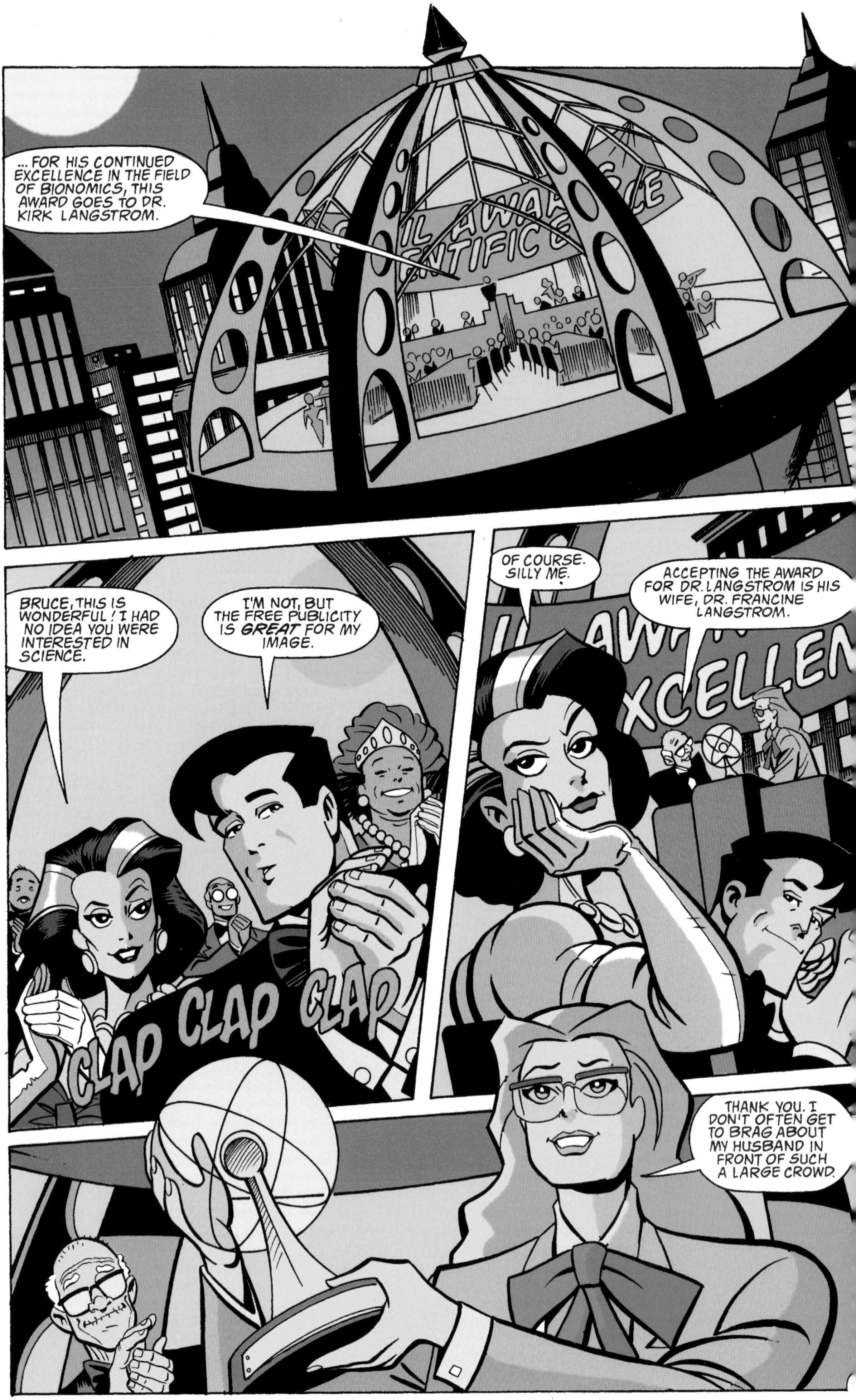
...FOR HIS CONTINUED EXCELLENCE IN THE FIELD OF BIONOMICS, THIS AWARD GOES TO DR. KIRK LANGSTROM.
BRUCE, THIS IS WONDERFUL! I HAD NO IDEA YOU WERE INTERESTED IN SCIENCE.
I'M NOT, BUT THE FREE PUBLICITY IS GREAT FOR MY IMAGE.
CLAP CLAP CLAP
OF COURSE. SILLY ME.
ACCEPTING THE AWARD FOR DR. LANGSTROM IS HIS WIFE, DR. FRANCINE LANGSTROM.
THANK YOU. I DON'T OFTEN GET TO BRAG ABOUT MY HUSBAND IN FRONT OF SUCH A LARGE CROWD.

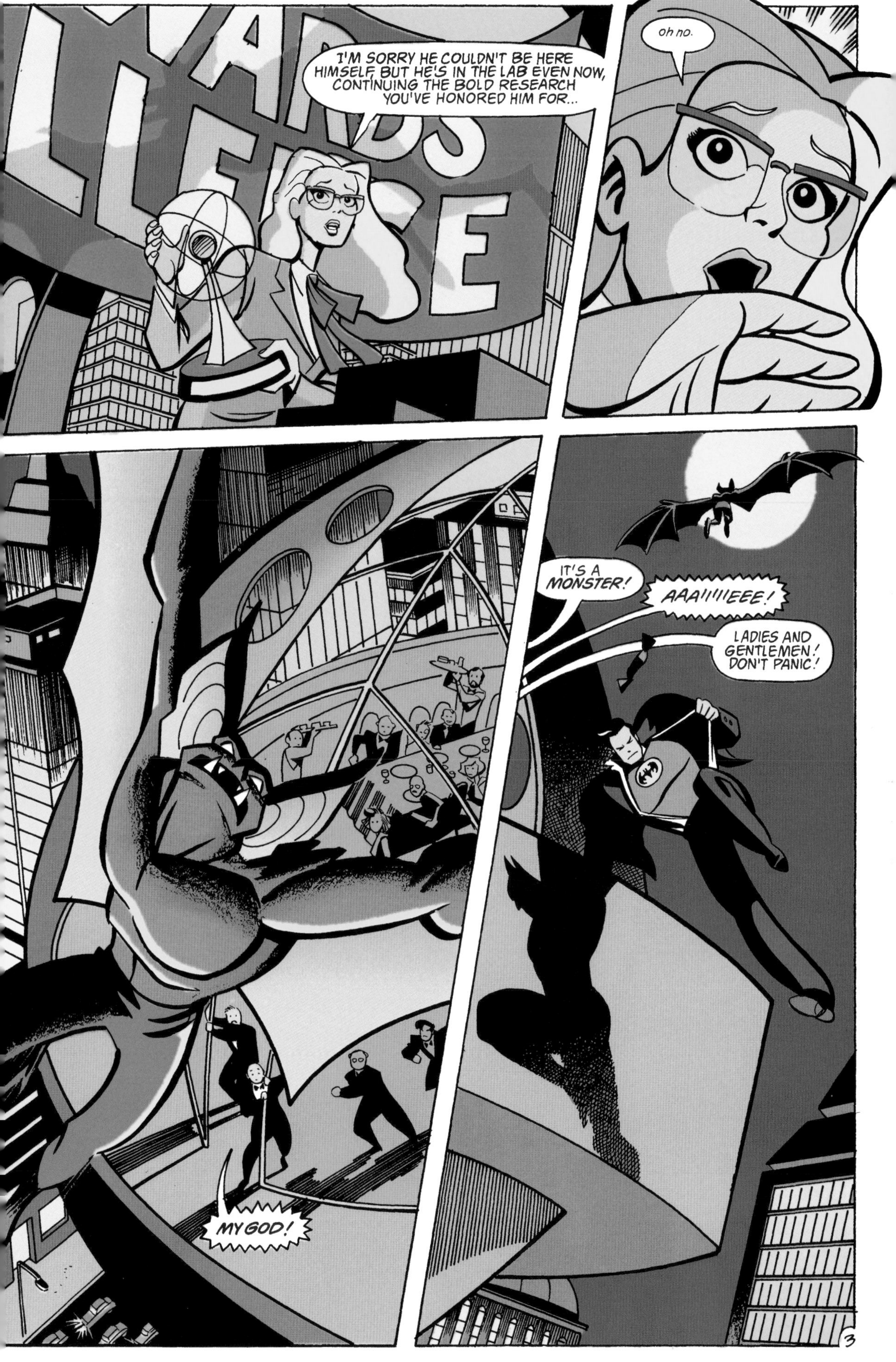
I'M SORRY HE COULDN'T BE HERE HIMSELF, BUT HE'S IN THE LAB EVEN NOW, CONTINUING THE BOLD RESEARCH YOU'VE HONORED HIM FOR...
oh no.
IT'S A MONSTER!
AAA!!!!EEE!
LADIES AND GENTLEMEN! DON'T PANIC!
MY GOD!
3

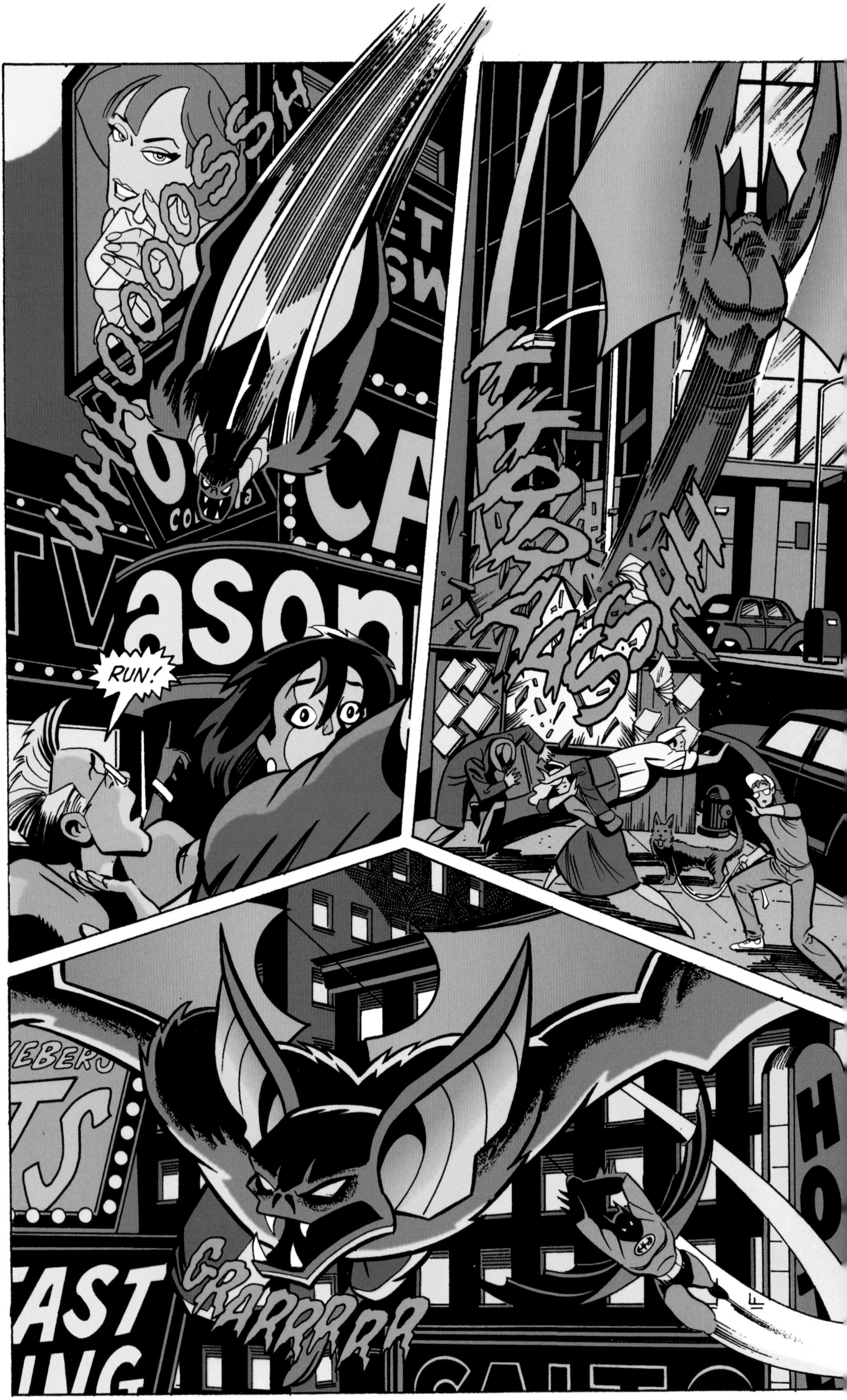
WHOOOOOSSH
RUN!
KRRAASSHH
GRARRRRRR

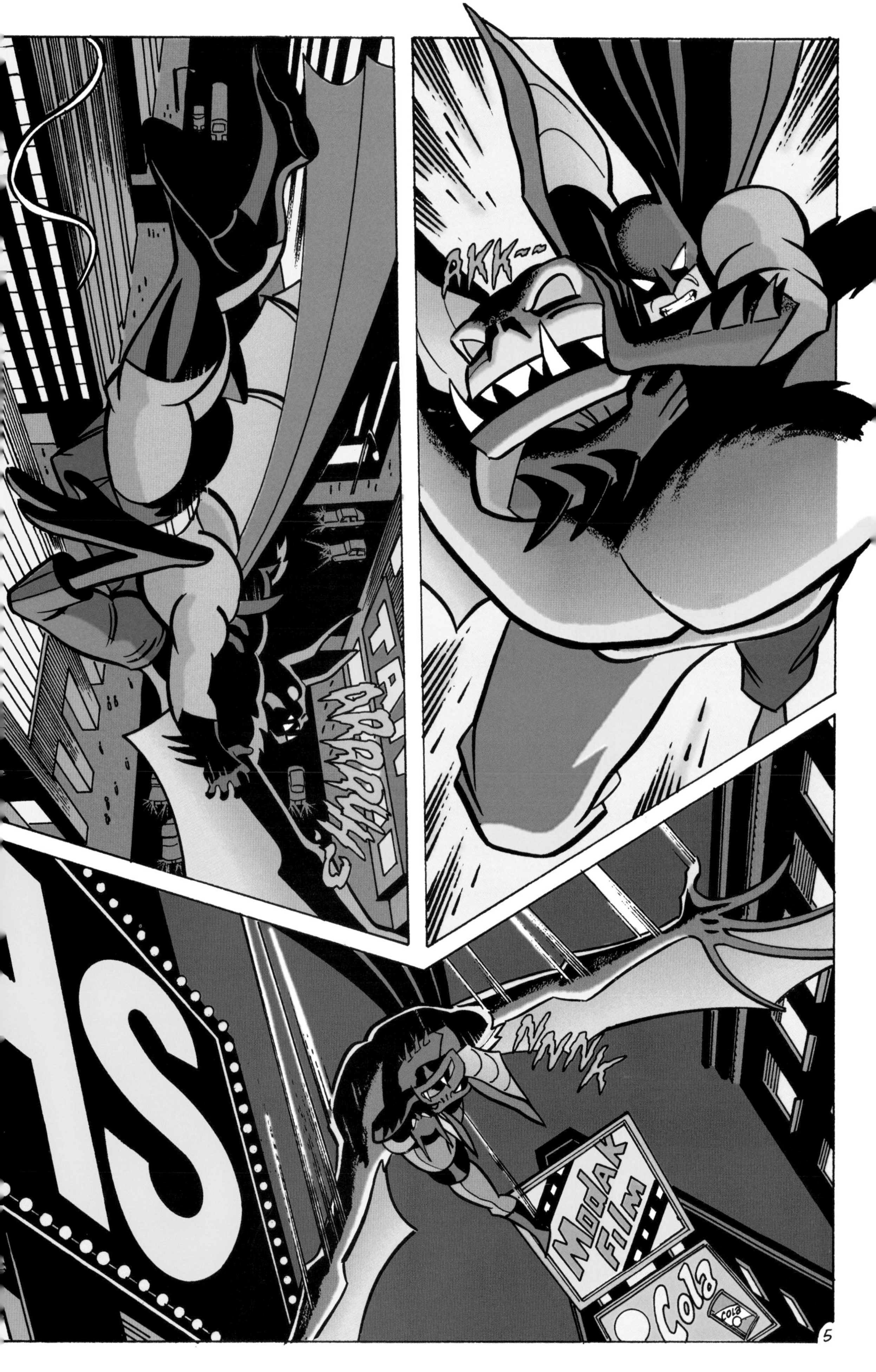
AKK--
NNNK
ModAK FILM
Cola
5

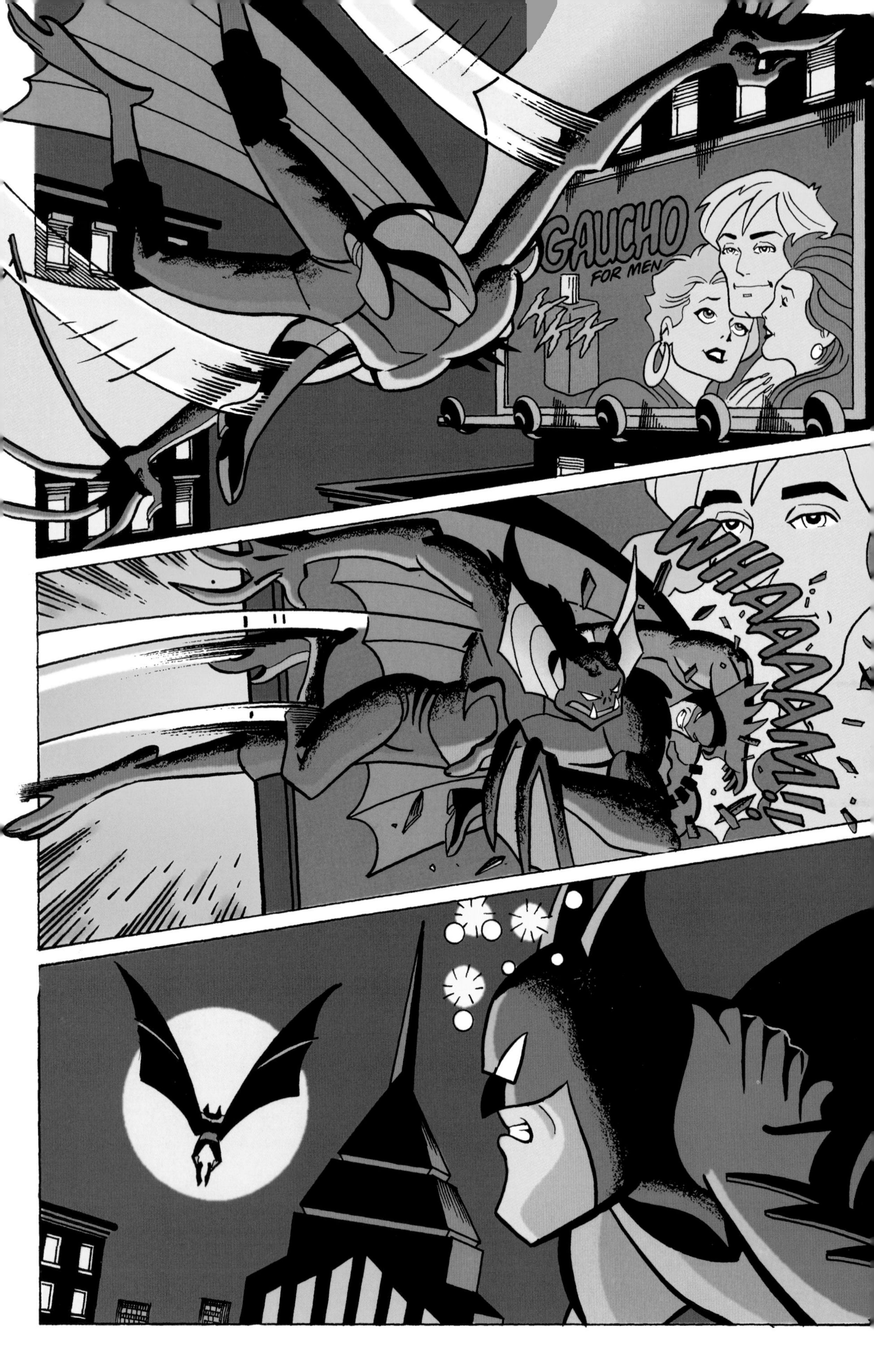
GAUCHO
FOR MEN
KKK
WHAAAAM!!

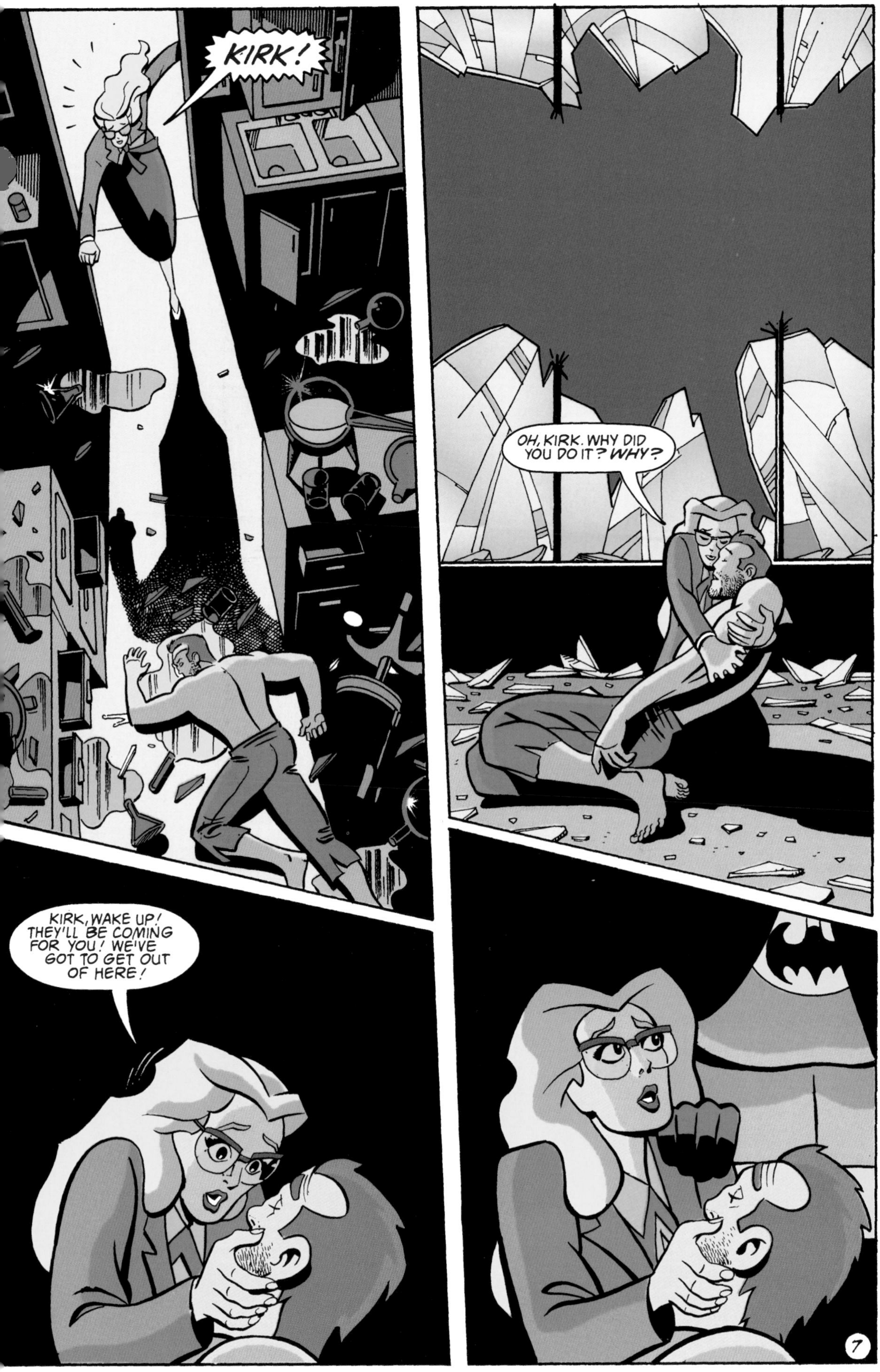
KIRK!
OH, KIRK. WHY DID YOU DO IT? WHY?
KIRK, WAKE UP! THEY'LL BE COMING FOR YOU! WE'VE GOT TO GET OUT OF HERE!
7

ACT 2: G.C.P.D.H.Q.!

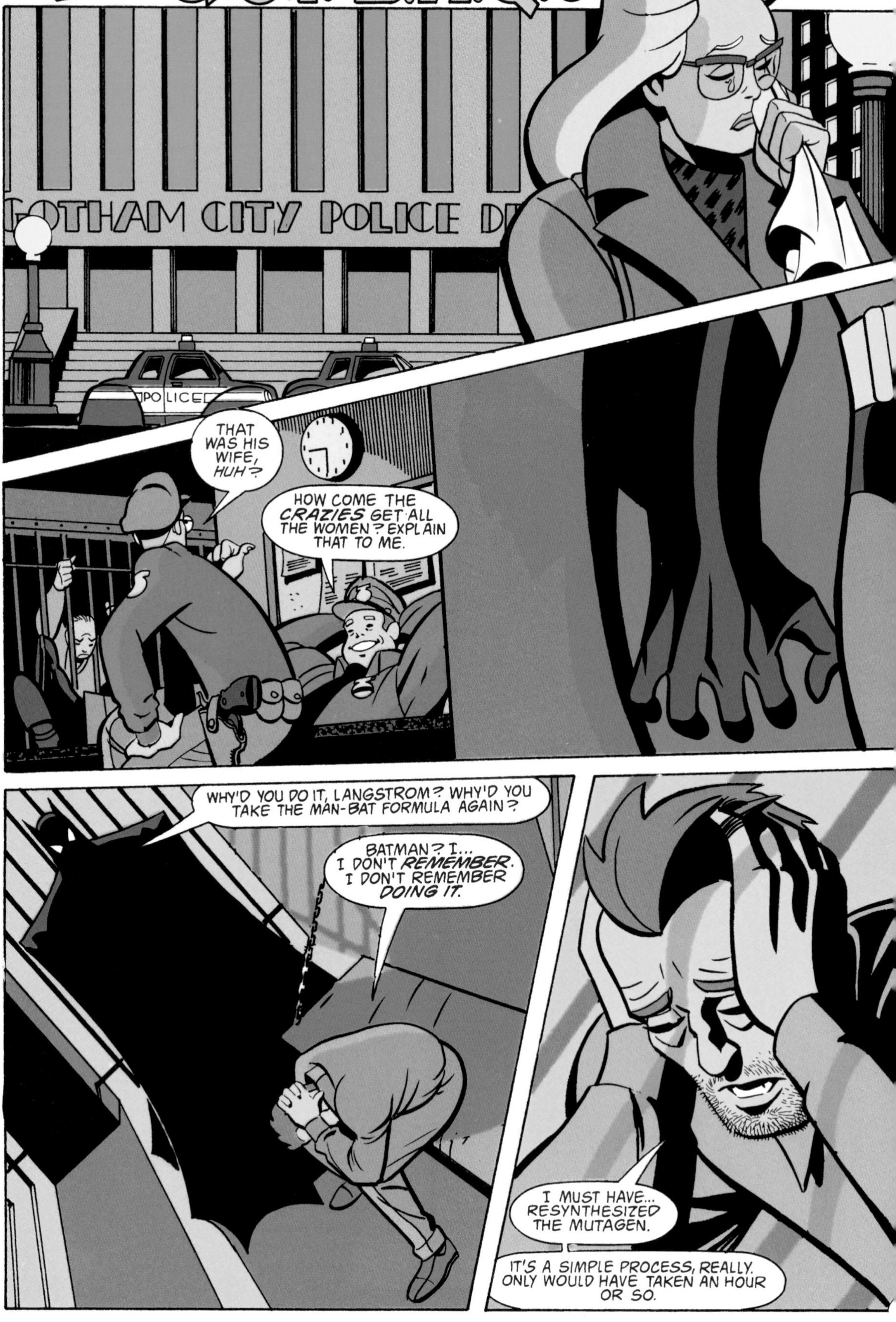

GOTHAM CITY POLICE DE
POLICE
THAT WAS HIS WIFE, HUH?
HOW COME THE CRAZIES GET ALL THE WOMEN? EXPLAIN THAT TO ME.
WHY'D YOU DO IT, LANGSTROM? WHY'D YOU TAKE THE MAN-BAT FORMULA AGAIN?
BATMAN? I... I DON'T REMEMBER. I DON'T REMEMBER DOING IT.
I MUST HAVE... RESYNTHESIZED THE MUTAGEN.
IT'S A SIMPLE PROCESS, REALLY. ONLY WOULD HAVE TAKEN AN HOUR OR SO.

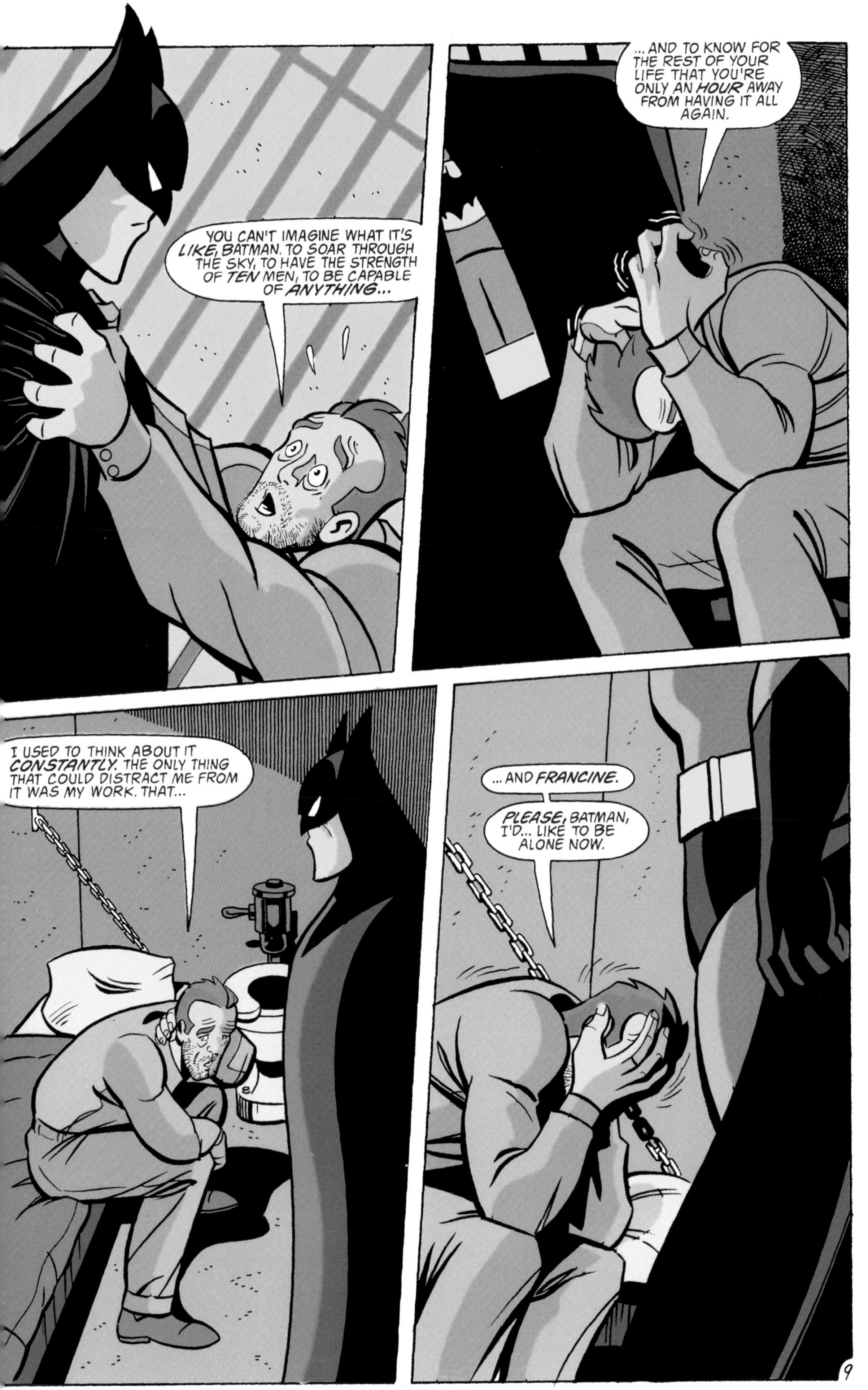
YOU CAN'T IMAGINE WHAT IT'S LIKE, BATMAN. TO SOAR THROUGH THE SKY, TO HAVE THE STRENGTH OF TEN MEN, TO BE CAPABLE OF ANYTHING...
...AND TO KNOW FOR THE REST OF YOUR LIFE THAT YOU'RE ONLY AN HOUR AWAY FROM HAVING IT ALL AGAIN.
I USED TO THINK ABOUT IT CONSTANTLY. THE ONLY THING THAT COULD DISTRACT ME FROM IT WAS MY WORK. THAT...
...AND FRANCINE.
PLEASE, BATMAN, I'D... LIKE TO BE ALONE NOW.
9

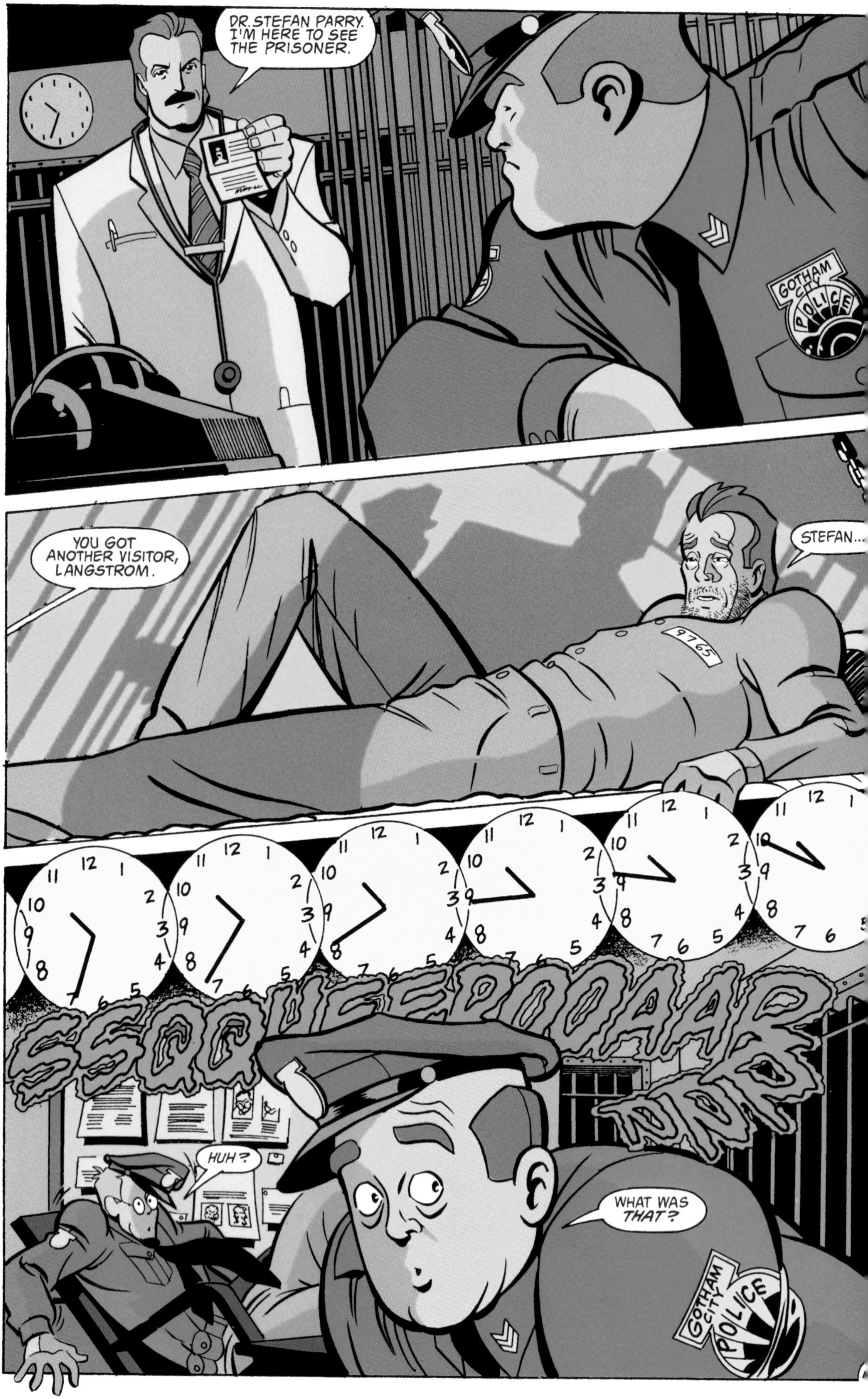

DR. STEFAN PARRY. I'M HERE TO SEE THE PRISONER.
GOTHAM CITY POLICE
YOU GOT ANOTHER VISITOR, LANGSTROM.
STEFAN...
9765
SSQQUEEDOOAAR
HUH?
WHAT WAS THAT?
GOTHAM CITY POLICE

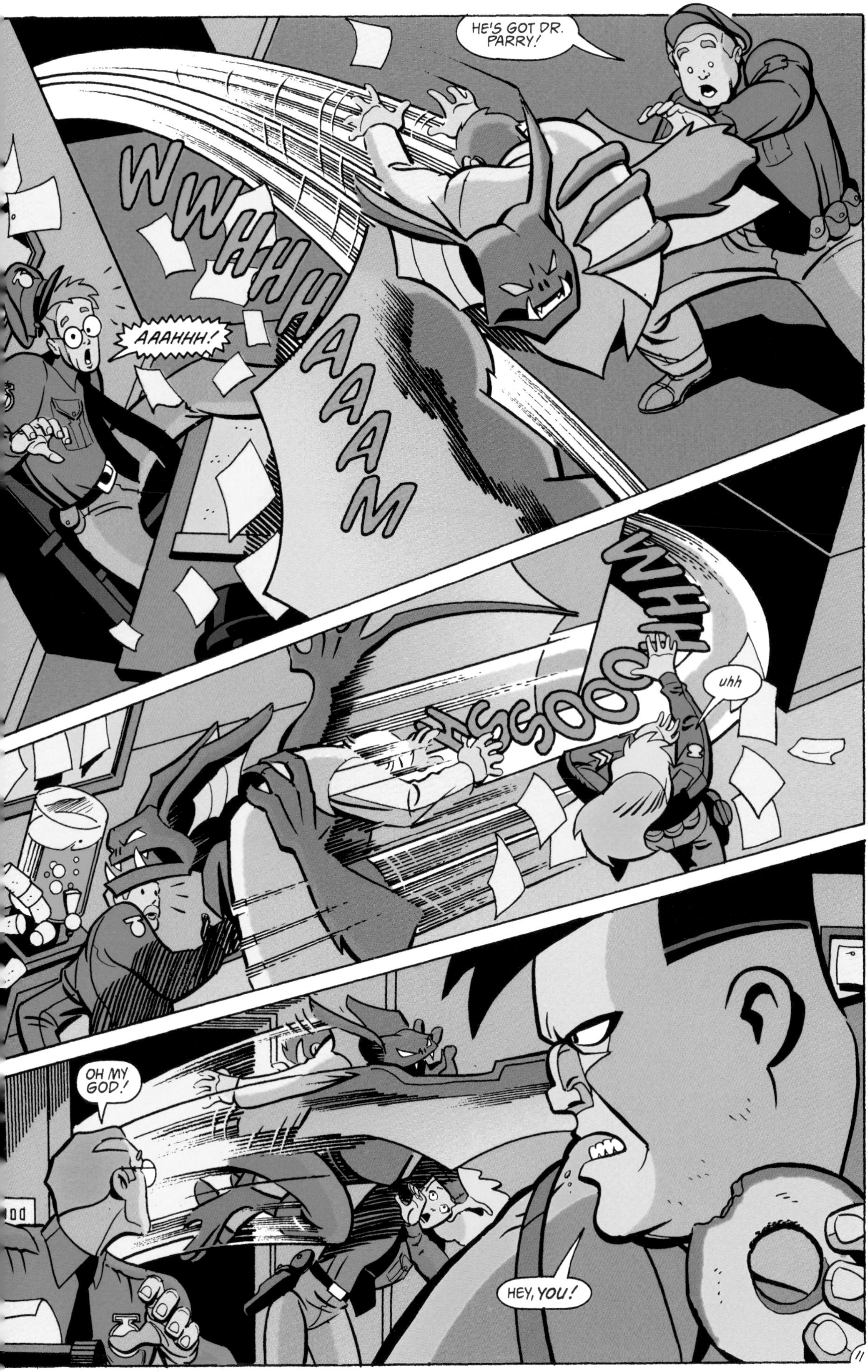
HE'S GOT DR. PARRY!
WWHHHAAAAM
AAAHHH!
WHHOOSSH
uhh
OH MY GOD!
HEY, YOU!
11

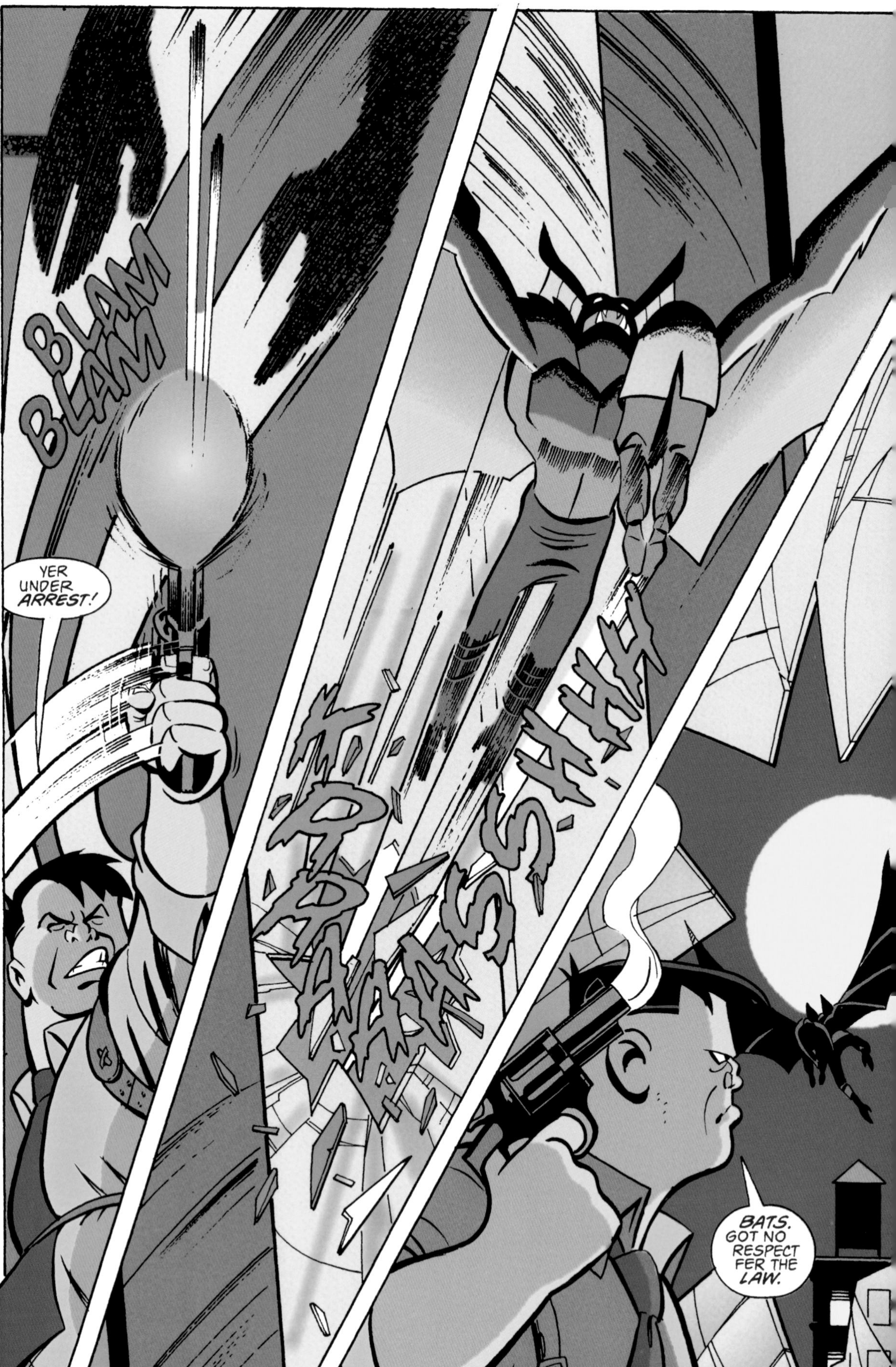
BLAM
BLAM
YER UNDER ARREST!
KRRAAASSHH
BATS. GOT NO RESPECT FER THE LAW.

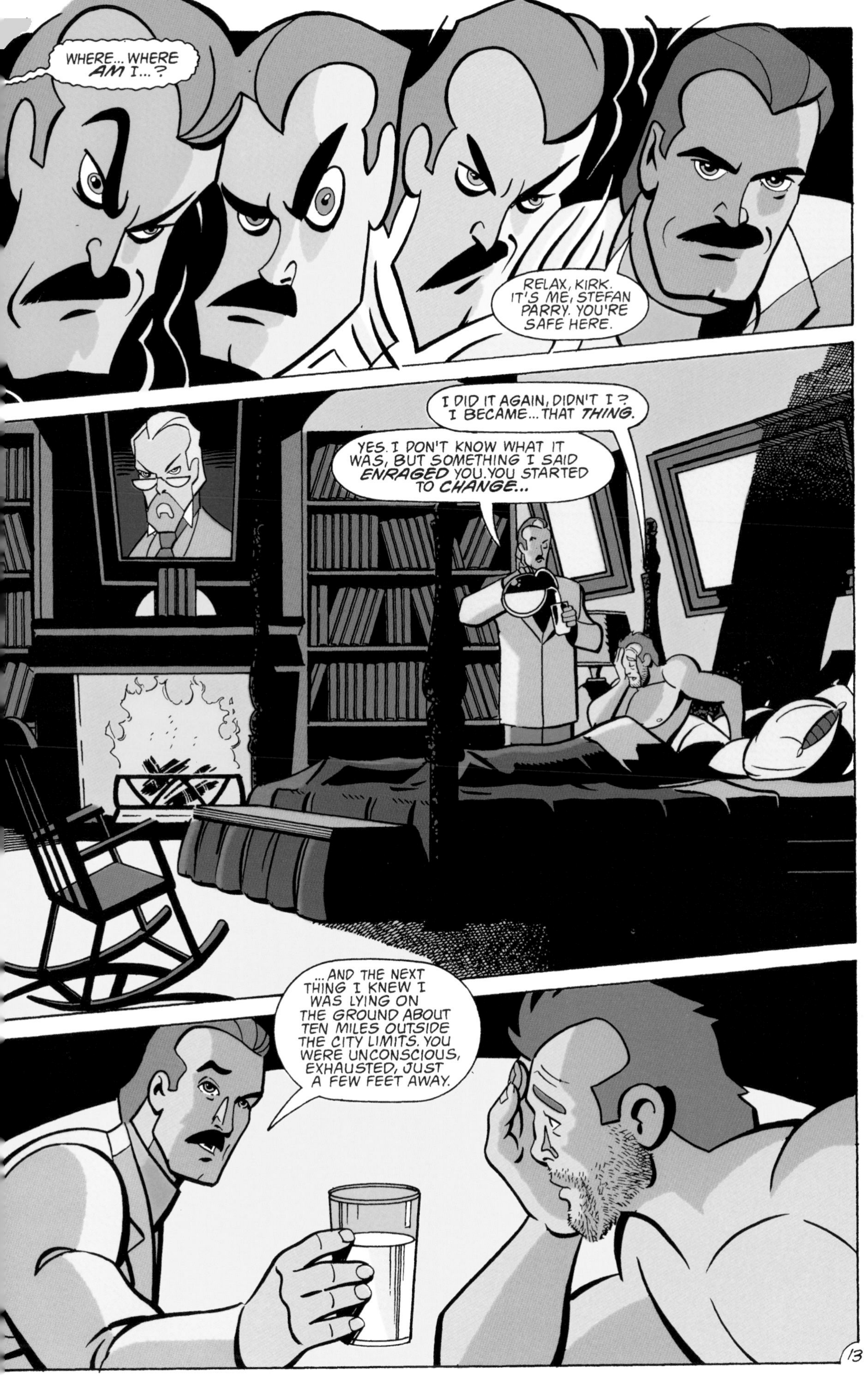
WHERE... WHERE AM I...?
RELAX, KIRK. IT'S ME, STEFAN PARRY. YOU'RE SAFE HERE.
I DID IT AGAIN, DIDN'T I? I BECAME... THAT THING.
YES. I DON'T KNOW WHAT IT WAS, BUT SOMETHING I SAID ENRAGED YOU. YOU STARTED TO CHANGE...
...AND THE NEXT THING I KNEW I WAS LYING ON THE GROUND ABOUT TEN MILES OUTSIDE THE CITY LIMITS. YOU WERE UNCONSCIOUS, EXHAUSTED, JUST A FEW FEET AWAY.
13

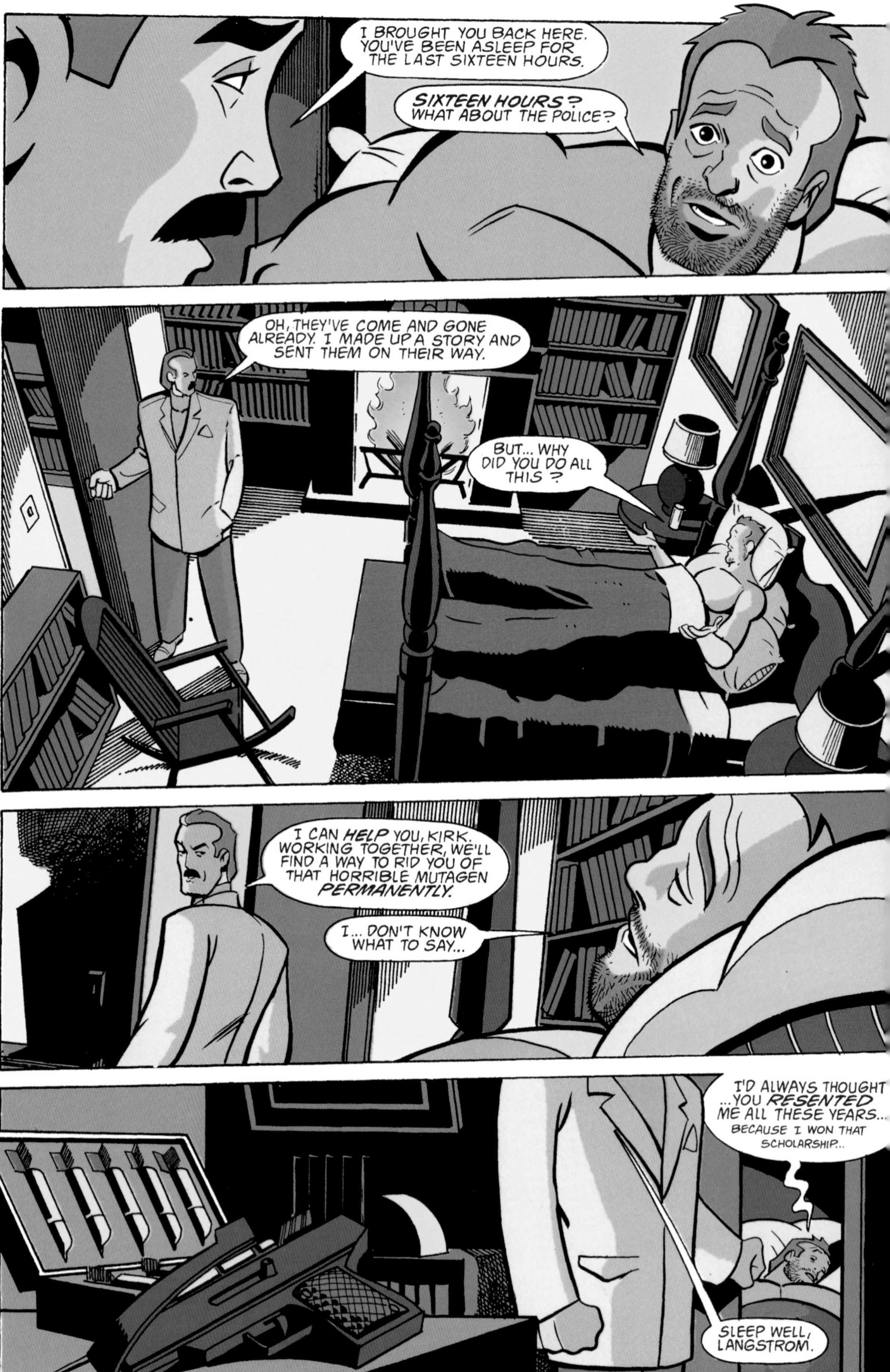
I BROUGHT YOU BACK HERE. YOU'VE BEEN ASLEEP FOR THE LAST SIXTEEN HOURS.
SIXTEEN HOURS? WHAT ABOUT THE POLICE?
OH, THEY'VE COME AND GONE ALREADY. I MADE UP A STORY AND SENT THEM ON THEIR WAY.
BUT... WHY DID YOU DO ALL THIS?
I CAN HELP YOU, KIRK. WORKING TOGETHER, WE'LL FIND A WAY TO RID YOU OF THAT HORRIBLE MUTAGEN PERMANENTLY.
I... DON'T KNOW WHAT TO SAY...
I'D ALWAYS THOUGHT ...YOU RESENTED ME ALL THESE YEARS... BECAUSE I WON THAT SCHOLARSHIP...
SLEEP WELL, LANGSTROM.
14

ACT THREE: THE AWFUL TRUTH!

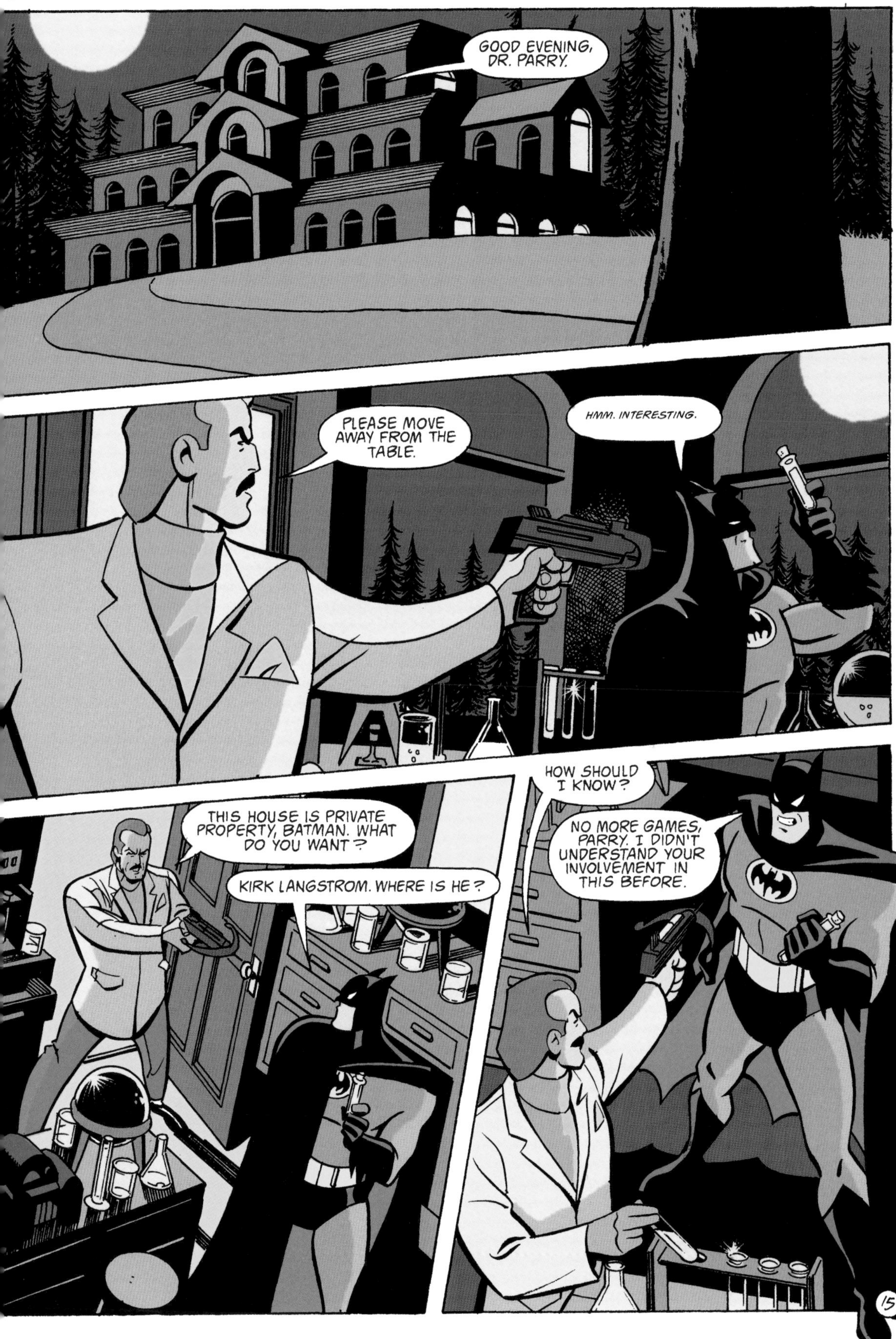
GOOD EVENING, DR. PARRY.
PLEASE MOVE AWAY FROM THE TABLE.
HMM. INTERESTING.
THIS HOUSE IS PRIVATE PROPERTY, BATMAN. WHAT DO YOU WANT?
KIRK LANGSTROM. WHERE IS HE?
HOW SHOULD I KNOW?
NO MORE GAMES, PARRY. I DIDN'T UNDERSTAND YOUR INVOLVEMENT IN THIS BEFORE.
15

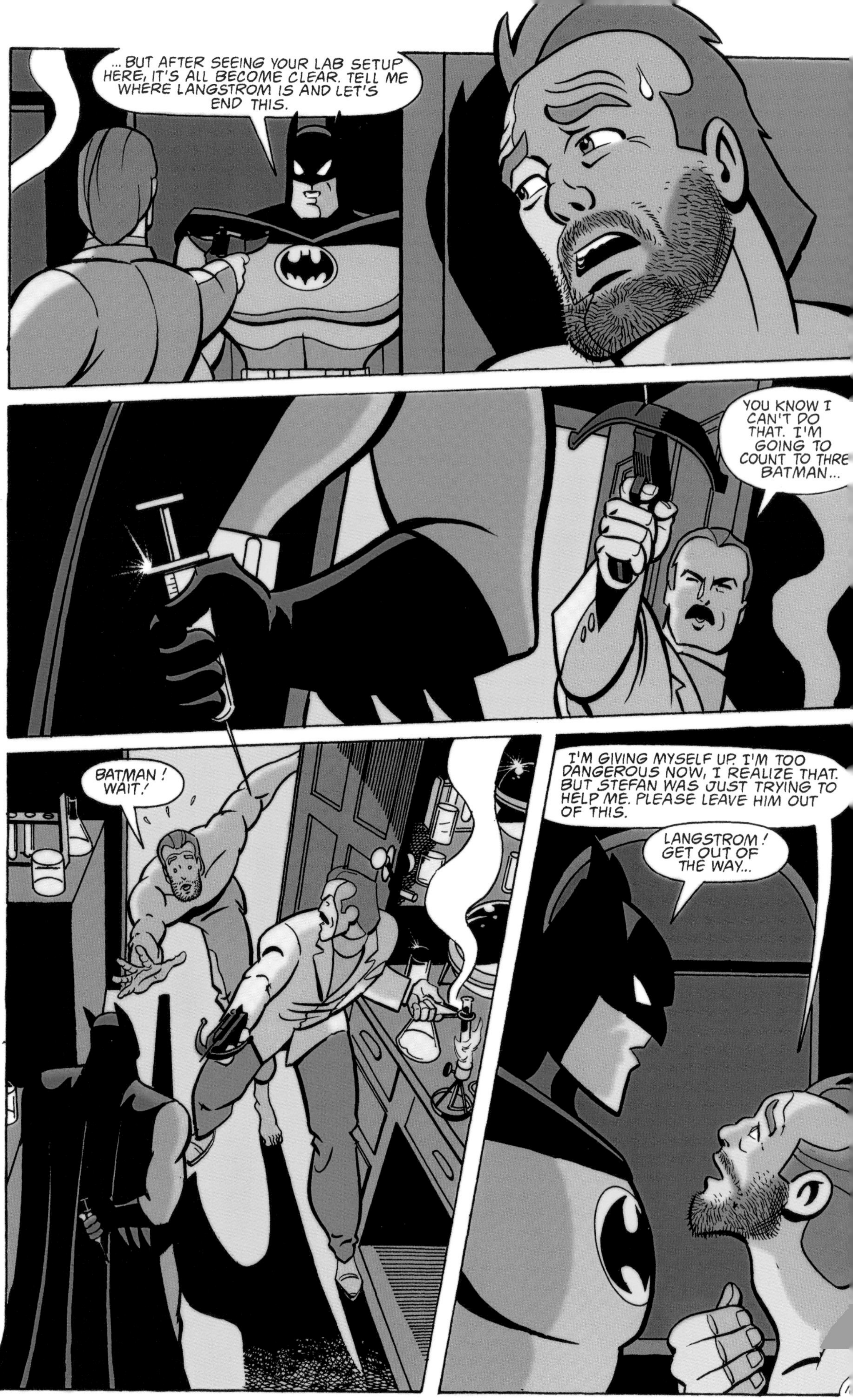
...BUT AFTER SEEING YOUR LAB SETUP HERE, IT'S ALL BECOME CLEAR. TELL ME WHERE LANGSTROM IS AND LET'S END THIS.
YOU KNOW I CAN'T DO THAT. I'M GOING TO COUNT TO THRE BATMAN...
BATMAN! WAIT!
I'M GIVING MYSELF UP. I'M TOO DANGEROUS NOW, I REALIZE THAT. BUT STEFAN WAS JUST TRYING TO HELP ME. PLEASE LEAVE HIM OUT OF THIS.
LANGSTROM! GET OUT OF THE WAY...

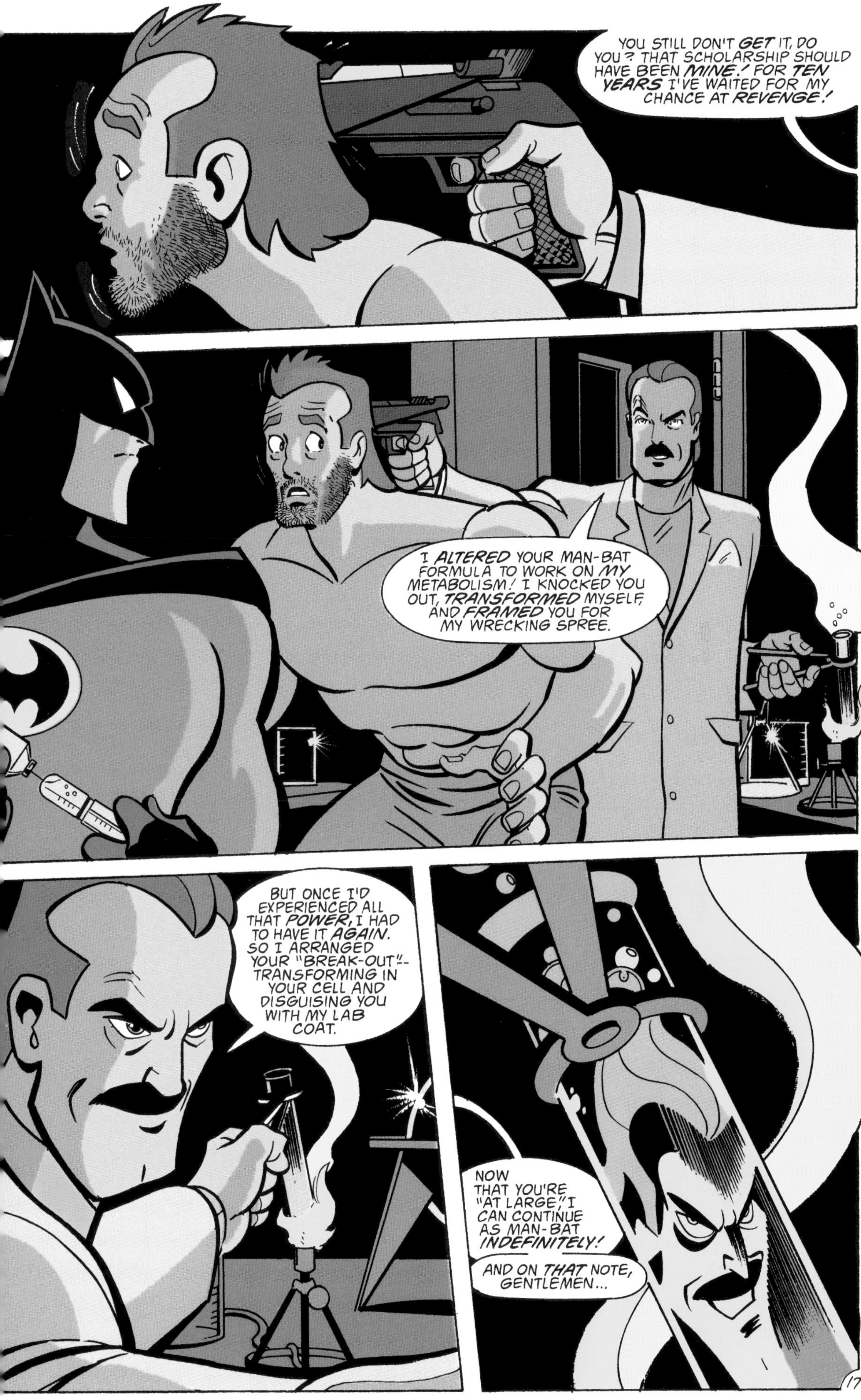

YOU STILL DON'T GET IT, DO YOU? THAT SCHOLARSHIP SHOULD HAVE BEEN MINE! FOR TEN YEARS I'VE WAITED FOR MY CHANCE AT REVENGE!
I ALTERED YOUR MAN-BAT FORMULA TO WORK ON MY METABOLISM! I KNOCKED YOU OUT, TRANSFORMED MYSELF, AND FRAMED YOU FOR MY WRECKING SPREE.
BUT ONCE I'D EXPERIENCED ALL THAT POWER, I HAD TO HAVE IT AGAIN. SO I ARRANGED YOUR "BREAK-OUT"-- TRANSFORMING IN YOUR CELL AND DISGUISING YOU WITH MY LAB COAT.
NOW THAT YOU'RE "AT LARGE," I CAN CONTINUE AS MAN-BAT INDEFINITELY!
AND ON THAT NOTE, GENTLEMEN...
17

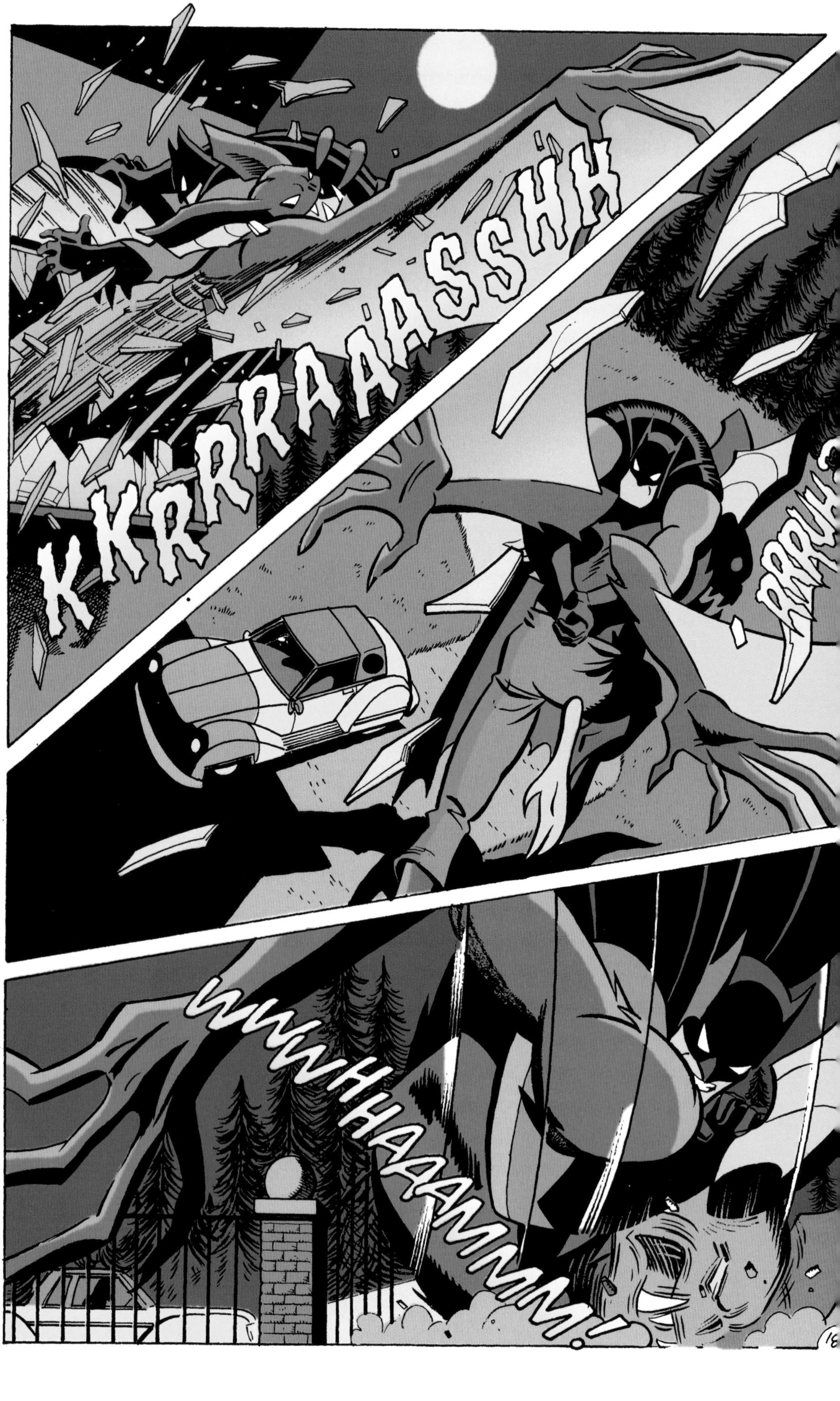
KKRRRAAASSHK
RRRUH
WWWHHAAAMMMM!

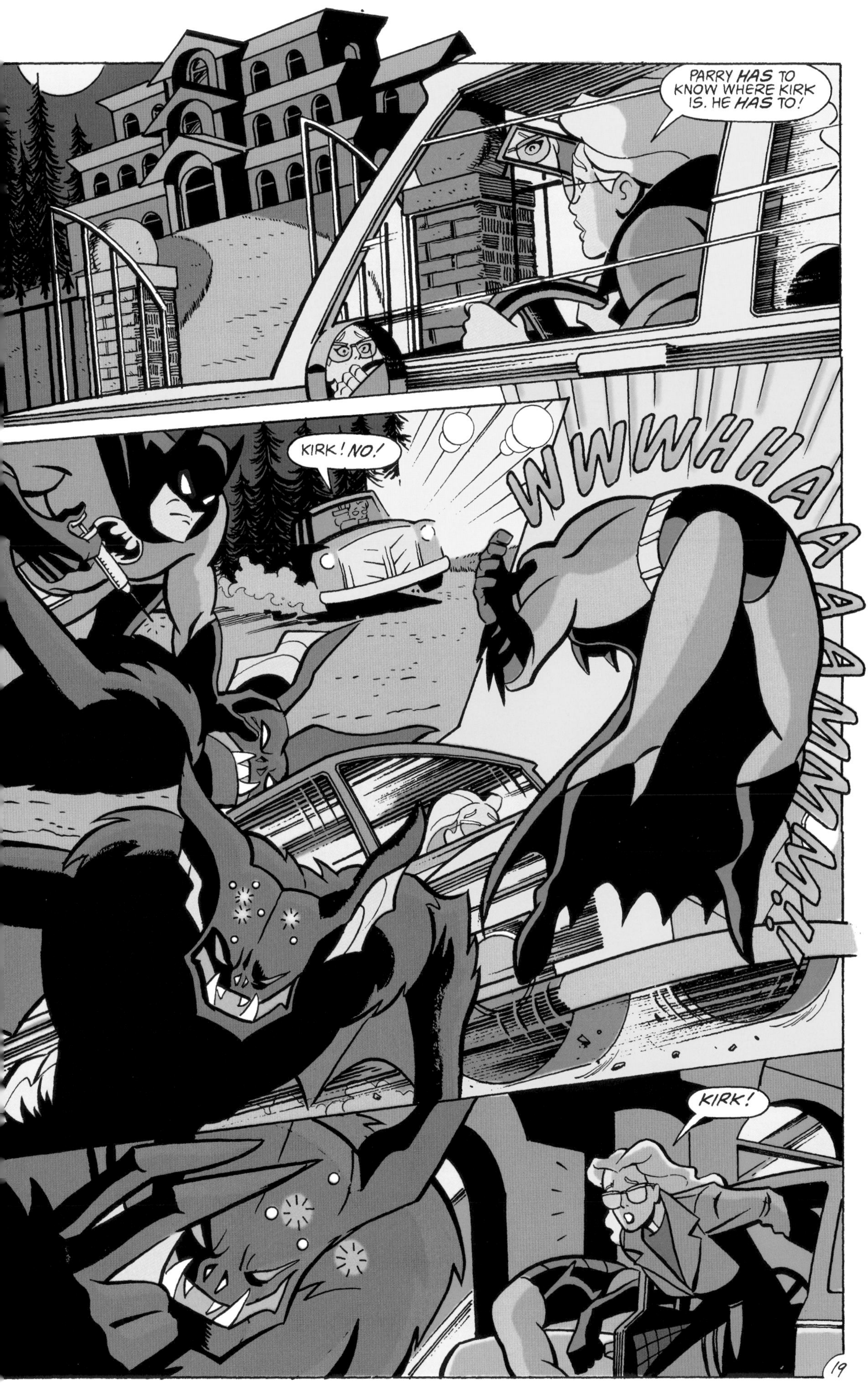
PARRY HAS TO KNOW WHERE KIRK IS. HE HAS TO!
KIRK! NO!
WWWHHAAAAAMMM!!
KIRK!
19

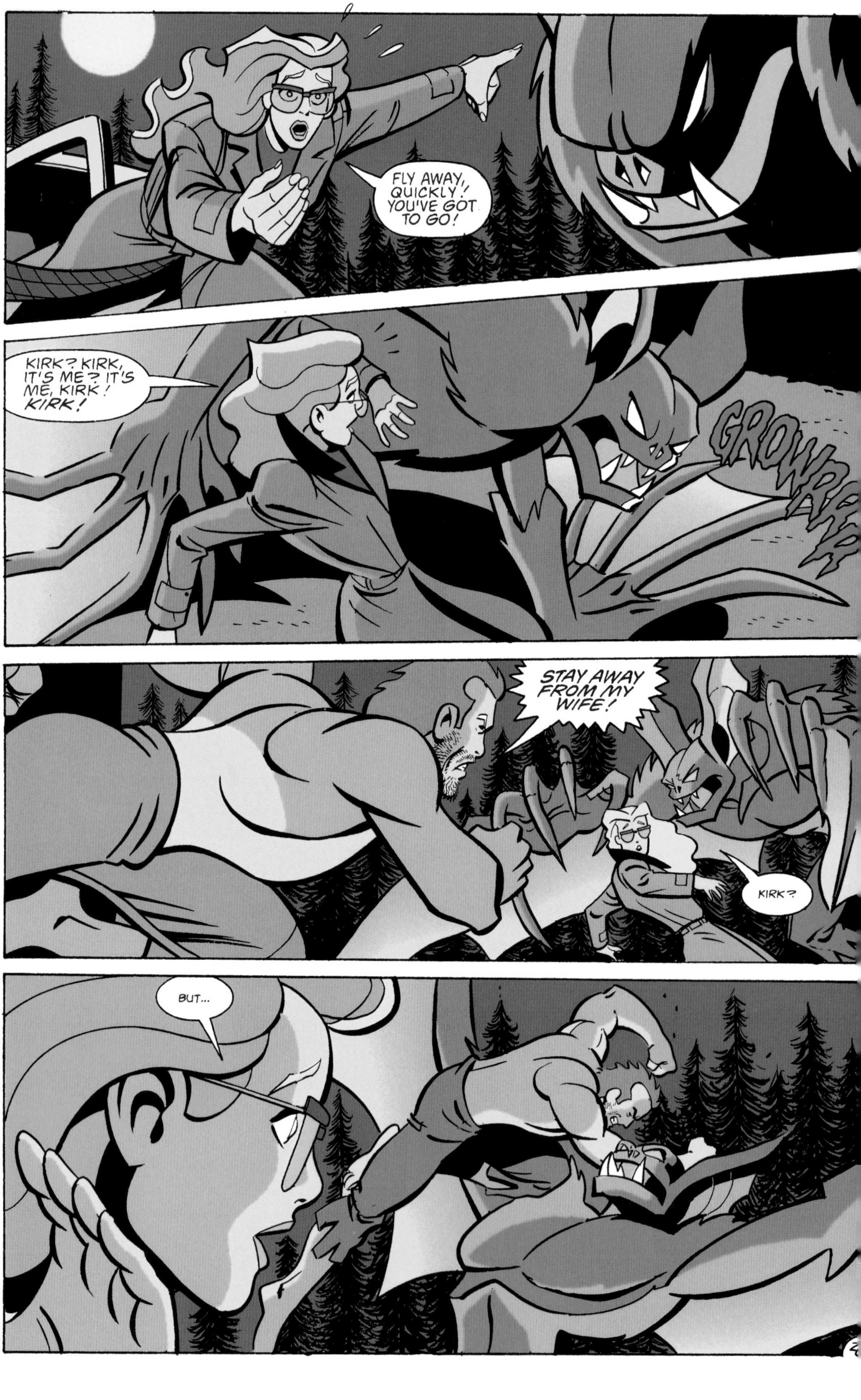
FLY AWAY, QUICKLY! YOU'VE GOT TO GO!
KIRK? KIRK, IT'S ME? IT'S ME, KIRK! KIRK!
GROWRRR
STAY AWAY FROM MY WIFE!
KIRK?
BUT...

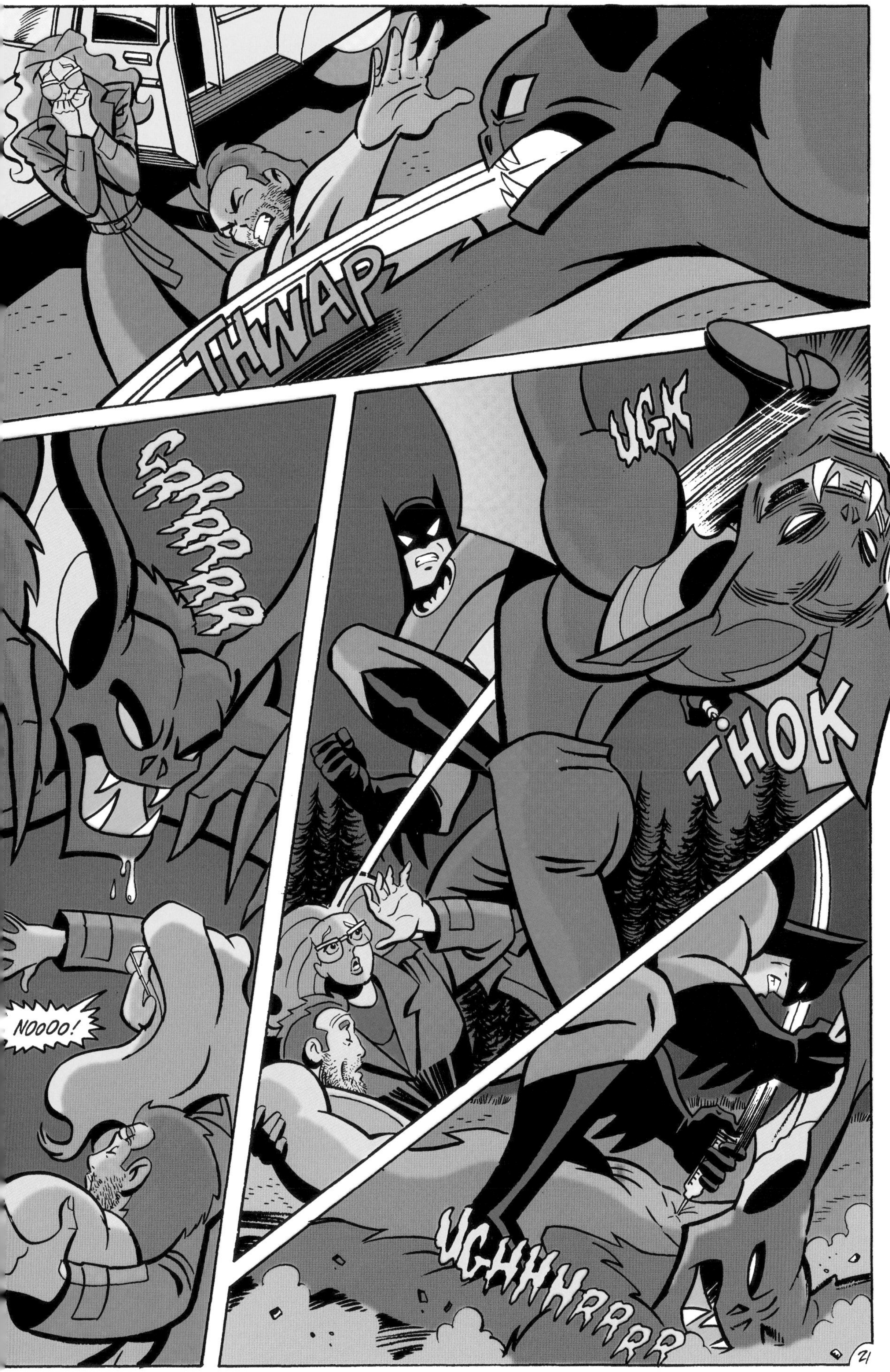
THWAP
GRRRRRR
UGK
THOK
NOOOO!
UGHHHRRRRR
21

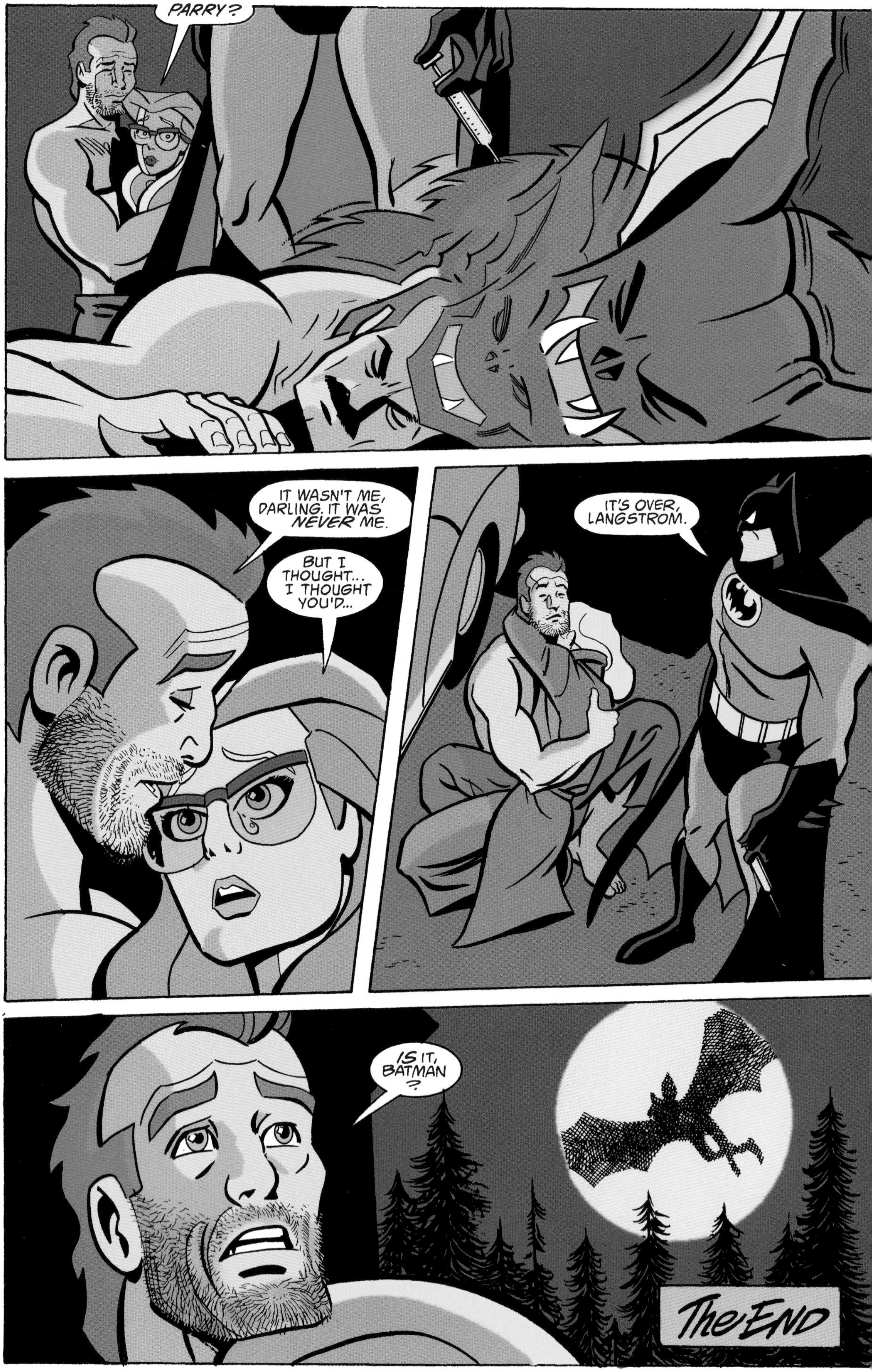
PARRY?
IT WASN'T ME, DARLING. IT WAS NEVER ME.
BUT I THOUGHT... I THOUGHT YOU'D...
IT'S OVER, LANGSTROM.
IS IT, BATMAN?
The End

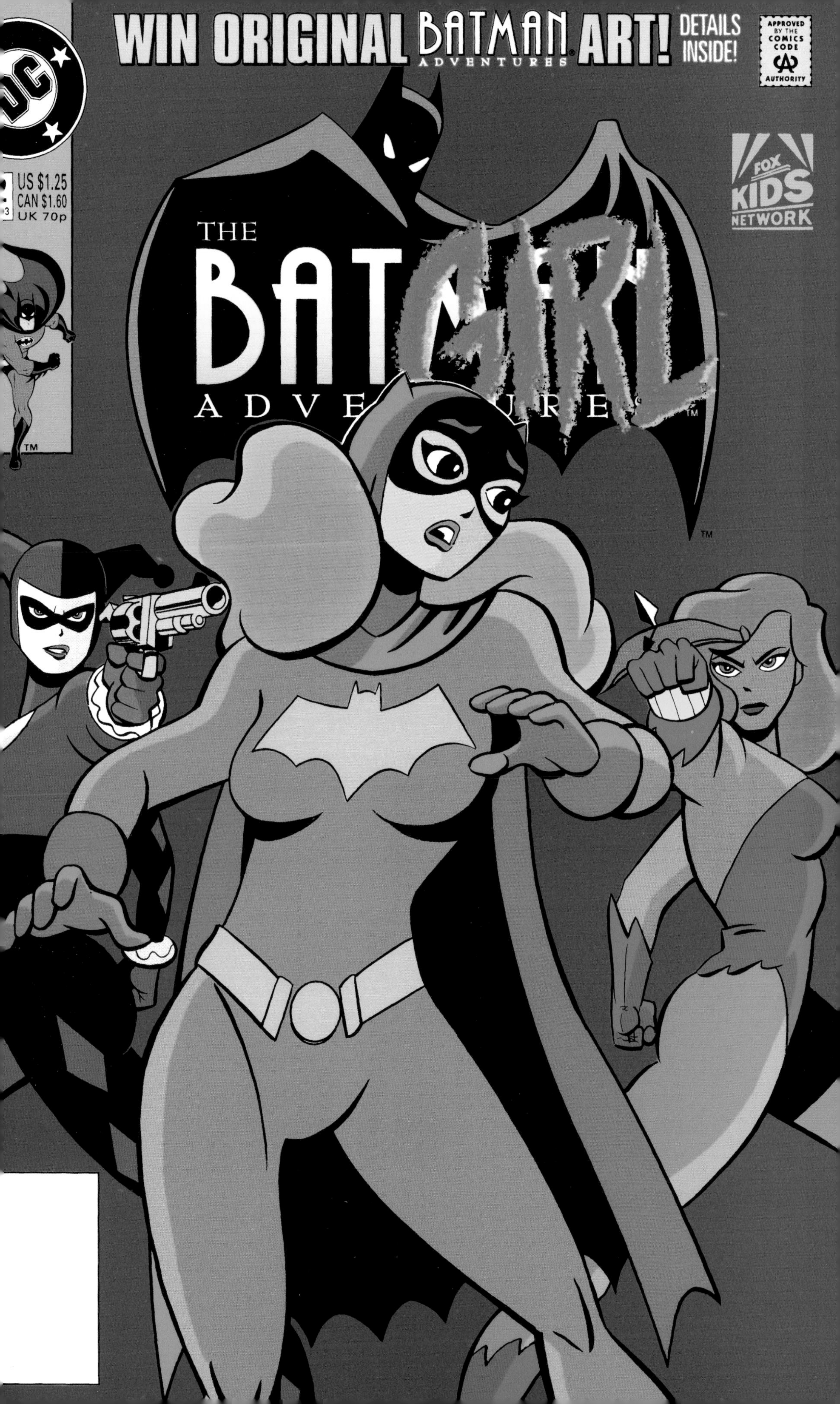

WIN ORIGINAL BATMAN ADVENTURES ART! DETAILS INSIDE!
APPROVED BY THE COMICS CODE AUTHORITY
DC
US $1.25
CAN $1.60
UK 70p
FOX KIDS NETWORK
THE BATGIRL ADVENTURES

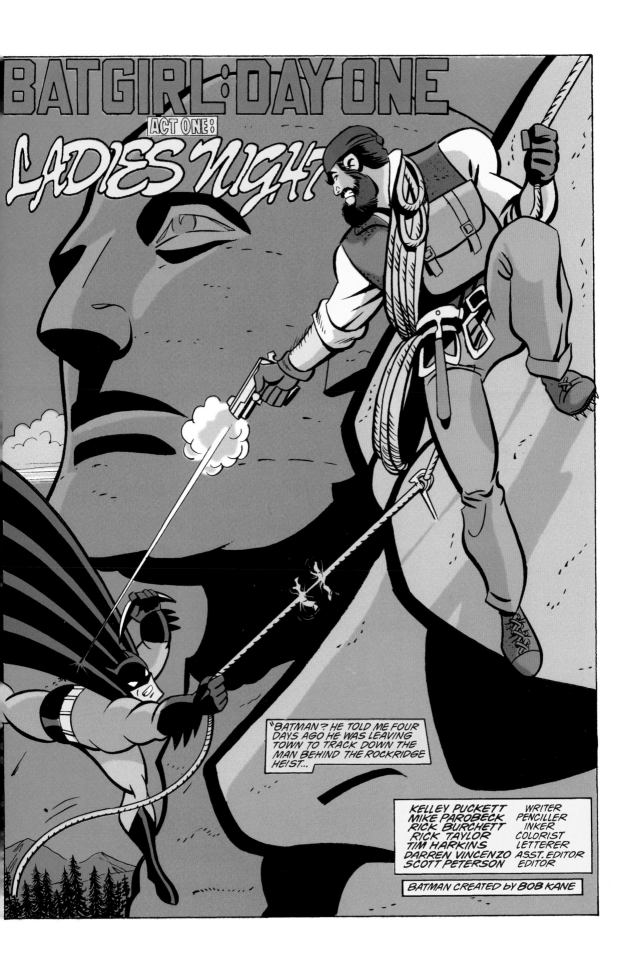

BATGIRL·DAY ONE

ACT ONE:

LADIES NIGHT

"BATMAN? HE TOLD ME FOUR DAYS AGO HE WAS LEAVING TOWN TO TRACK DOWN THE MAN BEHIND THE ROCKRIDGE HEIST..."

KELLEY PUCKETT — WRITER
MIKE PAROBECK — PENCILLER
RICK BURCHETT — INKER
RICK TAYLOR — COLORIST
TIM HARKINS — LETTERER
DARREN VINCENZO — ASST. EDITOR
SCOTT PETERSON — EDITOR

BATMAN CREATED BY BOB KANE

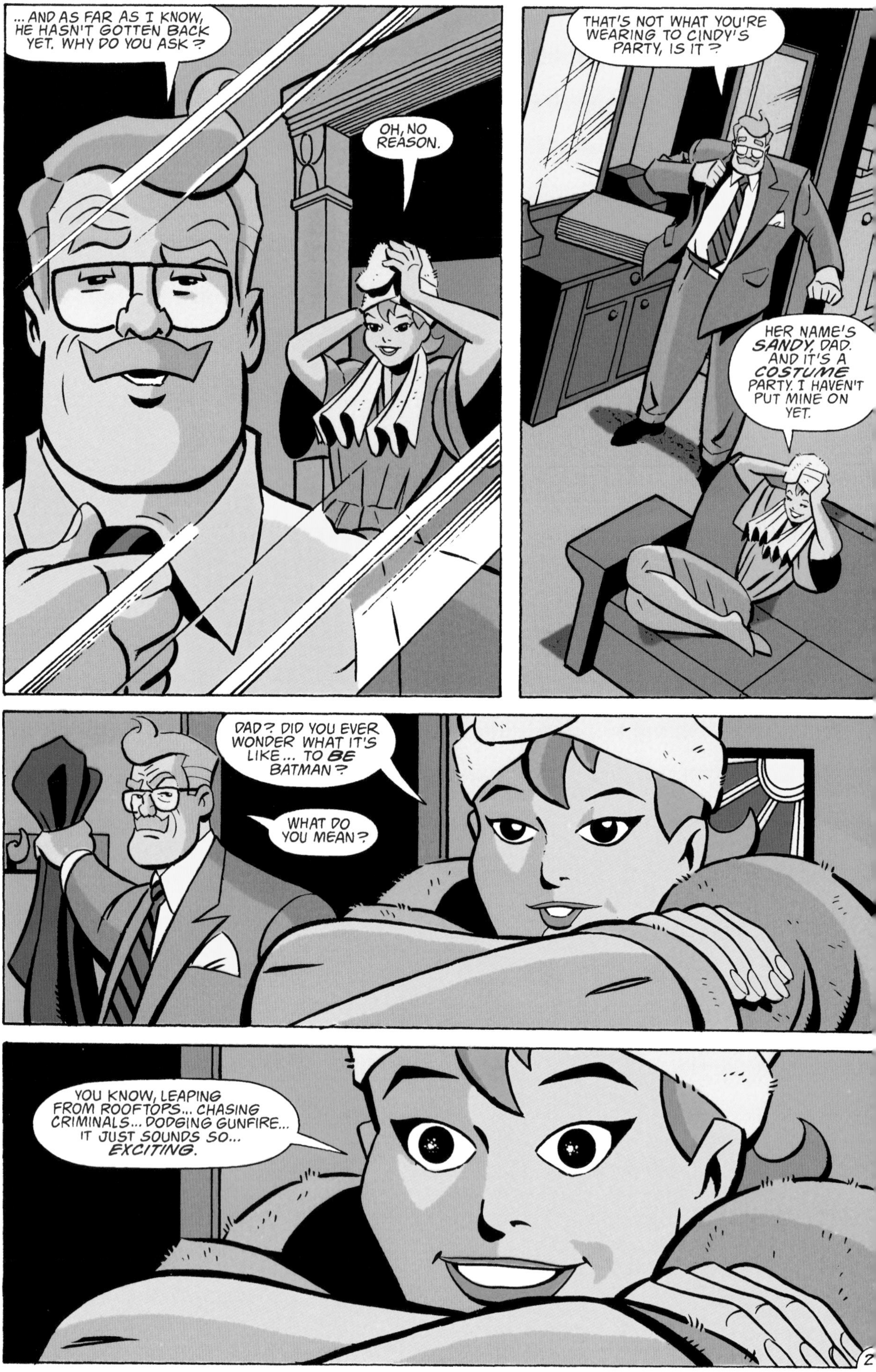
...AND AS FAR AS I KNOW, HE HASN'T GOTTEN BACK YET. WHY DO YOU ASK?
OH, NO REASON.
THAT'S NOT WHAT YOU'RE WEARING TO CINDY'S PARTY, IS IT?
HER NAME'S SANDY, DAD. AND IT'S A COSTUME PARTY. I HAVEN'T PUT MINE ON YET.
DAD? DID YOU EVER WONDER WHAT IT'S LIKE... TO BE BATMAN?
WHAT DO YOU MEAN?
YOU KNOW, LEAPING FROM ROOFTOPS... CHASING CRIMINALS... DODGING GUNFIRE... IT JUST SOUNDS SO... EXCITING.
2

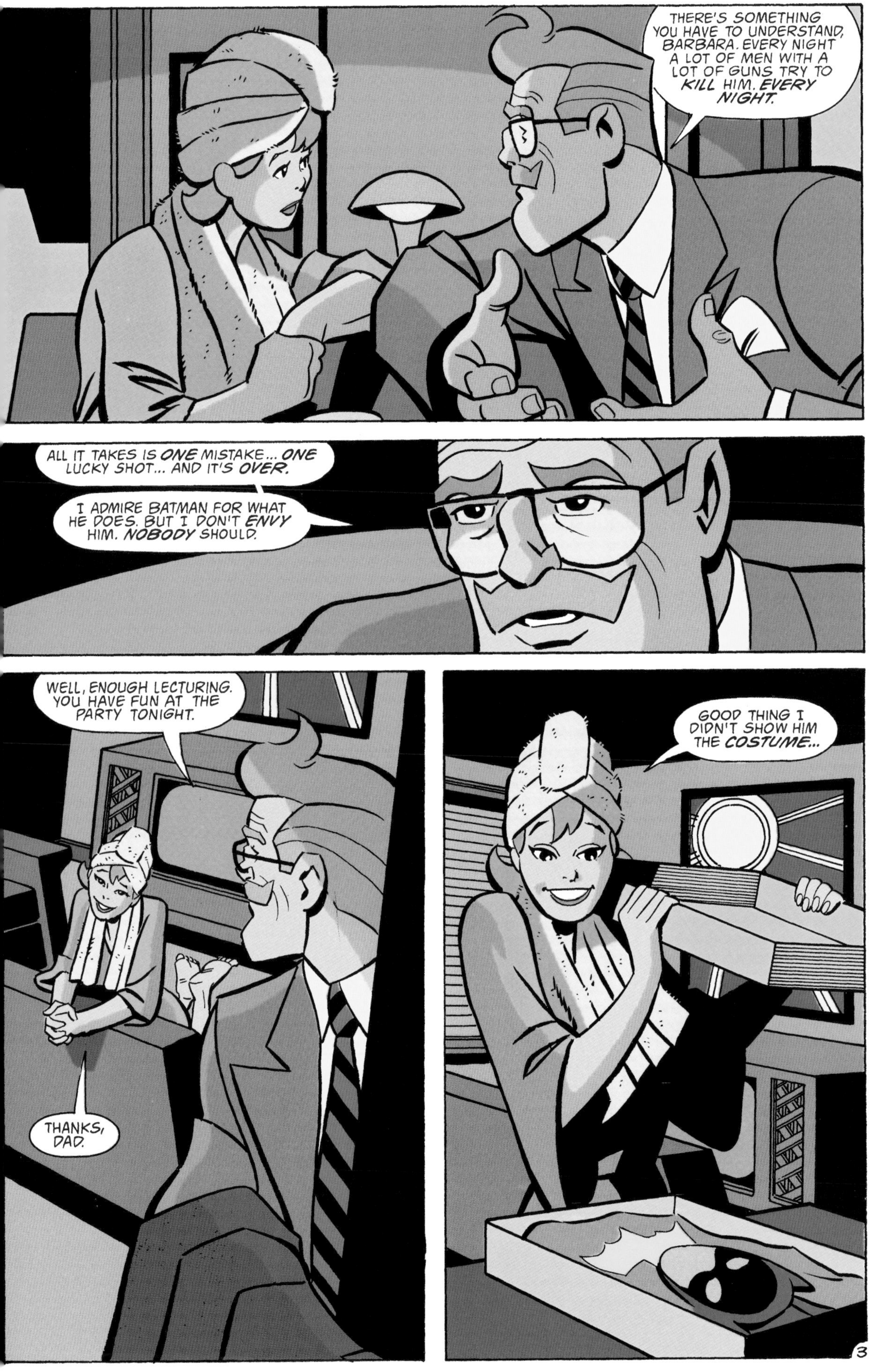
THERE'S SOMETHING YOU HAVE TO UNDERSTAND, BARBARA. EVERY NIGHT A LOT OF MEN WITH A LOT OF GUNS TRY TO KILL HIM. EVERY NIGHT.
ALL IT TAKES IS ONE MISTAKE... ONE LUCKY SHOT... AND IT'S OVER.
I ADMIRE BATMAN FOR WHAT HE DOES. BUT I DON'T ENVY HIM. NOBODY SHOULD.
WELL, ENOUGH LECTURING. YOU HAVE FUN AT THE PARTY TONIGHT.
THANKS, DAD.
GOOD THING I DIDN'T SHOW HIM THE COSTUME...
3

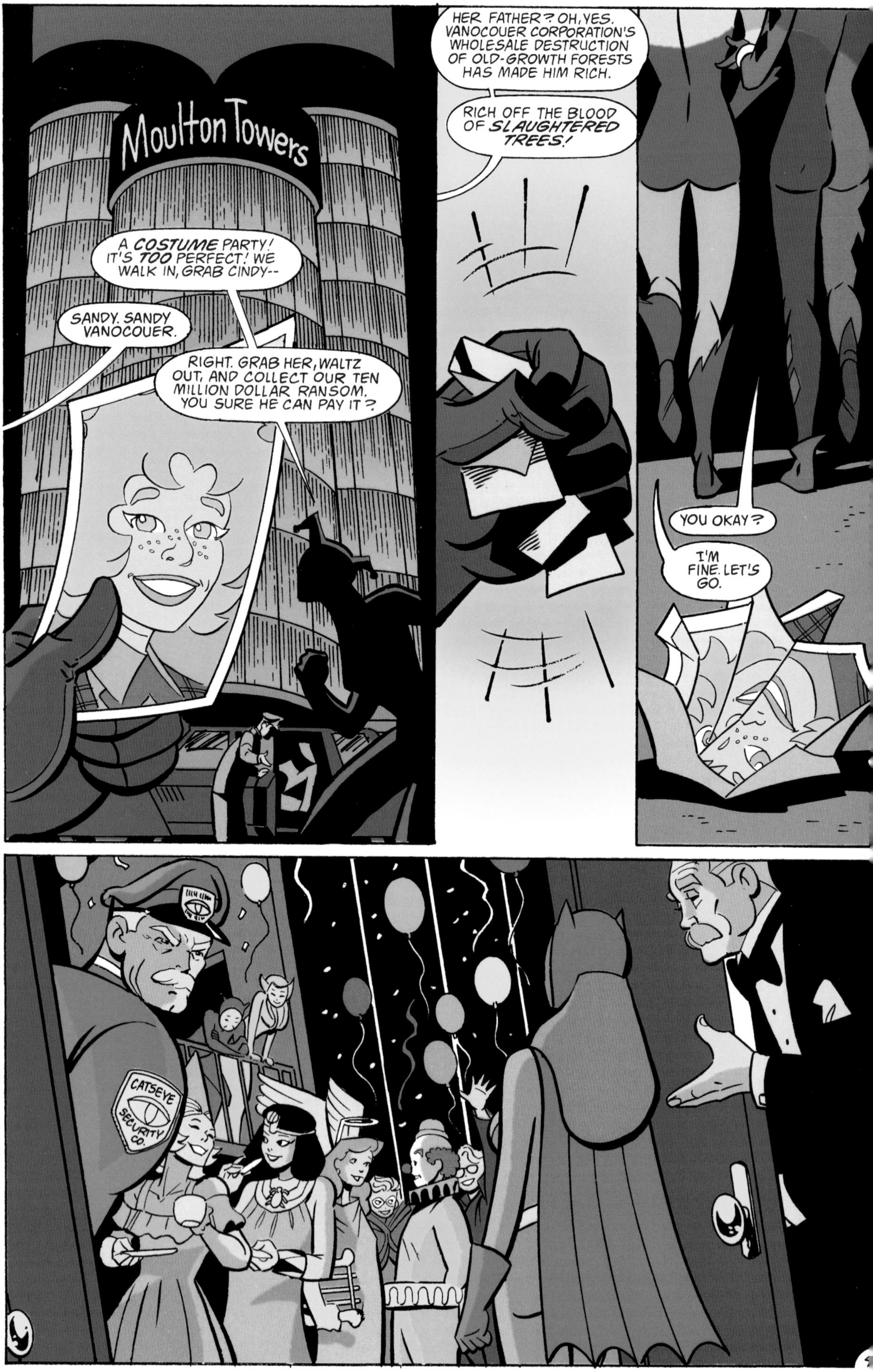
Moulton Towers
A COSTUME PARTY! IT'S TOO PERFECT! WE WALK IN, GRAB CINDY--
SANDY. SANDY VANOCOUER.
RIGHT. GRAB HER, WALTZ OUT, AND COLLECT OUR TEN MILLION DOLLAR RANSOM. YOU SURE HE CAN PAY IT?
HER FATHER? OH, YES. VANOCOUER CORPORATION'S WHOLESALE DESTRUCTION OF OLD-GROWTH FORESTS HAS MADE HIM RICH.
RICH OFF THE BLOOD OF SLAUGHTERED TREES!
YOU OKAY?
I'M FINE. LET'S GO.
CATSEYE SECURITY CO.

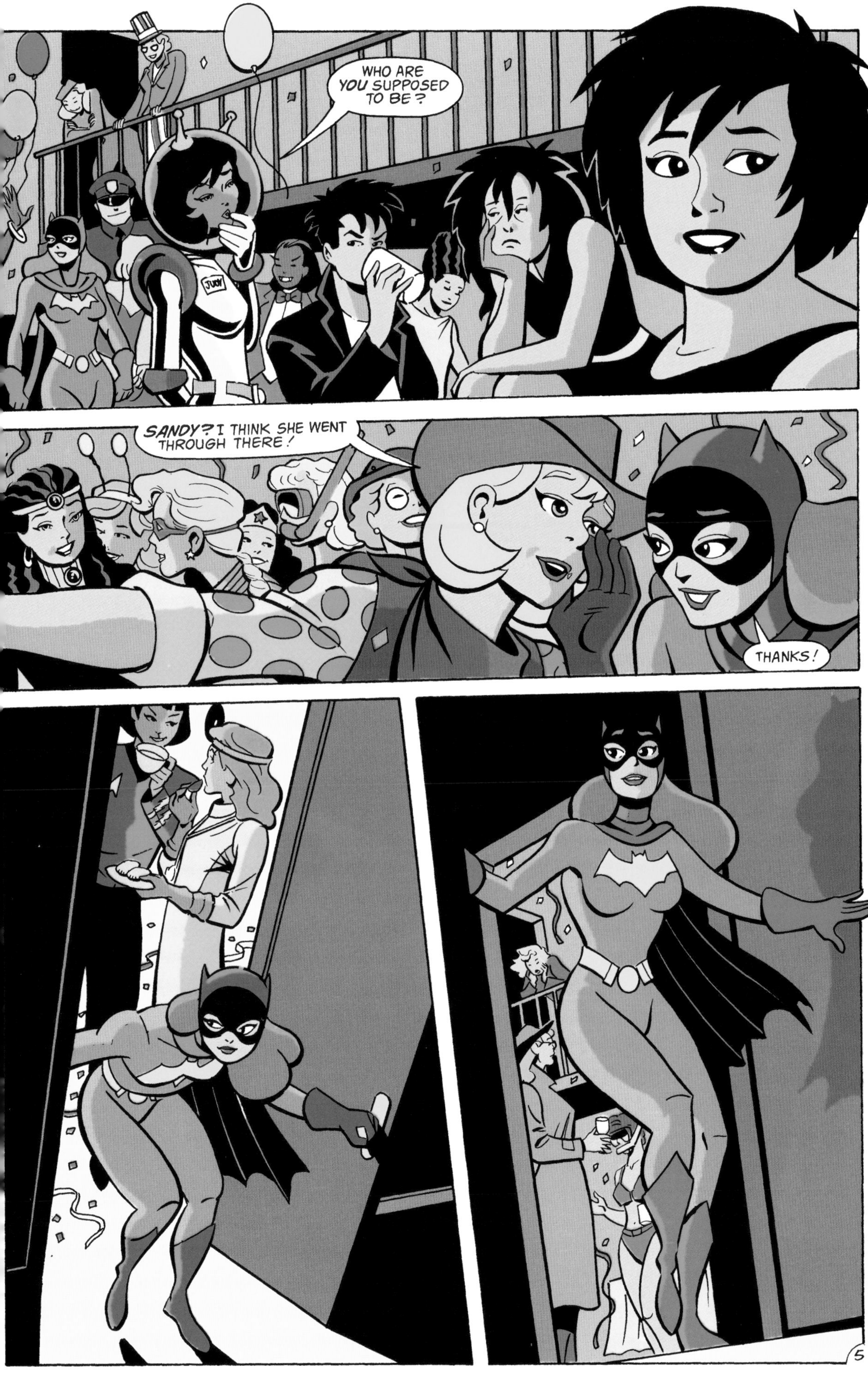
WHO ARE YOU SUPPOSED TO BE?
JUDY
SANDY? I THINK SHE WENT THROUGH THERE!
THANKS!
5

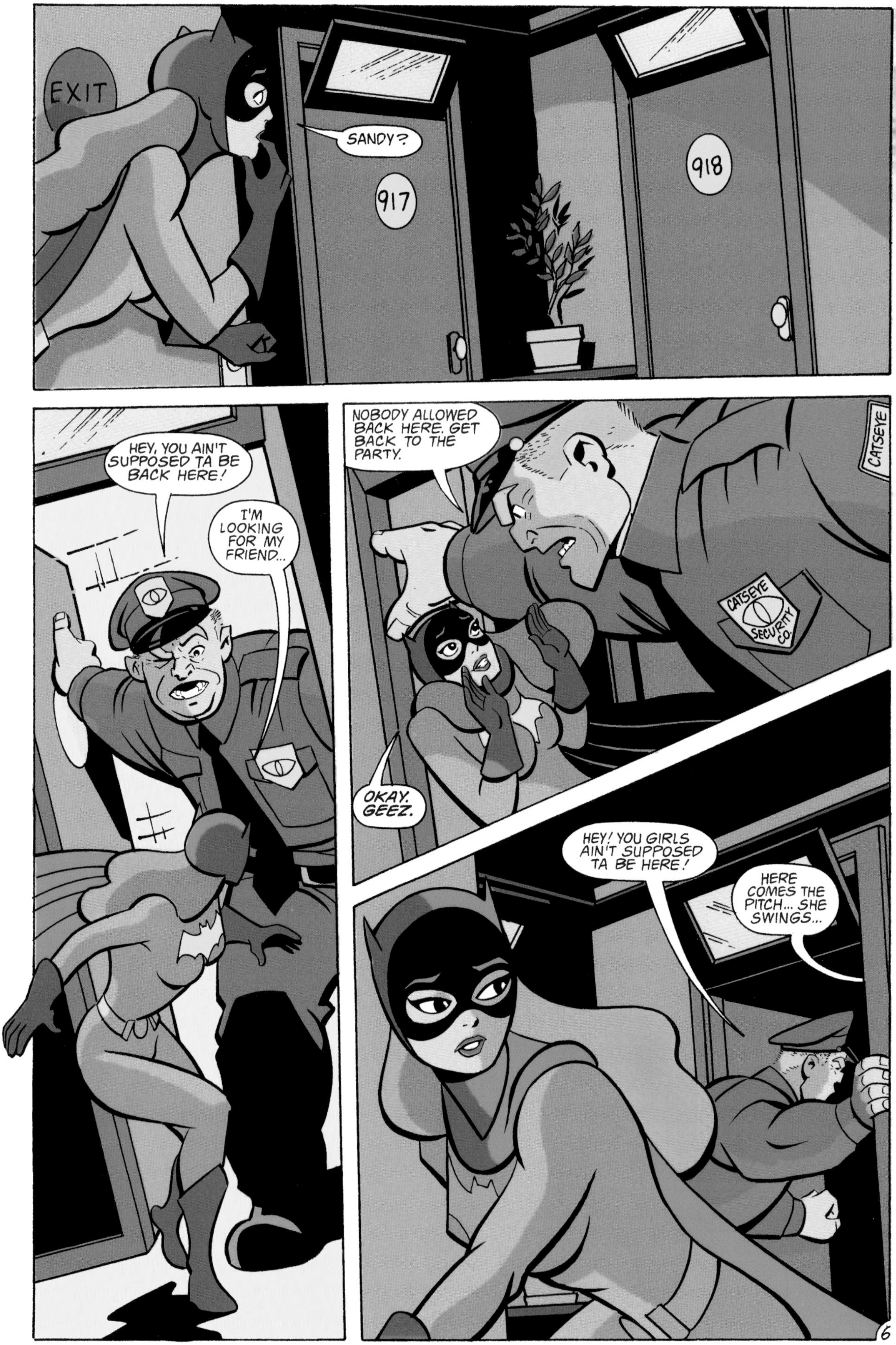
EXIT
SANDY?
917
918
HEY, YOU AIN'T SUPPOSED TA BE BACK HERE!
I'M LOOKING FOR MY FRIEND...
NOBODY ALLOWED BACK HERE. GET BACK TO THE PARTY.
CATSEYE
CATSEYE SECURITY CO.
OKAY. GEEZ.
HEY! YOU GIRLS AIN'T SUPPOSED TA BE HERE!
HERE COMES THE PITCH... SHE SWINGS...
6

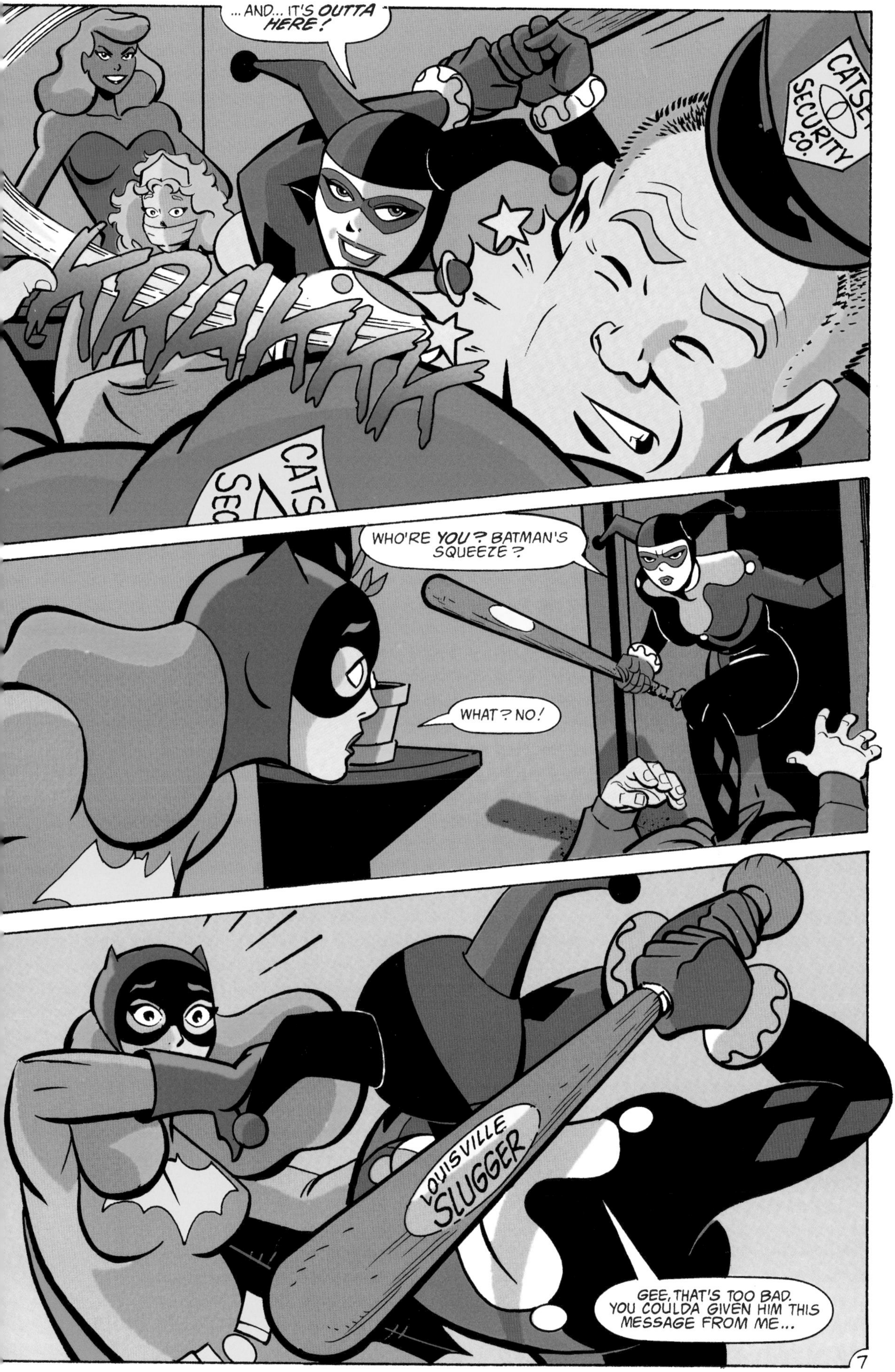

...AND... IT'S OUTTA HERE!
THWAKKK
CATSEYE SECURITY CO.
WHO'RE YOU? BATMAN'S SQUEEZE?
WHAT? NO!
LOUISVILLE SLUGGER
GEE, THAT'S TOO BAD. YOU COULDA GIVEN HIM THIS MESSAGE FROM ME...
7

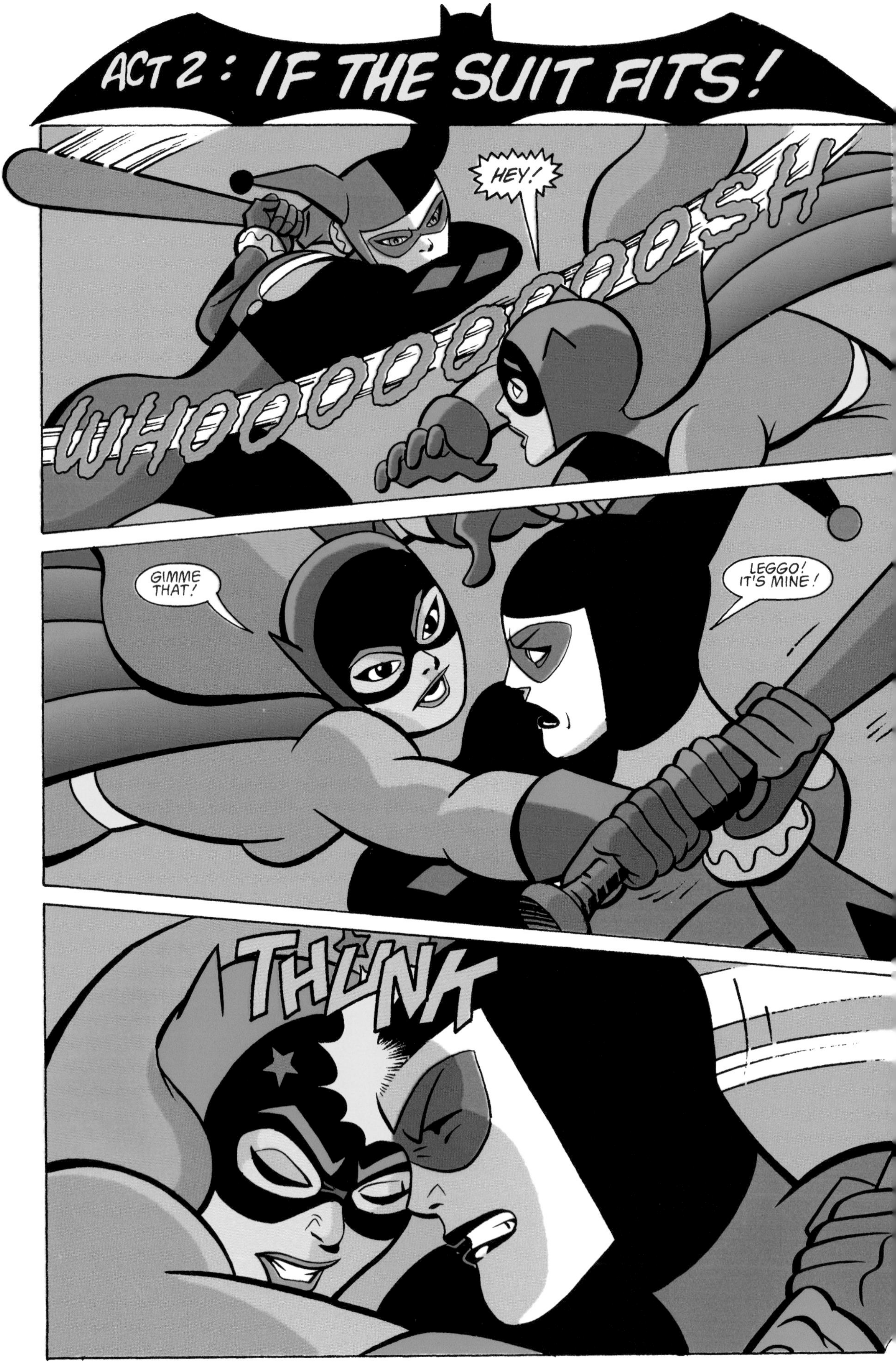
ACT 2 : IF THE SUIT FITS!
HEY!
WHOOOOOOOOOOOSH
GIMME THAT!
LEGGO! IT'S MINE!
THUNK

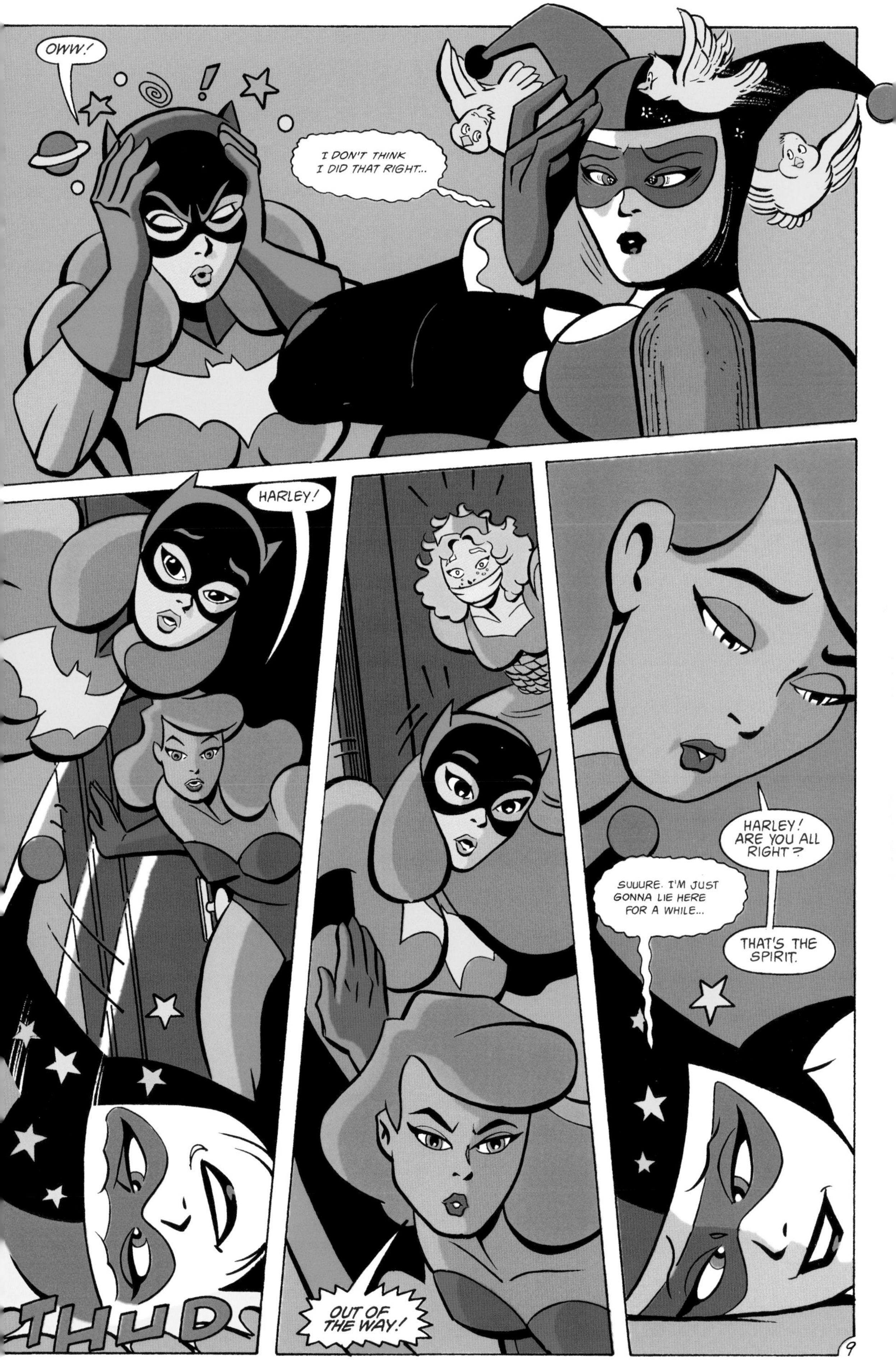

OWW!
I DON'T THINK I DID THAT RIGHT...
HARLEY!
THUD
OUT OF THE WAY!
HARLEY! ARE YOU ALL RIGHT?
SUUURE. I'M JUST GONNA LIE HERE FOR A WHILE...
THAT'S THE SPIRIT.
9

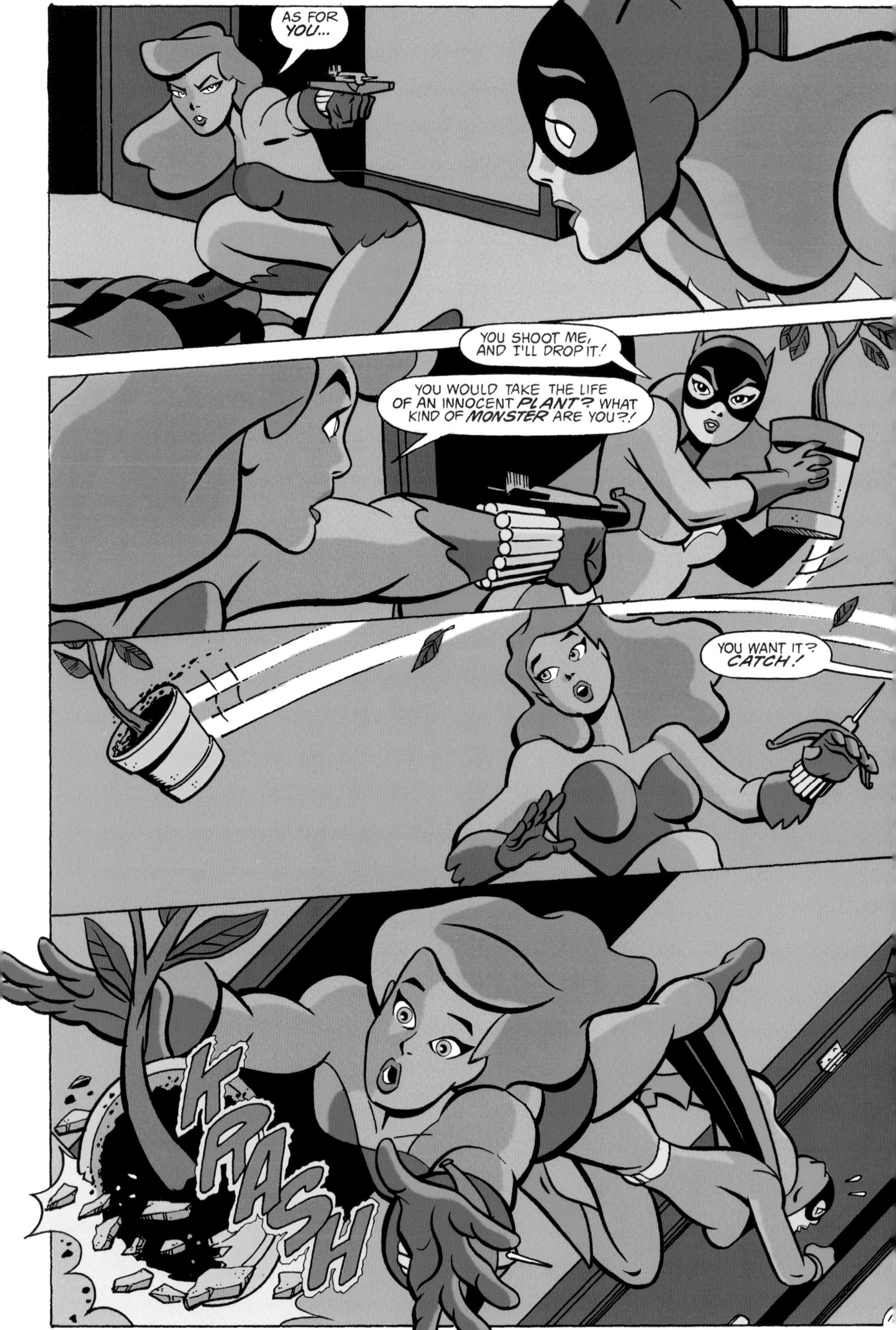

AS FOR YOU...
YOU SHOOT ME, AND I'LL DROP IT!
YOU WOULD TAKE THE LIFE OF AN INNOCENT PLANT? WHAT KIND OF MONSTER ARE YOU?!
YOU WANT IT? CATCH!
KRASH

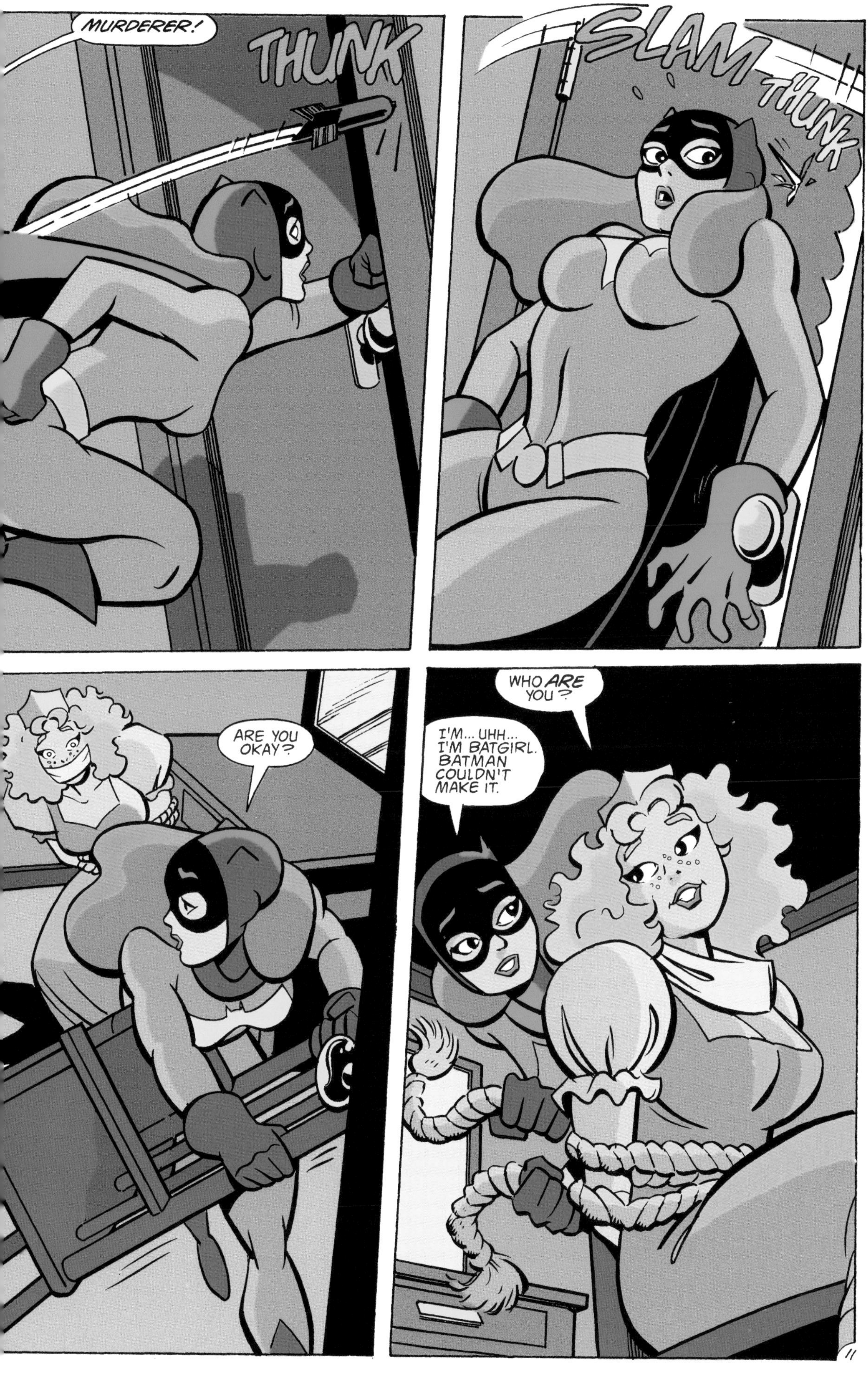
MURDERER!
THUNK
SLAM
THUNK
ARE YOU OKAY?
WHO ARE YOU?
I'M... UHH... I'M BATGIRL. BATMAN COULDN'T MAKE IT.
11

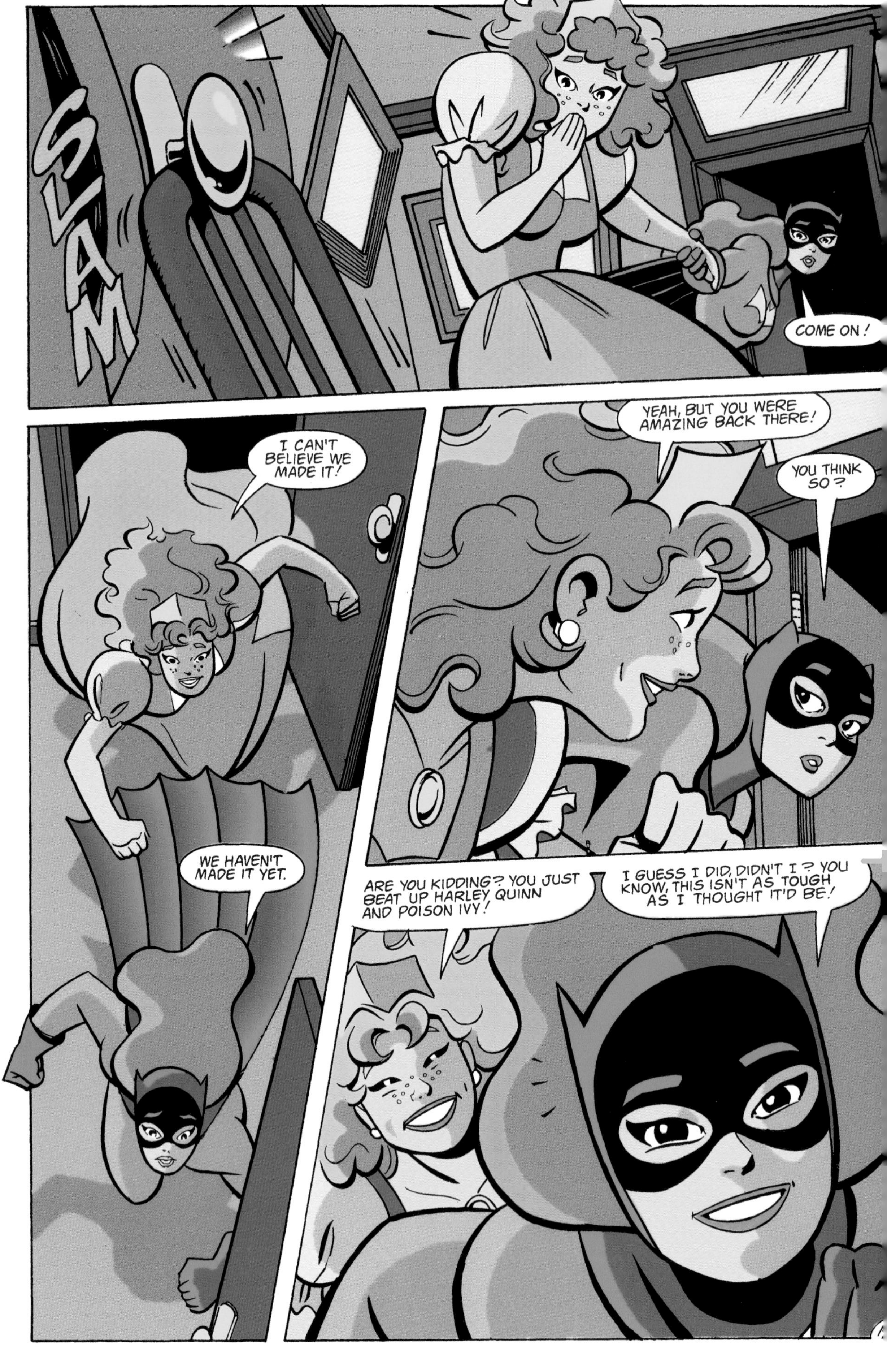
SLAM
COME ON!
I CAN'T BELIEVE WE MADE IT!
WE HAVEN'T MADE IT YET.
YEAH, BUT YOU WERE AMAZING BACK THERE!
YOU THINK SO?
ARE YOU KIDDING? YOU JUST BEAT UP HARLEY QUINN AND POISON IVY!
I GUESS I DID, DIDN'T I? YOU KNOW, THIS ISN'T AS TOUGH AS I THOUGHT IT'D BE!

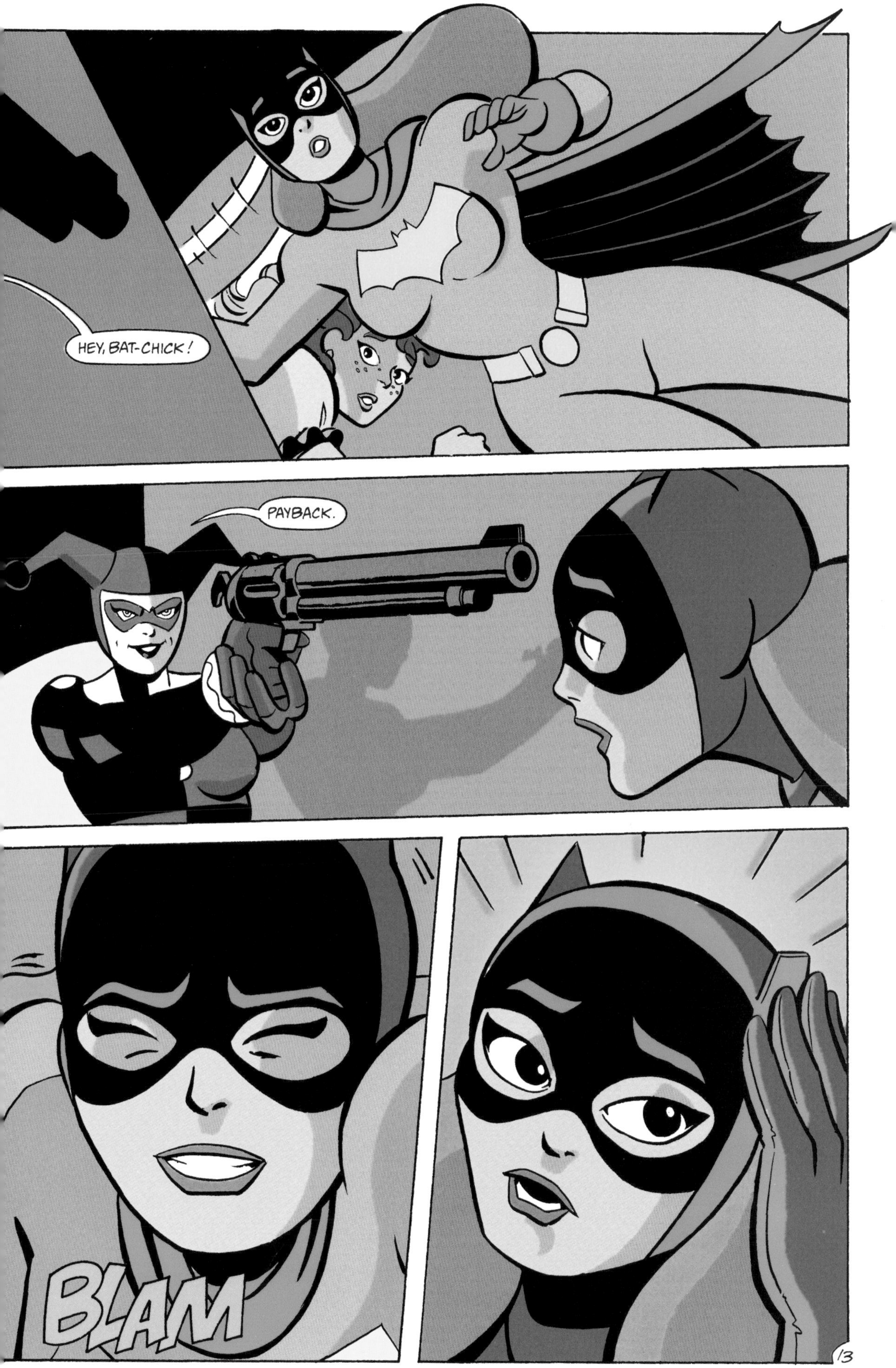
HEY, BAT-CHICK!
PAYBACK.
BLAM
13

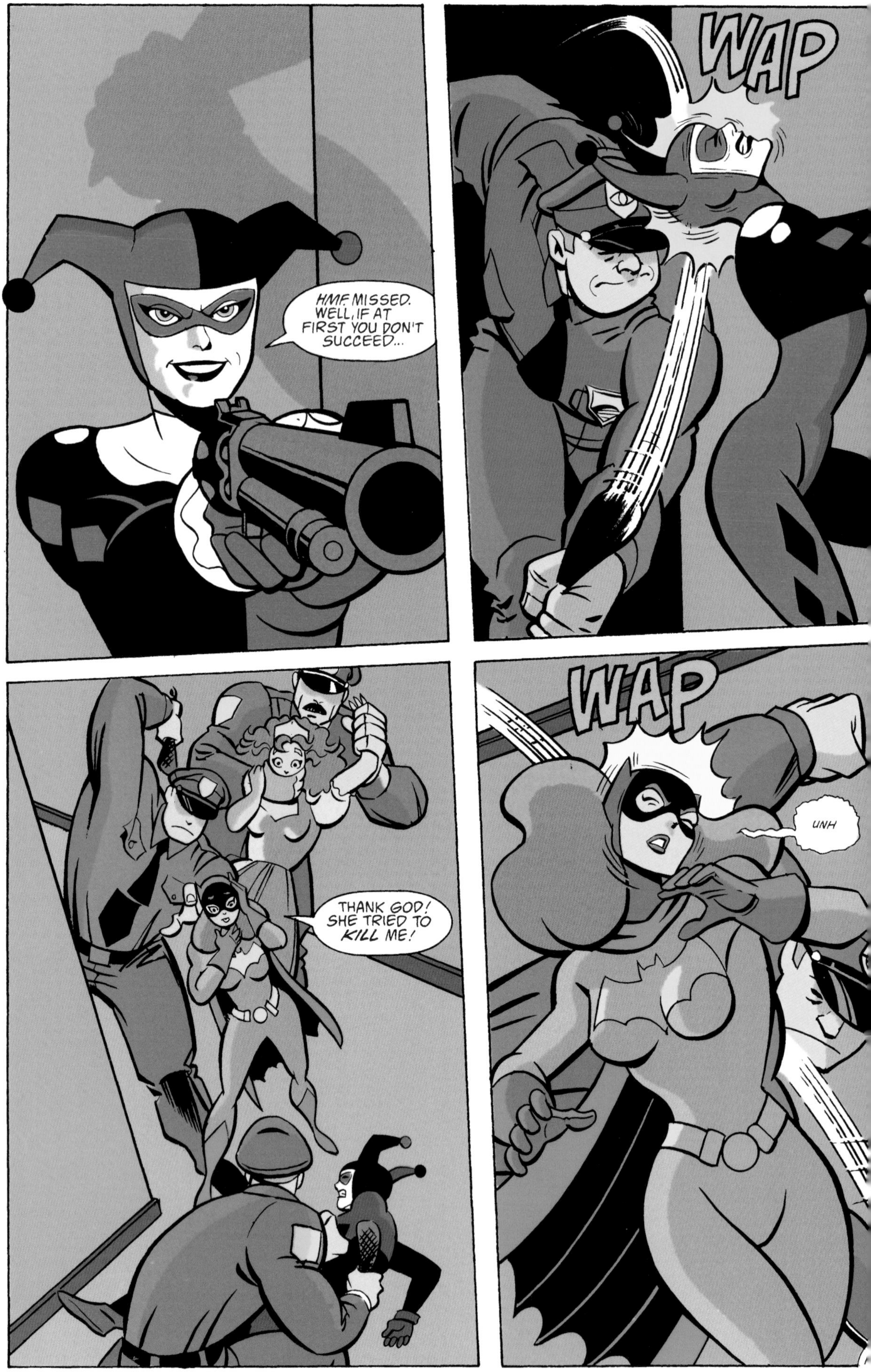
HMF. MISSED. WELL, IF AT FIRST YOU DON'T SUCCEED...
WAP
THANK GOD! SHE TRIED TO KILL ME!
WAP
UNH

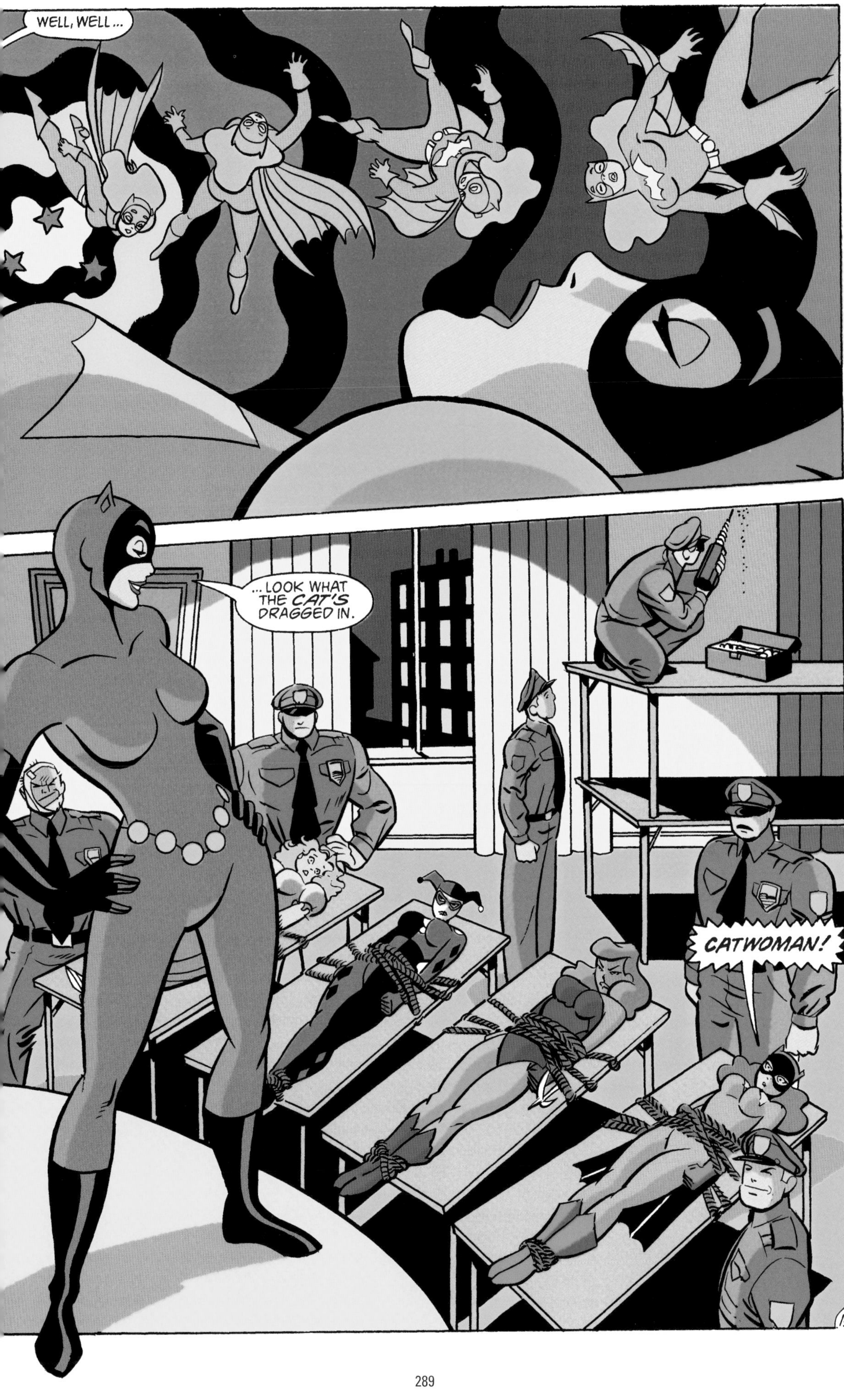

WELL, WELL...
...LOOK WHAT THE CAT'S DRAGGED IN.
CATWOMAN!
15

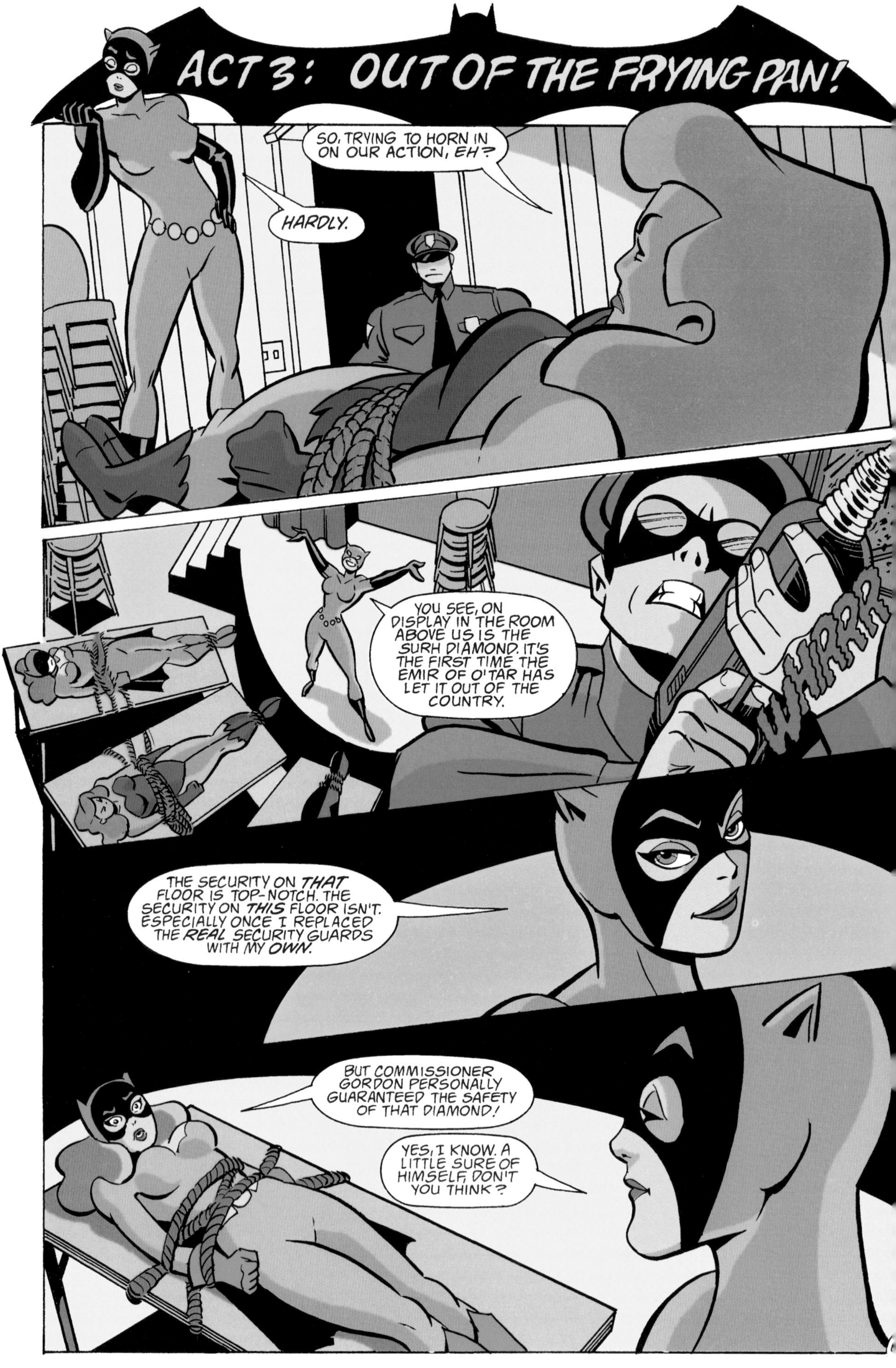
ACT 3: OUT OF THE FRYING PAN!
SO, TRYING TO HORN IN ON OUR ACTION, EH?
HARDLY.
YOU SEE, ON DISPLAY IN THE ROOM ABOVE US IS THE SURH DIAMOND. IT'S THE FIRST TIME THE EMIR OF O'TAR HAS LET IT OUT OF THE COUNTRY.
WHRRR
THE SECURITY ON THAT FLOOR IS TOP-NOTCH. THE SECURITY ON THIS FLOOR ISN'T. ESPECIALLY ONCE I REPLACED THE REAL SECURITY GUARDS WITH MY OWN.
BUT COMMISSIONER GORDON PERSONALLY GUARANTEED THE SAFETY OF THAT DIAMOND!
YES, I KNOW. A LITTLE SURE OF HIMSELF, DON'T YOU THINK?

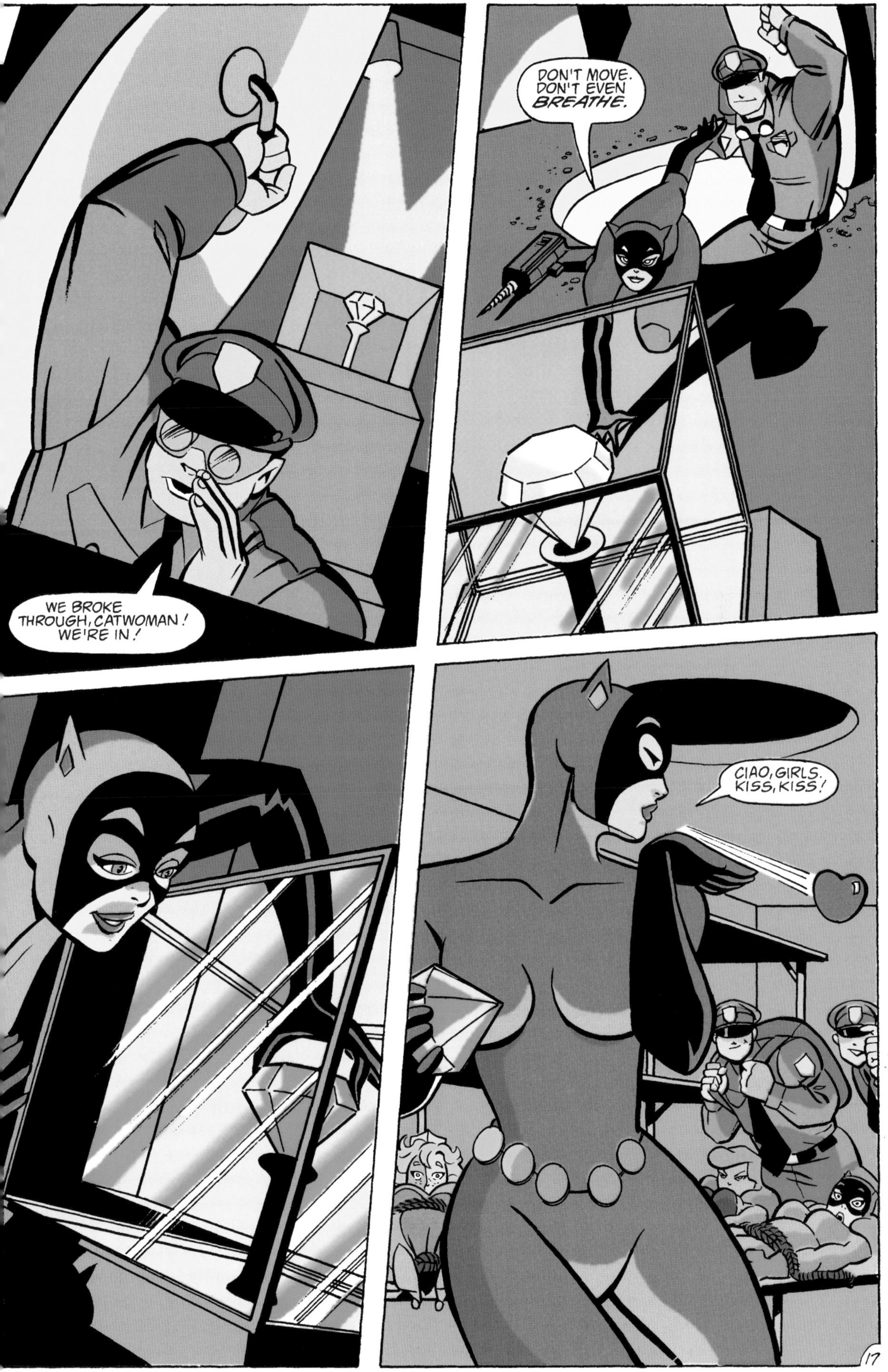
WE BROKE THROUGH, CATWOMAN! WE'RE IN!
DON'T MOVE. DON'T EVEN BREATHE.
CIAO, GIRLS. KISS, KISS!
17

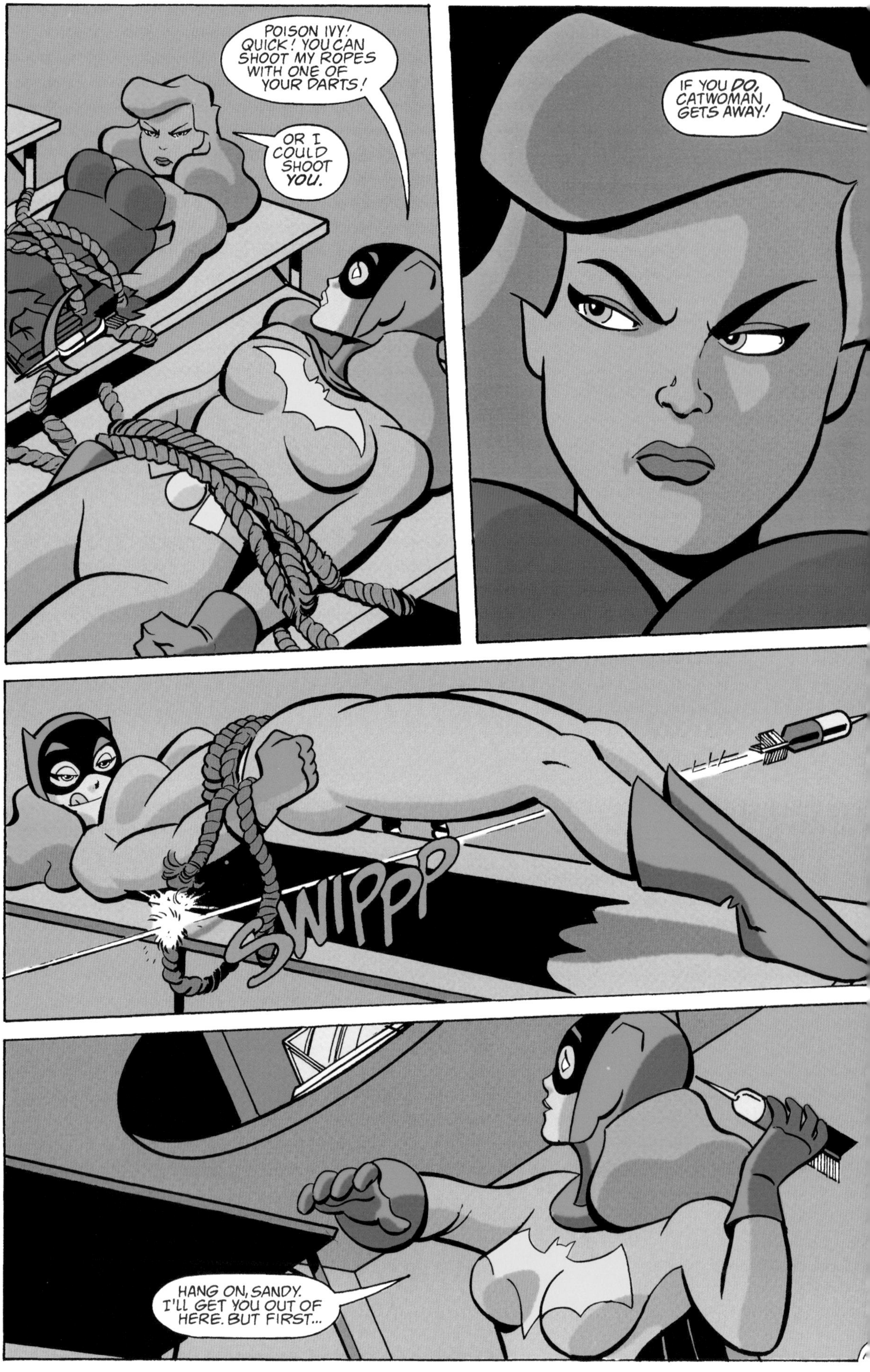
POISON IVY! QUICK! YOU CAN SHOOT MY ROPES WITH ONE OF YOUR DARTS!
OR I COULD SHOOT YOU.
IF YOU DO, CATWOMAN GETS AWAY!
SWIPPP
HANG ON, SANDY. I'LL GET YOU OUT OF HERE. BUT FIRST...

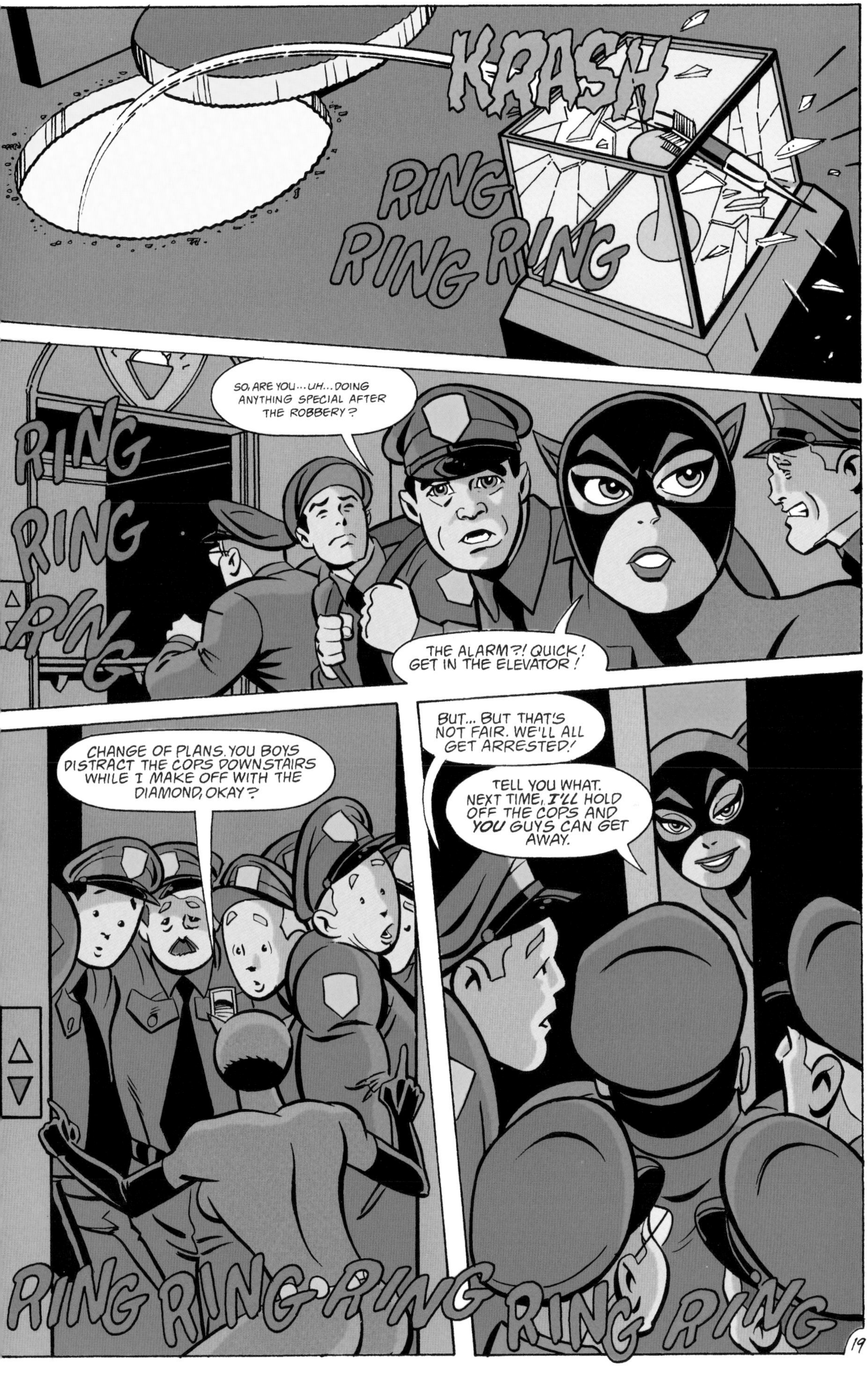
KRASH
RING
RING RING
RING
RING
RING
SO, ARE YOU...UH...DOING ANYTHING SPECIAL AFTER THE ROBBERY?
THE ALARM?! QUICK! GET IN THE ELEVATOR!
CHANGE OF PLANS. YOU BOYS DISTRACT THE COPS DOWNSTAIRS WHILE I MAKE OFF WITH THE DIAMOND, OKAY?
BUT... BUT THAT'S NOT FAIR. WE'LL ALL GET ARRESTED!
TELL YOU WHAT. NEXT TIME, *I'LL* HOLD OFF THE COPS AND *YOU* GUYS CAN GET AWAY.
RING RING RING RING RING RING
19

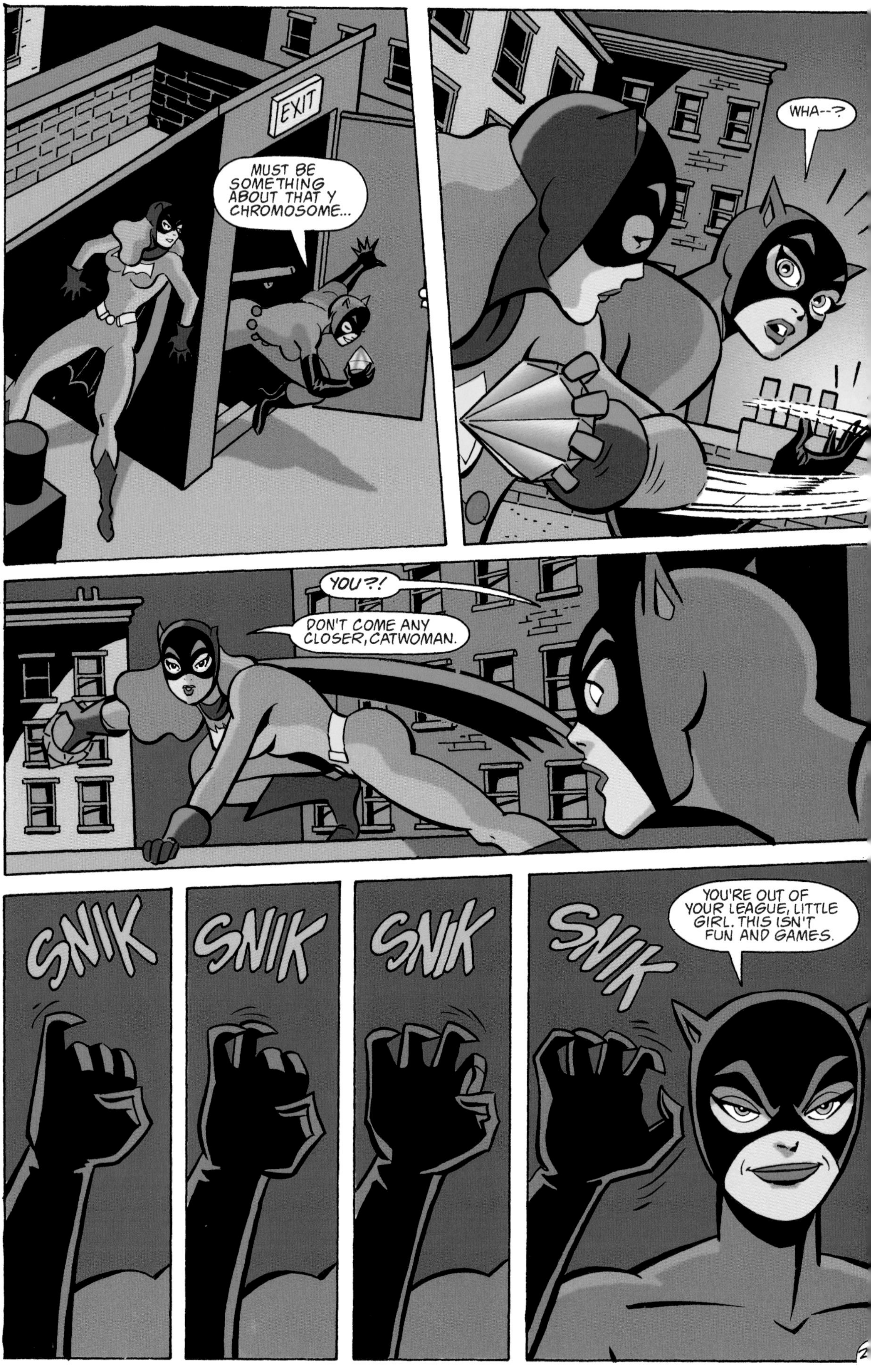
EXIT
MUST BE SOMETHING ABOUT THAT Y CHROMOSOME...
WHA--?
YOU?!
DON'T COME ANY CLOSER, CATWOMAN.
SNIK
SNIK
SNIK
SNIK
YOU'RE OUT OF YOUR LEAGUE, LITTLE GIRL. THIS ISN'T FUN AND GAMES.

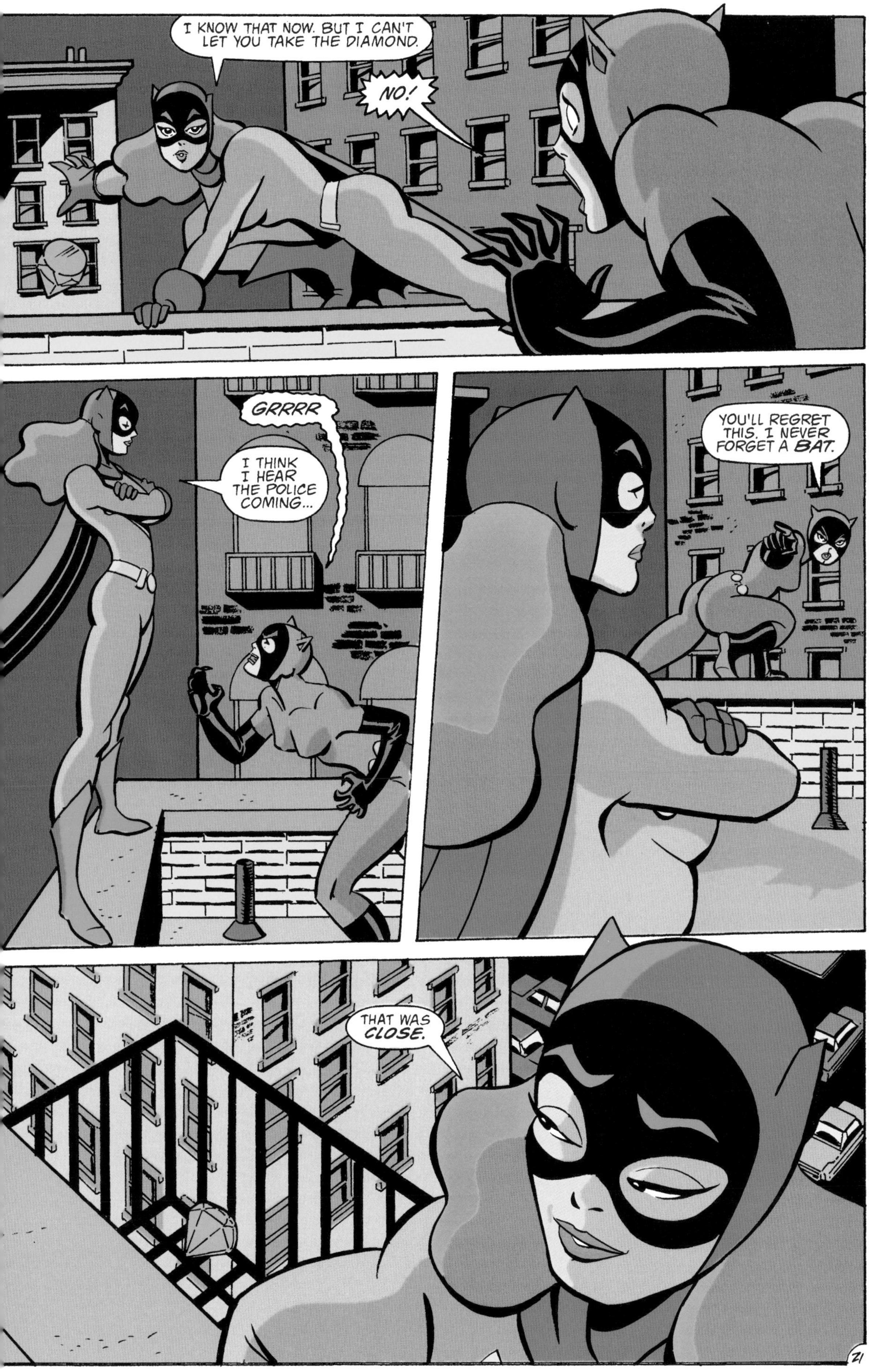
I KNOW THAT NOW. BUT I CAN'T LET YOU TAKE THE DIAMOND.
NO!
GRRRR
I THINK I HEAR THE POLICE COMING...
YOU'LL REGRET THIS. I NEVER FORGET A BAT.
THAT WAS CLOSE.
21

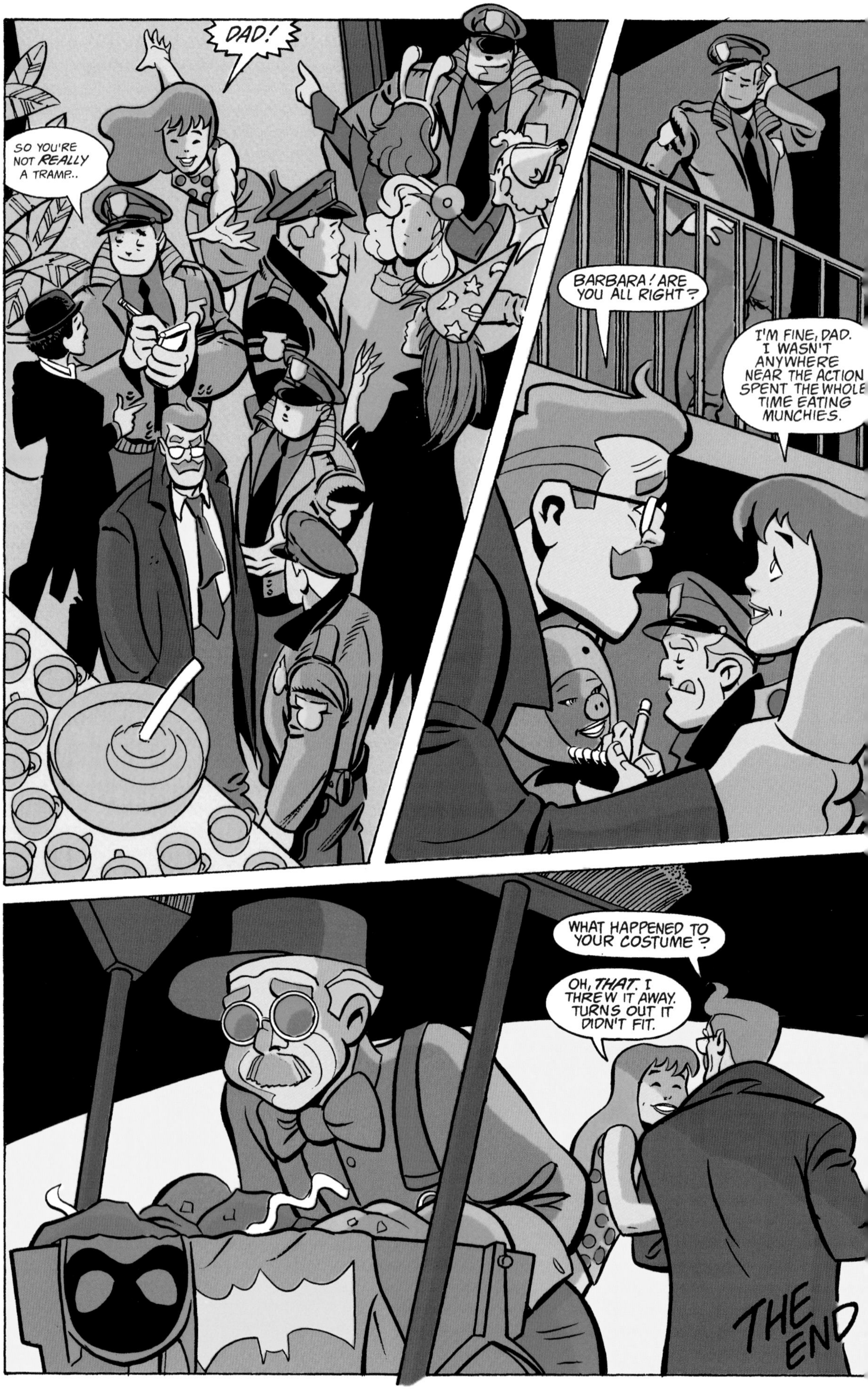
DAD!
SO YOU'RE NOT REALLY A TRAMP..
BARBARA! ARE YOU ALL RIGHT?
I'M FINE, DAD. I WASN'T ANYWHERE NEAR THE ACTION. SPENT THE WHOLE TIME EATING MUNCHIES.
WHAT HAPPENED TO YOUR COSTUME?
OH, THAT. I THREW IT AWAY. TURNS OUT IT DIDN'T FIT.
THE END

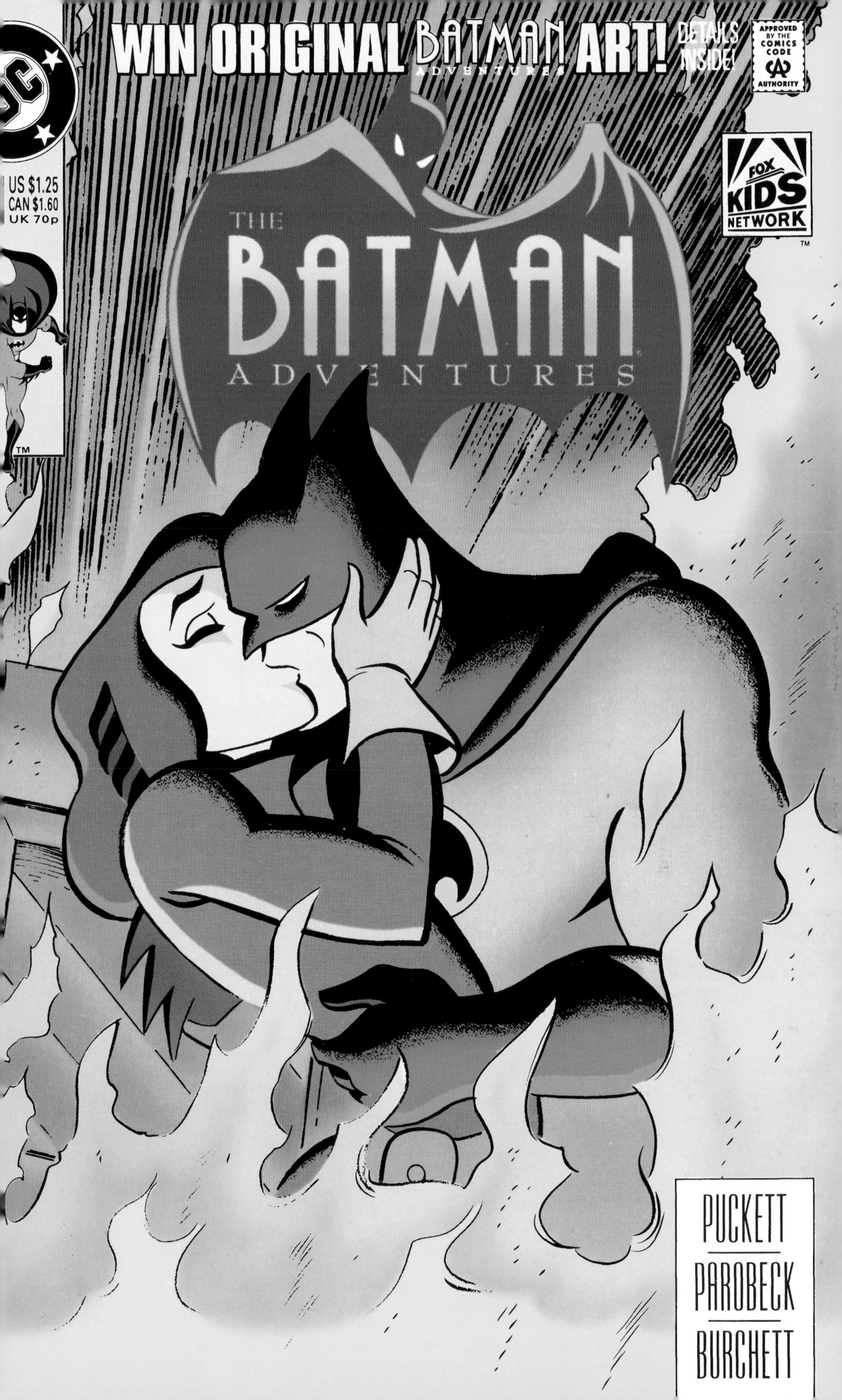
WIN ORIGINAL BATMAN ADVENTURES ART!
DETAILS INSIDE!
APPROVED BY THE COMICS CODE AUTHORITY
US $1.25
CAN $1.60
UK 70p
FOX KIDS NETWORK
THE BATMAN ADVENTURES
PUCKETT
PAROBECK
BURCHETT

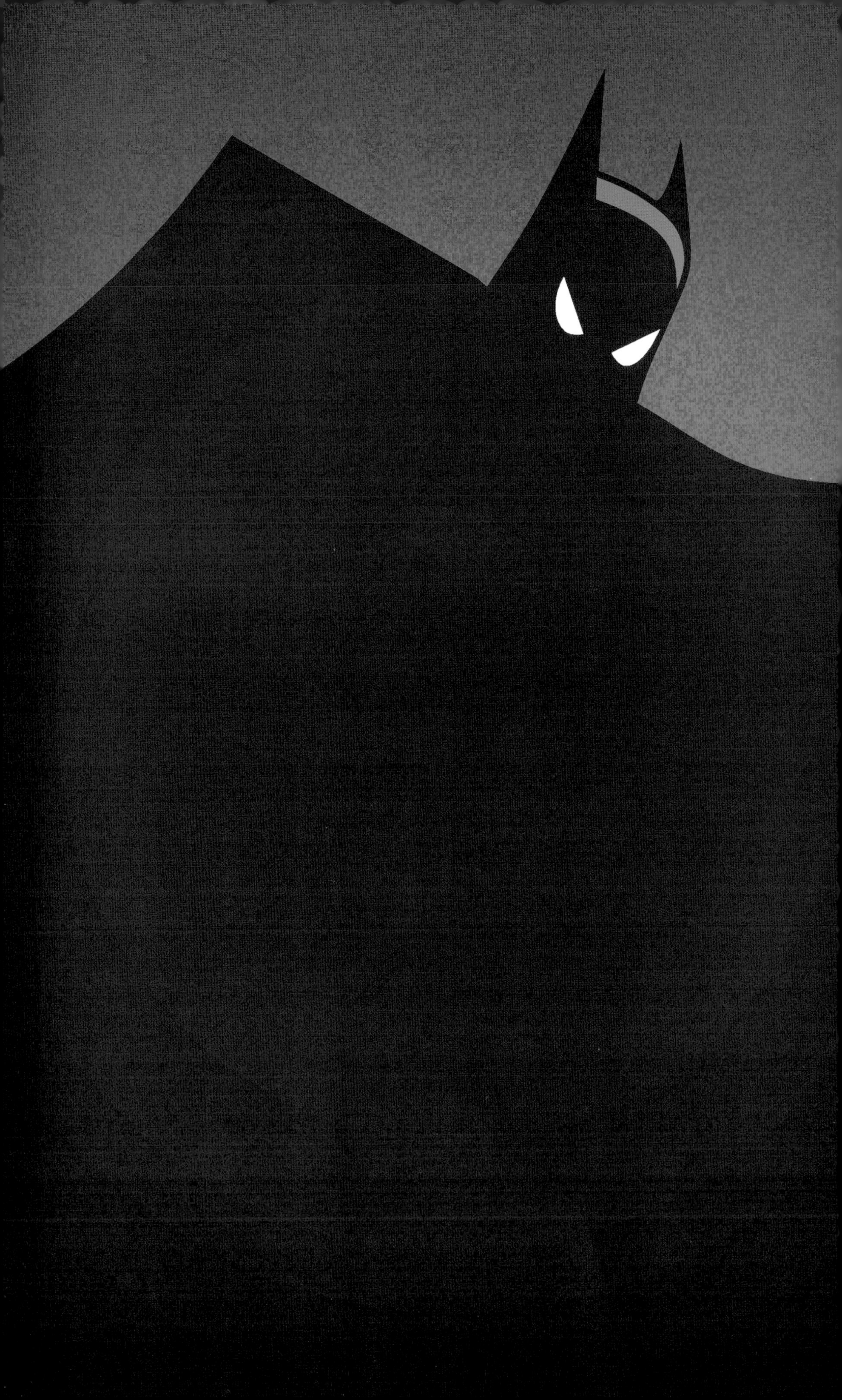

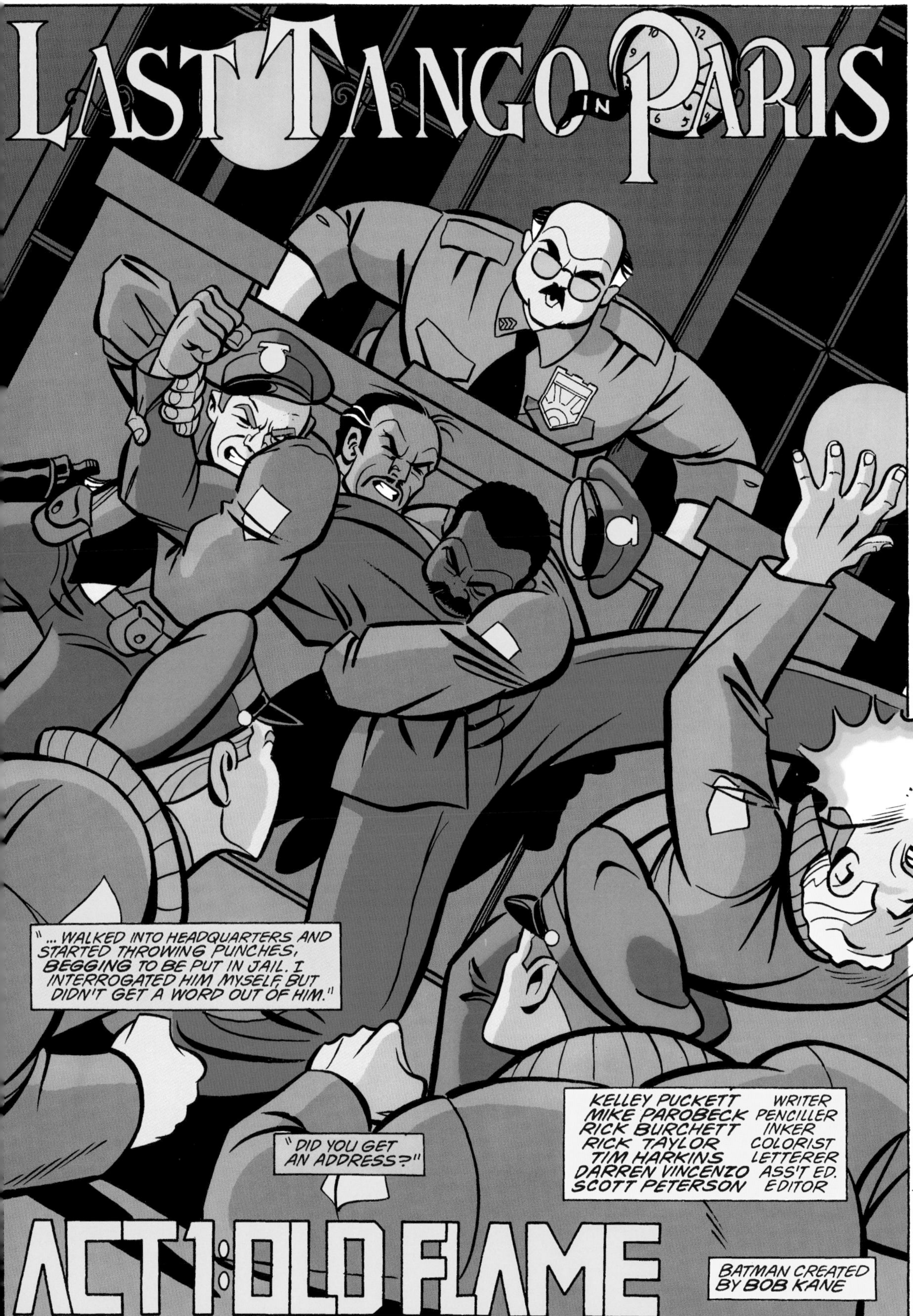
LAST TANGO IN PARIS
"...WALKED INTO HEADQUARTERS AND STARTED THROWING PUNCHES, BEGGING TO BE PUT IN JAIL. I INTERROGATED HIM MYSELF, BUT DIDN'T GET A WORD OUT OF HIM."
"DID YOU GET AN ADDRESS?"
KELLEY PUCKETT WRITER
MIKE PAROBECK PENCILLER
RICK BURCHETT INKER
RICK TAYLOR COLORIST
TIM HARKINS LETTERER
DARREN VINCENZO ASS'T ED.
SCOTT PETERSON EDITOR
ACT 1: OLD FLAME
BATMAN CREATED BY BOB KANE

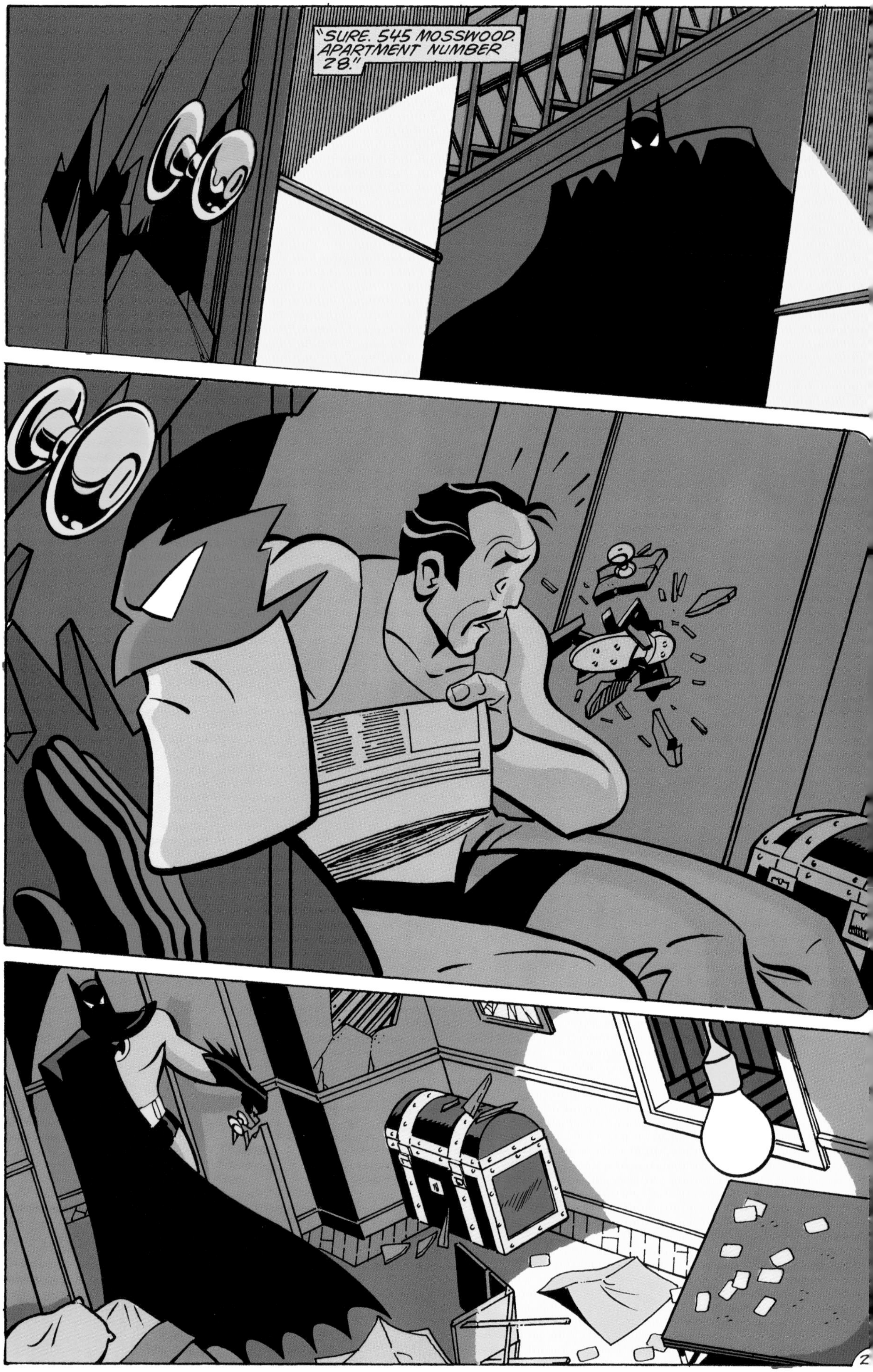
"SURE. 545 MOSSWOOD. APARTMENT NUMBER 28."

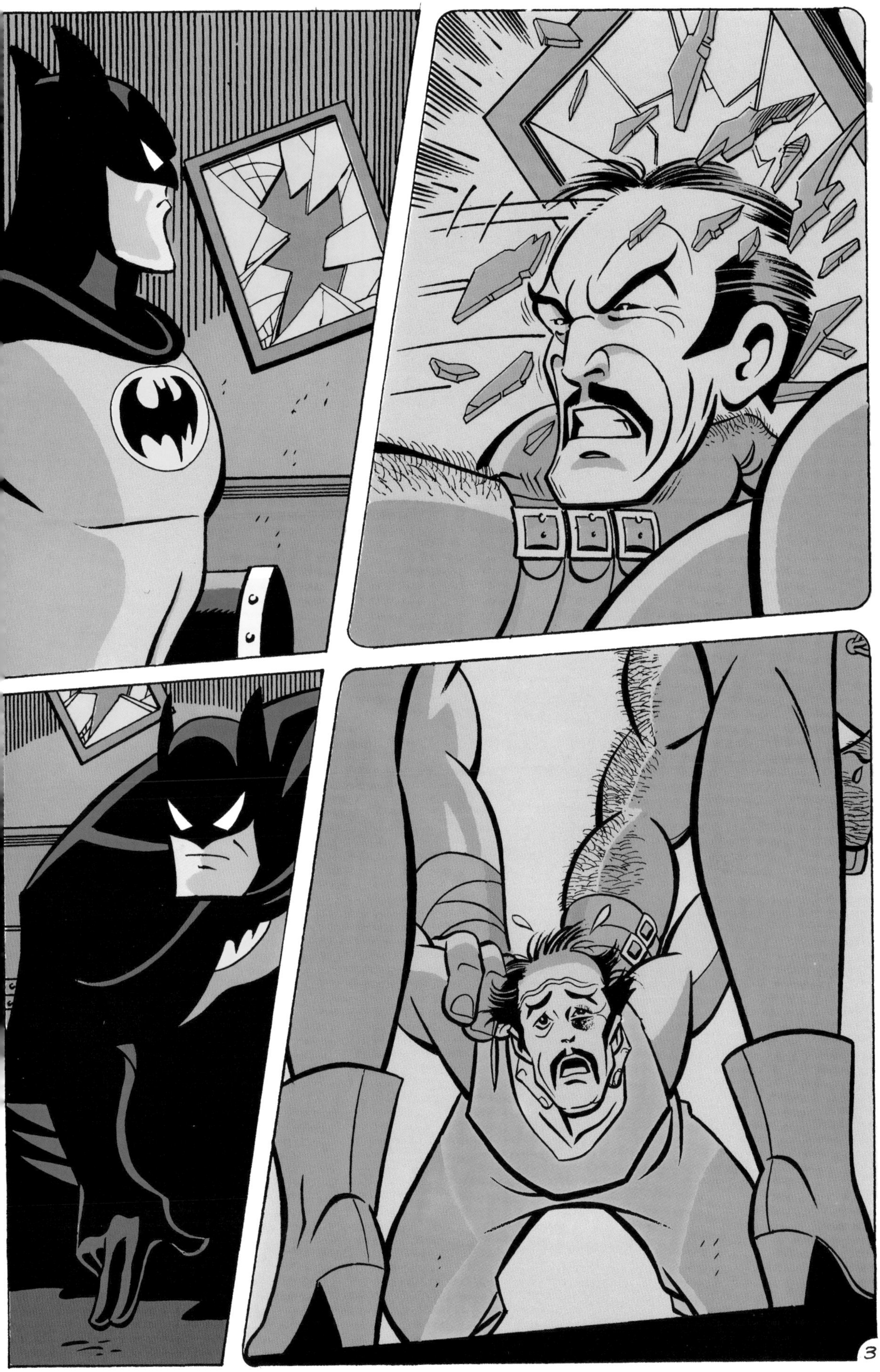
3

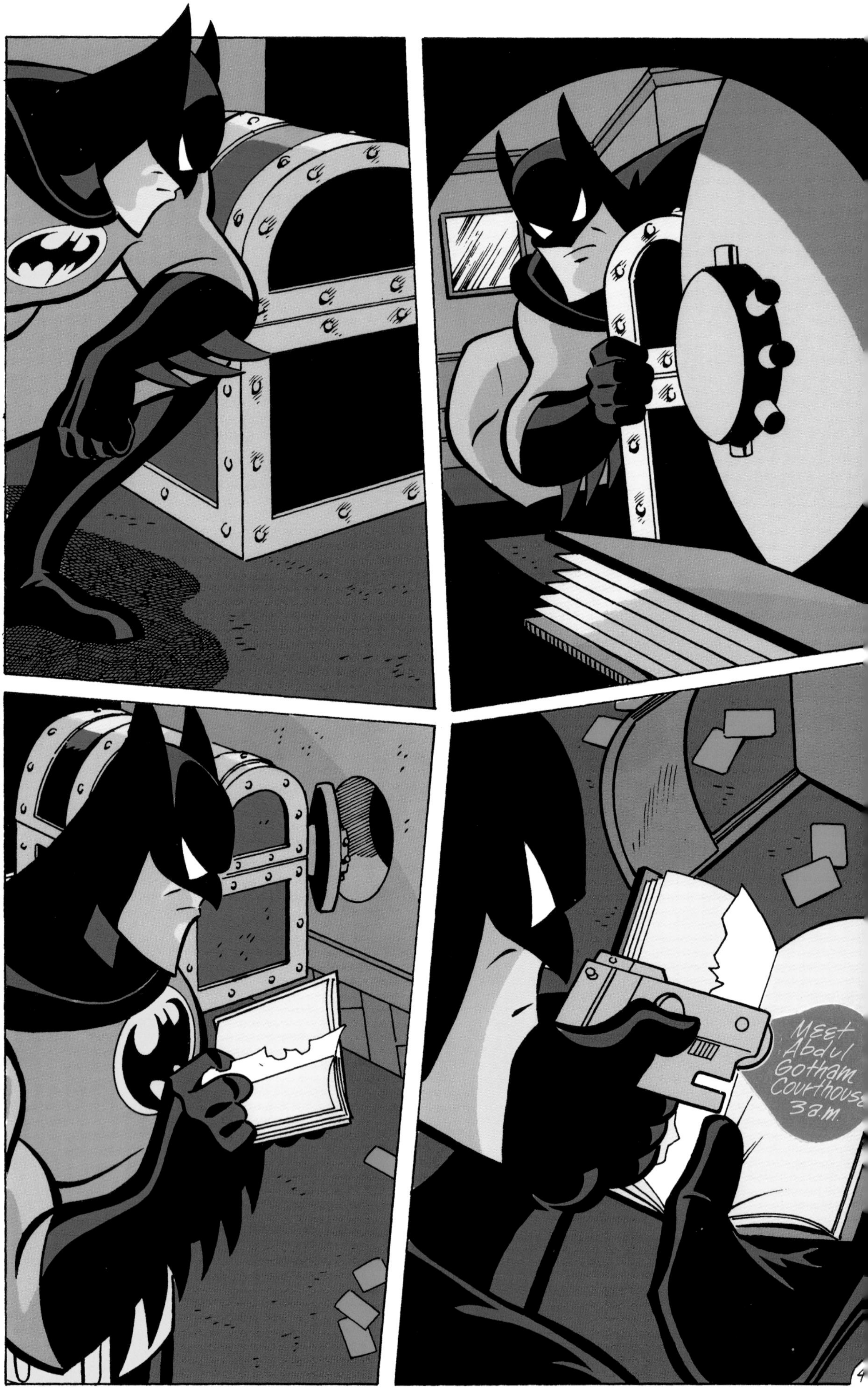

MEET
Abdul
Gotham
Courthouse
3 a.m.

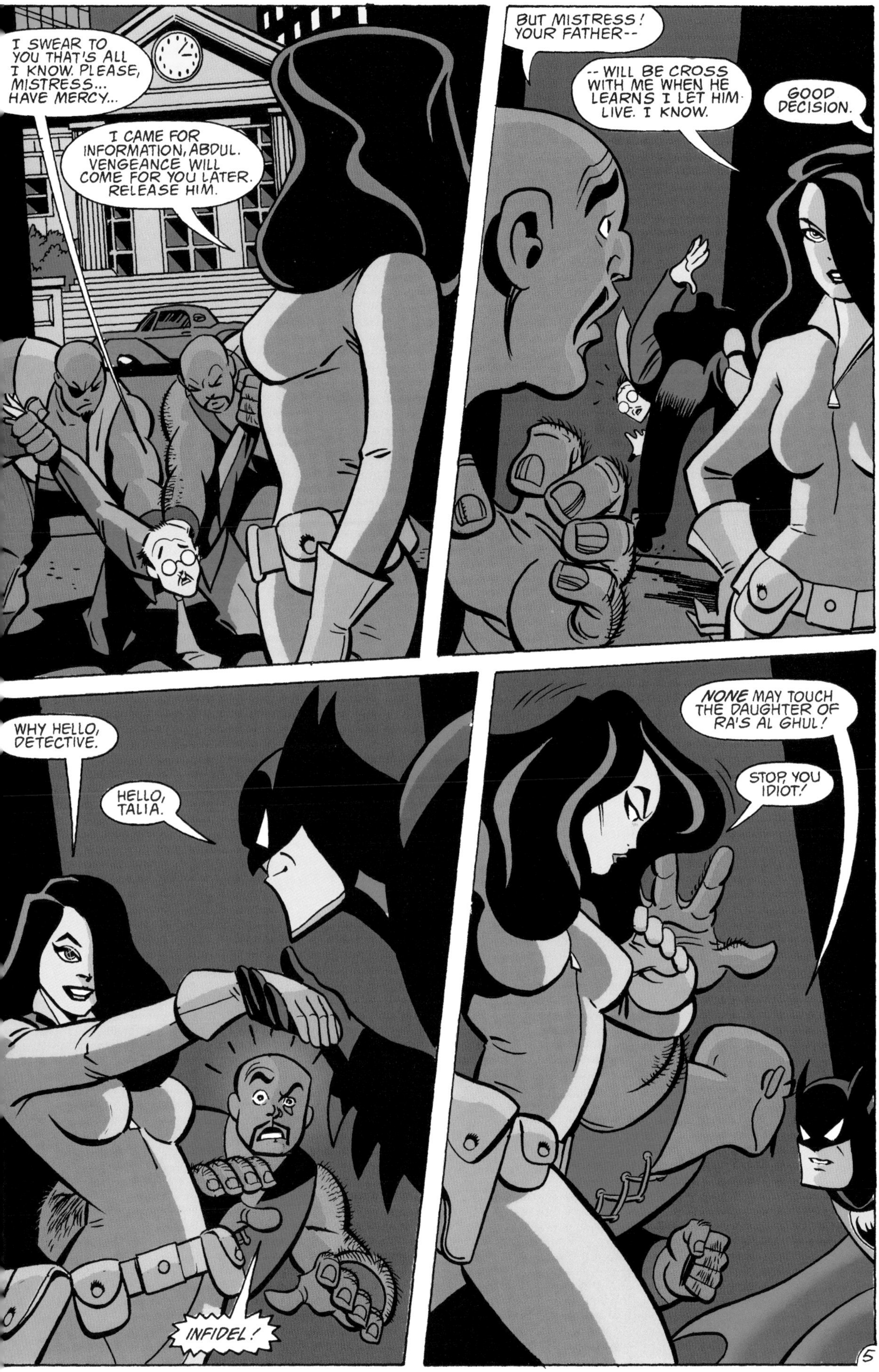

I SWEAR TO YOU THAT'S ALL I KNOW. PLEASE, MISTRESS... HAVE MERCY...
I CAME FOR INFORMATION, ABDUL. VENGEANCE WILL COME FOR YOU LATER. RELEASE HIM.
BUT MISTRESS! YOUR FATHER--
-- WILL BE CROSS WITH ME WHEN HE LEARNS I LET HIM LIVE. I KNOW.
GOOD DECISION.
WHY HELLO, DETECTIVE.
HELLO, TALIA.
INFIDEL!
NONE MAY TOUCH THE DAUGHTER OF RA'S AL GHUL!
STOP, YOU IDIOT!
5

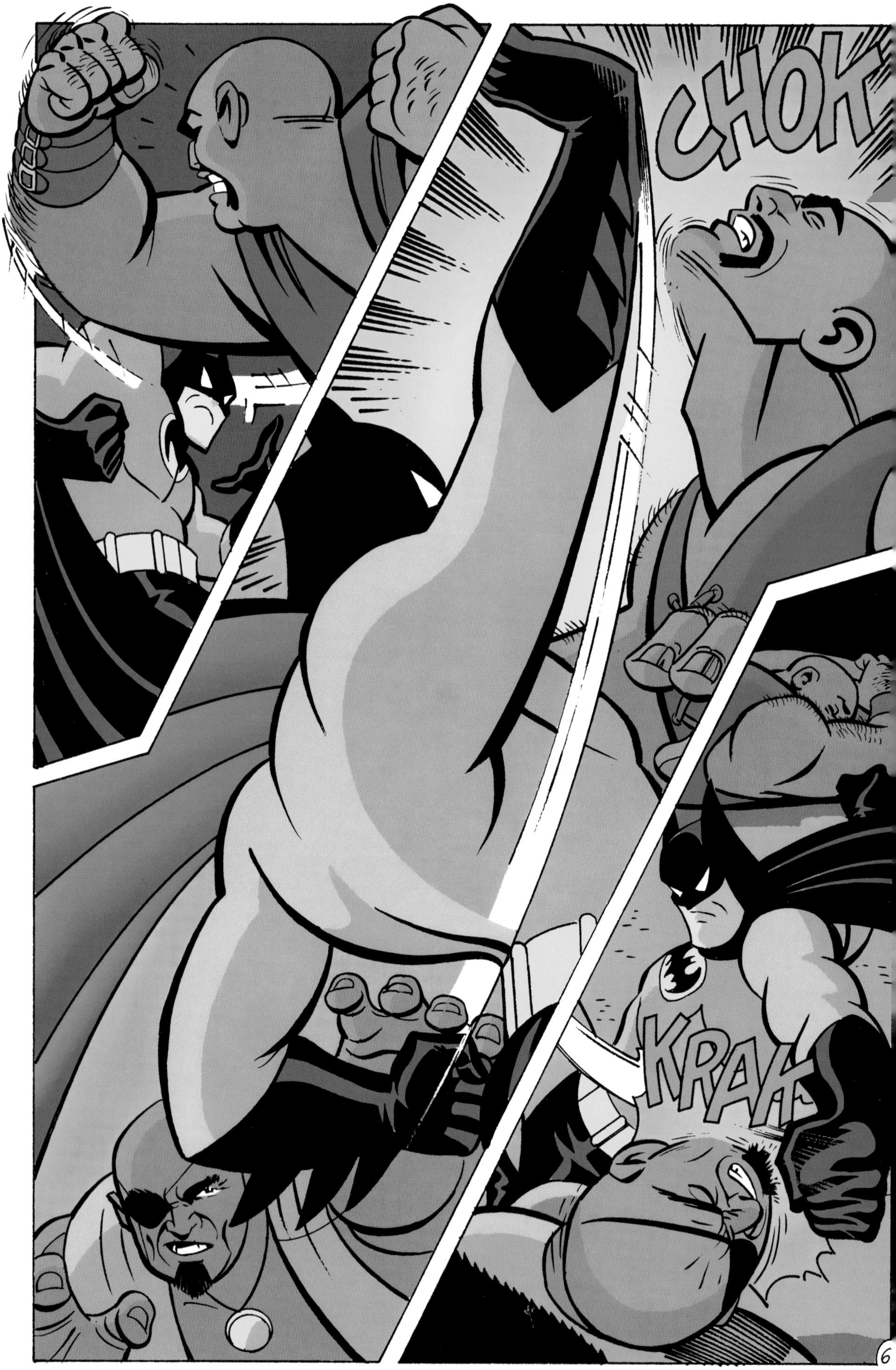

CHOK
KRAK
6

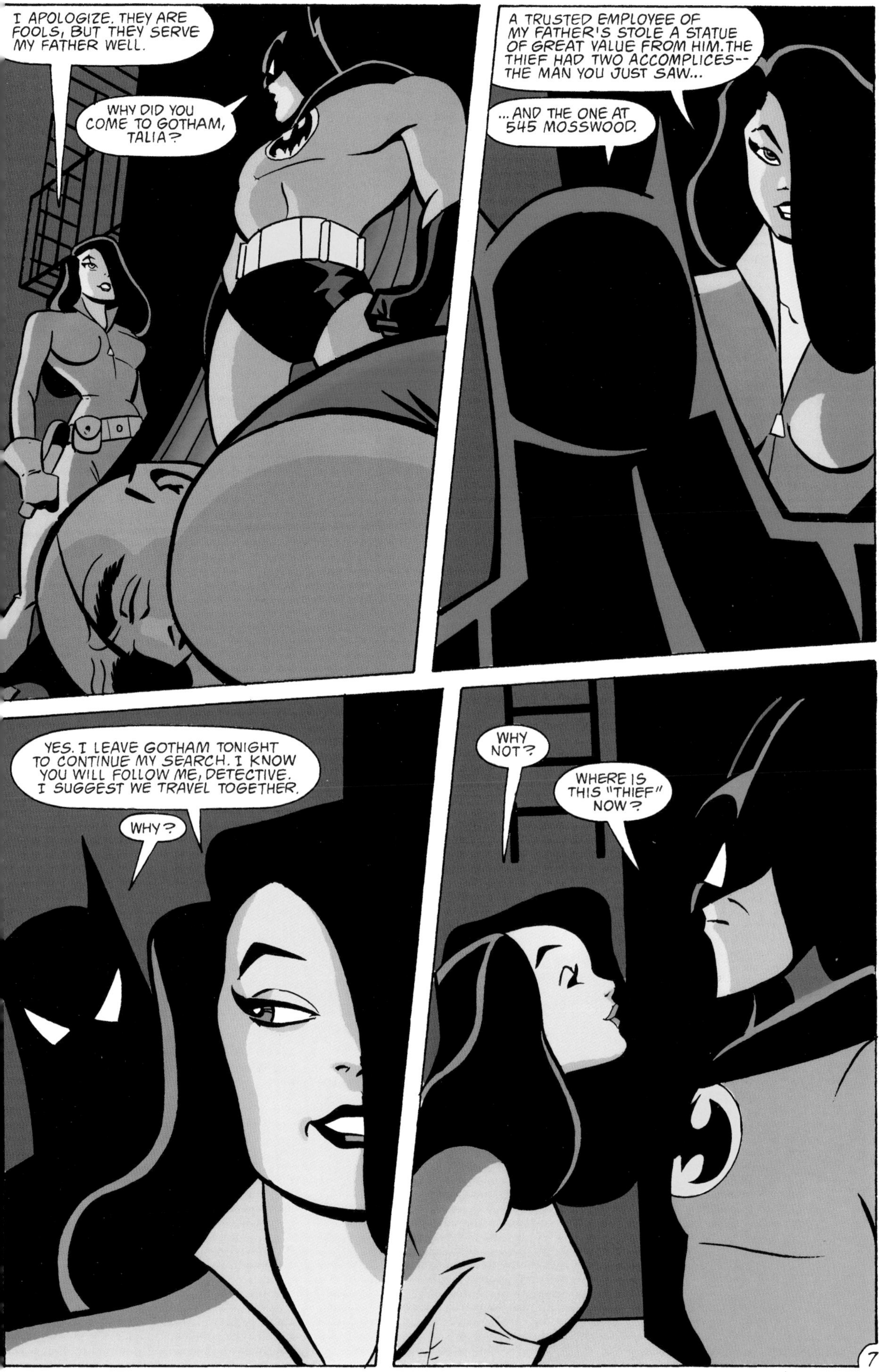

I APOLOGIZE. THEY ARE FOOLS, BUT THEY SERVE MY FATHER WELL.
WHY DID YOU COME TO GOTHAM, TALIA?
A TRUSTED EMPLOYEE OF MY FATHER'S STOLE A STATUE OF GREAT VALUE FROM HIM. THE THIEF HAD TWO ACCOMPLICES-- THE MAN YOU JUST SAW...
...AND THE ONE AT 545 MOSSWOOD.
YES. I LEAVE GOTHAM TONIGHT TO CONTINUE MY SEARCH. I KNOW YOU WILL FOLLOW ME, DETECTIVE. I SUGGEST WE TRAVEL TOGETHER.
WHY?
WHY NOT?
WHERE IS THIS "THIEF" NOW?
7

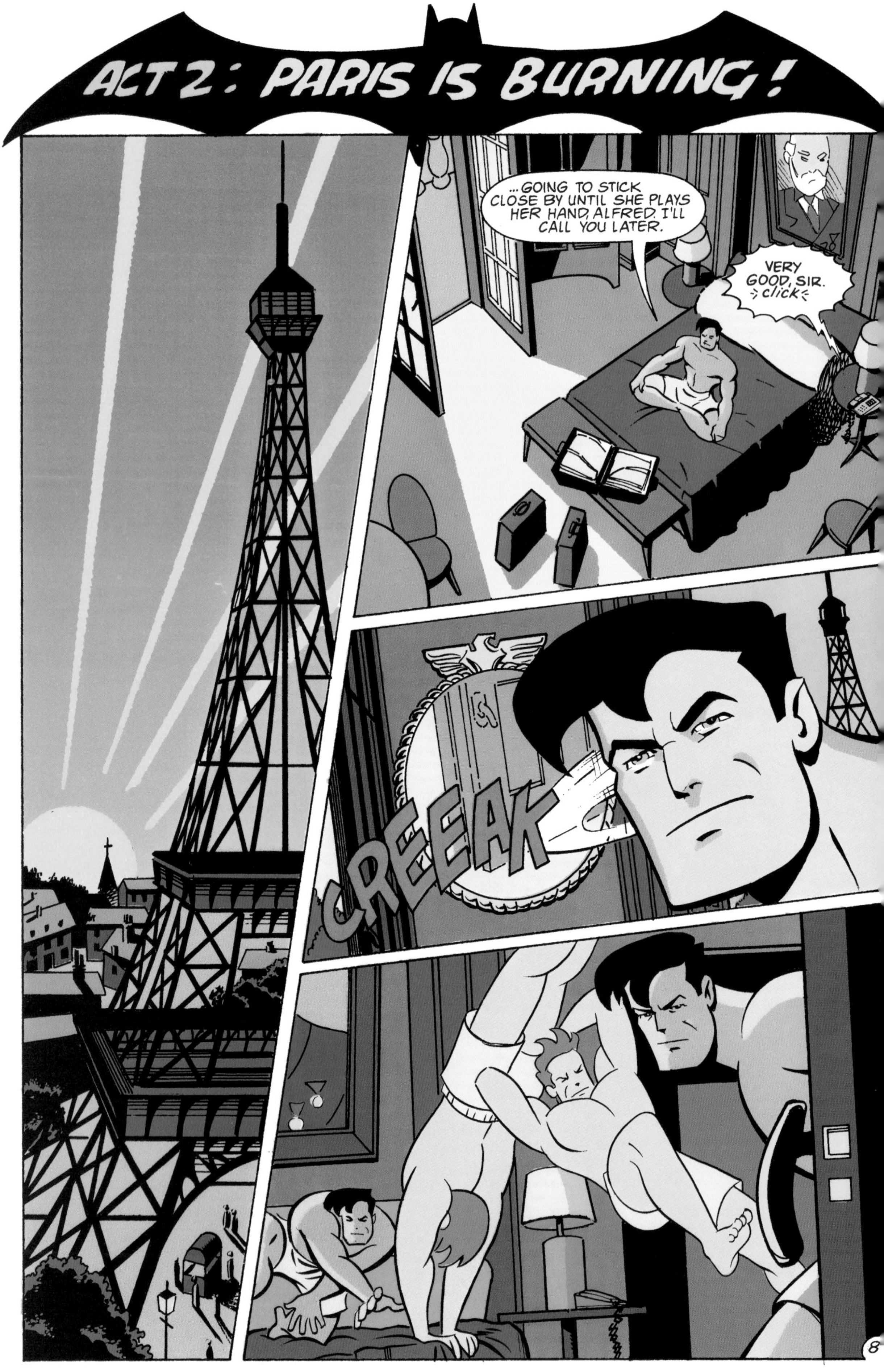
ACT 2: PARIS IS BURNING!
...GOING TO STICK CLOSE BY UNTIL SHE PLAYS HER HAND, ALFRED. I'LL CALL YOU LATER.
VERY GOOD, SIR.
click
CREEAK
8

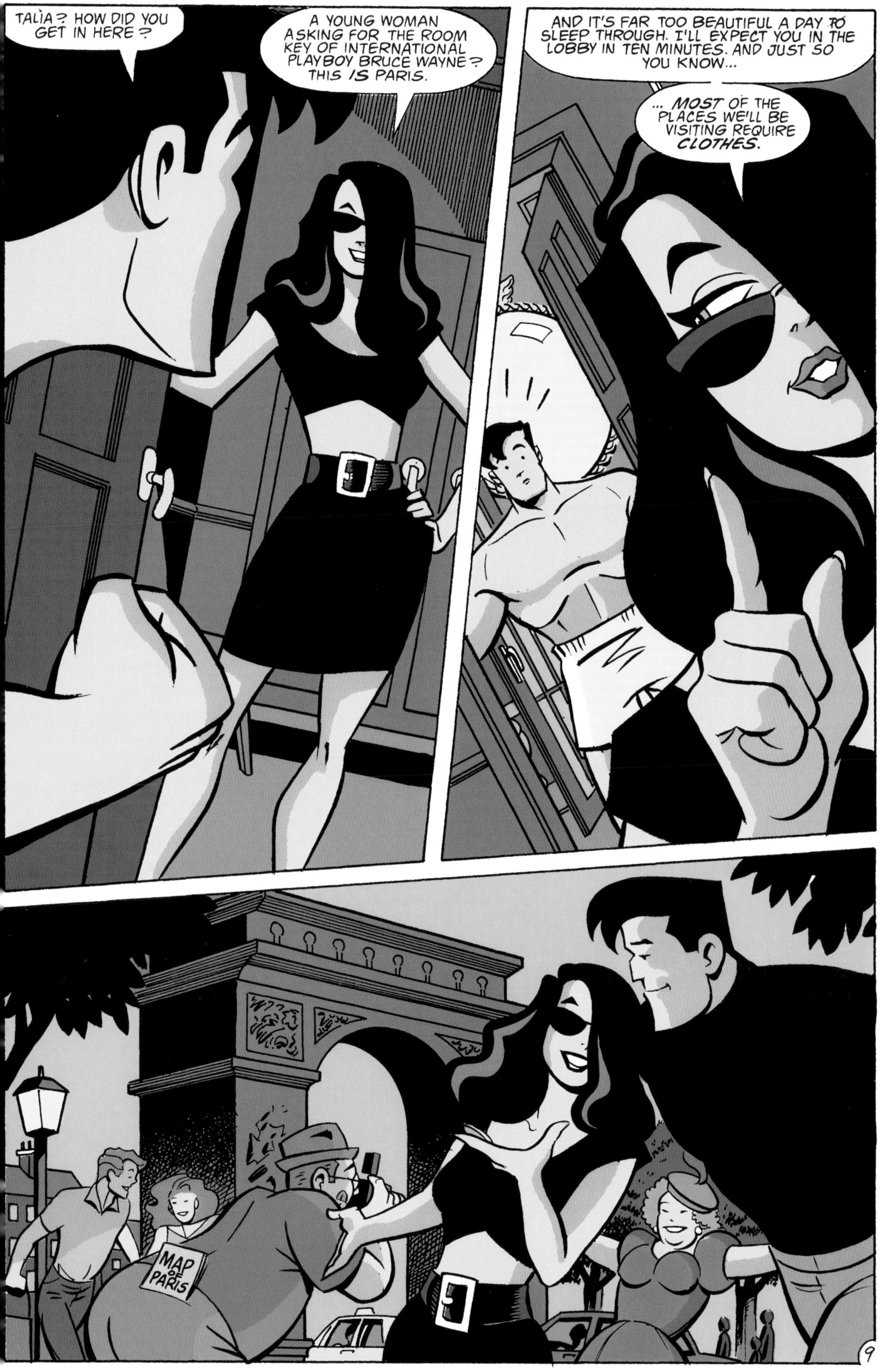
TALIA? HOW DID YOU GET IN HERE?
A YOUNG WOMAN ASKING FOR THE ROOM KEY OF INTERNATIONAL PLAYBOY BRUCE WAYNE? THIS IS PARIS.
AND IT'S FAR TOO BEAUTIFUL A DAY TO SLEEP THROUGH. I'LL EXPECT YOU IN THE LOBBY IN TEN MINUTES. AND JUST SO YOU KNOW...
... MOST OF THE PLACES WE'LL BE VISITING REQUIRE CLOTHES.
MAP OF PARIS
9

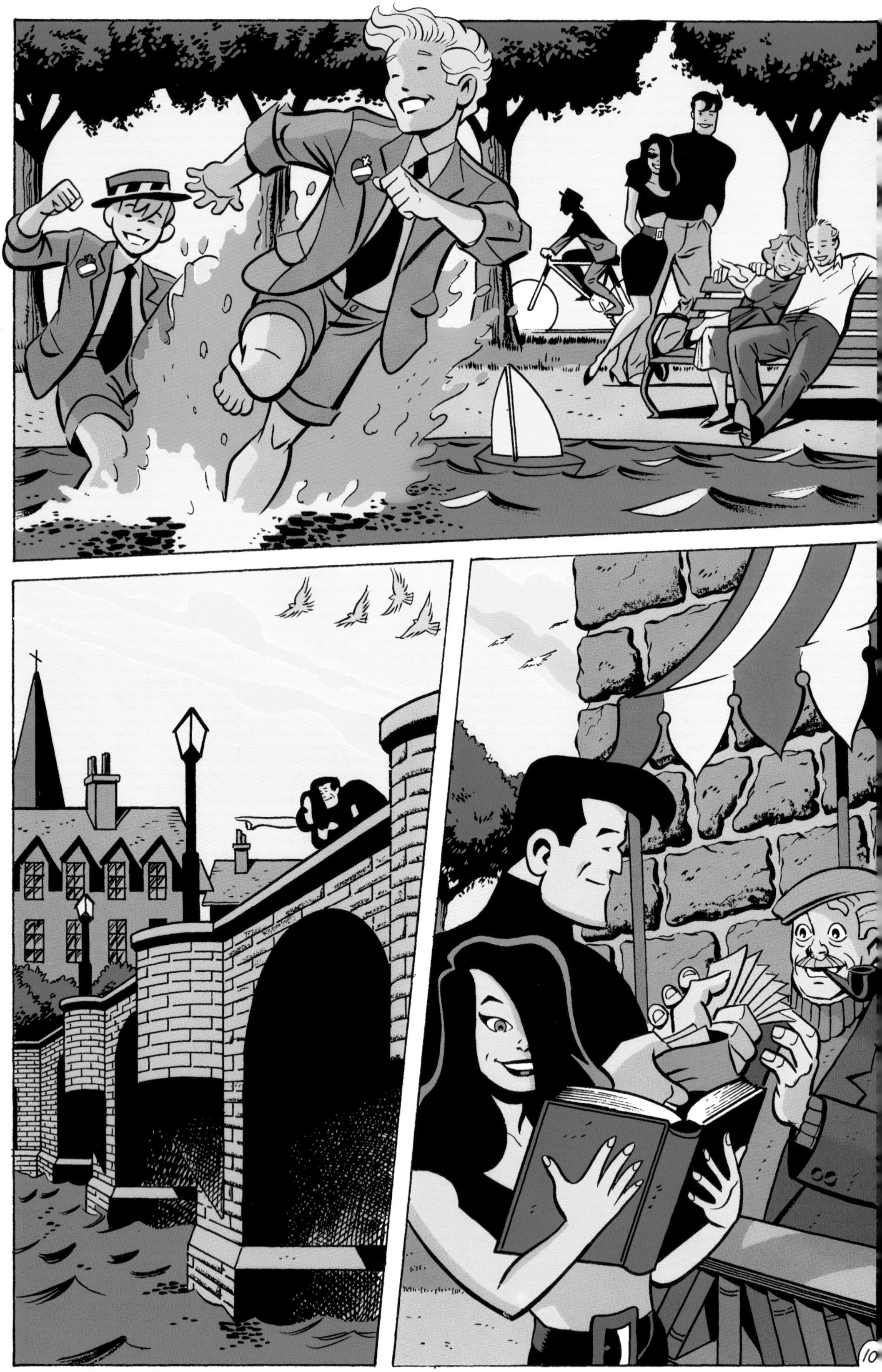
10

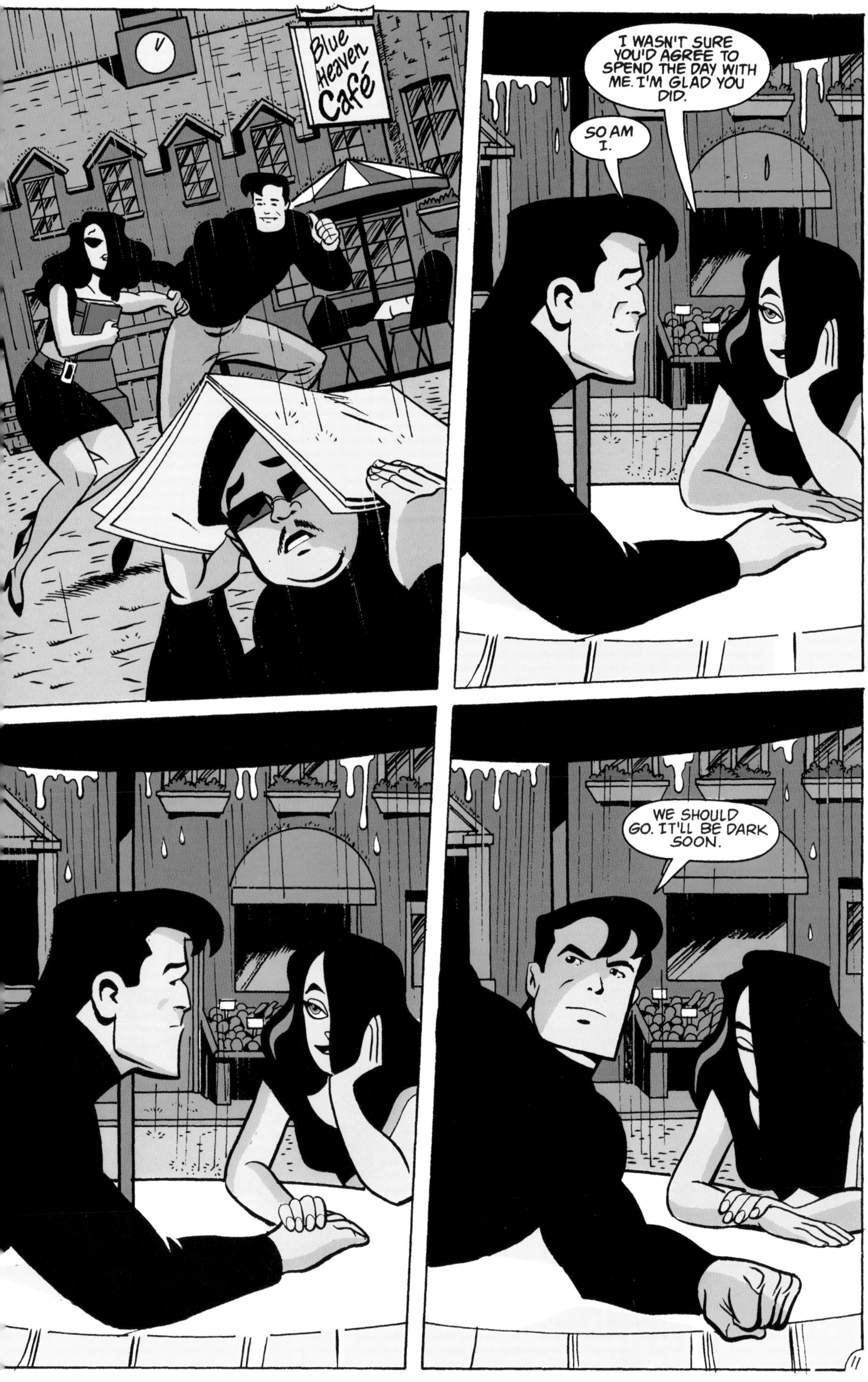
Blue Heaven Café
I WASN'T SURE YOU'D AGREE TO SPEND THE DAY WITH ME. I'M GLAD YOU DID.
SO AM I.
WE SHOULD GO. IT'LL BE DARK SOON.

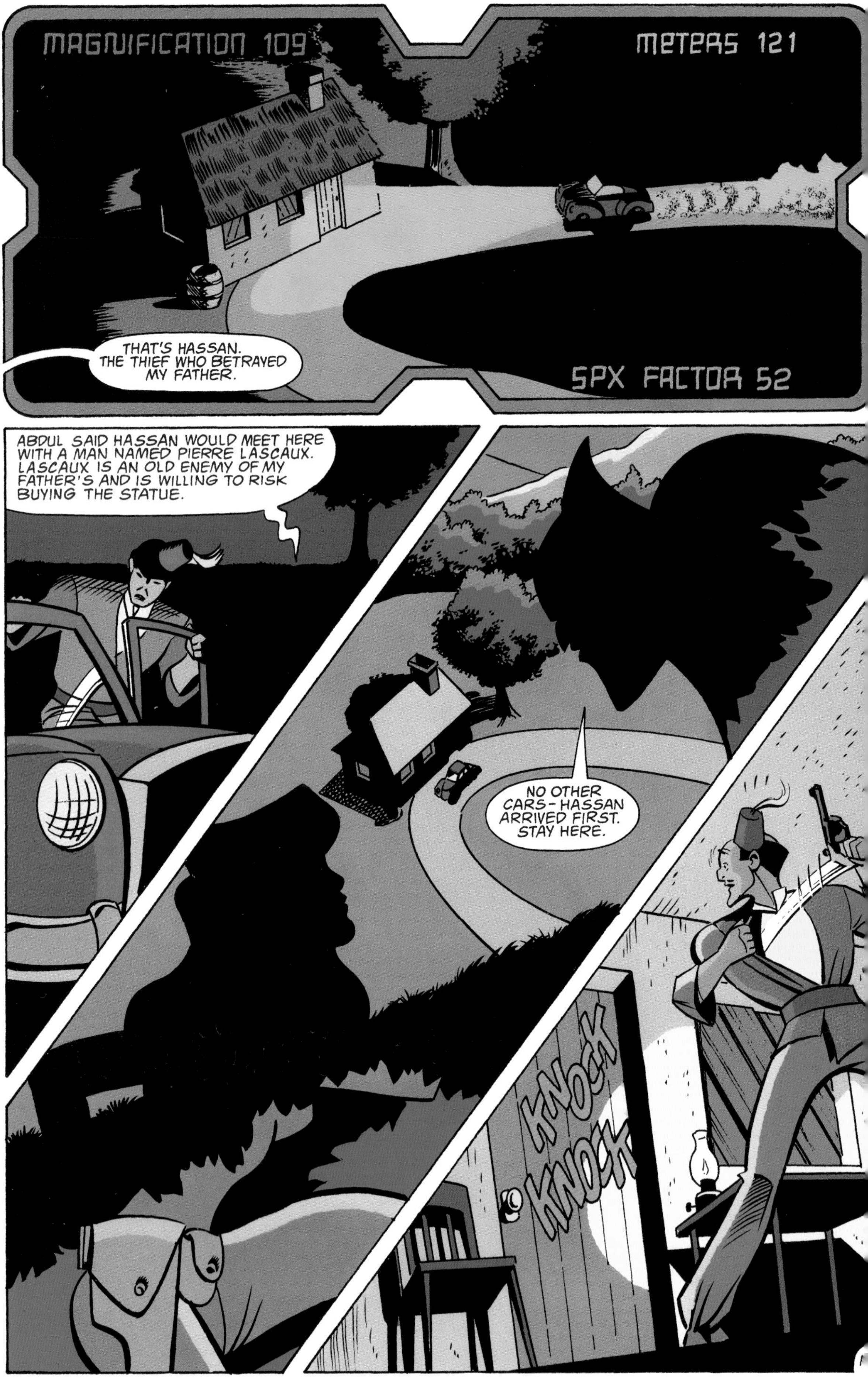
MAGNIFICATION 109
METERS 121
THAT'S HASSAN. THE THIEF WHO BETRAYED MY FATHER.
SPX FACTOR 52
ABDUL SAID HASSAN WOULD MEET HERE WITH A MAN NAMED PIERRE LASCAUX. LASCAUX IS AN OLD ENEMY OF MY FATHER'S AND IS WILLING TO RISK BUYING THE STATUE.
NO OTHER CARS- HASSAN ARRIVED FIRST. STAY HERE.
KNOCK KNOCK

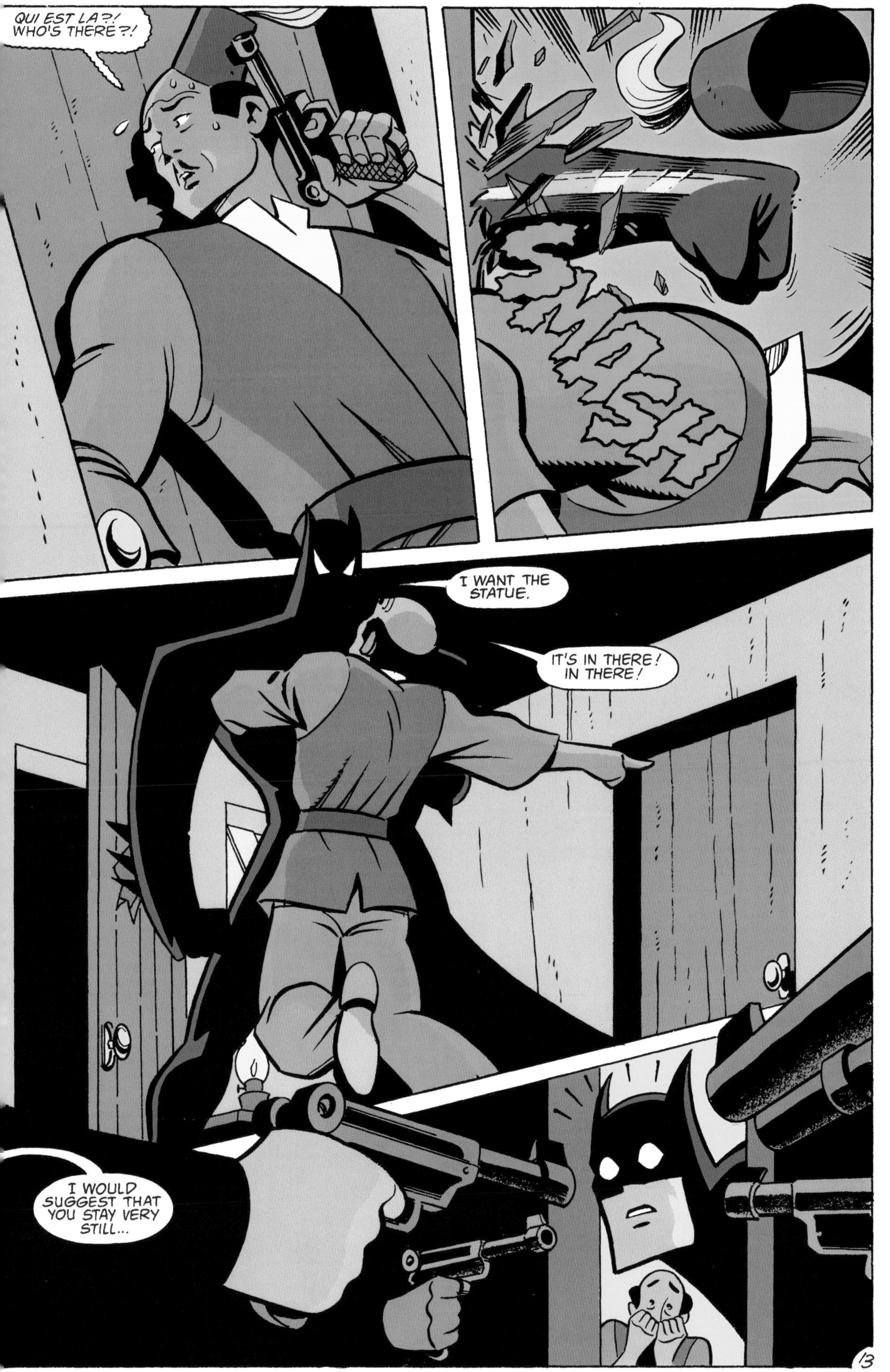
QUI EST LA?! WHO'S THERE?!
SMASH
I WANT THE STATUE.
IT'S IN THERE! IN THERE!
I WOULD SUGGEST THAT YOU STAY VERY STILL...
13

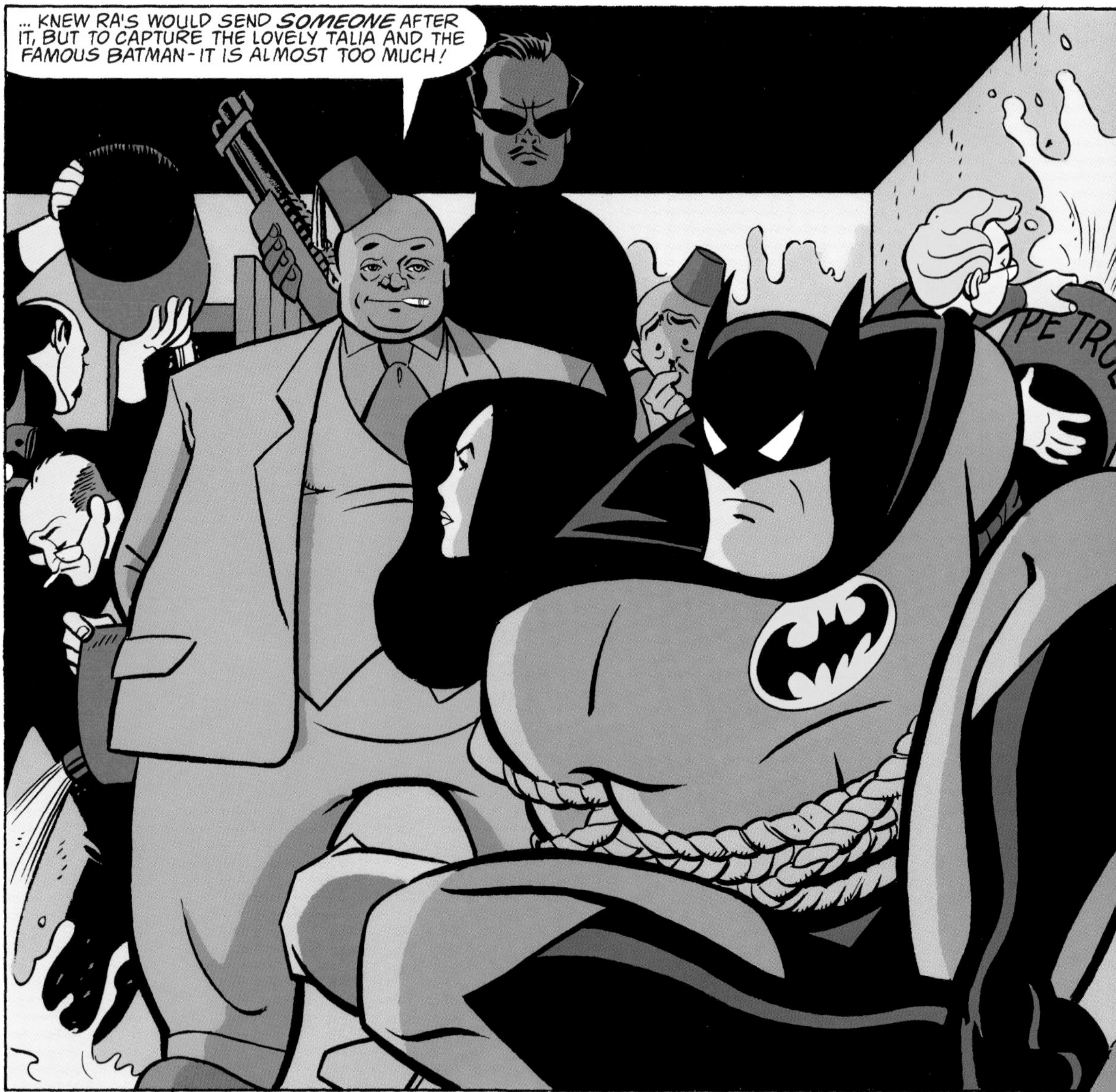
... KNEW RA'S WOULD SEND SOMEONE AFTER IT, BUT TO CAPTURE THE LOVELY TALIA AND THE FAMOUS BATMAN - IT IS ALMOST TOO MUCH!
PETRO

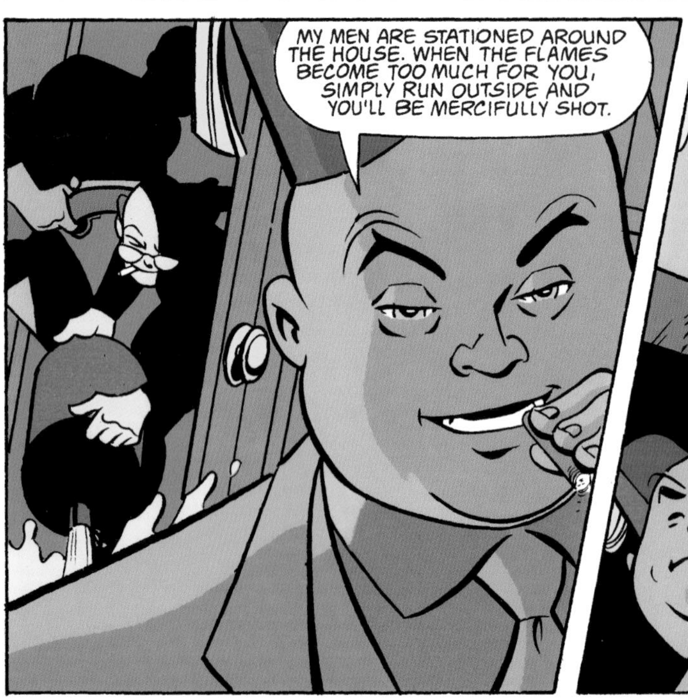
MY MEN ARE STATIONED AROUND THE HOUSE. WHEN THE FLAMES BECOME TOO MUCH FOR YOU, SIMPLY RUN OUTSIDE AND YOU'LL BE MERCIFULLY SHOT.

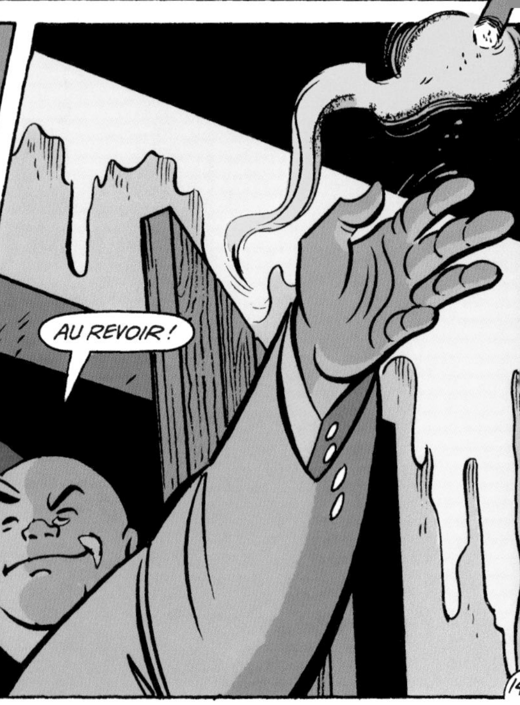
AU REVOIR!

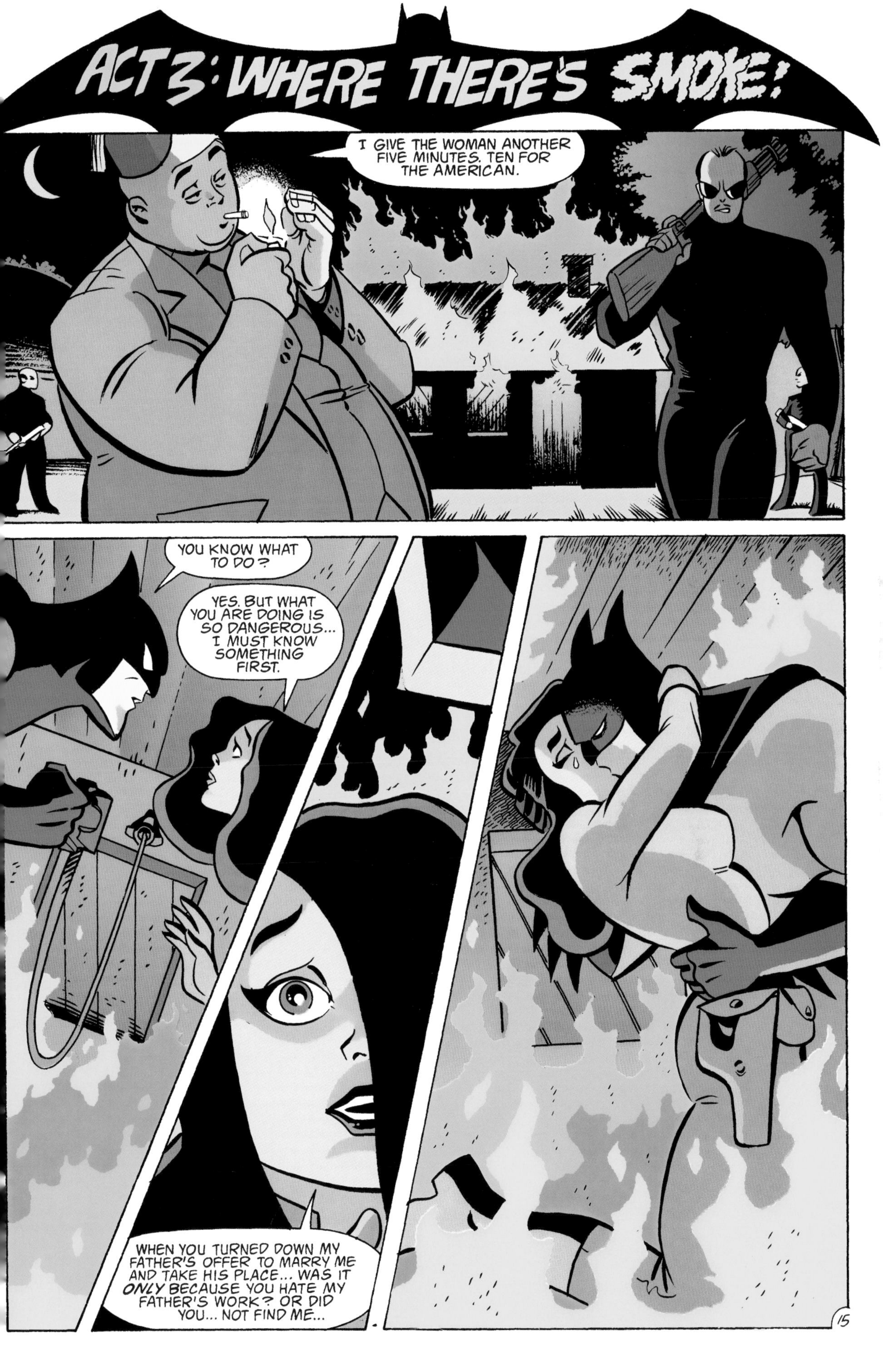

ACT 3: WHERE THERE'S SMOKE!
I GIVE THE WOMAN ANOTHER FIVE MINUTES. TEN FOR THE AMERICAN.
YOU KNOW WHAT TO DO?
YES. BUT WHAT YOU ARE DOING IS SO DANGEROUS... I MUST KNOW SOMETHING FIRST.
WHEN YOU TURNED DOWN MY FATHER'S OFFER TO MARRY ME AND TAKE HIS PLACE... WAS IT *ONLY* BECAUSE YOU HATE MY FATHER'S WORK? OR DID YOU... NOT FIND ME...
15

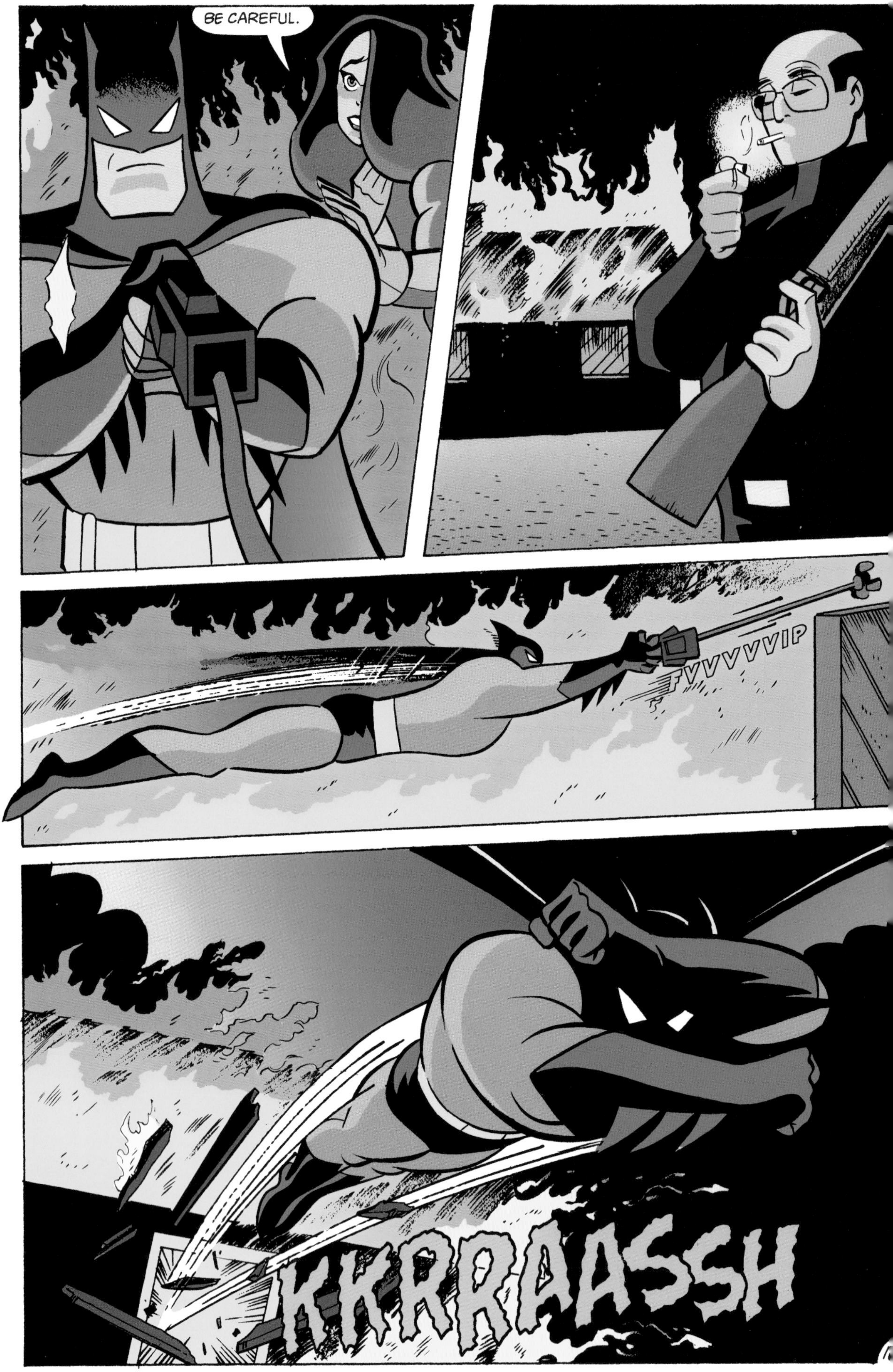
BE CAREFUL.
FVVVVVVIP
KKRRAASSH

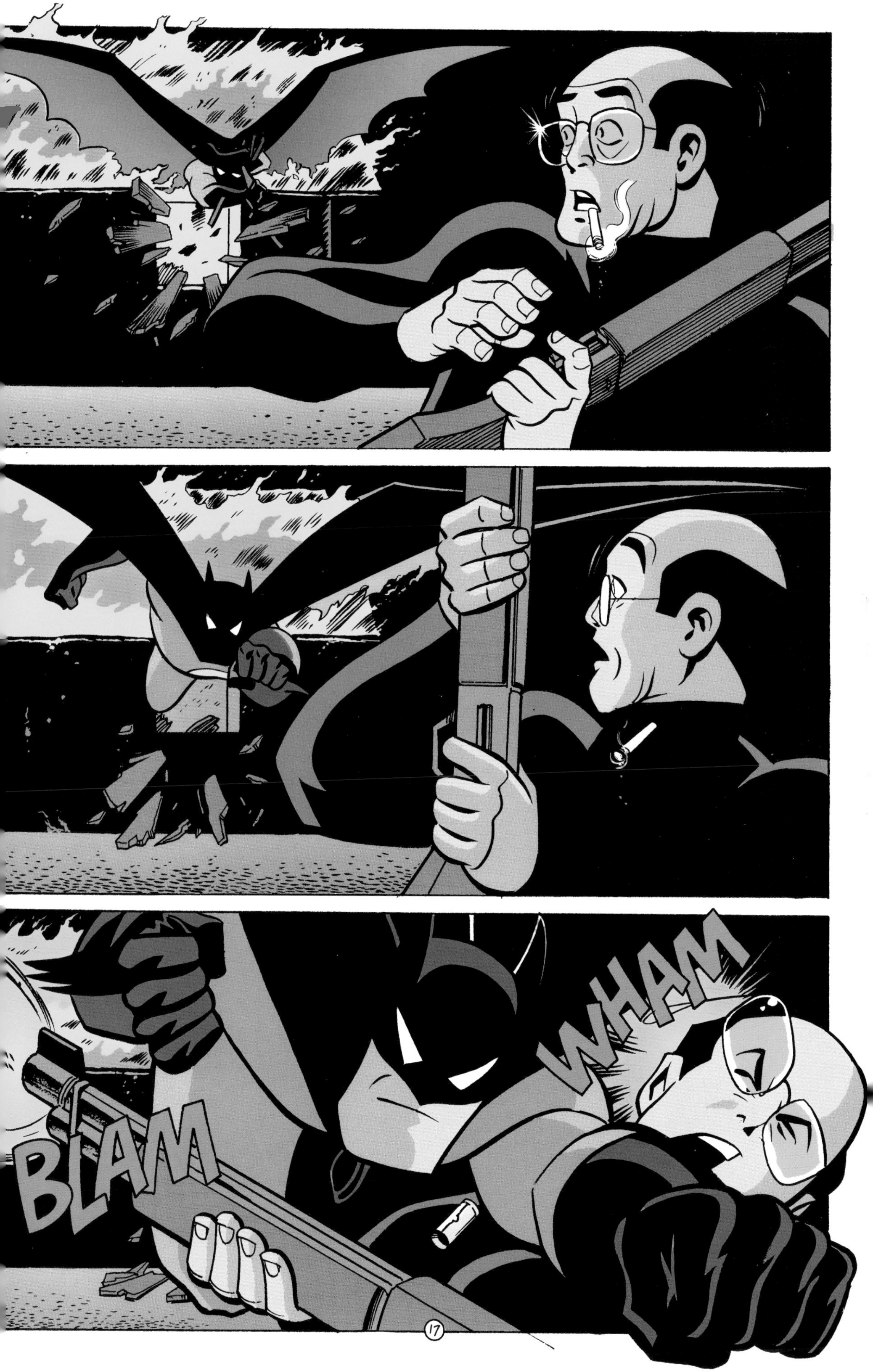
WHAM
BLAM
17

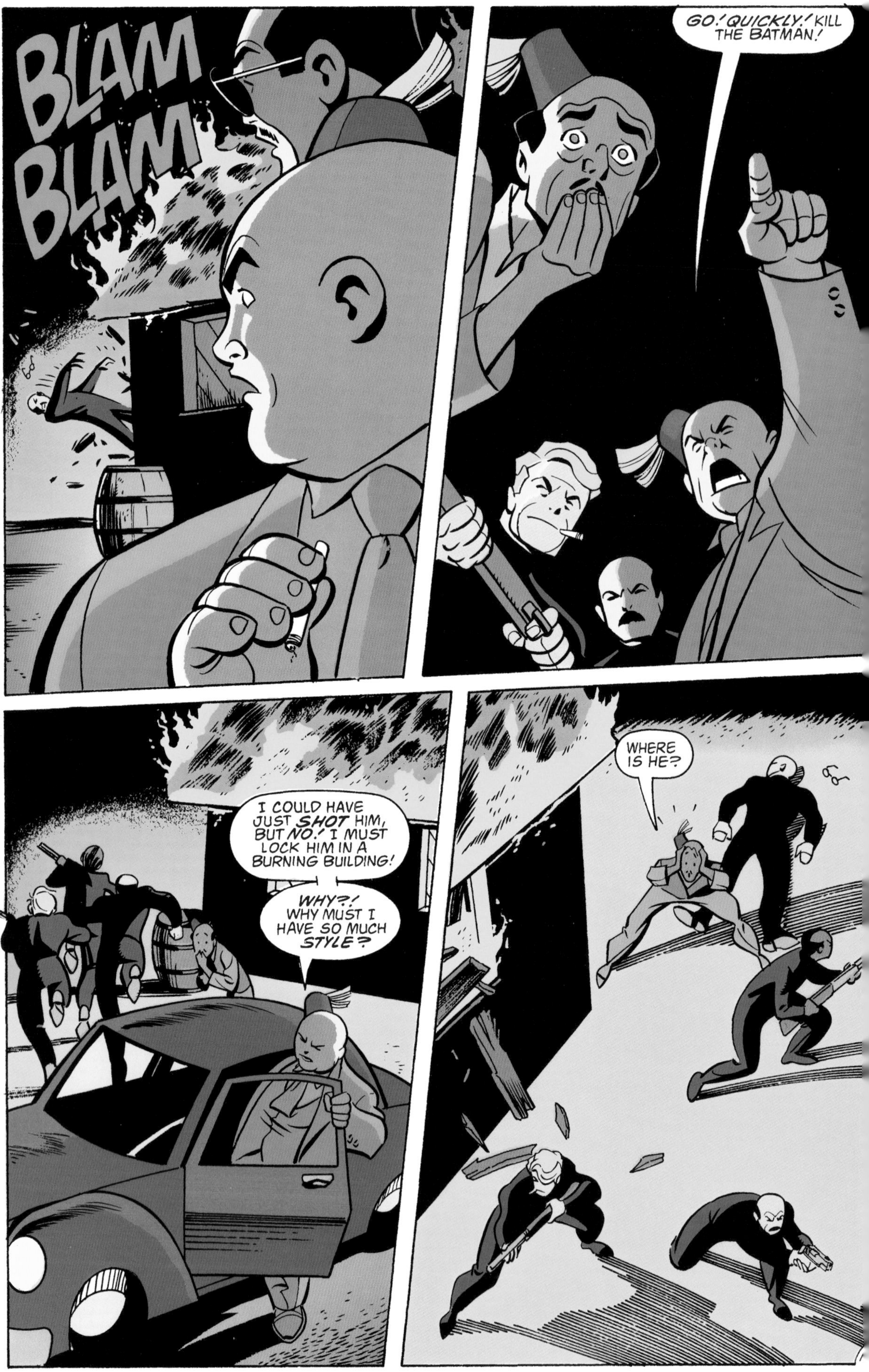
BLAM BLAM
GO! QUICKLY! KILL THE BATMAN!
I COULD HAVE JUST SHOT HIM, BUT NO! I MUST LOCK HIM IN A BURNING BUILDING!
WHY?! WHY MUST I HAVE SO MUCH STYLE?
WHERE IS HE?

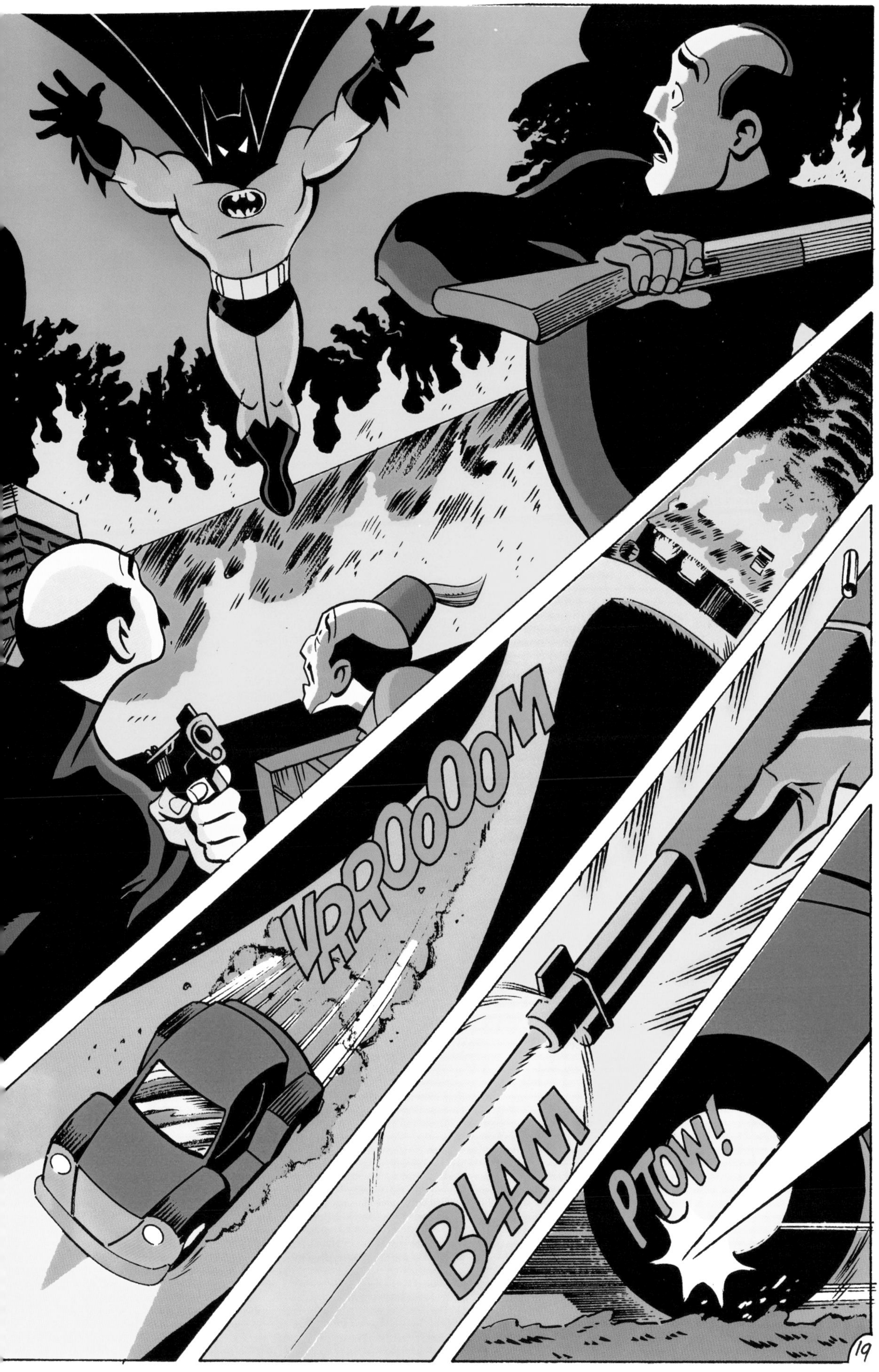
VRROOOOOM
BLAM
PTOW!
19

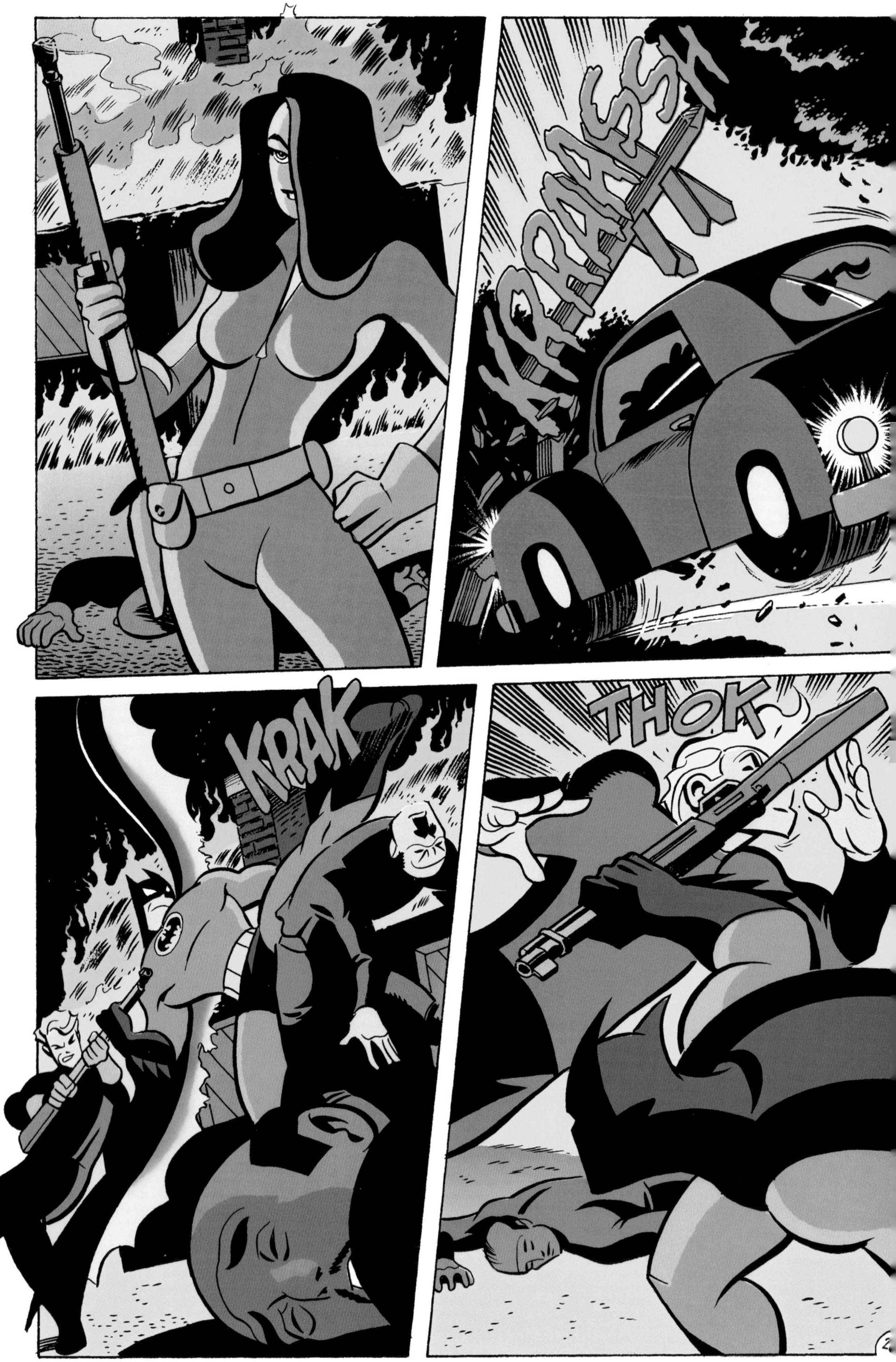
KRRAASSH
KRAK
THOK

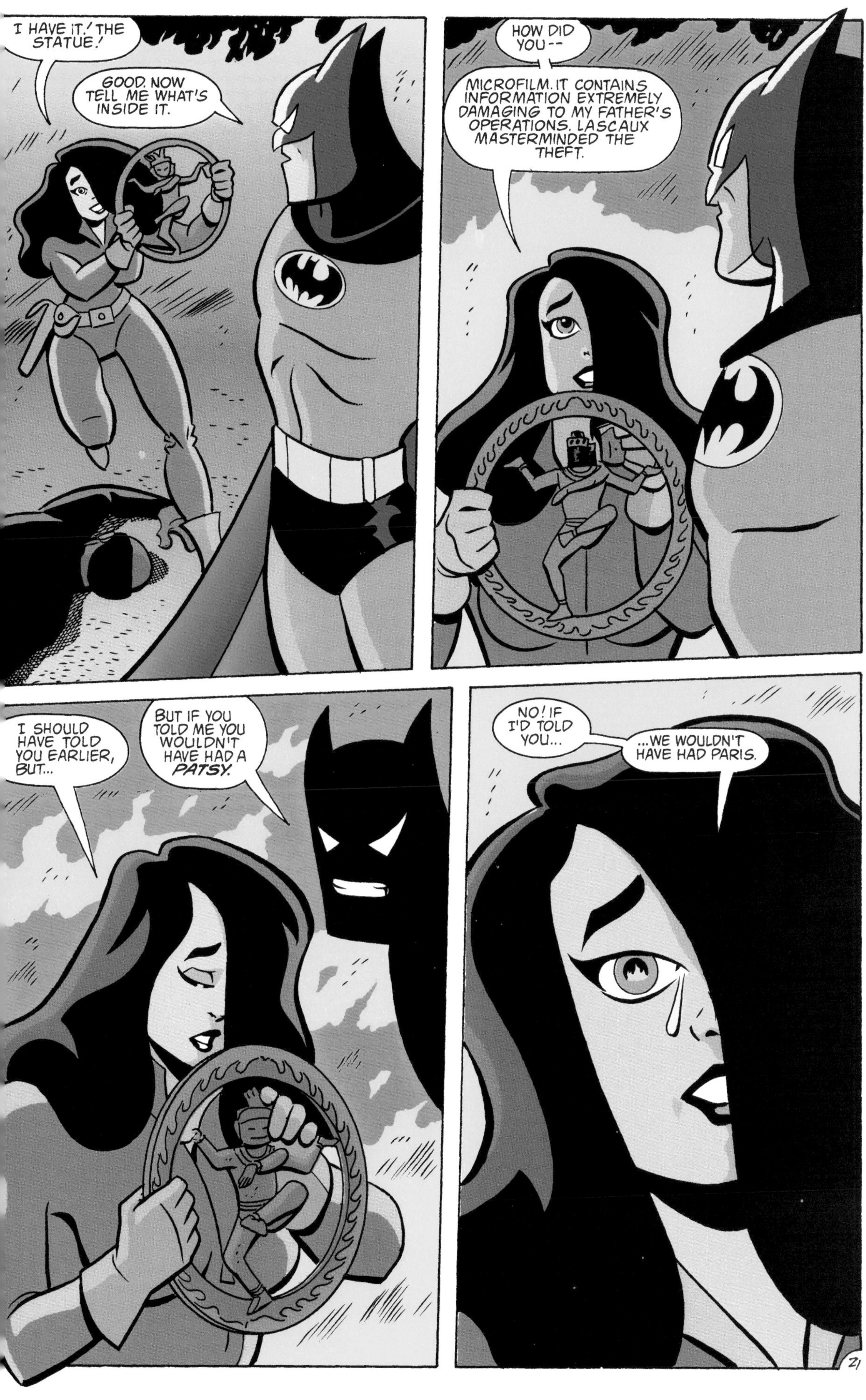
I HAVE IT! THE STATUE!
GOOD. NOW TELL ME WHAT'S INSIDE IT.
HOW DID YOU--
MICROFILM. IT CONTAINS INFORMATION EXTREMELY DAMAGING TO MY FATHER'S OPERATIONS. LASCAUX MASTERMINDED THE THEFT.
I SHOULD HAVE TOLD YOU EARLIER, BUT...
BUT IF YOU TOLD ME YOU WOULDN'T HAVE HAD A *PATSY.*
NO! IF I'D TOLD YOU...
...WE WOULDN'T HAVE HAD PARIS.
21

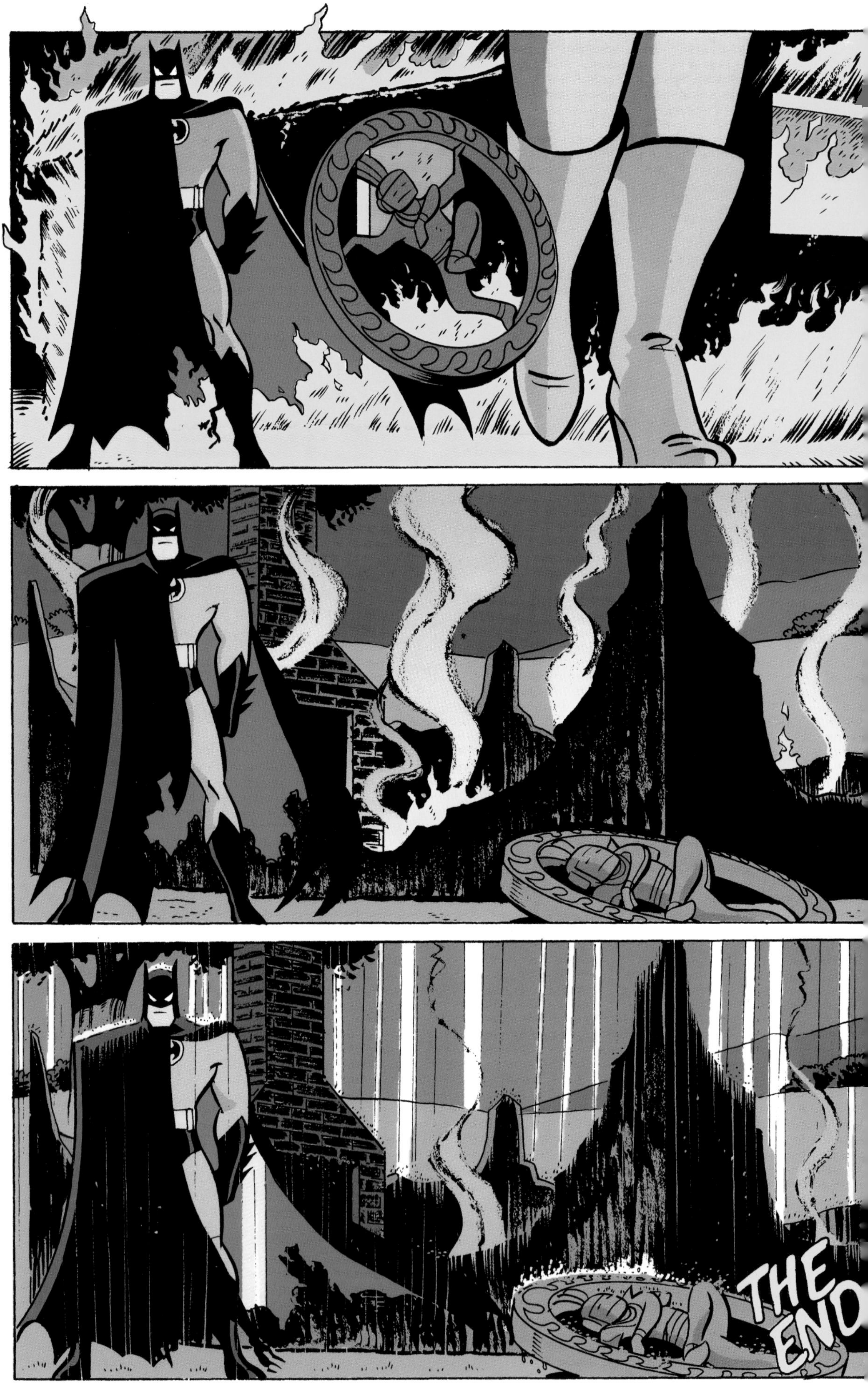
THE END

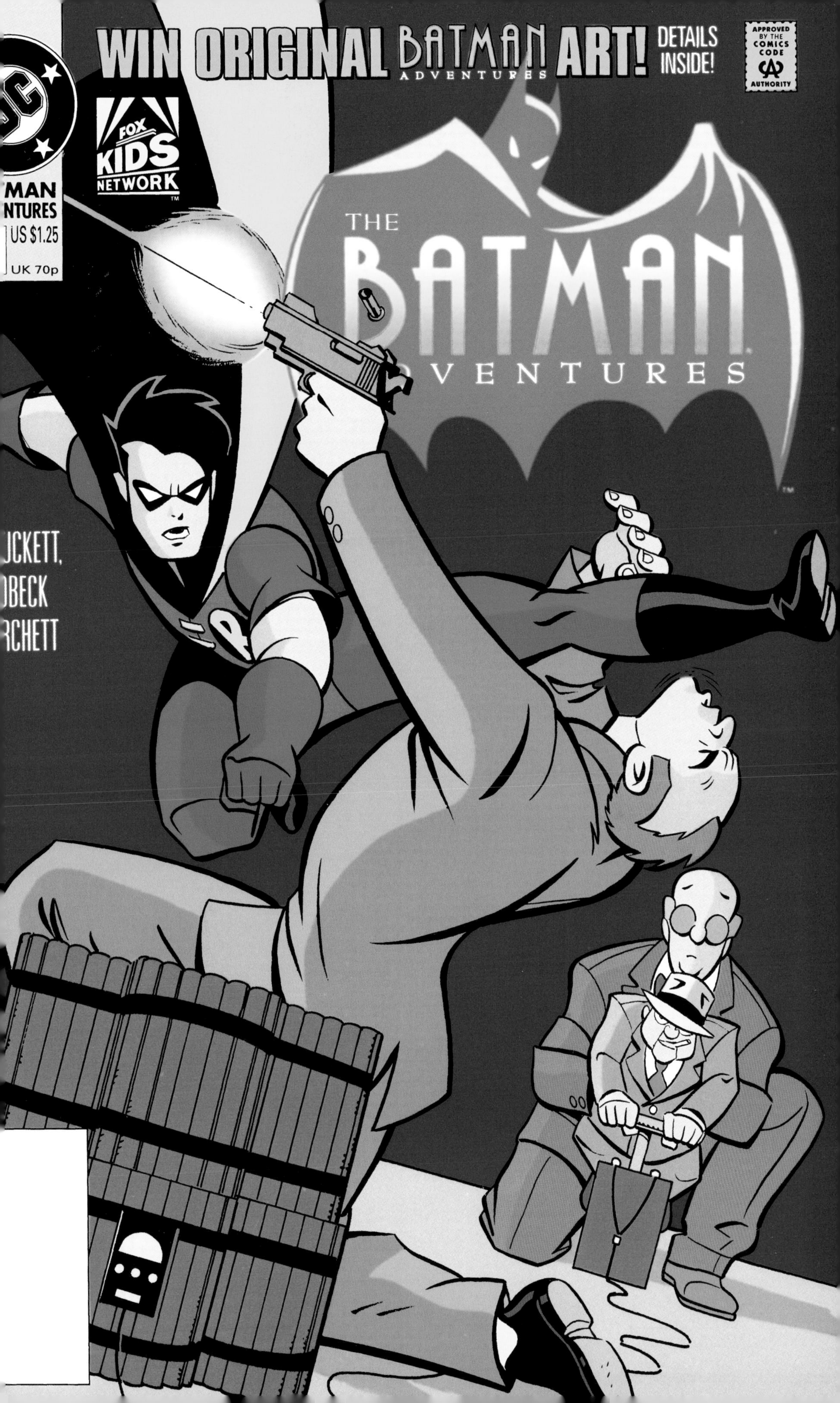

WIN ORIGINAL BATMAN ADVENTURES ART! DETAILS INSIDE!
APPROVED BY THE COMICS CODE AUTHORITY
DC
FOX KIDS NETWORK
MAN
NTURES
US $1.25
UK 70p
THE BATMAN ADVENTURES
CKETT,
BECK
RCHETT

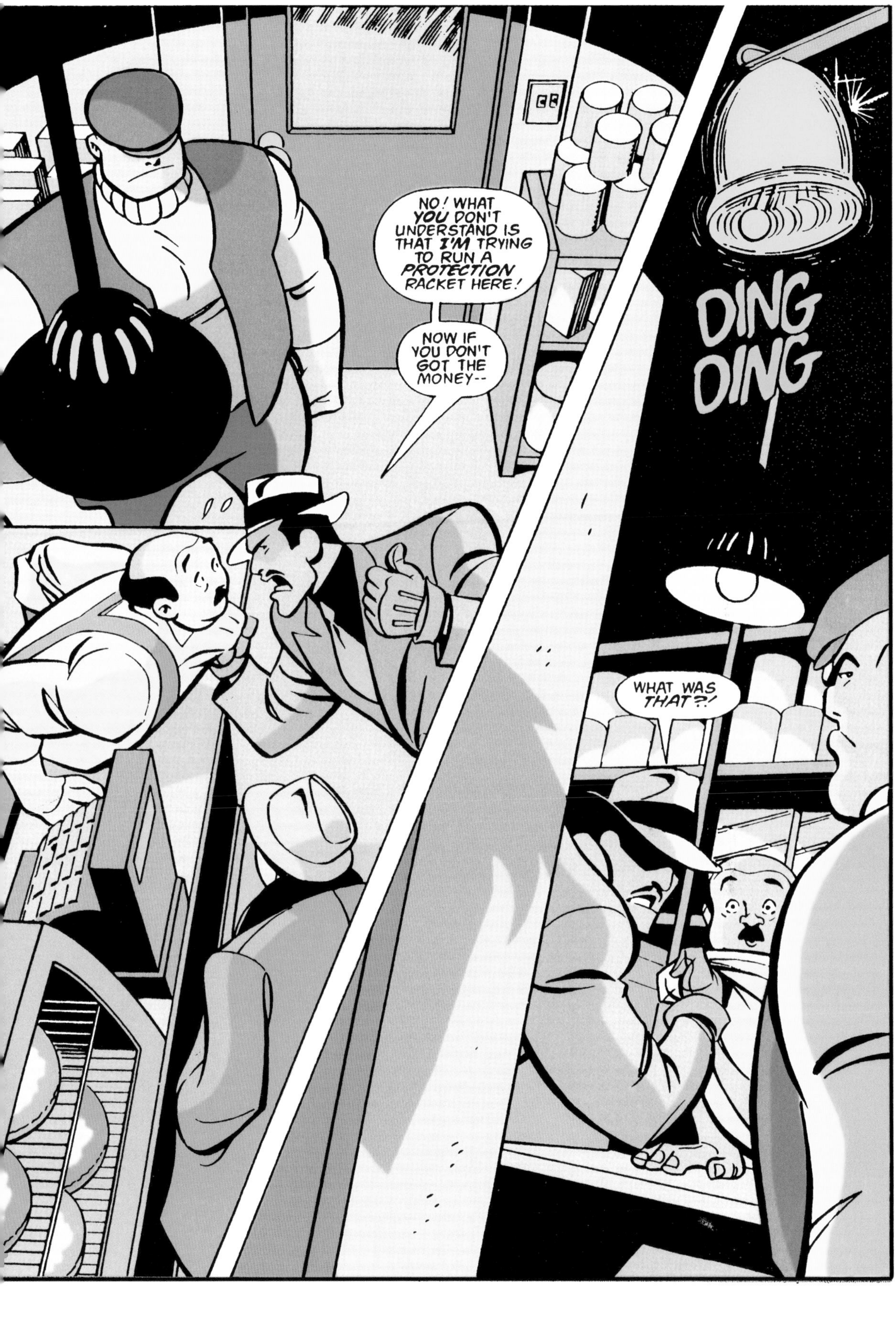
NO! WHAT YOU DON'T UNDERSTAND IS THAT I'M TRYING TO RUN A PROTECTION RACKET HERE!
NOW IF YOU DON'T GOT THE MONEY--
DING DING
WHAT WAS THAT?!

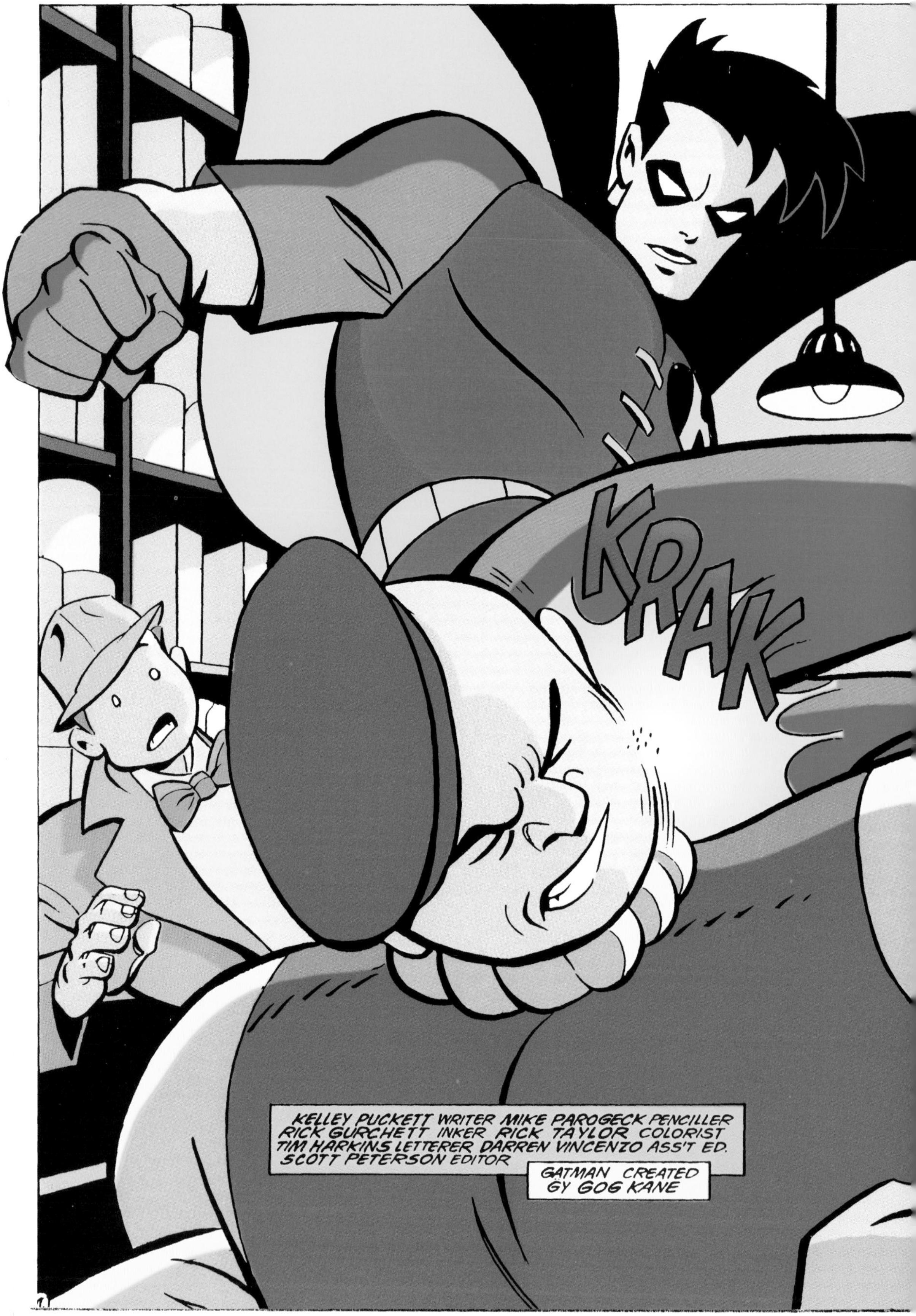
KRAK
KELLEY PUCKETT WRITER MIKE PAROGECK PENCILLER
RICK GURCHETT INKER RICK TAYLOR COLORIST
TIM HARKINS LETTERER DARREN VINCENZO ASS'T ED.
SCOTT PETERSON EDITOR
GATMAN CREATED GY GOG KANE

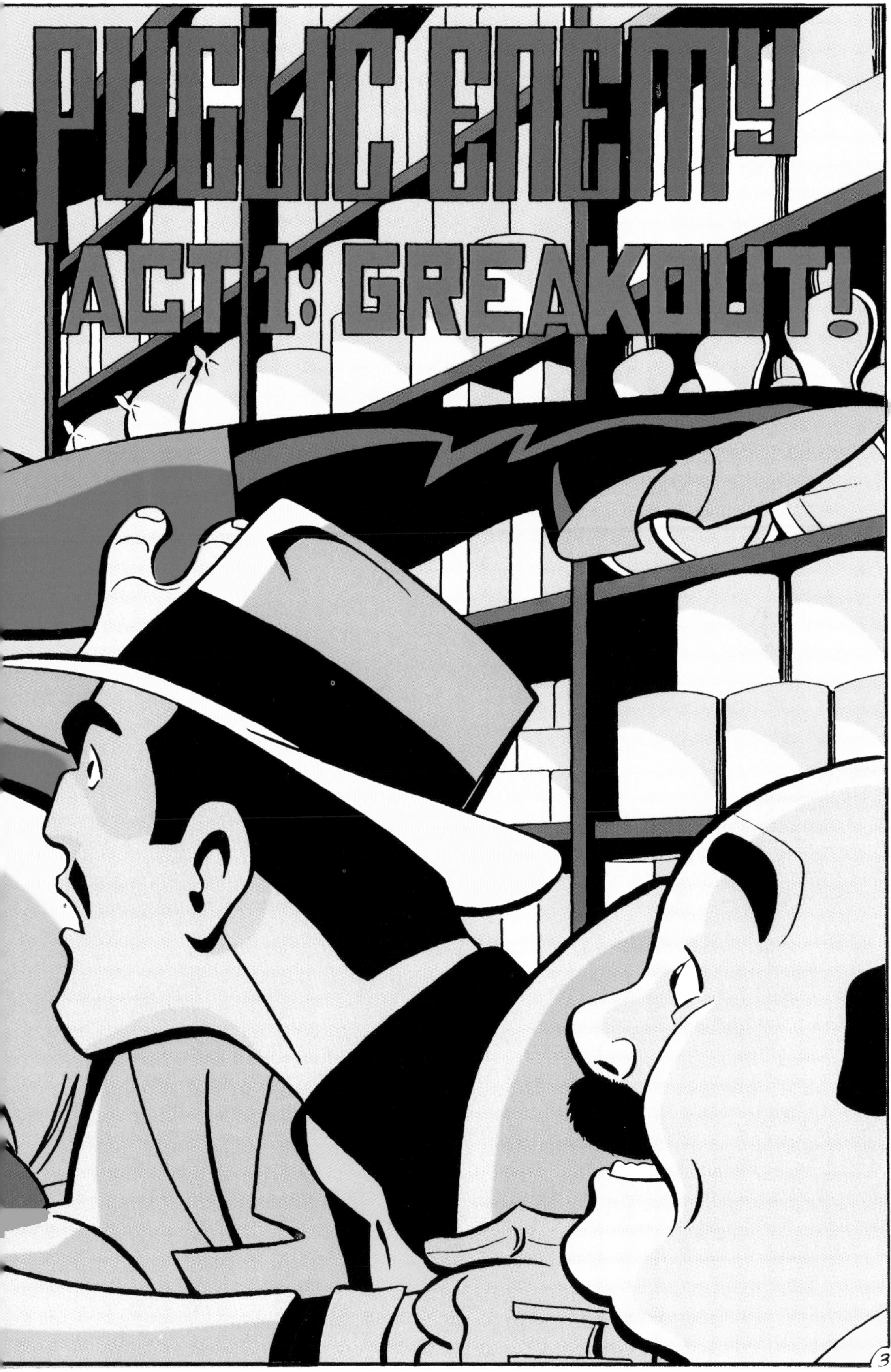
PUBLIC ENEMY
ACT 1: BREAKOUT!
3

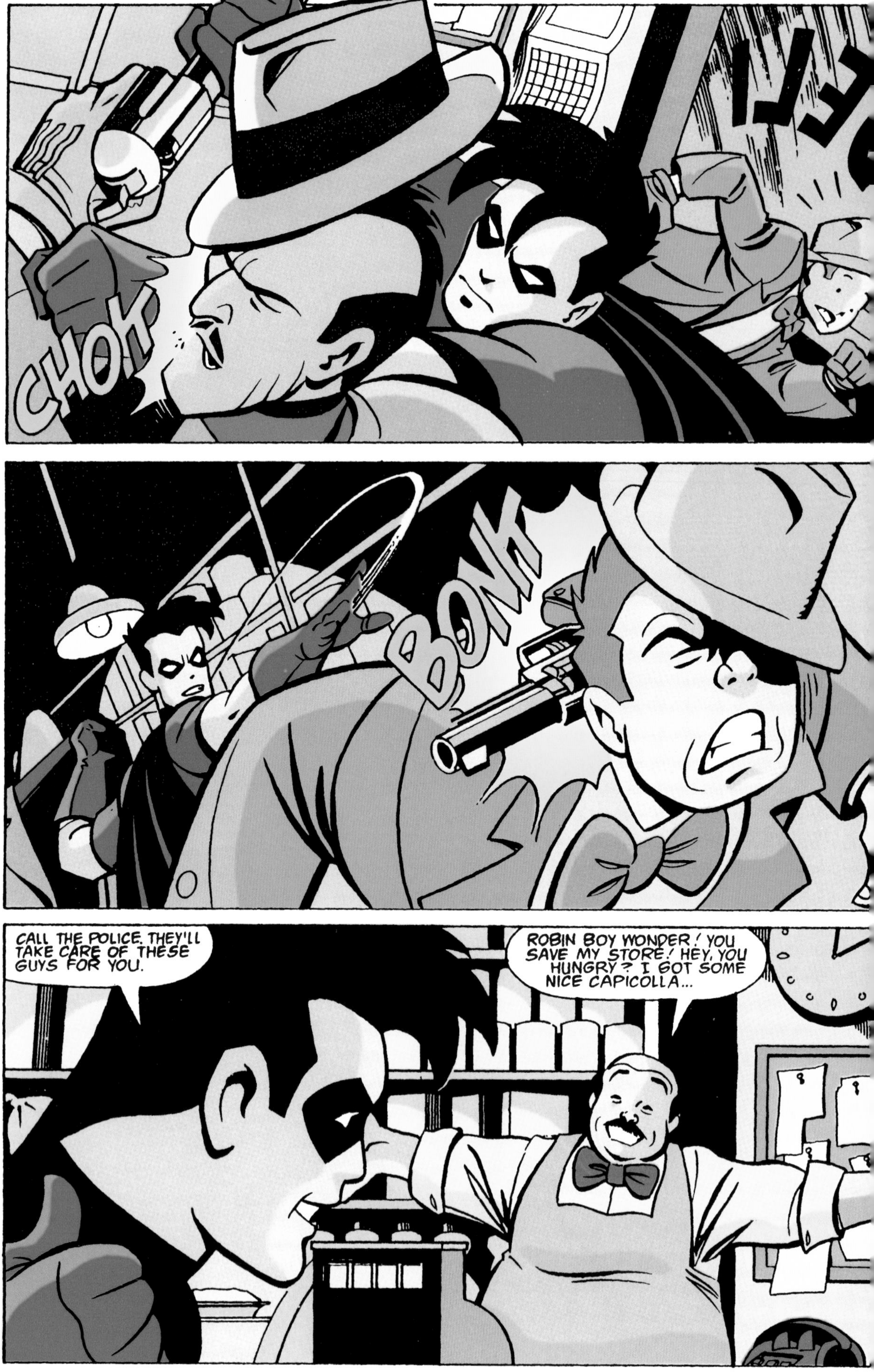

CHOK
BONK
CALL THE POLICE. THEY'LL TAKE CARE OF THESE GUYS FOR YOU.
ROBIN BOY WONDER! YOU SAVE MY STORE! HEY, YOU HUNGRY? I GOT SOME NICE CAPICOLLA...

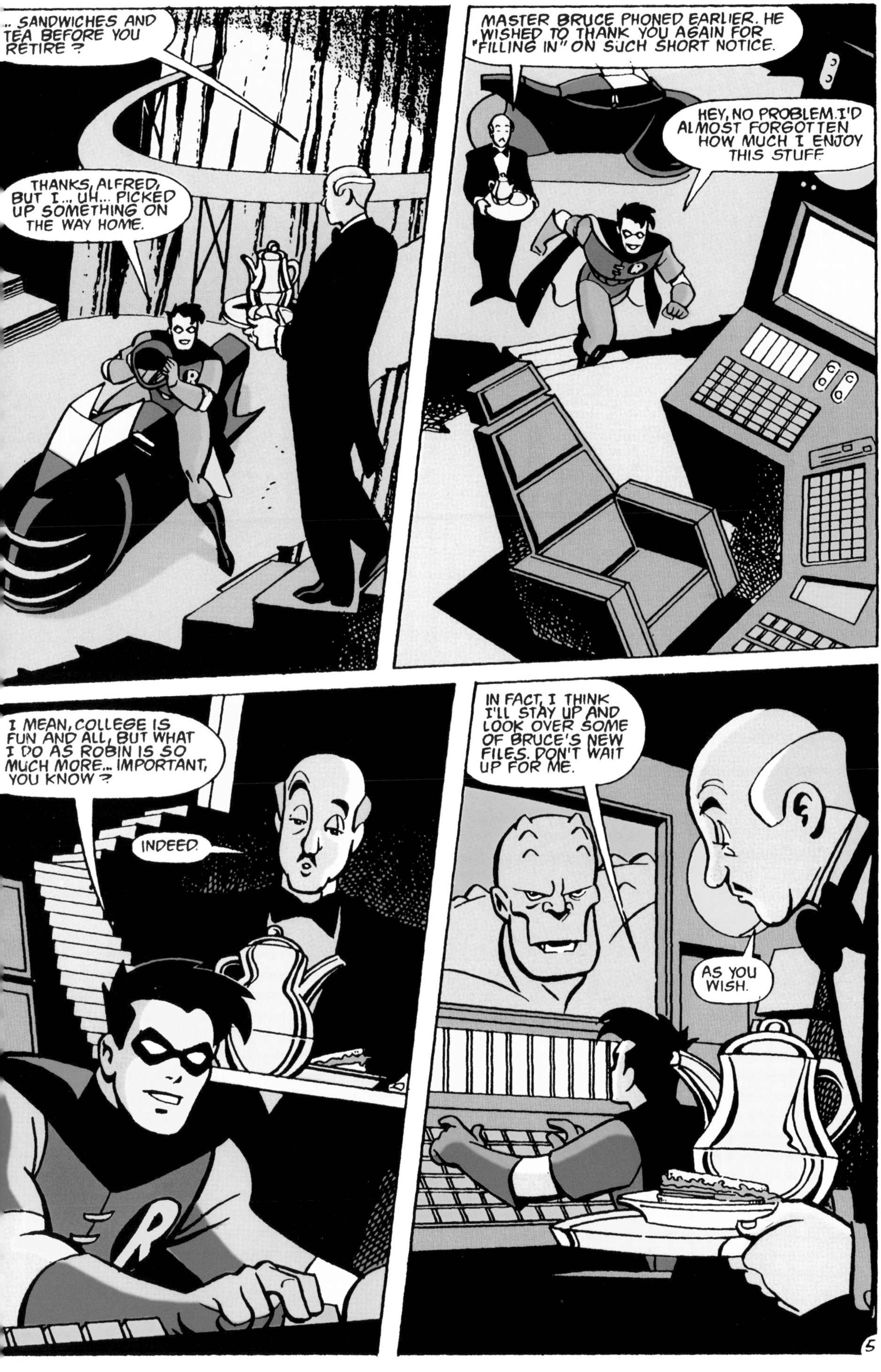
.. SANDWICHES AND TEA BEFORE YOU RETIRE ?
THANKS, ALFRED, BUT I... UH... PICKED UP SOMETHING ON THE WAY HOME.
MASTER BRUCE PHONED EARLIER. HE WISHED TO THANK YOU AGAIN FOR "FILLING IN" ON SUCH SHORT NOTICE.
HEY, NO PROBLEM. I'D ALMOST FORGOTTEN HOW MUCH I ENJOY THIS STUFF.
I MEAN, COLLEGE IS FUN AND ALL, BUT WHAT I DO AS ROBIN IS SO MUCH MORE... IMPORTANT, YOU KNOW ?
INDEED.
IN FACT, I THINK I'LL STAY UP AND LOOK OVER SOME OF BRUCE'S NEW FILES. DON'T WAIT UP FOR ME.
AS YOU WISH.
5

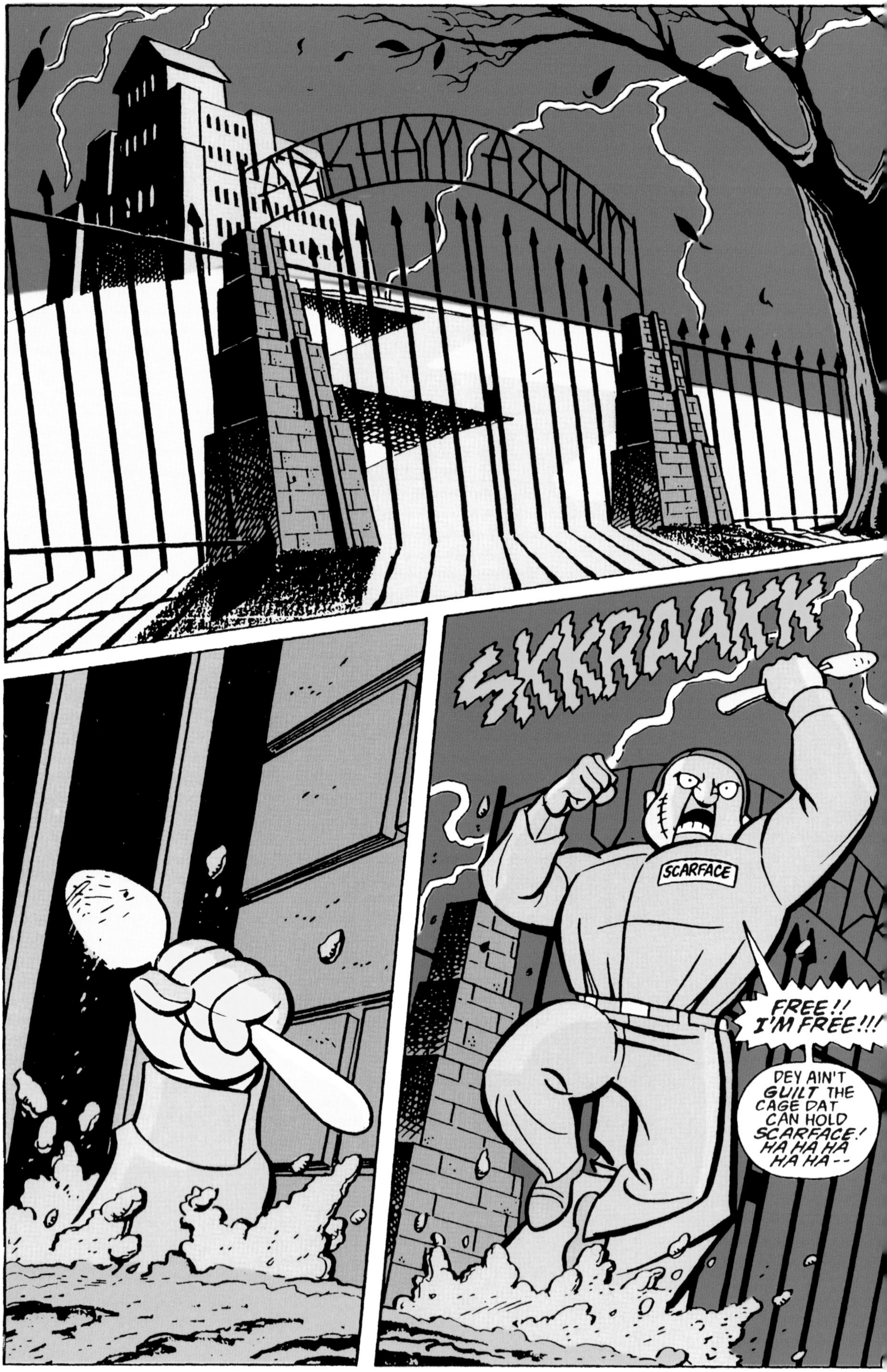
ARKHAM ASYLUM
SKKRAAKK
SCARFACE
FREE!! I'M FREE!!!
DEY AIN'T GUILT THE CAGE DAT CAN HOLD SCARFACE! HA HA HA HA HA--

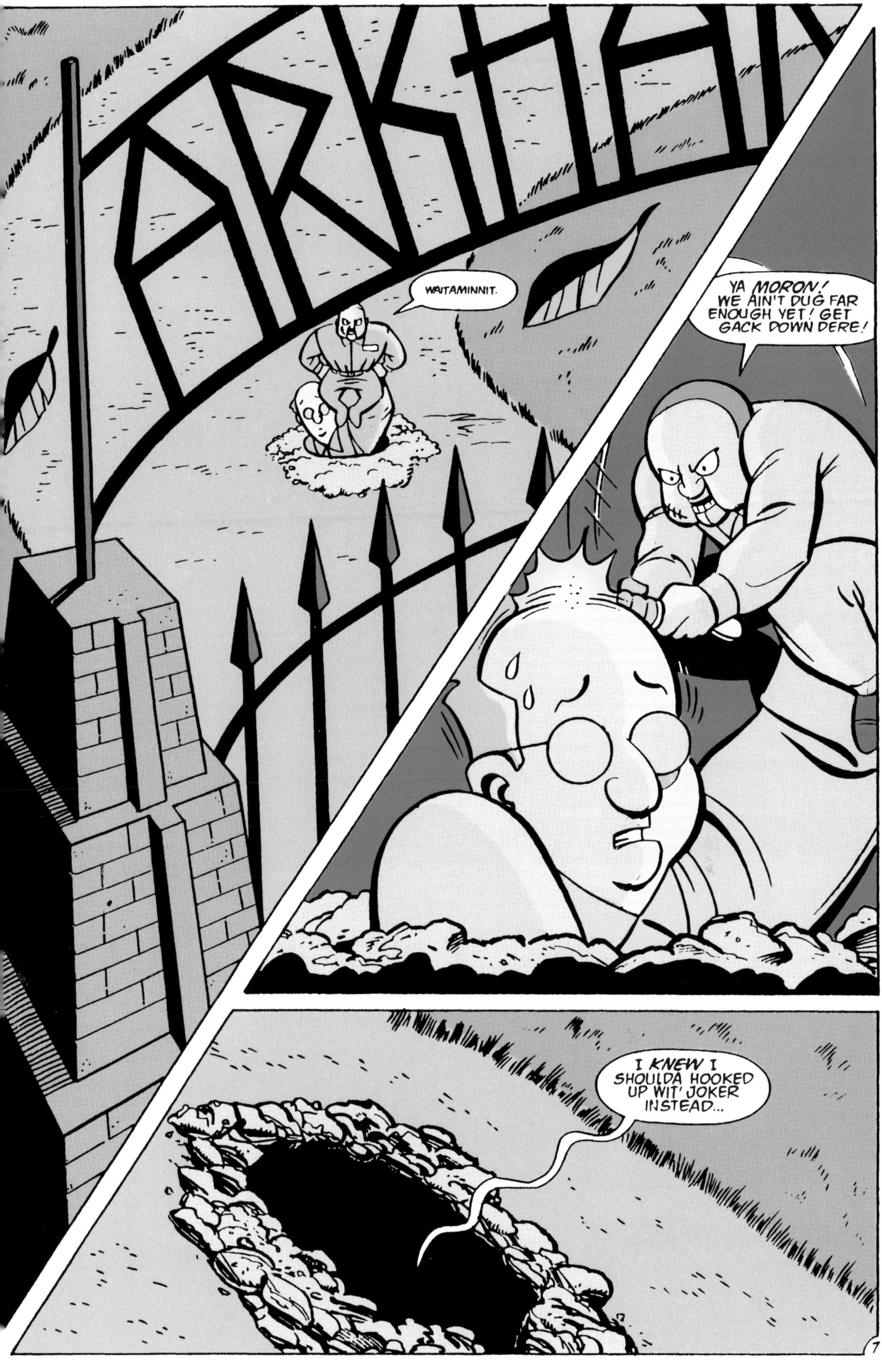

ARKHAM
WAITAMINNIT.
YA MORON! WE AIN'T DUG FAR ENOUGH YET! GET GACK DOWN DERE!
I KNEW I SHOULDA HOOKED UP WIT' JOKER INSTEAD...
7

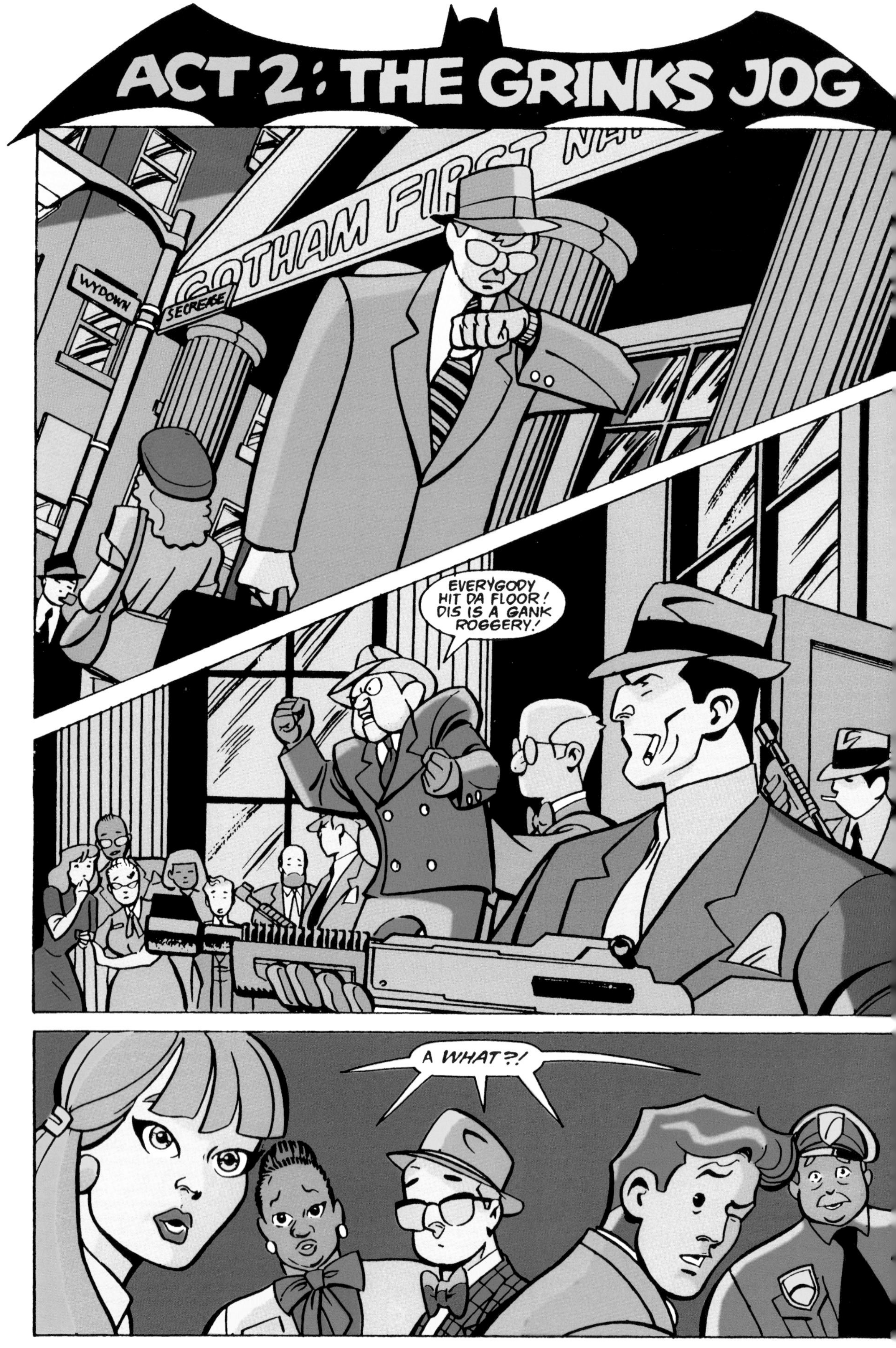
ACT 2: THE GRINKS JOG
GOTHAM FIRST NAT
WYDOWN
SECREASE
EVERYGODY HIT DA FLOOR! DIS IS A GANK ROGGERY!
A WHAT?!

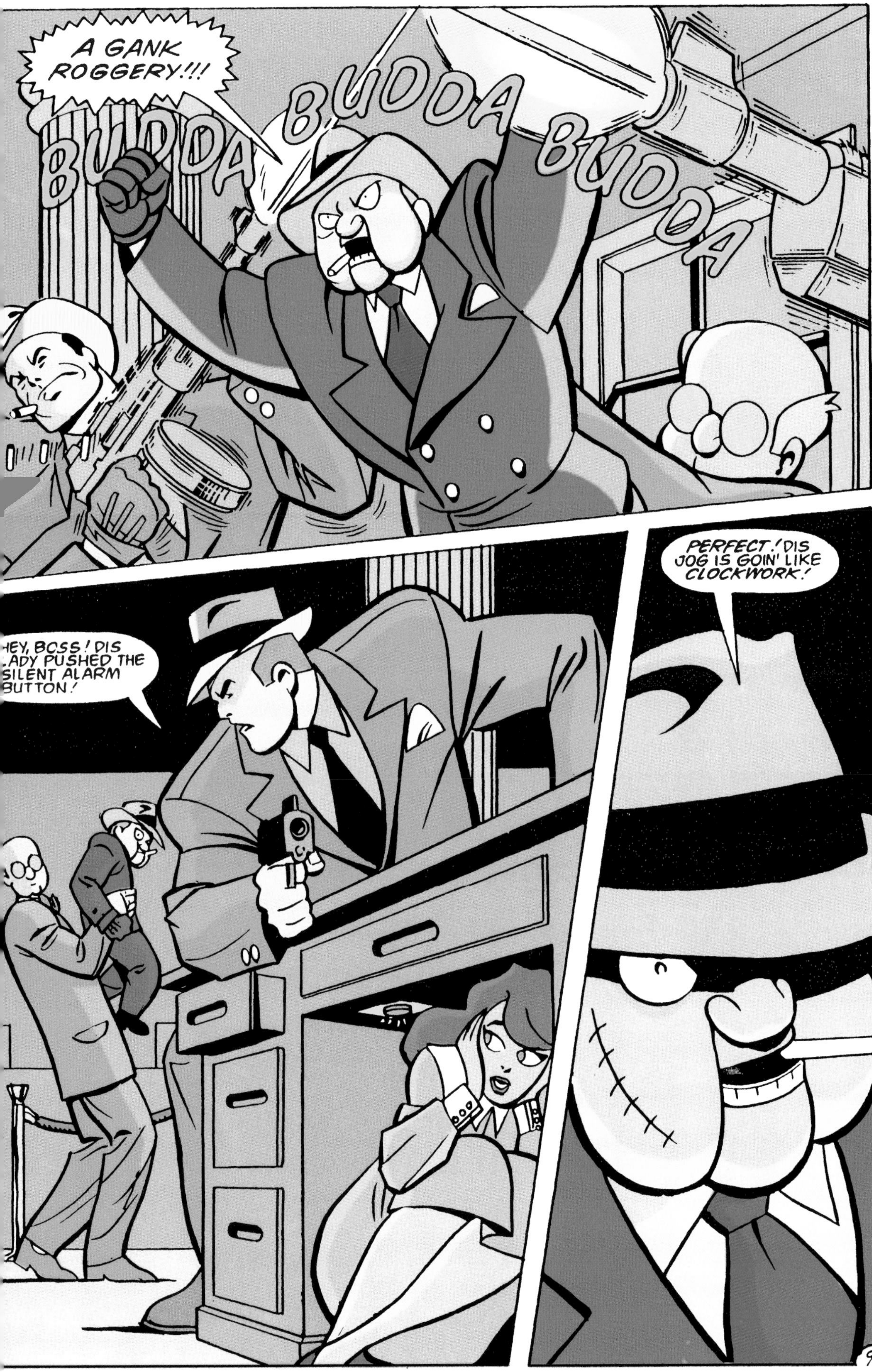
A GANK ROGGERY!!!
BUDDA BUDDA BUDDA BUDDA
HEY, BOSS! DIS LADY PUSHED THE SILENT ALARM BUTTON!
PERFECT! DIS JOG IS GOIN' LIKE CLOCKWORK!
9

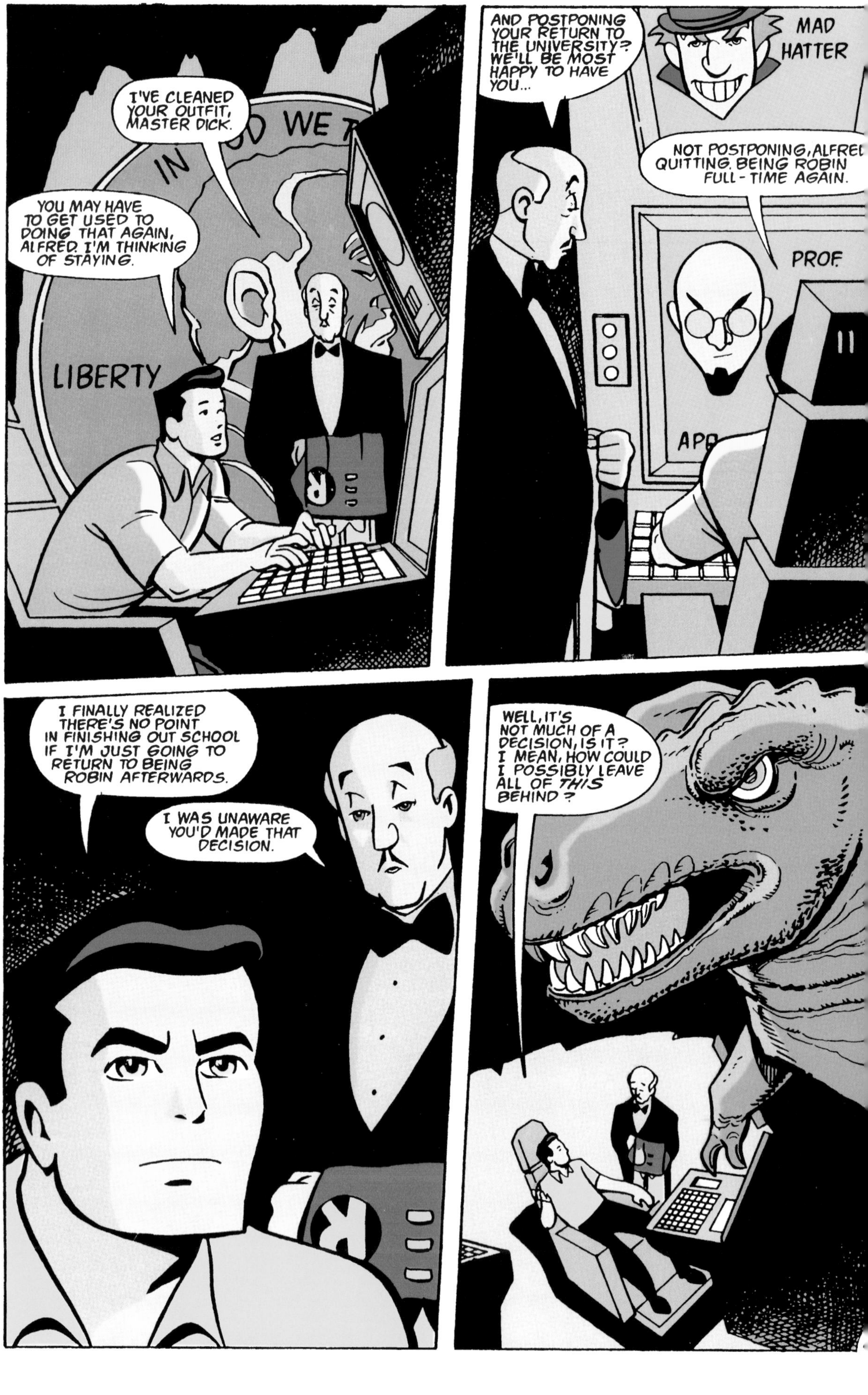
I'VE CLEANED YOUR OUTFIT, MASTER DICK.
IN GOD WE T
YOU MAY HAVE TO GET USED TO DOING THAT AGAIN, ALFRED. I'M THINKING OF STAYING.
LIBERTY
AND POSTPONING YOUR RETURN TO THE UNIVERSITY? WE'LL BE MOST HAPPY TO HAVE YOU...
MAD HATTER
NOT POSTPONING, ALFRED QUITTING. BEING ROBIN FULL-TIME AGAIN.
PROF.
APR
I FINALLY REALIZED THERE'S NO POINT IN FINISHING OUT SCHOOL IF I'M JUST GOING TO RETURN TO BEING ROBIN AFTERWARDS.
I WAS UNAWARE YOU'D MADE THAT DECISION.
WELL, IT'S NOT MUCH OF A DECISION, IS IT? I MEAN, HOW COULD I POSSIBLY LEAVE ALL OF THIS BEHIND?

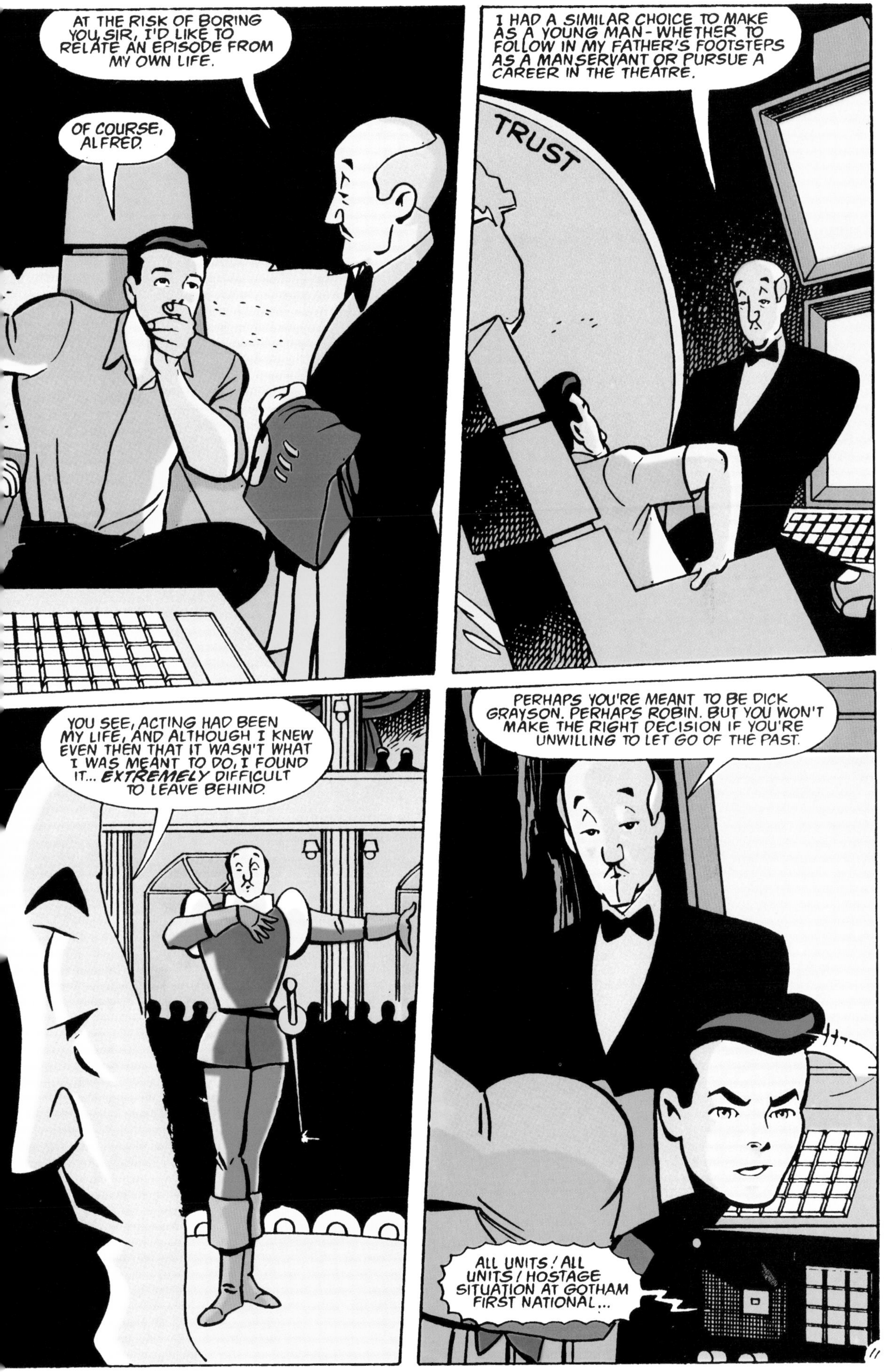
AT THE RISK OF BORING YOU, SIR, I'D LIKE TO RELATE AN EPISODE FROM MY OWN LIFE.
OF COURSE, ALFRED.
I HAD A SIMILAR CHOICE TO MAKE AS A YOUNG MAN - WHETHER TO FOLLOW IN MY FATHER'S FOOTSTEPS AS A MANSERVANT OR PURSUE A CAREER IN THE THEATRE.
TRUST
YOU SEE, ACTING HAD BEEN MY LIFE, AND ALTHOUGH I KNEW EVEN THEN THAT IT WASN'T WHAT I WAS MEANT TO DO, I FOUND IT... *EXTREMELY* DIFFICULT TO LEAVE BEHIND.
PERHAPS YOU'RE MEANT TO BE DICK GRAYSON. PERHAPS ROBIN. BUT YOU WON'T MAKE THE RIGHT DECISION IF YOU'RE UNWILLING TO LET GO OF THE PAST.
ALL UNITS! ALL UNITS! HOSTAGE SITUATION AT GOTHAM FIRST NATIONAL...

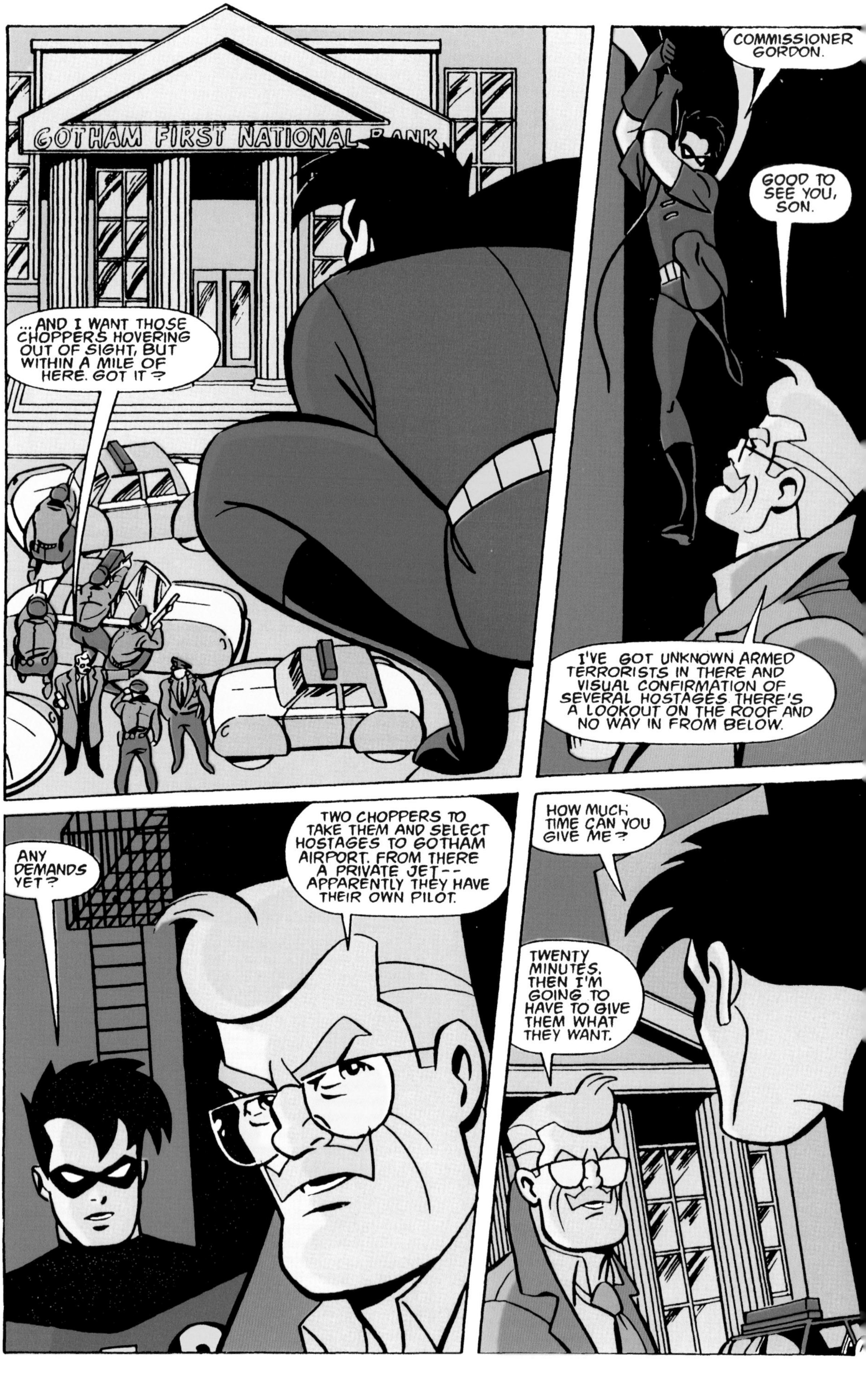
GOTHAM FIRST NATIONAL BANK
...AND I WANT THOSE CHOPPERS HOVERING OUT OF SIGHT, BUT WITHIN A MILE OF HERE. GOT IT?
COMMISSIONER GORDON.
GOOD TO SEE YOU, SON.
I'VE GOT UNKNOWN ARMED TERRORISTS IN THERE AND VISUAL CONFIRMATION OF SEVERAL HOSTAGES. THERE'S A LOOKOUT ON THE ROOF AND NO WAY IN FROM BELOW.
ANY DEMANDS YET?
TWO CHOPPERS TO TAKE THEM AND SELECT HOSTAGES TO GOTHAM AIRPORT. FROM THERE A PRIVATE JET-- APPARENTLY THEY HAVE THEIR OWN PILOT.
HOW MUCH TIME CAN YOU GIVE ME?
TWENTY MINUTES. THEN I'M GOING TO HAVE TO GIVE THEM WHAT THEY WANT.

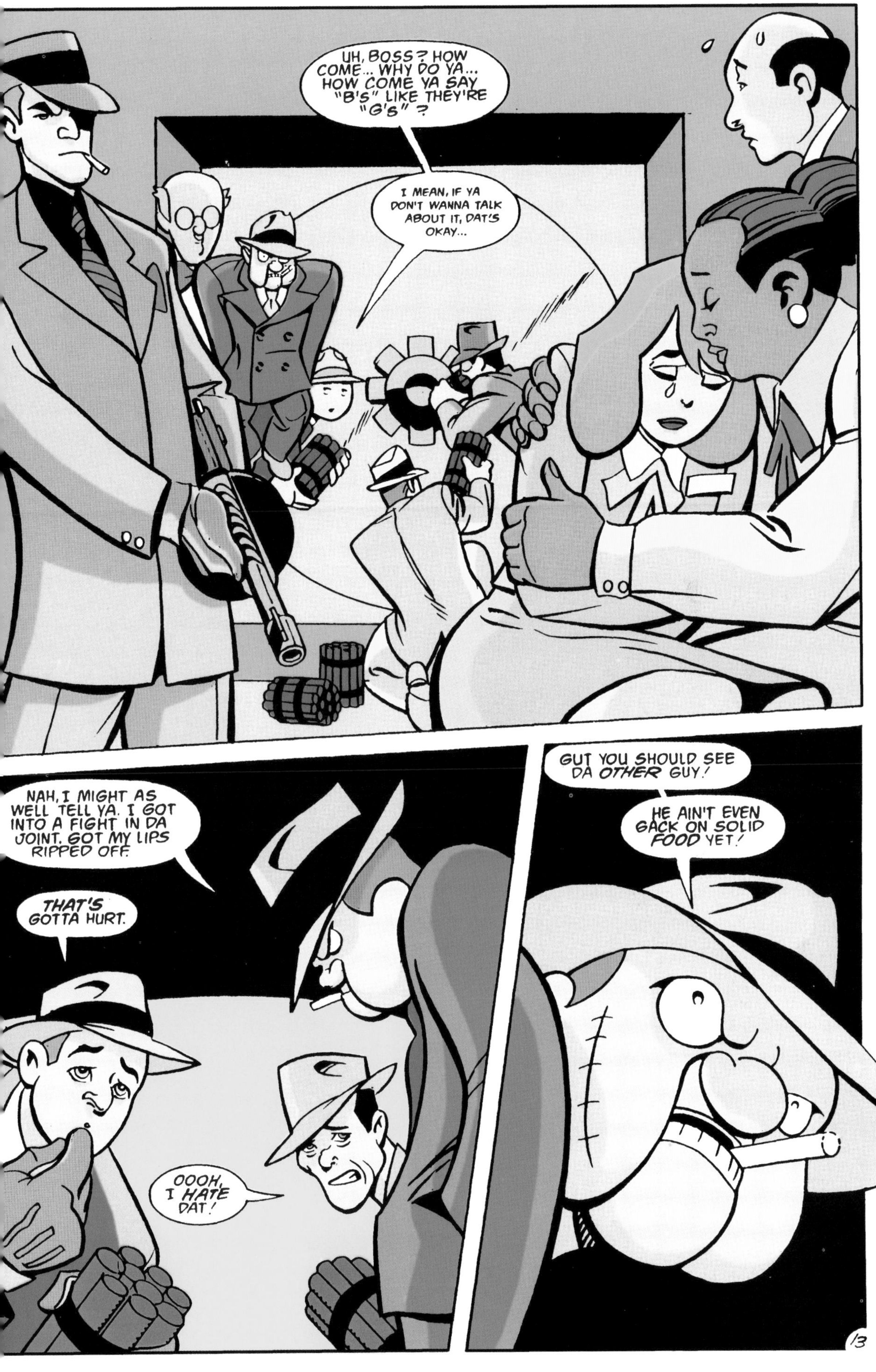
UH, BOSS? HOW COME... WHY DO YA... HOW COME YA SAY "B'S" LIKE THEY'RE "G'S"?
I MEAN, IF YA DON'T WANNA TALK ABOUT IT, DAT'S OKAY...
NAH, I MIGHT AS WELL TELL YA. I GOT INTO A FIGHT IN DA JOINT. GOT MY LIPS RIPPED OFF.
THAT'S GOTTA HURT.
OOOH, I HATE DAT!
GUT YOU SHOULD SEE DA OTHER GUY!
HE AIN'T EVEN GACK ON SOLID FOOD YET!
13

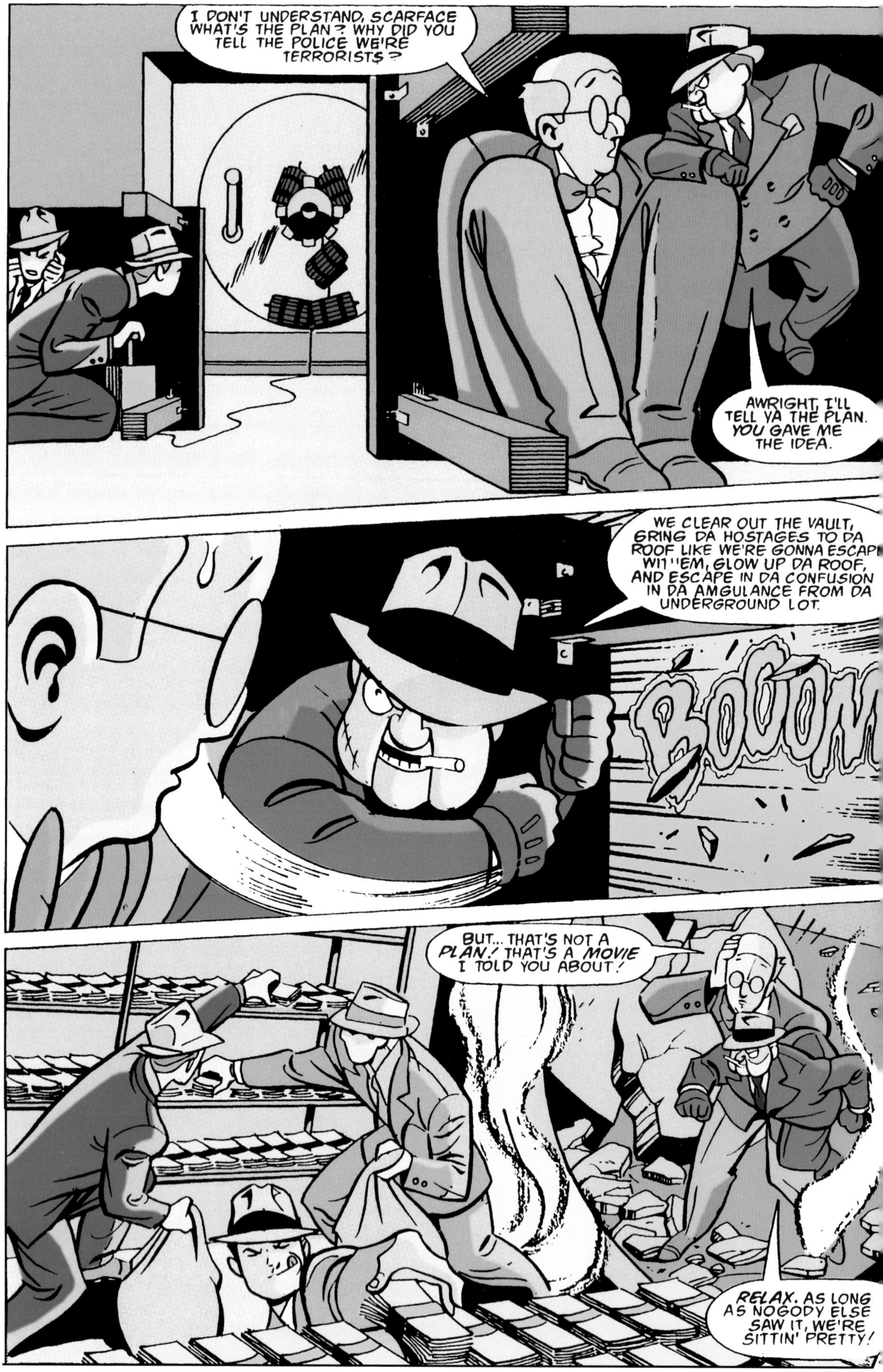
I DON'T UNDERSTAND, SCARFACE WHAT'S THE PLAN? WHY DID YOU TELL THE POLICE WE'RE TERRORIST$?
AWRIGHT, I'LL TELL YA THE PLAN. YOU GAVE ME THE IDEA.
WE CLEAR OUT THE VAULT, GRING DA HOSTAGES TO DA ROOF LIKE WE'RE GONNA ESCAPE WIT 'EM, GLOW UP DA ROOF, AND ESCAPE IN DA CONFUSION IN DA AMGULANCE FROM DA UNDERGROUND LOT.
BUT... THAT'S NOT A PLAN! THAT'S A MOVIE I TOLD YOU ABOUT!
RELAX. AS LONG AS NOGODY ELSE SAW IT, WE'RE SITTIN' PRETTY!

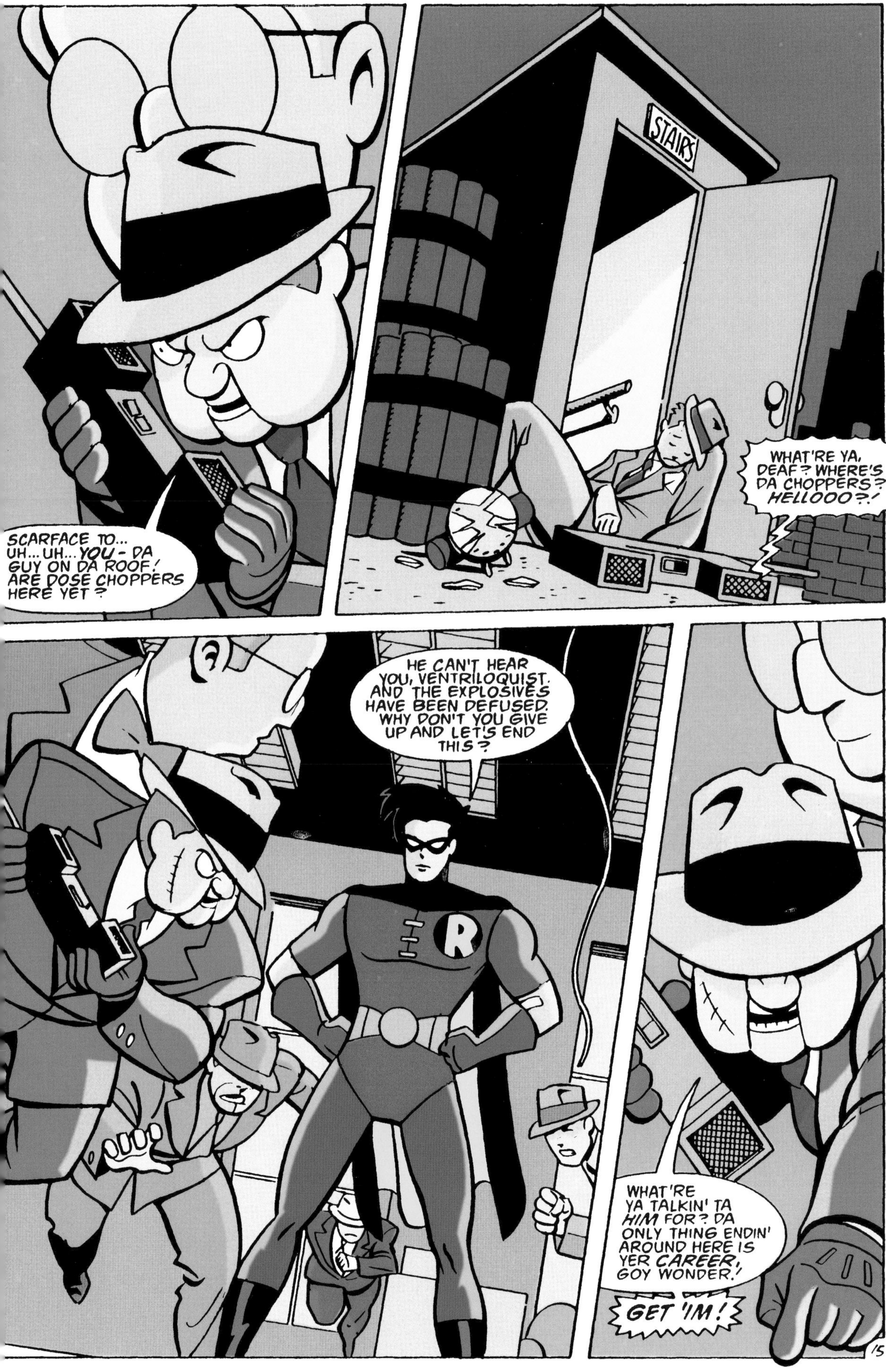
SCARFACE TO... UH... UH... YOU - DA GUY ON DA ROOF! ARE DOSE CHOPPERS HERE YET?
WHAT'RE YA, DEAF? WHERE'S DA CHOPPERS? HELLOOO?!
STAIRS
HE CAN'T HEAR YOU, VENTRILOQUIST. AND THE EXPLOSIVES HAVE BEEN DEFUSED. WHY DON'T YOU GIVE UP AND LET'S END THIS?
WHAT'RE YA TALKIN' TA HIM FOR? DA ONLY THING ENDIN' AROUND HERE IS YER CAREER, GOY WONDER!
GET 'IM!
15

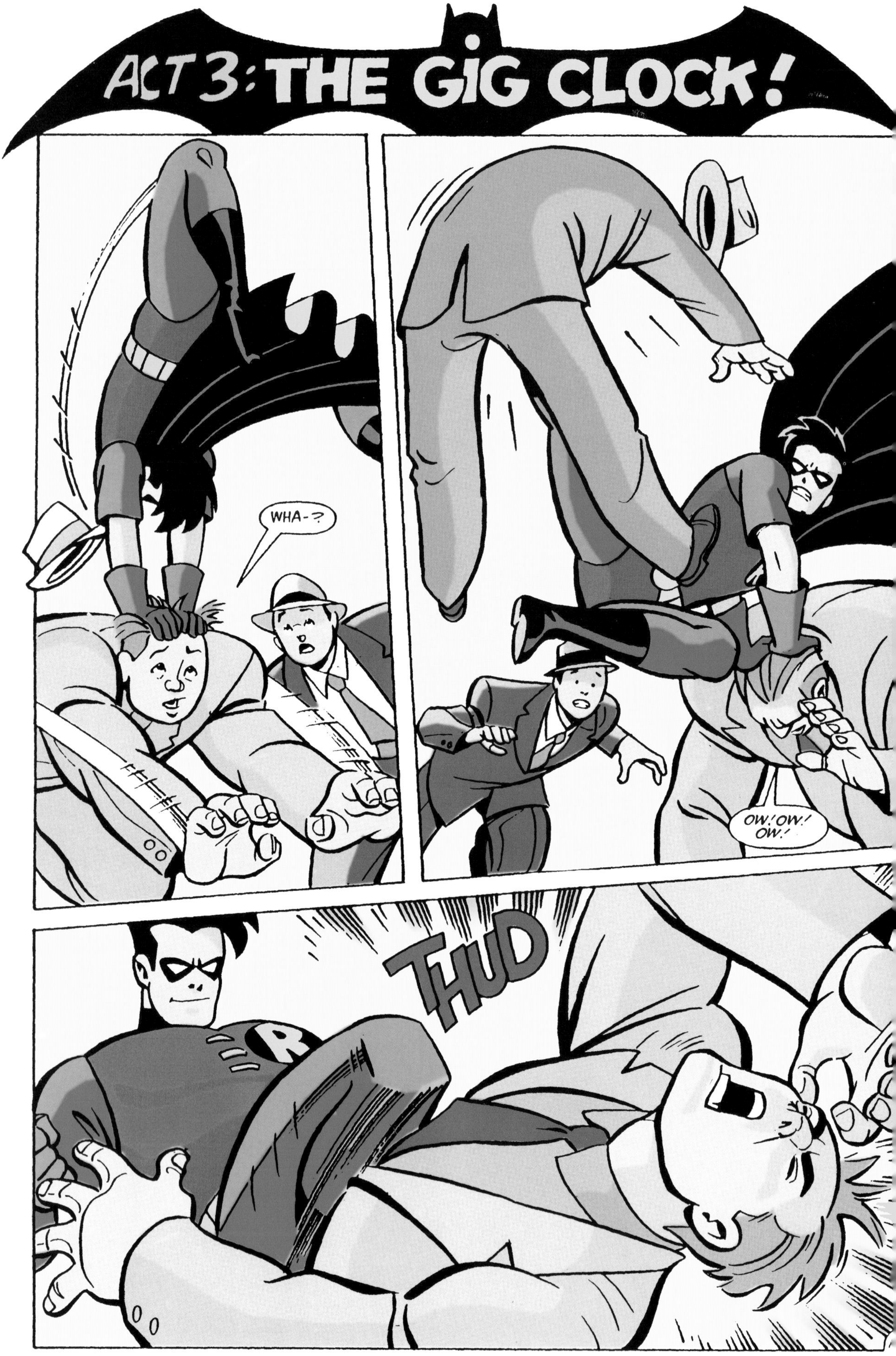
ACT 3: THE GIG CLOCK!
WHA-?
OW! OW! OW!
THUD

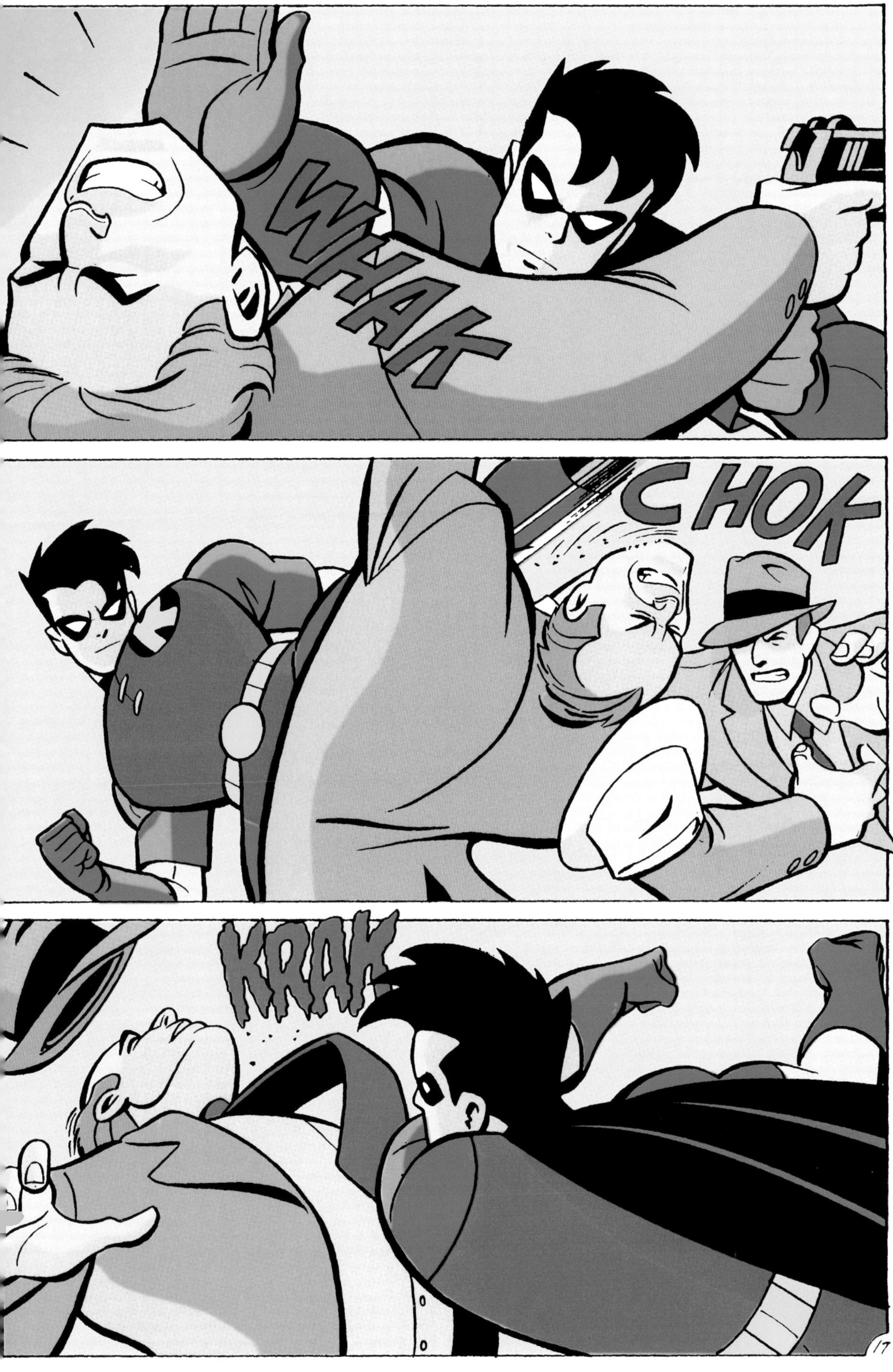
WHAK
CHOK
KRAK
17

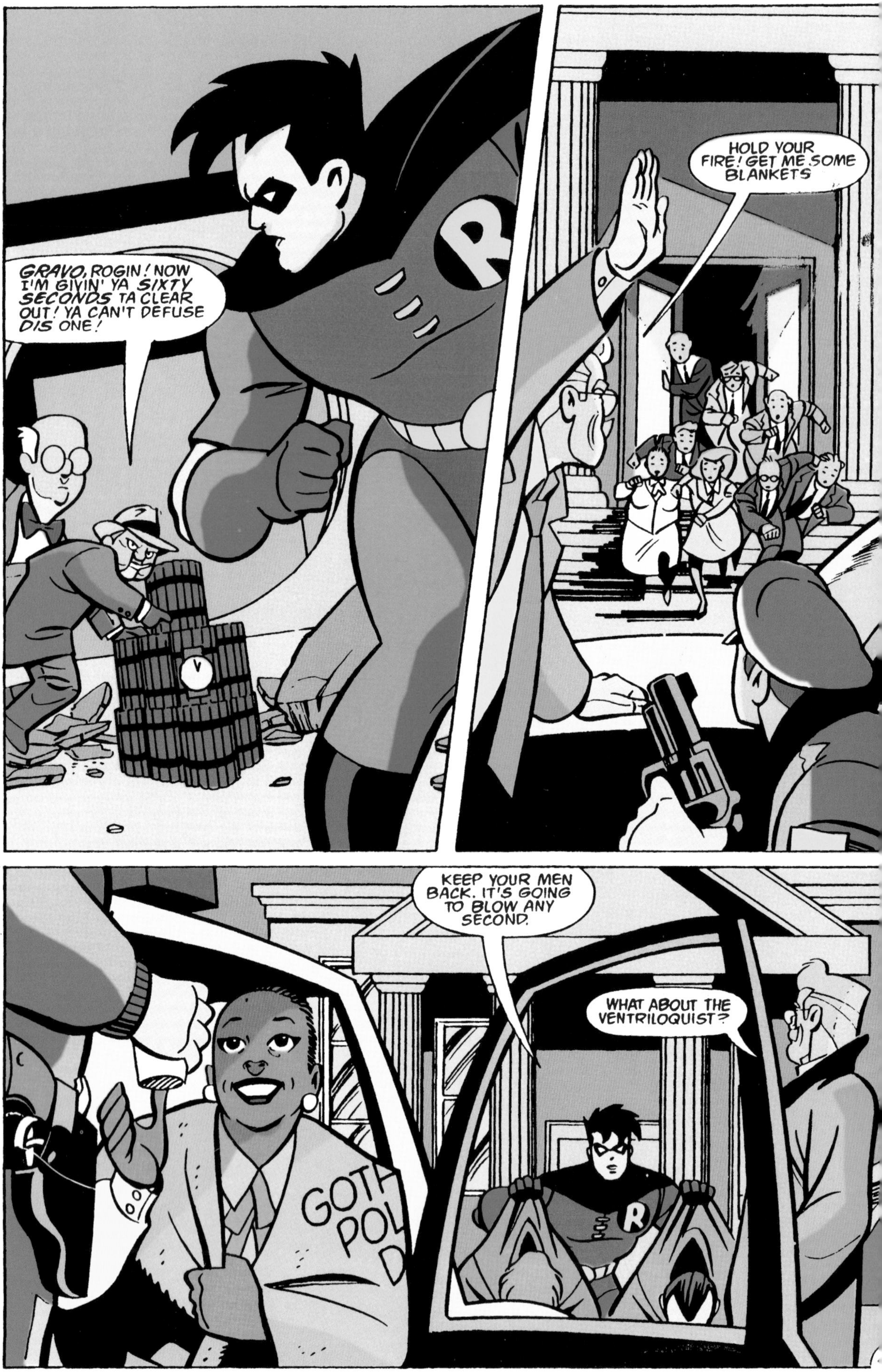
GRAVO, ROGIN! NOW I'M GIVIN' YA SIXTY SECONDS TA CLEAR OUT! YA CAN'T DEFUSE DIS ONE!
HOLD YOUR FIRE! GET ME SOME BLANKETS
KEEP YOUR MEN BACK. IT'S GOING TO BLOW ANY SECOND.
WHAT ABOUT THE VENTRILOQUIST?

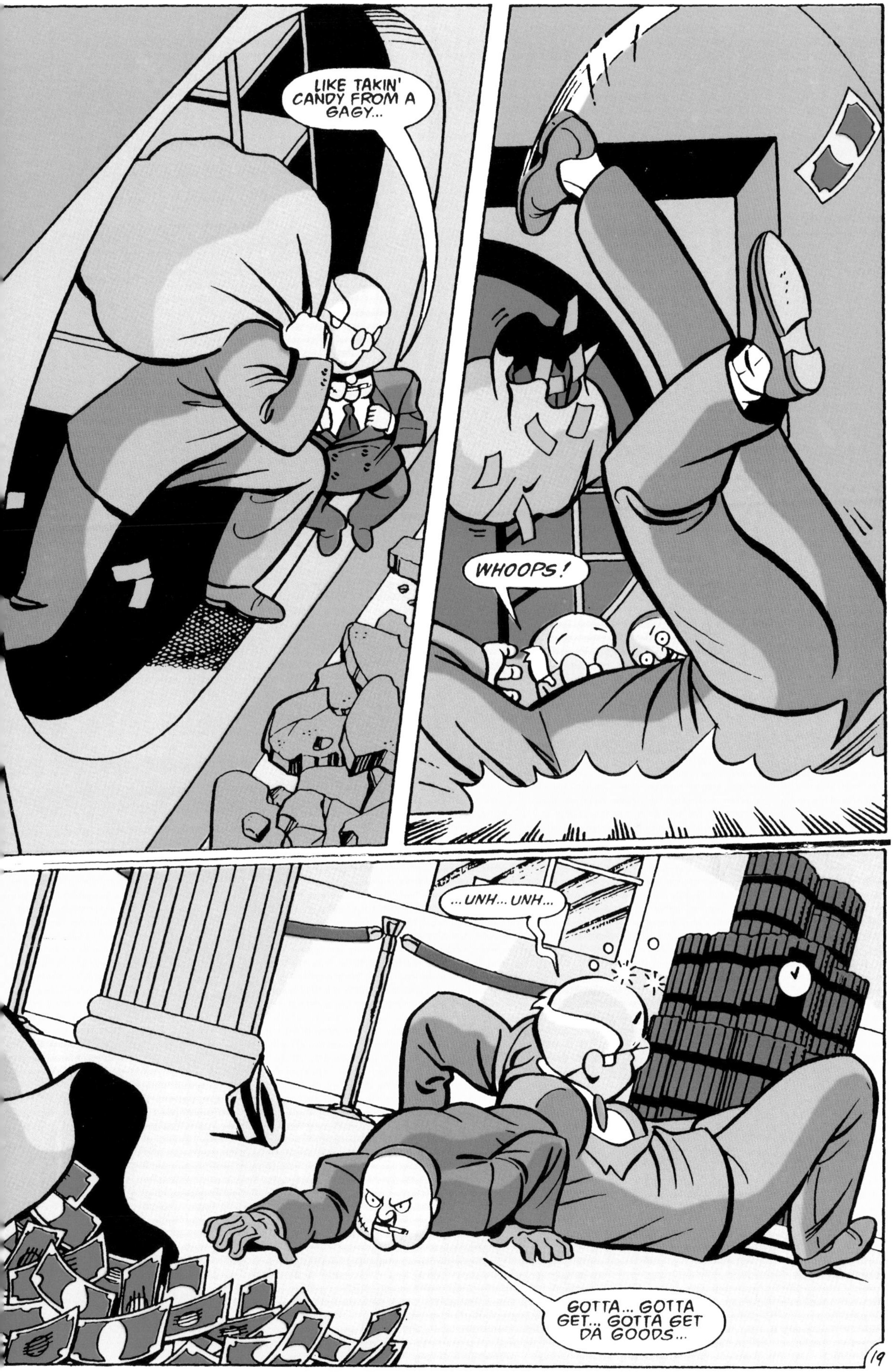
LIKE TAKIN' CANDY FROM A GAGY...
WHOOPS!
...UNH... UNH...
GOTTA... GOTTA GET... GOTTA GET DA GOODS...
19

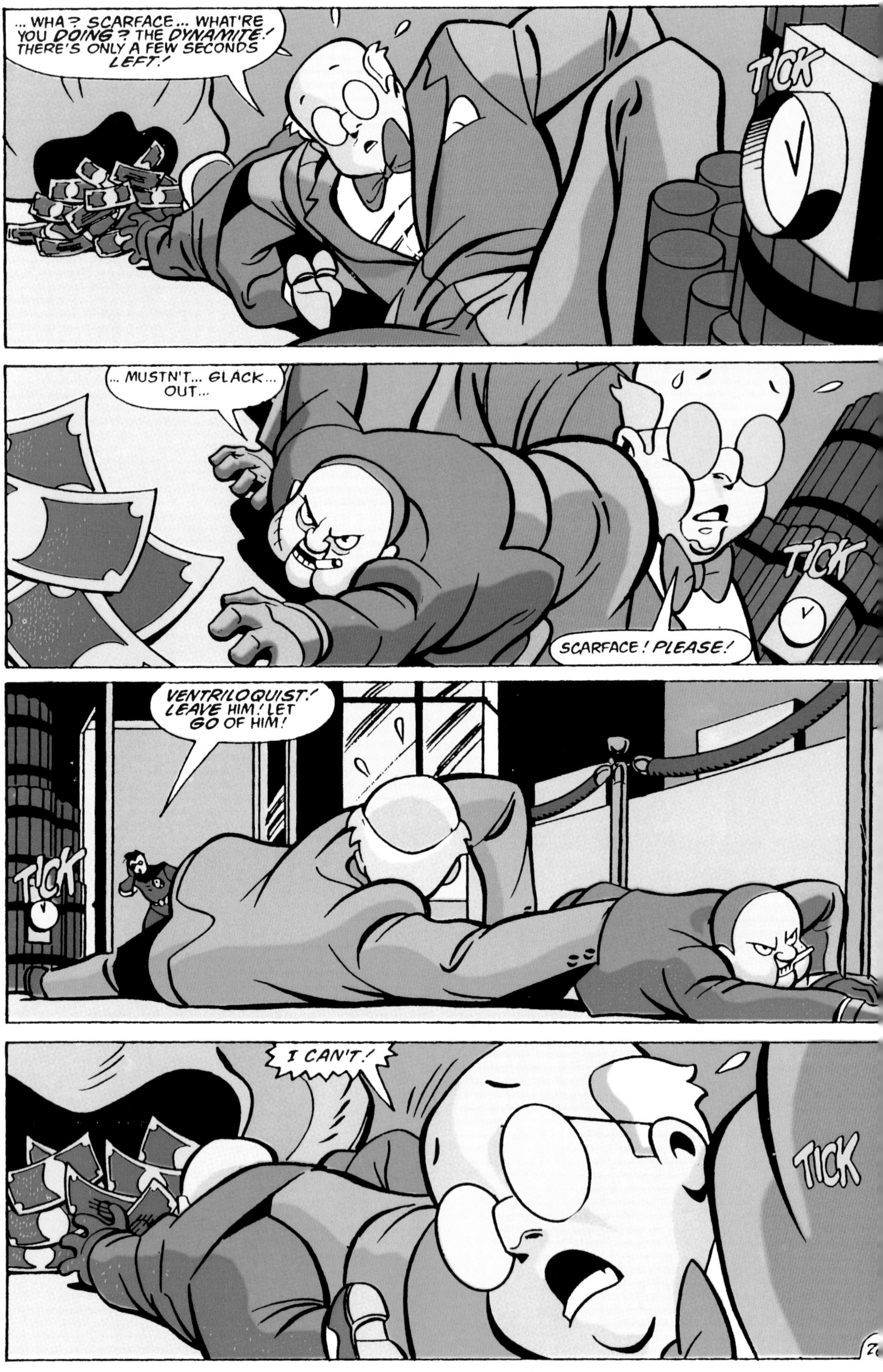
...WHA? SCARFACE... WHAT'RE YOU DOING? THE DYNAMITE! THERE'S ONLY A FEW SECONDS LEFT!
TICK
...MUSTN'T... GLACK... OUT...
TICK
SCARFACE! PLEASE!
VENTRILOQUIST! LEAVE HIM! LET GO OF HIM!
TICK
I CAN'T!
TICK

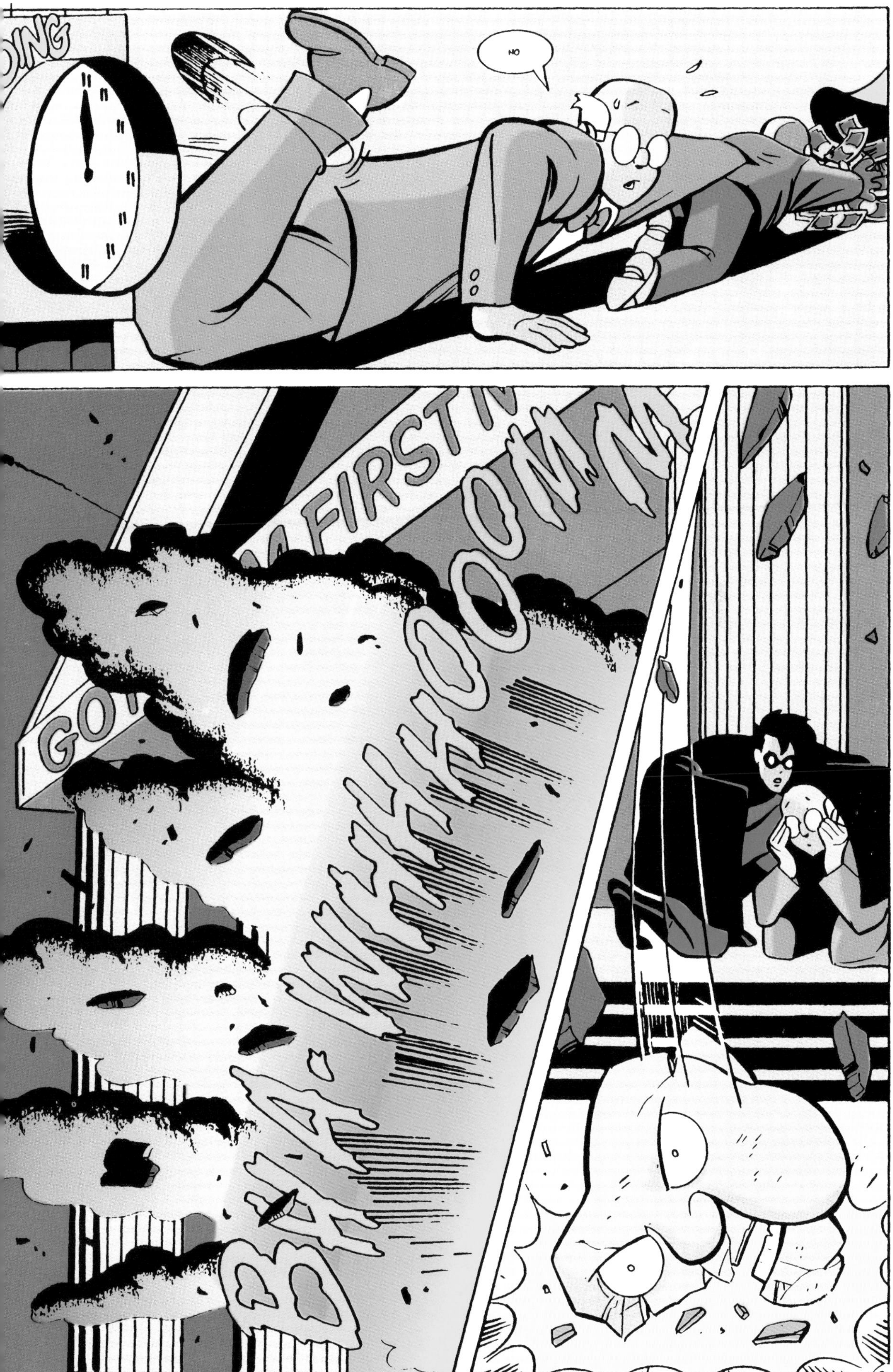
NO
FIRST
GOT
21

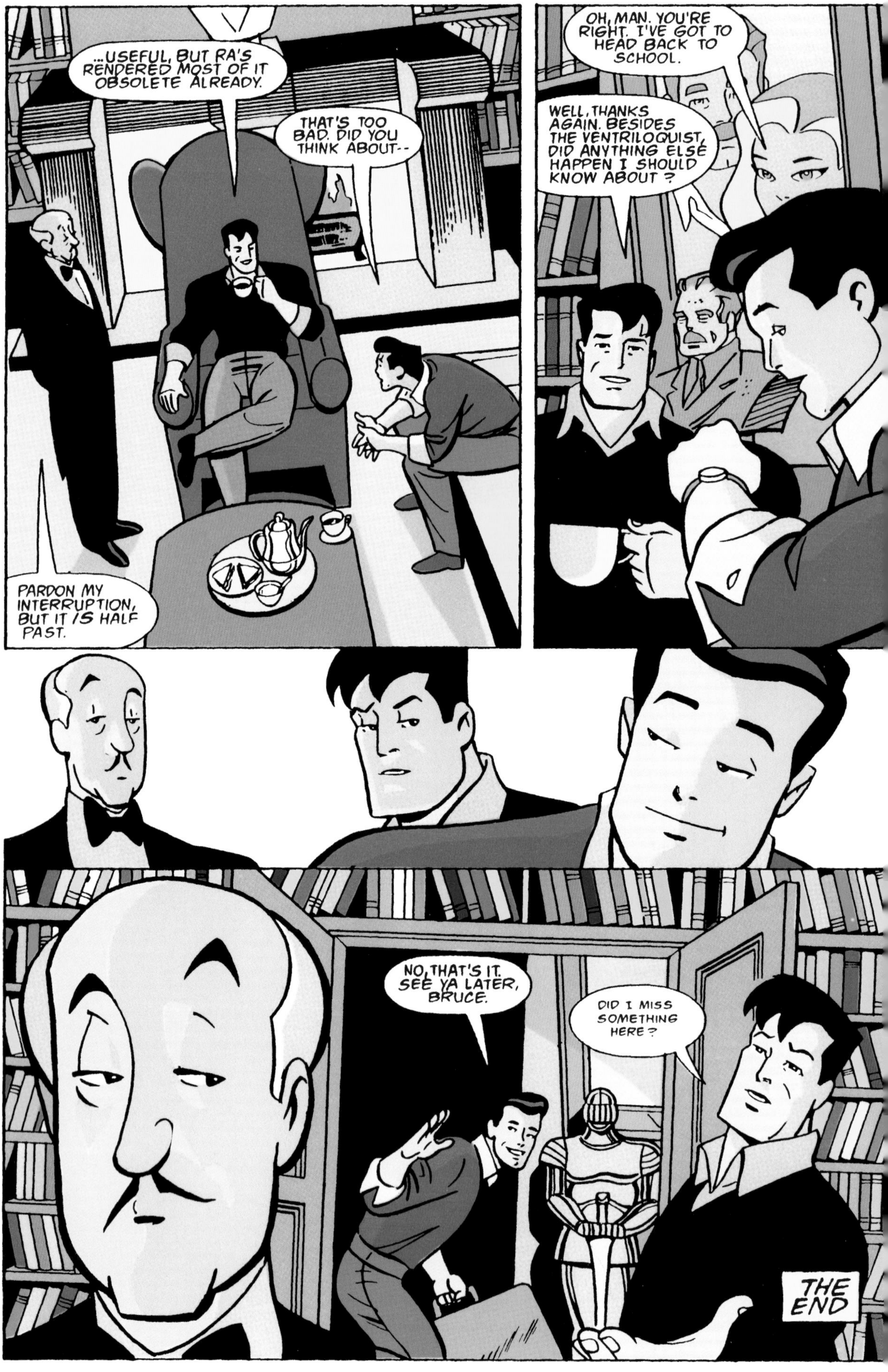
...USEFUL, BUT RA'S RENDERED MOST OF IT OBSOLETE ALREADY.
THAT'S TOO BAD. DID YOU THINK ABOUT--
PARDON MY INTERRUPTION, BUT IT IS HALF PAST.
OH, MAN. YOU'RE RIGHT. I'VE GOT TO HEAD BACK TO SCHOOL.
WELL, THANKS AGAIN. BESIDES THE VENTRILOQUIST, DID ANYTHING ELSE HAPPEN I SHOULD KNOW ABOUT?
NO, THAT'S IT. SEE YA LATER, BRUCE.
DID I MISS SOMETHING HERE?
THE END

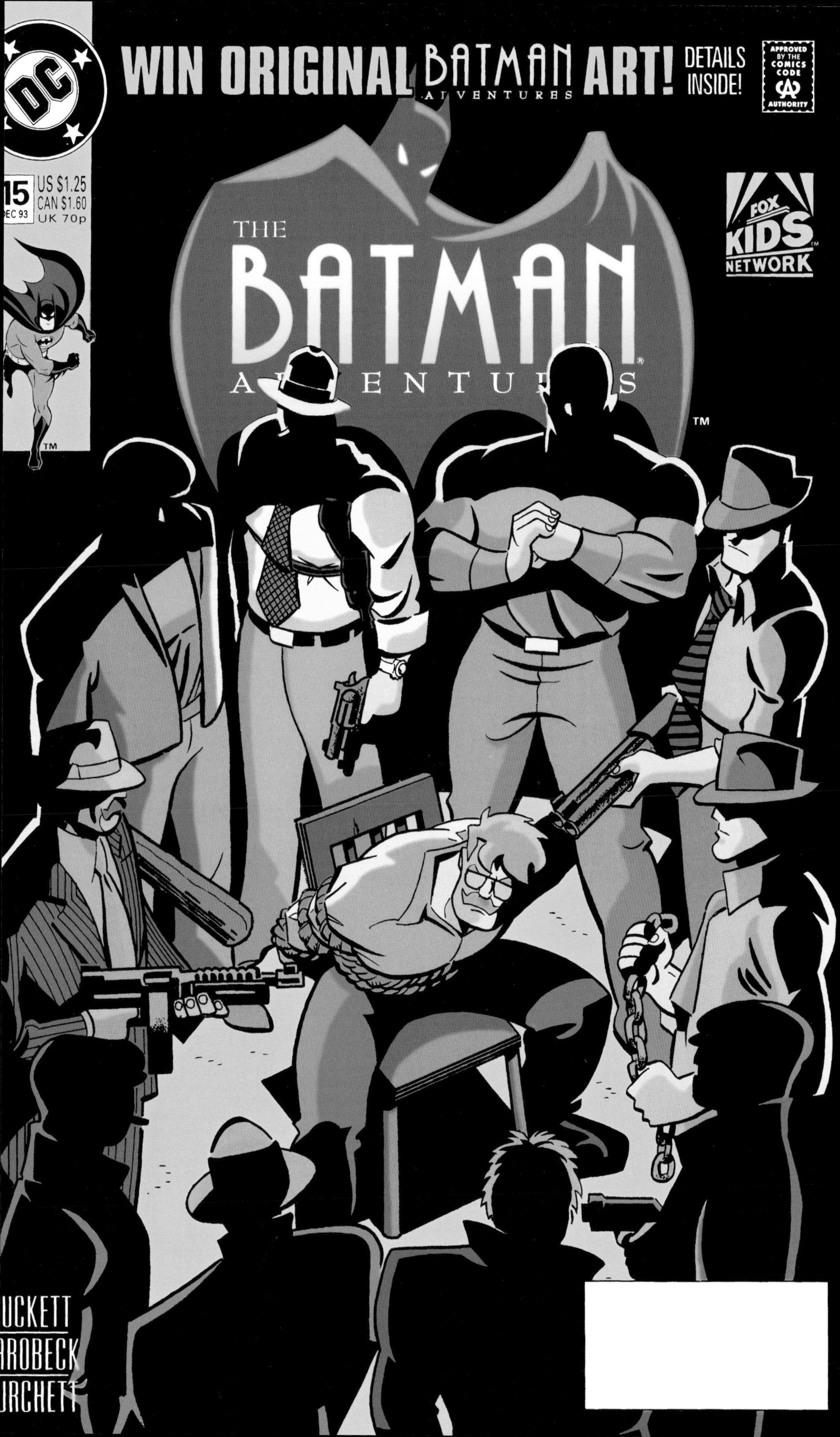

DC
WIN ORIGINAL BATMAN ADVENTURES ART!
DETAILS INSIDE!
APPROVED BY THE COMICS CODE AUTHORITY
15
DEC 93
US $1.25
CAN $1.60
UK 70p
THE BATMAN
FOX KIDS NETWORK
TM

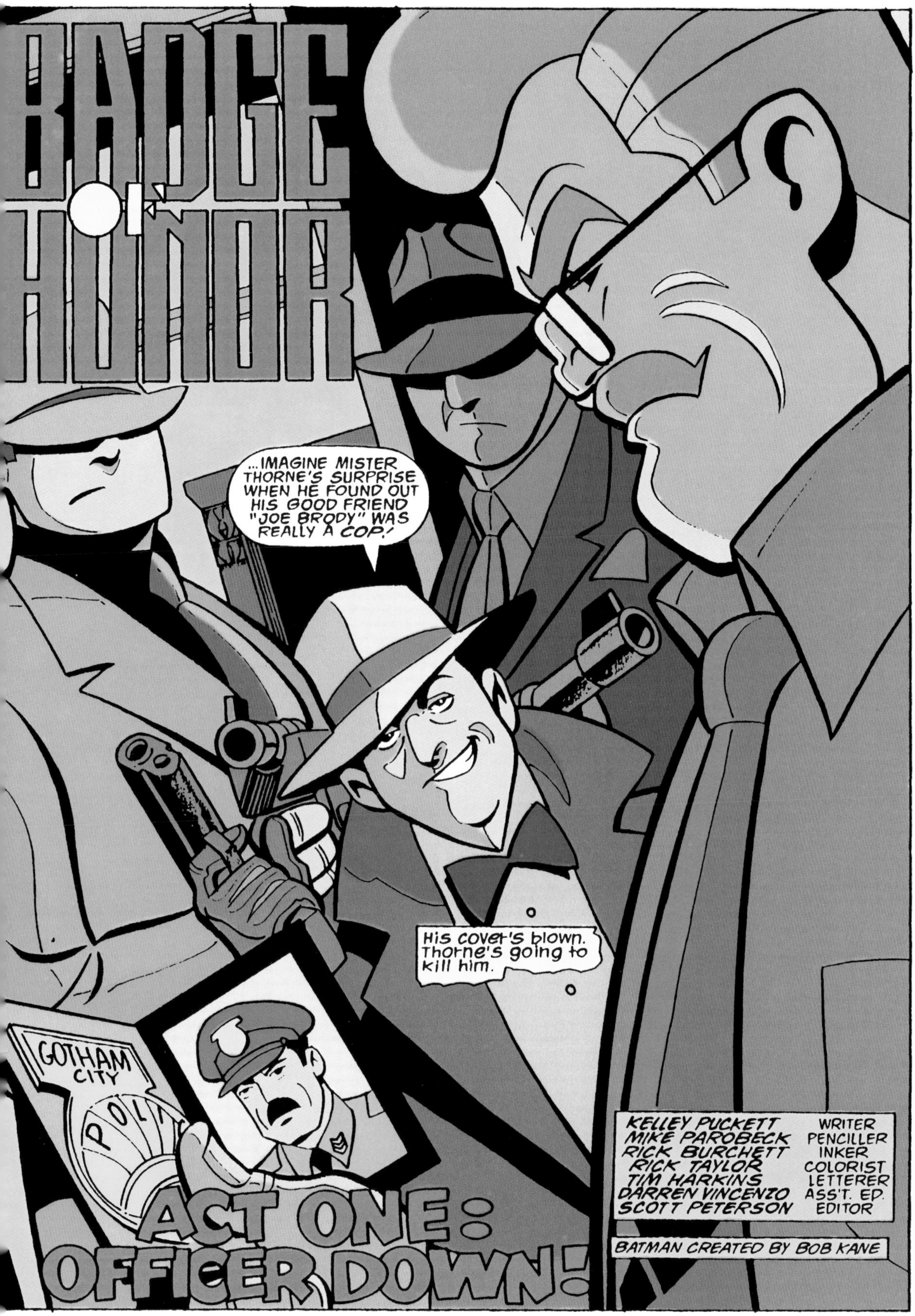
BADGE OF HONOR
...IMAGINE MISTER THORNE'S SURPRISE WHEN HE FOUND OUT HIS GOOD FRIEND "JOE BRODY" WAS REALLY A COP!
His cover's blown. Thorne's going to kill him.
GOTHAM CITY POLI
ACT ONE: OFFICER DOWN!
KELLEY PUCKETT WRITER
MIKE PAROBECK PENCILLER
RICK BURCHETT INKER
RICK TAYLOR COLORIST
TIM HARKINS LETTERER
DARREN VINCENZO ASS'T. ED.
SCOTT PETERSON EDITOR
BATMAN CREATED BY BOB KANE

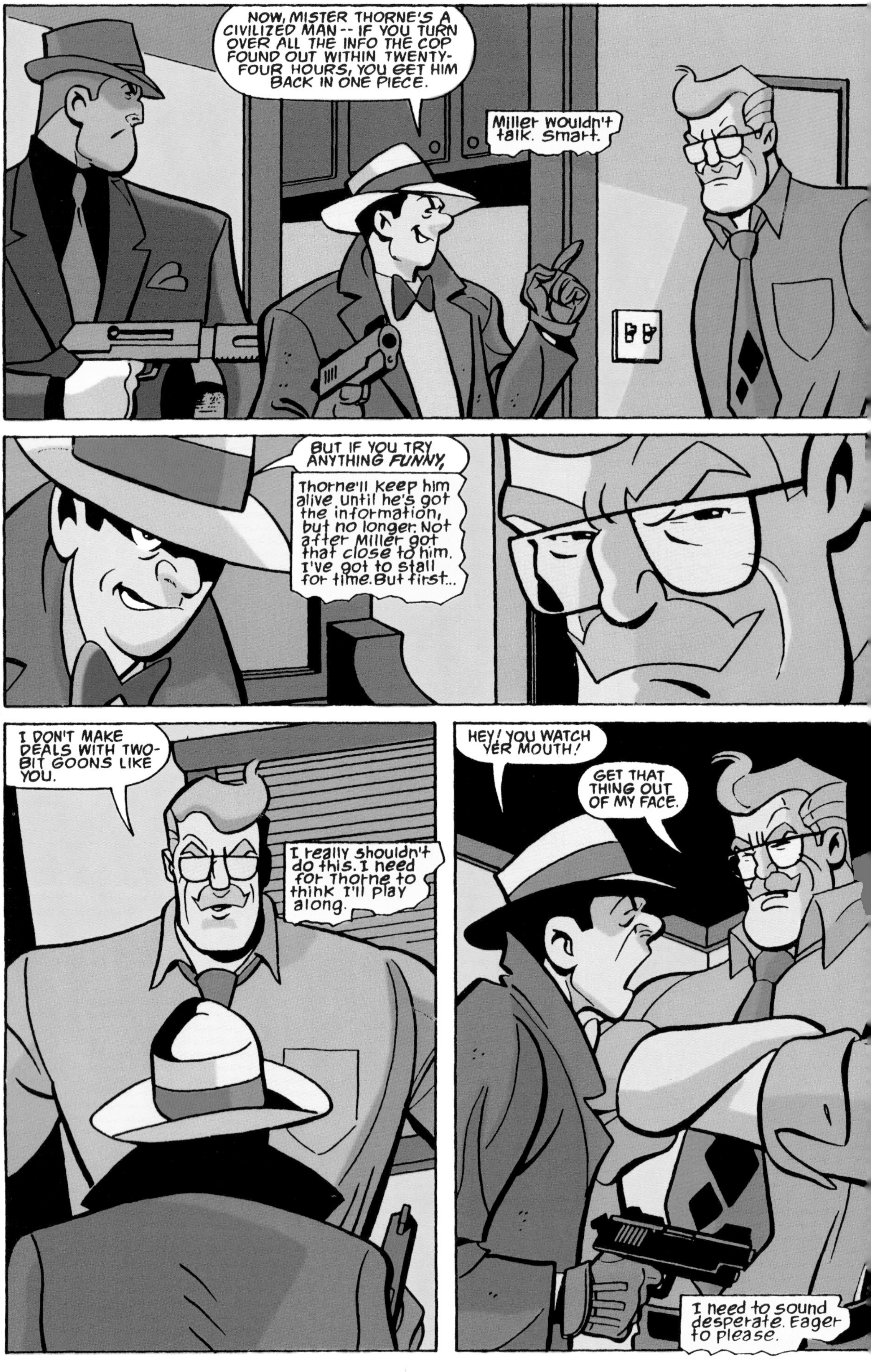
NOW, MISTER THORNE'S A CIVILIZED MAN -- IF YOU TURN OVER ALL THE INFO THE COP FOUND OUT WITHIN TWENTY-FOUR HOURS, YOU GET HIM BACK IN ONE PIECE.
Miller wouldn't talk. Smart.
BUT IF YOU TRY ANYTHING *FUNNY,*
Thorne'll keep him alive until he's got the information, but no longer. Not after Miller got that close to him. I've got to stall for time. But first...
I DON'T MAKE DEALS WITH TWO-BIT GOONS LIKE YOU.
I really shouldn't do this. I need for Thorne to think I'll play along.
HEY! YOU WATCH YER MOUTH!
GET THAT THING OUT OF MY FACE.
I need to sound desperate. Eager to please.

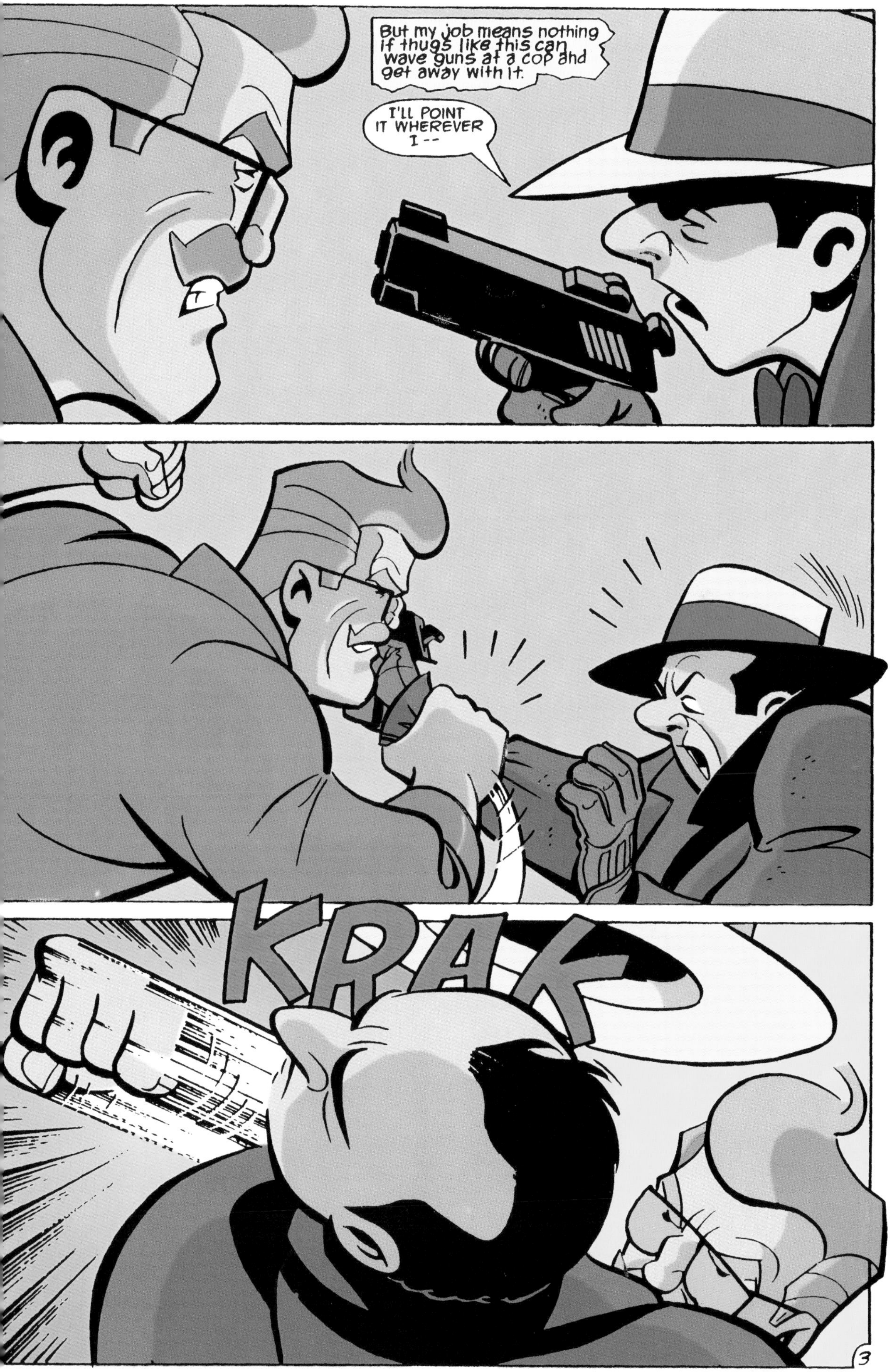

But my job means nothing if thugs like this can wave guns at a cop and get away with it.
I'LL POINT IT WHEREVER I --
KRAK
3

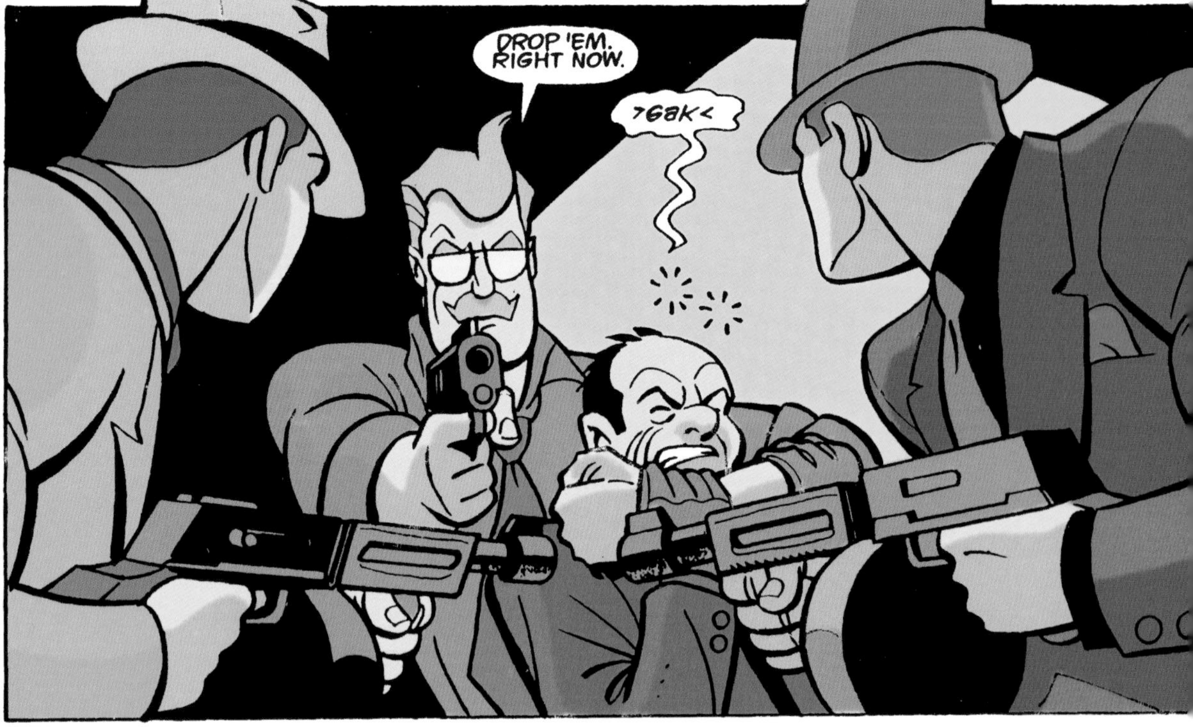

DROP 'EM. RIGHT NOW.
>GAK<

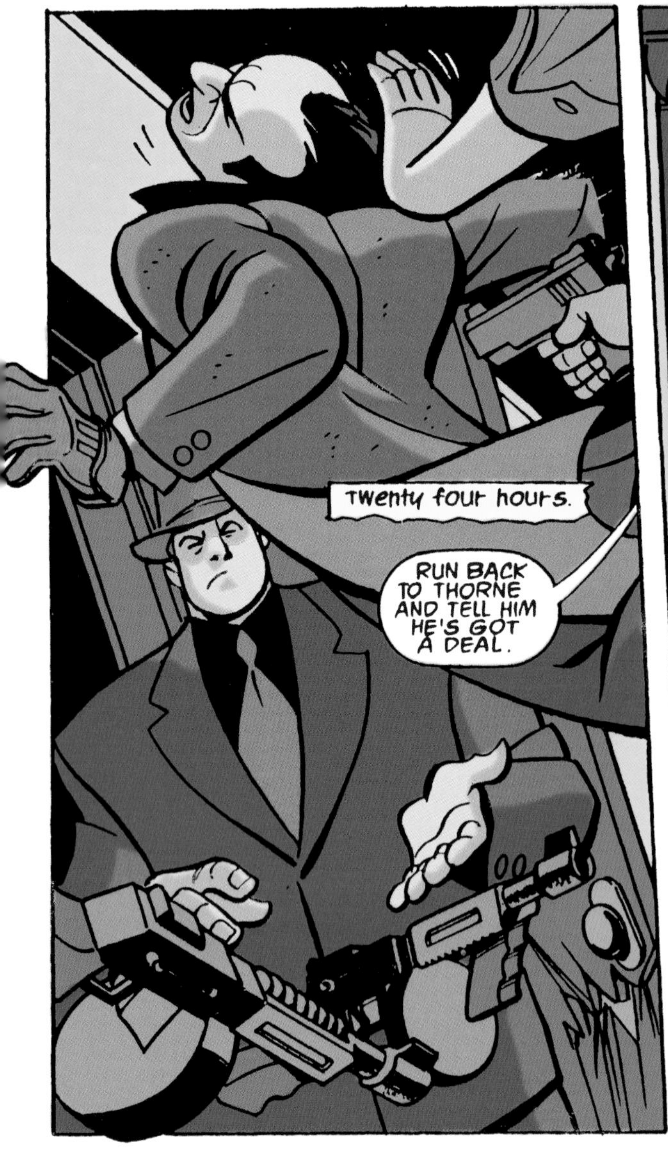

Twenty four hours.
RUN BACK TO THORNE AND TELL HIM HE'S GOT A DEAL.

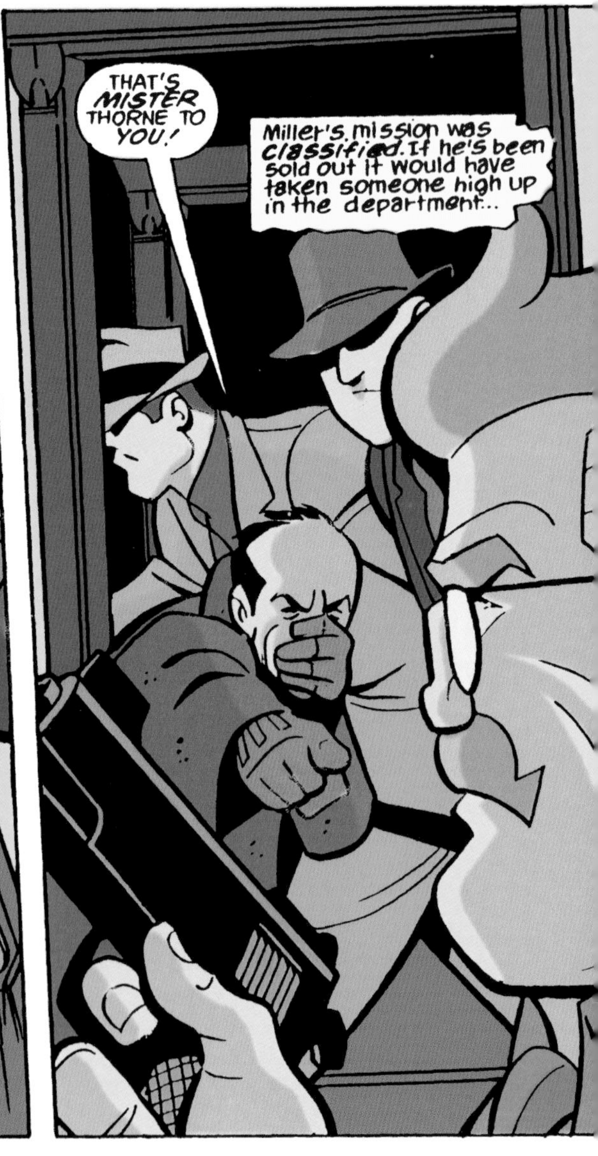

THAT'S MISTER THORNE TO YOU!
Miller's mission was classified. If he's been sold out it would have taken someone high up in the department...

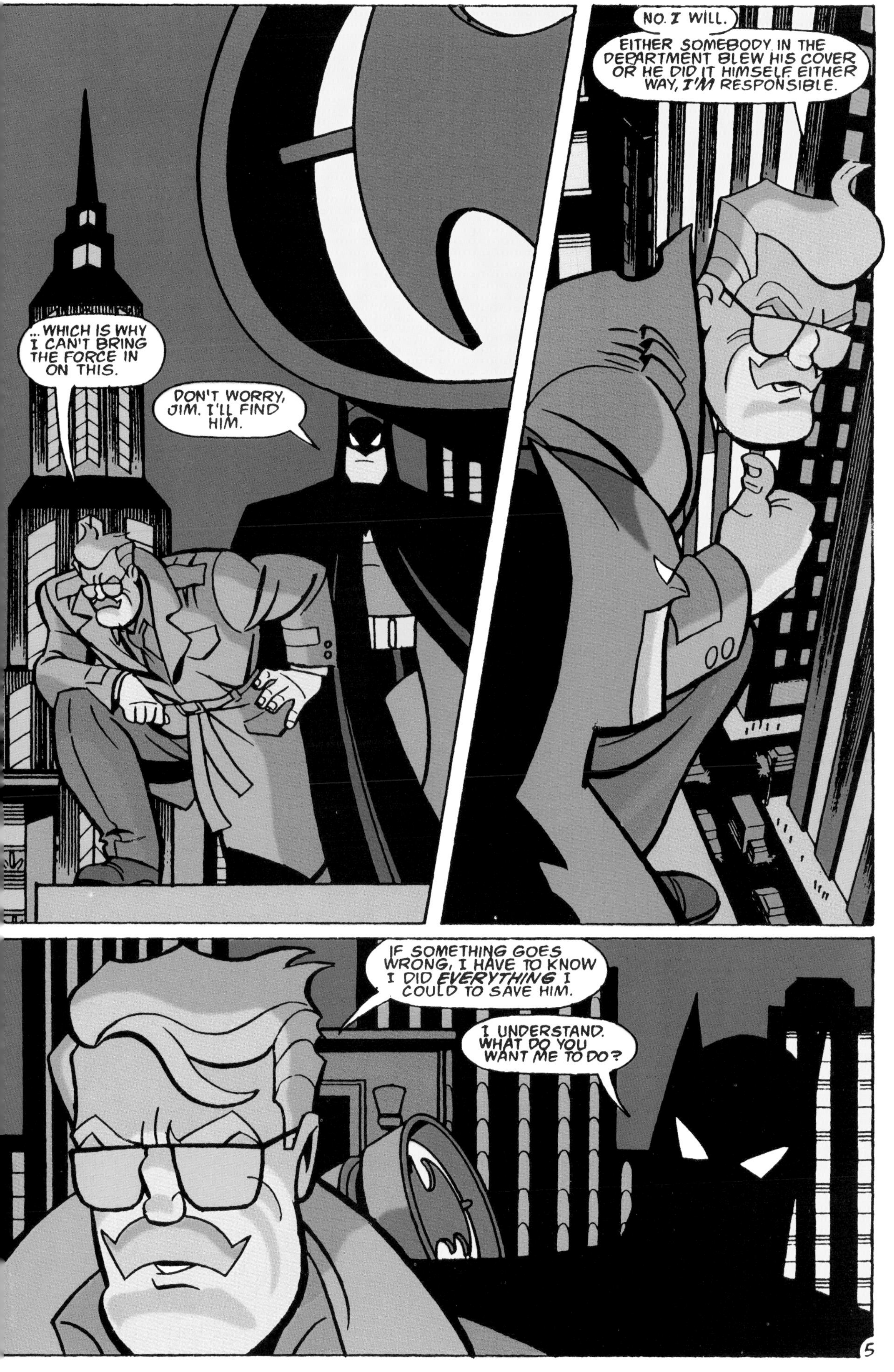
...WHICH IS WHY I CAN'T BRING THE FORCE IN ON THIS.
DON'T WORRY, JIM. I'LL FIND HIM.
NO. I WILL.
EITHER SOMEBODY IN THE DEPARTMENT BLEW HIS COVER OR HE DID IT HIMSELF. EITHER WAY, I'M RESPONSIBLE.
IF SOMETHING GOES WRONG, I HAVE TO KNOW I DID EVERYTHING I COULD TO SAVE HIM.
I UNDERSTAND. WHAT DO YOU WANT ME TO DO?
5

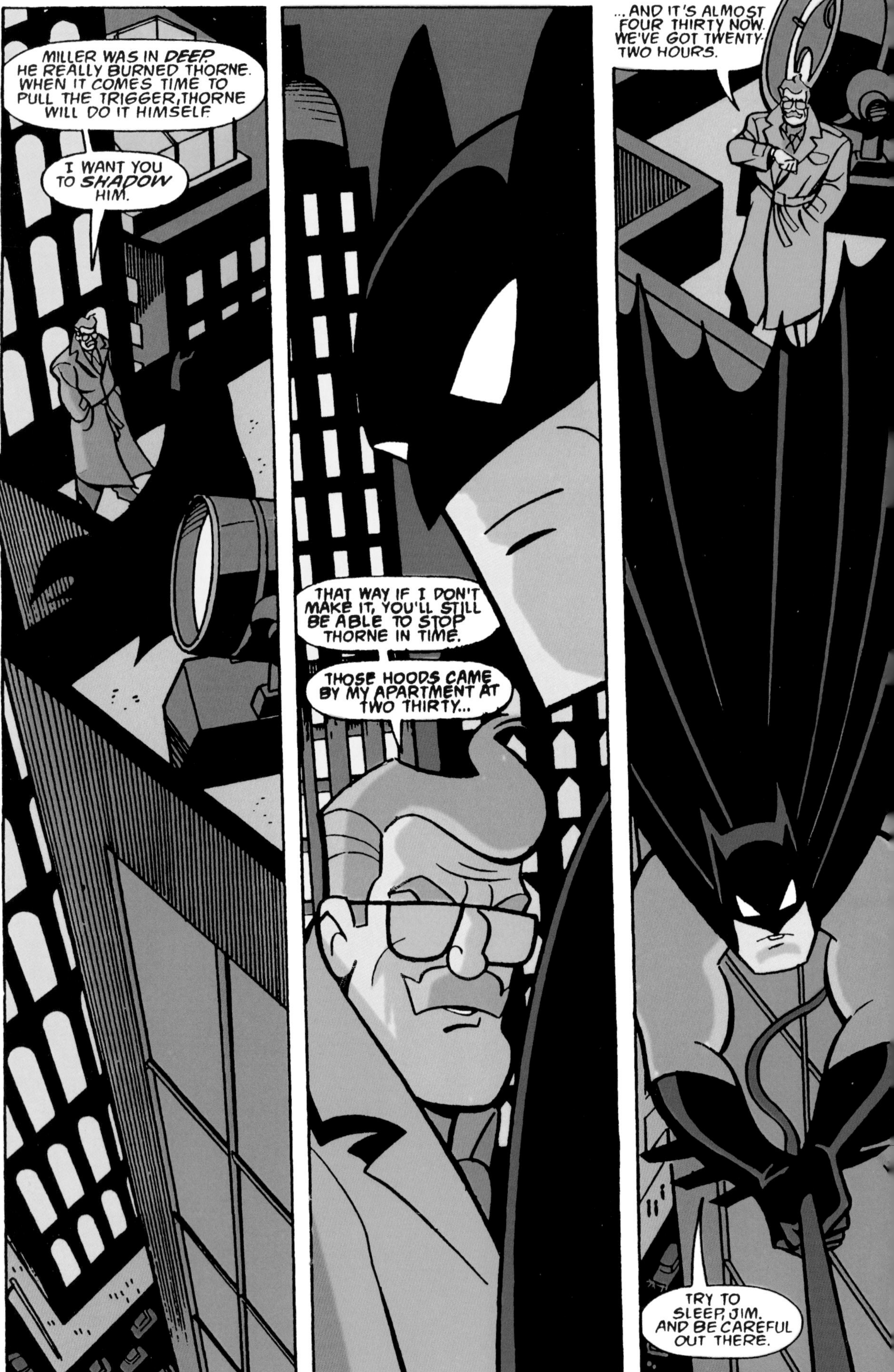

MILLER WAS IN DEEP. HE REALLY BURNED THORNE. WHEN IT COMES TIME TO PULL THE TRIGGER, THORNE WILL DO IT HIMSELF.
I WANT YOU TO SHADOW HIM.
THAT WAY IF I DON'T MAKE IT, YOU'LL STILL BE ABLE TO STOP THORNE IN TIME.
THOSE HOODS CAME BY MY APARTMENT AT TWO THIRTY...
...AND IT'S ALMOST FOUR THIRTY NOW. WE'VE GOT TWENTY-TWO HOURS.
TRY TO SLEEP, JIM. AND BE CAREFUL OUT THERE.

These files Miller got us are excellent police work. Perceptive. Observant. Detailed.

DET. ANTON MILLER

Tony Wiesel. My best shot at finding out where they're keeping him.

E: Tony Wiesel

K: Lieutenant. A mber of Thorne's er circle (see ow)

SPONSIBILITIES: Mostly numbers-run- ing and other low- profile activities, Wiesel also runs an underground nightclub (2nd Avenue and Fifth Street).

EVALUATION: Wiesel has made himself use- ful to Thorne by ratting out disloyal members of the organization, but his incompetence and cowardice weigh heavily against him. Thorne is openly contemptuous of him (calling him "weasel" in front of the others), and there are rumors of Wiesel's being "edged out" of the inner circle in the near future. This, combined with Wiesel's extreme fear of imprisonment (see page fo make him an ideal candidate for turning state's evidence in the future. Lament re- ...ality more painful tha open

...ounds made to order, but if ...iesel doesn't come through, ...don't know what I'll--

I'll think of something else. Find another way.

I'm not going to lose another good cop.

7

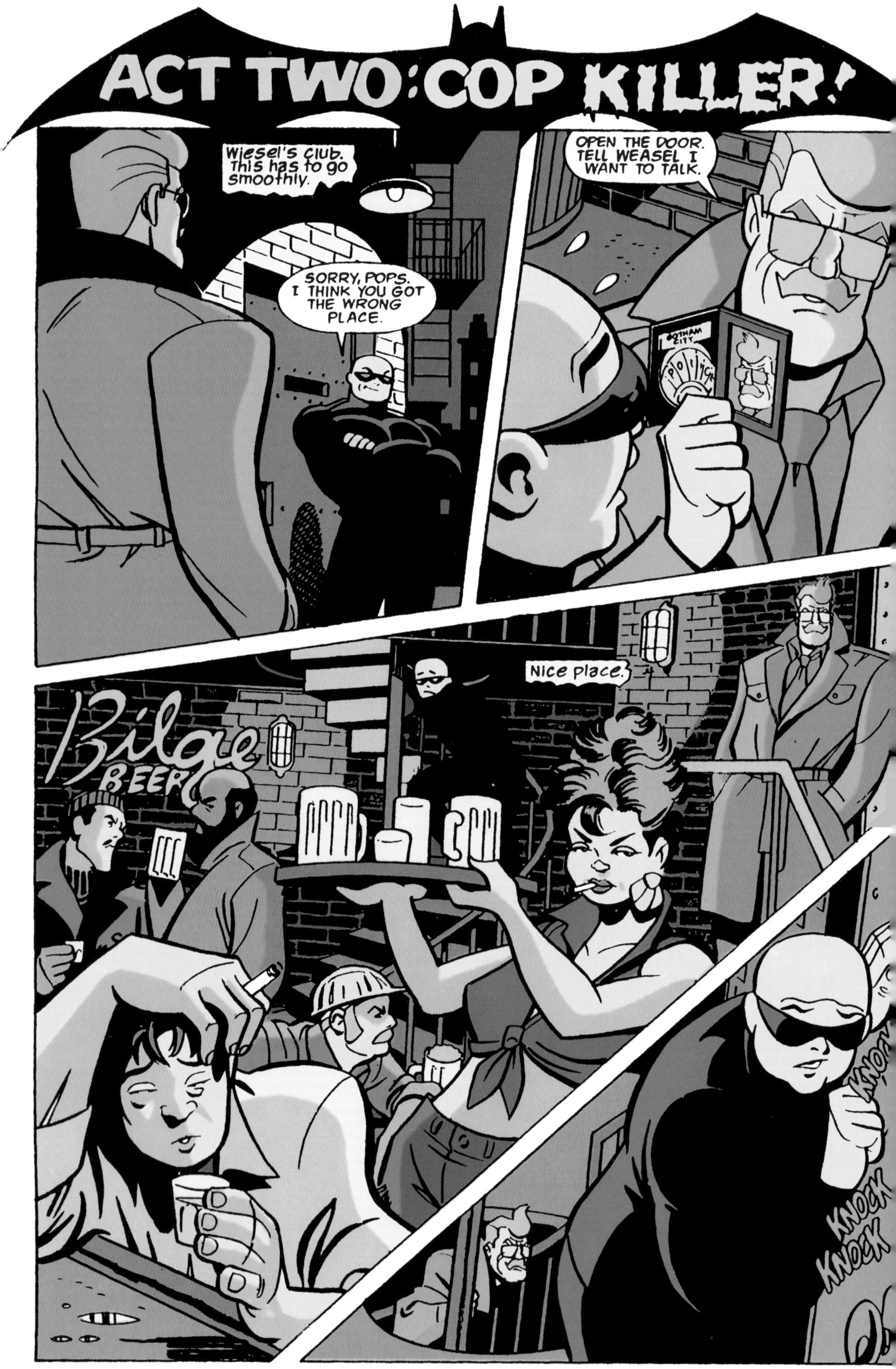

ACT TWO: COP KILLER!
Wiesel's club. This has to go smoothly.
SORRY, POPS. I THINK YOU GOT THE WRONG PLACE.
OPEN THE DOOR. TELL WEASEL I WANT TO TALK.
GOTHAM CITY POLICE
Nice place.
Bilge BEER
KNOCK
KNOCK KNOCK

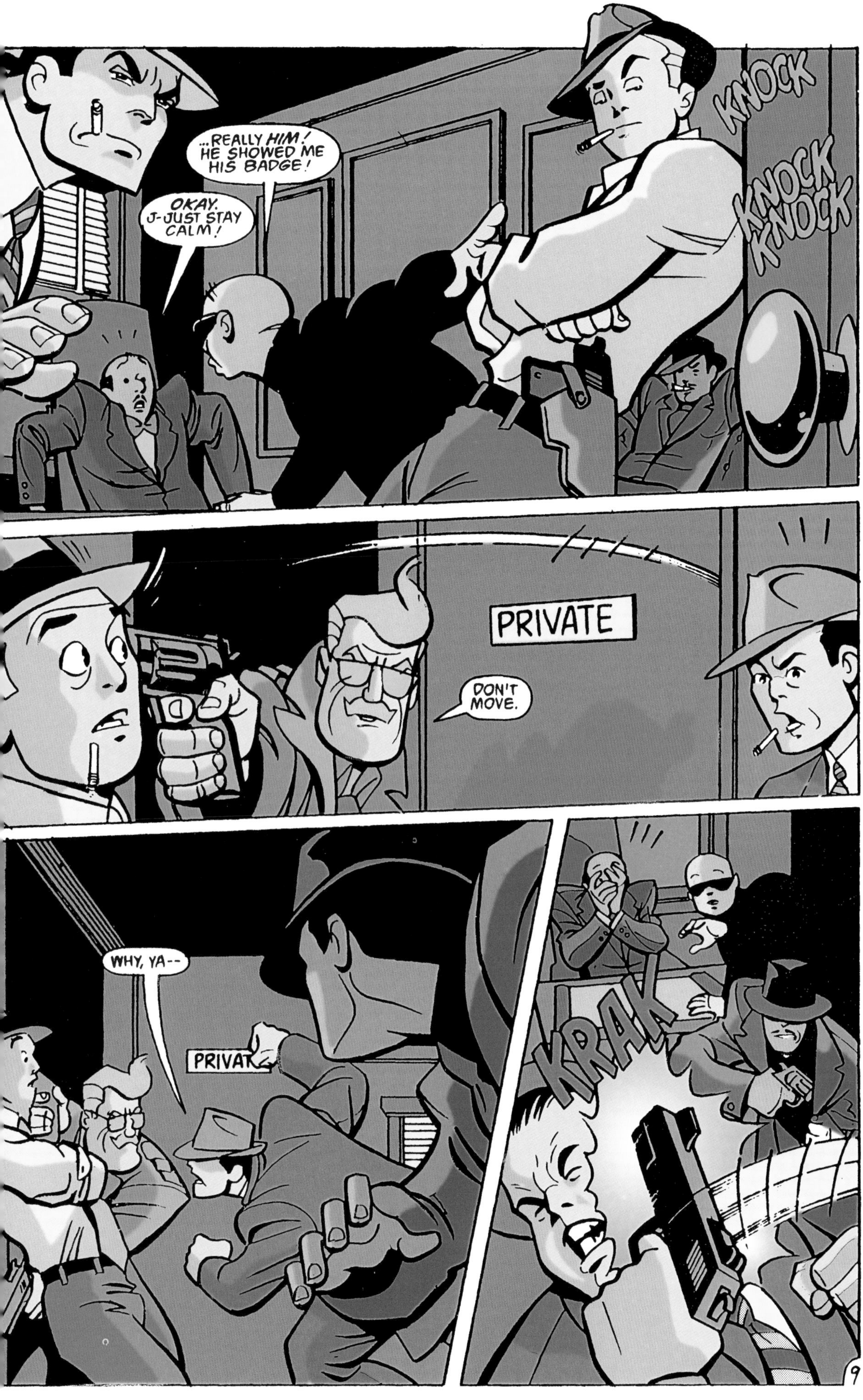
...REALLY HIM! HE SHOWED ME HIS BADGE!
OKAY. J-JUST STAY CALM!
KNOCK
KNOCK KNOCK
PRIVATE
DON'T MOVE.
WHY, YA--
PRIVAT
KRAK
9

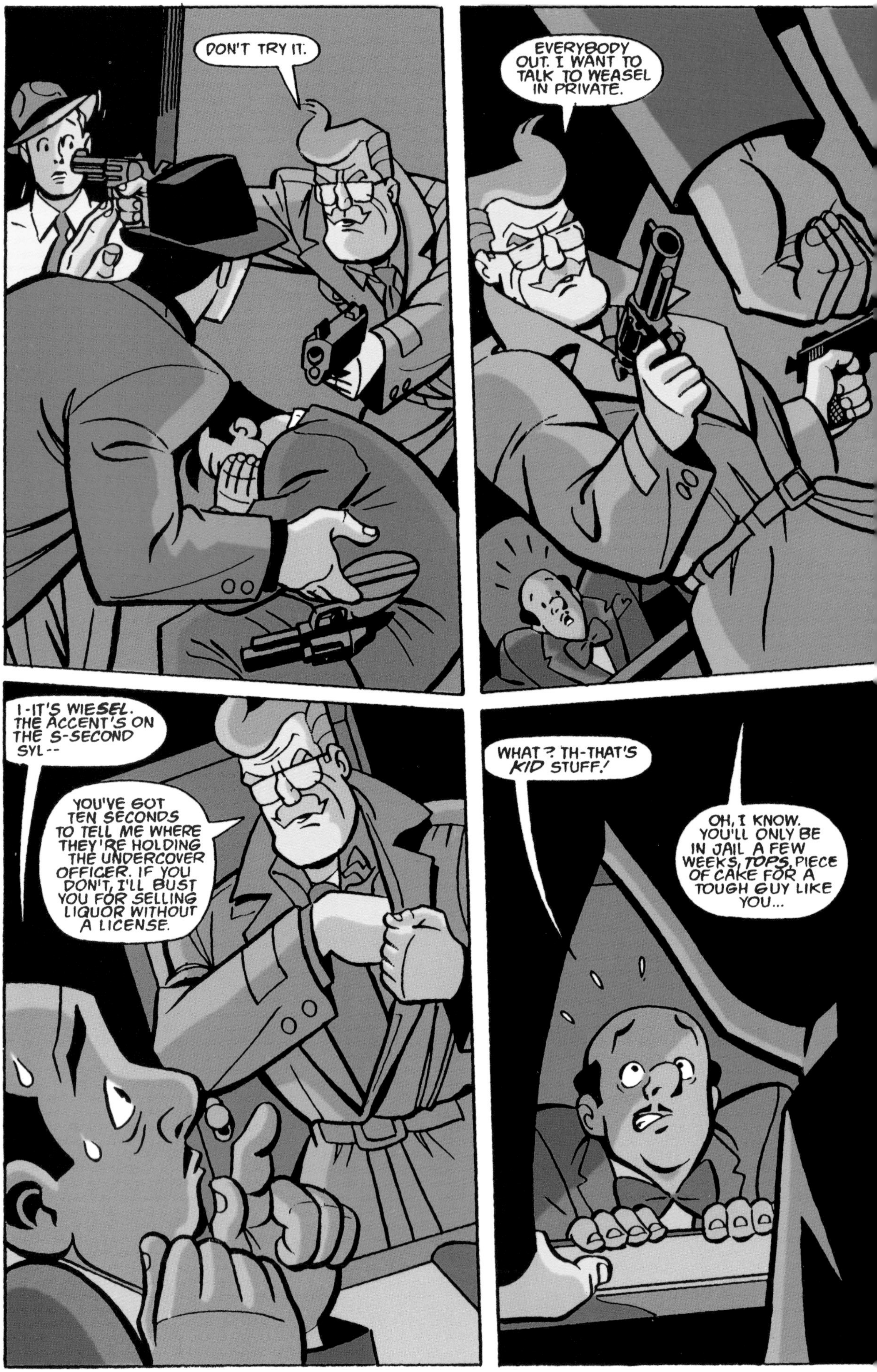

DON'T TRY IT.
EVERYBODY OUT. I WANT TO TALK TO WEASEL IN PRIVATE.
I-IT'S WIESEL. THE ACCENT'S ON THE S-SECOND SYL--
YOU'VE GOT TEN SECONDS TO TELL ME WHERE THEY'RE HOLDING THE UNDERCOVER OFFICER. IF YOU DON'T, I'LL BUST YOU FOR SELLING LIQUOR WITHOUT A LICENSE.
WHAT? TH-THAT'S KID STUFF!
OH, I KNOW. YOU'LL ONLY BE IN JAIL A FEW WEEKS, TOPS. PIECE OF CAKE FOR A TOUGH GUY LIKE YOU...

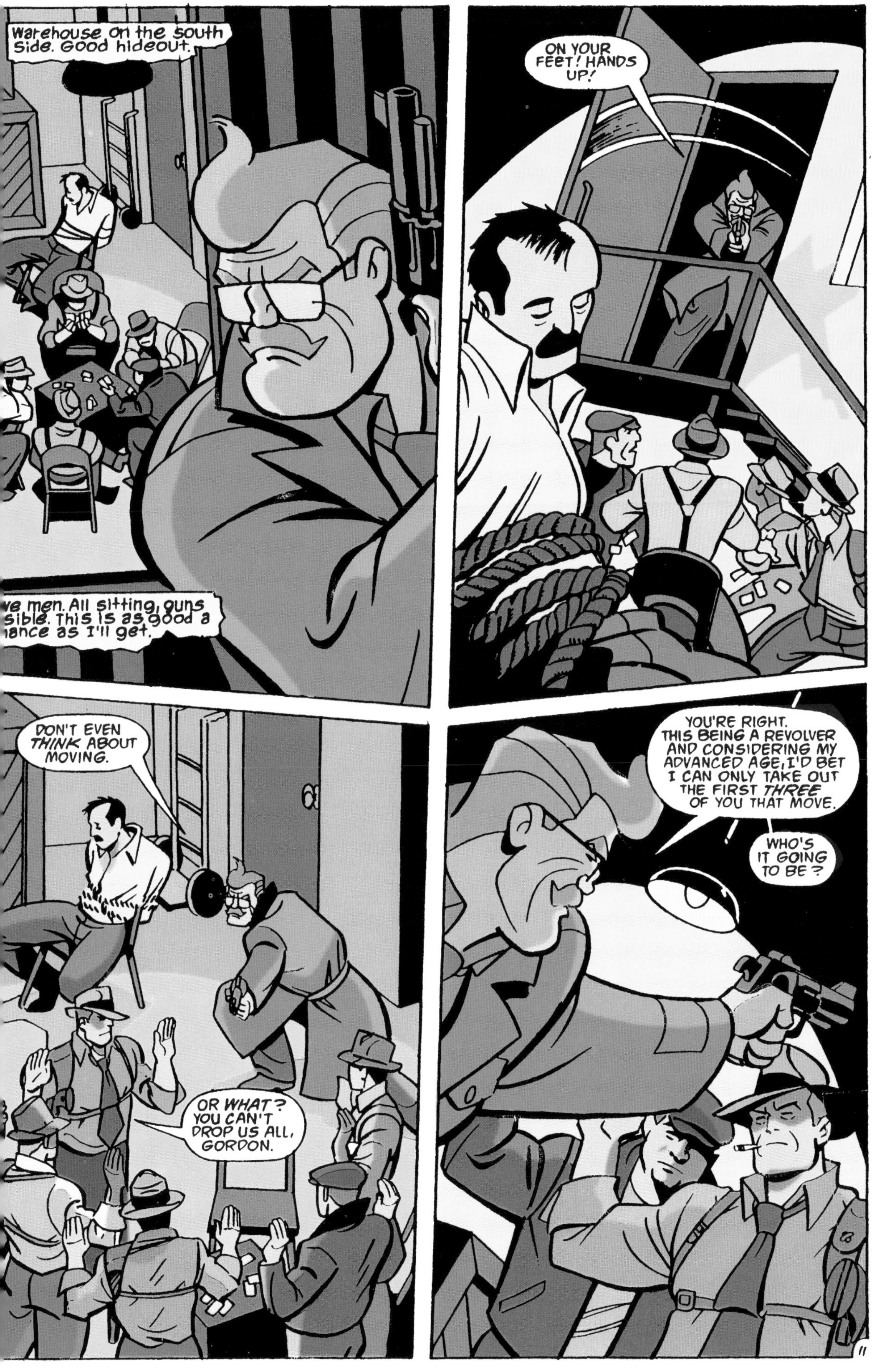

Warehouse on the south side. Good hideout.
ve men. All sitting, guns sible. This is as good a ance as I'll get.
ON YOUR FEET! HANDS UP!
DON'T EVEN *THINK* ABOUT MOVING.
OR *WHAT*? YOU CAN'T DROP US ALL, GORDON.
YOU'RE RIGHT. THIS BEING A REVOLVER AND CONSIDERING MY ADVANCED AGE, I'D BET I CAN ONLY TAKE OUT THE FIRST *THREE* OF YOU THAT MOVE.
WHO'S IT GOING TO BE?
11

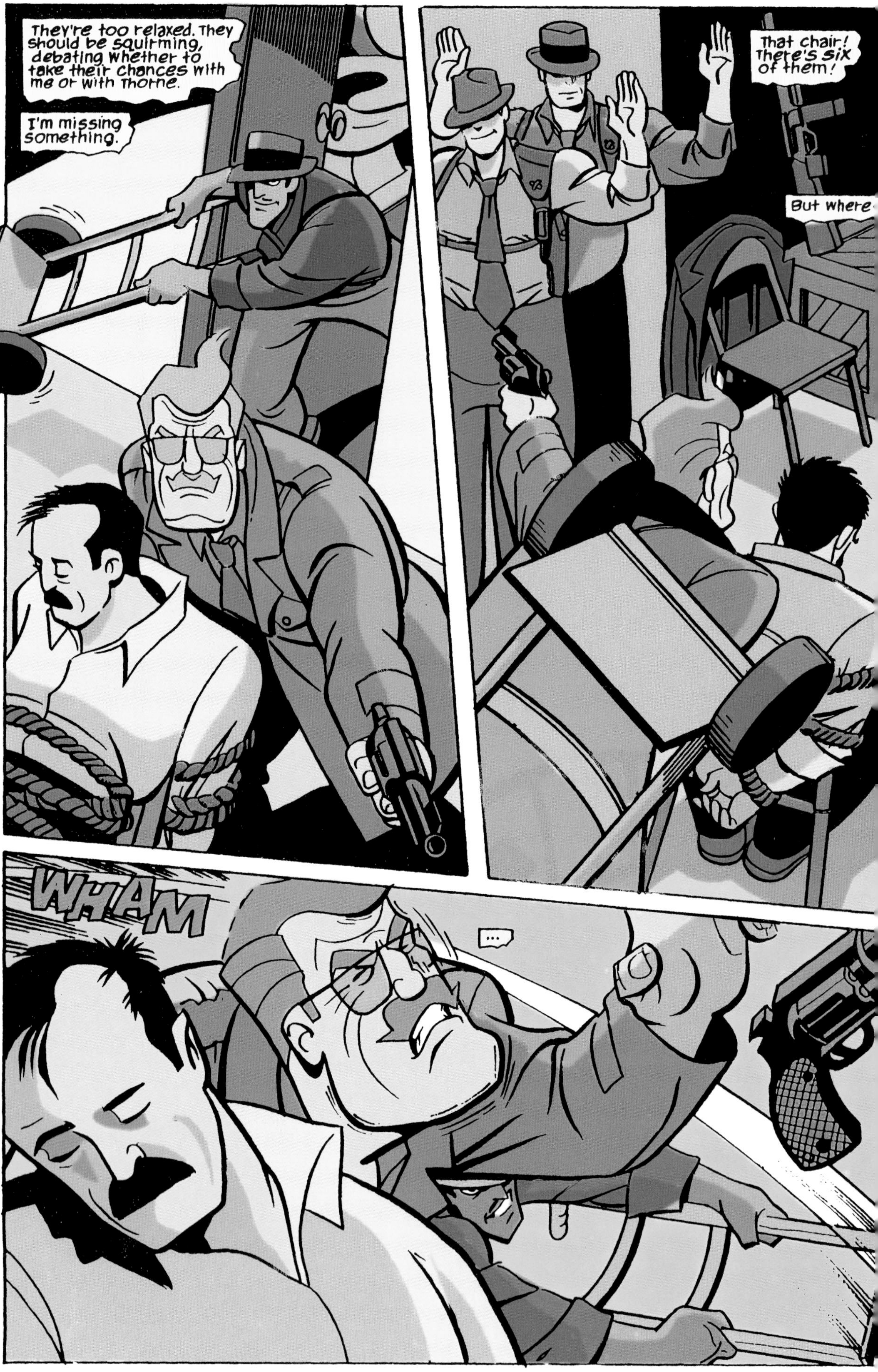
They're too relaxed. They should be squirming, debating whether to take their chances with me or with Thorne.
I'm missing something.
That chair! There's six of them!
But where
WHAM
...

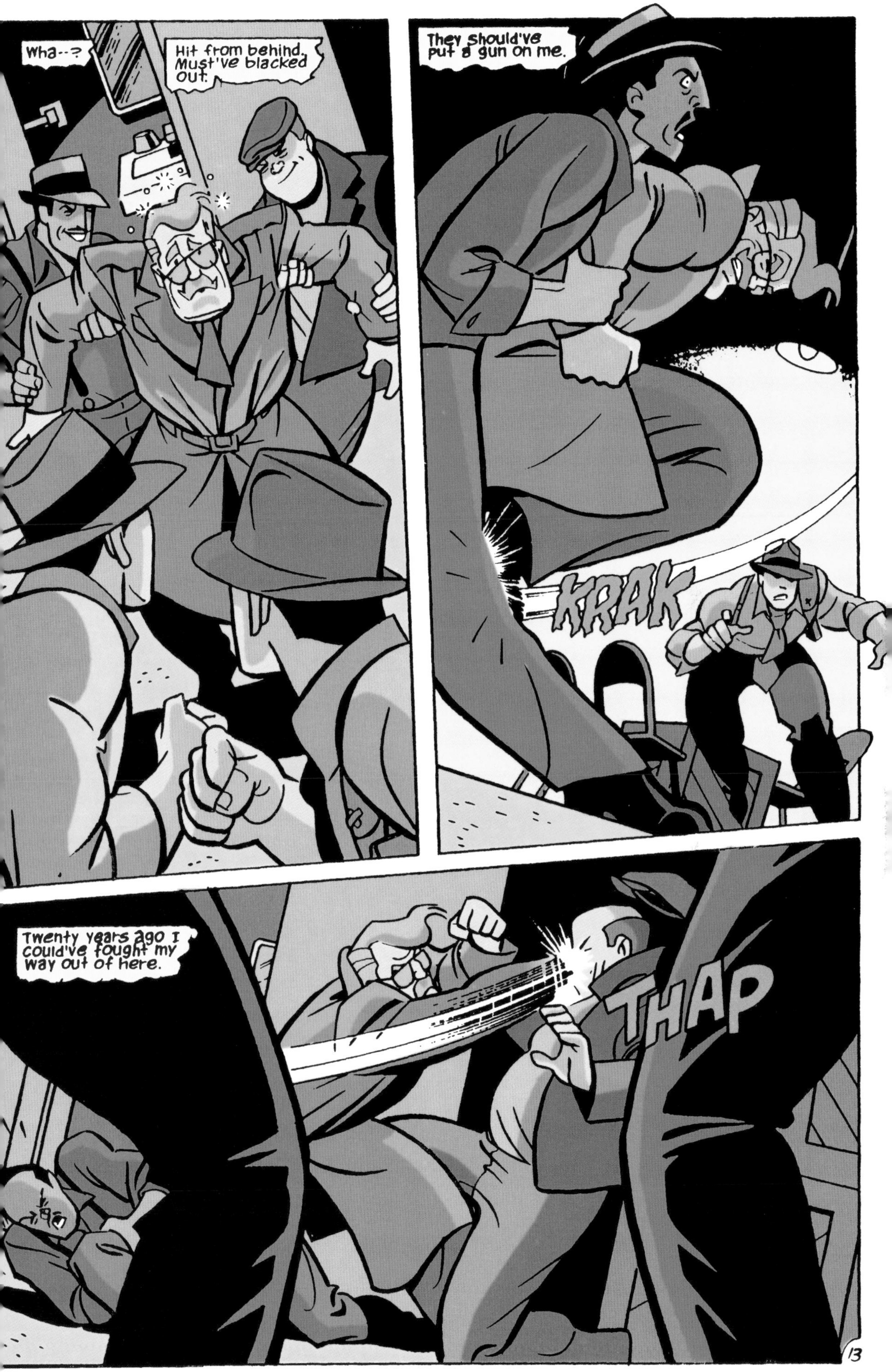

Wha--?
Hit from behind. Must've blacked out.
They should've put a gun on me.
KRAK
Twenty years ago I could've fought my way out of here.
THAP
13

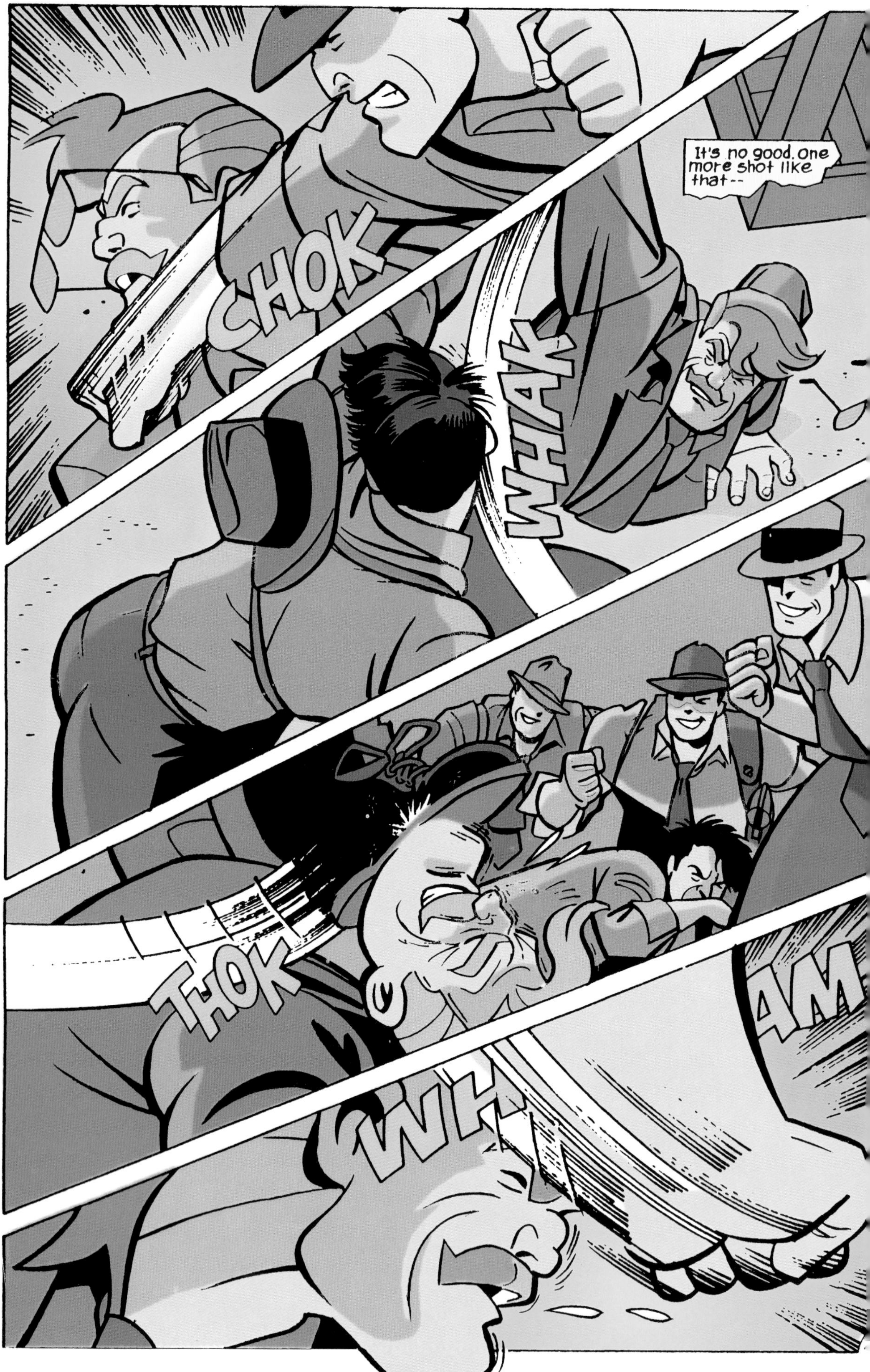
It's no good. One more shot like that--
CHOK
WHAK
THOK
WH
AM

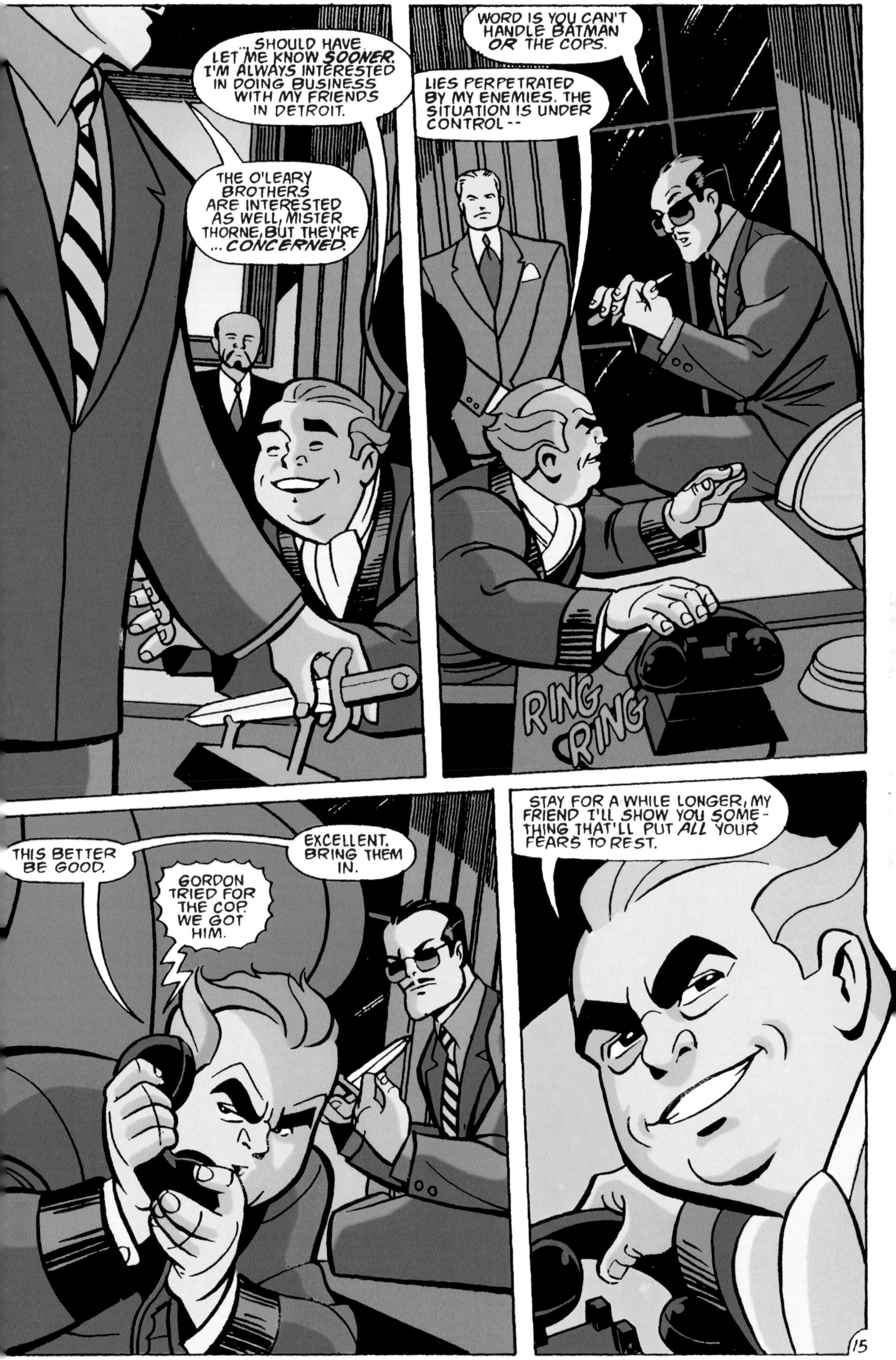
...SHOULD HAVE LET ME KNOW SOONER. I'M ALWAYS INTERESTED IN DOING BUSINESS WITH MY FRIENDS IN DETROIT.
THE O'LEARY BROTHERS ARE INTERESTED AS WELL, MISTER THORNE, BUT THEY'RE ...CONCERNED.
WORD IS YOU CAN'T HANDLE BATMAN OR THE COPS.
LIES PERPETRATED BY MY ENEMIES. THE SITUATION IS UNDER CONTROL--
RING RING
THIS BETTER BE GOOD.
GORDON TRIED FOR THE COP. WE GOT HIM.
EXCELLENT. BRING THEM IN.
STAY FOR A WHILE LONGER, MY FRIEND. I'LL SHOW YOU SOME-THING THAT'LL PUT ALL YOUR FEARS TO REST.
15

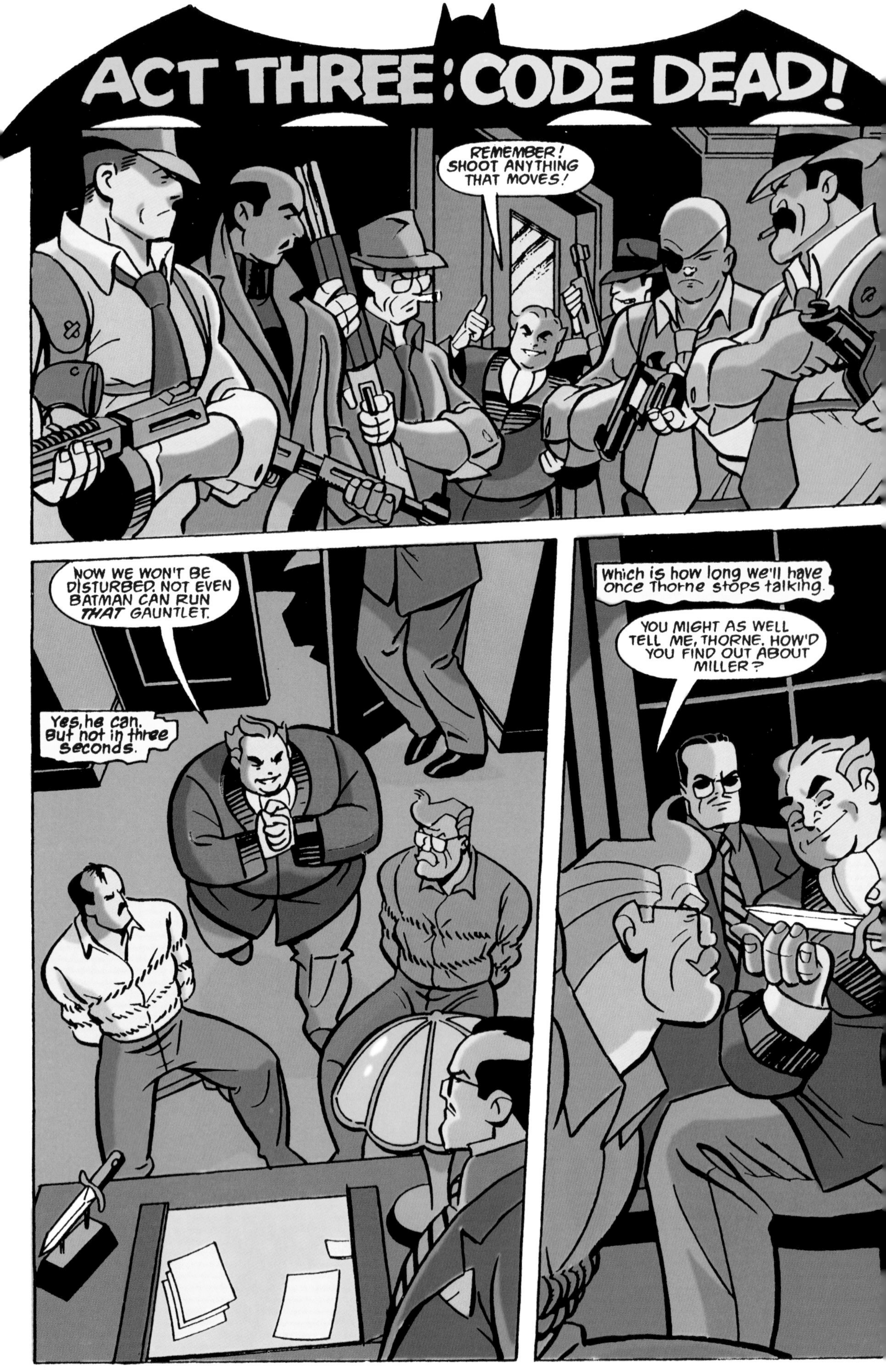
ACT THREE: CODE DEAD!
REMEMBER! SHOOT ANYTHING THAT MOVES!
NOW WE WON'T BE DISTURBED. NOT EVEN BATMAN CAN RUN *THAT* GAUNTLET.
Yes, he can. But not in three seconds.
Which is how long we'll have once Thorne stops talking.
YOU MIGHT AS WELL TELL ME, THORNE. HOW'D YOU FIND OUT ABOUT MILLER?

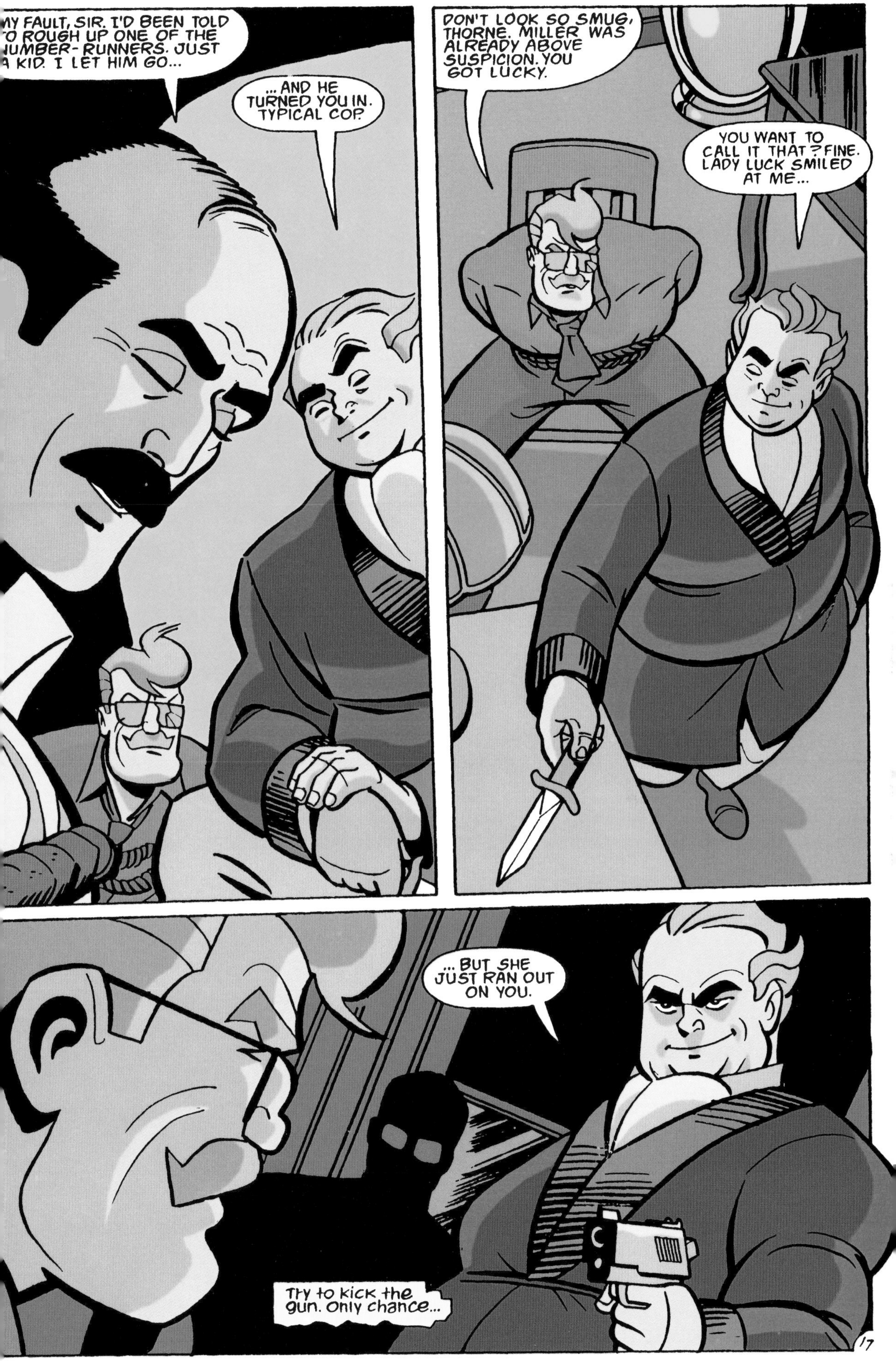
MY FAULT, SIR. I'D BEEN TOLD TO ROUGH UP ONE OF THE NUMBER-RUNNERS. JUST A KID. I LET HIM GO...
...AND HE TURNED YOU IN. TYPICAL COP.
DON'T LOOK SO SMUG, THORNE. MILLER WAS ALREADY ABOVE SUSPICION. YOU GOT LUCKY.
YOU WANT TO CALL IT THAT? FINE. LADY LUCK SMILED AT ME...
...BUT SHE JUST RAN OUT ON YOU.
Try to kick the gun. Only chance...
17

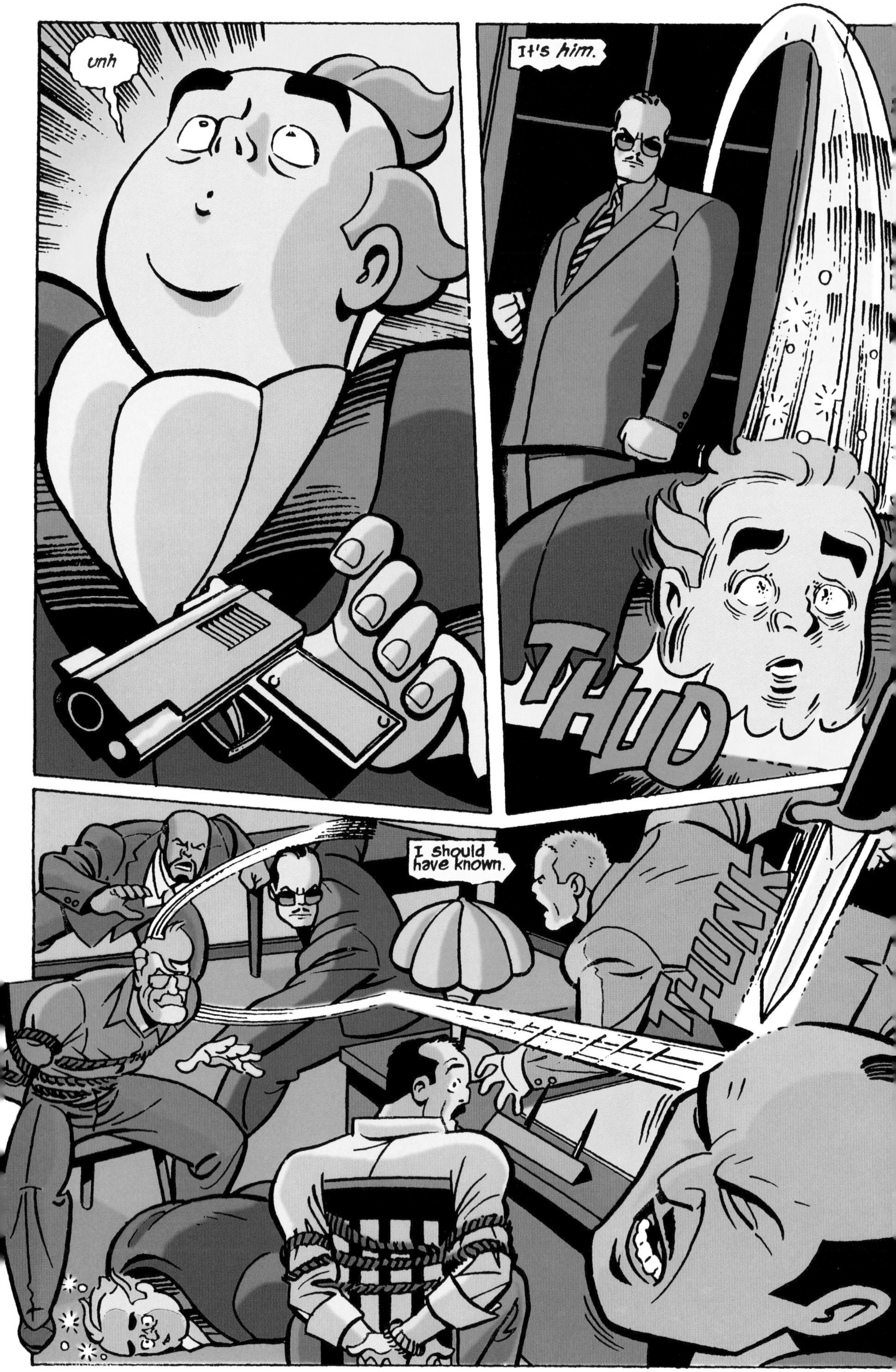
unh
It's him.
THUD
I should have known.
THUNK

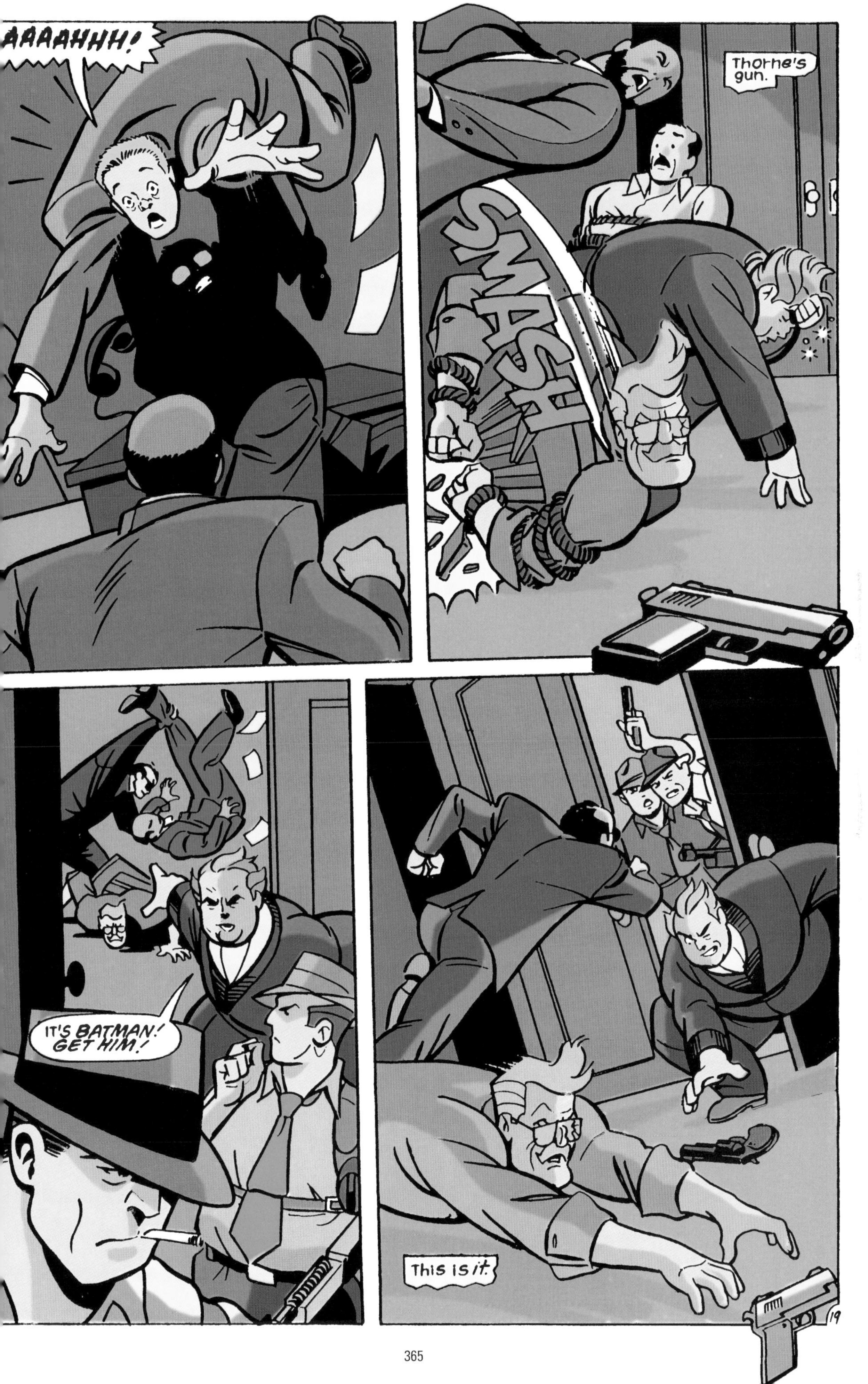
AAAAHHH!
SMASH
Thorne's gun.
IT'S BATMAN! GET HIM!
This is it.
19

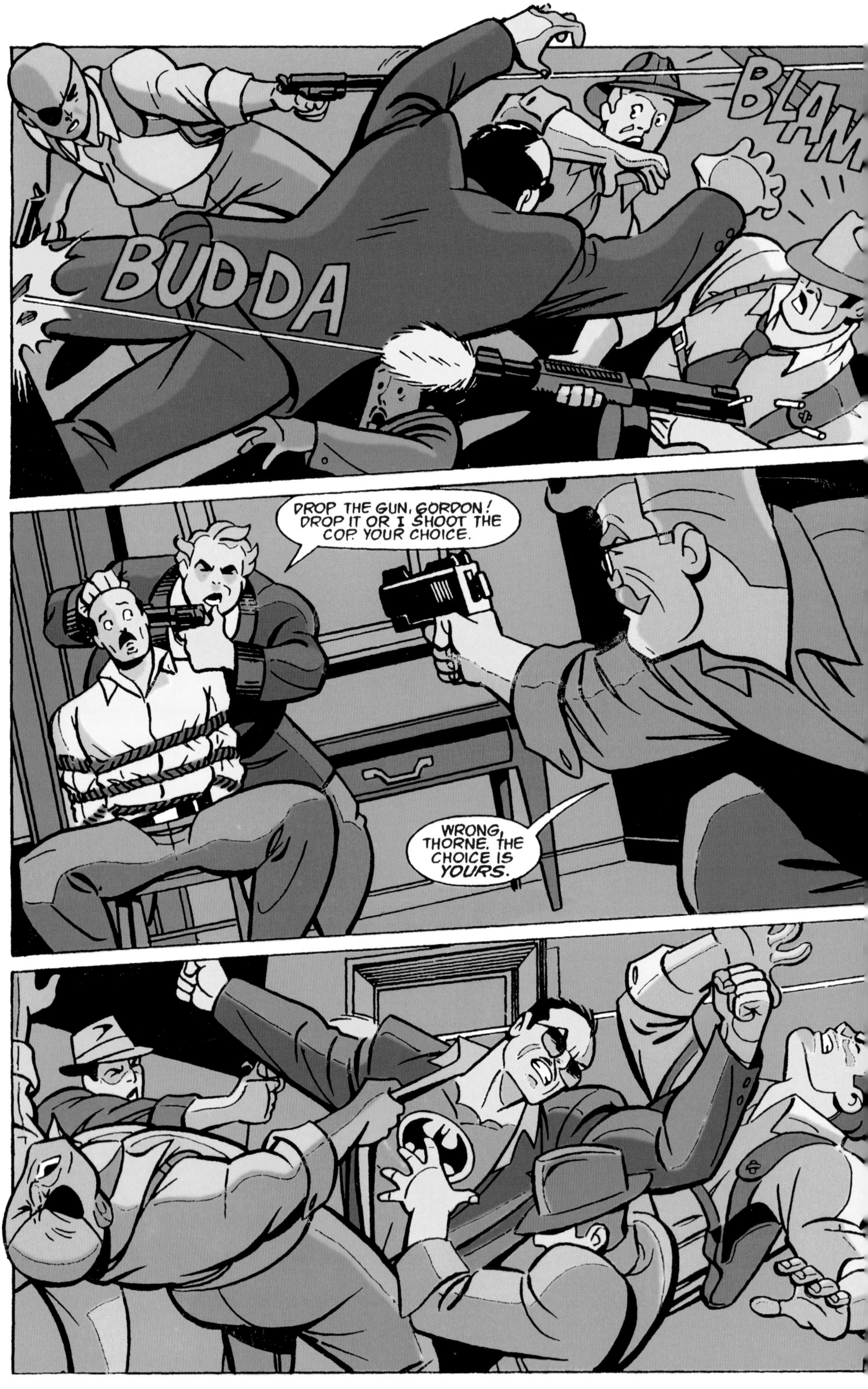
BLAM
BUDDA
DROP THE GUN, GORDON! DROP IT OR I SHOOT THE COP. YOUR CHOICE.
WRONG, THORNE. THE CHOICE IS YOURS.

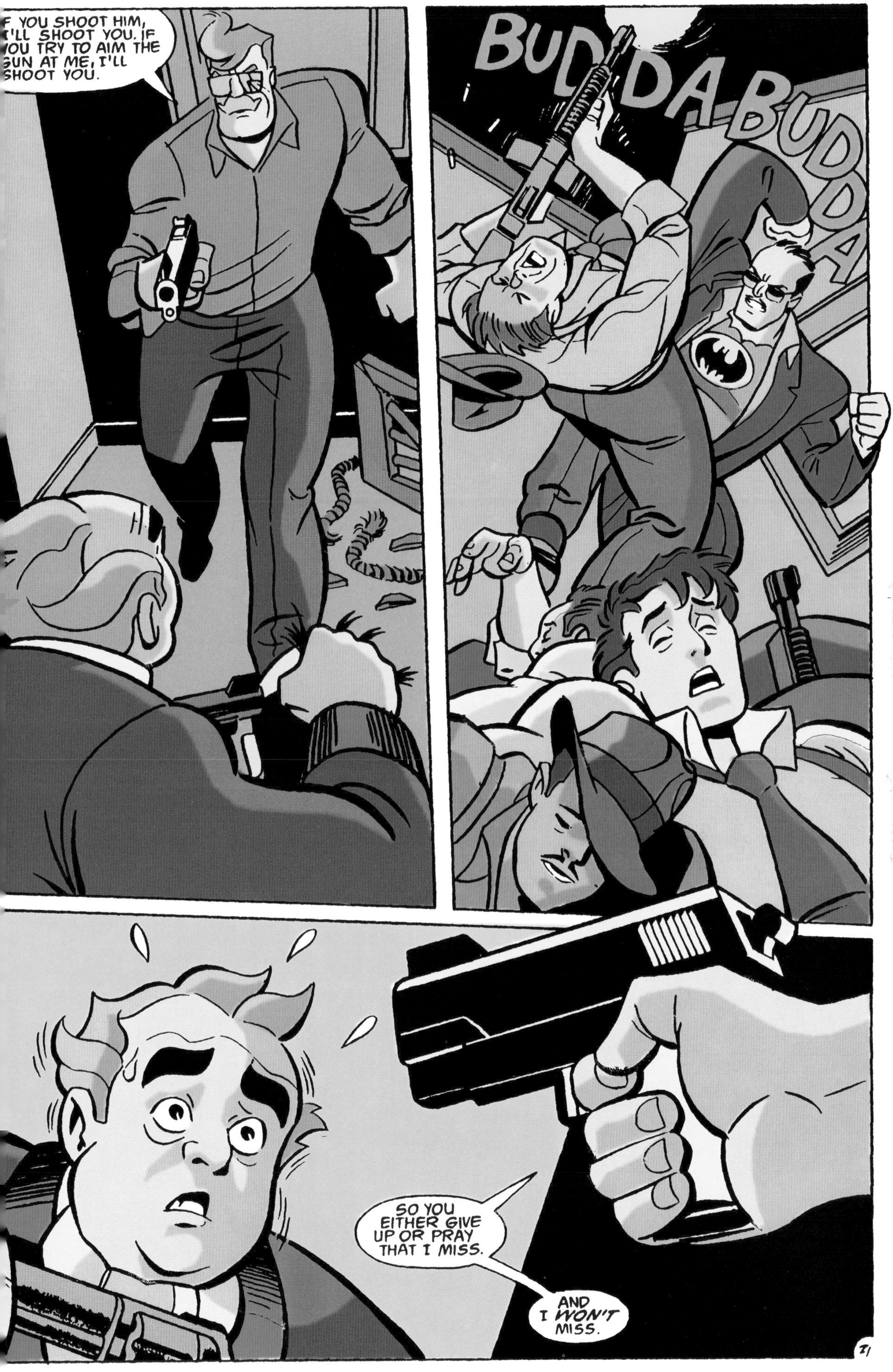
IF YOU SHOOT HIM, I'LL SHOOT YOU. IF YOU TRY TO AIM THE GUN AT ME, I'LL SHOOT YOU.
BUDDA BUDDA
SO YOU EITHER GIVE UP OR PRAY THAT I MISS.
AND I *WON'T* MISS.
21

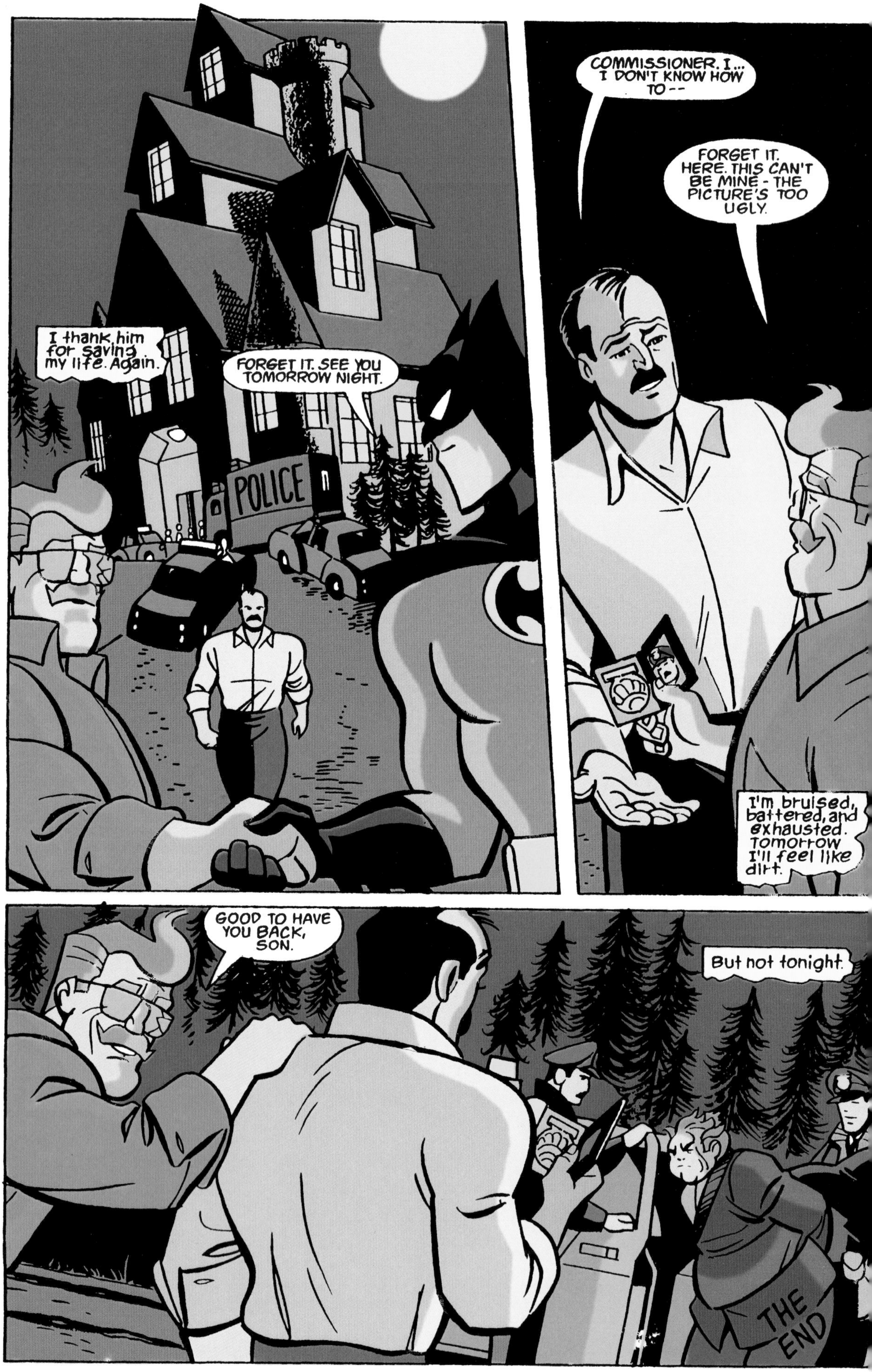
I thank him for saving my life. Again.
FORGET IT. SEE YOU TOMORROW NIGHT.
COMMISSIONER. I... I DON'T KNOW HOW TO --
FORGET IT. HERE. THIS CAN'T BE MINE - THE PICTURE'S TOO UGLY.
I'm bruised, battered, and exhausted. Tomorrow I'll feel like dirt.
GOOD TO HAVE YOU BACK, SON.
But not tonight.
THE END
POLICE

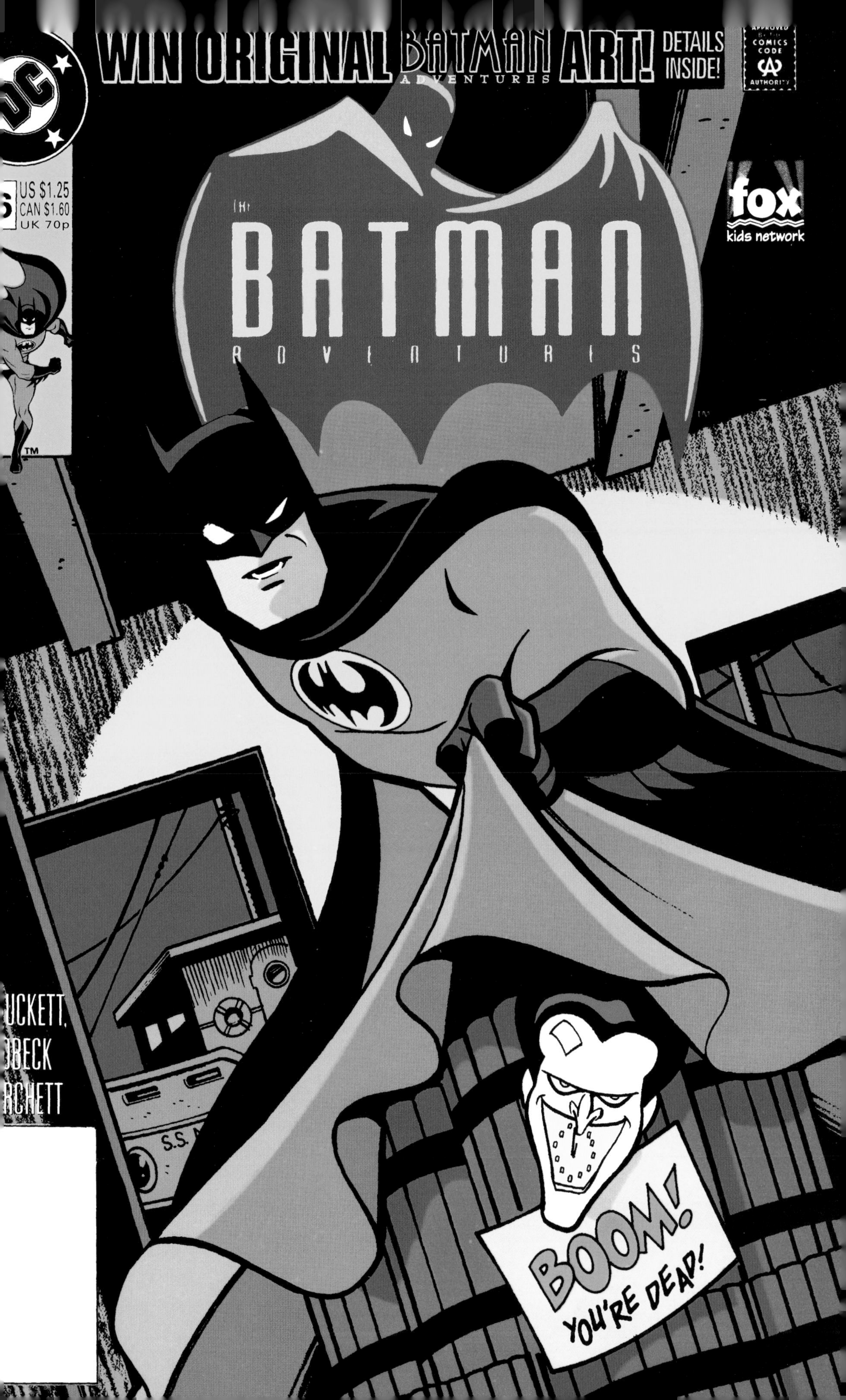

WIN ORIGINAL BATMAN ADVENTURES ART!
DETAILS INSIDE!
APPROVED BY THE COMICS CODE AUTHORITY
US $1.25
CAN $1.60
UK 70p
THE BATMAN ADVENTURES
fox kids network
S.S.
BOOM! YOU'RE DEAD!

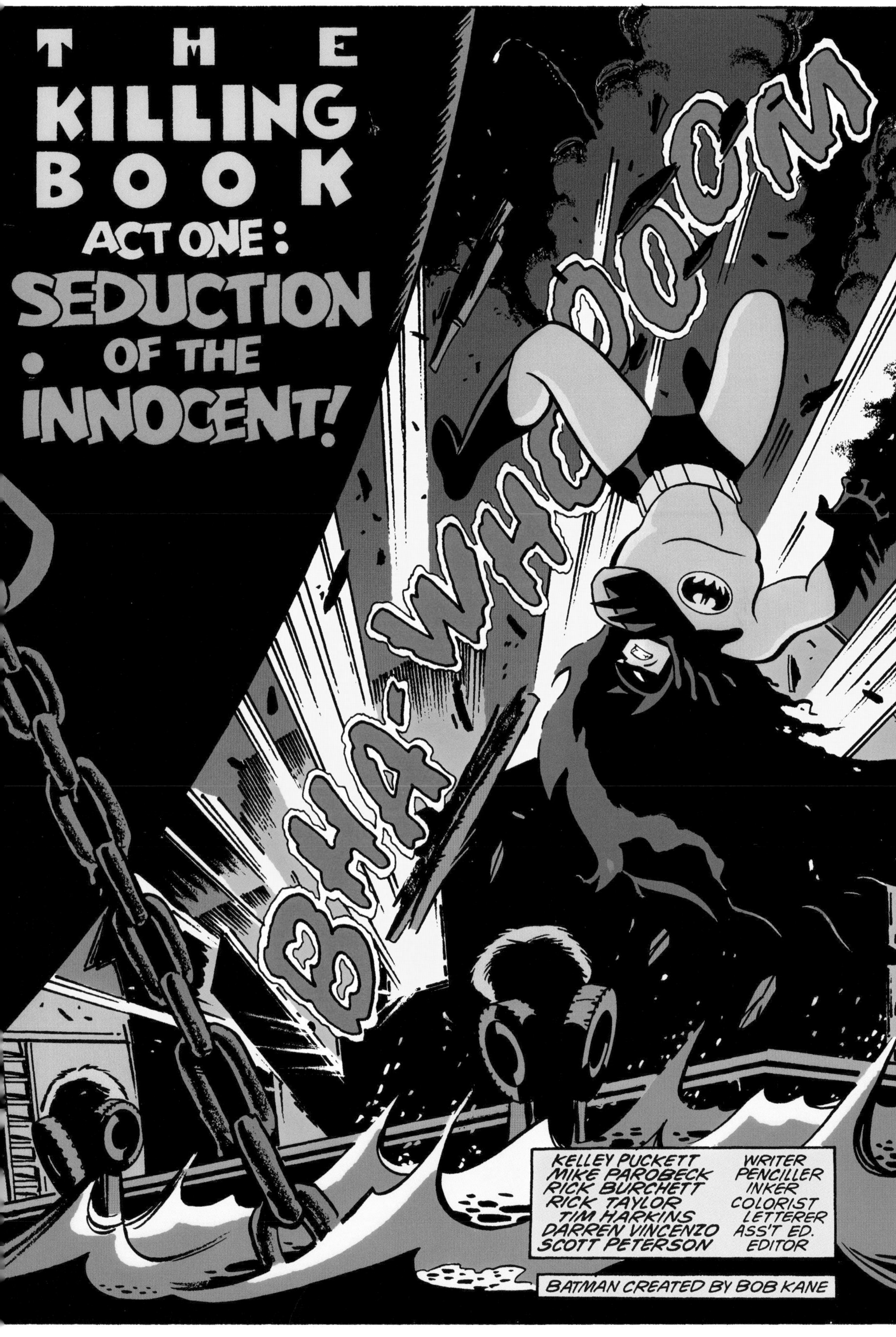
THE KILLING BOOK
ACT ONE:
SEDUCTION OF THE INNOCENT!
BBHA-WHOOOOM
KELLEY PUCKETT WRITER
MIKE PAROBECK PENCILLER
RICK BURCHETT INKER
RICK TAYLOR COLORIST
TIM HARKINS LETTERER
DARREN VINCENZO ASS'T ED.
SCOTT PETERSON EDITOR
BATMAN CREATED BY BOB KANE

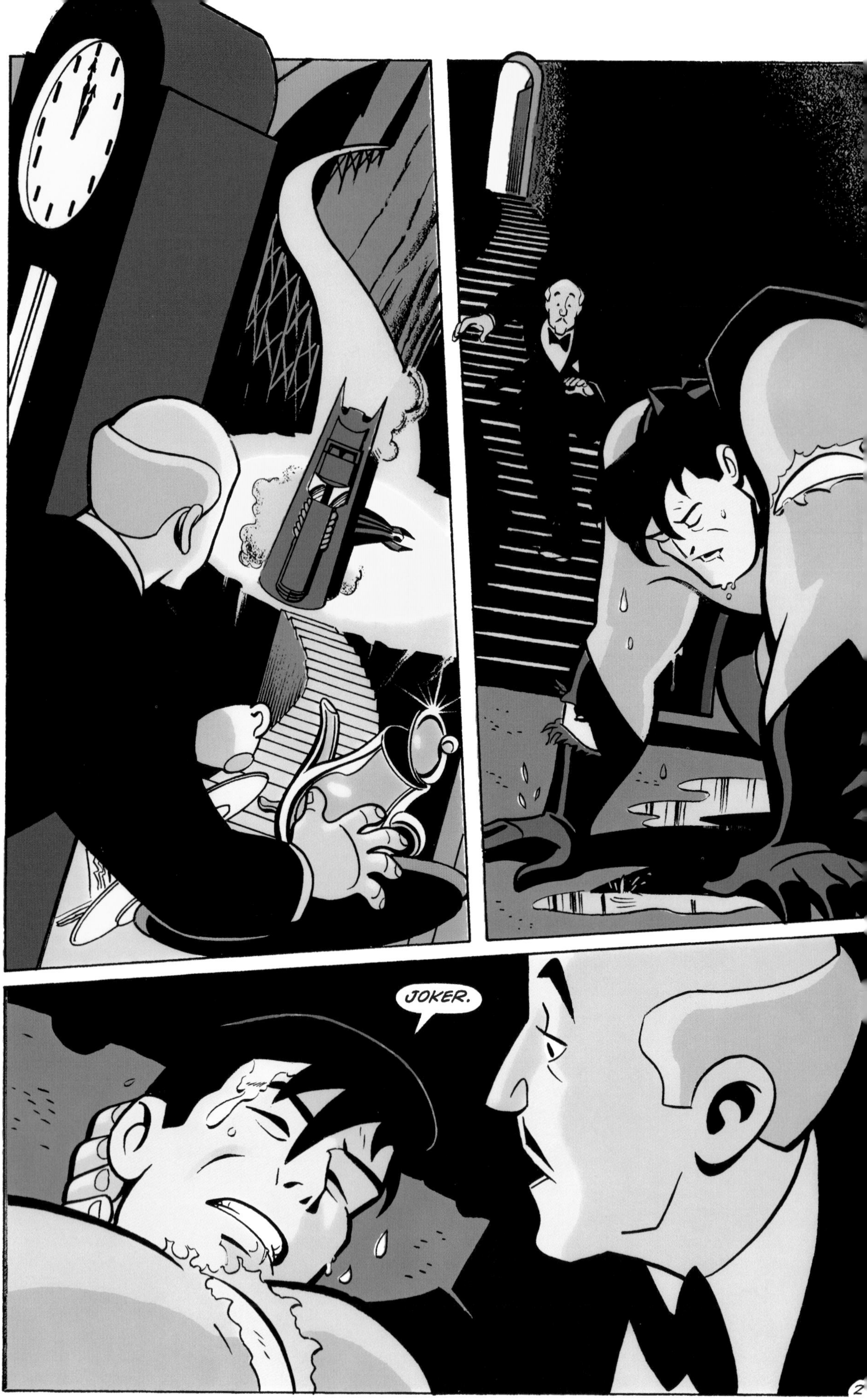
JOKER.
2

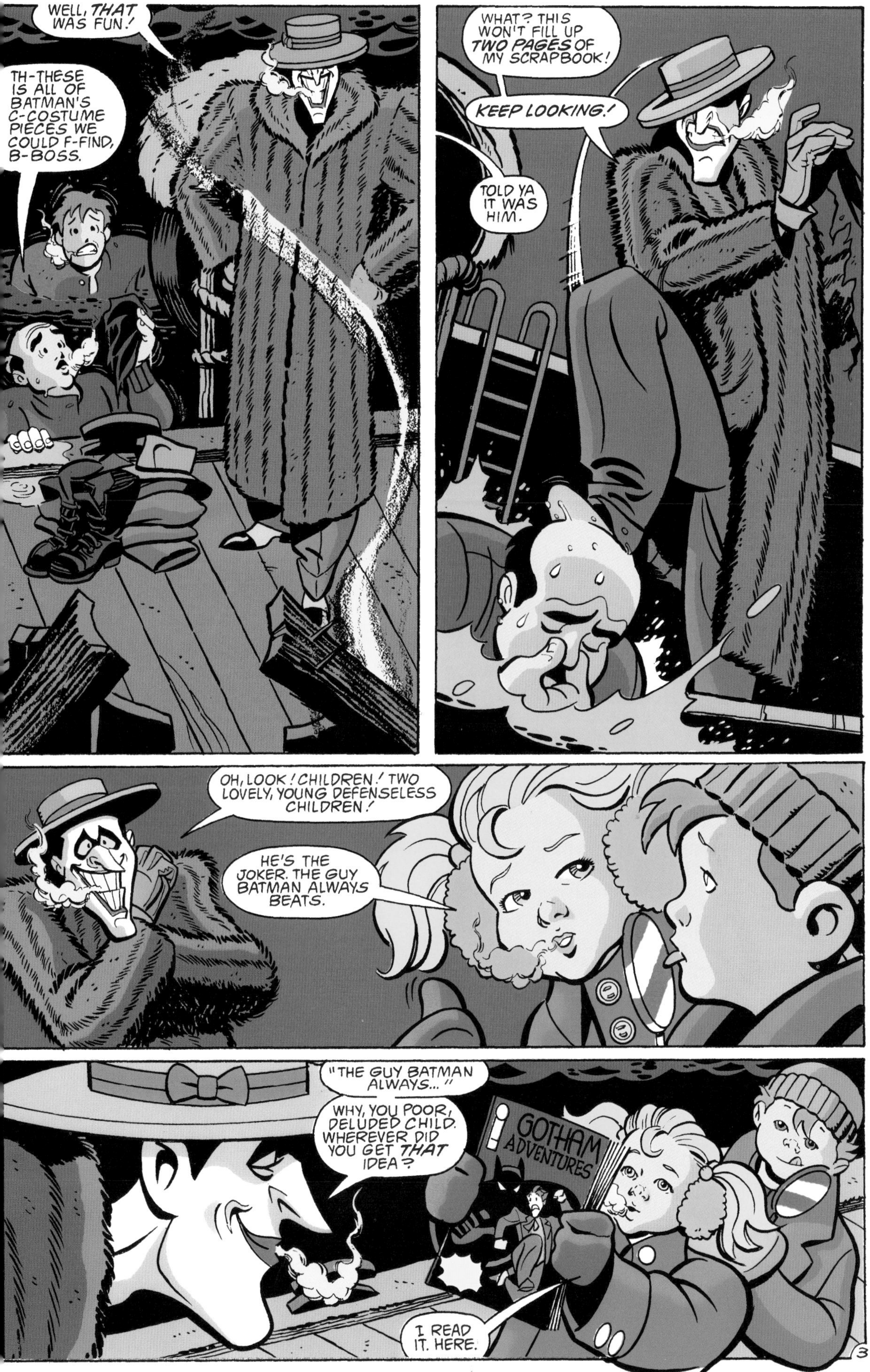
WELL, THAT WAS FUN!
TH-THESE IS ALL OF BATMAN'S C-COSTUME PIECES WE COULD F-FIND, B-BOSS.
WHAT? THIS WON'T FILL UP TWO PAGES OF MY SCRAPBOOK!
KEEP LOOKING!
TOLD YA IT WAS HIM.
OH, LOOK! CHILDREN! TWO LOVELY, YOUNG DEFENSELESS CHILDREN!
HE'S THE JOKER. THE GUY BATMAN ALWAYS BEATS.
"THE GUY BATMAN ALWAYS..."
WHY, YOU POOR, DELUDED CHILD. WHEREVER DID YOU GET THAT IDEA?
GOTHAM ADVENTURES
I READ IT. HERE.
3

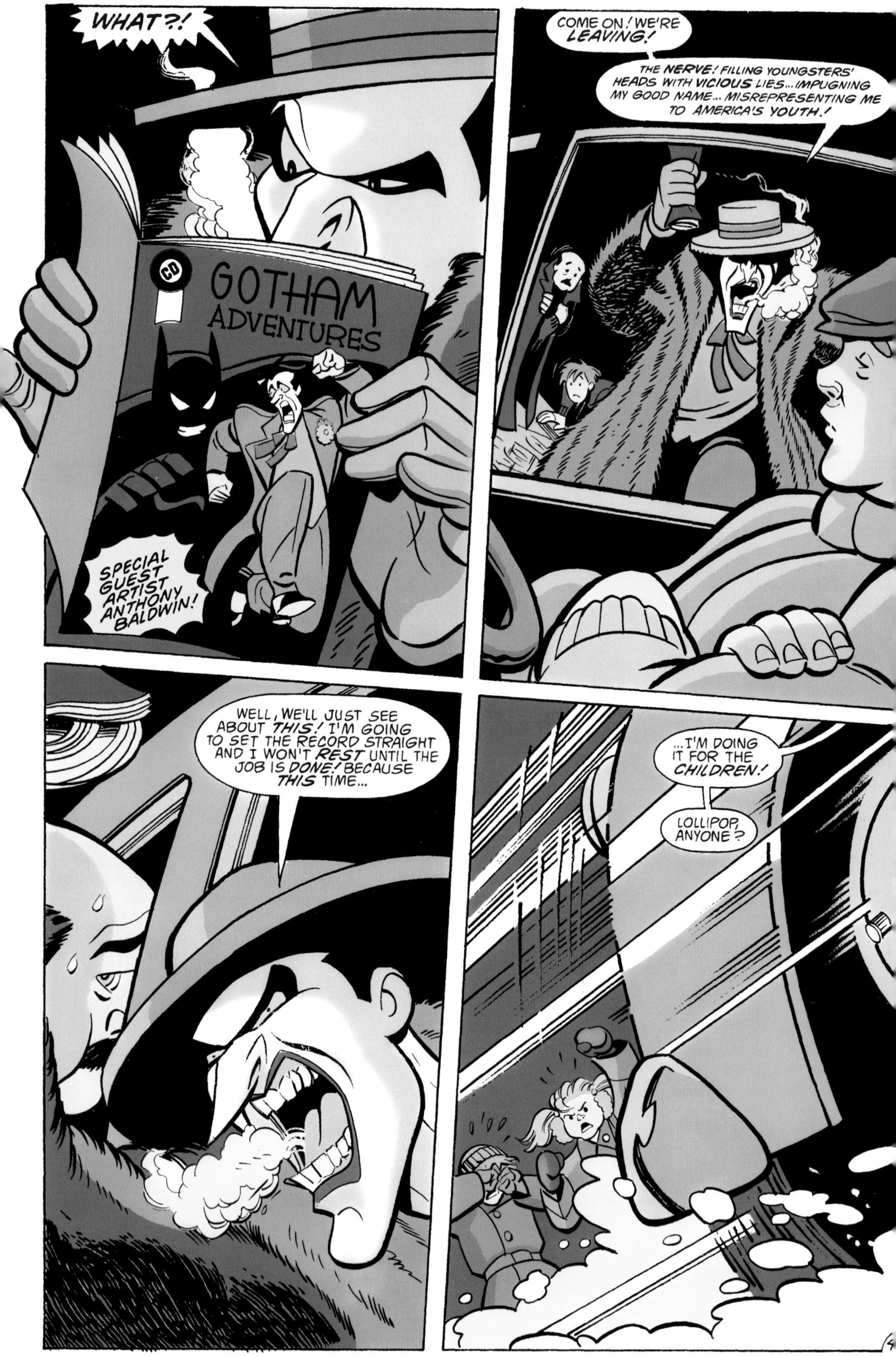
WHAT?!
GOTHAM ADVENTURES
SPECIAL GUEST ARTIST ANTHONY BALDWIN!
COME ON! WE'RE LEAVING!
THE NERVE! FILLING YOUNGSTERS' HEADS WITH VICIOUS LIES... IMPUGNING MY GOOD NAME... MISREPRESENTING ME TO AMERICA'S YOUTH!
WELL, WE'LL JUST SEE ABOUT THIS! I'M GOING TO SET THE RECORD STRAIGHT AND I WON'T REST UNTIL THE JOB IS DONE! BECAUSE THIS TIME...
...I'M DOING IT FOR THE CHILDREN!
LOLLIPOP, ANYONE?

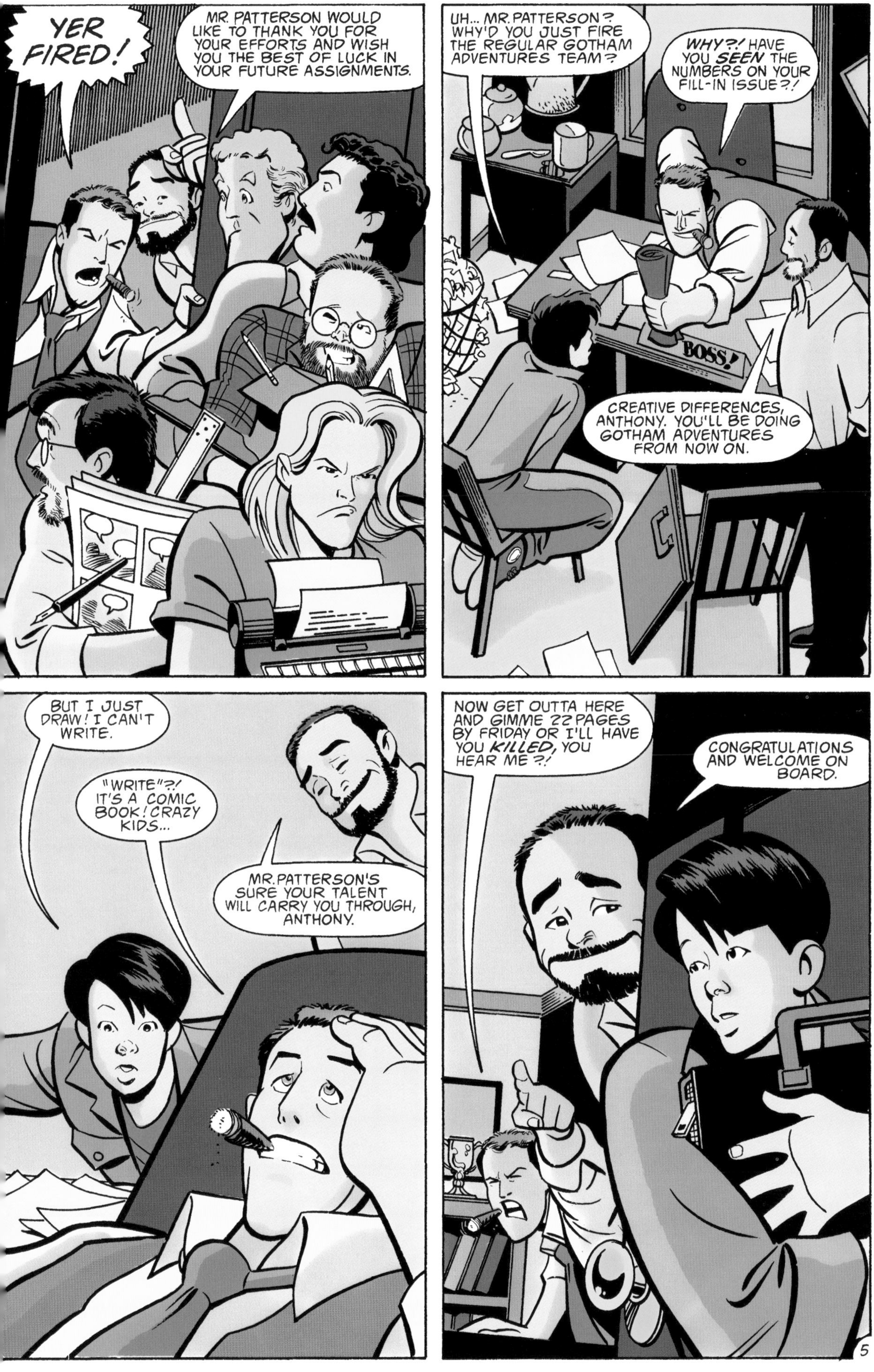
YER FIRED!
MR. PATTERSON WOULD LIKE TO THANK YOU FOR YOUR EFFORTS AND WISH YOU THE BEST OF LUCK IN YOUR FUTURE ASSIGNMENTS.
UH... MR. PATTERSON? WHY'D YOU JUST FIRE THE REGULAR GOTHAM ADVENTURES TEAM?
WHY?! HAVE YOU SEEN THE NUMBERS ON YOUR FILL-IN ISSUE?!
BOSS!
CREATIVE DIFFERENCES, ANTHONY. YOU'LL BE DOING GOTHAM ADVENTURES FROM NOW ON.
BUT I JUST DRAW! I CAN'T WRITE.
"WRITE"?! IT'S A COMIC BOOK! CRAZY KIDS...
MR. PATTERSON'S SURE YOUR TALENT WILL CARRY YOU THROUGH, ANTHONY.
NOW GET OUTTA HERE AND GIMME 22 PAGES BY FRIDAY OR I'LL HAVE YOU KILLED, YOU HEAR ME?!
CONGRATULATIONS AND WELCOME ON BOARD.
5

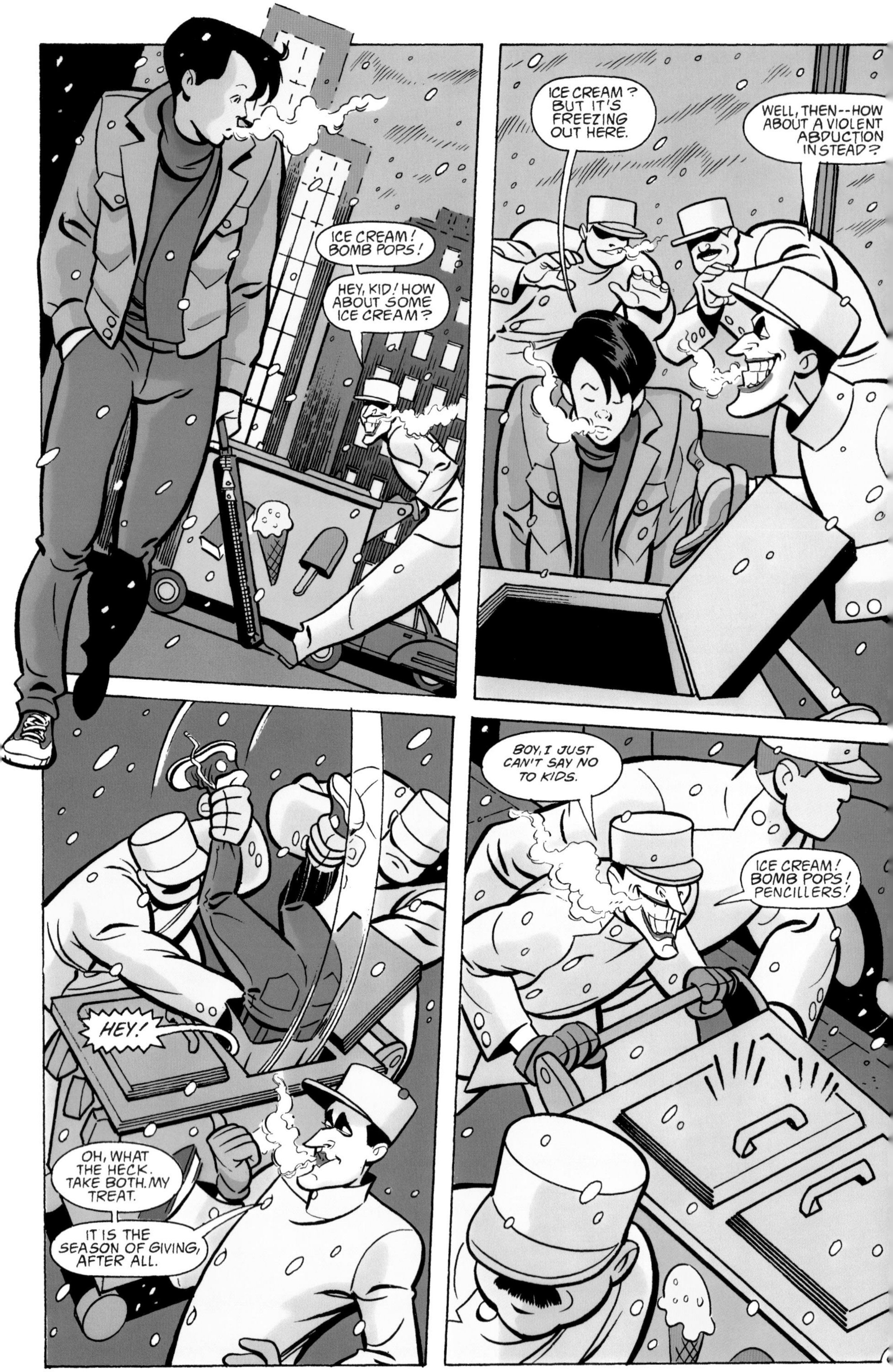
ICE CREAM! BOMB POPS!
HEY, KID! HOW ABOUT SOME ICE CREAM?
ICE CREAM? BUT IT'S FREEZING OUT HERE.
WELL, THEN--HOW ABOUT A VIOLENT ABDUCTION INSTEAD?
HEY!
OH, WHAT THE HECK. TAKE BOTH. MY TREAT.
IT IS THE SEASON OF GIVING, AFTER ALL.
BOY, I JUST CAN'T SAY NO TO KIDS.
ICE CREAM! BOMB POPS! PENCILLERS!

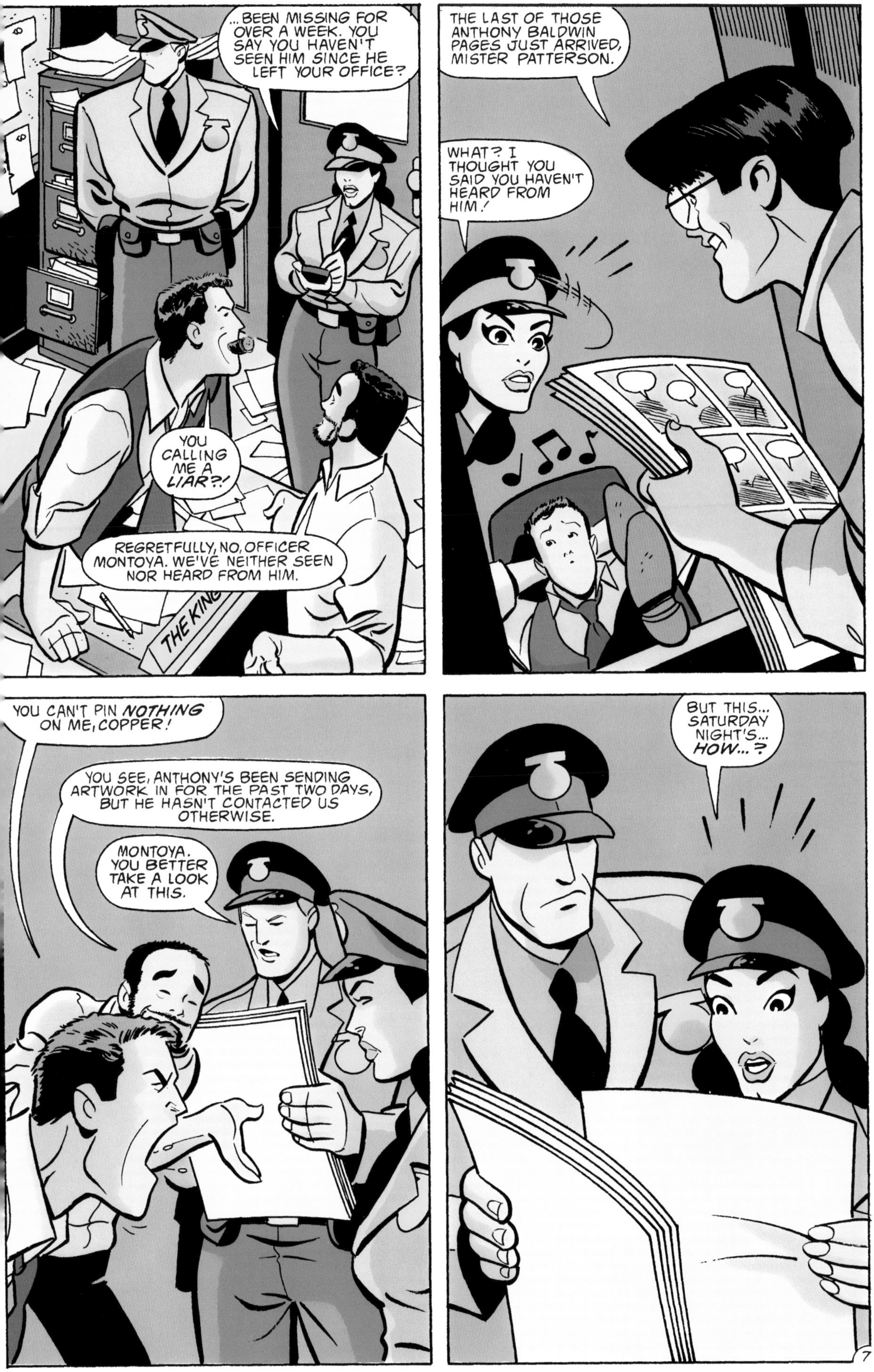
...BEEN MISSING FOR OVER A WEEK. YOU SAY YOU HAVEN'T SEEN HIM SINCE HE LEFT YOUR OFFICE?
YOU CALLING ME A LIAR?!
REGRETFULLY, NO, OFFICER MONTOYA. WE'VE NEITHER SEEN NOR HEARD FROM HIM.
THE KING
THE LAST OF THOSE ANTHONY BALDWIN PAGES JUST ARRIVED, MISTER PATTERSON.
WHAT? I THOUGHT YOU SAID YOU HAVEN'T HEARD FROM HIM!
YOU CAN'T PIN NOTHING ON ME, COPPER!
YOU SEE, ANTHONY'S BEEN SENDING ARTWORK IN FOR THE PAST TWO DAYS, BUT HE HASN'T CONTACTED US OTHERWISE.
MONTOYA. YOU BETTER TAKE A LOOK AT THIS.
BUT THIS... SATURDAY NIGHT'S... HOW...?
7

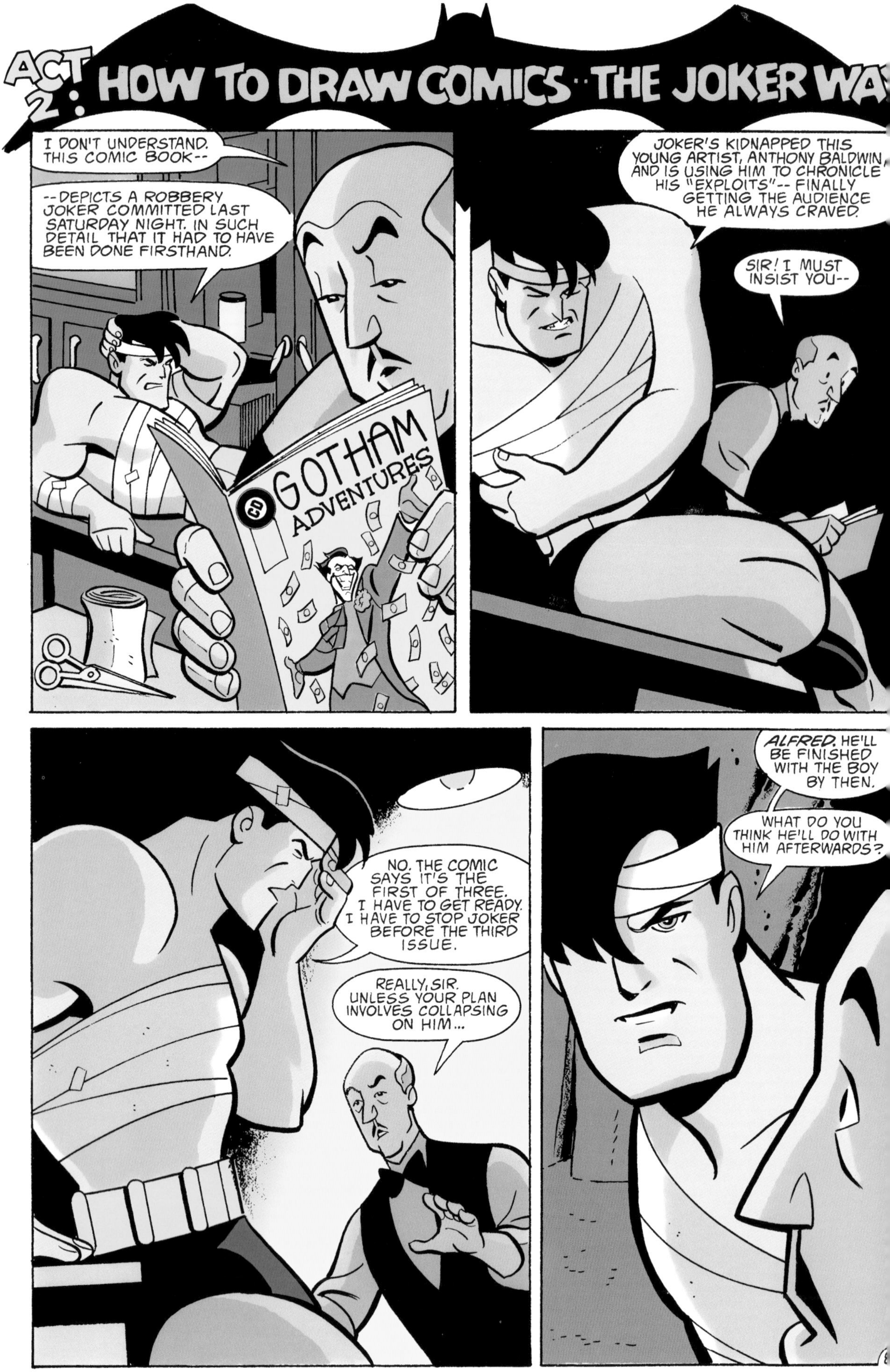
ACT 2: HOW TO DRAW COMICS · · THE JOKER WA
I DON'T UNDERSTAND. THIS COMIC BOOK--
--DEPICTS A ROBBERY JOKER COMMITTED LAST SATURDAY NIGHT. IN SUCH DETAIL THAT IT HAD TO HAVE BEEN DONE FIRSTHAND.
GOTHAM ADVENTURES
JOKER'S KIDNAPPED THIS YOUNG ARTIST, ANTHONY BALDWIN, AND IS USING HIM TO CHRONICLE HIS "EXPLOITS"-- FINALLY GETTING THE AUDIENCE HE ALWAYS CRAVED.
SIR! I MUST INSIST YOU--
NO. THE COMIC SAYS IT'S THE FIRST OF THREE. I HAVE TO GET READY. I HAVE TO STOP JOKER BEFORE THE THIRD ISSUE.
REALLY, SIR. UNLESS YOUR PLAN INVOLVES COLLAPSING ON HIM...
ALFRED. HE'LL BE FINISHED WITH THE BOY BY THEN.
WHAT DO YOU THINK HE'LL DO WITH HIM AFTERWARDS?

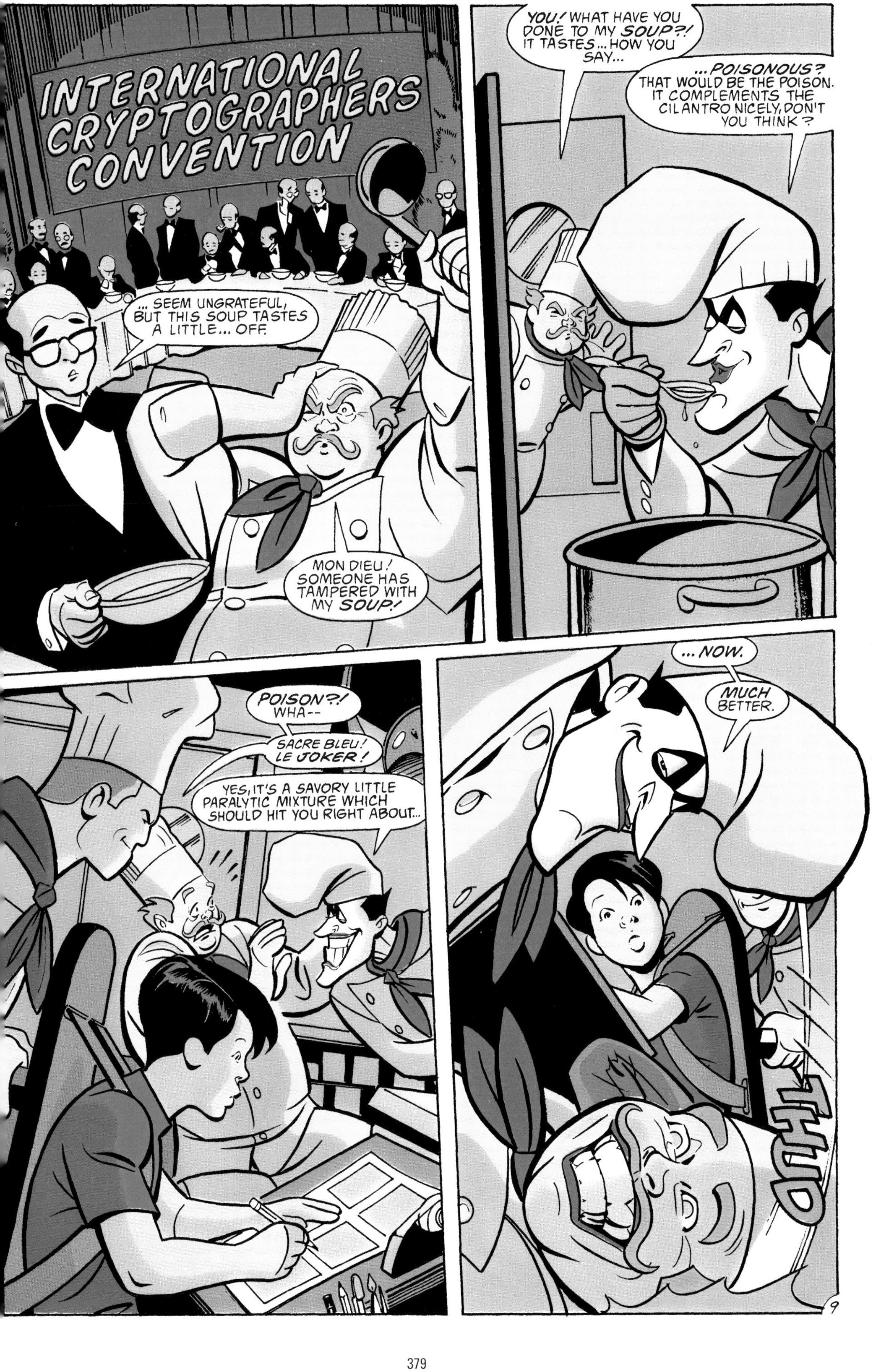
INTERNATIONAL CRYPTOGRAPHERS CONVENTION
... SEEM UNGRATEFUL, BUT THIS SOUP TASTES A LITTLE... OFF.
MON DIEU! SOMEONE HAS TAMPERED WITH MY SOUP!
YOU! WHAT HAVE YOU DONE TO MY SOUP?! IT TASTES... HOW YOU SAY...
...POISONOUS? THAT WOULD BE THE POISON. IT COMPLEMENTS THE CILANTRO NICELY, DON'T YOU THINK?
POISON?! WHA--
SACRE BLEU! LE JOKER!
YES, IT'S A SAVORY LITTLE PARALYTIC MIXTURE WHICH SHOULD HIT YOU RIGHT ABOUT...
...NOW.
MUCH BETTER.
THUD
9

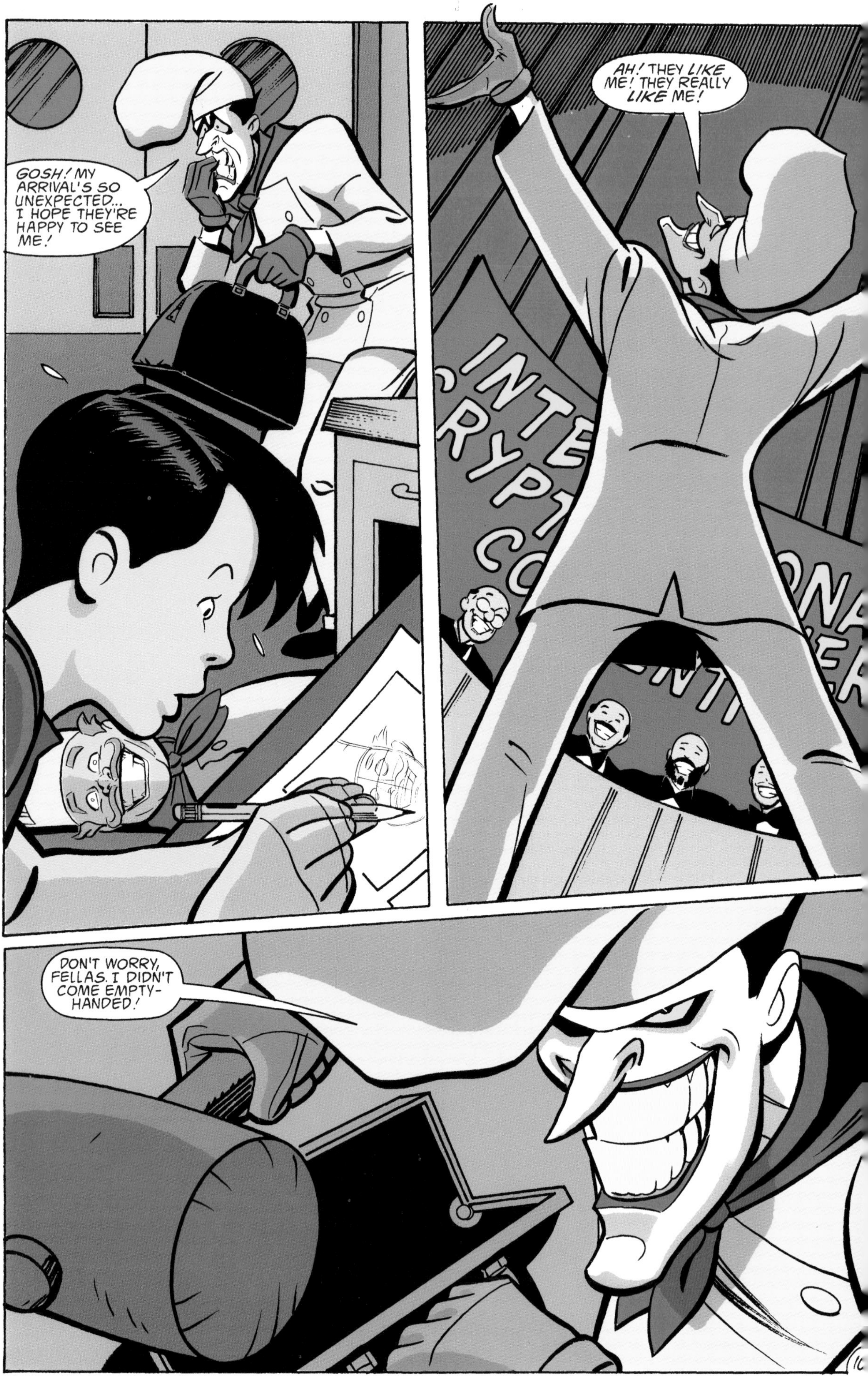
GOSH! MY ARRIVAL'S SO UNEXPECTED... I HOPE THEY'RE HAPPY TO SEE ME!
AH! THEY LIKE ME! THEY REALLY LIKE ME!
DON'T WORRY, FELLAS. I DIDN'T COME EMPTY-HANDED!

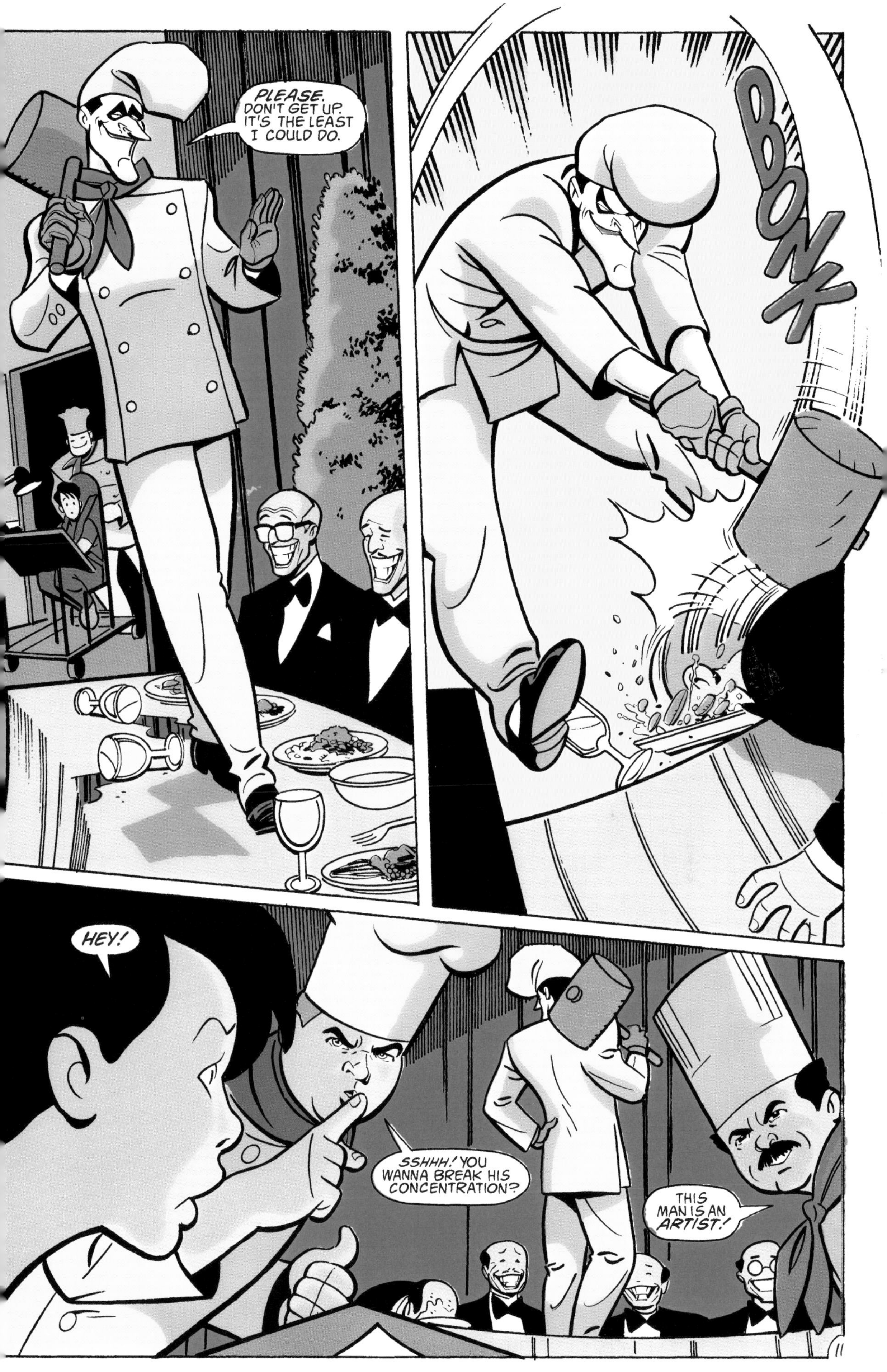
PLEASE. DON'T GET UP. IT'S THE LEAST I COULD DO.
BONK
HEY!
SSHHH! YOU WANNA BREAK HIS CONCENTRATION?
THIS MAN IS AN ARTIST!

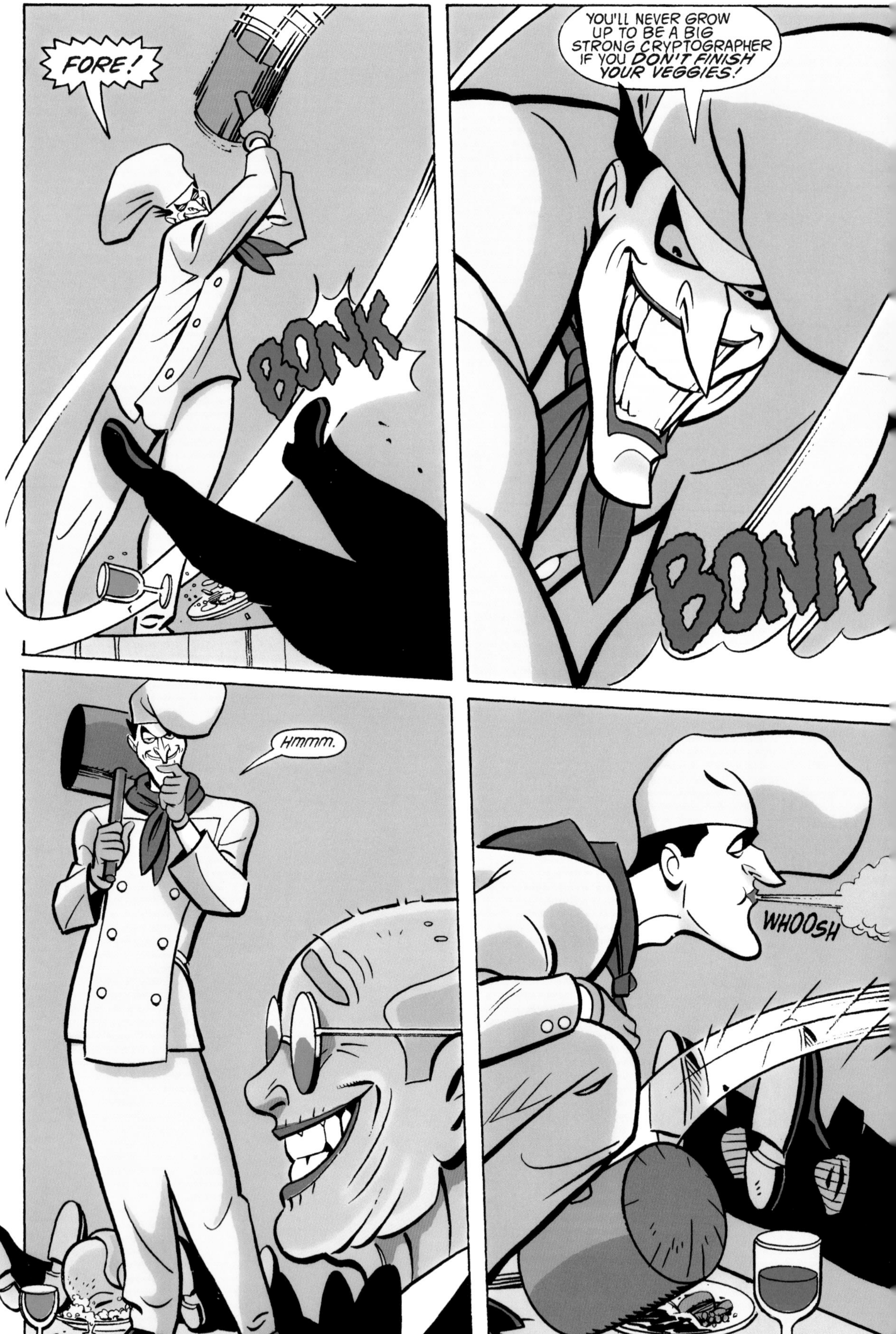
FORE!
BONK
YOU'LL NEVER GROW UP TO BE A BIG STRONG CRYPTOGRAPHER IF YOU DON'T FINISH YOUR VEGGIES!
BONK
HMMM.
WHOOSH

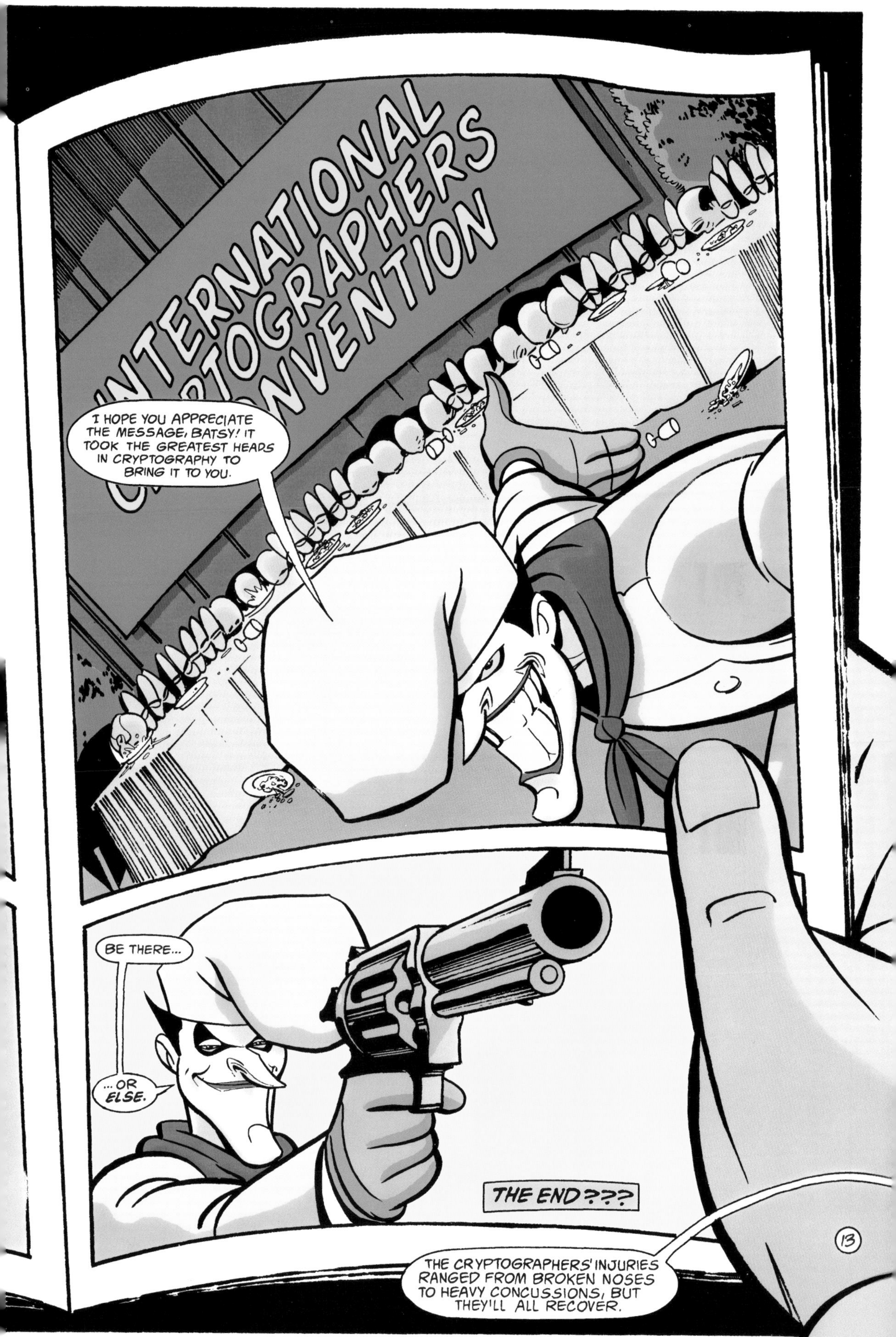

INTERNATIONAL CRYPTOGRAPHERS CONVENTION
I HOPE YOU APPRECIATE THE MESSAGE, BATSY! IT TOOK THE GREATEST HEADS IN CRYPTOGRAPHY TO BRING IT TO YOU.
BE THERE...
...OR ELSE.
THE END???
13
THE CRYPTOGRAPHERS' INJURIES RANGED FROM BROKEN NOSES TO HEAVY CONCUSSIONS, BUT THEY'LL ALL RECOVER.

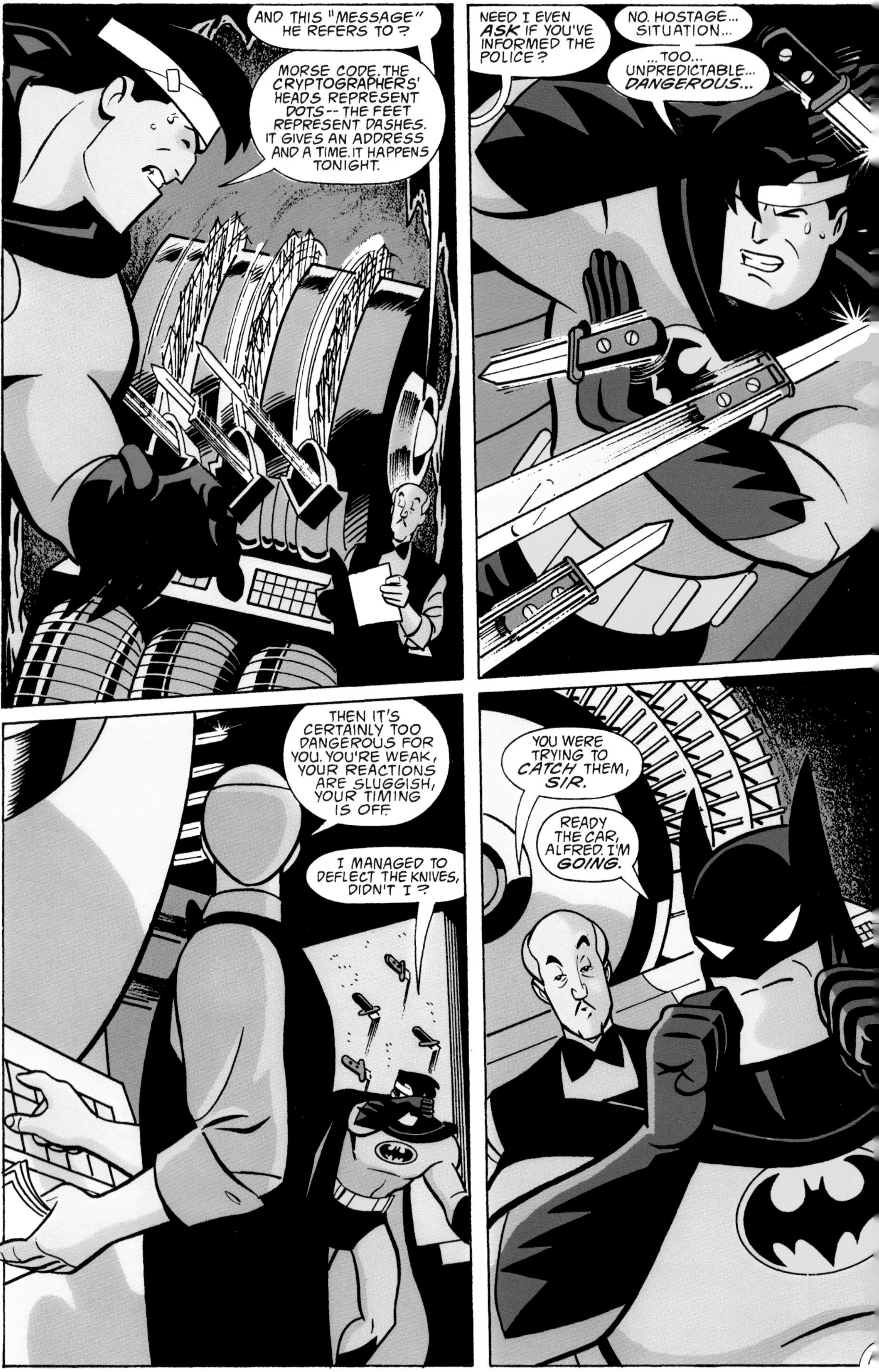
AND THIS "MESSAGE" HE REFERS TO?
MORSE CODE. THE CRYPTOGRAPHERS' HEADS REPRESENT DOTS-- THE FEET REPRESENT DASHES. IT GIVES AN ADDRESS AND A TIME. IT HAPPENS TONIGHT.
NEED I EVEN ASK IF YOU'VE INFORMED THE POLICE?
NO. HOSTAGE... SITUATION...
...TOO... UNPREDICTABLE... DANGEROUS...
THEN IT'S CERTAINLY TOO DANGEROUS FOR YOU. YOU'RE WEAK, YOUR REACTIONS ARE SLUGGISH, YOUR TIMING IS OFF.
I MANAGED TO DEFLECT THE KNIVES, DIDN'T I?
YOU WERE TRYING TO CATCH THEM, SIR.
READY THE CAR, ALFRED. I'M GOING.

ACT 3: COMICS AND SEQUENTIAL DEATH!

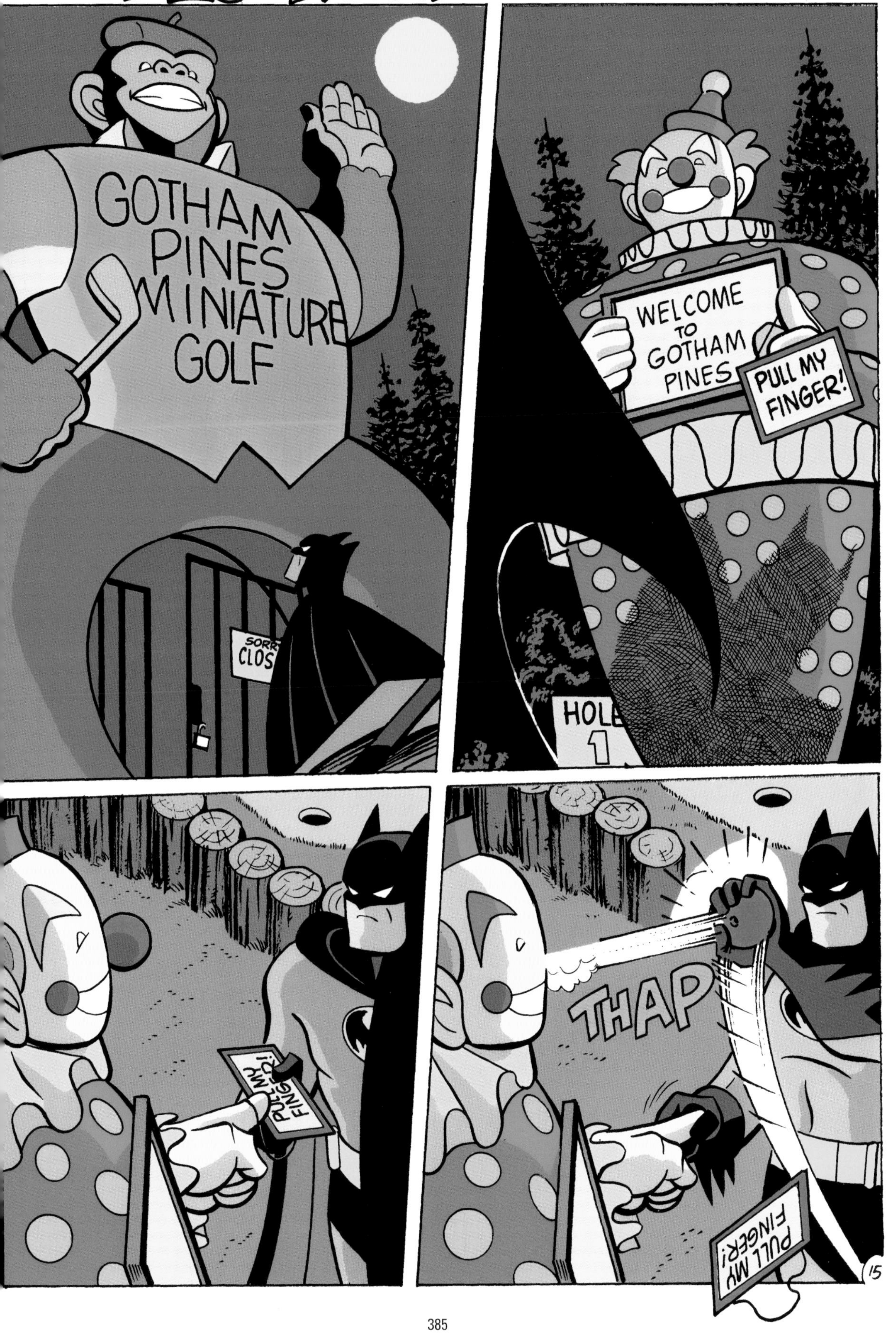

GOTHAM PINES MINIATURE GOLF
SORR
CLOS
WELCOME TO GOTHAM PINES
PULL MY FINGER!
HOLE 1
PULL MY FINGER!
THAP
PULL MY FINGER!
15

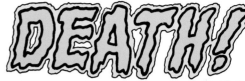

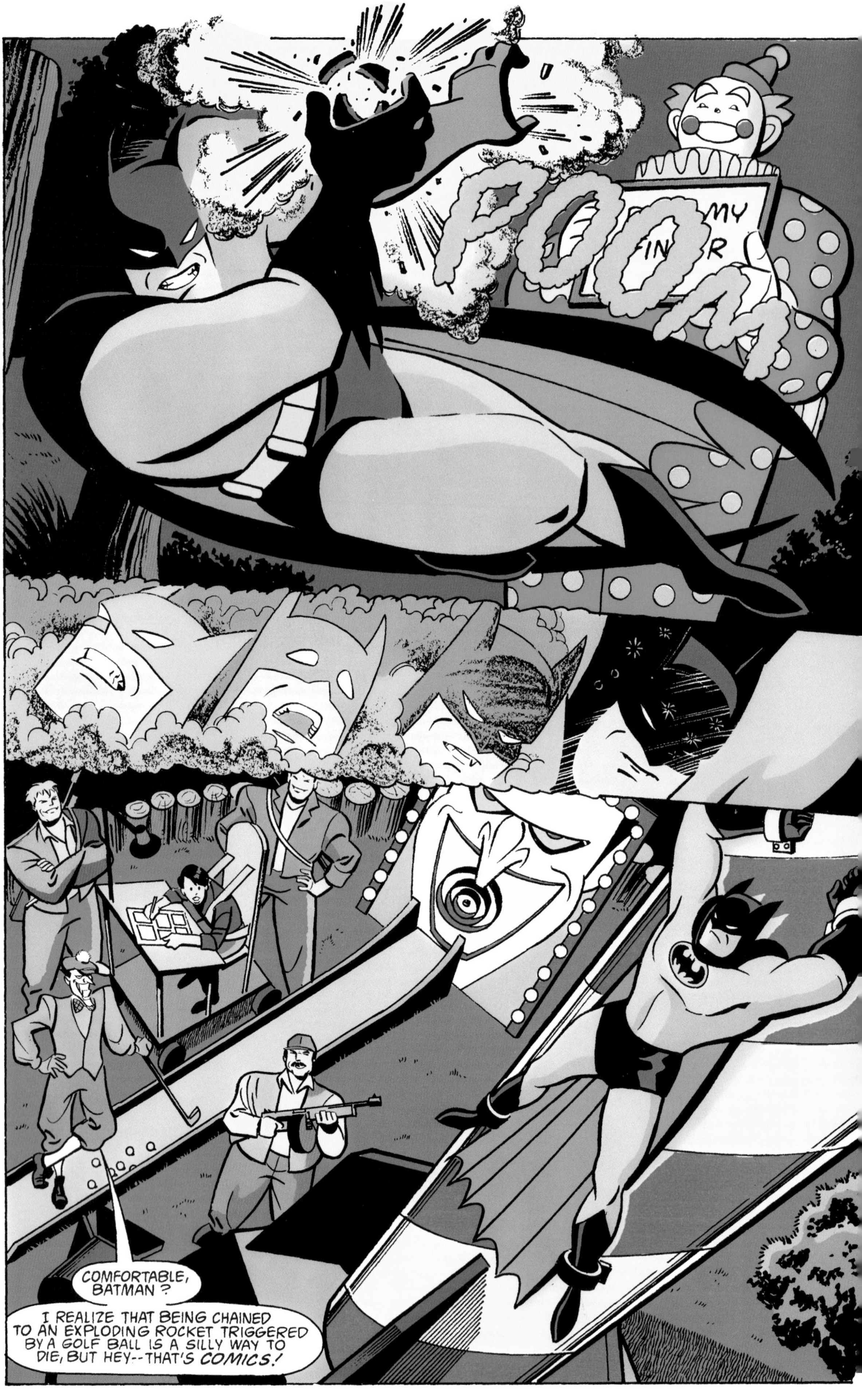
POOM
MY
FIN R
COMFORTABLE, BATMAN?
I REALIZE THAT BEING CHAINED TO AN EXPLODING ROCKET TRIGGERED BY A GOLF BALL IS A SILLY WAY TO DIE, BUT HEY--THAT'S COMICS!

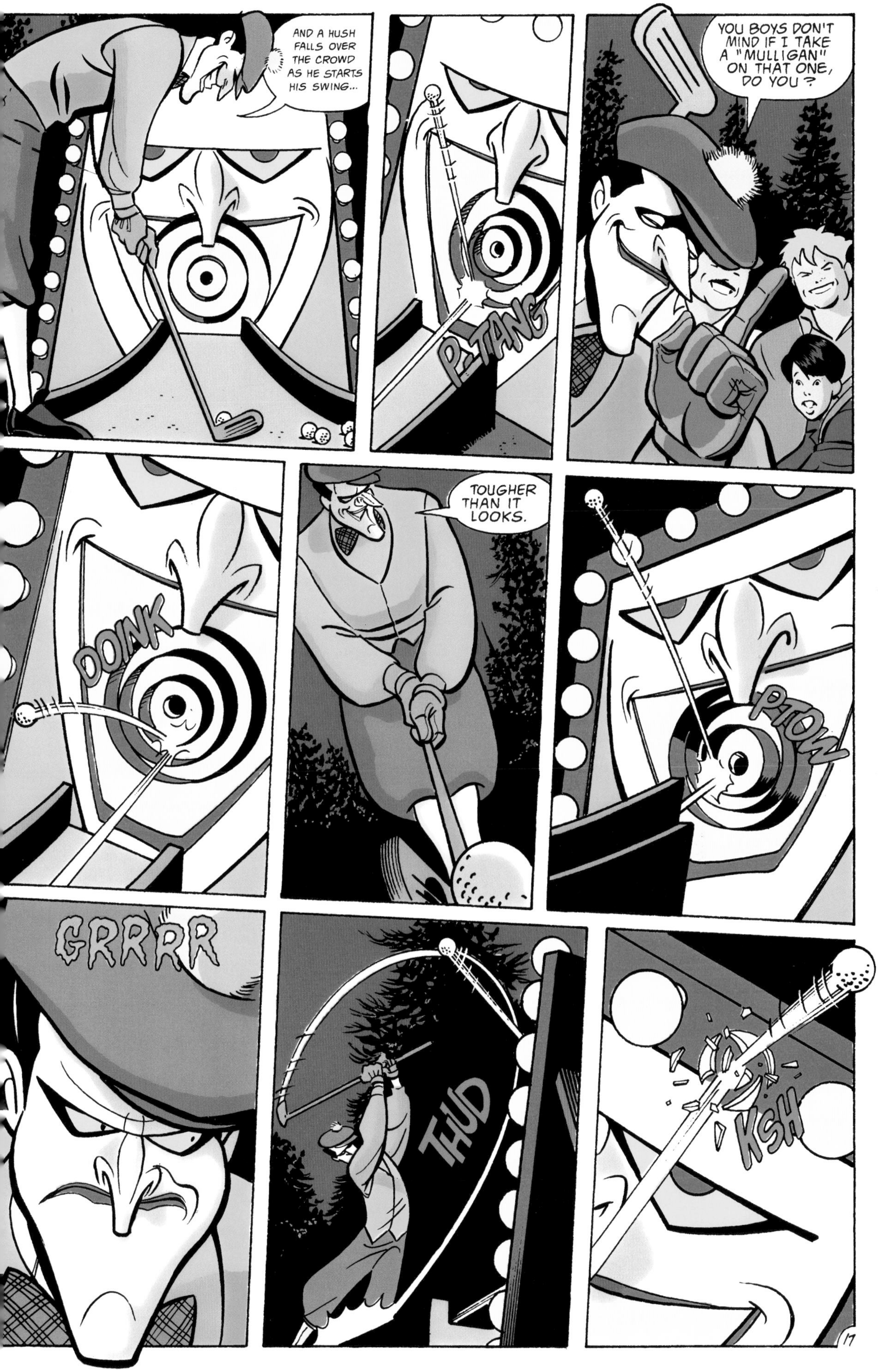

AND A HUSH FALLS OVER THE CROWD AS HE STARTS HIS SWING...
P-TANG
YOU BOYS DON'T MIND IF I TAKE A "MULLIGAN" ON THAT ONE, DO YOU?
DOINK
TOUGHER THAN IT LOOKS.
PTOW
GRRRR
THUD
KSH
17

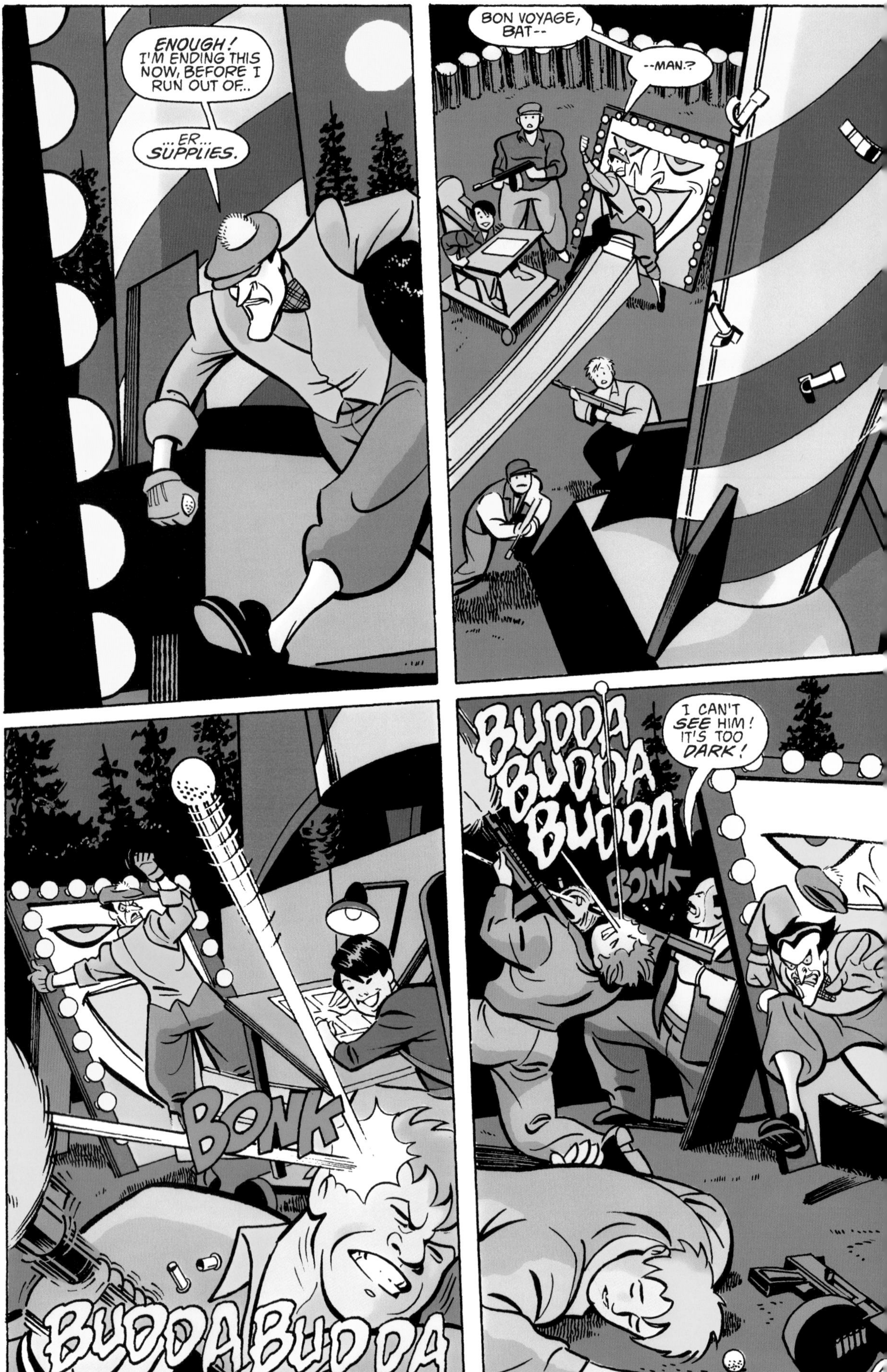
ENOUGH! I'M ENDING THIS NOW, BEFORE I RUN OUT OF...
...ER... SUPPLIES.
BON VOYAGE, BAT--
--MAN?
BONK
BUDDABUDDA
BUDDA BUDDA BUDDA
I CAN'T SEE HIM! IT'S TOO DARK!
BONK

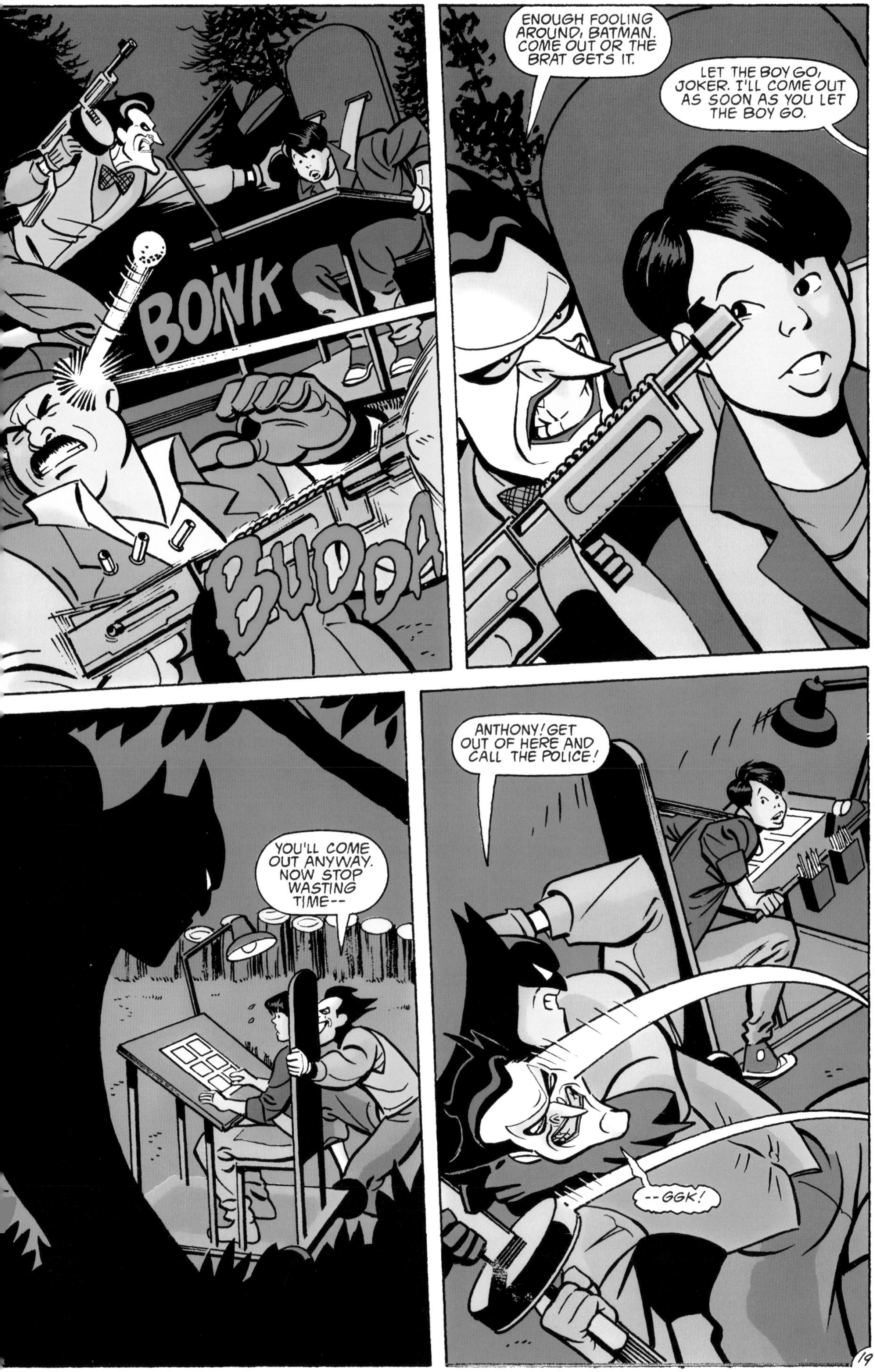
BONK
BUDDA
ENOUGH FOOLING AROUND, BATMAN. COME OUT OR THE BRAT GETS IT.
LET THE BOY GO, JOKER. I'LL COME OUT AS SOON AS YOU LET THE BOY GO.
YOU'LL COME OUT ANYWAY. NOW STOP WASTING TIME--
ANTHONY! GET OUT OF HERE AND CALL THE POLICE!
--GGK!
19

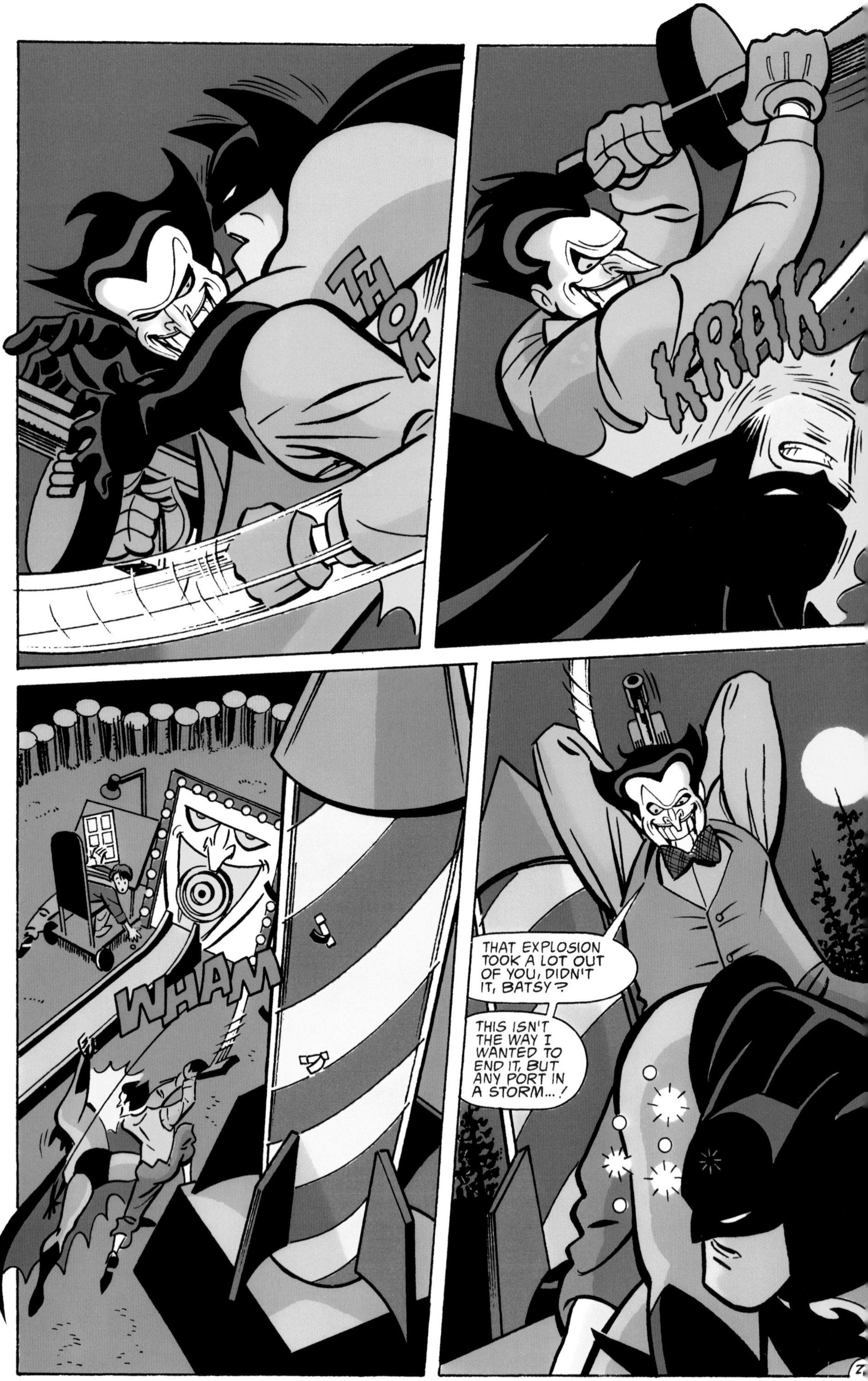
THOK
KRAK
WHAM
THAT EXPLOSION TOOK A LOT OUT OF YOU, DIDN'T IT, BATSY?
THIS ISN'T THE WAY I WANTED TO END IT, BUT ANY PORT IN A STORM...!

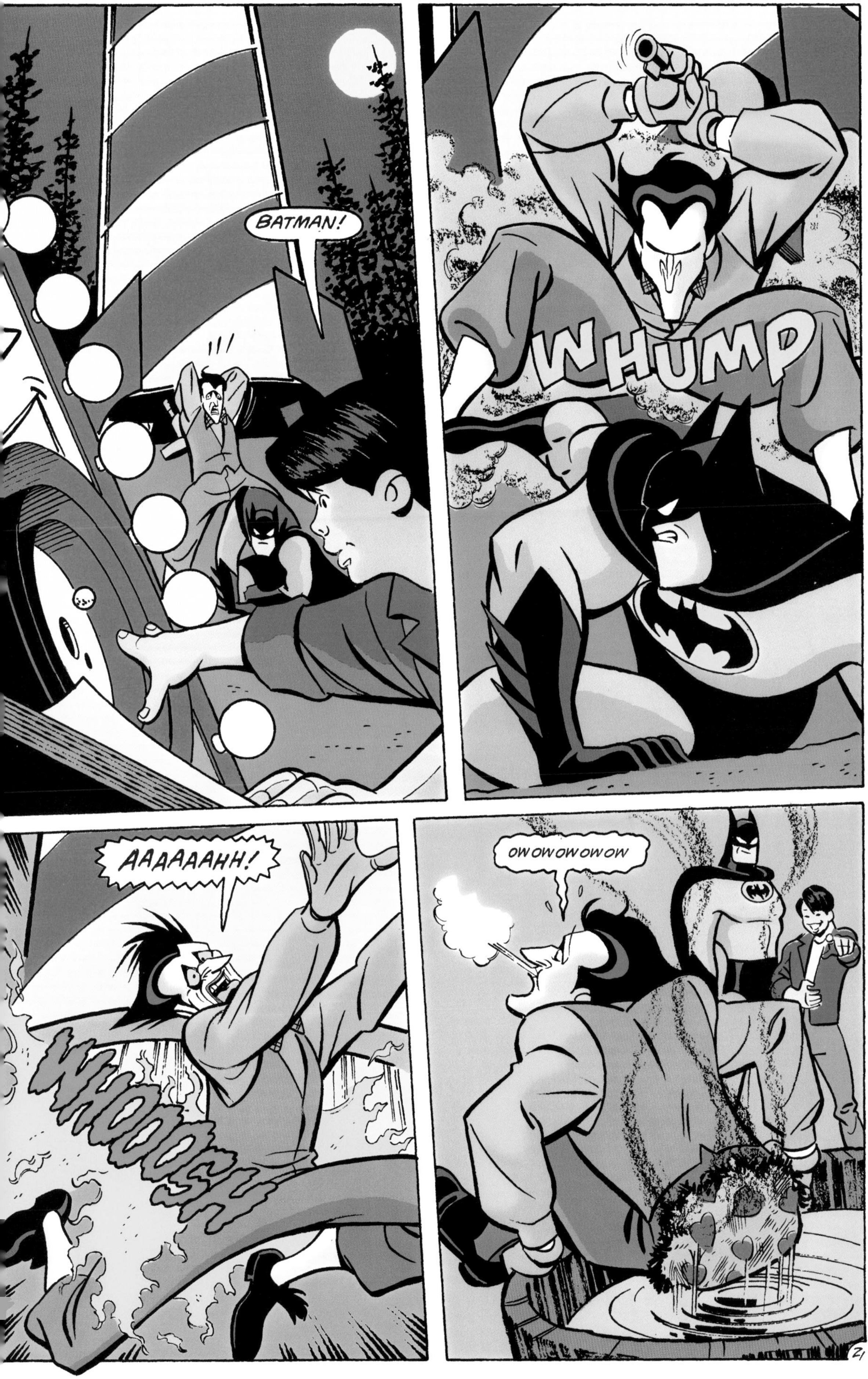
BATMAN!
WHUMP
AAAAAAHH!
WHOOSH
OWOWOWOWOW
21

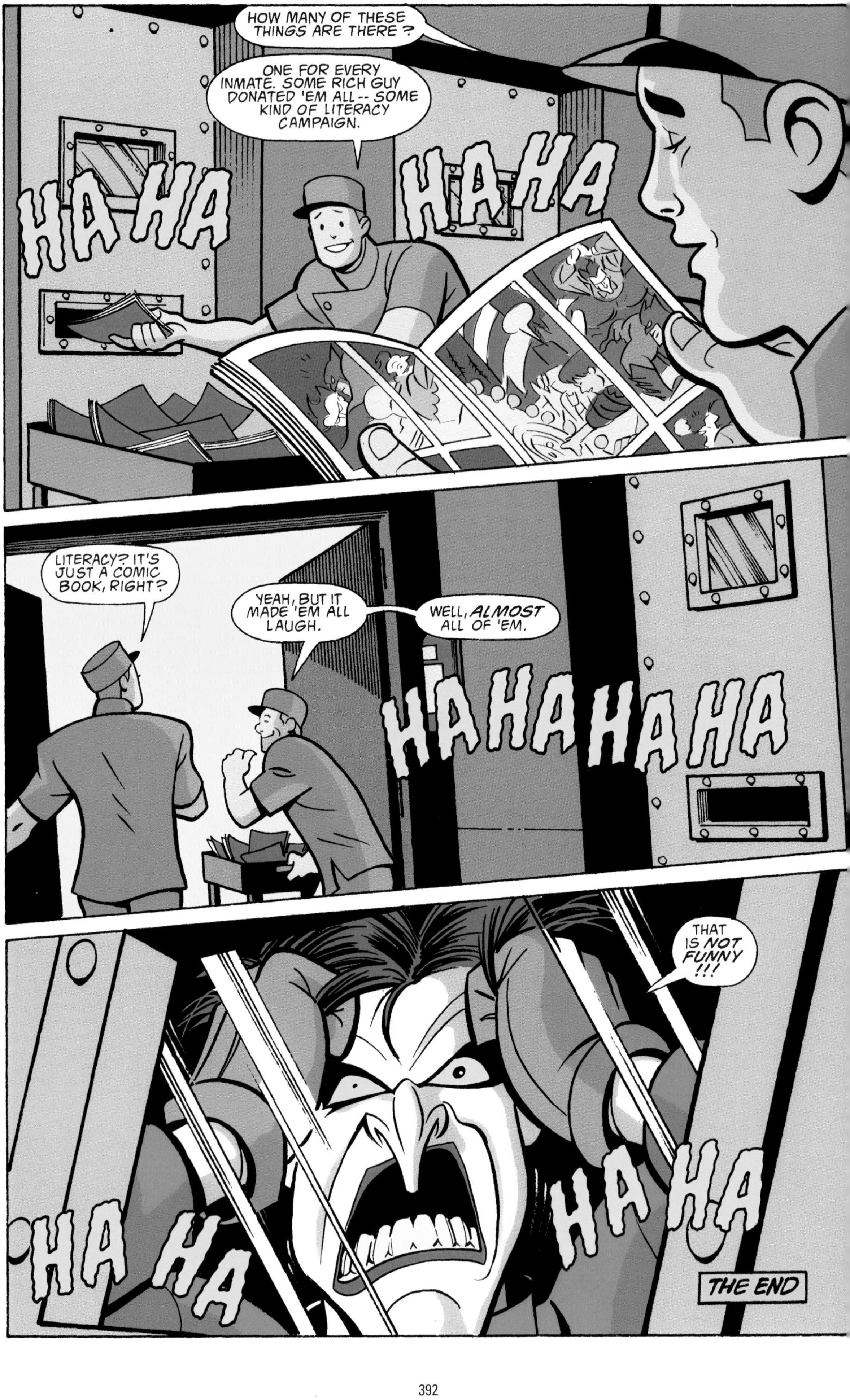
HOW MANY OF THESE THINGS ARE THERE ?
ONE FOR EVERY INMATE. SOME RICH GUY DONATED 'EM ALL -- SOME KIND OF LITERACY CAMPAIGN.
HA HA HA
HA HA HA
LITERACY? IT'S JUST A COMIC BOOK, RIGHT?
YEAH, BUT IT MADE 'EM ALL LAUGH.
WELL, ALMOST ALL OF 'EM.
HA HA HA HA HA
THAT IS NOT FUNNY !!!
HA HA HA
HA HA HA
THE END

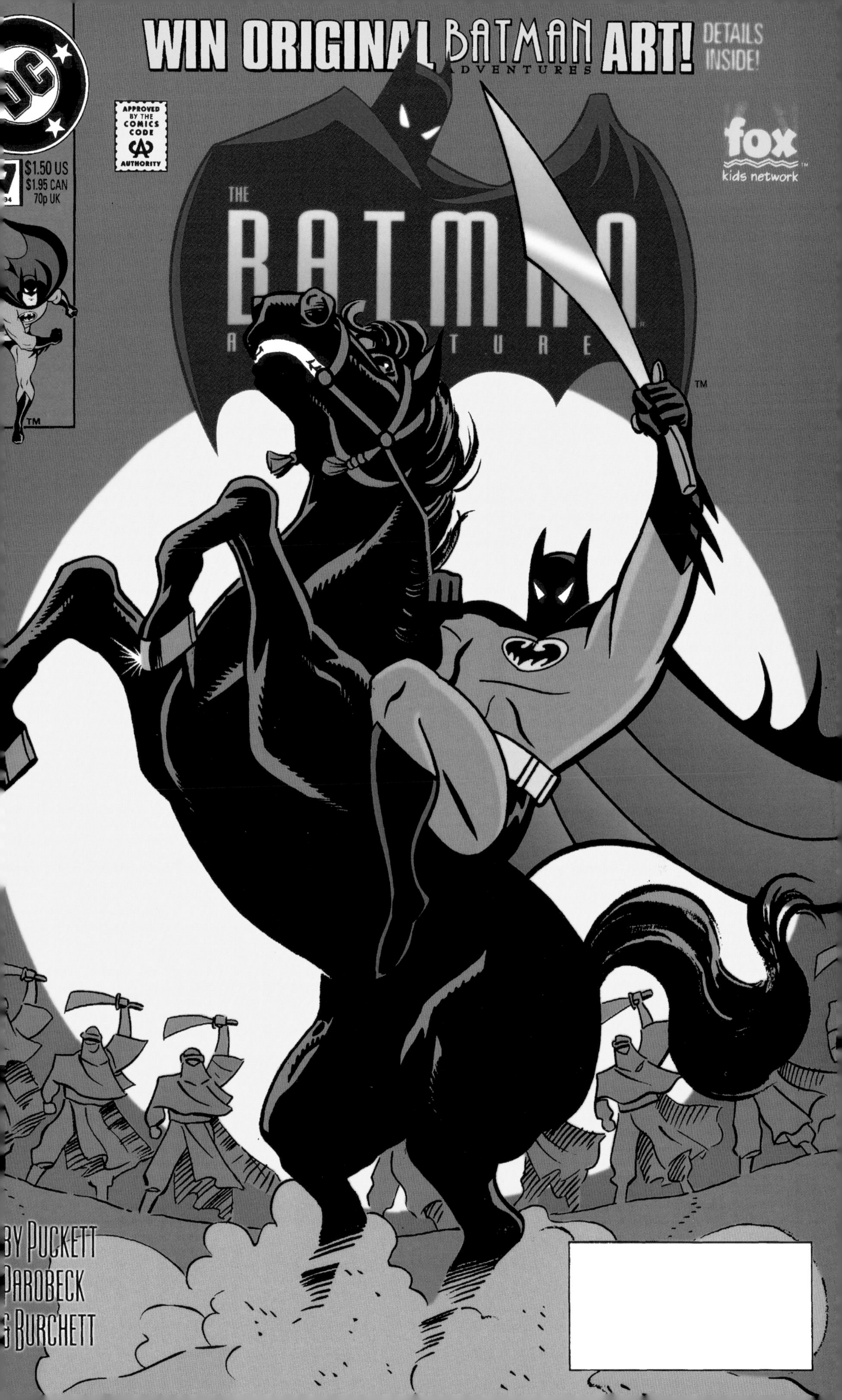
WIN ORIGINAL BATMAN ADVENTURES ART!
DETAILS INSIDE!
APPROVED BY THE COMICS CODE AUTHORITY
$1.50 US
$1.95 CAN
70p UK
THE BATMAN ADVENTURES
fox kids network
BY PUCKETT
PAROBECK
& BURCHETT

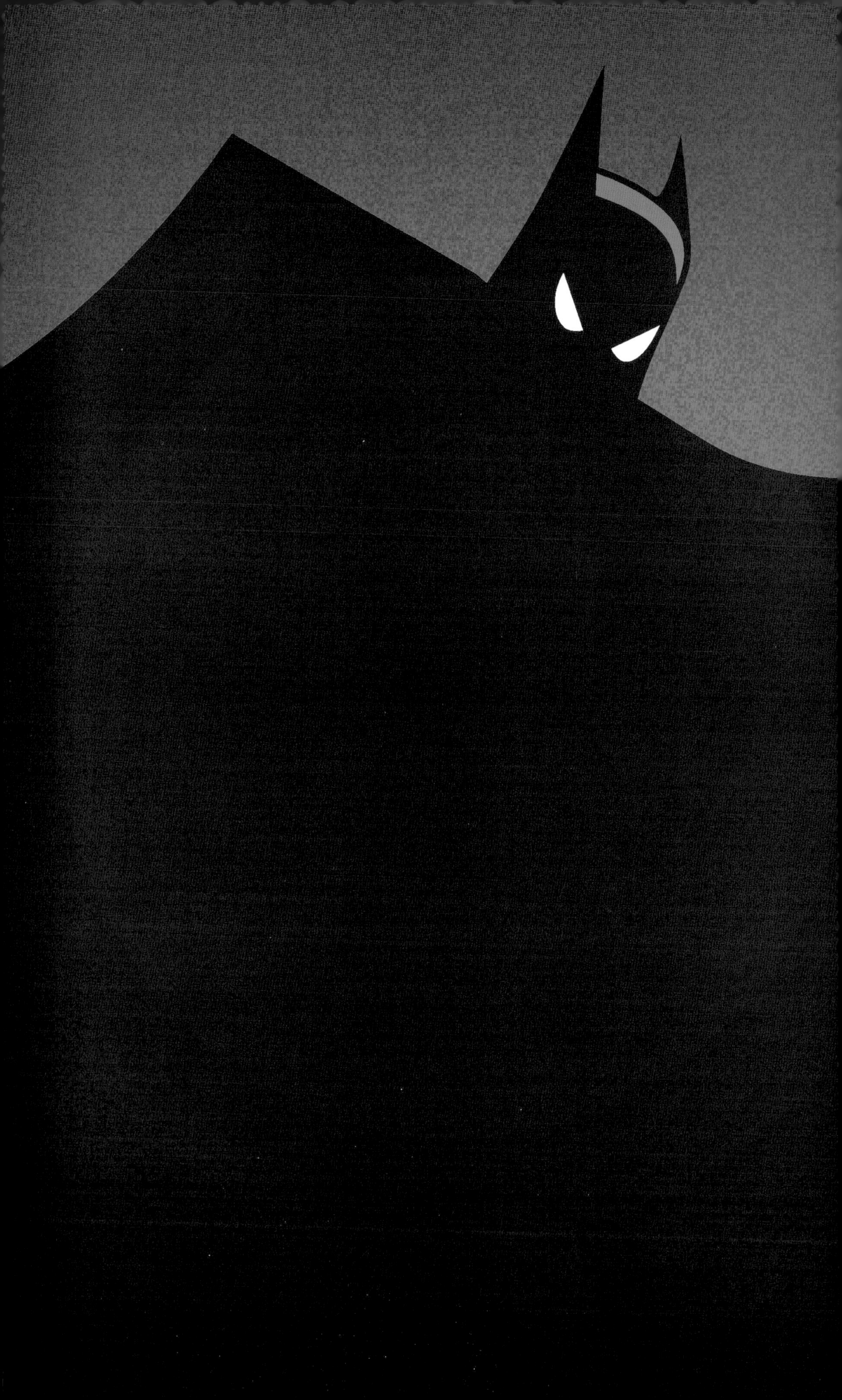

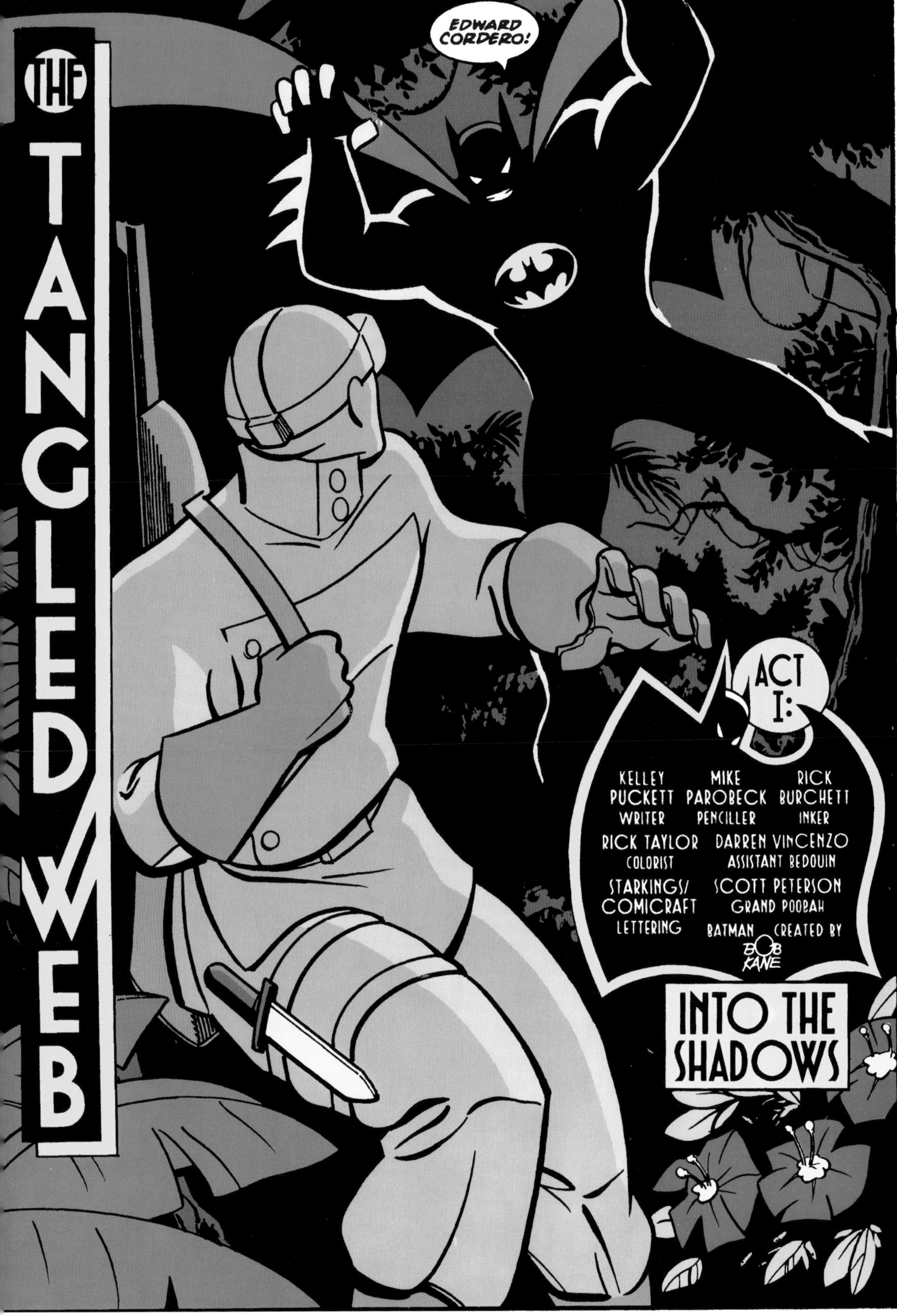

EDWARD CORDERO!
THE TANGLED WEB
ACT I:
KELLEY PUCKETT WRITER
MIKE PAROBECK PENCILLER
RICK BURCHETT INKER
RICK TAYLOR COLORIST
DARREN VINCENZO ASSISTANT BEDOUIN
STARKINGS/ COMICRAFT LETTERING
SCOTT PETERSON GRAND POOBAH
BATMAN CREATED BY BOB KANE
INTO THE SHADOWS

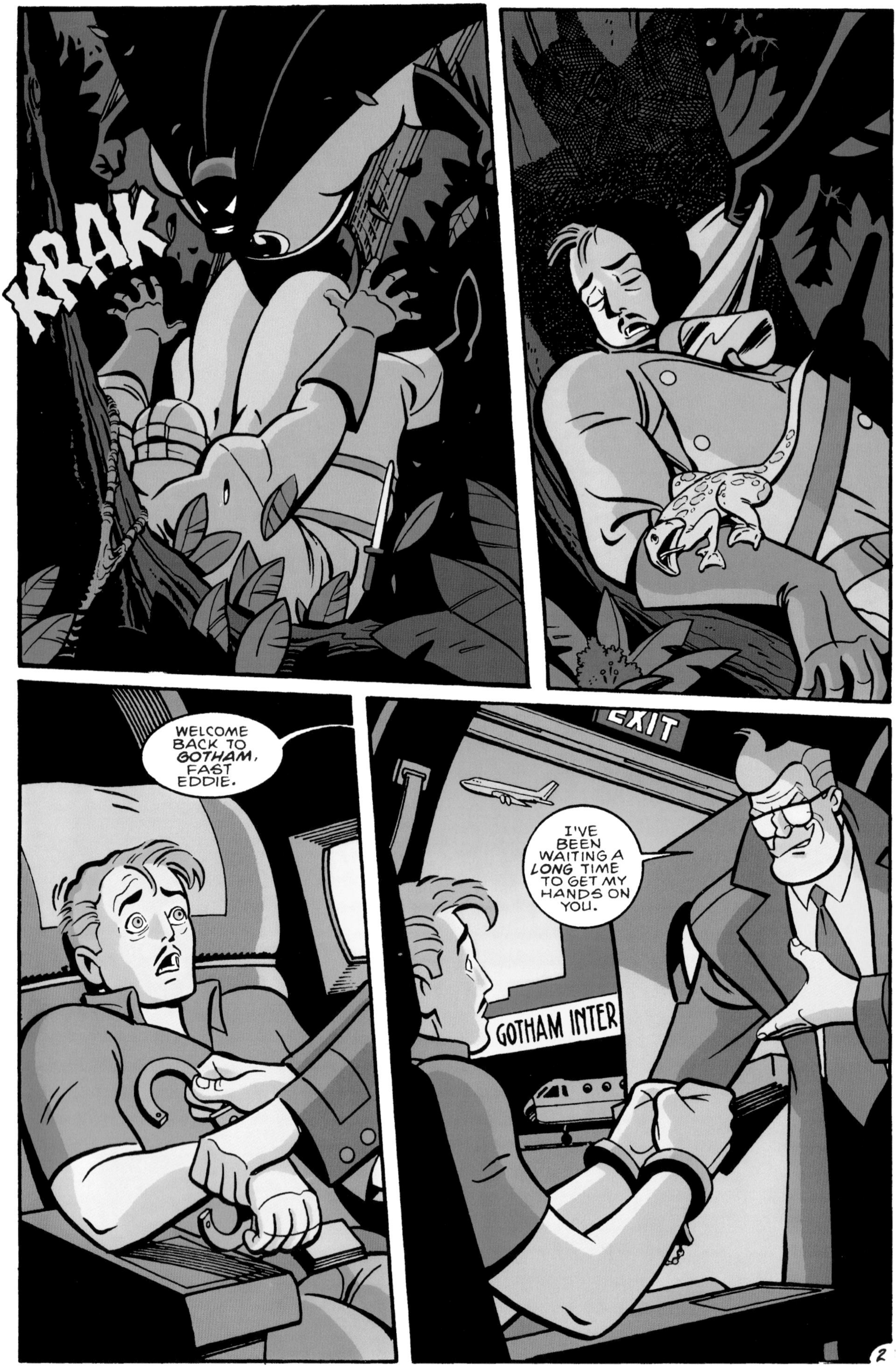
KRAK
WELCOME BACK TO GOTHAM, FAST EDDIE.
EXIT
I'VE BEEN WAITING A LONG TIME TO GET MY HANDS ON YOU.
GOTHAM INTER
2

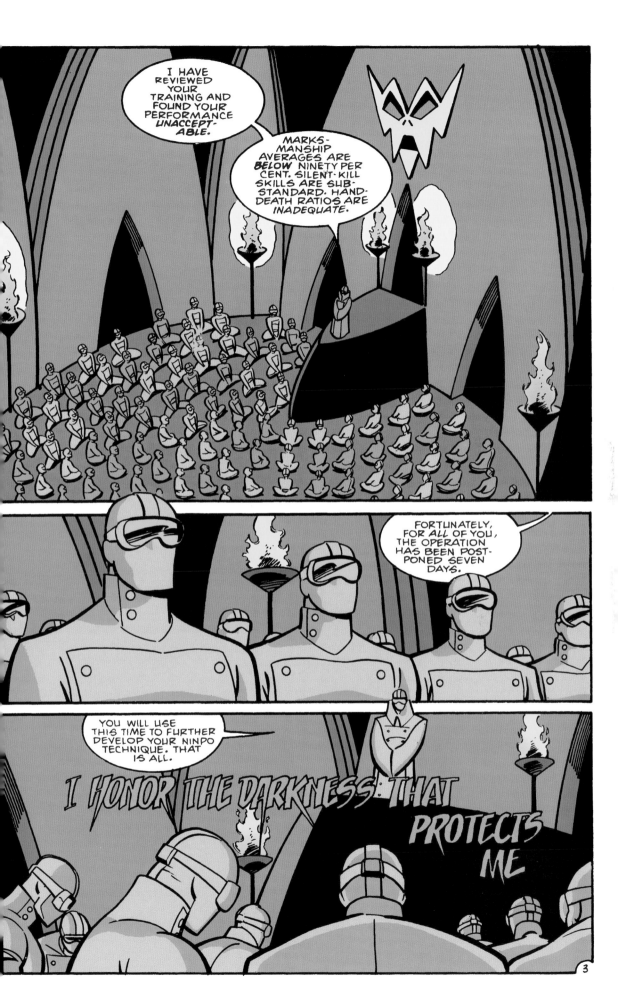

I HAVE REVIEWED YOUR TRAINING AND FOUND YOUR PERFORMANCE *UNACCEPT-ABLE.*

MARKS-MANSHIP AVERAGES ARE *BELOW* NINETY PER CENT. SILENT-KILL SKILLS ARE SUB-STANDARD. HAND-DEATH RATIOS ARE INADEQUATE.

FORTUNATELY, FOR *ALL* OF YOU, THE OPERATION HAS BEEN POST-PONED SEVEN DAYS.

YOU WILL USE THIS TIME TO FURTHER DEVELOP YOUR NINPO TECHNIQUE. THAT IS ALL.

I HONOR THE DARKNESS THAT PROTECTS ME

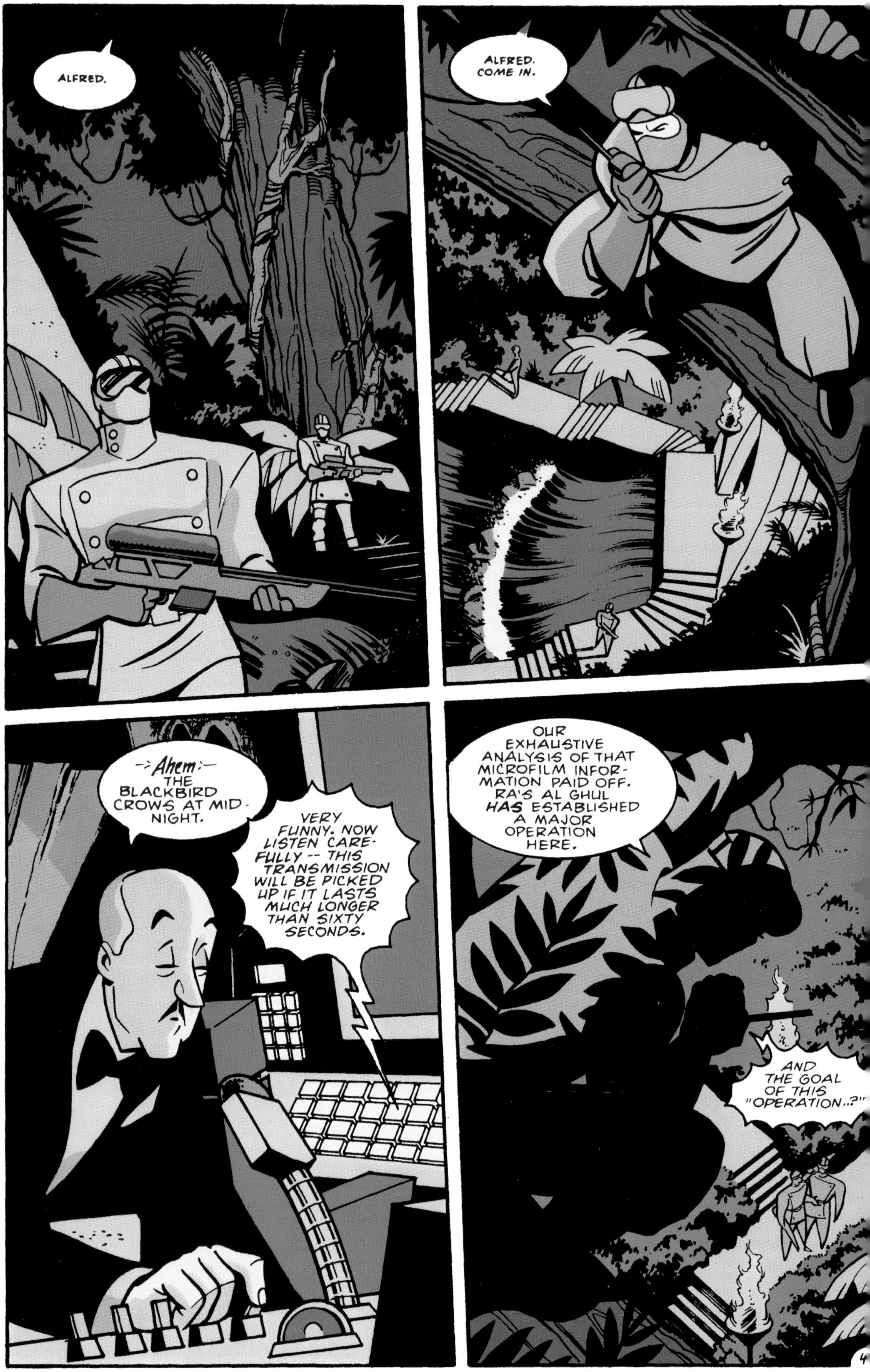

ALFRED.
ALFRED. COME IN.
-:- Ahem -:- THE BLACKBIRD CROWS AT MID-NIGHT.
VERY FUNNY. NOW LISTEN CARE-FULLY -- THIS TRANSMISSION WILL BE PICKED UP IF IT LASTS MUCH LONGER THAN SIXTY SECONDS.
OUR EXHAUSTIVE ANALYSIS OF THAT MICROFILM INFOR-MATION PAID OFF. RA'S AL GHUL HAS ESTABLISHED A MAJOR OPERATION HERE.
AND THE GOAL OF THIS "OPERATION..?"
4

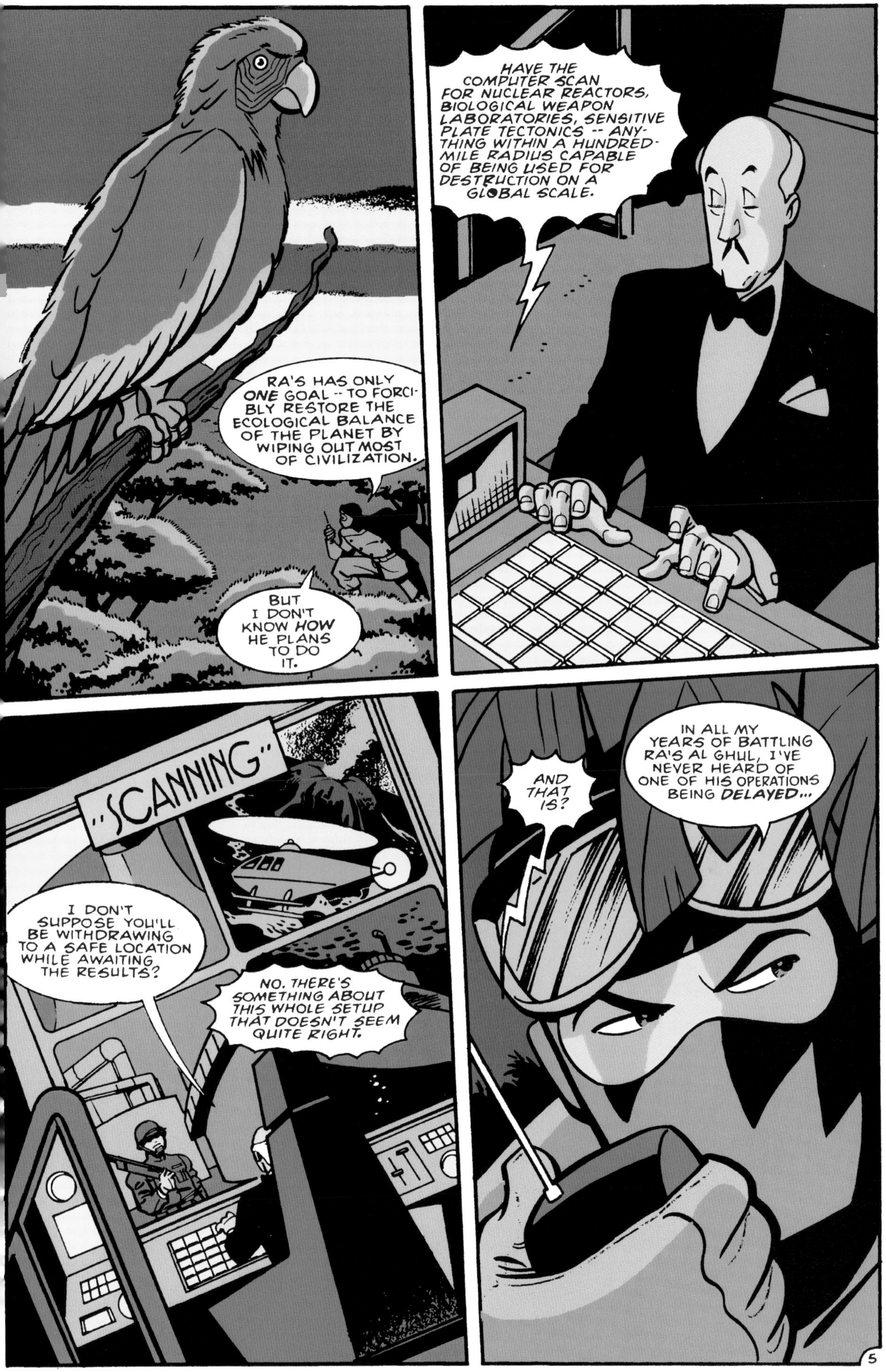
HAVE THE COMPUTER SCAN FOR NUCLEAR REACTORS, BIOLOGICAL WEAPON LABORATORIES, SENSITIVE PLATE TECTONICS -- ANYTHING WITHIN A HUNDRED-MILE RADIUS CAPABLE OF BEING USED FOR DESTRUCTION ON A GLOBAL SCALE.
RA'S HAS ONLY ONE GOAL -- TO FORCIBLY RESTORE THE ECOLOGICAL BALANCE OF THE PLANET BY WIPING OUT MOST OF CIVILIZATION.
BUT I DON'T KNOW HOW HE PLANS TO DO IT.
"SCANNING"
I DON'T SUPPOSE YOU'LL BE WITHDRAWING TO A SAFE LOCATION WHILE AWAITING THE RESULTS?
NO. THERE'S SOMETHING ABOUT THIS WHOLE SETUP THAT DOESN'T SEEM QUITE RIGHT.
AND THAT IS?
IN ALL MY YEARS OF BATTLING RA'S AL GHUL, I'VE NEVER HEARD OF ONE OF HIS OPERATIONS BEING DELAYED...
5

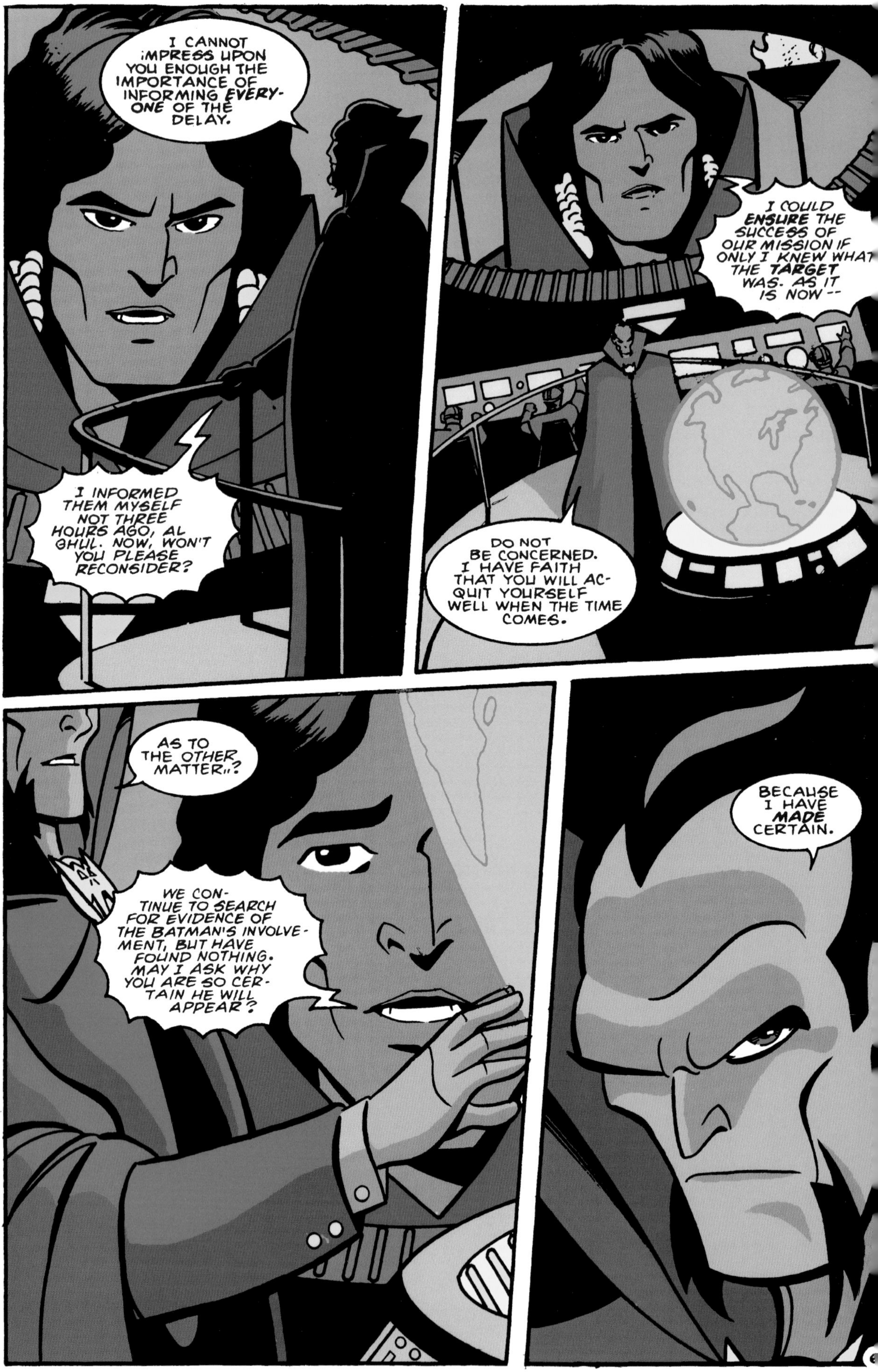
I CANNOT IMPRESS UPON YOU ENOUGH THE IMPORTANCE OF INFORMING EVERY-ONE OF THE DELAY.
I INFORMED THEM MYSELF NOT THREE HOURS AGO, AL GHUL. NOW, WON'T YOU PLEASE RECONSIDER?
I COULD ENSURE THE SUCCESS OF OUR MISSION IF ONLY I KNEW WHAT THE TARGET WAS. AS IT IS NOW --
DO NOT BE CONCERNED. I HAVE FAITH THAT YOU WILL AC-QUIT YOURSELF WELL WHEN THE TIME COMES.
AS TO THE OTHER MATTER..?
WE CON-TINUE TO SEARCH FOR EVIDENCE OF THE BATMAN'S INVOLVE-MENT, BUT HAVE FOUND NOTHING. MAY I ASK WHY YOU ARE SO CER-TAIN HE WILL APPEAR?
BECAUSE I HAVE MADE CERTAIN.

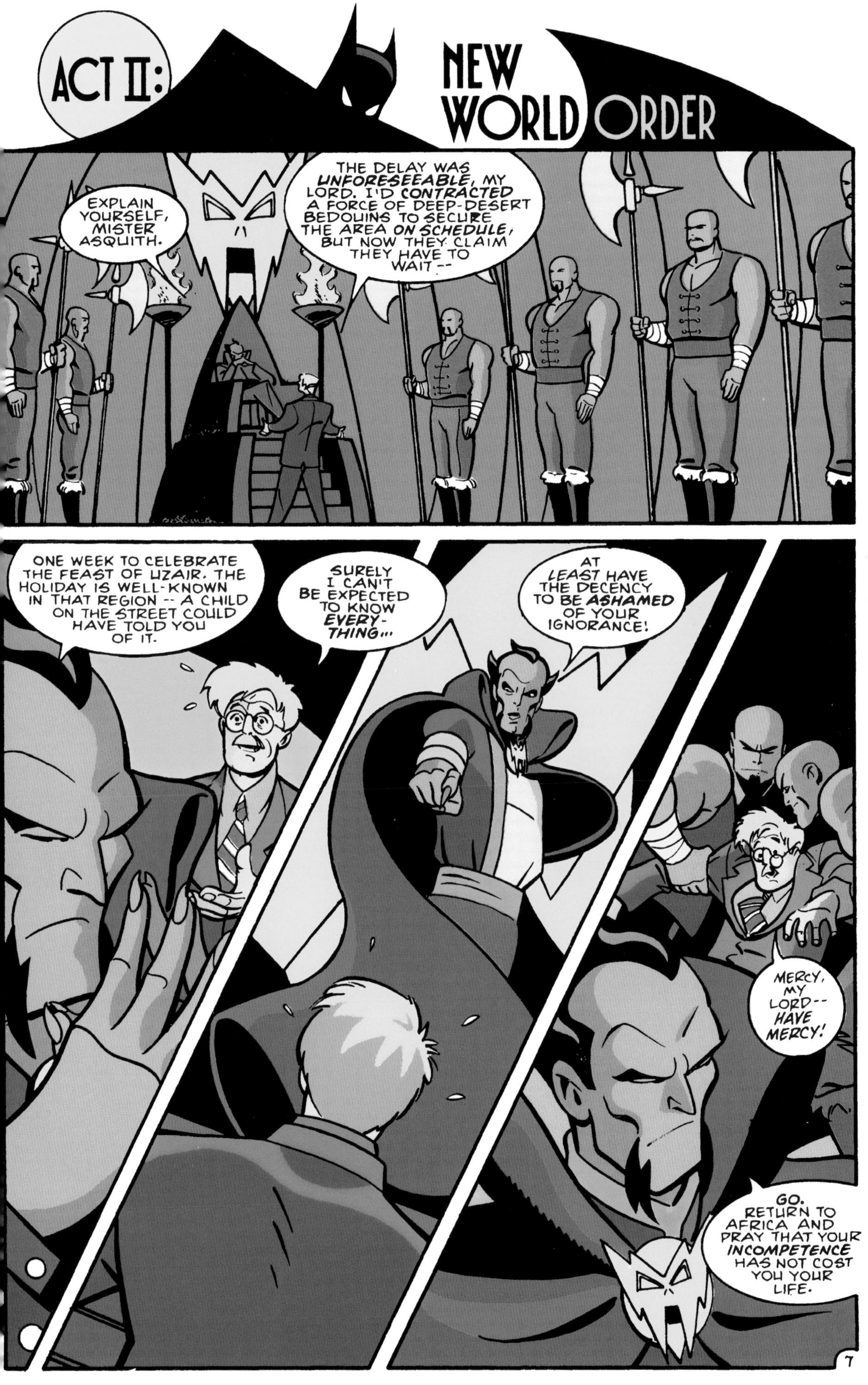
ACT II: NEW WORLD ORDER
EXPLAIN YOURSELF, MISTER ASQUITH.
THE DELAY WAS UNFORESEEABLE, MY LORD. I'D CONTRACTED A FORCE OF DEEP-DESERT BEDOUINS TO SECURE THE AREA ON SCHEDULE, BUT NOW THEY CLAIM THEY HAVE TO WAIT --
ONE WEEK TO CELEBRATE THE FEAST OF UZAIR. THE HOLIDAY IS WELL-KNOWN IN THAT REGION -- A CHILD ON THE STREET COULD HAVE TOLD YOU OF IT.
SURELY I CAN'T BE EXPECTED TO KNOW EVERYTHING...
AT LEAST HAVE THE DECENCY TO BE ASHAMED OF YOUR IGNORANCE!
MERCY, MY LORD-- HAVE MERCY!
GO. RETURN TO AFRICA AND PRAY THAT YOUR INCOMPETENCE HAS NOT COST YOU YOUR LIFE.
7

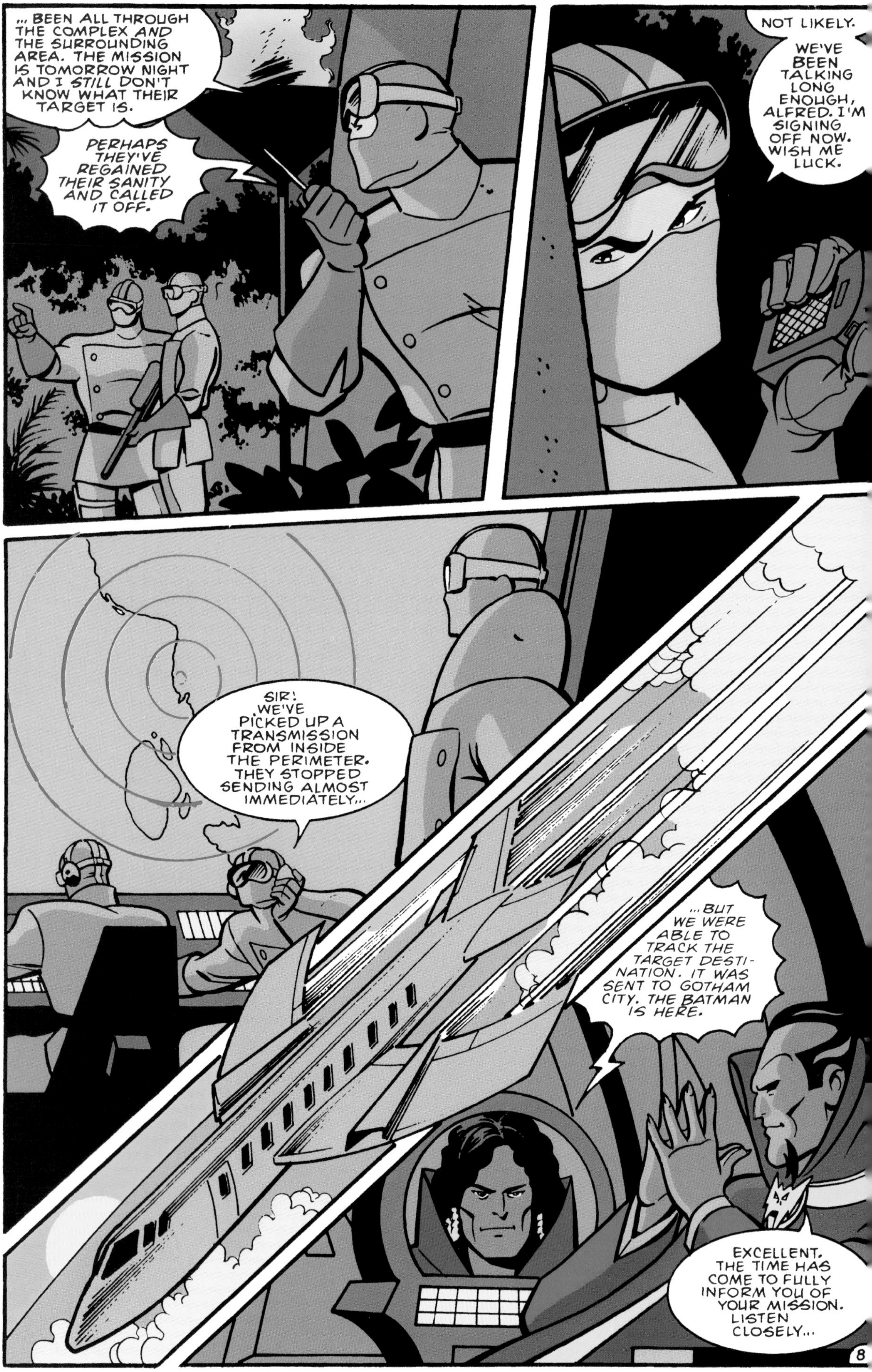

... BEEN ALL THROUGH THE COMPLEX AND THE SURROUNDING AREA. THE MISSION IS TOMORROW NIGHT AND I STILL DON'T KNOW WHAT THEIR TARGET IS.
PERHAPS THEY'VE REGAINED THEIR SANITY AND CALLED IT OFF.
NOT LIKELY.
WE'VE BEEN TALKING LONG ENOUGH, ALFRED. I'M SIGNING OFF NOW. WISH ME LUCK.
SIR! WE'VE PICKED UP A TRANSMISSION FROM INSIDE THE PERIMETER. THEY STOPPED SENDING ALMOST IMMEDIATELY...
...BUT WE WERE ABLE TO TRACK THE TARGET DESTI- NATION. IT WAS SENT TO GOTHAM CITY. THE BATMAN IS HERE.
EXCELLENT. THE TIME HAS COME TO FULLY INFORM YOU OF YOUR MISSION. LISTEN CLOSELY...
8

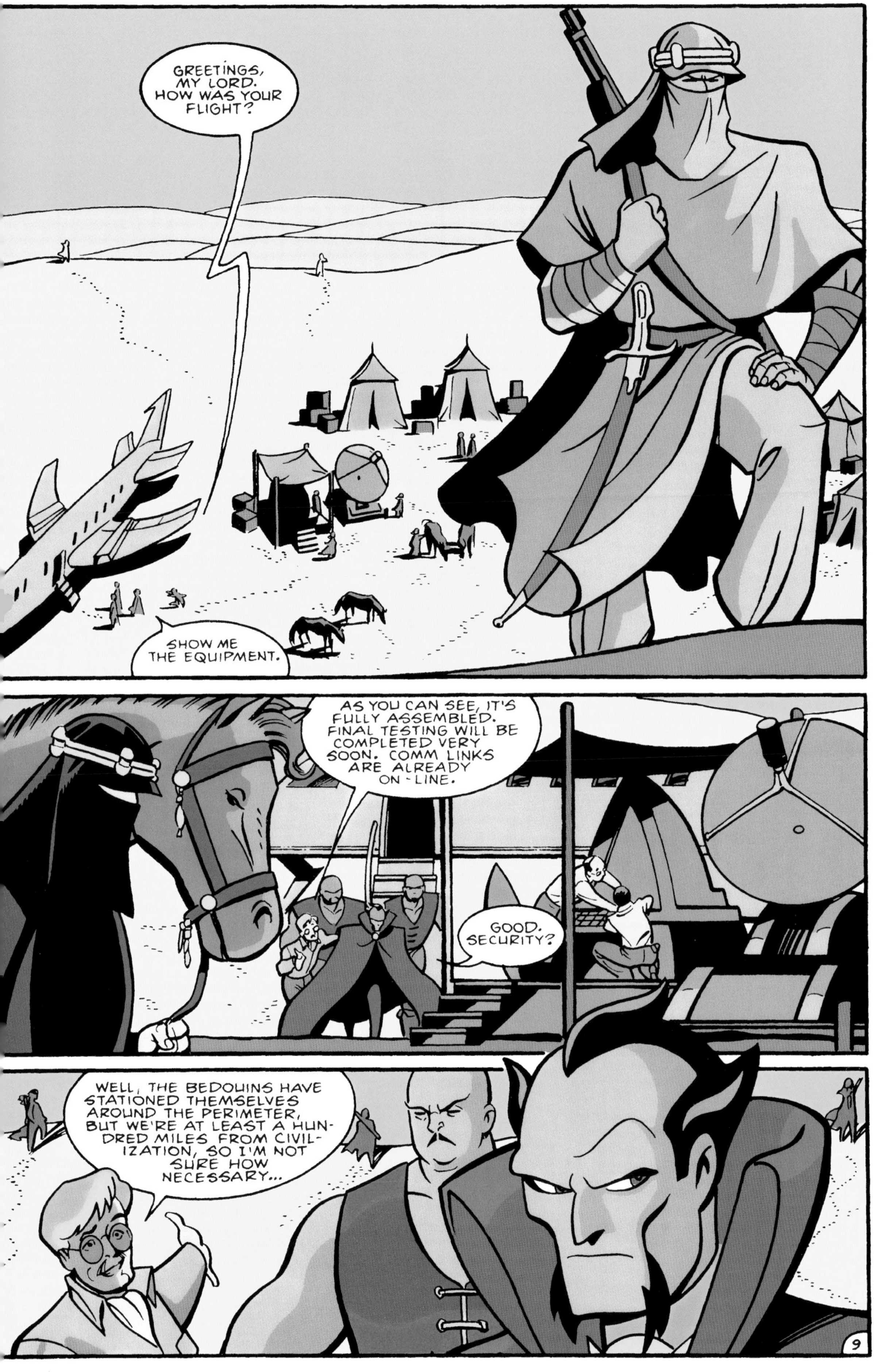

GREETINGS, MY LORD. HOW WAS YOUR FLIGHT?
SHOW ME THE EQUIPMENT.
AS YOU CAN SEE, IT'S FULLY ASSEMBLED. FINAL TESTING WILL BE COMPLETED VERY SOON. COMM LINKS ARE ALREADY ON-LINE.
GOOD. SECURITY?
WELL, THE BEDOUINS HAVE STATIONED THEMSELVES AROUND THE PERIMETER, BUT WE'RE AT LEAST A HUNDRED MILES FROM CIVILIZATION, SO I'M NOT SURE HOW NECESSARY...
9

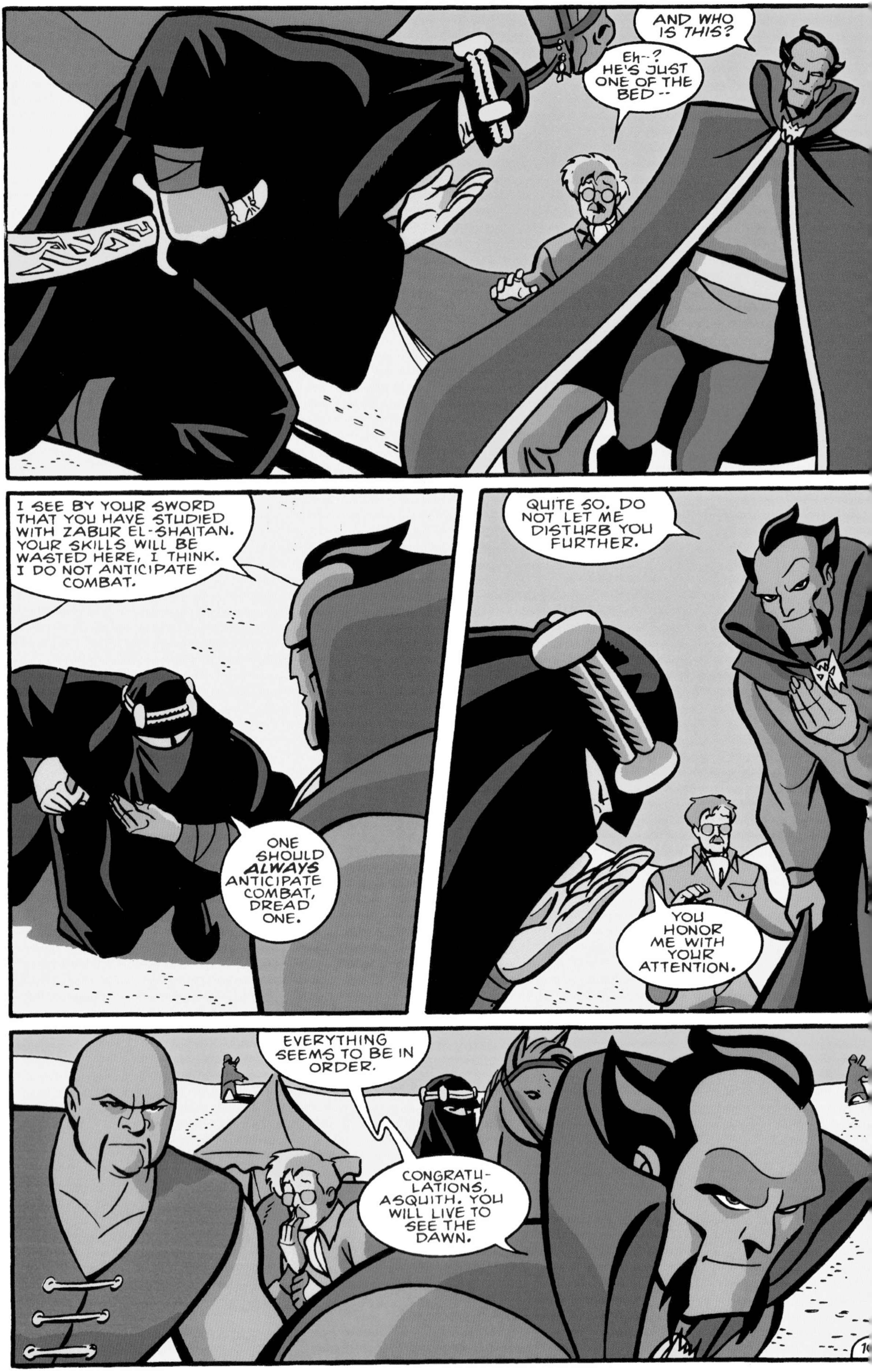
AND WHO IS THIS?
Eh--? HE'S JUST ONE OF THE BED --
I SEE BY YOUR SWORD THAT YOU HAVE STUDIED WITH ZABUR EL-SHAITAN. YOUR SKILLS WILL BE WASTED HERE, I THINK. I DO NOT ANTICIPATE COMBAT.
ONE SHOULD ALWAYS ANTICIPATE COMBAT, DREAD ONE.
QUITE SO. DO NOT LET ME DISTURB YOU FURTHER.
YOU HONOR ME WITH YOUR ATTENTION.
EVERYTHING SEEMS TO BE IN ORDER.
CONGRATU-LATIONS, ASQUITH. YOU WILL LIVE TO SEE THE DAWN.

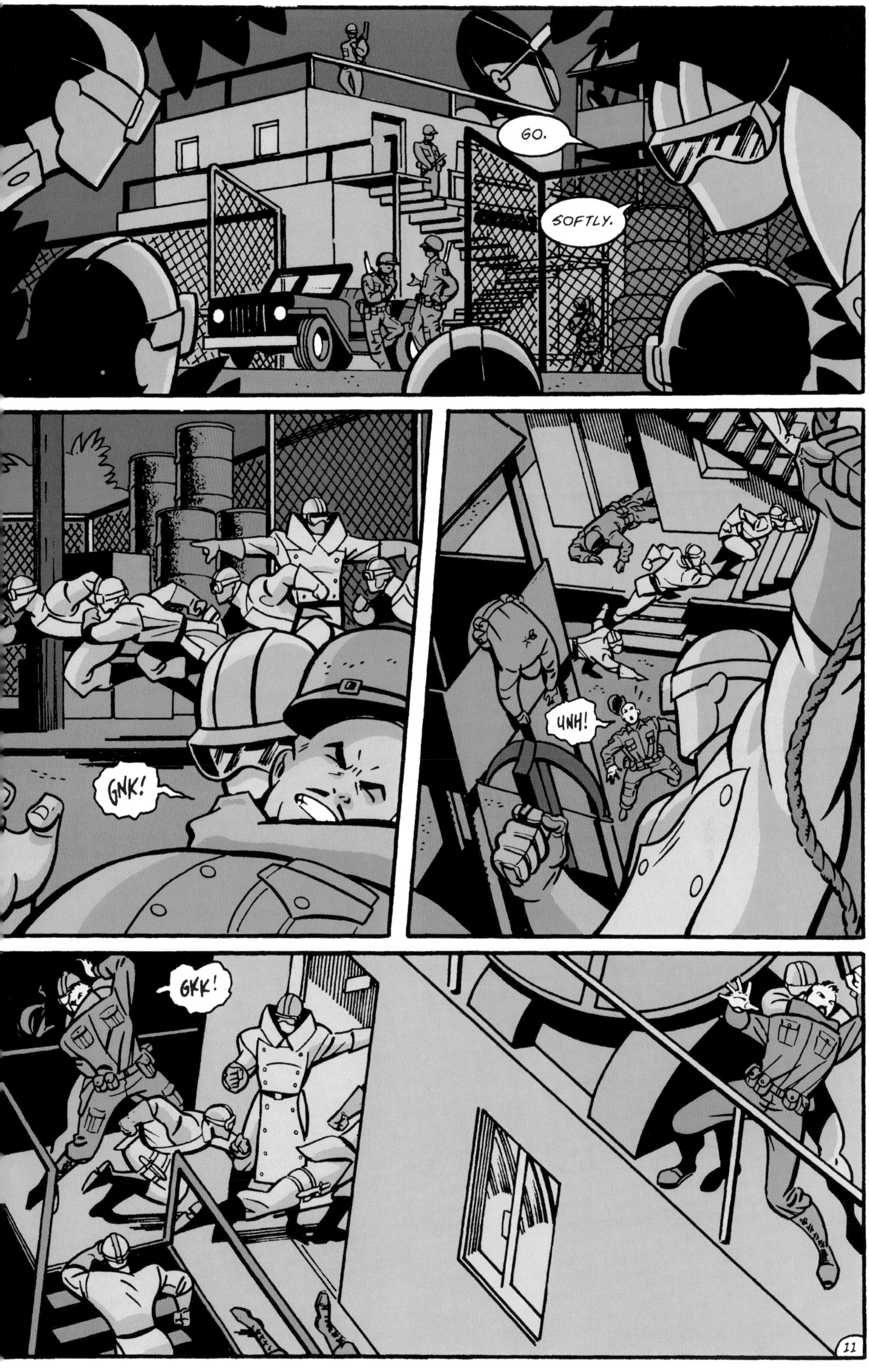
GO.
SOFTLY.
GNK!
UNH!
GKK!
11

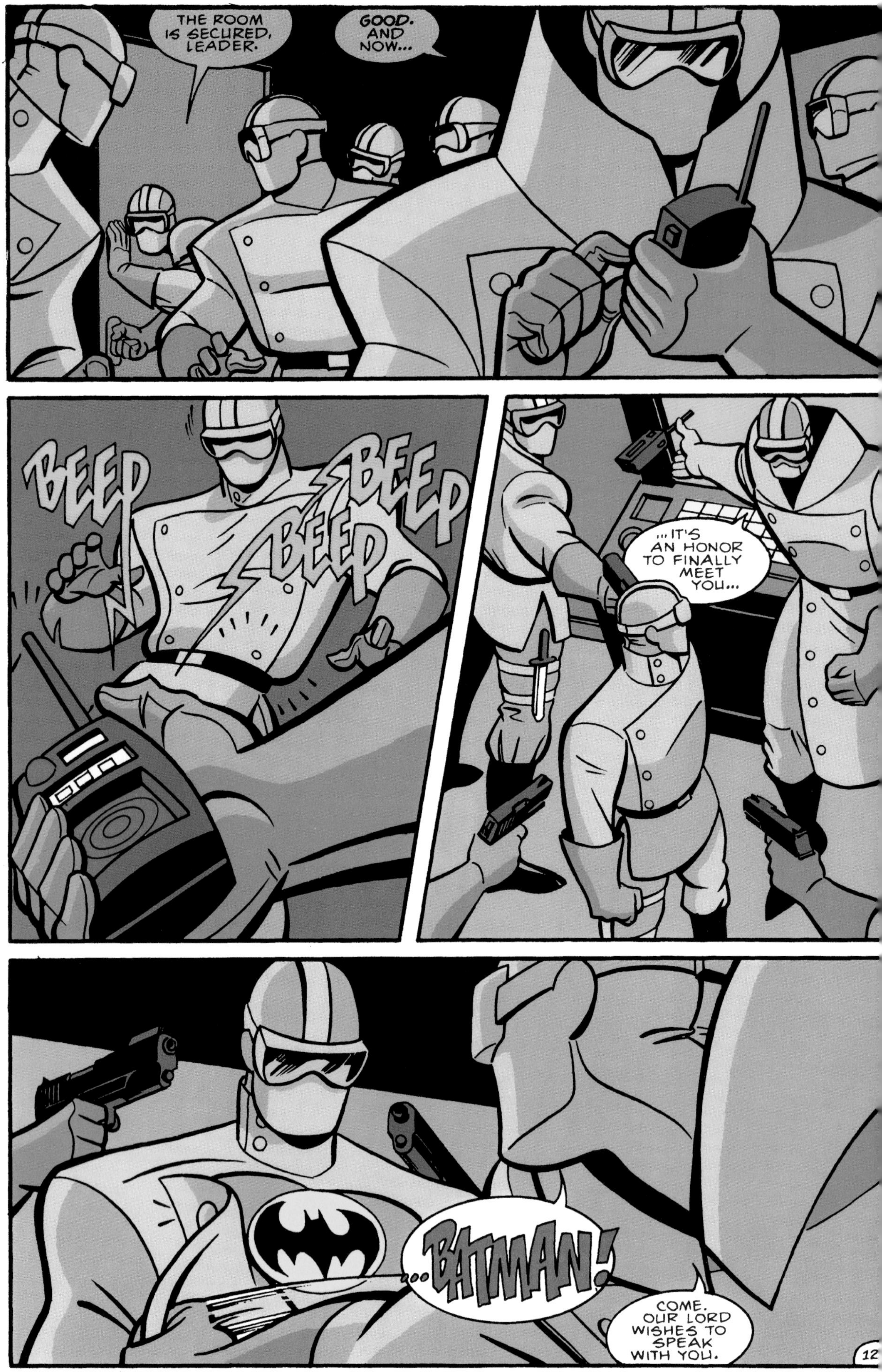
THE ROOM IS SECURED, LEADER.
GOOD. AND NOW...
BEEP
BEEP
BEEP
...IT'S AN HONOR TO FINALLY MEET YOU...
...BATMAN!
COME. OUR LORD WISHES TO SPEAK WITH YOU.
12

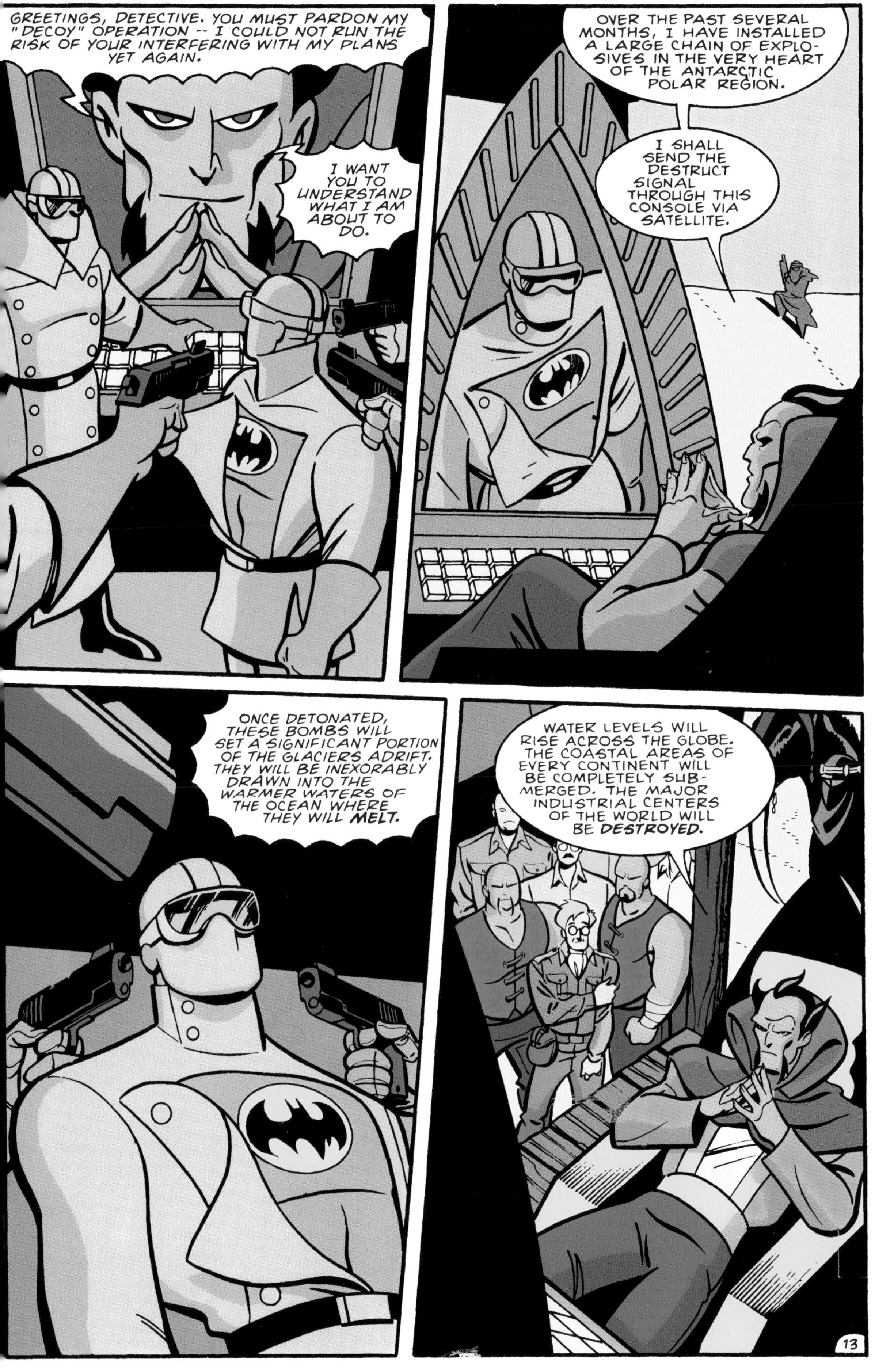
GREETINGS, DETECTIVE. YOU MUST PARDON MY "DECOY" OPERATION -- I COULD NOT RUN THE RISK OF YOUR INTERFERING WITH MY PLANS YET AGAIN.
I WANT YOU TO UNDERSTAND WHAT I AM ABOUT TO DO.
OVER THE PAST SEVERAL MONTHS, I HAVE INSTALLED A LARGE CHAIN OF EXPLOSIVES IN THE VERY HEART OF THE ANTARCTIC POLAR REGION.
I SHALL SEND THE DESTRUCT SIGNAL THROUGH THIS CONSOLE VIA SATELLITE.
ONCE DETONATED, THESE BOMBS WILL SET A SIGNIFICANT PORTION OF THE GLACIERS ADRIFT. THEY WILL BE INEXORABLY DRAWN INTO THE WARMER WATERS OF THE OCEAN WHERE THEY WILL MELT.
WATER LEVELS WILL RISE ACROSS THE GLOBE. THE COASTAL AREAS OF EVERY CONTINENT WILL BE COMPLETELY SUBMERGED. THE MAJOR INDUSTRIAL CENTERS OF THE WORLD WILL BE DESTROYED.
13

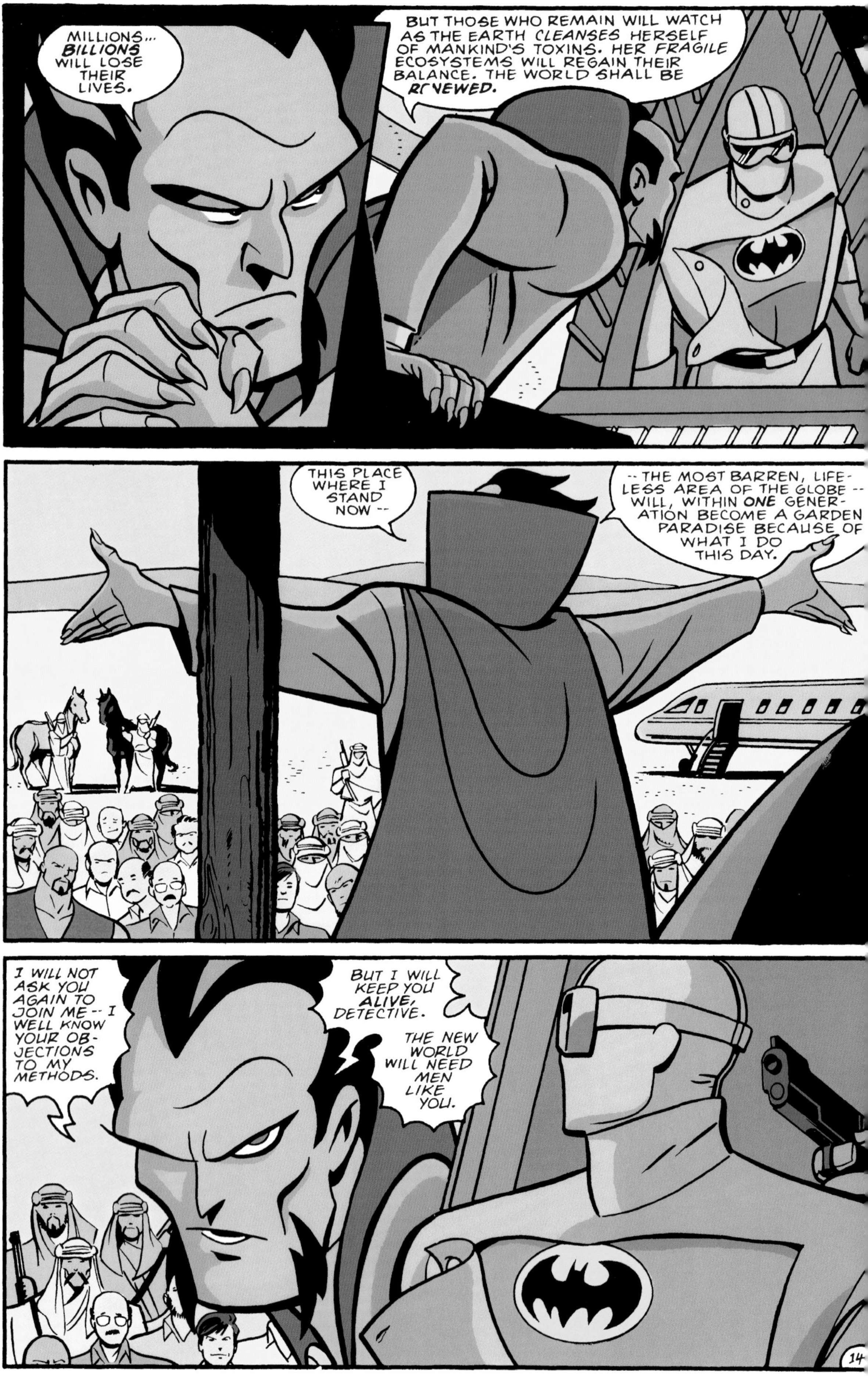
MILLIONS... BILLIONS WILL LOSE THEIR LIVES.
BUT THOSE WHO REMAIN WILL WATCH AS THE EARTH CLEANSES HERSELF OF MANKIND'S TOXINS. HER FRAGILE ECOSYSTEMS WILL REGAIN THEIR BALANCE. THE WORLD SHALL BE RENEWED.
THIS PLACE WHERE I STAND NOW --
-- THE MOST BARREN, LIFELESS AREA OF THE GLOBE -- WILL, WITHIN ONE GENERATION BECOME A GARDEN PARADISE BECAUSE OF WHAT I DO THIS DAY.
I WILL NOT ASK YOU AGAIN TO JOIN ME -- I WELL KNOW YOUR OBJECTIONS TO MY METHODS.
BUT I WILL KEEP YOU ALIVE, DETECTIVE.
THE NEW WORLD WILL NEED MEN LIKE YOU.
14

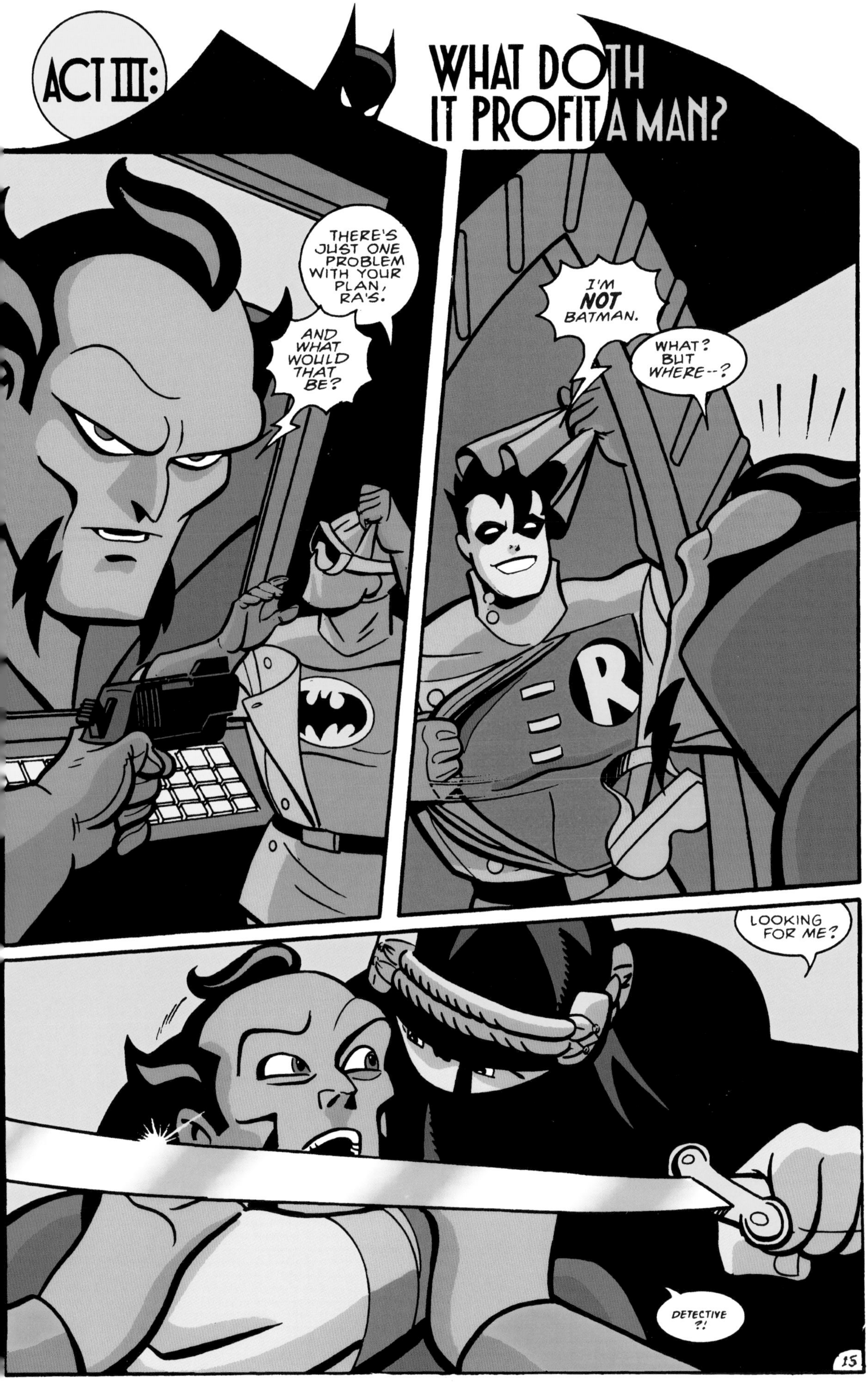
ACT III:
WHAT DOTH IT PROFIT A MAN?
THERE'S JUST ONE PROBLEM WITH YOUR PLAN, RA'S.
AND WHAT WOULD THAT BE?
I'M NOT BATMAN.
WHAT? BUT WHERE--?
LOOKING FOR ME?
DETECTIVE ?!
15

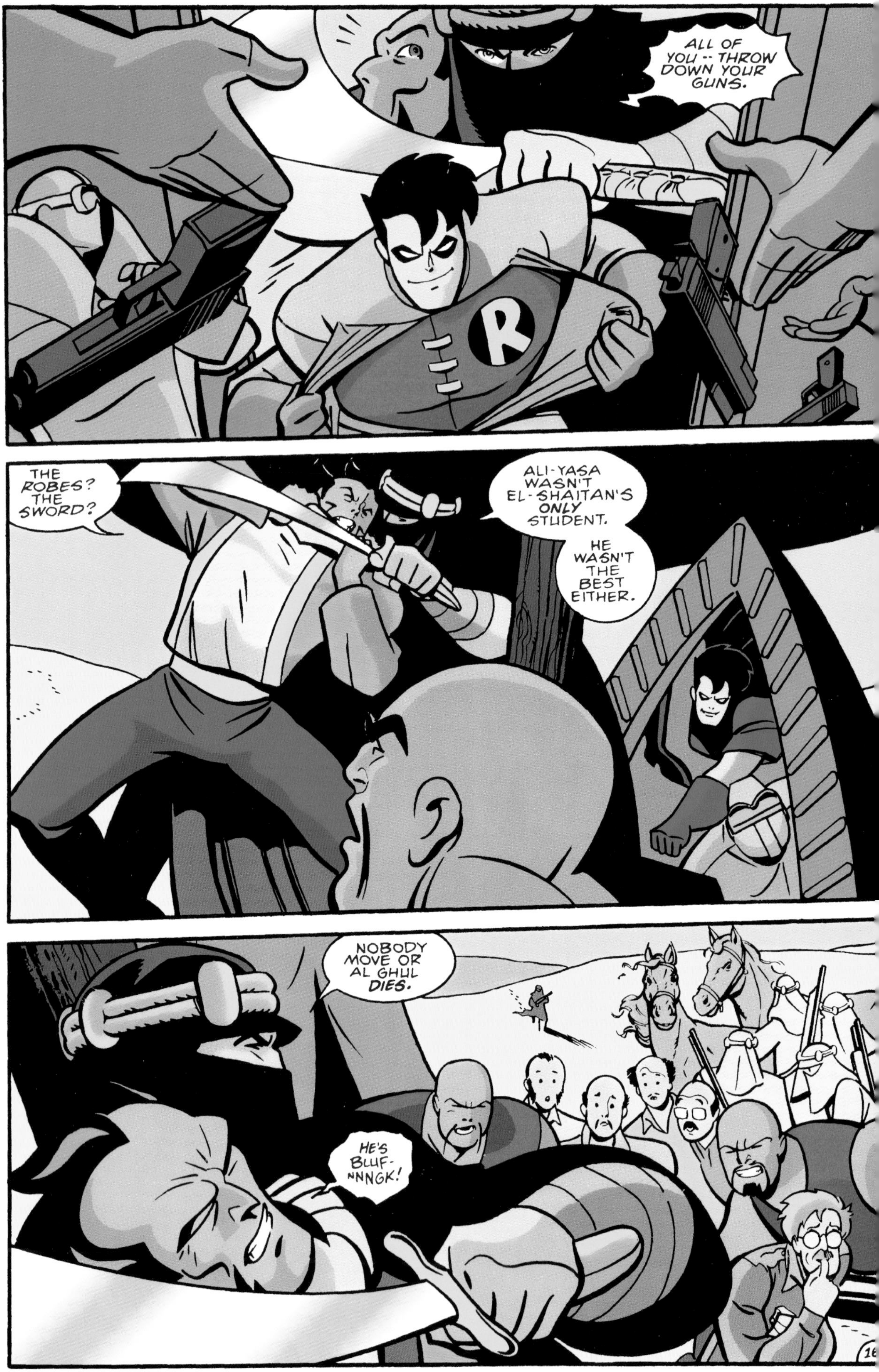
ALL OF YOU -- THROW DOWN YOUR GUNS.
THE ROBES? THE SWORD?
ALI-YASA WASN'T EL-SHAITAN'S ONLY STUDENT.
HE WASN'T THE BEST EITHER.
NOBODY MOVE OR AL GHUL DIES.
HE'S BLUF-NNNGK!

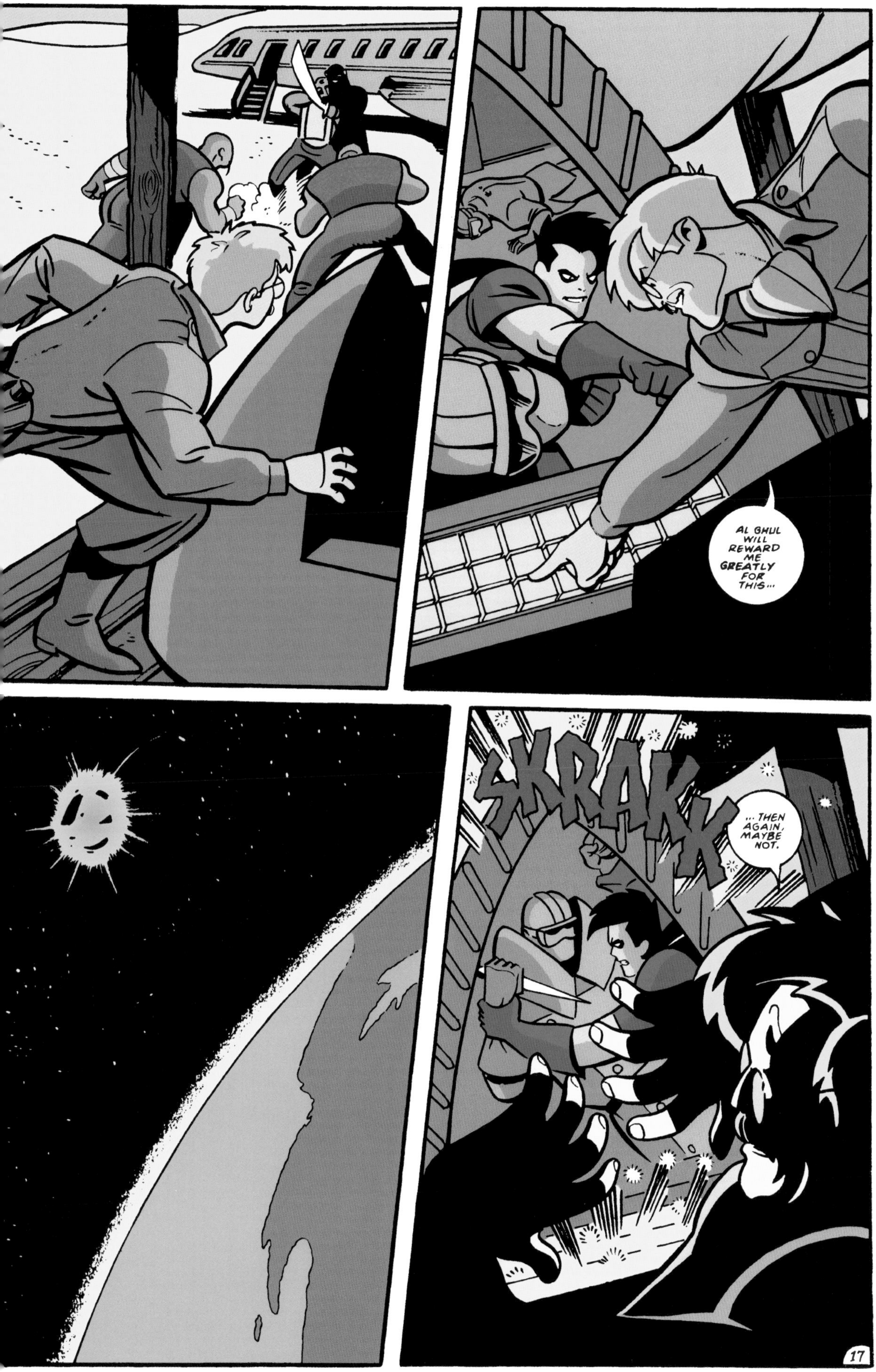

AL GHUL WILL REWARD ME GREATLY FOR THIS...
SKRAKK
...THEN AGAIN, MAYBE NOT.
17

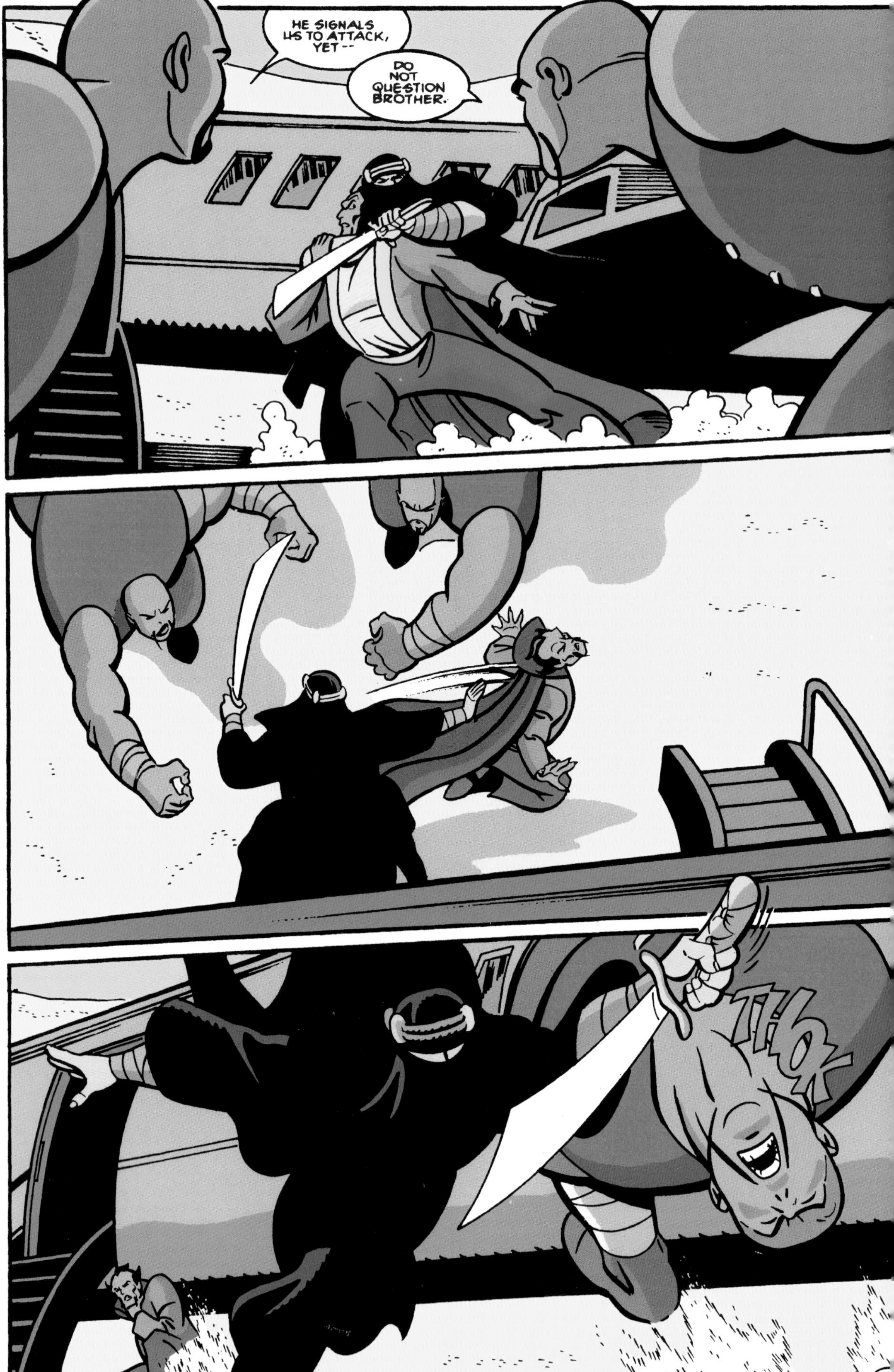
HE SIGNALS US TO ATTACK, YET --
DO NOT QUESTION BROTHER.
THOK
18

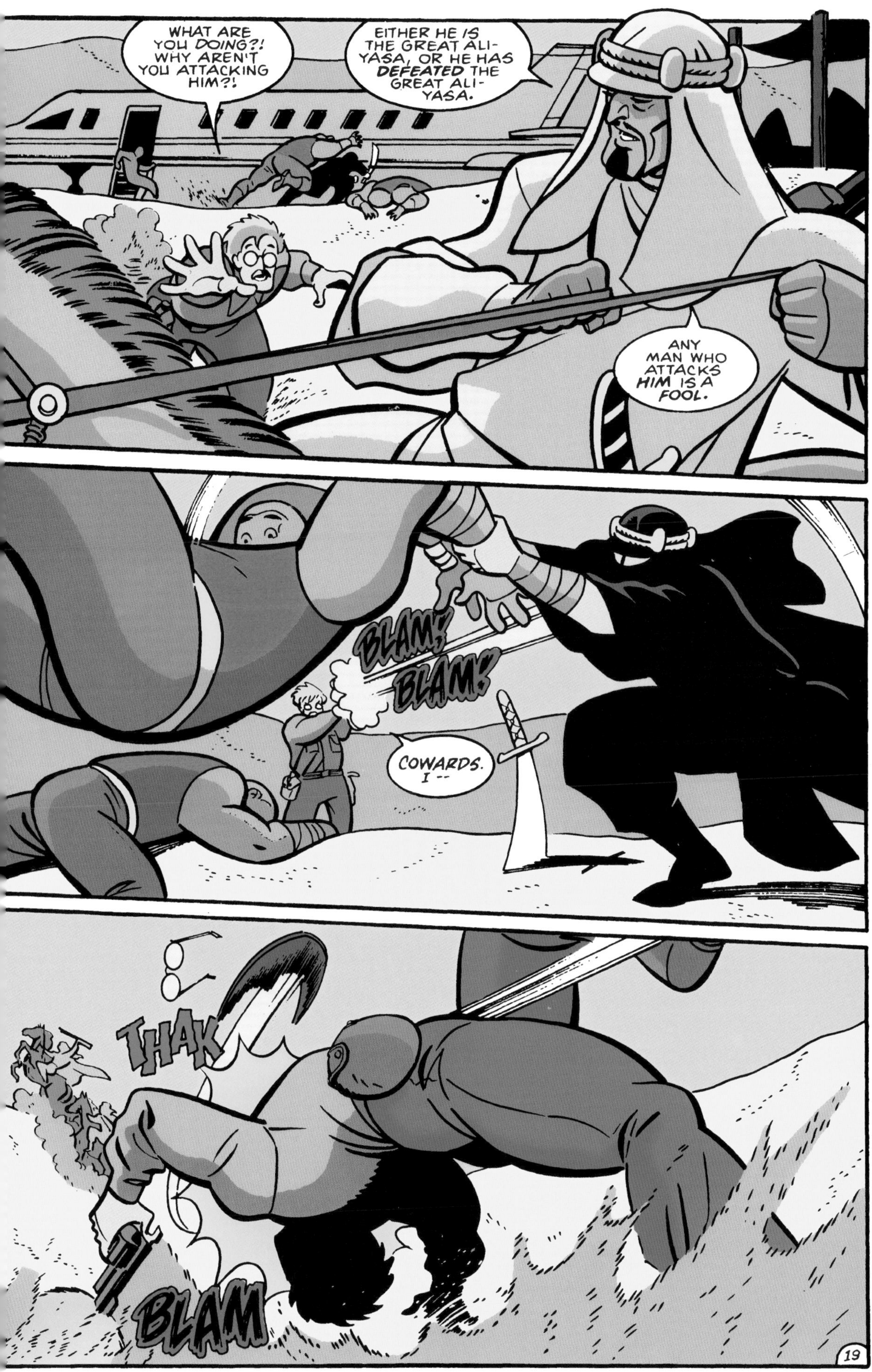
WHAT ARE YOU DOING?! WHY AREN'T YOU ATTACKING HIM?!
EITHER HE IS THE GREAT ALI-YASA, OR HE HAS DEFEATED THE GREAT ALI-YASA.
ANY MAN WHO ATTACKS HIM IS A FOOL.
BLAM!
BLAM!
COWARDS. I --
THAK
BLAM
19

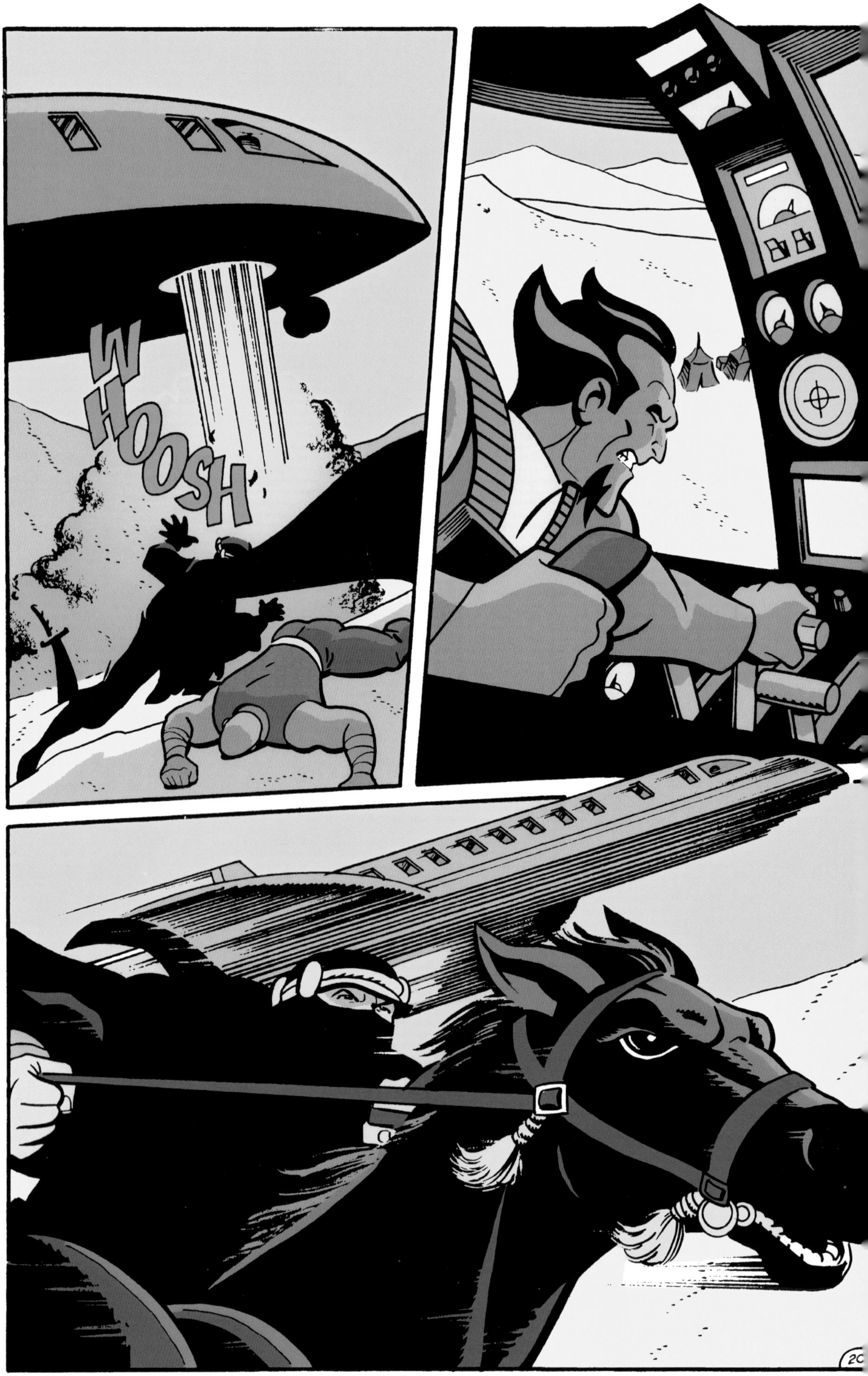
WHOOSH

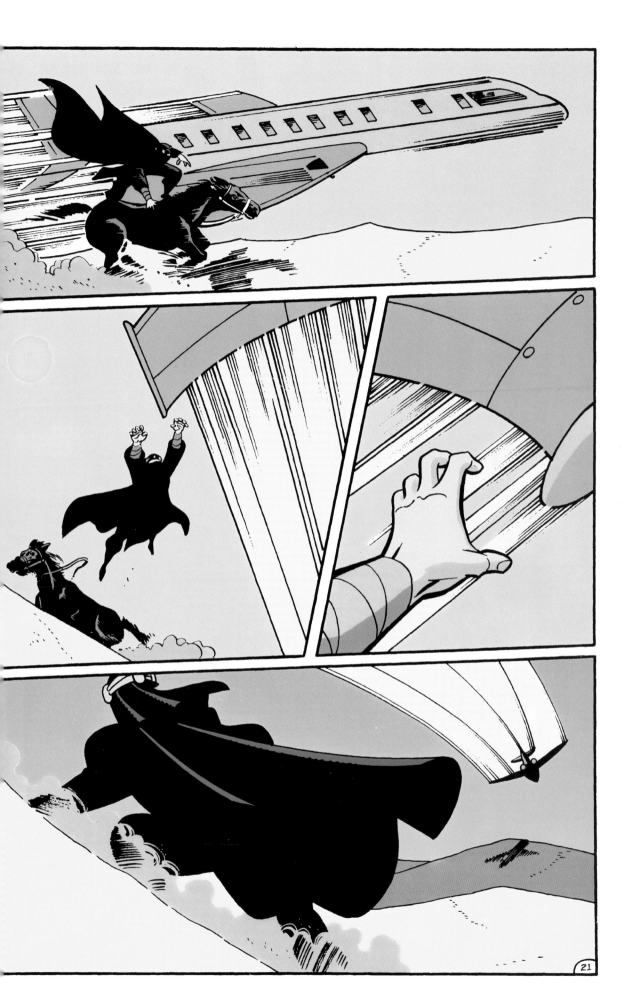

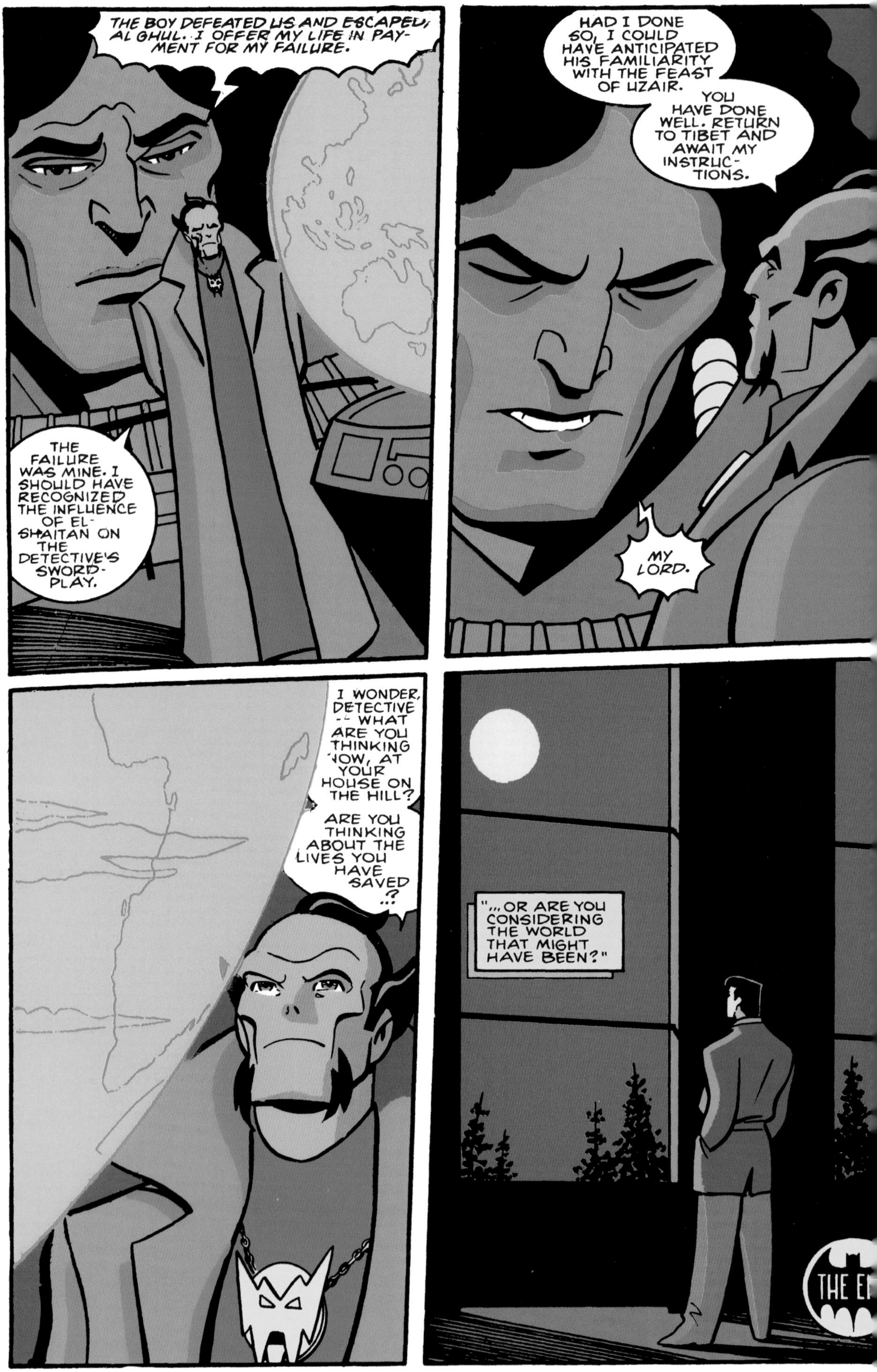
THE BOY DEFEATED US AND ESCAPED, AL GHUL. I OFFER MY LIFE IN PAYMENT FOR MY FAILURE.
THE FAILURE WAS MINE. I SHOULD HAVE RECOGNIZED THE INFLUENCE OF EL-SHAITAN ON THE DETECTIVE'S SWORDPLAY.
HAD I DONE SO, I COULD HAVE ANTICIPATED HIS FAMILIARITY WITH THE FEAST OF UZAIR.
YOU HAVE DONE WELL. RETURN TO TIBET AND AWAIT MY INSTRUCTIONS.
MY LORD.
I WONDER, DETECTIVE -- WHAT ARE YOU THINKING NOW, AT YOUR HOUSE ON THE HILL?
ARE YOU THINKING ABOUT THE LIVES YOU HAVE SAVED ...?
"...OR ARE YOU CONSIDERING THE WORLD THAT MIGHT HAVE BEEN?"

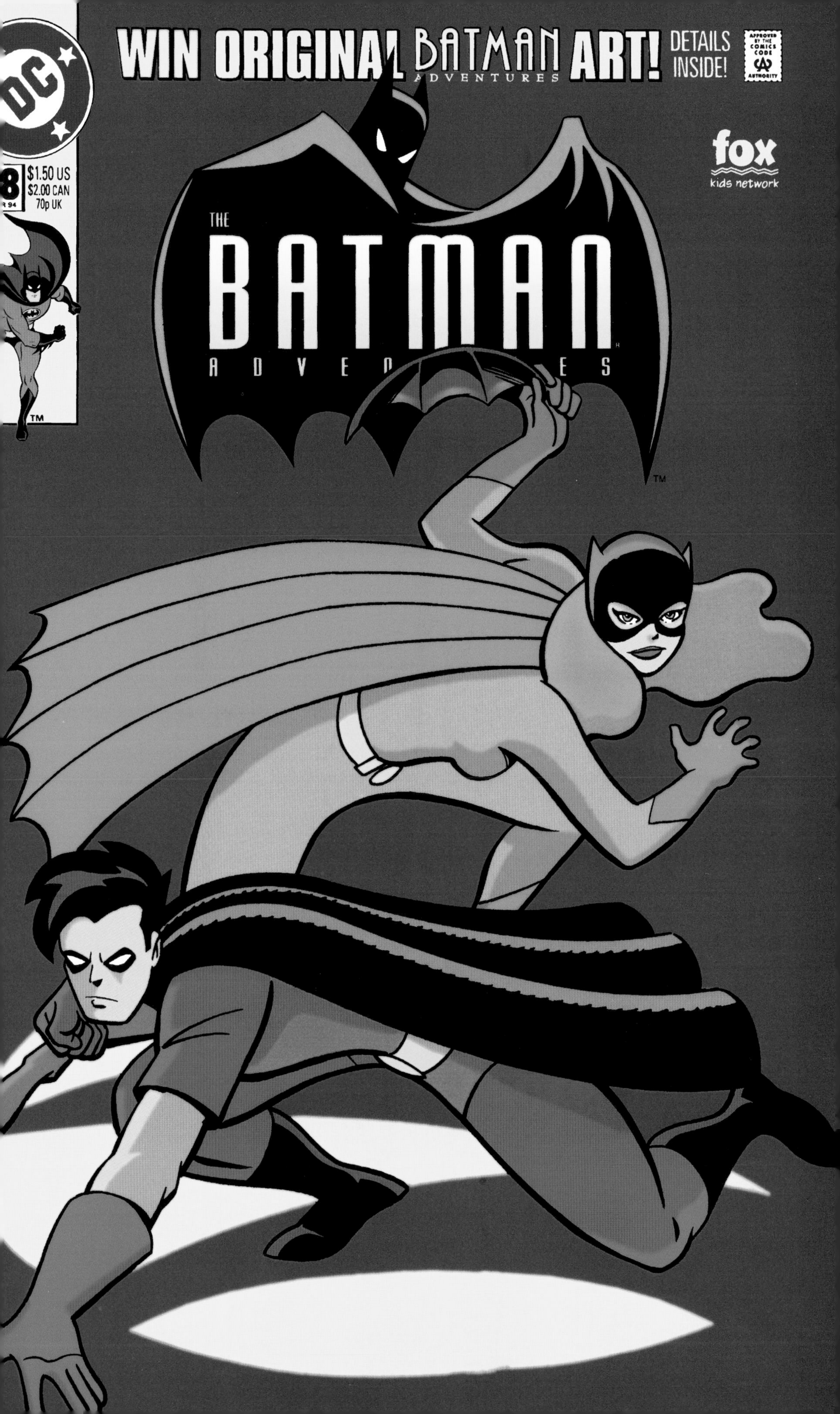
WIN ORIGINAL BATMAN ADVENTURES ART!
DETAILS INSIDE!
APPROVED BY THE COMICS CODE AUTHORITY
DC
$1.50 US
$2.00 CAN
70p UK
fox kids network
THE BATMAN ADVENTURES

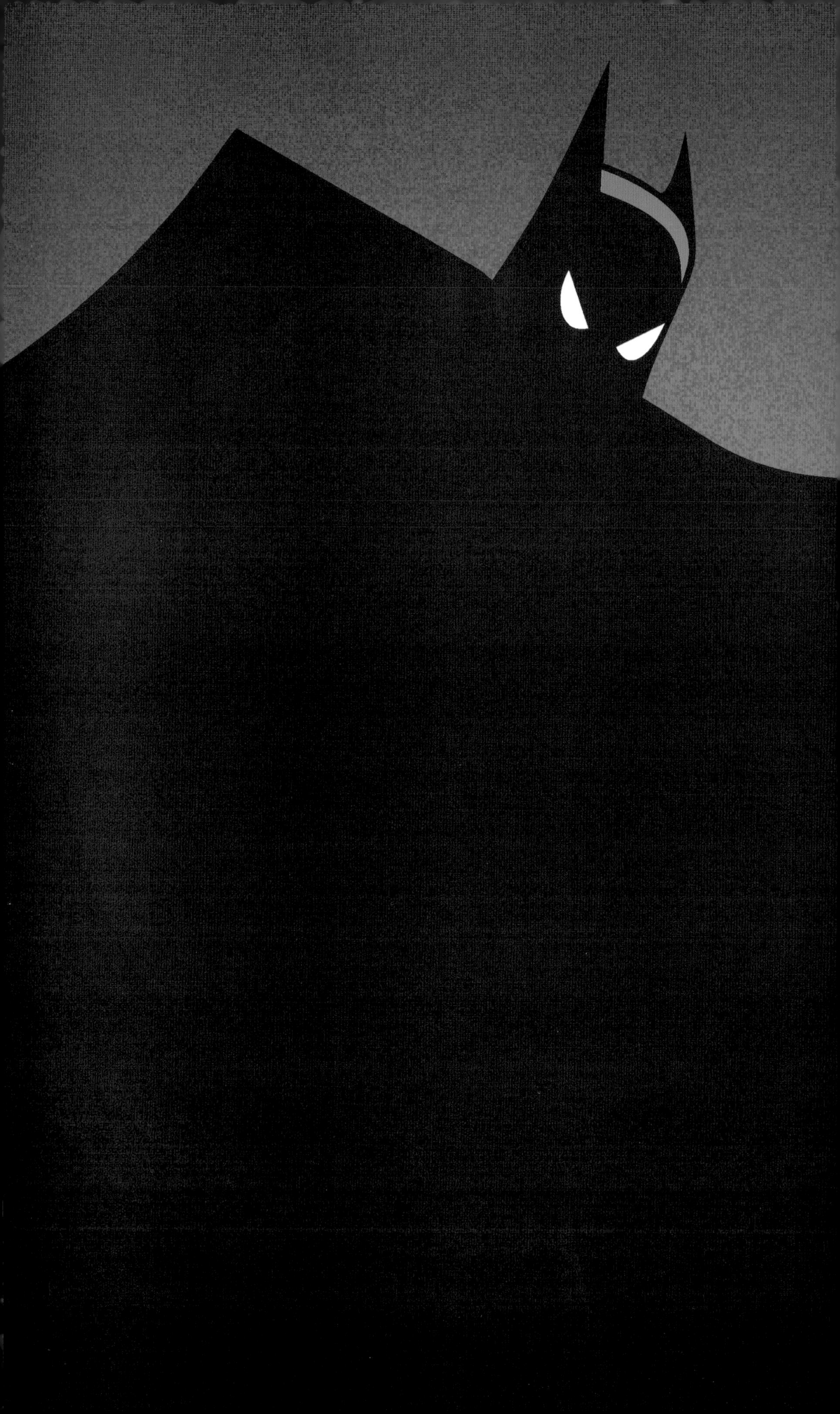

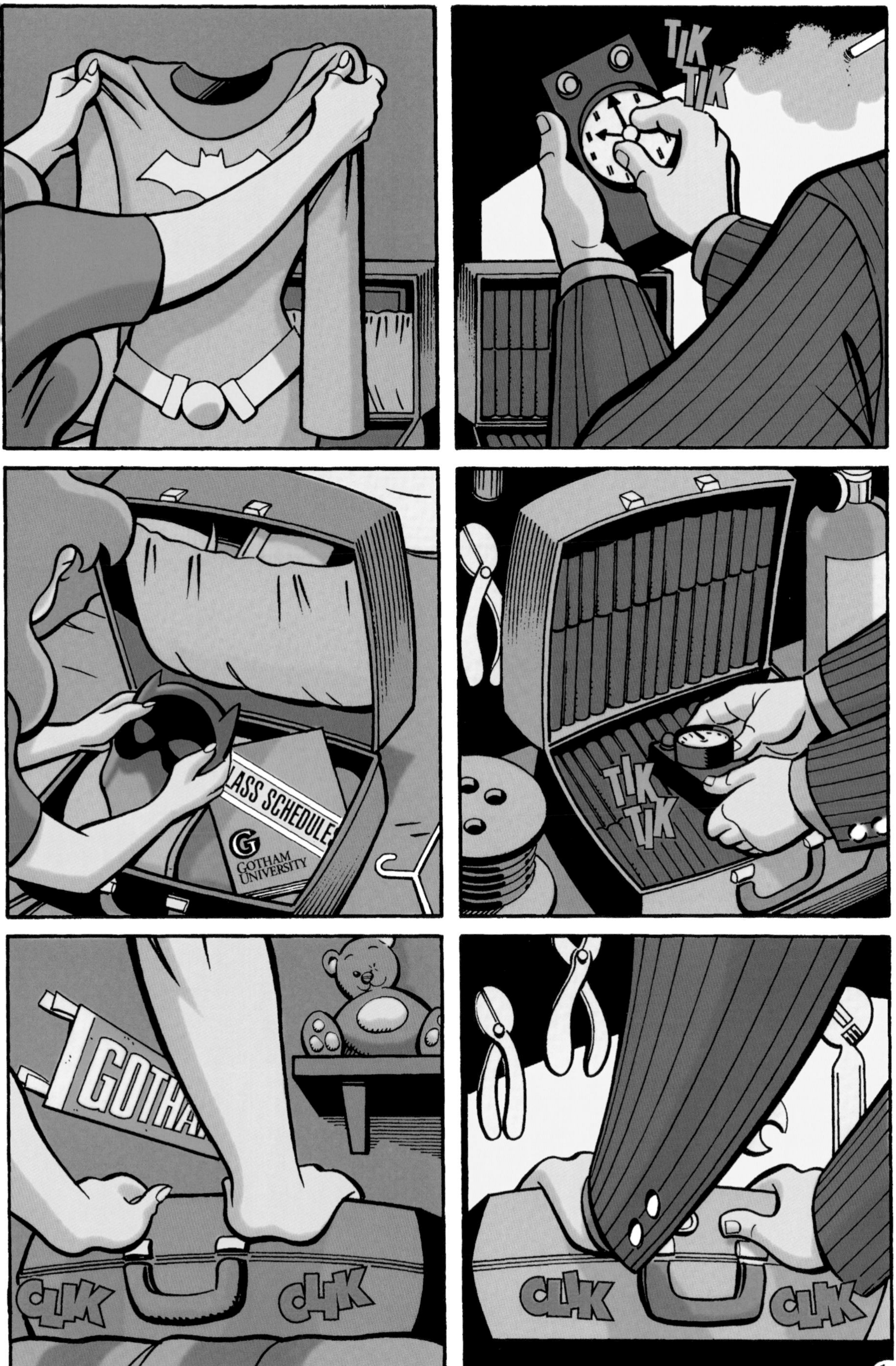
TIK
TIK
CLASS SCHEDULE
GOTHAM UNIVERSITY
TIK
TIK
GOTHA
CLIK
CLIK
CLIK
CLIK
1

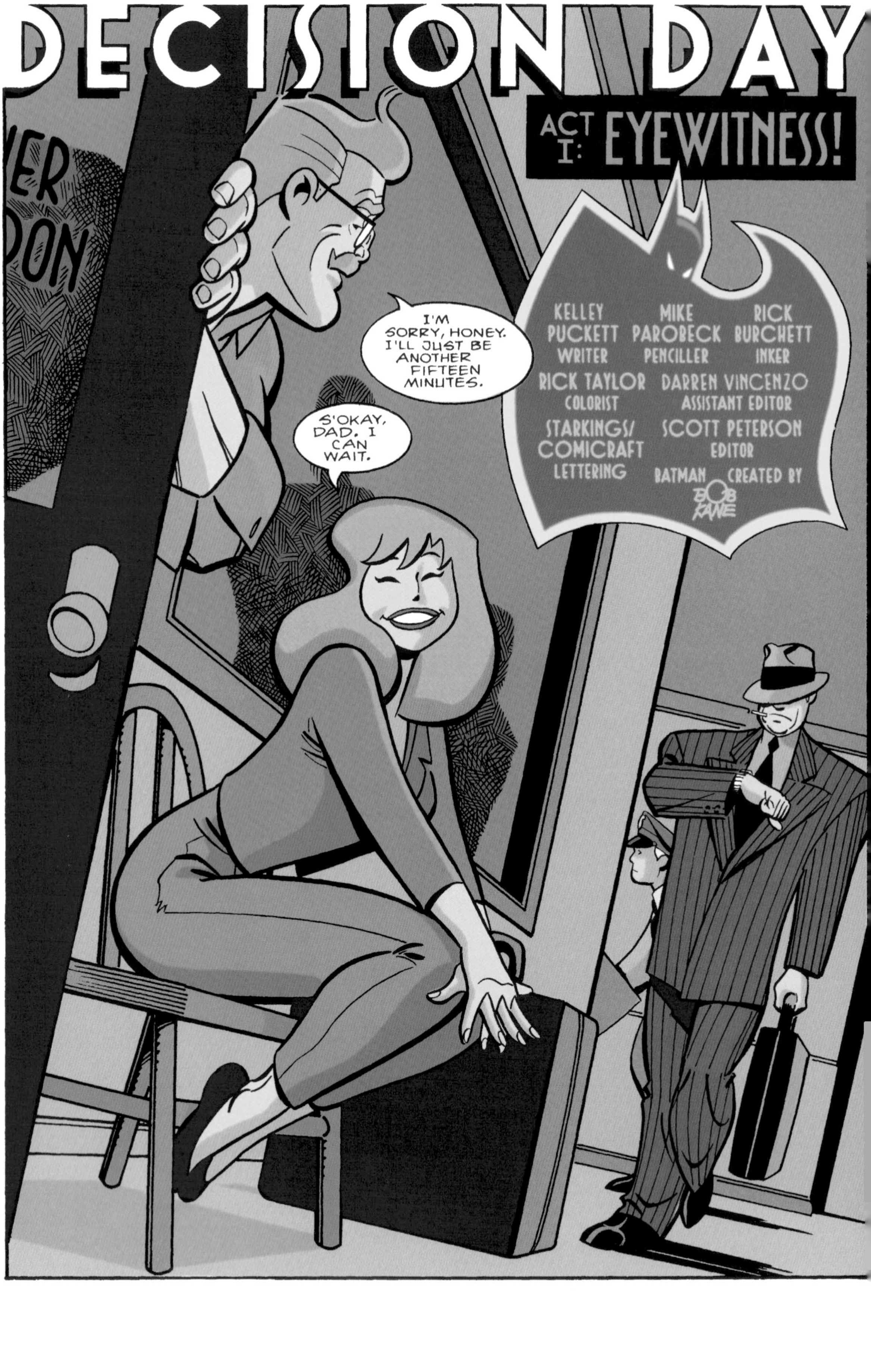

DECISION DAY
ACT I: EYEWITNESS!
I'M SORRY, HONEY. I'LL JUST BE ANOTHER FIFTEEN MINUTES.
S'OKAY, DAD. I CAN WAIT.
KELLEY PUCKETT WRITER
MIKE PAROBECK PENCILLER
RICK BURCHETT INKER
RICK TAYLOR COLORIST
DARREN VINCENZO ASSISTANT EDITOR
STARKINGS/ COMICRAFT LETTERING
SCOTT PETERSON EDITOR
BATMAN CREATED BY BOB KANE

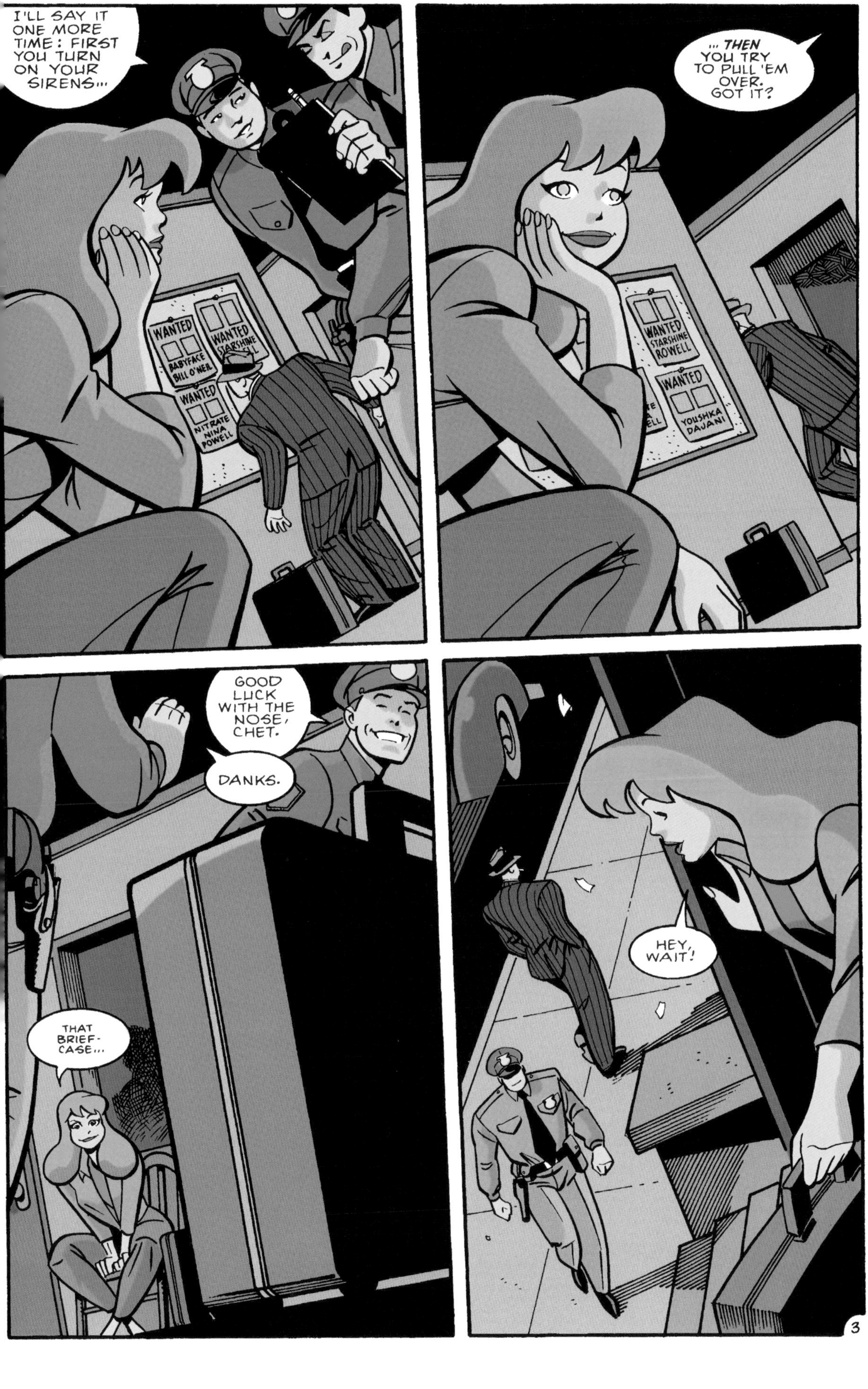
I'LL SAY IT ONE MORE TIME: FIRST YOU TURN ON YOUR SIRENS...
WANTED BABYFACE BILL O'NER
WANTED STARSHINE
WANTED NITRATE NINA POWELL
... THEN YOU TRY TO PULL 'EM OVER. GOT IT?
WANTED STARSHINE ROWELL
WANTED YOUSHKA DAJANI
GOOD LUCK WITH THE NOSE, CHET.
DANKS.
THAT BRIEF-CASE...
HEY, WAIT!
3

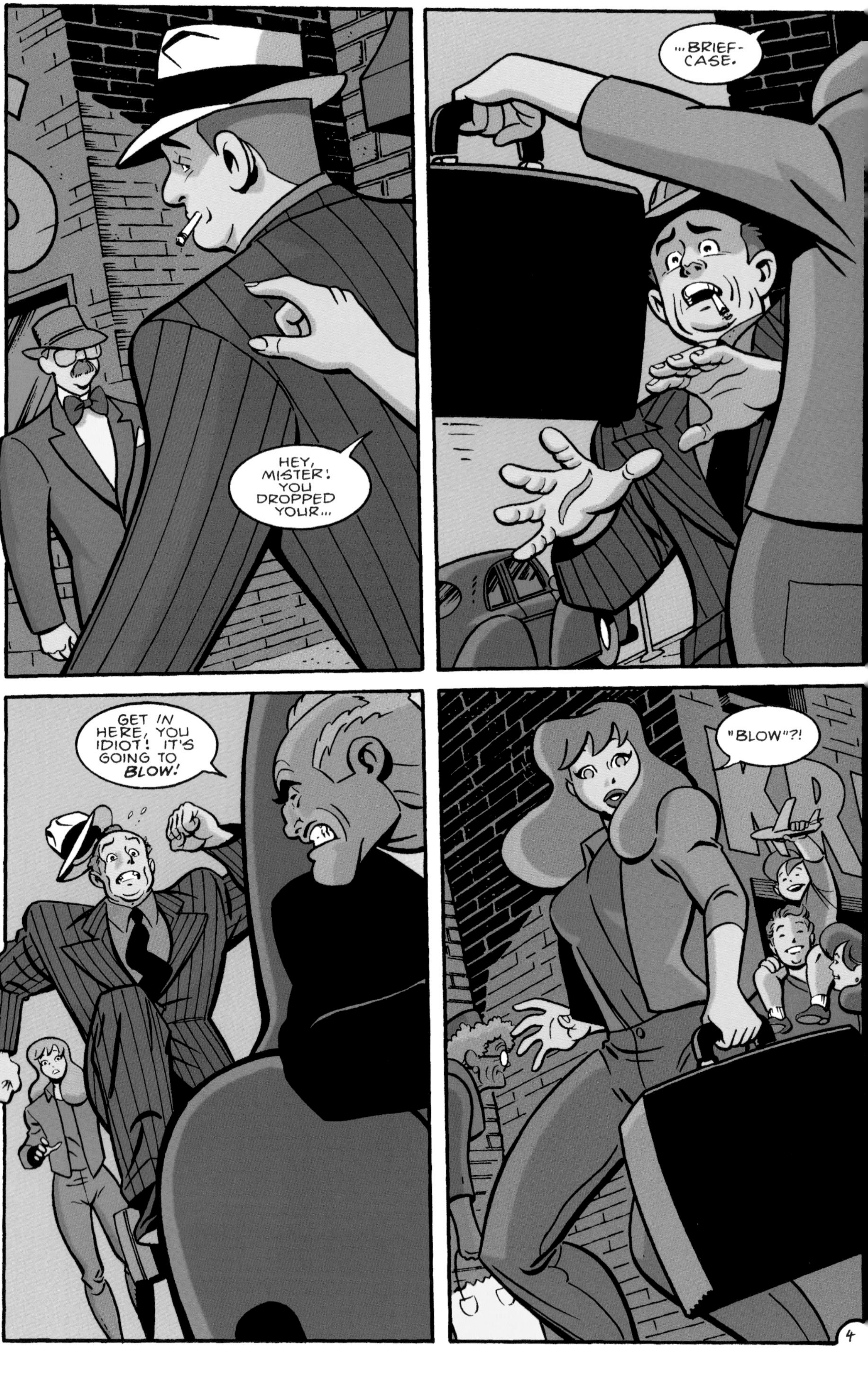

HEY, MISTER! YOU DROPPED YOUR...
...BRIEF-CASE.
GET IN HERE, YOU IDIOT! IT'S GOING TO BLOW!
"BLOW"?!
4

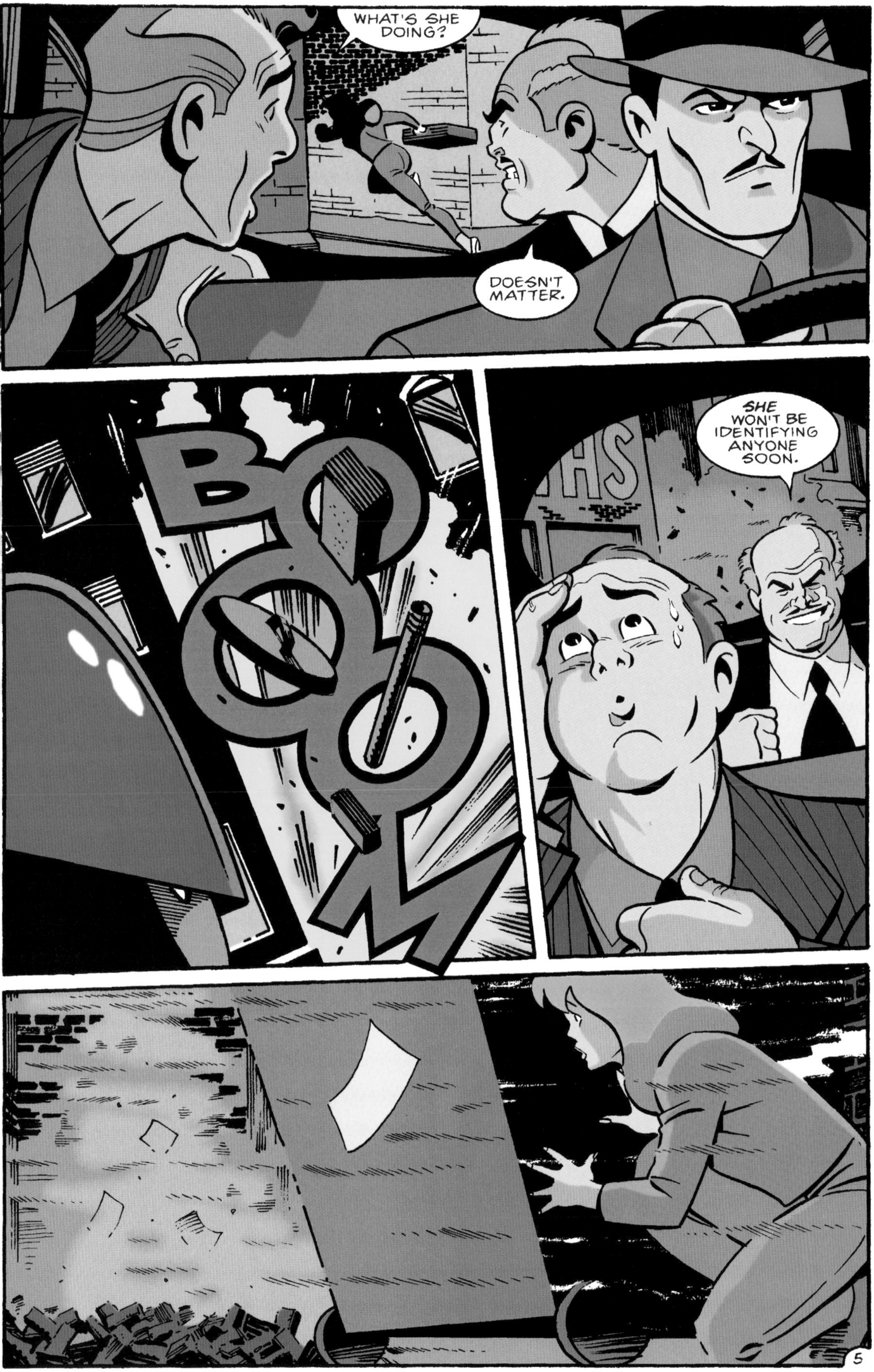
WHAT'S SHE DOING?
DOESN'T MATTER.
BOOM
SHE WON'T BE IDENTIFYING ANYONE SOON.
5

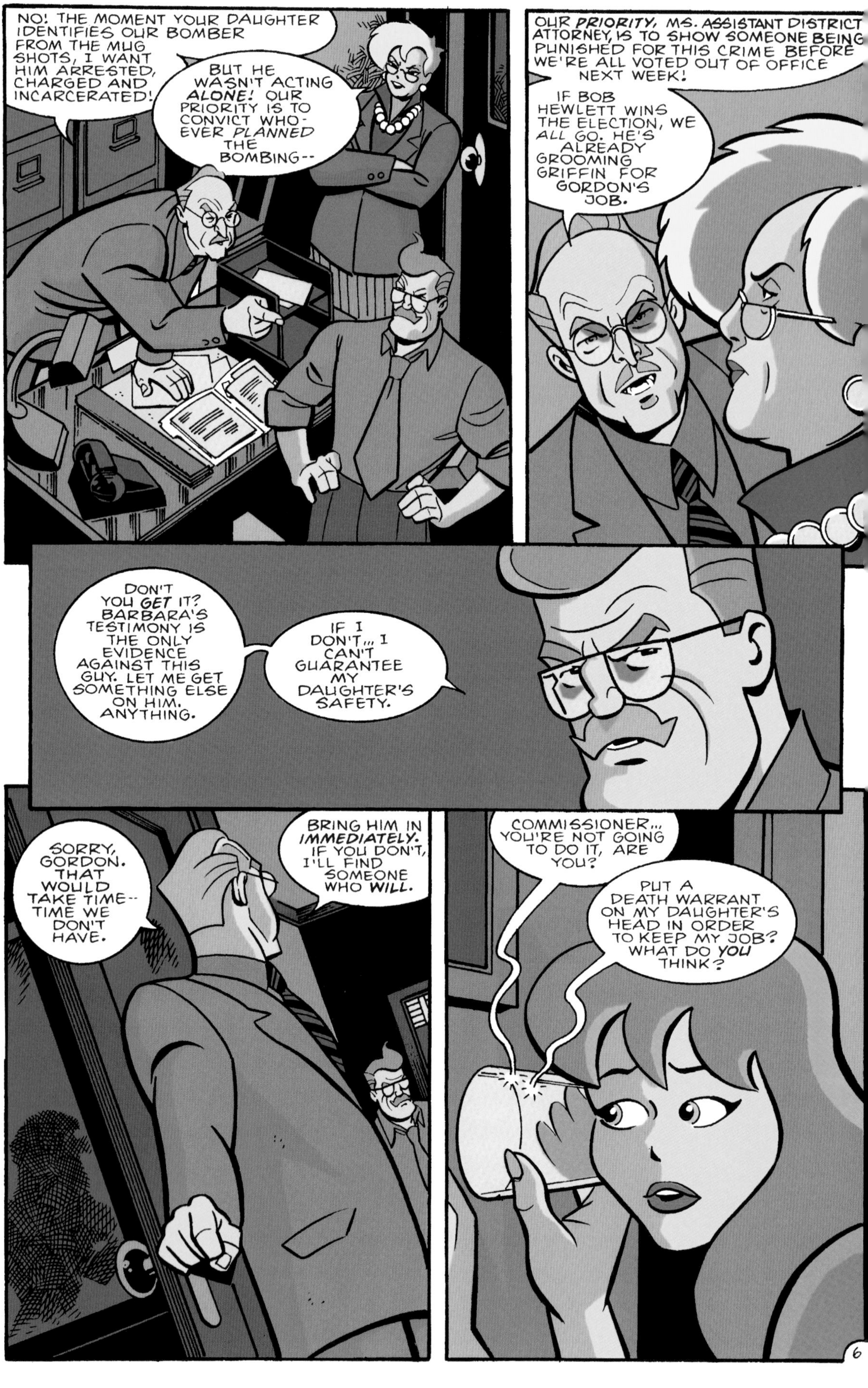
NO! THE MOMENT YOUR DAUGHTER IDENTIFIES OUR BOMBER FROM THE MUG SHOTS, I WANT HIM ARRESTED, CHARGED AND INCARCERATED!
BUT HE WASN'T ACTING *ALONE!* OUR PRIORITY IS TO CONVICT WHO-EVER *PLANNED* THE BOMBING--
OUR *PRIORITY,* MS. ASSISTANT DISTRICT ATTORNEY, IS TO SHOW SOMEONE BEING PUNISHED FOR THIS CRIME BEFORE WE'RE ALL VOTED OUT OF OFFICE NEXT WEEK!
IF BOB HEWLETT WINS THE ELECTION, WE *ALL* GO. HE'S ALREADY GROOMING GRIFFIN FOR GORDON'S JOB.
DON'T YOU *GET* IT? BARBARA'S TESTIMONY IS THE ONLY EVIDENCE AGAINST THIS GUY. LET ME GET SOMETHING ELSE ON HIM. ANYTHING.
IF I DON'T... I CAN'T GUARANTEE MY DAUGHTER'S SAFETY.
SORRY, GORDON. THAT WOULD TAKE TIME-- TIME WE DON'T HAVE.
BRING HIM IN *IMMEDIATELY.* IF YOU DON'T, I'LL FIND SOMEONE WHO *WILL.*
COMMISSIONER... YOU'RE NOT GOING TO DO IT, ARE YOU?
PUT A DEATH WARRANT ON MY DAUGHTER'S HEAD IN ORDER TO KEEP MY JOB? WHAT DO *YOU* THINK?
6

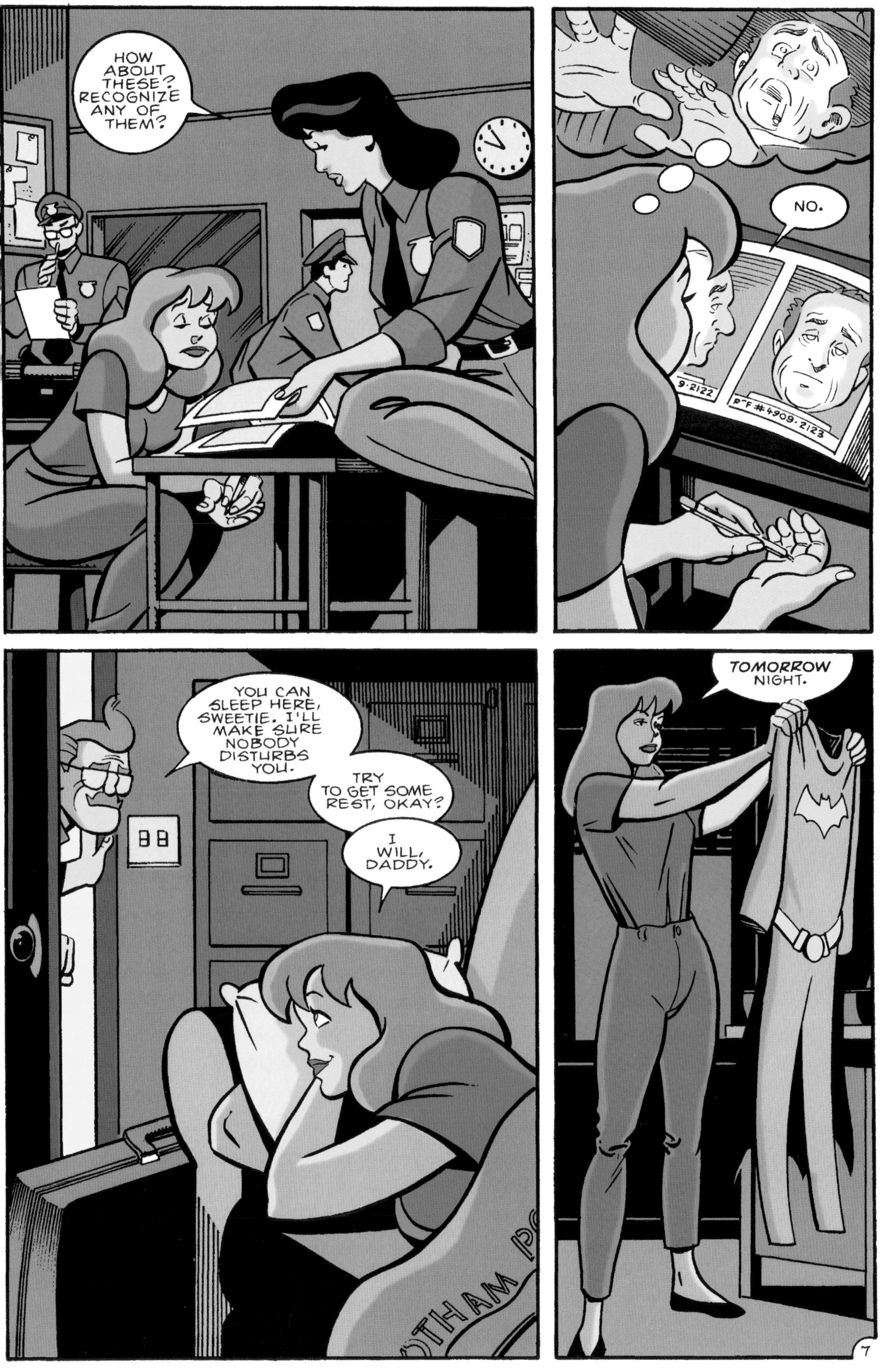
HOW ABOUT THESE? RECOGNIZE ANY OF THEM?
NO.
9·2122
R"F #4909·2123
YOU CAN SLEEP HERE, SWEETIE. I'LL MAKE SURE NOBODY DISTURBS YOU.
TRY TO GET SOME REST, OKAY?
I WILL, DADDY.
TOMORROW NIGHT.
7

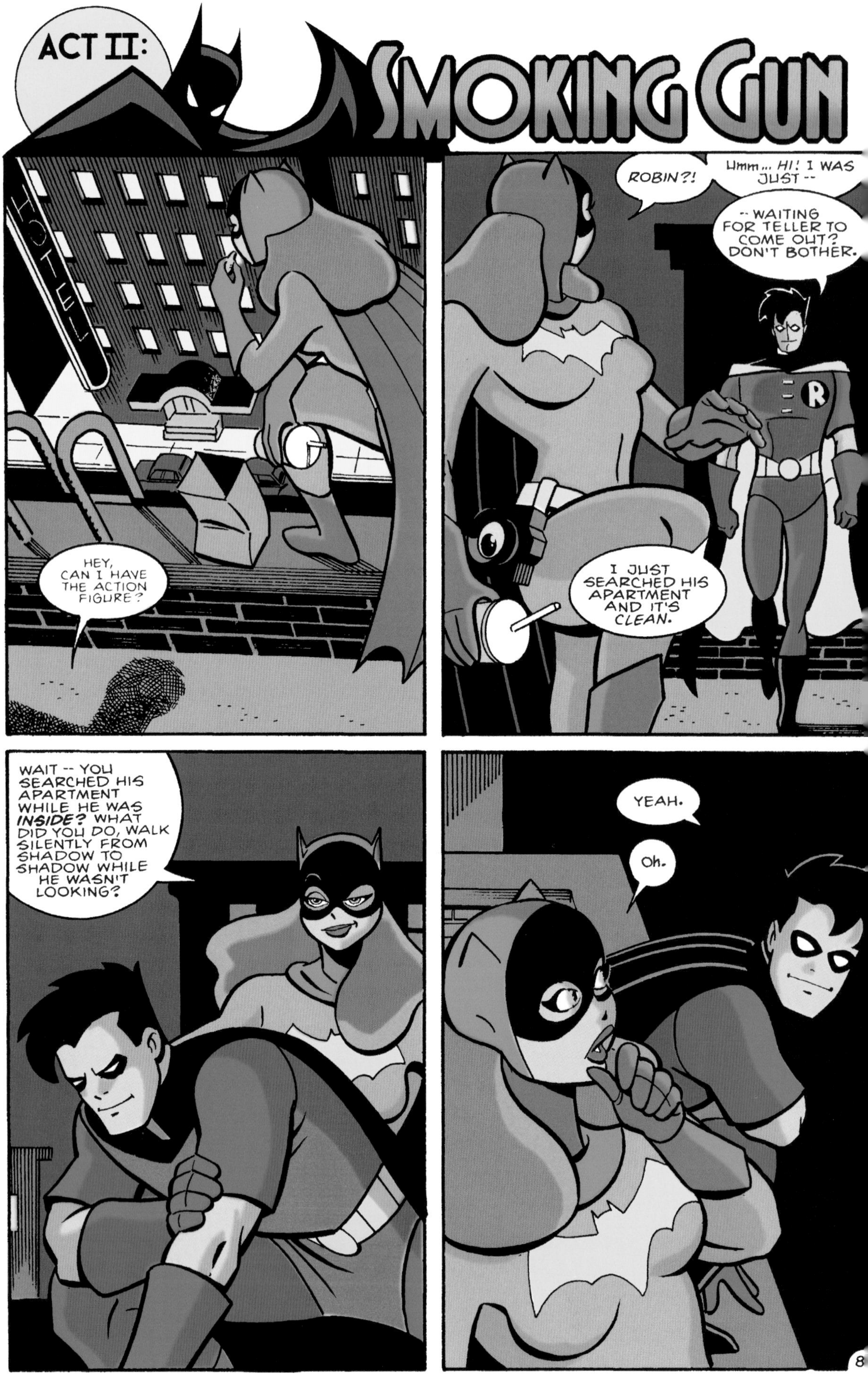
ACT II: SMOKING GUN
HOTEL
HEY, CAN I HAVE THE ACTION FIGURE?
ROBIN?!
Umm... HI! I WAS JUST --
-- WAITING FOR TELLER TO COME OUT? DON'T BOTHER.
I JUST SEARCHED HIS APARTMENT AND IT'S CLEAN.
WAIT -- YOU SEARCHED HIS APARTMENT WHILE HE WAS INSIDE? WHAT DID YOU DO, WALK SILENTLY FROM SHADOW TO SHADOW WHILE HE WASN'T LOOKING?
YEAH.
Oh.
8

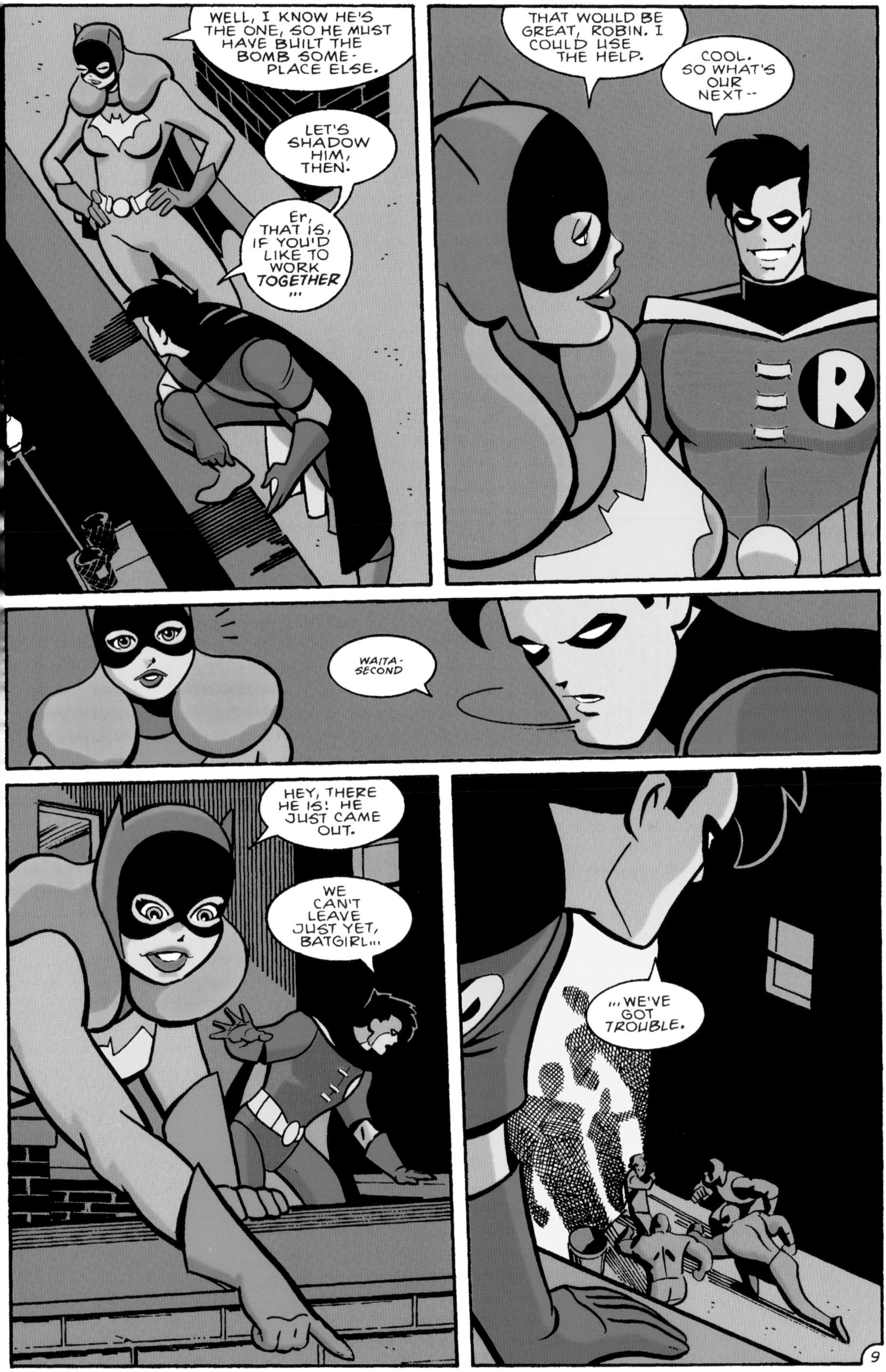
WELL, I KNOW HE'S THE ONE, SO HE MUST HAVE BUILT THE BOMB SOME-PLACE ELSE.
LET'S SHADOW HIM, THEN.
Er, THAT IS, IF YOU'D LIKE TO WORK TOGETHER...
THAT WOULD BE GREAT, ROBIN. I COULD USE THE HELP.
COOL. SO WHAT'S OUR NEXT--
WAITA-SECOND
HEY, THERE HE IS! HE JUST CAME OUT.
WE CAN'T LEAVE JUST YET, BATGIRL...
...WE'VE GOT TROUBLE.
9

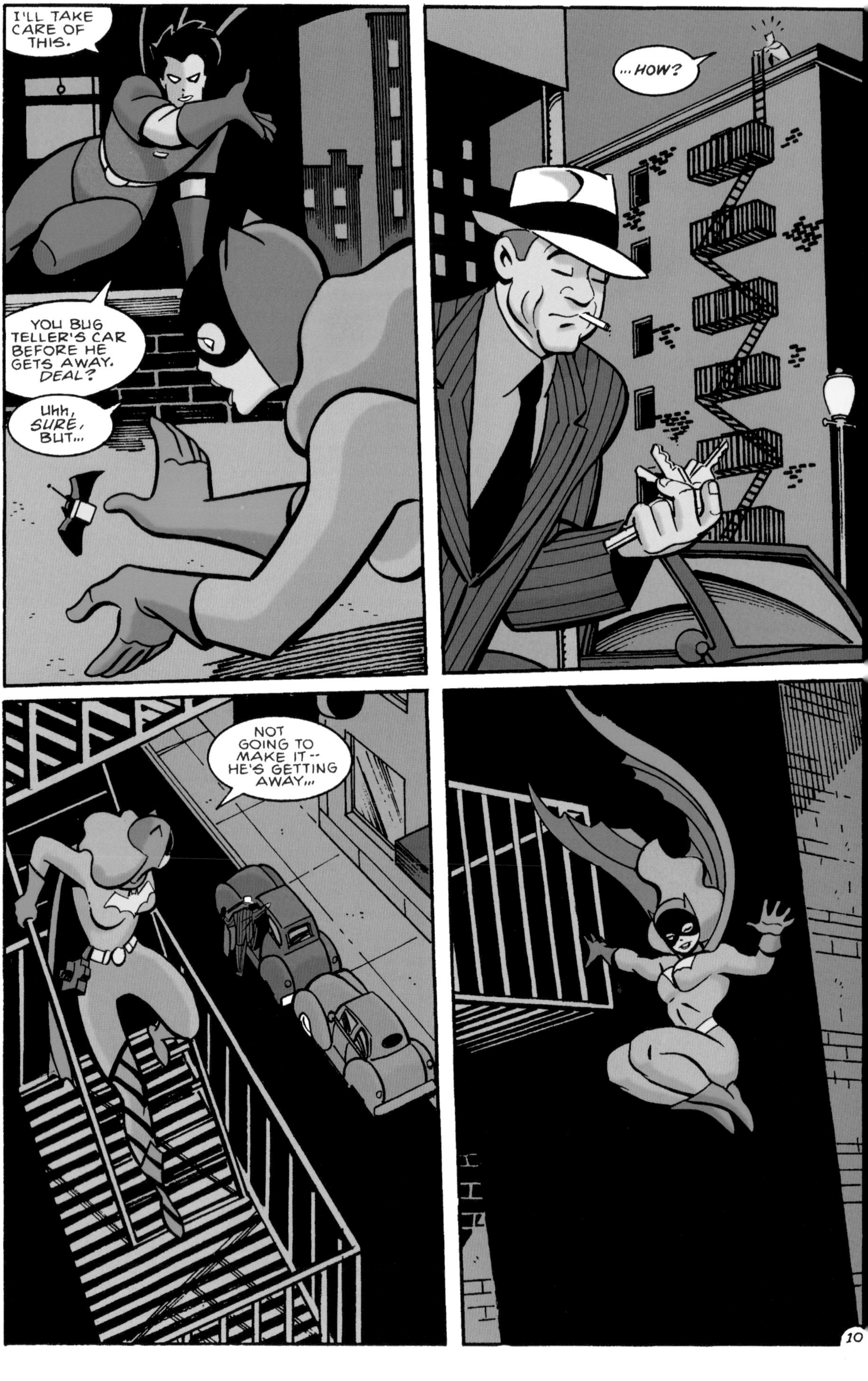

I'LL TAKE CARE OF THIS.
YOU BUG TELLER'S CAR BEFORE HE GETS AWAY. DEAL?
UHH, SURE, BUT...
...HOW?
NOT GOING TO MAKE IT -- HE'S GETTING AWAY...
10

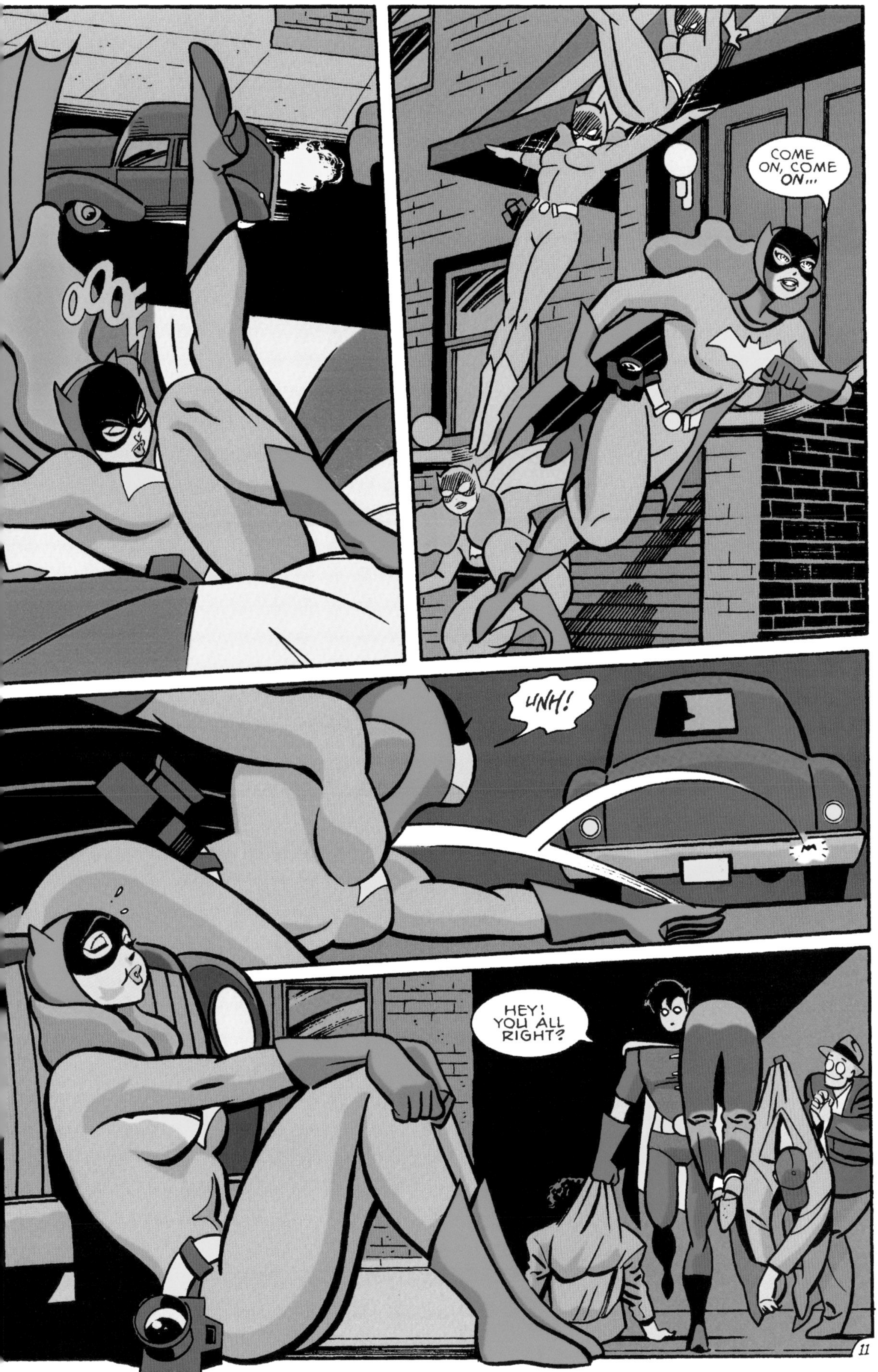
OOOF
COME ON, COME ON...
UNH!
HEY! YOU ALL RIGHT?
11

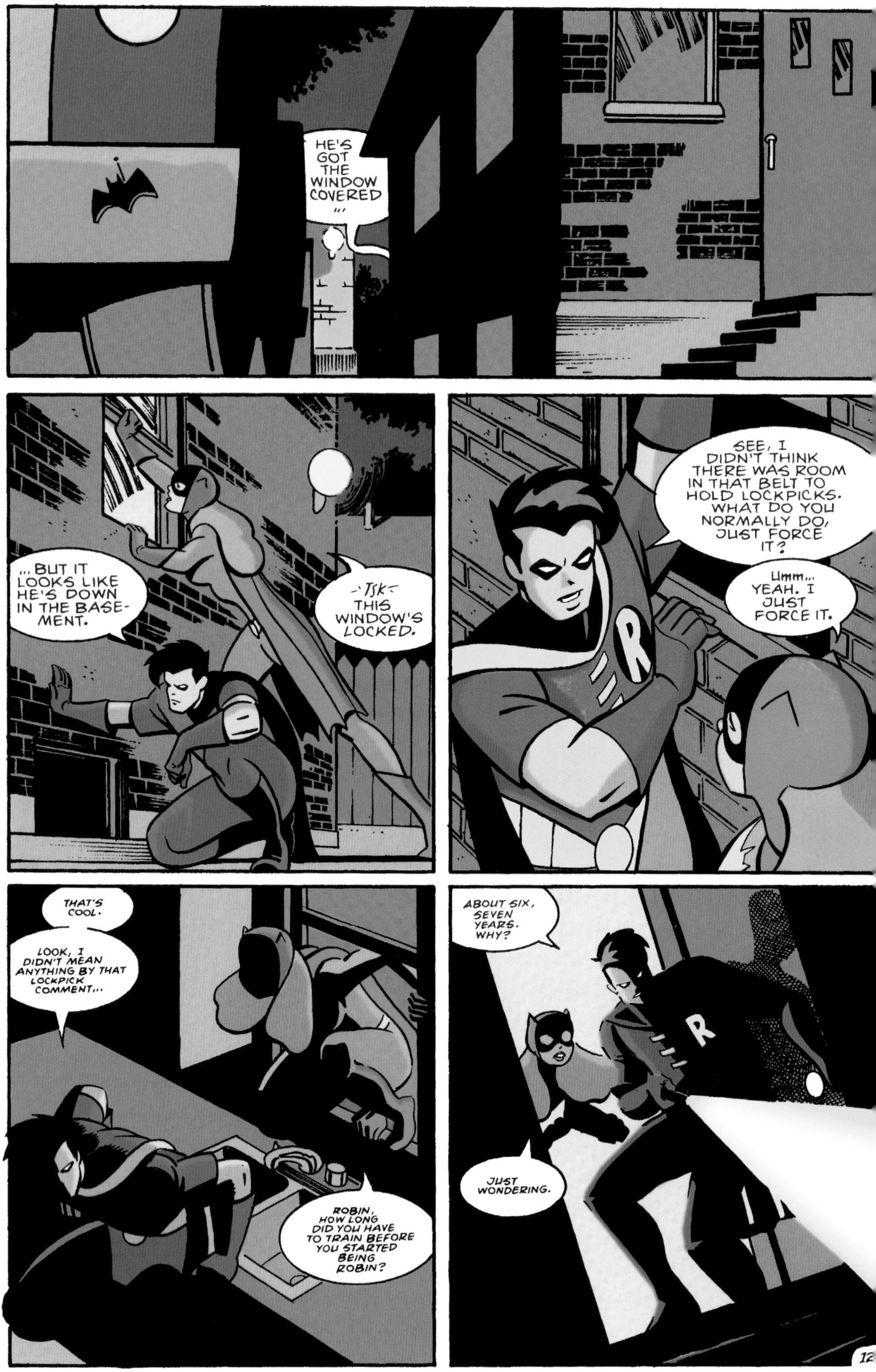
HE'S GOT THE WINDOW COVERED ...
...BUT IT LOOKS LIKE HE'S DOWN IN THE BASEMENT.
-TSK- THIS WINDOW'S LOCKED.
SEE, I DIDN'T THINK THERE WAS ROOM IN THAT BELT TO HOLD LOCKPICKS. WHAT DO YOU NORMALLY DO, JUST FORCE IT?
Umm... YEAH. I JUST FORCE IT.
THAT'S COOL.
LOOK, I DIDN'T MEAN ANYTHING BY THAT LOCKPICK COMMENT...
ROBIN, HOW LONG DID YOU HAVE TO TRAIN BEFORE YOU STARTED BEING ROBIN?
ABOUT SIX, SEVEN YEARS. WHY?
JUST WONDERING.
12

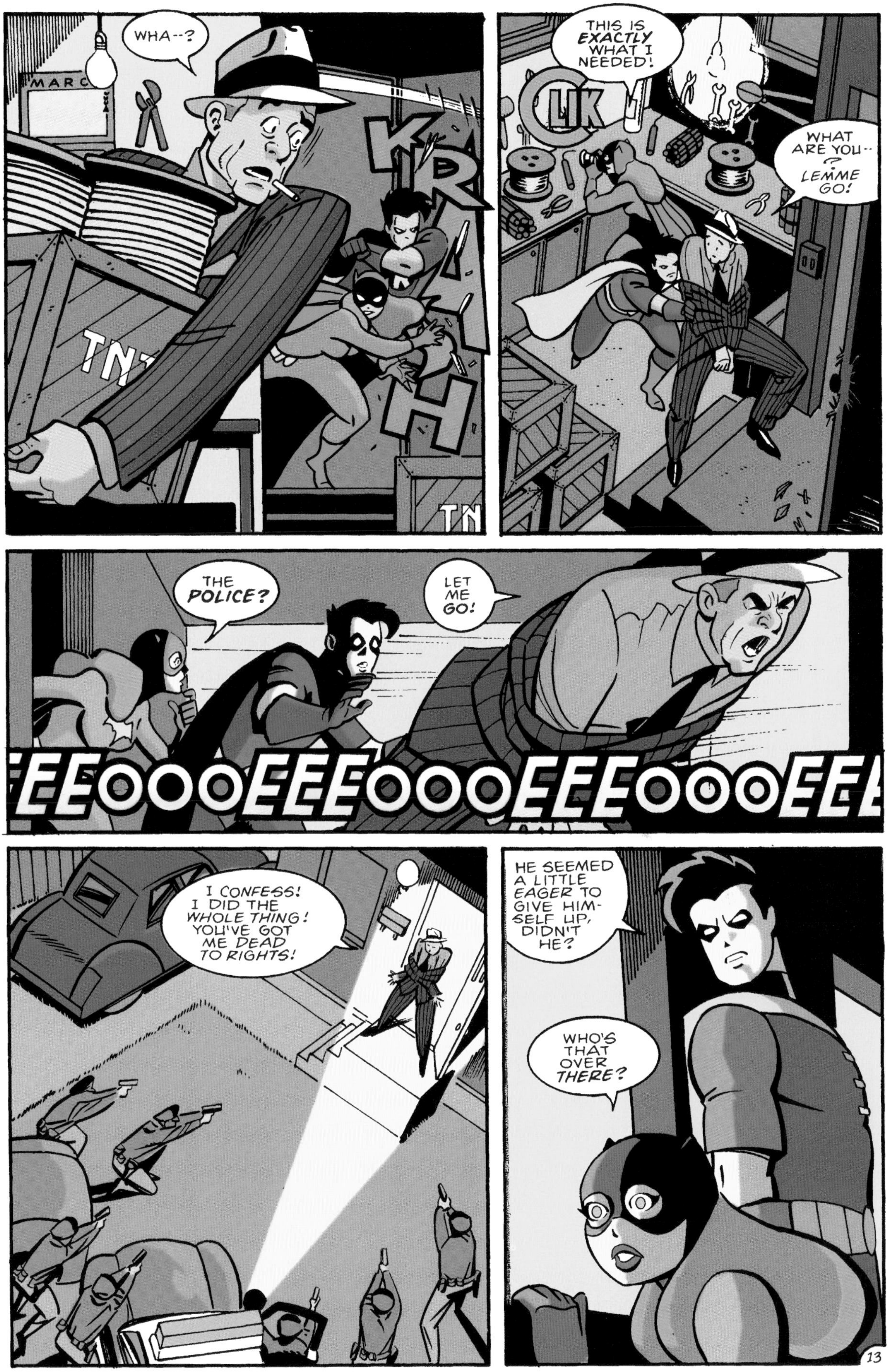
WHA--?
KRASH
THIS IS EXACTLY WHAT I NEEDED!
CLIK
WHAT ARE YOU--? LEMME GO!
THE POLICE?
LET ME GO!
EEOOOEEEOOOEEEOOOEEE
I CONFESS! I DID THE WHOLE THING! YOU'VE GOT ME DEAD TO RIGHTS!
HE SEEMED A LITTLE EAGER TO GIVE HIM-SELF UP, DIDN'T HE?
WHO'S THAT OVER THERE?
13

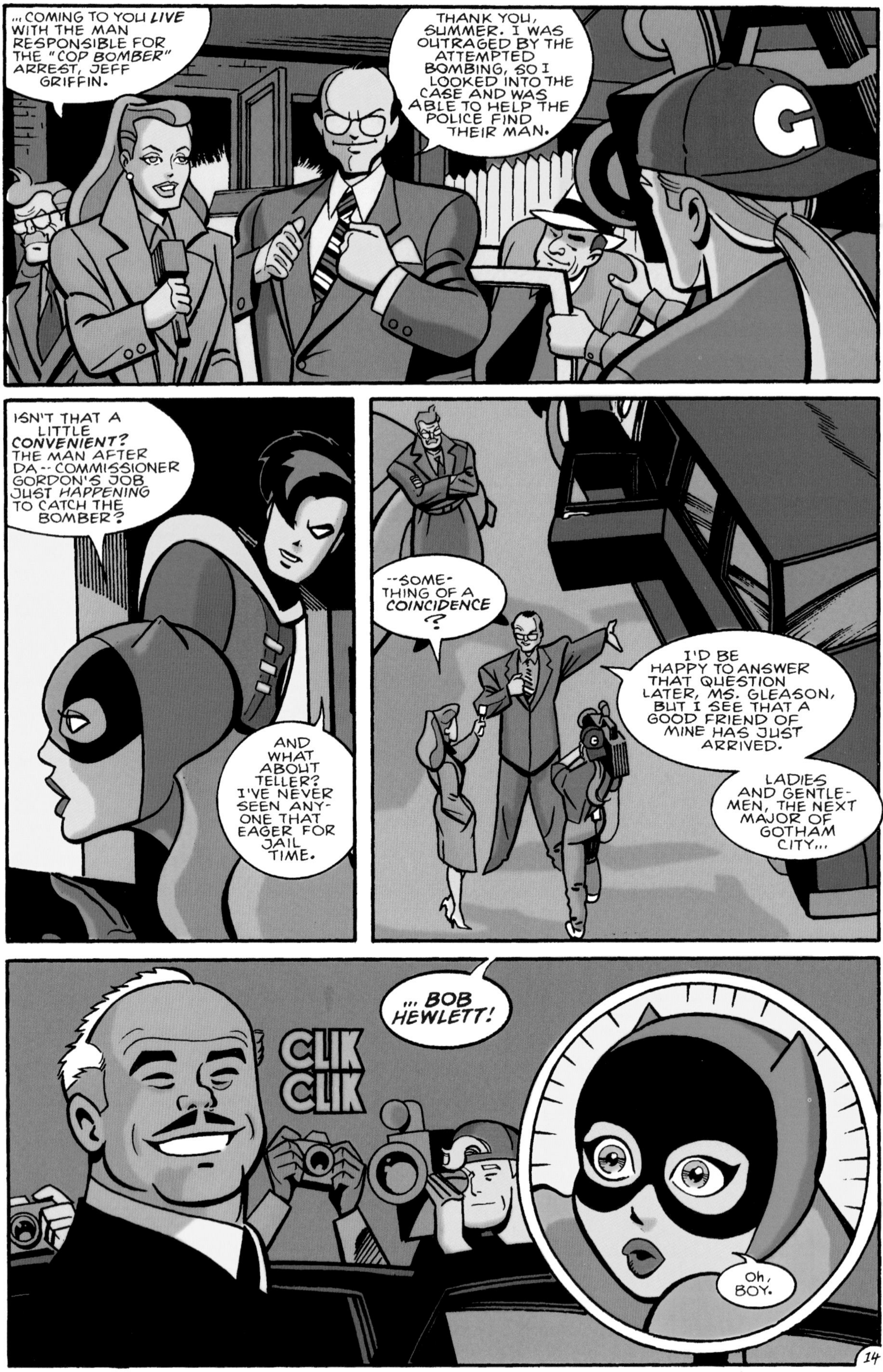
...COMING TO YOU LIVE WITH THE MAN RESPONSIBLE FOR THE "COP BOMBER" ARREST, JEFF GRIFFIN.
THANK YOU, SUMMER. I WAS OUTRAGED BY THE ATTEMPTED BOMBING, SO I LOOKED INTO THE CASE AND WAS ABLE TO HELP THE POLICE FIND THEIR MAN.
ISN'T THAT A LITTLE CONVENIENT? THE MAN AFTER DA--COMMISSIONER GORDON'S JOB JUST HAPPENING TO CATCH THE BOMBER?
AND WHAT ABOUT TELLER? I'VE NEVER SEEN ANYONE THAT EAGER FOR JAIL TIME.
--SOMETHING OF A COINCIDENCE?
I'D BE HAPPY TO ANSWER THAT QUESTION LATER, MS. GLEASON, BUT I SEE THAT A GOOD FRIEND OF MINE HAS JUST ARRIVED.
LADIES AND GENTLEMEN, THE NEXT MAJOR OF GOTHAM CITY...
...BOB HEWLETT!
CLIK CLIK
OH, BOY.
14

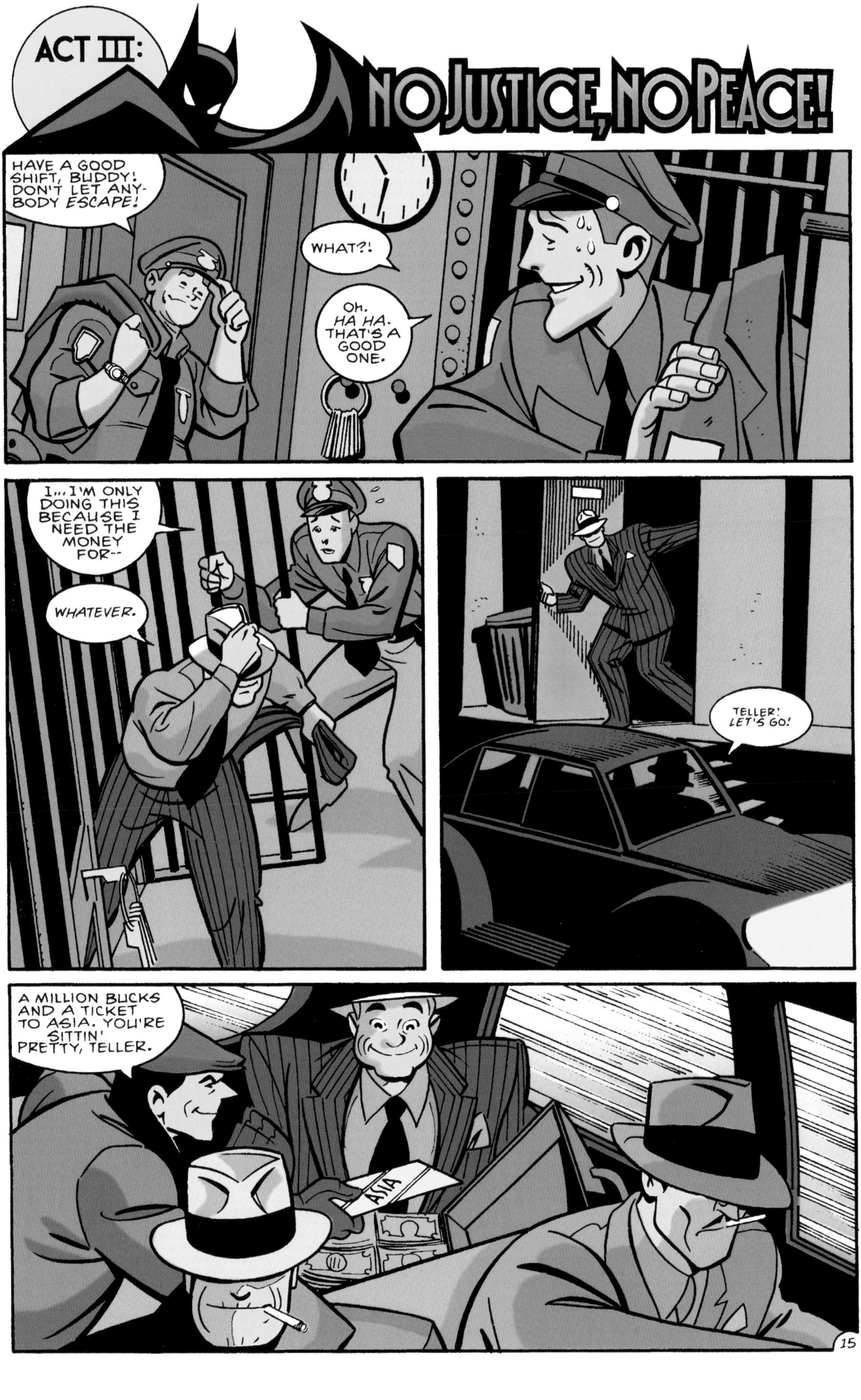
ACT III: NO JUSTICE, NO PEACE!
HAVE A GOOD SHIFT, BUDDY! DON'T LET ANYBODY ESCAPE!
WHAT?!
OH. HA HA. THAT'S A GOOD ONE.
I... I'M ONLY DOING THIS BECAUSE I NEED THE MONEY FOR--
WHATEVER.
TELLER! LET'S GO!
A MILLION BUCKS AND A TICKET TO ASIA. YOU'RE SITTIN' PRETTY, TELLER.
ASIA
15

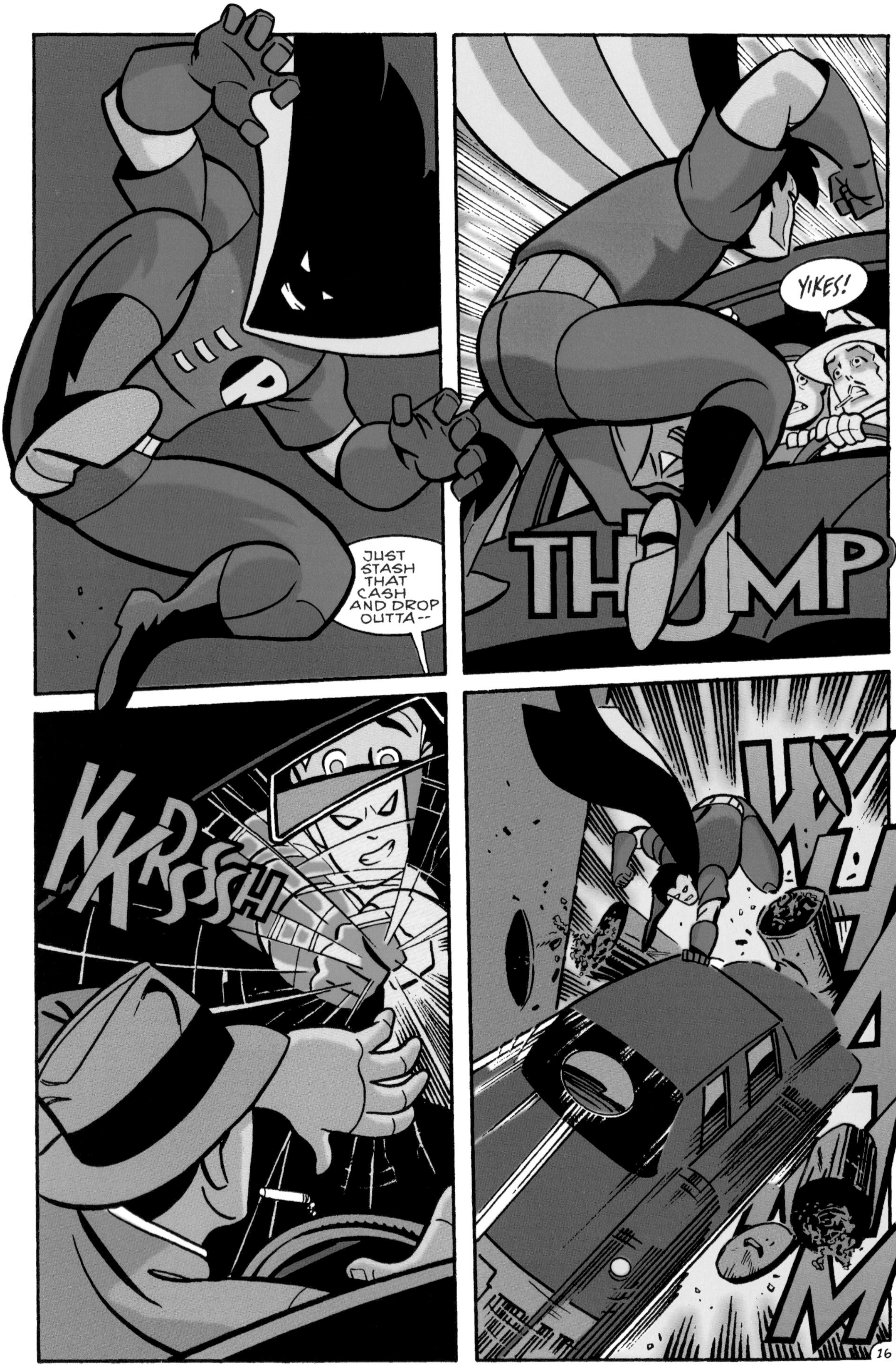
JUST STASH THAT CASH AND DROP OUTTA--
YIKES!
THUMP
KKRSSSH
16

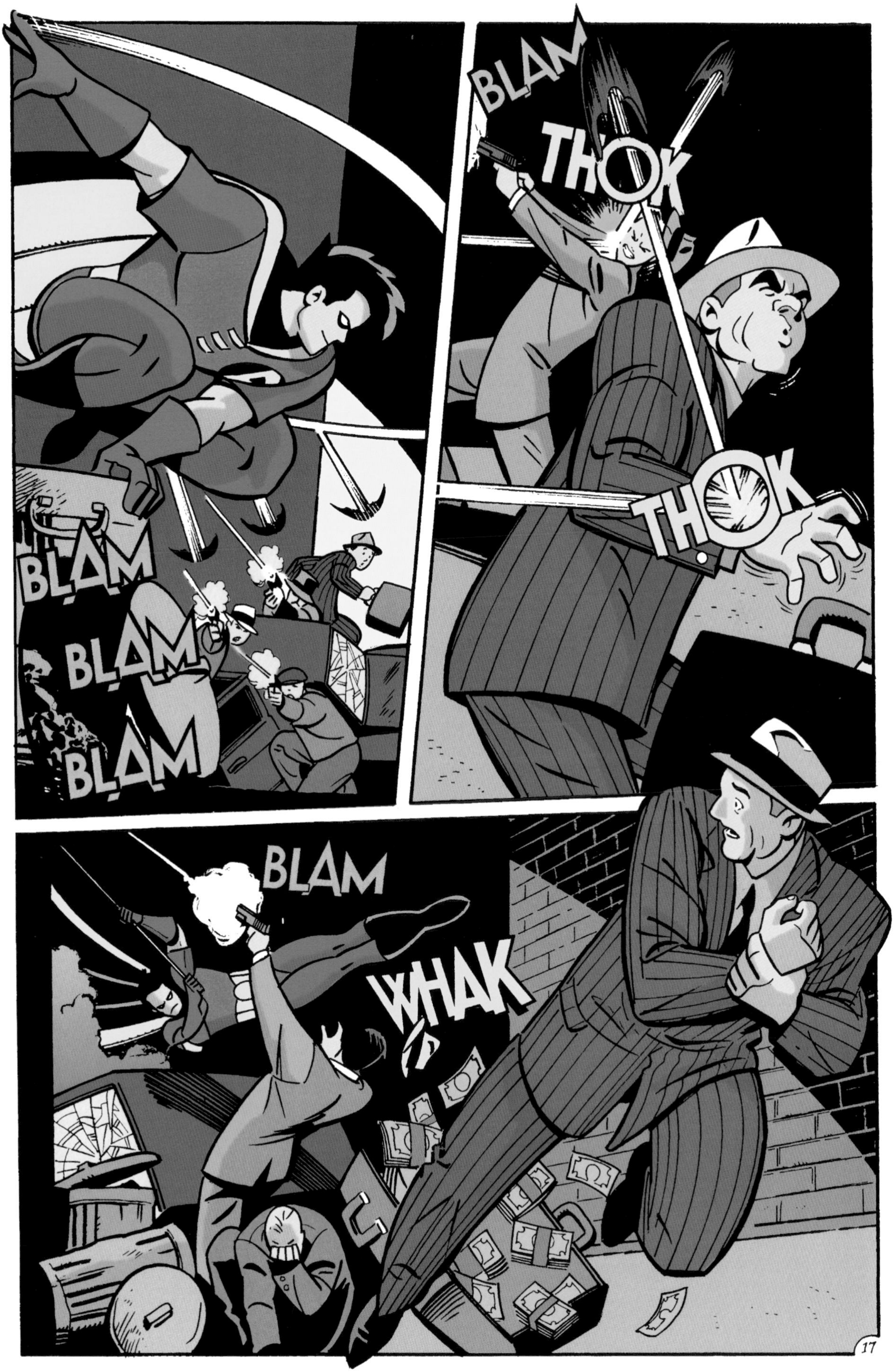
BLAM
BLAM
BLAM
BLAM
THOK
THOK
BLAM
WHAK
17

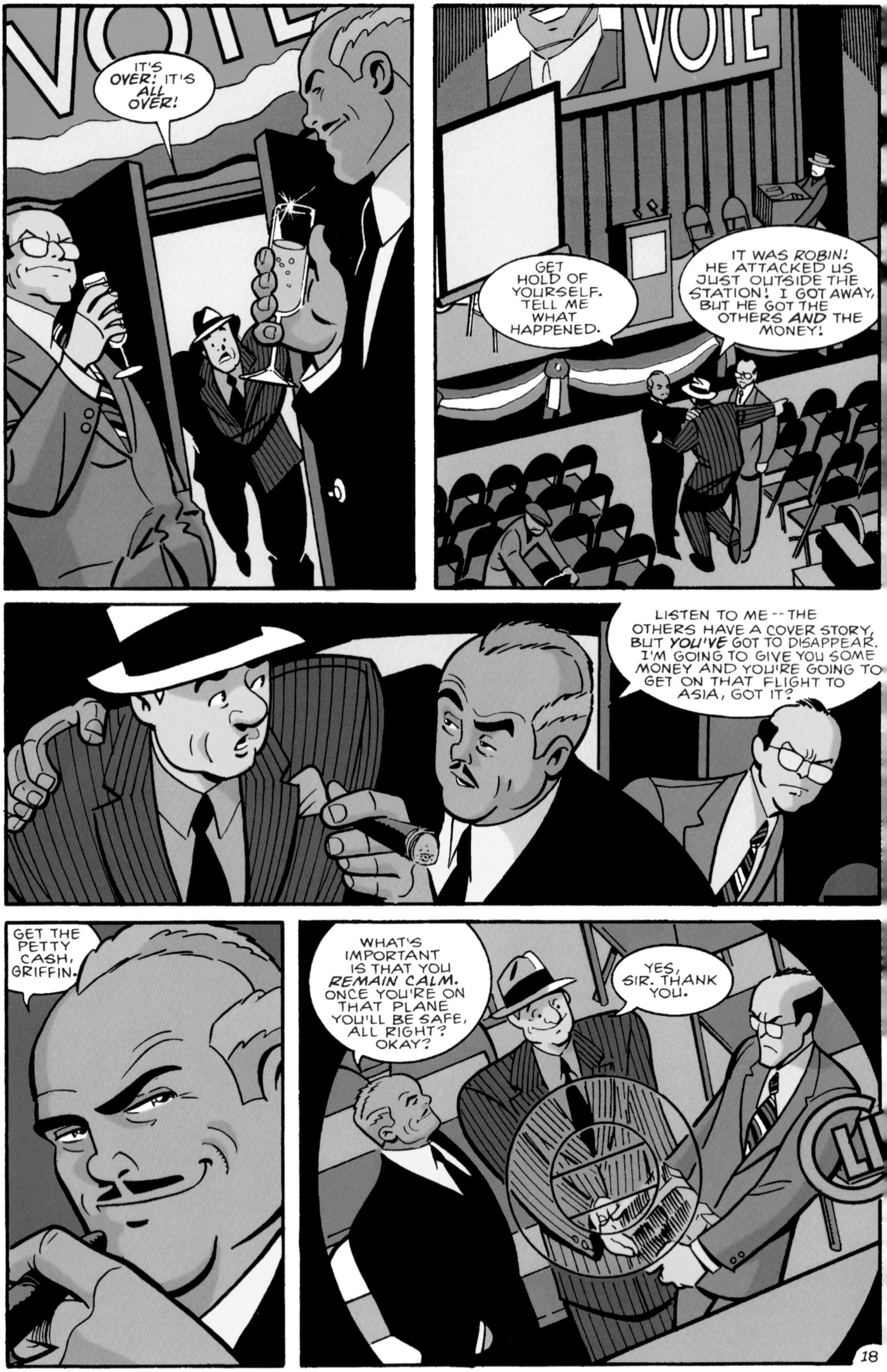
VOTE
IT'S OVER! IT'S ALL OVER!
VOTE
GET HOLD OF YOURSELF. TELL ME WHAT HAPPENED.
IT WAS ROBIN! HE ATTACKED US JUST OUTSIDE THE STATION! I GOT AWAY, BUT HE GOT THE OTHERS AND THE MONEY!
LISTEN TO ME -- THE OTHERS HAVE A COVER STORY, BUT YOU'VE GOT TO DISAPPEAR. I'M GOING TO GIVE YOU SOME MONEY AND YOU'RE GOING TO GET ON THAT FLIGHT TO ASIA, GOT IT?
GET THE PETTY CASH, GRIFFIN.
WHAT'S IMPORTANT IS THAT YOU REMAIN CALM. ONCE YOU'RE ON THAT PLANE YOU'LL BE SAFE, ALL RIGHT? OKAY?
YES, SIR. THANK YOU.
18

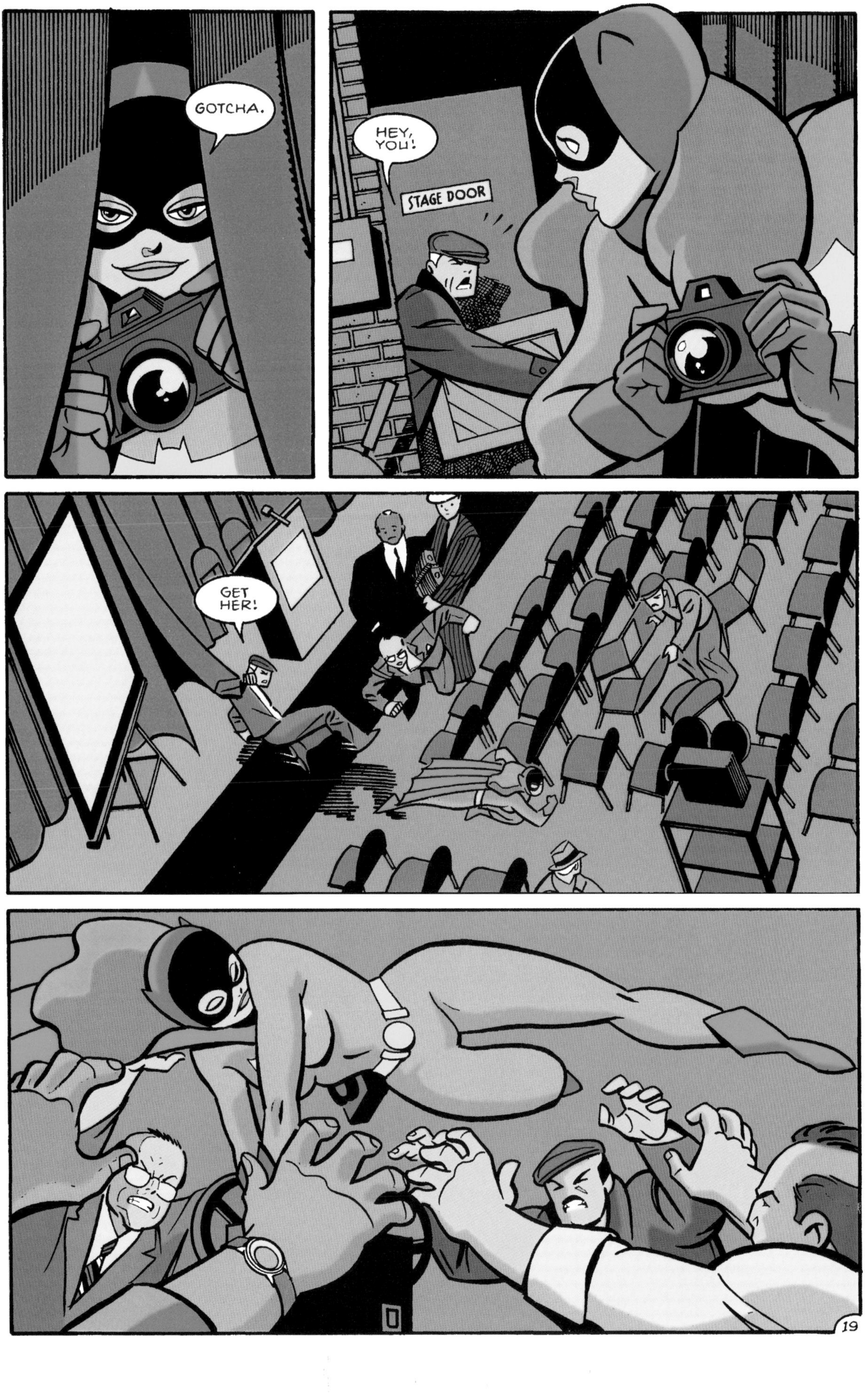
GOTCHA.
HEY, YOU!
STAGE DOOR
GET HER!
19

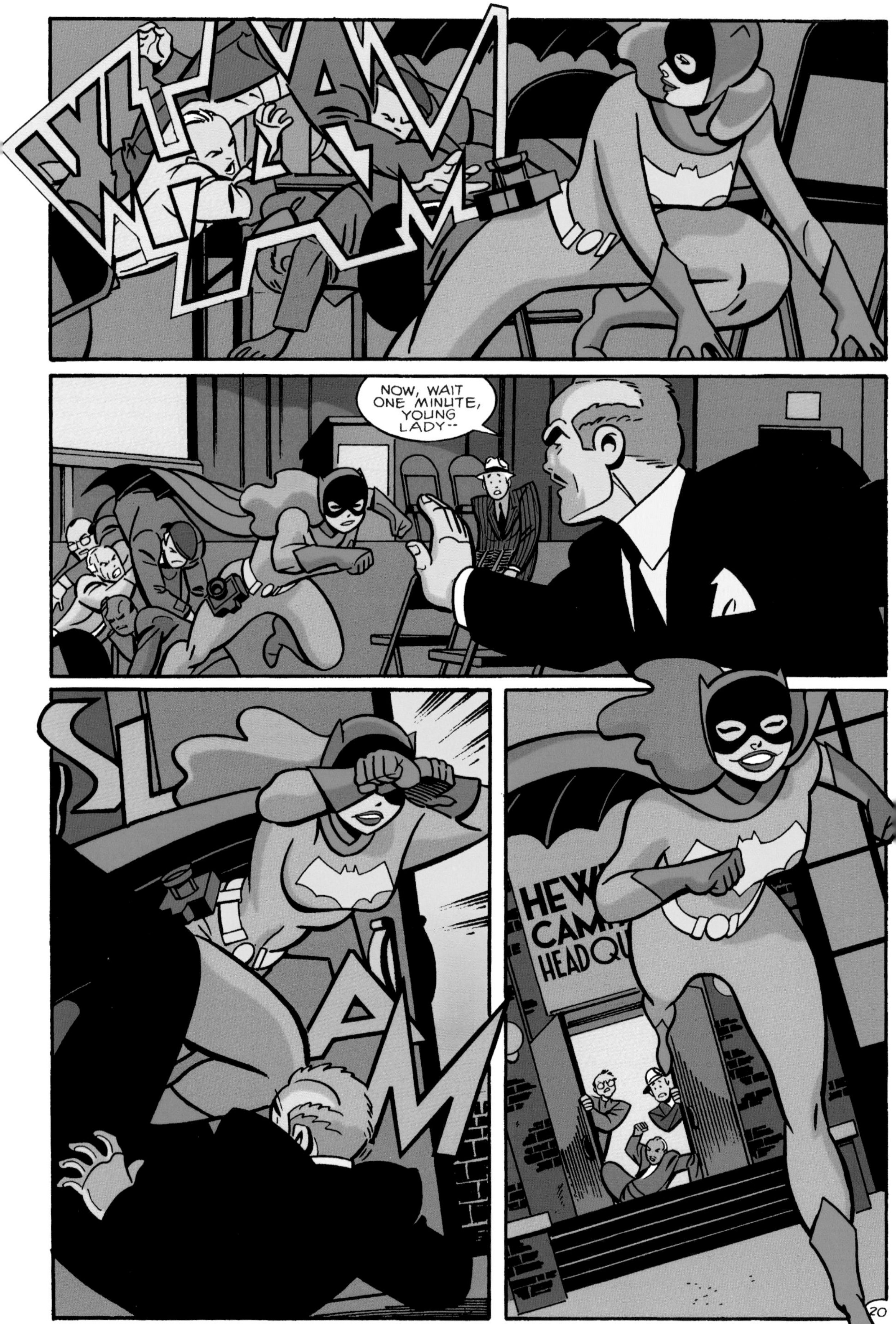
WHAM
NOW, WAIT ONE MINUTE, YOUNG LADY--
SLAM
HEW
CAM
HEADQU
20

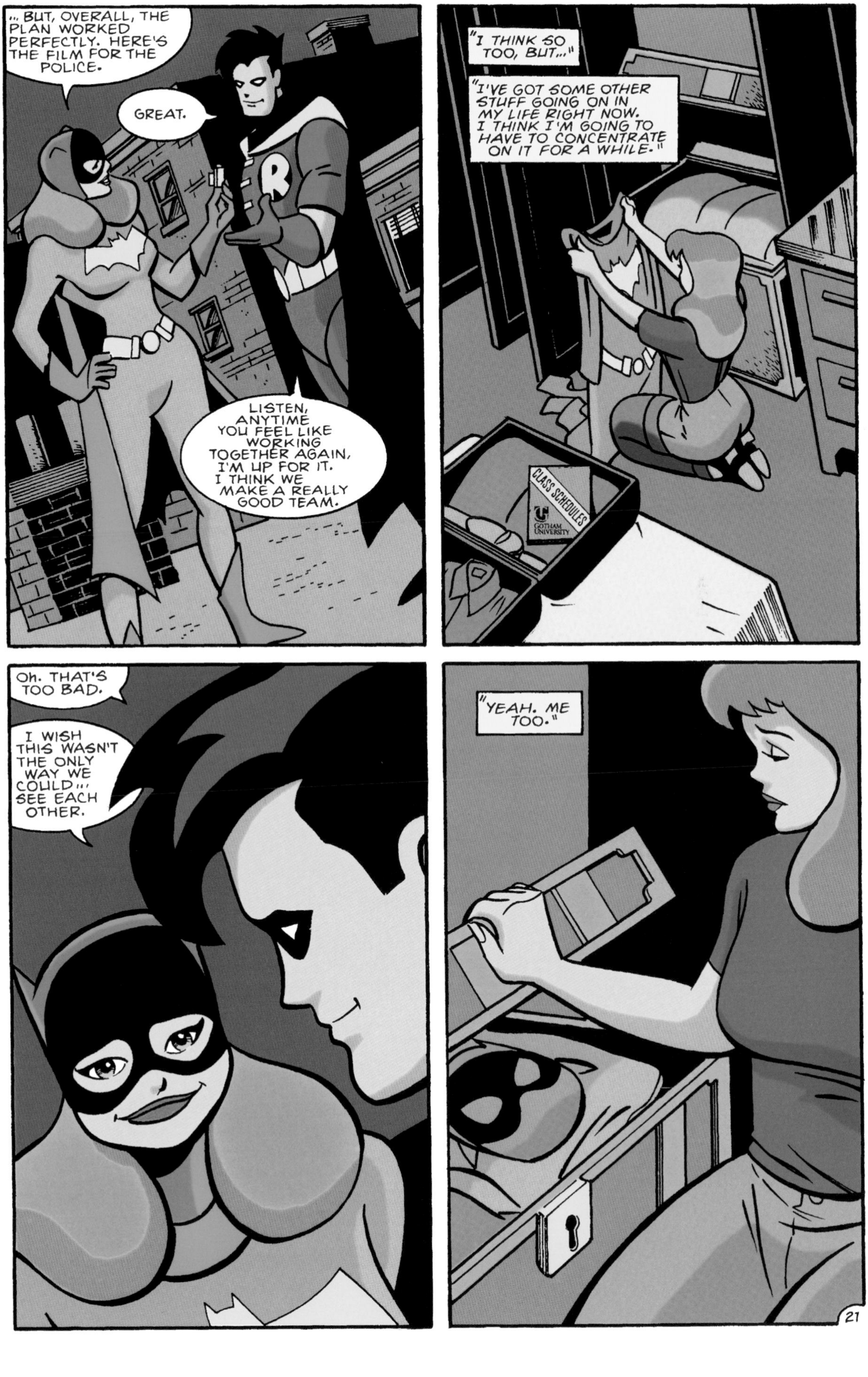
... BUT, OVERALL, THE PLAN WORKED PERFECTLY. HERE'S THE FILM FOR THE POLICE.
GREAT.
LISTEN, ANYTIME YOU FEEL LIKE WORKING TOGETHER AGAIN, I'M UP FOR IT. I THINK WE MAKE A REALLY GOOD TEAM.
"I THINK SO TOO, BUT..."
"I'VE GOT SOME OTHER STUFF GOING ON IN MY LIFE RIGHT NOW. I THINK I'M GOING TO HAVE TO CONCENTRATE ON IT FOR A WHILE."
CLASS SCHEDULES
GOTHAM UNIVERSITY
Oh. THAT'S TOO BAD.
I WISH THIS WASN'T THE ONLY WAY WE COULD... SEE EACH OTHER.
"YEAH. ME TOO."
21

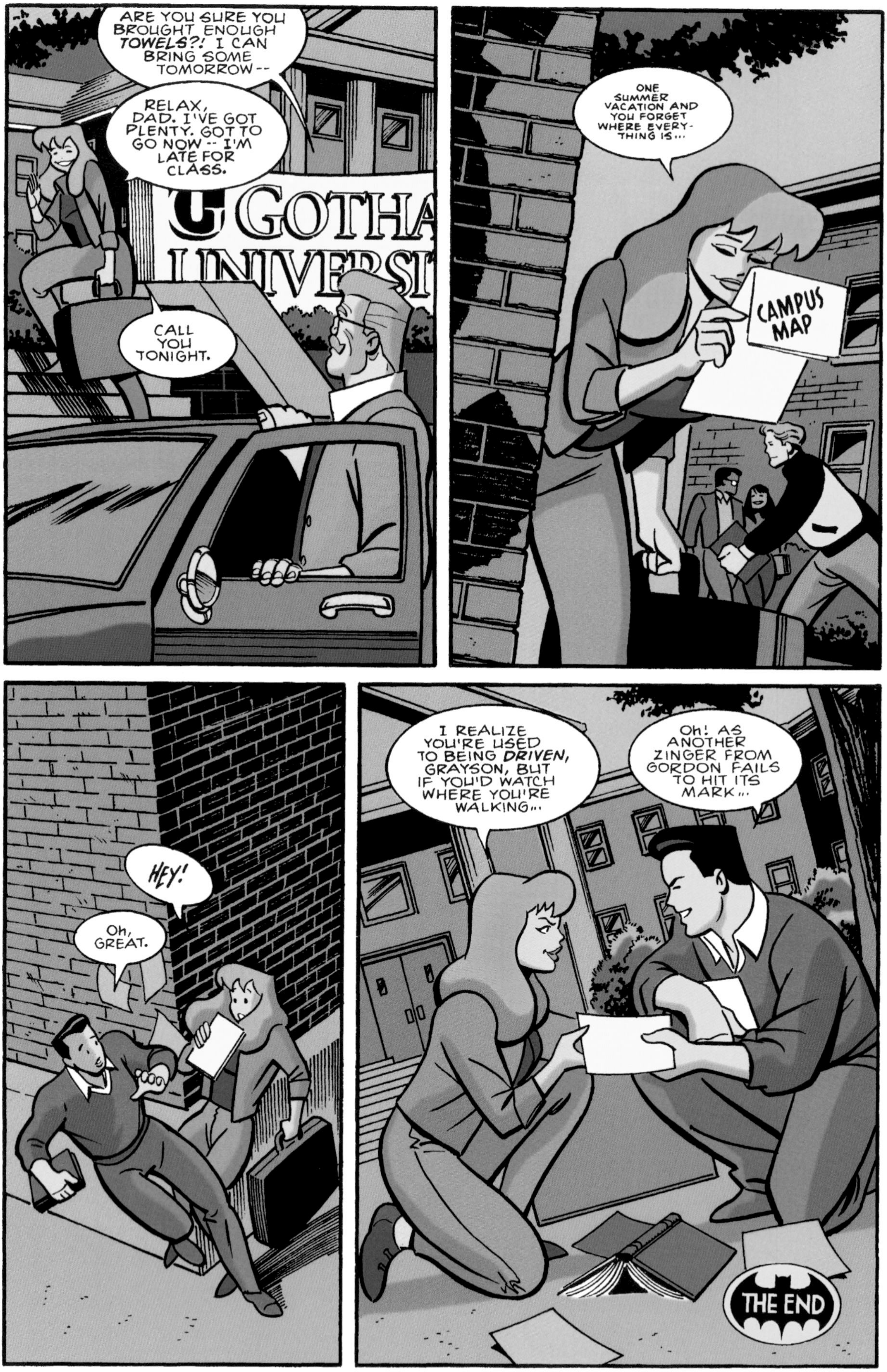
ARE YOU SURE YOU BROUGHT ENOUGH TOWELS?! I CAN BRING SOME TOMORROW --
RELAX, DAD. I'VE GOT PLENTY. GOT TO GO NOW -- I'M LATE FOR CLASS.
GOTHA
UNIVERSI
CALL YOU TONIGHT.
ONE SUMMER VACATION AND YOU FORGET WHERE EVERY-THING IS...
CAMPUS MAP
HEY!
Oh, GREAT.
I REALIZE YOU'RE USED TO BEING DRIVEN, GRAYSON, BUT IF YOU'D WATCH WHERE YOU'RE WALKING...
Oh! AS ANOTHER ZINGER FROM GORDON FAILS TO HIT ITS MARK...
THE END

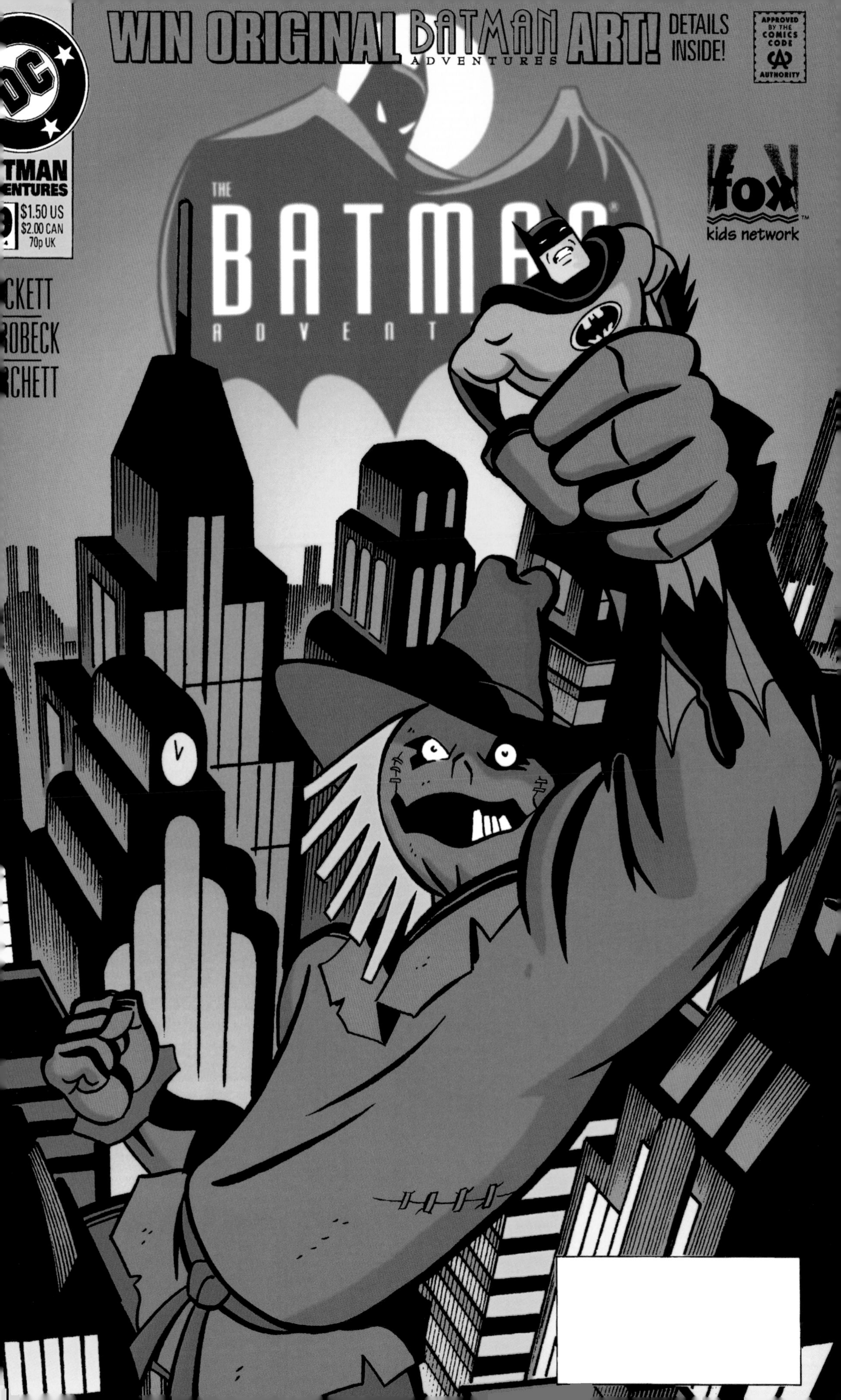
WIN ORIGINAL BATMAN ADVENTURES ART! DETAILS INSIDE!
APPROVED BY THE COMICS CODE AUTHORITY
DC
TMAN
ENTURES
$1.50 US
$2.00 CAN
70p UK
THE
BATMA
CKETT
OBECK
CHETT
fox
kids network

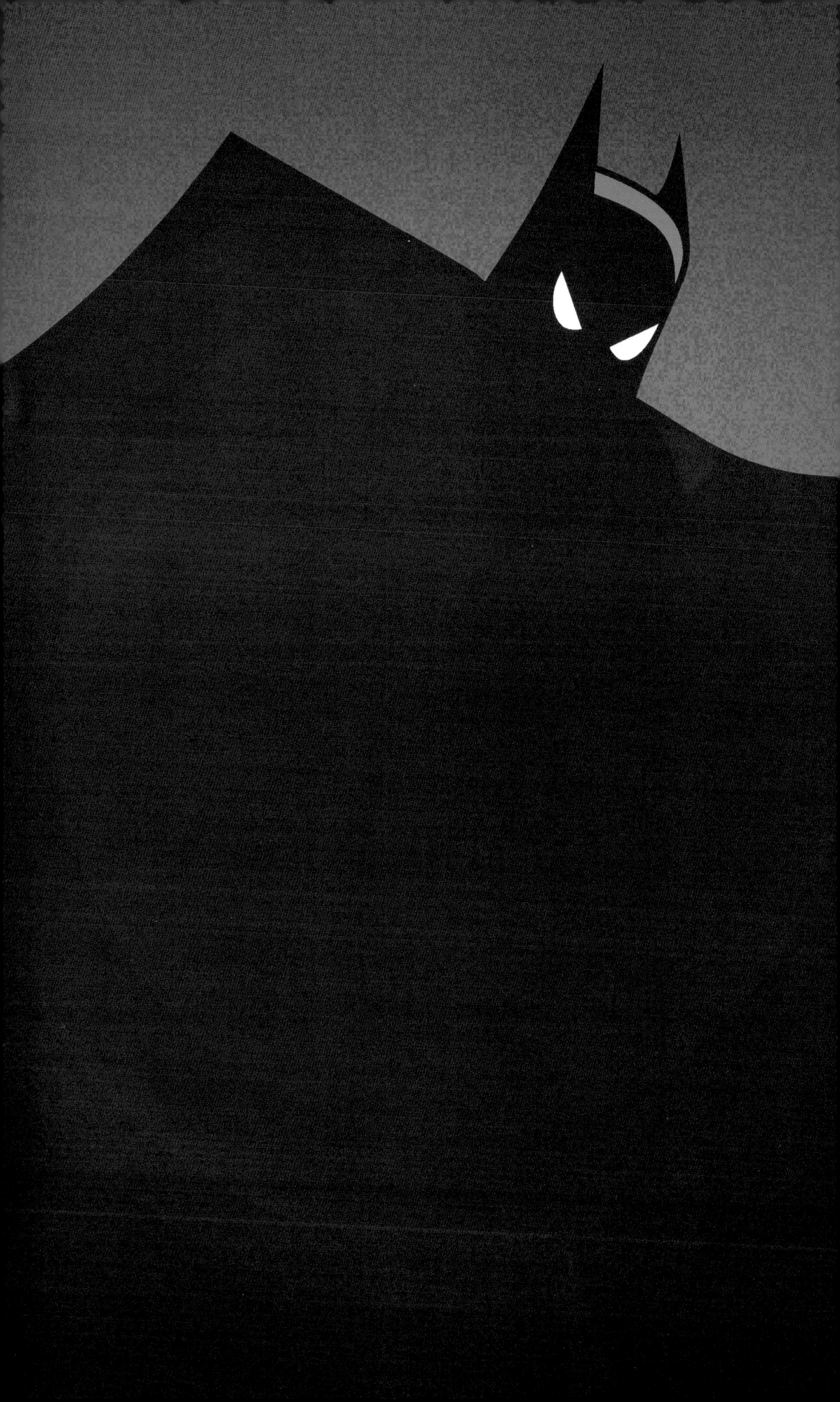

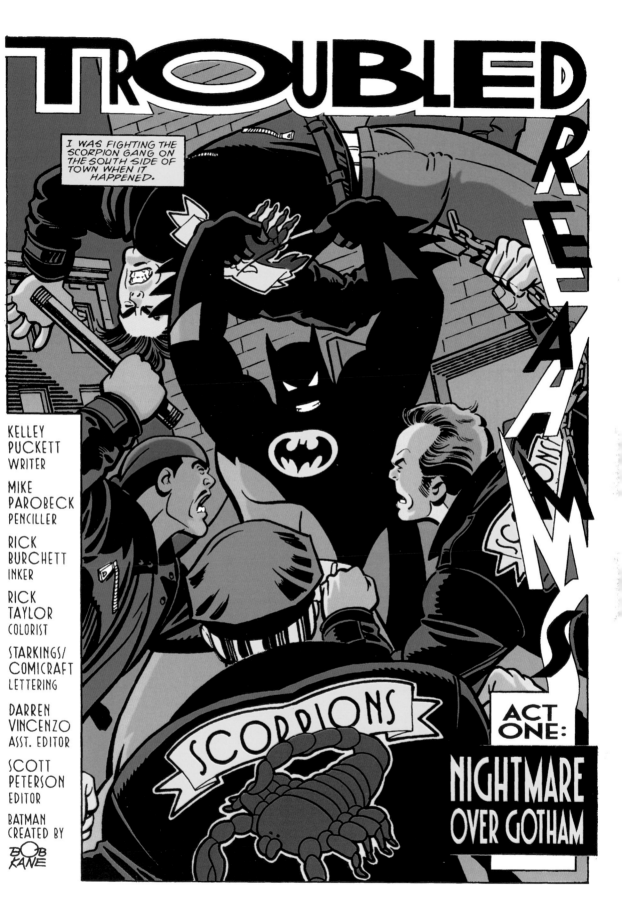

TROUBLED DREAMS

I WAS FIGHTING THE SCORPION GANG ON THE SOUTH SIDE OF TOWN WHEN IT HAPPENED.

KELLEY PUCKETT
WRITER

MIKE PAROBECK
PENCILLER

RICK BURCHETT
INKER

RICK TAYLOR
COLORIST

STARKINGS/ COMICRAFT
LETTERING

DARREN VINCENZO
ASST. EDITOR

SCOTT PETERSON
EDITOR

BATMAN CREATED BY
BOB KANE

SCORPIONS

ACT ONE:
NIGHTMARE OVER GOTHAM

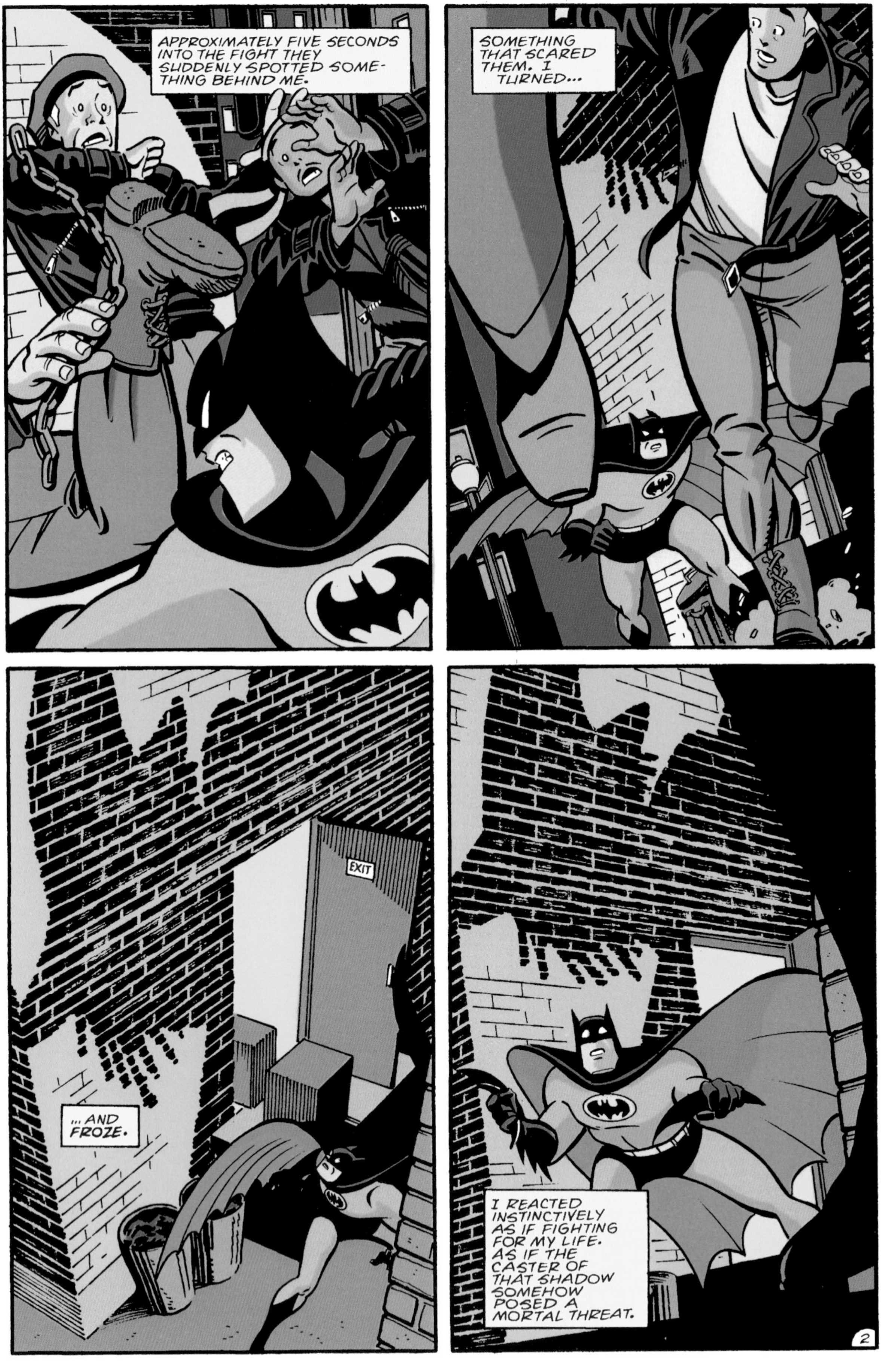
APPROXIMATELY FIVE SECONDS INTO THE FIGHT THEY SUDDENLY SPOTTED SOMETHING BEHIND ME.
SOMETHING THAT SCARED THEM. I TURNED...
EXIT
...AND FROZE.
I REACTED INSTINCTIVELY AS IF FIGHTING FOR MY LIFE. AS IF THE CASTER OF THAT SHADOW SOMEHOW POSED A MORTAL THREAT.
2

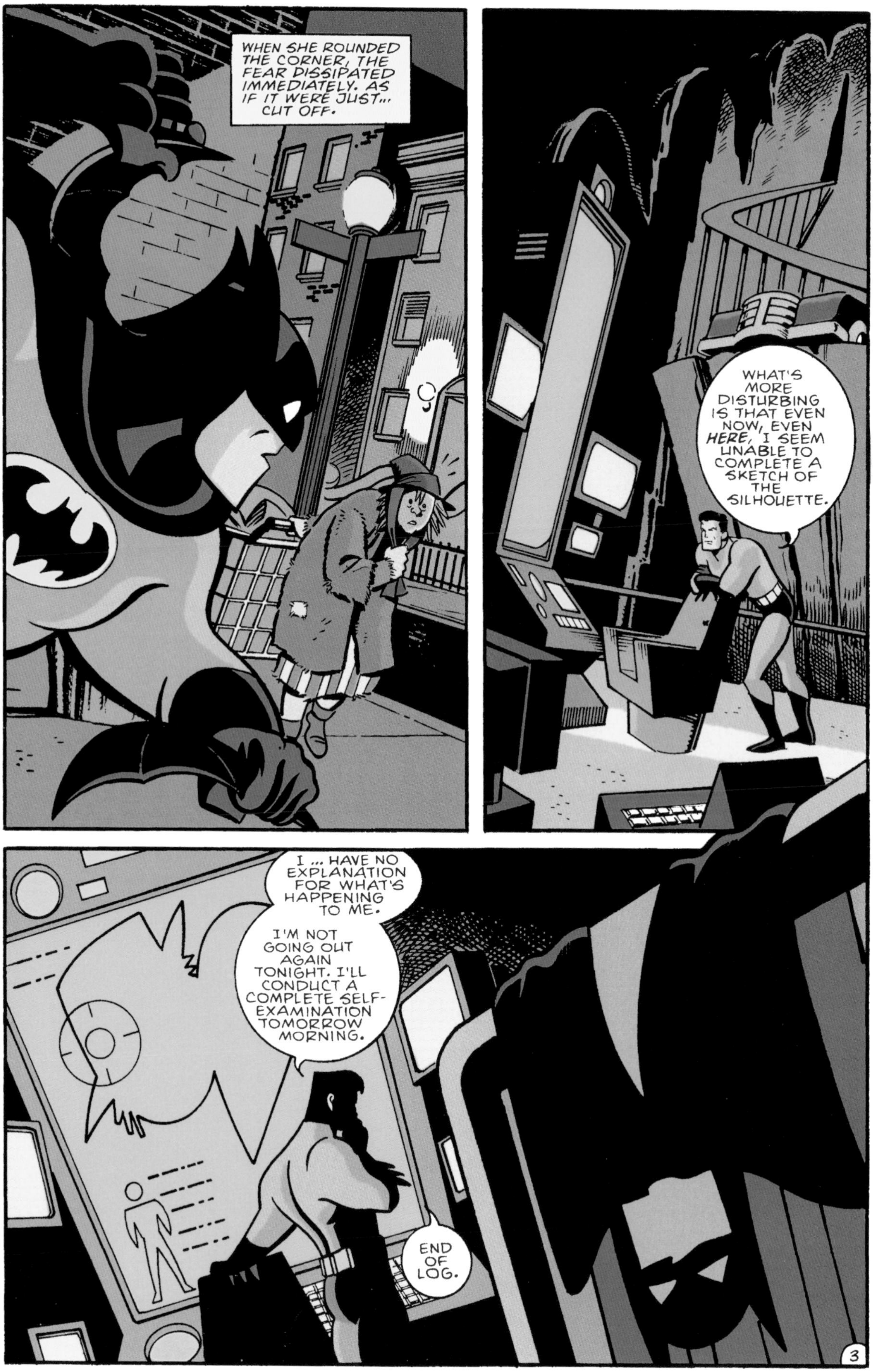
WHEN SHE ROUNDED THE CORNER, THE FEAR DISSIPATED IMMEDIATELY. AS IF IT WERE JUST... CUT OFF.
WHAT'S MORE DISTURBING IS THAT EVEN NOW, EVEN *HERE*, I SEEM UNABLE TO COMPLETE A SKETCH OF THE SILHOUETTE.
I ... HAVE NO EXPLANATION FOR WHAT'S HAPPENING TO ME.
I'M NOT GOING OUT AGAIN TONIGHT. I'LL CONDUCT A COMPLETE SELF-EXAMINATION TOMORROW MORNING.
END OF LOG.
3

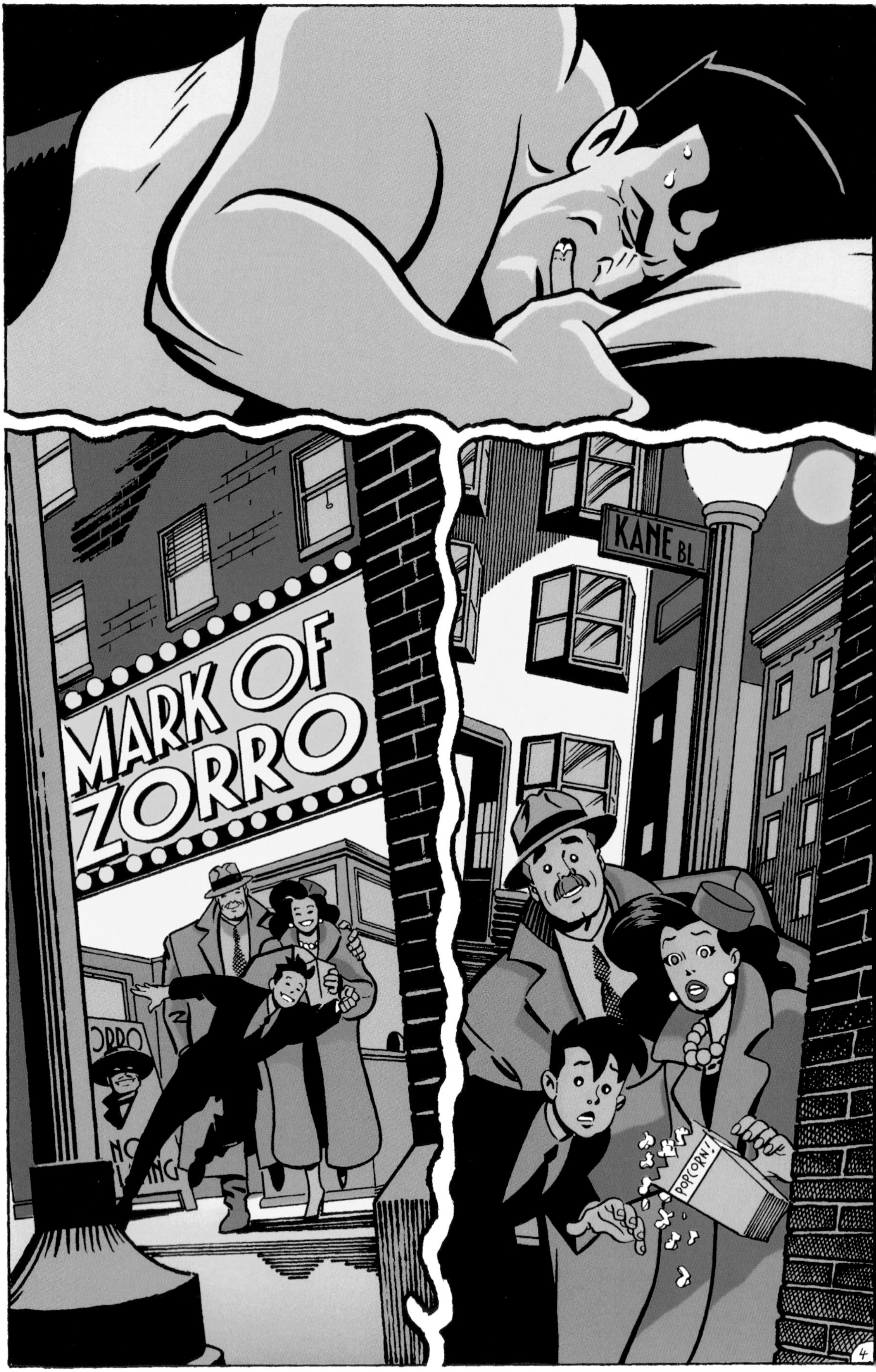
MARK OF ZORRO
KANE BL
POPCORN!

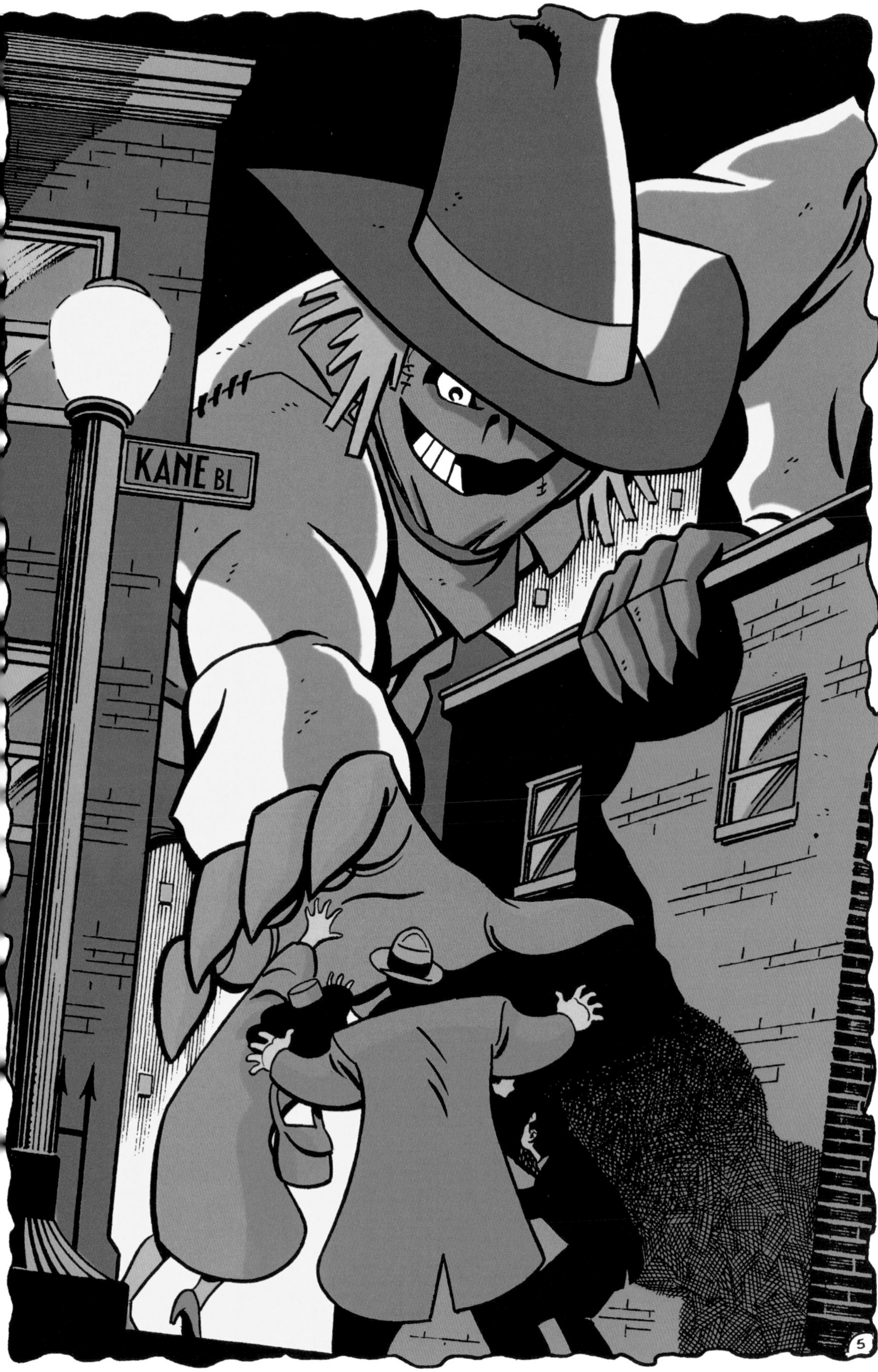
KANE BL
5

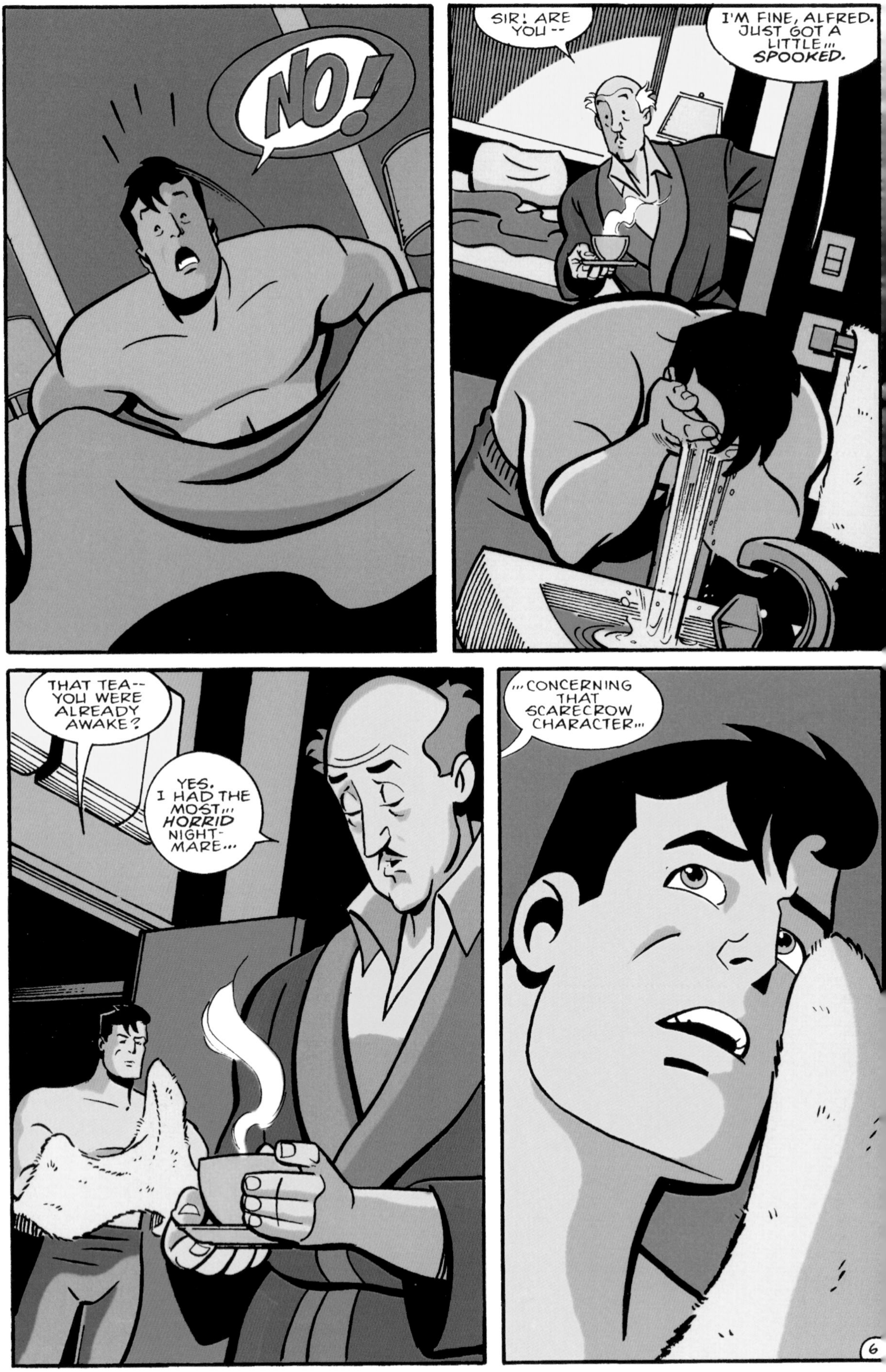
NO!
SIR! ARE YOU --
I'M FINE, ALFRED. JUST GOT A LITTLE... SPOOKED.
THAT TEA-- YOU WERE ALREADY AWAKE?
YES. I HAD THE MOST... HORRID NIGHTMARE...
...CONCERNING THAT SCARECROW CHARACTER...
6

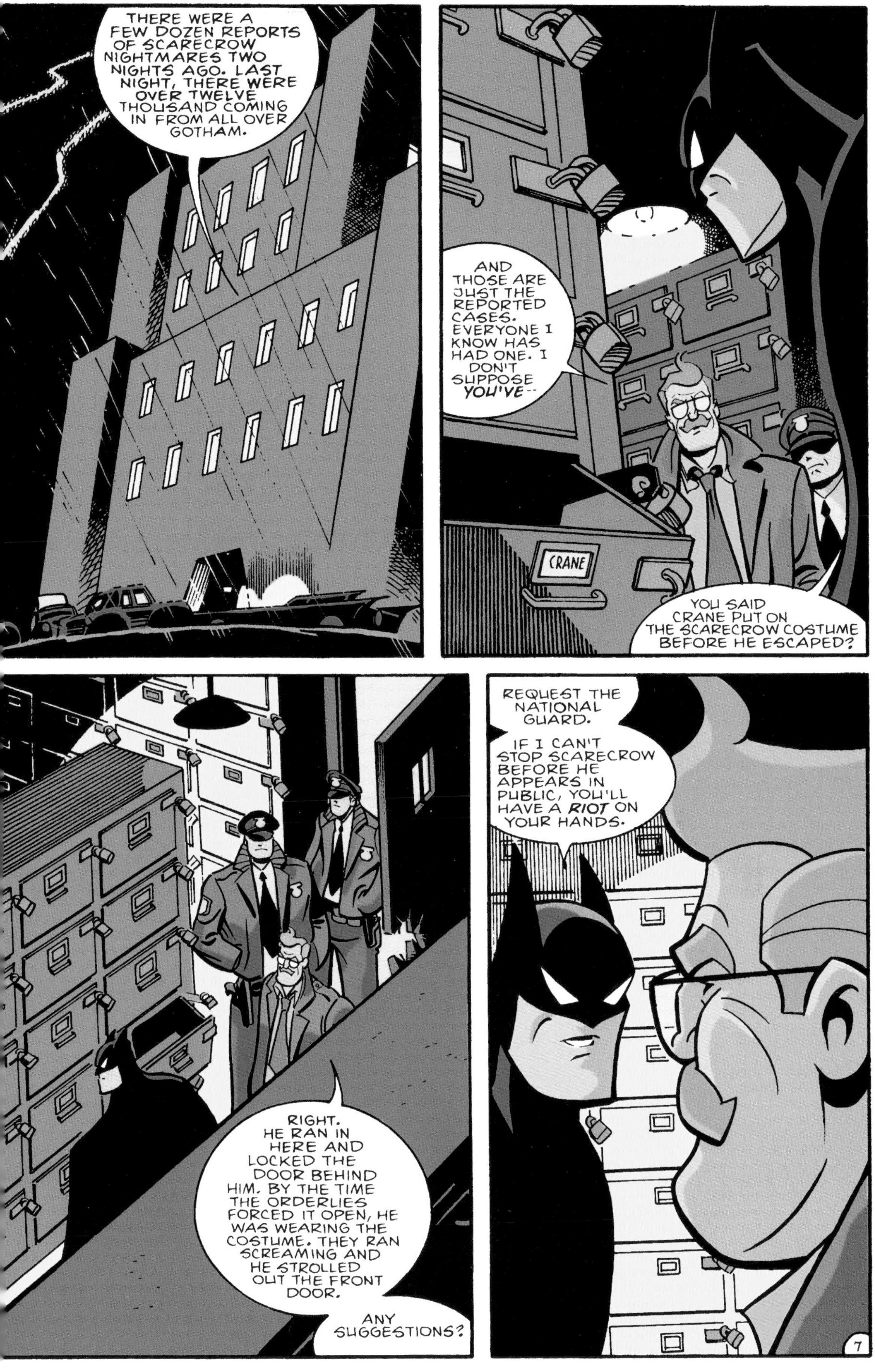
THERE WERE A FEW DOZEN REPORTS OF SCARECROW NIGHTMARES TWO NIGHTS AGO. LAST NIGHT, THERE WERE OVER TWELVE THOUSAND COMING IN FROM ALL OVER GOTHAM.
AND THOSE ARE JUST THE REPORTED CASES. EVERYONE I KNOW HAS HAD ONE. I DON'T SUPPOSE YOU'VE--
CRANE
YOU SAID CRANE PUT ON THE SCARECROW COSTUME BEFORE HE ESCAPED?
RIGHT. HE RAN IN HERE AND LOCKED THE DOOR BEHIND HIM. BY THE TIME THE ORDERLIES FORCED IT OPEN, HE WAS WEARING THE COSTUME. THEY RAN SCREAMING AND HE STROLLED OUT THE FRONT DOOR.
ANY SUGGESTIONS?
REQUEST THE NATIONAL GUARD.
IF I CAN'T STOP SCARECROW BEFORE HE APPEARS IN PUBLIC, YOU'LL HAVE A RIOT ON YOUR HANDS.
7

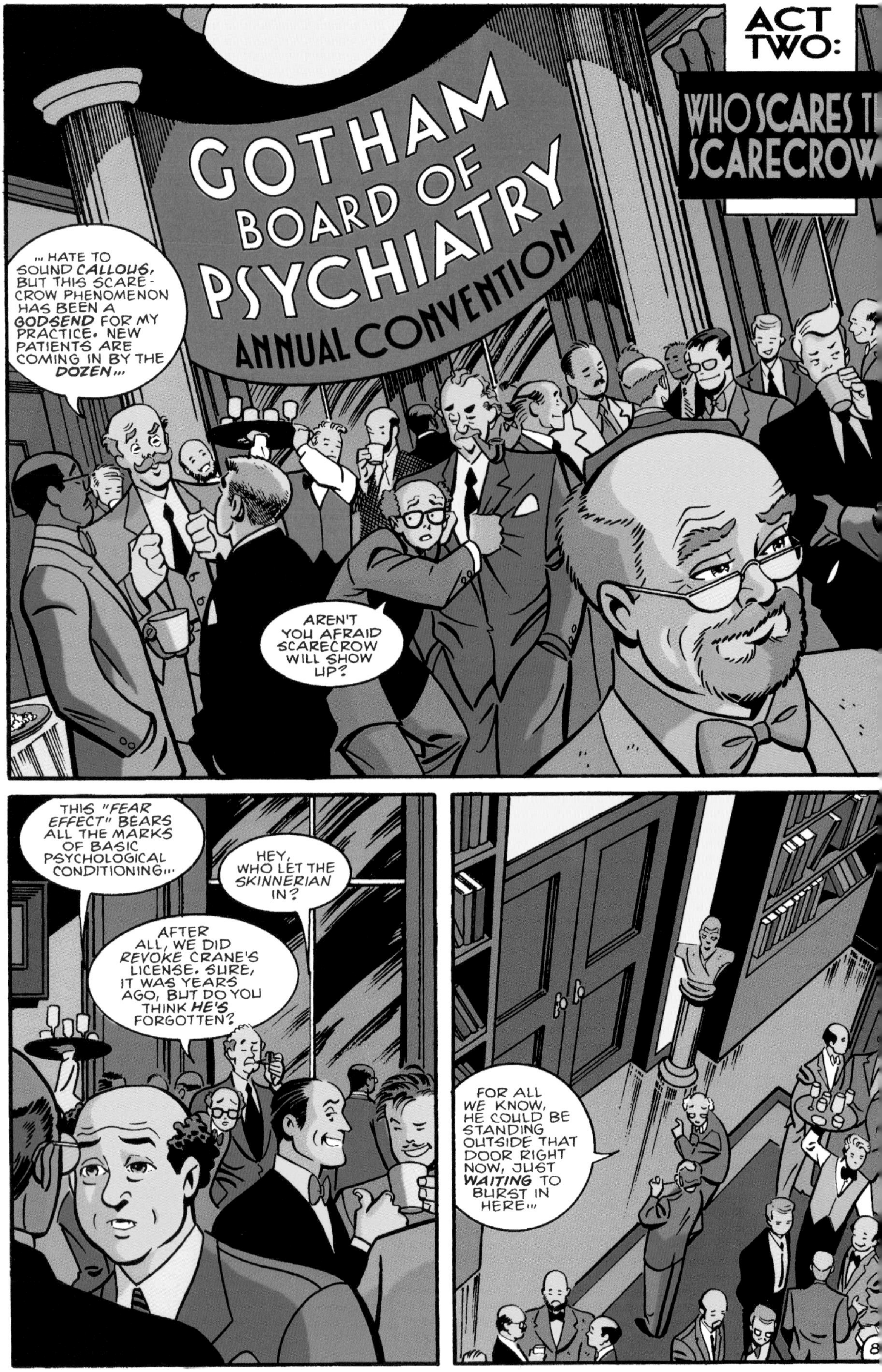
ACT TWO:
WHO SCARES T
SCARECROW
GOTHAM BOARD OF PSYCHIATRY ANNUAL CONVENTION
...HATE TO SOUND CALLOUS, BUT THIS SCARE-CROW PHENOMENON HAS BEEN A GODSEND FOR MY PRACTICE. NEW PATIENTS ARE COMING IN BY THE DOZEN...
AREN'T YOU AFRAID SCARECROW WILL SHOW UP?
THIS "FEAR EFFECT" BEARS ALL THE MARKS OF BASIC PSYCHOLOGICAL CONDITIONING...
HEY, WHO LET THE SKINNERIAN IN?
AFTER ALL, WE DID REVOKE CRANE'S LICENSE. SURE, IT WAS YEARS AGO, BUT DO YOU THINK HE'S FORGOTTEN?
FOR ALL WE KNOW, HE COULD BE STANDING OUTSIDE THAT DOOR RIGHT NOW, JUST WAITING TO BURST IN HERE...
8

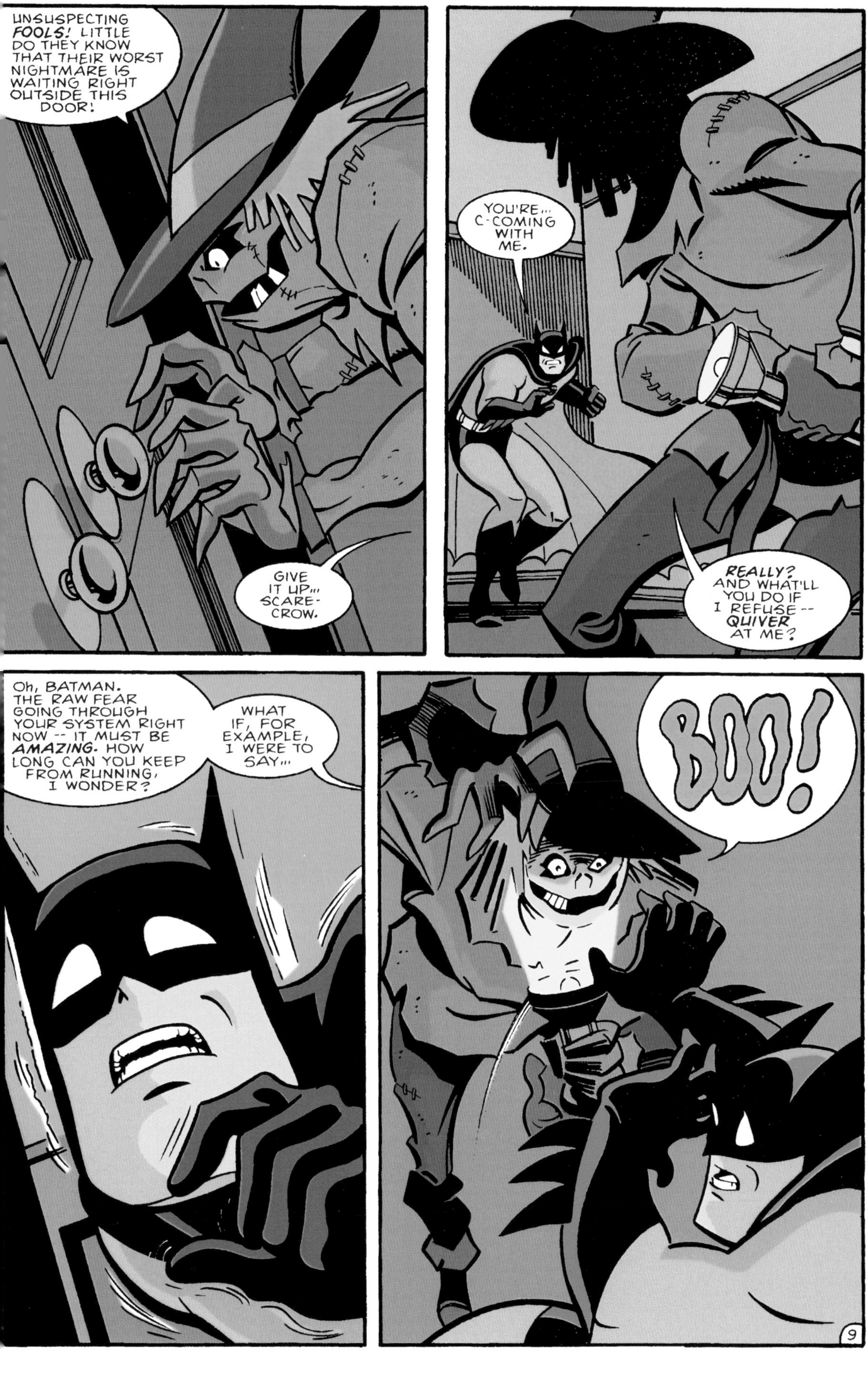
UNSUSPECTING FOOLS! LITTLE DO THEY KNOW THAT THEIR WORST NIGHTMARE IS WAITING RIGHT OUTSIDE THIS DOOR!
GIVE IT UP... SCARE-CROW.
YOU'RE... C-COMING WITH ME.
REALLY? AND WHAT'LL YOU DO IF I REFUSE -- QUIVER AT ME?
Oh, BATMAN. THE RAW FEAR GOING THROUGH YOUR SYSTEM RIGHT NOW -- IT MUST BE AMAZING. HOW LONG CAN YOU KEEP FROM RUNNING, I WONDER?
WHAT IF, FOR EXAMPLE, I WERE TO SAY...
BOO!
9

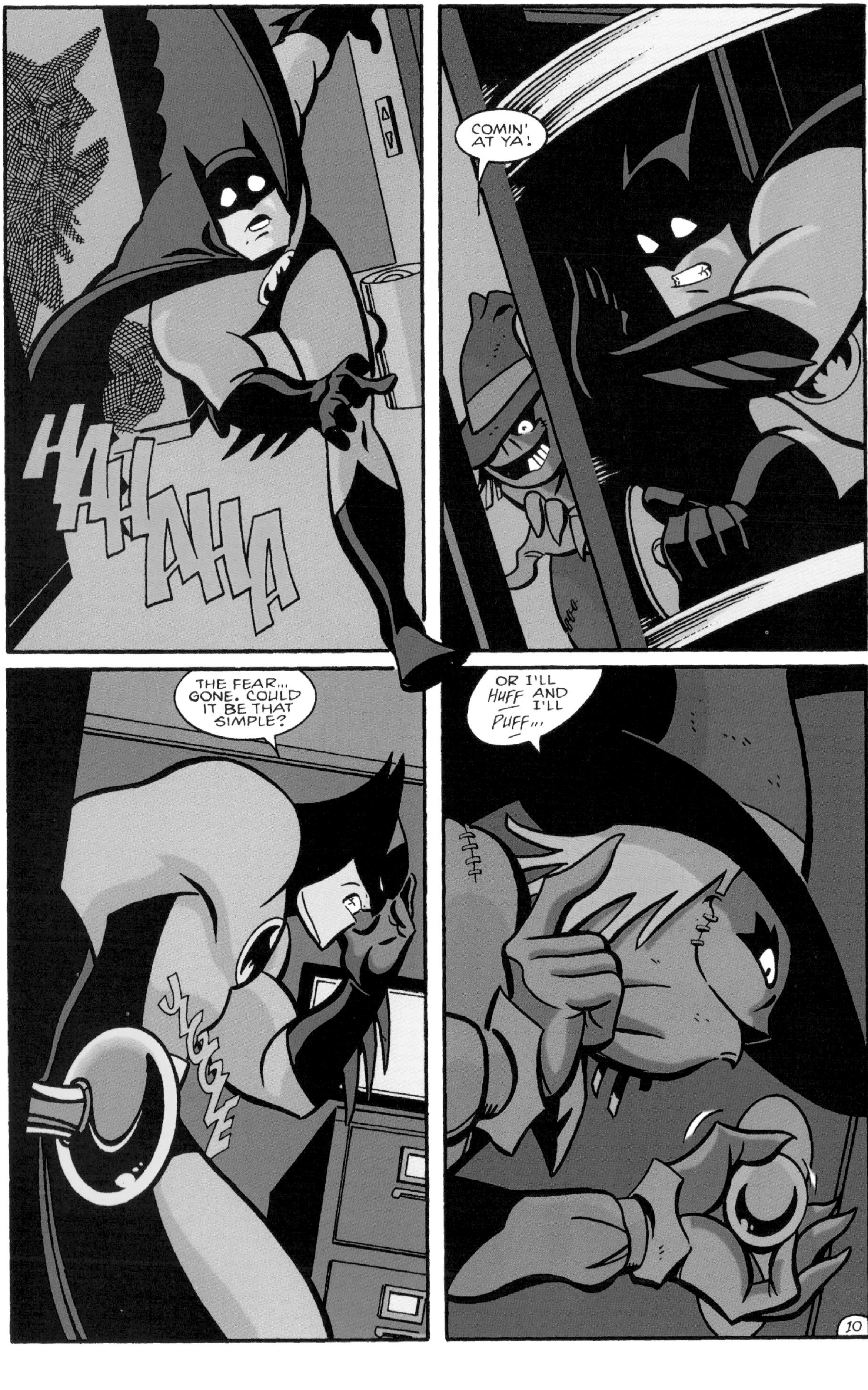
HAHAHAHA
COMIN' AT YA!
THE FEAR... GONE. COULD IT BE THAT SIMPLE?
OR I'LL HUFF AND I'LL PUFF...
10

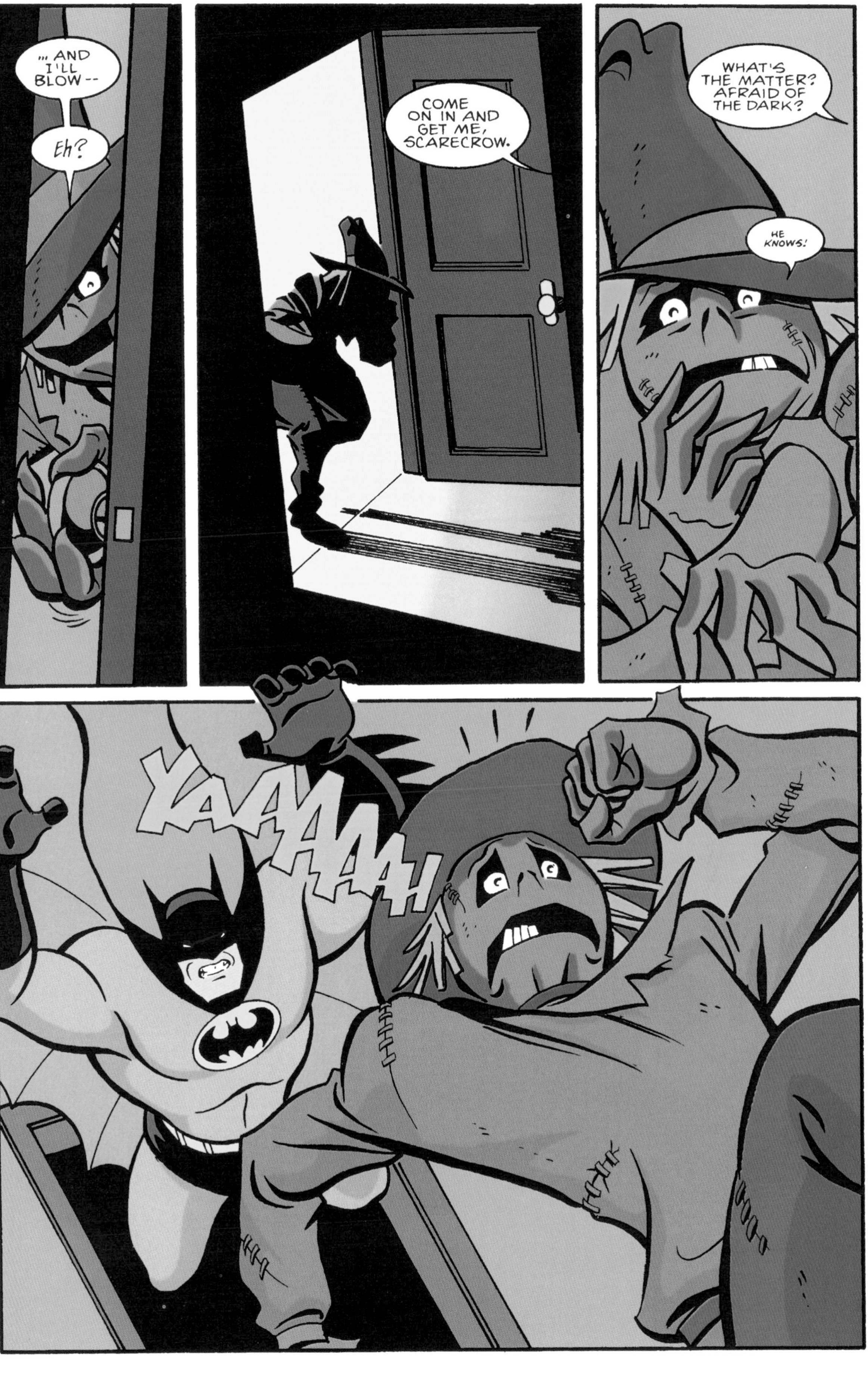
... AND I'LL BLOW --
Eh?
COME ON IN AND GET ME, SCARECROW.
WHAT'S THE MATTER? AFRAID OF THE DARK?
HE KNOWS!
YAAAAAAH

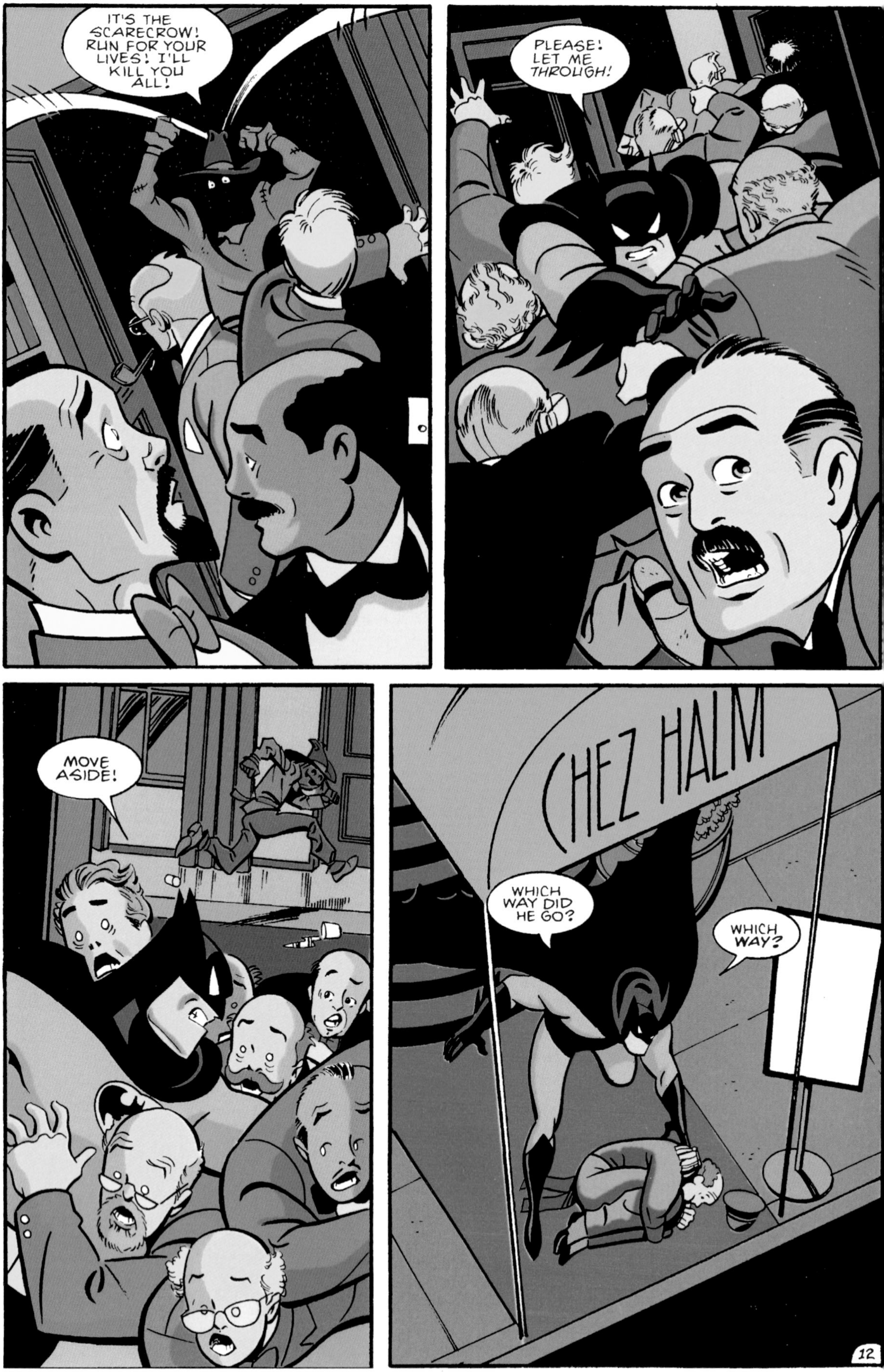
IT'S THE SCARECROW! RUN FOR YOUR LIVES! I'LL KILL YOU ALL!
PLEASE! LET ME THROUGH!
MOVE ASIDE!
CHEZ HALM
WHICH WAY DID HE GO?
WHICH WAY?
12

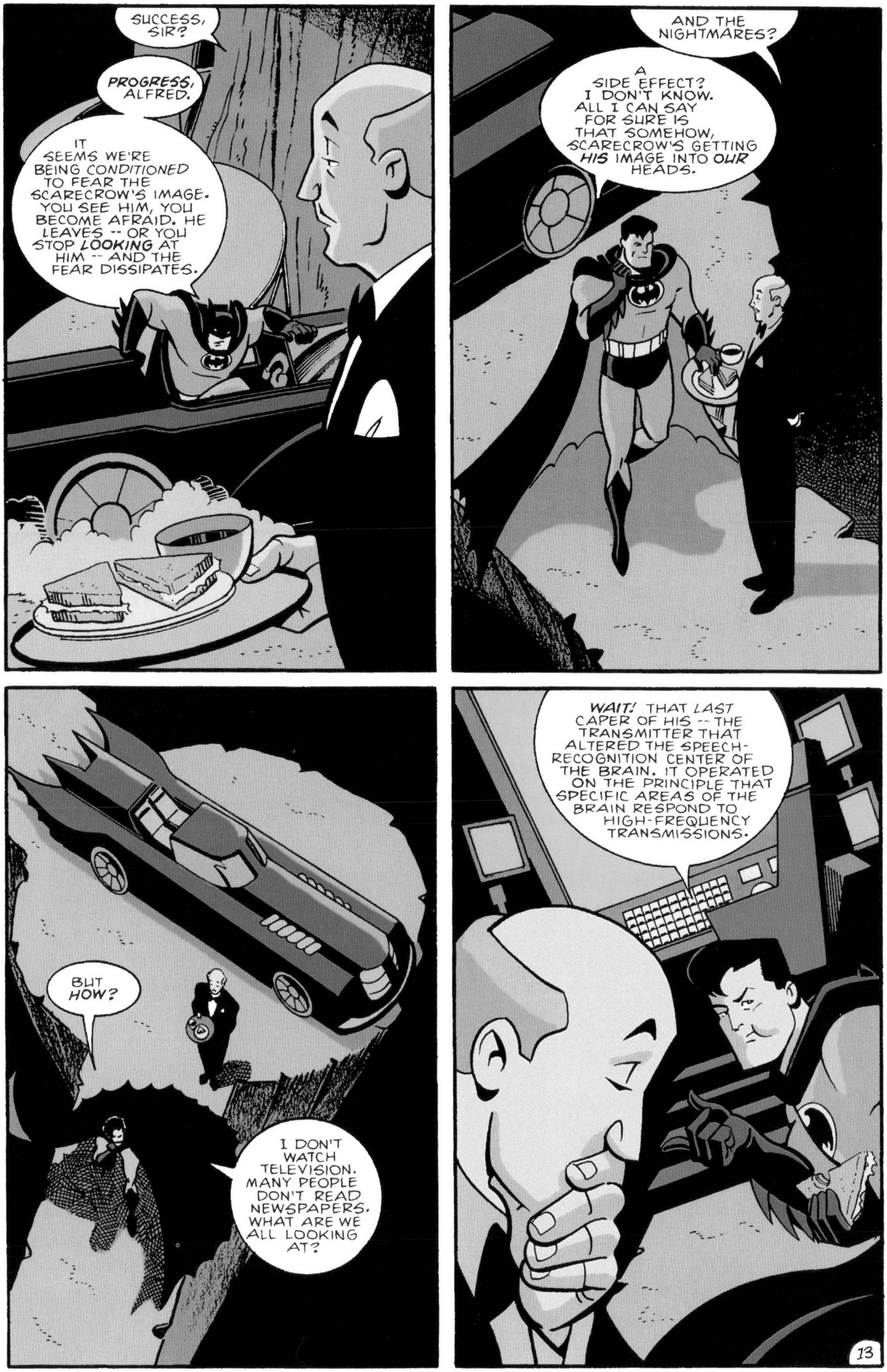

SUCCESS, SIR?
PROGRESS, ALFRED.
IT SEEMS WE'RE BEING CONDITIONED TO FEAR THE SCARECROW'S IMAGE. YOU SEE HIM, YOU BECOME AFRAID. HE LEAVES -- OR YOU STOP LOOKING AT HIM -- AND THE FEAR DISSIPATES.
AND THE NIGHTMARES?
A SIDE EFFECT? I DON'T KNOW. ALL I CAN SAY FOR SURE IS THAT SOMEHOW, SCARECROW'S GETTING HIS IMAGE INTO OUR HEADS.
BUT HOW?
I DON'T WATCH TELEVISION. MANY PEOPLE DON'T READ NEWSPAPERS. WHAT ARE WE ALL LOOKING AT?
WAIT! THAT LAST CAPER OF HIS -- THE TRANSMITTER THAT ALTERED THE SPEECH-RECOGNITION CENTER OF THE BRAIN. IT OPERATED ON THE PRINCIPLE THAT SPECIFIC AREAS OF THE BRAIN RESPOND TO HIGH-FREQUENCY TRANSMISSIONS.
13

COULD IT POSSIBLY HAVE BEEN REDESIGNED TO BEAM A SPECIFIC IMAGE *DIRECTLY* INTO OUR VISUAL CORTICES?

A SIGNAL OF THAT STRENGTH *SHOULD* BE EASILY DETECTABLE...

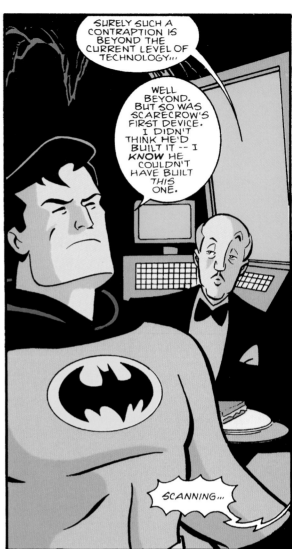

SURELY SUCH A CONTRAPTION IS BEYOND THE CURRENT LEVEL OF TECHNOLOGY...

WELL BEYOND. BUT SO WAS SCARECROW'S FIRST DEVICE. I DIDN'T THINK HE'D BUILT IT -- I *KNOW* HE COULDN'T HAVE BUILT *THIS* ONE.

SCANNING...

TRANSMISSION FOUND. TRACKING POINT OF ORIGIN...

GOT IT.

THANKS FOR DINNER, ALFRED.

->Ahem<- YOU'RE WELCOME, SIR.

ACT THREE: BENEATH THE MASK

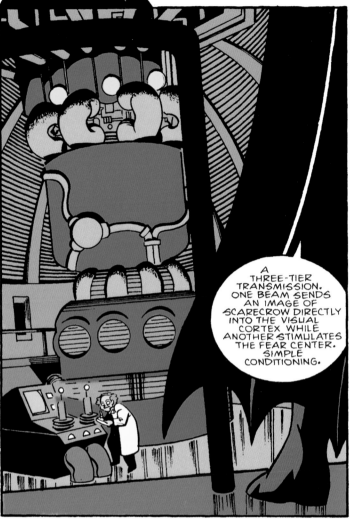

A THREE-TIER TRANSMISSION. ONE BEAM SENDS AN IMAGE OF SCARECROW DIRECTLY INTO THE VISUAL CORTEX WHILE ANOTHER STIMULATES THE FEAR CENTER. SIMPLE CONDITIONING.

YES, YES, AND THE THIRD BEAM STOPS THE FEAR RESPONSE AT THE BRAIN STEM SO THE SUBJECT IS UNAWARE OF THE PROCESS. DO YOU HAVE A *POINT*?!

CRANE DIDN'T BUILD THIS OR THE SPEECH DEVICE, DID HE?

OF COURSE NOT. THE INITIAL CONCEPT FOR IT, AS FOR *THIS* DEVICE, WAS CRANE'S, BUT THEY WERE JUST *IDEAS.* HE COULDN'T POSSIBLY HAVE BUILT THEM HIMSELF.

AND HE *NEVER* SAW THEIR *TRUE* POTENTIAL. WHERE IS HE NOW -- RUNNING AROUND TOWN, SCARING OLD LADIES? HOW *PATHETIC.*

MY *GREATEST* EXPERIMENT AND *HE* USES IT TO SUPPORT HIS FRAGILE EGO.

15

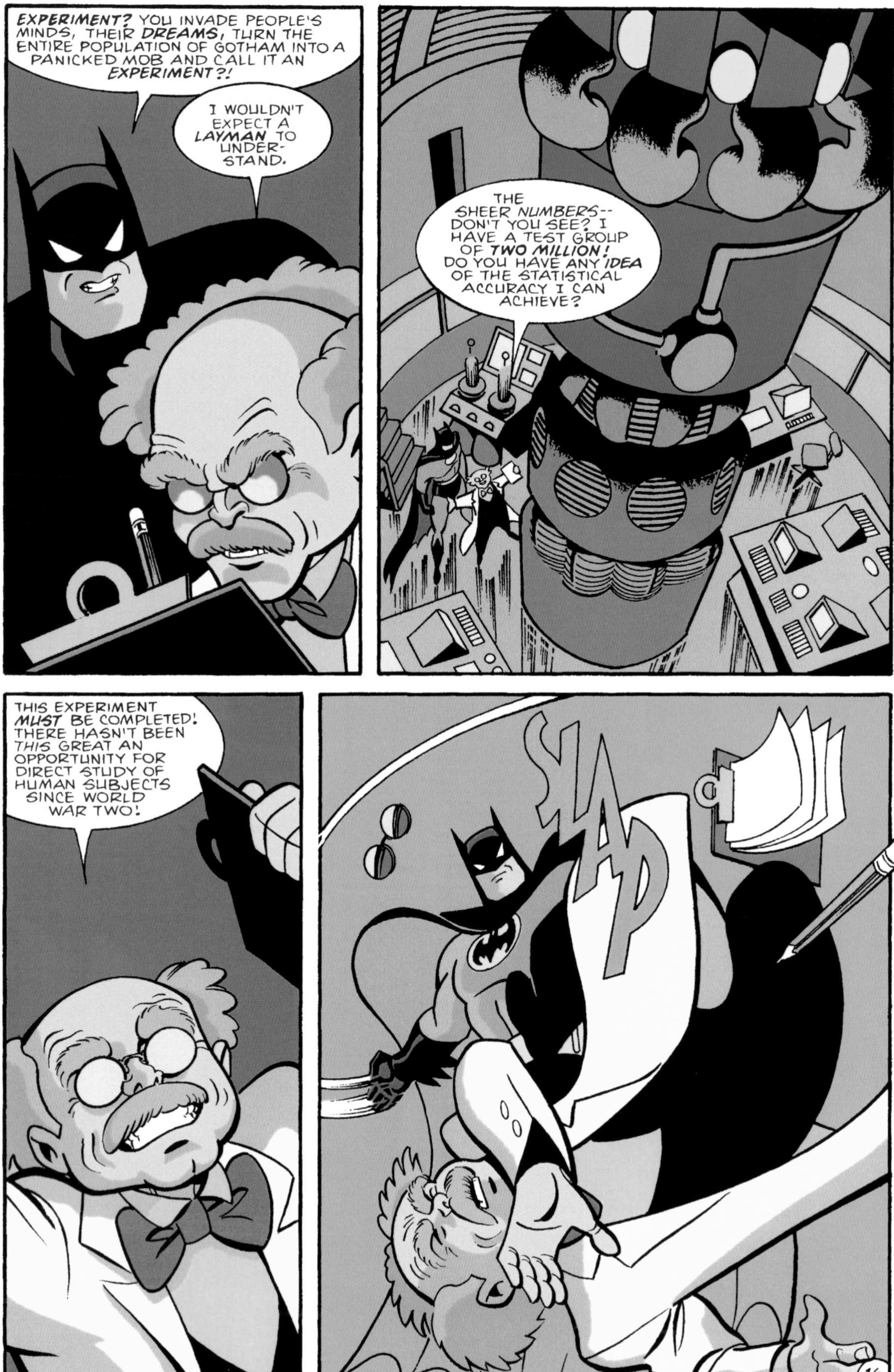
EXPERIMENT? YOU INVADE PEOPLE'S MINDS, THEIR DREAMS, TURN THE ENTIRE POPULATION OF GOTHAM INTO A PANICKED MOB AND CALL IT AN EXPERIMENT?!
I WOULDN'T EXPECT A LAYMAN TO UNDER-STAND.
THE SHEER NUMBERS-- DON'T YOU SEE? I HAVE A TEST GROUP OF TWO MILLION! DO YOU HAVE ANY IDEA OF THE STATISTICAL ACCURACY I CAN ACHIEVE?
THIS EXPERIMENT MUST BE COMPLETED! THERE HASN'T BEEN THIS GREAT AN OPPORTUNITY FOR DIRECT STUDY OF HUMAN SUBJECTS SINCE WORLD WAR TWO!
SLAP
16

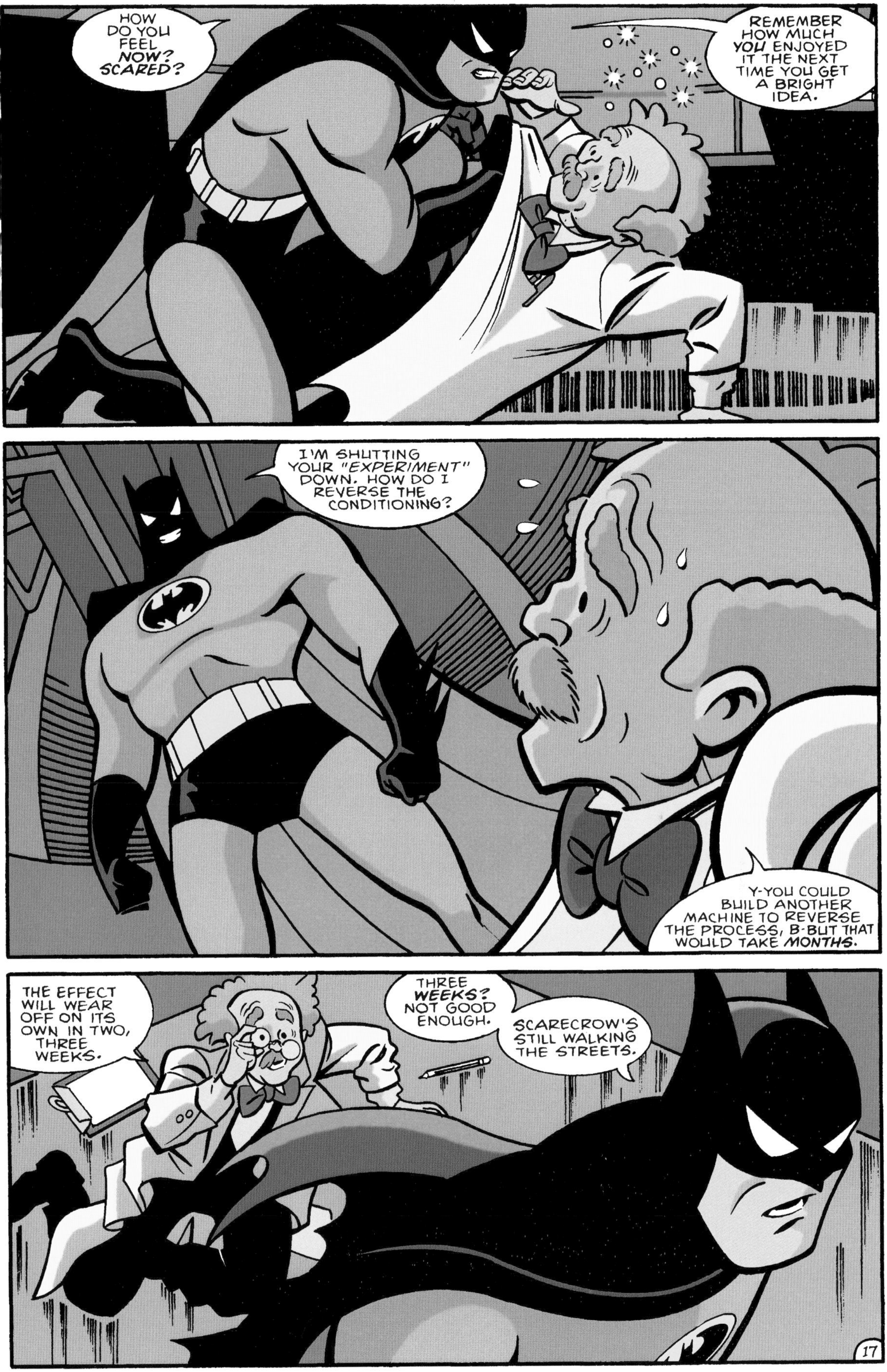
HOW DO YOU FEEL NOW? SCARED?
REMEMBER HOW MUCH YOU ENJOYED IT THE NEXT TIME YOU GET A BRIGHT IDEA.
I'M SHUTTING YOUR "EXPERIMENT" DOWN. HOW DO I REVERSE THE CONDITIONING?
Y-YOU COULD BUILD ANOTHER MACHINE TO REVERSE THE PROCESS, B-BUT THAT WOULD TAKE MONTHS.
THE EFFECT WILL WEAR OFF ON ITS OWN IN TWO, THREE WEEKS.
THREE WEEKS? NOT GOOD ENOUGH.
SCARECROW'S STILL WALKING THE STREETS.
17

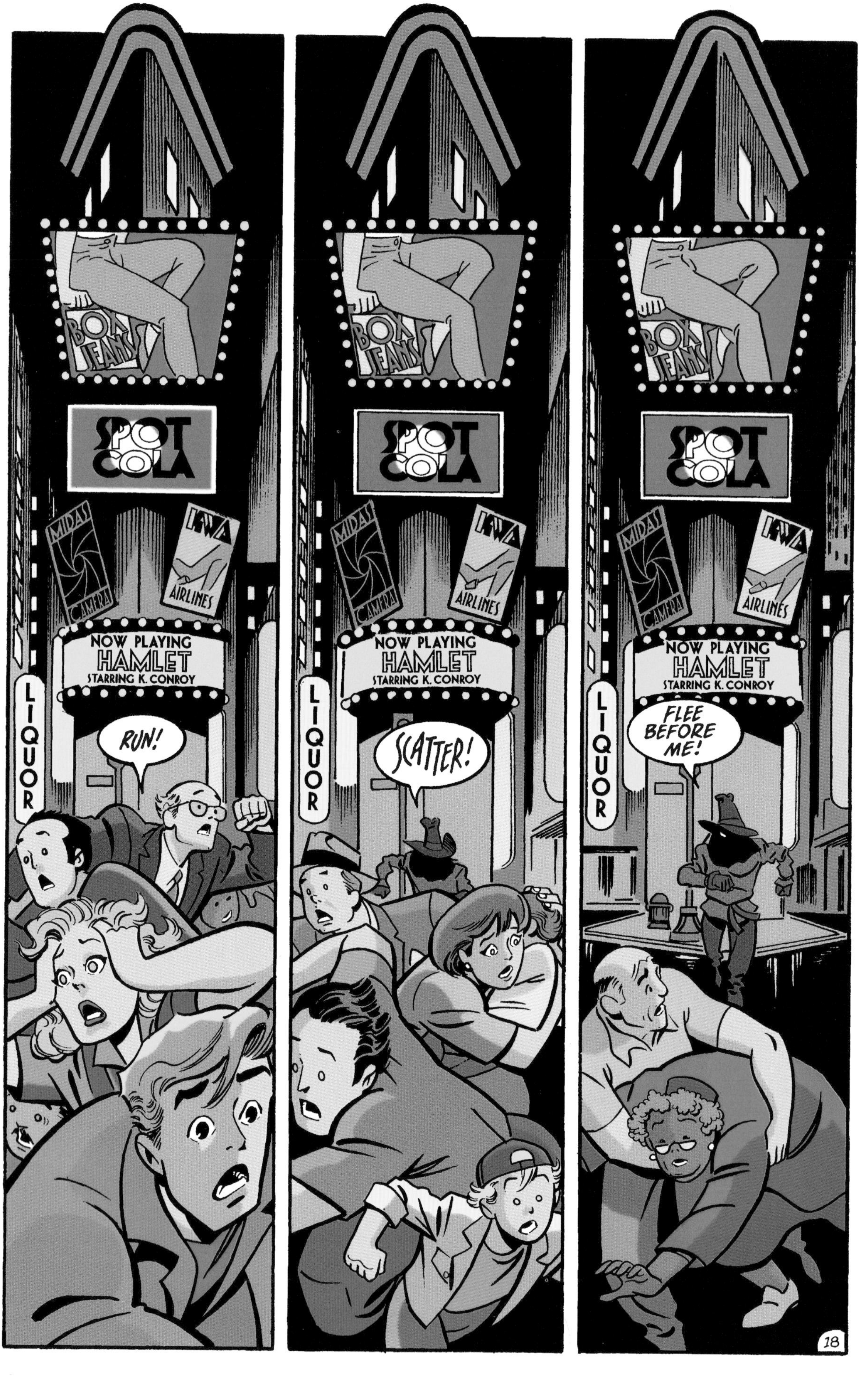

BOX JEANS
SPOT COLA
MIDAS CAMERA
AIRLINES
NOW PLAYING HAMLET STARRING K. CONROY
LIQUOR
RUN!
SCATTER!
FLEE BEFORE ME!
18

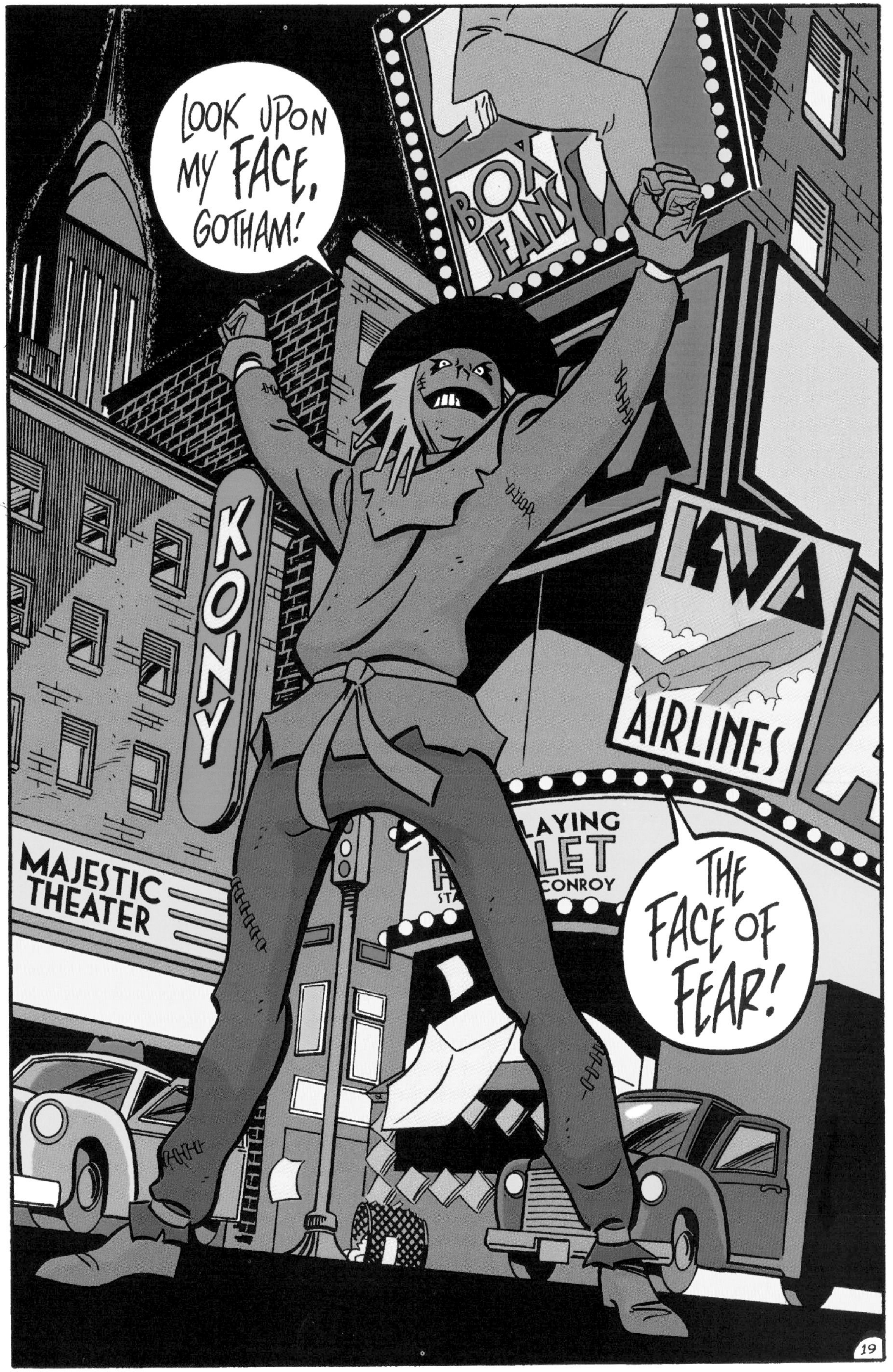

LOOK UPON MY FACE, GOTHAM!
BOX JEANS
KONY
KWA
AIRLINES
MAJESTIC THEATER
THE FACE OF FEAR!
19

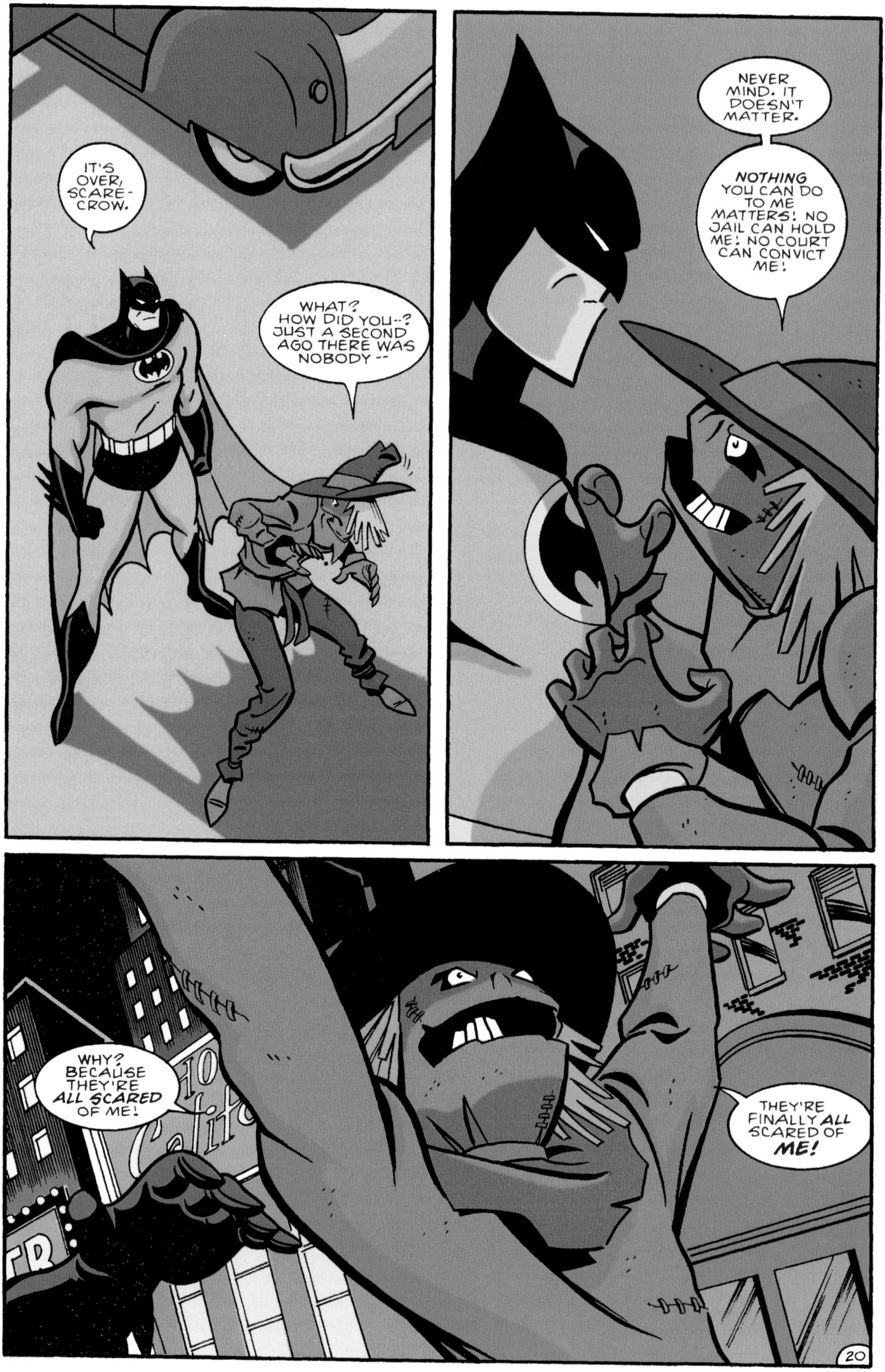
IT'S OVER, SCARE-CROW.
WHAT? HOW DID YOU--? JUST A SECOND AGO THERE WAS NOBODY --
NEVER MIND. IT DOESN'T MATTER.
NOTHING YOU CAN DO TO ME MATTERS! NO JAIL CAN HOLD ME! NO COURT CAN CONVICT ME!
WHY? BECAUSE THEY'RE ALL SCARED OF ME!
THEY'RE FINALLY ALL SCARED OF ME!
20

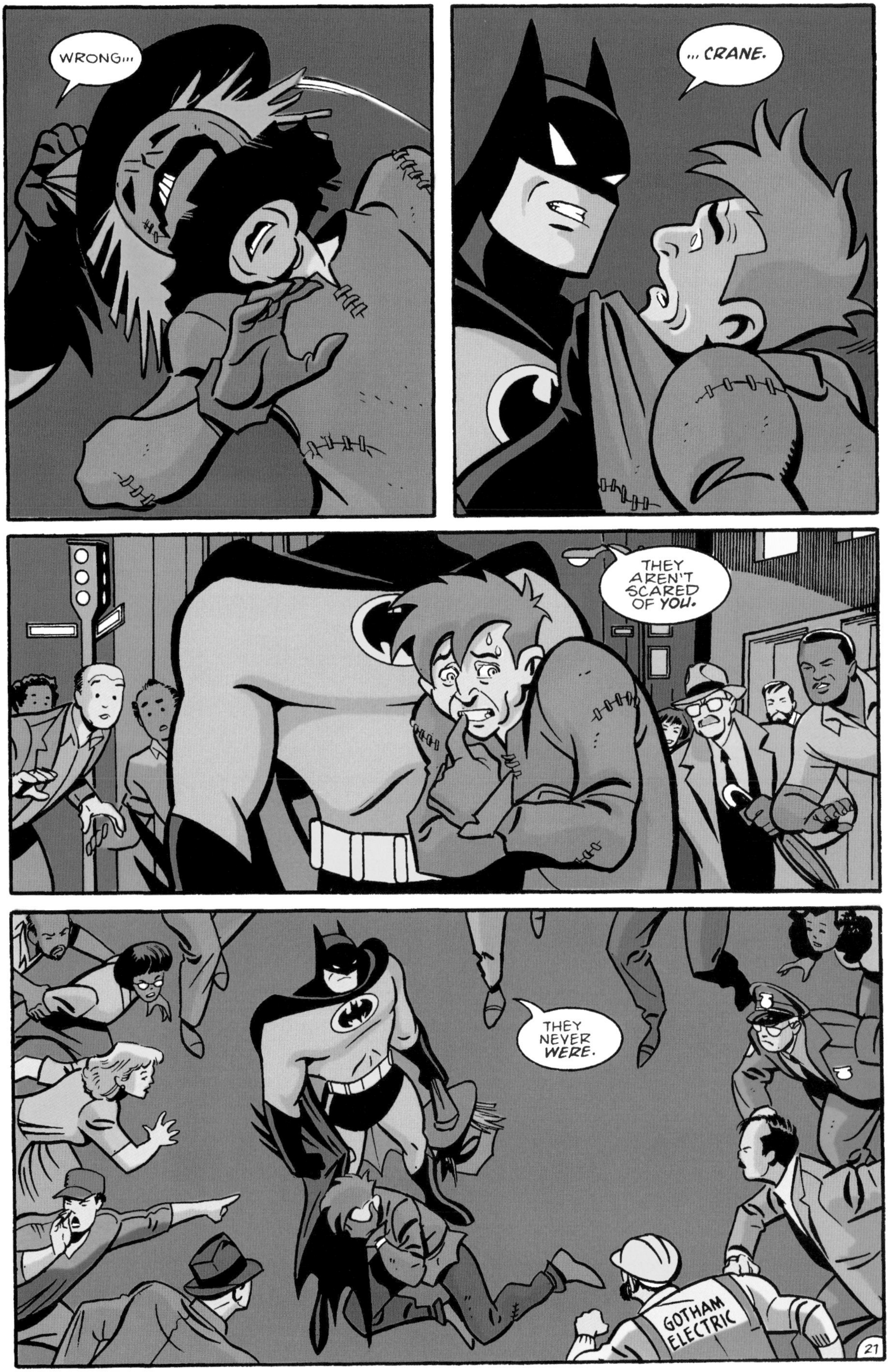
WRONG...
...CRANE.
THEY AREN'T SCARED OF YOU.
THEY NEVER WERE.
GOTHAM ELECTRIC
21

WELL, THINGS SEEM RELATIVELY BACK TO NORMAL.

GOTHAM GAZETTE

SCARECROW CAPTURED!

GOTHAM BREATHES EASIER

by STARSHINE ROWELL

Things are finally back to normal the recent attacks upon Gotham's populace by the notorious criminal Scarecrow. Police Commissioner Gordon was unavailable for comment but looked relieved at the recent court...

THE FEAR EFFECT SHOULD WEAR OFF COMPLETELY WITHIN THE WEEK.

AND NOT A MOMENT TOO SOON, FOR MY TASTE. NIGHTMARES EVERY NIGHT IS NO WAY TO LIVE ONE'S LIFE.

OH, DEAR.

I DO APOLOGIZE, SIR.

THAT'S... ALL RIGHT, ALFRED.

THE END

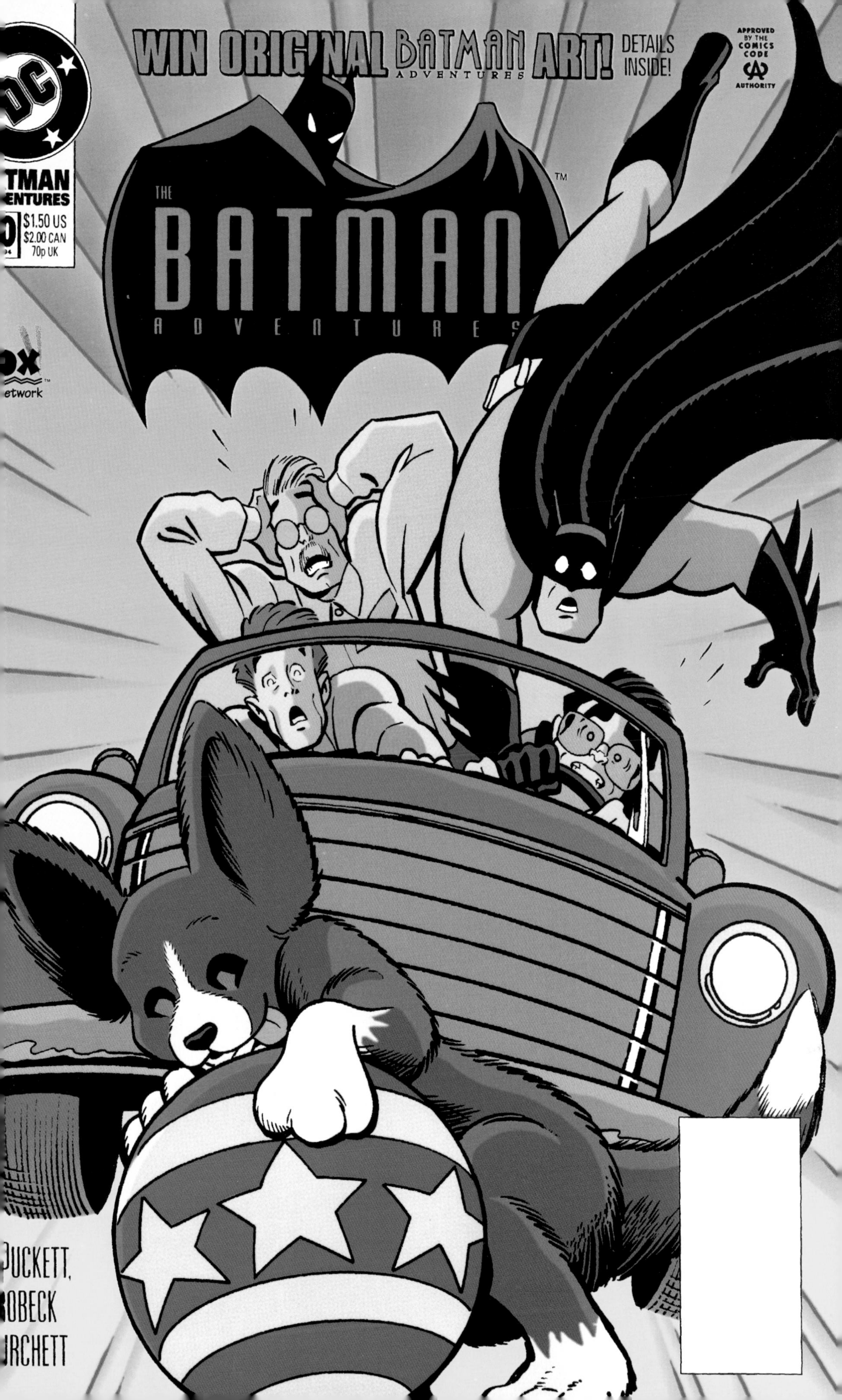

WIN ORIGINAL BATMAN ADVENTURES ART! DETAILS INSIDE!
APPROVED BY THE COMICS CODE AUTHORITY
DC
TMAN
ENTURES
$1.50 US
$2.00 CAN
70p UK
THE BATMAN ADVENTURES
etwork
UCKETT,
OBECK
RCHETT

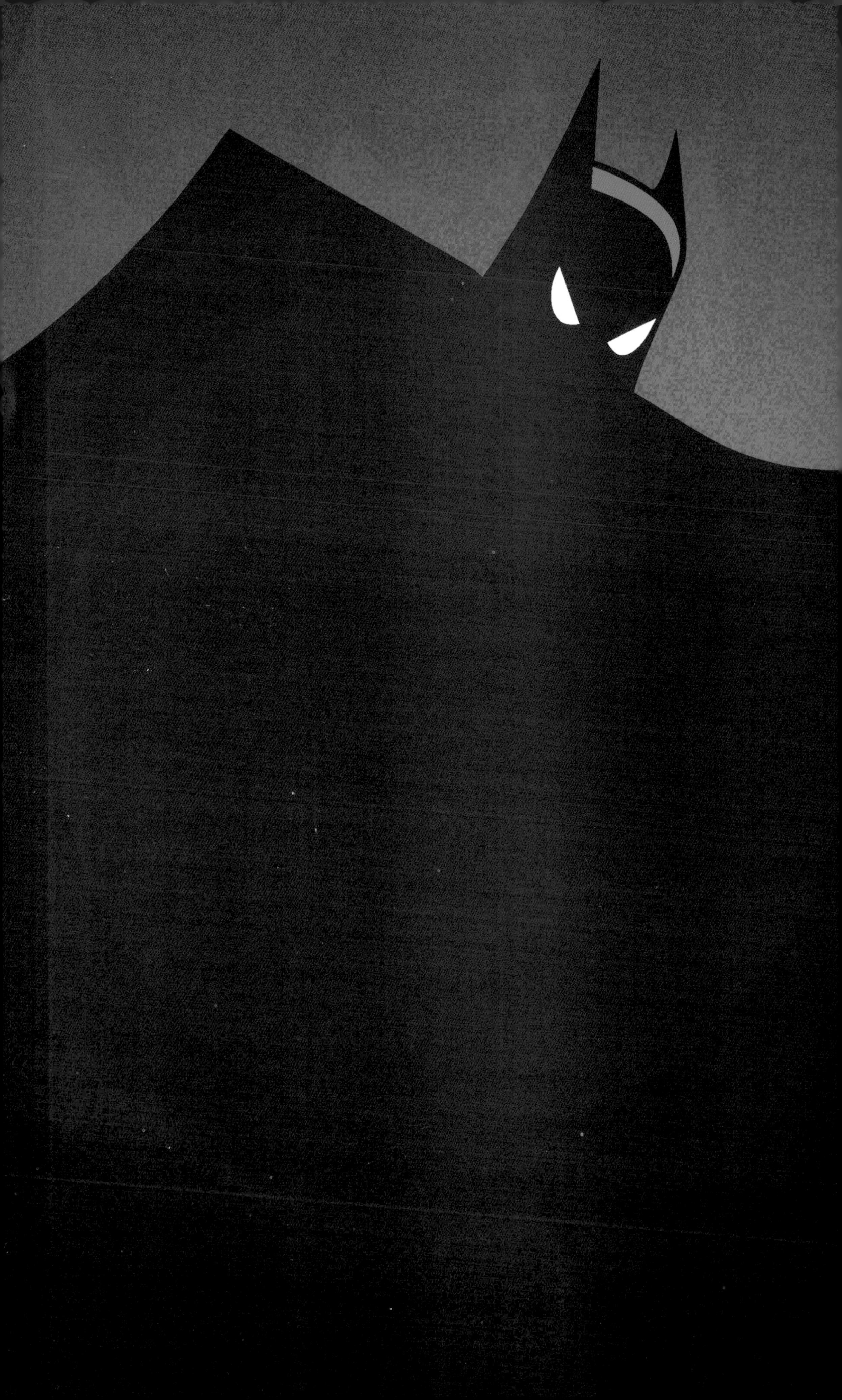

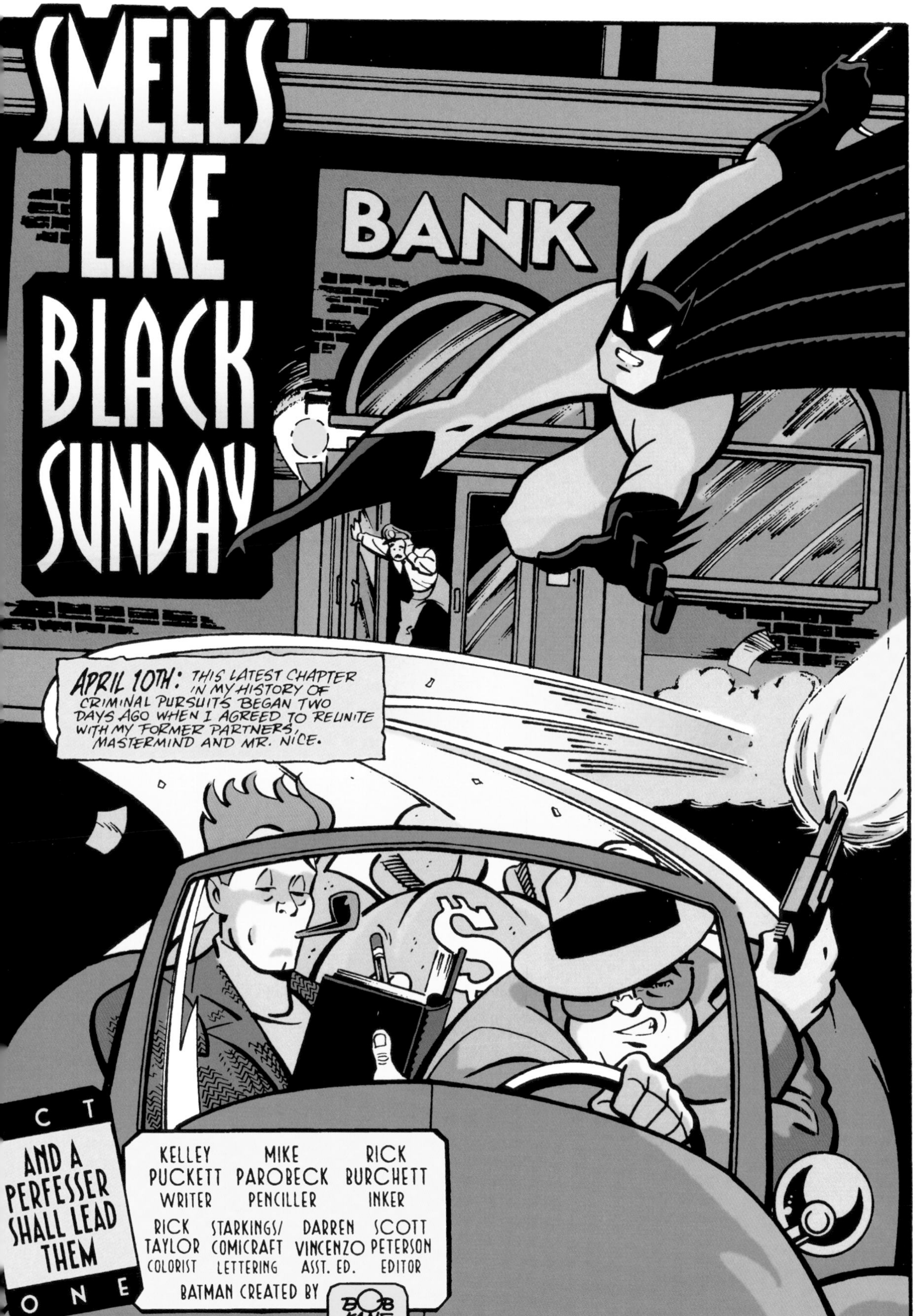
SMELLS LIKE BLACK SUNDAY
BANK
APRIL 10TH: THIS LATEST CHAPTER IN MY HISTORY OF CRIMINAL PURSUITS BEGAN TWO DAYS AGO WHEN I AGREED TO REUNITE WITH MY FORMER PARTNERS, MASTERMIND AND MR. NICE.
ACT ONE
AND A PERFESSER SHALL LEAD THEM
KELLEY PUCKETT WRITER
MIKE PAROBECK PENCILLER
RICK BURCHETT INKER
RICK TAYLOR COLORIST
STARKINGS/ COMICRAFT LETTERING
DARREN VINCENZO ASST. ED.
SCOTT PETERSON EDITOR
BATMAN CREATED BY BOB KANE

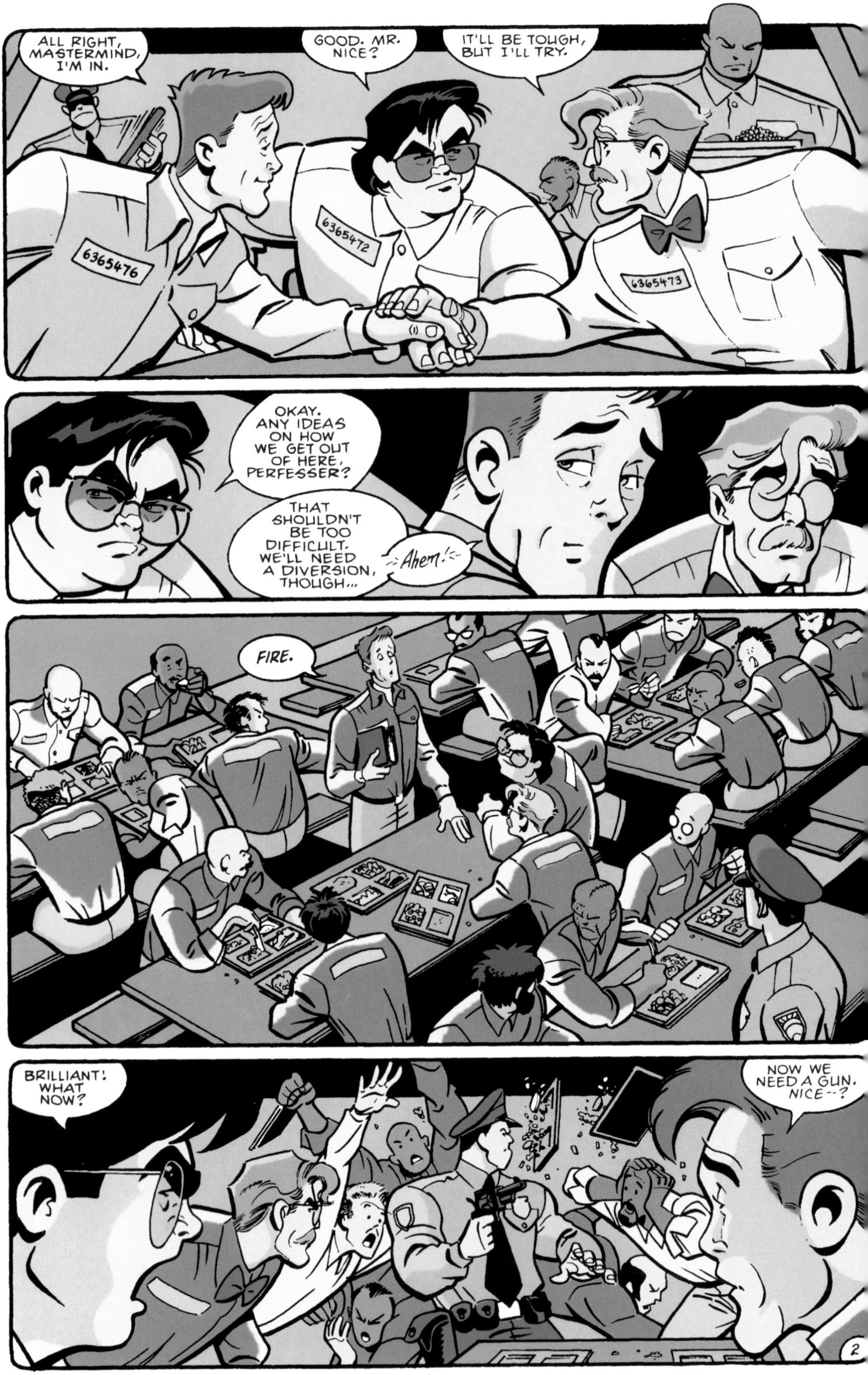
ALL RIGHT, MASTERMIND, I'M IN.
GOOD. MR. NICE?
IT'LL BE TOUGH, BUT I'LL TRY.
6365476
6365472
6365473
OKAY. ANY IDEAS ON HOW WE GET OUT OF HERE, PERFESSER?
THAT SHOULDN'T BE TOO DIFFICULT. WE'LL NEED A DIVERSION, THOUGH...
Ahem
FIRE.
BRILLIANT! WHAT NOW?
NOW WE NEED A GUN. NICE--?
2

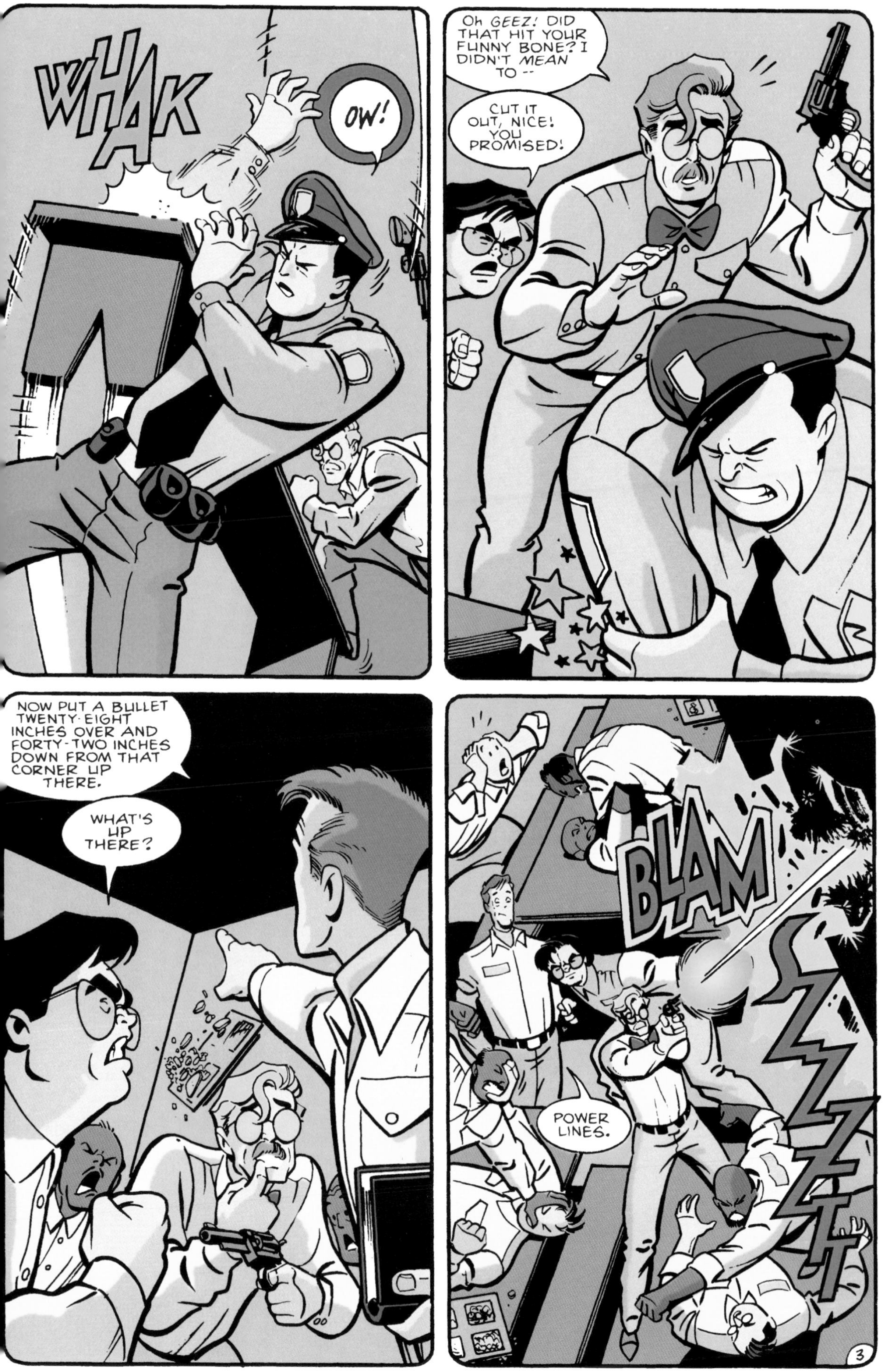
WHAK
OW!
Oh GEEZ! DID THAT HIT YOUR FUNNY BONE? I DIDN'T MEAN TO --
CUT IT OUT, NICE! YOU PROMISED!
NOW PUT A BULLET TWENTY-EIGHT INCHES OVER AND FORTY-TWO INCHES DOWN FROM THAT CORNER UP THERE.
WHAT'S UP THERE?
BLAM
POWER LINES.
ZZZZT
3

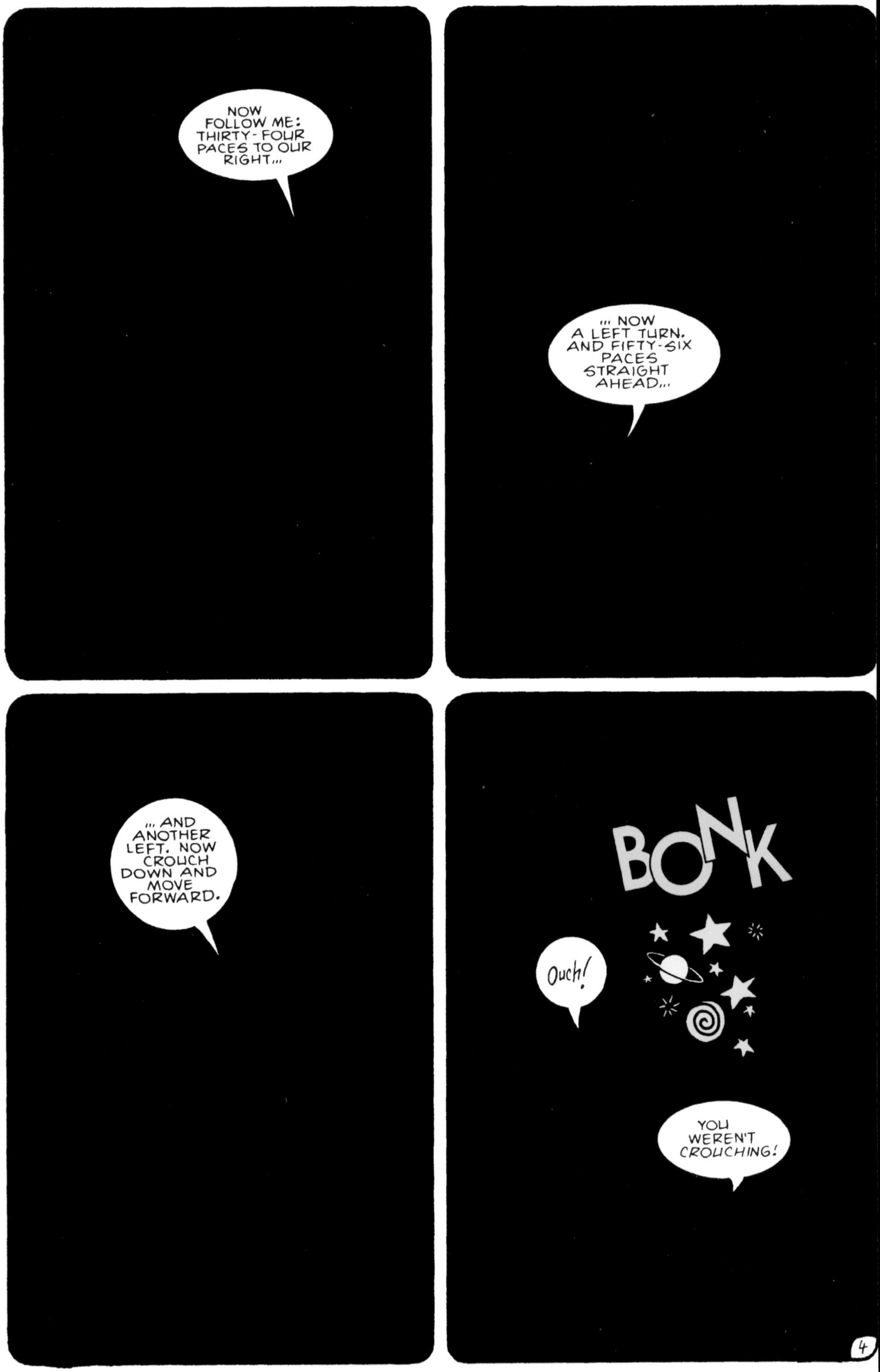

NOW FOLLOW ME: THIRTY-FOUR PACES TO OUR RIGHT...
... NOW A LEFT TURN. AND FIFTY-SIX PACES STRAIGHT AHEAD...
... AND ANOTHER LEFT. NOW CROUCH DOWN AND MOVE FORWARD.
BONK
Ouch!
YOU WEREN'T CROUCHING!
4

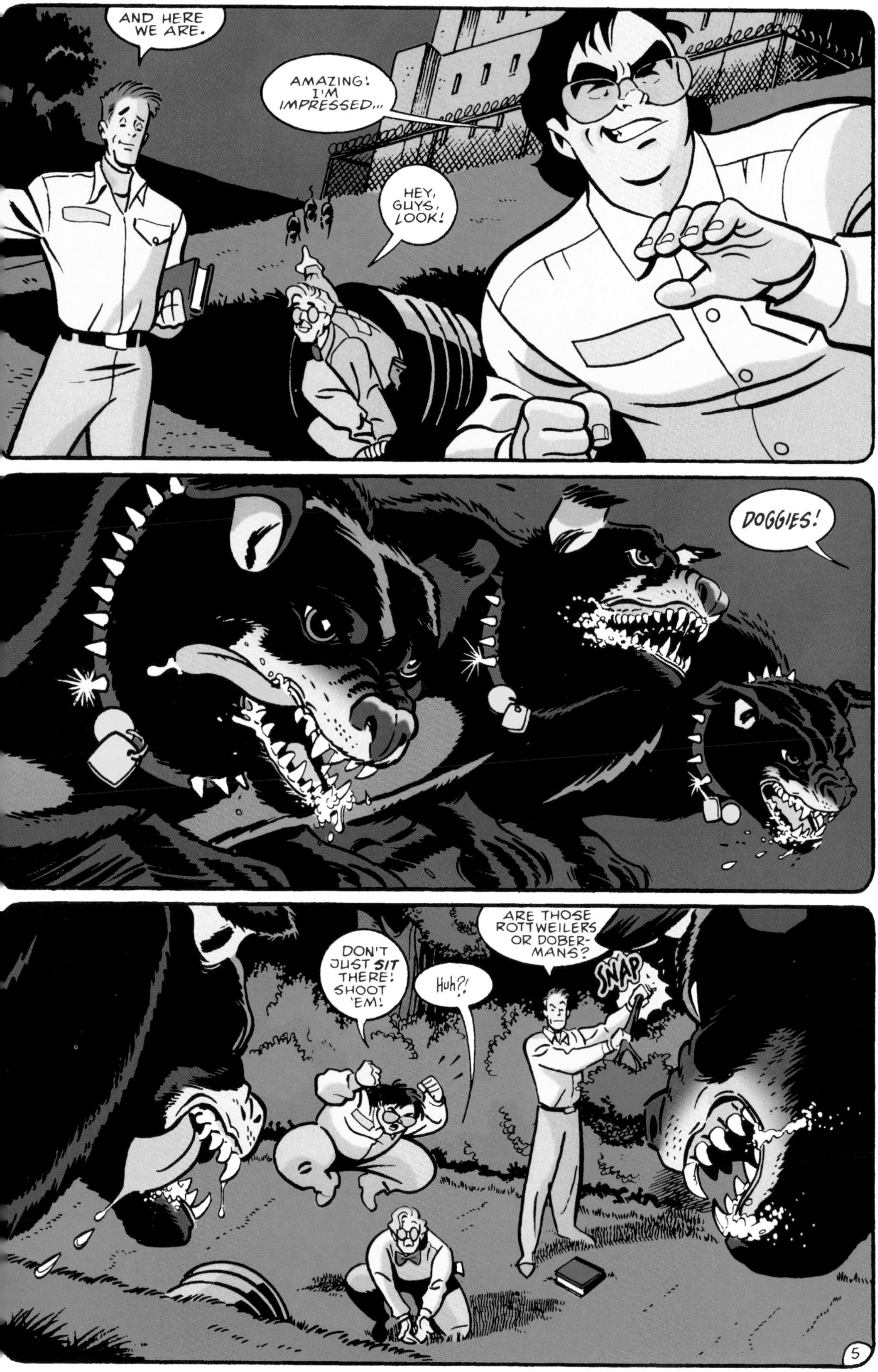
AND HERE WE ARE.
AMAZING! I'M IMPRESSED...
HEY, GUYS, LOOK!
DOGGIES!
DON'T JUST SIT THERE! SHOOT 'EM!
Huh?!
ARE THOSE ROTTWEILERS OR DOBER-MANS?
SNAP
5

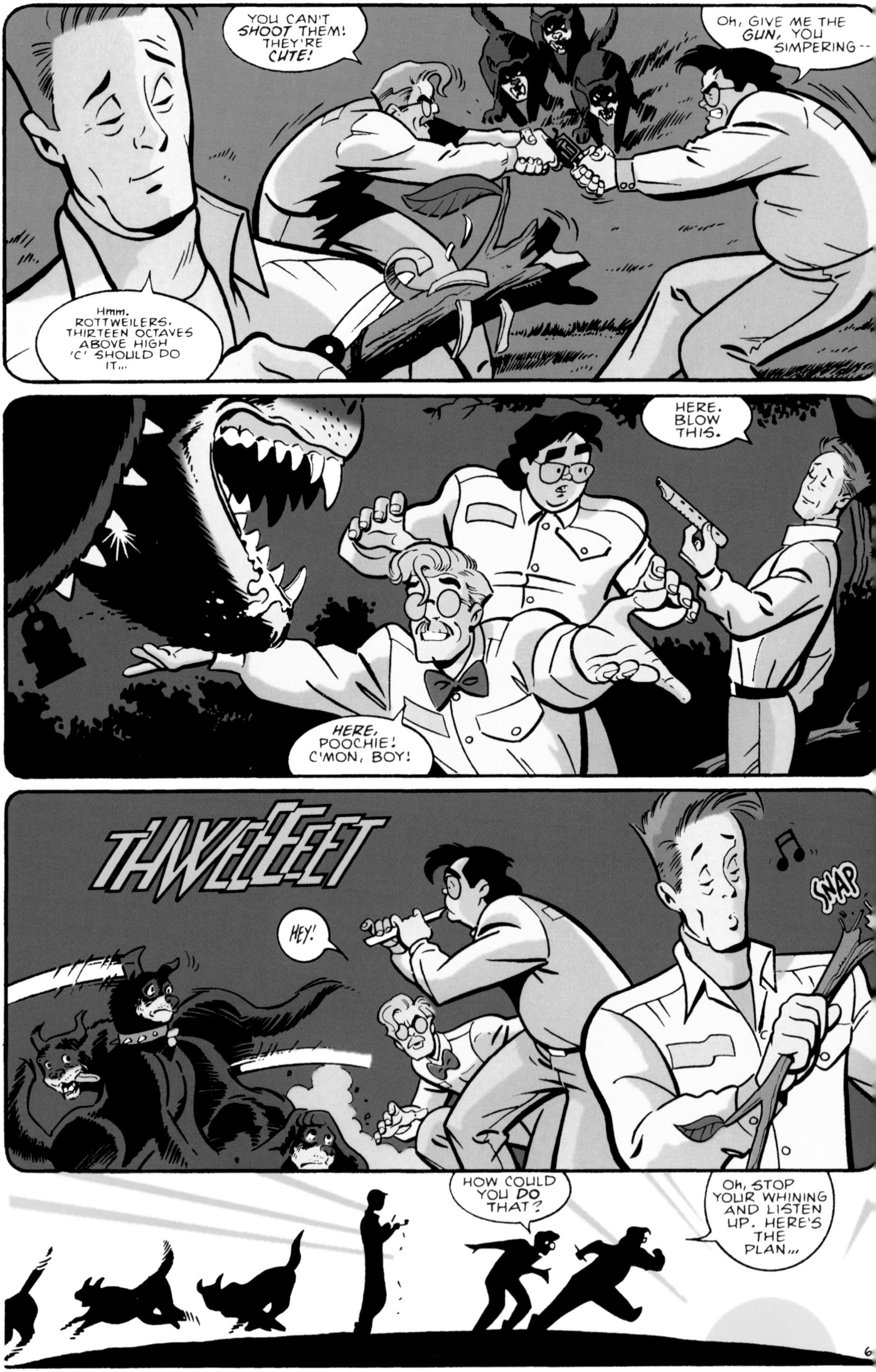
YOU CAN'T SHOOT THEM! THEY'RE CUTE!
Oh, GIVE ME THE GUN, YOU SIMPERING--
Hmm. ROTTWEILERS. THIRTEEN OCTAVES ABOVE HIGH 'C' SHOULD DO IT...
HERE. BLOW THIS.
HERE, POOCHIE! C'MON, BOY!
THWEEEEET
HEY!
SNAP
HOW COULD YOU DO THAT?
Oh, STOP YOUR WHINING AND LISTEN UP. HERE'S THE PLAN...
6

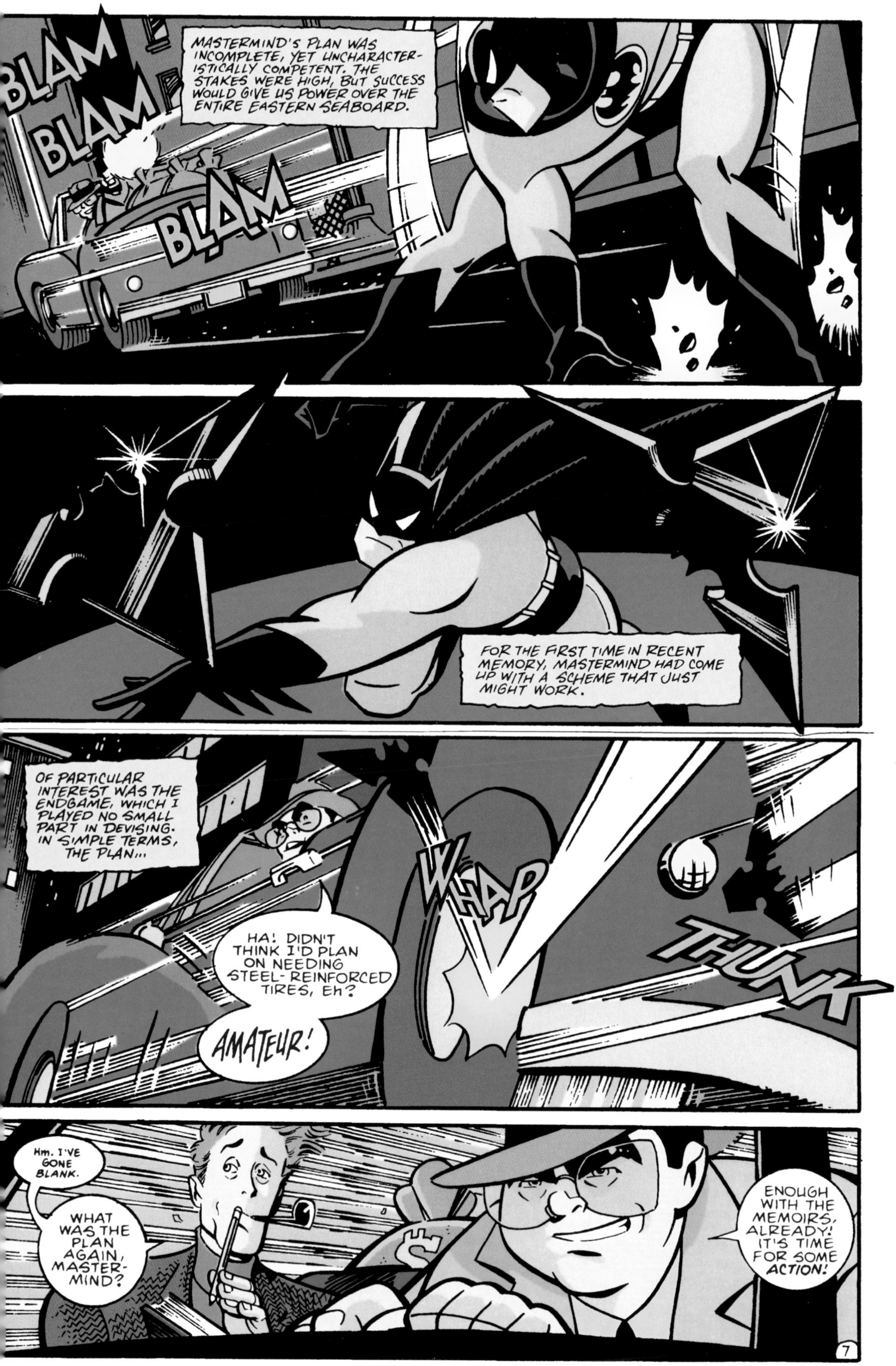
BLAM
BLAM
BLAM
MASTERMIND'S PLAN WAS INCOMPLETE, YET UNCHARACTER-ISTICALLY COMPETENT. THE STAKES WERE HIGH, BUT SUCCESS WOULD GIVE US POWER OVER THE ENTIRE EASTERN SEABOARD.
FOR THE FIRST TIME IN RECENT MEMORY, MASTERMIND HAD COME UP WITH A SCHEME THAT JUST MIGHT WORK.
OF PARTICULAR INTEREST WAS THE ENDGAME, WHICH I PLAYED NO SMALL PART IN DEVISING. IN SIMPLE TERMS, THE PLAN...
WHAP
THUNK
HA! DIDN'T THINK I'D PLAN ON NEEDING STEEL-REINFORCED TIRES, EH?
AMATEUR!
Hm. I'VE GONE BLANK.
WHAT WAS THE PLAN AGAIN, MASTER-MIND?
ENOUGH WITH THE MEMOIRS, ALREADY! IT'S TIME FOR SOME ACTION!
7

ACT FLYING BLIND WITH MASTERMIND TWO

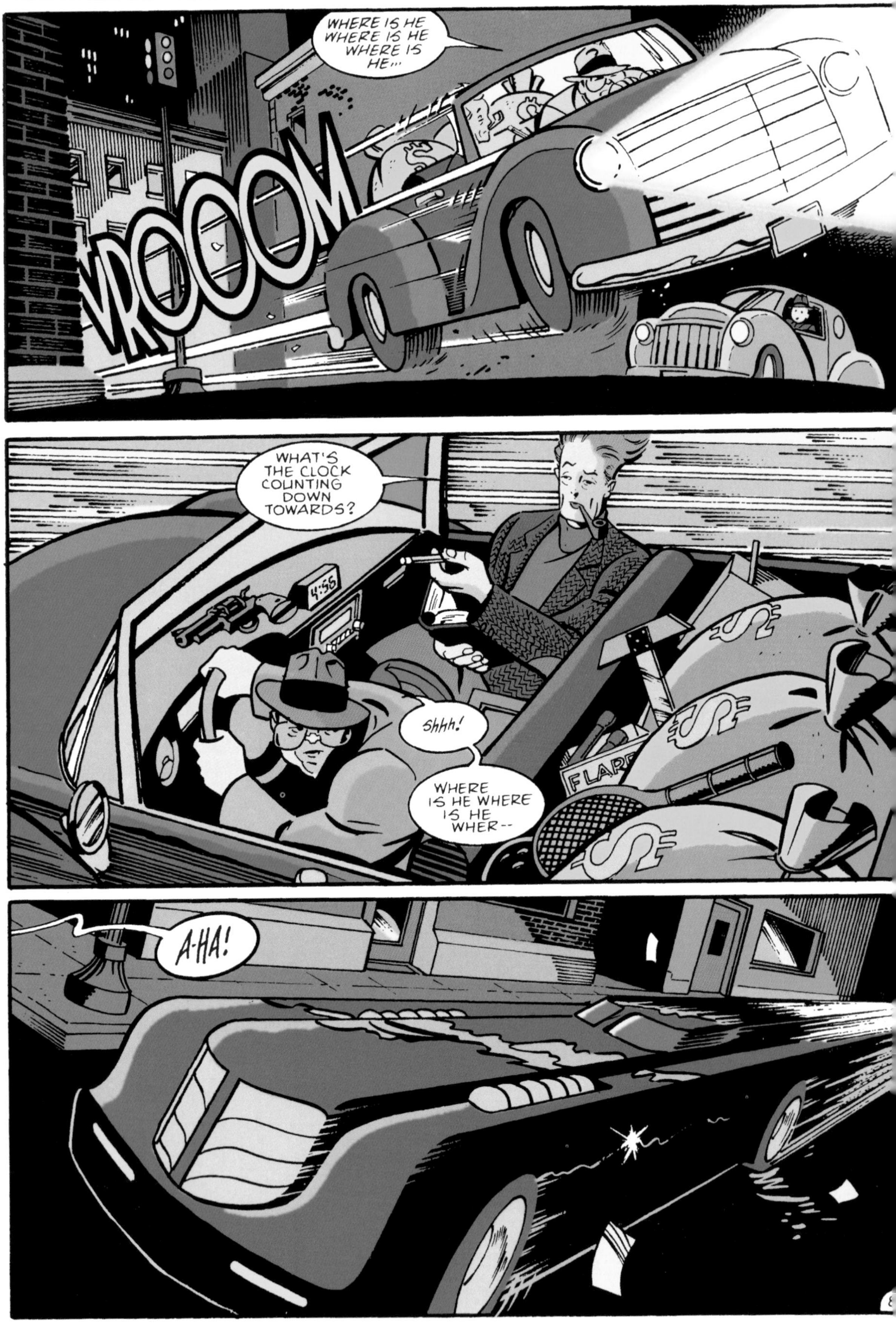

WHERE IS HE WHERE IS HE WHERE IS HE...
VROOOM
WHAT'S THE CLOCK COUNTING DOWN TOWARDS?
4:56
Shhh!
WHERE IS HE WHERE IS HE WHER--
FLAR
A-HA!

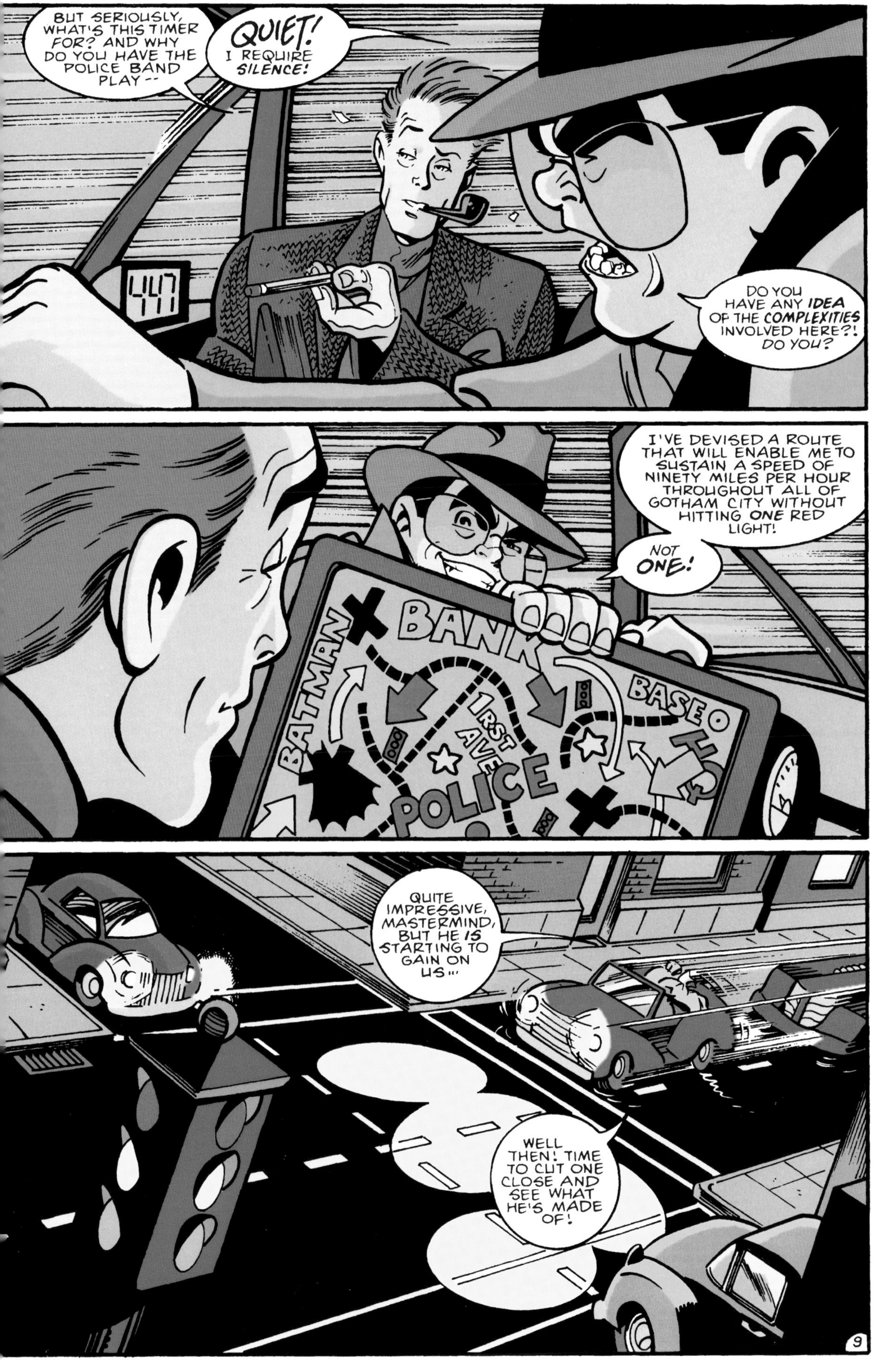
BUT SERIOUSLY, WHAT'S THIS TIMER FOR? AND WHY DO YOU HAVE THE POLICE BAND PLAY --
QUIET! I REQUIRE SILENCE!
447
DO YOU HAVE ANY IDEA OF THE COMPLEXITIES INVOLVED HERE?! DO YOU?
I'VE DEVISED A ROUTE THAT WILL ENABLE ME TO SUSTAIN A SPEED OF NINETY MILES PER HOUR THROUGHOUT ALL OF GOTHAM CITY WITHOUT HITTING ONE RED LIGHT!
NOT ONE!
BATMAN
BANK
IRST AVE
BASE
POLICE
HQ
QUITE IMPRESSIVE, MASTERMIND, BUT HE IS STARTING TO GAIN ON US...
WELL THEN! TIME TO CUT ONE CLOSE AND SEE WHAT HE'S MADE OF!
9

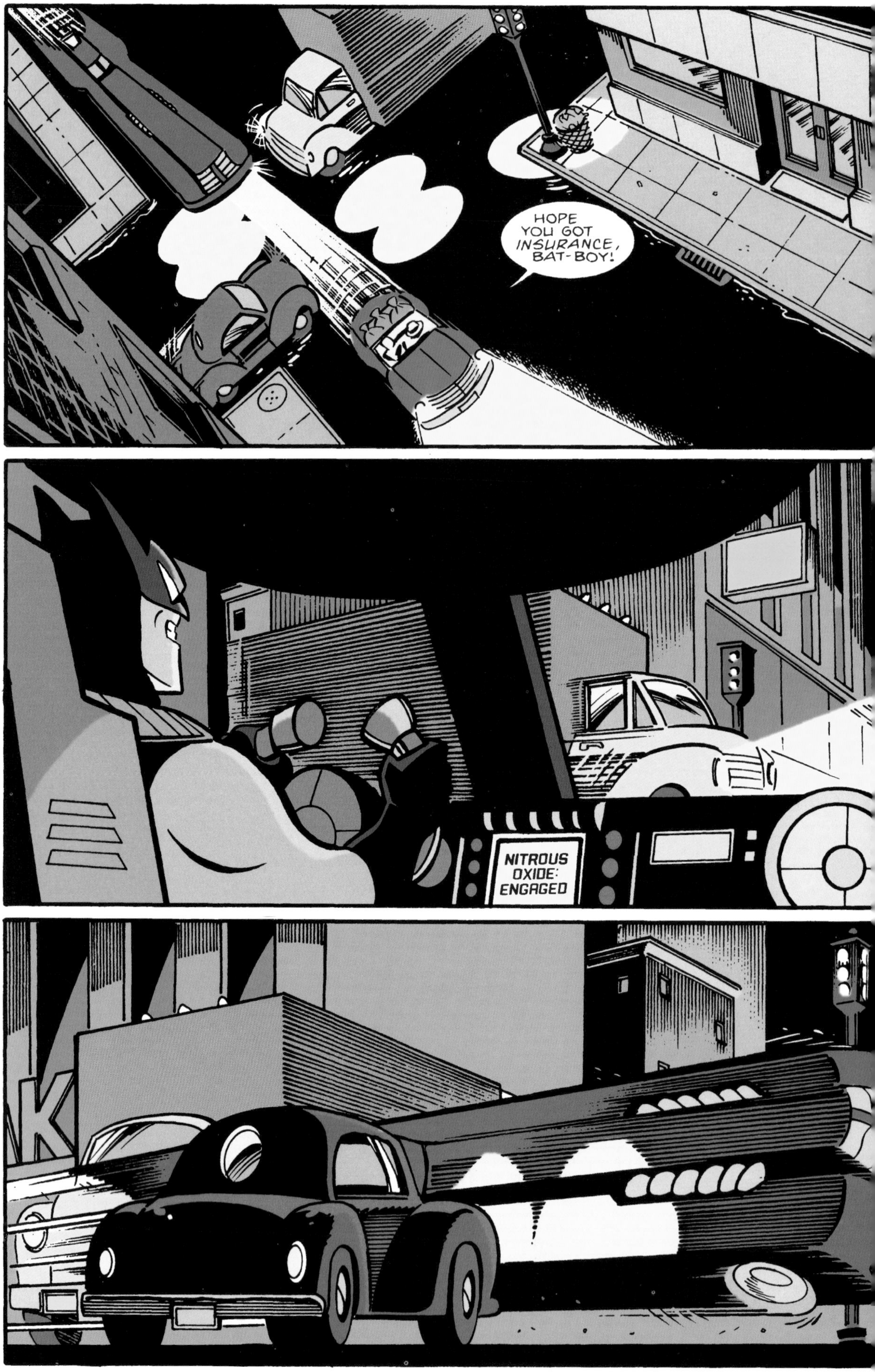
HOPE YOU GOT INSURANCE, BAT-BOY!
NITROUS OXIDE: ENGAGED

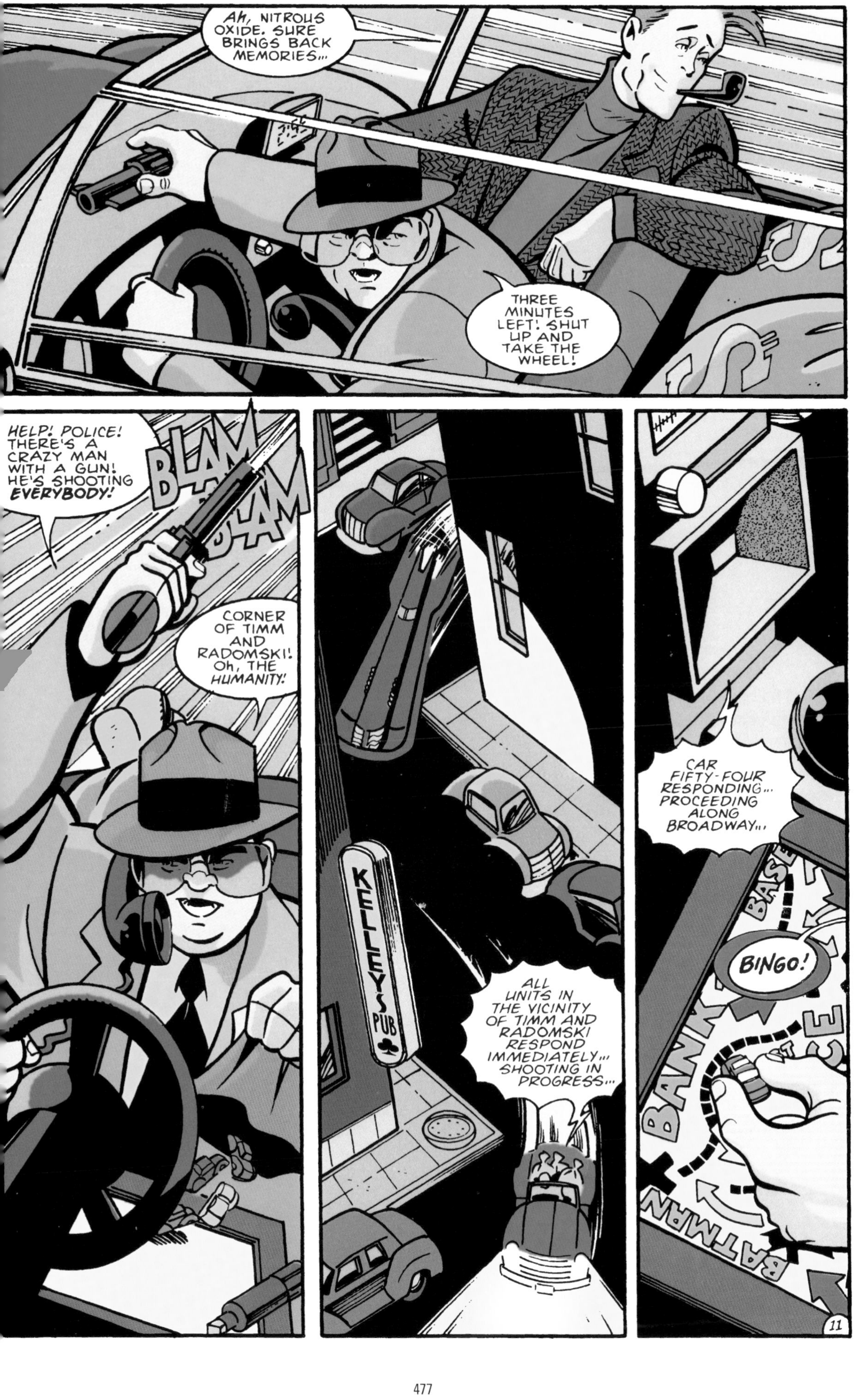
Ah, NITROUS OXIDE. SURE BRINGS BACK MEMORIES...
THREE MINUTES LEFT! SHUT UP AND TAKE THE WHEEL!
HELP! POLICE! THERE'S A CRAZY MAN WITH A GUN! HE'S SHOOTING EVERYBODY!
BLAM BLAM
CORNER OF TIMM AND RADOMSKI! Oh, THE HUMANITY!
KELLEY'S PUB
ALL UNITS IN THE VICINITY OF TIMM AND RADOMSKI RESPOND IMMEDIATELY... SHOOTING IN PROGRESS...
CAR FIFTY-FOUR RESPONDING... PROCEEDING ALONG BROADWAY...
BINGO!
BATMAN
BANK
BASE
11

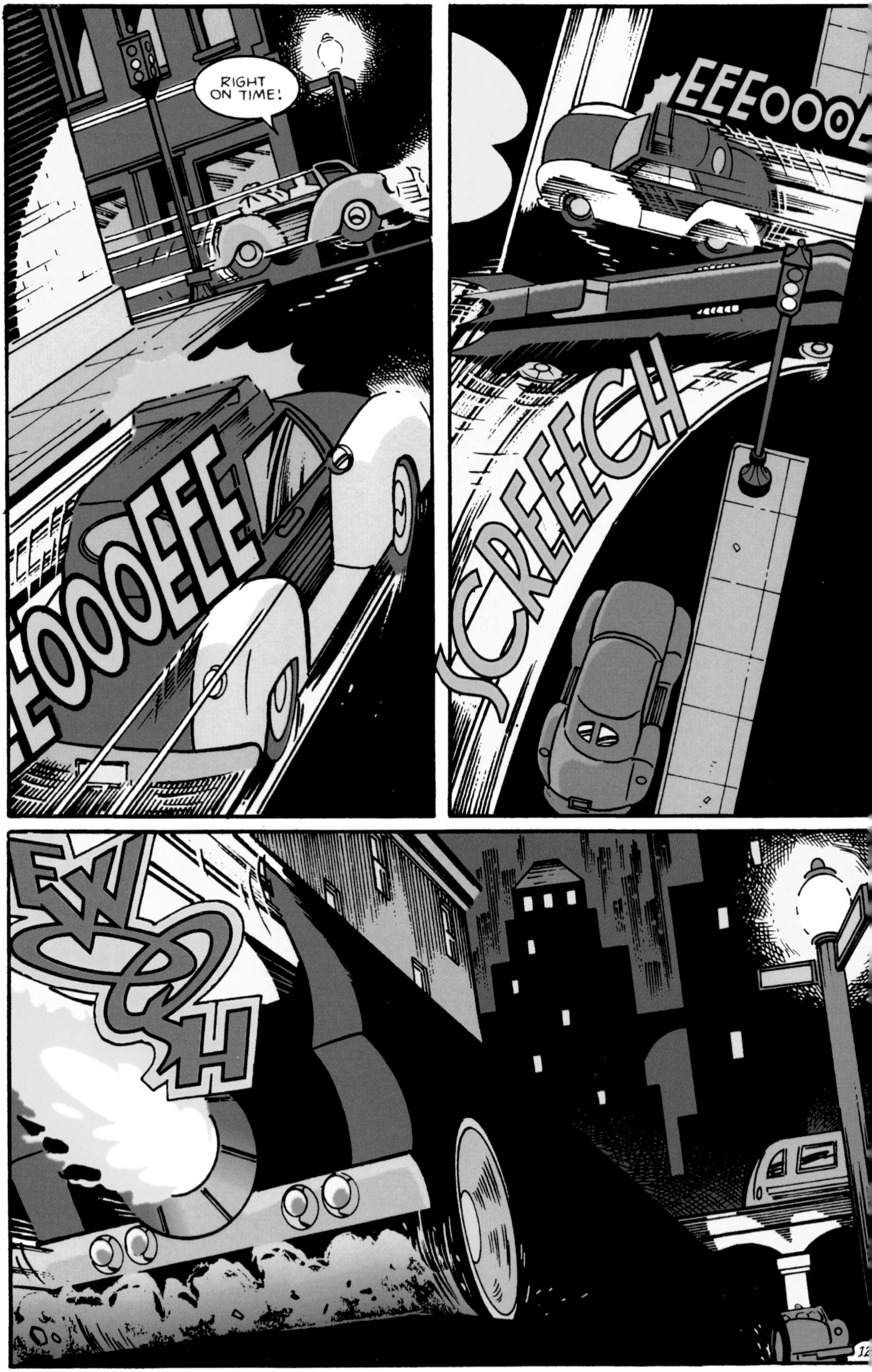
RIGHT ON TIME!
EOOOEEE
EEEOOOE
SCREEECH

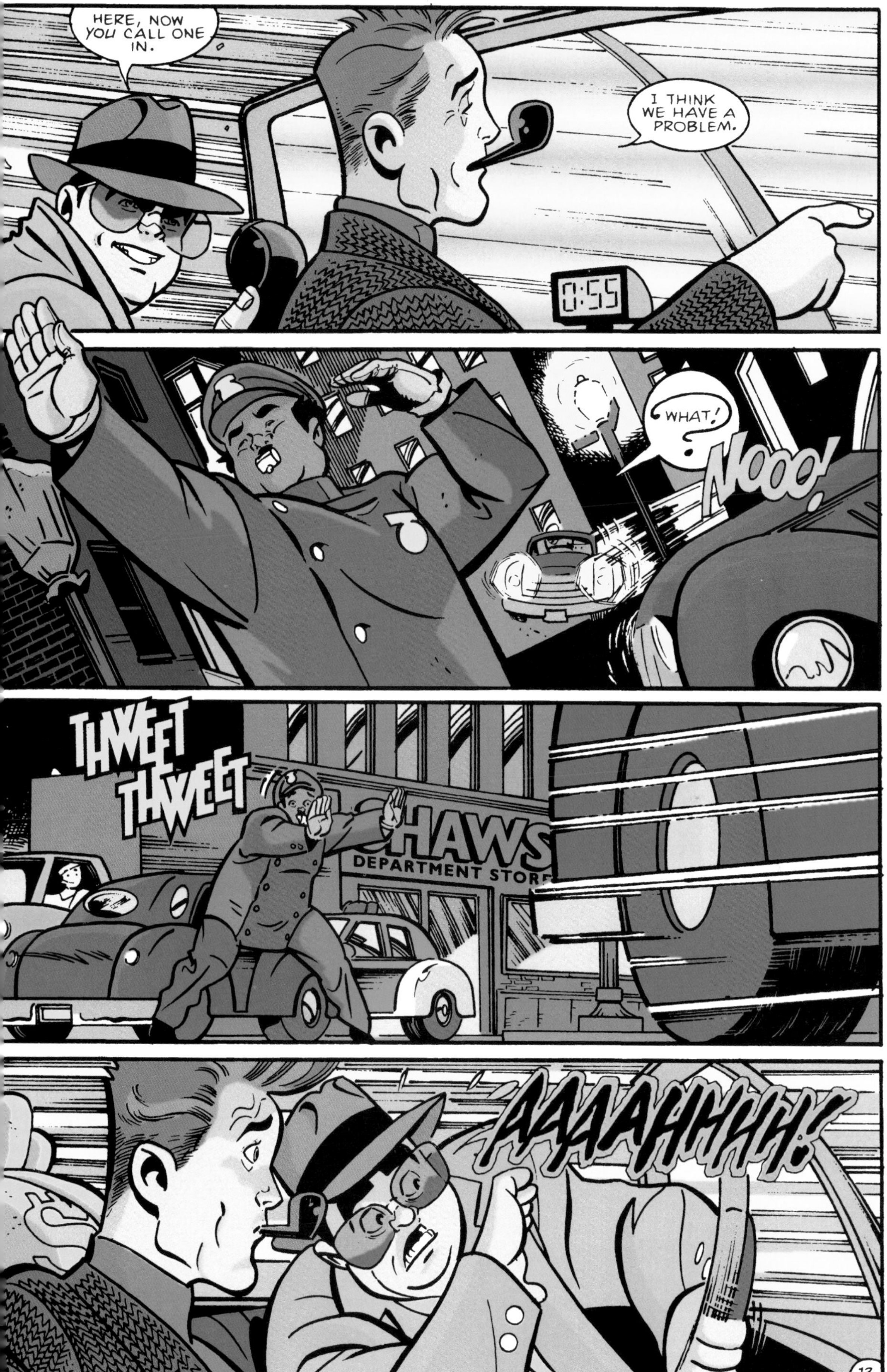
HERE, NOW YOU CALL ONE IN.
I THINK WE HAVE A PROBLEM.
0:55
WHAT?! NOOO!
THWEET THWEET
SHAWS DEPARTMENT STORE
AAAAHHHH!
13

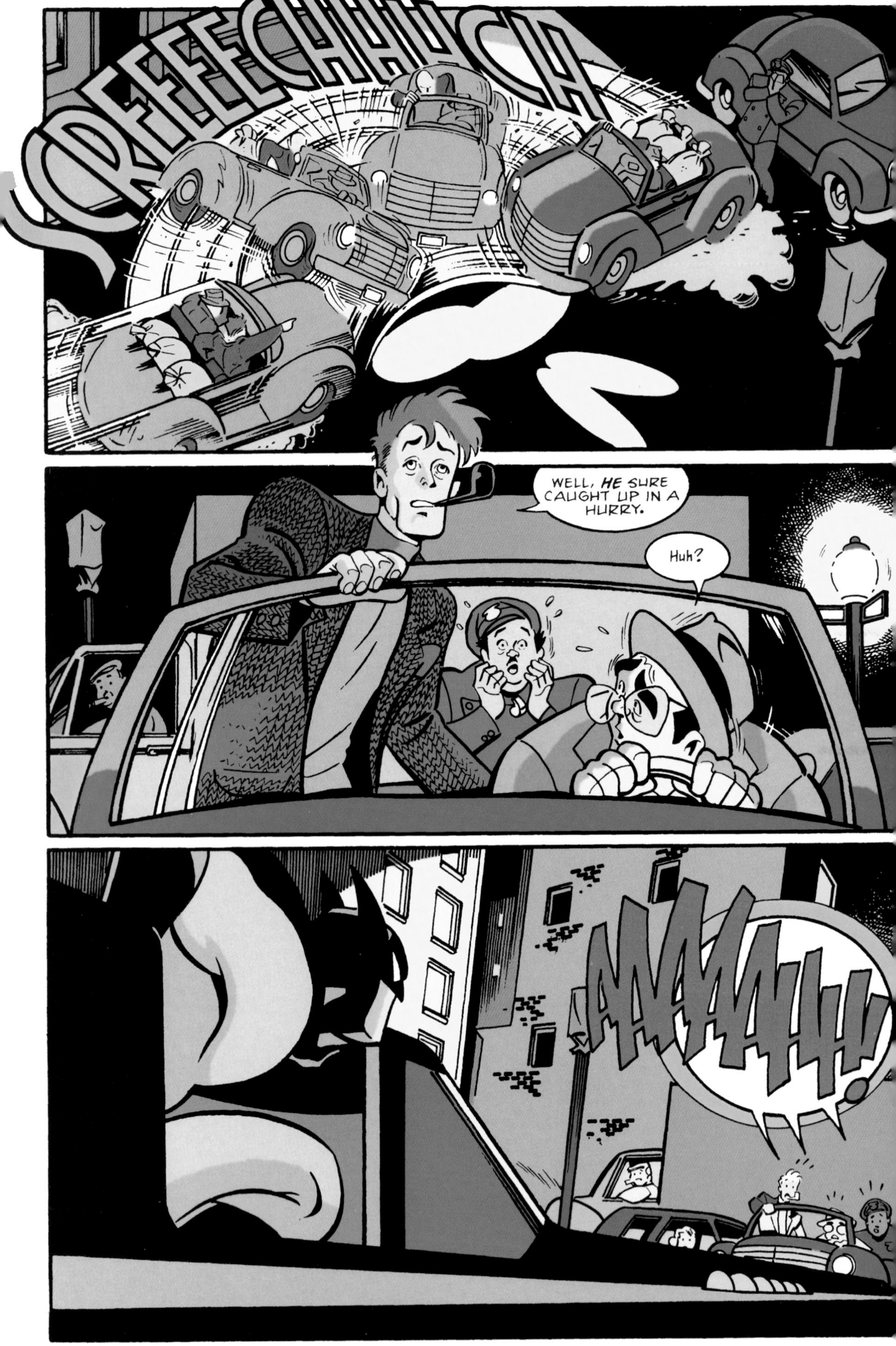
SCREEECHHHCLA
WELL, HE SURE CAUGHT UP IN A HURRY.
Huh?
AAAAAHHH!

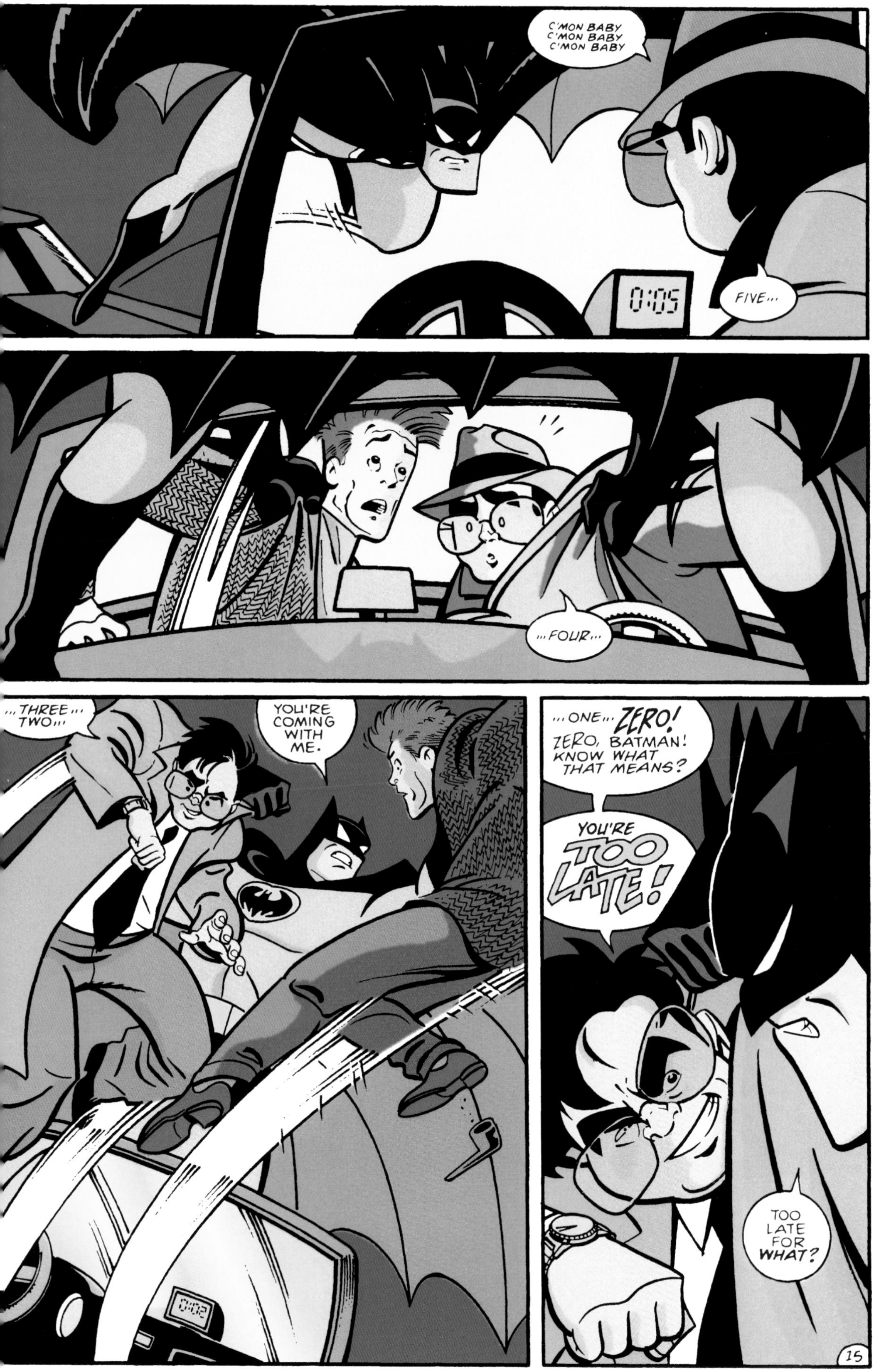
C'MON BABY
C'MON BABY
C'MON BABY
FIVE...
...FOUR...
...THREE... TWO...
YOU'RE COMING WITH ME.
...ONE... ZERO! ZERO, BATMAN! KNOW WHAT THAT MEANS?
YOU'RE TOO LATE!
TOO LATE FOR WHAT?
15

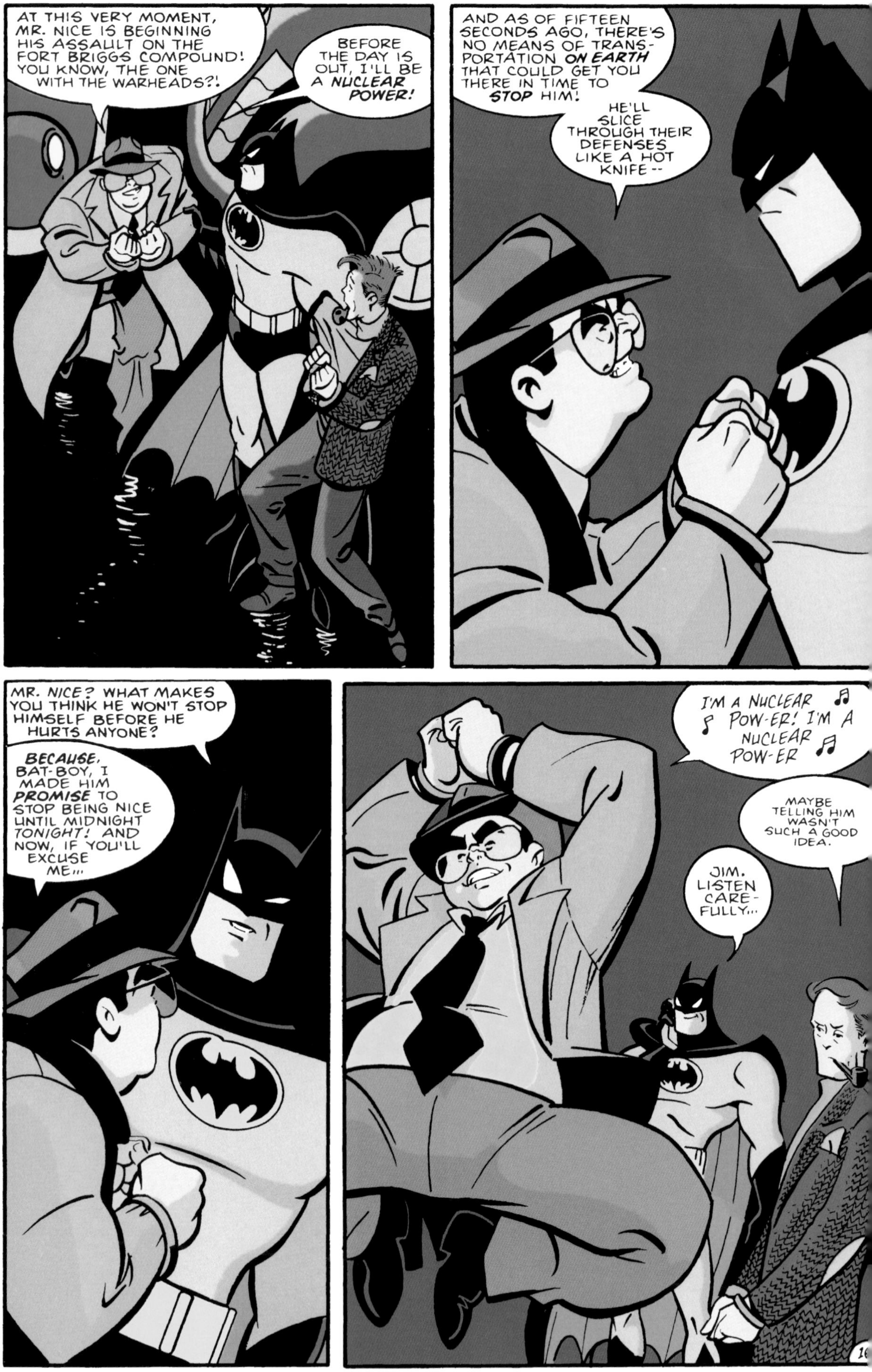

AT THIS VERY MOMENT, MR. NICE IS BEGINNING HIS ASSAULT ON THE FORT BRIGGS COMPOUND! YOU KNOW, THE ONE WITH THE WARHEADS?!
BEFORE THE DAY IS OUT, I'LL BE A NUCLEAR POWER!
AND AS OF FIFTEEN SECONDS AGO, THERE'S NO MEANS OF TRANSPORTATION ON EARTH THAT COULD GET YOU THERE IN TIME TO STOP HIM!
HE'LL SLICE THROUGH THEIR DEFENSES LIKE A HOT KNIFE --
MR. NICE? WHAT MAKES YOU THINK HE WON'T STOP HIMSELF BEFORE HE HURTS ANYONE?
BECAUSE, BAT-BOY, I MADE HIM PROMISE TO STOP BEING NICE UNTIL MIDNIGHT TONIGHT! AND NOW, IF YOU'LL EXCUSE ME...
I'M A NUCLEAR POW-ER! I'M A NUCLEAR POW-ER
MAYBE TELLING HIM WASN'T SUCH A GOOD IDEA.
JIM. LISTEN CAREFULLY...

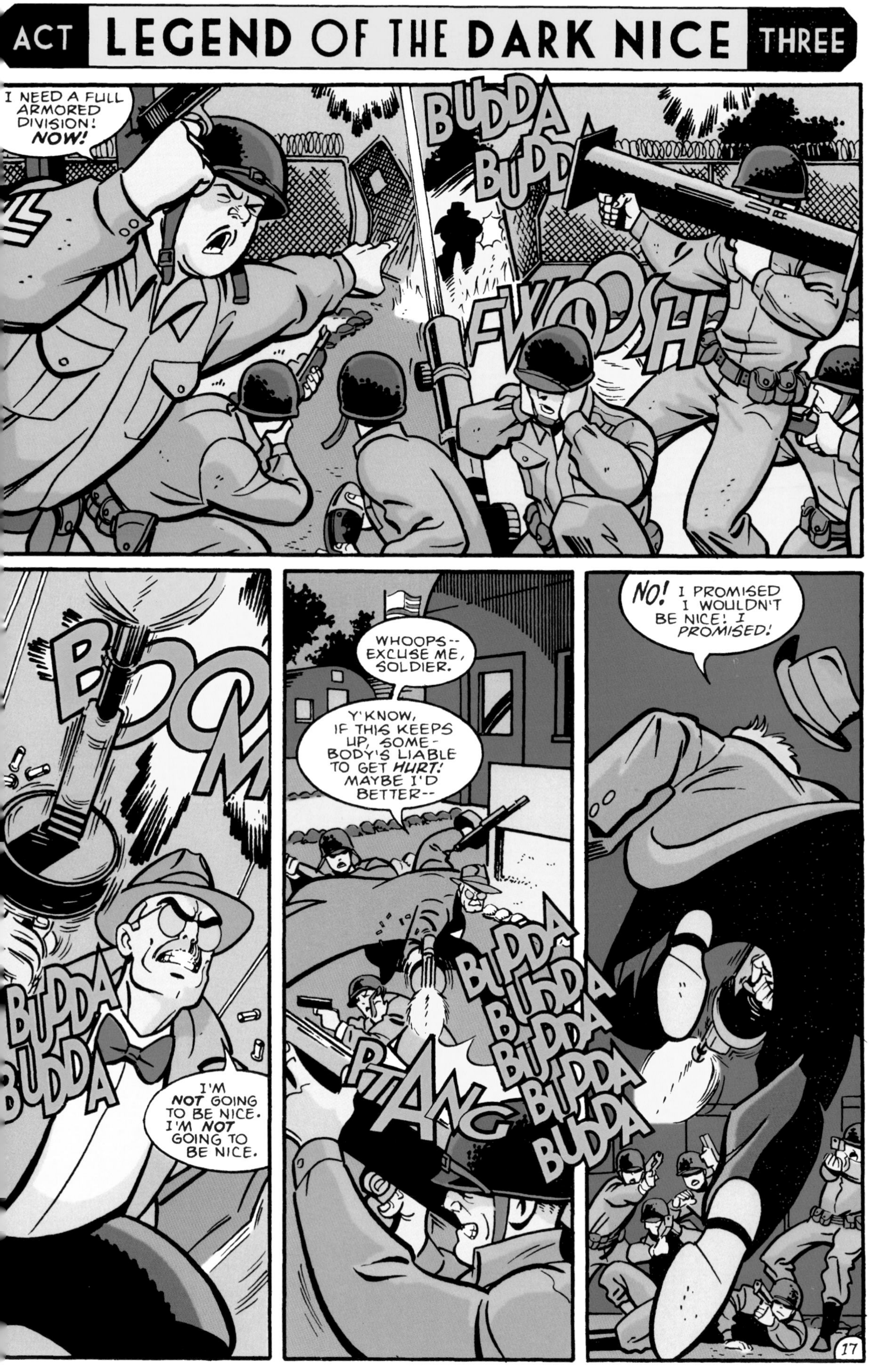

ACT LEGEND OF THE DARK NICE THREE
I NEED A FULL ARMORED DIVISION! NOW!
BUDDA BUDD
FWOOSH
BOOM
BUDDA BUDDA
I'M NOT GOING TO BE NICE. I'M NOT GOING TO BE NICE.
WHOOPS-- EXCUSE ME, SOLDIER.
Y'KNOW, IF THIS KEEPS UP, SOMEBODY'S LIABLE TO GET HURT! MAYBE I'D BETTER--
BUDDA BUDDA BUDDA BUDDA BUDDA BUDDA
PTANG
NO! I PROMISED I WOULDN'T BE NICE! I PROMISED!
17

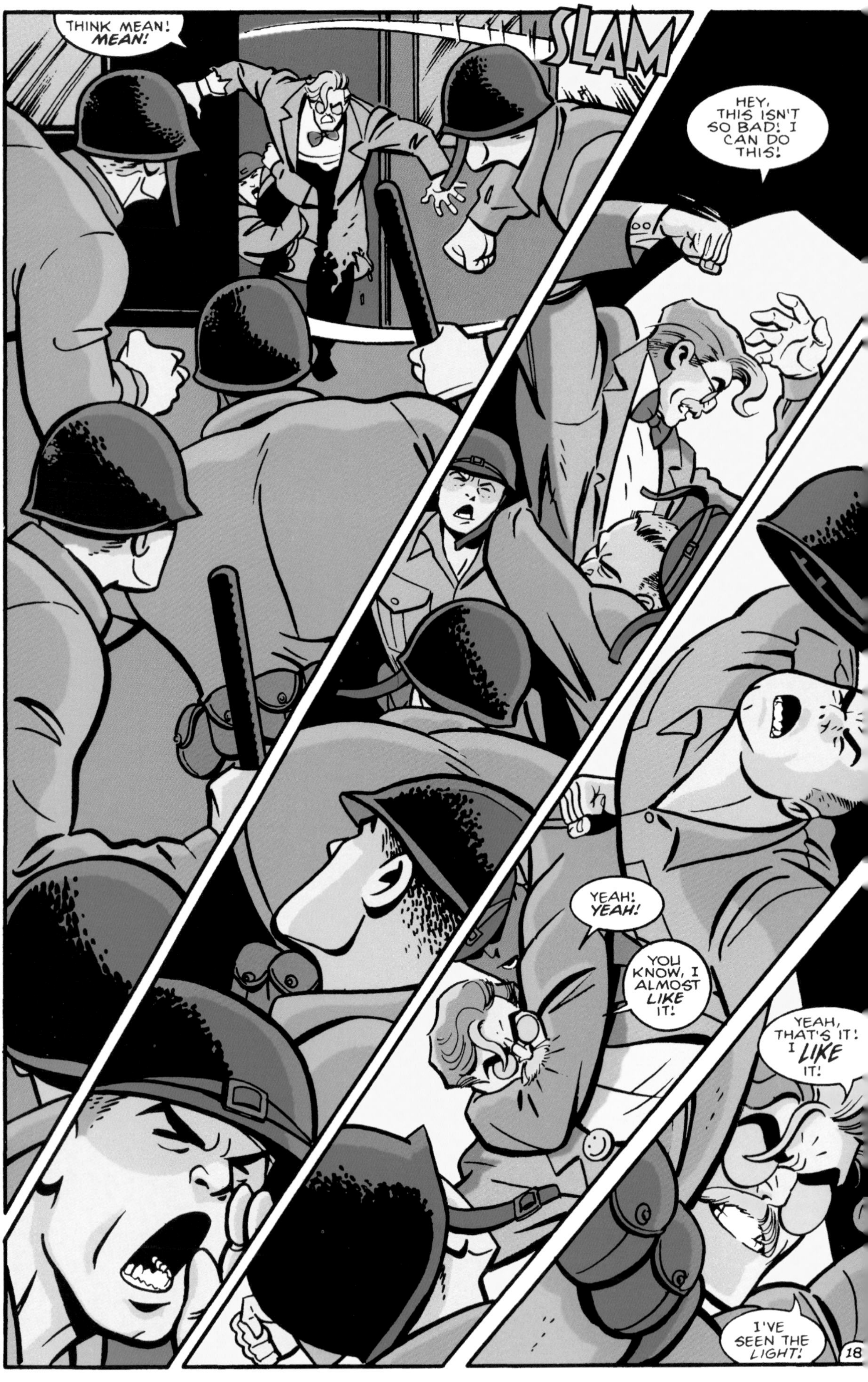
THINK MEAN! MEAN!
SLAM
HEY, THIS ISN'T SO BAD! I CAN DO THIS!
YEAH! YEAH!
YOU KNOW, I ALMOST LIKE IT!
YEAH, THAT'S IT! I LIKE IT!
I'VE SEEN THE LIGHT!
18

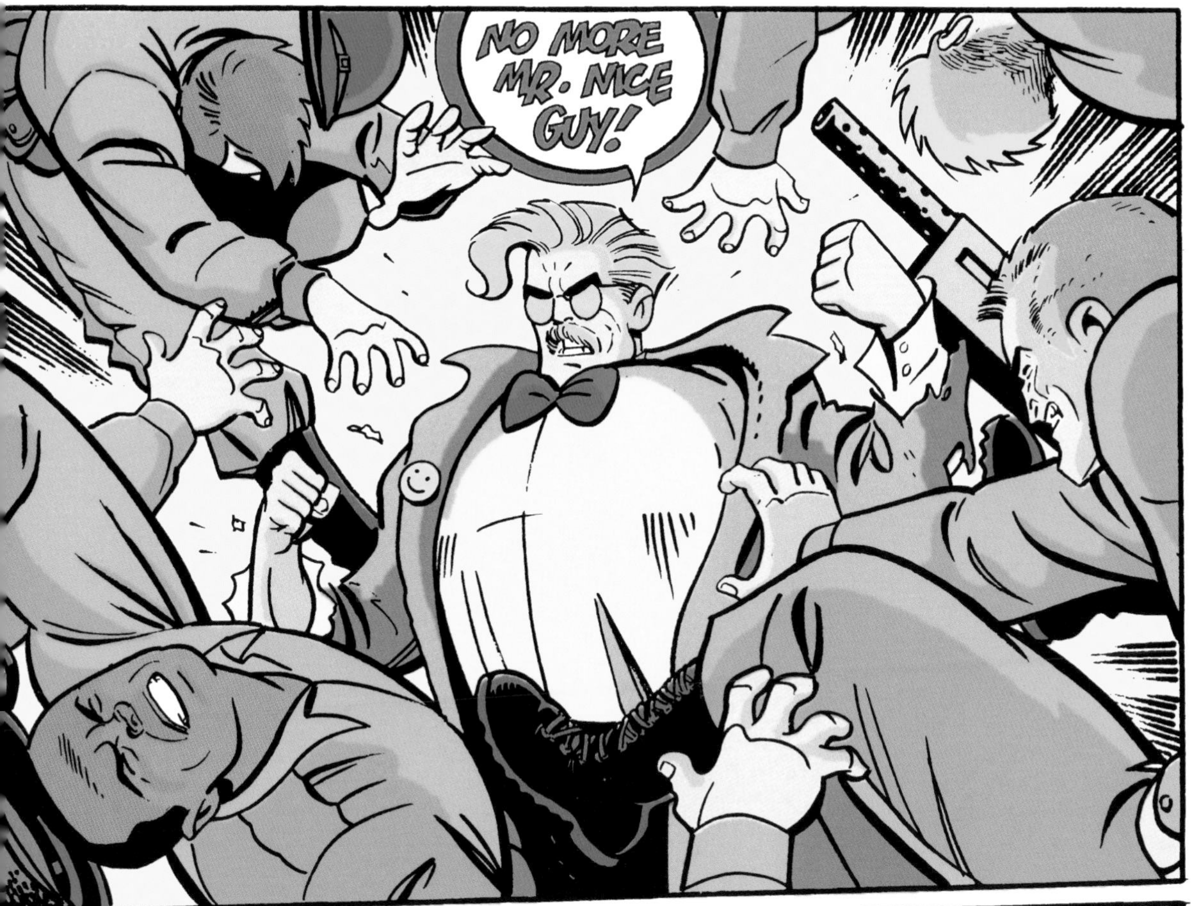
NO MORE MR. NICE GUY!

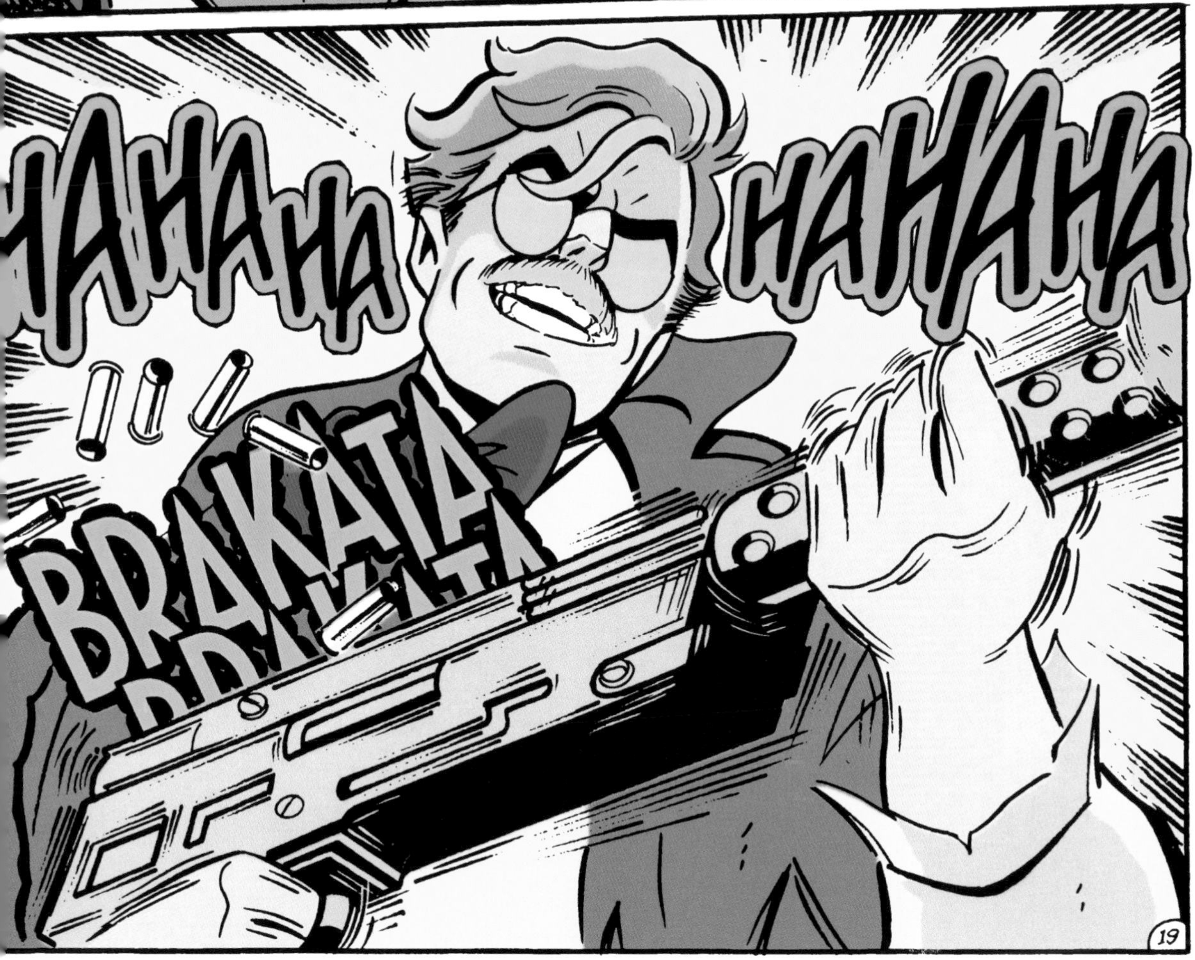
HAHAHA
HAHAHA
BRAKATA
19

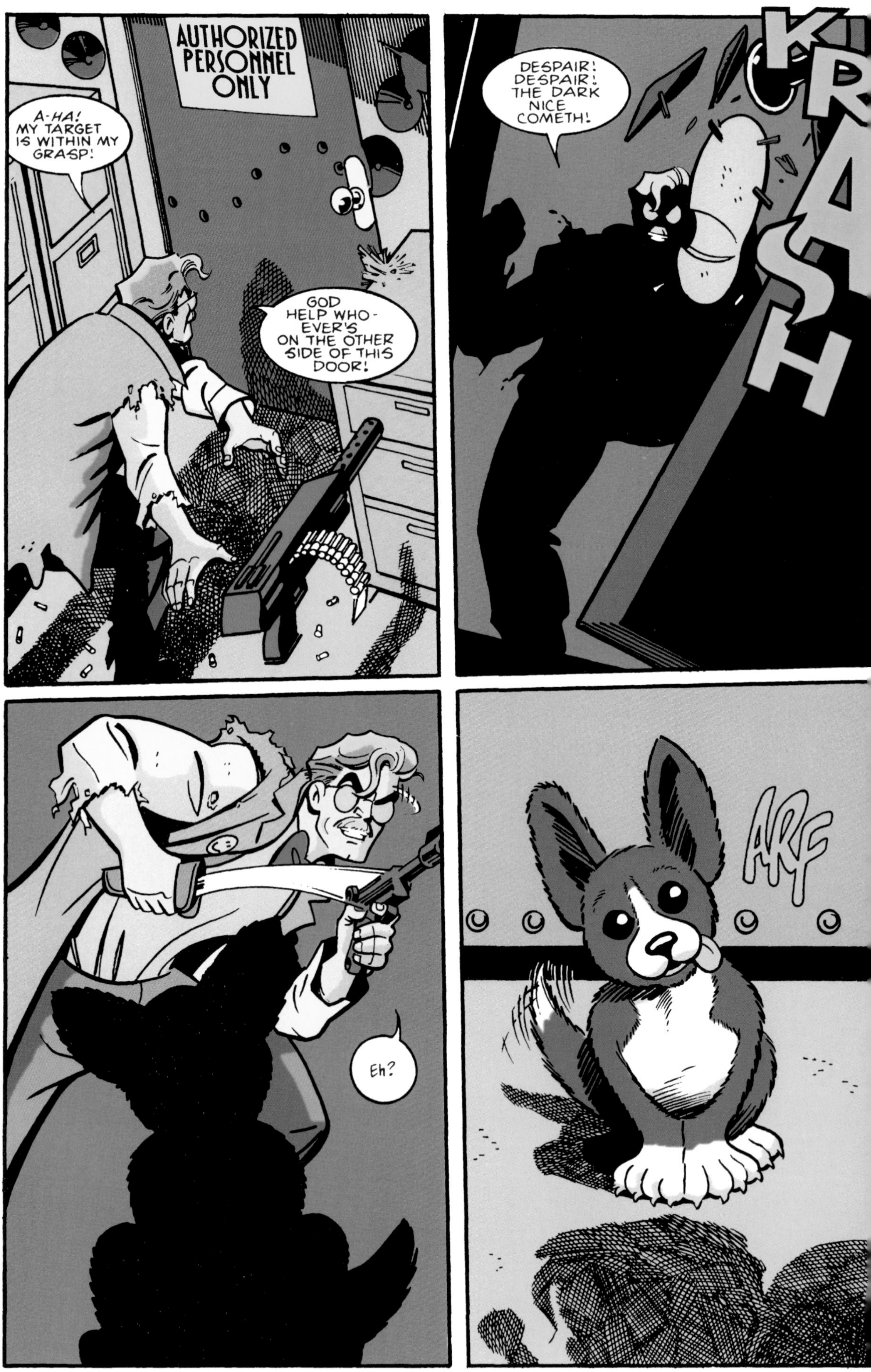
AUTHORIZED PERSONNEL ONLY
A-HA! MY TARGET IS WITHIN MY GRASP!
GOD HELP WHO-EVER'S ON THE OTHER SIDE OF THIS DOOR!
DESPAIR! DESPAIR! THE DARK NICE COMETH!
KRASH
Eh?
ARF

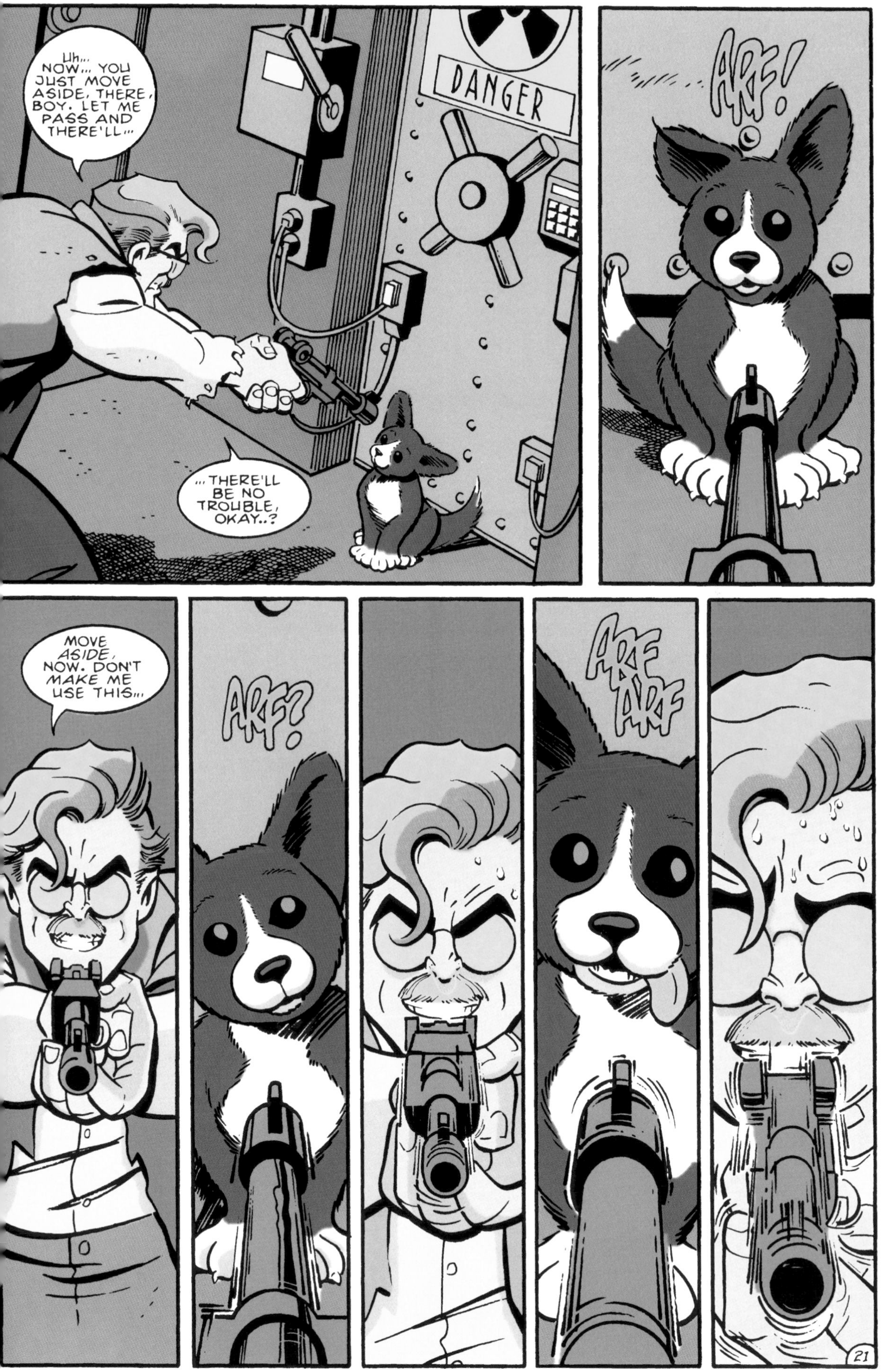

UH... NOW... YOU JUST MOVE ASIDE, THERE, BOY. LET ME PASS AND THERE'LL...
DANGER
...THERE'LL BE NO TROUBLE, OKAY..?
ARF!
MOVE ASIDE, NOW. DON'T MAKE ME USE THIS...
ARF?
ARF ARF
21

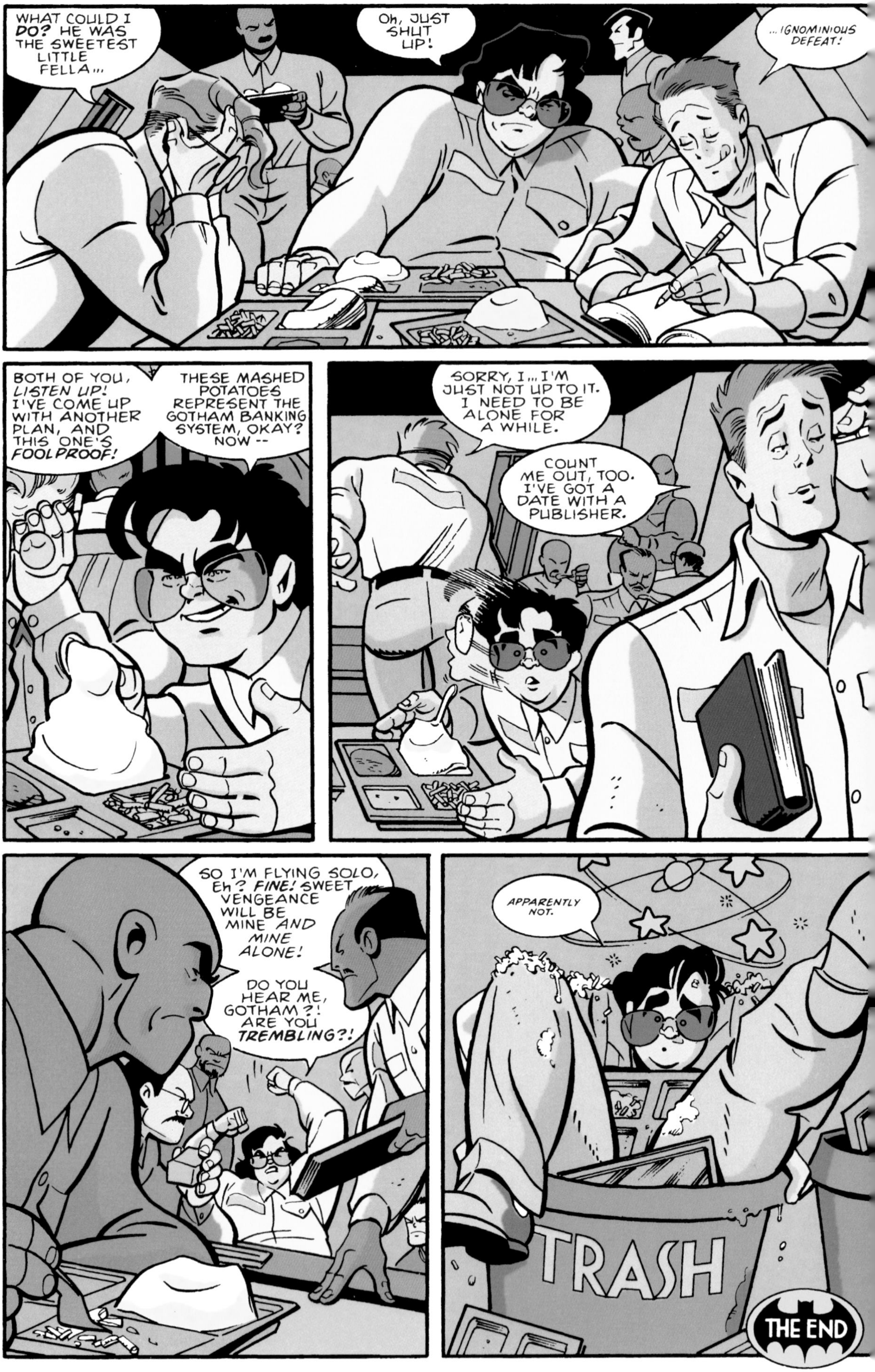
WHAT COULD I DO? HE WAS THE SWEETEST LITTLE FELLA...
Oh, JUST SHUT UP!
...IGNOMINIOUS DEFEAT!
BOTH OF YOU, LISTEN UP! I'VE COME UP WITH ANOTHER PLAN, AND THIS ONE'S FOOLPROOF!
THESE MASHED POTATOES REPRESENT THE GOTHAM BANKING SYSTEM, OKAY? NOW --
SORRY, I... I'M JUST NOT UP TO IT. I NEED TO BE ALONE FOR A WHILE.
COUNT ME OUT, TOO. I'VE GOT A DATE WITH A PUBLISHER.
SO I'M FLYING SOLO, Eh? FINE! SWEET VENGEANCE WILL BE MINE AND MINE ALONE!
DO YOU HEAR ME, GOTHAM?! ARE YOU TREMBLING?!
APPARENTLY NOT.
TRASH
THE END

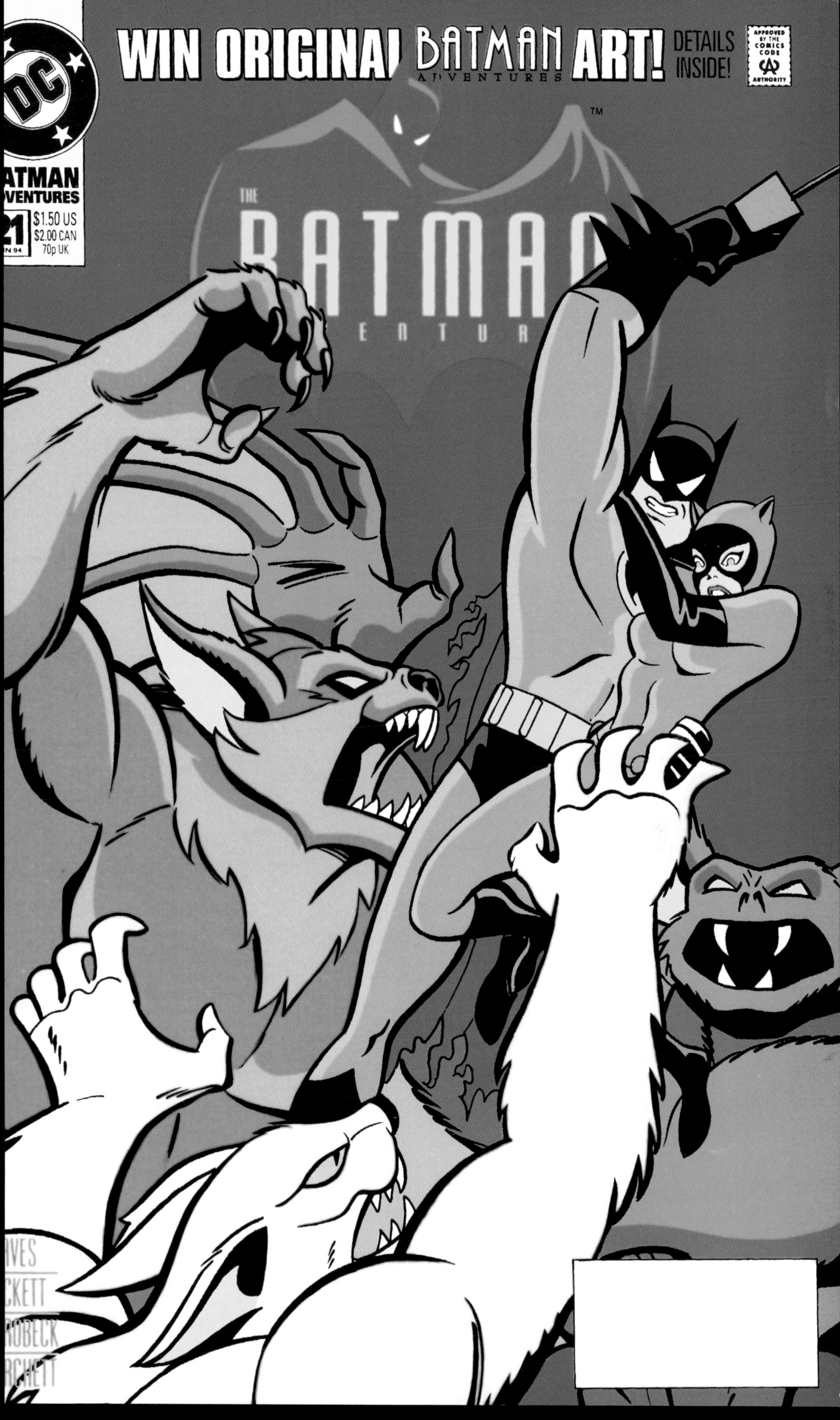
WIN ORIGINAL BATMAN ADVENTURES ART!
DETAILS INSIDE!
APPROVED BY THE COMICS CODE AUTHORITY
DC
ATMAN
VENTURES
21
$1.50 US
$2.00 CAN
70p UK
TM
THE BATMAN

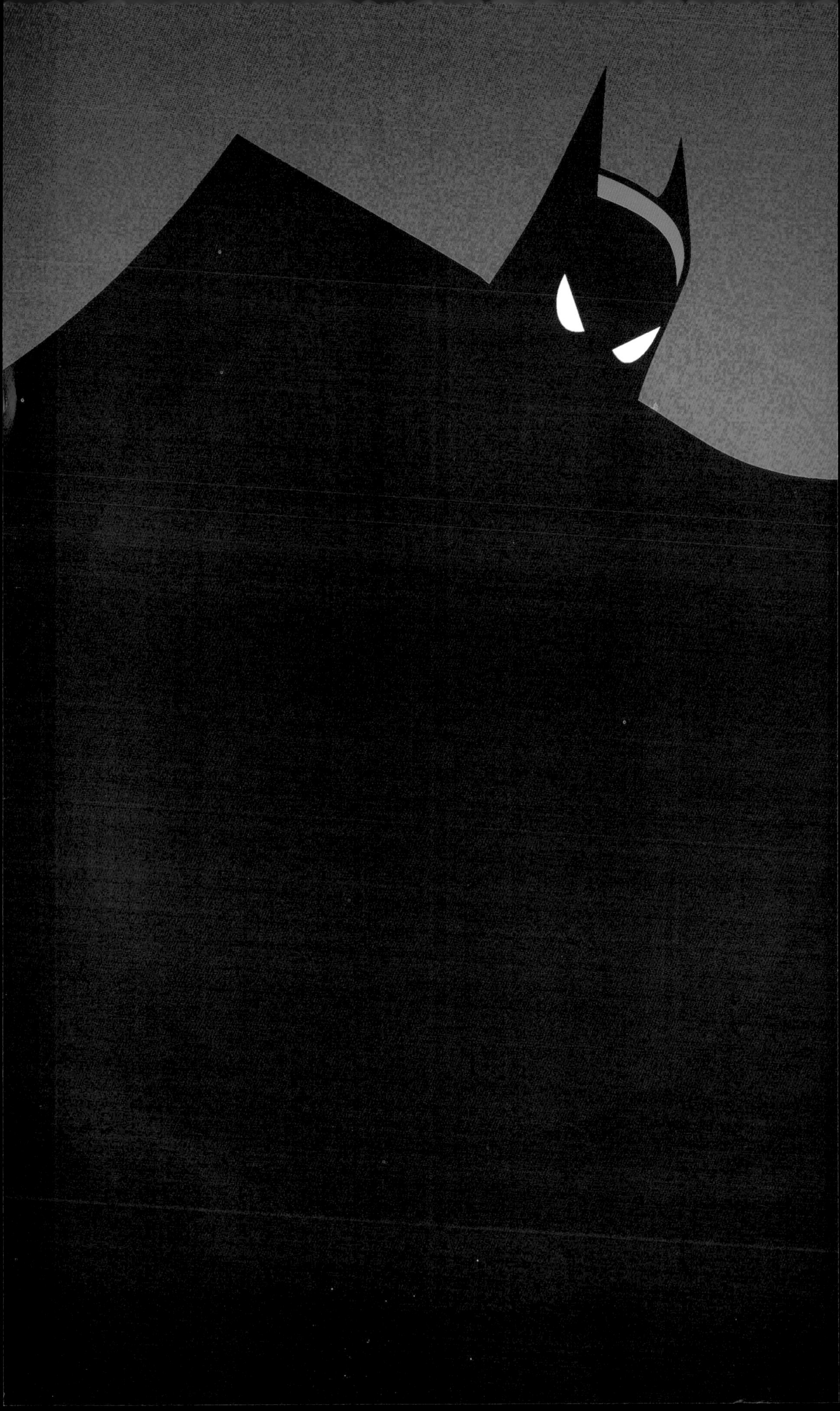

HOUSE OF DORIAN

MICHAEL REAVES STORY	KELLEY PUCKETT DIALOGUE	MIKE PAROBECK PENCILLER	RICK BURCHETT INKER	RICK TAYLOR COLORIST	STARKINGS/ COMICRAFT LETTERING	DARREN VINCENZO ASST. EDITOR	SCOTT PETERSON EDITOR	BATMAN CREATED BY BOB KANE

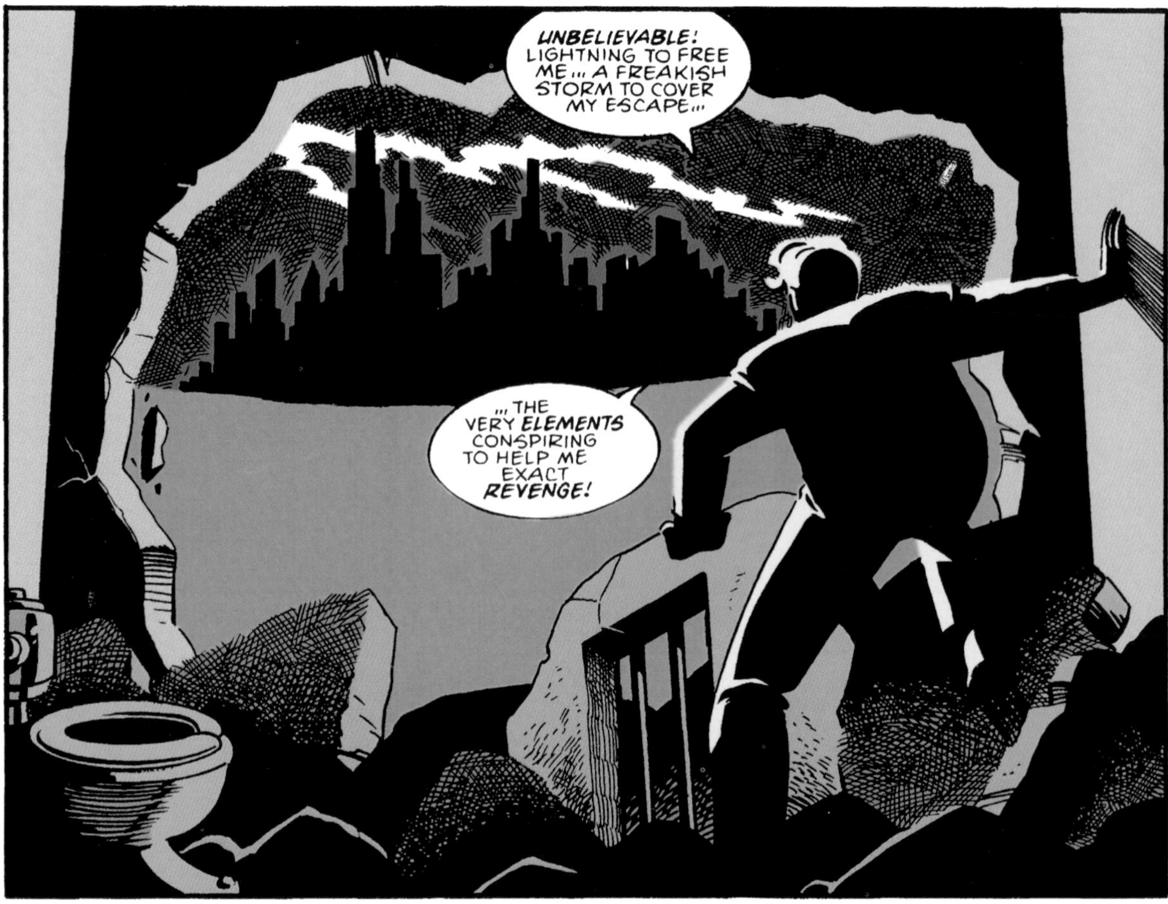
UNBELIEVABLE! LIGHTNING TO FREE ME... A FREAKISH STORM TO COVER MY ESCAPE...
...THE VERY ELEMENTS CONSPIRING TO HELP ME EXACT REVENGE!

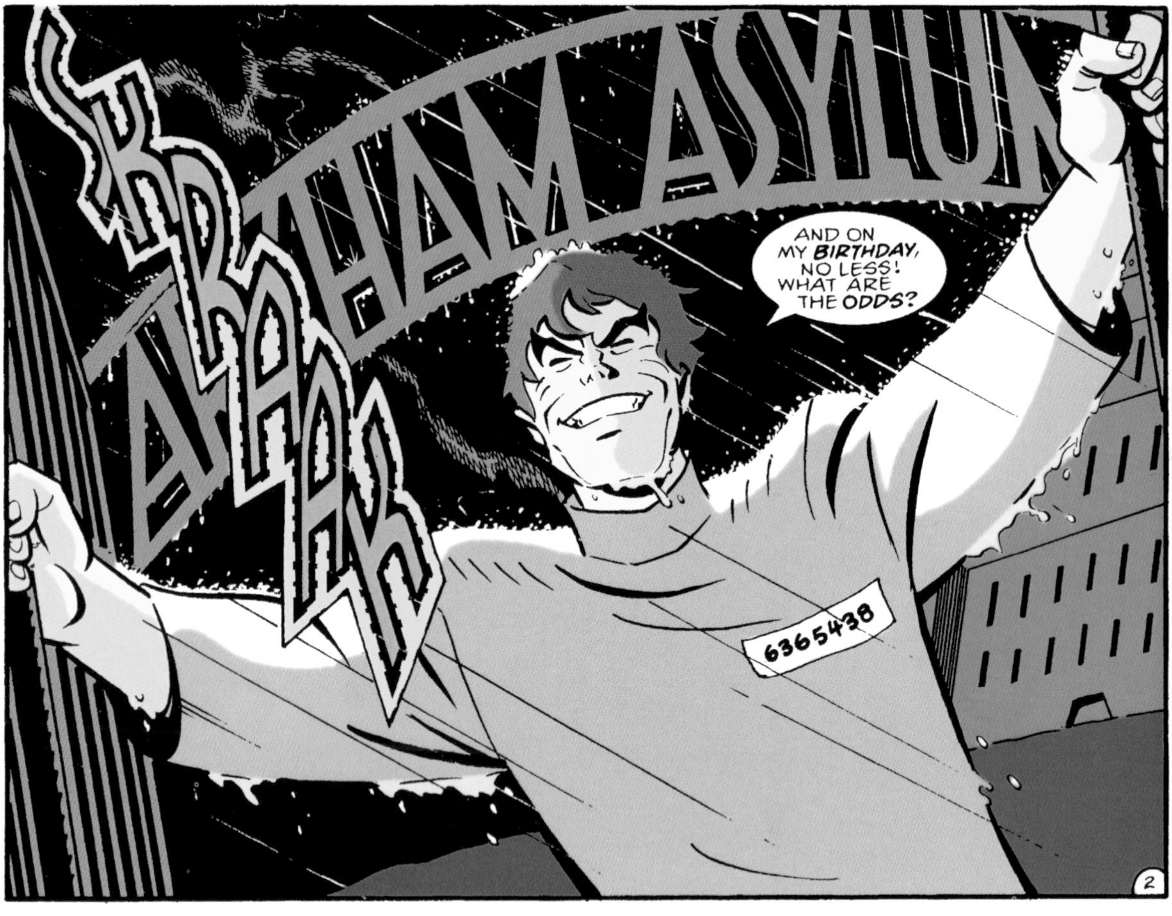
SKRAAAAK
ARKHAM ASYLUM
AND ON MY BIRTHDAY, NO LESS! WHAT ARE THE ODDS?
6365438
2

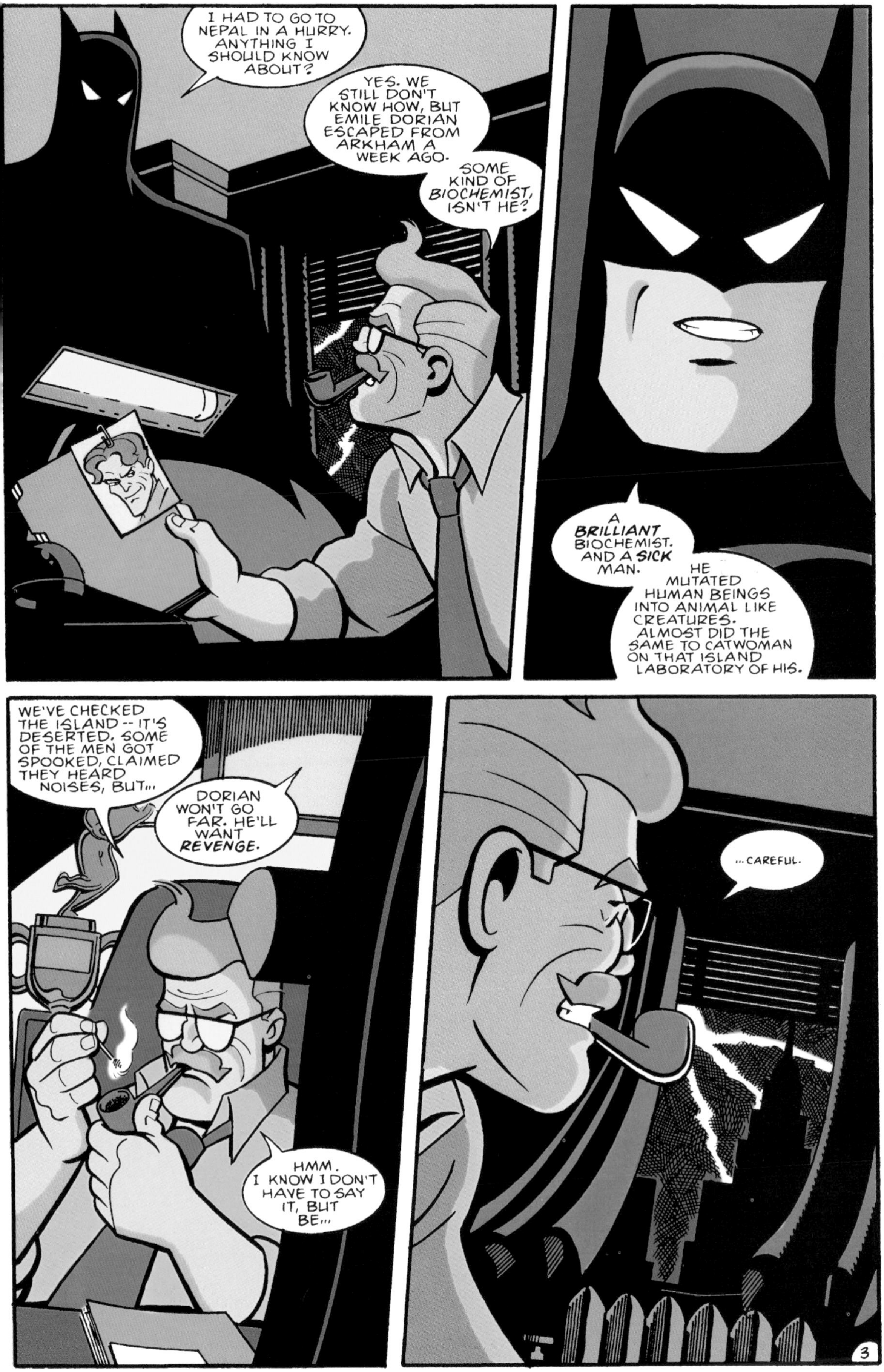
I HAD TO GO TO NEPAL IN A HURRY. ANYTHING I SHOULD KNOW ABOUT?
YES. WE STILL DON'T KNOW HOW, BUT EMILE DORIAN ESCAPED FROM ARKHAM A WEEK AGO.
SOME KIND OF BIOCHEMIST, ISN'T HE?
A BRILLIANT BIOCHEMIST. AND A SICK MAN.
HE MUTATED HUMAN BEINGS INTO ANIMAL LIKE CREATURES. ALMOST DID THE SAME TO CATWOMAN ON THAT ISLAND LABORATORY OF HIS.
WE'VE CHECKED THE ISLAND -- IT'S DESERTED. SOME OF THE MEN GOT SPOOKED, CLAIMED THEY HEARD NOISES, BUT...
DORIAN WON'T GO FAR. HE'LL WANT REVENGE.
HMM. I KNOW I DON'T HAVE TO SAY IT, BUT BE...
...CAREFUL.
3

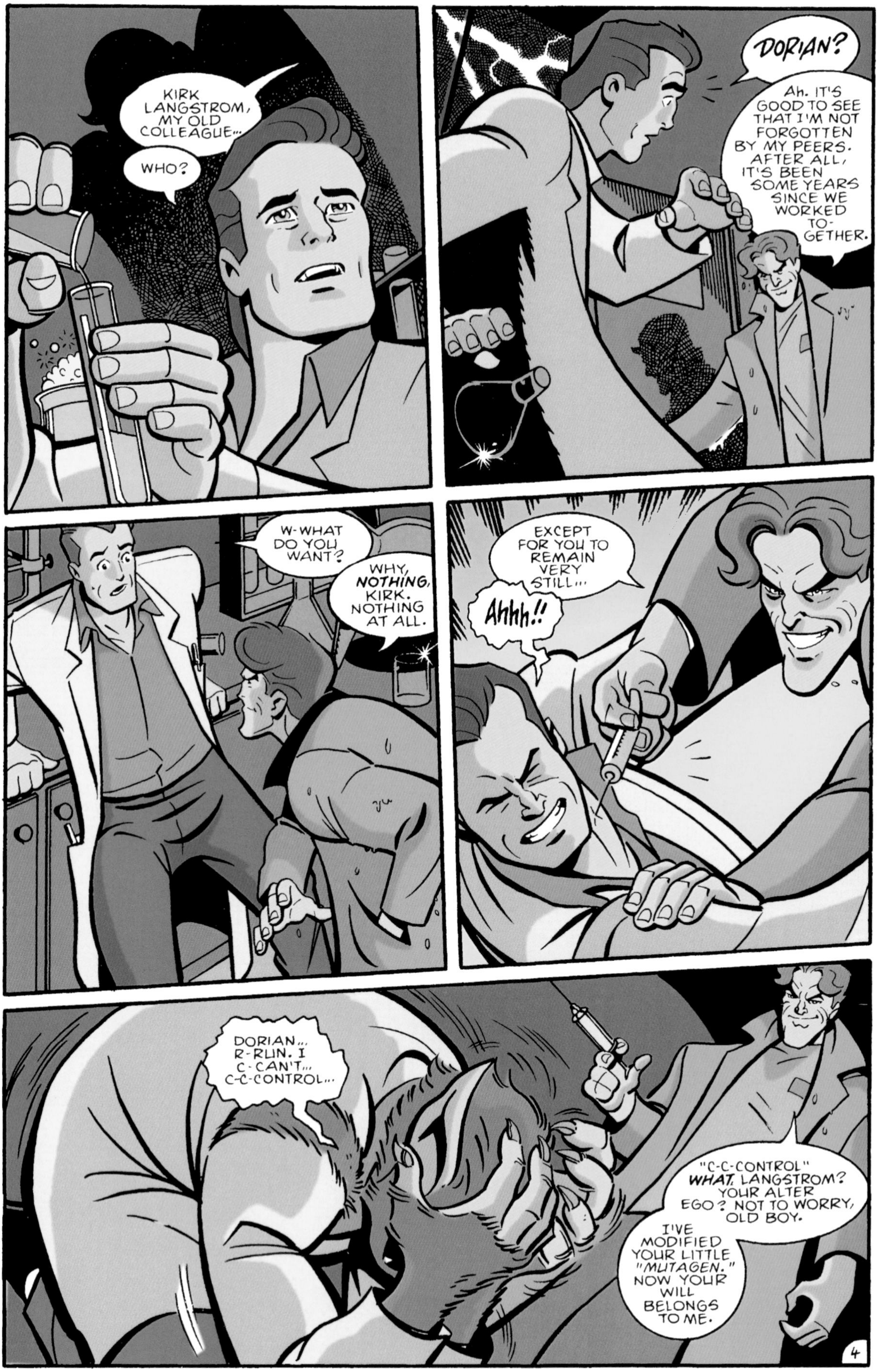
KIRK LANGSTROM, MY OLD COLLEAGUE...
WHO?
DORIAN?
Ah. IT'S GOOD TO SEE THAT I'M NOT FORGOTTEN BY MY PEERS. AFTER ALL, IT'S BEEN SOME YEARS SINCE WE WORKED TO-GETHER.
W-WHAT DO YOU WANT?
WHY, NOTHING, KIRK. NOTHING AT ALL.
EXCEPT FOR YOU TO REMAIN VERY STILL...
Ahhh!!
DORIAN... R-RUN. I C-CAN'T... C-C-CONTROL...
"C-C-CONTROL" WHAT, LANGSTROM? YOUR ALTER EGO? NOT TO WORRY, OLD BOY.
I'VE MODIFIED YOUR LITTLE "MUTAGEN." NOW YOUR WILL BELONGS TO ME.
4

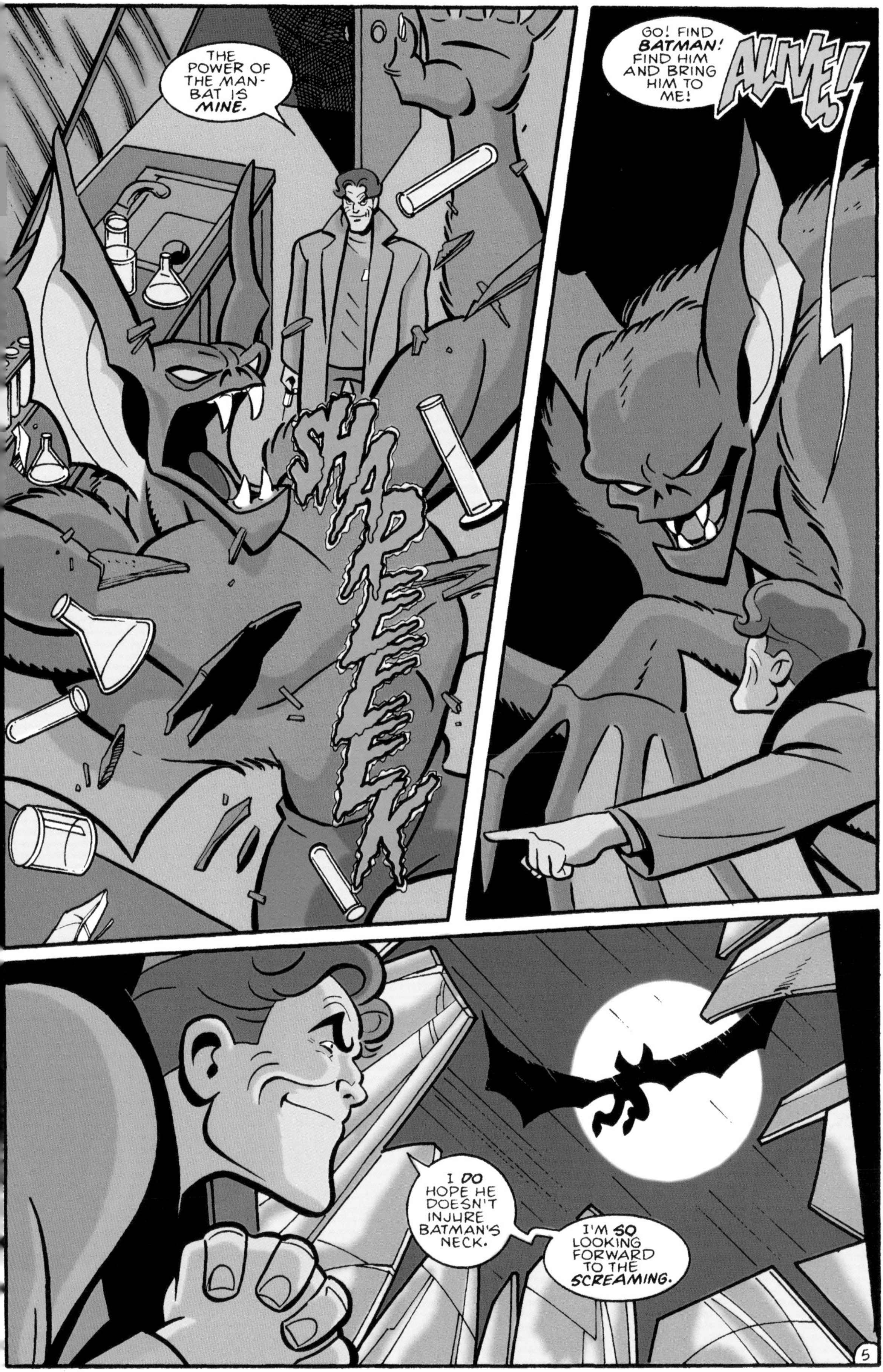
THE POWER OF THE MAN-BAT IS MINE.
SHATTEEEER
GO! FIND BATMAN! FIND HIM AND BRING HIM TO ME!
ALIVE!
I DO HOPE HE DOESN'T INJURE BATMAN'S NECK.
I'M SO LOOKING FORWARD TO THE SCREAMING.
5

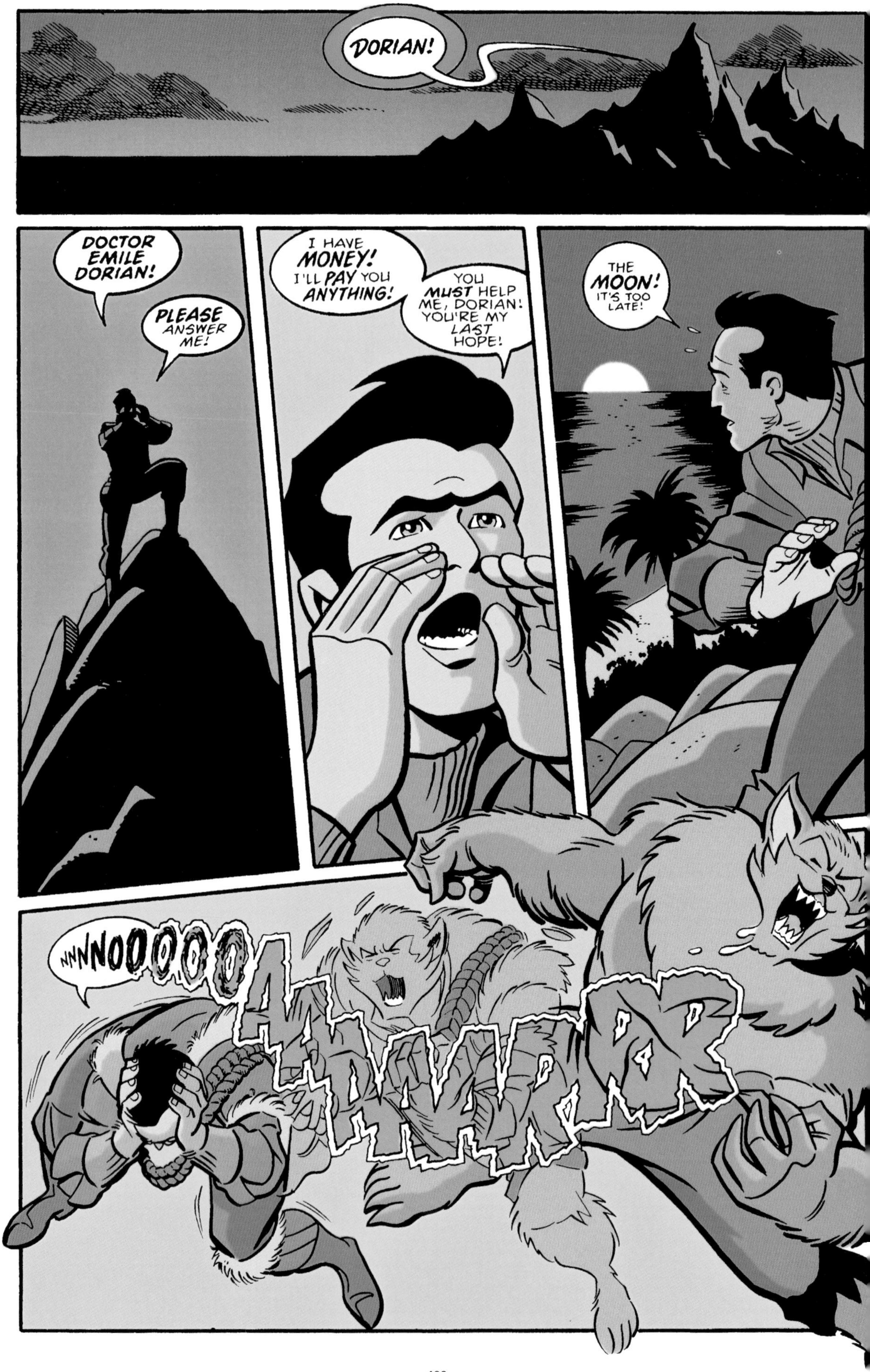
DORIAN!
DOCTOR EMILE DORIAN!
PLEASE ANSWER ME!
I HAVE MONEY! I'LL PAY YOU ANYTHING!
YOU MUST HELP ME, DORIAN! YOU'RE MY LAST HOPE!
THE MOON! IT'S TOO LATE!
NNNNOOOOO
AWWWROOOR

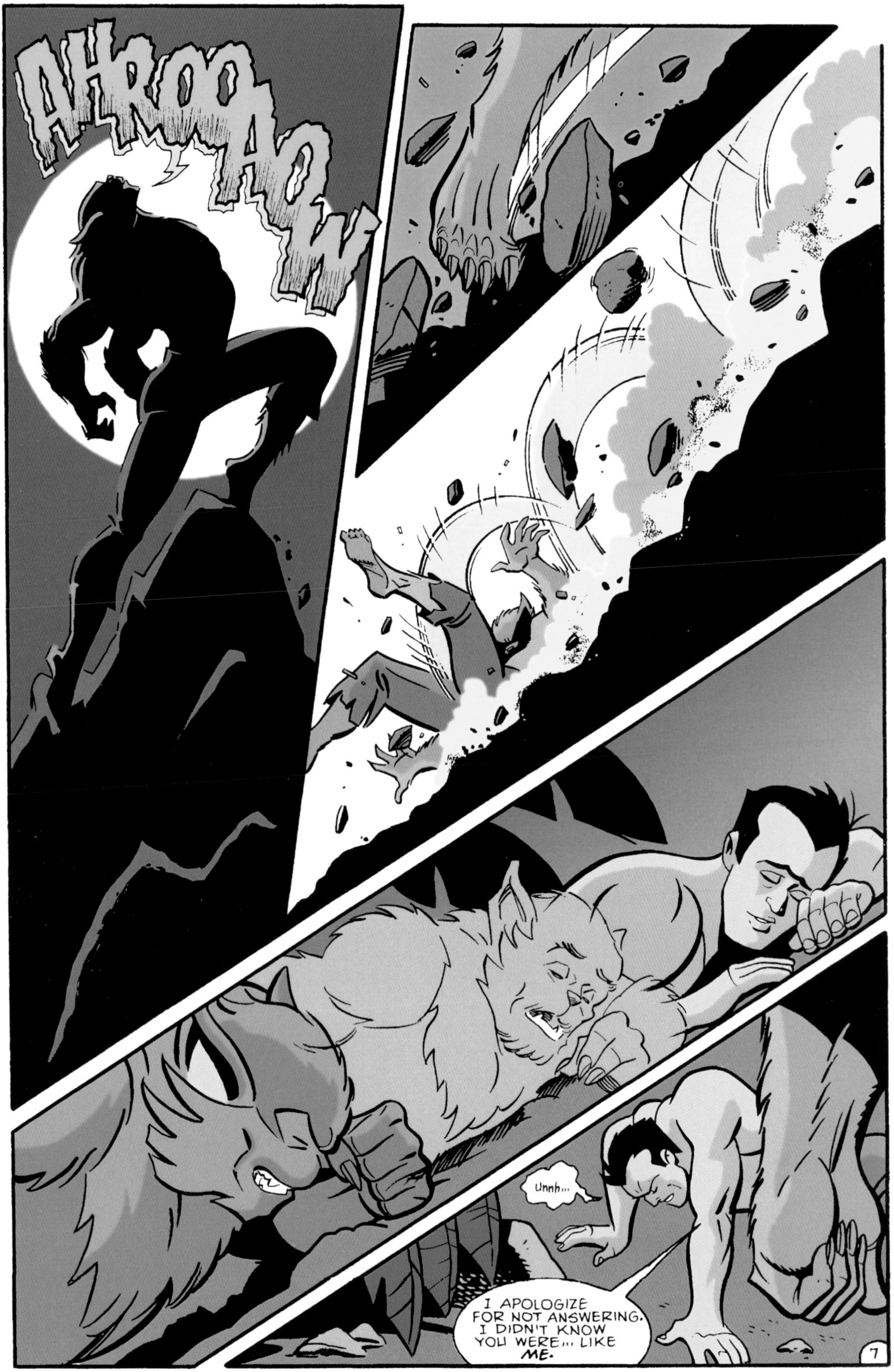
AHROOAOW
Unnh...
I APOLOGIZE FOR NOT ANSWERING. I DIDN'T KNOW YOU WERE... LIKE ME.
7

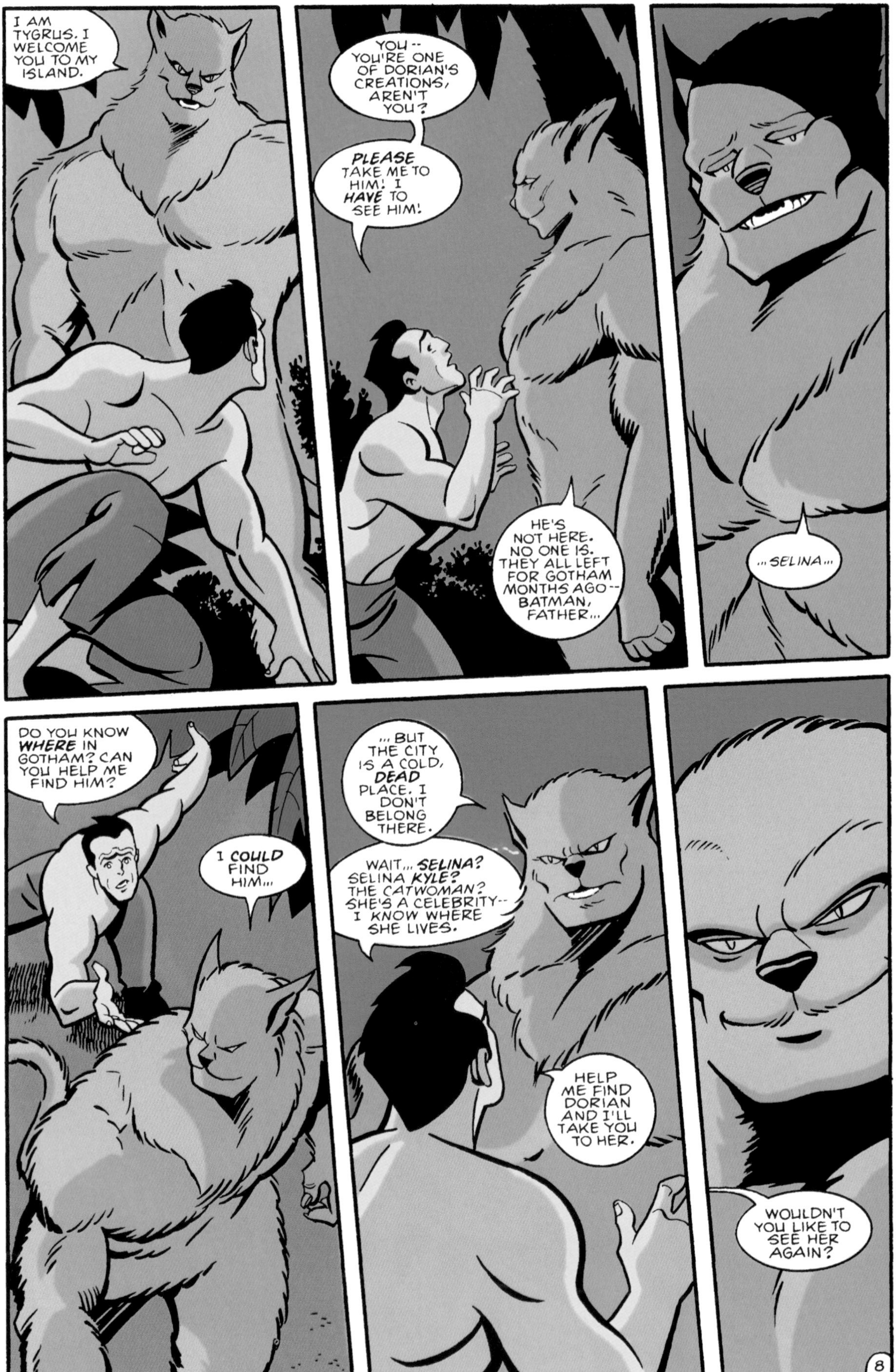
I AM TYGRUS. I WELCOME YOU TO MY ISLAND.
YOU -- YOU'RE ONE OF DORIAN'S CREATIONS, AREN'T YOU?
PLEASE TAKE ME TO HIM! I HAVE TO SEE HIM!
HE'S NOT HERE. NO ONE IS. THEY ALL LEFT FOR GOTHAM MONTHS AGO-- BATMAN, FATHER...
...SELINA...
DO YOU KNOW WHERE IN GOTHAM? CAN YOU HELP ME FIND HIM?
I COULD FIND HIM...
...BUT THE CITY IS A COLD, DEAD PLACE. I DON'T BELONG THERE.
WAIT... SELINA? SELINA KYLE? THE CATWOMAN? SHE'S A CELEBRITY-- I KNOW WHERE SHE LIVES.
HELP ME FIND DORIAN AND I'LL TAKE YOU TO HER.
WOULDN'T YOU LIKE TO SEE HER AGAIN?
8

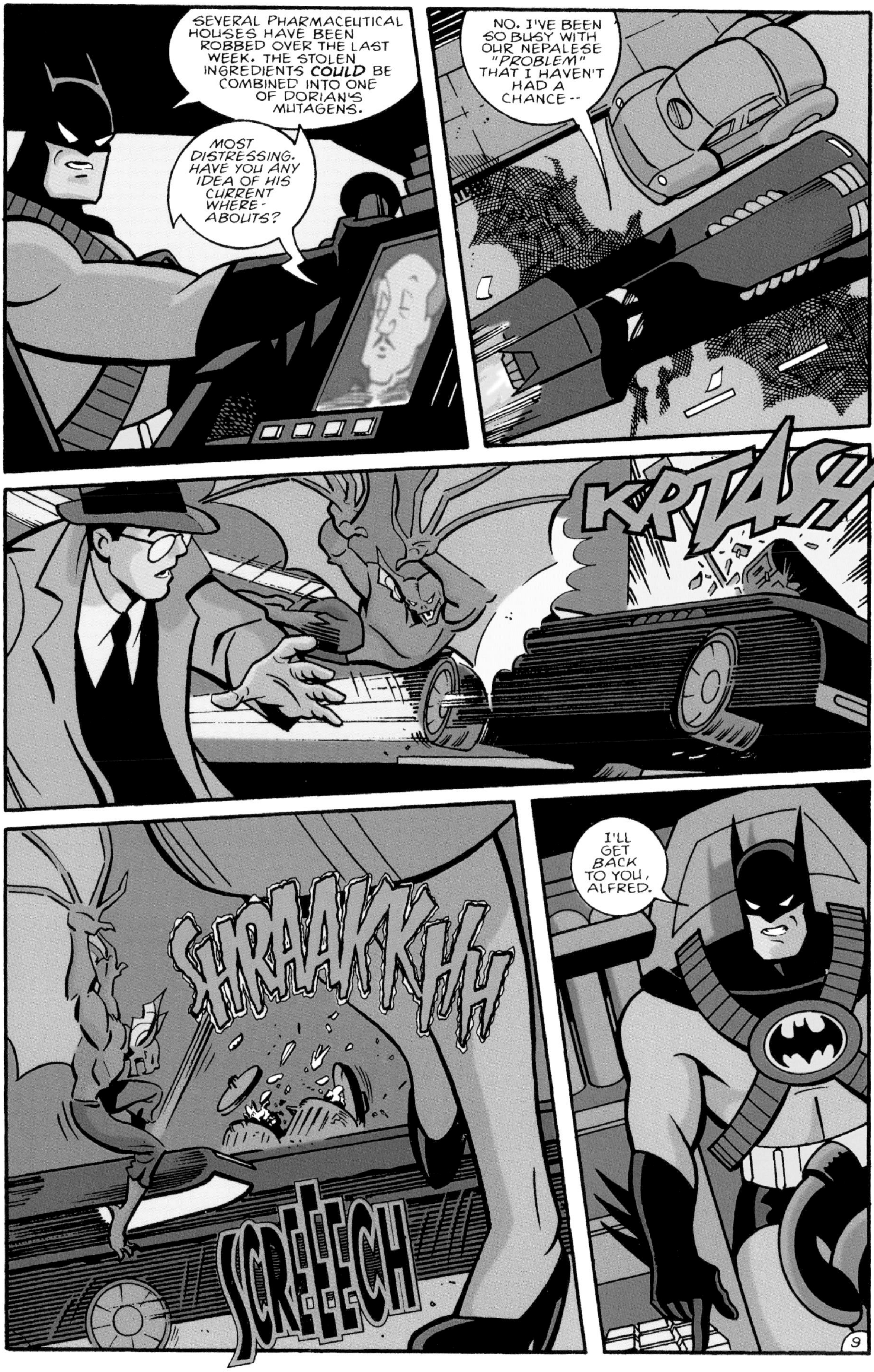
SEVERAL PHARMACEUTICAL HOUSES HAVE BEEN ROBBED OVER THE LAST WEEK. THE STOLEN INGREDIENTS **COULD** BE COMBINED INTO ONE OF DORIAN'S MUTAGENS.
MOST DISTRESSING. HAVE YOU ANY IDEA OF HIS CURRENT WHERE-ABOUTS?
NO. I'VE BEEN SO BUSY WITH OUR NEPALESE *"PROBLEM"* THAT I HAVEN'T HAD A CHANCE --
KRTASH
SHRAAKKHH
SCREEECH
I'LL GET *BACK* TO YOU, ALFRED.
9

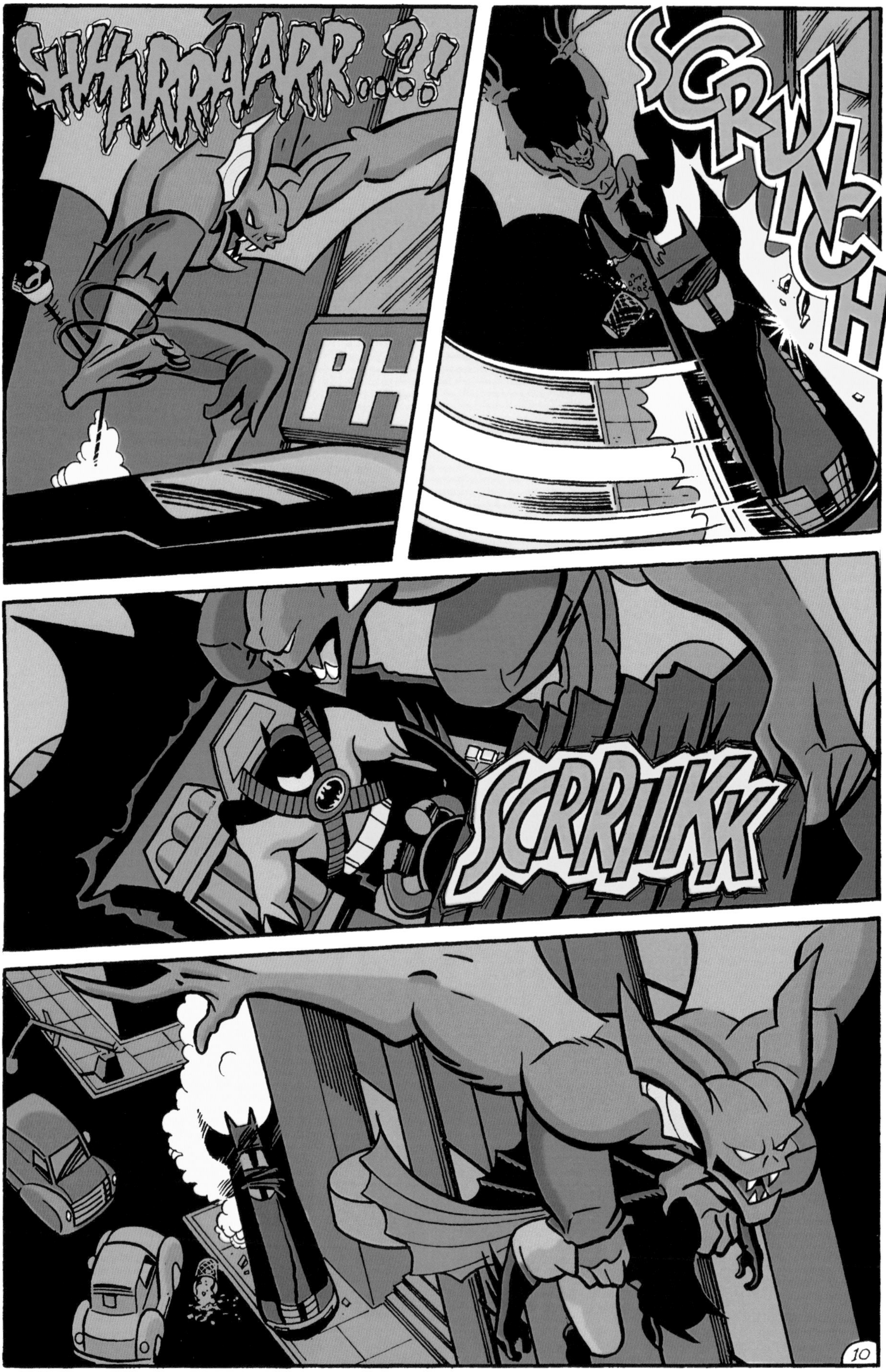
SHHARRAARR...?!
SCRUNCH
PH
SCRRIIKK
10

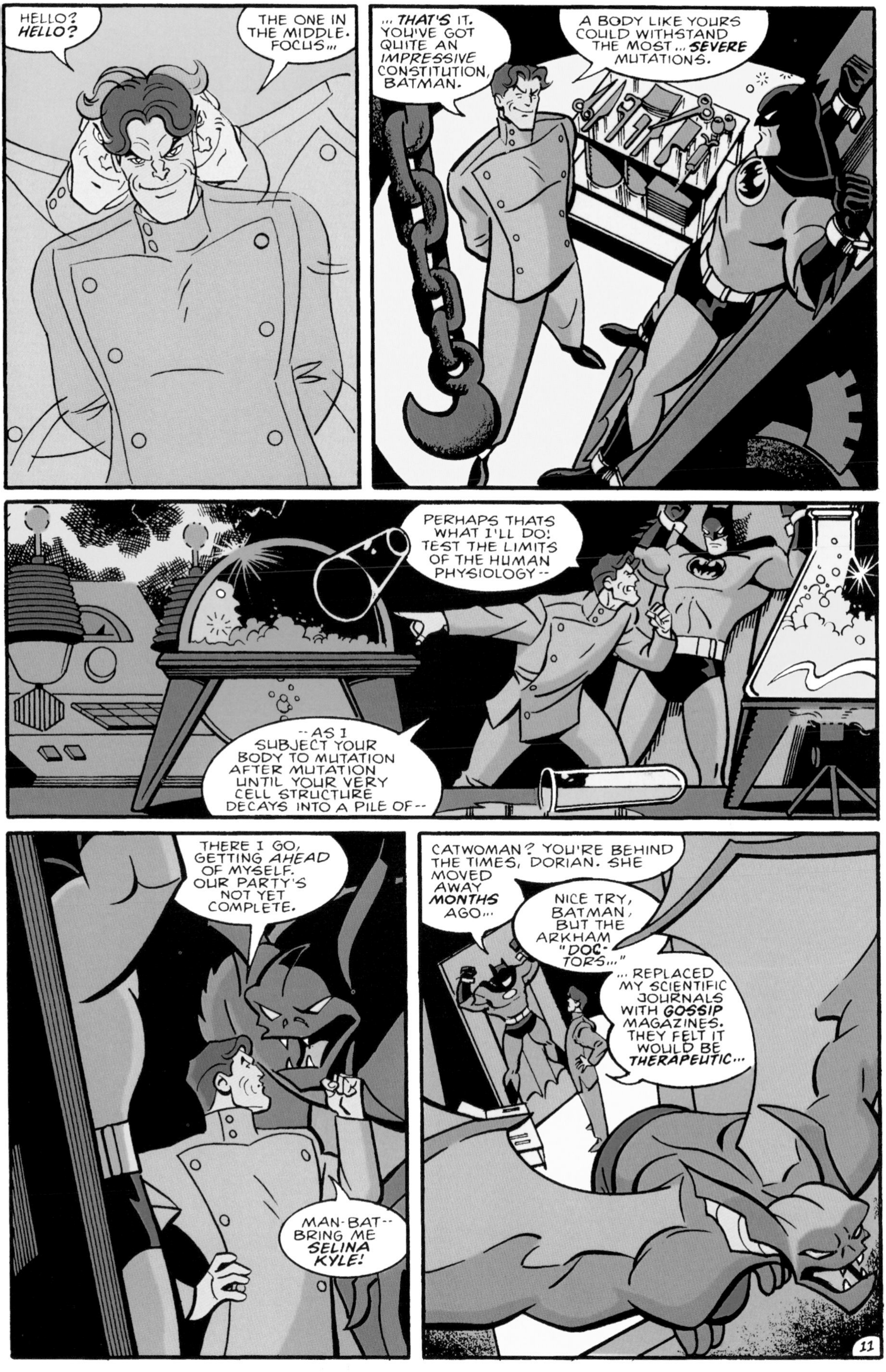
HELLO? HELLO?
THE ONE IN THE MIDDLE. FOCUS...
...THAT'S IT. YOU'VE GOT QUITE AN IMPRESSIVE CONSTITUTION, BATMAN.
A BODY LIKE YOURS COULD WITHSTAND THE MOST... SEVERE MUTATIONS.
PERHAPS THATS WHAT I'LL DO! TEST THE LIMITS OF THE HUMAN PHYSIOLOGY--
--AS I SUBJECT YOUR BODY TO MUTATION AFTER MUTATION UNTIL YOUR VERY CELL STRUCTURE DECAYS INTO A PILE OF--
THERE I GO, GETTING AHEAD OF MYSELF. OUR PARTY'S NOT YET COMPLETE.
MAN-BAT-- BRING ME SELINA KYLE!
CATWOMAN? YOU'RE BEHIND THE TIMES, DORIAN. SHE MOVED AWAY MONTHS AGO...
NICE TRY, BATMAN, BUT THE ARKHAM "DOC-TORS..."
...REPLACED MY SCIENTIFIC JOURNALS WITH GOSSIP MAGAZINES. THEY FELT IT WOULD BE THERAPEUTIC...
11

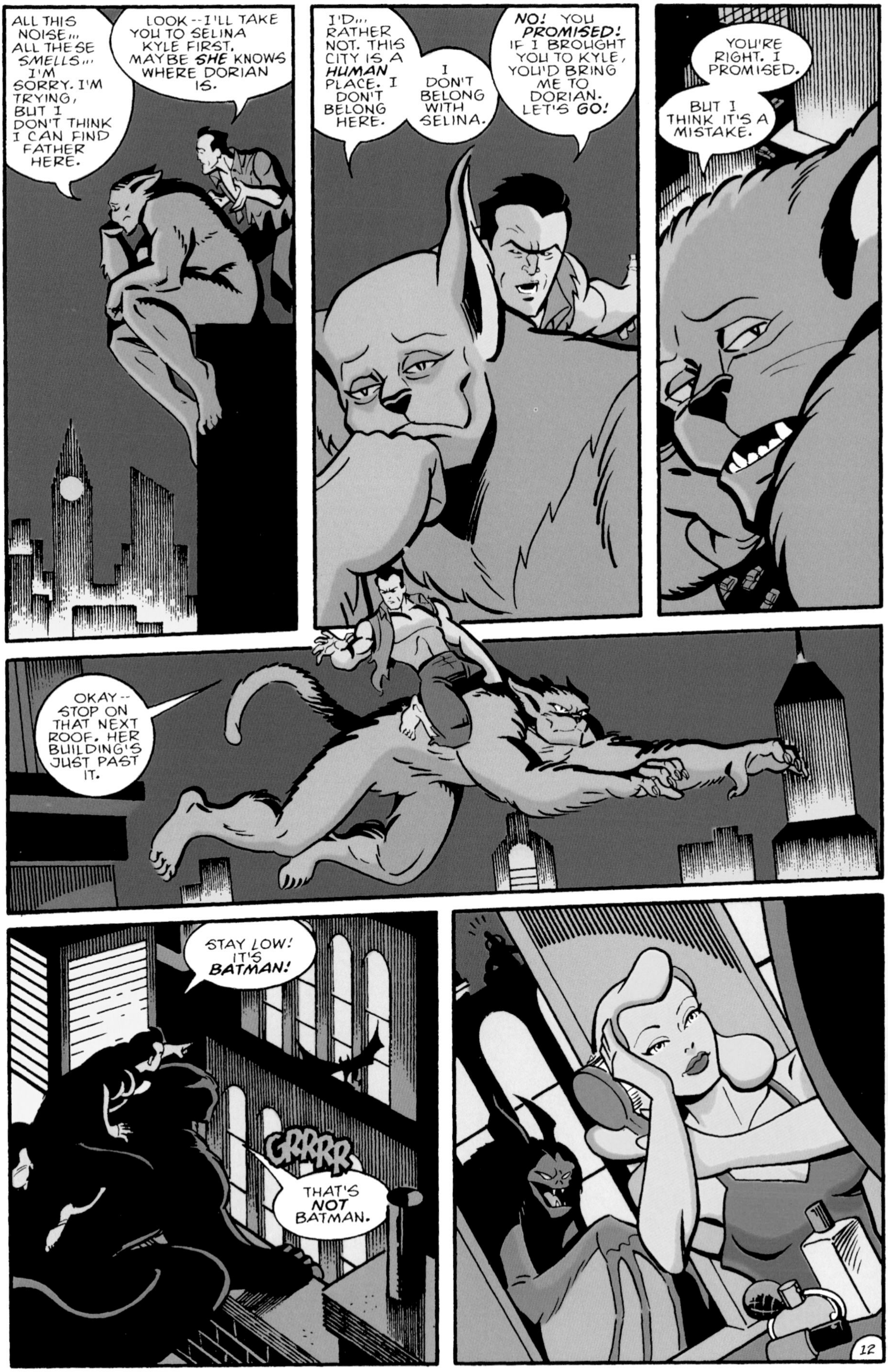
ALL THIS NOISE... ALL THESE SMELLS... I'M SORRY. I'M TRYING, BUT I DON'T THINK I CAN FIND FATHER HERE.
LOOK--I'LL TAKE YOU TO SELINA KYLE FIRST. MAYBE SHE KNOWS WHERE DORIAN IS.
I'D... RATHER NOT. THIS CITY IS A HUMAN PLACE. I DON'T BELONG HERE.
I DON'T BELONG WITH SELINA.
NO! YOU PROMISED! IF I BROUGHT YOU TO KYLE, YOU'D BRING ME TO DORIAN. LET'S GO!
YOU'RE RIGHT. I PROMISED.
BUT I THINK IT'S A MISTAKE.
OKAY-- STOP ON THAT NEXT ROOF. HER BUILDING'S JUST PAST IT.
STAY LOW! IT'S BATMAN!
GRRRR
THAT'S NOT BATMAN.
12

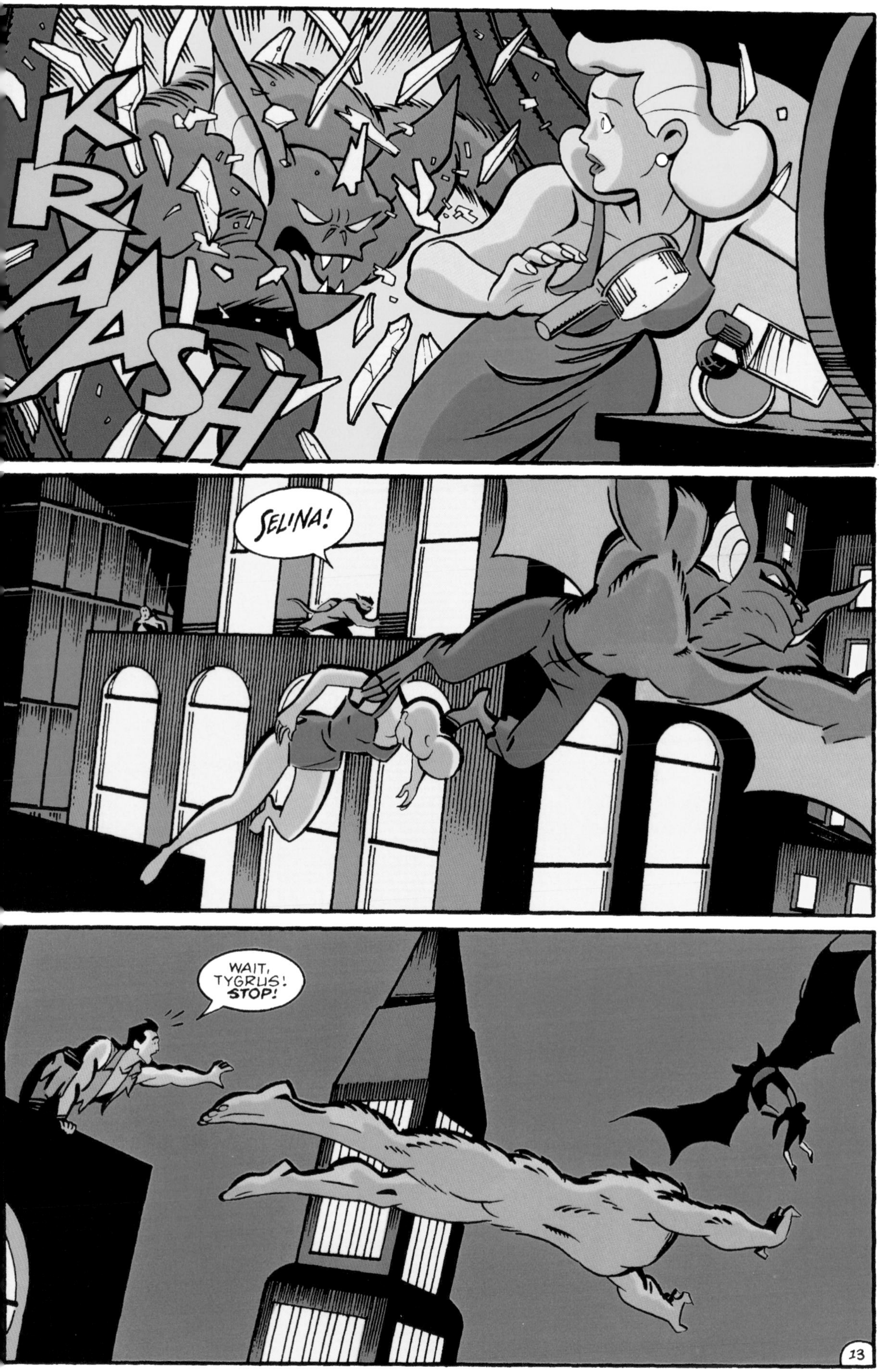
KRASH
SELINA!
WAIT, TYGRUS! STOP!
13

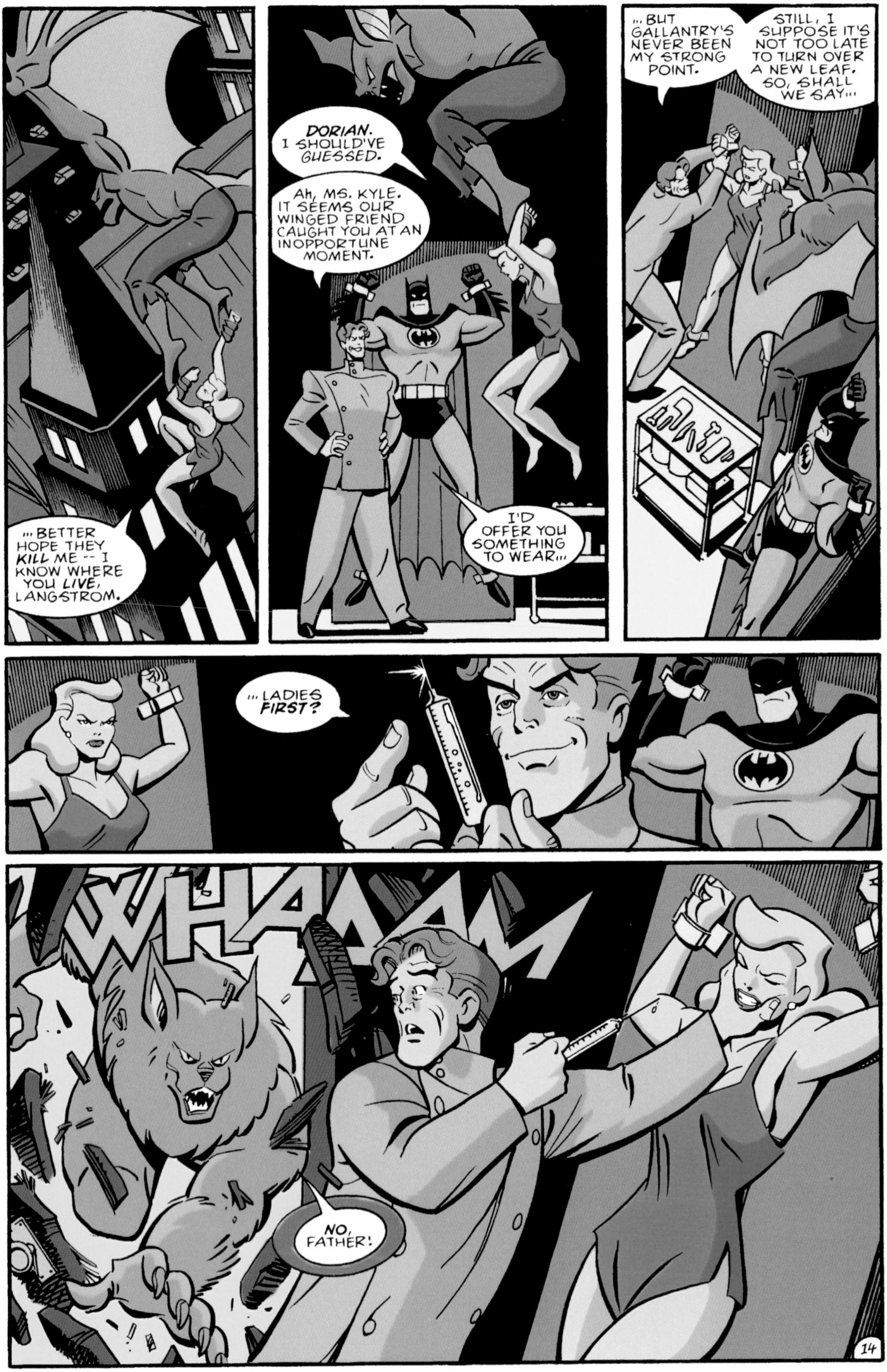
...BETTER HOPE THEY KILL ME -- I KNOW WHERE YOU LIVE, LANGSTROM.
DORIAN. I SHOULD'VE GUESSED.
Ah, MS. KYLE. IT SEEMS OUR WINGED FRIEND CAUGHT YOU AT AN INOPPORTUNE MOMENT.
I'D OFFER YOU SOMETHING TO WEAR...
...BUT GALLANTRY'S NEVER BEEN MY STRONG POINT.
STILL, I SUPPOSE IT'S NOT TOO LATE TO TURN OVER A NEW LEAF. SO, SHALL WE SAY...
...LADIES FIRST?
WHAAM
NO, FATHER!
14

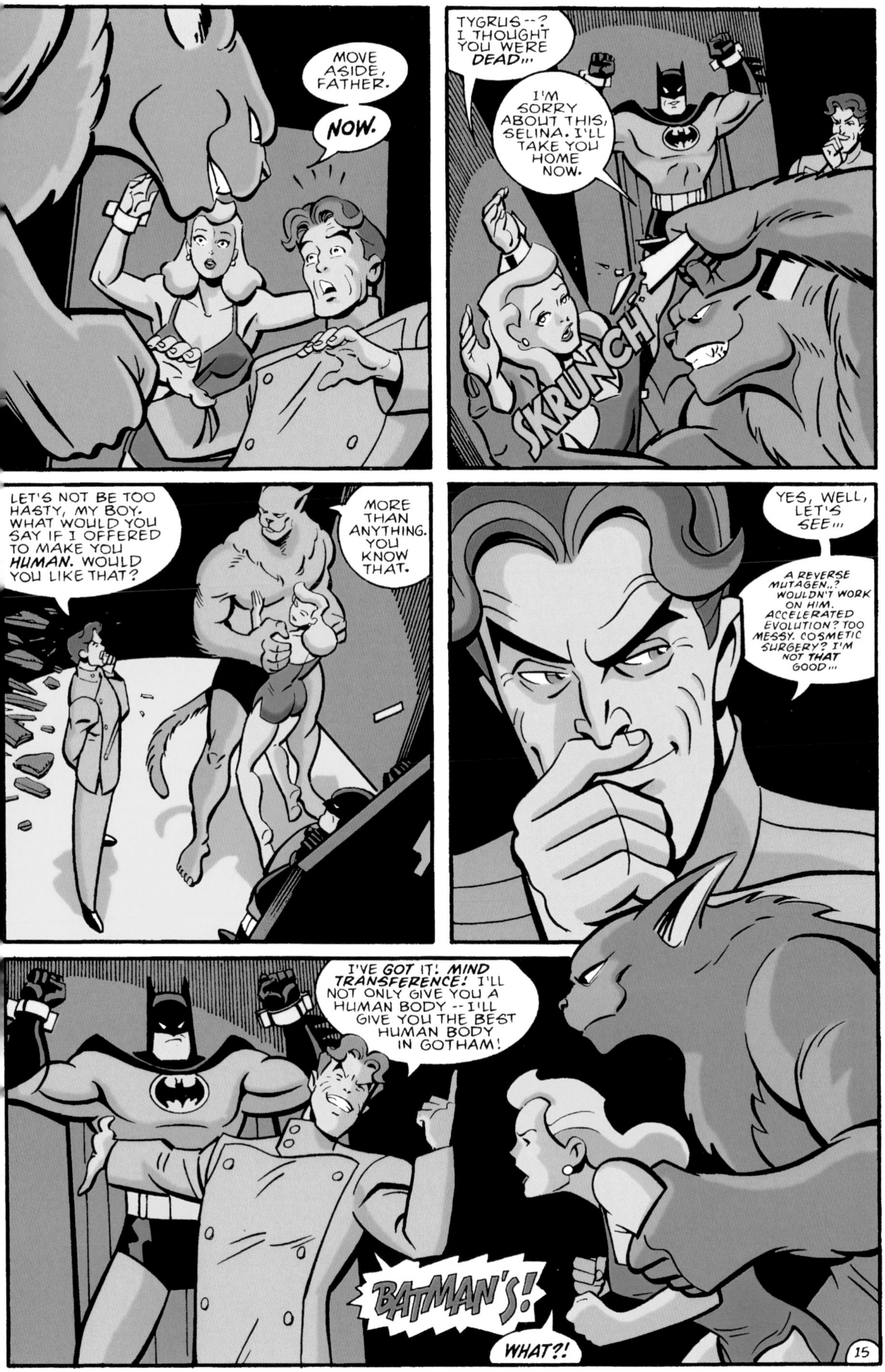
MOVE ASIDE, FATHER.
NOW.
TYGRUS--? I THOUGHT YOU WERE DEAD...
I'M SORRY ABOUT THIS, SELINA. I'LL TAKE YOU HOME NOW.
SKRUNCH
LET'S NOT BE TOO HASTY, MY BOY. WHAT WOULD YOU SAY IF I OFFERED TO MAKE YOU HUMAN. WOULD YOU LIKE THAT?
MORE THAN ANYTHING. YOU KNOW THAT.
YES, WELL, LET'S SEE...
A REVERSE MUTAGEN..? WOULDN'T WORK ON HIM. ACCELERATED EVOLUTION? TOO MESSY. COSMETIC SURGERY? I'M NOT THAT GOOD...
I'VE GOT IT! MIND TRANSFERENCE! I'LL NOT ONLY GIVE YOU A HUMAN BODY -- I'LL GIVE YOU THE BEST HUMAN BODY IN GOTHAM!
BATMAN'S!
WHAT?!
15

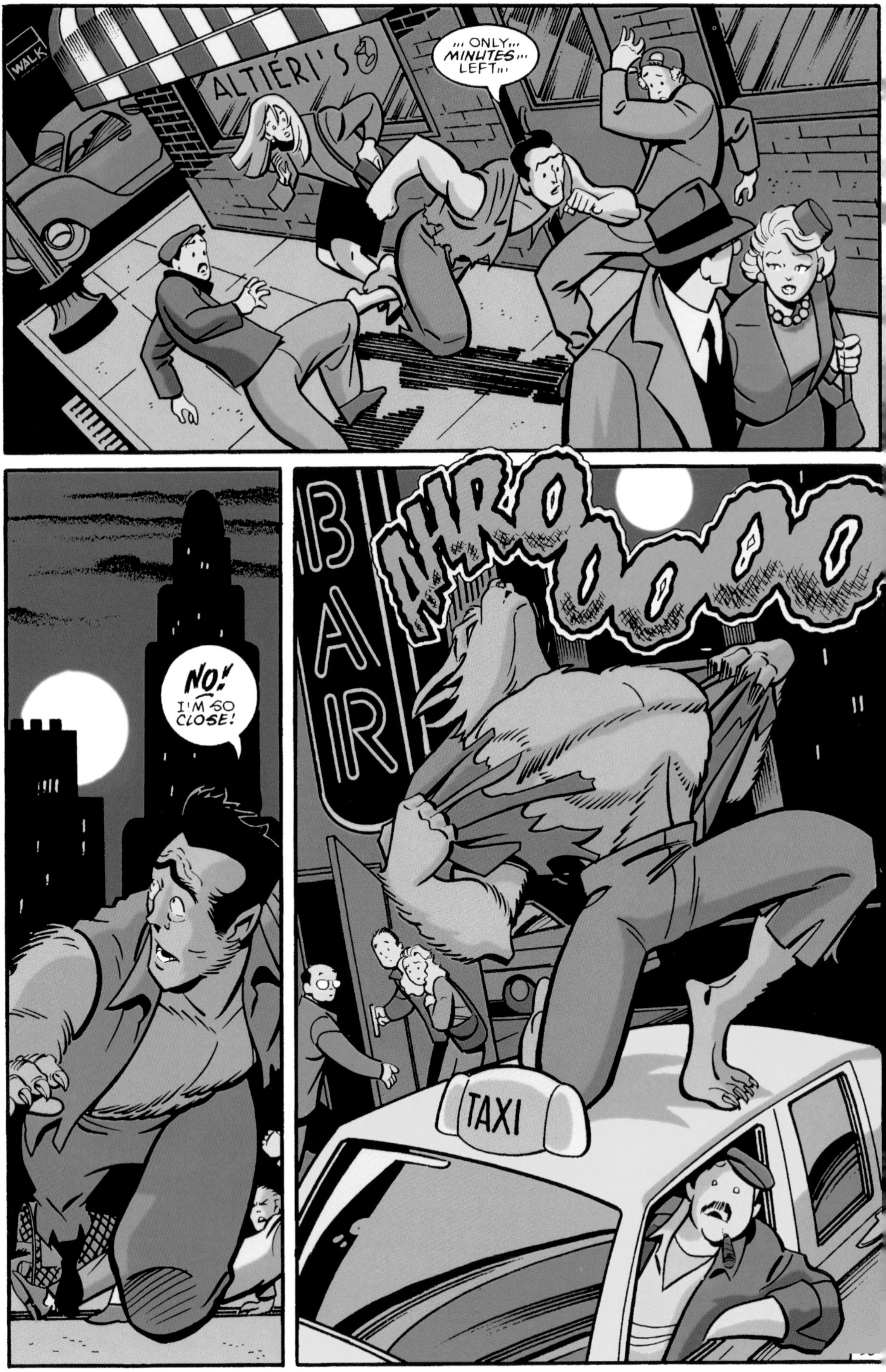
WALK
ALTIÉRI'S
... ONLY... MINUTES... LEFT...
NO! I'M SO CLOSE!
BAR
AHROOOOO
TAXI

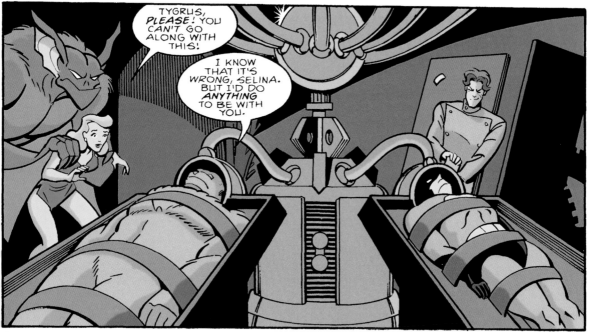

TYGRUS, *PLEASE!* YOU CAN'T GO ALONG WITH THIS!

I KNOW THAT IT'S WRONG, SELINA. BUT I'D DO *ANYTHING* TO BE WITH YOU.

BUT THIS IS *CRAZY!* I COULDN'T LOVE ANYONE WHO DID SOMETHING LIKE THIS!

PERHAPS. BUT I *KNOW* YOU COULDN'T LOVE SOMEONE WHO *LOOKS* LIKE THIS.

I'M KICKING MYSELF, BATMAN. MIND TRANSFERENCE SHOULD HAVE OCCURRED TO ME EARLIER. I WAS ONLY PLANNING ON A FEW *DAYS* OF TORTURE...

... BUT IN *TYGRUS'* BODY, YOU'LL LAST FOR *WEEKS.*

SHALL WE BEGIN"?

17

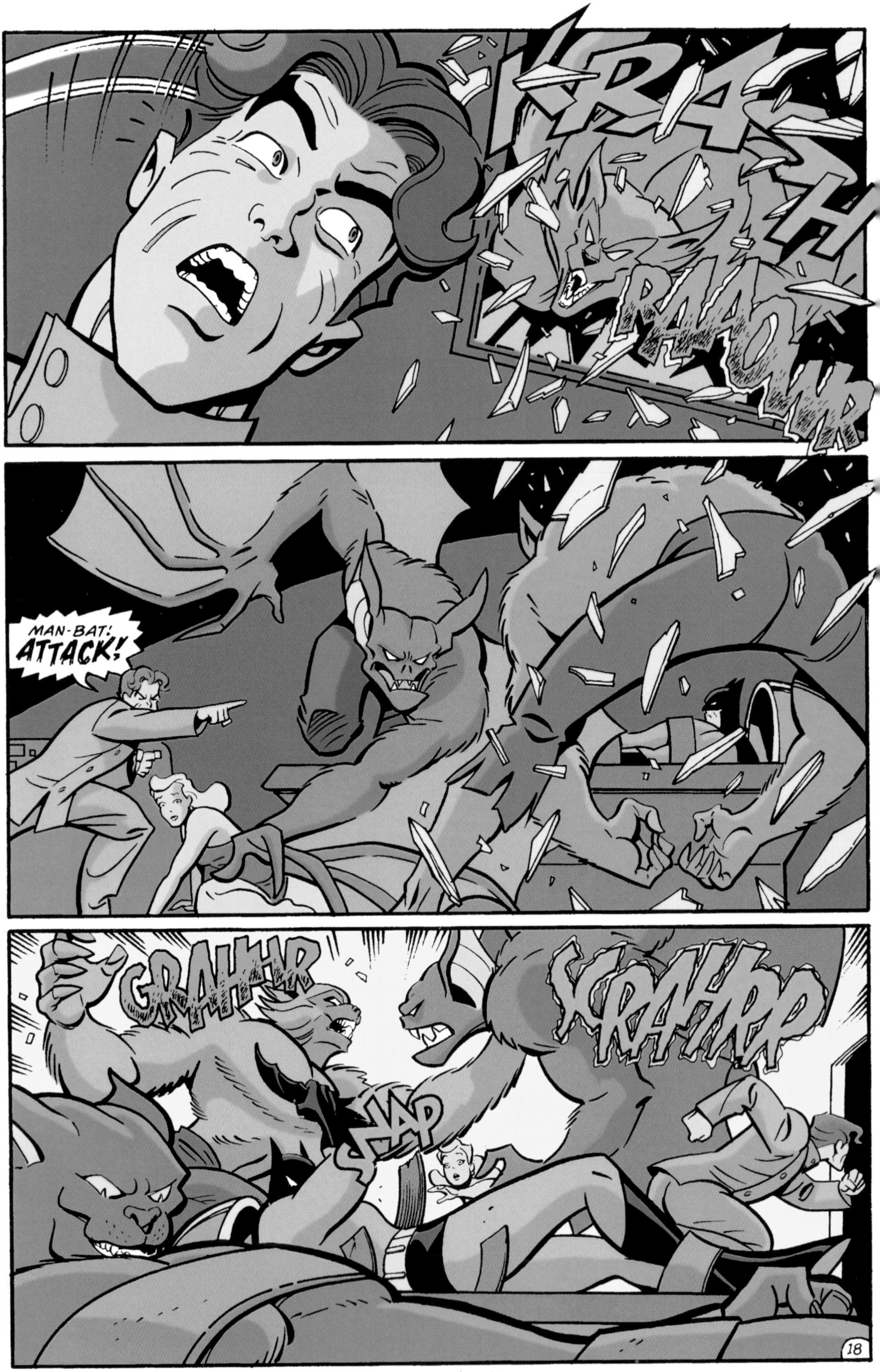

KRASH
RAAOWR
MAN-BAT! ATTACK!
GRAHHR
SCRAHRR
SHAP
18

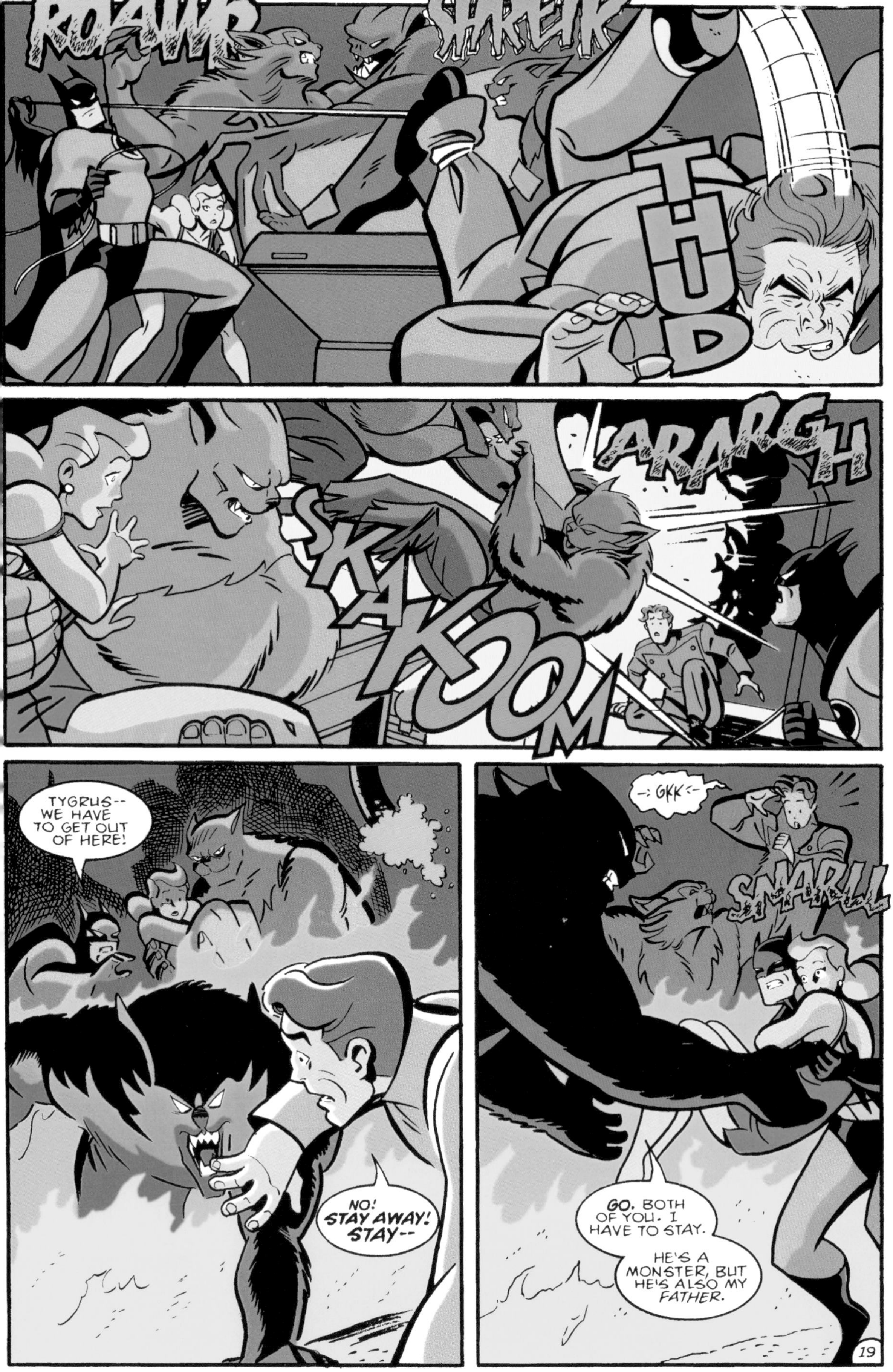
ROAWR
SHREIK
THUD
ARARGH
SKAKOOM
TYGRUS-- WE HAVE TO GET OUT OF HERE!
NO! STAY AWAY! STAY--
GKK
SNARLL
GO. BOTH OF YOU. I HAVE TO STAY.
HE'S A MONSTER, BUT HE'S ALSO MY FATHER.
19

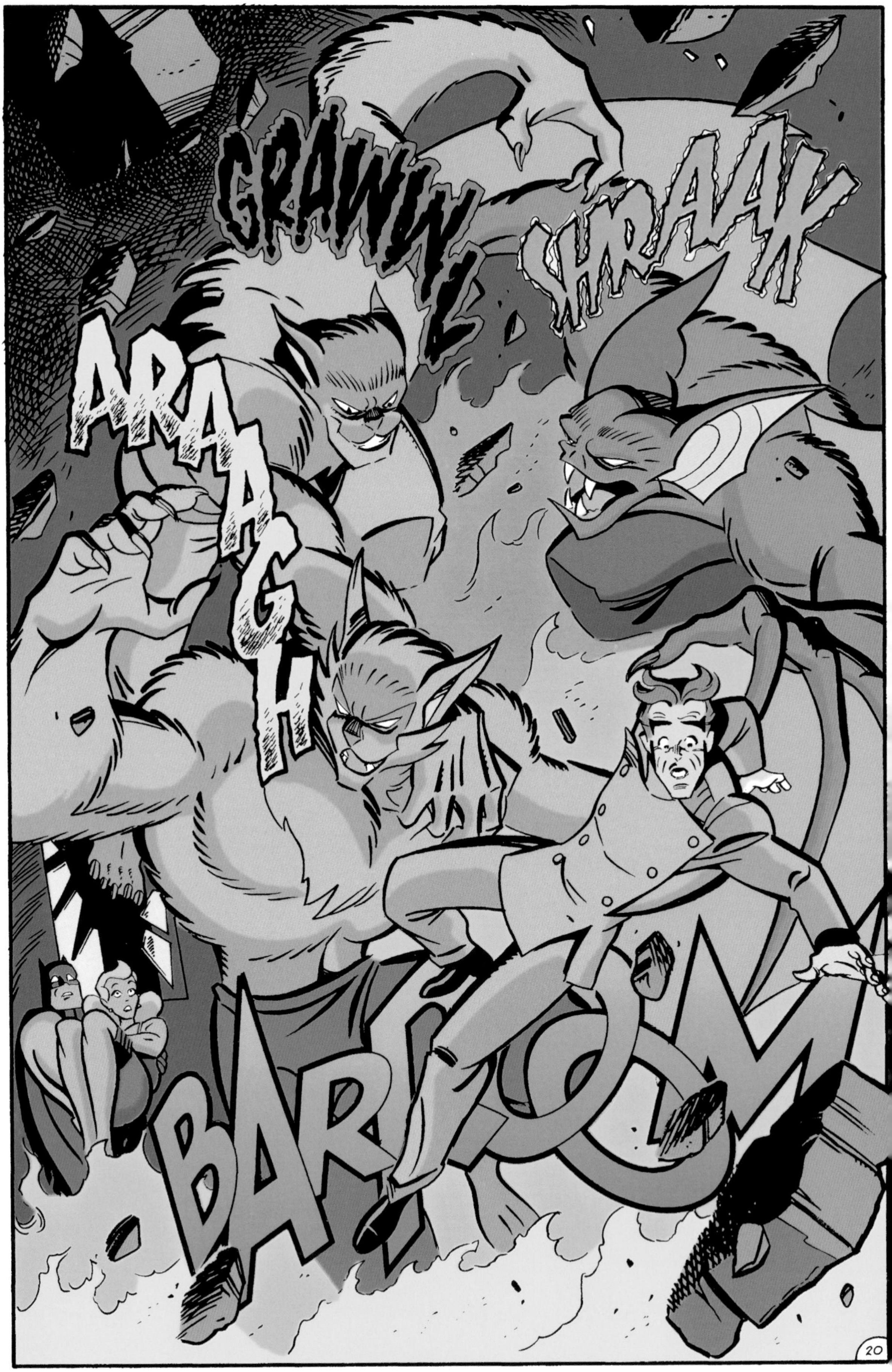
GRAWW
SHRAAK
ARAAGH
BARROOM
20

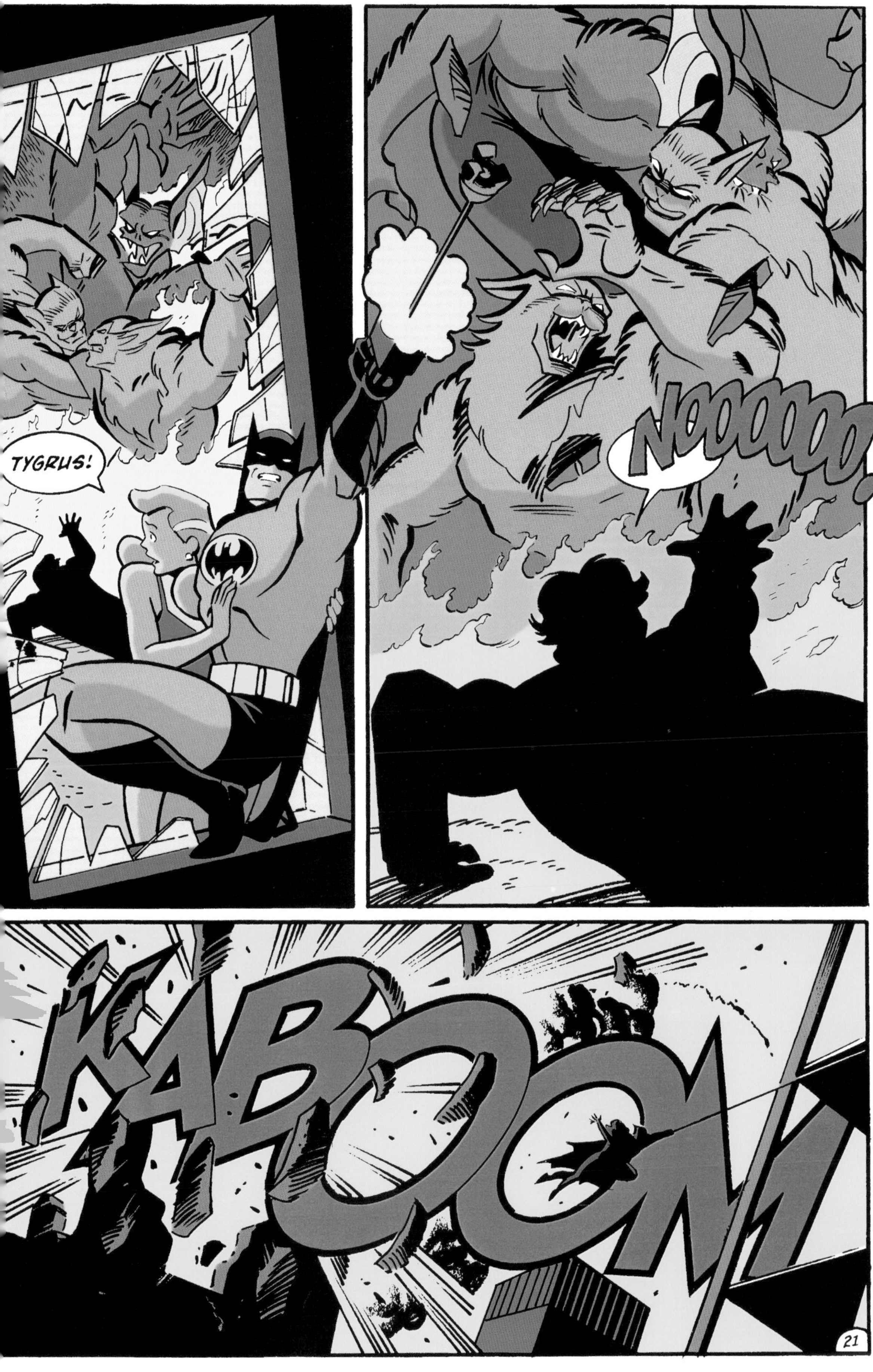
TYGRUS!
NOOOOOO!
KABOOM!
21

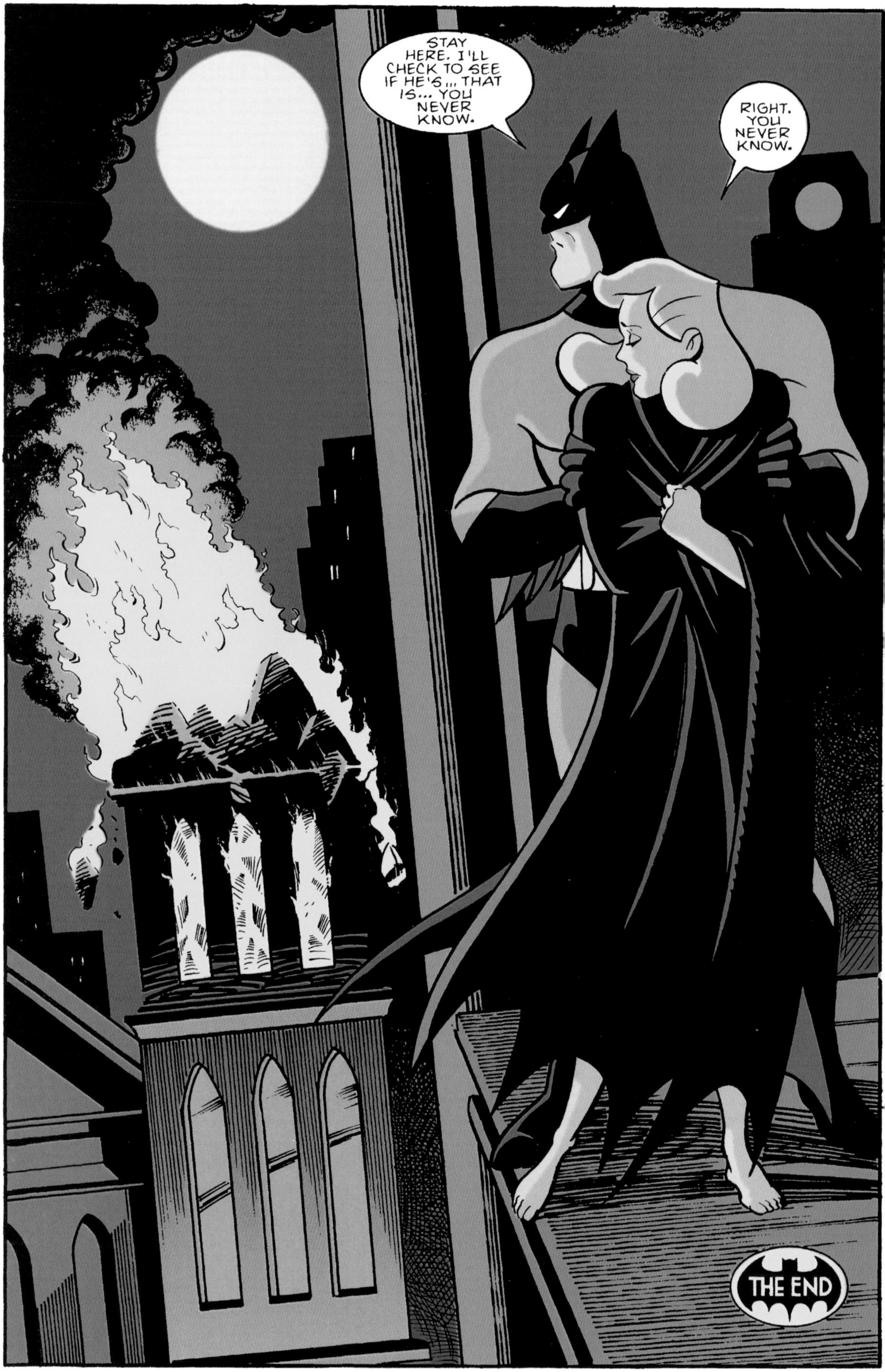
STAY HERE. I'LL CHECK TO SEE IF HE'S... THAT IS... YOU NEVER KNOW.
RIGHT. YOU NEVER KNOW.
THE END

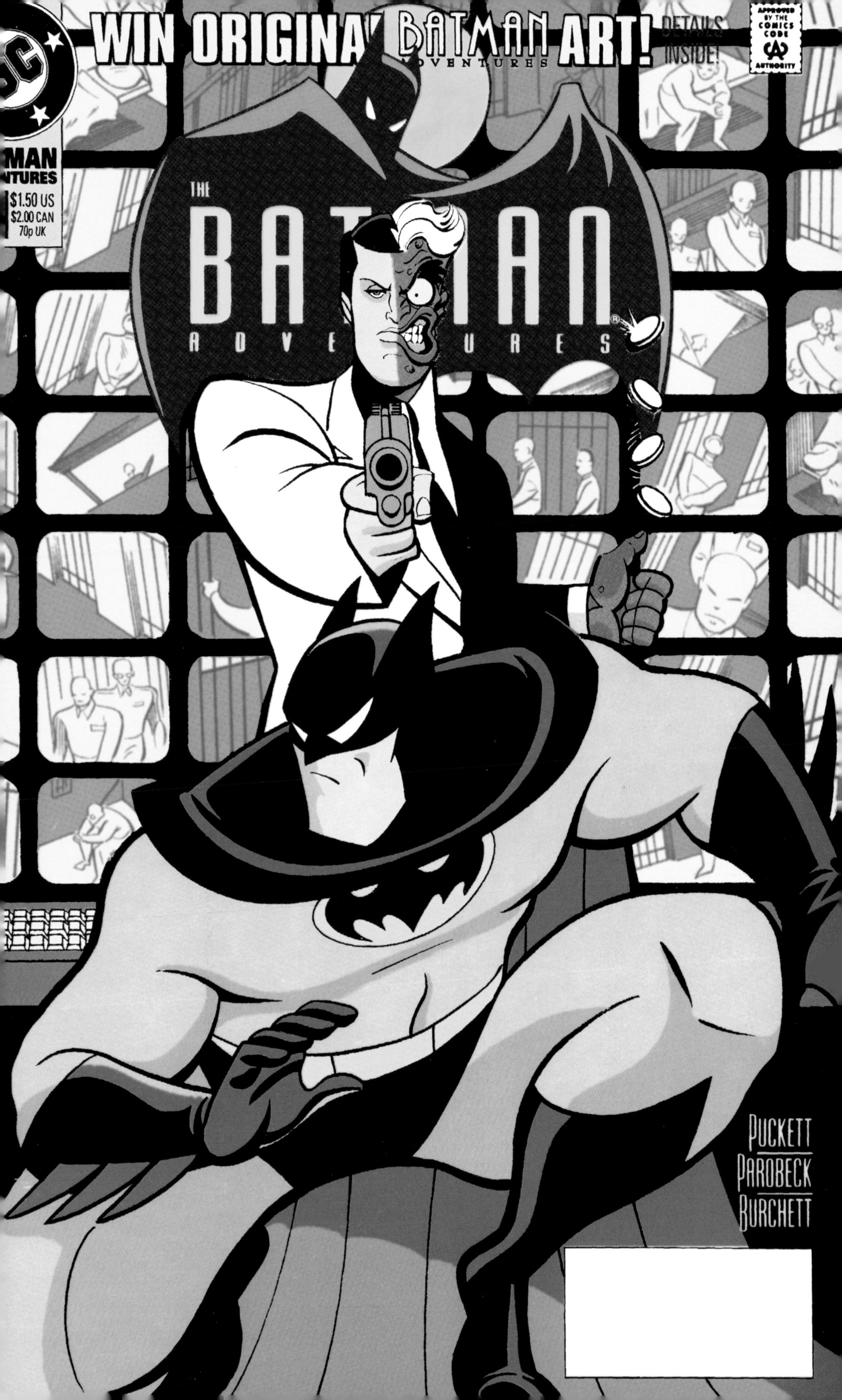

WIN ORIGINAL BATMAN ADVENTURES ART!
DETAILS INSIDE!
APPROVED BY THE COMICS CODE AUTHORITY
$1.50 US
$2.00 CAN
70p UK
THE BATMAN ADVENTURES
PUCKETT
PAROBECK
BURCHETT

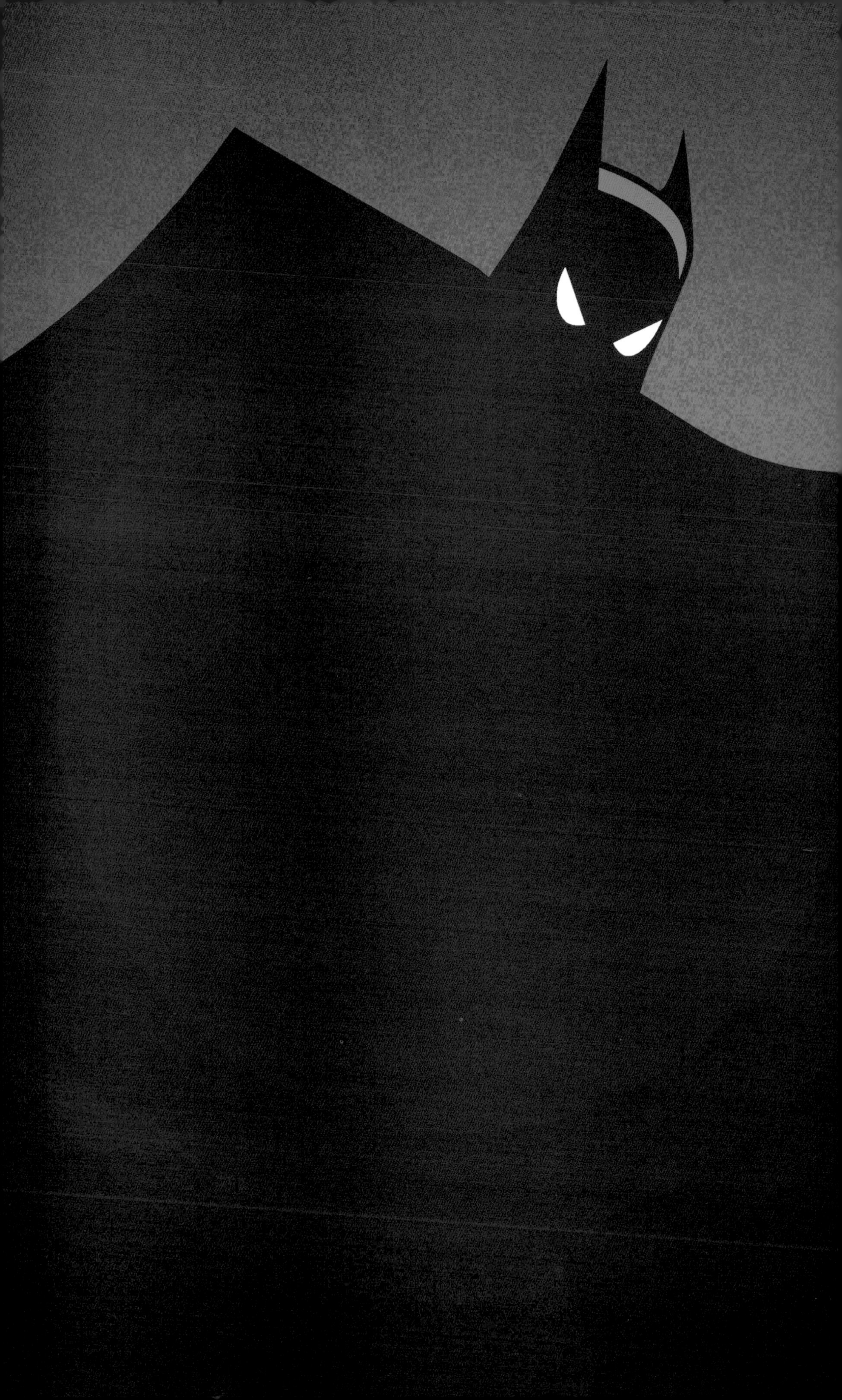

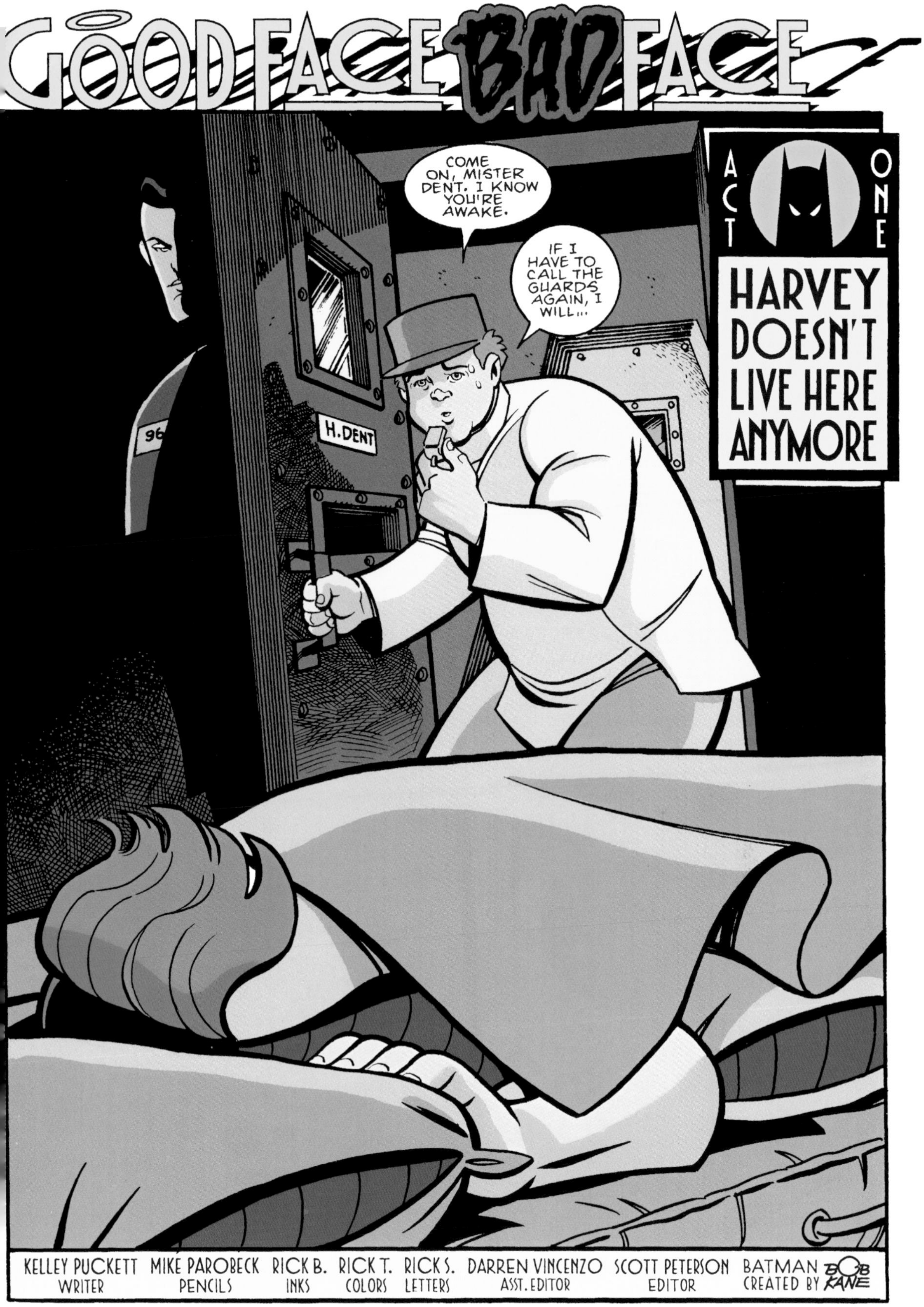
GOOD FACE BAD FACE
ACT ONE
HARVEY DOESN'T LIVE HERE ANYMORE
COME ON, MISTER DENT. I KNOW YOU'RE AWAKE.
IF I HAVE TO CALL THE GUARDS AGAIN, I WILL...
H. DENT
KELLEY PUCKETT WRITER
MIKE PAROBECK PENCILS
RICK B. INKS
RICK T. COLORS
RICK S. LETTERS
DARREN VINCENZO ASST. EDITOR
SCOTT PETERSON EDITOR
BATMAN CREATED BY BOB KANE

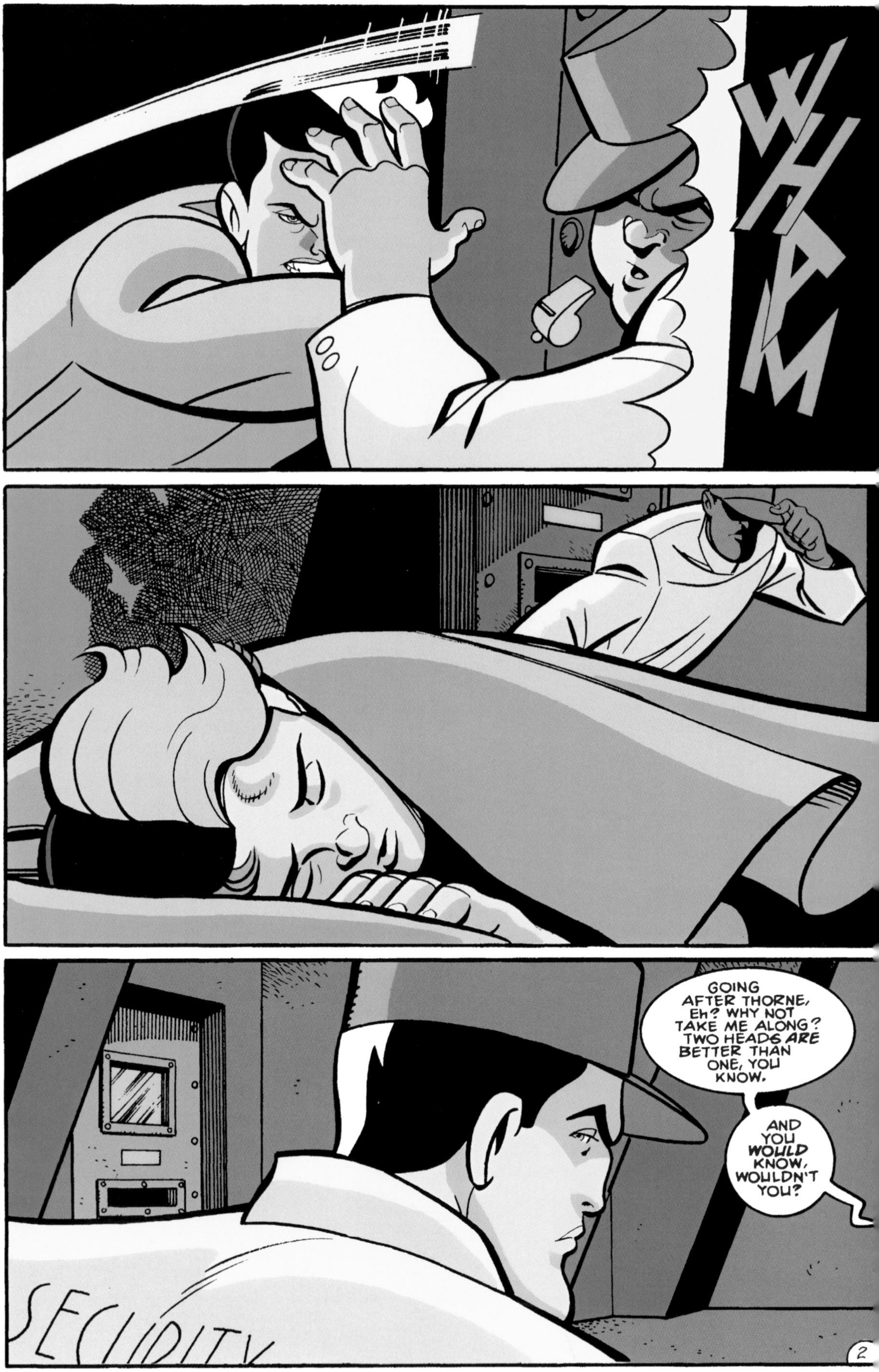
WHAM
GOING AFTER THORNE, Eh? WHY NOT TAKE ME ALONG? TWO HEADS ARE BETTER THAN ONE, YOU KNOW.
AND YOU WOULD KNOW, WOULDN'T YOU?
SECURITY
2

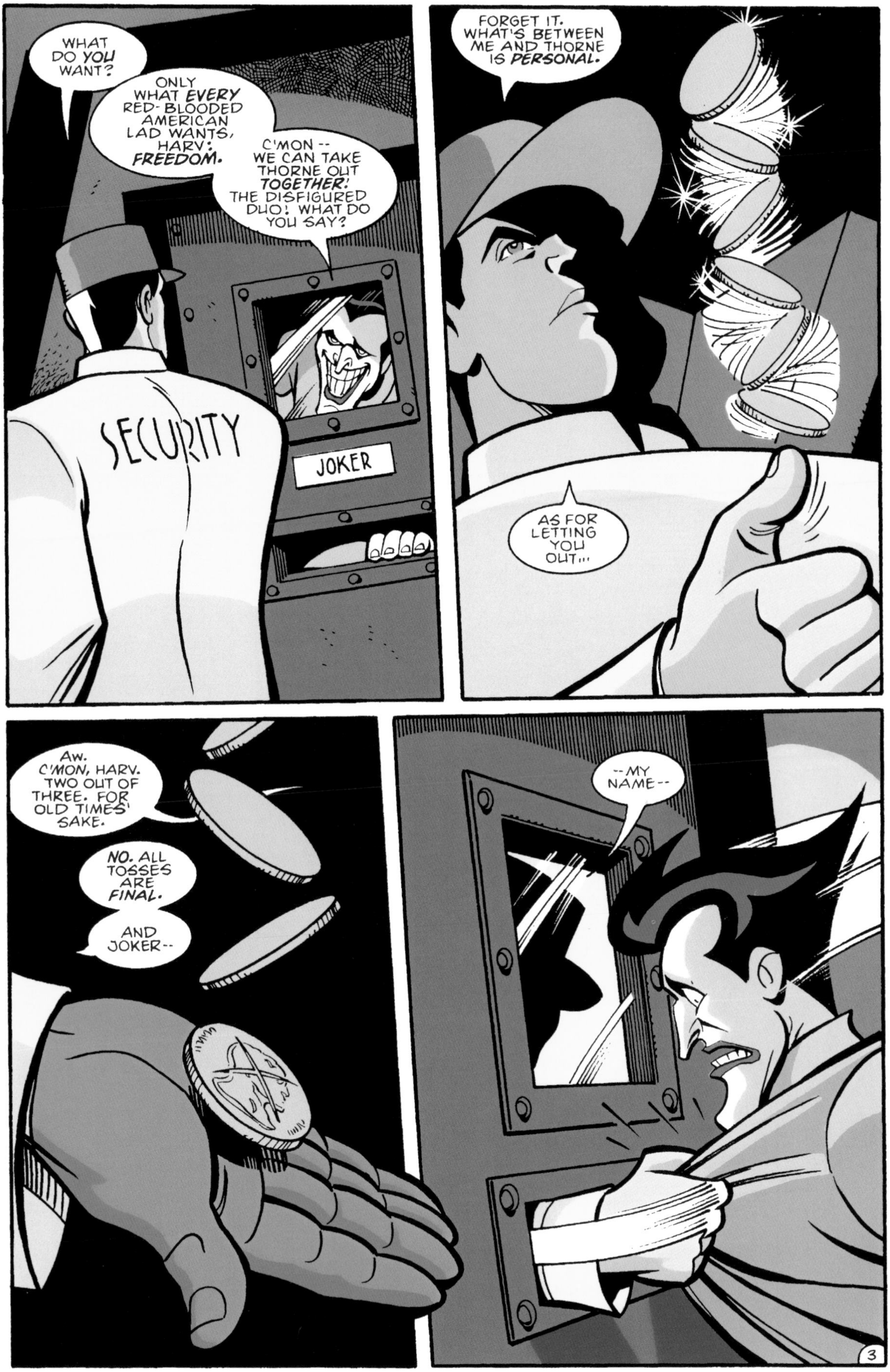
WHAT DO YOU WANT?
ONLY WHAT EVERY RED-BLOODED AMERICAN LAD WANTS, HARV: FREEDOM.
C'MON -- WE CAN TAKE THORNE OUT TOGETHER! THE DISFIGURED DUO! WHAT DO YOU SAY?
SECURITY
JOKER
FORGET IT. WHAT'S BETWEEN ME AND THORNE IS PERSONAL.
AS FOR LETTING YOU OUT...
AW. C'MON, HARV. TWO OUT OF THREE. FOR OLD TIMES' SAKE.
NO. ALL TOSSES ARE FINAL.
AND JOKER--
--MY NAME--
3

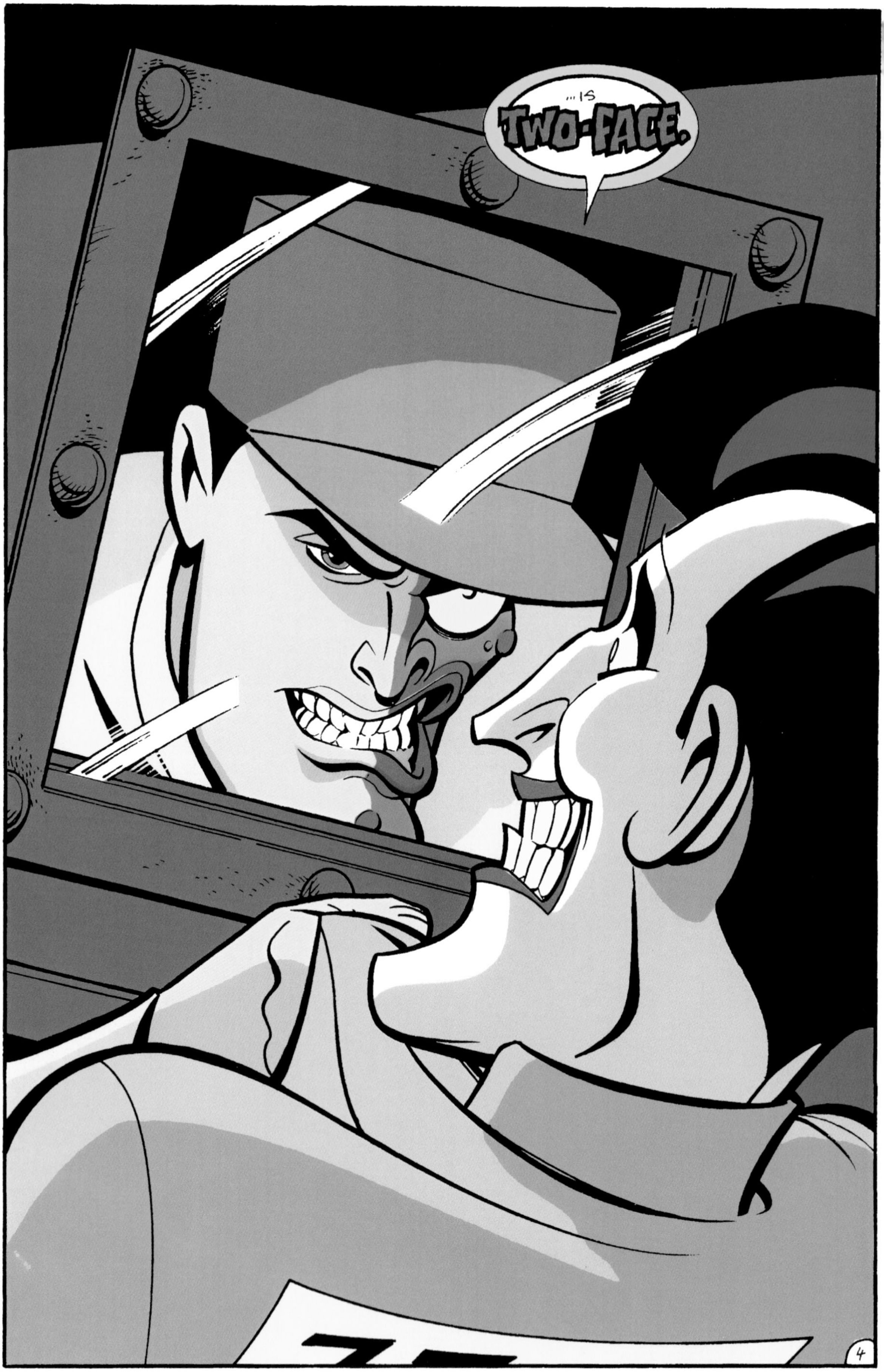
...IS
TWO-FACE.
4

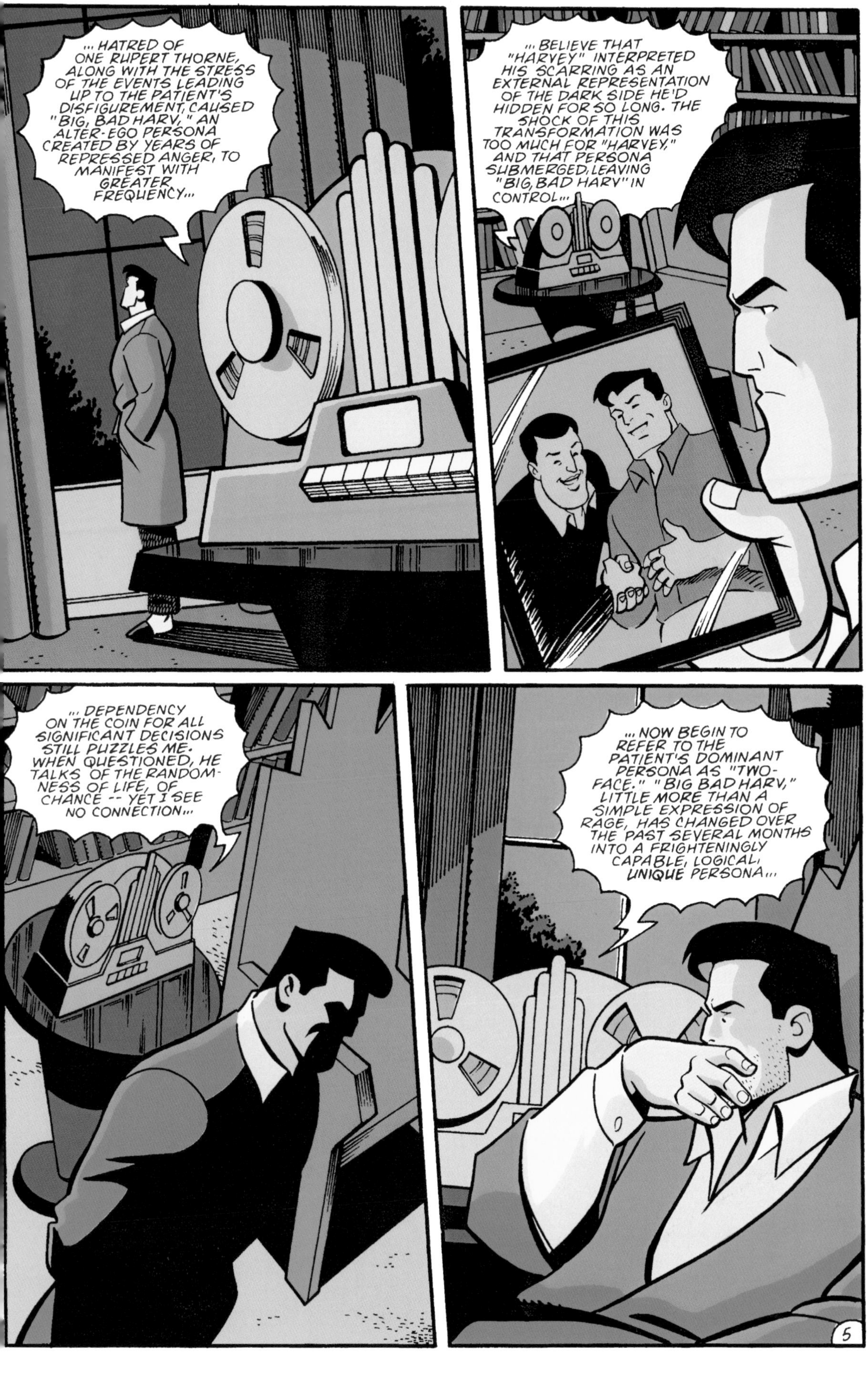
...HATRED OF ONE RUPERT THORNE, ALONG WITH THE STRESS OF THE EVENTS LEADING UP TO THE PATIENT'S DISFIGUREMENT, CAUSED "BIG, BAD HARV," AN ALTER-EGO PERSONA CREATED BY YEARS OF REPRESSED ANGER, TO MANIFEST WITH GREATER FREQUENCY...
...BELIEVE THAT "HARVEY" INTERPRETED HIS SCARRING AS AN EXTERNAL REPRESENTATION OF THE DARK SIDE HE'D HIDDEN FOR SO LONG. THE SHOCK OF THIS TRANSFORMATION WAS TOO MUCH FOR "HARVEY," AND THAT PERSONA SUBMERGED, LEAVING "BIG, BAD HARV" IN CONTROL...
...DEPENDENCY ON THE COIN FOR ALL SIGNIFICANT DECISIONS STILL PUZZLES ME. WHEN QUESTIONED, HE TALKS OF THE RANDOMNESS OF LIFE, OF CHANCE -- YET I SEE NO CONNECTION...
...NOW BEGIN TO REFER TO THE PATIENT'S DOMINANT PERSONA AS "TWO-FACE." "BIG BAD HARV," LITTLE MORE THAN A SIMPLE EXPRESSION OF RAGE, HAS CHANGED OVER THE PAST SEVERAL MONTHS INTO A FRIGHTENINGLY CAPABLE, LOGICAL, UNIQUE PERSONA...
5

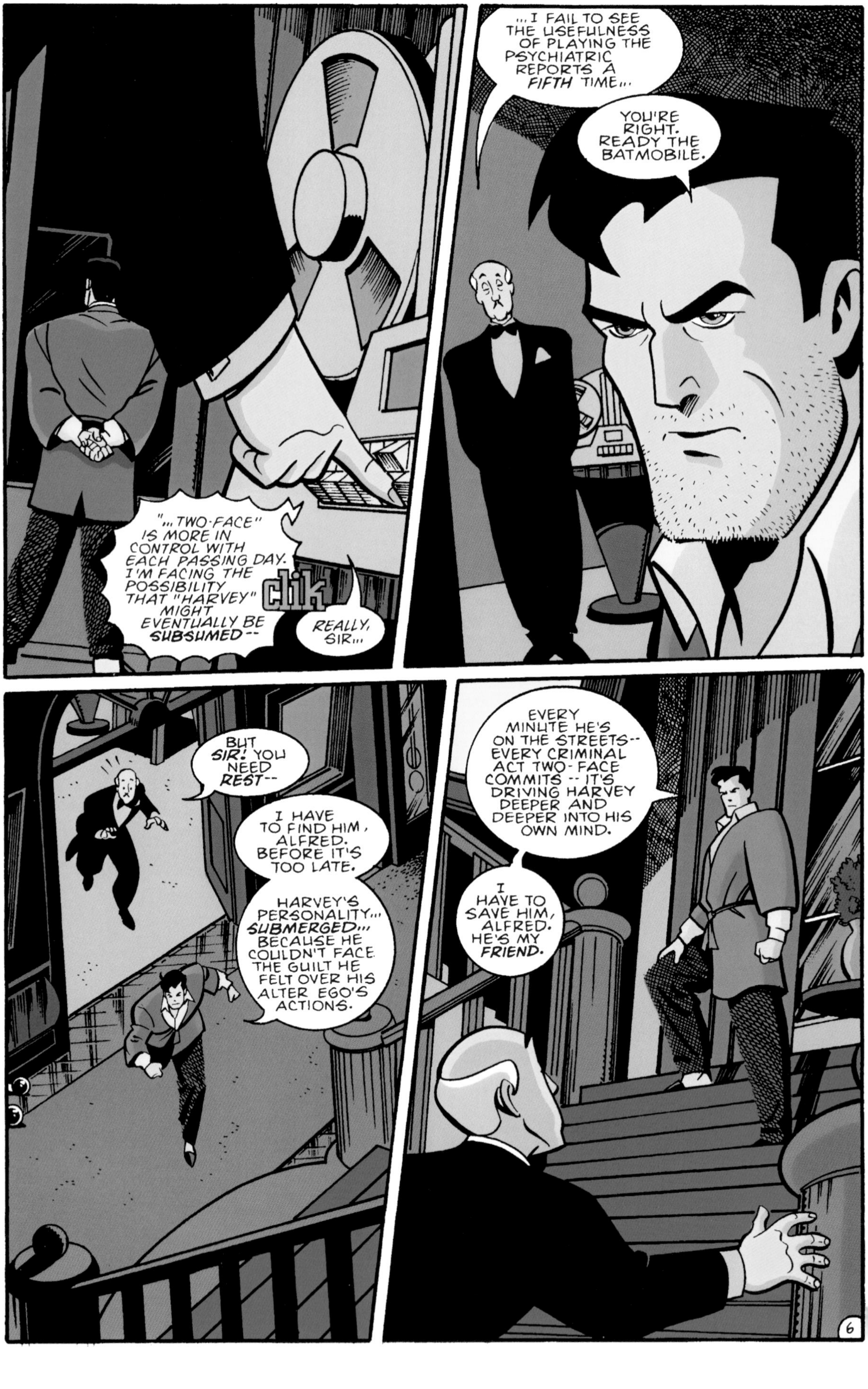
"...TWO-FACE" IS MORE IN CONTROL WITH EACH PASSING DAY. I'M FACING THE POSSIBILITY THAT "HARVEY" MIGHT EVENTUALLY BE SUBSUMED--
CLIK
REALLY, SIR...
...I FAIL TO SEE THE USEFULNESS OF PLAYING THE PSYCHIATRIC REPORTS A FIFTH TIME...
YOU'RE RIGHT. READY THE BATMOBILE.
BUT SIR! YOU NEED REST--
I HAVE TO FIND HIM, ALFRED. BEFORE IT'S TOO LATE.
HARVEY'S PERSONALITY... SUBMERGED... BECAUSE HE COULDN'T FACE THE GUILT HE FELT OVER HIS ALTER EGO'S ACTIONS.
EVERY MINUTE HE'S ON THE STREETS-- EVERY CRIMINAL ACT TWO-FACE COMMITS -- IT'S DRIVING HARVEY DEEPER AND DEEPER INTO HIS OWN MIND.
I HAVE TO SAVE HIM, ALFRED. HE'S MY FRIEND.
6

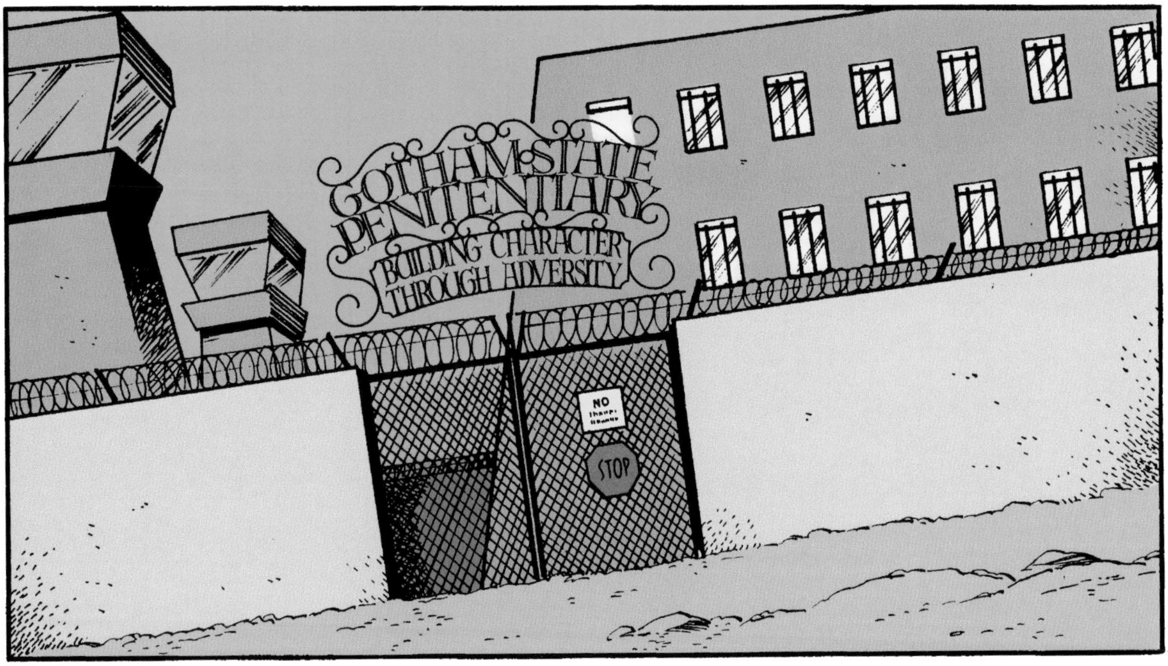
GOTHAM STATE
PENITENTIARY
BUILDING CHARACTER
THROUGH ADVERSITY
NO
STOP

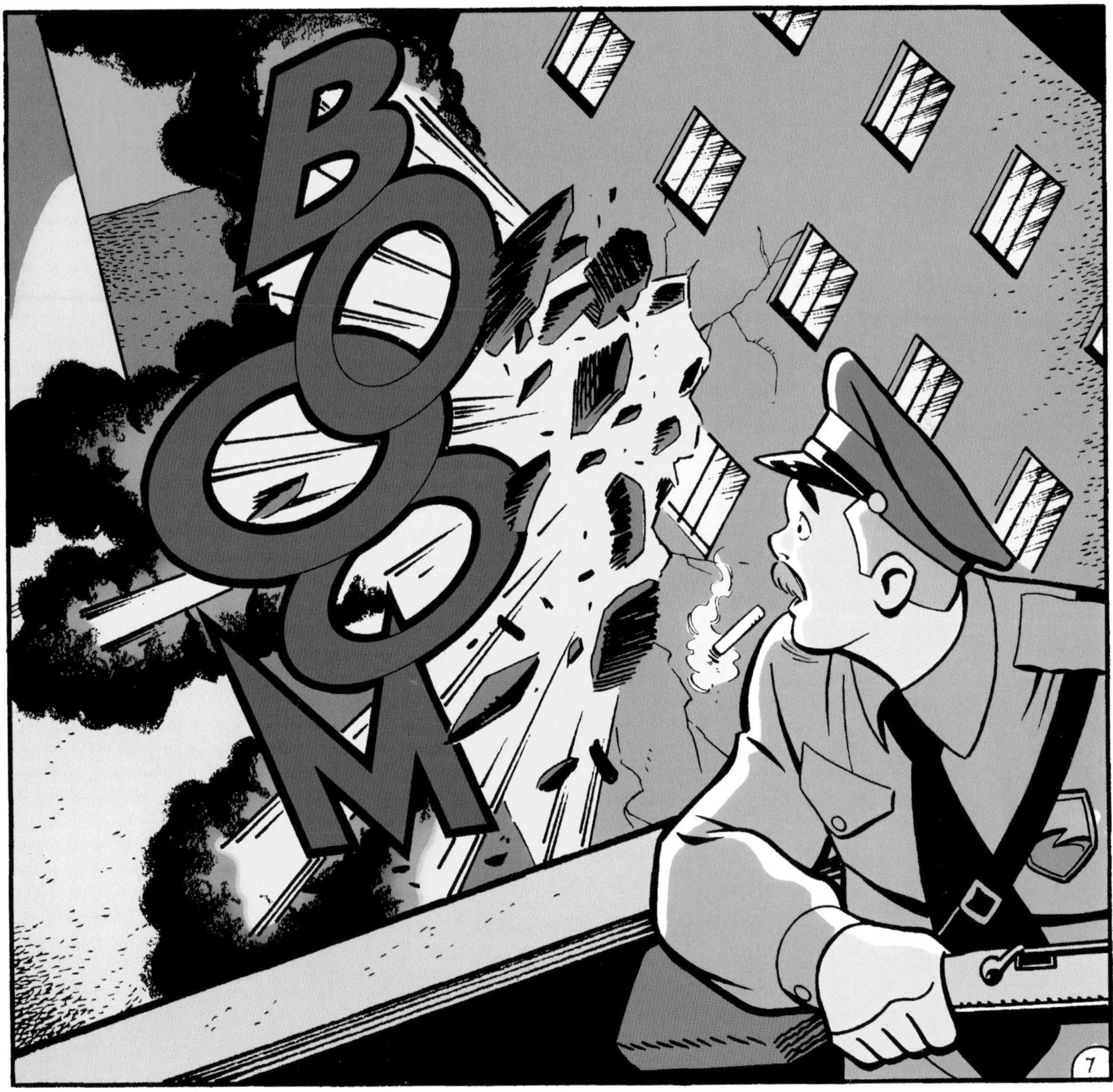
BOOM
7

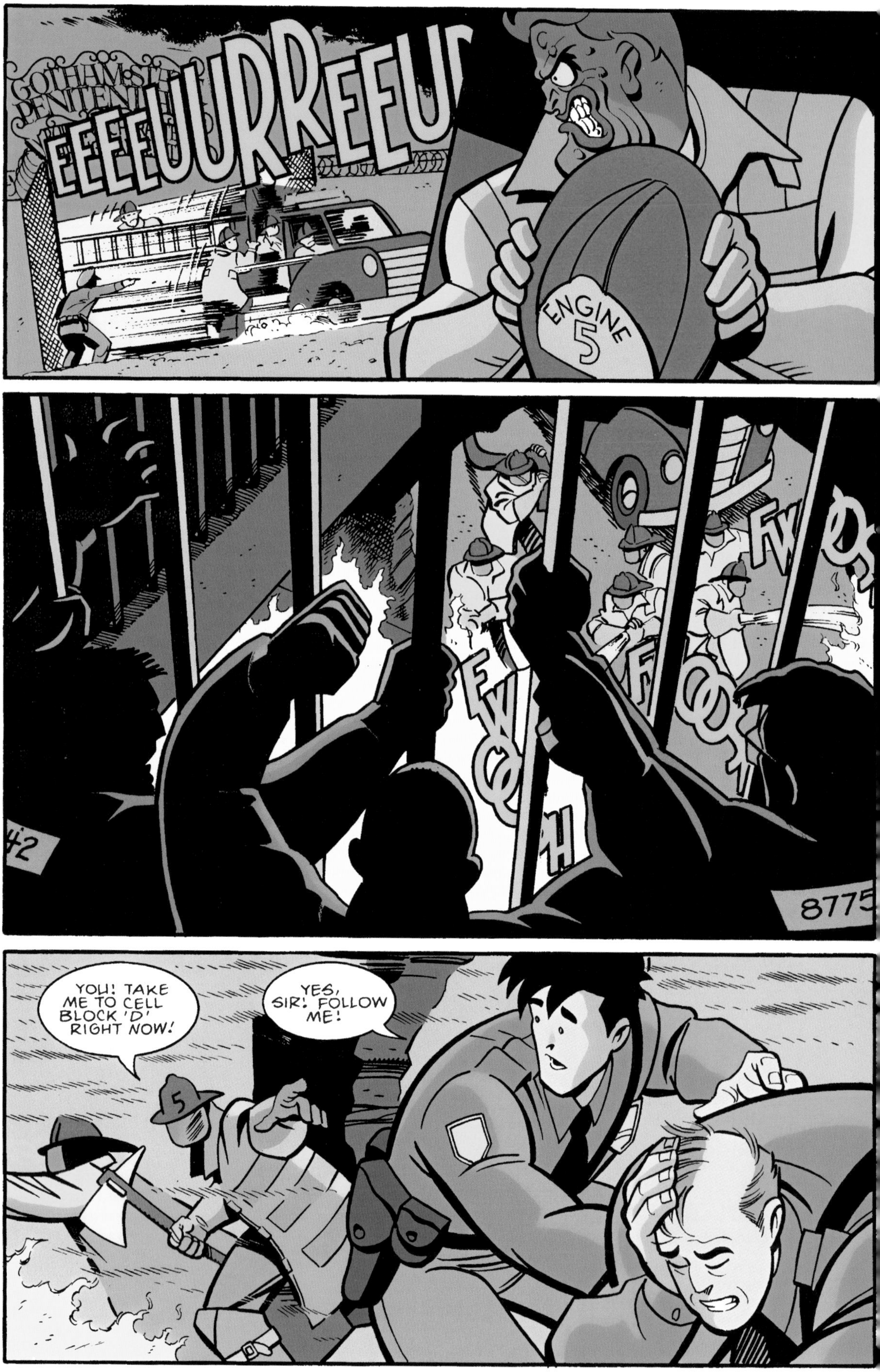
EEEEUURREEU
ENGINE 5
42
8775
YOU! TAKE ME TO CELL BLOCK 'D' RIGHT NOW!
YES, SIR! FOLLOW ME!

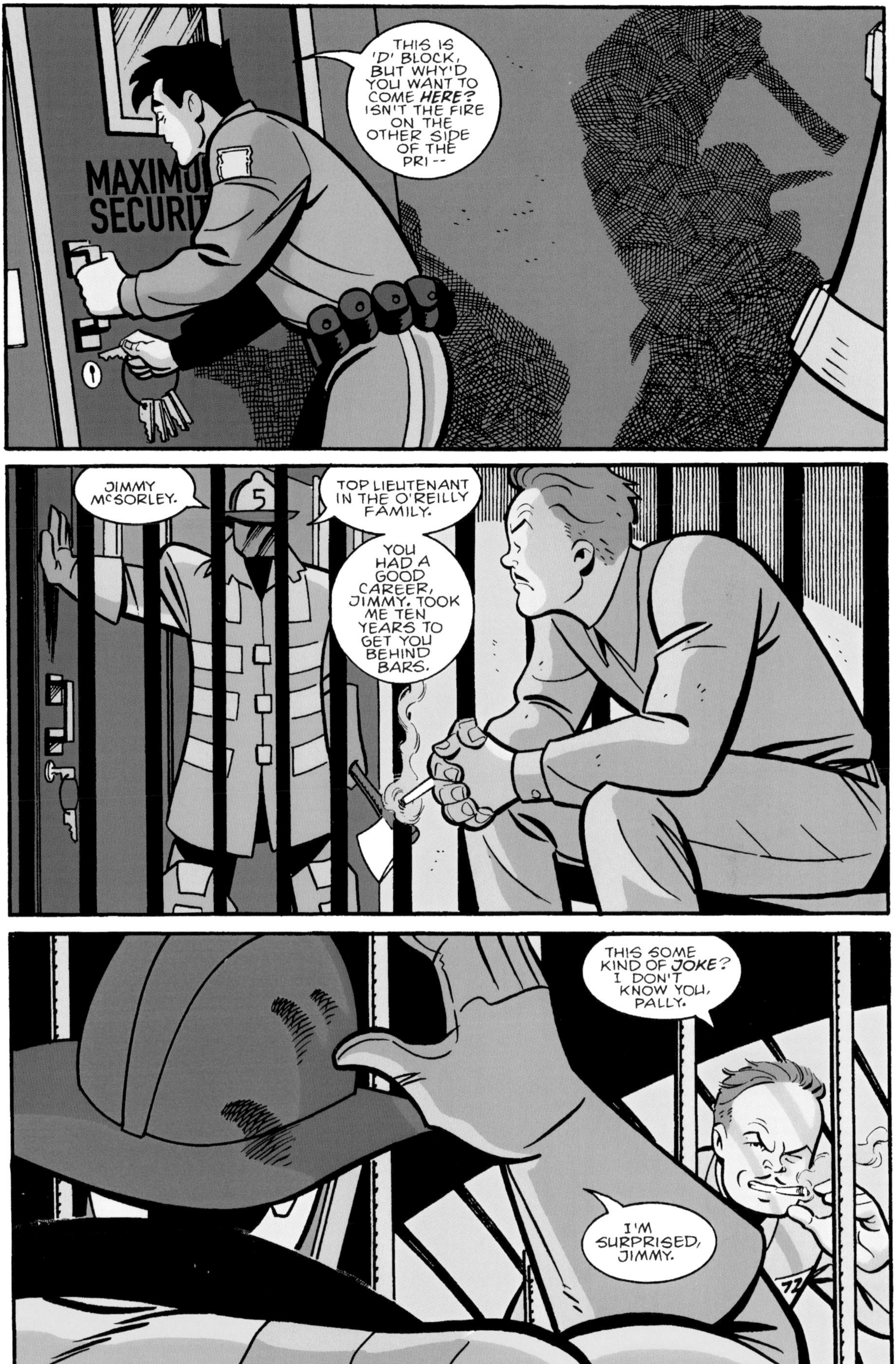
MAXIMUM SECURIT
THIS IS 'D' BLOCK, BUT WHY'D YOU WANT TO COME HERE? ISN'T THE FIRE ON THE OTHER SIDE OF THE PRI --
JIMMY McSORLEY.
TOP LIEUTENANT IN THE O'REILLY FAMILY.
YOU HAD A GOOD CAREER, JIMMY. TOOK ME TEN YEARS TO GET YOU BEHIND BARS.
THIS SOME KIND OF JOKE? I DON'T KNOW YOU, PALLY.
I'M SURPRISED, JIMMY.

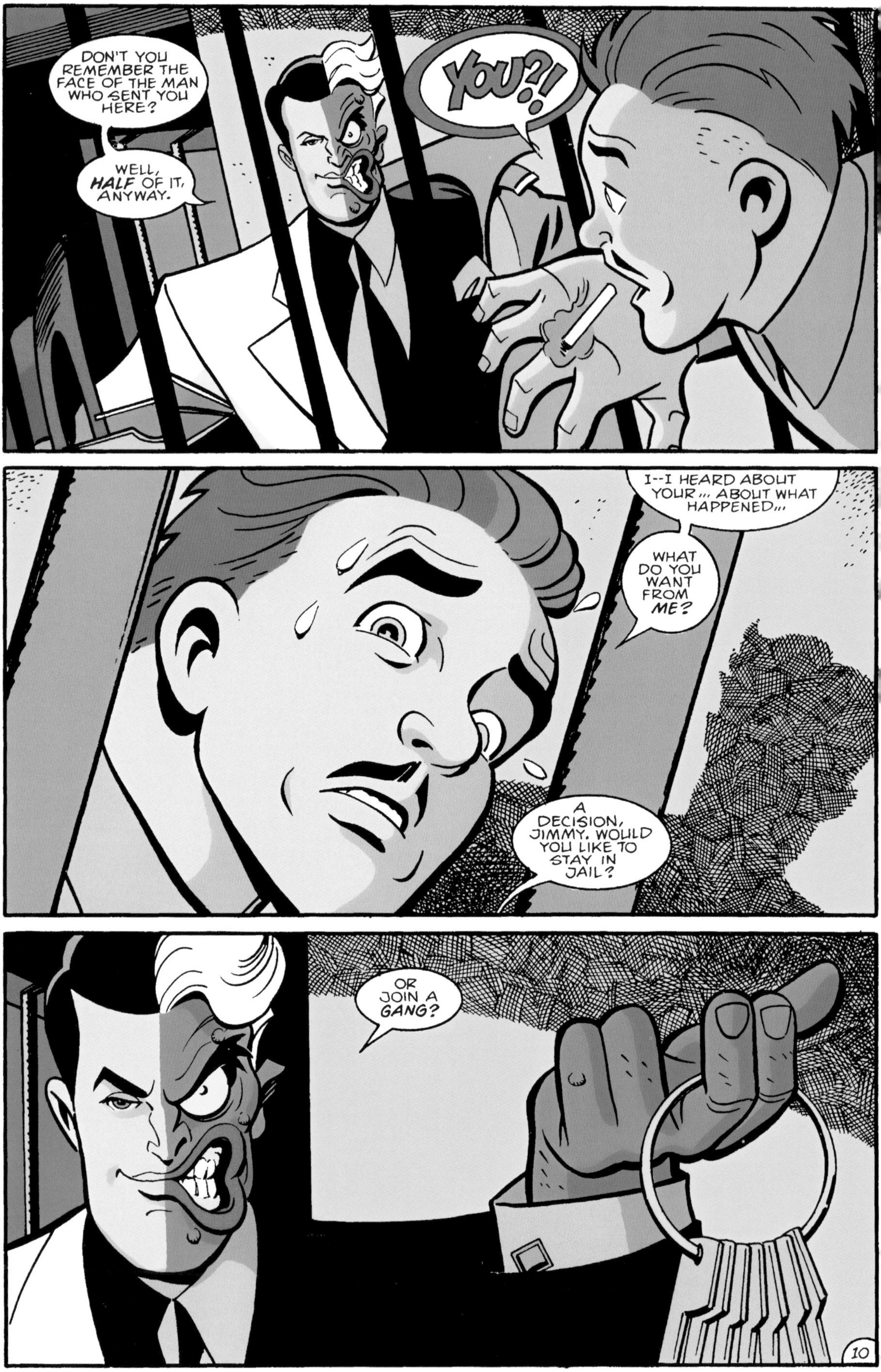

DON'T YOU REMEMBER THE FACE OF THE MAN WHO SENT YOU HERE?
WELL, HALF OF IT, ANYWAY.
YOU?!
I--I HEARD ABOUT YOUR... ABOUT WHAT HAPPENED...
WHAT DO YOU WANT FROM ME?
A DECISION, JIMMY. WOULD YOU LIKE TO STAY IN JAIL?
OR JOIN A GANG?
10

HOW GOES THE SLEEP DEPRIVATION, SIR? SEEING SPOTS YET?

HE'S STRUCK, ALFRED. HE WAS BEHIND THE GOTHAM STATE JAIL-BREAK.

ALL THE ESCAPED CONVICTS WERE SKILLED CAREER CRIMINALS, AND HARVEY PROSECUTED EVERY SINGLE ONE OF THEM.

DALTON KEVIERI

REEVE MICHAELS

RAY DOMSKI

PAUL D. NIEMAN

TIM BRUCE

KIRK BOYDLAND

PAS MA

BERNIE ALLEN

NONE WERE SIMPLE MUSCLE -- EACH POSSESSED A SKILL USEFUL TO A LARGE-SCALE CRIMINAL ORGANIZATION.

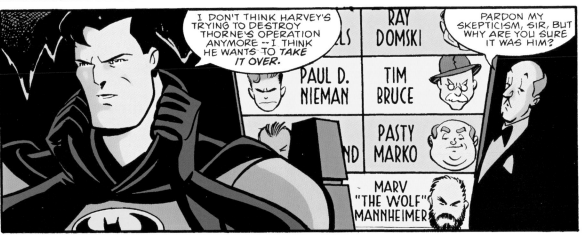

I DON'T THINK HARVEY'S TRYING TO DESTROY THORNE'S OPERATION ANYMORE -- I THINK HE WANTS TO *TAKE IT OVER.*

RAY DOMSKI

LS

PAUL D. NIEMAN

TIM BRUCE

ND

PASTY MARKO

MARV "THE WOLF" MANNHEIMER

PARDON MY SKEPTICISM, SIR, BUT WHY ARE YOU SURE IT WAS HIM?

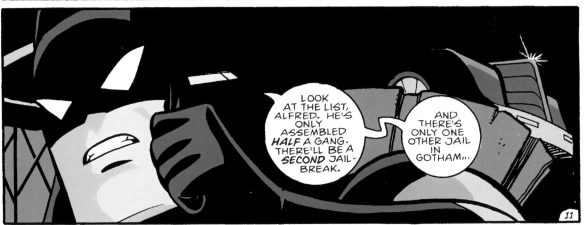

LOOK AT THE LIST, ALFRED. HE'S ONLY ASSEMBLED *HALF* A GANG. THERE'LL BE A *SECOND* JAIL-BREAK.

AND THERE'S ONLY ONE OTHER JAIL IN GOTHAM...

11

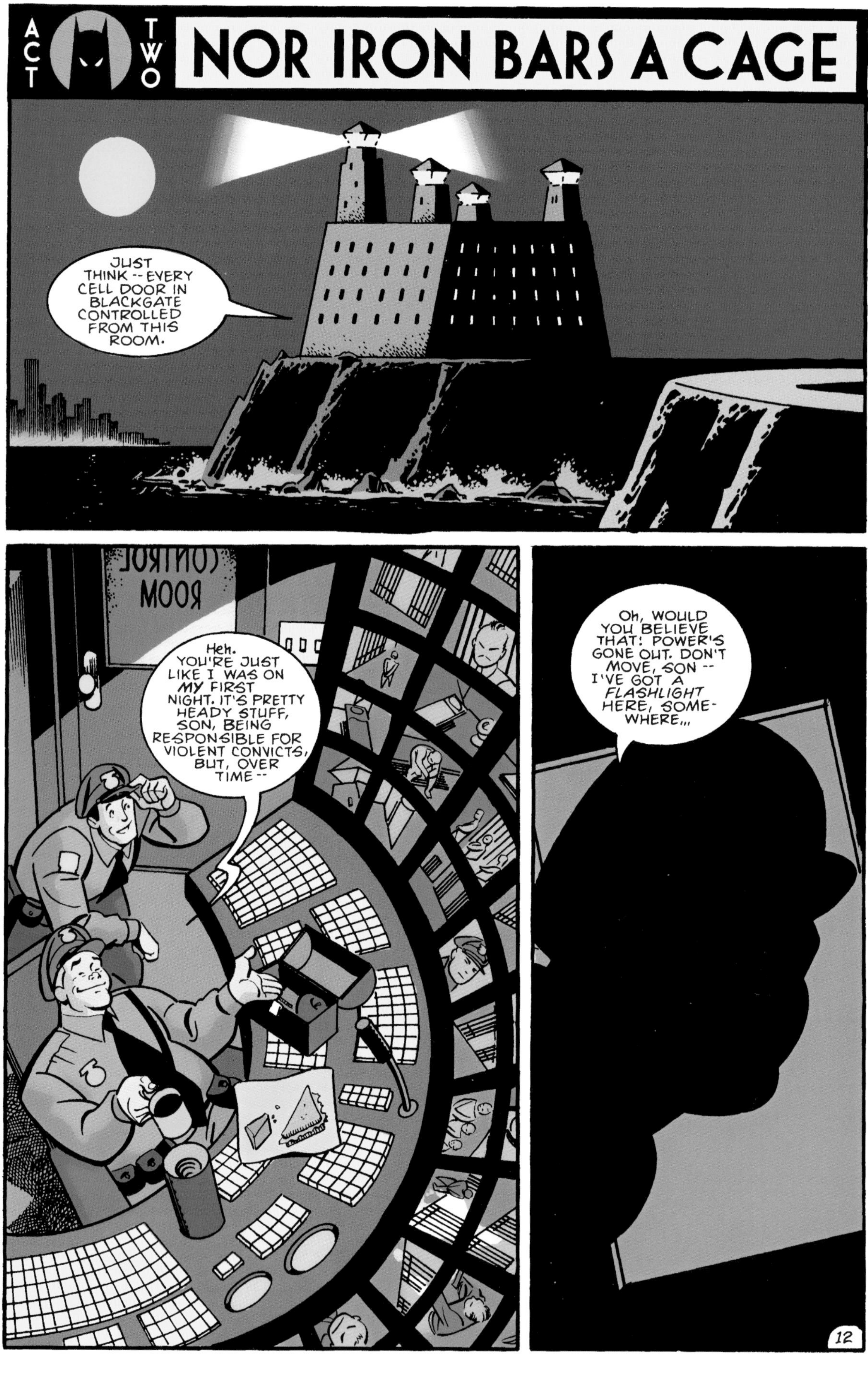
ACT TWO
NOR IRON BARS A CAGE
JUST THINK -- EVERY CELL DOOR IN BLACKGATE CONTROLLED FROM THIS ROOM.
CONTROL ROOM
Heh. YOU'RE JUST LIKE I WAS ON MY FIRST NIGHT. IT'S PRETTY HEADY STUFF, SON, BEING RESPONSIBLE FOR VIOLENT CONVICTS, BUT, OVER TIME --
Oh, WOULD YOU BELIEVE THAT: POWER'S GONE OUT. DON'T MOVE, SON -- I'VE GOT A FLASHLIGHT HERE, SOME-WHERE...
12

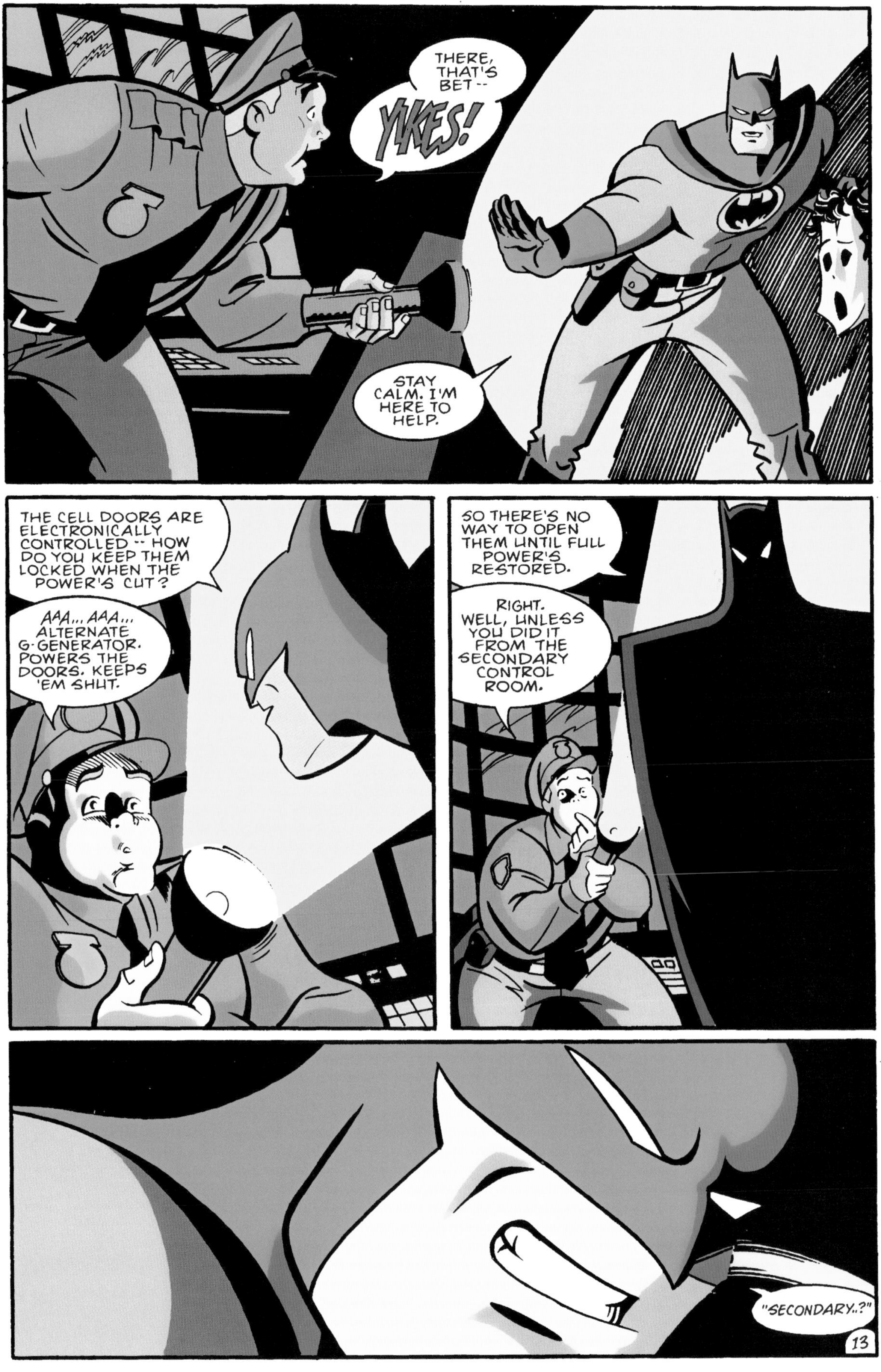
THERE, THAT'S BET--
YIKES!
STAY CALM. I'M HERE TO HELP.
THE CELL DOORS ARE ELECTRONICALLY CONTROLLED -- HOW DO YOU KEEP THEM LOCKED WHEN THE POWER'S CUT?
AAA... AAA... ALTERNATE G-GENERATOR. POWERS THE DOORS. KEEPS 'EM SHUT.
SO THERE'S NO WAY TO OPEN THEM UNTIL FULL POWER'S RESTORED.
RIGHT. WELL, UNLESS YOU DID IT FROM THE SECONDARY CONTROL ROOM.
"SECONDARY..?"
13

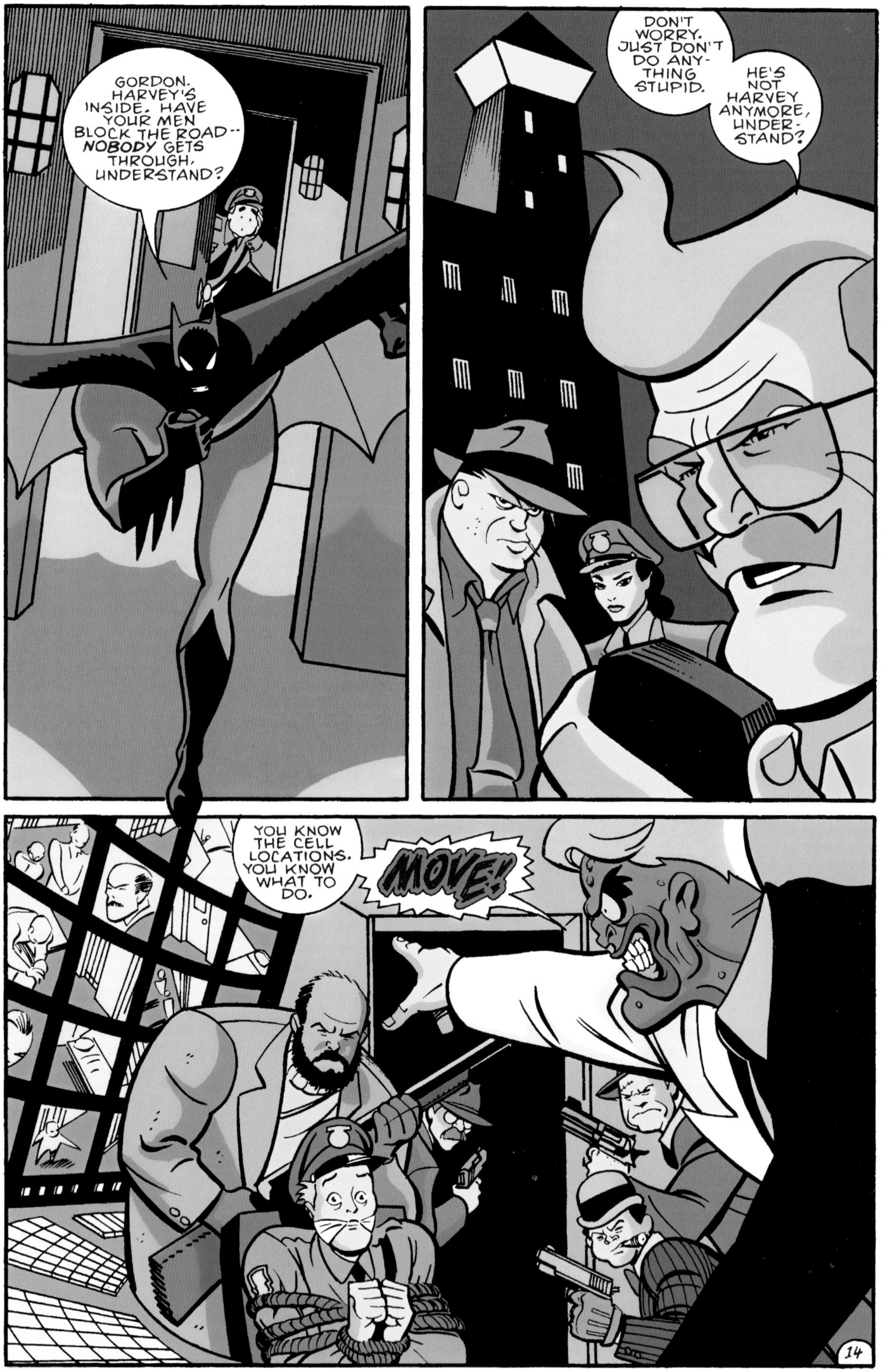
GORDON. HARVEY'S INSIDE. HAVE YOUR MEN BLOCK THE ROAD-- NOBODY GETS THROUGH, UNDERSTAND?
DON'T WORRY. JUST DON'T DO ANYTHING STUPID.
HE'S NOT HARVEY ANYMORE, UNDERSTAND?
YOU KNOW THE CELL LOCATIONS. YOU KNOW WHAT TO DO.
MOVE!
14

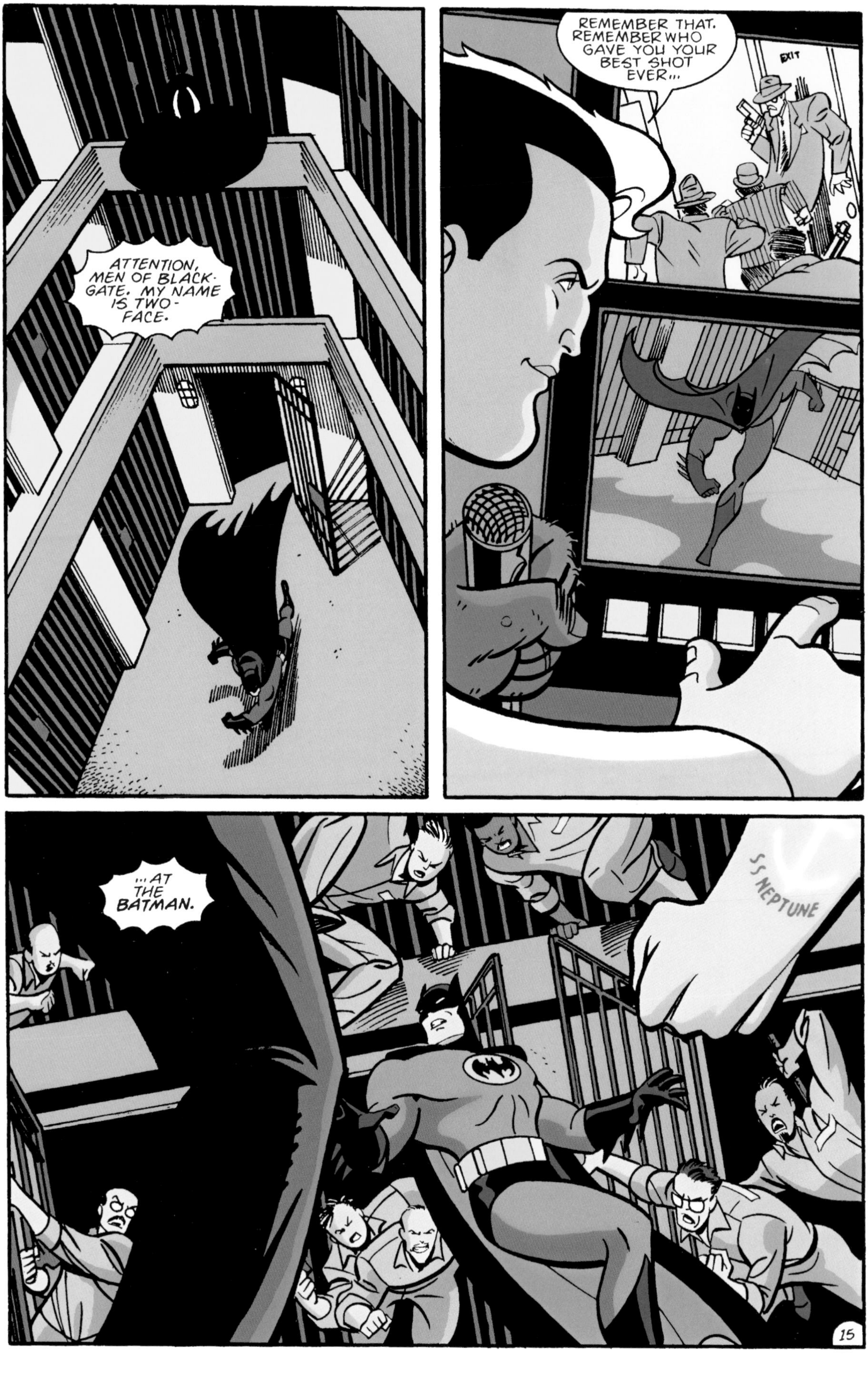

ATTENTION, MEN OF BLACKGATE. MY NAME IS TWO-FACE.
REMEMBER THAT. REMEMBER WHO GAVE YOU YOUR BEST SHOT EVER...
EXIT
...AT THE BATMAN.
SS NEPTUNE
15

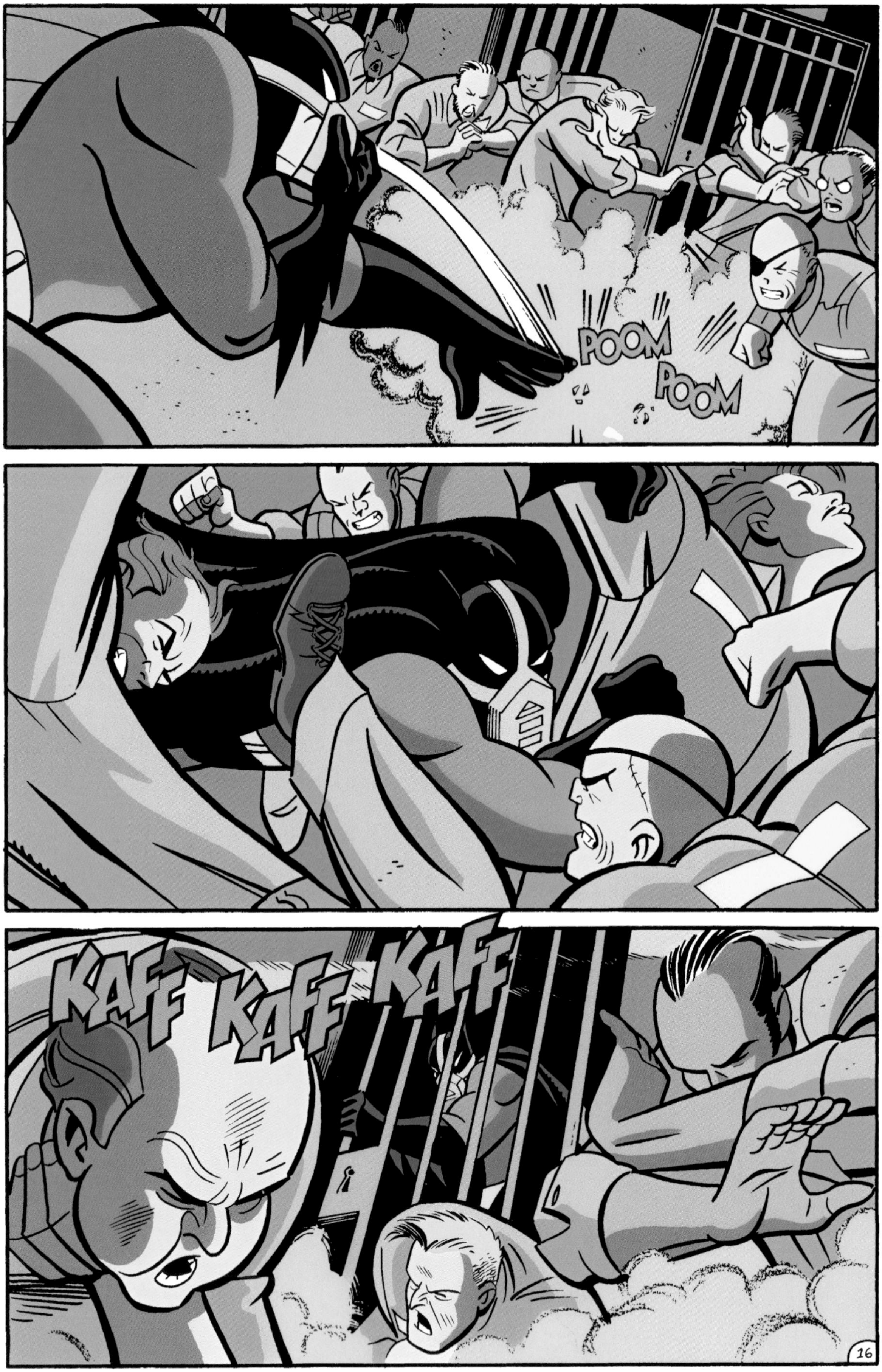
POOM
POOM
KAFF KAFF KAFF
16

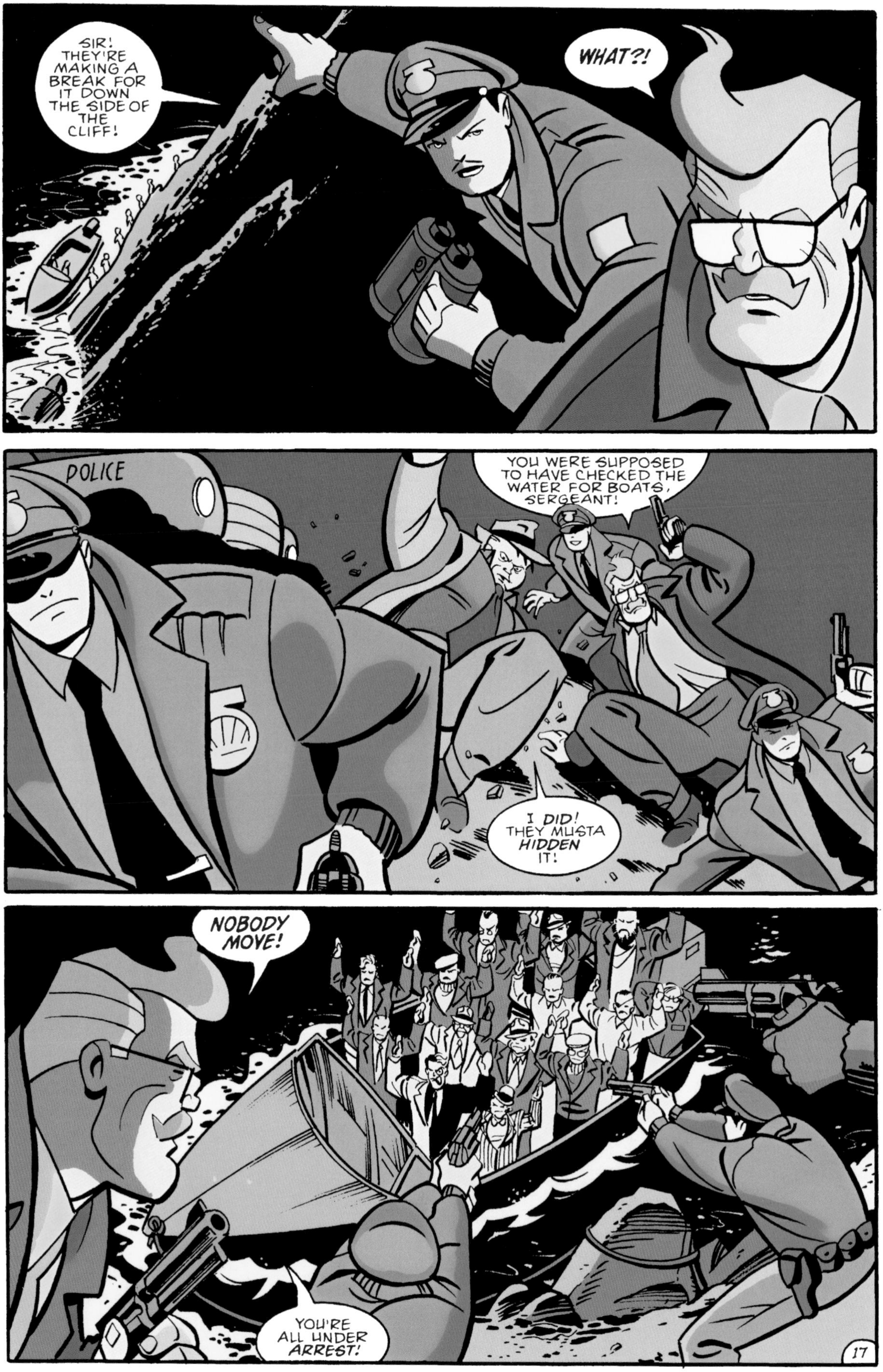
SIR! THEY'RE MAKING A BREAK FOR IT DOWN THE SIDE OF THE CLIFF!
WHAT?!
POLICE
YOU WERE SUPPOSED TO HAVE CHECKED THE WATER FOR BOATS, SERGEANT!
I DID! THEY MUSTA HIDDEN IT!
NOBODY MOVE!
YOU'RE ALL UNDER ARREST!
17

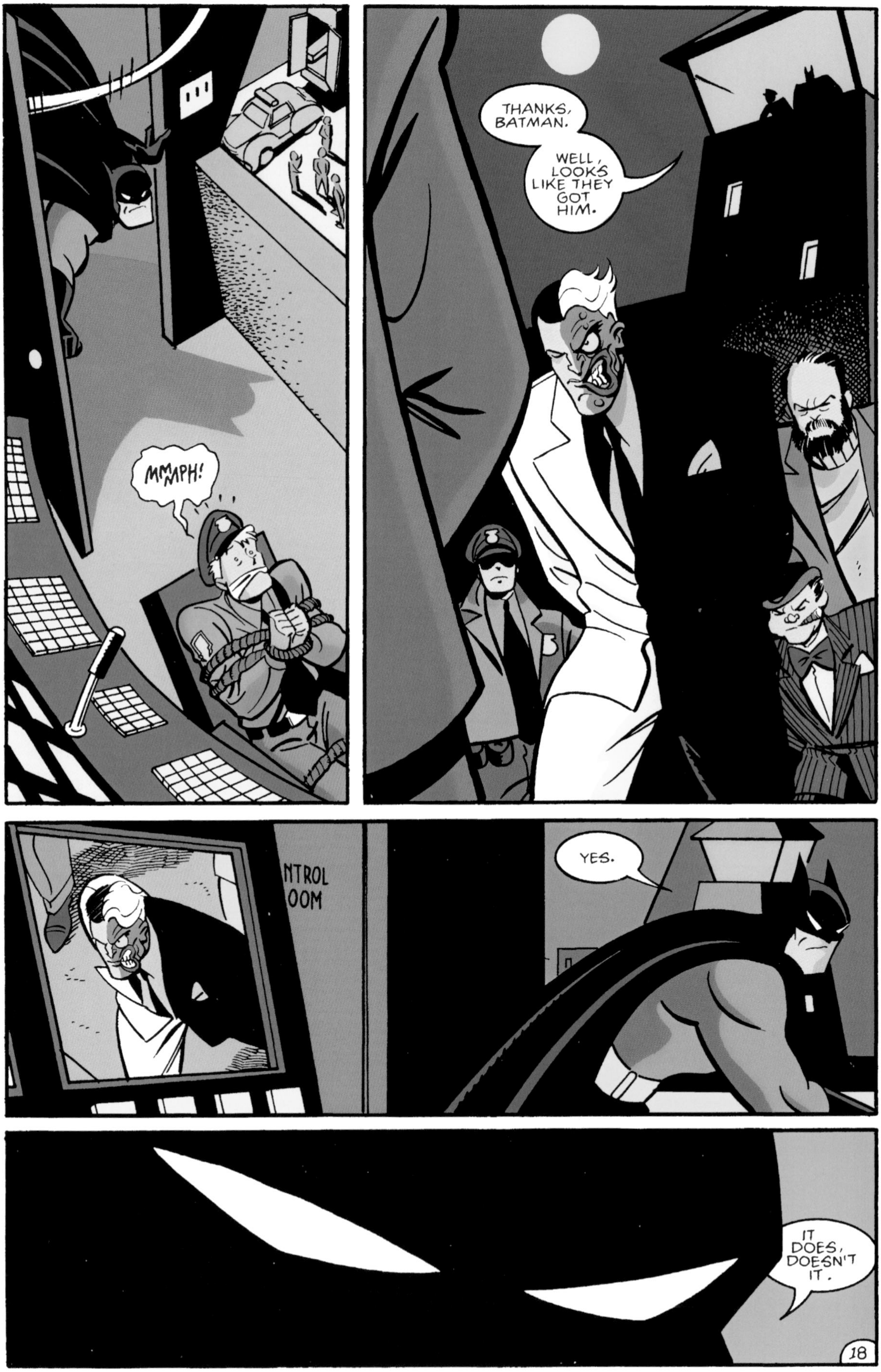
MMMPH!
THANKS, BATMAN.
WELL, LOOKS LIKE THEY GOT HIM.
NTROL
OOM
YES.
IT DOES, DOESN'T IT.
18

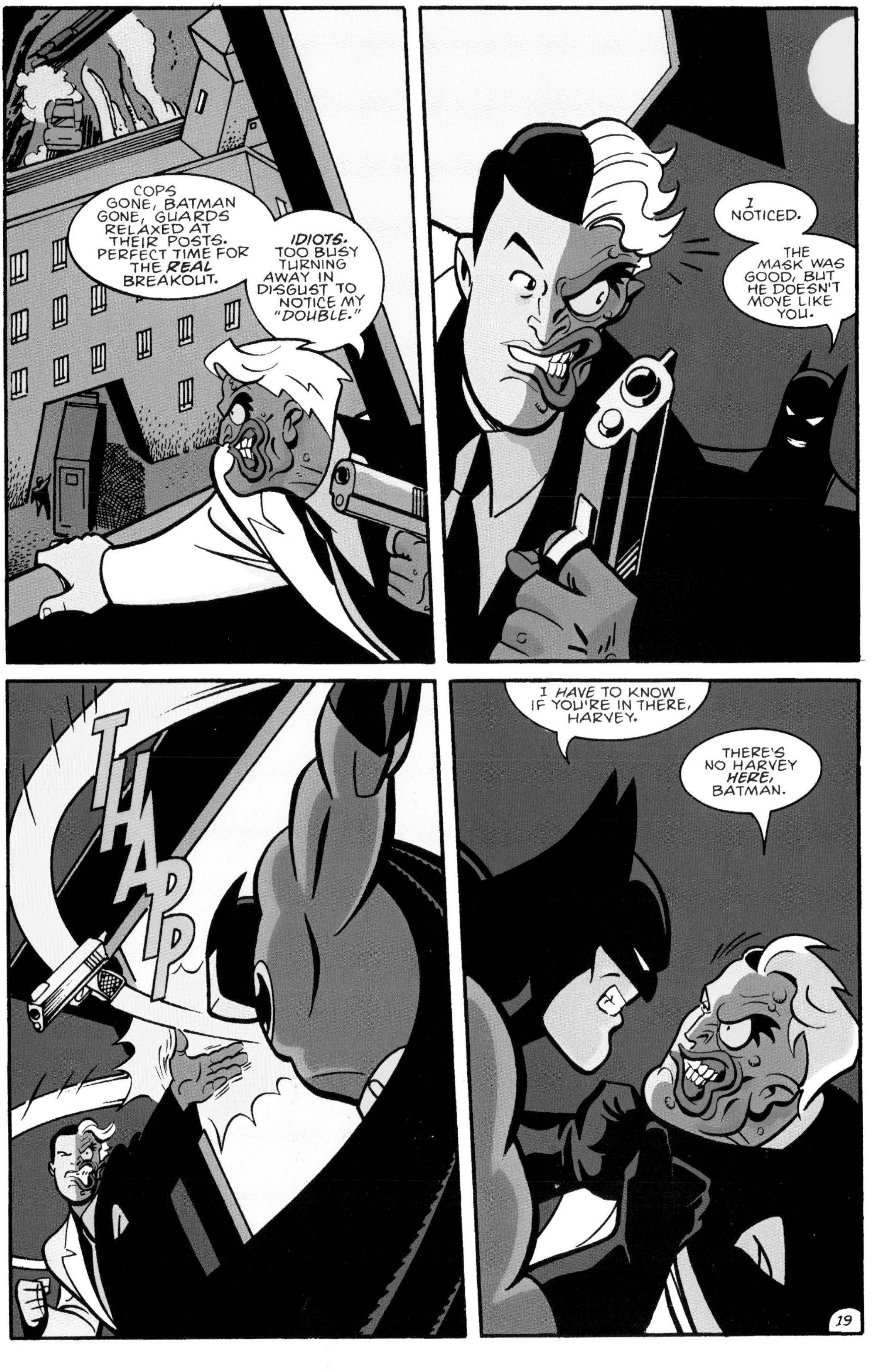

COPS GONE, BATMAN GONE, GUARDS RELAXED AT THEIR POSTS. PERFECT TIME FOR THE *REAL* BREAKOUT.
IDIOTS. TOO BUSY TURNING AWAY IN DISGUST TO NOTICE MY "*DOUBLE.*"
I NOTICED.
THE MASK WAS GOOD, BUT HE DOESN'T MOVE LIKE YOU.
THAPP
I *HAVE* TO KNOW IF YOU'RE IN THERE, HARVEY.
THERE'S NO HARVEY *HERE,* BATMAN.
19

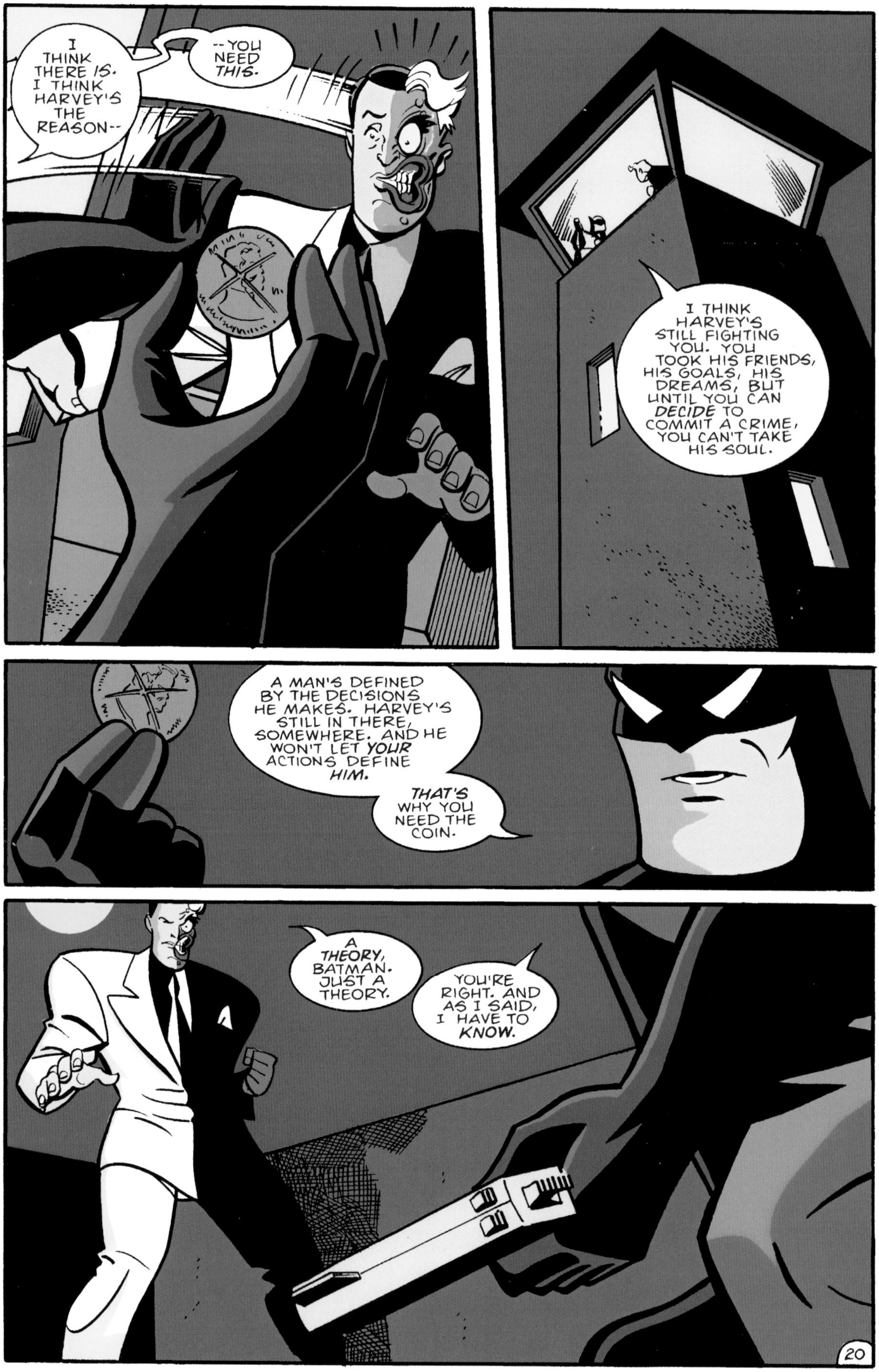
I THINK THERE IS. I THINK HARVEY'S THE REASON--
--YOU NEED THIS.
I THINK HARVEY'S STILL FIGHTING YOU. YOU TOOK HIS FRIENDS, HIS GOALS, HIS DREAMS, BUT UNTIL YOU CAN DECIDE TO COMMIT A CRIME, YOU CAN'T TAKE HIS SOUL.
A MAN'S DEFINED BY THE DECISIONS HE MAKES. HARVEY'S STILL IN THERE, SOMEWHERE. AND HE WON'T LET YOUR ACTIONS DEFINE HIM.
THAT'S WHY YOU NEED THE COIN.
A THEORY, BATMAN. JUST A THEORY.
YOU'RE RIGHT. AND AS I SAID, I HAVE TO KNOW.
20

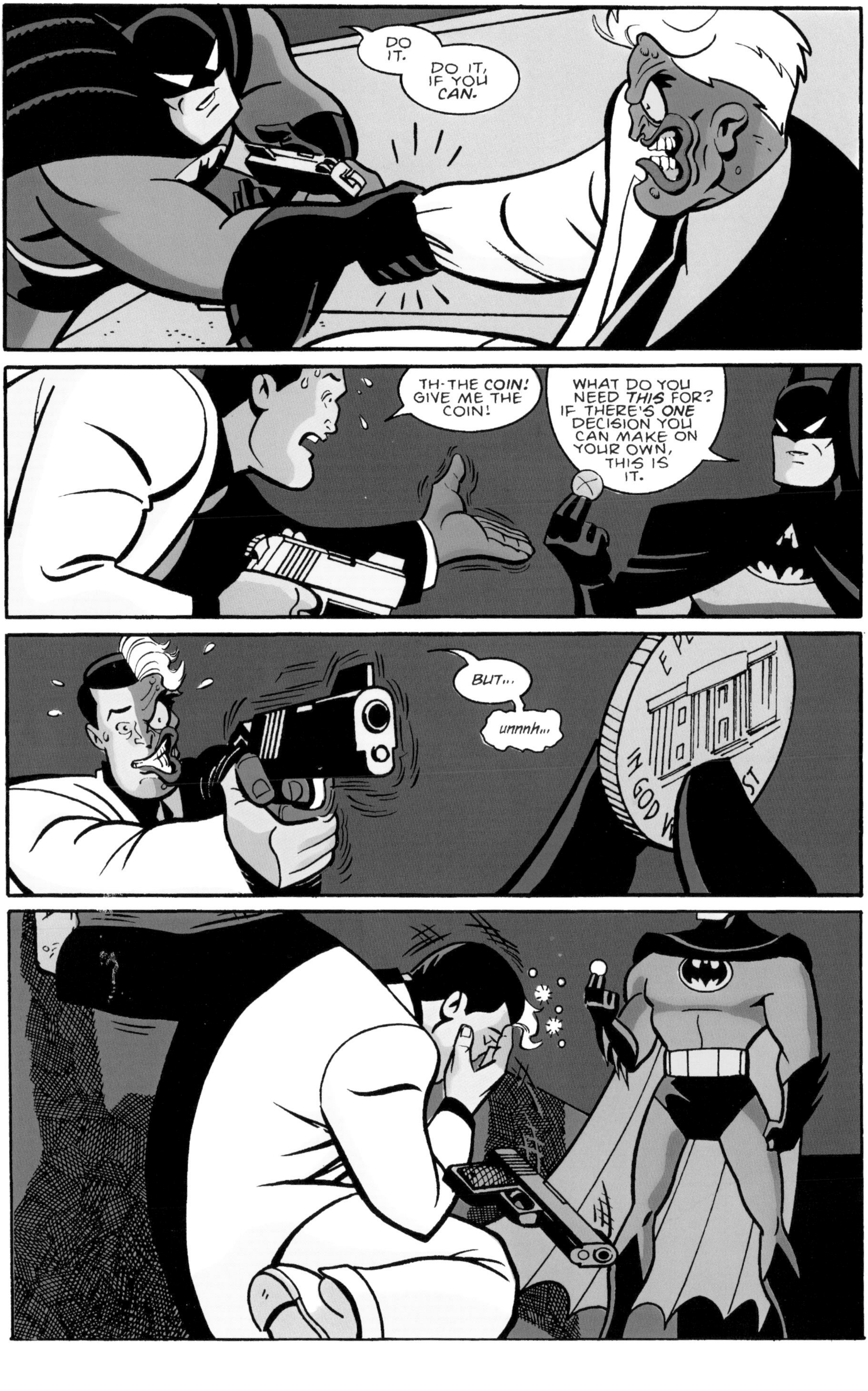
DO IT.
DO IT, IF YOU CAN.
TH-THE COIN! GIVE ME THE COIN!
WHAT DO YOU NEED THIS FOR? IF THERE'S ONE DECISION YOU CAN MAKE ON YOUR OWN, THIS IS IT.
BUT...
unnnh...

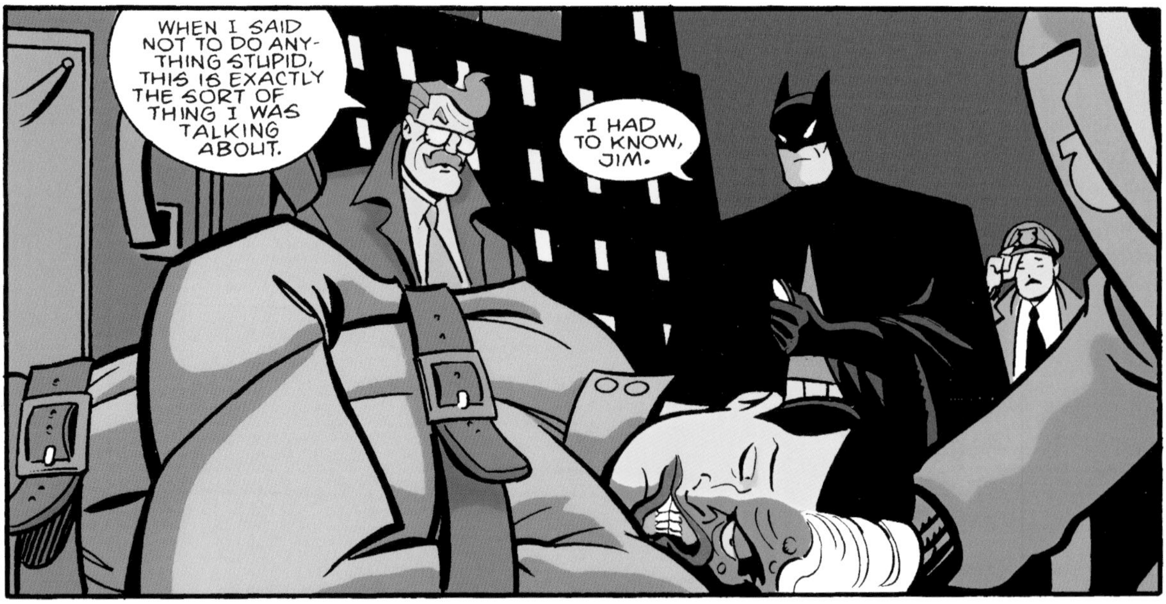
WHEN I SAID NOT TO DO ANY-THING STUPID, THIS IS EXACTLY THE SORT OF THING I WAS TALKING ABOUT.
I HAD TO KNOW, JIM.

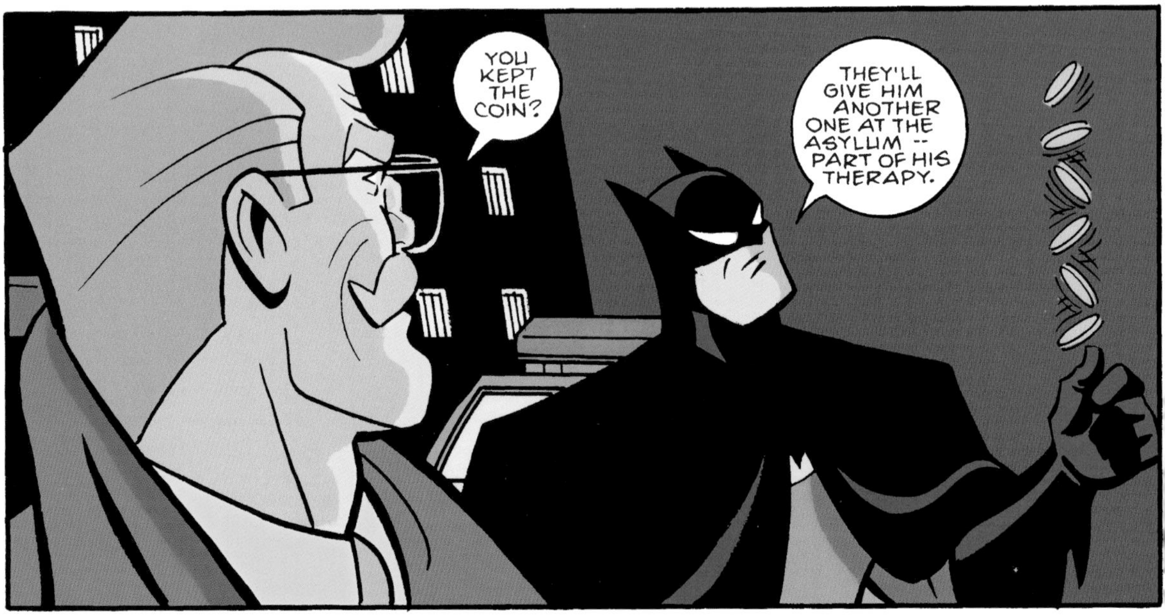
YOU KEPT THE COIN?
THEY'LL GIVE HIM ANOTHER ONE AT THE ASYLUM -- PART OF HIS THERAPY.

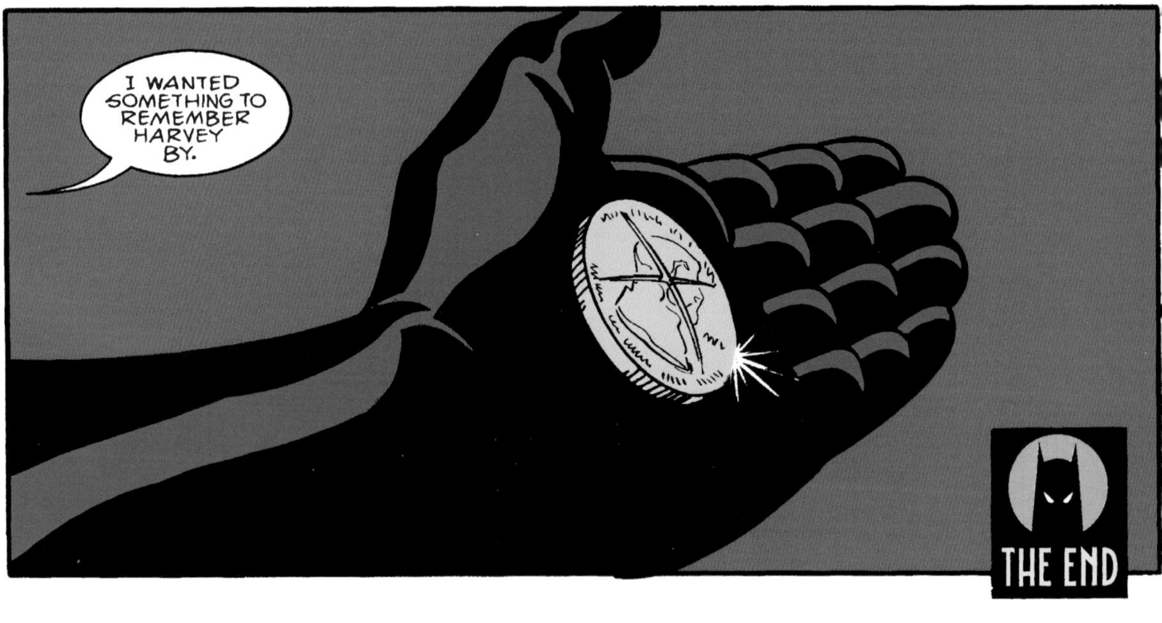
I WANTED SOMETHING TO REMEMBER HARVEY BY.
THE END

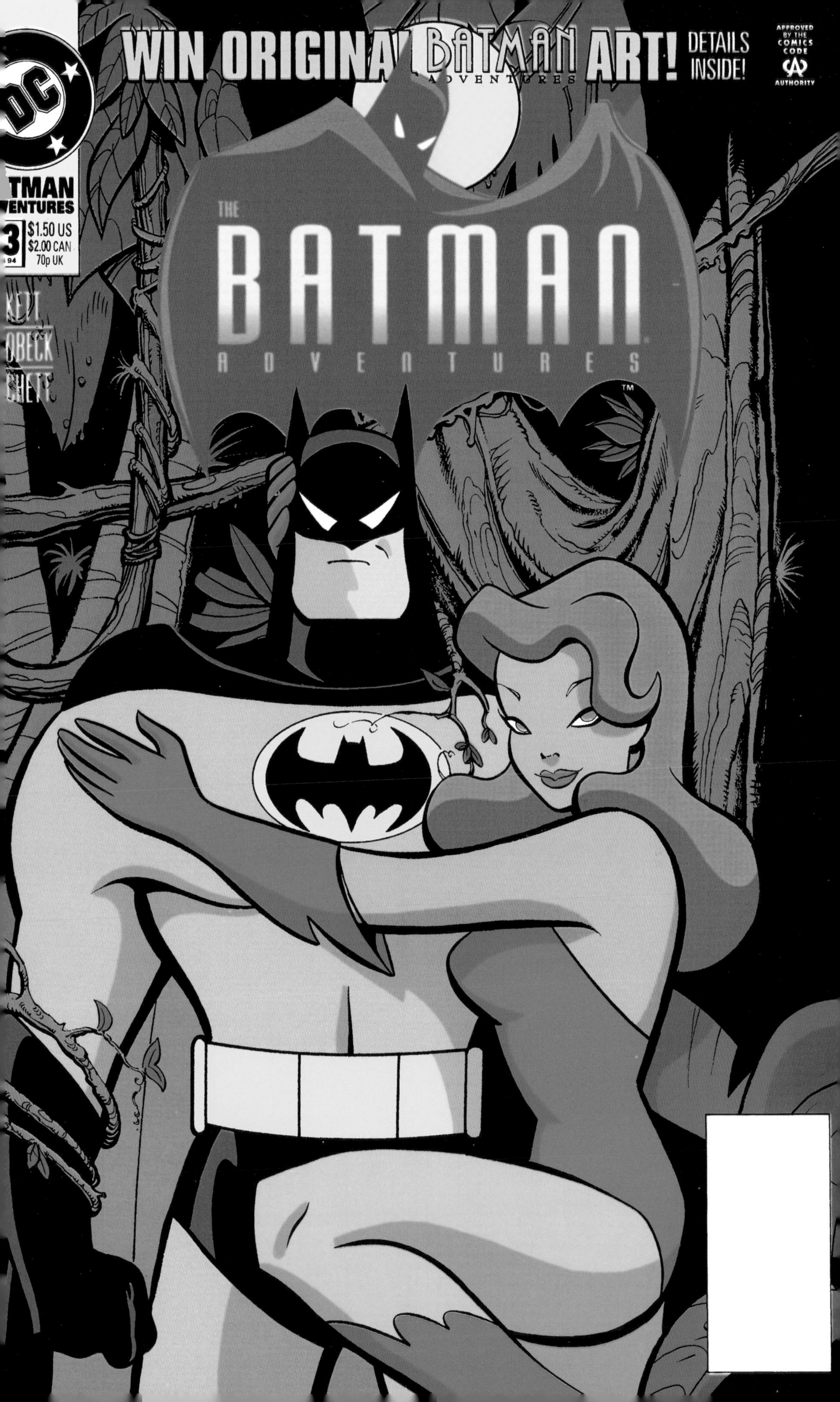

WIN ORIGINAL BATMAN ADVENTURES ART!
DETAILS INSIDE!
APPROVED BY THE COMICS CODE AUTHORITY
DC
TMAN
VENTURES
3
$1.50 US
$2.00 CAN
70p UK
THE
BATMAN
ADVENTURES

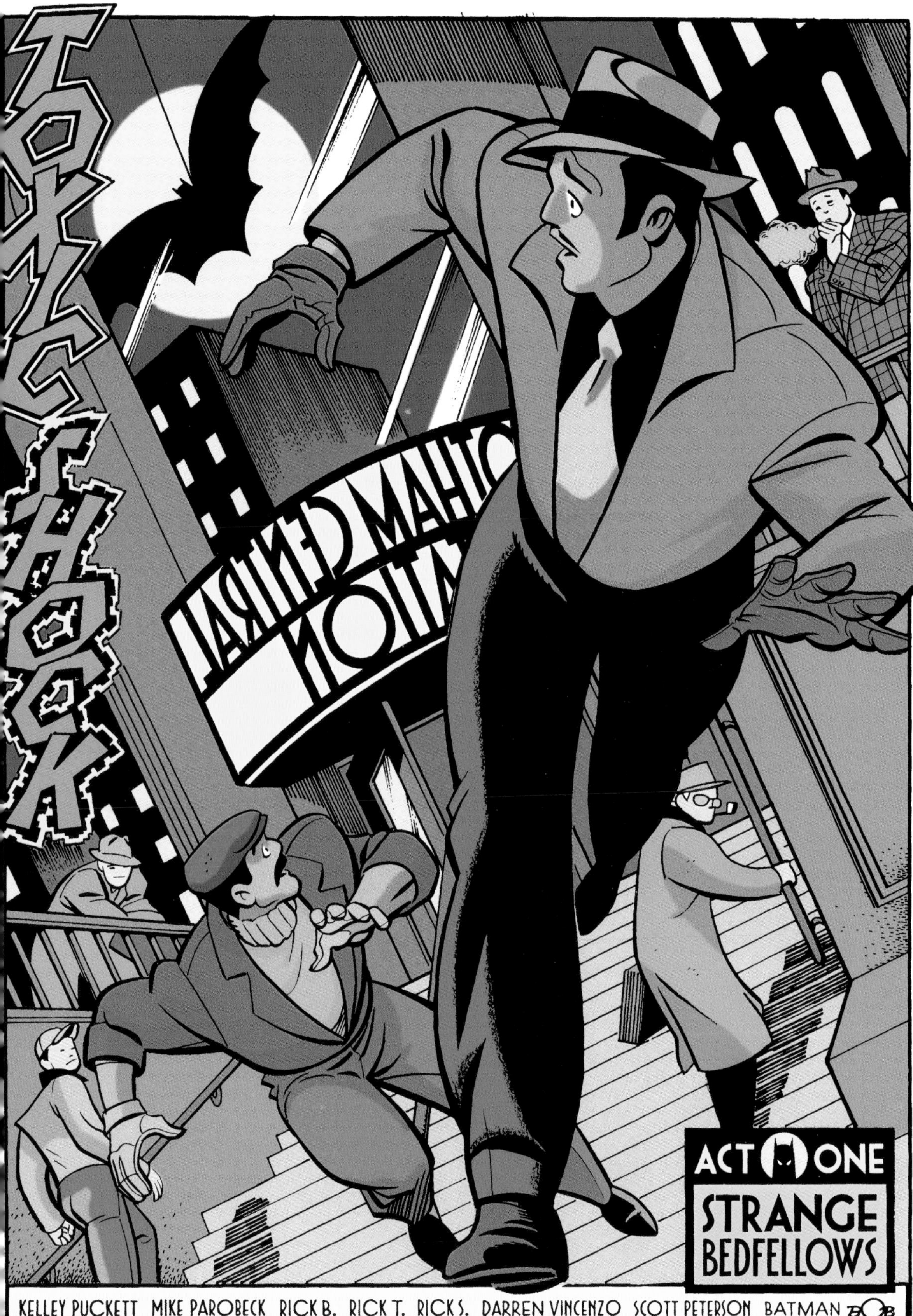
TOXIC SHOCK
ACT ONE
STRANGE BEDFELLOWS

KELLEY PUCKETT WRITES · MIKE PAROBECK PENCILS · RICK B. INKS · RICK T. COLORS · RICK S. LETTERS · DARREN VINCENZO ASSISTS · SCOTT PETERSON EDITS · BATMAN CREATED BY BOB KANE

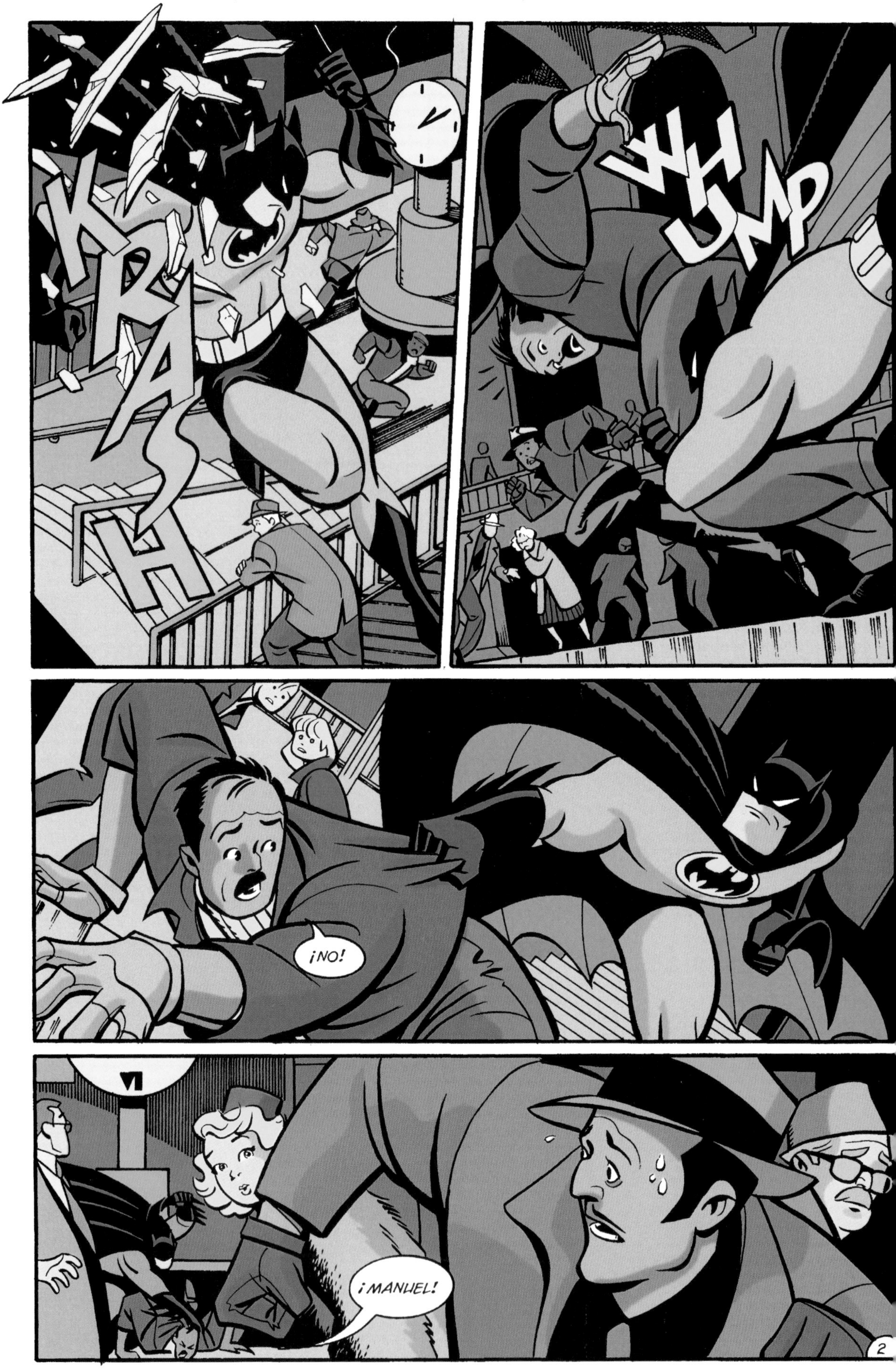
KRASH
WHUMP
¡NO!
¡MANUEL!
2

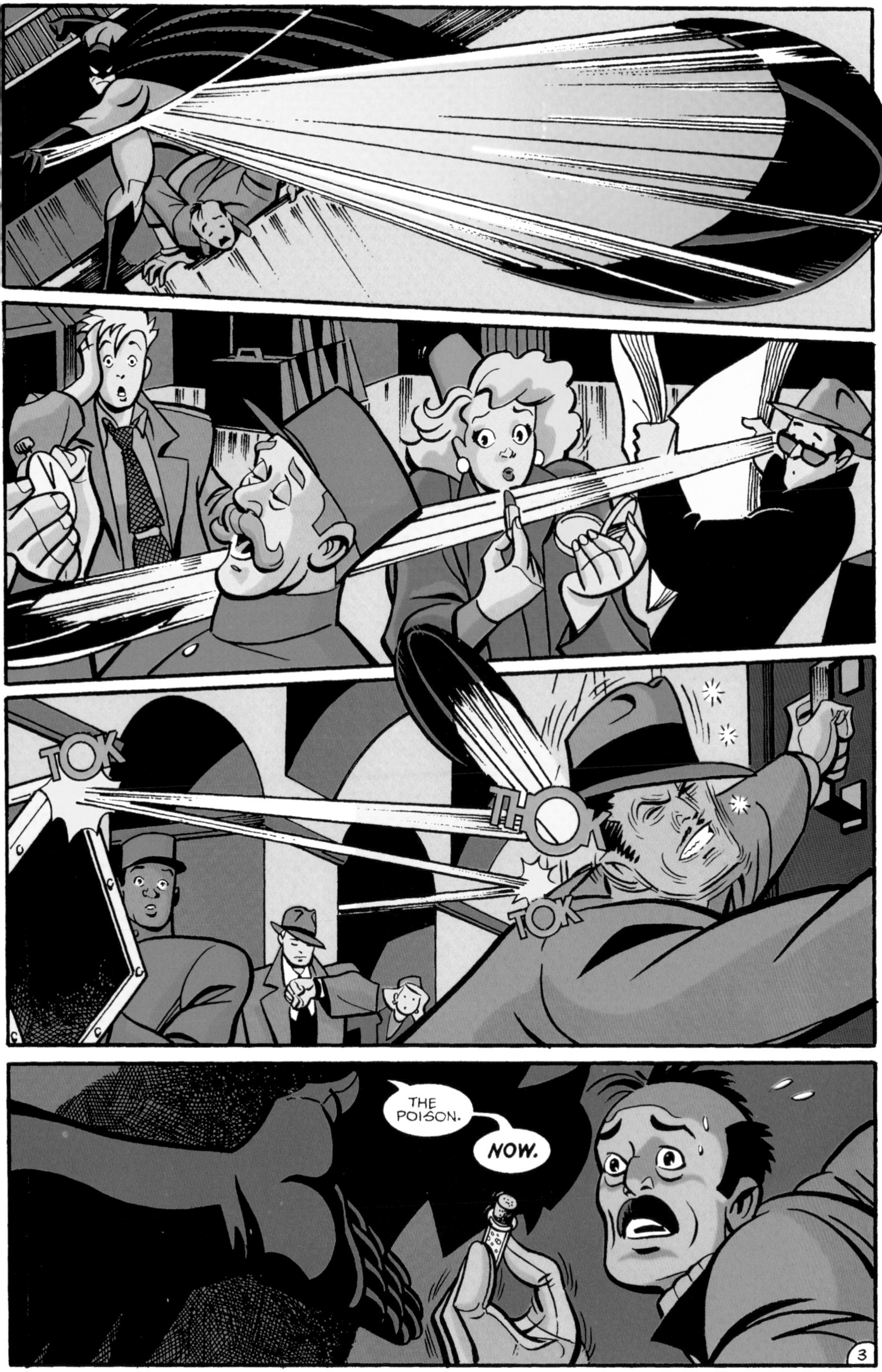
TOK
THOK
TOK
THE POISON.
NOW.
3

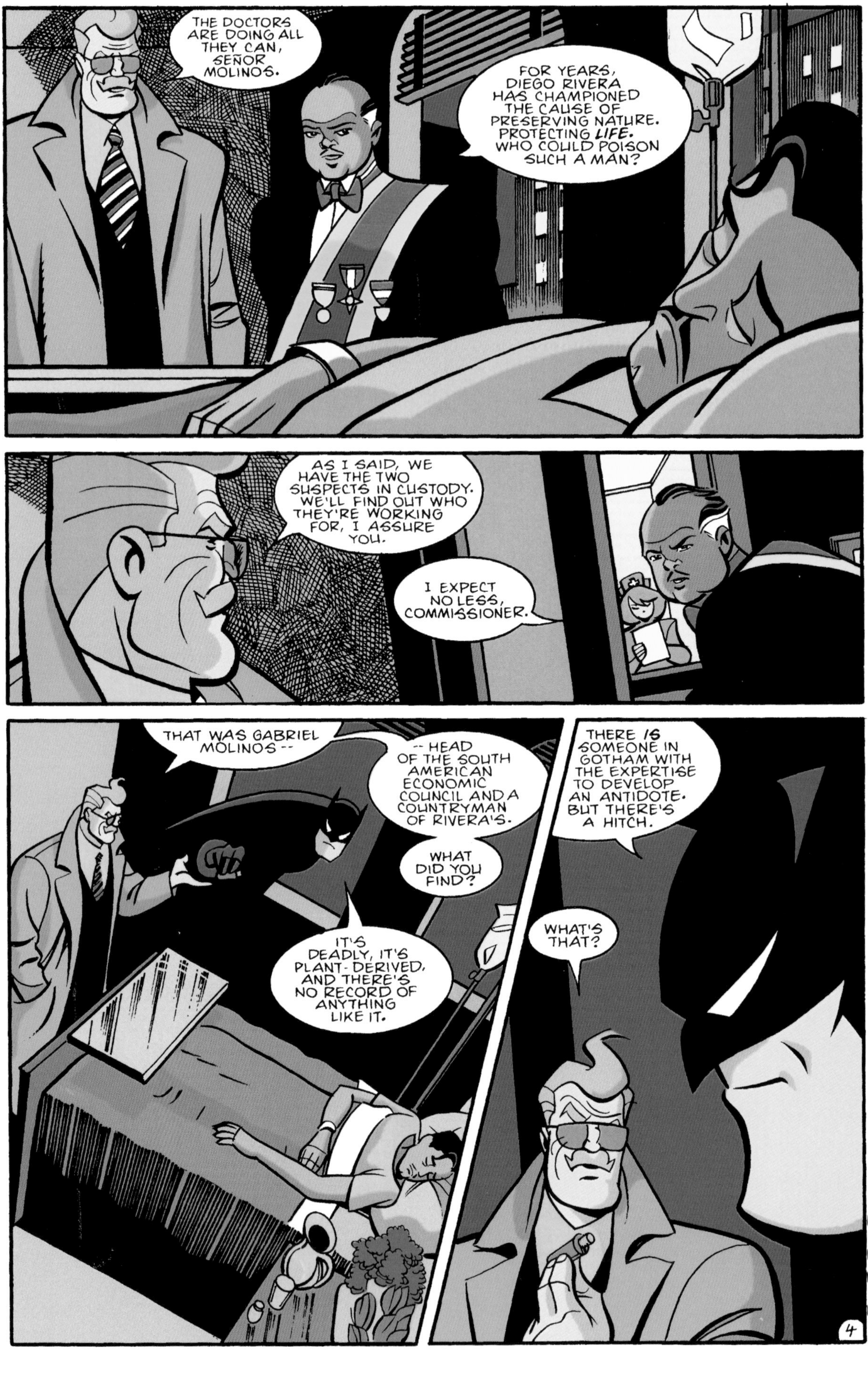
THE DOCTORS ARE DOING ALL THEY CAN, SEÑOR MOLINOS.
FOR YEARS, DIEGO RIVERA HAS CHAMPIONED THE CAUSE OF PRESERVING NATURE. PROTECTING LIFE. WHO COULD POISON SUCH A MAN?
AS I SAID, WE HAVE THE TWO SUSPECTS IN CUSTODY. WE'LL FIND OUT WHO THEY'RE WORKING FOR, I ASSURE YOU.
I EXPECT NO LESS, COMMISSIONER.
THAT WAS GABRIEL MOLINOS --
-- HEAD OF THE SOUTH AMERICAN ECONOMIC COUNCIL AND A COUNTRYMAN OF RIVERA'S.
WHAT DID YOU FIND?
IT'S DEADLY, IT'S PLANT-DERIVED, AND THERE'S NO RECORD OF ANYTHING LIKE IT.
THERE IS SOMEONE IN GOTHAM WITH THE EXPERTISE TO DEVELOP AN ANTIDOTE. BUT THERE'S A HITCH.
WHAT'S THAT?
4

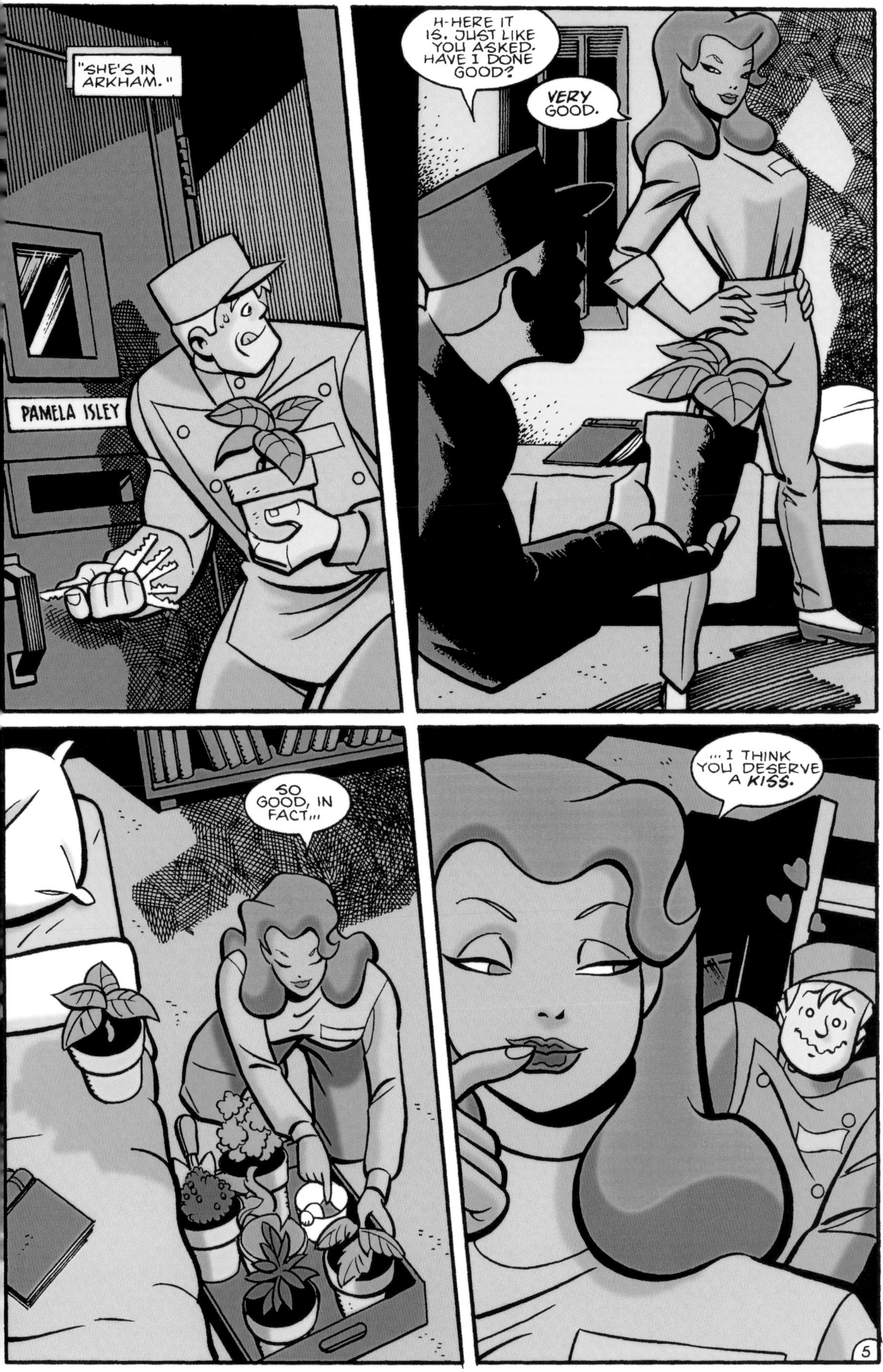
"SHE'S IN ARKHAM."
PAMELA ISLEY
H-HERE IT IS. JUST LIKE YOU ASKED. HAVE I DONE GOOD?
VERY GOOD.
SO GOOD, IN FACT...
...I THINK YOU DESERVE A KISS.
5

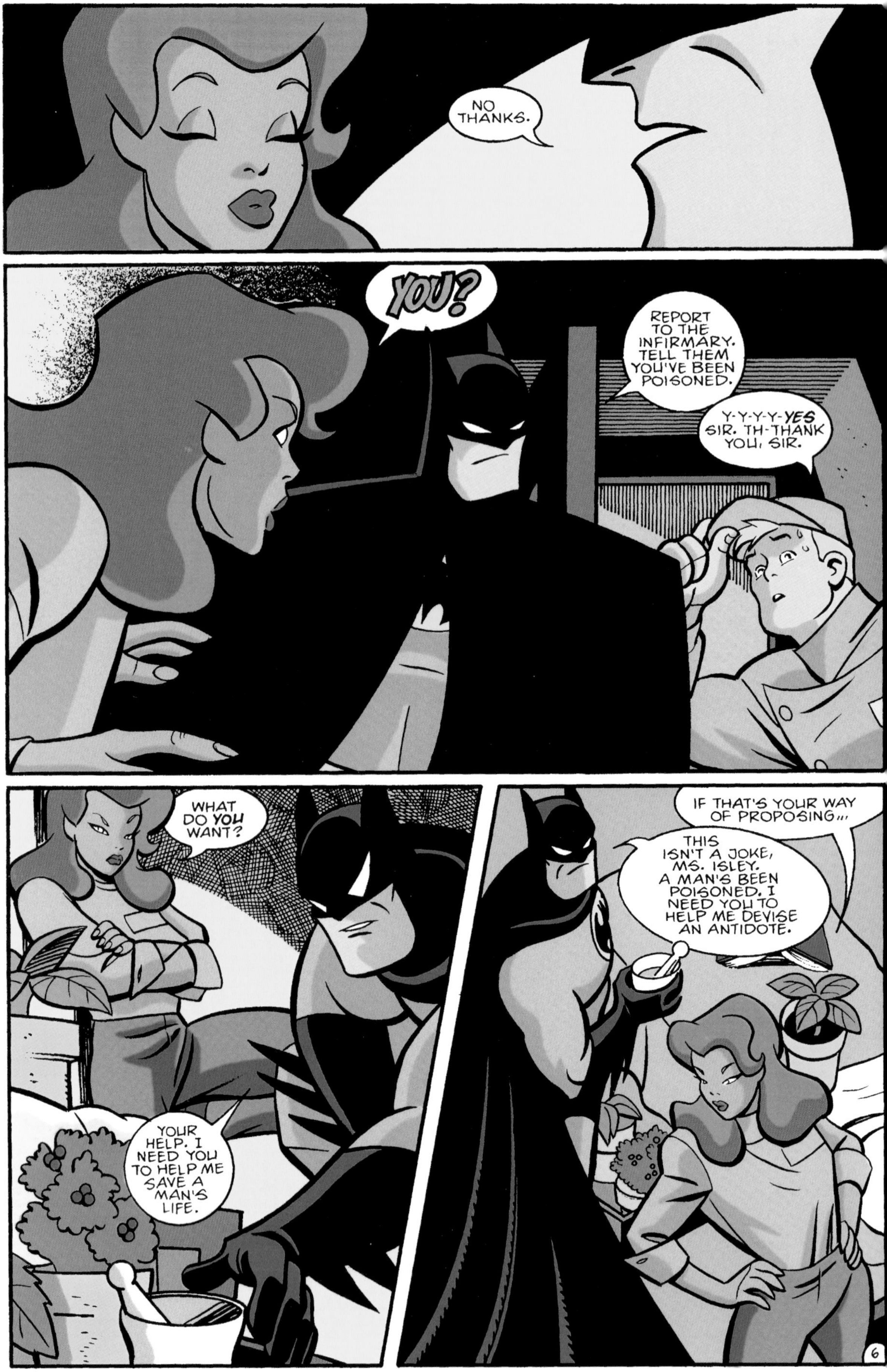
NO THANKS.
YOU?
REPORT TO THE INFIRMARY. TELL THEM YOU'VE BEEN POISONED.
Y-Y-Y-Y-YES SIR. TH-THANK YOU, SIR.
WHAT DO YOU WANT?
YOUR HELP. I NEED YOU TO HELP ME SAVE A MAN'S LIFE.
IF THAT'S YOUR WAY OF PROPOSING...
THIS ISN'T A JOKE, MS. ISLEY. A MAN'S BEEN POISONED. I NEED YOU TO HELP ME DEVISE AN ANTIDOTE.
6

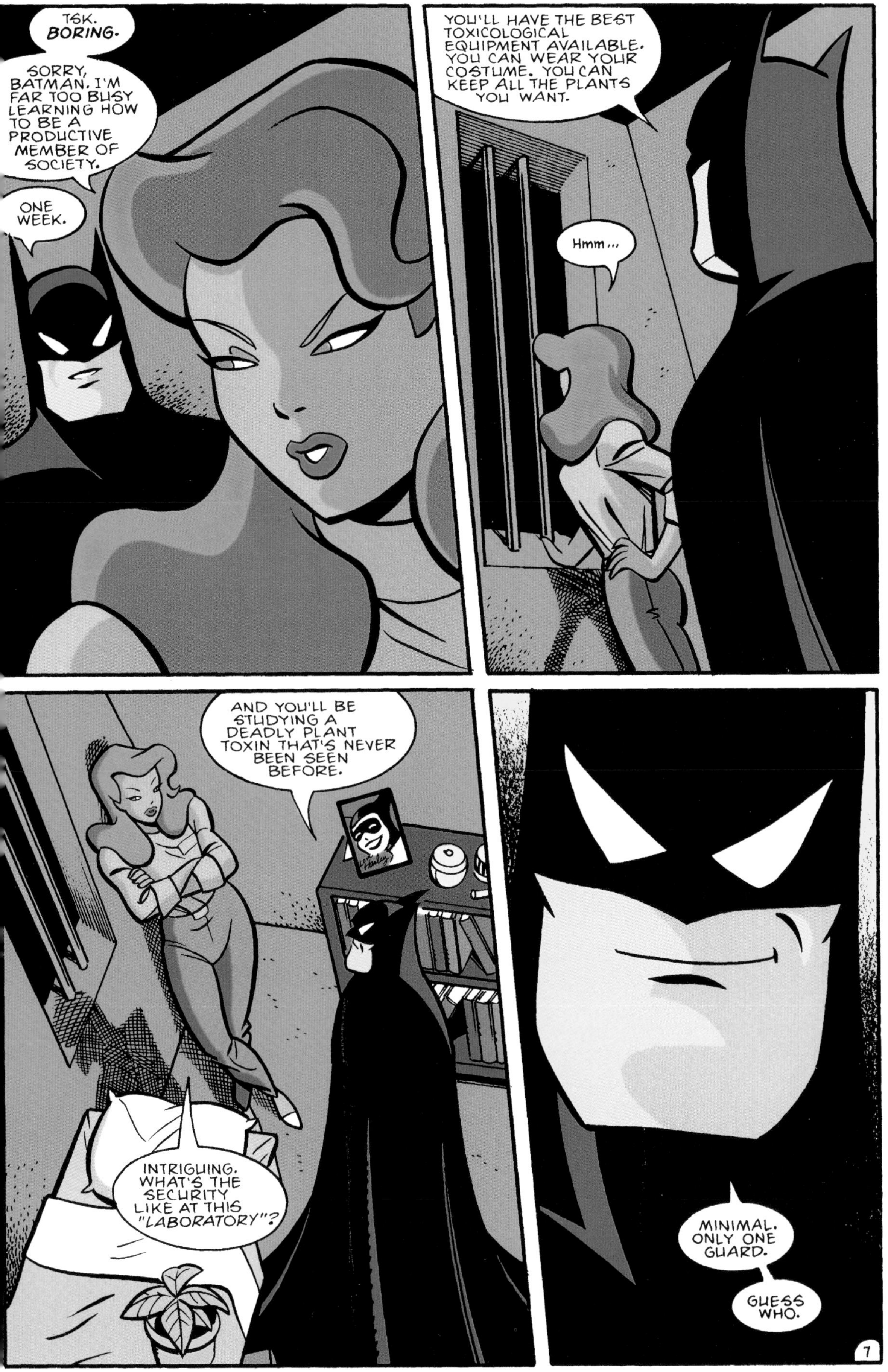

TSK. BORING.
SORRY, BATMAN. I'M FAR TOO BUSY LEARNING HOW TO BE A PRODUCTIVE MEMBER OF SOCIETY.
ONE WEEK.
YOU'LL HAVE THE BEST TOXICOLOGICAL EQUIPMENT AVAILABLE. YOU CAN WEAR YOUR COSTUME. YOU CAN KEEP ALL THE PLANTS YOU WANT.
Hmm...
AND YOU'LL BE STUDYING A DEADLY PLANT TOXIN THAT'S NEVER BEEN SEEN BEFORE.
INTRIGUING. WHAT'S THE SECURITY LIKE AT THIS "LABORATORY"?
MINIMAL. ONLY ONE GUARD.
GUESS WHO.
7

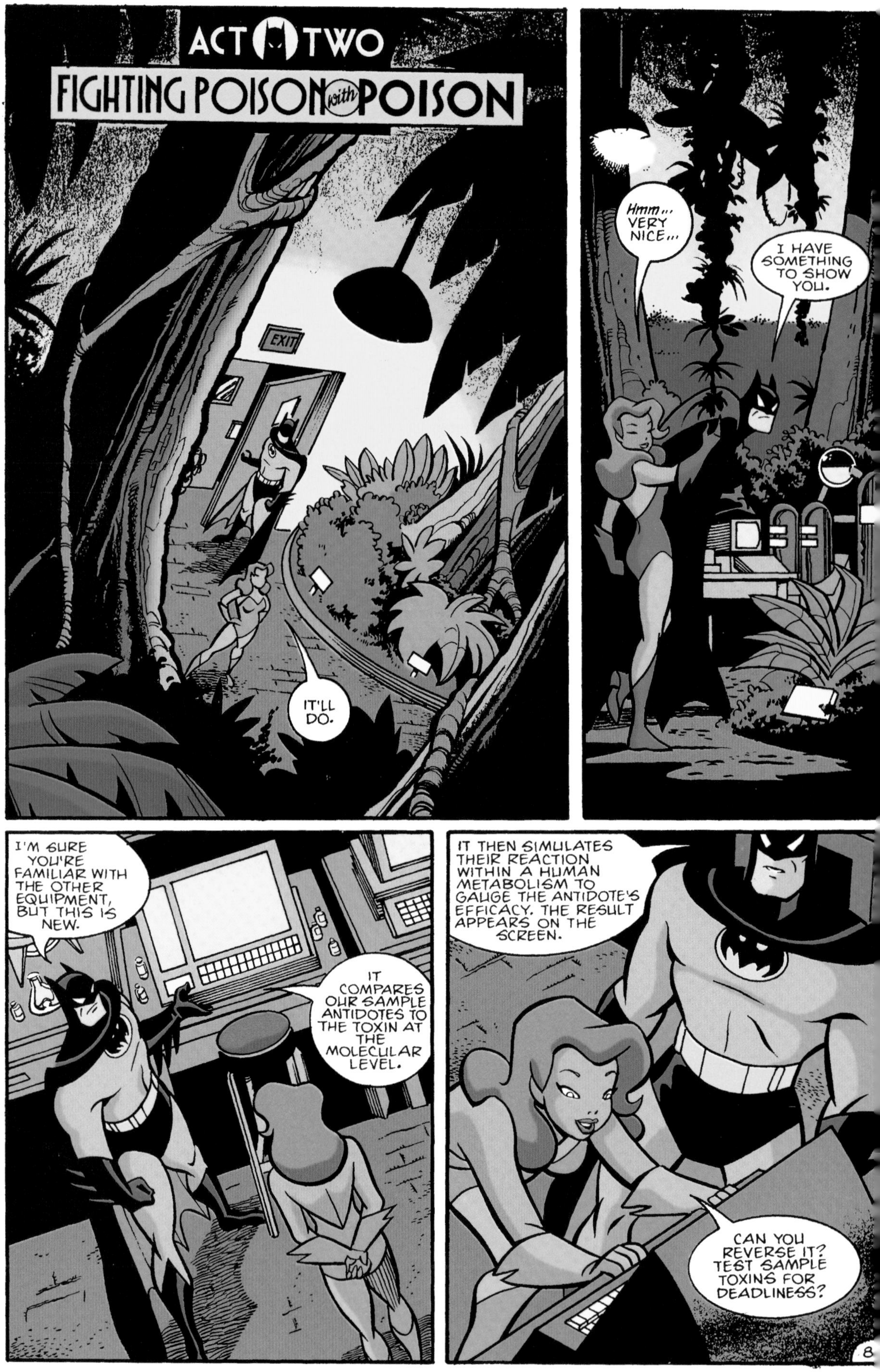
ACT TWO
FIGHTING POISON with POISON
EXIT
IT'LL DO.
Hmm... VERY NICE...
I HAVE SOMETHING TO SHOW YOU.
I'M SURE YOU'RE FAMILIAR WITH THE OTHER EQUIPMENT, BUT THIS IS NEW.
IT COMPARES OUR SAMPLE ANTIDOTES TO THE TOXIN AT THE MOLECULAR LEVEL.
IT THEN SIMULATES THEIR REACTION WITHIN A HUMAN METABOLISM TO GAUGE THE ANTIDOTE'S EFFICACY. THE RESULT APPEARS ON THE SCREEN.
CAN YOU REVERSE IT? TEST SAMPLE TOXINS FOR DEADLINESS?
8

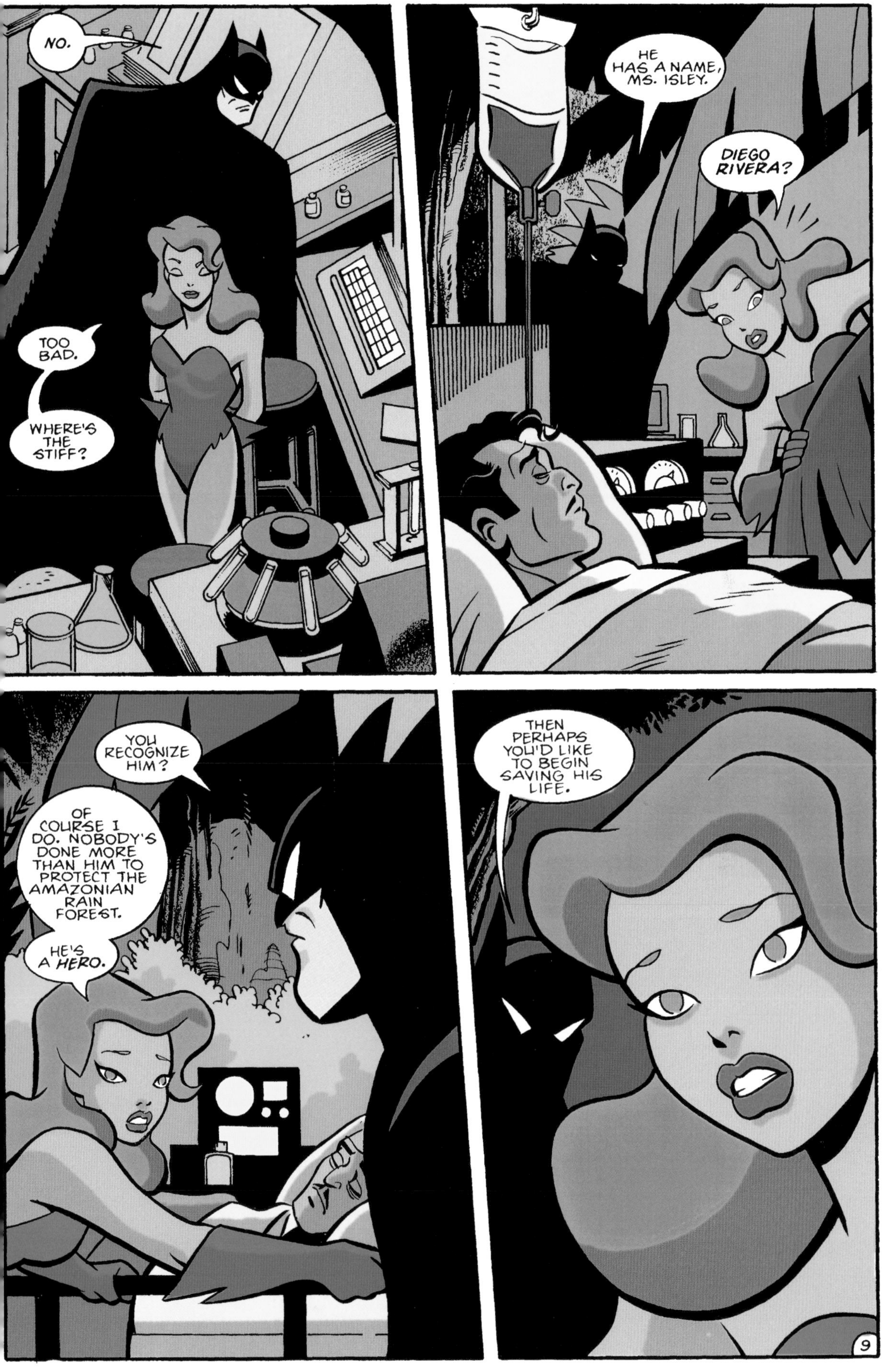
NO.
TOO BAD.
WHERE'S THE STIFF?
HE HAS A NAME, MS. ISLEY.
DIEGO RIVERA?
YOU RECOGNIZE HIM?
OF COURSE I DO. NOBODY'S DONE MORE THAN HIM TO PROTECT THE AMAZONIAN RAIN FOREST.
HE'S A HERO.
THEN PERHAPS YOU'D LIKE TO BEGIN SAVING HIS LIFE.
9

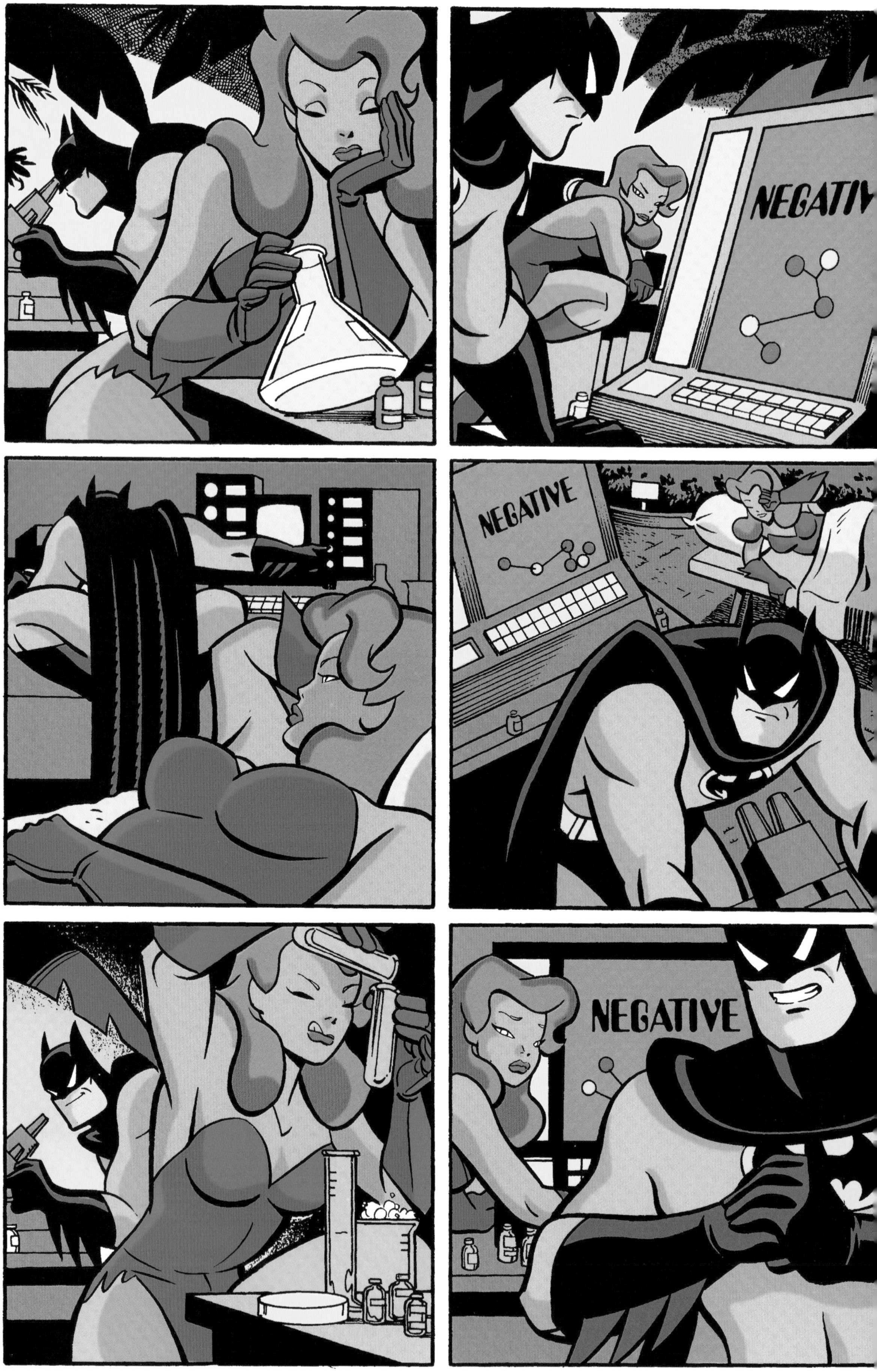
NEGATIV
NEGATIVE
NEGATIVE

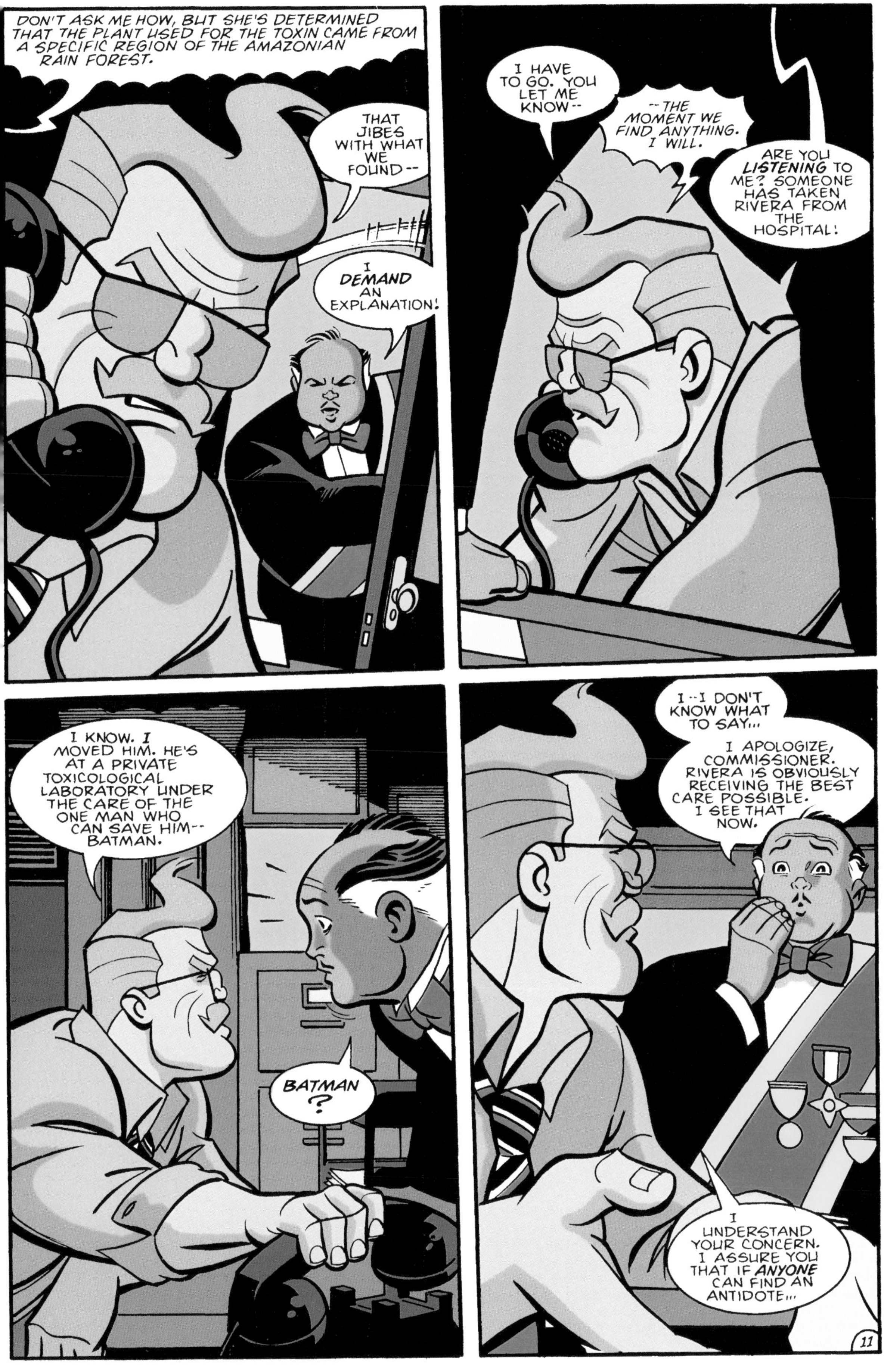
DON'T ASK ME HOW, BUT SHE'S DETERMINED THAT THE PLANT USED FOR THE TOXIN CAME FROM A SPECIFIC REGION OF THE AMAZONIAN RAIN FOREST.
THAT JIBES WITH WHAT WE FOUND--
I DEMAND AN EXPLANATION!
I HAVE TO GO. YOU LET ME KNOW--
--THE MOMENT WE FIND ANYTHING. I WILL.
ARE YOU LISTENING TO ME? SOMEONE HAS TAKEN RIVERA FROM THE HOSPITAL!
I KNOW. I MOVED HIM. HE'S AT A PRIVATE TOXICOLOGICAL LABORATORY UNDER THE CARE OF THE ONE MAN WHO CAN SAVE HIM--BATMAN.
BATMAN?
I--I DON'T KNOW WHAT TO SAY...
I APOLOGIZE, COMMISSIONER. RIVERA IS OBVIOUSLY RECEIVING THE BEST CARE POSSIBLE. I SEE THAT NOW.
I UNDERSTAND YOUR CONCERN. I ASSURE YOU THAT IF ANYONE CAN FIND AN ANTIDOTE...
11

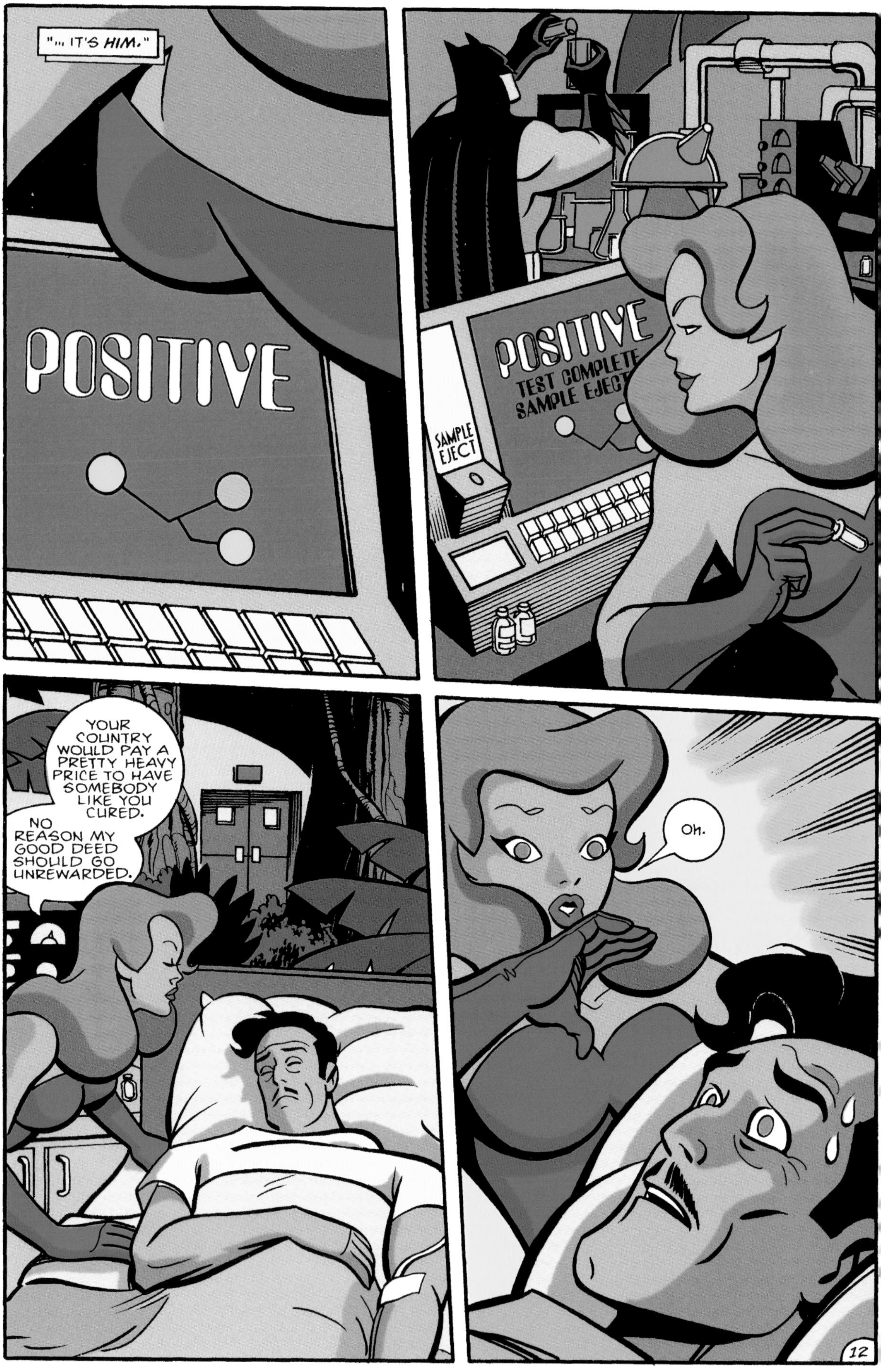
"... IT'S HIM."
POSITIVE
POSITIVE
TEST COMPLETE
SAMPLE EJECT
SAMPLE EJECT
YOUR COUNTRY WOULD PAY A PRETTY HEAVY PRICE TO HAVE SOMEBODY LIKE YOU CURED.
NO REASON MY GOOD DEED SHOULD GO UNREWARDED.
Oh.
12

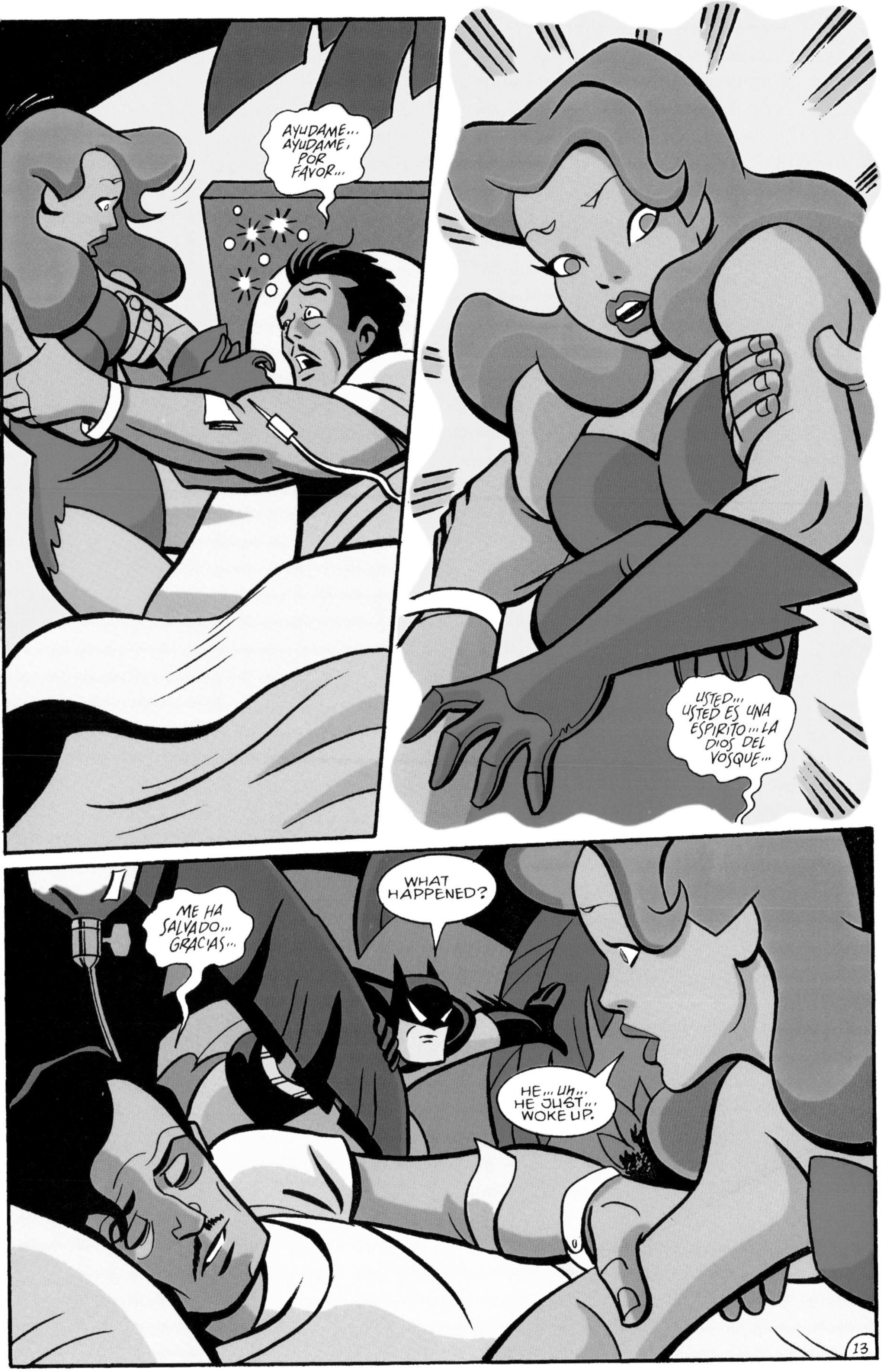

AYUDAME... AYUDAME, POR FAVOR...
USTED... USTED ES UNA ESPIRITO... LA DIOS DEL VOSQUE...
ME HA SALVADO... GRACIAS...
WHAT HAPPENED?
HE... UH... HE JUST... WOKE UP.
13

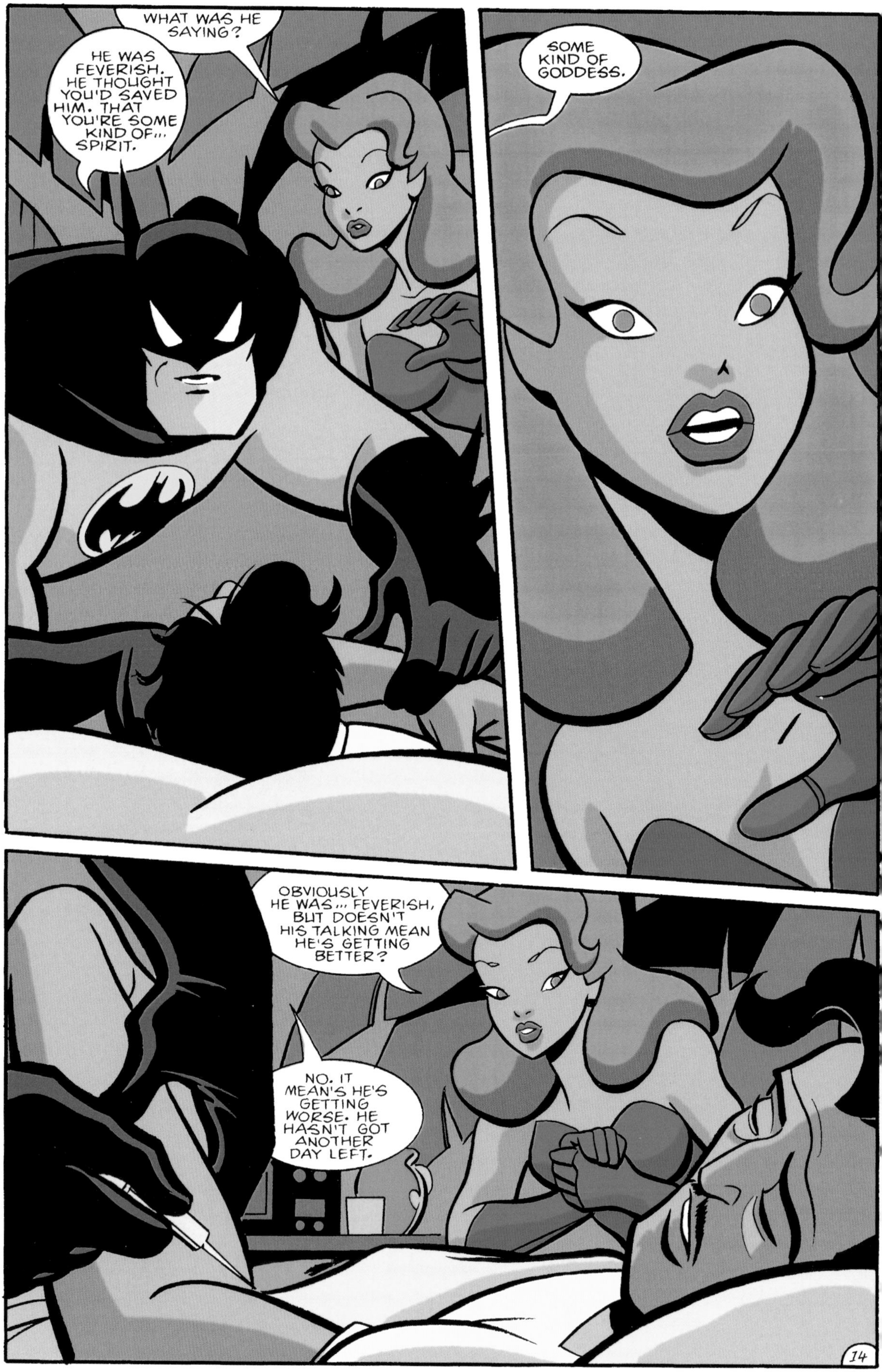
WHAT WAS HE SAYING?
HE WAS FEVERISH. HE THOUGHT YOU'D SAVED HIM. THAT YOU'RE SOME KIND OF... SPIRIT.
SOME KIND OF GODDESS.
OBVIOUSLY HE WAS... FEVERISH, BUT DOESN'T HIS TALKING MEAN HE'S GETTING BETTER?
NO. IT MEAN'S HE'S GETTING WORSE. HE HASN'T GOT ANOTHER DAY LEFT.
14

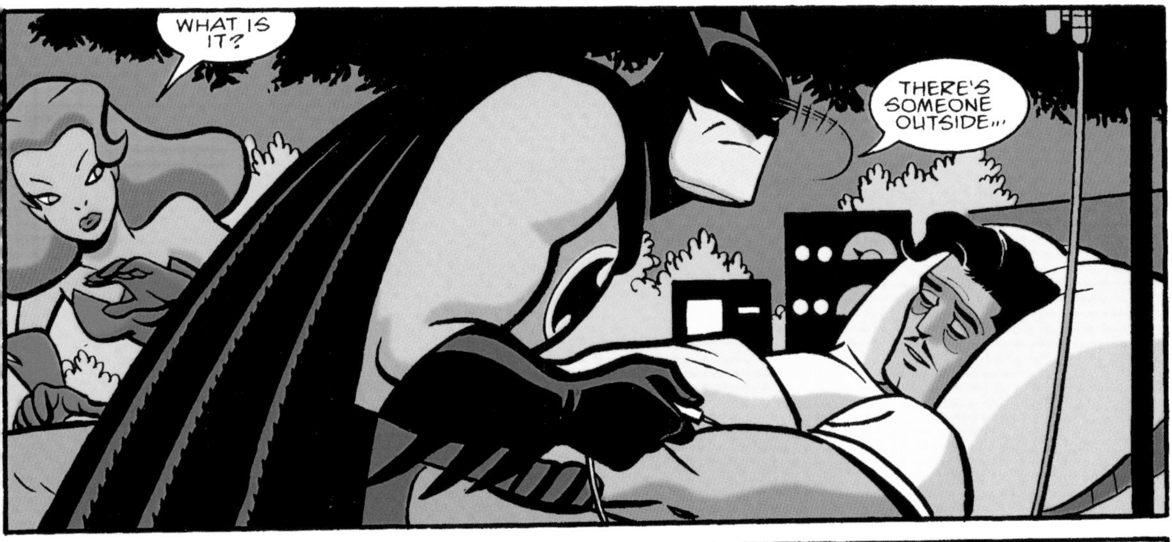
WHAT IS IT?
THERE'S SOMEONE OUTSIDE...

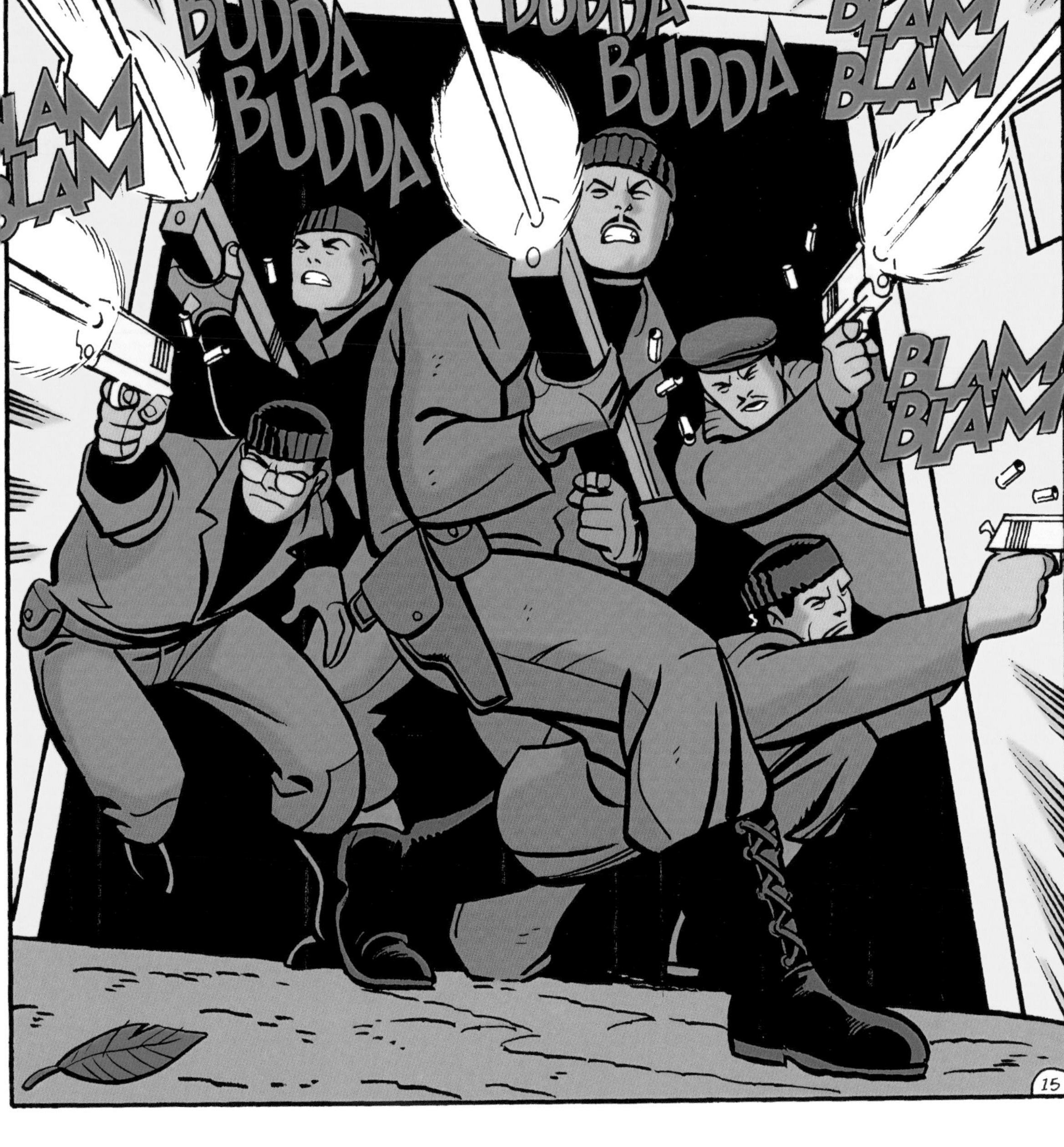
BLAM BLAM
BUDDA BUDDA
BUDDA BUDDA
BLAM BLAM
BLAM BLAM
15

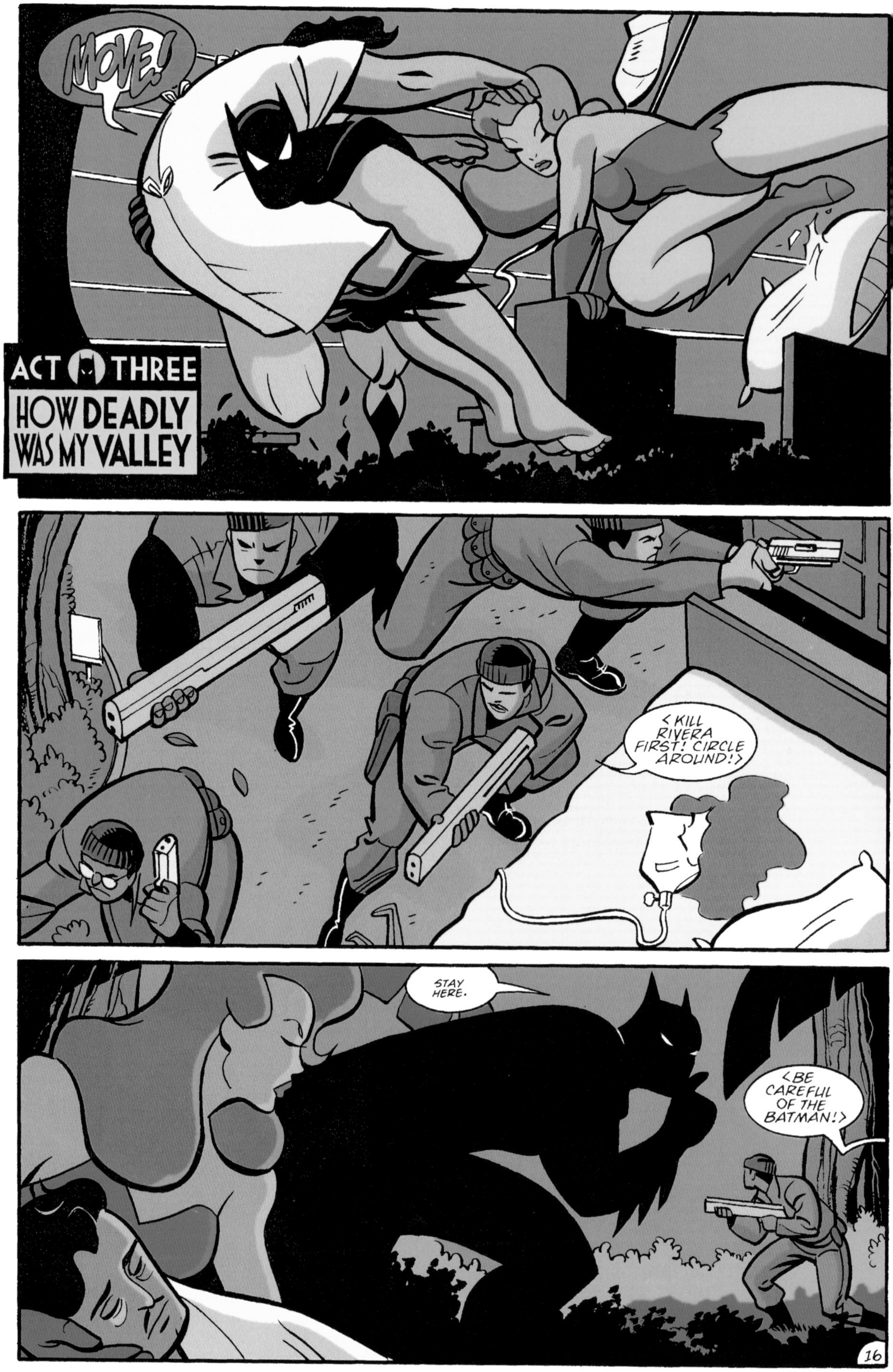
MOVE!
ACT THREE
HOW DEADLY WAS MY VALLEY
<KILL RIVERA FIRST! CIRCLE AROUND!>
STAY HERE.
<BE CAREFUL OF THE BATMAN!>
16

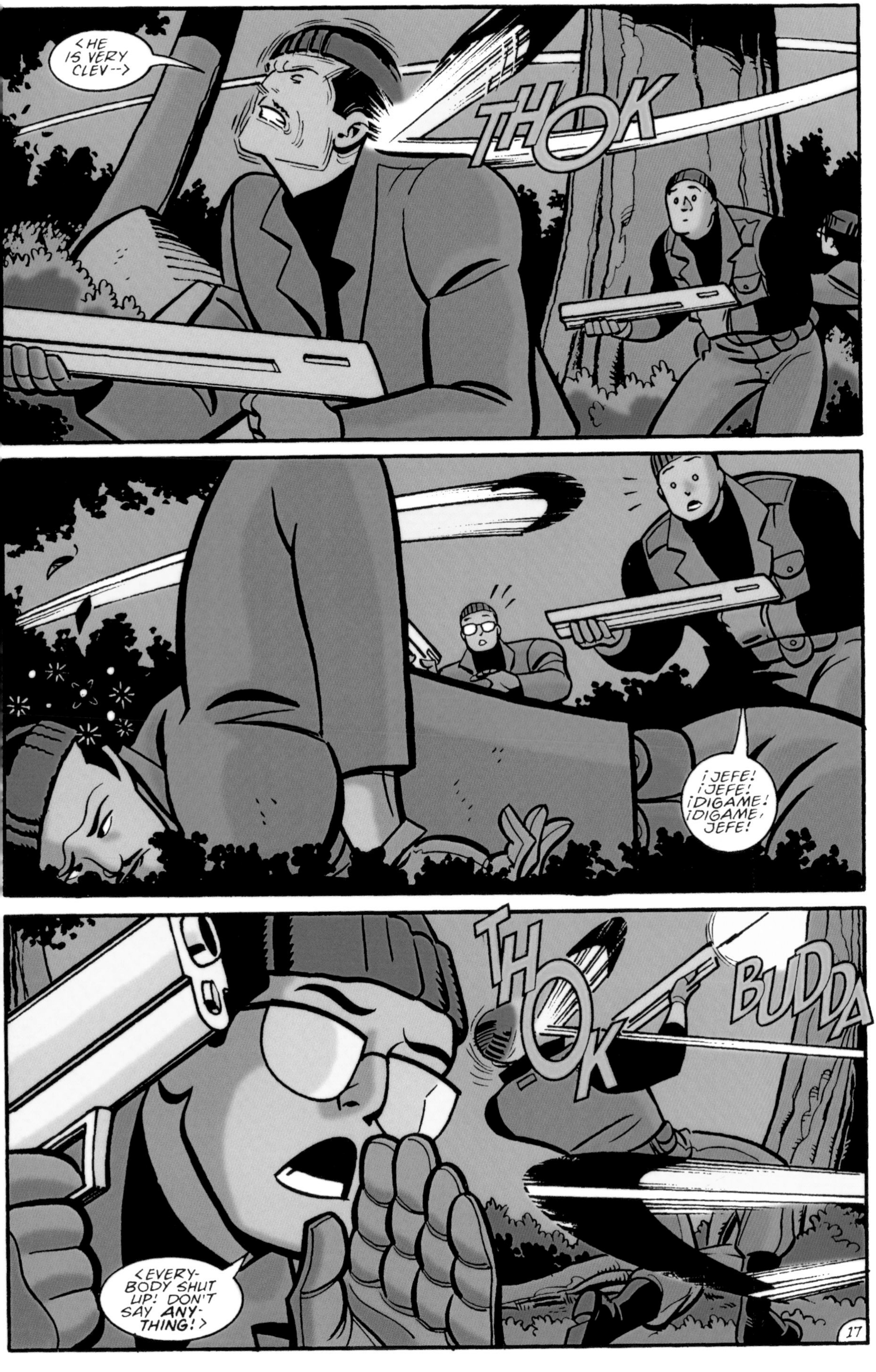

<HE IS VERY CLEV-->
THOK
¡JEFE! ¡JEFE! ¡DIGAME! ¡DIGAME, JEFE!
THOK
BUDDA
<EVERY-BODY SHUT UP! DON'T SAY ANY-THING!>
17

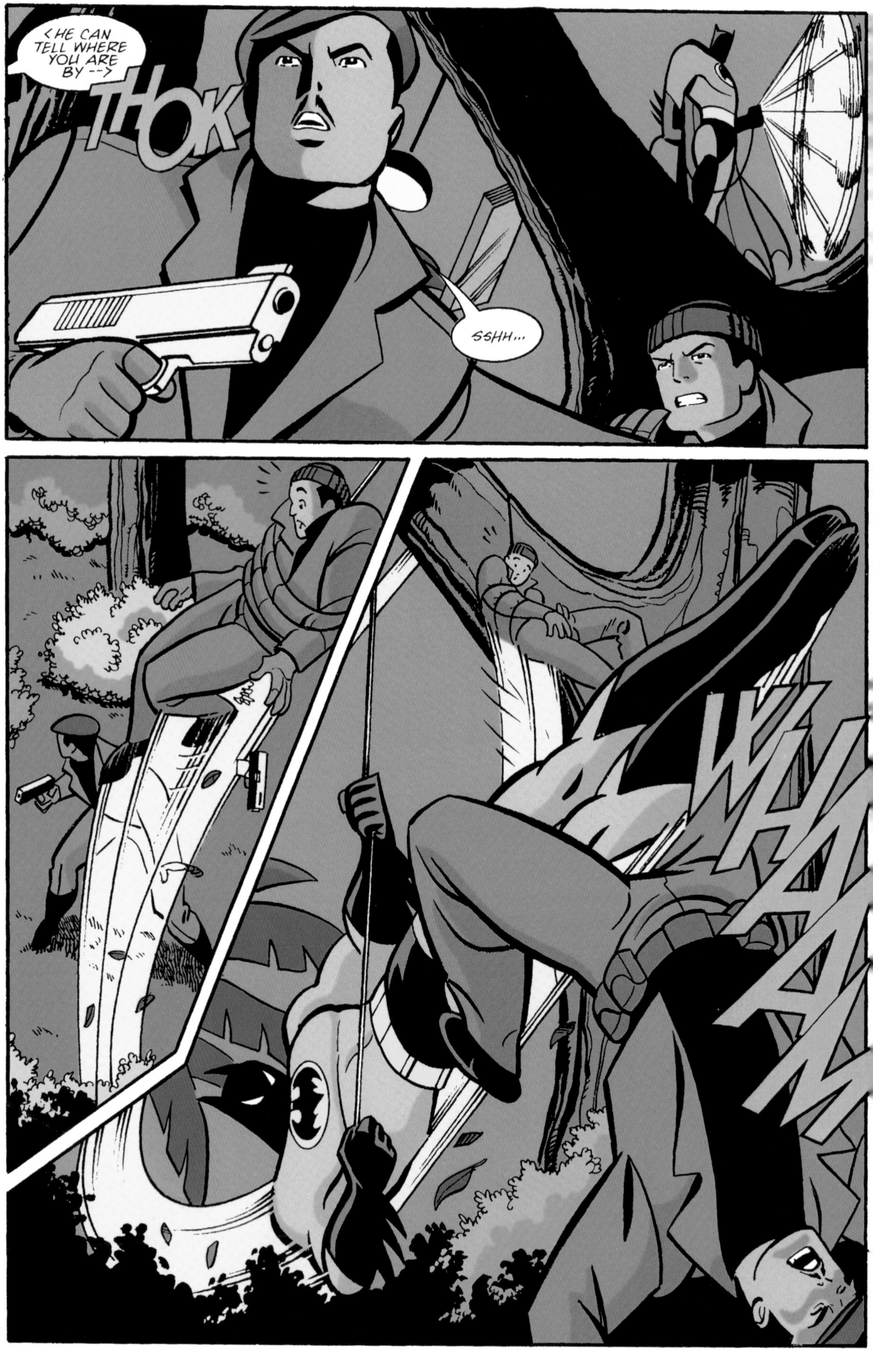

< HE CAN TELL WHERE YOU ARE BY -->
THOK
SSHH...
WHAM

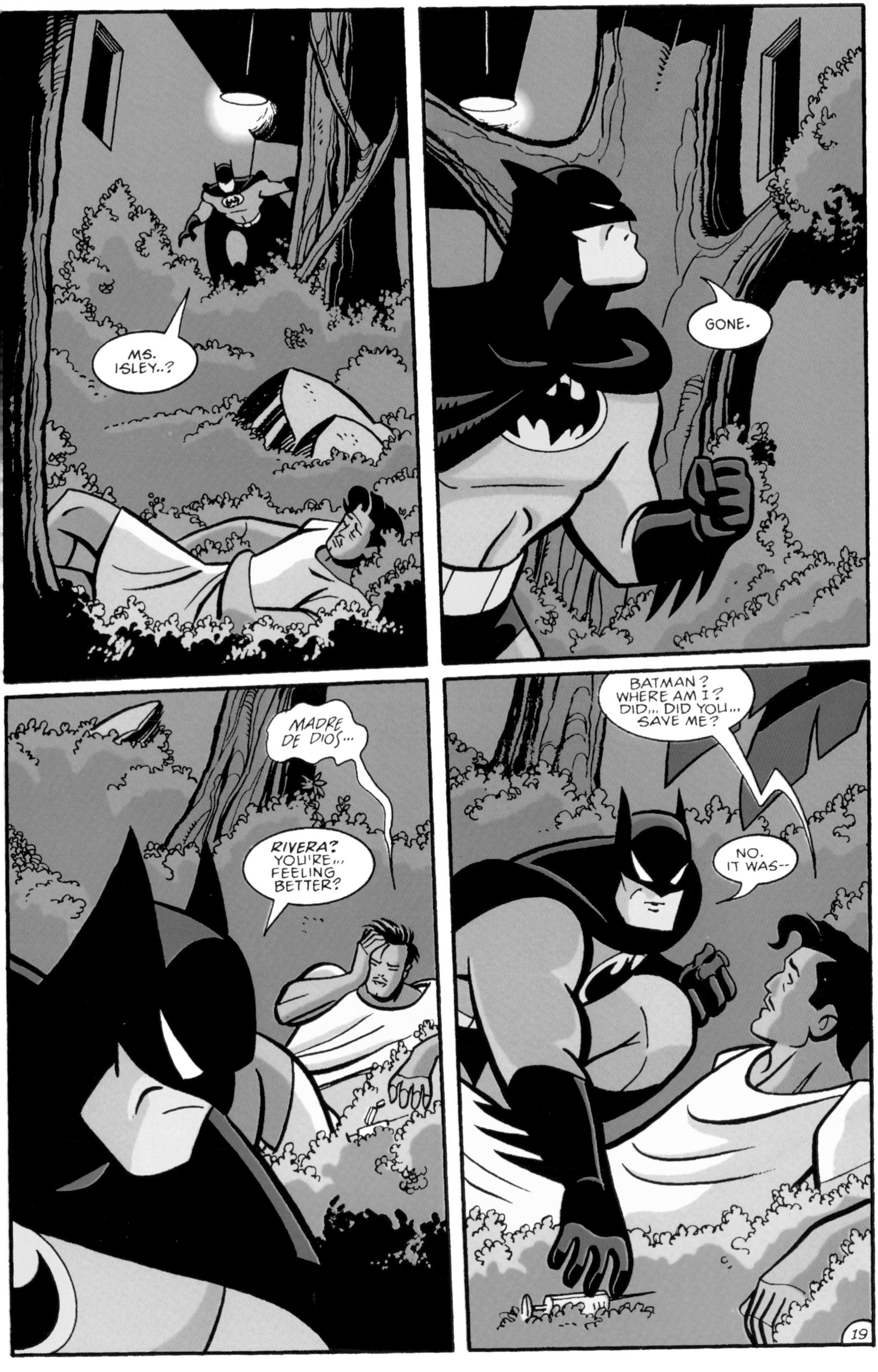
MS. ISLEY..?
GONE.
MADRE DE DIOS...
RIVERA? YOU'RE... FEELING BETTER?
BATMAN? WHERE AM I? DID... DID YOU... SAVE ME?
NO. IT WAS--
19

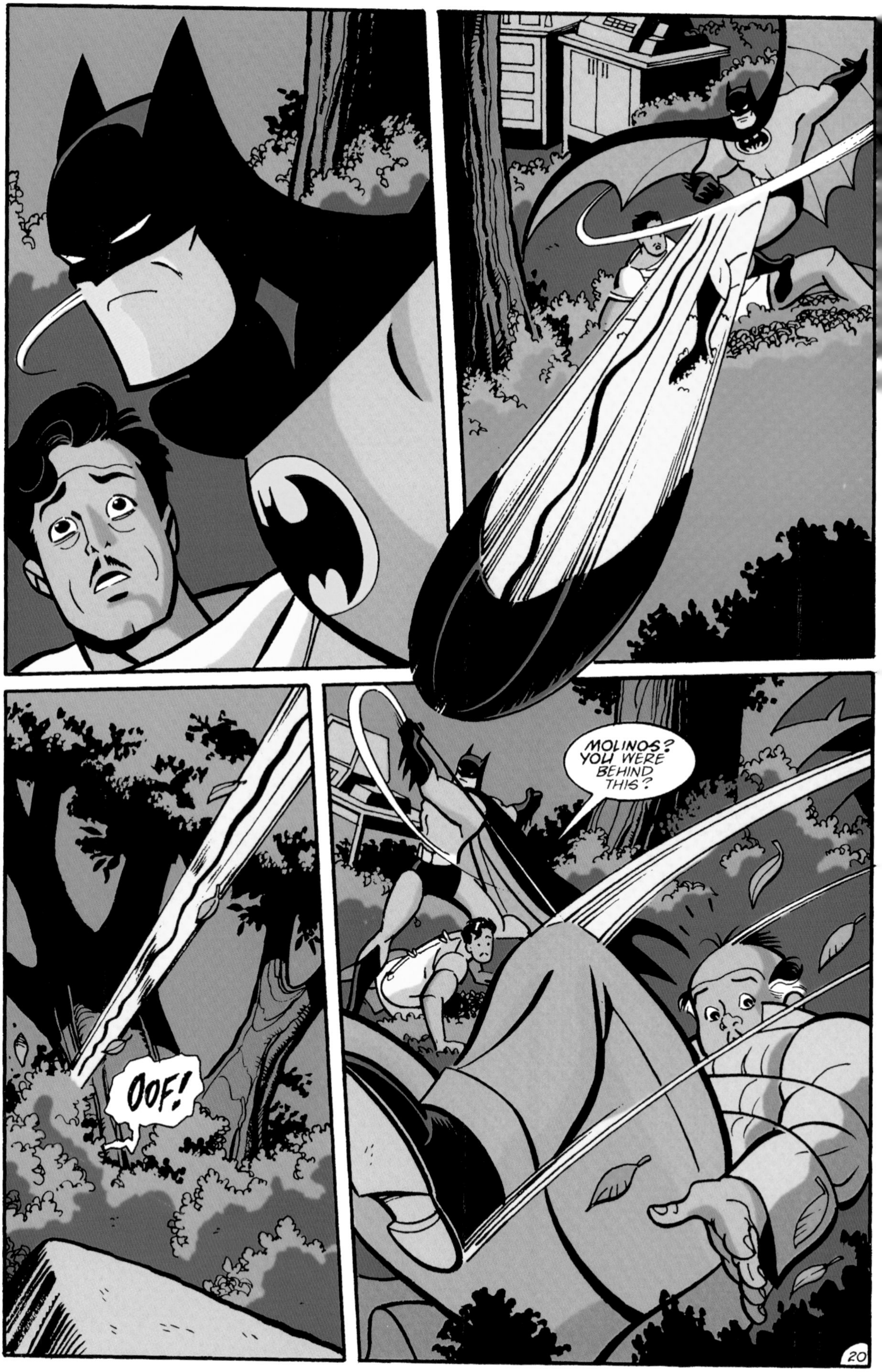

MOLINOS? YOU WERE BEHIND THIS?
OOF!
20

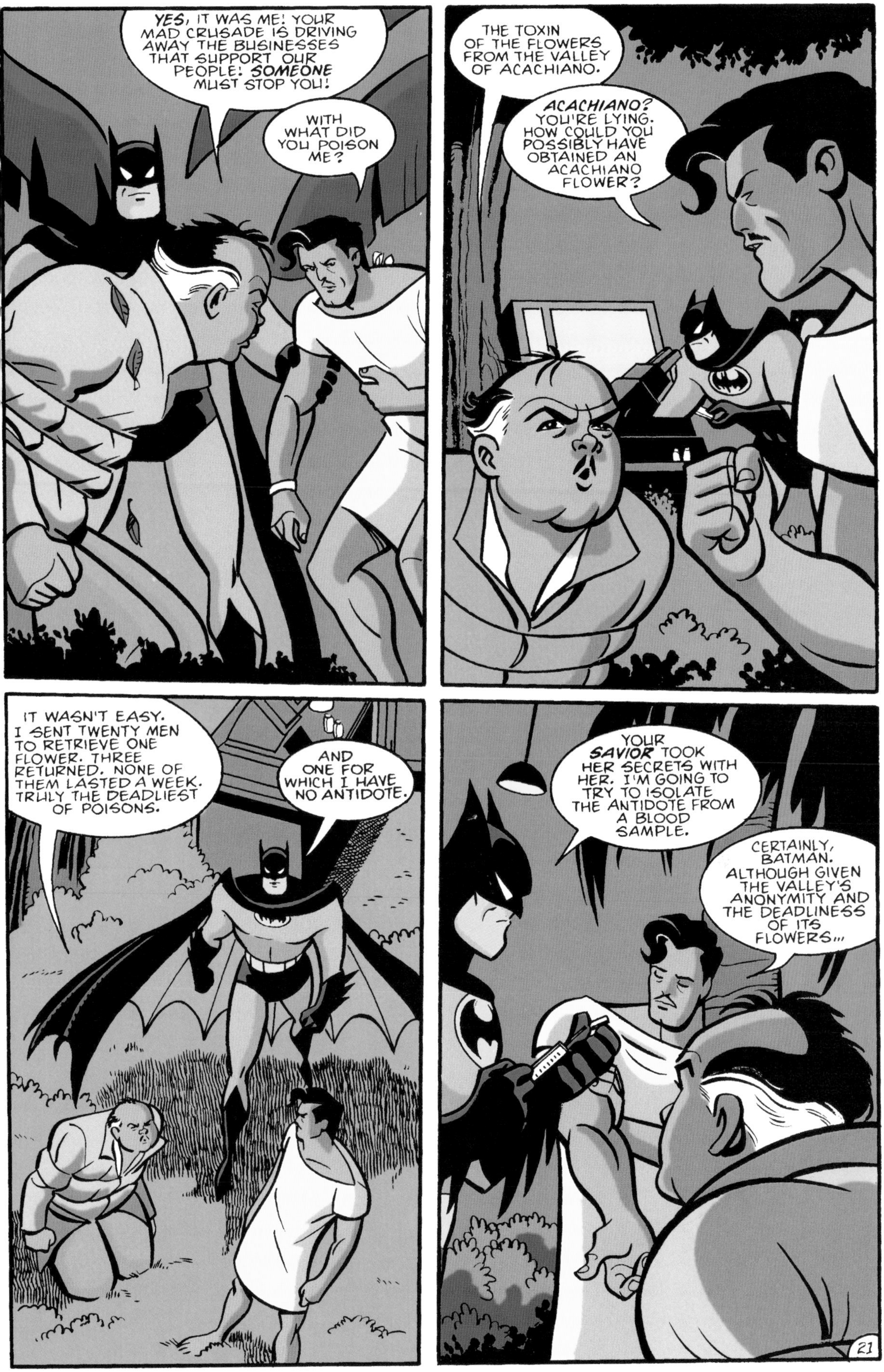

YES, IT WAS ME! YOUR MAD CRUSADE IS DRIVING AWAY THE BUSINESSES THAT SUPPORT OUR PEOPLE: SOMEONE MUST STOP YOU!
WITH WHAT DID YOU POISON ME?
THE TOXIN OF THE FLOWERS FROM THE VALLEY OF ACACHIANO.
ACACHIANO? YOU'RE LYING. HOW COULD YOU POSSIBLY HAVE OBTAINED AN ACACHIANO FLOWER?
IT WASN'T EASY. I SENT TWENTY MEN TO RETRIEVE ONE FLOWER. THREE RETURNED. NONE OF THEM LASTED A WEEK. TRULY THE DEADLIEST OF POISONS.
AND ONE FOR WHICH I HAVE NO ANTIDOTE.
YOUR SAVIOR TOOK HER SECRETS WITH HER. I'M GOING TO TRY TO ISOLATE THE ANTIDOTE FROM A BLOOD SAMPLE.
CERTAINLY, BATMAN. ALTHOUGH GIVEN THE VALLEY'S ANONYMITY AND THE DEADLINESS OF ITS FLOWERS...
21

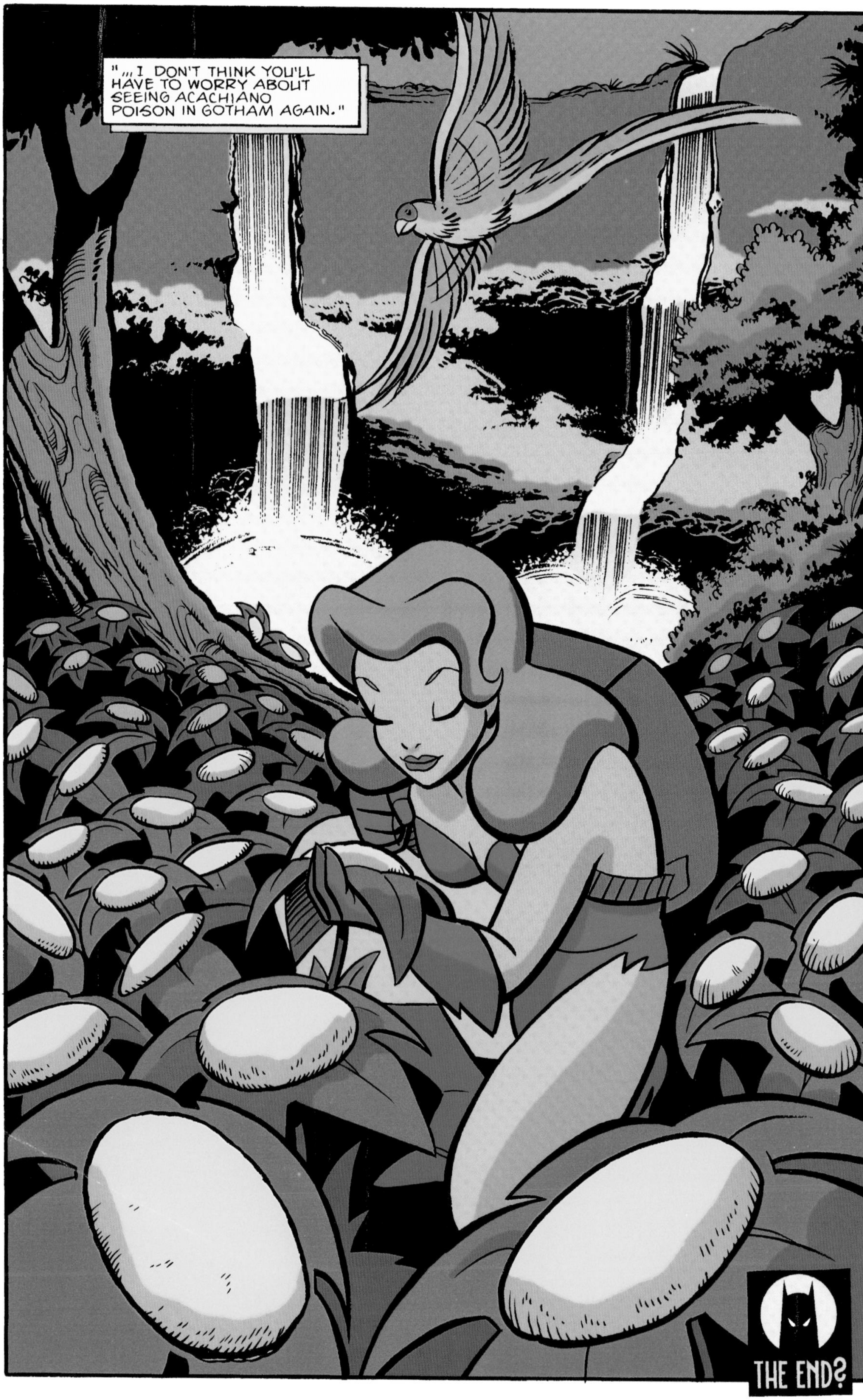
"...I DON'T THINK YOU'LL HAVE TO WORRY ABOUT SEEING ACACHIANO POISON IN GOTHAM AGAIN."
THE END?

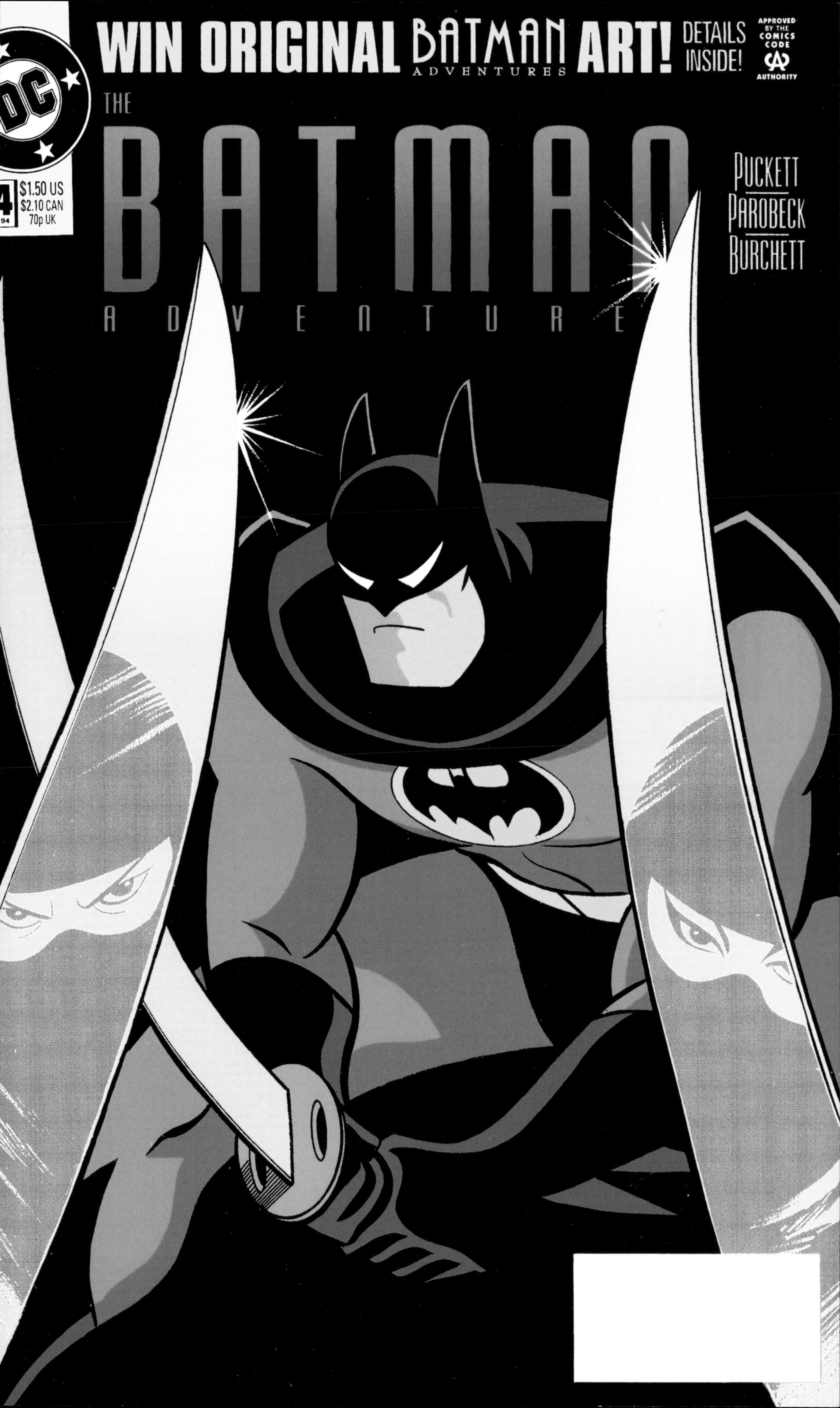
WIN ORIGINAL BATMAN ADVENTURES ART!
DETAILS INSIDE!
APPROVED BY THE COMICS CODE AUTHORITY
DC
4
$1.50 US
$2.10 CAN
70p UK
THE BATMAN ADVENTURES
PUCKETT
PAROBECK
BURCHETT

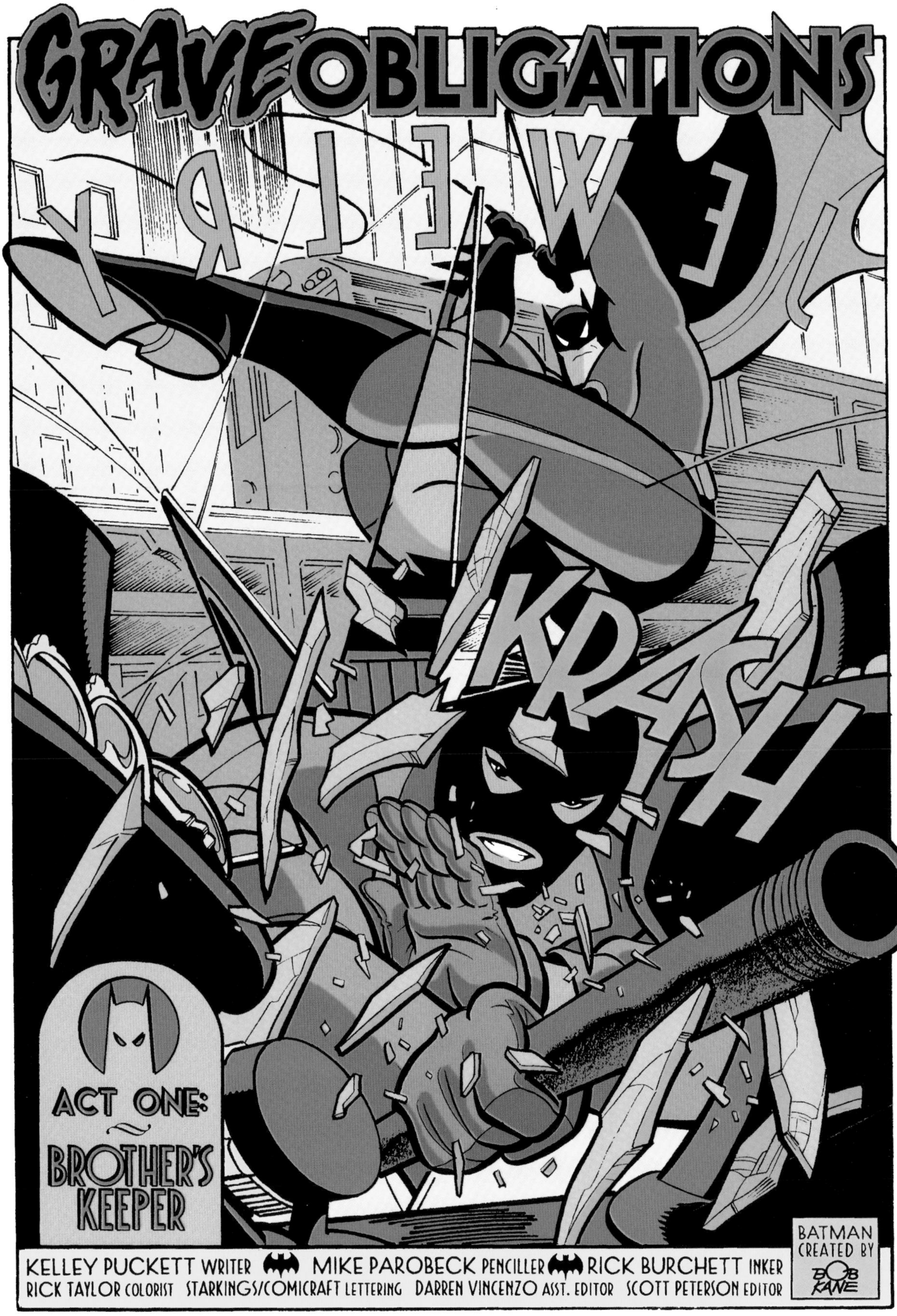
GRAVE OBLIGATIONS
KRASH
ACT ONE:
BROTHER'S KEEPER
KELLEY PUCKETT WRITER MIKE PAROBECK PENCILLER RICK BURCHETT INKER
RICK TAYLOR COLORIST STARKINGS/COMICRAFT LETTERING DARREN VINCENZO ASST. EDITOR SCOTT PETERSON EDITOR
BATMAN CREATED BY BOB KANE

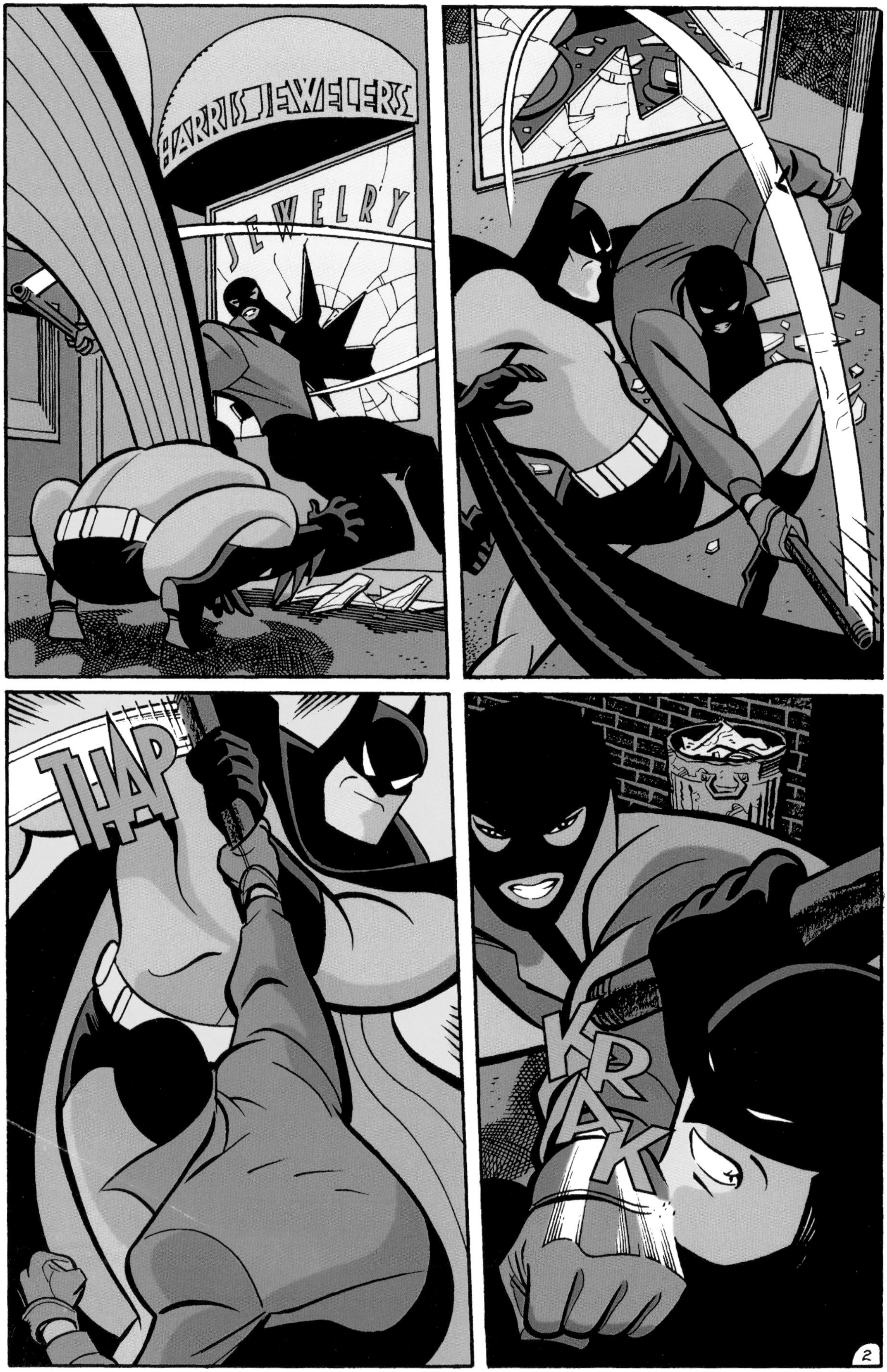
HARRIS JEWELERS
JEWELRY
THAP
KRAK
2

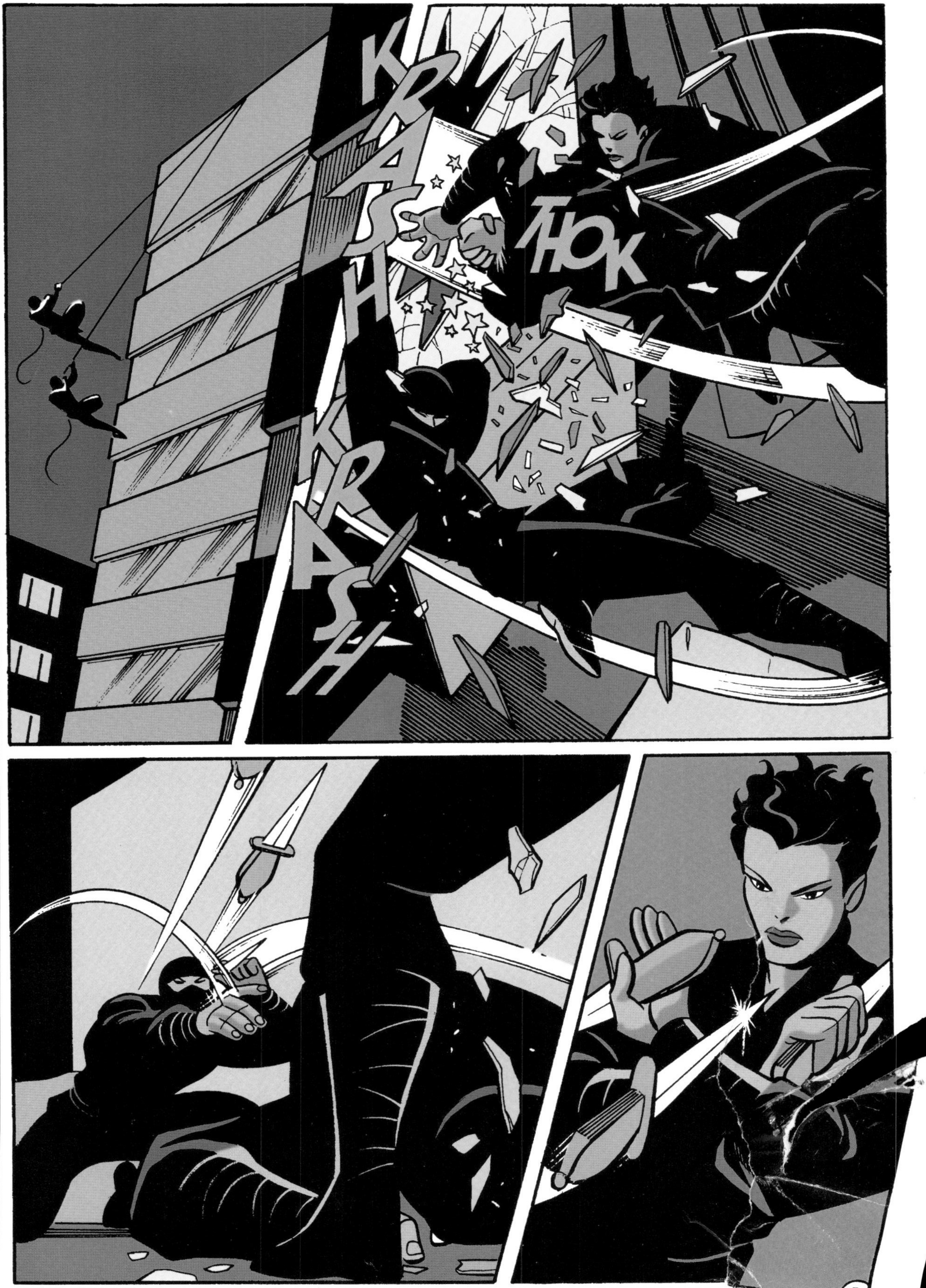
KRASH
THOK
KRASH
5

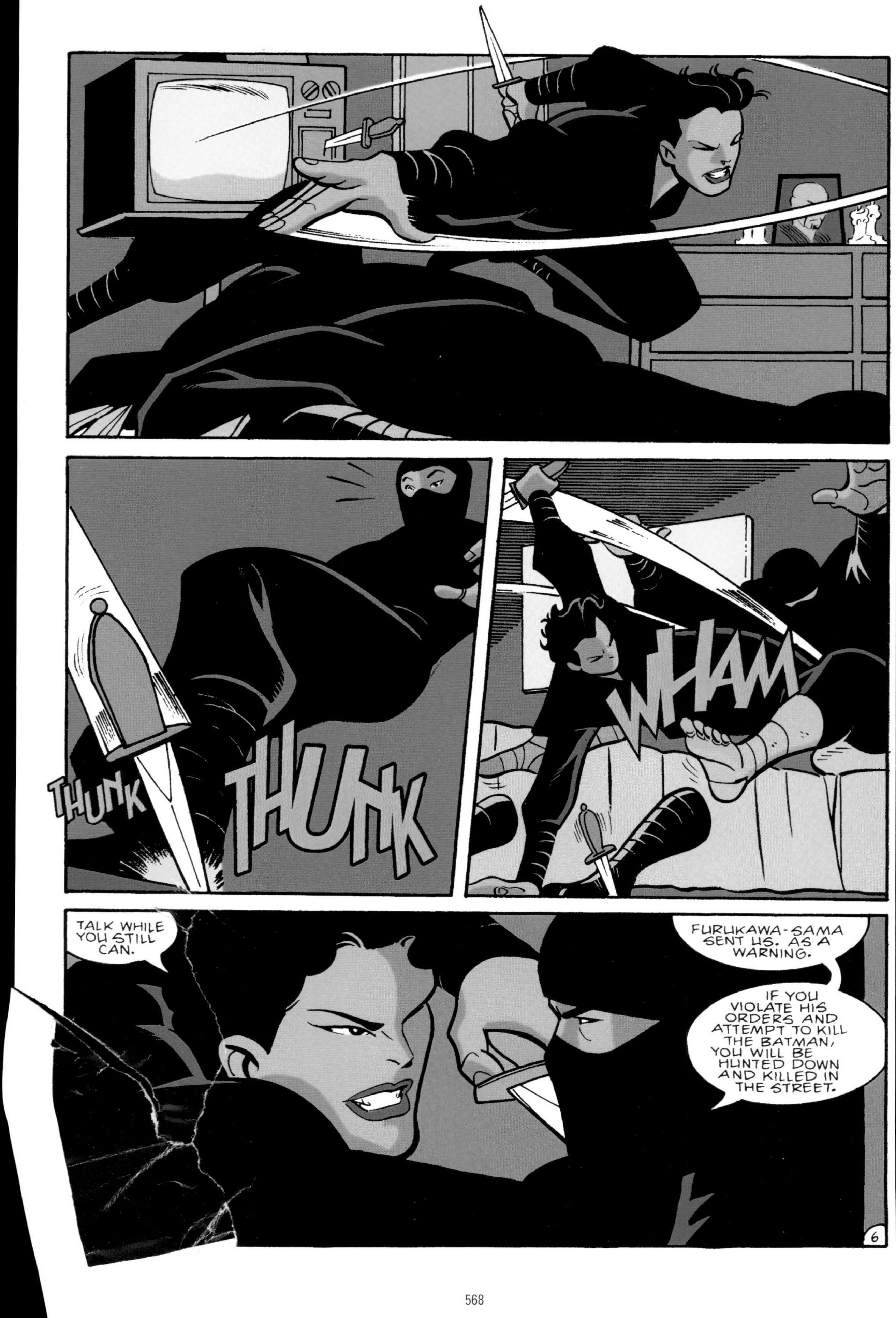
THUNK
THUNK
WHAM
TALK WHILE YOU STILL CAN.
FURUKAWA-SAMA SENT US. AS A WARNING.
IF YOU VIOLATE HIS ORDERS AND ATTEMPT TO KILL THE BATMAN, YOU WILL BE HUNTED DOWN AND KILLED IN THE STREET.
6

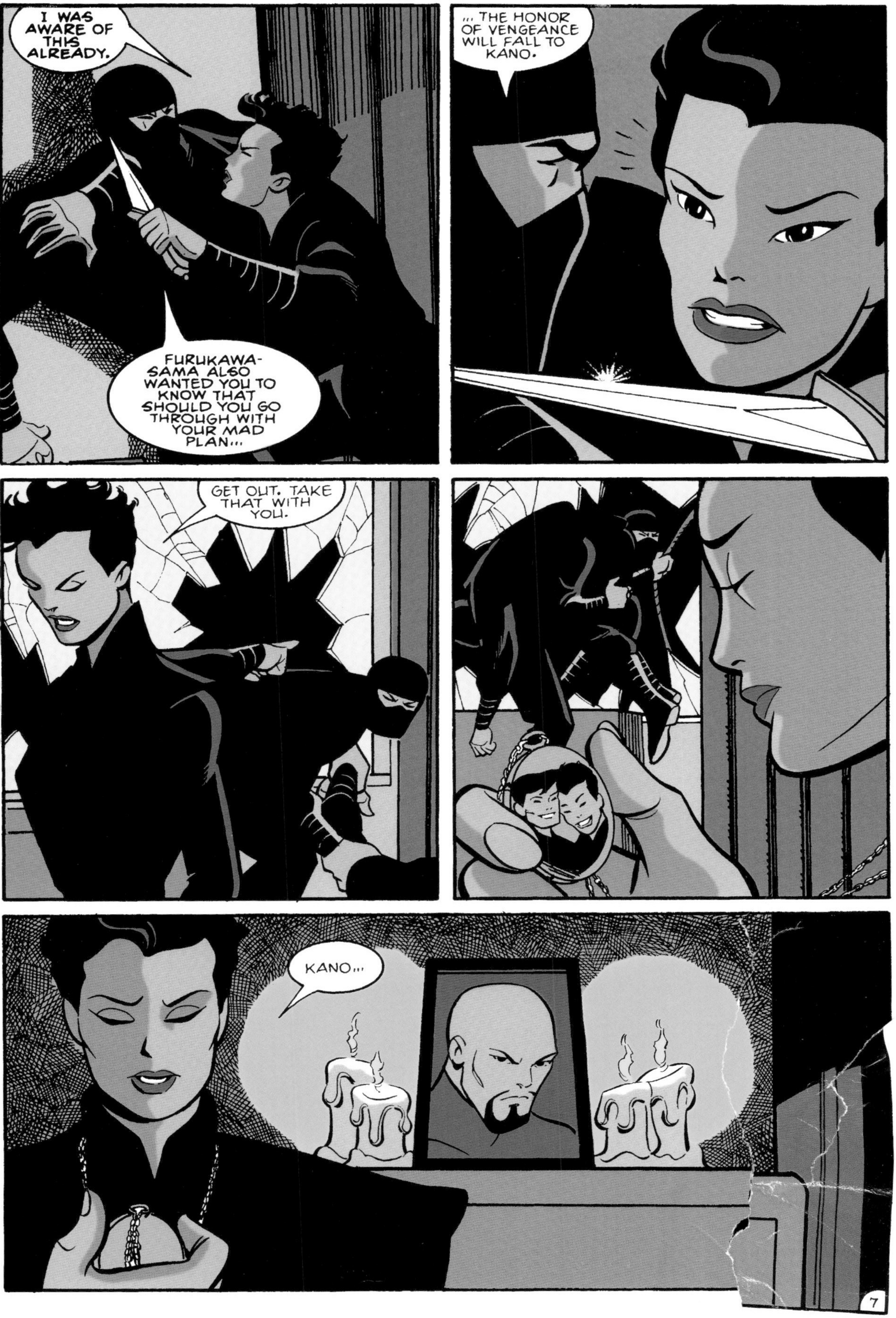

I WAS AWARE OF THIS ALREADY.
FURUKAWA-SAMA ALSO WANTED YOU TO KNOW THAT SHOULD YOU GO THROUGH WITH YOUR MAD PLAN...
... THE HONOR OF VENGEANCE WILL FALL TO KANO.
GET OUT. TAKE THAT WITH YOU.
KANO...
7

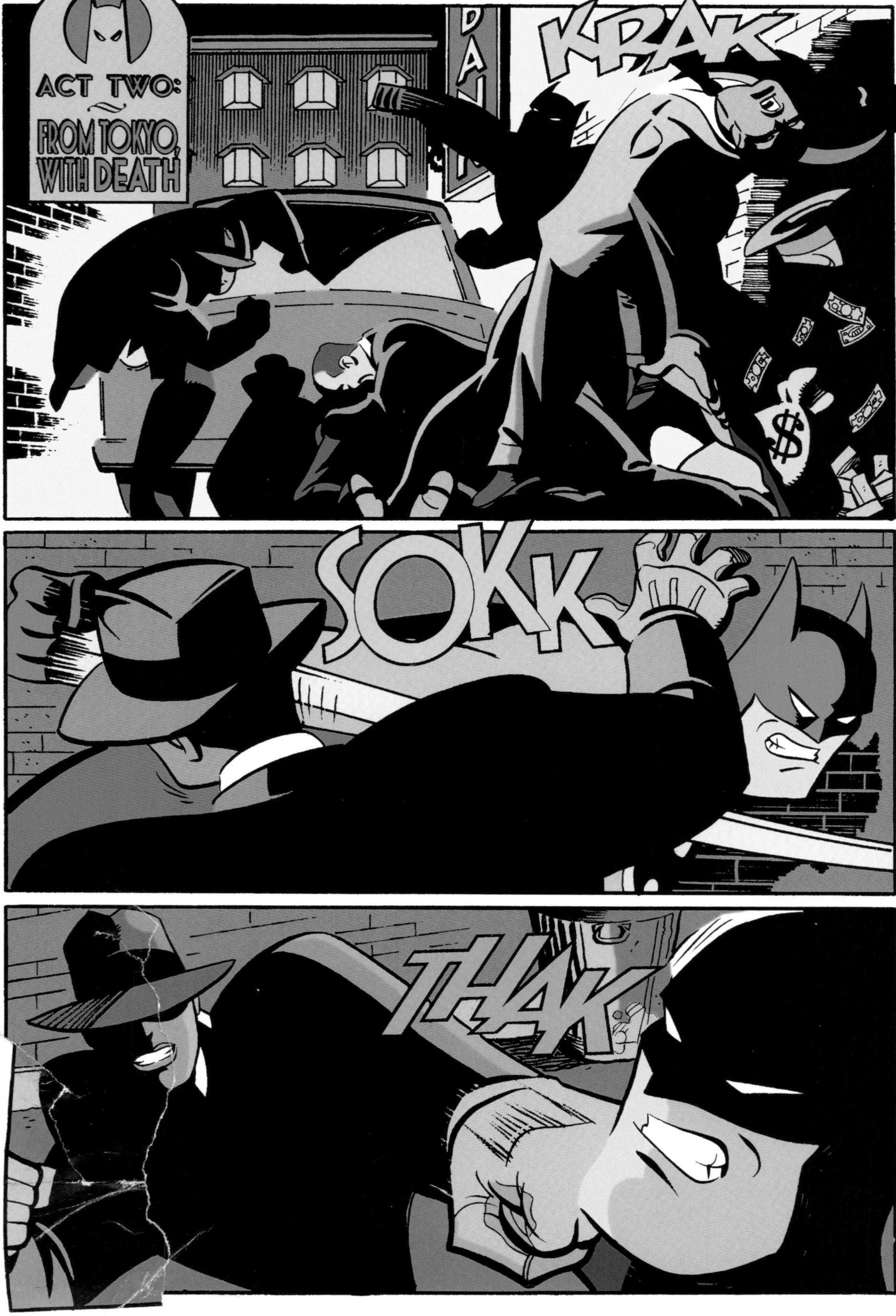

ACT TWO:
FROM TOKYO, WITH DEATH
KRAK
SOKK
THAK

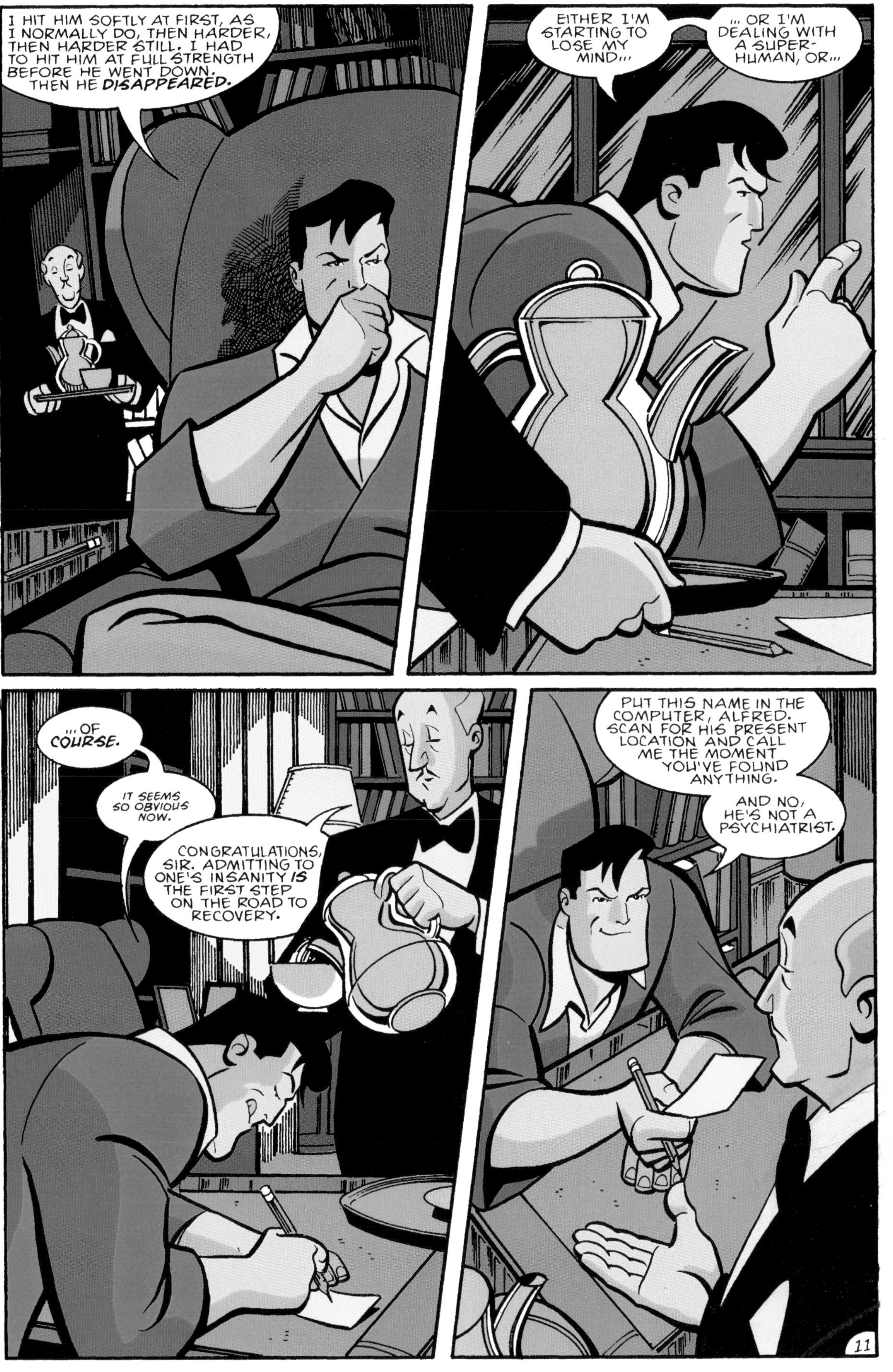

I HIT HIM SOFTLY AT FIRST, AS I NORMALLY DO, THEN HARDER, THEN HARDER STILL. I HAD TO HIT HIM AT FULL STRENGTH BEFORE HE WENT DOWN. THEN HE DISAPPEARED.
EITHER I'M STARTING TO LOSE MY MIND...
... OR I'M DEALING WITH A SUPER-HUMAN, OR...
...OF COURSE.
IT SEEMS SO OBVIOUS NOW.
CONGRATULATIONS, SIR. ADMITTING TO ONE'S INSANITY IS THE FIRST STEP ON THE ROAD TO RECOVERY.
PUT THIS NAME IN THE COMPUTER, ALFRED. SCAN FOR HIS PRESENT LOCATION AND CALL ME THE MOMENT YOU'VE FOUND ANYTHING.
AND NO, HE'S NOT A PSYCHIATRIST.
11

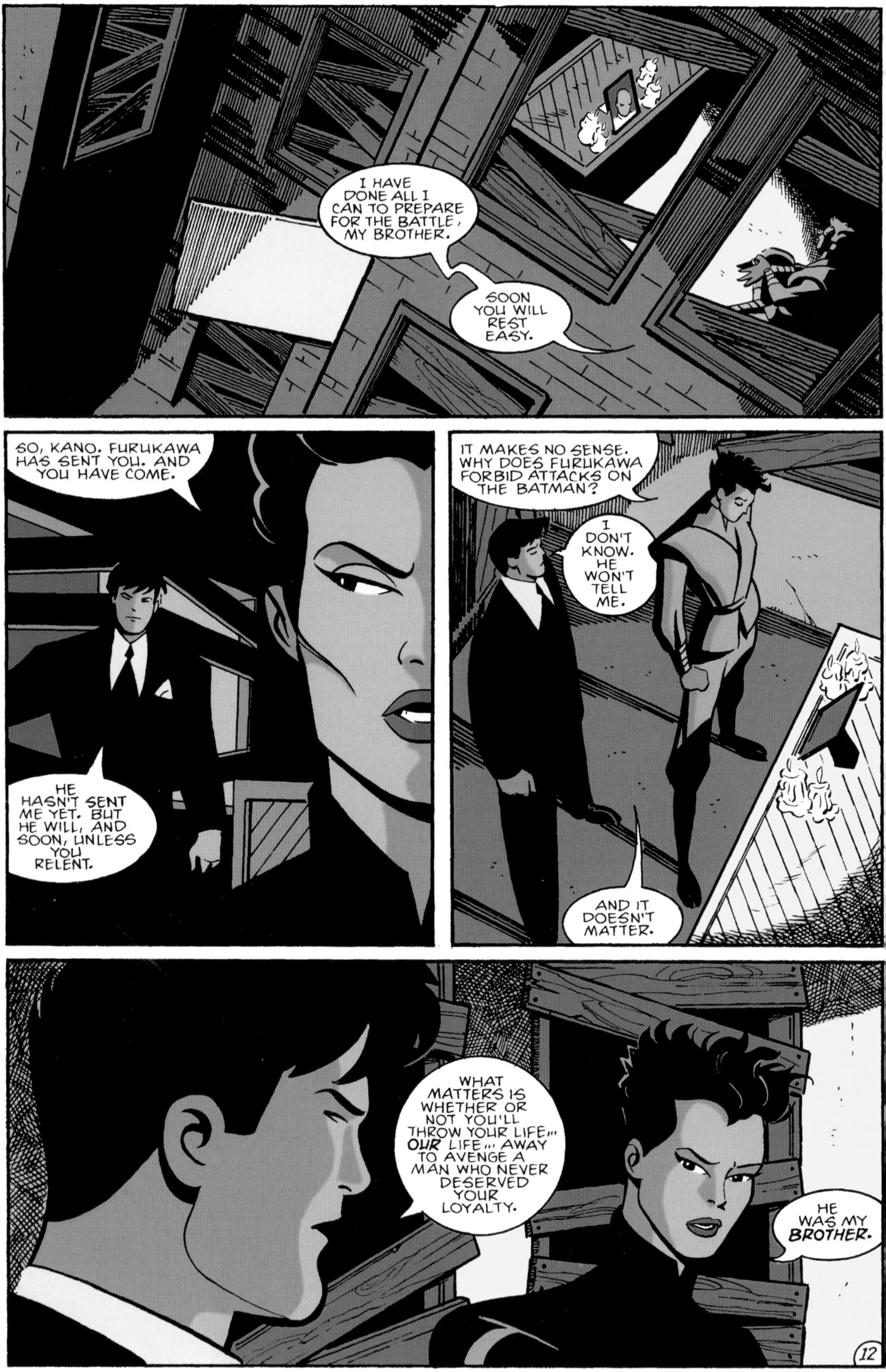
I HAVE DONE ALL I CAN TO PREPARE FOR THE BATTLE, MY BROTHER.
SOON YOU WILL REST EASY.
SO, KANO. FURUKAWA HAS SENT YOU. AND YOU HAVE COME.
HE HASN'T SENT ME YET. BUT HE WILL, AND SOON, UNLESS YOU RELENT.
IT MAKES NO SENSE. WHY DOES FURUKAWA FORBID ATTACKS ON THE BATMAN?
I DON'T KNOW. HE WON'T TELL ME.
AND IT DOESN'T MATTER.
WHAT MATTERS IS WHETHER OR NOT YOU'LL THROW YOUR LIFE... OUR LIFE... AWAY TO AVENGE A MAN WHO NEVER DESERVED YOUR LOYALTY.
HE WAS MY BROTHER.
12

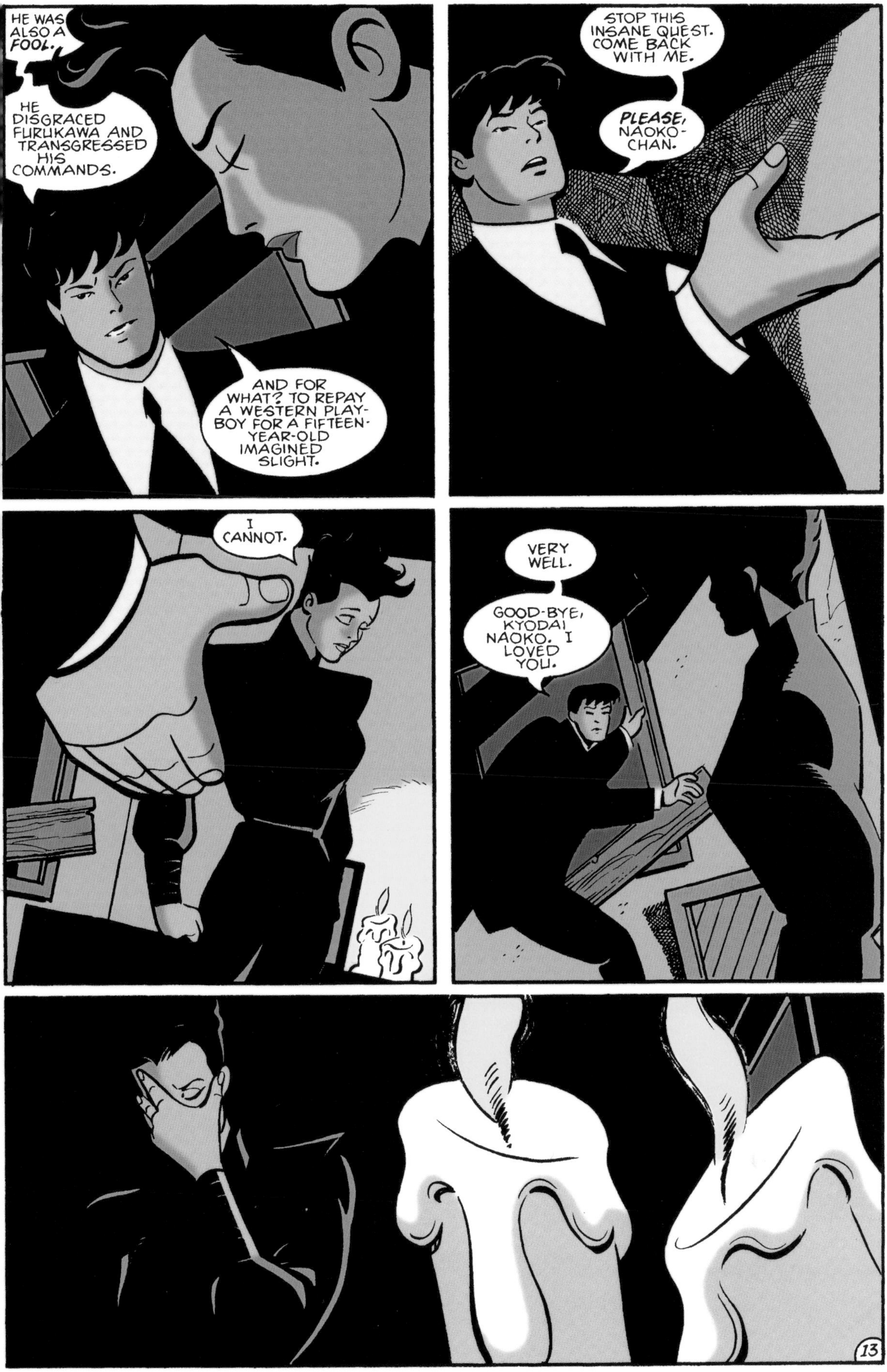
HE WAS ALSO A FOOL.
HE DISGRACED FURUKAWA AND TRANSGRESSED HIS COMMANDS.
AND FOR WHAT? TO REPAY A WESTERN PLAY-BOY FOR A FIFTEEN-YEAR-OLD IMAGINED SLIGHT.
STOP THIS INSANE QUEST. COME BACK WITH ME.
PLEASE, NAOKO-CHAN.
I CANNOT.
VERY WELL.
GOOD-BYE, KYODAI NAOKO. I LOVED YOU.
13

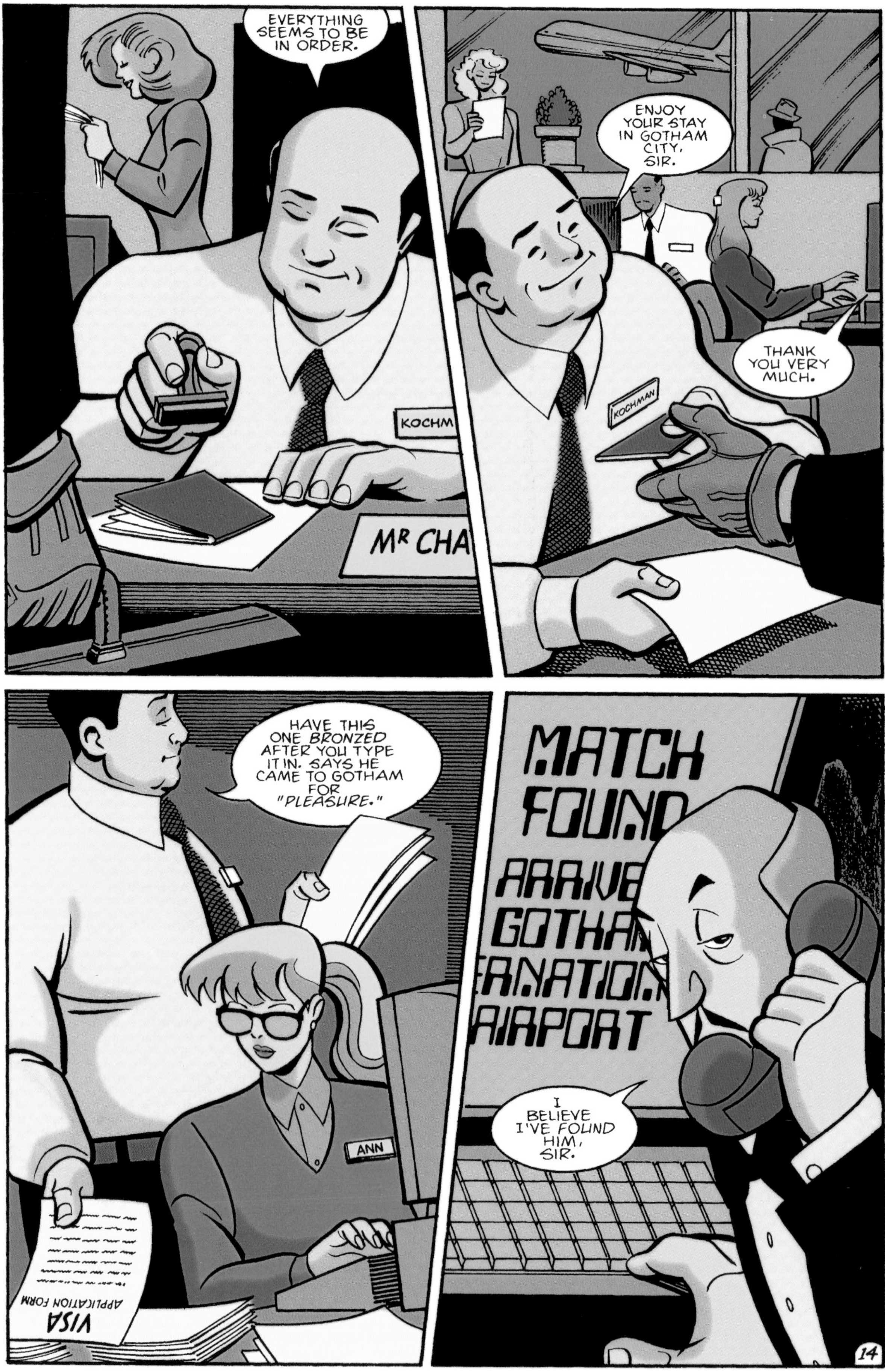
EVERYTHING SEEMS TO BE IN ORDER.
KOCHM
MR CHA
ENJOY YOUR STAY IN GOTHAM CITY, SIR.
THANK YOU VERY MUCH.
KOCHMAN
HAVE THIS ONE BRONZED AFTER YOU TYPE IT IN. SAYS HE CAME TO GOTHAM FOR "PLEASURE."
ANN
VISA
APPLICATION FORM
MATCH FOUND
ARRIVE
GOTHA
RNATIO
AIRPORT
I BELIEVE I'VE FOUND HIM, SIR.
14

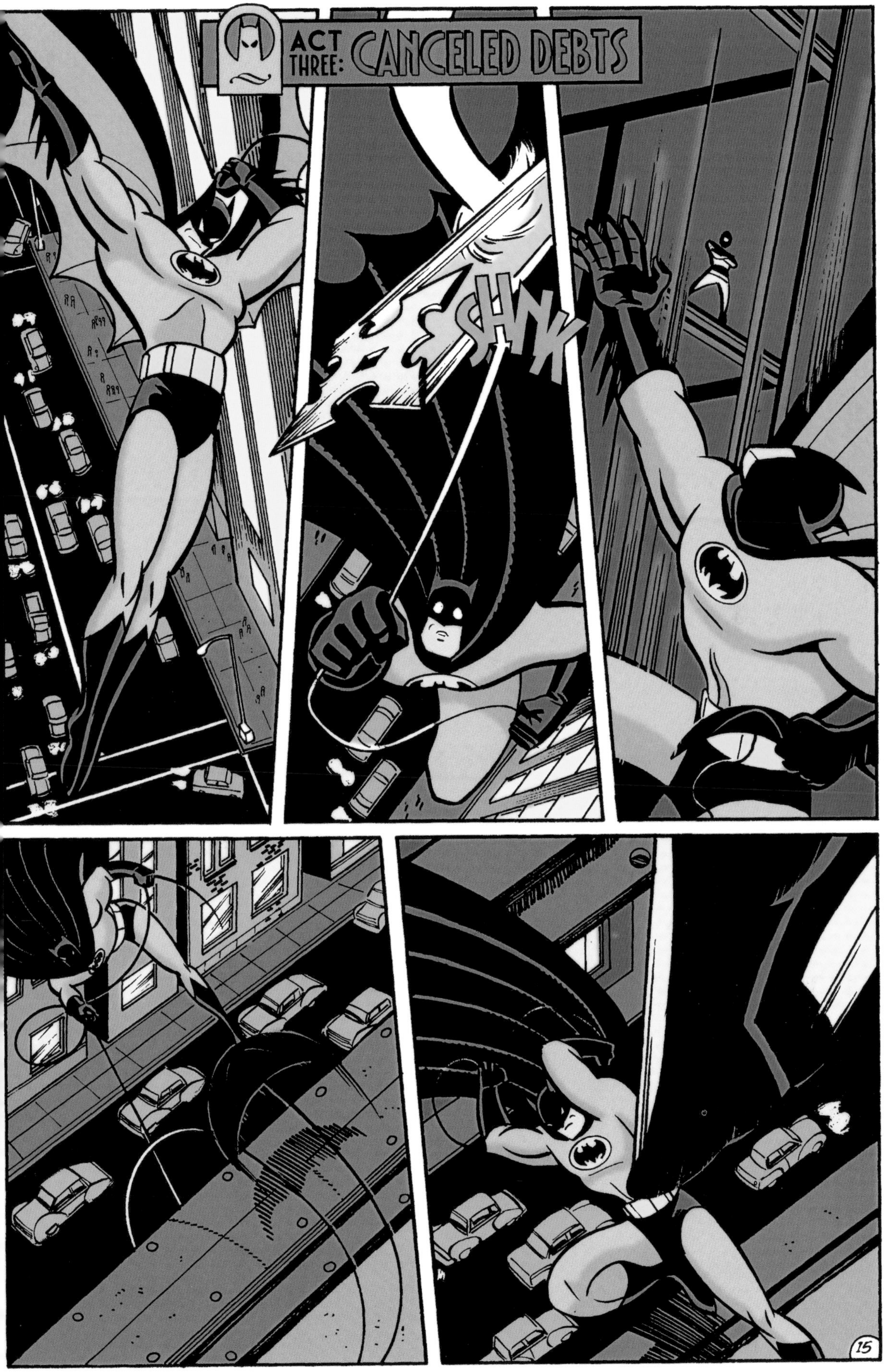

ACT THREE: CANCELED DEBTS
SHNK
15

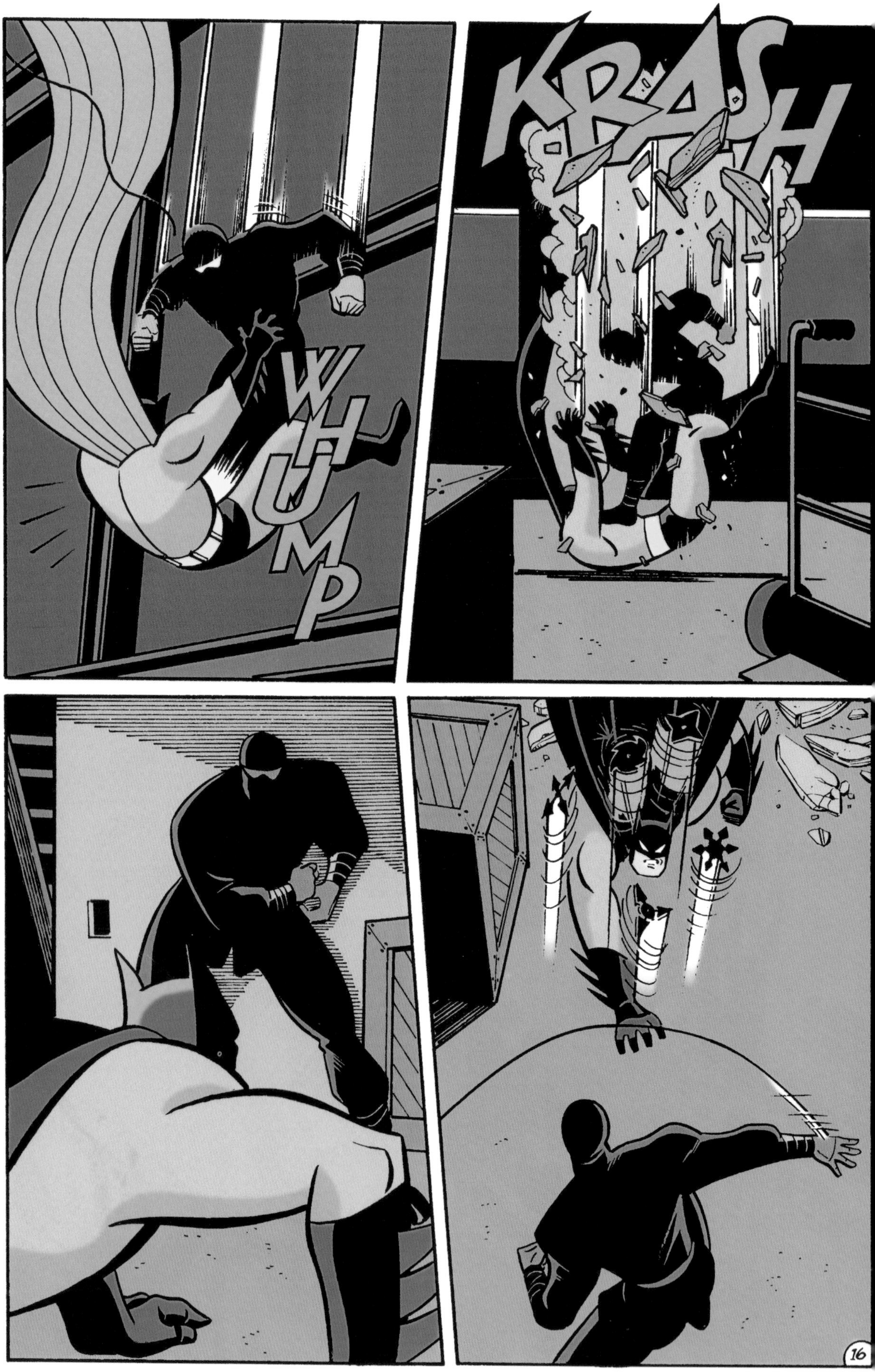
WHUMP
KRASH
16

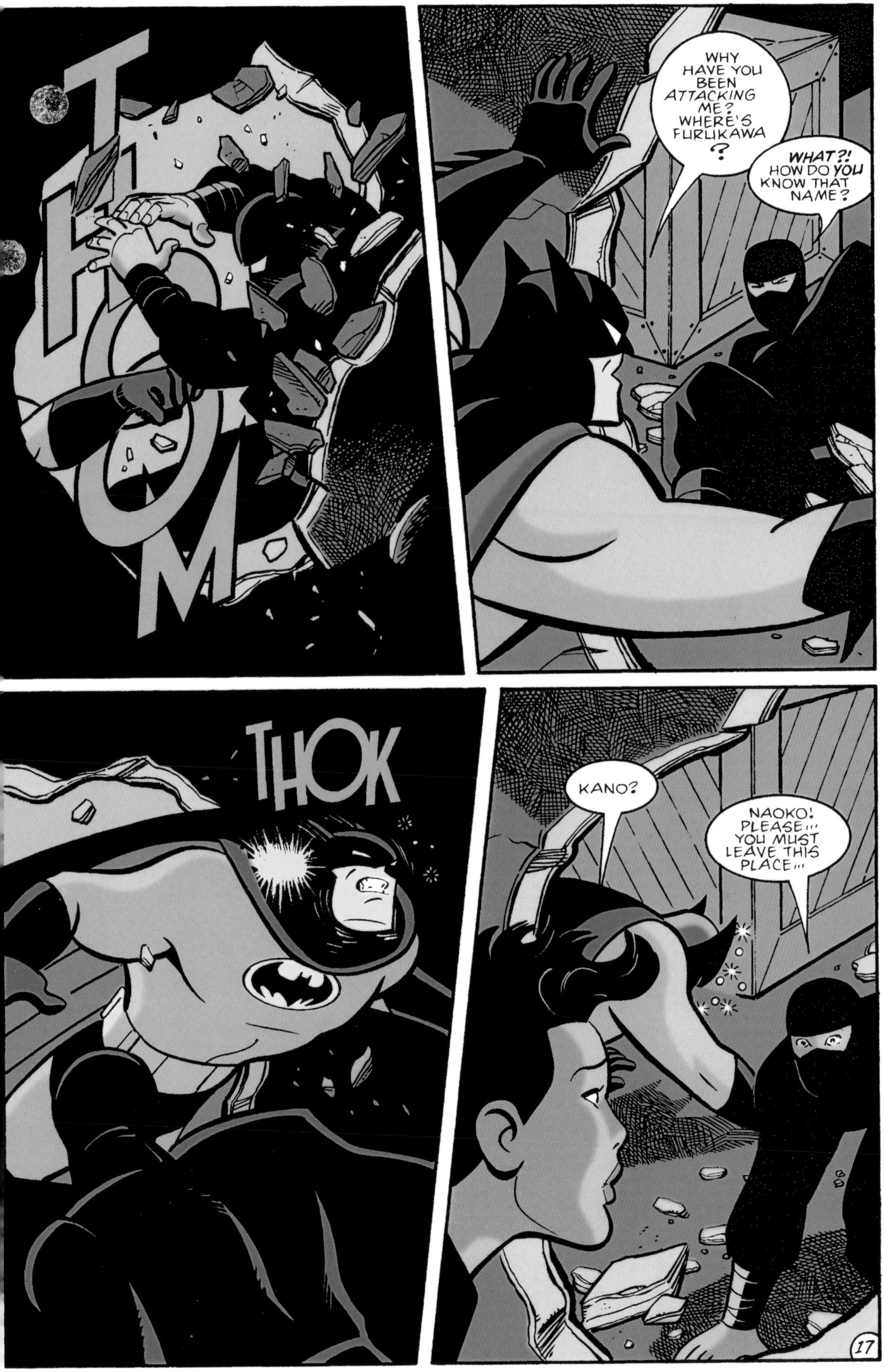
THOOM
WHY HAVE YOU BEEN ATTACKING ME? WHERE'S FURUKAWA?
WHAT?! HOW DO YOU KNOW THAT NAME?
THOK
KANO?
NAOKO! PLEASE... YOU MUST LEAVE THIS PLACE...
17

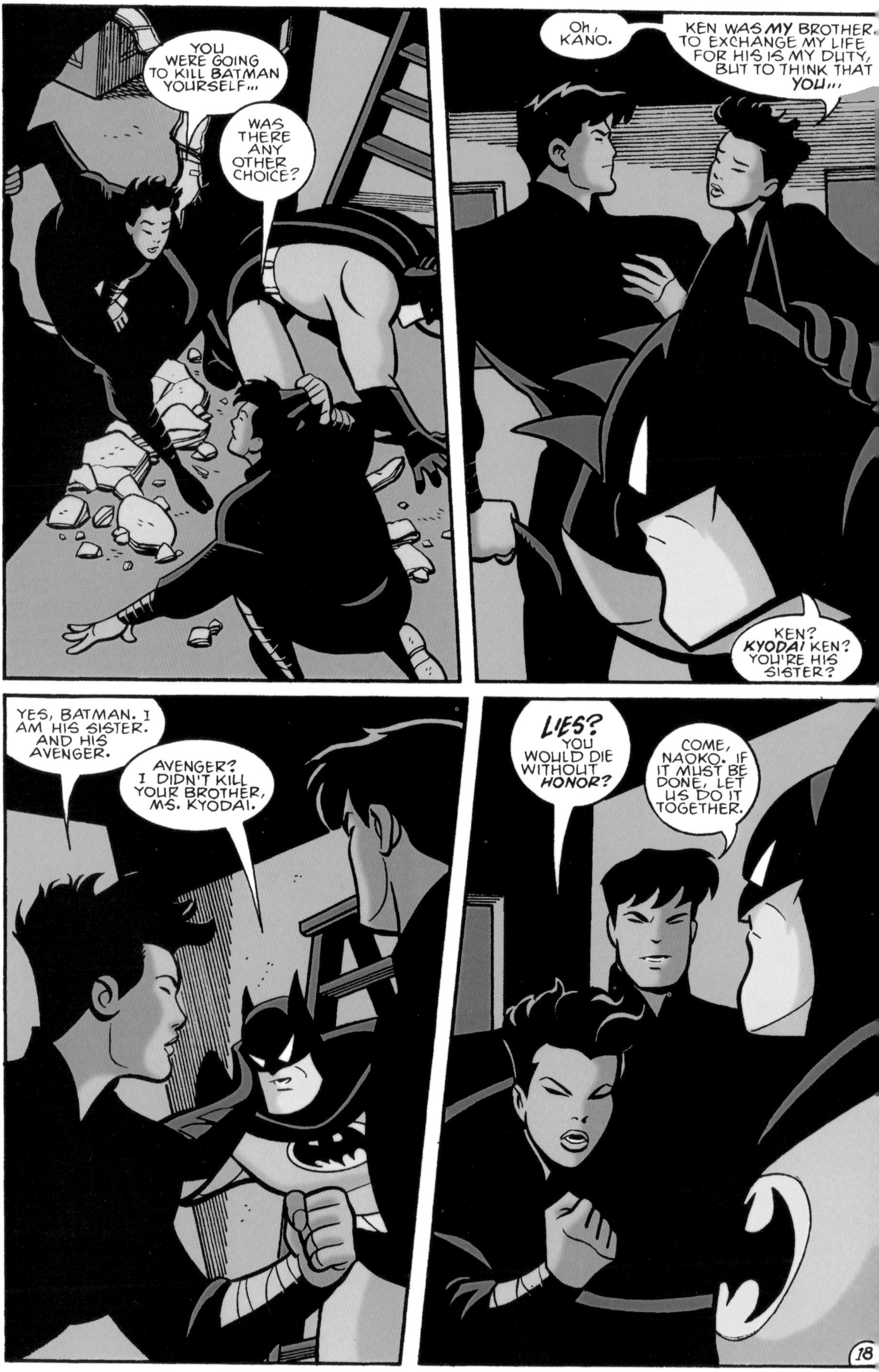

YOU WERE GOING TO KILL BATMAN YOURSELF...
WAS THERE ANY OTHER CHOICE?
Oh, KANO.
KEN WAS MY BROTHER. TO EXCHANGE MY LIFE FOR HIS IS MY DUTY, BUT TO THINK THAT YOU...
KEN? KYODAI KEN? YOU'RE HIS SISTER?
YES, BATMAN. I AM HIS SISTER. AND HIS AVENGER.
AVENGER? I DIDN'T KILL YOUR BROTHER, MS. KYODAI.
LIES? YOU WOULD DIE WITHOUT HONOR?
COME, NAOKO. IF IT MUST BE DONE, LET US DO IT TOGETHER.
18

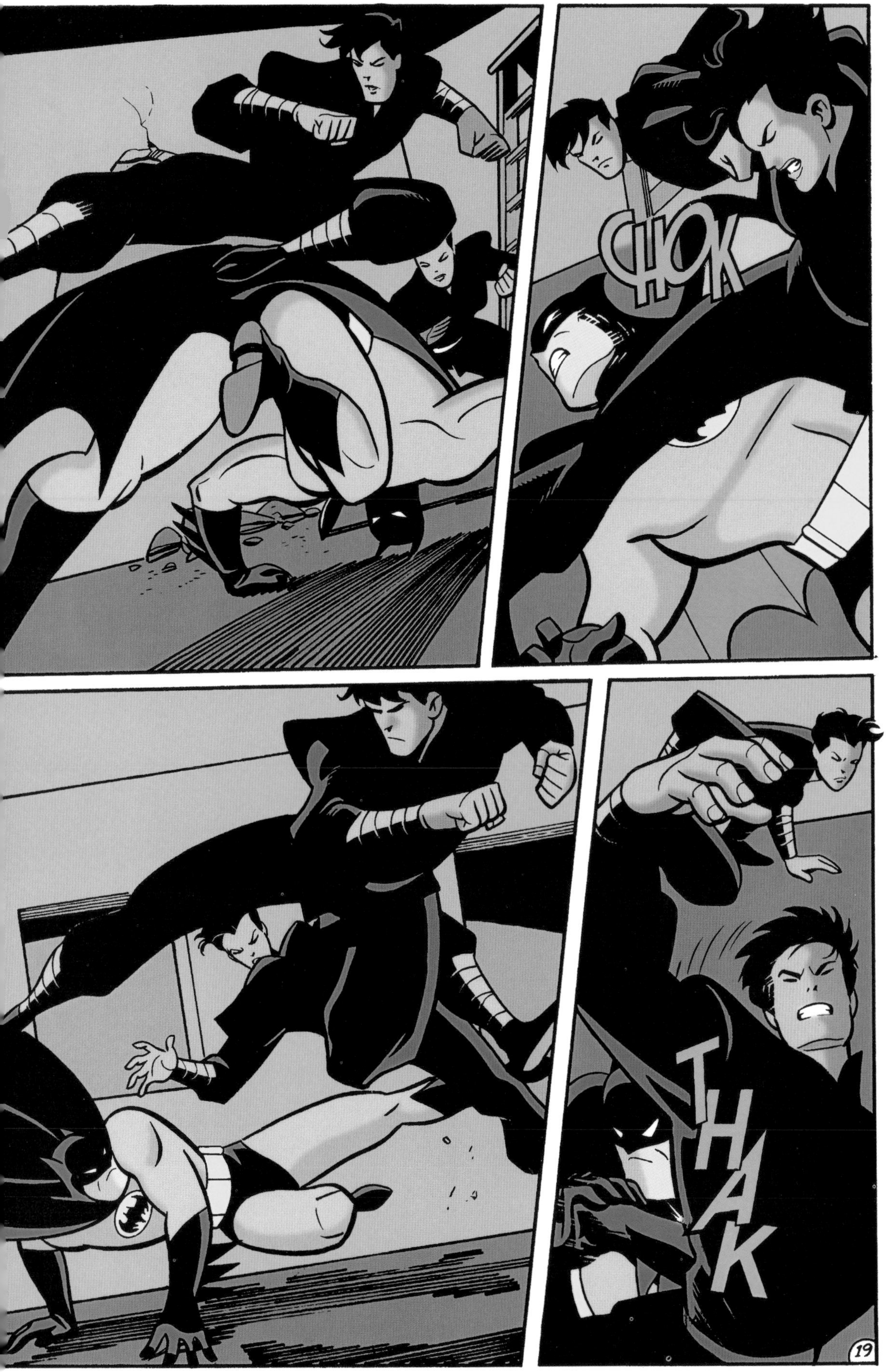
CHOK
THAK
19

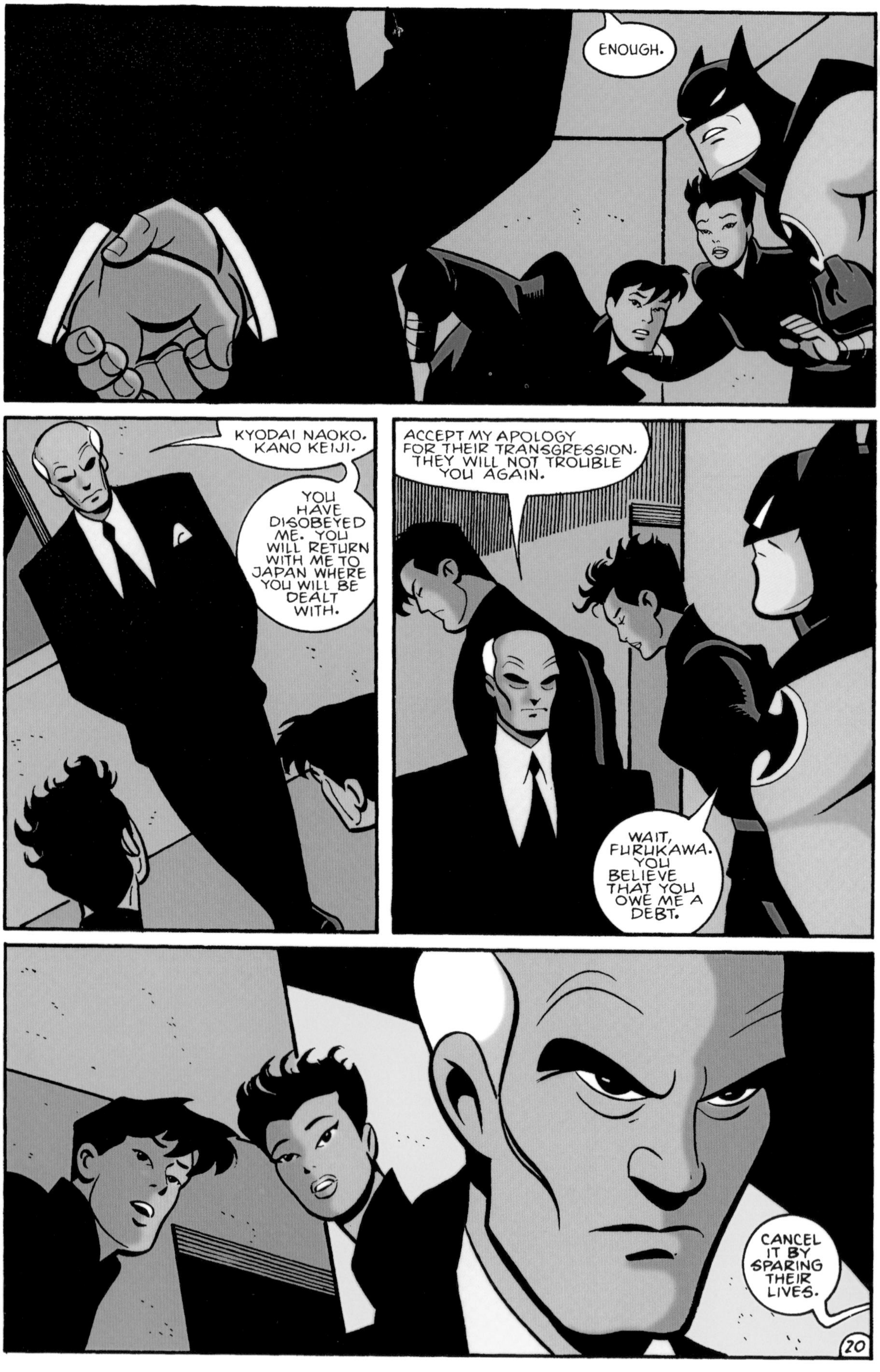
ENOUGH.
KYODAI NAOKO. KANO KEIJI.
YOU HAVE DISOBEYED ME. YOU WILL RETURN WITH ME TO JAPAN WHERE YOU WILL BE DEALT WITH.
ACCEPT MY APOLOGY FOR THEIR TRANSGRESSION. THEY WILL NOT TROUBLE YOU AGAIN.
WAIT, FURUKAWA. YOU BELIEVE THAT YOU OWE ME A DEBT.
CANCEL IT BY SPARING THEIR LIVES.
20

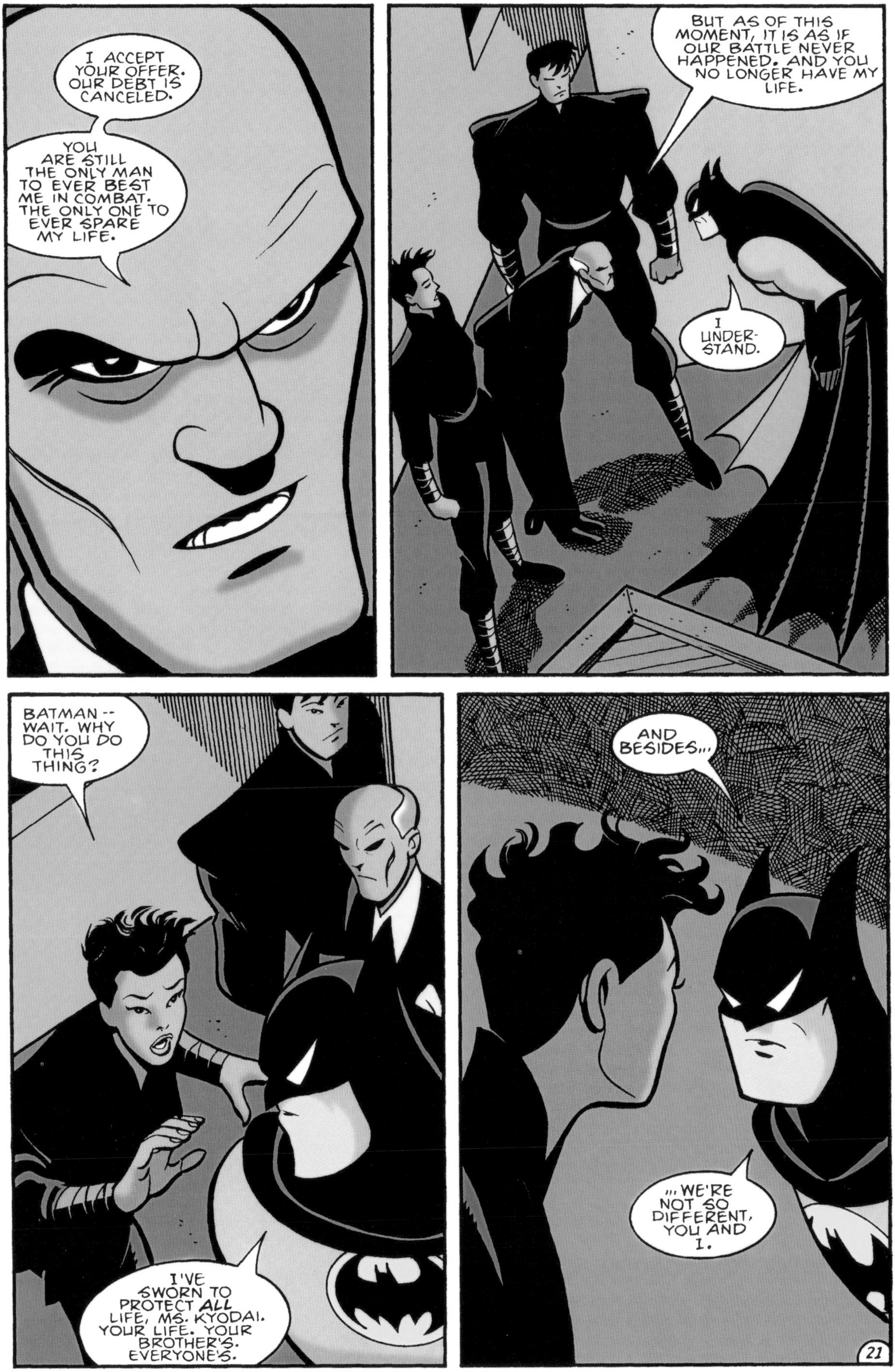
I ACCEPT YOUR OFFER. OUR DEBT IS CANCELED.
YOU ARE STILL THE ONLY MAN TO EVER BEST ME IN COMBAT. THE ONLY ONE TO EVER SPARE MY LIFE.
BUT AS OF THIS MOMENT, IT IS AS IF OUR BATTLE NEVER HAPPENED. AND YOU NO LONGER HAVE MY LIFE.
I UNDER-STAND.
BATMAN -- WAIT. WHY DO YOU DO THIS THING?
I'VE SWORN TO PROTECT ALL LIFE, MS. KYODAI. YOUR LIFE. YOUR BROTHER'S. EVERYONE'S.
AND BESIDES...
...WE'RE NOT SO DIFFERENT, YOU AND I.
21

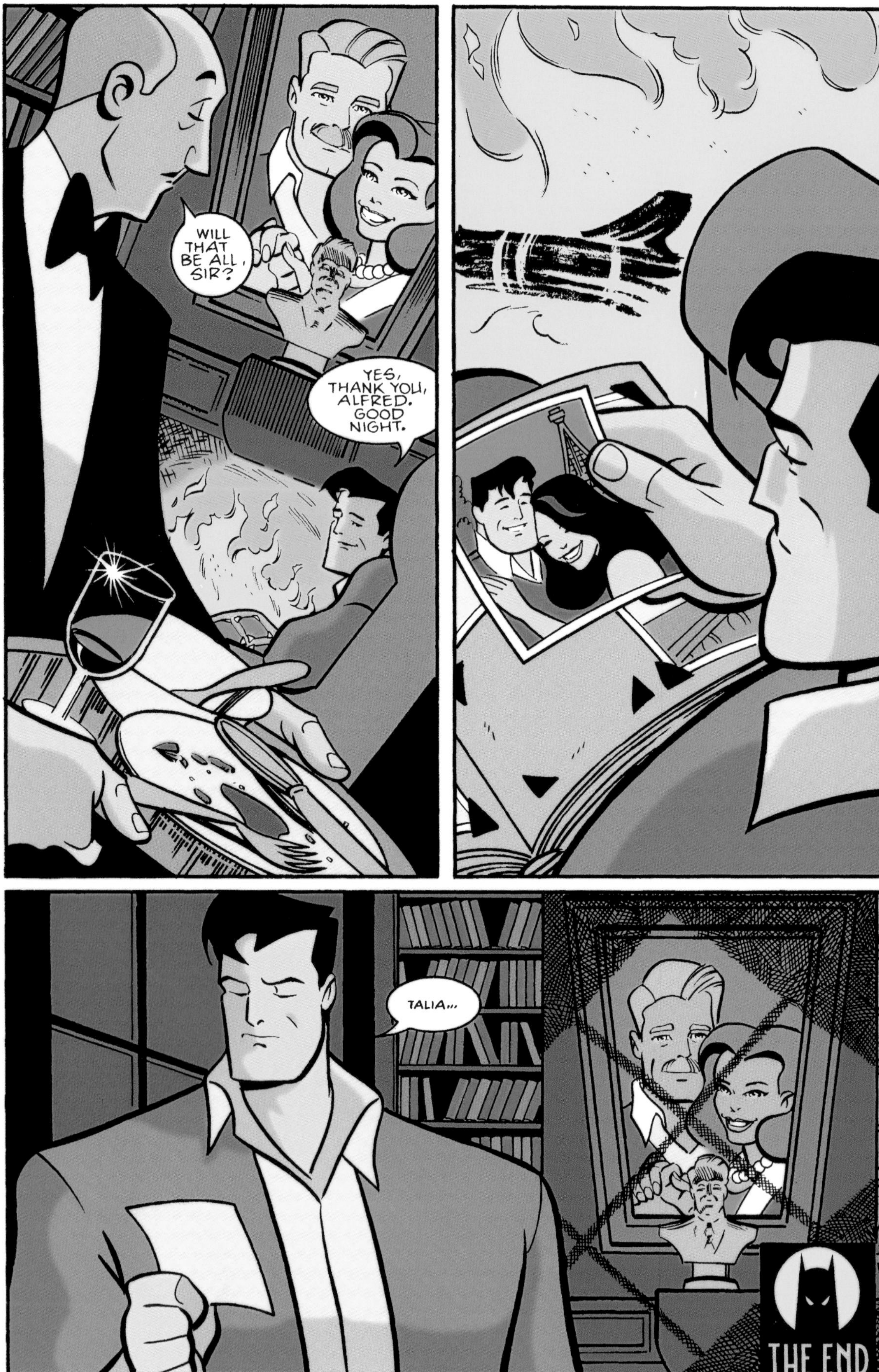
WILL THAT BE ALL, SIR?
YES, THANK YOU, ALFRED. GOOD NIGHT.
TALIA...
THE END

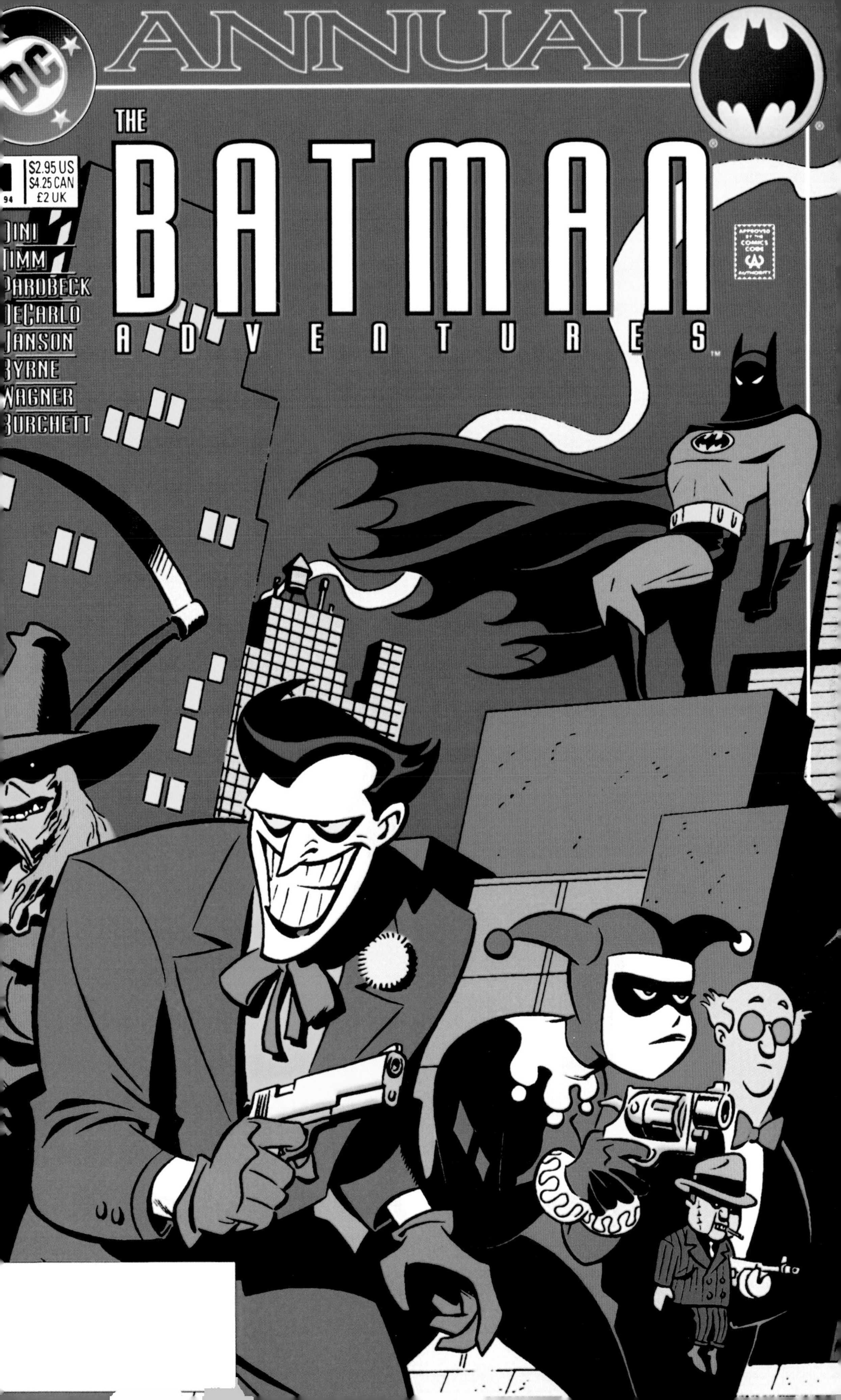

ANNUAL
THE BATMAN ADVENTURES
$2.95 US
$4.25 CAN
£2 UK
94
DINI
TIMM
PAROBECK
DECARLO
JANSON
BYRNE
WAGNER
BURCHETT
APPROVED BY THE COMICS CODE AUTHORITY

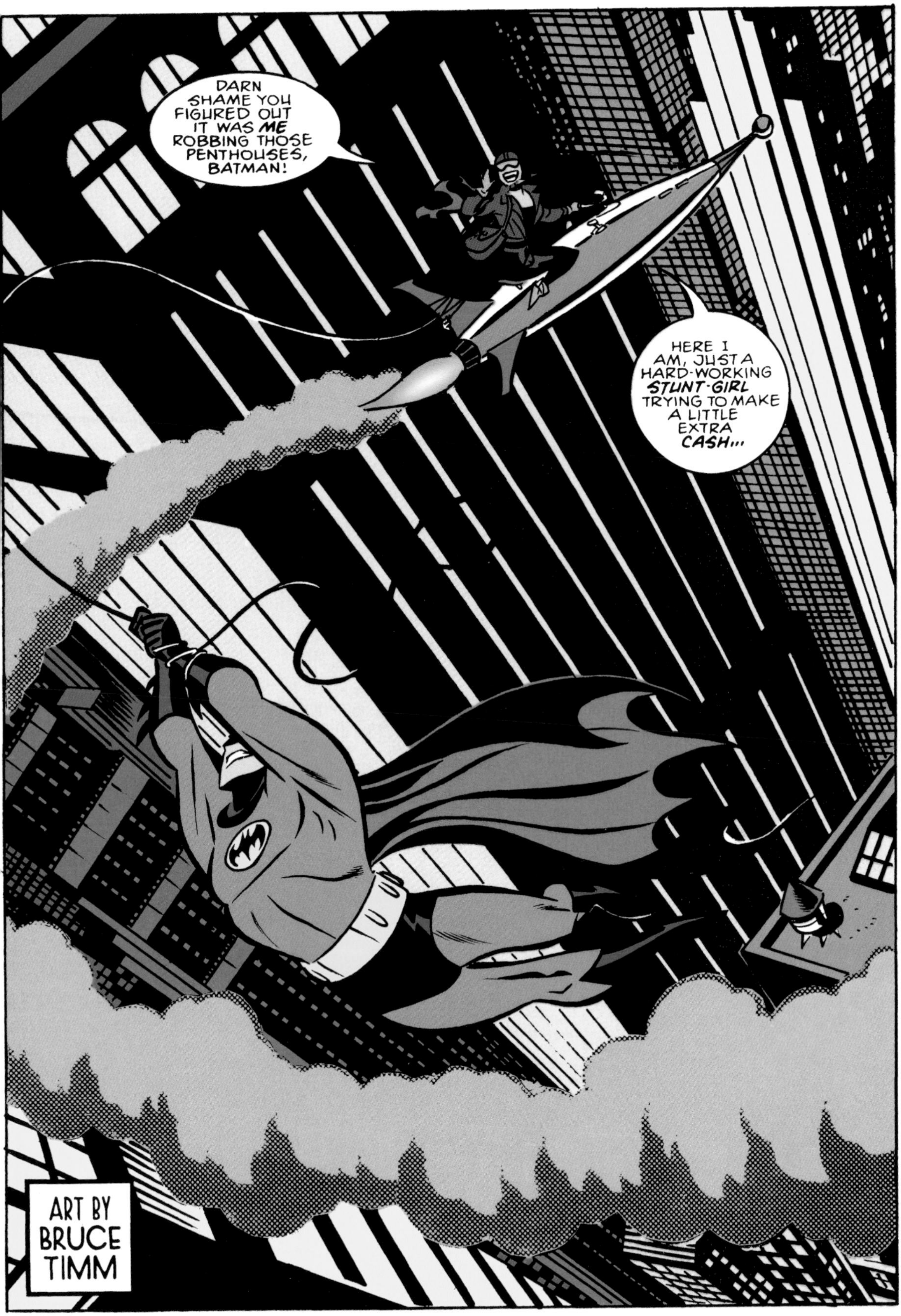
DARN SHAME YOU FIGURED OUT IT WAS ME ROBBING THOSE PENTHOUSES, BATMAN!
HERE I AM, JUST A HARD-WORKING STUNT-GIRL TRYING TO MAKE A LITTLE EXTRA CASH...
ART BY BRUCE TIMM

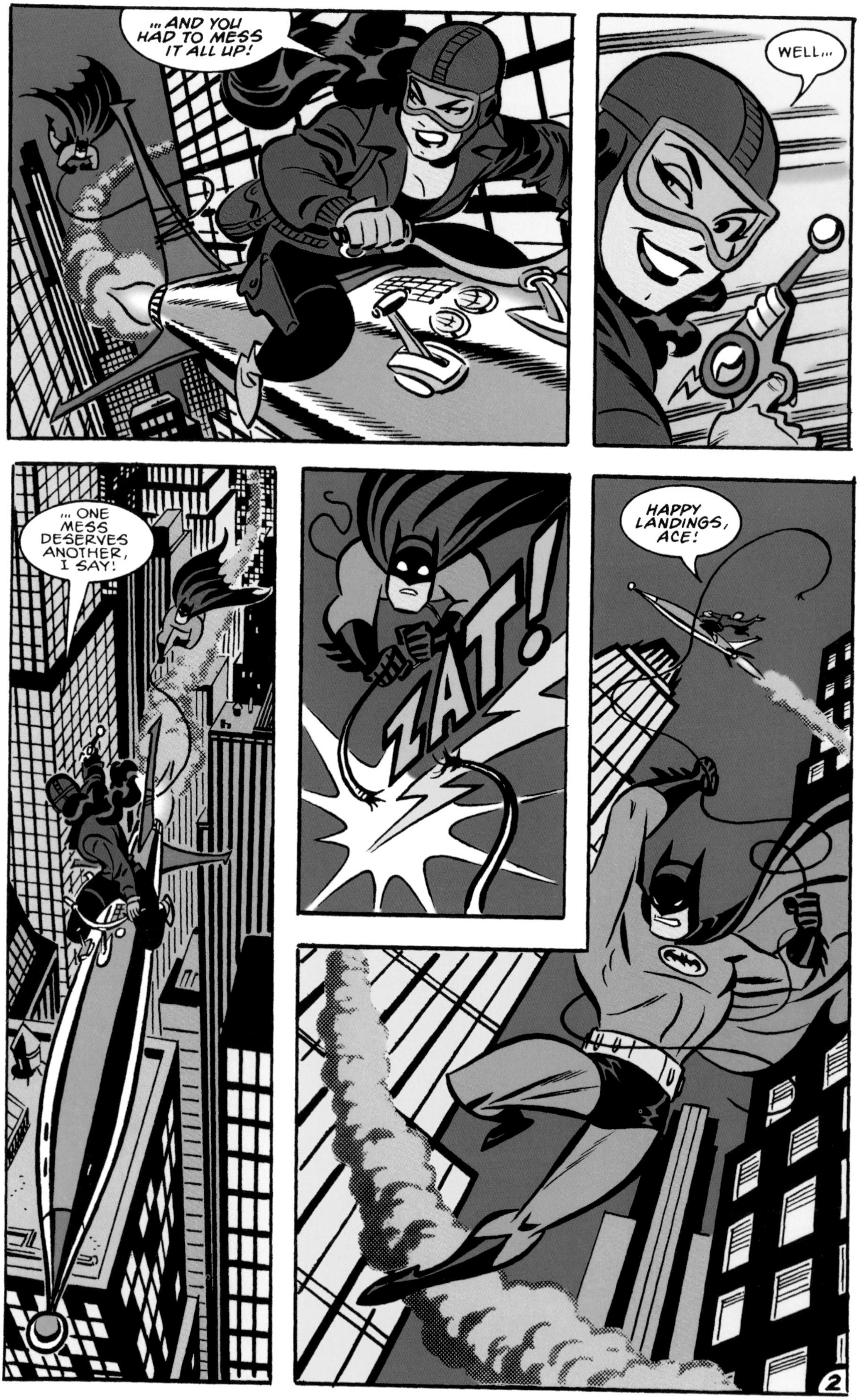
...AND YOU HAD TO MESS IT ALL UP!
WELL...
...ONE MESS DESERVES ANOTHER, I SAY!
ZAT!
HAPPY LANDINGS, ACE!
2

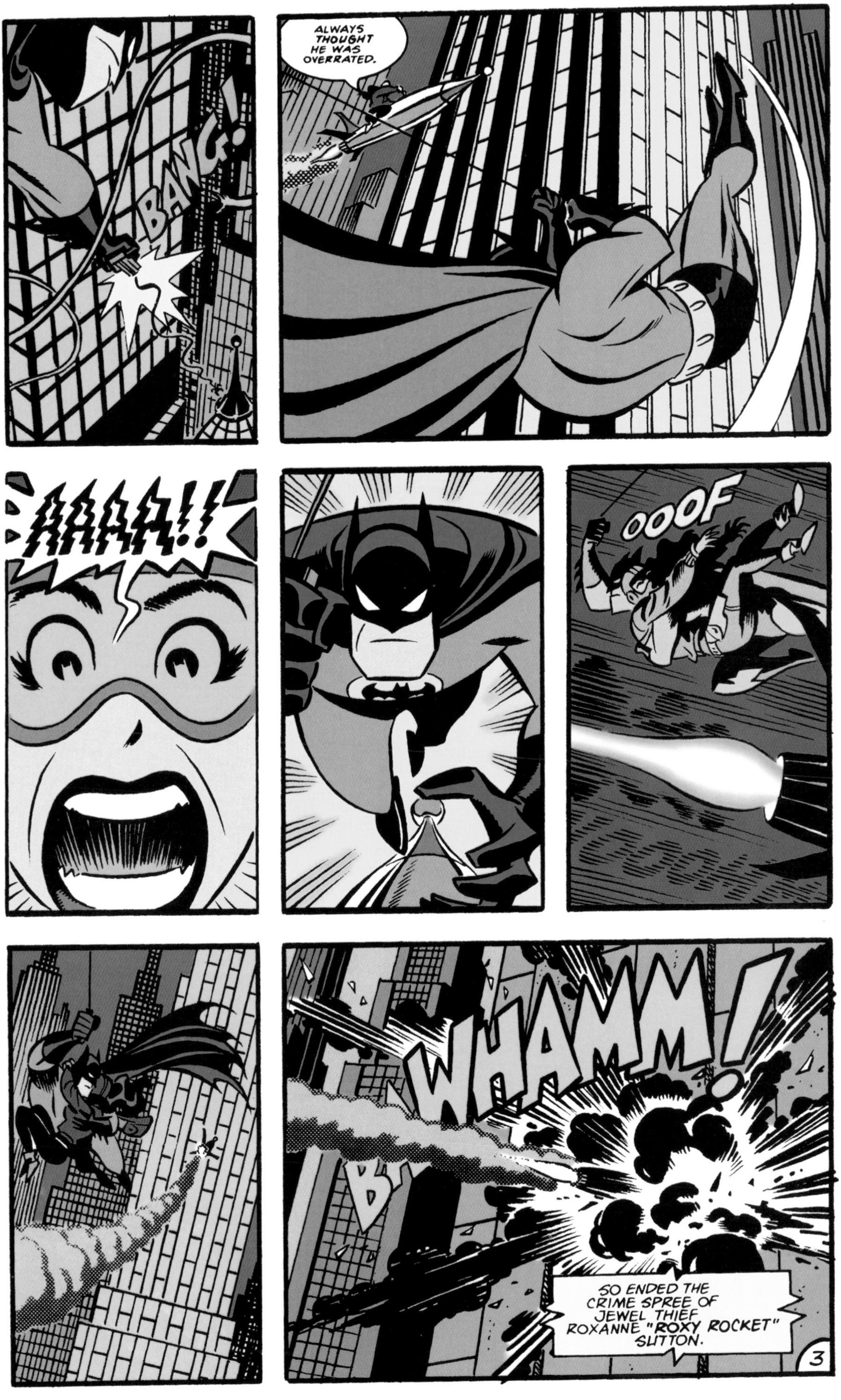

BANG!
ALWAYS THOUGHT HE WAS OVERRATED.
AAAA!!
OOOF
WHAMM!
SO ENDED THE CRIME SPREE OF JEWEL THIEF ROXANNE "ROXY ROCKET" SUTTON.
3

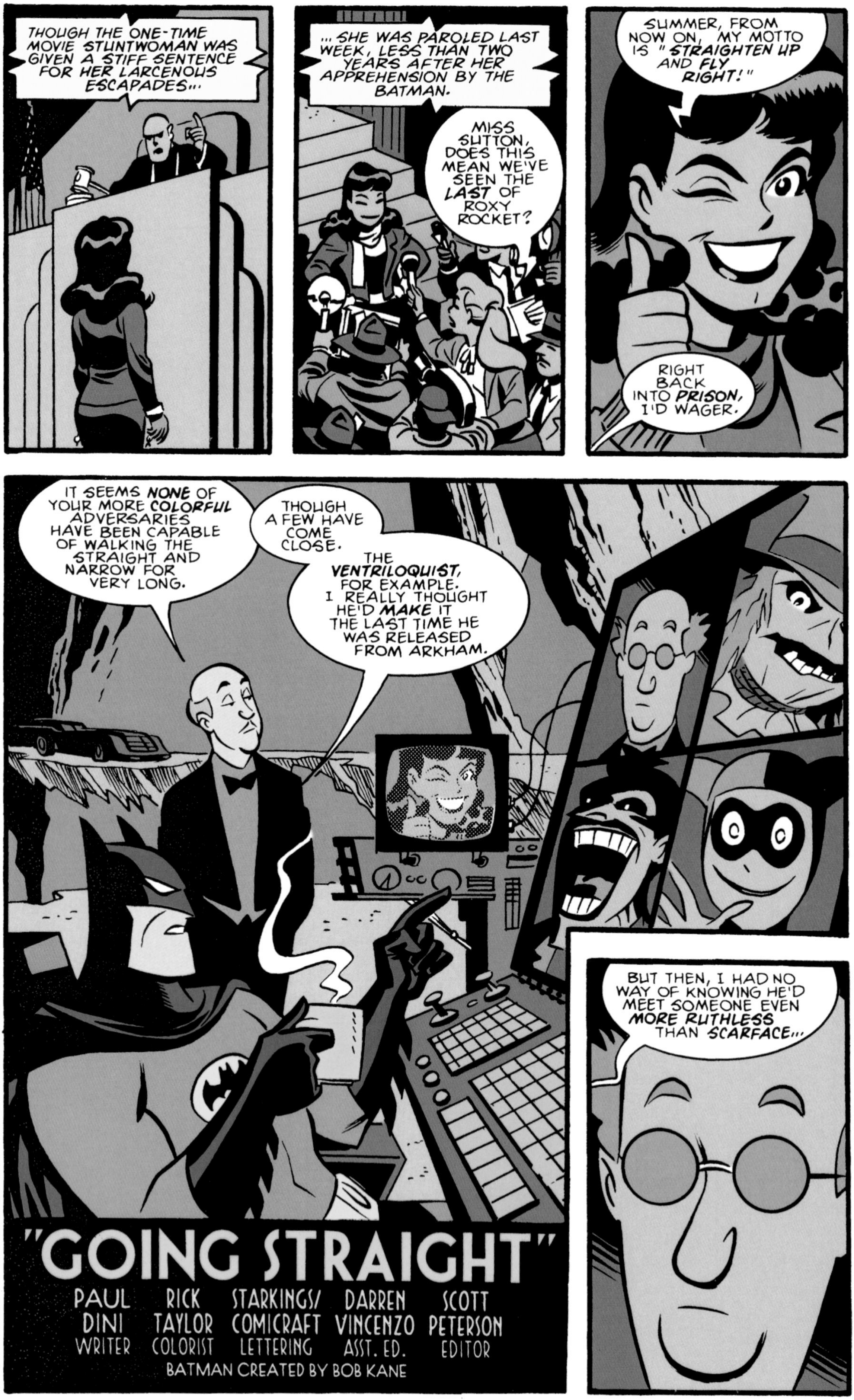

THOUGH THE ONE-TIME MOVIE STUNTWOMAN WAS GIVEN A STIFF SENTENCE FOR HER LARCENOUS ESCAPADES...
...SHE WAS PAROLED LAST WEEK, LESS THAN TWO YEARS AFTER HER APPREHENSION BY THE BATMAN.
MISS SUTTON, DOES THIS MEAN WE'VE SEEN THE LAST OF ROXY ROCKET?
SUMMER, FROM NOW ON, MY MOTTO IS "STRAIGHTEN UP AND FLY RIGHT!"
RIGHT BACK INTO PRISON, I'D WAGER.
IT SEEMS NONE OF YOUR MORE COLORFUL ADVERSARIES HAVE BEEN CAPABLE OF WALKING THE STRAIGHT AND NARROW FOR VERY LONG.
THOUGH A FEW HAVE COME CLOSE.
THE VENTRILOQUIST, FOR EXAMPLE. I REALLY THOUGHT HE'D MAKE IT THE LAST TIME HE WAS RELEASED FROM ARKHAM.
BUT THEN, I HAD NO WAY OF KNOWING HE'D MEET SOMEONE EVEN MORE RUTHLESS THAN SCARFACE...
"GOING STRAIGHT"
PAUL DINI WRITER
RICK TAYLOR COLORIST
STARKINGS/ COMICRAFT LETTERING
DARREN VINCENZO ASST. ED.
SCOTT PETERSON EDITOR
BATMAN CREATED BY BOB KANE

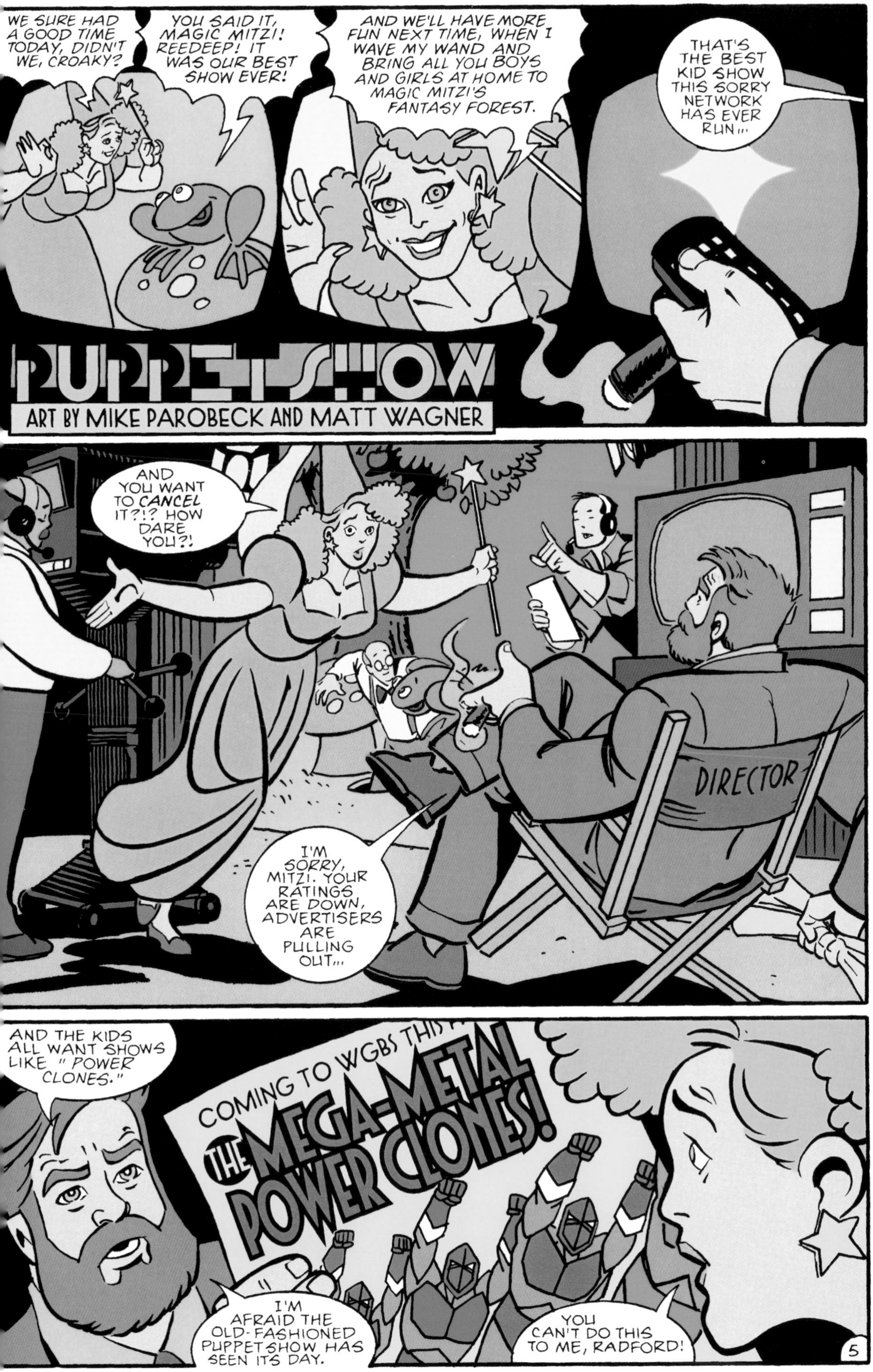
WE SURE HAD A GOOD TIME TODAY, DIDN'T WE, CROAKY?
YOU SAID IT, MAGIC MITZI! REEDEEP! IT WAS OUR BEST SHOW EVER!
AND WE'LL HAVE MORE FUN NEXT TIME, WHEN I WAVE MY WAND AND BRING ALL YOU BOYS AND GIRLS AT HOME TO MAGIC MITZI'S FANTASY FOREST.
THAT'S THE BEST KID SHOW THIS SORRY NETWORK HAS EVER RUN...
PUPPET SHOW
ART BY MIKE PAROBECK AND MATT WAGNER
AND YOU WANT TO CANCEL IT?!? HOW DARE YOU?!
DIRECTOR
I'M SORRY, MITZI. YOUR RATINGS ARE DOWN, ADVERTISERS ARE PULLING OUT...
AND THE KIDS ALL WANT SHOWS LIKE "POWER CLONES."
COMING TO WGBS THIS
THE MEGA-METAL POWER CLONES!
I'M AFRAID THE OLD-FASHIONED PUPPET SHOW HAS SEEN ITS DAY.
YOU CAN'T DO THIS TO ME, RADFORD!
5

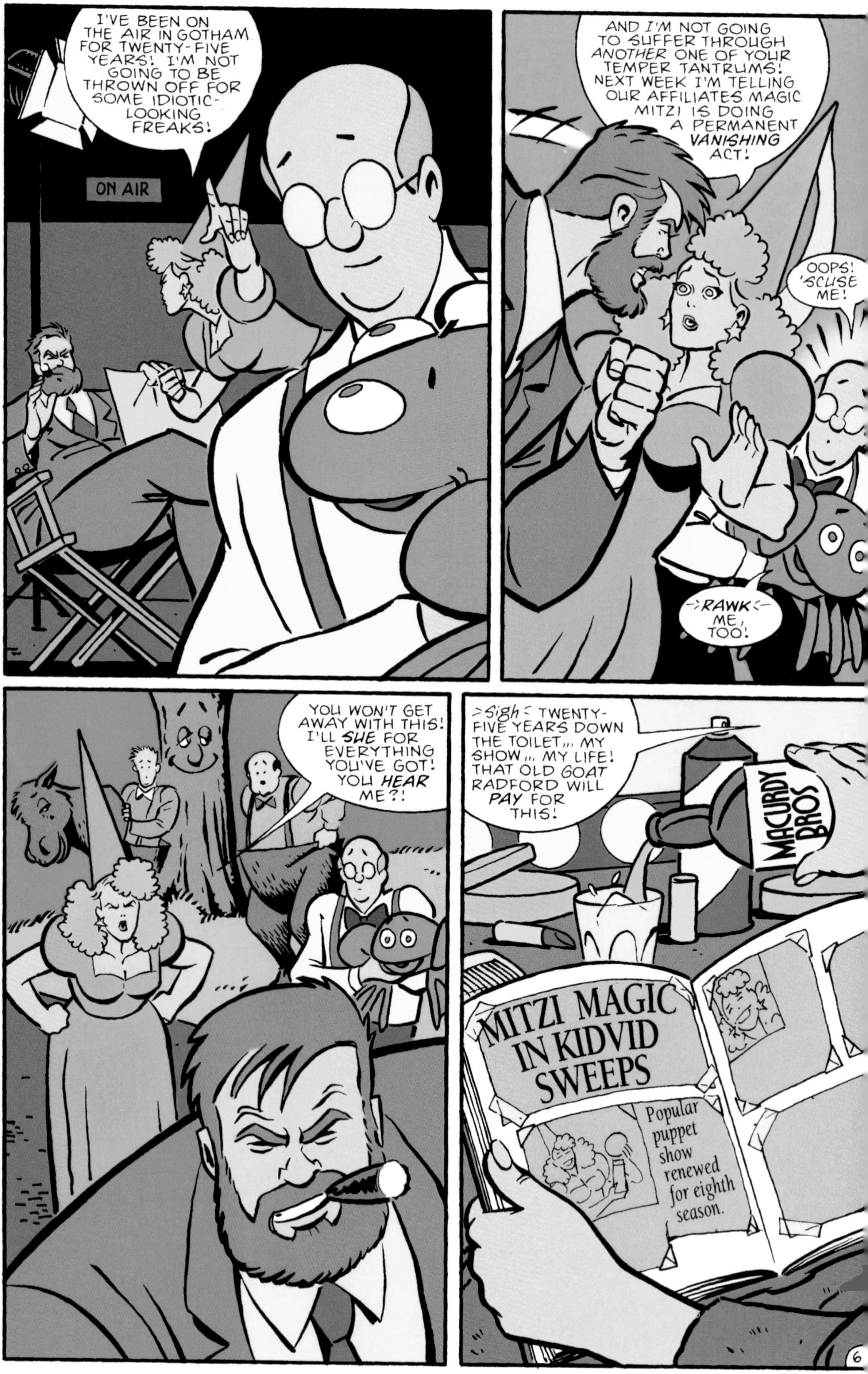
I'VE BEEN ON THE AIR IN GOTHAM FOR TWENTY-FIVE YEARS! I'M NOT GOING TO BE THROWN OFF FOR SOME IDIOTIC-LOOKING FREAKS!
ON AIR
AND I'M NOT GOING TO SUFFER THROUGH ANOTHER ONE OF YOUR TEMPER TANTRUMS! NEXT WEEK I'M TELLING OUR AFFILIATES MAGIC MITZI IS DOING A PERMANENT VANISHING ACT!
OOPS! 'SCUSE ME!
RAWK ME, TOO!
YOU WON'T GET AWAY WITH THIS! I'LL SUE FOR EVERYTHING YOU'VE GOT! YOU HEAR ME?!
SIGH TWENTY-FIVE YEARS DOWN THE TOILET... MY SHOW... MY LIFE! THAT OLD GOAT RADFORD WILL PAY FOR THIS!
MACURDY BROS
MITZI MAGIC IN KIDVID SWEEPS
Popular puppet show renewed for eighth season.
6

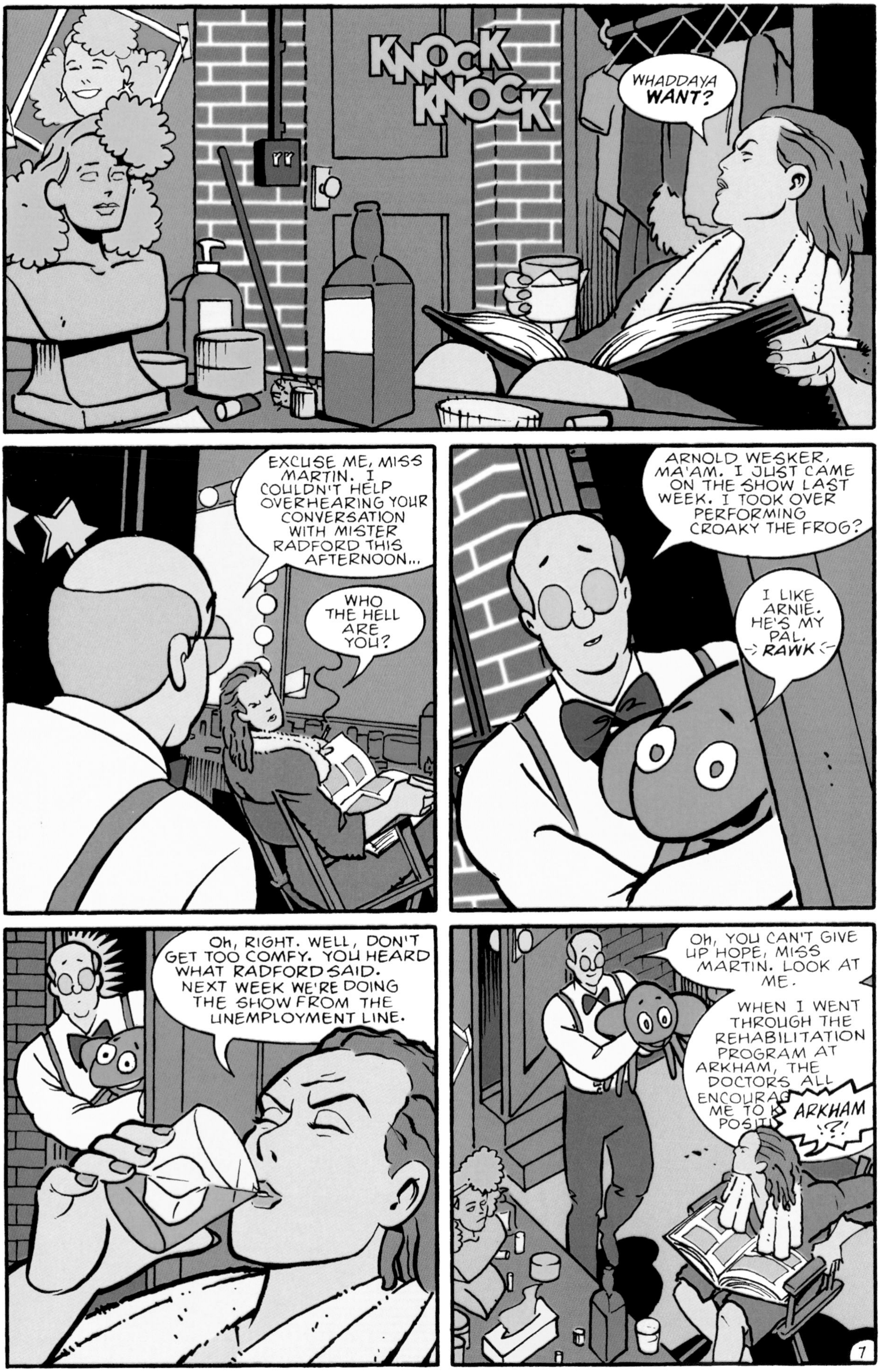
KNOCK KNOCK
WHADDAYA WANT?
EXCUSE ME, MISS MARTIN. I COULDN'T HELP OVERHEARING YOUR CONVERSATION WITH MISTER RADFORD THIS AFTERNOON...
WHO THE HELL ARE YOU?
ARNOLD WESKER, MA'AM. I JUST CAME ON THE SHOW LAST WEEK. I TOOK OVER PERFORMING CROAKY THE FROG?
I LIKE ARNIE. HE'S MY PAL. RAWK
OH, RIGHT. WELL, DON'T GET TOO COMFY. YOU HEARD WHAT RADFORD SAID. NEXT WEEK WE'RE DOING THE SHOW FROM THE UNEMPLOYMENT LINE.
OH, YOU CAN'T GIVE UP HOPE, MISS MARTIN. LOOK AT ME.
WHEN I WENT THROUGH THE REHABILITATION PROGRAM AT ARKHAM, THE DOCTORS ALL
ARKHAM !?!
7

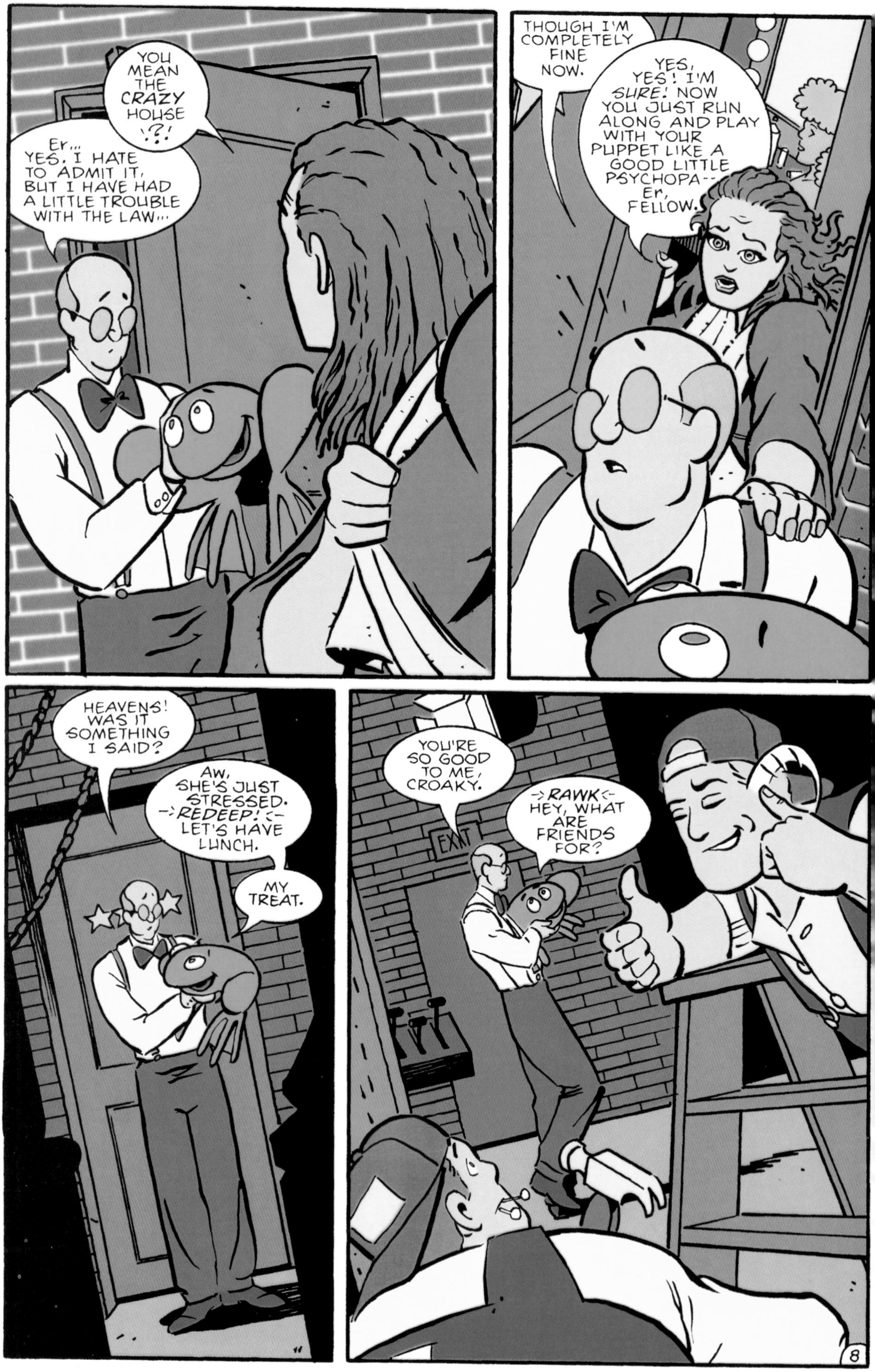
YOU MEAN THE CRAZY HOUSE !?!
Er... YES. I HATE TO ADMIT IT, BUT I HAVE HAD A LITTLE TROUBLE WITH THE LAW...
THOUGH I'M COMPLETELY FINE NOW.
YES, YES! I'M SURE! NOW YOU JUST RUN ALONG AND PLAY WITH YOUR PUPPET LIKE A GOOD LITTLE PSYCHOPA-- Er, FELLOW.
HEAVENS! WAS IT SOMETHING I SAID?
AW, SHE'S JUST STRESSED. ->REDEEP!<- LET'S HAVE LUNCH.
MY TREAT.
YOU'RE SO GOOD TO ME, CROAKY.
->RAWK<- HEY, WHAT ARE FRIENDS FOR?
EXIT
8

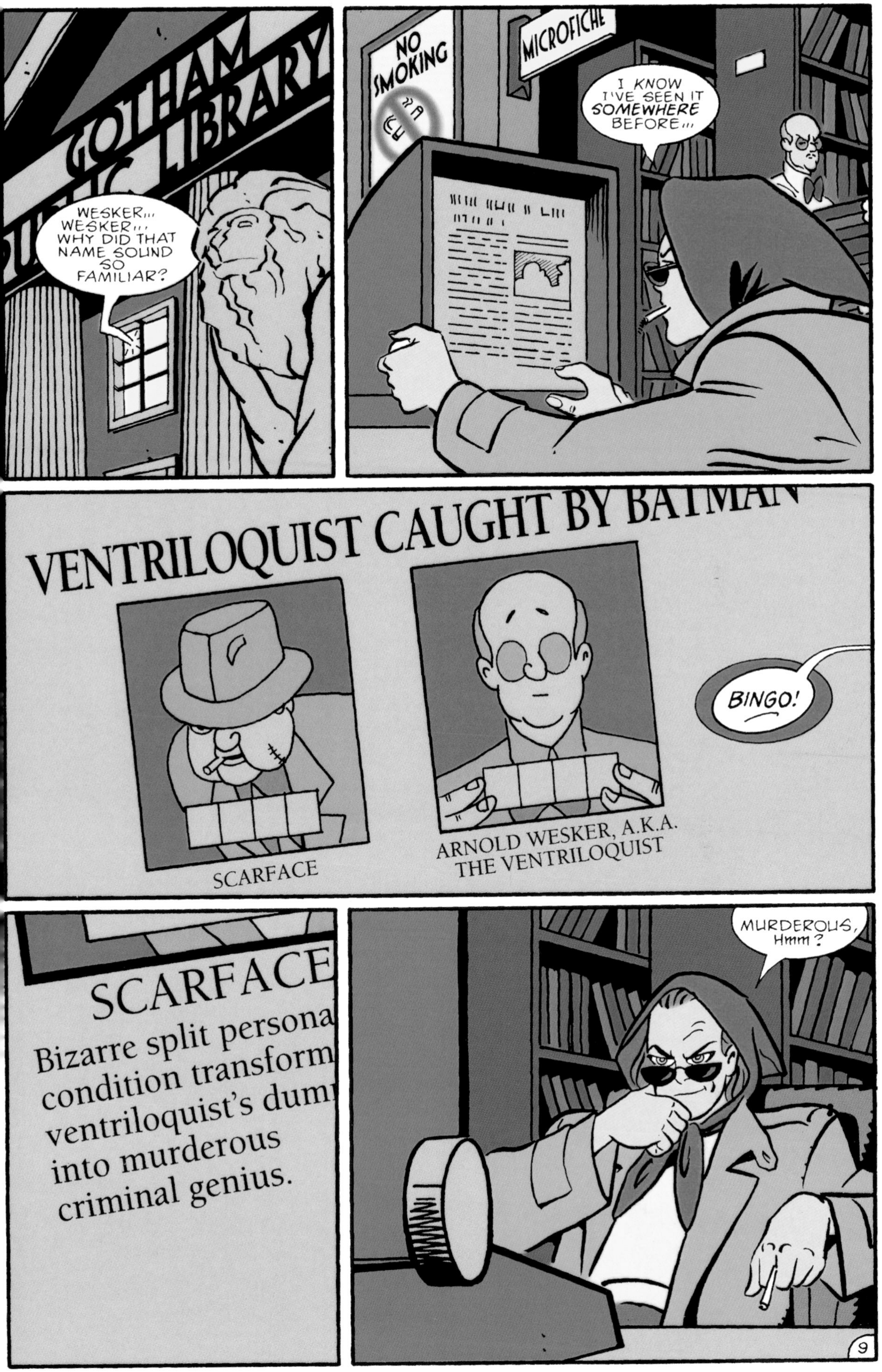
GOTHAM PUBLIC LIBRARY
WESKER... WESKER... WHY DID THAT NAME SOUND SO FAMILIAR?
NO SMOKING
MICROFICHE
I KNOW I'VE SEEN IT SOMEWHERE BEFORE...
VENTRILOQUIST CAUGHT BY BATMAN
SCARFACE
ARNOLD WESKER, A.K.A. THE VENTRILOQUIST
BINGO!
SCARFACE
Bizarre split persona
condition transform
ventriloquist's dum
into murderous
criminal genius.
MURDEROUS, Hmm?
9

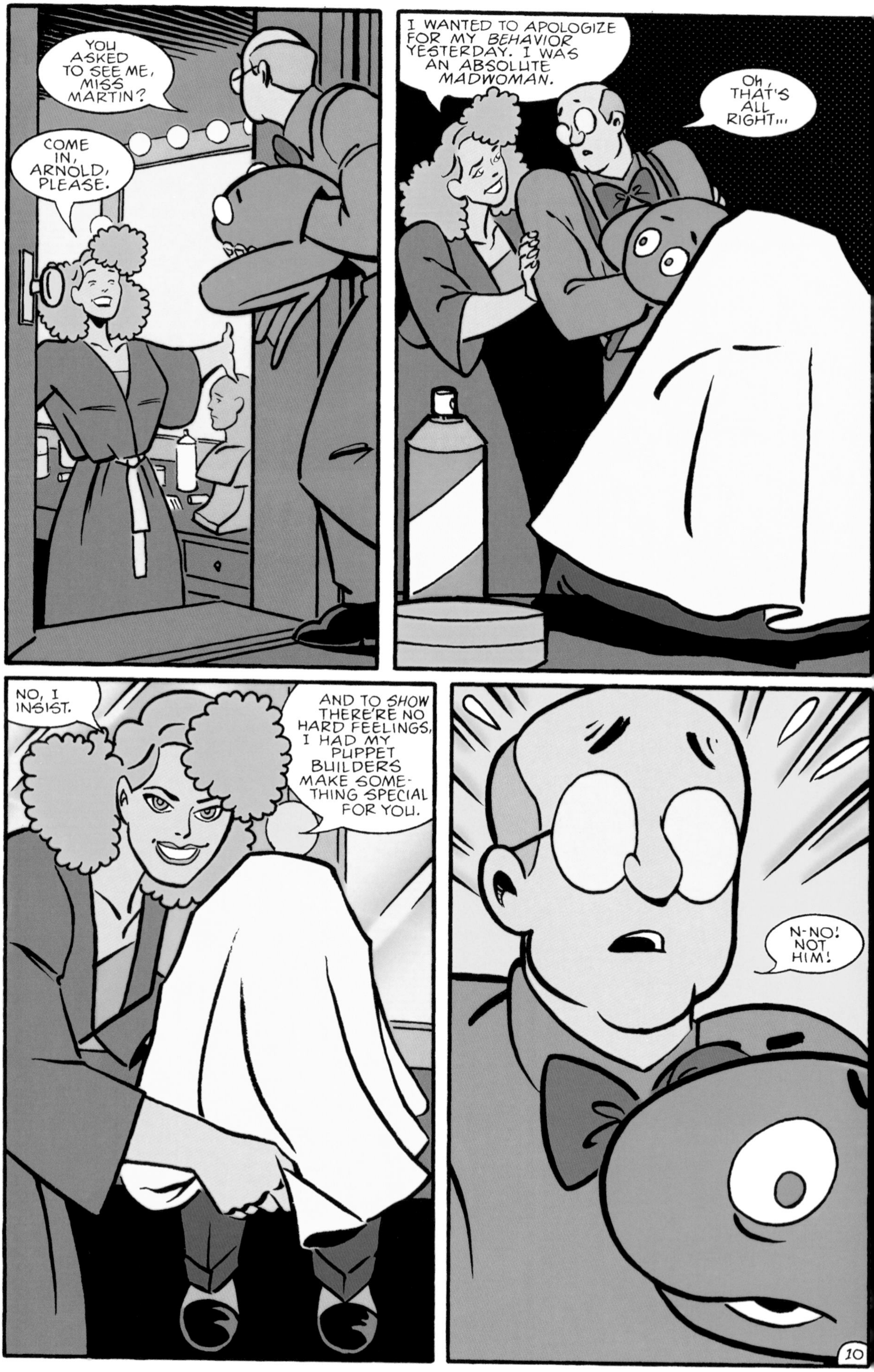
YOU ASKED TO SEE ME, MISS MARTIN?
COME IN, ARNOLD, PLEASE.
I WANTED TO APOLOGIZE FOR MY BEHAVIOR YESTERDAY. I WAS AN ABSOLUTE MADWOMAN.
OH, THAT'S ALL RIGHT...
NO, I INSIST.
AND TO SHOW THERE'RE NO HARD FEELINGS, I HAD MY PUPPET BUILDERS MAKE SOME-THING SPECIAL FOR YOU.
N-NO! NOT HIM!
10

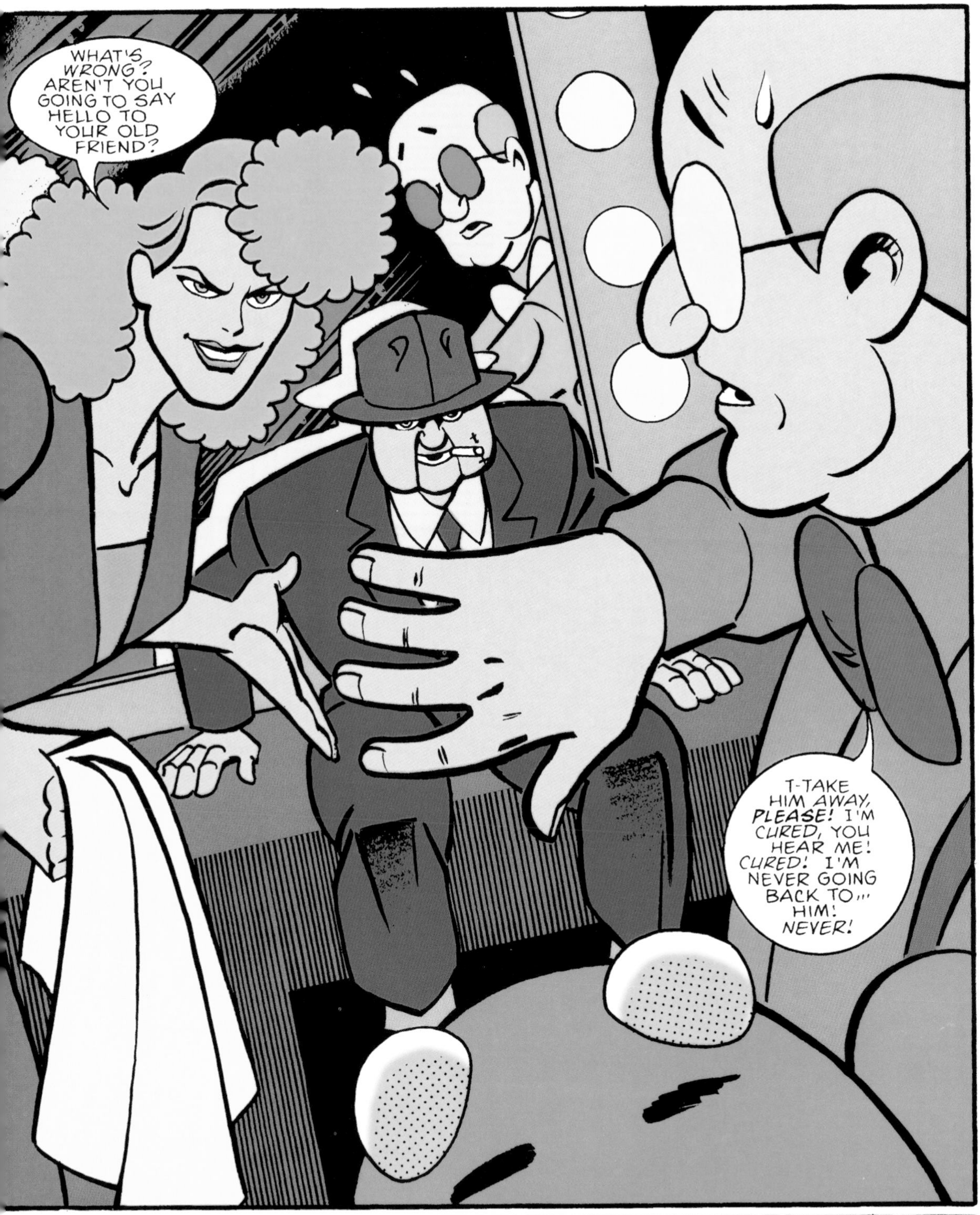

WHAT'S WRONG? AREN'T YOU GOING TO SAY HELLO TO YOUR OLD FRIEND?
T-TAKE HIM AWAY, PLEASE! I'M CURED, YOU HEAR ME! CURED! I'M NEVER GOING BACK TO... HIM! NEVER!

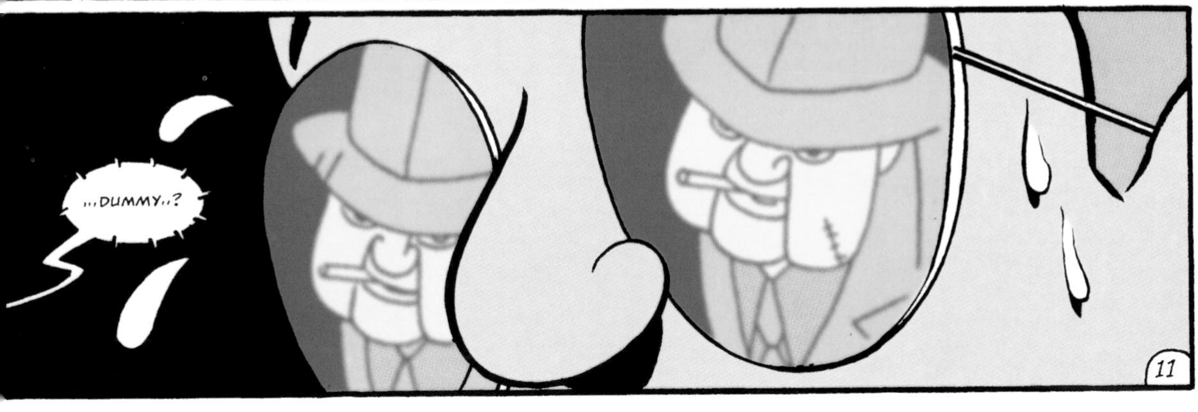

...DUMMY..?
11

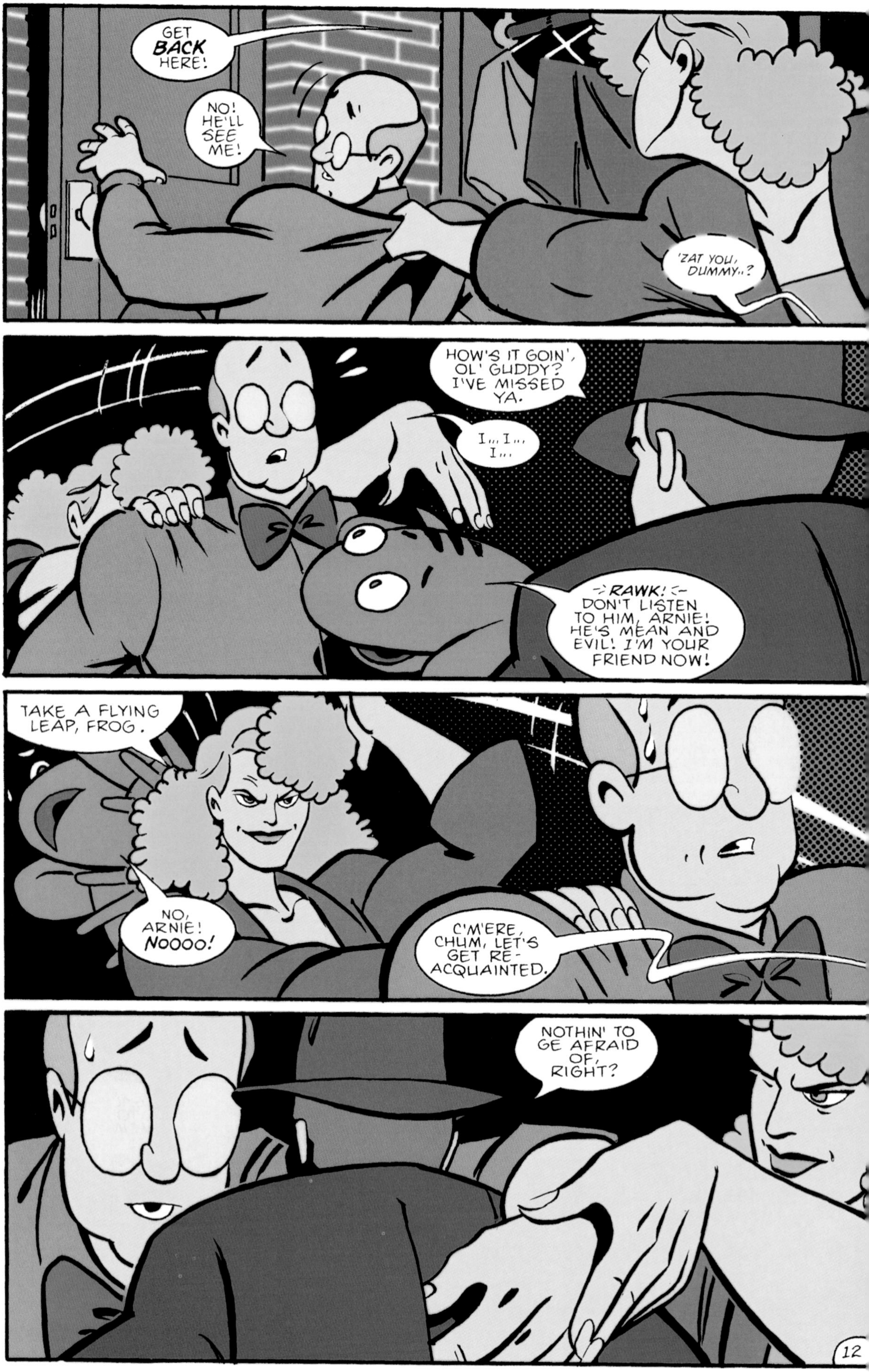
GET BACK HERE!
NO! HE'LL SEE ME!
'ZAT YOU, DUMMY..?
HOW'S IT GOIN', OL' GUDDY? I'VE MISSED YA.
I... I... I...
RAWK! DON'T LISTEN TO HIM, ARNIE! HE'S MEAN AND EVIL! I'M YOUR FRIEND NOW!
TAKE A FLYING LEAP, FROG.
NO, ARNIE! NOOOO!
C'M'ERE, CHUM, LET'S GET RE-ACQUAINTED.
NOTHIN' TO GE AFRAID OF, RIGHT?
12

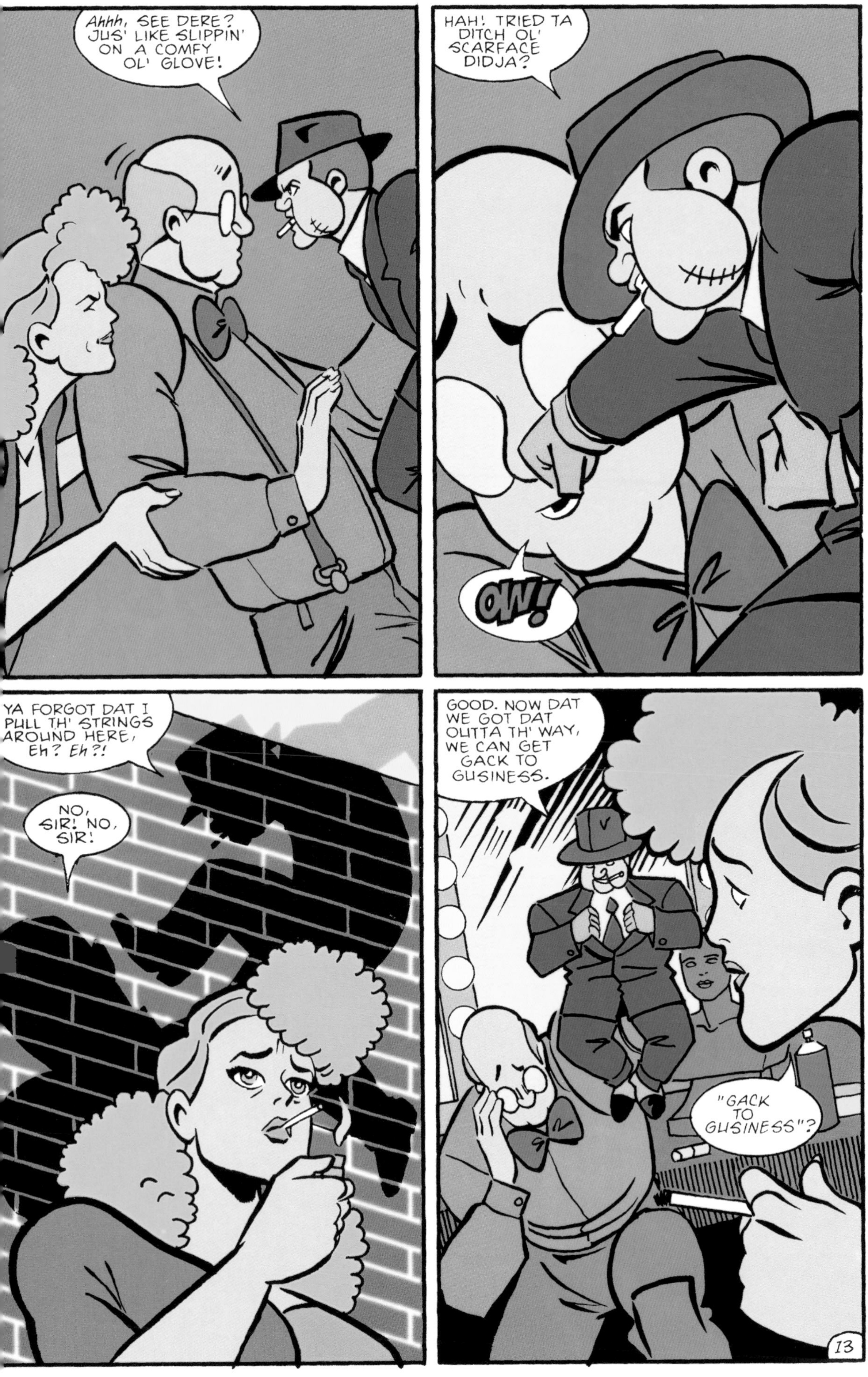
Ahhh, SEE DERE? JUS' LIKE SLIPPIN' ON A COMFY OL' GLOVE!
HAH! TRIED TA DITCH OL' SCARFACE DIDJA?
OW!
YA FORGOT DAT I PULL TH' STRINGS AROUND HERE, EH? EH?!
NO, SIR! NO, SIR!
GOOD. NOW DAT WE GOT DAT OUTTA TH' WAY, WE CAN GET GACK TO GUSINESS.
"GACK TO GUSINESS"?
13

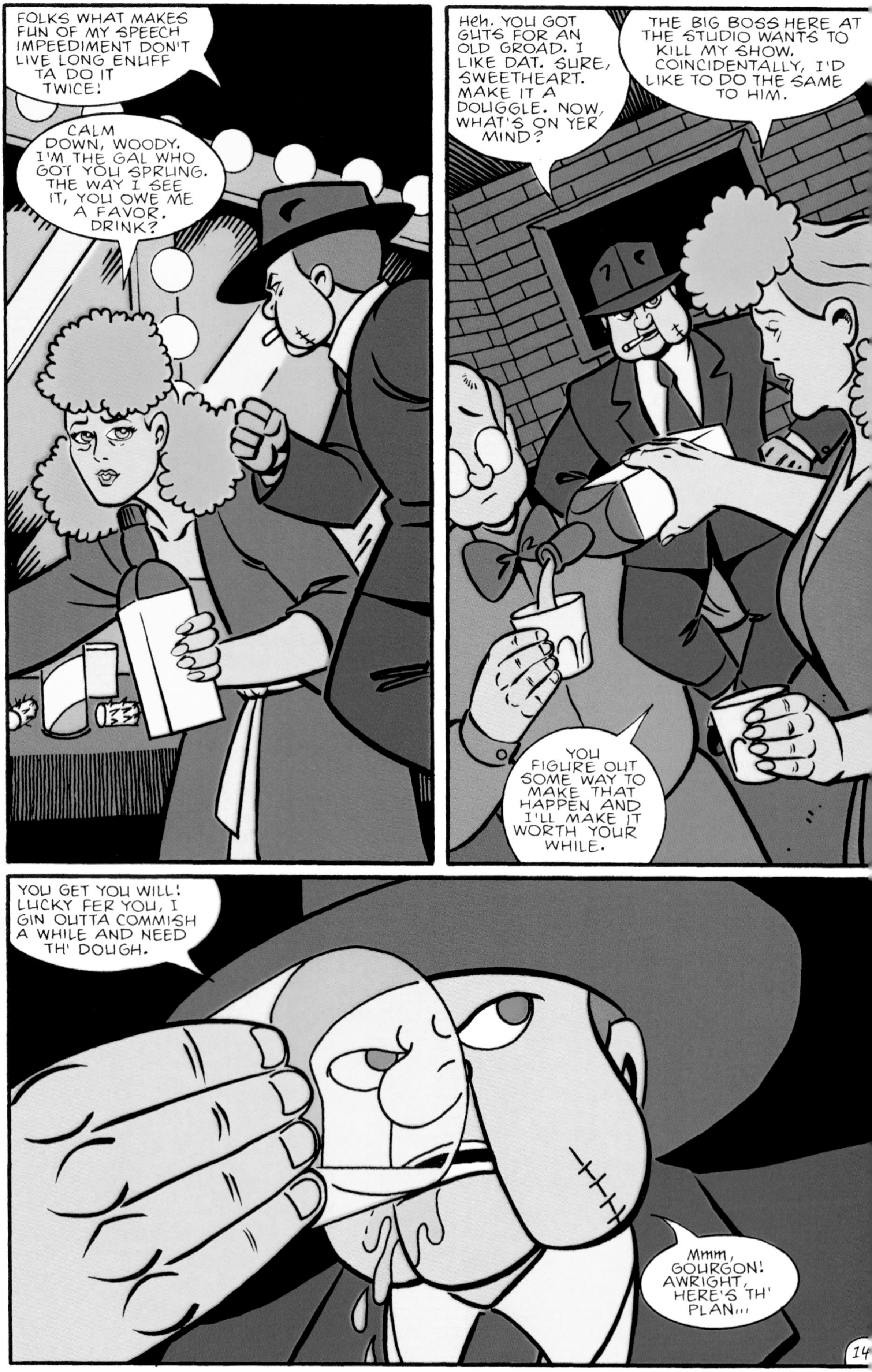
FOLKS WHAT MAKES FUN OF MY SPEECH IMPEEDIMENT DON'T LIVE LONG ENUFF TA DO IT TWICE!
CALM DOWN, WOODY. I'M THE GAL WHO GOT YOU SPRUNG. THE WAY I SEE IT, YOU OWE ME A FAVOR. DRINK?
Heh. YOU GOT GUTS FOR AN OLD GROAD. I LIKE DAT. SURE, SWEETHEART. MAKE IT A DOUGGLE. NOW, WHAT'S ON YER MIND?
THE BIG BOSS HERE AT THE STUDIO WANTS TO KILL MY SHOW. COINCIDENTALLY, I'D LIKE TO DO THE SAME TO HIM.
YOU FIGURE OUT SOME WAY TO MAKE THAT HAPPEN AND I'LL MAKE IT WORTH YOUR WHILE.
YOU GET YOU WILL! LUCKY FER YOU, I GIN OUTTA COMMISH A WHILE AND NEED TH' DOUGH.
Mmm, GOURGON! AWRIGHT, HERE'S TH' PLAN...
14

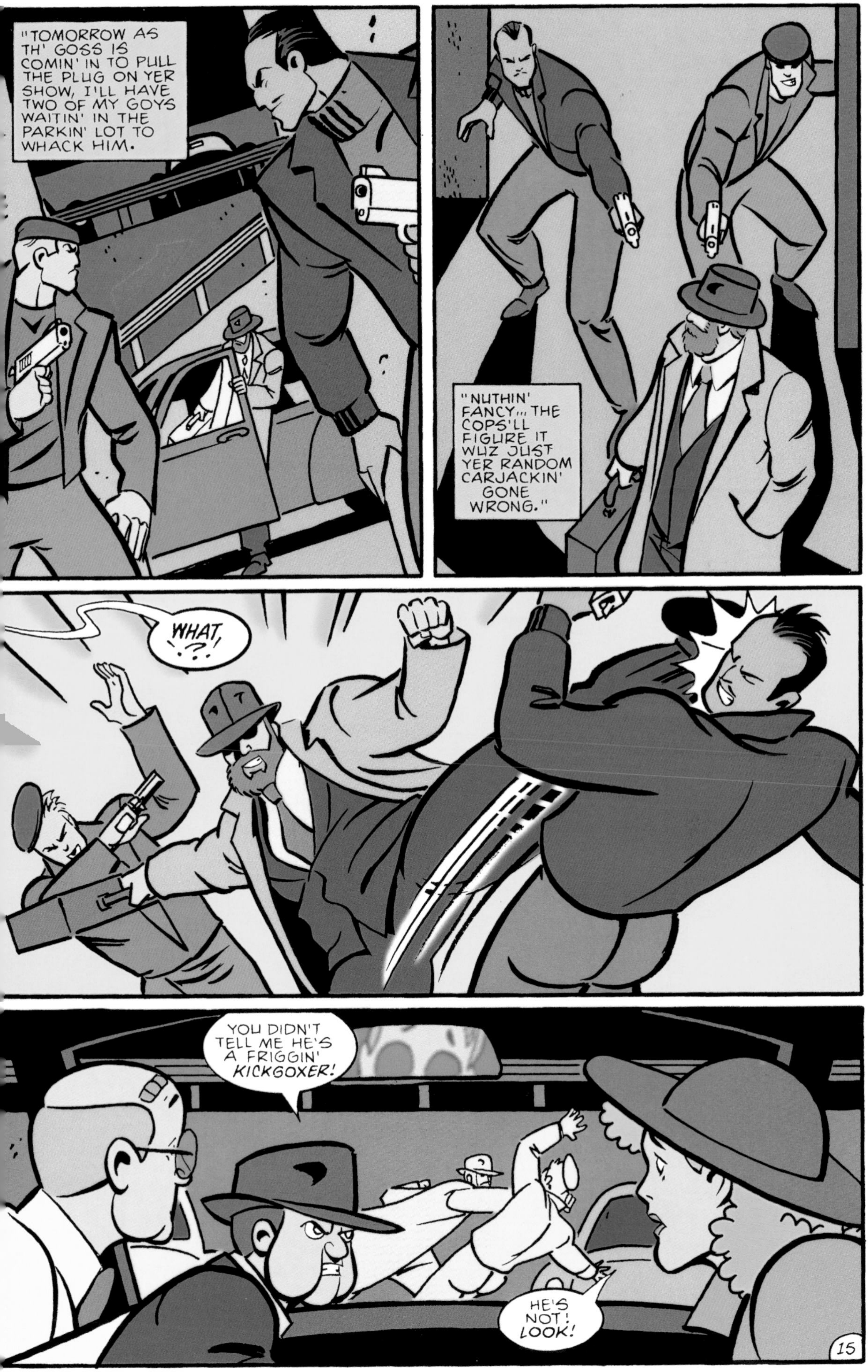
"TOMORROW AS TH' GOSS IS COMIN' IN TO PULL THE PLUG ON YER SHOW, I'LL HAVE TWO OF MY GOYS WAITIN' IN THE PARKIN' LOT TO WHACK HIM.
"NUTHIN' FANCY... THE COPS'LL FIGURE IT WUZ JUST YER RANDOM CARJACKIN' GONE WRONG."
WHAT, ?!
YOU DIDN'T TELL ME HE'S A FRIGGIN' KICKGOXER!
HE'S NOT! LOOK!
15

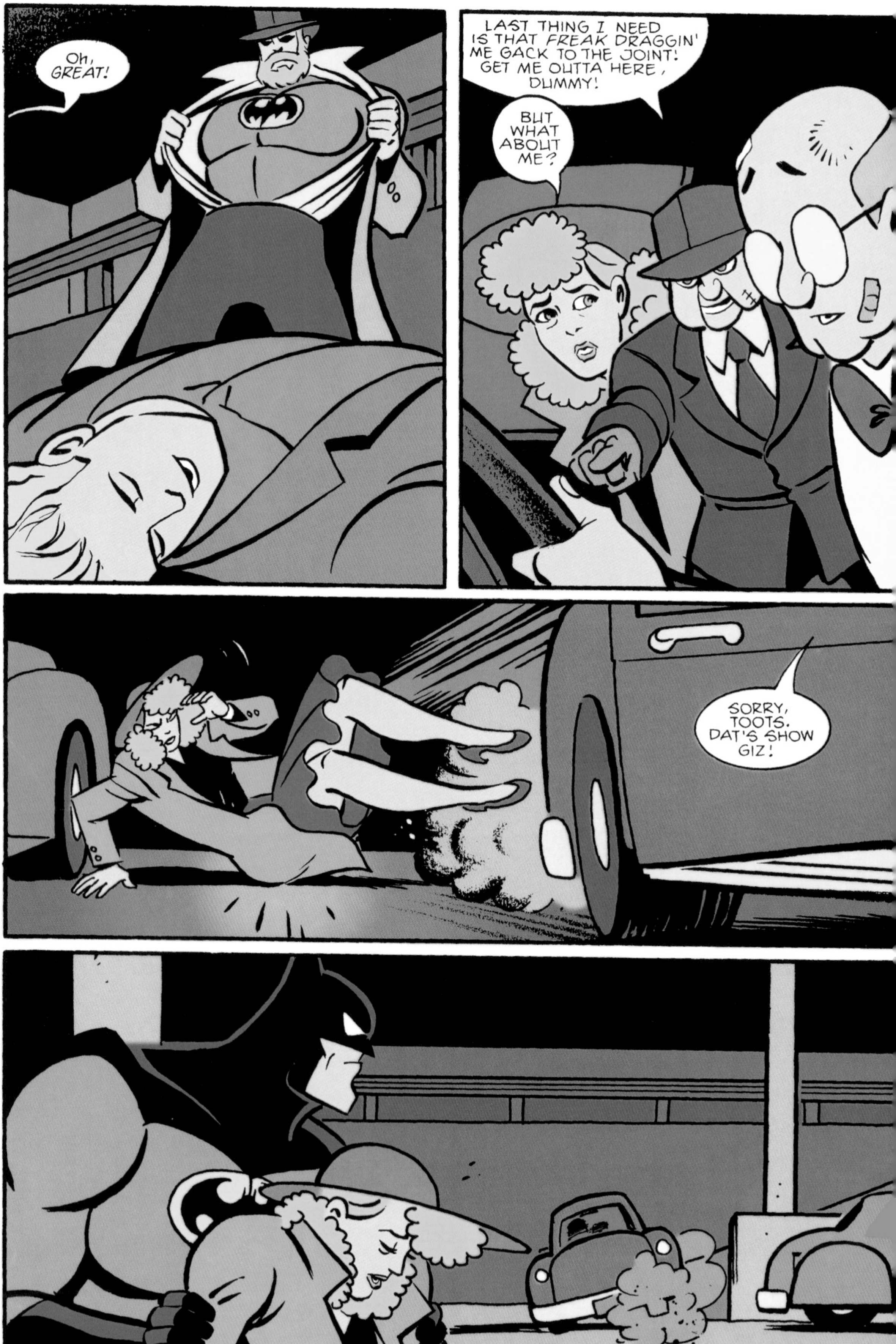

Oh, GREAT!
LAST THING I NEED IS THAT FREAK DRAGGIN' ME GACK TO THE JOINT! GET ME OUTTA HERE, DUMMY!
BUT WHAT ABOUT ME?
SORRY, TOOTS. DAT'S SHOW GIZ!
16

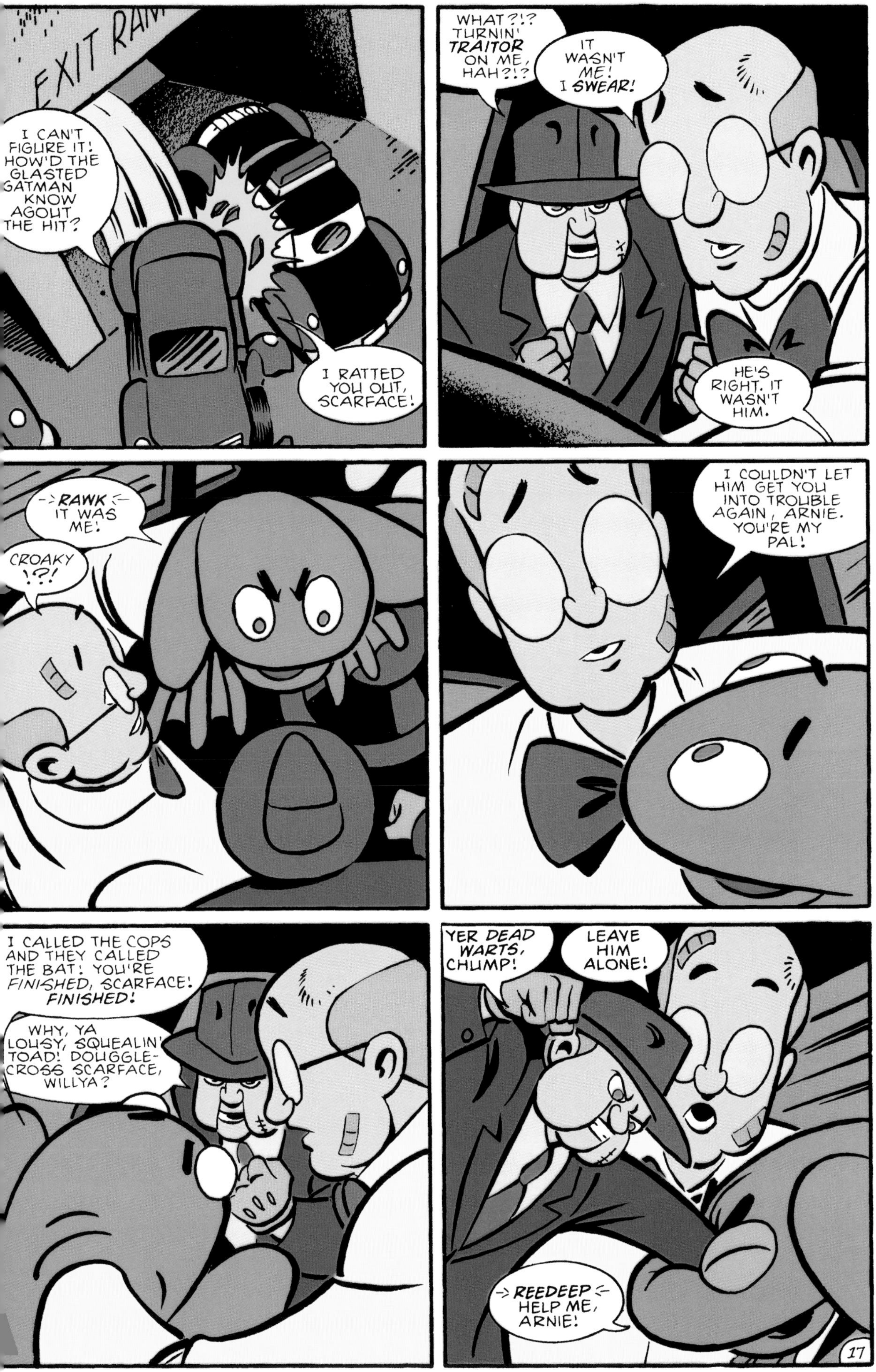
EXIT RAM
I CAN'T FIGURE IT! HOW'D THE GLASTED GATMAN KNOW AGOUT THE HIT?
I RATTED YOU OUT, SCARFACE!
WHAT?!? TURNIN' TRAITOR ON ME, HAH?!?
IT WASN'T ME! I SWEAR!
HE'S RIGHT. IT WASN'T HIM.
RAWK IT WAS ME!
CROAKY !?!
I COULDN'T LET HIM GET YOU INTO TROUBLE AGAIN, ARNIE. YOU'RE MY PAL!
I CALLED THE COPS AND THEY CALLED THE BAT! YOU'RE FINISHED, SCARFACE! FINISHED!
WHY, YA LOUSY, SQUEALIN' TOAD! DOUGGLE-CROSS SCARFACE, WILLYA?
YER DEAD WARTS, CHUMP!
LEAVE HIM ALONE!
REEDEEP HELP ME, ARNIE!
17

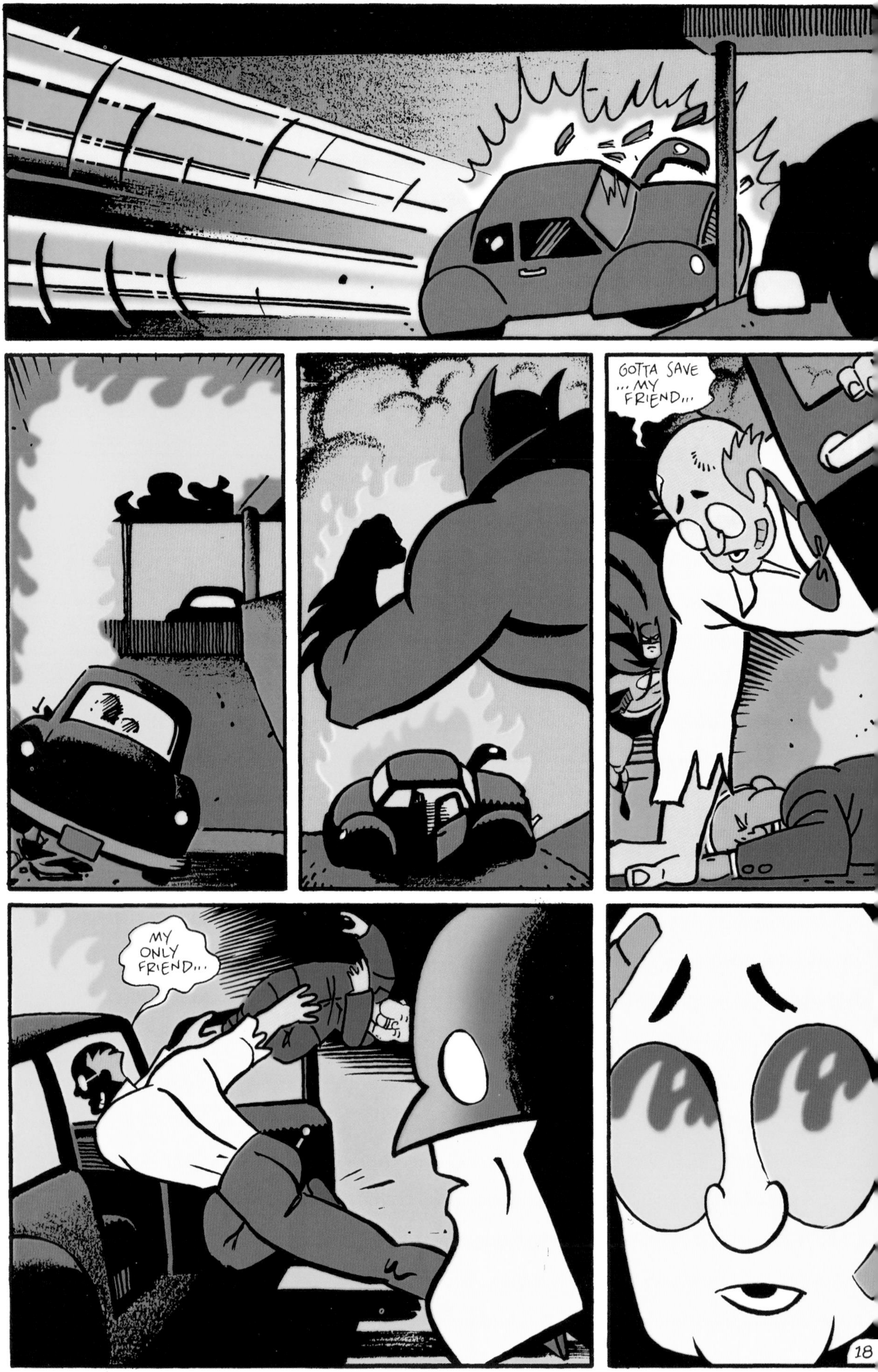
GOTTA SAVE ...MY FRIEND...
MY ONLY FRIEND...
18

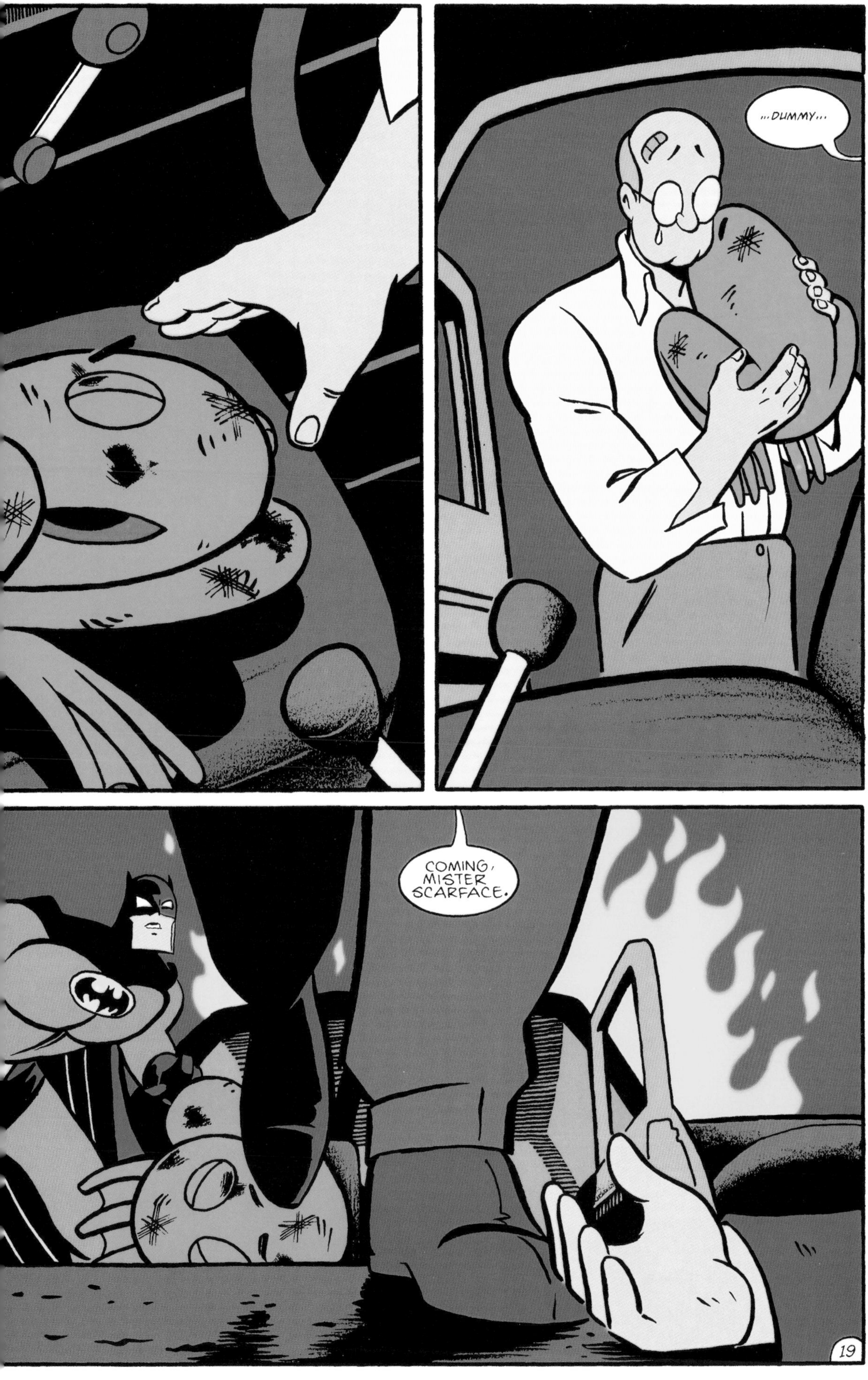
...DUMMY...
COMING, MISTER SCARFACE.
19

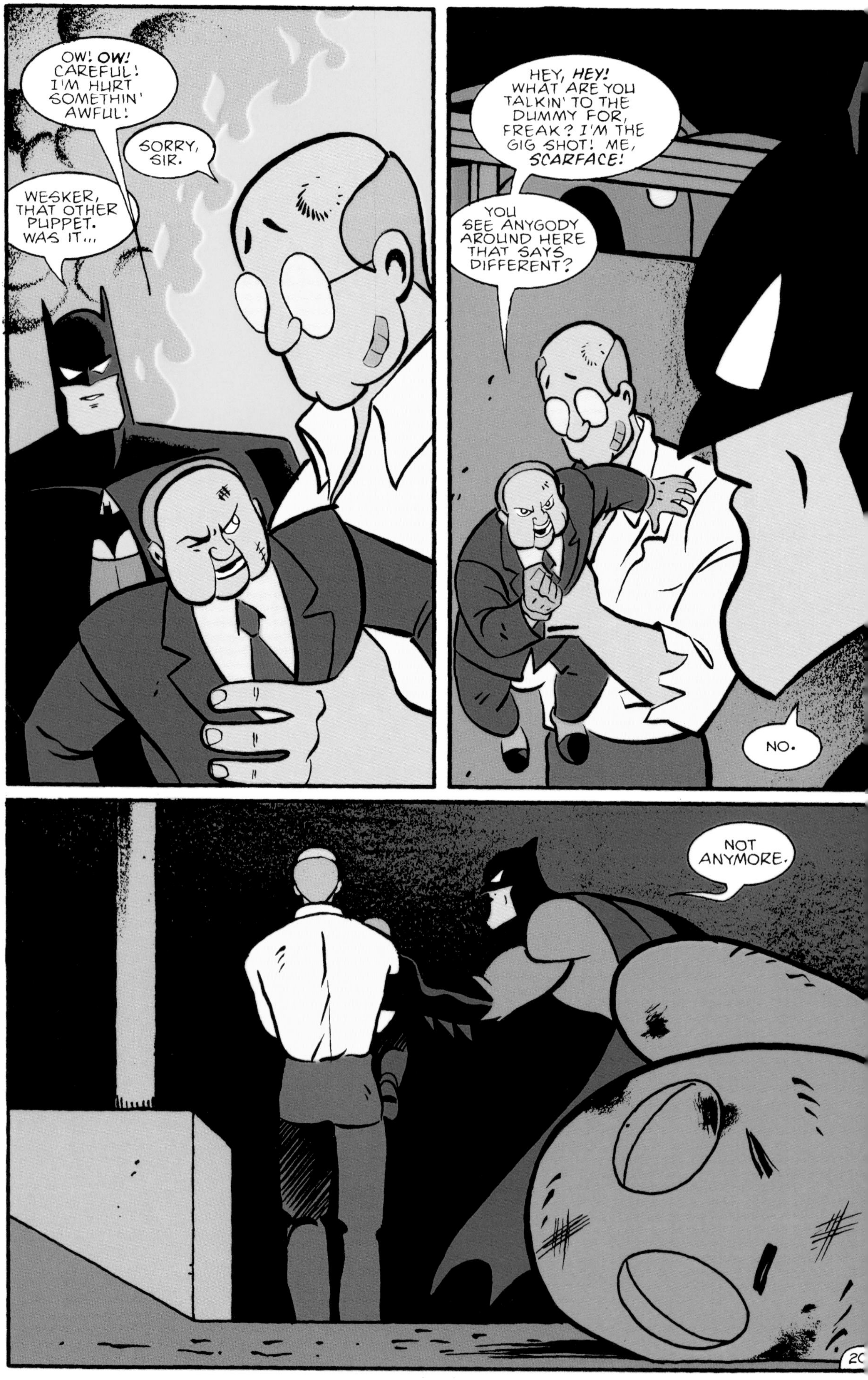
OW! OW! CAREFUL! I'M HURT SOMETHIN' AWFUL!
SORRY, SIR.
WESKER, THAT OTHER PUPPET. WAS IT...
HEY, HEY! WHAT ARE YOU TALKIN' TO THE DUMMY FOR, FREAK? I'M THE GIG SHOT! ME, SCARFACE!
YOU SEE ANYGODY AROUND HERE THAT SAYS DIFFERENT?
NO.
NOT ANYMORE.

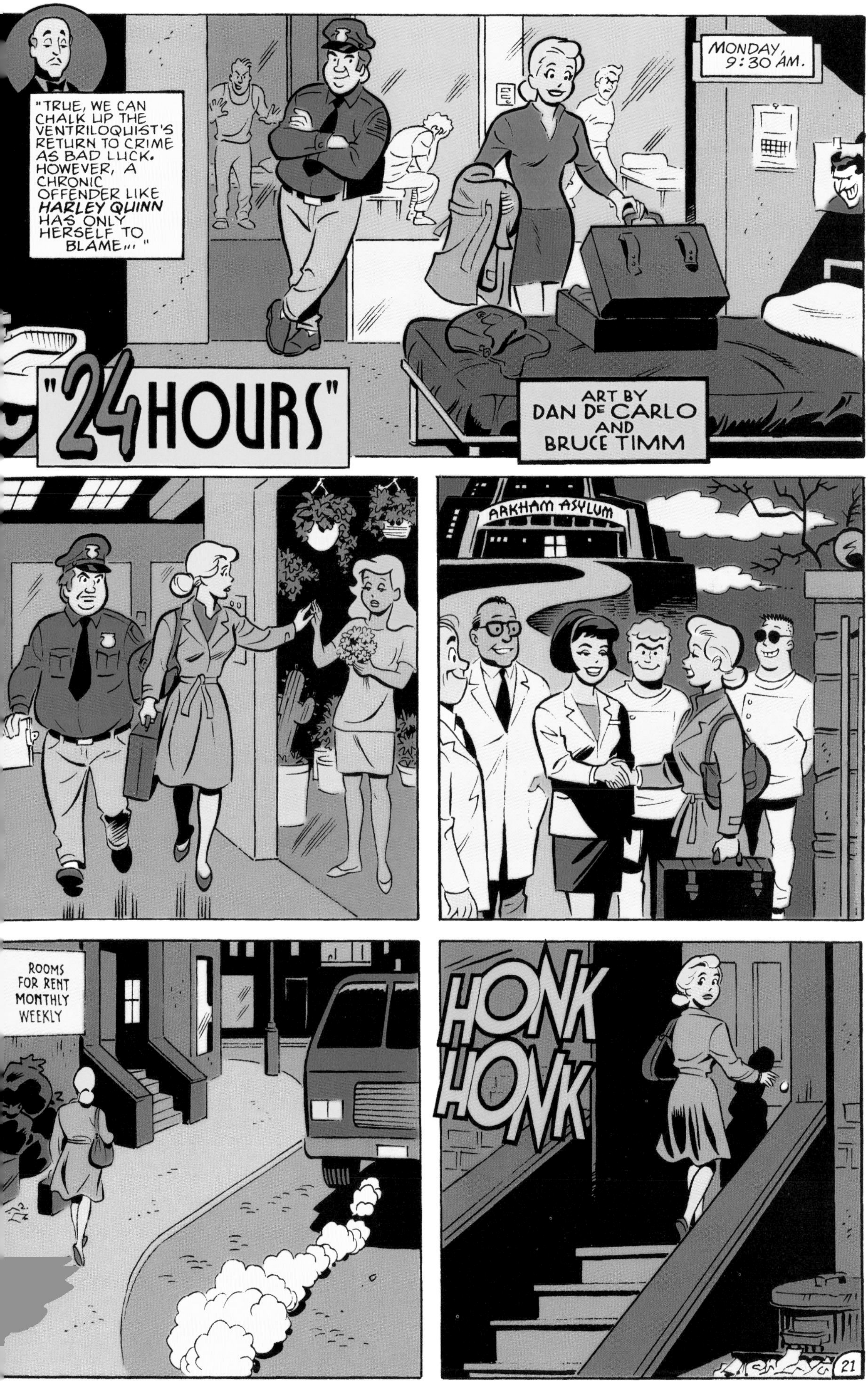

"TRUE, WE CAN CHALK UP THE VENTRILOQUIST'S RETURN TO CRIME AS BAD LUCK. HOWEVER, A CHRONIC OFFENDER LIKE HARLEY QUINN HAS ONLY HERSELF TO BLAME..."
MONDAY, 9:30 AM.
"24 HOURS"
ART BY DAN DE CARLO AND BRUCE TIMM
ARKHAM ASYLUM
ROOMS FOR RENT MONTHLY WEEKLY
HONK HONK
21

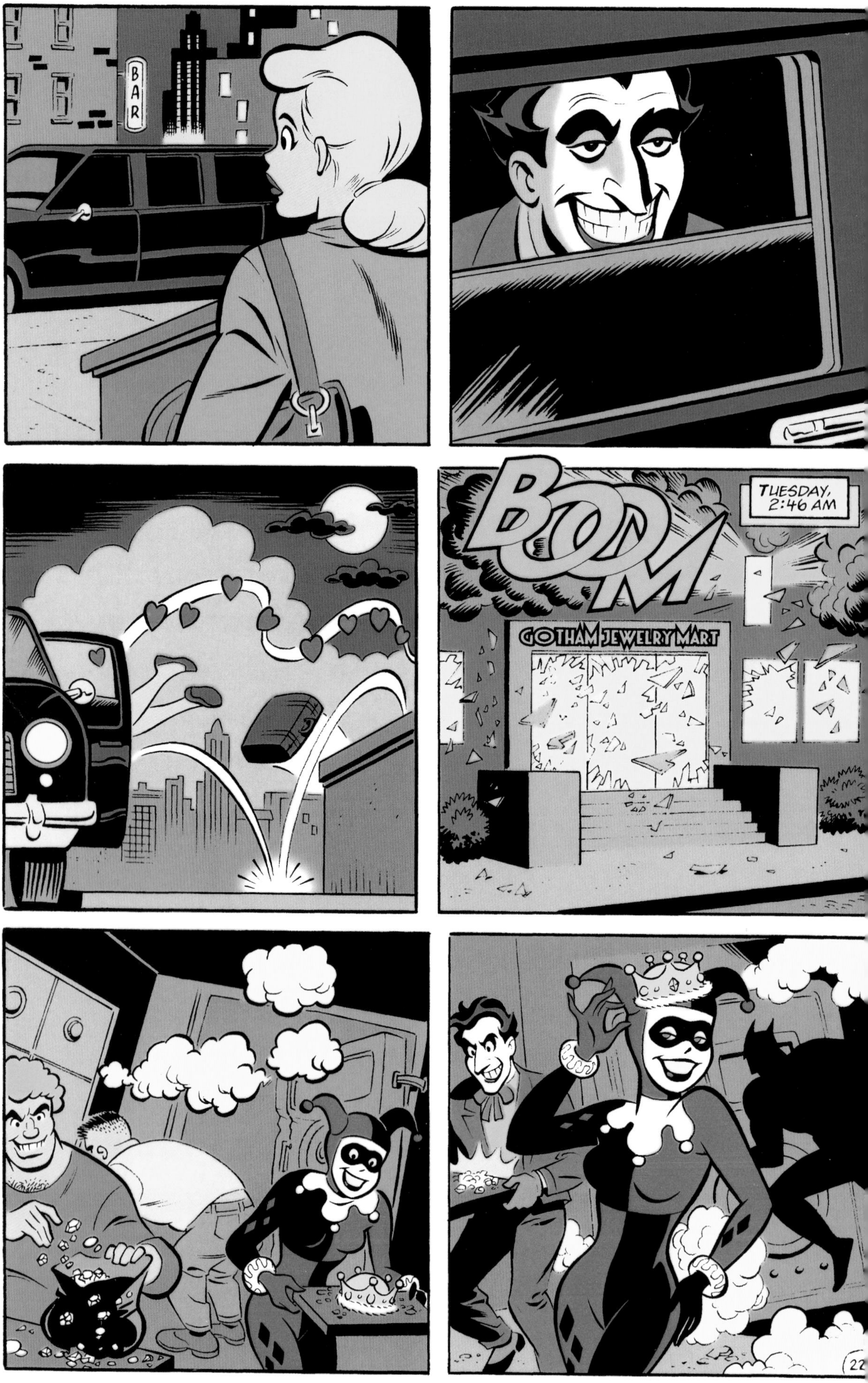
BAR
BOOM
TUESDAY, 2:46 AM
GOTHAM JEWELRY MART
22

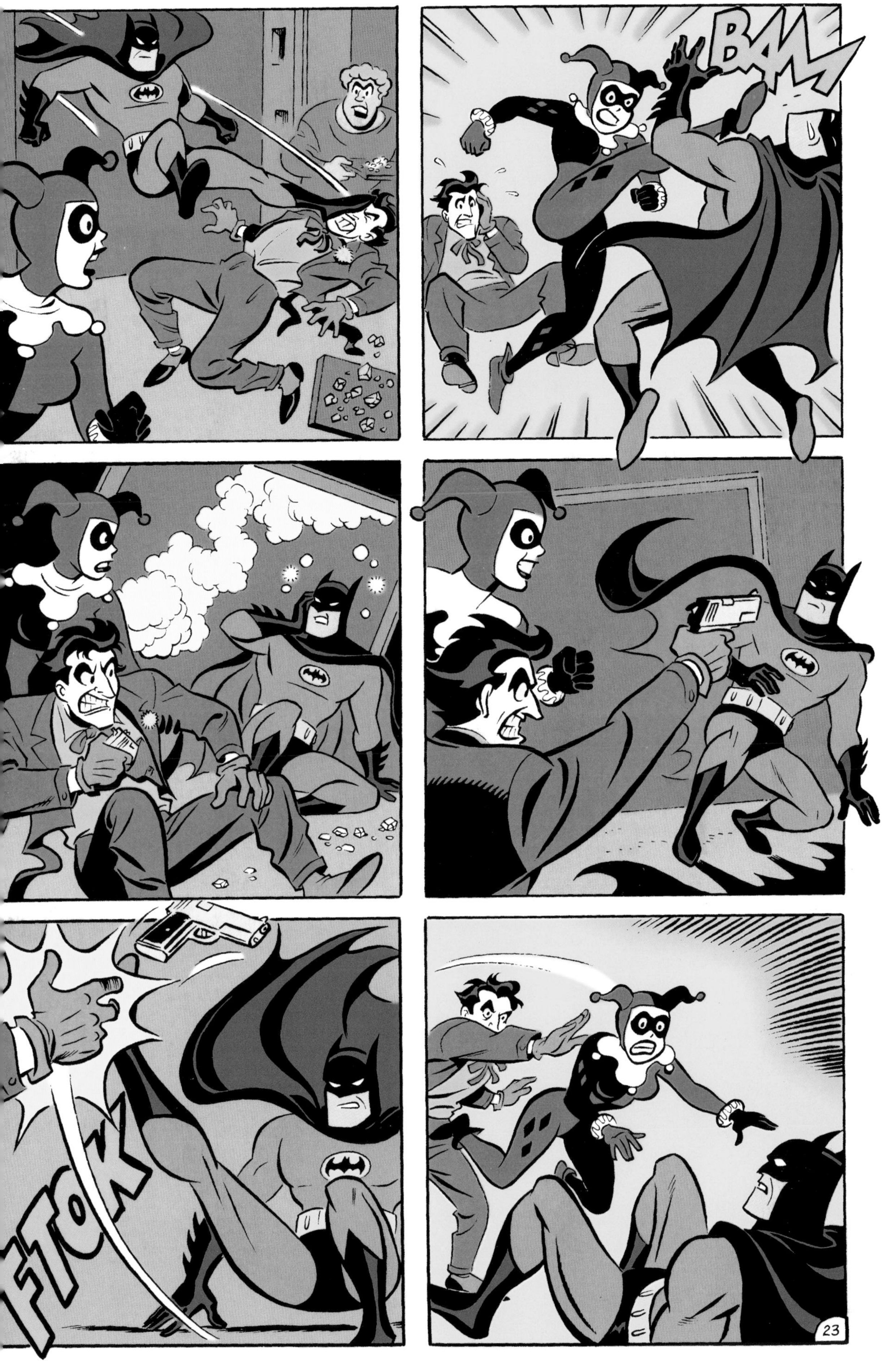
BAM
FTOK
23

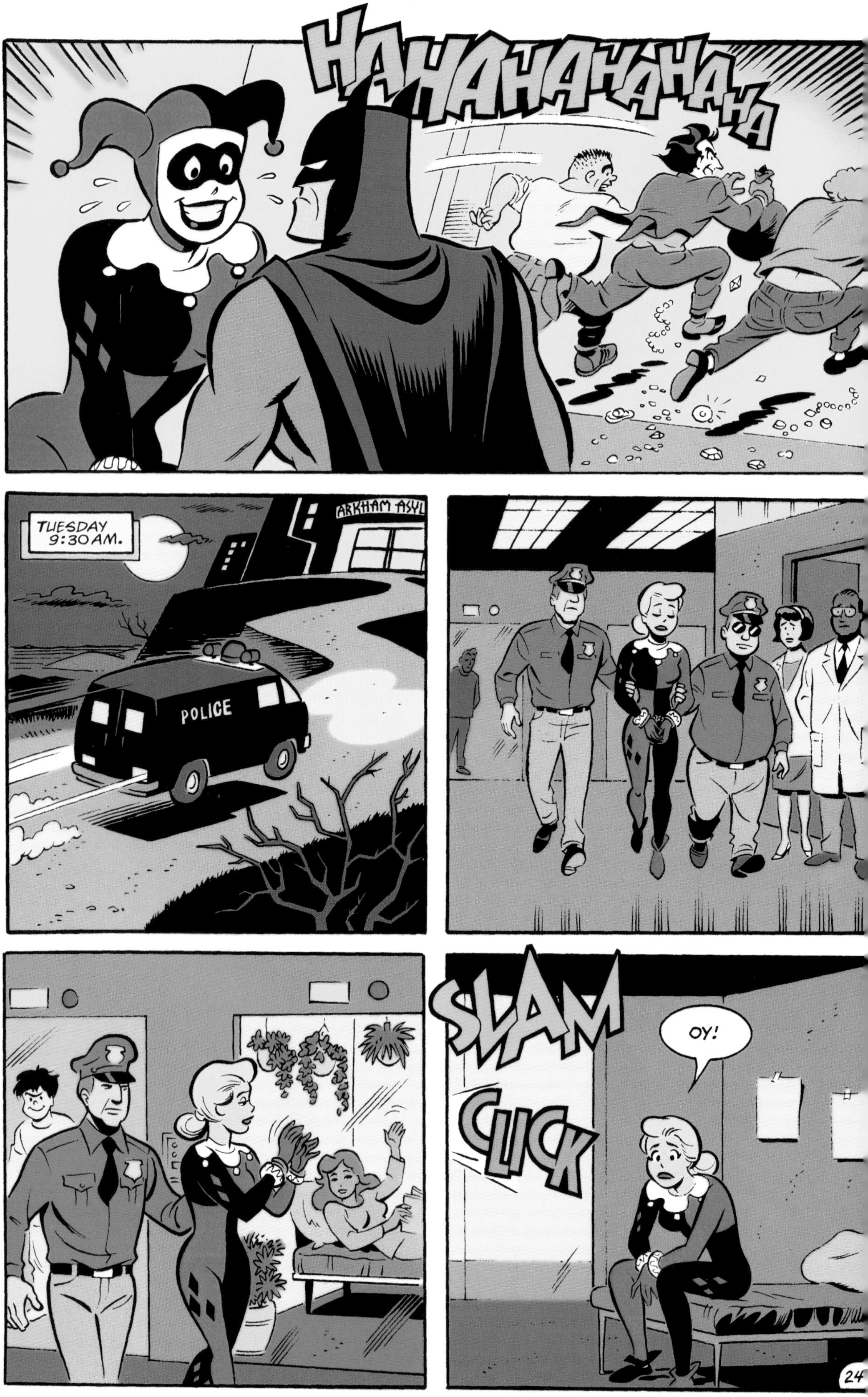
HAHAHAHAHAHAHA
TUESDAY 9:30 AM.
ARKHAM ASYL
POLICE
SLAM
CLICK
OY!
24

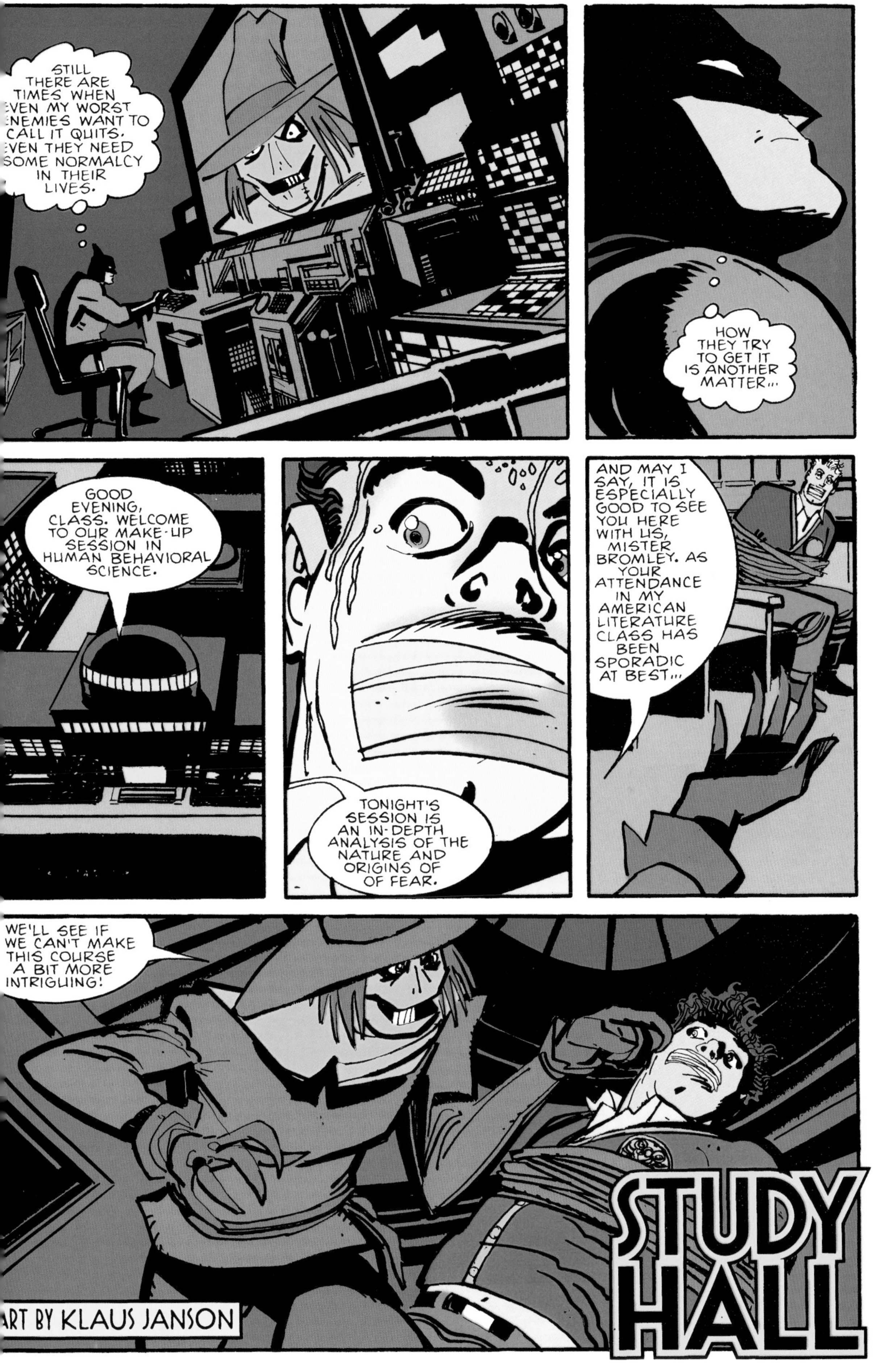
STILL THERE ARE TIMES WHEN EVEN MY WORST ENEMIES WANT TO CALL IT QUITS. EVEN THEY NEED SOME NORMALCY IN THEIR LIVES.
HOW THEY TRY TO GET IT IS ANOTHER MATTER...
GOOD EVENING, CLASS. WELCOME TO OUR MAKE-UP SESSION IN HUMAN BEHAVIORAL SCIENCE.
TONIGHT'S SESSION IS AN IN-DEPTH ANALYSIS OF THE NATURE AND ORIGINS OF OF FEAR.
AND MAY I SAY, IT IS ESPECIALLY GOOD TO SEE YOU HERE WITH US, MISTER BROMLEY. AS YOUR ATTENDANCE IN MY AMERICAN LITERATURE CLASS HAS BEEN SPORADIC AT BEST...
WE'LL SEE IF WE CAN'T MAKE THIS COURSE A BIT MORE INTRIGUING!
ART BY KLAUS JANSON
STUDY HALL

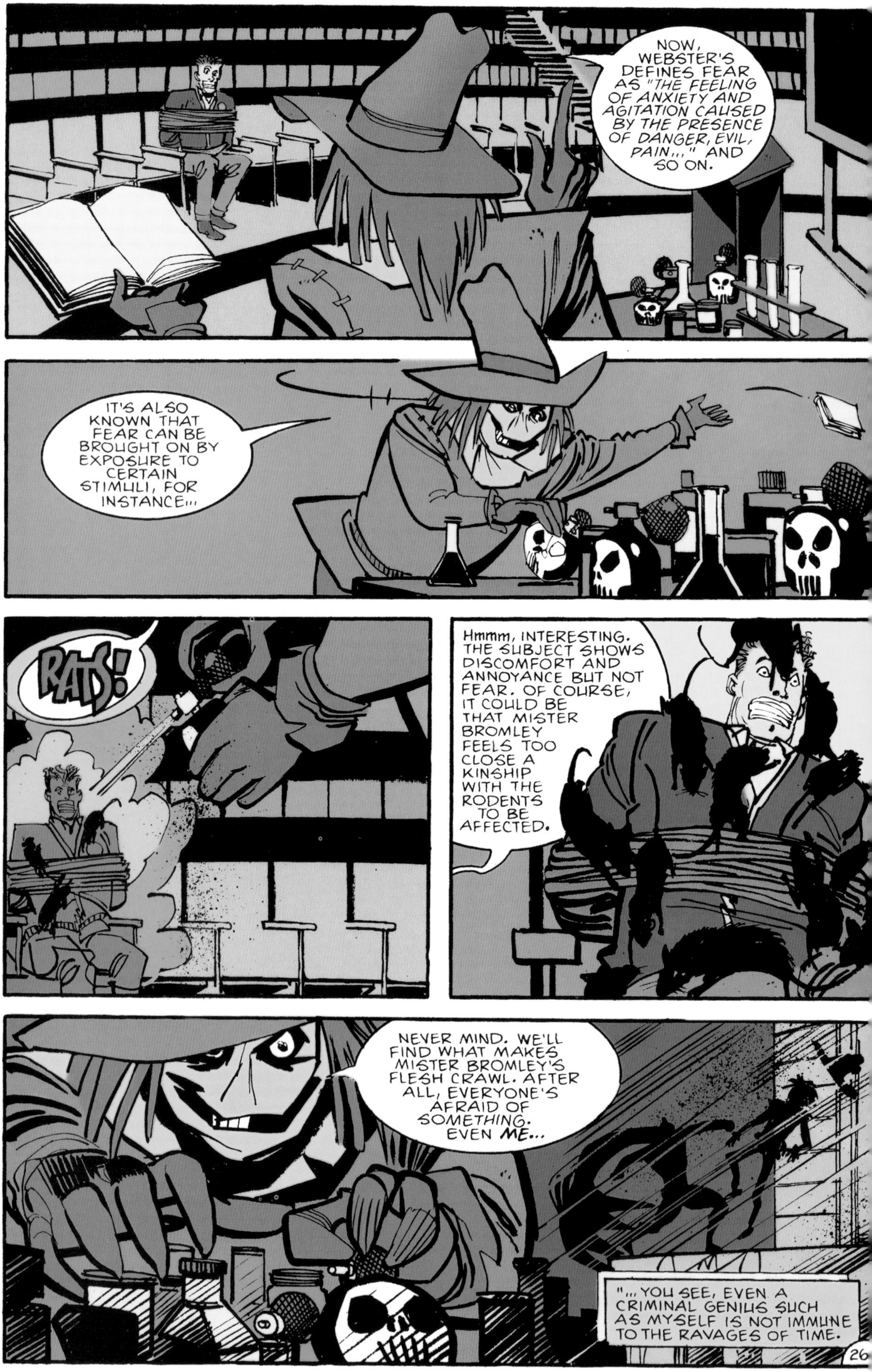

NOW, WEBSTER'S DEFINES FEAR AS "THE FEELING OF ANXIETY AND AGITATION CAUSED BY THE PRESENCE OF DANGER, EVIL, PAIN..." AND SO ON.
IT'S ALSO KNOWN THAT FEAR CAN BE BROUGHT ON BY EXPOSURE TO CERTAIN STIMULI, FOR INSTANCE...
RATS!
Hmmm, INTERESTING. THE SUBJECT SHOWS DISCOMFORT AND ANNOYANCE BUT NOT FEAR. OF COURSE, IT COULD BE THAT MISTER BROMLEY FEELS TOO CLOSE A KINSHIP WITH THE RODENTS TO BE AFFECTED.
NEVER MIND. WE'LL FIND WHAT MAKES MISTER BROMLEY'S FLESH CRAWL. AFTER ALL, EVERYONE'S AFRAID OF SOMETHING. EVEN ME...
"...YOU SEE, EVEN A CRIMINAL GENIUS SUCH AS MYSELF IS NOT IMMUNE TO THE RAVAGES OF TIME.
26

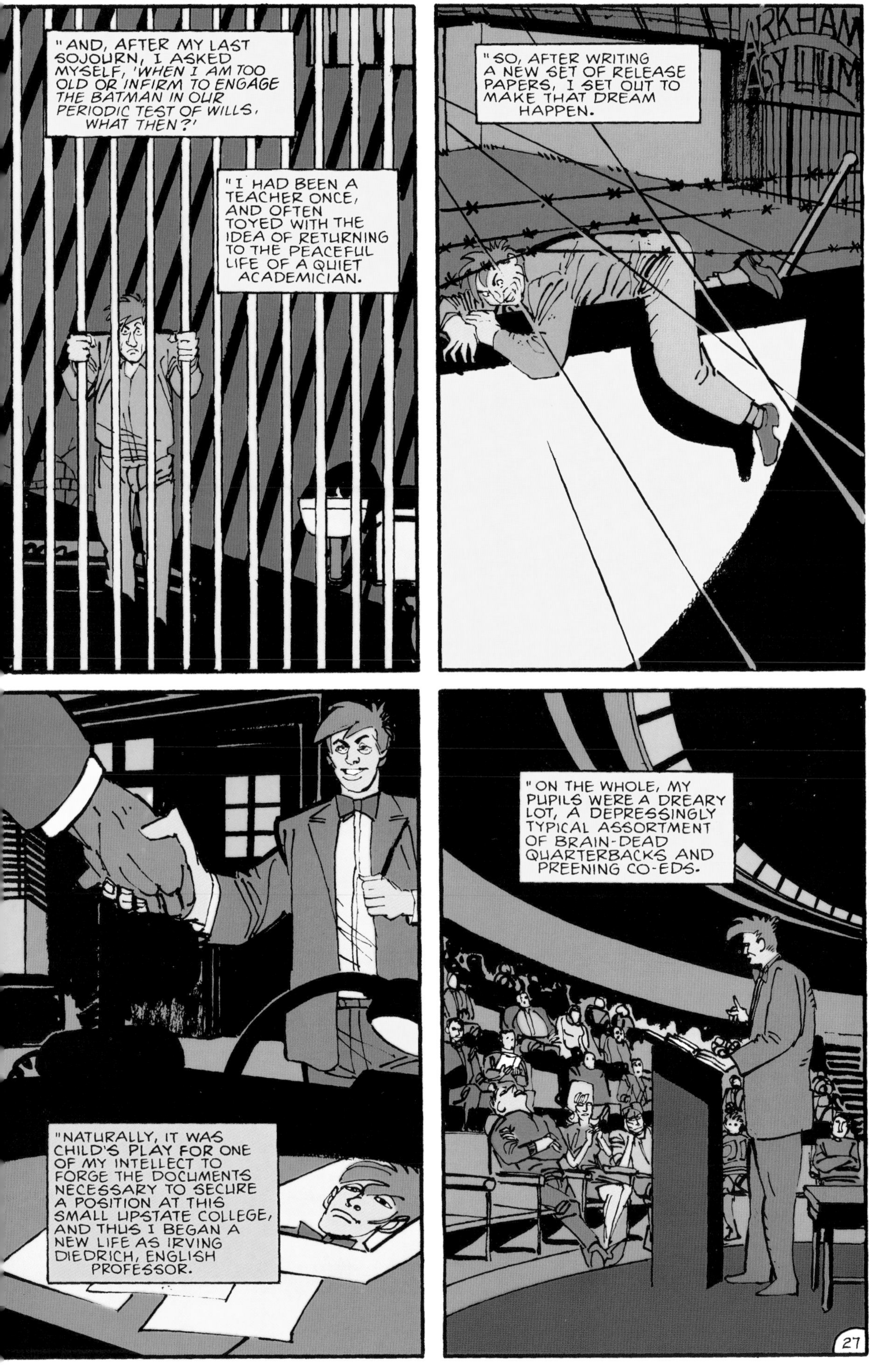

"AND, AFTER MY LAST SOJOURN, I ASKED MYSELF, 'WHEN I AM TOO OLD OR INFIRM TO ENGAGE THE BATMAN IN OUR PERIODIC TEST OF WILLS, WHAT THEN?'
"I HAD BEEN A TEACHER ONCE, AND OFTEN TOYED WITH THE IDEA OF RETURNING TO THE PEACEFUL LIFE OF A QUIET ACADEMICIAN.
"SO, AFTER WRITING A NEW SET OF RELEASE PAPERS, I SET OUT TO MAKE THAT DREAM HAPPEN.
"NATURALLY, IT WAS CHILD'S PLAY FOR ONE OF MY INTELLECT TO FORGE THE DOCUMENTS NECESSARY TO SECURE A POSITION AT THIS SMALL UPSTATE COLLEGE, AND THUS I BEGAN A NEW LIFE AS IRVING DIEDRICH, ENGLISH PROFESSOR.
"ON THE WHOLE, MY PUPILS WERE A DREARY LOT, A DEPRESSINGLY TYPICAL ASSORTMENT OF BRAIN-DEAD QUARTERBACKS AND PREENING CO-EDS.
27

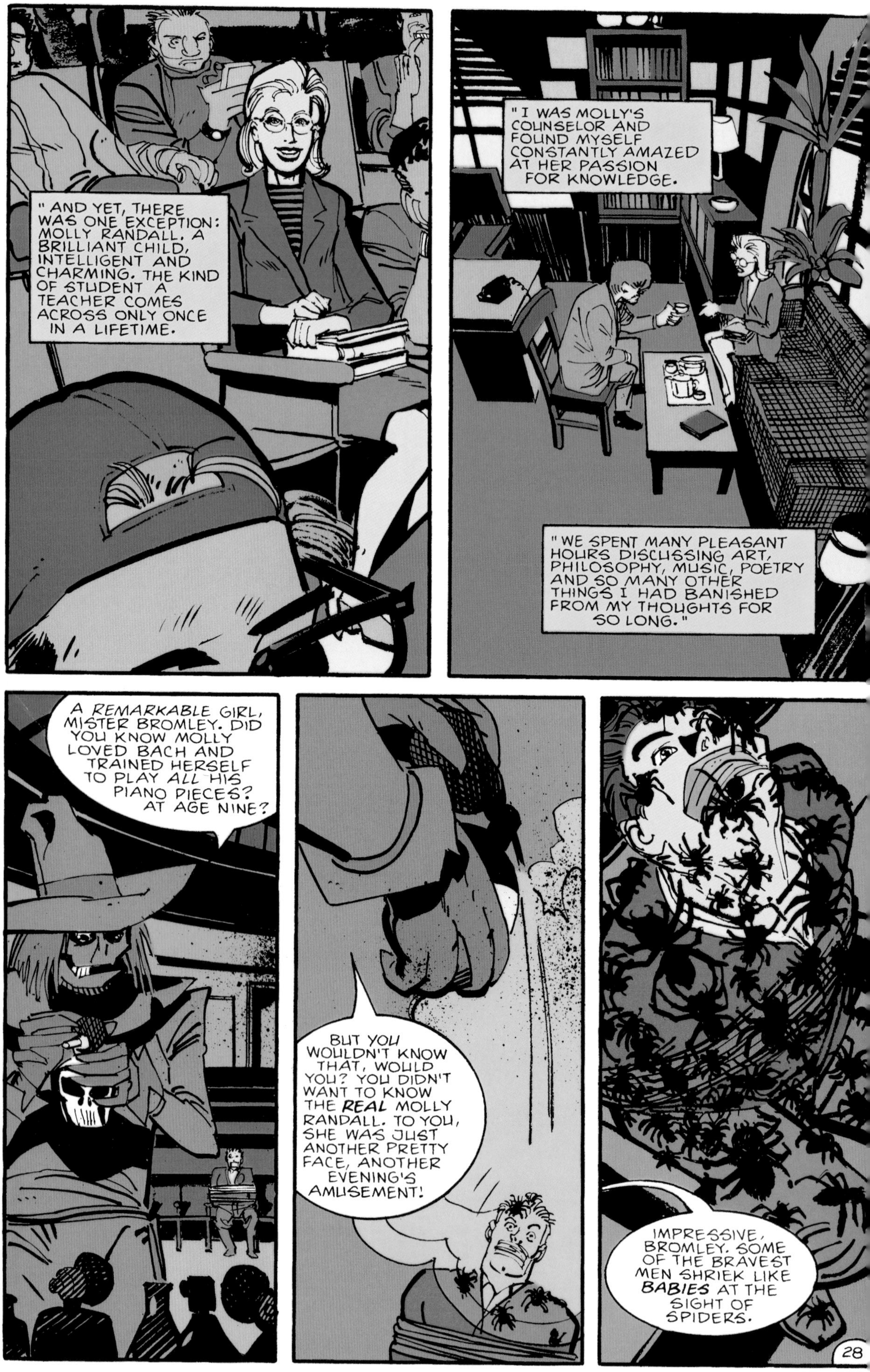
"AND YET, THERE WAS ONE EXCEPTION: MOLLY RANDALL. A BRILLIANT CHILD, INTELLIGENT AND CHARMING. THE KIND OF STUDENT A TEACHER COMES ACROSS ONLY ONCE IN A LIFETIME.
"I WAS MOLLY'S COUNSELOR AND FOUND MYSELF CONSTANTLY AMAZED AT HER PASSION FOR KNOWLEDGE.
"WE SPENT MANY PLEASANT HOURS DISCUSSING ART, PHILOSOPHY, MUSIC, POETRY AND SO MANY OTHER THINGS I HAD BANISHED FROM MY THOUGHTS FOR SO LONG."
A REMARKABLE GIRL, MISTER BROMLEY. DID YOU KNOW MOLLY LOVED BACH AND TRAINED HERSELF TO PLAY ALL HIS PIANO PIECES? AT AGE NINE?
BUT YOU WOULDN'T KNOW THAT, WOULD YOU? YOU DIDN'T WANT TO KNOW THE REAL MOLLY RANDALL. TO YOU, SHE WAS JUST ANOTHER PRETTY FACE, ANOTHER EVENING'S AMUSEMENT!
IMPRESSIVE, BROMLEY. SOME OF THE BRAVEST MEN SHRIEK LIKE BABIES AT THE SIGHT OF SPIDERS.
28

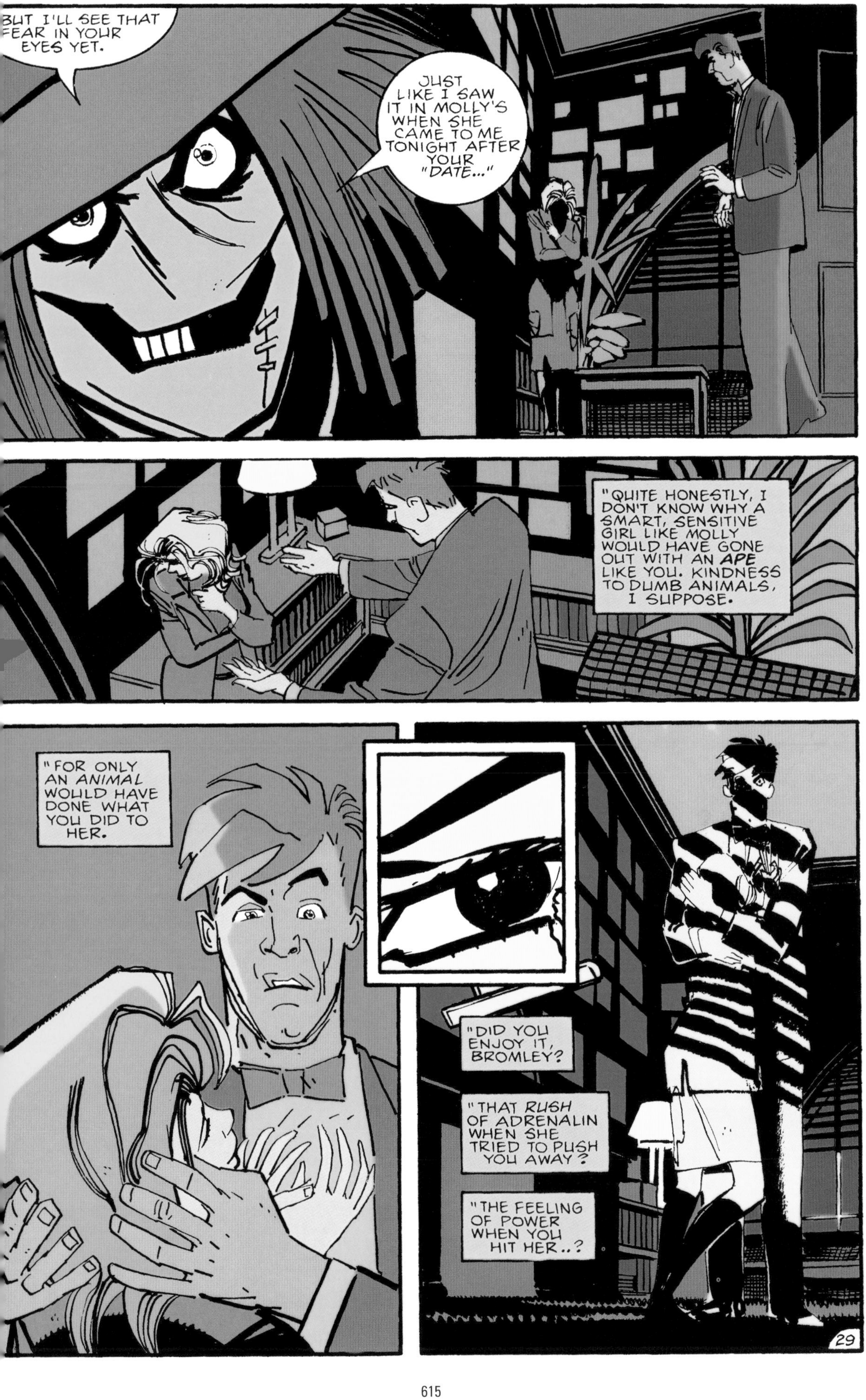
BUT I'LL SEE THAT FEAR IN YOUR EYES YET.
JUST LIKE I SAW IT IN MOLLY'S WHEN SHE CAME TO ME TONIGHT AFTER YOUR "DATE..."
"QUITE HONESTLY, I DON'T KNOW WHY A SMART, SENSITIVE GIRL LIKE MOLLY WOULD HAVE GONE OUT WITH AN APE LIKE YOU. KINDNESS TO DUMB ANIMALS, I SUPPOSE.
"FOR ONLY AN ANIMAL WOULD HAVE DONE WHAT YOU DID TO HER.
"DID YOU ENJOY IT, BROMLEY?
"THAT RUSH OF ADRENALIN WHEN SHE TRIED TO PUSH YOU AWAY?
"THE FEELING OF POWER WHEN YOU HIT HER..?
29

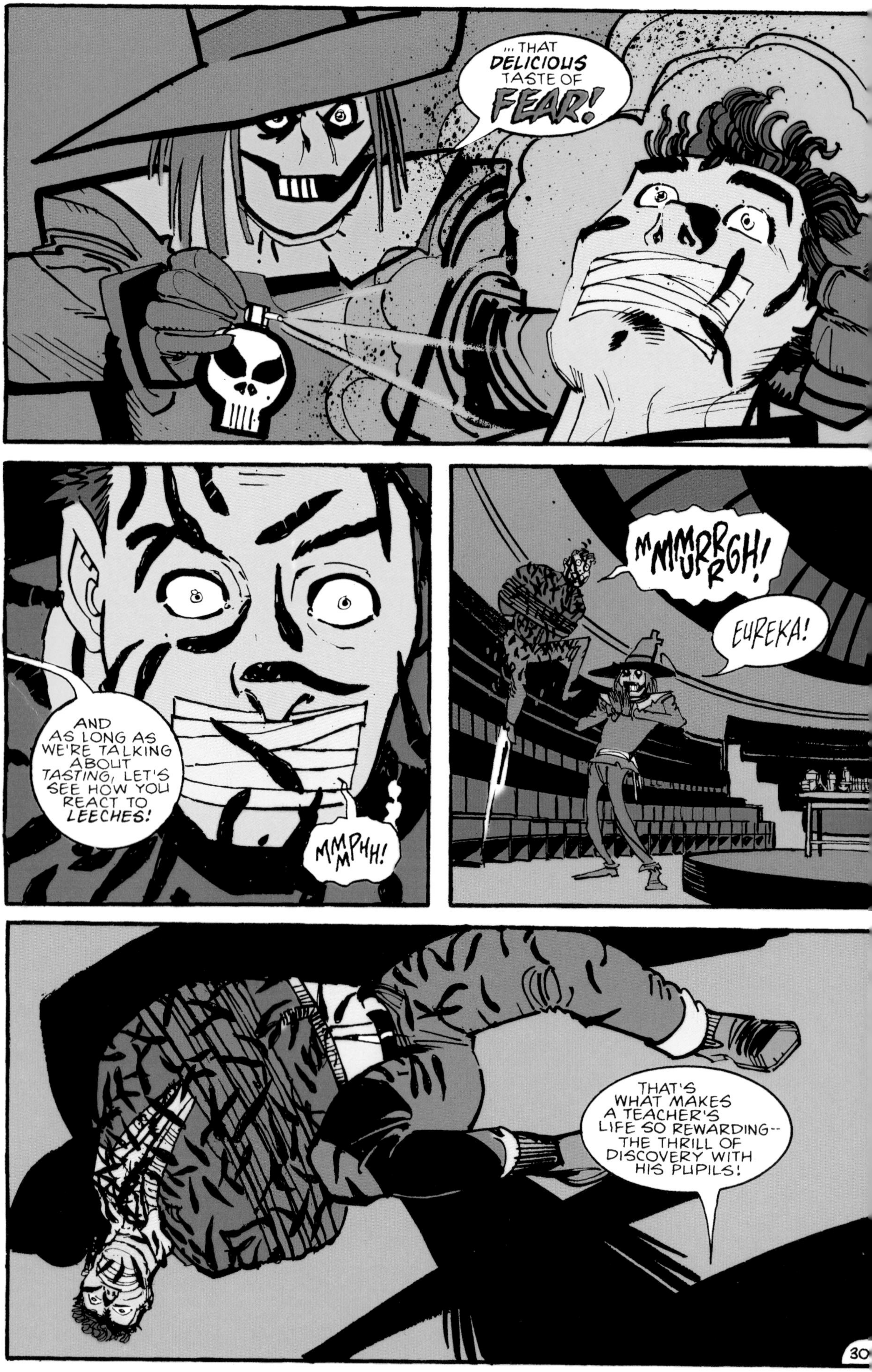
...THAT DELICIOUS TASTE OF FEAR!
AND AS LONG AS WE'RE TALKING ABOUT TASTING, LET'S SEE HOW YOU REACT TO LEECHES!
MMMPHH!
MMMURRRGH!
EUREKA!
THAT'S WHAT MAKES A TEACHER'S LIFE SO REWARDING-- THE THRILL OF DISCOVERY WITH HIS PUPILS!
30

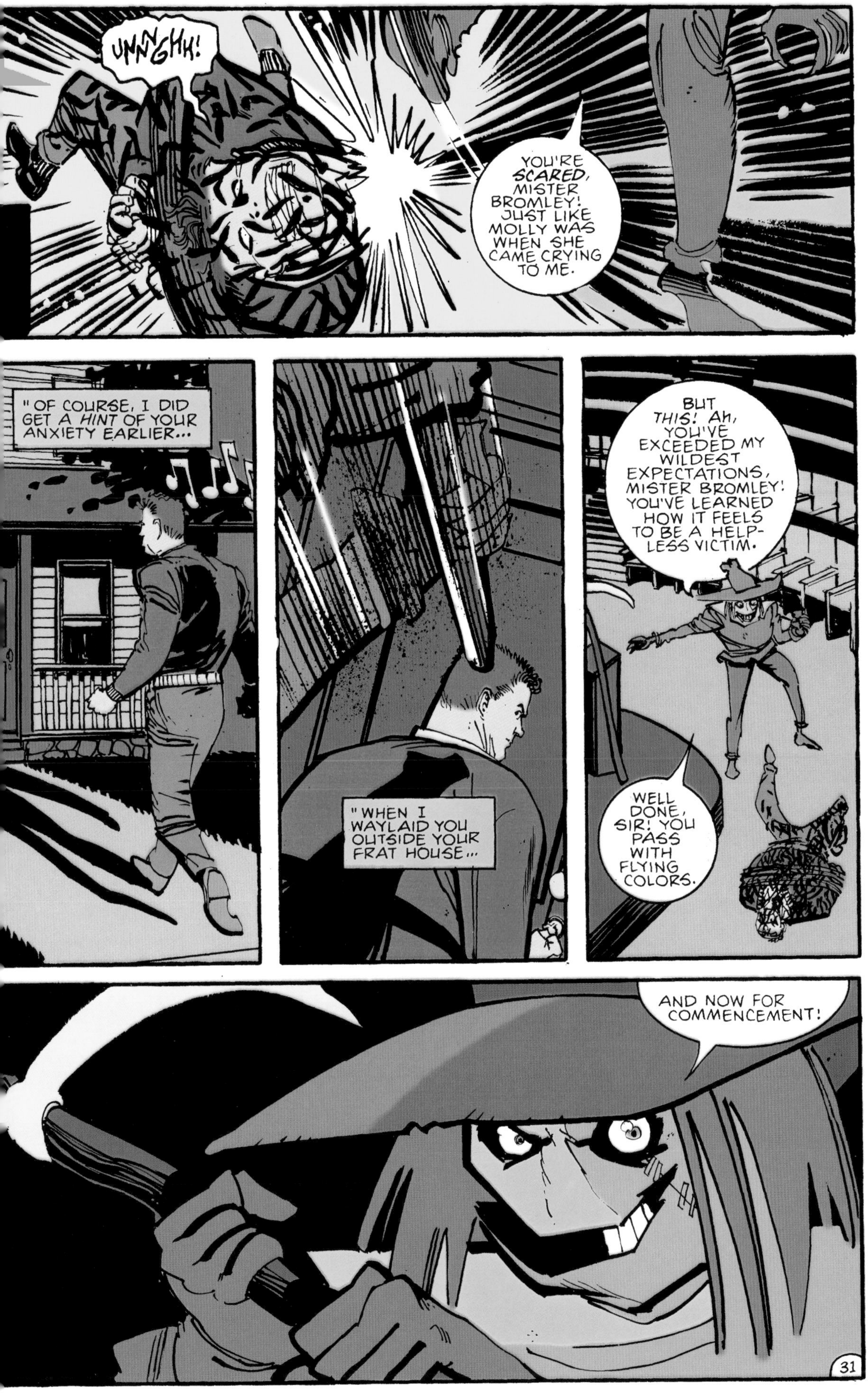
UNNNGHH!
YOU'RE SCARED, MISTER BROMLEY! JUST LIKE MOLLY WAS WHEN SHE CAME CRYING TO ME.
"OF COURSE, I DID GET A HINT OF YOUR ANXIETY EARLIER...
"WHEN I WAYLAID YOU OUTSIDE YOUR FRAT HOUSE...
BUT THIS! AH, YOU'VE EXCEEDED MY WILDEST EXPECTATIONS, MISTER BROMLEY! YOU'VE LEARNED HOW IT FEELS TO BE A HELPLESS VICTIM.
WELL DONE, SIR! YOU PASS WITH FLYING COLORS.
AND NOW FOR COMMENCEMENT!
31

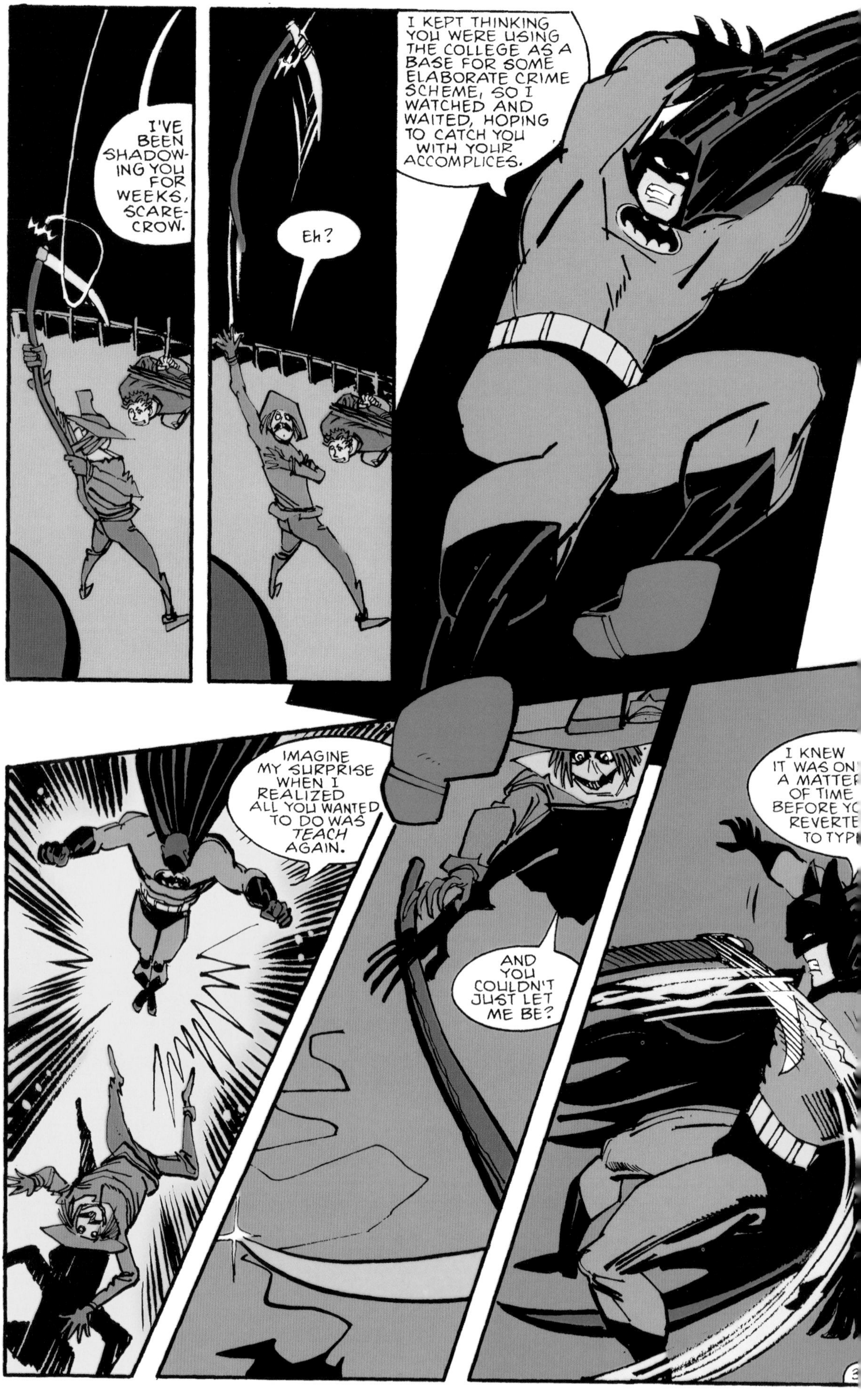
I'VE BEEN SHADOWING YOU FOR WEEKS, SCARECROW.
Eh?
I KEPT THINKING YOU WERE USING THE COLLEGE AS A BASE FOR SOME ELABORATE CRIME SCHEME, SO I WATCHED AND WAITED, HOPING TO CATCH YOU WITH YOUR ACCOMPLICES.
IMAGINE MY SURPRISE WHEN I REALIZED ALL YOU WANTED TO DO WAS *TEACH* AGAIN.
AND YOU COULDN'T JUST LET ME BE?
I KNEW IT WAS ON A MATTE OF TIME BEFORE YO REVERTE TO TYP

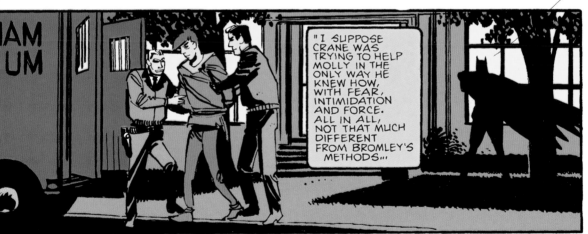

"I SUPPOSE CRANE WAS TRYING TO HELP MOLLY IN THE ONLY WAY HE KNEW HOW, WITH FEAR, INTIMIDATION AND FORCE. ALL IN ALL, NOT THAT MUCH DIFFERENT FROM BROMLEY'S METHODS..."

"EXCEPT CRANE HAS ALWAYS HAD THE DECENCY TO WEAR HIS MASK ON THE OUTSIDE."

33

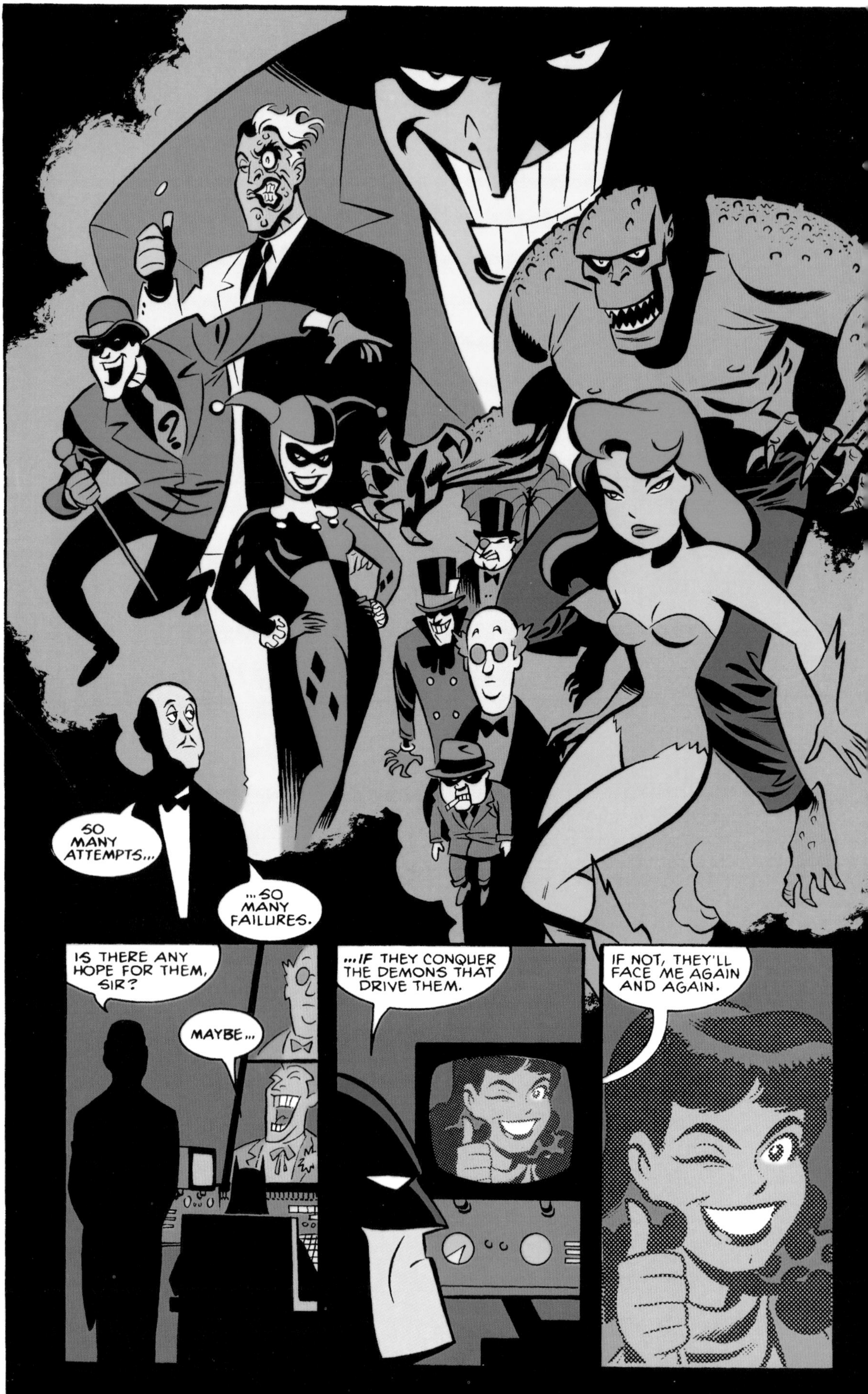
SO MANY ATTEMPTS...
...SO MANY FAILURES.
IS THERE ANY HOPE FOR THEM, SIR?
MAYBE...
...IF THEY CONQUER THE DEMONS THAT DRIVE THEM.
IF NOT, THEY'LL FACE ME AGAIN AND AGAIN.

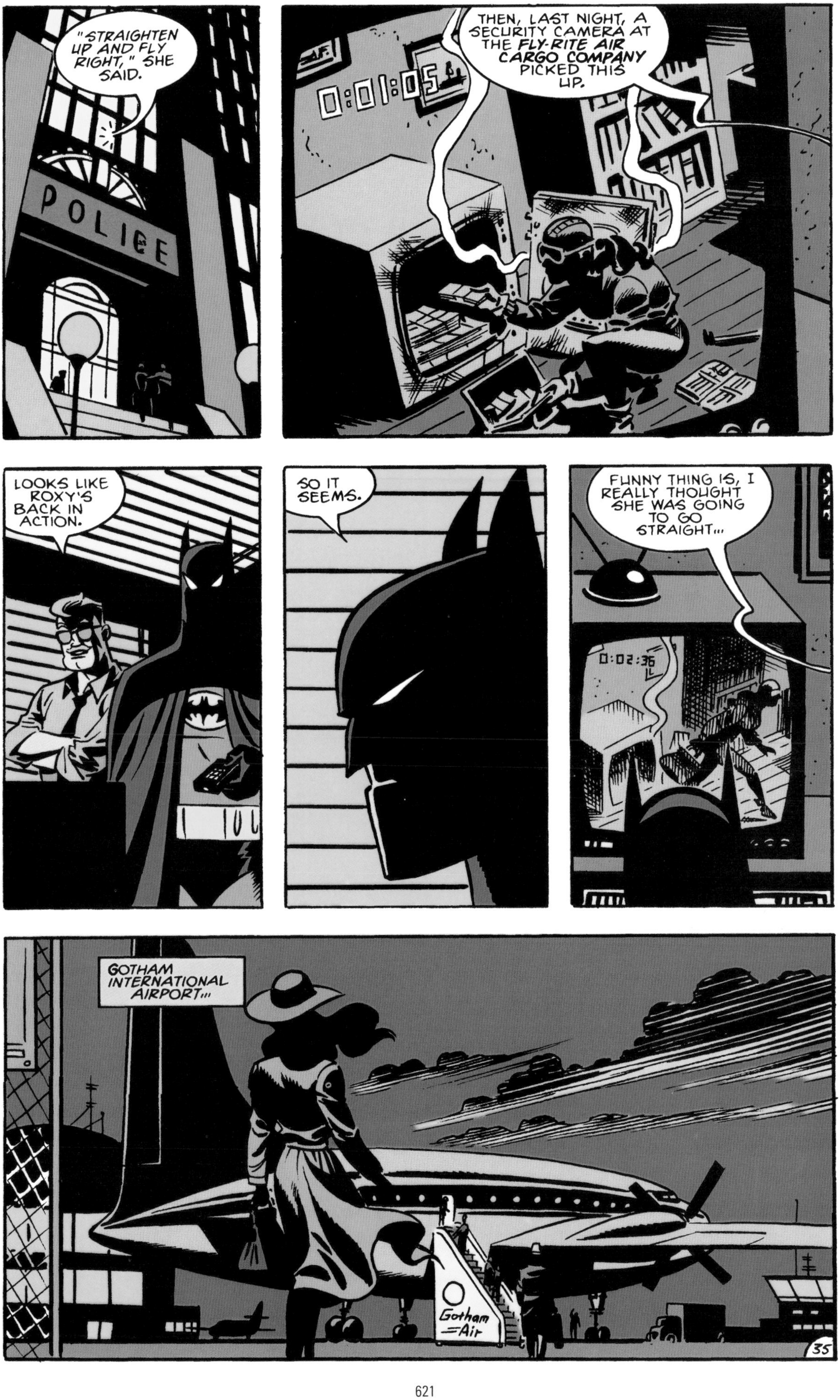
"STRAIGHTEN UP AND FLY RIGHT," SHE SAID.
POLICE
THEN, LAST NIGHT, A SECURITY CAMERA AT THE FLY-RITE AIR CARGO COMPANY PICKED THIS UP.
0:01:05
LOOKS LIKE ROXY'S BACK IN ACTION.
SO IT SEEMS.
FUNNY THING IS, I REALLY THOUGHT SHE WAS GOING TO GO STRAIGHT...
0:02:36
GOTHAM INTERNATIONAL AIRPORT...
Gotham Air
35

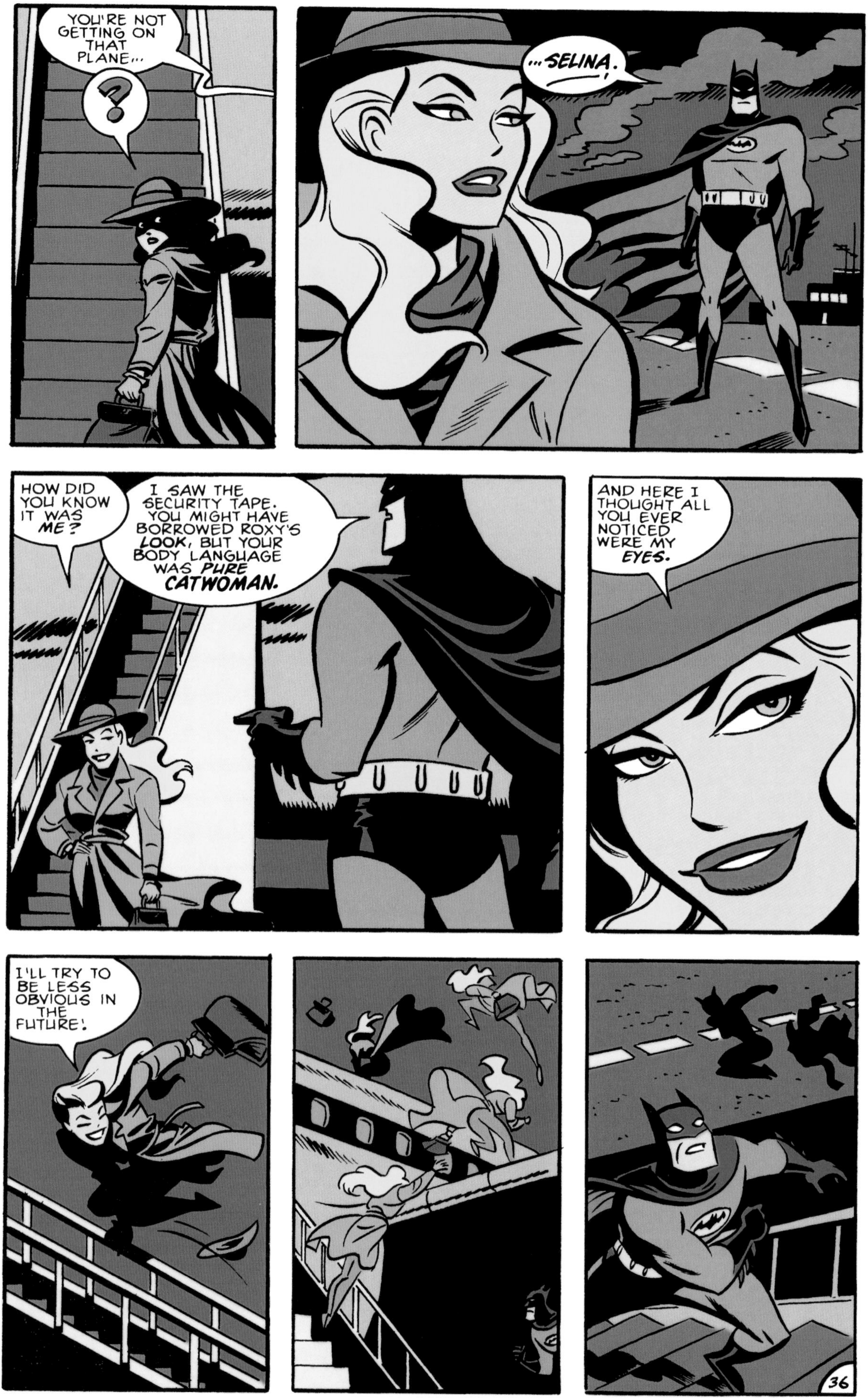

YOU'RE NOT GETTING ON THAT PLANE...
?
...SELINA.
HOW DID YOU KNOW IT WAS ME?
I SAW THE SECURITY TAPE. YOU MIGHT HAVE BORROWED ROXY'S LOOK, BUT YOUR BODY LANGUAGE WAS PURE CATWOMAN.
AND HERE I THOUGHT ALL YOU EVER NOTICED WERE MY EYES.
I'LL TRY TO BE LESS OBVIOUS IN THE FUTURE!
36

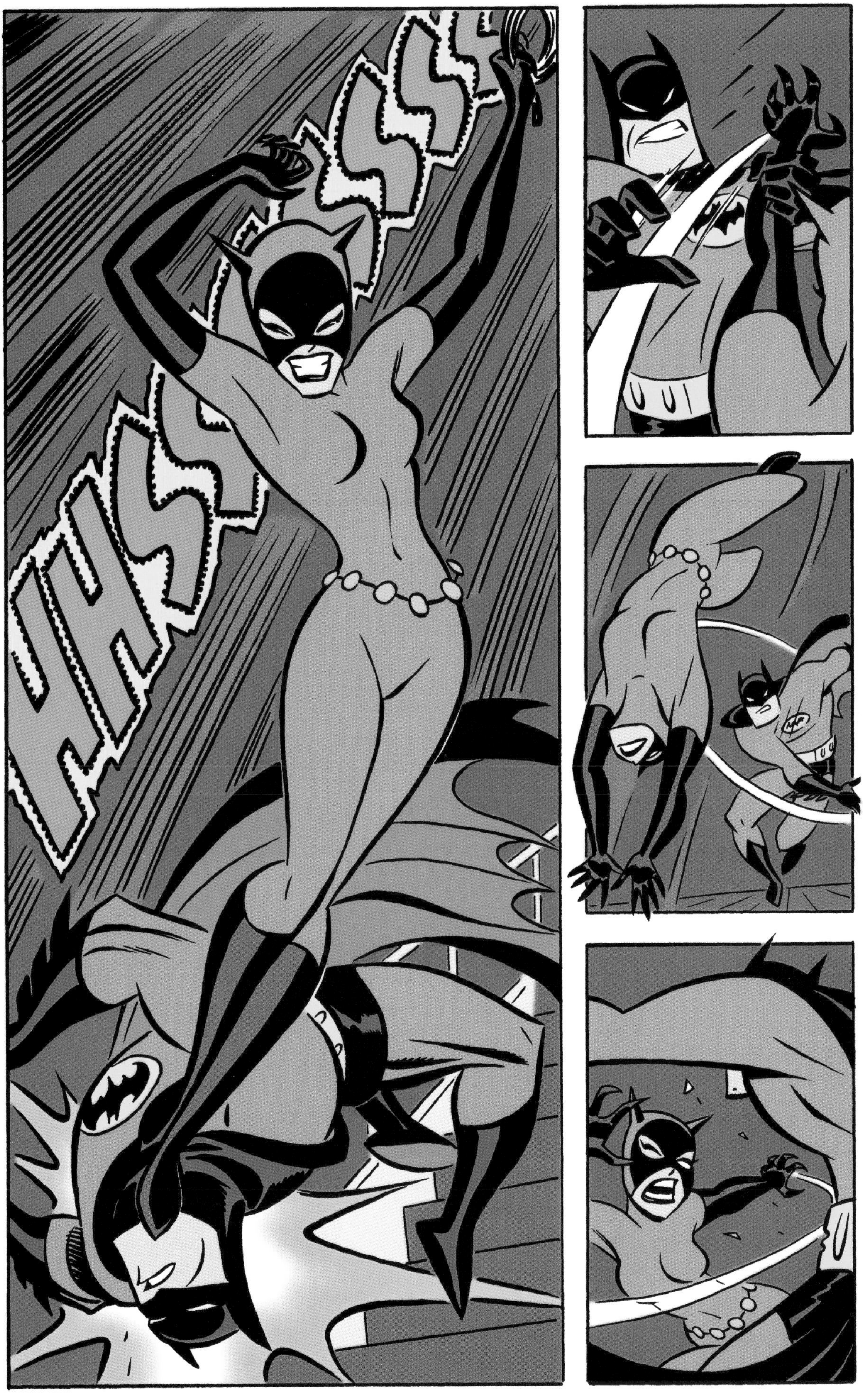

HHSSSSSS

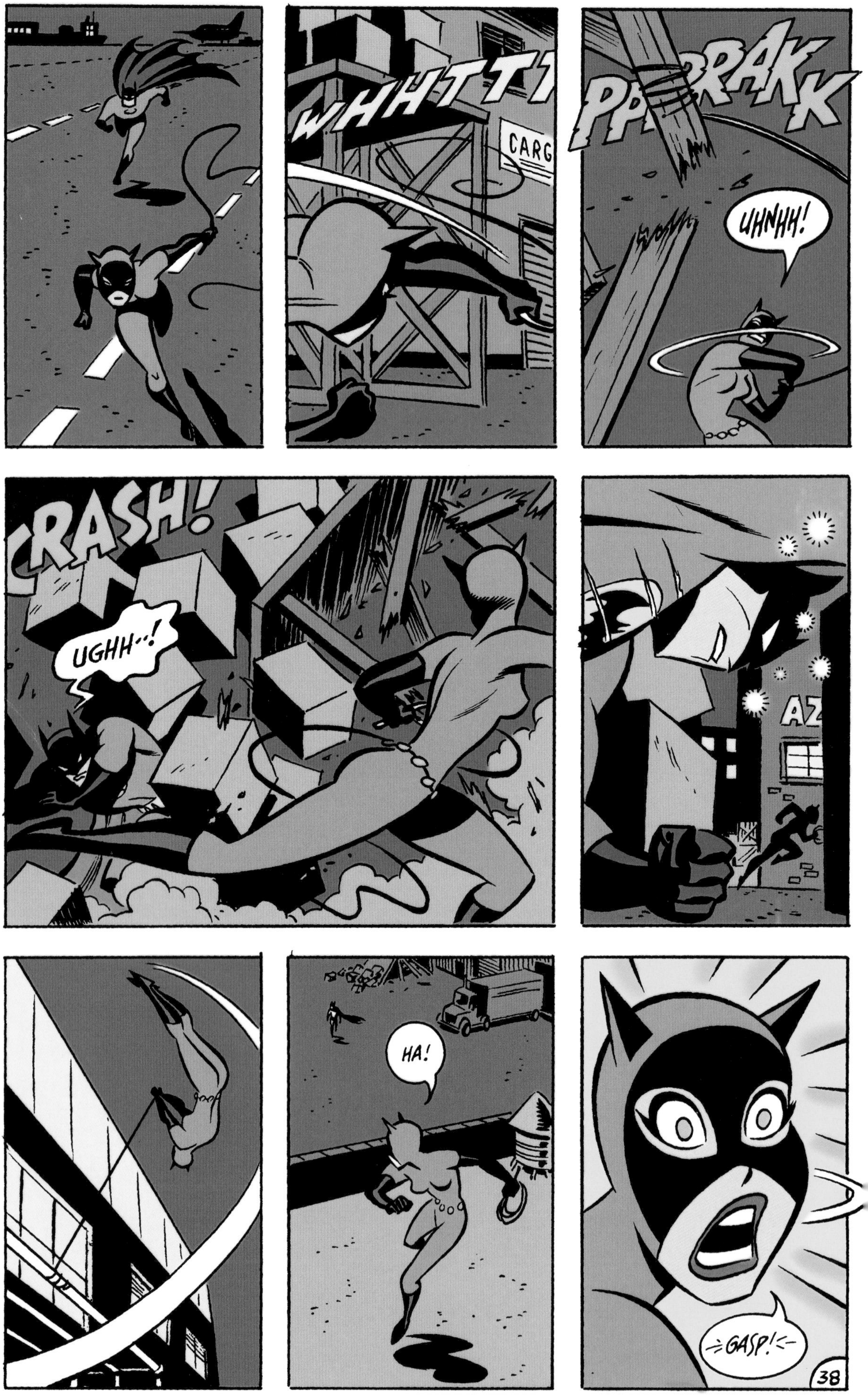
WHHTTT
CARG
PPPRAKK
UHNHH!
CRASH!
UGHH--!
AZ
HA!
GASP!
38

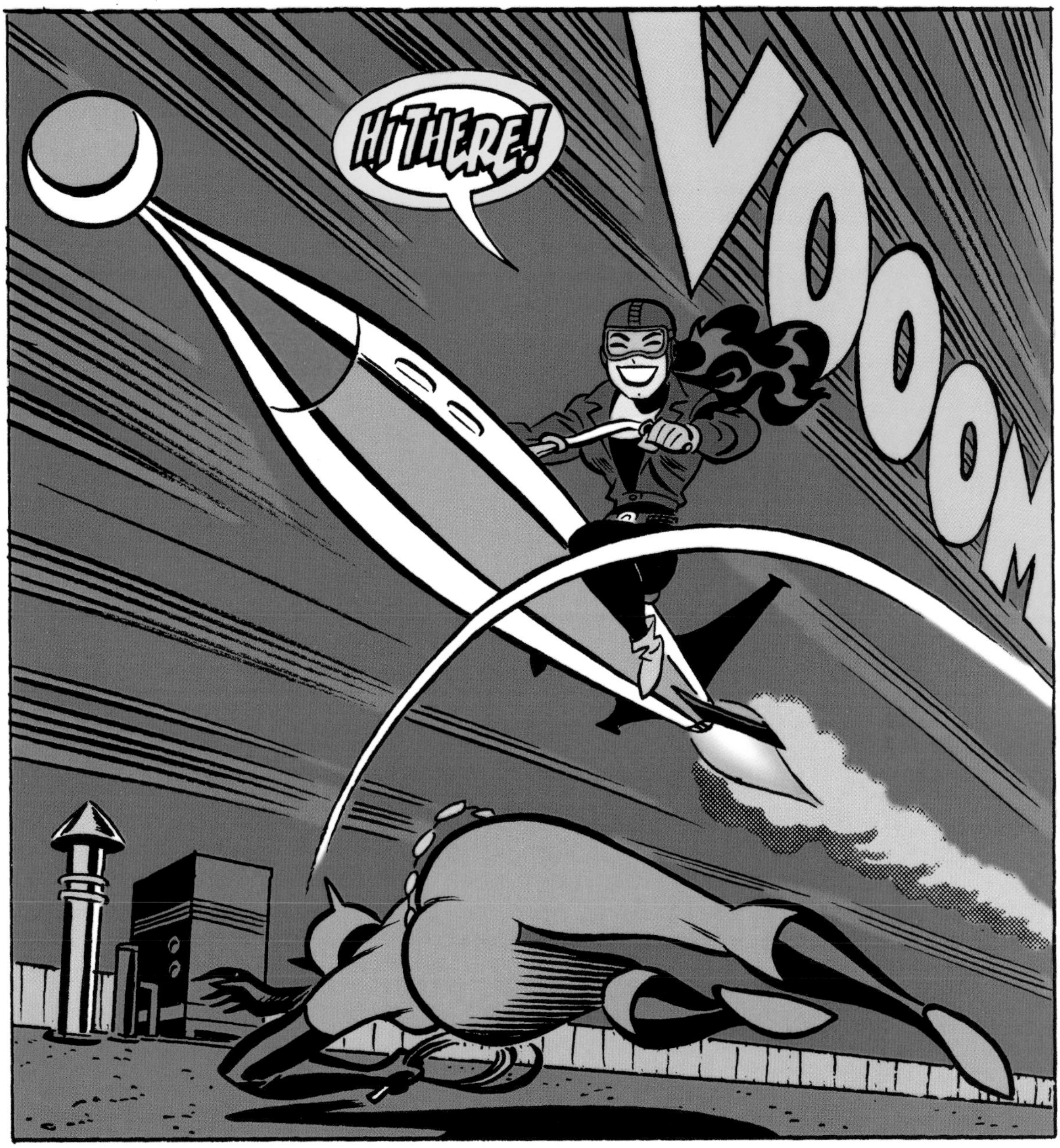
HI THERE!
VOOOOOM

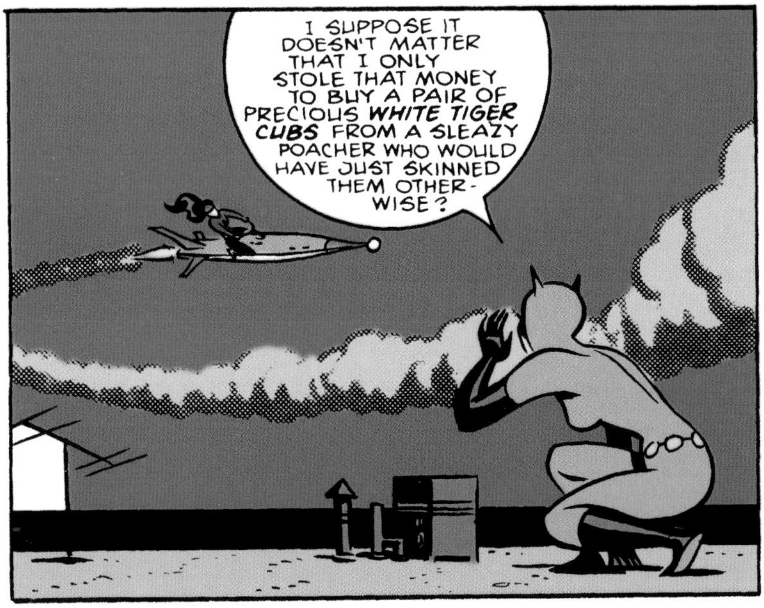
I SUPPOSE IT DOESN'T MATTER THAT I ONLY STOLE THAT MONEY TO BUY A PAIR OF PRECIOUS WHITE TIGER CUBS FROM A SLEAZY POACHER WHO WOULD HAVE JUST SKINNED THEM OTHER-WISE?

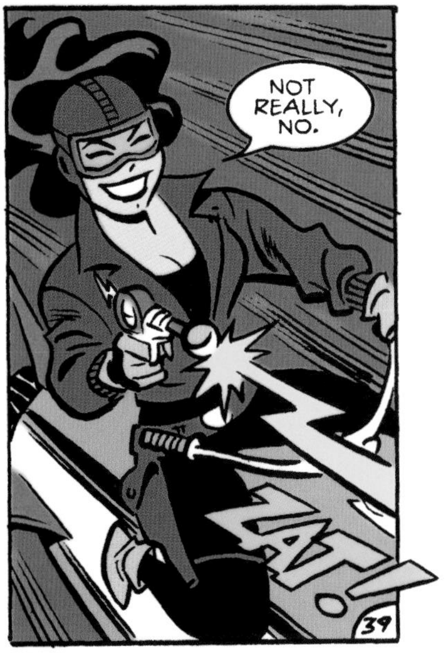
NOT REALLY, NO.
ZZAT!
39

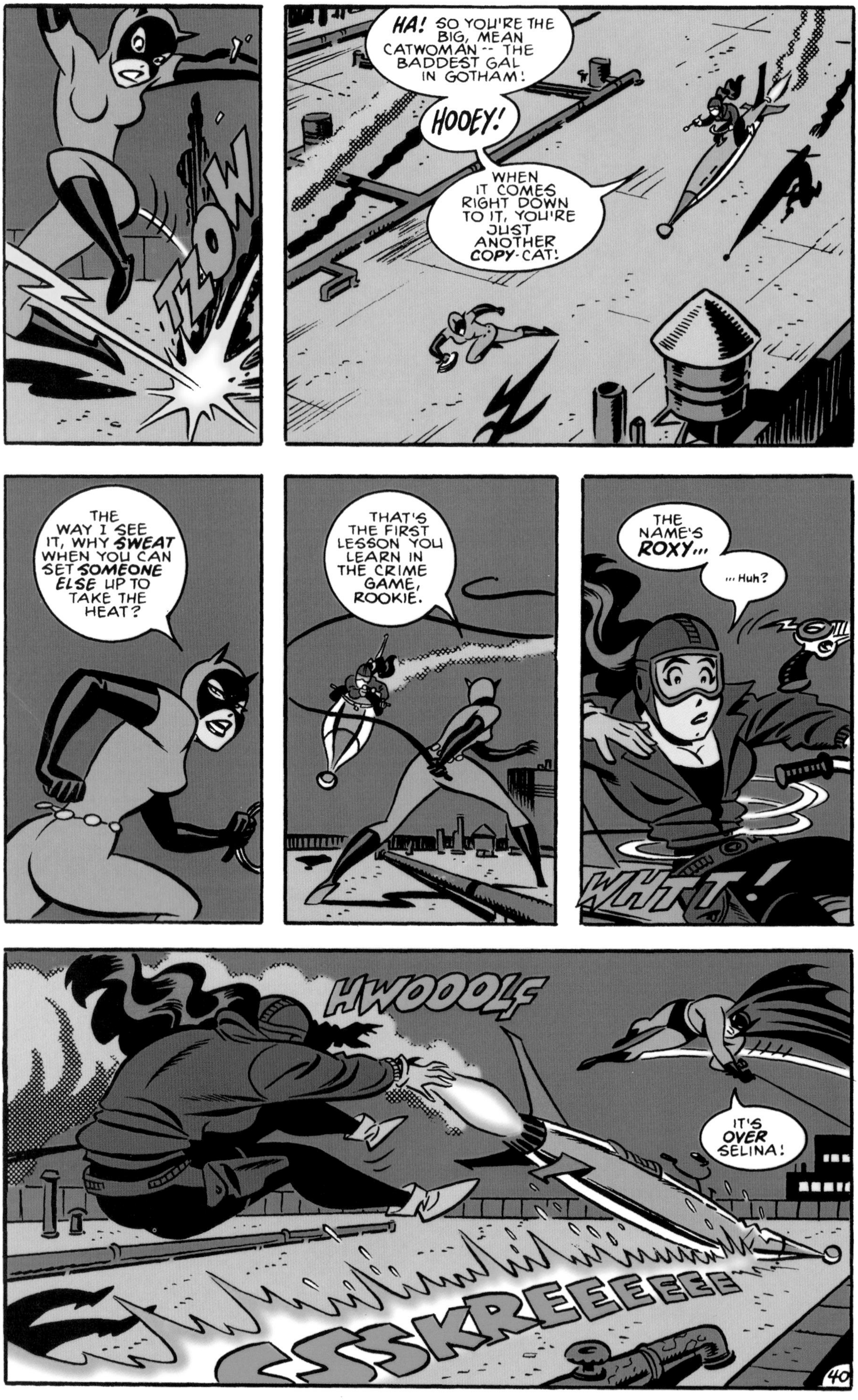
TZOW
HA! SO YOU'RE THE BIG, MEAN CATWOMAN -- THE BADDEST GAL IN GOTHAM!
HOOEY!
WHEN IT COMES RIGHT DOWN TO IT, YOU'RE JUST ANOTHER COPY-CAT!
THE WAY I SEE IT, WHY SWEAT WHEN YOU CAN SET SOMEONE ELSE UP TO TAKE THE HEAT?
THAT'S THE FIRST LESSON YOU LEARN IN THE CRIME GAME, ROOKIE.
THE NAME'S ROXY...
...Huh?
WHTT!
HWOOOLF
IT'S OVER SELINA!
SSKREEEEEEE
40

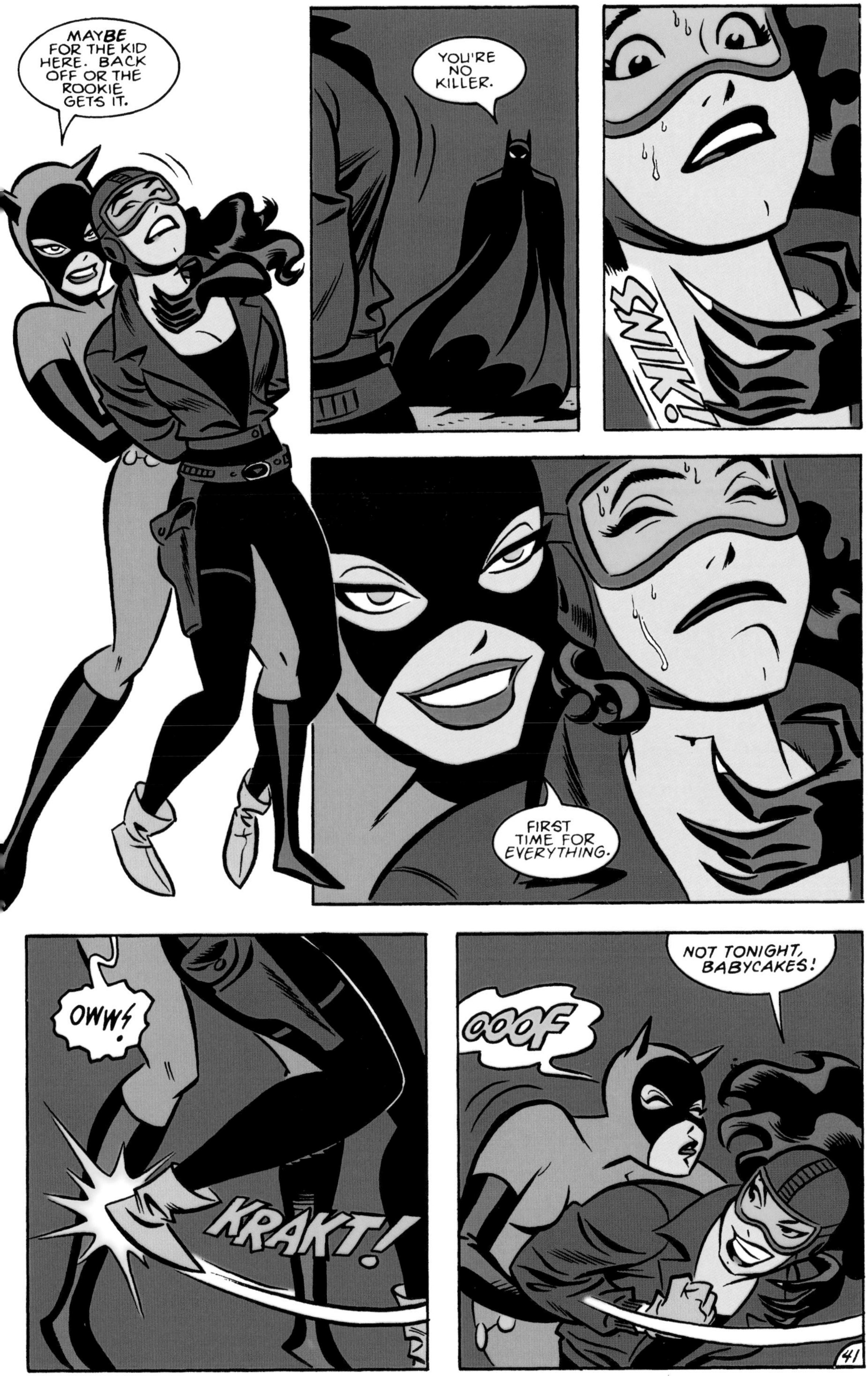
MAYBE FOR THE KID HERE. BACK OFF OR THE ROOKIE GETS IT.
YOU'RE NO KILLER.
SNIK!
FIRST TIME FOR EVERYTHING.
OWW!
KRAKT!
NOT TONIGHT, BABYCAKES!
OOOF
41

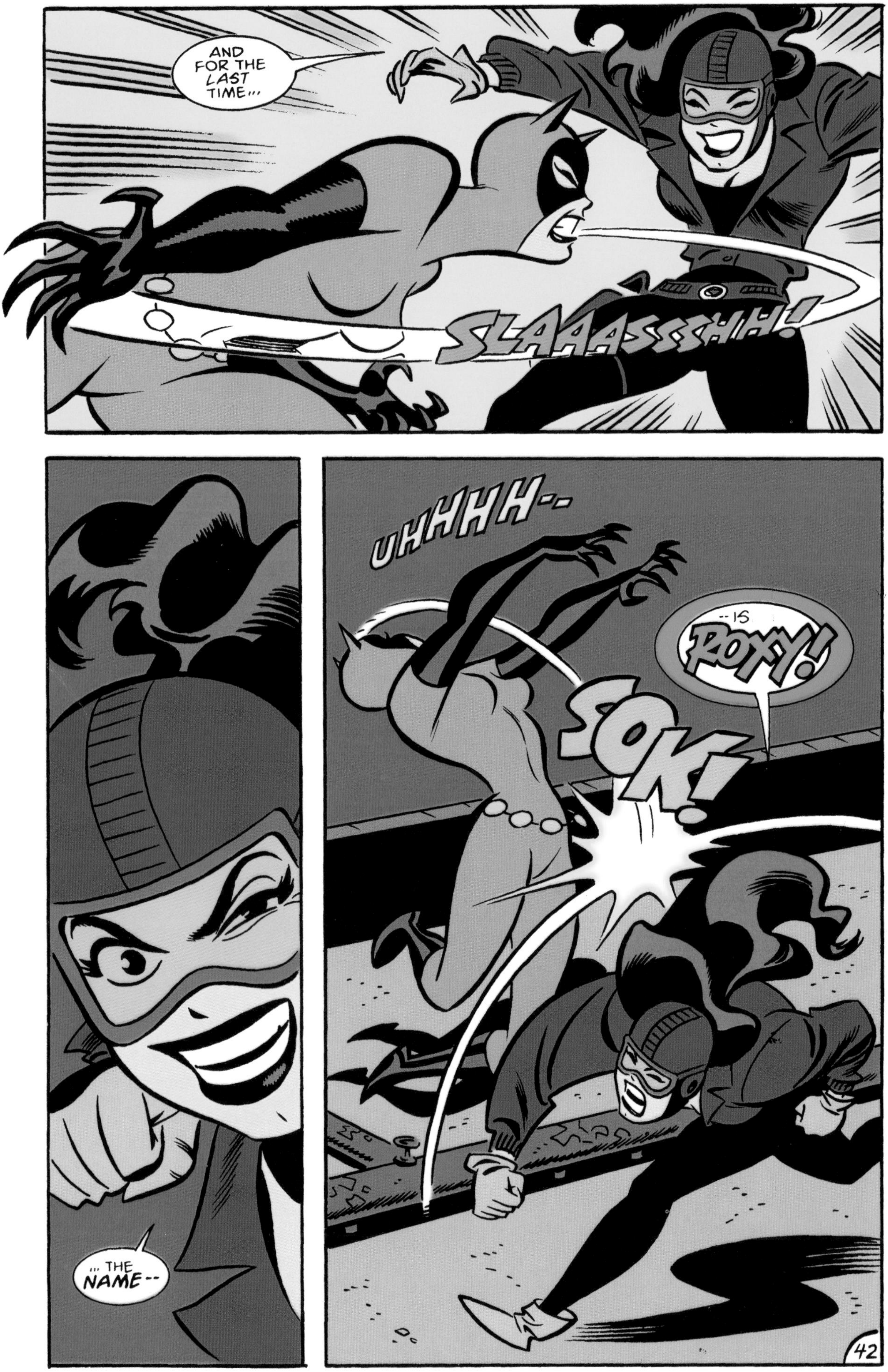
AND FOR THE LAST TIME...
SLAAASSSHH!
... THE NAME --
UHHHH --
-- IS ROXY!
SOK!
42

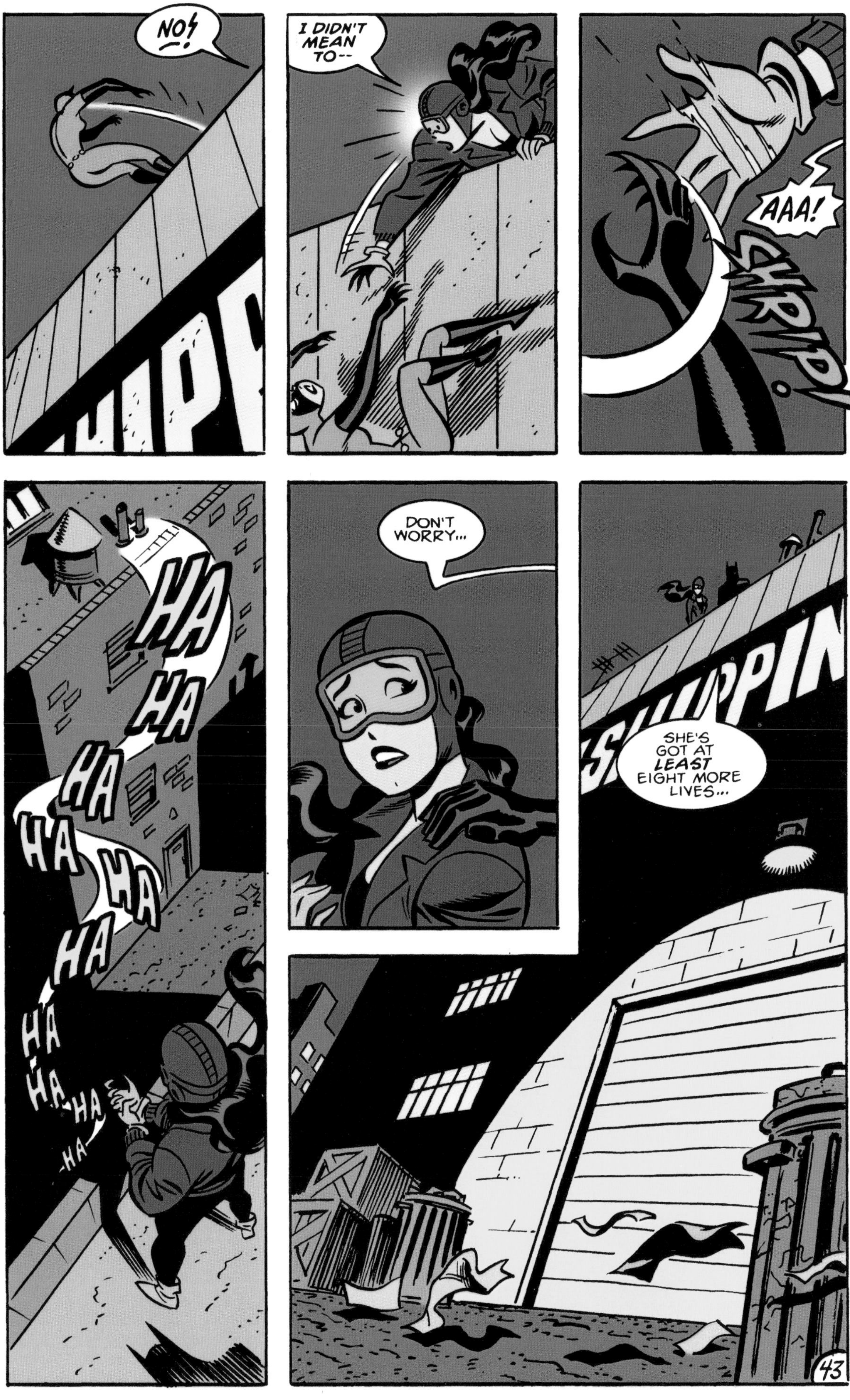
NO!
I DIDN'T MEAN TO--
AAA!
SHRIP!
HA HA HA HA HA HA HA HA HA HA -HA
DON'T WORRY...
SHE'S GOT AT LEAST EIGHT MORE LIVES...
43

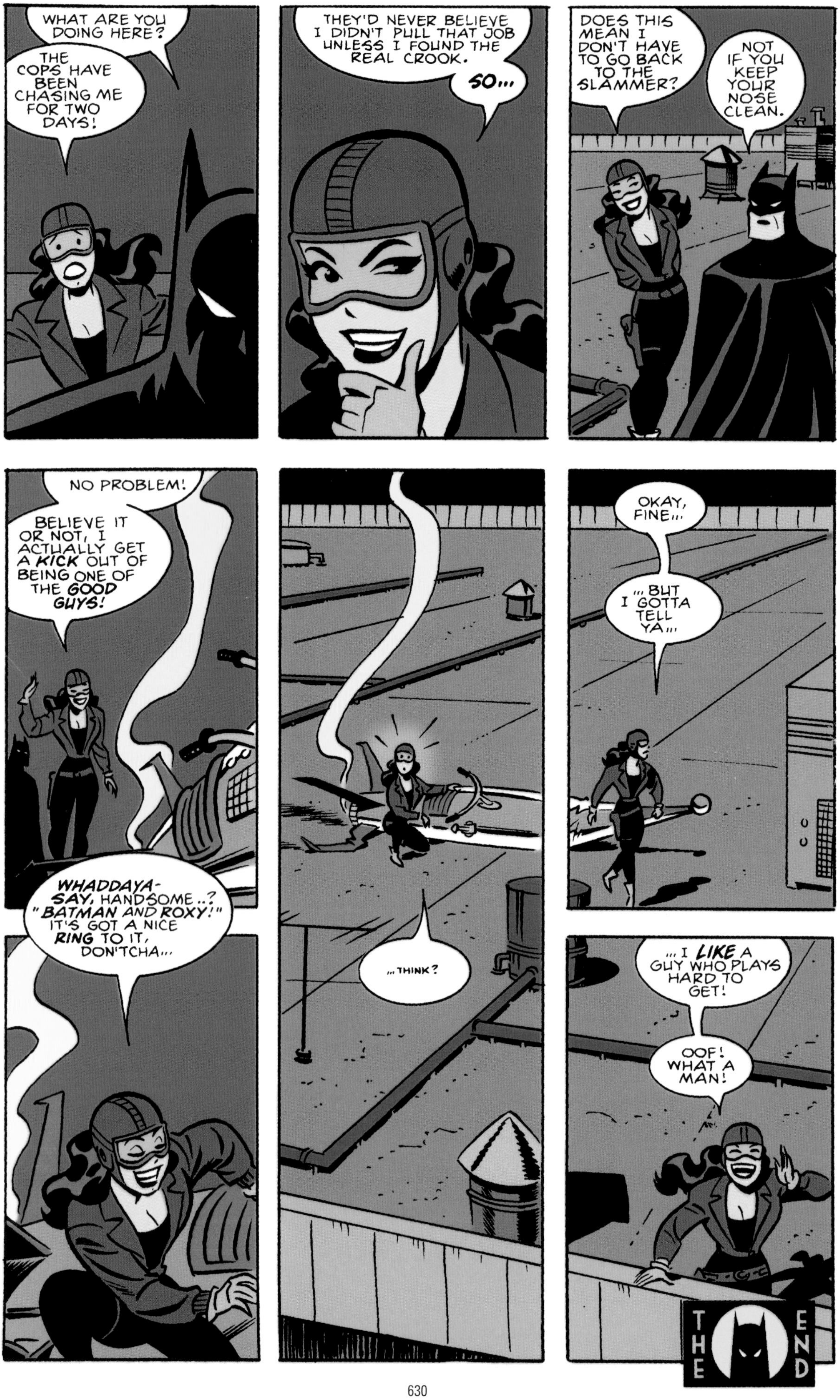

WHAT ARE YOU DOING HERE?
THE COPS HAVE BEEN CHASING ME FOR TWO DAYS!
THEY'D NEVER BELIEVE I DIDN'T PULL THAT JOB UNLESS I FOUND THE REAL CROOK.
SO...
DOES THIS MEAN I DON'T HAVE TO GO BACK TO THE SLAMMER?
NOT IF YOU KEEP YOUR NOSE CLEAN.
NO PROBLEM!
BELIEVE IT OR NOT, I ACTUALLY GET A KICK OUT OF BEING ONE OF THE GOOD GUYS!
WHADDAYA-SAY, HANDSOME..? "BATMAN AND ROXY!" IT'S GOT A NICE RING TO IT, DON'TCHA...
...THINK?
OKAY, FINE...
...BUT I GOTTA TELL YA...
...I LIKE A GUY WHO PLAYS HARD TO GET!
OOF! WHAT A MAN!
THE END

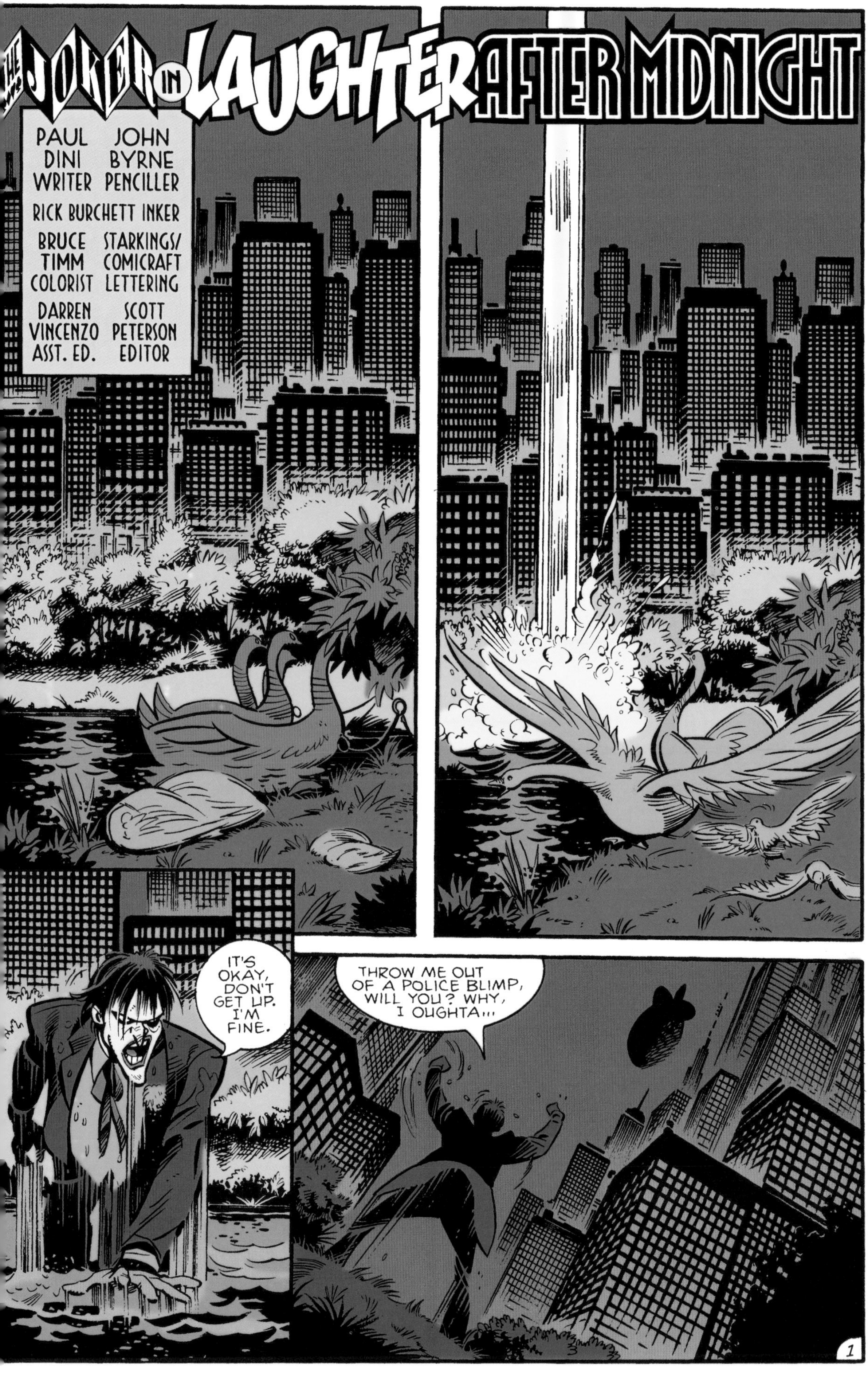
THE JOKER IN LAUGHTER AFTER MIDNIGHT
PAUL DINI WRITER
JOHN BYRNE PENCILLER
RICK BURCHETT INKER
BRUCE TIMM COLORIST
STARKINGS/ COMICRAFT LETTERING
DARREN VINCENZO ASST. ED.
SCOTT PETERSON EDITOR
IT'S OKAY, DON'T GET UP. I'M FINE.
THROW ME OUT OF A POLICE BLIMP, WILL YOU? WHY, I OUGHTA...
1

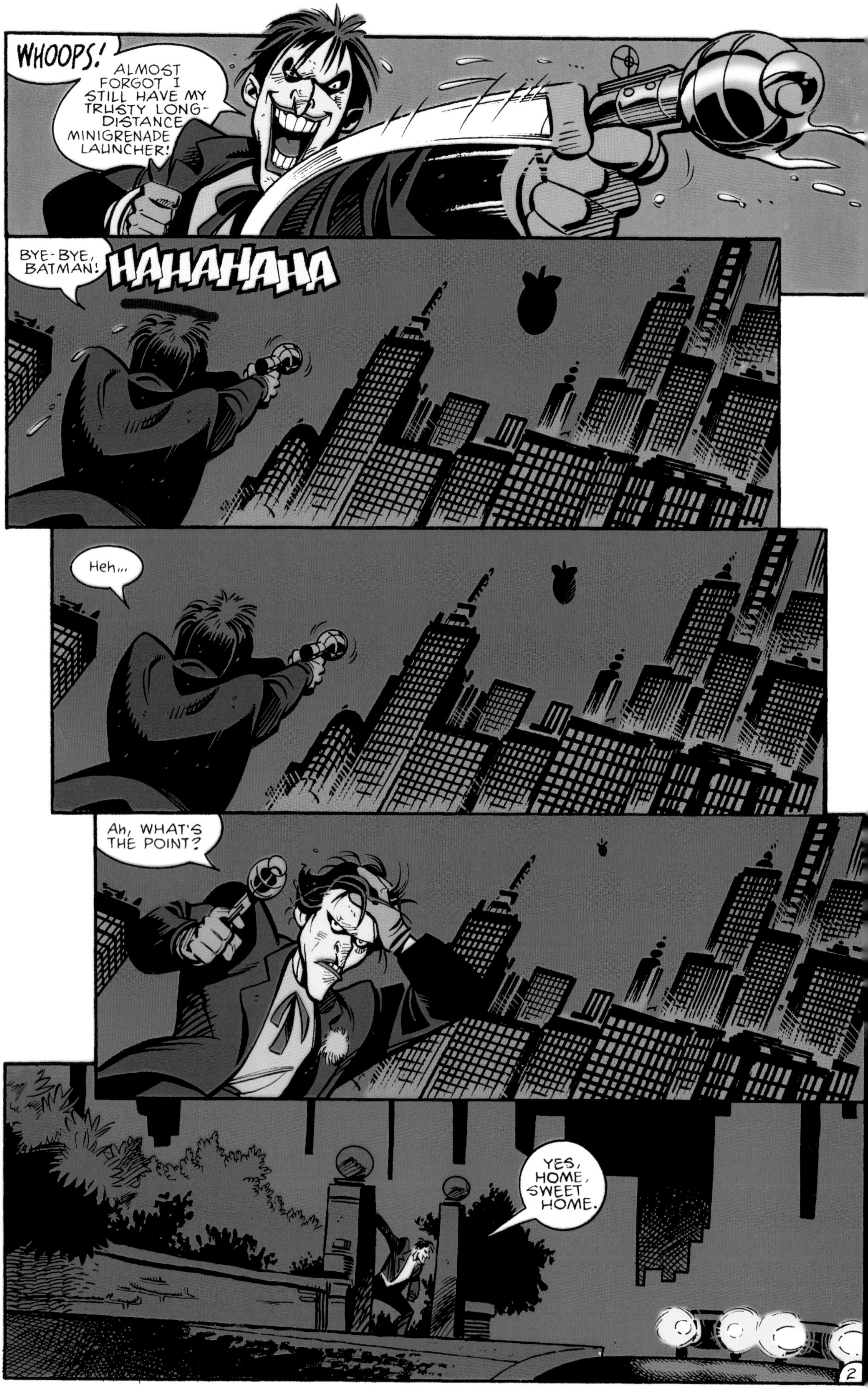
WHOOPS!
ALMOST FORGOT I STILL HAVE MY TRUSTY LONG-DISTANCE MINIGRENADE LAUNCHER!
BYE-BYE, BATMAN!
HAHAHAHA
Heh...
Ah, WHAT'S THE POINT?
YES, HOME, SWEET HOME.
2

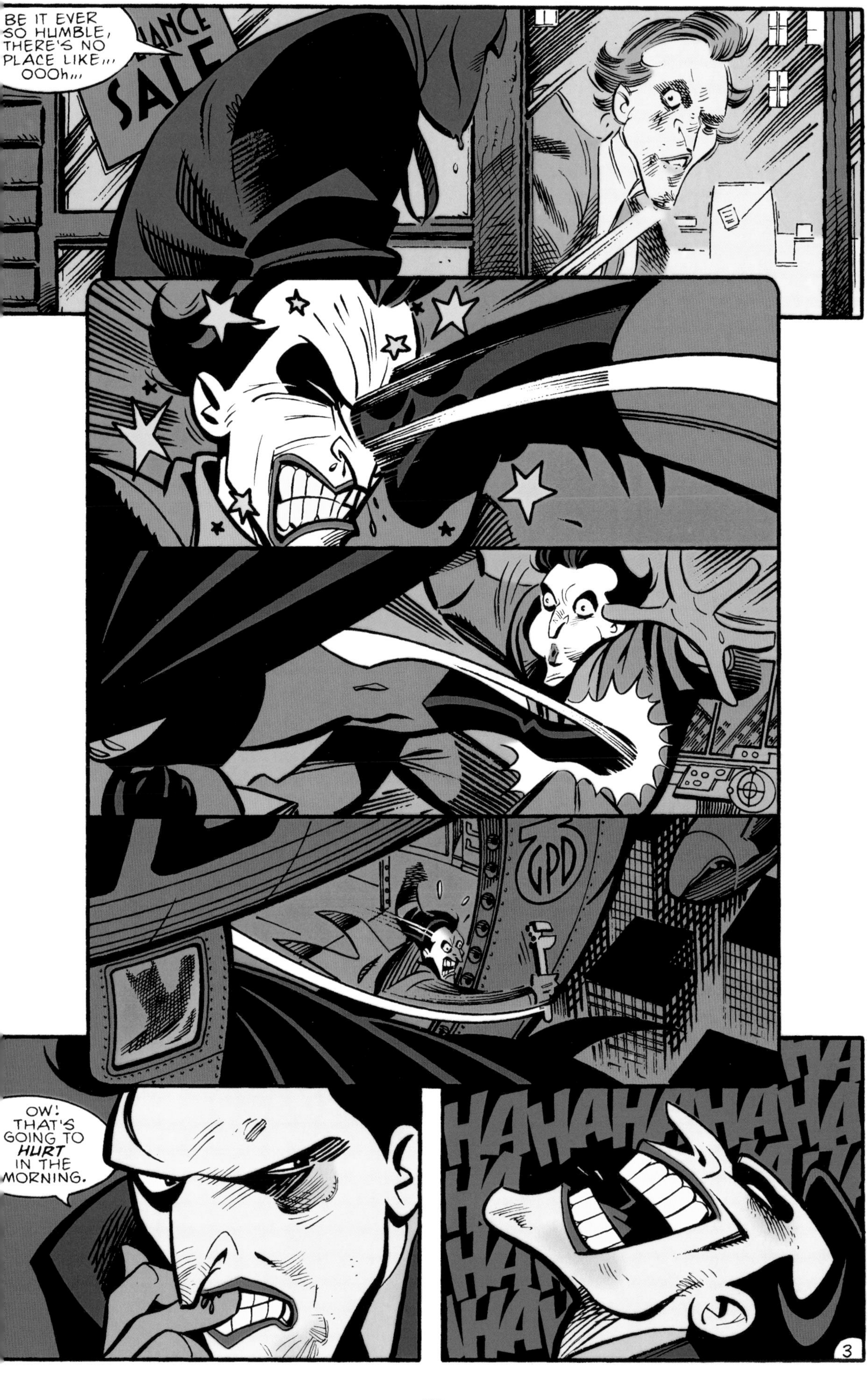
BE IT EVER SO HUMBLE, THERE'S NO PLACE LIKE,,, OOOh,,,
SALE
GPD
OW! THAT'S GOING TO *HURT* IN THE MORNING.
HAHAHAHAHAHA
3

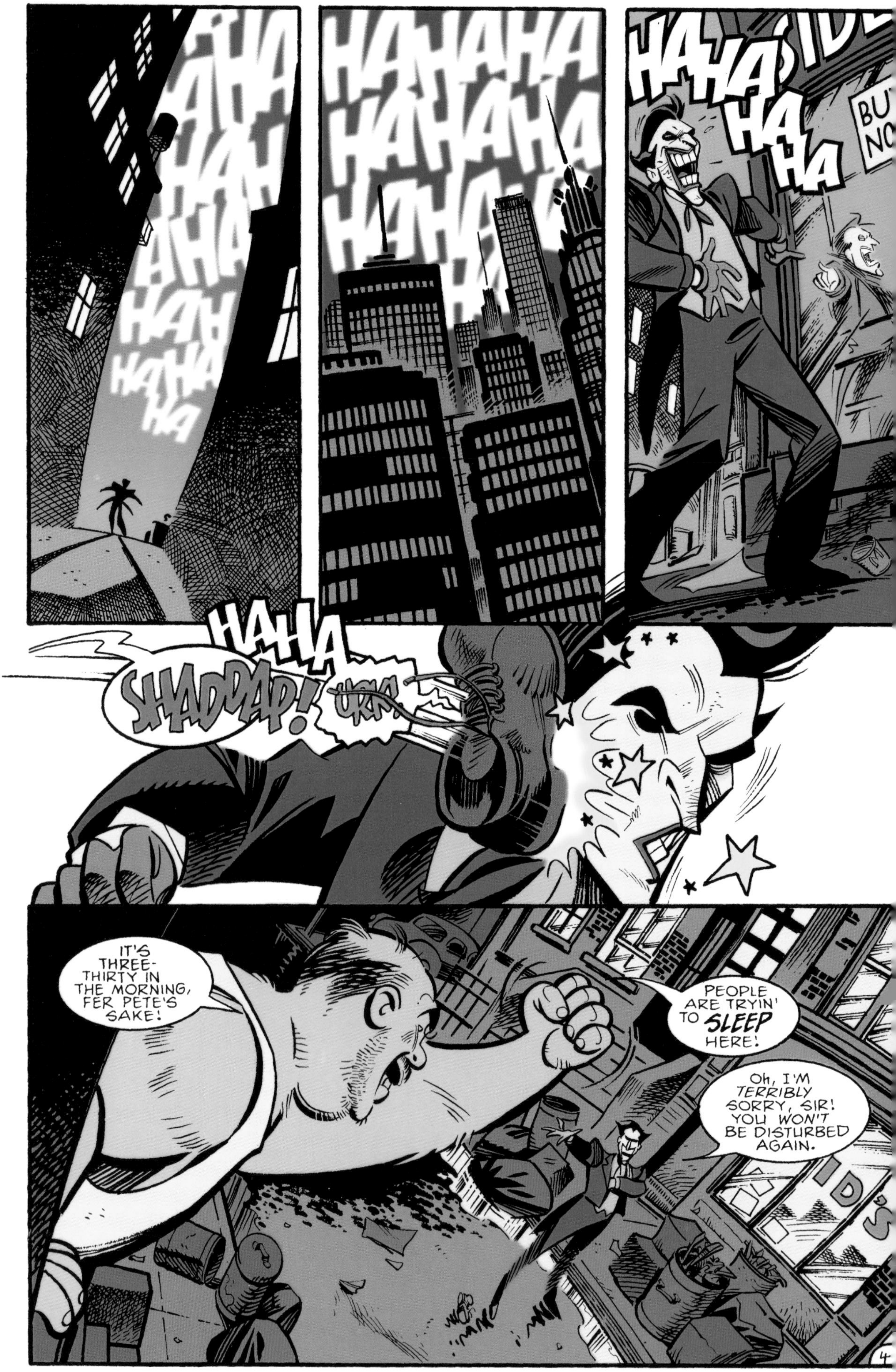
HAHA HAHA HAHA HAHA HAHA HAHA HA
HAHAHAHA HAHAHAHA HAHAHA
HAHA HA HA HA
HAHA
SHADDAP!
URK!
IT'S THREE-THIRTY IN THE MORNING, FER PETE'S SAKE!
PEOPLE ARE TRYIN' TO SLEEP HERE!
Oh, I'M TERRIBLY SORRY, SIR! YOU WON'T BE DISTURBED AGAIN.
4

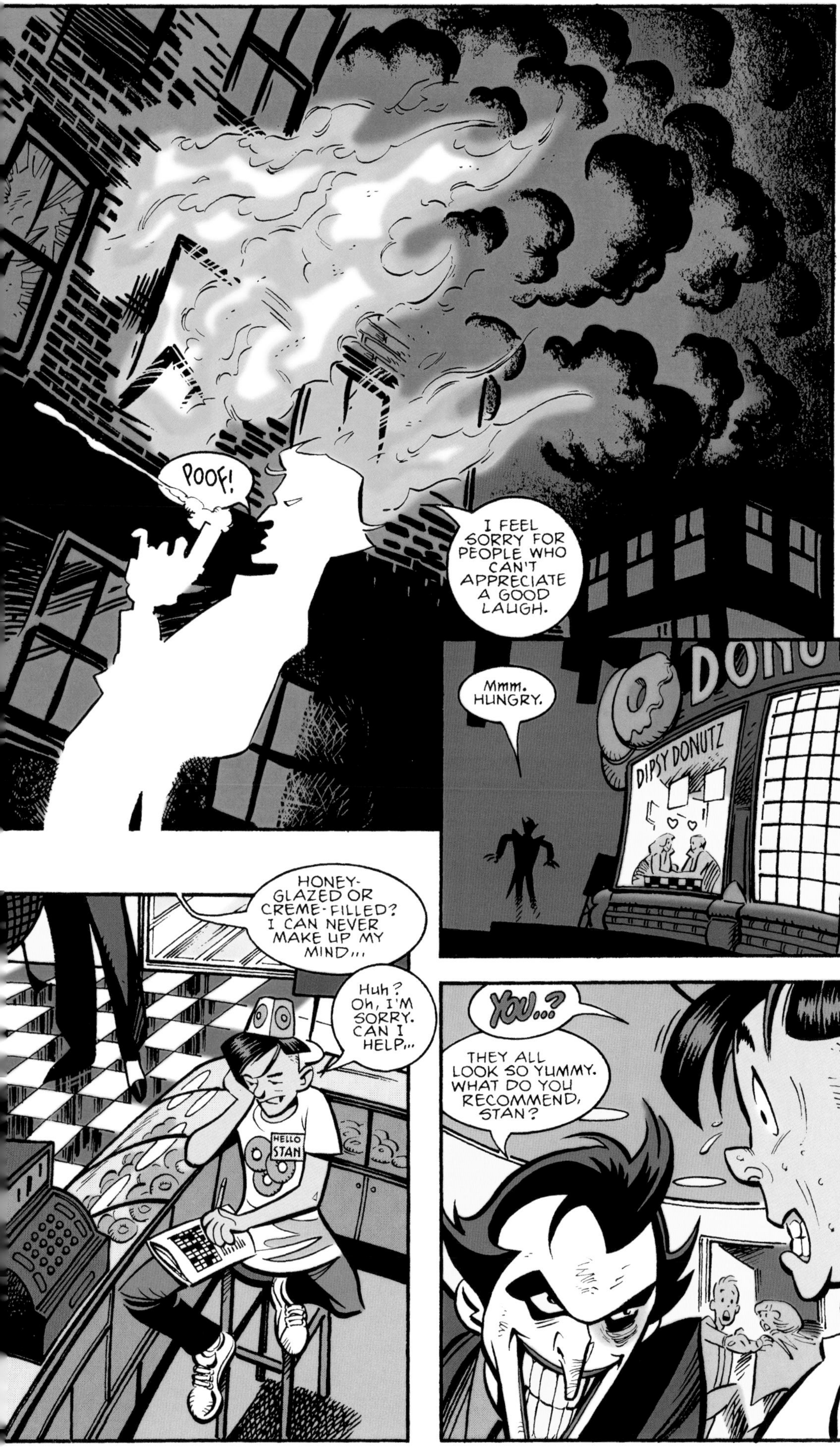
POOF!
I FEEL SORRY FOR PEOPLE WHO CAN'T APPRECIATE A GOOD LAUGH.
DONUTZ
Mmm. HUNGRY.
DIPSY DONUTZ
PRIV
HONEY-GLAZED OR CREME-FILLED? I CAN NEVER MAKE UP MY MIND...
Huh? Oh, I'M SORRY. CAN I HELP...
HELLO STAN
YOU..?
THEY ALL LOOK SO YUMMY. WHAT DO YOU RECOMMEND, STAN?
5

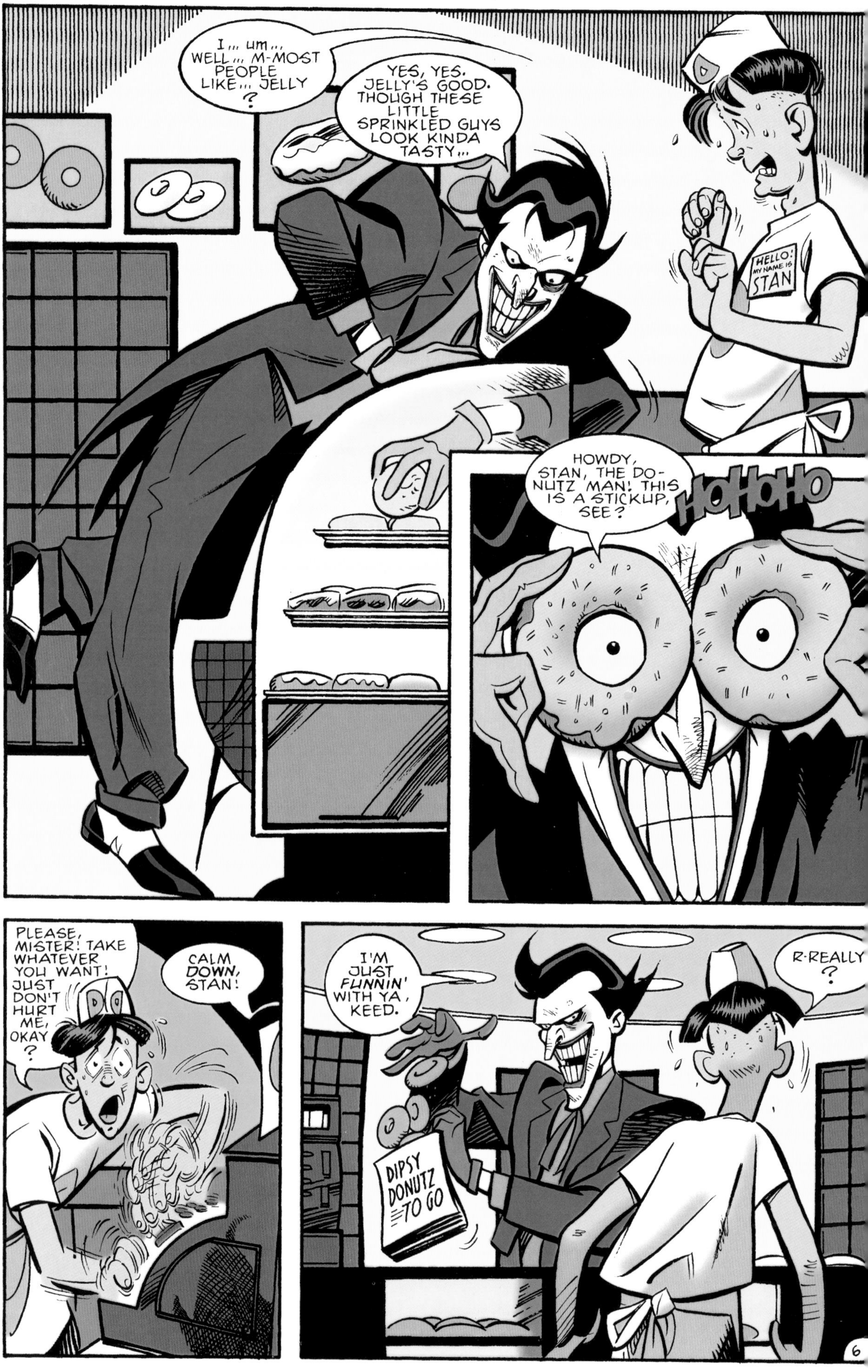
I... um...
WELL... M-MOST PEOPLE LIKE... JELLY?
YES, YES. JELLY'S GOOD. THOUGH THESE LITTLE SPRINKLED GUYS LOOK KINDA TASTY...
HELLO! MY NAME IS STAN
HOWDY, STAN, THE DO-NUTZ MAN! THIS IS A STICKUP, SEE?
HOHOHO
PLEASE, MISTER! TAKE WHATEVER YOU WANT! JUST DON'T HURT ME, OKAY?
CALM DOWN, STAN!
I'M JUST FUNNIN' WITH YA, KEED.
R-REALLY?
DIPSY DONUTZ TO GO
6

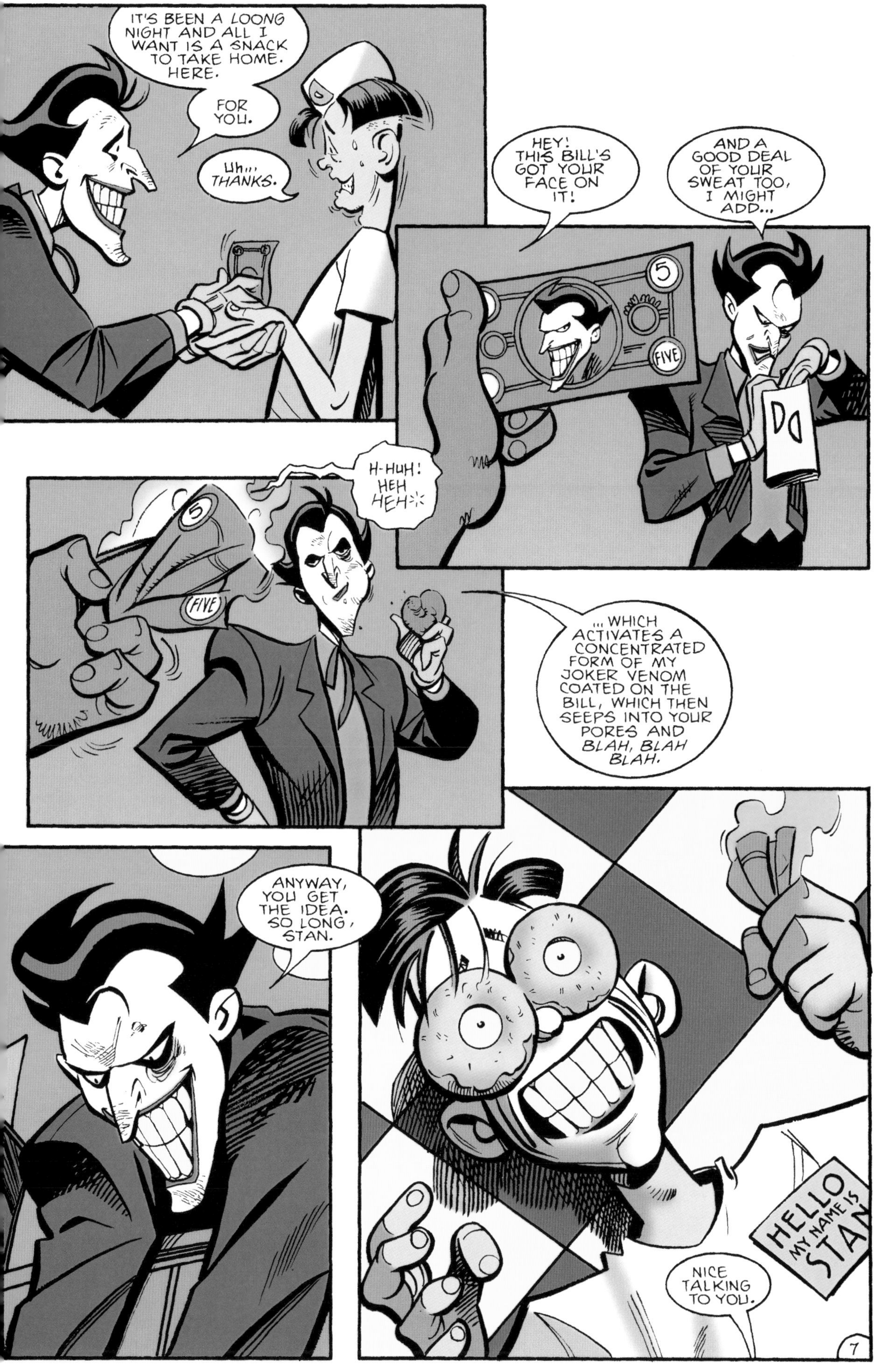
IT'S BEEN A LOONG NIGHT AND ALL I WANT IS A SNACK TO TAKE HOME. HERE.
FOR YOU.
UH... THANKS.
HEY! THIS BILL'S GOT YOUR FACE ON IT!
AND A GOOD DEAL OF YOUR SWEAT TOO, I MIGHT ADD...
5
FIVE
H-HUH! HEH HEH!
...WHICH ACTIVATES A CONCENTRATED FORM OF MY JOKER VENOM COATED ON THE BILL, WHICH THEN SEEPS INTO YOUR PORES AND BLAH, BLAH BLAH.
ANYWAY, YOU GET THE IDEA. SO LONG, STAN.
HELLO MY NAME IS STAN
NICE TALKING TO YOU.
7

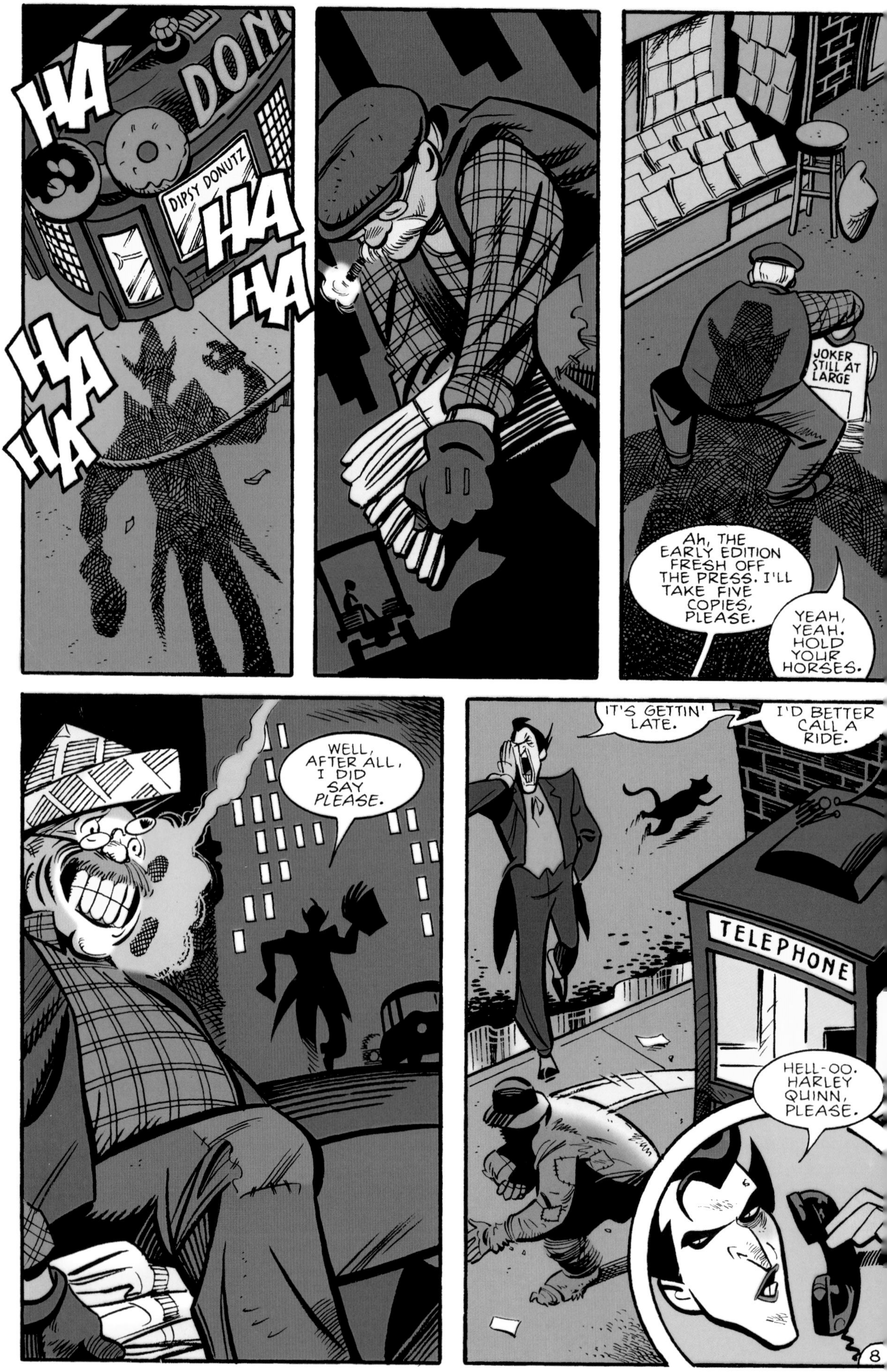
DONU
HA
DIPSY DONUTZ
HA
HA
HA
HA
HA
JOKER STILL AT LARGE
Ah, THE EARLY EDITION FRESH OFF THE PRESS. I'LL TAKE FIVE COPIES, PLEASE.
YEAH, YEAH. HOLD YOUR HORSES.
WELL, AFTER ALL, I DID SAY PLEASE.
IT'S GETTIN' LATE.
I'D BETTER CALL A RIDE.
TELEPHONE
HELL-OO. HARLEY QUINN, PLEASE.
8

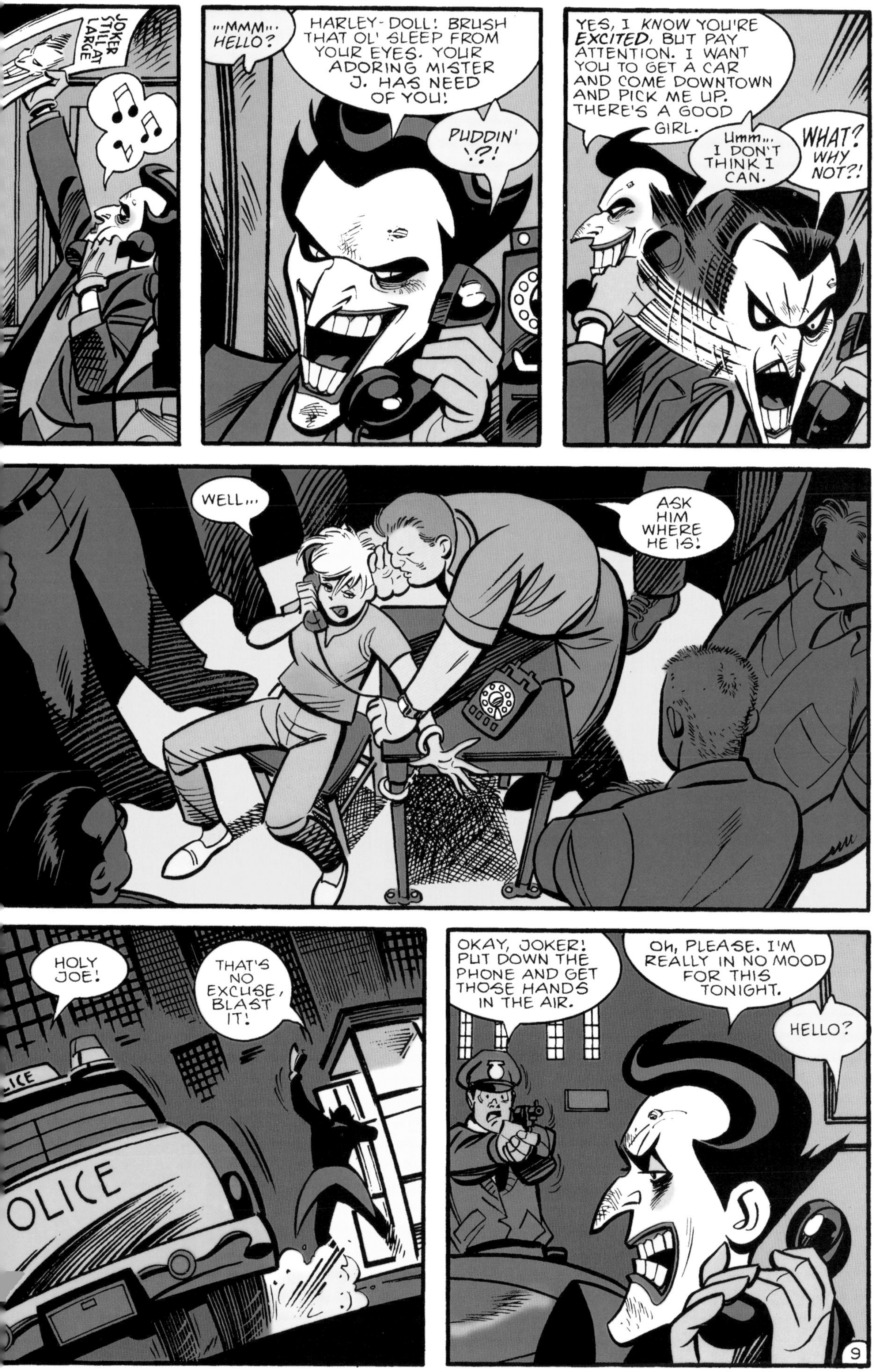
JOKER STILL AT LARGE
...MMM... HELLO?
HARLEY-DOLL! BRUSH THAT OL' SLEEP FROM YOUR EYES. YOUR ADORING MISTER J. HAS NEED OF YOU!
PUDDIN' !?!
YES, I KNOW YOU'RE EXCITED, BUT PAY ATTENTION. I WANT YOU TO GET A CAR AND COME DOWNTOWN AND PICK ME UP. THERE'S A GOOD GIRL.
Umm... I DON'T THINK I CAN.
WHAT? WHY NOT?!
WELL...
ASK HIM WHERE HE IS!
HOLY JOE!
THAT'S NO EXCUSE, BLAST IT!
POLICE
OLICE
OKAY, JOKER! PUT DOWN THE PHONE AND GET THOSE HANDS IN THE AIR.
Oh, PLEASE. I'M REALLY IN NO MOOD FOR THIS TONIGHT.
HELLO?
9

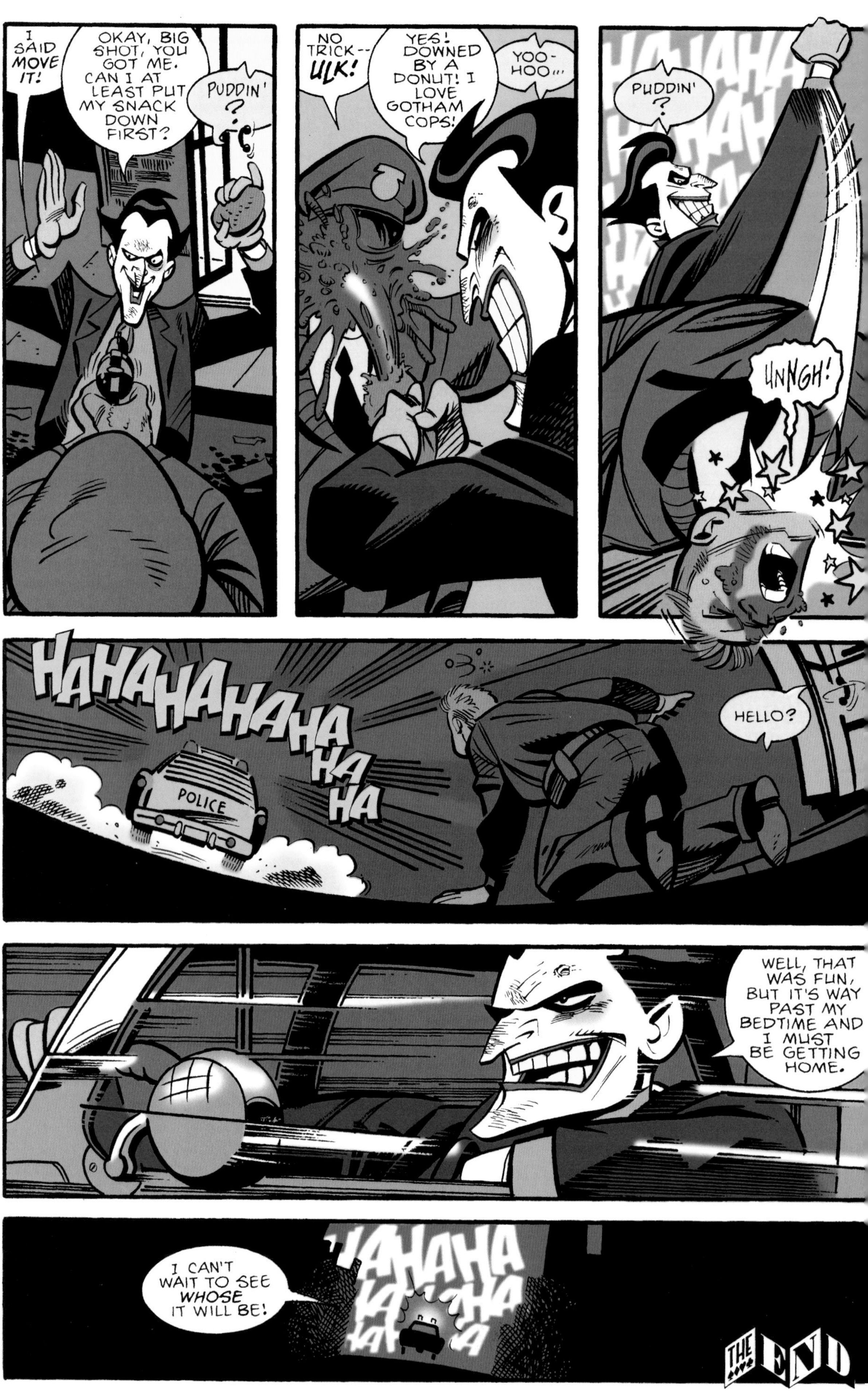
I SAID MOVE IT!
OKAY, BIG SHOT, YOU GOT ME. CAN I AT LEAST PUT MY SNACK DOWN FIRST?
PUDDIN' ?
NO TRICK-- ULK!
YES! DOWNED BY A DONUT! I LOVE GOTHAM COPS!
YOO-HOO...
HAHAHAHA
PUDDIN' ?
UNNGH!
HAHAHAHAHAHAHAHA
POLICE
HELLO?
WELL, THAT WAS FUN, BUT IT'S WAY PAST MY BEDTIME AND I MUST BE GETTING HOME.
I CAN'T WAIT TO SEE WHOSE IT WILL BE!
HAHAHA HAHAHA
THE END

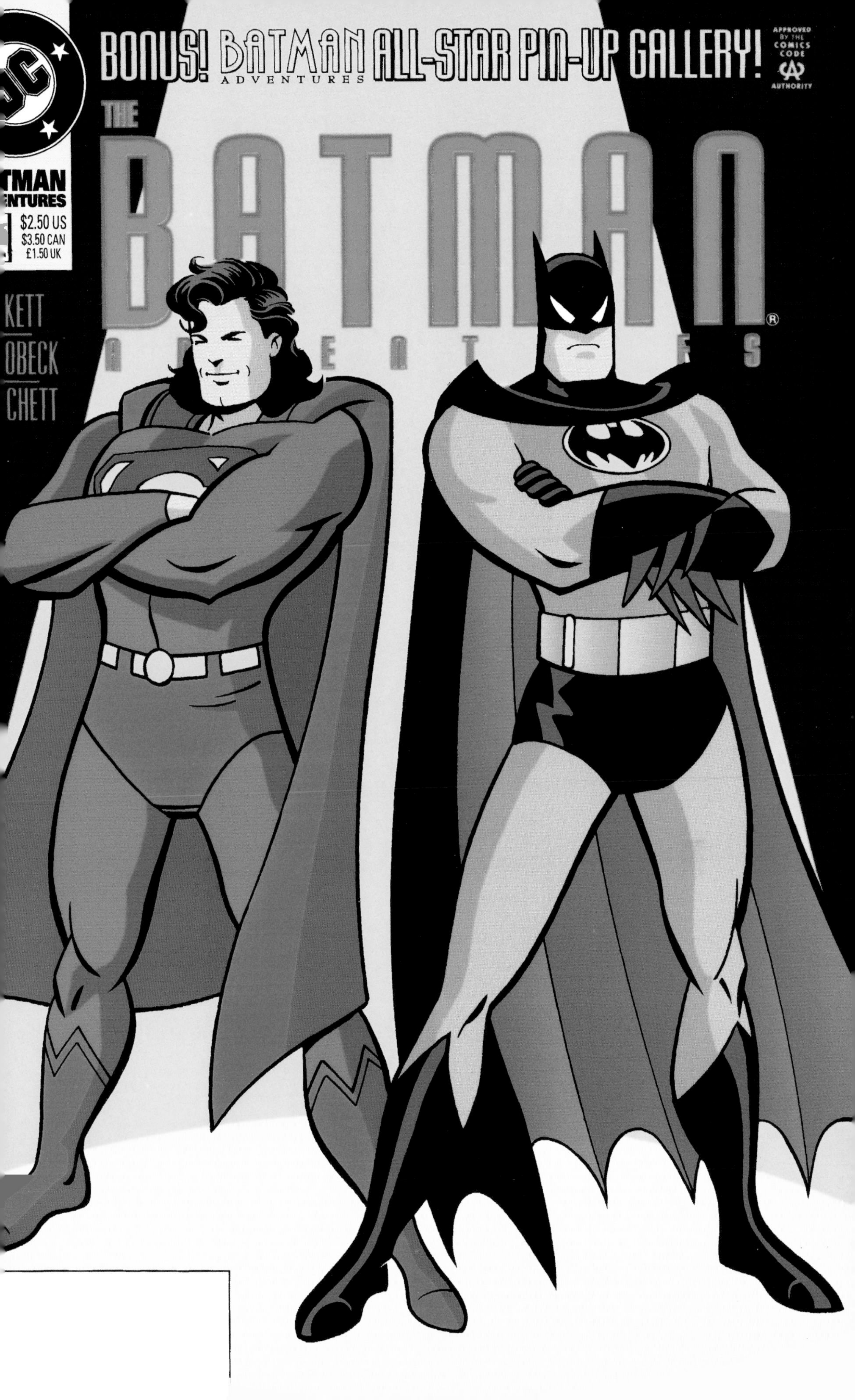
BONUS! BATMAN ADVENTURES ALL-STAR PIN-UP GALLERY!
APPROVED BY THE COMICS CODE AUTHORITY
THE BATMAN ADVENTURES
$2.50 US
$3.50 CAN
£1.50 UK

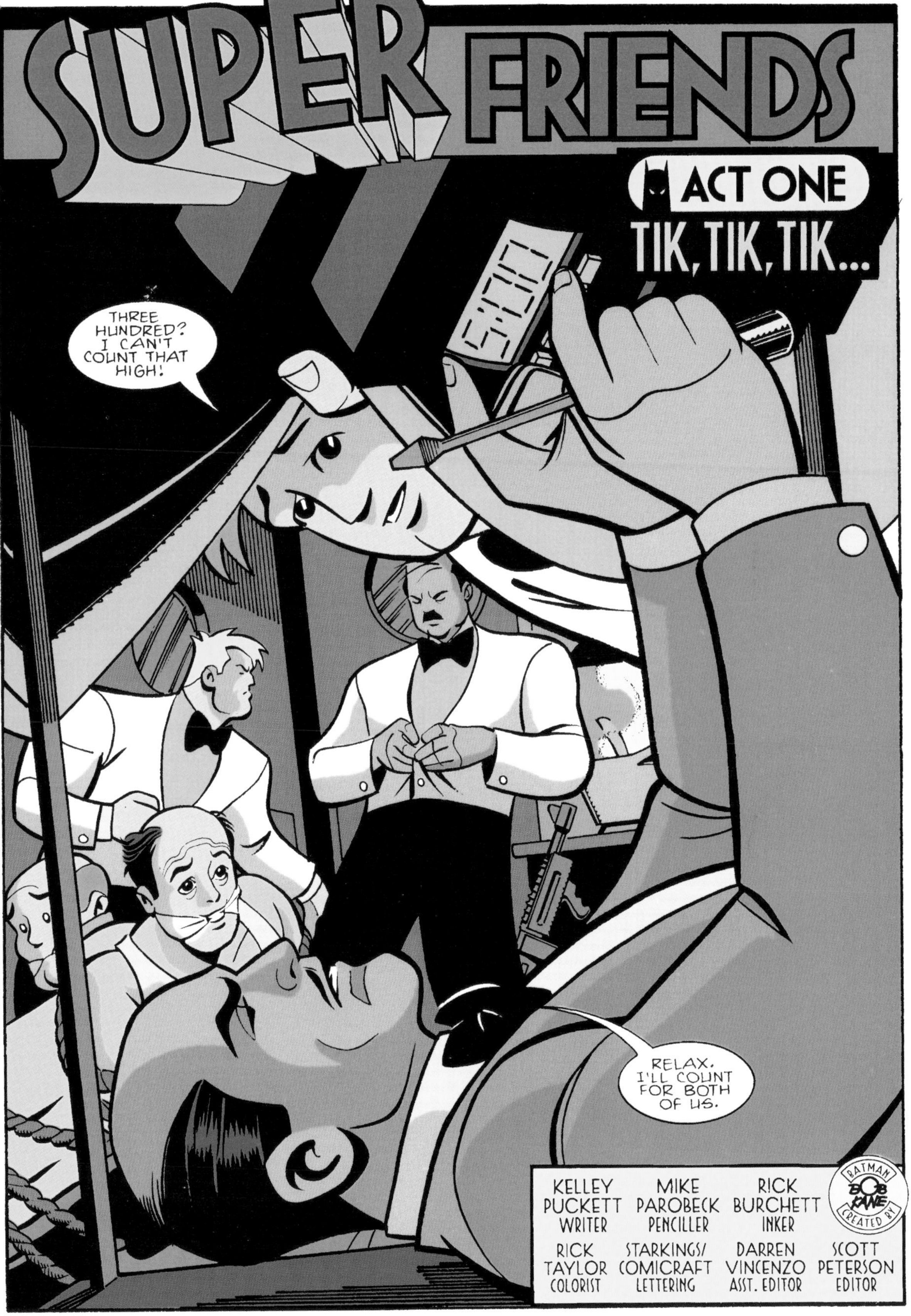
SUPER FRIENDS
ACT ONE
TIK, TIK, TIK...
THREE HUNDRED? I CAN'T COUNT THAT HIGH!
RELAX. I'LL COUNT FOR BOTH OF US.
KELLEY PUCKETT WRITER
MIKE PAROBECK PENCILLER
RICK BURCHETT INKER
RICK TAYLOR COLORIST
STARKINGS/ COMICRAFT LETTERING
DARREN VINCENZO ASST. EDITOR
SCOTT PETERSON EDITOR
BATMAN CREATED BY BOB KANE

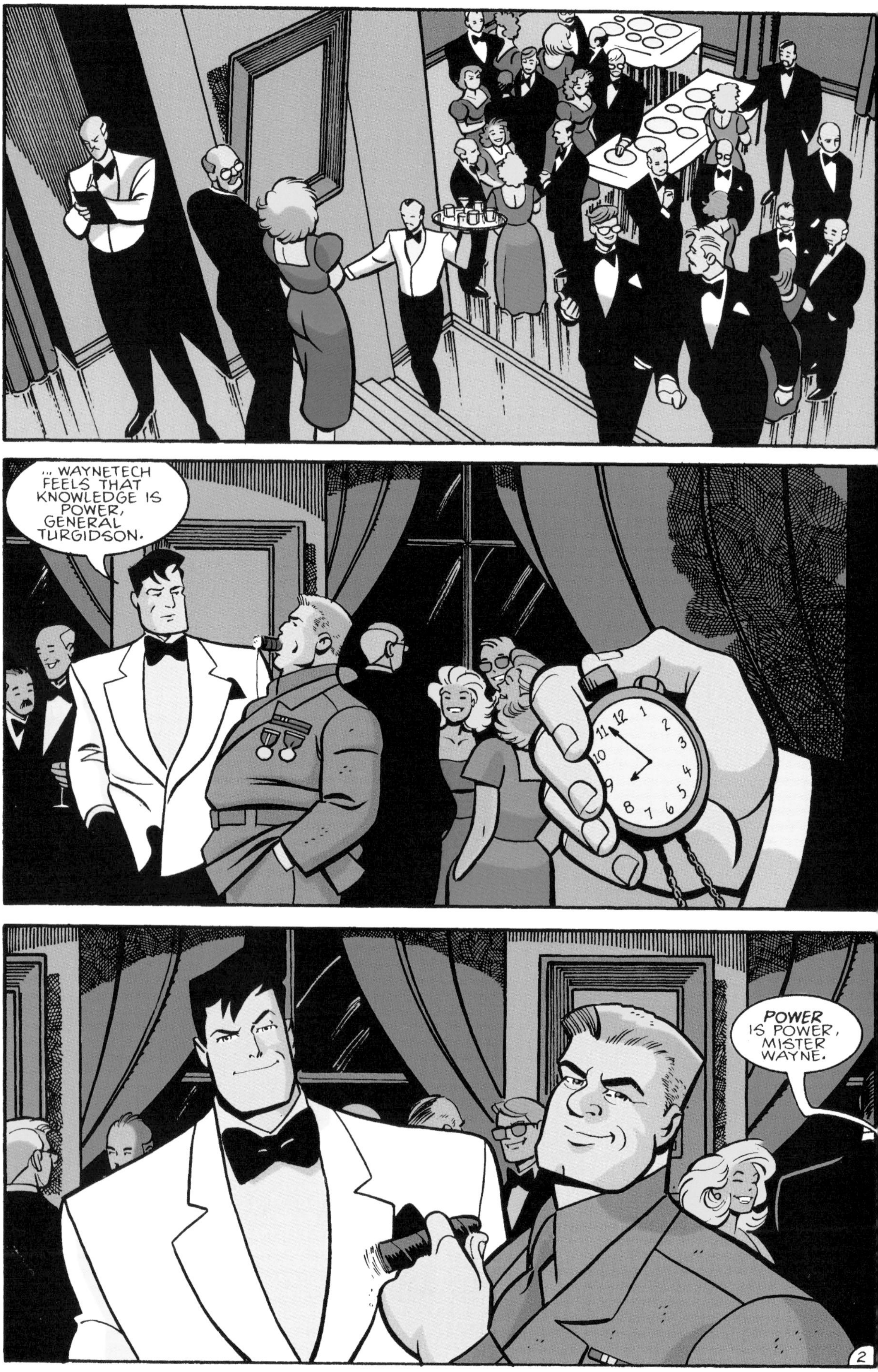

... WAYNETECH FEELS THAT KNOWLEDGE IS POWER, GENERAL TURGIDSON.
POWER IS POWER, MISTER WAYNE.
2

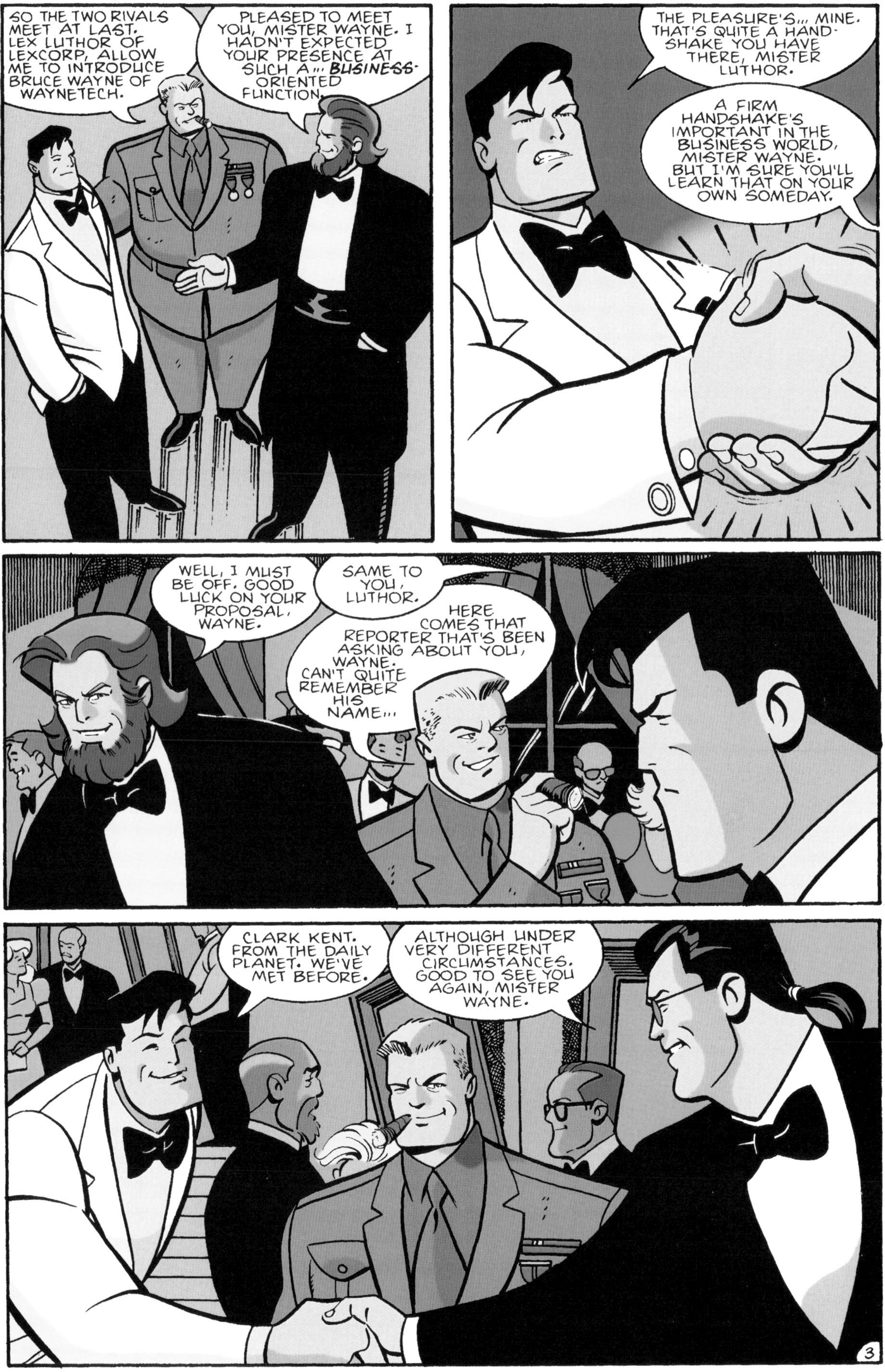
SO THE TWO RIVALS MEET AT LAST. LEX LUTHOR OF LEXCORP, ALLOW ME TO INTRODUCE BRUCE WAYNE OF WAYNETECH.
PLEASED TO MEET YOU, MISTER WAYNE. I HADN'T EXPECTED YOUR PRESENCE AT SUCH A... BUSINESS-ORIENTED FUNCTION.
THE PLEASURE'S... MINE. THAT'S QUITE A HAND-SHAKE YOU HAVE THERE, MISTER LUTHOR.
A FIRM HANDSHAKE'S IMPORTANT IN THE BUSINESS WORLD, MISTER WAYNE. BUT I'M SURE YOU'LL LEARN THAT ON YOUR OWN SOMEDAY.
WELL, I MUST BE OFF. GOOD LUCK ON YOUR PROPOSAL, WAYNE.
SAME TO YOU, LUTHOR.
HERE COMES THAT REPORTER THAT'S BEEN ASKING ABOUT YOU, WAYNE. CAN'T QUITE REMEMBER HIS NAME...
CLARK KENT. FROM THE DAILY PLANET. WE'VE MET BEFORE.
ALTHOUGH UNDER VERY DIFFERENT CIRCUMSTANCES. GOOD TO SEE YOU AGAIN, MISTER WAYNE.
3

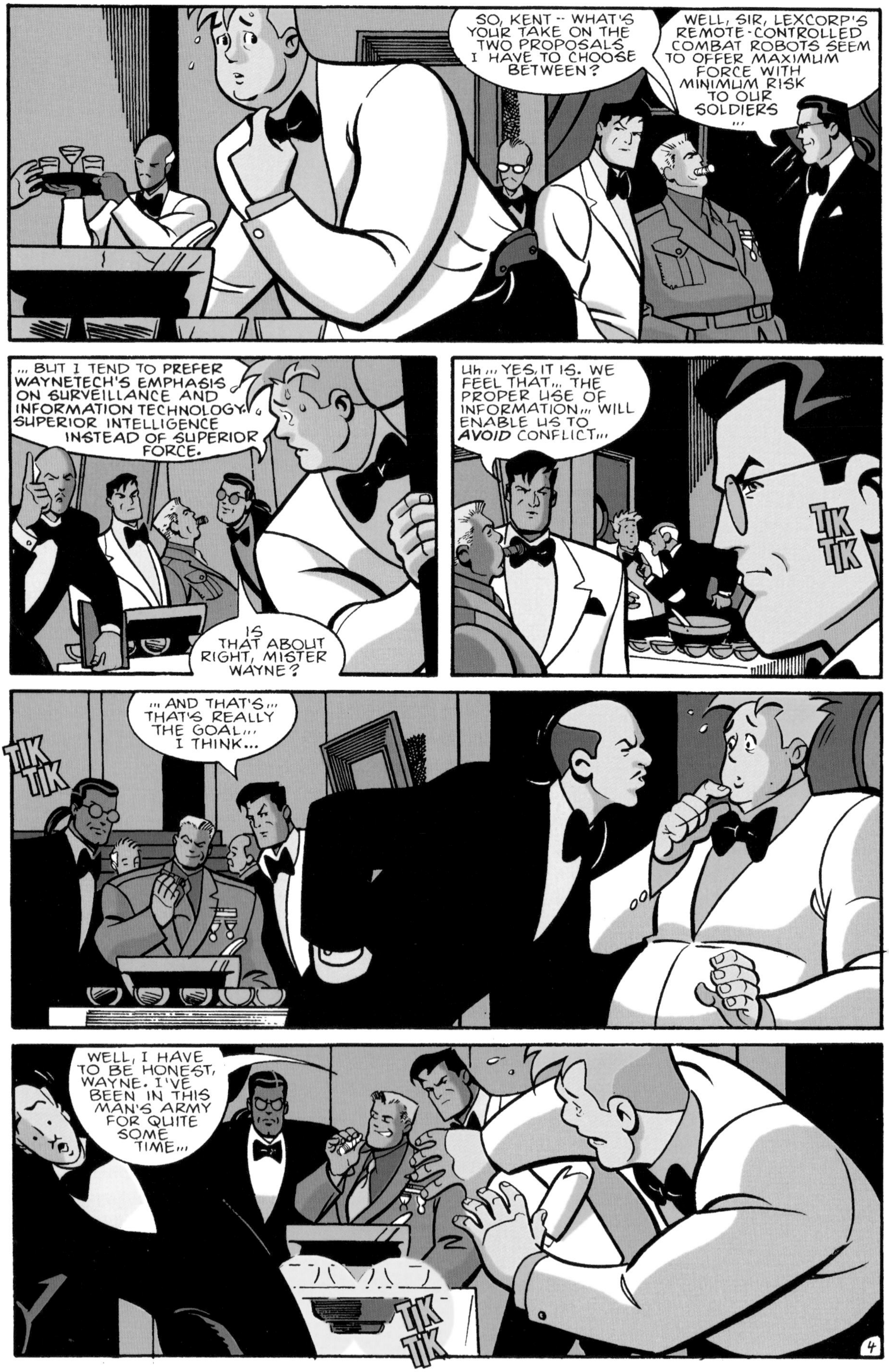
SO, KENT -- WHAT'S YOUR TAKE ON THE TWO PROPOSALS I HAVE TO CHOOSE BETWEEN?
WELL, SIR, LEXCORP'S REMOTE-CONTROLLED COMBAT ROBOTS SEEM TO OFFER MAXIMUM FORCE WITH MINIMUM RISK TO OUR SOLDIERS ...
... BUT I TEND TO PREFER WAYNETECH'S EMPHASIS ON SURVEILLANCE AND INFORMATION TECHNOLOGY. SUPERIOR INTELLIGENCE INSTEAD OF SUPERIOR FORCE.
IS THAT ABOUT RIGHT, MISTER WAYNE?
UH ... YES, IT IS. WE FEEL THAT... THE PROPER USE OF INFORMATION... WILL ENABLE US TO AVOID CONFLICT...
TIK TIK
TIK TIK
... AND THAT'S... THAT'S REALLY THE GOAL... I THINK...
WELL, I HAVE TO BE HONEST, WAYNE. I'VE BEEN IN THIS MAN'S ARMY FOR QUITE SOME TIME...
TIK TIK
4

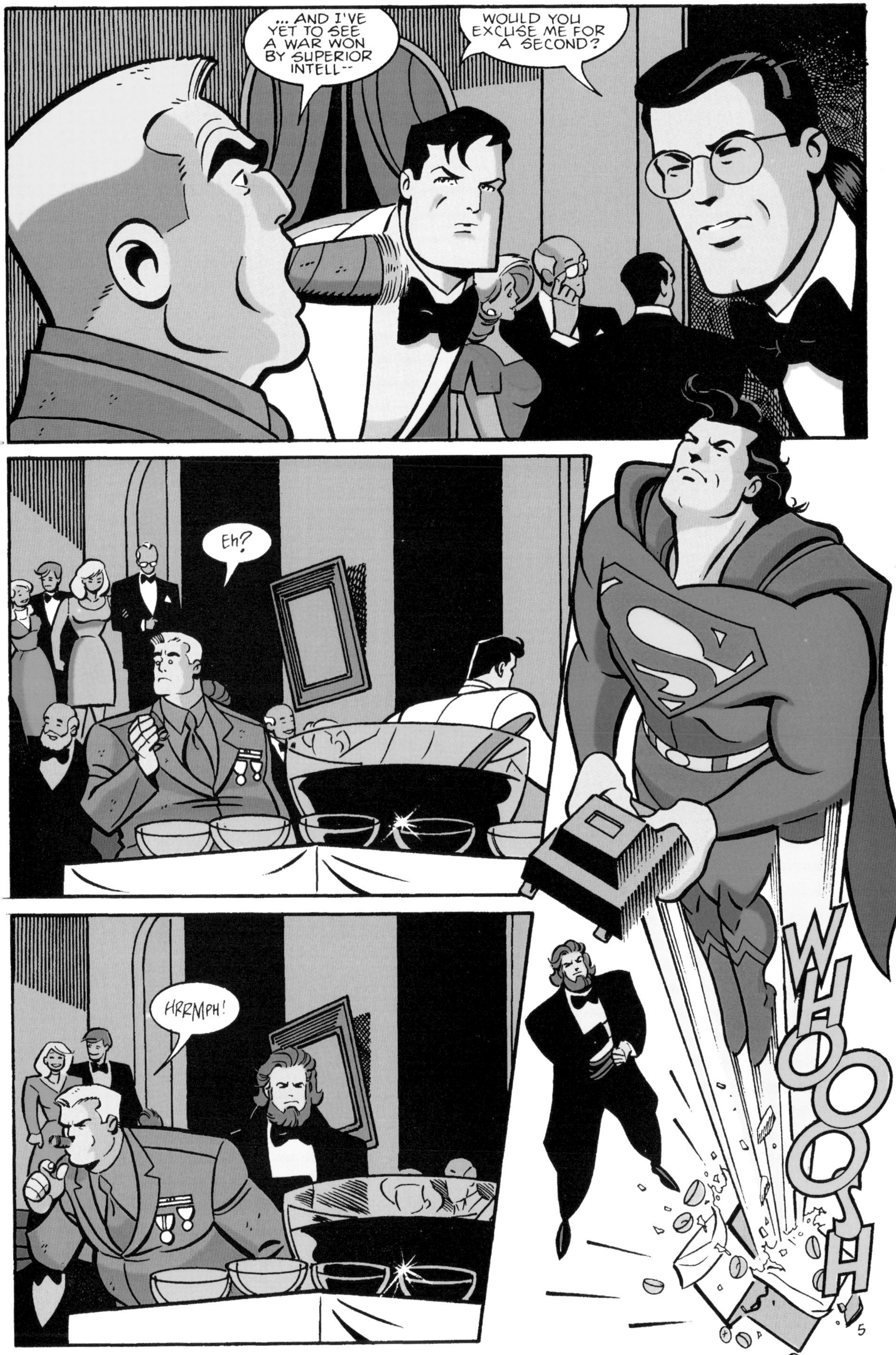
...AND I'VE YET TO SEE A WAR WON BY SUPERIOR INTELL--
WOULD YOU EXCUSE ME FOR A SECOND?
Eh?
HRRMPH!
WHOOOOSH
5

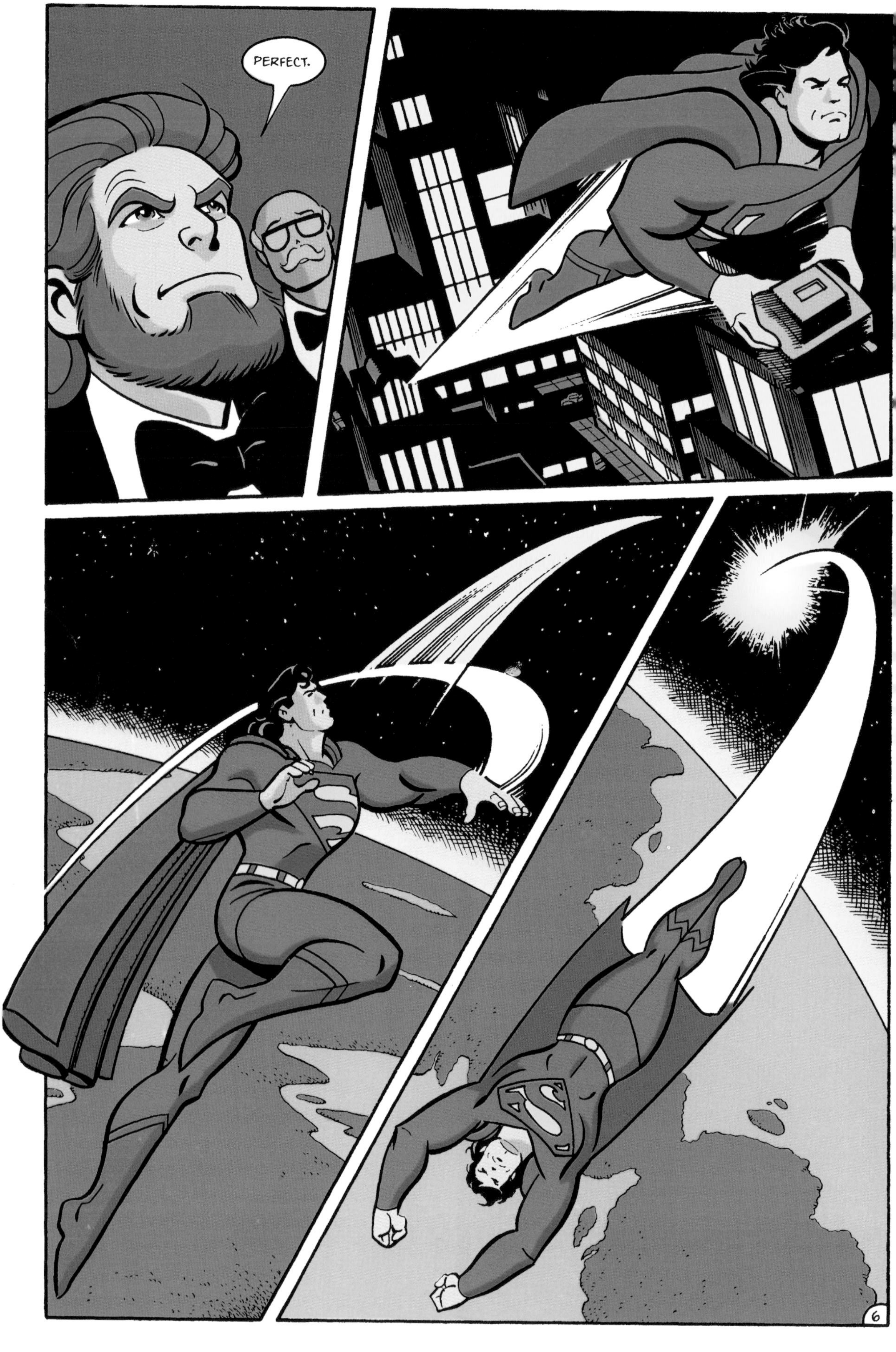
PERFECT.
6

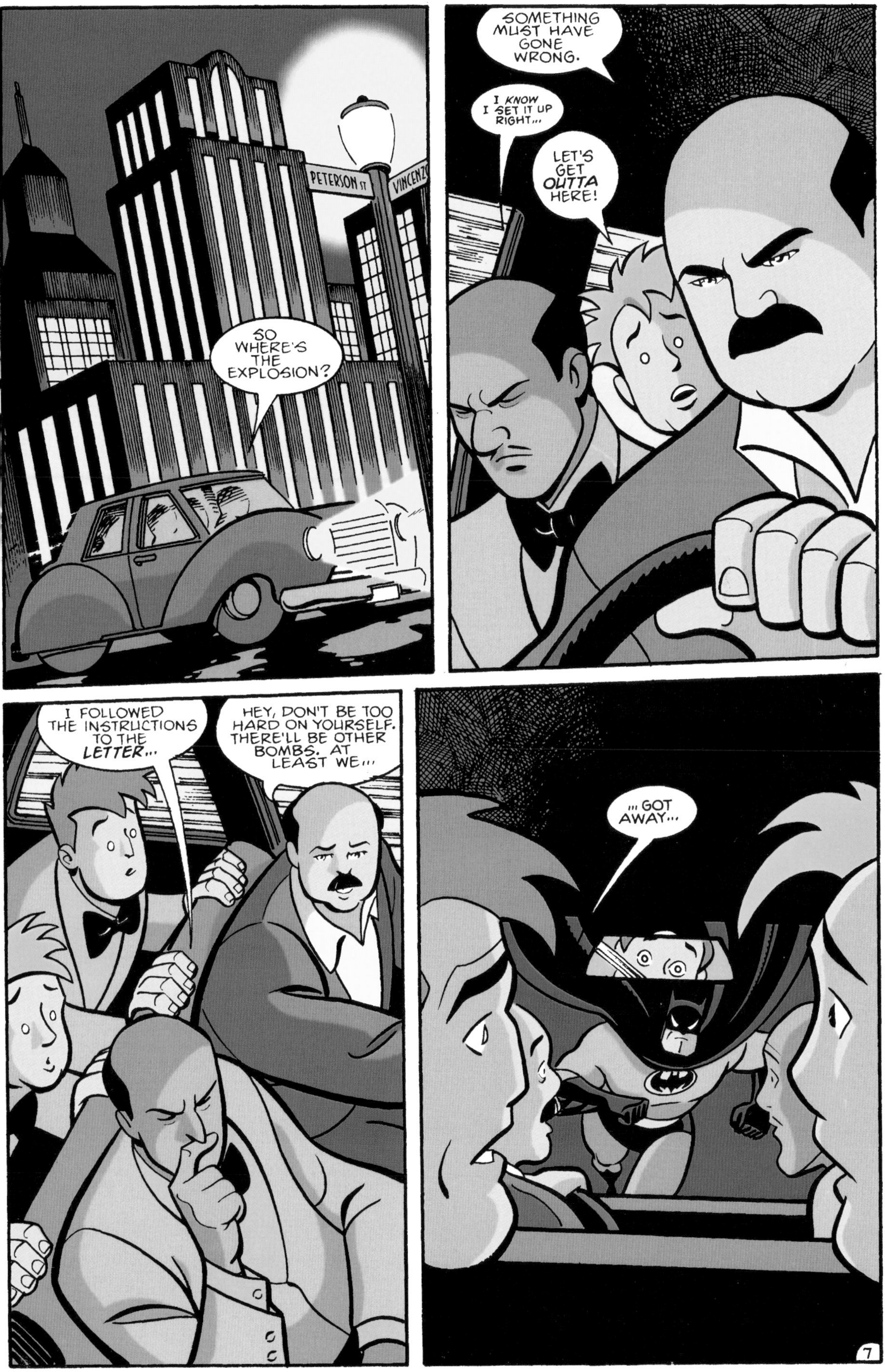
PETERSON ST
VINCENZO
SO WHERE'S THE EXPLOSION?
SOMETHING MUST HAVE GONE WRONG.
I KNOW I SET IT UP RIGHT...
LET'S GET OUTTA HERE!
I FOLLOWED THE INSTRUCTIONS TO THE LETTER...
HEY, DON'T BE TOO HARD ON YOURSELF. THERE'LL BE OTHER BOMBS. AT LEAST WE...
...GOT AWAY...
7

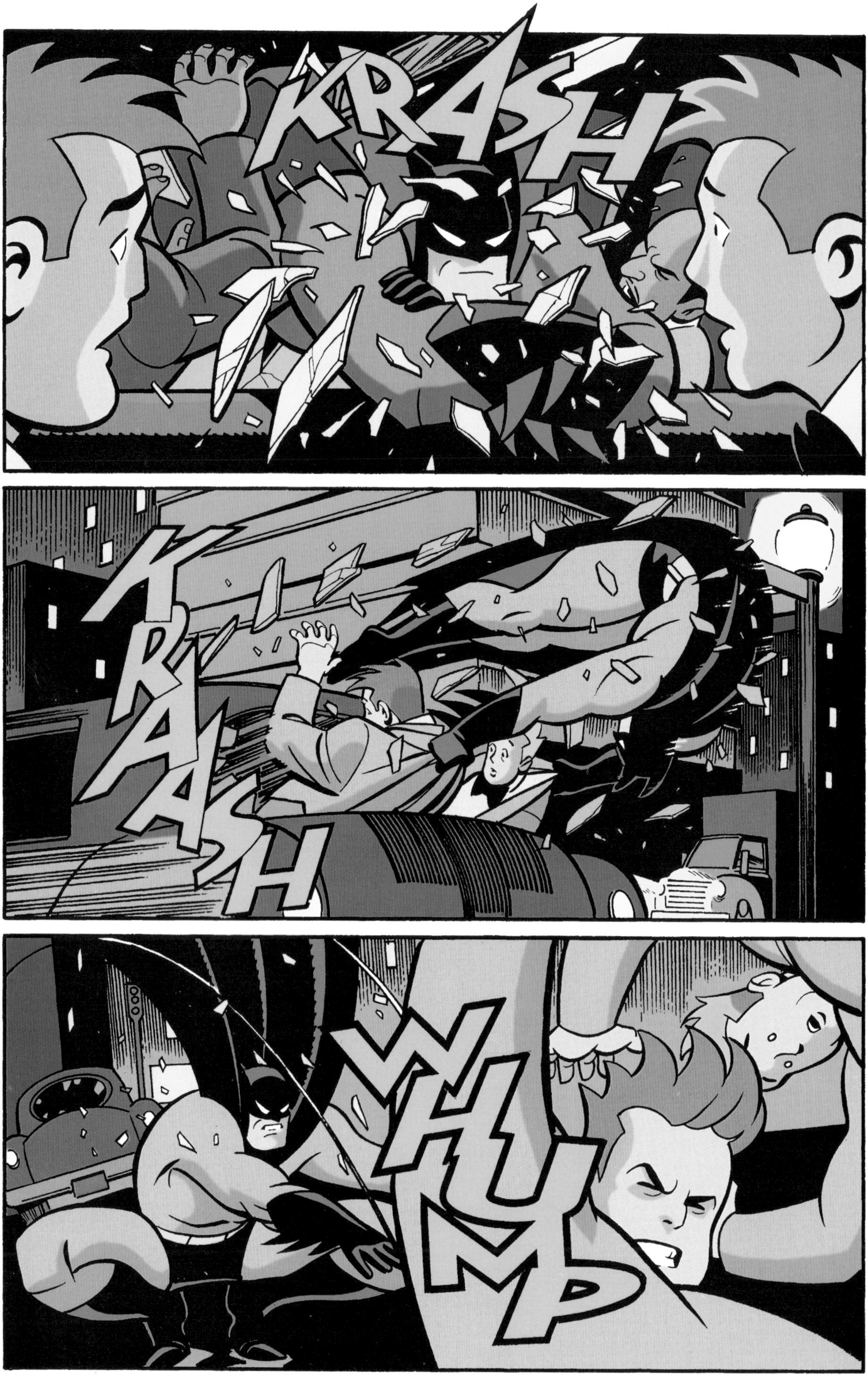
KRASH
KRASH
WHUMP

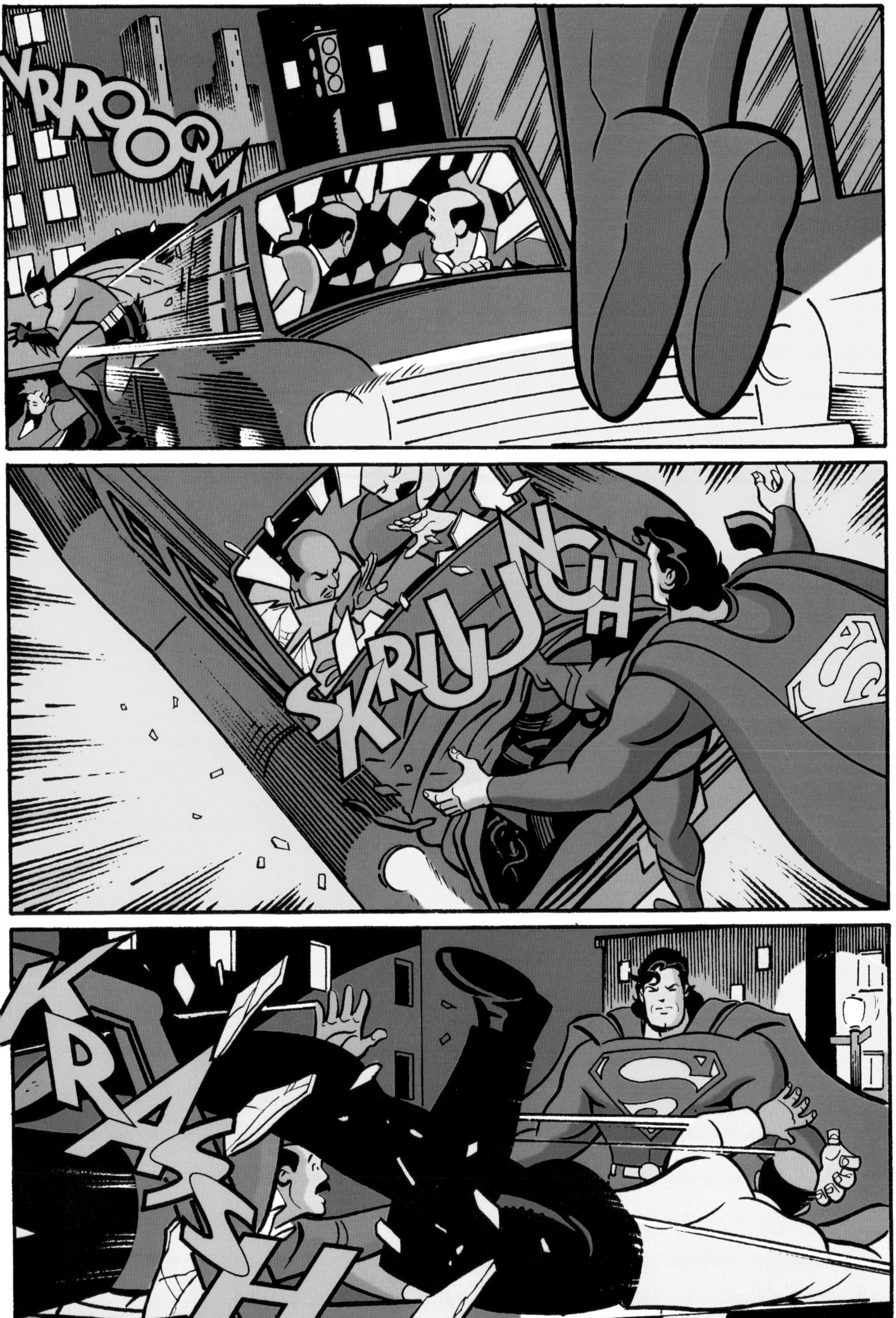
VRROOOM
SKRUUNCH
KRASSH
9

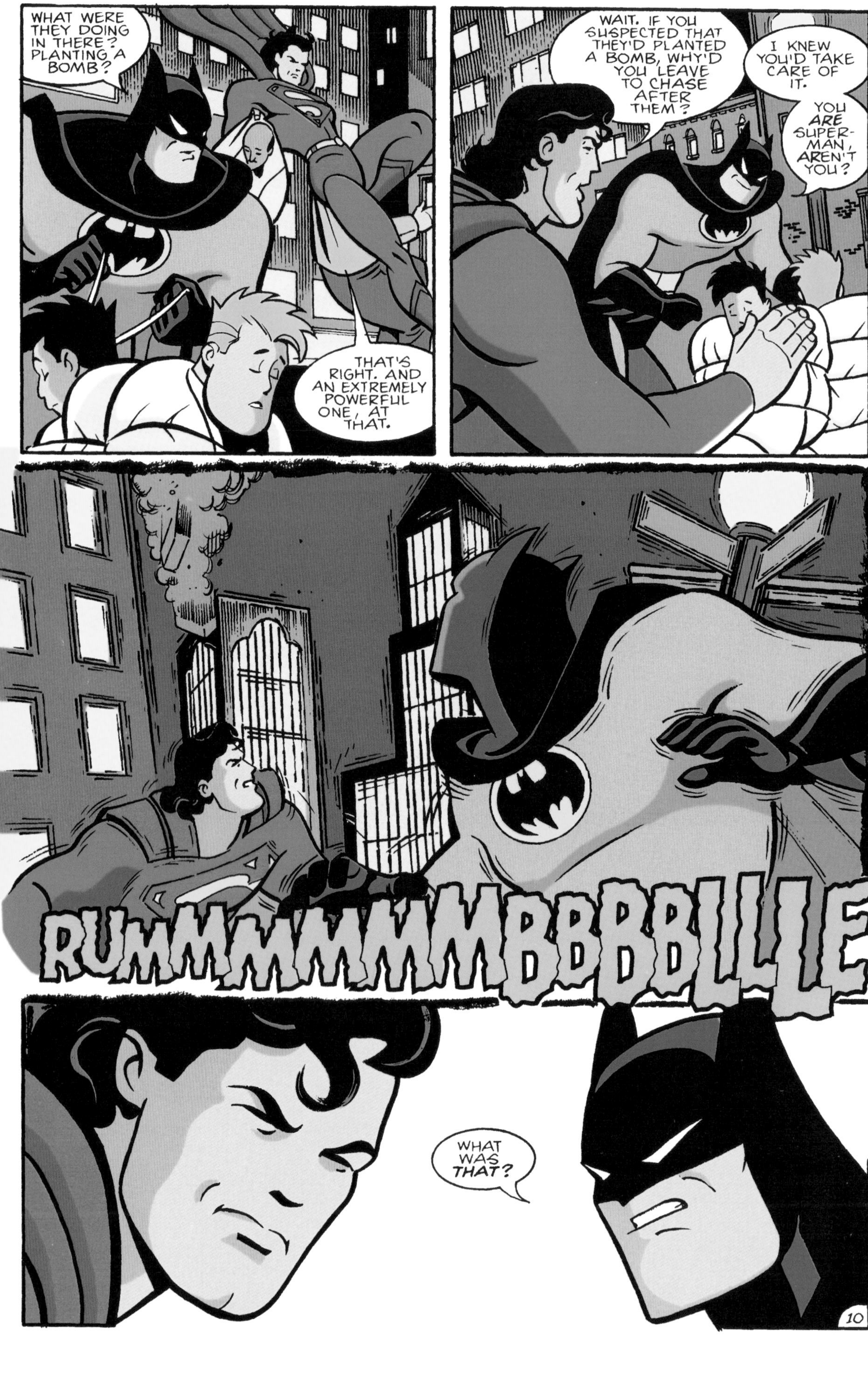
WHAT WERE THEY DOING IN THERE? PLANTING A BOMB?
THAT'S RIGHT. AND AN EXTREMELY POWERFUL ONE, AT THAT.
WAIT. IF YOU SUSPECTED THAT THEY'D PLANTED A BOMB, WHY'D YOU LEAVE TO CHASE AFTER THEM?
I KNEW YOU'D TAKE CARE OF IT.
YOU *ARE* SUPERMAN, AREN'T YOU?
RUMMMMMMMBBBBLLLE
WHAT WAS *THAT*?
10

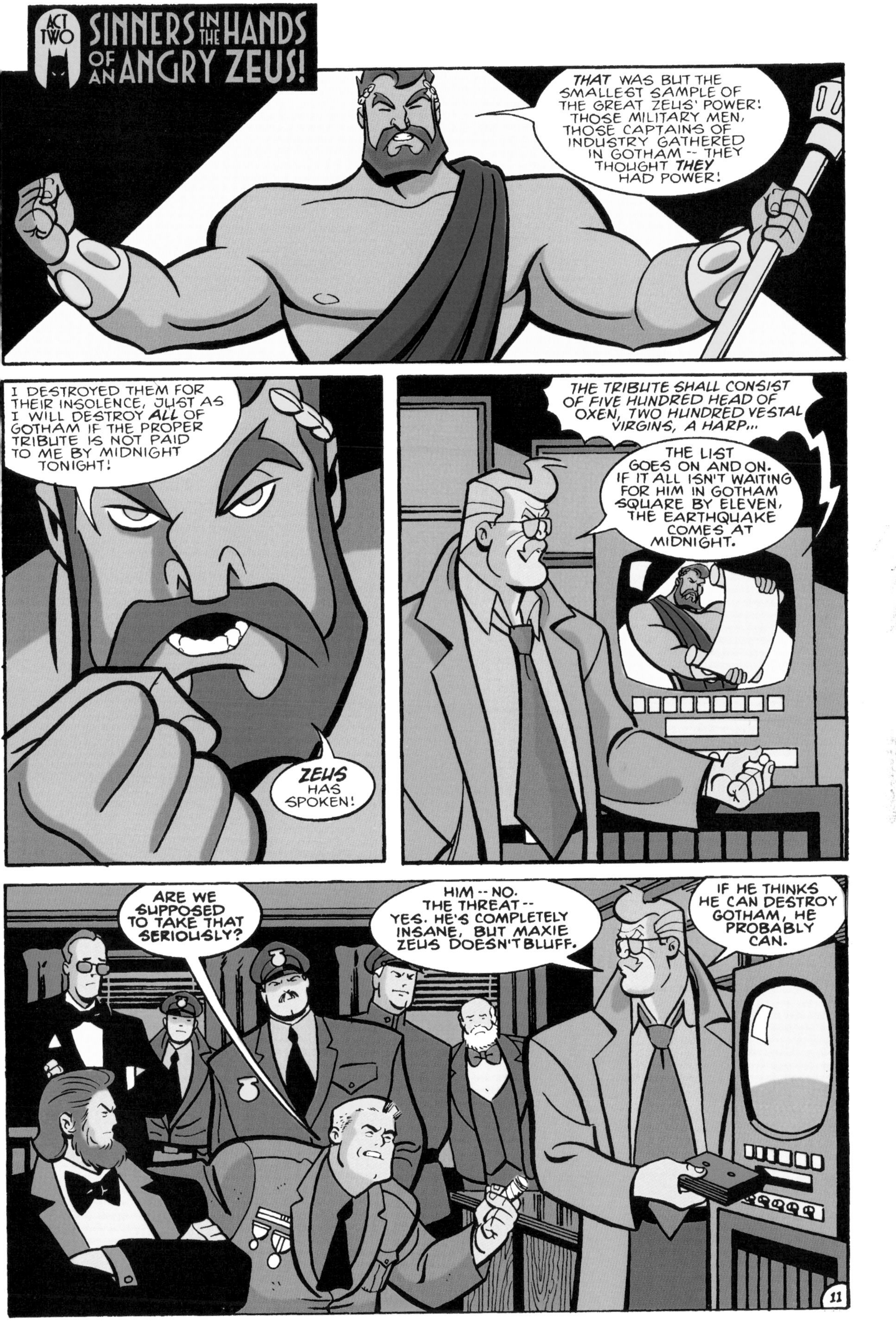
ACT TWO
SINNERS IN THE HANDS OF AN ANGRY ZEUS!
THAT WAS BUT THE SMALLEST SAMPLE OF THE GREAT ZEUS' POWER: THOSE MILITARY MEN, THOSE CAPTAINS OF INDUSTRY GATHERED IN GOTHAM -- THEY THOUGHT THEY HAD POWER!
I DESTROYED THEM FOR THEIR INSOLENCE, JUST AS I WILL DESTROY ALL OF GOTHAM IF THE PROPER TRIBUTE IS NOT PAID TO ME BY MIDNIGHT TONIGHT!
ZEUS HAS SPOKEN!
THE TRIBUTE SHALL CONSIST OF FIVE HUNDRED HEAD OF OXEN, TWO HUNDRED VESTAL VIRGINS, A HARP...
THE LIST GOES ON AND ON. IF IT ALL ISN'T WAITING FOR HIM IN GOTHAM SQUARE BY ELEVEN, THE EARTHQUAKE COMES AT MIDNIGHT.
ARE WE SUPPOSED TO TAKE THAT SERIOUSLY?
HIM -- NO. THE THREAT -- YES. HE'S COMPLETELY INSANE, BUT MAXIE ZEUS DOESN'T BLUFF.
IF HE THINKS HE CAN DESTROY GOTHAM, HE PROBABLY CAN.
11

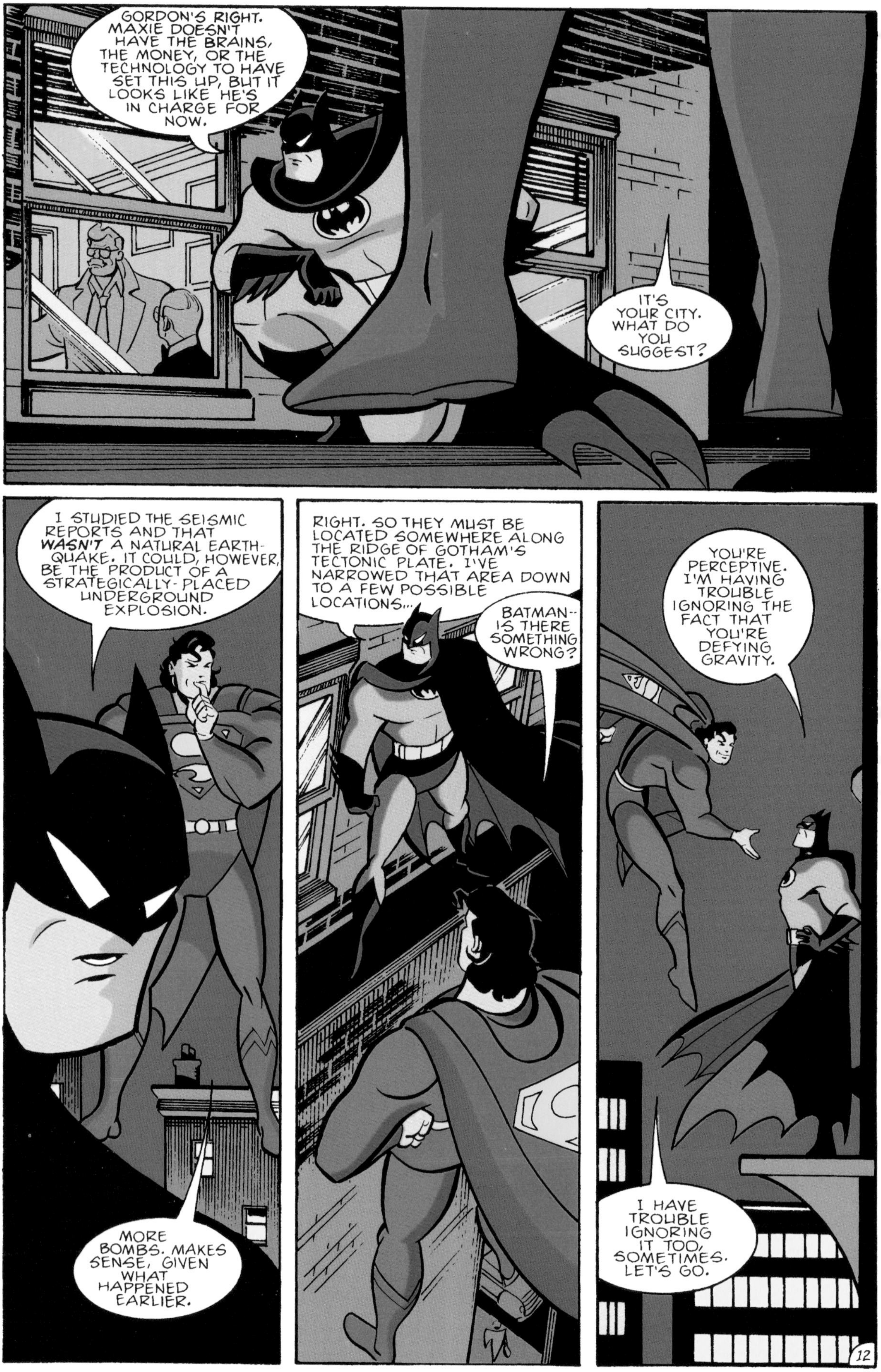
GORDON'S RIGHT. MAXIE DOESN'T HAVE THE BRAINS, THE MONEY, OR THE TECHNOLOGY TO HAVE SET THIS UP, BUT IT LOOKS LIKE HE'S IN CHARGE FOR NOW.
IT'S YOUR CITY. WHAT DO YOU SUGGEST?
I STUDIED THE SEISMIC REPORTS AND THAT WASN'T A NATURAL EARTHQUAKE. IT COULD, HOWEVER, BE THE PRODUCT OF A STRATEGICALLY-PLACED UNDERGROUND EXPLOSION.
MORE BOMBS. MAKES SENSE, GIVEN WHAT HAPPENED EARLIER.
RIGHT. SO THEY MUST BE LOCATED SOMEWHERE ALONG THE RIDGE OF GOTHAM'S TECTONIC PLATE. I'VE NARROWED THAT AREA DOWN TO A FEW POSSIBLE LOCATIONS...
BATMAN-- IS THERE SOMETHING WRONG?
YOU'RE PERCEPTIVE. I'M HAVING TROUBLE IGNORING THE FACT THAT YOU'RE DEFYING GRAVITY.
I HAVE TROUBLE IGNORING IT TOO, SOMETIMES. LET'S GO.
12

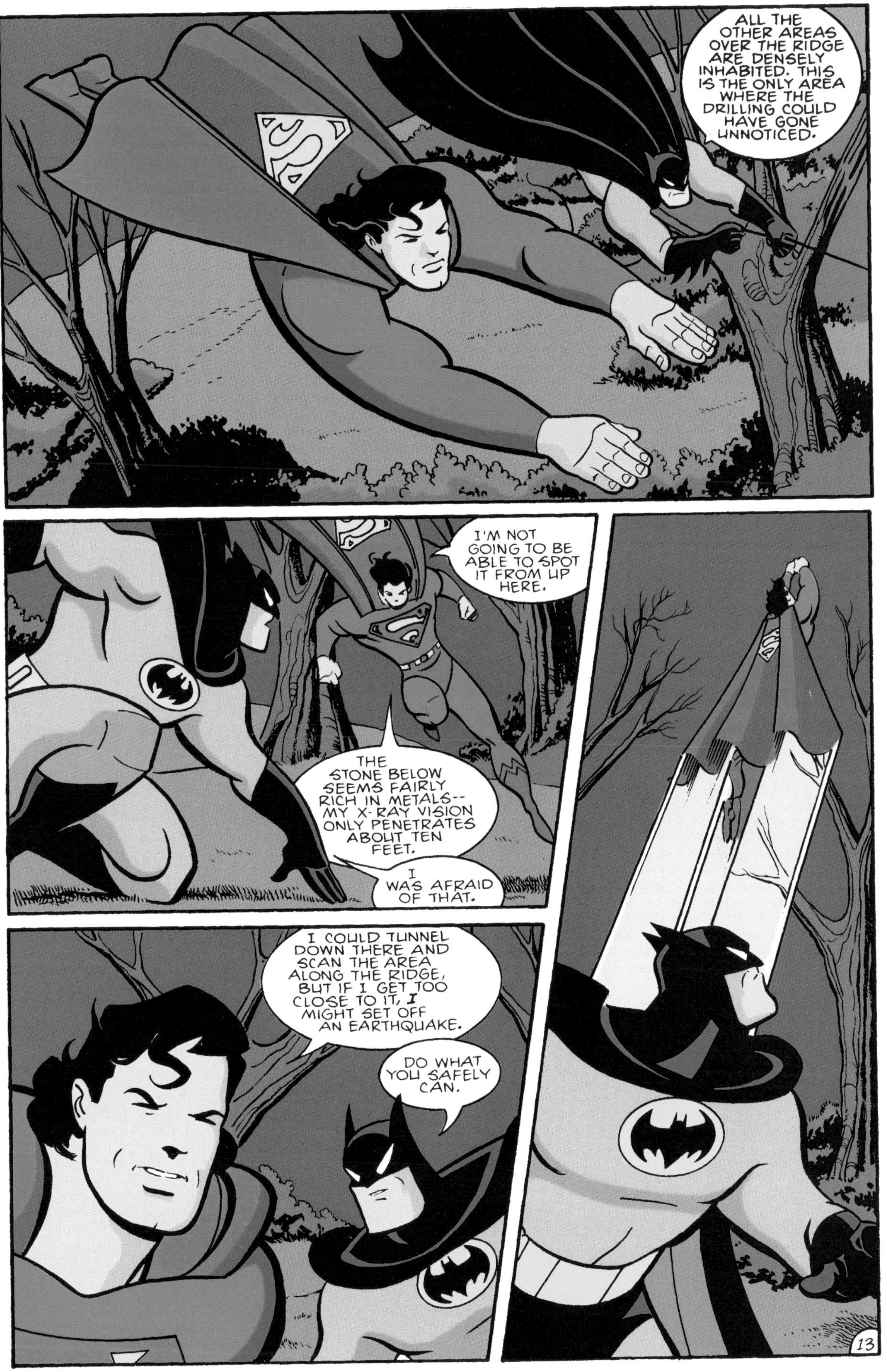
ALL THE OTHER AREAS OVER THE RIDGE ARE DENSELY INHABITED. THIS IS THE ONLY AREA WHERE THE DRILLING COULD HAVE GONE UNNOTICED.
I'M NOT GOING TO BE ABLE TO SPOT IT FROM UP HERE.
THE STONE BELOW SEEMS FAIRLY RICH IN METALS-- MY X-RAY VISION ONLY PENETRATES ABOUT TEN FEET.
I WAS AFRAID OF THAT.
I COULD TUNNEL DOWN THERE AND SCAN THE AREA ALONG THE RIDGE, BUT IF I GET TOO CLOSE TO IT, I MIGHT SET OFF AN EARTHQUAKE.
DO WHAT YOU SAFELY CAN.
13

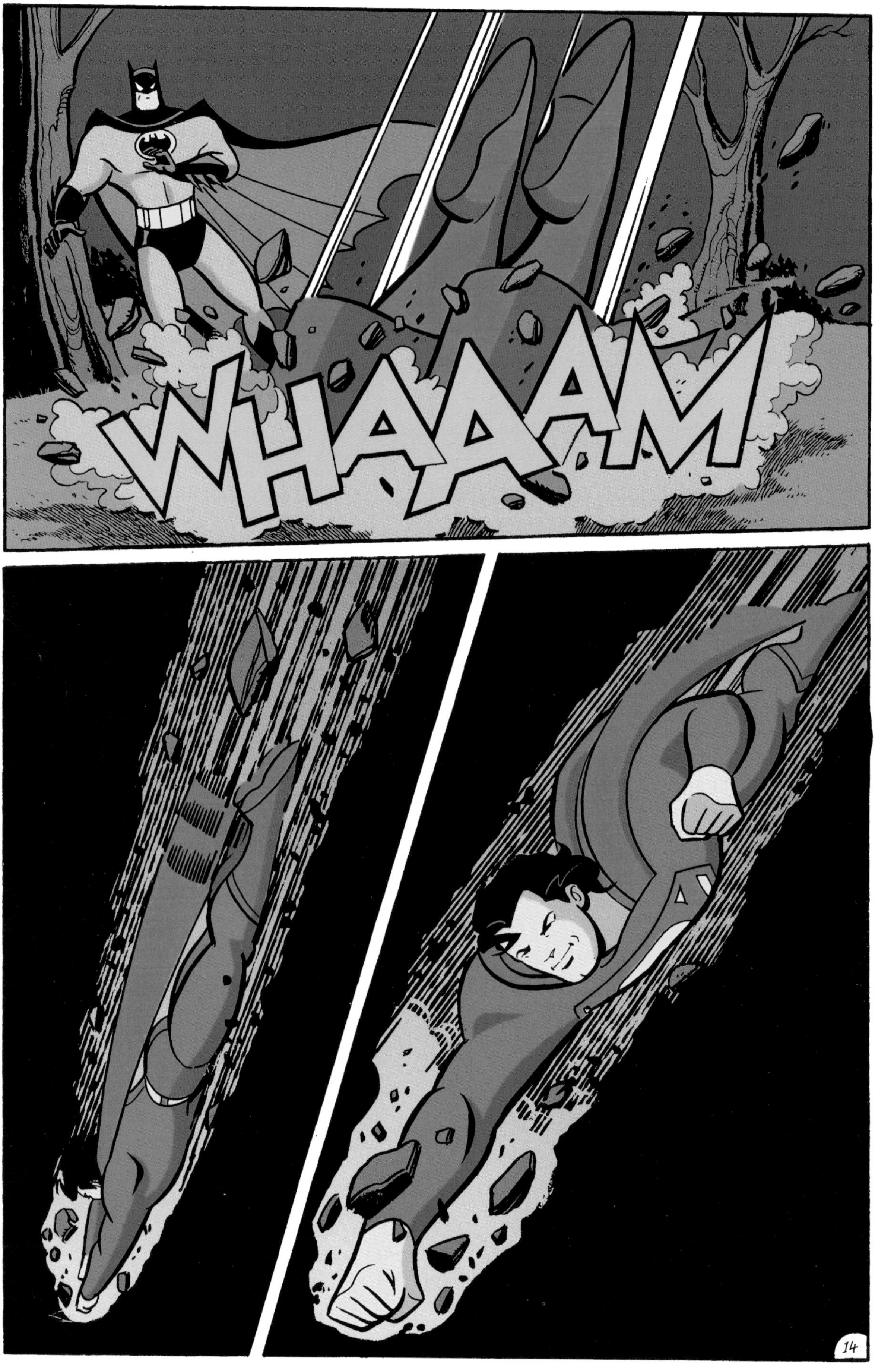
WHAAAM
14

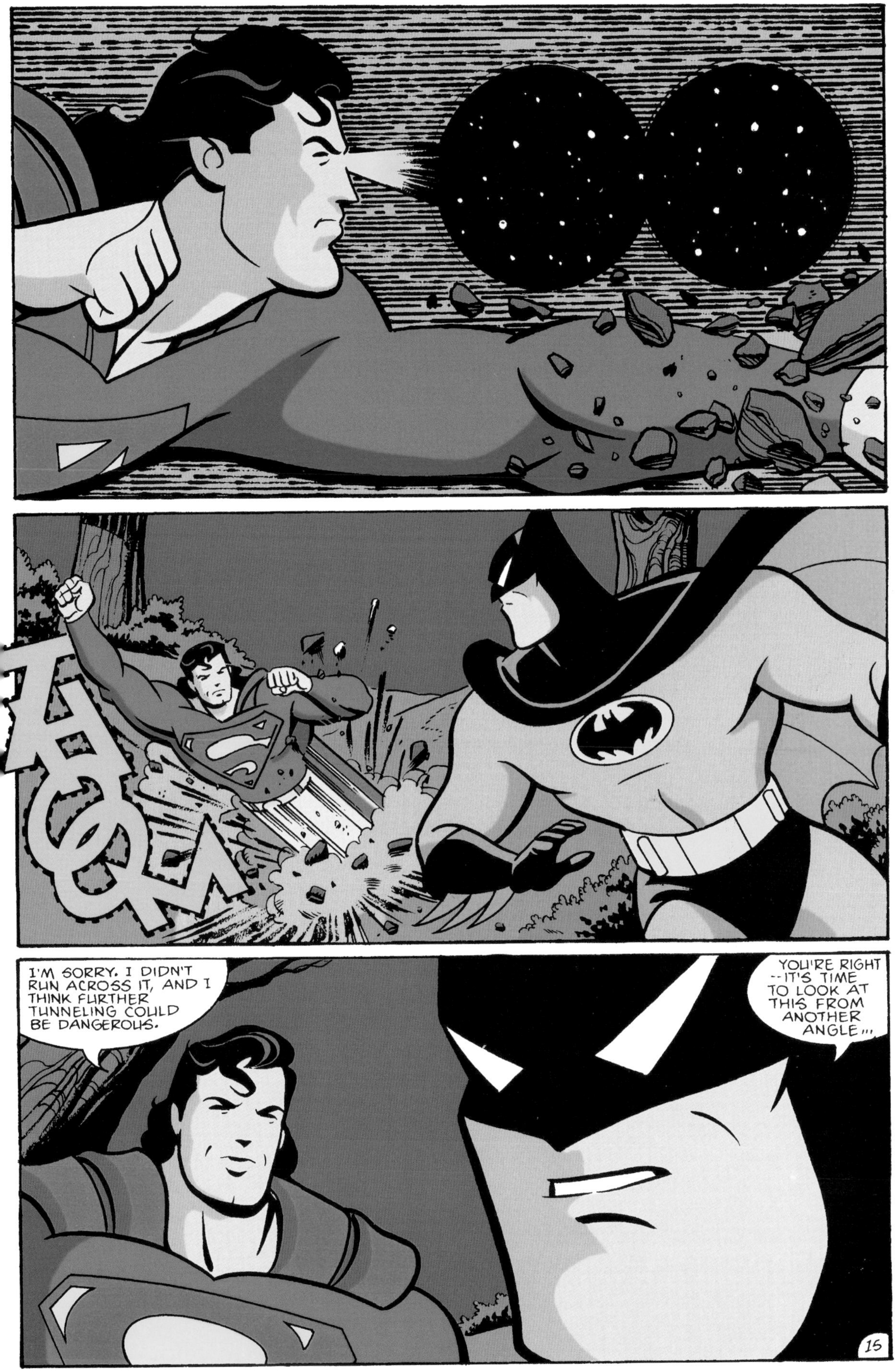

FOOM
I'M SORRY. I DIDN'T RUN ACROSS IT, AND I THINK FURTHER TUNNELING COULD BE DANGEROUS.
YOU'RE RIGHT --IT'S TIME TO LOOK AT THIS FROM ANOTHER ANGLE...
15

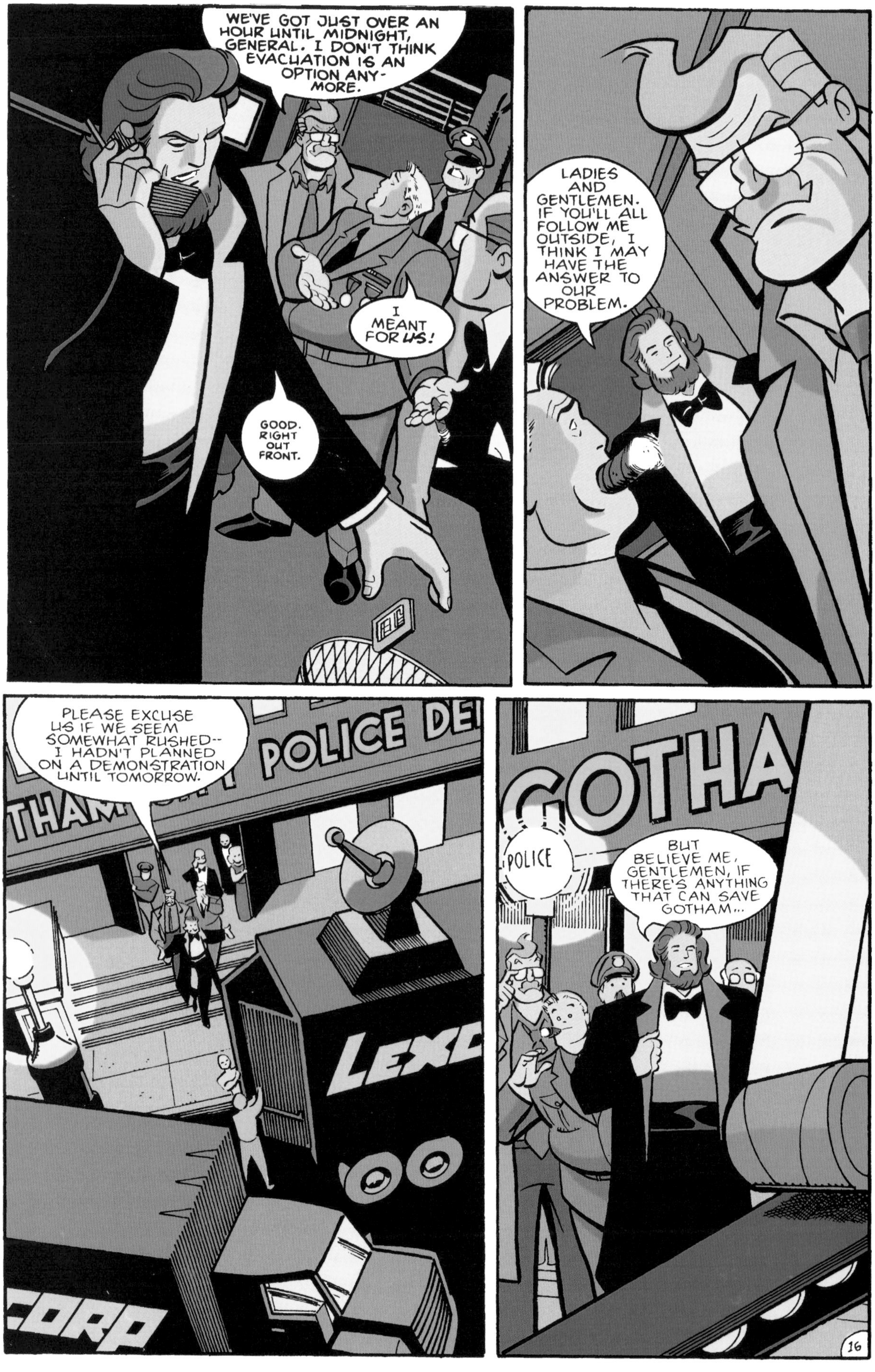
WE'VE GOT JUST OVER AN HOUR UNTIL MIDNIGHT, GENERAL. I DON'T THINK EVACUATION IS AN OPTION ANY-MORE.
I MEANT FOR US!
GOOD. RIGHT OUT FRONT.
LADIES AND GENTLEMEN. IF YOU'LL ALL FOLLOW ME OUTSIDE, I THINK I MAY HAVE THE ANSWER TO OUR PROBLEM.
PLEASE EXCUSE US IF WE SEEM SOMEWHAT RUSHED-- I HADN'T PLANNED ON A DEMONSTRATION UNTIL TOMORROW.
POLICE DE
LEXC
CORP
GOTHA
POLICE
BUT BELIEVE ME, GENTLEMEN, IF THERE'S ANYTHING THAT CAN SAVE GOTHAM...
16

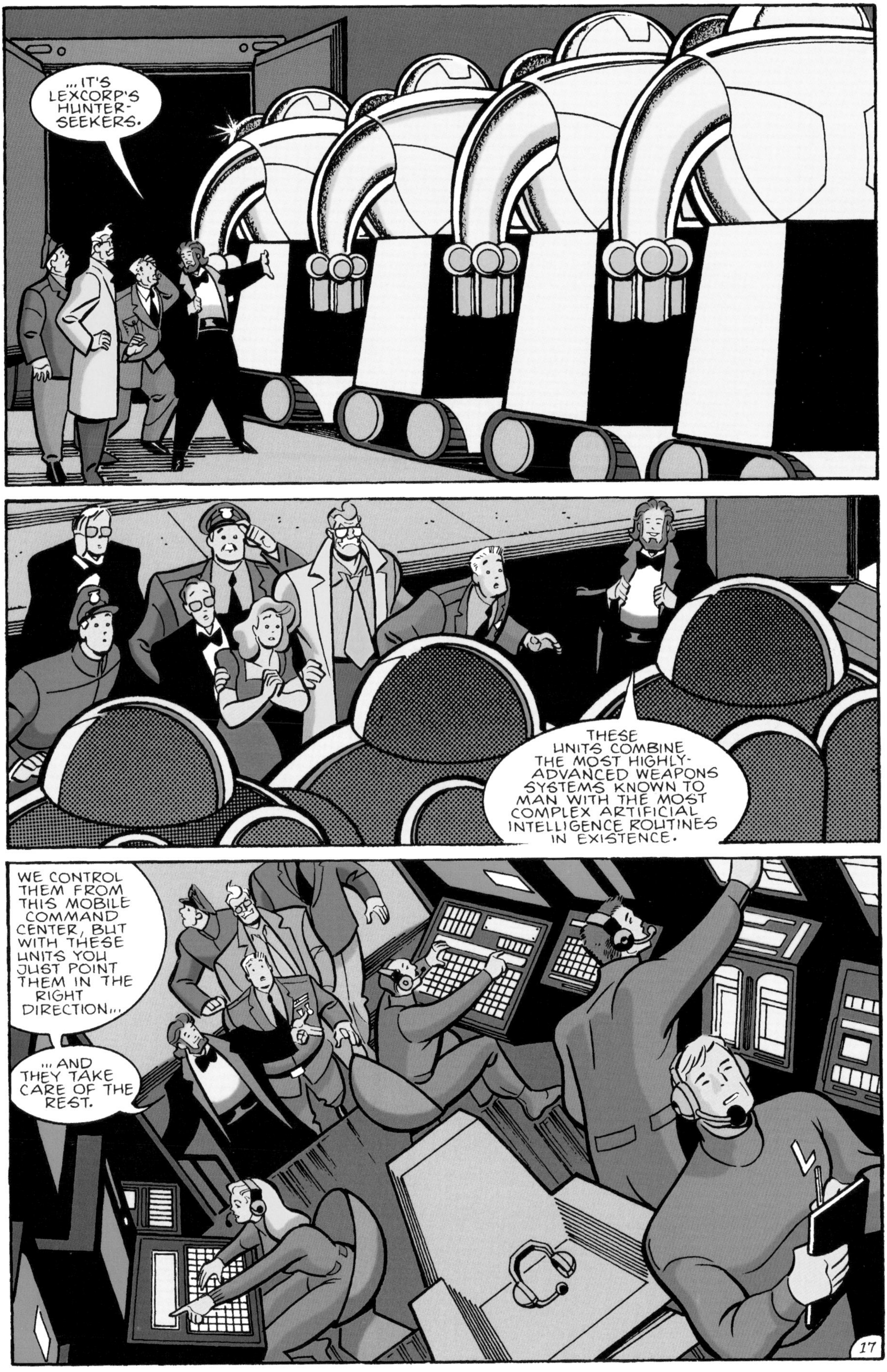
...IT'S LEXCORP'S HUNTER-SEEKERS.
THESE UNITS COMBINE THE MOST HIGHLY-ADVANCED WEAPONS SYSTEMS KNOWN TO MAN WITH THE MOST COMPLEX ARTIFICIAL INTELLIGENCE ROUTINES IN EXISTENCE.
WE CONTROL THEM FROM THIS MOBILE COMMAND CENTER, BUT WITH THESE UNITS YOU JUST POINT THEM IN THE RIGHT DIRECTION...
...AND THEY TAKE CARE OF THE REST.
17

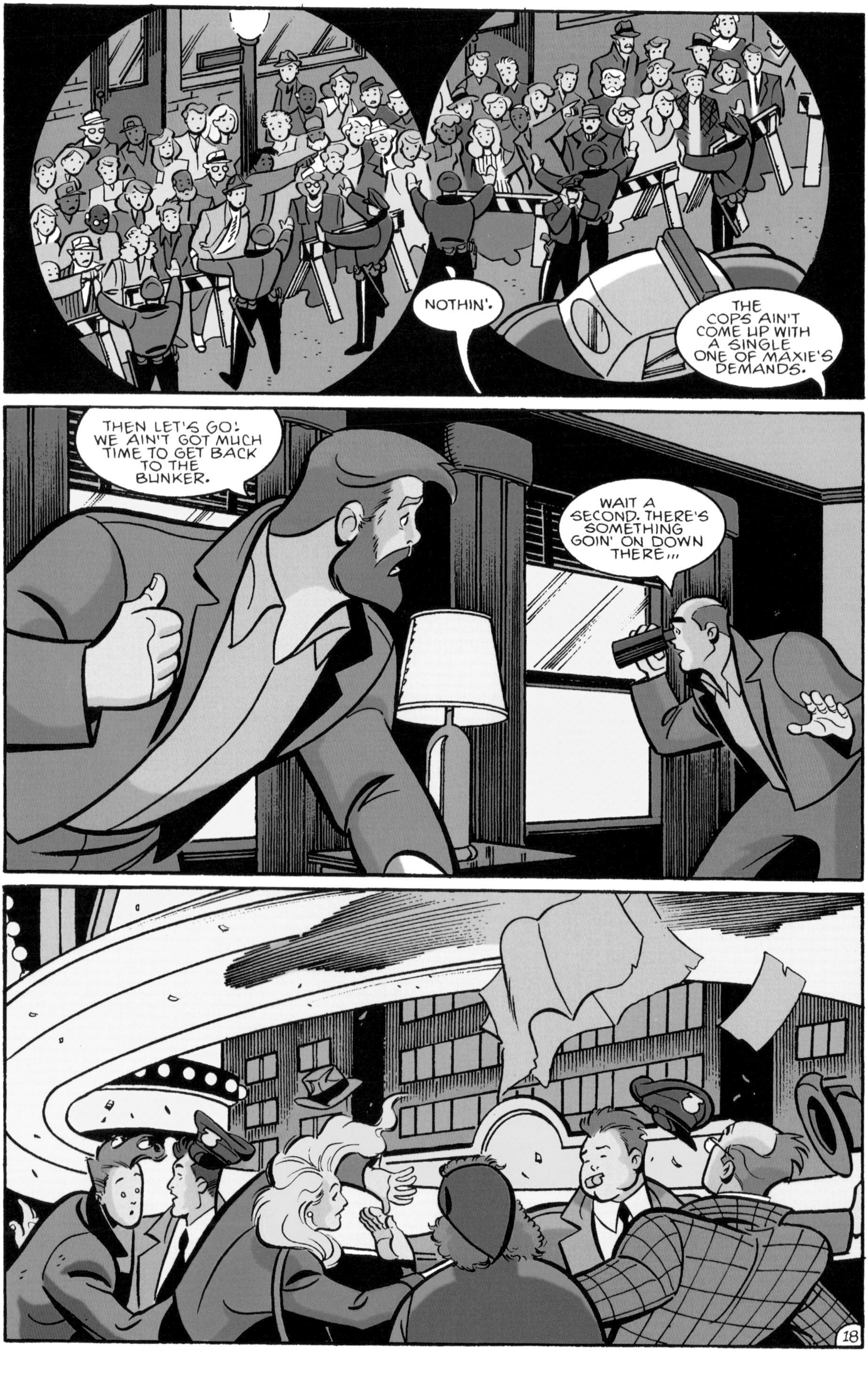
NOTHIN'.
THE COPS AIN'T COME UP WITH A SINGLE ONE OF MAXIE'S DEMANDS.
THEN LET'S GO! WE AIN'T GOT MUCH TIME TO GET BACK TO THE BUNKER.
WAIT A SECOND. THERE'S SOMETHING GOIN' ON DOWN THERE...
18

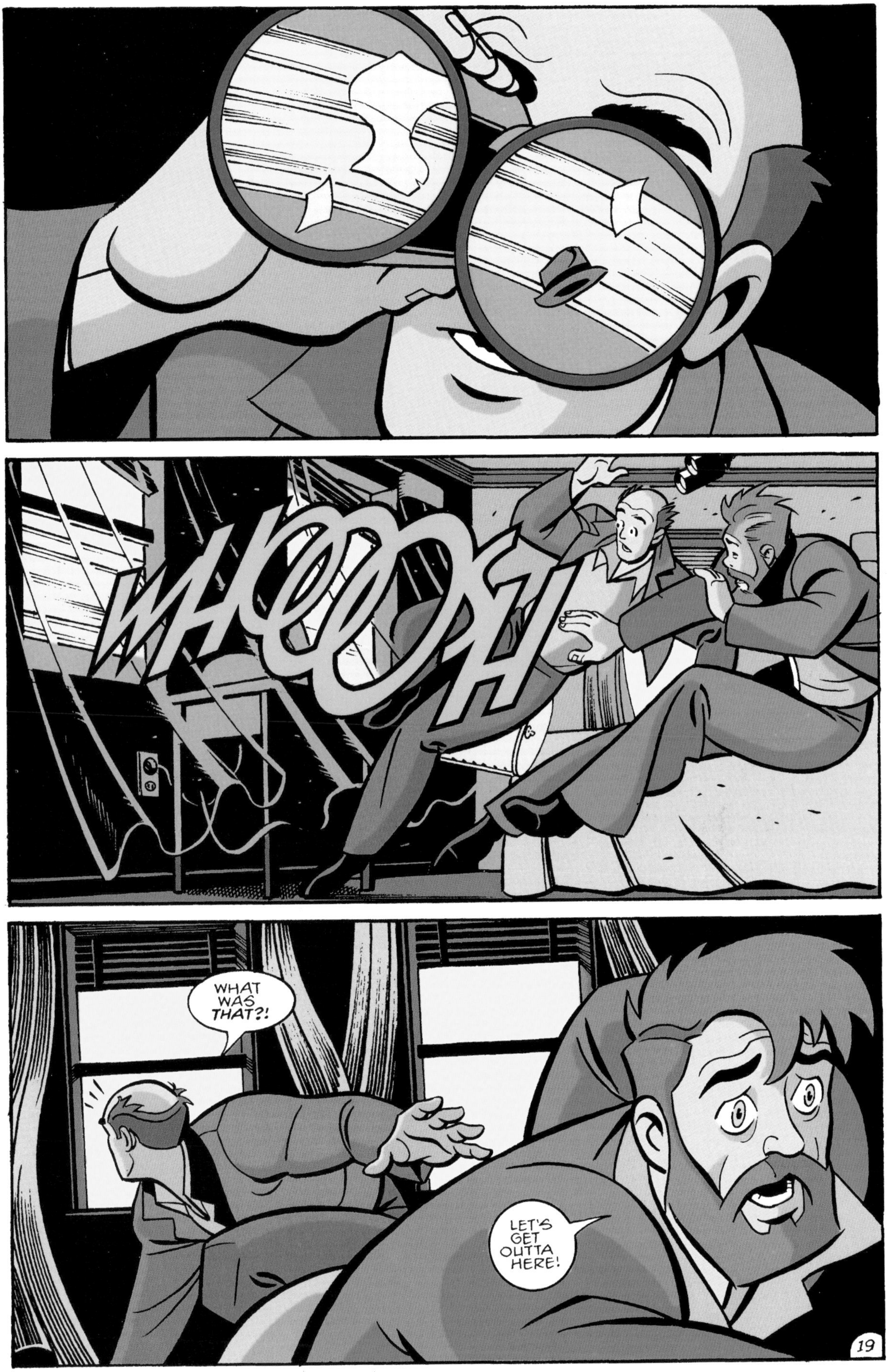
WHOOSH
WHAT WAS *THAT?!*
LET'S GET OUTTA HERE!
19

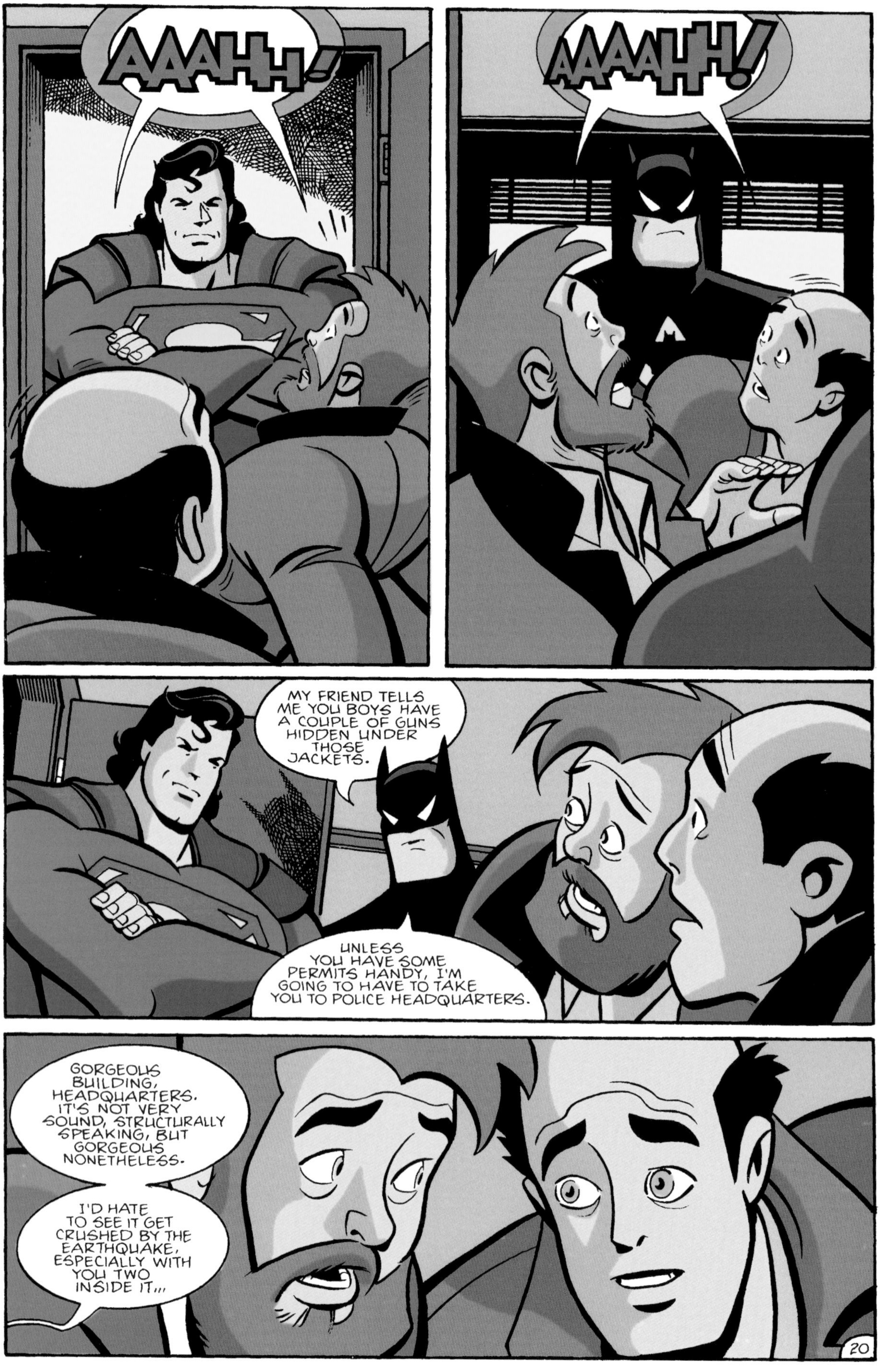
AAAHH!
AAAAHH!
MY FRIEND TELLS ME YOU BOYS HAVE A COUPLE OF GUNS HIDDEN UNDER THOSE JACKETS.
UNLESS YOU HAVE SOME PERMITS HANDY, I'M GOING TO HAVE TO TAKE YOU TO POLICE HEADQUARTERS.
GORGEOUS BUILDING, HEADQUARTERS. IT'S NOT VERY SOUND, STRUCTURALLY SPEAKING, BUT GORGEOUS NONETHELESS.
I'D HATE TO SEE IT GET CRUSHED BY THE EARTHQUAKE, ESPECIALLY WITH YOU TWO INSIDE IT...
20

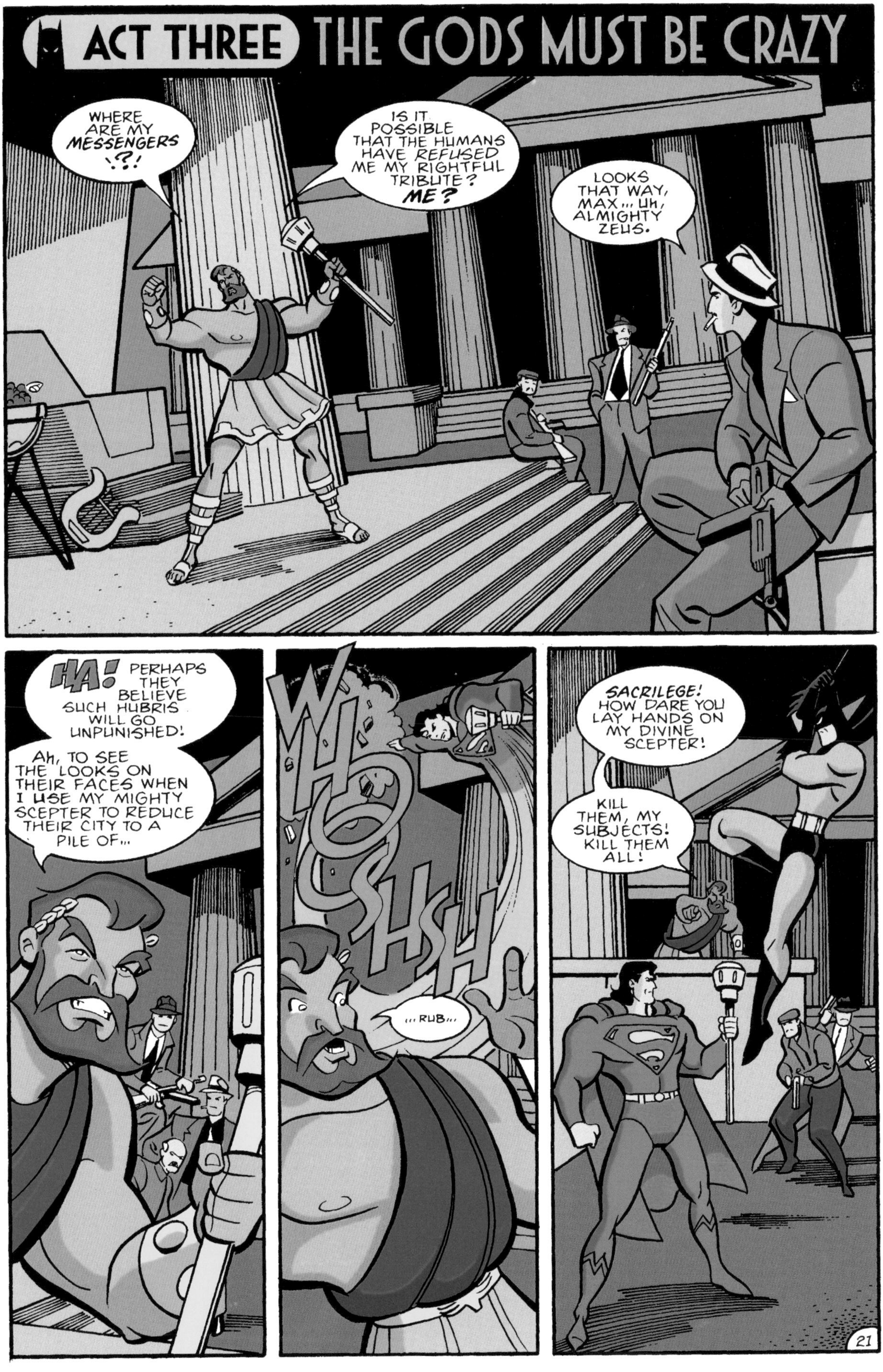
ACT THREE
THE GODS MUST BE CRAZY
WHERE ARE MY MESSENGERS !?!
IS IT POSSIBLE THAT THE HUMANS HAVE REFUSED ME MY RIGHTFUL TRIBUTE? ME?
LOOKS THAT WAY, MAX... UH, ALMIGHTY ZEUS.
HA! PERHAPS THEY BELIEVE SUCH HUBRIS WILL GO UNPUNISHED!
AH, TO SEE THE LOOKS ON THEIR FACES WHEN I USE MY MIGHTY SCEPTER TO REDUCE THEIR CITY TO A PILE OF...
WHOOSHSH
...RUB...
SACRILEGE! HOW DARE YOU LAY HANDS ON MY DIVINE SCEPTER!
KILL THEM, MY SUBJECTS! KILL THEM ALL!
21

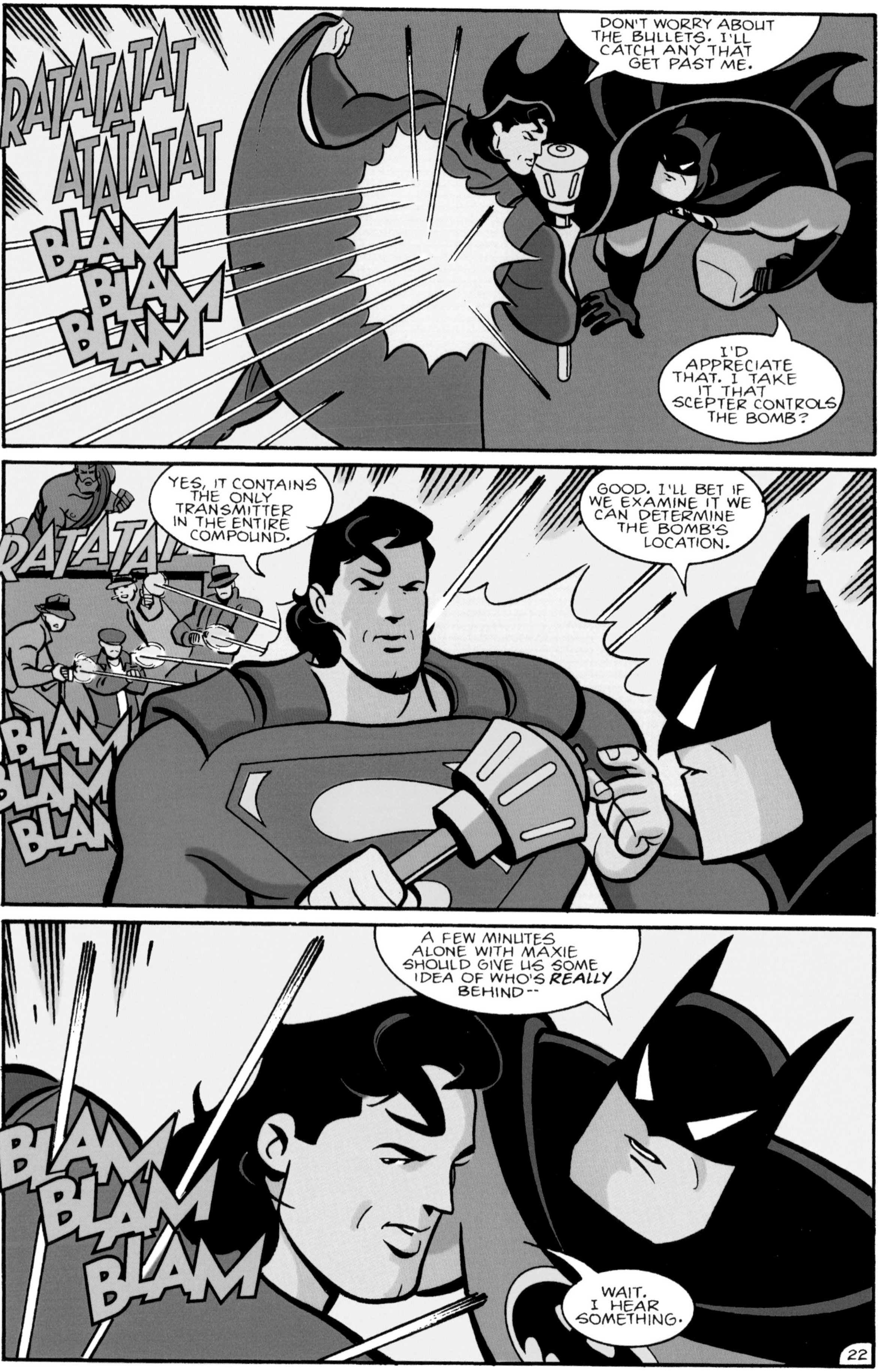
RATATATAT ATATATAT
BLAM BLAM BLAM
DON'T WORRY ABOUT THE BULLETS. I'LL CATCH ANY THAT GET PAST ME.
I'D APPRECIATE THAT. I TAKE IT THAT SCEPTER CONTROLS THE BOMB?
RATATAT
YES, IT CONTAINS THE ONLY TRANSMITTER IN THE ENTIRE COMPOUND.
GOOD. I'LL BET IF WE EXAMINE IT WE CAN DETERMINE THE BOMB'S LOCATION.
BLAM BLAM BLAM
A FEW MINUTES ALONE WITH MAXIE SHOULD GIVE US SOME IDEA OF WHO'S *REALLY* BEHIND--
BLAM BLAM BLAM
WAIT. I HEAR SOMETHING.
22

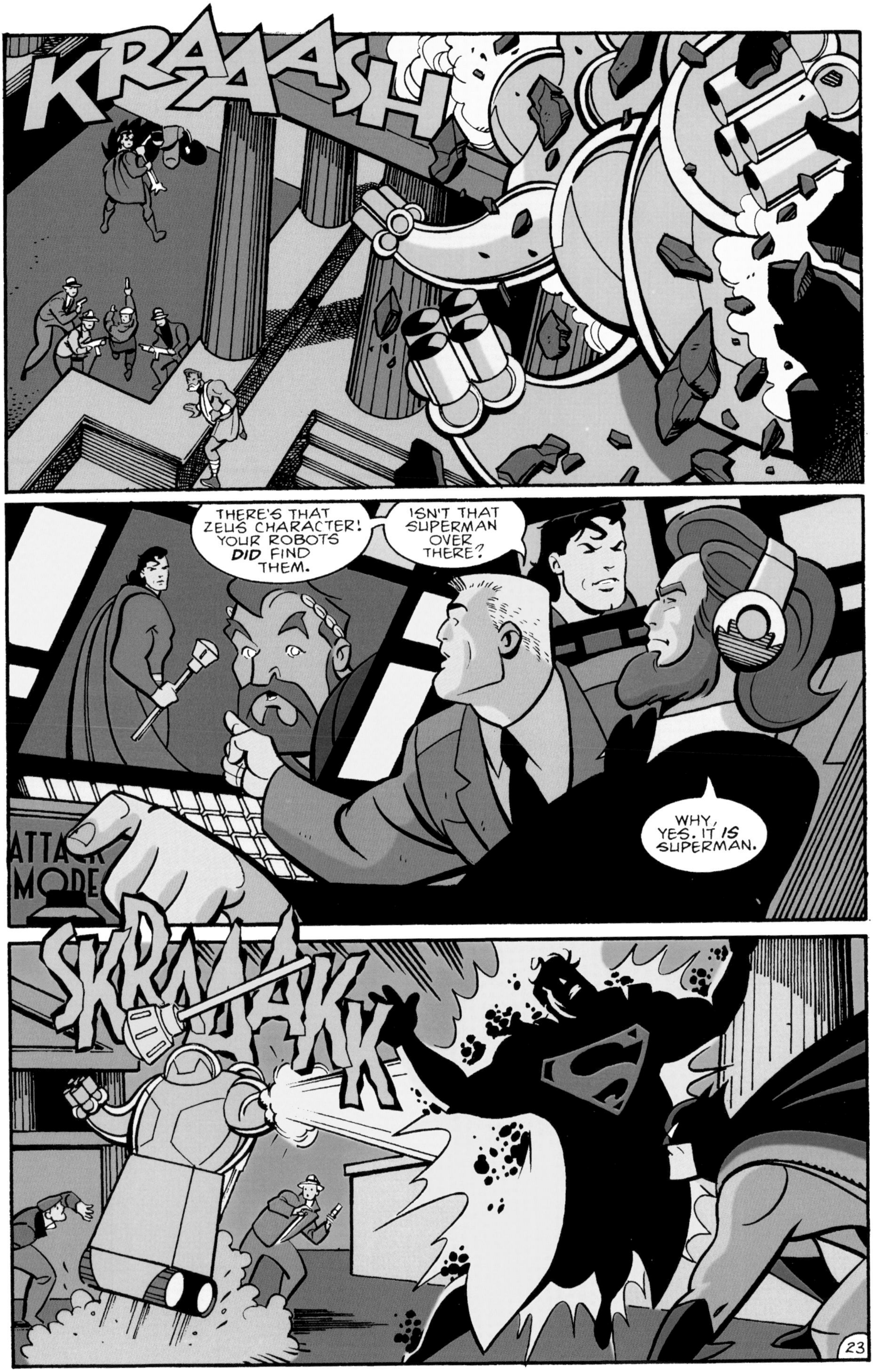
KRAAASH
THERE'S THAT ZEUS CHARACTER! YOUR ROBOTS DID FIND THEM.
ISN'T THAT SUPERMAN OVER THERE?
WHY, YES. IT IS SUPERMAN.
23

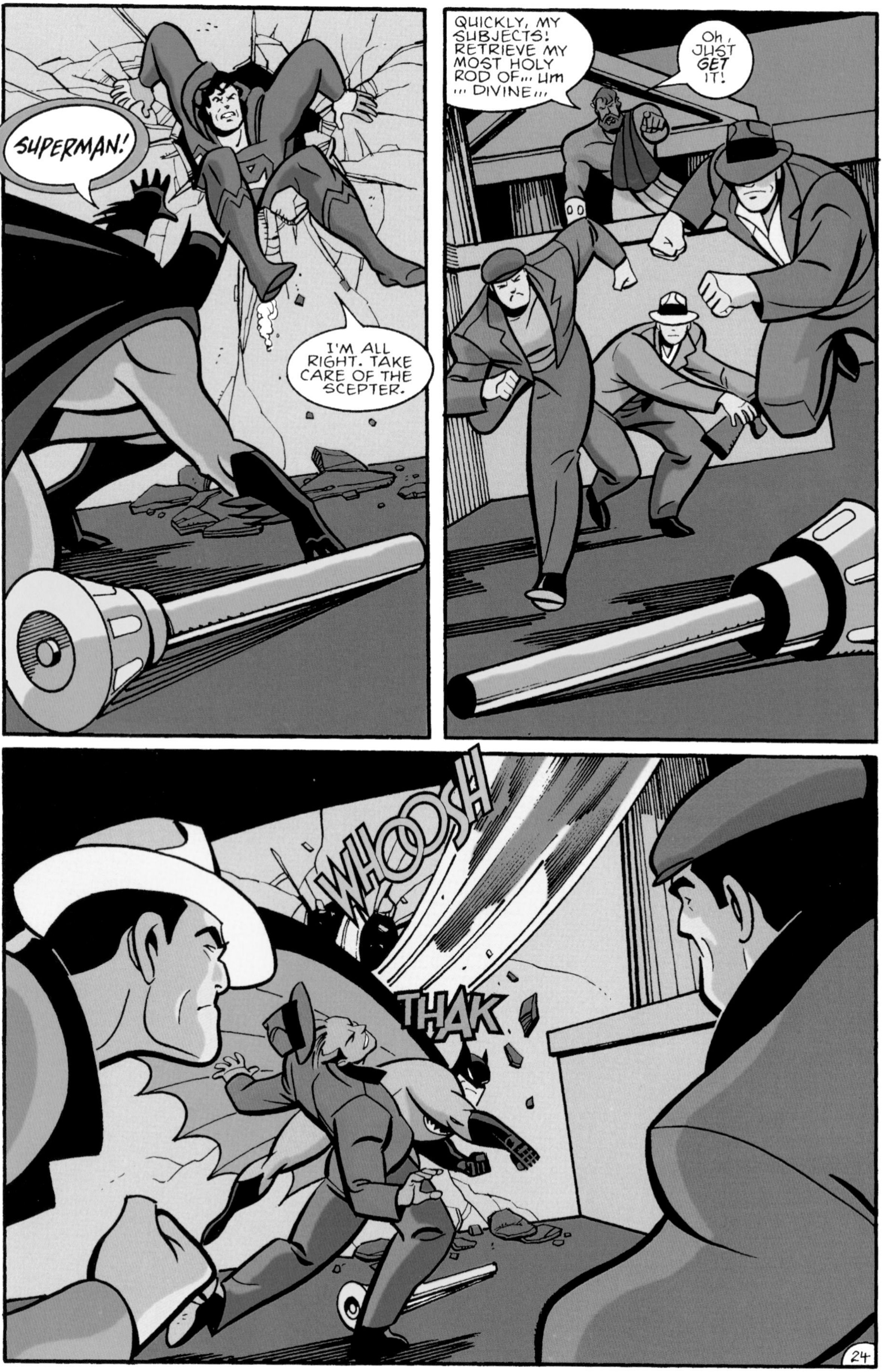
SUPERMAN!
I'M ALL RIGHT. TAKE CARE OF THE SCEPTER.
QUICKLY, MY SUBJECTS! RETRIEVE MY MOST HOLY ROD OF... um ... DIVINE...
Oh, JUST GET IT!
WHOOSH
THAK
24

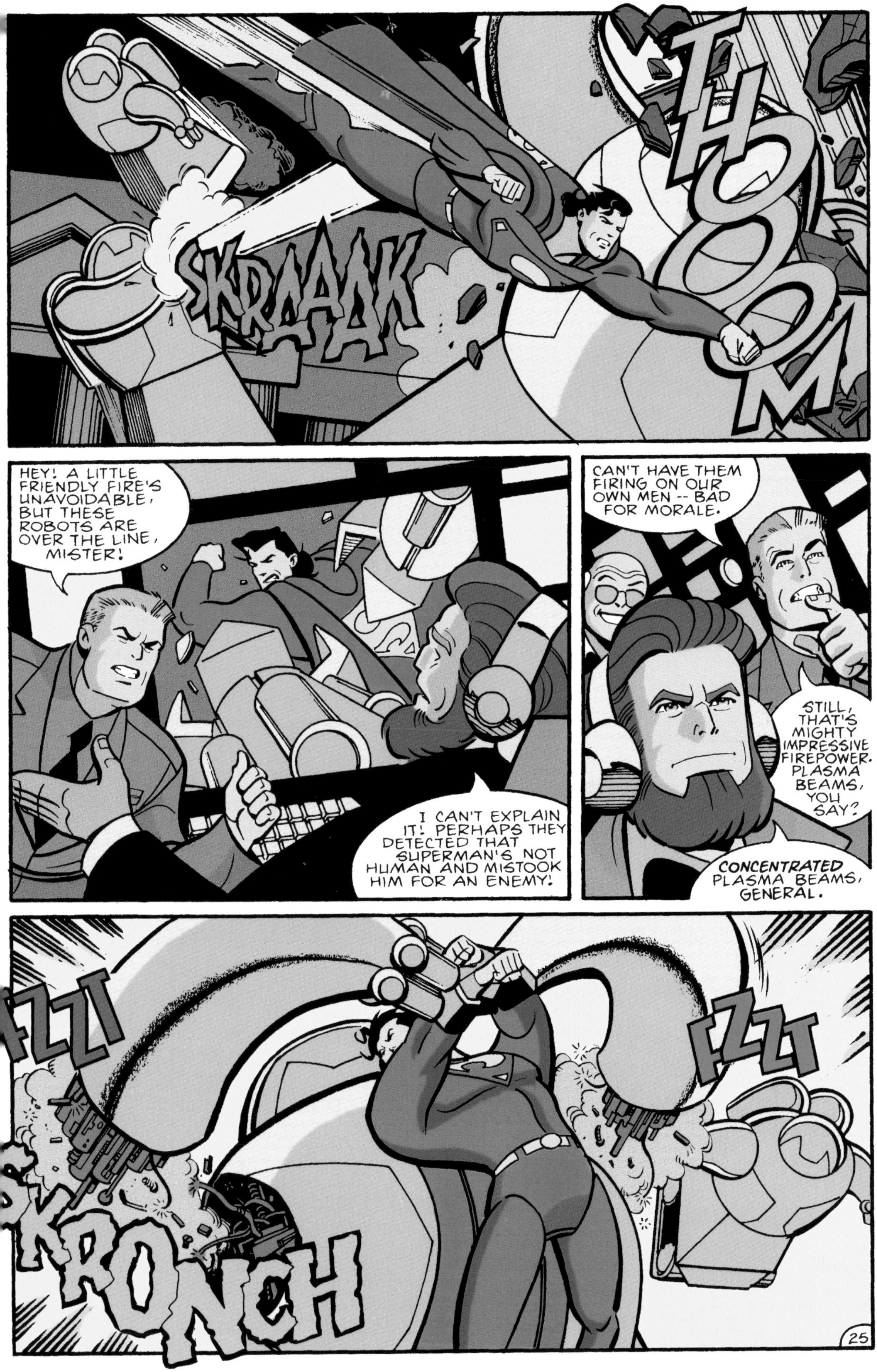
SKRAAAK
THOOOM
HEY! A LITTLE FRIENDLY FIRE'S UNAVOIDABLE, BUT THESE ROBOTS ARE OVER THE LINE, MISTER!
I CAN'T EXPLAIN IT! PERHAPS THEY DETECTED THAT SUPERMAN'S NOT HUMAN AND MISTOOK HIM FOR AN ENEMY!
CAN'T HAVE THEM FIRING ON OUR OWN MEN -- BAD FOR MORALE.
STILL, THAT'S MIGHTY IMPRESSIVE FIREPOWER. PLASMA BEAMS, YOU SAY?
CONCENTRATED PLASMA BEAMS, GENERAL.
FZZT
FZZT
SKRONCH
25

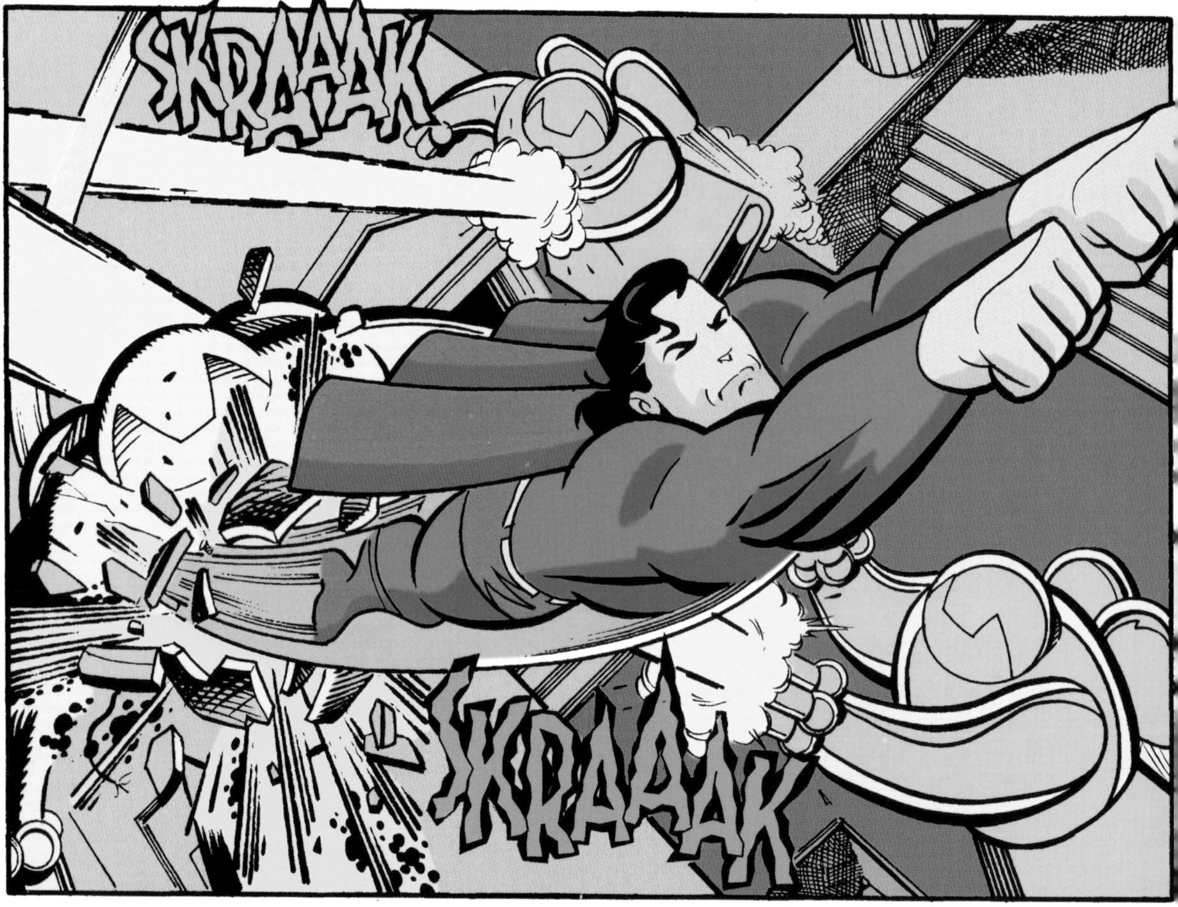
SKRAAAK
SKRAAAK

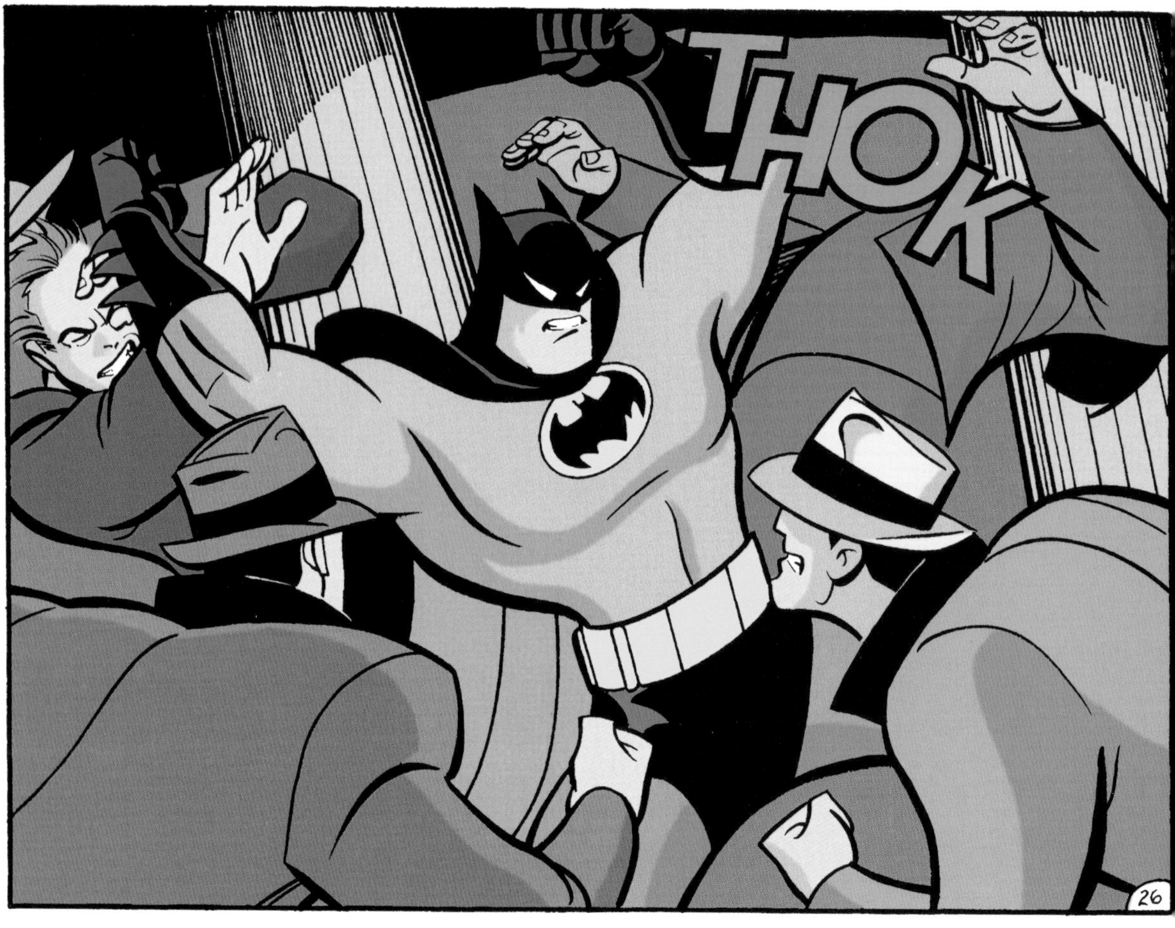
THOK
26

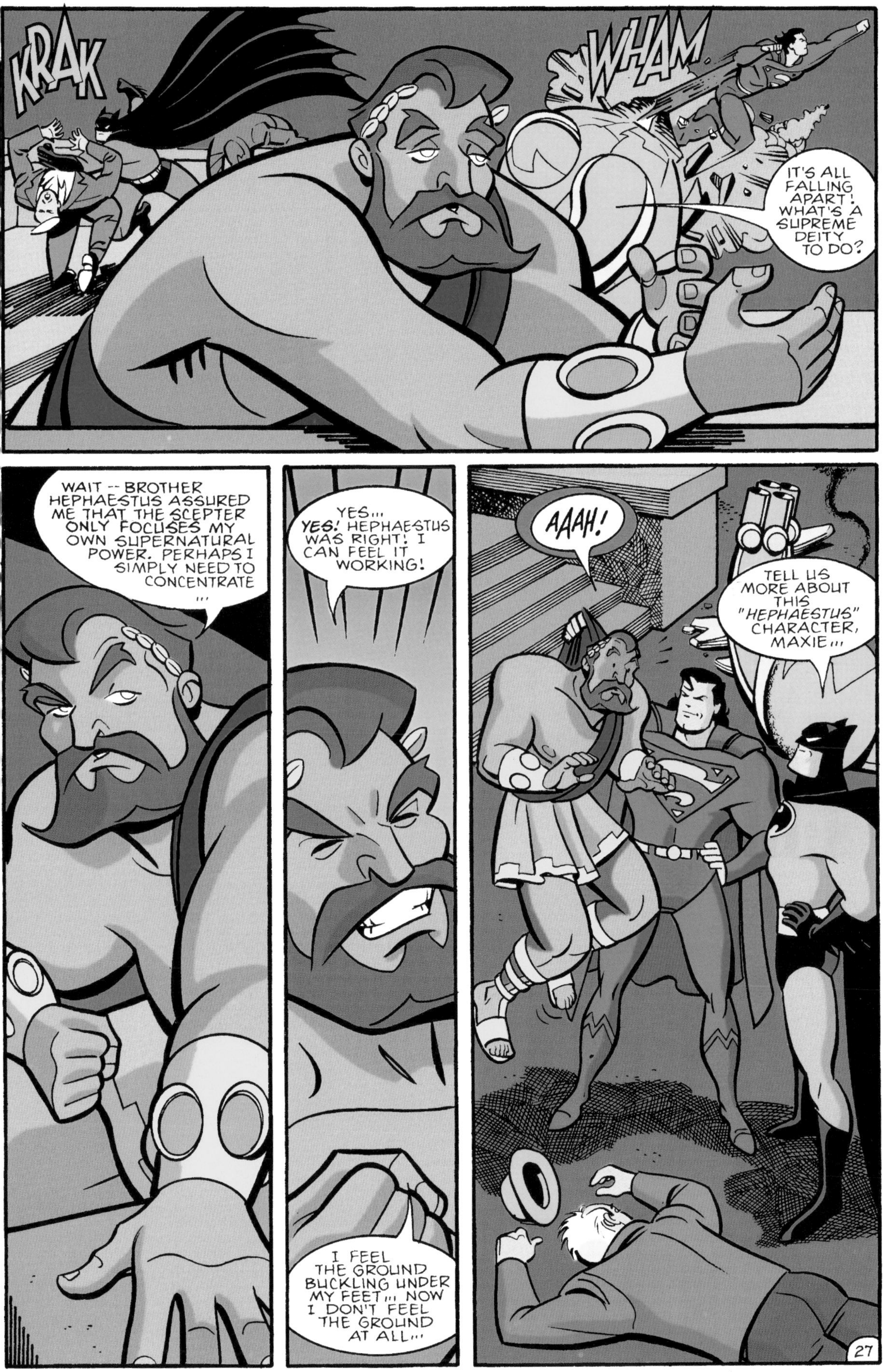
KRAK
WHAM
IT'S ALL FALLING APART! WHAT'S A SUPREME DEITY TO DO?
WAIT -- BROTHER HEPHAESTUS ASSURED ME THAT THE SCEPTER ONLY FOCUSES MY OWN SUPERNATURAL POWER. PERHAPS I SIMPLY NEED TO CONCENTRATE ...
YES... *YES!* HEPHAESTUS WAS RIGHT! I CAN FEEL IT WORKING!
I FEEL THE GROUND BUCKLING UNDER MY FEET... NOW I DON'T FEEL THE GROUND AT ALL...
AAAH!
TELL US MORE ABOUT THIS "*HEPHAESTUS*" CHARACTER, MAXIE...
27

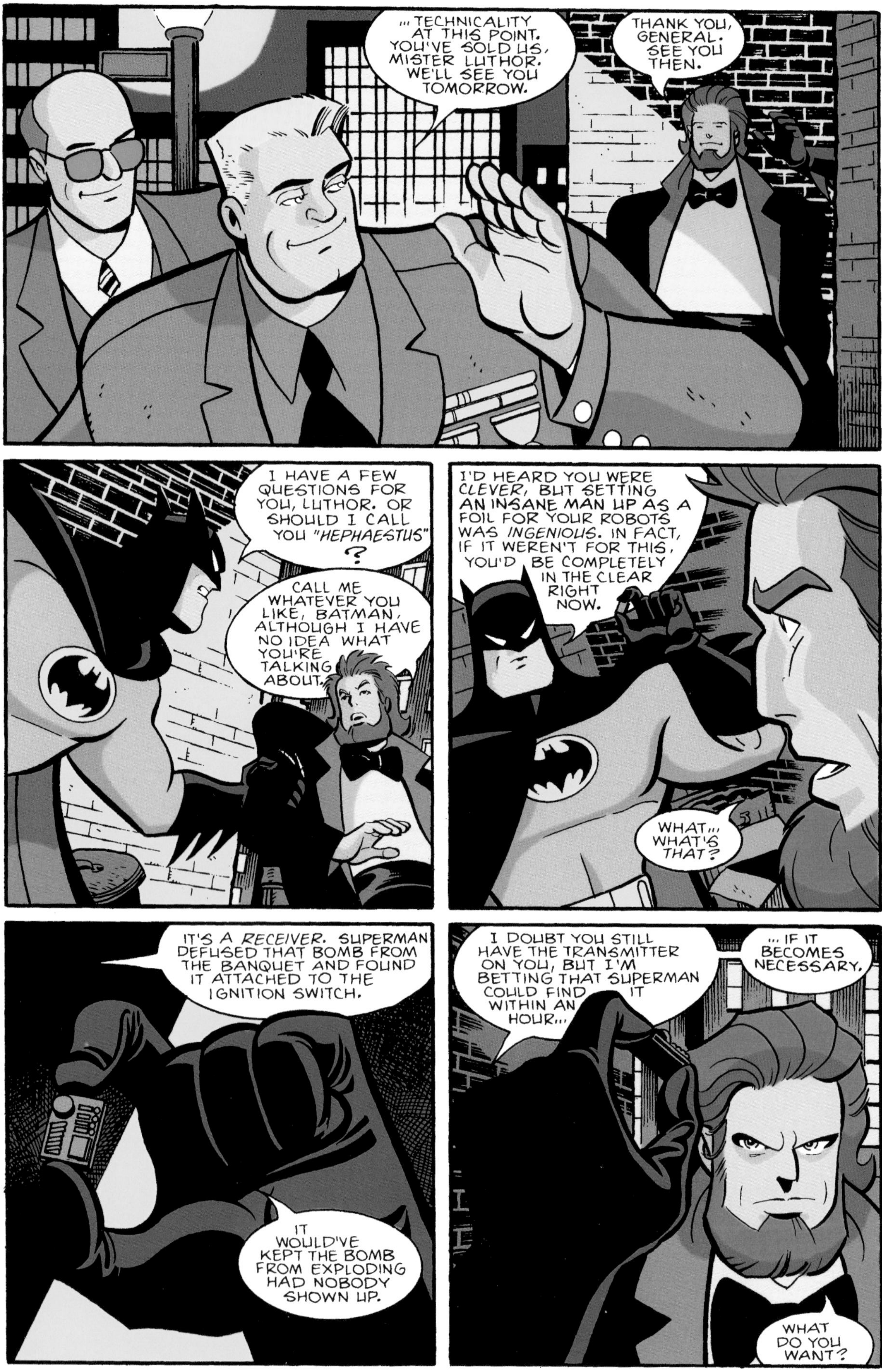
...TECHNICALITY AT THIS POINT. YOU'VE SOLD US, MISTER LUTHOR. WE'LL SEE YOU TOMORROW.
THANK YOU, GENERAL. SEE YOU THEN.
I HAVE A FEW QUESTIONS FOR YOU, LUTHOR. OR SHOULD I CALL YOU "HEPHAESTUS"?
CALL ME WHATEVER YOU LIKE, BATMAN, ALTHOUGH I HAVE NO IDEA WHAT YOU'RE TALKING ABOUT.
I'D HEARD YOU WERE CLEVER, BUT SETTING AN INSANE MAN UP AS A FOIL FOR YOUR ROBOTS WAS INGENIOUS. IN FACT, IF IT WEREN'T FOR THIS, YOU'D BE COMPLETELY IN THE CLEAR RIGHT NOW.
WHAT... WHAT'S THAT?
IT'S A RECEIVER. SUPERMAN DEFUSED THAT BOMB FROM THE BANQUET AND FOUND IT ATTACHED TO THE IGNITION SWITCH.
IT WOULD'VE KEPT THE BOMB FROM EXPLODING HAD NOBODY SHOWN UP.
I DOUBT YOU STILL HAVE THE TRANSMITTER ON YOU, BUT I'M BETTING THAT SUPERMAN COULD FIND IT WITHIN AN HOUR...
...IF IT BECOMES NECESSARY.
WHAT DO YOU WANT?

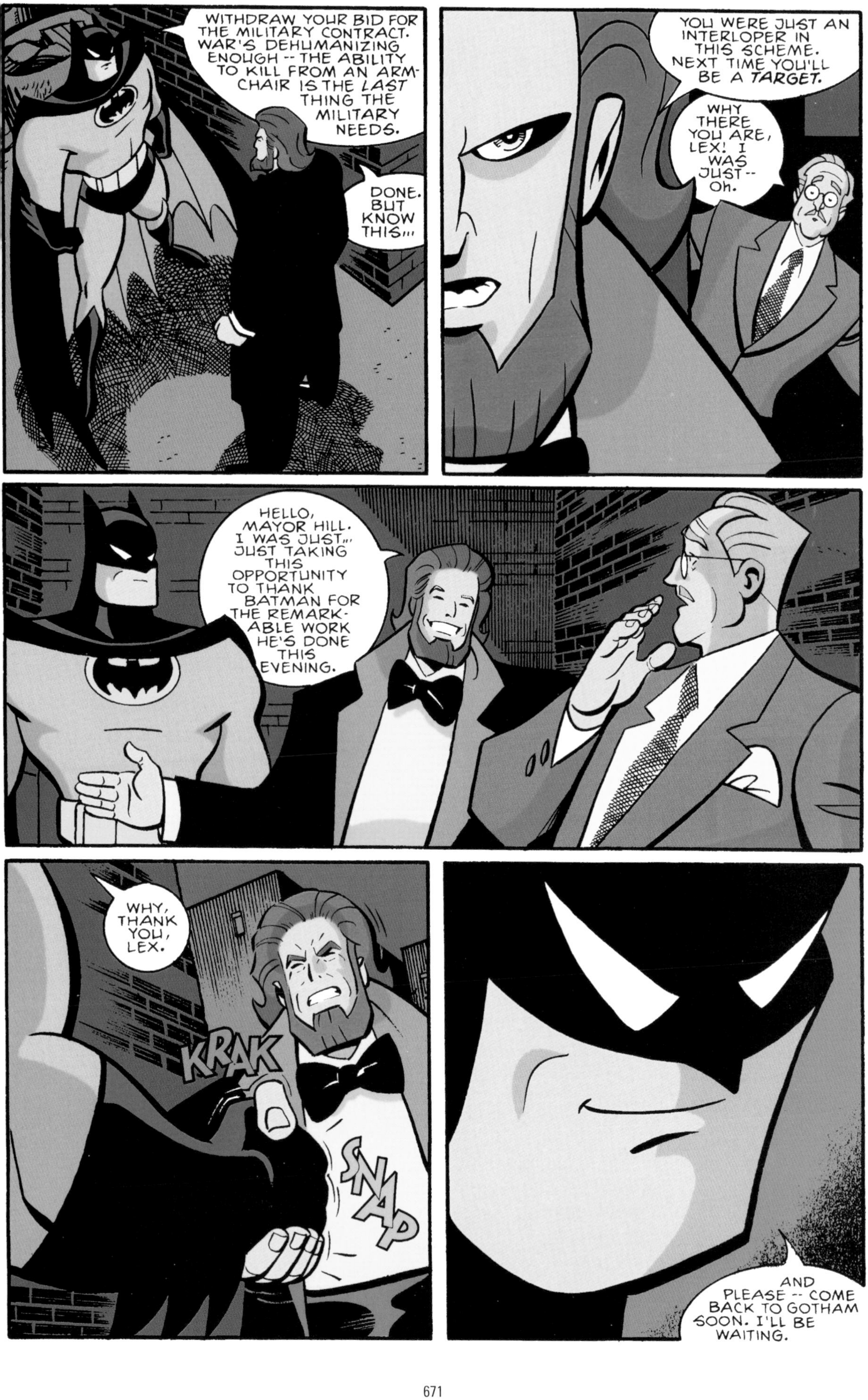
WITHDRAW YOUR BID FOR THE MILITARY CONTRACT. WAR'S DEHUMANIZING ENOUGH -- THE ABILITY TO KILL FROM AN ARM-CHAIR IS THE *LAST* THING THE MILITARY NEEDS.
DONE. BUT KNOW THIS...
YOU WERE JUST AN INTERLOPER IN THIS SCHEME. NEXT TIME YOU'LL BE A *TARGET.*
WHY THERE YOU ARE, LEX! I WAS JUST -- Oh.
HELLO, MAYOR HILL. I WAS JUST... JUST TAKING THIS OPPORTUNITY TO THANK BATMAN FOR THE REMARK-ABLE WORK HE'S DONE THIS EVENING.
WHY, THANK YOU, LEX.
KRAK
SNAP
AND PLEASE -- COME BACK TO GOTHAM SOON. I'LL BE WAITING.

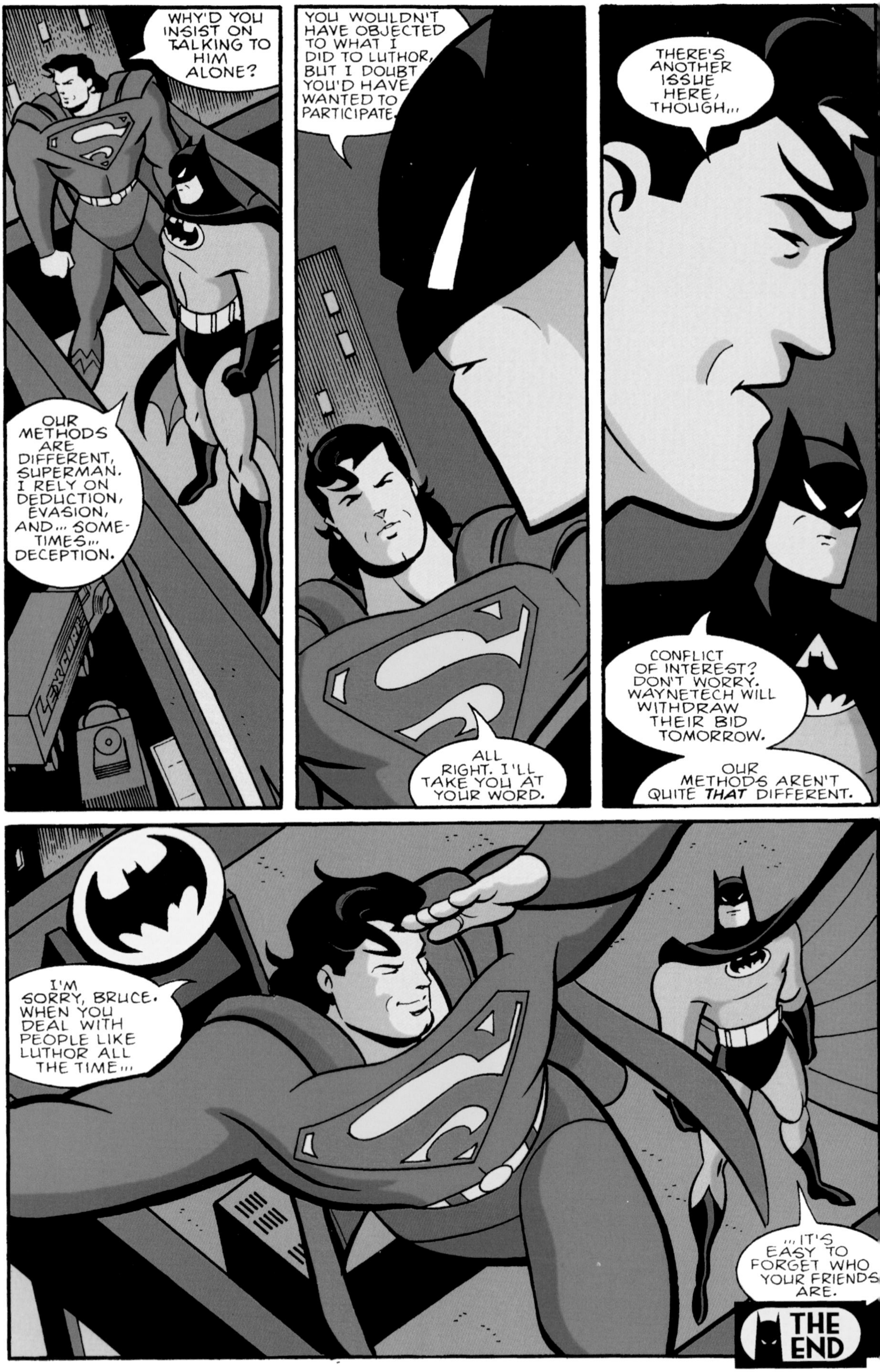
WHY'D YOU INSIST ON TALKING TO HIM ALONE?
OUR METHODS ARE DIFFERENT, SUPERMAN. I RELY ON DEDUCTION, EVASION, AND... SOME-TIMES... DECEPTION.
YOU WOULDN'T HAVE OBJECTED TO WHAT I DID TO LUTHOR, BUT I DOUBT YOU'D HAVE WANTED TO PARTICIPATE.
ALL RIGHT. I'LL TAKE YOU AT YOUR WORD.
THERE'S ANOTHER ISSUE HERE, THOUGH...
CONFLICT OF INTEREST? DON'T WORRY. WAYNETECH WILL WITHDRAW THEIR BID TOMORROW.
OUR METHODS AREN'T QUITE THAT DIFFERENT.
I'M SORRY, BRUCE. WHEN YOU DEAL WITH PEOPLE LIKE LUTHOR ALL THE TIME...
...IT'S EASY TO FORGET WHO YOUR FRIENDS ARE.
THE END

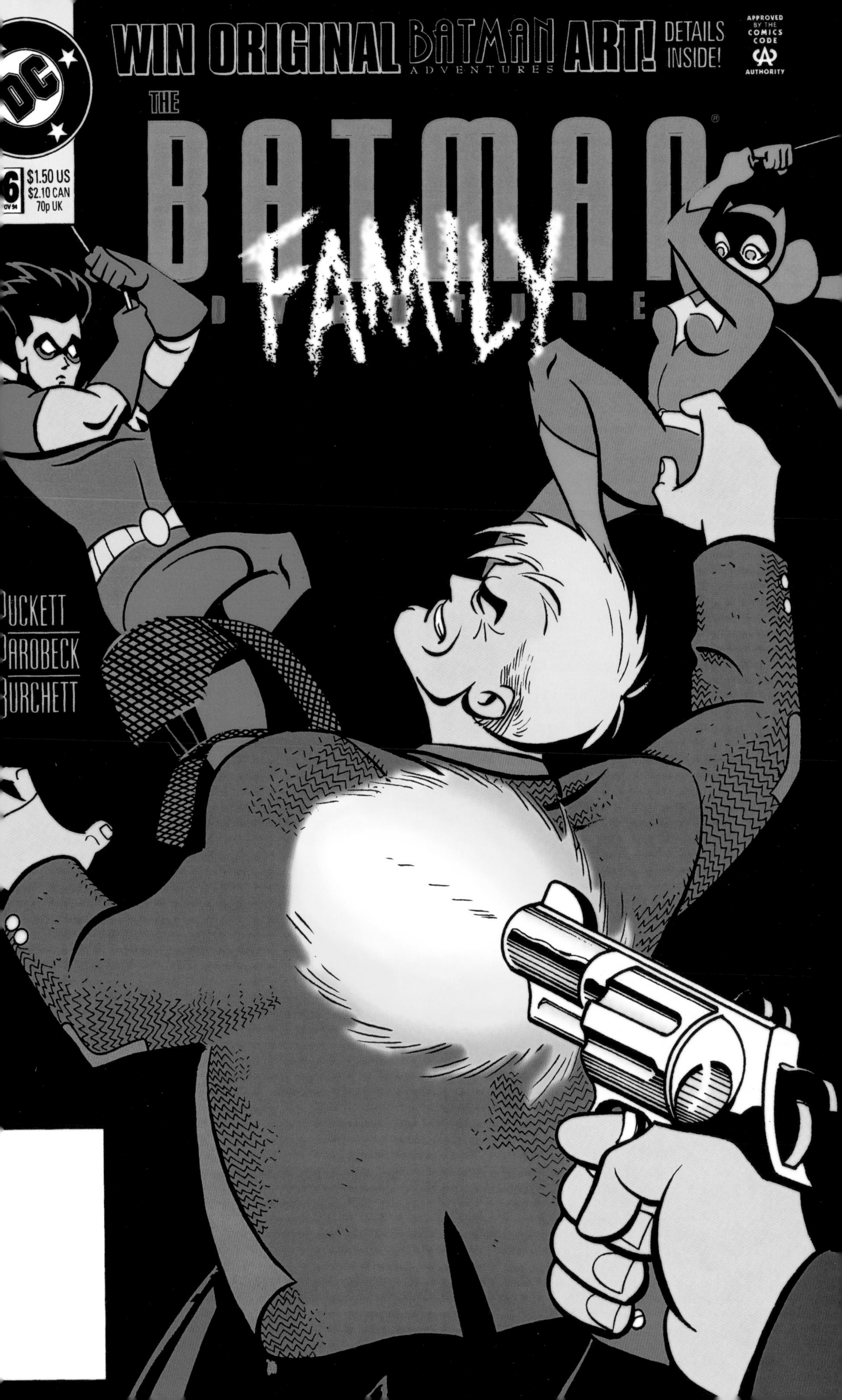
WIN ORIGINAL BATMAN ADVENTURES ART! DETAILS INSIDE!
APPROVED BY THE COMICS CODE AUTHORITY
DC
THE BATMAN ADVENTURES
FAMILY
6
$1.50 US
$2.10 CAN
70p UK
PUCKETT
PAROBECK
BURCHETT

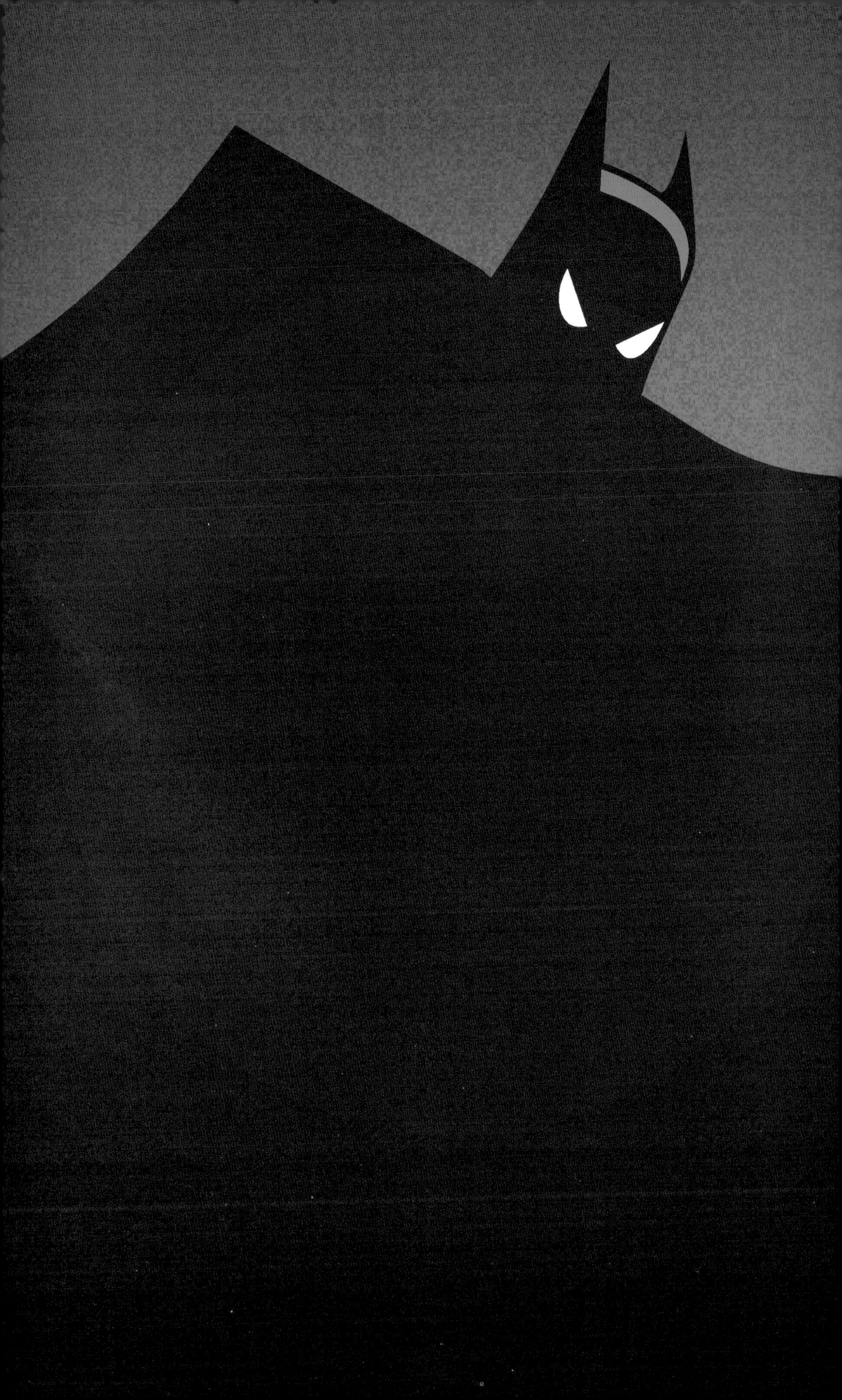

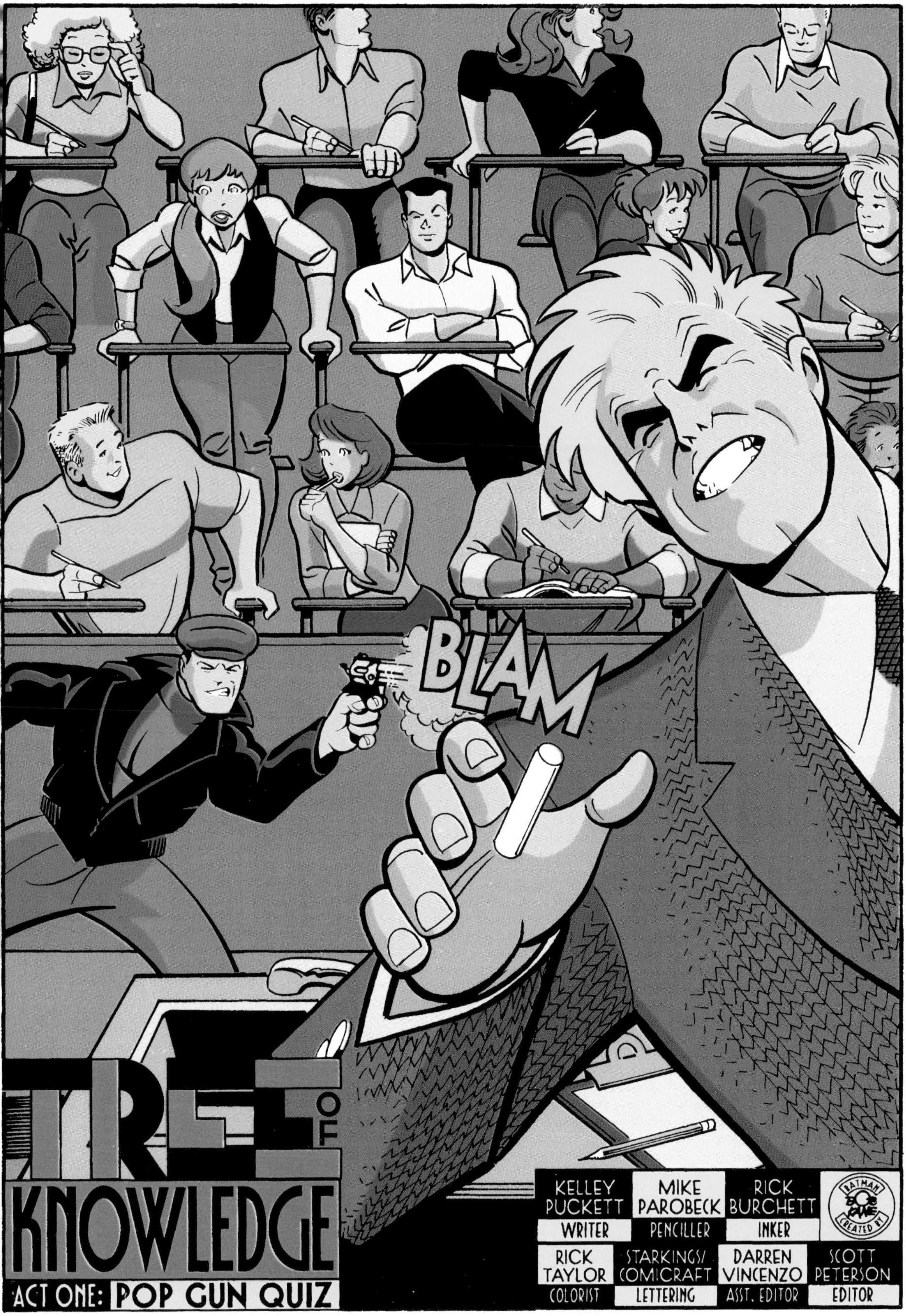
BLAM
TREE OF KNOWLEDGE
ACT ONE: POP GUN QUIZ
KELLEY PUCKETT WRITER
MIKE PAROBECK PENCILLER
RICK BURCHETT INKER
BATMAN CREATED BY BOB KANE
RICK TAYLOR COLORIST
STARKINGS/ COMICRAFT LETTERING
DARREN VINCENZO ASST. EDITOR
SCOTT PETERSON EDITOR

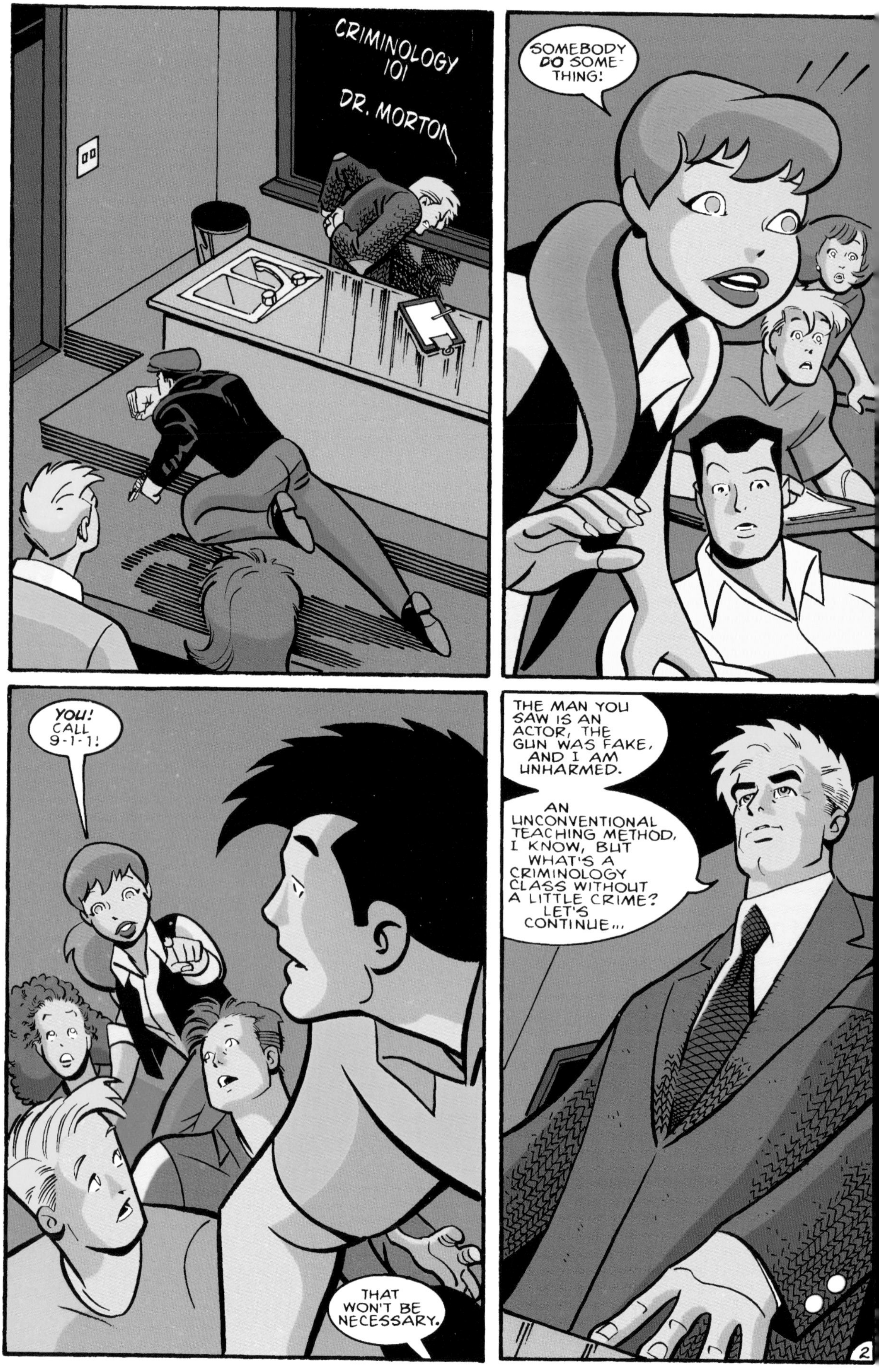
CRIMINOLOGY 101
DR. MORTON
SOMEBODY DO SOME-THING!
YOU! CALL 9-1-1!
THAT WON'T BE NECESSARY.
THE MAN YOU SAW IS AN ACTOR, THE GUN WAS FAKE, AND I AM UNHARMED.
AN UNCONVENTIONAL TEACHING METHOD, I KNOW, BUT WHAT'S A CRIMINOLOGY CLASS WITHOUT A LITTLE CRIME? LET'S CONTINUE...
2

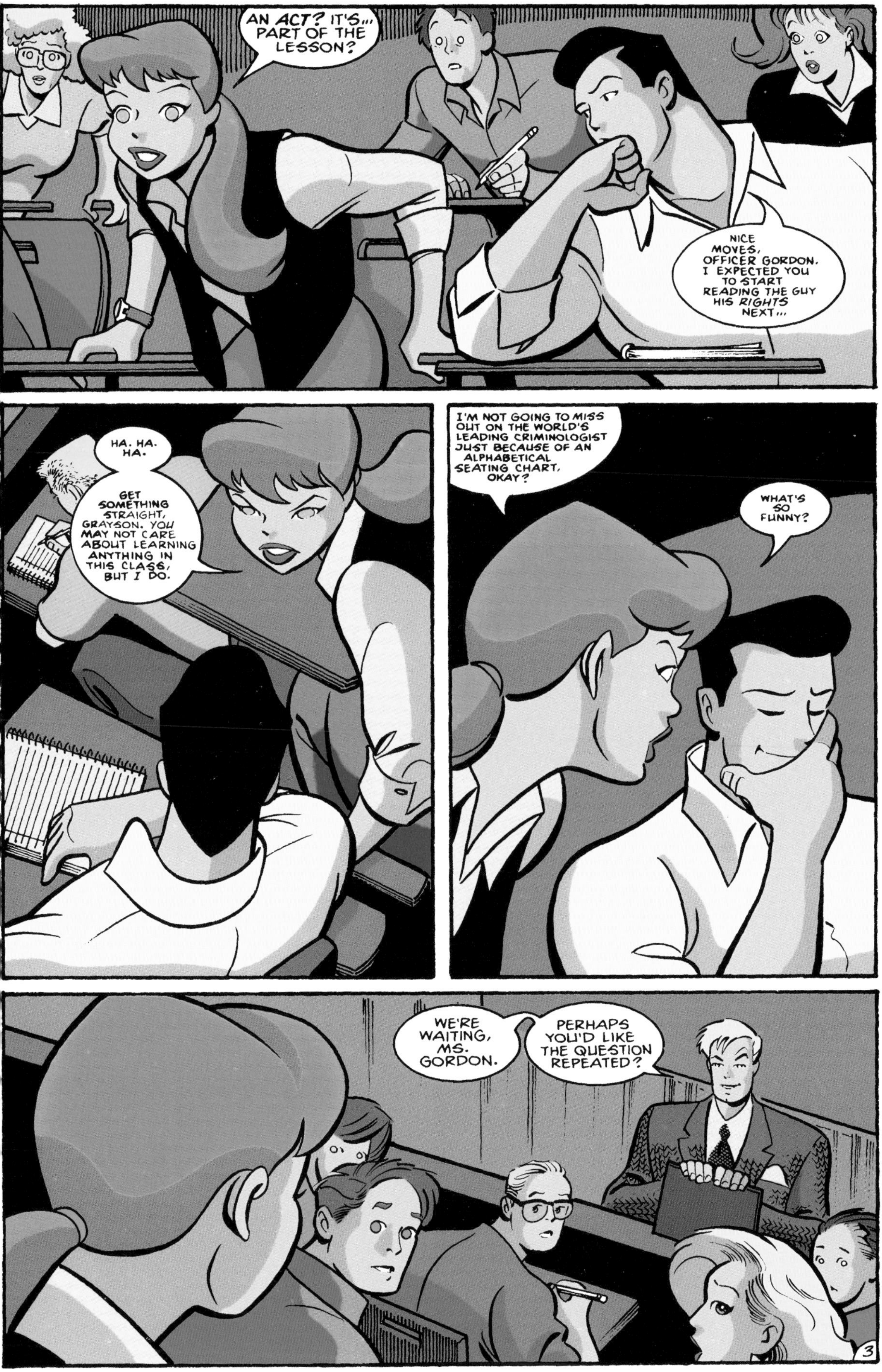

AN ACT? IT'S... PART OF THE LESSON?
NICE MOVES, OFFICER GORDON. I EXPECTED YOU TO START READING THE GUY HIS RIGHTS NEXT...
HA. HA. HA.
GET SOMETHING STRAIGHT, GRAYSON. YOU MAY NOT CARE ABOUT LEARNING ANYTHING IN THIS CLASS, BUT I DO.
I'M NOT GOING TO MISS OUT ON THE WORLD'S LEADING CRIMINOLOGIST JUST BECAUSE OF AN ALPHABETICAL SEATING CHART, OKAY?
WHAT'S SO FUNNY?
WE'RE WAITING, MS. GORDON.
PERHAPS YOU'D LIKE THE QUESTION REPEATED?
3

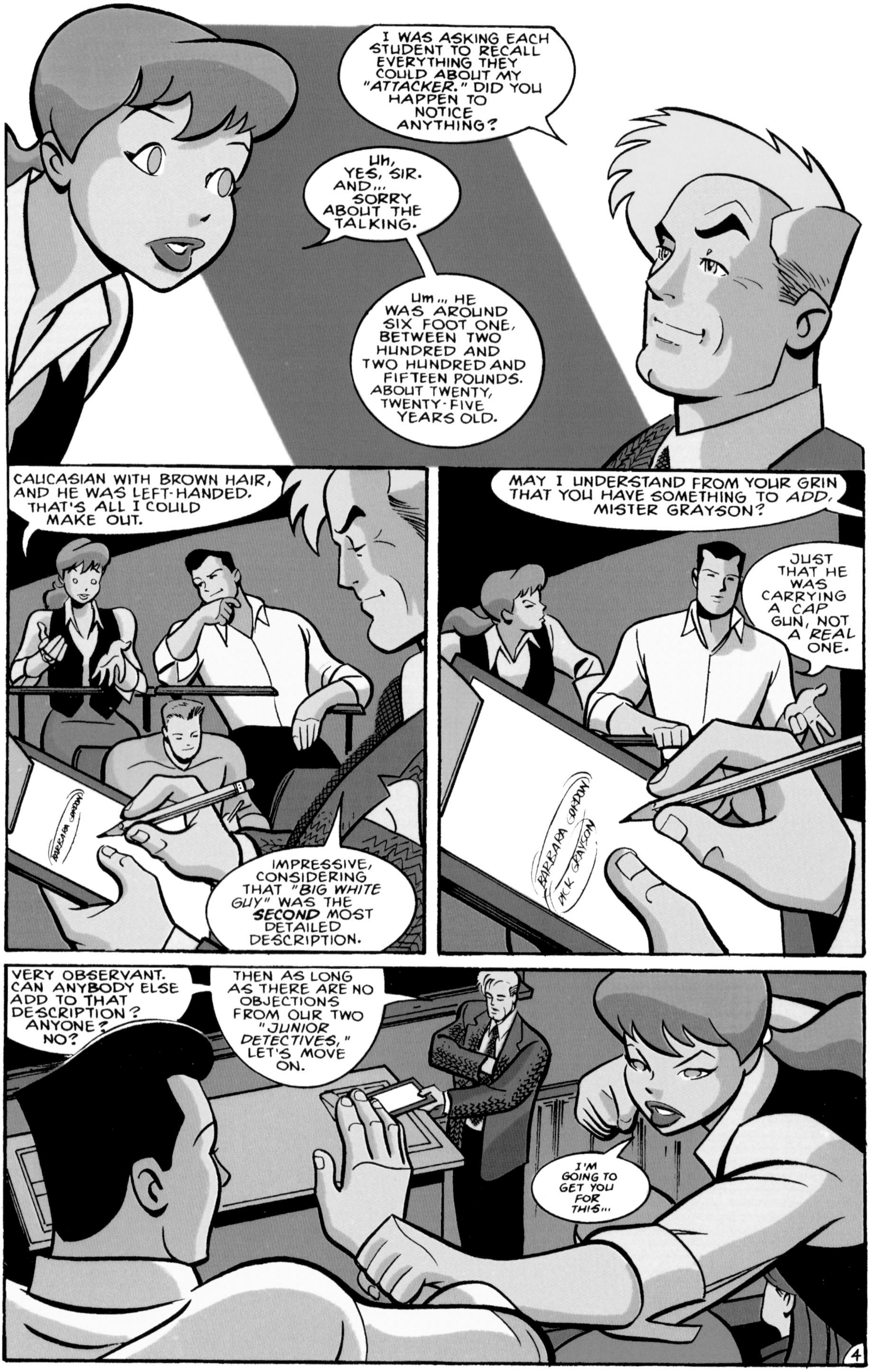
I WAS ASKING EACH STUDENT TO RECALL EVERYTHING THEY COULD ABOUT MY "ATTACKER." DID YOU HAPPEN TO NOTICE ANYTHING?
UH, YES, SIR. AND... SORRY ABOUT THE TALKING.
UM... HE WAS AROUND SIX FOOT ONE, BETWEEN TWO HUNDRED AND TWO HUNDRED AND FIFTEEN POUNDS. ABOUT TWENTY, TWENTY-FIVE YEARS OLD.
CAUCASIAN WITH BROWN HAIR, AND HE WAS LEFT-HANDED. THAT'S ALL I COULD MAKE OUT.
BARBARA GORDON
IMPRESSIVE, CONSIDERING THAT "BIG WHITE GUY" WAS THE SECOND MOST DETAILED DESCRIPTION.
MAY I UNDERSTAND FROM YOUR GRIN THAT YOU HAVE SOMETHING TO ADD, MISTER GRAYSON?
JUST THAT HE WAS CARRYING A CAP GUN, NOT A REAL ONE.
BARBARA GORDON
DICK GRAYSON
VERY OBSERVANT. CAN ANYBODY ELSE ADD TO THAT DESCRIPTION? ANYONE? NO?
THEN AS LONG AS THERE ARE NO OBJECTIONS FROM OUR TWO "JUNIOR DETECTIVES," LET'S MOVE ON.
I'M GOING TO GET YOU FOR THIS...
4

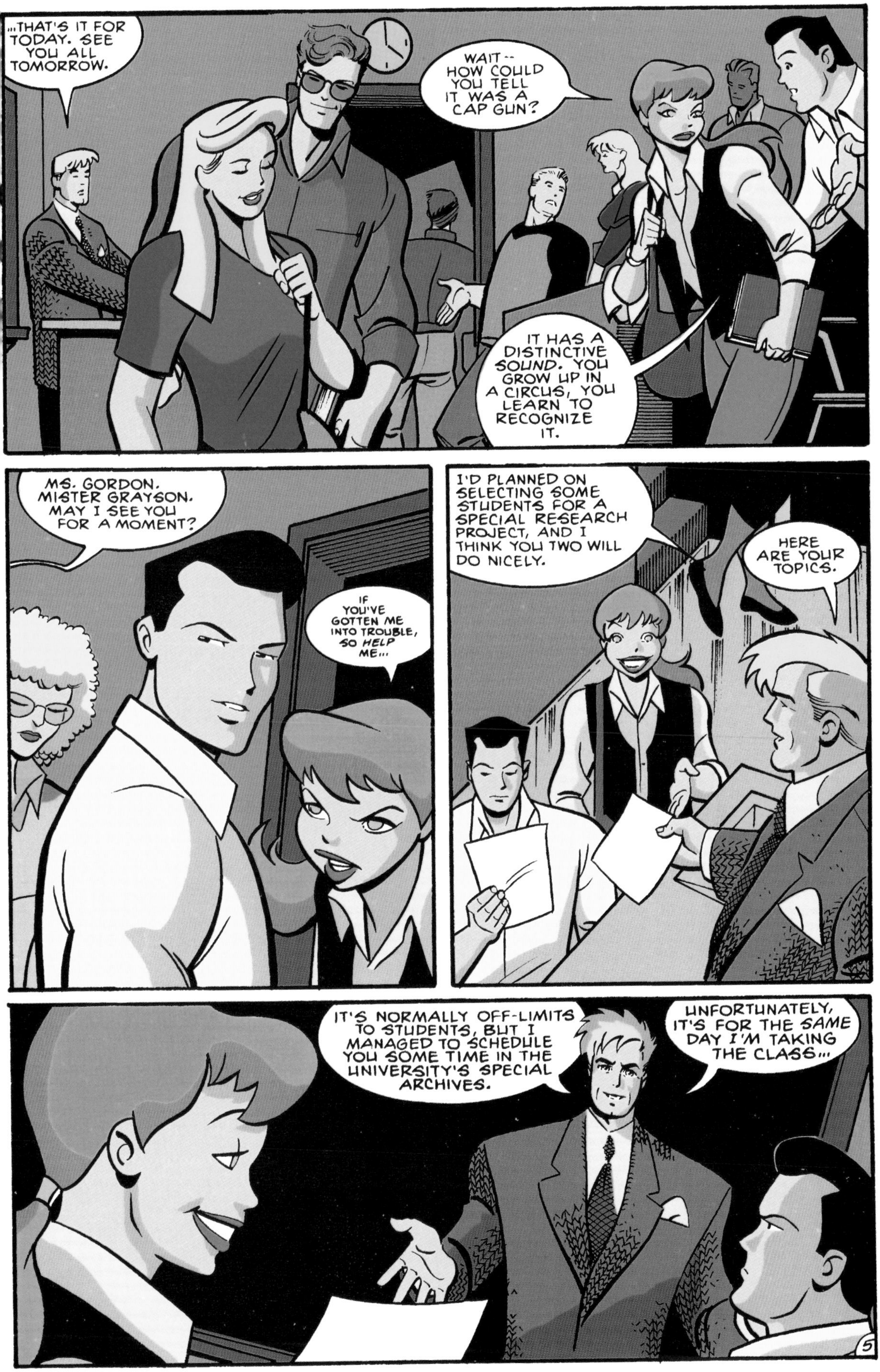
...THAT'S IT FOR TODAY. SEE YOU ALL TOMORROW.
WAIT -- HOW COULD YOU TELL IT WAS A CAP GUN?
IT HAS A DISTINCTIVE SOUND. YOU GROW UP IN A CIRCUS, YOU LEARN TO RECOGNIZE IT.
MS. GORDON. MISTER GRAYSON. MAY I SEE YOU FOR A MOMENT?
IF YOU'VE GOTTEN ME INTO TROUBLE, SO HELP ME...
I'D PLANNED ON SELECTING SOME STUDENTS FOR A SPECIAL RESEARCH PROJECT, AND I THINK YOU TWO WILL DO NICELY.
HERE ARE YOUR TOPICS.
IT'S NORMALLY OFF-LIMITS TO STUDENTS, BUT I MANAGED TO SCHEDULE YOU SOME TIME IN THE UNIVERSITY'S SPECIAL ARCHIVES.
UNFORTUNATELY, IT'S FOR THE SAME DAY I'M TAKING THE CLASS...
5

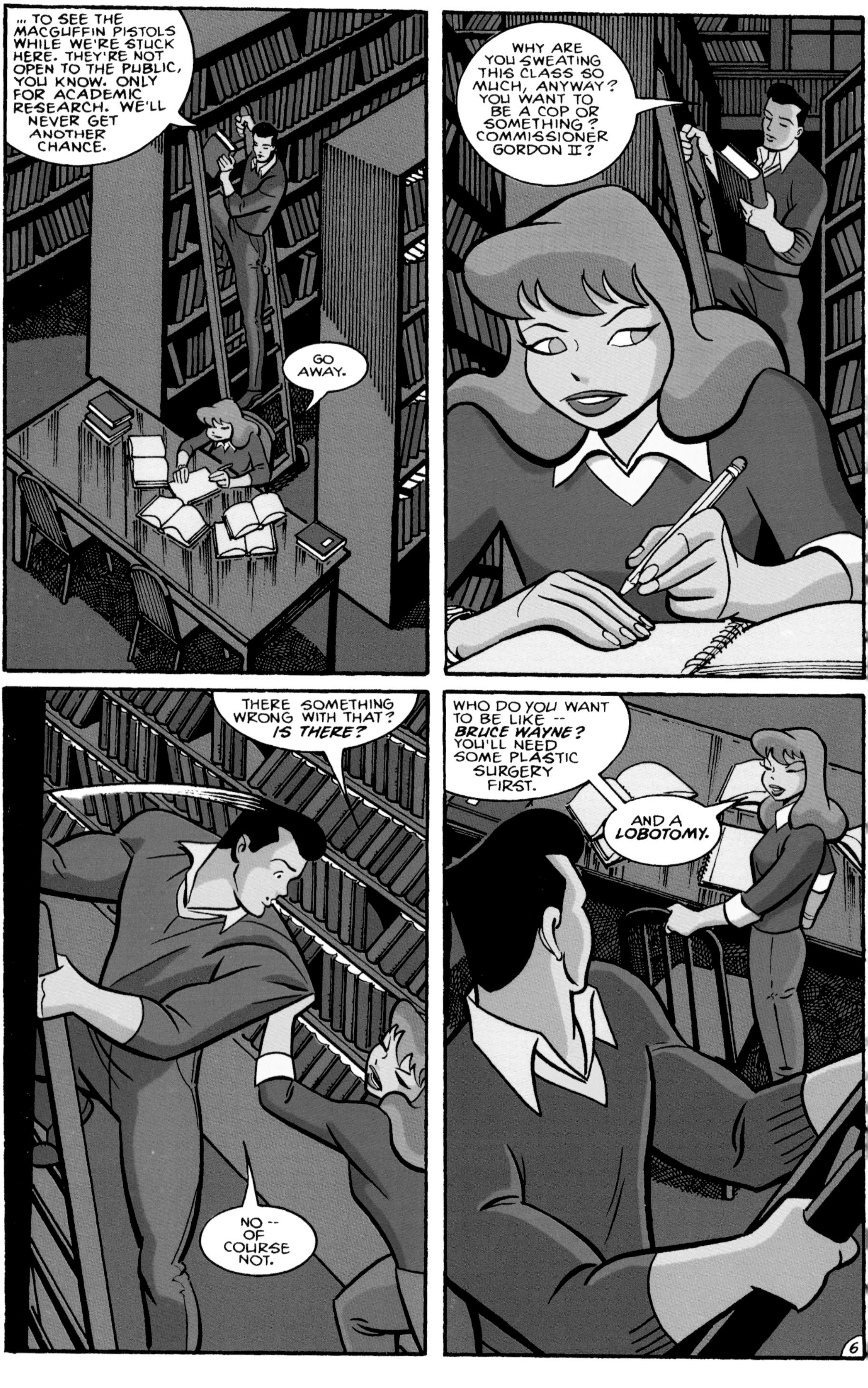
... TO SEE THE MACGUFFIN PISTOLS WHILE WE'RE STUCK HERE. THEY'RE NOT OPEN TO THE PUBLIC, YOU KNOW. ONLY FOR ACADEMIC RESEARCH. WE'LL NEVER GET ANOTHER CHANCE.
GO AWAY.
WHY ARE YOU SWEATING THIS CLASS SO MUCH, ANYWAY? YOU WANT TO BE A COP OR SOMETHING? COMMISSIONER GORDON II?
THERE SOMETHING WRONG WITH THAT? IS THERE?
NO -- OF COURSE NOT.
WHO DO YOU WANT TO BE LIKE -- BRUCE WAYNE? YOU'LL NEED SOME PLASTIC SURGERY FIRST.
AND A LOBOTOMY.
6

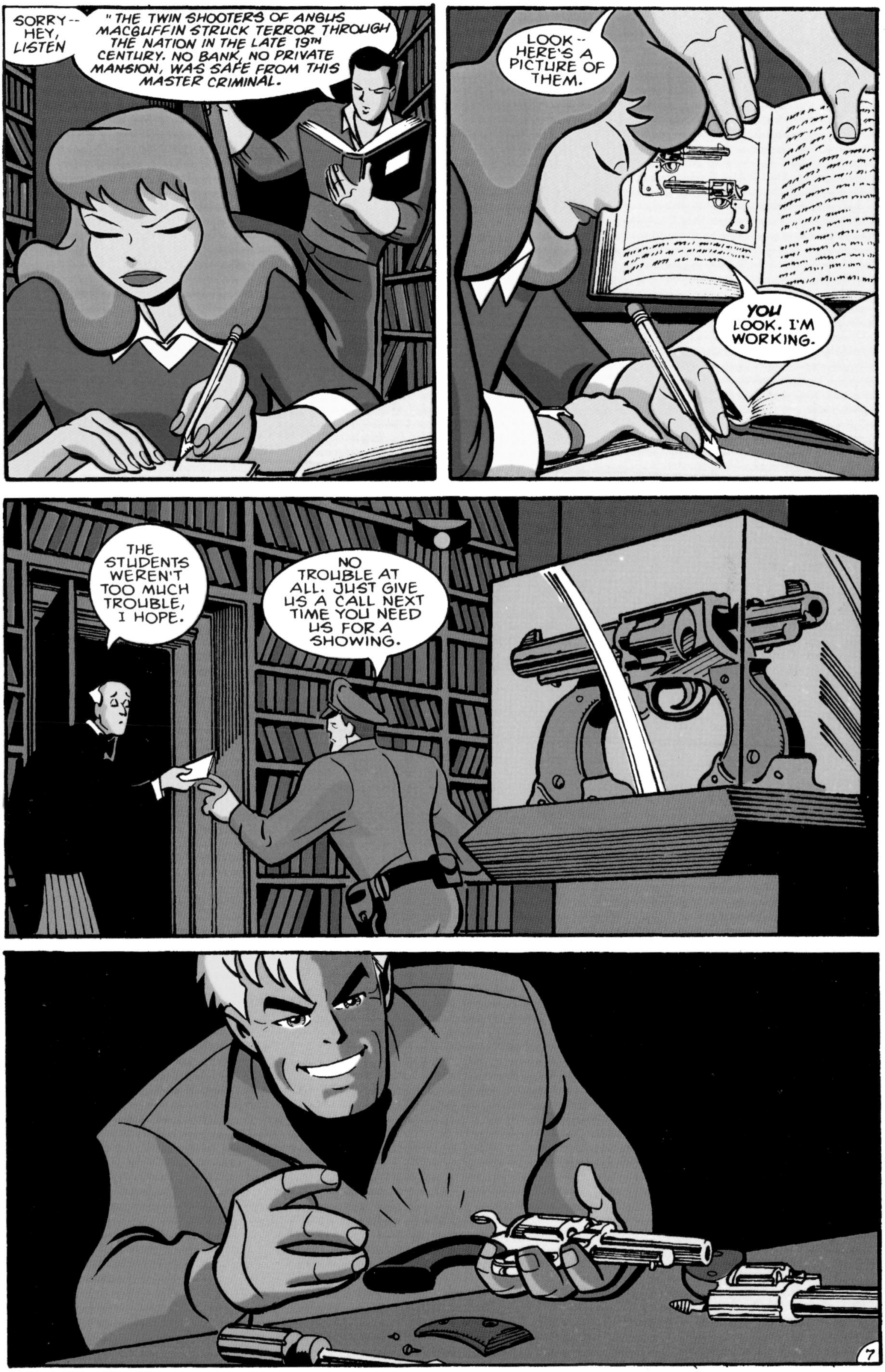
SORRY-- HEY, LISTEN
"THE TWIN SHOOTERS OF ANGUS MACGUFFIN STRUCK TERROR THROUGH THE NATION IN THE LATE 19TH CENTURY. NO BANK, NO PRIVATE MANSION, WAS SAFE FROM THIS MASTER CRIMINAL.
LOOK-- HERE'S A PICTURE OF THEM.
YOU LOOK. I'M WORKING.
THE STUDENTS WEREN'T TOO MUCH TROUBLE, I HOPE.
NO TROUBLE AT ALL. JUST GIVE US A CALL NEXT TIME YOU NEED US FOR A SHOWING.
7

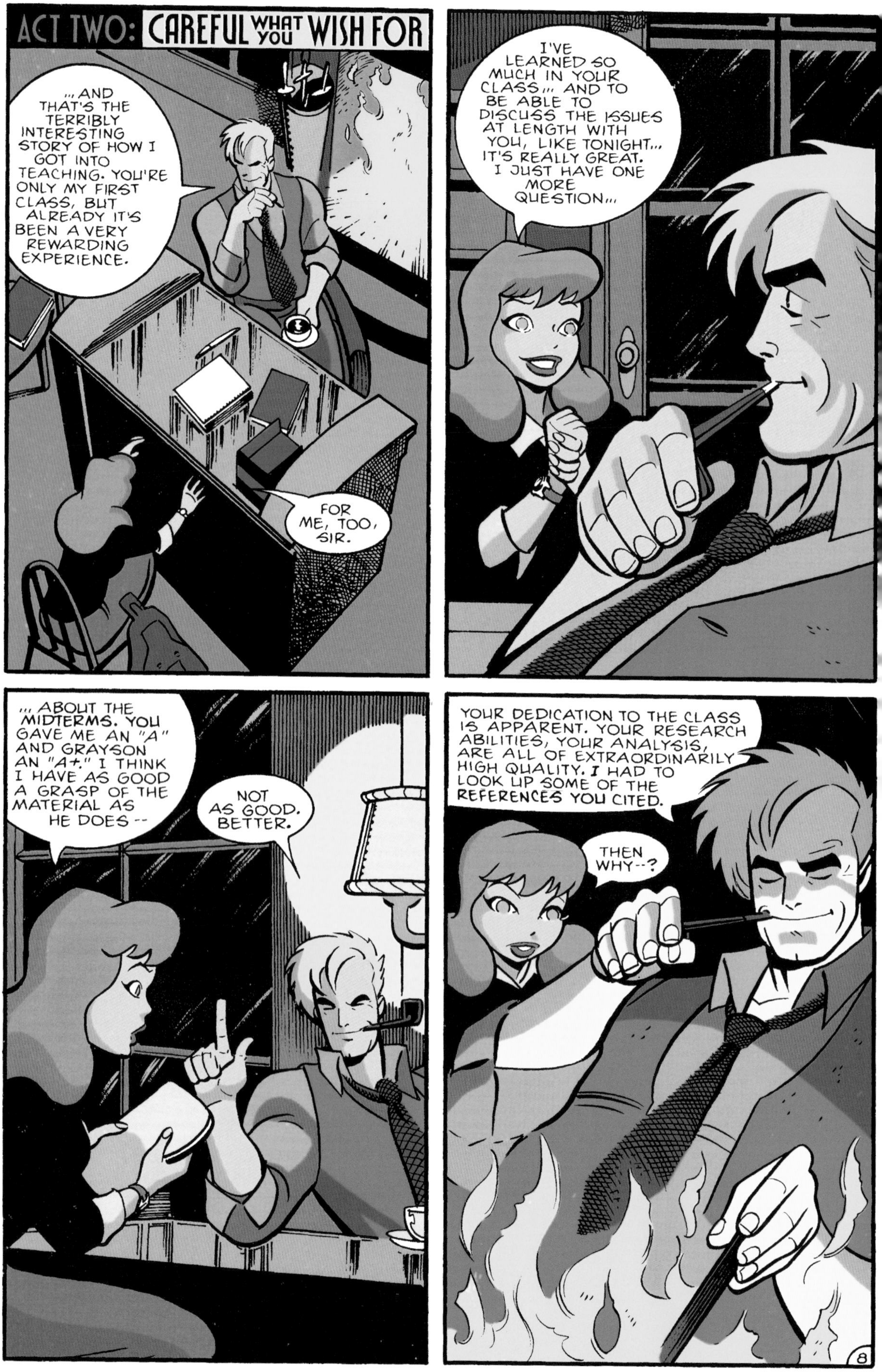

ACT TWO: CAREFUL WHAT YOU WISH FOR
...AND THAT'S THE TERRIBLY INTERESTING STORY OF HOW I GOT INTO TEACHING. YOU'RE ONLY MY FIRST CLASS, BUT ALREADY IT'S BEEN A VERY REWARDING EXPERIENCE.
FOR ME, TOO, SIR.
I'VE LEARNED SO MUCH IN YOUR CLASS... AND TO BE ABLE TO DISCUSS THE ISSUES AT LENGTH WITH YOU, LIKE TONIGHT... IT'S REALLY GREAT. I JUST HAVE ONE MORE QUESTION...
...ABOUT THE MIDTERMS. YOU GAVE ME AN "A" AND GRAYSON AN "A+." I THINK I HAVE AS GOOD A GRASP OF THE MATERIAL AS HE DOES --
NOT AS GOOD. BETTER.
YOUR DEDICATION TO THE CLASS IS APPARENT. YOUR RESEARCH ABILITIES, YOUR ANALYSIS, ARE ALL OF EXTRAORDINARILY HIGH QUALITY. I HAD TO LOOK UP SOME OF THE REFERENCES YOU CITED.
THEN WHY--?
8

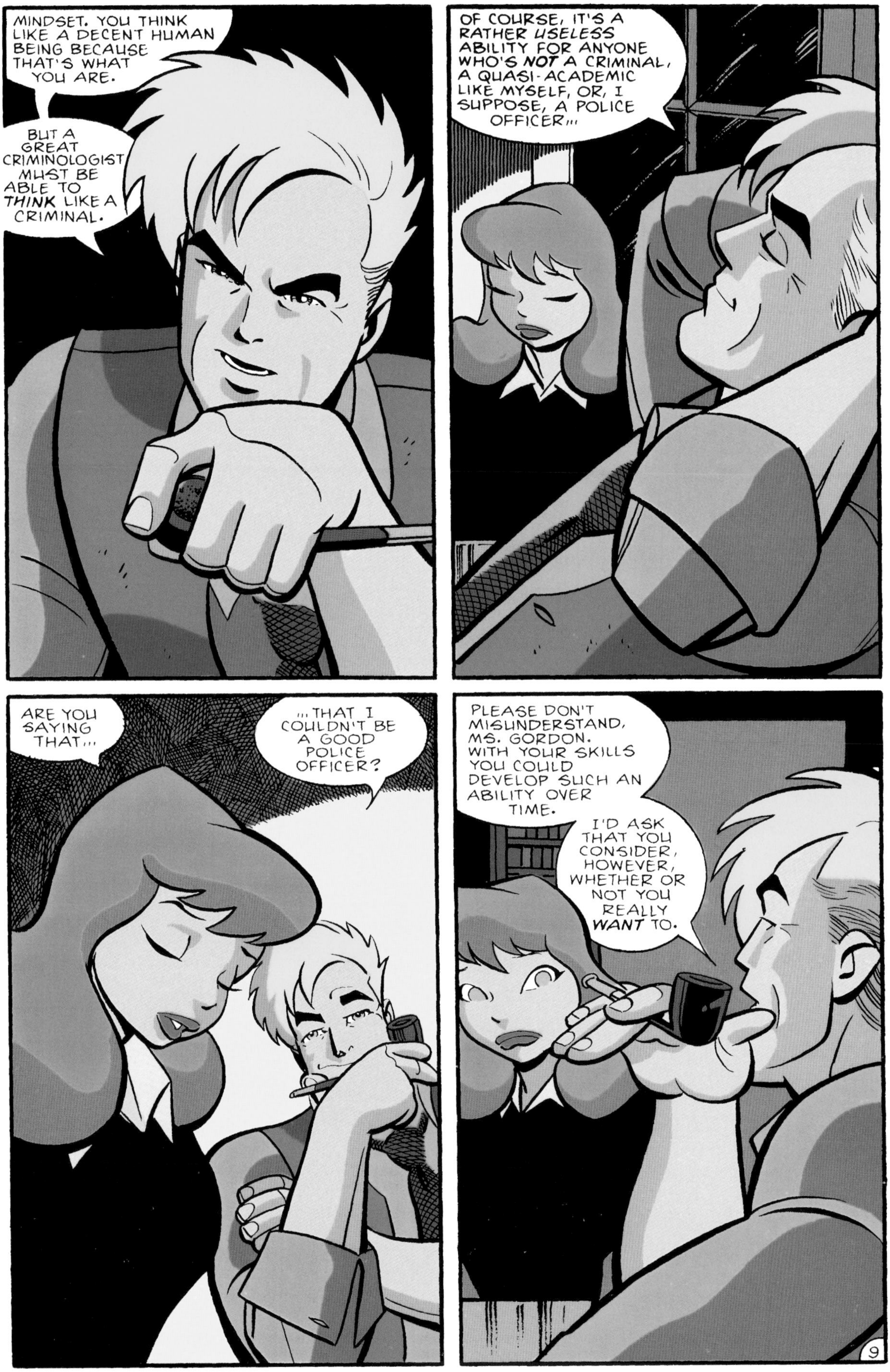
MINDSET. YOU THINK LIKE A DECENT HUMAN BEING BECAUSE THAT'S WHAT YOU ARE.
BUT A GREAT CRIMINOLOGIST MUST BE ABLE TO THINK LIKE A CRIMINAL.
OF COURSE, IT'S A RATHER USELESS ABILITY FOR ANYONE WHO'S NOT A CRIMINAL, A QUASI-ACADEMIC LIKE MYSELF, OR, I SUPPOSE, A POLICE OFFICER...
ARE YOU SAYING THAT...
...THAT I COULDN'T BE A GOOD POLICE OFFICER?
PLEASE DON'T MISUNDERSTAND, MS. GORDON. WITH YOUR SKILLS YOU COULD DEVELOP SUCH AN ABILITY OVER TIME.
I'D ASK THAT YOU CONSIDER, HOWEVER, WHETHER OR NOT YOU REALLY WANT TO.
9

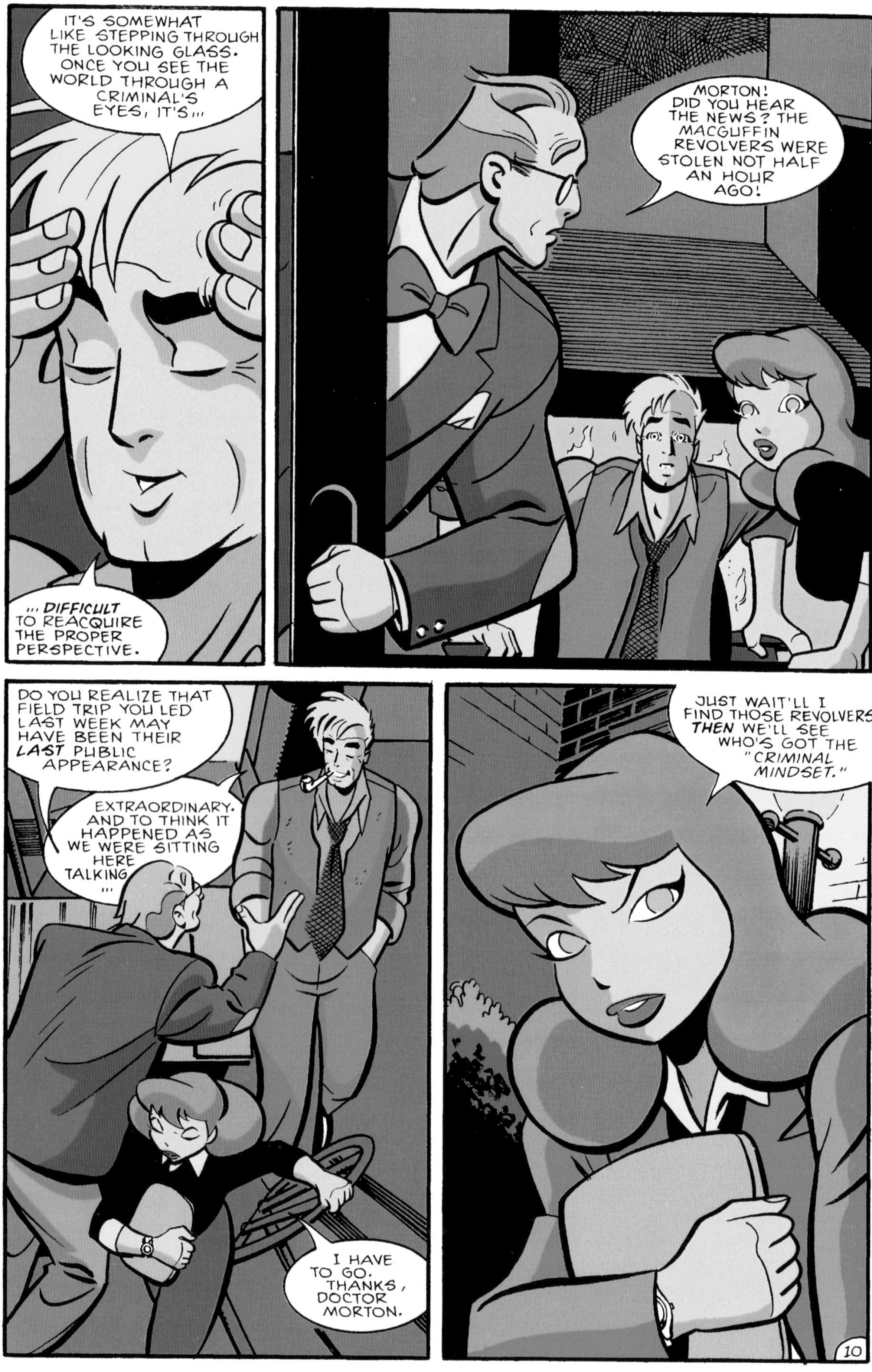

IT'S SOMEWHAT LIKE STEPPING THROUGH THE LOOKING GLASS. ONCE YOU SEE THE WORLD THROUGH A CRIMINAL'S EYES, IT'S...
...DIFFICULT TO REACQUIRE THE PROPER PERSPECTIVE.
MORTON! DID YOU HEAR THE NEWS? THE MACGUFFIN REVOLVERS WERE STOLEN NOT HALF AN HOUR AGO!
DO YOU REALIZE THAT FIELD TRIP YOU LED LAST WEEK MAY HAVE BEEN THEIR LAST PUBLIC APPEARANCE?
EXTRAORDINARY. AND TO THINK IT HAPPENED AS WE WERE SITTING HERE TALKING...
I HAVE TO GO. THANKS, DOCTOR MORTON.
JUST WAIT'LL I FIND THOSE REVOLVERS. THEN WE'LL SEE WHO'S GOT THE "CRIMINAL MINDSET."
10

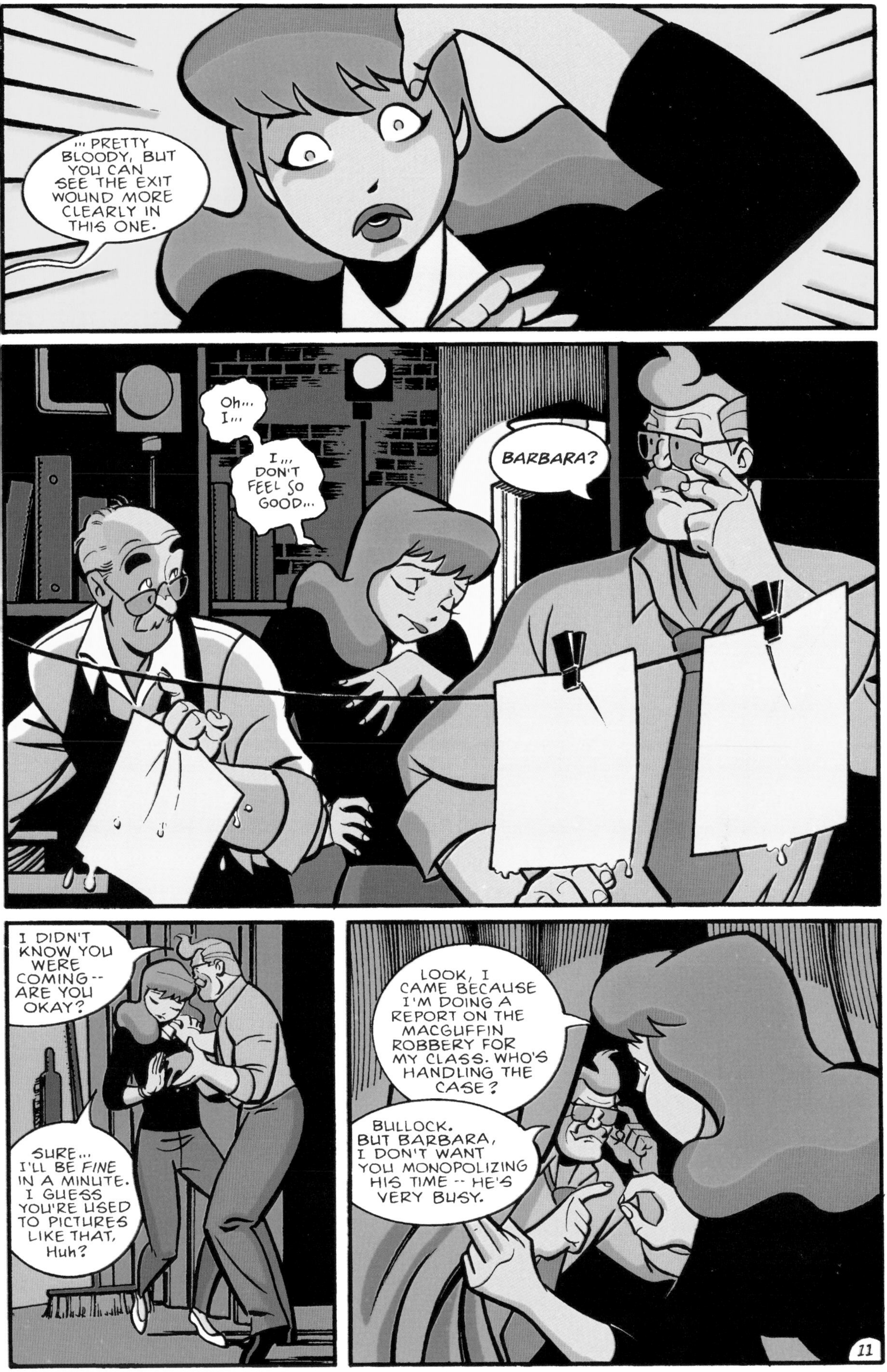
...PRETTY BLOODY, BUT YOU CAN SEE THE EXIT WOUND MORE CLEARLY IN THIS ONE.
Oh... I...
I... DON'T FEEL SO GOOD...
BARBARA?
I DIDN'T KNOW YOU WERE COMING-- ARE YOU OKAY?
SURE... I'LL BE FINE IN A MINUTE. I GUESS YOU'RE USED TO PICTURES LIKE THAT, Huh?
LOOK, I CAME BECAUSE I'M DOING A REPORT ON THE MACGUFFIN ROBBERY FOR MY CLASS. WHO'S HANDLING THE CASE?
BULLOCK. BUT BARBARA, I DON'T WANT YOU MONOPOLIZING HIS TIME -- HE'S VERY BUSY.
11

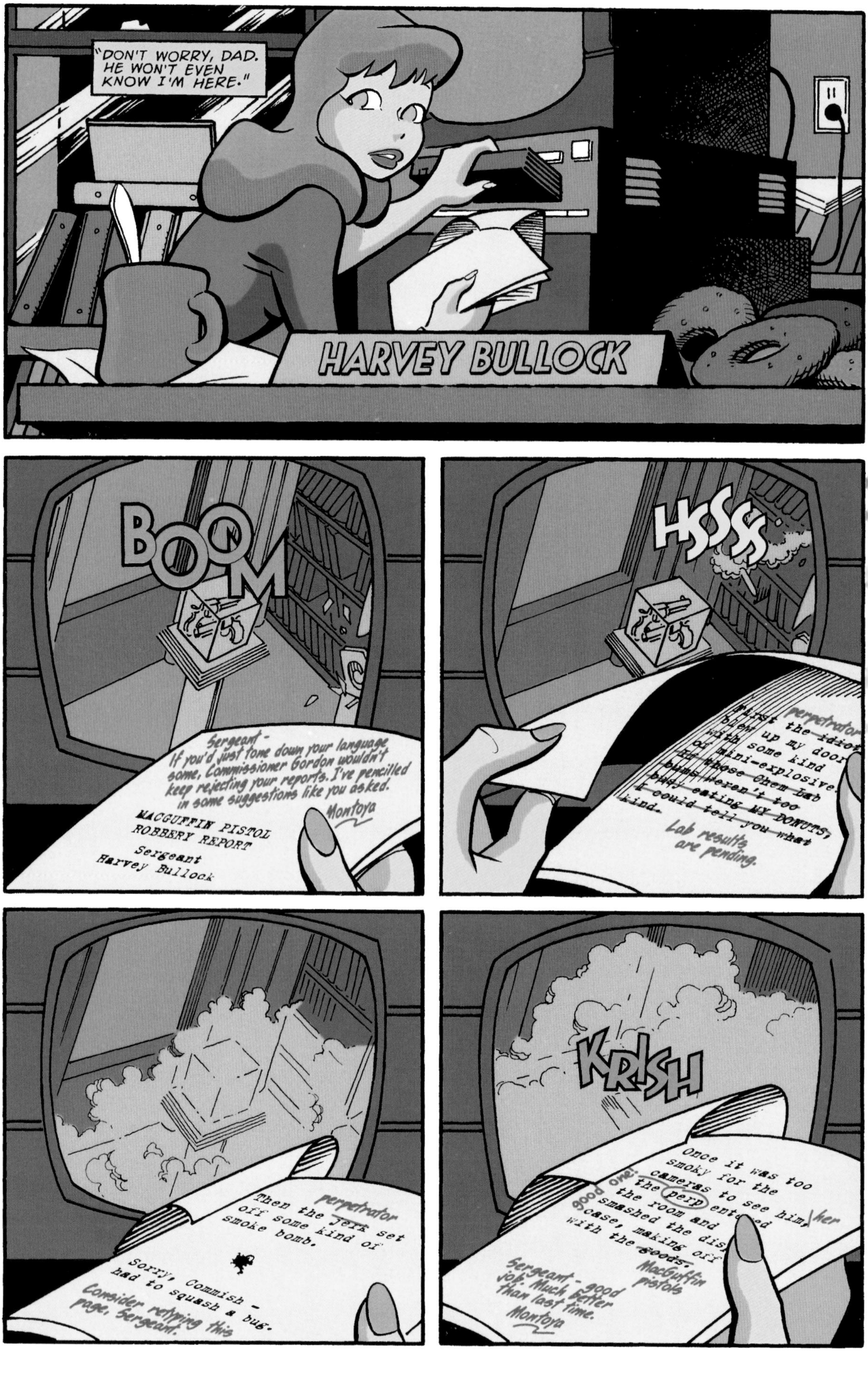
"DON'T WORRY, DAD. HE WON'T EVEN KNOW I'M HERE."
HARVEY BULLOCK
BOOM
Sergeant - If you'd just tone down your language some, Commissioner Gordon wouldn't keep rejecting your reports. I've pencilled in some suggestions like you asked.
Montoya
MACGUFFIN PISTOL ROBBERY REPORT
Sergeant Harvey Bullock
HSSSS
First the idiot blew up my door with some kind of mini-explosive. If those Chem Lab bums weren't too busy eating MY DONUTS, I could tell you what kind.
perpetrator
Lab results are pending.
Then the jerk set off some kind of smoke bomb.
perpetrator
Sorry, Commish - had to squash a bug.
Consider retyping this page, Sergeant.
KRISH
Once it was too smoky for the cameras to see him, the perp entered the room and smashed the display case, making off with the goods.
her
good one!
MacGuffin pistols
Sergeant - good job. Much better than last time.
Montoya

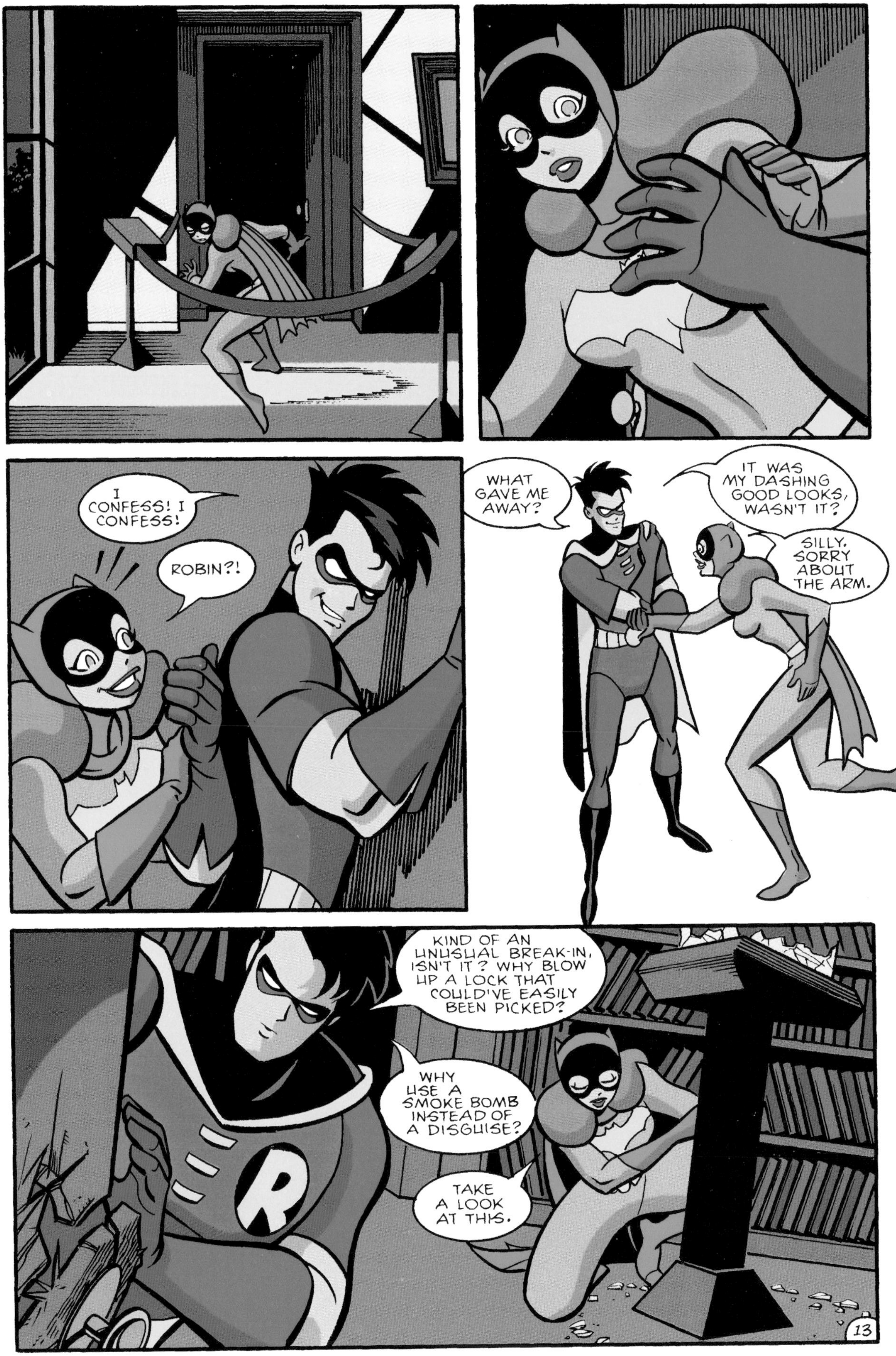
I CONFESS! I CONFESS!
ROBIN?!
WHAT GAVE ME AWAY?
IT WAS MY DASHING GOOD LOOKS, WASN'T IT?
SILLY. SORRY ABOUT THE ARM.
KIND OF AN UNUSUAL BREAK-IN, ISN'T IT? WHY BLOW UP A LOCK THAT COULD'VE EASILY BEEN PICKED?
WHY USE A SMOKE BOMB INSTEAD OF A DISGUISE?
TAKE A LOOK AT THIS.
13

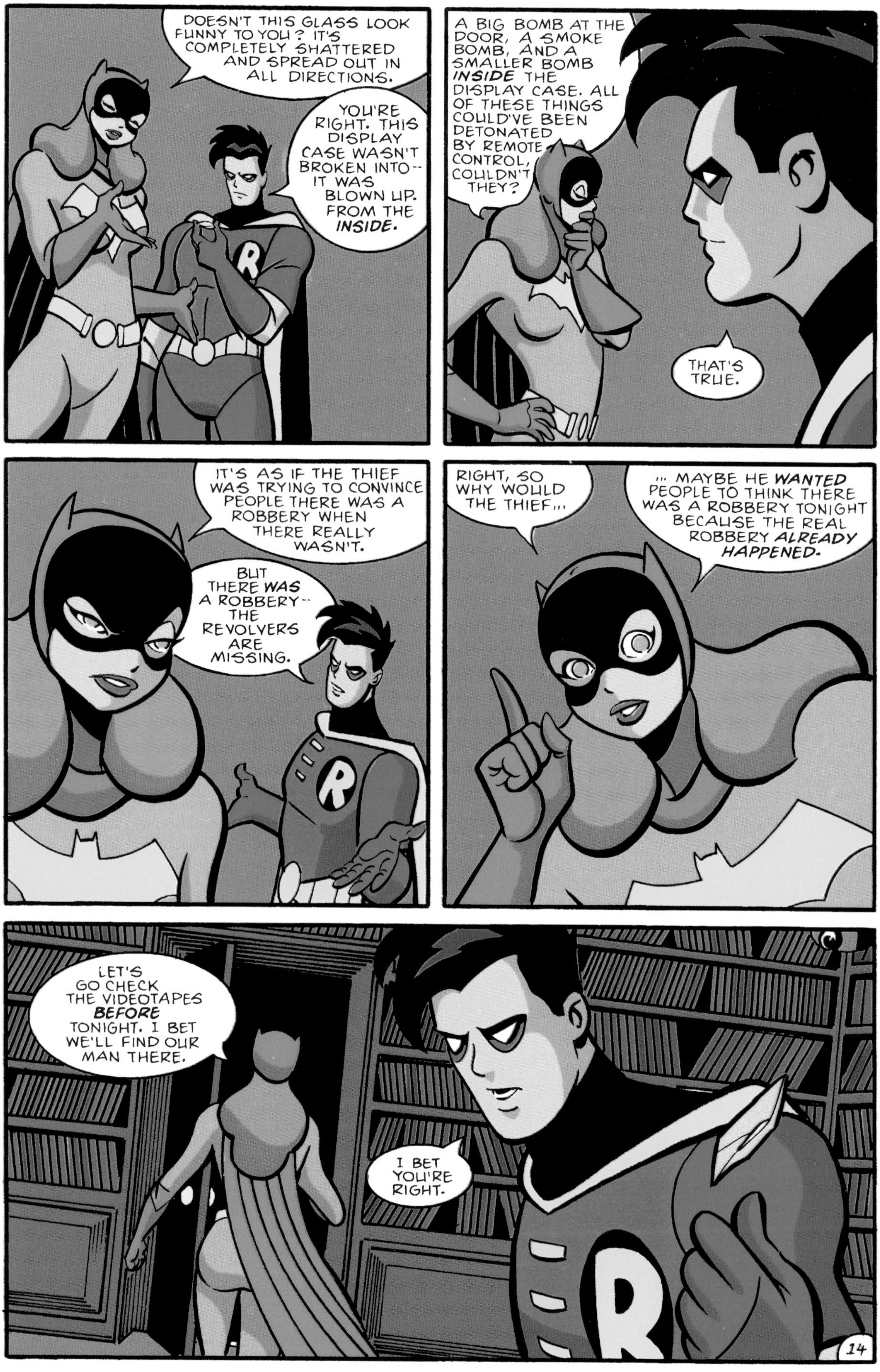
DOESN'T THIS GLASS LOOK FUNNY TO YOU? IT'S COMPLETELY SHATTERED AND SPREAD OUT IN ALL DIRECTIONS.
YOU'RE RIGHT. THIS DISPLAY CASE WASN'T BROKEN INTO-- IT WAS BLOWN UP. FROM THE INSIDE.
A BIG BOMB AT THE DOOR, A SMOKE BOMB, AND A SMALLER BOMB INSIDE THE DISPLAY CASE. ALL OF THESE THINGS COULD'VE BEEN DETONATED BY REMOTE CONTROL, COULDN'T THEY?
THAT'S TRUE.
IT'S AS IF THE THIEF WAS TRYING TO CONVINCE PEOPLE THERE WAS A ROBBERY WHEN THERE REALLY WASN'T.
BUT THERE WAS A ROBBERY-- THE REVOLVERS ARE MISSING.
RIGHT, SO WHY WOULD THE THIEF...
... MAYBE HE WANTED PEOPLE TO THINK THERE WAS A ROBBERY TONIGHT BECAUSE THE REAL ROBBERY ALREADY HAPPENED.
LET'S GO CHECK THE VIDEOTAPES BEFORE TONIGHT. I BET WE'LL FIND OUR MAN THERE.
I BET YOU'RE RIGHT.
14

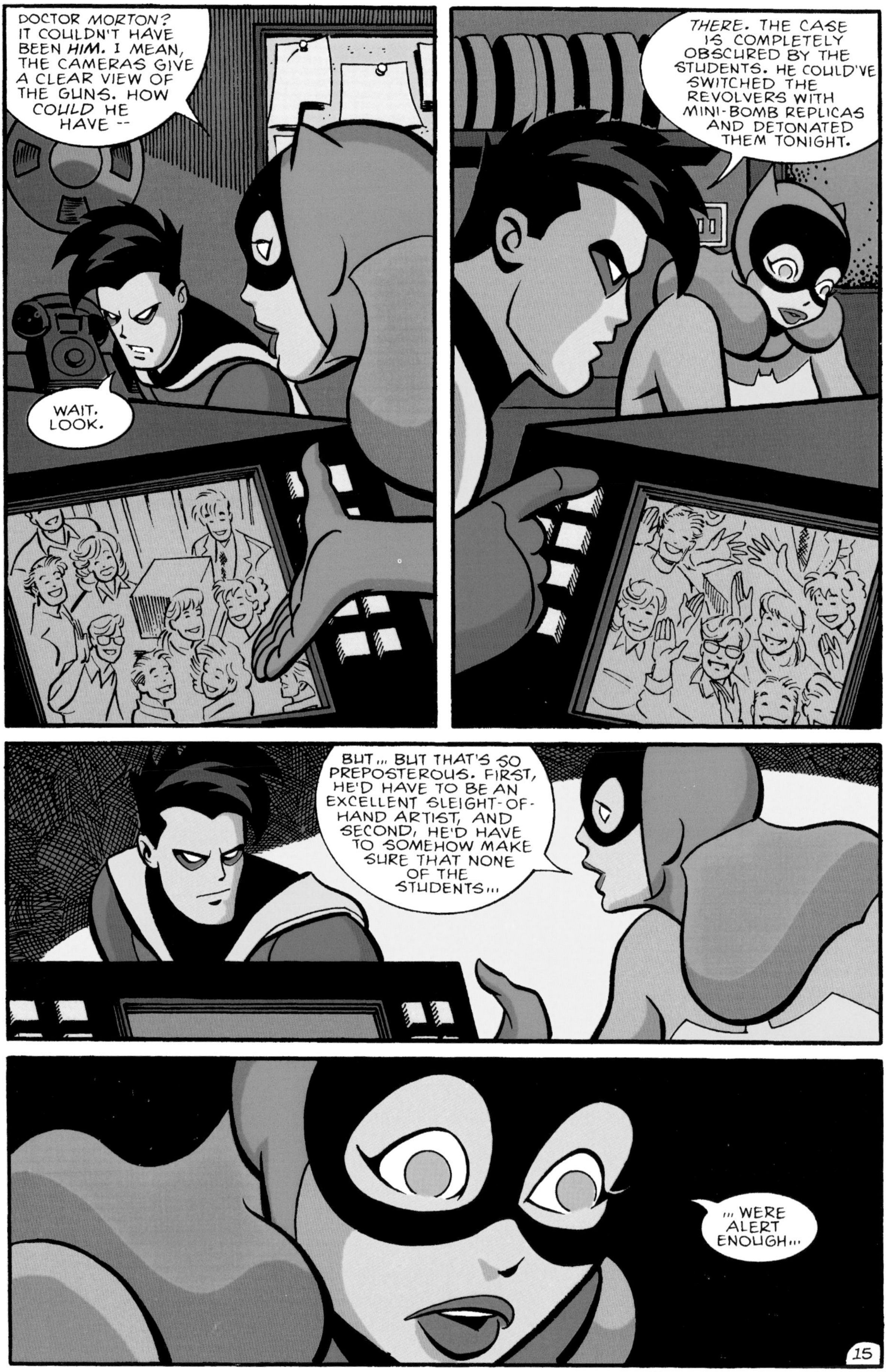
DOCTOR MORTON? IT COULDN'T HAVE BEEN HIM. I MEAN, THE CAMERAS GIVE A CLEAR VIEW OF THE GUNS. HOW COULD HE HAVE --
WAIT. LOOK.
THERE. THE CASE IS COMPLETELY OBSCURED BY THE STUDENTS. HE COULD'VE SWITCHED THE REVOLVERS WITH MINI-BOMB REPLICAS AND DETONATED THEM TONIGHT.
BUT... BUT THAT'S SO PREPOSTEROUS. FIRST, HE'D HAVE TO BE AN EXCELLENT SLEIGHT-OF-HAND ARTIST, AND SECOND, HE'D HAVE TO SOMEHOW MAKE SURE THAT NONE OF THE STUDENTS...
... WERE ALERT ENOUGH...
15

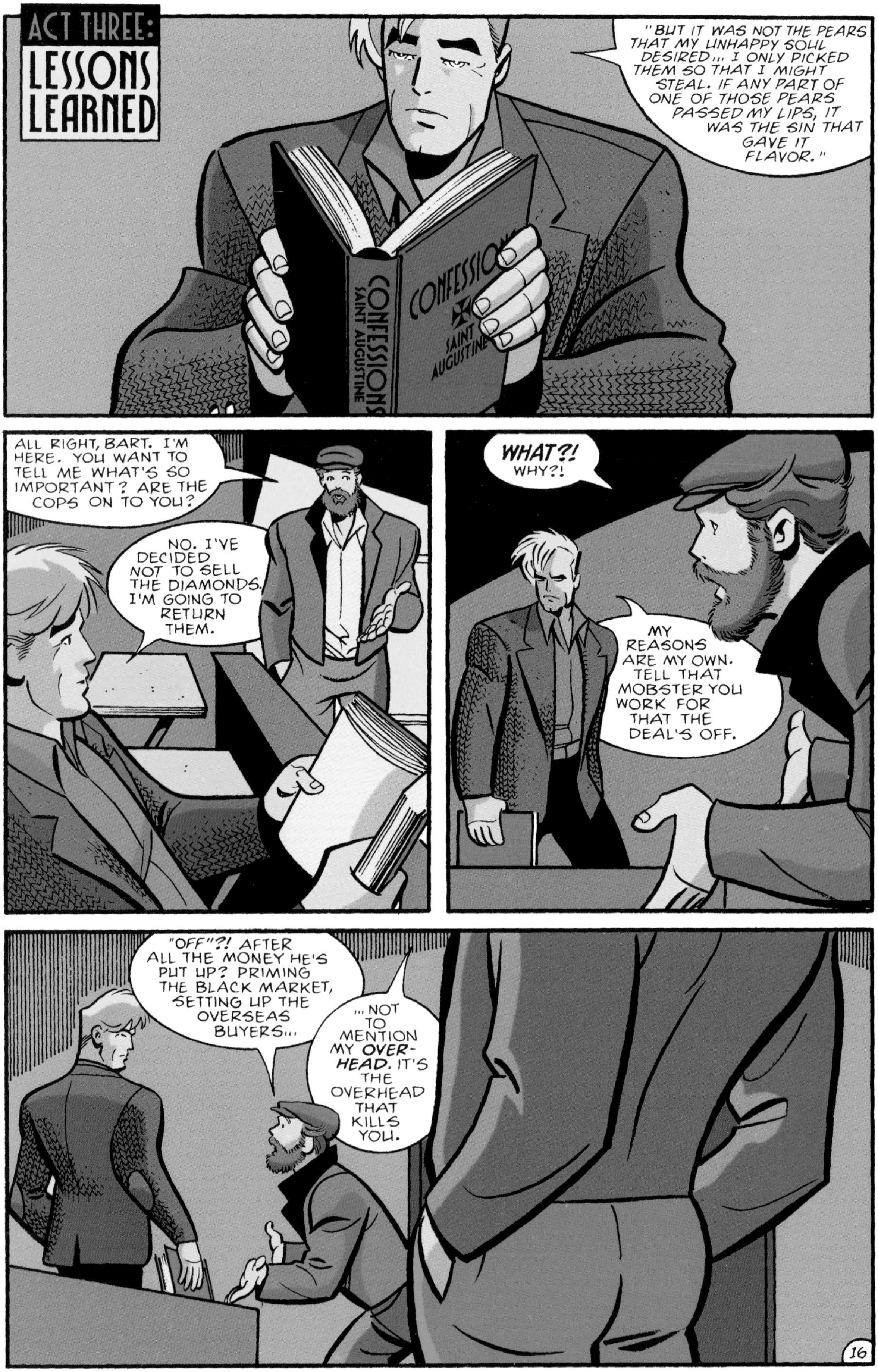
ACT THREE:
LESSONS LEARNED
"BUT IT WAS NOT THE PEARS THAT MY UNHAPPY SOUL DESIRED... I ONLY PICKED THEM SO THAT I MIGHT STEAL. IF ANY PART OF ONE OF THOSE PEARS PASSED MY LIPS, IT WAS THE SIN THAT GAVE IT FLAVOR."
CONFESSIONS SAINT AUGUSTINE
ALL RIGHT, BART. I'M HERE. YOU WANT TO TELL ME WHAT'S SO IMPORTANT? ARE THE COPS ON TO YOU?
NO. I'VE DECIDED NOT TO SELL THE DIAMONDS. I'M GOING TO RETURN THEM.
WHAT?! WHY?!
MY REASONS ARE MY OWN. TELL THAT MOBSTER YOU WORK FOR THAT THE DEAL'S OFF.
"OFF"?! AFTER ALL THE MONEY HE'S PUT UP? PRIMING THE BLACK MARKET, SETTING UP THE OVERSEAS BUYERS...
...NOT TO MENTION MY OVERHEAD. IT'S THE OVERHEAD THAT KILLS YOU.
16

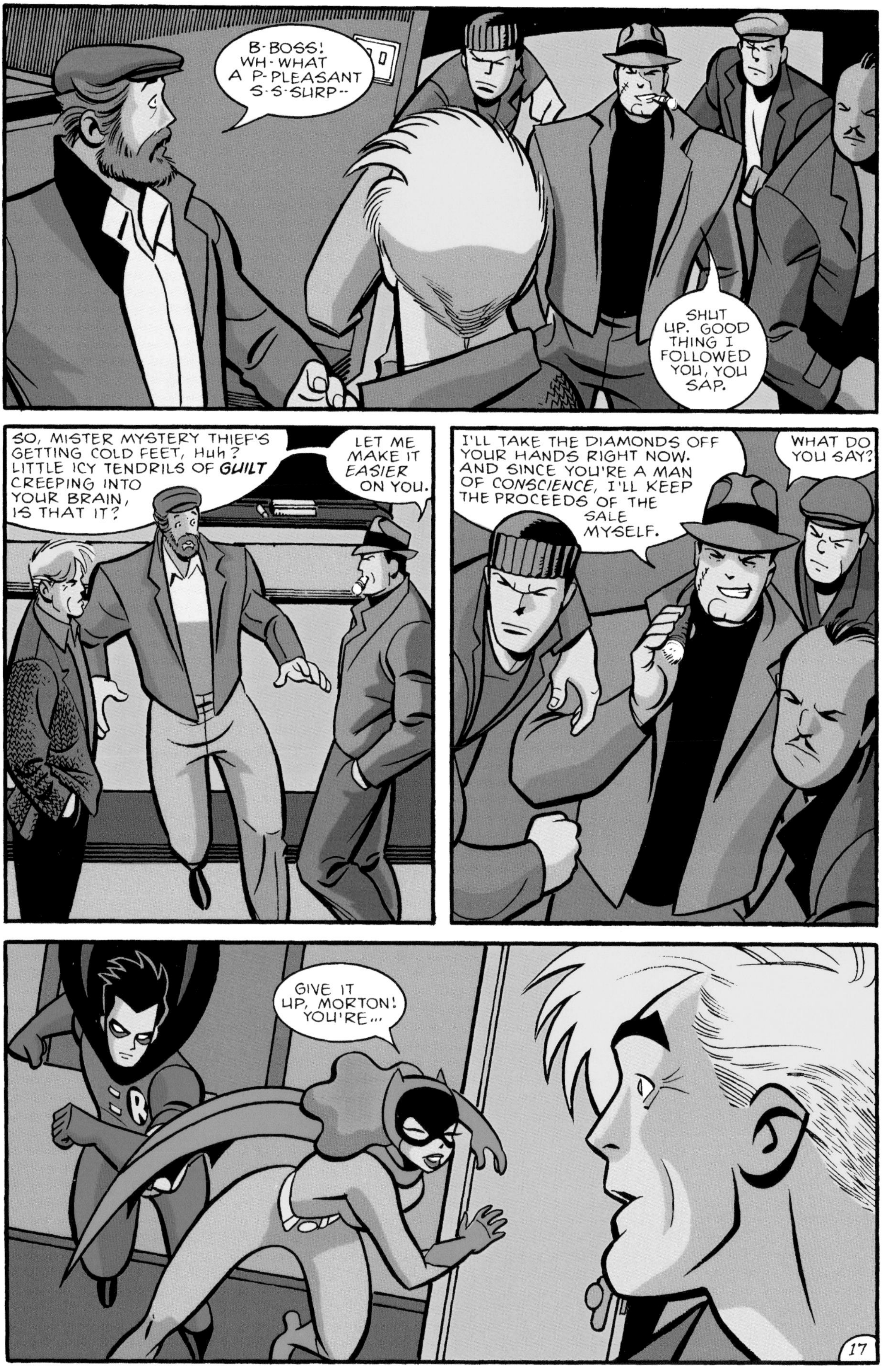
B-BOSS! WH-WHAT A P-PLEASANT S-S-SURP--
SHUT UP. GOOD THING I FOLLOWED YOU, YOU SAP.
SO, MISTER MYSTERY THIEF'S GETTING COLD FEET, Huh? LITTLE ICY TENDRILS OF GUILT CREEPING INTO YOUR BRAIN, IS THAT IT?
LET ME MAKE IT EASIER ON YOU.
I'LL TAKE THE DIAMONDS OFF YOUR HANDS RIGHT NOW. AND SINCE YOU'RE A MAN OF CONSCIENCE, I'LL KEEP THE PROCEEDS OF THE SALE MYSELF.
WHAT DO YOU SAY?
GIVE IT UP, MORTON! YOU'RE...
17

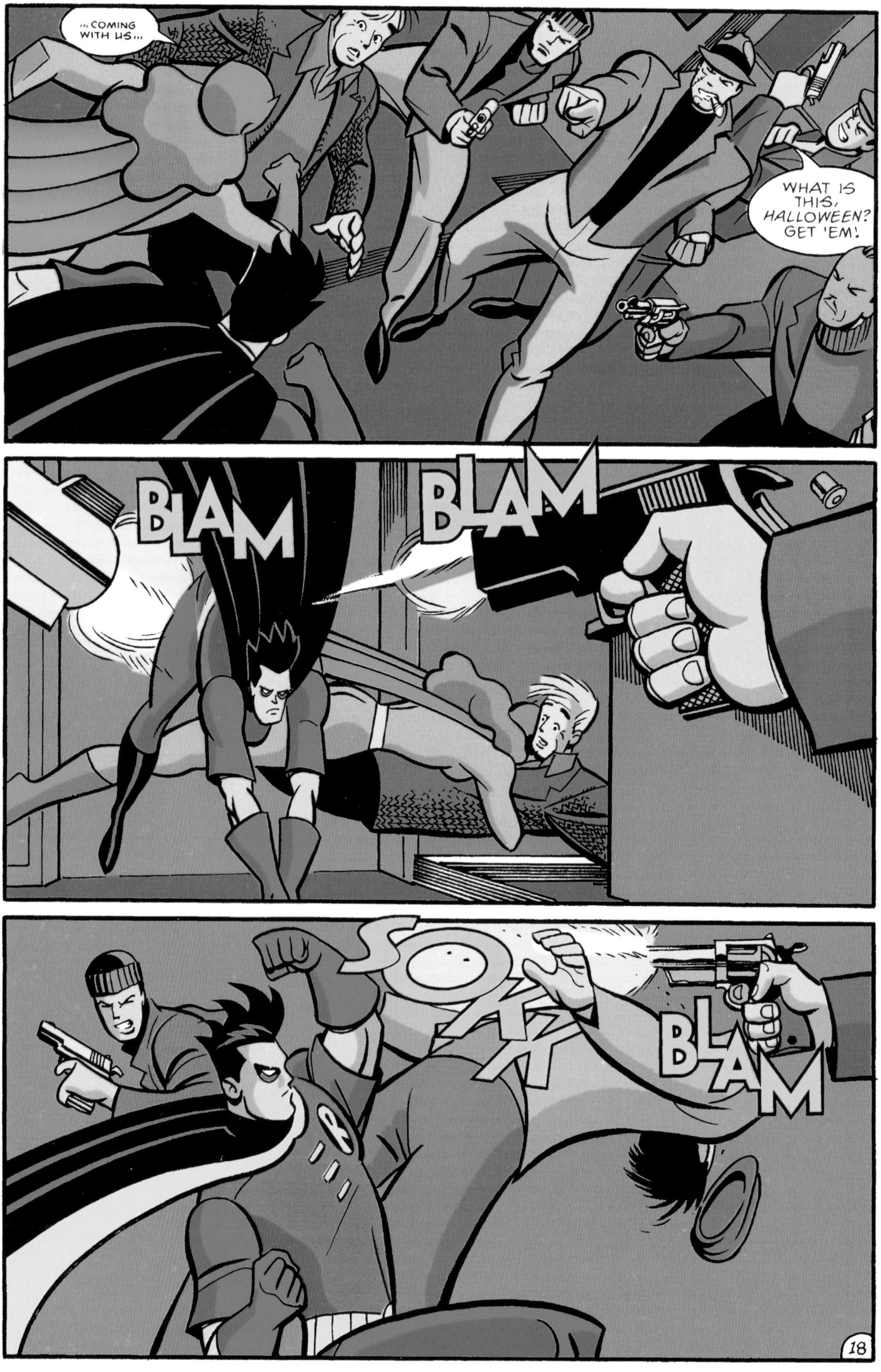
...COMING WITH US...
WHAT IS THIS, HALLOWEEN? GET 'EM!
BLAM
BLAM
SOKK
BLAM
18

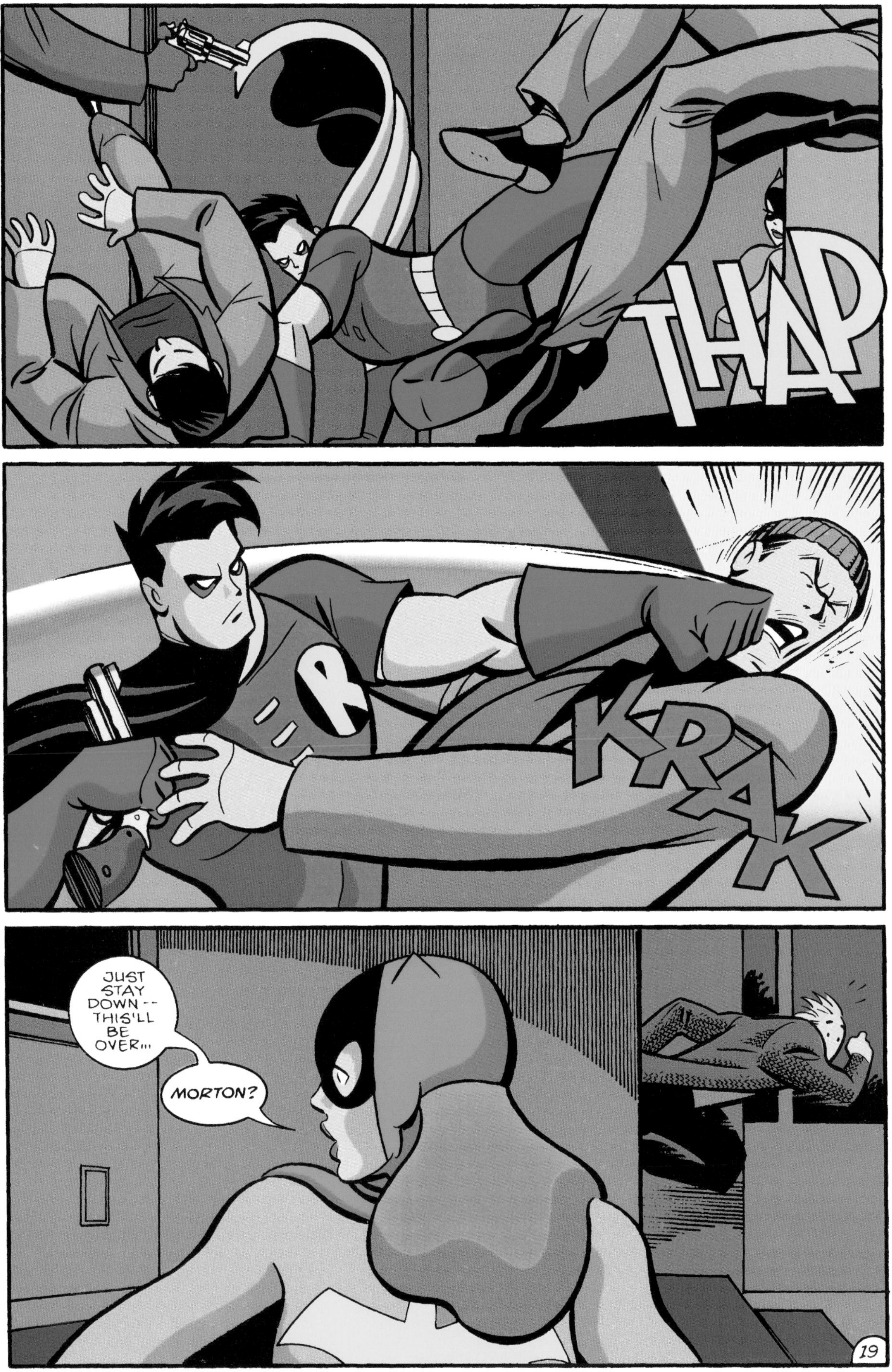
THAP
KRAK
JUST STAY DOWN -- THIS'LL BE OVER...
MORTON?
19

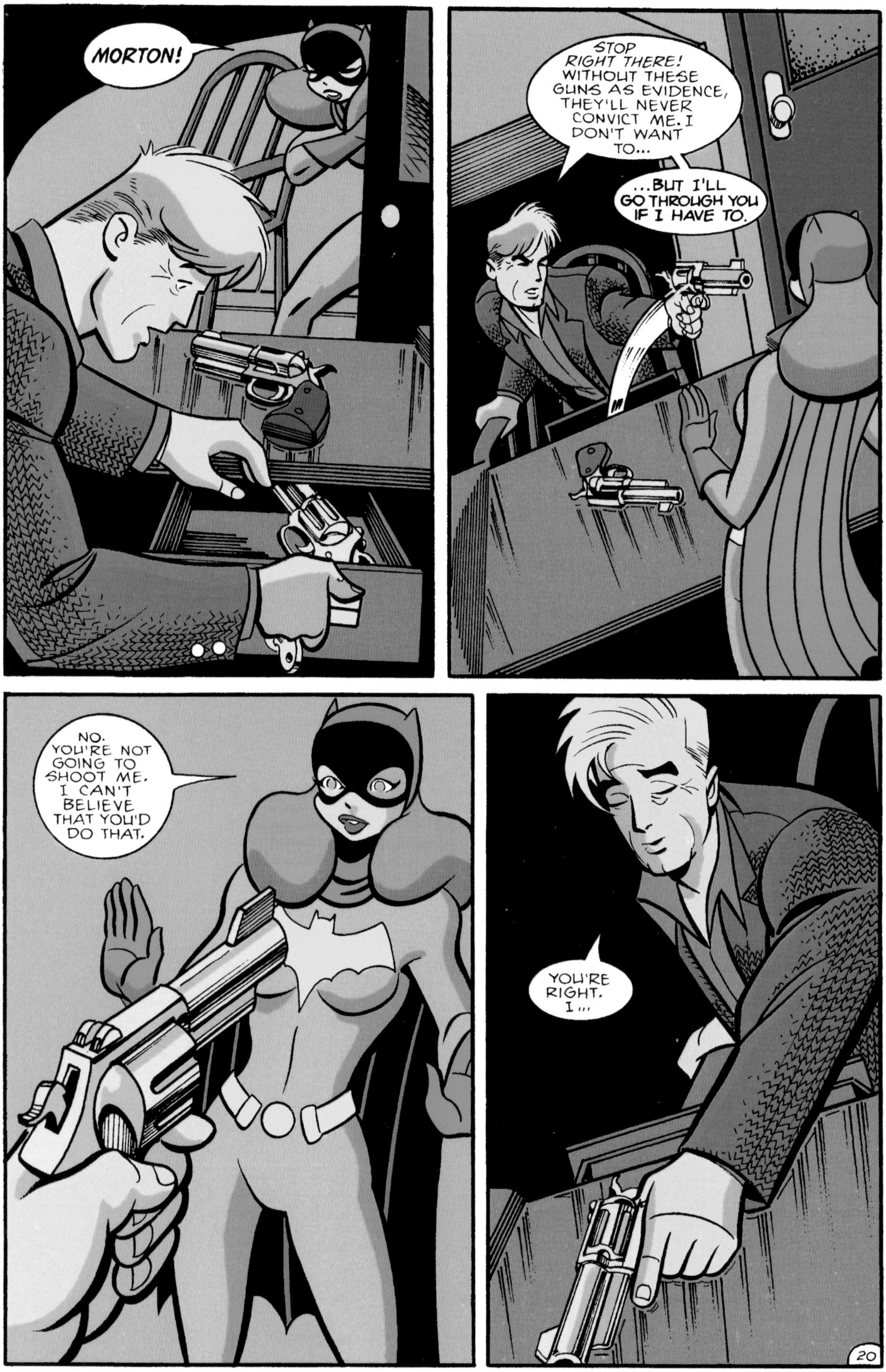
MORTON!
STOP RIGHT THERE! WITHOUT THESE GUNS AS EVIDENCE, THEY'LL NEVER CONVICT ME. I DON'T WANT TO...
...BUT I'LL GO THROUGH YOU IF I HAVE TO.
NO. YOU'RE NOT GOING TO SHOOT ME. I CAN'T BELIEVE THAT YOU'D DO THAT.
YOU'RE RIGHT. I...
20

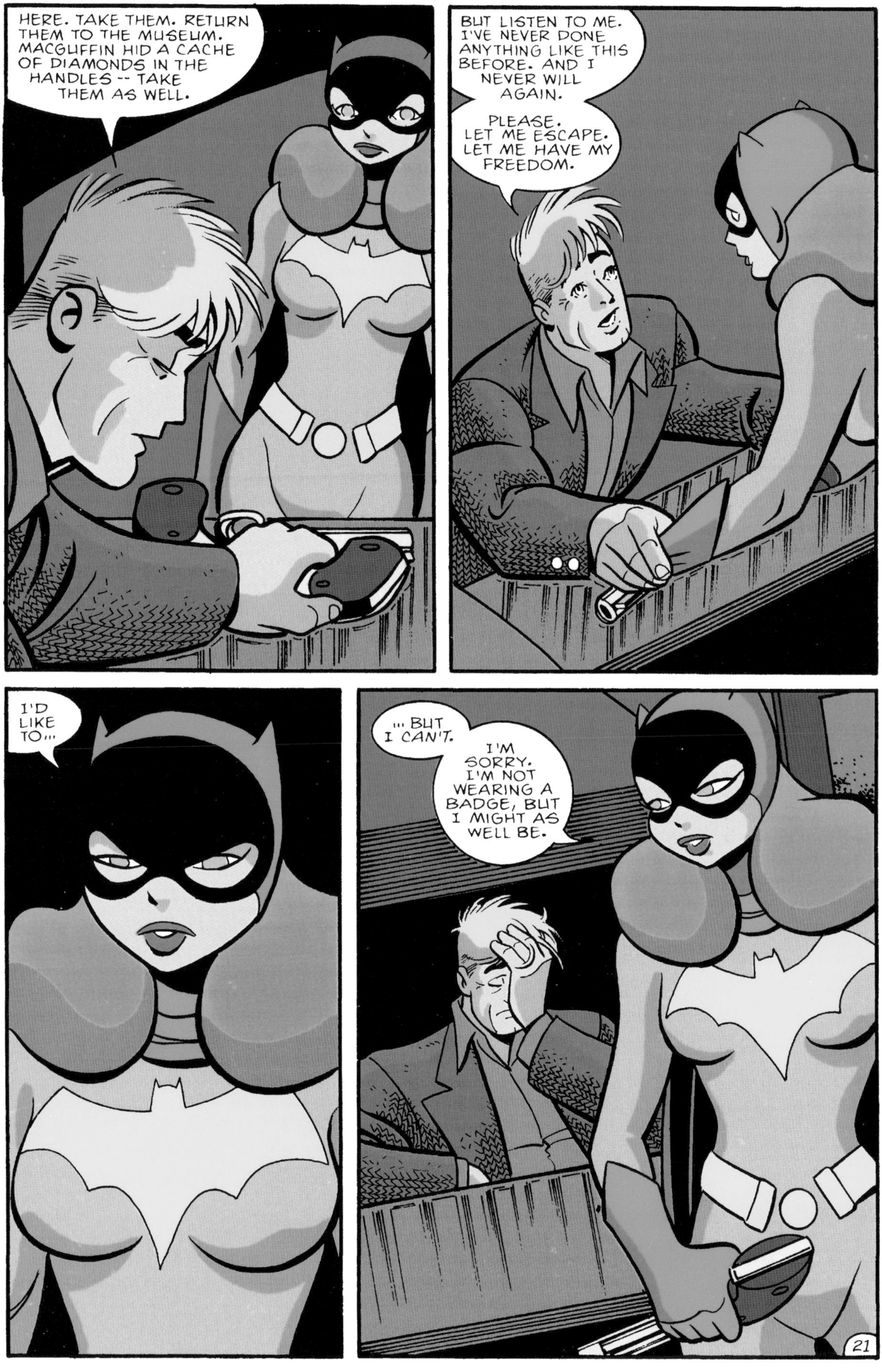
HERE. TAKE THEM. RETURN THEM TO THE MUSEUM. MACGUFFIN HID A CACHE OF DIAMONDS IN THE HANDLES -- TAKE THEM AS WELL.
BUT LISTEN TO ME. I'VE NEVER DONE ANYTHING LIKE THIS BEFORE. AND I NEVER WILL AGAIN.
PLEASE. LET ME ESCAPE. LET ME HAVE MY FREEDOM.
I'D LIKE TO...
...BUT I CAN'T.
I'M SORRY. I'M NOT WEARING A BADGE, BUT I MIGHT AS WELL BE.
21

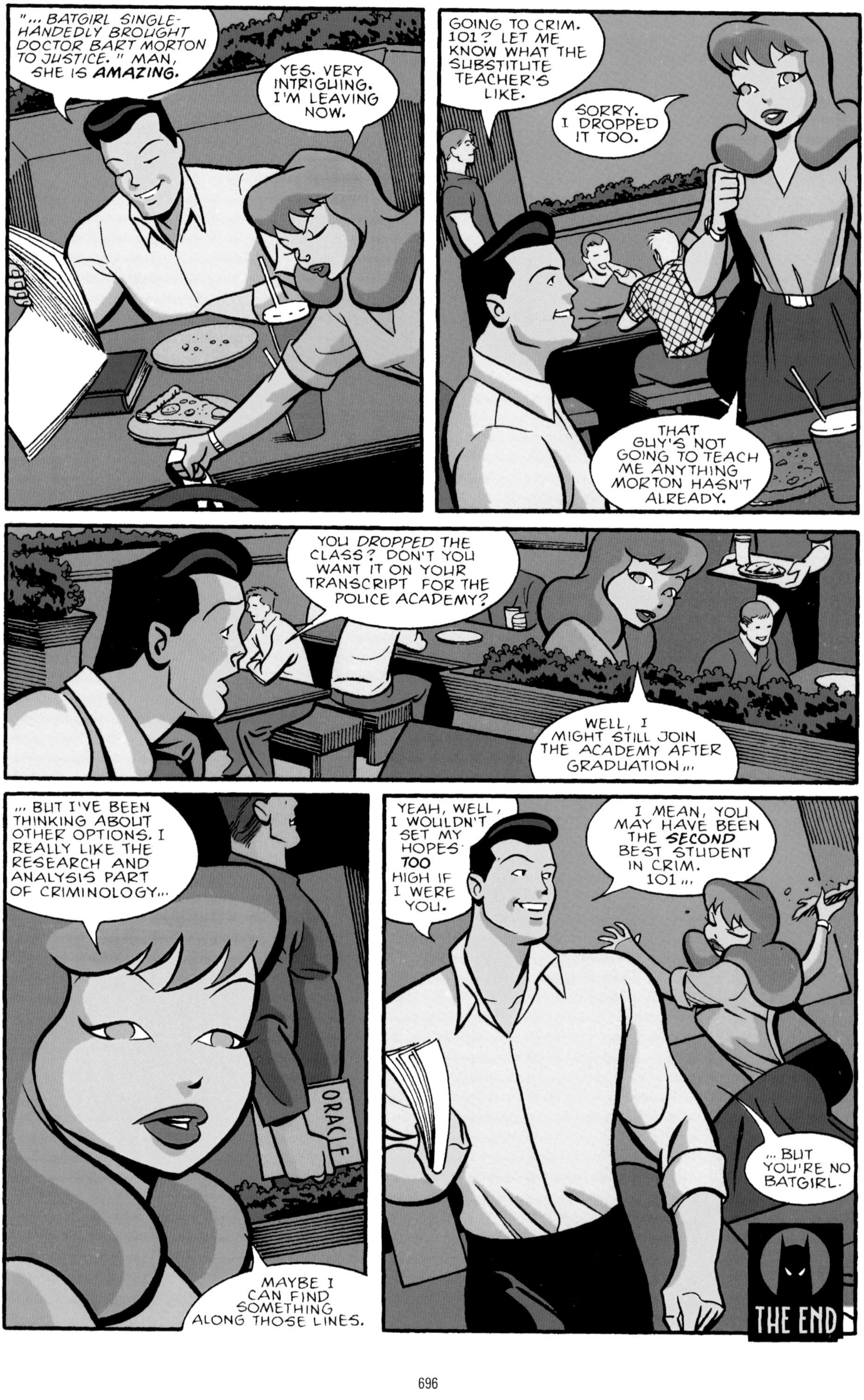
"... BATGIRL SINGLE-HANDEDLY BROUGHT DOCTOR BART MORTON TO JUSTICE." MAN, SHE IS **AMAZING**.
YES. VERY INTRIGUING. I'M LEAVING NOW.
GOING TO CRIM. 101? LET ME KNOW WHAT THE SUBSTITUTE TEACHER'S LIKE.
SORRY. I DROPPED IT TOO.
THAT GUY'S NOT GOING TO TEACH ME ANYTHING MORTON HASN'T ALREADY.
YOU *DROPPED* THE CLASS? DON'T YOU WANT IT ON YOUR TRANSCRIPT FOR THE POLICE ACADEMY?
WELL, I MIGHT STILL JOIN THE ACADEMY AFTER GRADUATION...
... BUT I'VE BEEN THINKING ABOUT OTHER OPTIONS. I REALLY LIKE THE RESEARCH AND ANALYSIS PART OF CRIMINOLOGY...
ORACLE
MAYBE I CAN FIND SOMETHING ALONG THOSE LINES.
YEAH, WELL, I WOULDN'T SET MY HOPES **TOO** HIGH IF I WERE YOU.
I MEAN, YOU MAY HAVE BEEN THE **SECOND** BEST STUDENT IN CRIM. 101...
... BUT YOU'RE NO BATGIRL.
THE END

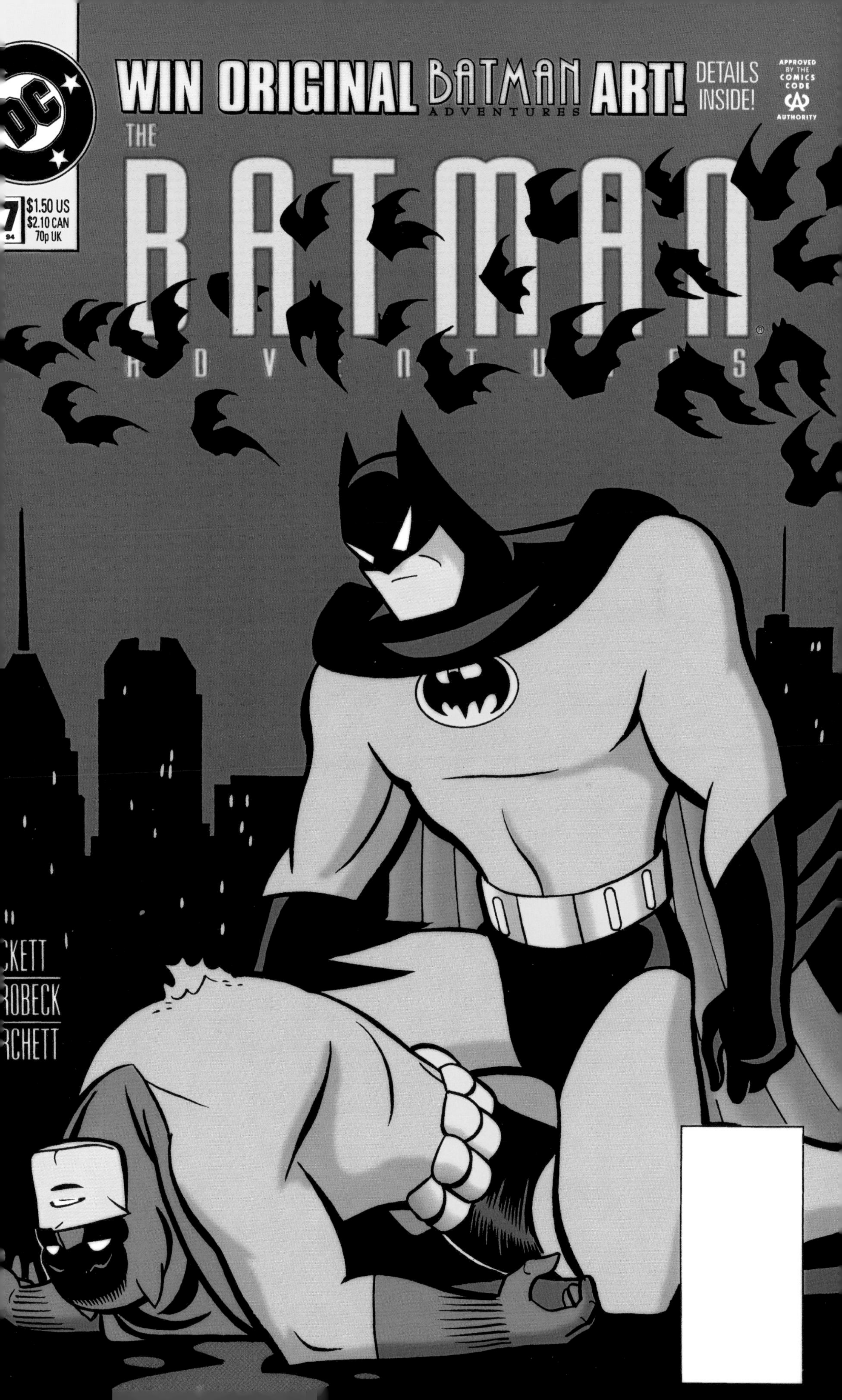
WIN ORIGINAL BATMAN ADVENTURES ART! DETAILS INSIDE!
APPROVED BY THE COMICS CODE AUTHORITY
DC
$1.50 US
$2.10 CAN
70p UK
THE BATMAN ADVENTURES
CKETT
ROBECK
RCHETT

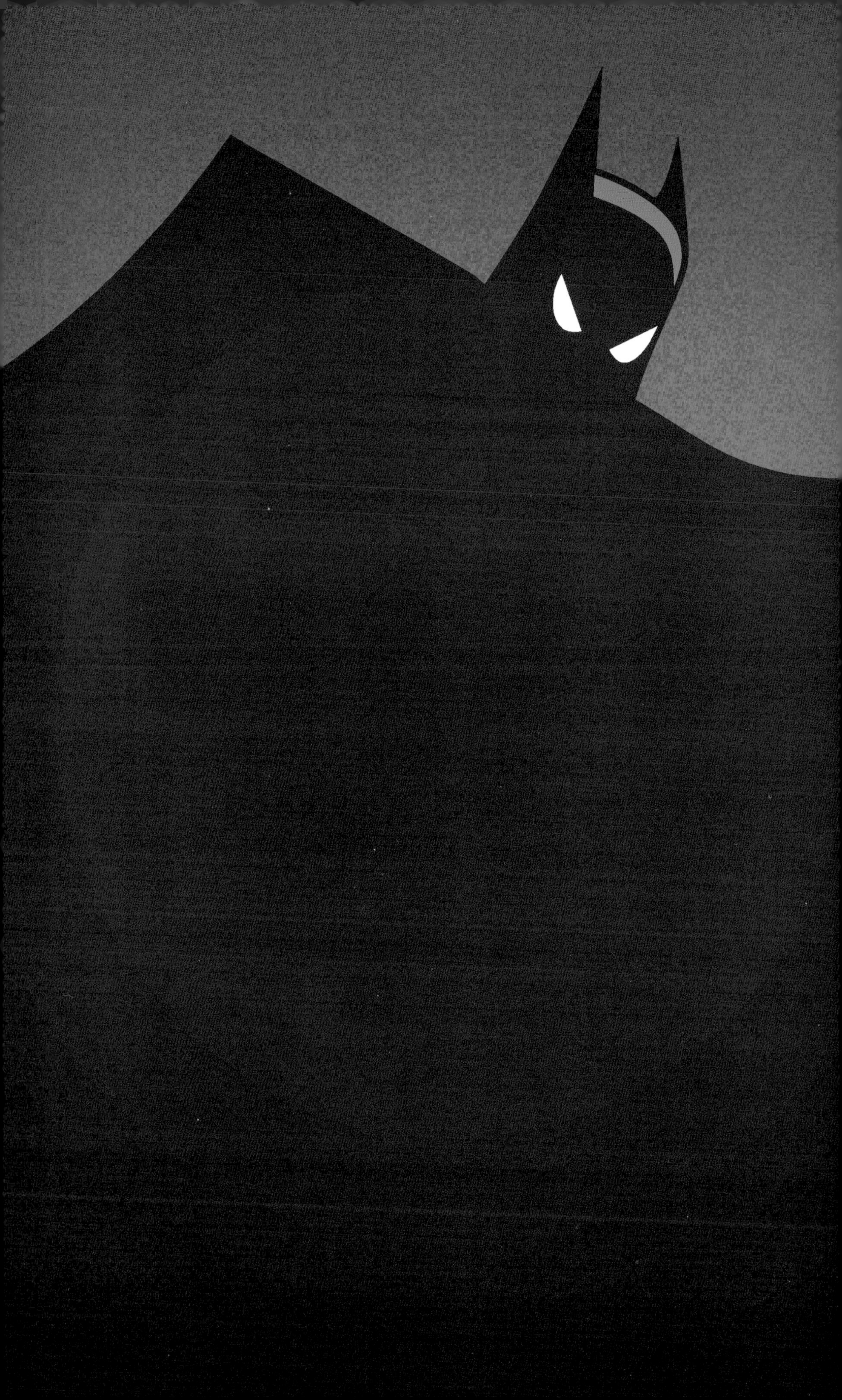

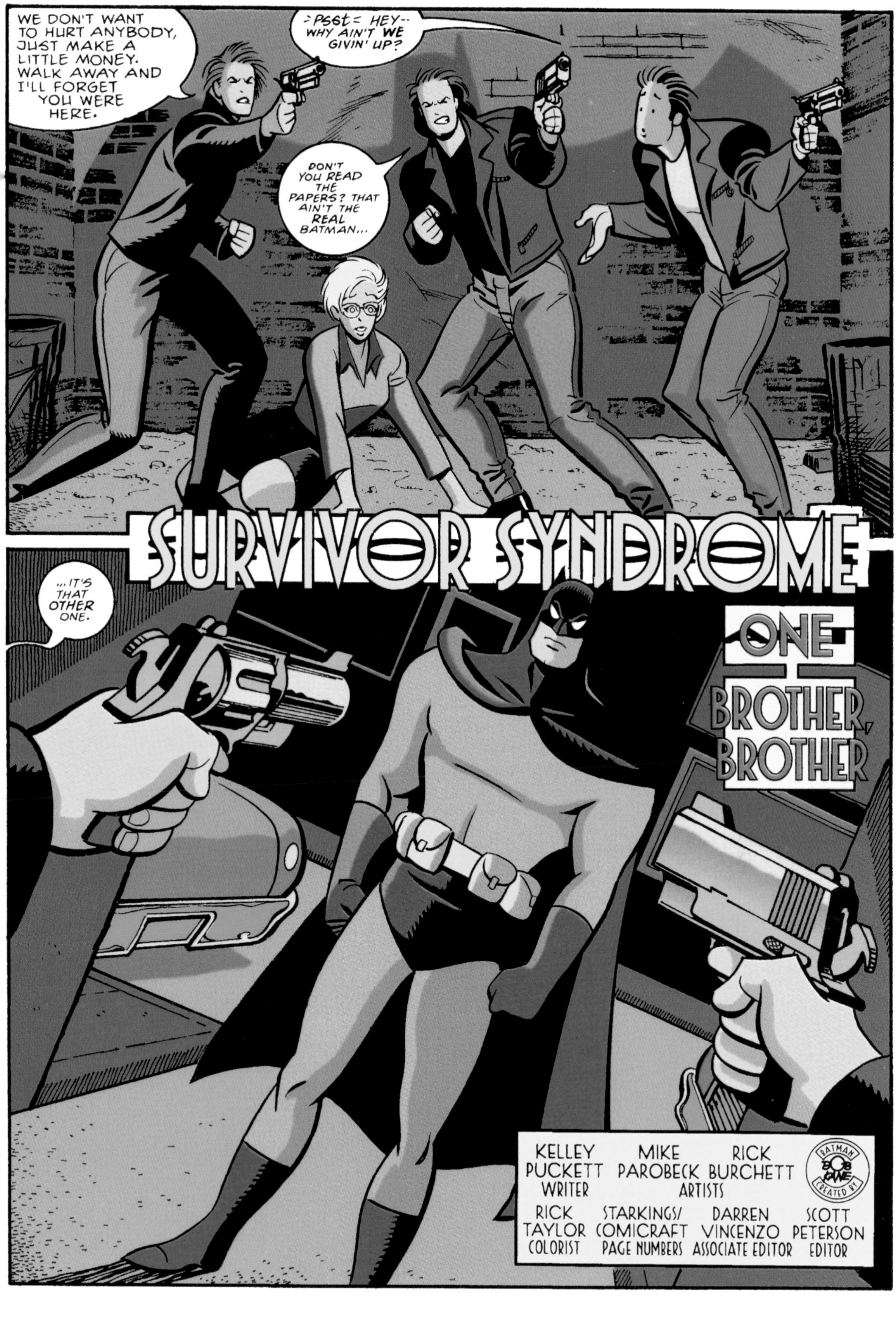
WE DON'T WANT TO HURT ANYBODY, JUST MAKE A LITTLE MONEY. WALK AWAY AND I'LL FORGET YOU WERE HERE.
=PSST= HEY-- WHY AIN'T WE GIVIN' UP?
DON'T YOU READ THE PAPERS? THAT AIN'T THE REAL BATMAN...
SURVIVOR SYNDROME
...IT'S THAT OTHER ONE.
ONE
BROTHER, BROTHER
KELLEY PUCKETT WRITER
MIKE PAROBECK RICK BURCHETT ARTISTS
RICK TAYLOR COLORIST
STARKINGS/ COMICRAFT PAGE NUMBERS
DARREN VINCENZO ASSOCIATE EDITOR
SCOTT PETERSON EDITOR
BATMAN CREATED BY BOB KANE

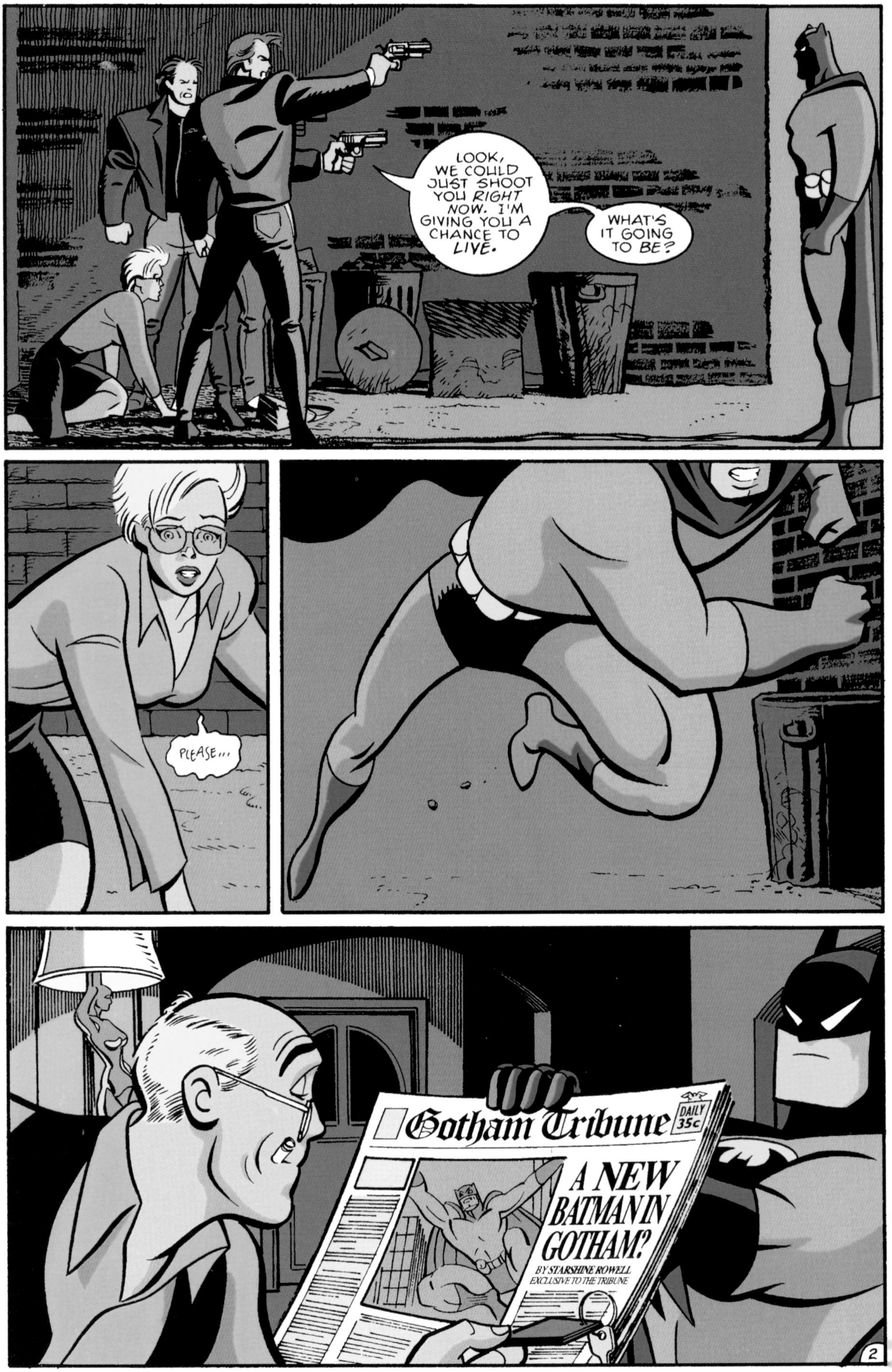

LOOK, WE COULD JUST SHOOT YOU RIGHT NOW. I'M GIVING YOU A CHANCE TO LIVE.
WHAT'S IT GOING TO BE?
PLEASE...
Gotham Tribune
DAILY 35c
A NEW BATMAN IN GOTHAM?
BY STARSHINE ROWELL
EXCLUSIVE TO THE TRIBUNE
2

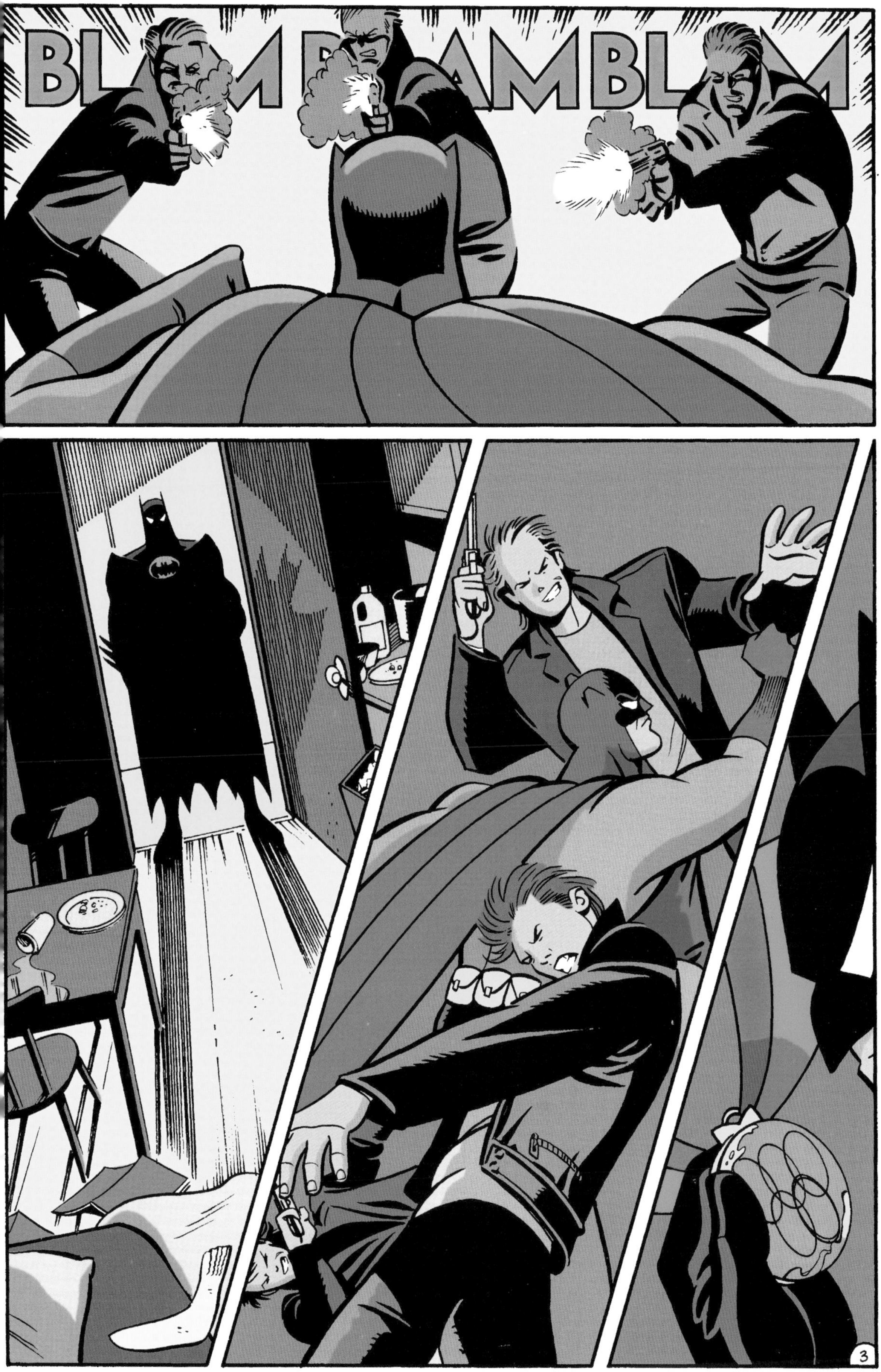

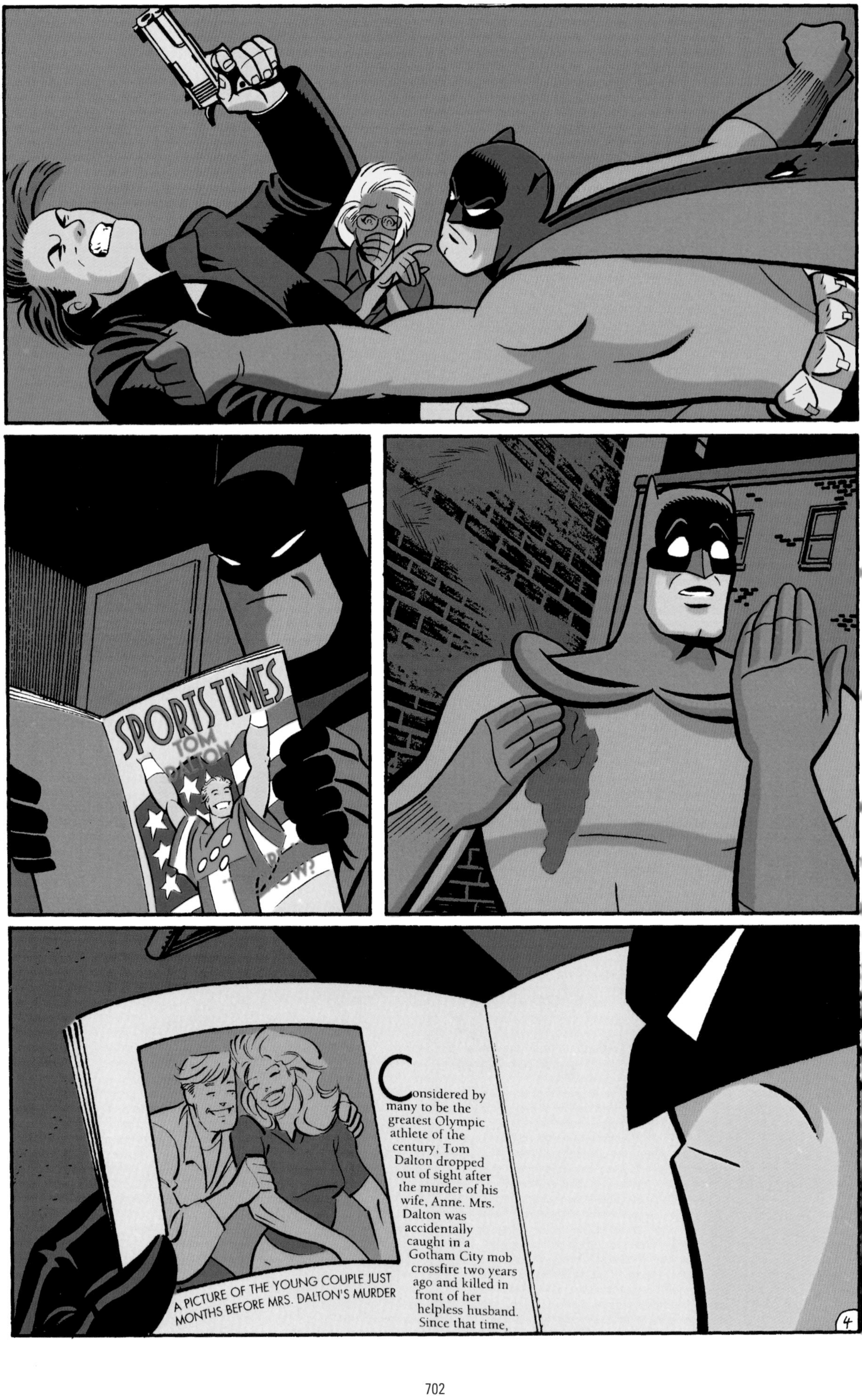
SPORTS TIMES
TOM DALTON
Considered by many to be the greatest Olympic athlete of the century, Tom Dalton dropped out of sight after the murder of his wife, Anne. Mrs. Dalton was accidentally caught in a Gotham City mob crossfire two years ago and killed in front of her helpless husband. Since that time,
A PICTURE OF THE YOUNG COUPLE JUST MONTHS BEFORE MRS. DALTON'S MURDER
4

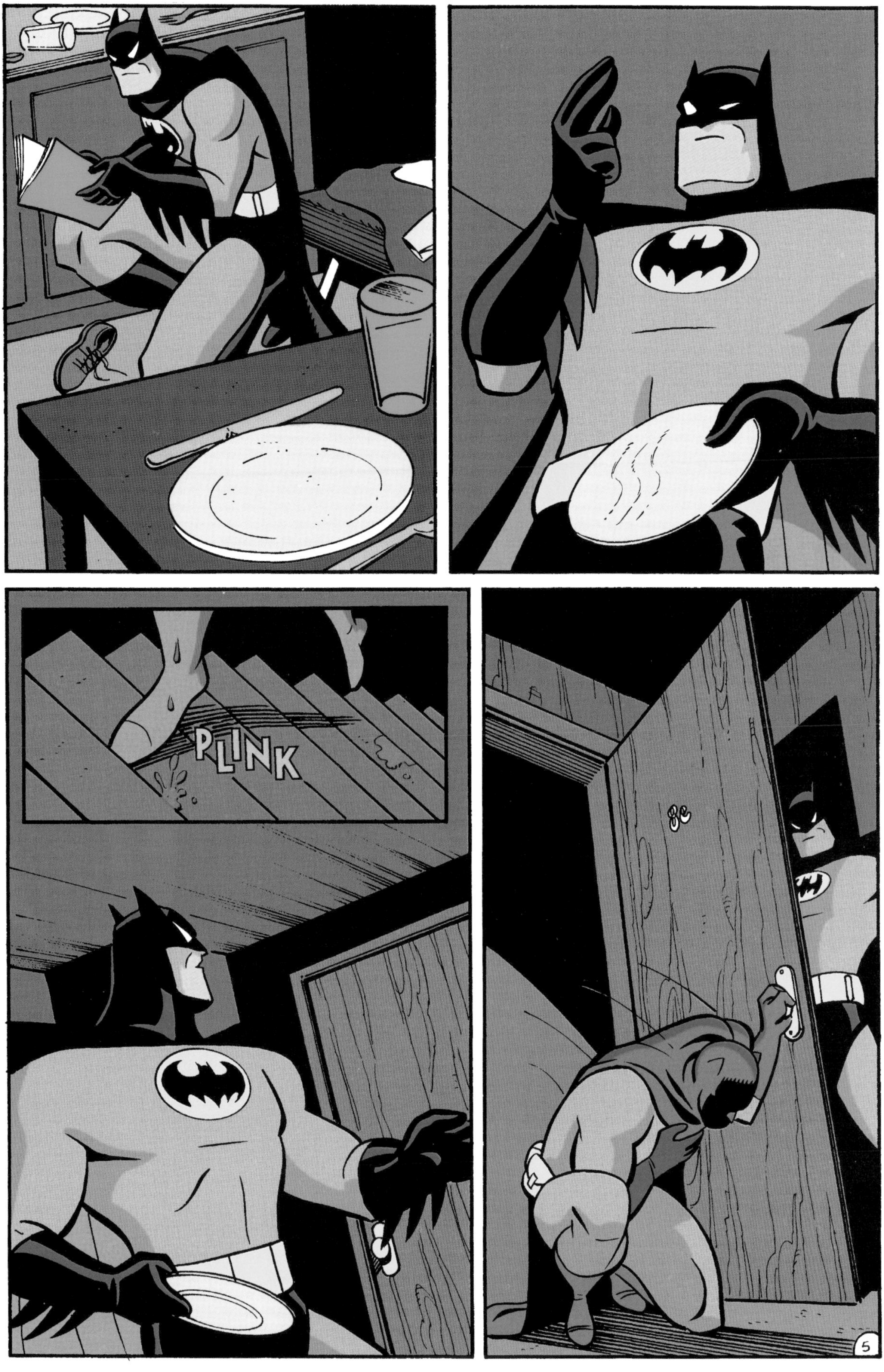
PLINK
5

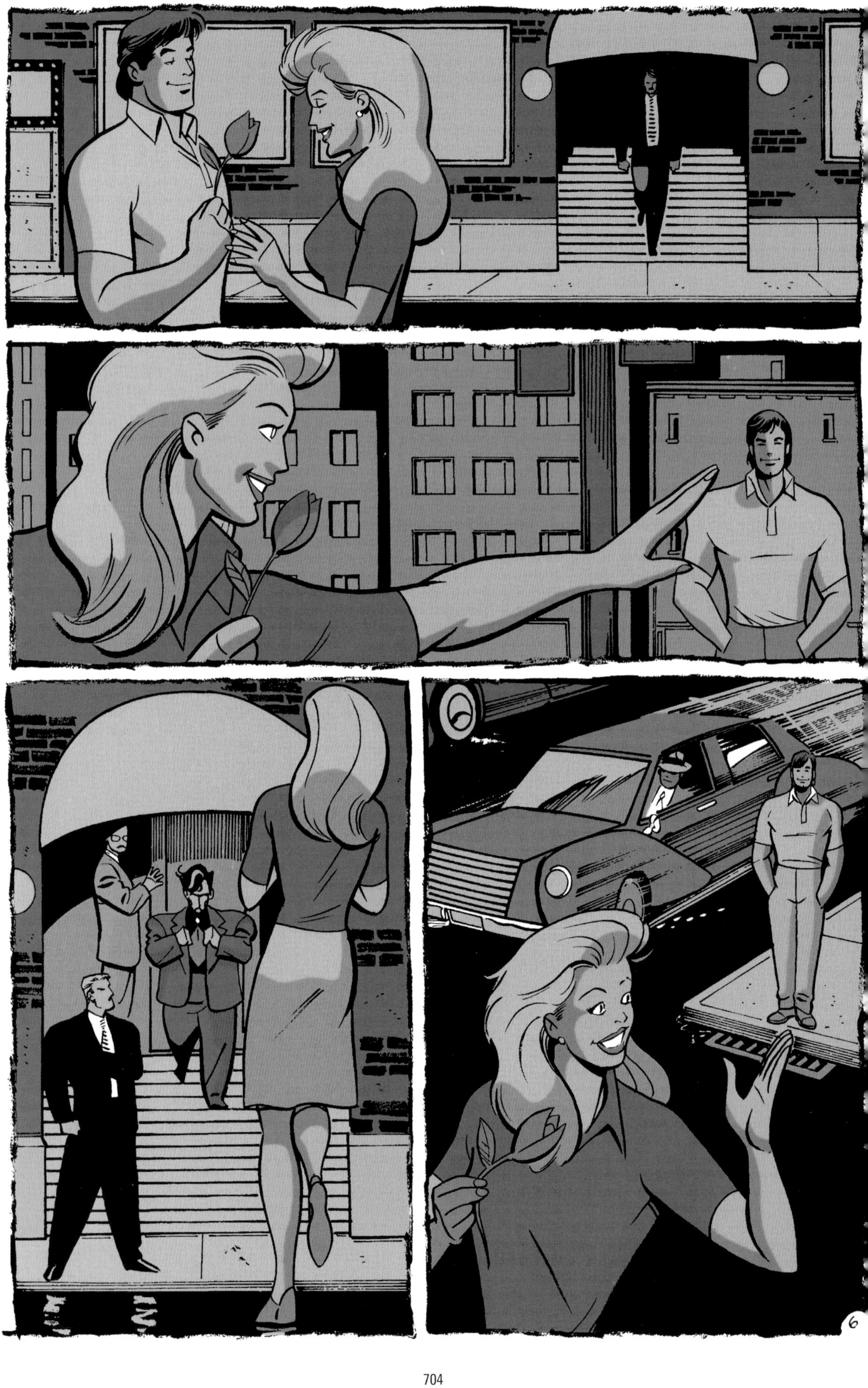

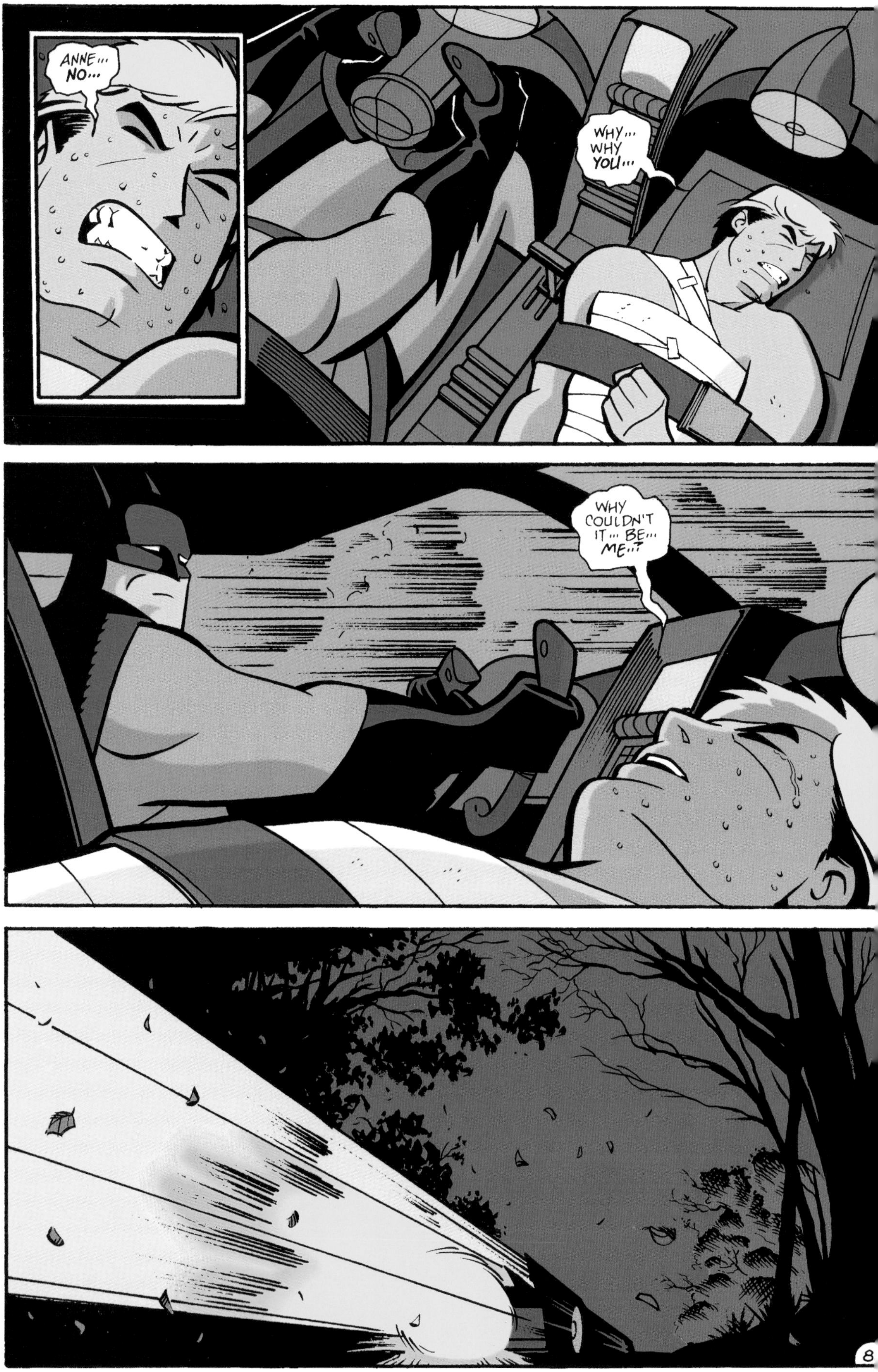
ANNE... NO...
WHY... WHY YOU...
WHY COULDN'T IT... BE... ME...?
8

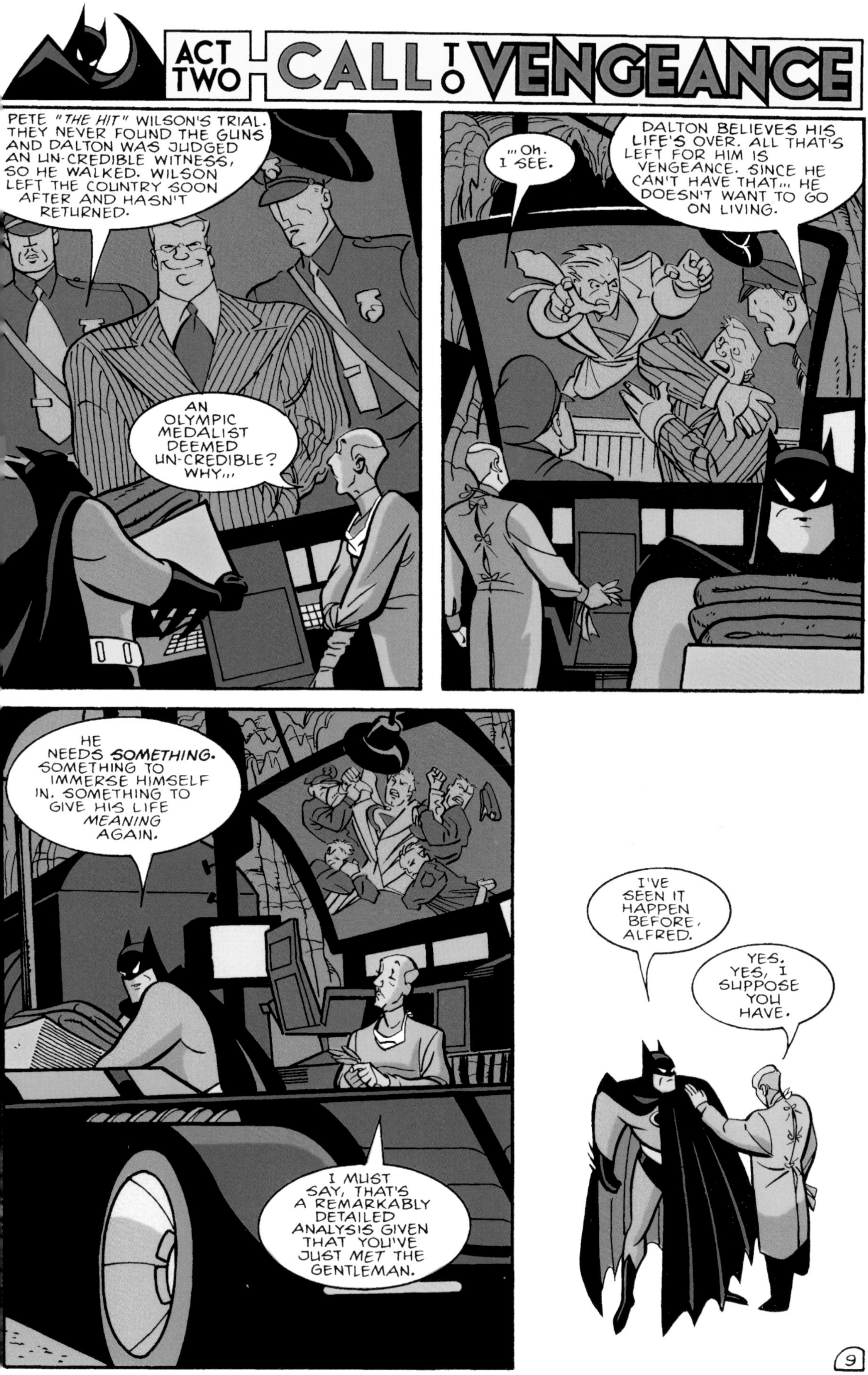
ACT TWO
CALL TO VENGEANCE
PETE "THE HIT" WILSON'S TRIAL. THEY NEVER FOUND THE GUNS AND DALTON WAS JUDGED AN UN-CREDIBLE WITNESS, SO HE WALKED. WILSON LEFT THE COUNTRY SOON AFTER AND HASN'T RETURNED.
AN OLYMPIC MEDALIST DEEMED UN-CREDIBLE? WHY...
...OH. I SEE.
DALTON BELIEVES HIS LIFE'S OVER. ALL THAT'S LEFT FOR HIM IS VENGEANCE. SINCE HE CAN'T HAVE THAT... HE DOESN'T WANT TO GO ON LIVING.
HE NEEDS SOMETHING. SOMETHING TO IMMERSE HIMSELF IN. SOMETHING TO GIVE HIS LIFE MEANING AGAIN.
I MUST SAY, THAT'S A REMARKABLY DETAILED ANALYSIS GIVEN THAT YOU'VE JUST MET THE GENTLEMAN.
I'VE SEEN IT HAPPEN BEFORE, ALFRED.
YES. YES, I SUPPOSE YOU HAVE.
9

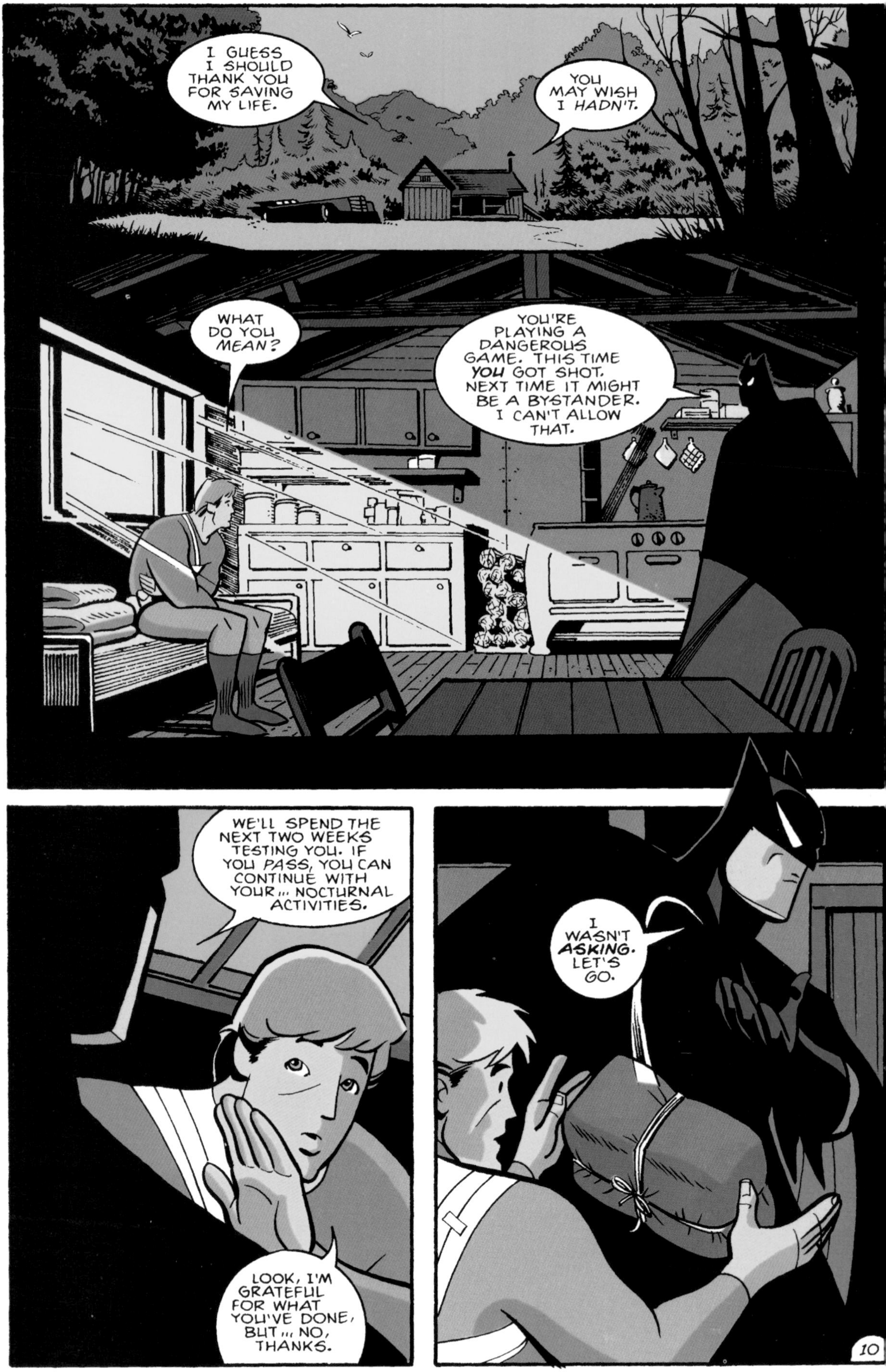
I GUESS I SHOULD THANK YOU FOR SAVING MY LIFE.
YOU MAY WISH I HADN'T.
WHAT DO YOU MEAN?
YOU'RE PLAYING A DANGEROUS GAME. THIS TIME YOU GOT SHOT. NEXT TIME IT MIGHT BE A BYSTANDER. I CAN'T ALLOW THAT.
WE'LL SPEND THE NEXT TWO WEEKS TESTING YOU. IF YOU PASS, YOU CAN CONTINUE WITH YOUR... NOCTURNAL ACTIVITIES.
LOOK, I'M GRATEFUL FOR WHAT YOU'VE DONE, BUT... NO, THANKS.
I WASN'T ASKING. LET'S GO.
10

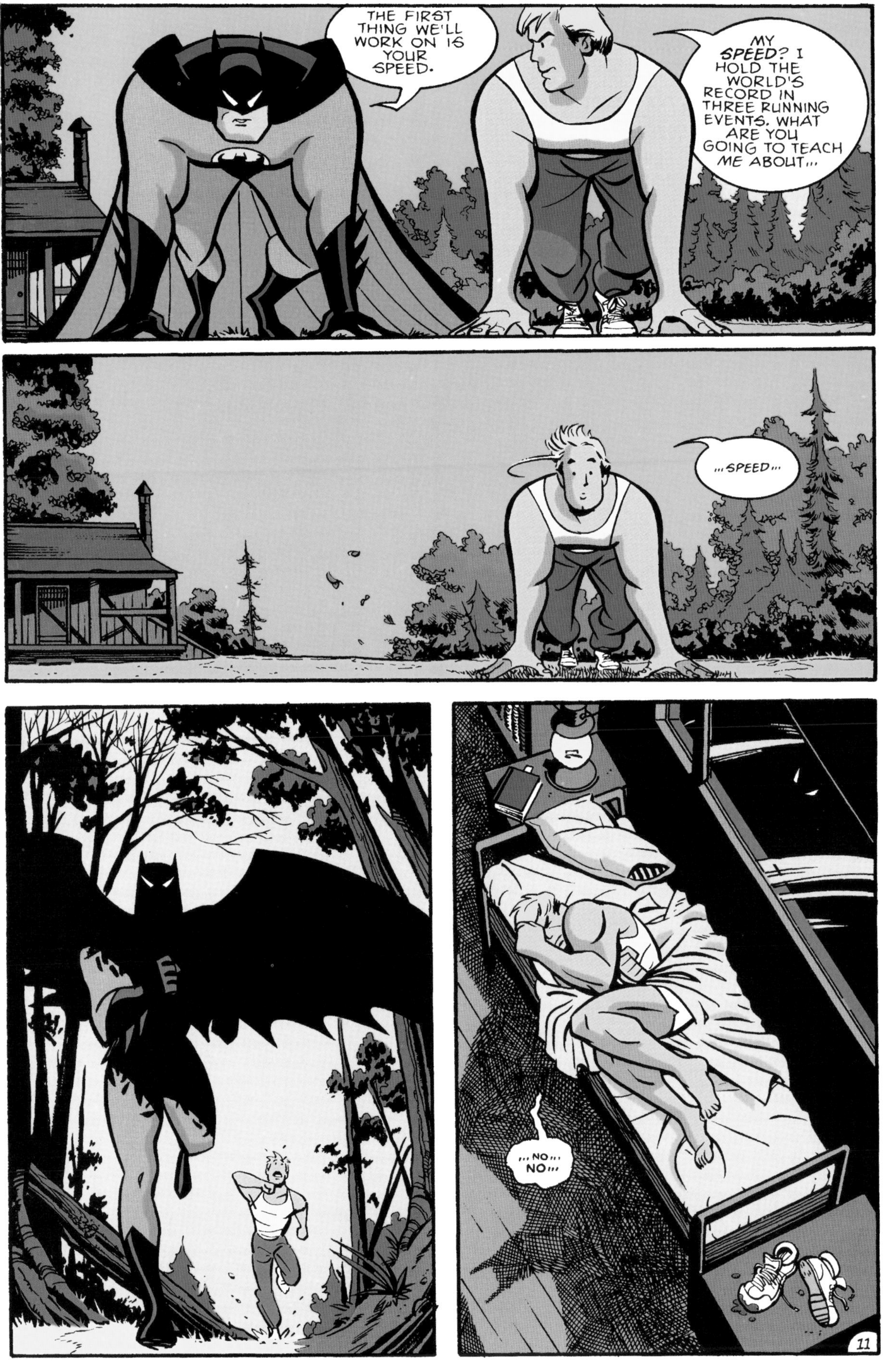
THE FIRST THING WE'LL WORK ON IS YOUR SPEED.
MY SPEED? I HOLD THE WORLD'S RECORD IN THREE RUNNING EVENTS. WHAT ARE YOU GOING TO TEACH ME ABOUT...
...SPEED...
...NO... NO...
11

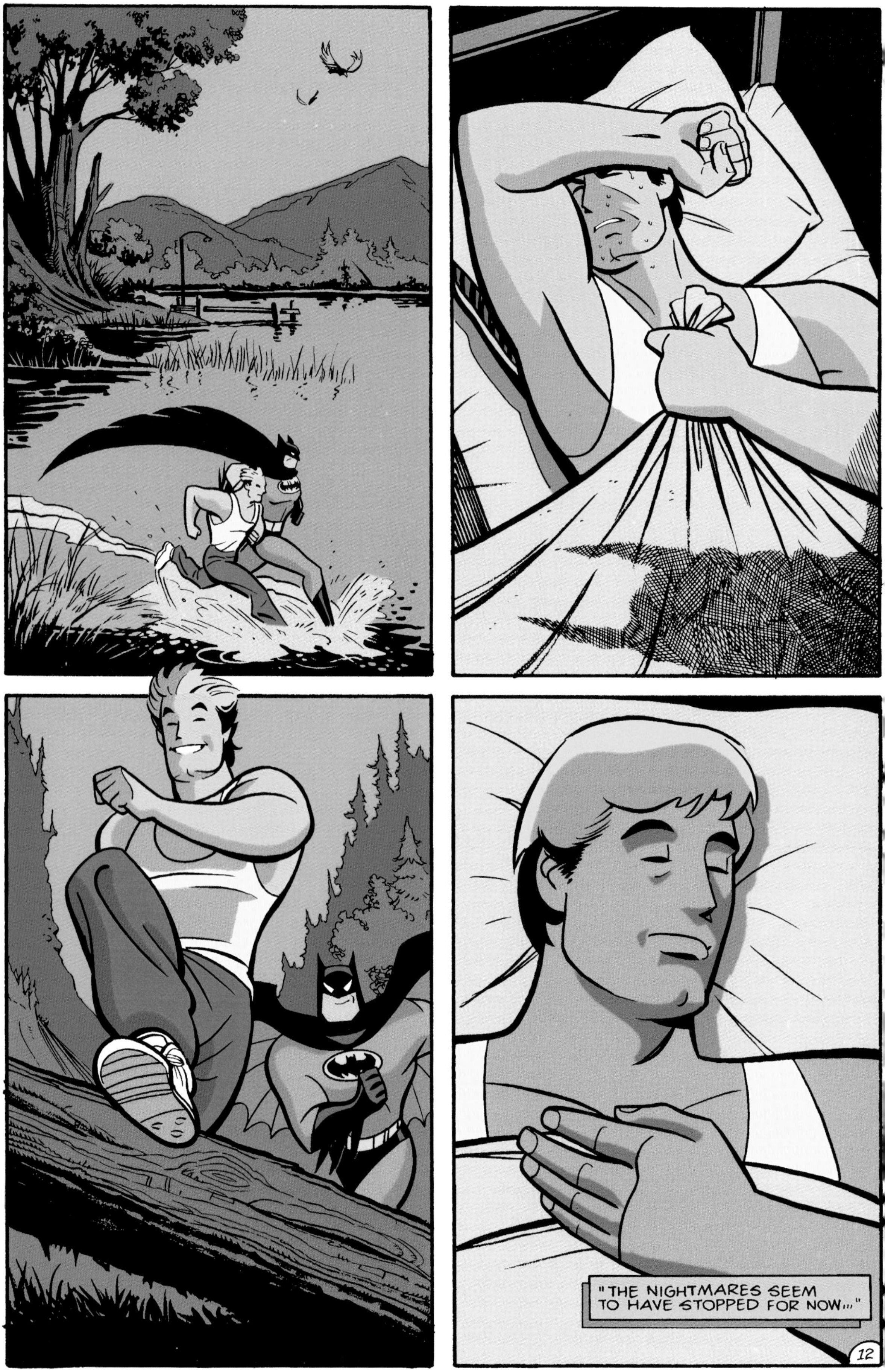
"THE NIGHTMARES SEEM
TO HAVE STOPPED FOR NOW..."
12

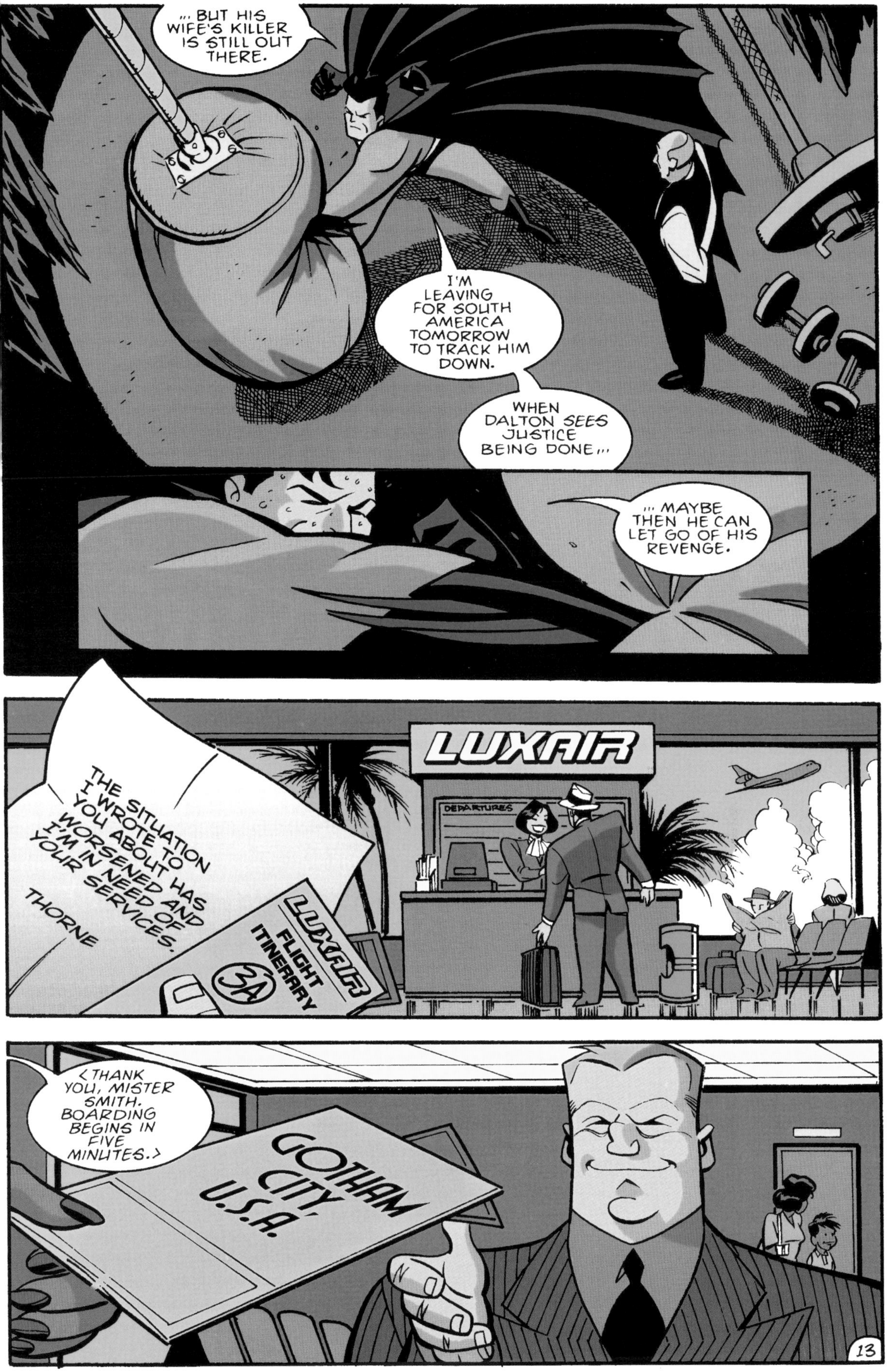
...BUT HIS WIFE'S KILLER IS STILL OUT THERE.
I'M LEAVING FOR SOUTH AMERICA TOMORROW TO TRACK HIM DOWN.
WHEN DALTON SEES JUSTICE BEING DONE...
...MAYBE THEN HE CAN LET GO OF HIS REVENGE.
THE SITUATION I WROTE TO YOU ABOUT HAS WORSENED AND I'M IN NEED OF YOUR SERVICES.
THORNE
LUXAIR
FLIGHT ITINERARY
3A
LUXAIR
DEPARTURES
<THANK YOU, MISTER SMITH. BOARDING BEGINS IN FIVE MINUTES.>
GOTHAM CITY, U.S.A.
13

IMPRESSIVE.

TAKE A LOOK.

BUT THAT'S JUST SEVEN SECONDS SLOWER THAN MY *RECORD!* ON A *LEVEL* TRACK I COULD *EASILY* SHAVE THAT TIME OFF,,,

MAYBE, BUT THAT'S NOT MUCH USE IN FIGHTING *CRIME*, IS IT?

NO,,, I SUPPOSE NOT,,,

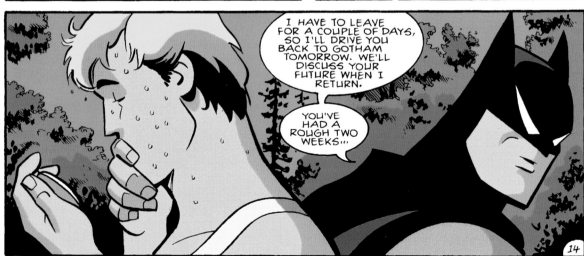

I HAVE TO LEAVE FOR A COUPLE OF DAYS, SO I'LL DRIVE YOU BACK TO GOTHAM TOMORROW. WE'LL DISCUSS YOUR FUTURE WHEN I RETURN.

YOU'VE HAD A ROUGH TWO WEEKS,,,

14

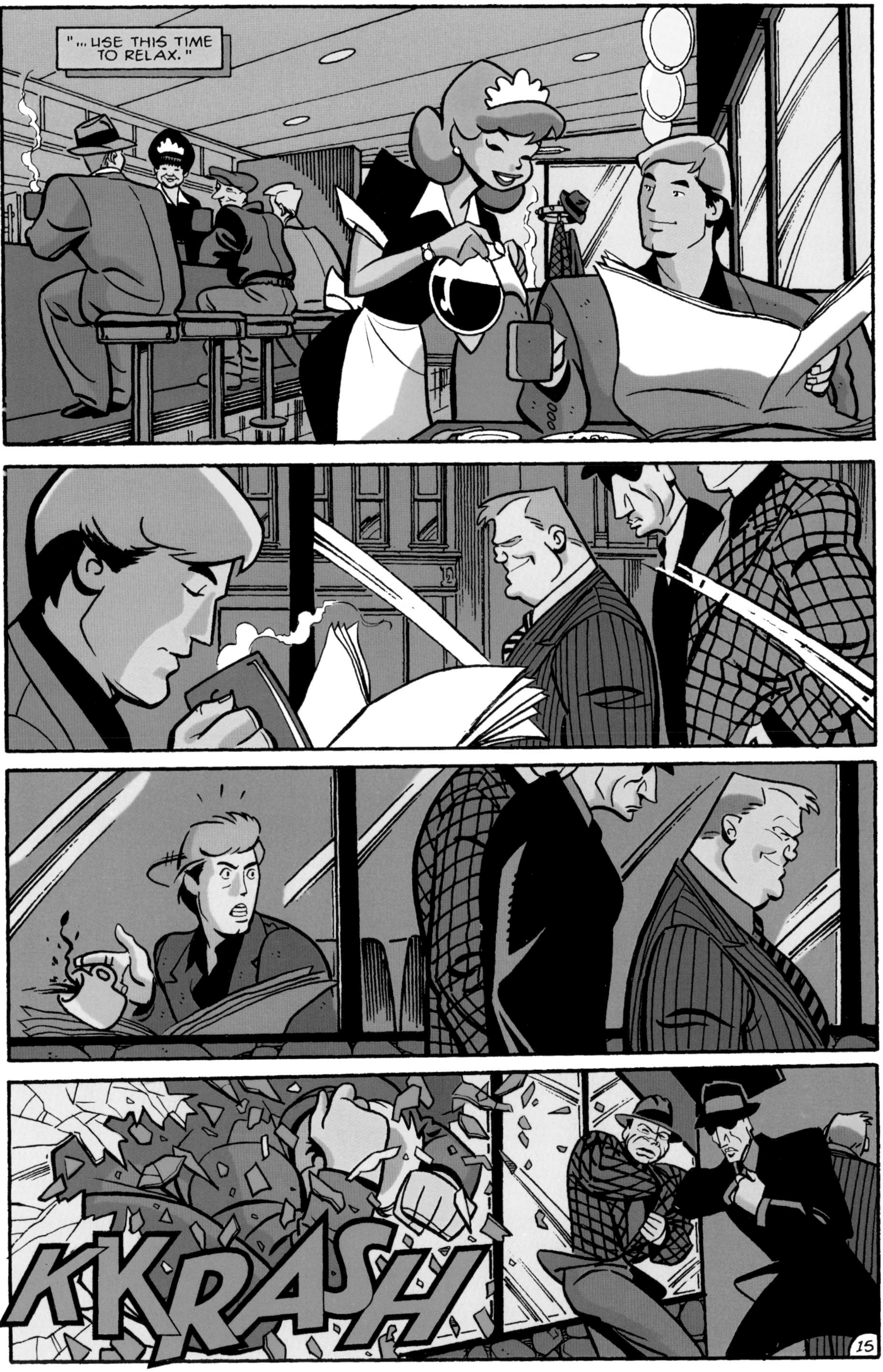
"... USE THIS TIME TO RELAX."
KKRASH
15

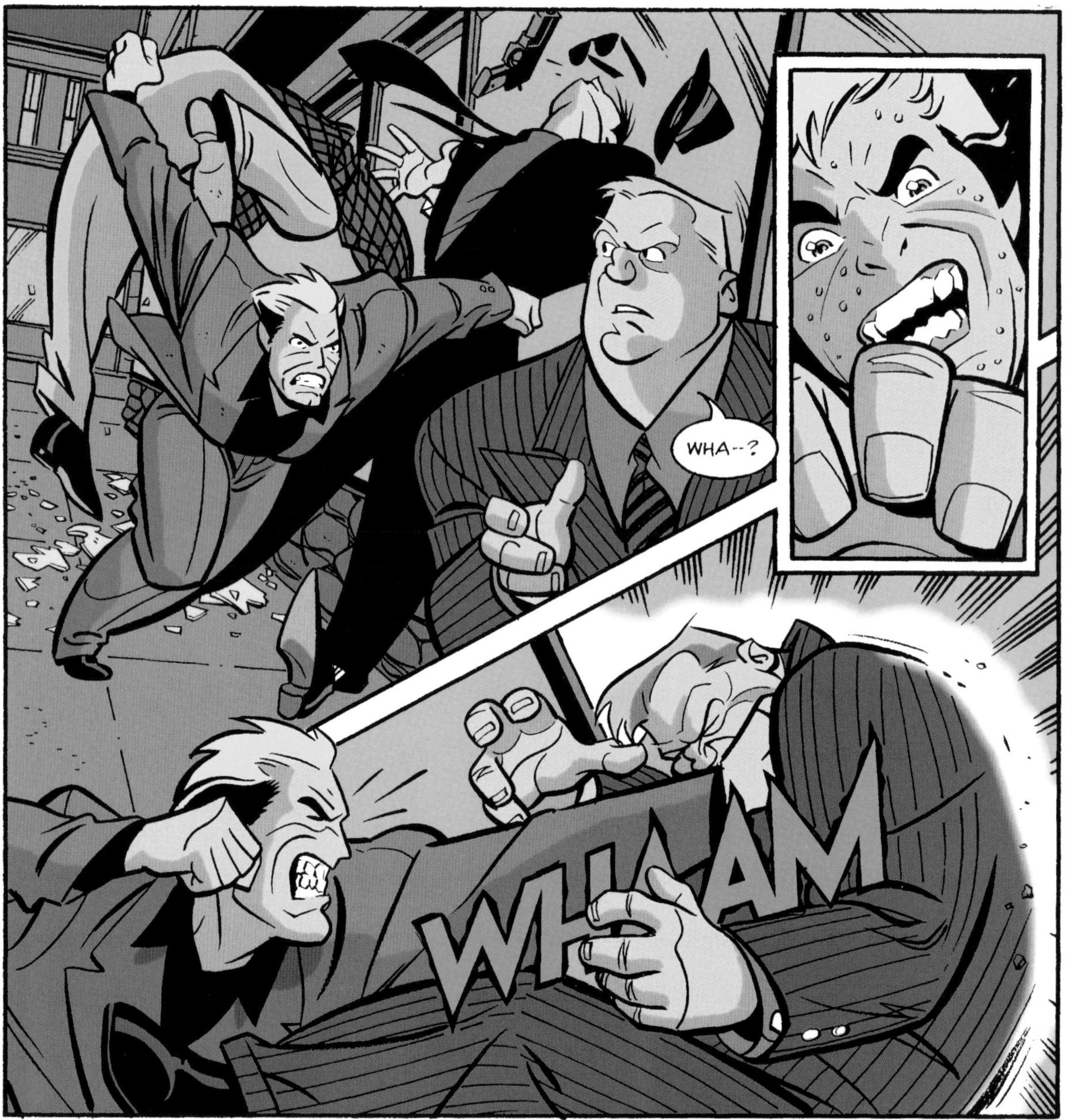
WHA--?
WHAM

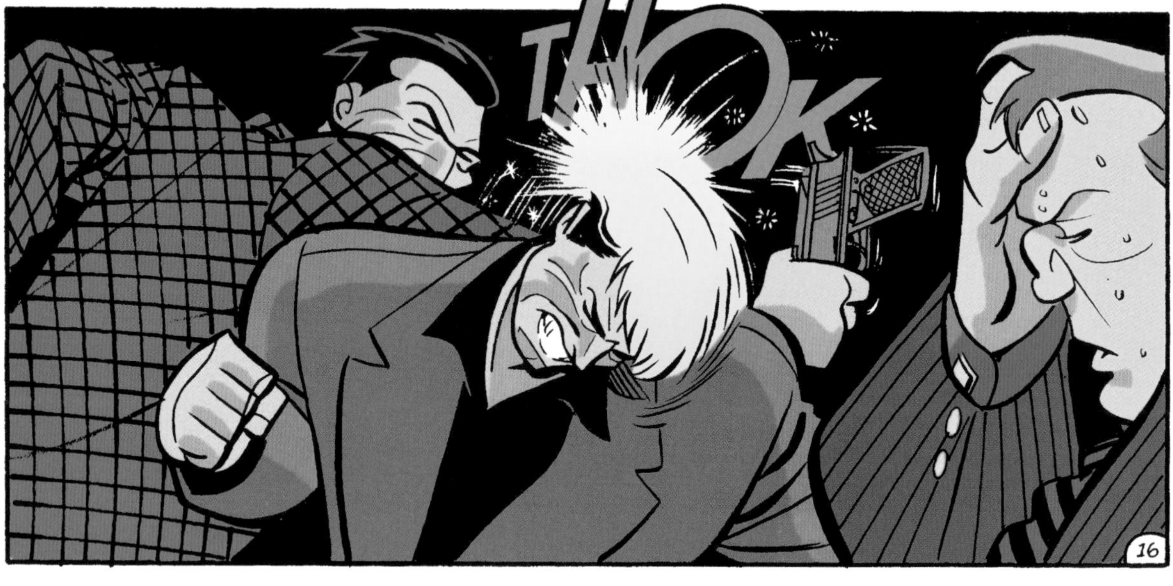
THOK
16

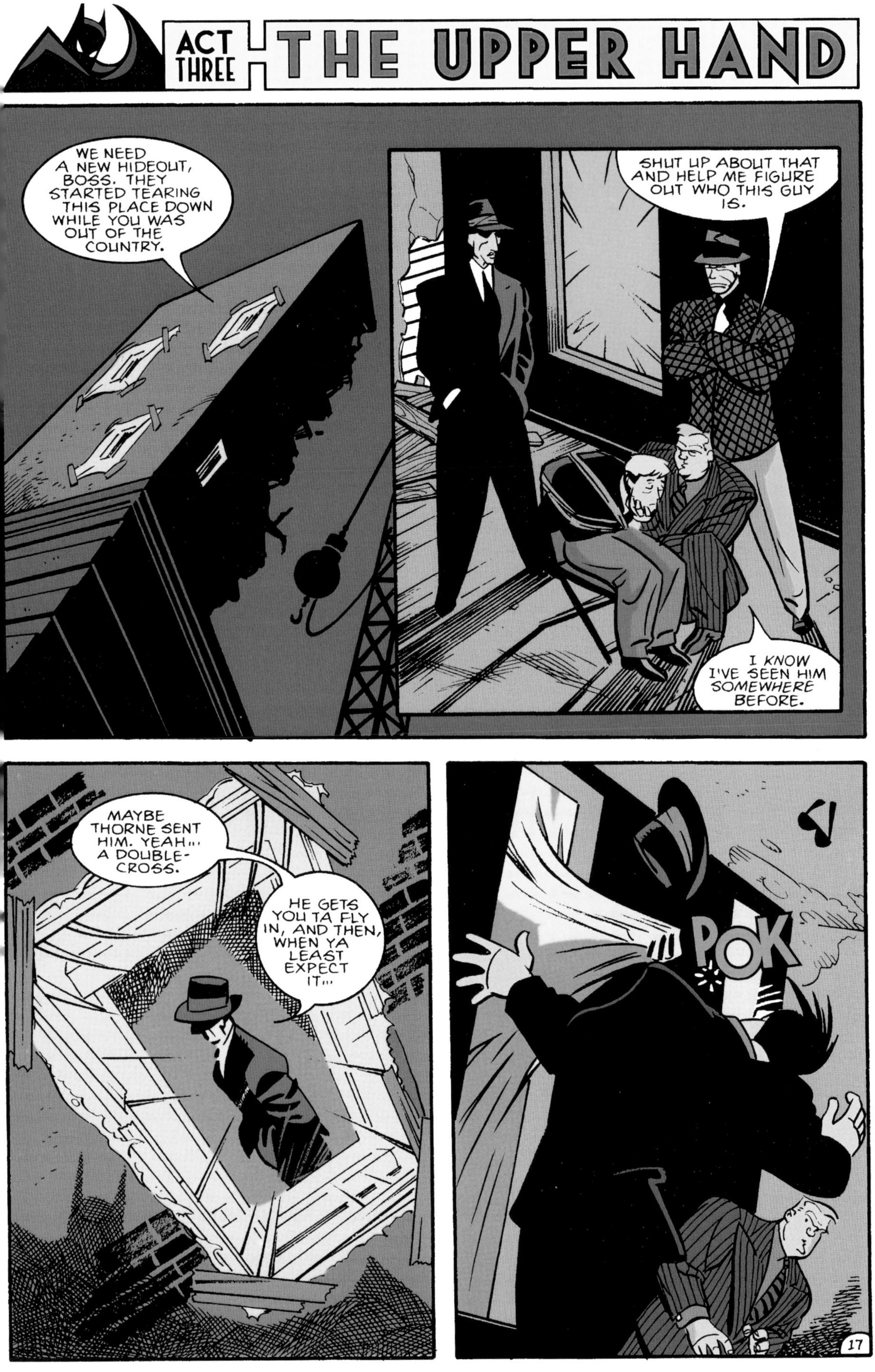
ACT THREE
THE UPPER HAND
WE NEED A NEW HIDEOUT, BOSS. THEY STARTED TEARING THIS PLACE DOWN WHILE YOU WAS OUT OF THE COUNTRY.
SHUT UP ABOUT THAT AND HELP ME FIGURE OUT WHO THIS GUY IS.
I KNOW I'VE SEEN HIM SOMEWHERE BEFORE.
MAYBE THORNE SENT HIM. YEAH... A DOUBLE-CROSS.
HE GETS YOU TA FLY IN, AND THEN, WHEN YA LEAST EXPECT IT...
POK
17

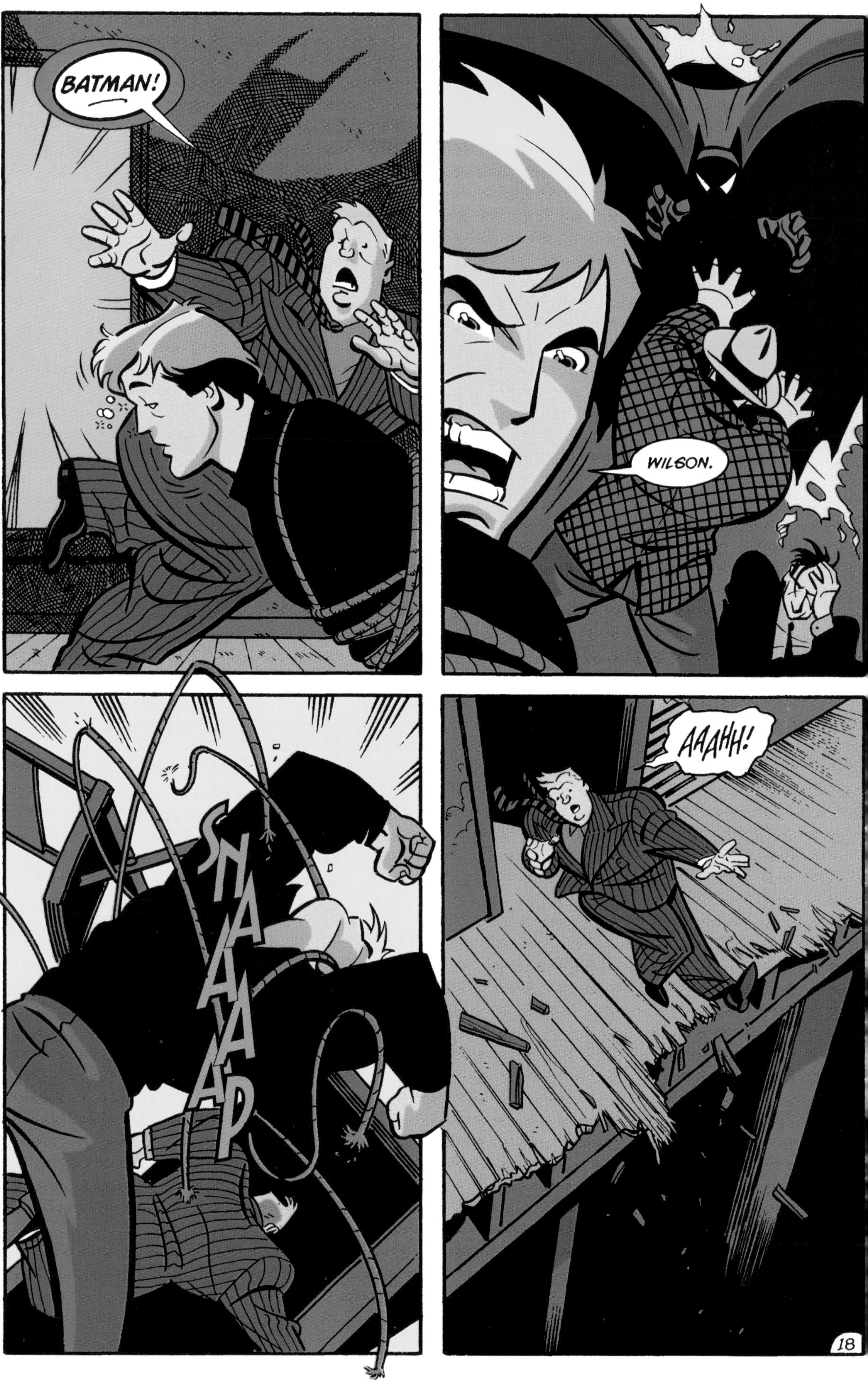
BATMAN!
WILSON.
SNAAAAP
AAAHH!
18

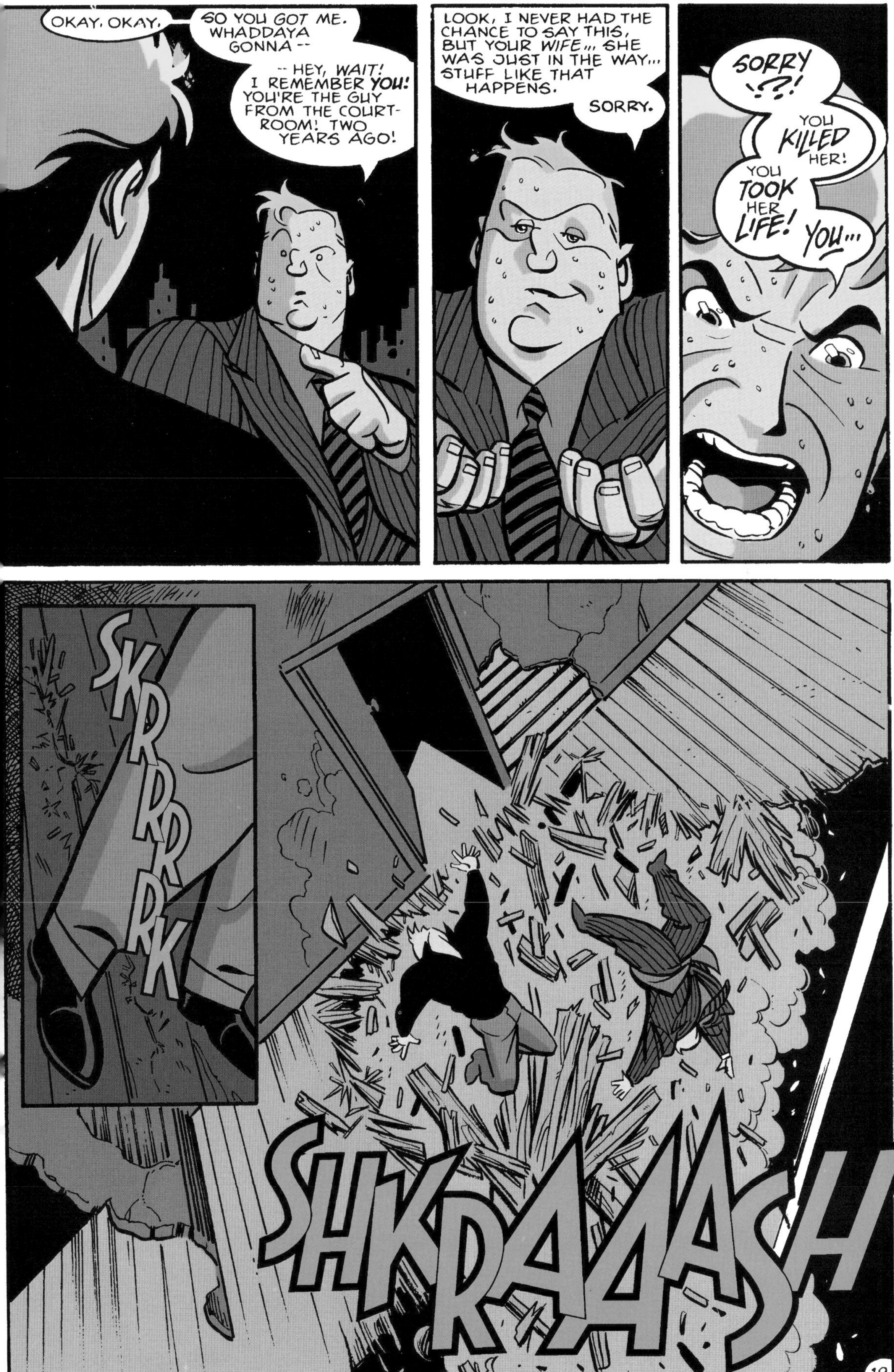
OKAY, OKAY,
SO YOU GOT ME. WHADDAYA GONNA --
-- HEY, WAIT! I REMEMBER YOU! YOU'RE THE GUY FROM THE COURTROOM! TWO YEARS AGO!
LOOK, I NEVER HAD THE CHANCE TO SAY THIS, BUT YOUR WIFE... SHE WAS JUST IN THE WAY... STUFF LIKE THAT HAPPENS.
SORRY.
SORRY !?!
YOU KILLED HER!
YOU TOOK HER LIFE!
YOU...
SKRRRRRK
SHKRAAASH
19

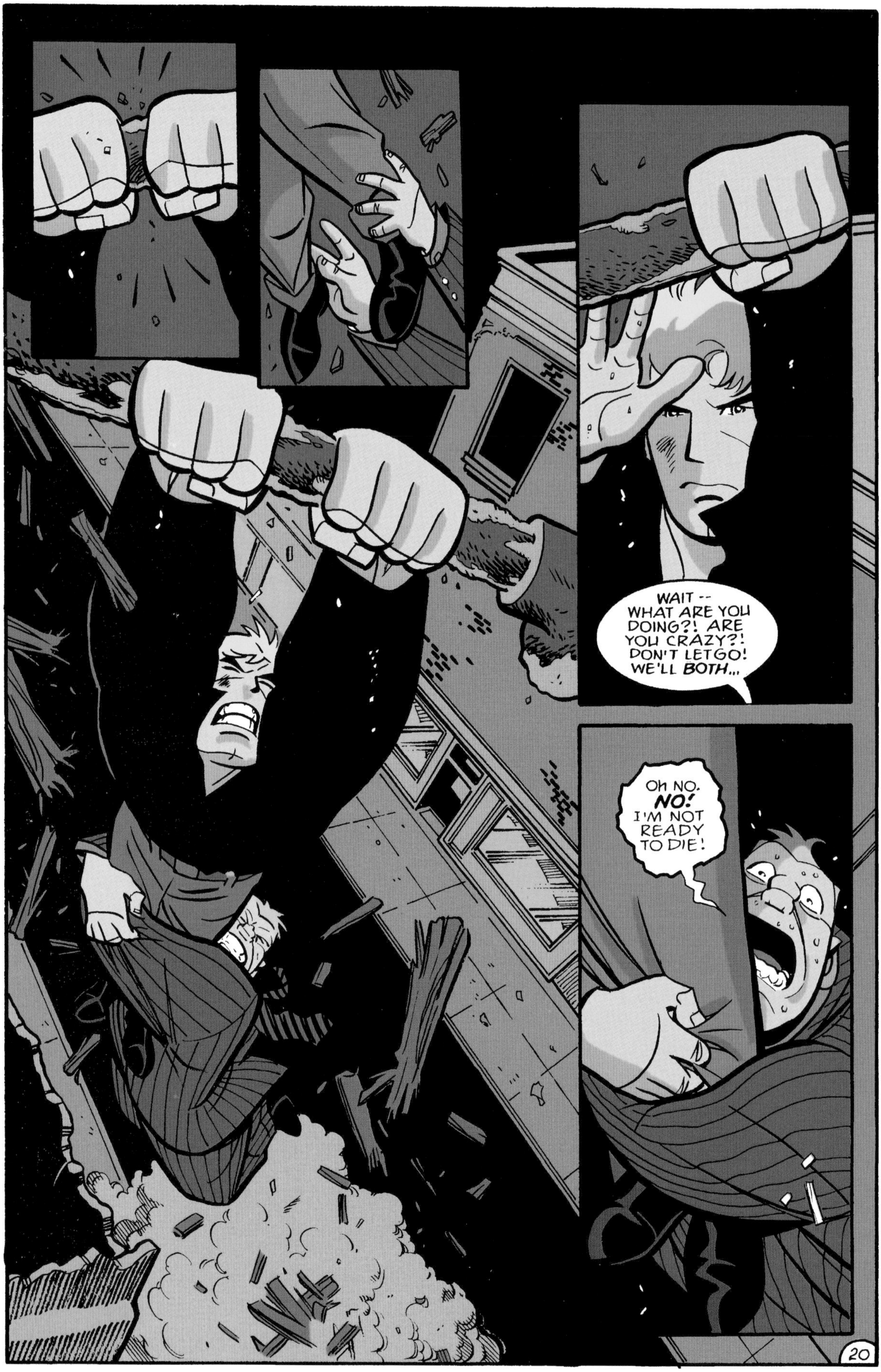
WAIT -- WHAT ARE YOU DOING?! ARE YOU CRAZY?! DON'T LETGO! WE'LL *BOTH*...
Oh NO. **NO!** I'M NOT READY TO DIE!
20

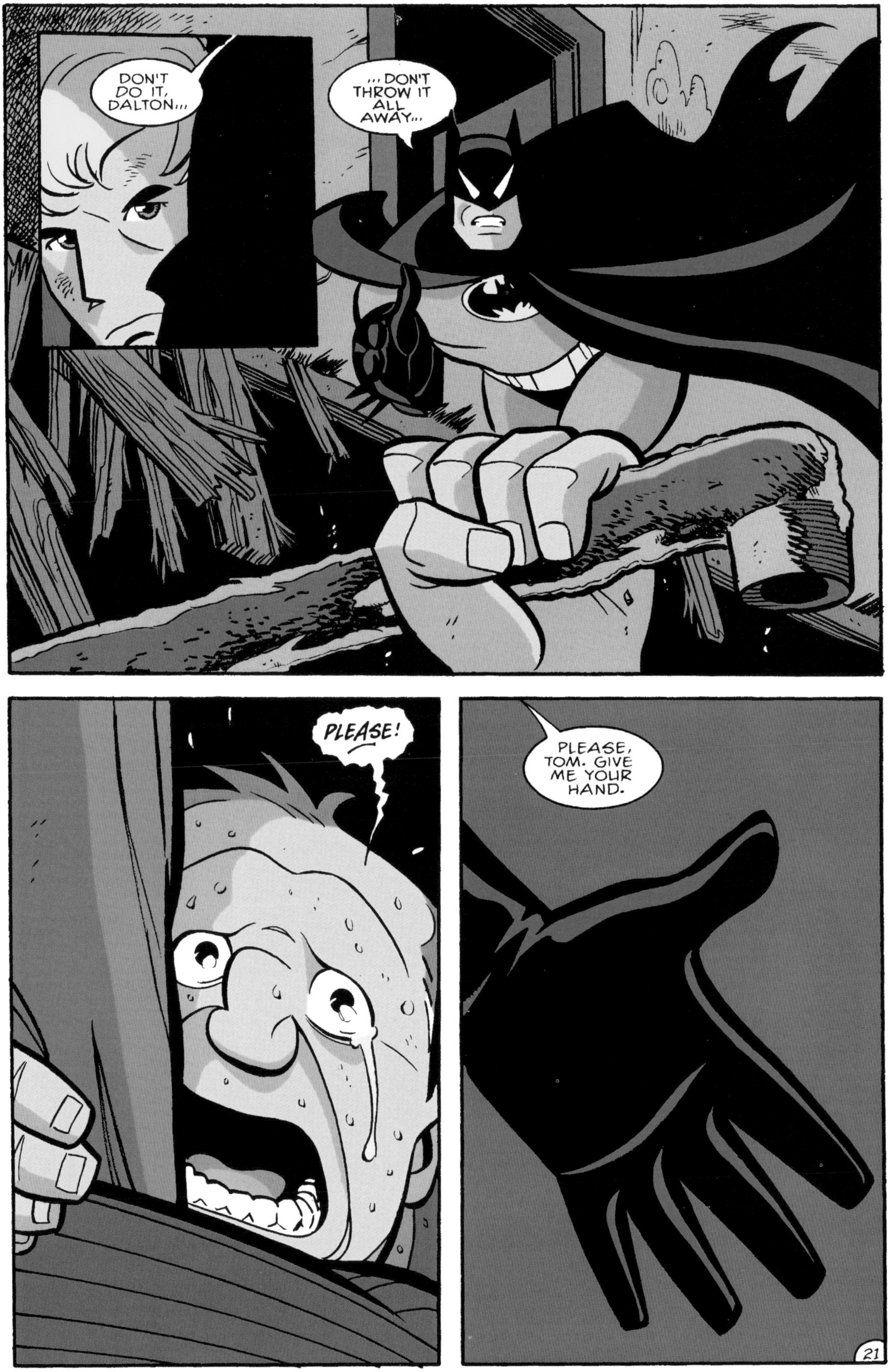
DON'T DO IT, DALTON...
...DON'T THROW IT ALL AWAY...
PLEASE!
PLEASE, TOM. GIVE ME YOUR HAND.
21

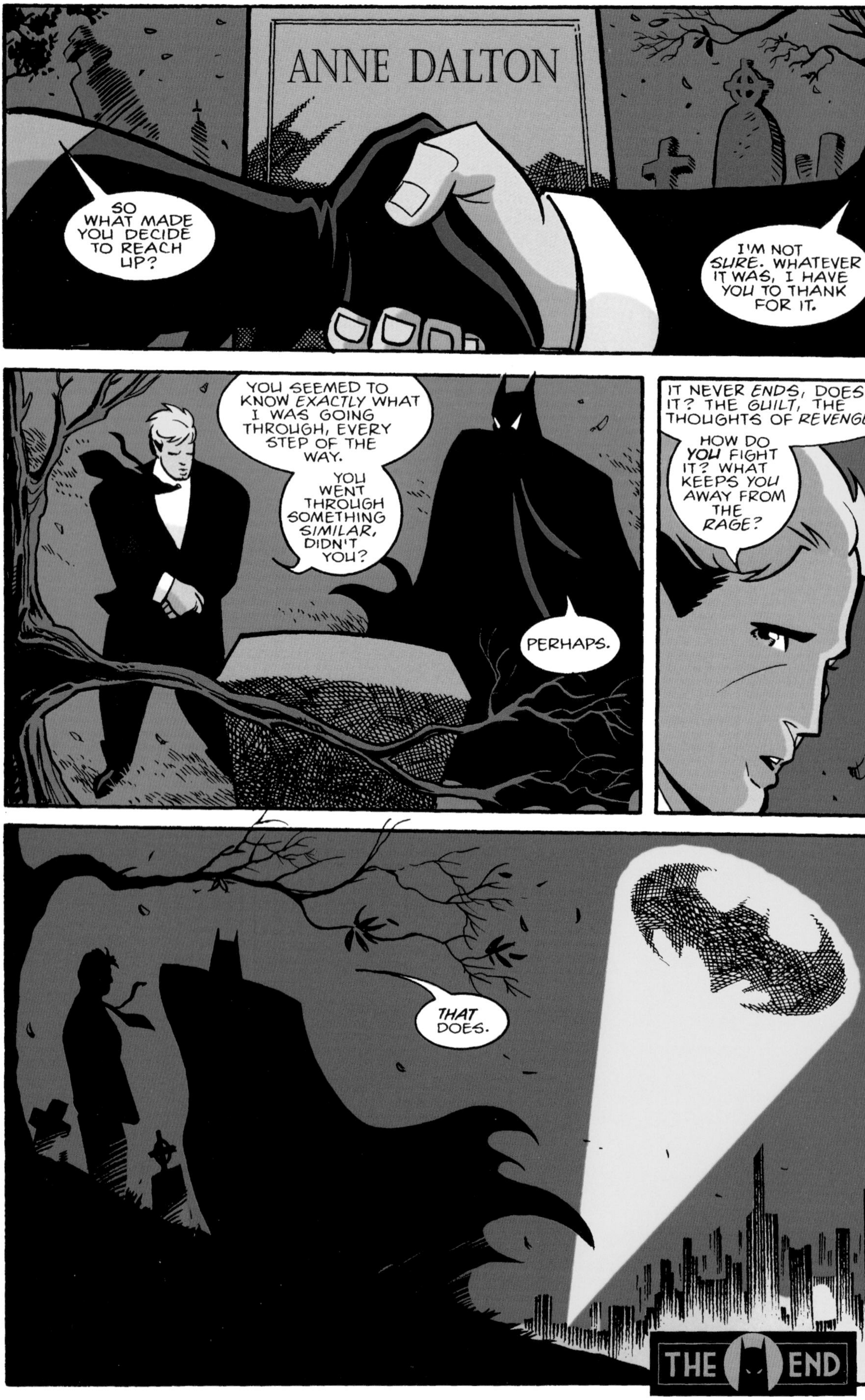
ANNE DALTON
SO WHAT MADE YOU DECIDE TO REACH UP?
I'M NOT SURE. WHATEVER IT WAS, I HAVE YOU TO THANK FOR IT.
YOU SEEMED TO KNOW EXACTLY WHAT I WAS GOING THROUGH, EVERY STEP OF THE WAY.
YOU WENT THROUGH SOMETHING SIMILAR, DIDN'T YOU?
PERHAPS.
IT NEVER ENDS, DOES IT? THE GUILT, THE THOUGHTS OF REVENGE.
HOW DO YOU FIGHT IT? WHAT KEEPS YOU AWAY FROM THE RAGE?
THAT DOES.
THE END

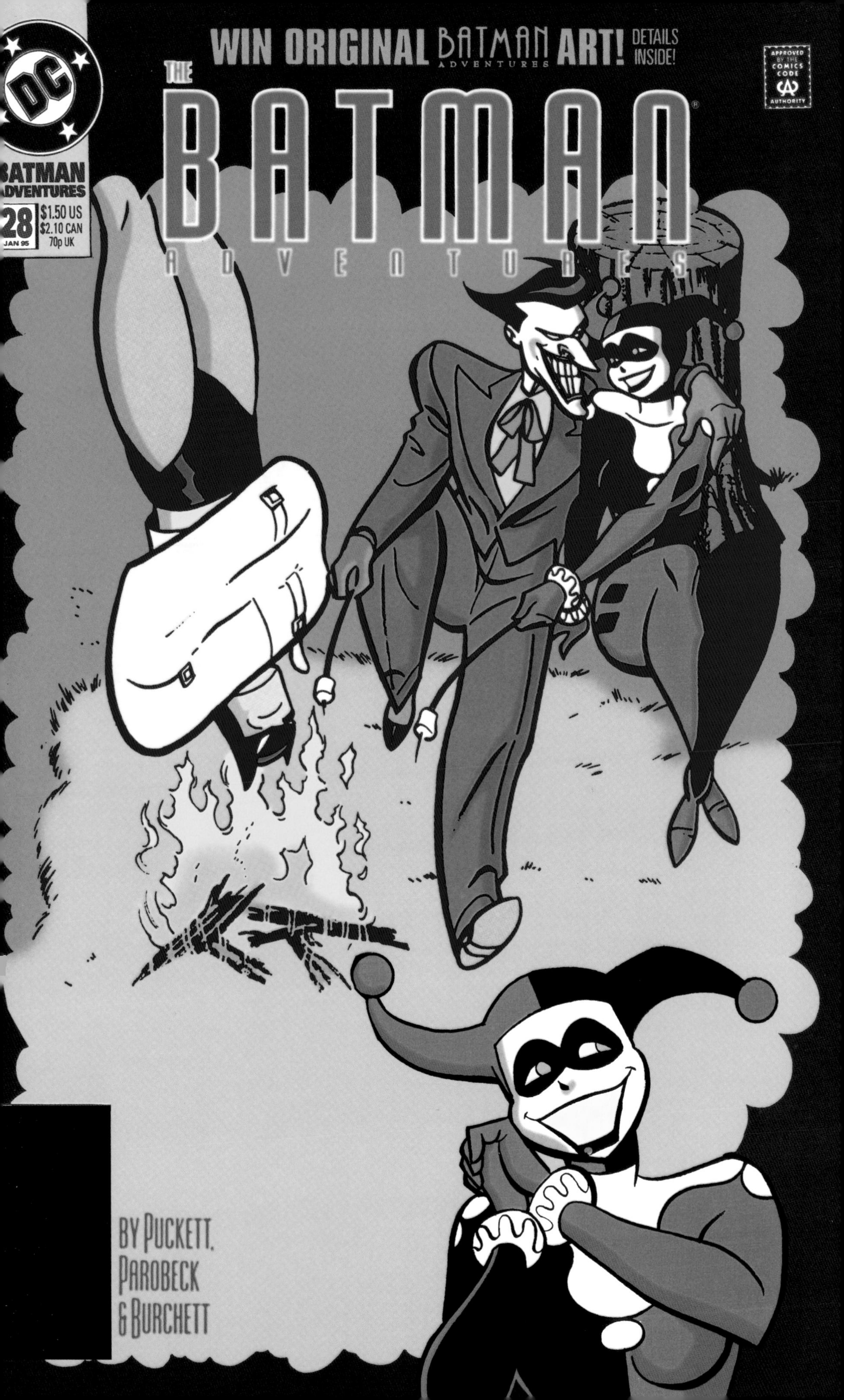

WIN ORIGINAL BATMAN ADVENTURES ART!
DETAILS INSIDE!
DC
APPROVED BY THE COMICS CODE AUTHORITY
THE BATMAN ADVENTURES
BATMAN ADVENTURES
28
$1.50 US
$2.10 CAN
70p UK
JAN 95
BY PUCKETT, PAROBECK & BURCHETT

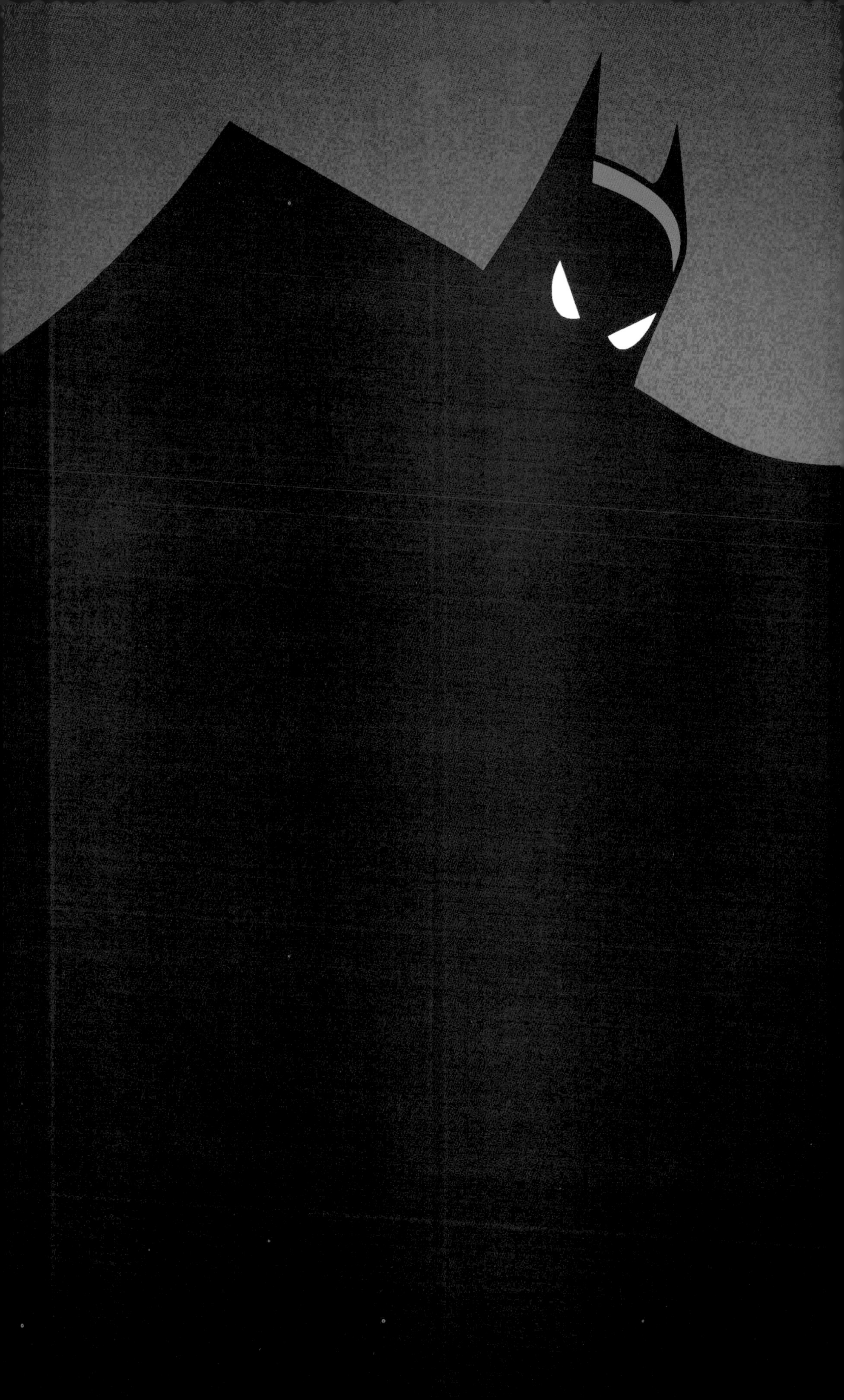

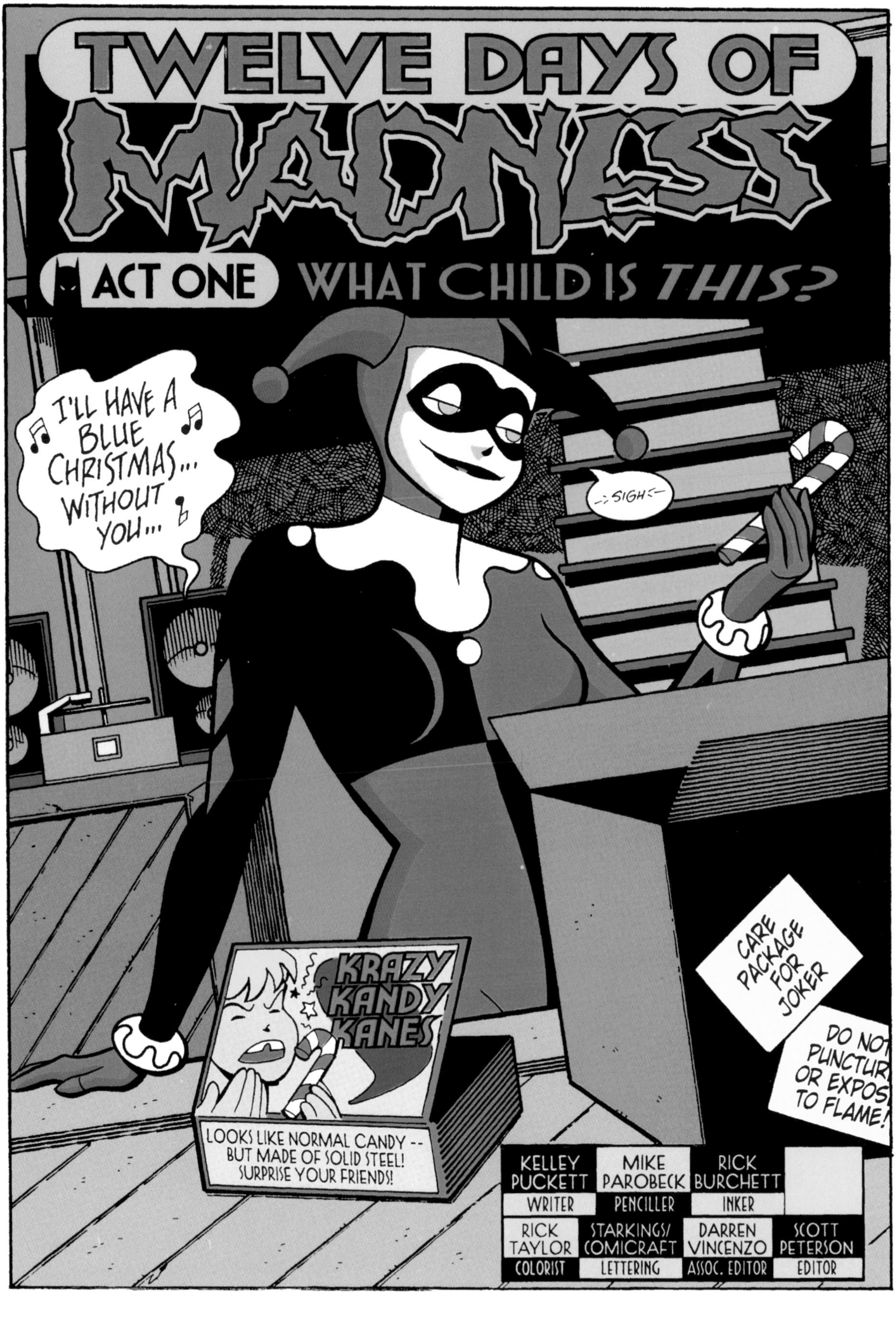

TWELVE DAYS OF MADNESS
ACT ONE WHAT CHILD IS THIS?
I'LL HAVE A BLUE CHRISTMAS... WITHOUT YOU...
SIGH
KRAZY KANDY KANES
LOOKS LIKE NORMAL CANDY -- BUT MADE OF SOLID STEEL! SURPRISE YOUR FRIENDS!
CARE PACKAGE FOR JOKER
DO NOT PUNCTURE OR EXPOSE TO FLAME!
KELLEY PUCKETT WRITER
MIKE PAROBECK PENCILLER
RICK BURCHETT INKER
RICK TAYLOR COLORIST
STARKINGS/ COMICRAFT LETTERING
DARREN VINCENZO ASSOC. EDITOR
SCOTT PETERSON EDITOR

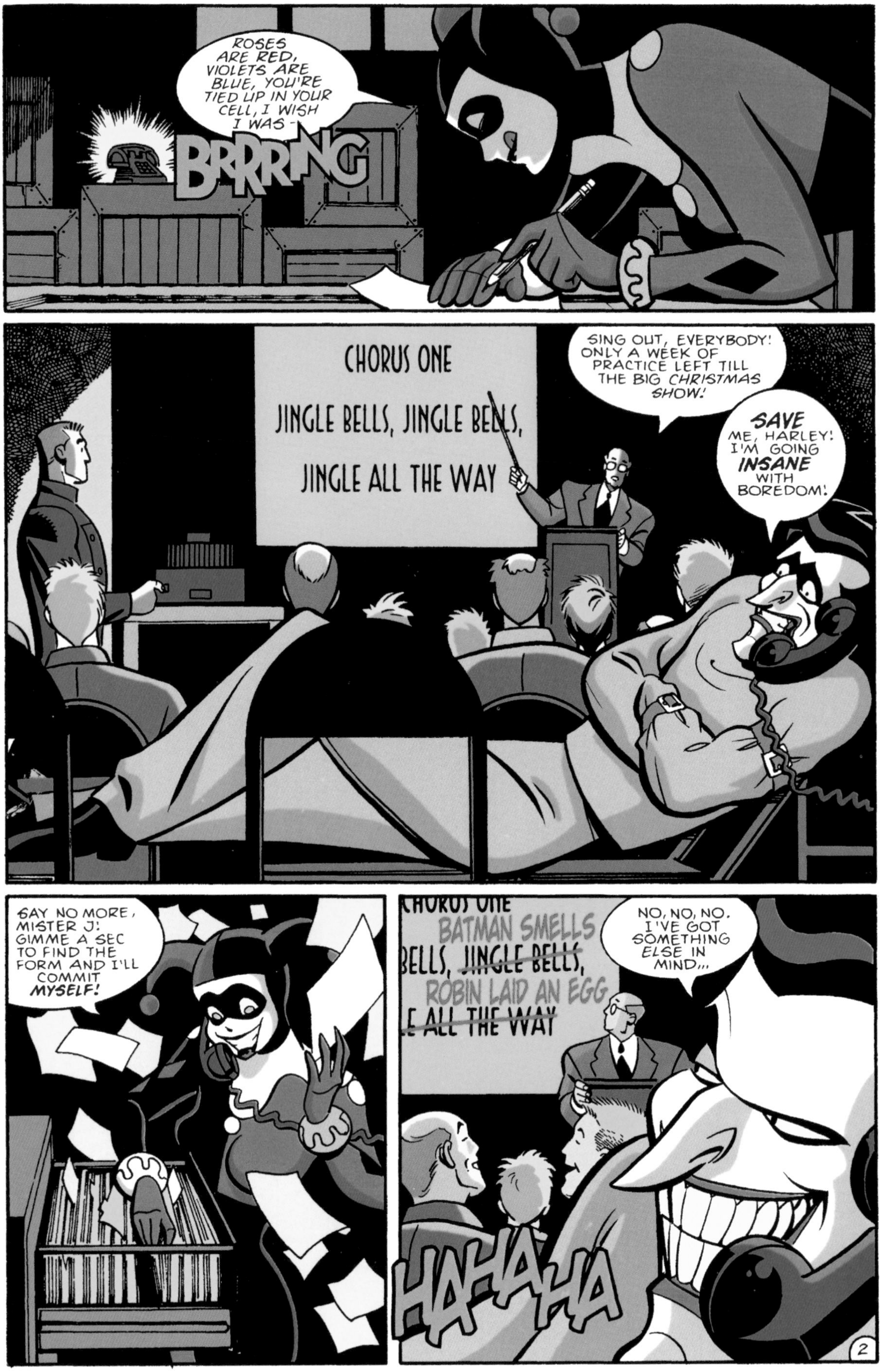
ROSES ARE RED, VIOLETS ARE BLUE, YOU'RE TIED UP IN YOUR CELL, I WISH I WAS -
BRRRING
CHORUS ONE
JINGLE BELLS, JINGLE BELLS,
JINGLE ALL THE WAY
SING OUT, EVERYBODY! ONLY A WEEK OF PRACTICE LEFT TILL THE BIG *CHRISTMAS* SHOW!
SAVE ME, HARLEY! I'M GOING ***INSANE*** WITH BOREDOM!
SAY NO MORE, MISTER J: GIMME A SEC TO FIND THE FORM AND I'LL COMMIT ***MYSELF!***
CHORUS ONE
BATMAN SMELLS
BELLS, JINGLE BELLS,
ROBIN LAID AN EGG
E ALL THE WAY
NO, NO, NO. I'VE GOT SOMETHING *ELSE* IN MIND...
HAHAHAHA
2

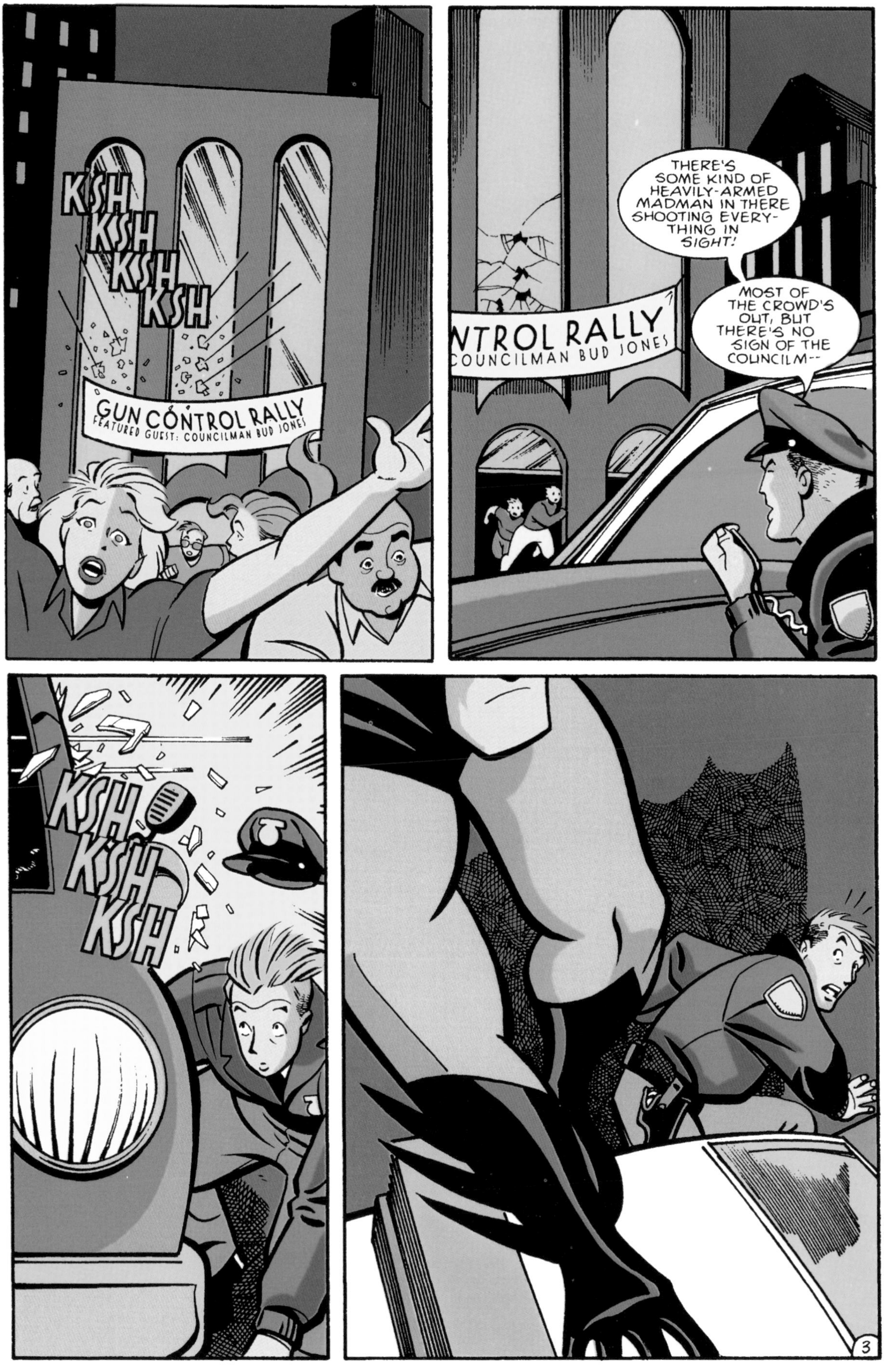
KSH KSH KSH KSH
GUN CONTROL RALLY
FEATURED GUEST: COUNCILMAN BUD JONES
NTROL RALLY
COUNCILMAN BUD JONES
THERE'S SOME KIND OF HEAVILY-ARMED MADMAN IN THERE SHOOTING EVERY-THING IN SIGHT!
MOST OF THE CROWD'S OUT, BUT THERE'S NO SIGN OF THE COUNCILM--
KSH KSH KSH
3

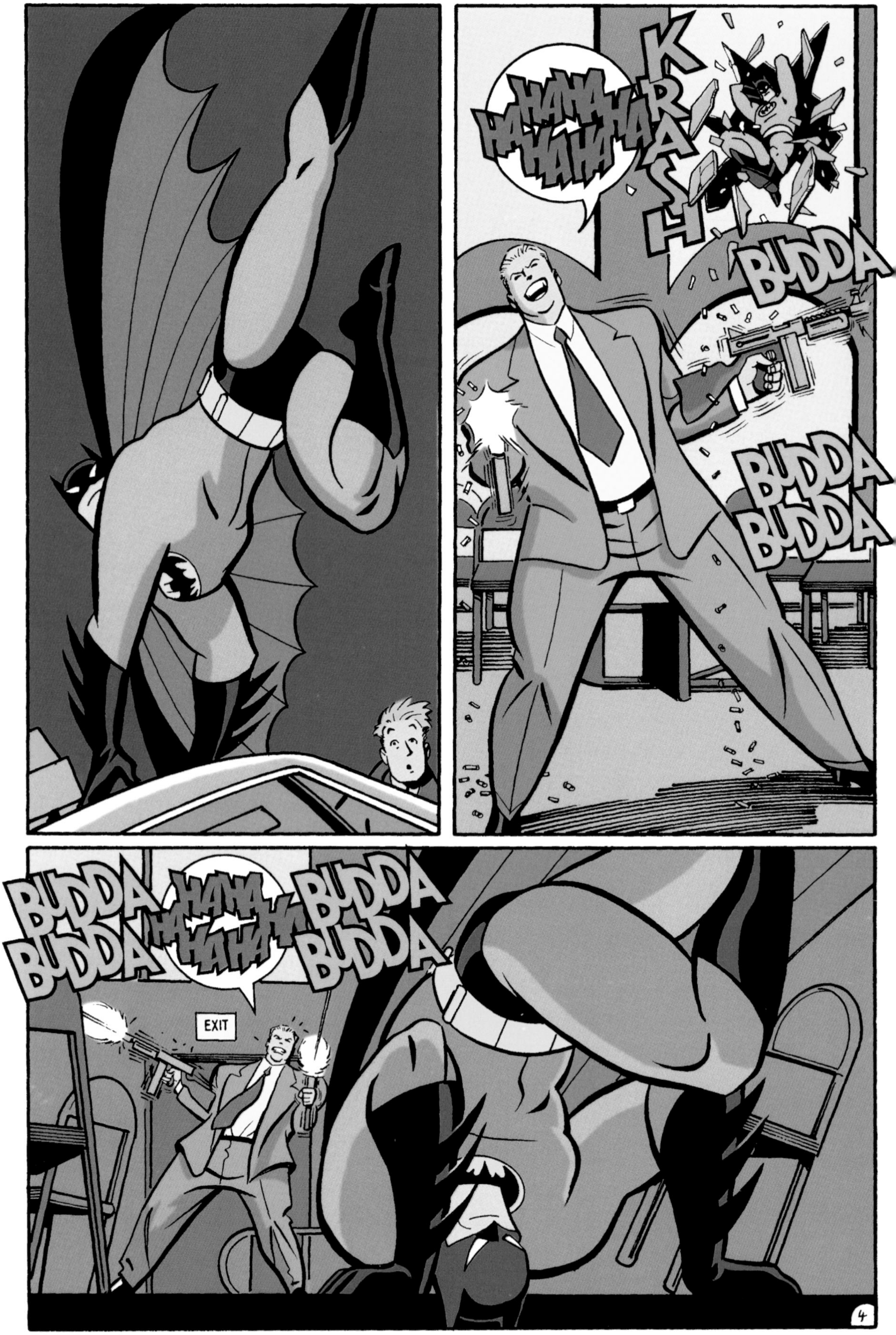
HAHAHAHAHA HAHAHA
KRASH
BUDDA
BUDDA BUDDA
BUDDA BUDDA
HAHAHAHAHA HAHAHA
BUDDA BUDDA
EXIT
4

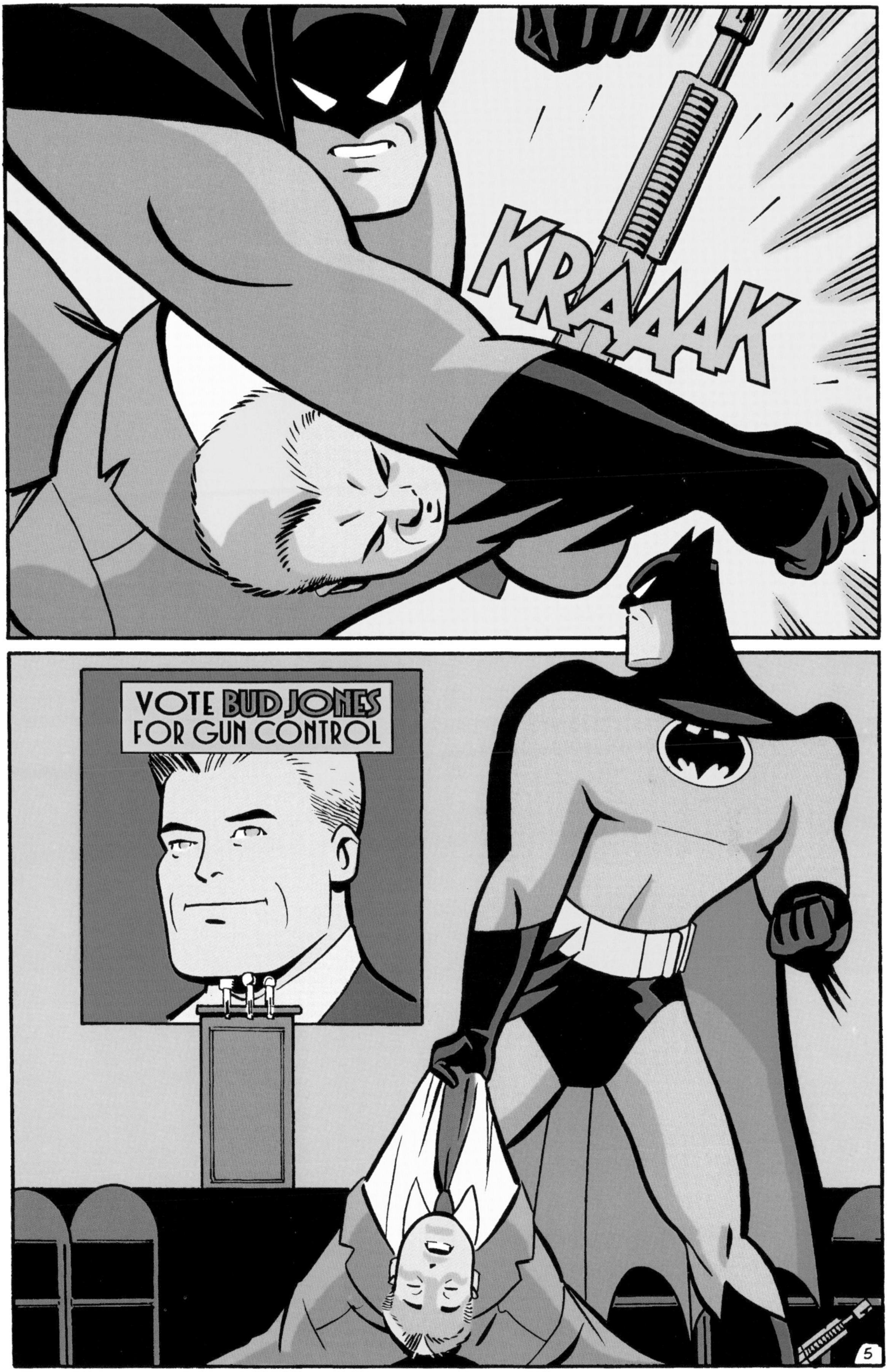
KRAAAK
VOTE BUD JONES
FOR GUN CONTROL
5

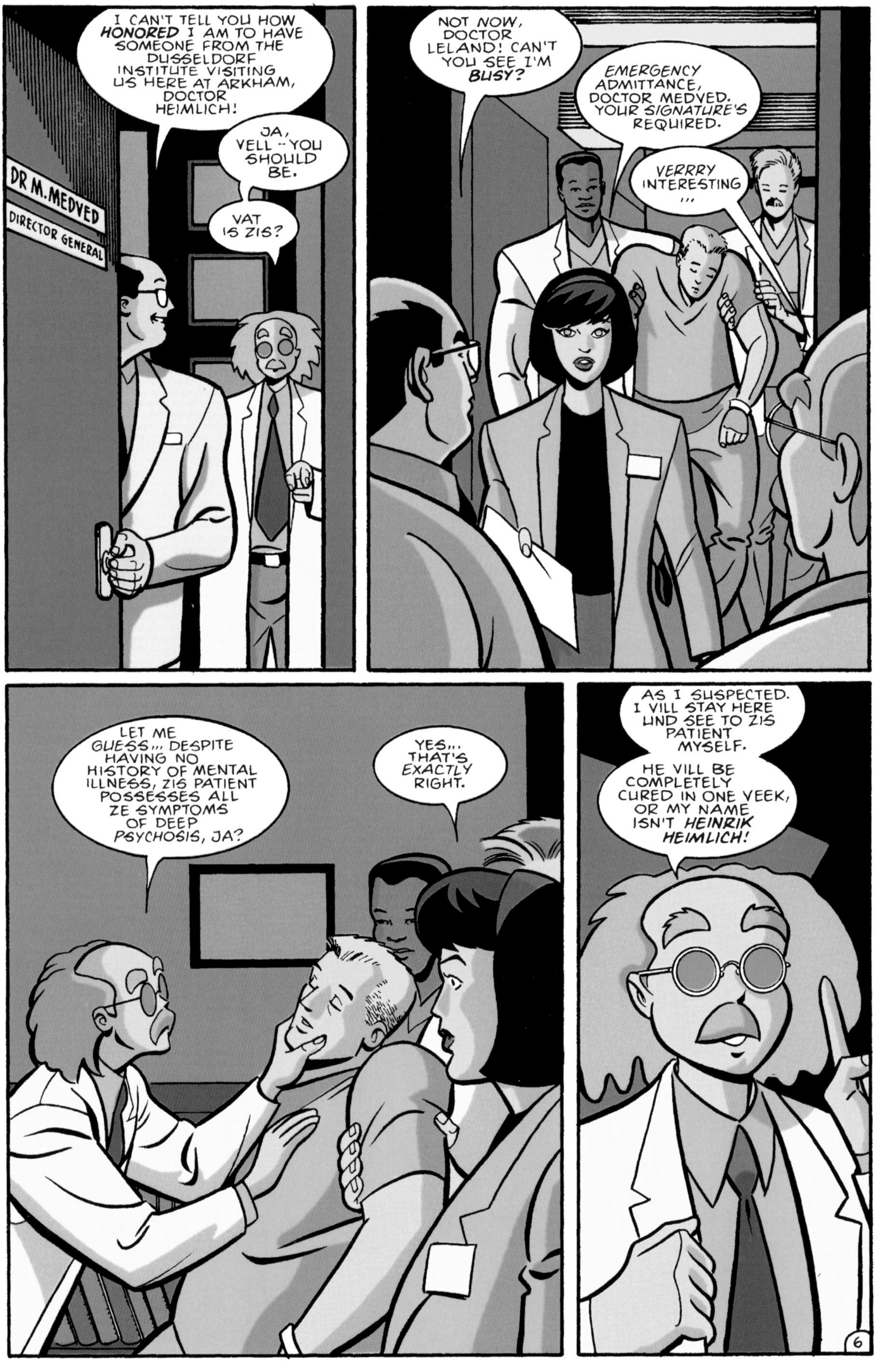
I CAN'T TELL YOU HOW HONORED I AM TO HAVE SOMEONE FROM THE DUSSELDORF INSTITUTE VISITING US HERE AT ARKHAM, DOCTOR HEIMLICH!
JA, VELL -- YOU SHOULD BE.
VAT IS ZIS?
DR M. MEDVED
DIRECTOR GENERAL
NOT NOW, DOCTOR LELAND! CAN'T YOU SEE I'M BUSY?
EMERGENCY ADMITTANCE, DOCTOR MEDVED. YOUR SIGNATURE'S REQUIRED.
VERRRY INTERESTING ...
LET ME GUESS... DESPITE HAVING NO HISTORY OF MENTAL ILLNESS, ZIS PATIENT POSSESSES ALL ZE SYMPTOMS OF DEEP PSYCHOSIS, JA?
YES... THAT'S EXACTLY RIGHT.
AS I SUSPECTED. I VILL STAY HERE UND SEE TO ZIS PATIENT MYSELF.
HE VILL BE COMPLETELY CURED IN ONE VEEK, OR MY NAME ISN'T HEINRIK HEIMLICH!
6

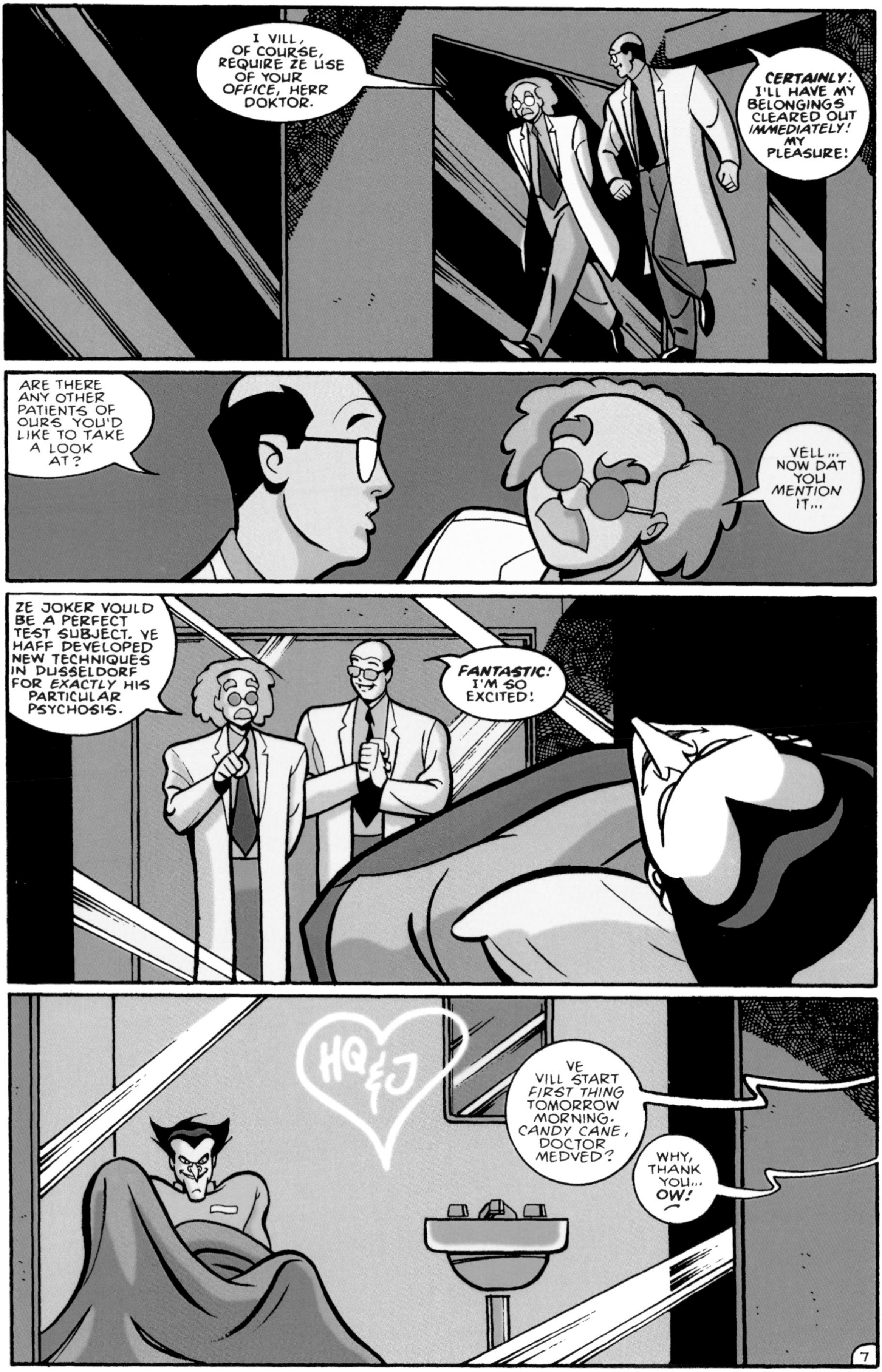

I VILL, OF COURSE, REQUIRE ZE USE OF YOUR OFFICE, HERR DOKTOR.
CERTAINLY! I'LL HAVE MY BELONGINGS CLEARED OUT IMMEDIATELY! MY PLEASURE!
ARE THERE ANY OTHER PATIENTS OF OURS YOU'D LIKE TO TAKE A LOOK AT?
VELL... NOW DAT YOU MENTION IT...
ZE JOKER VOULD BE A PERFECT TEST SUBJECT. VE HAFF DEVELOPED NEW TECHNIQUES IN DUSSELDORF FOR EXACTLY HIS PARTICULAR PSYCHOSIS.
FANTASTIC! I'M SO EXCITED!
HQ&J
VE VILL START FIRST THING TOMORROW MORNING. CANDY CANE, DOCTOR MEDVED?
WHY, THANK YOU... OW!
7

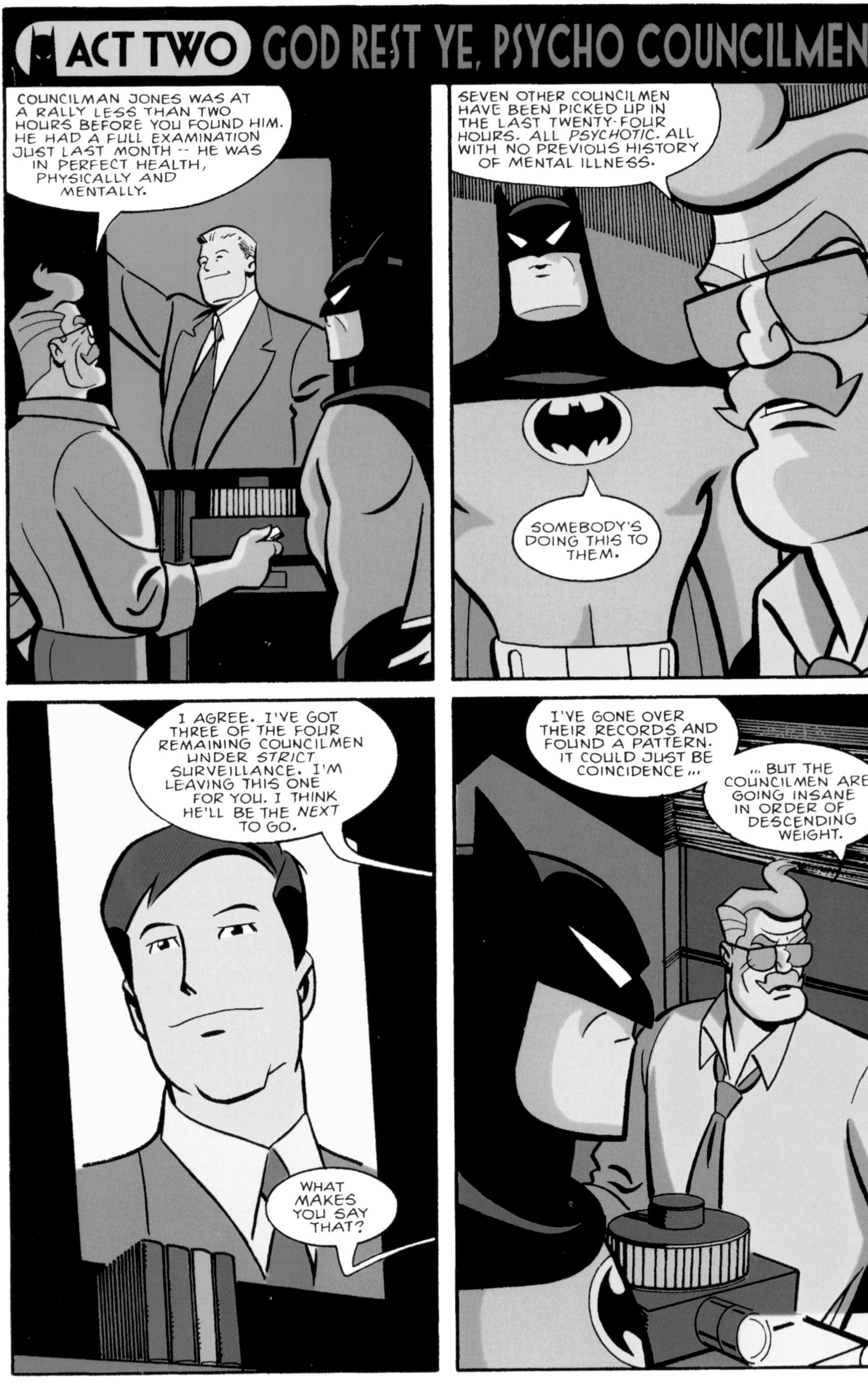

ACT TWO GOD REST YE, PSYCHO COUNCILMEN
COUNCILMAN JONES WAS AT A RALLY LESS THAN TWO HOURS BEFORE YOU FOUND HIM. HE HAD A FULL EXAMINATION JUST LAST MONTH -- HE WAS IN PERFECT HEALTH, PHYSICALLY AND MENTALLY.
SEVEN OTHER COUNCILMEN HAVE BEEN PICKED UP IN THE LAST TWENTY-FOUR HOURS. ALL PSYCHOTIC. ALL WITH NO PREVIOUS HISTORY OF MENTAL ILLNESS.
SOMEBODY'S DOING THIS TO THEM.
I AGREE. I'VE GOT THREE OF THE FOUR REMAINING COUNCILMEN UNDER STRICT SURVEILLANCE. I'M LEAVING THIS ONE FOR YOU. I THINK HE'LL BE THE NEXT TO GO.
WHAT MAKES YOU SAY THAT?
I'VE GONE OVER THEIR RECORDS AND FOUND A PATTERN. IT COULD JUST BE COINCIDENCE...
... BUT THE COUNCILMEN ARE GOING INSANE IN ORDER OF DESCENDING WEIGHT.
8

PEOPLE, **PEOPLE!**

WE'RE *FOUR* DAYS AWAY FROM OPENING NIGHT!

YOU FOUR ON THE BOTTOM SHOULD HAVE THIS *DOWN* BY NOW!

REALLY, DOCTOR MEDVED. THESE PATIENTS NEED *COUNSELING*, NOT REHEARSALS.

BUT JUST LOOK AT HOW *MOTIVATED* THEY ARE. I DON'T PRETEND TO UNDERSTAND DOCTOR HEIMLICH'S METHODS, BUT YOU CAN'T ARGUE WITH HIS RESULTS!

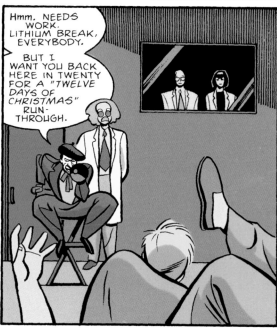

Hmm. NEEDS WORK. LITHIUM BREAK, EVERYBODY.

BUT I WANT YOU BACK HERE IN TWENTY FOR A *"TWELVE DAYS OF CHRISTMAS"* RUN-THROUGH.

THAT'S *FULL DRESS*, PEOPLE! PRACTICE YOUR KICK-TURNS!

YOU'RE DOING JUST GREAT, PUDDIN'. YOU'LL KNOCK 'EM DEAD.

WELL ... THAT GOES WITHOUT SAYING, DOESN'T IT?

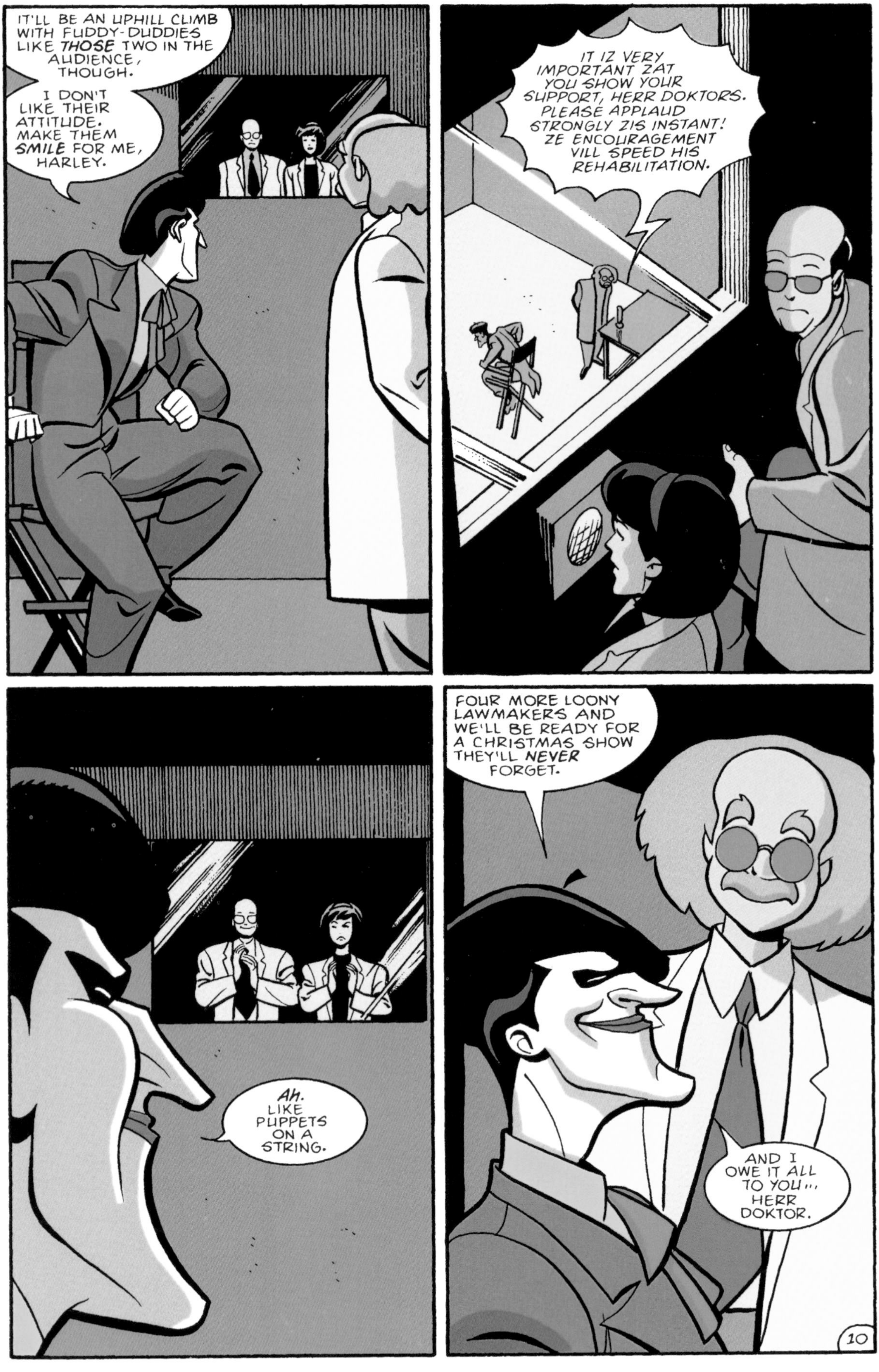
IT'LL BE AN UPHILL CLIMB WITH FUDDY-DUDDIES LIKE THOSE TWO IN THE AUDIENCE, THOUGH.
I DON'T LIKE THEIR ATTITUDE. MAKE THEM SMILE FOR ME, HARLEY.
IT IZ VERY IMPORTANT ZAT YOU SHOW YOUR SUPPORT, HERR DOKTORS. PLEASE APPLAUD STRONGLY ZIS INSTANT! ZE ENCOURAGEMENT VILL SPEED HIS REHABILITATION.
AH. LIKE PUPPETS ON A STRING.
FOUR MORE LOONY LAWMAKERS AND WE'LL BE READY FOR A CHRISTMAS SHOW THEY'LL NEVER FORGET.
AND I OWE IT ALL TO YOU... HERR DOKTOR.
10

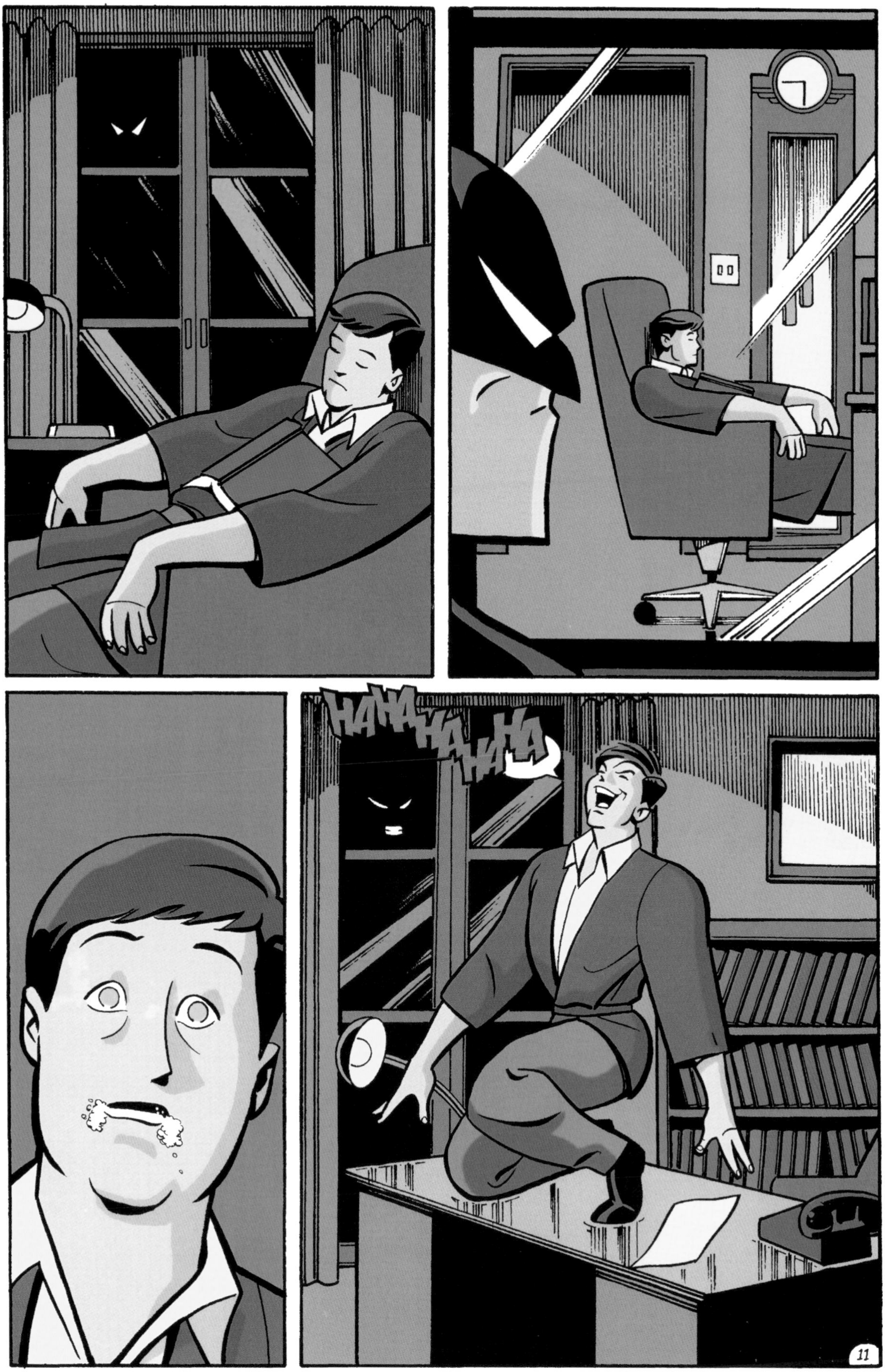
HA HA HA HA HA HA
11

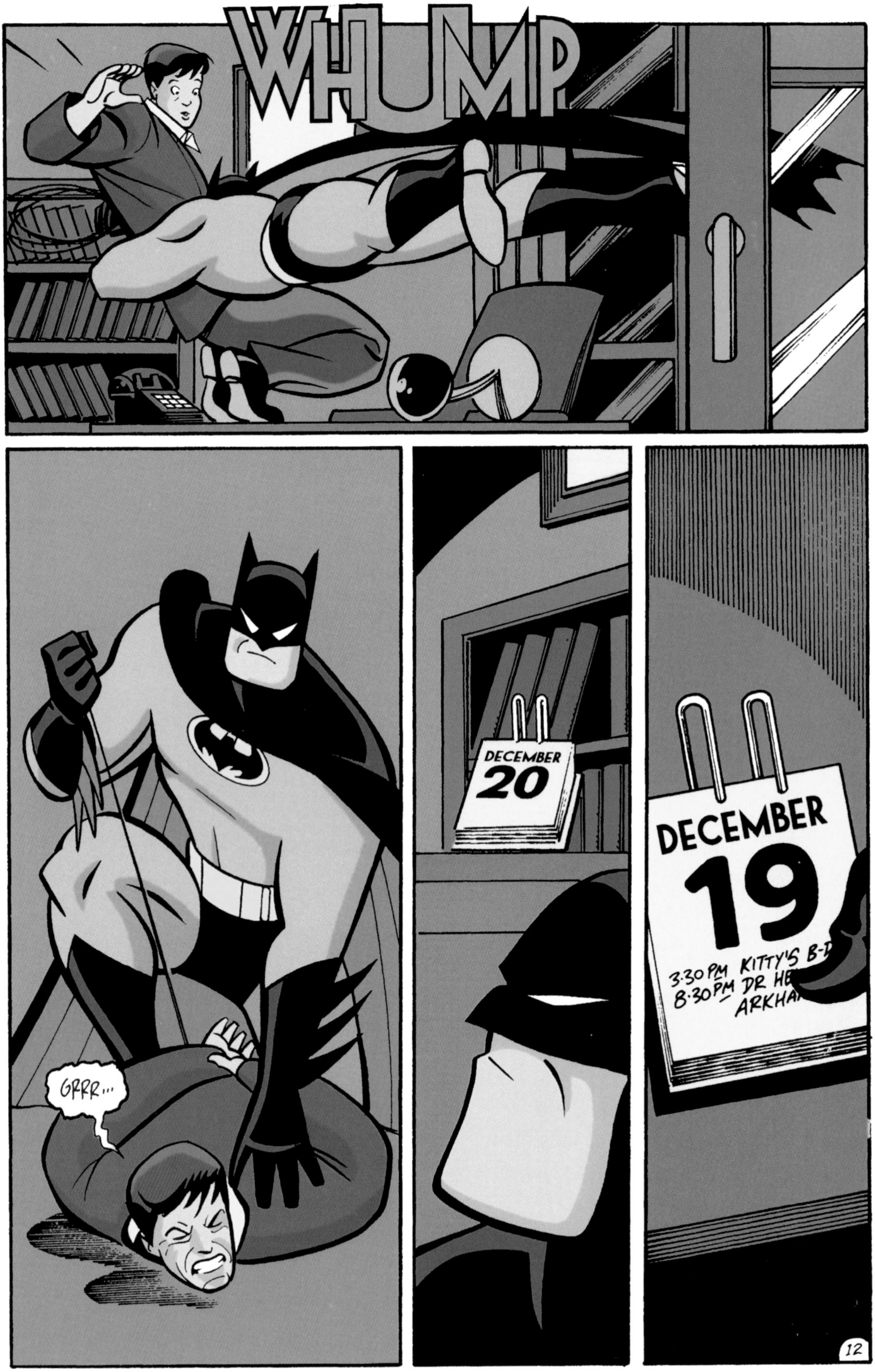
WHUMP
GRRR...
DECEMBER
20
DECEMBER
19
3:30 PM KITTY'S B-D
8:30 PM DR HE
ARKHA
12

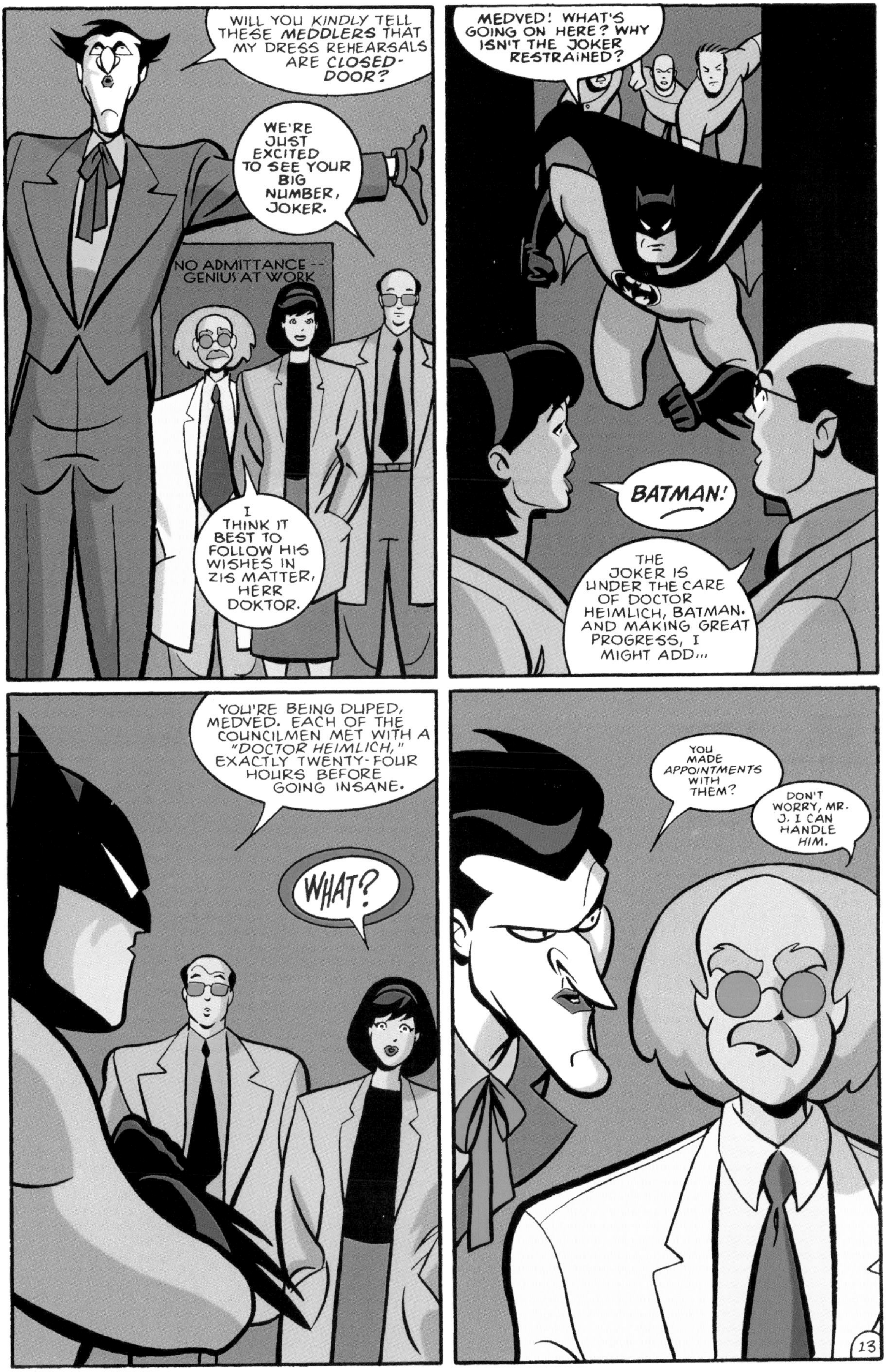
WILL YOU KINDLY TELL THESE MEDDLERS THAT MY DRESS REHEARSALS ARE CLOSED-DOOR?
WE'RE JUST EXCITED TO SEE YOUR BIG NUMBER, JOKER.
NO ADMITTANCE -- GENIUS AT WORK
I THINK IT BEST TO FOLLOW HIS WISHES IN ZIS MATTER, HERR DOKTOR.
MEDVED! WHAT'S GOING ON HERE? WHY ISN'T THE JOKER RESTRAINED?
BATMAN!
THE JOKER IS UNDER THE CARE OF DOCTOR HEIMLICH, BATMAN. AND MAKING GREAT PROGRESS, I MIGHT ADD...
YOU'RE BEING DUPED, MEDVED. EACH OF THE COUNCILMEN MET WITH A "DOCTOR HEIMLICH," EXACTLY TWENTY-FOUR HOURS BEFORE GOING INSANE.
WHAT?
YOU MADE APPOINTMENTS WITH THEM?
DON'T WORRY, MR. J. I CAN HANDLE HIM.
13

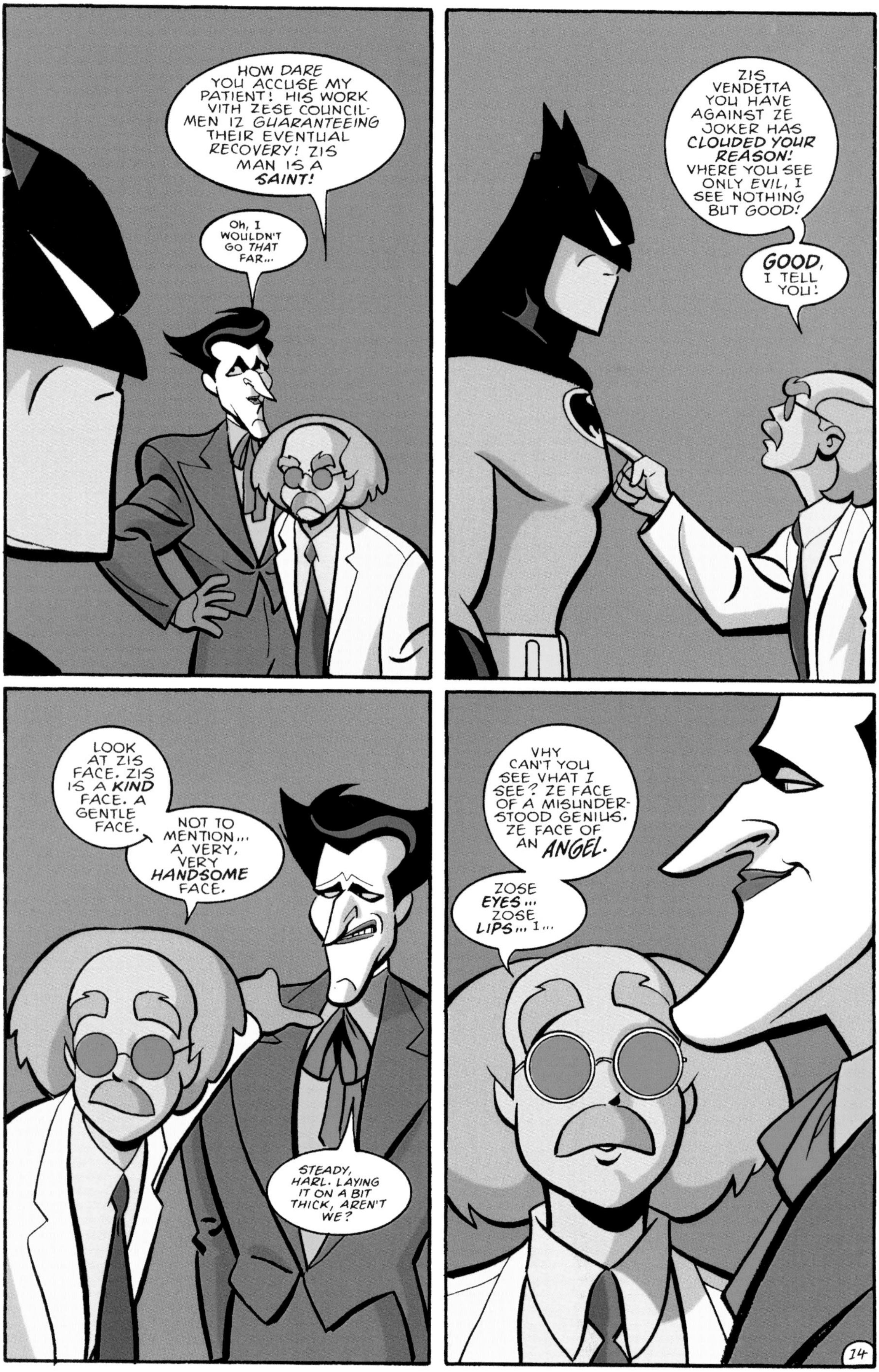
HOW DARE YOU ACCUSE MY PATIENT! HIS WORK VITH ZESE COUNCILMEN IZ GUARANTEEING THEIR EVENTUAL RECOVERY! ZIS MAN IS A SAINT!
Oh, I WOULDN'T GO THAT FAR...
ZIS VENDETTA YOU HAVE AGAINST ZE JOKER HAS CLOUDED YOUR REASON! VHERE YOU SEE ONLY EVIL, I SEE NOTHING BUT GOOD!
GOOD, I TELL YOU!
LOOK AT ZIS FACE. ZIS IS A KIND FACE. A GENTLE FACE.
NOT TO MENTION... A VERY, VERY HANDSOME FACE.
STEADY, HARL. LAYING IT ON A BIT THICK, AREN'T WE?
VHY CAN'T YOU SEE VHAT I SEE? ZE FACE OF A MISUNDERSTOOD GENIUS. ZE FACE OF AN ANGEL.
ZOSE EYES... ZOSE LIPS... I...
14

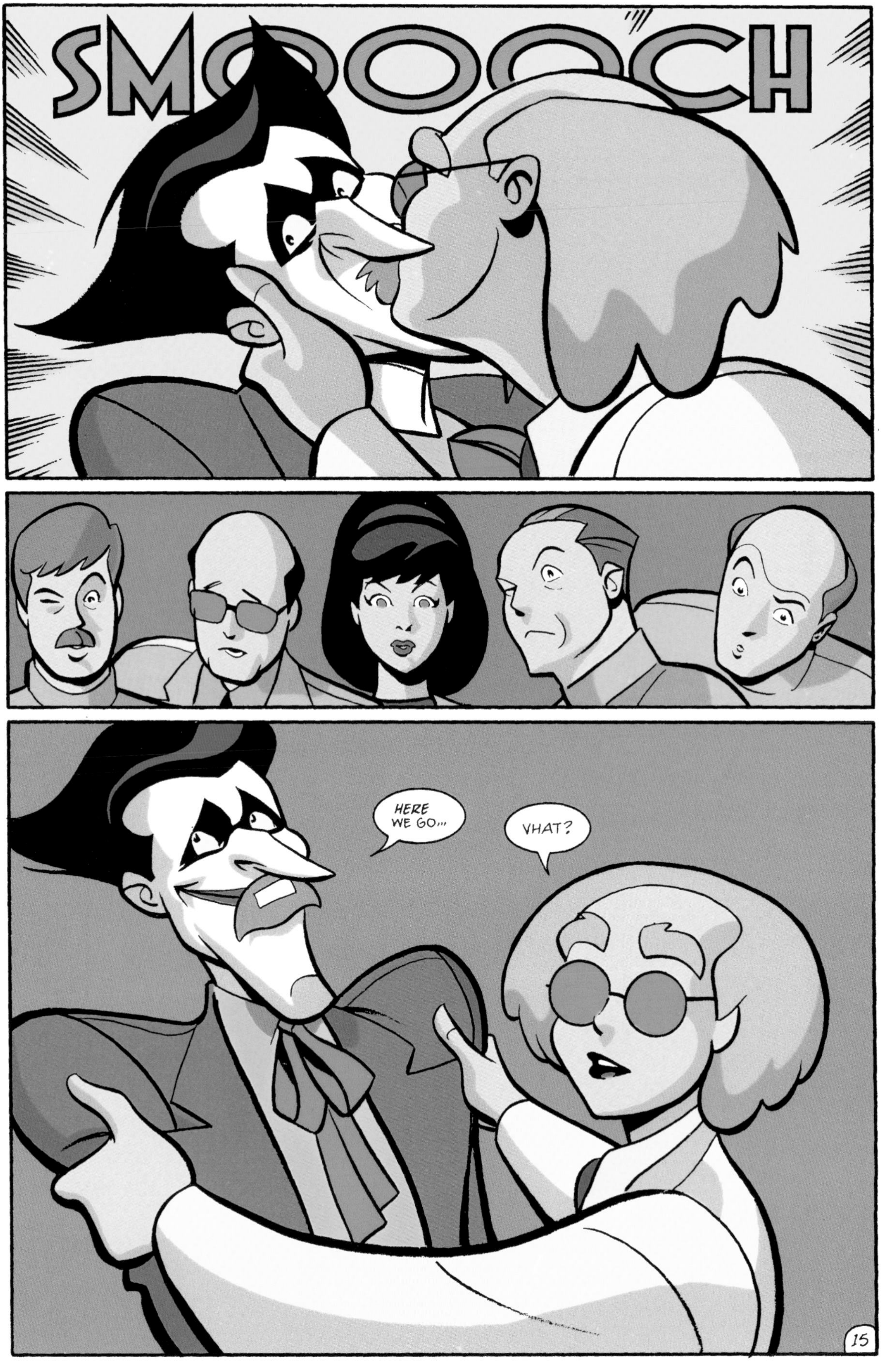
SMOOOCH
HERE WE GO...
VHAT?
15

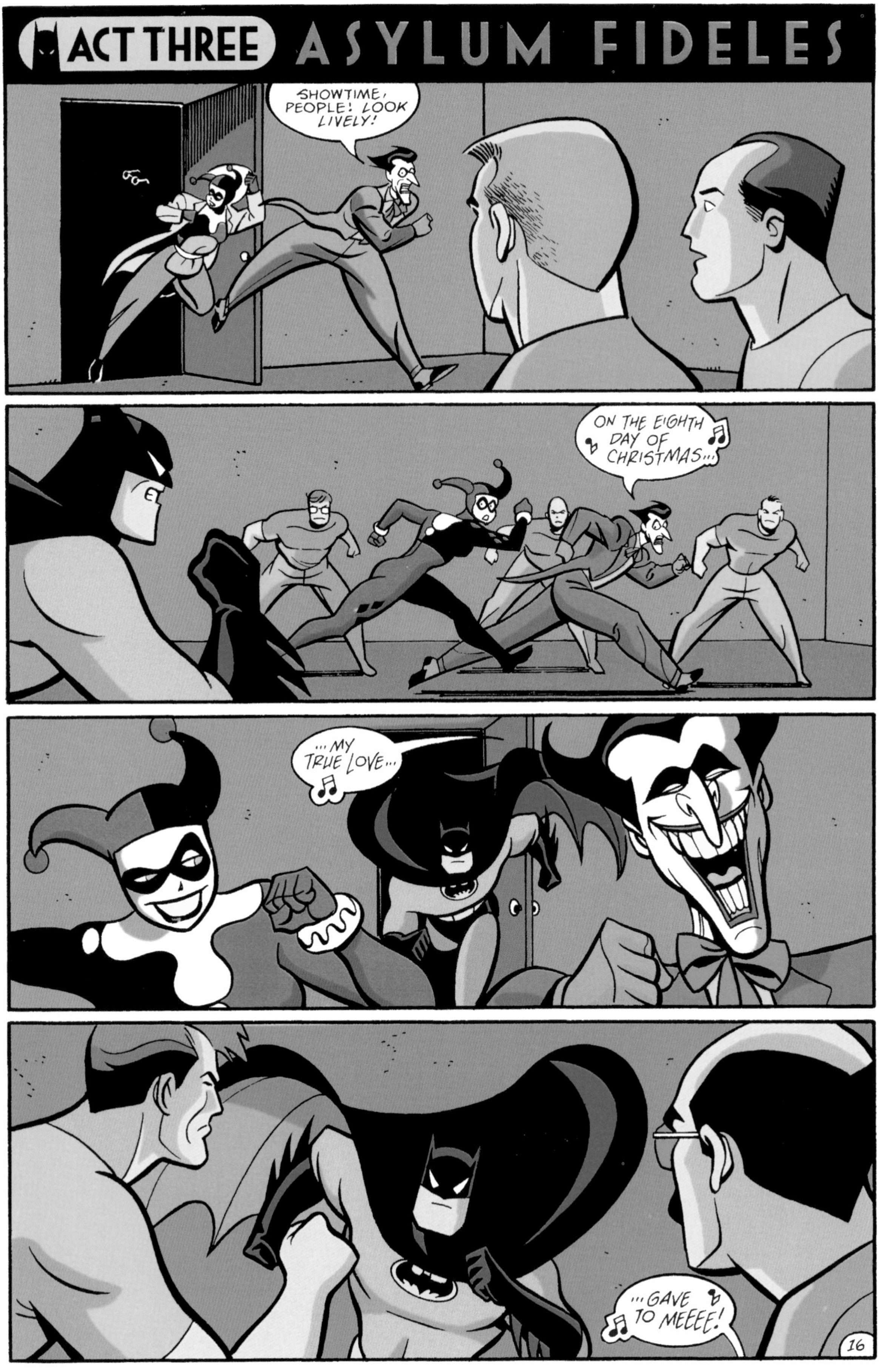
ACT THREE
ASYLUM FIDELES
SHOWTIME, PEOPLE! LOOK LIVELY!
ON THE EIGHTH DAY OF CHRISTMAS...
...MY TRUE LOVE...
...GAVE TO MEEEE!
16

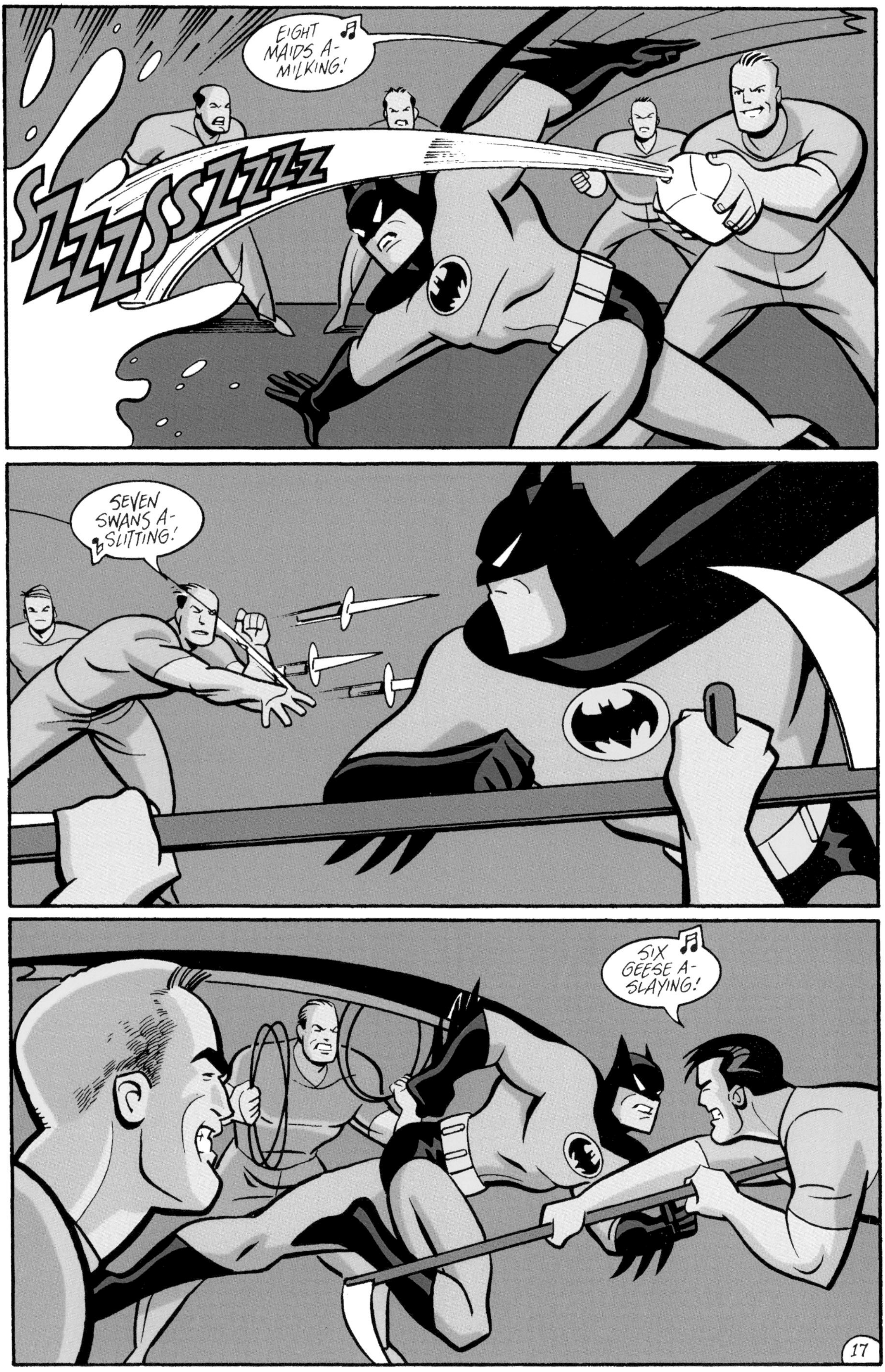
EIGHT MAIDS A-MILKING!
SZZZSSZZZZ
SEVEN SWANS A-SLITTING!
SIX GEESE A-SLAYING!
17

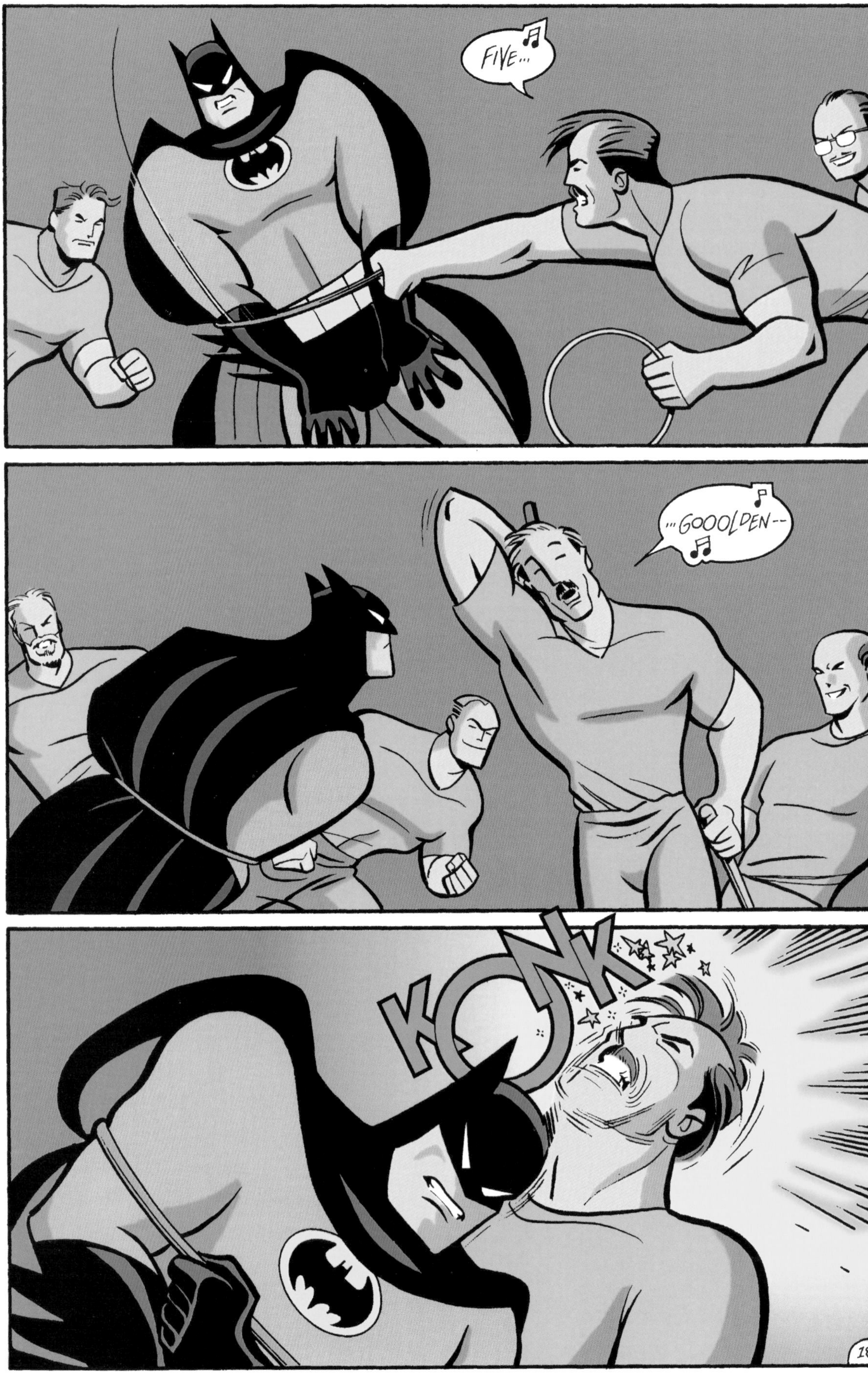
FIVE...
...GOOOLDEN--
KONK
18

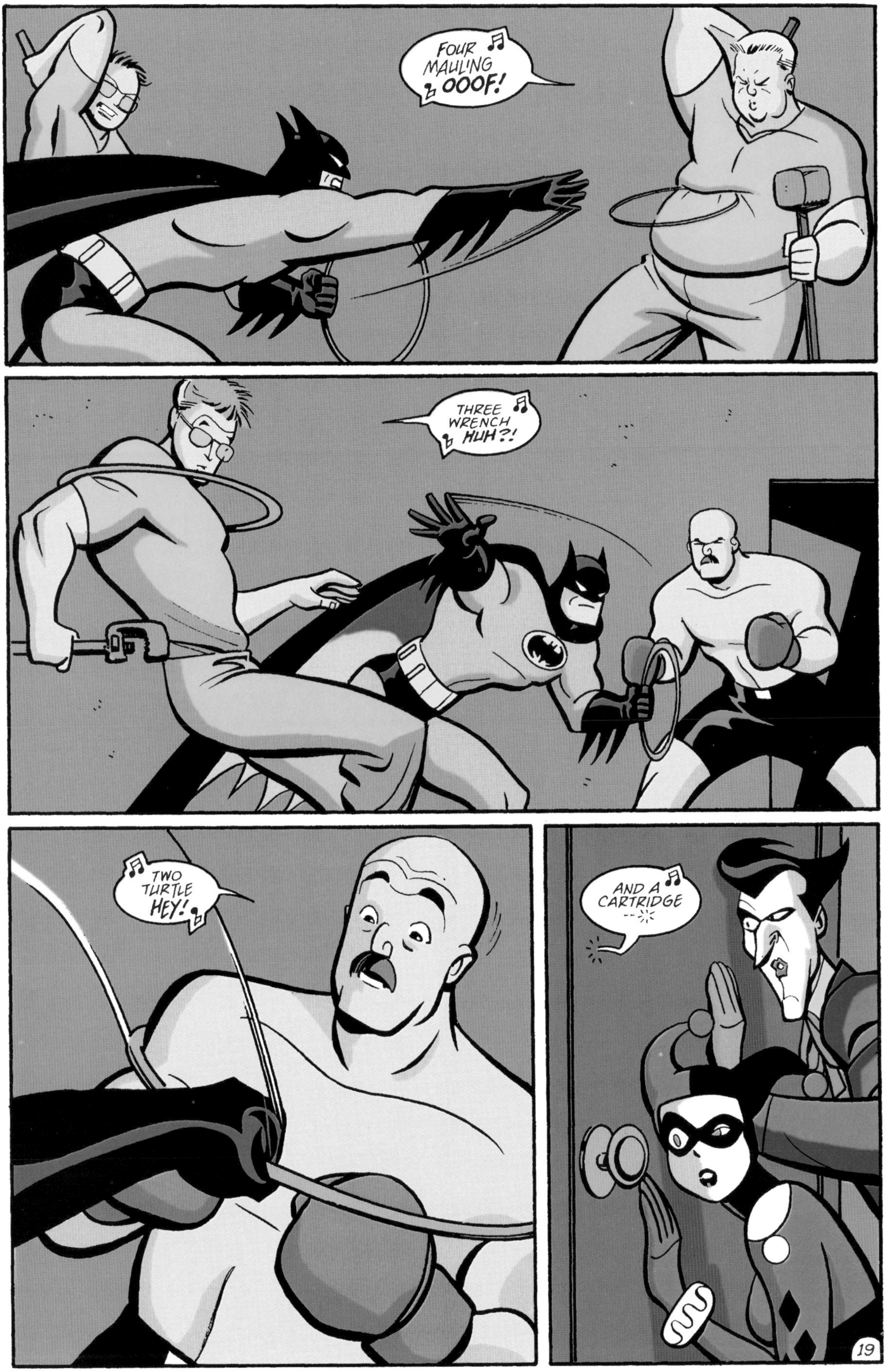
FOUR MAULING OOOF!
THREE WRENCH HUH?!
TWO TURTLE HEY!
AND A CARTRIDGE
19

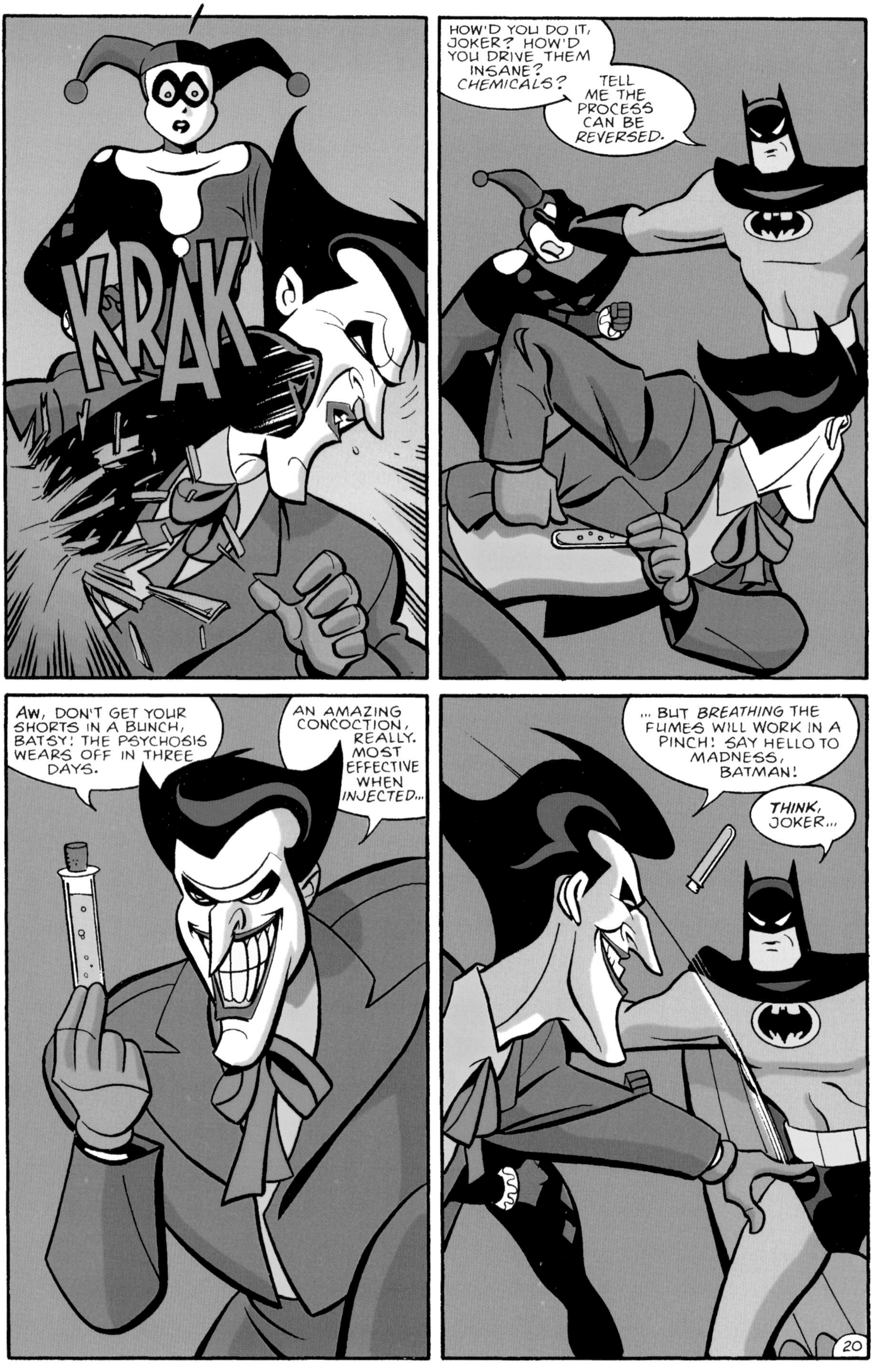
KRAK
HOW'D YOU DO IT, JOKER? HOW'D YOU DRIVE THEM INSANE? CHEMICALS?
TELL ME THE PROCESS CAN BE REVERSED.
AW, DON'T GET YOUR SHORTS IN A BUNCH, BATSY: THE PSYCHOSIS WEARS OFF IN THREE DAYS.
AN AMAZING CONCOCTION, REALLY. MOST EFFECTIVE WHEN INJECTED...
... BUT BREATHING THE FUMES WILL WORK IN A PINCH! SAY HELLO TO MADNESS, BATMAN!
THINK, JOKER...
20

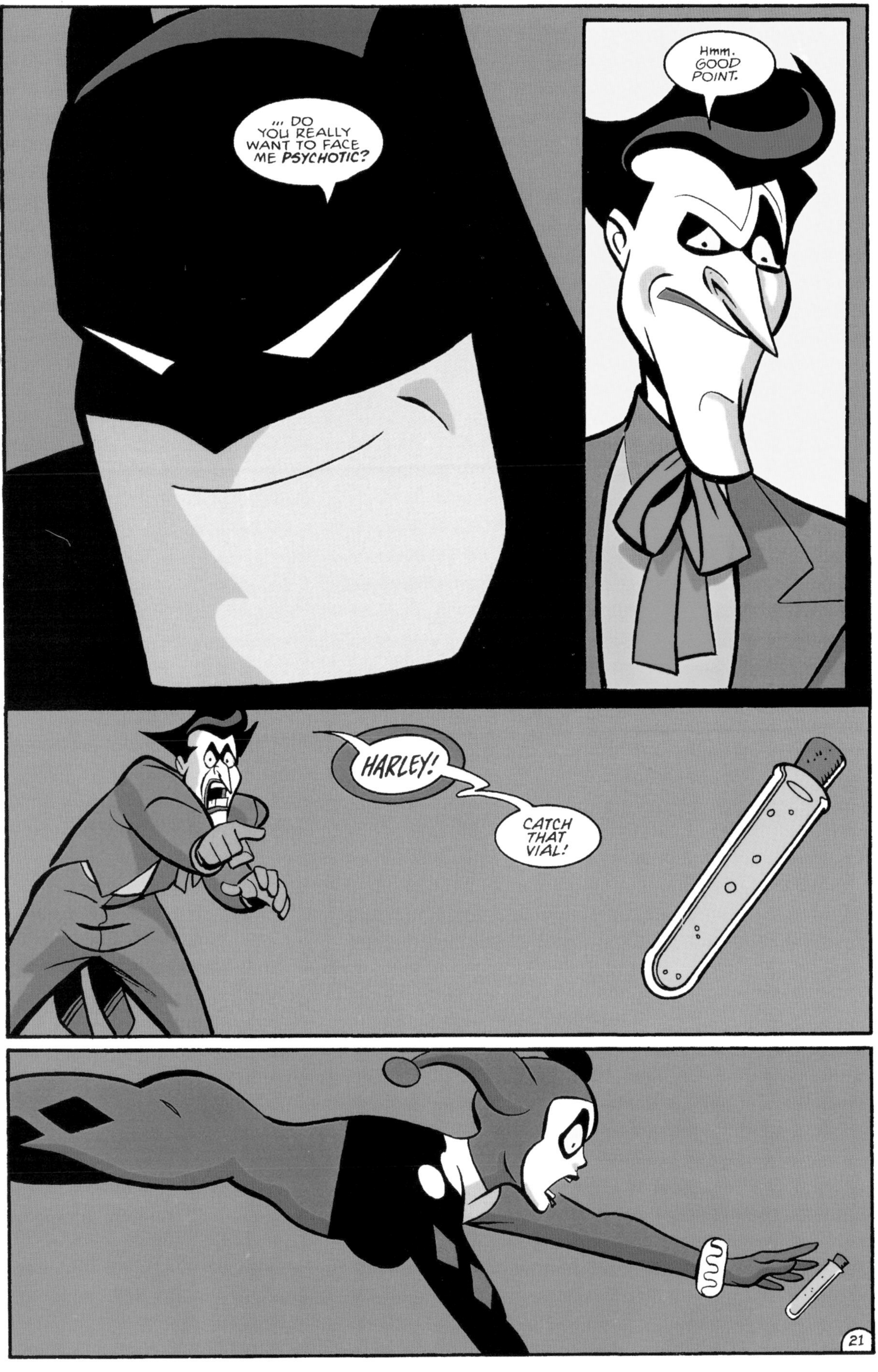
... DO YOU REALLY WANT TO FACE ME PSYCHOTIC?
Hmm. GOOD POINT.
HARLEY!
CATCH THAT VIAL!
21

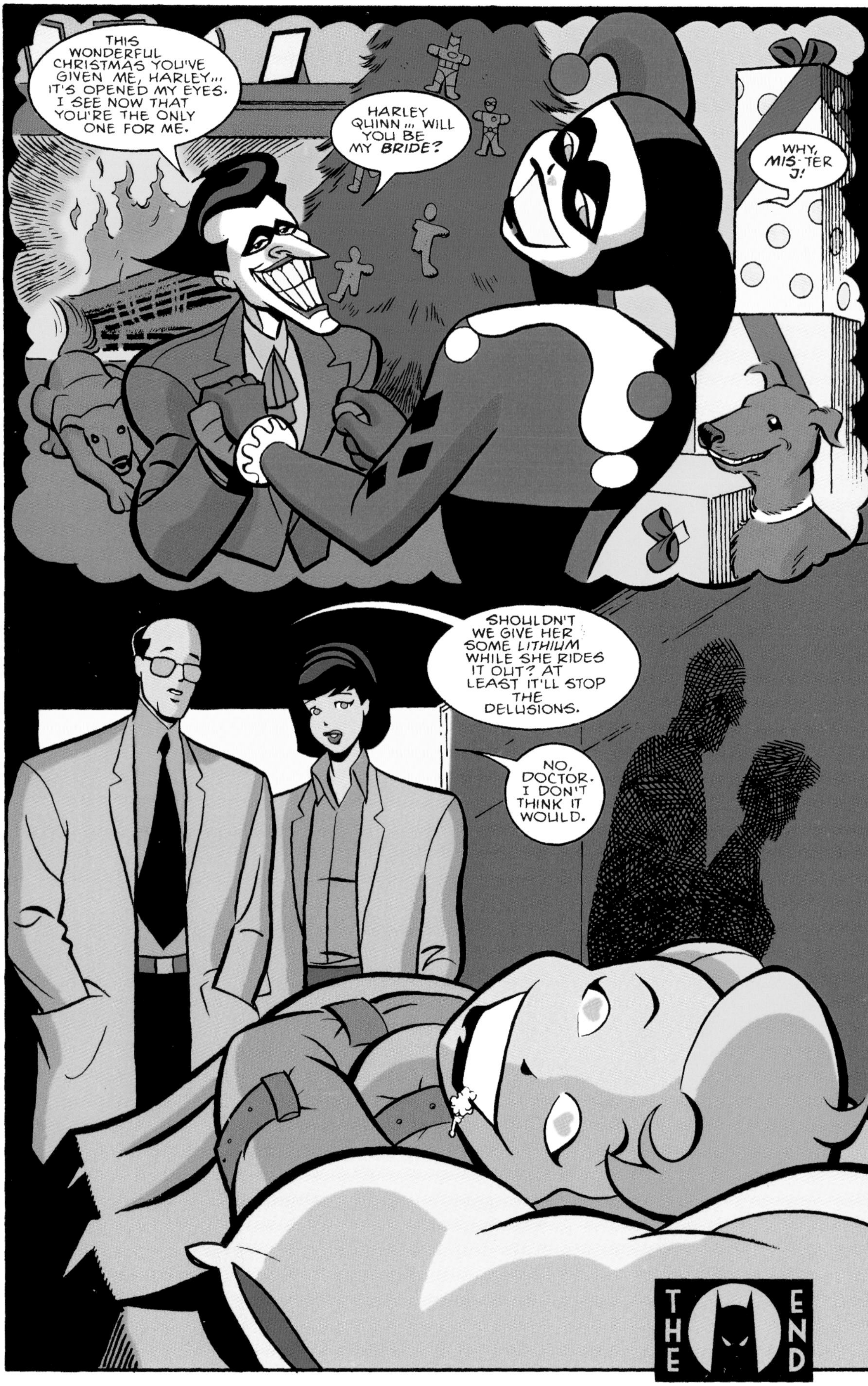

THIS WONDERFUL CHRISTMAS YOU'VE GIVEN ME, HARLEY... IT'S OPENED MY EYES. I SEE NOW THAT YOU'RE THE ONLY ONE FOR ME.
HARLEY QUINN... WILL YOU BE MY BRIDE?
WHY, MIS-TER J!
SHOULDN'T WE GIVE HER SOME LITHIUM WHILE SHE RIDES IT OUT? AT LEAST IT'LL STOP THE DELUSIONS.
NO, DOCTOR. I DON'T THINK IT WOULD.
THE END

HOLIDAY SPECIAL
THE
BATMAN
ADVENTURES
$2.95 US
$4.25 CAN
£2 UK
DINI
TIMM
ALTIERI
MURAKAMI
RIBA
B.T.

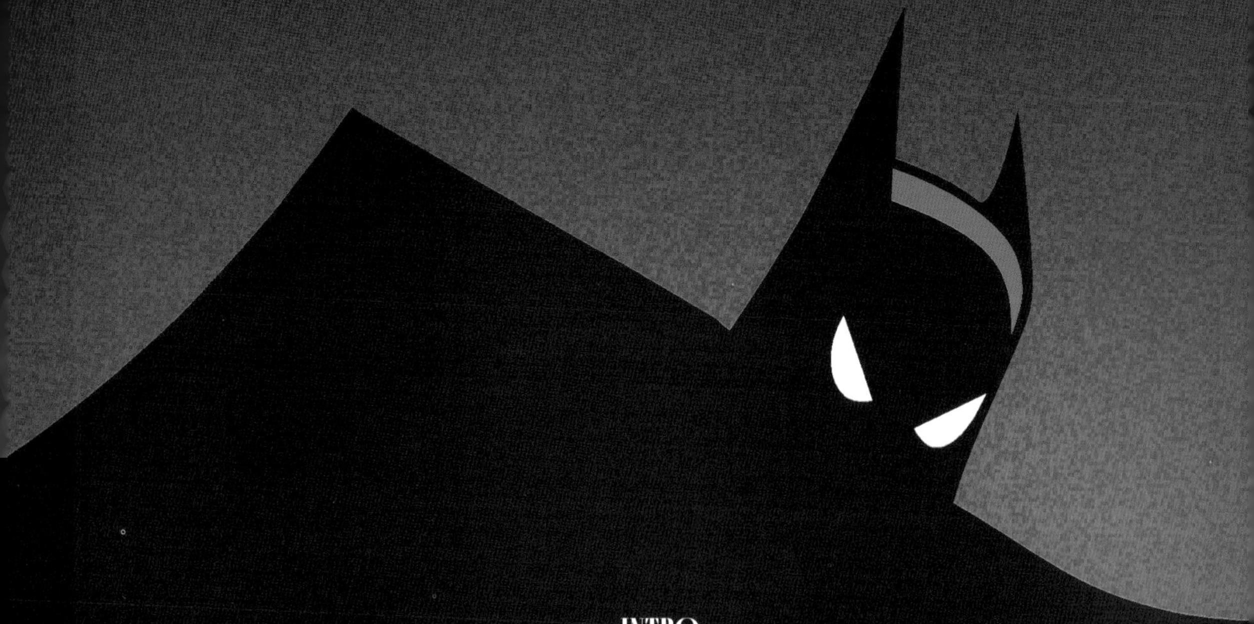

INTRO
written by PAUL DINI
art by DAN RIBA
colored by BRUCE TIMM
lettered by RICHARD STARKINGS/COMICRAFT

"JOLLY OL' ST. NICHOLAS"
written by PAUL DINI and BRUCE TIMM
art and color by BRUCE TIMM
lettered by RICHARD STARKINGS/COMICRAFT

"THE HARLEY AND THE IVY"
story by PAUL DINI and RONNIE DEL CARMEN
written by PAUL DINI
art and color by RONNIE DEL CARMEN
lettered by RICHARD STARKINGS/COMICRAFT

"WHITE CHRISTMAS"
written by PAUL DINI
art and color by GLEN MURAKAMI
lettered by RICHARD STARKINGS/COMICRAFT

"WHAT ARE YOU DOING NEW YEAR'S EVE?"
story by PAUL DINI and BRUCE TIMM
written by PAUL DINI
art by KEVIN ALTIERI and BUTCH LUKIC
colored by GLEN MURAKAMI
lettered by RICHARD STARKINGS/COMICRAFT

"SHOULD OLD ACQUAINTANCE BE FORGOT"
written by PAUL DINI
art by DAN RIBA
colored by BRUCE TIMM
lettered by RICHARD STARKINGS/COMICRAFT

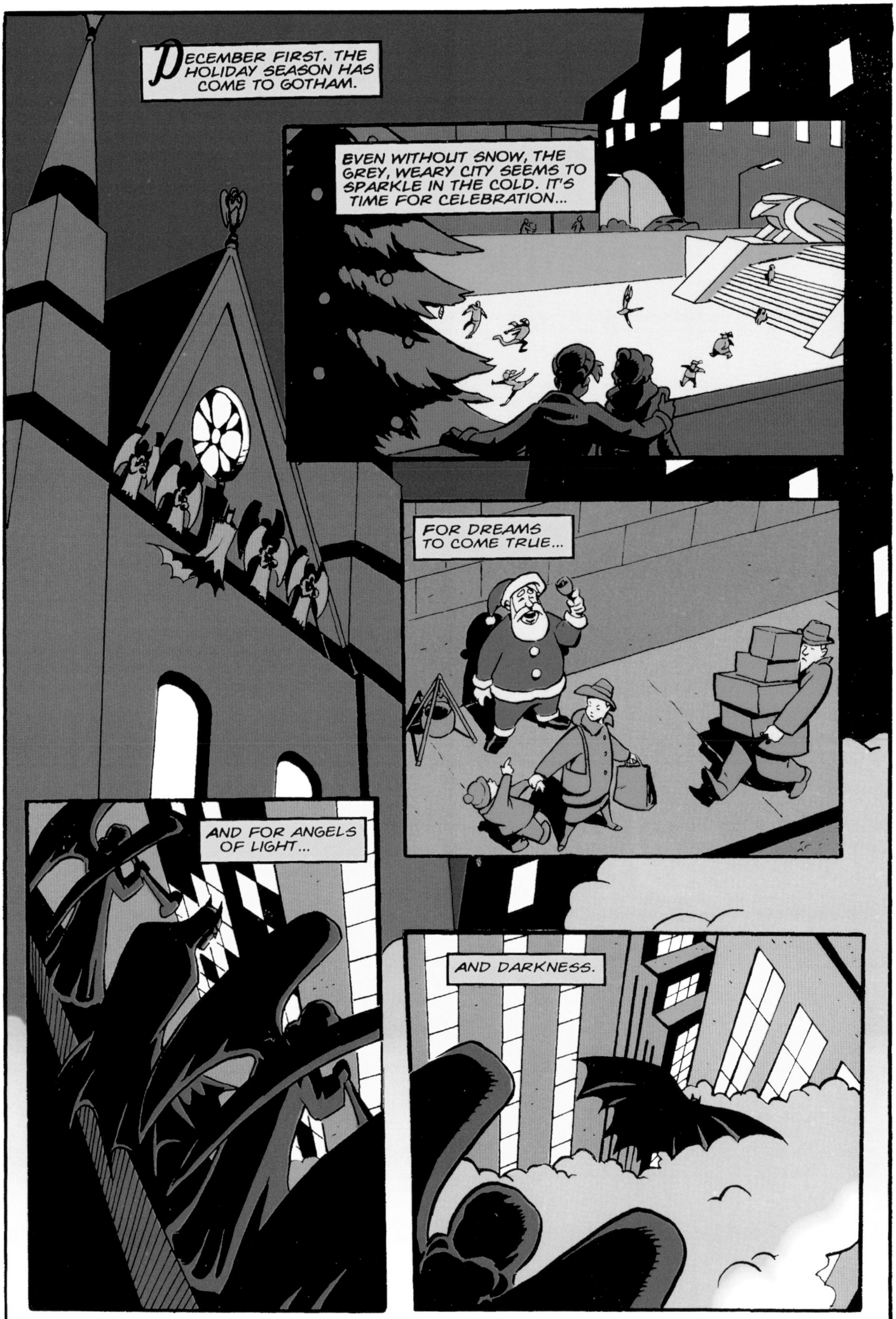
DECEMBER FIRST. THE HOLIDAY SEASON HAS COME TO GOTHAM.
EVEN WITHOUT SNOW, THE GREY, WEARY CITY SEEMS TO SPARKLE IN THE COLD. IT'S TIME FOR CELEBRATION...
FOR DREAMS TO COME TRUE...
AND FOR ANGELS OF LIGHT...
AND DARKNESS.

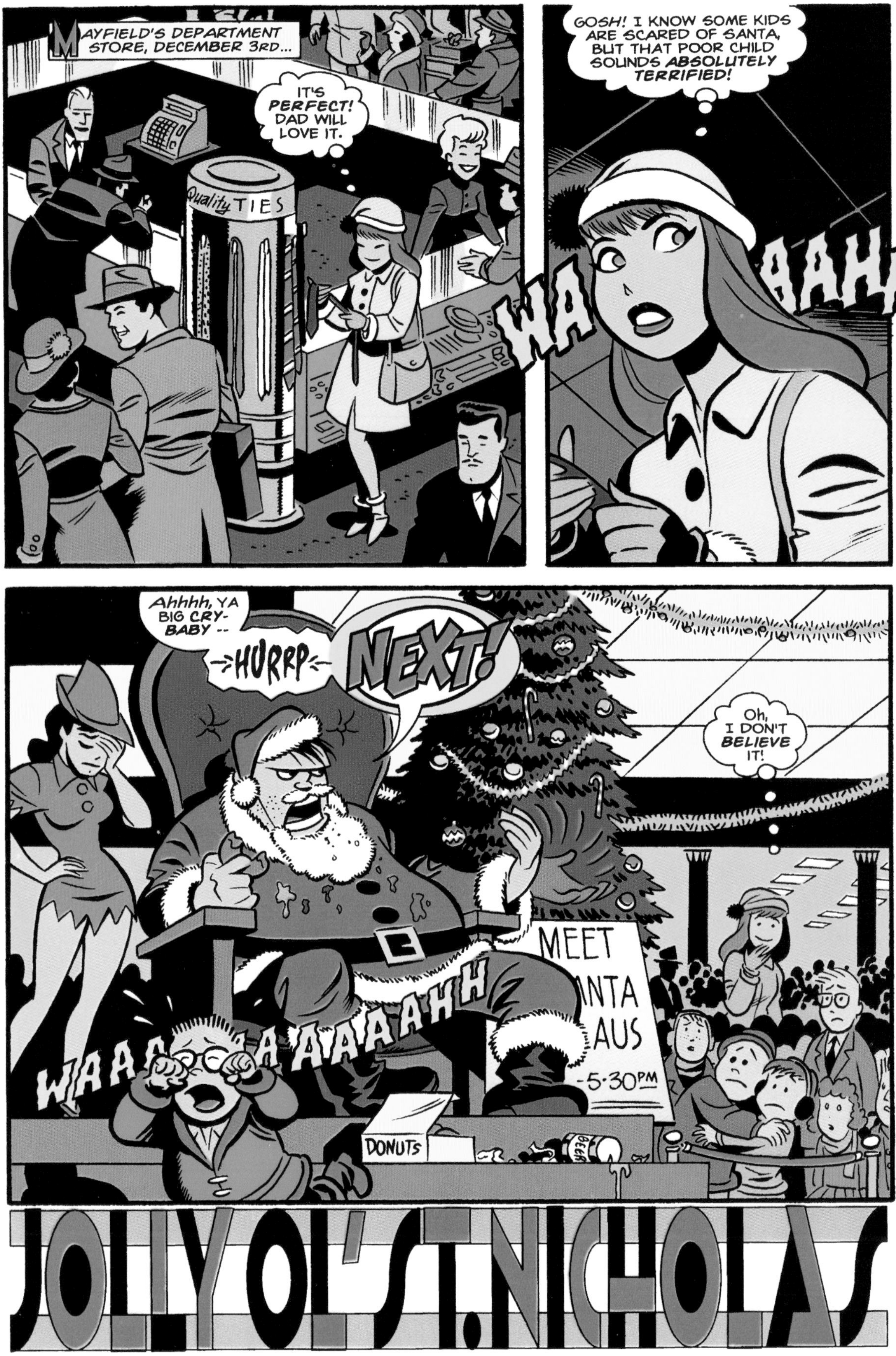
MAYFIELD'S DEPARTMENT STORE, DECEMBER 3RD...
IT'S PERFECT! DAD WILL LOVE IT.
Quality TIES
GOSH! I KNOW SOME KIDS ARE SCARED OF SANTA, BUT THAT POOR CHILD SOUNDS ABSOLUTELY TERRIFIED!
Ahhhh, YA BIG CRY-BABY --
-HURRP-
NEXT!
Oh, I DON'T BELIEVE IT!
MEET
-5:30PM
DONUTS
JOLLY OL' ST. NICHOLAS

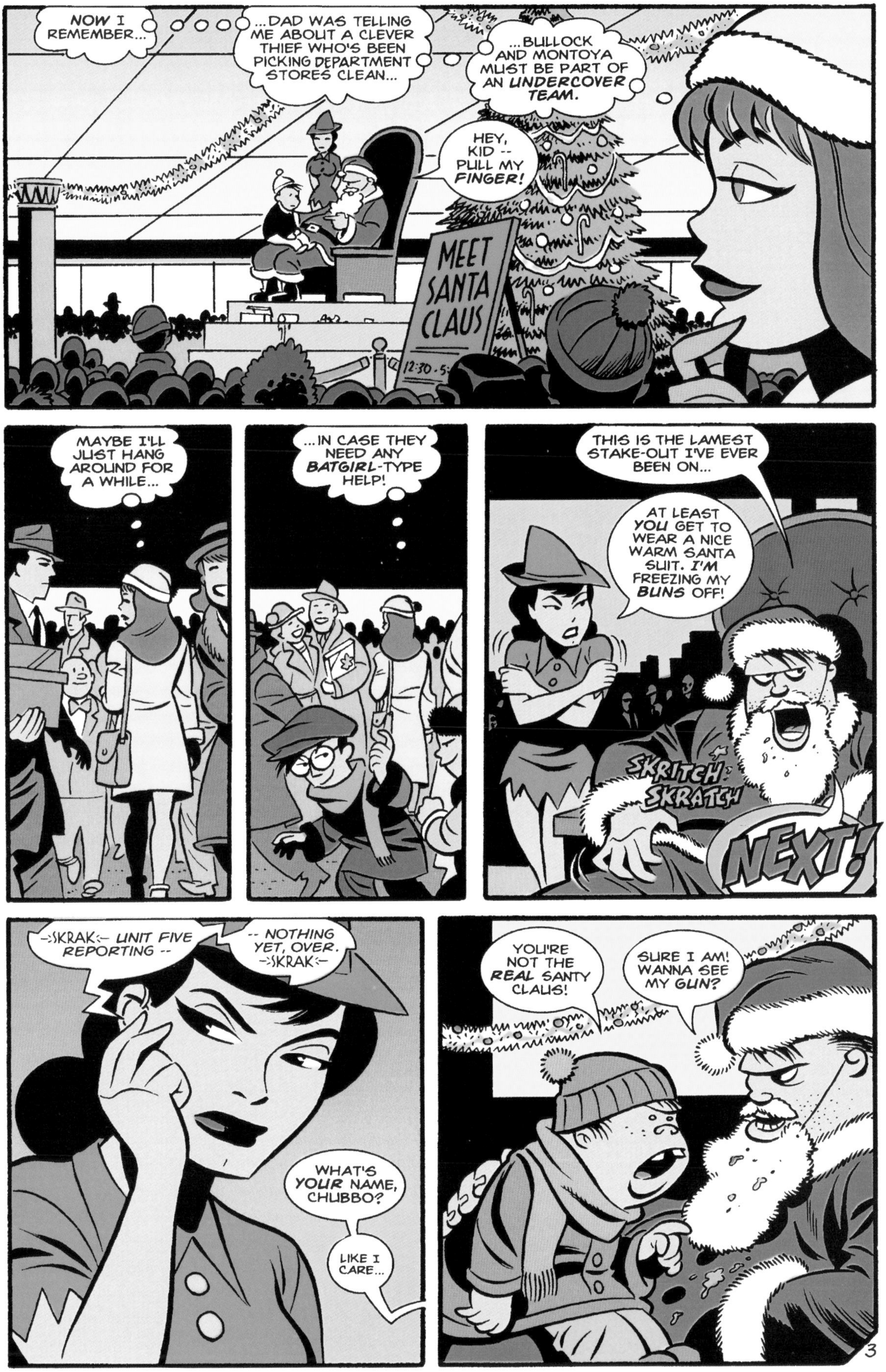
NOW I REMEMBER...
...DAD WAS TELLING ME ABOUT A CLEVER THIEF WHO'S BEEN PICKING DEPARTMENT STORES CLEAN...
...BULLOCK AND MONTOYA MUST BE PART OF AN UNDERCOVER TEAM.
HEY, KID -- PULL MY FINGER!
MEET SANTA CLAUS
12:30-5
MAYBE I'LL JUST HANG AROUND FOR A WHILE...
...IN CASE THEY NEED ANY BATGIRL-TYPE HELP!
THIS IS THE LAMEST STAKE-OUT I'VE EVER BEEN ON...
AT LEAST YOU GET TO WEAR A NICE WARM SANTA SUIT. I'M FREEZING MY BUNS OFF!
SKRITCH SKRATCH
NEXT!
-SKRAK- UNIT FIVE REPORTING --
-- NOTHING YET, OVER. -SKRAK-
WHAT'S YOUR NAME, CHUBBO?
LIKE I CARE...
YOU'RE NOT THE REAL SANTY CLAUS!
SURE I AM! WANNA SEE MY GUN?
3

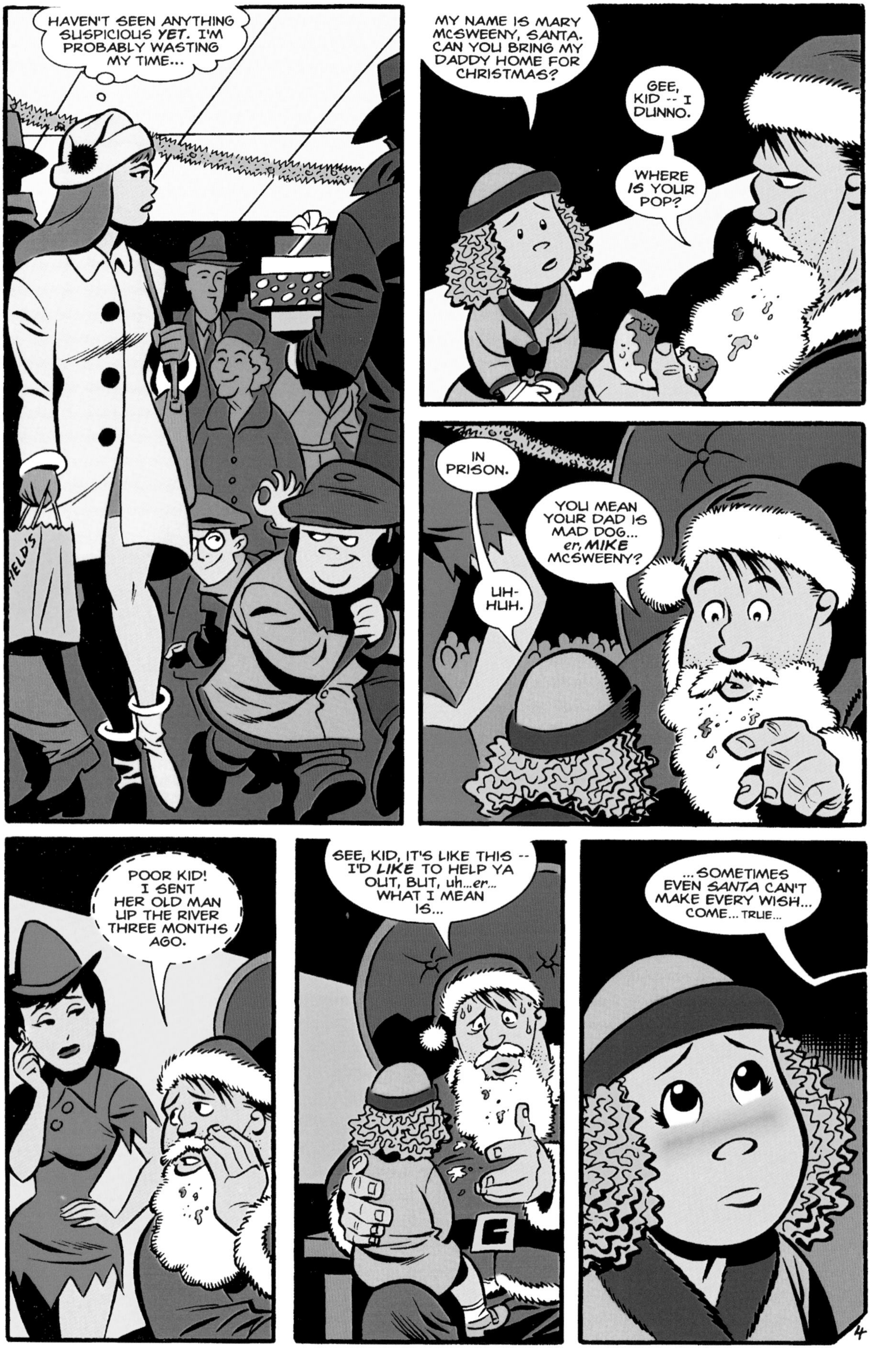
HAVEN'T SEEN ANYTHING SUSPICIOUS YET. I'M PROBABLY WASTING MY TIME...
HELD'S
MY NAME IS MARY MCSWEENY, SANTA. CAN YOU BRING MY DADDY HOME FOR CHRISTMAS?
GEE, KID -- I DUNNO.
WHERE IS YOUR POP?
IN PRISON.
YOU MEAN YOUR DAD IS MAD DOG... er, MIKE MCSWEENY?
UH-HUH.
POOR KID! I SENT HER OLD MAN UP THE RIVER THREE MONTHS AGO.
SEE, KID, IT'S LIKE THIS -- I'D LIKE TO HELP YA OUT, BUT, uh...er... WHAT I MEAN IS...
...SOMETIMES EVEN SANTA CAN'T MAKE EVERY WISH... COME... TRUE...
4

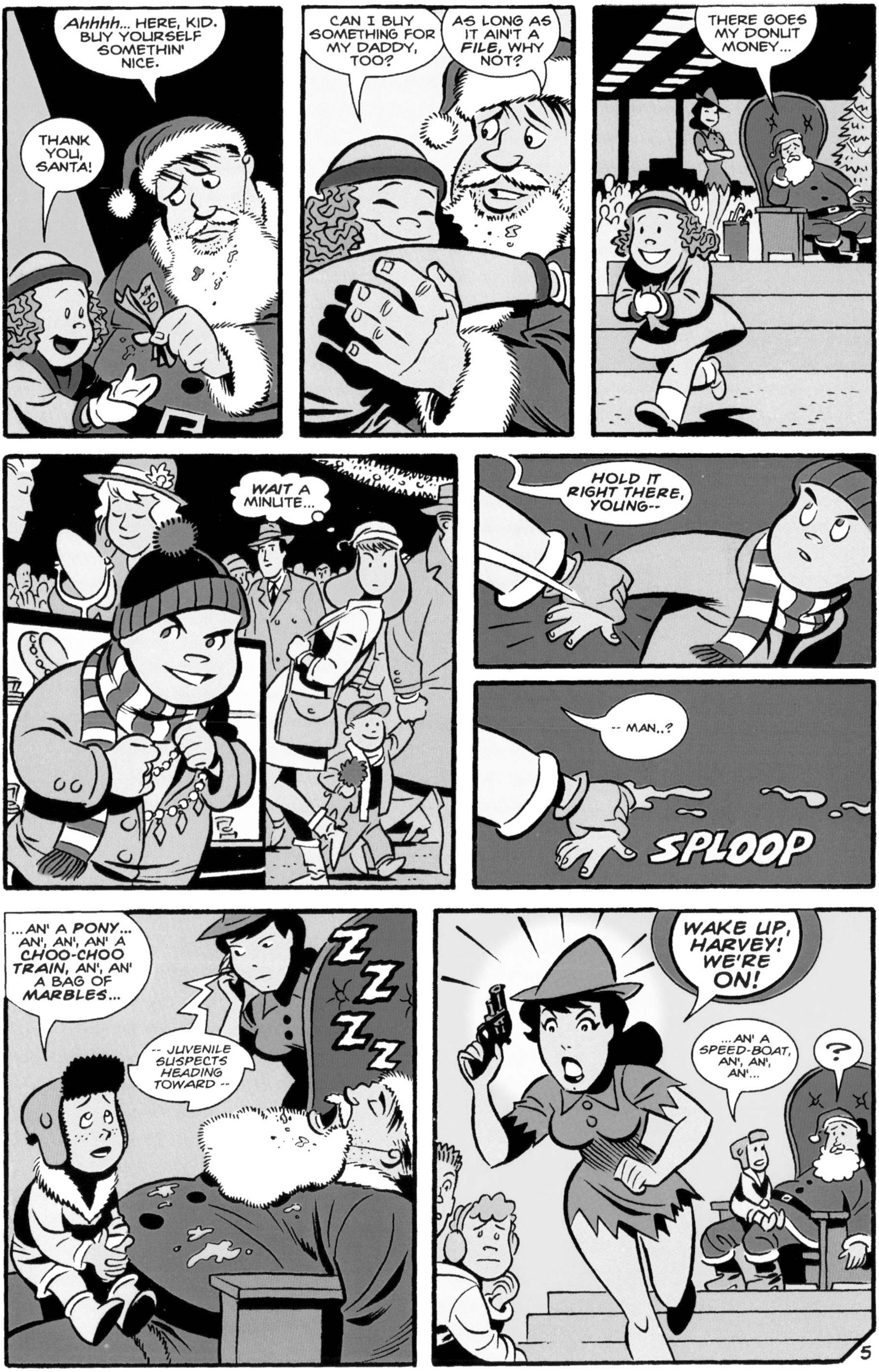
Ahhhh... HERE, KID. BUY YOURSELF SOMETHIN' NICE.
THANK YOU, SANTA!
$50
CAN I BUY SOMETHING FOR MY DADDY, TOO?
AS LONG AS IT AIN'T A FILE, WHY NOT?
THERE GOES MY DONUT MONEY...
WAIT A MINUTE...
HOLD IT RIGHT THERE, YOUNG--
-- MAN..?
SPLOOP
...AN' A PONY... AN', AN', AN' A CHOO-CHOO TRAIN, AN', AN' A BAG OF MARBLES...
-- JUVENILE SUSPECTS HEADING TOWARD --
Z Z Z Z
WAKE UP, HARVEY! WE'RE ON!
...AN' A SPEED-BOAT, AN', AN', AN'...
?
5

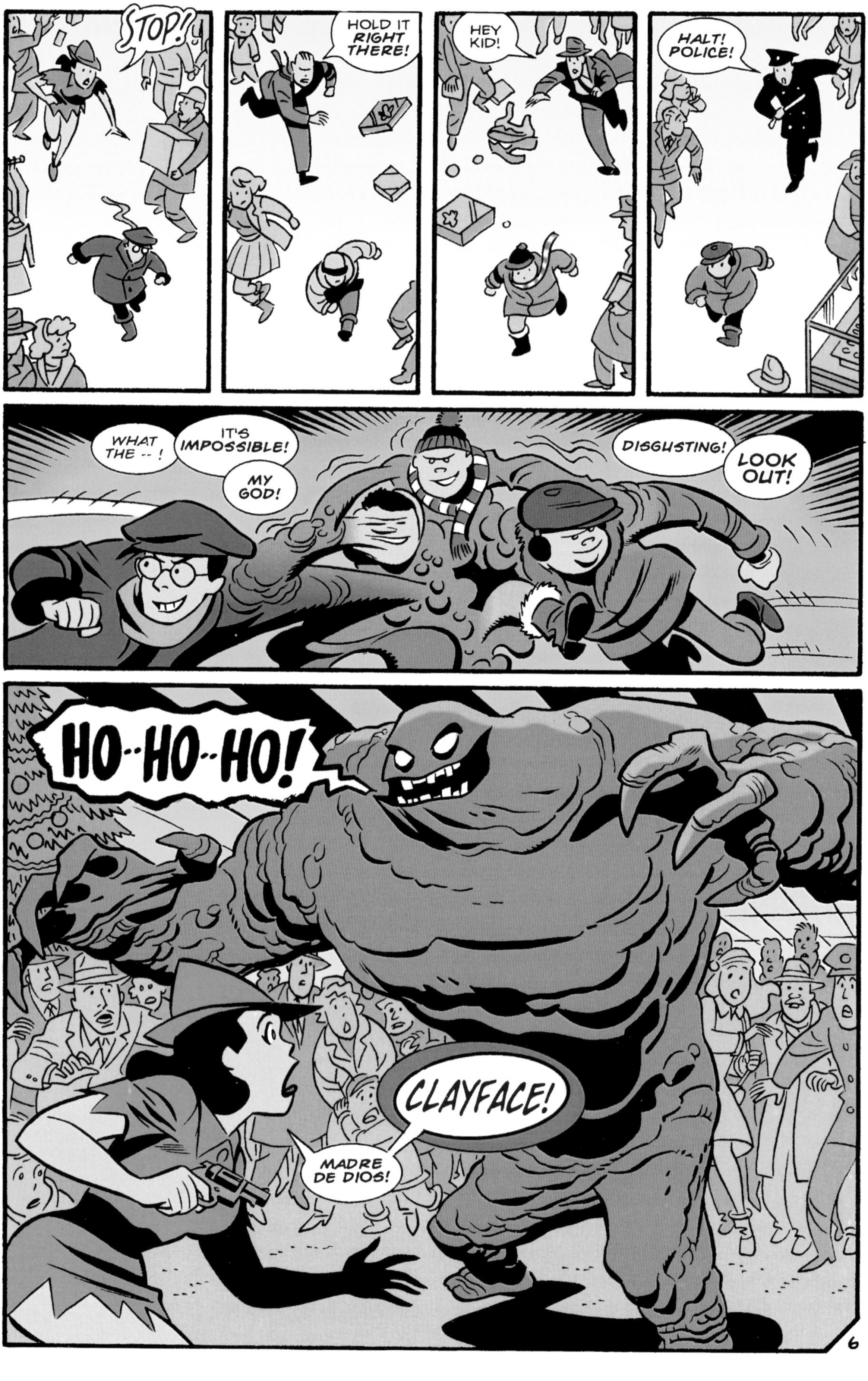
STOP!
HOLD IT RIGHT THERE!
HEY KID!
HALT! POLICE!
WHAT THE -- !
IT'S IMPOSSIBLE!
MY GOD!
DISGUSTING!
LOOK OUT!
HO-HO-HO!
CLAYFACE!
MADRE DE DIOS!
6

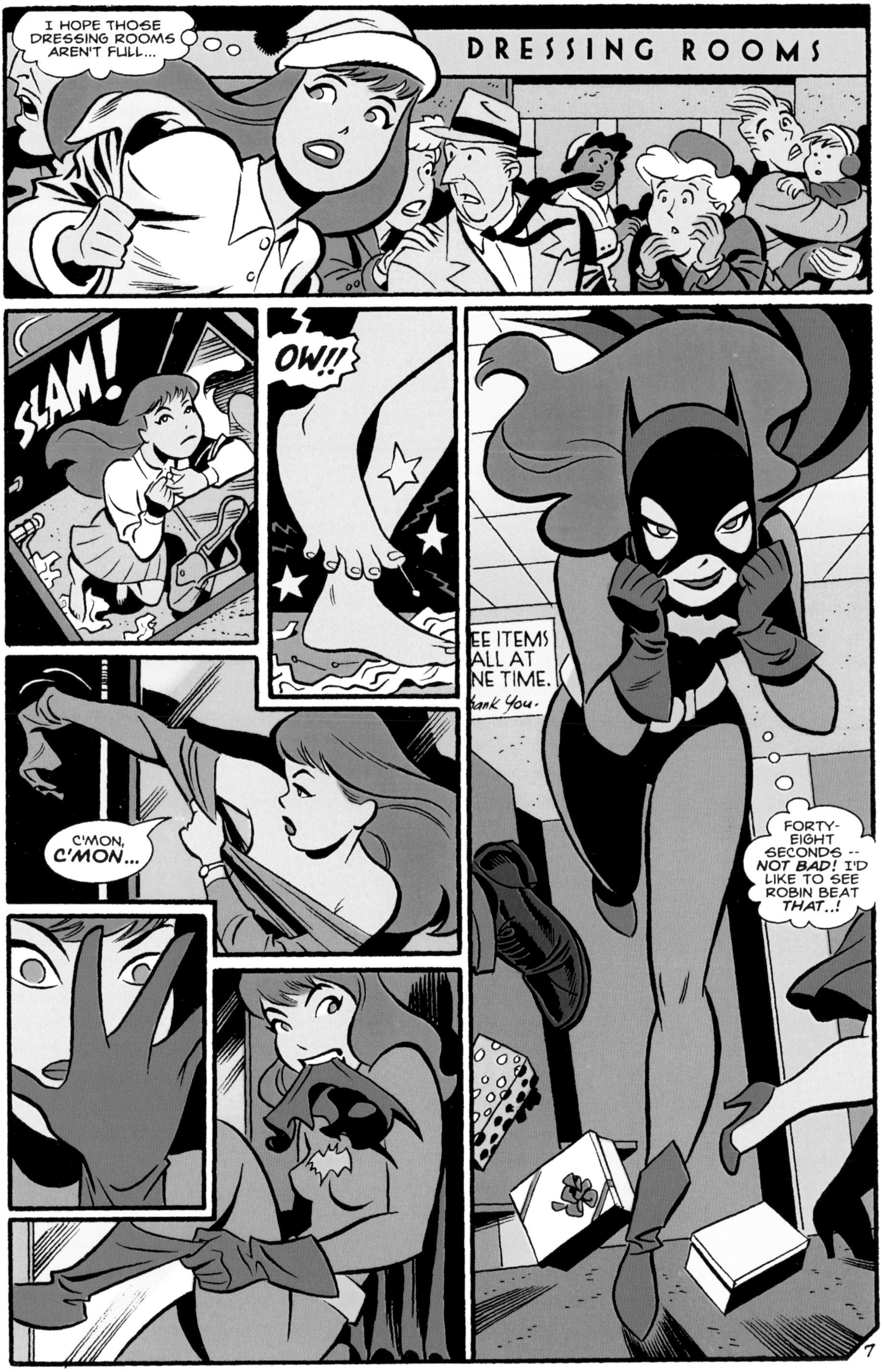

I HOPE THOSE DRESSING ROOMS AREN'T FULL...
DRESSING ROOMS
SLAM!
OW!!
SEE ITEMS
ALL AT
NE TIME.
hank You.
C'MON, C'MON...
FORTY-EIGHT SECONDS -- NOT BAD! I'D LIKE TO SEE ROBIN BEAT THAT..!
7

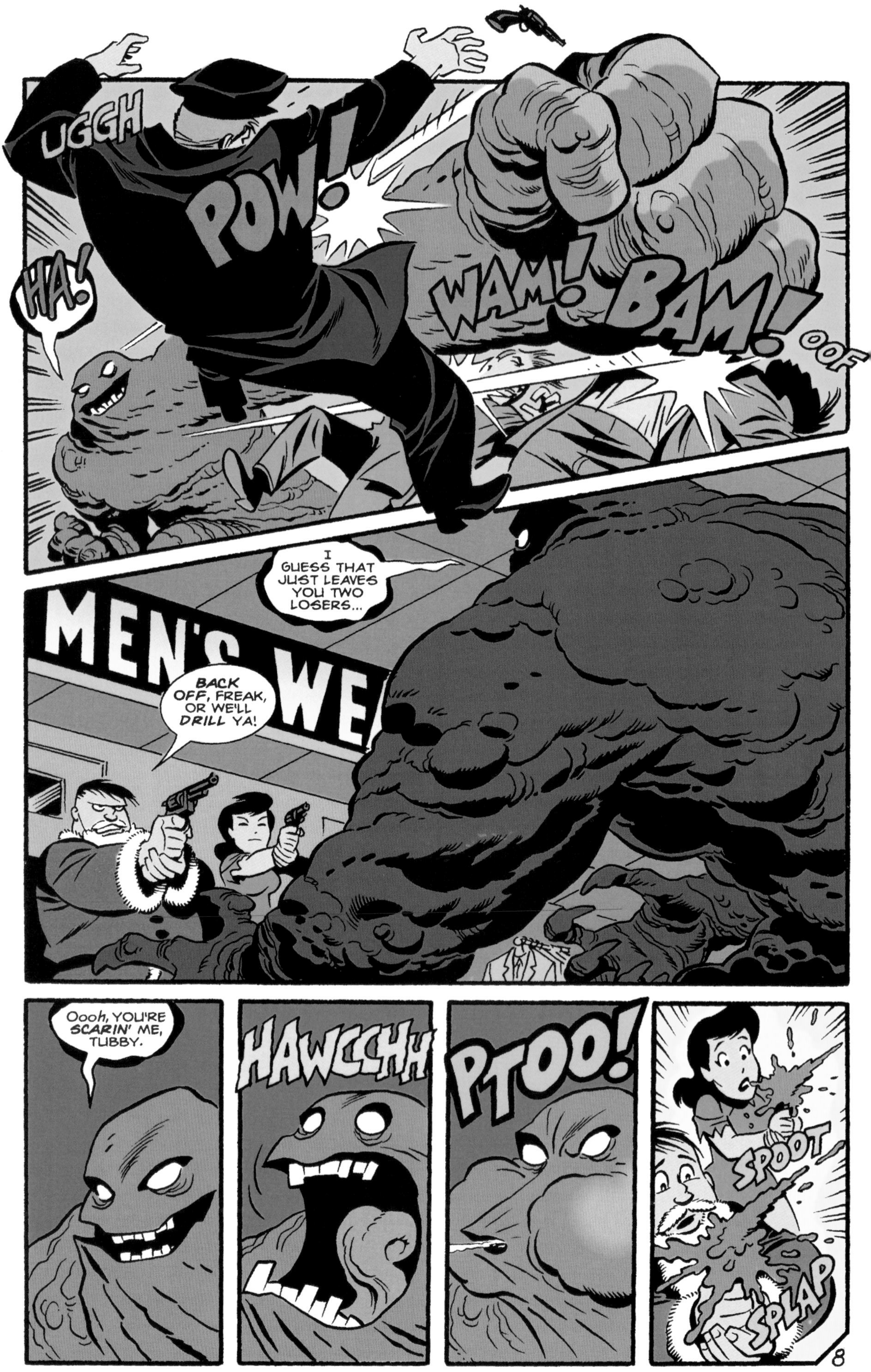
UGGH
POW!
HA!
WAM! BAM!
OOF
I GUESS THAT JUST LEAVES YOU TWO LOSERS...
MEN'S WE
BACK OFF, FREAK, OR WE'LL DRILL YA!
Oooh, YOU'RE SCARIN' ME, TUBBY.
HAWCCHH
PTOO!
!
SPOOT
SPLAP
8

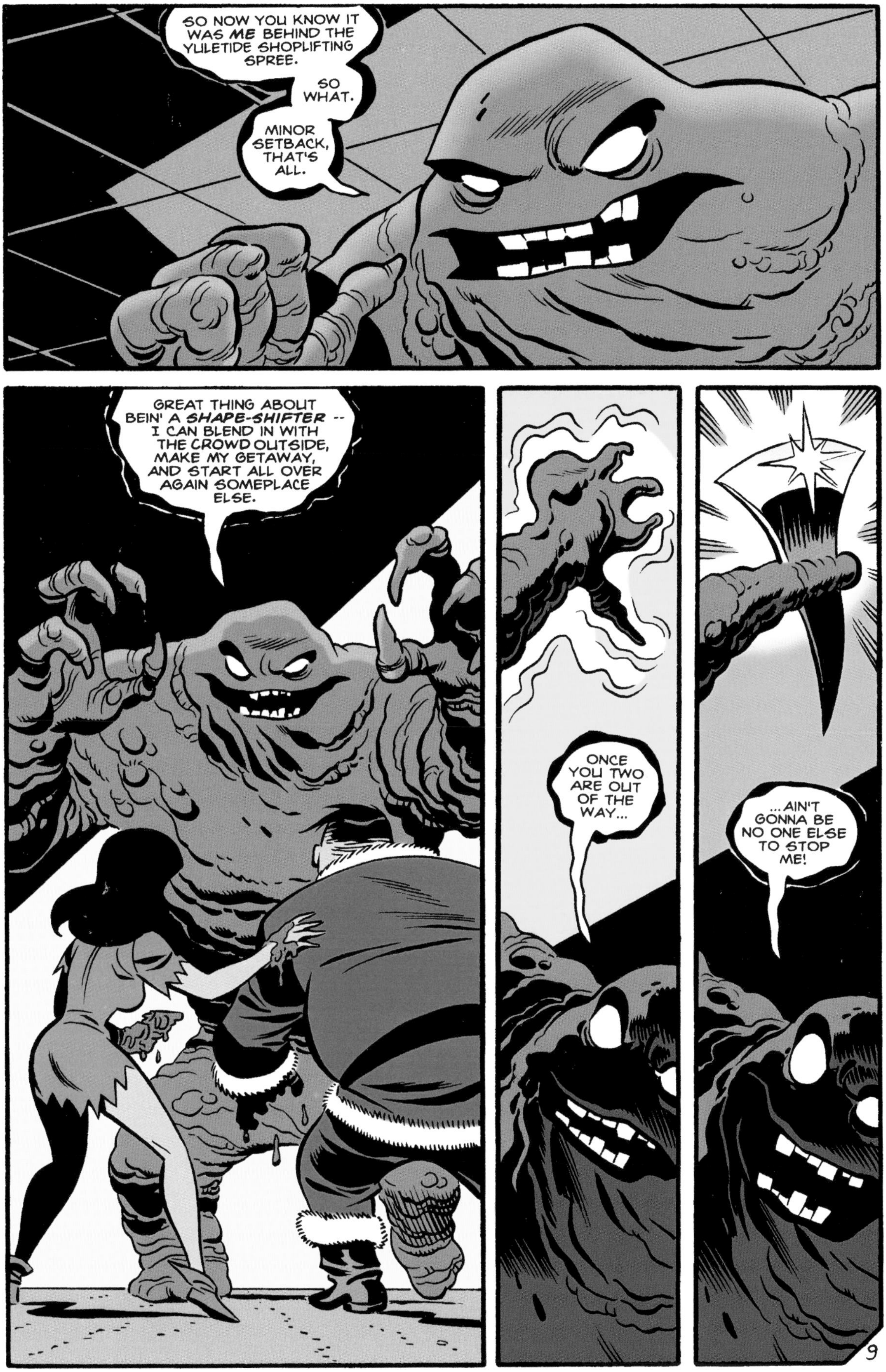
SO NOW YOU KNOW IT WAS ME BEHIND THE YULETIDE SHOPLIFTING SPREE.
SO WHAT.
MINOR SETBACK, THAT'S ALL.
GREAT THING ABOUT BEIN' A SHAPE-SHIFTER -- I CAN BLEND IN WITH THE CROWD OUTSIDE, MAKE MY GETAWAY, AND START ALL OVER AGAIN SOMEPLACE ELSE.
ONCE YOU TWO ARE OUT OF THE WAY...
...AIN'T GONNA BE NO ONE ELSE TO STOP ME!
9

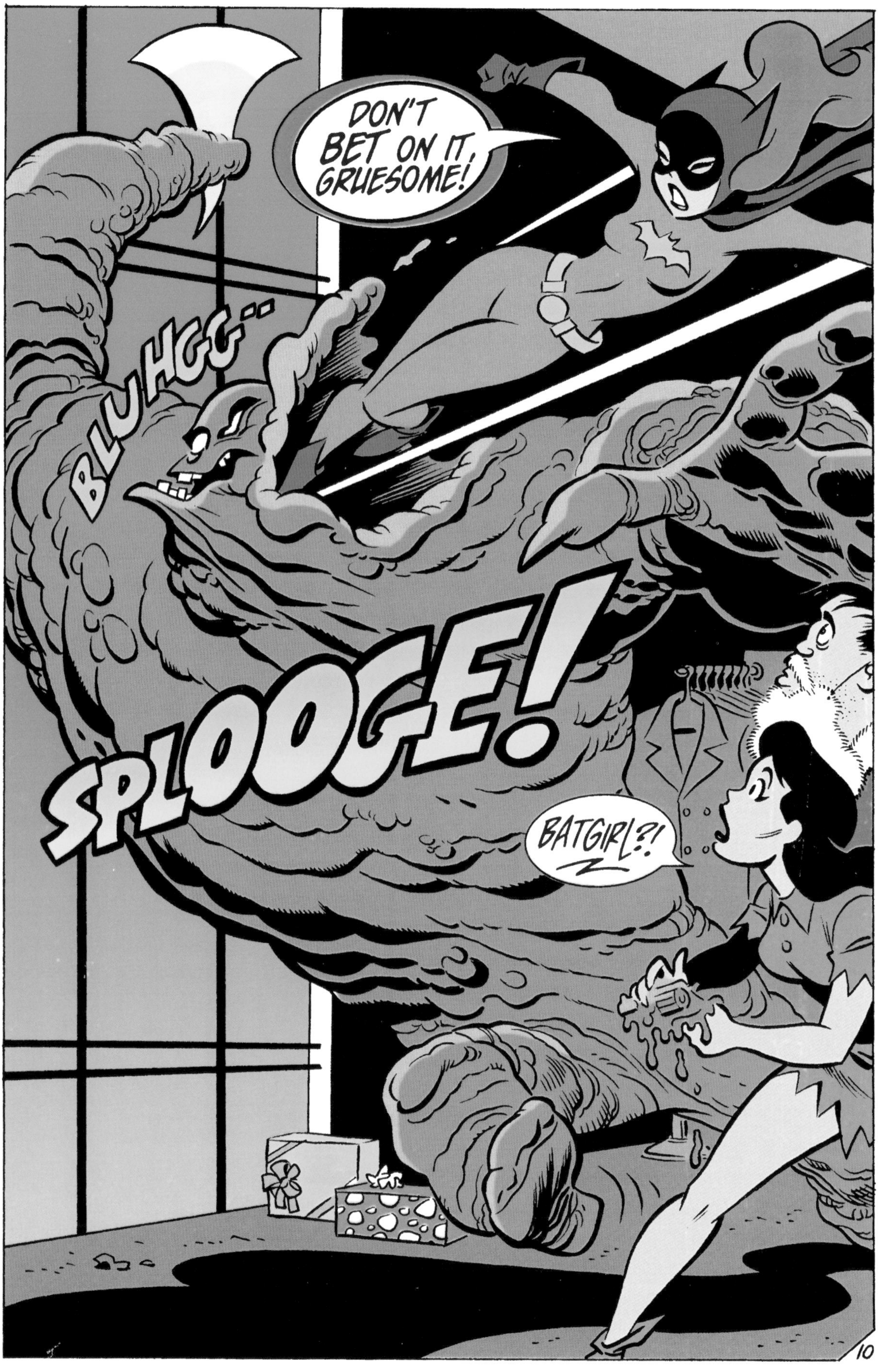
DON'T BET ON IT, GRUESOME!
BLUHGG--
SPLOOGE!
BATGIRL?!
10

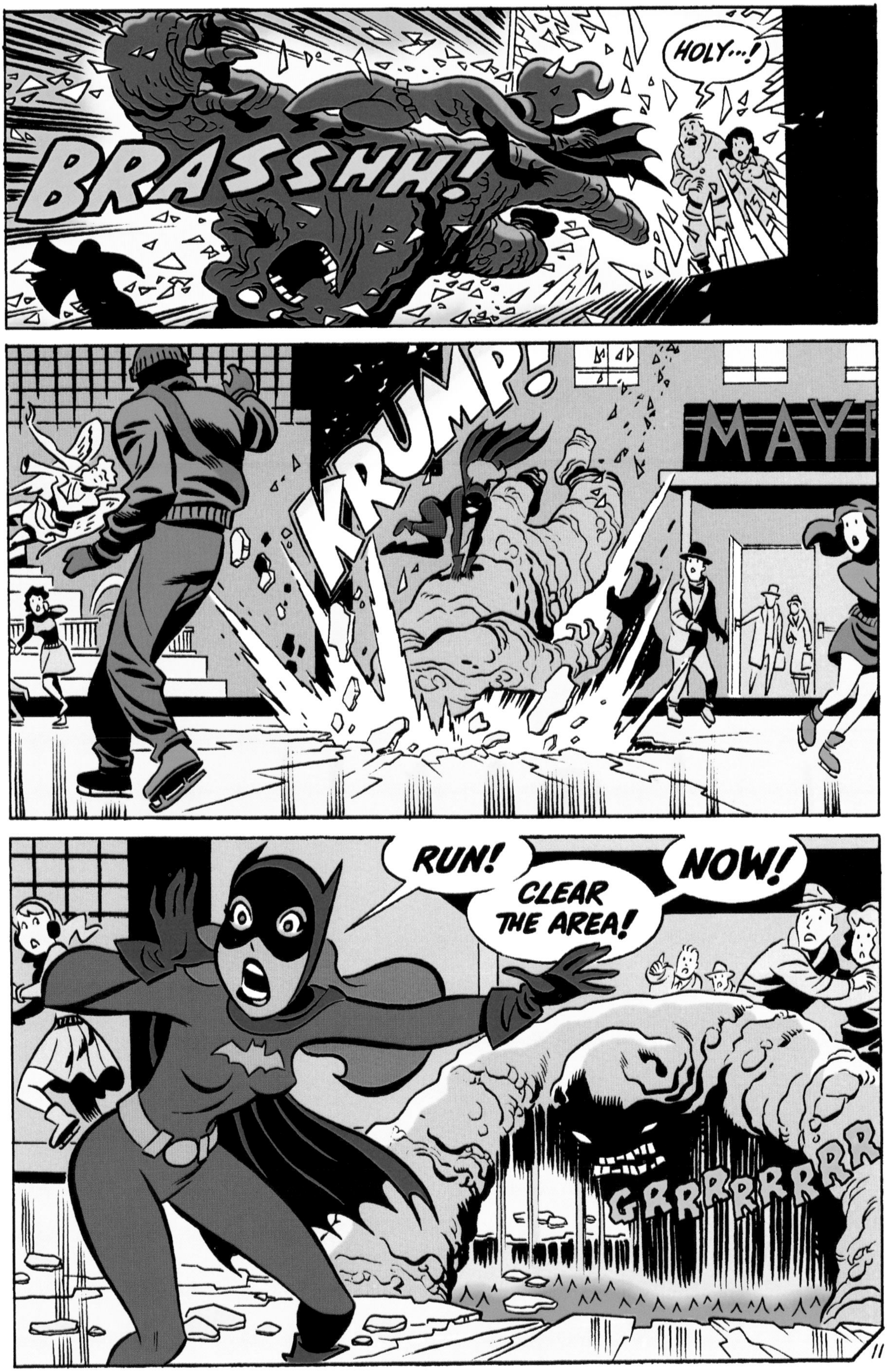

HOLY...!
BRASSHH!
KRUMP!
MAYF
RUN!
CLEAR THE AREA!
NOW!
GRRRRRRRRRR
11

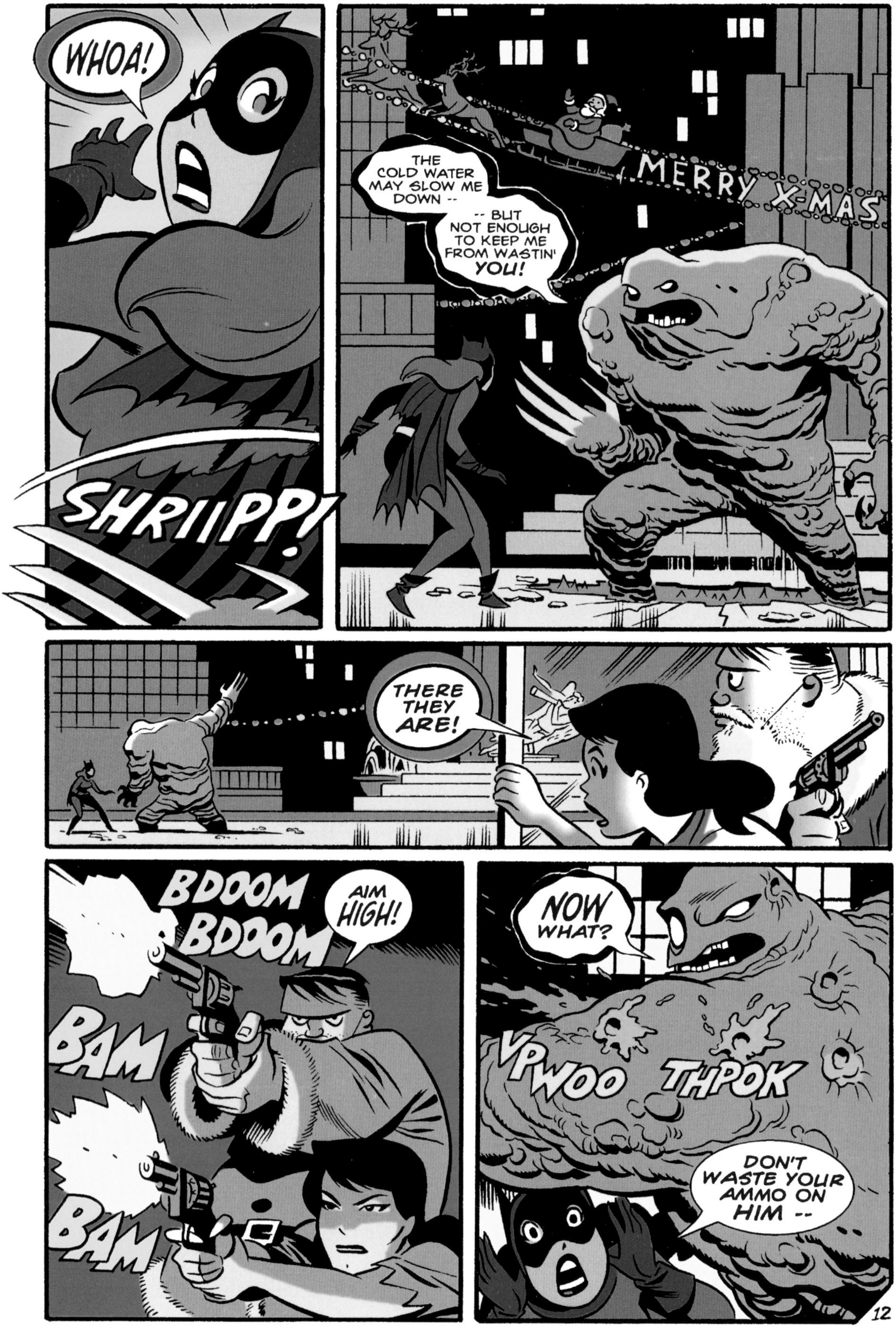
WHOA!
SHRIIPP!
MERRY X-MAS
THE COLD WATER MAY SLOW ME DOWN --
-- BUT NOT ENOUGH TO KEEP ME FROM WASTIN' YOU!
THERE THEY ARE!
BDOOM
BDOOM
AIM HIGH!
BAM
BAM
NOW WHAT?
VPWOO
THPOK
DON'T WASTE YOUR AMMO ON HIM --
12

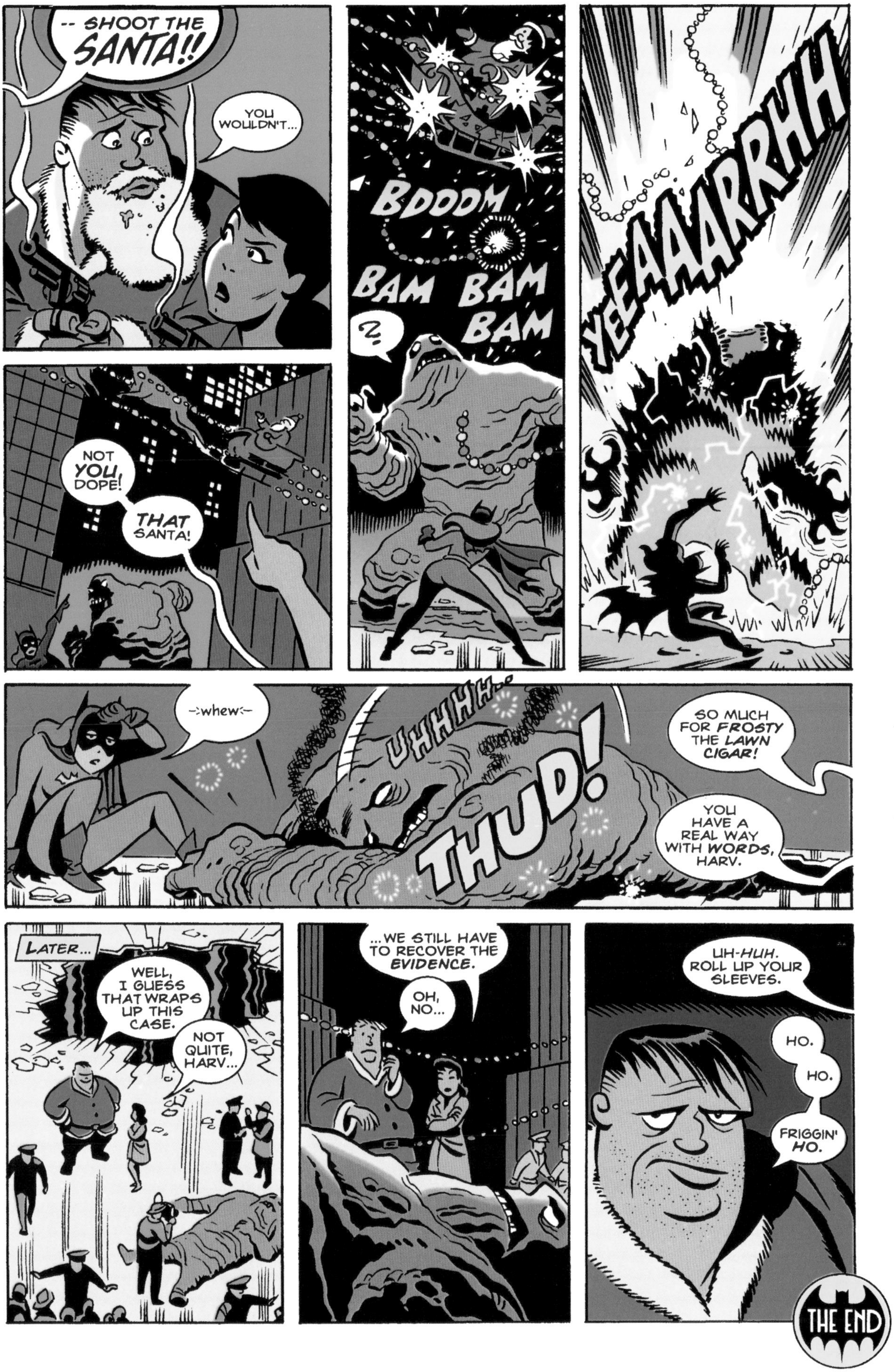
-- SHOOT THE SANTA!!
YOU WOULDN'T...
NOT YOU, DOPE!
THAT SANTA!
BDOOM
BAM BAM BAM
?
YEEAAARRHH
-:-whew-:-
UHHHHH...
THUD!
SO MUCH FOR FROSTY THE LAWN CIGAR!
YOU HAVE A REAL WAY WITH WORDS, HARV.
LATER...
WELL, I GUESS THAT WRAPS UP THIS CASE.
NOT QUITE, HARV...
...WE STILL HAVE TO RECOVER THE EVIDENCE.
OH, NO...
UH-HUH. ROLL UP YOUR SLEEVES.
HO.
HO.
FRIGGIN' HO.
THE END

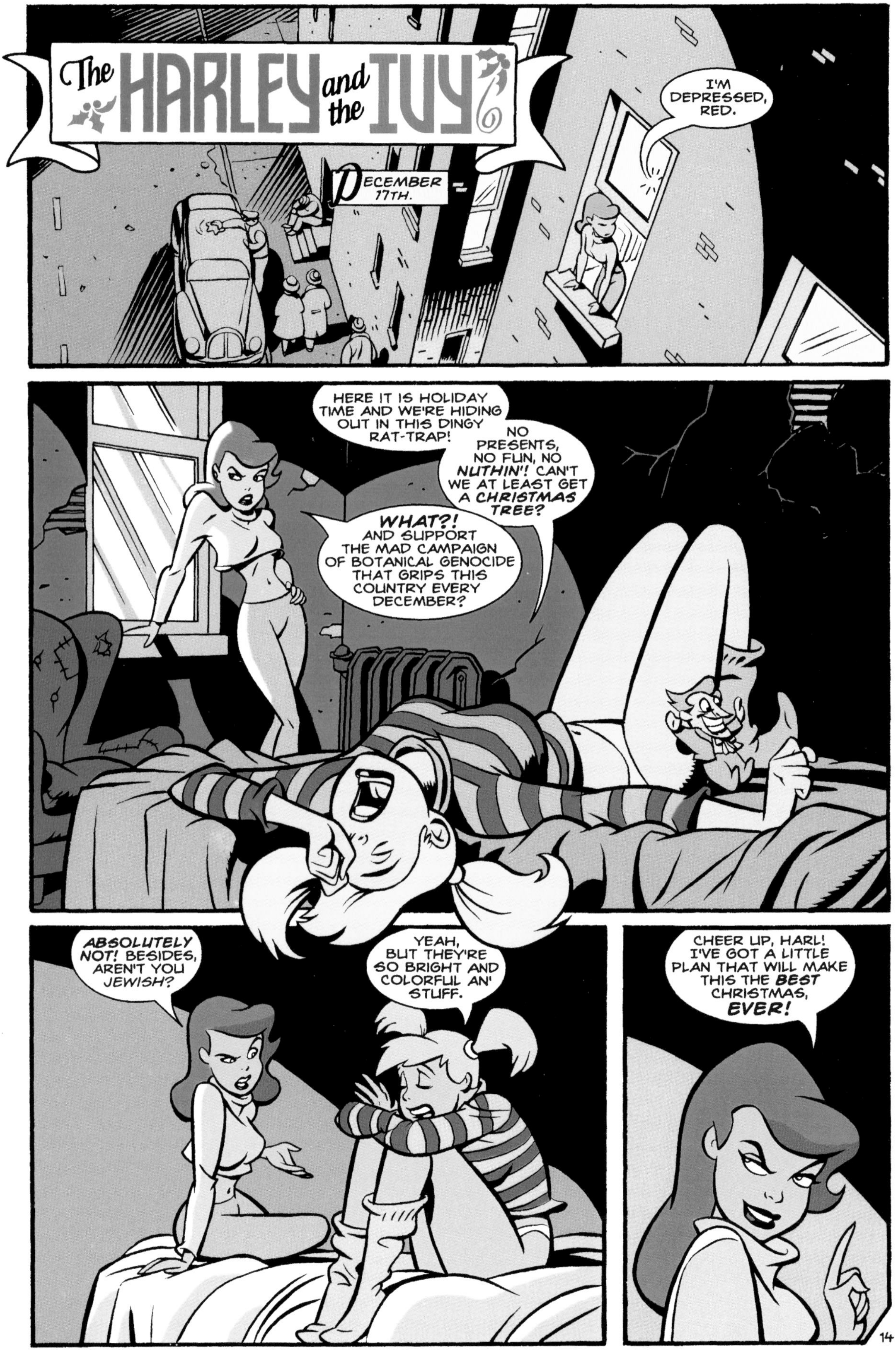

The HARLEY and the IVY
DECEMBER 17TH.
I'M DEPRESSED, RED.
HERE IT IS HOLIDAY TIME AND WE'RE HIDING OUT IN THIS DINGY RAT-TRAP!
NO PRESENTS, NO FUN, NO NUTHIN'! CAN'T WE AT LEAST GET A CHRISTMAS TREE?
WHAT?! AND SUPPORT THE MAD CAMPAIGN OF BOTANICAL GENOCIDE THAT GRIPS THIS COUNTRY EVERY DECEMBER?
ABSOLUTELY NOT! BESIDES, AREN'T YOU JEWISH?
YEAH, BUT THEY'RE SO BRIGHT AND COLORFUL AN' STUFF.
CHEER UP, HARL! I'VE GOT A LITTLE PLAN THAT WILL MAKE THIS THE BEST CHRISTMAS, EVER!
14

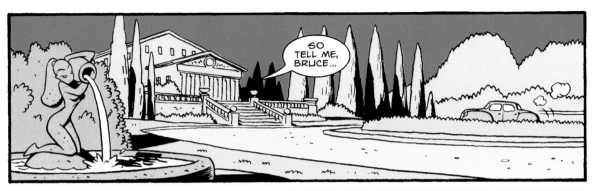

SO TELL ME, BRUCE...

WHICH LUCKY GIRL IS GOING TO SPEND THE HOLIDAYS WITH GOTHAM'S MOST ELIGIBLE BACHELOR?

ACTUALLY, I WAS PLANNING ON A QUIET CHRISTMAS ALONE, VERONICA.

REALLY? I WOULDN'T TELL *THEM* THAT.

WHO'S *"THEM"*?

BRUCIE!

YOU'RE STANDING UNDER THE MISTLETOE!

15

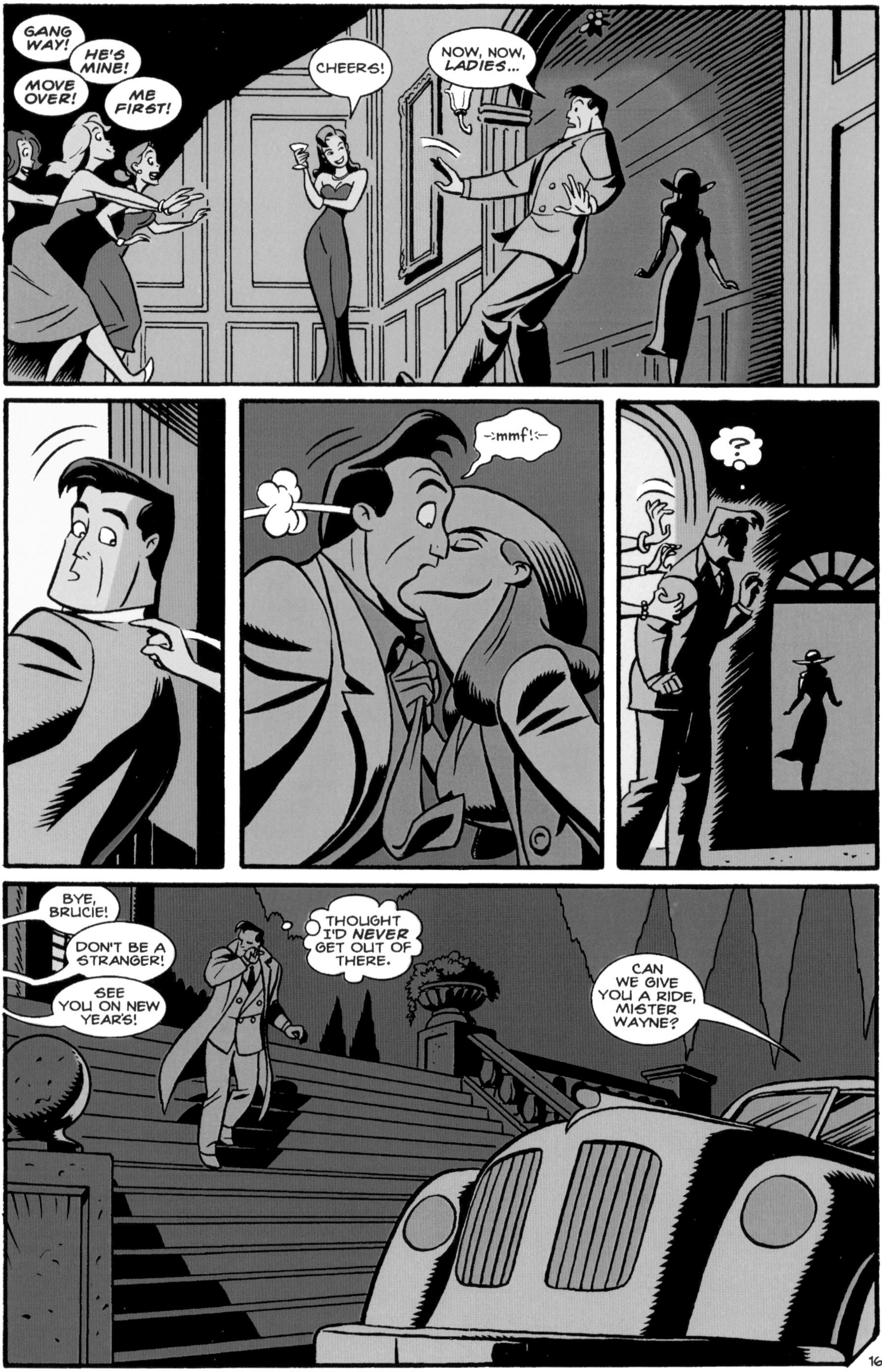
GANG WAY!
HE'S MINE!
MOVE OVER!
ME FIRST!
CHEERS!
NOW, NOW, LADIES...
mmf!
?
BYE, BRUCIE!
DON'T BE A STRANGER!
SEE YOU ON NEW YEAR'S!
THOUGHT I'D NEVER GET OUT OF THERE.
CAN WE GIVE YOU A RIDE, MISTER WAYNE?
16

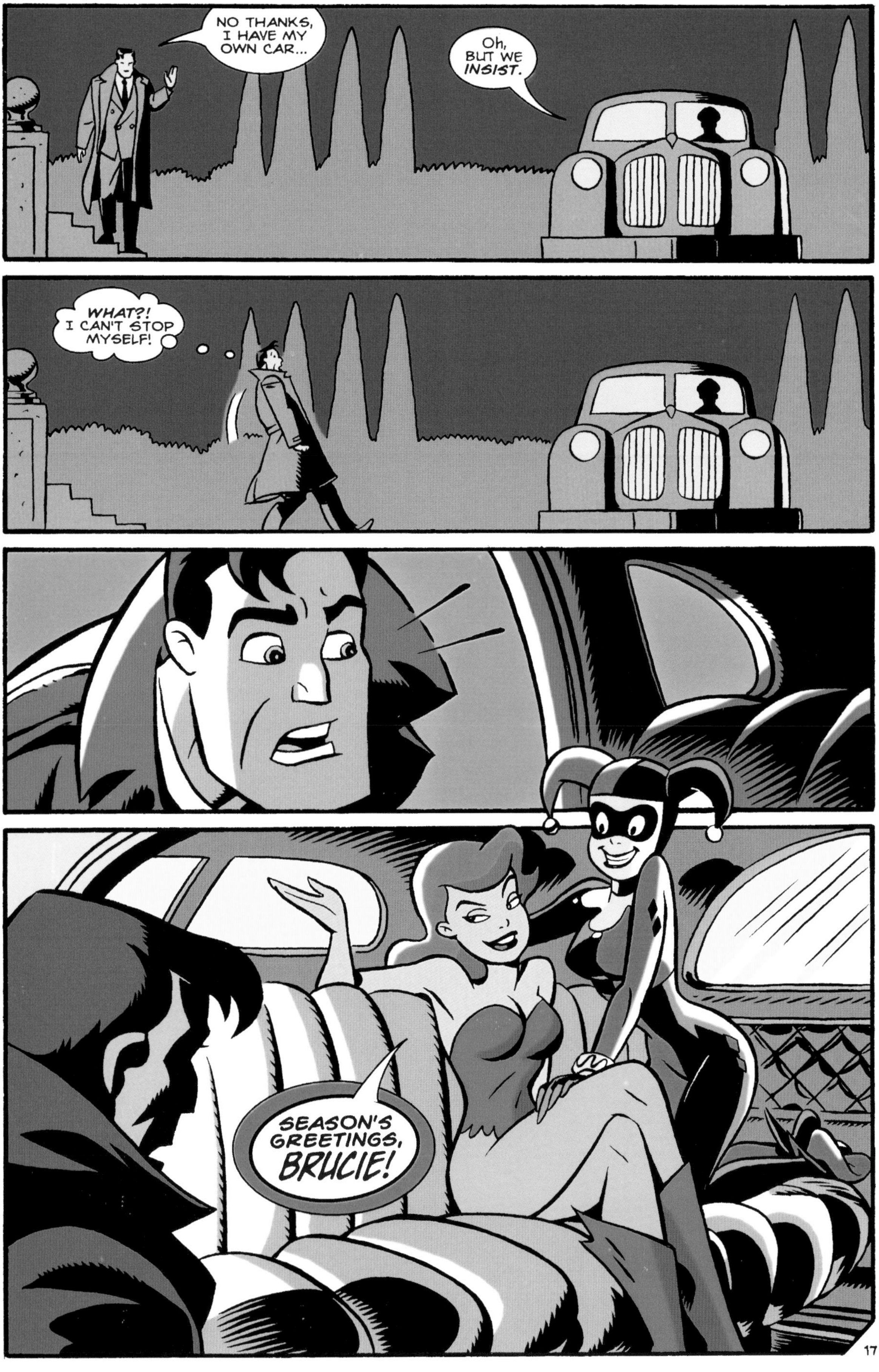
NO THANKS, I HAVE MY OWN CAR...
Oh, BUT WE *INSIST*.
WHAT?! I CAN'T STOP MYSELF!
SEASON'S GREETINGS, *BRUCIE!*
17

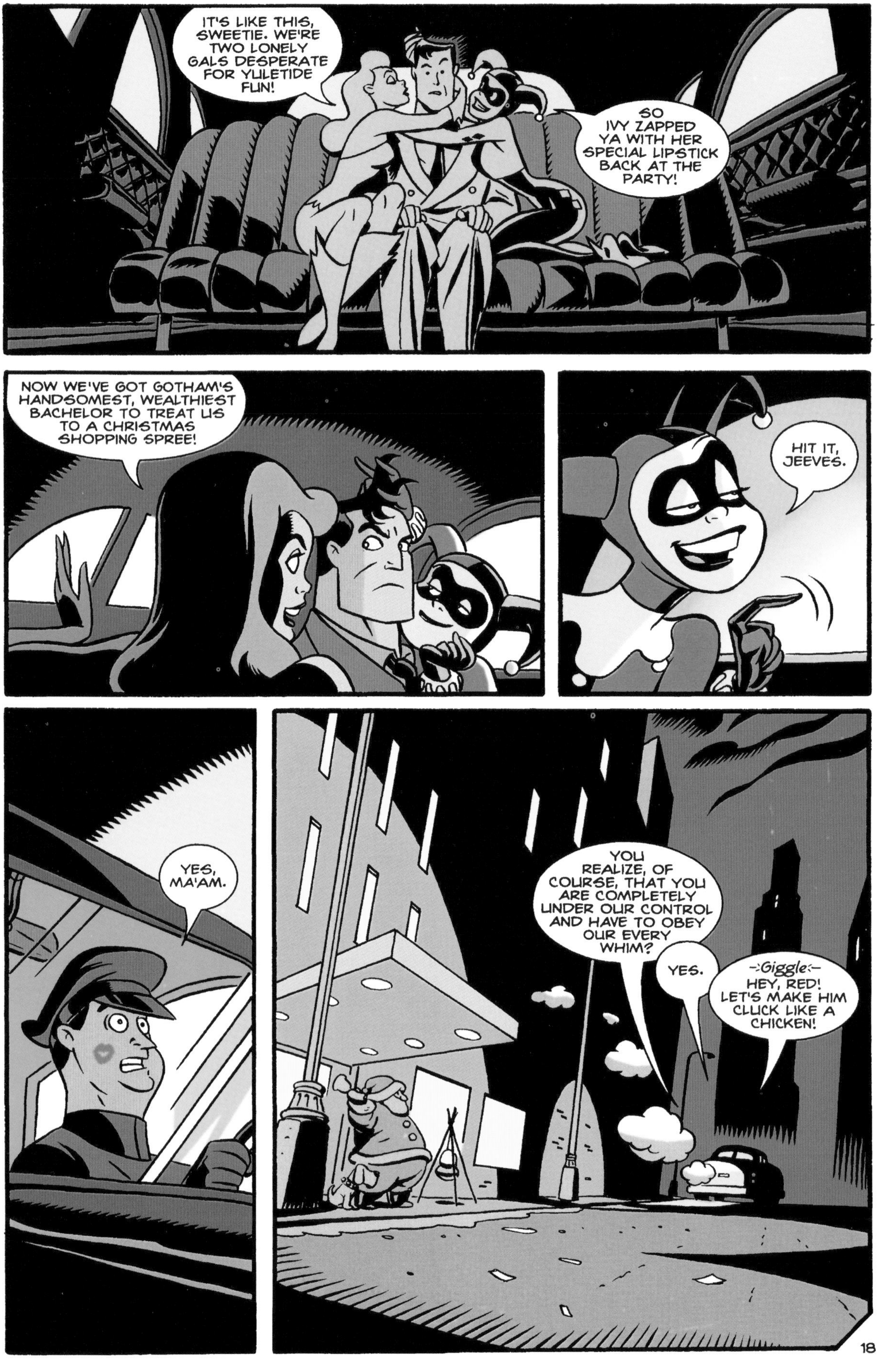

IT'S LIKE THIS, SWEETIE. WE'RE TWO LONELY GALS DESPERATE FOR YULETIDE FUN!
SO IVY ZAPPED YA WITH HER SPECIAL LIPSTICK BACK AT THE PARTY!
NOW WE'VE GOT GOTHAM'S HANDSOMEST, WEALTHIEST BACHELOR TO TREAT US TO A CHRISTMAS SHOPPING SPREE!
HIT IT, JEEVES.
YES, MA'AM.
YOU REALIZE, OF COURSE, THAT YOU ARE COMPLETELY UNDER OUR CONTROL AND HAVE TO OBEY OUR EVERY WHIM?
YES.
-Giggle-
HEY, RED! LET'S MAKE HIM CLUCK LIKE A CHICKEN!
18

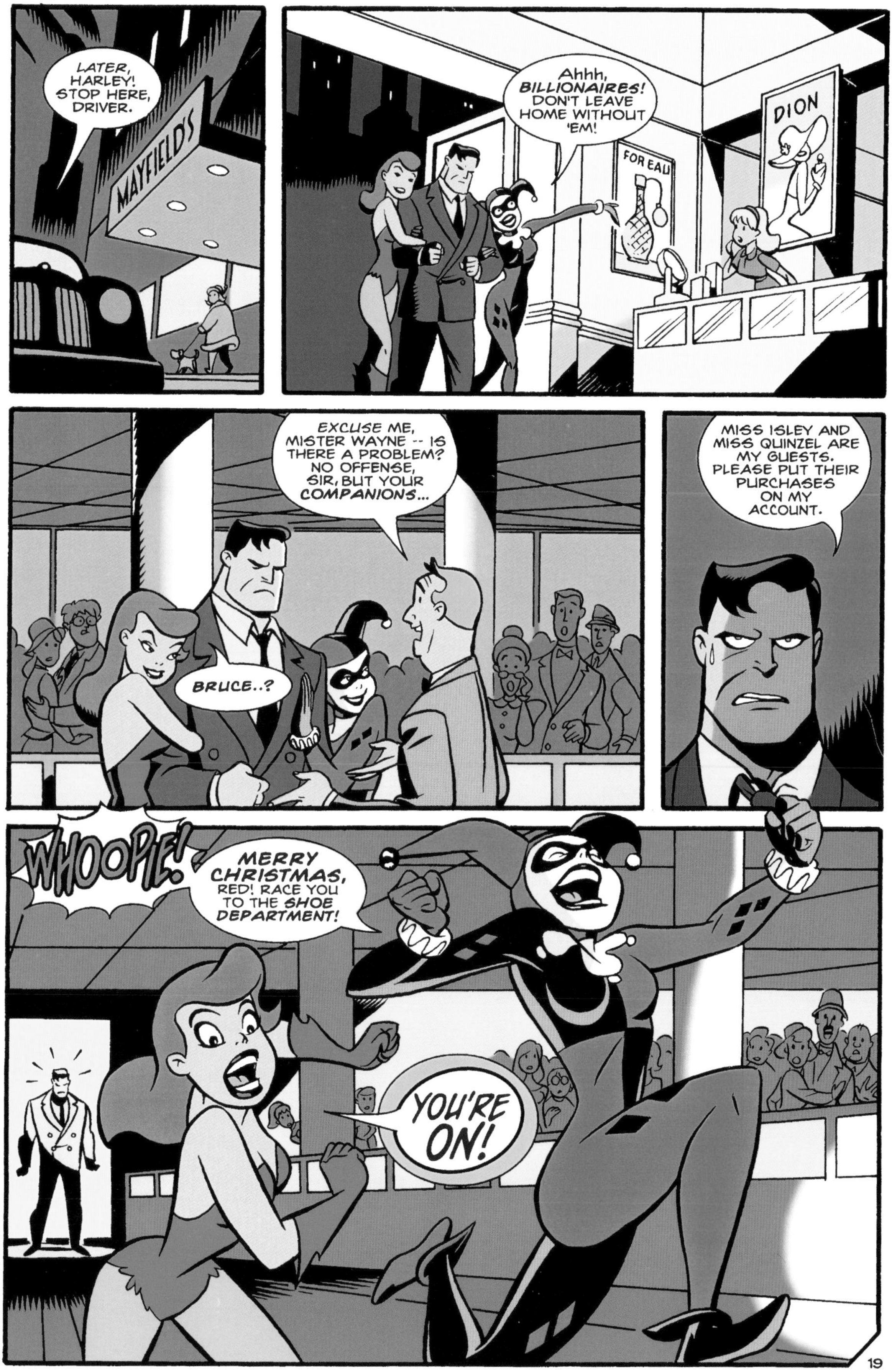
LATER, HARLEY! STOP HERE, DRIVER.
MAYFIELD'S
Ahhh, BILLIONAIRES! DON'T LEAVE HOME WITHOUT 'EM!
FOR EAU
DION
EXCUSE ME, MISTER WAYNE -- IS THERE A PROBLEM? NO OFFENSE, SIR, BUT YOUR COMPANIONS...
BRUCE..?
MISS ISLEY AND MISS QUINZEL ARE MY GUESTS. PLEASE PUT THEIR PURCHASES ON MY ACCOUNT.
WHOOPIE!
MERRY CHRISTMAS, RED! RACE YOU TO THE SHOE DEPARTMENT!
YOU'RE ON!
19

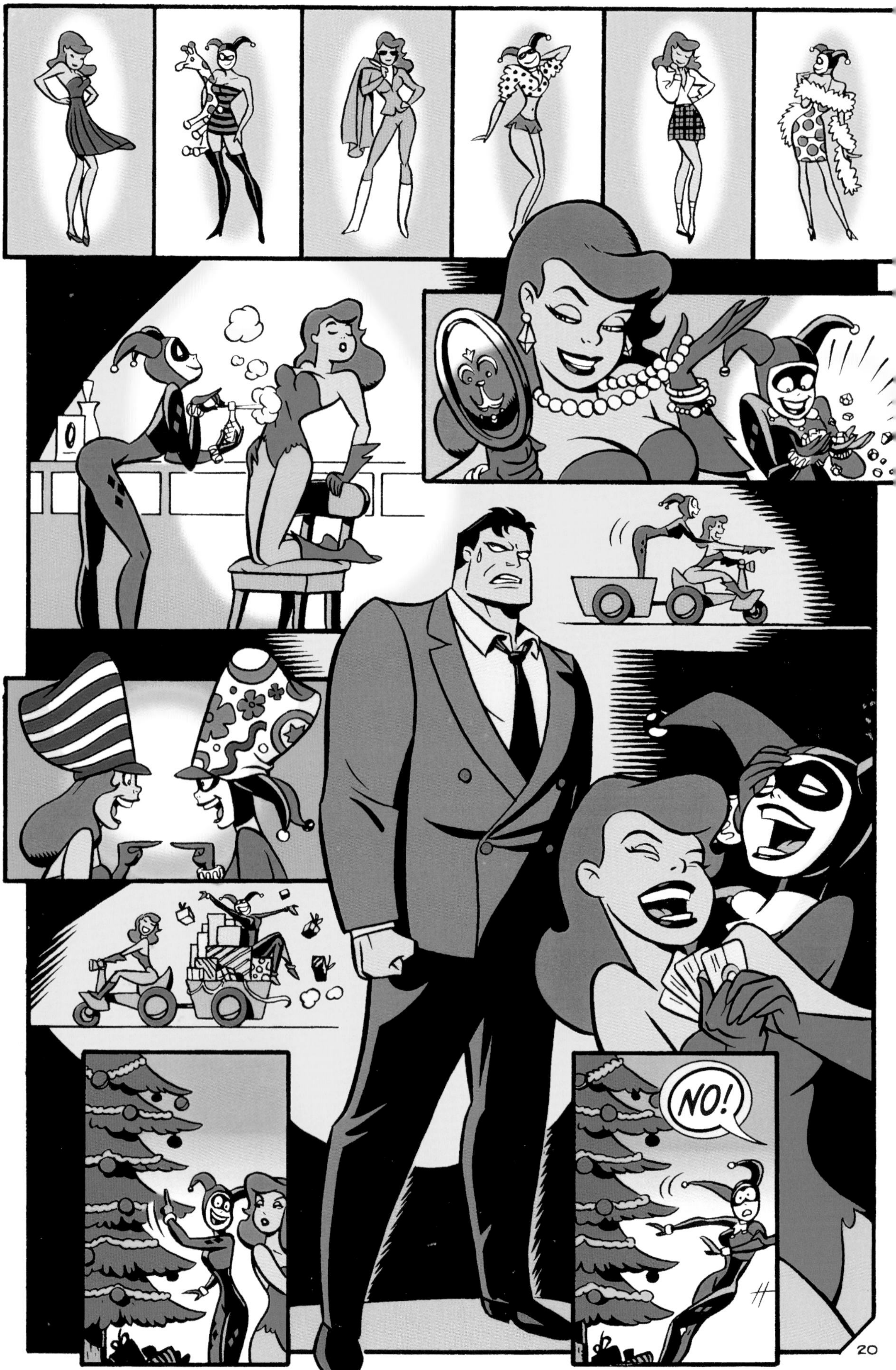
NO!
20

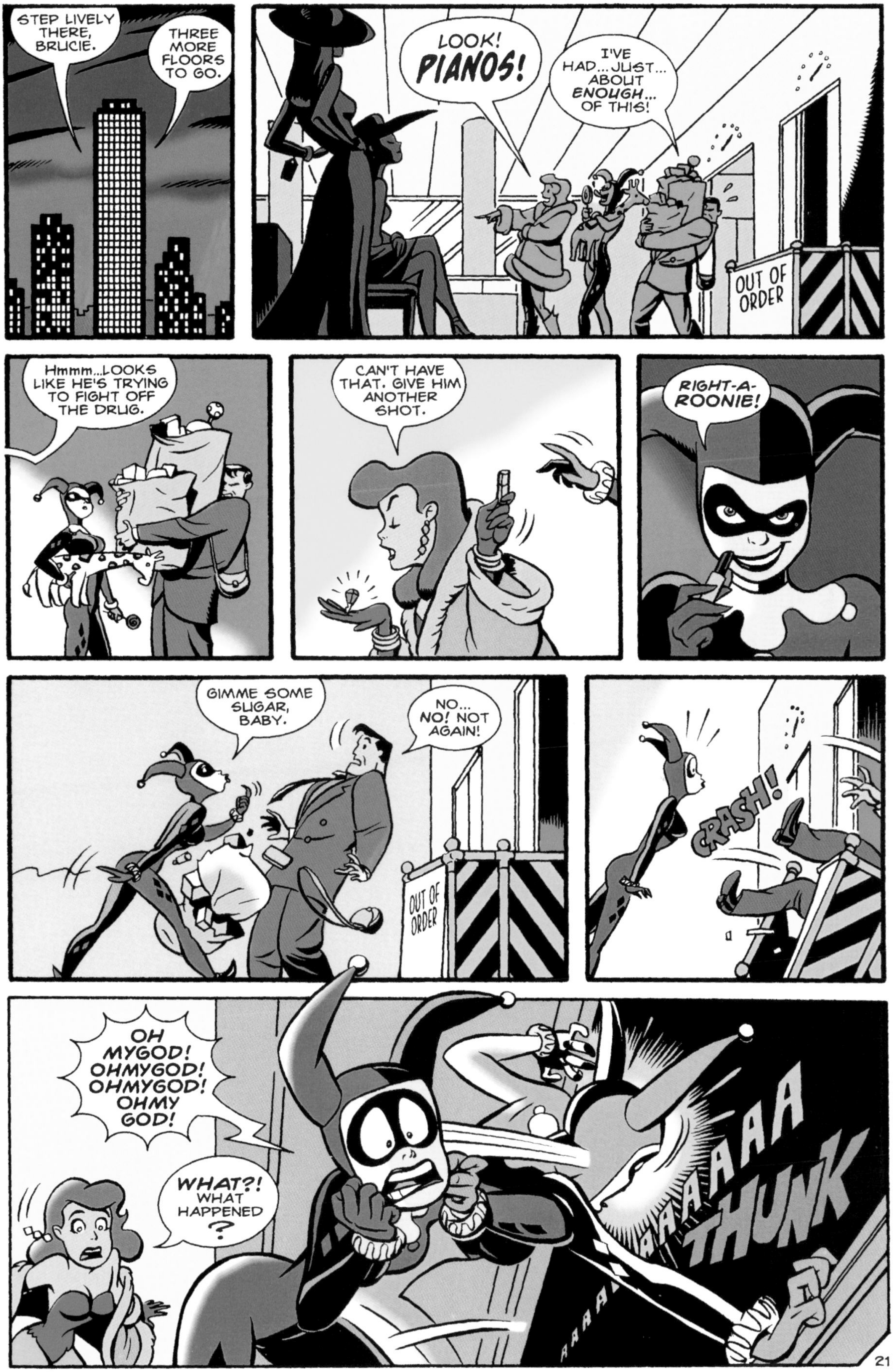
STEP LIVELY THERE, BRUCIE.
THREE MORE FLOORS TO GO.
LOOK! PIANOS!
I'VE HAD... JUST... ABOUT ENOUGH... OF THIS!
OUT OF ORDER
Hmmm...LOOKS LIKE HE'S TRYING TO FIGHT OFF THE DRUG.
CAN'T HAVE THAT. GIVE HIM ANOTHER SHOT.
RIGHT-A-ROONIE!
GIMME SOME SUGAR, BABY.
NO... NO! NOT AGAIN!
OUT OF ORDER
CRASH!
OH MYGOD! OHMYGOD! OHMYGOD! OHMY GOD!
WHAT?! WHAT HAPPENED?
AAAAAAAAAAAA
THUNK
21

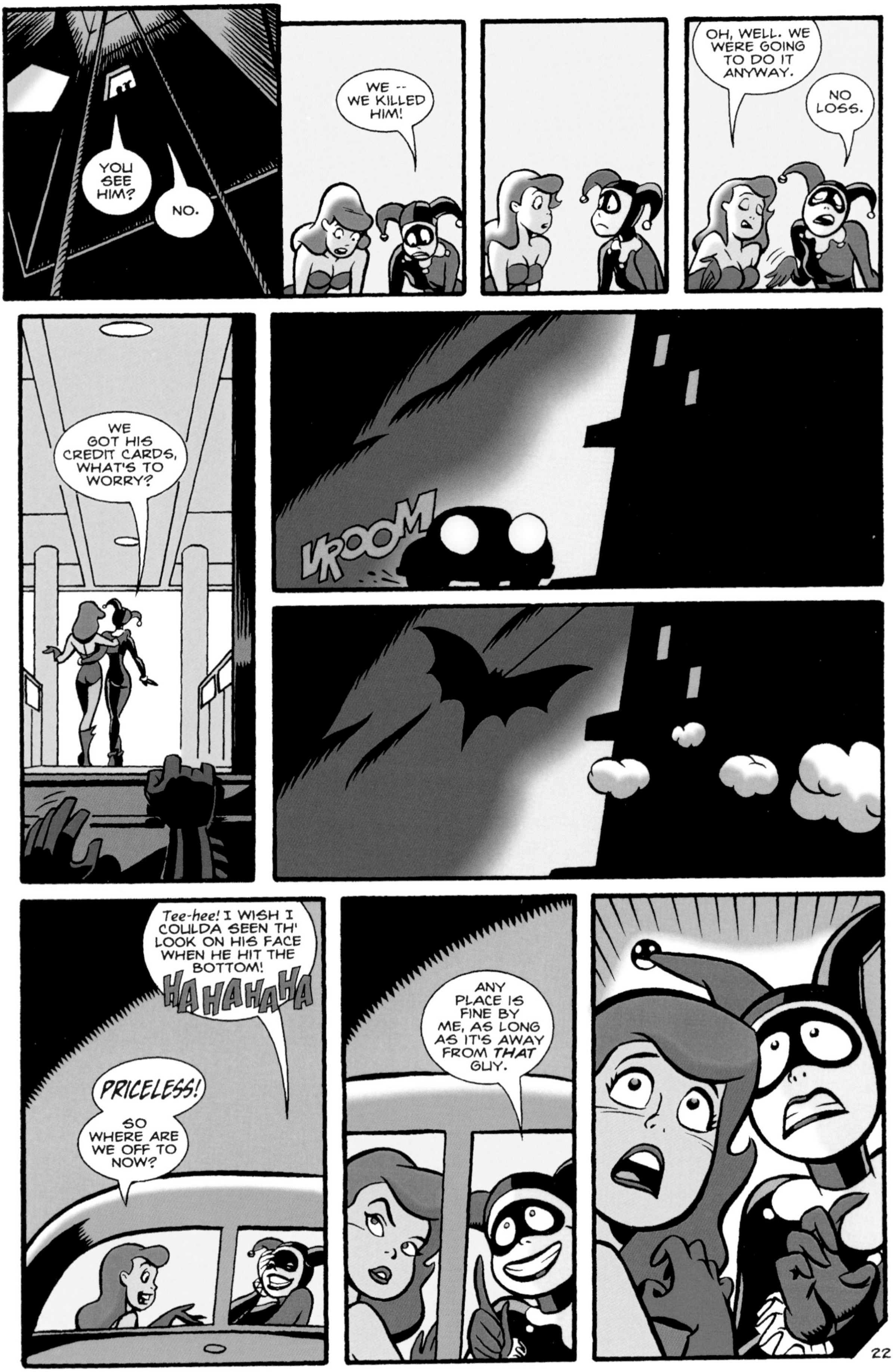
YOU SEE HIM?
NO.
WE -- WE KILLED HIM!
OH, WELL. WE WERE GOING TO DO IT ANYWAY.
NO LOSS.
WE GOT HIS CREDIT CARDS, WHAT'S TO WORRY?
VROOM
Tee-hee! I WISH I COULDA SEEN TH' LOOK ON HIS FACE WHEN HE HIT THE BOTTOM!
HAHAHAHAHA
PRICELESS!
SO WHERE ARE WE OFF TO NOW?
ANY PLACE IS FINE BY ME, AS LONG AS IT'S AWAY FROM THAT GUY.
22

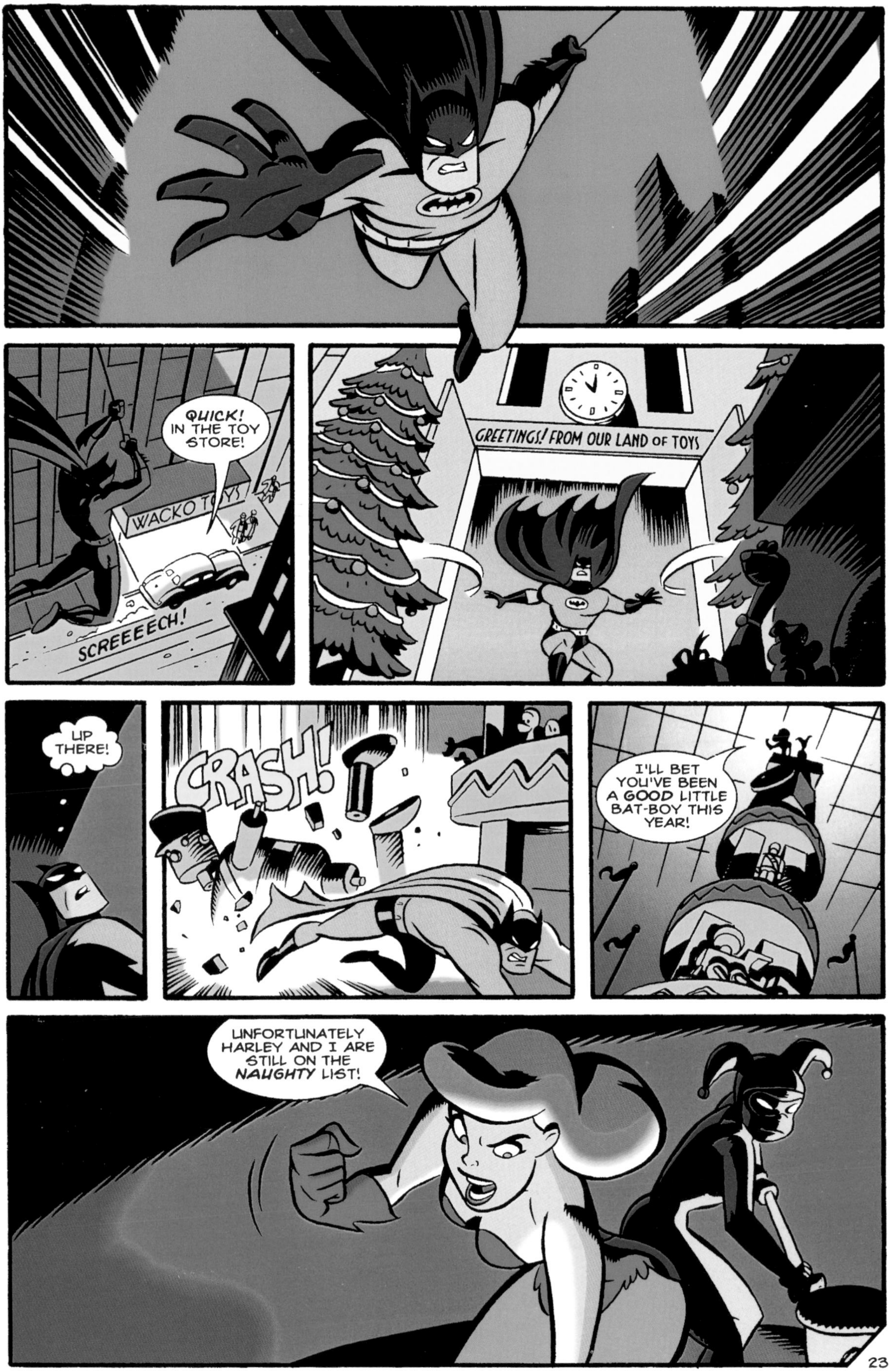
QUICK! IN THE TOY STORE!
WACKO TOYS
SCREEEECH!
GREETINGS! FROM OUR LAND OF TOYS
UP THERE!
CRASH!
I'LL BET YOU'VE BEEN A GOOD LITTLE BAT-BOY THIS YEAR!
UNFORTUNATELY HARLEY AND I ARE STILL ON THE NAUGHTY LIST!
23

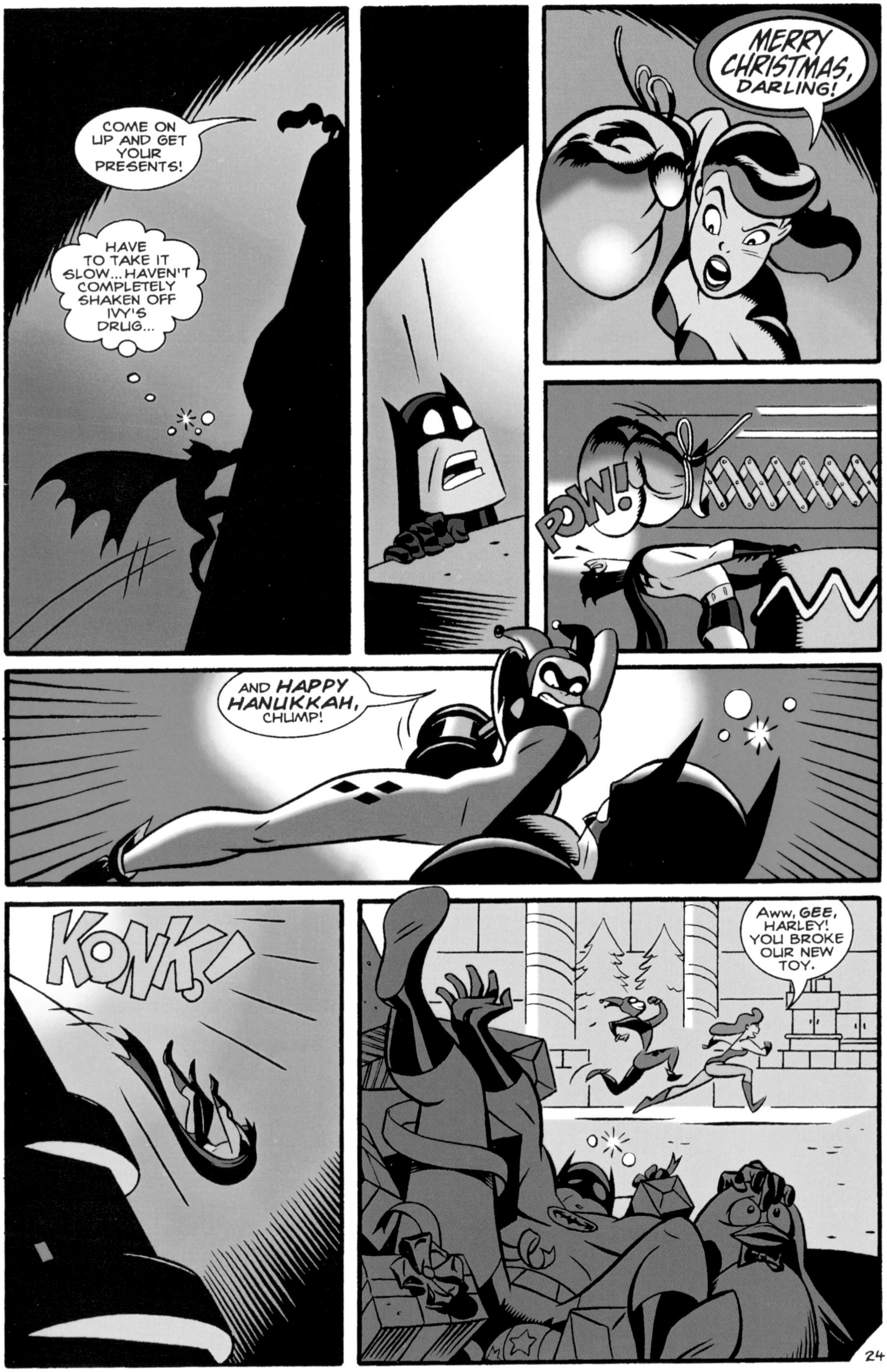
COME ON UP AND GET YOUR PRESENTS!
HAVE TO TAKE IT SLOW... HAVEN'T COMPLETELY SHAKEN OFF IVY'S DRUG...
MERRY CHRISTMAS, DARLING!
POW!
AND HAPPY HANUKKAH, CHUMP!
KONK!
AWW, GEE, HARLEY! YOU BROKE OUR NEW TOY.
24

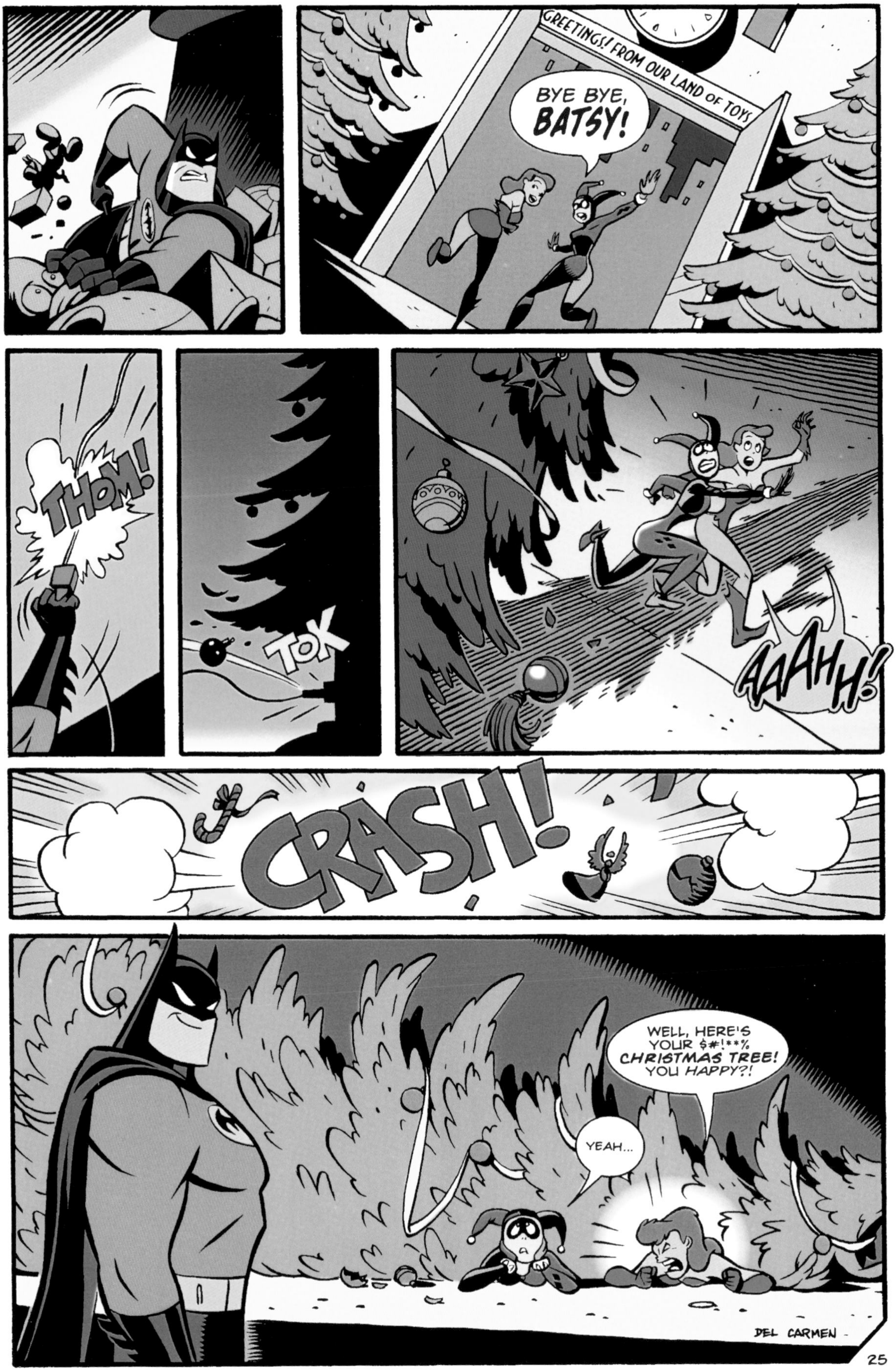
GREETINGS! FROM OUR LAND OF TOYS
BYE BYE, BATSY!
THOM!
TOK
AAAHH!
CRASH!
WELL, HERE'S YOUR $#!**% CHRISTMAS TREE! YOU HAPPY?!
YEAH...
DEL CARMEN
25

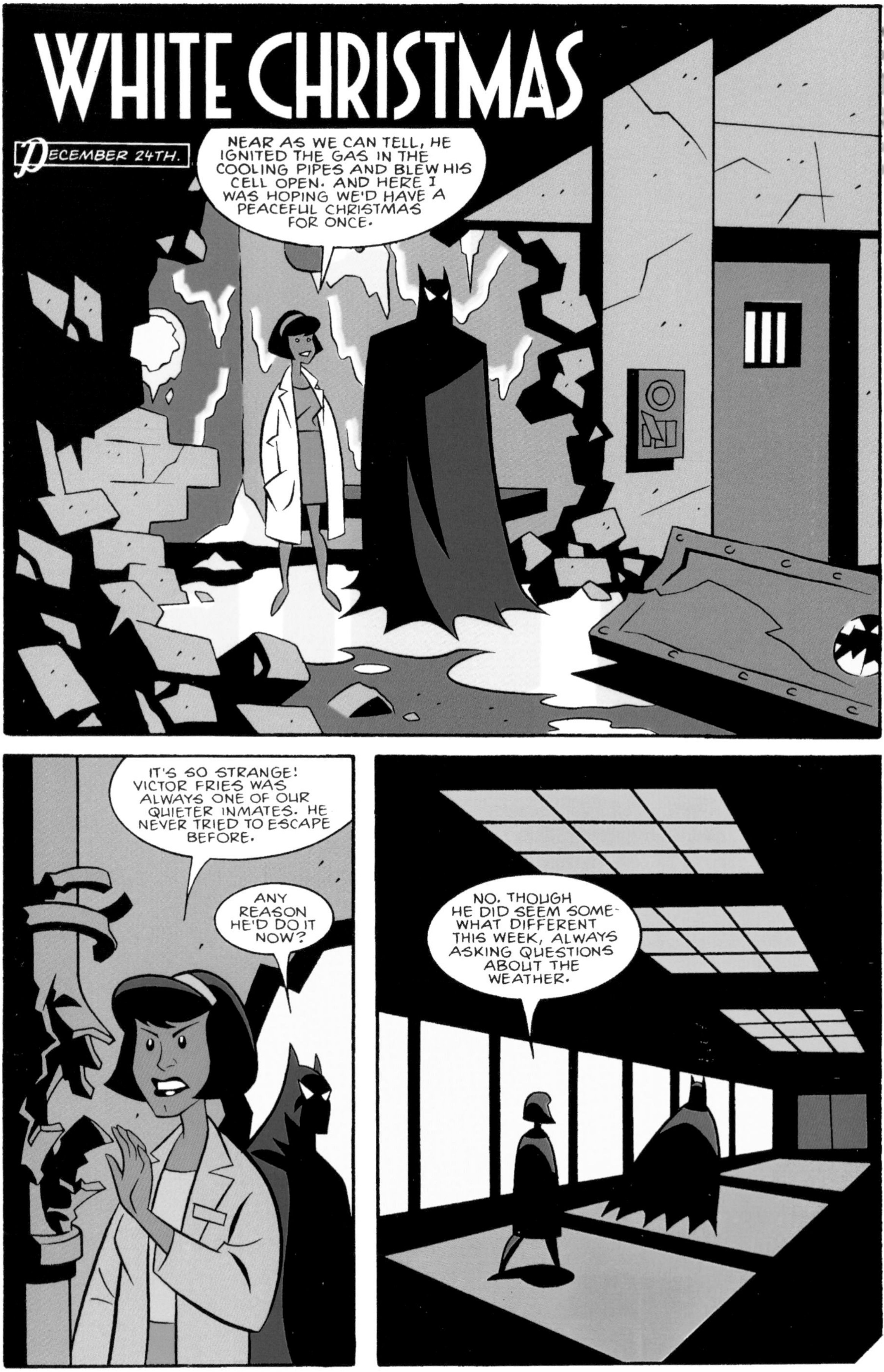
WHITE CHRISTMAS
DECEMBER 24TH.
NEAR AS WE CAN TELL, HE IGNITED THE GAS IN THE COOLING PIPES AND BLEW HIS CELL OPEN. AND HERE I WAS HOPING WE'D HAVE A PEACEFUL CHRISTMAS FOR ONCE.
IT'S SO STRANGE! VICTOR FRIES WAS ALWAYS ONE OF OUR QUIETER INMATES. HE NEVER TRIED TO ESCAPE BEFORE.
ANY REASON HE'D DO IT NOW?
NO. THOUGH HE DID SEEM SOME-WHAT DIFFERENT THIS WEEK, ALWAYS ASKING QUESTIONS ABOUT THE WEATHER.

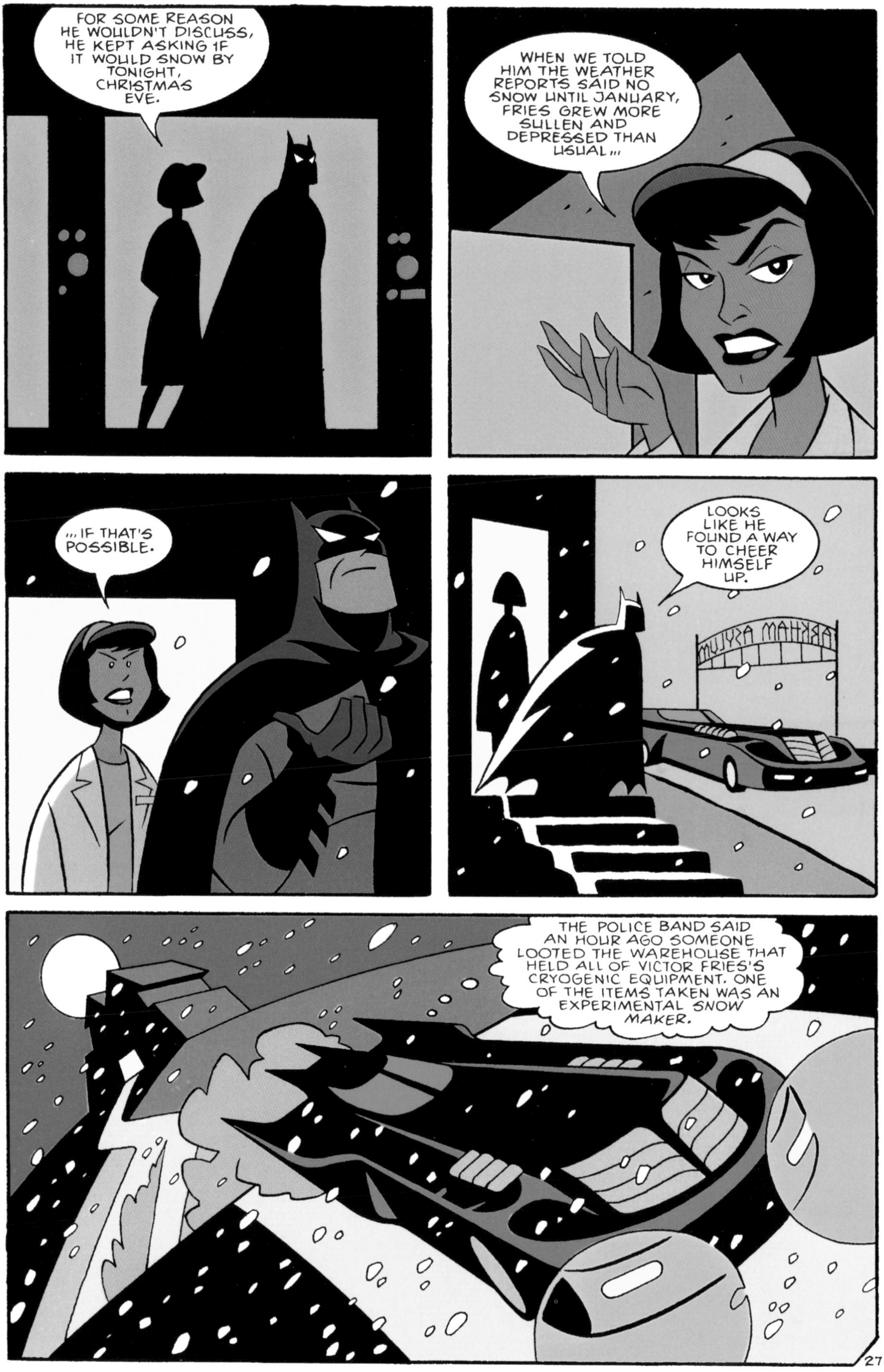

FOR SOME REASON HE WOULDN'T DISCUSS, HE KEPT ASKING IF IT WOULD SNOW BY TONIGHT, CHRISTMAS EVE.
WHEN WE TOLD HIM THE WEATHER REPORTS SAID NO SNOW UNTIL JANUARY, FRIES GREW MORE SULLEN AND DEPRESSED THAN USUAL...
...IF THAT'S POSSIBLE.
LOOKS LIKE HE FOUND A WAY TO CHEER HIMSELF UP.
ARKHAM ASYLUM
THE POLICE BAND SAID AN HOUR AGO SOMEONE LOOTED THE WAREHOUSE THAT HELD ALL OF VICTOR FRIES'S CRYOGENIC EQUIPMENT. ONE OF THE ITEMS TAKEN WAS AN EXPERIMENTAL SNOW MAKER.
27

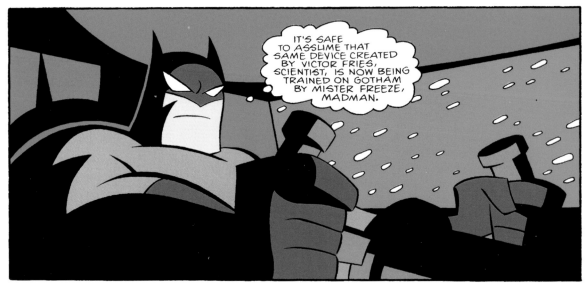

IT'S SAFE TO ASSUME THAT SAME DEVICE CREATED BY VICTOR FRIES, SCIENTIST, IS NOW BEING TRAINED ON GOTHAM BY MISTER FREEZE, MADMAN.

" IN THE ENSUING STRUGGLE, VICTOR FRIES WAS EXPOSED TO HIS OWN SUPER-COOLANT, WHICH RENDERED HIM UNABLE TO LIVE OUT OF A SUBZERO ENVIRONMENT.

" FREEZE'S STORY IS AS TRAGIC AS THEY COME. A *BRILLIANT* INVENTOR, HE CREATED A UNIQUE WAY OF FREEZING THE TERMINALLY ILL, UNTIL A *CURE* COULD BE FOUND. HIS FIRST PATIENT WAS HIS OWN WIFE, WHO HAD BEEN STRICKEN WITH INOPERABLE CANCER. BUT THE HEARTLESS CORPO- RATION FUNDING THE PROJECT DEEMED IT TOO COSTLY AND ORDERED IT SHUT DOWN.

" HIS WIFE'S BODY WAS LOST IN THE EXPLOSION.

" WITH HIS ONLY REASON FOR LIVING GONE, MR. FREEZE NOW CLAIMS TO BE DEAD TO HUMAN EMOTION.

" ANYONE WHO'D CALL DOWN A BLIZZARD LIKE THIS ON CHRISTMAS EVE WOULD HAVE TO BE.

28

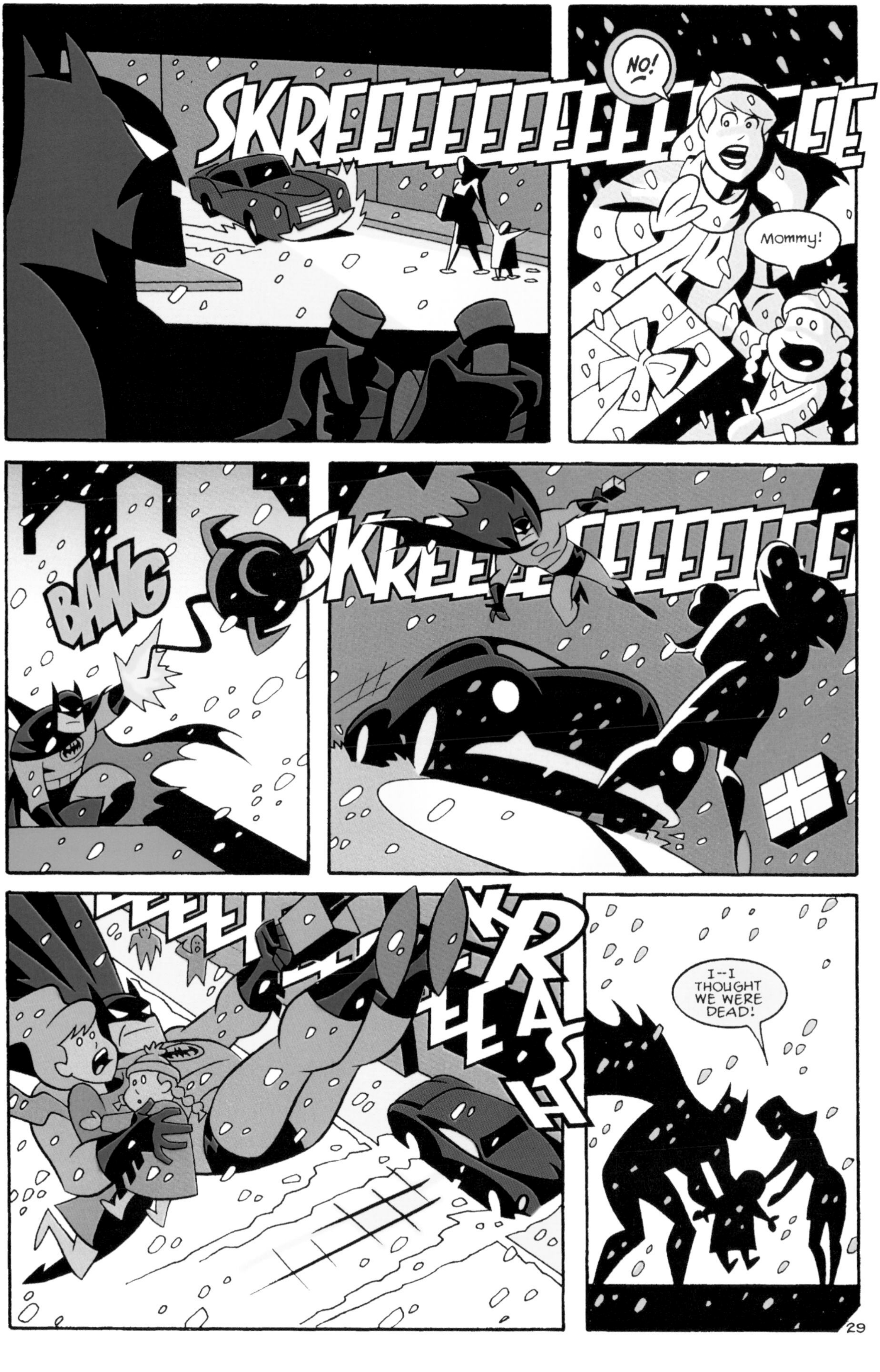

SKREEEEEEEEEEEEEEEE
NO!
Mommy!
BANG
SKREEEEEEEEEEEE
KRASH
I--I THOUGHT WE WERE DEAD!
29

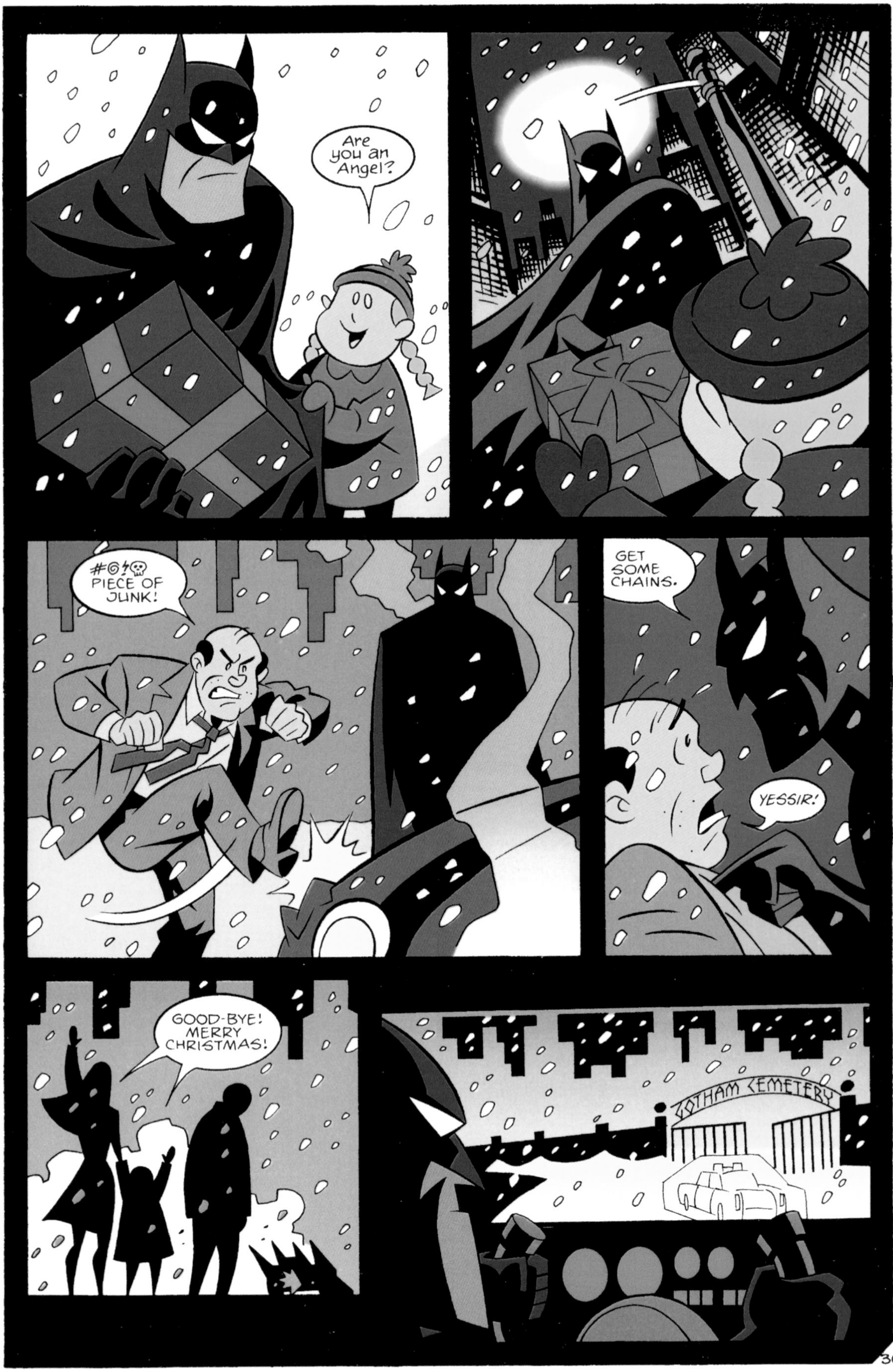
Are you an Angel?
#@!☠ PIECE OF JUNK!
GET SOME CHAINS.
YESSIR!
GOOD-BYE! MERRY CHRISTMAS!
GOTHAM CEMETERY
30

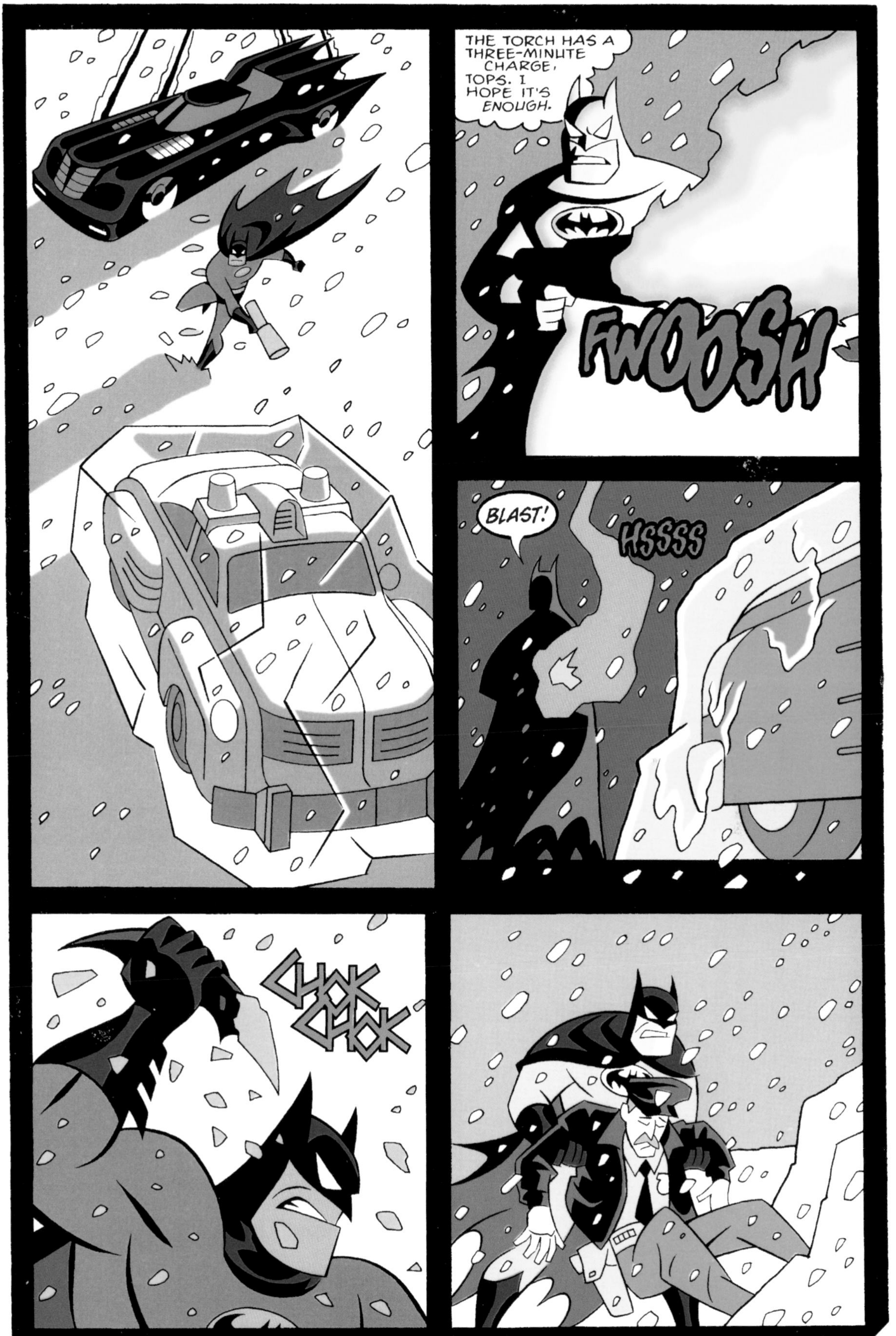
THE TORCH HAS A THREE-MINUTE CHARGE, TOPS. I HOPE IT'S ENOUGH.
FWOOSH
BLAST!
HSSSS
CHOK CHOK
31

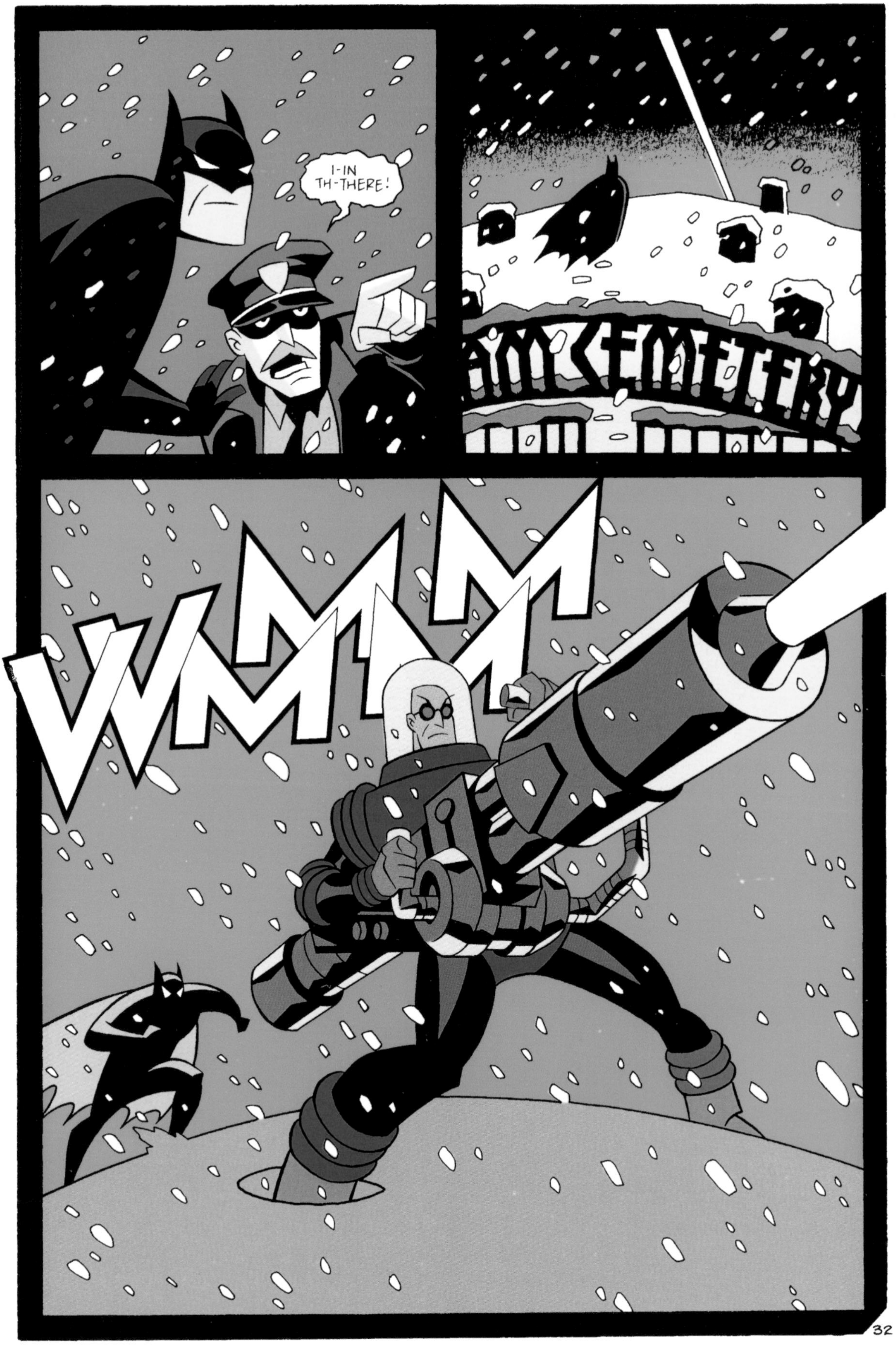
I-IN TH-THERE!
...AM CEMETERY
VVMMMM
32

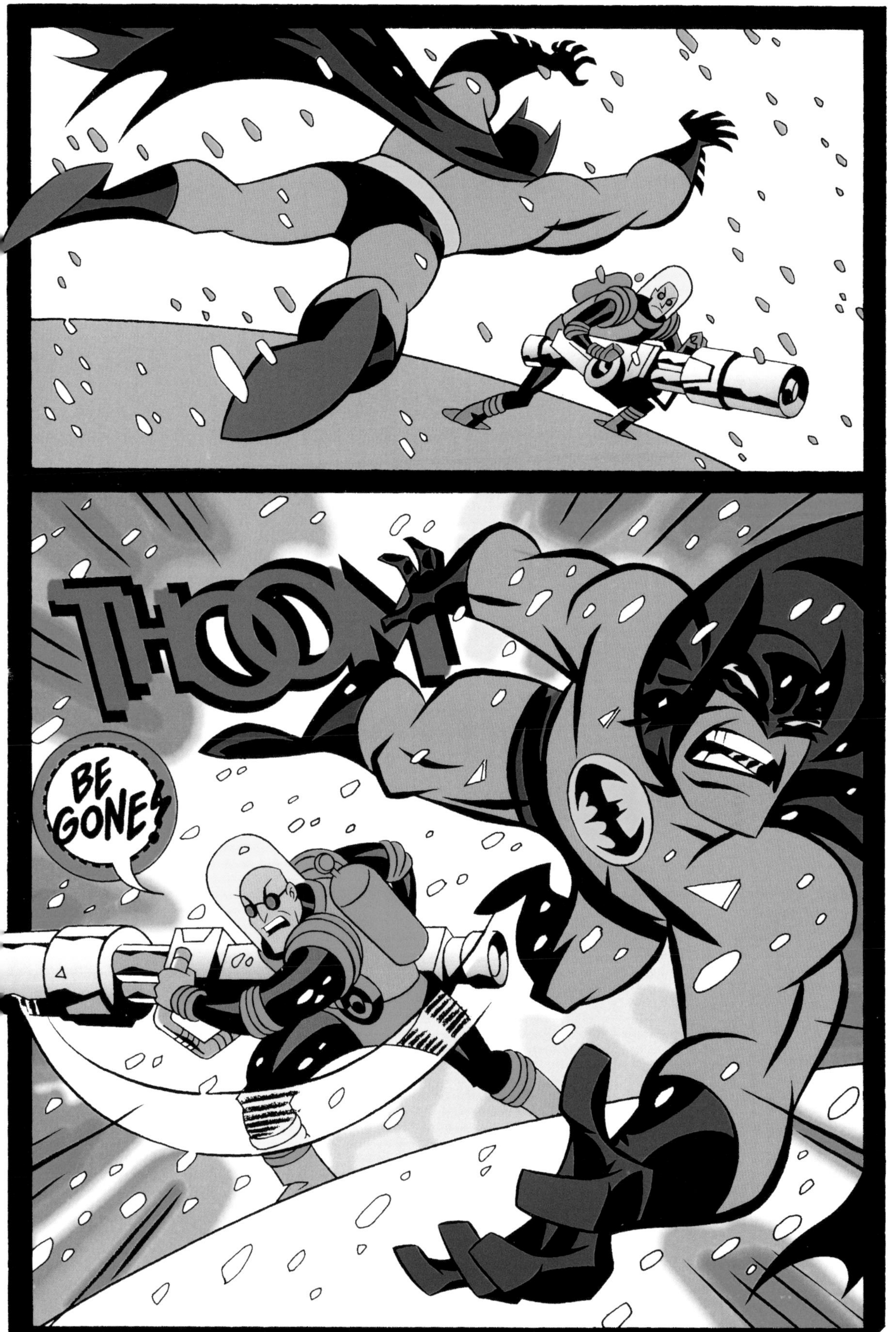
THOOM
BE GONE!
33

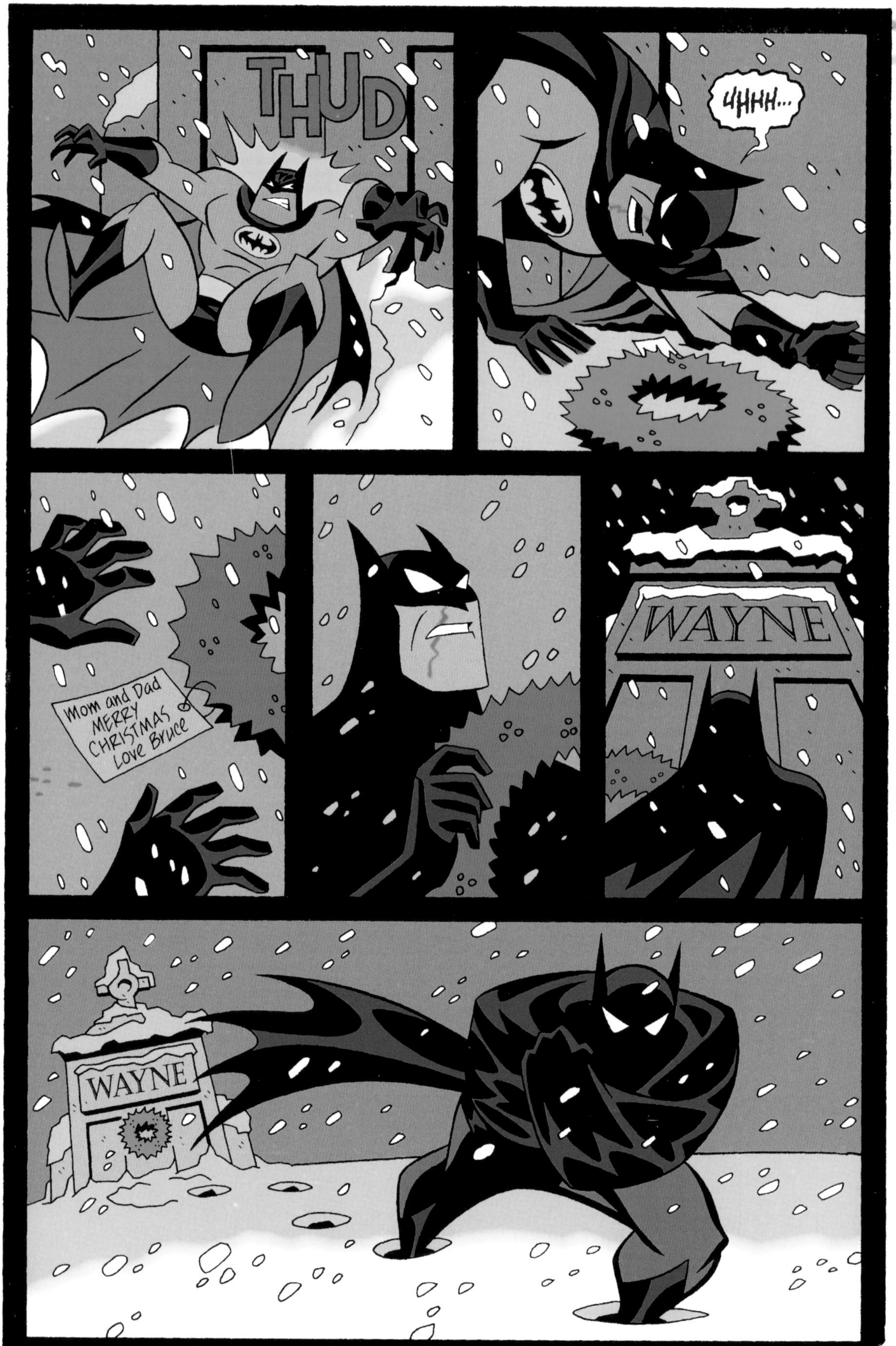
THUD
UHHH...
Mom and Dad MERRY CHRISTMAS Love Bruce
WAYNE
WAYNE
34

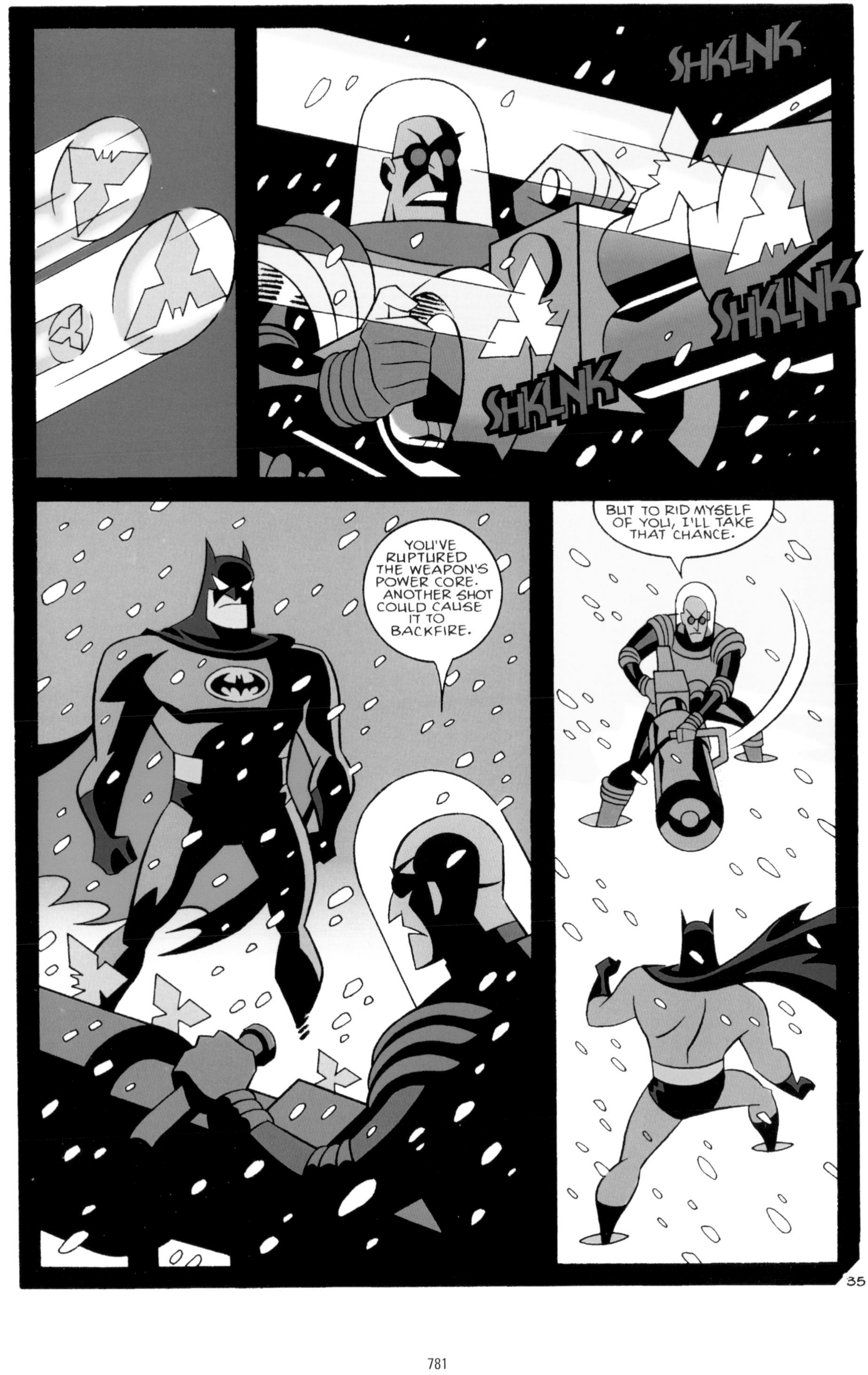
SHKLNK
SHKLNK
SHKLNK
YOU'VE RUPTURED THE WEAPON'S POWER CORE. ANOTHER SHOT COULD CAUSE IT TO BACKFIRE.
BUT TO RID MYSELF OF YOU, I'LL TAKE THAT CHANCE.
35

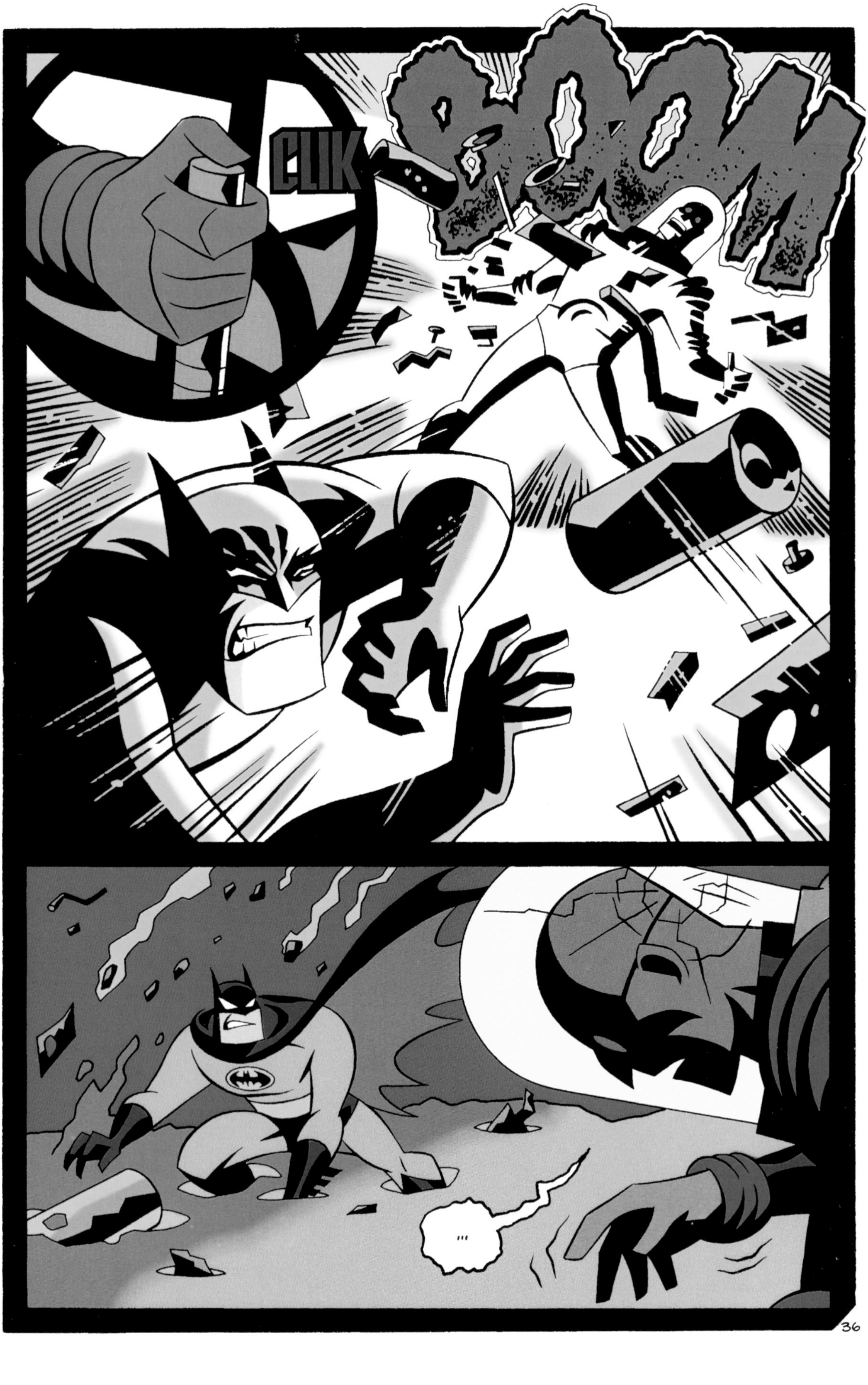
CLIK
BOOM
...

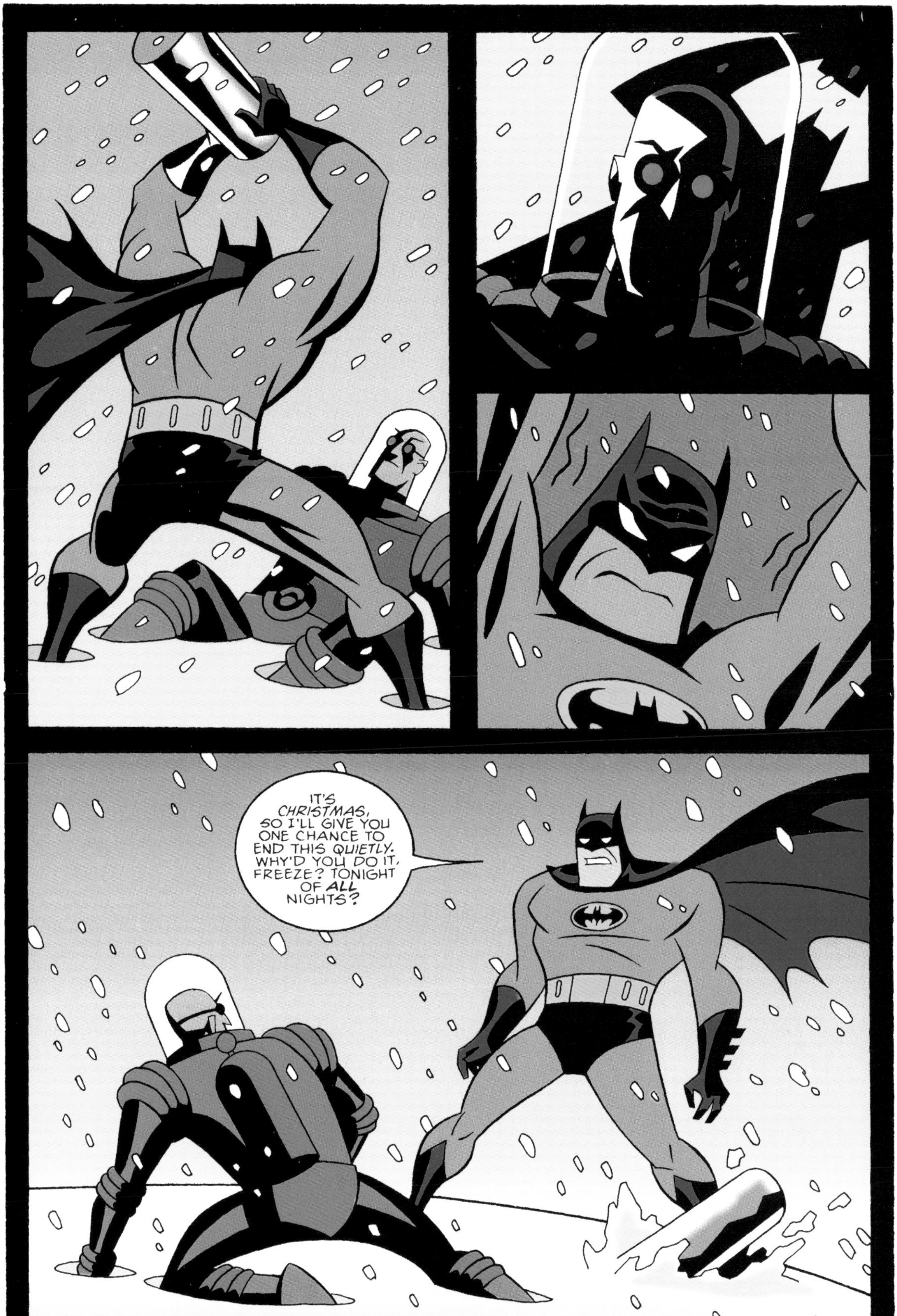
IT'S CHRISTMAS, SO I'LL GIVE YOU ONE CHANCE TO END THIS QUIETLY. WHY'D YOU DO IT, FREEZE? TONIGHT OF ALL NIGHTS?
37

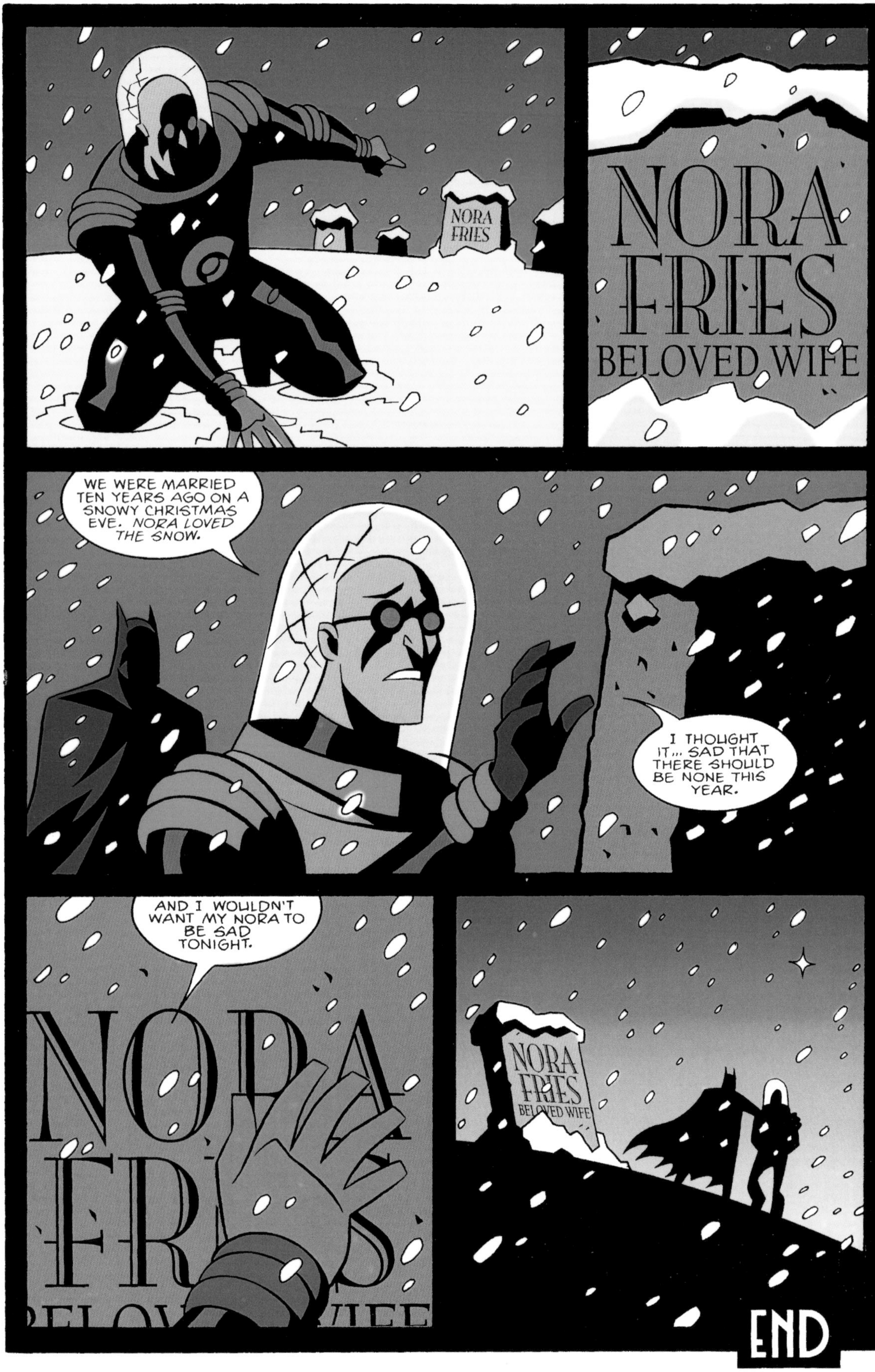
NORA FRIES
NORA FRIES BELOVED WIFE
WE WERE MARRIED TEN YEARS AGO ON A SNOWY CHRISTMAS EVE. NORA LOVED THE SNOW.
I THOUGHT IT... SAD THAT THERE SHOULD BE NONE THIS YEAR.
AND I WOULDN'T WANT MY NORA TO BE SAD TONIGHT.
NORA FRIES BELOVED WIFE
END

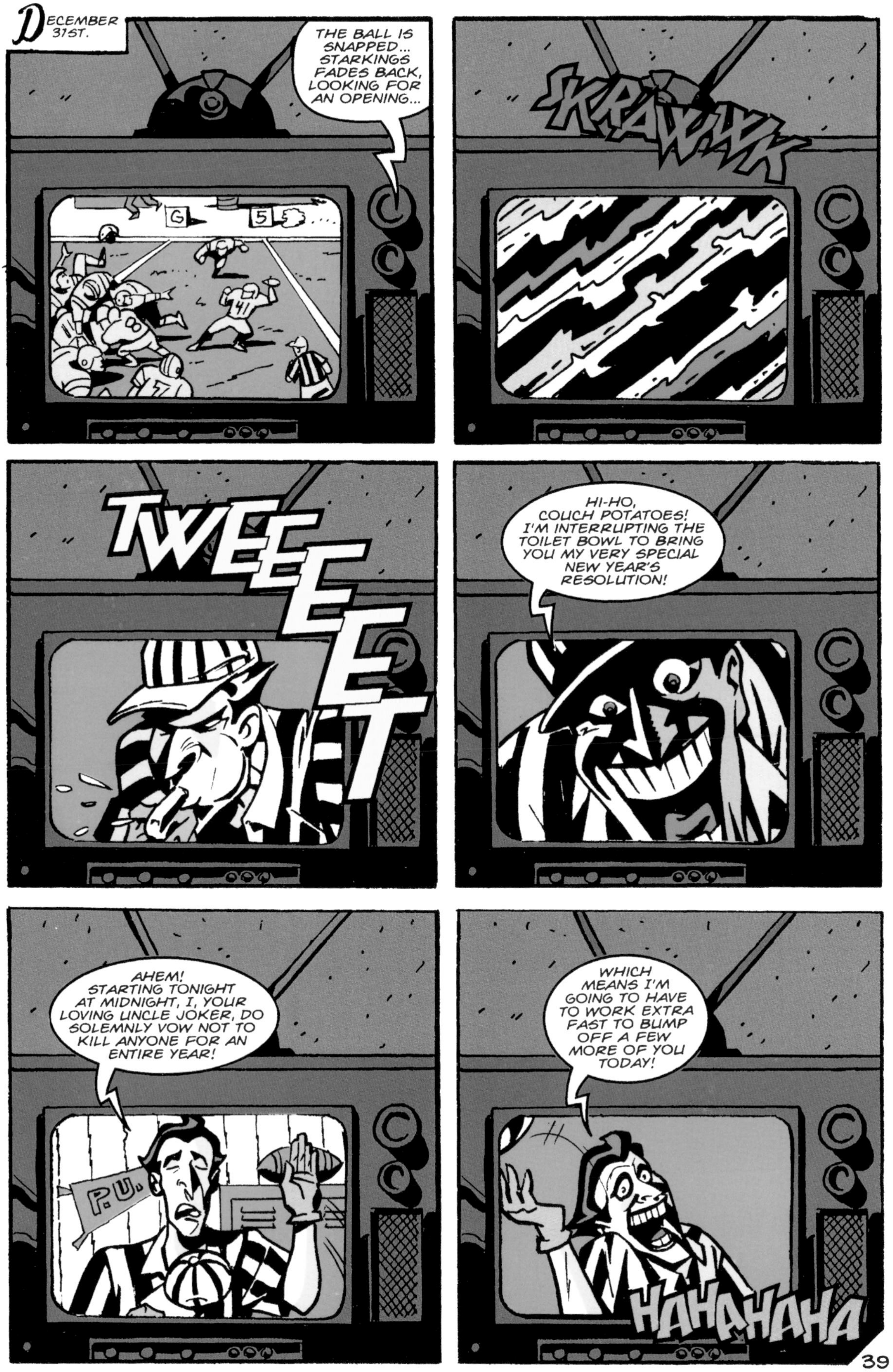
DECEMBER 31ST.
THE BALL IS SNAPPED... STARKINGS FADES BACK, LOOKING FOR AN OPENING...
SKRAWWK
TWEEEEET
HI-HO, COUCH POTATOES! I'M INTERRUPTING THE TOILET BOWL TO BRING YOU MY VERY SPECIAL NEW YEAR'S RESOLUTION!
AHEM! STARTING TONIGHT AT MIDNIGHT, I, YOUR LOVING UNCLE JOKER, DO SOLEMNLY VOW NOT TO KILL ANYONE FOR AN ENTIRE YEAR!
P.U.
WHICH MEANS I'M GOING TO HAVE TO WORK EXTRA FAST TO BUMP OFF A FEW MORE OF YOU TODAY!
HAHAHAHA
39

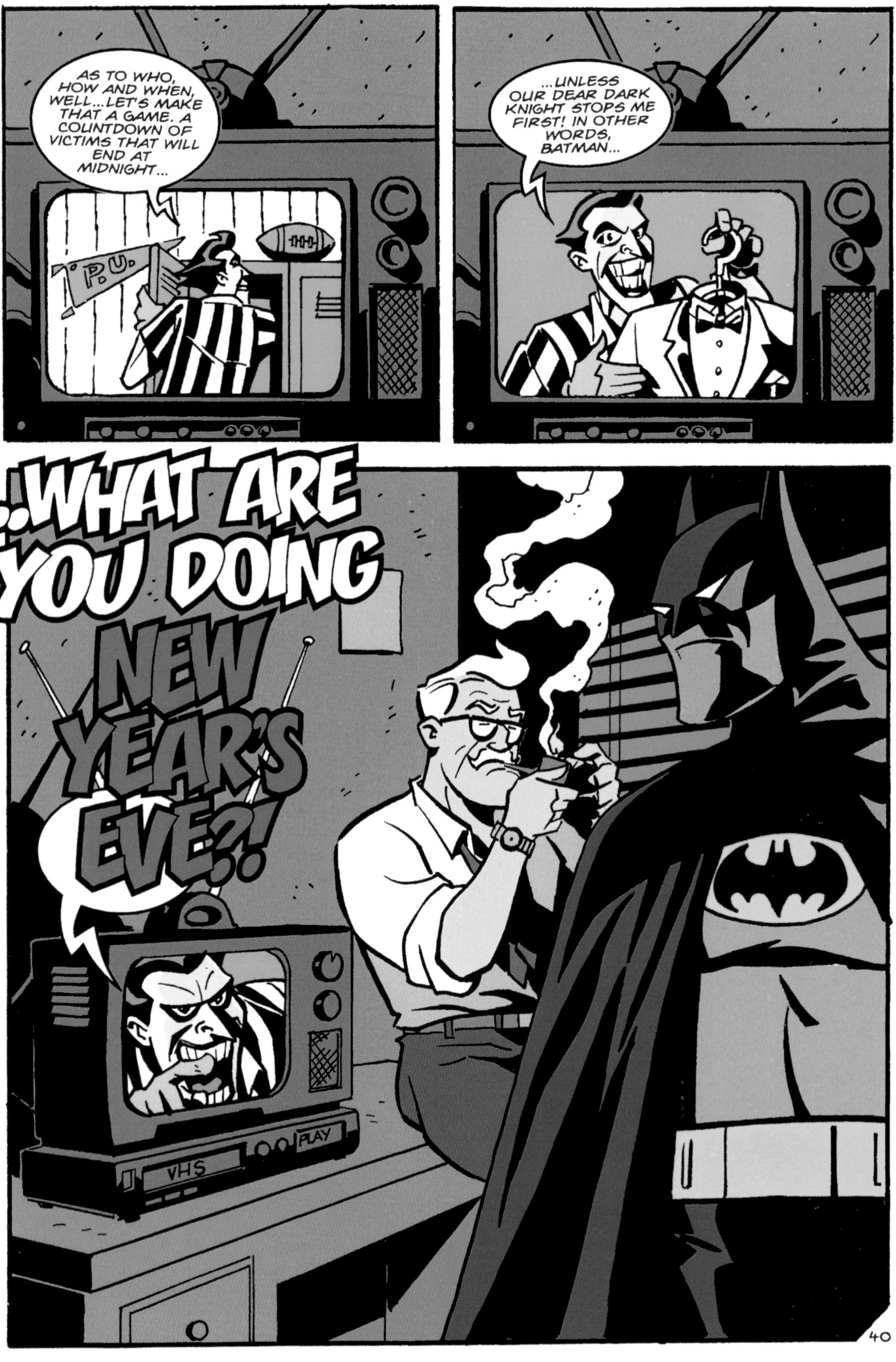
AS TO WHO, HOW AND WHEN, WELL...LET'S MAKE THAT A GAME. A COUNTDOWN OF VICTIMS THAT WILL END AT MIDNIGHT...
P.U.
...UNLESS OUR DEAR DARK KNIGHT STOPS ME FIRST! IN OTHER WORDS, BATMAN...
...WHAT ARE YOU DOING NEW YEAR'S EVE?!
PLAY
VHS
40

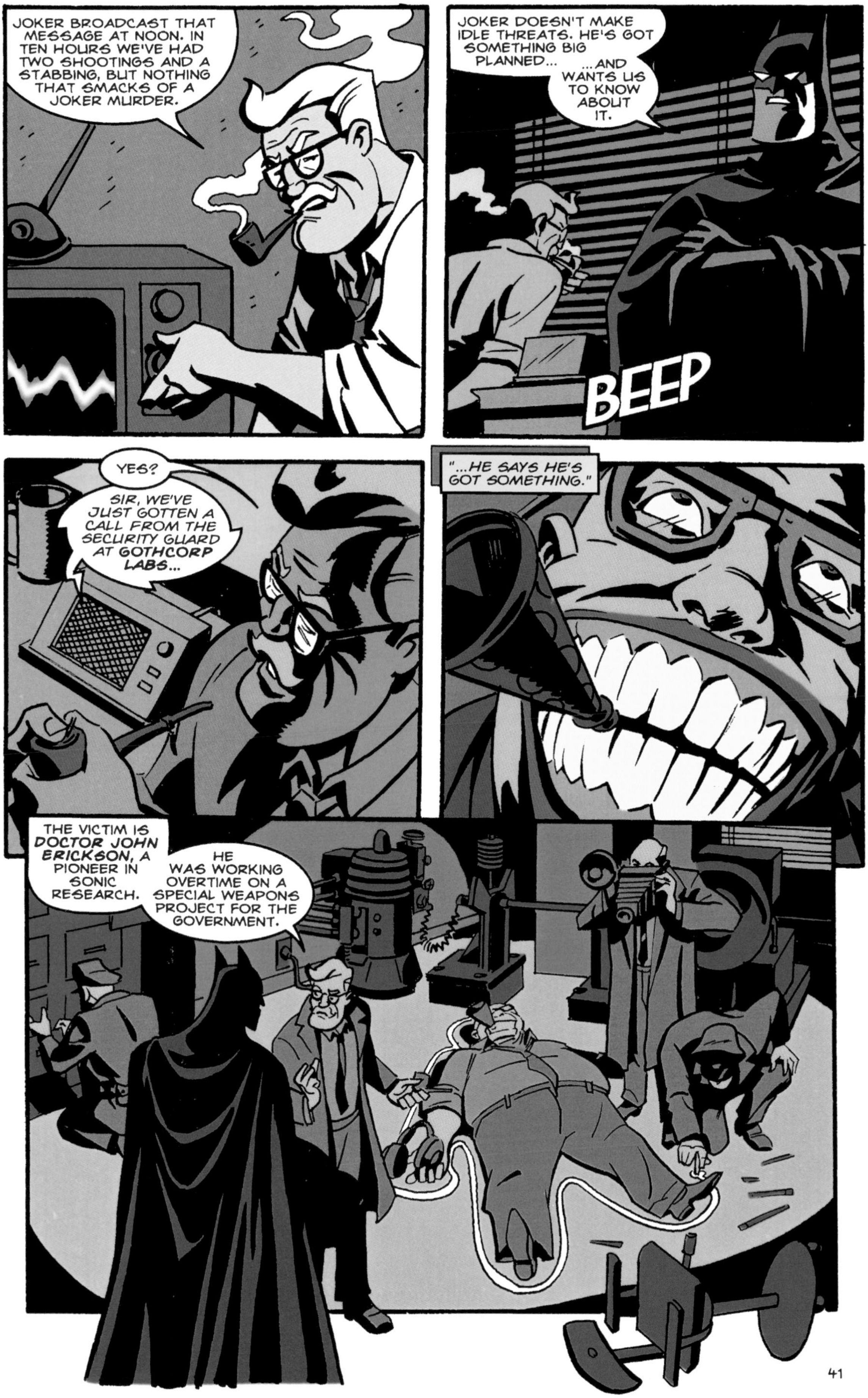

JOKER BROADCAST THAT MESSAGE AT NOON. IN TEN HOURS WE'VE HAD TWO SHOOTINGS AND A STABBING, BUT NOTHING THAT SMACKS OF A JOKER MURDER.
JOKER DOESN'T MAKE IDLE THREATS. HE'S GOT SOMETHING BIG PLANNED...
...AND WANTS US TO KNOW ABOUT IT.
BEEP
YES?
SIR, WE'VE JUST GOTTEN A CALL FROM THE SECURITY GUARD AT GOTHCORP LABS...
"...HE SAYS HE'S GOT SOMETHING."
THE VICTIM IS DOCTOR JOHN ERICKSON, A PIONEER IN SONIC RESEARCH.
HE WAS WORKING OVERTIME ON A SPECIAL WEAPONS PROJECT FOR THE GOVERNMENT.
41

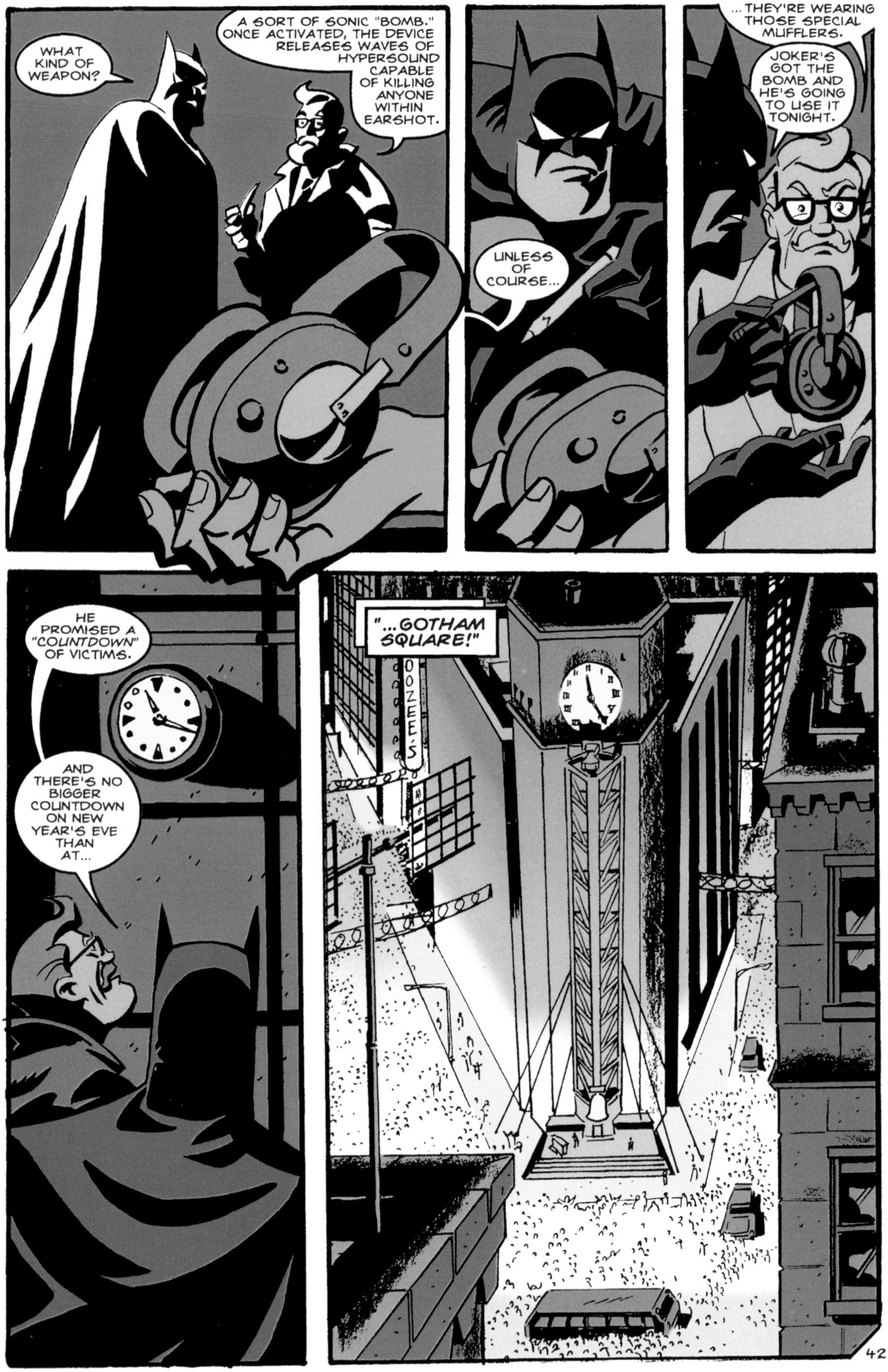
WHAT KIND OF WEAPON?
A SORT OF SONIC "BOMB." ONCE ACTIVATED, THE DEVICE RELEASES WAVES OF HYPERSOUND CAPABLE OF KILLING ANYONE WITHIN EARSHOT.
UNLESS OF COURSE...
...THEY'RE WEARING THOSE SPECIAL MUFFLERS.
JOKER'S GOT THE BOMB AND HE'S GOING TO USE IT TONIGHT.
HE PROMISED A "COUNTDOWN" OF VICTIMS.
AND THERE'S NO BIGGER COUNTDOWN ON NEW YEAR'S EVE THAN AT...
"...GOTHAM SQUARE!"
OOZEE'S
42

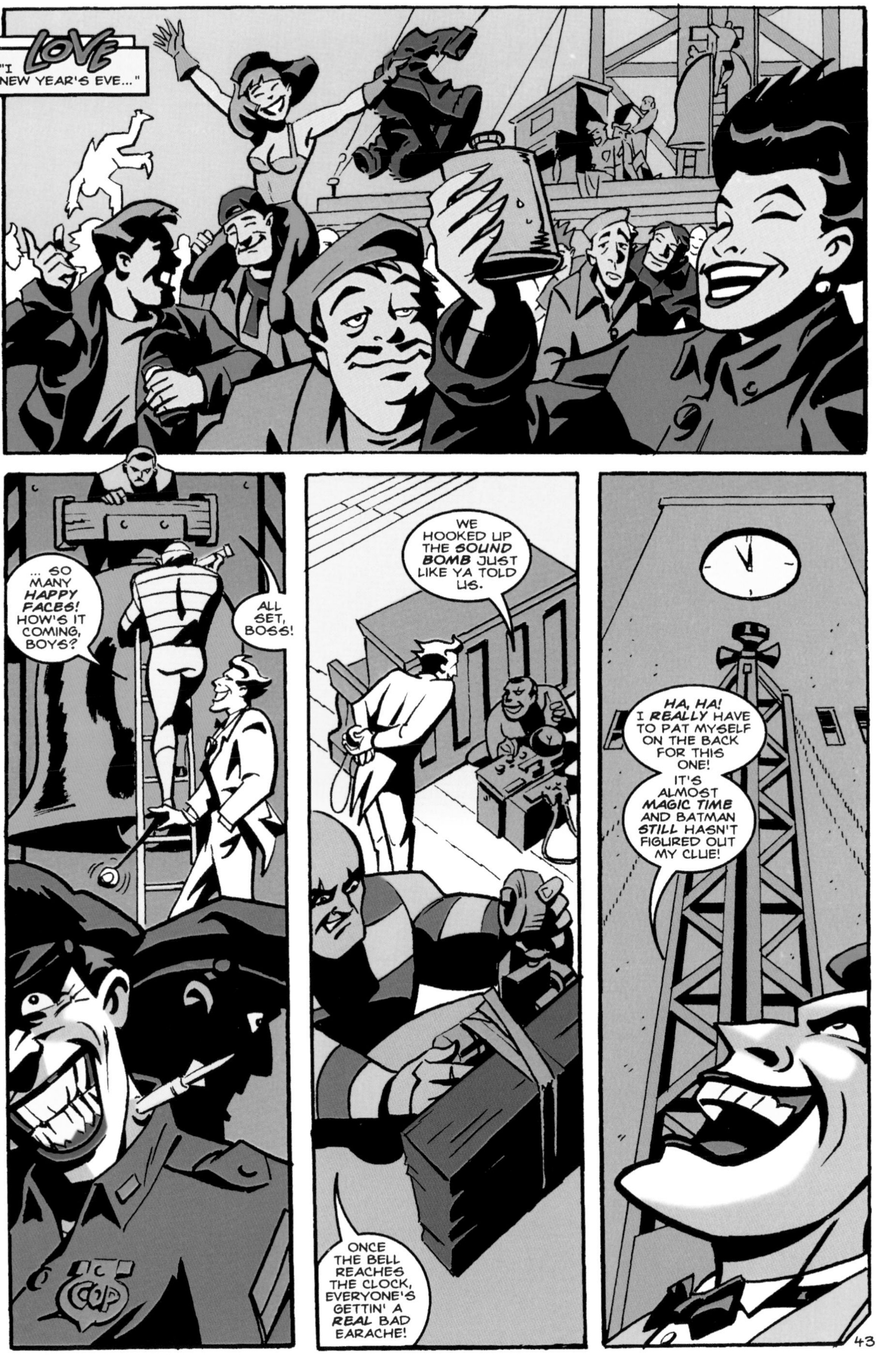

"I LOVE NEW YEAR'S EVE..."
... SO MANY HAPPY FACES! HOW'S IT COMING, BOYS?
ALL SET, BOSS!
WE HOOKED UP THE SOUND BOMB JUST LIKE YA TOLD US.
ONCE THE BELL REACHES THE CLOCK, EVERYONE'S GETTIN' A REAL BAD EARACHE!
HA, HA! I REALLY HAVE TO PAT MYSELF ON THE BACK FOR THIS ONE!
IT'S ALMOST MAGIC TIME AND BATMAN STILL HASN'T FIGURED OUT MY CLUE!
COP
43

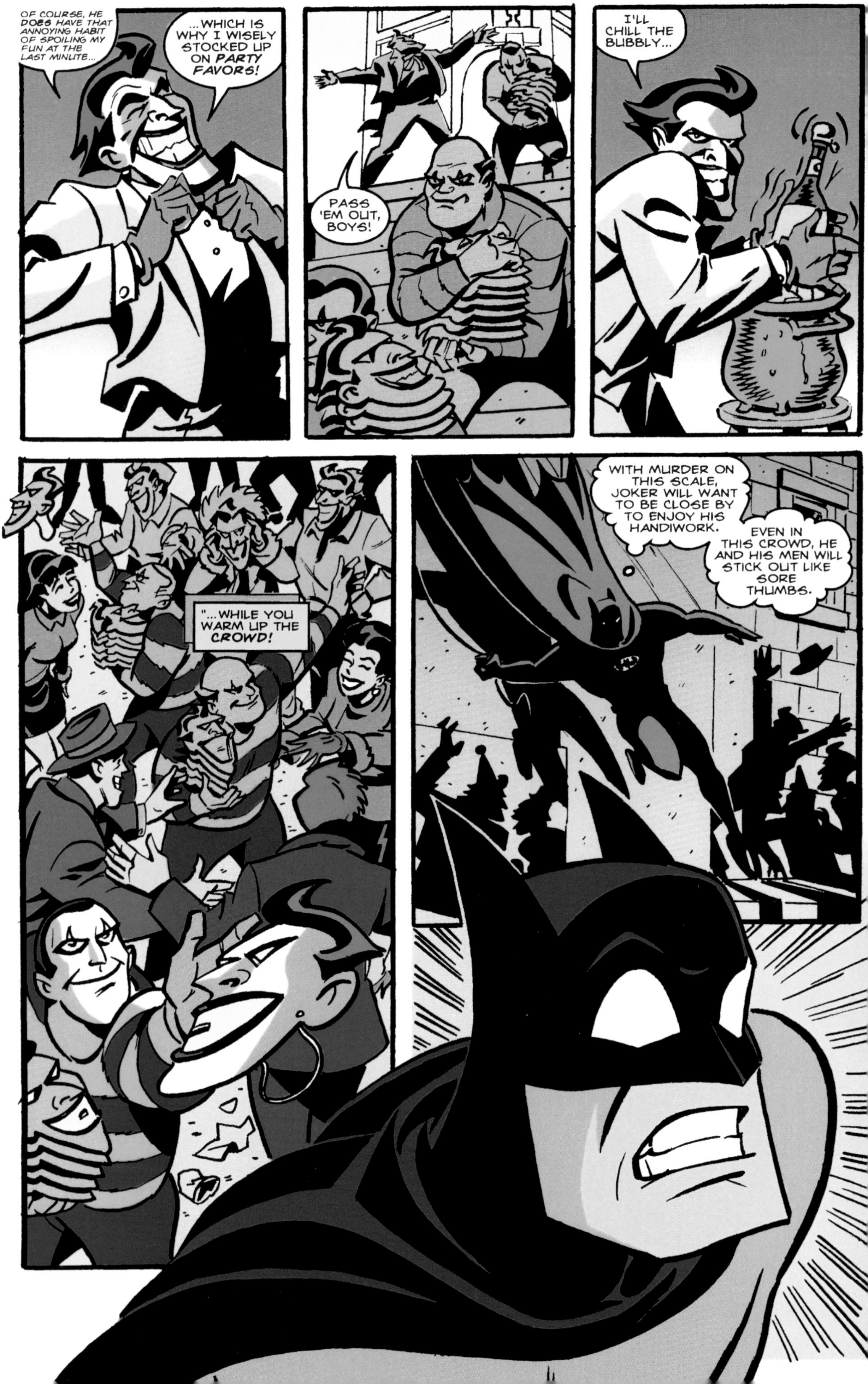
OF COURSE, HE DOES HAVE THAT ANNOYING HABIT OF SPOILING MY FUN AT THE LAST MINUTE...
...WHICH IS WHY I WISELY STOCKED UP ON PARTY FAVORS!
PASS 'EM OUT, BOYS!
I'LL CHILL THE BUBBLY...
"...WHILE YOU WARM UP THE CROWD!
WITH MURDER ON THIS SCALE, JOKER WILL WANT TO BE CLOSE BY TO ENJOY HIS HANDIWORK.
EVEN IN THIS CROWD, HE AND HIS MEN WILL STICK OUT LIKE SORE THUMBS.

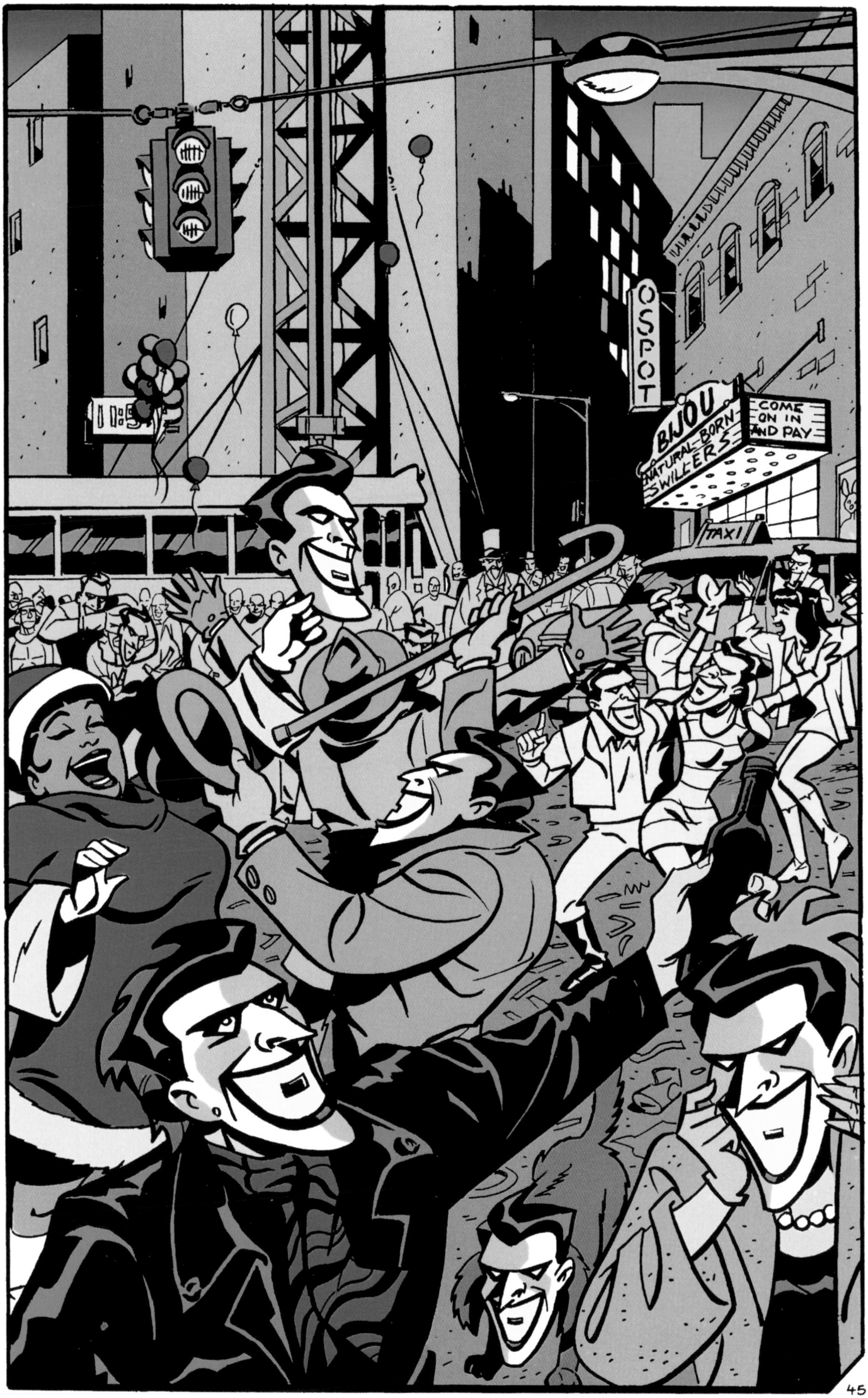
OSPOT
BIJOU
NATURAL-BORN SWILLERS
COME ON IN AND PAY
TAXI

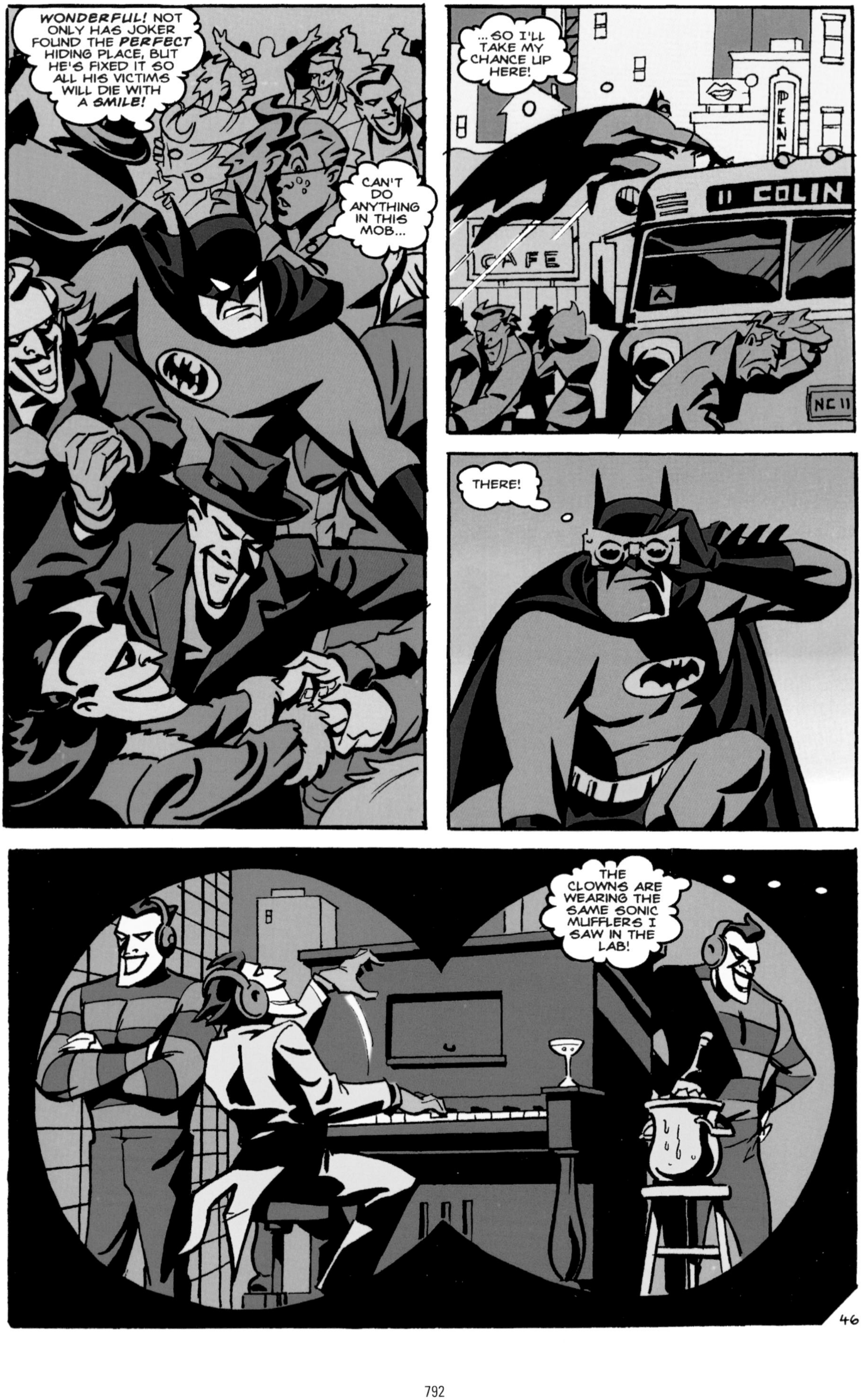
WONDERFUL! NOT ONLY HAS JOKER FOUND THE PERFECT HIDING PLACE, BUT HE'S FIXED IT SO ALL HIS VICTIMS WILL DIE WITH A SMILE!
CAN'T DO ANYTHING IN THIS MOB...
...SO I'LL TAKE MY CHANCE UP HERE!
PEN
11 COLIN
CAFE
NC 11
THERE!
THE CLOWNS ARE WEARING THE SAME SONIC MUFFLERS I SAW IN THE LAB!
46

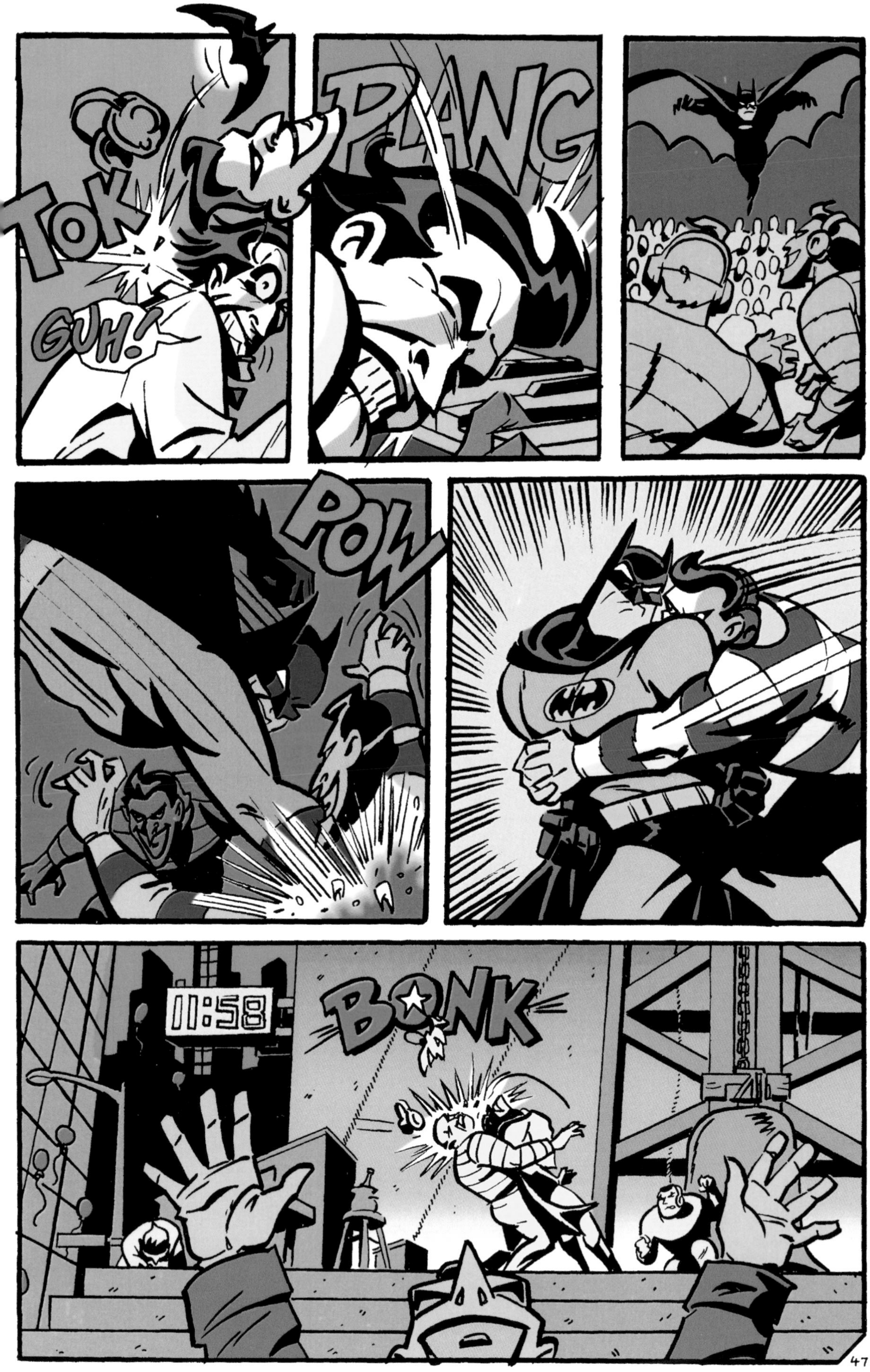
TOK
GUH!
PLANG
POW
11:58
BONK
47

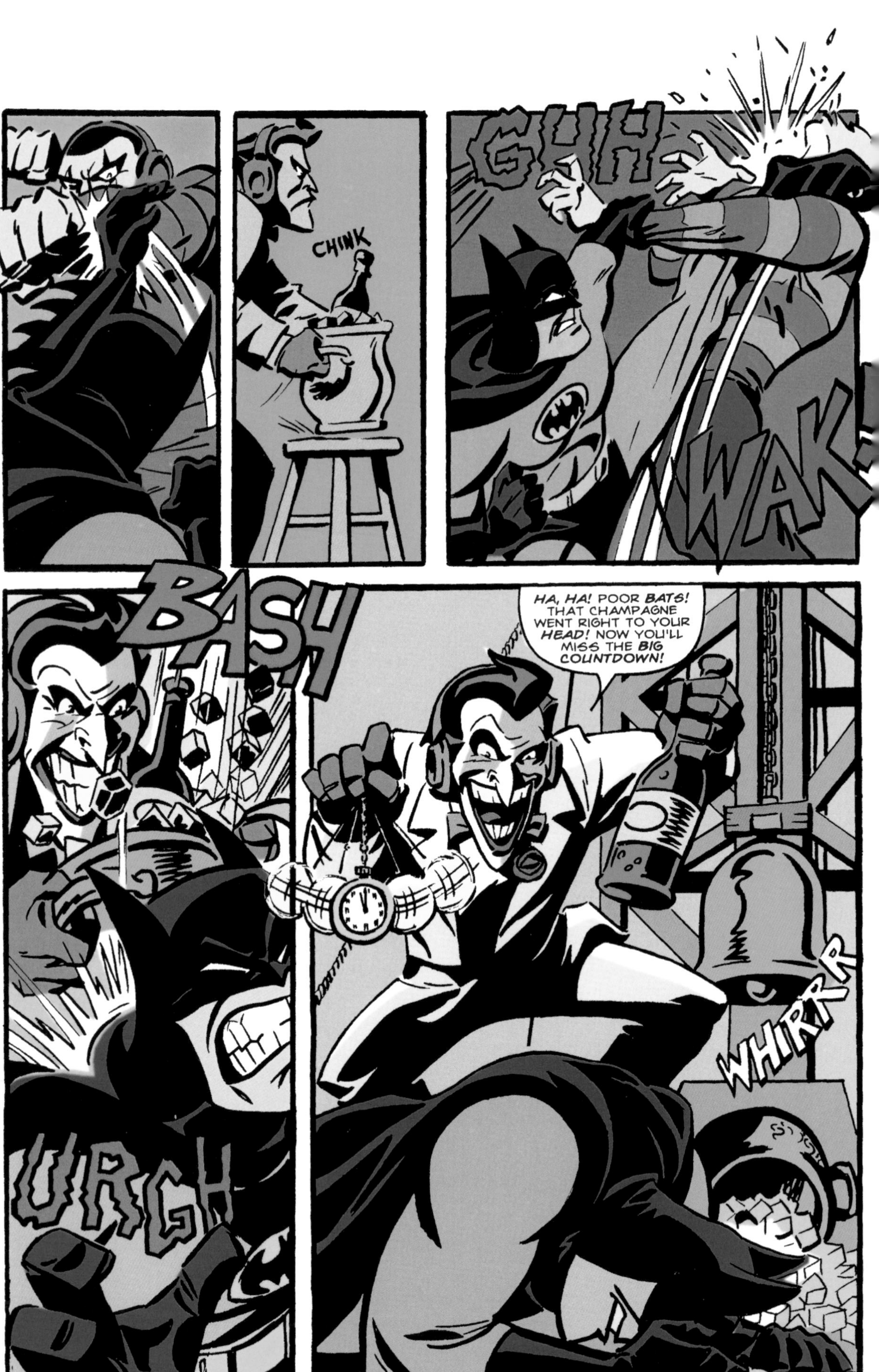

CHINK
GUH
WAK!
BASH
HA, HA! POOR BATS! THAT CHAMPAGNE WENT RIGHT TO YOUR HEAD! NOW YOU'LL MISS THE BIG COUNTDOWN!
WHIRRR
URGH
48

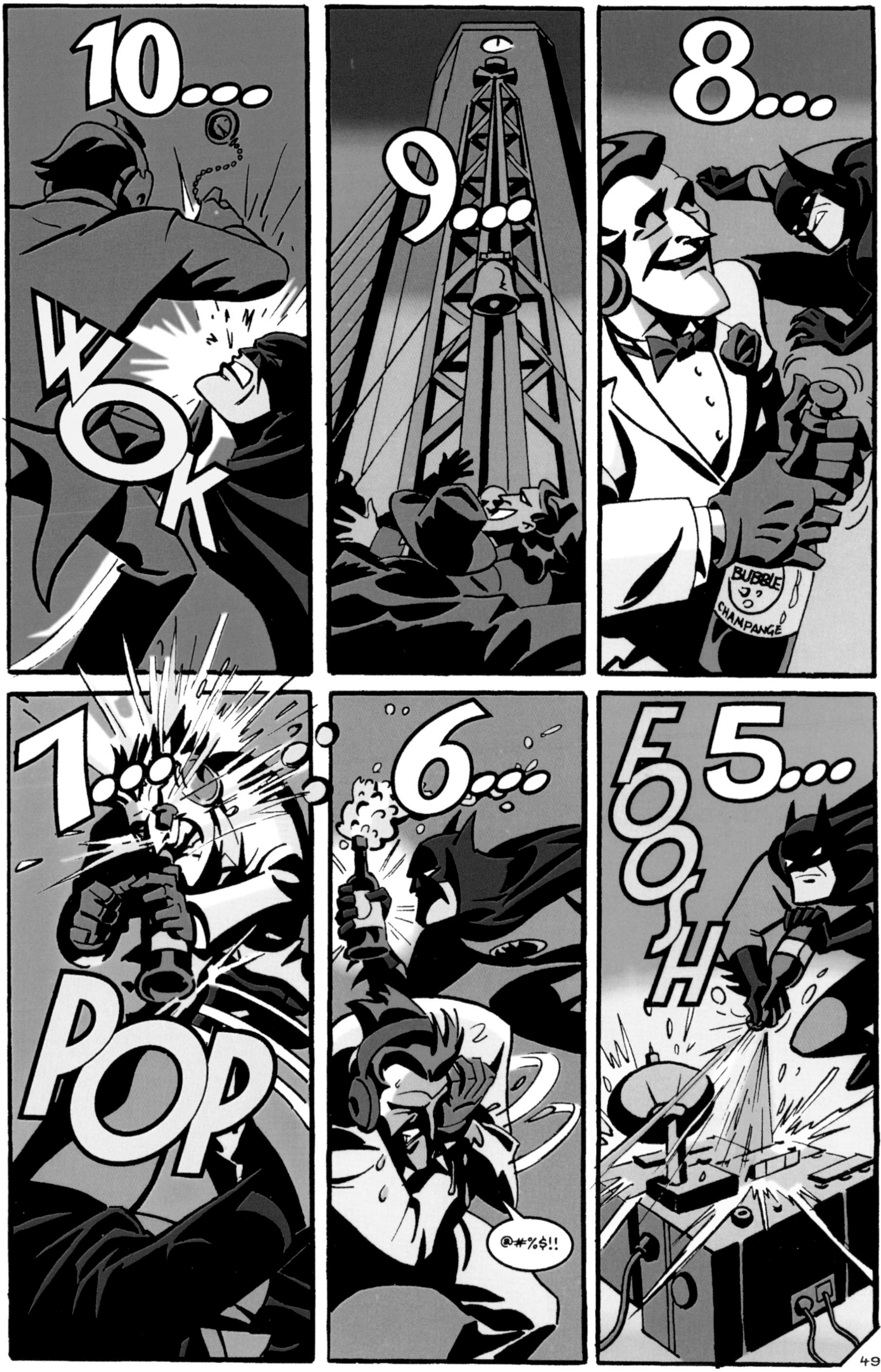
10...
WOK
9...
8...
BUBBLE
CHAMPANGE
7...
POP
6...
@#%$!!
FOOSH
5...

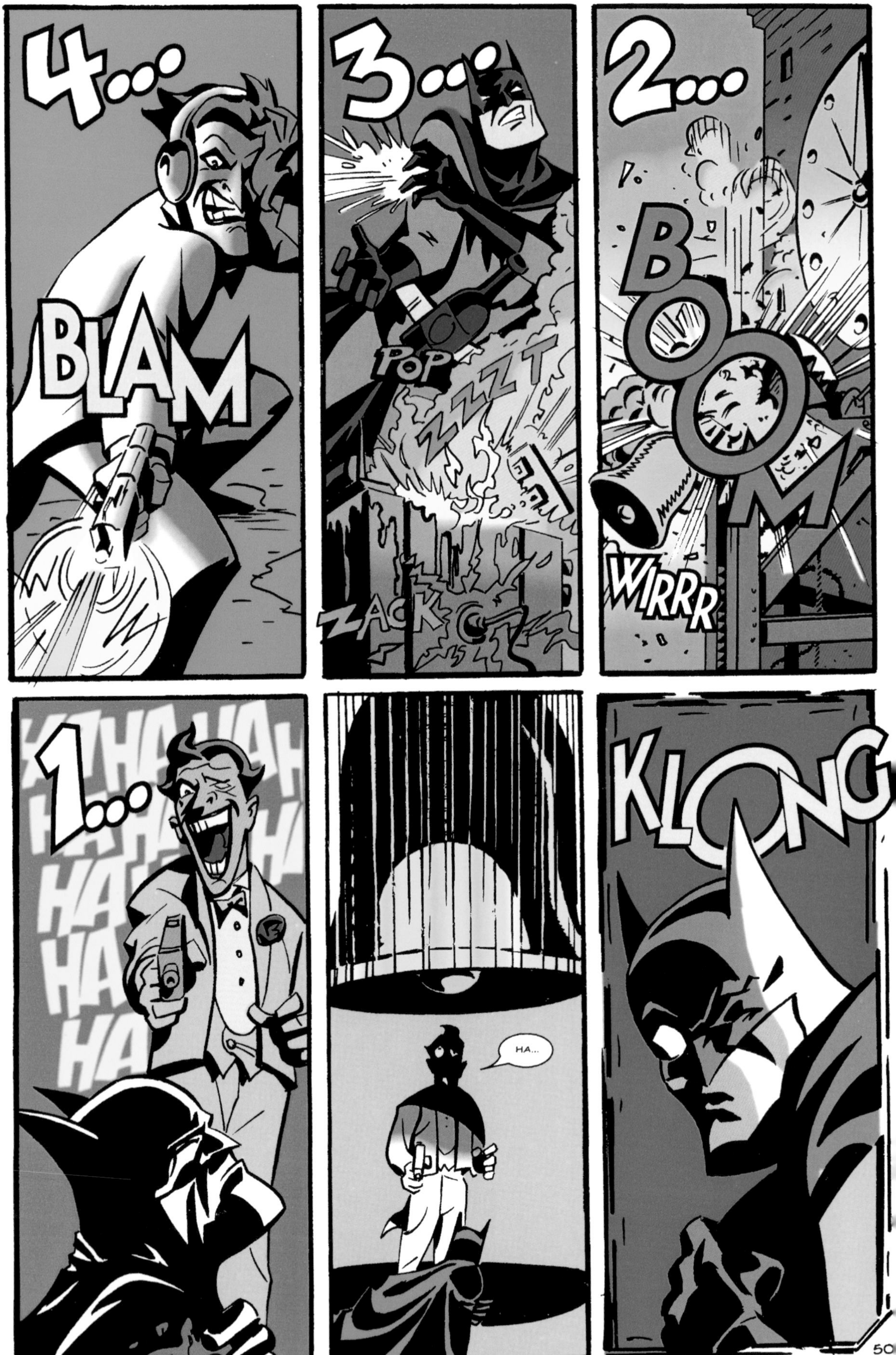
4...
BLAM
3...
POP
ZZZZT
ZACK
2...
BOOM
WIRRR
1...
HA HA HA HA HA HA HA HA
HA...
KLONG
50

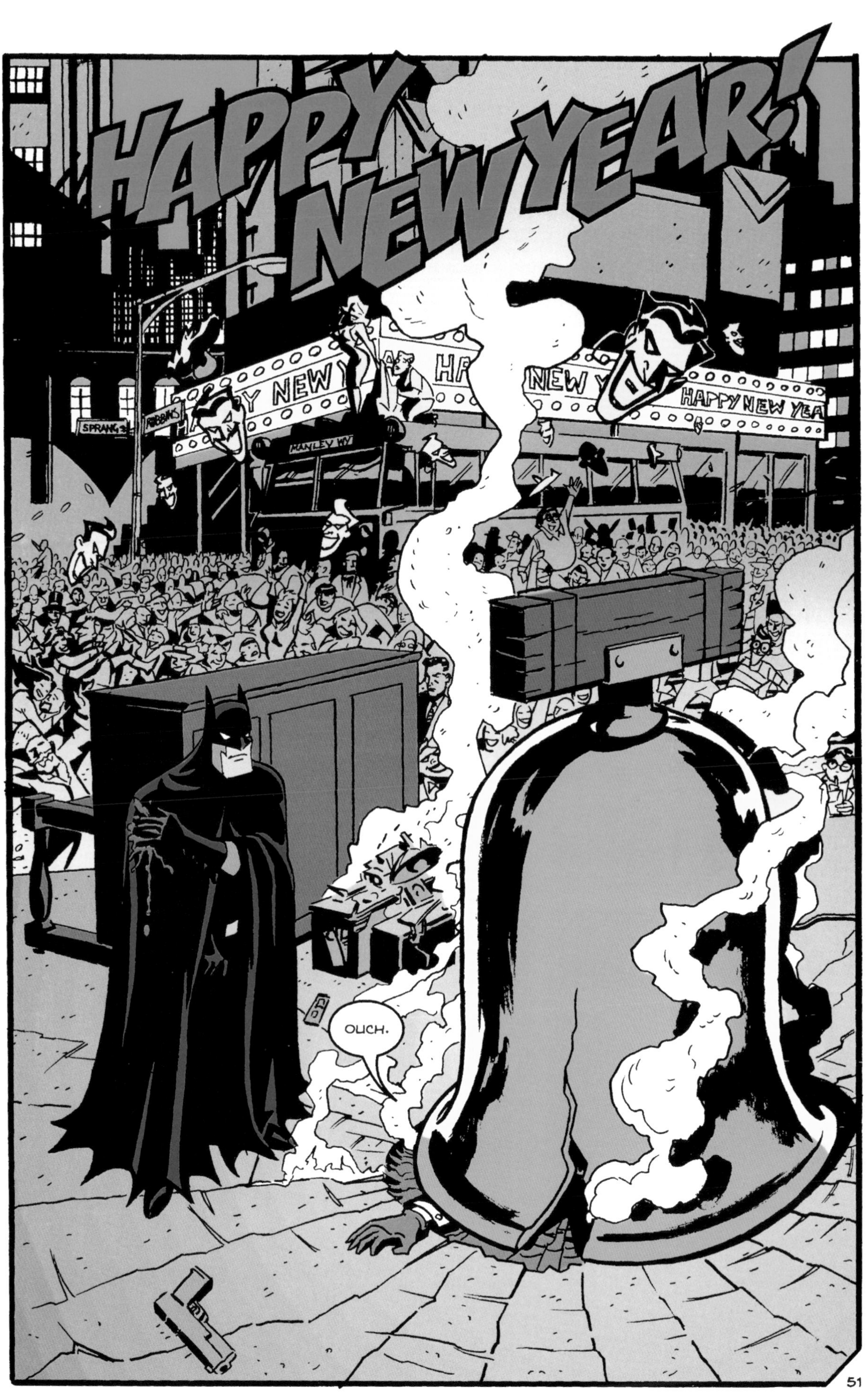
HAPPY NEW YEAR!
HAPPY NEW YEA
SPRANG
ROBBINS
MANLEY WY
OUCH.

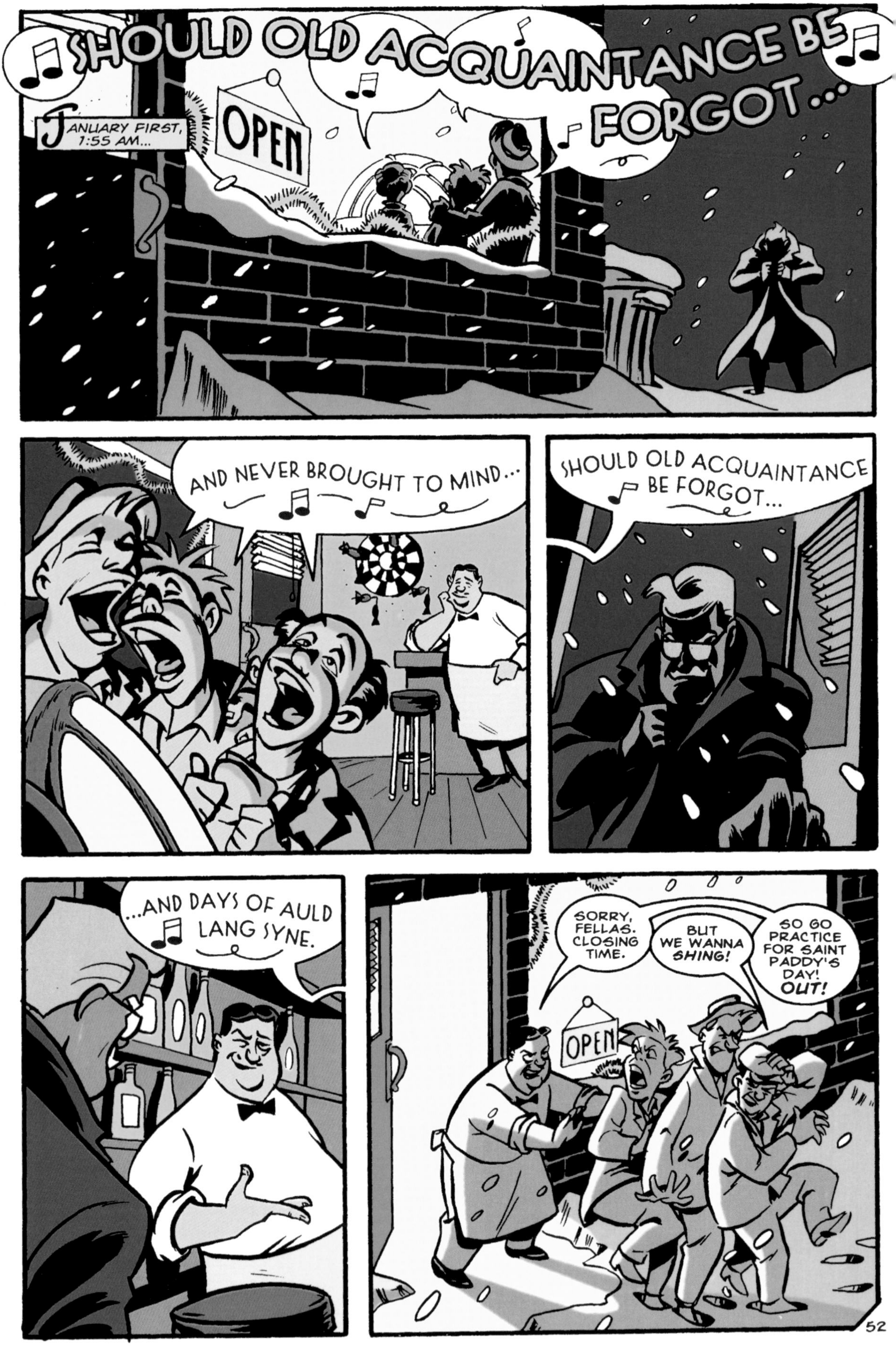
SHOULD OLD ACQUAINTANCE BE FORGOT...
JANUARY FIRST, 1:55 AM...
OPEN
AND NEVER BROUGHT TO MIND...
SHOULD OLD ACQUAINTANCE BE FORGOT...
...AND DAYS OF AULD LANG SYNE.
SORRY, FELLAS. CLOSING TIME.
BUT WE WANNA SHING!
SO GO PRACTICE FOR SAINT PADDY'S DAY! OUT!
OPEN
52

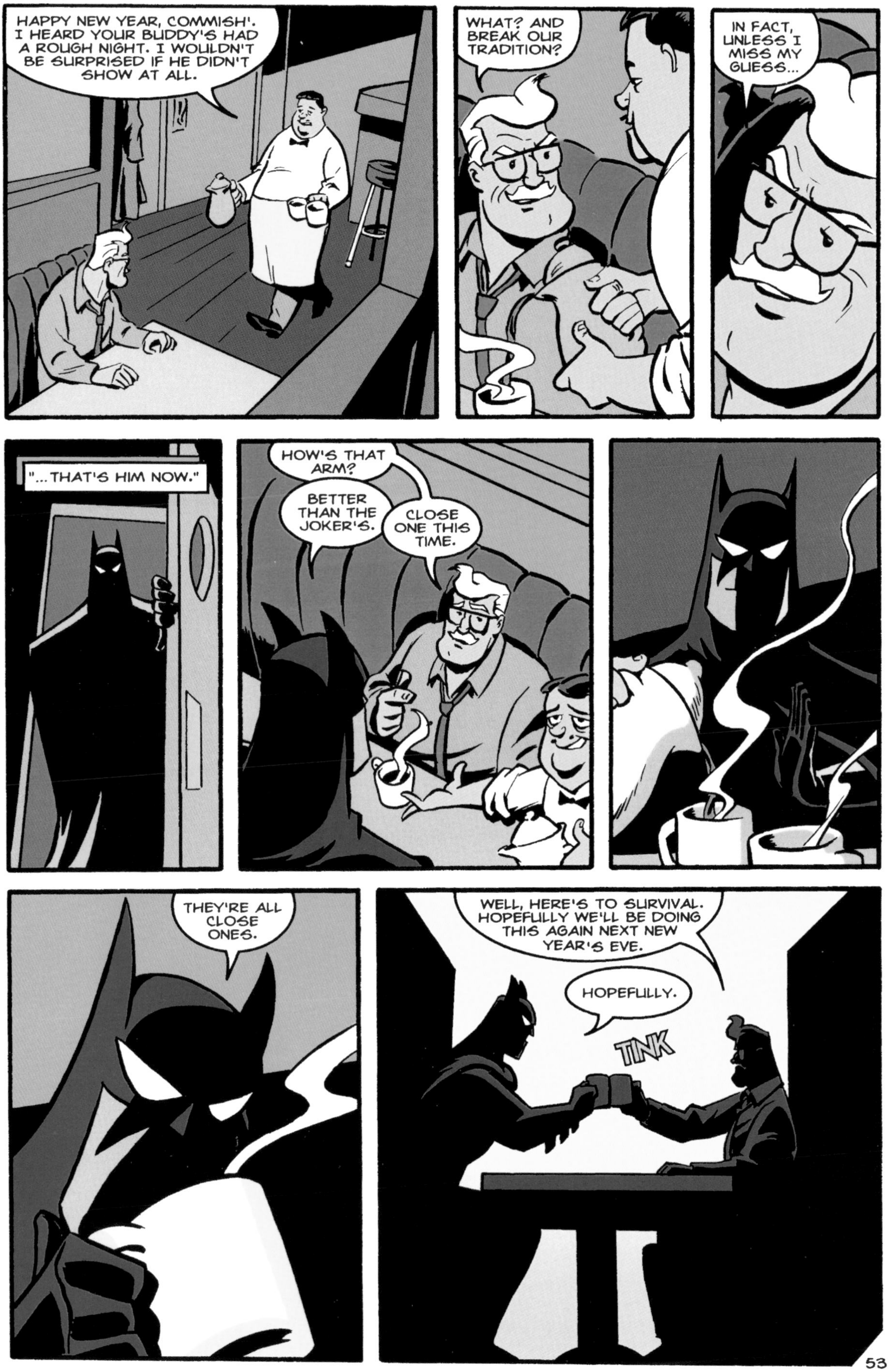

HAPPY NEW YEAR, COMMISH'. I HEARD YOUR BUDDY'S HAD A ROUGH NIGHT. I WOULDN'T BE SURPRISED IF HE DIDN'T SHOW AT ALL.
WHAT? AND BREAK OUR TRADITION?
IN FACT, UNLESS I MISS MY GUESS...
"...THAT'S HIM NOW."
HOW'S THAT ARM?
BETTER THAN THE JOKER'S.
CLOSE ONE THIS TIME.
THEY'RE ALL CLOSE ONES.
WELL, HERE'S TO SURVIVAL. HOPEFULLY WE'LL BE DOING THIS AGAIN NEXT NEW YEAR'S EVE.
HOPEFULLY.
TINK
53

AND NOW, JOE, IF I COULD GET ONE OF YOUR FAMOUS CHEESE STEAKS TO GO, I'LL BE READY TO CALL IT A NIGHT.

ANYTHING FOR YOU?

Hmm. ONE OF THESE YEARS I'M GOING TO BEAT HIM TO THE CHECK.

HAPPY NEW YEAR, JOE.

CLOSED

AND TO YOU TOO, OLD FRIEND.

SEASON'S GREETINGS

Paul Dini
BUTCH LUKIC Rdel Carmen
B.T.
GLEN MURAKAMI

Dan Riba
Kevin Altieri

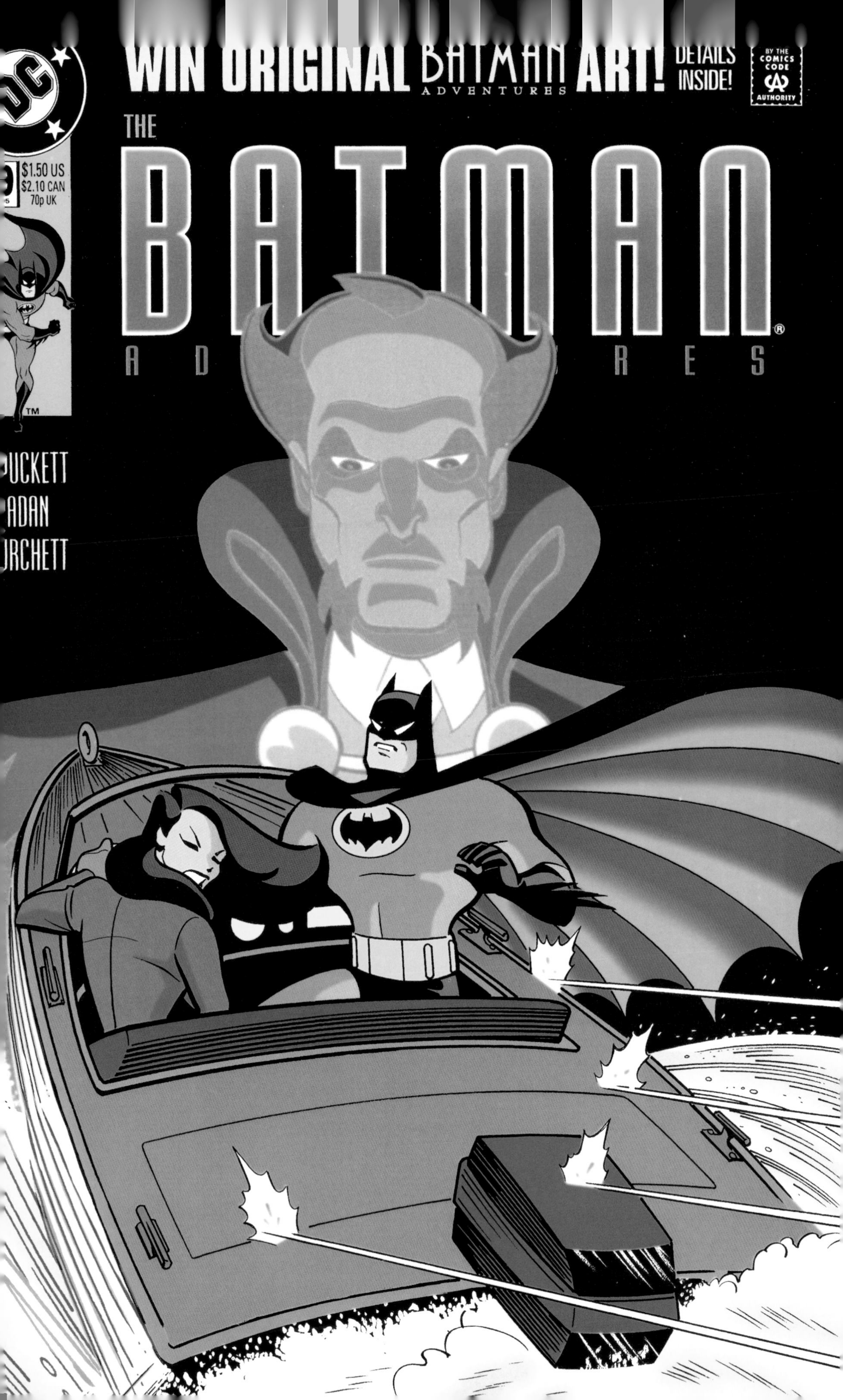

WIN ORIGINAL BATMAN ADVENTURES ART!
DETAILS INSIDE!
BY THE COMICS CODE AUTHORITY
THE BATMAN ADVENTURES
$1.50 US
$2.10 CAN
70p UK
UCKETT
ADAN
URCHETT

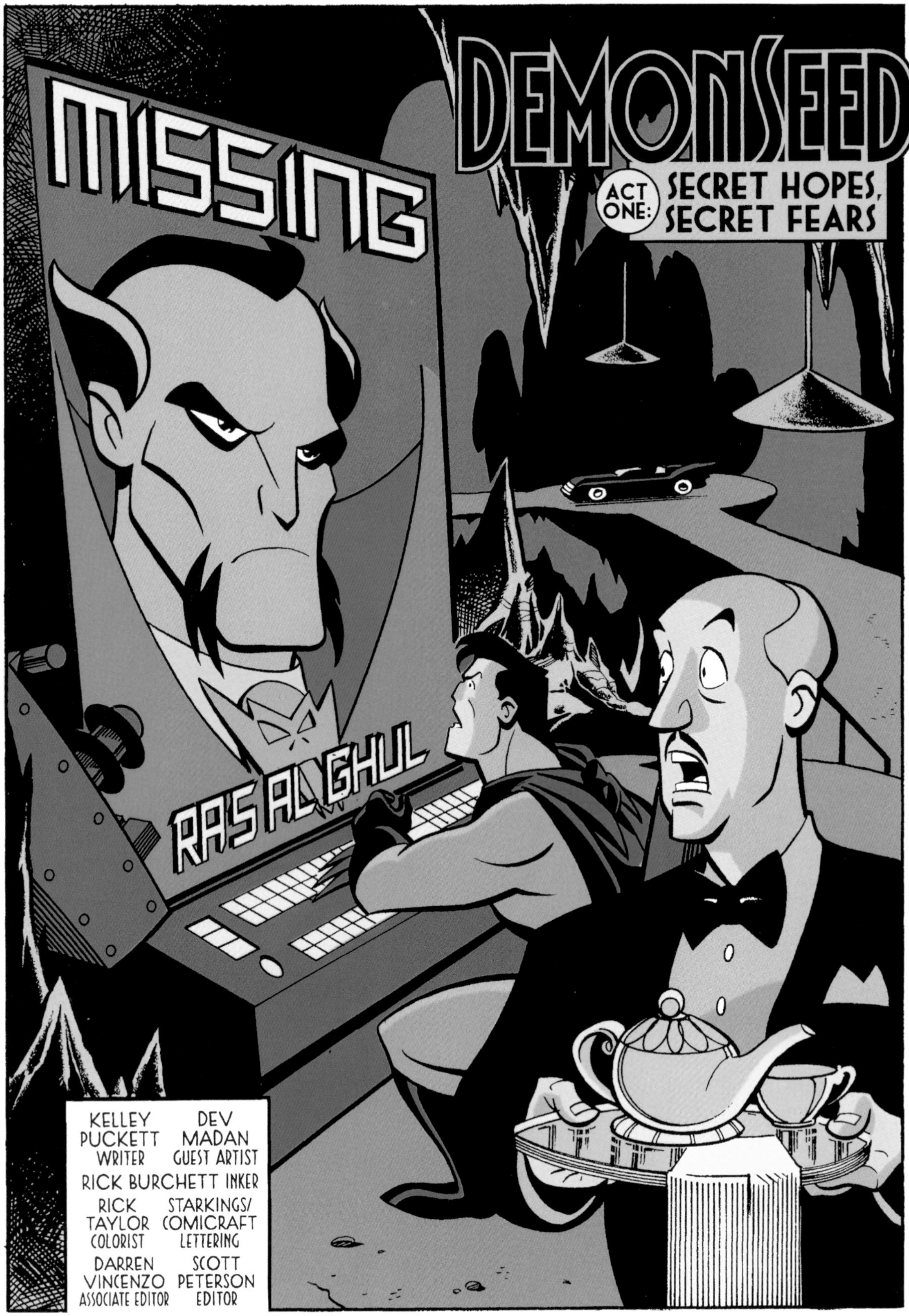
MISSING
DEMONSEED
ACT ONE: SECRET HOPES, SECRET FEARS
RA'S AL GHUL
KELLEY PUCKETT WRITER
DEV MADAN GUEST ARTIST
RICK BURCHETT INKER
RICK TAYLOR COLORIST
STARKINGS/ COMICRAFT LETTERING
DARREN VINCENZO ASSOCIATE EDITOR
SCOTT PETERSON EDITOR

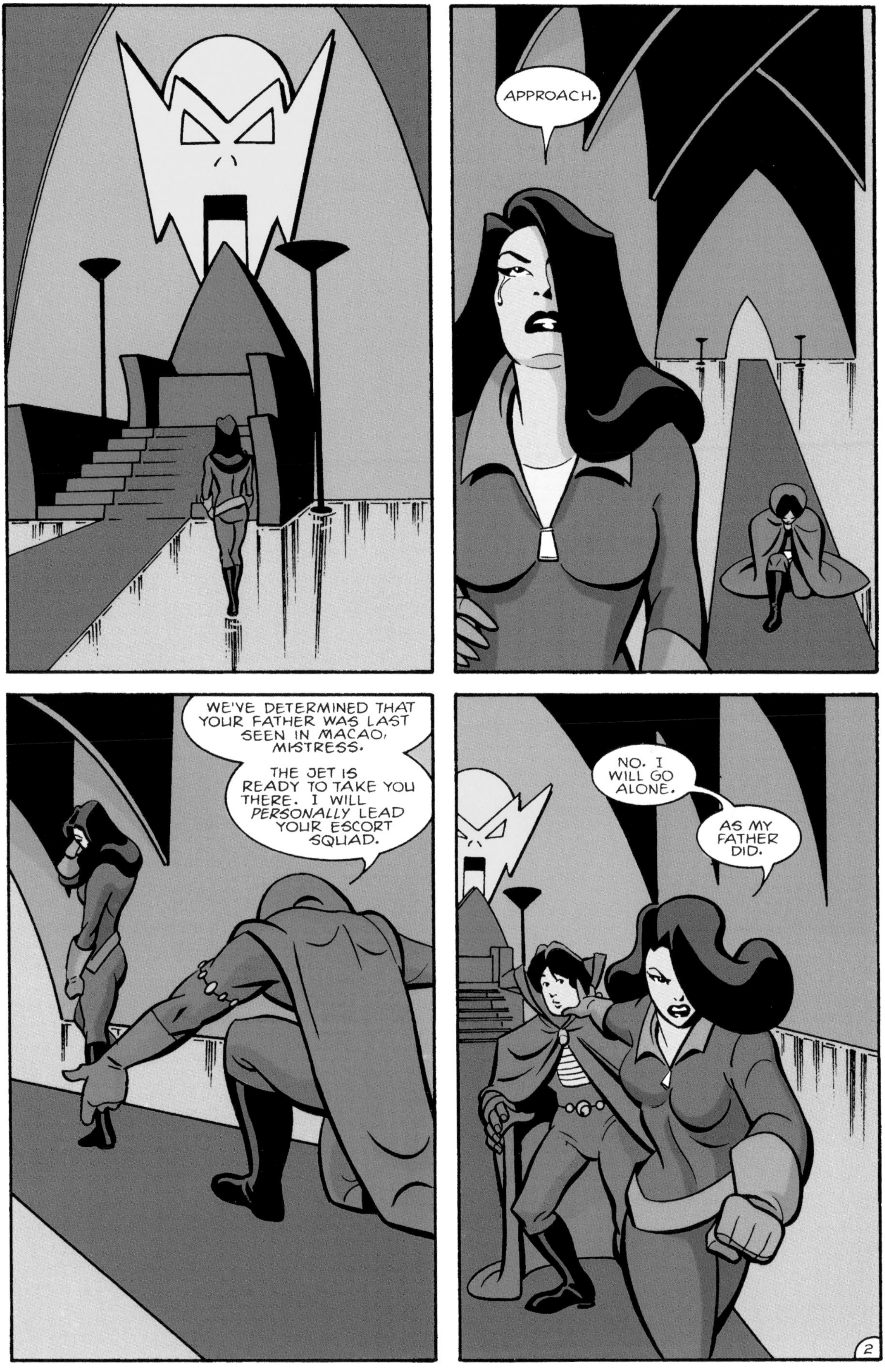
APPROACH.
WE'VE DETERMINED THAT YOUR FATHER WAS LAST SEEN IN MACAO, MISTRESS.
THE JET IS READY TO TAKE YOU THERE. I WILL *PERSONALLY* LEAD YOUR ESCORT SQUAD.
NO. I WILL GO ALONE.
AS MY FATHER DID.
2

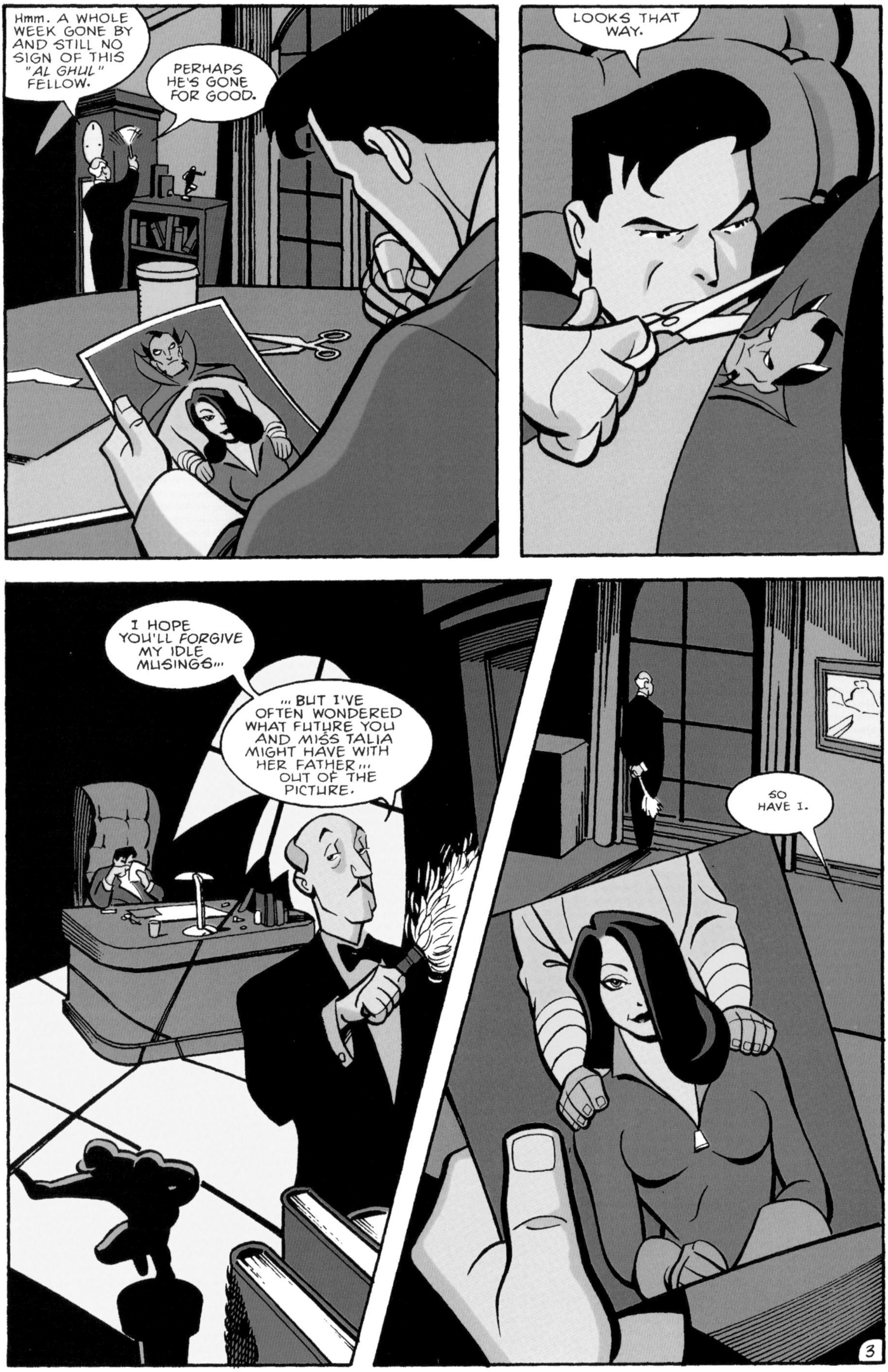
Hmm. A WHOLE WEEK GONE BY AND STILL NO SIGN OF THIS "AL GHUL" FELLOW.
PERHAPS HE'S GONE FOR GOOD.
LOOKS THAT WAY.
I HOPE YOU'LL FORGIVE MY IDLE MUSINGS...
...BUT I'VE OFTEN WONDERED WHAT FUTURE YOU AND MISS TALIA MIGHT HAVE WITH HER FATHER... OUT OF THE PICTURE.
SO HAVE I.
3

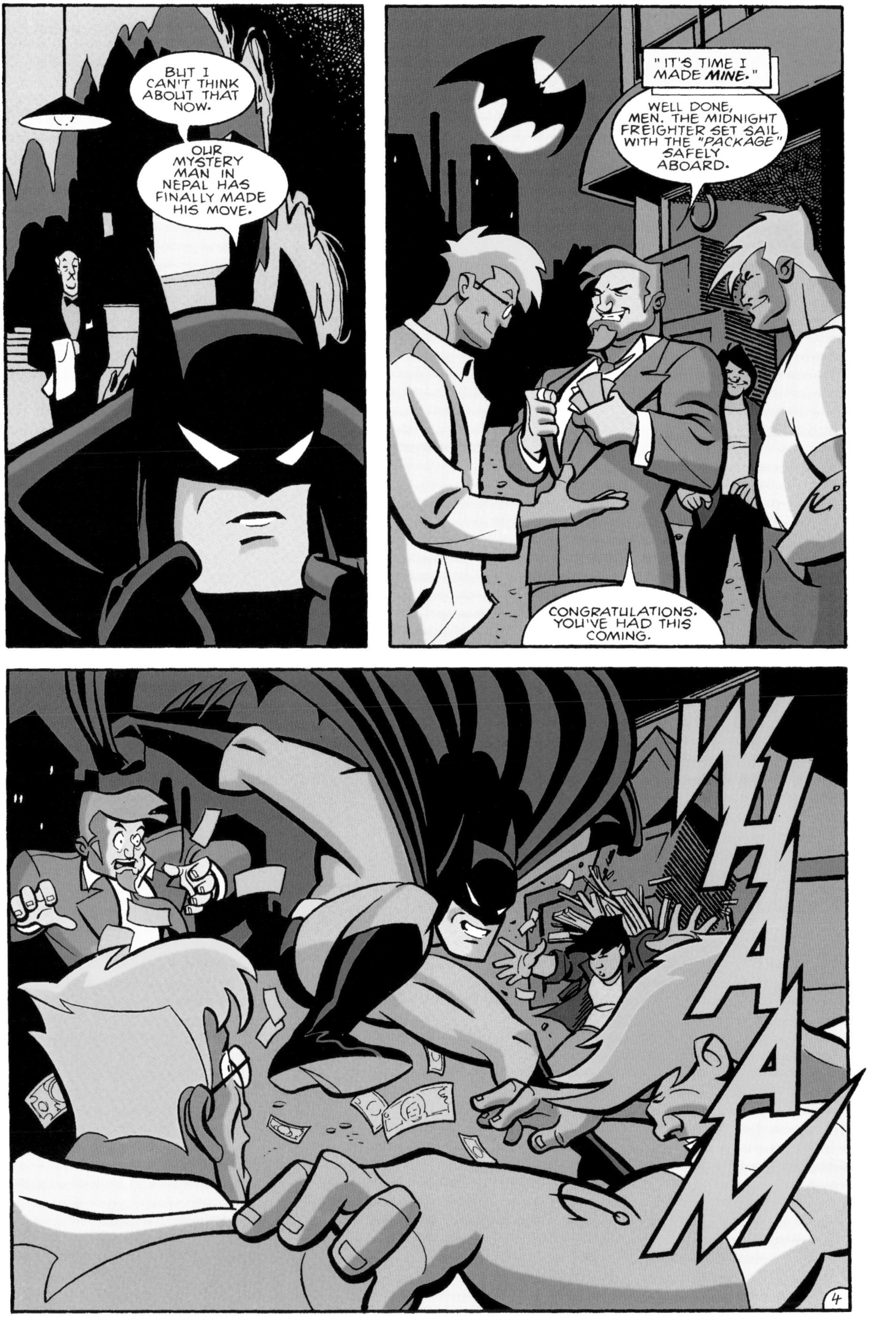
BUT I CAN'T THINK ABOUT THAT NOW.
OUR MYSTERY MAN IN NEPAL HAS FINALLY MADE HIS MOVE.
"IT'S TIME I MADE MINE."
WELL DONE, MEN. THE MIDNIGHT FREIGHTER SET SAIL WITH THE "PACKAGE" SAFELY ABOARD.
CONGRATULATIONS. YOU'VE HAD THIS COMING.
WHAAM
4

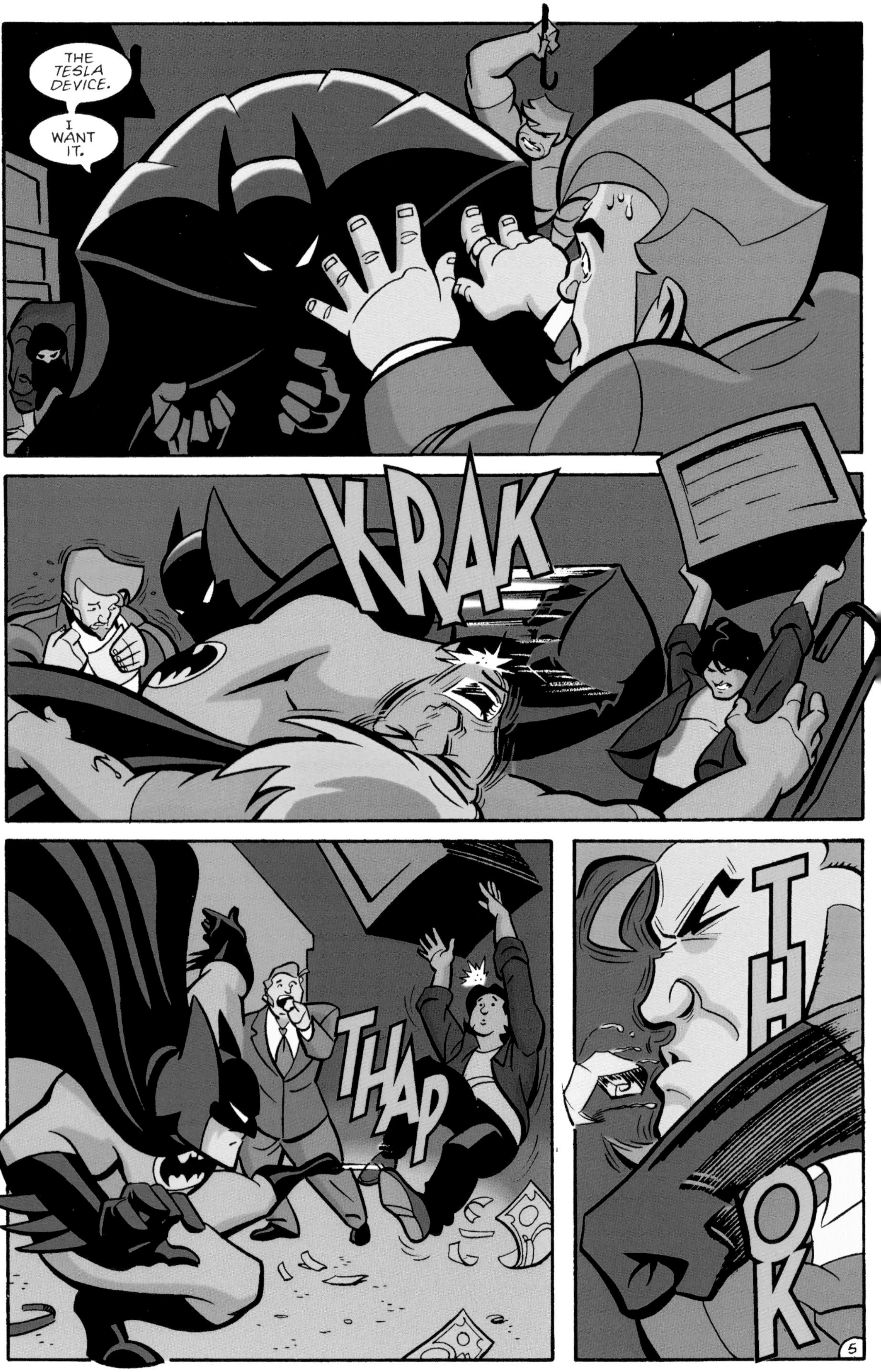
THE TESLA DEVICE.
I WANT IT.
KRAK
THAP
THOK
5

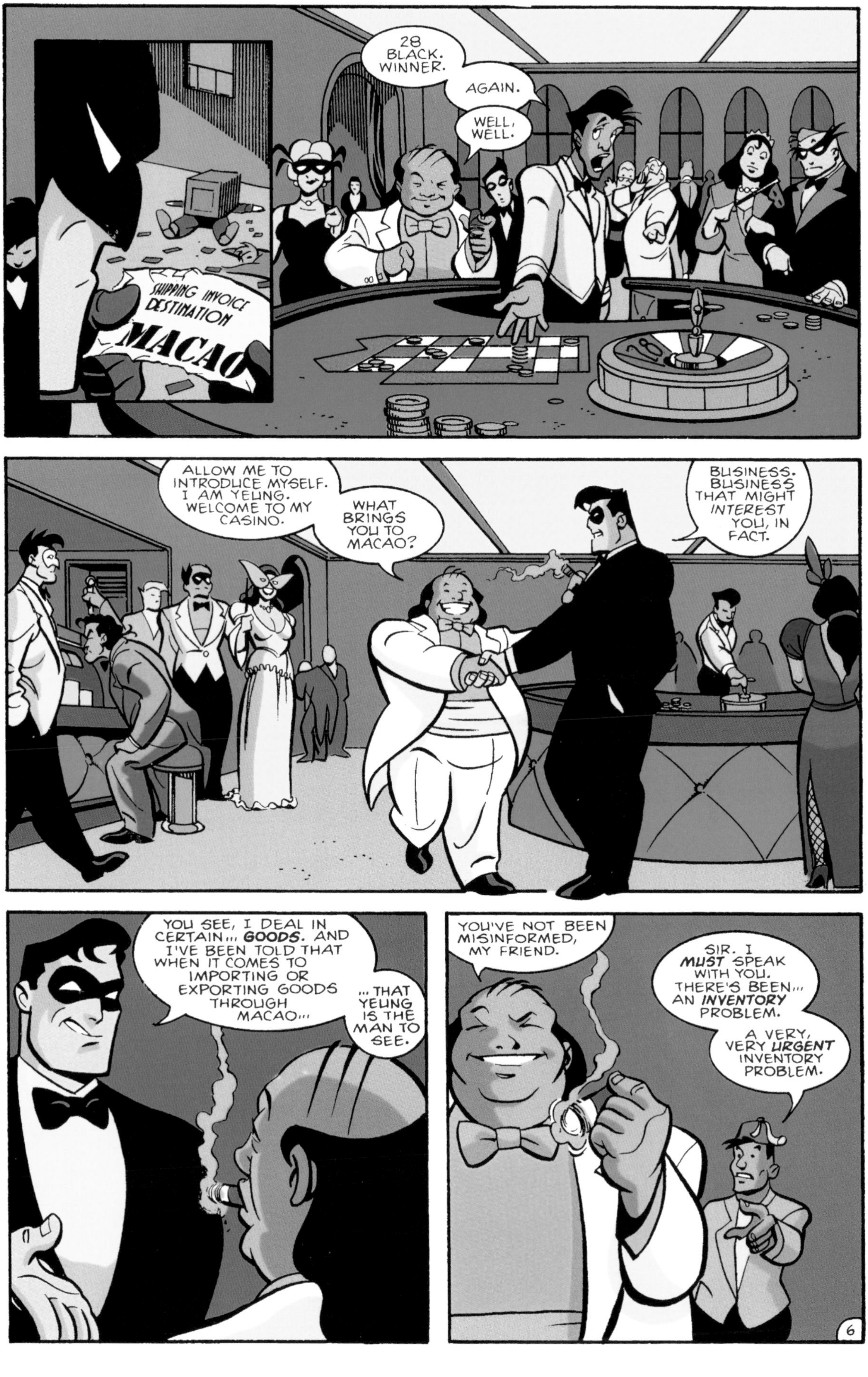

SHIPPING INVOICE
DESTINATION
MACAO
28 BLACK. WINNER.
AGAIN.
WELL, WELL.
ALLOW ME TO INTRODUCE MYSELF. I AM YEUNG. WELCOME TO MY CASINO.
WHAT BRINGS YOU TO MACAO?
BUSINESS. BUSINESS THAT MIGHT INTEREST YOU, IN FACT.
YOU SEE, I DEAL IN CERTAIN... GOODS. AND I'VE BEEN TOLD THAT WHEN IT COMES TO IMPORTING OR EXPORTING GOODS THROUGH MACAO...
...THAT YEUNG IS THE MAN TO SEE.
YOU'VE NOT BEEN MISINFORMED, MY FRIEND.
SIR. I MUST SPEAK WITH YOU. THERE'S BEEN... AN INVENTORY PROBLEM.
A VERY, VERY URGENT INVENTORY PROBLEM.
6

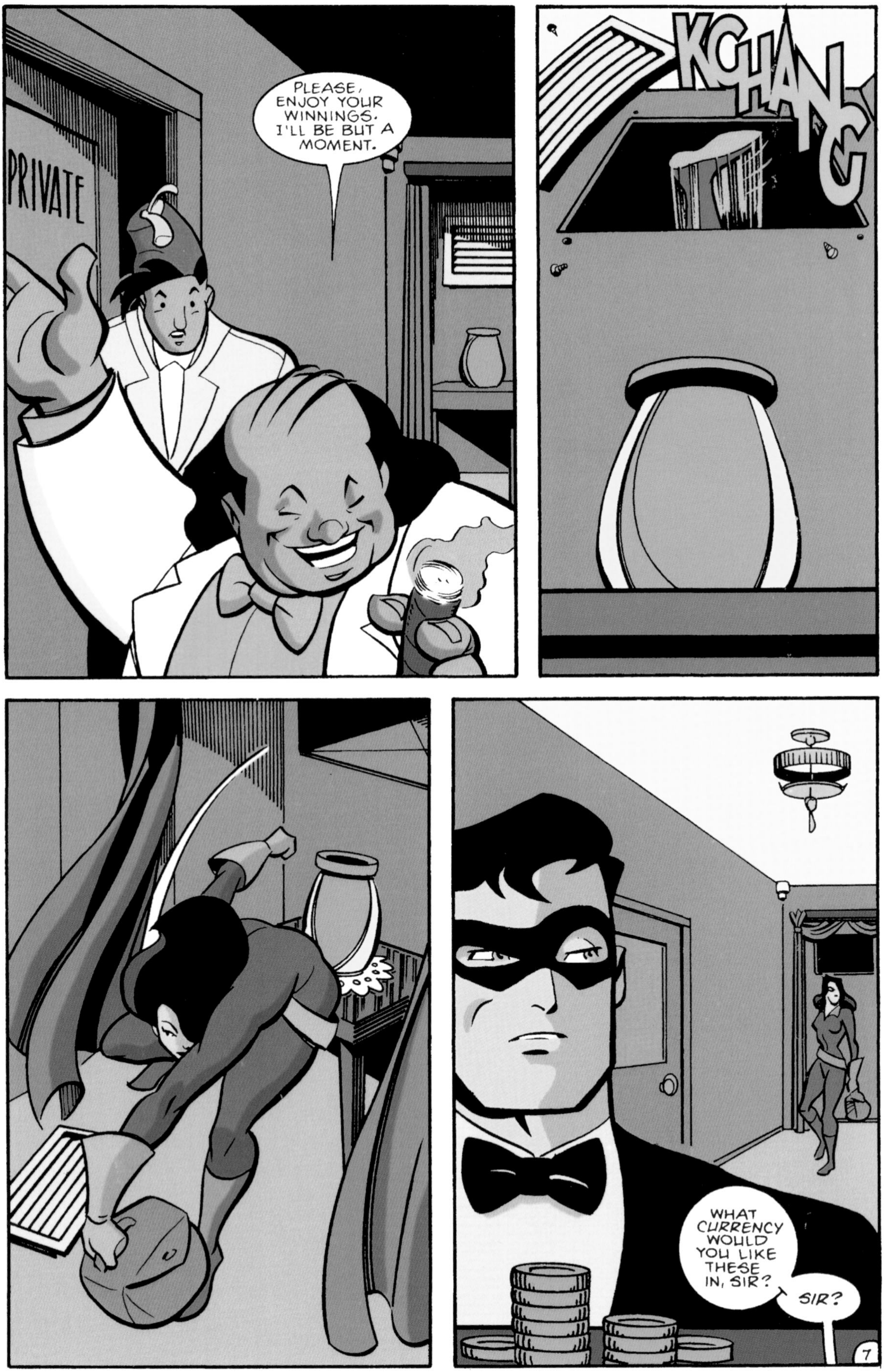
PLEASE, ENJOY YOUR WINNINGS. I'LL BE BUT A MOMENT.
PRIVATE
KCHANG
WHAT CURRENCY WOULD YOU LIKE THESE IN, SIR?
SIR?
7

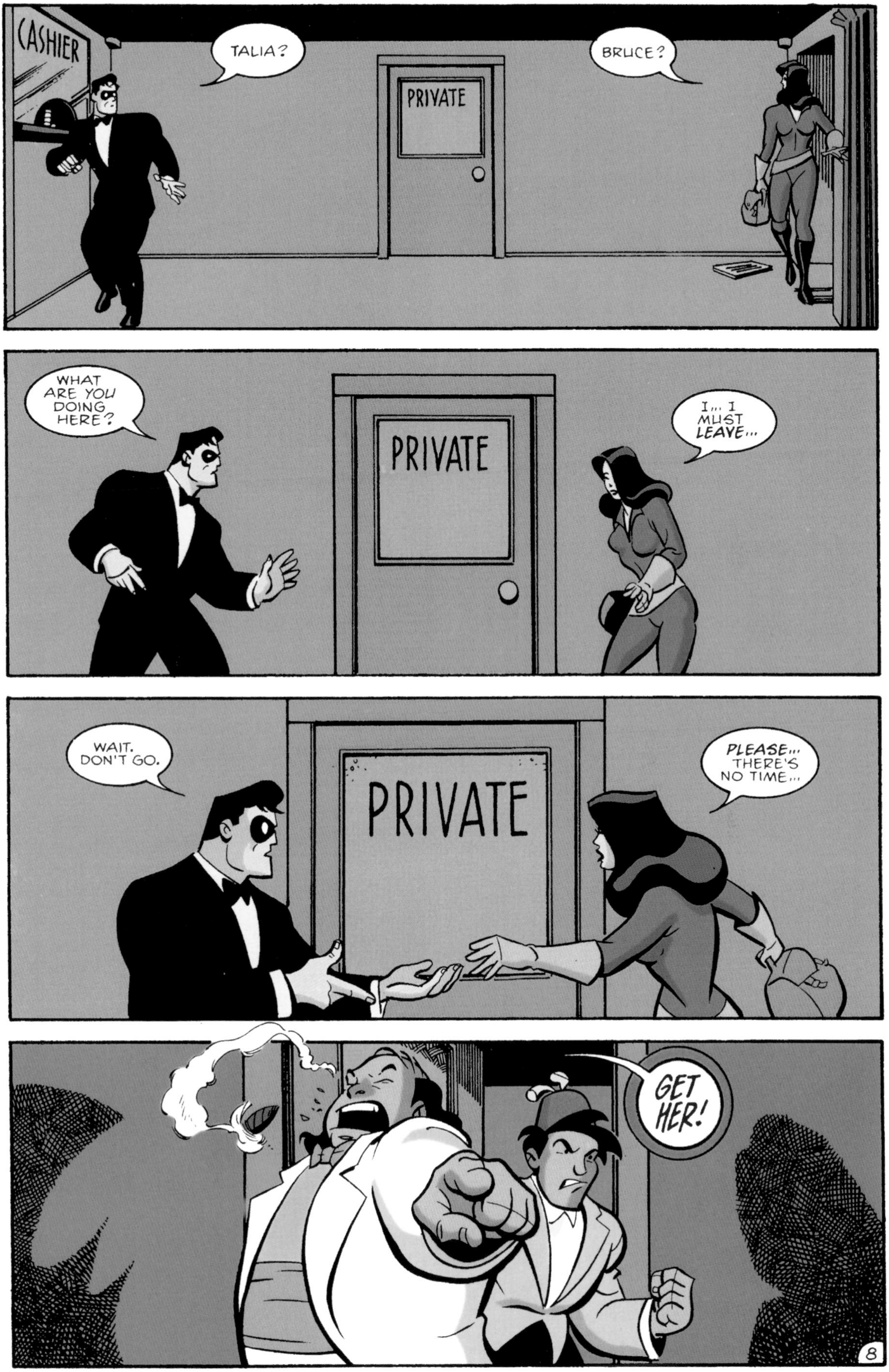
CASHIER
TALIA?
BRUCE?
PRIVATE
WHAT ARE YOU DOING HERE?
I... I MUST LEAVE...
PRIVATE
WAIT. DON'T GO.
PLEASE... THERE'S NO TIME...
PRIVATE
GET HER!
8

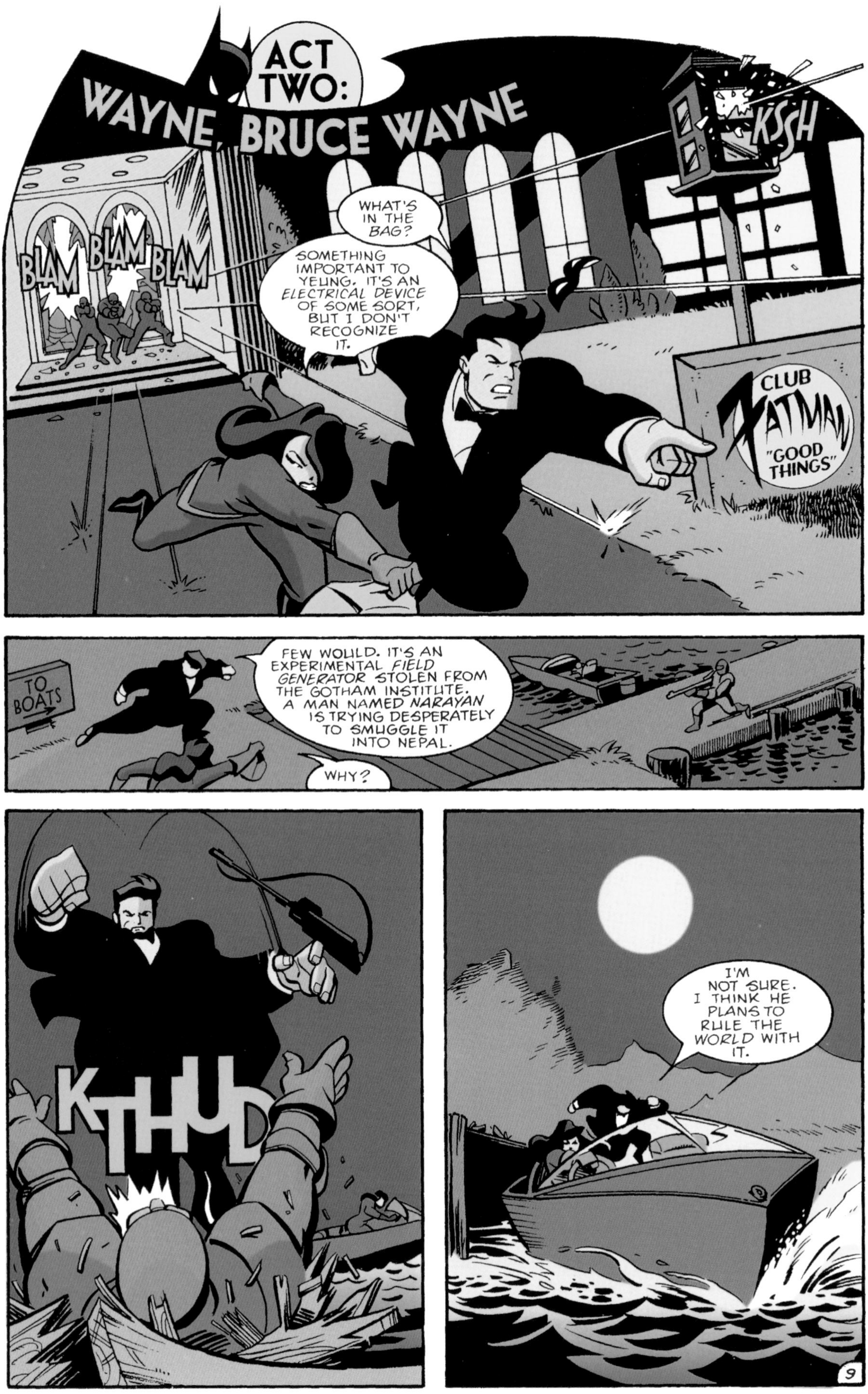
ACT TWO:
WAYNE, BRUCE WAYNE
KSSH
BLAM BLAM BLAM
WHAT'S IN THE BAG?
SOMETHING IMPORTANT TO YEUNG. IT'S AN ELECTRICAL DEVICE OF SOME SORT, BUT I DON'T RECOGNIZE IT.
CLUB BATMAN "GOOD THINGS"
TO BOATS
FEW WOULD. IT'S AN EXPERIMENTAL FIELD GENERATOR STOLEN FROM THE GOTHAM INSTITUTE. A MAN NAMED NARAYAN IS TRYING DESPERATELY TO SMUGGLE IT INTO NEPAL.
WHY?
KTHUD
I'M NOT SURE. I THINK HE PLANS TO RULE THE WORLD WITH IT.
9

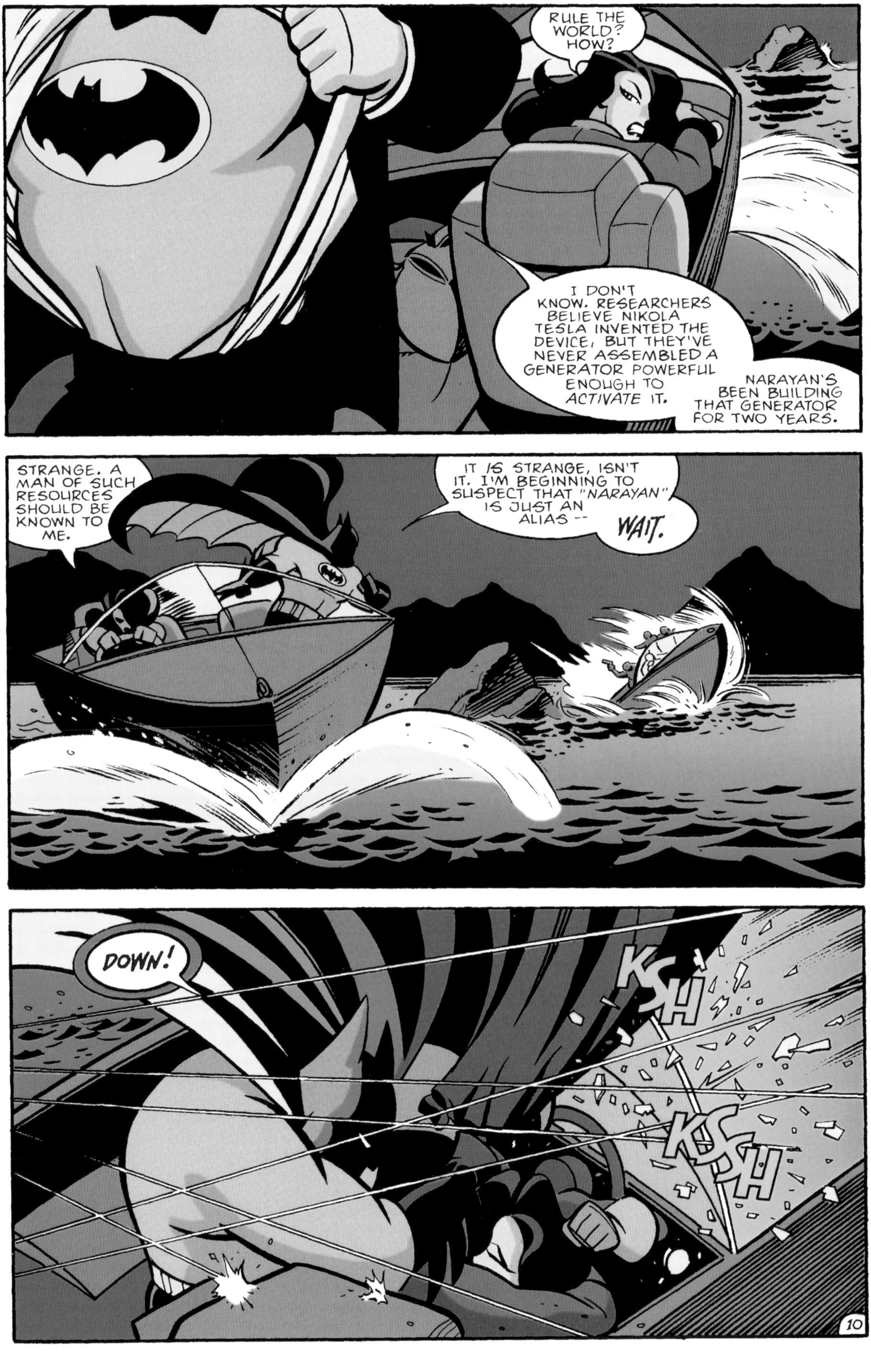
RULE THE WORLD? HOW?
I DON'T KNOW. RESEARCHERS BELIEVE NIKOLA TESLA INVENTED THE DEVICE, BUT THEY'VE NEVER ASSEMBLED A GENERATOR POWERFUL ENOUGH TO ACTIVATE IT.
NARAYAN'S BEEN BUILDING THAT GENERATOR FOR TWO YEARS.
STRANGE. A MAN OF SUCH RESOURCES SHOULD BE KNOWN TO ME.
IT IS STRANGE, ISN'T IT. I'M BEGINNING TO SUSPECT THAT "NARAYAN" IS JUST AN ALIAS --
WAIT.
DOWN!
KSH
KSSH
10

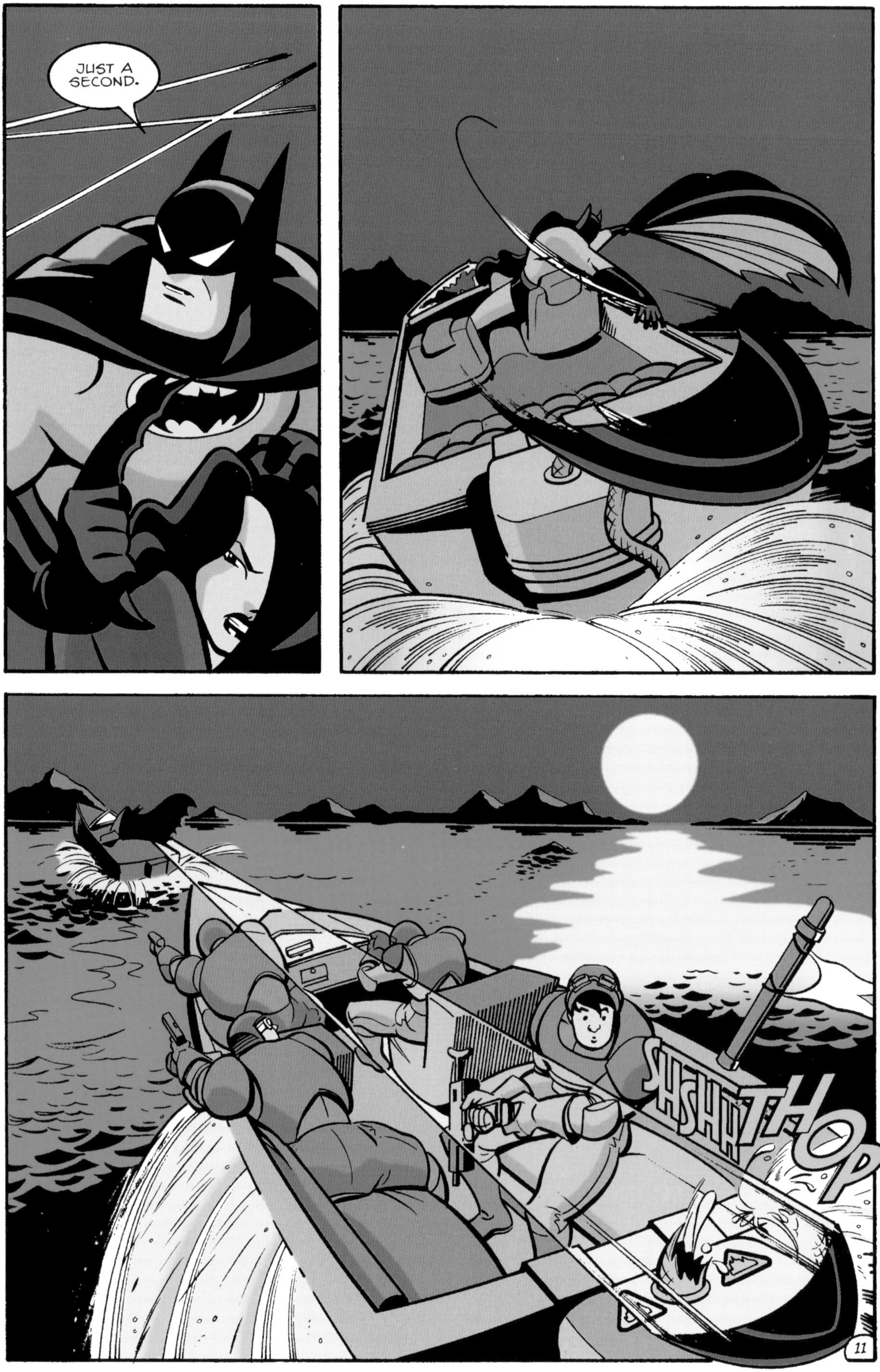

JUST A SECOND.
SHSHHTHOP
11

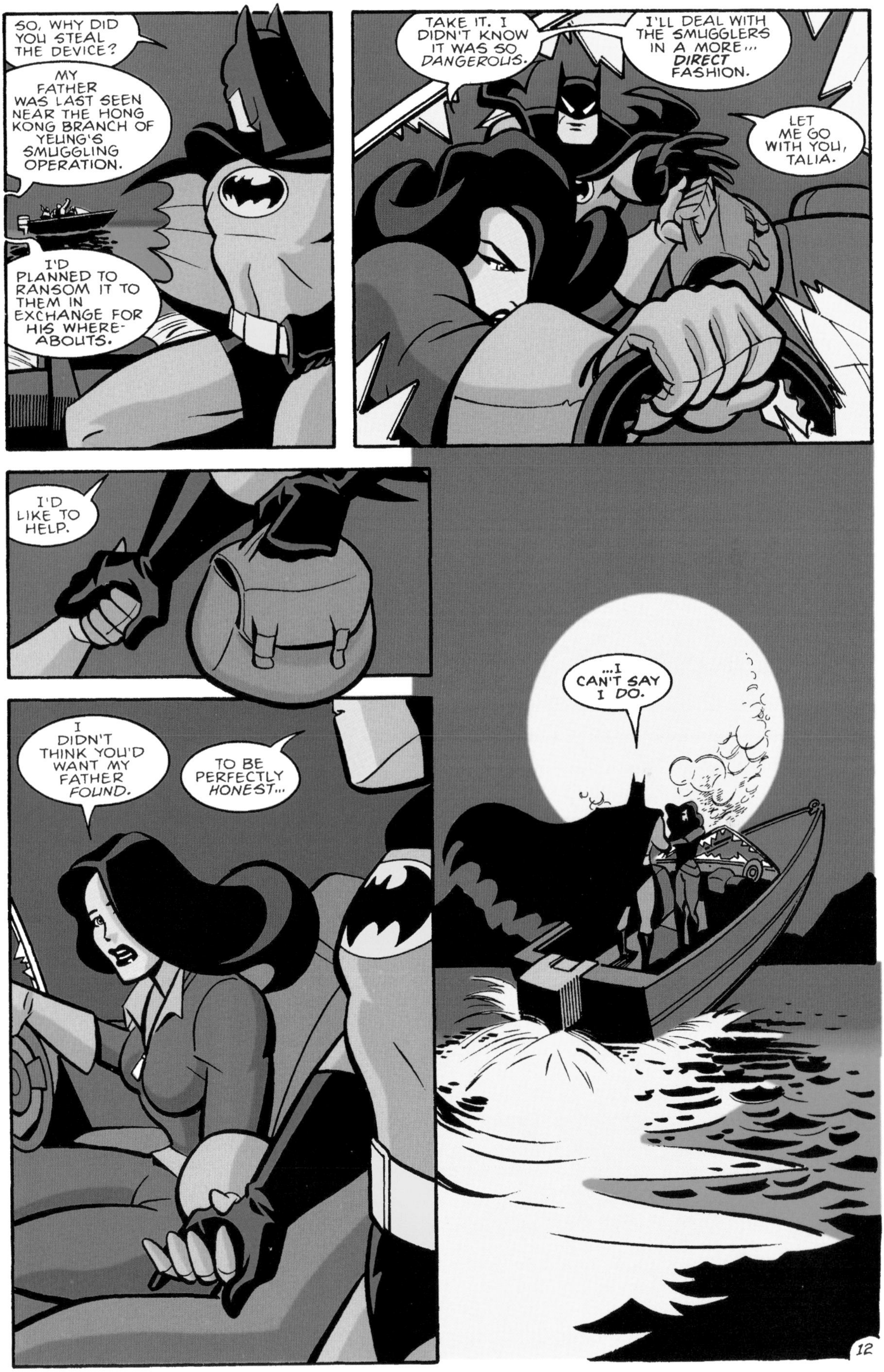

SO, WHY DID YOU STEAL THE DEVICE?
MY FATHER WAS LAST SEEN NEAR THE HONG KONG BRANCH OF YEUNG'S SMUGGLING OPERATION.
I'D PLANNED TO RANSOM IT TO THEM IN EXCHANGE FOR HIS WHERE-ABOUTS.
TAKE IT. I DIDN'T KNOW IT WAS SO DANGEROUS.
I'LL DEAL WITH THE SMUGGLERS IN A MORE... DIRECT FASHION.
LET ME GO WITH YOU, TALIA.
I'D LIKE TO HELP.
I DIDN'T THINK YOU'D WANT MY FATHER FOUND.
TO BE PERFECTLY HONEST...
...I CAN'T SAY I DO.
12

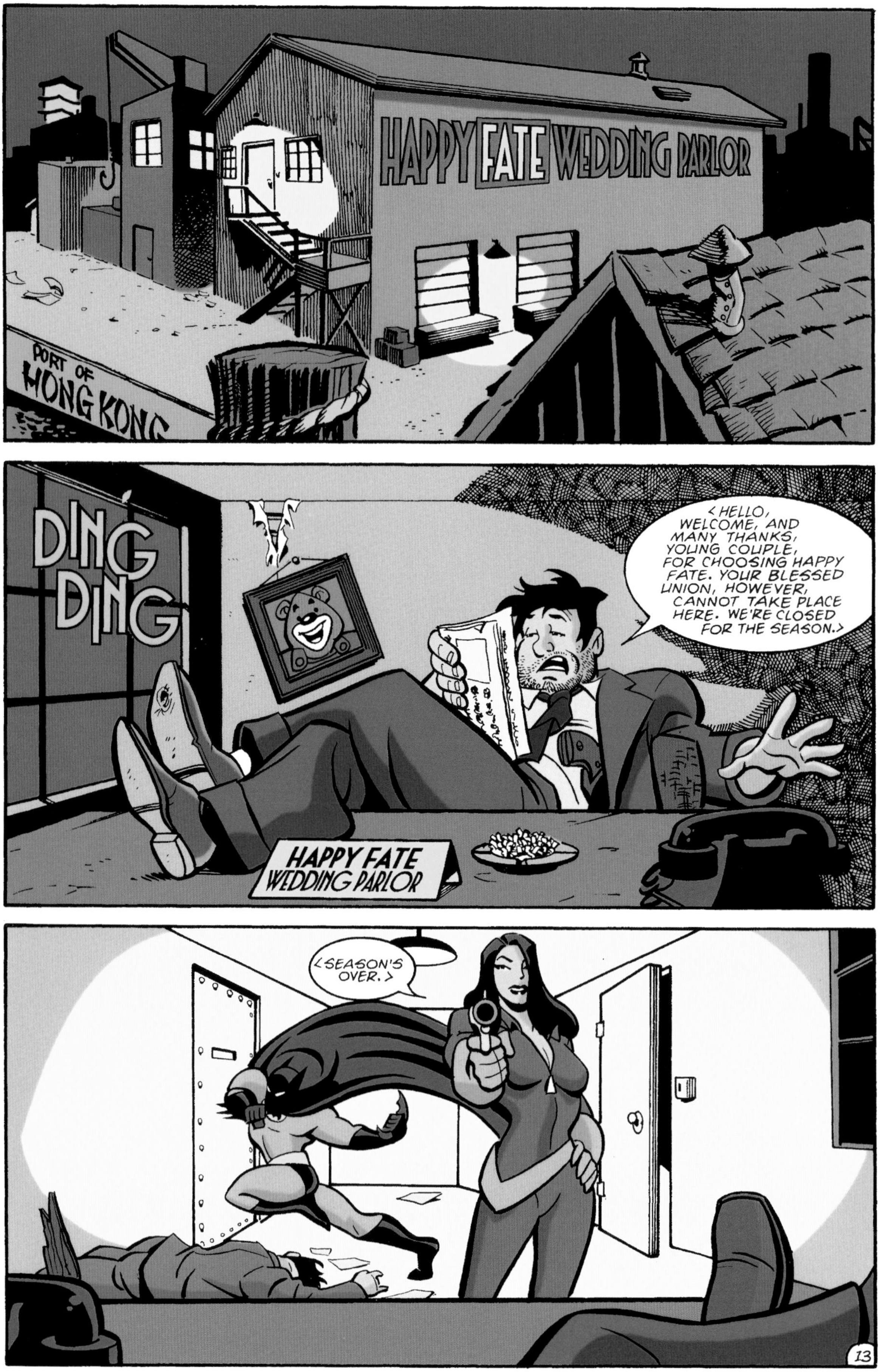
HAPPY FATE WEDDING PARLOR
PORT OF HONG KONG
DING DING
<HELLO, WELCOME, AND MANY THANKS, YOUNG COUPLE, FOR CHOOSING HAPPY FATE. YOUR BLESSED UNION, HOWEVER, CANNOT TAKE PLACE HERE. WE'RE CLOSED FOR THE SEASON.>
HAPPY FATE WEDDING PARLOR
<SEASON'S OVER.>
13

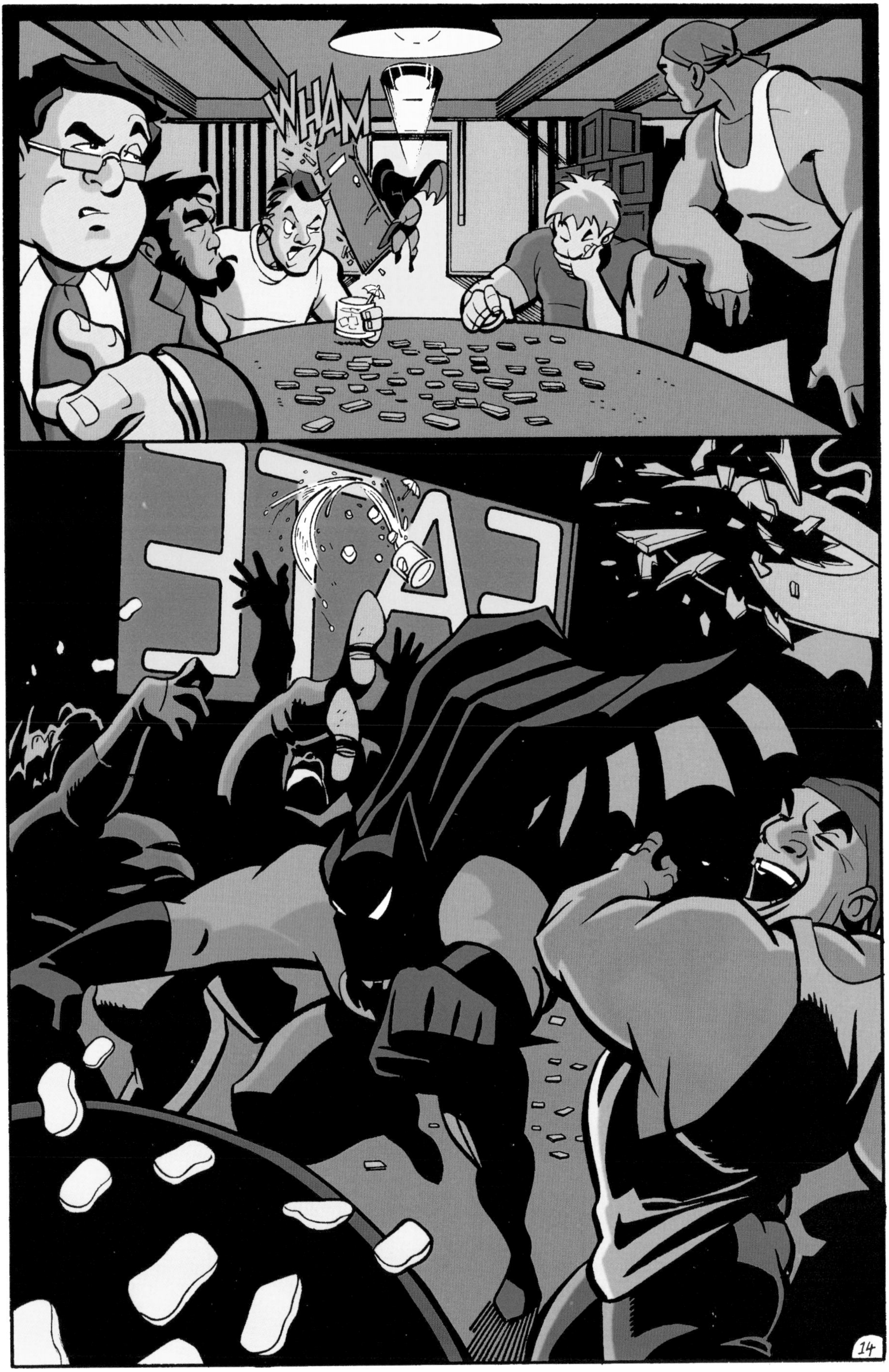
WHAM
14

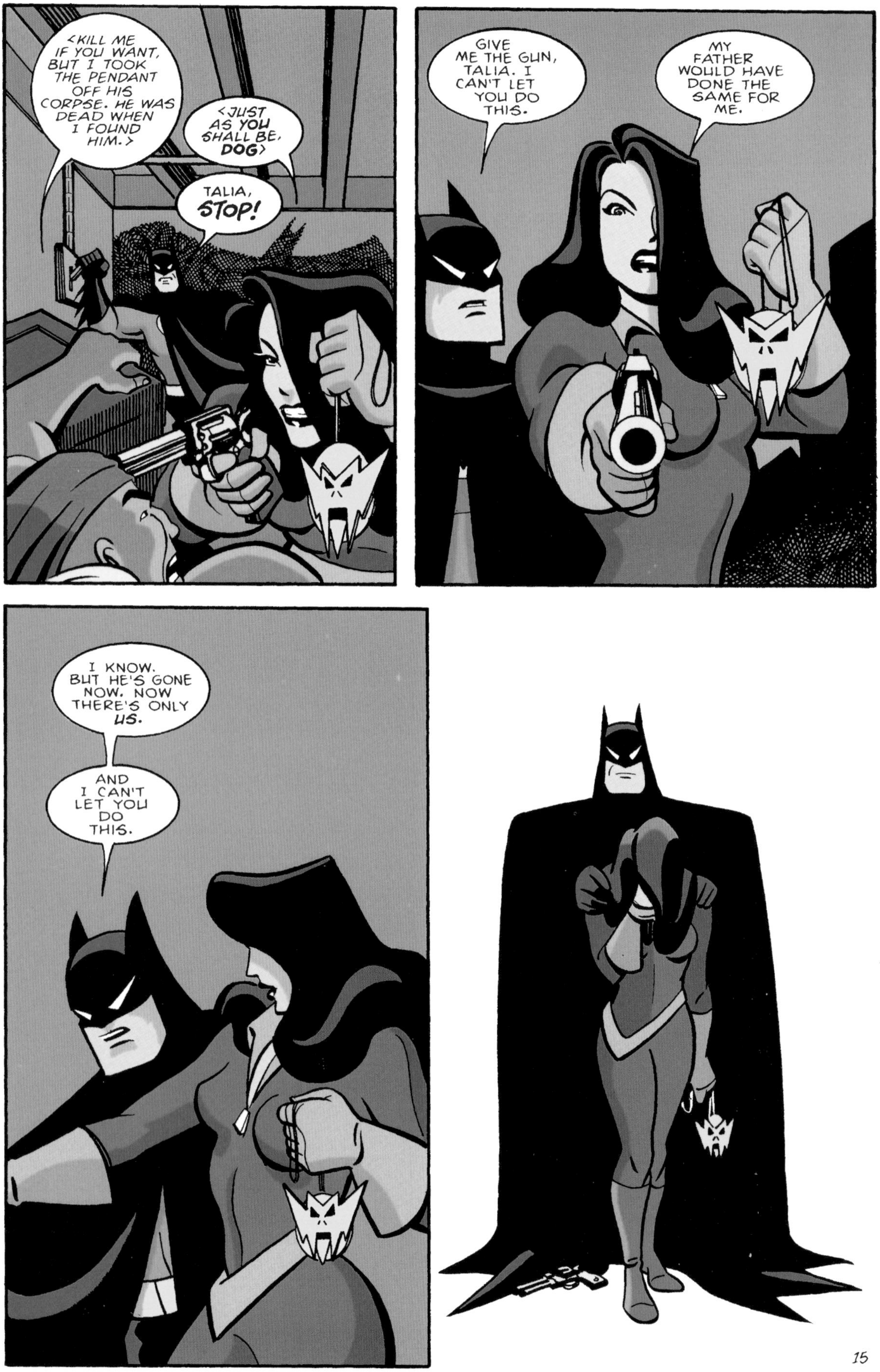

<KILL ME IF YOU WANT, BUT I TOOK THE PENDANT OFF HIS CORPSE. HE WAS DEAD WHEN I FOUND HIM.>
<JUST AS YOU SHALL BE, DOG>
TALIA, STOP!
GIVE ME THE GUN, TALIA. I CAN'T LET YOU DO THIS.
MY FATHER WOULD HAVE DONE THE SAME FOR ME.
I KNOW. BUT HE'S GONE NOW. NOW THERE'S ONLY US.
AND I CAN'T LET YOU DO THIS.

15

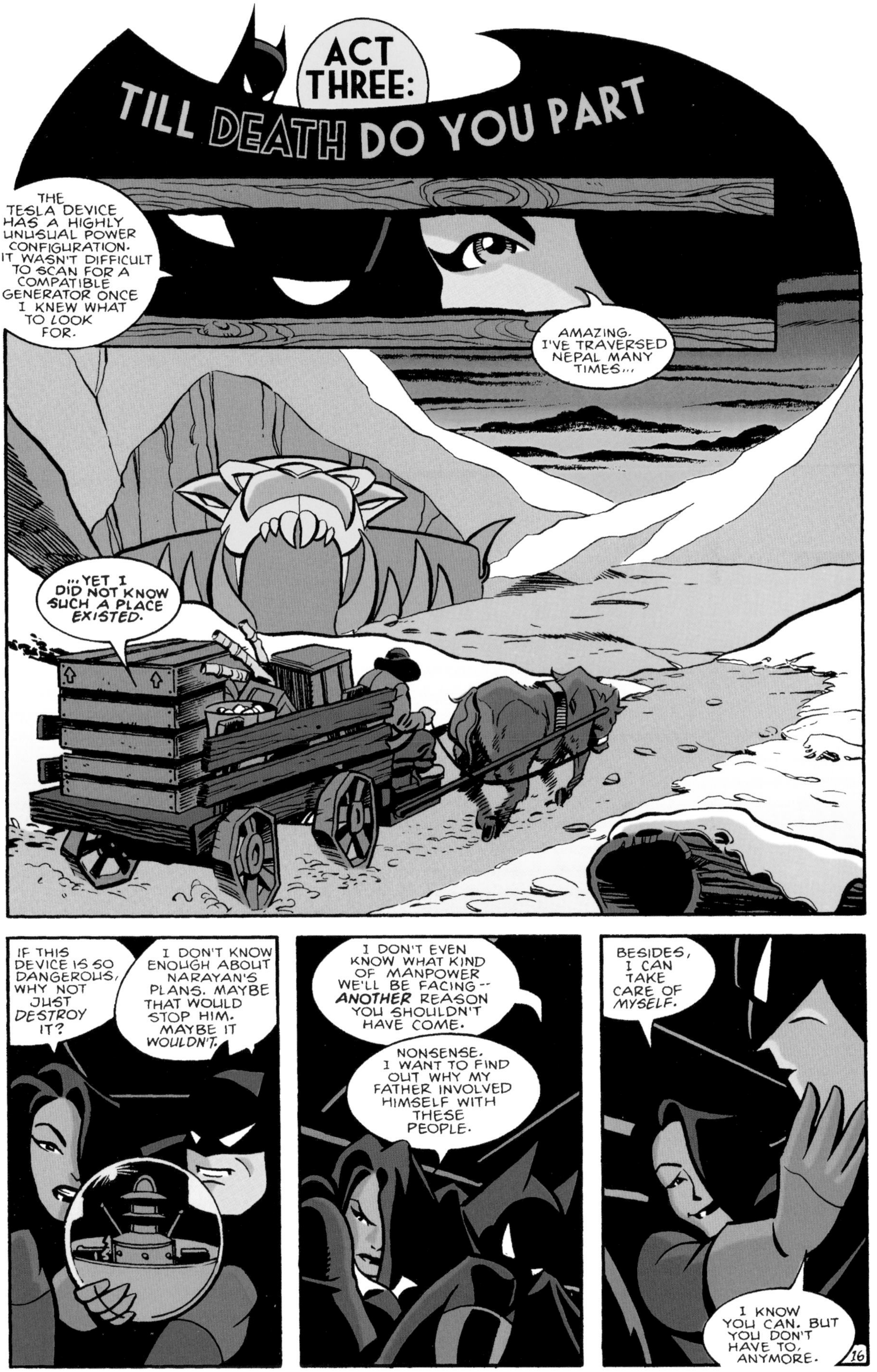
ACT THREE:
TILL DEATH DO YOU PART
THE TESLA DEVICE HAS A HIGHLY UNUSUAL POWER CONFIGURATION. IT WASN'T DIFFICULT TO SCAN FOR A COMPATIBLE GENERATOR ONCE I KNEW WHAT TO LOOK FOR.
AMAZING. I'VE TRAVERSED NEPAL MANY TIMES...
...YET I DID NOT KNOW SUCH A PLACE EXISTED.
IF THIS DEVICE IS SO DANGEROUS, WHY NOT JUST DESTROY IT?
I DON'T KNOW ENOUGH ABOUT NARAYAN'S PLANS. MAYBE THAT WOULD STOP HIM. MAYBE IT WOULDN'T.
I DON'T EVEN KNOW WHAT KIND OF MANPOWER WE'LL BE FACING-- ANOTHER REASON YOU SHOULDN'T HAVE COME.
NONSENSE. I WANT TO FIND OUT WHY MY FATHER INVOLVED HIMSELF WITH THESE PEOPLE.
BESIDES, I CAN TAKE CARE OF MYSELF.
I KNOW YOU CAN. BUT YOU DON'T HAVE TO, ANYMORE.
16

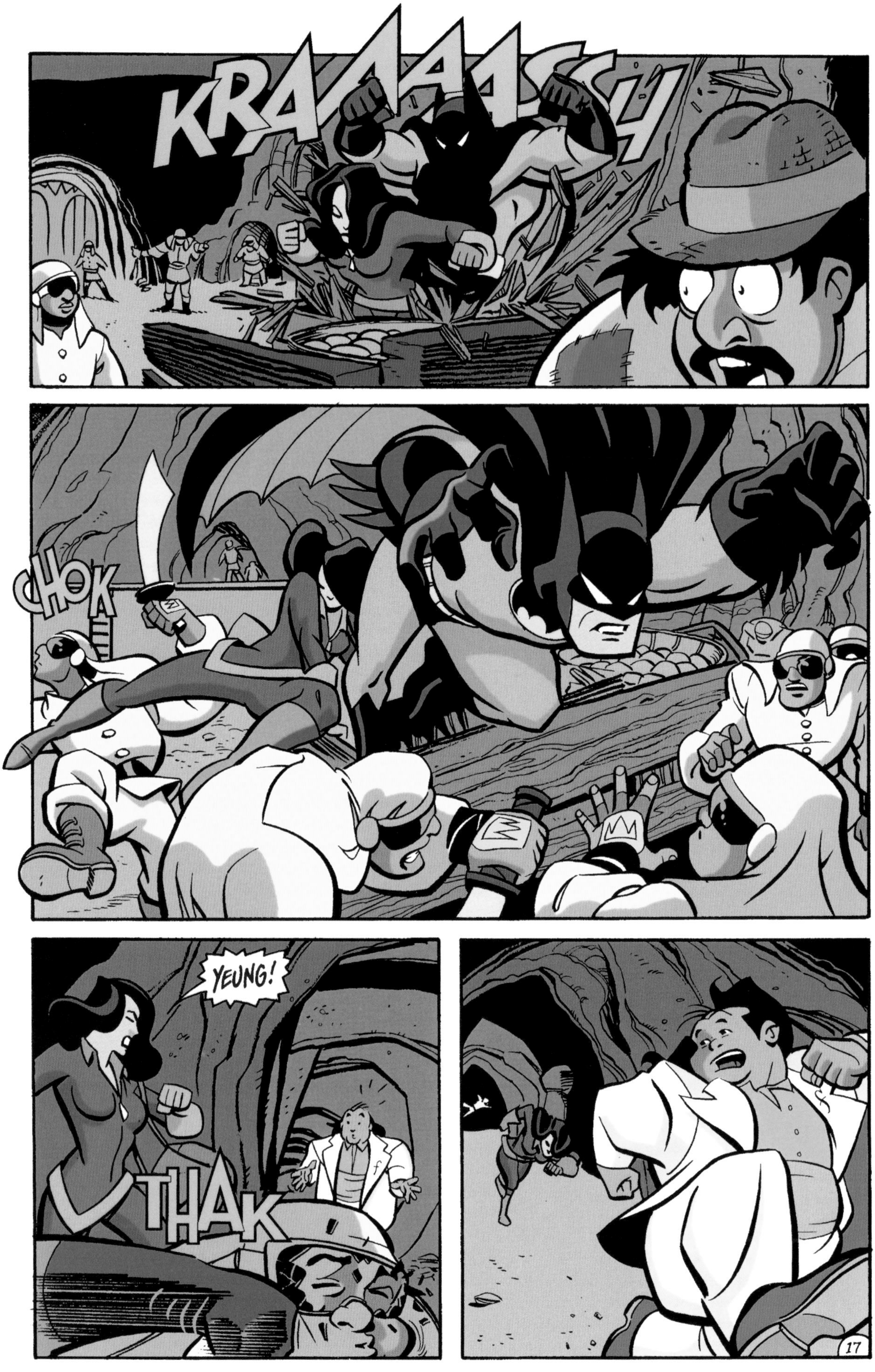
KRAAAASCH
CHOK
YEUNG!
THAK
17

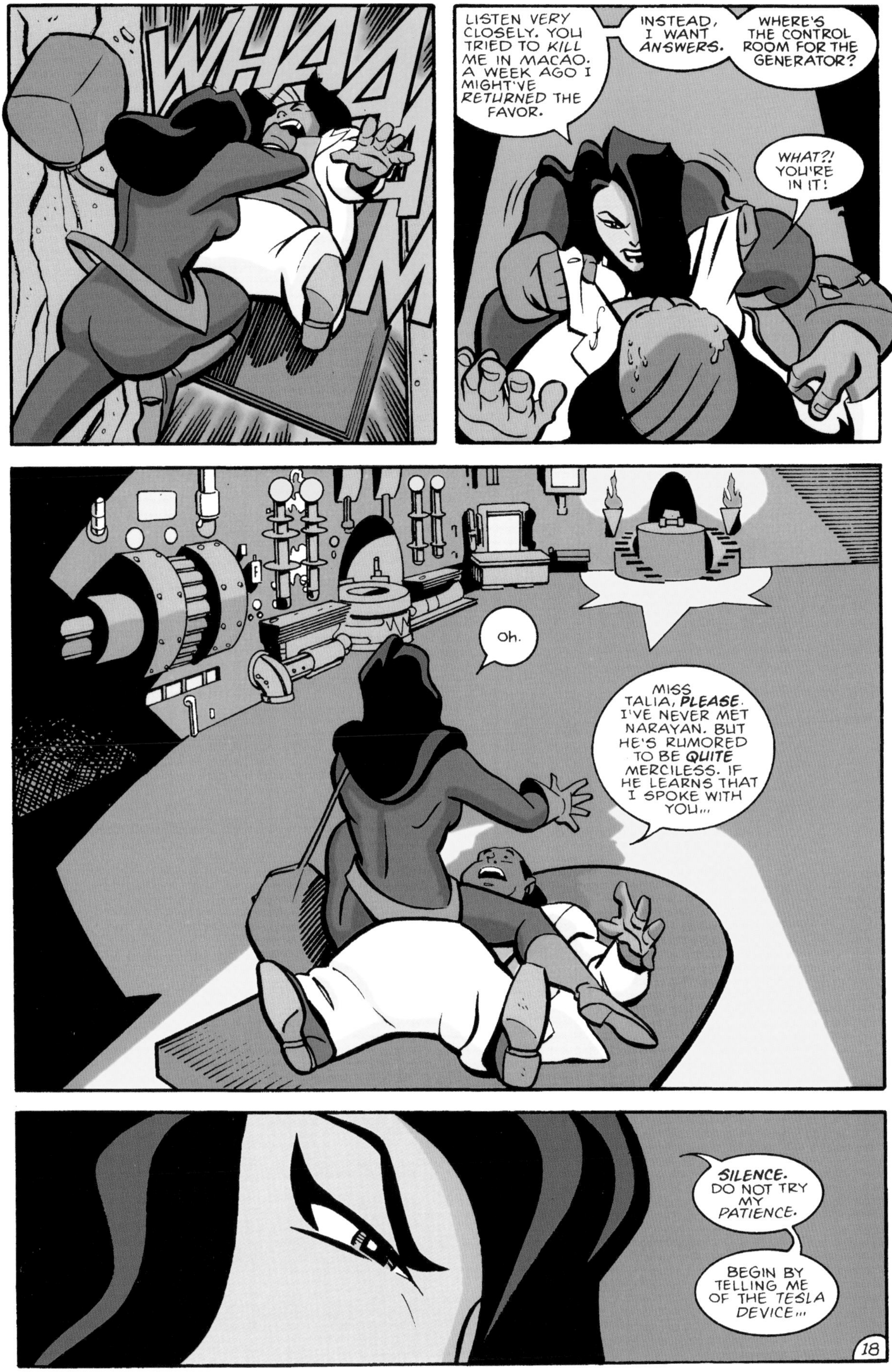
WHAAM
LISTEN VERY CLOSELY. YOU TRIED TO KILL ME IN MACAO. A WEEK AGO I MIGHT'VE RETURNED THE FAVOR.
INSTEAD, I WANT ANSWERS.
WHERE'S THE CONTROL ROOM FOR THE GENERATOR?
WHAT?! YOU'RE IN IT!
Oh.
MISS TALIA, PLEASE. I'VE NEVER MET NARAYAN. BUT HE'S RUMORED TO BE QUITE MERCILESS. IF HE LEARNS THAT I SPOKE WITH YOU...
SILENCE. DO NOT TRY MY PATIENCE.
BEGIN BY TELLING ME OF THE TESLA DEVICE...
18

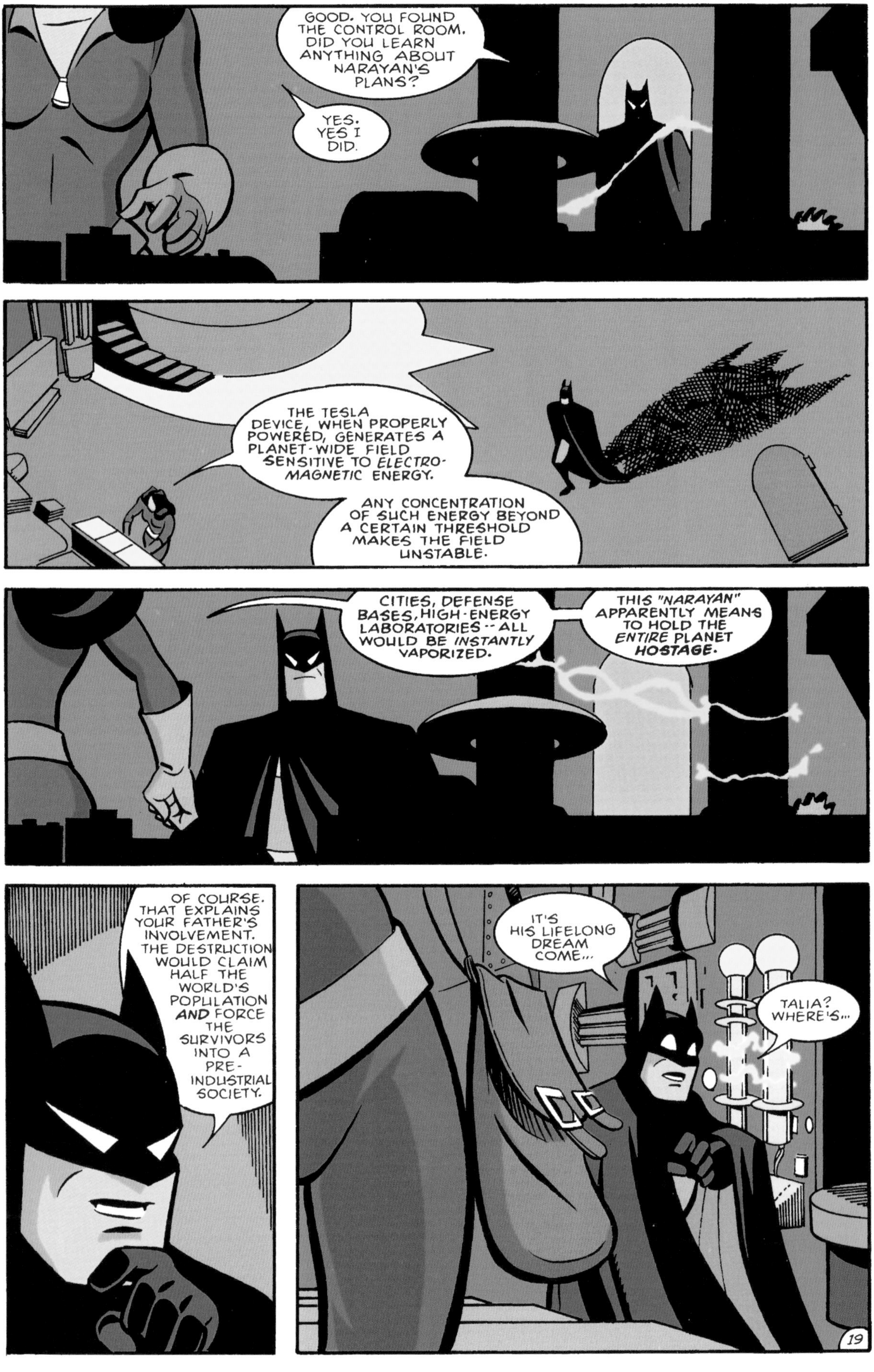
GOOD. YOU FOUND THE CONTROL ROOM. DID YOU LEARN ANYTHING ABOUT NARAYAN'S PLANS?
YES. YES I DID.
THE TESLA DEVICE, WHEN PROPERLY POWERED, GENERATES A PLANET-WIDE FIELD SENSITIVE TO ELECTRO-MAGNETIC ENERGY.
ANY CONCENTRATION OF SUCH ENERGY BEYOND A CERTAIN THRESHOLD MAKES THE FIELD UNSTABLE.
CITIES, DEFENSE BASES, HIGH-ENERGY LABORATORIES -- ALL WOULD BE INSTANTLY VAPORIZED.
THIS "NARAYAN" APPARENTLY MEANS TO HOLD THE ENTIRE PLANET HOSTAGE.
OF COURSE. THAT EXPLAINS YOUR FATHER'S INVOLVEMENT. THE DESTRUCTION WOULD CLAIM HALF THE WORLD'S POPULATION AND FORCE THE SURVIVORS INTO A PRE-INDUSTRIAL SOCIETY.
IT'S HIS LIFELONG DREAM COME...
TALIA? WHERE'S...
19

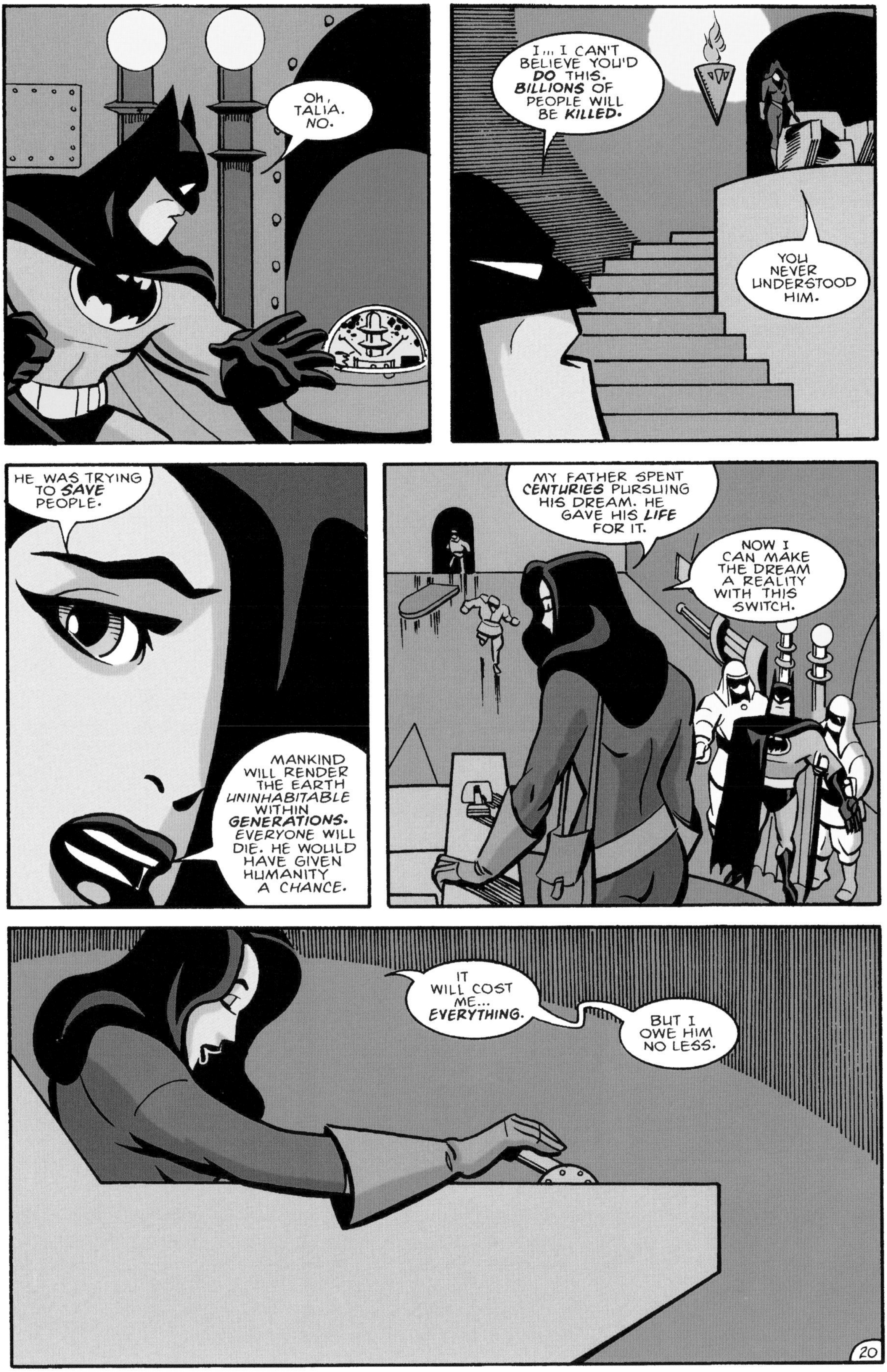

OH, TALIA. NO.
I... I CAN'T BELIEVE YOU'D DO THIS. BILLIONS OF PEOPLE WILL BE KILLED.
YOU NEVER UNDERSTOOD HIM.
HE WAS TRYING TO SAVE PEOPLE.
MANKIND WILL RENDER THE EARTH UNINHABITABLE WITHIN GENERATIONS. EVERYONE WILL DIE. HE WOULD HAVE GIVEN HUMANITY A CHANCE.
MY FATHER SPENT CENTURIES PURSUING HIS DREAM. HE GAVE HIS LIFE FOR IT.
NOW I CAN MAKE THE DREAM A REALITY WITH THIS SWITCH.
IT WILL COST ME... EVERYTHING.
BUT I OWE HIM NO LESS.
20

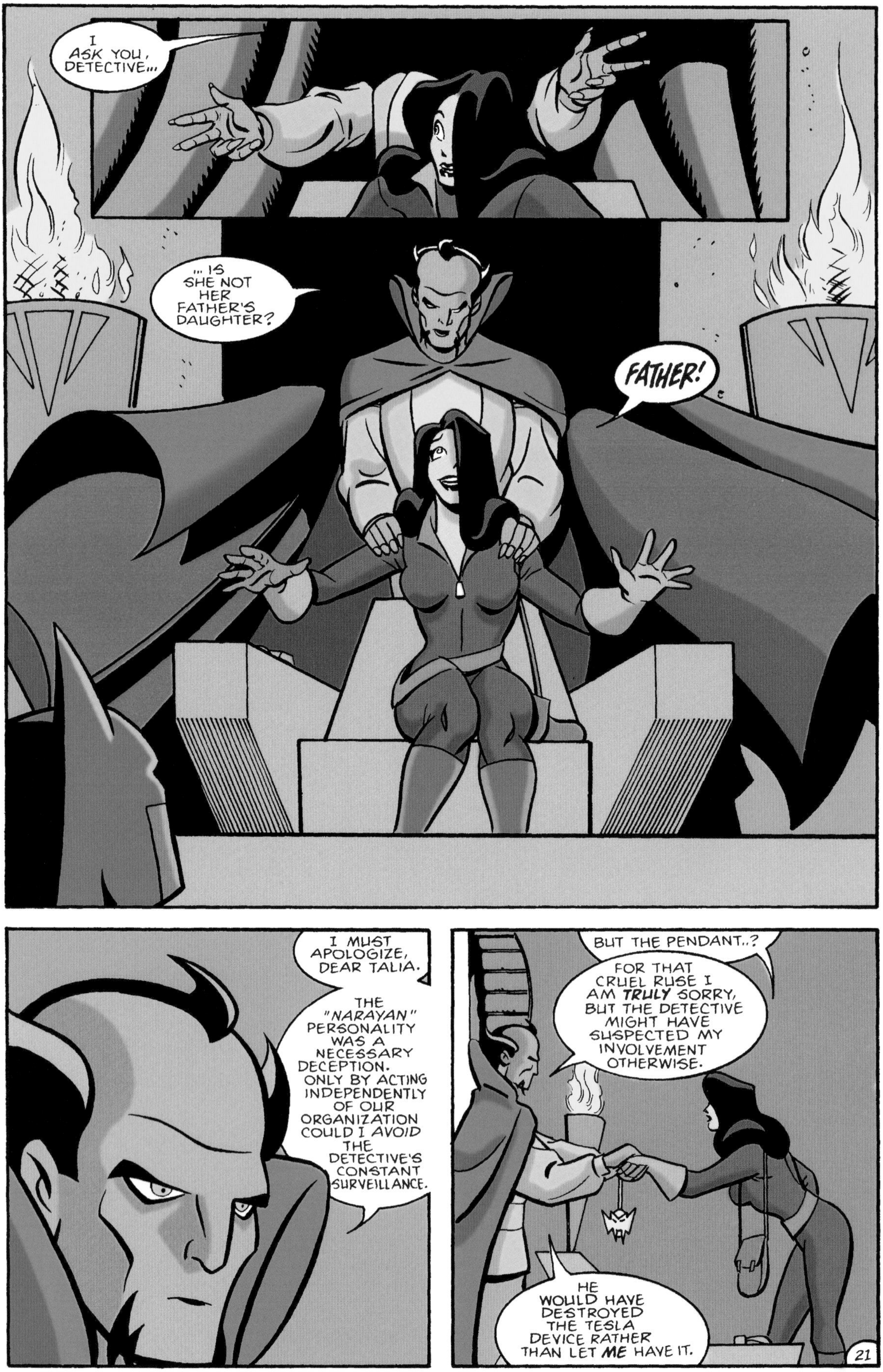
I ASK YOU, DETECTIVE...
...IS SHE NOT HER FATHER'S DAUGHTER?
FATHER!
I MUST APOLOGIZE, DEAR TALIA.
THE "NARAYAN" PERSONALITY WAS A NECESSARY DECEPTION. ONLY BY ACTING INDEPENDENTLY OF OUR ORGANIZATION COULD I AVOID THE DETECTIVE'S CONSTANT SURVEILLANCE.
BUT THE PENDANT..?
FOR THAT CRUEL RUSE I AM TRULY SORRY, BUT THE DETECTIVE MIGHT HAVE SUSPECTED MY INVOLVEMENT OTHERWISE.
HE WOULD HAVE DESTROYED THE TESLA DEVICE RATHER THAN LET ME HAVE IT.
21

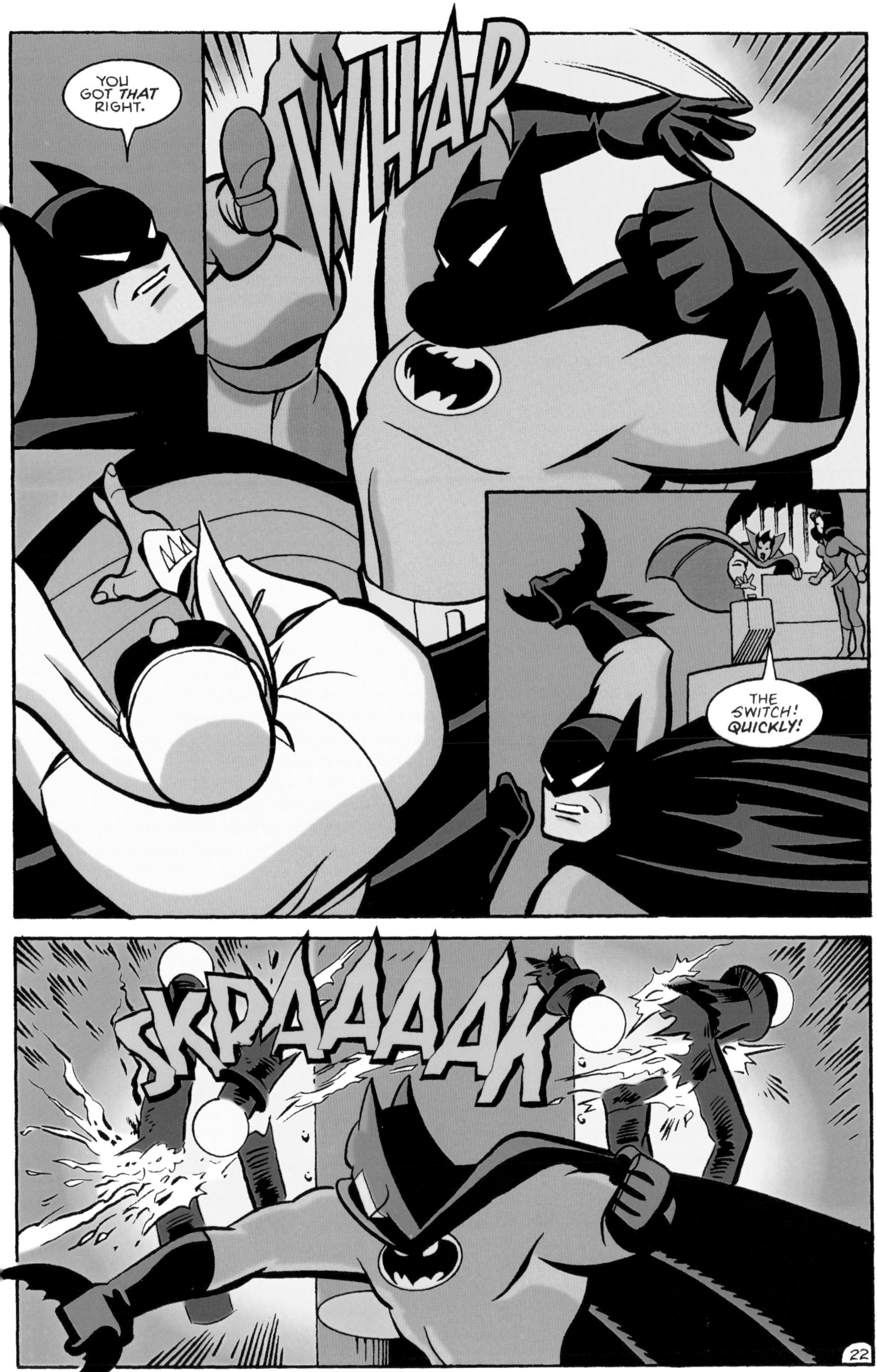
YOU GOT THAT RIGHT.
WHAP
THE SWITCH! QUICKLY!
SKRAAAAK
22

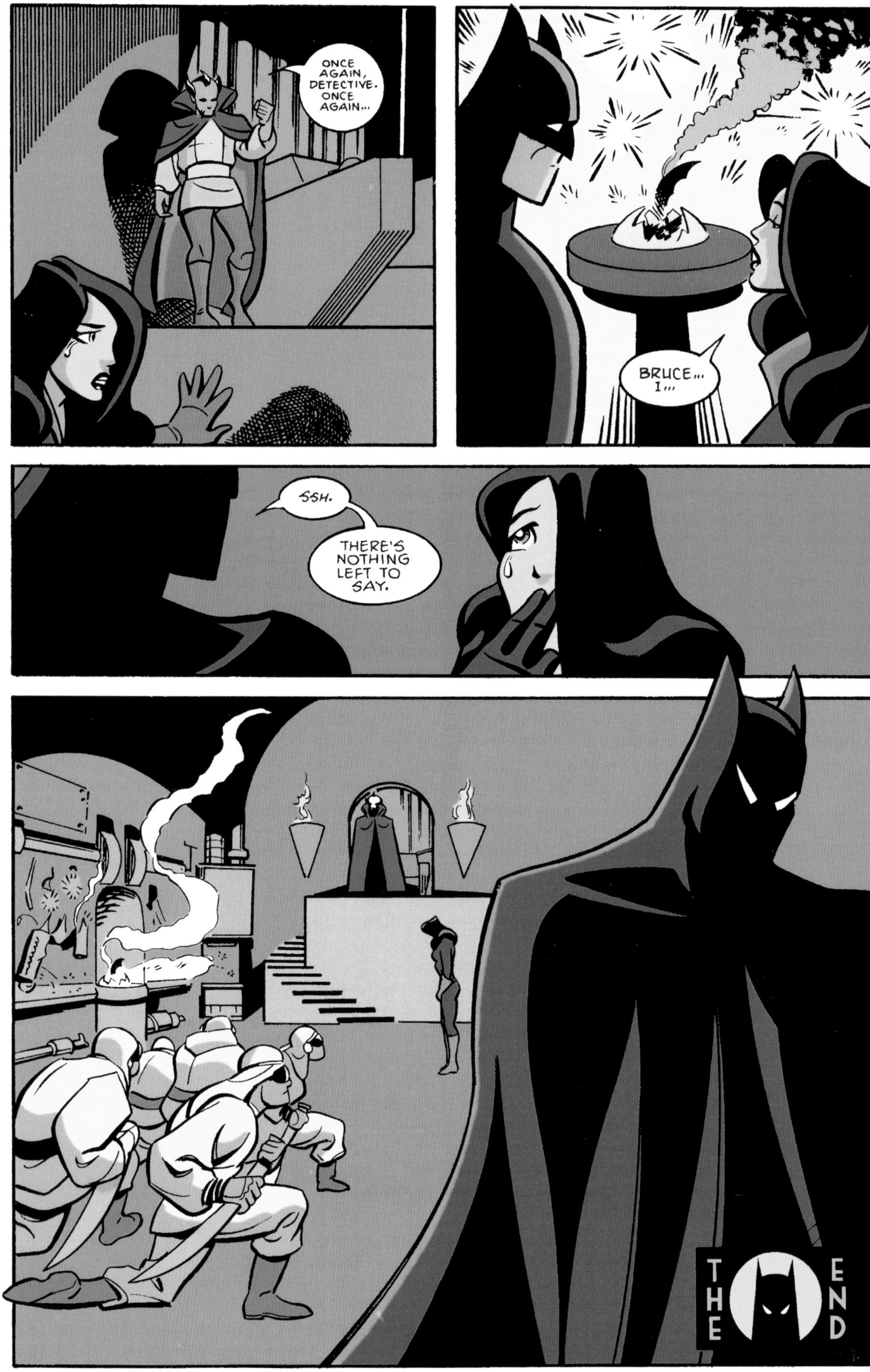
ONCE AGAIN, DETECTIVE. ONCE AGAIN...
BRUCE... I...
SSH.
THERE'S NOTHING LEFT TO SAY.
THE END

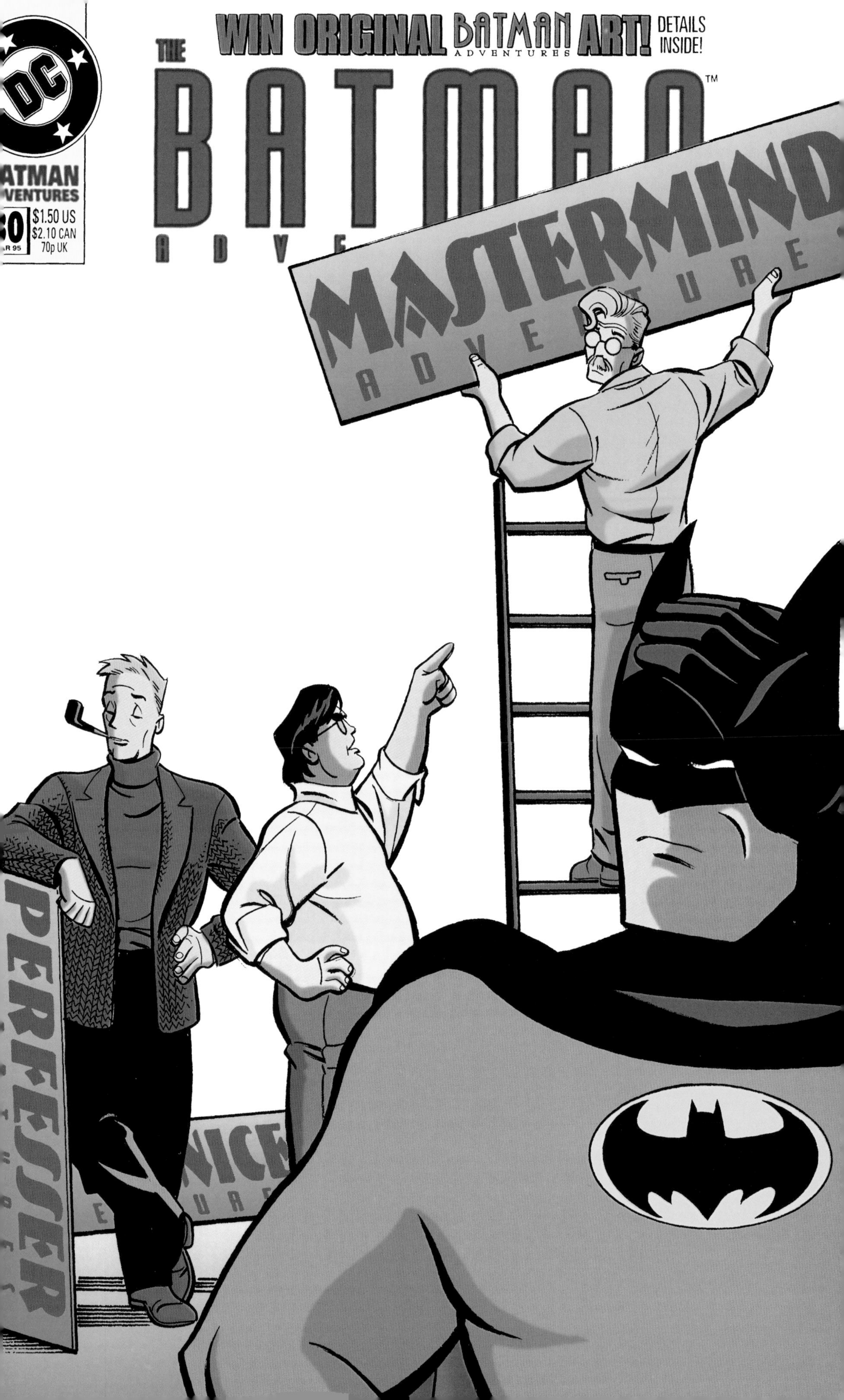
WIN ORIGINAL BATMAN ADVENTURES ART! DETAILS INSIDE!
THE BATMAN™ ADVE
ATMAN VENTURES
$1.50 US
$2.10 CAN
70p UK
MASTERMIND
ADVE TURES
PERFESSER
NICE

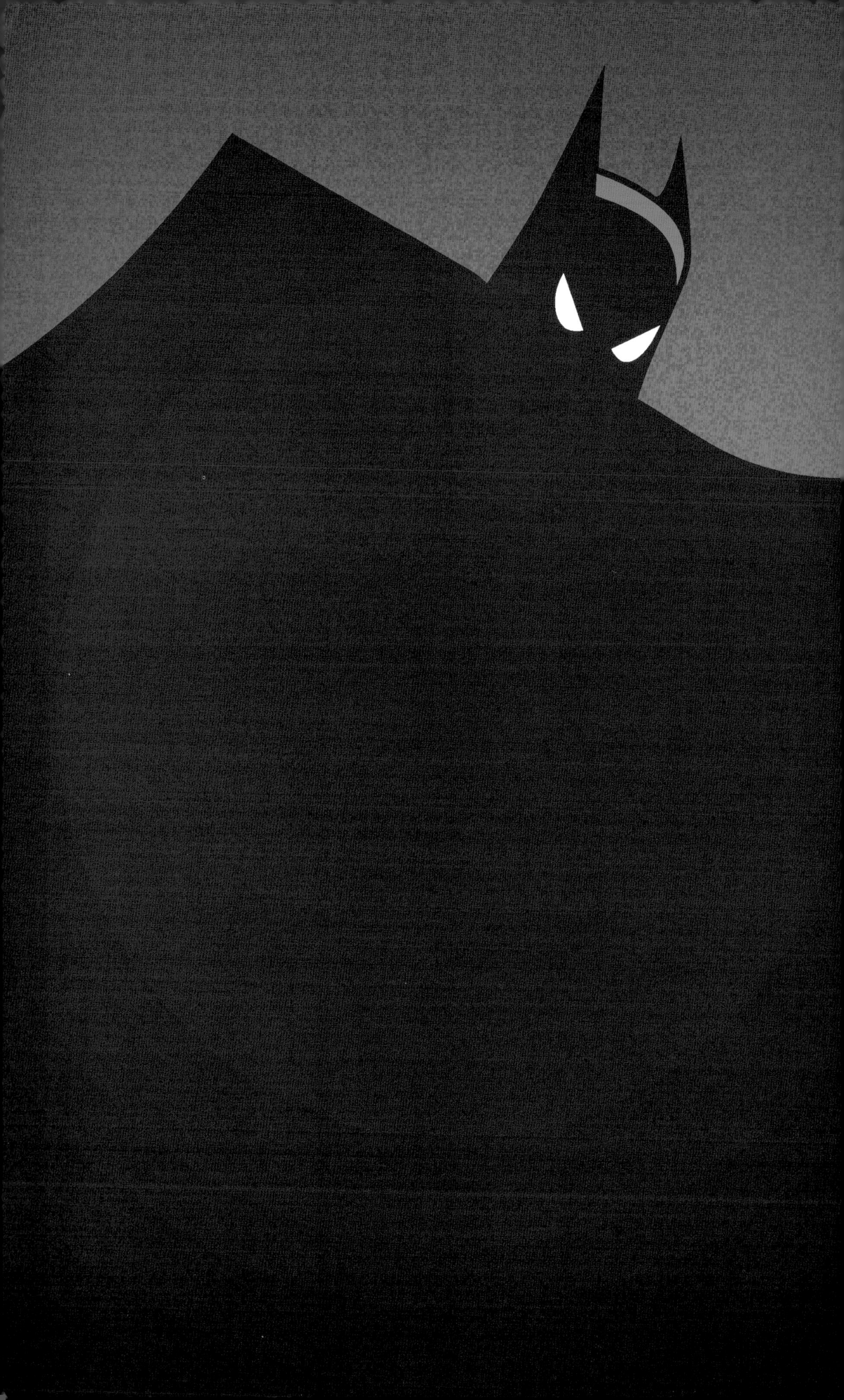

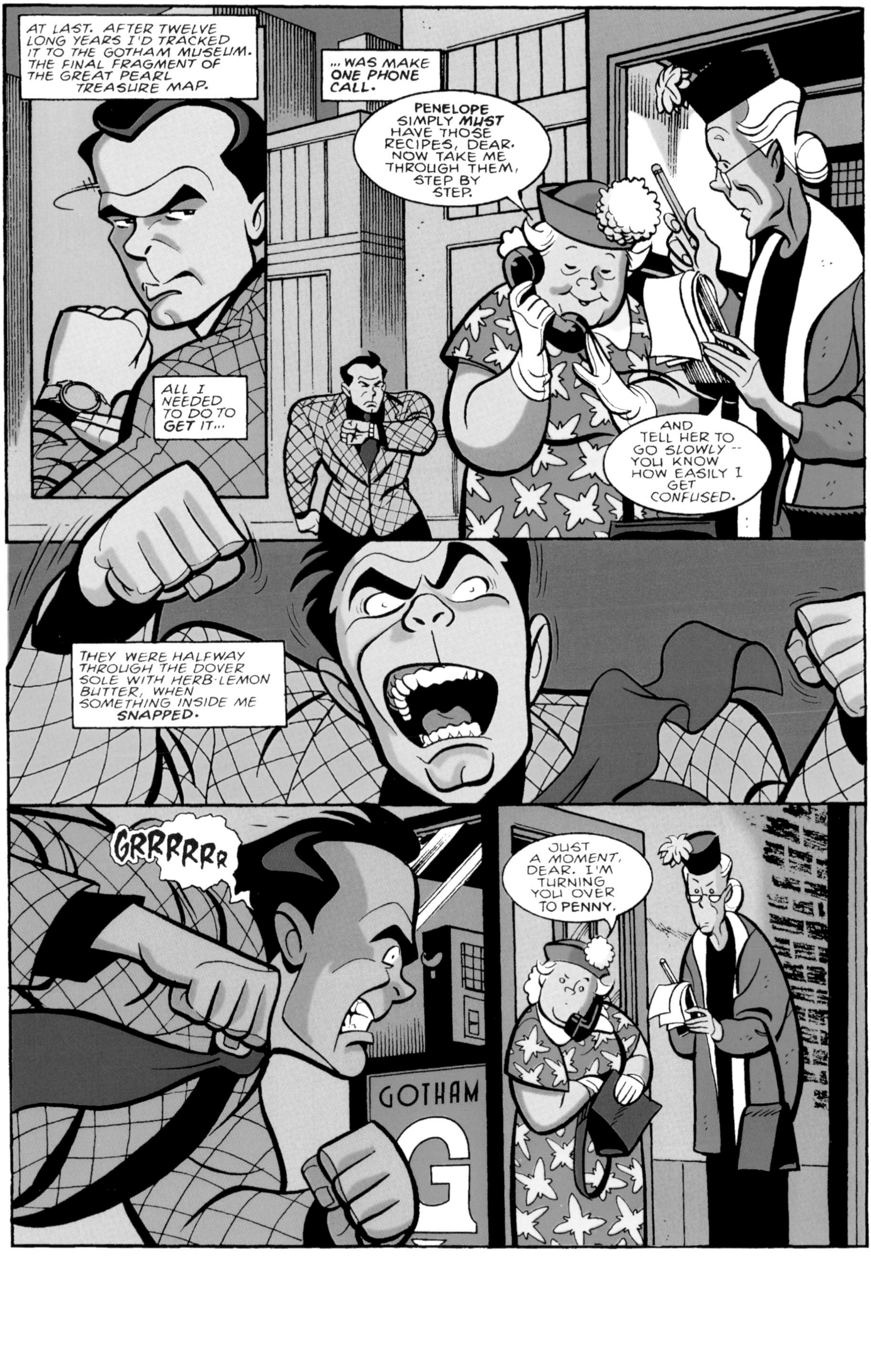
AT LAST. AFTER TWELVE LONG YEARS I'D TRACKED IT TO THE GOTHAM MUSEUM. THE FINAL FRAGMENT OF THE GREAT PEARL TREASURE MAP.
ALL I NEEDED TO DO TO GET IT...
...WAS MAKE ONE PHONE CALL.
PENELOPE SIMPLY MUST HAVE THOSE RECIPES, DEAR. NOW TAKE ME THROUGH THEM, STEP BY STEP.
AND TELL HER TO GO SLOWLY -- YOU KNOW HOW EASILY I GET CONFUSED.
THEY WERE HALFWAY THROUGH THE DOVER SOLE WITH HERB-LEMON BUTTER, WHEN SOMETHING INSIDE ME SNAPPED.
GRRRRRR
JUST A MOMENT, DEAR. I'M TURNING YOU OVER TO PENNY.
GOTHAM
G

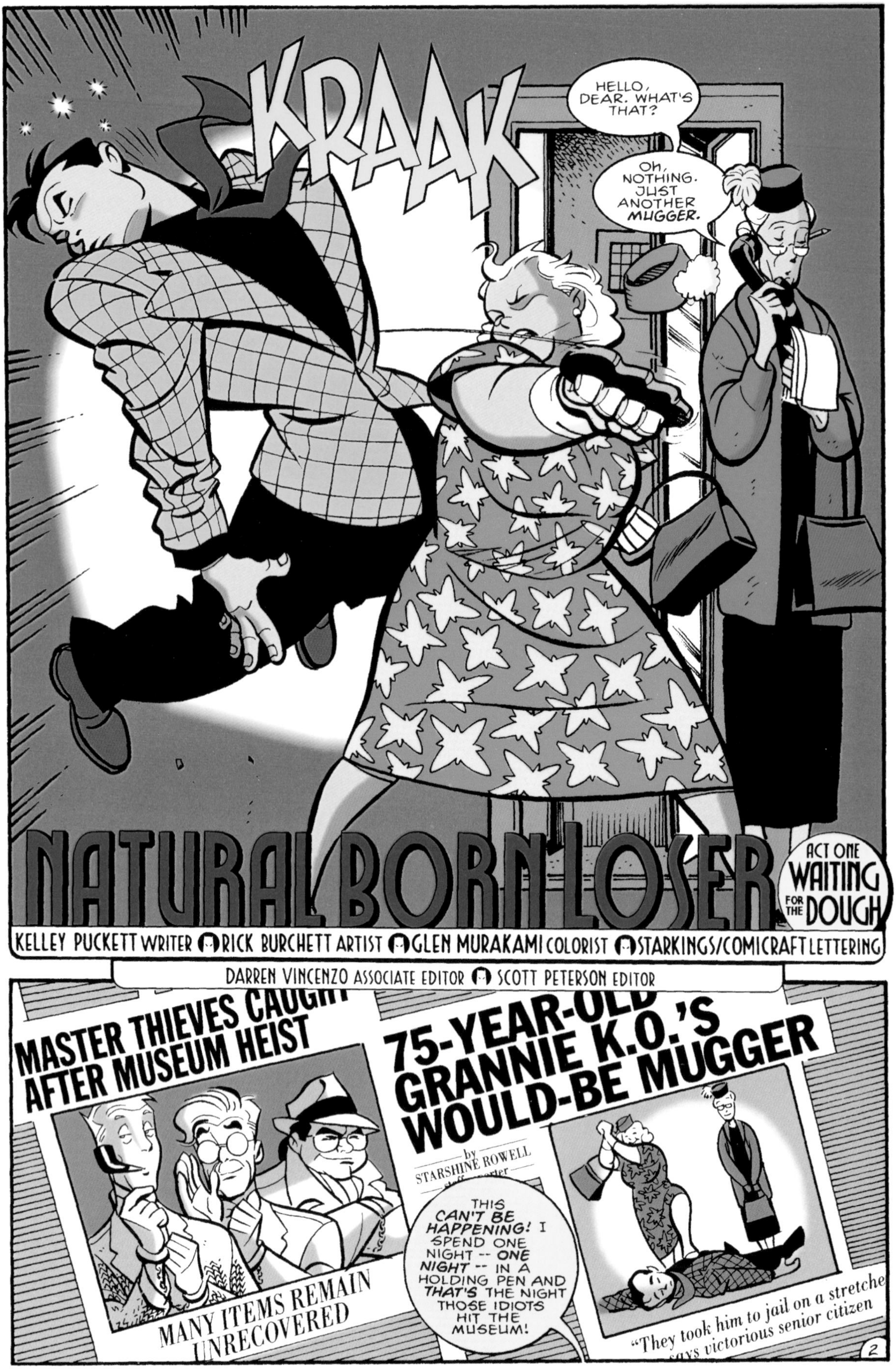
KRAAK
HELLO, DEAR. WHAT'S THAT?
OH, NOTHING. JUST ANOTHER MUGGER.
NATURAL BORN LOSER
ACT ONE WAITING FOR THE DOUGH
KELLEY PUCKETT WRITER RICK BURCHETT ARTIST GLEN MURAKAMI COLORIST STARKINGS/COMICRAFT LETTERING
DARREN VINCENZO ASSOCIATE EDITOR SCOTT PETERSON EDITOR
MASTER THIEVES CAUGH
AFTER MUSEUM HEIST
MANY ITEMS REMAIN UNRECOVERED
75-YEAR-OLD GRANNIE K.O.'S WOULD-BE MUGGER
by STARSHINE ROWELL
THIS CAN'T BE HAPPENING! I SPEND ONE NIGHT -- ONE NIGHT -- IN A HOLDING PEN AND THAT'S THE NIGHT THOSE IDIOTS HIT THE MUSEUM!
"They took him to jail on a stretche
says victorious senior citizen
2

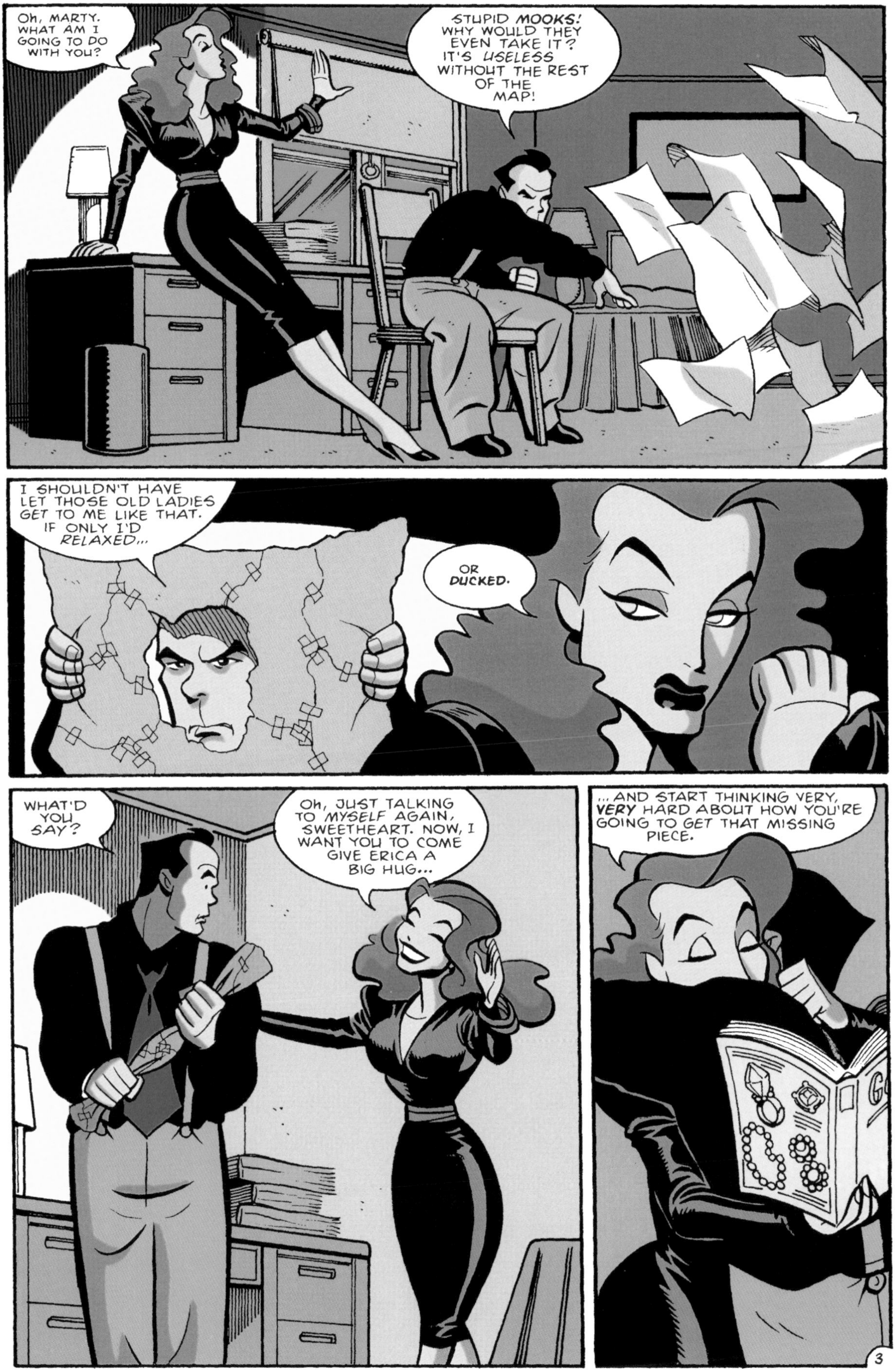
Oh, MARTY. WHAT AM I GOING TO DO WITH YOU?
STUPID MOOKS! WHY WOULD THEY EVEN TAKE IT? IT'S USELESS WITHOUT THE REST OF THE MAP!
I SHOULDN'T HAVE LET THOSE OLD LADIES GET TO ME LIKE THAT. IF ONLY I'D RELAXED...
OR DUCKED.
WHAT'D YOU SAY?
Oh, JUST TALKING TO MYSELF AGAIN, SWEETHEART. NOW, I WANT YOU TO COME GIVE ERICA A BIG HUG...
...AND START THINKING VERY, VERY HARD ABOUT HOW YOU'RE GOING TO GET THAT MISSING PIECE.
3

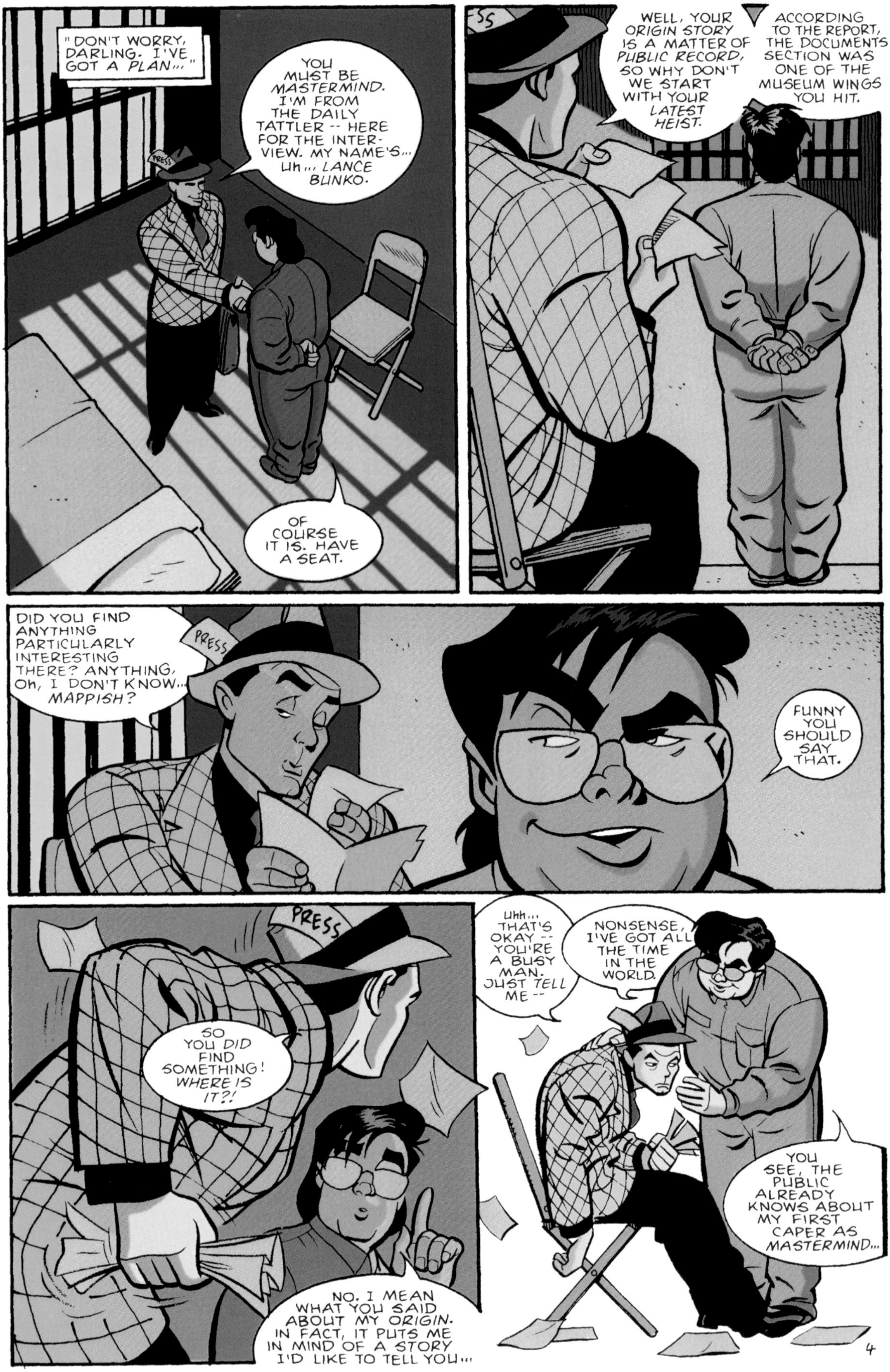
"DON'T WORRY, DARLING. I'VE GOT A PLAN..."
YOU MUST BE MASTERMIND. I'M FROM THE DAILY TATTLER -- HERE FOR THE INTER-VIEW. MY NAME'S... UH... LANCE BUNKO.
OF COURSE IT IS. HAVE A SEAT.
PRESS
WELL, YOUR ORIGIN STORY IS A MATTER OF PUBLIC RECORD, SO WHY DON'T WE START WITH YOUR LATEST HEIST.
ACCORDING TO THE REPORT, THE DOCUMENTS SECTION WAS ONE OF THE MUSEUM WINGS YOU HIT.
DID YOU FIND ANYTHING PARTICULARLY INTERESTING THERE? ANYTHING, OH, I DON'T KNOW... MAPPISH?
PRESS
FUNNY YOU SHOULD SAY THAT.
PRESS
SO YOU DID FIND SOMETHING! WHERE IS IT?!
NO. I MEAN WHAT YOU SAID ABOUT MY ORIGIN. IN FACT, IT PUTS ME IN MIND OF A STORY I'D LIKE TO TELL YOU...
UHH... THAT'S OKAY -- YOU'RE A BUSY MAN. JUST TELL ME --
NONSENSE, I'VE GOT ALL THE TIME IN THE WORLD.
YOU SEE, THE PUBLIC ALREADY KNOWS ABOUT MY FIRST CAPER AS MASTERMIND...
4

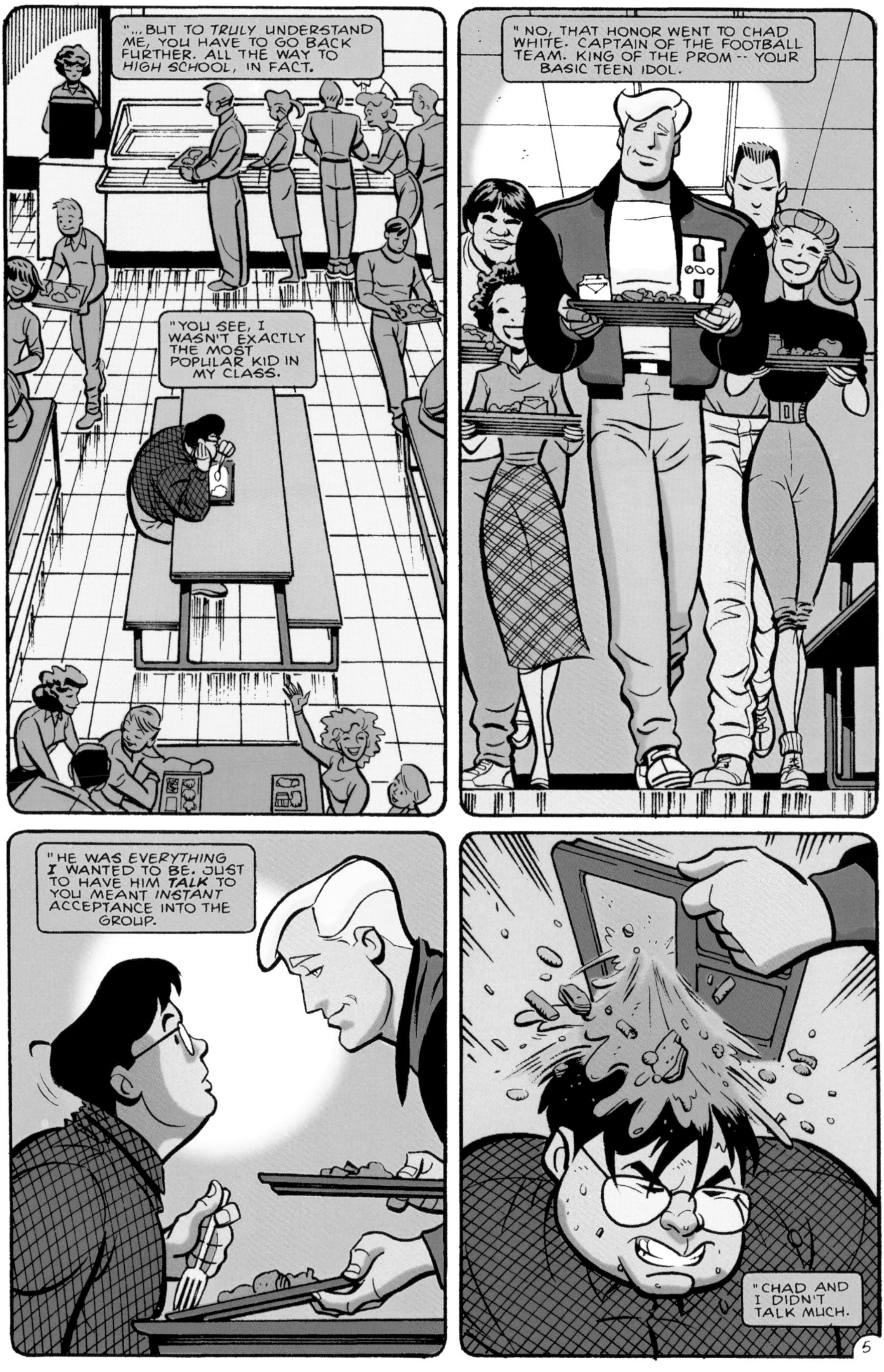
"...BUT TO TRULY UNDERSTAND ME, YOU HAVE TO GO BACK FURTHER. ALL THE WAY TO HIGH SCHOOL, IN FACT.
"YOU SEE, I WASN'T EXACTLY THE MOST POPULAR KID IN MY CLASS.
"NO, THAT HONOR WENT TO CHAD WHITE. CAPTAIN OF THE FOOTBALL TEAM. KING OF THE PROM -- YOUR BASIC TEEN IDOL.
"HE WAS EVERYTHING I WANTED TO BE. JUST TO HAVE HIM TALK TO YOU MEANT INSTANT ACCEPTANCE INTO THE GROUP.
"CHAD AND I DIDN'T TALK MUCH.
5

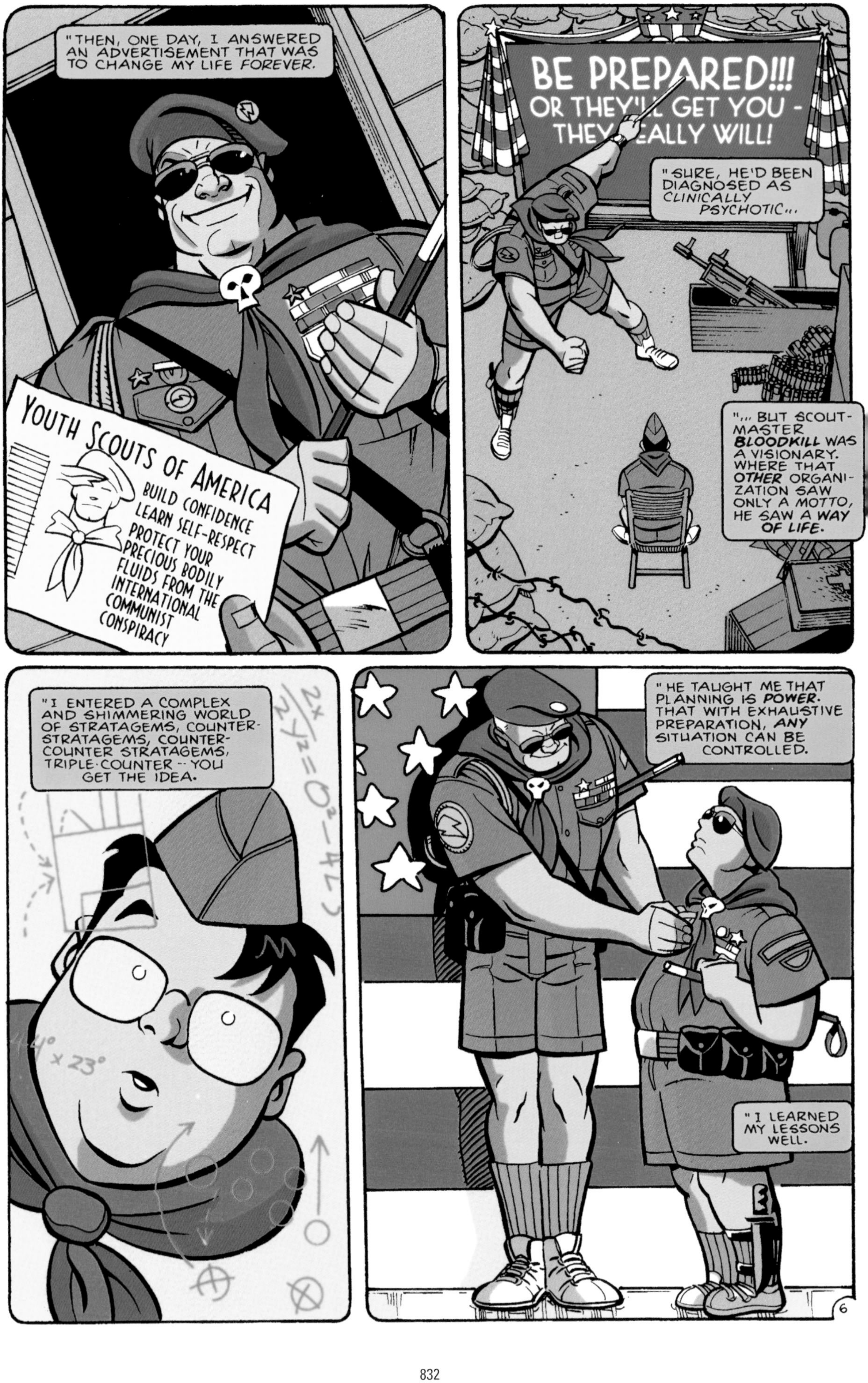
"THEN, ONE DAY, I ANSWERED AN ADVERTISEMENT THAT WAS TO CHANGE MY LIFE *FOREVER*.
YOUTH SCOUTS OF AMERICA
BUILD CONFIDENCE
LEARN SELF-RESPECT
PROTECT YOUR PRECIOUS BODILY FLUIDS FROM THE INTERNATIONAL COMMUNIST CONSPIRACY
BE PREPARED!!!
OR THEY'LL GET YOU - THEY REALLY WILL!
"SURE, HE'D BEEN DIAGNOSED AS *CLINICALLY PSYCHOTIC*...
"... BUT SCOUTMASTER **BLOODKILL** WAS A VISIONARY. WHERE THAT **OTHER** ORGANIZATION SAW ONLY A *MOTTO*, HE SAW A **WAY OF LIFE**.
"I ENTERED A COMPLEX AND SHIMMERING WORLD OF STRATAGEMS, COUNTER-STRATAGEMS, COUNTER-COUNTER STRATAGEMS, TRIPLE-COUNTER -- YOU GET THE IDEA.
"HE TAUGHT ME THAT PLANNING IS **POWER**. THAT WITH EXHAUSTIVE PREPARATION, **ANY** SITUATION CAN BE CONTROLLED.
"I LEARNED MY LESSONS WELL.
6

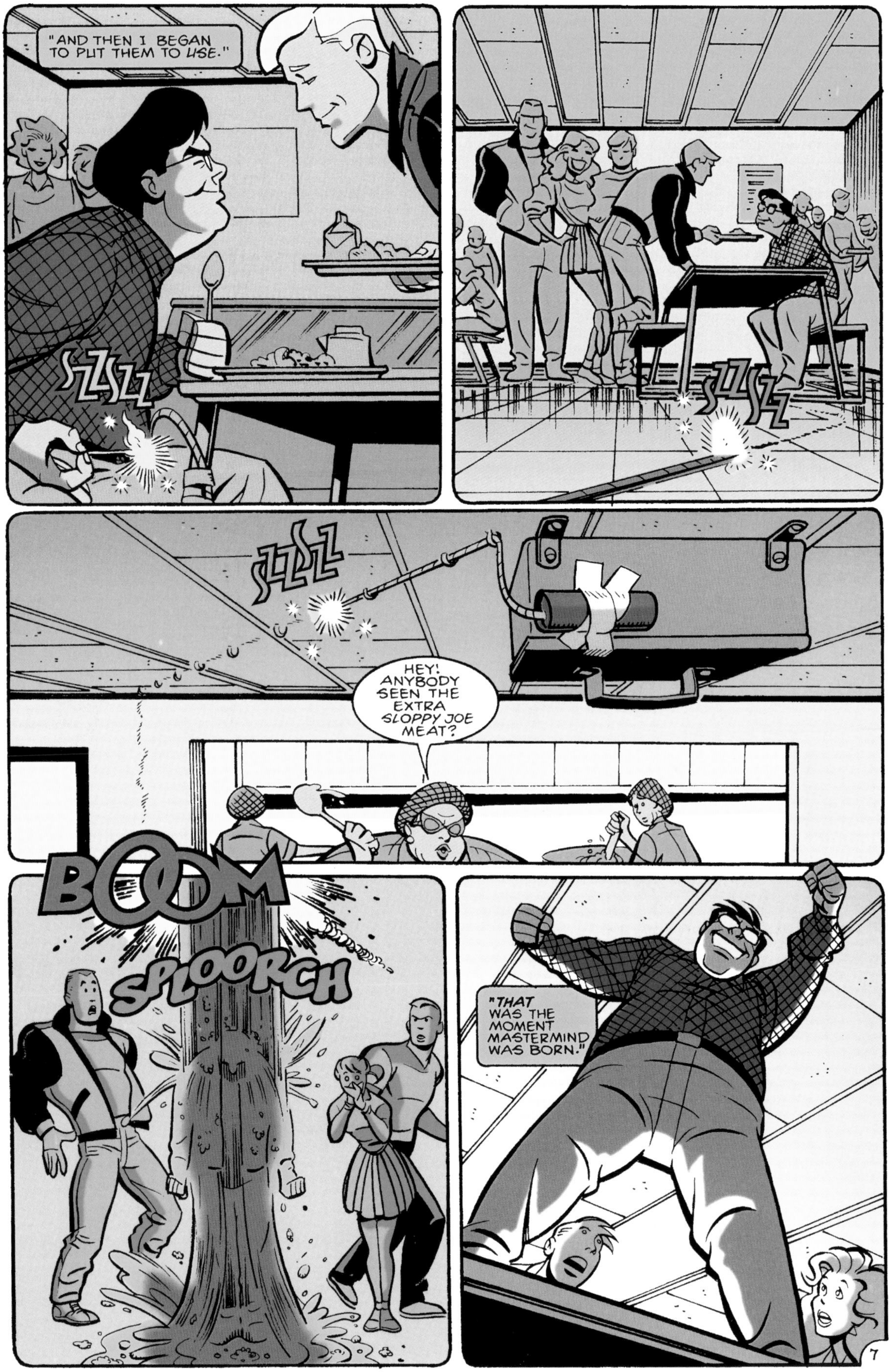
"AND THEN I BEGAN TO PUT THEM TO USE."
SZZSZZ
SZZSZZ
SZZSZZ
HEY! ANYBODY SEEN THE EXTRA SLOPPY JOE MEAT?
BOOM
SPLOORCH
"THAT WAS THE MOMENT MASTERMIND WAS BORN."
7

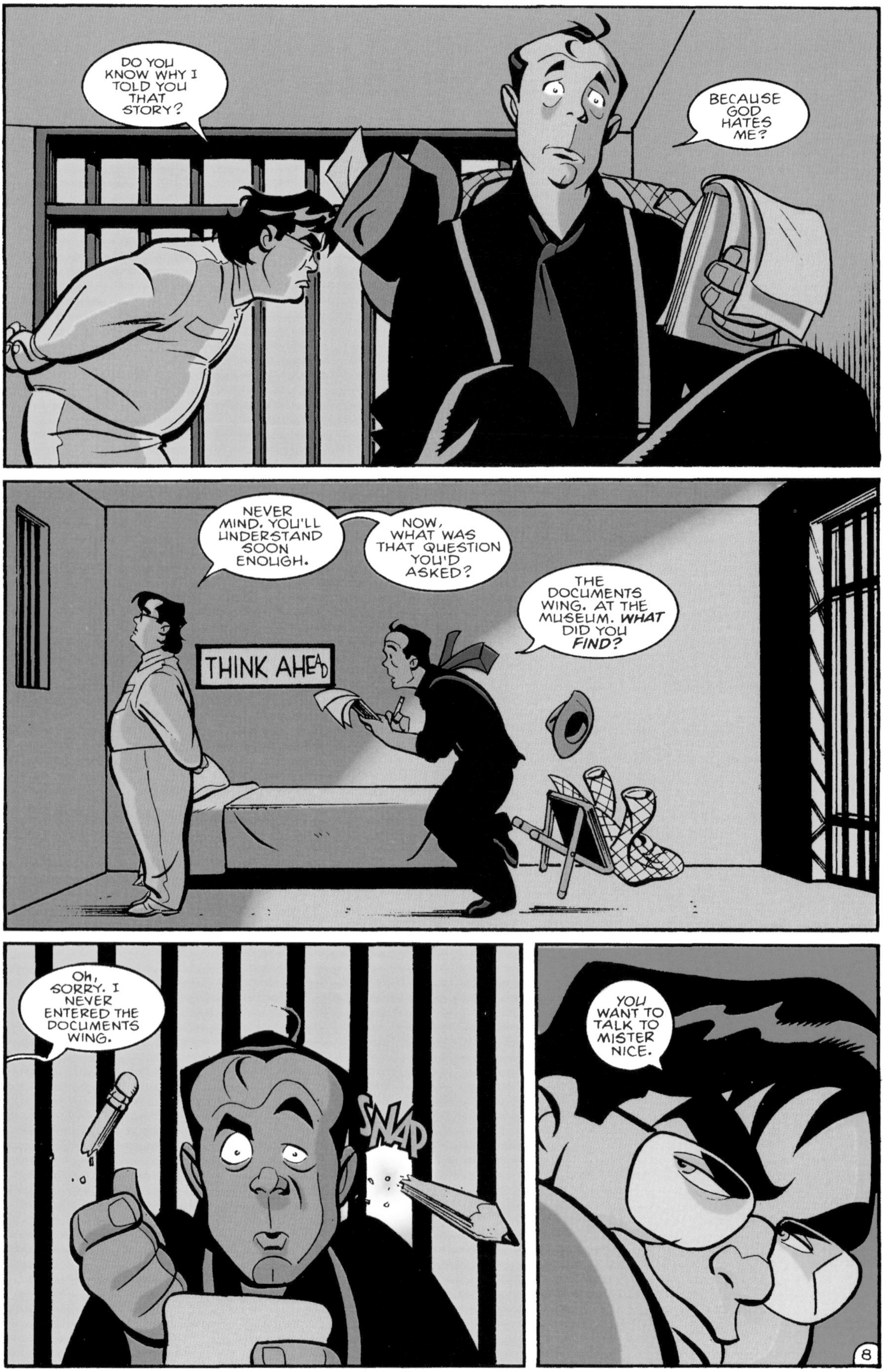
DO YOU KNOW WHY I TOLD YOU THAT STORY?
BECAUSE GOD HATES ME?
NEVER MIND. YOU'LL UNDERSTAND SOON ENOUGH.
NOW, WHAT WAS THAT QUESTION YOU'D ASKED?
THINK AHEAD
THE DOCUMENTS WING. AT THE MUSEUM. WHAT DID YOU FIND?
Oh, SORRY. I NEVER ENTERED THE DOCUMENTS WING.
SNAP
YOU WANT TO TALK TO MISTER NICE.
8

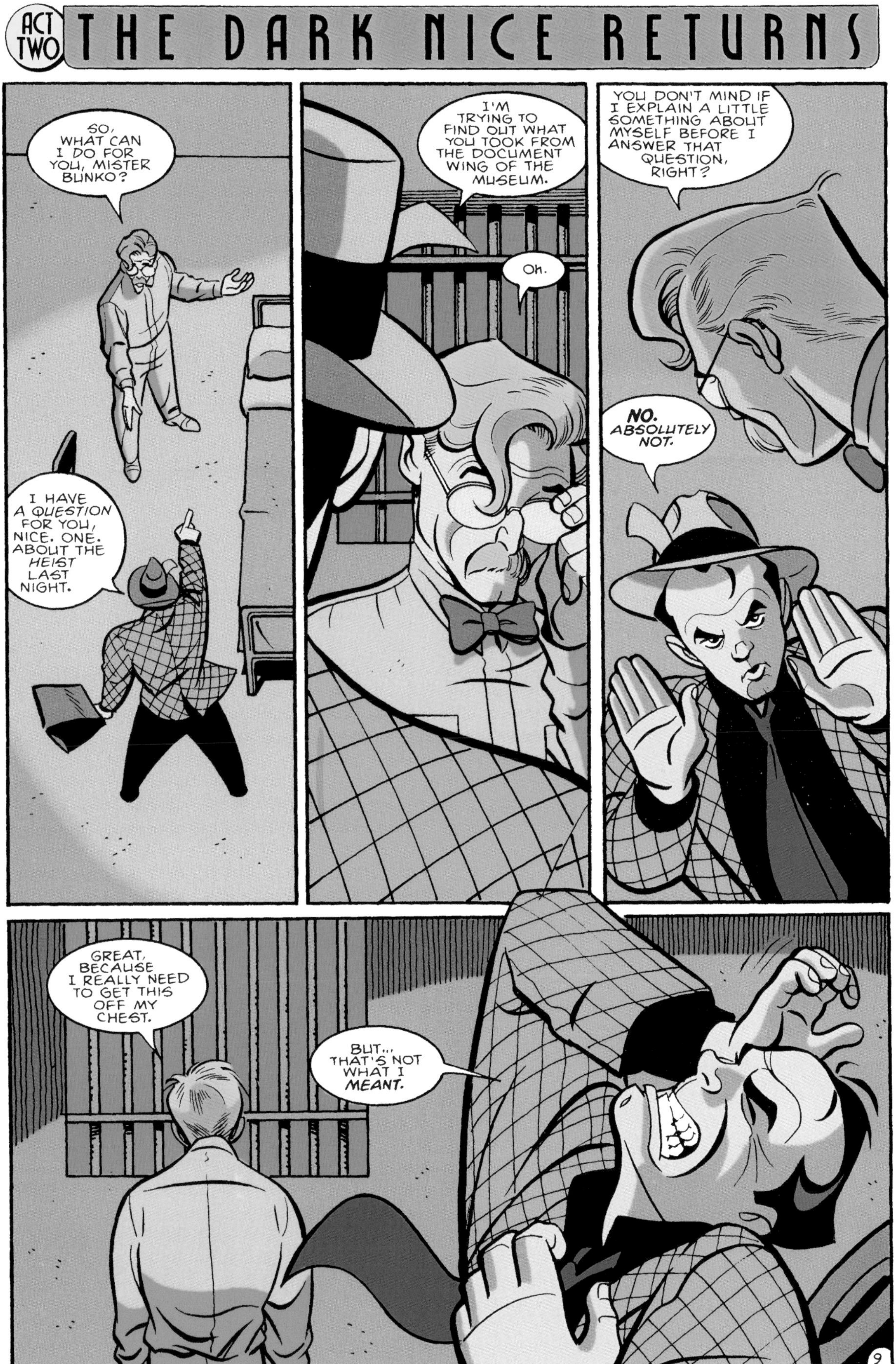
ACT TWO
THE DARK NICE RETURNS
SO, WHAT CAN I DO FOR YOU, MISTER BUNKO?
I HAVE A QUESTION FOR YOU, NICE. ONE. ABOUT THE HEIST LAST NIGHT.
I'M TRYING TO FIND OUT WHAT YOU TOOK FROM THE DOCUMENT WING OF THE MUSEUM.
Oh.
YOU DON'T MIND IF I EXPLAIN A LITTLE SOMETHING ABOUT MYSELF BEFORE I ANSWER THAT QUESTION, RIGHT?
NO. ABSOLUTELY NOT.
GREAT, BECAUSE I REALLY NEED TO GET THIS OFF MY CHEST.
BUT... THAT'S NOT WHAT I MEANT.
9

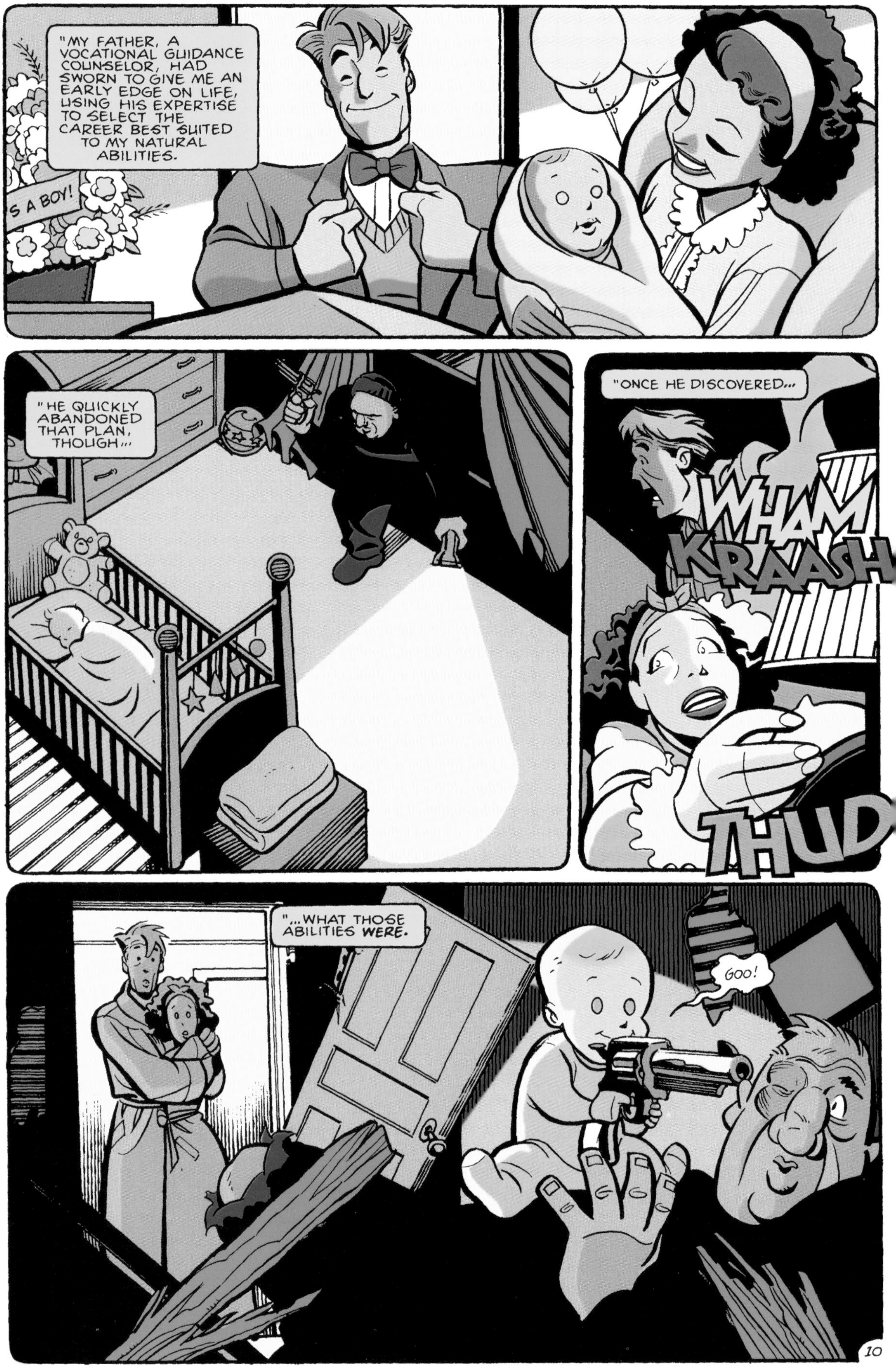
"MY FATHER, A VOCATIONAL GUIDANCE COUNSELOR, HAD SWORN TO GIVE ME AN EARLY EDGE ON LIFE, USING HIS EXPERTISE TO SELECT THE CAREER BEST SUITED TO MY NATURAL ABILITIES.
S A BOY!
"HE QUICKLY ABANDONED THAT PLAN, THOUGH...
"ONCE HE DISCOVERED...
WHAM
KRAASH
THUD
"...WHAT THOSE ABILITIES WERE.
GOO!
10

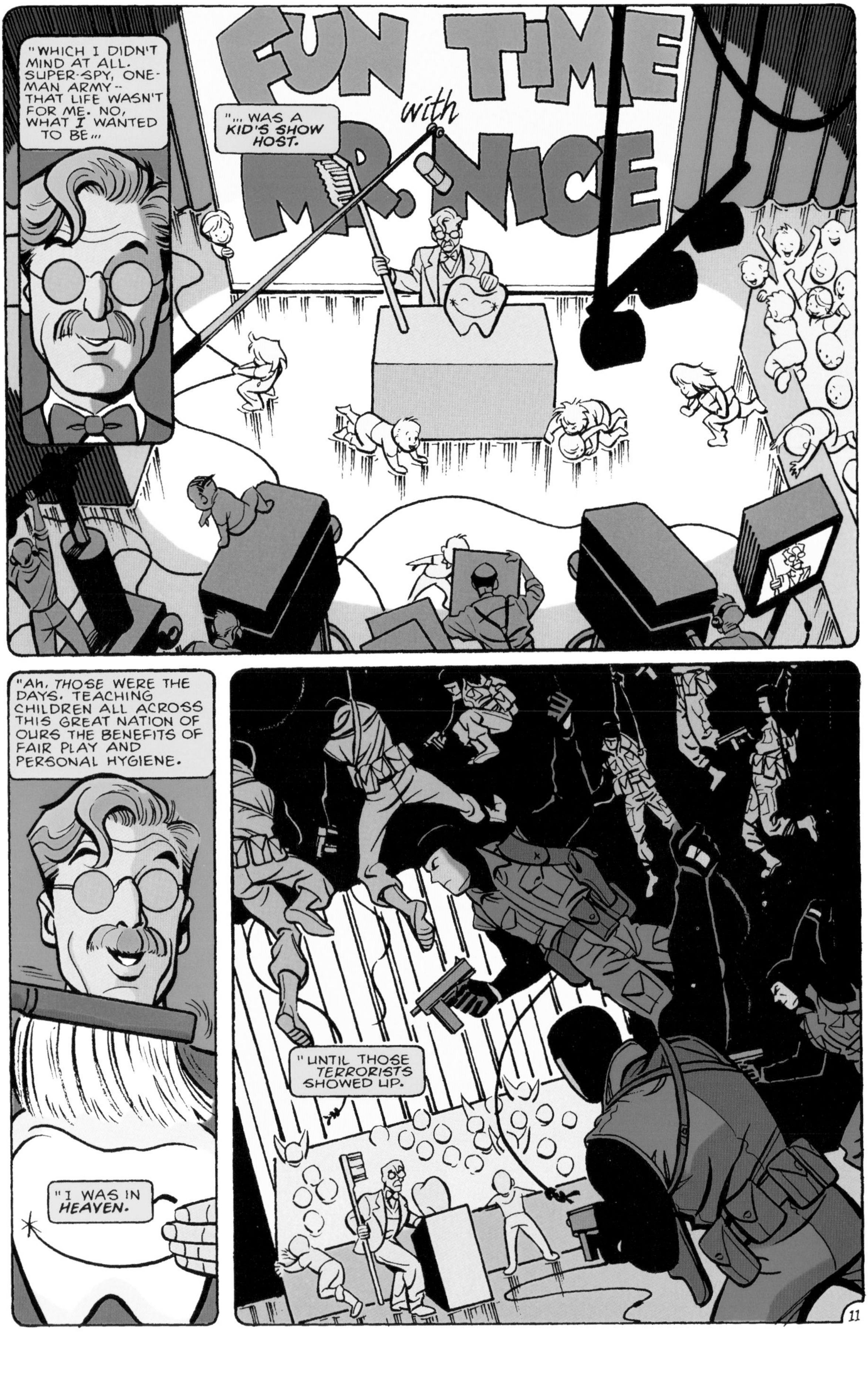
"WHICH I DIDN'T MIND AT ALL. SUPER-SPY, ONE-MAN ARMY-- THAT LIFE WASN'T FOR ME. NO, WHAT I WANTED TO BE...
FUN TIME with MR. NICE
"... WAS A KID'S SHOW HOST.
"Ah, THOSE WERE THE DAYS. TEACHING CHILDREN ALL ACROSS THIS GREAT NATION OF OURS THE BENEFITS OF FAIR PLAY AND PERSONAL HYGIENE.
"I WAS IN HEAVEN.
"UNTIL THOSE TERRORISTS SHOWED UP.
11

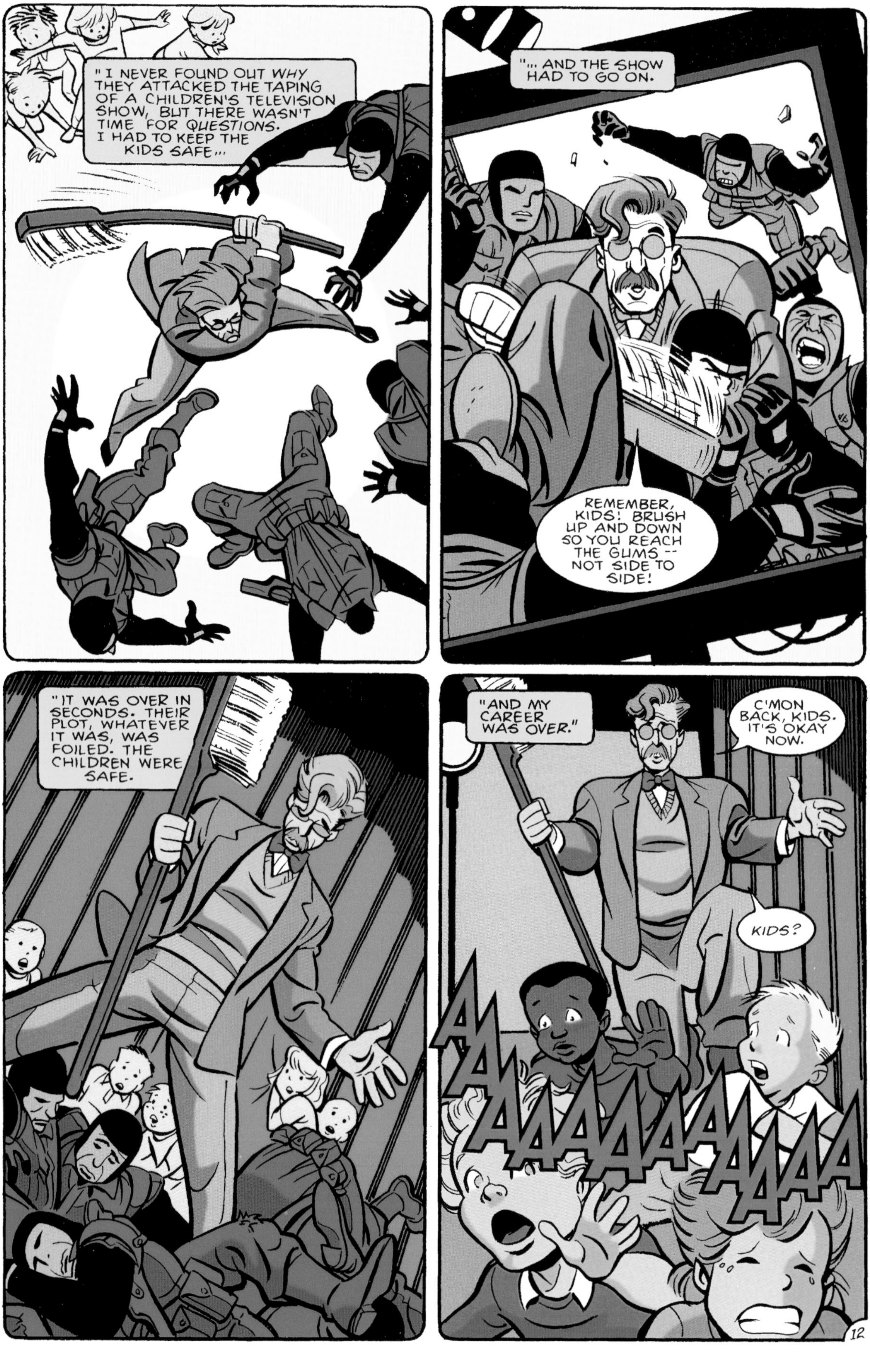
"I NEVER FOUND OUT WHY THEY ATTACKED THE TAPING OF A CHILDREN'S TELEVISION SHOW, BUT THERE WASN'T TIME FOR QUESTIONS. I HAD TO KEEP THE KIDS SAFE...
"... AND THE SHOW HAD TO GO ON.
REMEMBER, KIDS! BRUSH UP AND DOWN SO YOU REACH THE GUMS -- NOT SIDE TO SIDE!
"IT WAS OVER IN SECONDS. THEIR PLOT, WHATEVER IT WAS, WAS FOILED. THE CHILDREN WERE SAFE.
"AND MY CAREER WAS OVER."
C'MON BACK, KIDS. IT'S OKAY NOW.
KIDS?
AAAAAAAAAAAAAA
12

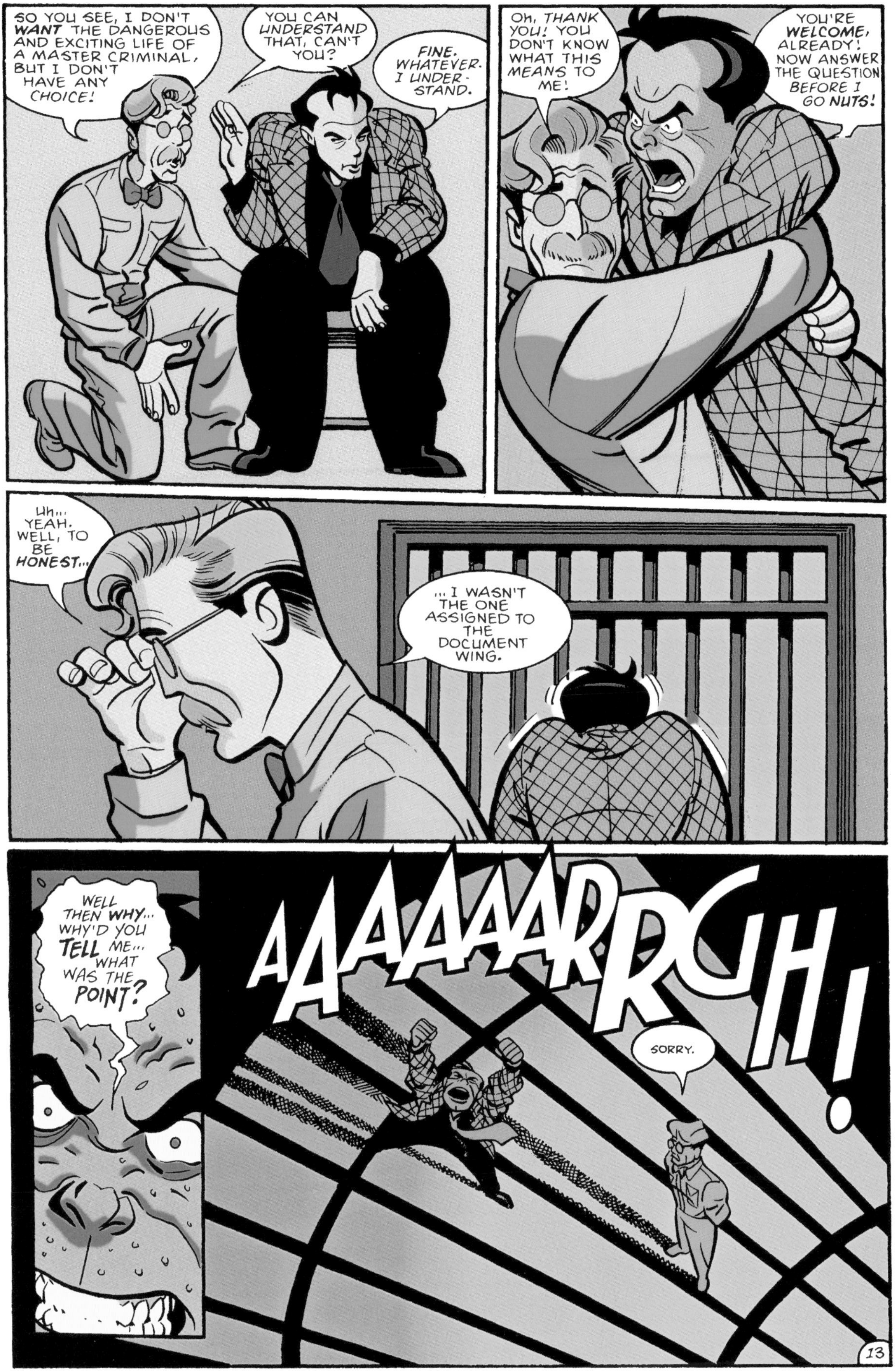
SO YOU SEE, I DON'T WANT THE DANGEROUS AND EXCITING LIFE OF A MASTER CRIMINAL, BUT I DON'T HAVE ANY CHOICE!
YOU CAN UNDERSTAND THAT, CAN'T YOU?
FINE. WHATEVER. I UNDER-STAND.
OH, THANK YOU! YOU DON'T KNOW WHAT THIS MEANS TO ME!
YOU'RE WELCOME, ALREADY! NOW ANSWER THE QUESTION BEFORE I GO NUTS!
UH... YEAH. WELL, TO BE HONEST...
...I WASN'T THE ONE ASSIGNED TO THE DOCUMENT WING.
WELL THEN WHY... WHY'D YOU TELL ME... WHAT WAS THE POINT?
AAAAAARRGH!
SORRY.
13

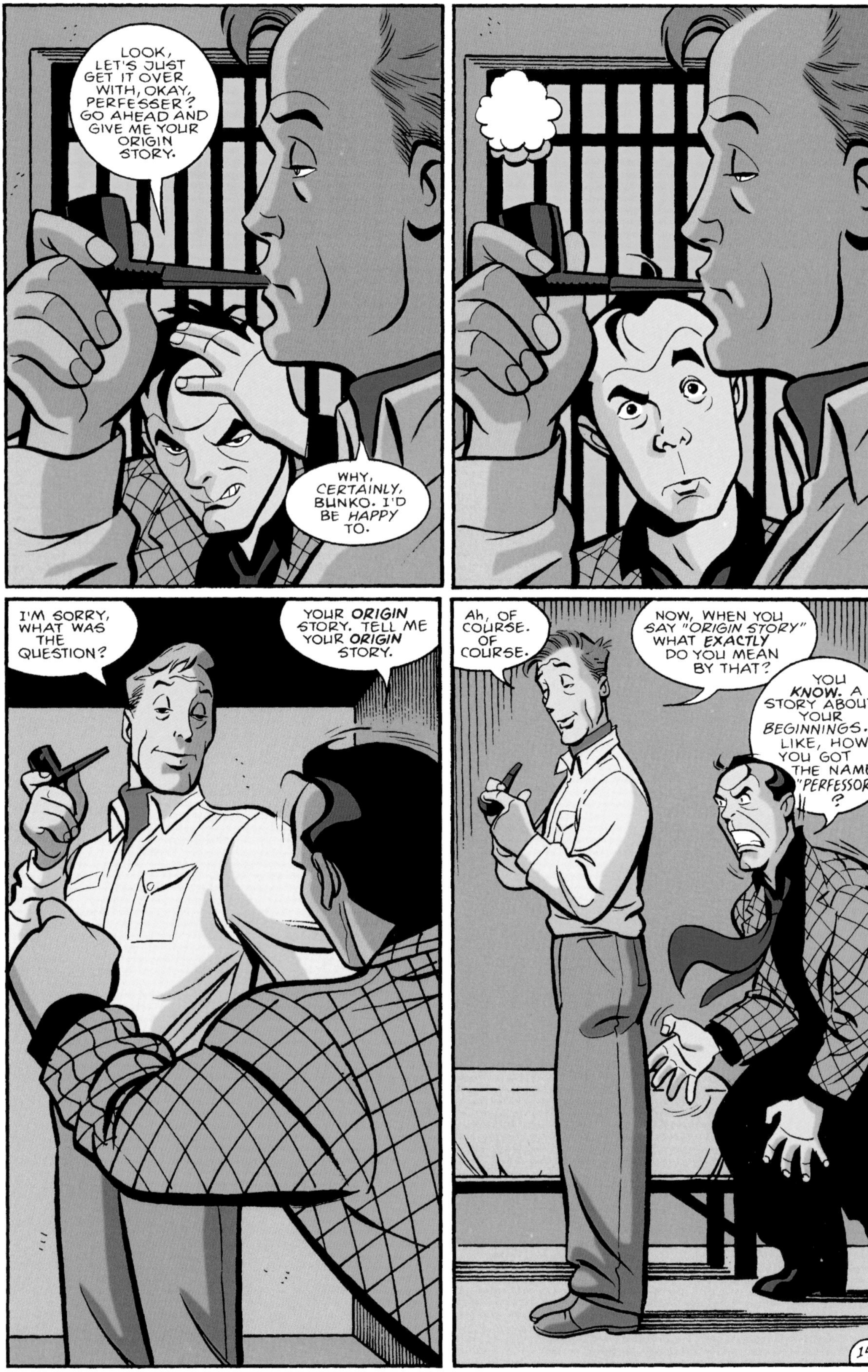
LOOK, LET'S JUST GET IT OVER WITH, OKAY, PERFESSER? GO AHEAD AND GIVE ME YOUR ORIGIN STORY.
WHY, CERTAINLY, BUNKO. I'D BE *HAPPY* TO.
I'M SORRY, WHAT WAS THE QUESTION?
YOUR **ORIGIN** STORY. TELL ME YOUR **ORIGIN** STORY.
Ah, OF COURSE. OF COURSE.
NOW, WHEN YOU SAY *"ORIGIN STORY"* WHAT **EXACTLY** DO YOU MEAN BY THAT?
YOU **KNOW.** A STORY ABOUT YOUR *BEGINNINGS.* LIKE, HOW YOU GOT THE NAME, *"PERFESSOR"*?
14

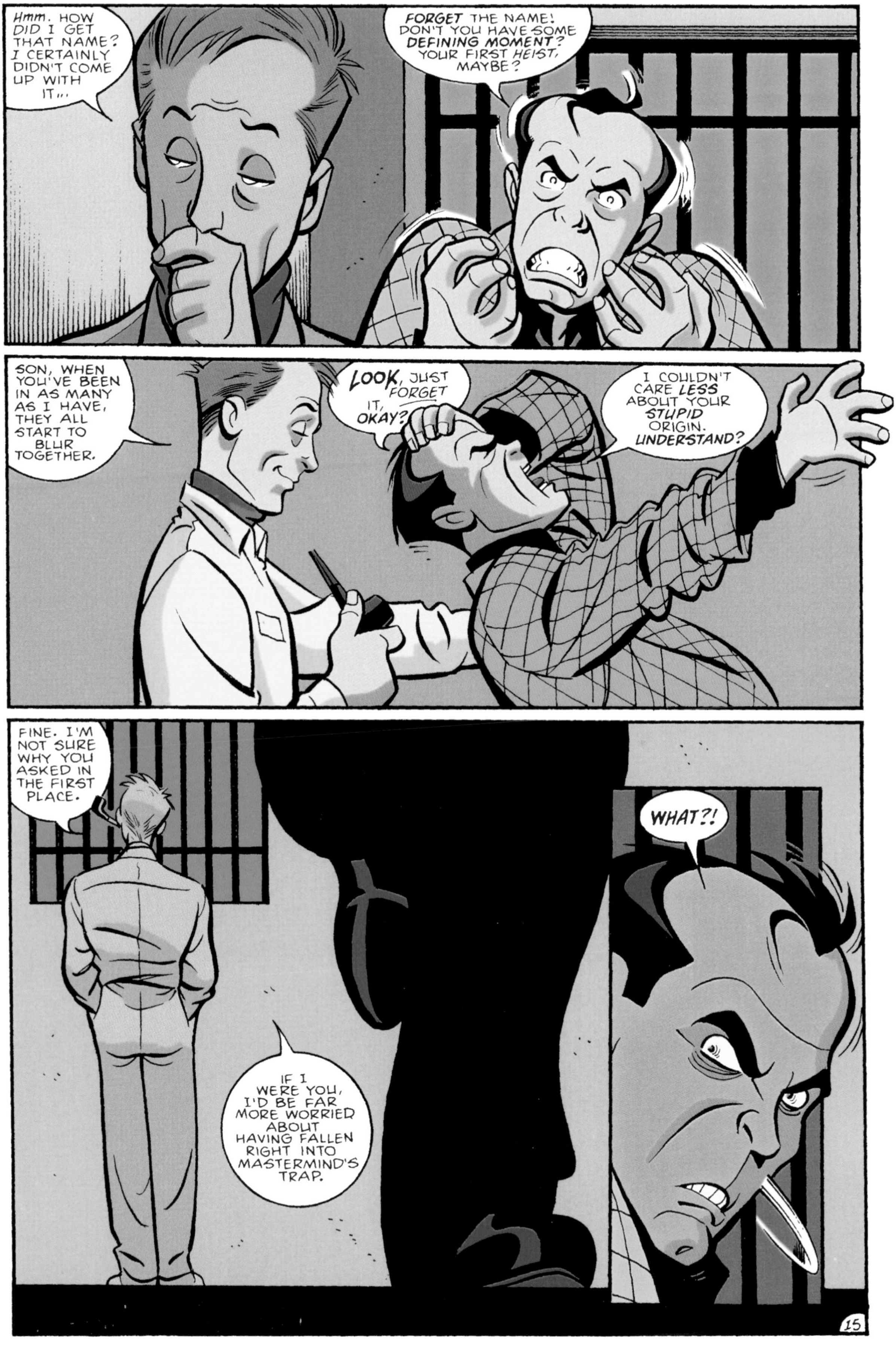
Hmm. HOW DID I GET THAT NAME? I CERTAINLY DIDN'T COME UP WITH IT...
FORGET THE NAME! DON'T YOU HAVE SOME DEFINING MOMENT? YOUR FIRST HEIST, MAYBE?
SON, WHEN YOU'VE BEEN IN AS MANY AS I HAVE, THEY ALL START TO BLUR TOGETHER.
LOOK, JUST FORGET IT, OKAY?
I COULDN'T CARE LESS ABOUT YOUR STUPID ORIGIN. UNDERSTAND?
FINE. I'M NOT SURE WHY YOU ASKED IN THE FIRST PLACE.
WHAT?!
IF I WERE YOU, I'D BE FAR MORE WORRIED ABOUT HAVING FALLEN RIGHT INTO MASTERMIND'S TRAP.
15

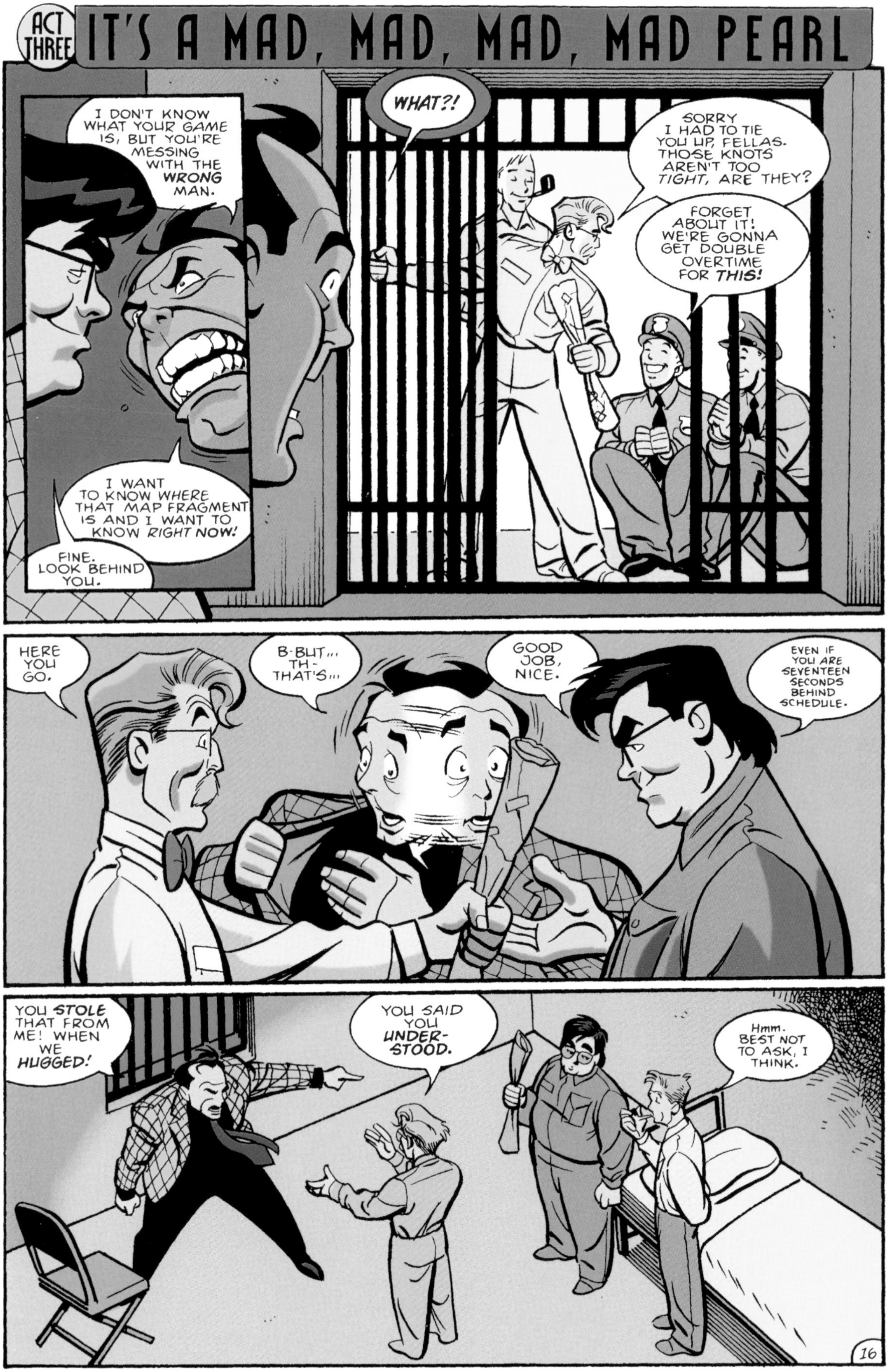
ACT THREE
IT'S A MAD, MAD, MAD, MAD PEARL
I DON'T KNOW WHAT YOUR GAME IS, BUT YOU'RE MESSING WITH THE WRONG MAN.
I WANT TO KNOW WHERE THAT MAP FRAGMENT IS AND I WANT TO KNOW RIGHT NOW!
FINE. LOOK BEHIND YOU.
WHAT?!
SORRY I HAD TO TIE YOU UP, FELLAS. THOSE KNOTS AREN'T TOO TIGHT, ARE THEY?
FORGET ABOUT IT! WE'RE GONNA GET DOUBLE OVERTIME FOR THIS!
HERE YOU GO.
B-BUT... TH-THAT'S...
GOOD JOB, NICE.
EVEN IF YOU ARE SEVENTEEN SECONDS BEHIND SCHEDULE.
YOU STOLE THAT FROM ME! WHEN WE HUGGED!
YOU SAID YOU UNDER-STOOD.
Hmm. BEST NOT TO ASK, I THINK.
16

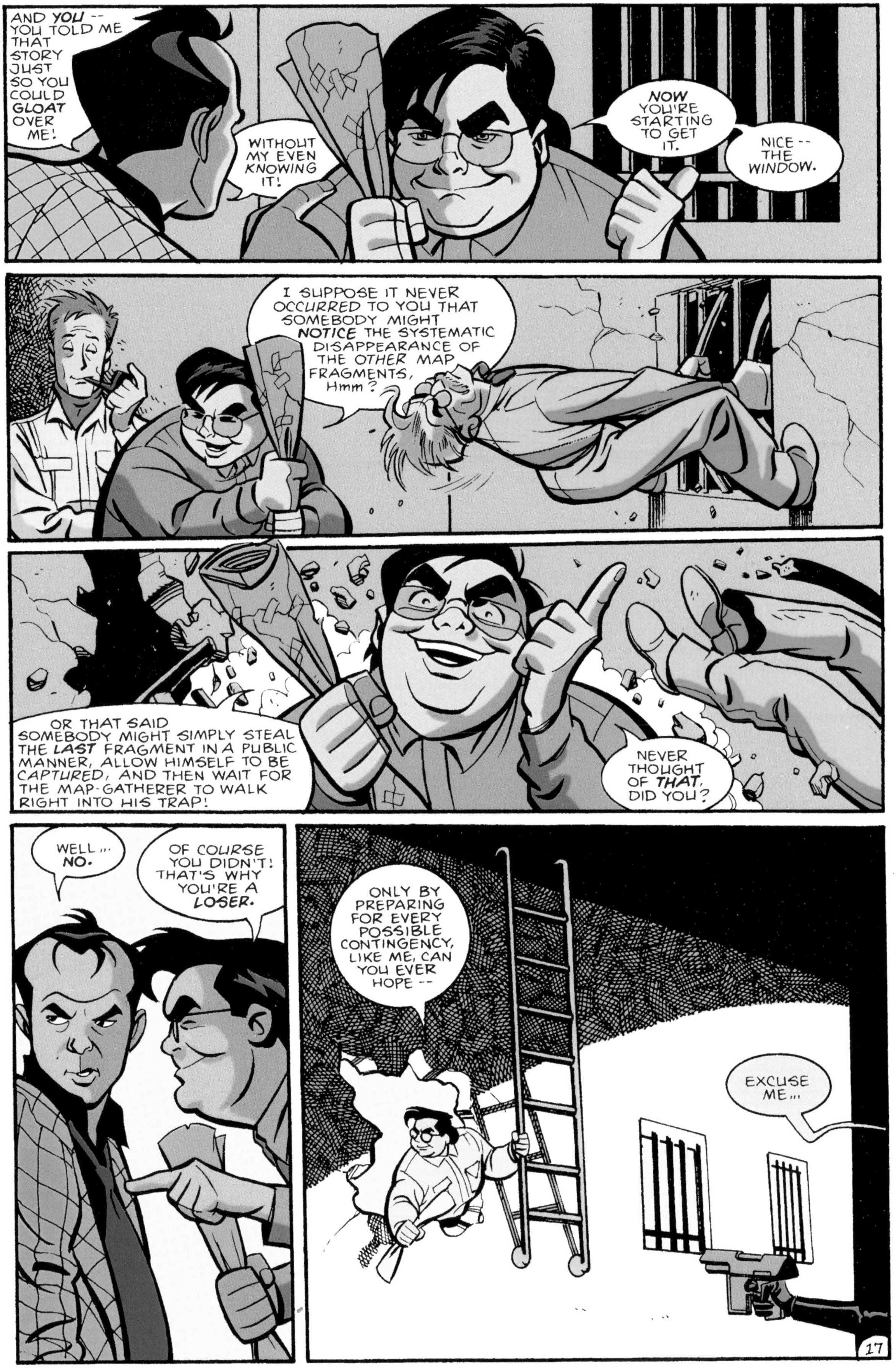
AND YOU -- YOU TOLD ME THAT STORY JUST SO YOU COULD GLOAT OVER ME!
WITHOUT MY EVEN KNOWING IT!
NOW YOU'RE STARTING TO GET IT.
NICE -- THE WINDOW.
I SUPPOSE IT NEVER OCCURRED TO YOU THAT SOMEBODY MIGHT NOTICE THE SYSTEMATIC DISAPPEARANCE OF THE OTHER MAP FRAGMENTS, Hmm?
OR THAT SAID SOMEBODY MIGHT SIMPLY STEAL THE LAST FRAGMENT IN A PUBLIC MANNER, ALLOW HIMSELF TO BE CAPTURED, AND THEN WAIT FOR THE MAP-GATHERER TO WALK RIGHT INTO HIS TRAP!
NEVER THOUGHT OF THAT, DID YOU?
WELL... NO.
OF COURSE YOU DIDN'T! THAT'S WHY YOU'RE A LOSER.
ONLY BY PREPARING FOR EVERY POSSIBLE CONTINGENCY, LIKE ME, CAN YOU EVER HOPE --
EXCUSE ME...
17

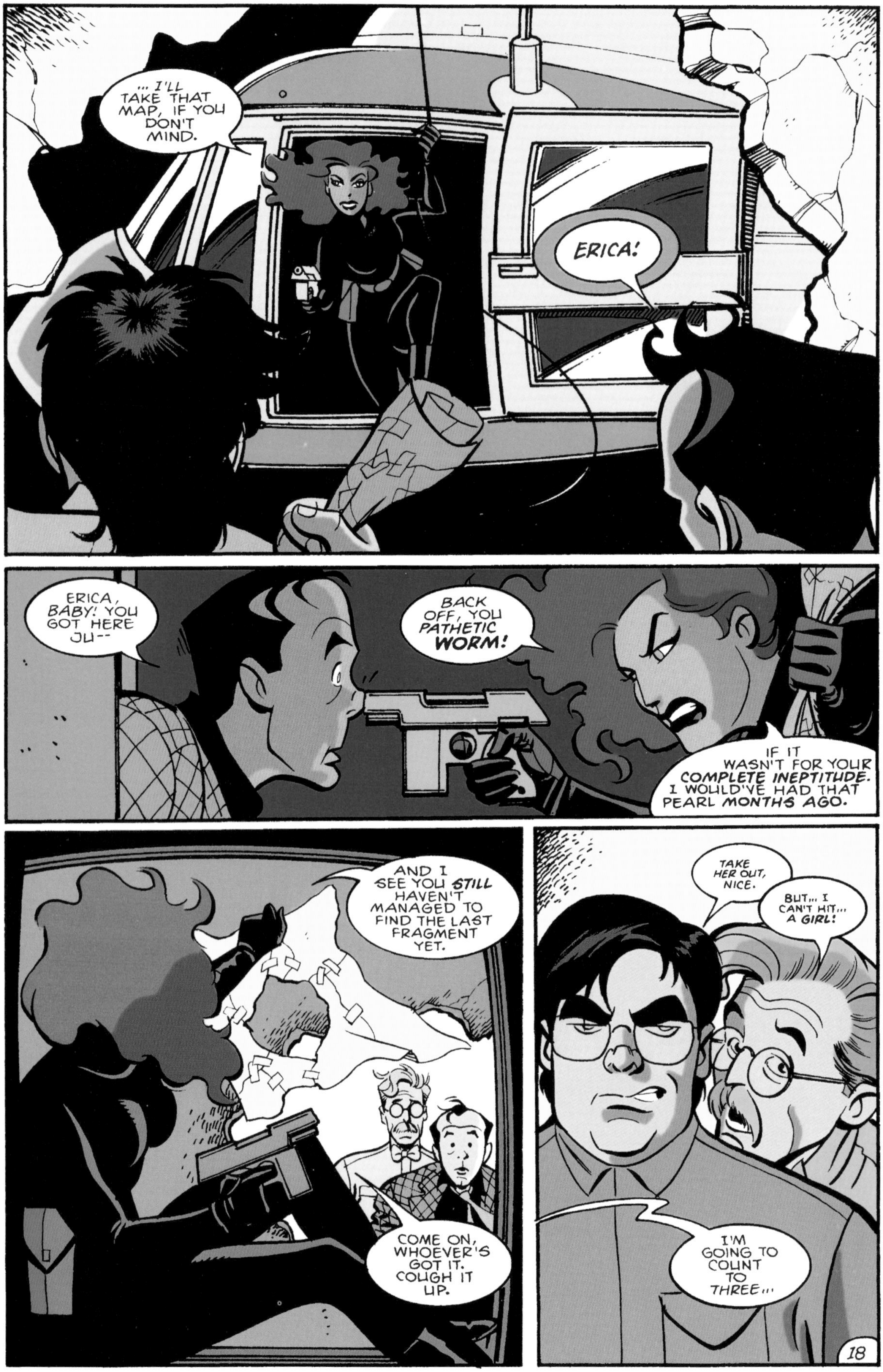

...I'LL TAKE THAT MAP, IF YOU DON'T MIND.
ERICA!
ERICA, BABY! YOU GOT HERE JU--
BACK OFF, YOU PATHETIC WORM!
IF IT WASN'T FOR YOUR COMPLETE INEPTITUDE, I WOULD'VE HAD THAT PEARL MONTHS AGO.
AND I SEE YOU STILL HAVEN'T MANAGED TO FIND THE LAST FRAGMENT YET.
COME ON, WHOEVER'S GOT IT. COUGH IT UP.
TAKE HER OUT, NICE.
BUT... I CAN'T HIT... A GIRL!
I'M GOING TO COUNT TO THREE...
18

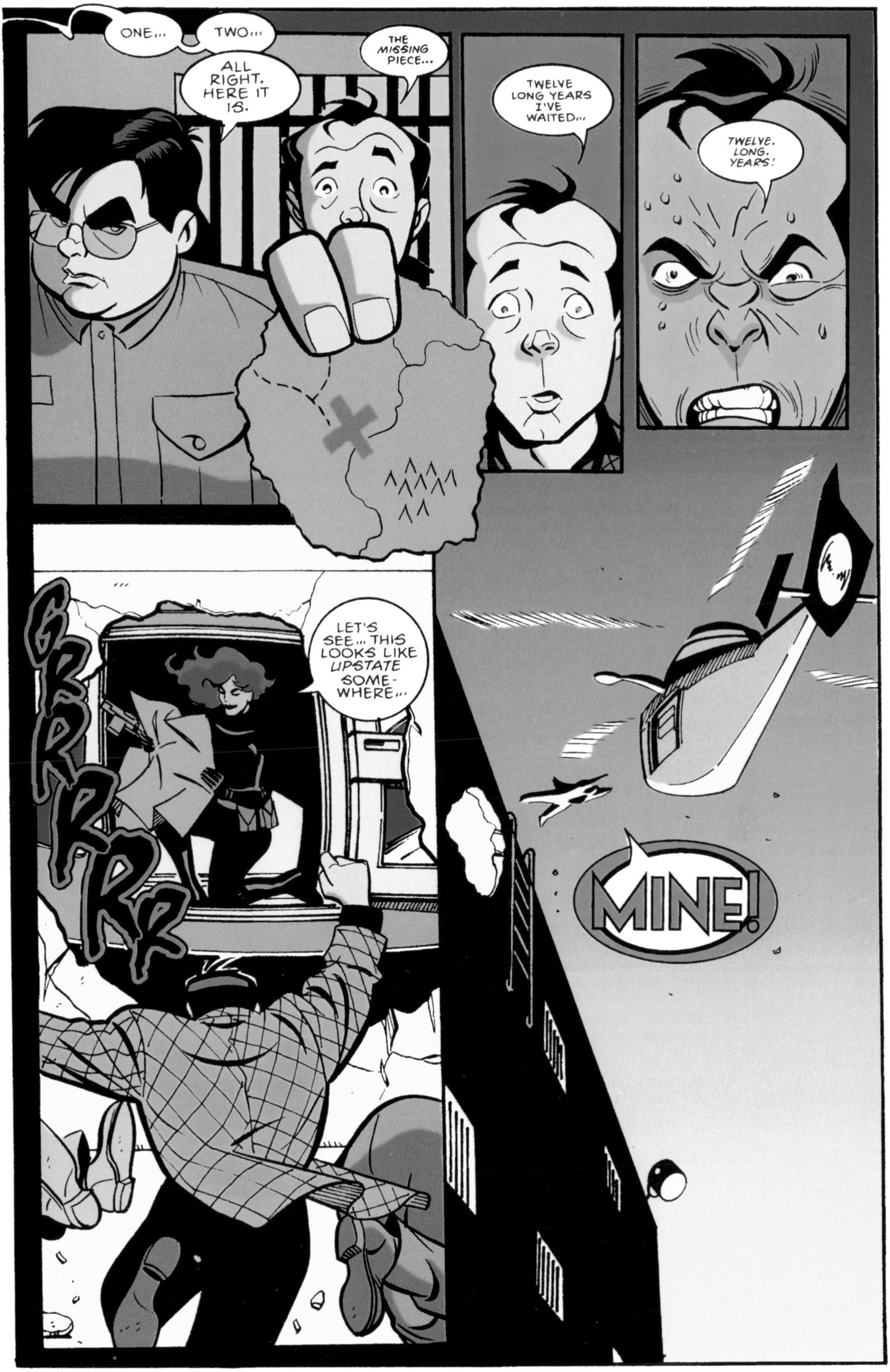
ONE...
TWO...
ALL RIGHT. HERE IT IS.
THE MISSING PIECE...
TWELVE LONG YEARS I'VE WAITED...
TWELVE. LONG. YEARS!
GRRRRRR
LET'S SEE... THIS LOOKS LIKE UPSTATE SOME-WHERE...
MINE!

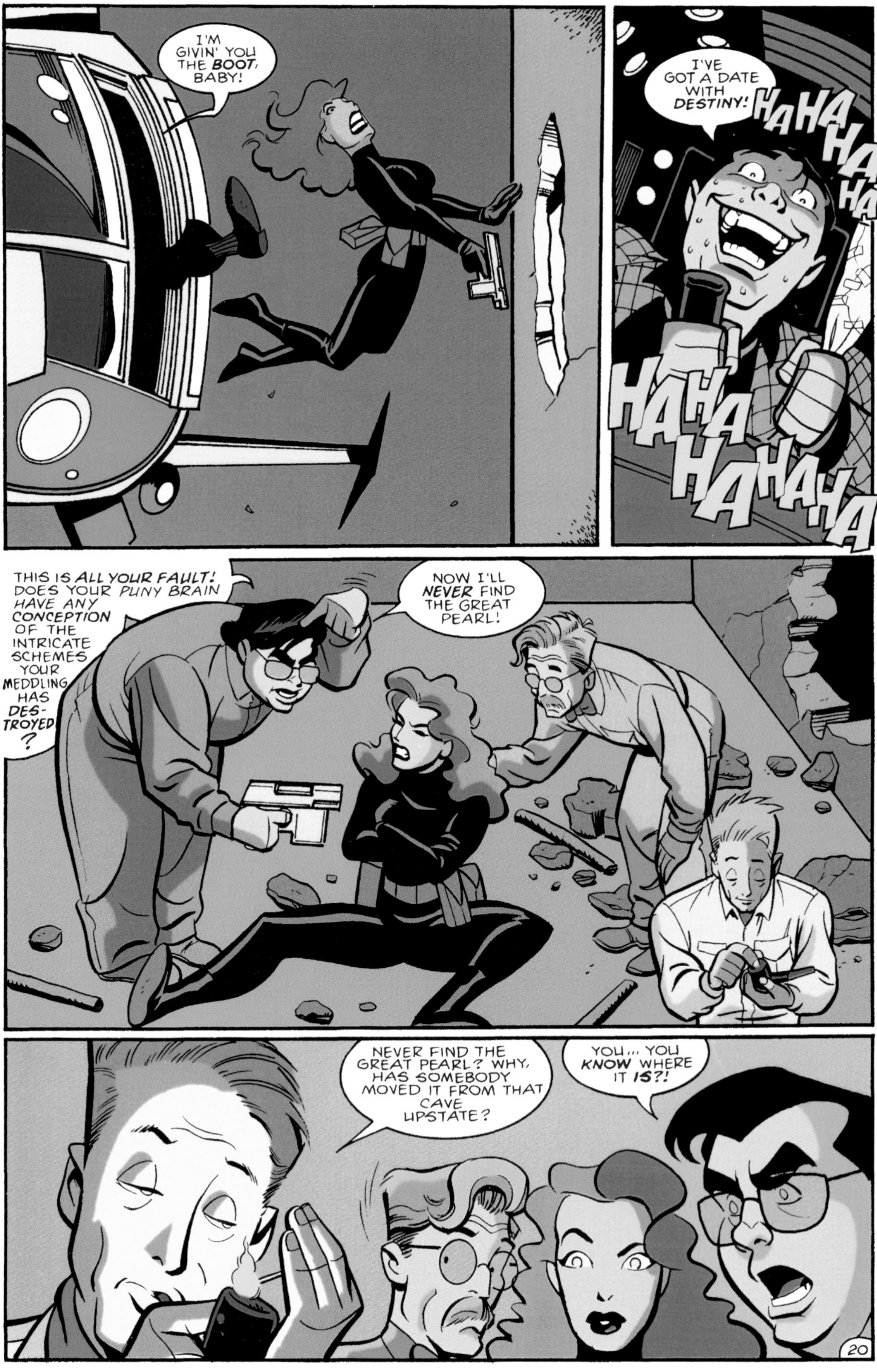
I'M GIVIN' YOU THE BOOT, BABY!
I'VE GOT A DATE WITH DESTINY!
HAHAHAHA
HAHAHA
HAHAHAHAHA
THIS IS ALL YOUR FAULT! DOES YOUR PUNY BRAIN HAVE ANY CONCEPTION OF THE INTRICATE SCHEMES YOUR MEDDLING HAS DESTROYED?
NOW I'LL NEVER FIND THE GREAT PEARL!
NEVER FIND THE GREAT PEARL? WHY, HAS SOMEBODY MOVED IT FROM THAT CAVE UPSTATE?
YOU... YOU KNOW WHERE IT IS?!
20

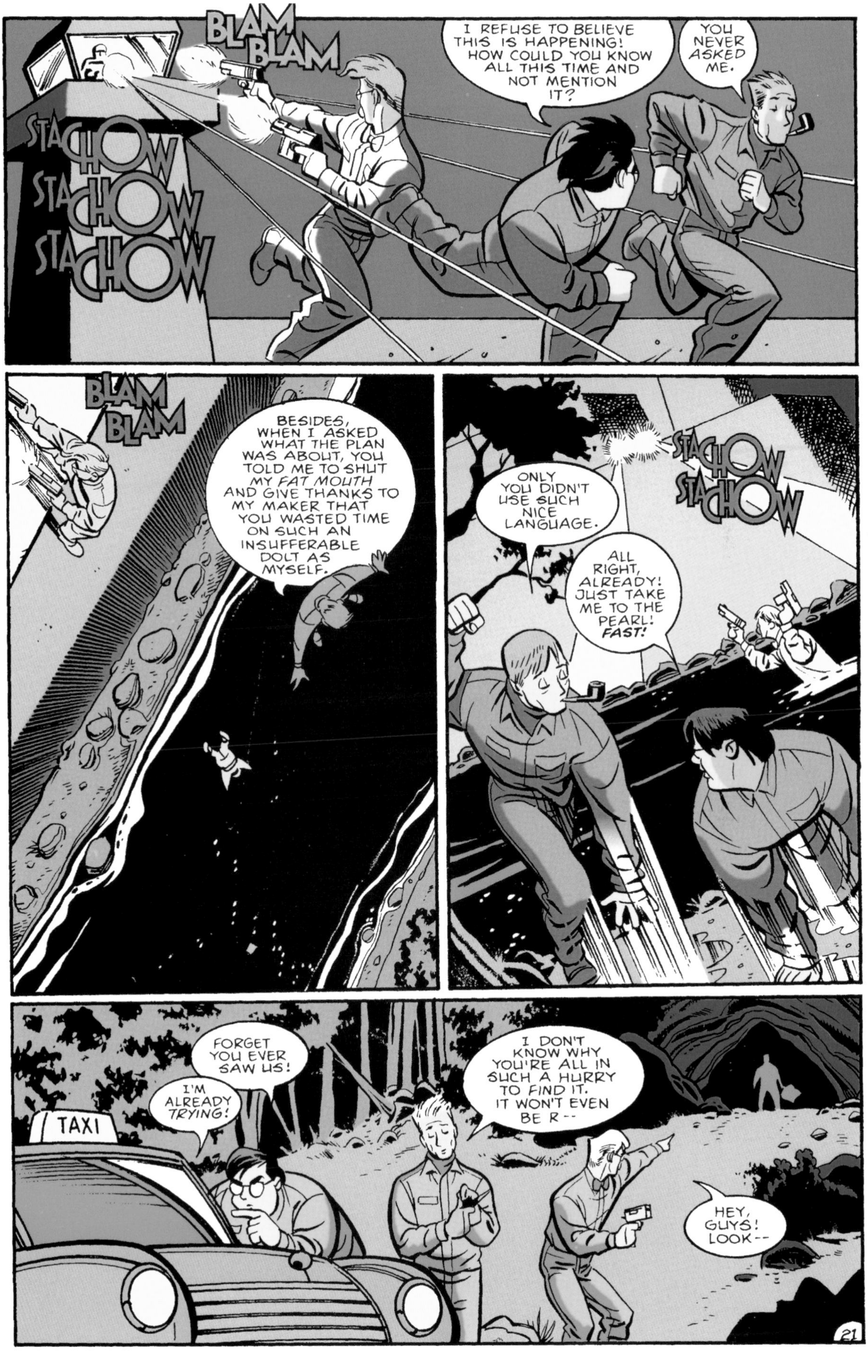
BLAM BLAM
STACHOW STACHOW STACHOW
I REFUSE TO BELIEVE THIS IS HAPPENING! HOW COULD YOU KNOW ALL THIS TIME AND NOT MENTION IT?
YOU NEVER ASKED ME.
BLAM BLAM
BESIDES, WHEN I ASKED WHAT THE PLAN WAS ABOUT, YOU TOLD ME TO SHUT MY FAT MOUTH AND GIVE THANKS TO MY MAKER THAT YOU WASTED TIME ON SUCH AN INSUFFERABLE DOLT AS MYSELF.
STACHOW STACHOW
ONLY YOU DIDN'T USE SUCH NICE LANGUAGE.
ALL RIGHT, ALREADY! JUST TAKE ME TO THE PEARL! FAST!
TAXI
FORGET YOU EVER SAW US!
I'M ALREADY TRYING!
I DON'T KNOW WHY YOU'RE ALL IN SUCH A HURRY TO FIND IT. IT WON'T EVEN BE R--
HEY, GUYS! LOOK--
21

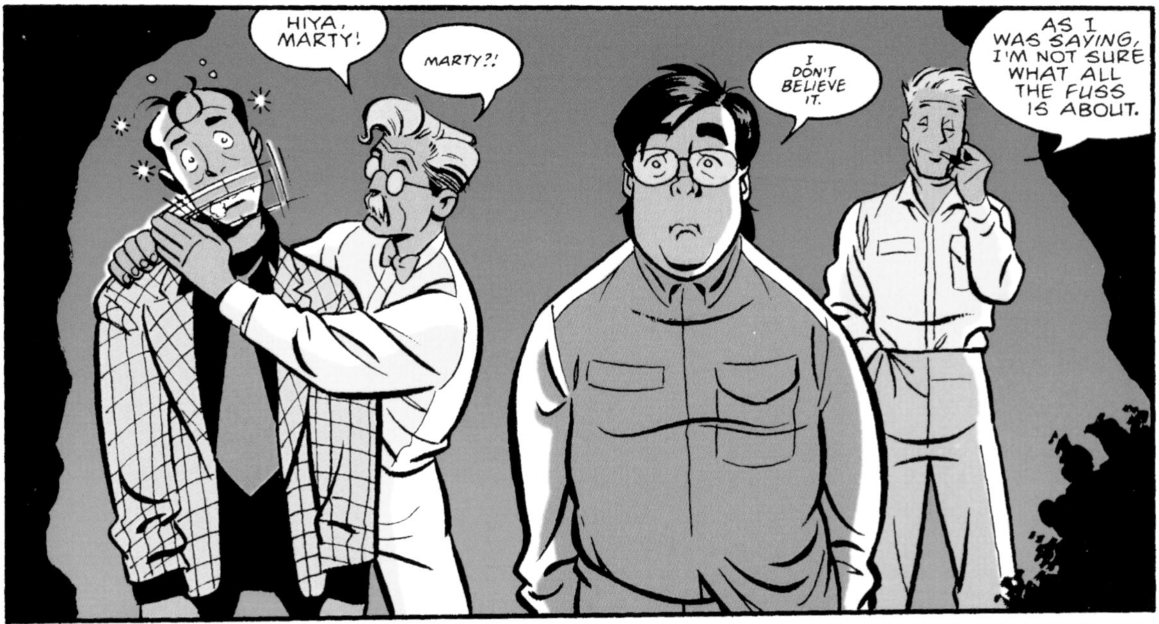
HIYA, MARTY!
MARTY?!
I DON'T BELIEVE IT.
AS I WAS SAYING, I'M NOT SURE WHAT ALL THE FUSS IS ABOUT.

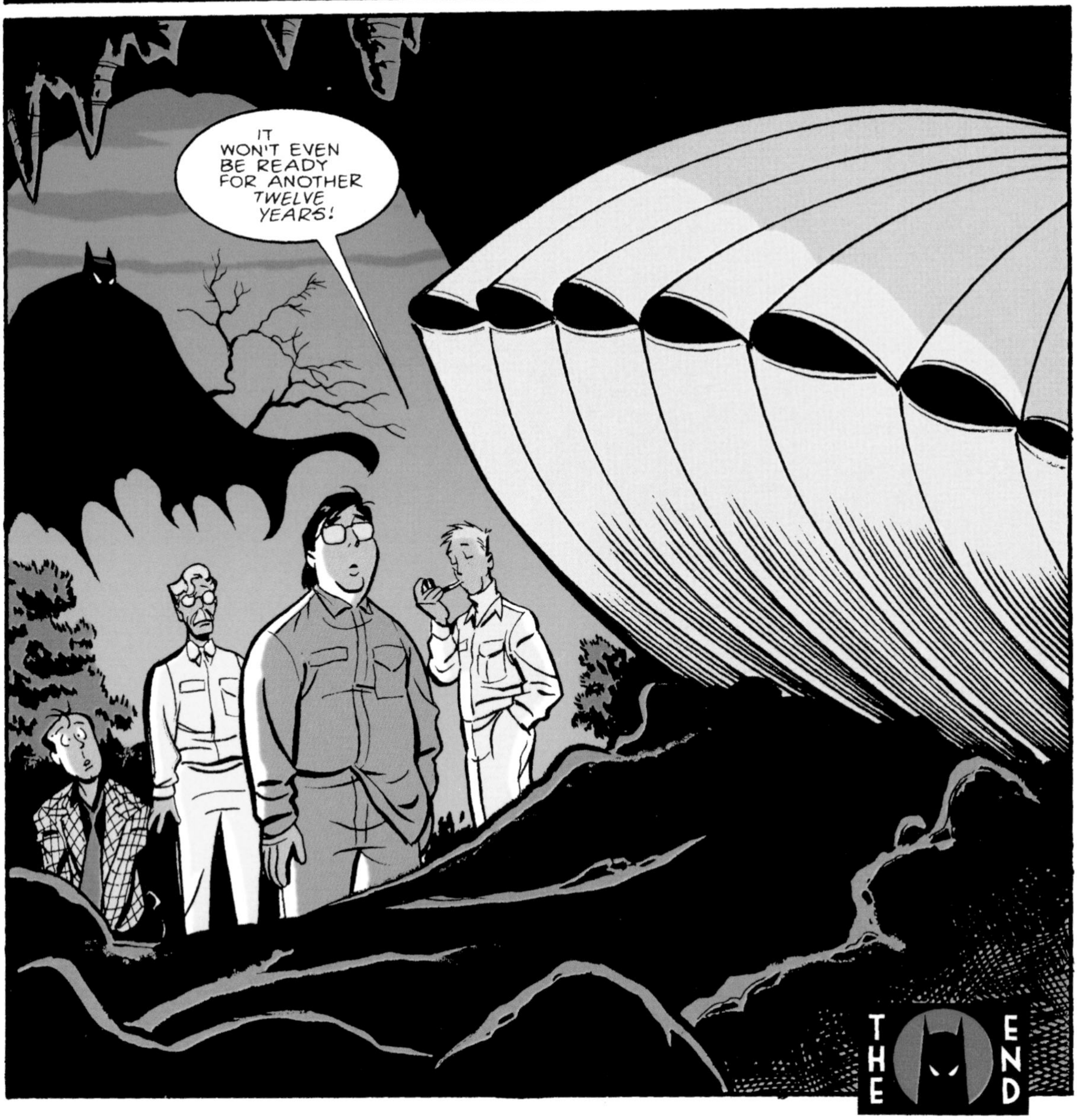
IT WON'T EVEN BE READY FOR ANOTHER TWELVE YEARS!
THE END

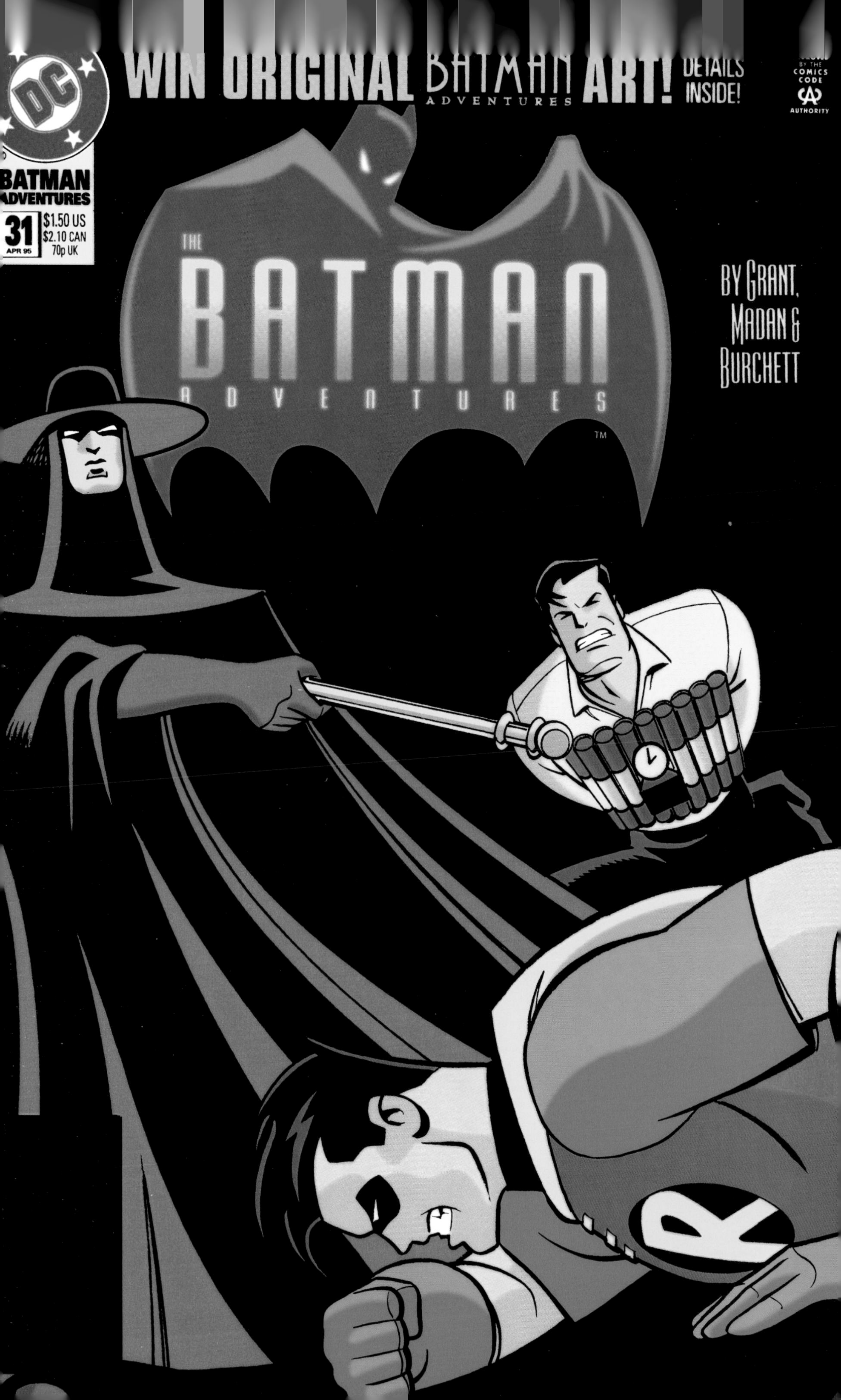

WIN ORIGINAL BATMAN ADVENTURES ART! DETAILS INSIDE!
BY THE COMICS CODE AUTHORITY
DC
BATMAN ADVENTURES
31
APR 95
$1.50 US
$2.10 CAN
70p UK
THE BATMAN ADVENTURES
TM
BY GRANT, MADAN & BURCHETT

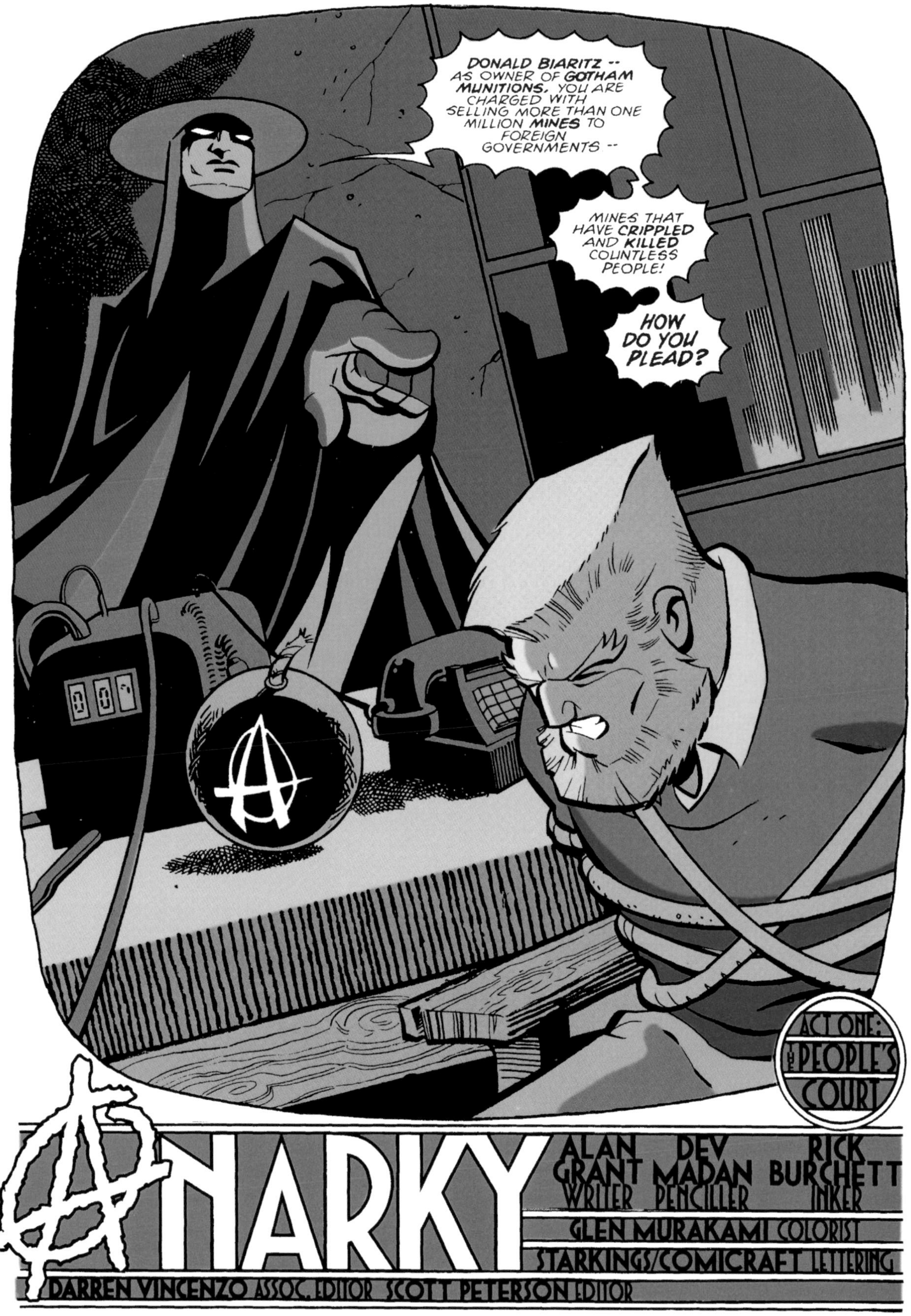
DONALD BIARITZ -- AS OWNER OF GOTHAM MUNITIONS, YOU ARE CHARGED WITH SELLING MORE THAN ONE MILLION MINES TO FOREIGN GOVERNMENTS --
MINES THAT HAVE CRIPPLED AND KILLED COUNTLESS PEOPLE!
HOW DO YOU PLEAD?
ACT ONE: THE PEOPLE'S COURT
ANARKY
ALAN GRANT WRITER
DEV MADAN PENCILLER
RICK BURCHETT INKER
GLEN MURAKAMI COLORIST
STARKINGS/COMICRAFT LETTERING
DARREN VINCENZO ASSOC. EDITOR SCOTT PETERSON EDITOR

THIS IS **RIDICULOUS!** I RUN A LEGITIMATE CORPORATION! I PAY MY TAXES! I'VE COMMITTED NO CRIME!

HUMANITY MIGHT BEG TO **DIFFER,** DONALD!

HE'S **JAMMING** OUR SIGNAL AND FORCING THROUGH HIS OWN.

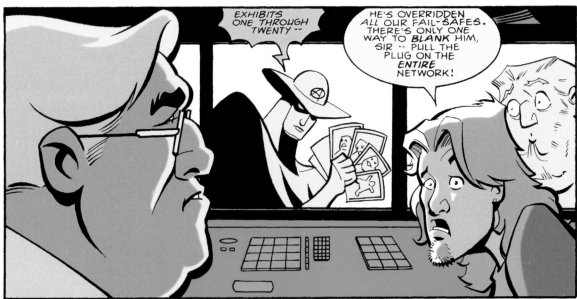

EXHIBITS ONE **THROUGH** TWENTY --

HE'S **OVERRIDDEN** ALL OUR **FAIL-SAFES.** THERE'S ONLY ONE WAY TO **BLANK** HIM, SIR -- PULL THE PLUG ON THE **ENTIRE** NETWORK!

-- CIVILIANS INJURED BY **YOUR** MINES!

ARE YOU **CRAZY!** VIGILANTE ACTION **LIVE** ON TV?!

WE'RE IN **RATINGS HEAVEN!**

2

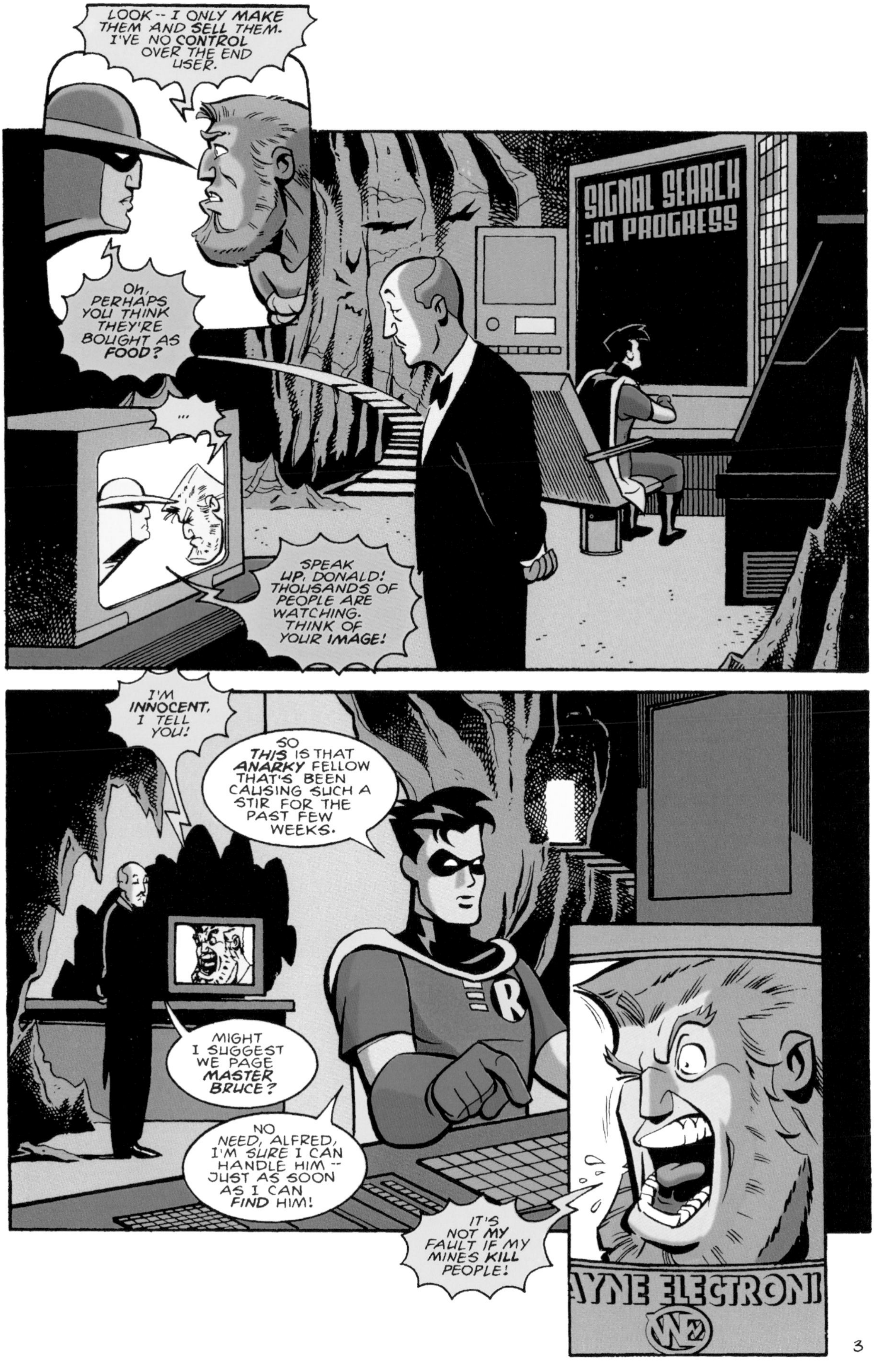
LOOK -- I ONLY MAKE THEM AND SELL THEM. I'VE NO CONTROL OVER THE END USER.
SIGNAL SEARCH :IN PROGRESS
Oh, PERHAPS YOU THINK THEY'RE BOUGHT AS FOOD?
...
SPEAK UP, DONALD! THOUSANDS OF PEOPLE ARE WATCHING. THINK OF YOUR IMAGE!
I'M INNOCENT, I TELL YOU!
SO THIS IS THAT ANARKY FELLOW THAT'S BEEN CAUSING SUCH A STIR FOR THE PAST FEW WEEKS.
MIGHT I SUGGEST WE PAGE MASTER BRUCE?
NO NEED, ALFRED, I'M SURE I CAN HANDLE HIM -- JUST AS SOON AS I CAN FIND HIM!
IT'S NOT MY FAULT IF MY MINES KILL PEOPLE!
AYNE ELECTRONI

3

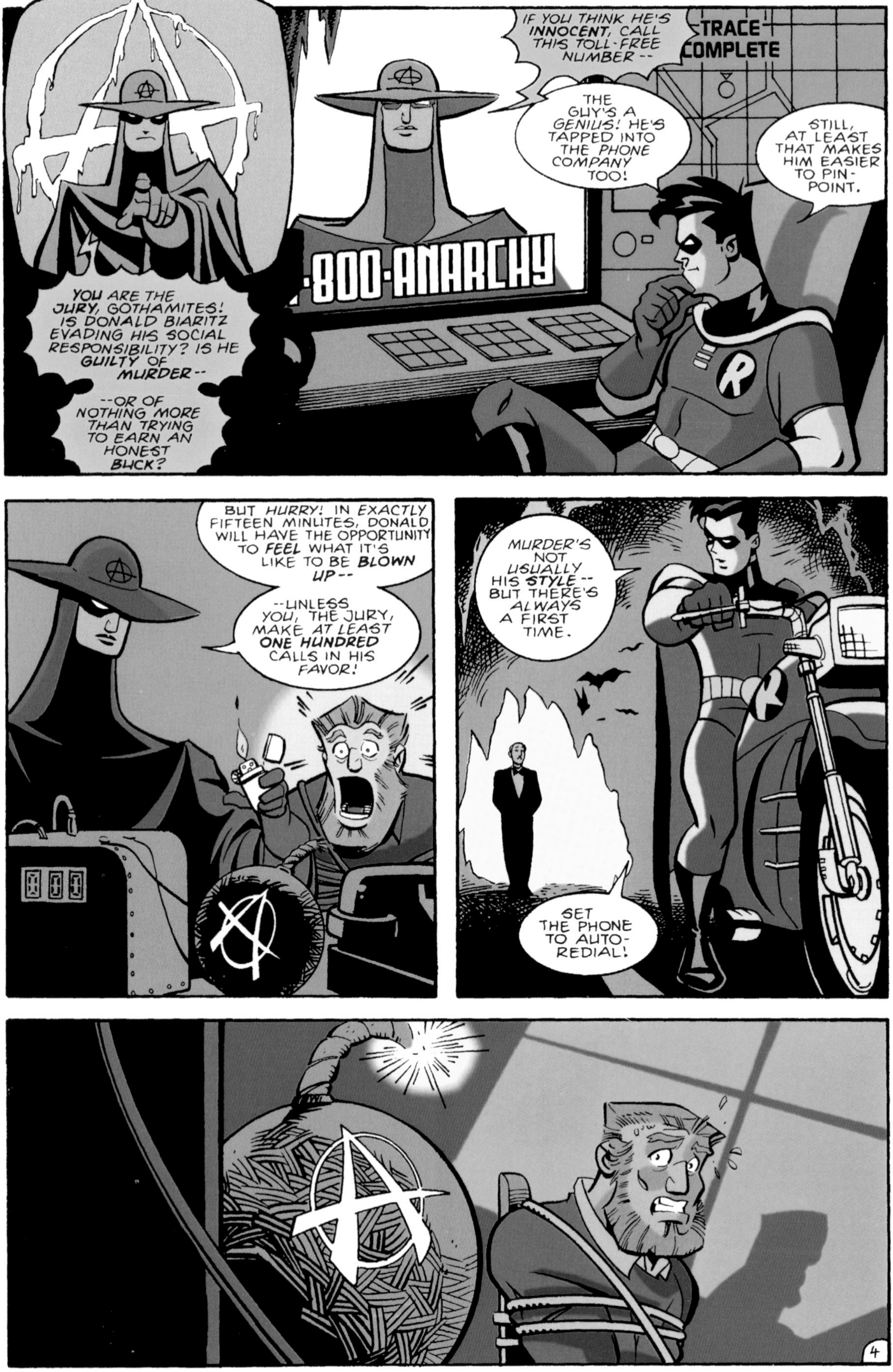
YOU ARE THE JURY, GOTHAMITES! IS DONALD BIARITZ EVADING HIS SOCIAL RESPONSIBILITY? IS HE GUILTY OF MURDER--
--OR OF NOTHING MORE THAN TRYING TO EARN AN HONEST BUCK?
IF YOU THINK HE'S INNOCENT, CALL THIS TOLL-FREE NUMBER --
-800-ANARCHY
TRACE COMPLETE
THE GUY'S A GENIUS! HE'S TAPPED INTO THE PHONE COMPANY TOO!
STILL, AT LEAST THAT MAKES HIM EASIER TO PIN-POINT.
BUT HURRY! IN EXACTLY FIFTEEN MINUTES, DONALD WILL HAVE THE OPPORTUNITY TO FEEL WHAT IT'S LIKE TO BE BLOWN UP--
--UNLESS YOU, THE JURY, MAKE AT LEAST ONE HUNDRED CALLS IN HIS FAVOR!
MURDER'S NOT USUALLY HIS STYLE-- BUT THERE'S ALWAYS A FIRST TIME.
SET THE PHONE TO AUTO-REDIAL!
4

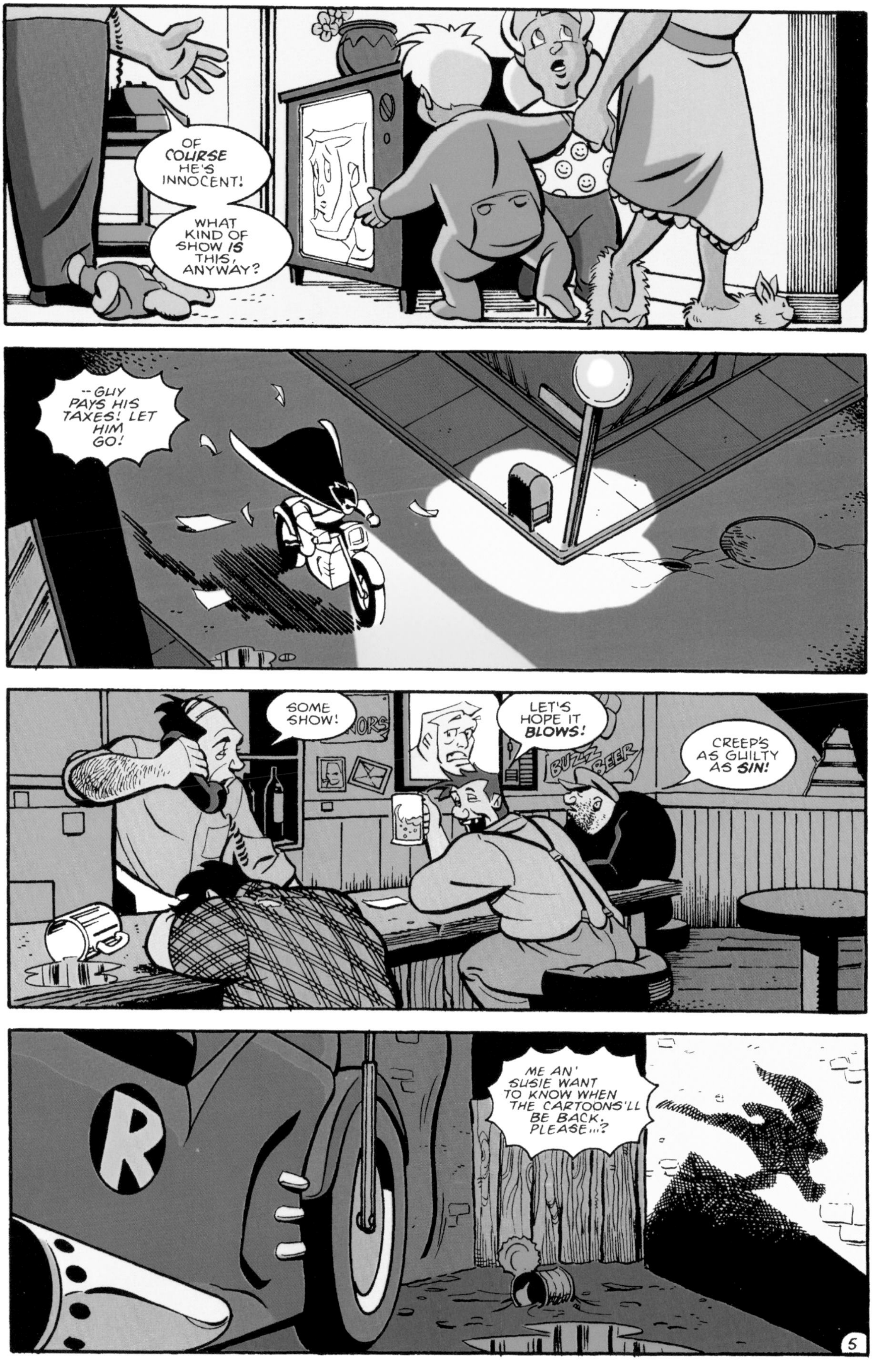
OF COURSE HE'S INNOCENT!
WHAT KIND OF SHOW IS THIS, ANYWAY?
--GUY PAYS HIS TAXES! LET HIM GO!
SOME SHOW!
LET'S HOPE IT BLOWS!
BUZZ BEER
CREEP'S AS GUILTY AS SIN!
ME AN' SUSIE WANT TO KNOW WHEN THE CARTOONS'LL BE BACK. PLEASE...?
5

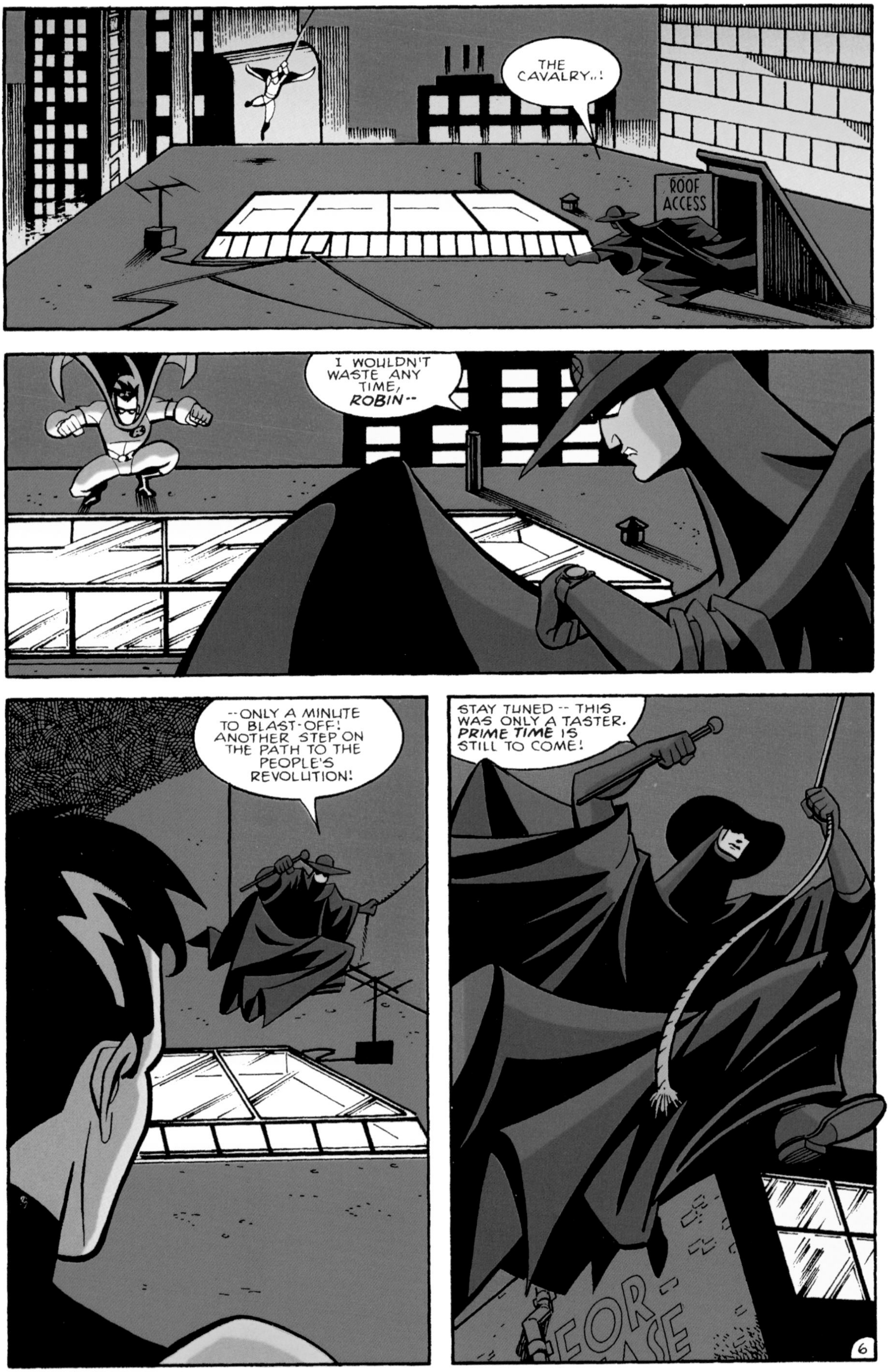
THE CAVALRY..!
ROOF ACCESS
I WOULDN'T WASTE ANY TIME, ROBIN--
--ONLY A MINUTE TO BLAST-OFF! ANOTHER STEP ON THE PATH TO THE PEOPLE'S REVOLUTION!
STAY TUNED -- THIS WAS ONLY A TASTER. PRIME TIME IS STILL TO COME!
6

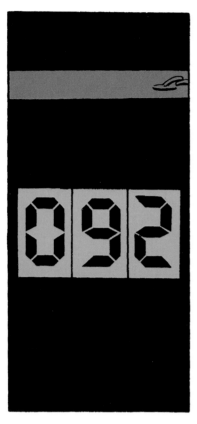

SKA KRASH

857

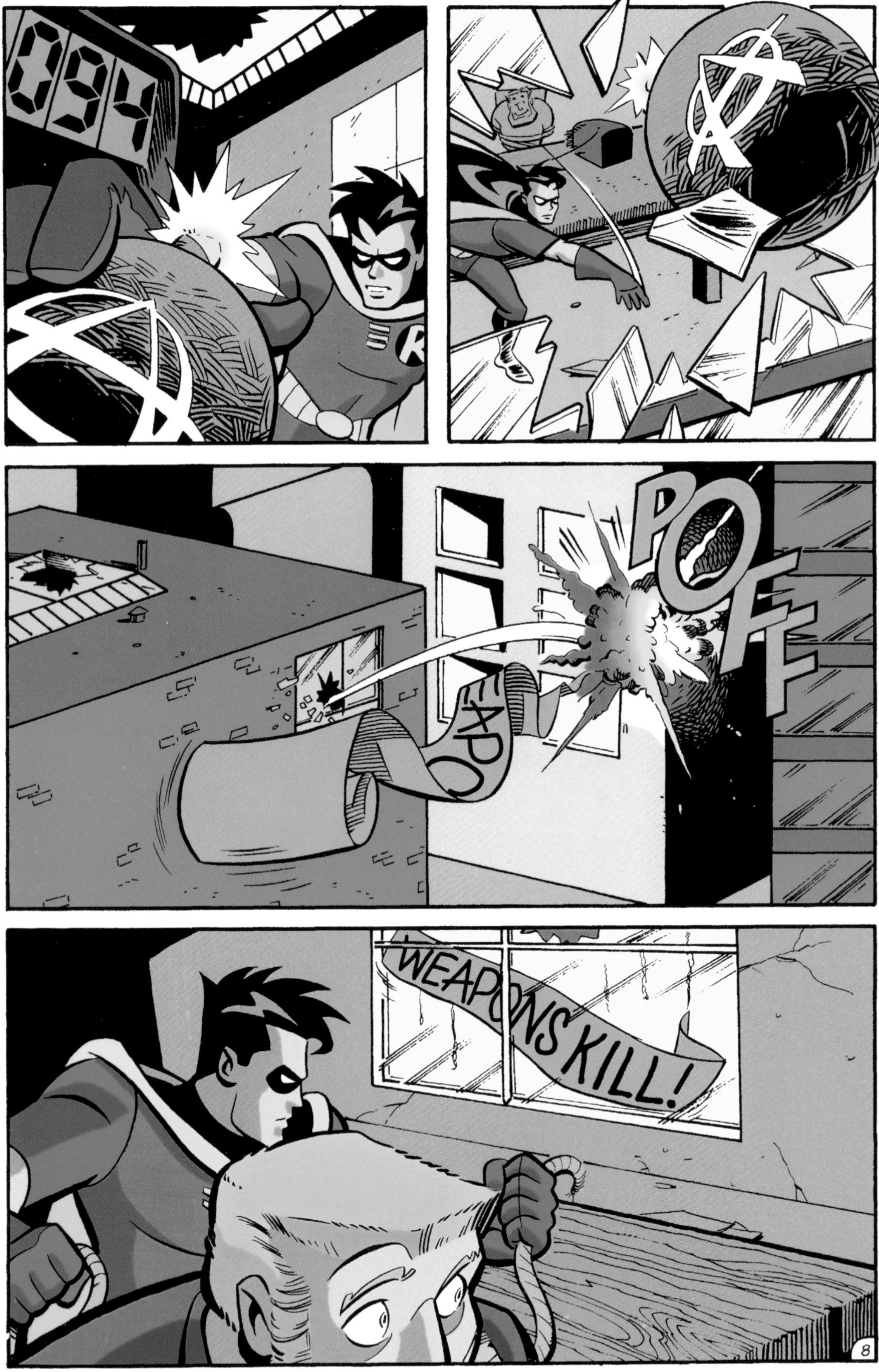
094
POFF
EAPO
WEAPONS KILL!
8

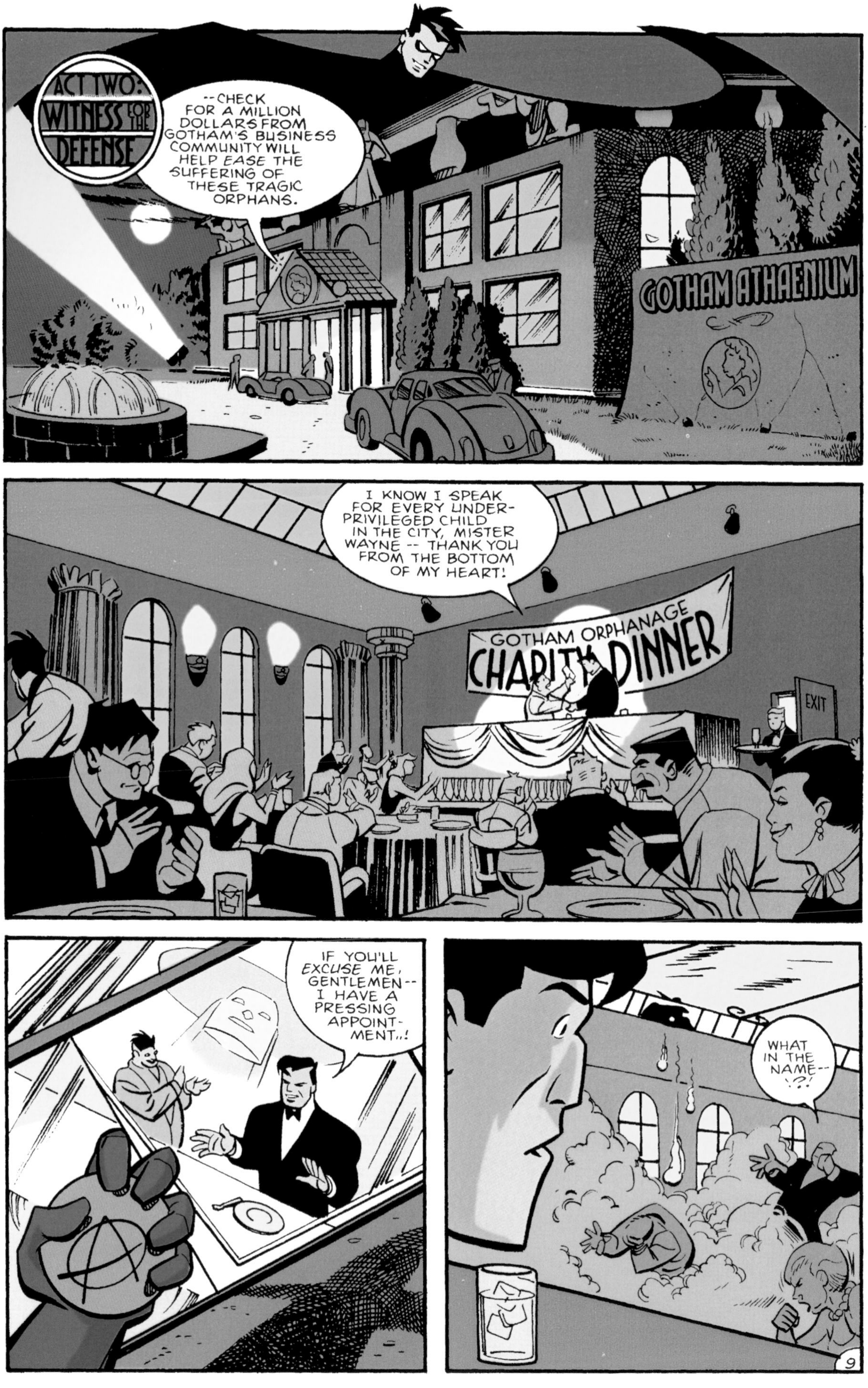

ACT TWO: WITNESS FOR THE DEFENSE
--CHECK FOR A MILLION DOLLARS FROM GOTHAM'S BUSINESS COMMUNITY WILL HELP *EASE* THE SUFFERING OF THESE TRAGIC ORPHANS.
GOTHAM ATHAENIUM
I KNOW I SPEAK FOR EVERY UNDER-PRIVILEGED CHILD IN THE CITY, MISTER WAYNE -- THANK YOU FROM THE BOTTOM OF MY HEART!
GOTHAM ORPHANAGE CHARITY DINNER
EXIT
IF YOU'LL *EXCUSE* ME, GENTLEMEN-- I HAVE A PRESSING APPOINT-MENT..!
WHAT IN THE NAME-- !?!
9

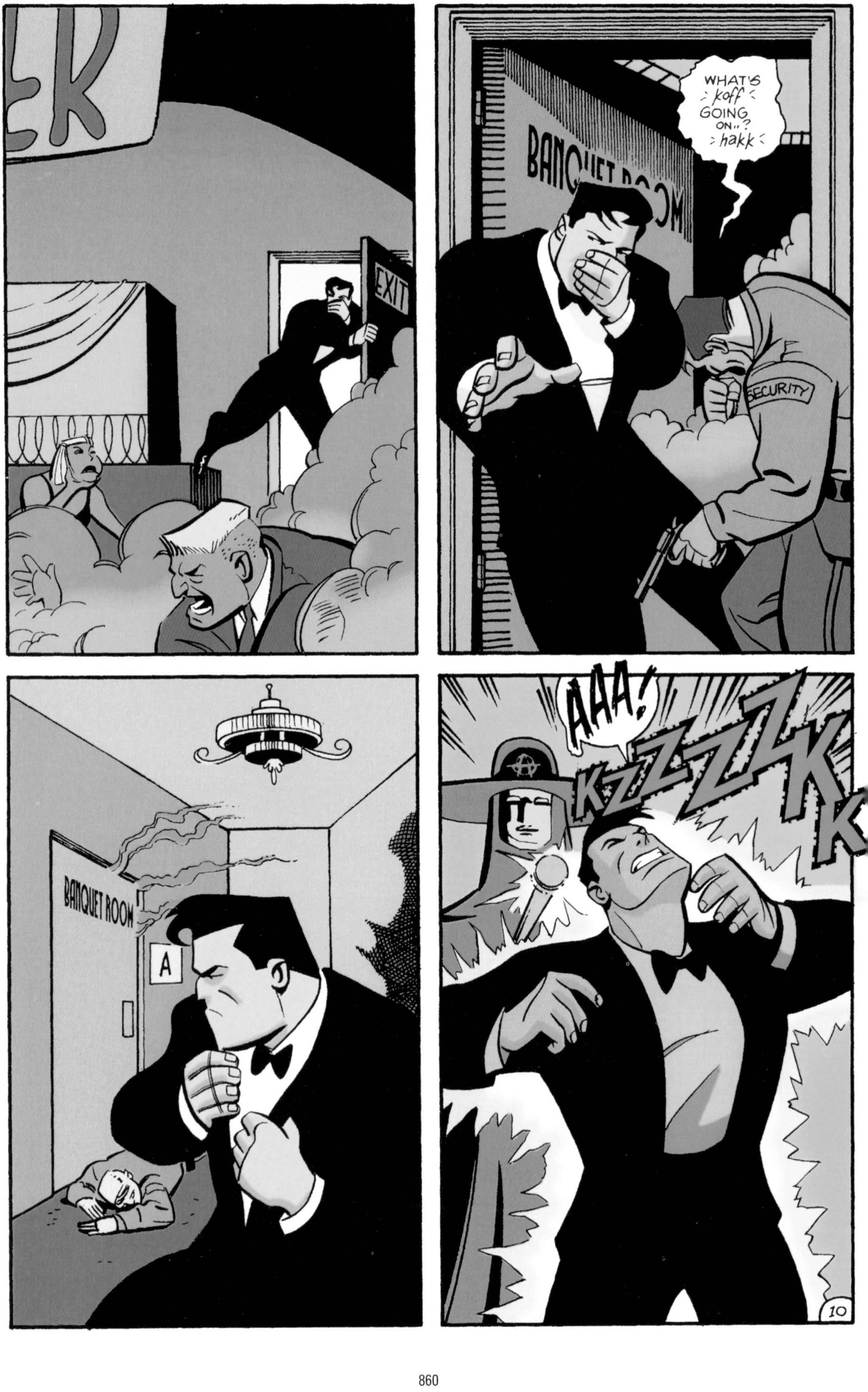
EXIT
BANQUET ROOM
WHAT'S
koff
GOING ON..?
hakk
SECURITY
BANQUET ROOM
A
AAA!
KZZZZK
10

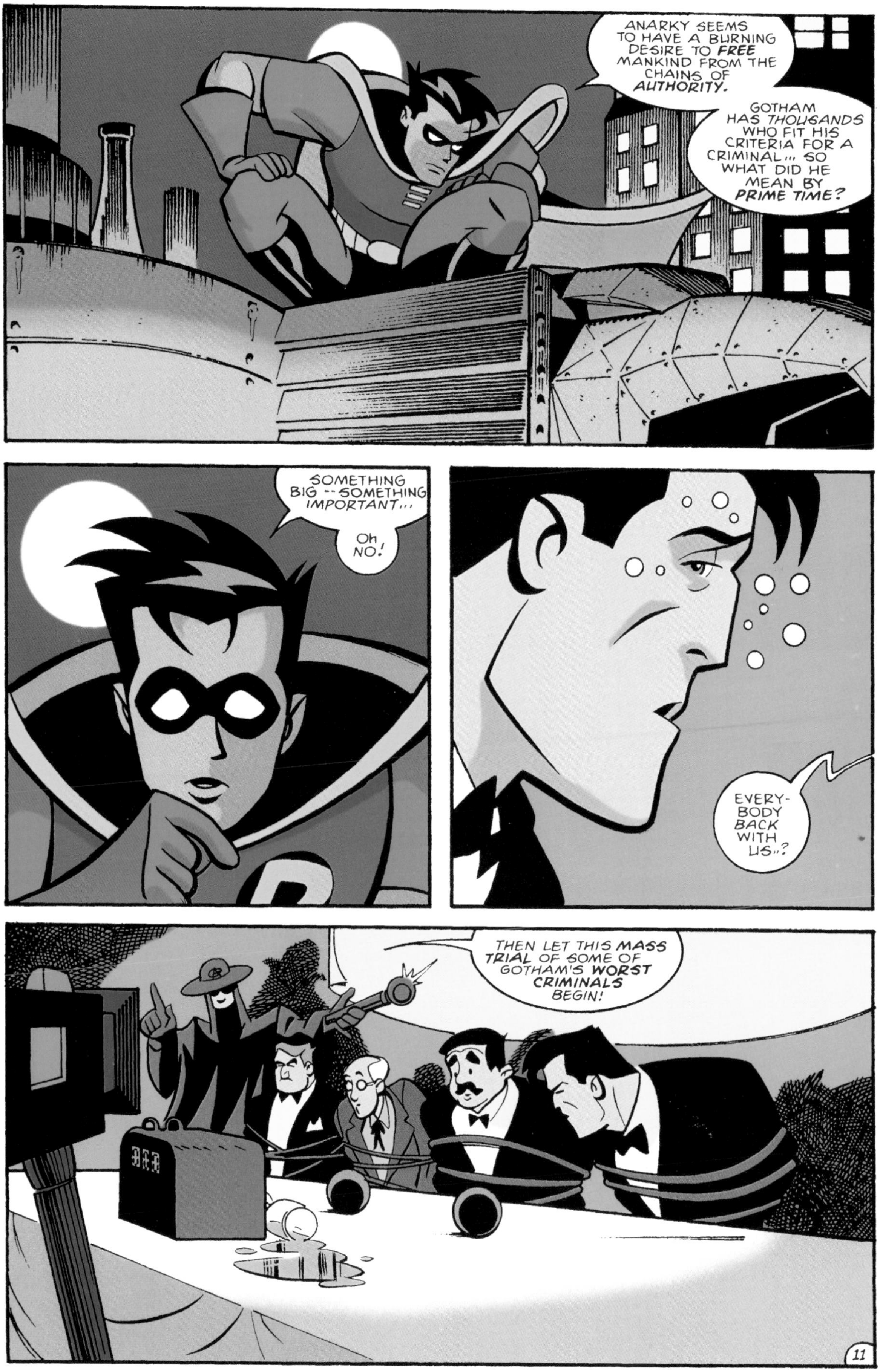
ANARKY SEEMS TO HAVE A BURNING DESIRE TO FREE MANKIND FROM THE CHAINS OF AUTHORITY.
GOTHAM HAS THOUSANDS WHO FIT HIS CRITERIA FOR A CRIMINAL... SO WHAT DID HE MEAN BY PRIME TIME?
SOMETHING BIG -- SOMETHING IMPORTANT...
Oh NO!
EVERY-BODY BACK WITH US..?
THEN LET THIS MASS TRIAL OF SOME OF GOTHAM'S WORST CRIMINALS BEGIN!
11

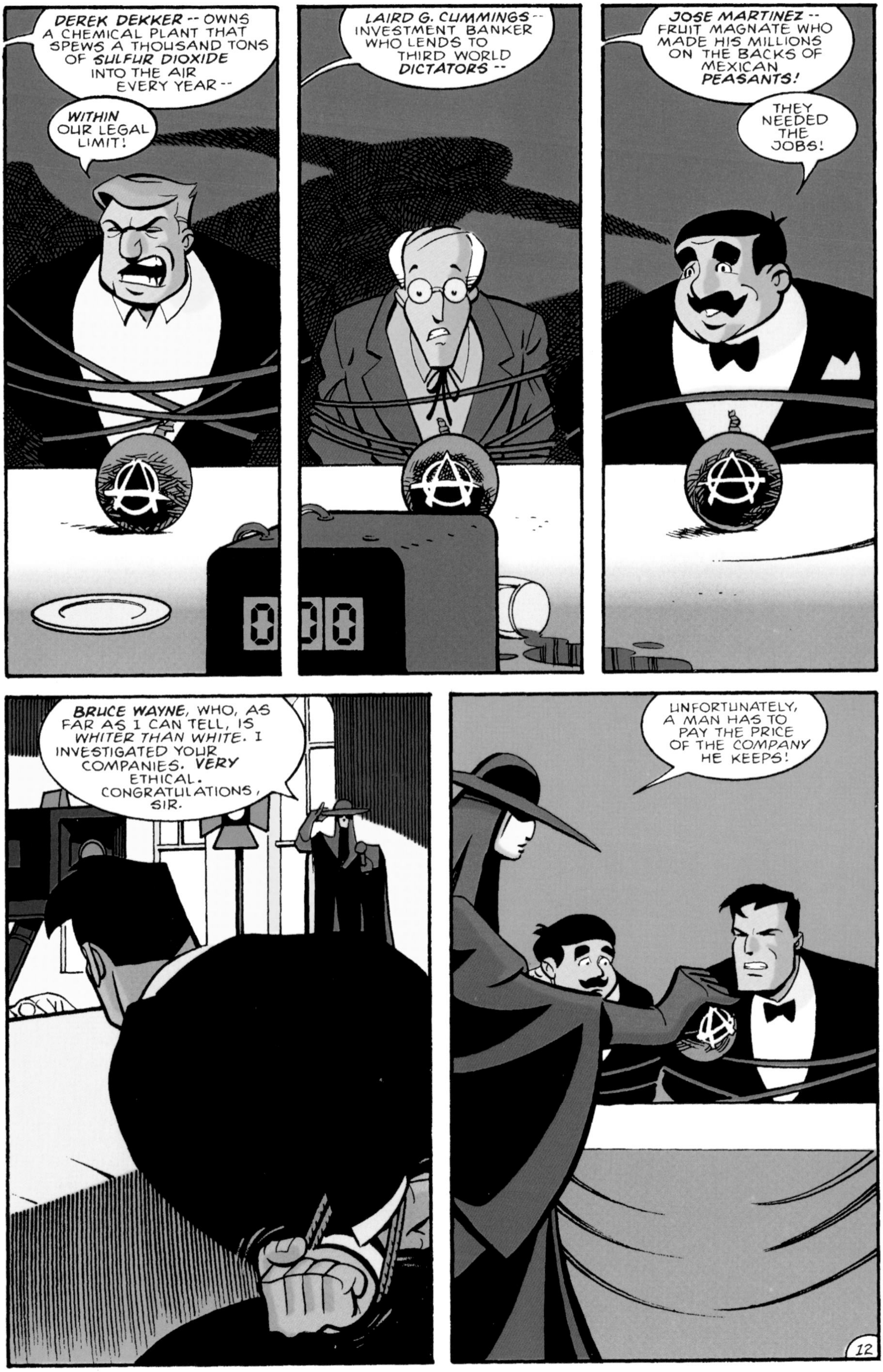
DEREK DEKKER -- OWNS A CHEMICAL PLANT THAT SPEWS A THOUSAND TONS OF SULFUR DIOXIDE INTO THE AIR EVERY YEAR --
WITHIN OUR LEGAL LIMIT!
LAIRD G. CUMMINGS -- INVESTMENT BANKER WHO LENDS TO THIRD WORLD DICTATORS --
JOSE MARTINEZ -- FRUIT MAGNATE WHO MADE HIS MILLIONS ON THE BACKS OF MEXICAN PEASANTS!
THEY NEEDED THE JOBS!
BRUCE WAYNE, WHO, AS FAR AS I CAN TELL, IS WHITER THAN WHITE. I INVESTIGATED YOUR COMPANIES. VERY ETHICAL. CONGRATULATIONS, SIR.
UNFORTUNATELY, A MAN HAS TO PAY THE PRICE OF THE COMPANY HE KEEPS!
12

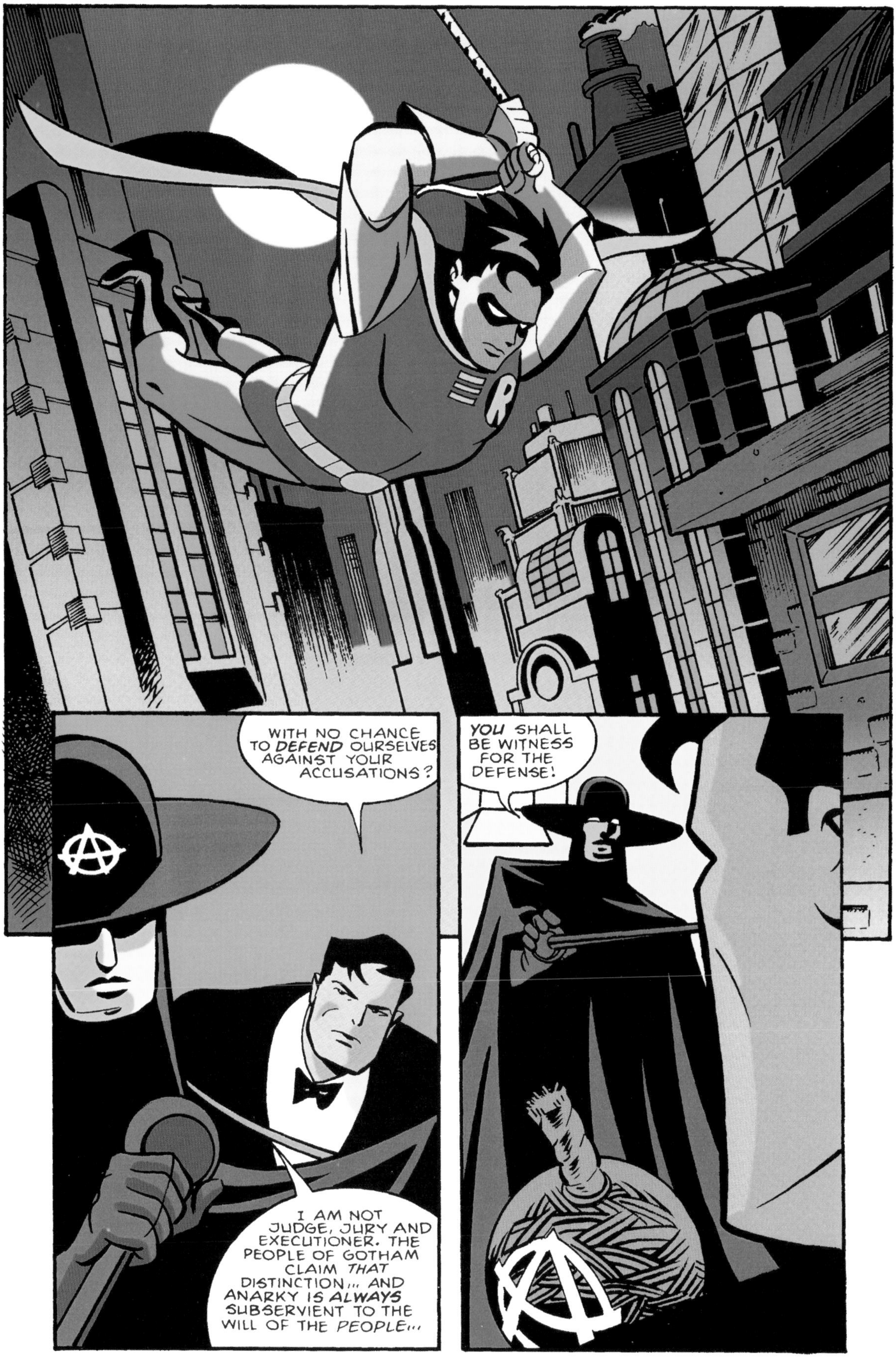
WITH NO CHANCE TO DEFEND OURSELVES AGAINST YOUR ACCUSATIONS?
I AM NOT JUDGE, JURY AND EXECUTIONER. THE PEOPLE OF GOTHAM CLAIM THAT DISTINCTION... AND ANARKY IS ALWAYS SUBSERVIENT TO THE WILL OF THE PEOPLE...
YOU SHALL BE WITNESS FOR THE DEFENSE!

13

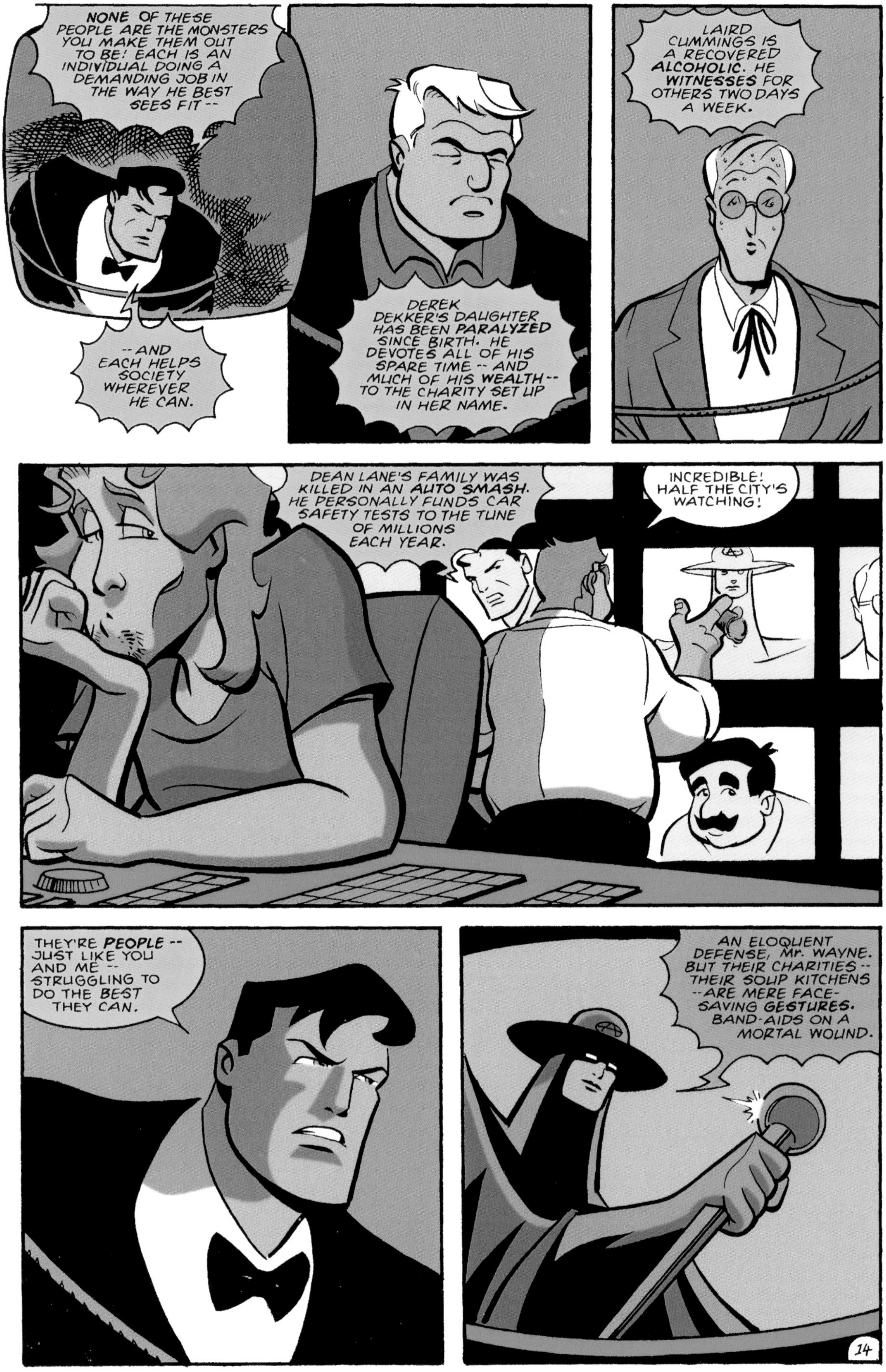
NONE OF THESE PEOPLE ARE THE MONSTERS YOU MAKE THEM OUT TO BE! EACH IS AN INDIVIDUAL DOING A DEMANDING JOB IN THE WAY HE BEST SEES FIT --
-- AND EACH HELPS SOCIETY WHEREVER HE CAN.
DEREK DEKKER'S DAUGHTER HAS BEEN PARALYZED SINCE BIRTH. HE DEVOTES ALL OF HIS SPARE TIME -- AND MUCH OF HIS WEALTH -- TO THE CHARITY SET UP IN HER NAME.
LAIRD CUMMINGS IS A RECOVERED ALCOHOLIC. HE WITNESSES FOR OTHERS TWO DAYS A WEEK.
DEAN LANE'S FAMILY WAS KILLED IN AN AUTO SMASH. HE PERSONALLY FUNDS CAR SAFETY TESTS TO THE TUNE OF MILLIONS EACH YEAR.
INCREDIBLE! HALF THE CITY'S WATCHING!
THEY'RE PEOPLE -- JUST LIKE YOU AND ME -- STRUGGLING TO DO THE BEST THEY CAN.
AN ELOQUENT DEFENSE, MR. WAYNE. BUT THEIR CHARITIES -- THEIR SOUP KITCHENS -- ARE MERE FACE-SAVING GESTURES. BAND-AIDS ON A MORTAL WOUND.
14

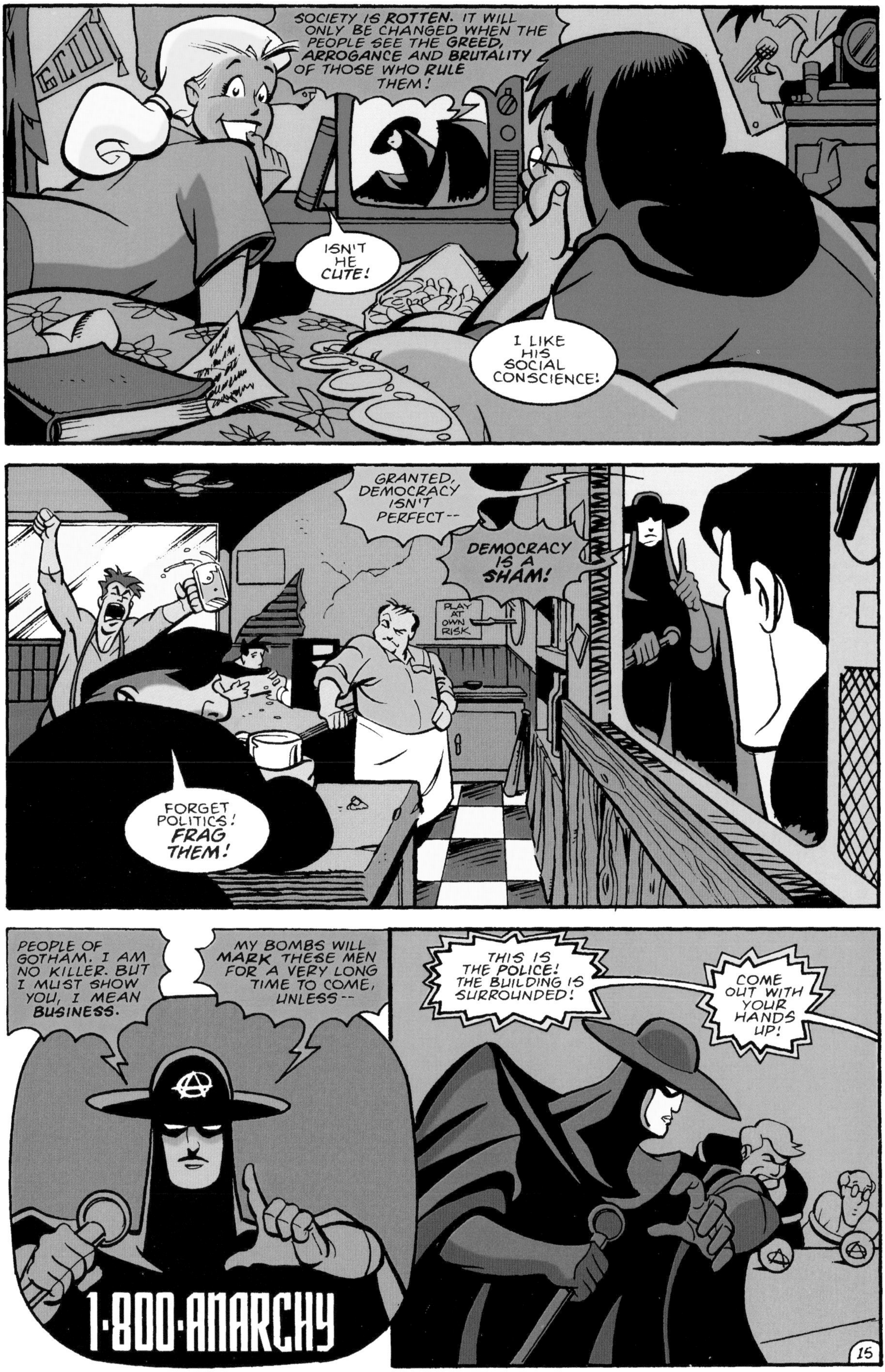

SOCIETY IS ROTTEN. IT WILL ONLY BE CHANGED WHEN THE PEOPLE SEE THE GREED, ARROGANCE AND BRUTALITY OF THOSE WHO RULE THEM!
ISN'T HE CUTE!
I LIKE HIS SOCIAL CONSCIENCE!
GRANTED, DEMOCRACY ISN'T PERFECT--
DEMOCRACY IS A SHAM!
PLAY AT OWN RISK
FORGET POLITICS! FRAG THEM!
PEOPLE OF GOTHAM. I AM NO KILLER. BUT I MUST SHOW YOU, I MEAN BUSINESS.
MY BOMBS WILL MARK THESE MEN FOR A VERY LONG TIME TO COME, UNLESS--
1-800-ANARCHY
THIS IS THE POLICE! THE BUILDING IS SURROUNDED!
COME OUT WITH YOUR HANDS UP!
15

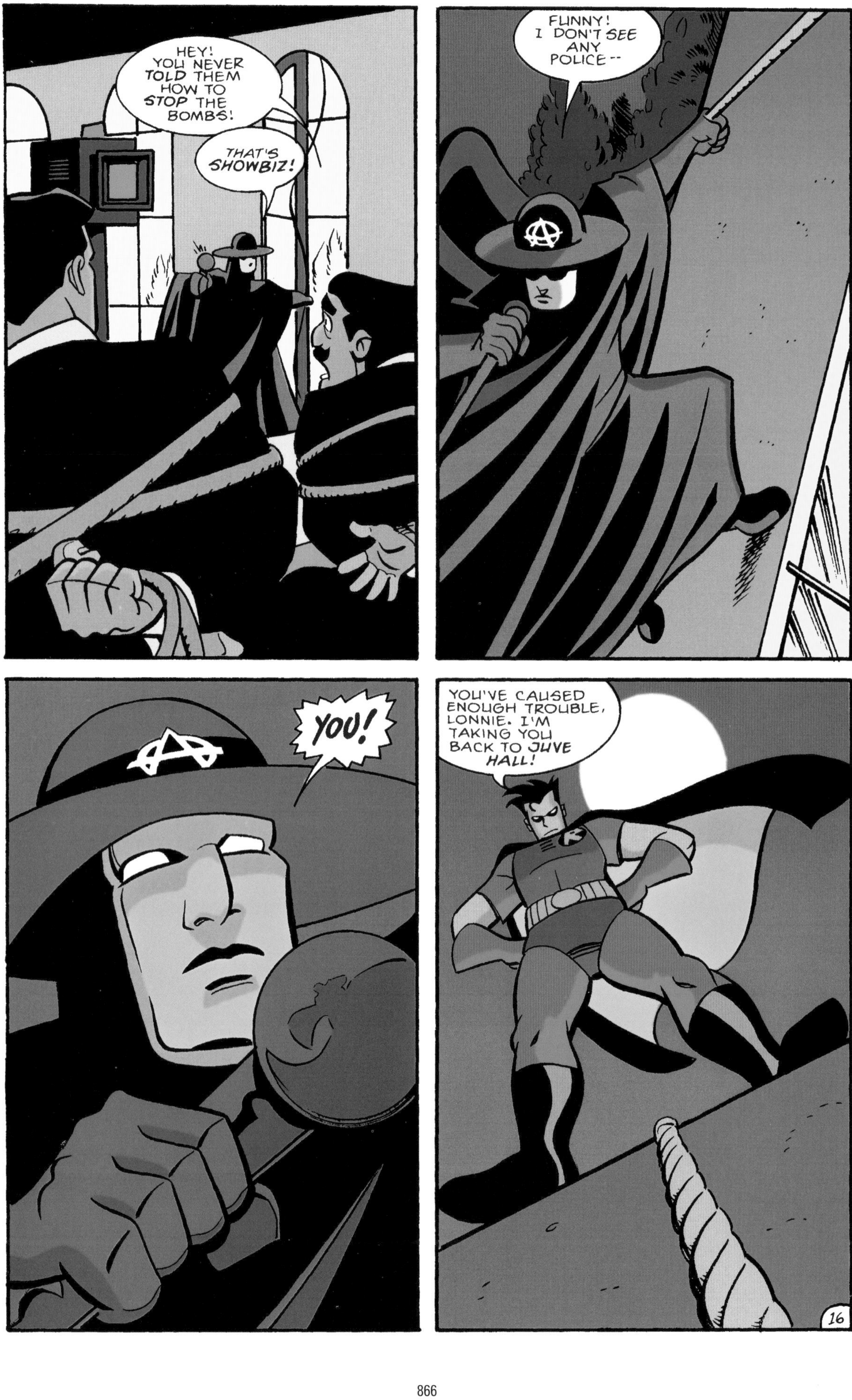
HEY! YOU NEVER TOLD THEM HOW TO STOP THE BOMBS!
THAT'S SHOWBIZ!
FUNNY! I DON'T SEE ANY POLICE --
YOU!
YOU'VE CAUSED ENOUGH TROUBLE, LONNIE. I'M TAKING YOU BACK TO JUVE HALL!
16

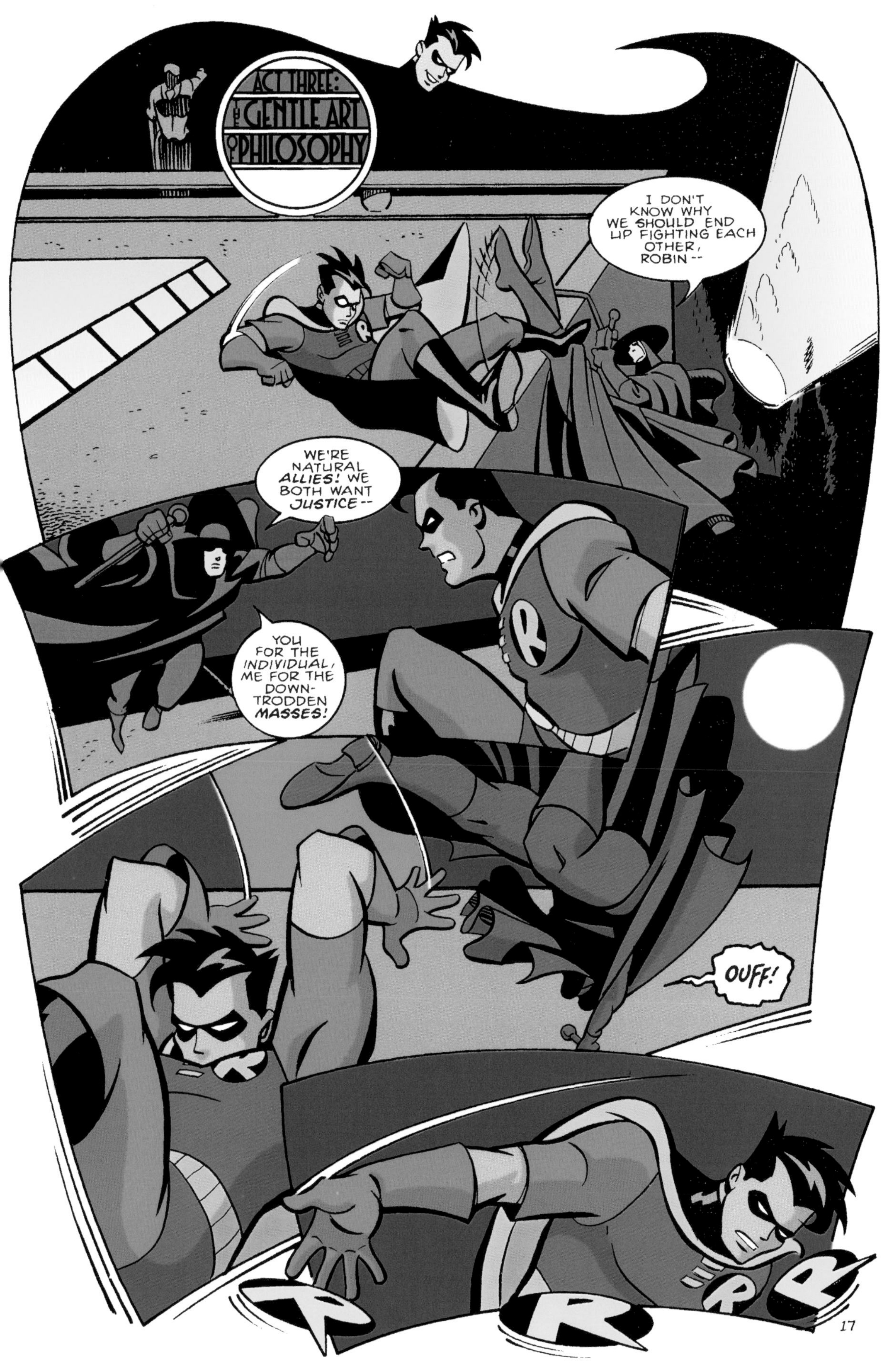

ACT THREE: THE GENTLE ART OF PHILOSOPHY
I DON'T KNOW WHY WE SHOULD END UP FIGHTING EACH OTHER, ROBIN--
WE'RE NATURAL ALLIES! WE BOTH WANT JUSTICE--
YOU FOR THE INDIVIDUAL, ME FOR THE DOWN-TRODDEN MASSES!
OUFF!
17

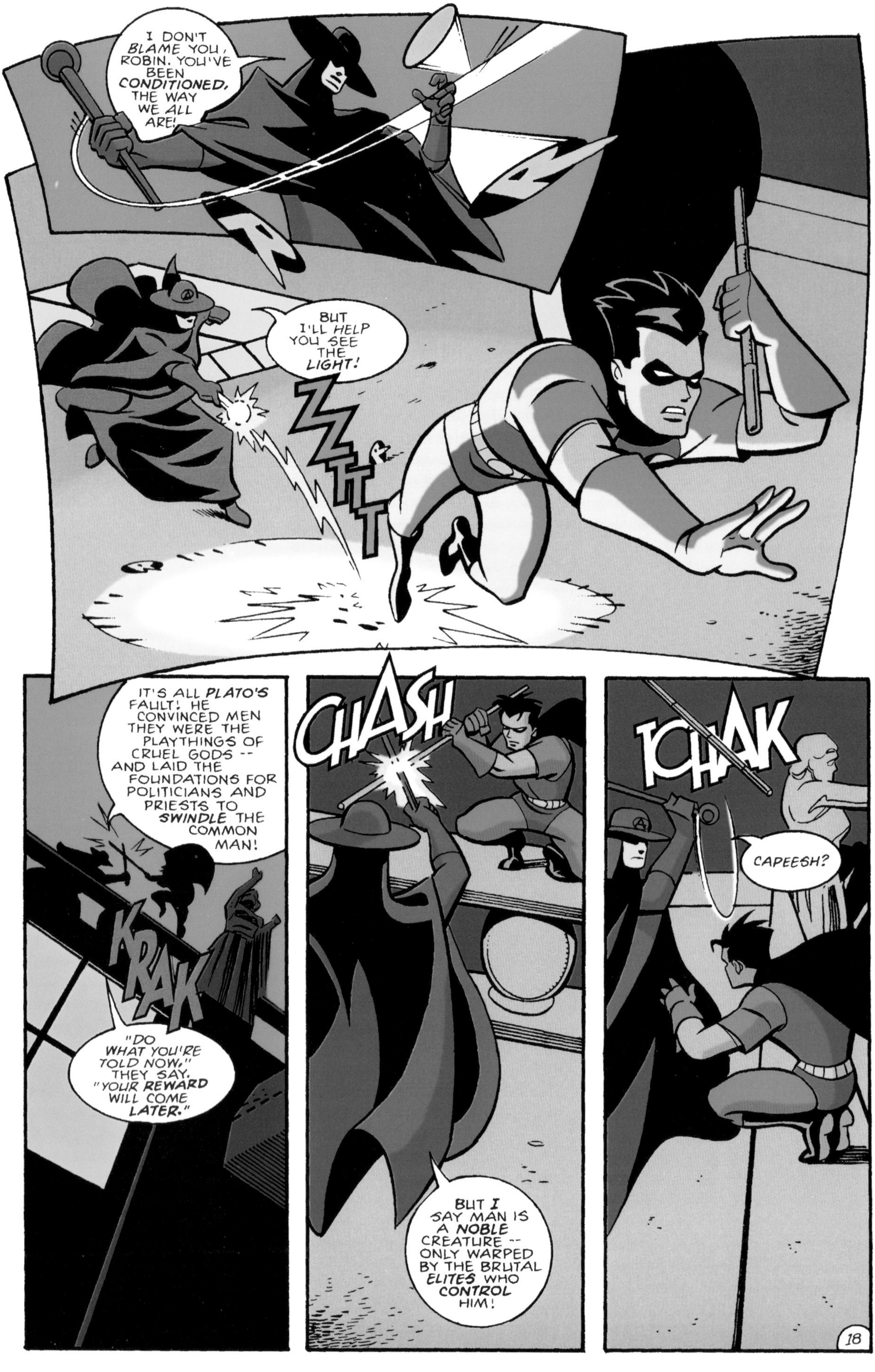

I DON'T BLAME YOU, ROBIN. YOU'VE BEEN CONDITIONED, THE WAY WE ALL ARE!
BUT I'LL HELP YOU SEE THE LIGHT!
ZZTTTT
IT'S ALL PLATO'S FAULT! HE CONVINCED MEN THEY WERE THE PLAYTHINGS OF CRUEL GODS -- AND LAID THE FOUNDATIONS FOR POLITICIANS AND PRIESTS TO SWINDLE THE COMMON MAN!
KRAK
"DO WHAT YOU'RE TOLD NOW," THEY SAY. "YOUR REWARD WILL COME LATER."
CHASH
BUT I SAY MAN IS A NOBLE CREATURE -- ONLY WARPED BY THE BRUTAL ELITES WHO CONTROL HIM!
TCHAK
CAPEESH?
18

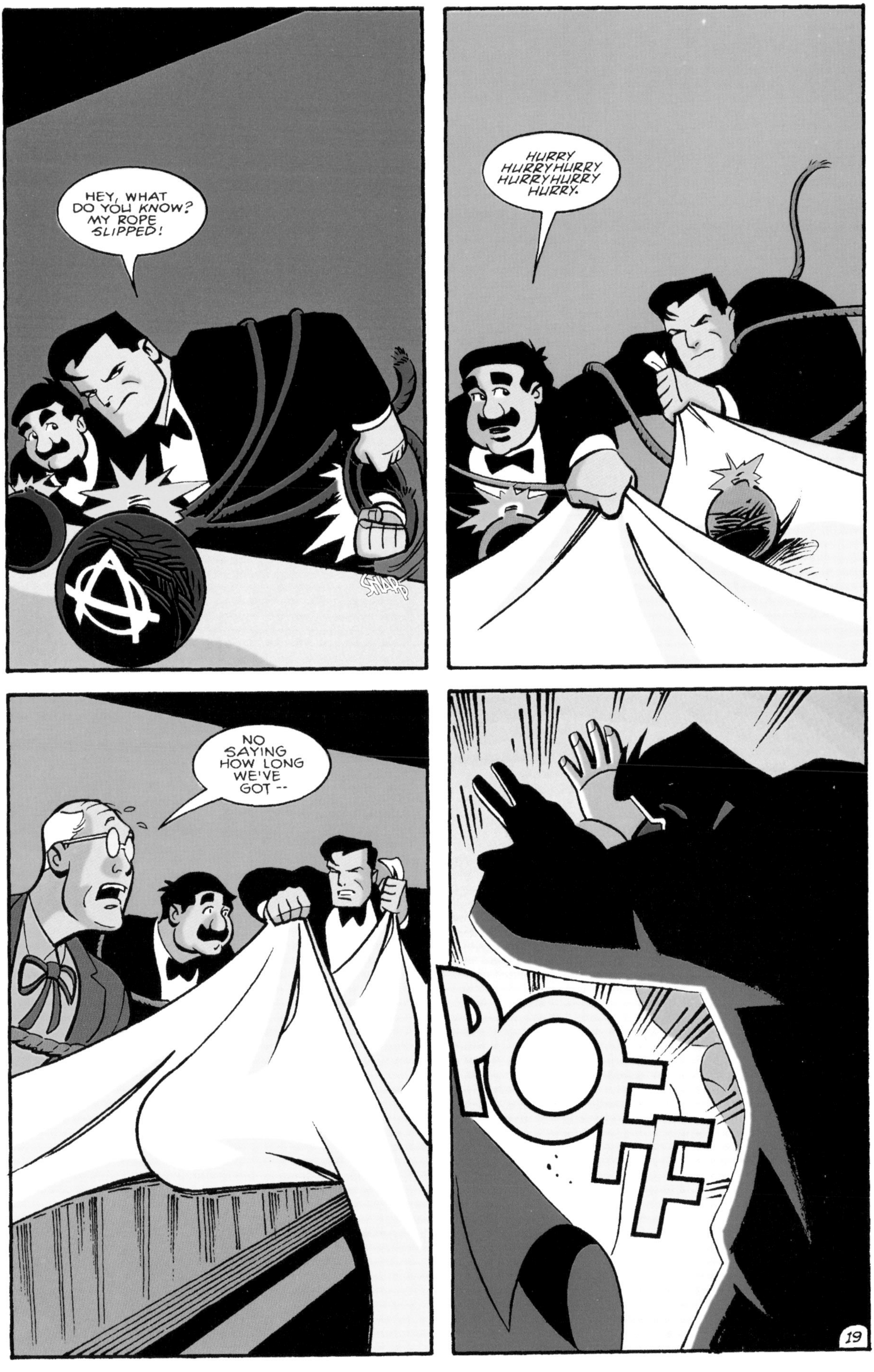
HEY, WHAT DO YOU KNOW? MY ROPE SLIPPED!
HURRY HURRYHURRY HURRYHURRY HURRY.
NO SAYING HOW LONG WE'VE GOT --
POFF
19

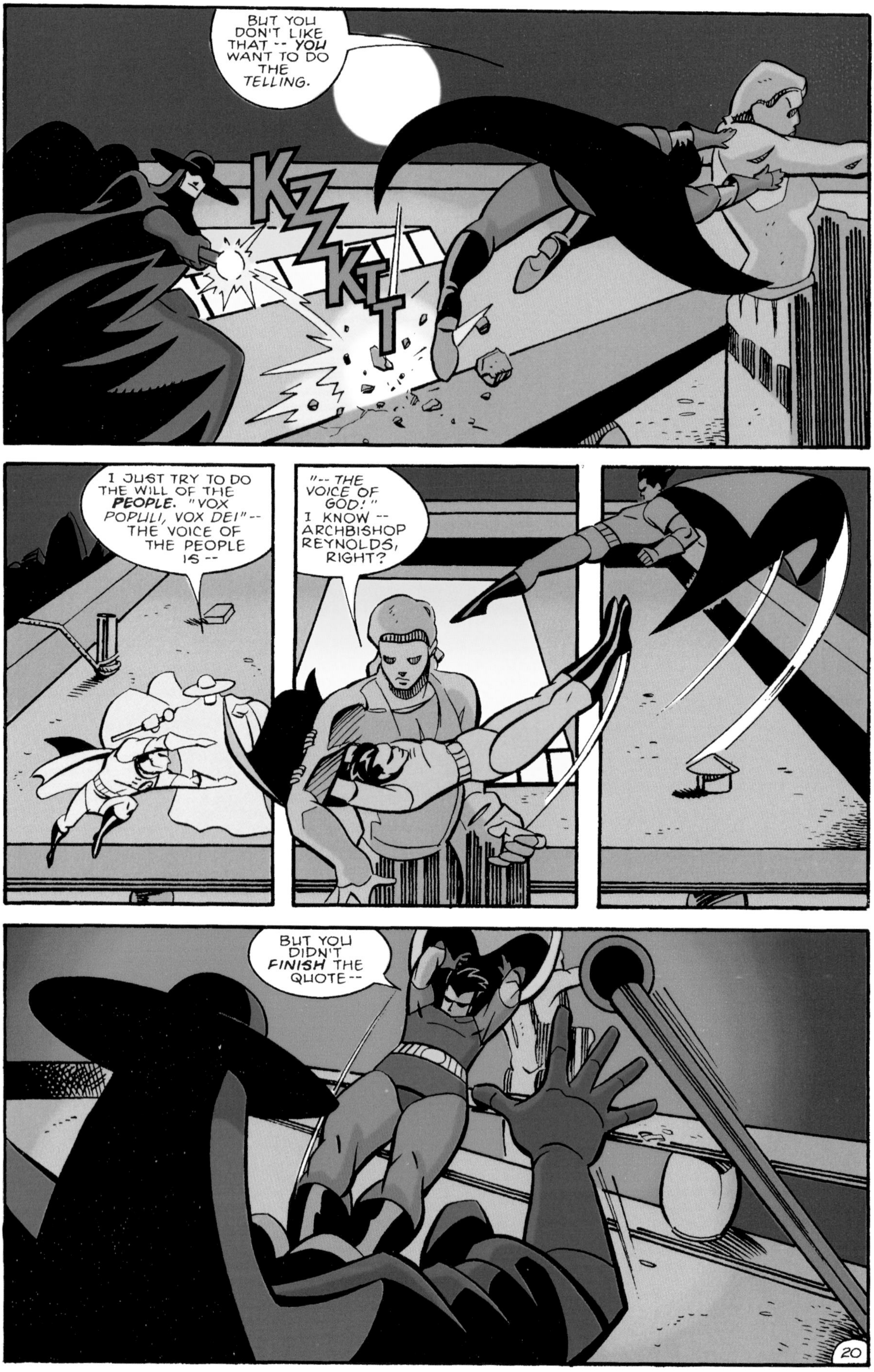
BUT YOU DON'T LIKE THAT -- YOU WANT TO DO THE TELLING.
KZZKTT
I JUST TRY TO DO THE WILL OF THE PEOPLE. "VOX POPULI, VOX DEI" -- THE VOICE OF THE PEOPLE IS --
"-- THE VOICE OF GOD!" I KNOW -- ARCHBISHOP REYNOLDS, RIGHT?
BUT YOU DIDN'T FINISH THE QUOTE --
20

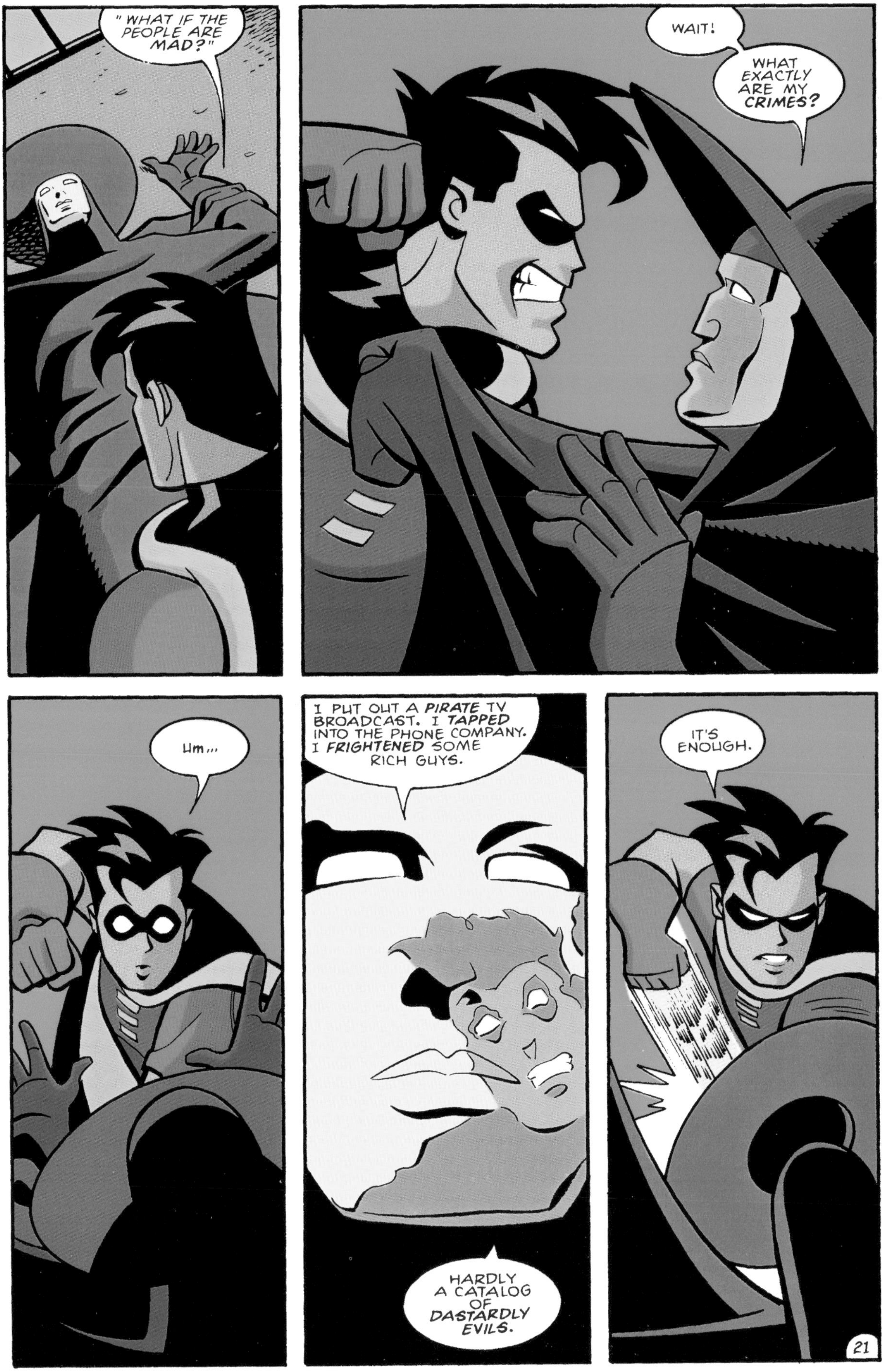
"WHAT IF THE PEOPLE ARE MAD?"
WAIT!
WHAT EXACTLY ARE MY CRIMES?
UM...
I PUT OUT A PIRATE TV BROADCAST. I TAPPED INTO THE PHONE COMPANY. I FRIGHTENED SOME RICH GUYS.
HARDLY A CATALOG OF DASTARDLY EVILS.
IT'S ENOUGH.
21

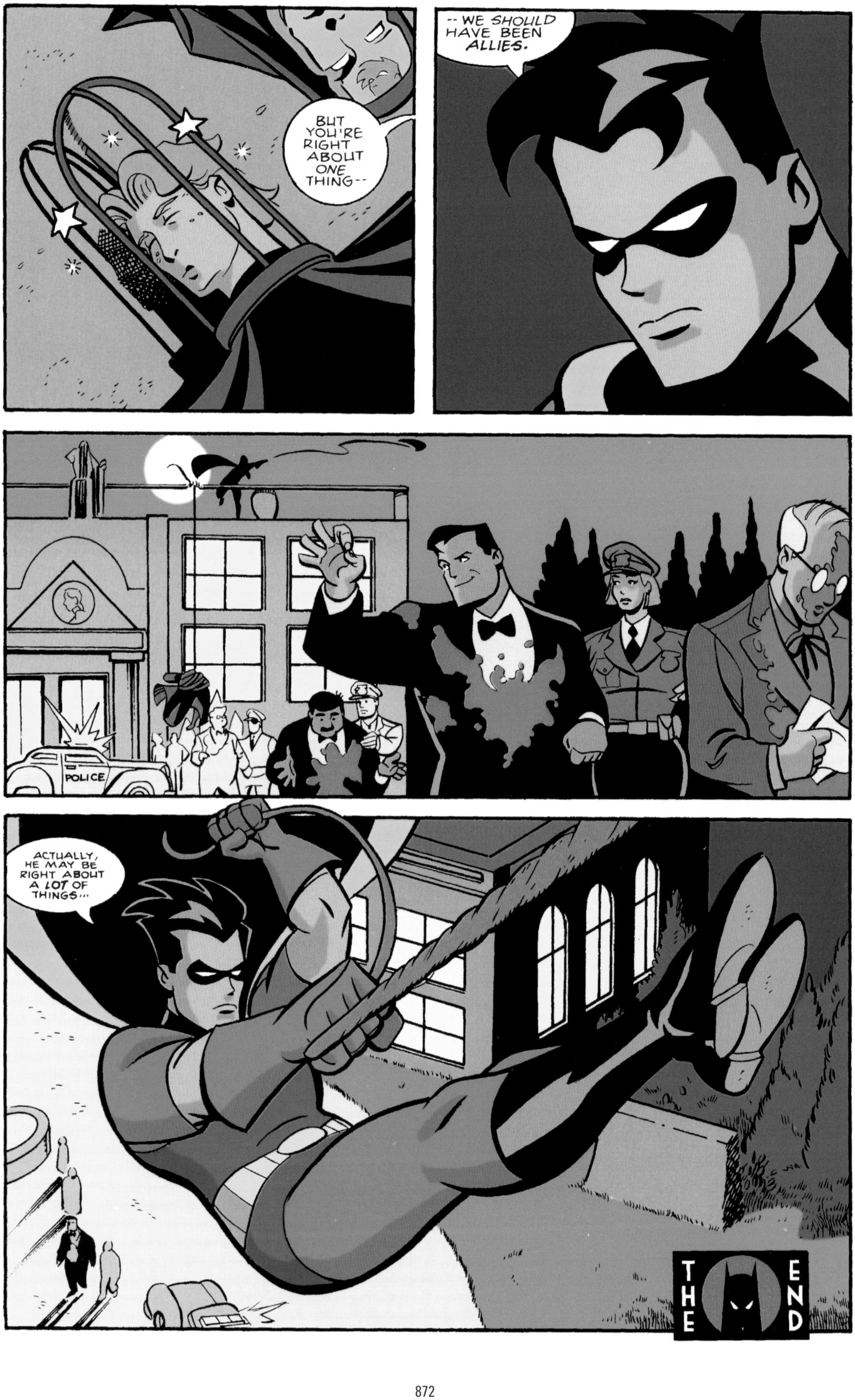
BUT YOU'RE RIGHT ABOUT ONE THING--
--WE SHOULD HAVE BEEN ALLIES.
POLICE
ACTUALLY, HE MAY BE RIGHT ABOUT A LOT OF THINGS...
THE END

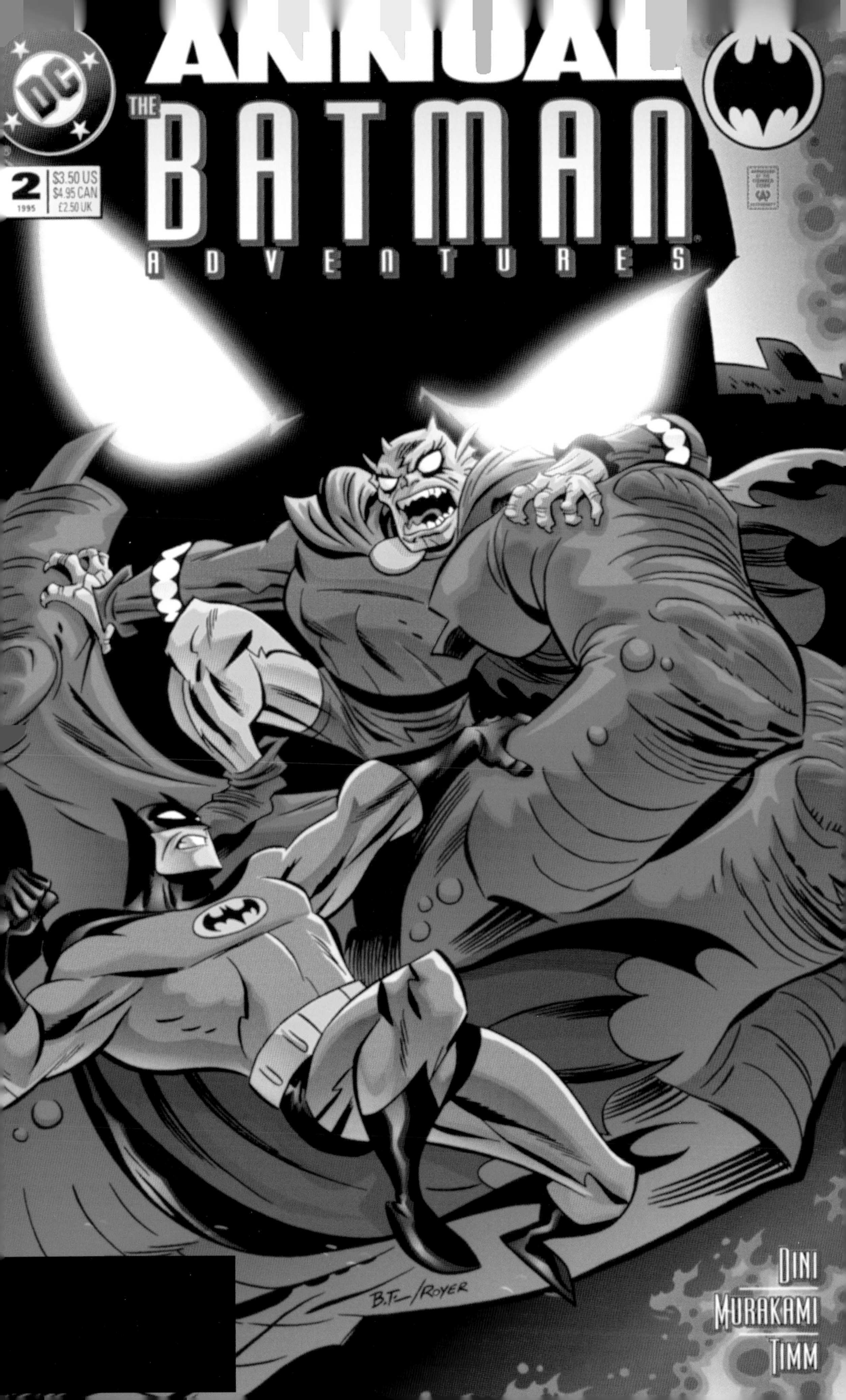
ANNUAL
DC
THE BATMAN ADVENTURES
2
1995
$3.50 US
$4.95 CAN
£2.50 UK
B.T.—/ROYER
DINI
MURAKAMI
TIMM

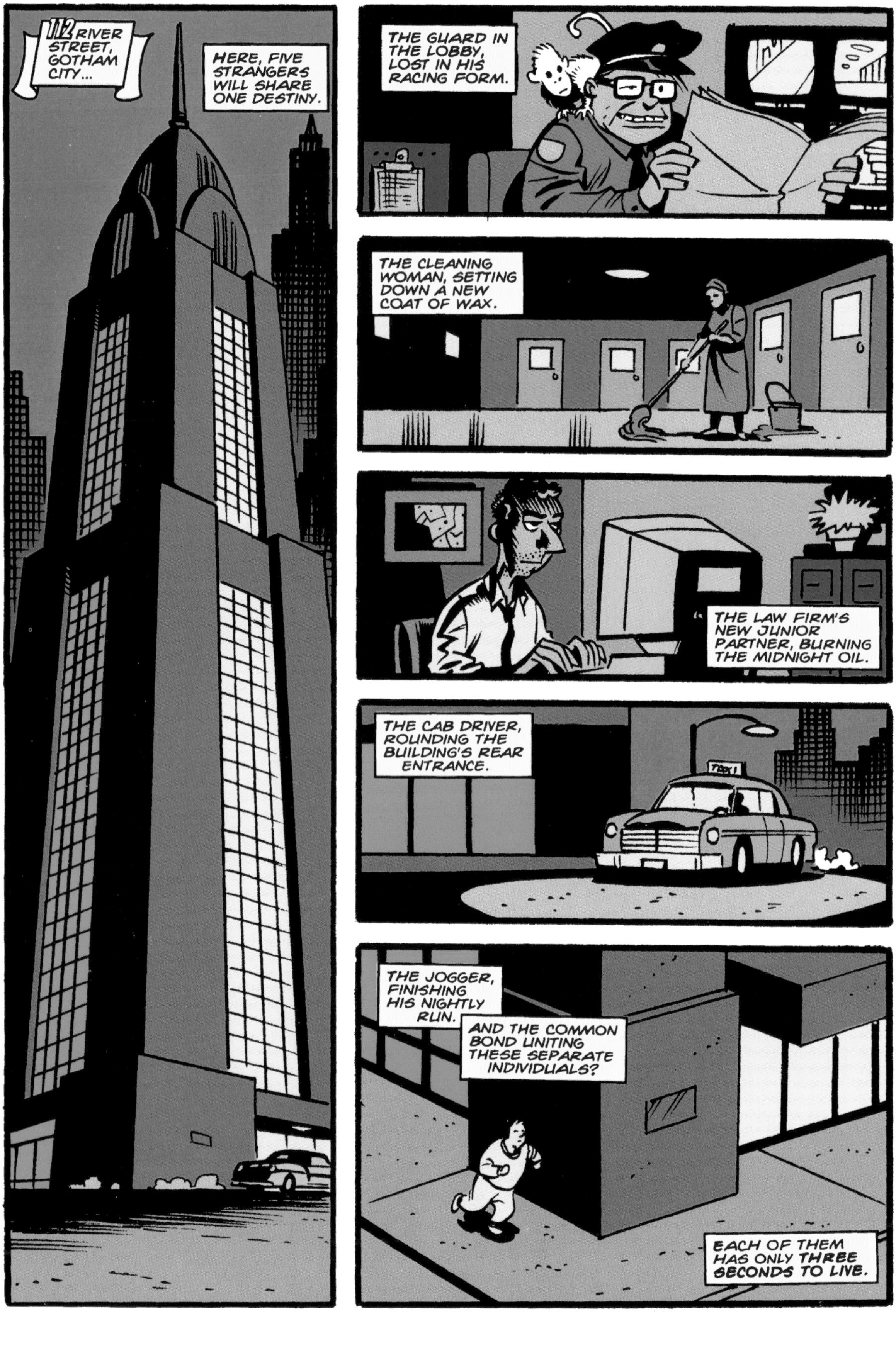
112 RIVER STREET, GOTHAM CITY...
HERE, FIVE STRANGERS WILL SHARE ONE DESTINY.
THE GUARD IN THE LOBBY, LOST IN HIS RACING FORM.
THE CLEANING WOMAN, SETTING DOWN A NEW COAT OF WAX.
THE LAW FIRM'S NEW JUNIOR PARTNER, BURNING THE MIDNIGHT OIL.
THE CAB DRIVER, ROUNDING THE BUILDING'S REAR ENTRANCE.
TAXI
THE JOGGER, FINISHING HIS NIGHTLY RUN.
AND THE COMMON BOND UNITING THESE SEPARATE INDIVIDUALS?
EACH OF THEM HAS ONLY THREE SECONDS TO LIVE.

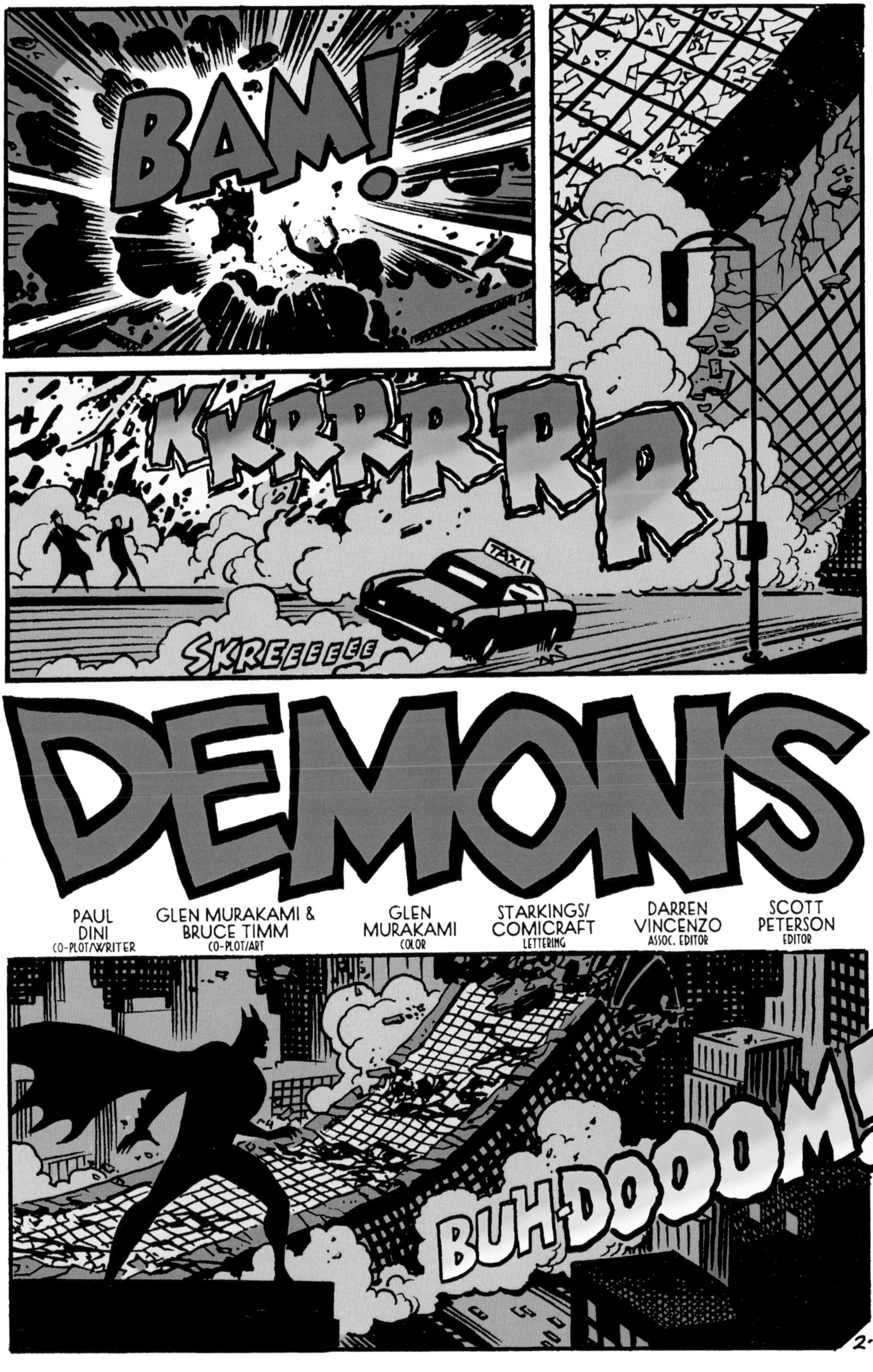

BAM!
KKRRRRR
TAXI
SKREEEEEE
DEMONS
PAUL DINI CO-PLOT/WRITER
GLEN MURAKAMI & BRUCE TIMM CO-PLOT/ART
GLEN MURAKAMI COLOR
STARKINGS/ COMICRAFT LETTERING
DARREN VINCENZO ASSOC. EDITOR
SCOTT PETERSON EDITOR
BUH-DOOOM!
2.

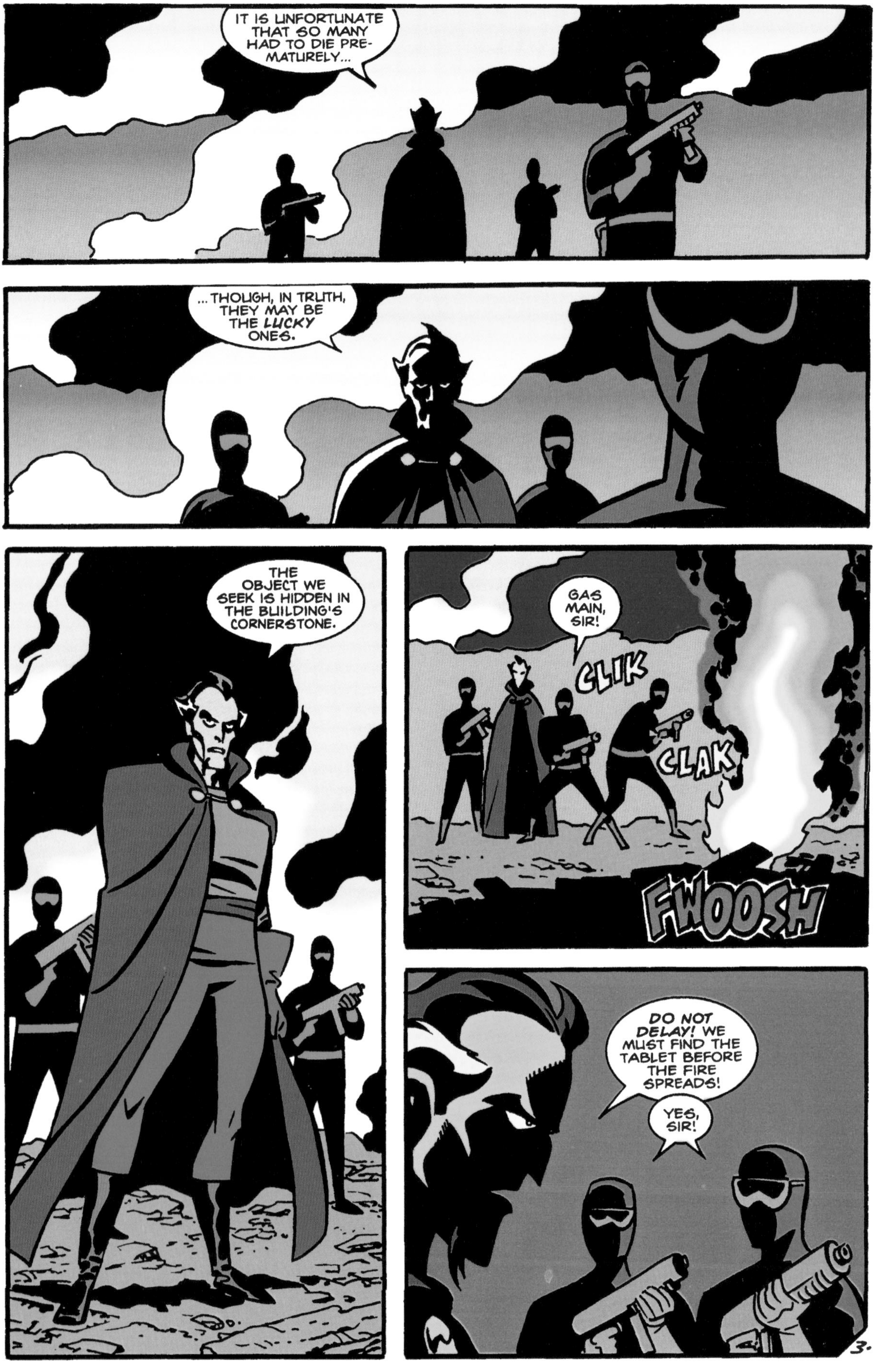
IT IS UNFORTUNATE THAT SO MANY HAD TO DIE PRE-MATURELY...
...THOUGH, IN TRUTH, THEY MAY BE THE LUCKY ONES.
THE OBJECT WE SEEK IS HIDDEN IN THE BUILDING'S CORNERSTONE.
GAS MAIN, SIR!
CLIK
CLAK
FWOOSH
DO NOT DELAY! WE MUST FIND THE TABLET BEFORE THE FIRE SPREADS!
YES, SIR!
3.

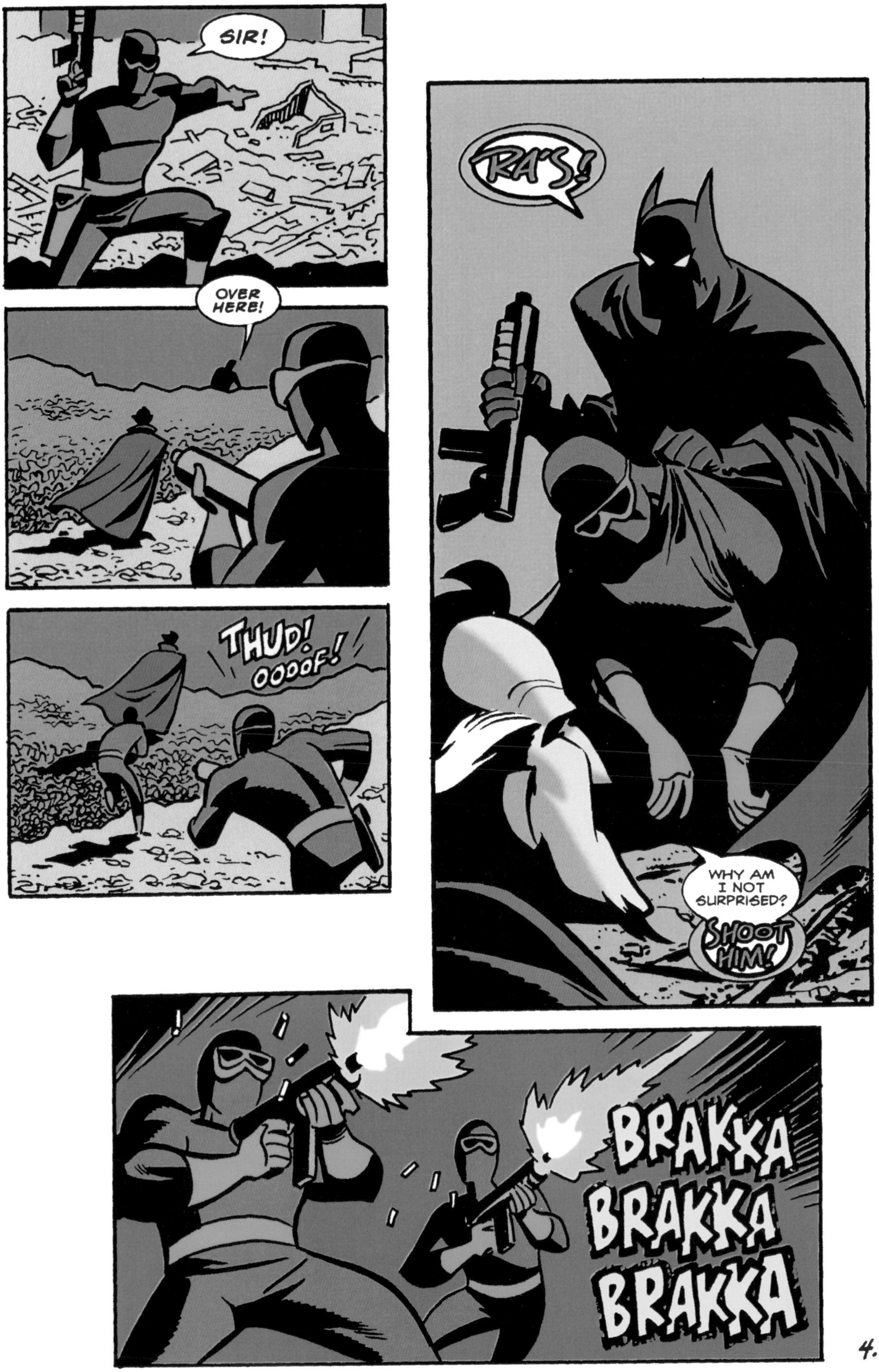
SIR!
OVER HERE!
THUD! OOOOF!
RA'S!
WHY AM I NOT SURPRISED?
SHOOT HIM!
!
BRAKKA BRAKKA BRAKKA
4.

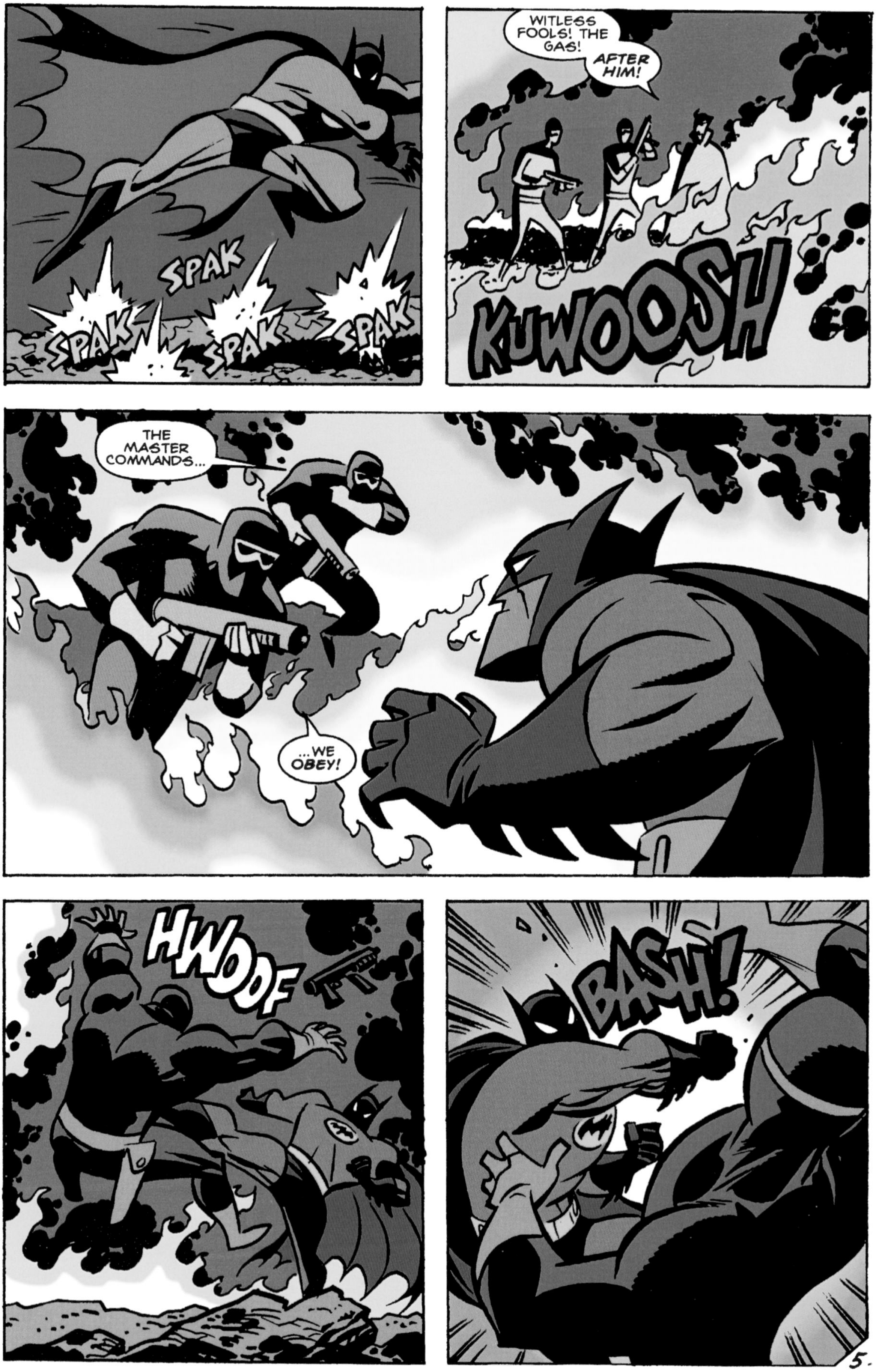
SPAK
SPAK
SPAK
SPAK
WITLESS FOOLS! THE GAS!
AFTER HIM!
KUWOOSH
THE MASTER COMMANDS...
...WE OBEY!
HWOOF
BASH!
5.

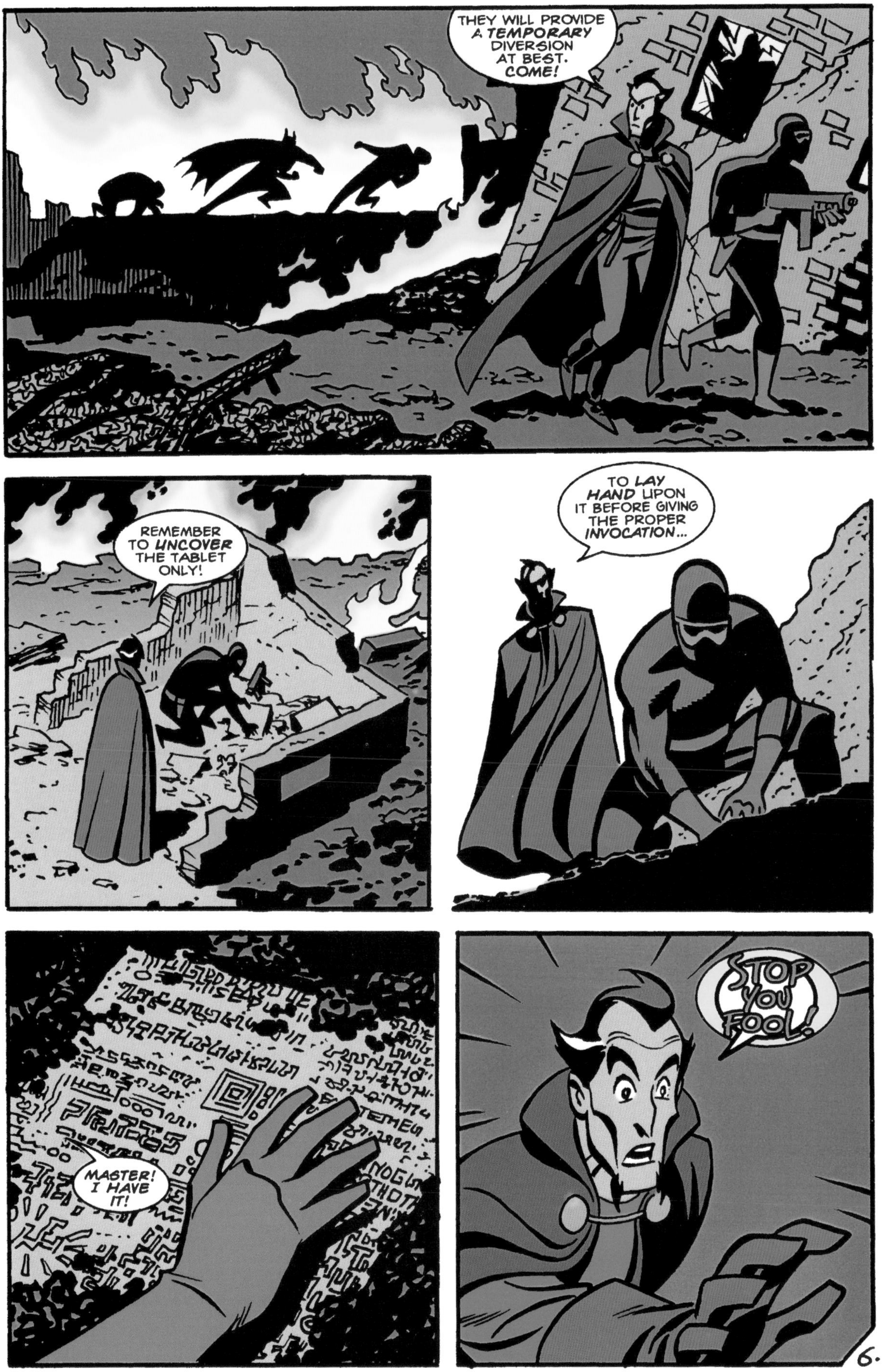
THEY WILL PROVIDE A TEMPORARY DIVERSION AT BEST. COME!
REMEMBER TO UNCOVER THE TABLET ONLY!
TO LAY HAND UPON IT BEFORE GIVING THE PROPER INVOCATION...
MASTER! I HAVE IT!
STOP YOU FOOL!
6.

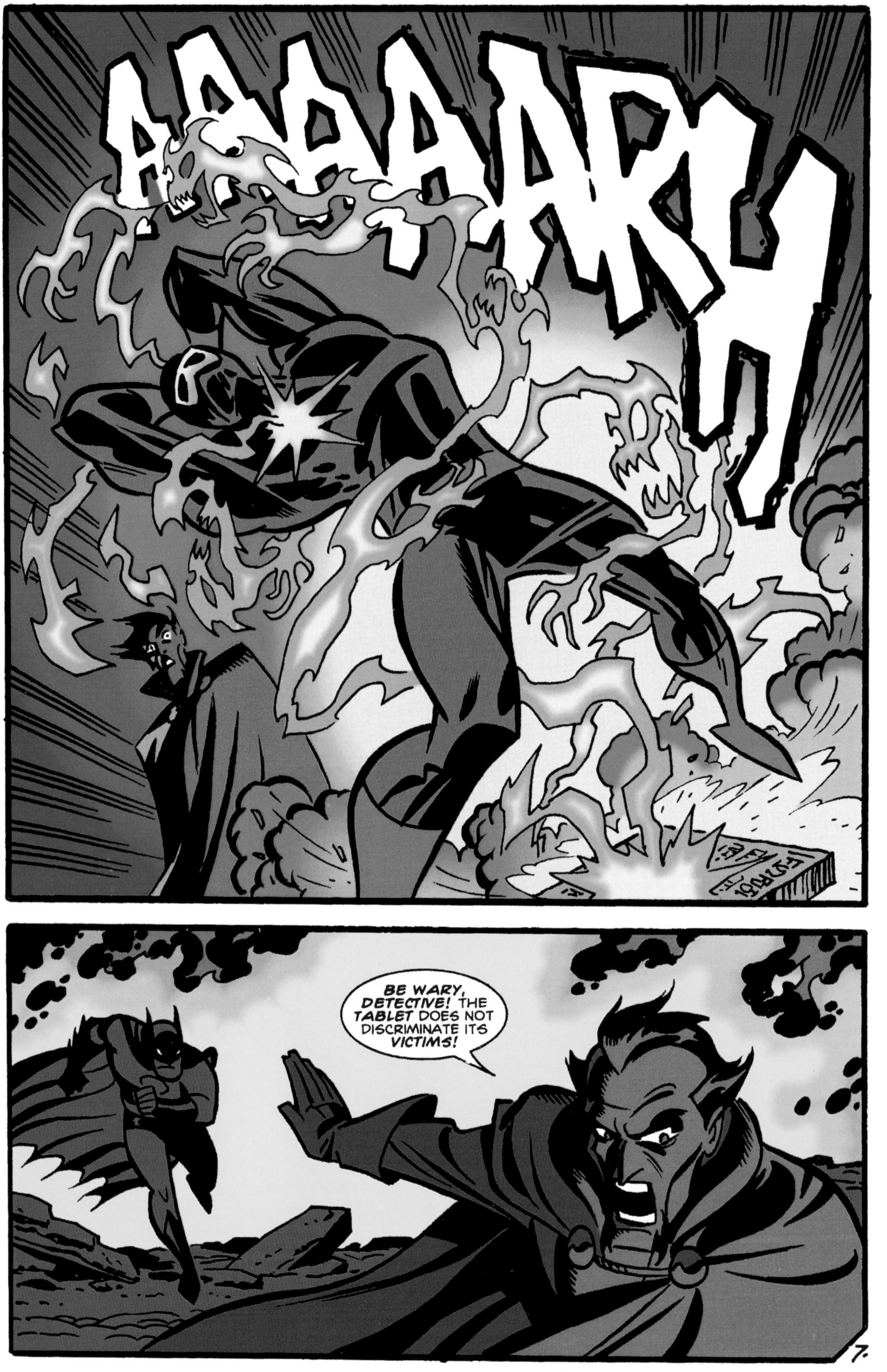
AAAAARH
BE WARY, DETECTIVE! THE TABLET DOES NOT DISCRIMINATE ITS VICTIMS!
7.

TABLET?

BWAK!

AH-NAHL-NATHRACH...

OOTH-BA-SPETHUTH...

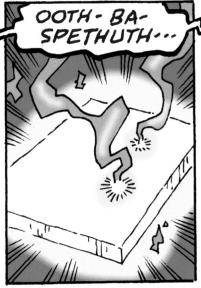

DOH-HIL-NIELDRE!

HA! IT'S MINE!

AFTER TWO HUNDRED YEARS!

YOU MURDERED INNOCENT PEOPLE FOR A WORTHLESS PIECE OF STONE?

8.

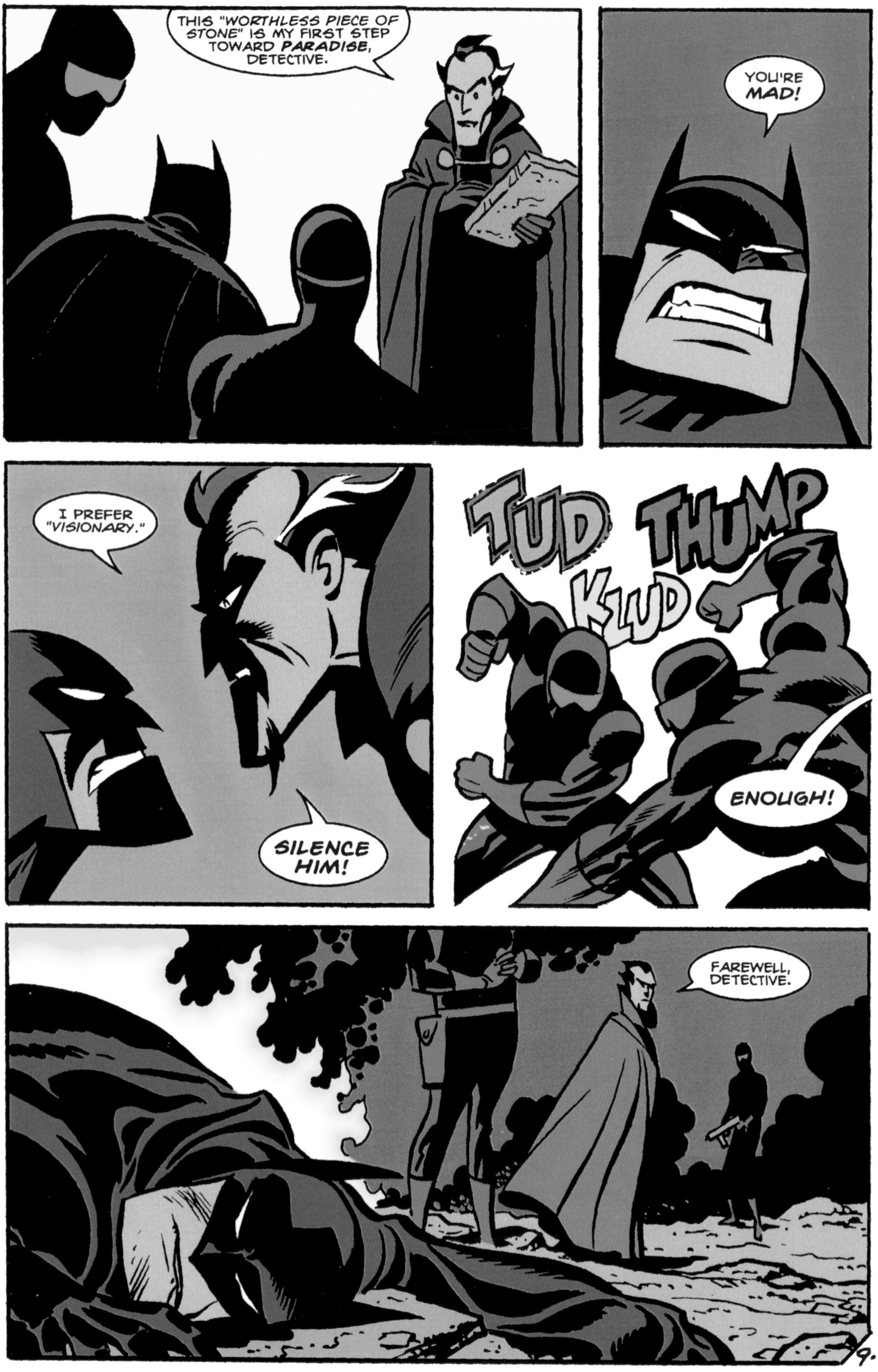
THIS "WORTHLESS PIECE OF STONE" IS MY FIRST STEP TOWARD PARADISE, DETECTIVE.
YOU'RE MAD!
I PREFER "VISIONARY."
SILENCE HIM!
TUD
THUMP
KLUD
ENOUGH!
FAREWELL, DETECTIVE.
9.

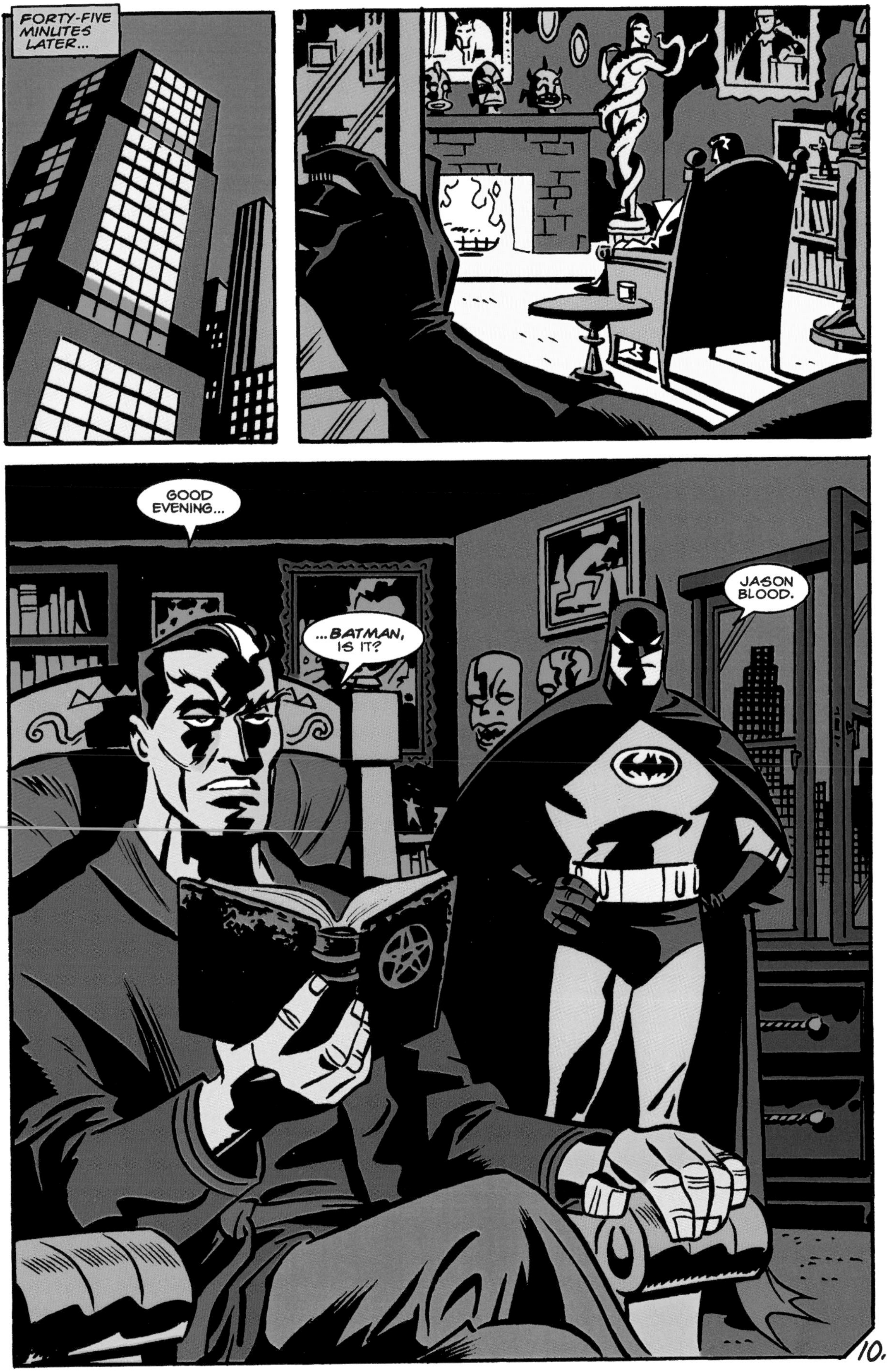
FORTY-FIVE MINUTES LATER...
GOOD EVENING...
...BATMAN, IS IT?
JASON BLOOD.
10.

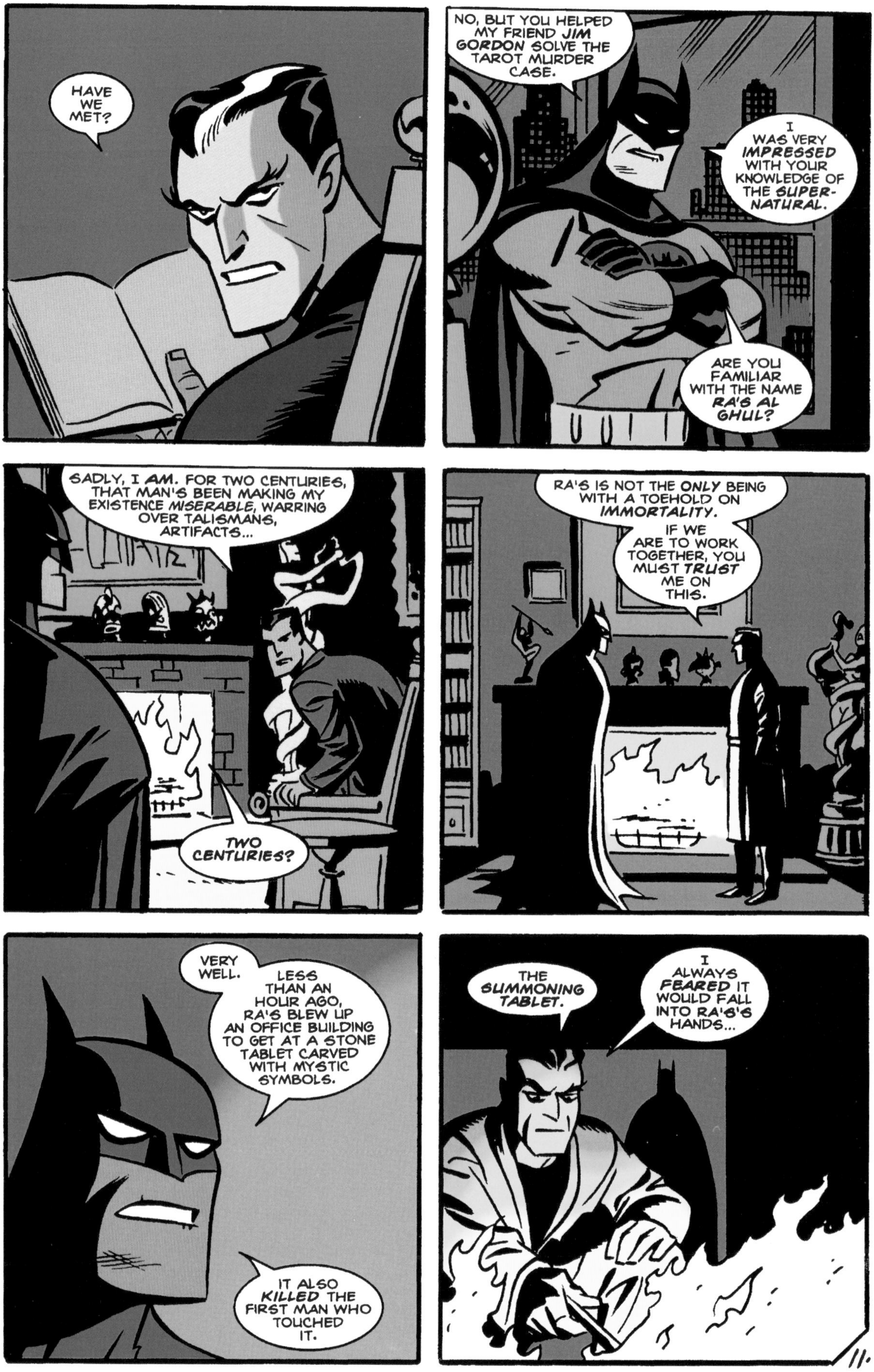

HAVE WE MET?
NO, BUT YOU HELPED MY FRIEND JIM GORDON SOLVE THE TAROT MURDER CASE.
I WAS VERY IMPRESSED WITH YOUR KNOWLEDGE OF THE SUPER-NATURAL.
ARE YOU FAMILIAR WITH THE NAME RA'S AL GHUL?
SADLY, I AM. FOR TWO CENTURIES, THAT MAN'S BEEN MAKING MY EXISTENCE MISERABLE, WARRING OVER TALISMANS, ARTIFACTS...
TWO CENTURIES?
RA'S IS NOT THE ONLY BEING WITH A TOEHOLD ON IMMORTALITY.
IF WE ARE TO WORK TOGETHER, YOU MUST TRUST ME ON THIS.
VERY WELL.
LESS THAN AN HOUR AGO, RA'S BLEW UP AN OFFICE BUILDING TO GET AT A STONE TABLET CARVED WITH MYSTIC SYMBOLS.
IT ALSO KILLED THE FIRST MAN WHO TOUCHED IT.
THE SUMMONING TABLET.
I ALWAYS FEARED IT WOULD FALL INTO RA'S'S HANDS...

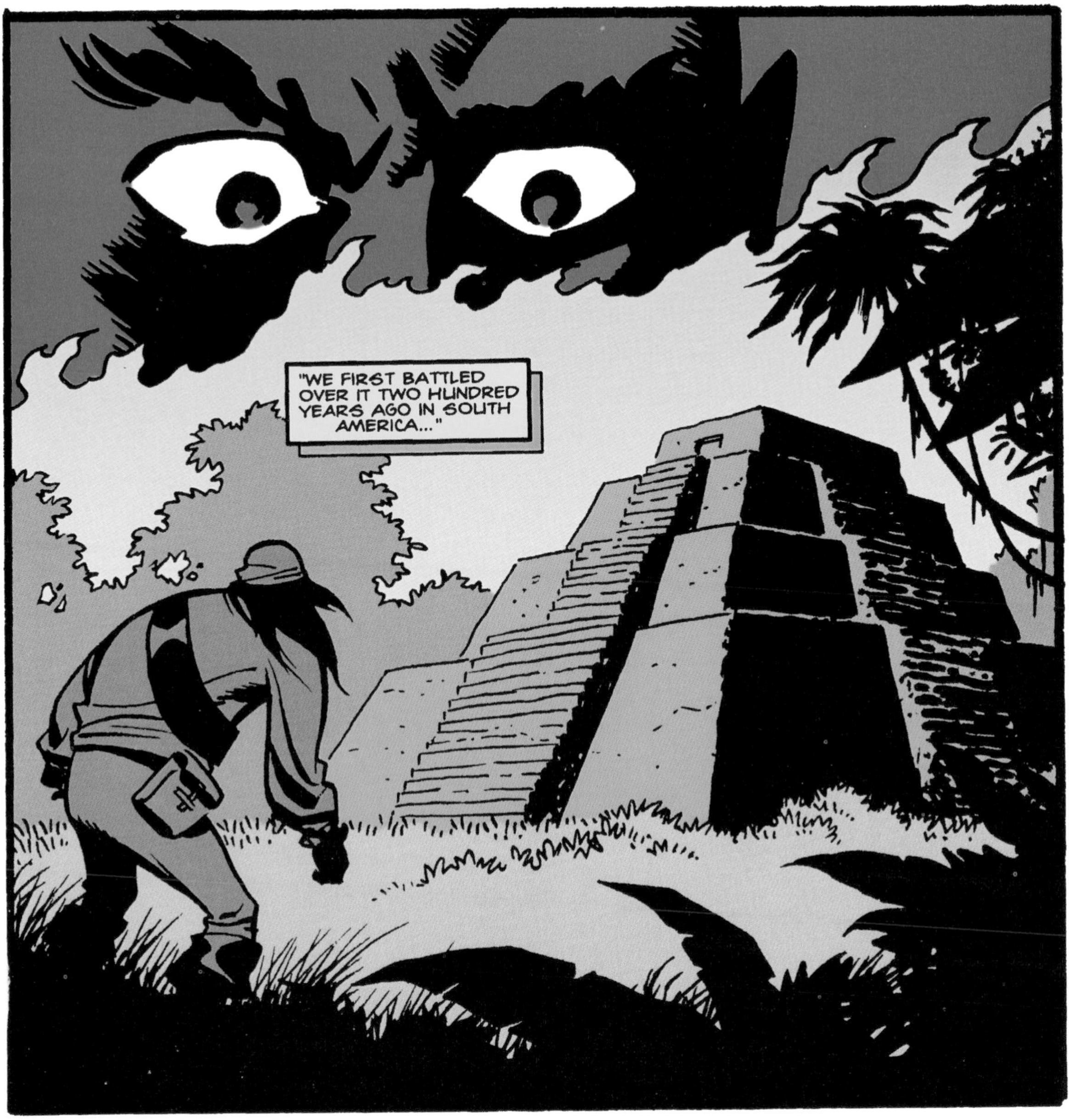
"WE FIRST BATTLED OVER IT TWO HUNDRED YEARS AGO IN SOUTH AMERICA..."

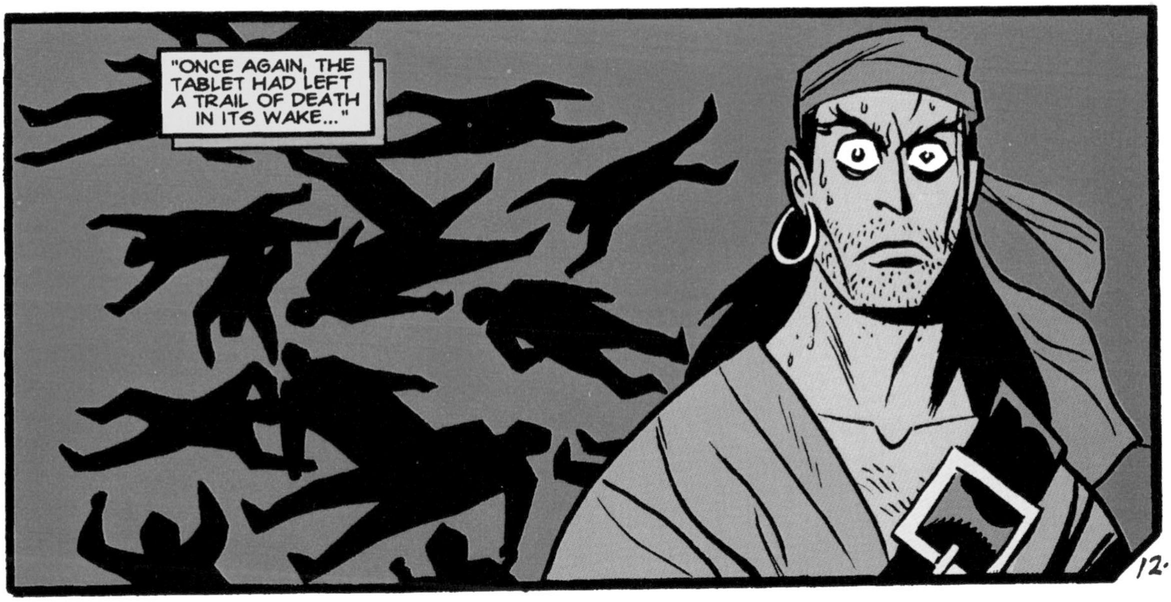
"ONCE AGAIN, THE TABLET HAD LEFT A TRAIL OF DEATH IN ITS WAKE..."
12.

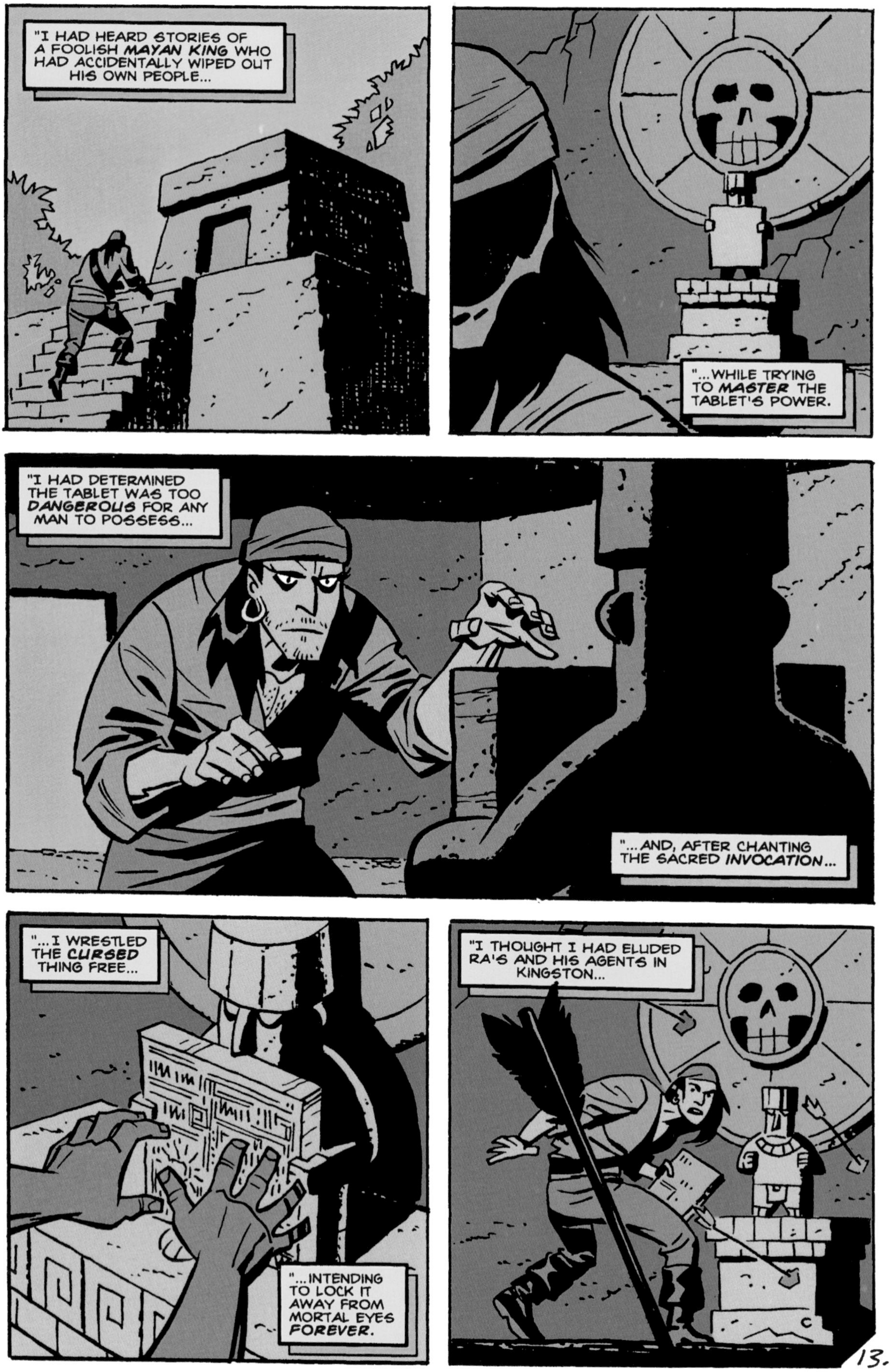
"I HAD HEARD STORIES OF A FOOLISH MAYAN KING WHO HAD ACCIDENTALLY WIPED OUT HIS OWN PEOPLE...
"...WHILE TRYING TO MASTER THE TABLET'S POWER.
"I HAD DETERMINED THE TABLET WAS TOO DANGEROUS FOR ANY MAN TO POSSESS...
"...AND, AFTER CHANTING THE SACRED INVOCATION...
"...I WRESTLED THE CURSED THING FREE...
"...INTENDING TO LOCK IT AWAY FROM MORTAL EYES FOREVER.
"I THOUGHT I HAD ELUDED RA'S AND HIS AGENTS IN KINGSTON...
13.

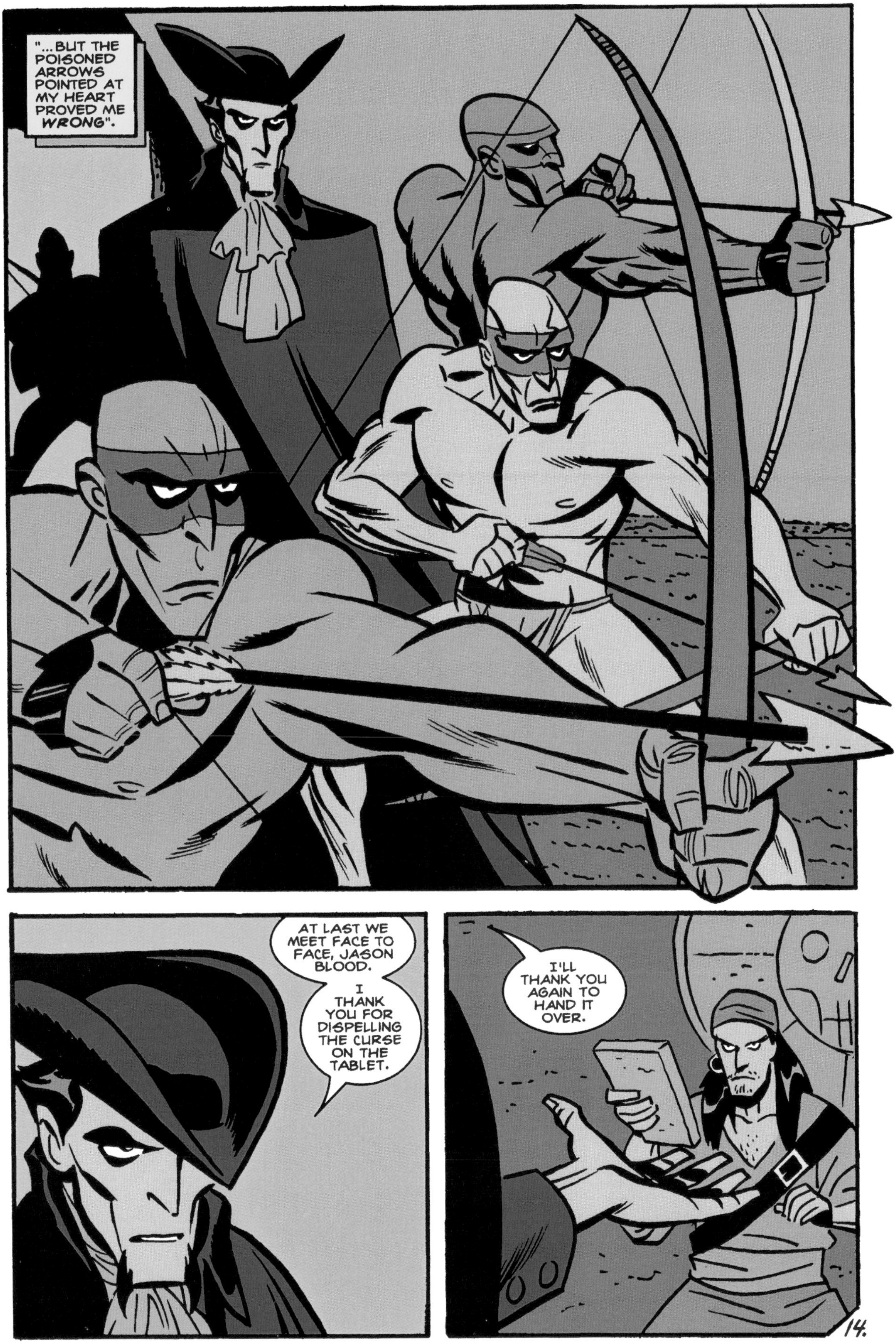
"...BUT THE POISONED ARROWS POINTED AT MY HEART PROVED ME *WRONG*".
AT LAST WE MEET FACE TO FACE, JASON BLOOD.
I THANK YOU FOR DISPELLING THE CURSE ON THE TABLET.
I'LL THANK YOU AGAIN TO HAND IT OVER.
14.

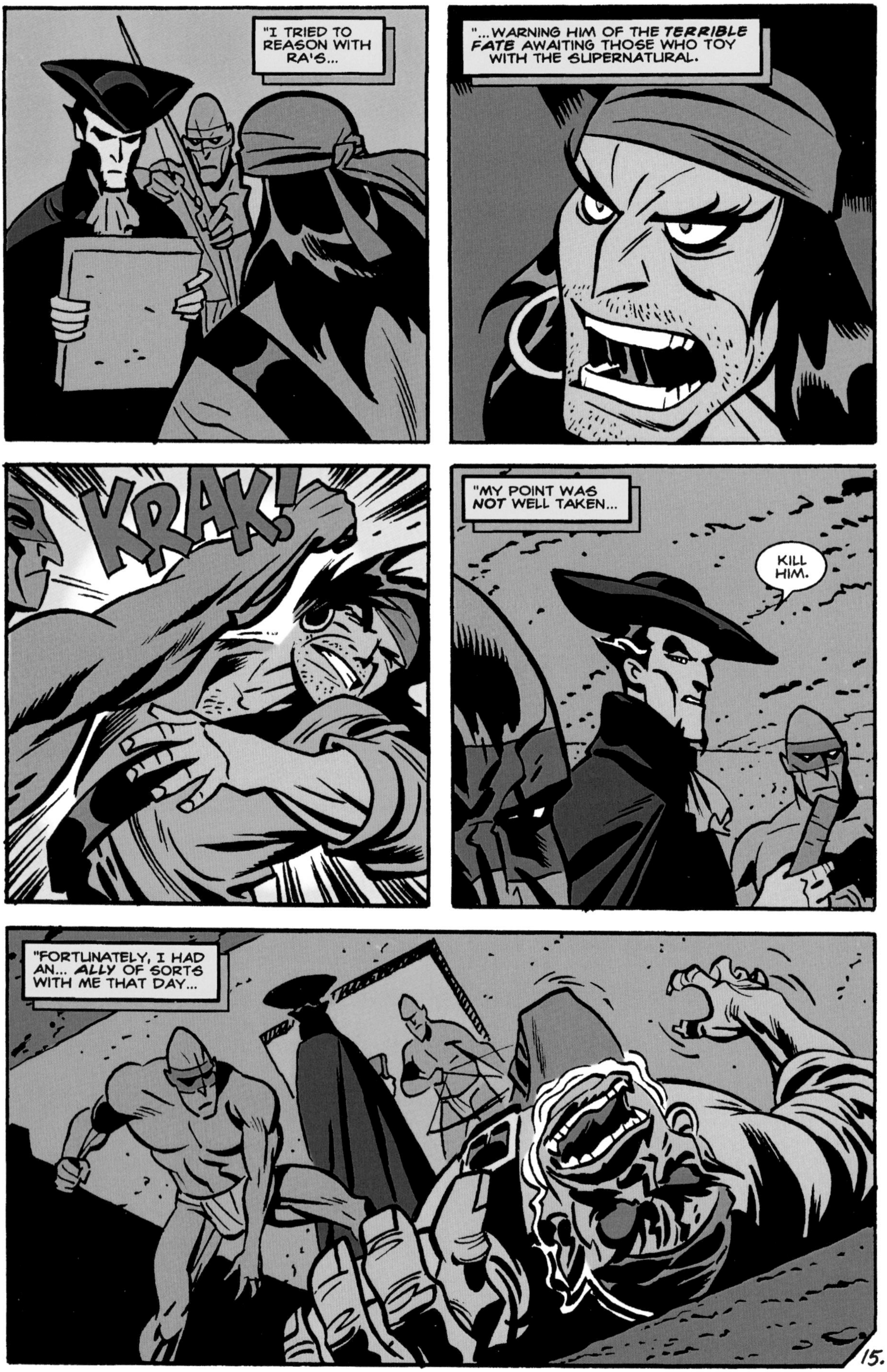
"I TRIED TO REASON WITH RA'S...
"...WARNING HIM OF THE TERRIBLE FATE AWAITING THOSE WHO TOY WITH THE SUPERNATURAL.
KRAK!
"MY POINT WAS NOT WELL TAKEN...
KILL HIM.
"FORTUNATELY, I HAD AN... ALLY OF SORTS WITH ME THAT DAY...
15.

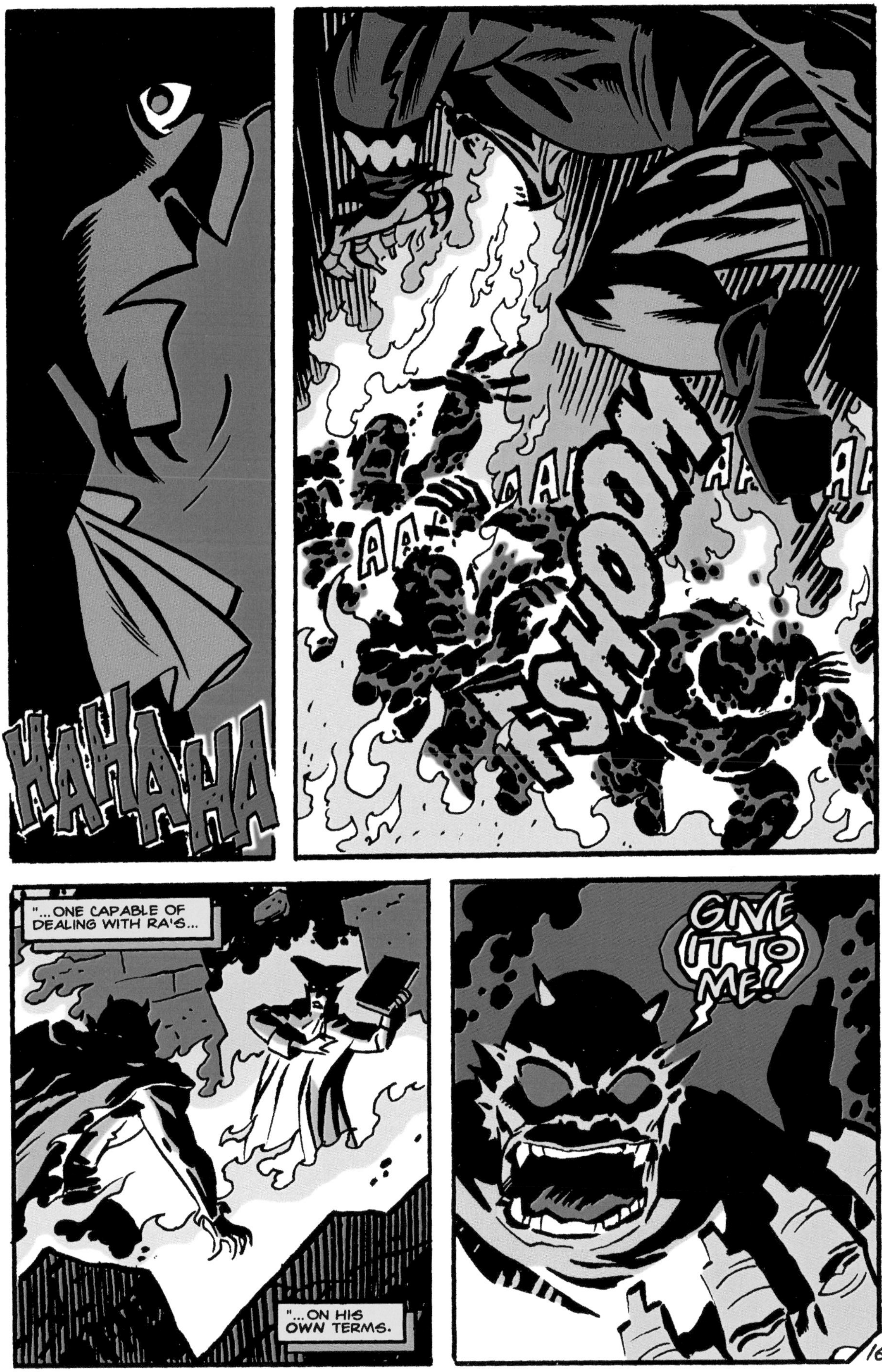
HAHAHA
AAA
AA
AA
FSHOOM
AA
"...ONE CAPABLE OF DEALING WITH RA'S...
"...ON HIS OWN TERMS.
GIVE IT TO ME!
16.

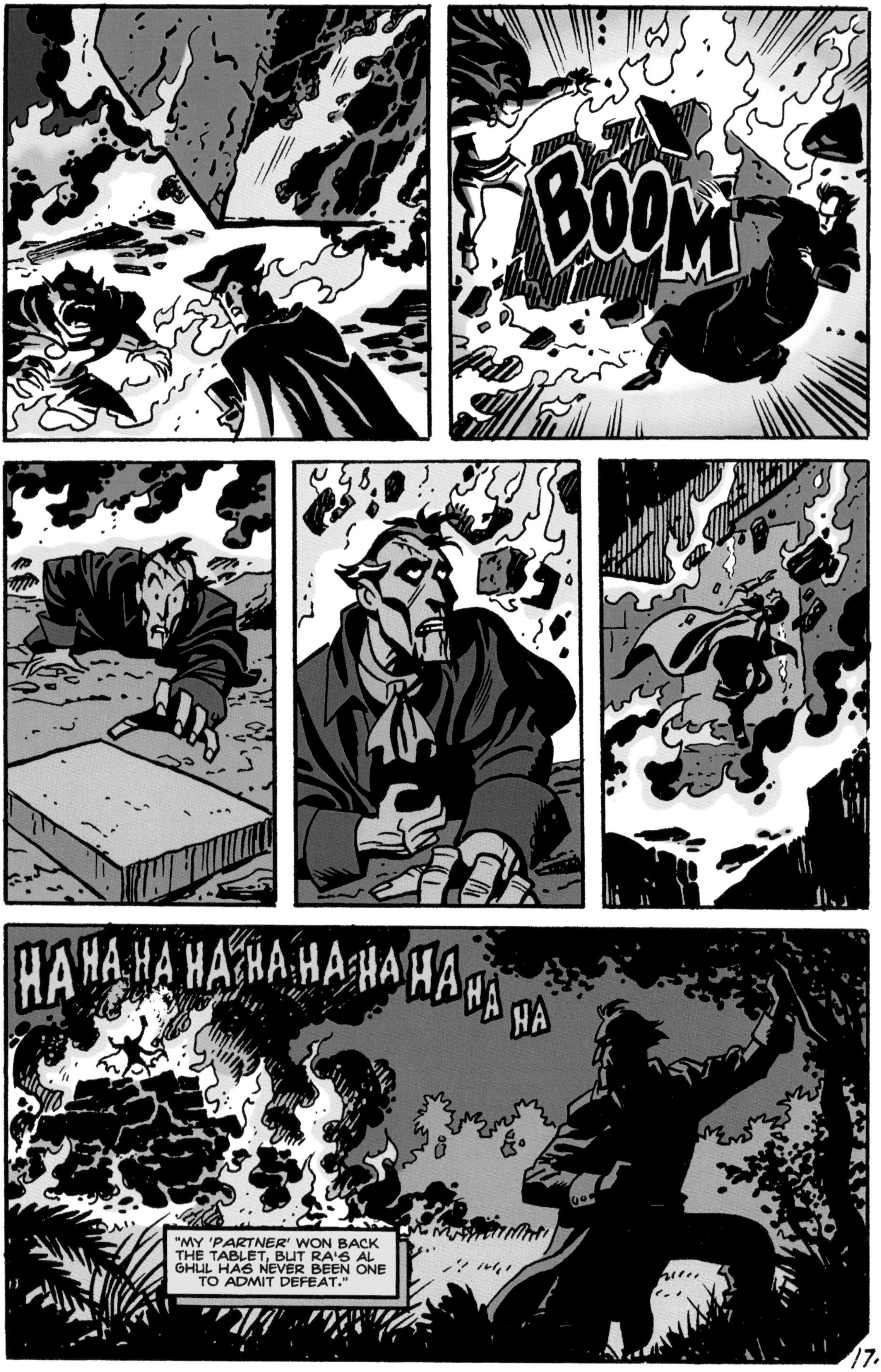
BOOM
HA HA HA HA HA HA HA HA HA HA HA HA
"MY 'PARTNER' WON BACK THE TABLET, BUT RA'S AL GHUL HAS NEVER BEEN ONE TO ADMIT DEFEAT."
17.

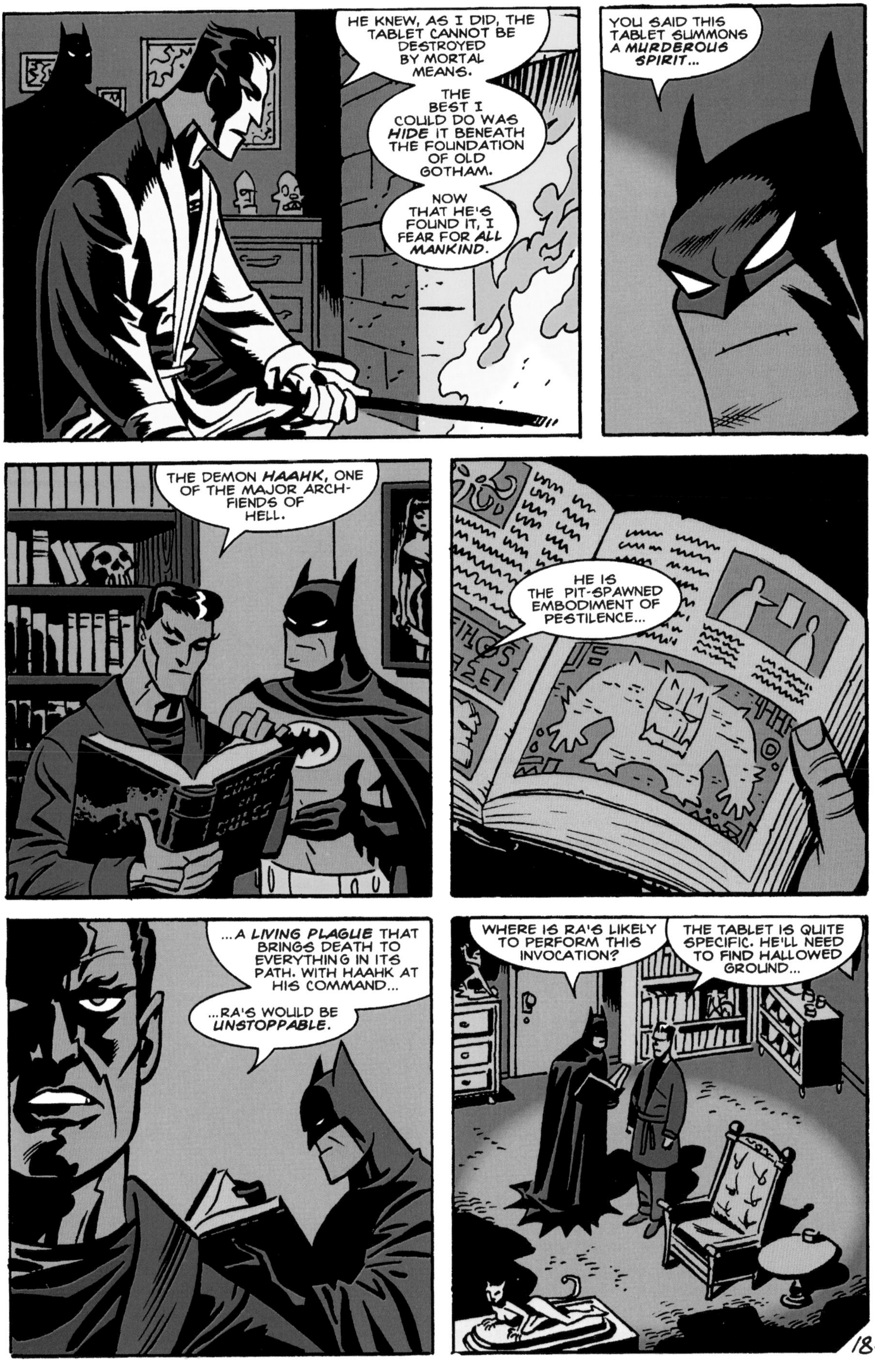
HE KNEW, AS I DID, THE TABLET CANNOT BE DESTROYED BY MORTAL MEANS.
THE BEST I COULD DO WAS HIDE IT BENEATH THE FOUNDATION OF OLD GOTHAM.
NOW THAT HE'S FOUND IT, I FEAR FOR ALL MANKIND.
YOU SAID THIS TABLET SUMMONS A MURDEROUS SPIRIT...
THE DEMON HAAHK, ONE OF THE MAJOR ARCH-FIENDS OF HELL.
HE IS THE PIT-SPAWNED EMBODIMENT OF PESTILENCE...
...A LIVING PLAGUE THAT BRINGS DEATH TO EVERYTHING IN ITS PATH. WITH HAAHK AT HIS COMMAND...
...RA'S WOULD BE UNSTOPPABLE.
WHERE IS RA'S LIKELY TO PERFORM THIS INVOCATION?
THE TABLET IS QUITE SPECIFIC. HE'LL NEED TO FIND HALLOWED GROUND...
18.

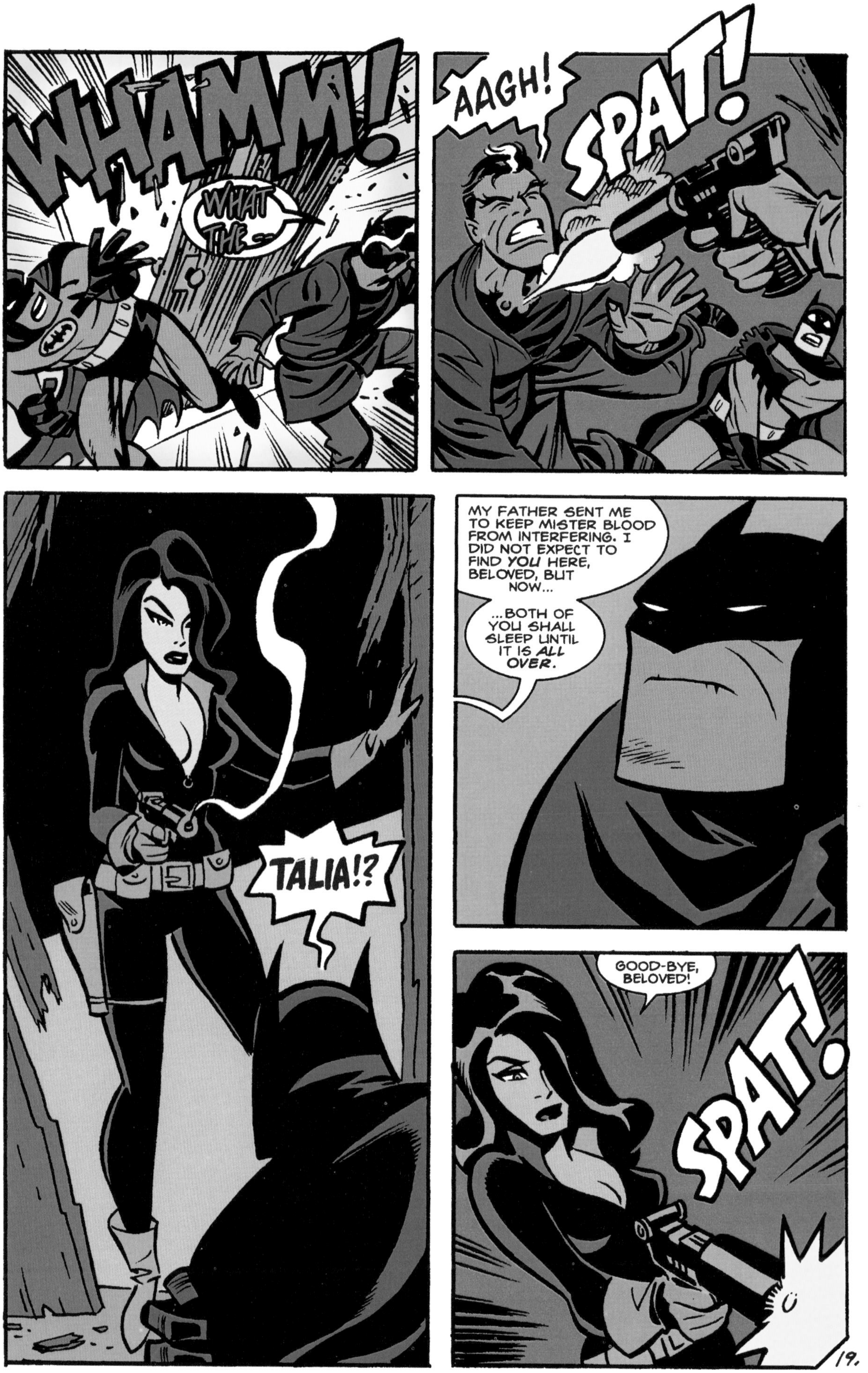
WHAMM!
WHAT THE--
AAGH!
SPAT!
TALIA!?
MY FATHER SENT ME TO KEEP MISTER BLOOD FROM INTERFERING. I DID NOT EXPECT TO FIND YOU HERE, BELOVED, BUT NOW...
...BOTH OF YOU SHALL SLEEP UNTIL IT IS ALL OVER.
GOOD-BYE, BELOVED!
SPAT!
19.

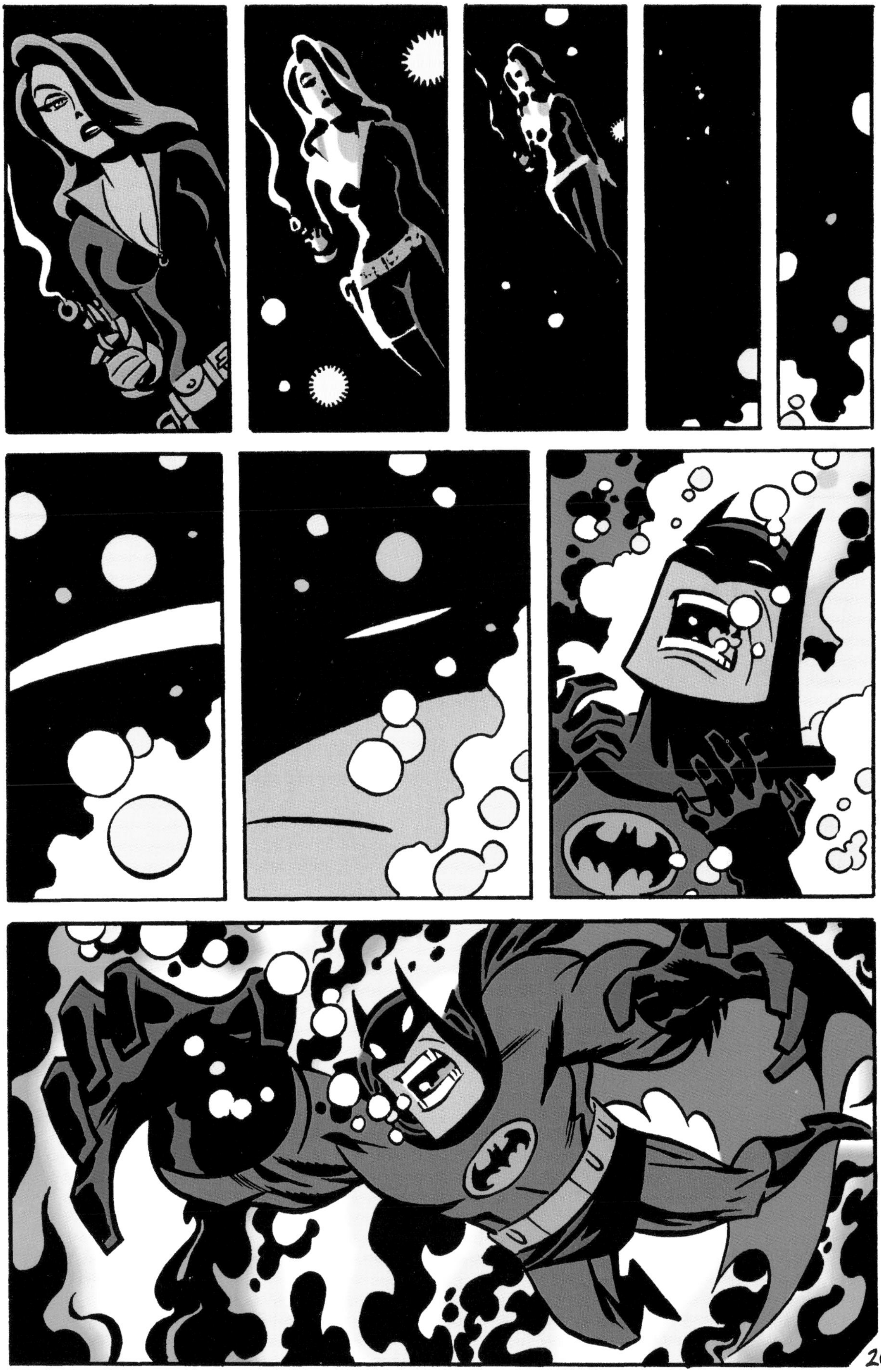
20.

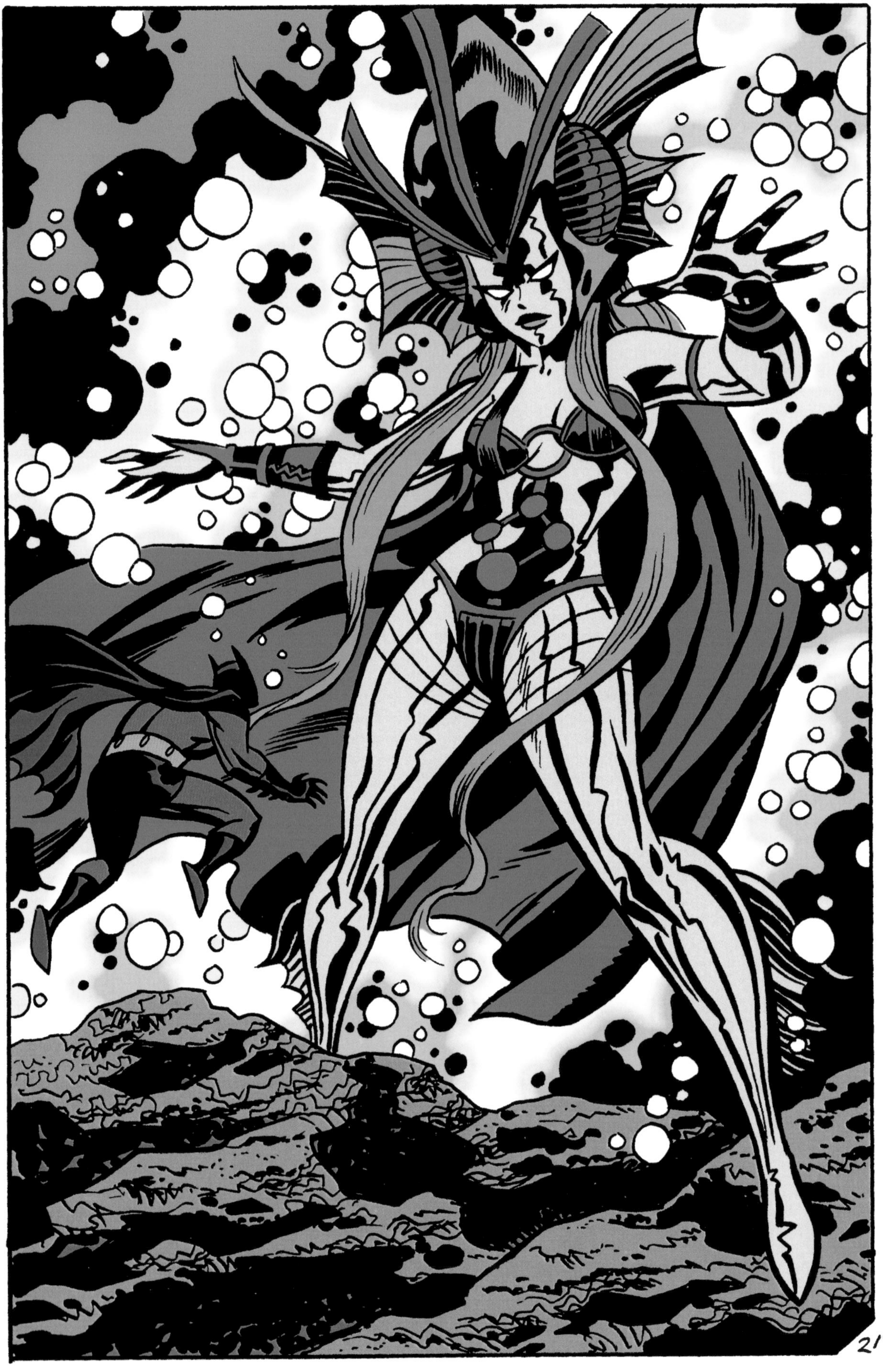
21

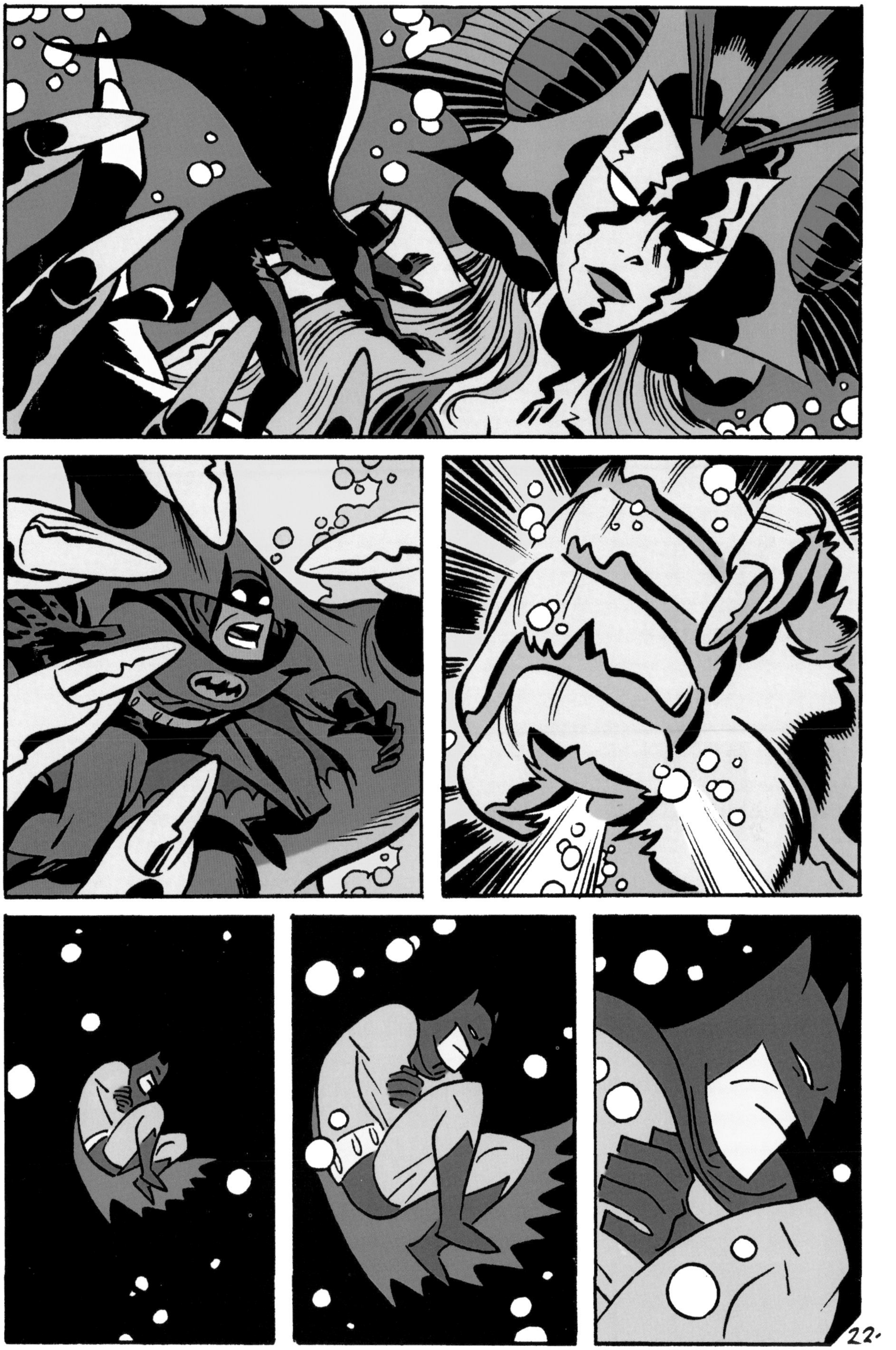
22.

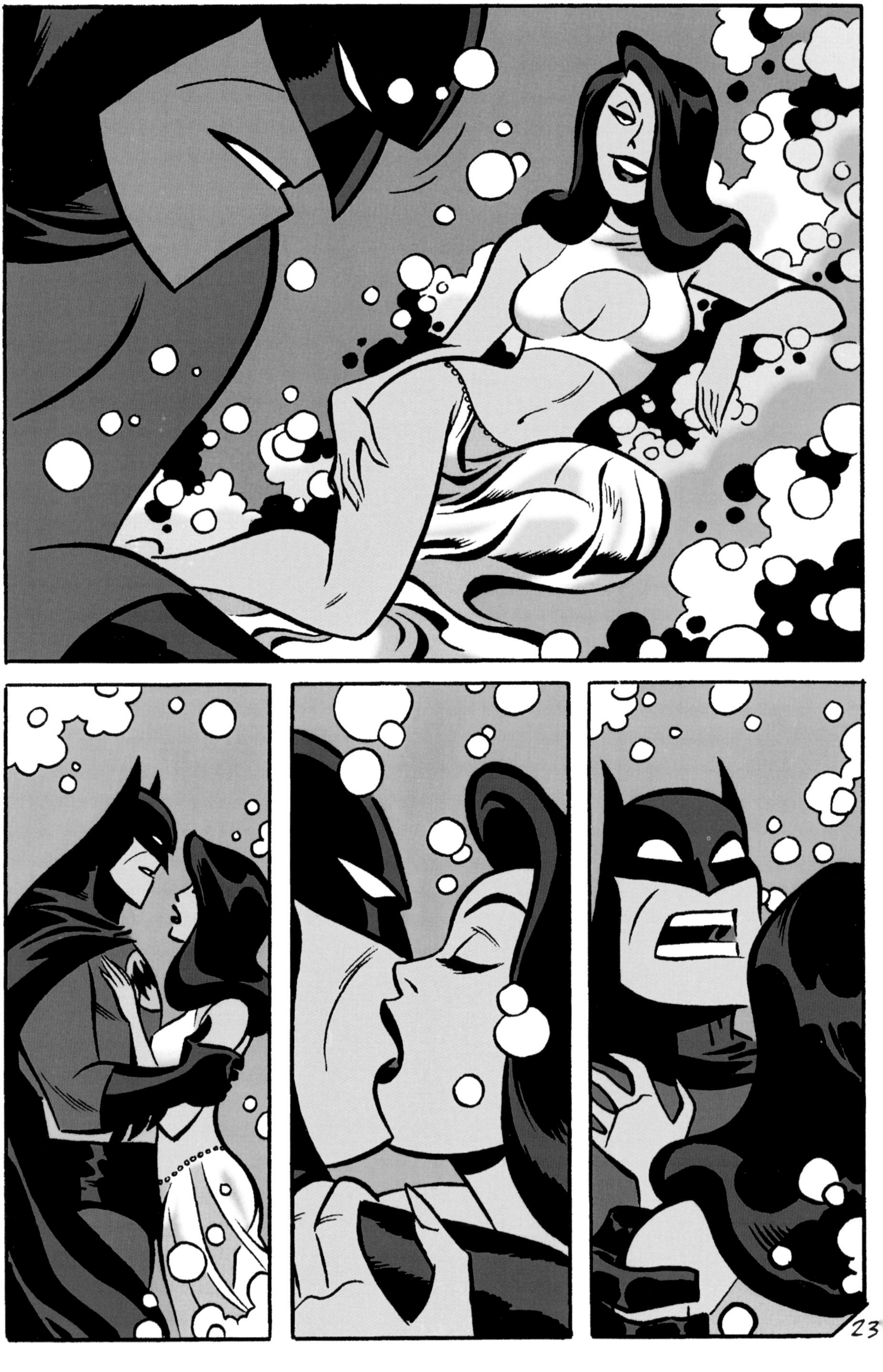
23

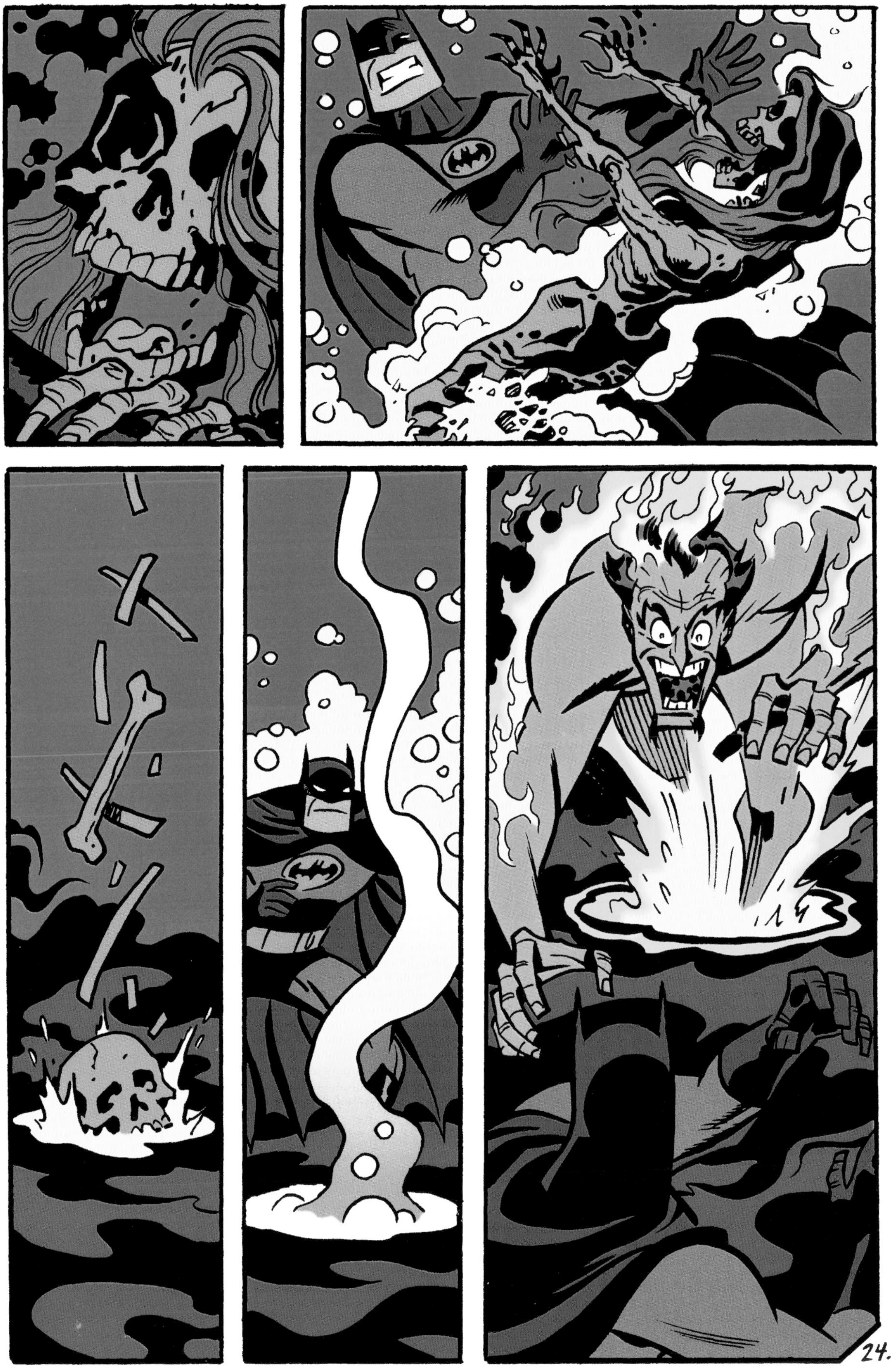
24.

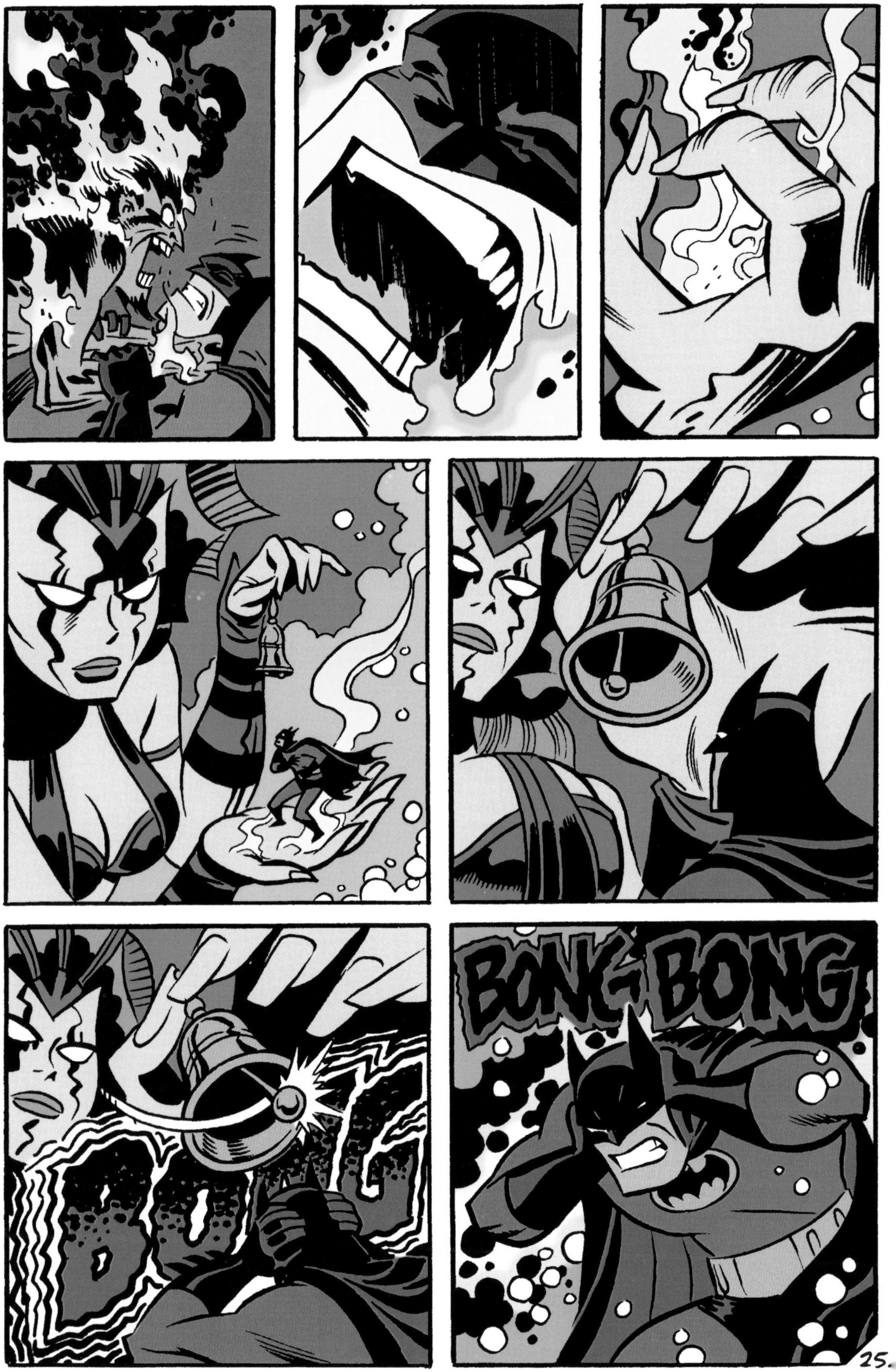
BONG BONG
25.

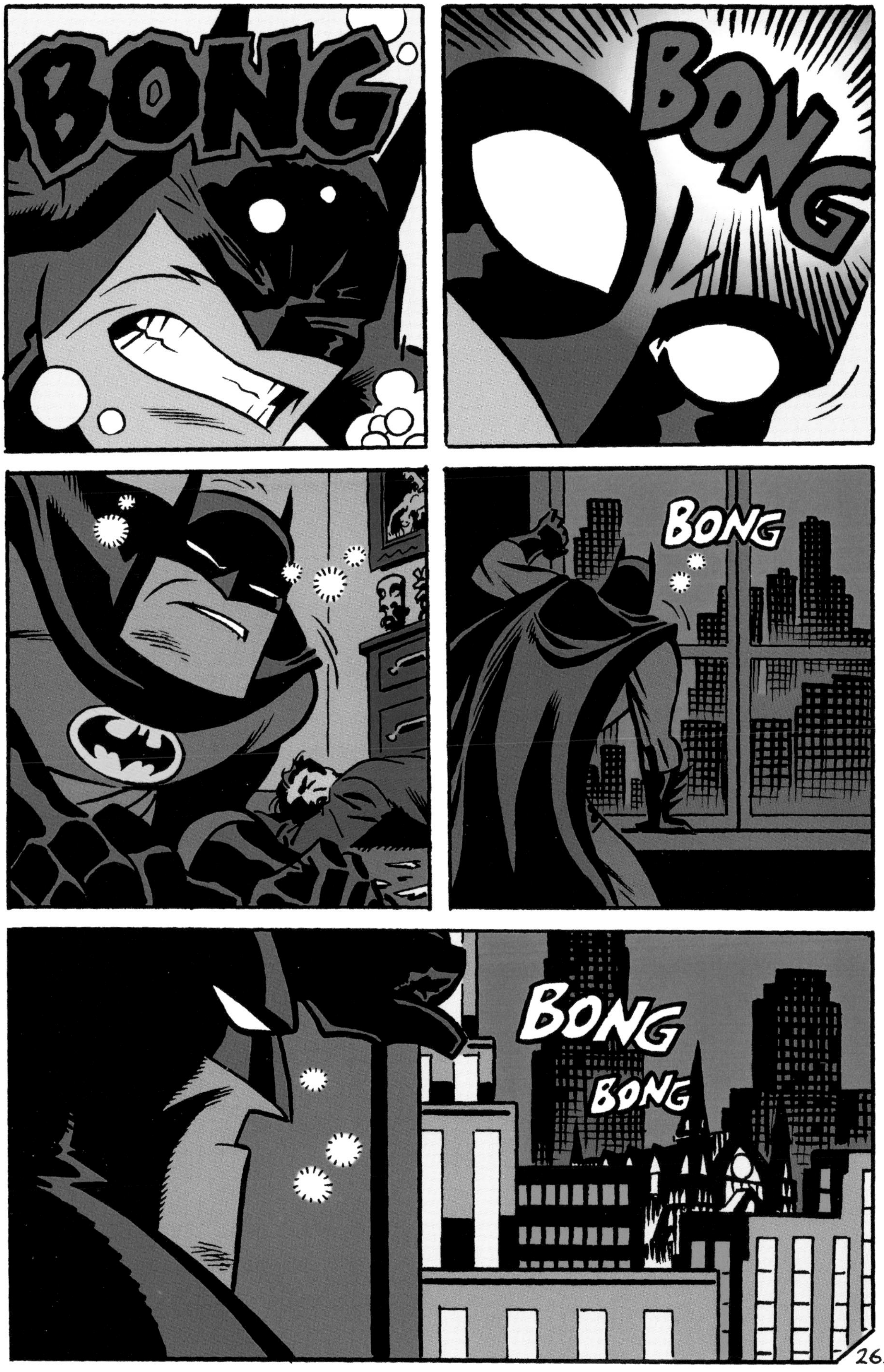
BONG
BONG
BONG
BONG
BONG
26.

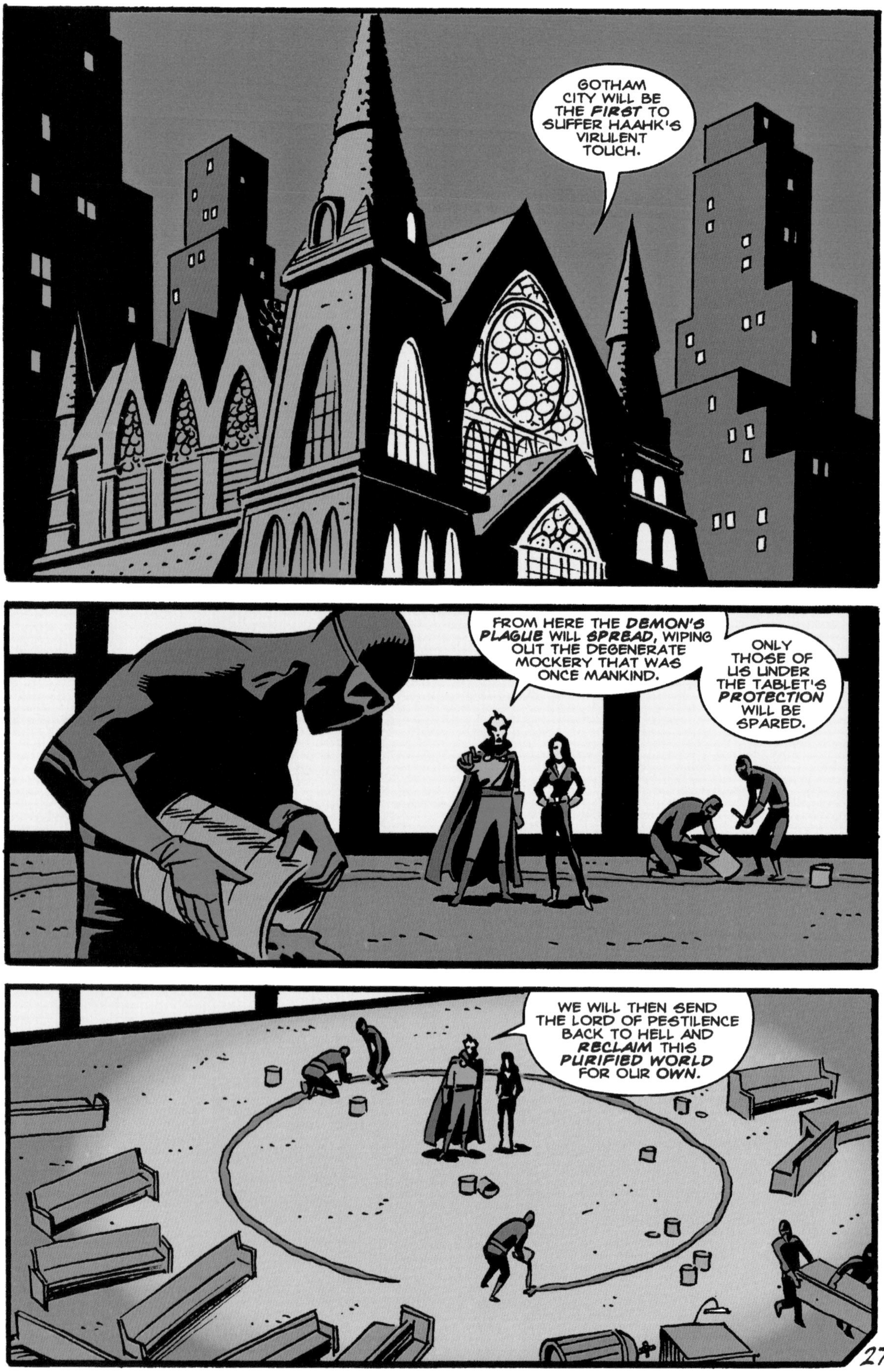
GOTHAM CITY WILL BE THE FIRST TO SUFFER HAAHK'S VIRULENT TOUCH.
FROM HERE THE DEMON'S PLAGUE WILL SPREAD, WIPING OUT THE DEGENERATE MOCKERY THAT WAS ONCE MANKIND.
ONLY THOSE OF US UNDER THE TABLET'S PROTECTION WILL BE SPARED.
WE WILL THEN SEND THE LORD OF PESTILENCE BACK TO HELL AND RECLAIM THIS PURIFIED WORLD FOR OUR OWN.
27.

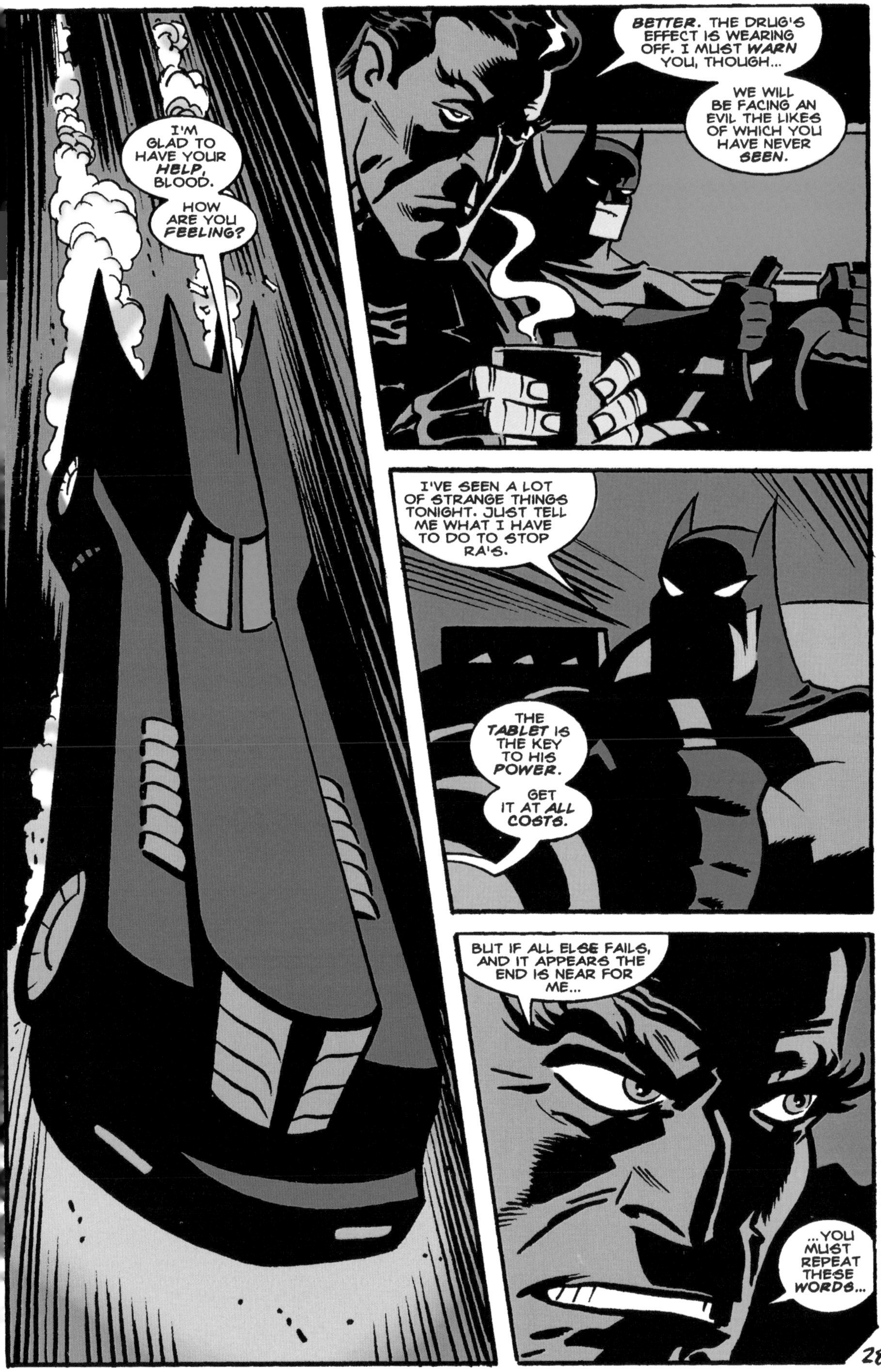

I'M GLAD TO HAVE YOUR HELP, BLOOD.
HOW ARE YOU FEELING?
BETTER. THE DRUG'S EFFECT IS WEARING OFF. I MUST WARN YOU, THOUGH...
WE WILL BE FACING AN EVIL THE LIKES OF WHICH YOU HAVE NEVER SEEN.
I'VE SEEN A LOT OF STRANGE THINGS TONIGHT. JUST TELL ME WHAT I HAVE TO DO TO STOP RA'S.
THE TABLET IS THE KEY TO HIS POWER.
GET IT AT ALL COSTS.
BUT IF ALL ELSE FAILS, AND IT APPEARS THE END IS NEAR FOR ME...
...YOU MUST REPEAT THESE WORDS...
28.

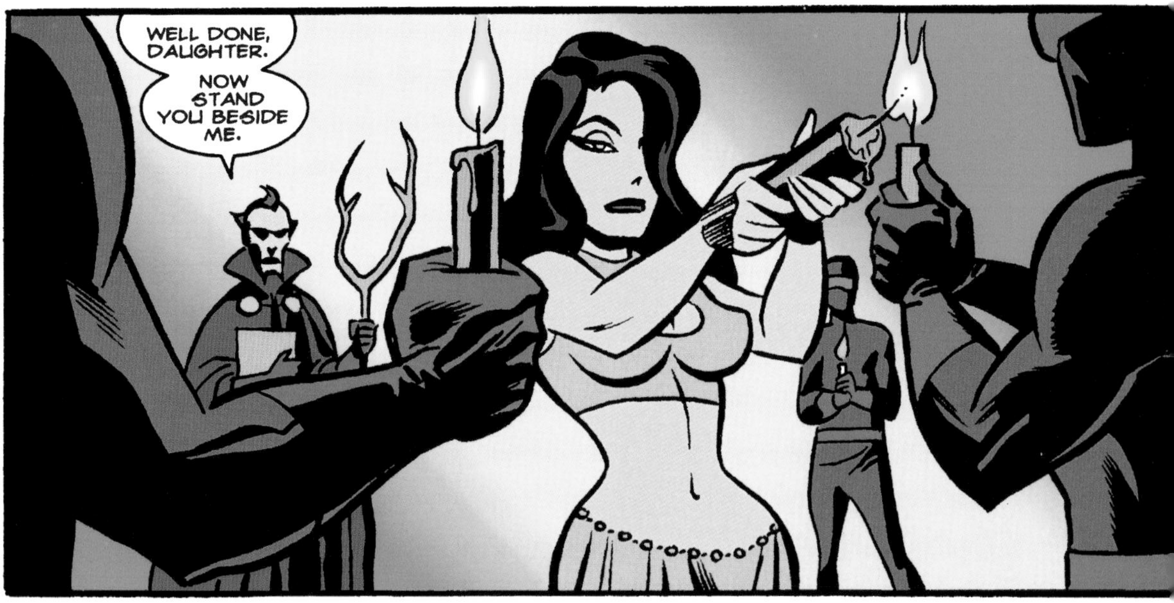
WELL DONE, DAUGHTER.
NOW STAND YOU BESIDE ME.

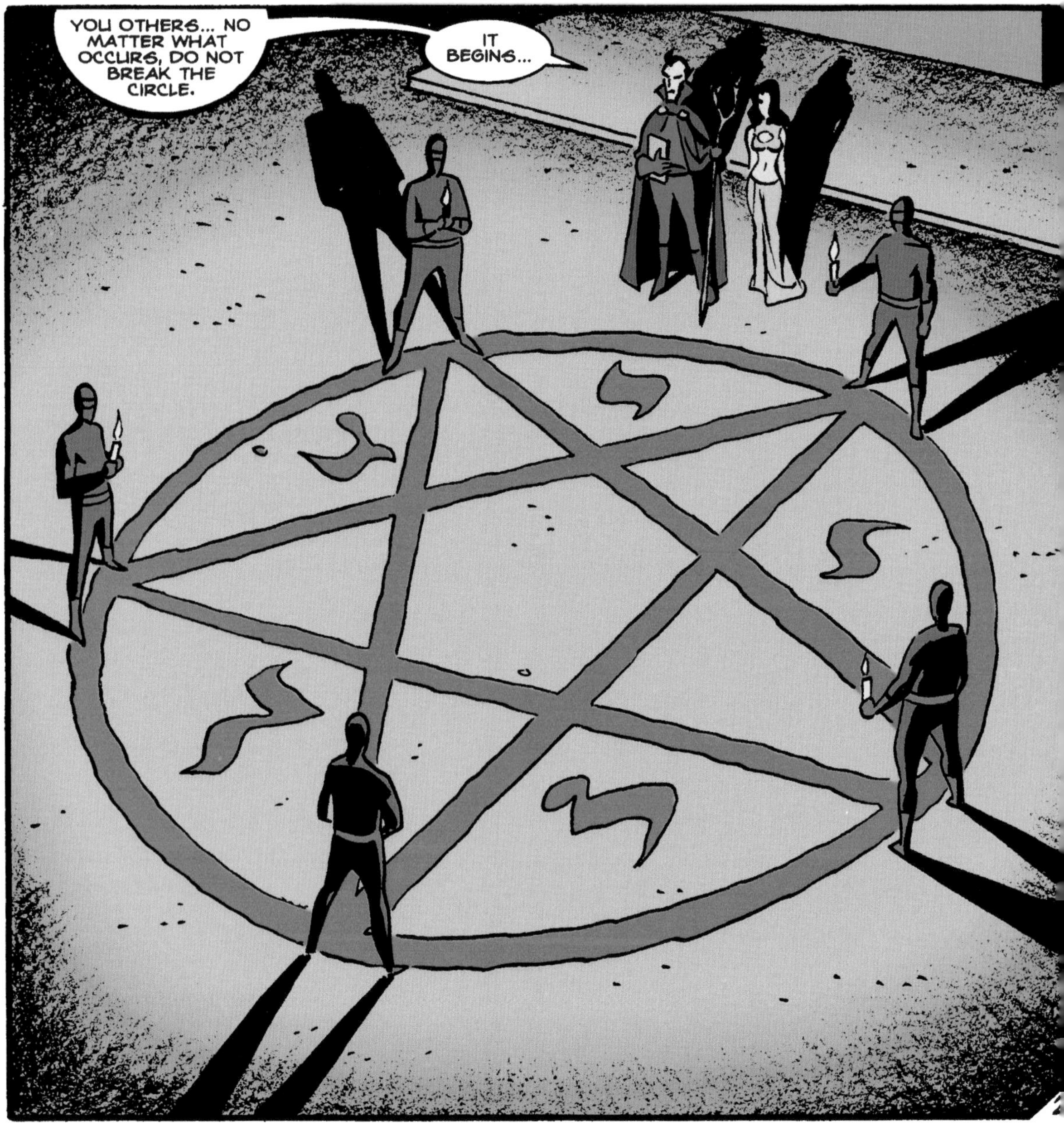
YOU OTHERS... NO MATTER WHAT OCCURS, DO NOT BREAK THE CIRCLE.
IT BEGINS...

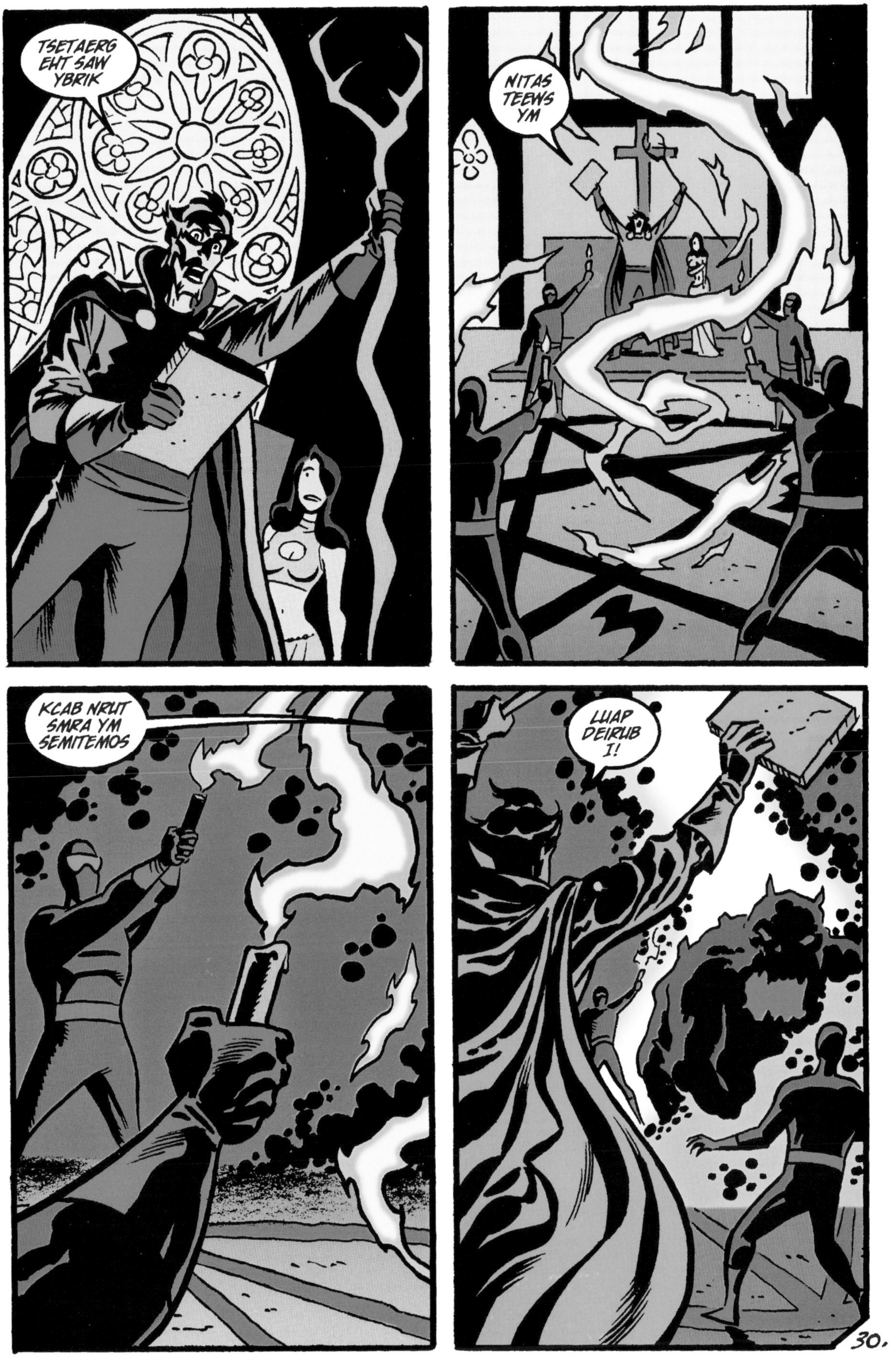
TSETAERG EHT SAW YBRIK
NITAS TEEWS YM
KCAB NRUT SMRA YM SEMITEMOS
LUAP DEIRUB I!
30.

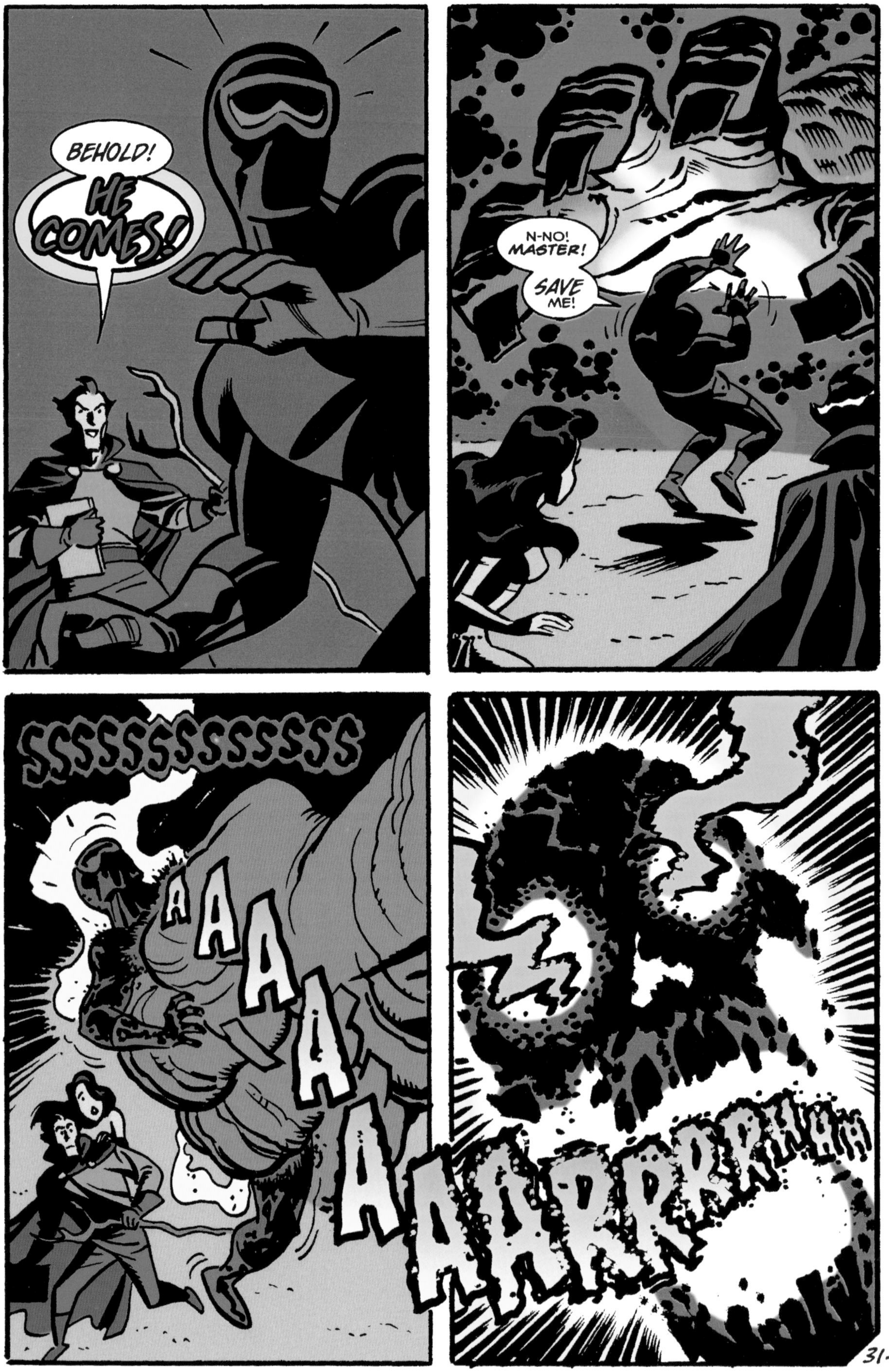
BEHOLD!
HE COMES!
N-NO! MASTER!
SAVE ME!
SSSSSSSSSSSSSS
AAAAAAARRRRHHH
31.

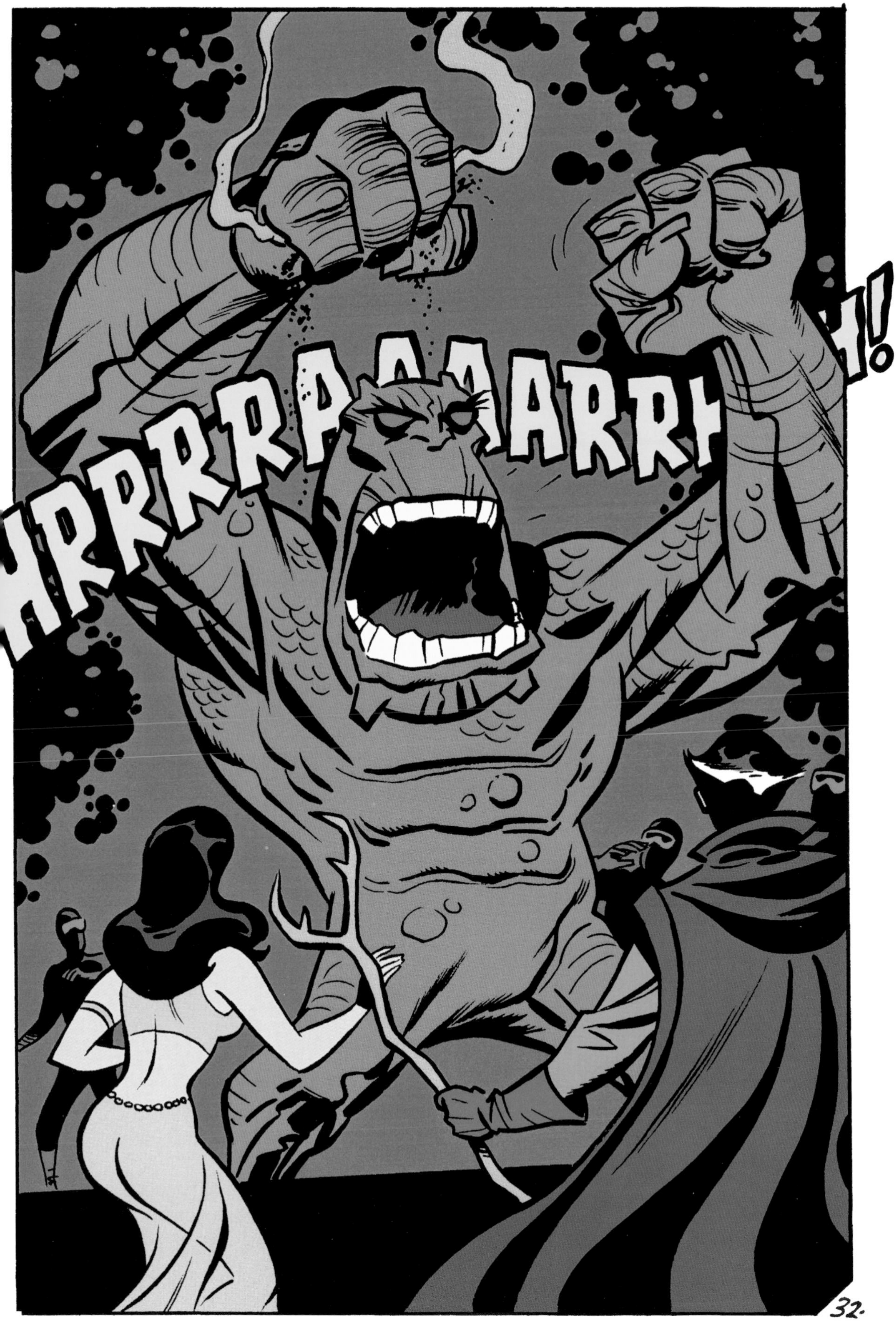
HRRRAAAAARRRH!
32.

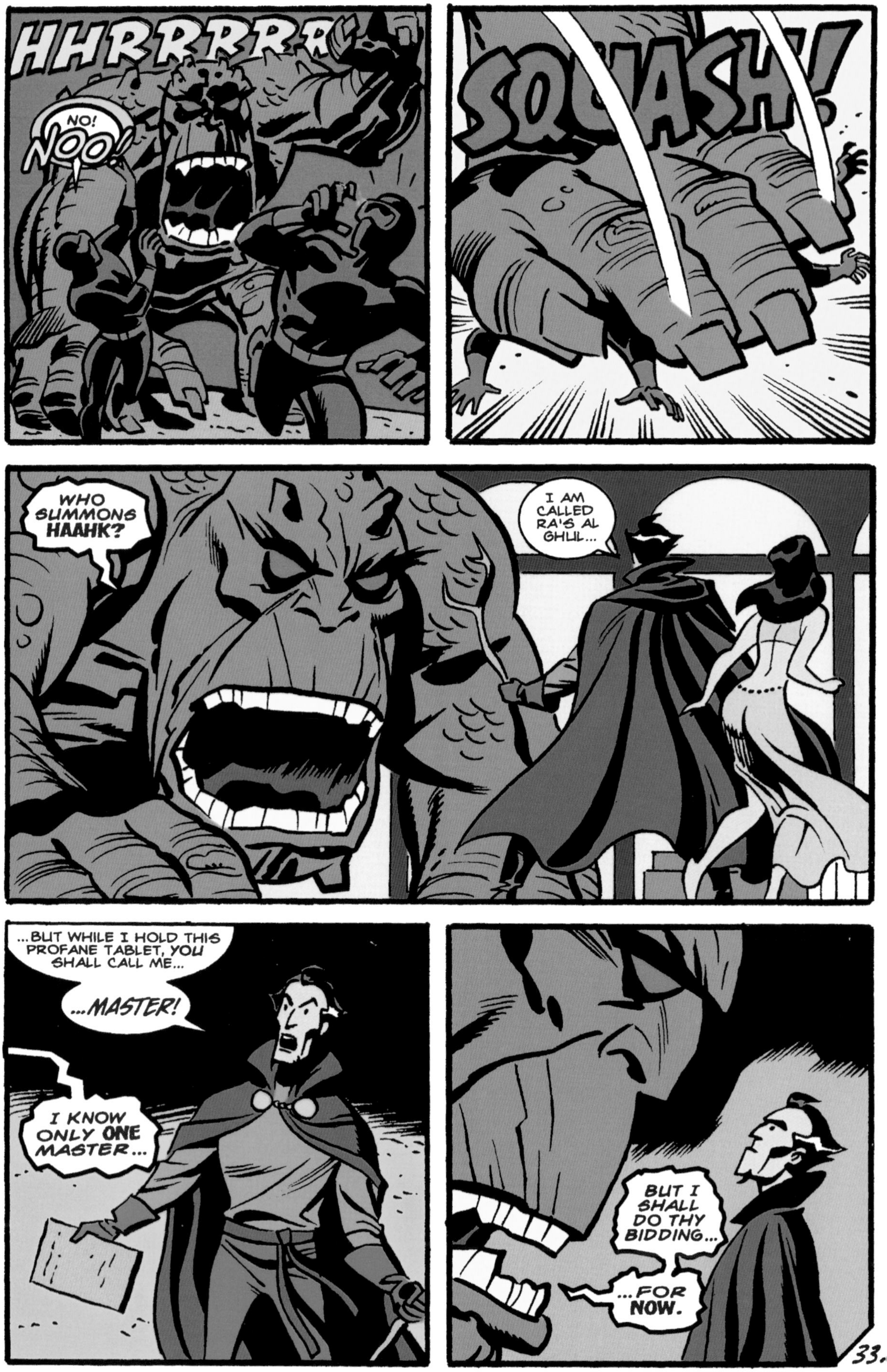
HHRRRRR
NO! NOO!
SQUASH!
WHO SUMMONS HAAHK?
I AM CALLED RA'S AL GHUL...
...BUT WHILE I HOLD THIS PROFANE TABLET, YOU SHALL CALL ME...
...MASTER!
I KNOW ONLY ONE MASTER...
BUT I SHALL DO THY BIDDING...
...FOR NOW.
33.

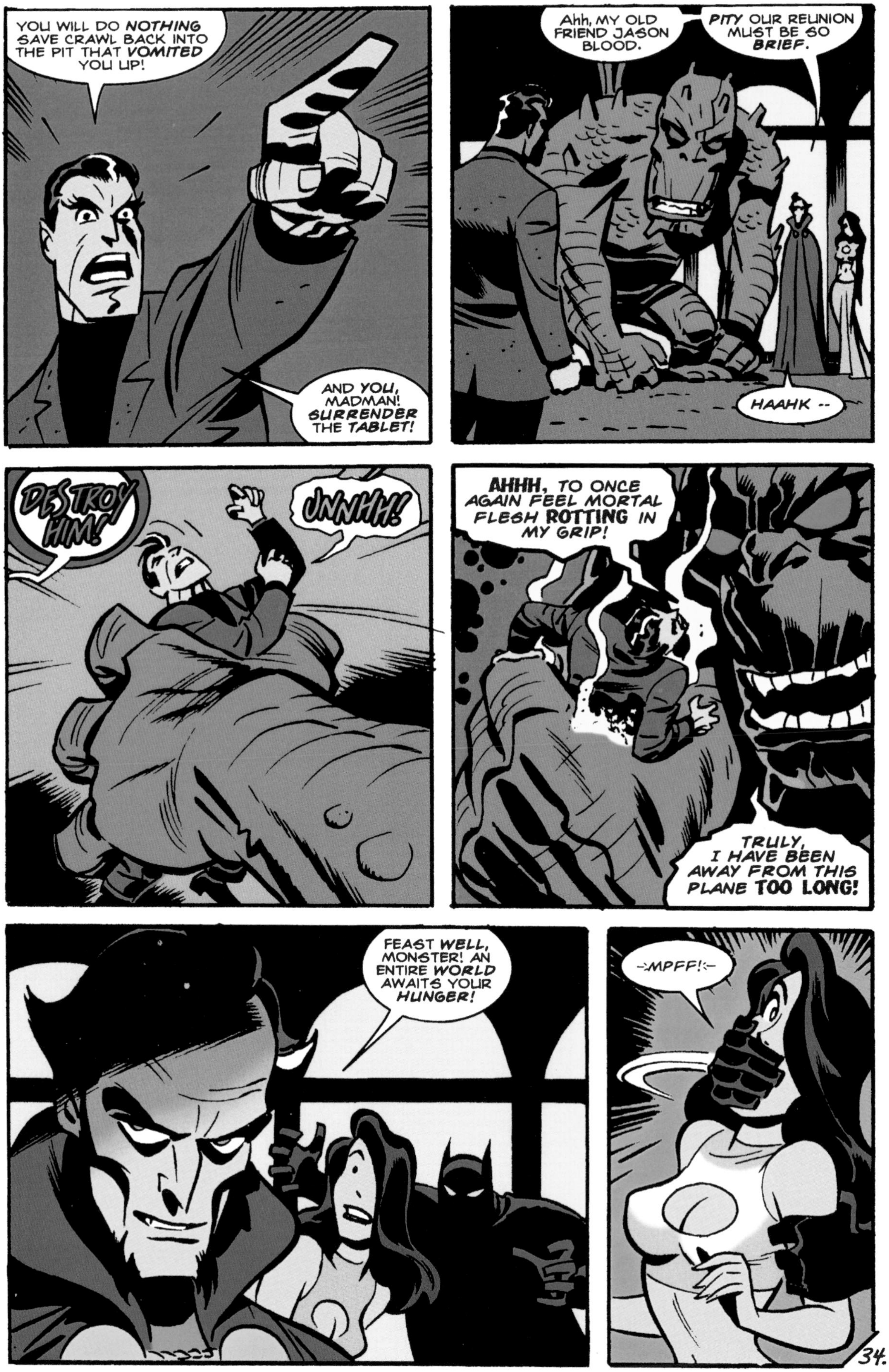
YOU WILL DO NOTHING SAVE CRAWL BACK INTO THE PIT THAT VOMITED YOU UP!
AND YOU, MADMAN! SURRENDER THE TABLET!
Ahh, MY OLD FRIEND JASON BLOOD.
PITY OUR REUNION MUST BE SO BRIEF.
HAAHK --
DESTROY HIM!
UNNHH!
AHHH, TO ONCE AGAIN FEEL MORTAL FLESH ROTTING IN MY GRIP!
TRULY, I HAVE BEEN AWAY FROM THIS PLANE TOO LONG!
FEAST WELL, MONSTER! AN ENTIRE WORLD AWAITS YOUR HUNGER!
-MPFF!-
34.

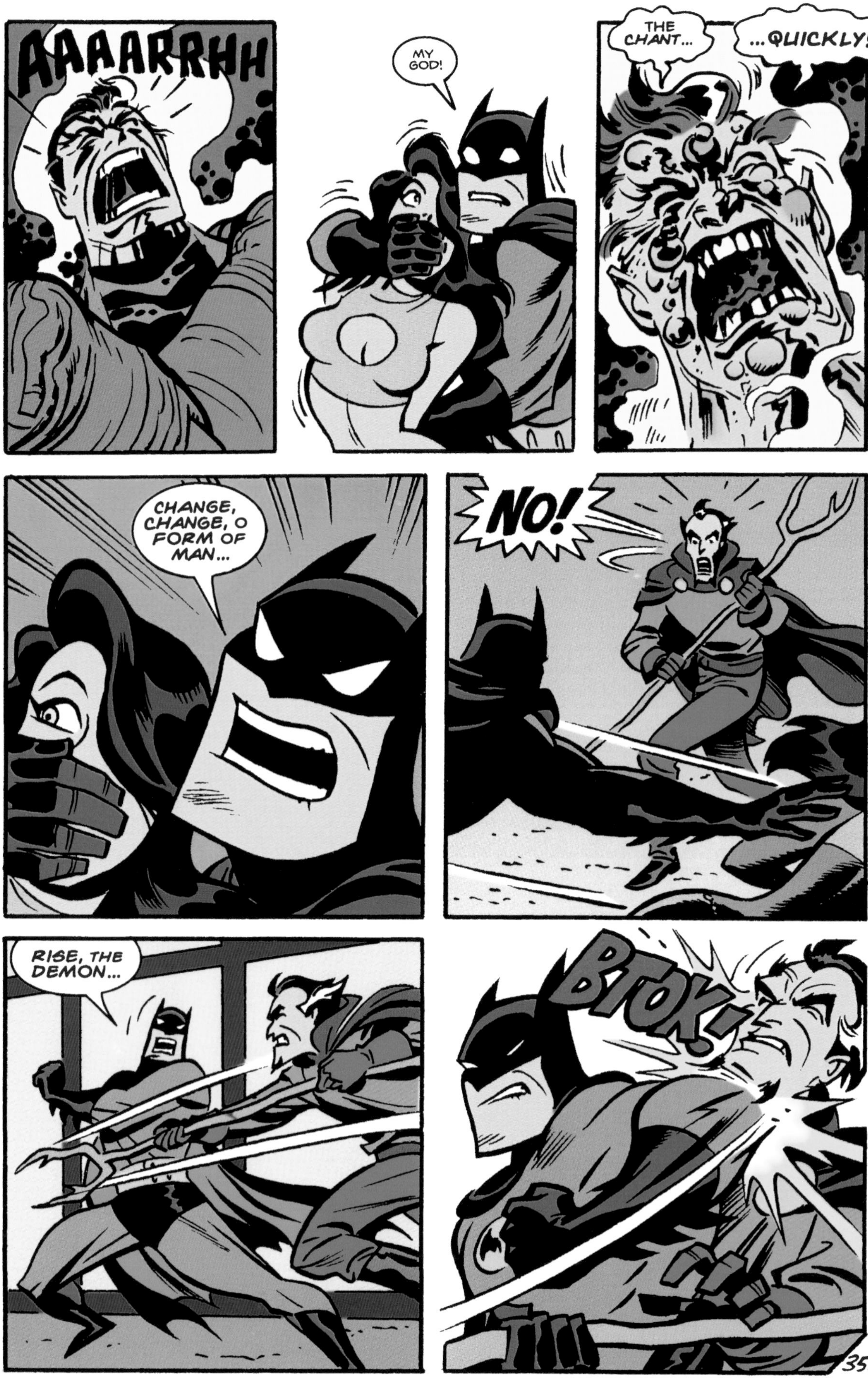
AAAARRHH
MY GOD!
THE CHANT...
...QUICKLY!
CHANGE, CHANGE, O FORM OF MAN...
NO!
RISE, THE DEMON...
BTOK!
35.

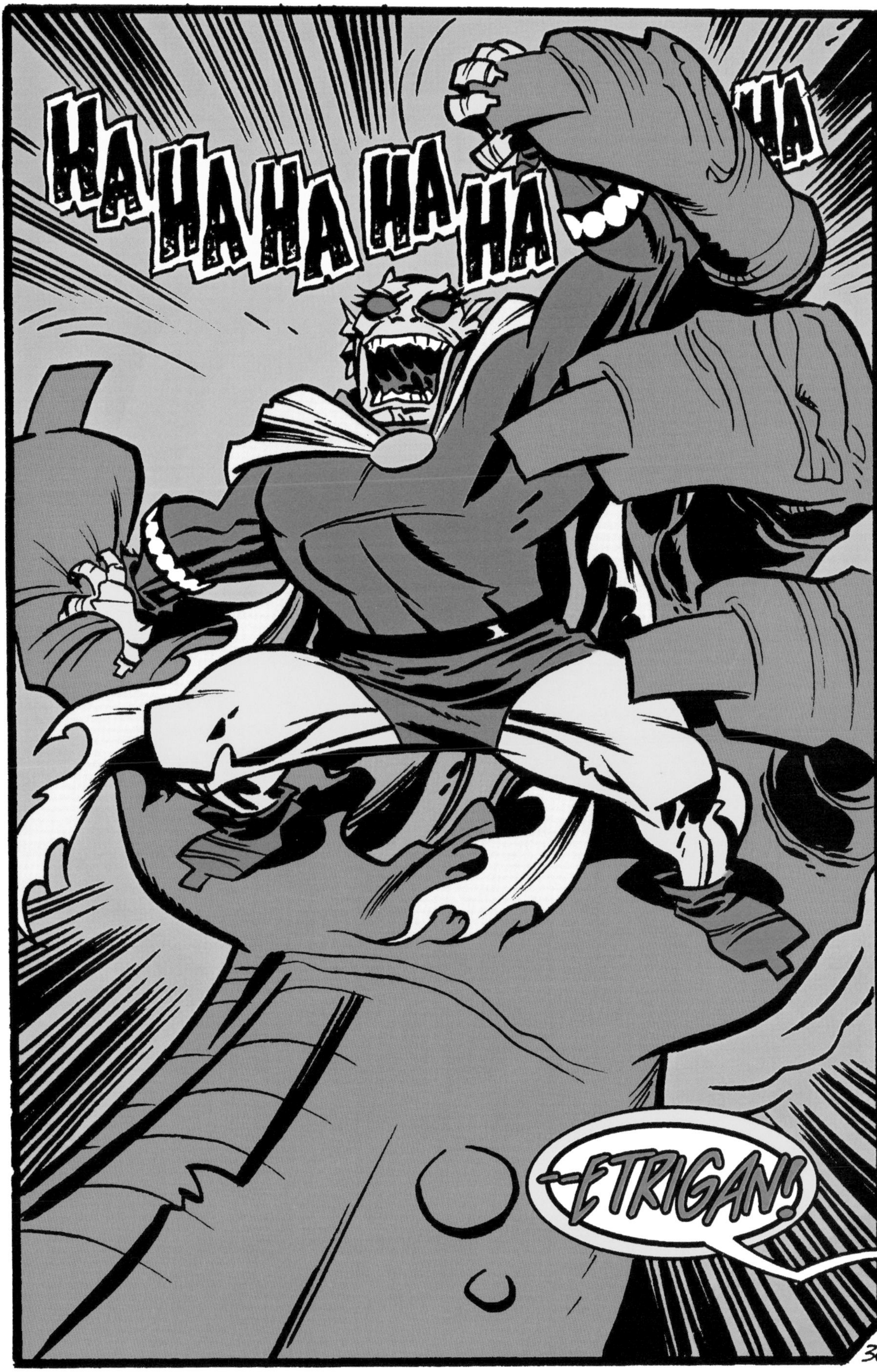
HA HA HA HA HA HA HA
-ETRIGAN!
36.

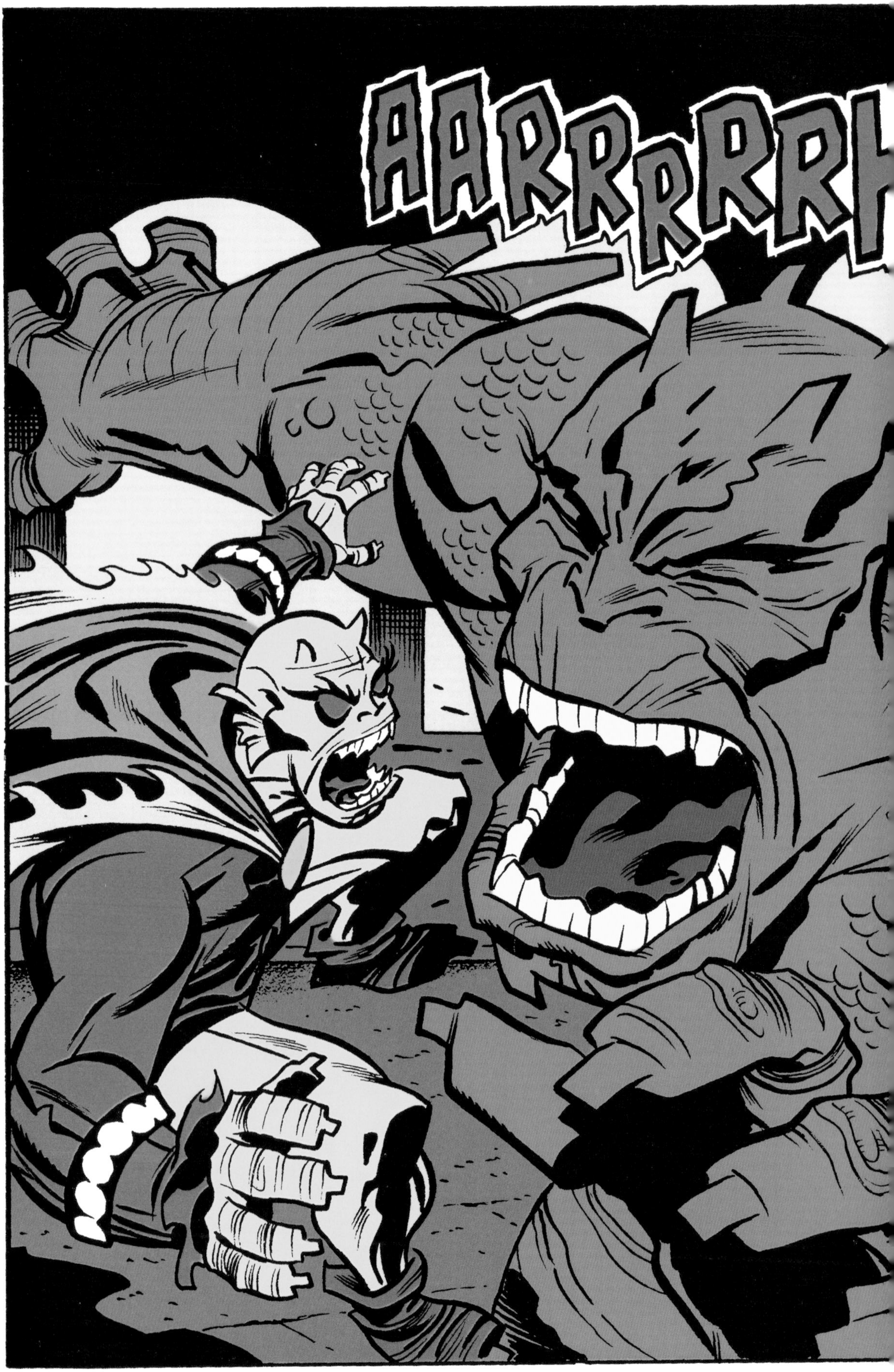
AARRRRR

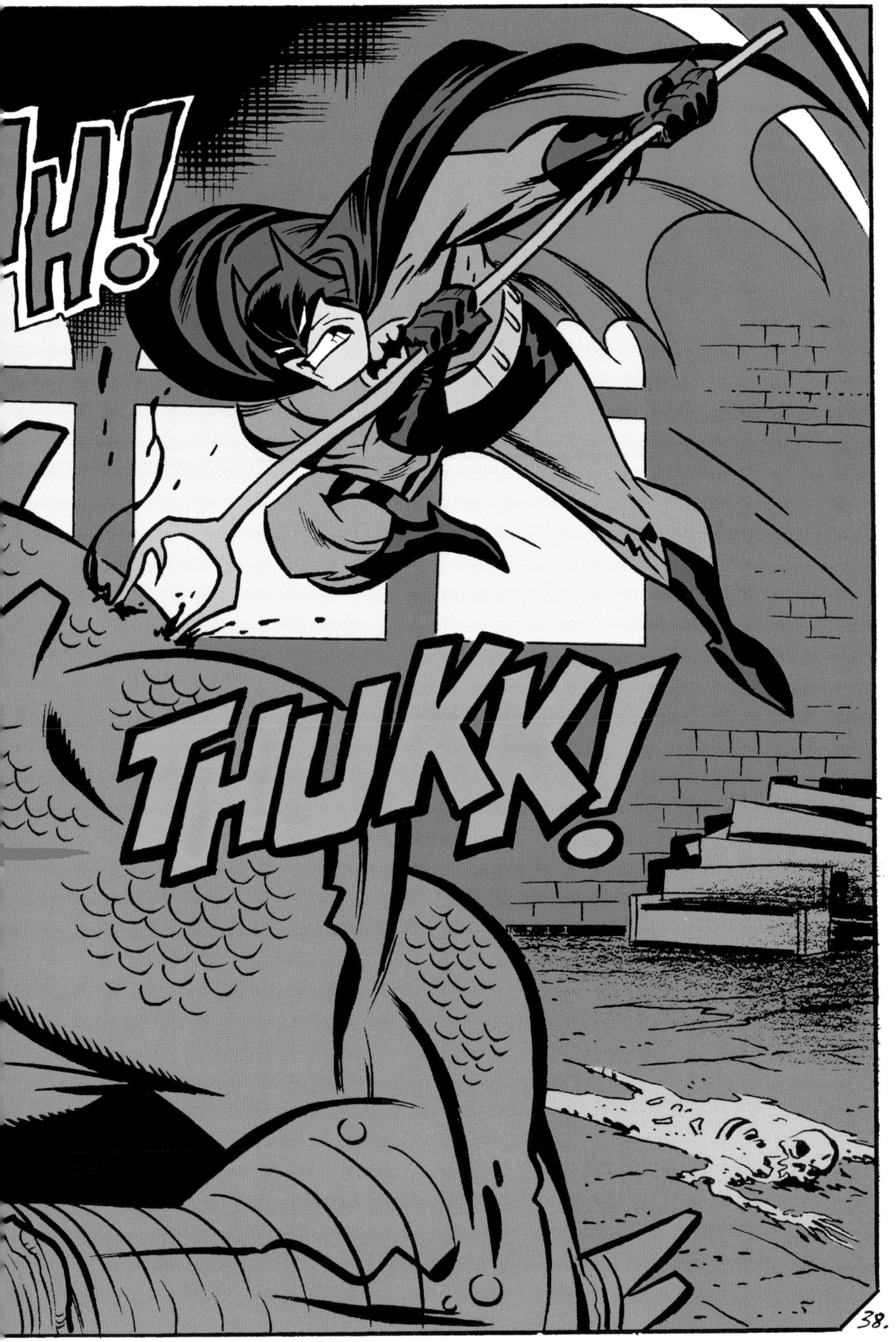
H!
THUKK!
38.

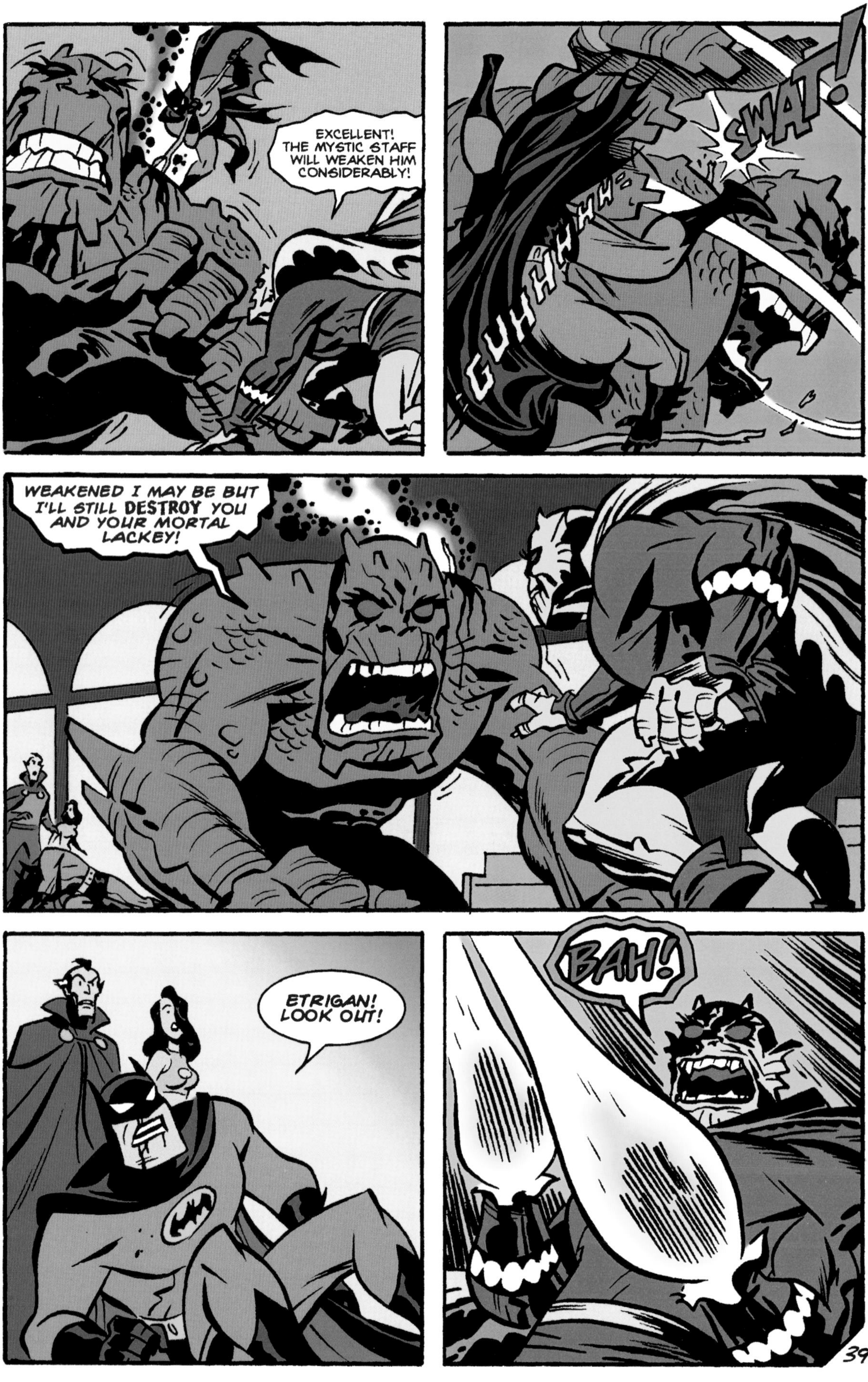
EXCELLENT! THE MYSTIC STAFF WILL WEAKEN HIM CONSIDERABLY!
GUHHHHHH-
SWAT!
WEAKENED I MAY BE BUT I'LL STILL DESTROY YOU AND YOUR MORTAL LACKEY!
ETRIGAN! LOOK OUT!
BAH!
39.

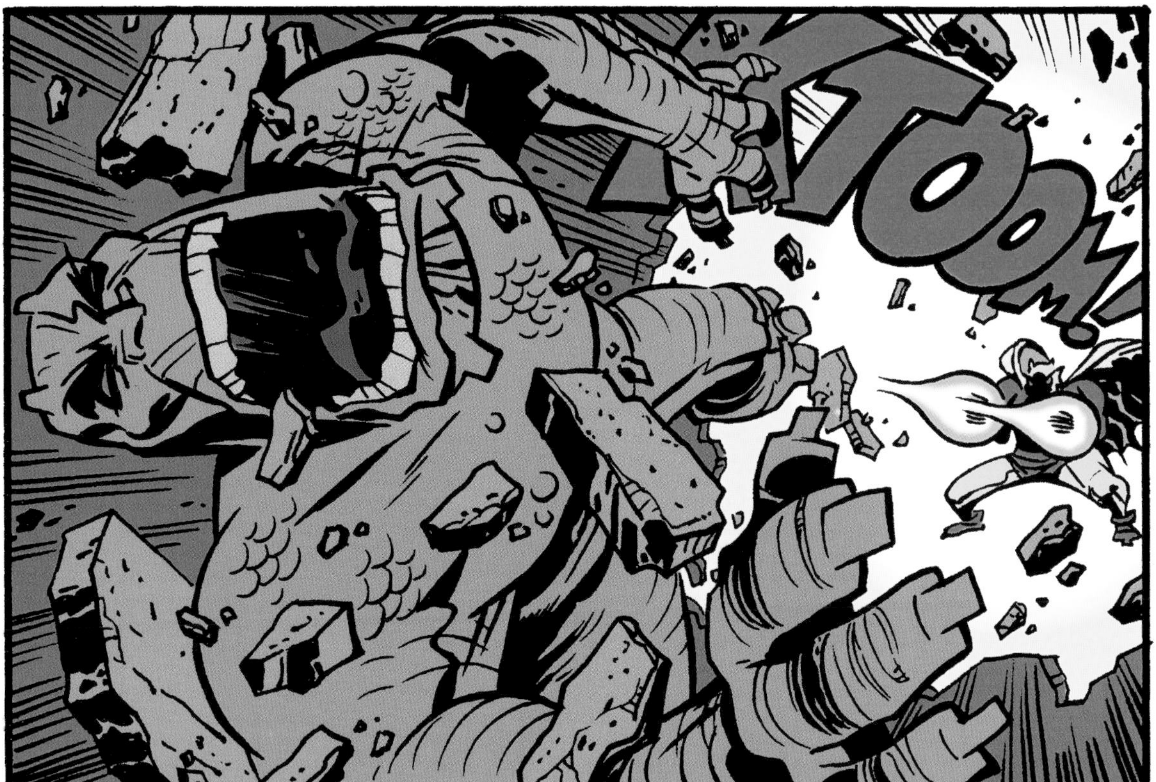
TOOOM!

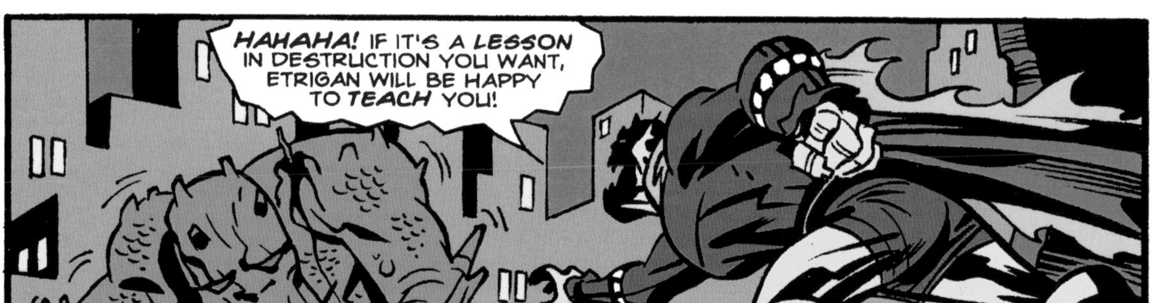
HAHAHA! IF IT'S A LESSON IN DESTRUCTION YOU WANT, ETRIGAN WILL BE HAPPY TO TEACH YOU!

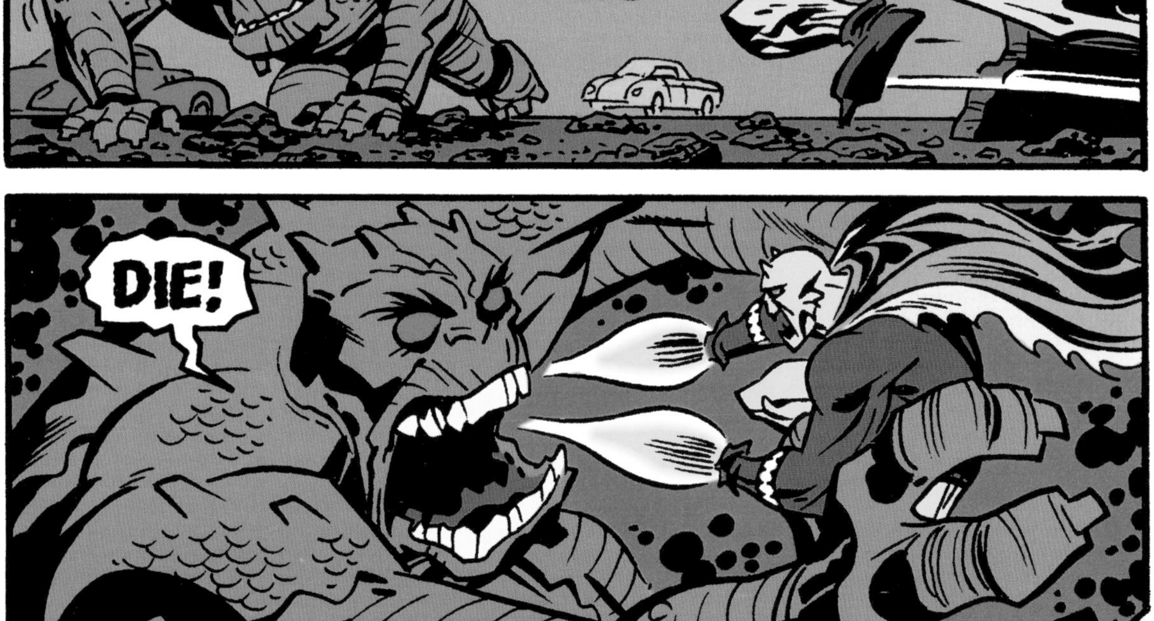
DIE!
40.

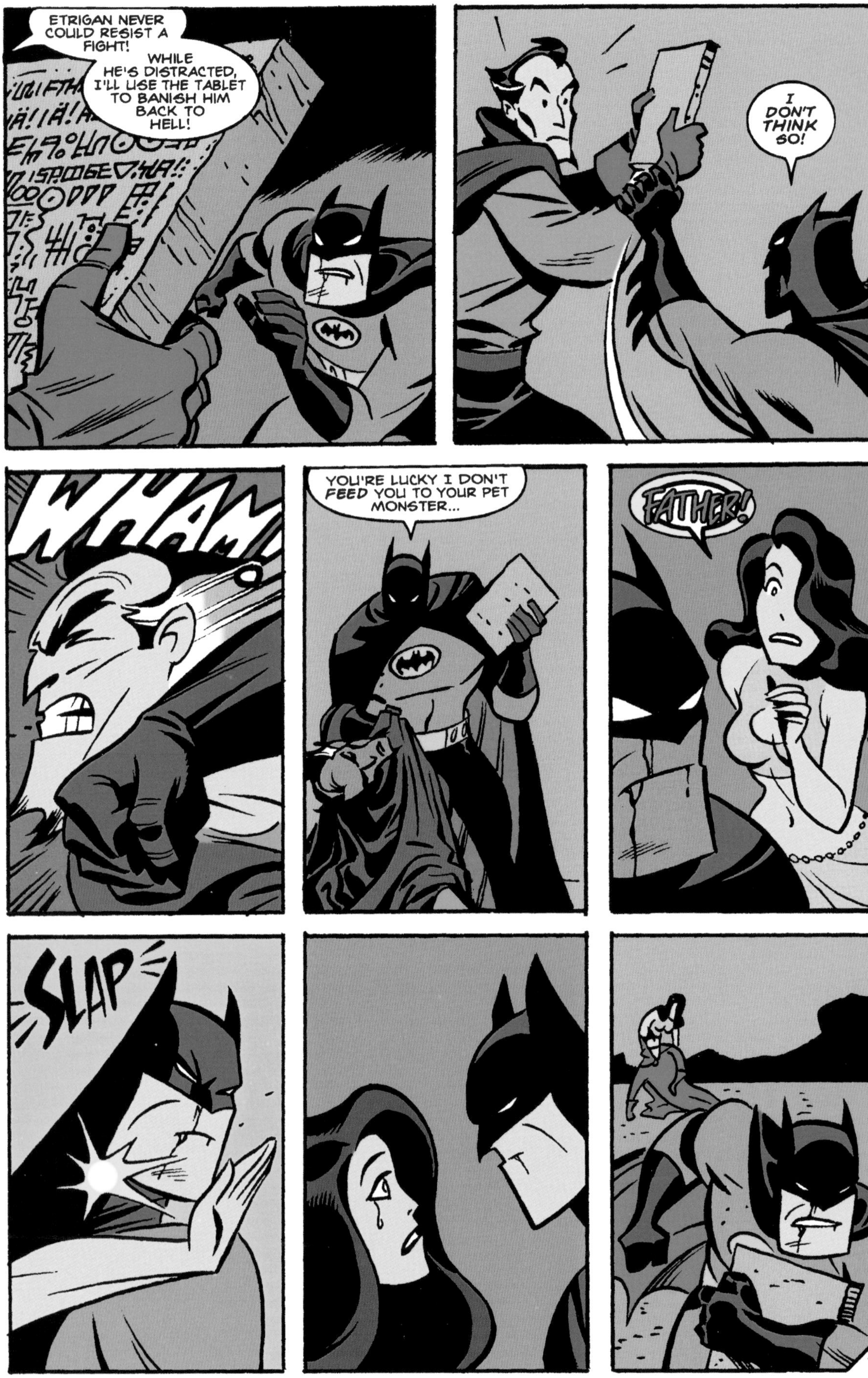
ETRIGAN NEVER COULD RESIST A FIGHT!
WHILE HE'S DISTRACTED, I'LL USE THE TABLET TO BANISH HIM BACK TO HELL!
I DON'T THINK SO!
WHAM!
YOU'RE LUCKY I DON'T FEED YOU TO YOUR PET MONSTER...
FATHER!
SLAP
41.

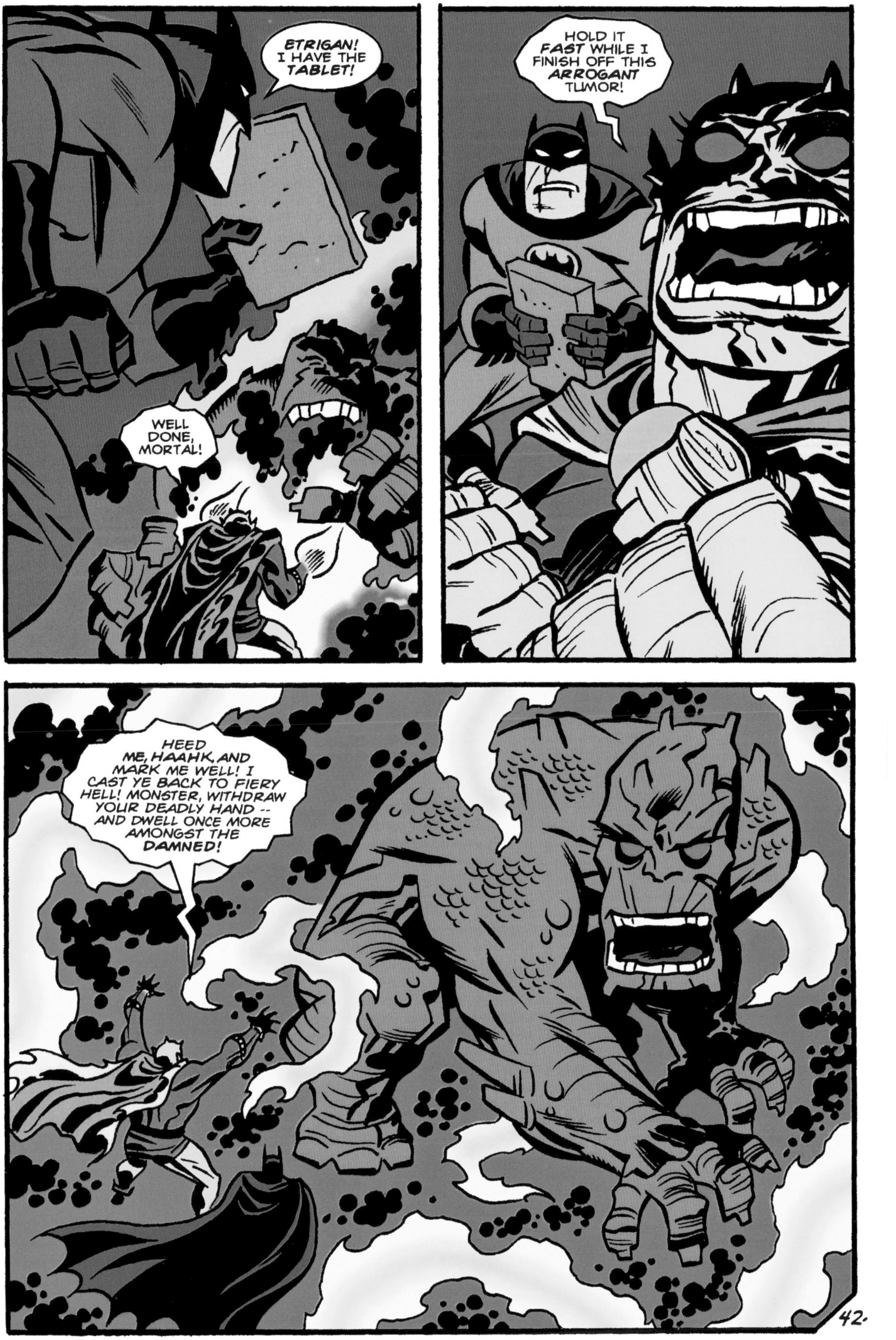
ETRIGAN! I HAVE THE TABLET!
WELL DONE, MORTAL!
HOLD IT FAST WHILE I FINISH OFF THIS ARROGANT TUMOR!
HEED ME, HAAHK, AND MARK ME WELL! I CAST YE BACK TO FIERY HELL! MONSTER, WITHDRAW YOUR DEADLY HAND -- AND DWELL ONCE MORE AMONGST THE DAMNED!
42.

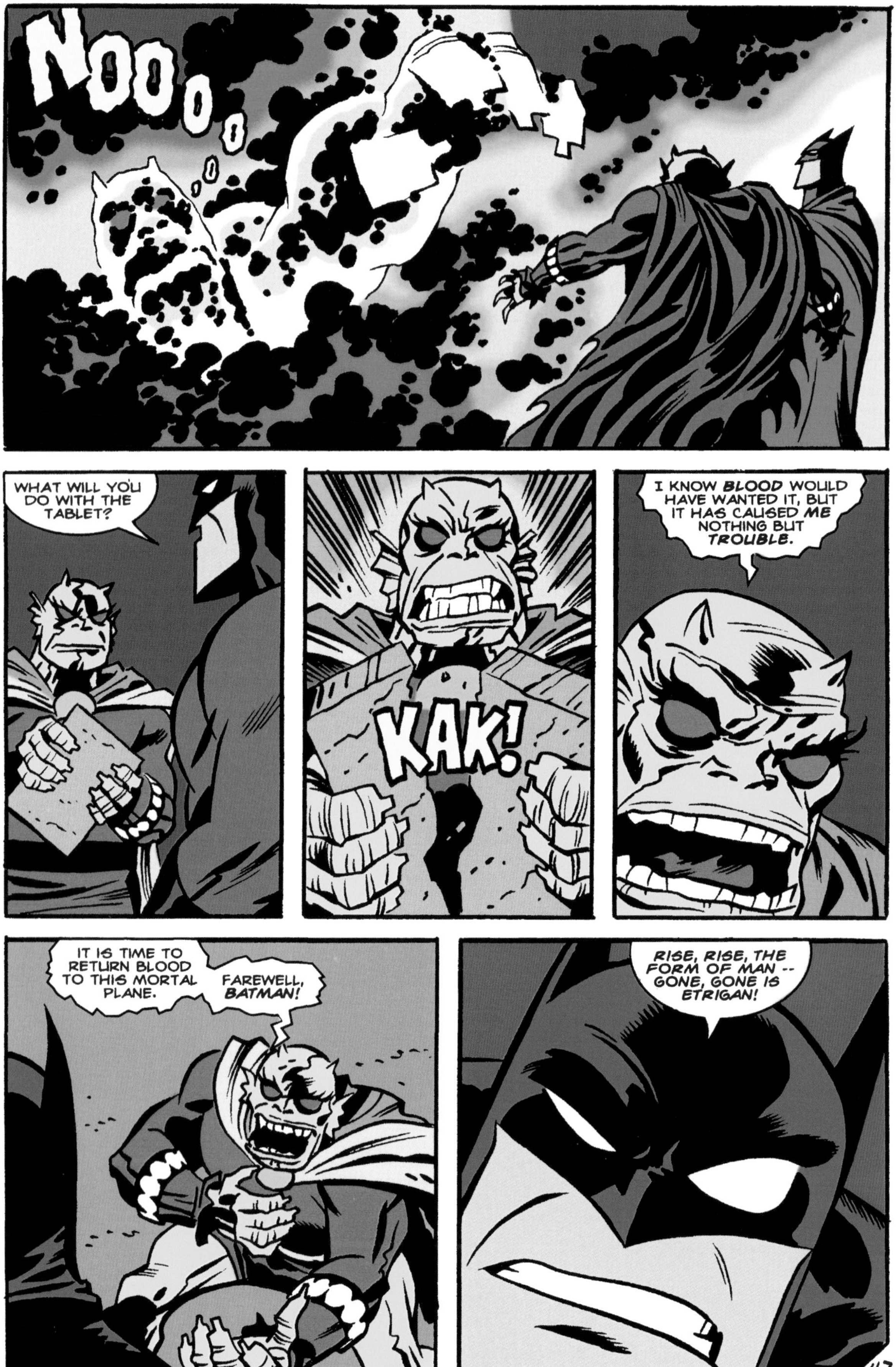
NOOOOO
WHAT WILL YOU DO WITH THE TABLET?
KAK!
I KNOW BLOOD WOULD HAVE WANTED IT, BUT IT HAS CAUSED ME NOTHING BUT TROUBLE.
IT IS TIME TO RETURN BLOOD TO THIS MORTAL PLANE.
FAREWELL, BATMAN!
RISE, RISE, THE FORM OF MAN -- GONE, GONE IS ETRIGAN!
43.

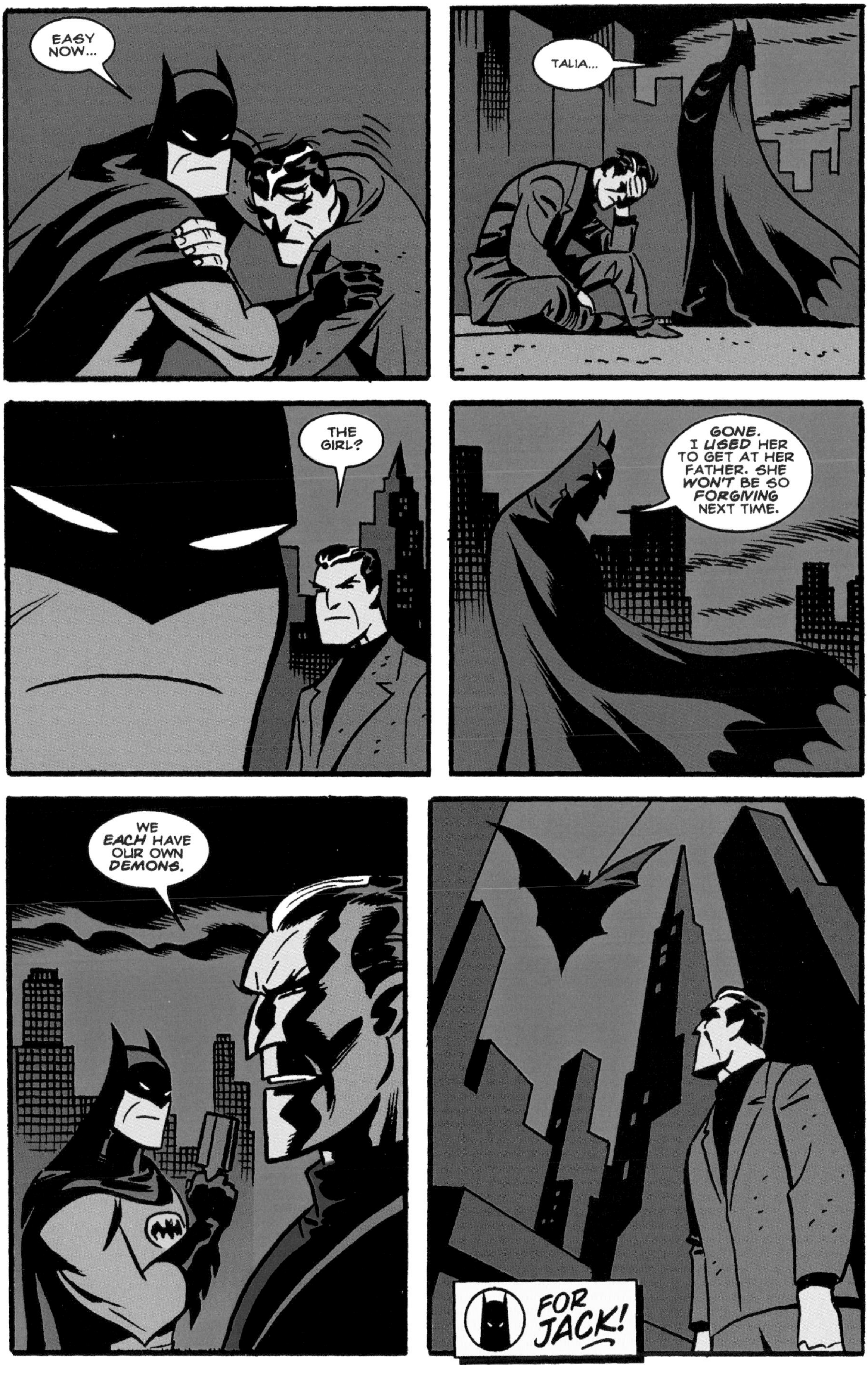
EASY NOW...
TALIA...
THE GIRL?
GONE. I USED HER TO GET AT HER FATHER. SHE WON'T BE SO FORGIVING NEXT TIME.
WE EACH HAVE OUR OWN DEMONS.
FOR JACK!

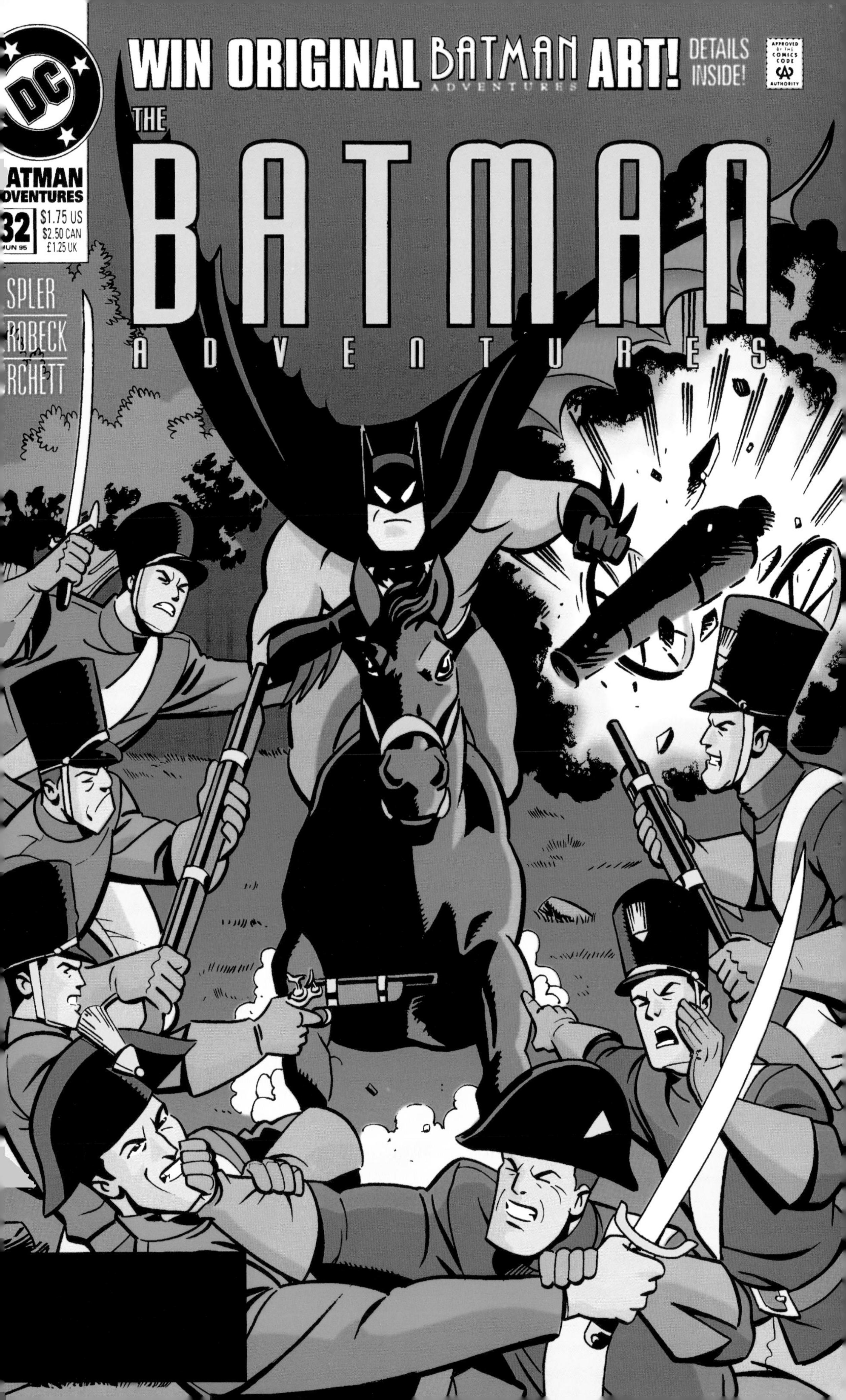

WIN ORIGINAL BATMAN ADVENTURES ART! DETAILS INSIDE!
APPROVED BY THE COMICS CODE AUTHORITY
DC
ATMAN
DVENTURES
32
UN 95
$1.75 US
$2.50 CAN
£1.25 UK
THE
BATMAN
ADVENTURES
SPLER
ROBECK
RCHETT

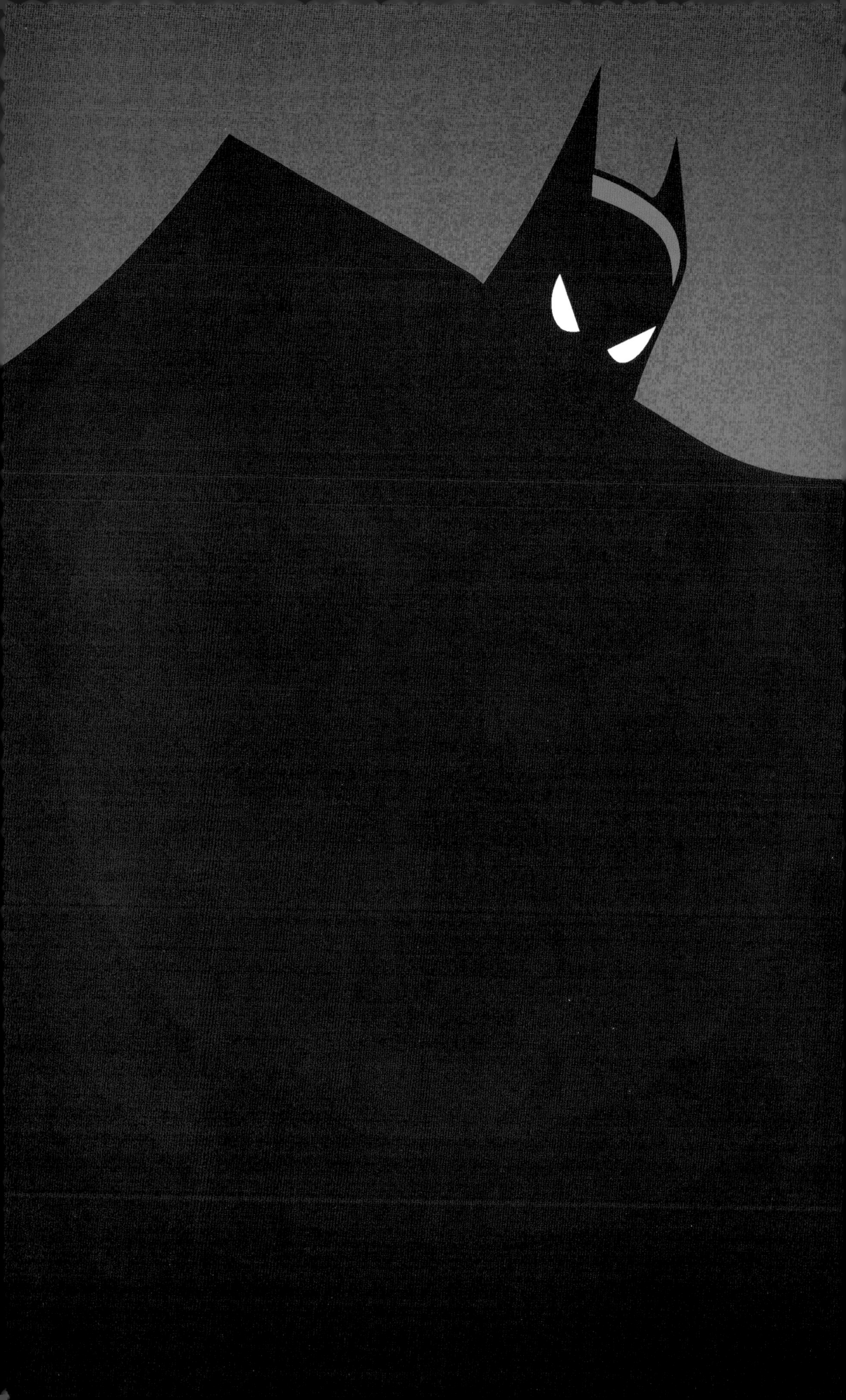

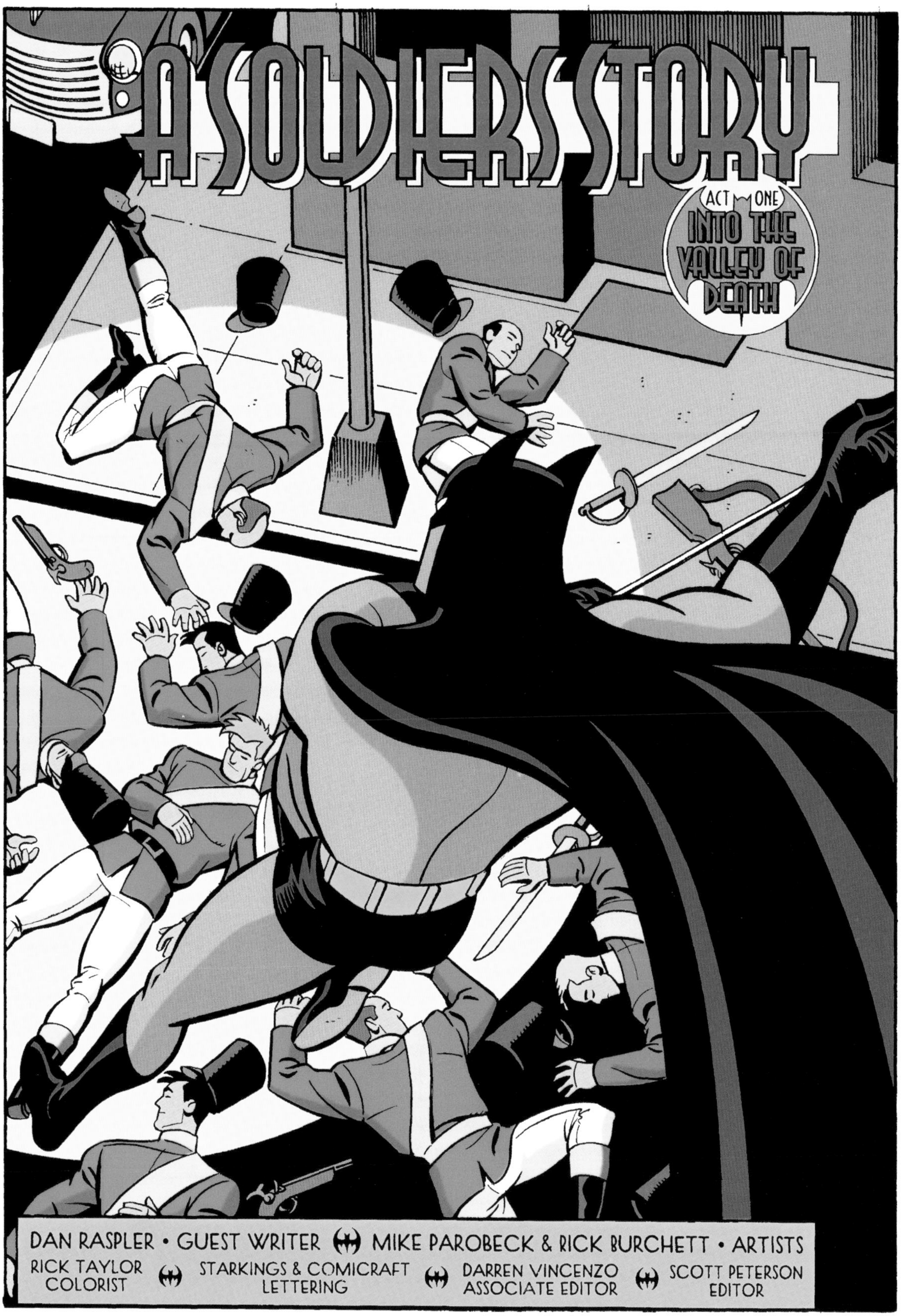
A SOLDIER'S STORY
ACT ONE
INTO THE VALLEY OF DEATH
DAN RASPLER • GUEST WRITER
MIKE PAROBECK & RICK BURCHETT • ARTISTS
RICK TAYLOR COLORIST
STARKINGS & COMICRAFT LETTERING
DARREN VINCENZO ASSOCIATE EDITOR
SCOTT PETERSON EDITOR

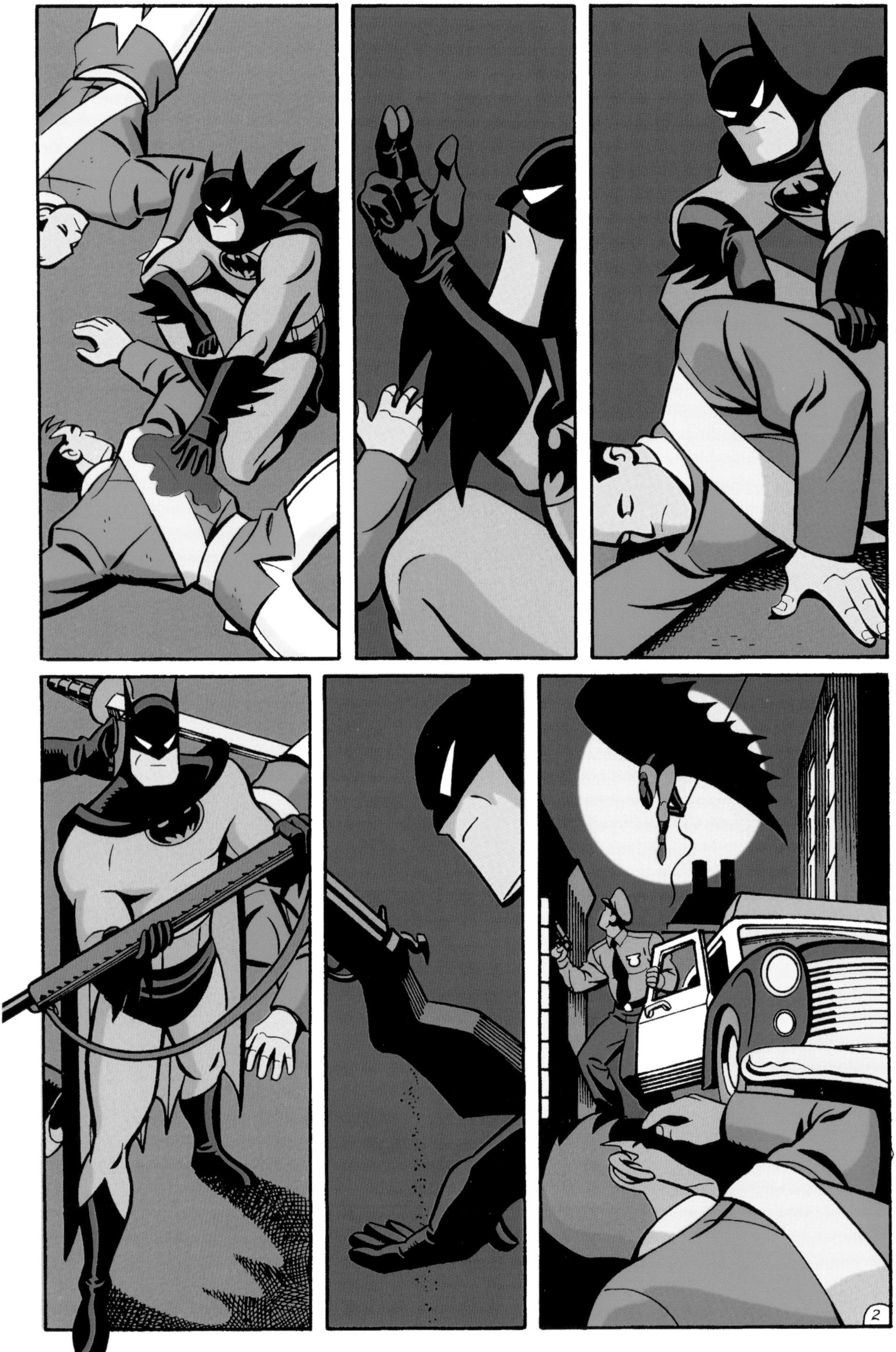
2

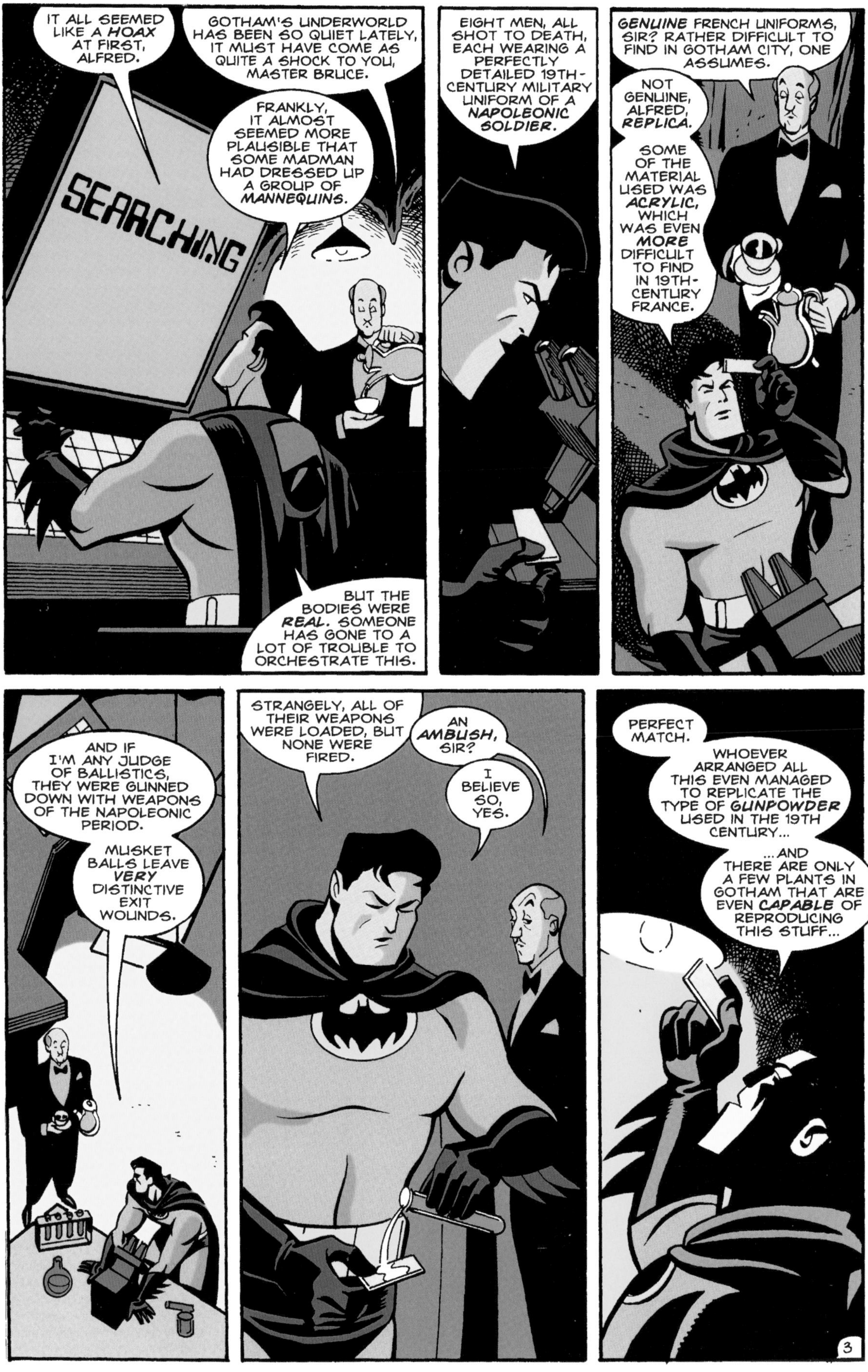
IT ALL SEEMED LIKE A HOAX AT FIRST, ALFRED.
GOTHAM'S UNDERWORLD HAS BEEN SO QUIET LATELY, IT MUST HAVE COME AS QUITE A SHOCK TO YOU, MASTER BRUCE.
FRANKLY, IT ALMOST SEEMED MORE PLAUSIBLE THAT SOME MADMAN HAD DRESSED UP A GROUP OF MANNEQUINS.
SEARCHING
BUT THE BODIES WERE REAL. SOMEONE HAS GONE TO A LOT OF TROUBLE TO ORCHESTRATE THIS.
EIGHT MEN, ALL SHOT TO DEATH, EACH WEARING A PERFECTLY DETAILED 19TH-CENTURY MILITARY UNIFORM OF A NAPOLEONIC SOLDIER.
GENUINE FRENCH UNIFORMS, SIR? RATHER DIFFICULT TO FIND IN GOTHAM CITY, ONE ASSUMES.
NOT GENUINE, ALFRED, REPLICA.
SOME OF THE MATERIAL USED WAS ACRYLIC, WHICH WAS EVEN MORE DIFFICULT TO FIND IN 19TH-CENTURY FRANCE.
AND IF I'M ANY JUDGE OF BALLISTICS, THEY WERE GUNNED DOWN WITH WEAPONS OF THE NAPOLEONIC PERIOD.
MUSKET BALLS LEAVE VERY DISTINCTIVE EXIT WOUNDS.
STRANGELY, ALL OF THEIR WEAPONS WERE LOADED, BUT NONE WERE FIRED.
AN AMBUSH, SIR?
I BELIEVE SO, YES.
PERFECT MATCH.
WHOEVER ARRANGED ALL THIS EVEN MANAGED TO REPLICATE THE TYPE OF GUNPOWDER USED IN THE 19TH CENTURY...
...AND THERE ARE ONLY A FEW PLANTS IN GOTHAM THAT ARE EVEN CAPABLE OF REPRODUCING THIS STUFF...
3

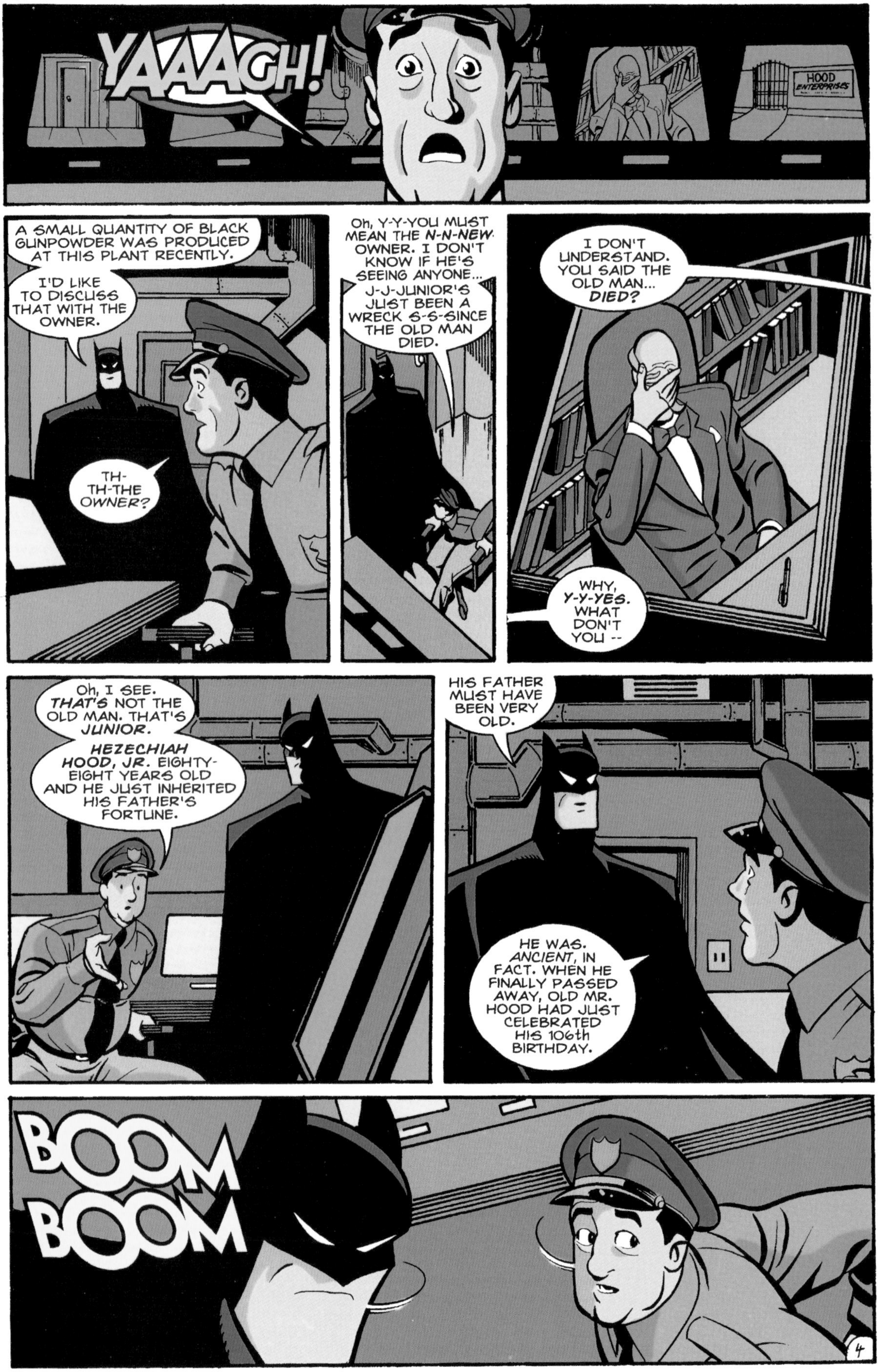

YAAAGH!
HOOD ENTERPRISES
A SMALL QUANTITY OF BLACK GUNPOWDER WAS PRODUCED AT THIS PLANT RECENTLY.
I'D LIKE TO DISCUSS THAT WITH THE OWNER.
TH-TH-THE OWNER?
Oh, Y-Y-YOU MUST MEAN THE N-N-NEW OWNER. I DON'T KNOW IF HE'S SEEING ANYONE...
J-J-JUNIOR'S JUST BEEN A WRECK S-S-SINCE THE OLD MAN DIED.
I DON'T UNDERSTAND. YOU SAID THE OLD MAN... DIED?
WHY, Y-Y-YES. WHAT DON'T YOU --
Oh, I SEE. THAT'S NOT THE OLD MAN. THAT'S JUNIOR.
HEZECHIAH HOOD, JR. EIGHTY-EIGHT YEARS OLD AND HE JUST INHERITED HIS FATHER'S FORTUNE.
HIS FATHER MUST HAVE BEEN VERY OLD.
HE WAS. ANCIENT, IN FACT. WHEN HE FINALLY PASSED AWAY, OLD MR. HOOD HAD JUST CELEBRATED HIS 106th BIRTHDAY.
BOOM BOOM
4

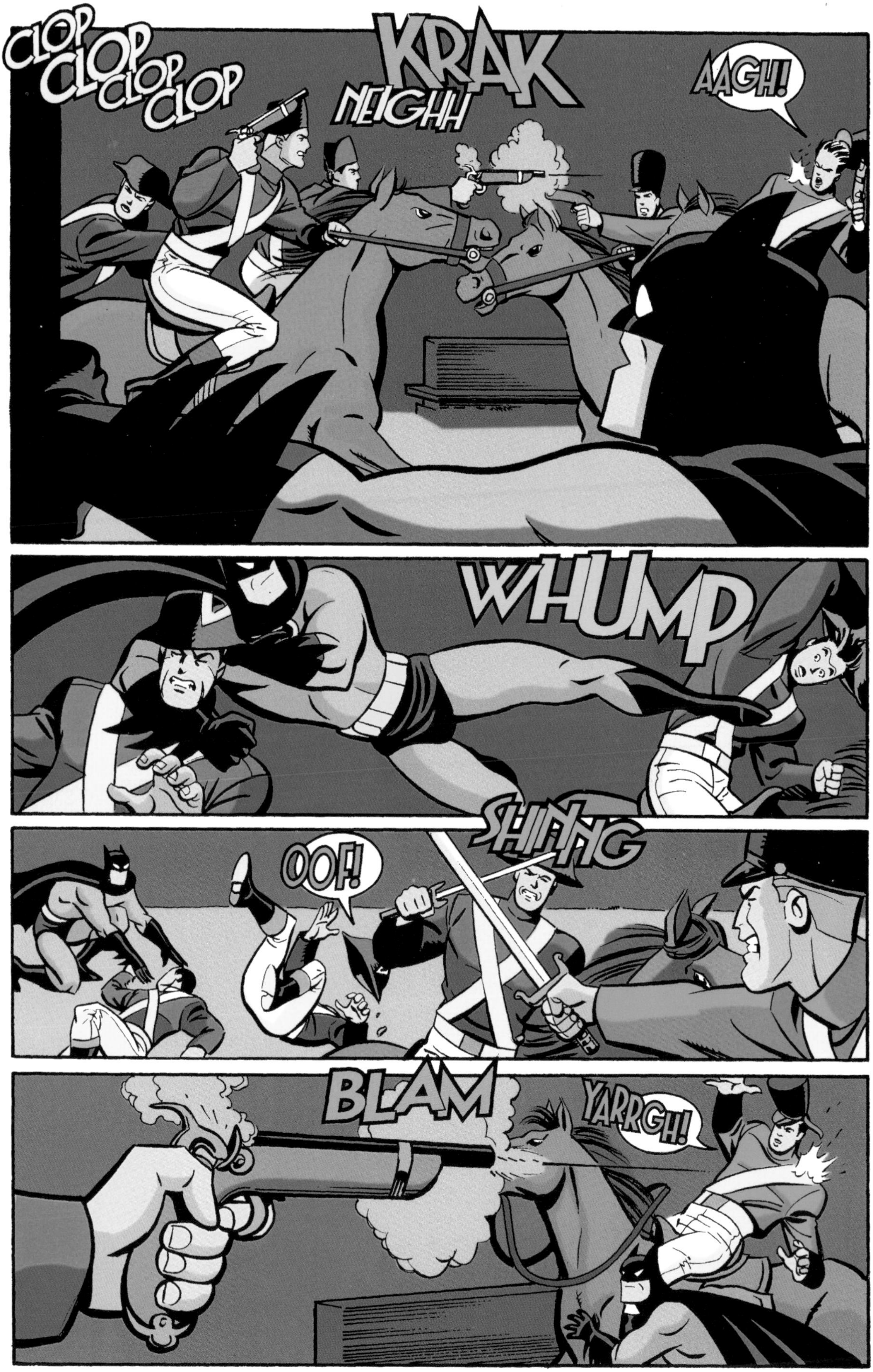
CLOP
CLOP
CLOP
CLOP
KRAK
NEIGHH
AAGH!
WHUMP
SHINNG
OOF!
BLAM
YARRGH!

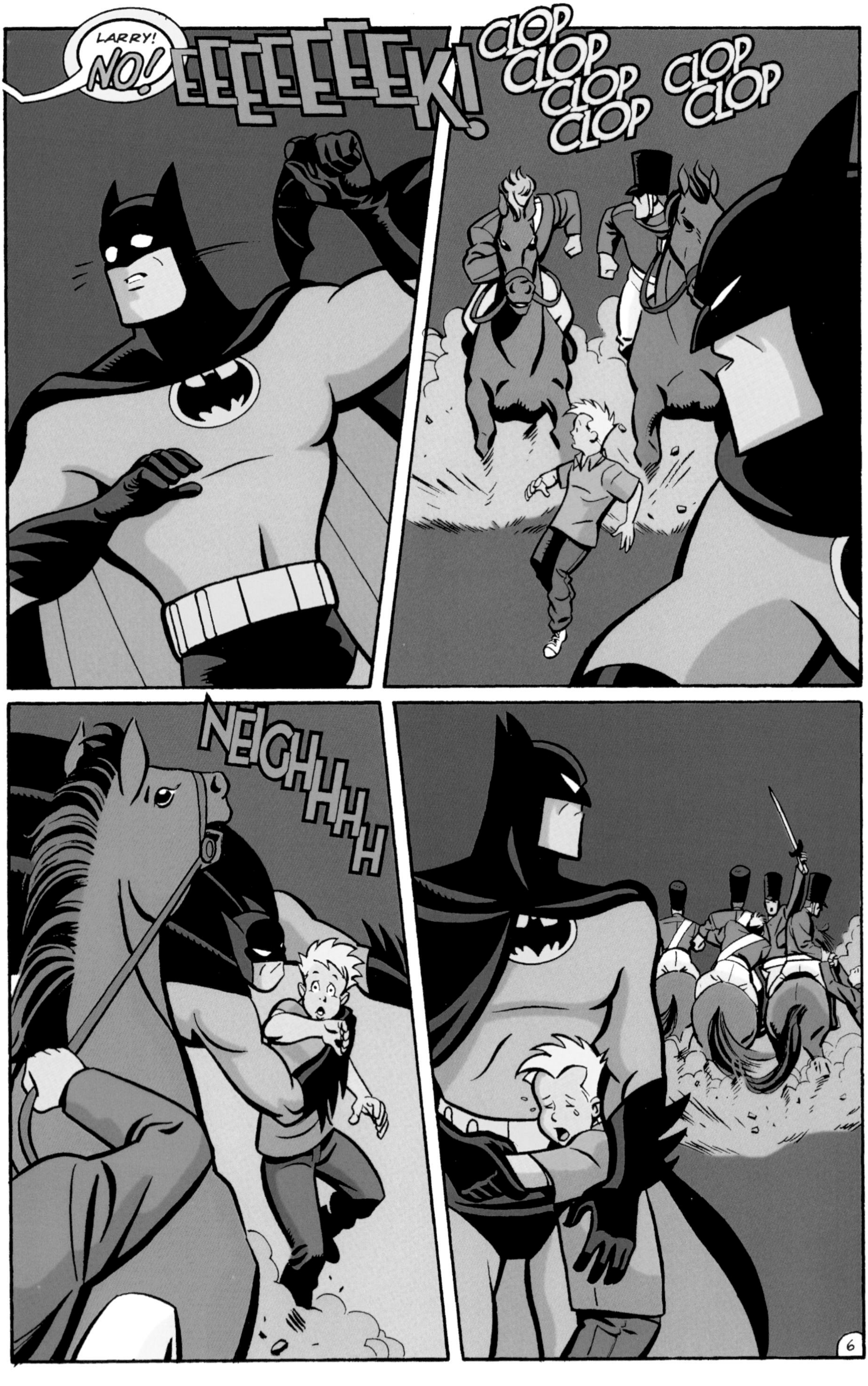
LARRY! NO!
EEEEEEEK!
CLOP CLOP CLOP CLOP
CLOP CLOP
NEIGHHHHH
6

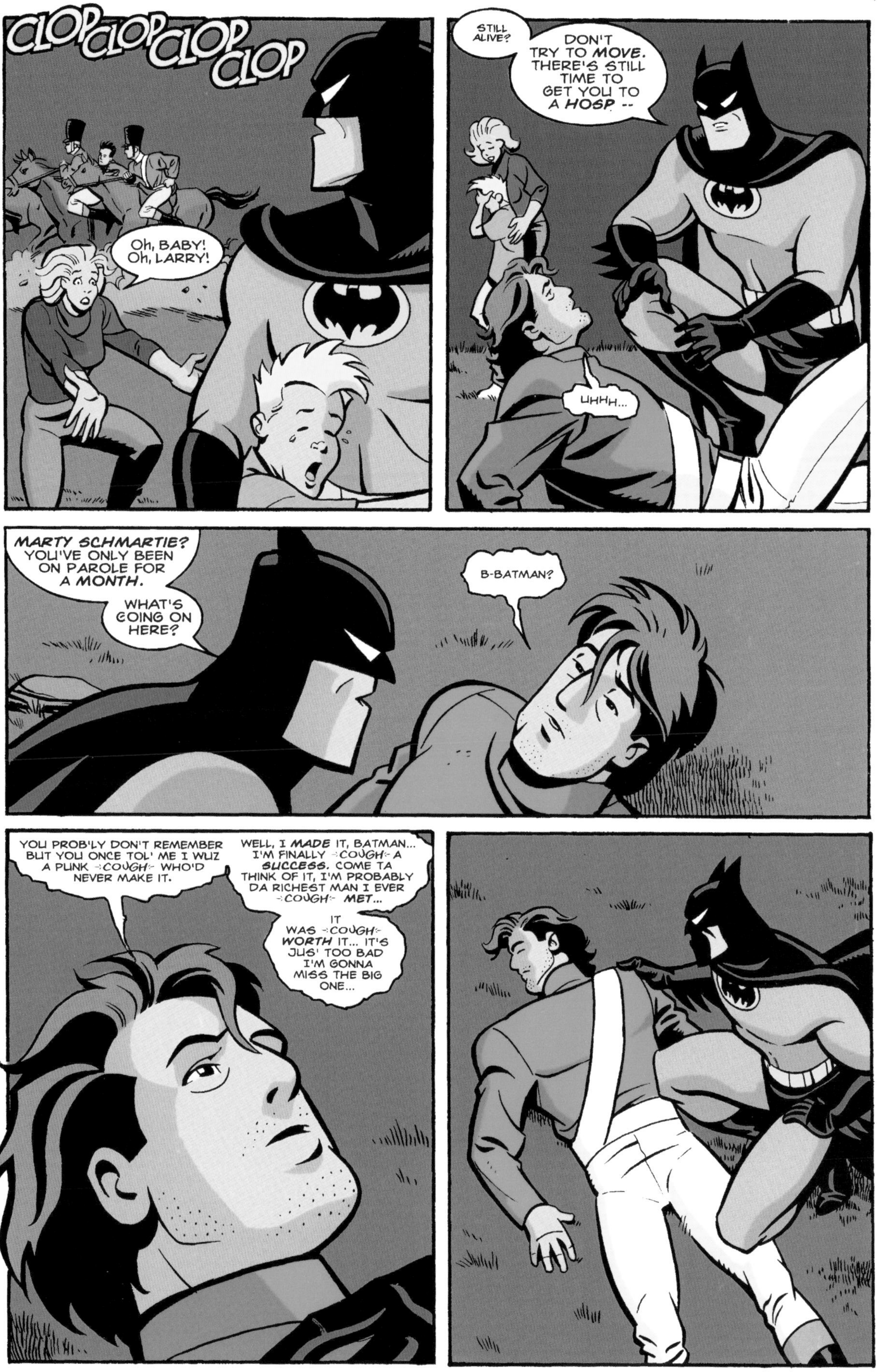
CLOP CLOP CLOP CLOP
Oh, BABY! Oh, LARRY!
STILL ALIVE?
DON'T TRY TO MOVE. THERE'S STILL TIME TO GET YOU TO A HOSP --
UHHH...
MARTY SCHMARTIE? YOU'VE ONLY BEEN ON PAROLE FOR A MONTH.
WHAT'S GOING ON HERE?
B-BATMAN?
YOU PROB'LY DON'T REMEMBER BUT YOU ONCE TOL' ME I WUZ A PUNK -COUGH- WHO'D NEVER MAKE IT.
WELL, I MADE IT, BATMAN... I'M FINALLY -COUGH- A SUCCESS. COME TA THINK OF IT, I'M PROBABLY DA RICHEST MAN I EVER -COUGH- MET...
IT WAS -COUGH- WORTH IT... IT'S JUS' TOO BAD I'M GONNA MISS THE BIG ONE...

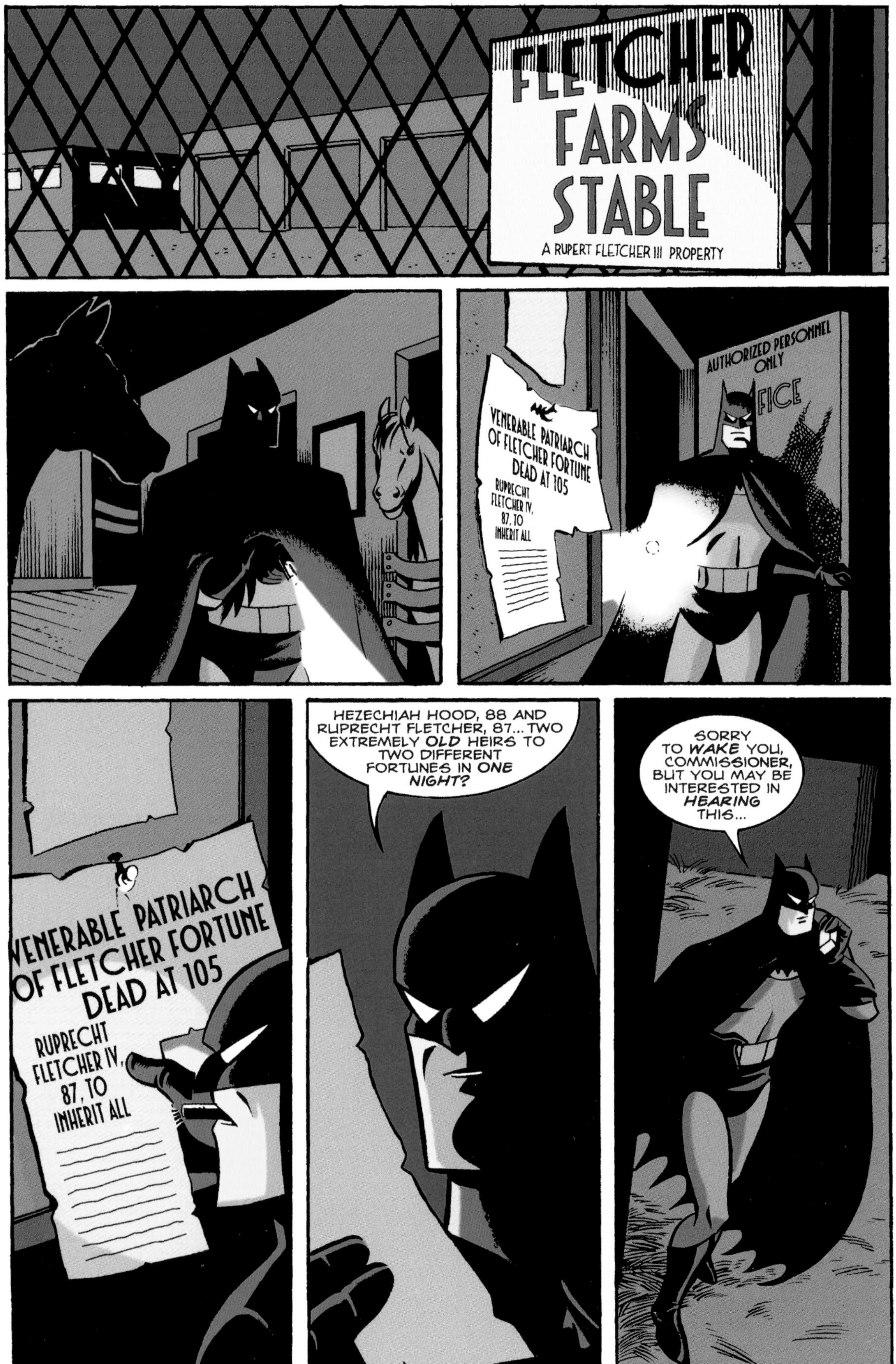
FLETCHER FARMS STABLE
A RUPERT FLETCHER III PROPERTY
VENERABLE PATRIARCH OF FLETCHER FORTUNE DEAD AT 105
RUPRECHT FLETCHER IV, 87, TO INHERIT ALL
AUTHORIZED PERSONNEL ONLY
FICE
VENERABLE PATRIARCH OF FLETCHER FORTUNE DEAD AT 105
RUPRECHT FLETCHER IV, 87, TO INHERIT ALL
HEZECHIAH HOOD, 88 AND RUPRECHT FLETCHER, 87... TWO EXTREMELY OLD HEIRS TO TWO DIFFERENT FORTUNES IN ONE NIGHT?
SORRY TO WAKE YOU, COMMISSIONER, BUT YOU MAY BE INTERESTED IN HEARING THIS...

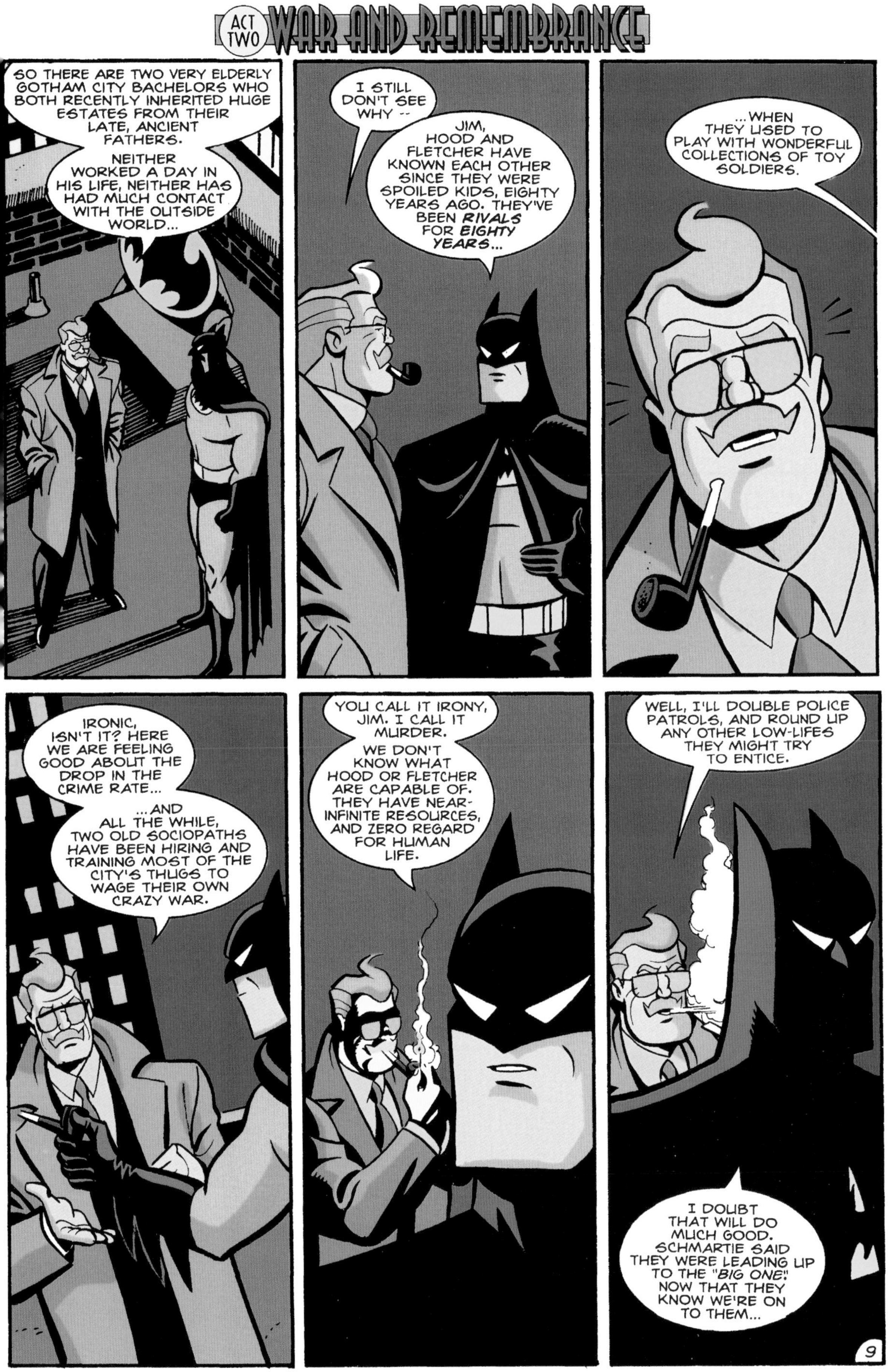
ACT TWO WAR AND REMEMBRANCE
SO THERE ARE TWO VERY ELDERLY GOTHAM CITY BACHELORS WHO BOTH RECENTLY INHERITED HUGE ESTATES FROM THEIR LATE, ANCIENT FATHERS.
NEITHER WORKED A DAY IN HIS LIFE, NEITHER HAS HAD MUCH CONTACT WITH THE OUTSIDE WORLD...
I STILL DON'T SEE WHY --
JIM, HOOD AND FLETCHER HAVE KNOWN EACH OTHER SINCE THEY WERE SPOILED KIDS, EIGHTY YEARS AGO. THEY'VE BEEN RIVALS FOR EIGHTY YEARS...
...WHEN THEY USED TO PLAY WITH WONDERFUL COLLECTIONS OF TOY SOLDIERS.
IRONIC, ISN'T IT? HERE WE ARE FEELING GOOD ABOUT THE DROP IN THE CRIME RATE...
...AND ALL THE WHILE, TWO OLD SOCIOPATHS HAVE BEEN HIRING AND TRAINING MOST OF THE CITY'S THUGS TO WAGE THEIR OWN CRAZY WAR.
YOU CALL IT IRONY, JIM. I CALL IT MURDER.
WE DON'T KNOW WHAT HOOD OR FLETCHER ARE CAPABLE OF. THEY HAVE NEAR-INFINITE RESOURCES, AND ZERO REGARD FOR HUMAN LIFE.
WELL, I'LL DOUBLE POLICE PATROLS, AND ROUND UP ANY OTHER LOW-LIFES THEY MIGHT TRY TO ENTICE.
I DOUBT THAT WILL DO MUCH GOOD. SCHMARTIE SAID THEY WERE LEADING UP TO THE "BIG ONE." NOW THAT THEY KNOW WE'RE ON TO THEM...
9

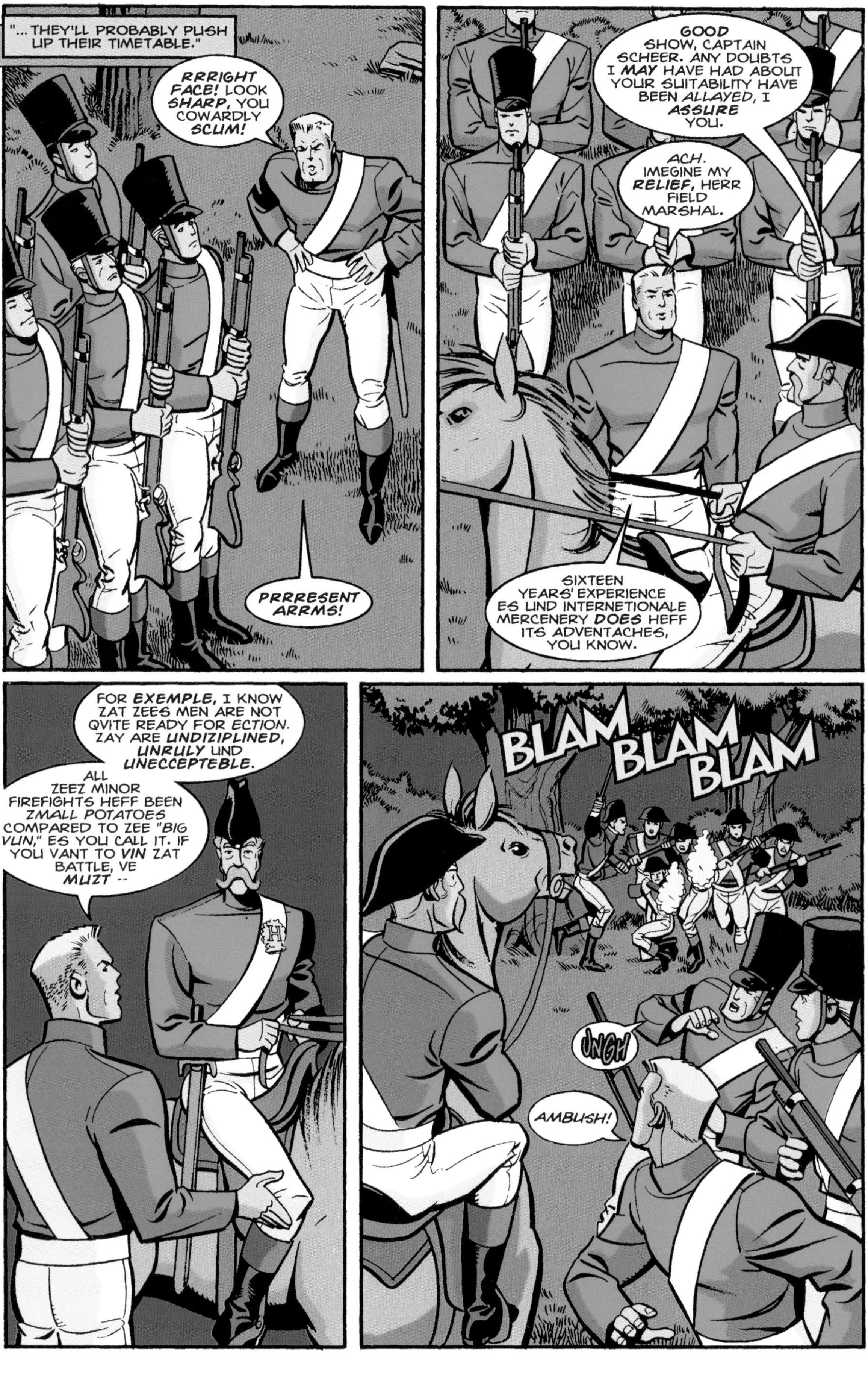

"...THEY'LL PROBABLY PUSH UP THEIR TIMETABLE."
RRRIGHT FACE! LOOK SHARP, YOU COWARDLY SCUM!
PRRRESENT ARRMS!
GOOD SHOW, CAPTAIN SCHEER. ANY DOUBTS I MAY HAVE HAD ABOUT YOUR SUITABILITY HAVE BEEN ALLAYED, I ASSURE YOU.
ACH. IMEGINE MY RELIEF, HERR FIELD MARSHAL.
SIXTEEN YEARS' EXPERIENCE ES UND INTERNETIONALE MERCENERY DOES HEFF ITS ADVENTACHES, YOU KNOW.
FOR EXEMPLE, I KNOW ZAT ZEES MEN ARE NOT QVITE READY FOR ECTION. ZAY ARE UNDIZIPLINED, UNRULY UND UNECCEPTEBLE.
ALL ZEEZ MINOR FIREFIGHTS HEFF BEEN ZMALL POTATOES COMPARED TO ZEE "BIG VUN," ES YOU CALL IT. IF YOU VANT TO VIN ZAT BATTLE, VE MUZT --
BLAM BLAM BLAM
UNGH
AMBUSH!

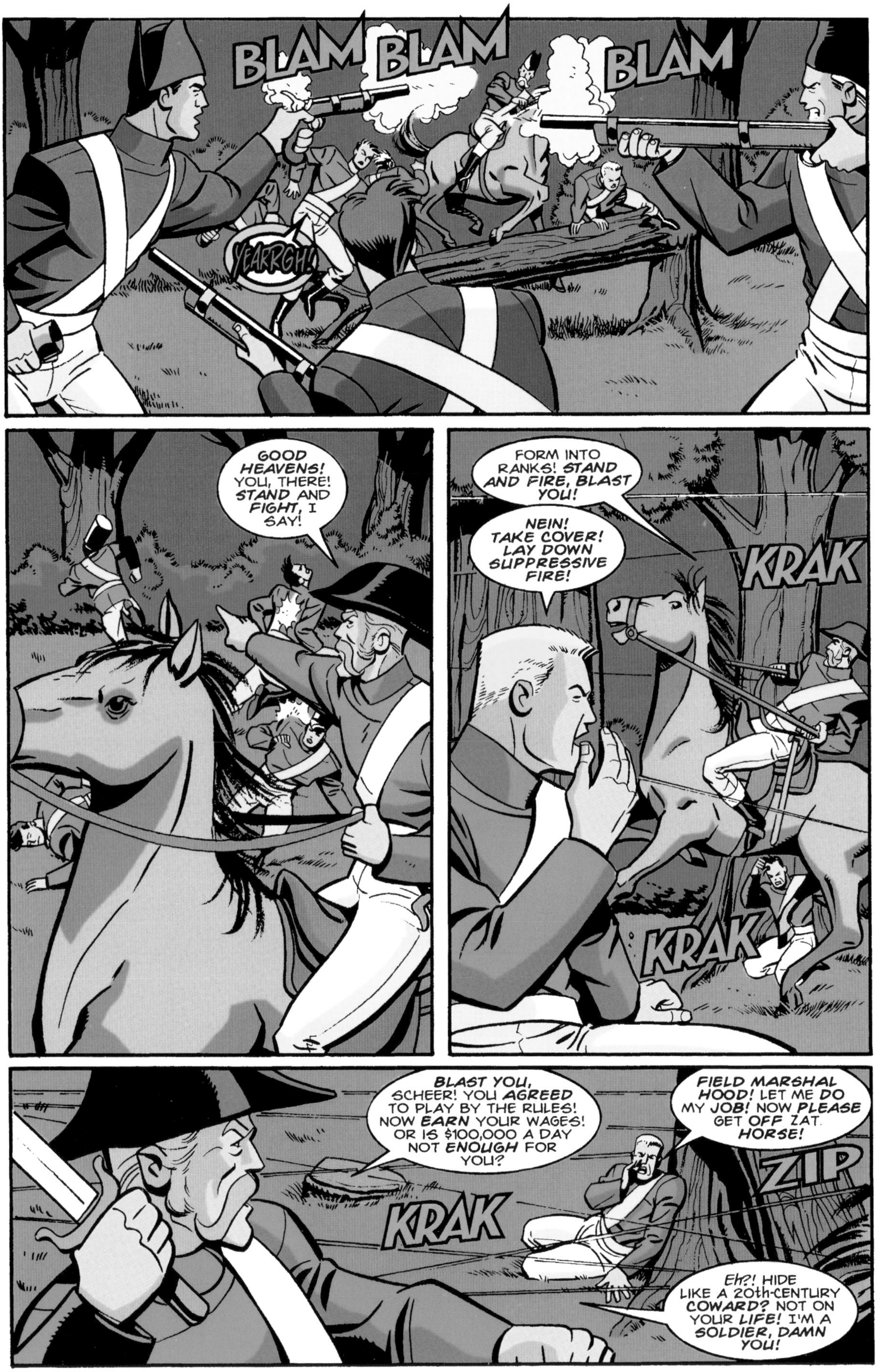
BLAM BLAM
BLAM
YEARRGH!
GOOD HEAVENS! YOU, THERE! STAND AND FIGHT, I SAY!
FORM INTO RANKS! STAND AND FIRE, BLAST YOU!
NEIN! TAKE COVER! LAY DOWN SUPPRESSIVE FIRE!
KRAK
KRAK
BLAST YOU, SCHEER! YOU AGREED TO PLAY BY THE RULES! NOW EARN YOUR WAGES! OR IS $100,000 A DAY NOT ENOUGH FOR YOU?
FIELD MARSHAL HOOD! LET ME DO MY JOB! NOW PLEASE GET OFF ZAT HORSE!
ZIP
KRAK
Eh?! HIDE LIKE A 20th-CENTURY COWARD? NOT ON YOUR LIFE! I'M A SOLDIER, DAMN YOU!

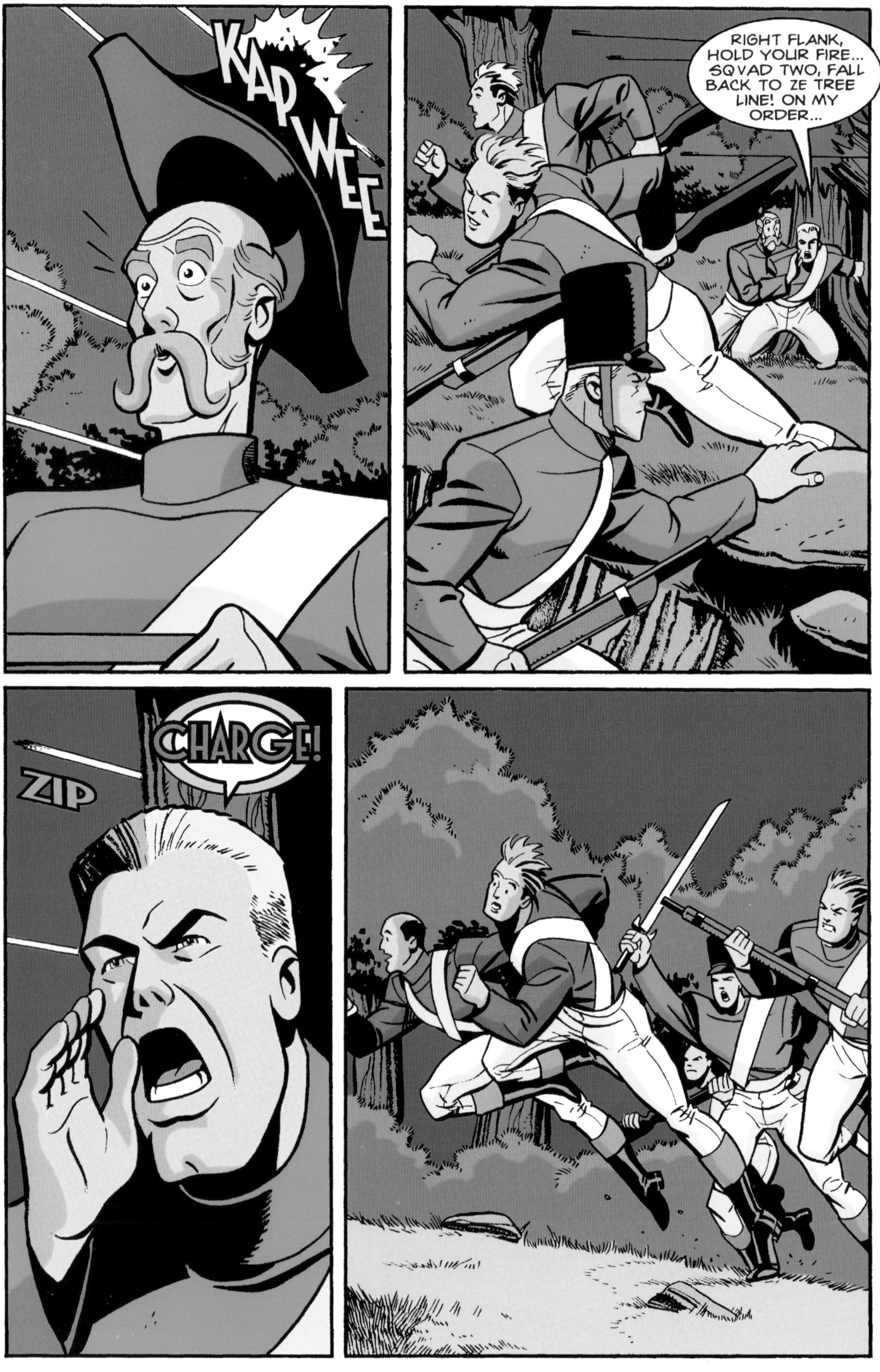
KAPWEEE
RIGHT FLANK, HOLD YOUR FIRE... SQVAD TWO, FALL BACK TO ZE TREE LINE! ON MY ORDER...
CHARGE!
ZIP

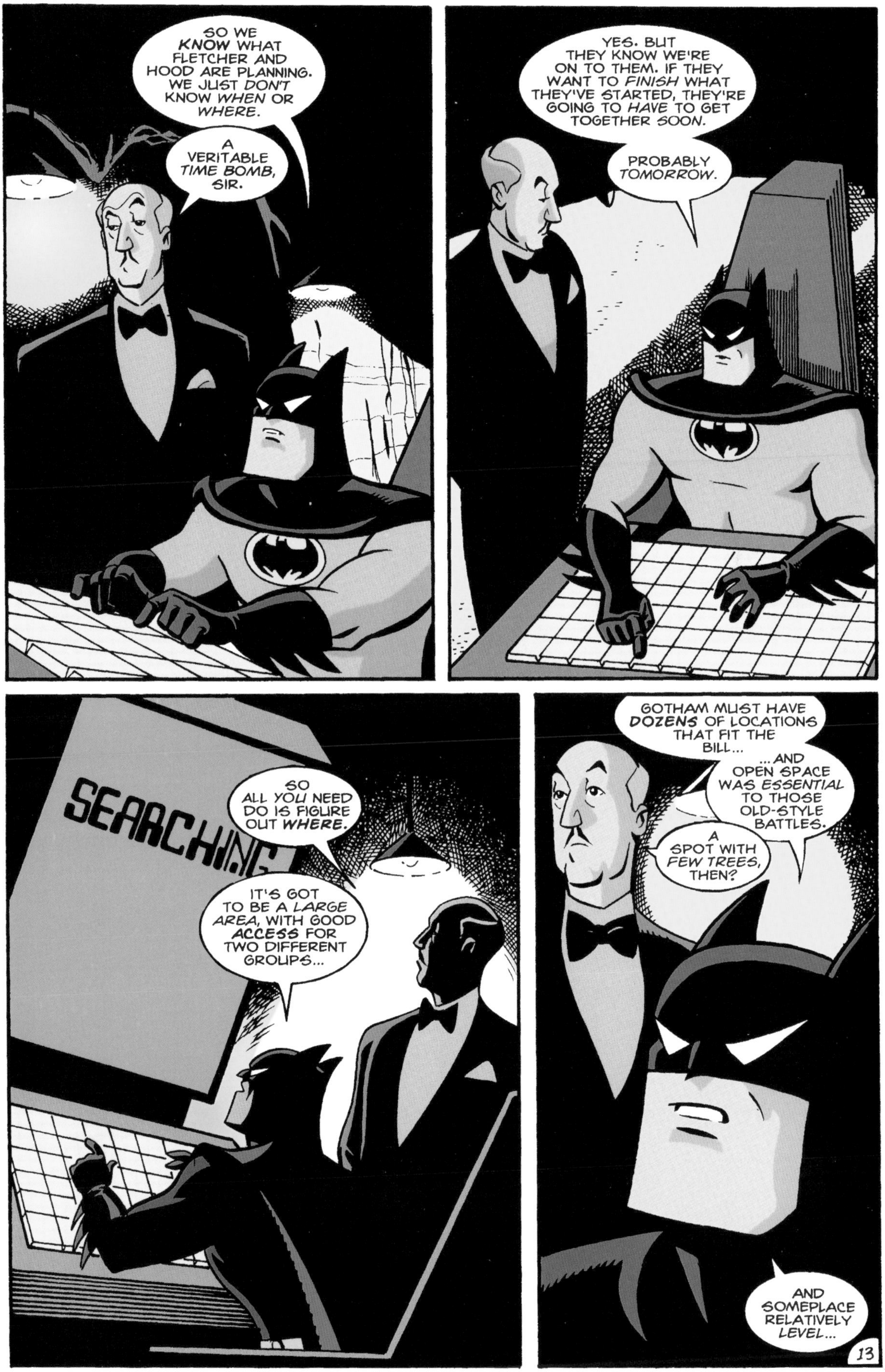
SO WE KNOW WHAT FLETCHER AND HOOD ARE PLANNING. WE JUST DON'T KNOW WHEN OR WHERE.
A VERITABLE TIME BOMB, SIR.
YES. BUT THEY KNOW WE'RE ON TO THEM. IF THEY WANT TO FINISH WHAT THEY'VE STARTED, THEY'RE GOING TO HAVE TO GET TOGETHER SOON.
PROBABLY TOMORROW.
SEARCHING
SO ALL YOU NEED DO IS FIGURE OUT WHERE.
IT'S GOT TO BE A LARGE AREA, WITH GOOD ACCESS FOR TWO DIFFERENT GROUPS...
GOTHAM MUST HAVE DOZENS OF LOCATIONS THAT FIT THE BILL...
...AND OPEN SPACE WAS ESSENTIAL TO THOSE OLD-STYLE BATTLES.
A SPOT WITH FEW TREES, THEN?
AND SOMEPLACE RELATIVELY LEVEL...
13

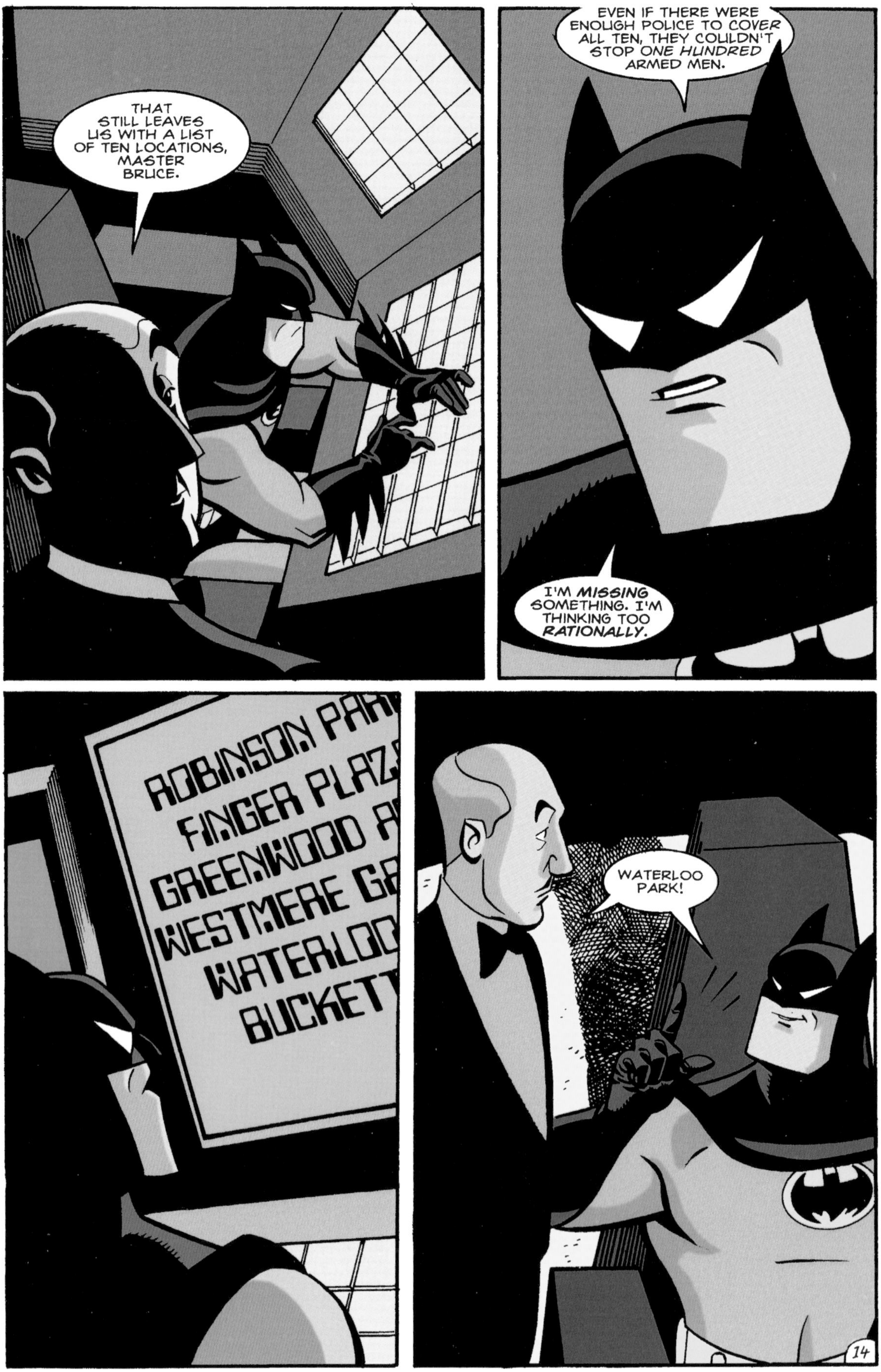
THAT STILL LEAVES US WITH A LIST OF TEN LOCATIONS, MASTER BRUCE.
EVEN IF THERE WERE ENOUGH POLICE TO COVER ALL TEN, THEY COULDN'T STOP ONE HUNDRED ARMED MEN.
I'M MISSING SOMETHING. I'M THINKING TOO RATIONALLY.
ROBINSON PAR
FINGER PLAZ
GREENWOOD A
WESTMERE GE
WATERLOO
BUCKETT
WATERLOO PARK!
14

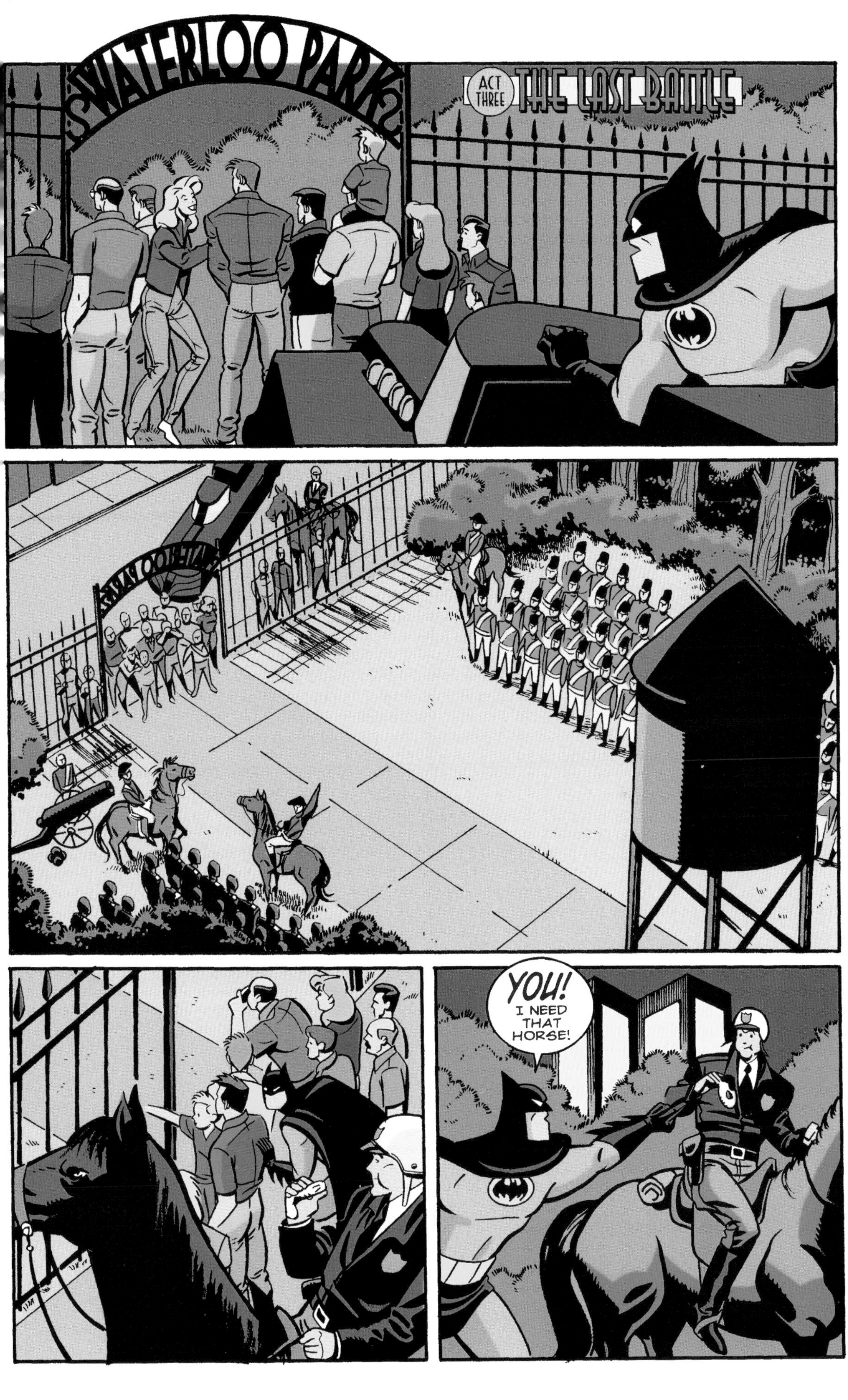
WATERLOO PARK
ACT THREE
THE LAST BATTLE
WATERLOO PARK
YOU!
I NEED THAT HORSE!

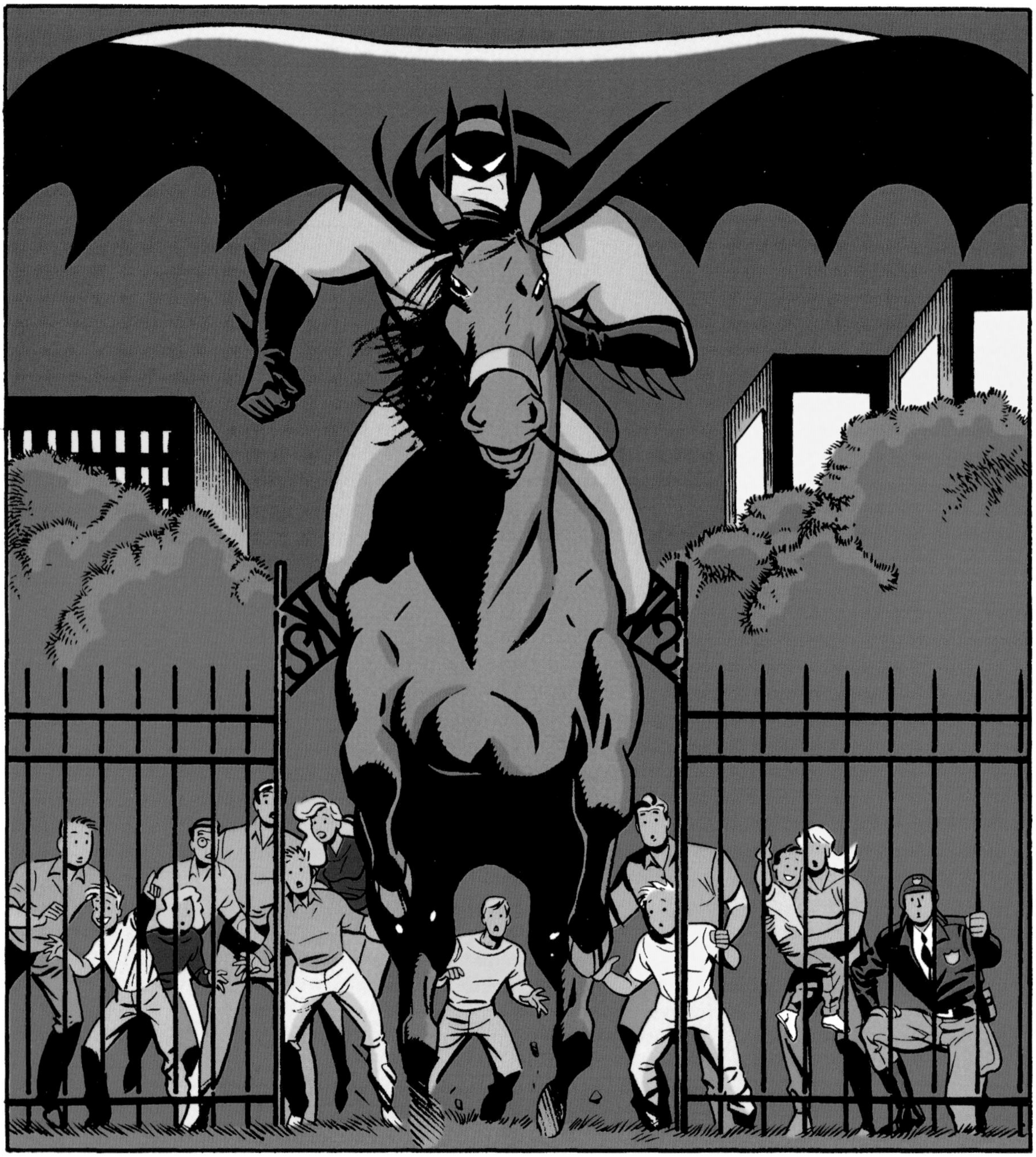

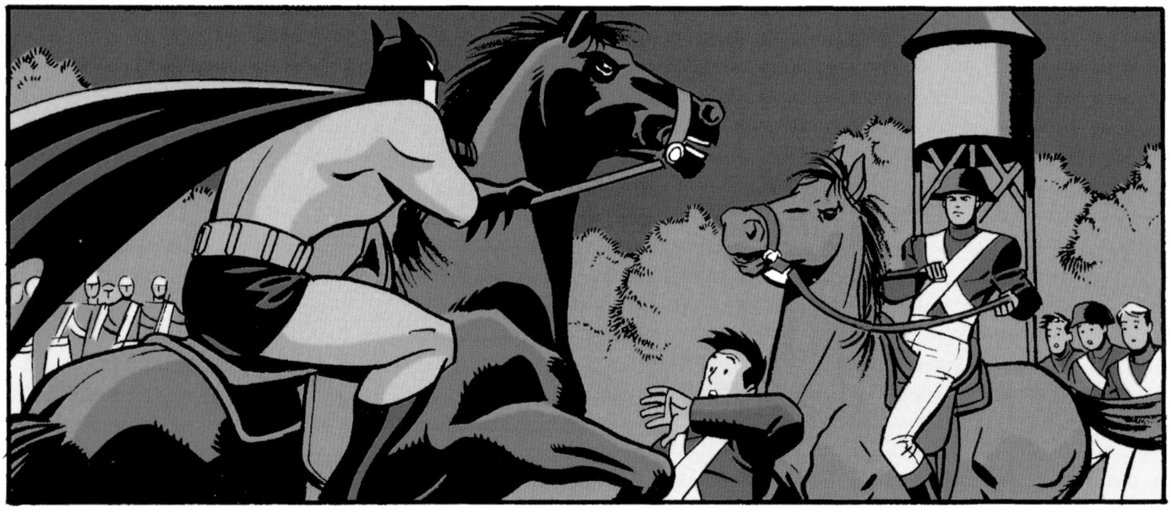

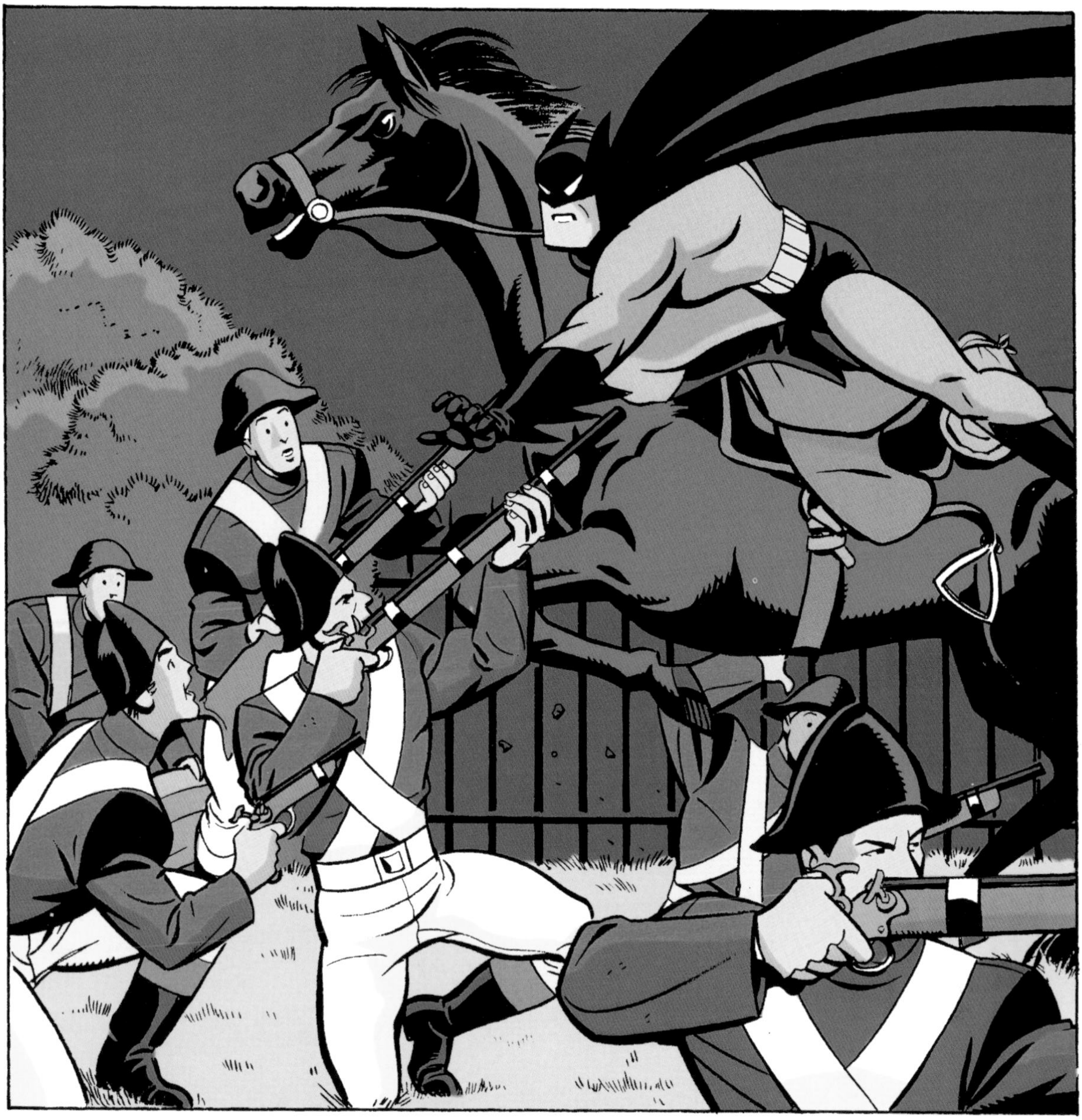

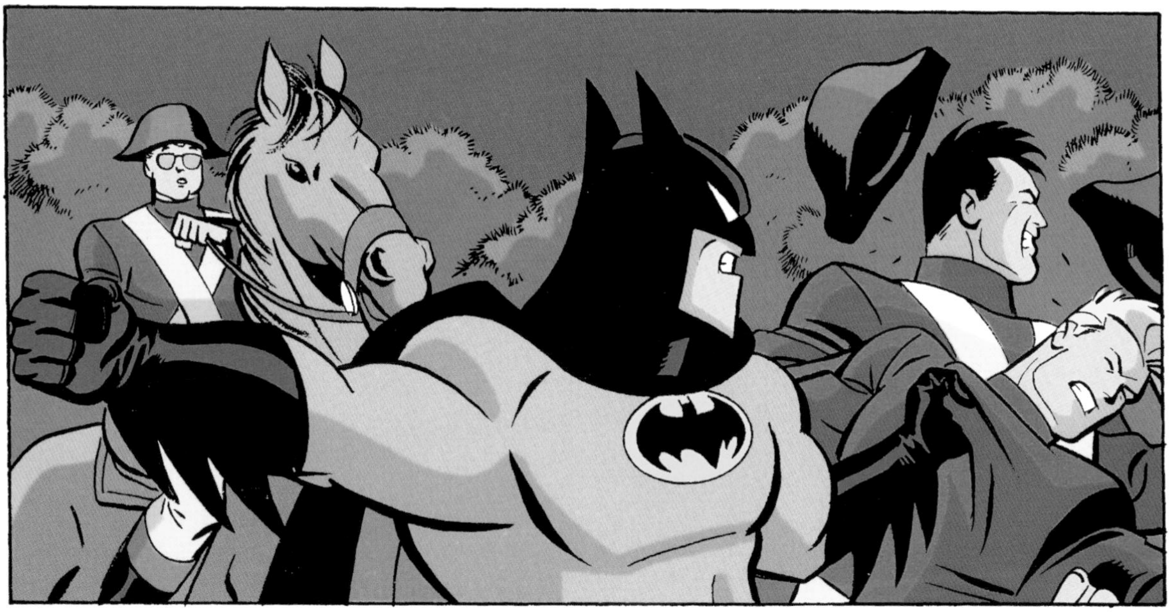

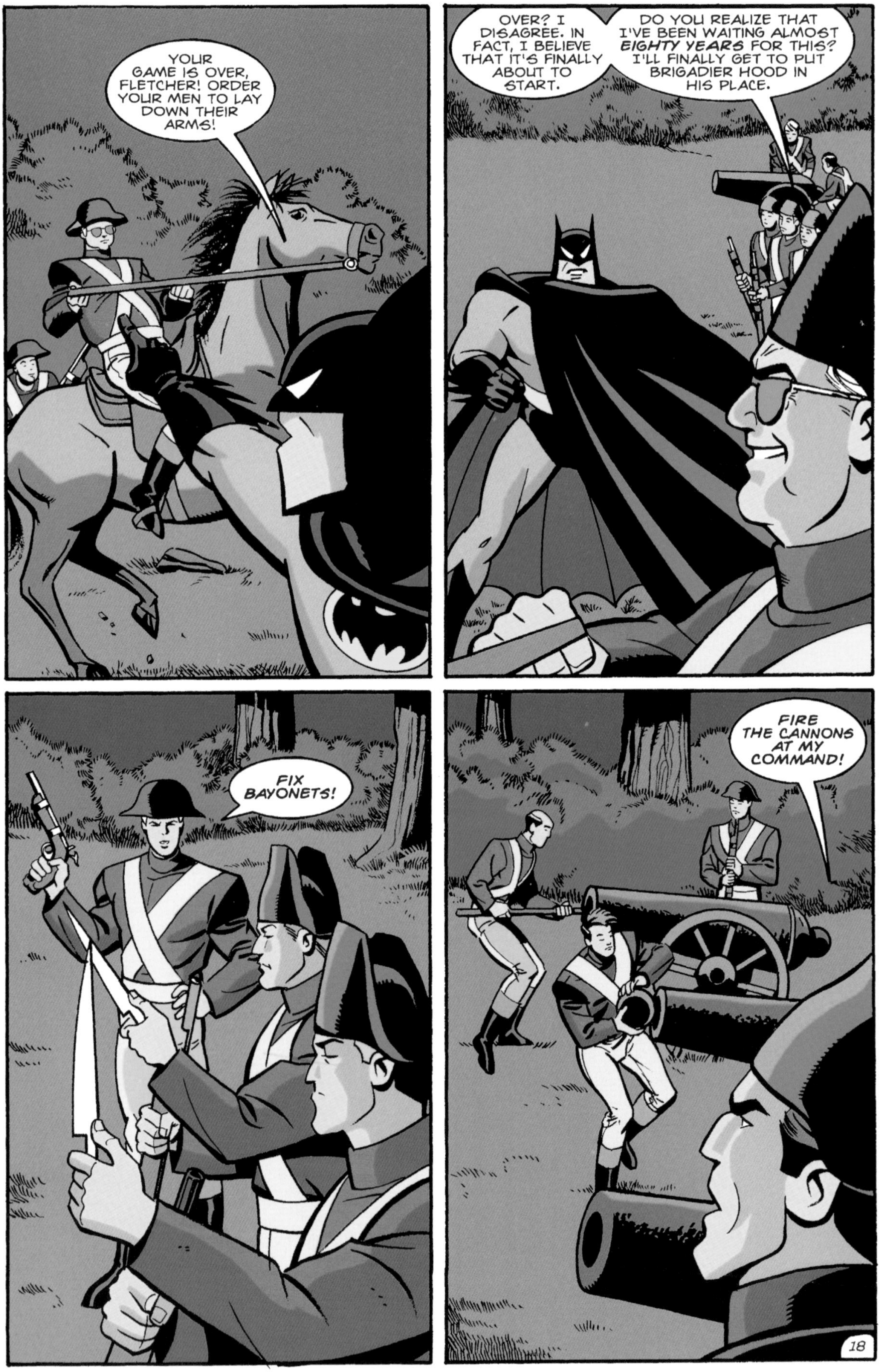
YOUR GAME IS OVER, FLETCHER! ORDER YOUR MEN TO LAY DOWN THEIR ARMS!
OVER? I DISAGREE. IN FACT, I BELIEVE THAT IT'S FINALLY ABOUT TO START.
DO YOU REALIZE THAT I'VE BEEN WAITING ALMOST *EIGHTY YEARS* FOR THIS? I'LL FINALLY GET TO PUT BRIGADIER HOOD IN HIS PLACE.
FIX BAYONETS!
FIRE THE CANNONS AT MY COMMAND!
18

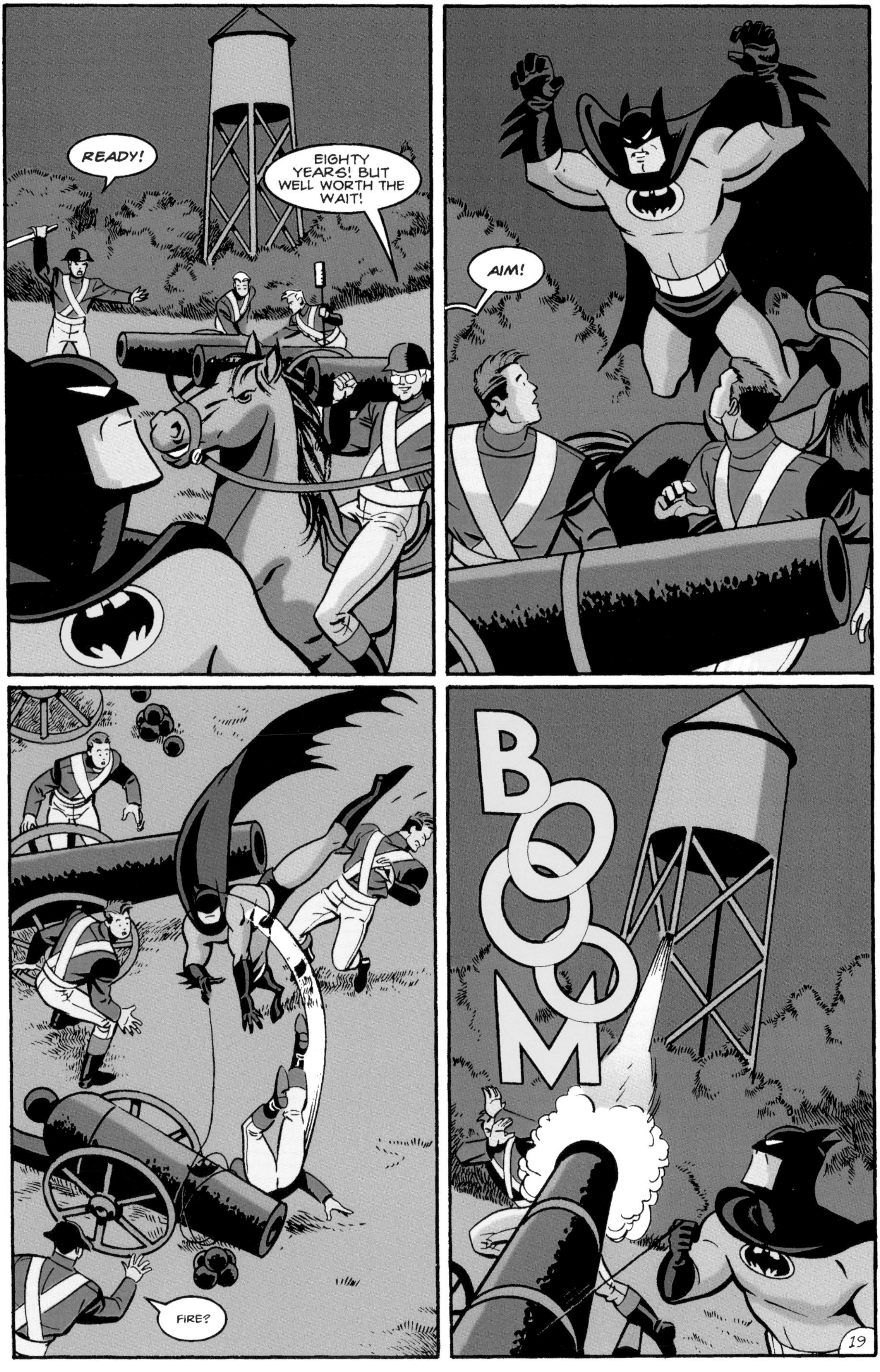
READY!
EIGHTY YEARS! BUT WELL WORTH THE WAIT!
AIM!
FIRE?
BOOOOM
19

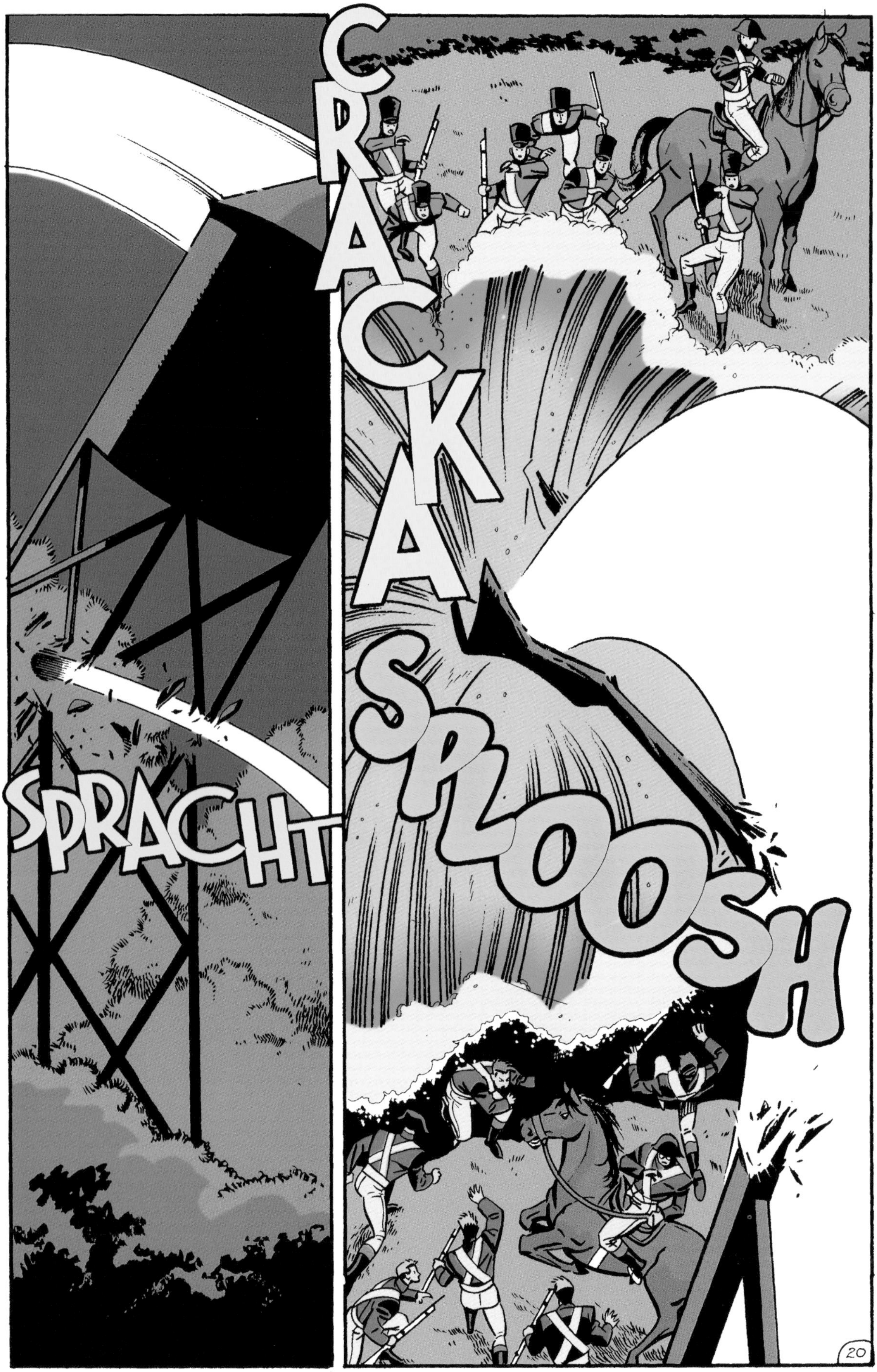

SPRACHT
CRACKA
SPLOOSH
20

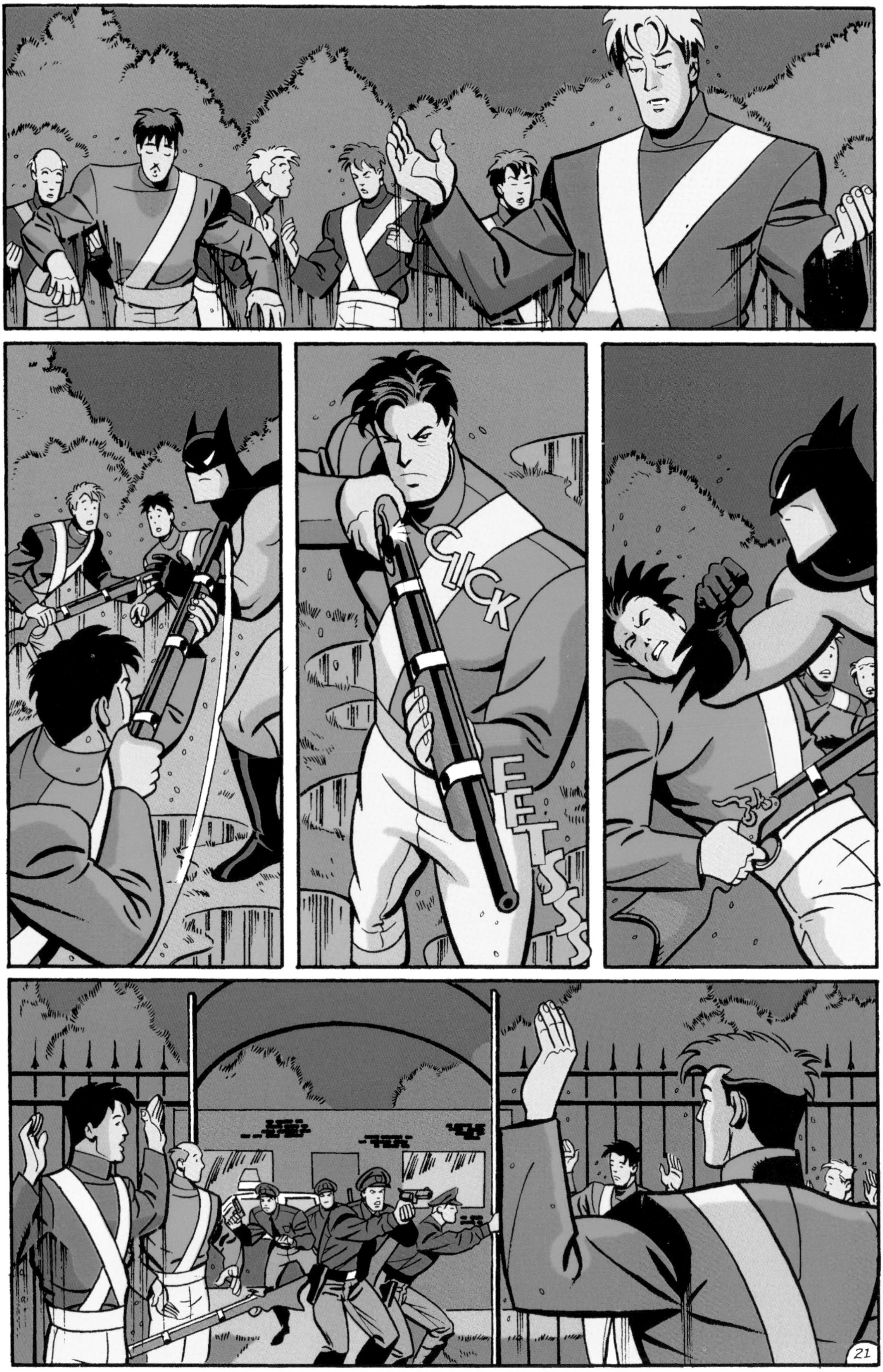
CLICK
FFTSSS
21

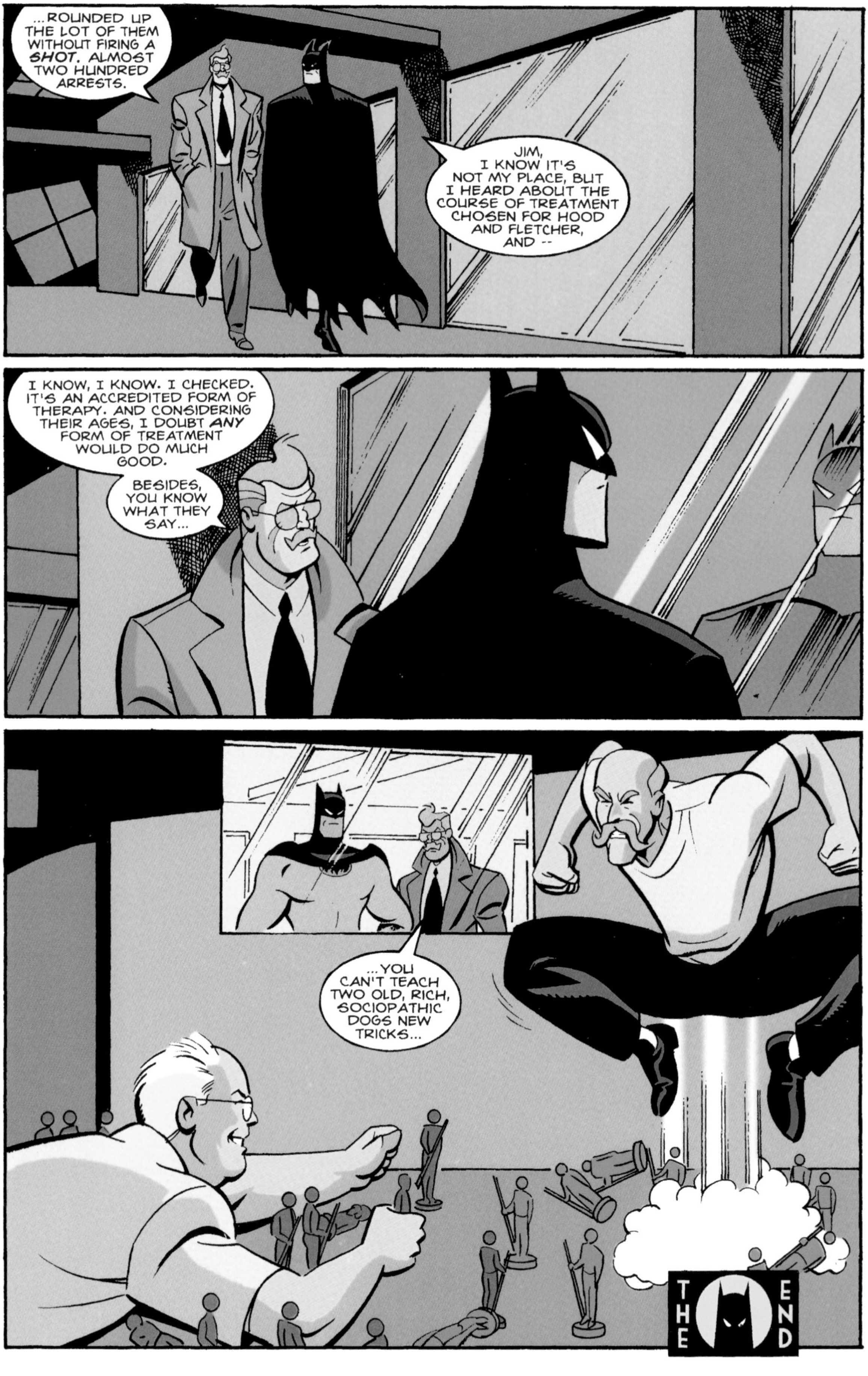
...ROUNDED UP THE LOT OF THEM WITHOUT FIRING A SHOT. ALMOST TWO HUNDRED ARRESTS.
JIM, I KNOW IT'S NOT MY PLACE, BUT I HEARD ABOUT THE COURSE OF TREATMENT CHOSEN FOR HOOD AND FLETCHER, AND --
I KNOW, I KNOW. I CHECKED. IT'S AN ACCREDITED FORM OF THERAPY. AND CONSIDERING THEIR AGES, I DOUBT ANY FORM OF TREATMENT WOULD DO MUCH GOOD.
BESIDES, YOU KNOW WHAT THEY SAY...
...YOU CAN'T TEACH TWO OLD, RICH, SOCIOPATHIC DOGS NEW TRICKS...
THE END

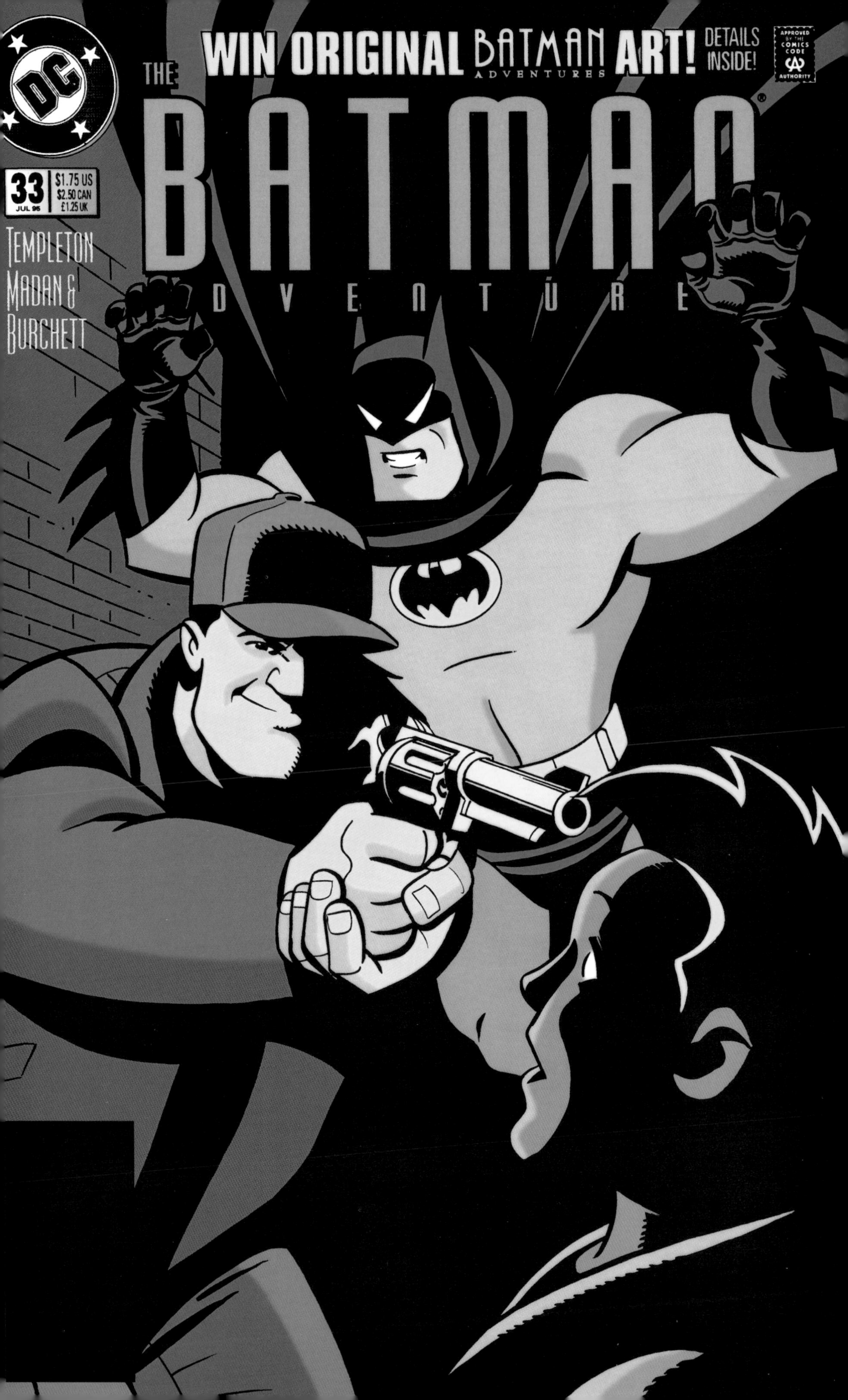

WIN ORIGINAL BATMAN ADVENTURES ART!
DETAILS INSIDE!
APPROVED BY THE COMICS CODE AUTHORITY
THE BATMAN ADVENTURES
33
JUL 95
$1.75 US
$2.50 CAN
£1.25 UK
TEMPLETON
MADAN &
BURCHETT

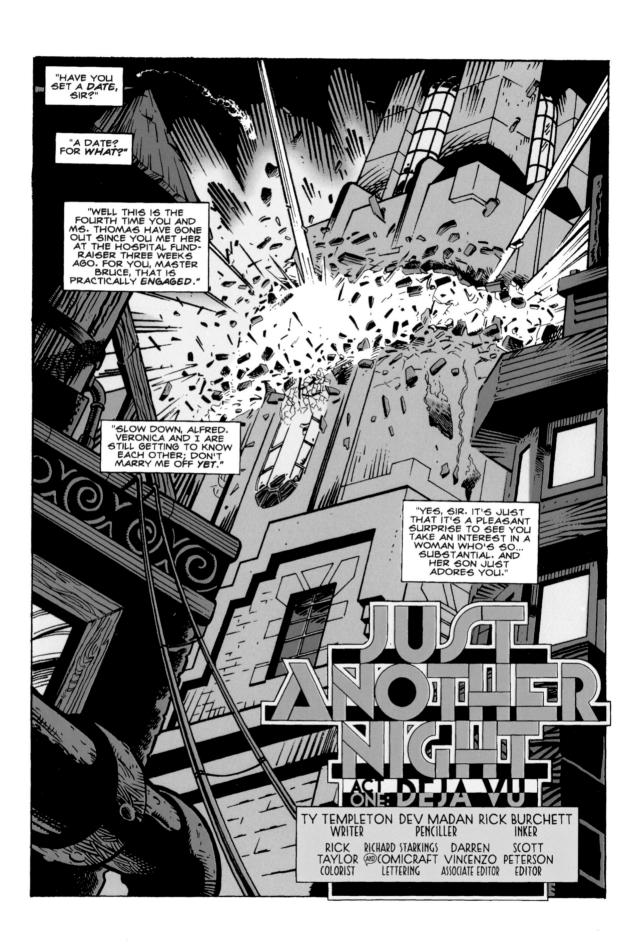

"HAVE YOU SET A *DATE*, SIR?"

"A DATE? FOR *WHAT*?"

"WELL THIS IS THE FOURTH TIME YOU AND MS. THOMAS HAVE GONE OUT SINCE YOU MET HER AT THE HOSPITAL FUND-RAISER THREE WEEKS AGO. FOR YOU, MASTER BRUCE, THAT IS PRACTICALLY *ENGAGED*."

"SLOW DOWN, ALFRED. VERONICA AND I ARE STILL GETTING TO KNOW EACH OTHER; DON'T MARRY ME OFF *YET*."

"YES, SIR. IT'S JUST THAT IT'S A PLEASANT SURPRISE TO SEE YOU TAKE AN INTEREST IN A WOMAN WHO'S SO... SUBSTANTIAL. AND HER SON JUST ADORES YOU."

JUST ANOTHER NIGHT

ACT ONE: DEJA VU

TY TEMPLETON
WRITER

DEV MADAN
PENCILLER

RICK BURCHETT
INKER

RICK TAYLOR
COLORIST

RICHARD STARKINGS *AND* COMICRAFT
LETTERING

DARREN VINCENZO
ASSOCIATE EDITOR

SCOTT PETERSON
EDITOR

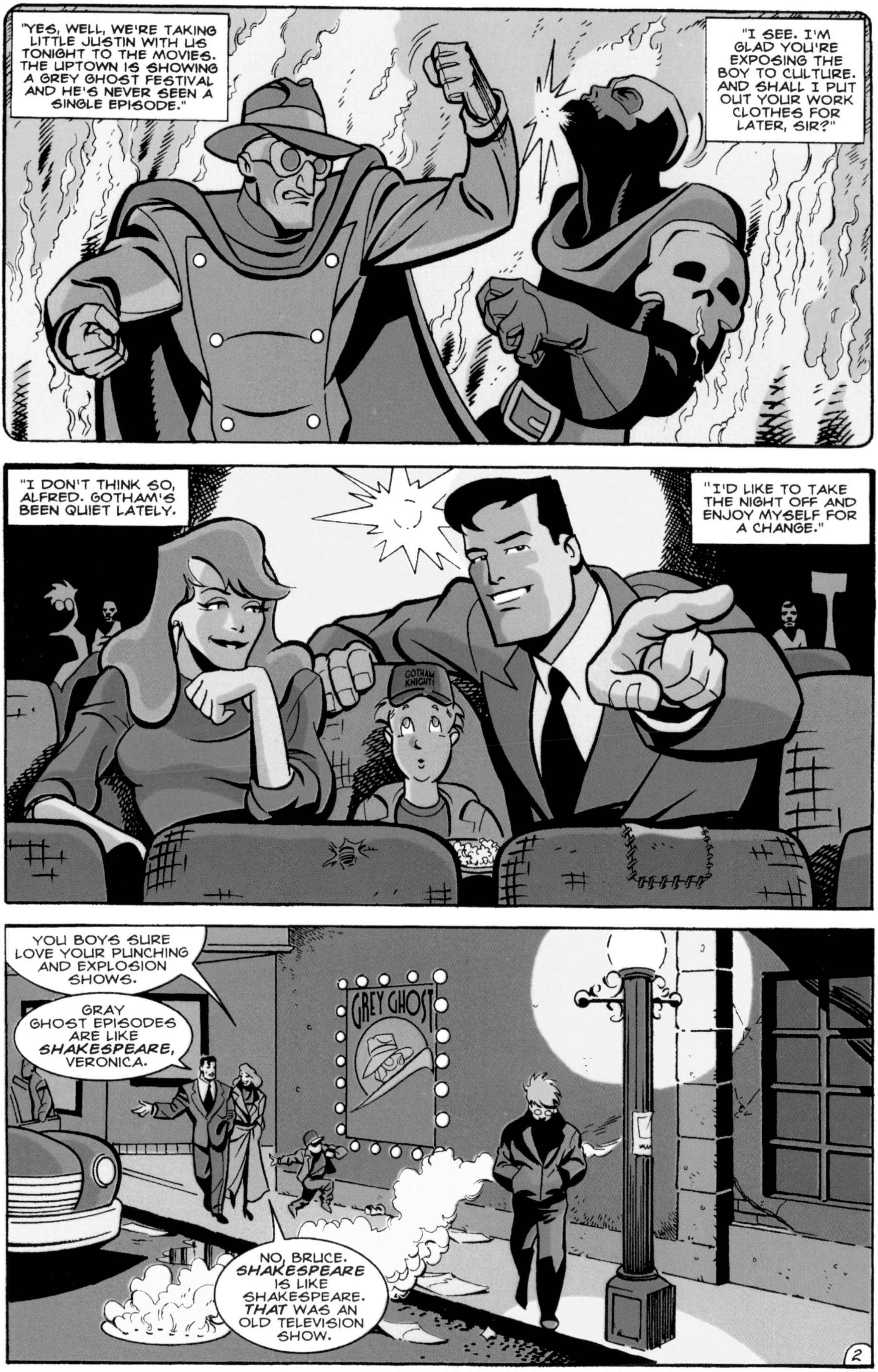
"YES, WELL, WE'RE TAKING LITTLE JUSTIN WITH US TONIGHT TO THE MOVIES. THE UPTOWN IS SHOWING A GREY GHOST FESTIVAL AND HE'S NEVER SEEN A SINGLE EPISODE."
"I SEE. I'M GLAD YOU'RE EXPOSING THE BOY TO CULTURE. AND SHALL I PUT OUT YOUR WORK CLOTHES FOR LATER, SIR?"
"I DON'T THINK SO, ALFRED. GOTHAM'S BEEN QUIET LATELY.
"I'D LIKE TO TAKE THE NIGHT OFF AND ENJOY MYSELF FOR A CHANGE."
GOTHAM KNIGHTS
YOU BOYS SURE LOVE YOUR PUNCHING AND EXPLOSION SHOWS.
GRAY GHOST EPISODES ARE LIKE ***SHAKESPEARE***, VERONICA.
GREY GHOST
NO, BRUCE. ***SHAKESPEARE*** IS LIKE SHAKESPEARE. ***THAT*** WAS AN OLD TELEVISION SHOW.
2

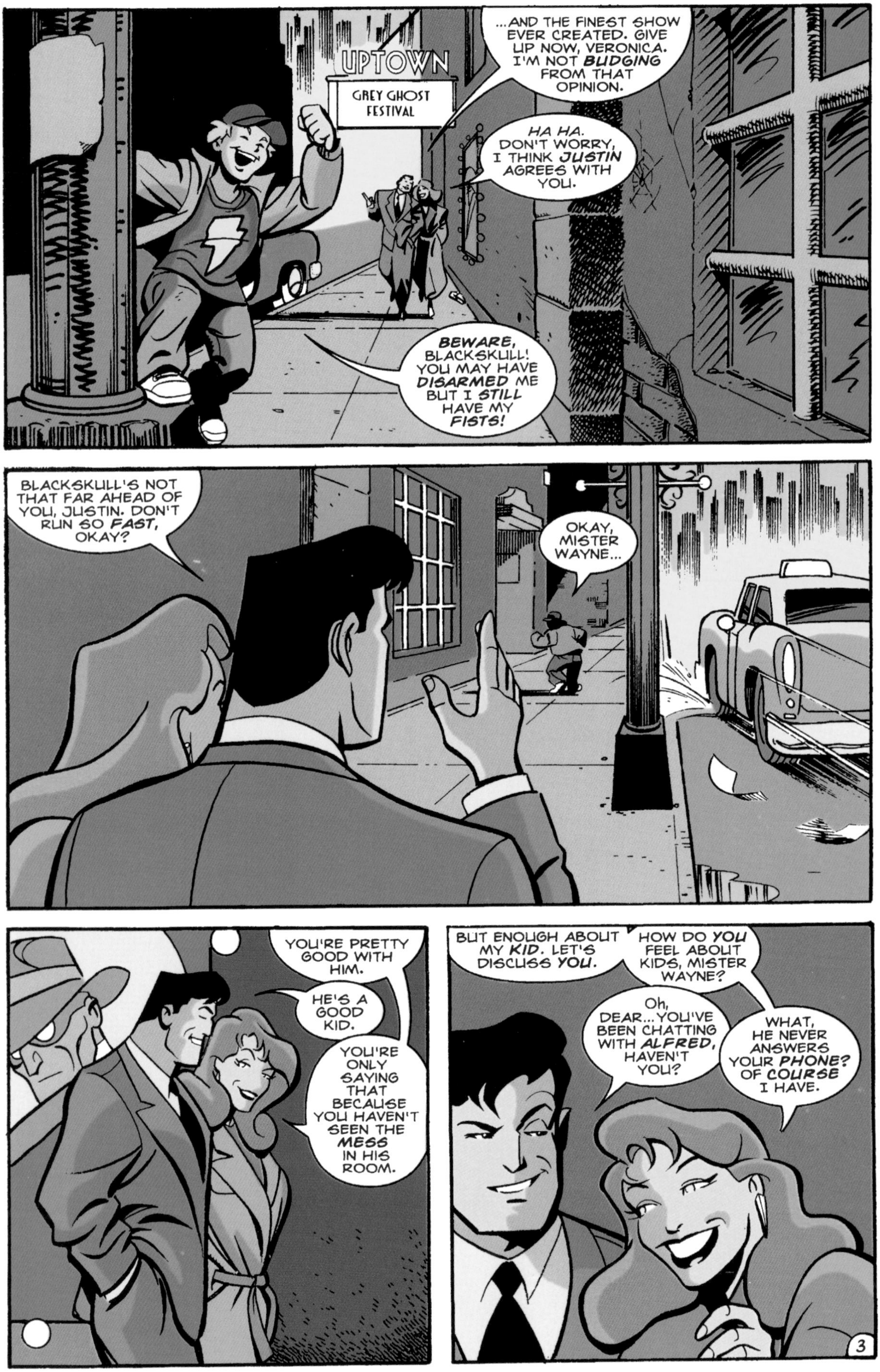
UPTOWN
GREY GHOST FESTIVAL
...AND THE FINEST SHOW EVER CREATED. GIVE UP NOW, VERONICA. I'M NOT BUDGING FROM THAT OPINION.
HA HA. DON'T WORRY, I THINK JUSTIN AGREES WITH YOU.
BEWARE, BLACKSKULL! YOU MAY HAVE DISARMED ME BUT I STILL HAVE MY FISTS!
BLACKSKULL'S NOT THAT FAR AHEAD OF YOU, JUSTIN. DON'T RUN SO FAST, OKAY?
OKAY, MISTER WAYNE...
YOU'RE PRETTY GOOD WITH HIM.
HE'S A GOOD KID.
YOU'RE ONLY SAYING THAT BECAUSE YOU HAVEN'T SEEN THE MESS IN HIS ROOM.
BUT ENOUGH ABOUT MY KID. LET'S DISCUSS YOU.
HOW DO YOU FEEL ABOUT KIDS, MISTER WAYNE?
Oh, DEAR...YOU'VE BEEN CHATTING WITH ALFRED, HAVEN'T YOU?
WHAT, HE NEVER ANSWERS YOUR PHONE? OF COURSE I HAVE.
3

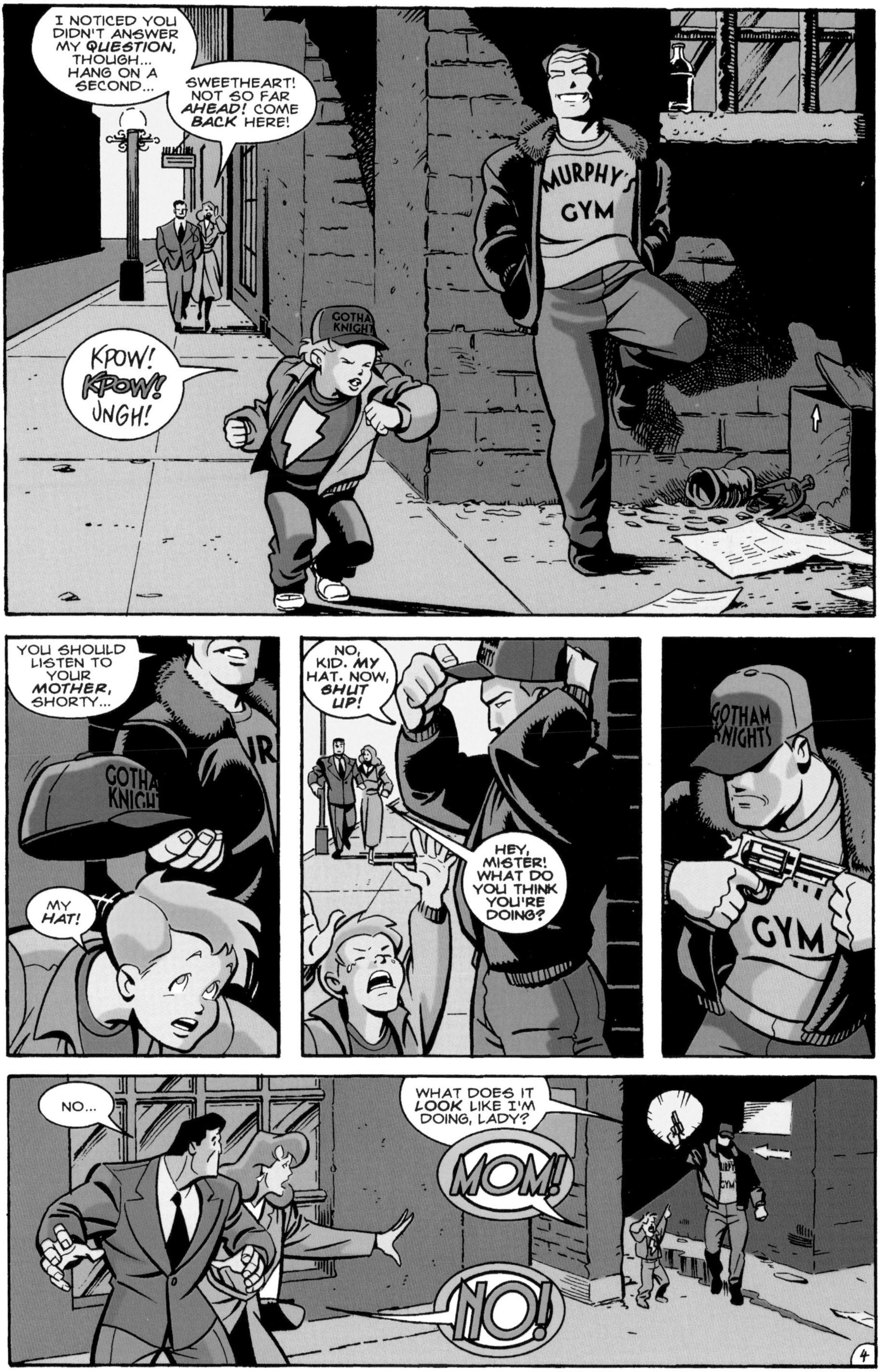
I NOTICED YOU DIDN'T ANSWER MY QUESTION, THOUGH... HANG ON A SECOND...
SWEETHEART! NOT SO FAR AHEAD! COME BACK HERE!
MURPHY'S GYM
GOTHAM KNIGHT
KPOW! KPOW! UNGH!
YOU SHOULD LISTEN TO YOUR MOTHER, SHORTY...
GOTHAM KNIGHT
MY HAT!
NO, KID. MY HAT. NOW, SHUT UP!
HEY, MISTER! WHAT DO YOU THINK YOU'RE DOING?
GOTHAM KNIGHTS
GYM
NO...
WHAT DOES IT LOOK LIKE I'M DOING, LADY?
MOM!
NO!
4

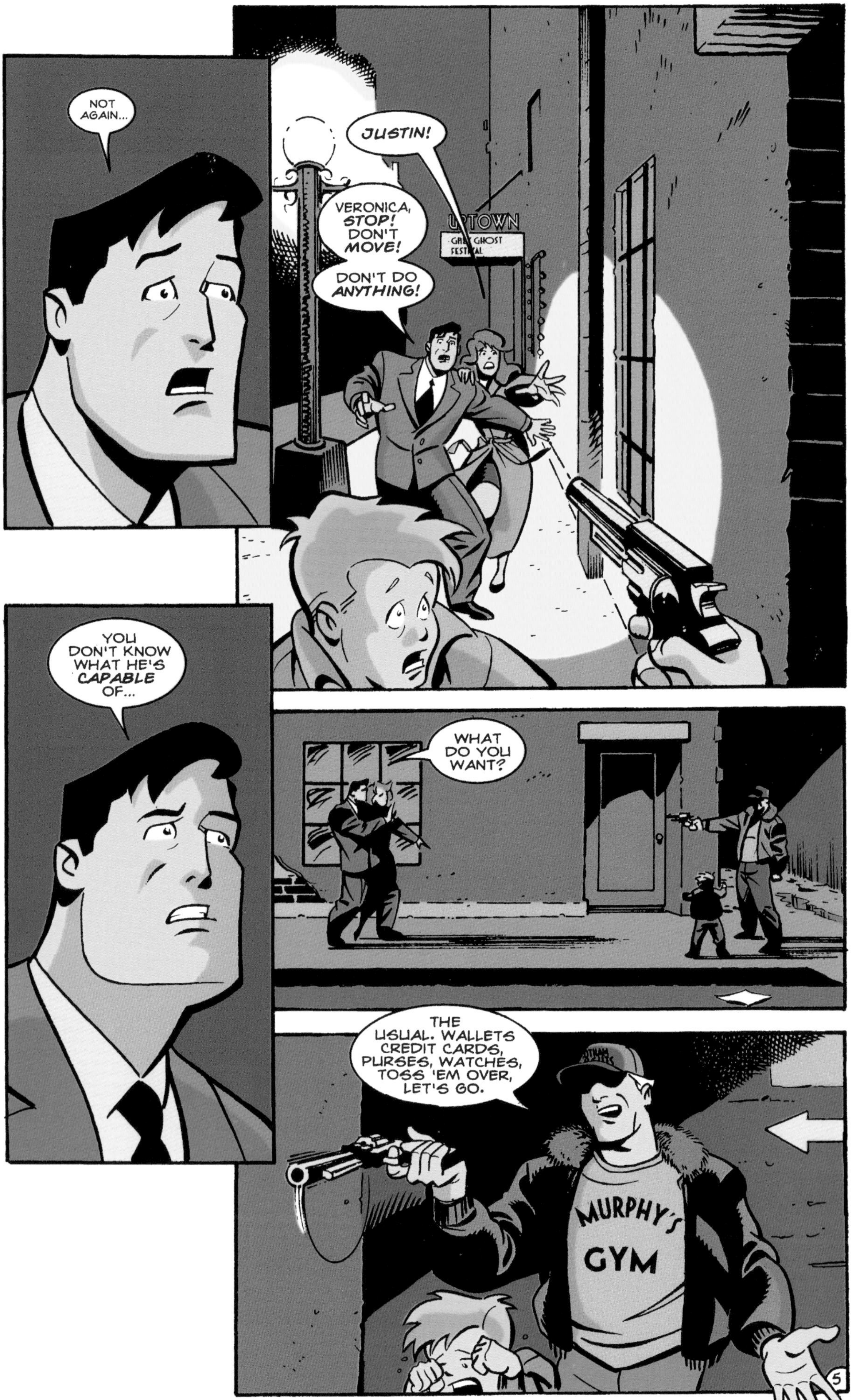
NOT AGAIN...
JUSTIN!
VERONICA, STOP! DON'T MOVE!
DON'T DO ANYTHING!
UPTOWN
GREY GHOST FESTIVAL
YOU DON'T KNOW WHAT HE'S CAPABLE OF...
WHAT DO YOU WANT?
THE USUAL. WALLETS CREDIT CARDS, PURSES, WATCHES, TOSS 'EM OVER, LET'S GO.
MURPHY'S GYM
5

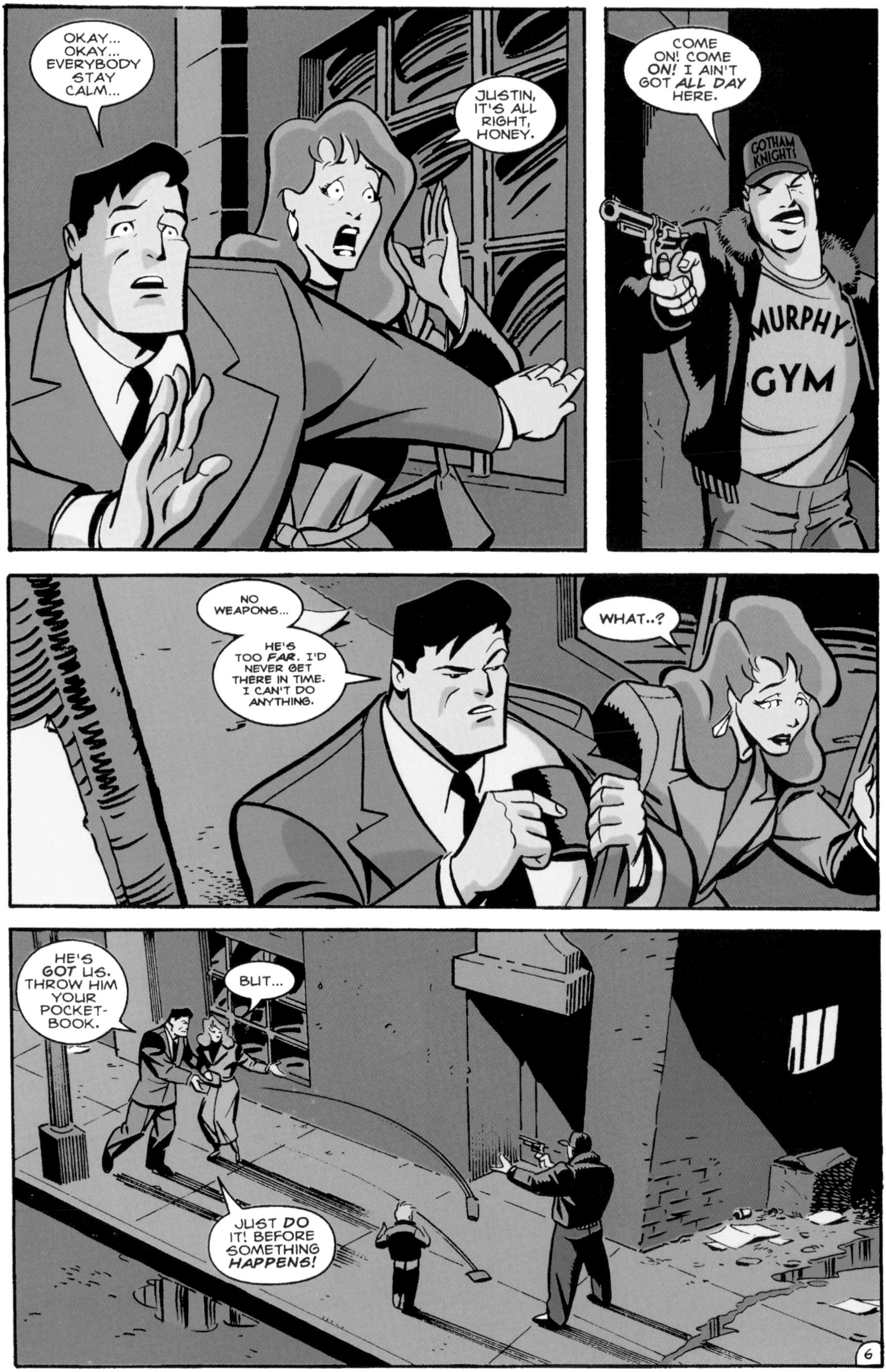
OKAY... OKAY... EVERYBODY STAY CALM...
JUSTIN, IT'S ALL RIGHT, HONEY.
COME ON! COME ON! I AIN'T GOT ALL DAY HERE.
GOTHAM KNIGHTS
MURPHY'S GYM
NO WEAPONS...
HE'S TOO FAR. I'D NEVER GET THERE IN TIME. I CAN'T DO ANYTHING.
WHAT..?
HE'S GOT US. THROW HIM YOUR POCKET-BOOK.
BUT...
JUST DO IT! BEFORE SOMETHING HAPPENS!
6

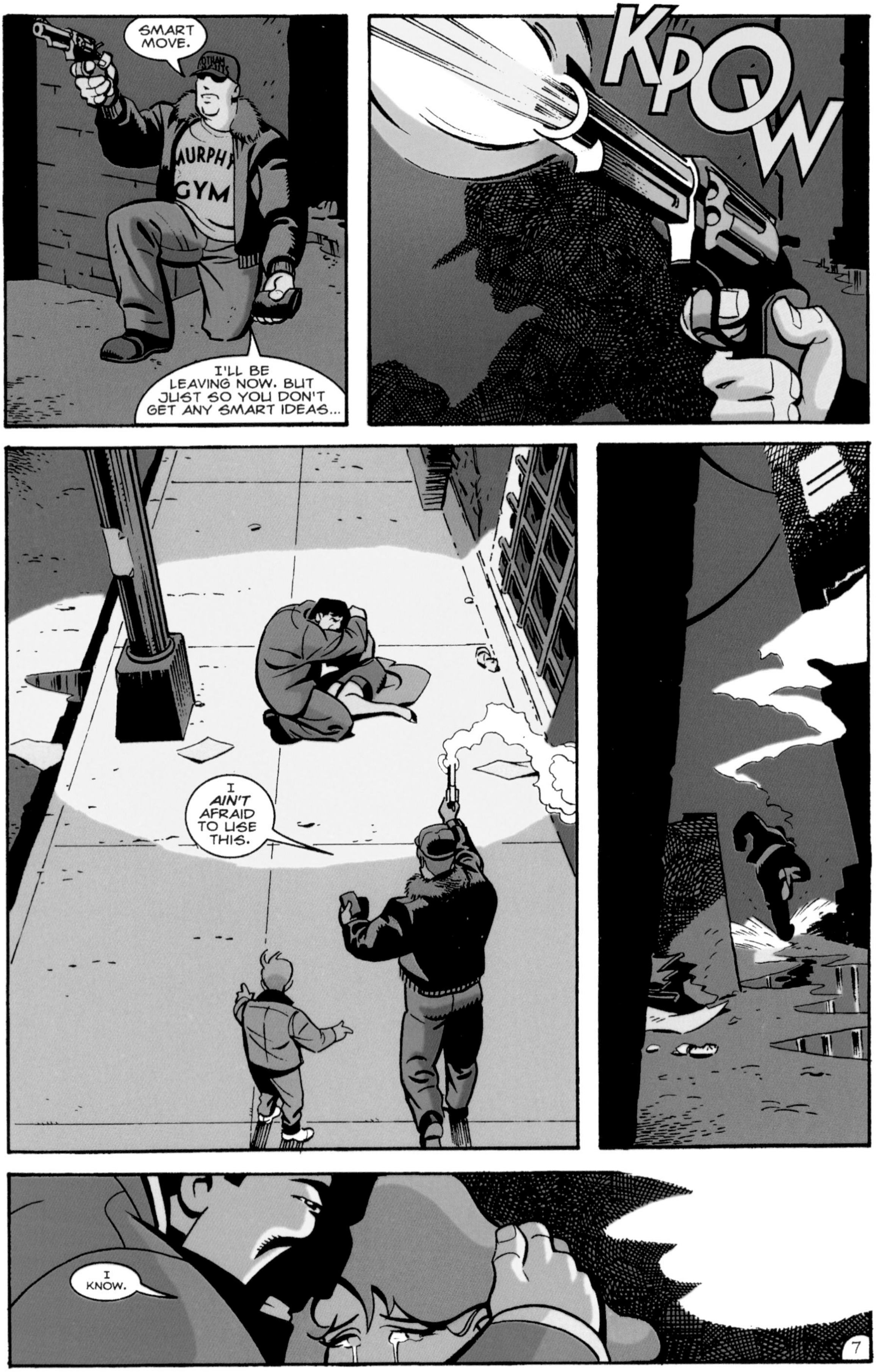
SMART MOVE.
I'LL BE LEAVING NOW. BUT JUST SO YOU DON'T GET ANY SMART IDEAS...
MURPHY GYM
KPOW
I AIN'T AFRAID TO USE THIS.
I KNOW.
7

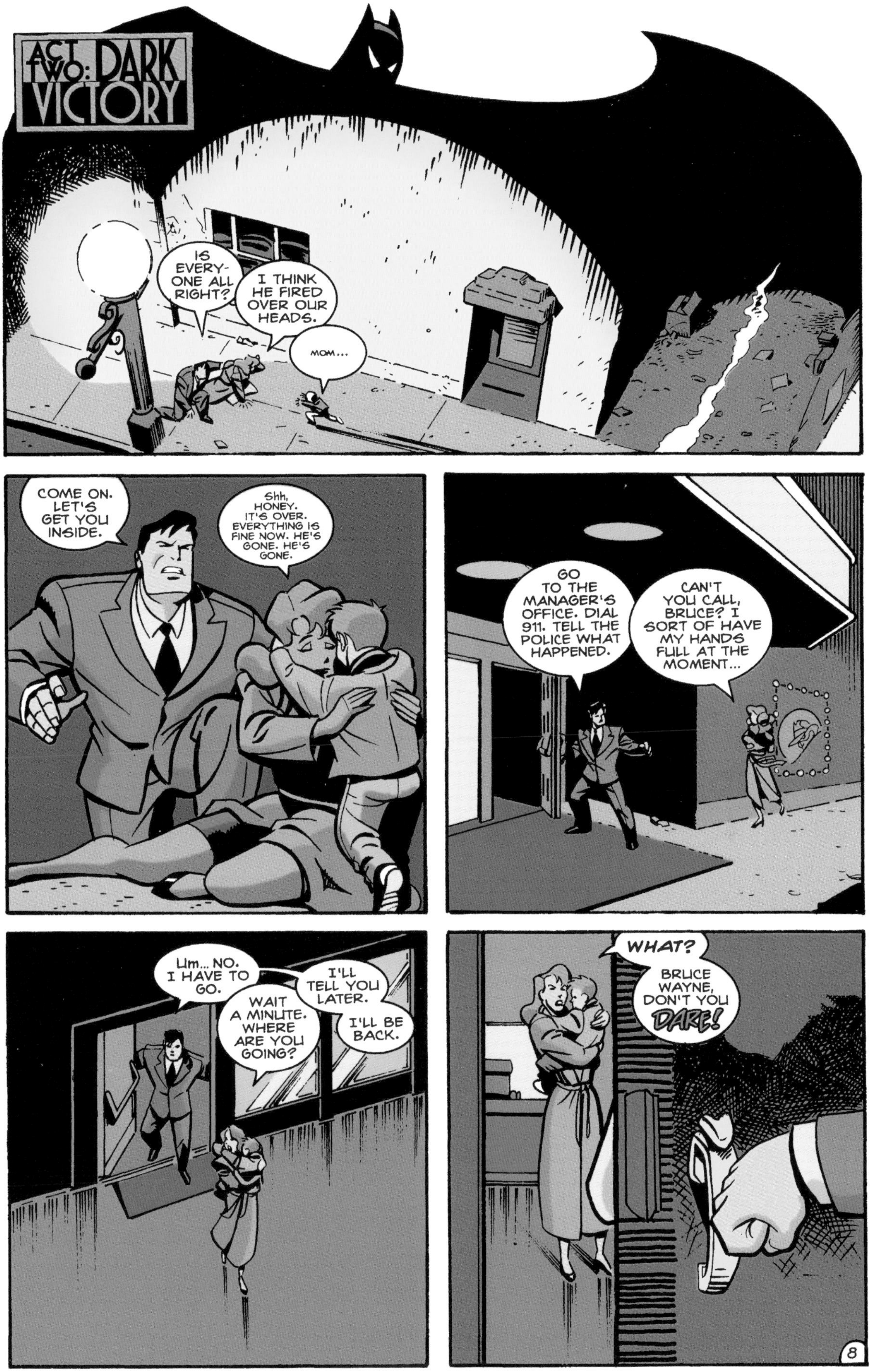
ACT TWO: DARK VICTORY
IS EVERY-ONE ALL RIGHT?
I THINK HE FIRED OVER OUR HEADS.
MOM...
COME ON. LET'S GET YOU INSIDE.
Shh, HONEY. IT'S OVER. EVERYTHING IS FINE NOW. HE'S GONE. HE'S GONE.
GO TO THE MANAGER'S OFFICE. DIAL 911. TELL THE POLICE WHAT HAPPENED.
CAN'T YOU CALL, BRUCE? I SORT OF HAVE MY HANDS FULL AT THE MOMENT...
Um... NO. I HAVE TO GO.
WAIT A MINUTE. WHERE ARE YOU GOING?
I'LL TELL YOU LATER.
I'LL BE BACK.
WHAT?
BRUCE WAYNE, DON'T YOU DARE!
8

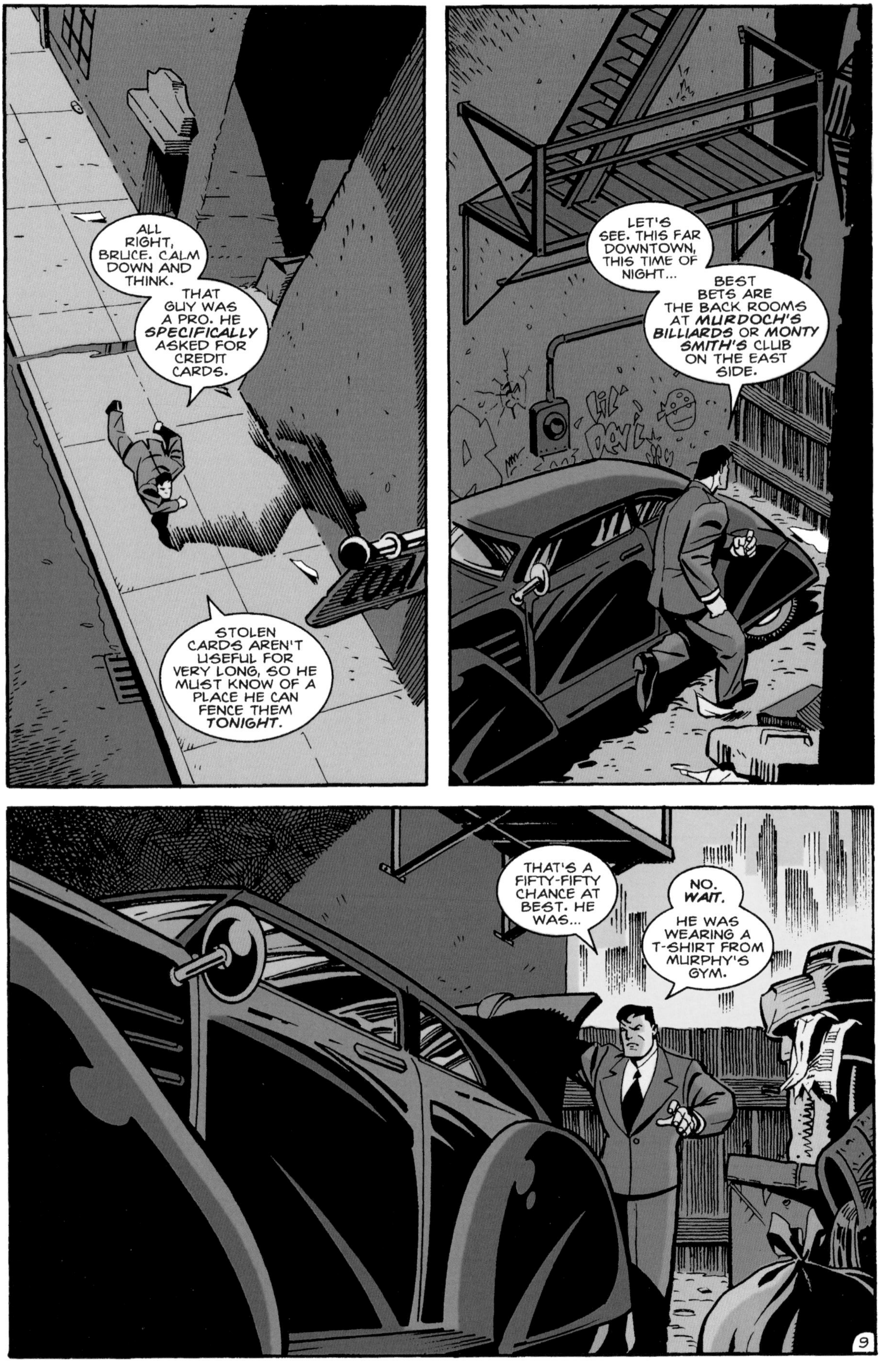
ALL RIGHT, BRUCE. CALM DOWN AND THINK.
THAT GUY WAS A PRO. HE *SPECIFICALLY* ASKED FOR CREDIT CARDS.
STOLEN CARDS AREN'T USEFUL FOR VERY LONG, SO HE MUST KNOW OF A PLACE HE CAN FENCE THEM *TONIGHT*.
LET'S SEE. THIS FAR DOWNTOWN, THIS TIME OF NIGHT...
BEST BETS ARE THE BACK ROOMS AT *MURDOCH'S BILLIARDS* OR *MONTY SMITH'S* CLUB ON THE EAST SIDE.
THAT'S A FIFTY-FIFTY CHANCE AT BEST. HE WAS...
NO. *WAIT.*
HE WAS WEARING A T-SHIRT FROM MURPHY'S GYM.
9

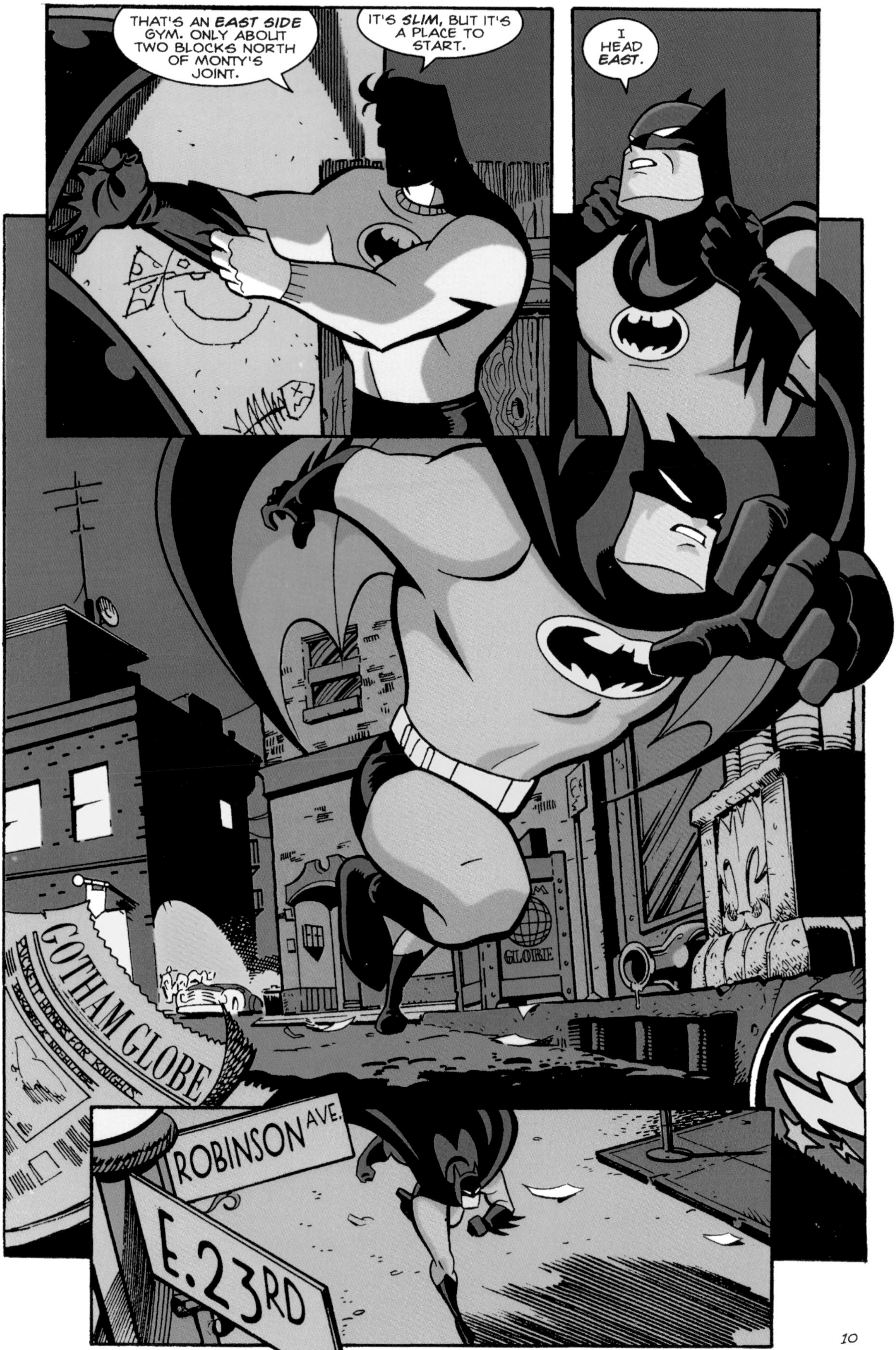
THAT'S AN EAST SIDE GYM. ONLY ABOUT TWO BLOCKS NORTH OF MONTY'S JOINT.
IT'S SLIM, BUT IT'S A PLACE TO START.
I HEAD EAST.
GOTHAM GLOBE
GLOBE
ROBINSON AVE.
E.23RD

10

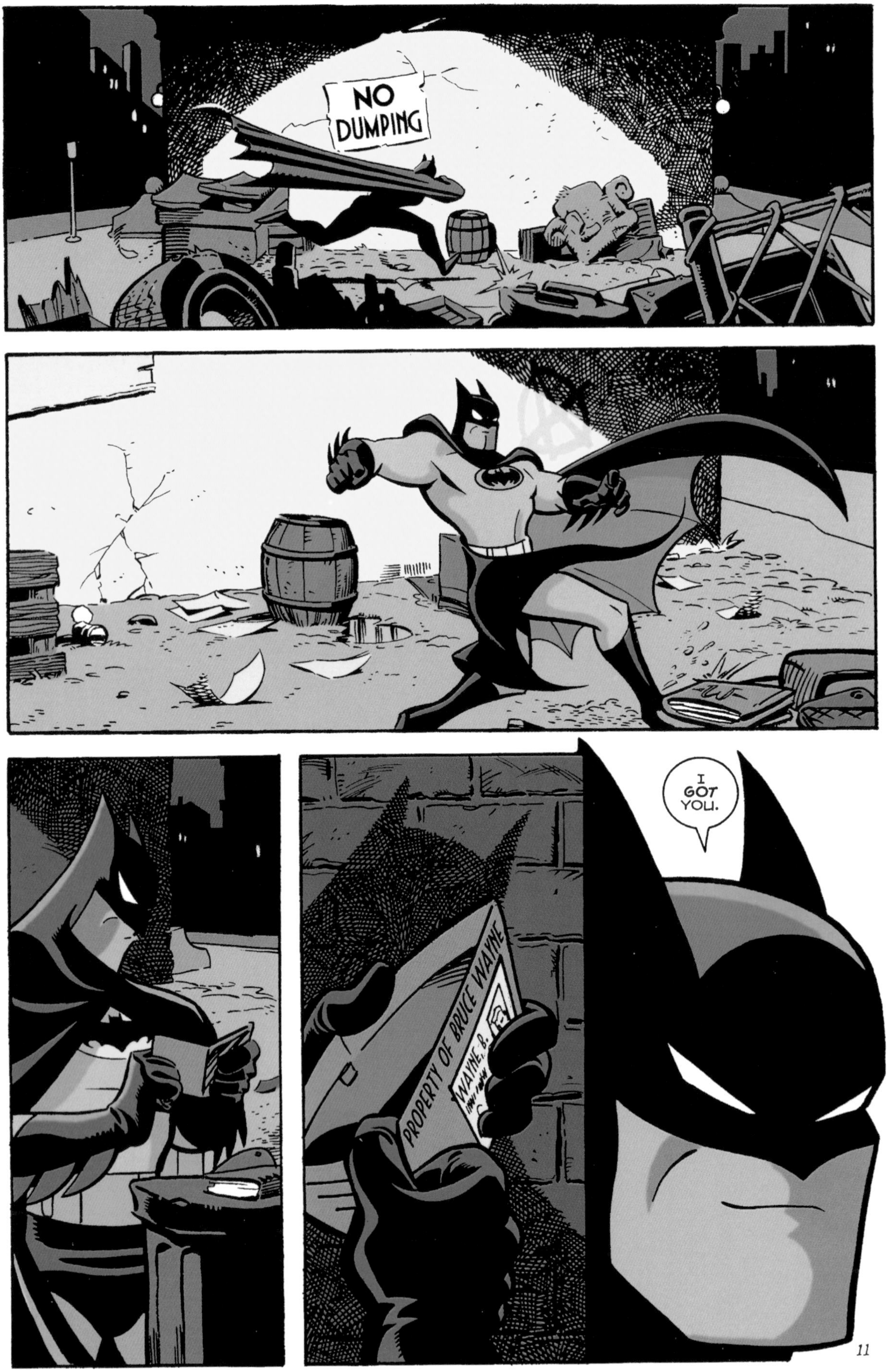
NO DUMPING
PROPERTY OF BRUCE WAYNE
WAYNE, B.
I GOT YOU.
11

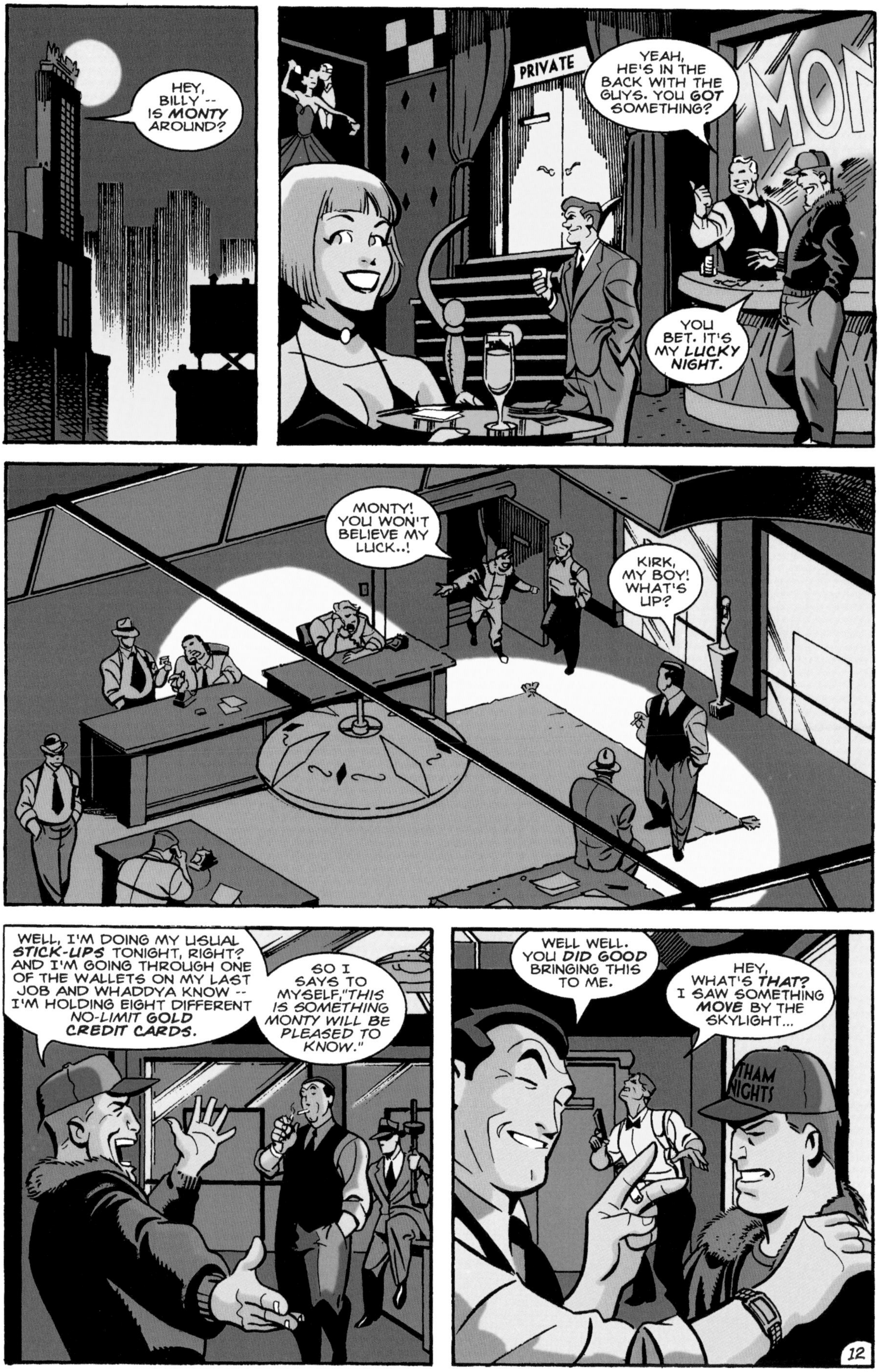
HEY, BILLY -- IS MONTY AROUND?
YEAH, HE'S IN THE BACK WITH THE GUYS. YOU GOT SOMETHING?
YOU BET. IT'S MY LUCKY NIGHT.
PRIVATE
MONTY! YOU WON'T BELIEVE MY LUCK..!
KIRK, MY BOY! WHAT'S UP?
WELL, I'M DOING MY USUAL STICK-UPS TONIGHT, RIGHT? AND I'M GOING THROUGH ONE OF THE WALLETS ON MY LAST JOB AND WHADDYA KNOW -- I'M HOLDING EIGHT DIFFERENT NO-LIMIT GOLD CREDIT CARDS.
SO I SAYS TO MYSELF, "THIS IS SOMETHING MONTY WILL BE PLEASED TO KNOW."
WELL WELL. YOU DID GOOD BRINGING THIS TO ME.
HEY, WHAT'S THAT? I SAW SOMETHING MOVE BY THE SKYLIGHT...
12

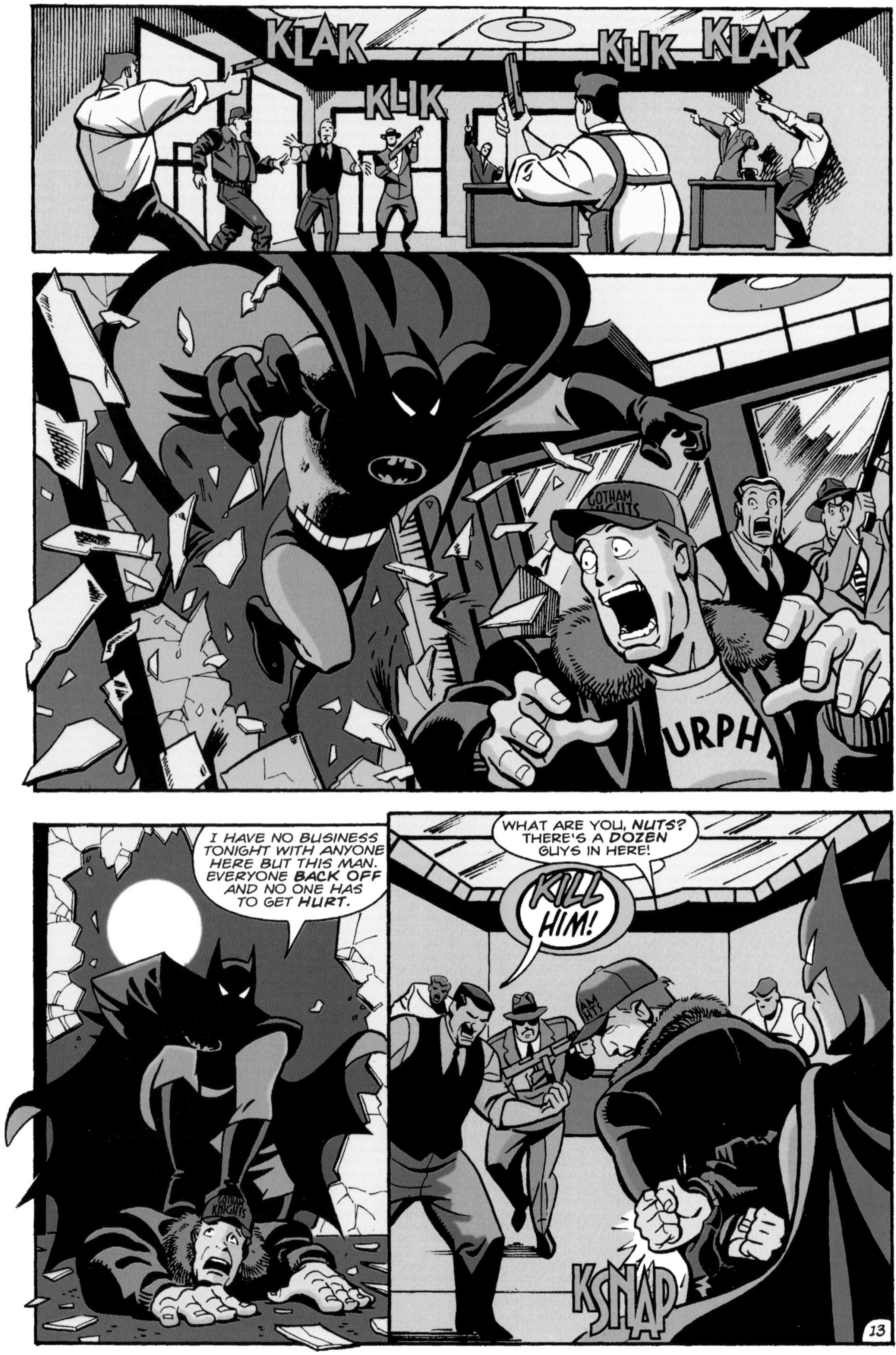
KLAK
KLIK
KLIK KLAK
GOTHAM KNIGHTS
URPH
I HAVE NO BUSINESS TONIGHT WITH ANYONE HERE BUT THIS MAN. EVERYONE BACK OFF AND NO ONE HAS TO GET HURT.
GOTHAM KNIGHTS
WHAT ARE YOU, NUTS? THERE'S A DOZEN GUYS IN HERE!
KILL HIM!
KSNAP
13

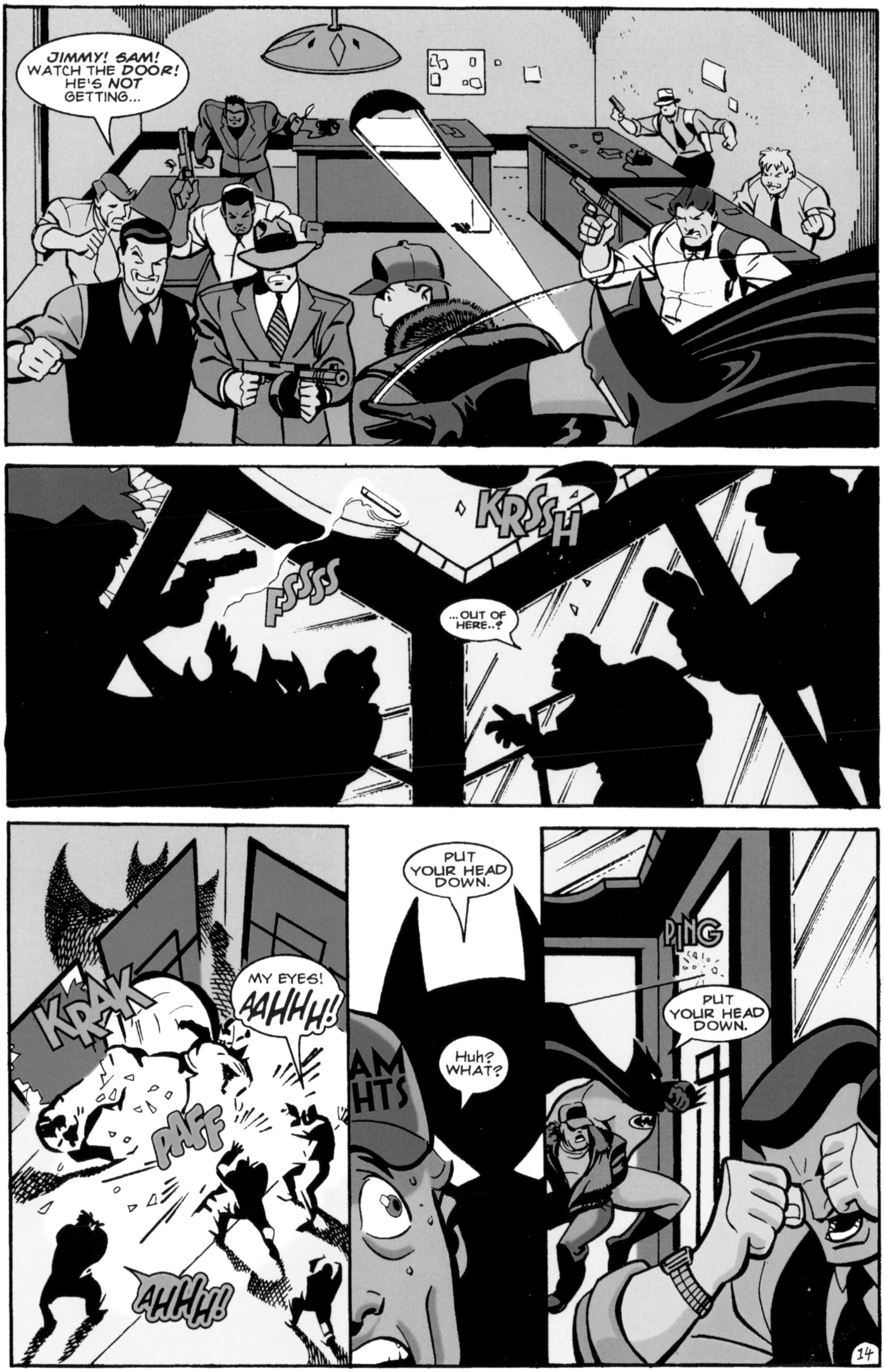
JIMMY! SAM! WATCH THE DOOR! HE'S NOT GETTING...
KRSSH
FSSSS
...OUT OF HERE..?
KRAK
MY EYES! AAHHH!
PAFF
AHHH!
PUT YOUR HEAD DOWN.
Huh? WHAT?
PING
PUT YOUR HEAD DOWN.
14

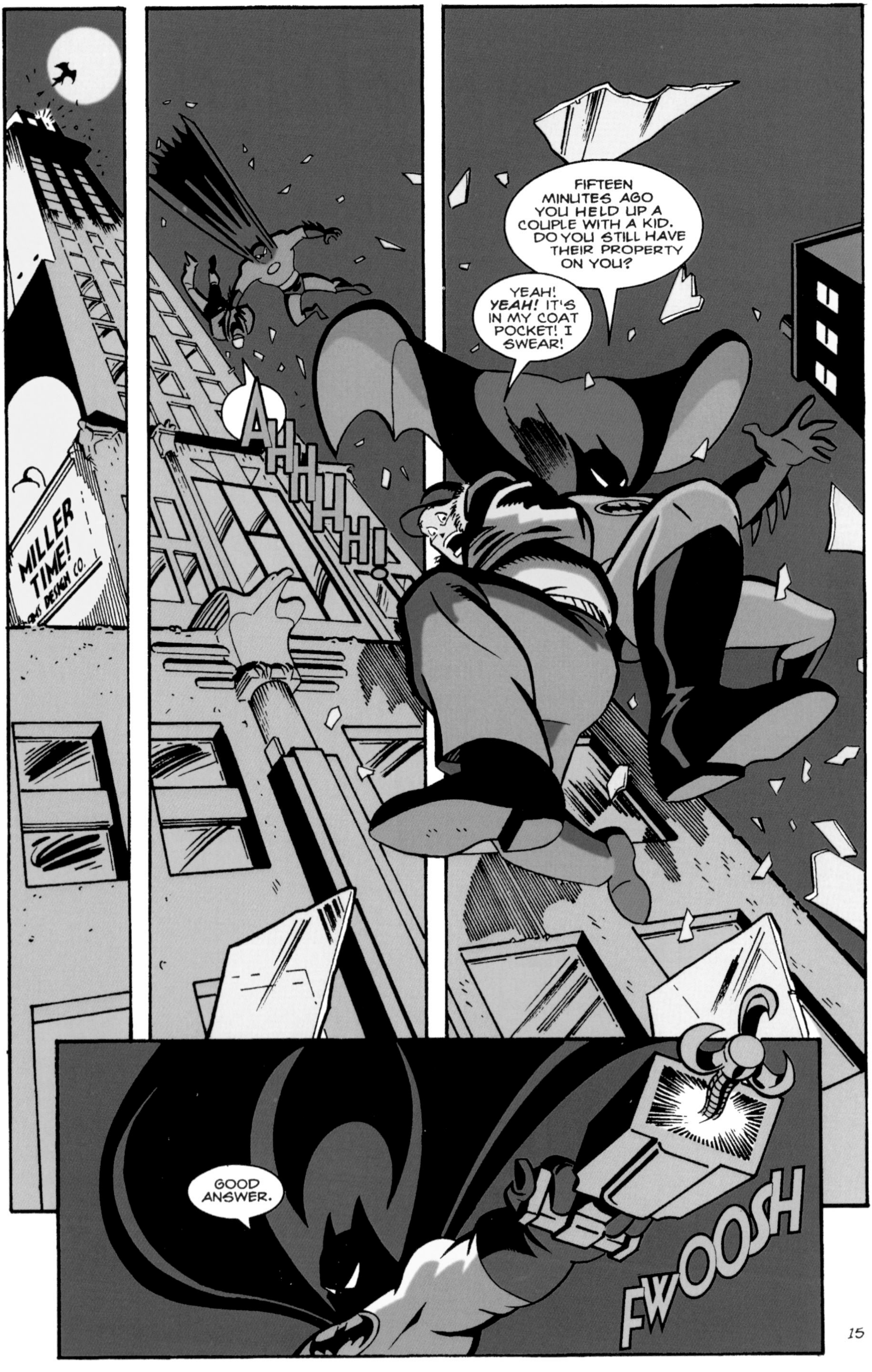
MILLER TIME!
AHHHHHH!
FIFTEEN MINUTES AGO YOU HELD UP A COUPLE WITH A KID. DO YOU STILL HAVE THEIR PROPERTY ON YOU?
YEAH! *YEAH!* IT'S IN MY COAT POCKET! I SWEAR!
GOOD ANSWER.
FWOOSH
15

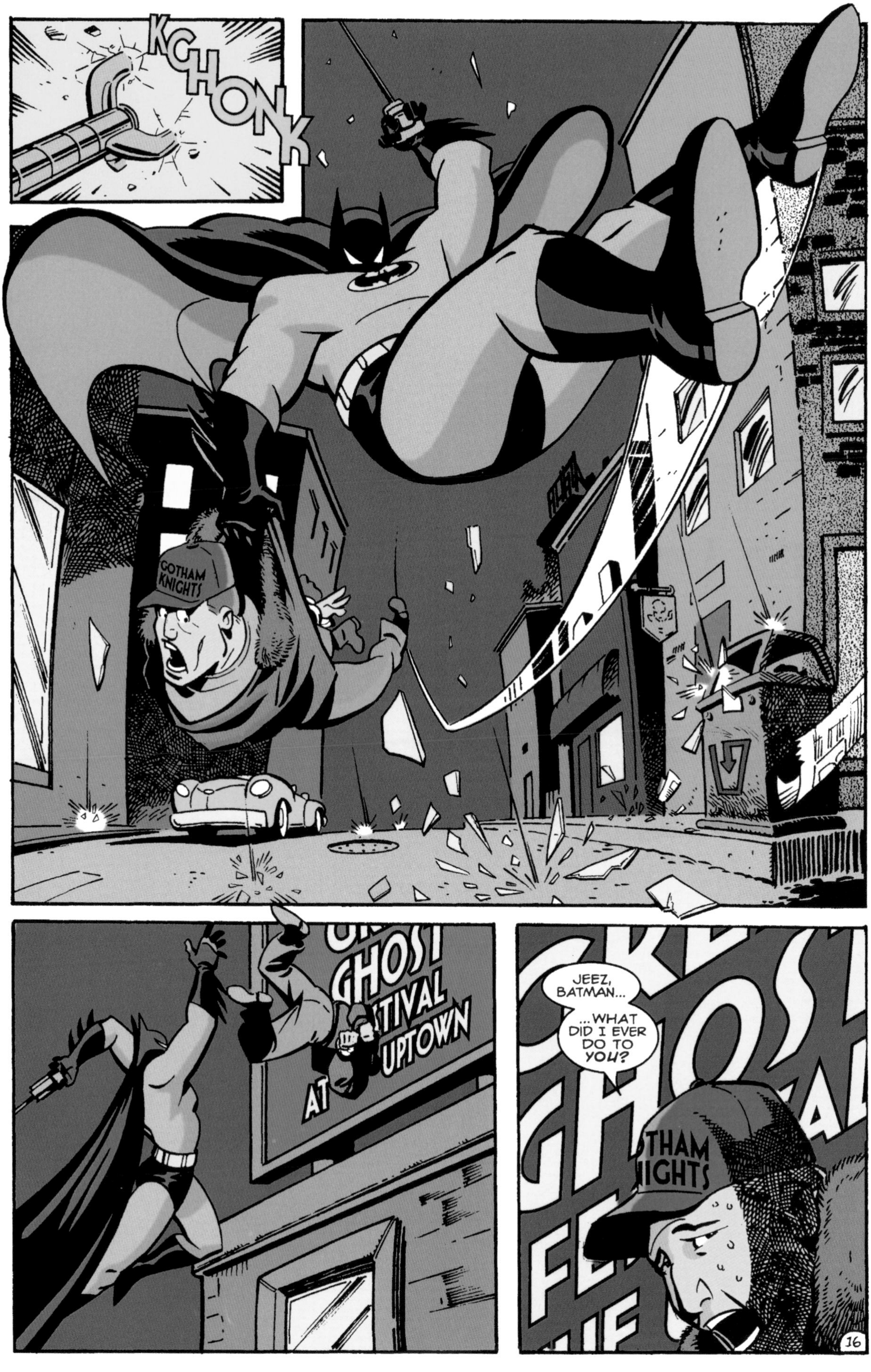
KCHONK
GOTHAM KNIGHTS
GHOST
TIVAL
AT
UPTOWN
JEEZ, BATMAN...
...WHAT DID I EVER DO TO YOU?
16

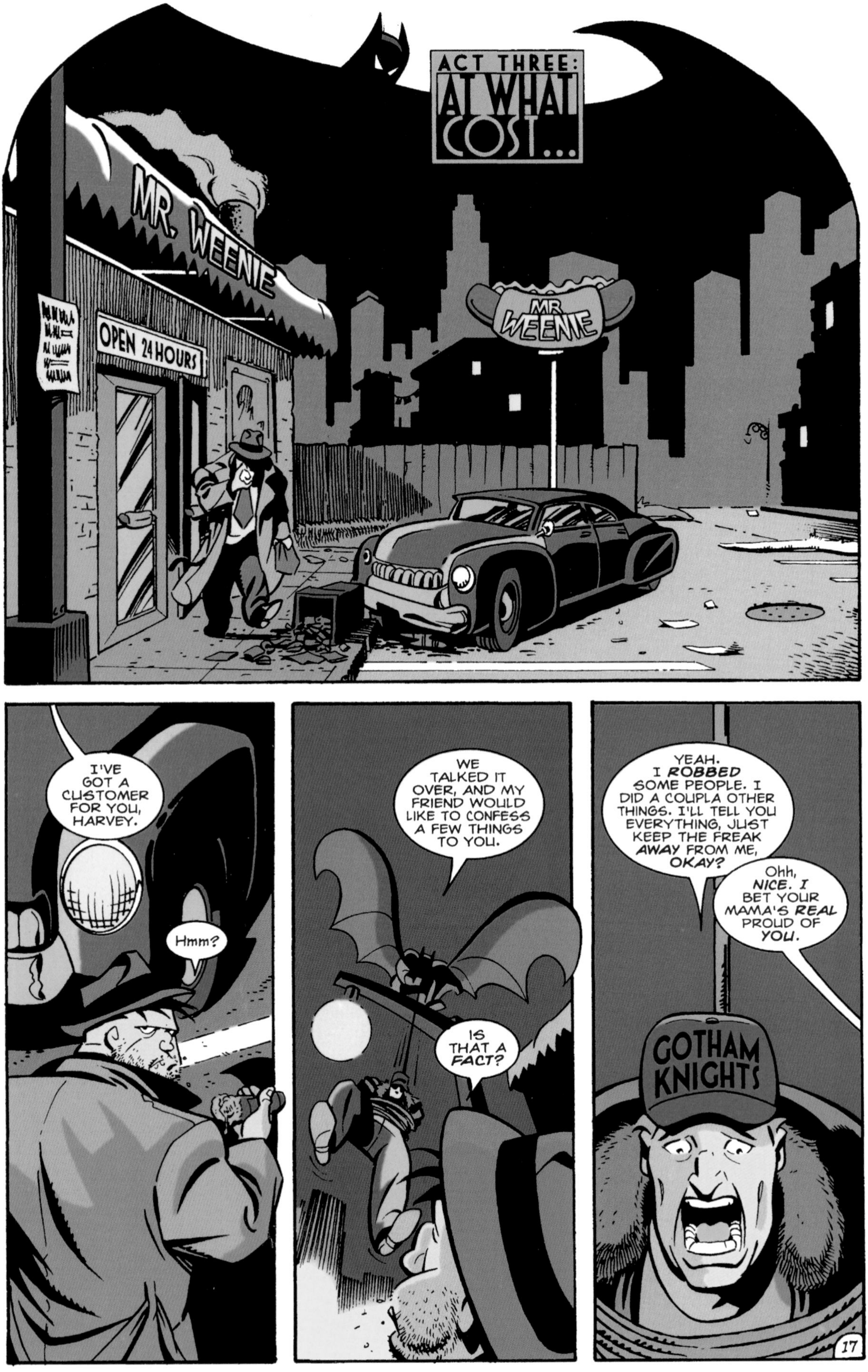
ACT THREE:
AT WHAT COST...
MR. WEENIE
OPEN 24 HOURS
MR WEENIE
I'VE GOT A CUSTOMER FOR YOU, HARVEY.
Hmm?
WE TALKED IT OVER, AND MY FRIEND WOULD LIKE TO CONFESS A FEW THINGS TO YOU.
IS THAT A FACT?
YEAH. I ROBBED SOME PEOPLE. I DID A COUPLA OTHER THINGS. I'LL TELL YOU EVERYTHING, JUST KEEP THE FREAK AWAY FROM ME, OKAY?
Ohh, NICE. I BET YOUR MAMA'S REAL PROUD OF YOU.
GOTHAM KNIGHTS
17

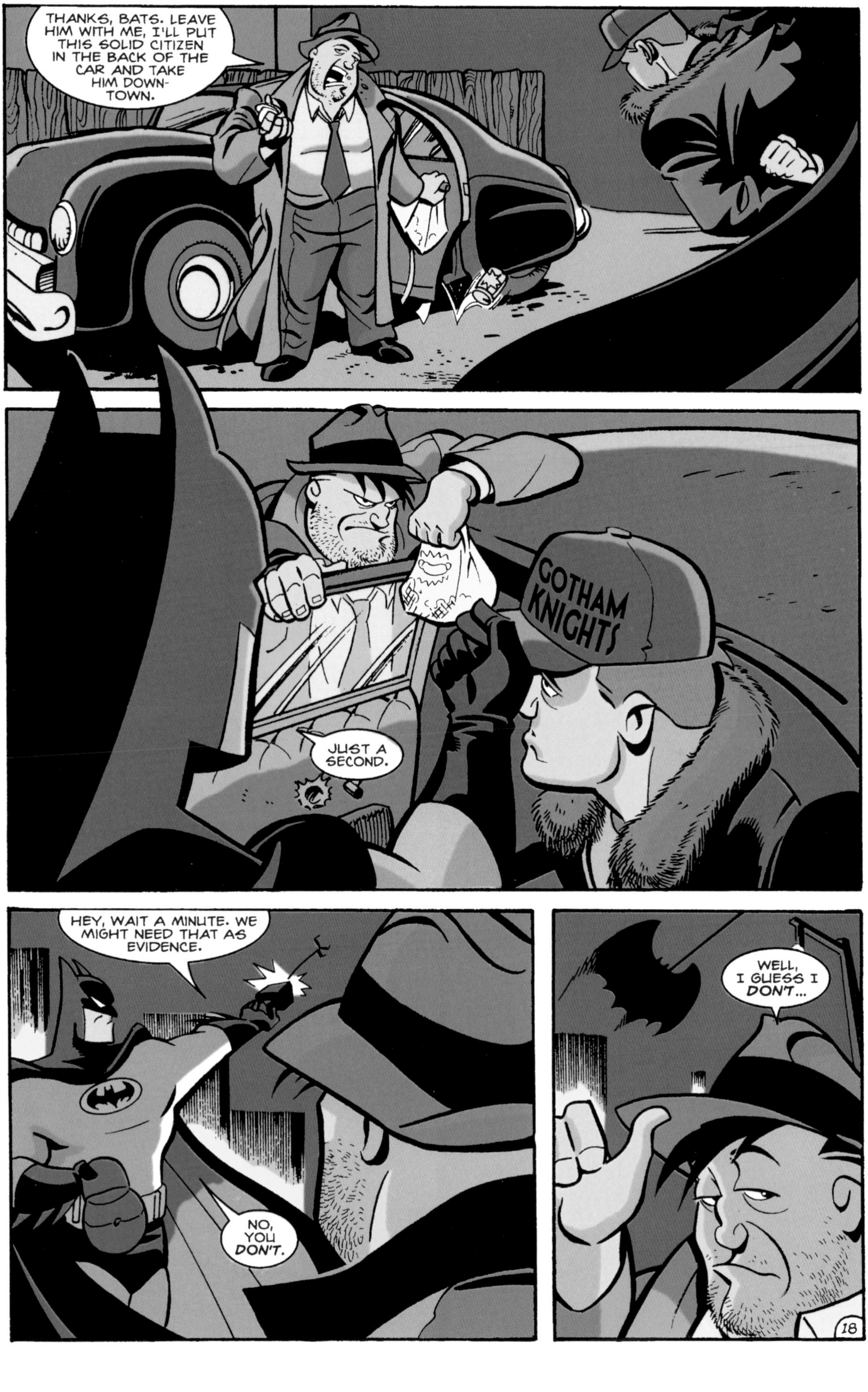
THANKS, BATS. LEAVE HIM WITH ME, I'LL PUT THIS SOLID CITIZEN IN THE BACK OF THE CAR AND TAKE HIM DOWN-TOWN.
GOTHAM KNIGHTS
JUST A SECOND.
HEY, WAIT A MINUTE. WE MIGHT NEED THAT AS EVIDENCE.
NO, YOU DON'T.
WELL, I GUESS I DON'T...
18

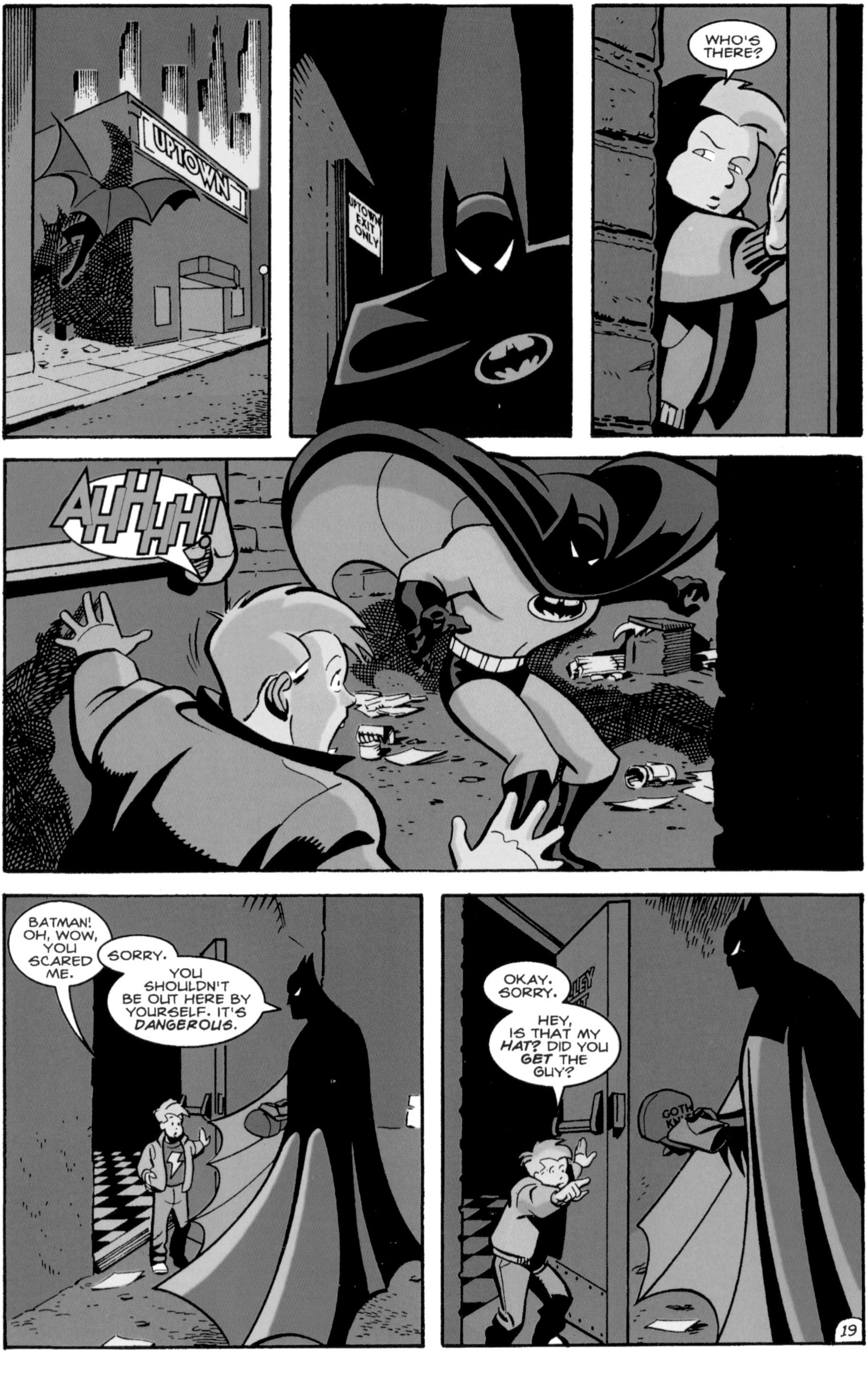

UPTOWN
UPTOWN EXIT ONLY
WHO'S THERE?
AHHHH!
BATMAN! OH, WOW, YOU SCARED ME.
SORRY.
YOU SHOULDN'T BE OUT HERE BY YOURSELF. IT'S DANGEROUS.
OKAY. SORRY.
HEY, IS THAT MY HAT? DID YOU GET THE GUY?
19

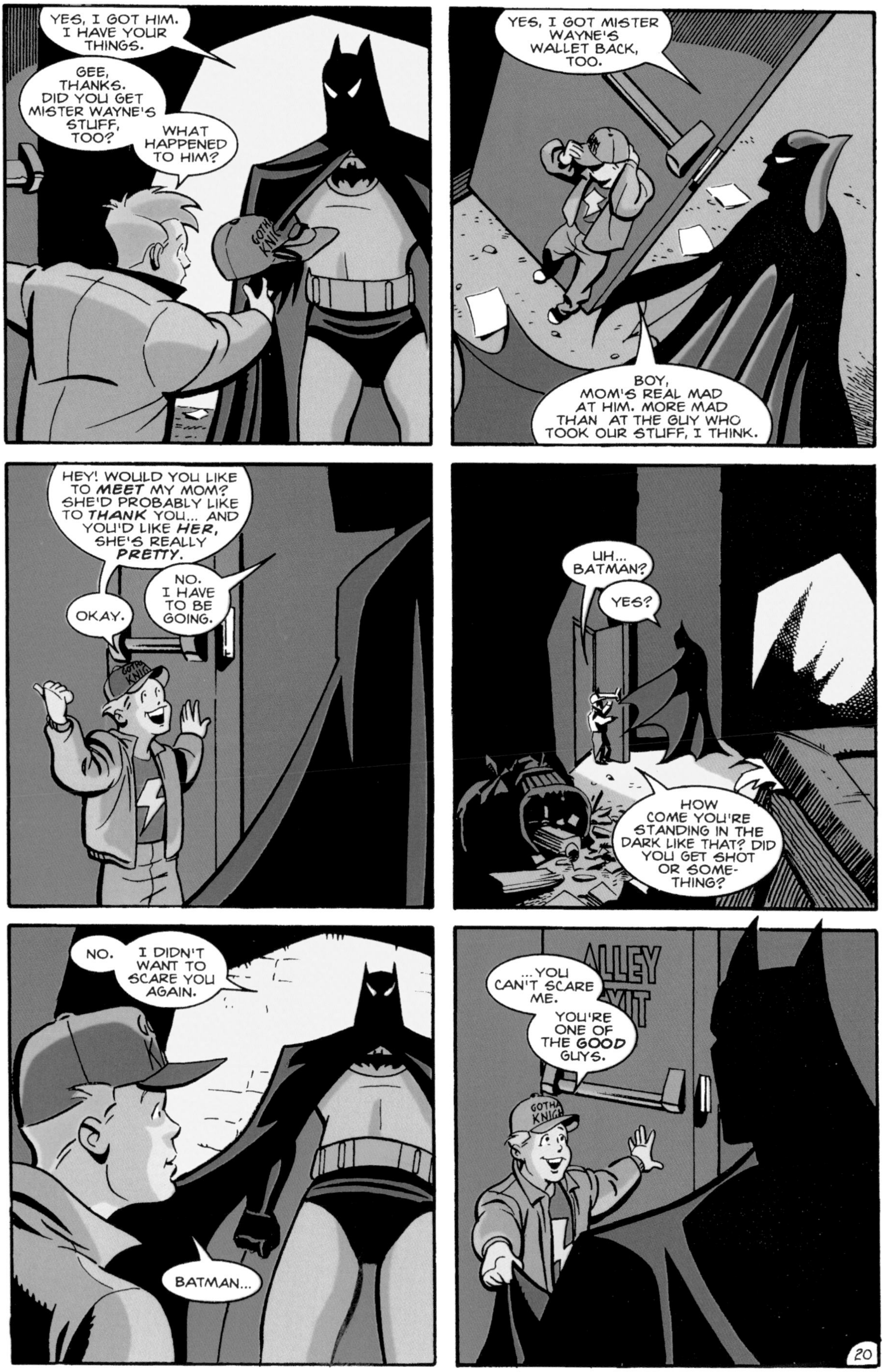
YES, I GOT HIM. I HAVE YOUR THINGS.
GEE, THANKS. DID YOU GET MISTER WAYNE'S STUFF, TOO?
WHAT HAPPENED TO HIM?
YES, I GOT MISTER WAYNE'S WALLET BACK, TOO.
BOY, MOM'S REAL MAD AT HIM. MORE MAD THAN AT THE GUY WHO TOOK OUR STUFF, I THINK.
HEY! WOULD YOU LIKE TO MEET MY MOM? SHE'D PROBABLY LIKE TO THANK YOU... AND YOU'D LIKE HER, SHE'S REALLY PRETTY.
NO. I HAVE TO BE GOING.
OKAY.
UH... BATMAN?
YES?
HOW COME YOU'RE STANDING IN THE DARK LIKE THAT? DID YOU GET SHOT OR SOME-THING?
NO.
I DIDN'T WANT TO SCARE YOU AGAIN.
BATMAN...
...YOU CAN'T SCARE ME.
YOU'RE ONE OF THE GOOD GUYS.
ALLEY EXIT
20

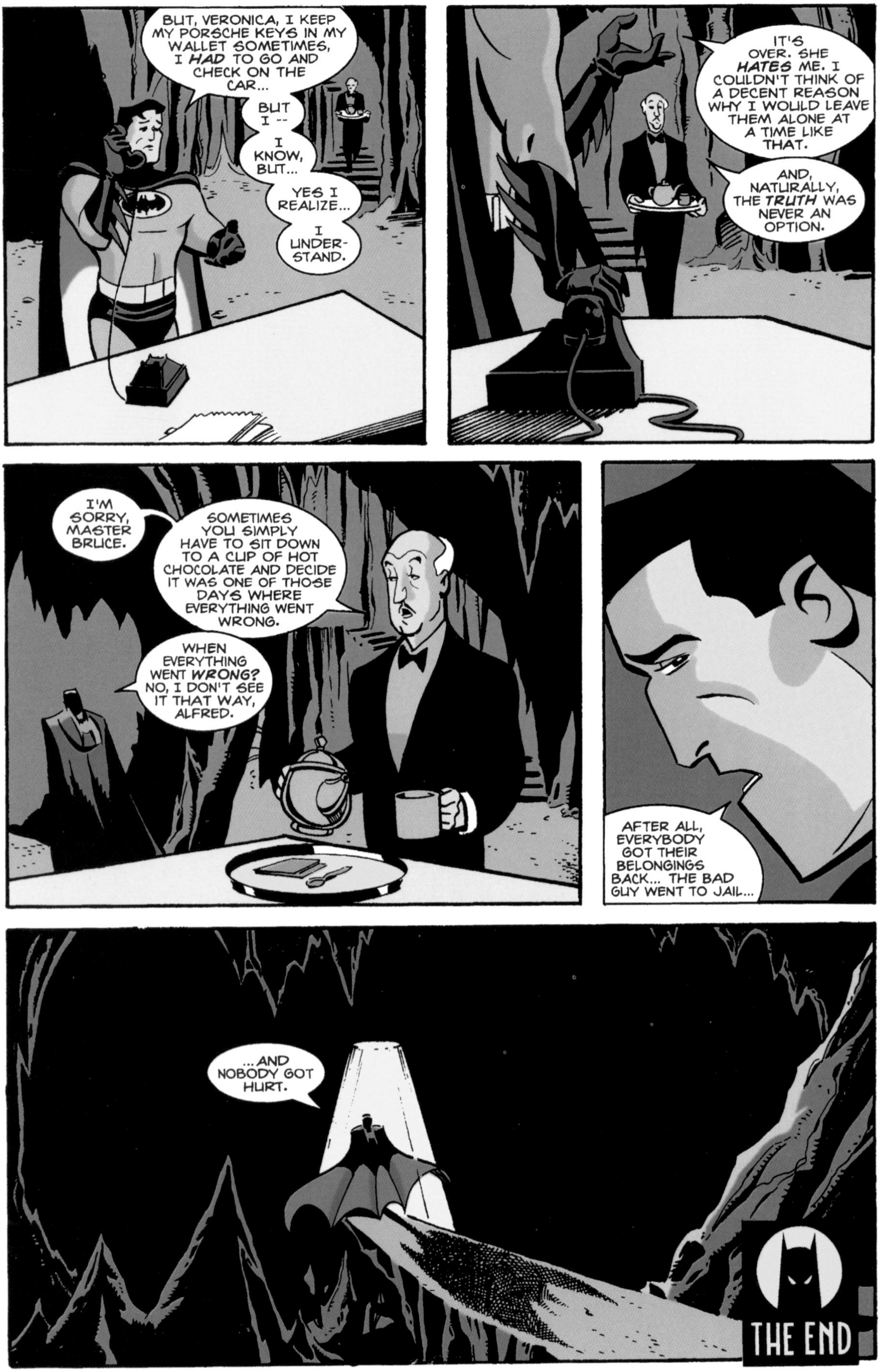
BUT, VERONICA, I KEEP MY PORSCHE KEYS IN MY WALLET SOMETIMES, I HAD TO GO AND CHECK ON THE CAR...
BUT I --
I KNOW, BUT...
YES I REALIZE...
I UNDER-STAND.
IT'S OVER. SHE HATES ME. I COULDN'T THINK OF A DECENT REASON WHY I WOULD LEAVE THEM ALONE AT A TIME LIKE THAT.
AND, NATURALLY, THE TRUTH WAS NEVER AN OPTION.
I'M SORRY, MASTER BRUCE.
SOMETIMES YOU SIMPLY HAVE TO SIT DOWN TO A CUP OF HOT CHOCOLATE AND DECIDE IT WAS ONE OF THOSE DAYS WHERE EVERYTHING WENT WRONG.
WHEN EVERYTHING WENT WRONG? NO, I DON'T SEE IT THAT WAY, ALFRED.
AFTER ALL, EVERYBODY GOT THEIR BELONGINGS BACK... THE BAD GUY WENT TO JAIL...
...AND NOBODY GOT HURT.
THE END

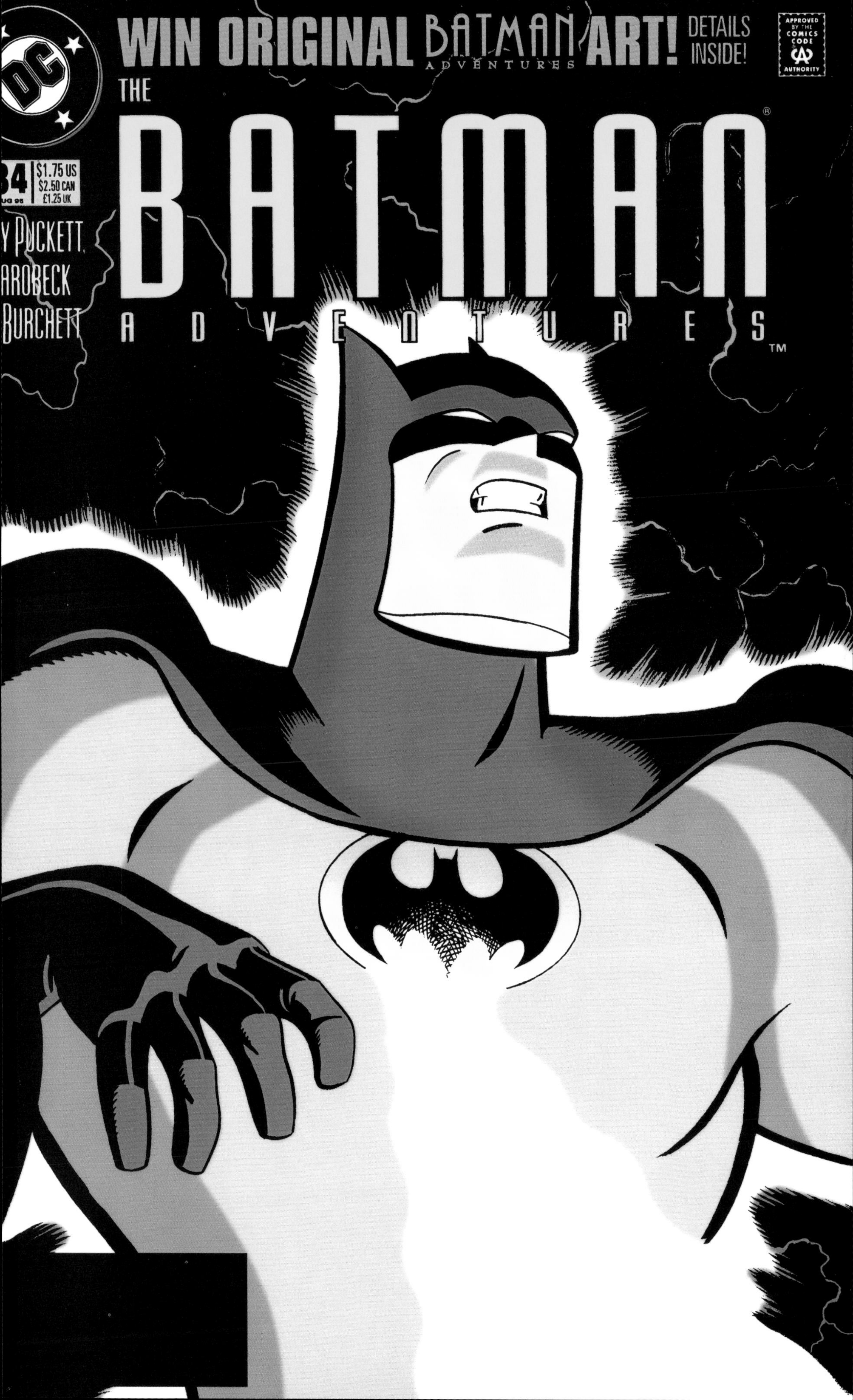

WIN ORIGINAL BATMAN ADVENTURES ART!
DETAILS INSIDE!
APPROVED BY THE COMICS CODE AUTHORITY
DC
THE BATMAN ADVENTURES
34
$1.75 US
$2.50 CAN
£1.25 UK
UG 95
Y PUCKETT
AROBECK
BURCHETT

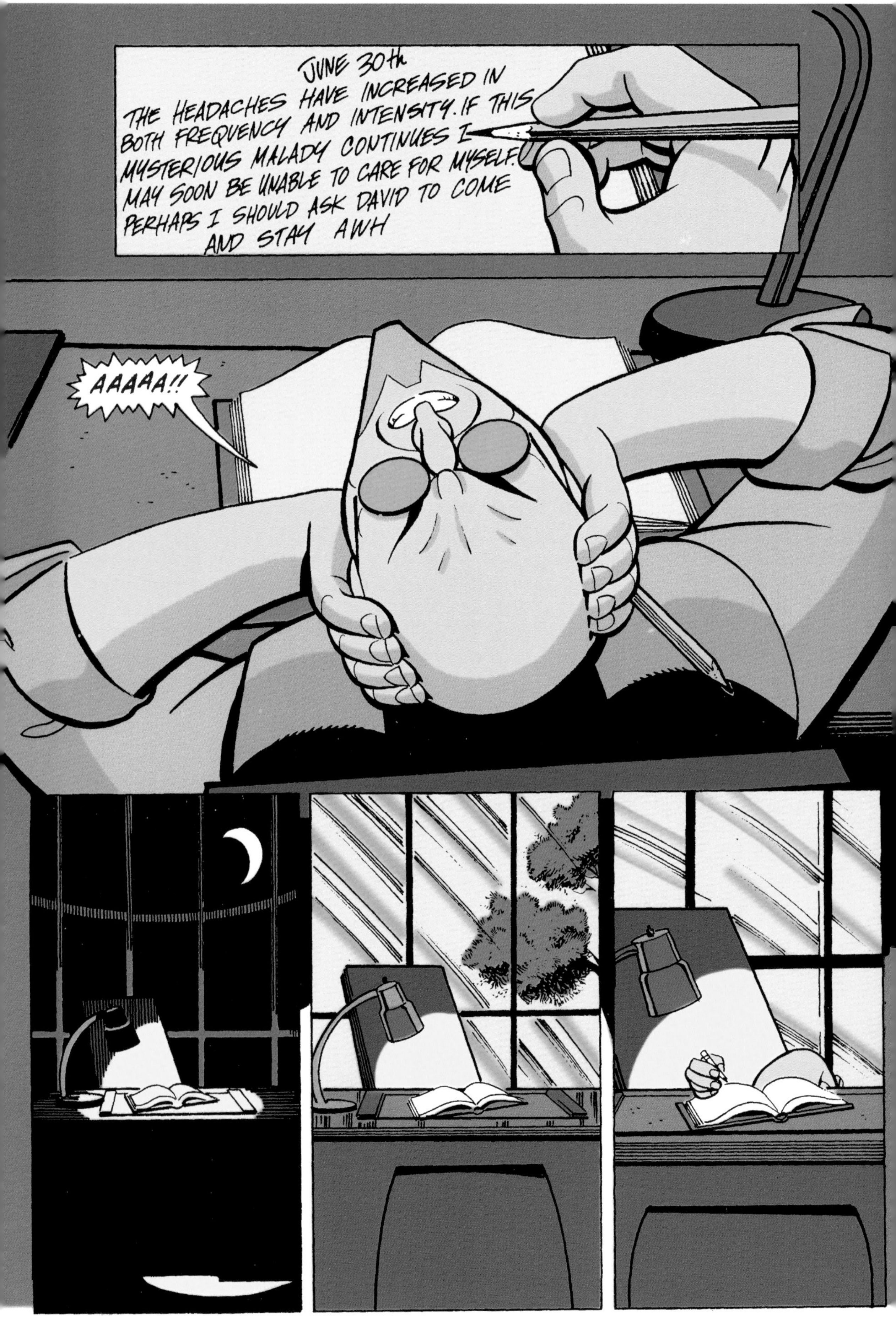
JUNE 30th
THE HEADACHES HAVE INCREASED IN BOTH FREQUENCY AND INTENSITY. IF THIS MYSTERIOUS MALADY CONTINUES I MAY SOON BE UNABLE TO CARE FOR MYSELF. PERHAPS I SHOULD ASK DAVID TO COME AND STAY AWH
AAAAA!!

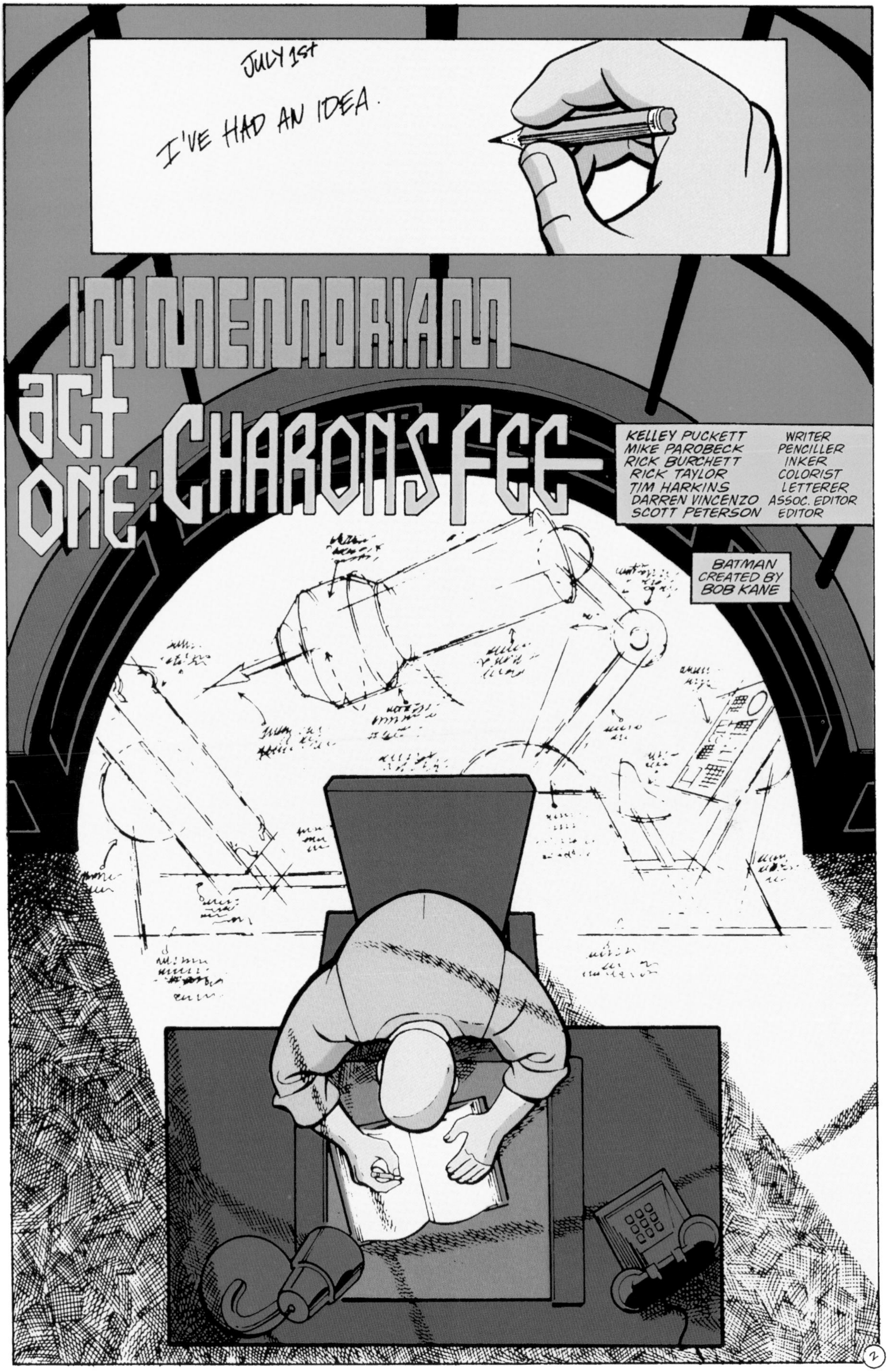
JULY 1st
I'VE HAD AN IDEA.
IN MEMORIAM
act ONE: CHARONS FEE
KELLEY PUCKETT WRITER
MIKE PAROBECK PENCILLER
RICK BURCHETT INKER
RICK TAYLOR COLORIST
TIM HARKINS LETTERER
DARREN VINCENZO ASSOC. EDITOR
SCOTT PETERSON EDITOR
BATMAN CREATED BY BOB KANE
2

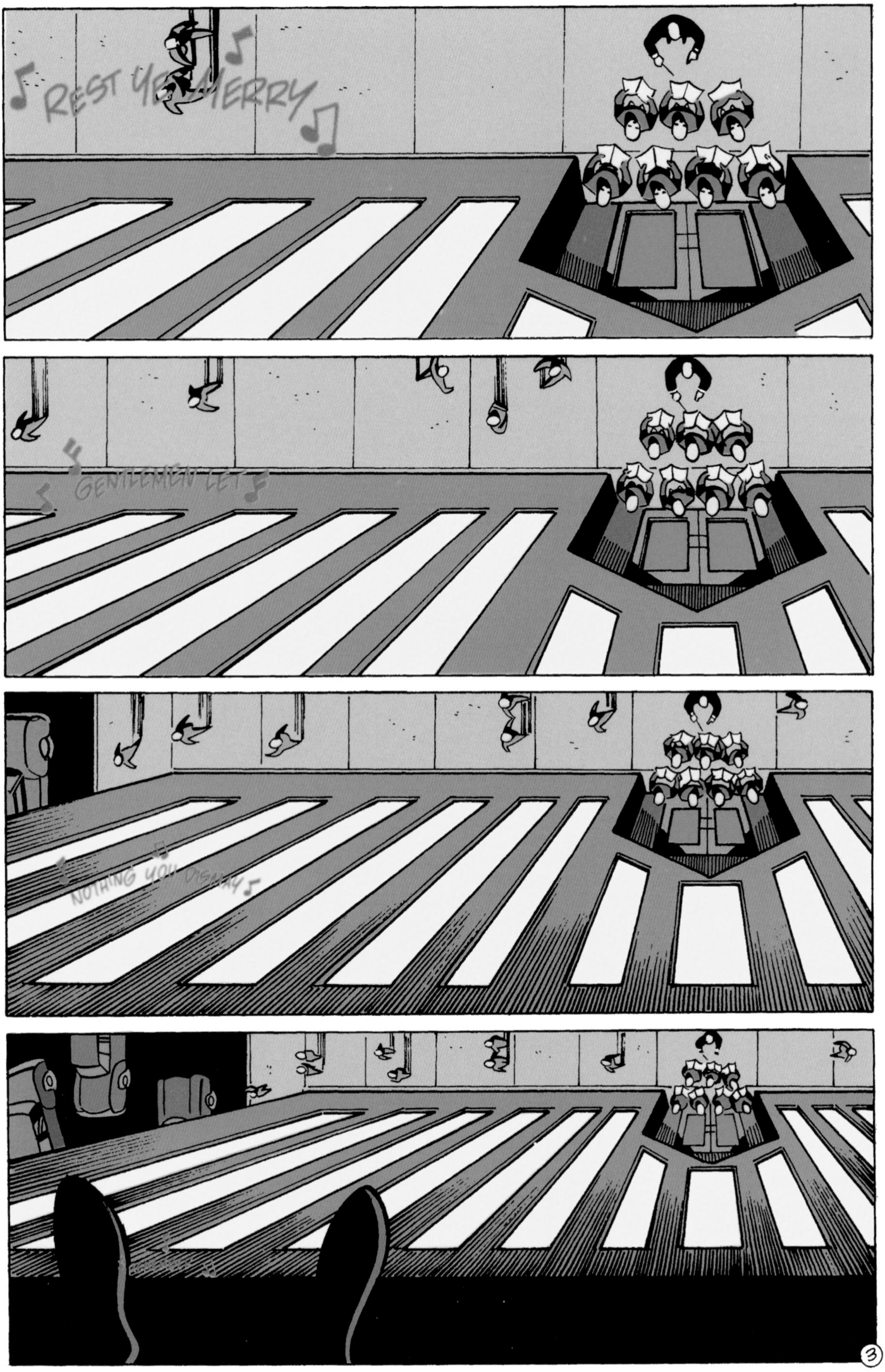
REST YE MERRY
GENTLEMEN LET
NOTHING YOU DISMAY
3

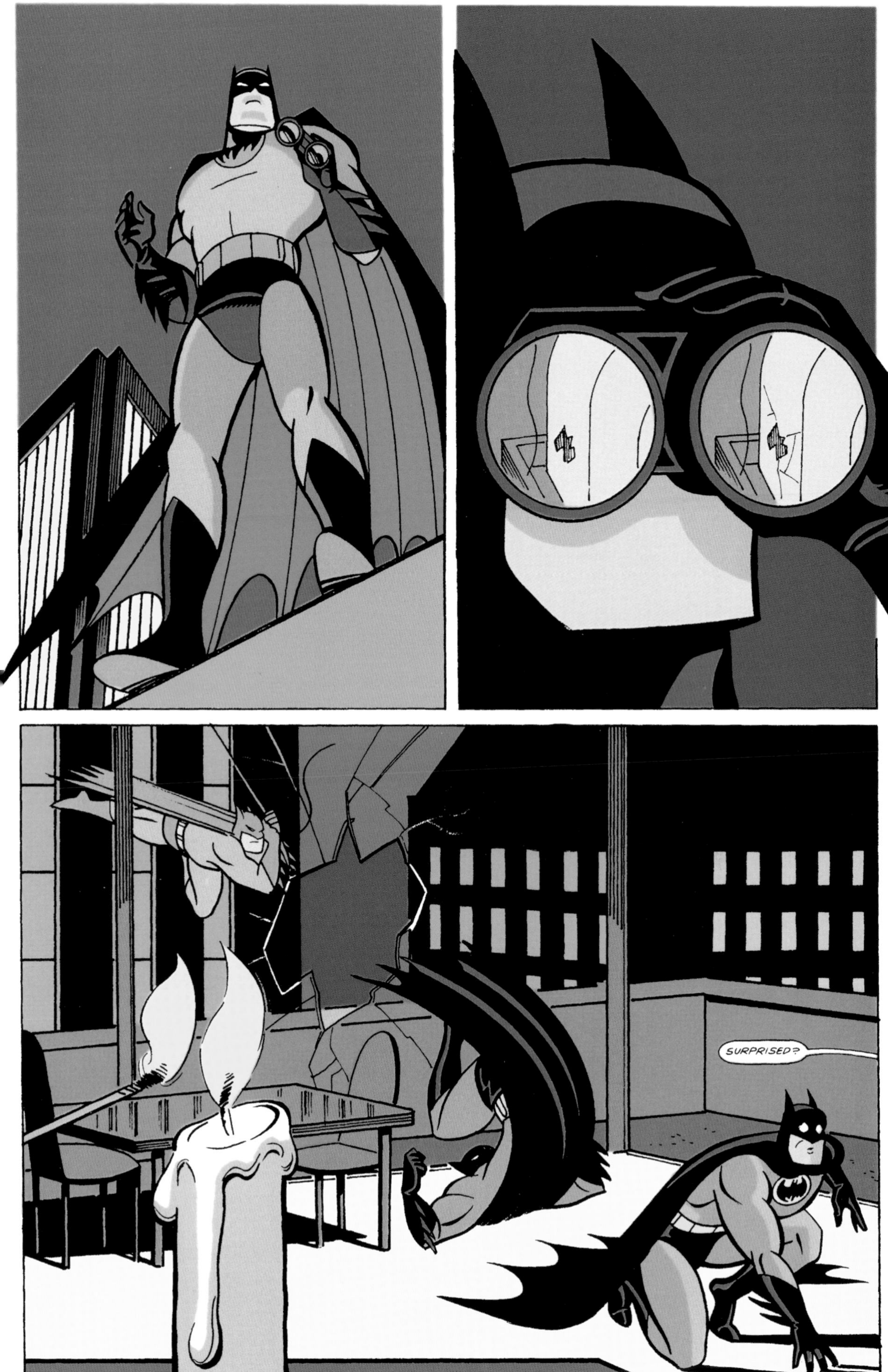
SURPRISED?
4

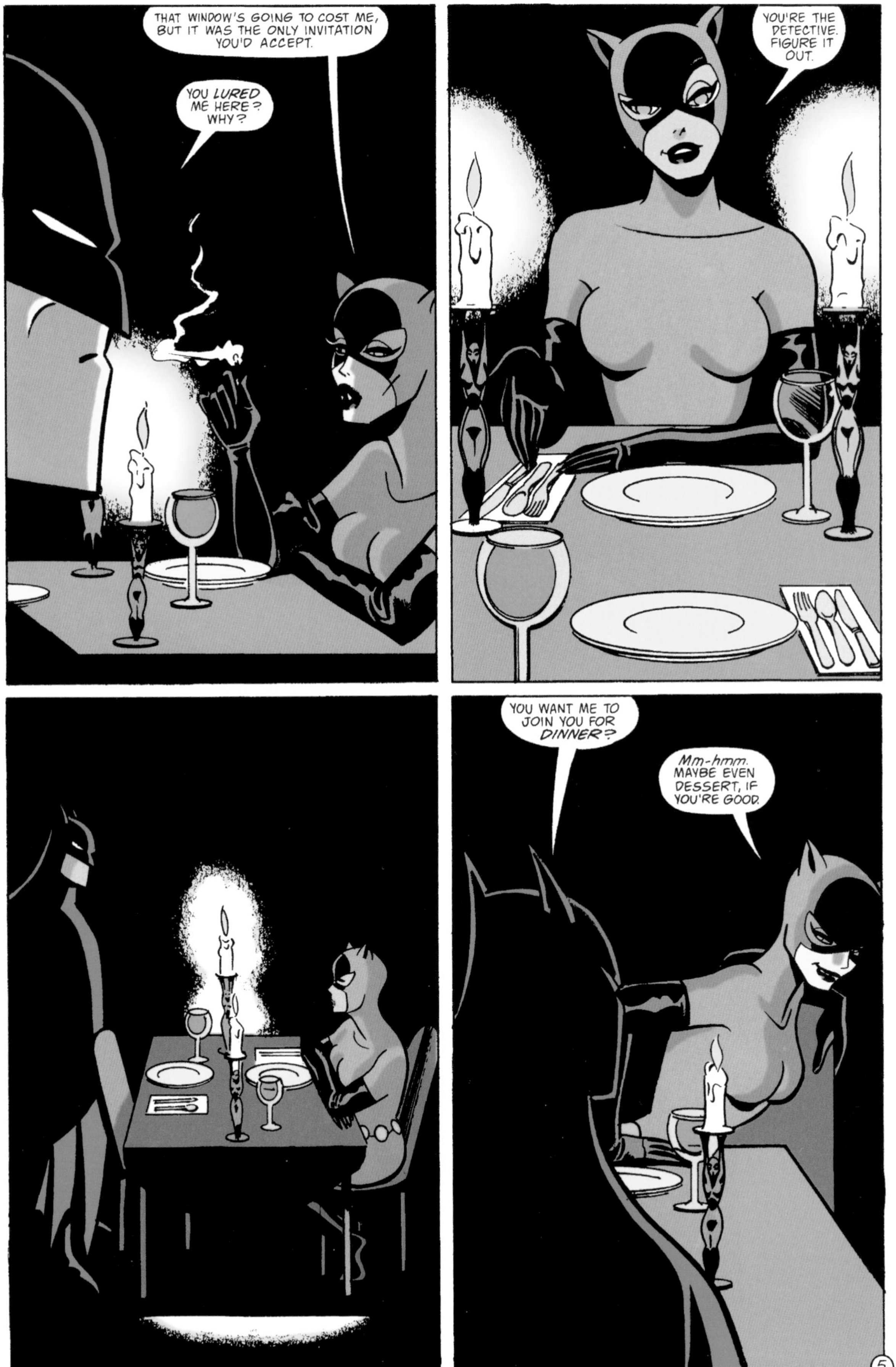
THAT WINDOW'S GOING TO COST ME, BUT IT WAS THE ONLY INVITATION YOU'D ACCEPT.
YOU *LURED* ME HERE? WHY?
YOU'RE THE DETECTIVE. FIGURE IT OUT.
YOU WANT ME TO JOIN YOU FOR *DINNER*?
Mm-hmm. MAYBE EVEN DESSERT, IF YOU'RE GOOD.
5

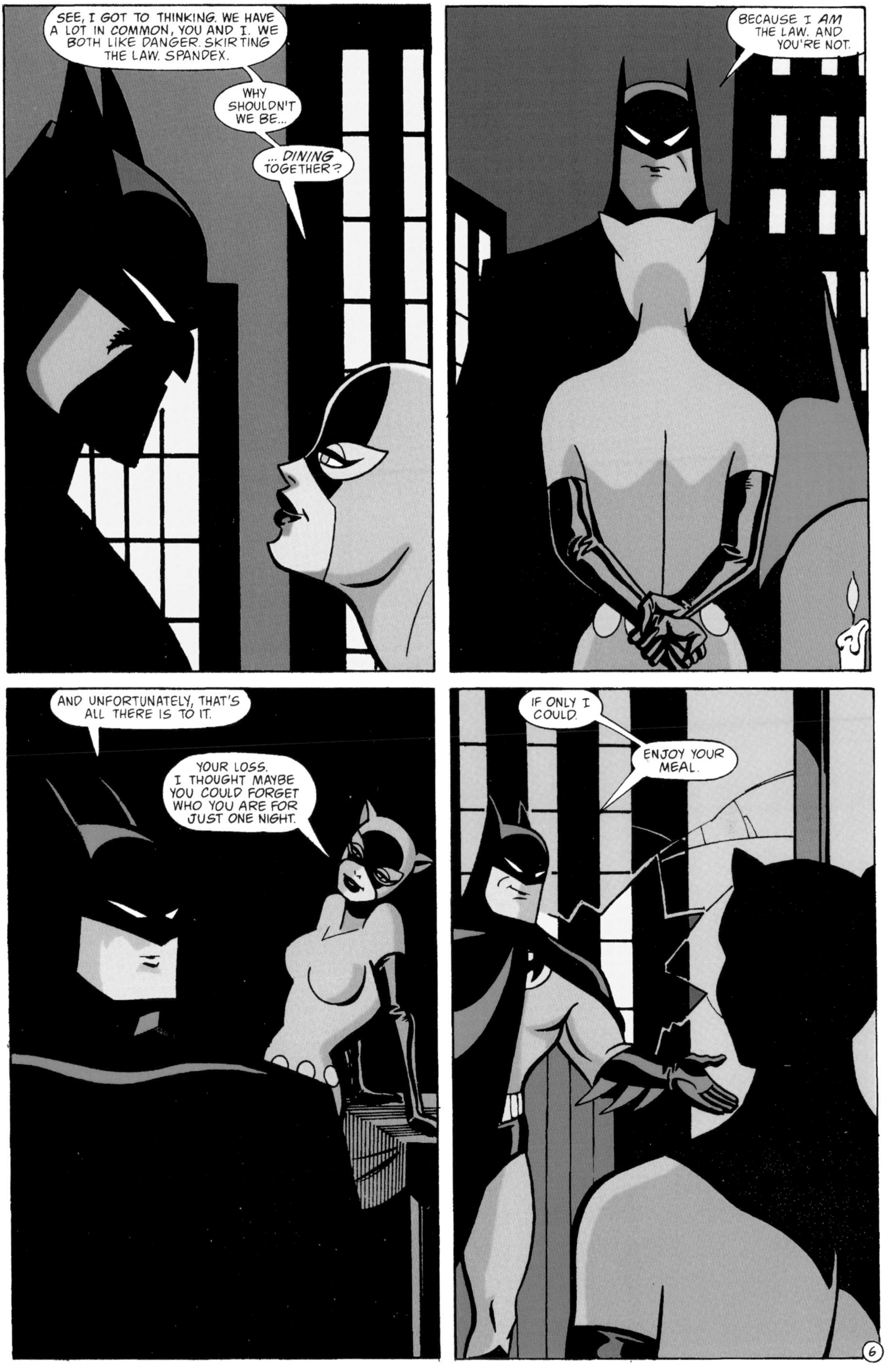
SEE, I GOT TO THINKING. WE HAVE A LOT IN COMMON, YOU AND I. WE BOTH LIKE DANGER. SKIRTING THE LAW. SPANDEX.
WHY SHOULDN'T WE BE...
...DINING TOGETHER?
BECAUSE I AM THE LAW. AND YOU'RE NOT.
AND UNFORTUNATELY, THAT'S ALL THERE IS TO IT.
YOUR LOSS. I THOUGHT MAYBE YOU COULD FORGET WHO YOU ARE FOR JUST ONE NIGHT.
IF ONLY I COULD.
ENJOY YOUR MEAL.
6

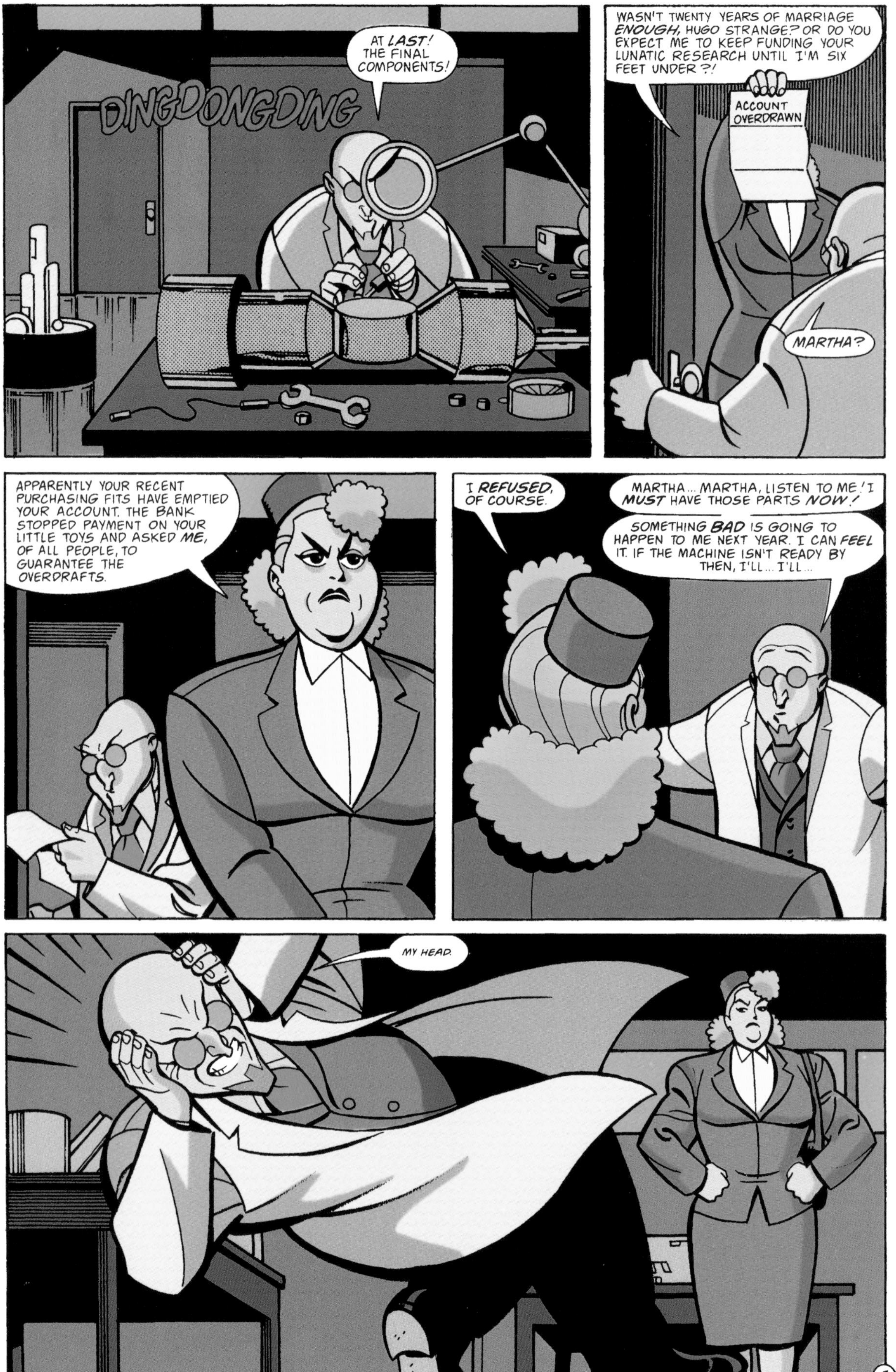
DINGDONGDING
AT LAST! THE FINAL COMPONENTS!
WASN'T TWENTY YEARS OF MARRIAGE ENOUGH, HUGO STRANGE? OR DO YOU EXPECT ME TO KEEP FUNDING YOUR LUNATIC RESEARCH UNTIL I'M SIX FEET UNDER?!
ACCOUNT OVERDRAWN
MARTHA?
APPARENTLY YOUR RECENT PURCHASING FITS HAVE EMPTIED YOUR ACCOUNT. THE BANK STOPPED PAYMENT ON YOUR LITTLE TOYS AND ASKED ME, OF ALL PEOPLE, TO GUARANTEE THE OVERDRAFTS.
I REFUSED, OF COURSE.
MARTHA... MARTHA, LISTEN TO ME! I MUST HAVE THOSE PARTS NOW!
SOMETHING BAD IS GOING TO HAPPEN TO ME NEXT YEAR. I CAN FEEL IT. IF THE MACHINE ISN'T READY BY THEN, I'LL... I'LL...
MY HEAD.
7

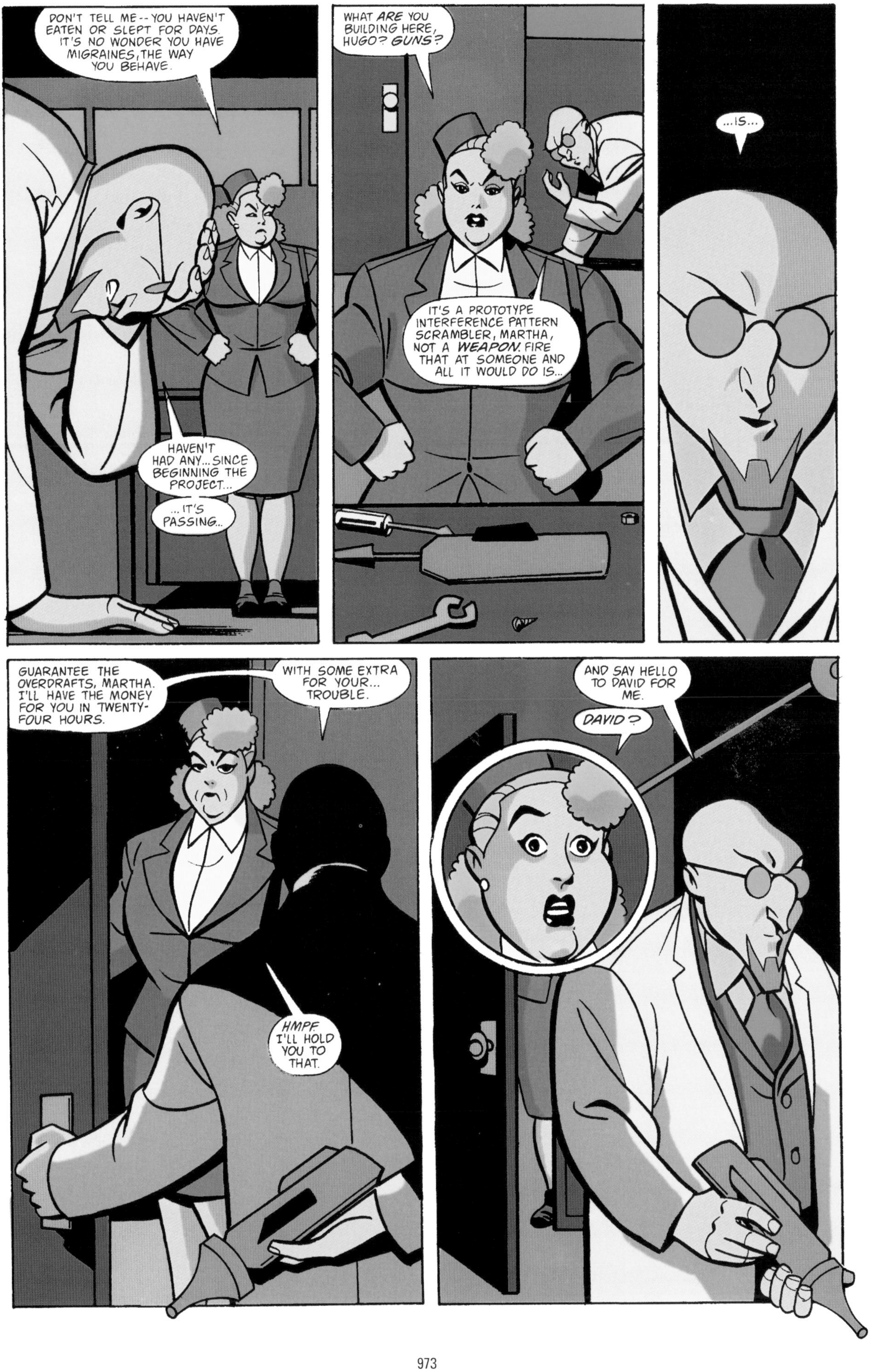

DON'T TELL ME--YOU HAVEN'T EATEN OR SLEPT FOR DAYS. IT'S NO WONDER YOU HAVE MIGRAINES, THE WAY YOU BEHAVE.
HAVEN'T HAD ANY...SINCE BEGINNING THE PROJECT...
...IT'S PASSING...
WHAT ARE YOU BUILDING HERE, HUGO? GUNS?
IT'S A PROTOTYPE INTERFERENCE PATTERN SCRAMBLER, MARTHA, NOT A WEAPON. FIRE THAT AT SOMEONE AND ALL IT WOULD DO IS...
...IS...
GUARANTEE THE OVERDRAFTS, MARTHA. I'LL HAVE THE MONEY FOR YOU IN TWENTY-FOUR HOURS.
WITH SOME EXTRA FOR YOUR... TROUBLE.
HMPF I'LL HOLD YOU TO THAT.
AND SAY HELLO TO DAVID FOR ME.
DAVID?

ACT 2: Filling In The GAPS

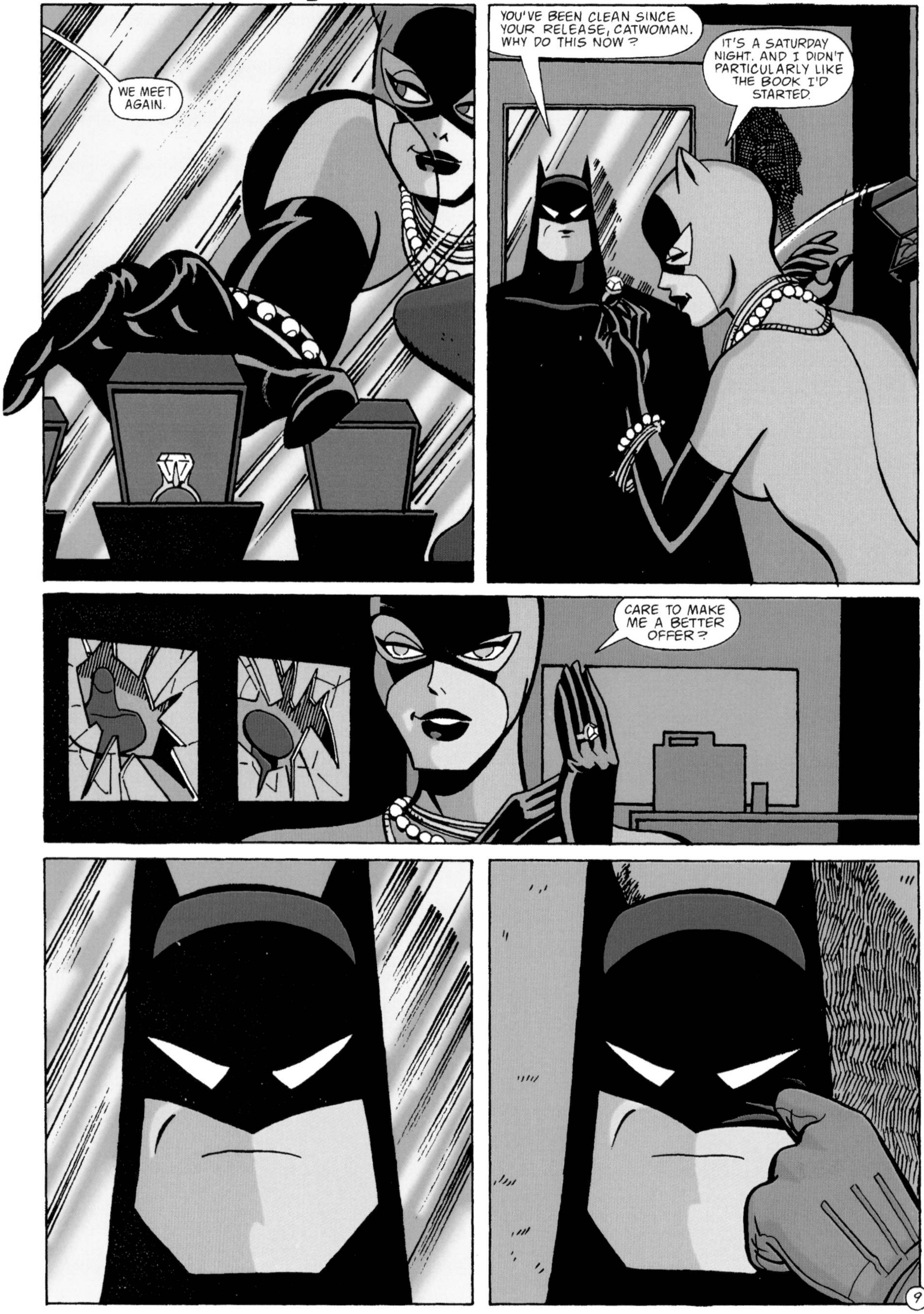
WE MEET AGAIN.
YOU'VE BEEN CLEAN SINCE YOUR RELEASE, CATWOMAN. WHY DO THIS NOW?
IT'S A SATURDAY NIGHT. AND I DIDN'T PARTICULARLY LIKE THE BOOK I'D STARTED.
CARE TO MAKE ME A BETTER OFFER?
9

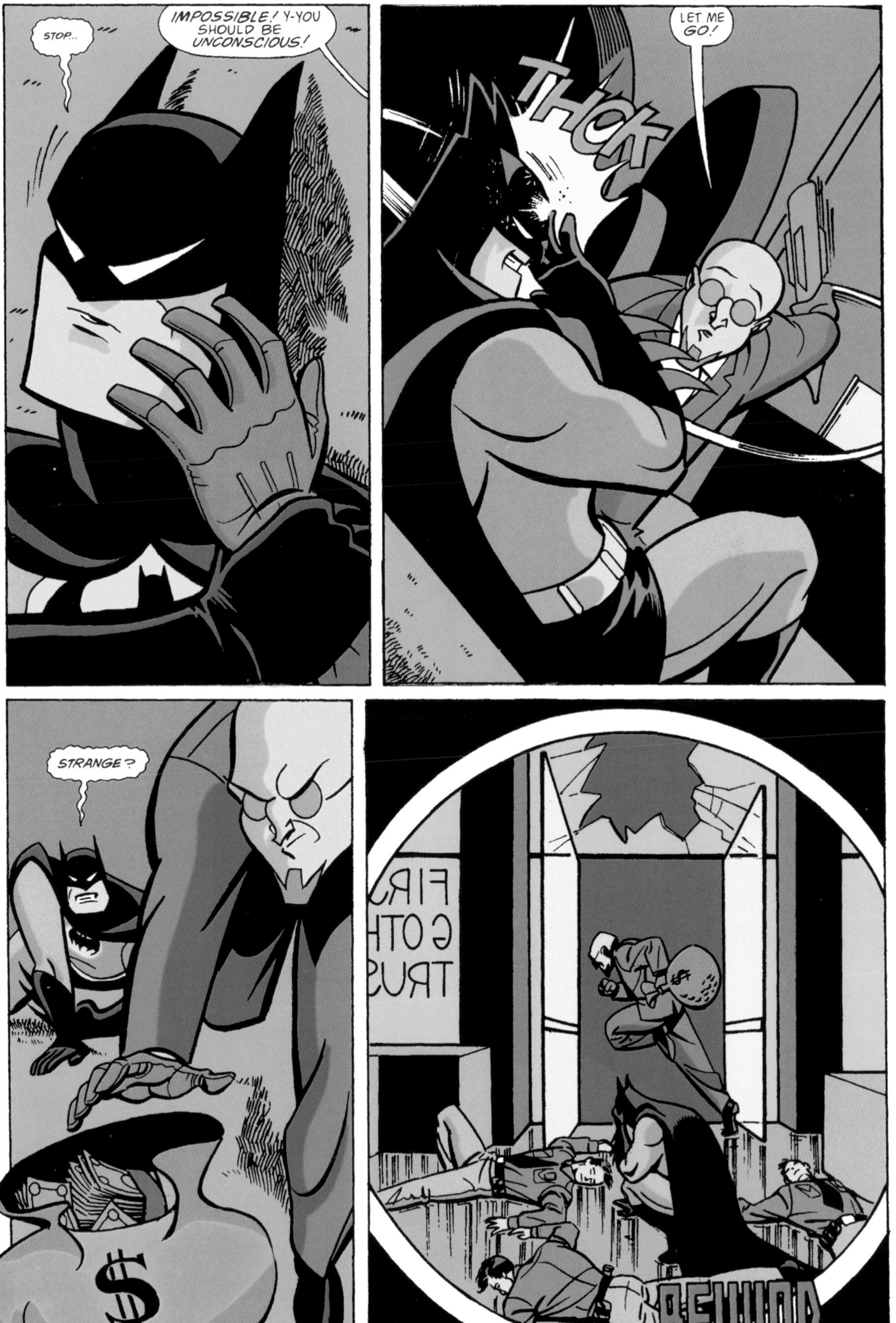
STOP...
IMPOSSIBLE! Y-YOU SHOULD BE UNCONSCIOUS!
THOK
LET ME GO!
STRANGE?
REWIND
10

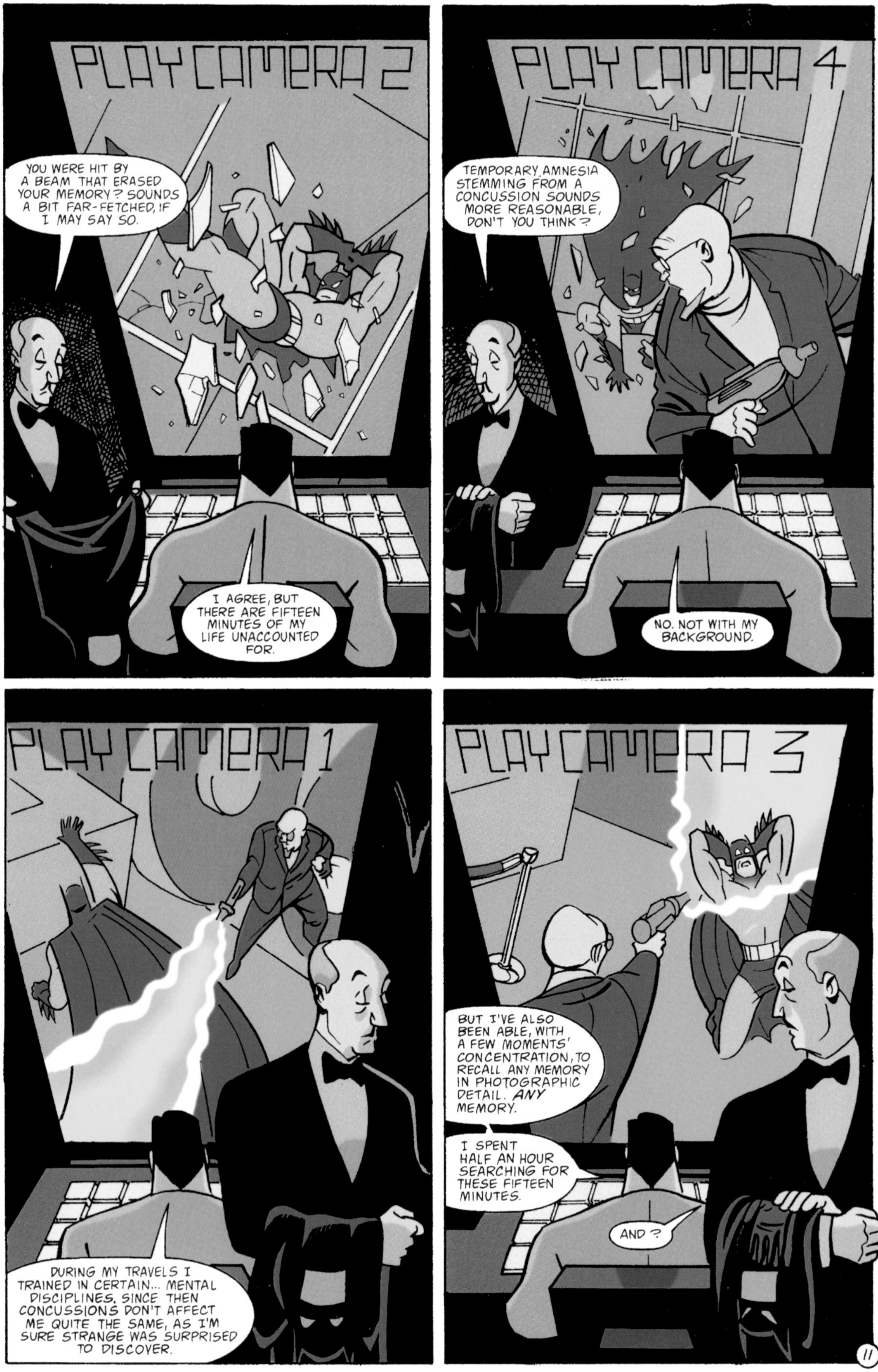
PLAY CAMERA 2
YOU WERE HIT BY A BEAM THAT ERASED YOUR MEMORY? SOUNDS A BIT FAR-FETCHED, IF I MAY SAY SO.
I AGREE, BUT THERE ARE FIFTEEN MINUTES OF MY LIFE UNACCOUNTED FOR.
PLAY CAMERA 4
TEMPORARY AMNESIA STEMMING FROM A CONCUSSION SOUNDS MORE REASONABLE, DON'T YOU THINK?
NO. NOT WITH MY BACKGROUND.
PLAY CAMERA 1
DURING MY TRAVELS I TRAINED IN CERTAIN... MENTAL DISCIPLINES. SINCE THEN CONCUSSIONS DON'T AFFECT ME QUITE THE SAME, AS I'M SURE STRANGE WAS SURPRISED TO DISCOVER.
PLAY CAMERA 3
BUT I'VE ALSO BEEN ABLE, WITH A FEW MOMENTS' CONCENTRATION, TO RECALL ANY MEMORY IN PHOTOGRAPHIC DETAIL. *ANY* MEMORY.
I SPENT HALF AN HOUR SEARCHING FOR THESE FIFTEEN MINUTES.
AND?
11

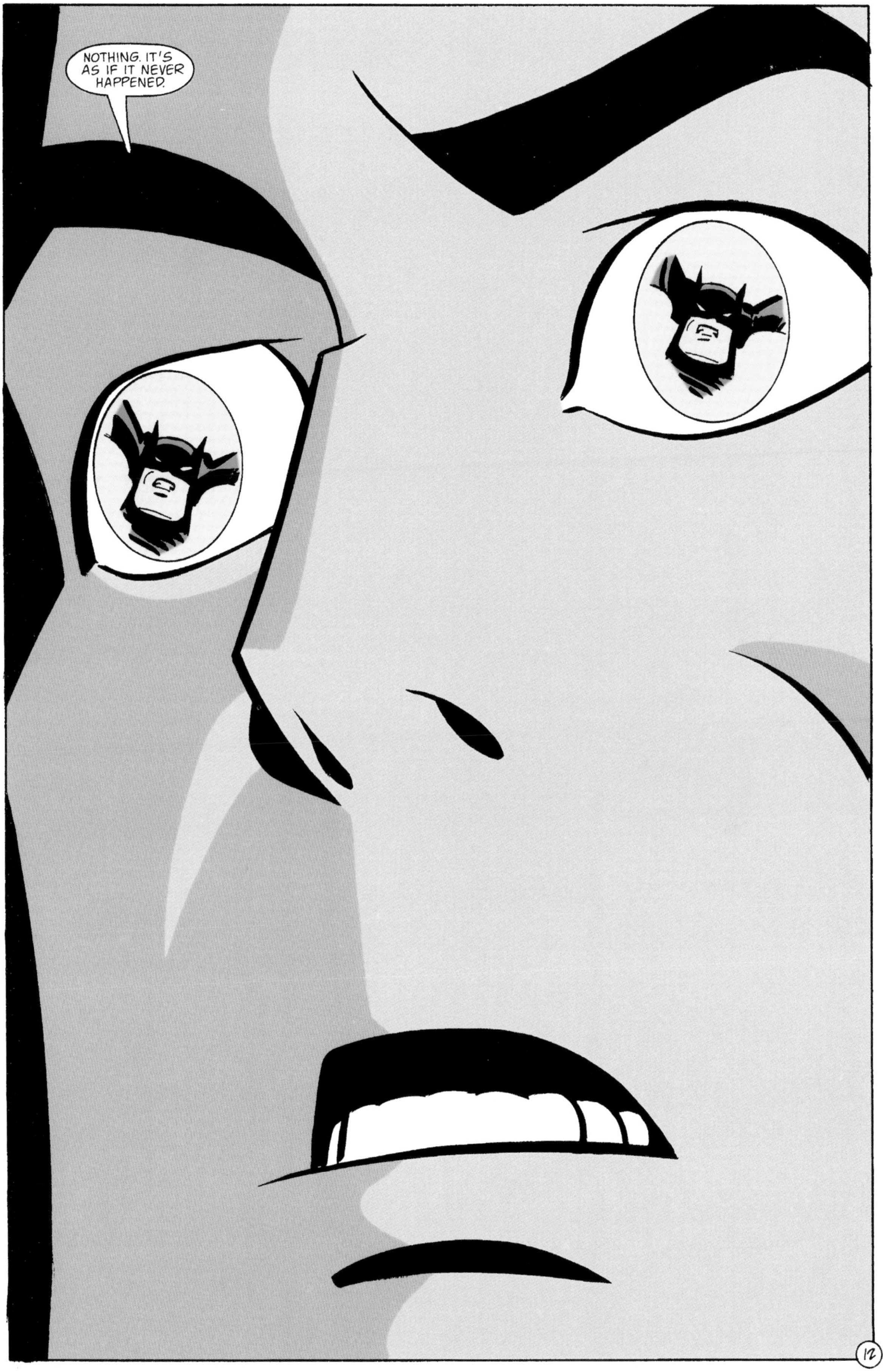
NOTHING. IT'S AS IF IT NEVER HAPPENED.
12

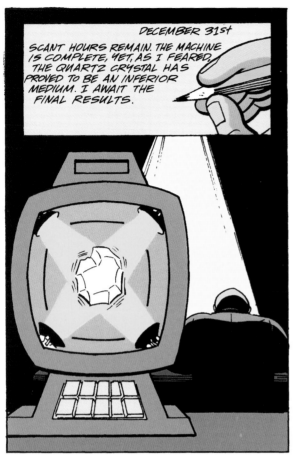

DECEMBER 31st

SCANT HOURS REMAIN. THE MACHINE IS COMPLETE, YET, AS I FEARED, THE QUARTZ CRYSTAL HAS PROVED TO BE AN INFERIOR MEDIUM. I AWAIT THE FINAL RESULTS.

HOW STRANGE IT SEEMS TO ME NOW. THIS FEVERISH RACE AGAINST TIME. THIS CERTAINTY OF AN UNKNOWN, UNTHINKABLE DOOM SHOULD I FAIL.

I WONDER... IS THIS HOW IT FEELS TO GO *MAD* ??

SKKRAASSK

NO. MAD OR NOT, I *WILL* SUCCEED.

THE QUARTZ WAS TOO WEAK. I MUST FIND SOMETHING *STRONGER.*

13

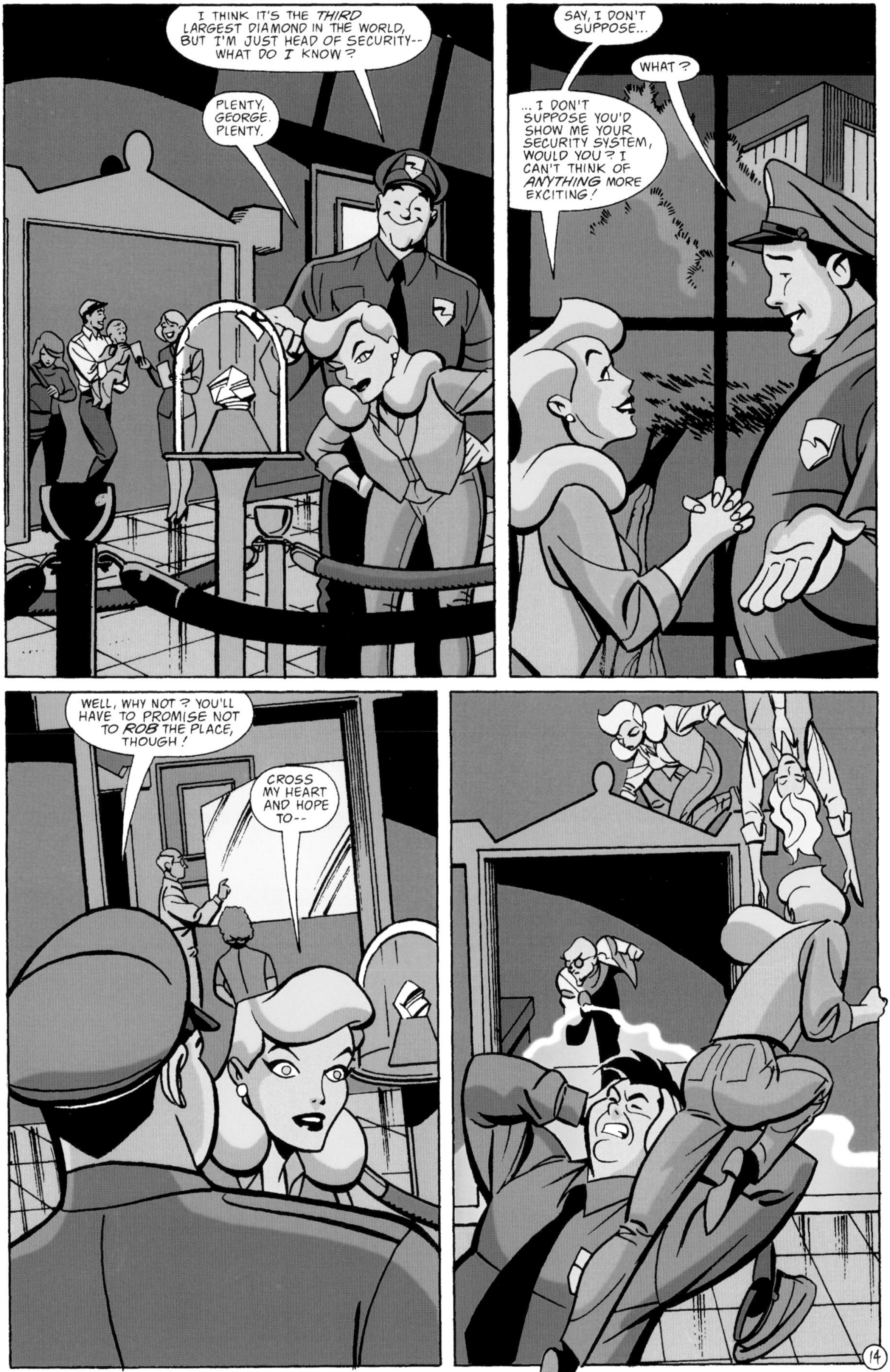

I THINK IT'S THE THIRD LARGEST DIAMOND IN THE WORLD, BUT I'M JUST HEAD OF SECURITY-- WHAT DO I KNOW?
PLENTY, GEORGE. PLENTY.
SAY, I DON'T SUPPOSE...
WHAT?
...I DON'T SUPPOSE YOU'D SHOW ME YOUR SECURITY SYSTEM, WOULD YOU? I CAN'T THINK OF ANYTHING MORE EXCITING!
WELL, WHY NOT? YOU'LL HAVE TO PROMISE NOT TO ROB THE PLACE, THOUGH!
CROSS MY HEART AND HOPE TO--
14

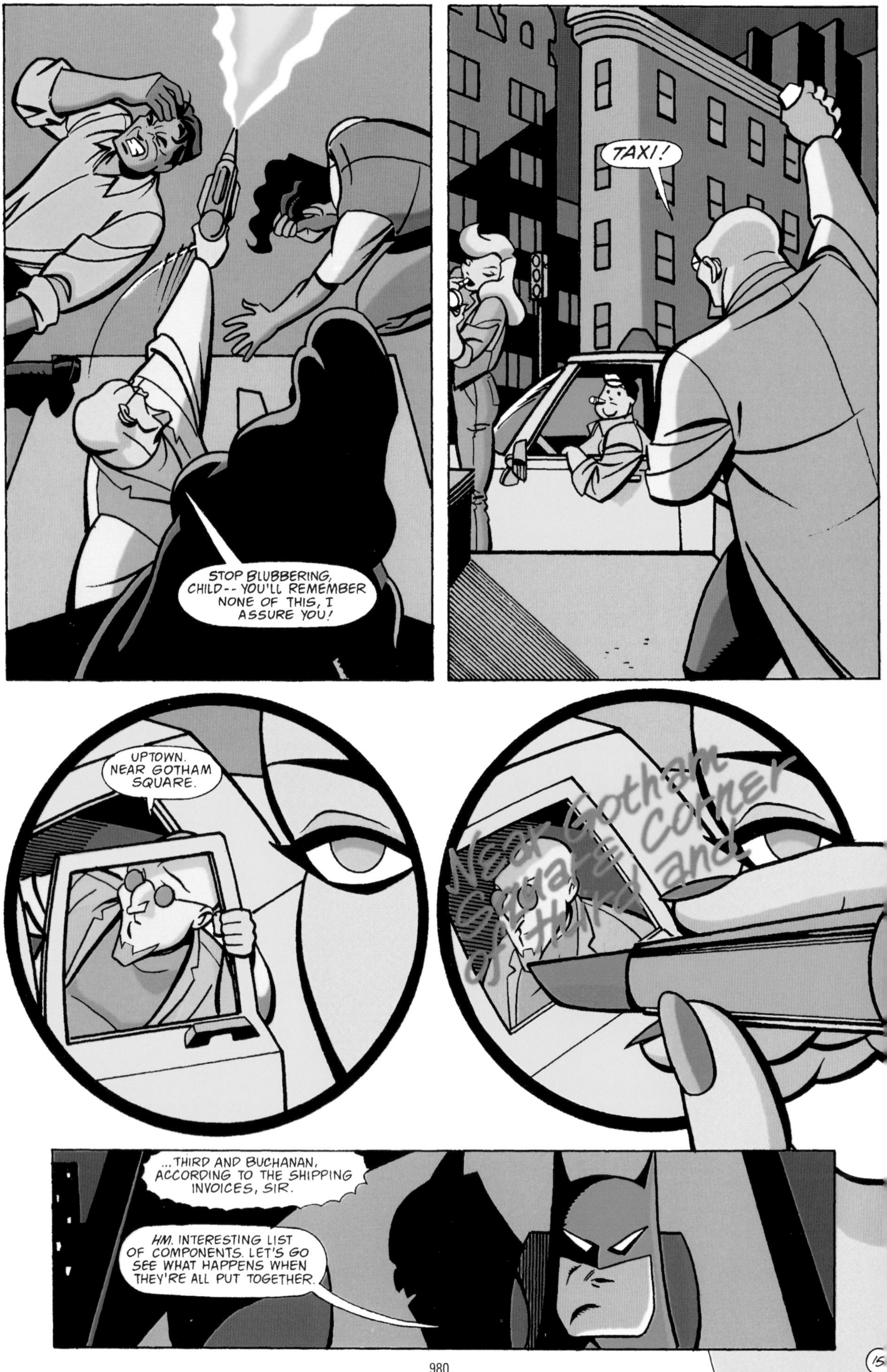
STOP BLUBBERING, CHILD-- YOU'LL REMEMBER NONE OF THIS, I ASSURE YOU!
TAXI!
UPTOWN. NEAR GOTHAM SQUARE.
Near Gotham
Square Corner
of third and
...THIRD AND BUCHANAN, ACCORDING TO THE SHIPPING INVOICES, SIR.
HM. INTERESTING LIST OF COMPONENTS. LET'S GO SEE WHAT HAPPENS WHEN THEY'RE ALL PUT TOGETHER.

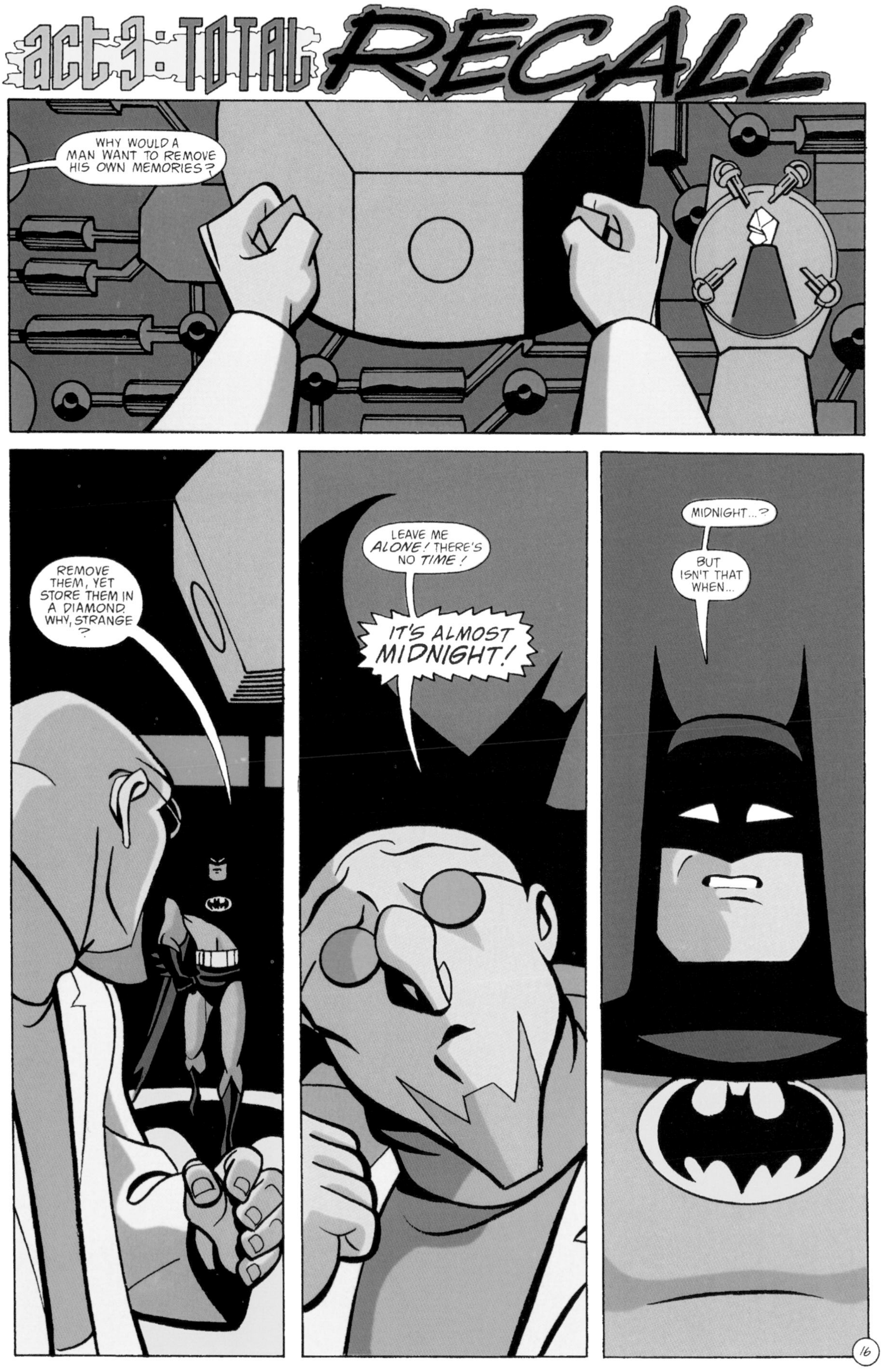

act 3: TOTAL RECALL
WHY WOULD A MAN WANT TO REMOVE HIS OWN MEMORIES?
REMOVE THEM, YET STORE THEM IN A DIAMOND. WHY, STRANGE?
LEAVE ME ALONE! THERE'S NO TIME!
IT'S ALMOST MIDNIGHT!
MIDNIGHT...?
BUT ISN'T THAT WHEN...
16

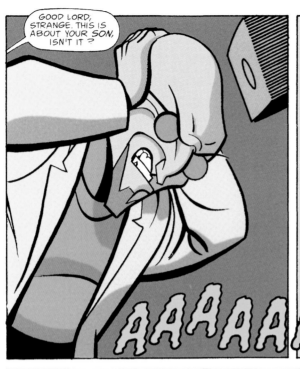

GOOD LORD, STRANGE. THIS IS ABOUT YOUR *SON*, ISN'T IT?

AAAAAAAAAA!

eh?

NO!

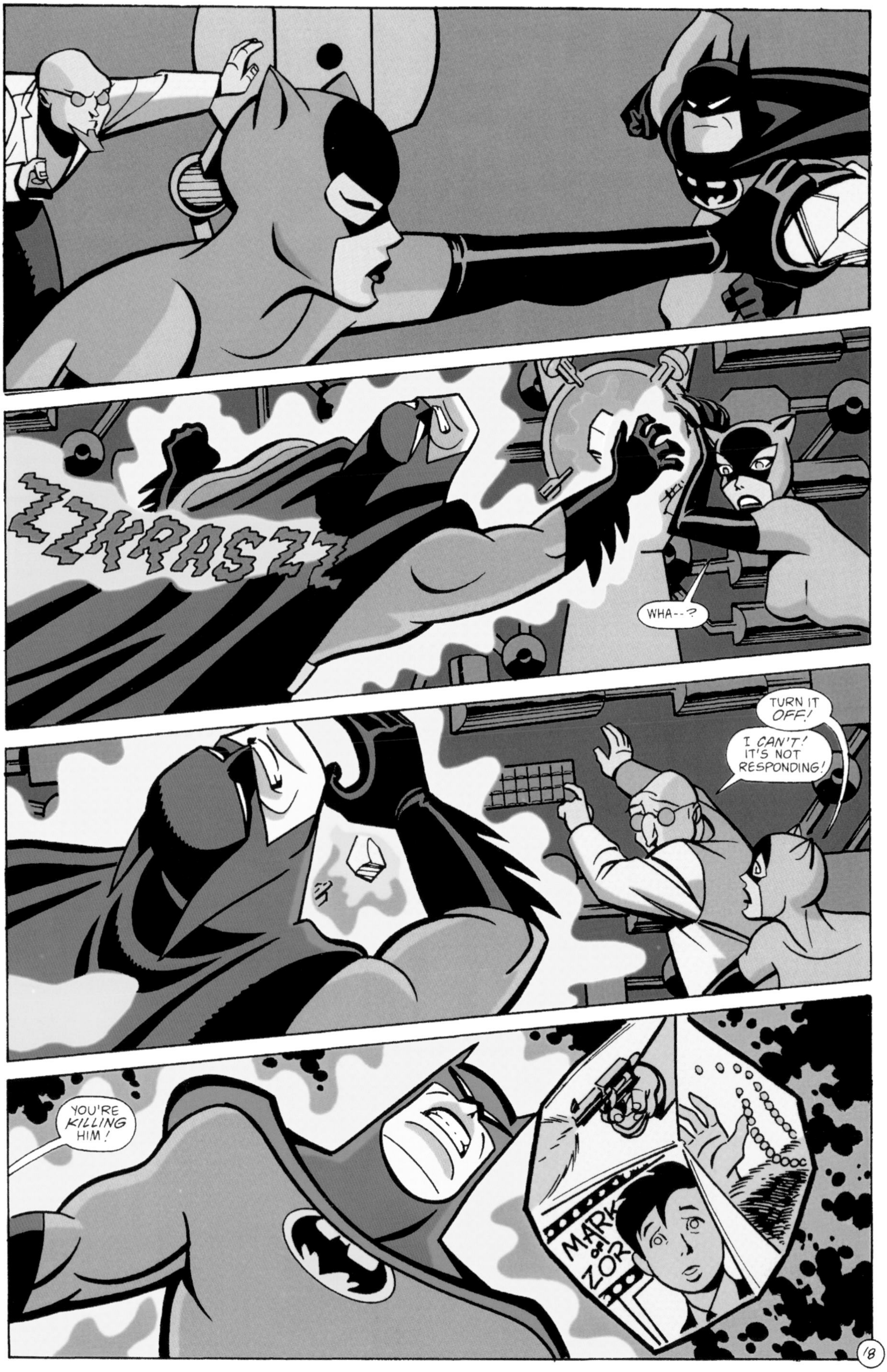
ZZKRASZZ
WHA--?
TURN IT OFF!
I CAN'T! IT'S NOT RESPONDING!
YOU'RE KILLING HIM!
MARK OF ZORRO
18

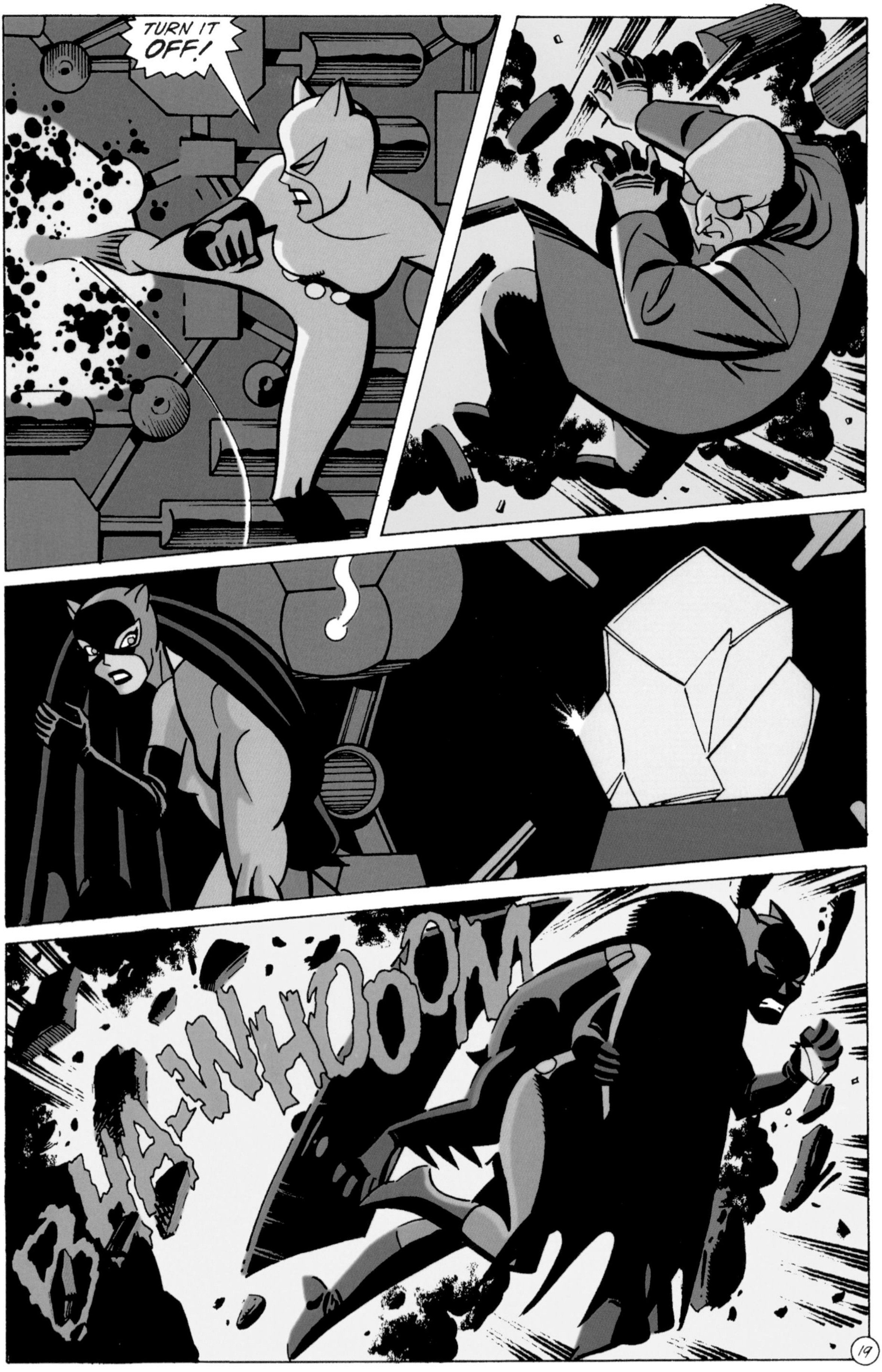

TURN IT OFF!
BA-WHOOOM
19

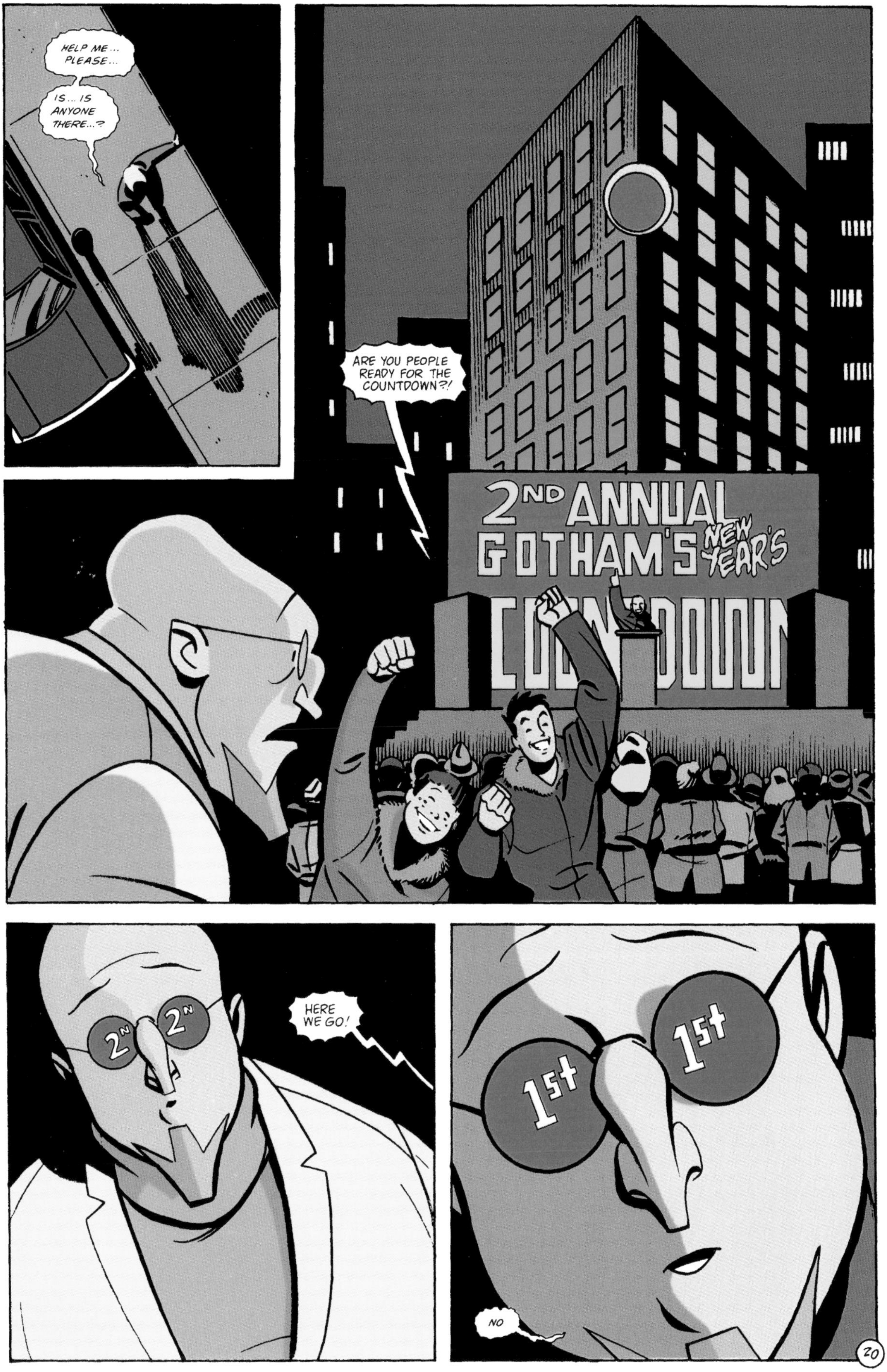
HELP ME... PLEASE...
IS... IS ANYONE THERE...?
ARE YOU PEOPLE READY FOR THE COUNTDOWN?!
2ND ANNUAL GOTHAM'S NEW YEAR'S COUNTDOWN
HERE WE GO!
NO
20

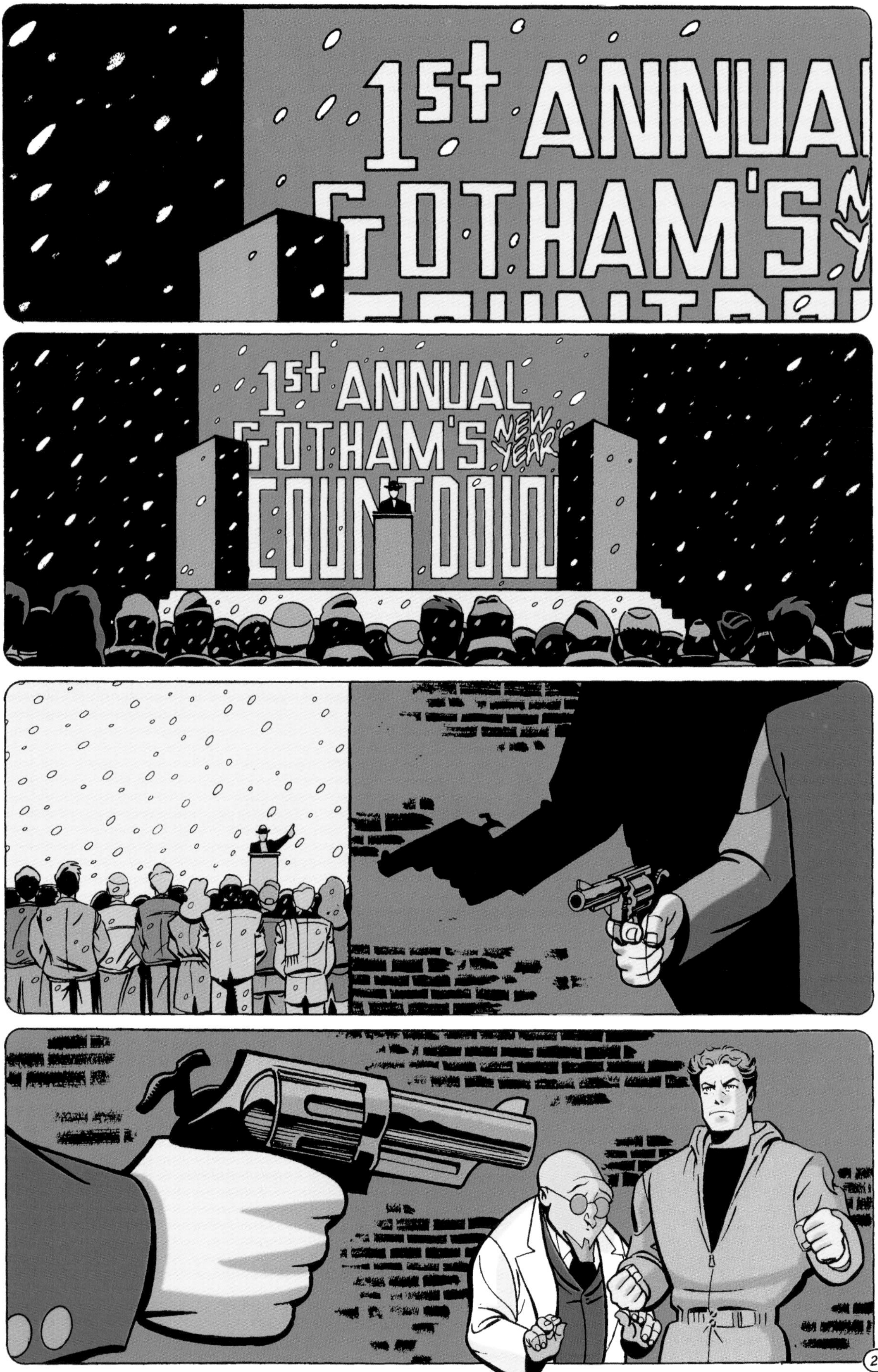
1st ANNUAL
GOTHAM'S
1st ANNUAL
GOTHAM'S
NEW YEAR

21

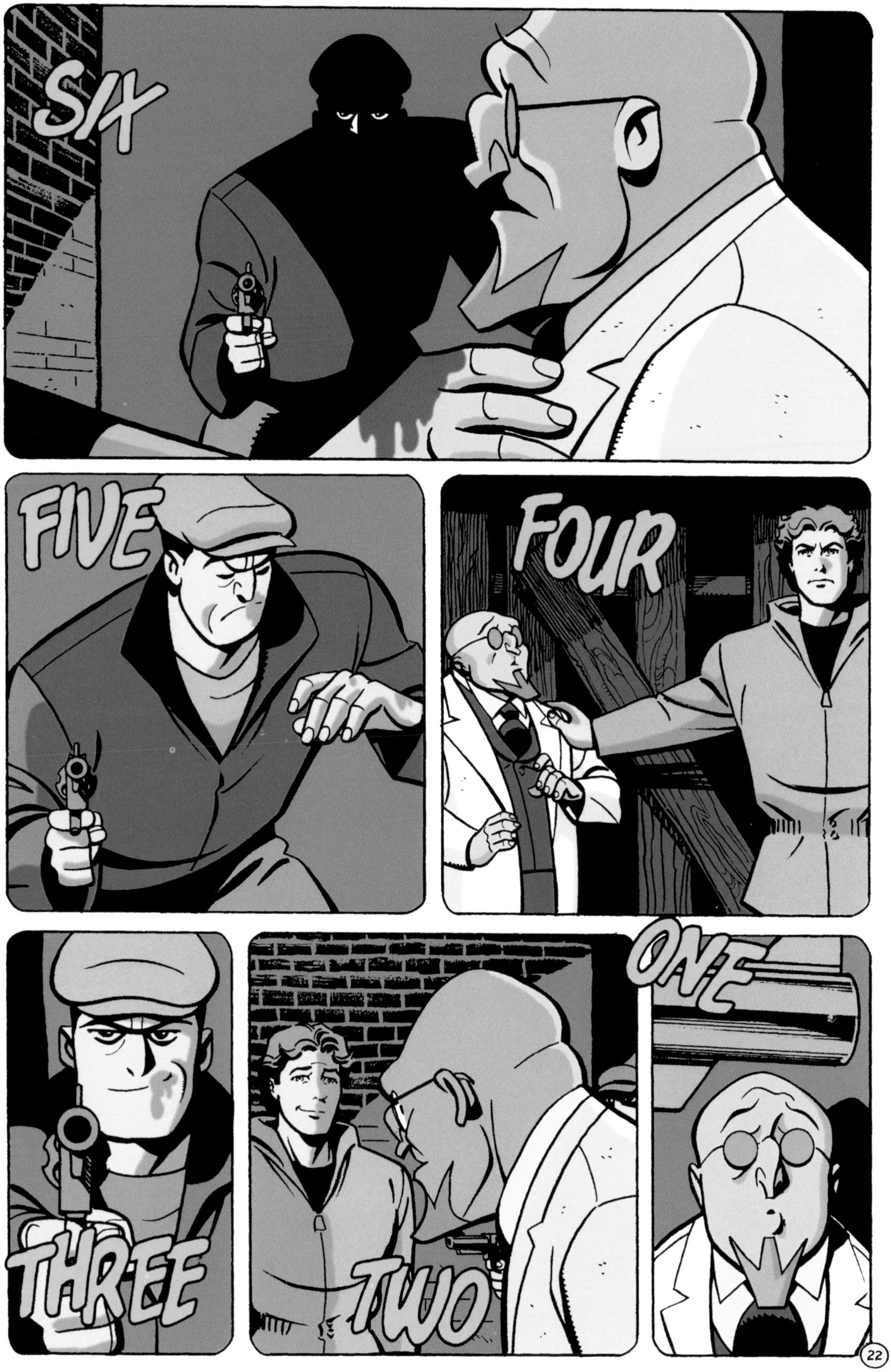
SIX
FIVE
FOUR
THREE
TWO
ONE
22

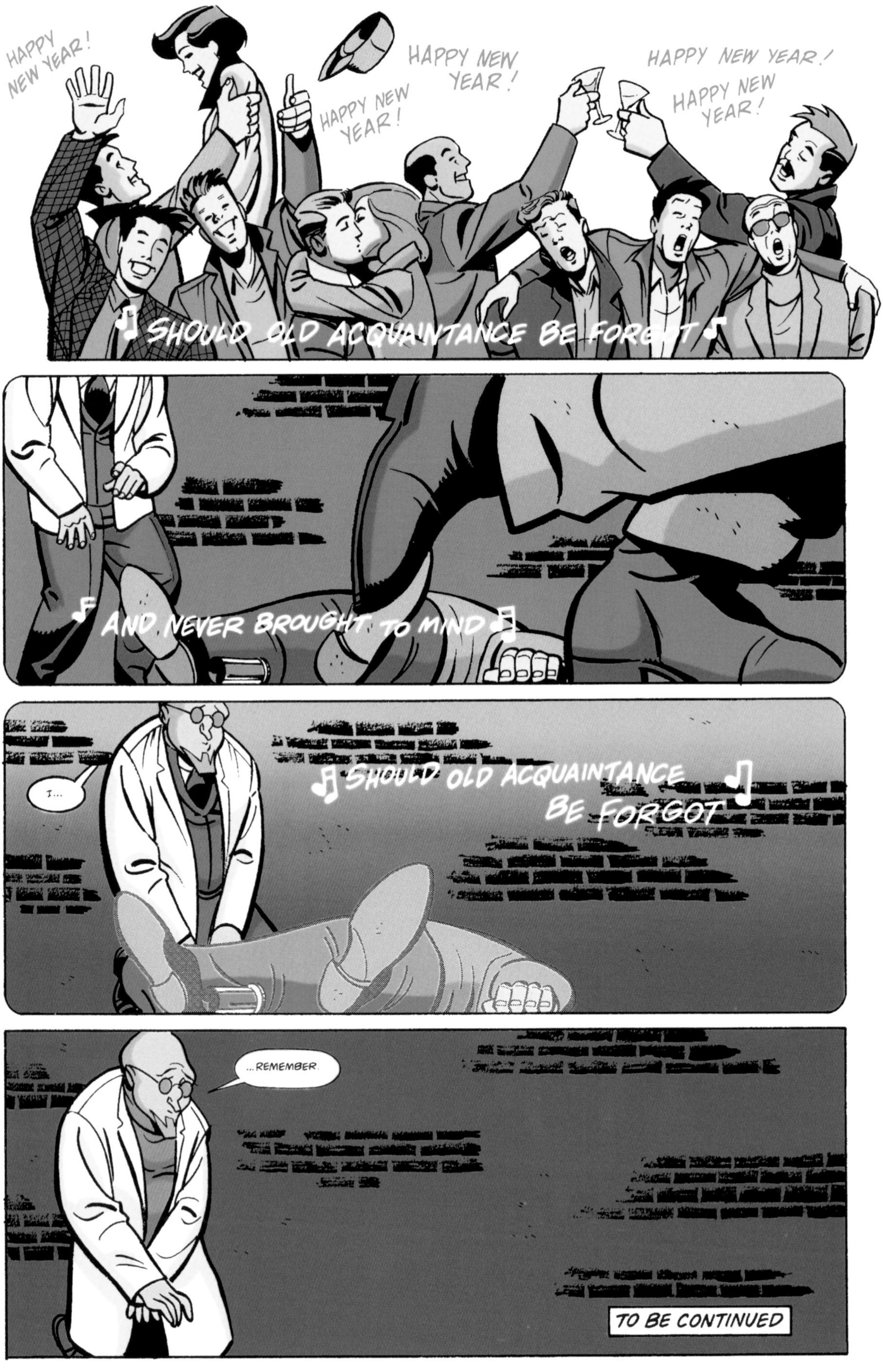
HAPPY NEW YEAR!
HAPPY NEW YEAR!
HAPPY NEW YEAR!
HAPPY NEW YEAR!
HAPPY NEW YEAR!
SHOULD OLD ACQUAINTANCE BE FORGOT
AND NEVER BROUGHT TO MIND
I...
SHOULD OLD ACQUAINTANCE BE FORGOT
...REMEMBER.
TO BE CONTINUED

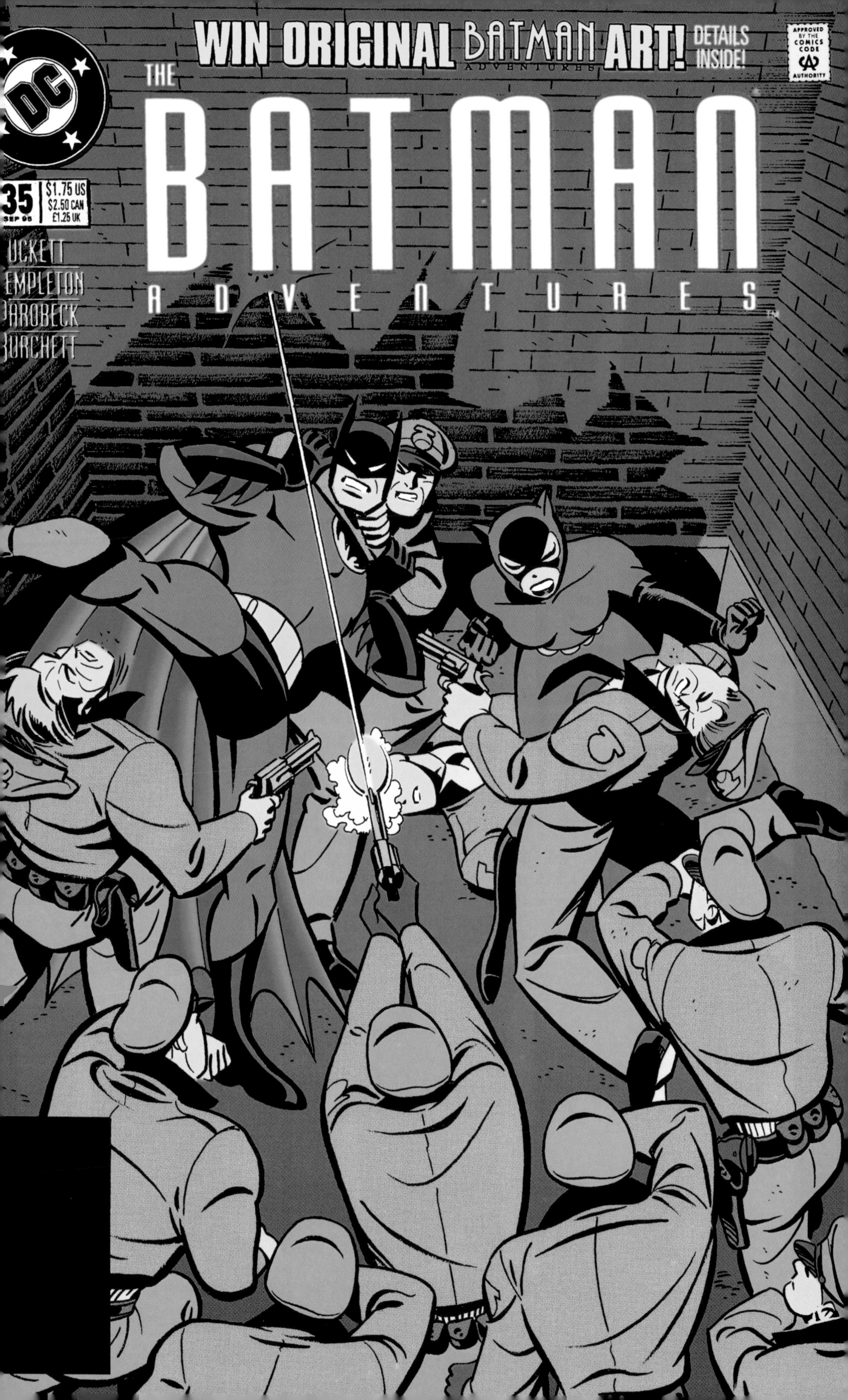
WIN ORIGINAL BATMAN ADVENTURES ART!
DETAILS INSIDE!
APPROVED BY THE COMICS CODE AUTHORITY
DC
THE BATMAN ADVENTURES
35
SEP 95
$1.75 US
$2.50 CAN
£1.25 UK
UCKETT
EMPLETON
AROBECK
URCHETT

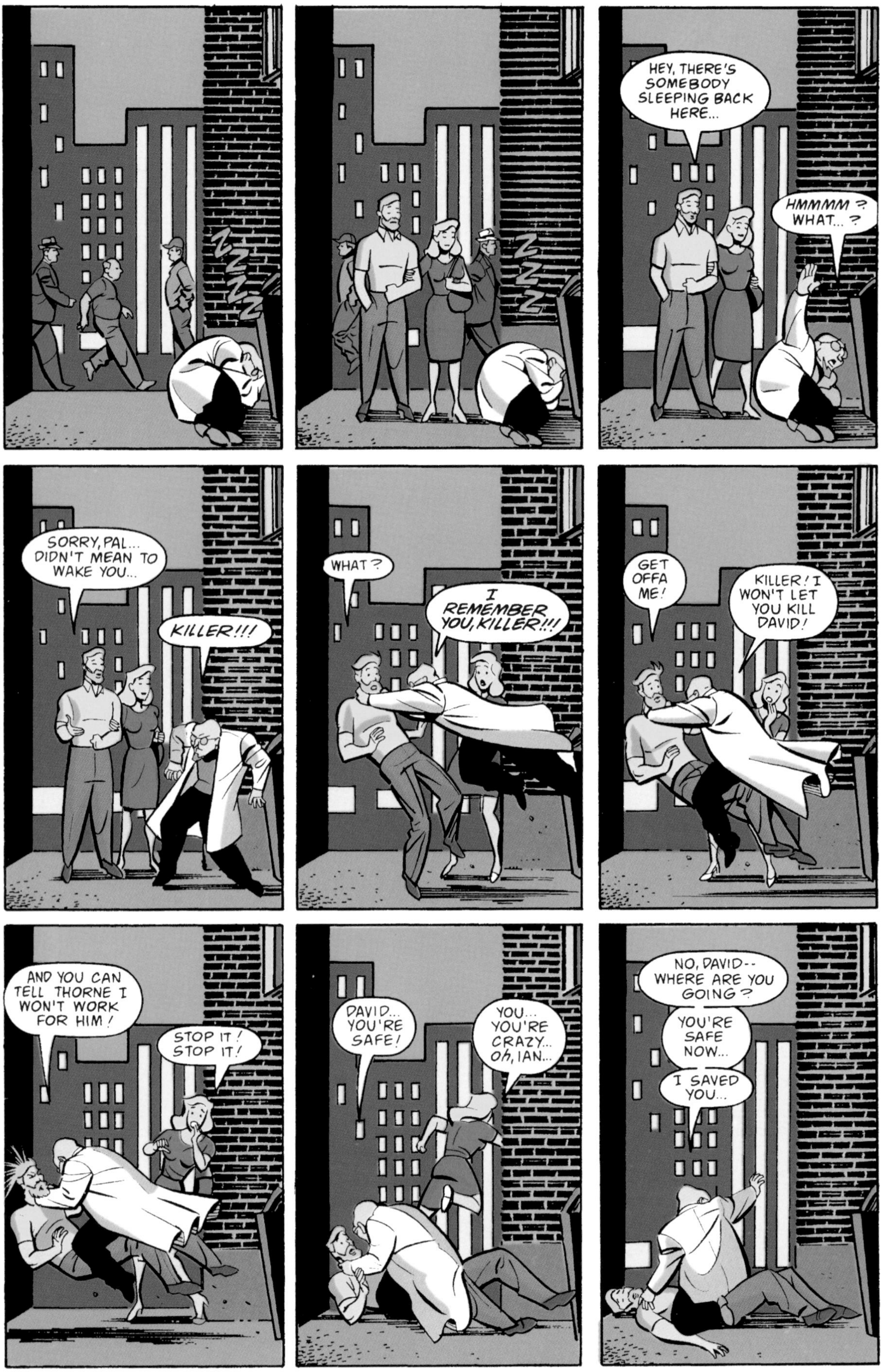
Z Z Z
Z Z Z
HEY, THERE'S SOMEBODY SLEEPING BACK HERE...
HMMMM? WHAT...?
SORRY, PAL... DIDN'T MEAN TO WAKE YOU...
KILLER!!!
WHAT?
I REMEMBER YOU, KILLER!!!
GET OFFA ME!
KILLER! I WON'T LET YOU KILL DAVID!
AND YOU CAN TELL THORNE I WON'T WORK FOR HIM!
STOP IT! STOP IT!
DAVID... YOU'RE SAFE!
YOU... YOU'RE CRAZY... oh, IAN...
NO, DAVID-- WHERE ARE YOU GOING?
YOU'RE SAFE NOW...
I SAVED YOU...

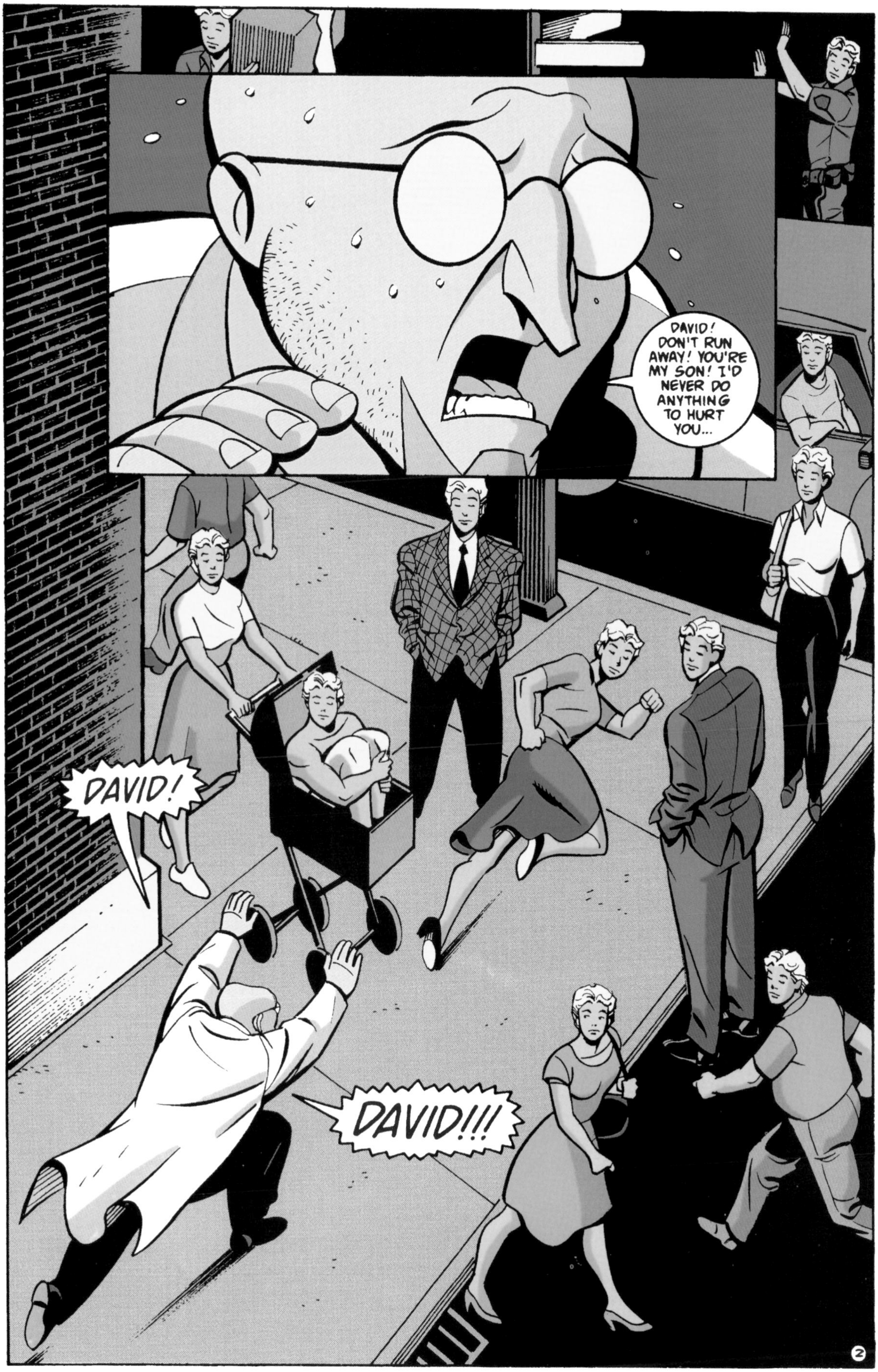
DAVID! DON'T RUN AWAY! YOU'RE MY SON! I'D NEVER DO ANYTHING TO HURT YOU...
DAVID!
DAVID!!!
2

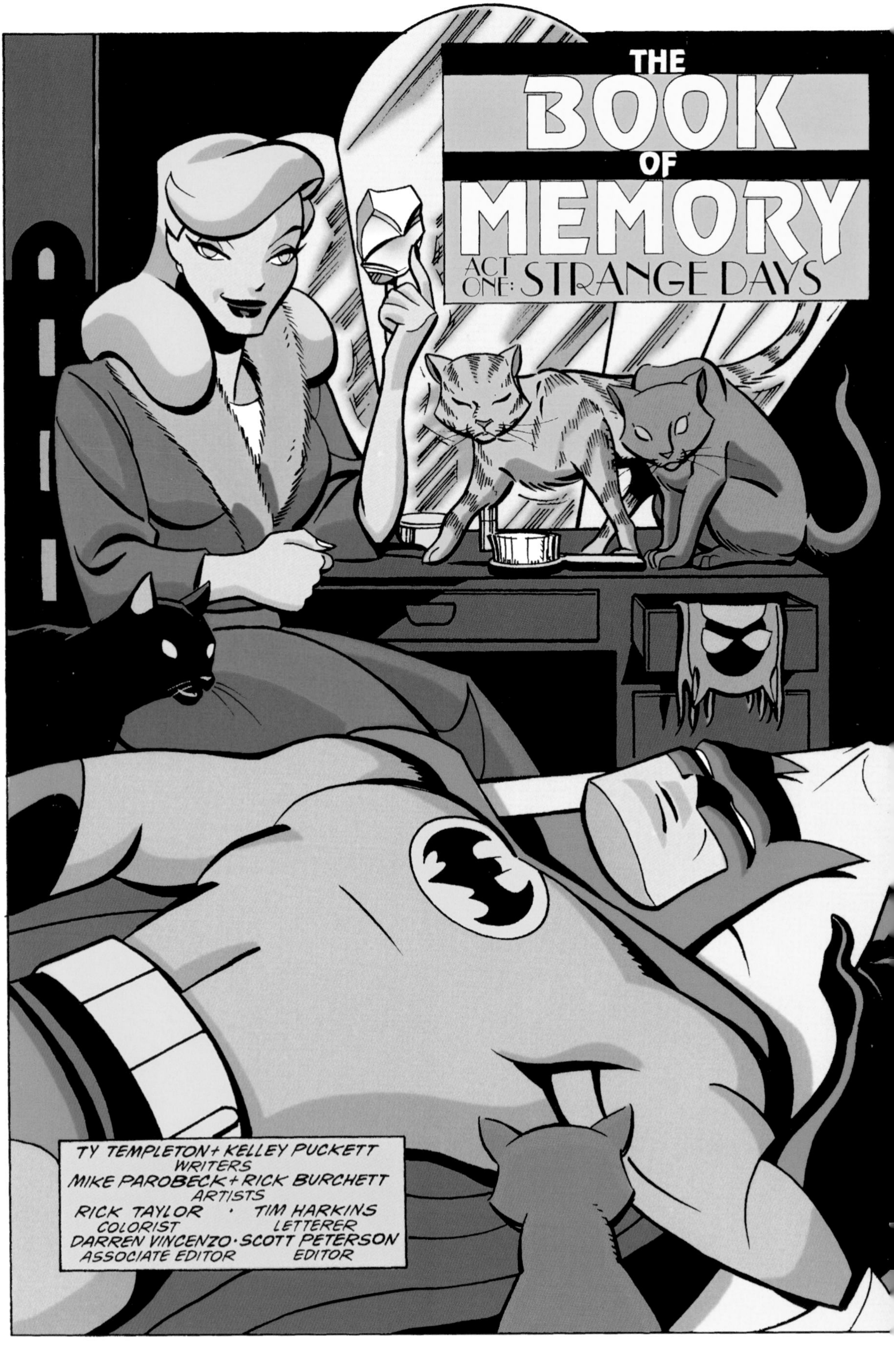
THE BOOK OF MEMORY
ACT ONE: STRANGE DAYS
TY TEMPLETON + KELLEY PUCKETT
WRITERS
MIKE PAROBECK + RICK BURCHETT
ARTISTS
RICK TAYLOR · TIM HARKINS
COLORIST LETTERER
DARREN VINCENZO · SCOTT PETERSON
ASSOCIATE EDITOR EDITOR

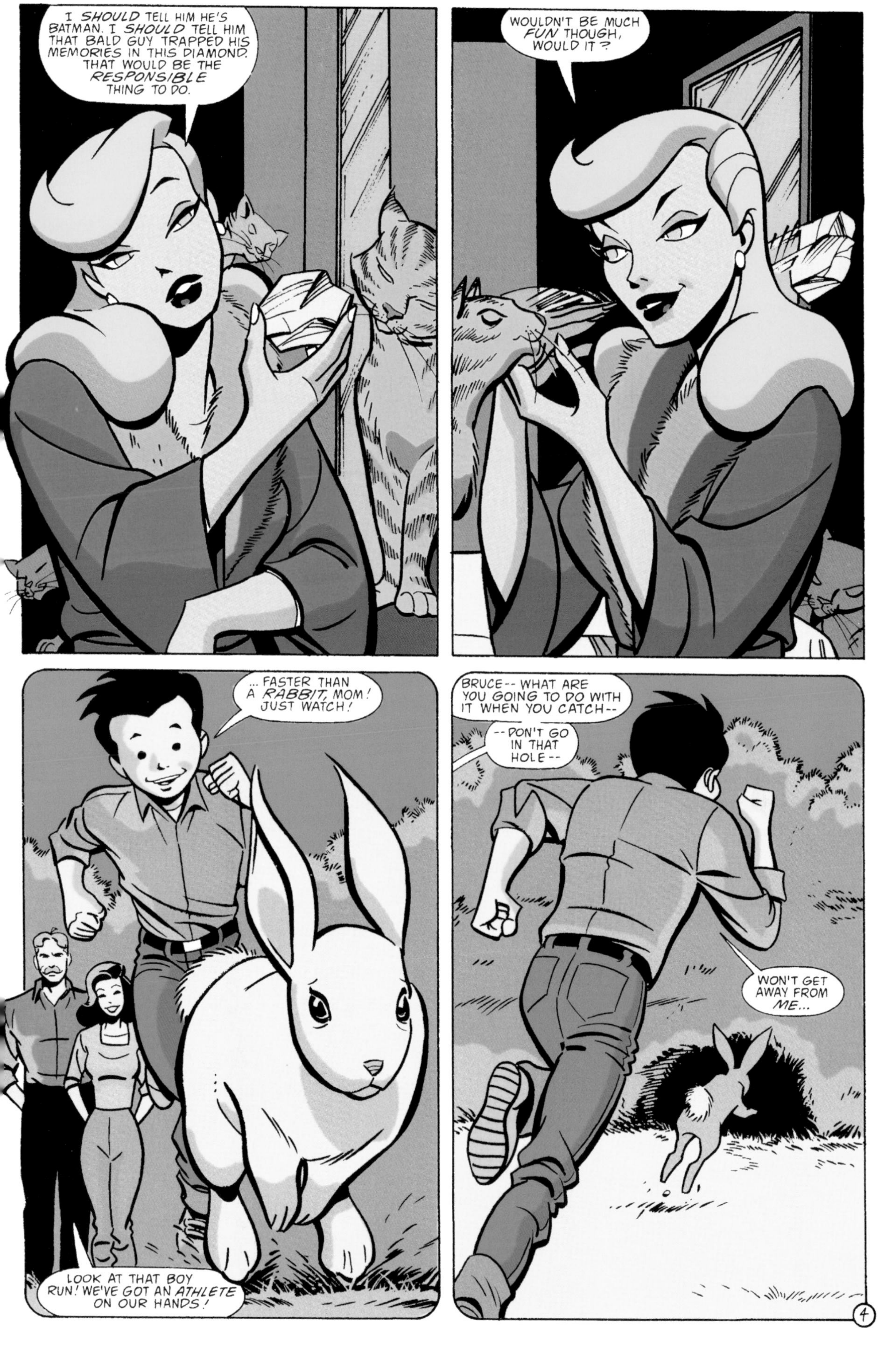
I SHOULD TELL HIM HE'S BATMAN. I SHOULD TELL HIM THAT BALD GUY TRAPPED HIS MEMORIES IN THIS DIAMOND. THAT WOULD BE THE RESPONSIBLE THING TO DO.
WOULDN'T BE MUCH FUN THOUGH, WOULD IT?
...FASTER THAN A RABBIT, MOM! JUST WATCH!
LOOK AT THAT BOY RUN! WE'VE GOT AN ATHLETE ON OUR HANDS!
BRUCE-- WHAT ARE YOU GOING TO DO WITH IT WHEN YOU CATCH--
--DON'T GO IN THAT HOLE--
WON'T GET AWAY FROM ME...
4

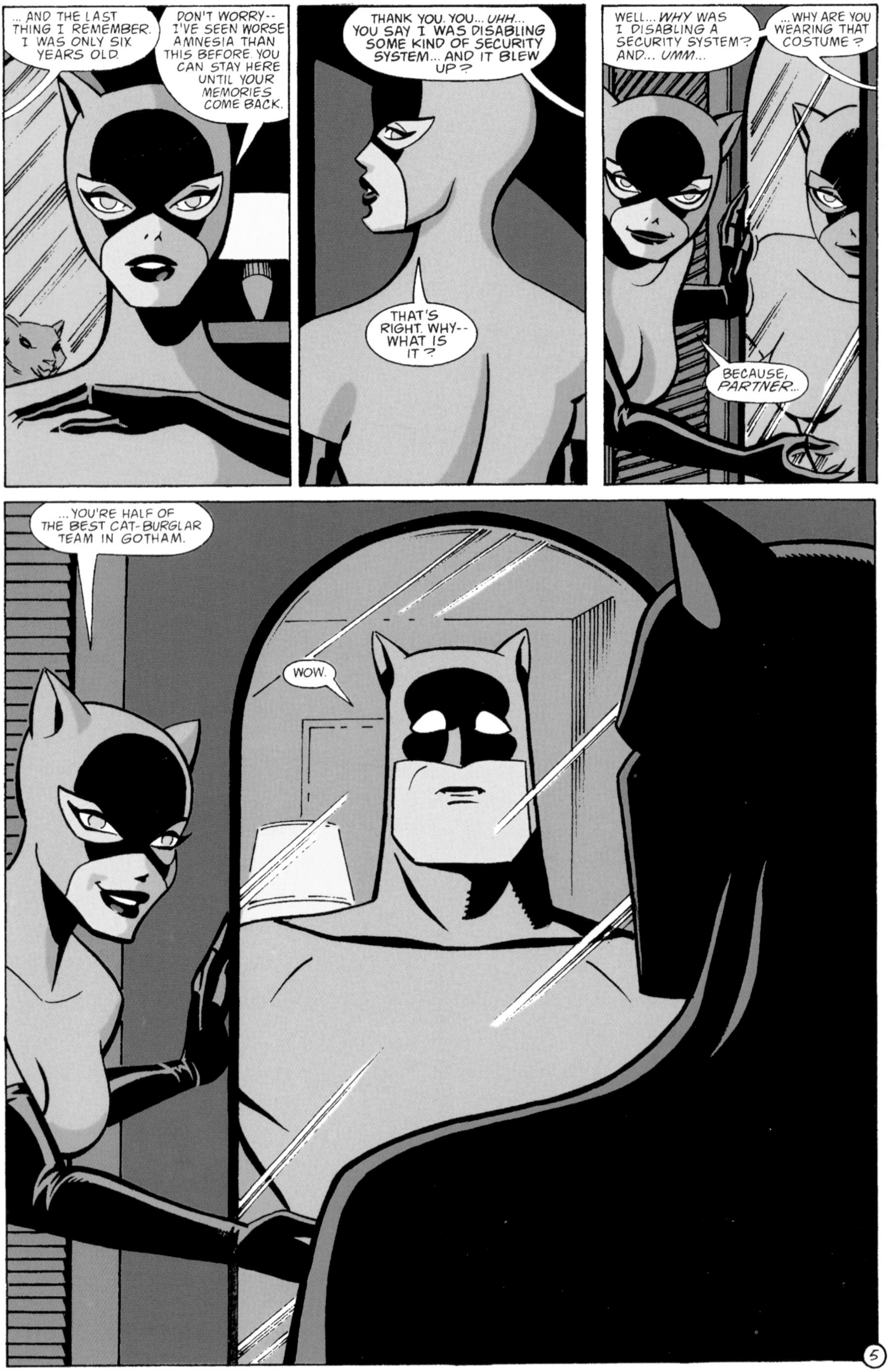
... AND THE LAST THING I REMEMBER. I WAS ONLY SIX YEARS OLD.
DON'T WORRY-- I'VE SEEN WORSE AMNESIA THAN THIS BEFORE. YOU CAN STAY HERE UNTIL YOUR MEMORIES COME BACK.
THANK YOU. YOU... UHH... YOU SAY I WAS DISABLING SOME KIND OF SECURITY SYSTEM... AND IT BLEW UP?
THAT'S RIGHT. WHY-- WHAT IS IT?
WELL... WHY WAS I DISABLING A SECURITY SYSTEM? AND... UMM...
...WHY ARE YOU WEARING THAT COSTUME?
BECAUSE, PARTNER...
...YOU'RE HALF OF THE BEST CAT-BURGLAR TEAM IN GOTHAM.
WOW.
5

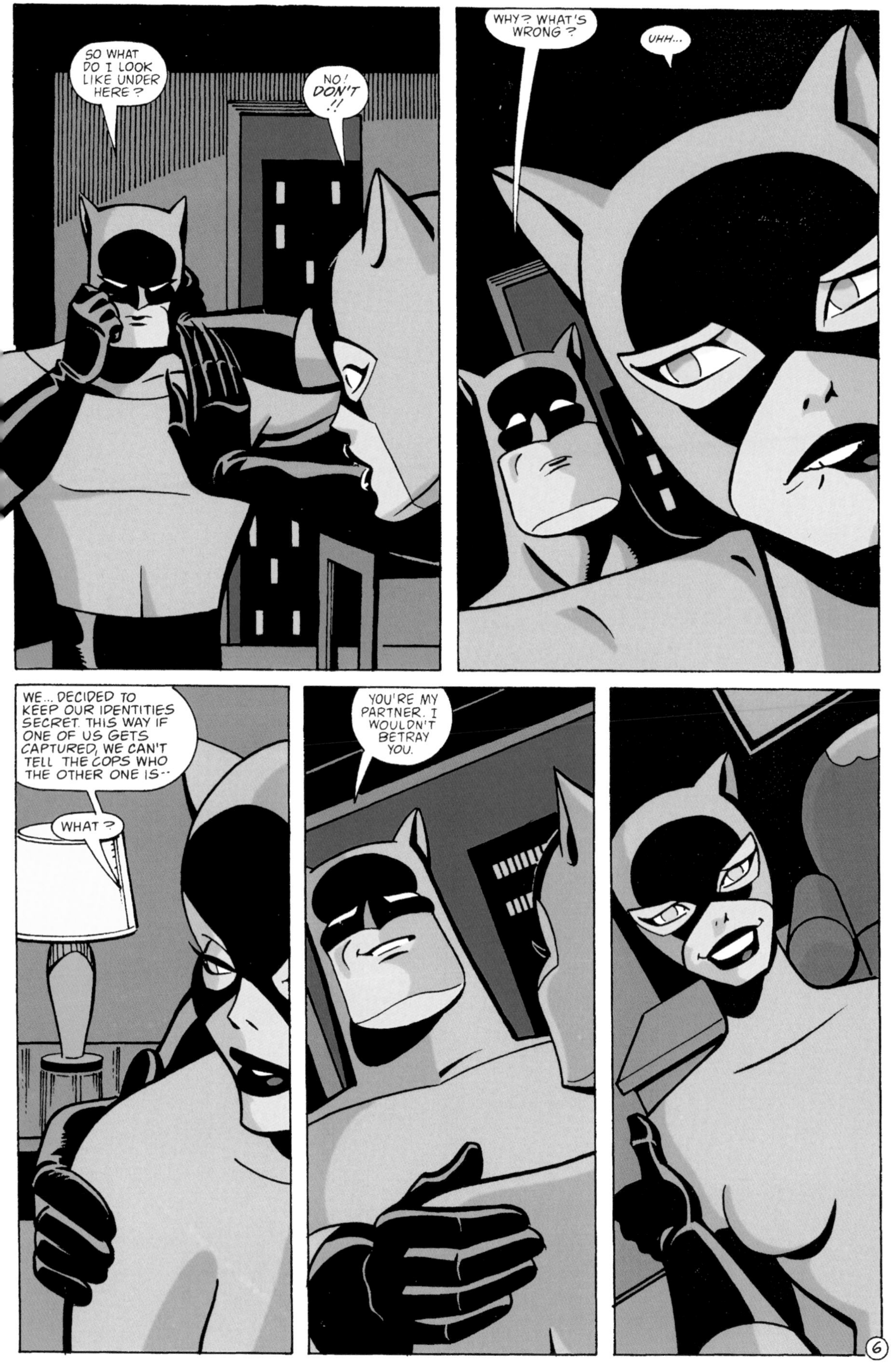
SO WHAT DO I LOOK LIKE UNDER HERE?
NO! DON'T !!
WHY? WHAT'S WRONG?
UHH...
WE... DECIDED TO KEEP OUR IDENTITIES SECRET. THIS WAY IF ONE OF US GETS CAPTURED, WE CAN'T TELL THE COPS WHO THE OTHER ONE IS--
WHAT?
YOU'RE MY PARTNER. I WOULDN'T BETRAY YOU.
6

OKAY-- THE IDEA'S SIMPLE. GET FROM HERE TO THERE WITHOUT TOUCHING A BEAM. NOW, WITH A FIELD THIS COMPLEX, YOU HAVE TO GO *VERY* SLOWLY AND TAKE IT ONE STEP AT A TIME.

HERBERT ROTHSCHILD MEMORIAL EXH...

WHY BOTHER?

WHAT? *HEY!*

PIECE OF CAKE.

THIS IS *GREAT.* IT'S LIKE... I JUST *KNOW* WHAT TO DO. I DON'T EVEN HAVE TO *THINK* ABOUT IT!

IN *FACT...*

WAIT! WHAT'RE YOU--?

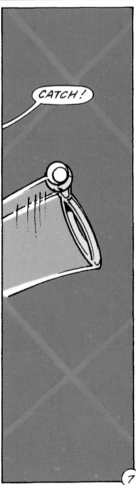

CATCH!

7

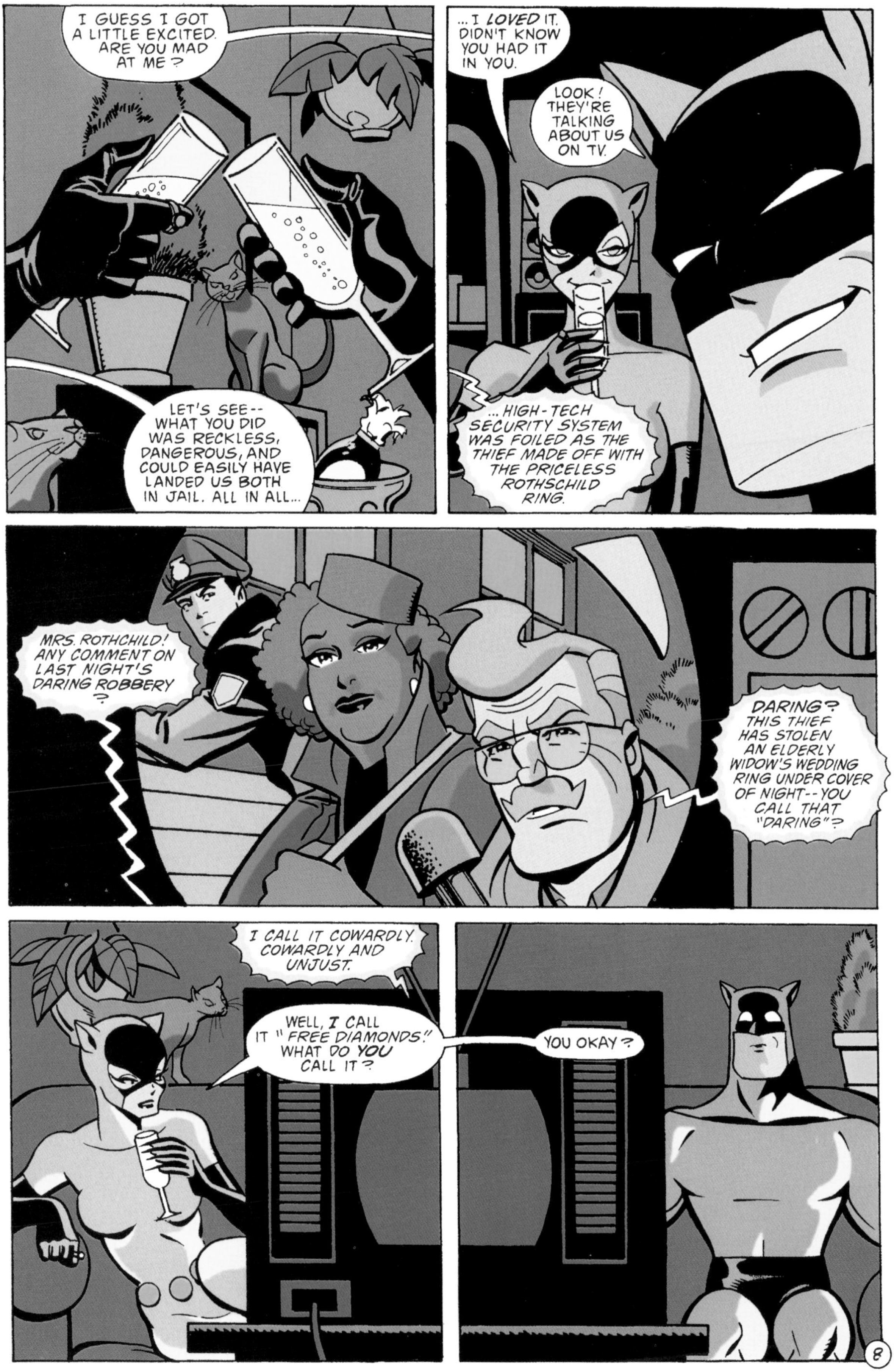
I GUESS I GOT A LITTLE EXCITED. ARE YOU MAD AT ME?
LET'S SEE-- WHAT YOU DID WAS RECKLESS, DANGEROUS, AND COULD EASILY HAVE LANDED US BOTH IN JAIL. ALL IN ALL...
...I LOVED IT. DIDN'T KNOW YOU HAD IT IN YOU.
LOOK! THEY'RE TALKING ABOUT US ON TV.
...HIGH-TECH SECURITY SYSTEM WAS FOILED AS THE THIEF MADE OFF WITH THE PRICELESS ROTHSCHILD RING.
MRS. ROTHCHILD! ANY COMMENT ON LAST NIGHT'S DARING ROBBERY?
DARING? THIS THIEF HAS STOLEN AN ELDERLY WIDOW'S WEDDING RING UNDER COVER OF NIGHT--YOU CALL THAT "DARING"?
I CALL IT COWARDLY. COWARDLY AND UNJUST.
WELL, I CALL IT "FREE DIAMONDS." WHAT DO YOU CALL IT?
YOU OKAY?
8

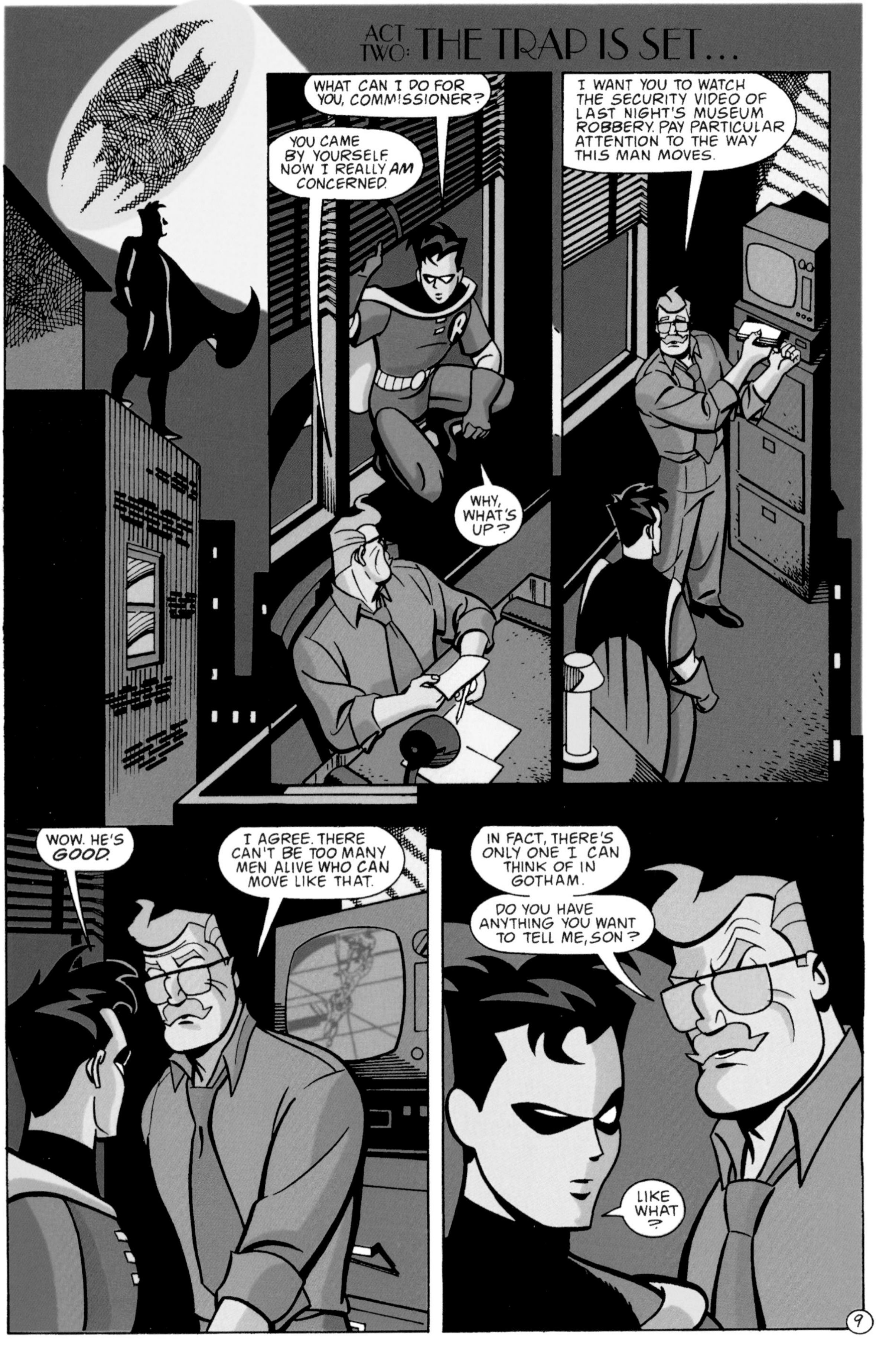
ACT TWO: THE TRAP IS SET...
WHAT CAN I DO FOR YOU, COMMISSIONER?
YOU CAME BY YOURSELF. NOW I REALLY AM CONCERNED.
WHY, WHAT'S UP?
I WANT YOU TO WATCH THE SECURITY VIDEO OF LAST NIGHT'S MUSEUM ROBBERY. PAY PARTICULAR ATTENTION TO THE WAY THIS MAN MOVES.
WOW. HE'S GOOD.
I AGREE. THERE CAN'T BE TOO MANY MEN ALIVE WHO CAN MOVE LIKE THAT.
IN FACT, THERE'S ONLY ONE I CAN THINK OF IN GOTHAM.
DO YOU HAVE ANYTHING YOU WANT TO TELL ME, SON?
LIKE WHAT?
9

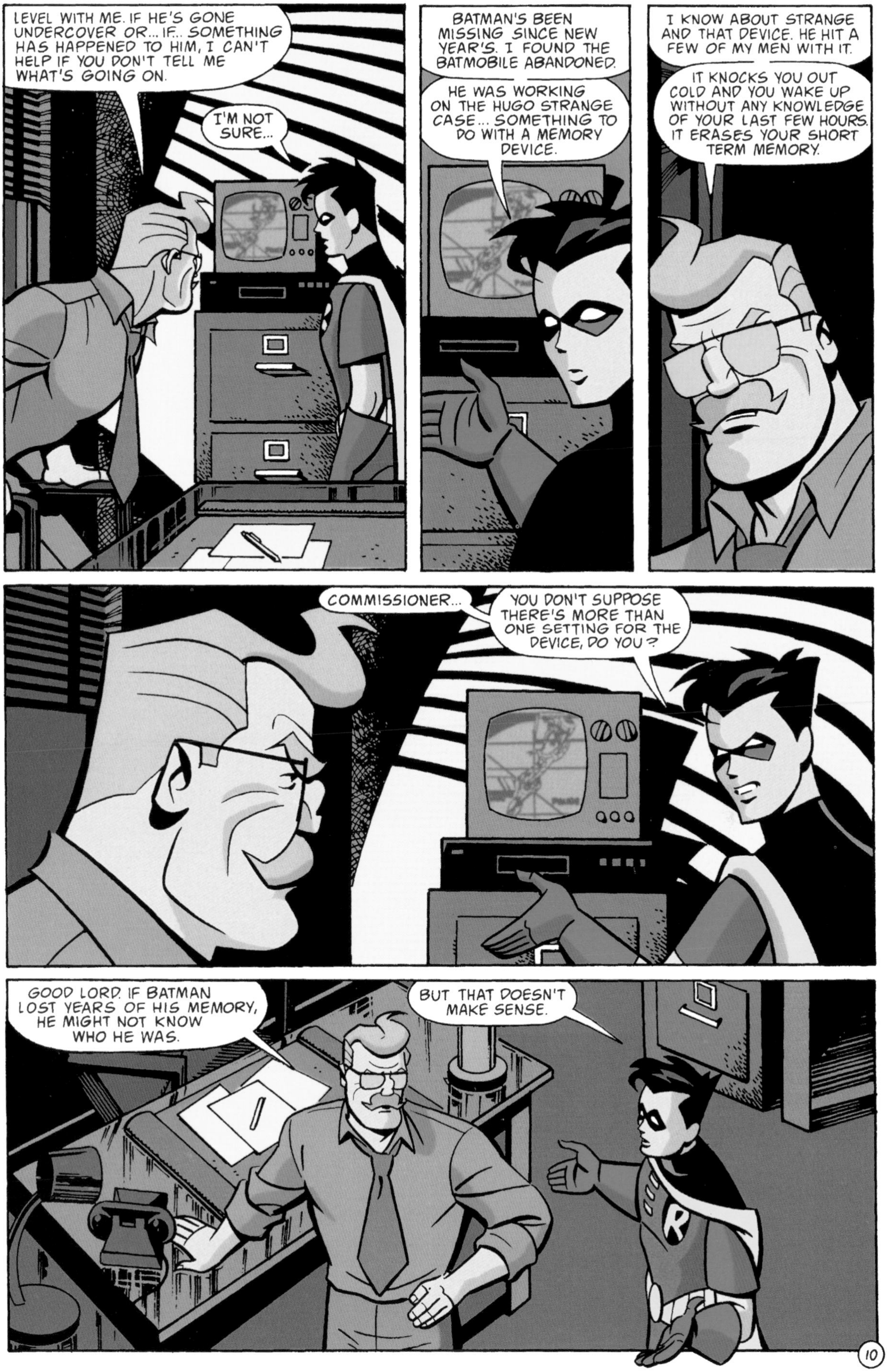
LEVEL WITH ME. IF HE'S GONE UNDERCOVER OR... IF... SOMETHING HAS HAPPENED TO HIM, I CAN'T HELP IF YOU DON'T TELL ME WHAT'S GOING ON.
I'M NOT SURE...
BATMAN'S BEEN MISSING SINCE NEW YEAR'S. I FOUND THE BATMOBILE ABANDONED.
HE WAS WORKING ON THE HUGO STRANGE CASE... SOMETHING TO DO WITH A MEMORY DEVICE.
I KNOW ABOUT STRANGE AND THAT DEVICE. HE HIT A FEW OF MY MEN WITH IT.
IT KNOCKS YOU OUT COLD AND YOU WAKE UP WITHOUT ANY KNOWLEDGE OF YOUR LAST FEW HOURS. IT ERASES YOUR SHORT TERM MEMORY.
COMMISSIONER...
YOU DON'T SUPPOSE THERE'S MORE THAN ONE SETTING FOR THE DEVICE, DO YOU?
GOOD LORD. IF BATMAN LOST YEARS OF HIS MEMORY, HE MIGHT NOT KNOW WHO HE WAS.
BUT THAT DOESN'T MAKE SENSE.
10

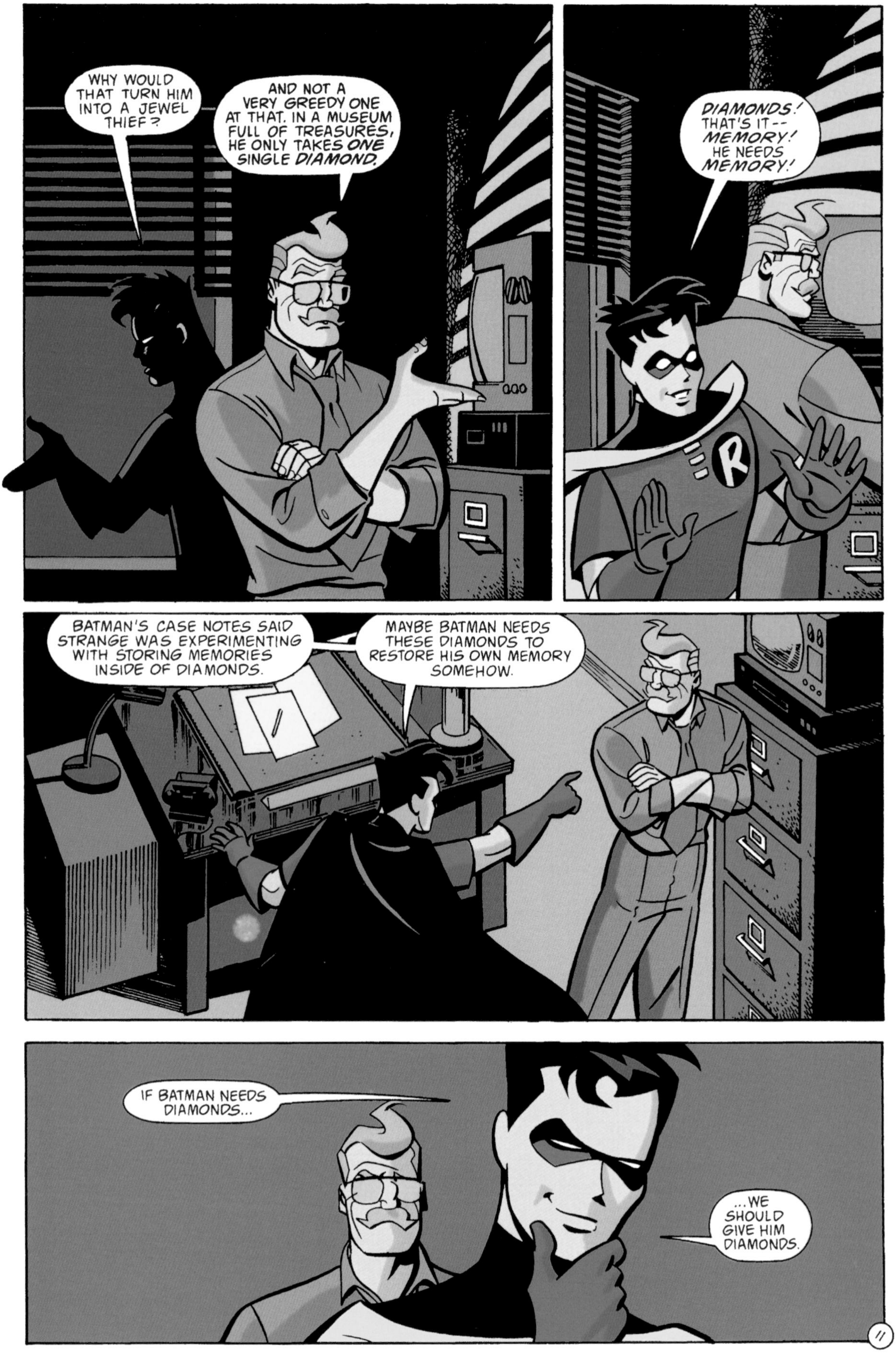
WHY WOULD THAT TURN HIM INTO A JEWEL THIEF?
AND NOT A VERY GREEDY ONE AT THAT. IN A MUSEUM FULL OF TREASURES, HE ONLY TAKES ONE SINGLE DIAMOND.
DIAMONDS! THAT'S IT-- MEMORY! HE NEEDS MEMORY!
BATMAN'S CASE NOTES SAID STRANGE WAS EXPERIMENTING WITH STORING MEMORIES INSIDE OF DIAMONDS.
MAYBE BATMAN NEEDS THESE DIAMONDS TO RESTORE HIS OWN MEMORY SOMEHOW.
IF BATMAN NEEDS DIAMONDS...
...WE SHOULD GIVE HIM DIAMONDS.
11

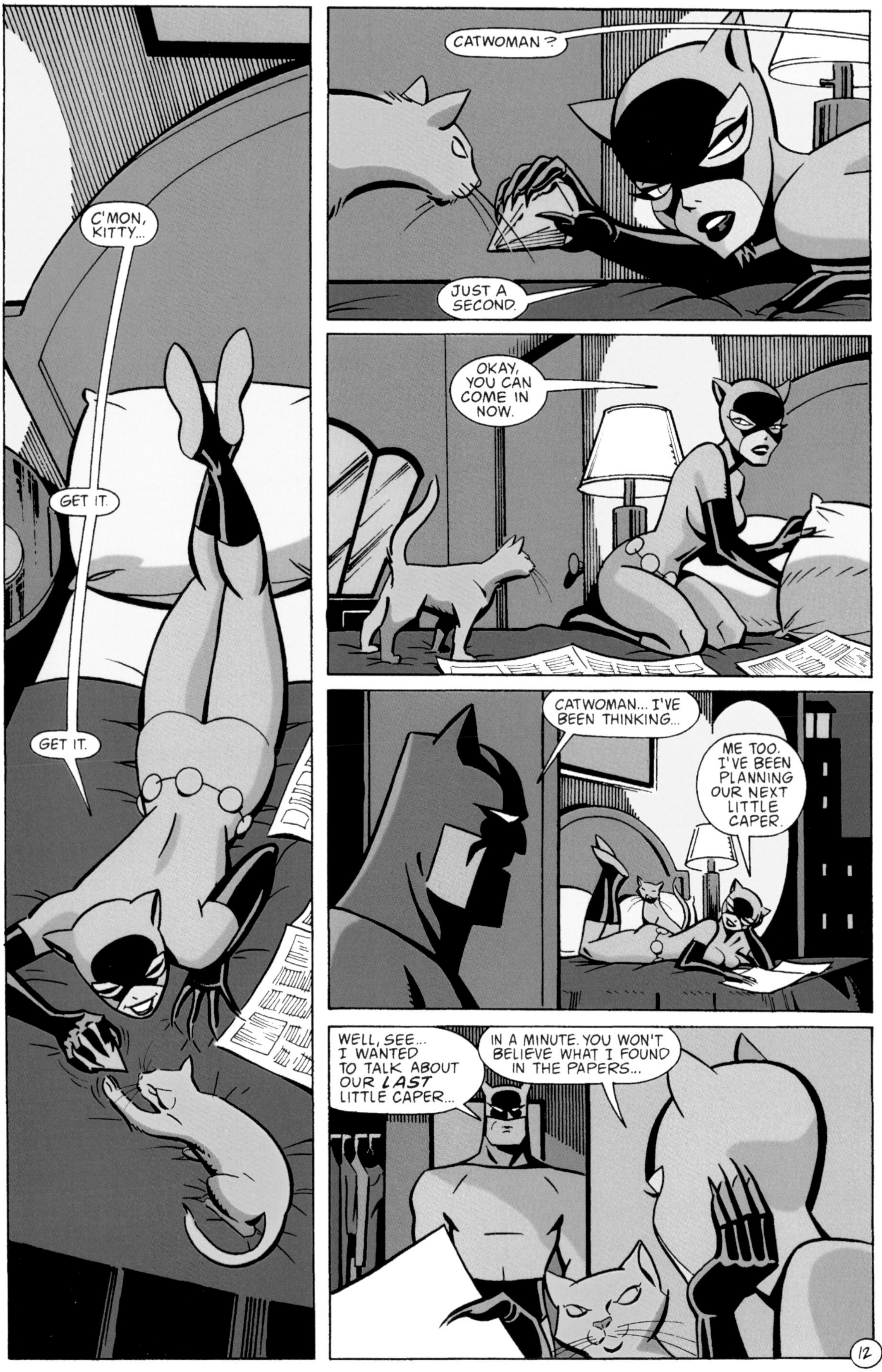
C'MON, KITTY...
GET IT.
GET IT.
CATWOMAN?
JUST A SECOND.
OKAY, YOU CAN COME IN NOW.
CATWOMAN... I'VE BEEN THINKING...
ME TOO. I'VE BEEN PLANNING OUR NEXT LITTLE CAPER.
WELL, SEE... I WANTED TO TALK ABOUT OUR LAST LITTLE CAPER...
IN A MINUTE. YOU WON'T BELIEVE WHAT I FOUND IN THE PAPERS...
12

LISTEN, MAYBE WE SHOULDN'T BE...

OH, JUST HUSH UP AND LISTEN TO THIS.

"A JEWEL-ENCRUSTED STATUE OF THE AZTEC GOD QUIPUXATCHLI IS BEING PUT ON DISPLAY IN THE LOBBY OF THE UPTOWN THEATER IN GOTHAM'S FASHIONABLE WEST SIDE TO PROMOTE THE PREMIERE OF THEIR NEW HORROR MOVIE, 'LAND OF BLOOD...'"

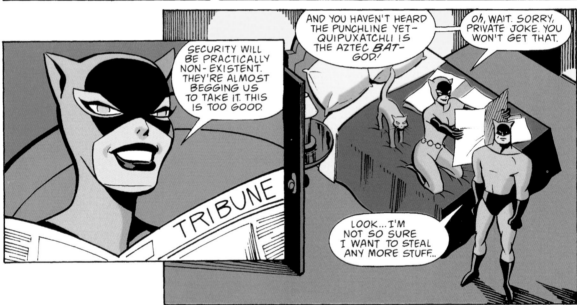

SECURITY WILL BE PRACTICALLY NON-EXISTENT. THEY'RE ALMOST BEGGING US TO TAKE IT. THIS IS TOO GOOD.

TRIBUNE

AND YOU HAVEN'T HEARD THE PUNCHLINE YET—QUIPUXATCHLI IS THE AZTEC *BAT-GOD!*

OH, WAIT. SORRY, PRIVATE JOKE. YOU WON'T GET THAT.

LOOK... I'M NOT SO SURE I WANT TO STEAL ANY MORE STUFF...

THE MORE I THINK ABOUT IT, THE MORE I GET TO THINKING IT'S NOT WHAT MOM AND DAD TAUGHT ME WAS RIGHT...

MAYBE WE JUST *SHOULDN'T*, IS ALL.

THAT'S THE *AMNESIA* TALKING. YOU'LL FEEL BETTER AFTER A NICE JEWEL-COVERED AZTEC TREASURE.

13

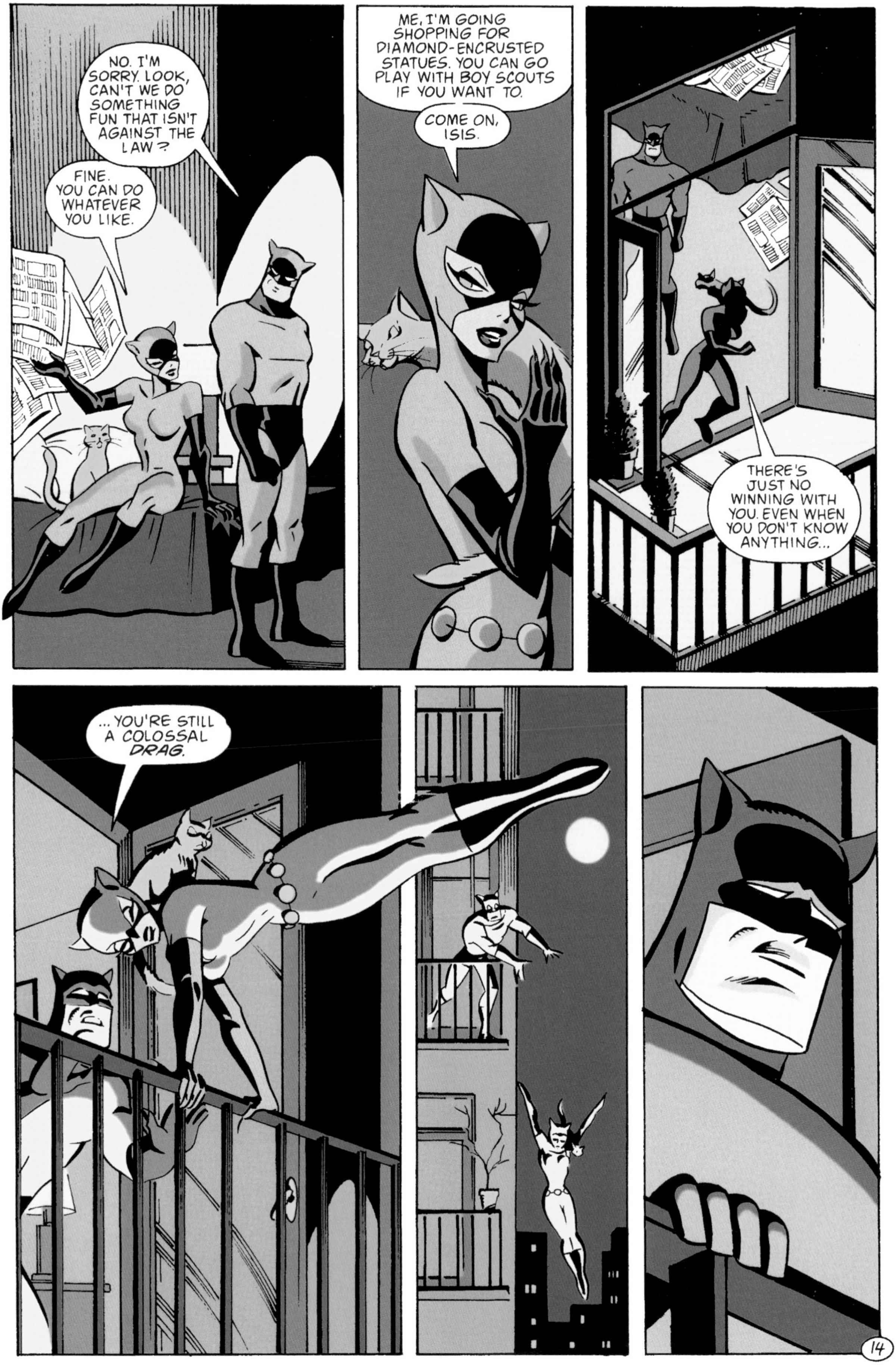

NO. I'M SORRY. LOOK, CAN'T WE DO SOMETHING FUN THAT ISN'T AGAINST THE LAW?
FINE. YOU CAN DO WHATEVER YOU LIKE.
ME, I'M GOING SHOPPING FOR DIAMOND-ENCRUSTED STATUES. YOU CAN GO PLAY WITH BOY SCOUTS IF YOU WANT TO.
COME ON, ISIS.
THERE'S JUST NO WINNING WITH YOU. EVEN WHEN YOU DON'T KNOW ANYTHING...
...YOU'RE STILL A COLOSSAL DRAG.
14

HEY! HEY, PUT THAT DOWN!

I GO TO THE BATHROOM FOR TWO MINUTES AND THIS CLOWN STARTS EATING OFF MY PLATE...

Mmm? WHAT?

Oh, NO... I'M SORRY, LADY.

MRF! MRF! MUNCH!

LOOK, BUDDY, IF YOU'RE HUNGRY THERE'S A MISSION TWO BLOCKS FROM HERE, BUT YOU CAN'T COME IN HERE AND DO THIS SORT OF THING.

Mmmmph... GOOD FOOD. EVEN THORNE CAN'T STOP ME FROM EATING...

NO, BUT I CAN. DON'T MAKE ME GET ROUGH WITH YOU.

WHAM!

ahhh! KILLER! KILLER!

YOU MADE ME DROP MY CHICKEN LEG, KILLER! BUT I STOPPED YOU FROM HURTING DAVID, DIDN'T I?

15

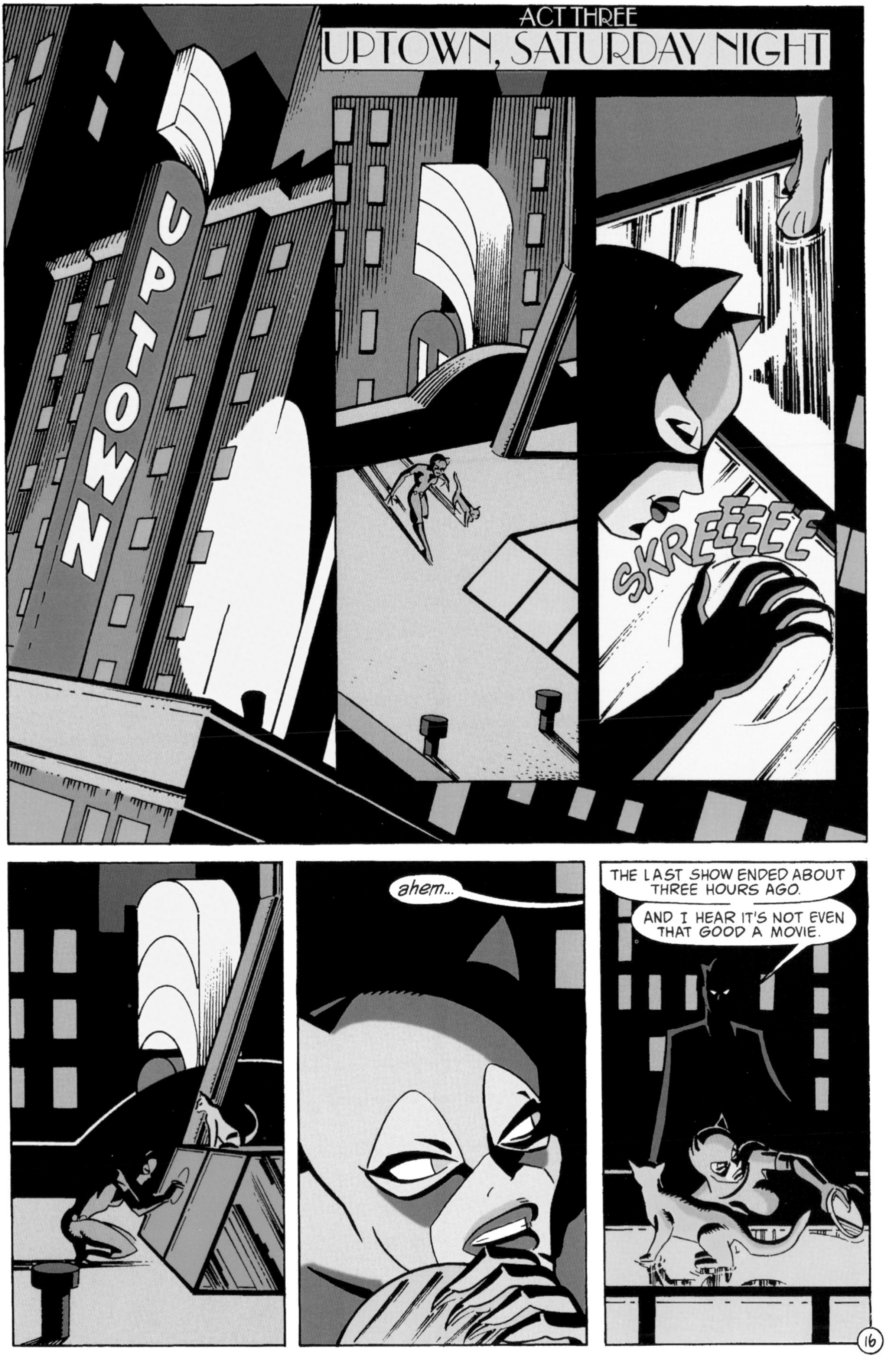
ACT THREE
UPTOWN, SATURDAY NIGHT
UPTOWN
SKREEEEEE
ahem...
THE LAST SHOW ENDED ABOUT THREE HOURS AGO.
AND I HEAR IT'S NOT EVEN THAT GOOD A MOVIE.
16

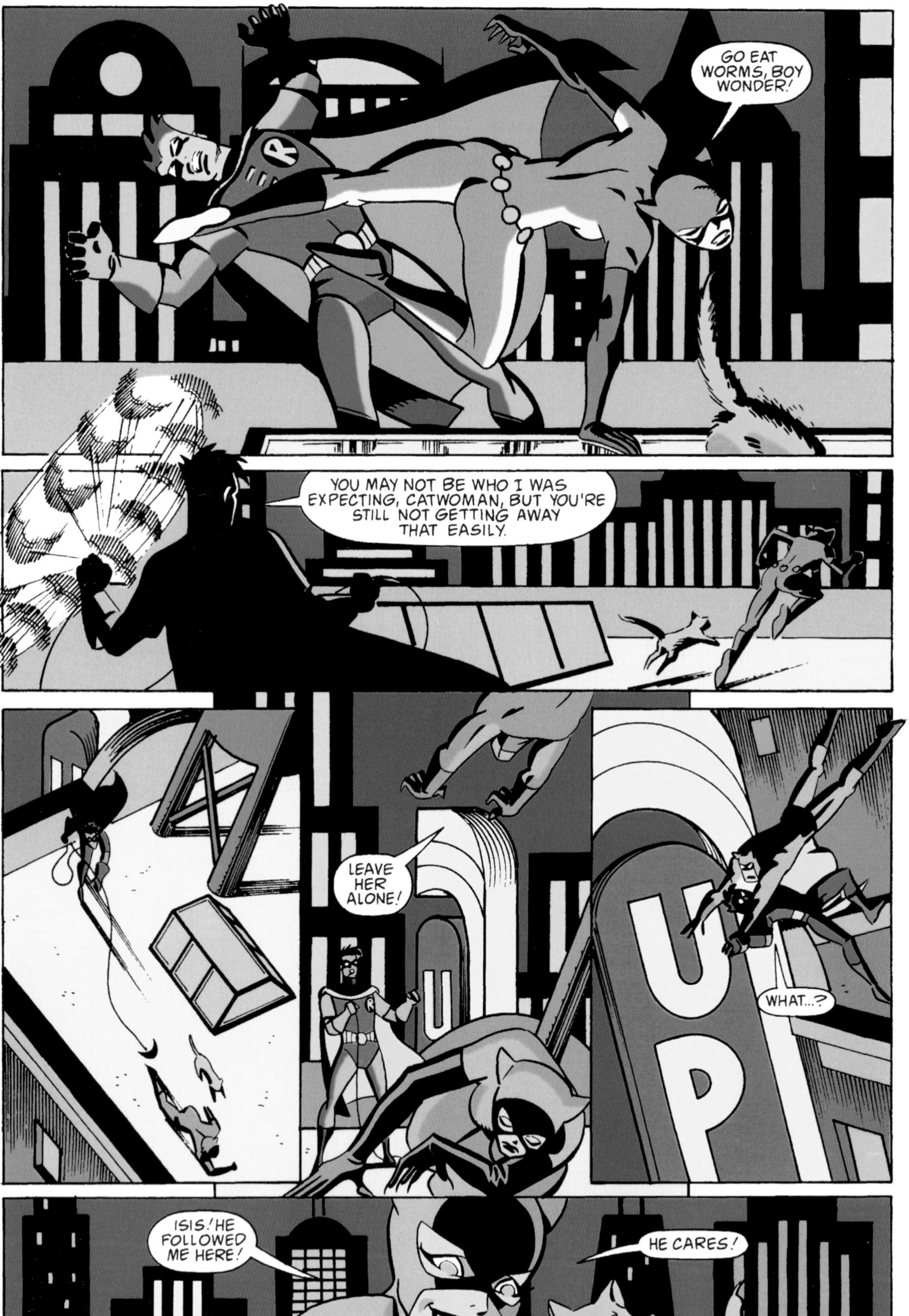
GO EAT WORMS, BOY WONDER!
YOU MAY NOT BE WHO I WAS EXPECTING, CATWOMAN, BUT YOU'RE STILL NOT GETTING AWAY THAT EASILY.
LEAVE HER ALONE!
WHAT...?
ISIS! HE FOLLOWED ME HERE!
HE CARES!
17

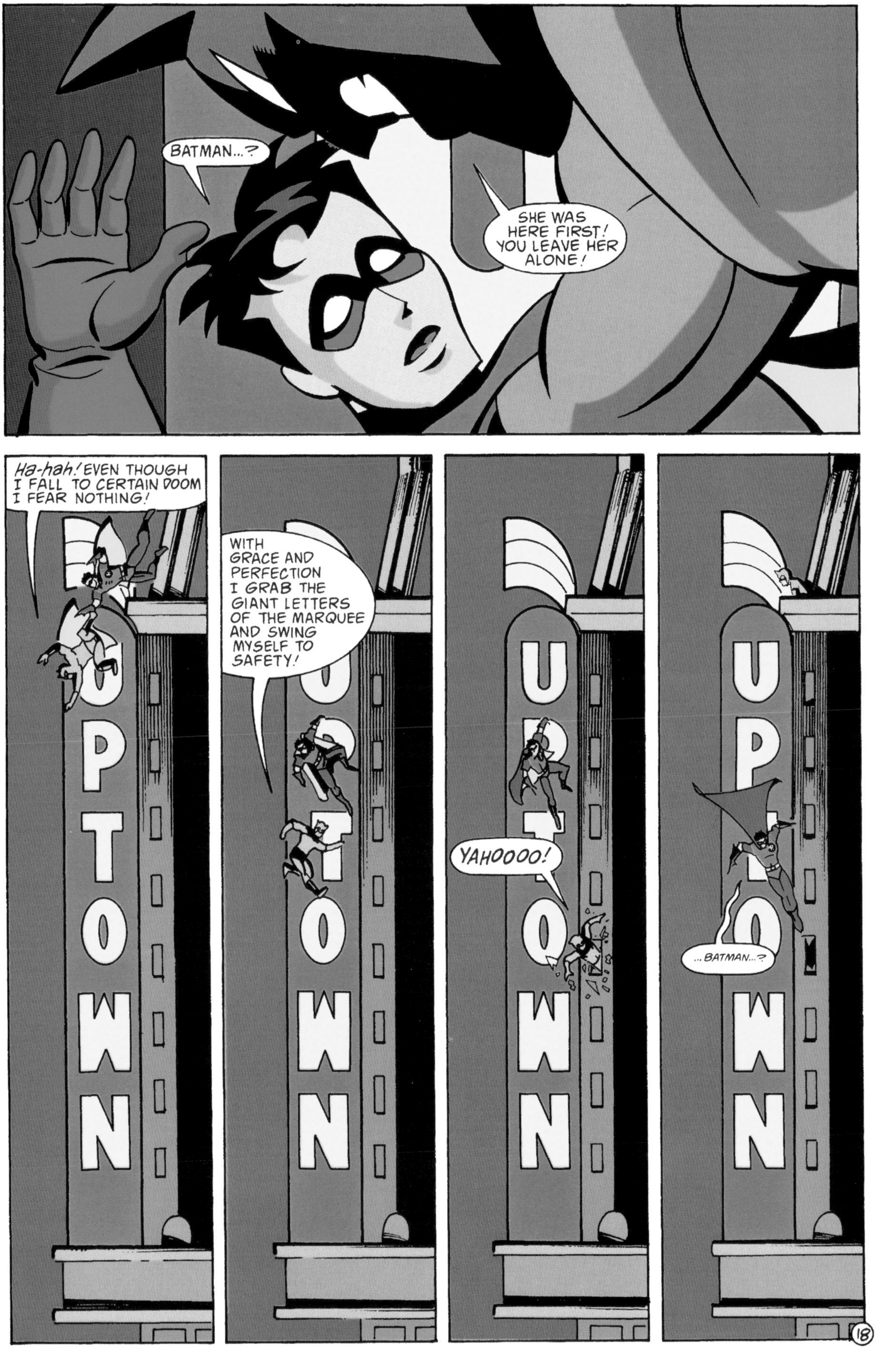
BATMAN...?
SHE WAS HERE FIRST! YOU LEAVE HER ALONE!
Ha-hah! EVEN THOUGH I FALL TO CERTAIN DOOM I FEAR NOTHING!
UPTOWN
WITH GRACE AND PERFECTION I GRAB THE GIANT LETTERS OF THE MARQUEE AND SWING MYSELF TO SAFETY!
YAHOOOO!
...BATMAN...?
18

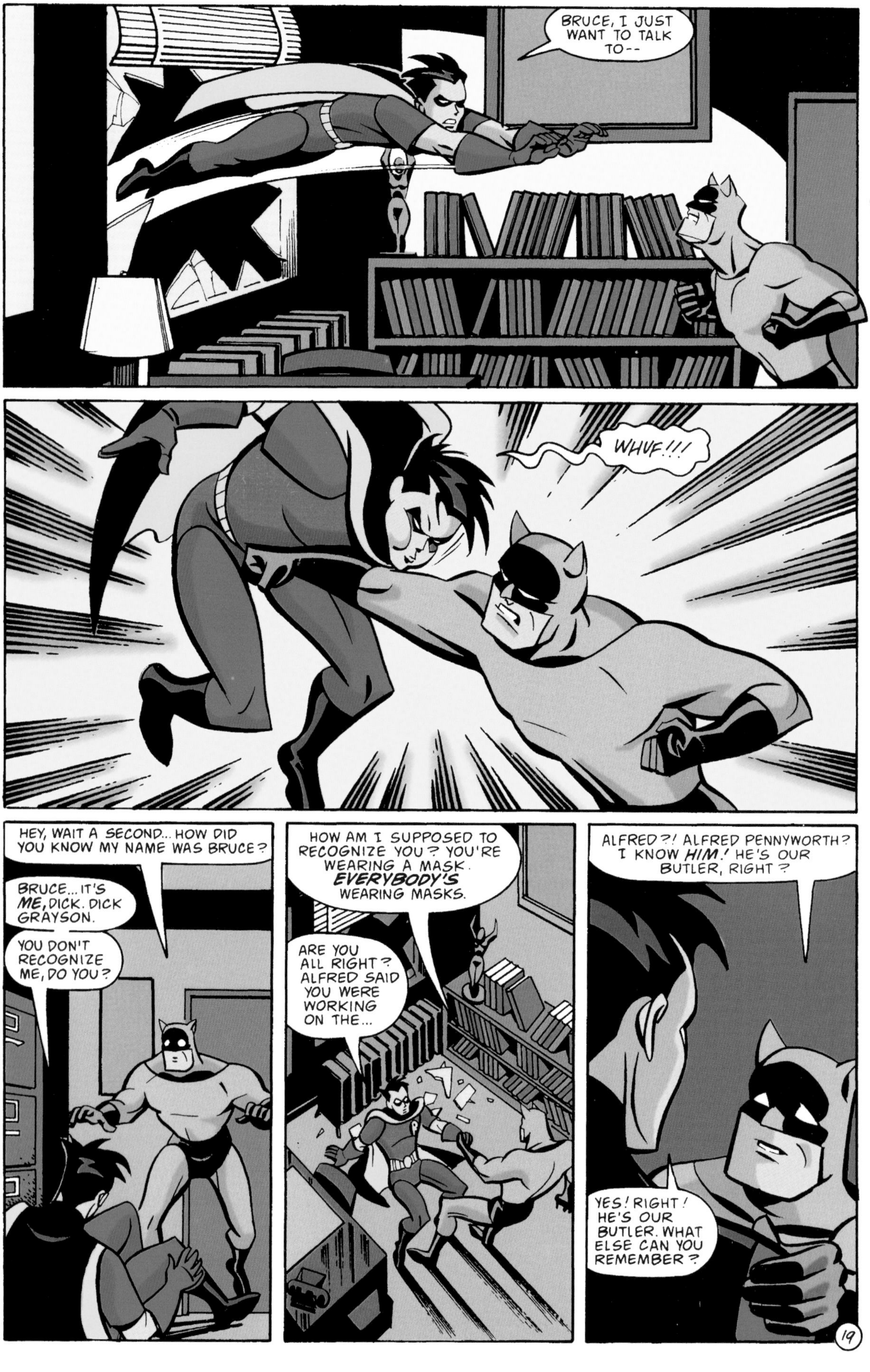
BRUCE, I JUST WANT TO TALK TO--
WHUF!!!
HEY, WAIT A SECOND... HOW DID YOU KNOW MY NAME WAS BRUCE?
BRUCE... IT'S ME, DICK. DICK GRAYSON.
YOU DON'T RECOGNIZE ME, DO YOU?
HOW AM I SUPPOSED TO RECOGNIZE YOU? YOU'RE WEARING A MASK. EVERYBODY'S WEARING MASKS.
ARE YOU ALL RIGHT? ALFRED SAID YOU WERE WORKING ON THE...
ALFRED?! ALFRED PENNYWORTH? I KNOW HIM! HE'S OUR BUTLER, RIGHT?
YES! RIGHT! HE'S OUR BUTLER. WHAT ELSE CAN YOU REMEMBER?
19

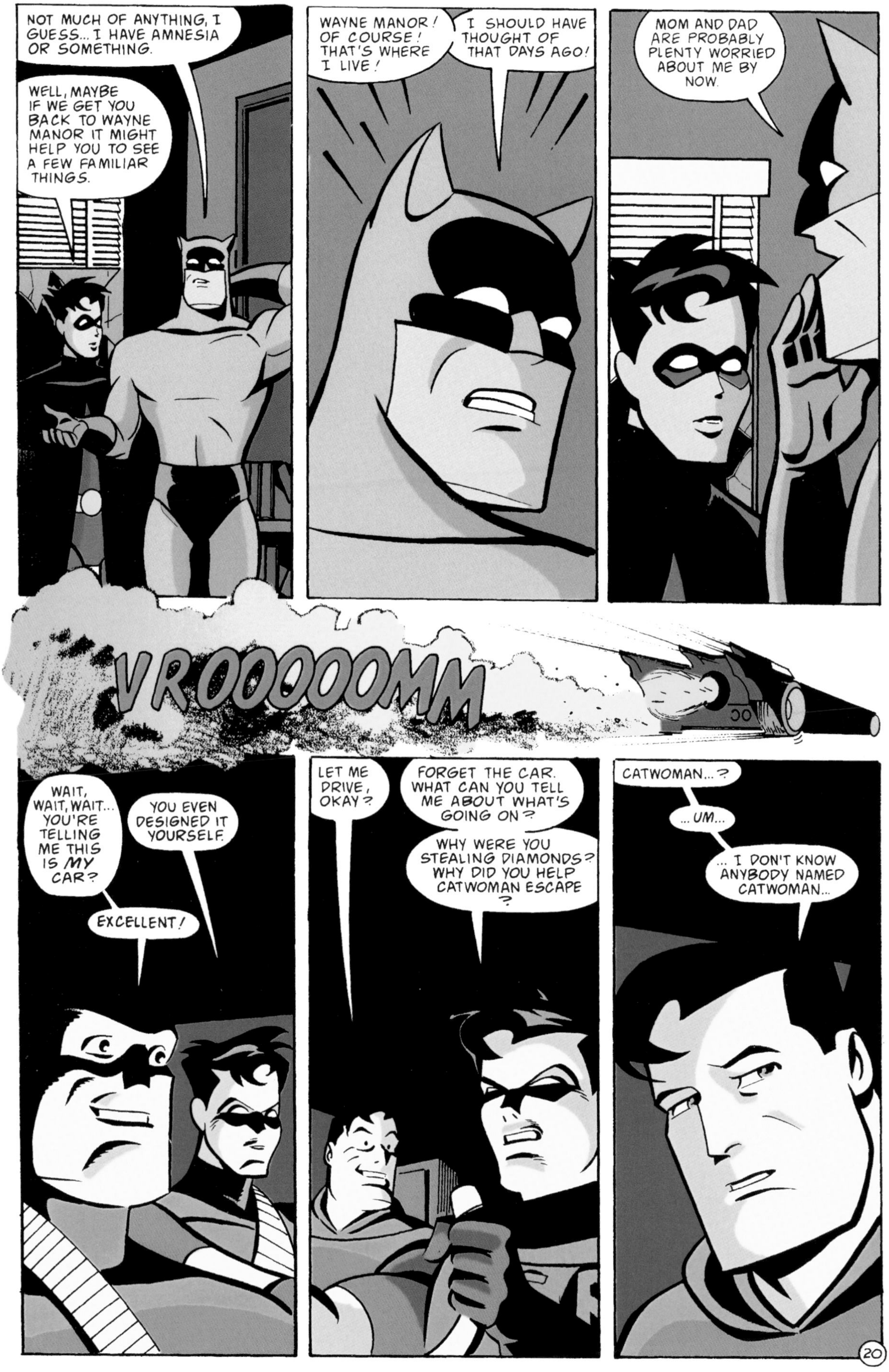
NOT MUCH OF ANYTHING, I GUESS... I HAVE AMNESIA OR SOMETHING.
WELL, MAYBE IF WE GET YOU BACK TO WAYNE MANOR IT MIGHT HELP YOU TO SEE A FEW FAMILIAR THINGS.
WAYNE MANOR! OF COURSE! THAT'S WHERE I LIVE!
I SHOULD HAVE THOUGHT OF THAT DAYS AGO!
MOM AND DAD ARE PROBABLY PLENTY WORRIED ABOUT ME BY NOW.
VROOOOOMM
WAIT, WAIT, WAIT... YOU'RE TELLING ME THIS IS MY CAR?
YOU EVEN DESIGNED IT YOURSELF.
EXCELLENT!
LET ME DRIVE, OKAY?
FORGET THE CAR. WHAT CAN YOU TELL ME ABOUT WHAT'S GOING ON?
WHY WERE YOU STEALING DIAMONDS? WHY DID YOU HELP CATWOMAN ESCAPE?
CATWOMAN...?
...UM...
...I DON'T KNOW ANYBODY NAMED CATWOMAN...
20

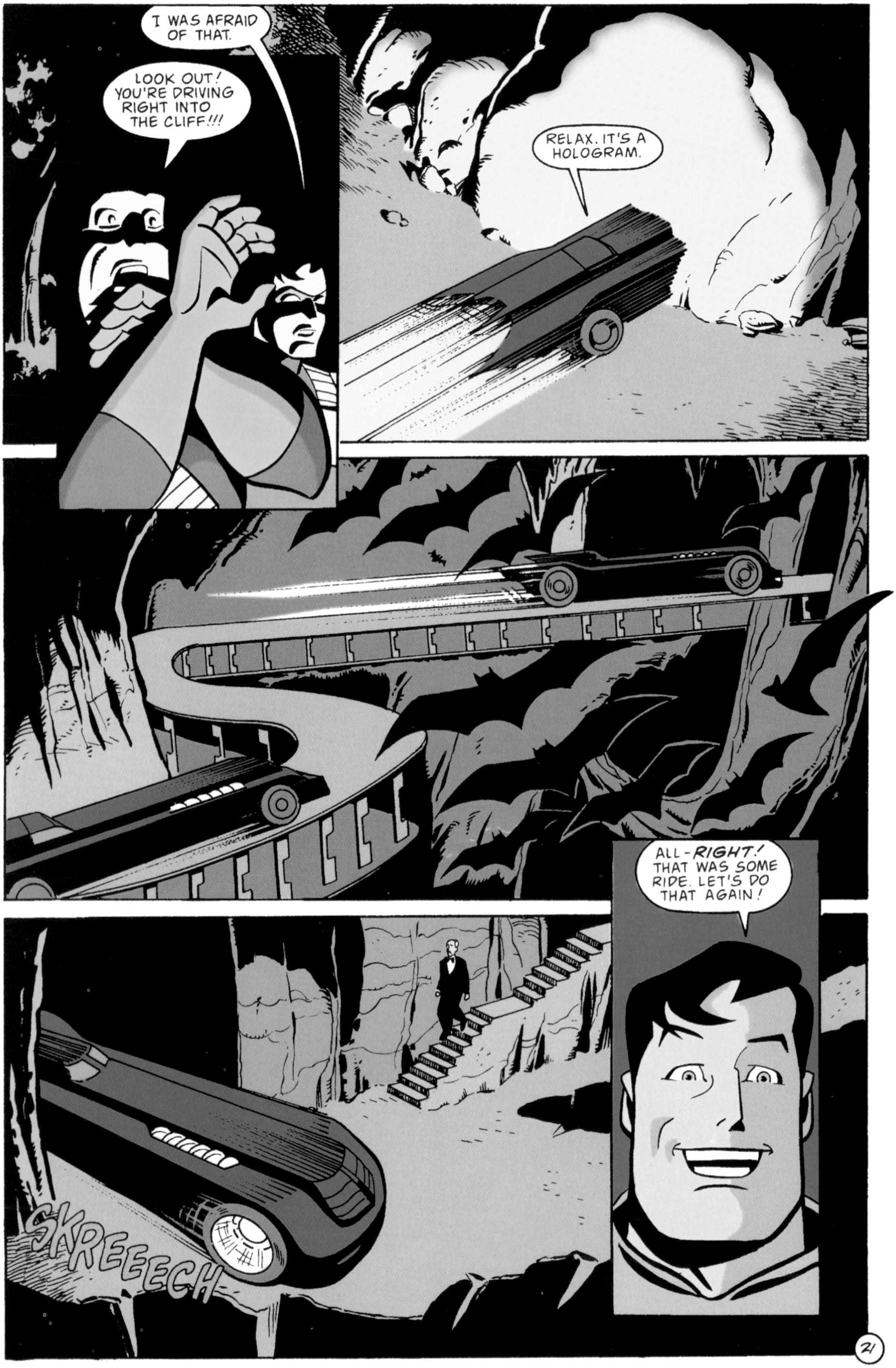
I WAS AFRAID OF THAT.
LOOK OUT! YOU'RE DRIVING RIGHT INTO THE CLIFF!!!
RELAX. IT'S A HOLOGRAM.
ALL-RIGHT! THAT WAS SOME RIDE. LET'S DO THAT AGAIN!
SKREEECH
21

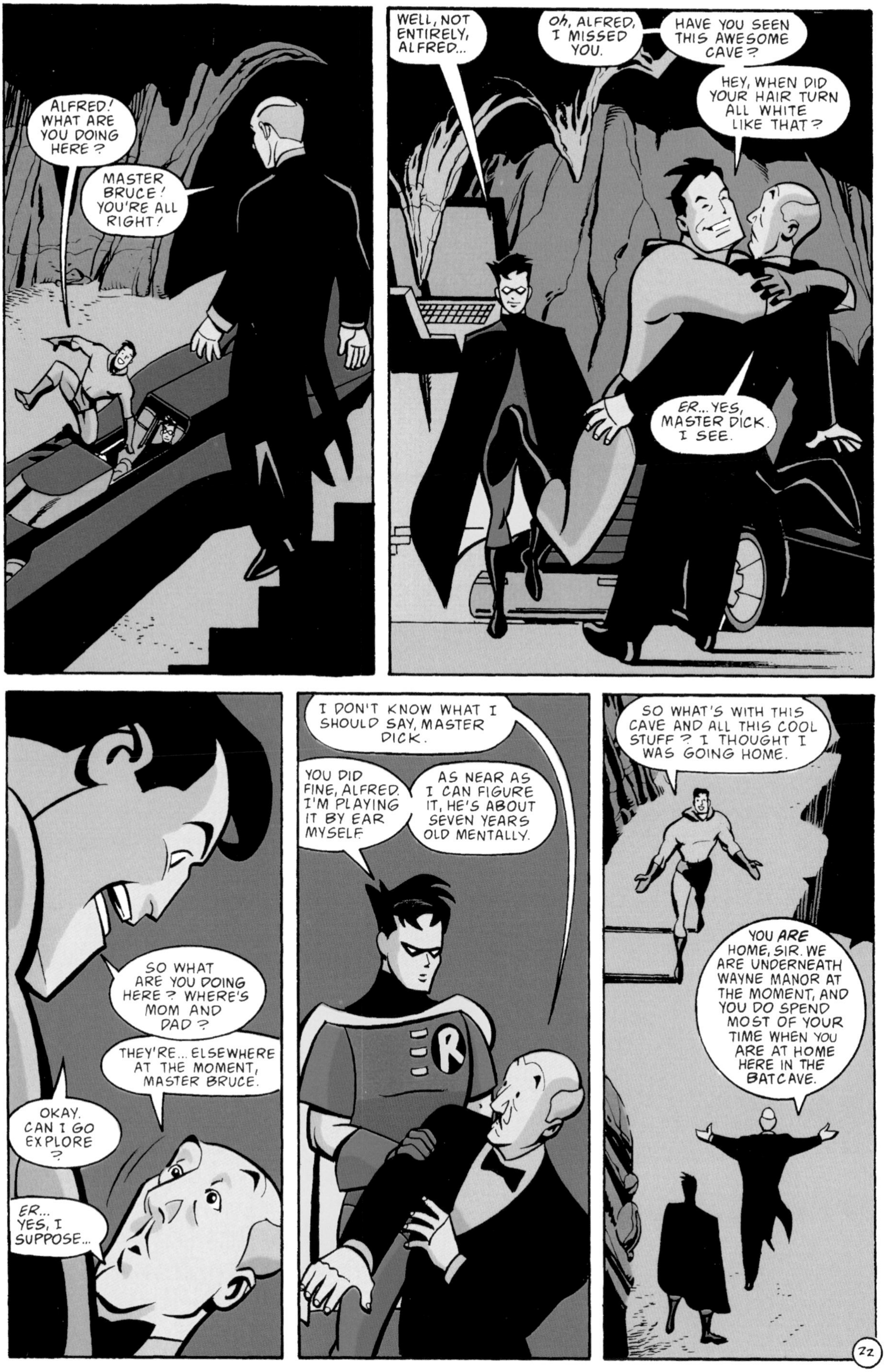
ALFRED! WHAT ARE YOU DOING HERE?
MASTER BRUCE! YOU'RE ALL RIGHT!
WELL, NOT ENTIRELY, ALFRED...
Oh, ALFRED, I MISSED YOU.
HAVE YOU SEEN THIS AWESOME CAVE?
HEY, WHEN DID YOUR HAIR TURN ALL WHITE LIKE THAT?
ER... YES, MASTER DICK. I SEE.
SO WHAT ARE YOU DOING HERE? WHERE'S MOM AND DAD?
THEY'RE... ELSEWHERE AT THE MOMENT, MASTER BRUCE.
OKAY. CAN I GO EXPLORE?
ER... YES, I SUPPOSE...
I DON'T KNOW WHAT I SHOULD SAY, MASTER DICK.
YOU DID FINE, ALFRED. I'M PLAYING IT BY EAR MYSELF.
AS NEAR AS I CAN FIGURE IT, HE'S ABOUT SEVEN YEARS OLD MENTALLY.
SO WHAT'S WITH THIS CAVE AND ALL THIS COOL STUFF? I THOUGHT I WAS GOING HOME.
YOU ARE HOME, SIR. WE ARE UNDERNEATH WAYNE MANOR AT THE MOMENT, AND YOU DO SPEND MOST OF YOUR TIME WHEN YOU ARE AT HOME HERE IN THE BATCAVE.
22

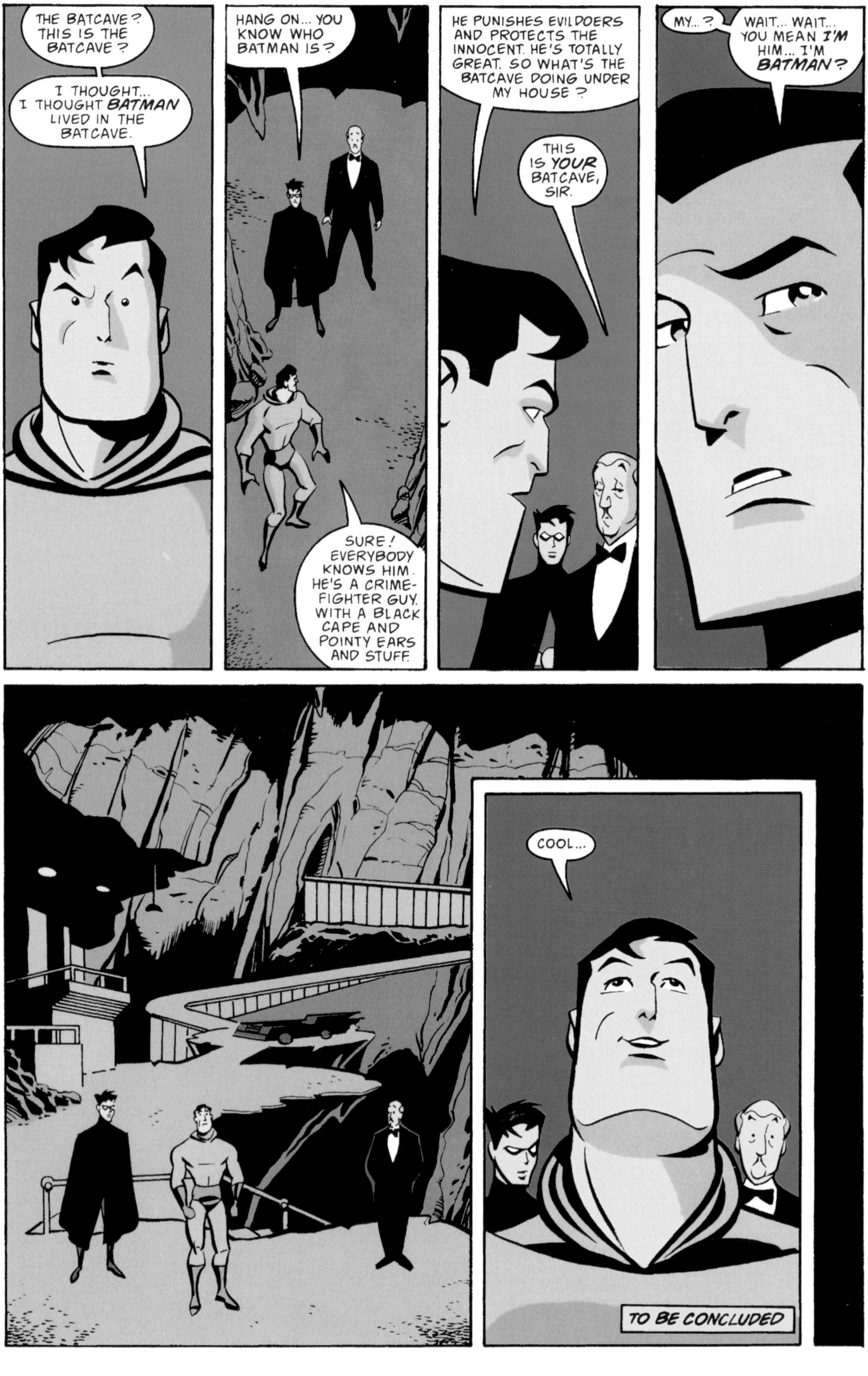
THE BATCAVE? THIS IS THE BATCAVE?
I THOUGHT... I THOUGHT BATMAN LIVED IN THE BATCAVE.
HANG ON... YOU KNOW WHO BATMAN IS?
SURE! EVERYBODY KNOWS HIM. HE'S A CRIME-FIGHTER GUY. WITH A BLACK CAPE AND POINTY EARS AND STUFF.
HE PUNISHES EVILDOERS AND PROTECTS THE INNOCENT. HE'S TOTALLY GREAT. SO WHAT'S THE BATCAVE DOING UNDER MY HOUSE?
THIS IS YOUR BATCAVE, SIR.
MY...?
WAIT... WAIT... YOU MEAN I'M HIM... I'M BATMAN?
COOL...
TO BE CONCLUDED

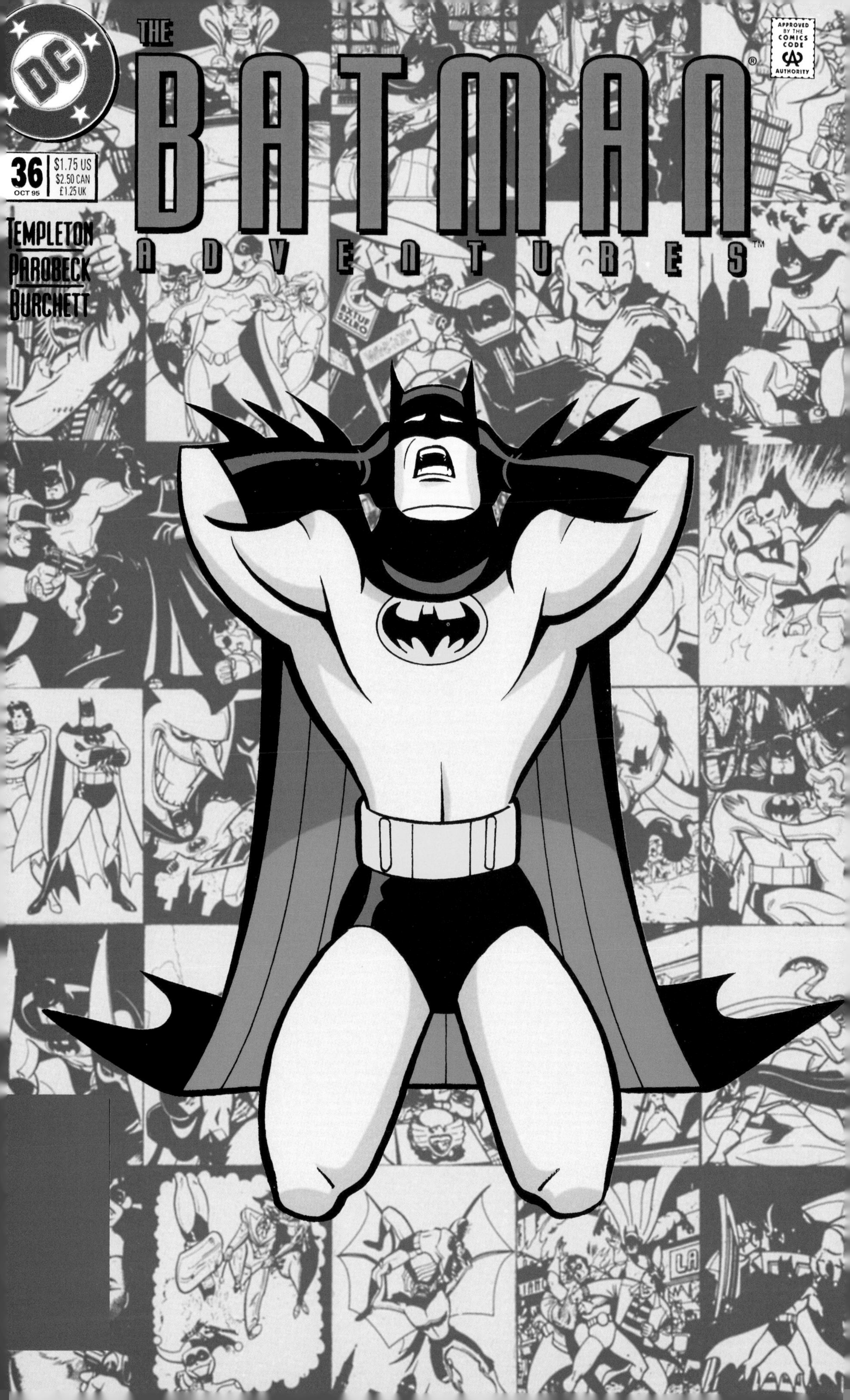
DC
THE BATMAN® ADVENTURES™
36
OCT 95
$1.75 US
$2.50 CAN
£1.25 UK
APPROVED BY THE COMICS CODE AUTHORITY
TEMPLETON
PAROBECK
BURCHETT

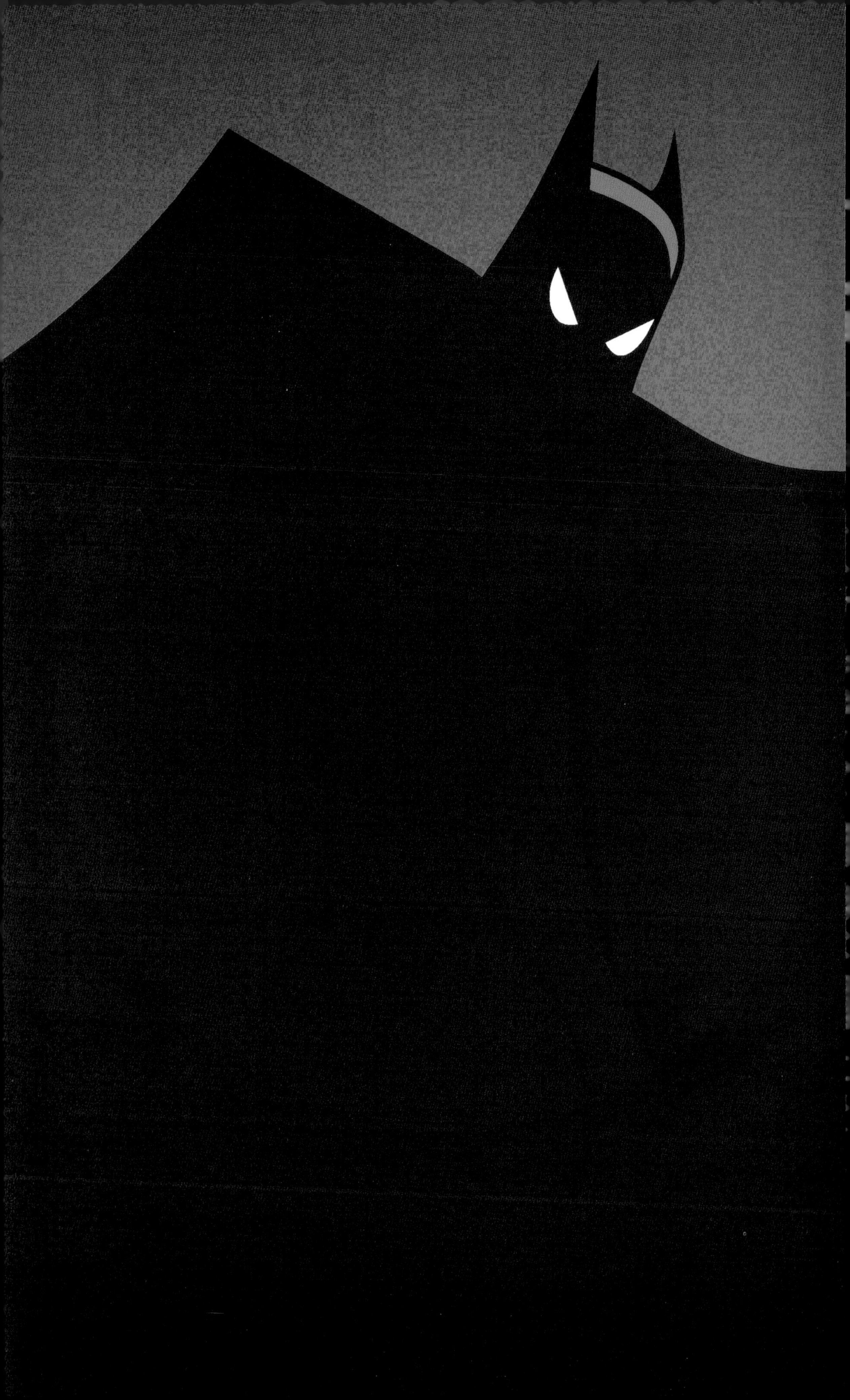

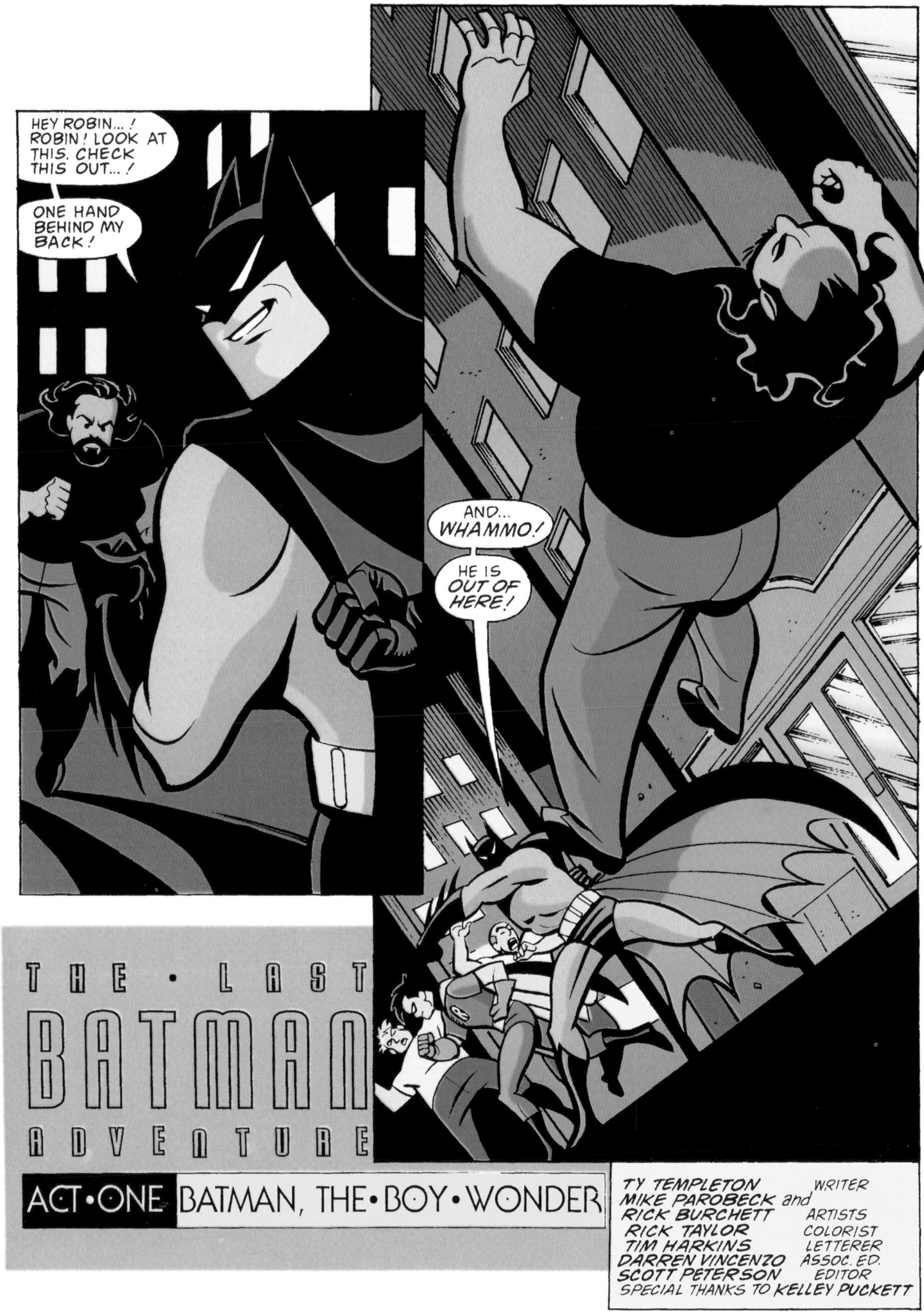
HEY ROBIN...! ROBIN! LOOK AT THIS. CHECK THIS OUT...!
ONE HAND BEHIND MY BACK!
AND... WHAMMO!
HE IS OUT OF HERE!
THE · LAST BATMAN ADVENTURE
ACT · ONE BATMAN, THE · BOY · WONDER
TY TEMPLETON WRITER
MIKE PAROBECK and RICK BURCHETT ARTISTS
RICK TAYLOR COLORIST
TIM HARKINS LETTERER
DARREN VINCENZO ASSOC. ED.
SCOTT PETERSON EDITOR
SPECIAL THANKS TO KELLEY PUCKETT

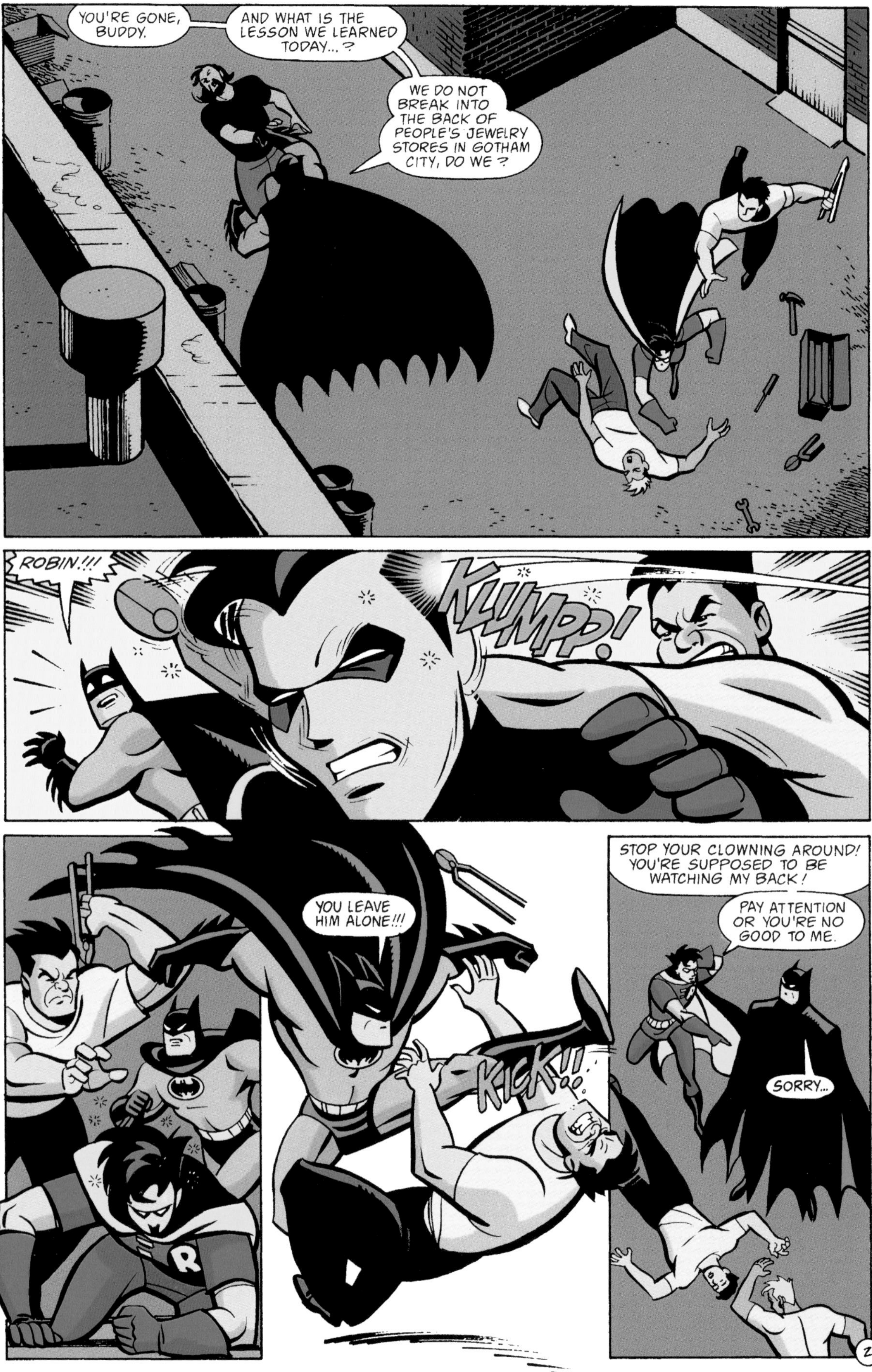
YOU'RE GONE, BUDDY.
AND WHAT IS THE LESSON WE LEARNED TODAY...?
WE DO NOT BREAK INTO THE BACK OF PEOPLE'S JEWELRY STORES IN GOTHAM CITY, DO WE?
ROBIN!!!
KLUMPP!
YOU LEAVE HIM ALONE!!!
KICK!!
STOP YOUR CLOWNING AROUND! YOU'RE SUPPOSED TO BE WATCHING MY BACK!
PAY ATTENTION OR YOU'RE NO GOOD TO ME.
SORRY...
2

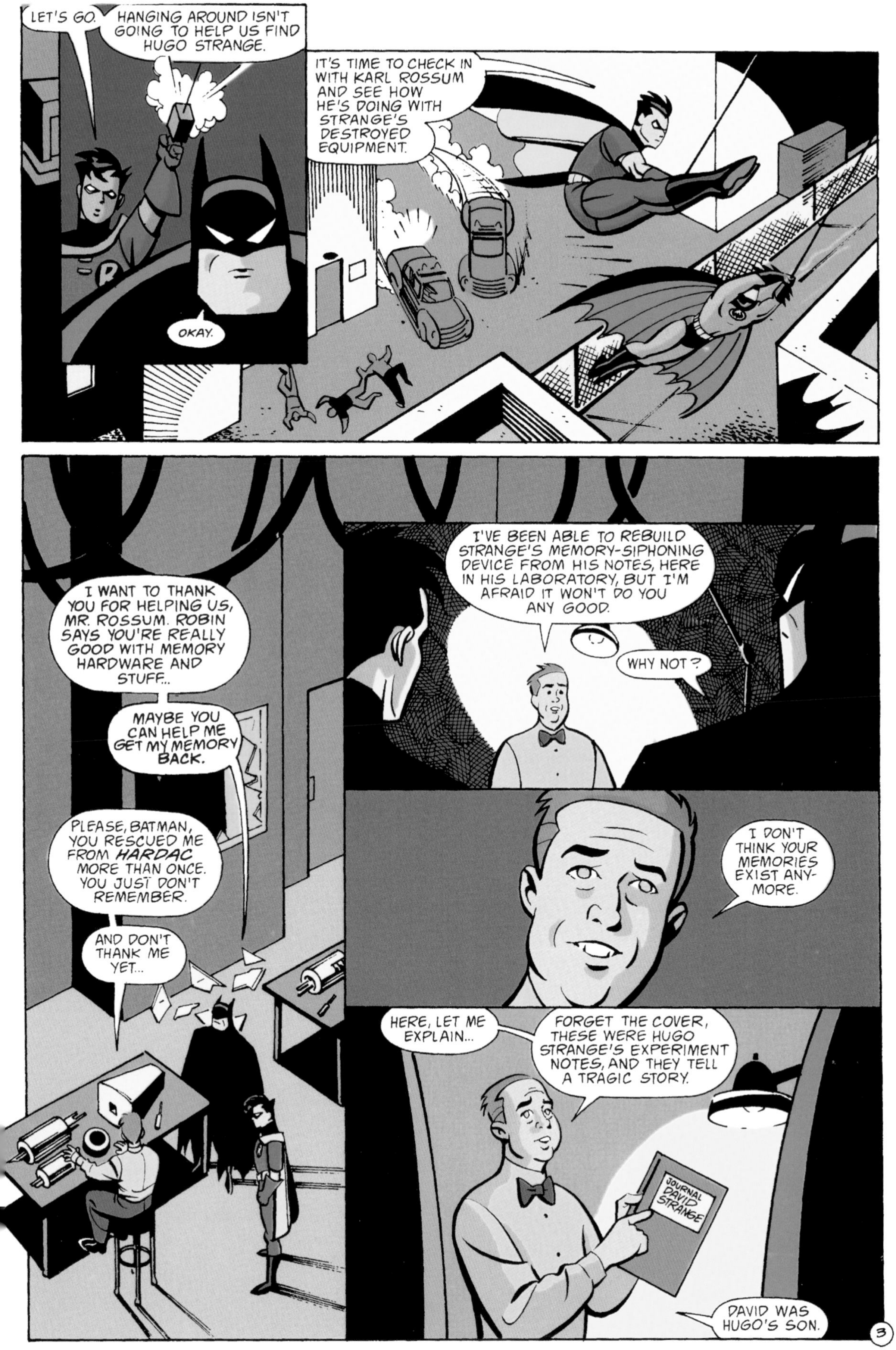
LET'S GO.
HANGING AROUND ISN'T GOING TO HELP US FIND HUGO STRANGE.
OKAY.
IT'S TIME TO CHECK IN WITH KARL ROSSUM AND SEE HOW HE'S DOING WITH STRANGE'S DESTROYED EQUIPMENT.
I WANT TO THANK YOU FOR HELPING US, MR. ROSSUM. ROBIN SAYS YOU'RE REALLY GOOD WITH MEMORY HARDWARE AND STUFF...
MAYBE YOU CAN HELP ME GET MY MEMORY BACK.
PLEASE, BATMAN, YOU RESCUED ME FROM HARDAC MORE THAN ONCE. YOU JUST DON'T REMEMBER.
AND DON'T THANK ME YET...
I'VE BEEN ABLE TO REBUILD STRANGE'S MEMORY-SIPHONING DEVICE FROM HIS NOTES, HERE IN HIS LABORATORY, BUT I'M AFRAID IT WON'T DO YOU ANY GOOD.
WHY NOT?
I DON'T THINK YOUR MEMORIES EXIST ANY-MORE.
HERE, LET ME EXPLAIN...
FORGET THE COVER, THESE WERE HUGO STRANGE'S EXPERIMENT NOTES, AND THEY TELL A TRAGIC STORY.
JOURNAL DAVID STRANGE
DAVID WAS HUGO'S SON.
3

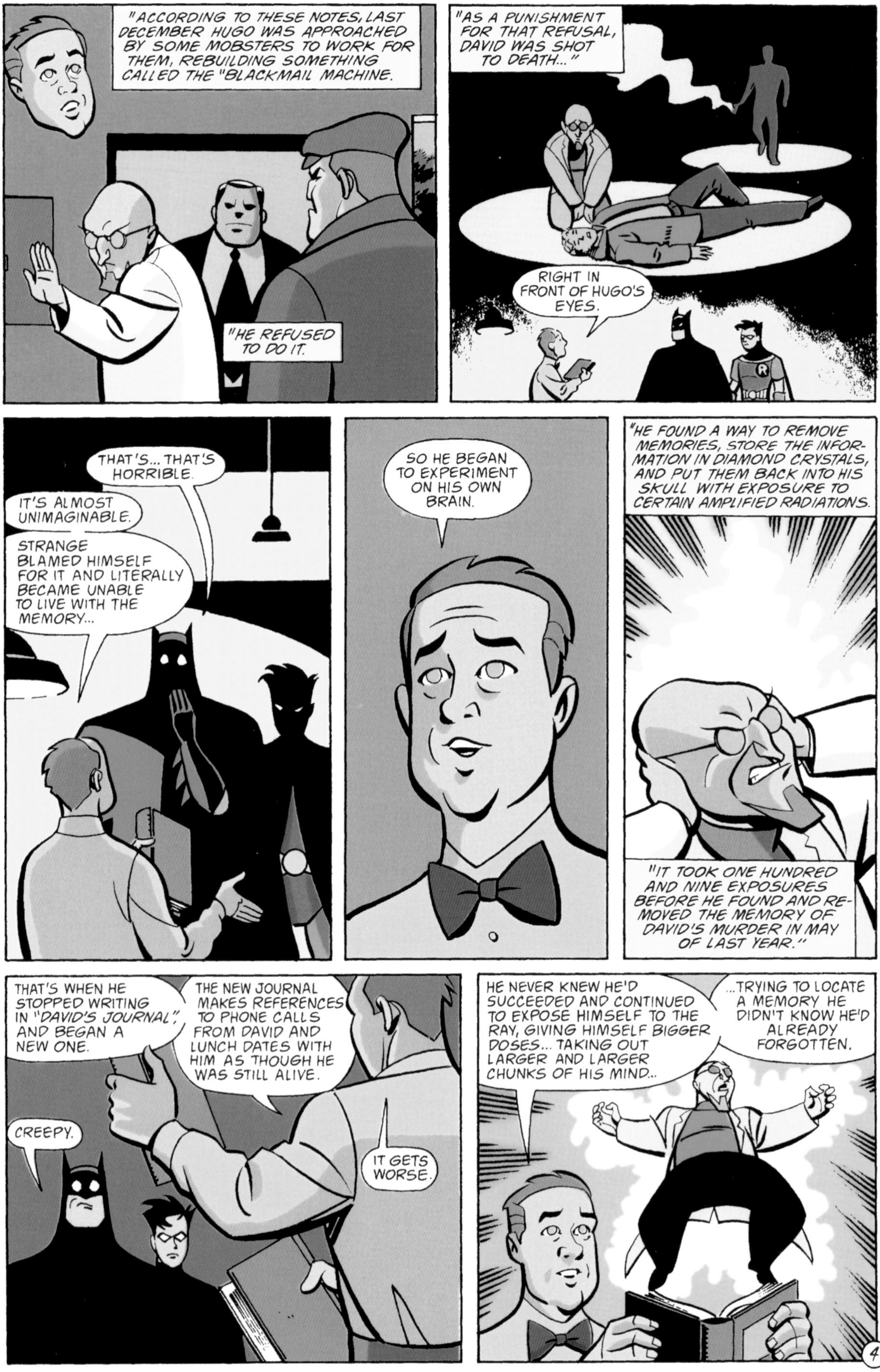
"ACCORDING TO THESE NOTES, LAST DECEMBER HUGO WAS APPROACHED BY SOME MOBSTERS TO WORK FOR THEM, REBUILDING SOMETHING CALLED THE "BLACKMAIL MACHINE.
"HE REFUSED TO DO IT.
"AS A PUNISHMENT FOR THAT REFUSAL, DAVID WAS SHOT TO DEATH..."
RIGHT IN FRONT OF HUGO'S EYES.
THAT'S... THAT'S HORRIBLE.
IT'S ALMOST UNIMAGINABLE.
STRANGE BLAMED HIMSELF FOR IT AND LITERALLY BECAME UNABLE TO LIVE WITH THE MEMORY...
SO HE BEGAN TO EXPERIMENT ON HIS OWN BRAIN.
"HE FOUND A WAY TO REMOVE MEMORIES, STORE THE INFORMATION IN DIAMOND CRYSTALS, AND PUT THEM BACK INTO HIS SKULL WITH EXPOSURE TO CERTAIN AMPLIFIED RADIATIONS.
"IT TOOK ONE HUNDRED AND NINE EXPOSURES BEFORE HE FOUND AND REMOVED THE MEMORY OF DAVID'S MURDER IN MAY OF LAST YEAR."
THAT'S WHEN HE STOPPED WRITING IN "DAVID'S JOURNAL", AND BEGAN A NEW ONE.
THE NEW JOURNAL MAKES REFERENCES TO PHONE CALLS FROM DAVID AND LUNCH DATES WITH HIM AS THOUGH HE WAS STILL ALIVE.
CREEPY.
IT GETS WORSE.
HE NEVER KNEW HE'D SUCCEEDED AND CONTINUED TO EXPOSE HIMSELF TO THE RAY, GIVING HIMSELF BIGGER DOSES... TAKING OUT LARGER AND LARGER CHUNKS OF HIS MIND...
...TRYING TO LOCATE A MEMORY HE DIDN'T KNOW HE'D ALREADY FORGOTTEN.
4

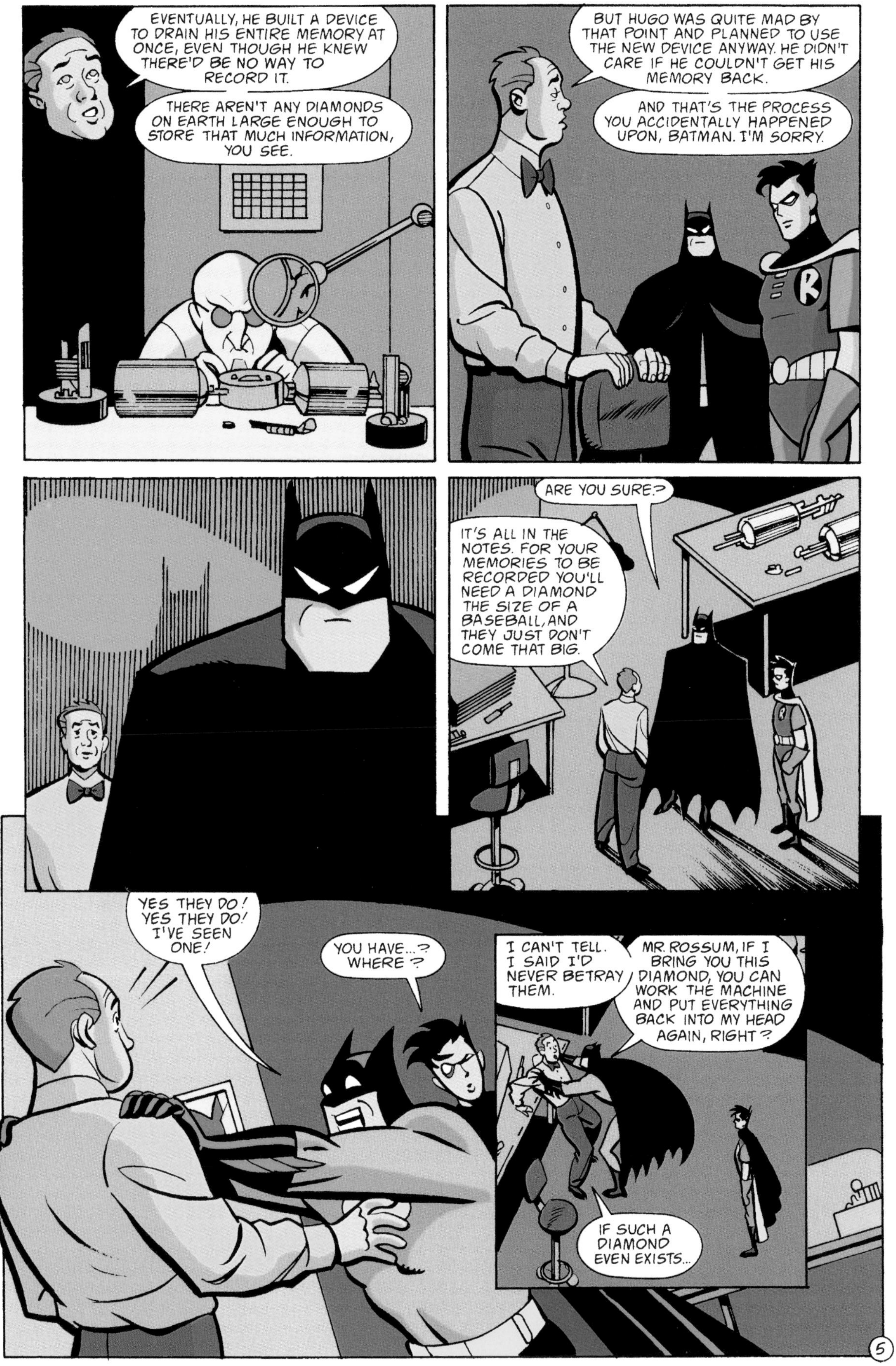

EVENTUALLY, HE BUILT A DEVICE TO DRAIN HIS ENTIRE MEMORY AT ONCE, EVEN THOUGH HE KNEW THERE'D BE NO WAY TO RECORD IT.
THERE AREN'T ANY DIAMONDS ON EARTH LARGE ENOUGH TO STORE THAT MUCH INFORMATION, YOU SEE.
BUT HUGO WAS QUITE MAD BY THAT POINT AND PLANNED TO USE THE NEW DEVICE ANYWAY. HE DIDN'T CARE IF HE COULDN'T GET HIS MEMORY BACK.
AND THAT'S THE PROCESS YOU ACCIDENTALLY HAPPENED UPON, BATMAN. I'M SORRY.
ARE YOU SURE?
IT'S ALL IN THE NOTES. FOR YOUR MEMORIES TO BE RECORDED YOU'LL NEED A DIAMOND THE SIZE OF A BASEBALL, AND THEY JUST DON'T COME THAT BIG.
YES THEY DO! YES THEY DO! I'VE SEEN ONE!
YOU HAVE...? WHERE?
I CAN'T TELL. I SAID I'D NEVER BETRAY THEM.
MR. ROSSUM, IF I BRING YOU THIS DIAMOND, YOU CAN WORK THE MACHINE AND PUT EVERYTHING BACK INTO MY HEAD AGAIN, RIGHT?
IF SUCH A DIAMOND EVEN EXISTS...
5

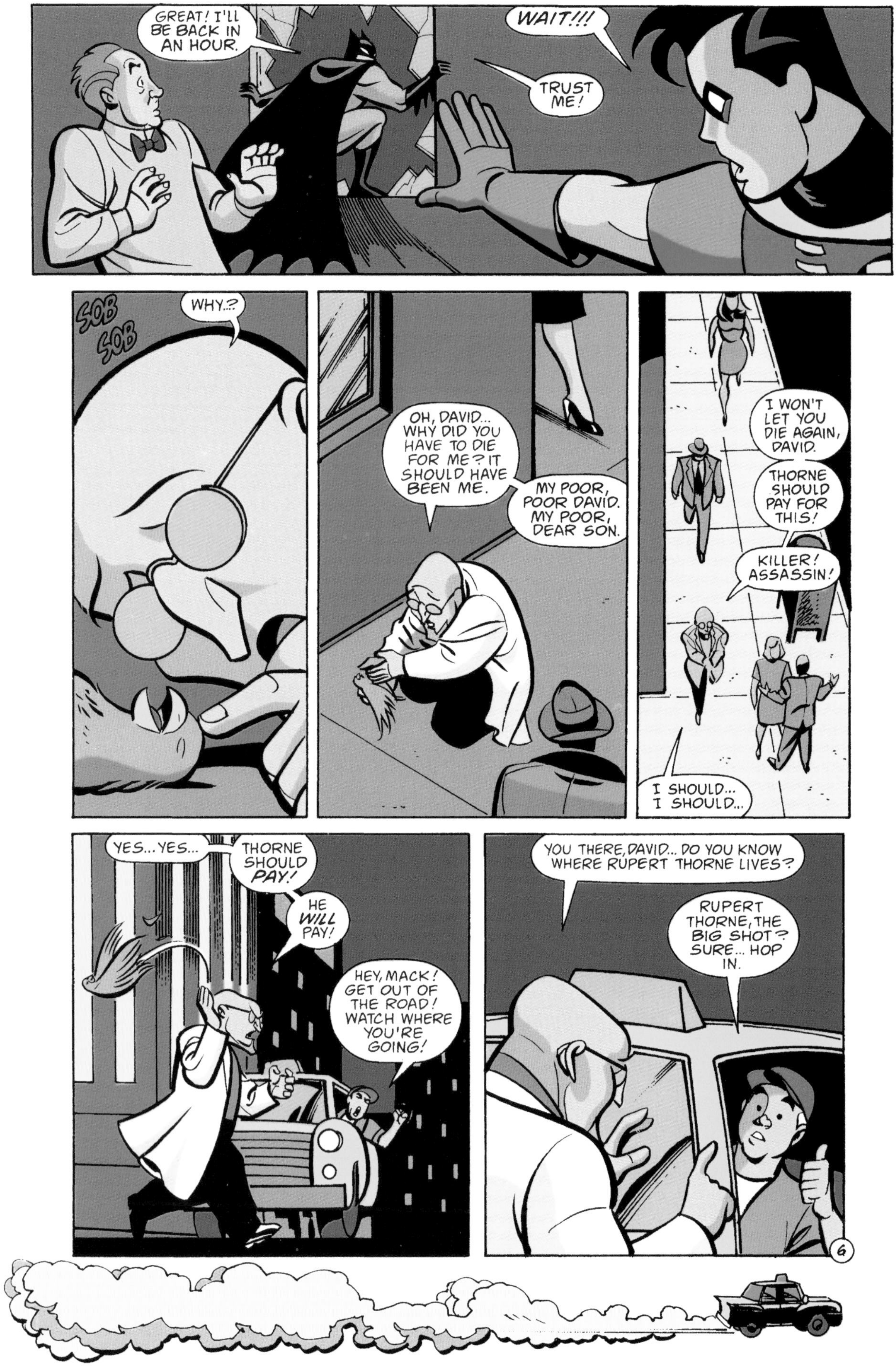
GREAT! I'LL BE BACK IN AN HOUR.
WAIT!!!
TRUST ME!
SOB SOB
WHY..?
OH, DAVID... WHY DID YOU HAVE TO DIE FOR ME? IT SHOULD HAVE BEEN ME.
MY POOR, POOR DAVID. MY POOR, DEAR SON.
I WON'T LET YOU DIE AGAIN, DAVID.
THORNE SHOULD PAY FOR THIS!
KILLER! ASSASSIN!
I SHOULD... I SHOULD...
YES... YES...
THORNE SHOULD PAY!
HE WILL PAY!
HEY, MACK! GET OUT OF THE ROAD! WATCH WHERE YOU'RE GOING!
YOU THERE, DAVID... DO YOU KNOW WHERE RUPERT THORNE LIVES?
RUPERT THORNE, THE BIG SHOT? SURE... HOP IN.
6

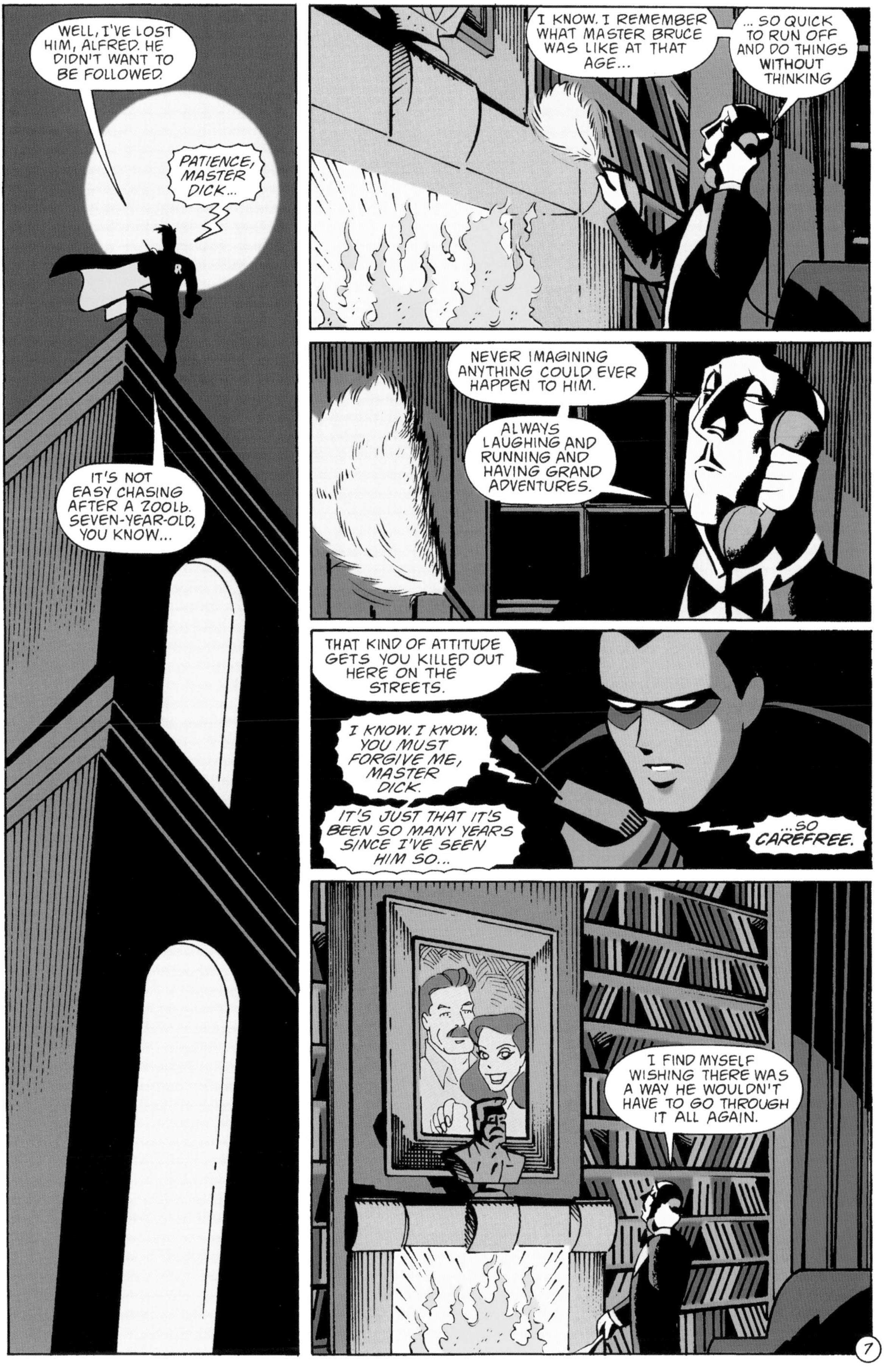
WELL, I'VE LOST HIM, ALFRED. HE DIDN'T WANT TO BE FOLLOWED.
PATIENCE, MASTER DICK...
IT'S NOT EASY CHASING AFTER A 200lb. SEVEN-YEAR-OLD, YOU KNOW...
I KNOW. I REMEMBER WHAT MASTER BRUCE WAS LIKE AT THAT AGE...
... SO QUICK TO RUN OFF AND DO THINGS WITHOUT THINKING
NEVER IMAGINING ANYTHING COULD EVER HAPPEN TO HIM.
ALWAYS LAUGHING AND RUNNING AND HAVING GRAND ADVENTURES.
THAT KIND OF ATTITUDE GETS YOU KILLED OUT HERE ON THE STREETS.
I KNOW. I KNOW. YOU MUST FORGIVE ME, MASTER DICK.
IT'S JUST THAT IT'S BEEN SO MANY YEARS SINCE I'VE SEEN HIM SO...
...SO CAREFREE.
I FIND MYSELF WISHING THERE WAS A WAY HE WOULDN'T HAVE TO GO THROUGH IT ALL AGAIN.
7

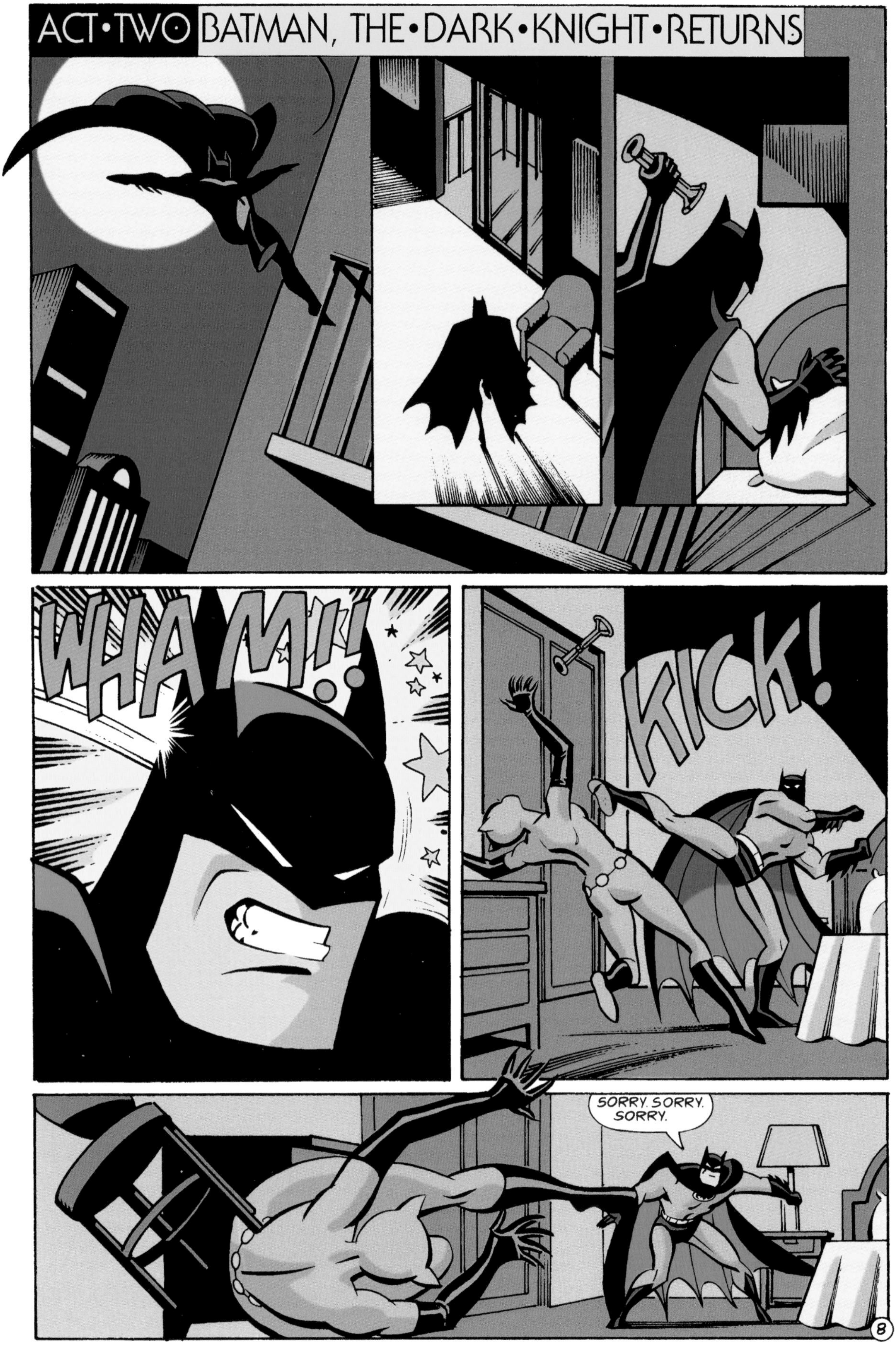
ACT•TWO BATMAN, THE•DARK•KNIGHT•RETURNS
WHAM!!
KICK!
SORRY. SORRY. SORRY.
8

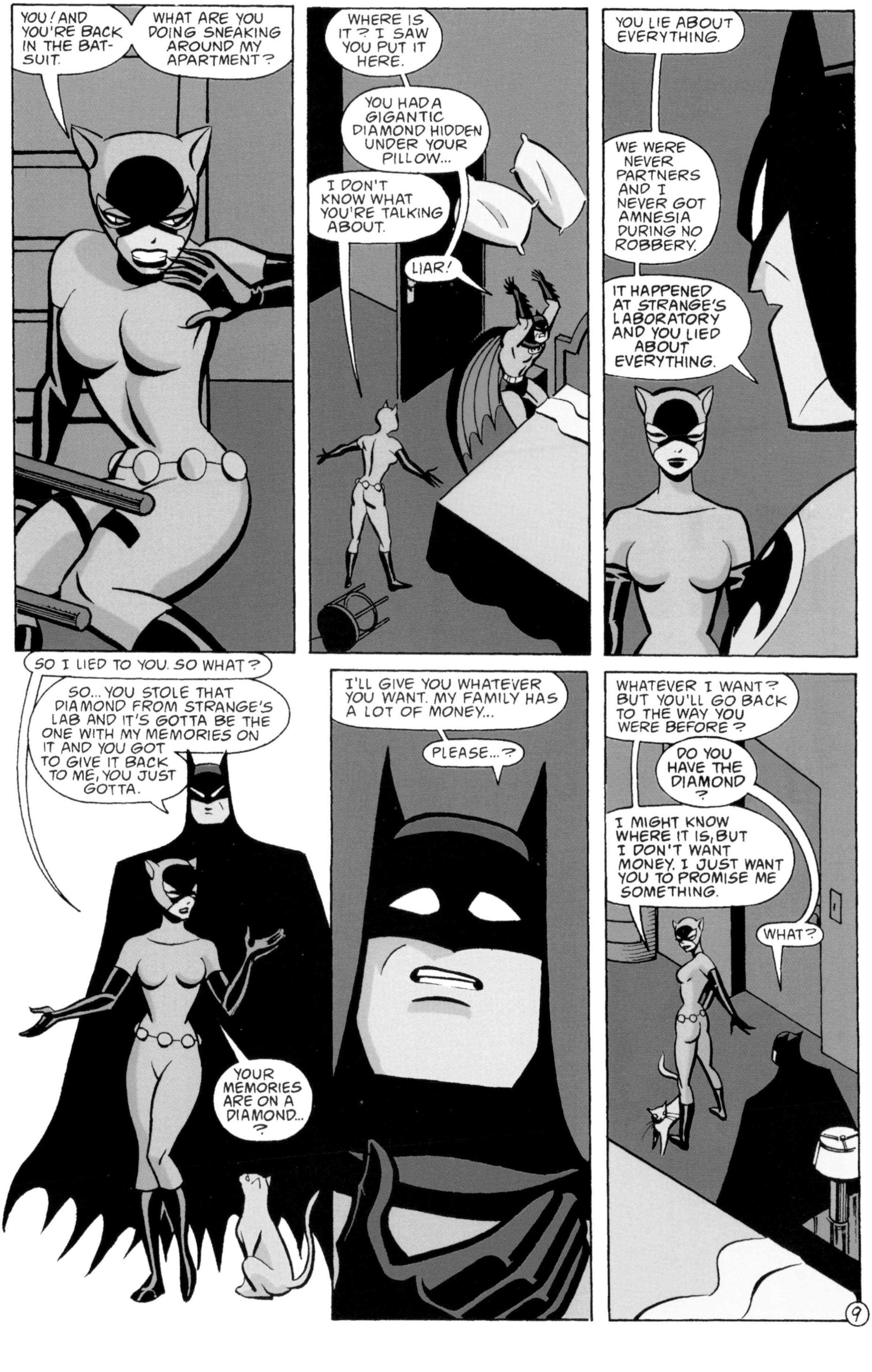
YOU! AND YOU'RE BACK IN THE BAT-SUIT.
WHAT ARE YOU DOING SNEAKING AROUND MY APARTMENT?
WHERE IS IT? I SAW YOU PUT IT HERE.
YOU HAD A GIGANTIC DIAMOND HIDDEN UNDER YOUR PILLOW...
I DON'T KNOW WHAT YOU'RE TALKING ABOUT.
LIAR!
YOU LIE ABOUT EVERYTHING.
WE WERE NEVER PARTNERS AND I NEVER GOT AMNESIA DURING NO ROBBERY.
IT HAPPENED AT STRANGE'S LABORATORY AND YOU LIED ABOUT EVERYTHING.
SO I LIED TO YOU. SO WHAT?
SO... YOU STOLE THAT DIAMOND FROM STRANGE'S LAB AND IT'S GOTTA BE THE ONE WITH MY MEMORIES ON IT AND YOU GOT TO GIVE IT BACK TO ME, YOU JUST GOTTA.
YOUR MEMORIES ARE ON A DIAMOND...?
I'LL GIVE YOU WHATEVER YOU WANT. MY FAMILY HAS A LOT OF MONEY...
PLEASE...?
WHATEVER I WANT? BUT YOU'LL GO BACK TO THE WAY YOU WERE BEFORE?
DO YOU HAVE THE DIAMOND?
I MIGHT KNOW WHERE IT IS, BUT I DON'T WANT MONEY. I JUST WANT YOU TO PROMISE ME SOMETHING.
WHAT?
9

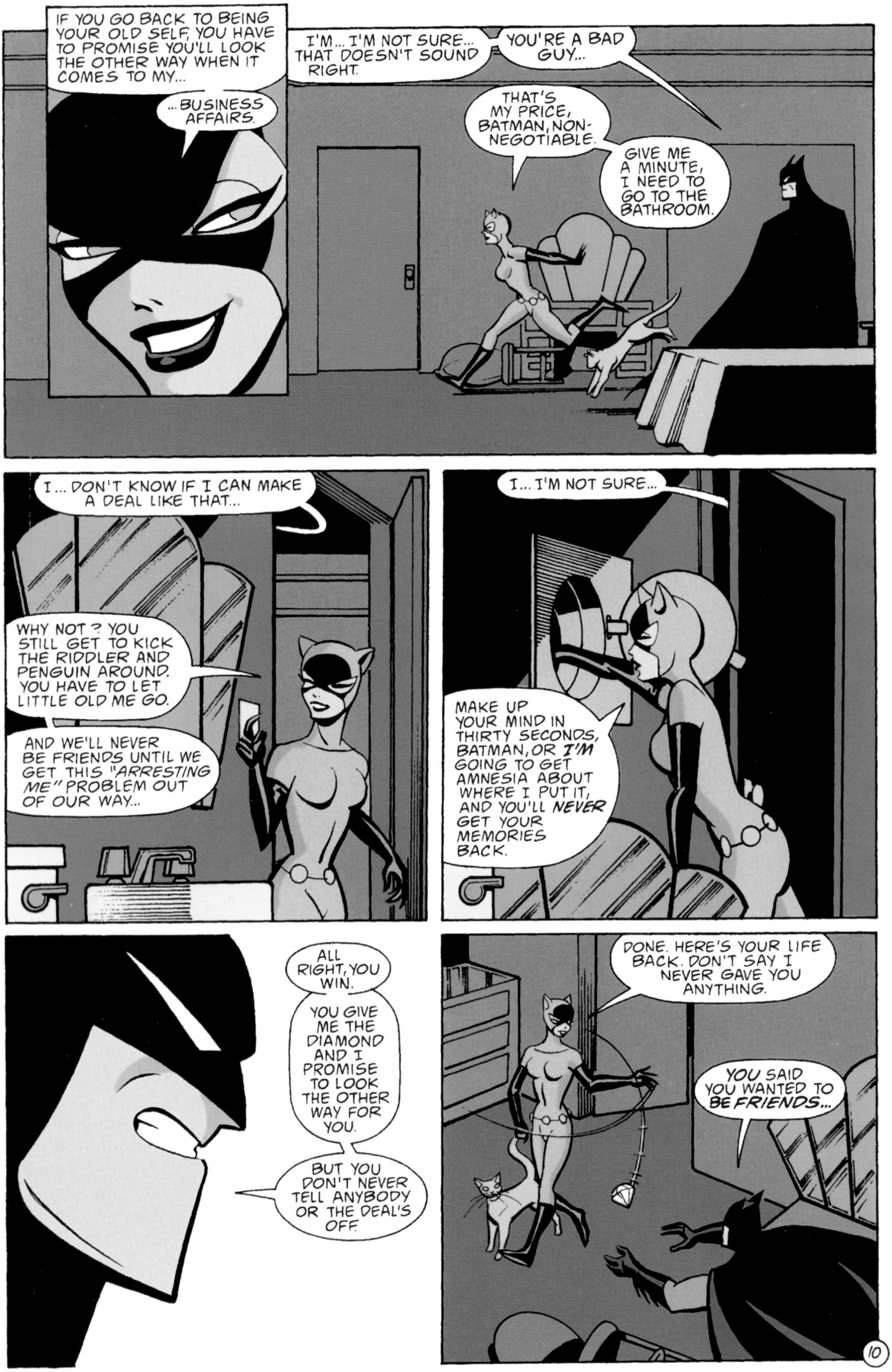
IF YOU GO BACK TO BEING YOUR OLD SELF, YOU HAVE TO PROMISE YOU'LL LOOK THE OTHER WAY WHEN IT COMES TO MY...
...BUSINESS AFFAIRS.
I'M... I'M NOT SURE... THAT DOESN'T SOUND RIGHT.
YOU'RE A BAD GUY...
THAT'S MY PRICE, BATMAN, NON-NEGOTIABLE.
GIVE ME A MINUTE, I NEED TO GO TO THE BATHROOM.
I... DON'T KNOW IF I CAN MAKE A DEAL LIKE THAT...
WHY NOT? YOU STILL GET TO KICK THE RIDDLER AND PENGUIN AROUND. YOU HAVE TO LET LITTLE OLD ME GO.
AND WE'LL NEVER BE FRIENDS UNTIL WE GET THIS "ARRESTING ME" PROBLEM OUT OF OUR WAY...
I... I'M NOT SURE...
MAKE UP YOUR MIND IN THIRTY SECONDS, BATMAN, OR I'M GOING TO GET AMNESIA ABOUT WHERE I PUT IT, AND YOU'LL NEVER GET YOUR MEMORIES BACK.
ALL RIGHT, YOU WIN.
YOU GIVE ME THE DIAMOND AND I PROMISE TO LOOK THE OTHER WAY FOR YOU.
BUT YOU DON'T NEVER TELL ANYBODY OR THE DEAL'S OFF.
DONE. HERE'S YOUR LIFE BACK. DON'T SAY I NEVER GAVE YOU ANYTHING.
YOU SAID YOU WANTED TO BE FRIENDS...
10

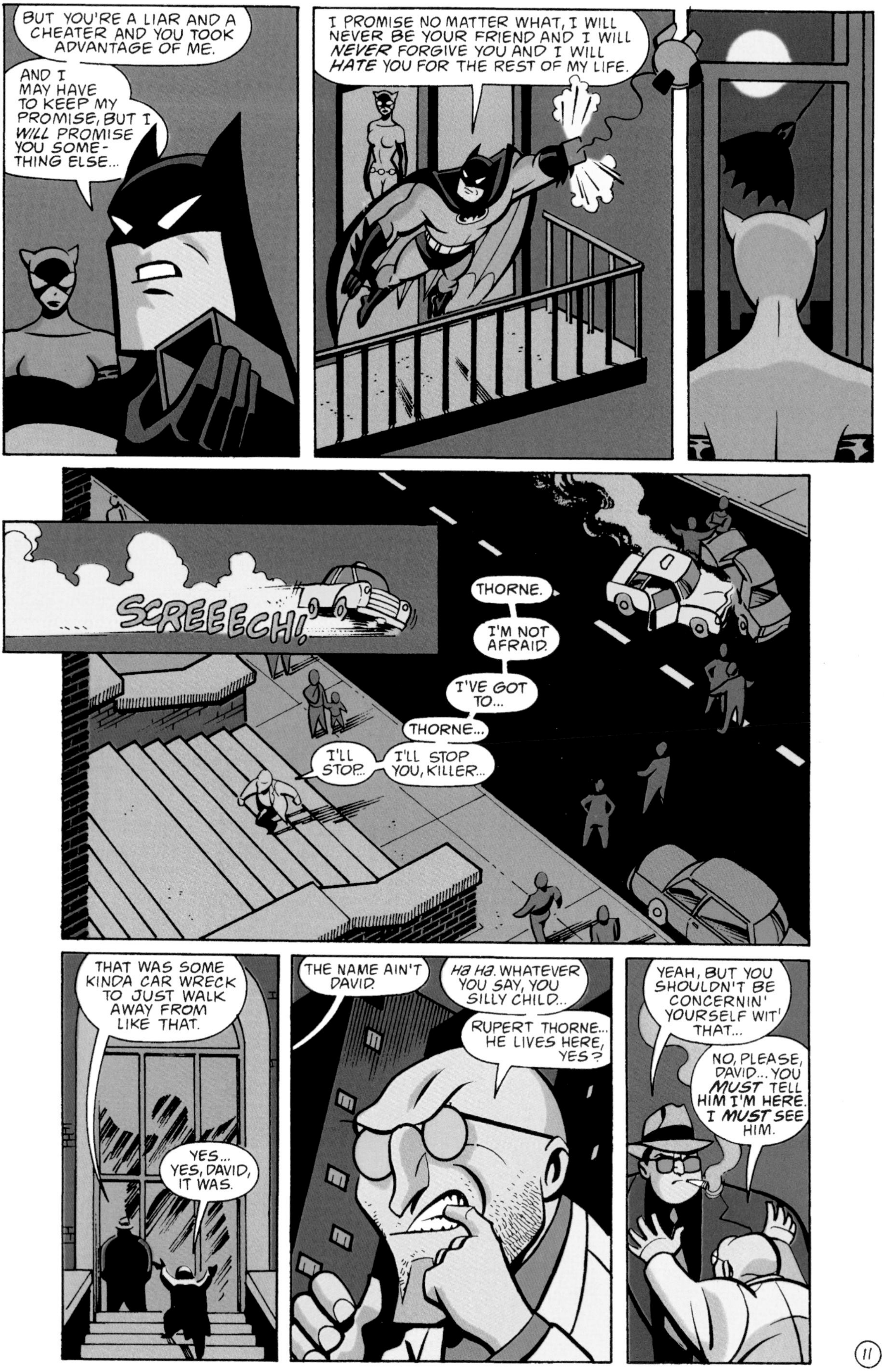
BUT YOU'RE A LIAR AND A CHEATER AND YOU TOOK ADVANTAGE OF ME.
AND I MAY HAVE TO KEEP MY PROMISE, BUT I *WILL* PROMISE YOU SOME-THING ELSE...
I PROMISE NO MATTER WHAT, I WILL NEVER BE YOUR FRIEND AND I WILL *NEVER* FORGIVE YOU AND I WILL *HATE* YOU FOR THE REST OF MY LIFE.
SCREEEECH!
THORNE.
I'M NOT AFRAID.
I'VE GOT TO...
THORNE...
I'LL STOP...
I'LL STOP YOU, KILLER...
THAT WAS SOME KINDA CAR WRECK TO JUST WALK AWAY FROM LIKE THAT.
YES... YES, DAVID, IT WAS.
THE NAME AIN'T DAVID.
Ha Ha. WHATEVER YOU SAY, YOU SILLY CHILD...
RUPERT THORNE... HE LIVES HERE, YES?
YEAH, BUT YOU SHOULDN'T BE CONCERNIN' YOURSELF WIT' THAT...
NO, PLEASE, DAVID... YOU *MUST* TELL HIM I'M HERE. I *MUST* SEE HIM.
11

HUGO STRANGE, YOU SAY?

BY ALL MEANS, SEND HIM UP, SEND HIM UP.

THIS SHOULD BE INTERESTING. I WONDER WHAT THE OLD WEIRDO WANTS...

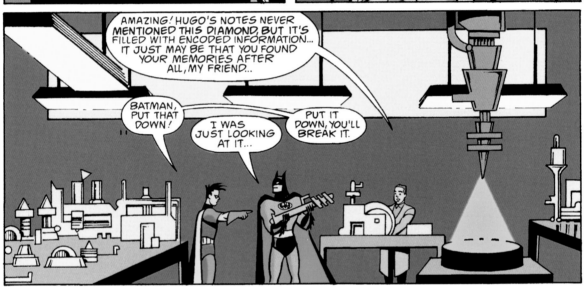

AMAZING! HUGO'S NOTES NEVER MENTIONED THIS DIAMOND, BUT IT'S FILLED WITH ENCODED INFORMATION... IT JUST MAY BE THAT YOU FOUND YOUR MEMORIES AFTER ALL, MY FRIEND...

BATMAN, PUT THAT DOWN!

I WAS JUST LOOKING AT IT...

PUT IT DOWN, YOU'LL BREAK IT.

uh, LISTEN, MR. ROSSUM... NOT EVERYTHING BATMAN'S GOING TO REMEMBER IS GOING TO BE THAT... *NICE.*

CAN HE HANDLE IT ALL COMING BACK AT ONCE LIKE THIS?

I DON'T KNOW. THIS HAS NEVER BEEN TRIED BEFORE...

I'M NOT SCARED, MR. ROSSUM, I DON'T MIND THE RISK...

I'M A PRETTY LOUSY BATMAN WITH MY MIND LIKE THIS.

I DON'T KNOW ANYTHING... I KEEP MESSING UP...

12

1026

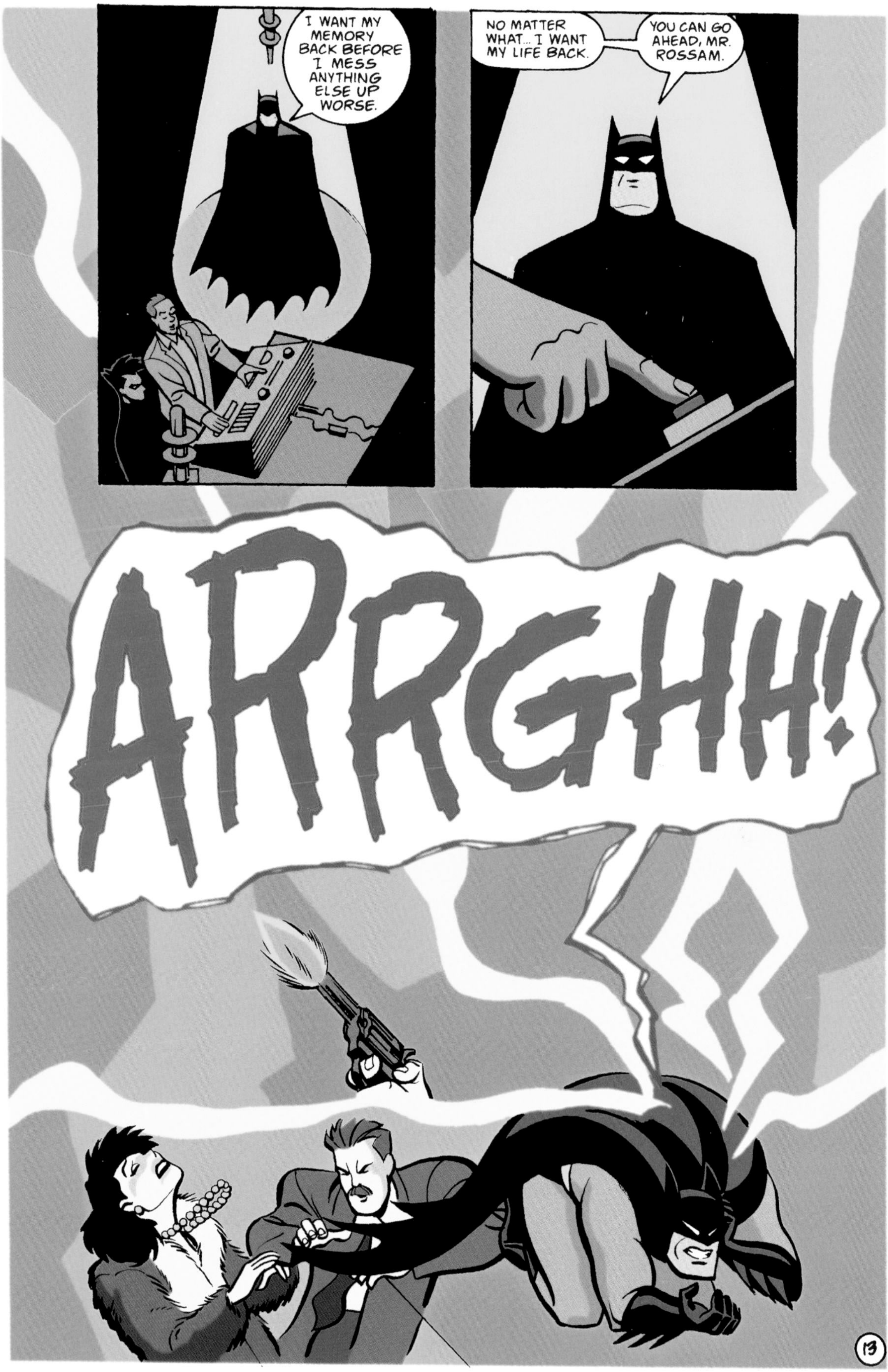
I WANT MY MEMORY BACK BEFORE I MESS ANYTHING ELSE UP WORSE.
NO MATTER WHAT... I WANT MY LIFE BACK.
YOU CAN GO AHEAD, MR. ROSSAM.
ARRGHH!
13

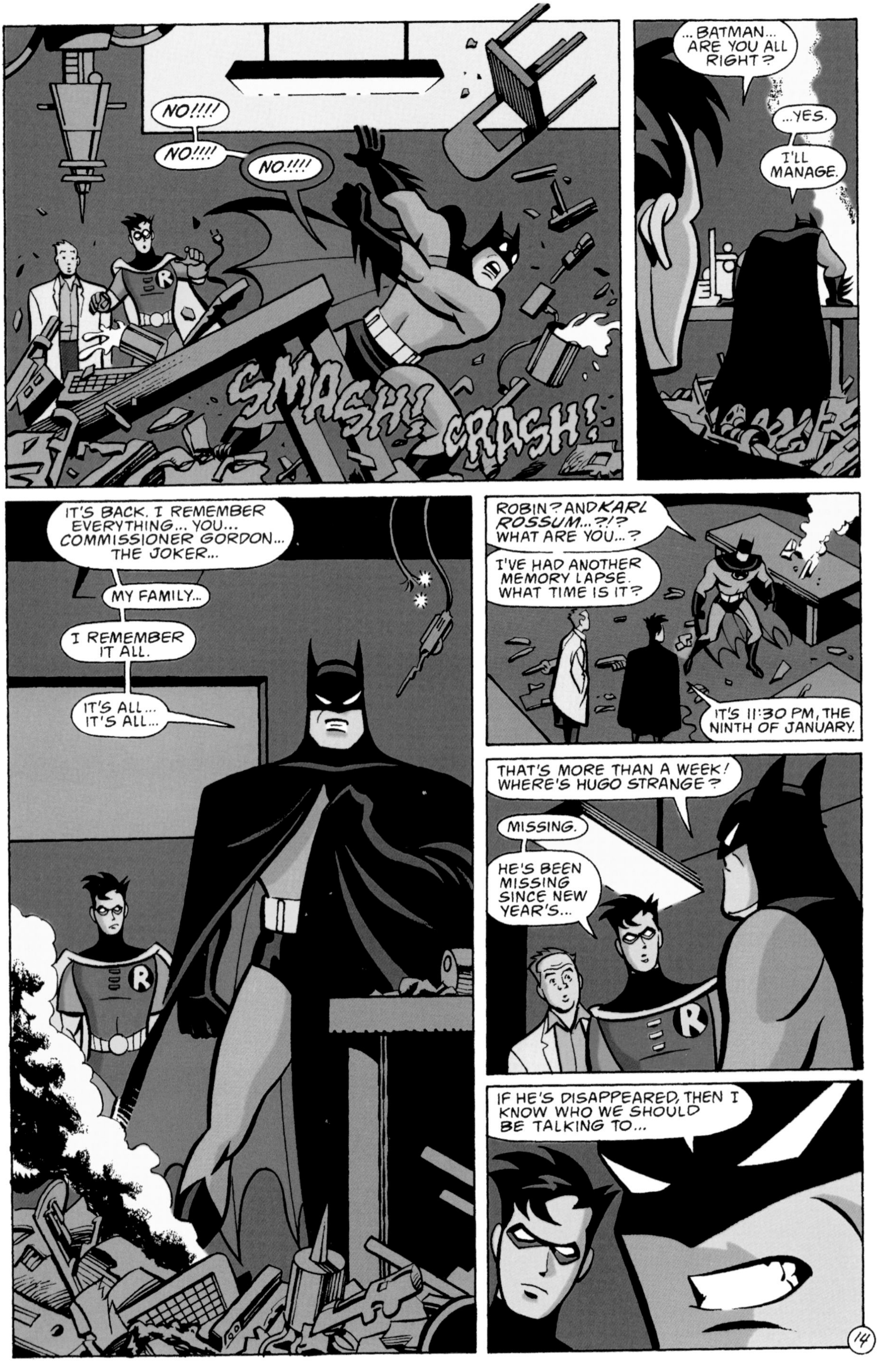
NO!!!!
NO!!!!
NO!!!!
SMASH!
CRASH!
...BATMAN... ARE YOU ALL RIGHT?
...YES.
I'LL MANAGE.
IT'S BACK. I REMEMBER EVERYTHING... YOU... COMMISSIONER GORDON... THE JOKER...
MY FAMILY...
I REMEMBER IT ALL.
IT'S ALL... IT'S ALL...
ROBIN? AND KARL ROSSUM...?!? WHAT ARE YOU...?
I'VE HAD ANOTHER MEMORY LAPSE. WHAT TIME IS IT?
IT'S 11:30 PM, THE NINTH OF JANUARY.
THAT'S MORE THAN A WEEK! WHERE'S HUGO STRANGE?
MISSING.
HE'S BEEN MISSING SINCE NEW YEAR'S...
IF HE'S DISAPPEARED, THEN I KNOW WHO WE SHOULD BE TALKING TO...
14

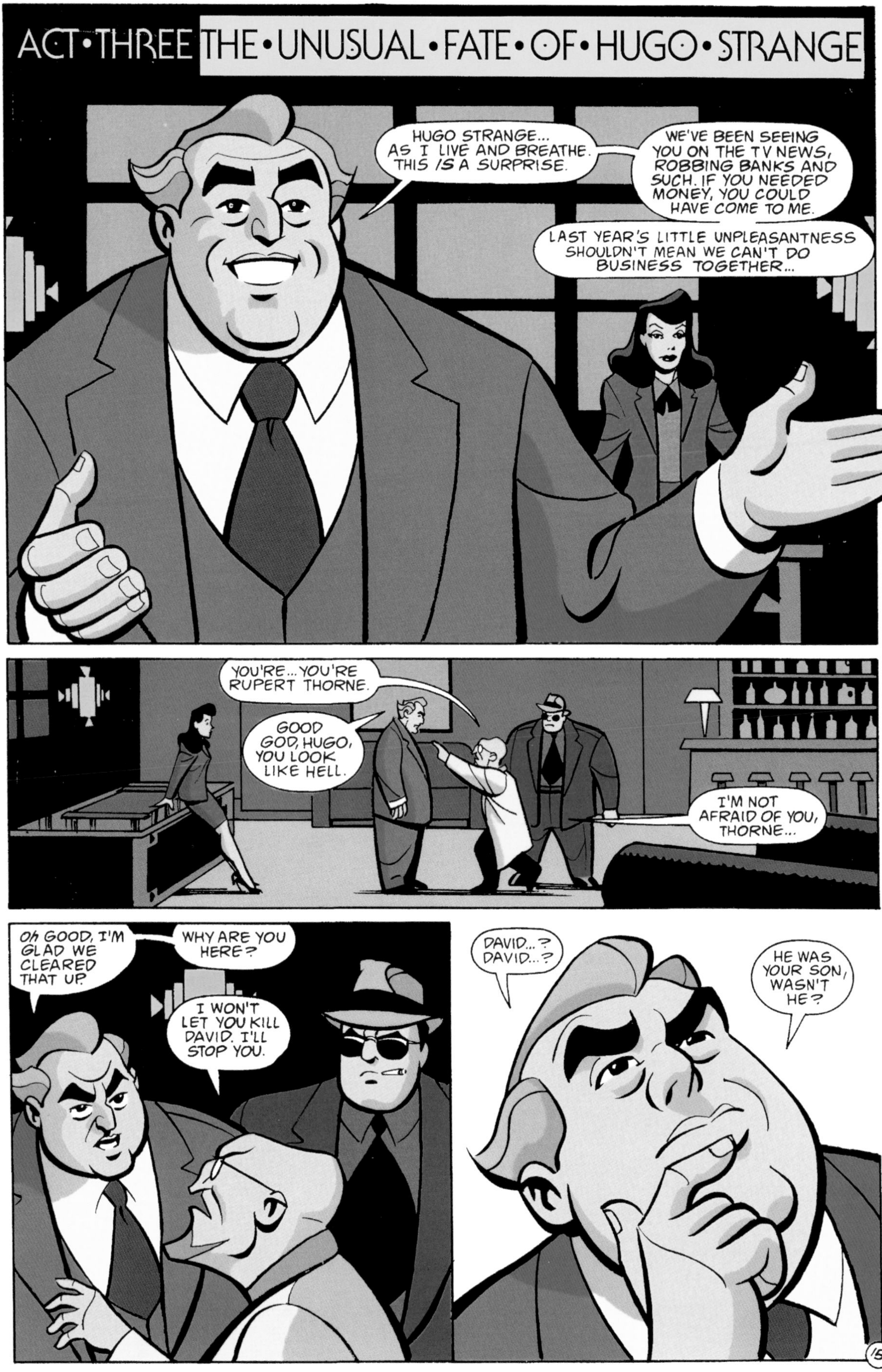
ACT • THREE THE • UNUSUAL • FATE • OF • HUGO • STRANGE
HUGO STRANGE... AS I LIVE AND BREATHE. THIS *IS* A SURPRISE.
WE'VE BEEN SEEING YOU ON THE TV NEWS, ROBBING BANKS AND SUCH. IF YOU NEEDED MONEY, YOU COULD HAVE COME TO ME.
LAST YEAR'S LITTLE UNPLEASANTNESS SHOULDN'T MEAN WE CAN'T DO BUSINESS TOGETHER...
YOU'RE... YOU'RE RUPERT THORNE.
GOOD GOD, HUGO, YOU LOOK LIKE HELL.
I'M NOT AFRAID OF YOU, THORNE...
Oh GOOD, I'M GLAD WE CLEARED THAT UP.
WHY ARE YOU HERE?
I WON'T LET YOU KILL DAVID. I'LL STOP YOU.
DAVID...? DAVID...?
HE WAS YOUR SON, WASN'T HE?
15

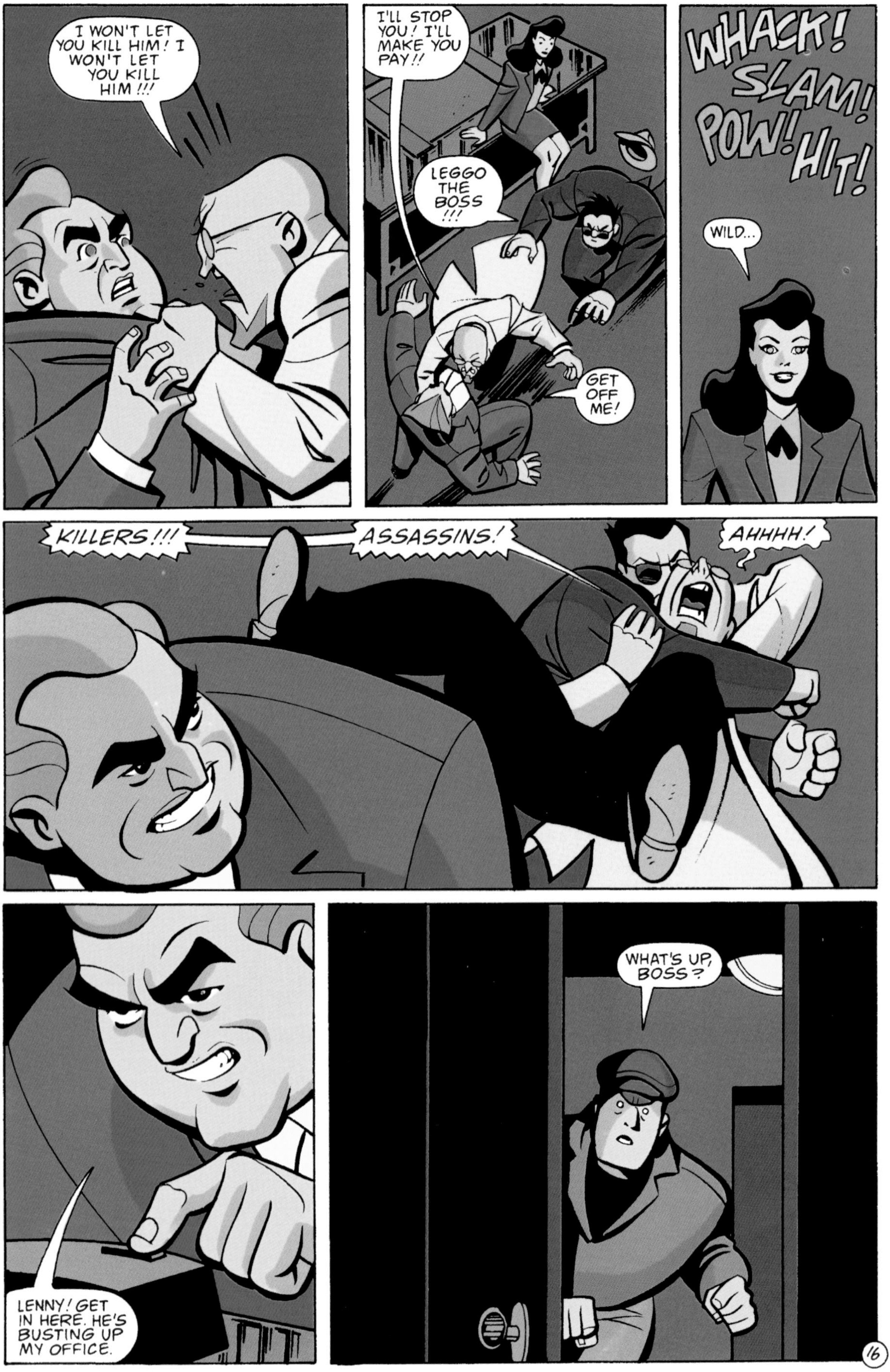

I WON'T LET YOU KILL HIM! I WON'T LET YOU KILL HIM!!!
I'LL STOP YOU! I'LL MAKE YOU PAY!!
LEGGO THE BOSS!!!
GET OFF ME!
WHACK! SLAM! POW! HIT!
WILD...
KILLERS!!!
ASSASSINS!
AHHHH!
LENNY! GET IN HERE. HE'S BUSTING UP MY OFFICE.
WHAT'S UP, BOSS?
16

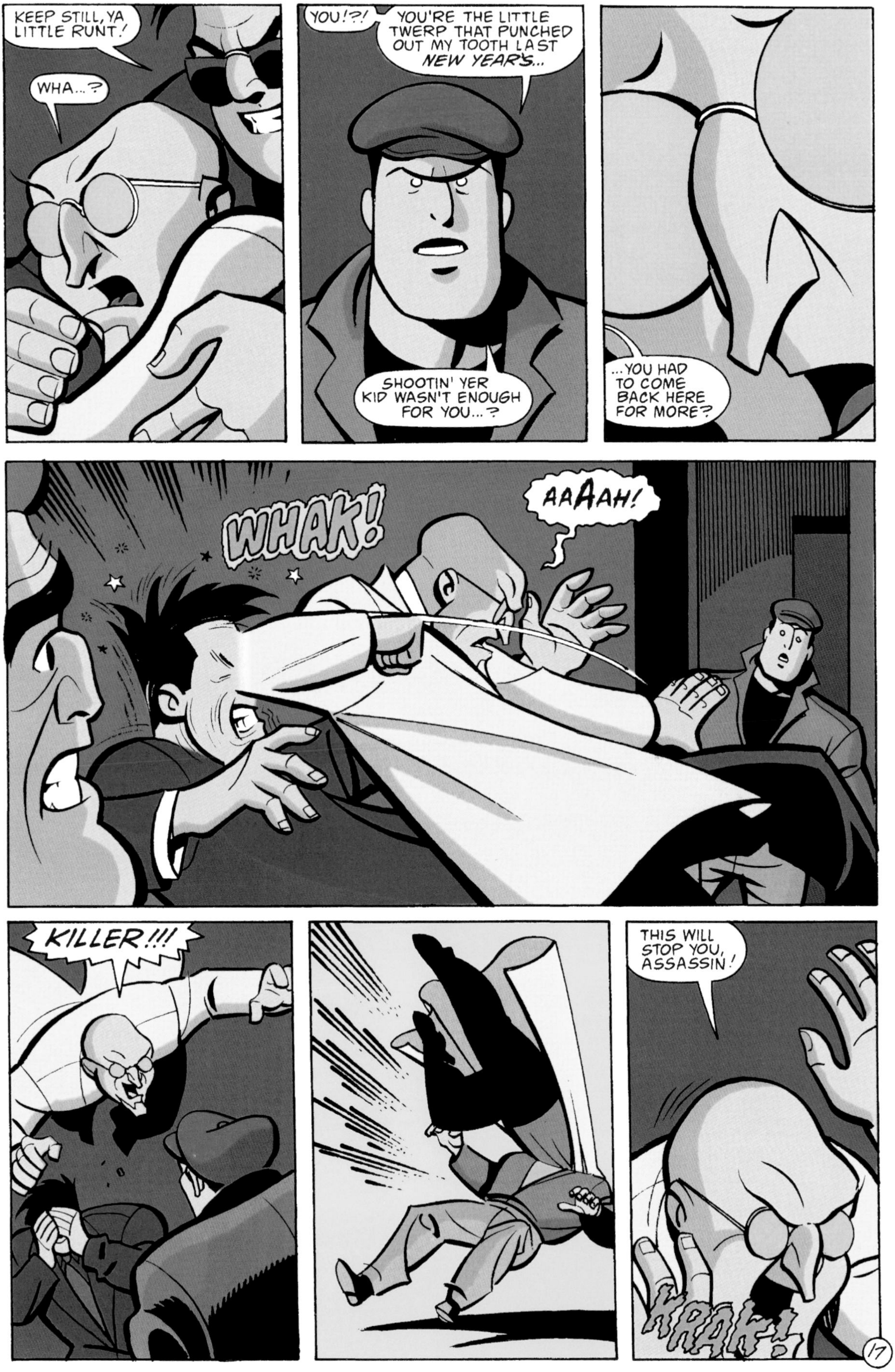
KEEP STILL, YA LITTLE RUNT!
WHA...?
YOU!?!
YOU'RE THE LITTLE TWERP THAT PUNCHED OUT MY TOOTH LAST NEW YEAR'S...
SHOOTIN' YER KID WASN'T ENOUGH FOR YOU...?
...YOU HAD TO COME BACK HERE FOR MORE?
WHAK!
AAAAH!
KILLER!!!
THIS WILL STOP YOU, ASSASSIN!
KRAK!
17

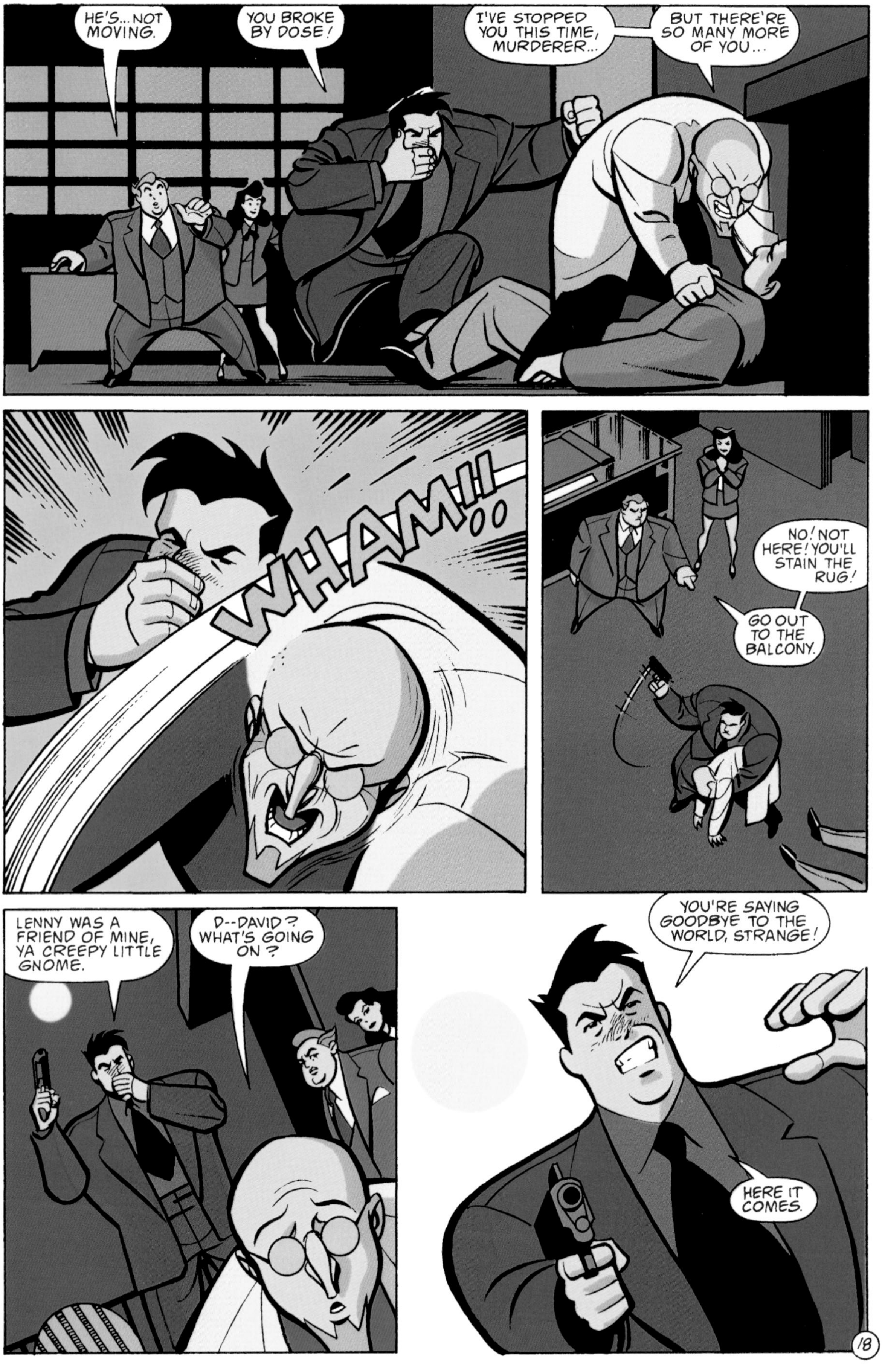

HE'S...NOT MOVING.
YOU BROKE BY DOSE!
I'VE STOPPED YOU THIS TIME, MURDERER...
BUT THERE'RE SO MANY MORE OF YOU...
WHAM!!
NO! NOT HERE! YOU'LL STAIN THE RUG!
GO OUT TO THE BALCONY.
LENNY WAS A FRIEND OF MINE, YA CREEPY LITTLE GNOME.
D--DAVID? WHAT'S GOING ON?
YOU'RE SAYING GOODBYE TO THE WORLD, STRANGE!
HERE IT COMES.
18

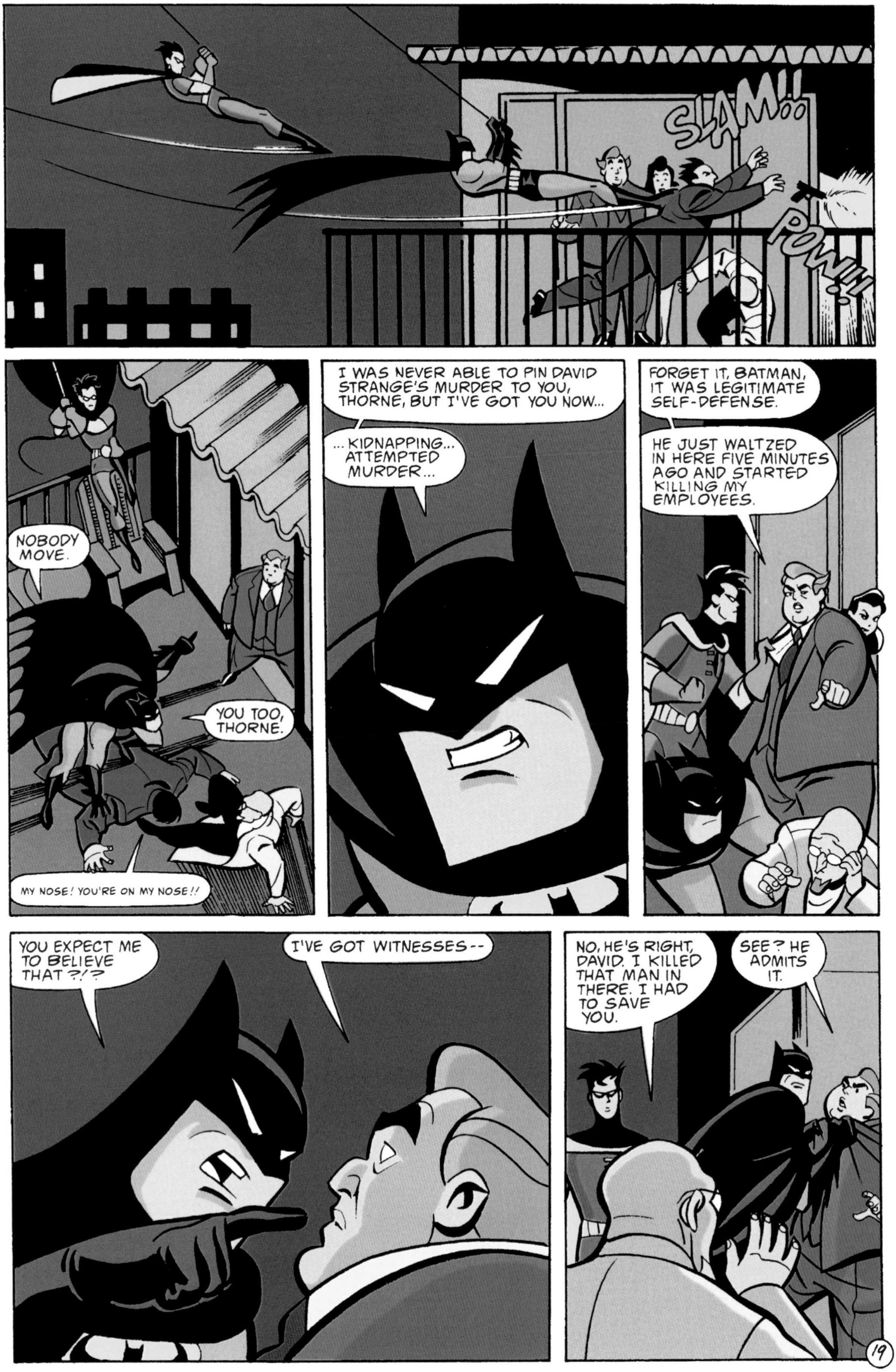
SLAM!!
POW!!
NOBODY MOVE.
YOU TOO, THORNE.
MY NOSE! YOU'RE ON MY NOSE!!
I WAS NEVER ABLE TO PIN DAVID STRANGE'S MURDER TO YOU, THORNE, BUT I'VE GOT YOU NOW...
...KIDNAPPING... ATTEMPTED MURDER...
FORGET IT, BATMAN, IT WAS LEGITIMATE SELF-DEFENSE.
HE JUST WALTZED IN HERE FIVE MINUTES AGO AND STARTED KILLING MY EMPLOYEES.
YOU EXPECT ME TO BELIEVE THAT?!?
I'VE GOT WITNESSES--
NO, HE'S RIGHT, DAVID. I KILLED THAT MAN IN THERE. I HAD TO SAVE YOU.
SEE? HE ADMITS IT.
19

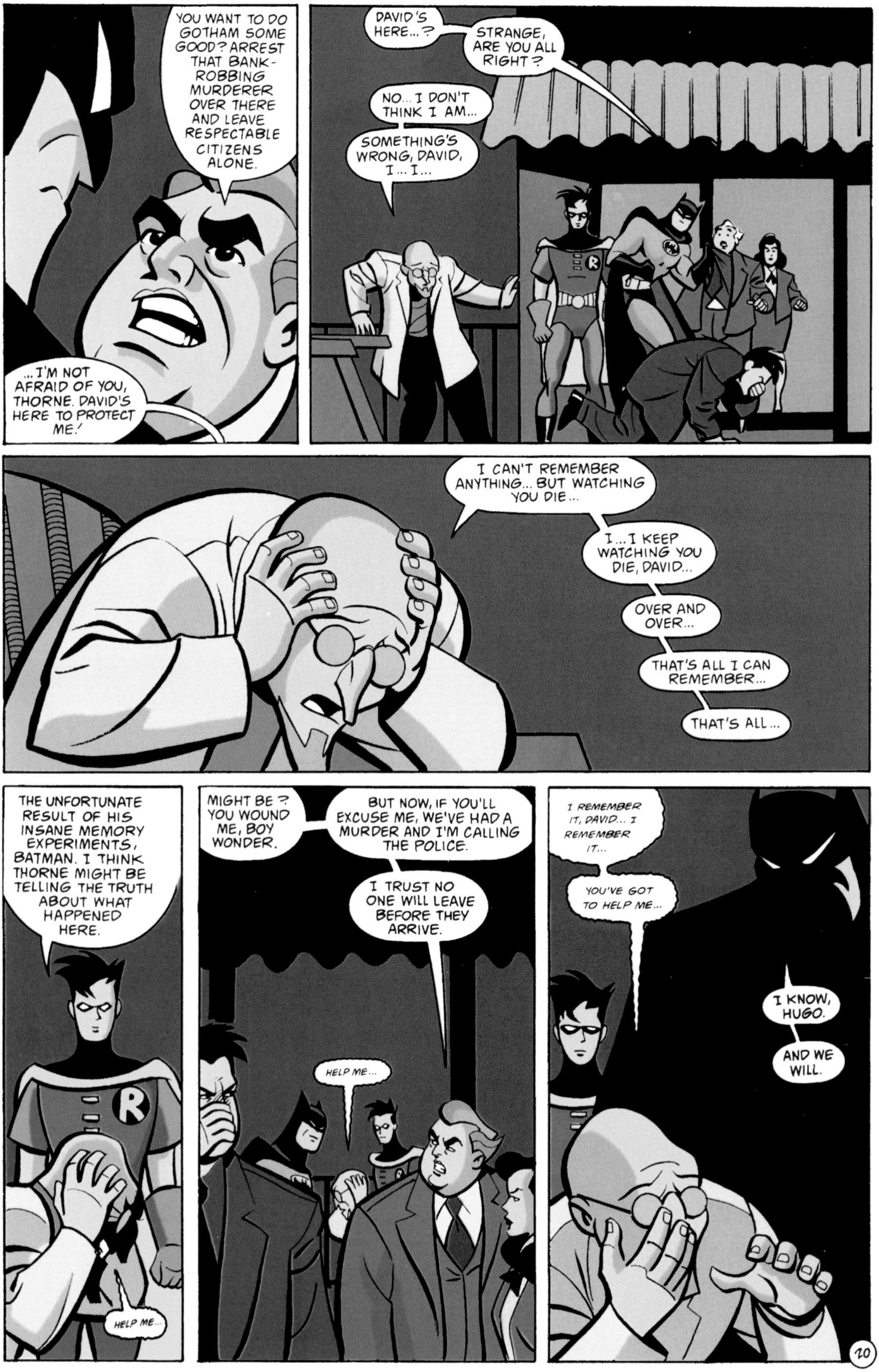
YOU WANT TO DO GOTHAM SOME GOOD? ARREST THAT BANK-ROBBING MURDERER OVER THERE AND LEAVE RESPECTABLE CITIZENS ALONE.
...I'M NOT AFRAID OF YOU, THORNE. DAVID'S HERE TO PROTECT ME!
DAVID'S HERE...?
STRANGE, ARE YOU ALL RIGHT?
NO... I DON'T THINK I AM...
SOMETHING'S WRONG, DAVID, I... I...
I CAN'T REMEMBER ANYTHING... BUT WATCHING YOU DIE...
I... I KEEP WATCHING YOU DIE, DAVID...
OVER AND OVER...
THAT'S ALL I CAN REMEMBER...
THAT'S ALL...
THE UNFORTUNATE RESULT OF HIS INSANE MEMORY EXPERIMENTS, BATMAN. I THINK THORNE MIGHT BE TELLING THE TRUTH ABOUT WHAT HAPPENED HERE.
HELP ME...
MIGHT BE? YOU WOUND ME, BOY WONDER.
BUT NOW, IF YOU'LL EXCUSE ME, WE'VE HAD A MURDER AND I'M CALLING THE POLICE.
I TRUST NO ONE WILL LEAVE BEFORE THEY ARRIVE.
HELP ME...
I REMEMBER IT, DAVID... I REMEMBER IT...
YOU'VE GOT TO HELP ME...
I KNOW, HUGO.
AND WE WILL.
20

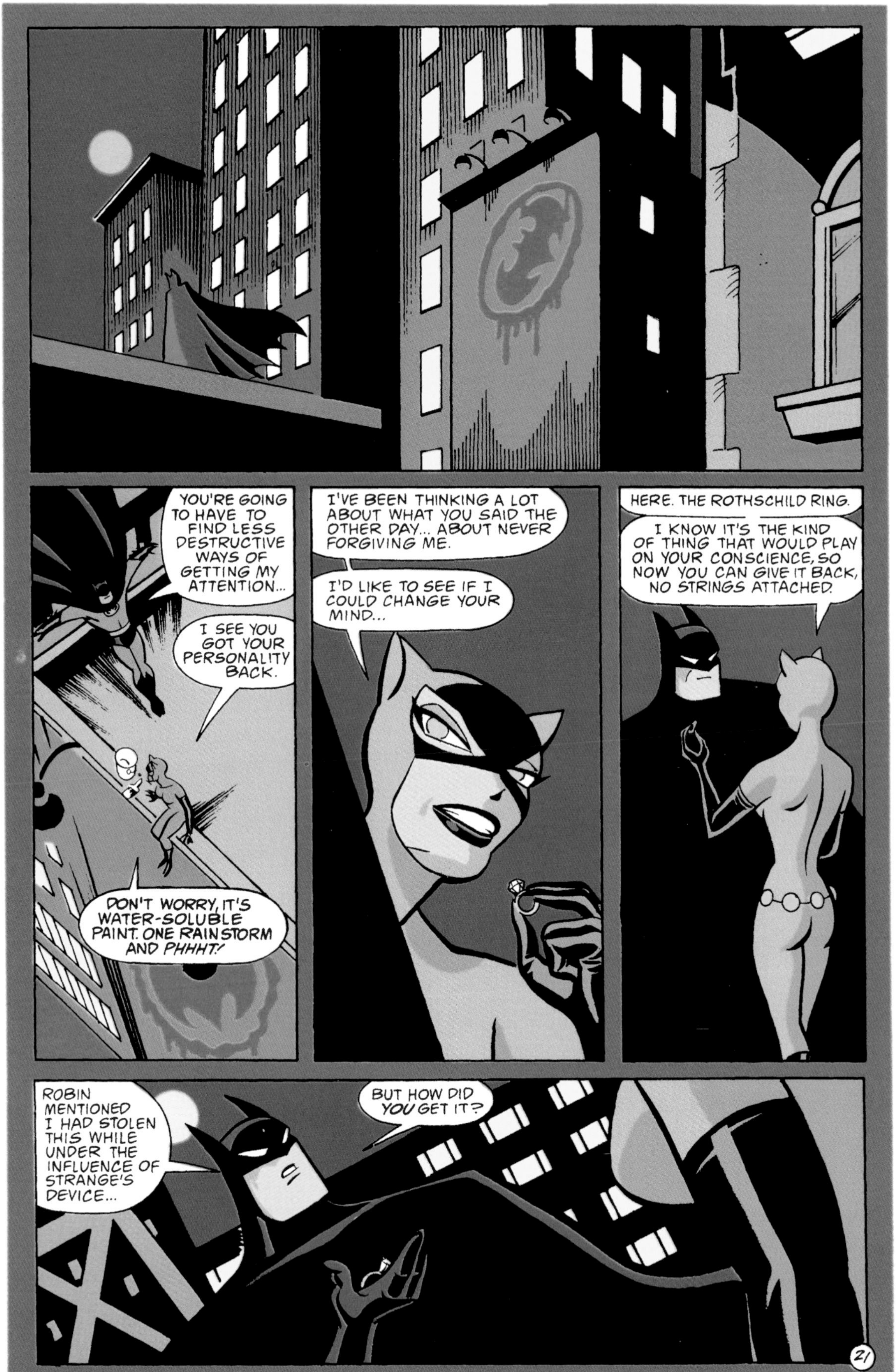
YOU'RE GOING TO HAVE TO FIND LESS DESTRUCTIVE WAYS OF GETTING MY ATTENTION...
I SEE YOU GOT YOUR PERSONALITY BACK.
DON'T WORRY, IT'S WATER-SOLUBLE PAINT. ONE RAINSTORM AND PHHHT!
I'VE BEEN THINKING A LOT ABOUT WHAT YOU SAID THE OTHER DAY... ABOUT NEVER FORGIVING ME.
I'D LIKE TO SEE IF I COULD CHANGE YOUR MIND...
HERE. THE ROTHSCHILD RING.
I KNOW IT'S THE KIND OF THING THAT WOULD PLAY ON YOUR CONSCIENCE, SO NOW YOU CAN GIVE IT BACK, NO STRINGS ATTACHED.
ROBIN MENTIONED I HAD STOLEN THIS WHILE UNDER THE INFLUENCE OF STRANGE'S DEVICE...
BUT HOW DID YOU GET IT?
21

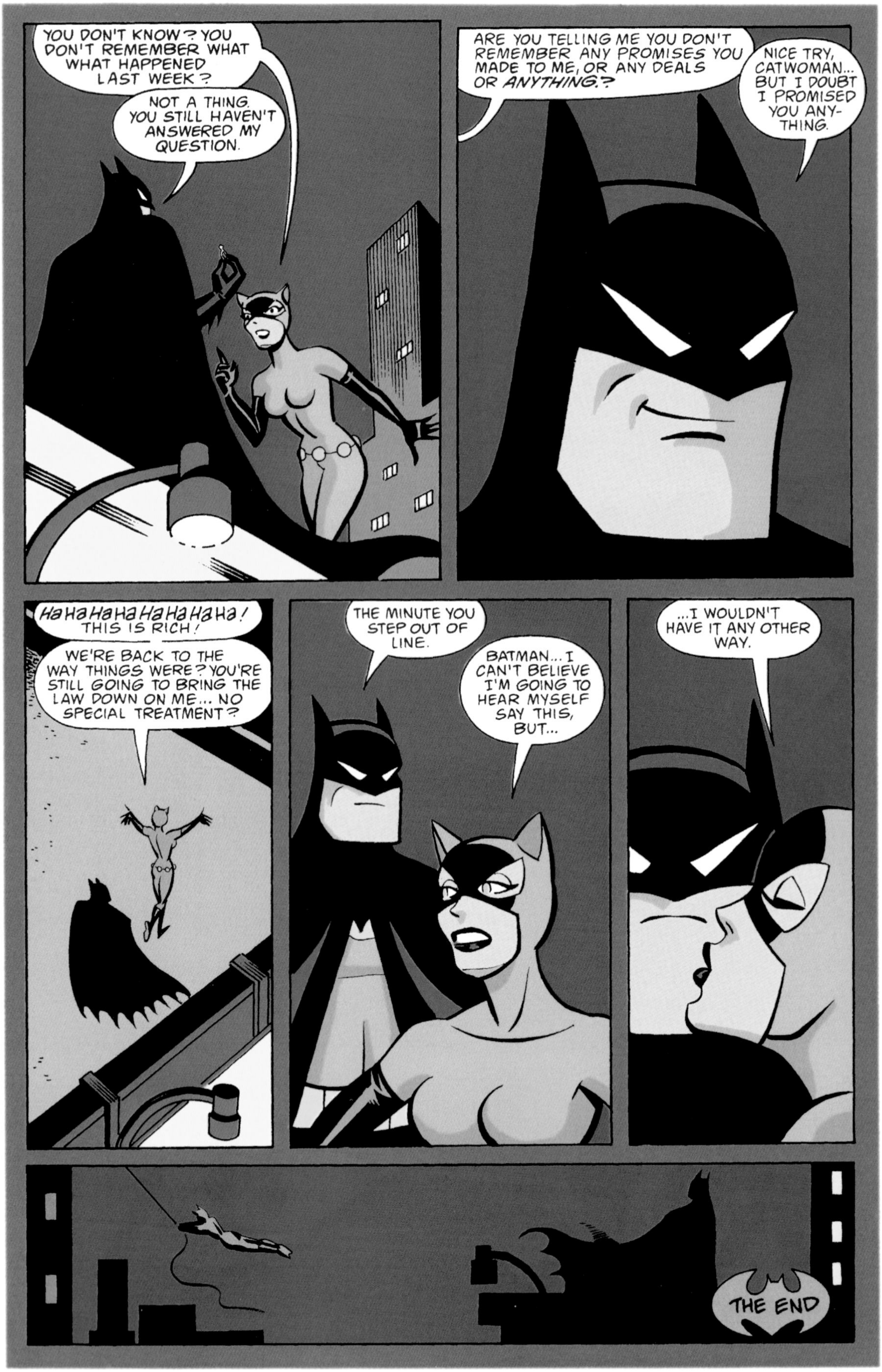
YOU DON'T KNOW? YOU DON'T REMEMBER WHAT WHAT HAPPENED LAST WEEK?
NOT A THING. YOU STILL HAVEN'T ANSWERED MY QUESTION.
ARE YOU TELLING ME YOU DON'T REMEMBER ANY PROMISES YOU MADE TO ME, OR ANY DEALS OR *ANYTHING*?
NICE TRY, CATWOMAN... BUT I DOUBT I PROMISED YOU ANY-THING.
HA HA HA HA HA HA HA HA HA! THIS IS RICH!
WE'RE BACK TO THE WAY THINGS WERE? YOU'RE STILL GOING TO BRING THE LAW DOWN ON ME... NO SPECIAL TREATMENT?
THE MINUTE YOU STEP OUT OF LINE.
BATMAN... I CAN'T BELIEVE I'M GOING TO HEAR MYSELF SAY THIS, BUT...
...I WOULDN'T HAVE IT ANY OTHER WAY.
THE END

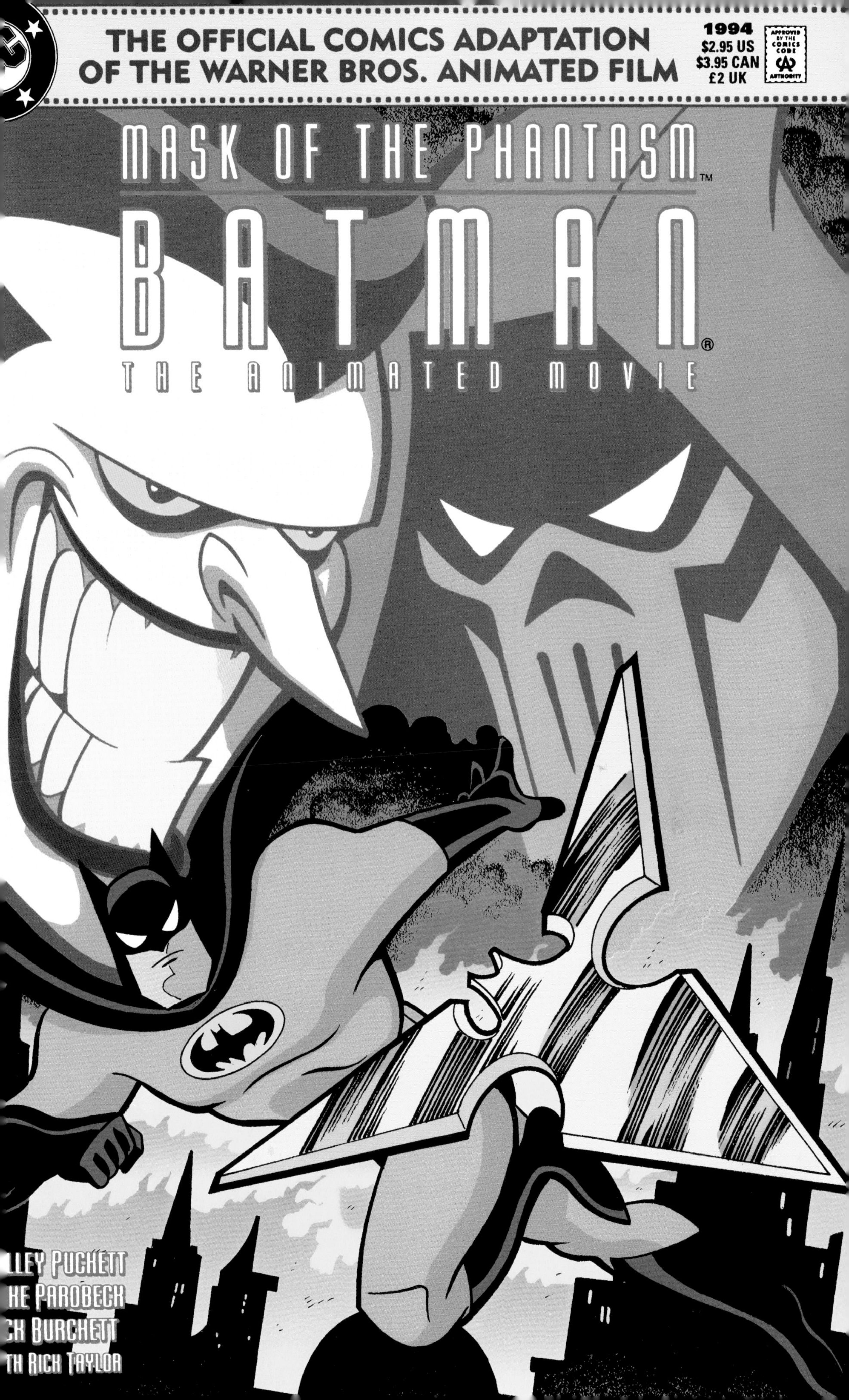
THE OFFICIAL COMICS ADAPTATION
OF THE WARNER BROS. ANIMATED FILM
1994
$2.95 US
$3.95 CAN
£2 UK
APPROVED BY THE COMICS CODE AUTHORITY
MASK OF THE PHANTASM™
BATMAN®
THE ANIMATED MOVIE
LLEY PUCKETT
KE PAROBECK
CK BURCHETT
TH RICK TAYLOR

A STRING OF
MURDERS

A LOVE
REKINDLED

AN ENEMY
RETURNED

A HERO
ACCUSED

A DUEL OF
MASKS

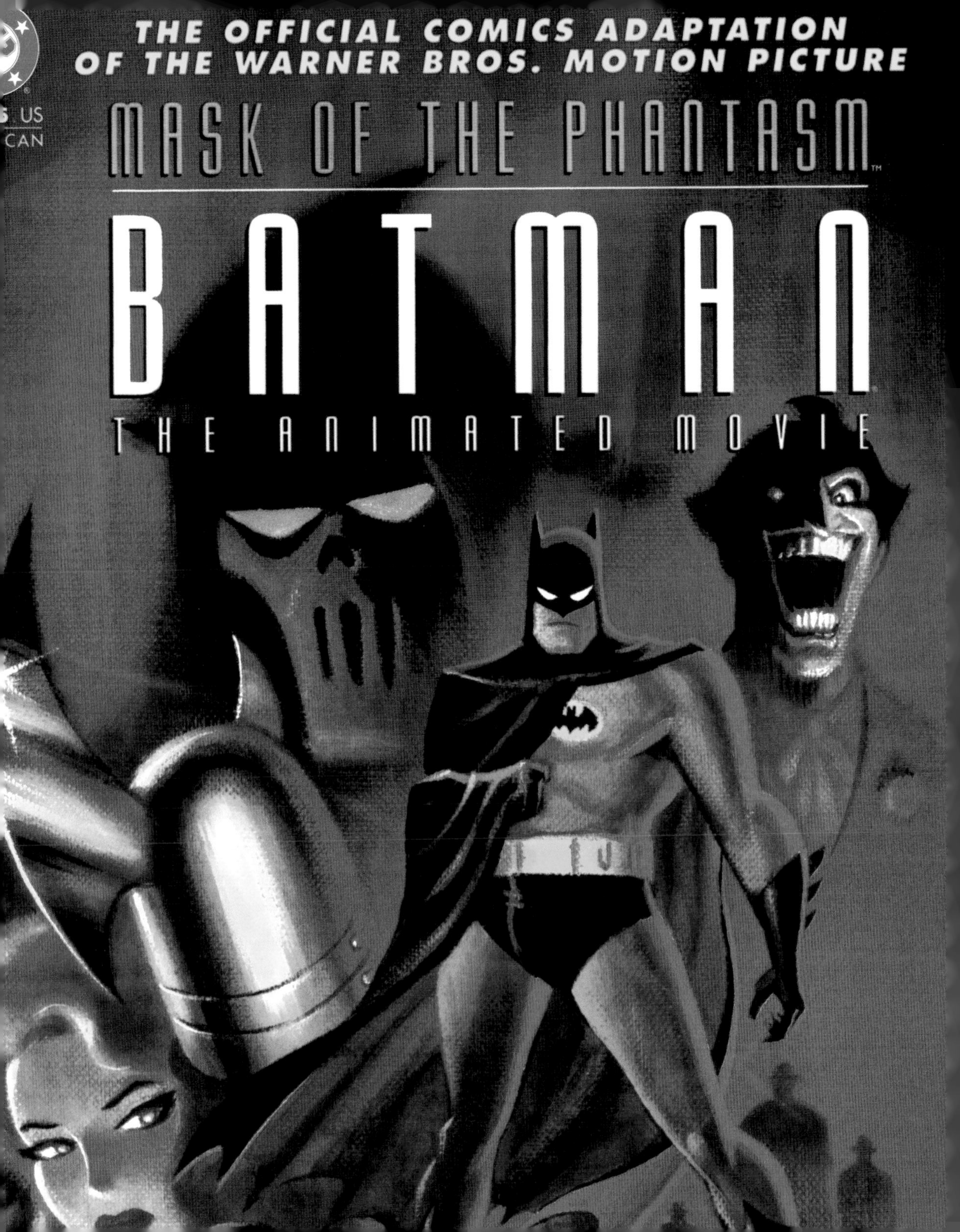
THE OFFICIAL COMICS ADAPTATION
OF THE WARNER BROS. MOTION PICTURE
US
CAN
MASK OF THE PHANTASM
BATMAN
THE ANIMATED MOVIE

MASK OF THE PHANTASM

BATMAN

THE ANIMATED MOVIE

WRITTEN BY
KELLEY PUCKETT

PENCILLED BY
MIKE PAROBECK

INKED BY
RICK BURCHETT

COLORED BY RICK TAYLOR
LETTERED BY TIM HARKINS

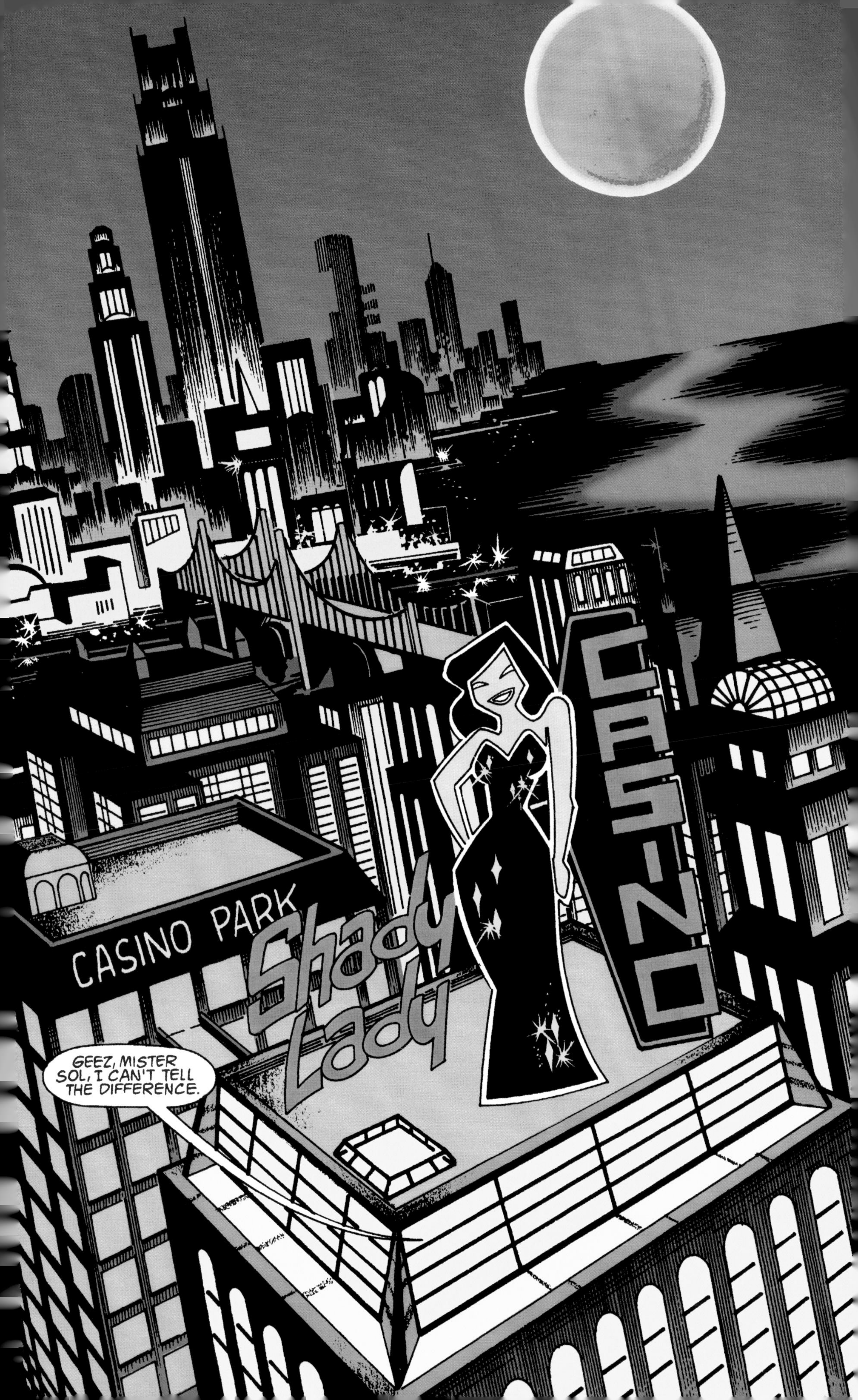
CASINO
CASINO PARK
Shady Lady
GEEZ, MISTER SOL, I CAN'T TELL THE DIFFERENCE.

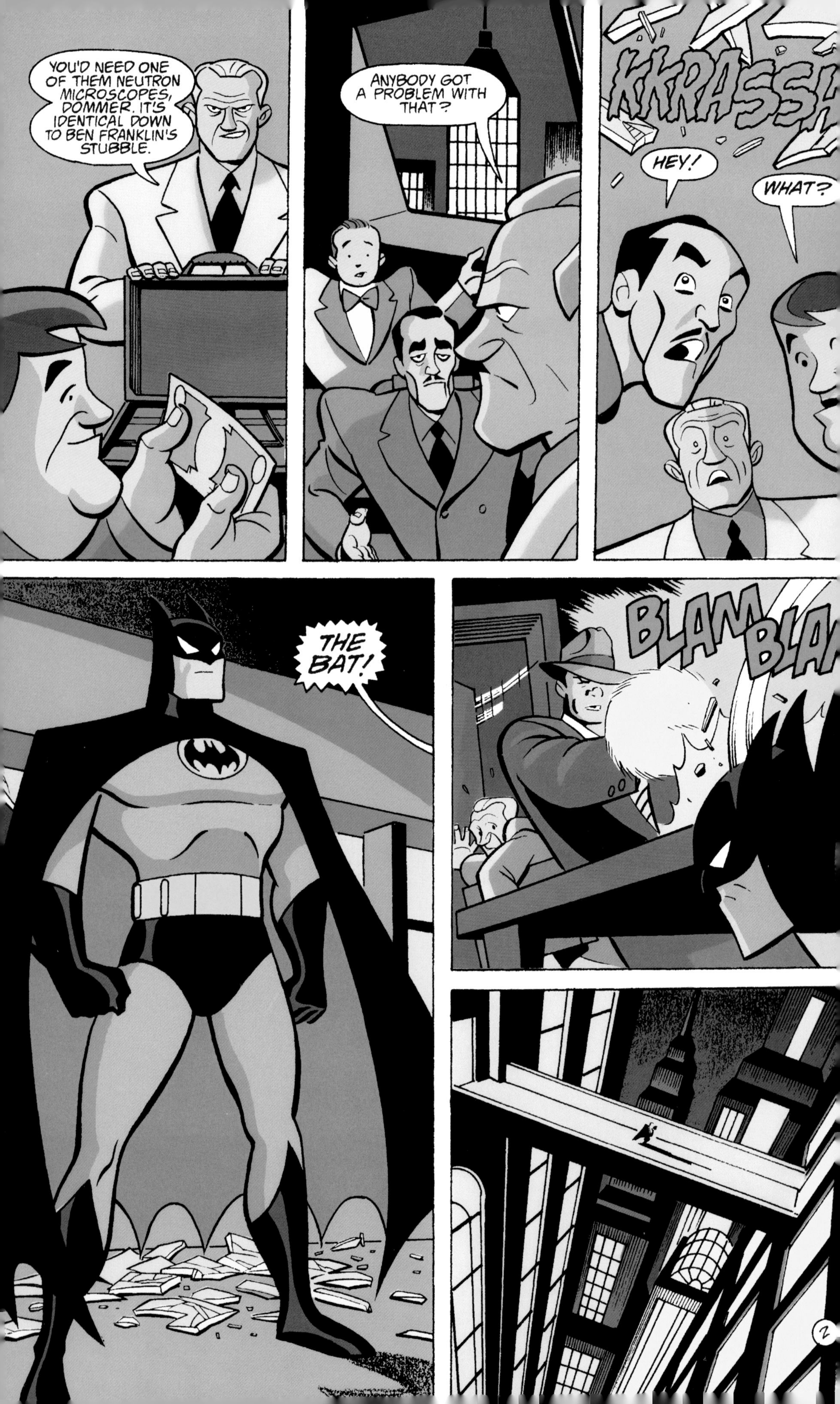
YOU'D NEED ONE OF THEM NEUTRON MICROSCOPES, DOMMER. IT'S IDENTICAL DOWN TO BEN FRANKLIN'S STUBBLE.
ANYBODY GOT A PROBLEM WITH THAT?
KKRASSH
HEY!
WHAT?
THE BAT!
BLAM
BLAM
2

CHUCKIE SOL...

BATMAN!

BLAM BLAM BLAM

CLICK CLICK

YOUR ANGEL OF DEATH AWAITS.

YOU AIN'T THE BATMAN!

WH-WHO ARE YOU? WHADDAYA WANT?

I WANT YOU, CHUCKIE BOY.

KRAAASSSSSHH!

③

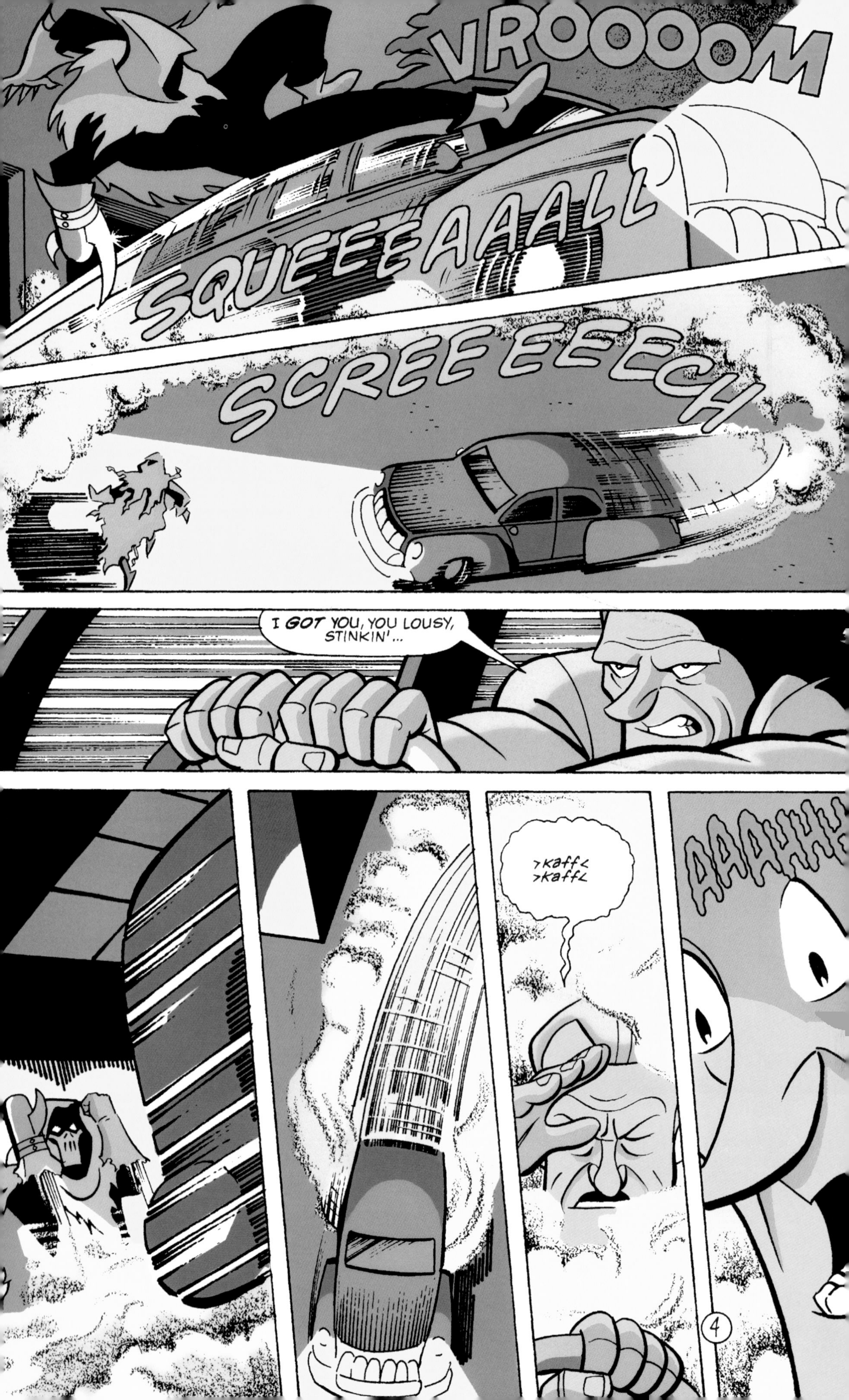
VROOOOM
SQUEEEAAALL
SCREEEEEECH
I GOT YOU, YOU LOUSY, STINKIN'...
>kaff< >kaff<
AAAHH
4

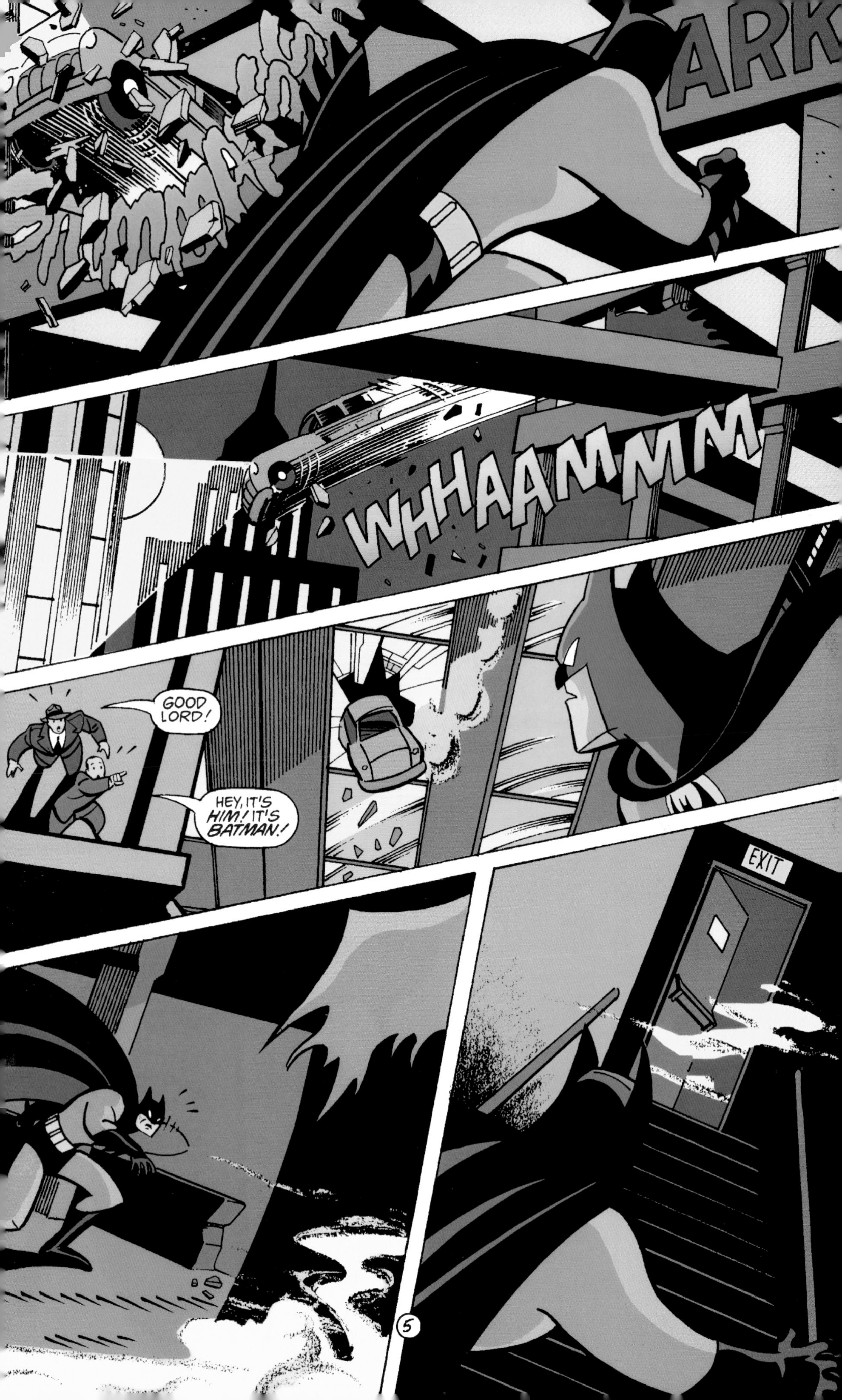
SMMAASH
ARK
WHHAAMMMM
GOOD LORD!
HEY, IT'S HIM! IT'S BATMAN!
EXIT

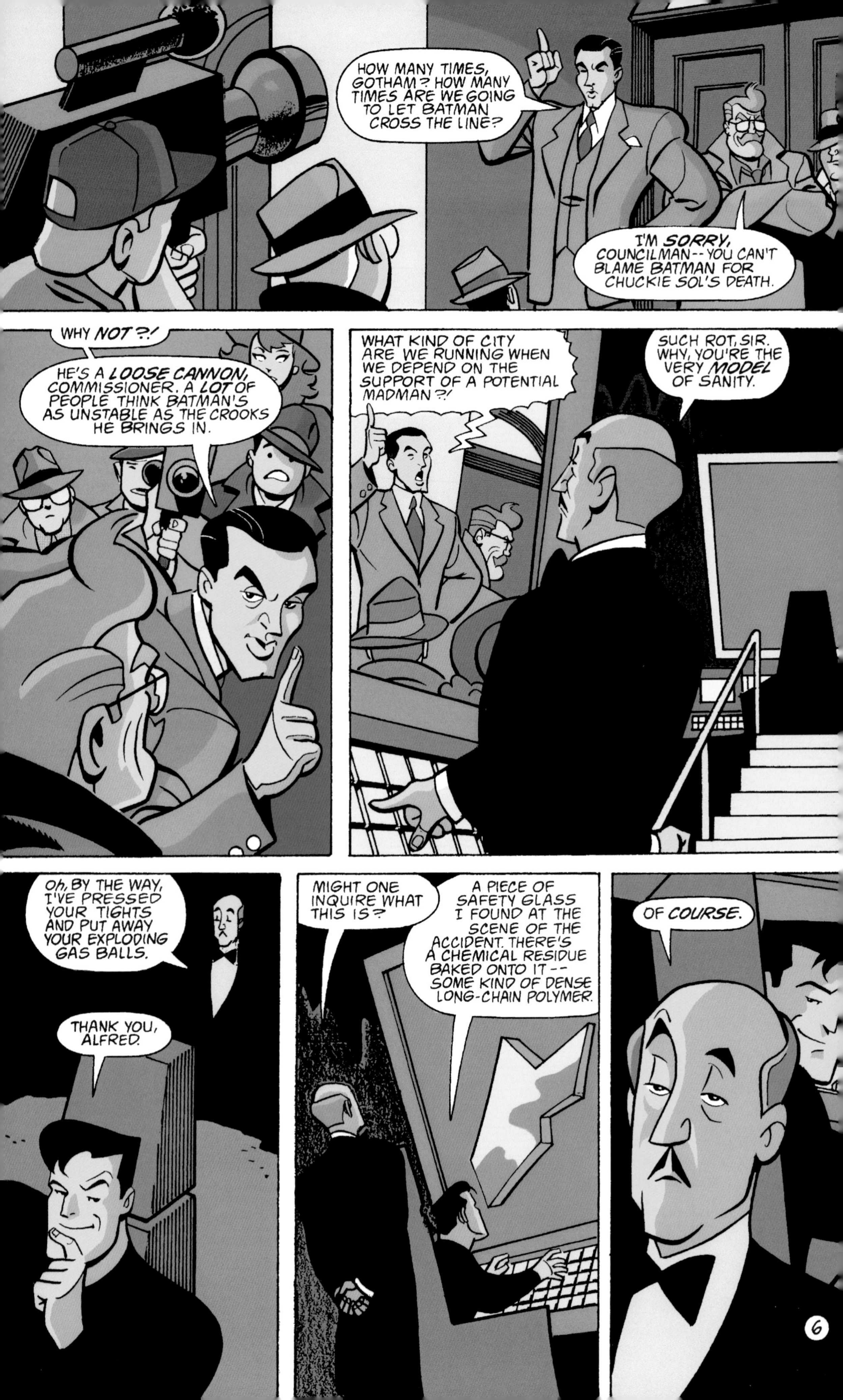
HOW MANY TIMES, GOTHAM? HOW MANY TIMES ARE WE GOING TO LET BATMAN CROSS THE LINE?
I'M SORRY, COUNCILMAN-- YOU CAN'T BLAME BATMAN FOR CHUCKIE SOL'S DEATH.
WHY NOT?!
HE'S A LOOSE CANNON, COMMISSIONER. A LOT OF PEOPLE THINK BATMAN'S AS UNSTABLE AS THE CROOKS HE BRINGS IN.
WHAT KIND OF CITY ARE WE RUNNING WHEN WE DEPEND ON THE SUPPORT OF A POTENTIAL MADMAN?!
SUCH ROT, SIR. WHY, YOU'RE THE VERY MODEL OF SANITY.
Oh, BY THE WAY, I'VE PRESSED YOUR TIGHTS AND PUT AWAY YOUR EXPLODING GAS BALLS.
THANK YOU, ALFRED.
MIGHT ONE INQUIRE WHAT THIS IS?
A PIECE OF SAFETY GLASS I FOUND AT THE SCENE OF THE ACCIDENT. THERE'S A CHEMICAL RESIDUE BAKED ONTO IT -- SOME KIND OF DENSE LONG-CHAIN POLYMER.
OF COURSE.

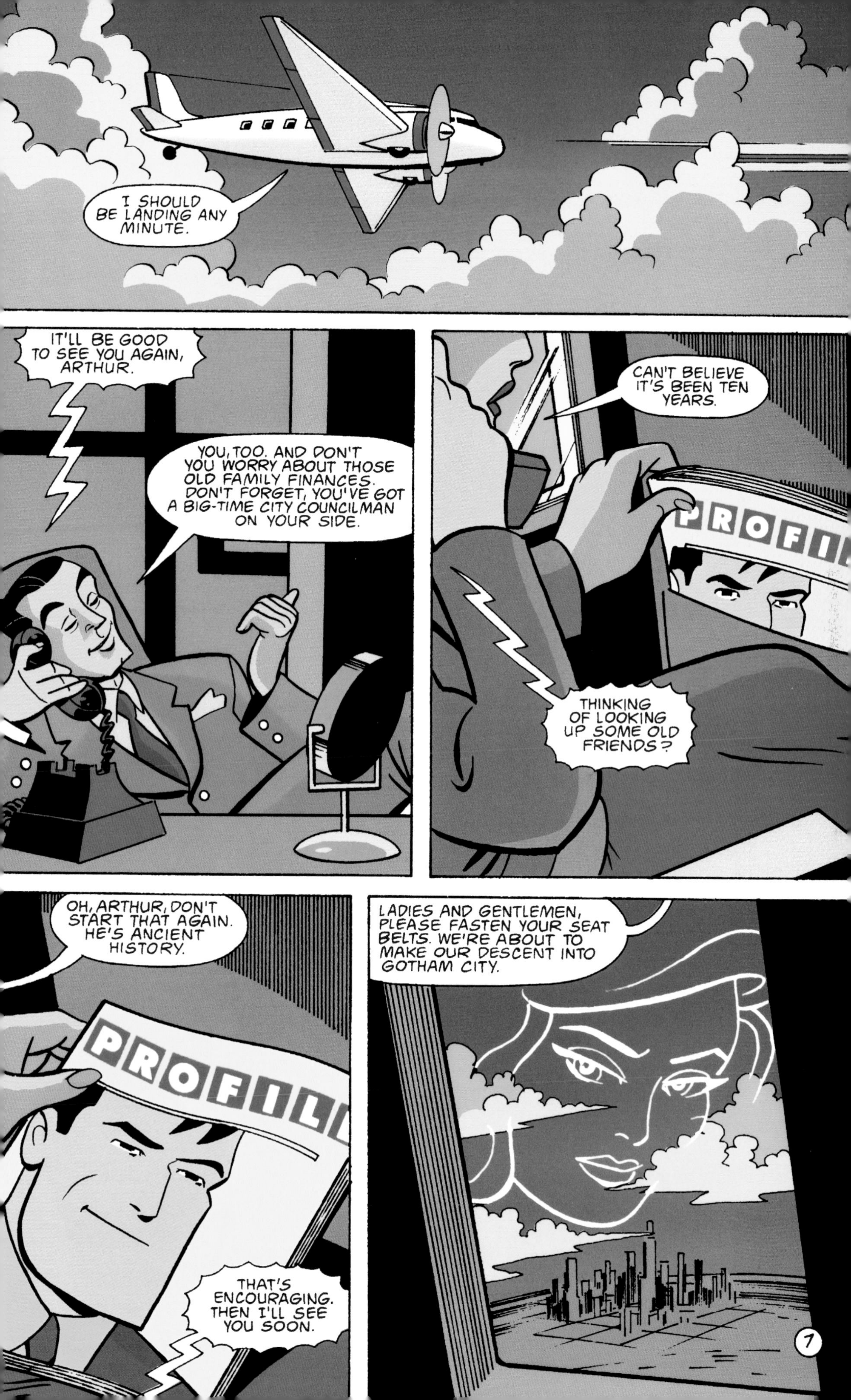

I SHOULD BE LANDING ANY MINUTE.
IT'LL BE GOOD TO SEE YOU AGAIN, ARTHUR.
YOU, TOO. AND DON'T YOU WORRY ABOUT THOSE OLD FAMILY FINANCES. DON'T FORGET, YOU'VE GOT A BIG-TIME CITY COUNCILMAN ON YOUR SIDE.
CAN'T BELIEVE IT'S BEEN TEN YEARS.
PROFIL
THINKING OF LOOKING UP SOME OLD FRIENDS?
OH, ARTHUR, DON'T START THAT AGAIN. HE'S ANCIENT HISTORY.
PROFILE
THAT'S ENCOURAGING. THEN I'LL SEE YOU SOON.
LADIES AND GENTLEMEN, PLEASE FASTEN YOUR SEAT BELTS. WE'RE ABOUT TO MAKE OUR DESCENT INTO GOTHAM CITY.

COME *ON*, BRUCE. ALL ALONE IN THIS BIG MANSION. HAVEN'T YOU EVER THOUGHT ABOUT MARRIAGE, EVEN *ONCE?*

OH, NEVER SAY THE "M" WORD IN FRONT OF BRUCE. IT MAKES HIM *NERVOUS.*

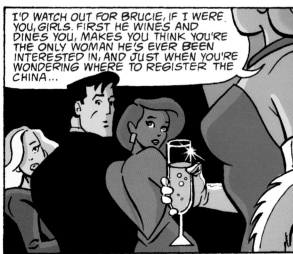

I'D WATCH OUT FOR BRUCIE, IF I WERE YOU, GIRLS. FIRST HE WINES AND DINES YOU, MAKES YOU THINK YOU'RE THE ONLY WOMAN HE'S EVER BEEN INTERESTED IN, AND JUST WHEN YOU'RE WONDERING WHERE TO REGISTER THE CHINA...

...HE FORGETS YOUR PHONE NUMBER. *THAT'S* BRUCE WAYNE'S STYLE.

REALLY, BRUCE, IT'S ALMOST AS IF YOU PICK THEM BECAUSE YOU *KNOW* THERE'S NO CHANCE FOR A SERIOUS RELATIONSHIP.

COUNCILMAN REEVES.

AT LEAST SINCE THAT ONE GIRL... WHAT WAS HER NAME? ANNE... ANDI... *ANDREA.*

8

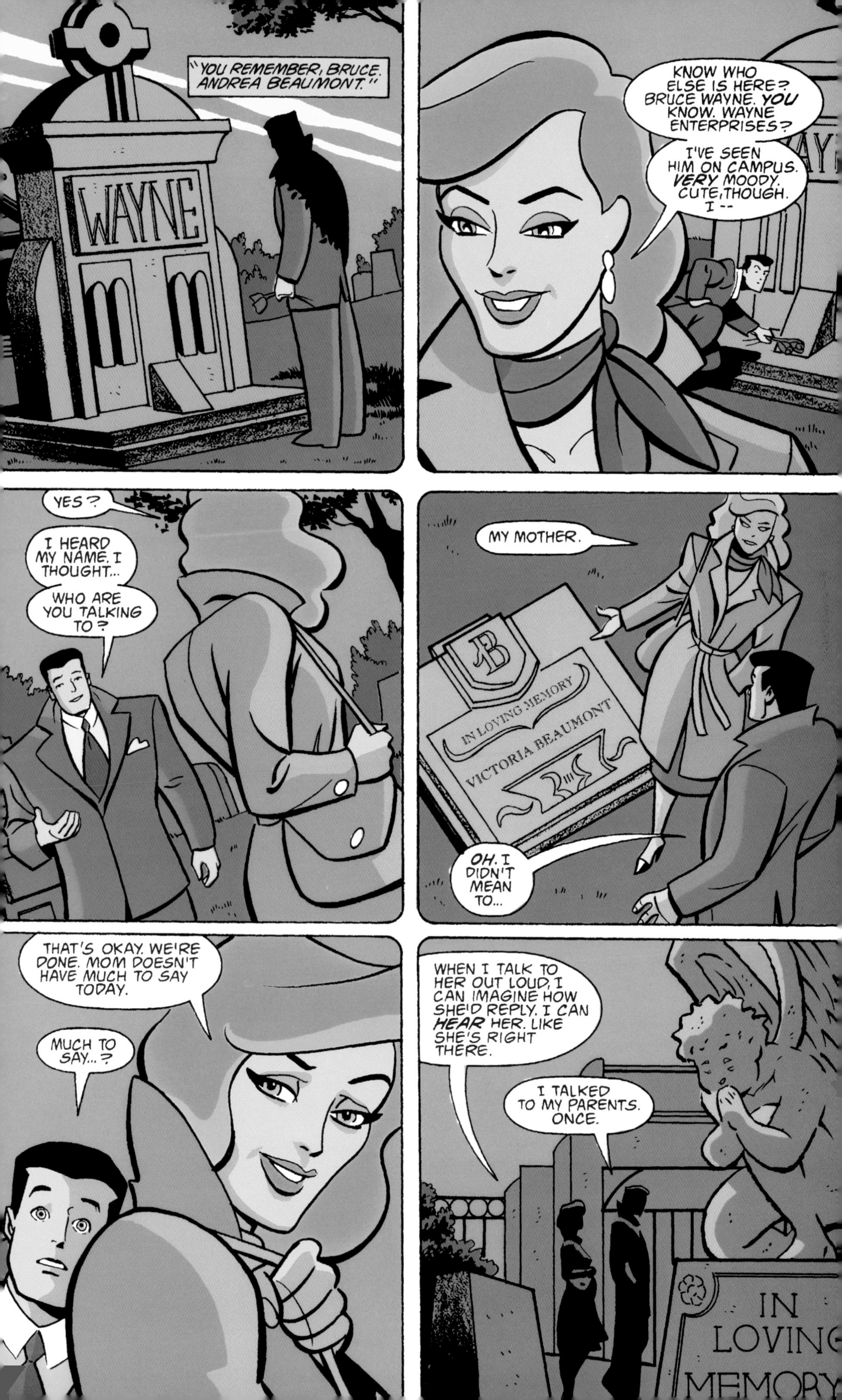
"YOU REMEMBER, BRUCE. ANDREA BEAUMONT."
WAYNE
KNOW WHO ELSE IS HERE? BRUCE WAYNE. YOU KNOW. WAYNE ENTERPRISES?
I'VE SEEN HIM ON CAMPUS. VERY MOODY. CUTE, THOUGH. I --
YES?
I HEARD MY NAME. I THOUGHT...
WHO ARE YOU TALKING TO?
MY MOTHER.
IN LOVING MEMORY
VICTORIA BEAUMONT
OH. I DIDN'T MEAN TO...
THAT'S OKAY. WE'RE DONE. MOM DOESN'T HAVE MUCH TO SAY TODAY.
MUCH TO SAY...?
WHEN I TALK TO HER OUT LOUD, I CAN IMAGINE HOW SHE'D REPLY. I CAN HEAR HER. LIKE SHE'S RIGHT THERE.
I TALKED TO MY PARENTS. ONCE.
IN LOVING MEMORY

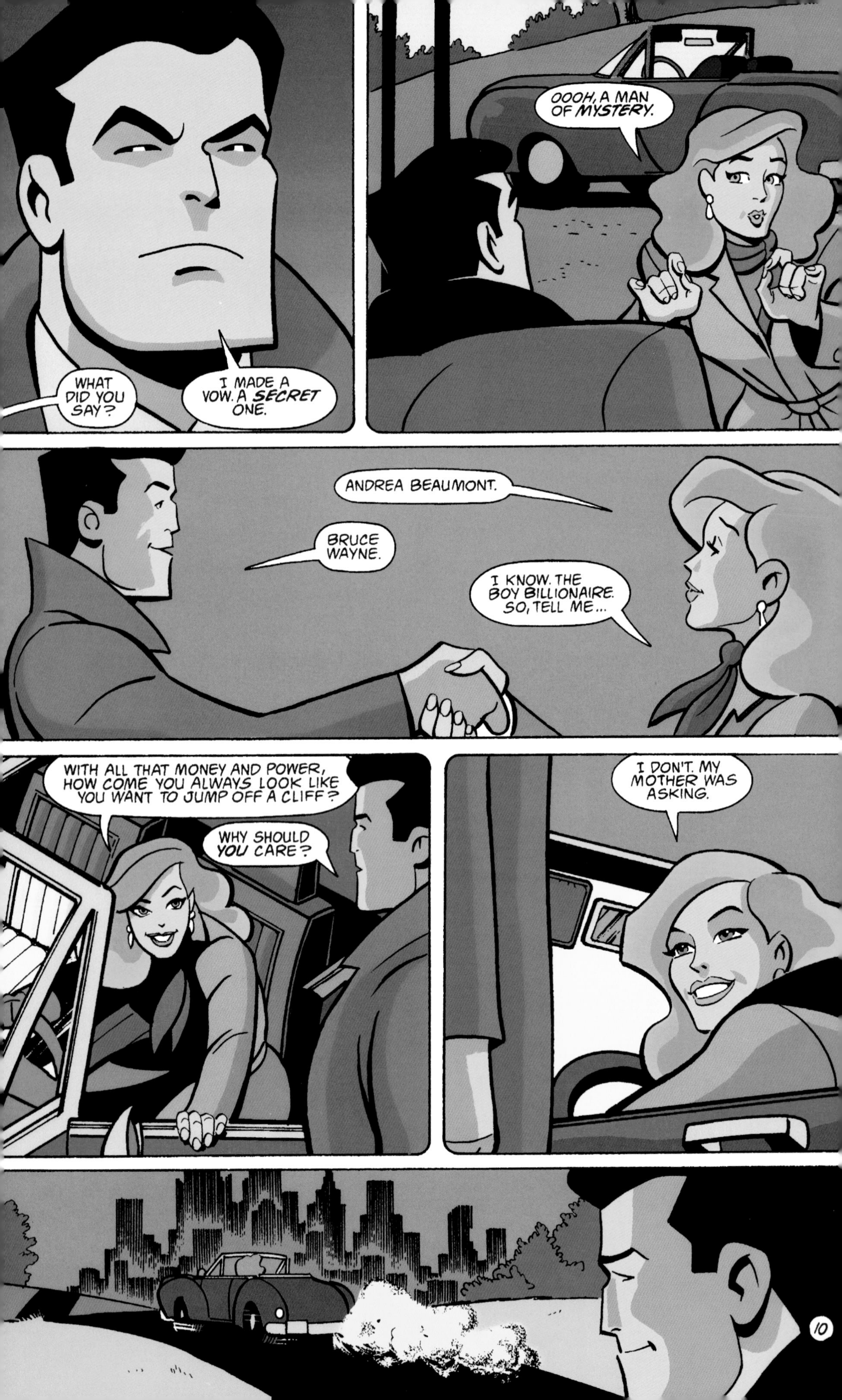
WHAT DID YOU SAY?
I MADE A VOW. A SECRET ONE.
OOOH, A MAN OF MYSTERY.
ANDREA BEAUMONT.
BRUCE WAYNE.
I KNOW. THE BOY BILLIONAIRE. SO, TELL ME...
WITH ALL THAT MONEY AND POWER, HOW COME YOU ALWAYS LOOK LIKE YOU WANT TO JUMP OFF A CLIFF?
WHY SHOULD YOU CARE?
I DON'T. MY MOTHER WAS ASKING.
10

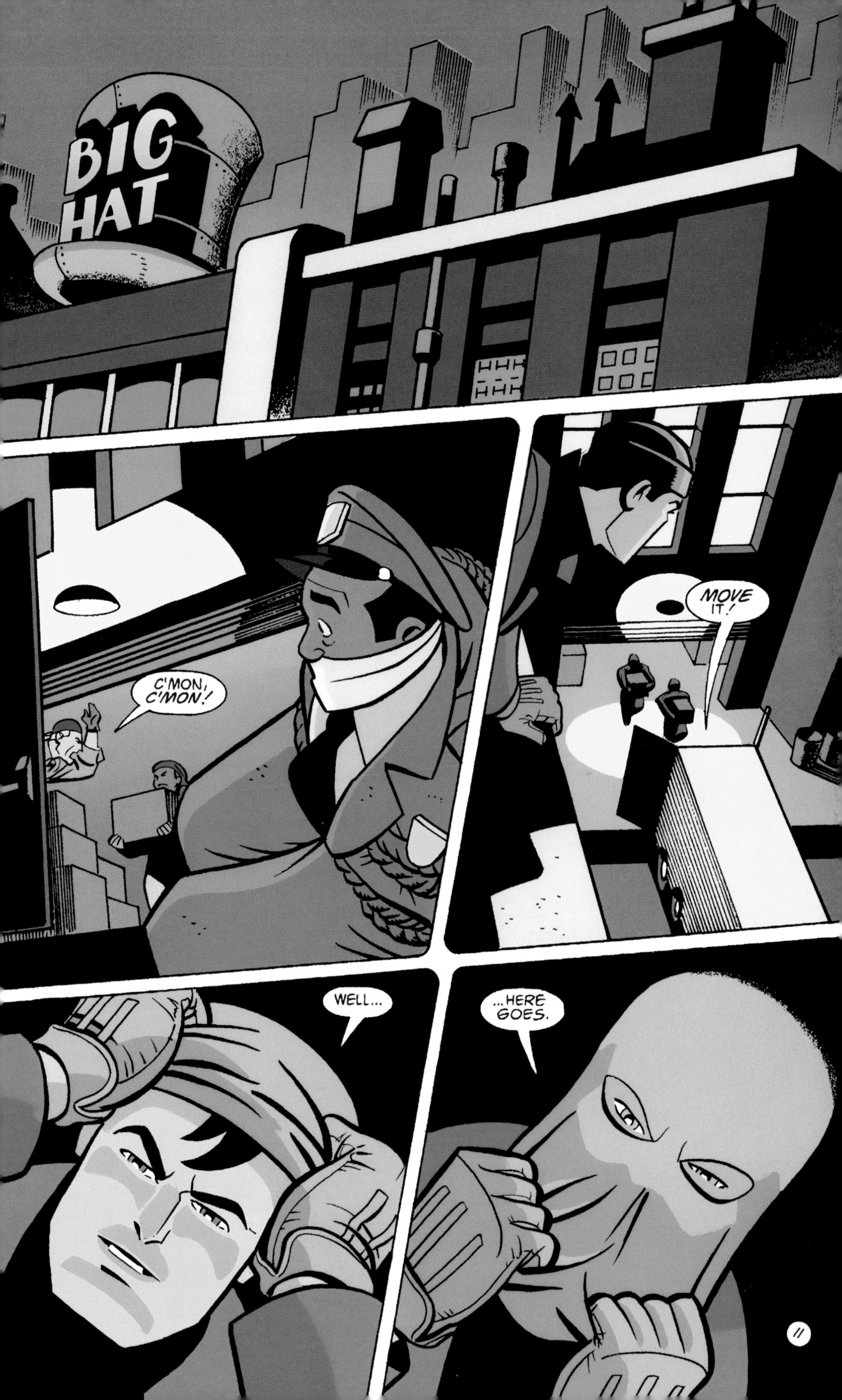
BIG HAT
C'MON, C'MON!
MOVE IT!
WELL...
...HERE GOES.

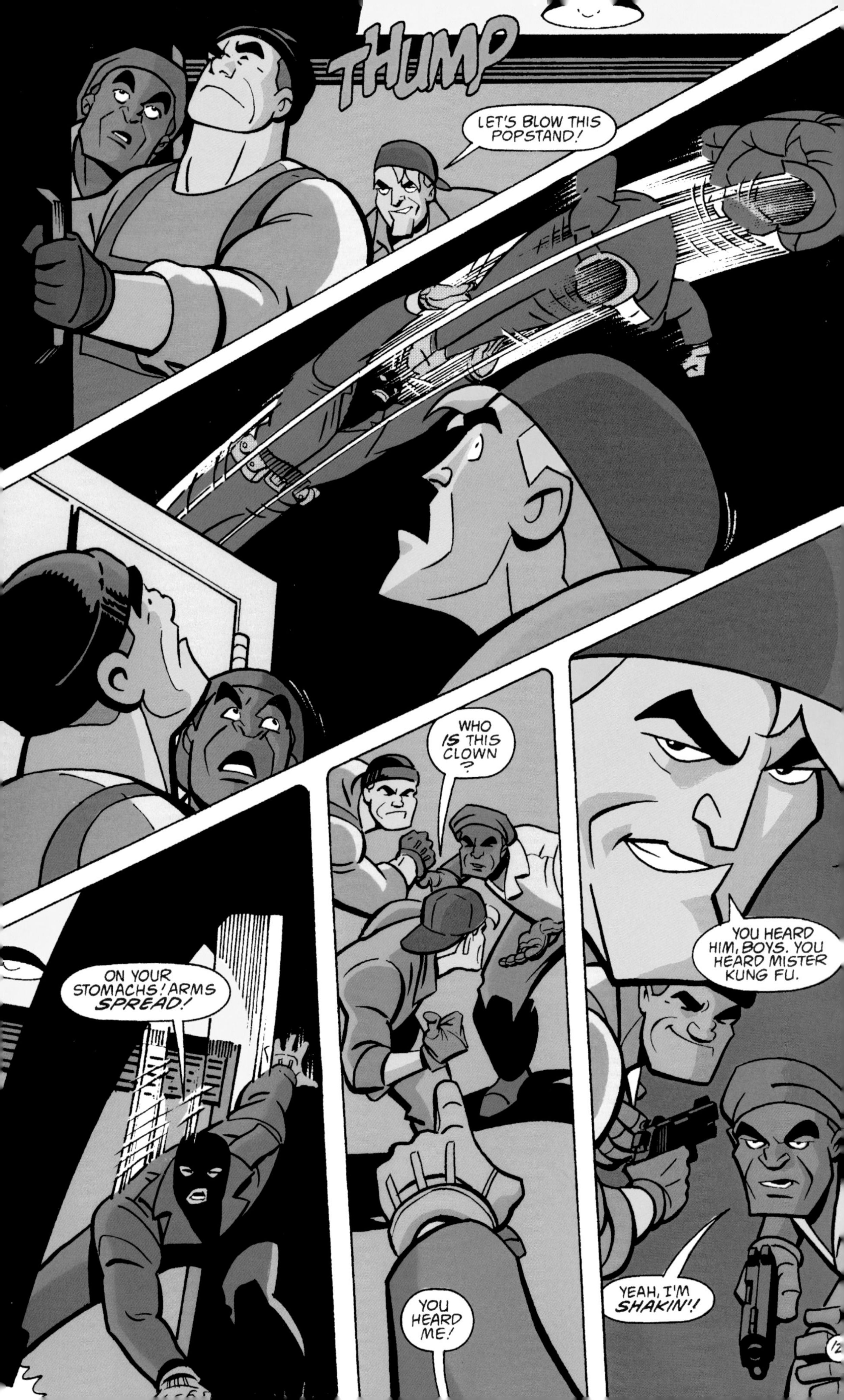
THUMP
LET'S BLOW THIS POPSTAND!
WHO IS THIS CLOWN?
YOU HEARD HIM, BOYS. YOU HEARD MISTER KUNG FU.
ON YOUR STOMACHS! ARMS SPREAD!
YOU HEARD ME!
YEAH, I'M SHAKIN'!

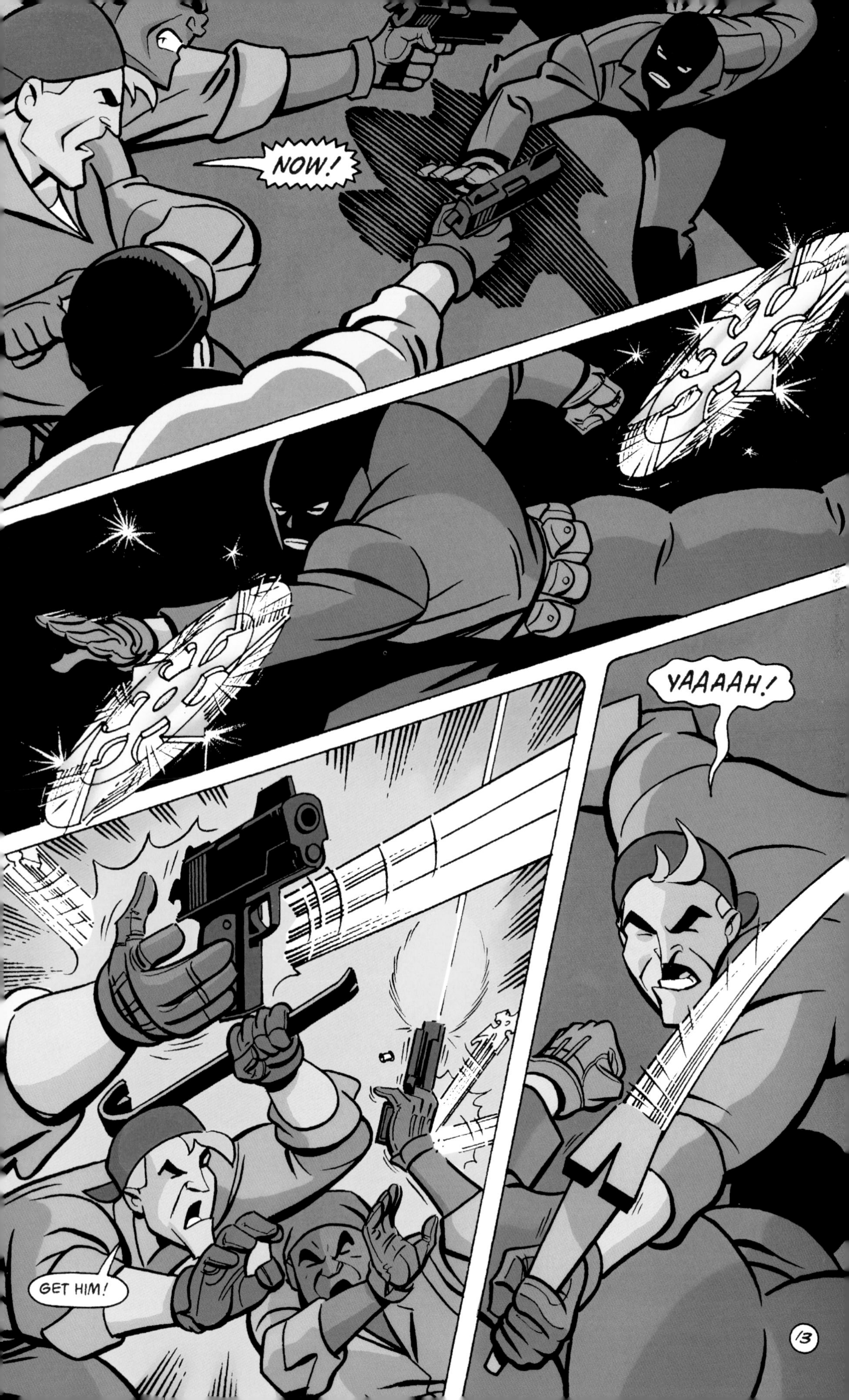
NOW!
YAAAAH!
GET HIM!

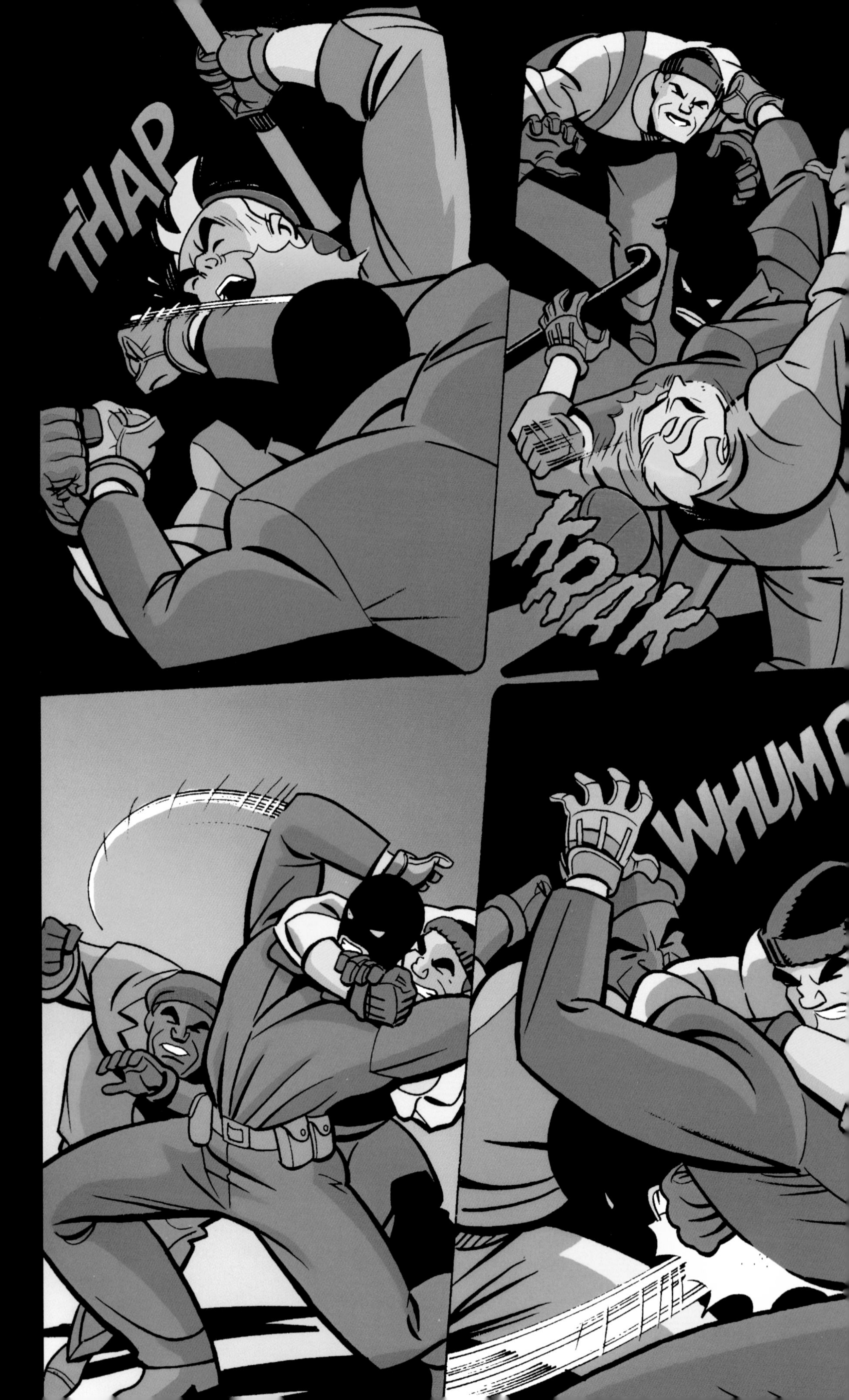
THAP
KRAK
WHUM

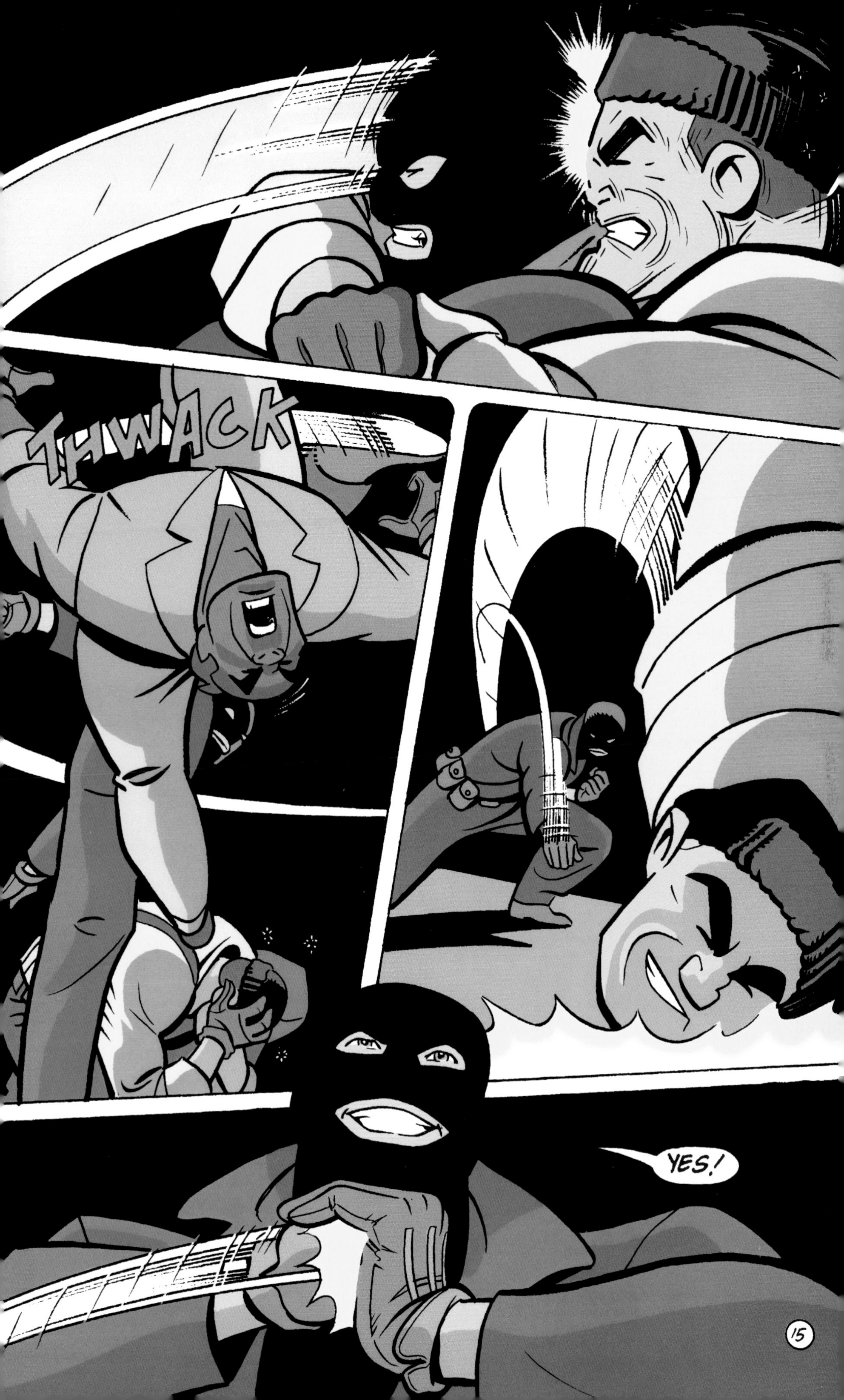
THWACK
YES!

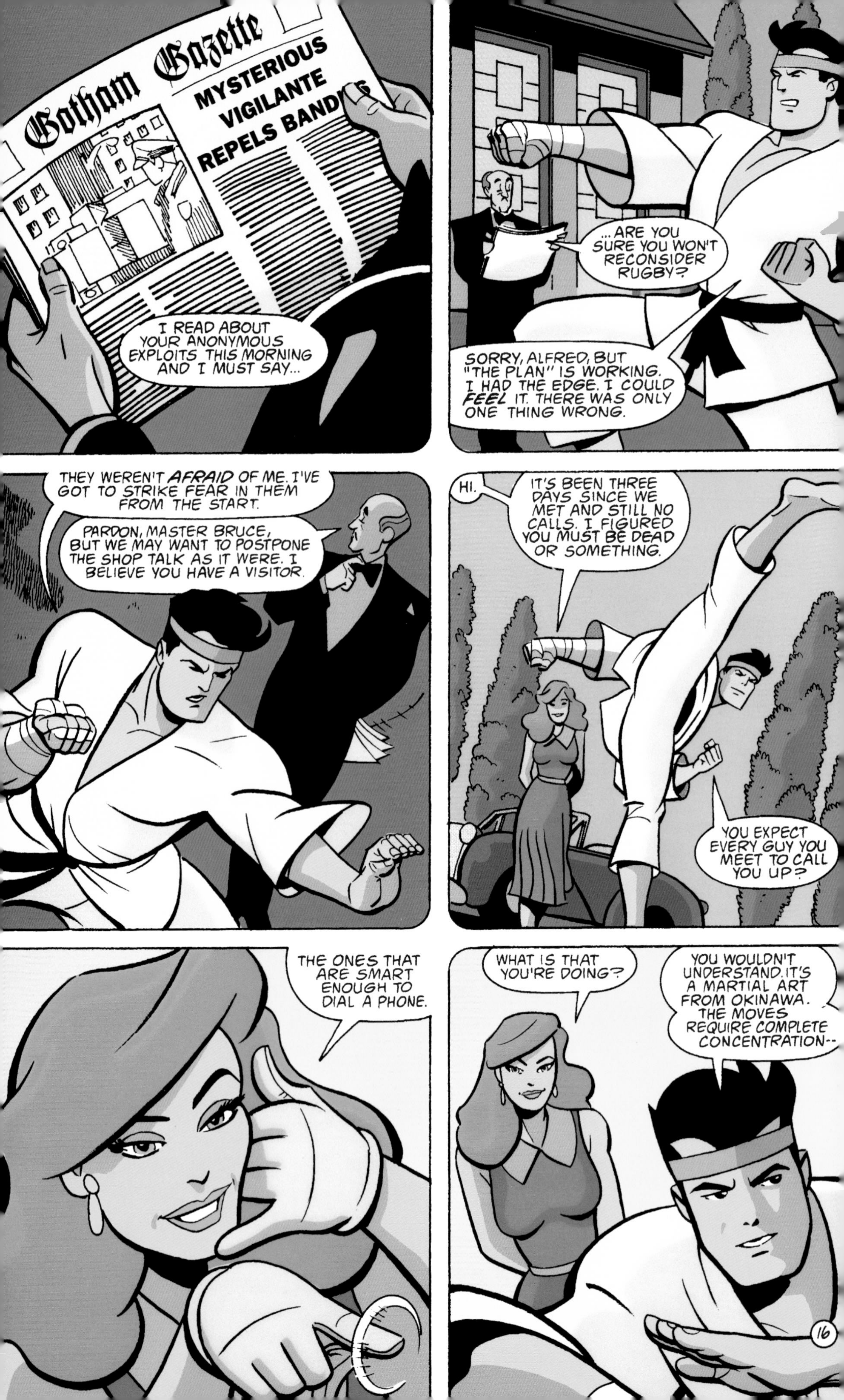
Gotham Gazette
MYSTERIOUS VIGILANTE REPELS BANDITS
I READ ABOUT YOUR ANONYMOUS EXPLOITS THIS MORNING AND I MUST SAY...
...ARE YOU SURE YOU WON'T RECONSIDER RUGBY?
SORRY, ALFRED, BUT "THE PLAN" IS WORKING. I HAD THE EDGE. I COULD *FEEL* IT. THERE WAS ONLY ONE THING WRONG.
THEY WEREN'T *AFRAID* OF ME. I'VE GOT TO STRIKE FEAR IN THEM FROM THE START.
PARDON, MASTER BRUCE, BUT WE MAY WANT TO POSTPONE THE SHOP TALK AS IT WERE. I BELIEVE YOU HAVE A VISITOR.
HI.
IT'S BEEN THREE DAYS SINCE WE MET AND STILL NO CALLS. I FIGURED YOU MUST BE DEAD OR SOMETHING.
YOU EXPECT EVERY GUY YOU MEET TO CALL YOU UP?
THE ONES THAT ARE SMART ENOUGH TO DIAL A PHONE.
WHAT IS THAT YOU'RE DOING?
YOU WOULDN'T UNDERSTAND. IT'S A MARTIAL ART FROM OKINAWA. THE MOVES REQUIRE COMPLETE CONCENTRATION--
16

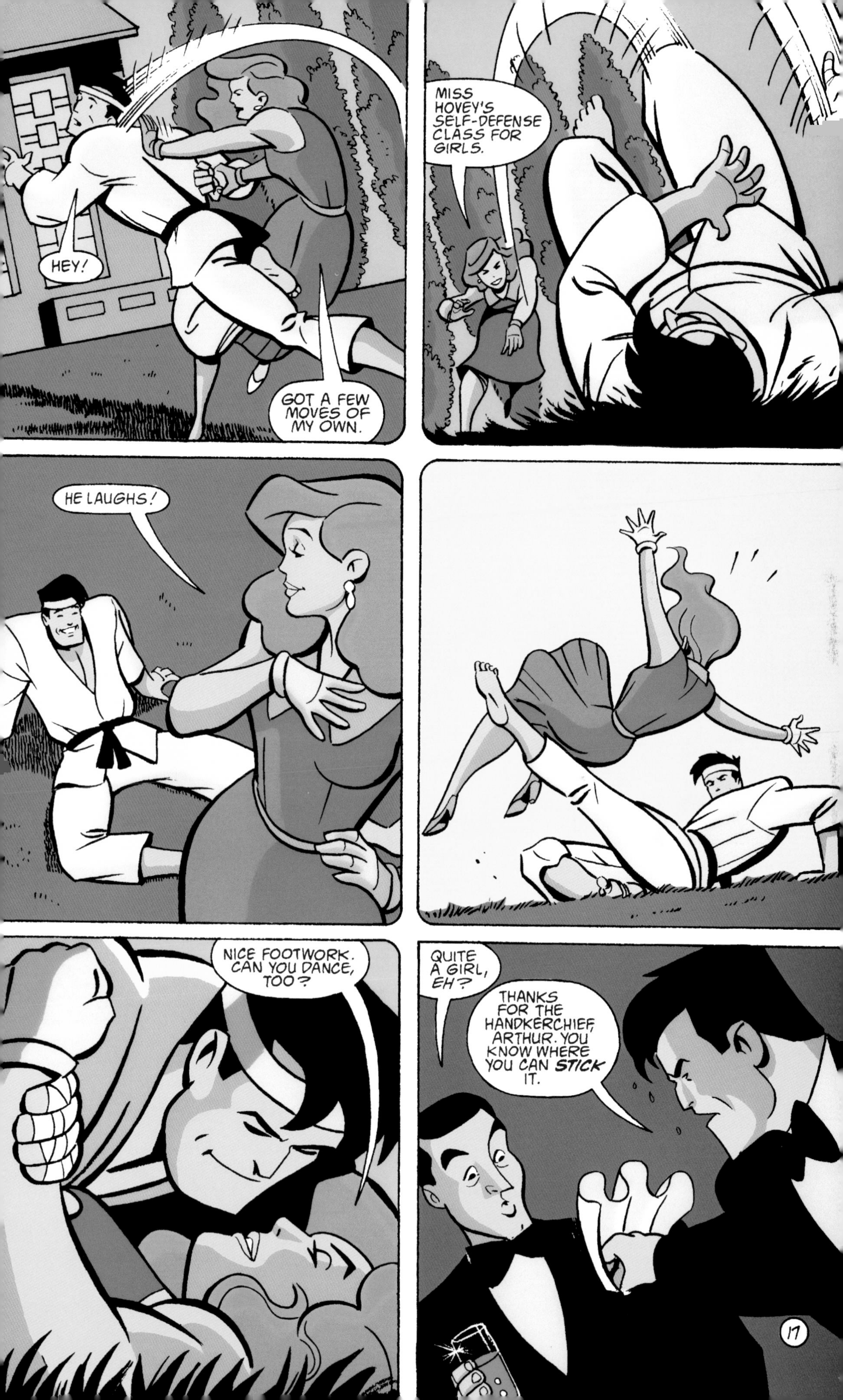
HEY!
GOT A FEW MOVES OF MY OWN.
MISS HOVEY'S SELF-DEFENSE CLASS FOR GIRLS.
HE LAUGHS!
NICE FOOTWORK. CAN YOU DANCE, TOO?
QUITE A GIRL, EH?
THANKS FOR THE HANDKERCHIEF, ARTHUR. YOU KNOW WHERE YOU CAN STICK IT.
17

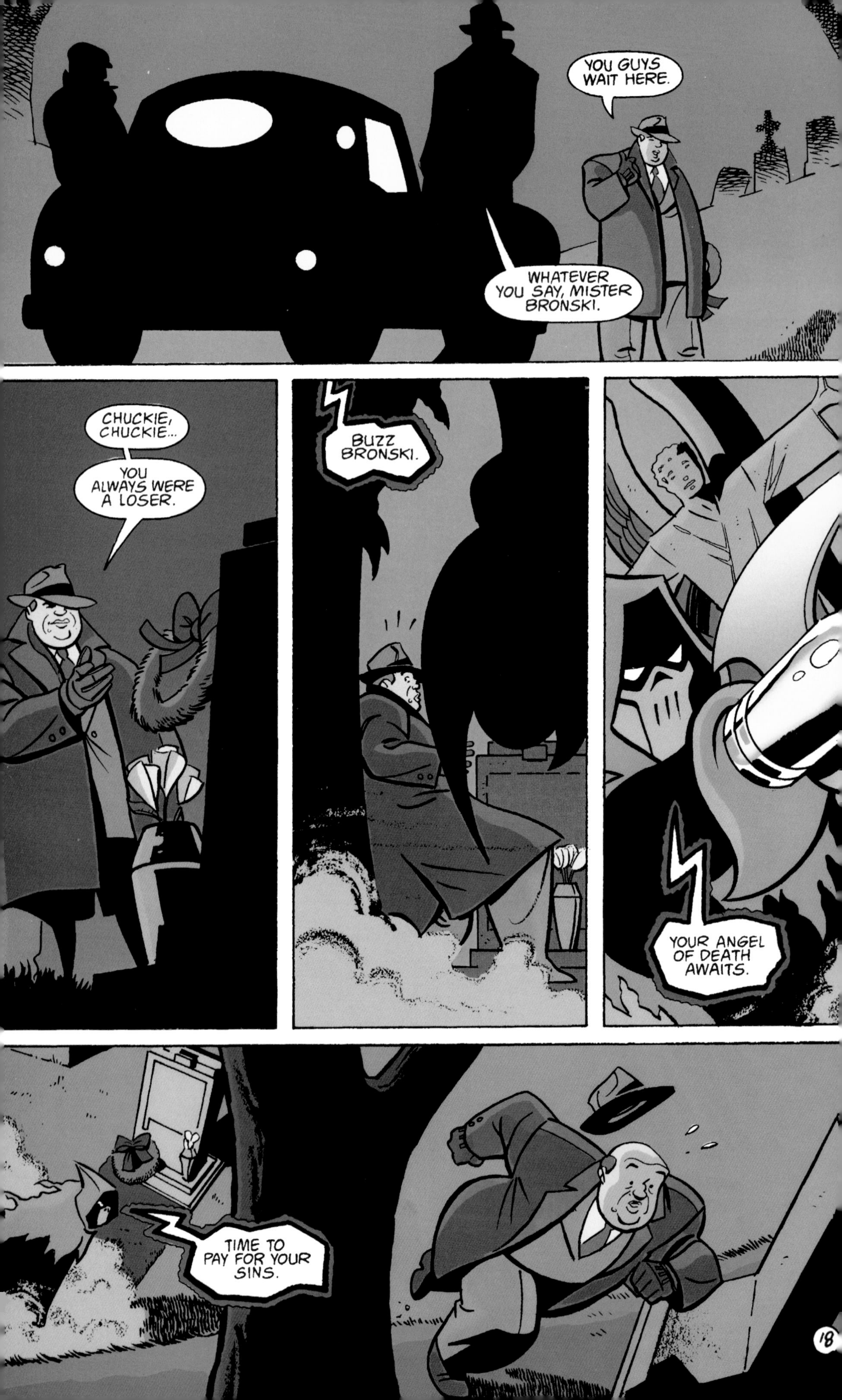
YOU GUYS WAIT HERE.
WHATEVER YOU SAY, MISTER BRONSKI.
CHUCKIE, CHUCKIE...
YOU ALWAYS WERE A LOSER.
BUZZ BRONSKI.
YOUR ANGEL OF DEATH AWAITS.
TIME TO PAY FOR YOUR SINS.

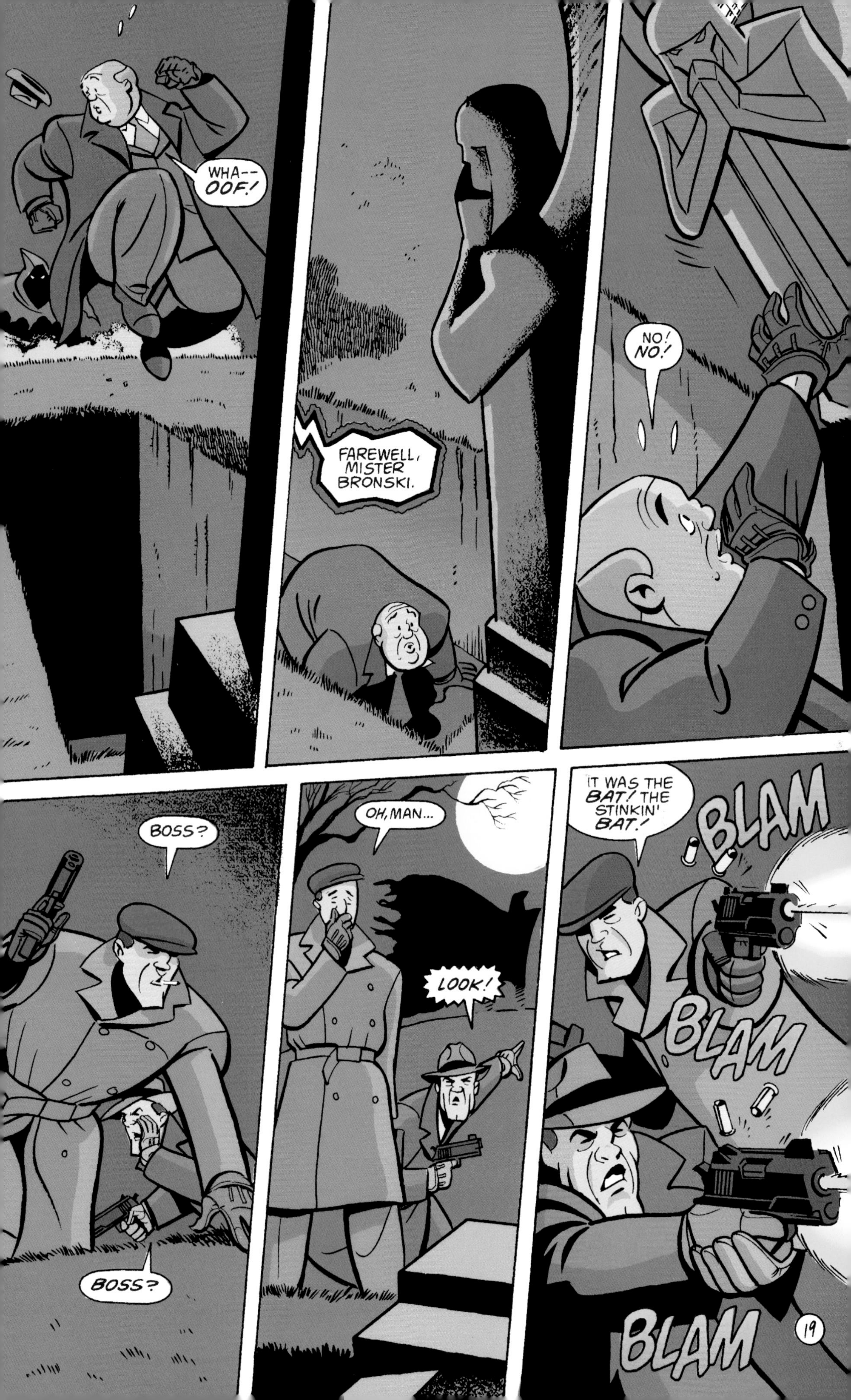
WHA--
OOF!
FAREWELL, MISTER BRONSKI.
NO! NO!
BOSS?
BOSS?
OH, MAN...
LOOK!
IT WAS THE BAT! THE STINKIN' BAT!
BLAM
BLAM
BLAM
19

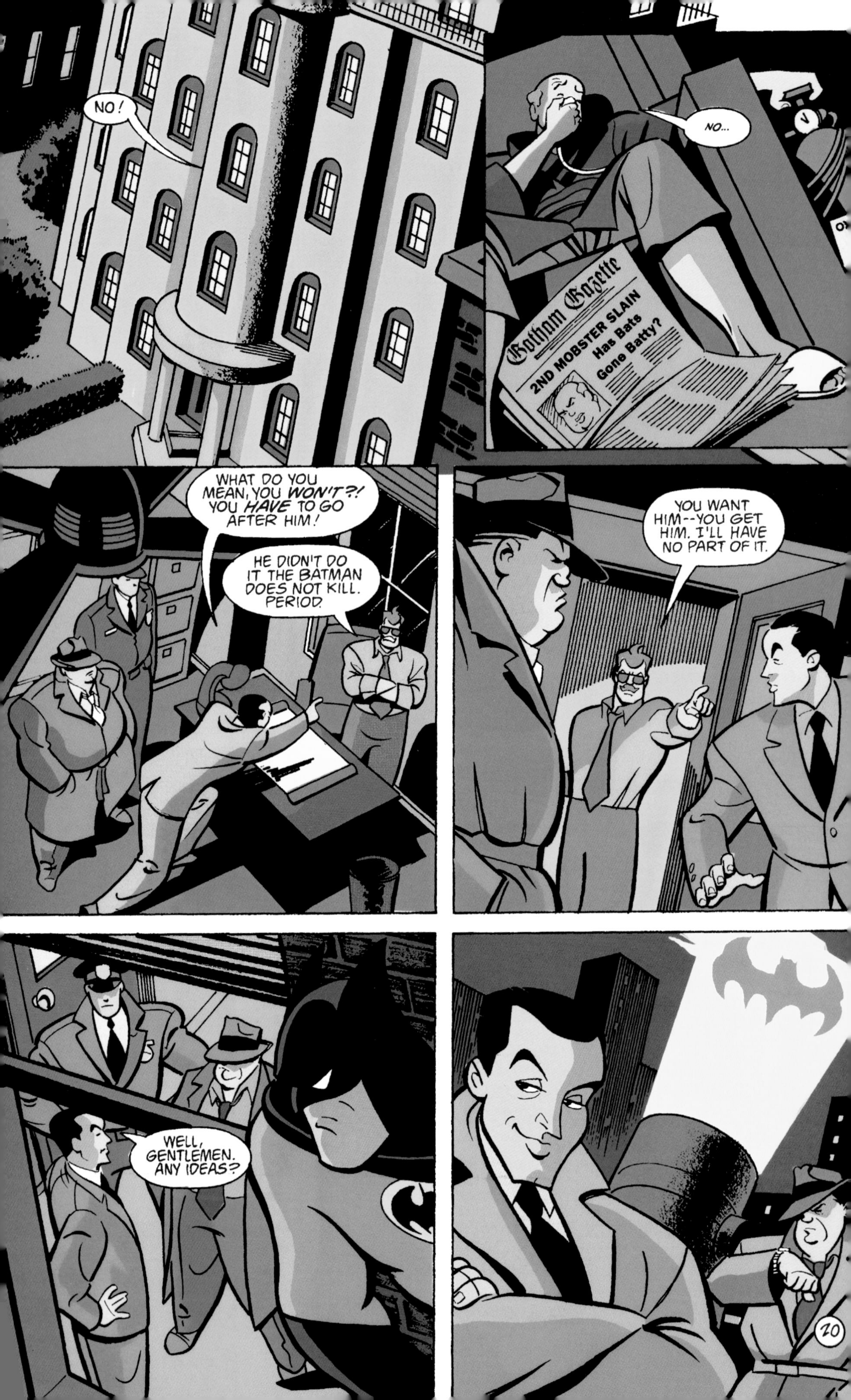
NO!
NO...
Gotham Gazette
2ND MOBSTER SLAIN
Has Bats Gone Batty?
WHAT DO YOU MEAN, YOU WON'T?! YOU HAVE TO GO AFTER HIM!
HE DIDN'T DO IT THE BATMAN DOES NOT KILL. PERIOD.
YOU WANT HIM--YOU GET HIM. I'LL HAVE NO PART OF IT.
WELL, GENTLEMEN. ANY IDEAS?
20

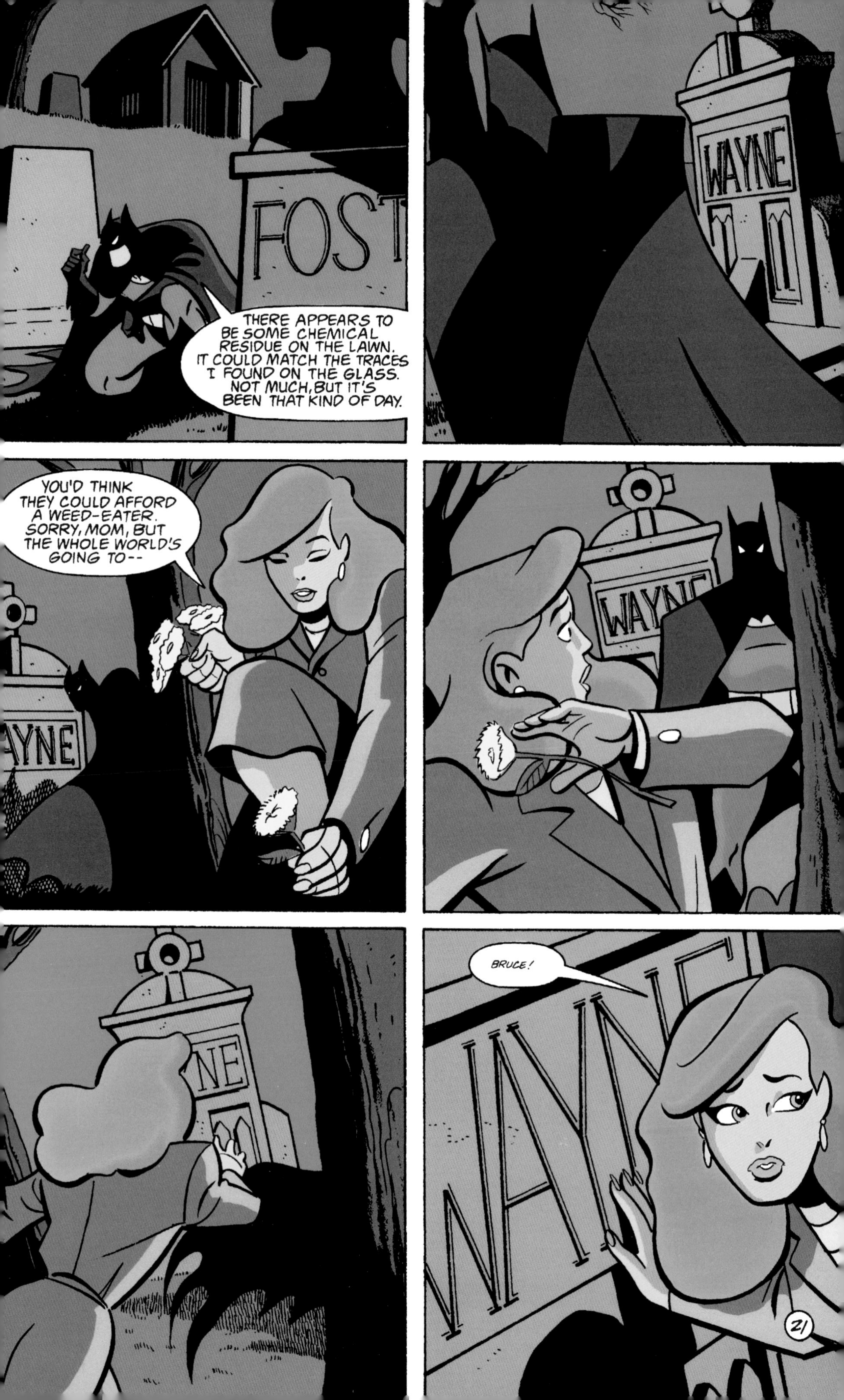
THERE APPEARS TO BE SOME CHEMICAL RESIDUE ON THE LAWN. IT COULD MATCH THE TRACES I FOUND ON THE GLASS. NOT MUCH, BUT IT'S BEEN THAT KIND OF DAY.
FOST
WAYNE
YOU'D THINK THEY COULD AFFORD A WEED-EATER. SORRY, MOM, BUT THE WHOLE WORLD'S GOING TO--
BRUCE!
21

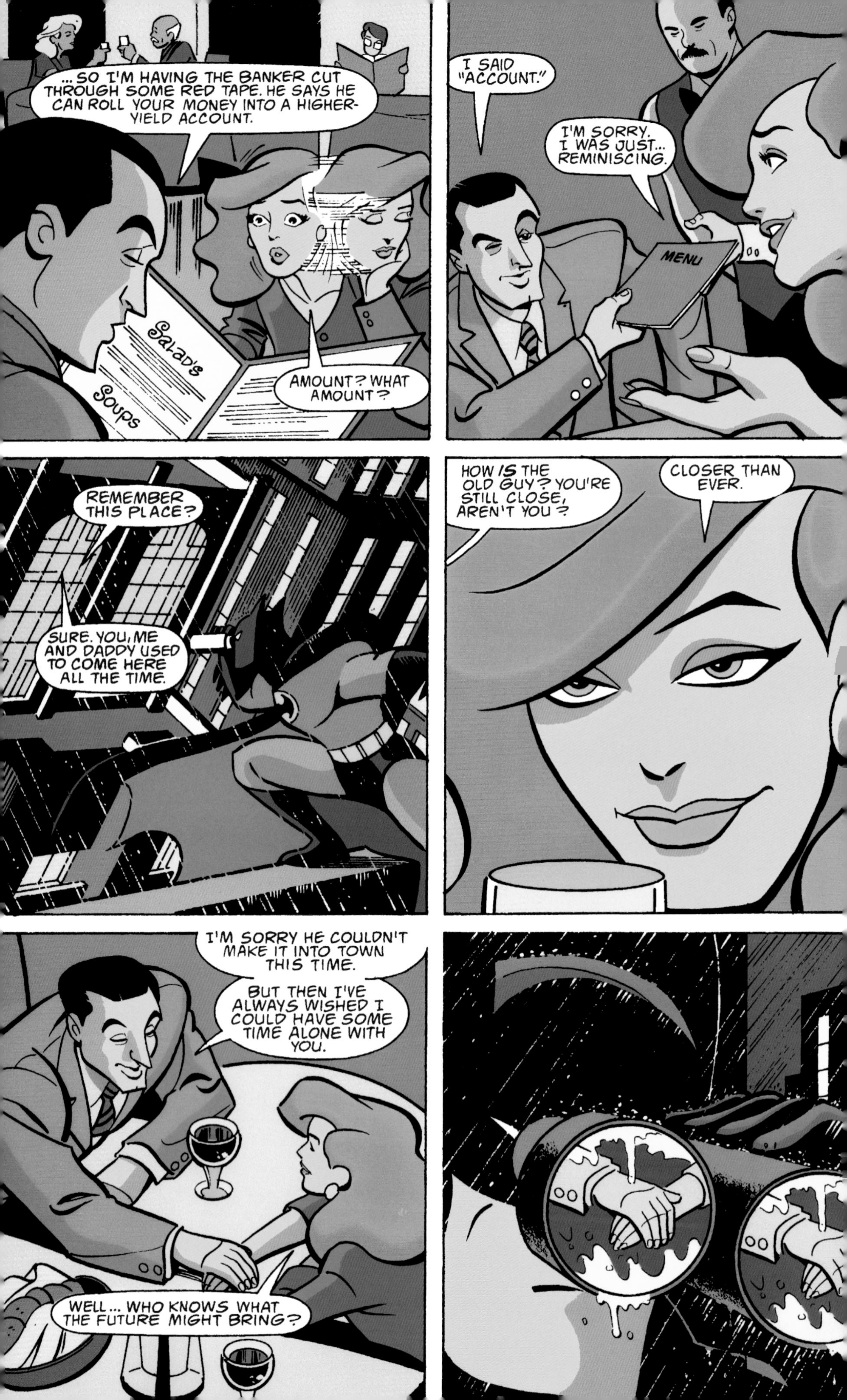
...SO I'M HAVING THE BANKER CUT THROUGH SOME RED TAPE. HE SAYS HE CAN ROLL YOUR MONEY INTO A HIGHER-YIELD ACCOUNT.
Salad's
Soups
AMOUNT? WHAT AMOUNT?
I SAID "ACCOUNT."
I'M SORRY. I WAS JUST... REMINISCING.
MENU
REMEMBER THIS PLACE?
SURE. YOU, ME AND DADDY USED TO COME HERE ALL THE TIME.
HOW *IS* THE OLD GUY? YOU'RE STILL CLOSE, AREN'T YOU?
CLOSER THAN EVER.
I'M SORRY HE COULDN'T MAKE IT INTO TOWN THIS TIME.
BUT THEN I'VE ALWAYS WISHED I COULD HAVE SOME TIME ALONE WITH YOU.
WELL... WHO KNOWS WHAT THE FUTURE MIGHT BRING?

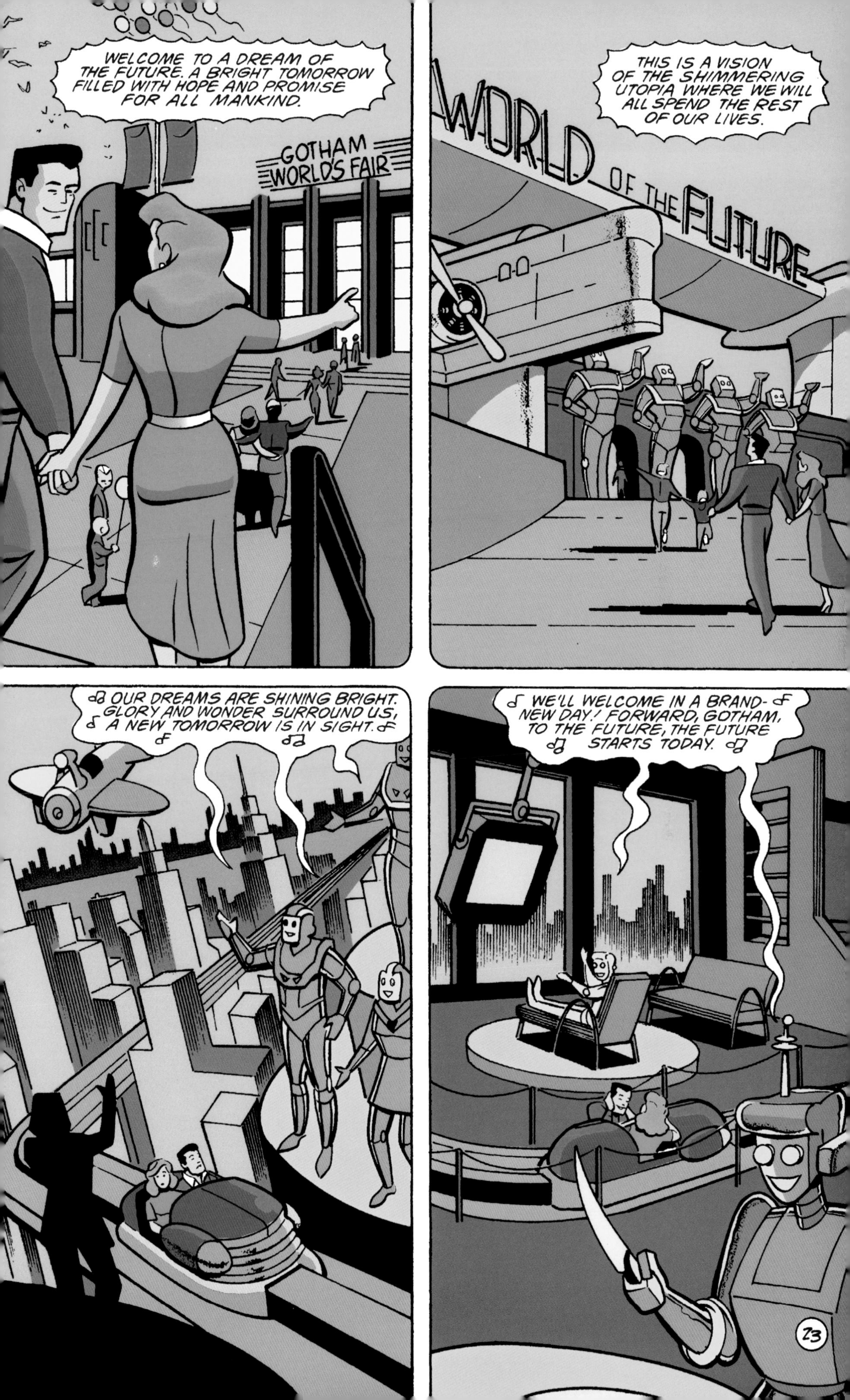

WELCOME TO A DREAM OF THE FUTURE. A BRIGHT TOMORROW FILLED WITH HOPE AND PROMISE FOR ALL MANKIND.
GOTHAM WORLD'S FAIR
THIS IS A VISION OF THE SHIMMERING UTOPIA WHERE WE WILL ALL SPEND THE REST OF OUR LIVES.
WORLD OF THE FUTURE
OUR DREAMS ARE SHINING BRIGHT. GLORY AND WONDER SURROUND US, A NEW TOMORROW IS IN SIGHT.
WE'LL WELCOME IN A BRAND-NEW DAY! FORWARD, GOTHAM, TO THE FUTURE, THE FUTURE STARTS TODAY.
23

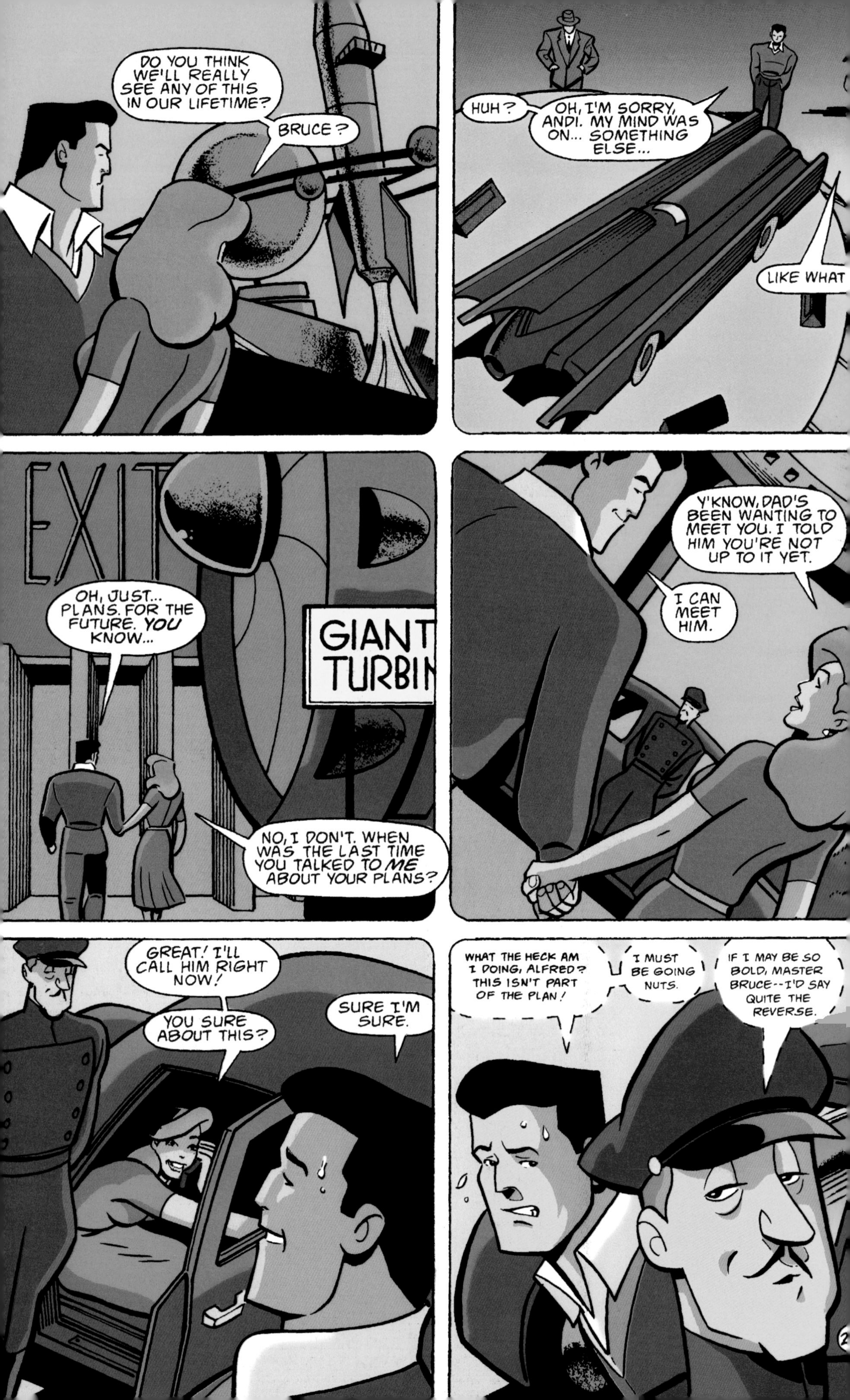
DO YOU THINK WE'LL REALLY SEE ANY OF THIS IN OUR LIFETIME?
BRUCE?
HUH?
OH, I'M SORRY, ANDI. MY MIND WAS ON... SOMETHING ELSE...
LIKE WHAT
EXIT
OH, JUST... PLANS. FOR THE FUTURE. YOU KNOW...
GIANT TURBIN
NO, I DON'T. WHEN WAS THE LAST TIME YOU TALKED TO ME ABOUT YOUR PLANS?
Y'KNOW, DAD'S BEEN WANTING TO MEET YOU. I TOLD HIM YOU'RE NOT UP TO IT YET.
I CAN MEET HIM.
GREAT! I'LL CALL HIM RIGHT NOW!
YOU SURE ABOUT THIS?
SURE I'M SURE.
WHAT THE HECK AM I DOING, ALFRED? THIS ISN'T PART OF THE PLAN!
I MUST BE GOING NUTS.
IF I MAY BE SO BOLD, MASTER BRUCE--I'D SAY QUITE THE REVERSE.

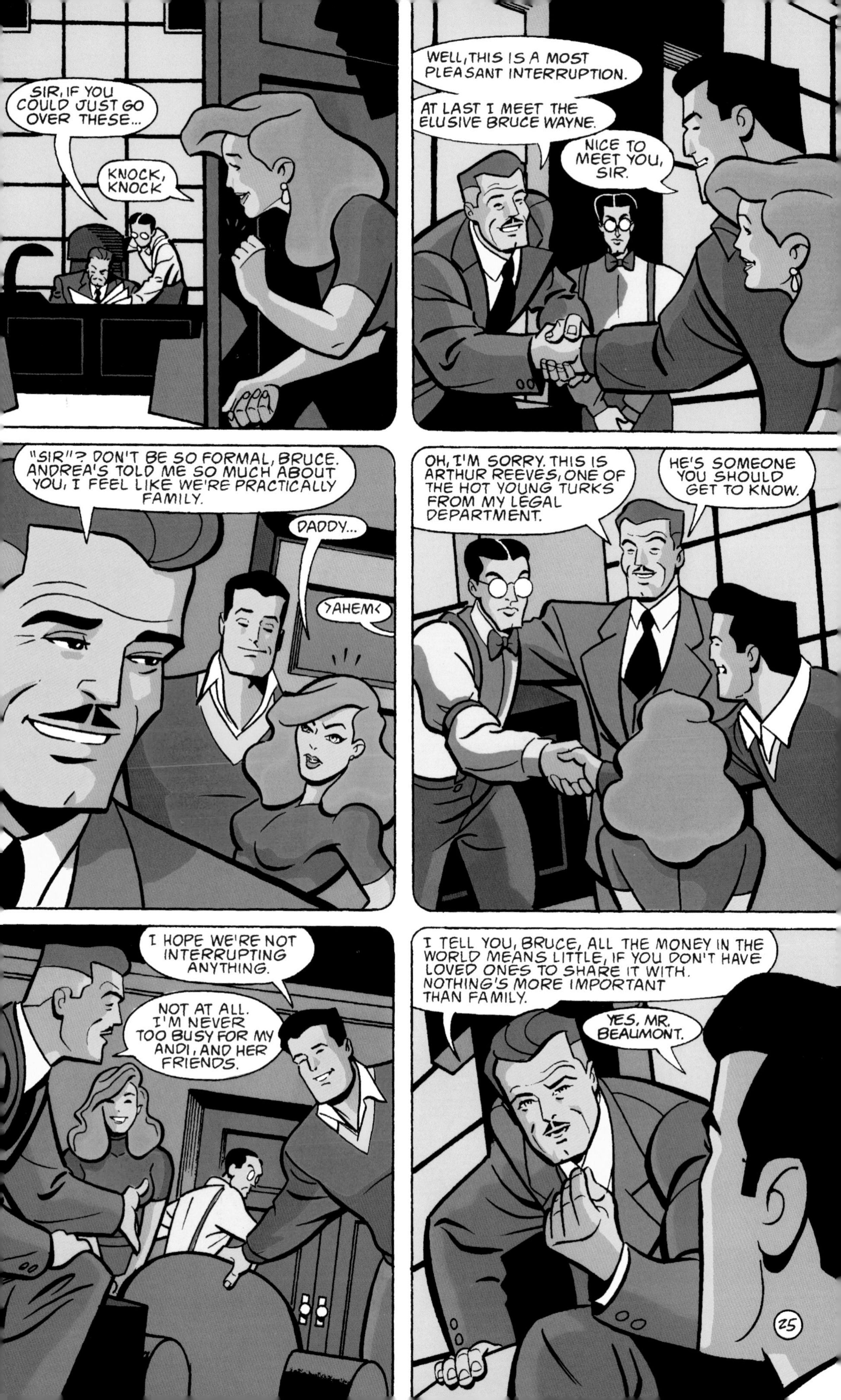

SIR, IF YOU COULD JUST GO OVER THESE...
KNOCK, KNOCK
WELL, THIS IS A MOST PLEASANT INTERRUPTION.
AT LAST I MEET THE ELUSIVE BRUCE WAYNE.
NICE TO MEET YOU, SIR.
"SIR"? DON'T BE SO FORMAL, BRUCE. ANDREA'S TOLD ME SO MUCH ABOUT YOU, I FEEL LIKE WE'RE PRACTICALLY FAMILY.
DADDY...
>AHEM<
OH, I'M SORRY. THIS IS ARTHUR REEVES, ONE OF THE HOT YOUNG TURKS FROM MY LEGAL DEPARTMENT.
HE'S SOMEONE YOU SHOULD GET TO KNOW.
I HOPE WE'RE NOT INTERRUPTING ANYTHING.
NOT AT ALL. I'M NEVER TOO BUSY FOR MY ANDI, AND HER FRIENDS.
I TELL YOU, BRUCE, ALL THE MONEY IN THE WORLD MEANS LITTLE, IF YOU DON'T HAVE LOVED ONES TO SHARE IT WITH. NOTHING'S MORE IMPORTANT THAN FAMILY.
YES, MR. BEAUMONT.

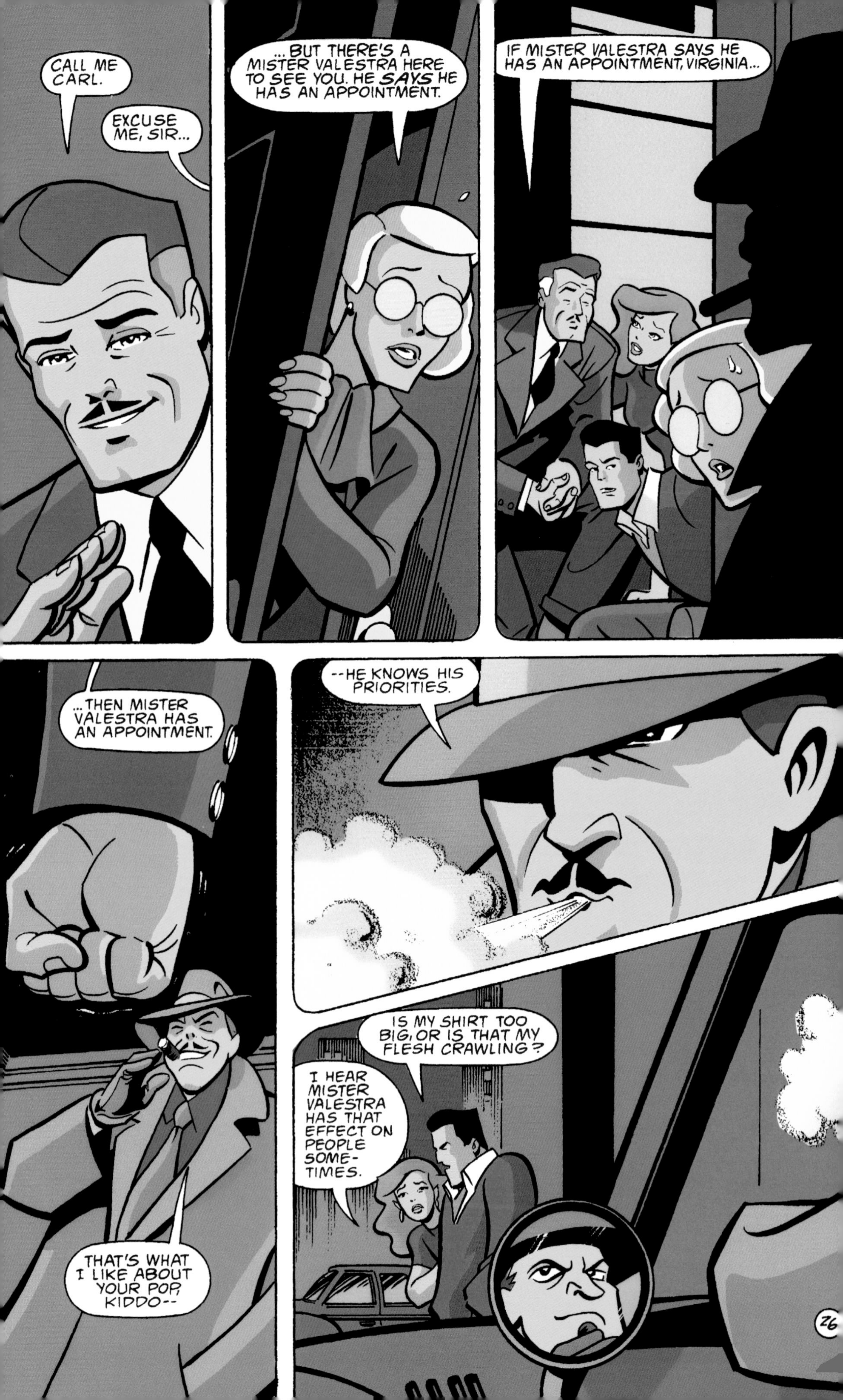
CALL ME CARL.
EXCUSE ME, SIR...
... BUT THERE'S A MISTER VALESTRA HERE TO SEE YOU. HE SAYS HE HAS AN APPOINTMENT.
IF MISTER VALESTRA SAYS HE HAS AN APPOINTMENT, VIRGINIA...
...THEN MISTER VALESTRA HAS AN APPOINTMENT.
THAT'S WHAT I LIKE ABOUT YOUR POP, KIDDO--
--HE KNOWS HIS PRIORITIES.
IS MY SHIRT TOO BIG, OR IS THAT MY FLESH CRAWLING?
I HEAR MISTER VALESTRA HAS THAT EFFECT ON PEOPLE SOME-TIMES.
26

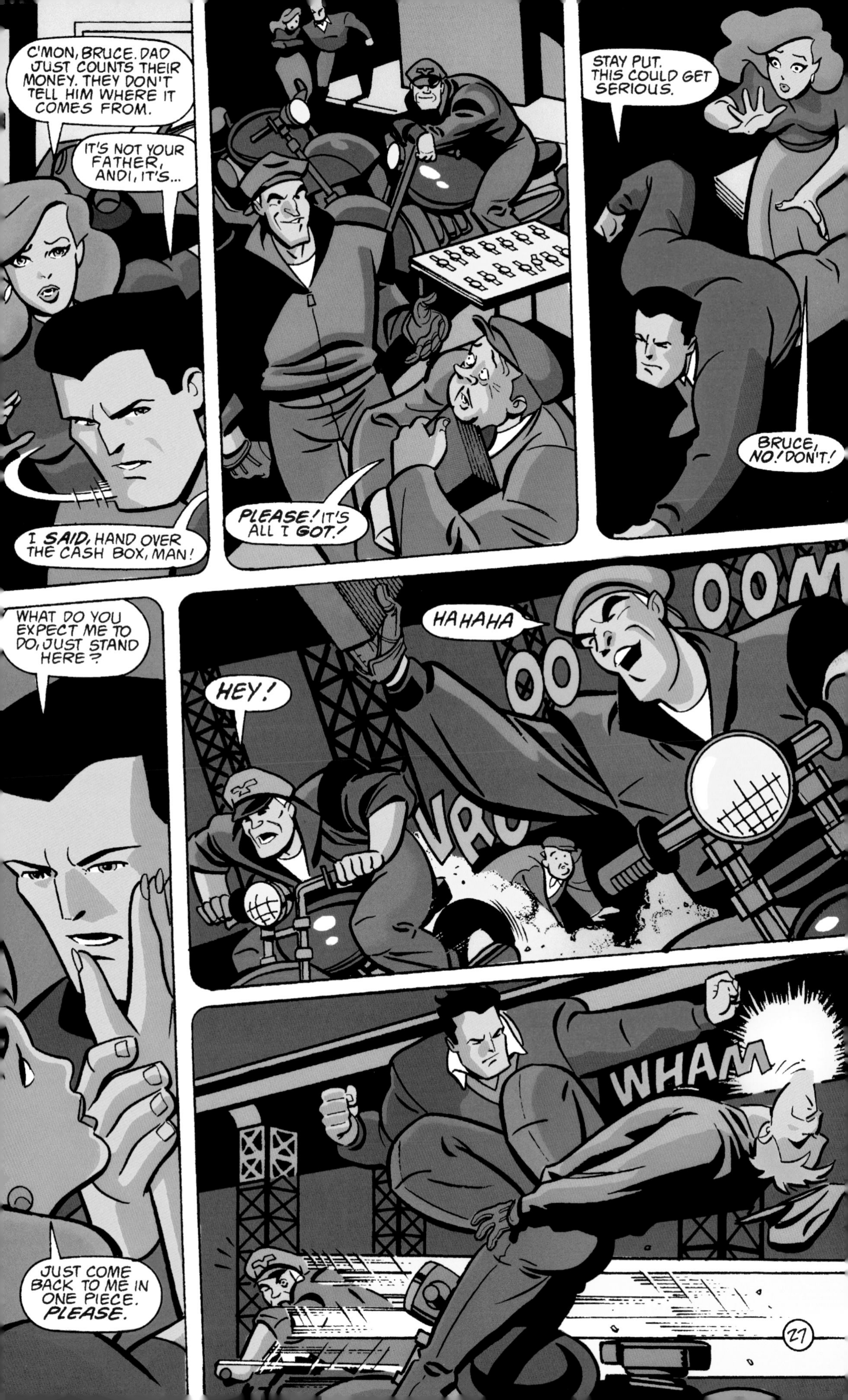

C'MON, BRUCE. DAD JUST COUNTS THEIR MONEY. THEY DON'T TELL HIM WHERE IT COMES FROM.
IT'S NOT YOUR FATHER, ANDI, IT'S...
I SAID, HAND OVER THE CASH BOX, MAN!
PLEASE! IT'S ALL I GOT!
STAY PUT. THIS COULD GET SERIOUS.
BRUCE, NO! DON'T!
WHAT DO YOU EXPECT ME TO DO, JUST STAND HERE?
JUST COME BACK TO ME IN ONE PIECE. PLEASE.
HAHAHA
HEY!
VROOOOOM
WHAM
27

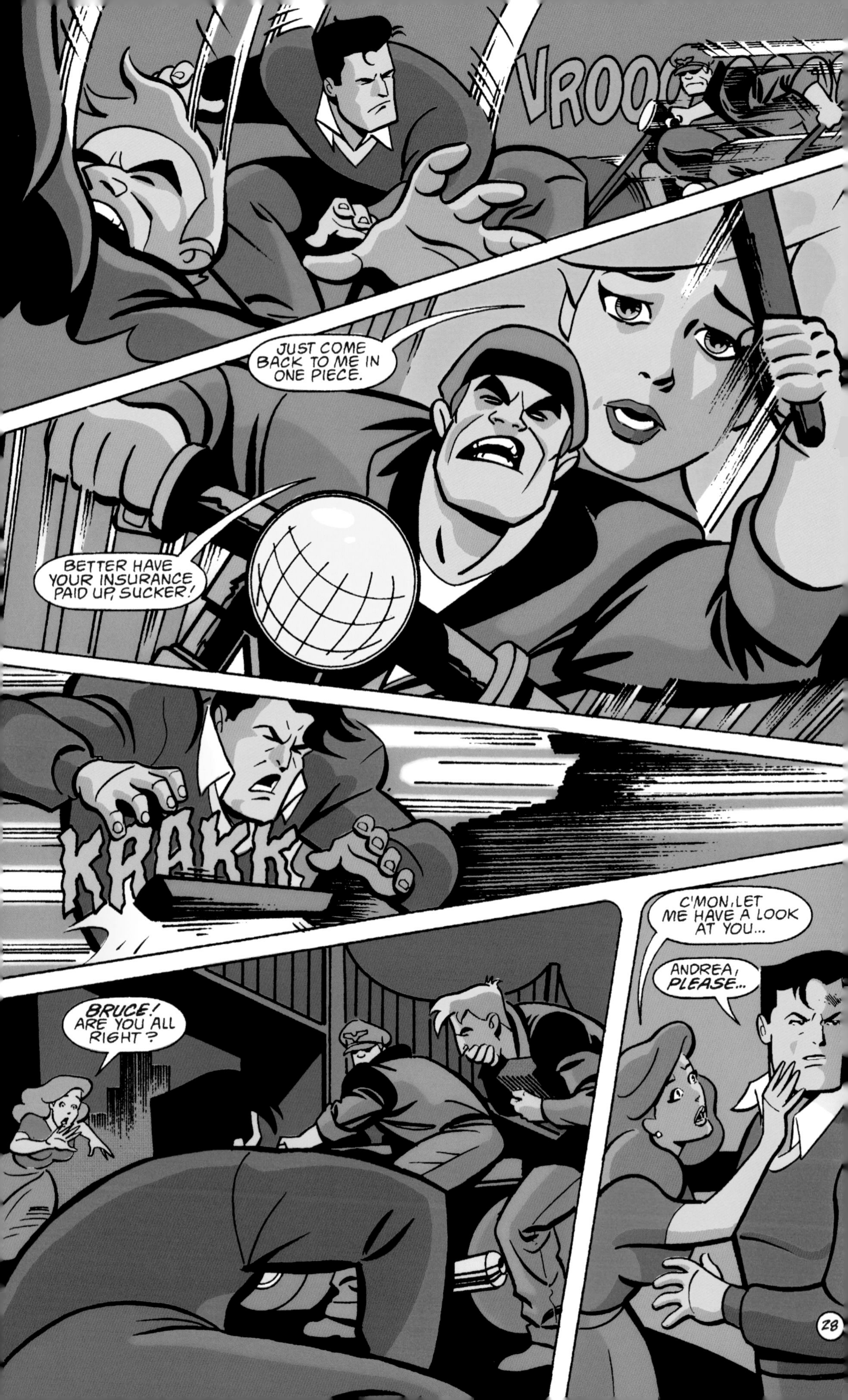
VROOOOOOOOM
JUST COME BACK TO ME IN ONE PIECE.
BETTER HAVE YOUR INSURANCE PAID UP, SUCKER!
KRAKK
BRUCE! ARE YOU ALL RIGHT?
C'MON, LET ME HAVE A LOOK AT YOU...
ANDREA, PLEASE...

WHAT AM I STILL DOING THIS FOR?
IT'S GOTTA BE ONE OR THE OTHER-- I CAN'T HAVE IT BOTH WAYS. I CAN'T PUT MYSELF ON THE LINE AS LONG AS THERE'S SOMEONE WAITING FOR ME TO COME HOME.
MISS BEAUMONT WOULD BE GLAD TO KNOW YOU FEEL THAT WAY, MASTER BRUCE.
SHE'S HOLDING ON LINE ONE.
ALFRED, I CAN'T. NOT NOW.
WHAT SHALL I SAY?
I DON'T KNOW. I JUST DON'T KNOW.
THUD

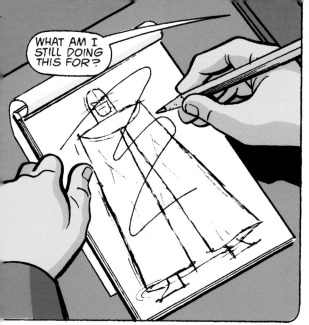

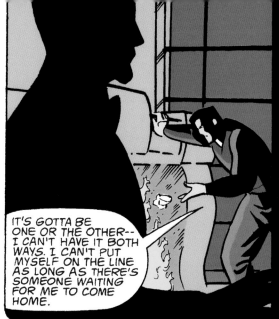

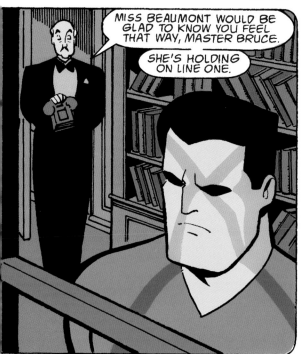

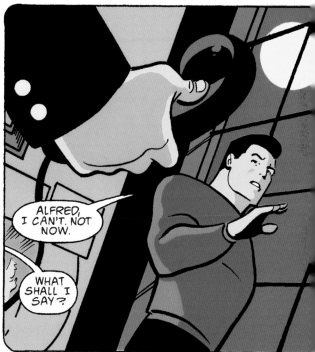

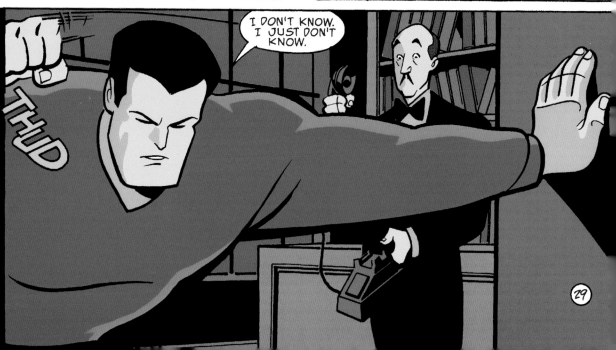

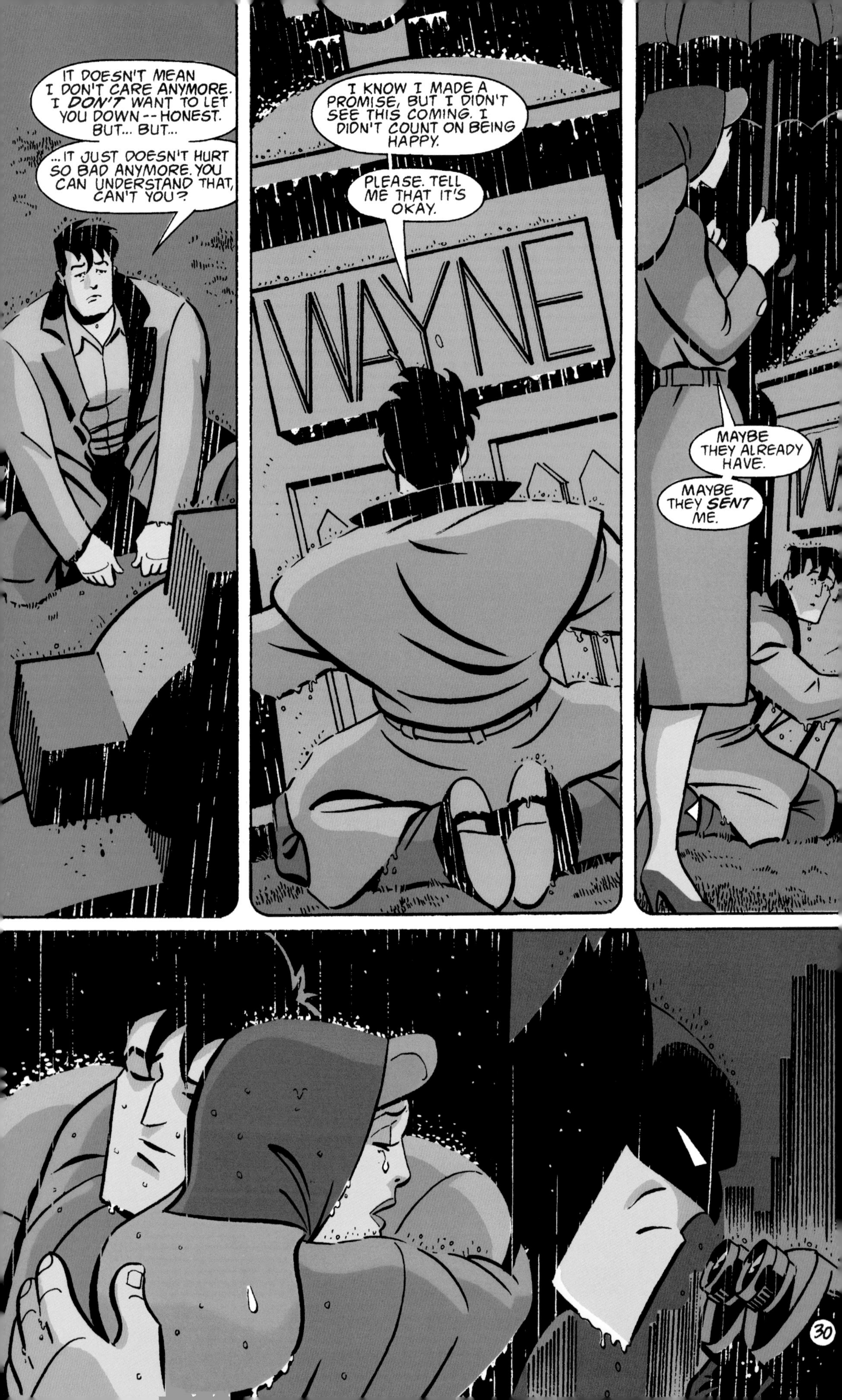
IT DOESN'T MEAN I DON'T CARE ANYMORE. I DON'T WANT TO LET YOU DOWN--HONEST. BUT... BUT...
...IT JUST DOESN'T HURT SO BAD ANYMORE. YOU CAN UNDERSTAND THAT, CAN'T YOU?
I KNOW I MADE A PROMISE, BUT I DIDN'T SEE THIS COMING. I DIDN'T COUNT ON BEING HAPPY.
PLEASE. TELL ME THAT IT'S OKAY.
WAYNE
MAYBE THEY ALREADY HAVE.
MAYBE THEY SENT ME.

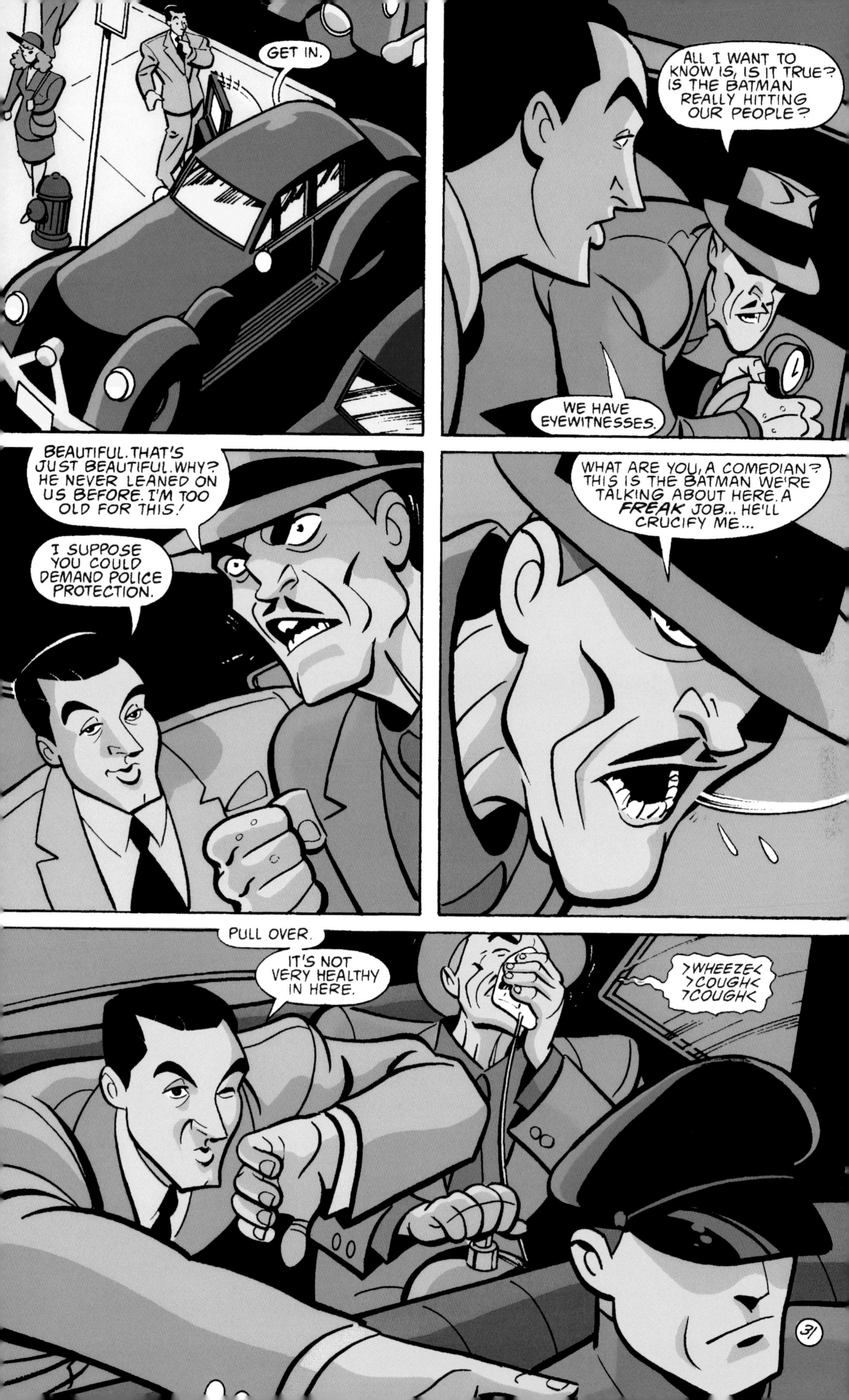
GET IN.
ALL I WANT TO KNOW IS, IS IT TRUE? IS THE BATMAN REALLY HITTING OUR PEOPLE?
WE HAVE EYEWITNESSES.
BEAUTIFUL. THAT'S JUST BEAUTIFUL. WHY? HE NEVER LEANED ON US BEFORE. I'M TOO OLD FOR THIS!
I SUPPOSE YOU COULD DEMAND POLICE PROTECTION.
WHAT ARE YOU, A COMEDIAN? THIS IS THE BATMAN WE'RE TALKING ABOUT HERE. A FREAK JOB... HE'LL CRUCIFY ME...
PULL OVER.
IT'S NOT VERY HEALTHY IN HERE.
>WHEEZE<
>COUGH<
>COUGH<

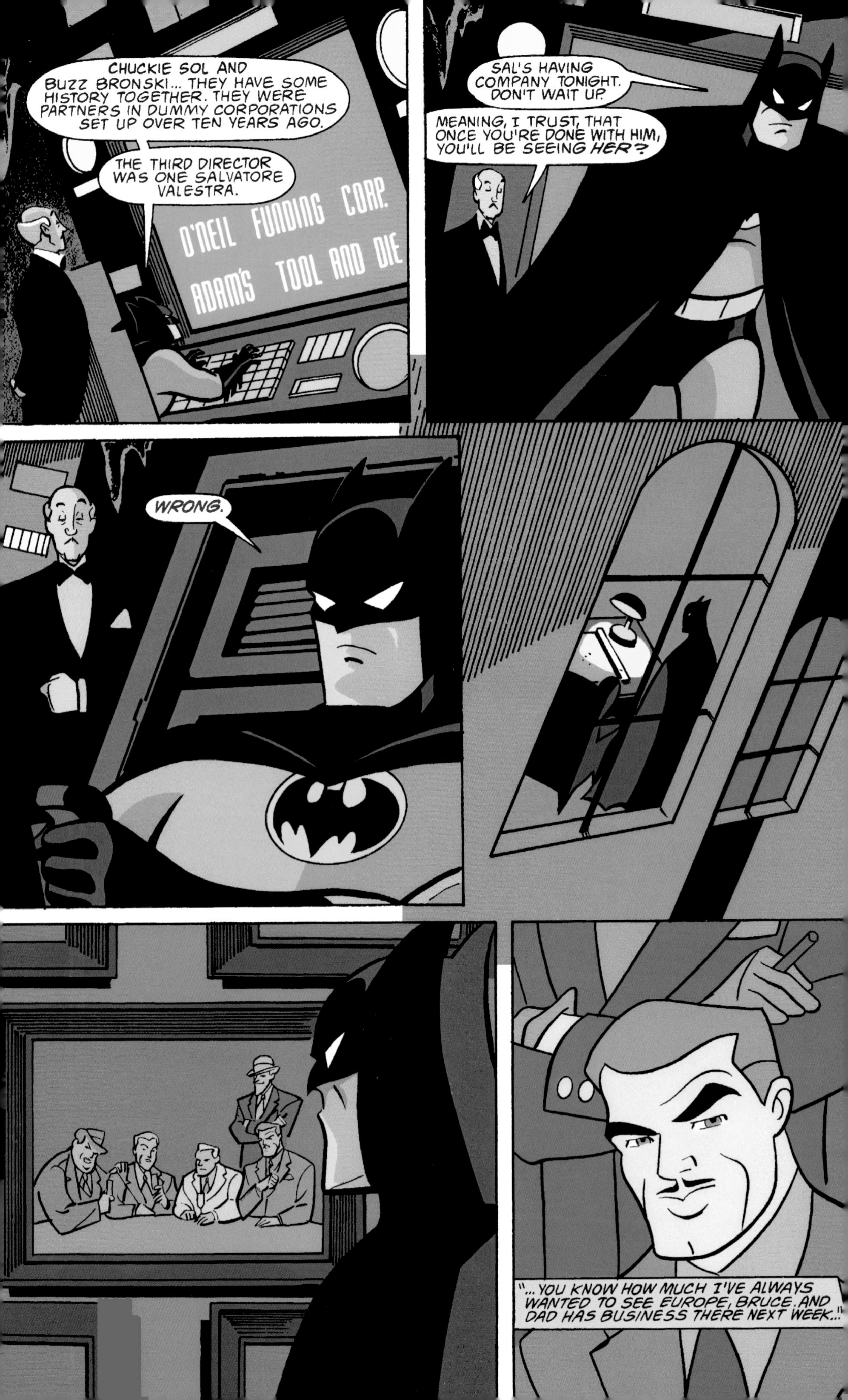
CHUCKIE SOL AND BUZZ BRONSKI... THEY HAVE SOME HISTORY TOGETHER. THEY WERE PARTNERS IN DUMMY CORPORATIONS SET UP OVER TEN YEARS AGO.
THE THIRD DIRECTOR WAS ONE SALVATORE VALESTRA.
O'NEIL FUNDING CORP.
ADAM'S TOOL AND DIE
SAL'S HAVING COMPANY TONIGHT. DON'T WAIT UP.
MEANING, I TRUST, THAT ONCE YOU'RE DONE WITH HIM, YOU'LL BE SEEING *HER*?
WRONG.
"...YOU KNOW HOW MUCH I'VE ALWAYS WANTED TO SEE EUROPE, BRUCE. AND DAD HAS BUSINESS THERE NEXT WEEK..."

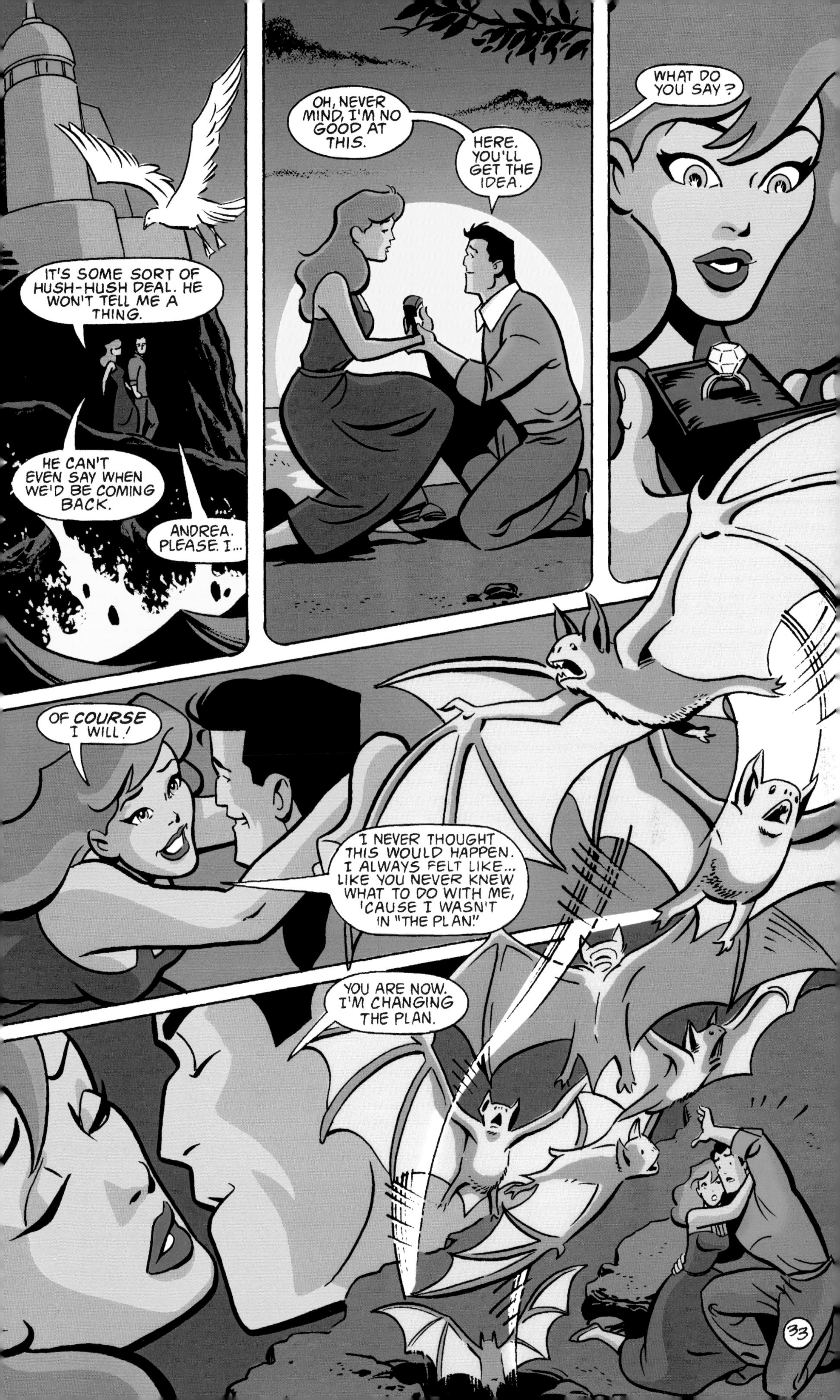
IT'S SOME SORT OF HUSH-HUSH DEAL. HE WON'T TELL ME A THING.
HE CAN'T EVEN SAY WHEN WE'D BE COMING BACK.
ANDREA. PLEASE. I...
OH, NEVER MIND, I'M NO GOOD AT THIS.
HERE. YOU'LL GET THE IDEA.
WHAT DO YOU SAY?
OF COURSE I WILL!
I NEVER THOUGHT THIS WOULD HAPPEN. I ALWAYS FELT LIKE... LIKE YOU NEVER KNEW WHAT TO DO WITH ME, 'CAUSE I WASN'T IN "THE PLAN."
YOU ARE NOW. I'M CHANGING THE PLAN.
33

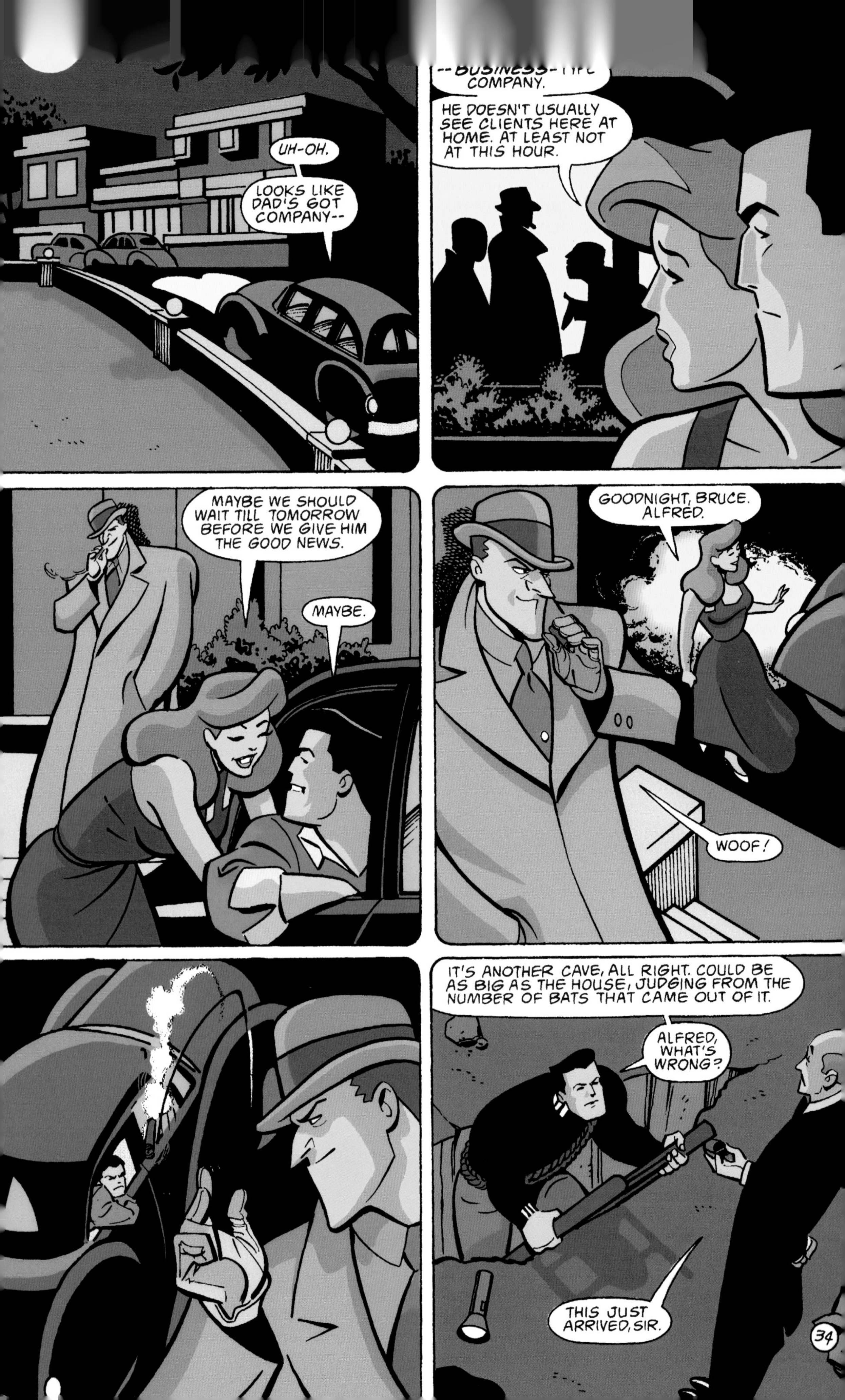
UH-OH.
LOOKS LIKE DAD'S GOT COMPANY--
COMPANY.
HE DOESN'T USUALLY SEE CLIENTS HERE AT HOME. AT LEAST NOT AT THIS HOUR.
MAYBE WE SHOULD WAIT TILL TOMORROW BEFORE WE GIVE HIM THE GOOD NEWS.
MAYBE.
GOODNIGHT, BRUCE. ALFRED.
WOOF!
IT'S ANOTHER CAVE, ALL RIGHT. COULD BE AS BIG AS THE HOUSE, JUDGING FROM THE NUMBER OF BATS THAT CAME OUT OF IT.
ALFRED, WHAT'S WRONG?
THIS JUST ARRIVED, SIR.

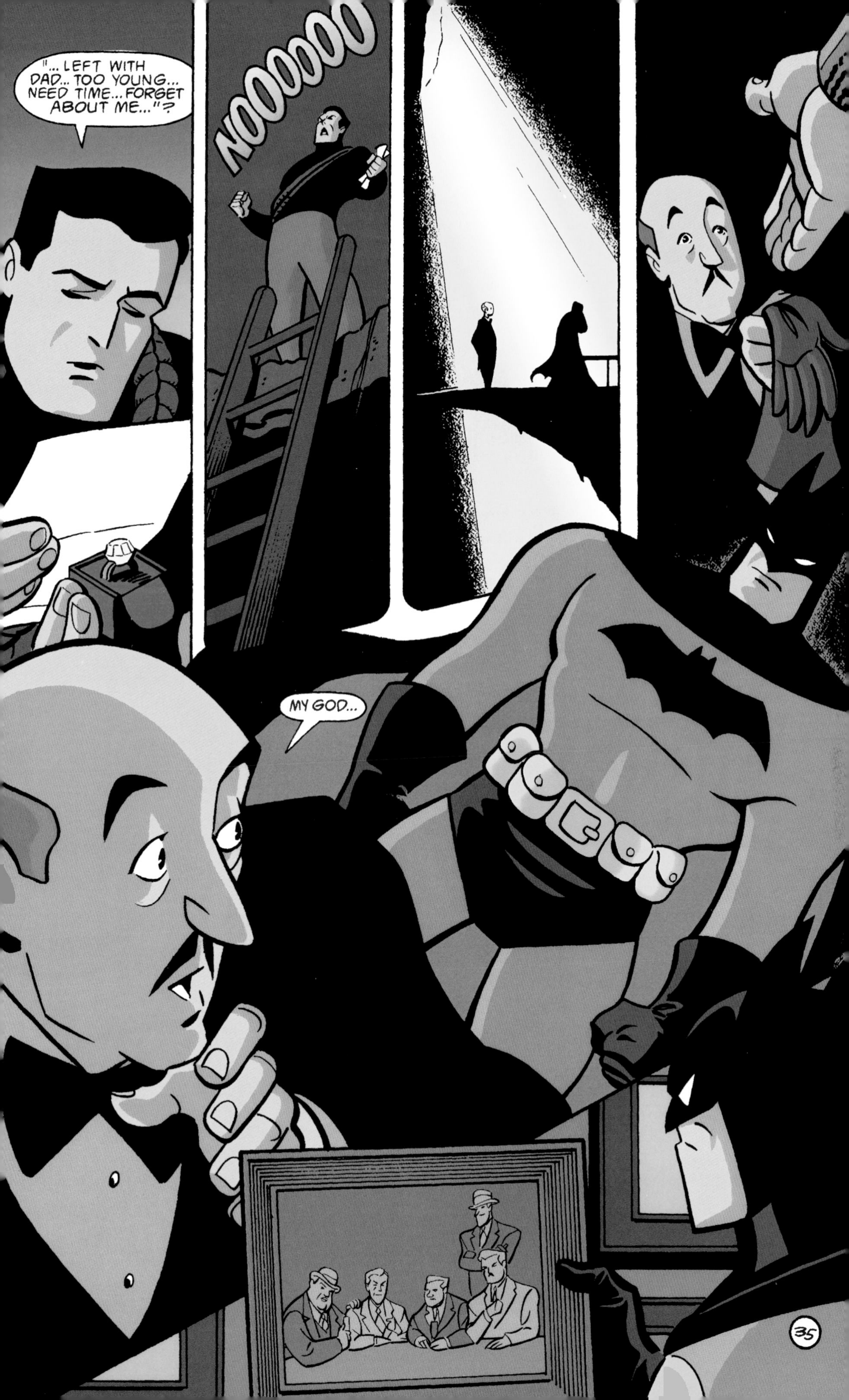
"... LEFT WITH DAD... TOO YOUNG... NEED TIME... FORGET ABOUT ME..."?
NOOOOOO
MY GOD...

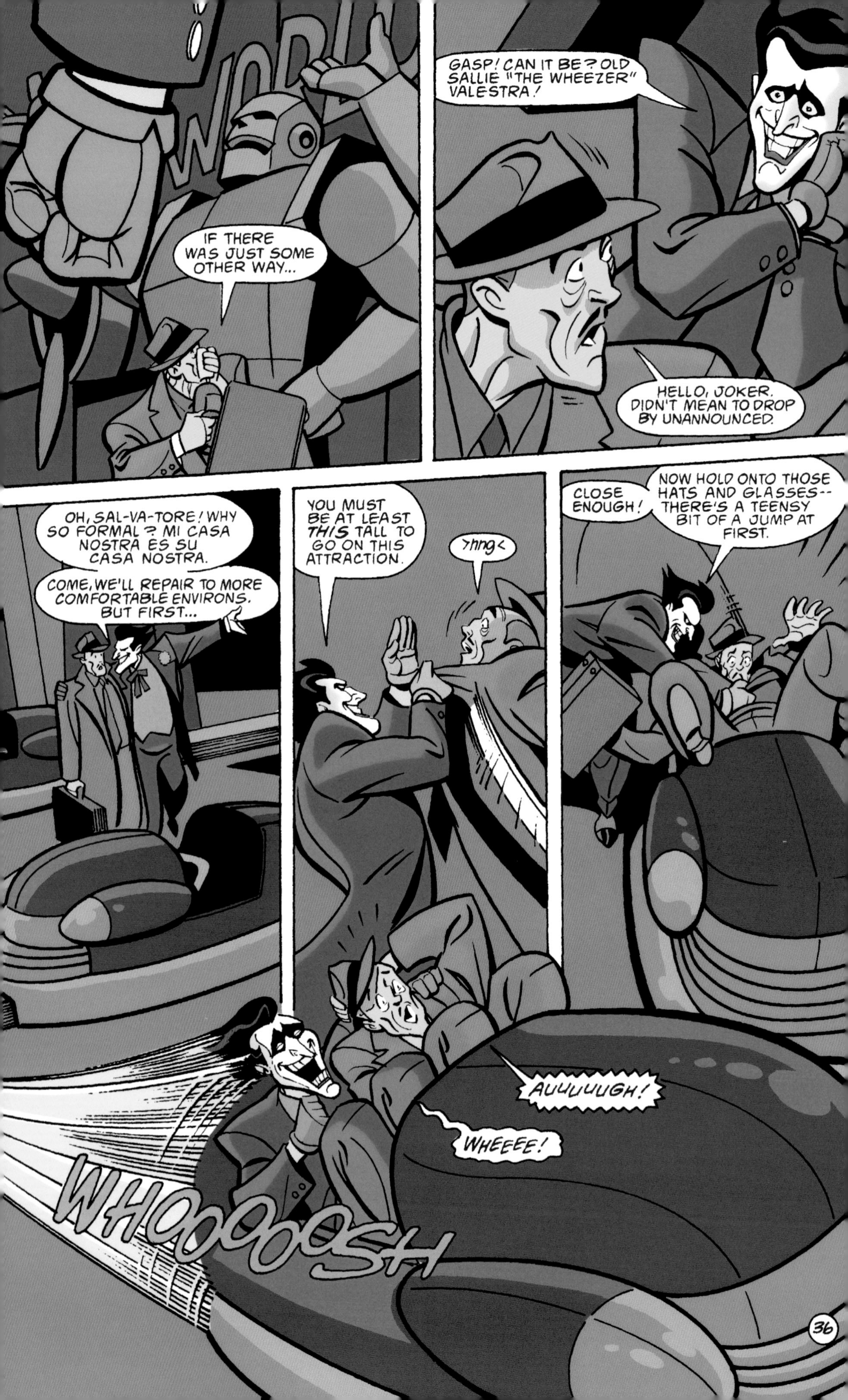
WOOD
IF THERE WAS JUST SOME OTHER WAY...
GASP! CAN IT BE? OLD SALLIE "THE WHEEZER" VALESTRA!
HELLO, JOKER. DIDN'T MEAN TO DROP BY UNANNOUNCED.
OH, SAL-VA-TORE! WHY SO FORMAL? MI CASA NOSTRA ES SU CASA NOSTRA.
COME, WE'LL REPAIR TO MORE COMFORTABLE ENVIRONS. BUT FIRST...
YOU MUST BE AT LEAST *THIS* TALL TO GO ON THIS ATTRACTION.
>hng<
CLOSE ENOUGH!
NOW HOLD ONTO THOSE HATS AND GLASSES-- THERE'S A TEENSY BIT OF A JUMP AT FIRST.
AUUUUUGH!
WHEEEE!
WHOOOOOSH

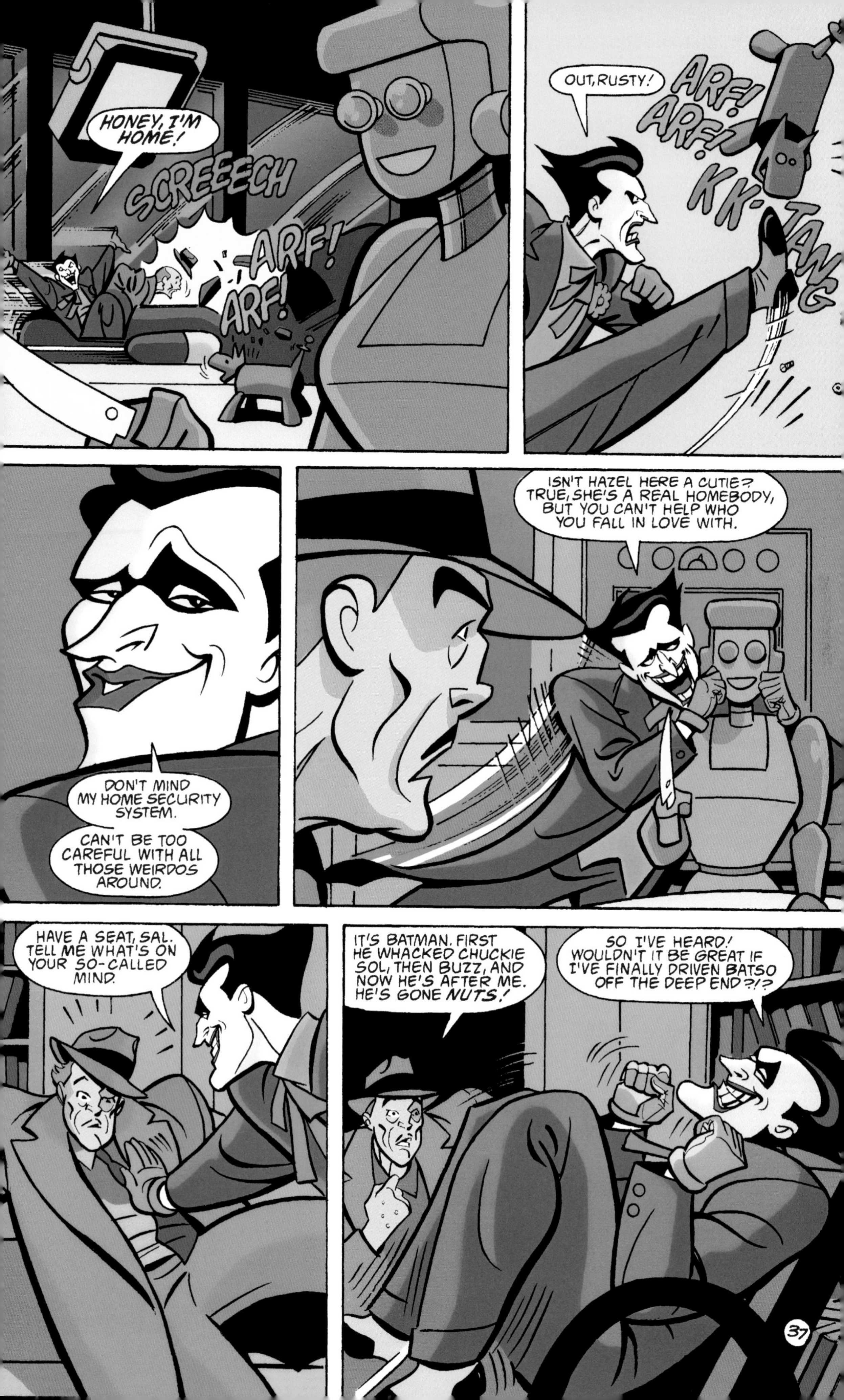
HONEY, I'M HOME!
SCREEEECH
ARF!
ARF!
OUT, RUSTY!
ARF!
ARF!
KK-TANG
DON'T MIND MY HOME SECURITY SYSTEM.
CAN'T BE TOO CAREFUL WITH ALL THOSE WEIRDOS AROUND.
ISN'T HAZEL HERE A CUTIE? TRUE, SHE'S A REAL HOMEBODY, BUT YOU CAN'T HELP WHO YOU FALL IN LOVE WITH.
HAVE A SEAT, SAL. TELL ME WHAT'S ON YOUR SO-CALLED MIND.
IT'S BATMAN. FIRST HE WHACKED CHUCKIE SOL, THEN BUZZ, AND NOW HE'S AFTER ME. HE'S GONE *NUTS*!
SO I'VE HEARD! WOULDN'T IT BE GREAT IF I'VE FINALLY DRIVEN BATSO OFF THE DEEP END?!?
37

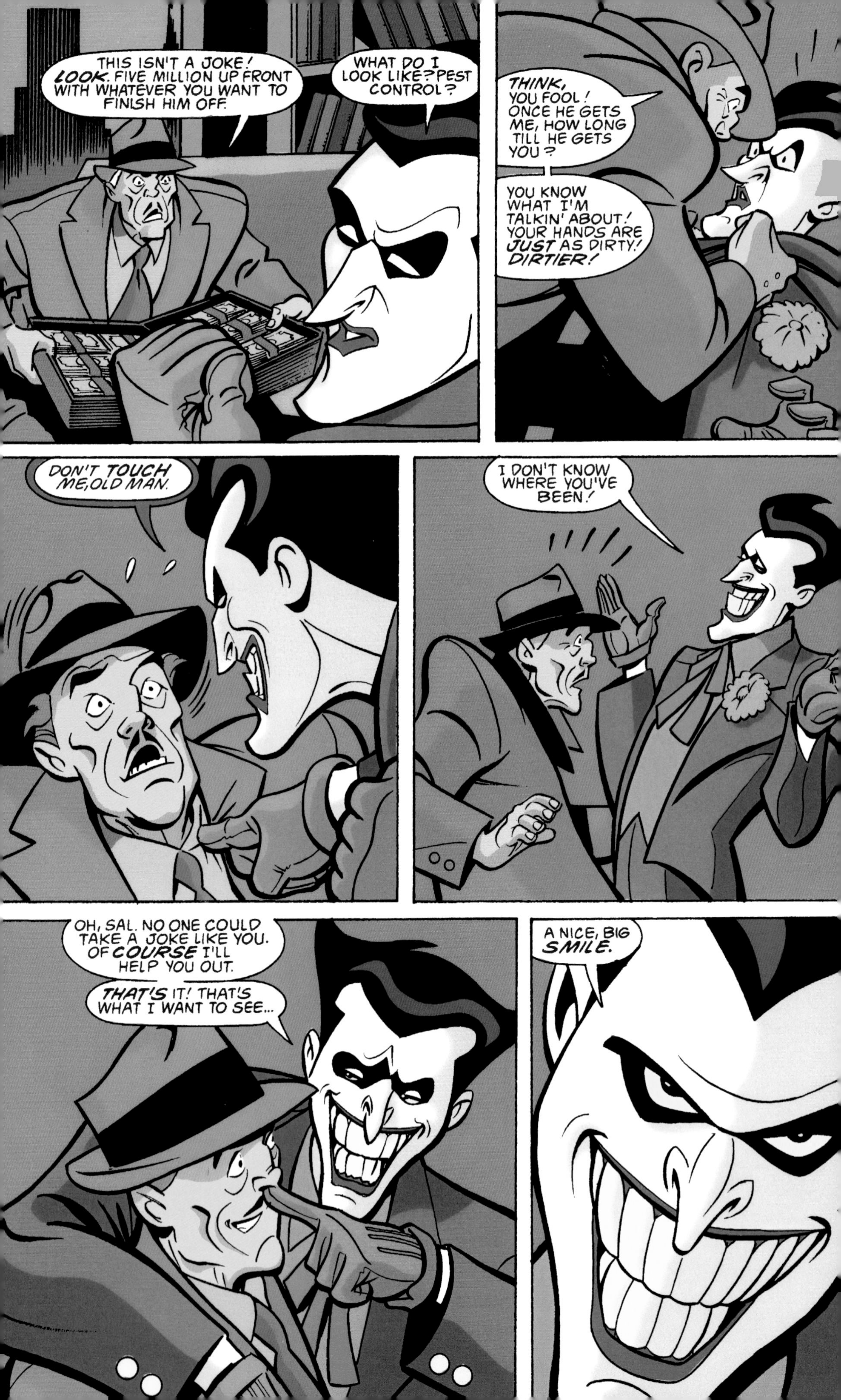
THIS ISN'T A JOKE! LOOK. FIVE MILLION UP FRONT WITH WHATEVER YOU WANT TO FINISH HIM OFF.
WHAT DO I LOOK LIKE? PEST CONTROL?
THINK, YOU FOOL! ONCE HE GETS ME, HOW LONG TILL HE GETS YOU?
YOU KNOW WHAT I'M TALKIN' ABOUT! YOUR HANDS ARE JUST AS DIRTY! DIRTIER!
DON'T TOUCH ME, OLD MAN.
I DON'T KNOW WHERE YOU'VE BEEN!
OH, SAL. NO ONE COULD TAKE A JOKE LIKE YOU. OF COURSE I'LL HELP YOU OUT.
THAT'S IT! THAT'S WHAT I WANT TO SEE...
A NICE, BIG SMILE.

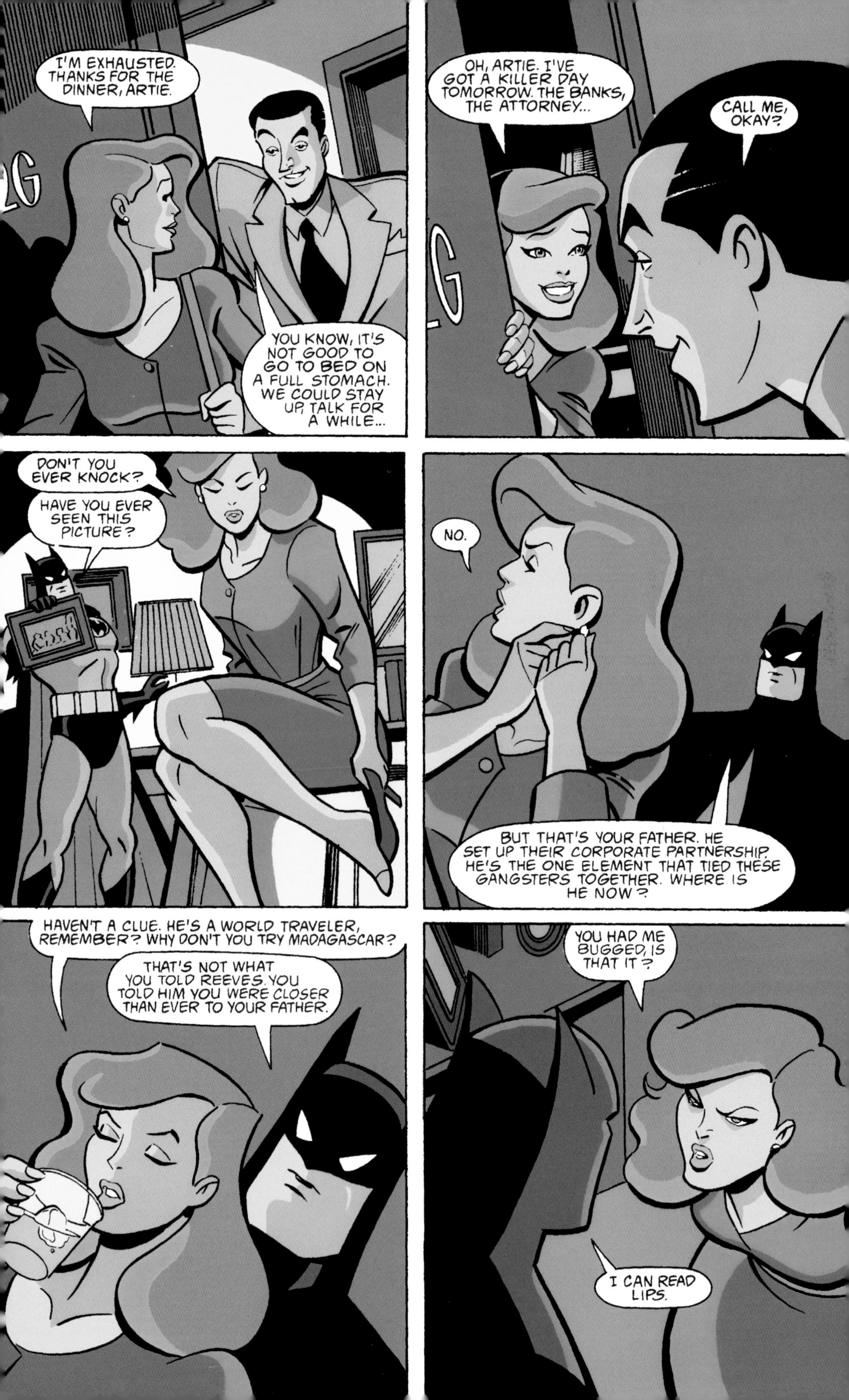
I'M EXHAUSTED. THANKS FOR THE DINNER, ARTIE.
YOU KNOW, IT'S NOT GOOD TO GO TO BED ON A FULL STOMACH. WE COULD STAY UP, TALK FOR A WHILE...
OH, ARTIE. I'VE GOT A KILLER DAY TOMORROW. THE BANKS, THE ATTORNEY...
CALL ME, OKAY?
DON'T YOU EVER KNOCK?
HAVE YOU EVER SEEN THIS PICTURE?
NO.
BUT THAT'S YOUR FATHER. HE SET UP THEIR CORPORATE PARTNERSHIP. HE'S THE ONE ELEMENT THAT TIED THESE GANGSTERS TOGETHER. WHERE IS HE NOW?
HAVEN'T A CLUE. HE'S A WORLD TRAVELER, REMEMBER? WHY DON'T YOU TRY MADAGASCAR?
THAT'S NOT WHAT YOU TOLD REEVES. YOU TOLD HIM YOU WERE CLOSER THAN EVER TO YOUR FATHER.
YOU HAD ME BUGGED, IS THAT IT?
I CAN READ LIPS.

THEN READ THEM NOW. *GET OUT.*

WHY WON'T YOU TELL ME WHERE HE IS? ARE YOU STILL FOLLOWING HIS ORDERS?

THE WAY I SEE IT, THE ONLY ONE IN THIS ROOM CONTROLLED BY THEIR PARENTS IS *YOU.*

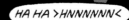
HA HA >HNNNNNN<

HA HA >HNNNNN<

HA HA >HNNNNN<

40

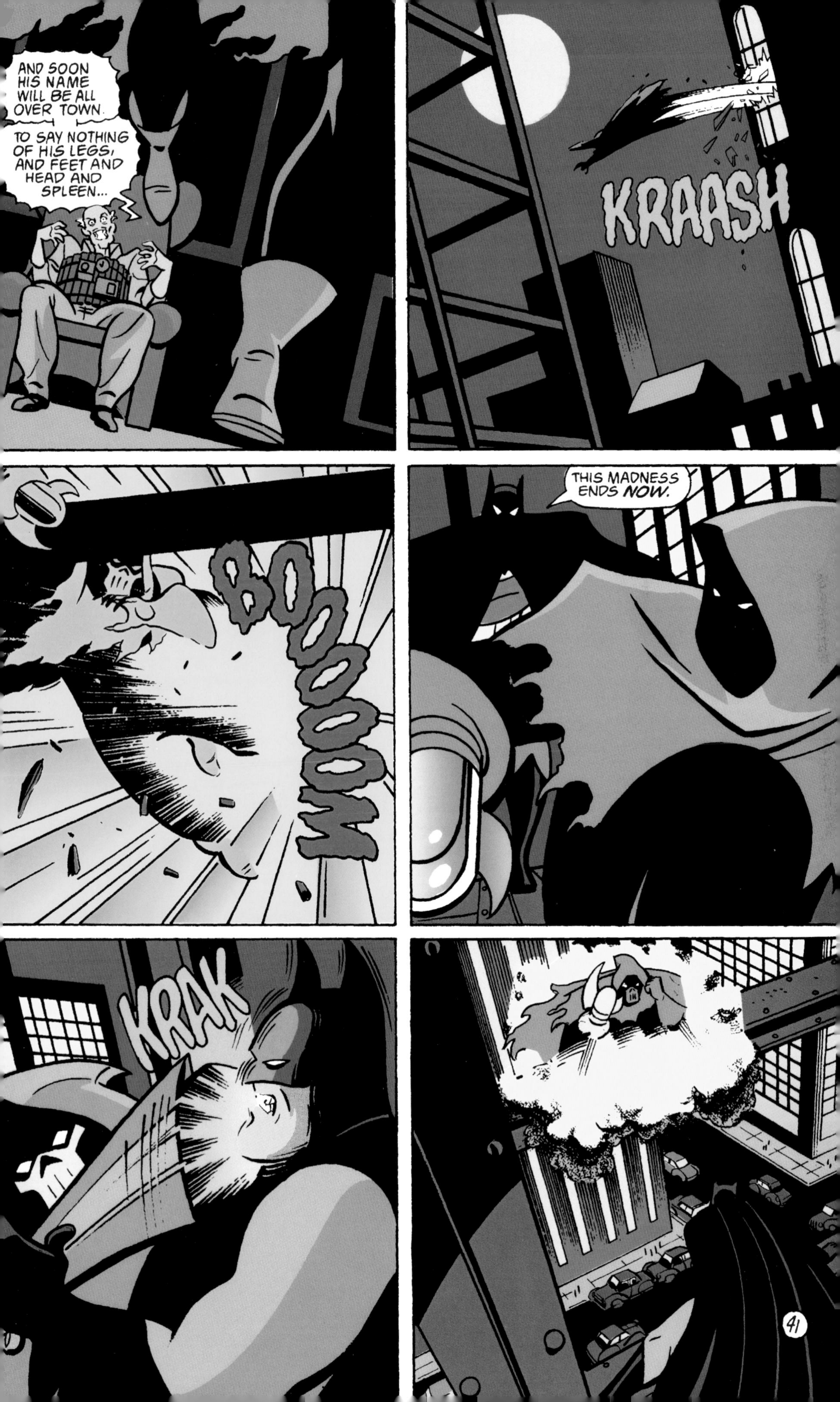
AND SOON HIS NAME WILL BE ALL OVER TOWN.
TO SAY NOTHING OF HIS LEGS, AND FEET AND HEAD AND SPLEEN...
KRAASH
BOOOOOOM
THIS MADNESS ENDS NOW.
KRAK

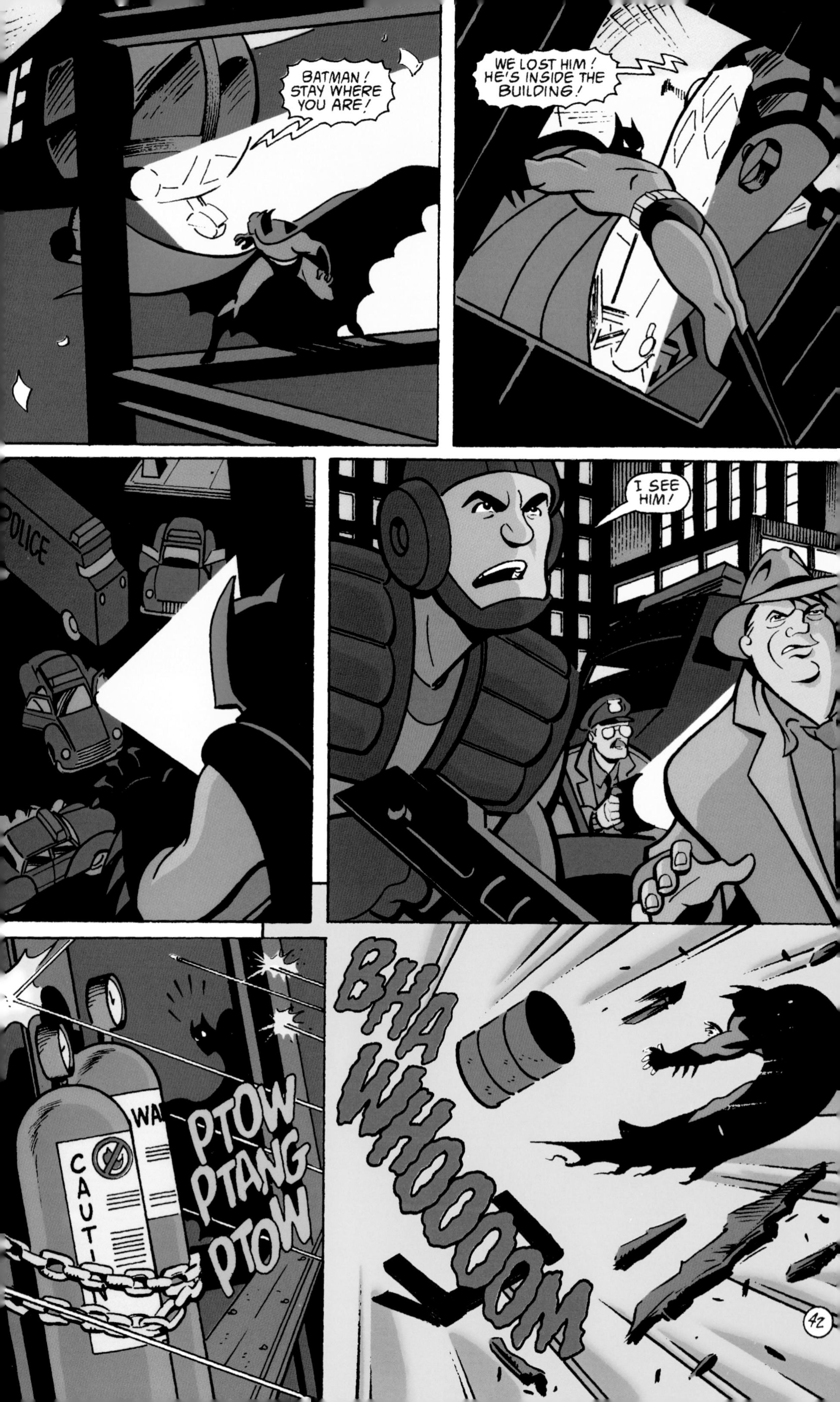
BATMAN! STAY WHERE YOU ARE!
WE LOST HIM! HE'S INSIDE THE BUILDING!
POLICE
I SEE HIM!
CAUTI
PTOW
PTANG
PTOW
BHA WHOOOOM
42

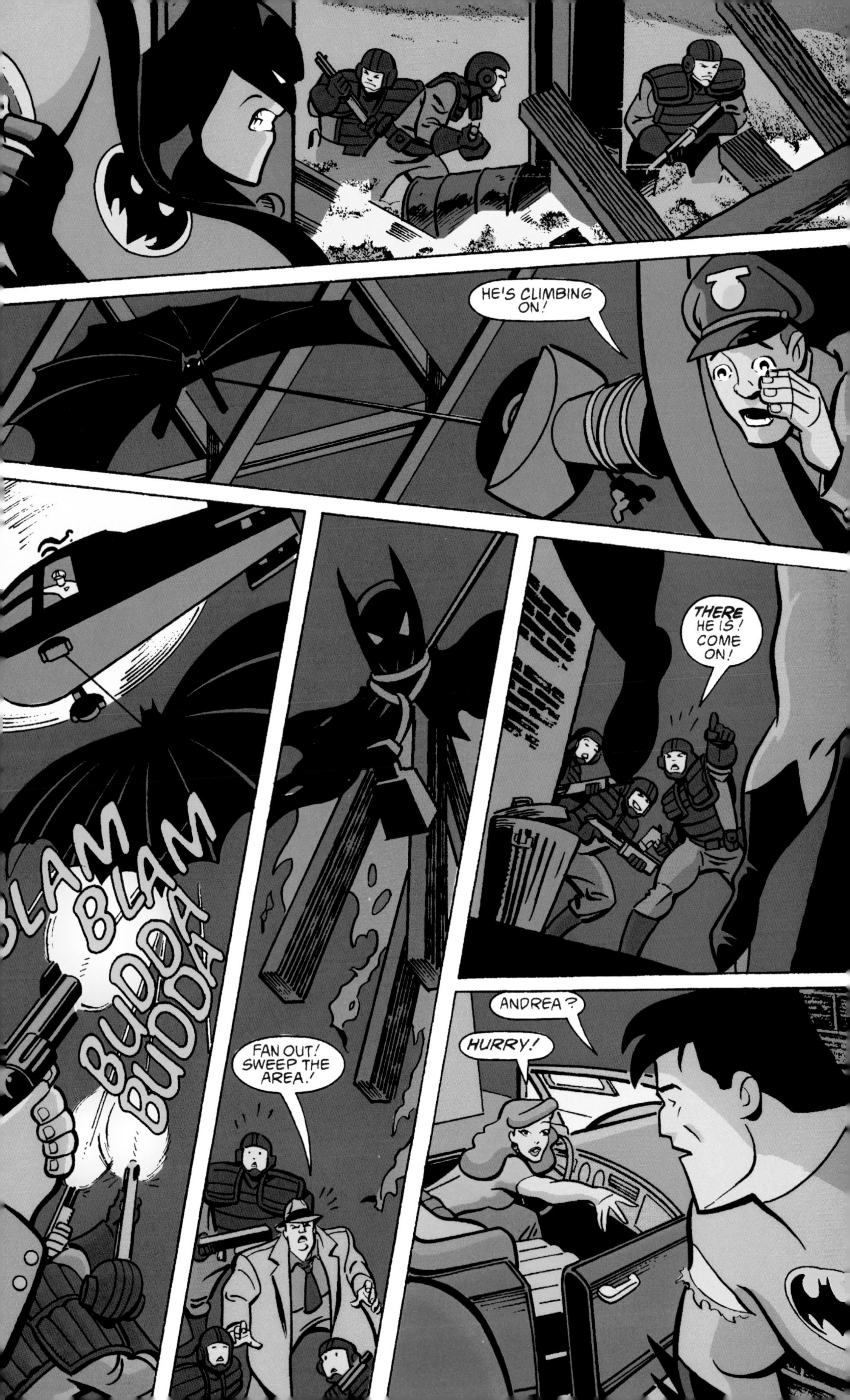

HE'S CLIMBING ON!
BLAM BLAM BUDDA BUDDA
FAN OUT! SWEEP THE AREA.!
THERE HE IS! COME ON!
ANDREA?
HURRY!

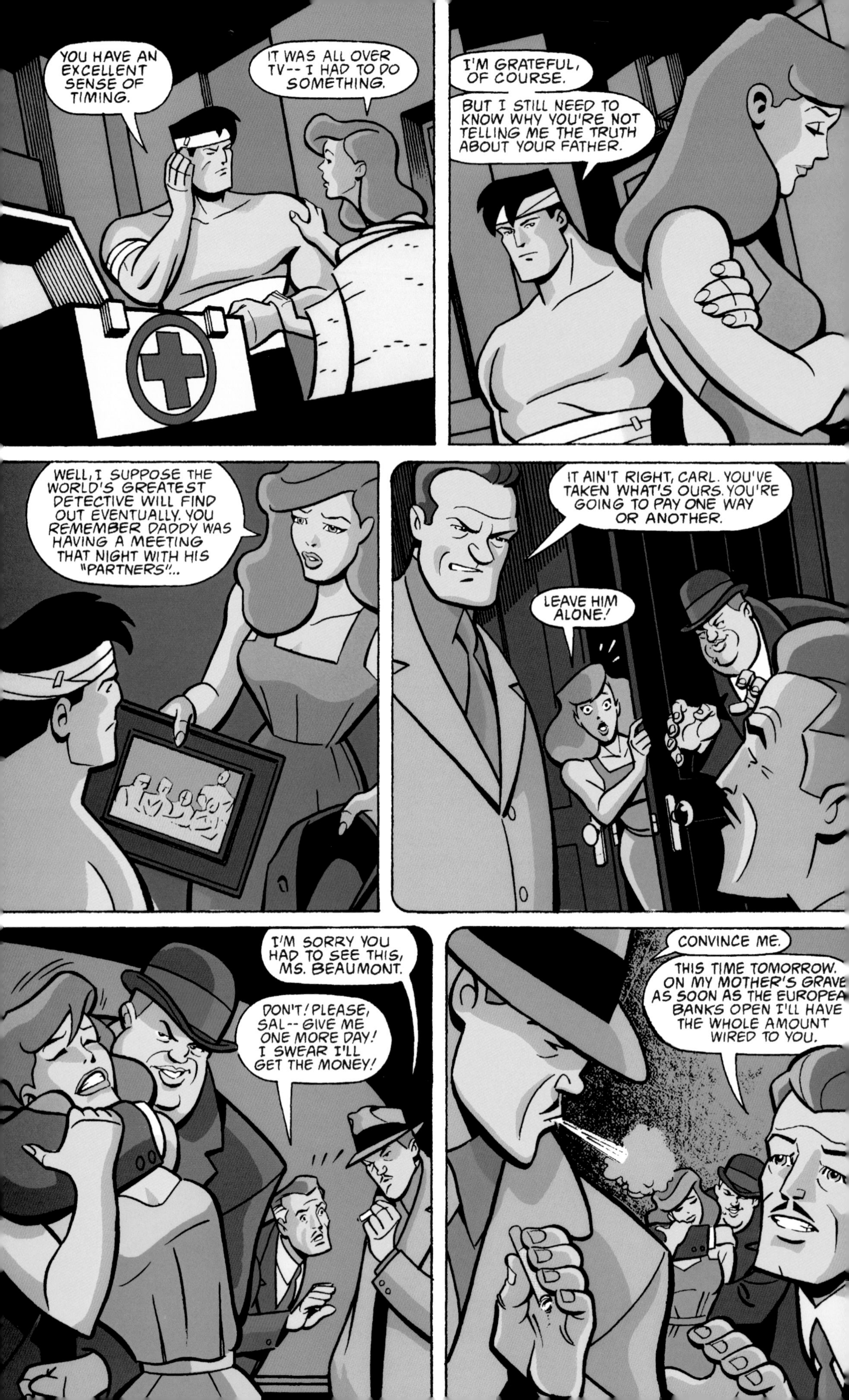
YOU HAVE AN EXCELLENT SENSE OF TIMING.
IT WAS ALL OVER TV-- I HAD TO DO SOMETHING.
I'M GRATEFUL, OF COURSE.
BUT I STILL NEED TO KNOW WHY YOU'RE NOT TELLING ME THE TRUTH ABOUT YOUR FATHER.
WELL, I SUPPOSE THE WORLD'S GREATEST DETECTIVE WILL FIND OUT EVENTUALLY. YOU REMEMBER DADDY WAS HAVING A MEETING THAT NIGHT WITH HIS "PARTNERS"...
IT AIN'T RIGHT, CARL. YOU'VE TAKEN WHAT'S OURS. YOU'RE GOING TO PAY ONE WAY OR ANOTHER.
LEAVE HIM ALONE!
I'M SORRY YOU HAD TO SEE THIS, MS. BEAUMONT.
DON'T! PLEASE, SAL-- GIVE ME ONE MORE DAY! I SWEAR I'LL GET THE MONEY!
CONVINCE ME.
THIS TIME TOMORROW. ON MY MOTHER'S GRAVE AS SOON AS THE EUROPEA BANKS OPEN I'LL HAVE THE WHOLE AMOUNT WIRED TO YOU.

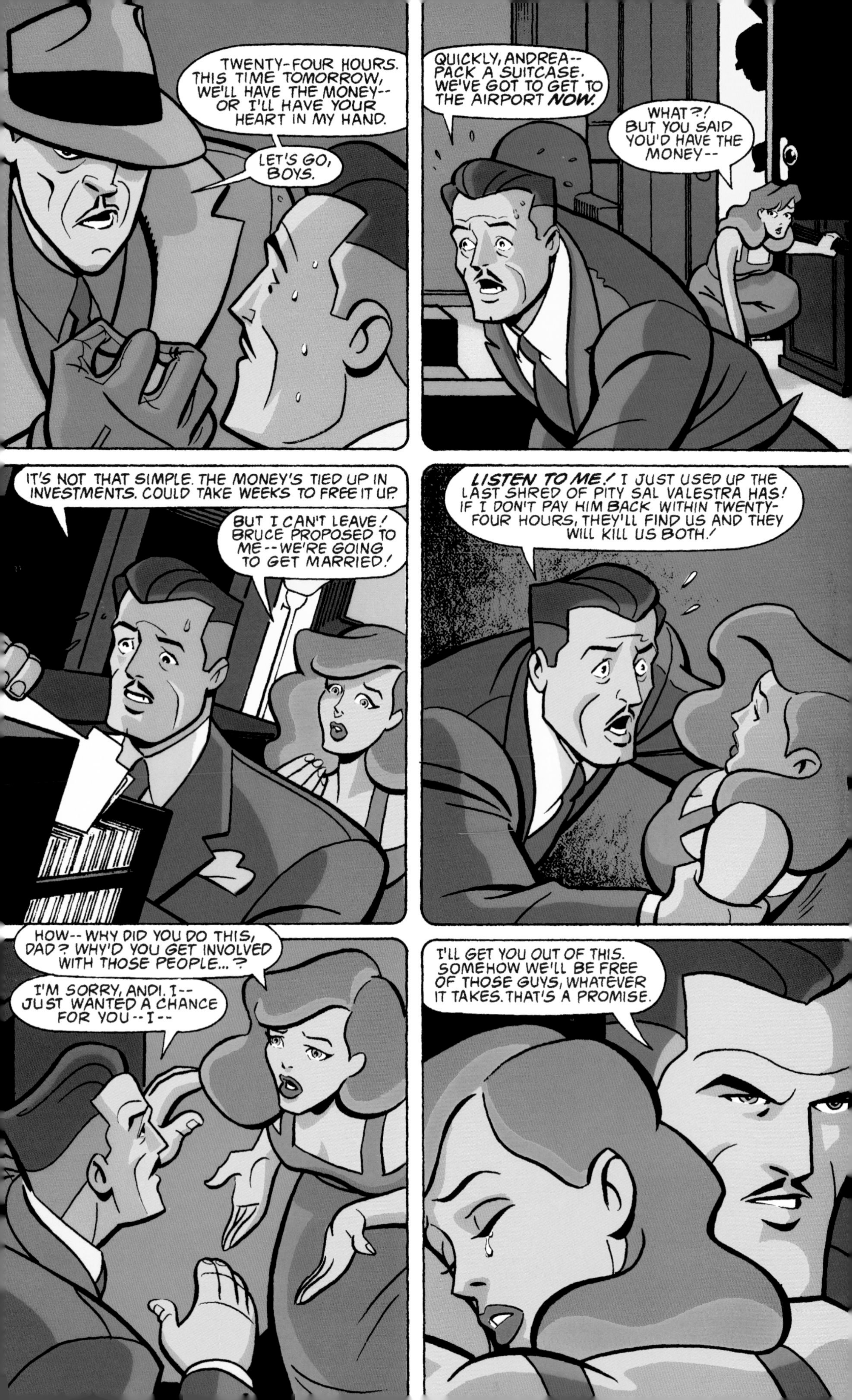
TWENTY-FOUR HOURS. THIS TIME TOMORROW, WE'LL HAVE THE MONEY-- OR I'LL HAVE YOUR HEART IN MY HAND.
LET'S GO, BOYS.
QUICKLY, ANDREA-- PACK A SUITCASE. WE'VE GOT TO GET TO THE AIRPORT NOW.
WHAT?! BUT YOU SAID YOU'D HAVE THE MONEY--
IT'S NOT THAT SIMPLE. THE MONEY'S TIED UP IN INVESTMENTS. COULD TAKE WEEKS TO FREE IT UP.
BUT I CAN'T LEAVE! BRUCE PROPOSED TO ME--WE'RE GOING TO GET MARRIED!
LISTEN TO ME! I JUST USED UP THE LAST SHRED OF PITY SAL VALESTRA HAS! IF I DON'T PAY HIM BACK WITHIN TWENTY-FOUR HOURS, THEY'LL FIND US AND THEY WILL KILL US BOTH!
HOW--WHY DID YOU DO THIS, DAD? WHY'D YOU GET INVOLVED WITH THOSE PEOPLE...?
I'M SORRY, ANDI. I-- JUST WANTED A CHANCE FOR YOU--I--
I'LL GET YOU OUT OF THIS. SOMEHOW WE'LL BE FREE OF THOSE GUYS, WHATEVER IT TAKES. THAT'S A PROMISE.

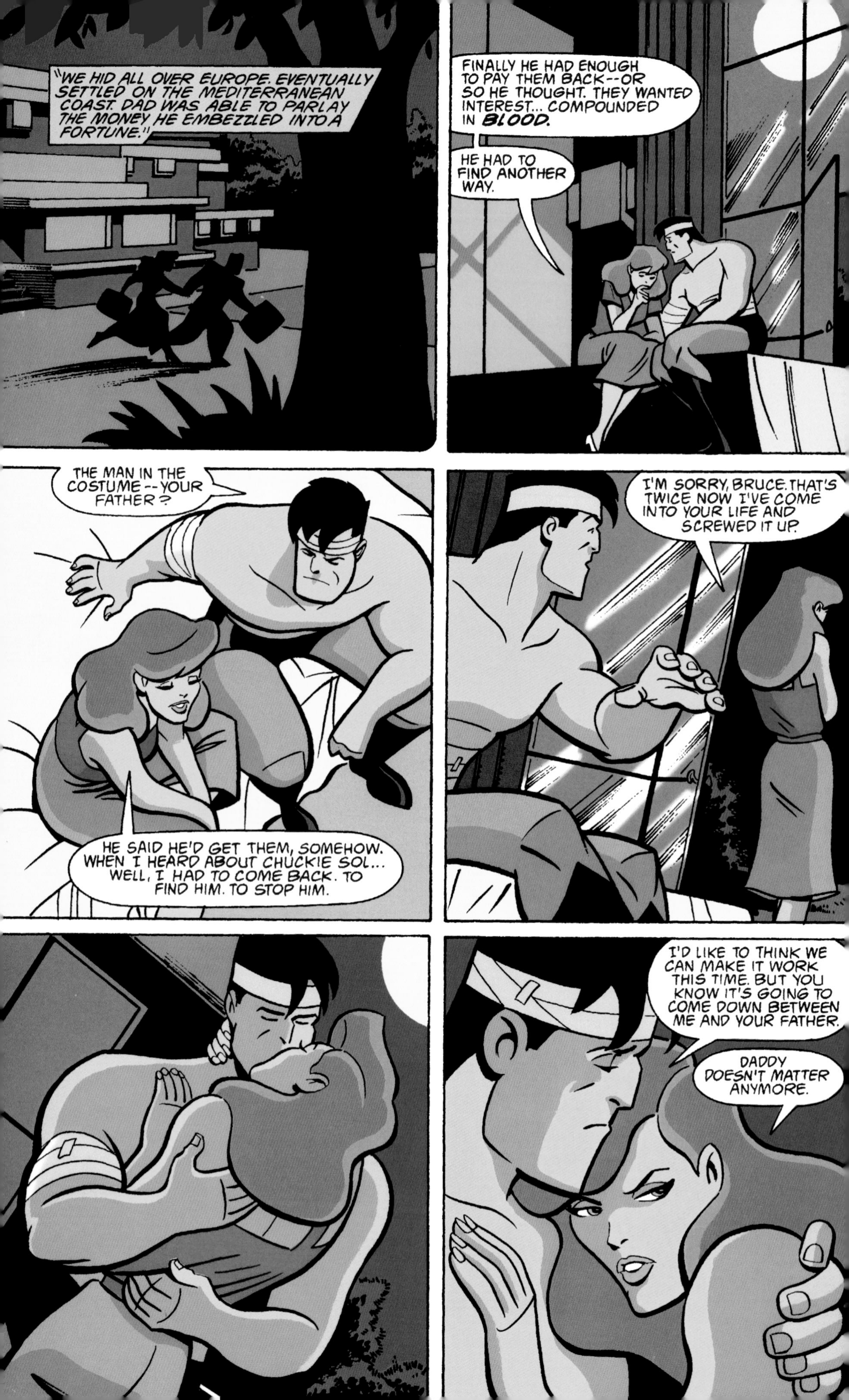
"WE HID ALL OVER EUROPE. EVENTUALLY SETTLED ON THE MEDITERRANEAN COAST. DAD WAS ABLE TO PARLAY THE MONEY HE EMBEZZLED INTO A FORTUNE."
FINALLY HE HAD ENOUGH TO PAY THEM BACK--OR SO HE THOUGHT. THEY WANTED INTEREST... COMPOUNDED IN BLOOD.
HE HAD TO FIND ANOTHER WAY.
THE MAN IN THE COSTUME--YOUR FATHER?
HE SAID HE'D GET THEM, SOMEHOW. WHEN I HEARD ABOUT CHUCKIE SOL... WELL, I HAD TO COME BACK. TO FIND HIM. TO STOP HIM.
I'M SORRY, BRUCE. THAT'S TWICE NOW I'VE COME INTO YOUR LIFE AND SCREWED IT UP.
I'D LIKE TO THINK WE CAN MAKE IT WORK THIS TIME. BUT YOU KNOW IT'S GOING TO COME DOWN BETWEEN ME AND YOUR FATHER.
DADDY DOESN'T MATTER ANYMORE.

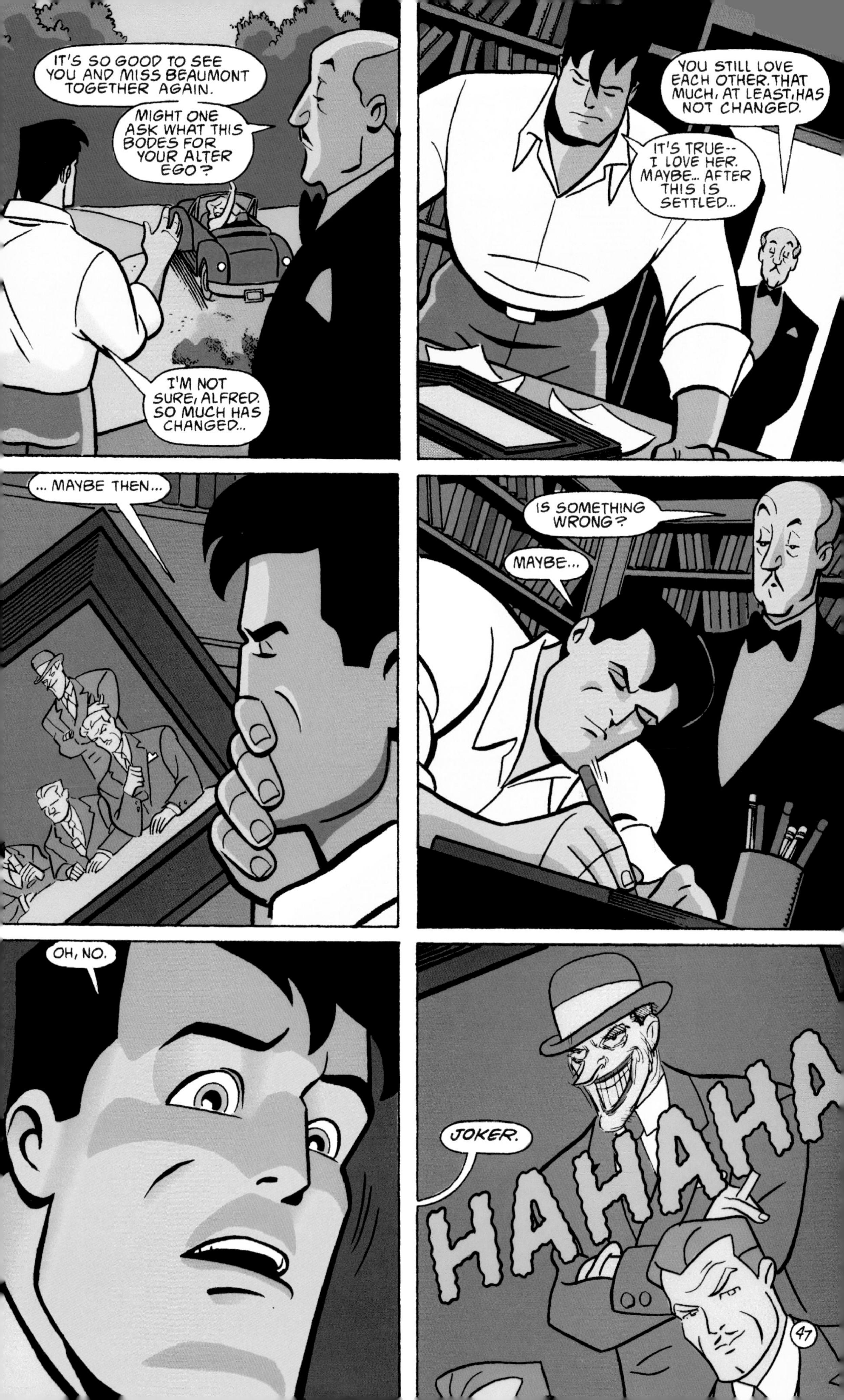

IT'S SO GOOD TO SEE YOU AND MISS BEAUMONT TOGETHER AGAIN.
MIGHT ONE ASK WHAT THIS BODES FOR YOUR ALTER EGO?
I'M NOT SURE, ALFRED. SO MUCH HAS CHANGED...
YOU STILL LOVE EACH OTHER. THAT MUCH, AT LEAST, HAS NOT CHANGED.
IT'S TRUE-- I LOVE HER. MAYBE... AFTER THIS IS SETTLED...
... MAYBE THEN...
IS SOMETHING WRONG?
MAYBE...
OH, NO.
JOKER.
HAHAHA

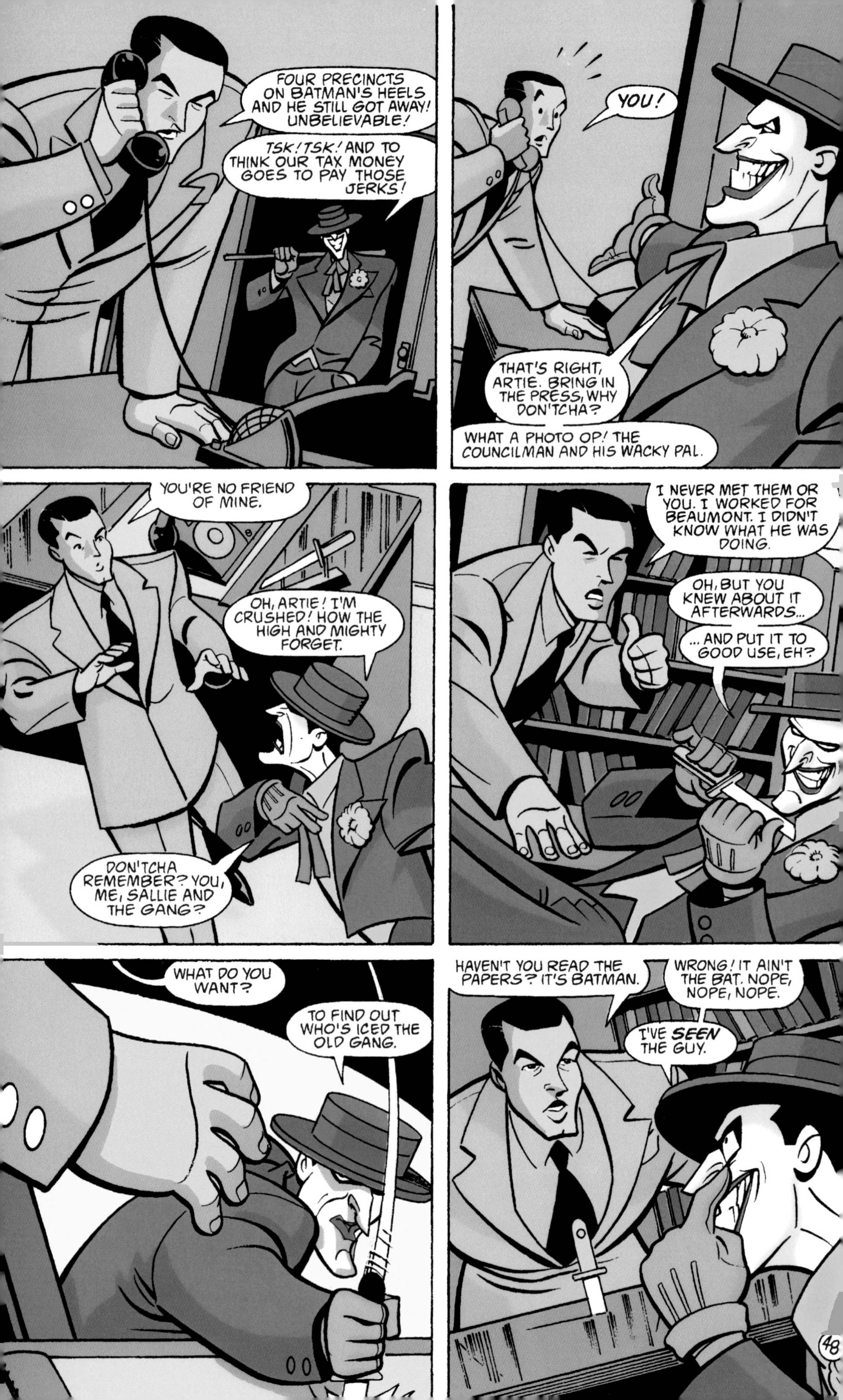
FOUR PRECINCTS ON BATMAN'S HEELS AND HE STILL GOT AWAY! UNBELIEVABLE!
TSK! TSK! AND TO THINK OUR TAX MONEY GOES TO PAY THOSE JERKS!
YOU!
THAT'S RIGHT, ARTIE. BRING IN THE PRESS, WHY DON'TCHA?
WHAT A PHOTO OP! THE COUNCILMAN AND HIS WACKY PAL.
YOU'RE NO FRIEND OF MINE.
OH, ARTIE! I'M CRUSHED! HOW THE HIGH AND MIGHTY FORGET.
DON'TCHA REMEMBER? YOU, ME, SALLIE AND THE GANG?
I NEVER MET THEM OR YOU. I WORKED FOR BEAUMONT. I DIDN'T KNOW WHAT HE WAS DOING.
OH, BUT YOU KNEW ABOUT IT AFTERWARDS...
...AND PUT IT TO GOOD USE, EH?
WHAT DO YOU WANT?
TO FIND OUT WHO'S ICED THE OLD GANG.
HAVEN'T YOU READ THE PAPERS? IT'S BATMAN.
WRONG! IT AIN'T THE BAT. NOPE, NOPE, NOPE.
I'VE SEEN THE GUY.

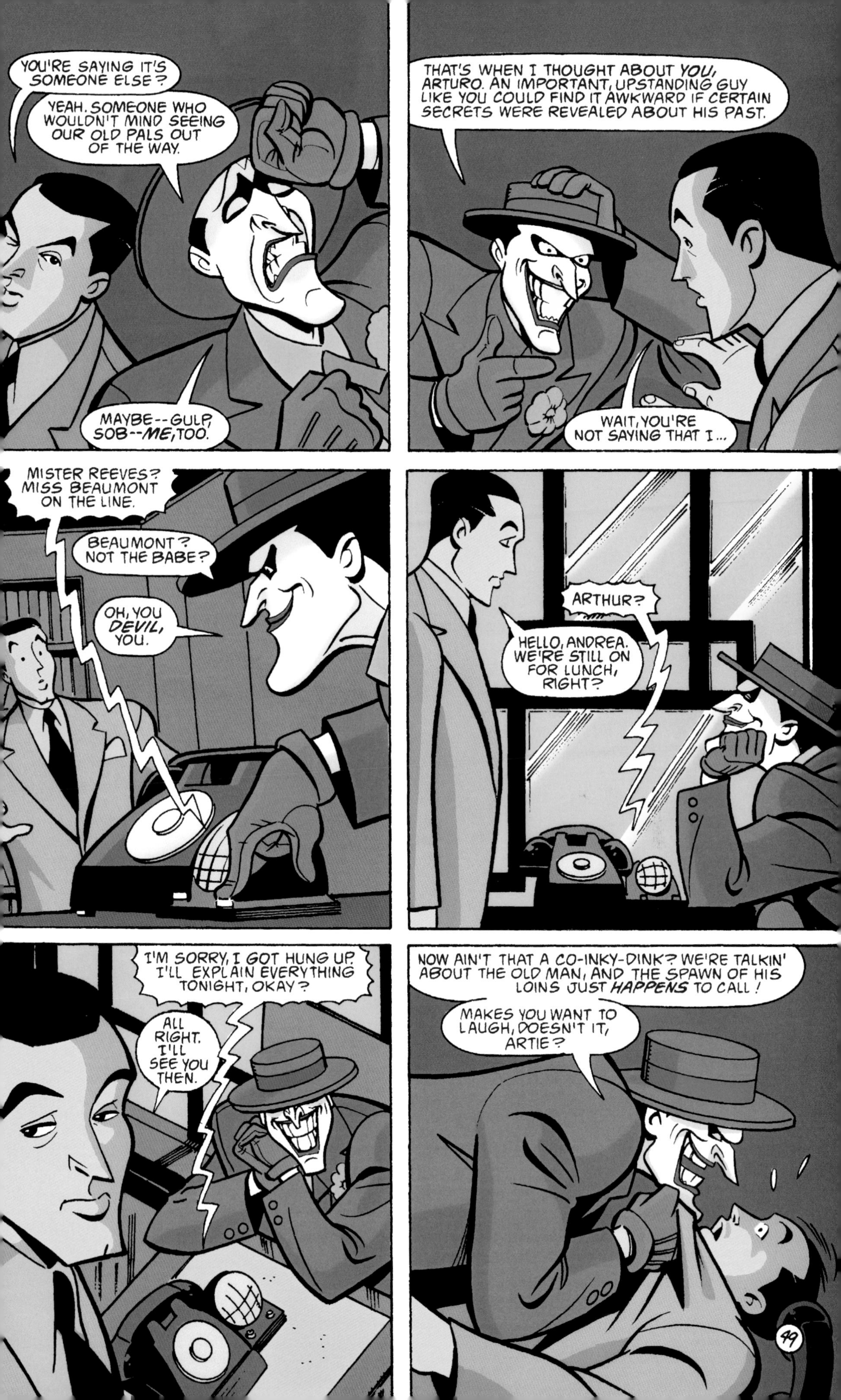
YOU'RE SAYING IT'S SOMEONE ELSE?
YEAH. SOMEONE WHO WOULDN'T MIND SEEING OUR OLD PALS OUT OF THE WAY.
MAYBE--GULP, SOB--*ME*, TOO.
THAT'S WHEN I THOUGHT ABOUT *YOU*, ARTURO. AN IMPORTANT, UPSTANDING GUY LIKE YOU COULD FIND IT AWKWARD IF CERTAIN SECRETS WERE REVEALED ABOUT HIS PAST.
WAIT, YOU'RE NOT SAYING THAT I...
MISTER REEVES? MISS BEAUMONT ON THE LINE.
BEAUMONT? NOT THE BABE?
OH, YOU *DEVIL*, YOU.
ARTHUR?
HELLO, ANDREA. WE'RE STILL ON FOR LUNCH, RIGHT?
I'M SORRY, I GOT HUNG UP. I'LL EXPLAIN EVERYTHING TONIGHT, OKAY?
ALL RIGHT. I'LL SEE YOU THEN.
NOW AIN'T THAT A CO-INKY-DINK? WE'RE TALKIN' ABOUT THE OLD MAN, AND THE SPAWN OF HIS LOINS JUST *HAPPENS* TO CALL!
MAKES YOU WANT TO LAUGH, DOESN'T IT, ARTIE?

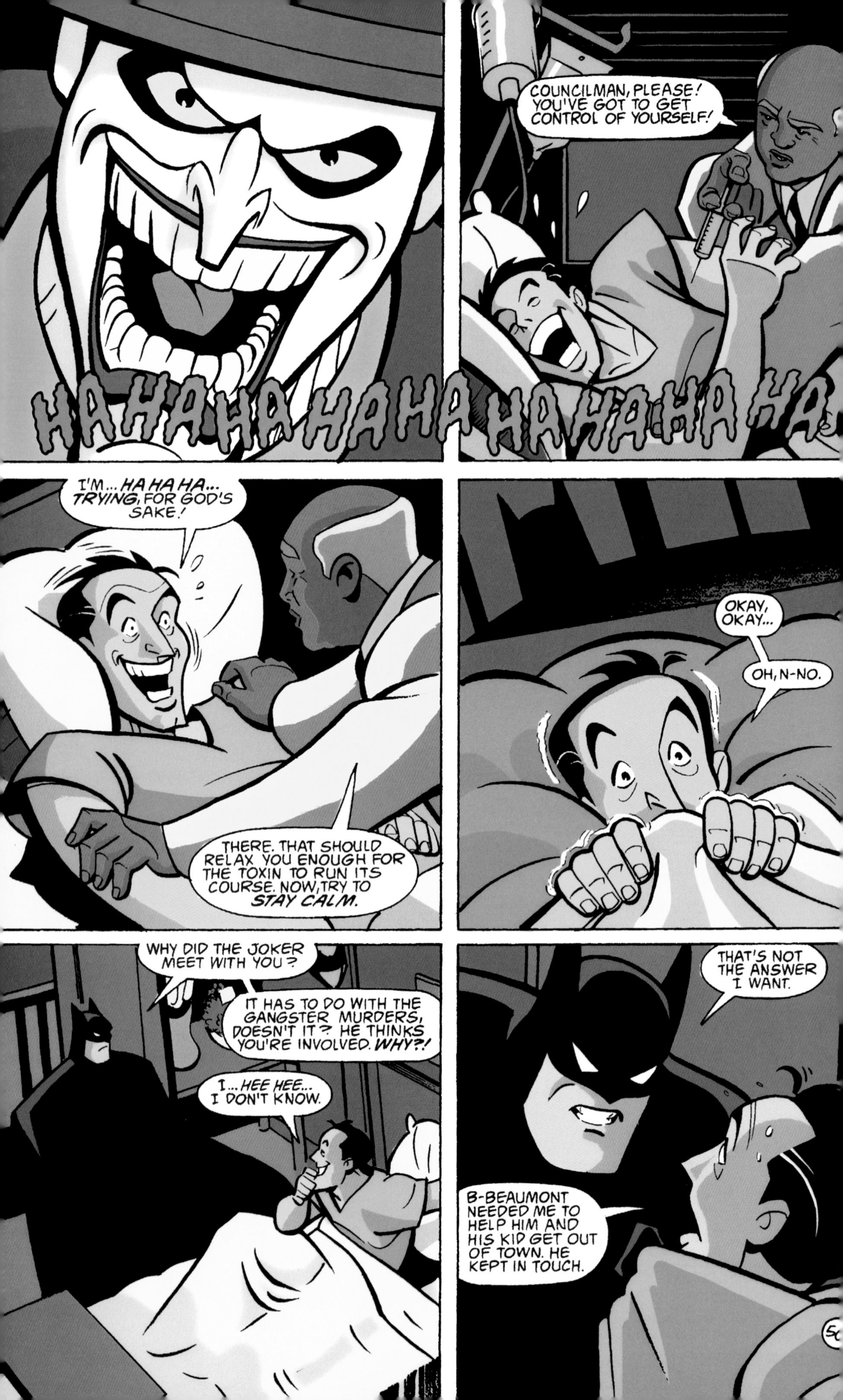
COUNCILMAN, PLEASE! YOU'VE GOT TO GET CONTROL OF YOURSELF!
HA HA HA HA HA HA HA HA HA HA HA
I'M... HA HA HA... TRYING, FOR GOD'S SAKE!
THERE. THAT SHOULD RELAX YOU ENOUGH FOR THE TOXIN TO RUN ITS COURSE. NOW, TRY TO STAY CALM.
OKAY, OKAY...
OH, N-NO.
WHY DID THE JOKER MEET WITH YOU?
IT HAS TO DO WITH THE GANGSTER MURDERS, DOESN'T IT? HE THINKS YOU'RE INVOLVED. WHY?!
I... HEE HEE... I DON'T KNOW.
THAT'S NOT THE ANSWER I WANT.
B-BEAUMONT NEEDED ME TO HELP HIM AND HIS KID GET OUT OF TOWN. HE KEPT IN TOUCH.

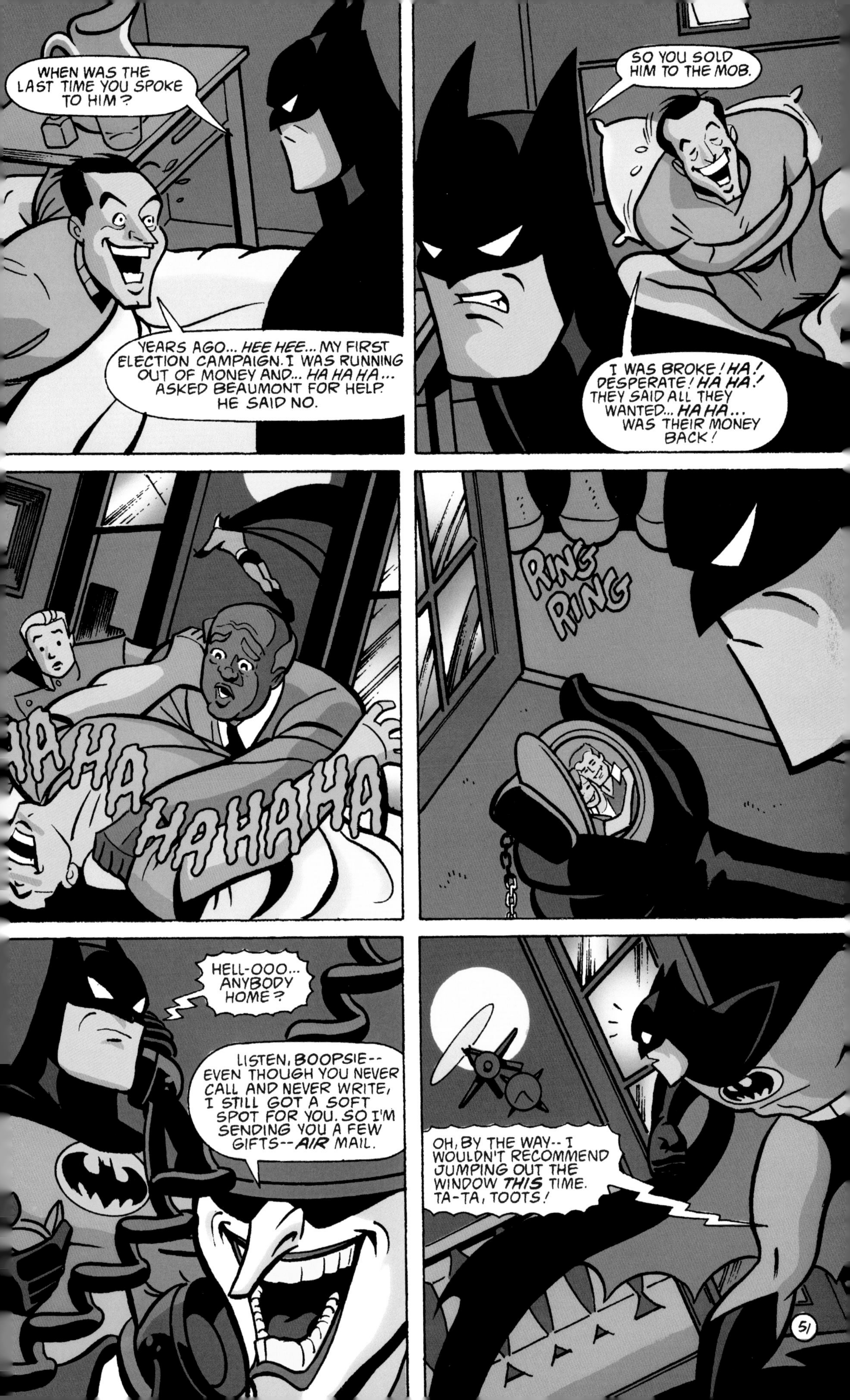

WHEN WAS THE LAST TIME YOU SPOKE TO HIM?
YEARS AGO... HEE HEE... MY FIRST ELECTION CAMPAIGN. I WAS RUNNING OUT OF MONEY AND... HA HA HA... ASKED BEAUMONT FOR HELP. HE SAID NO.
SO YOU SOLD HIM TO THE MOB.
I WAS BROKE! HA! DESPERATE! HA HA! THEY SAID ALL THEY WANTED... HA HA... WAS THEIR MONEY BACK!
HAHA HAHAHAHA
RING RING
HELL-OOO... ANYBODY HOME?
LISTEN, BOOPSIE-- EVEN THOUGH YOU NEVER CALL AND NEVER WRITE, I STILL GOT A SOFT SPOT FOR YOU. SO I'M SENDING YOU A FEW GIFTS--AIR MAIL.
OH, BY THE WAY-- I WOULDN'T RECOMMEND JUMPING OUT THE WINDOW THIS TIME. TA-TA, TOOTS!

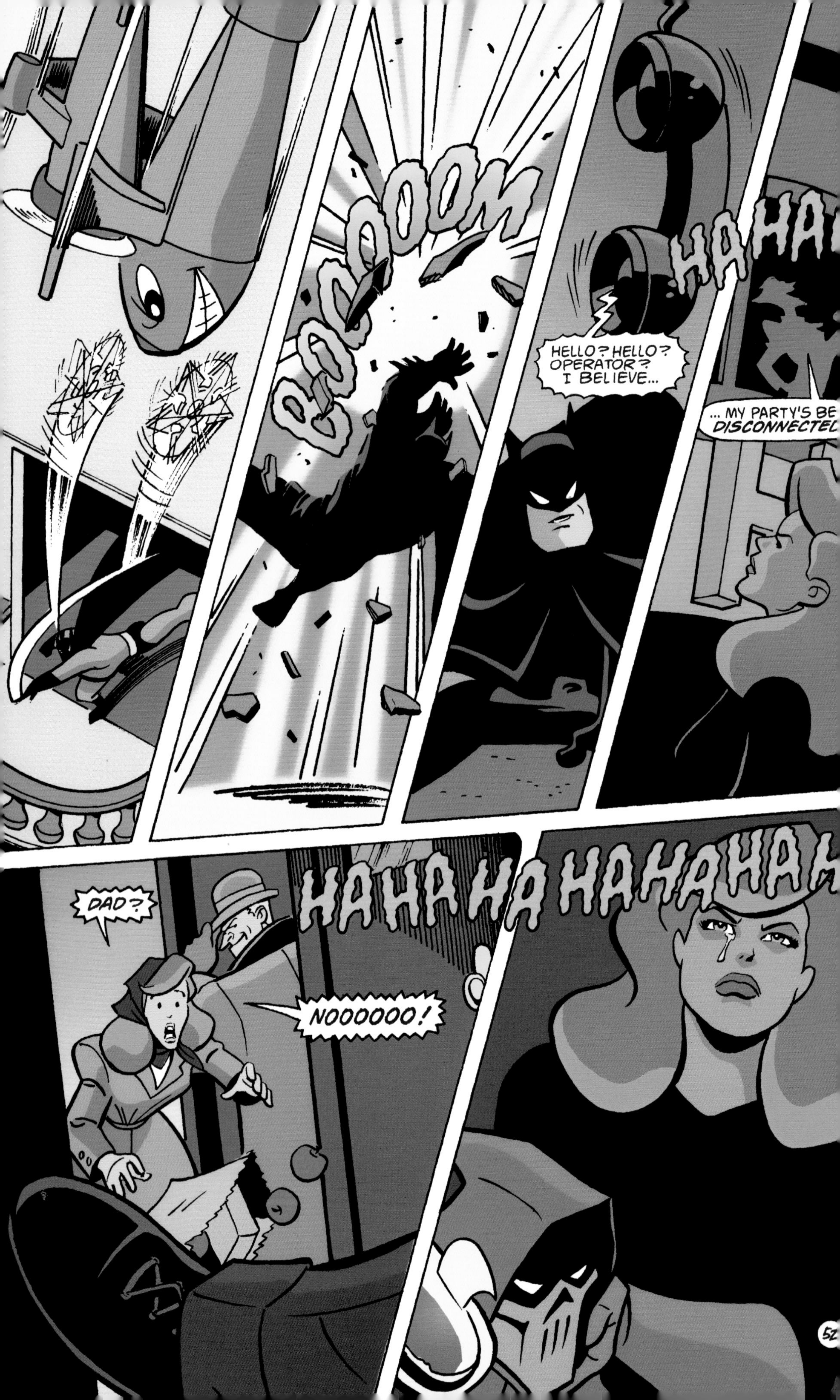
BOOOOOOM
HELLO? HELLO? OPERATOR? I BELIEVE...
HAHAHA
... MY PARTY'S BE
DISCONNECTEL
DAD?
HAHAHAHA HAHAHAHAH
NOOOOOO!

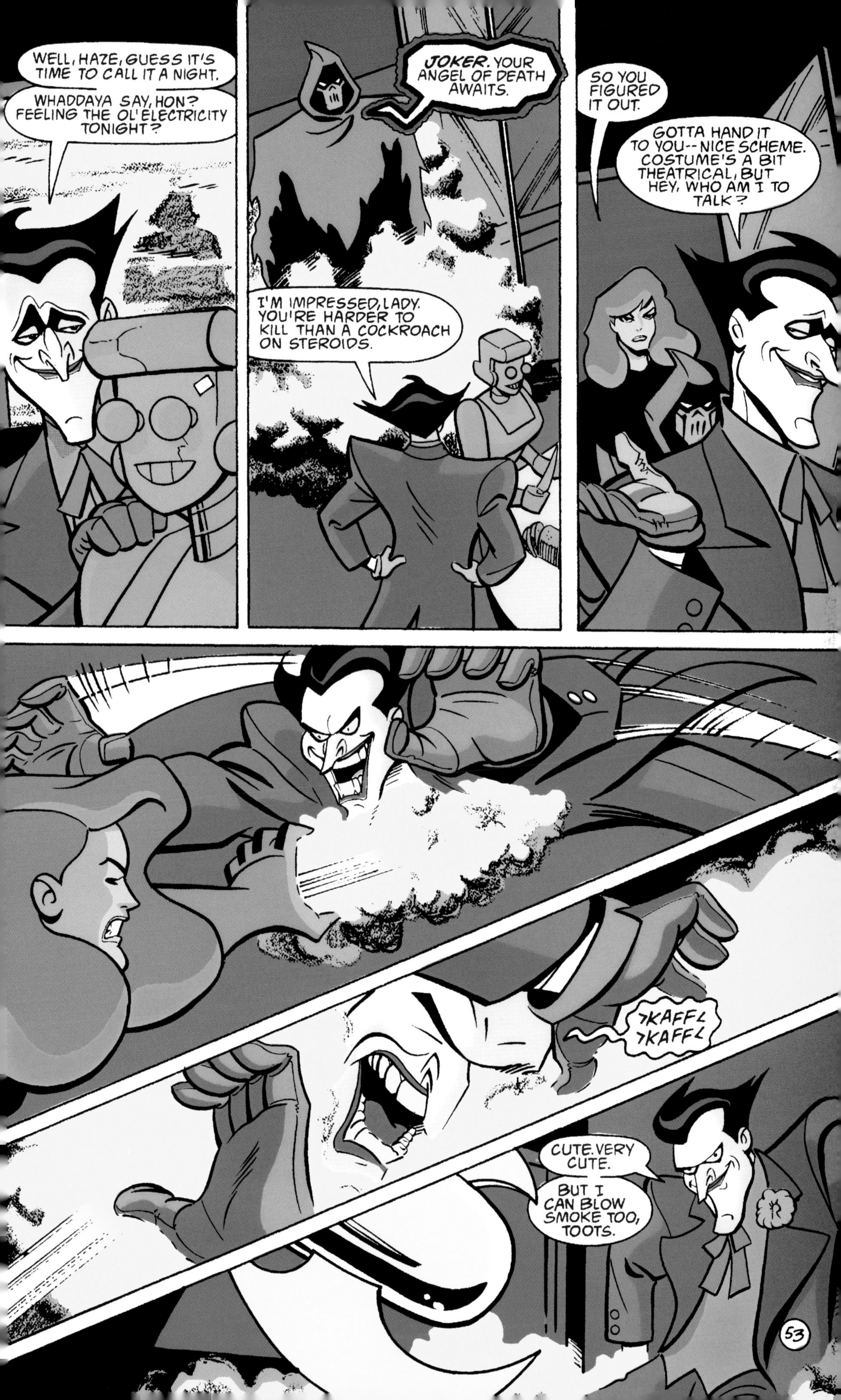
WELL, HAZE, GUESS IT'S TIME TO CALL IT A NIGHT.
WHADDAYA SAY, HON? FEELING THE OL' ELECTRICITY TONIGHT?
JOKER. YOUR ANGEL OF DEATH AWAITS.
I'M IMPRESSED, LADY. YOU'RE HARDER TO KILL THAN A COCKROACH ON STEROIDS.
SO YOU FIGURED IT OUT.
GOTTA HAND IT TO YOU--NICE SCHEME. COSTUME'S A BIT THEATRICAL, BUT HEY, WHO AM I TO TALK?
>KAFF<
>KAFF<
CUTE. VERY CUTE.
BUT I CAN BLOW SMOKE TOO, TOOTS.
53

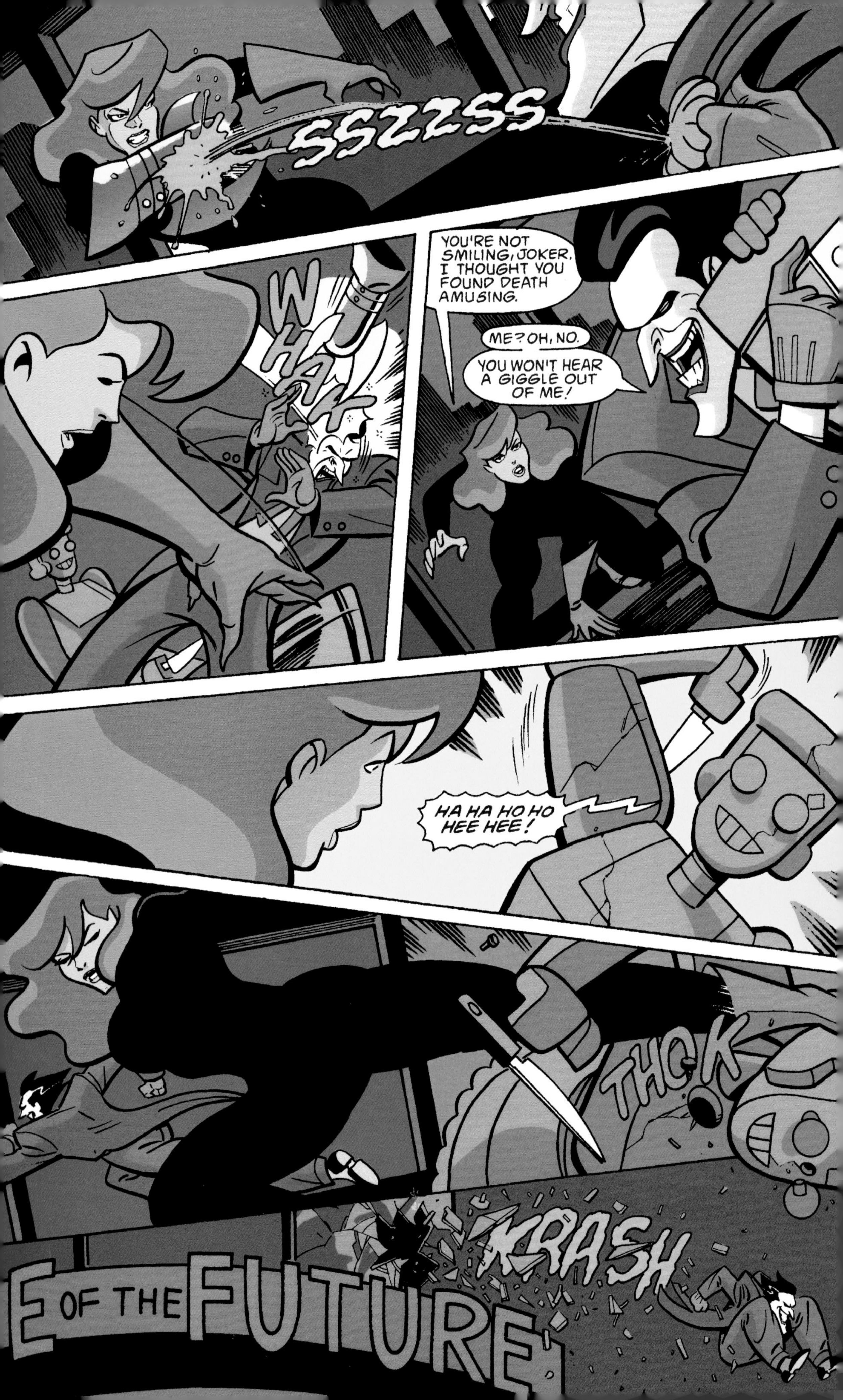
SSZZSS
WHAK
YOU'RE NOT SMILING, JOKER. I THOUGHT YOU FOUND DEATH AMUSING.
ME? OH, NO.
YOU WON'T HEAR A GIGGLE OUT OF ME!
HA HA HO HO HEE HEE!
THOK
KRASH
E OF THE FUTURE

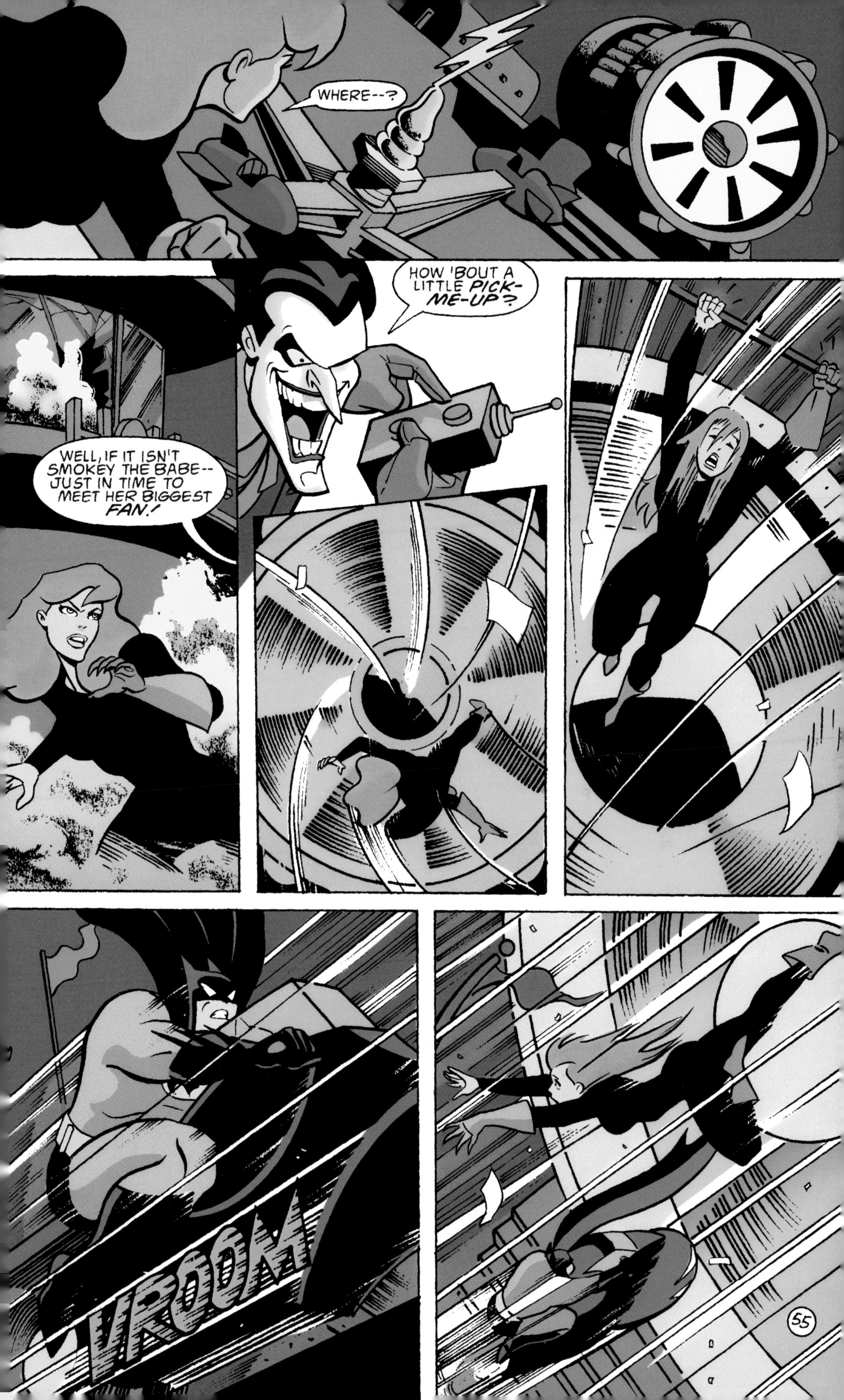

WHERE--?
WELL, IF IT ISN'T SMOKEY THE BABE-- JUST IN TIME TO MEET HER BIGGEST FAN!
HOW 'BOUT A LITTLE PICK-ME-UP?
VROOM
55

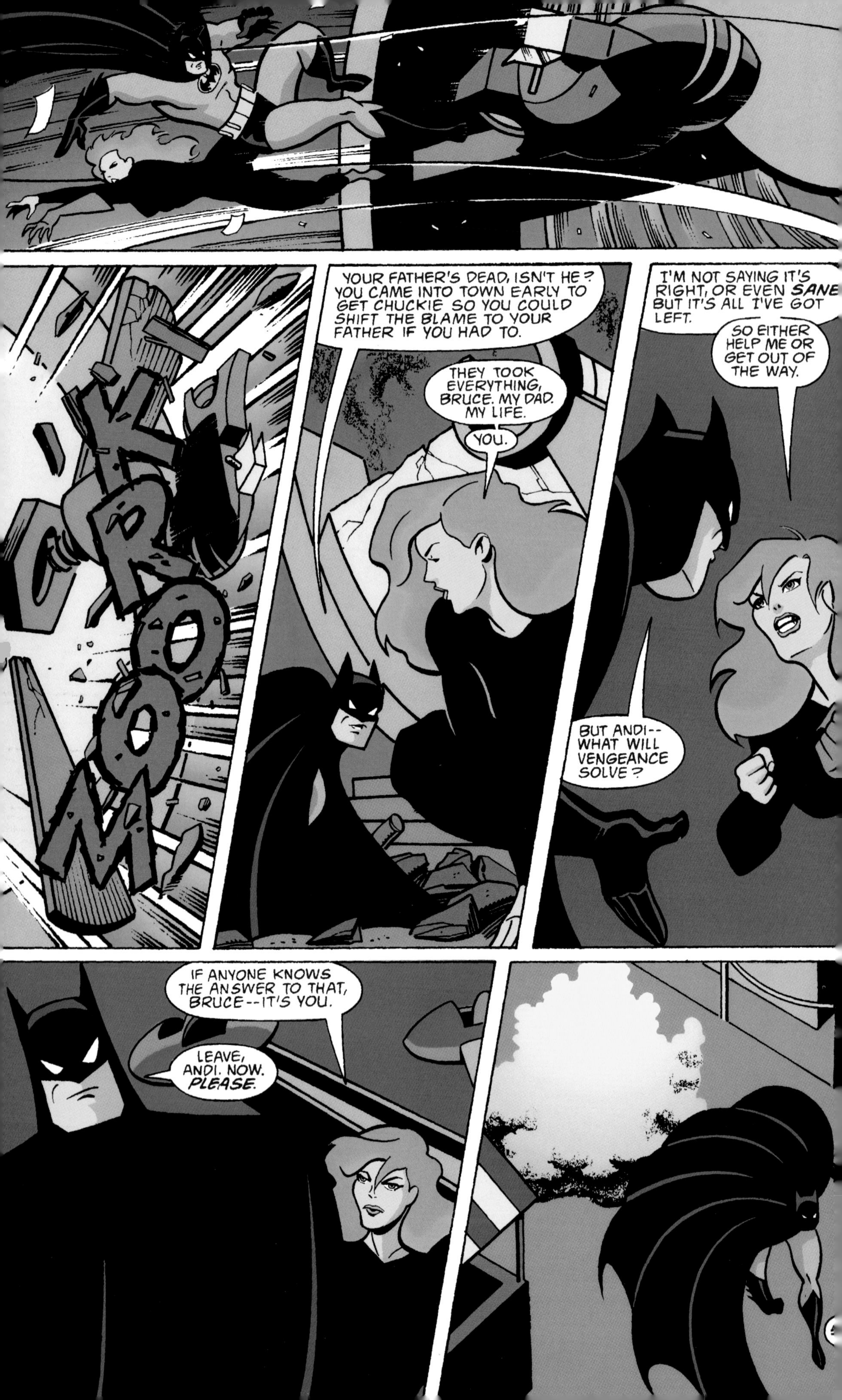
KRRROOOM
YOUR FATHER'S DEAD, ISN'T HE? YOU CAME INTO TOWN EARLY TO GET CHUCKIE SO YOU COULD SHIFT THE BLAME TO YOUR FATHER IF YOU HAD TO.
THEY TOOK EVERYTHING, BRUCE. MY DAD. MY LIFE.
YOU.
I'M NOT SAYING IT'S RIGHT, OR EVEN SANE BUT IT'S ALL I'VE GOT LEFT.
SO EITHER HELP ME OR GET OUT OF THE WAY.
BUT ANDI-- WHAT WILL VENGEANCE SOLVE?
IF ANYONE KNOWS THE ANSWER TO THAT, BRUCE--IT'S YOU.
LEAVE, ANDI. NOW. PLEASE.

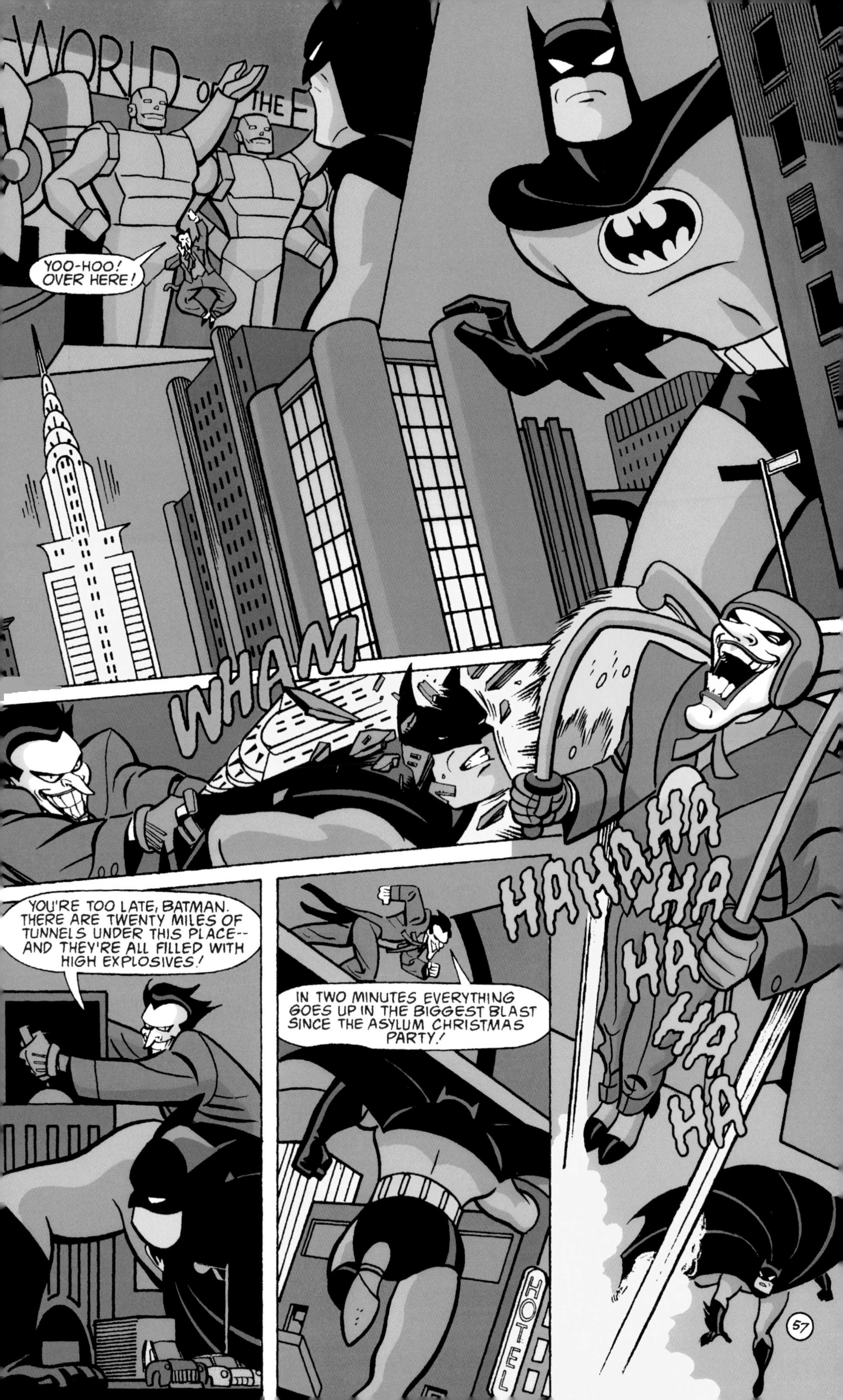
WORLD OF THE F
YOO-HOO! OVER HERE!
WHAM
YOU'RE TOO LATE, BATMAN. THERE ARE TWENTY MILES OF TUNNELS UNDER THIS PLACE-- AND THEY'RE ALL FILLED WITH HIGH EXPLOSIVES!
IN TWO MINUTES EVERYTHING GOES UP IN THE BIGGEST BLAST SINCE THE ASYLUM CHRISTMAS PARTY!
HAHAHAHA HA HA HA HA HA
HOTEL

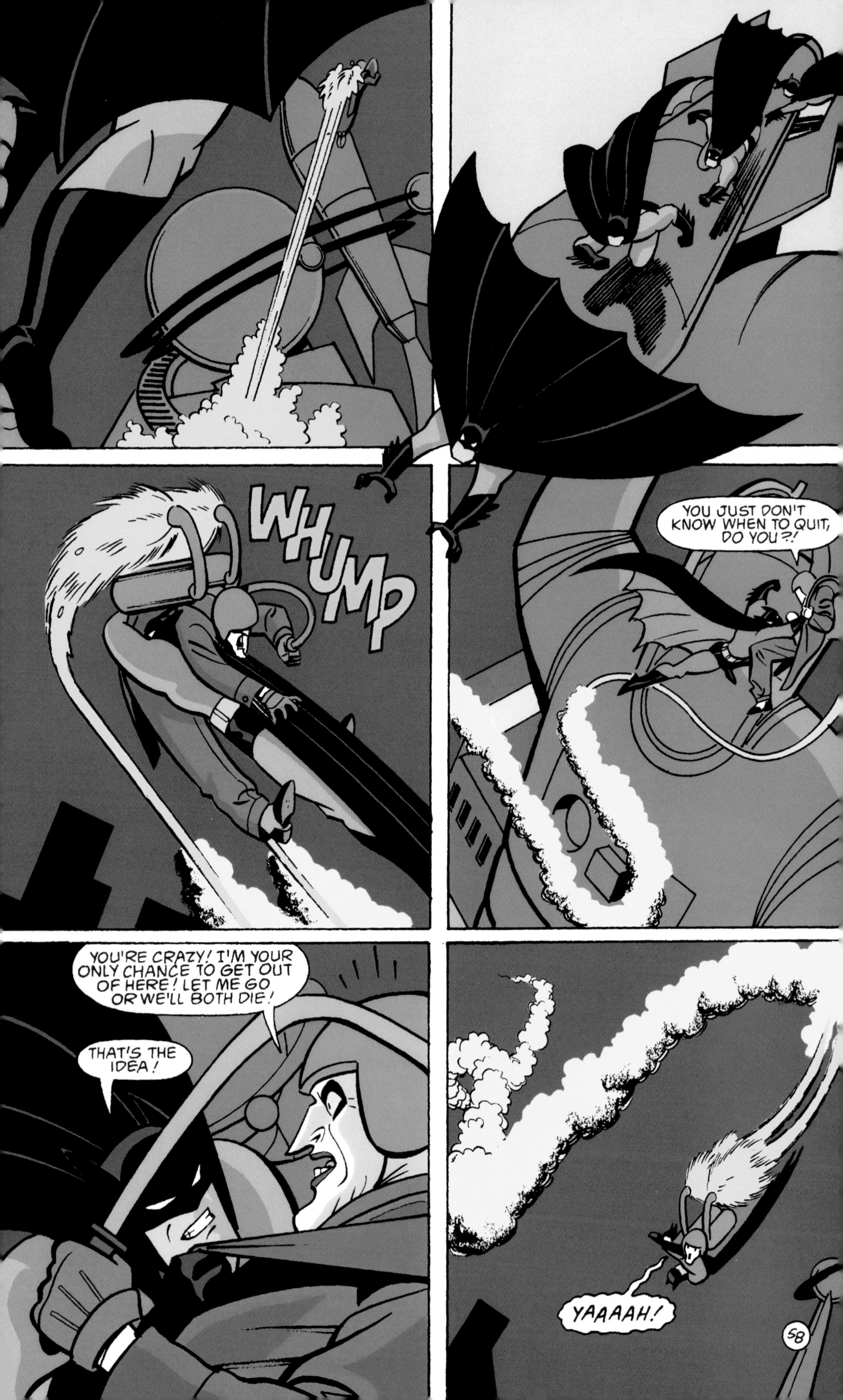
WHUMP
YOU JUST DON'T KNOW WHEN TO QUIT, DO YOU?!
YOU'RE CRAZY! I'M YOUR ONLY CHANCE TO GET OUT OF HERE! LET ME GO OR WE'LL BOTH DIE!
THAT'S THE IDEA!
YAAAAH!

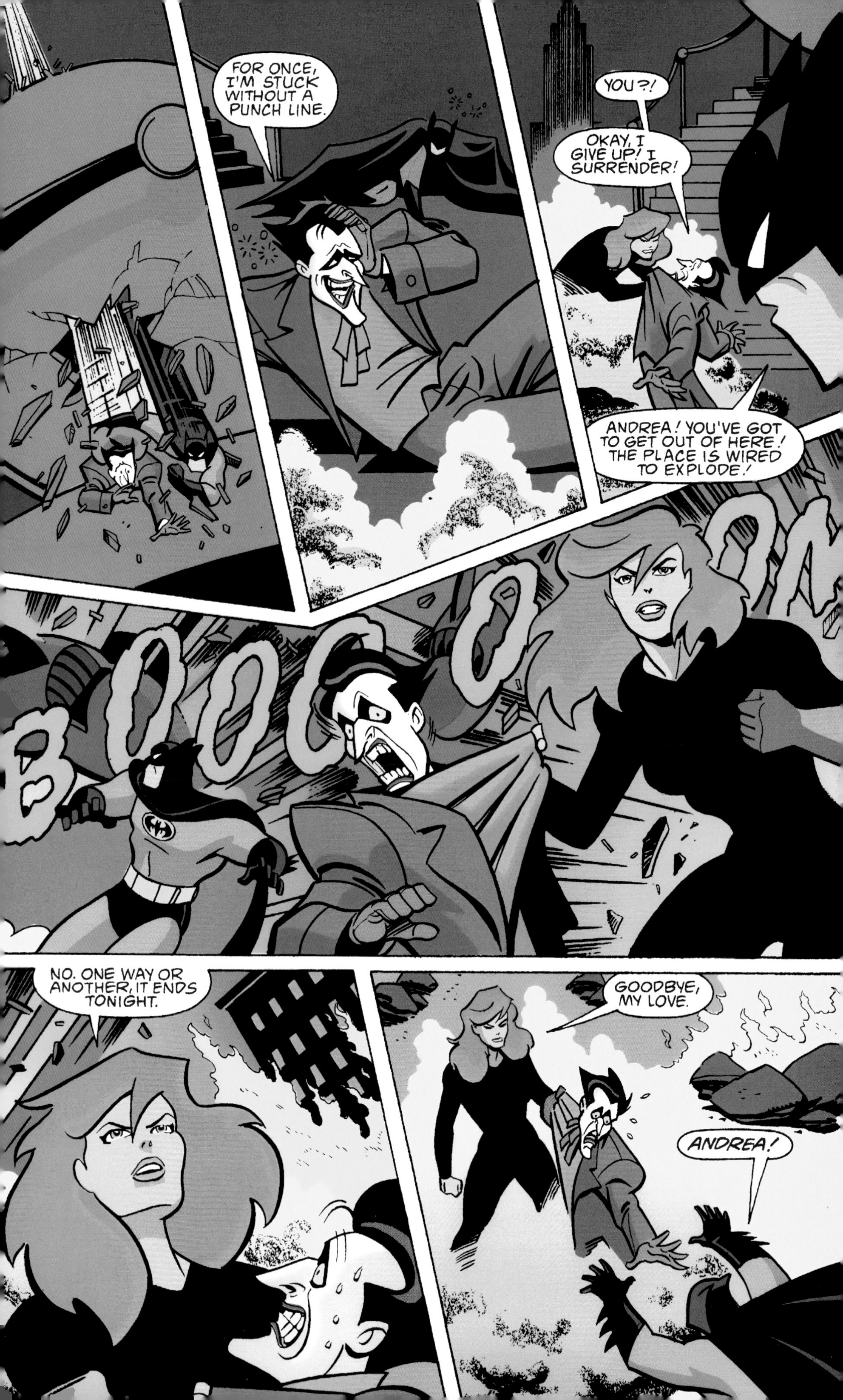

FOR ONCE, I'M STUCK WITHOUT A PUNCH LINE.
YOU?!
OKAY, I GIVE UP! I SURRENDER!
ANDREA! YOU'VE GOT TO GET OUT OF HERE! THE PLACE IS WIRED TO EXPLODE!
BOOOOOOM
NO. ONE WAY OR ANOTHER, IT ENDS TONIGHT.
GOODBYE, MY LOVE.
ANDREA!

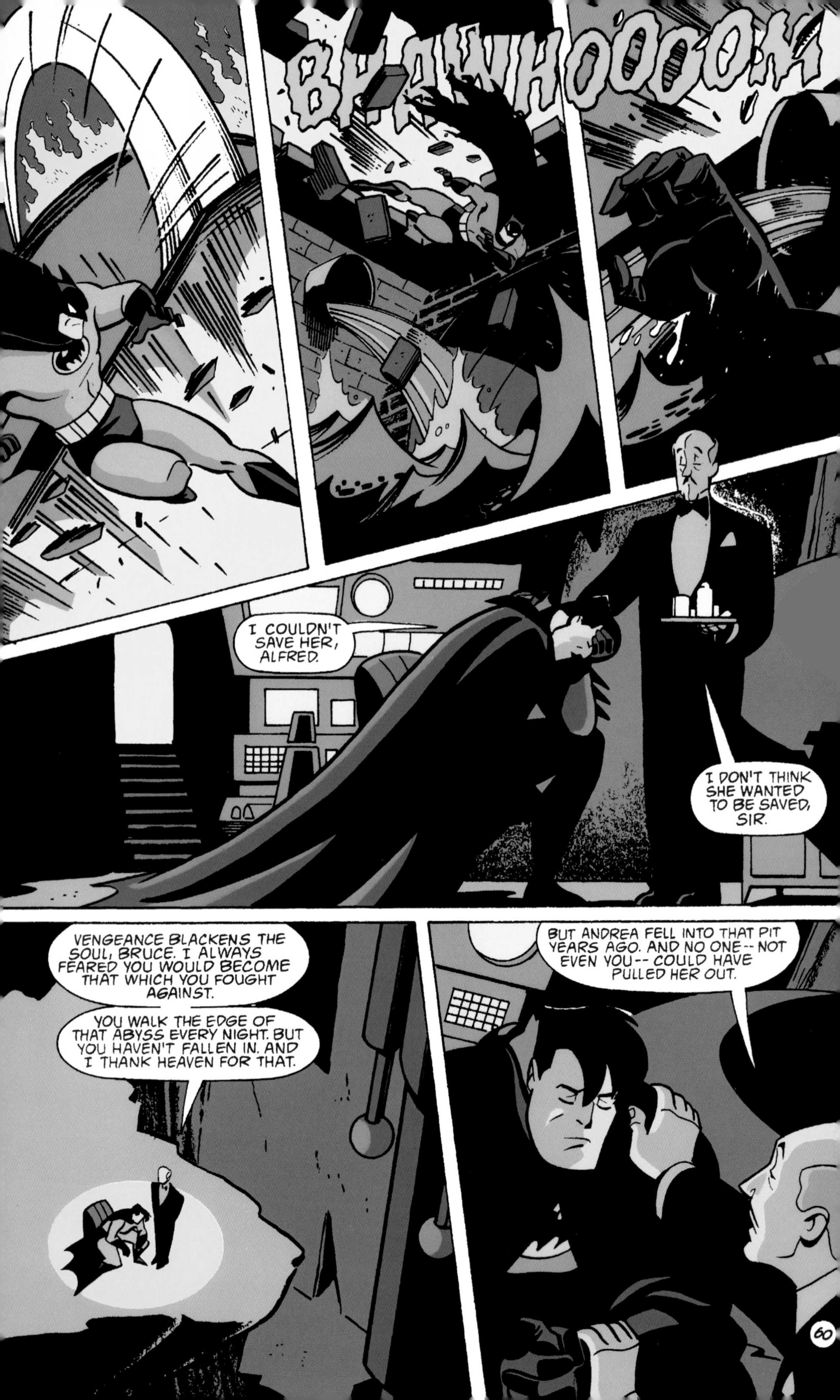
BRAWHOOOOOM
I COULDN'T SAVE HER, ALFRED.
I DON'T THINK SHE WANTED TO BE SAVED, SIR.
VENGEANCE BLACKENS THE SOUL, BRUCE. I ALWAYS FEARED YOU WOULD BECOME THAT WHICH YOU FOUGHT AGAINST.
YOU WALK THE EDGE OF THAT ABYSS EVERY NIGHT. BUT YOU HAVEN'T FALLEN IN. AND I THANK HEAVEN FOR THAT.
BUT ANDREA FELL INTO THAT PIT YEARS AGO. AND NO ONE-- NOT EVEN YOU-- COULD HAVE PULLED HER OUT.

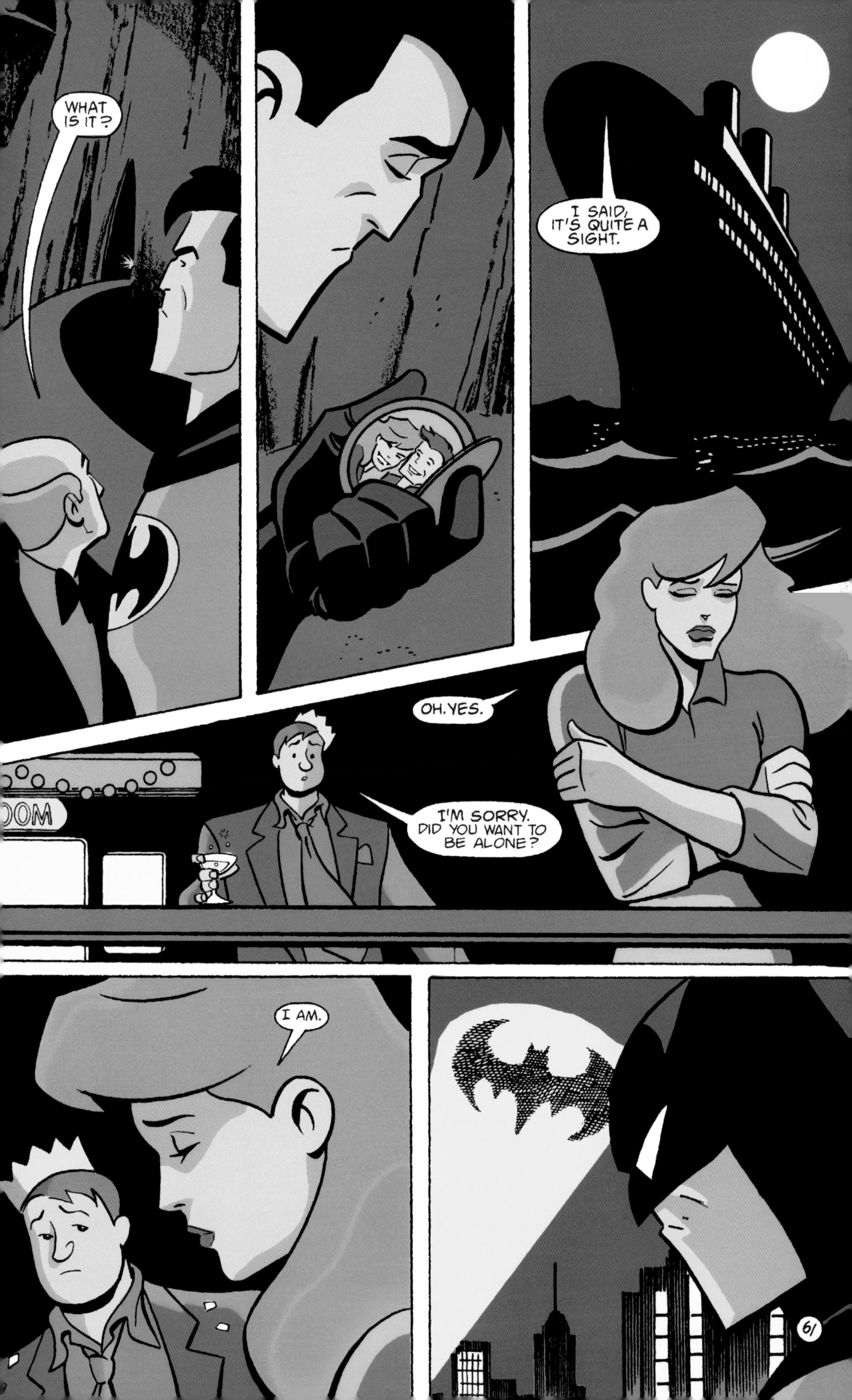
WHAT IS IT?
I SAID, IT'S QUITE A SIGHT.
OH. YES.
I'M SORRY. DID YOU WANT TO BE ALONE?
I AM.
61

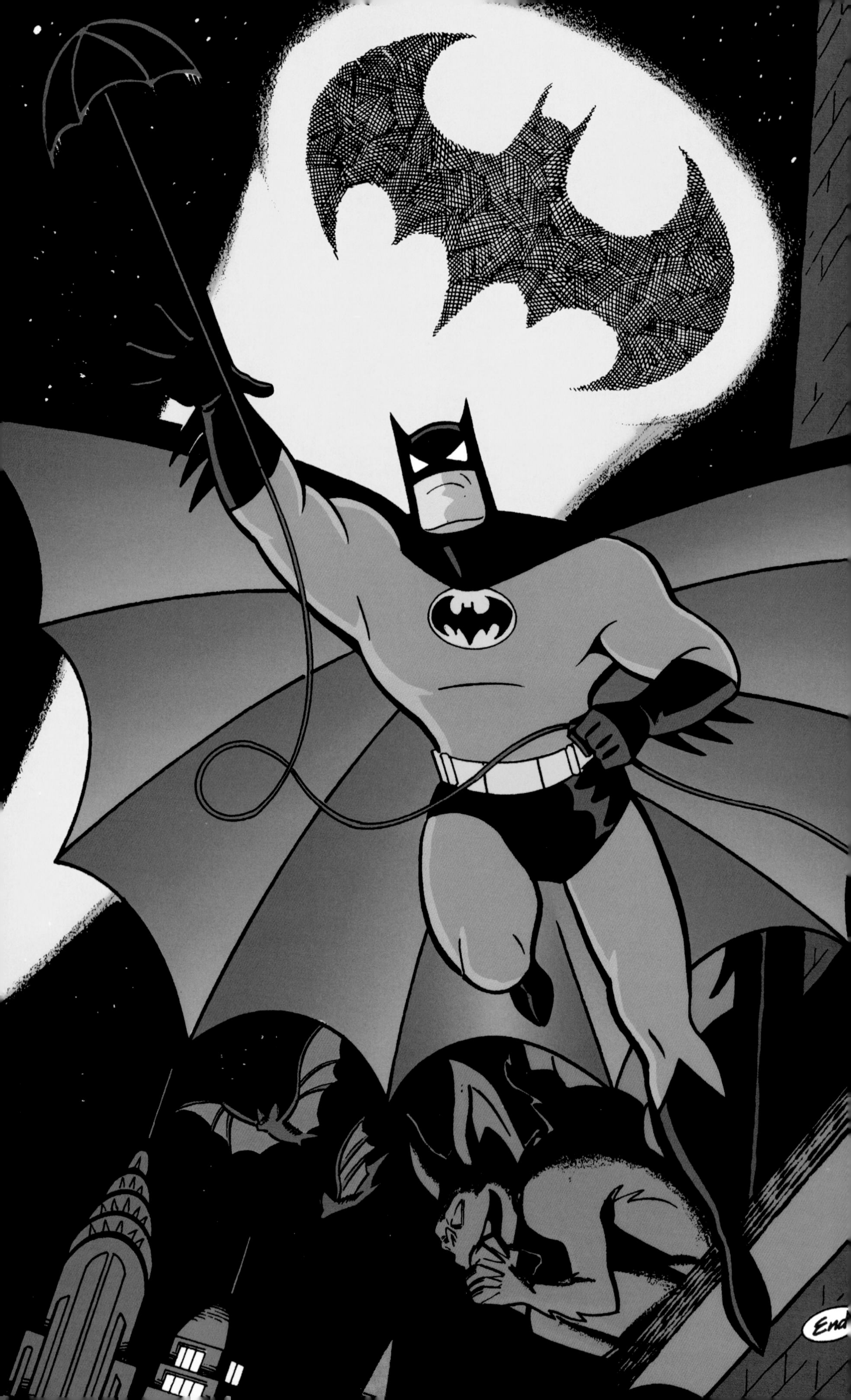
End

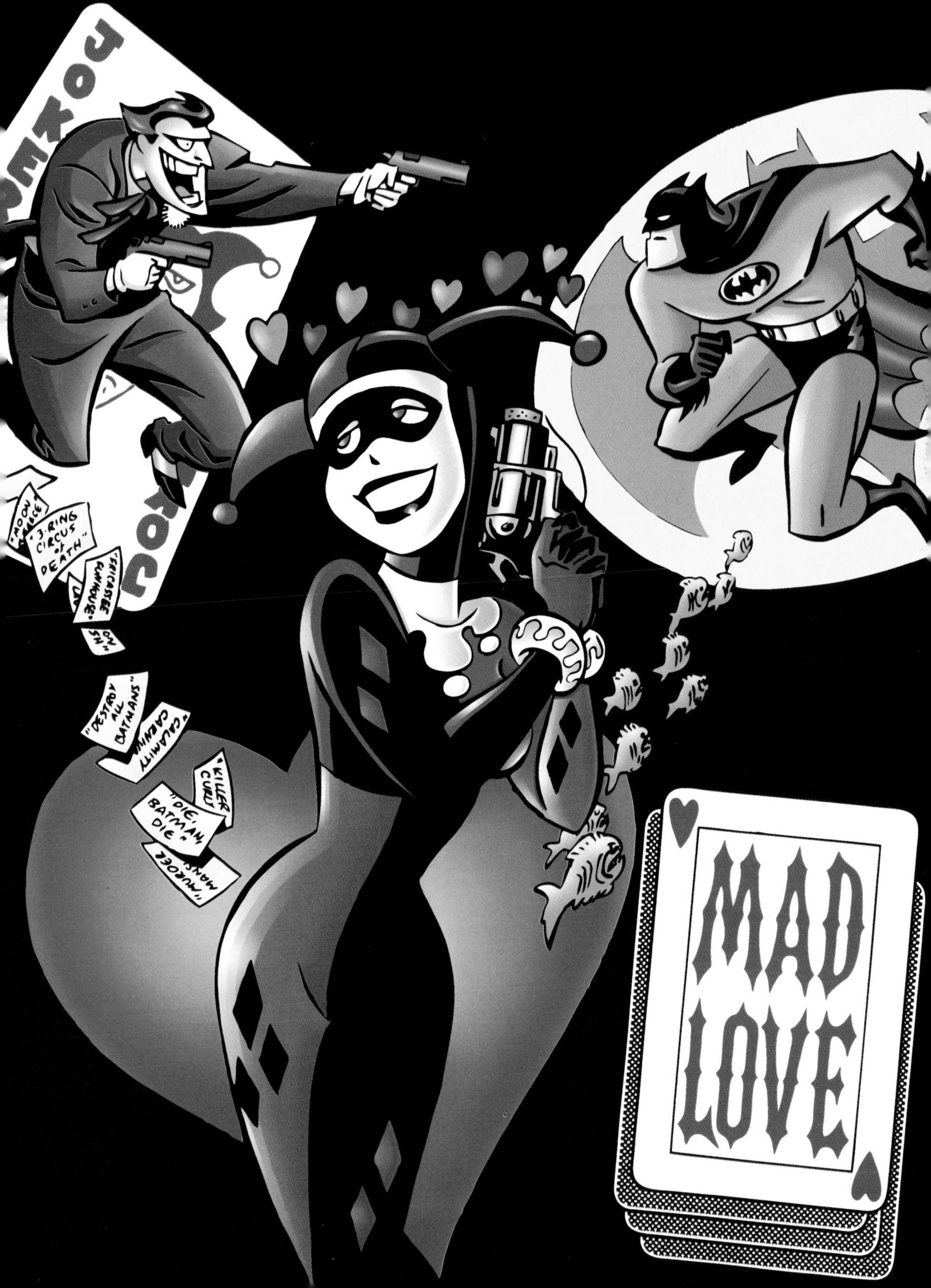
"3-RING CIRCUS of DEATH"
"FRICASSEE FUNHOUSE"
"DESTROY ALL BATMANS"
"DIE, BATMAN, DIE"
MAD LOVE

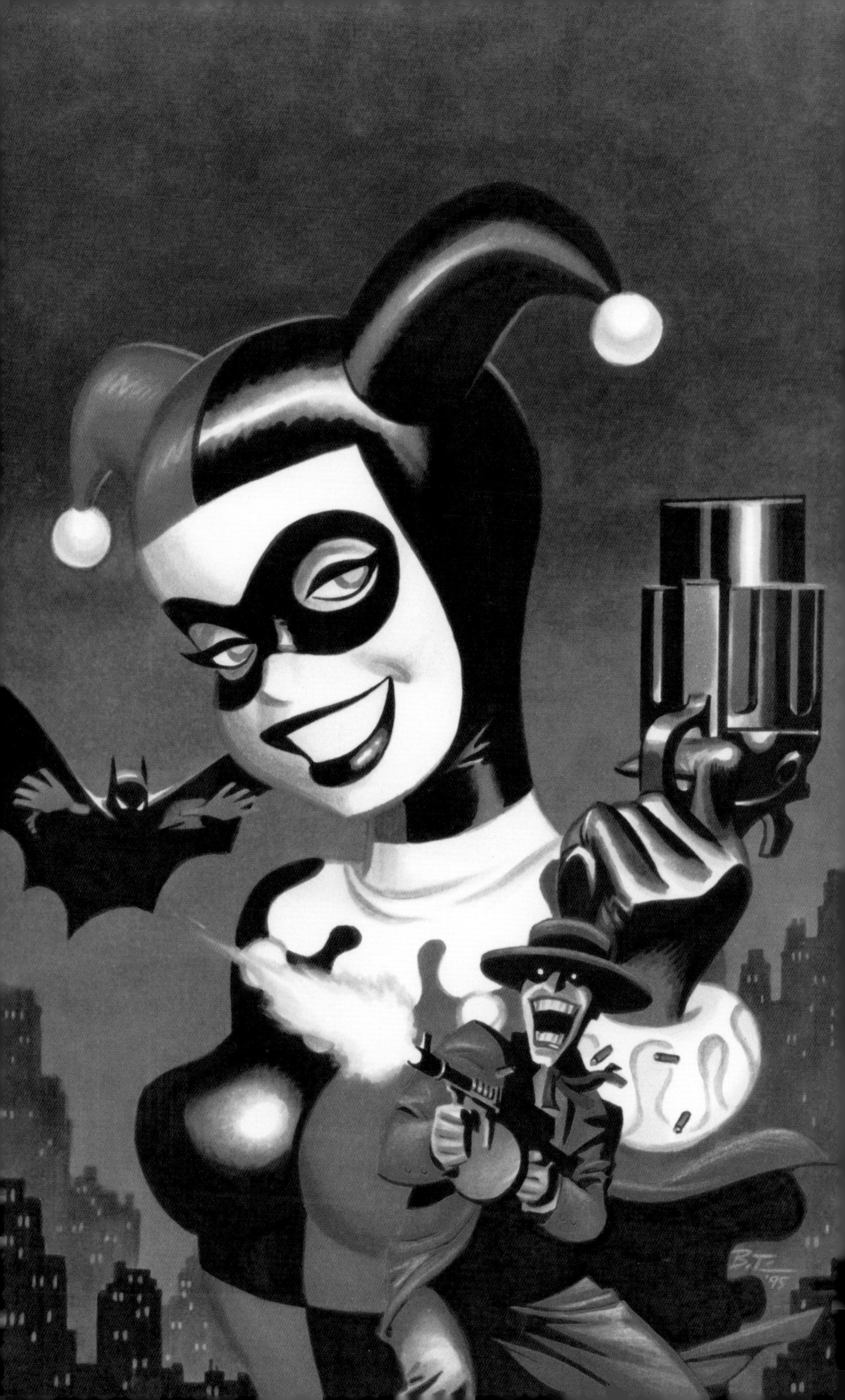
B.T. '95

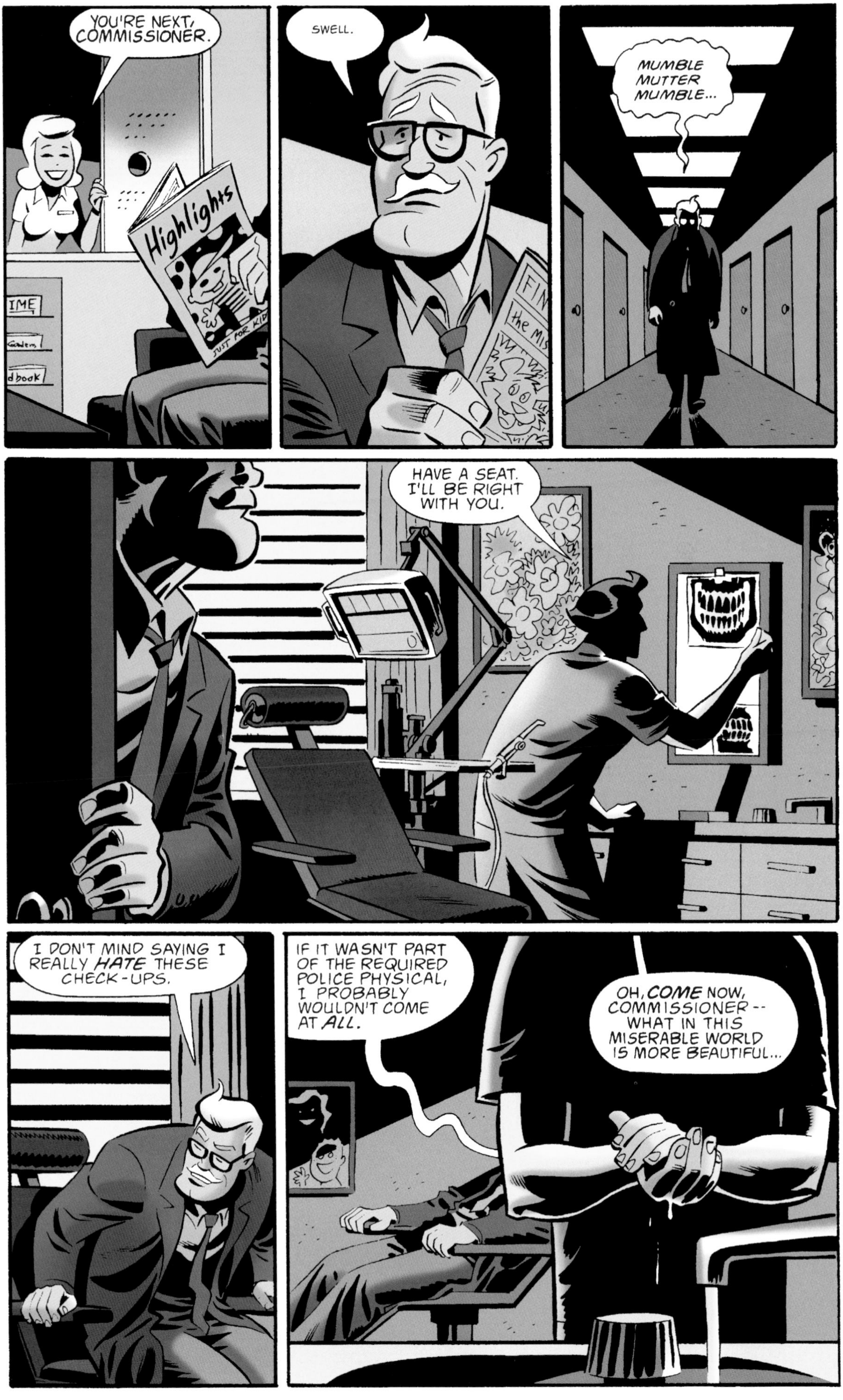
YOU'RE NEXT, COMMISSIONER.
Highlights
JUST FOR KIDS
SWELL.
MUMBLE MUTTER MUMBLE...
HAVE A SEAT. I'LL BE RIGHT WITH YOU.
I DON'T MIND SAYING I REALLY *HATE* THESE CHECK-UPS.
IF IT WASN'T PART OF THE REQUIRED POLICE PHYSICAL, I PROBABLY WOULDN'T COME AT *ALL*.
OH, *COME* NOW, COMMISSIONER -- WHAT IN THIS MISERABLE WORLD IS MORE BEAUTIFUL...

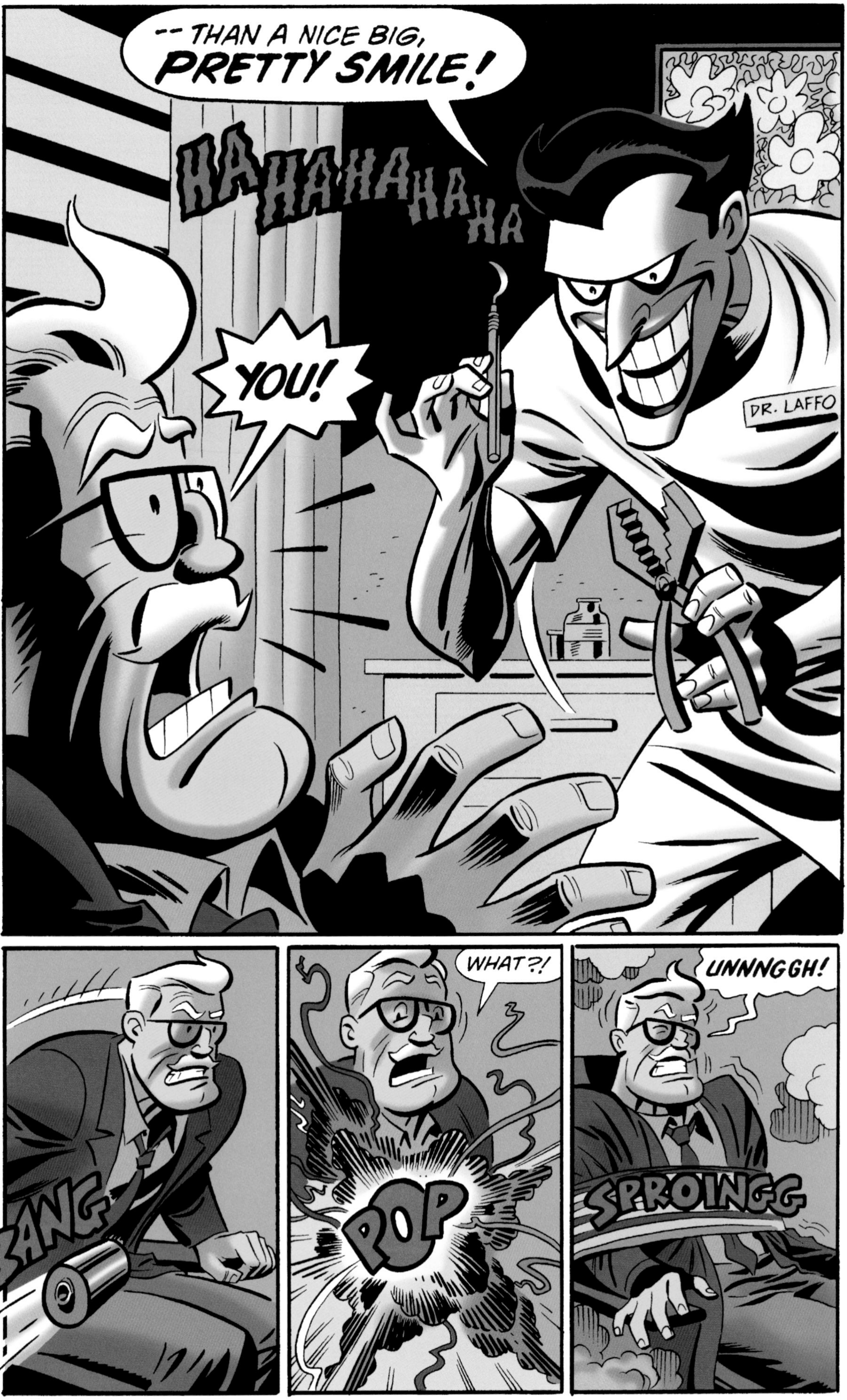
-- THAN A NICE BIG, PRETTY SMILE!
HAHAHAHAHAHA
YOU!
DR. LAFFO
BANG
WHAT?!
POP
UNNNGGH!
SPROINGG

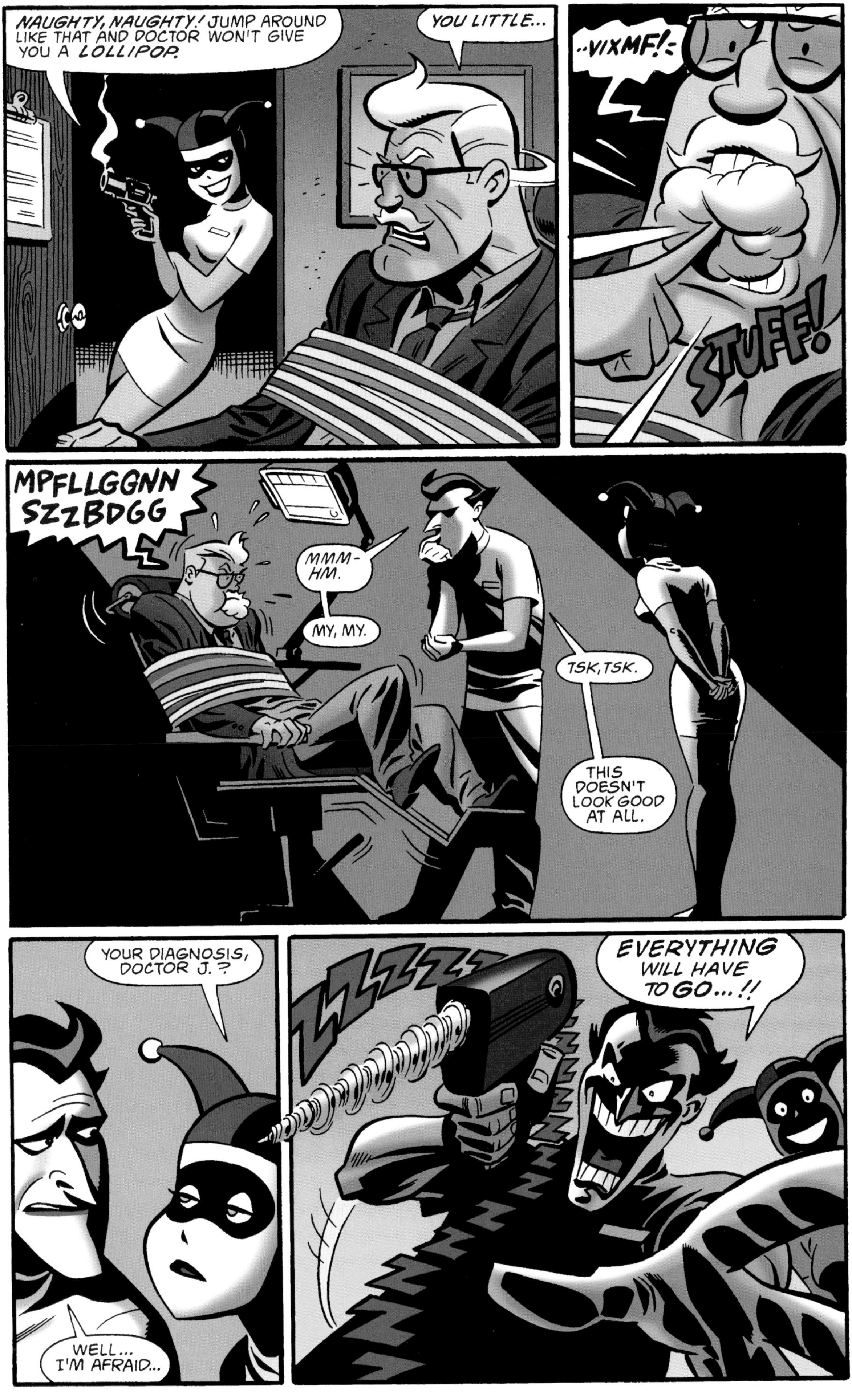
NAUGHTY, NAUGHTY! JUMP AROUND LIKE THAT AND DOCTOR WON'T GIVE YOU A LOLLIPOP.
YOU LITTLE...
..VIXMF!..
STUFF!
MPFLLGGNN SZZBDGG
MMM-HM.
MY, MY.
TSK, TSK.
THIS DOESN'T LOOK GOOD AT ALL.
YOUR DIAGNOSIS, DOCTOR J.?
WELL... I'M AFRAID...
EVERYTHING WILL HAVE TO GO...!!

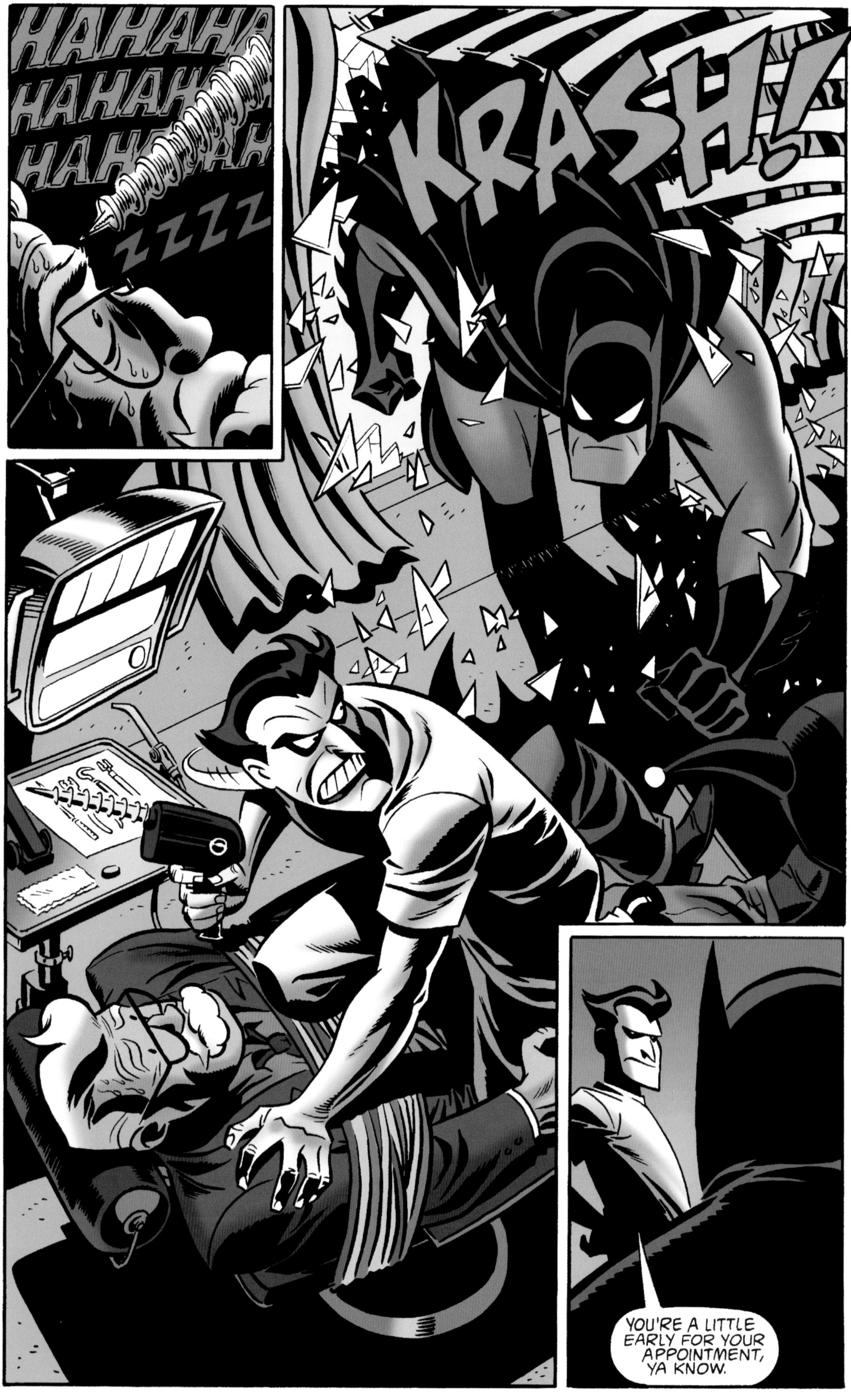
HAHAHA
HAHAHA
HAHAHA
ZZZZ
KRASH!
YOU'RE A LITTLE EARLY FOR YOUR APPOINTMENT, YA KNOW.

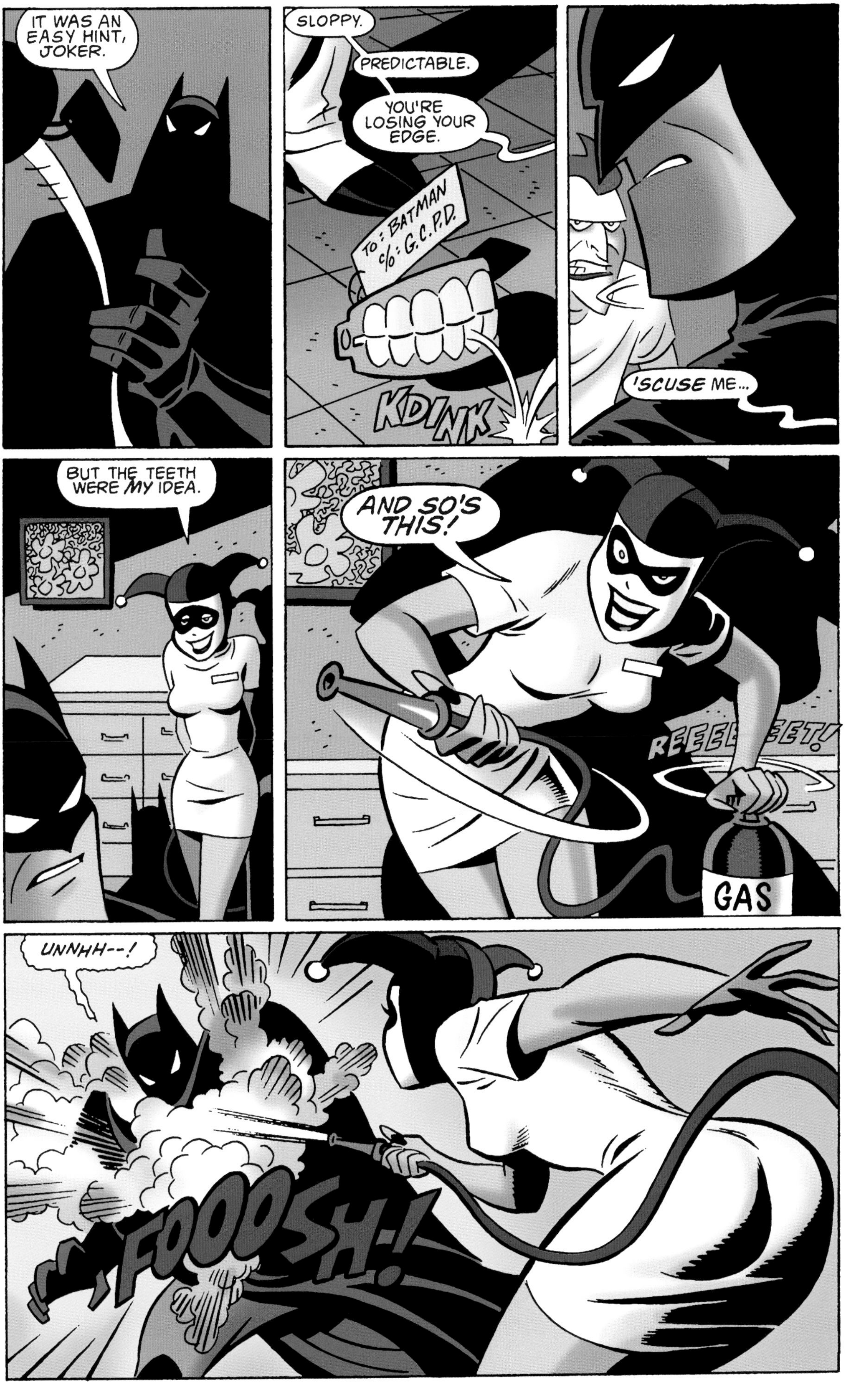

IT WAS AN EASY HINT, JOKER.
SLOPPY.
PREDICTABLE.
YOU'RE LOSING YOUR EDGE.
TO: BATMAN c/o: G.C.P.D.
KDINK
'SCUSE ME...
BUT THE TEETH WERE MY IDEA.
AND SO'S THIS!
REEEEEEET!
GAS
UNNHH--!
FOOOSH!

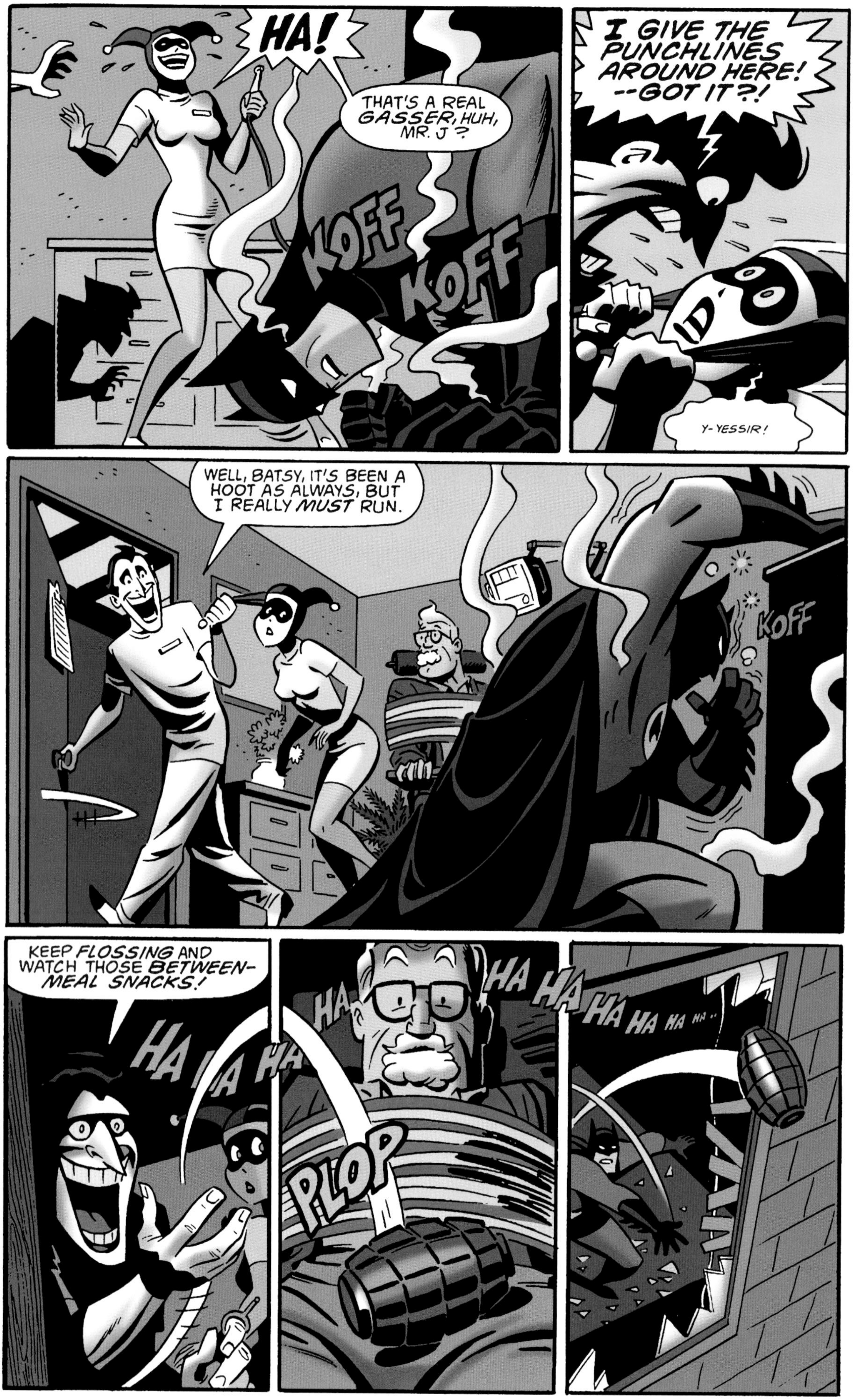
HA!
THAT'S A REAL GASSER, HUH, MR. J?
KOFF KOFF
I GIVE THE PUNCHLINES AROUND HERE! --GOT IT?!
Y-YESSIR!
WELL, BATSY, IT'S BEEN A HOOT AS ALWAYS, BUT I REALLY MUST RUN.
KOFF
KEEP FLOSSING AND WATCH THOSE BETWEEN-MEAL SNACKS!
HA HA HA HA
PLOP
HA HA HA HA HA HA HA HA

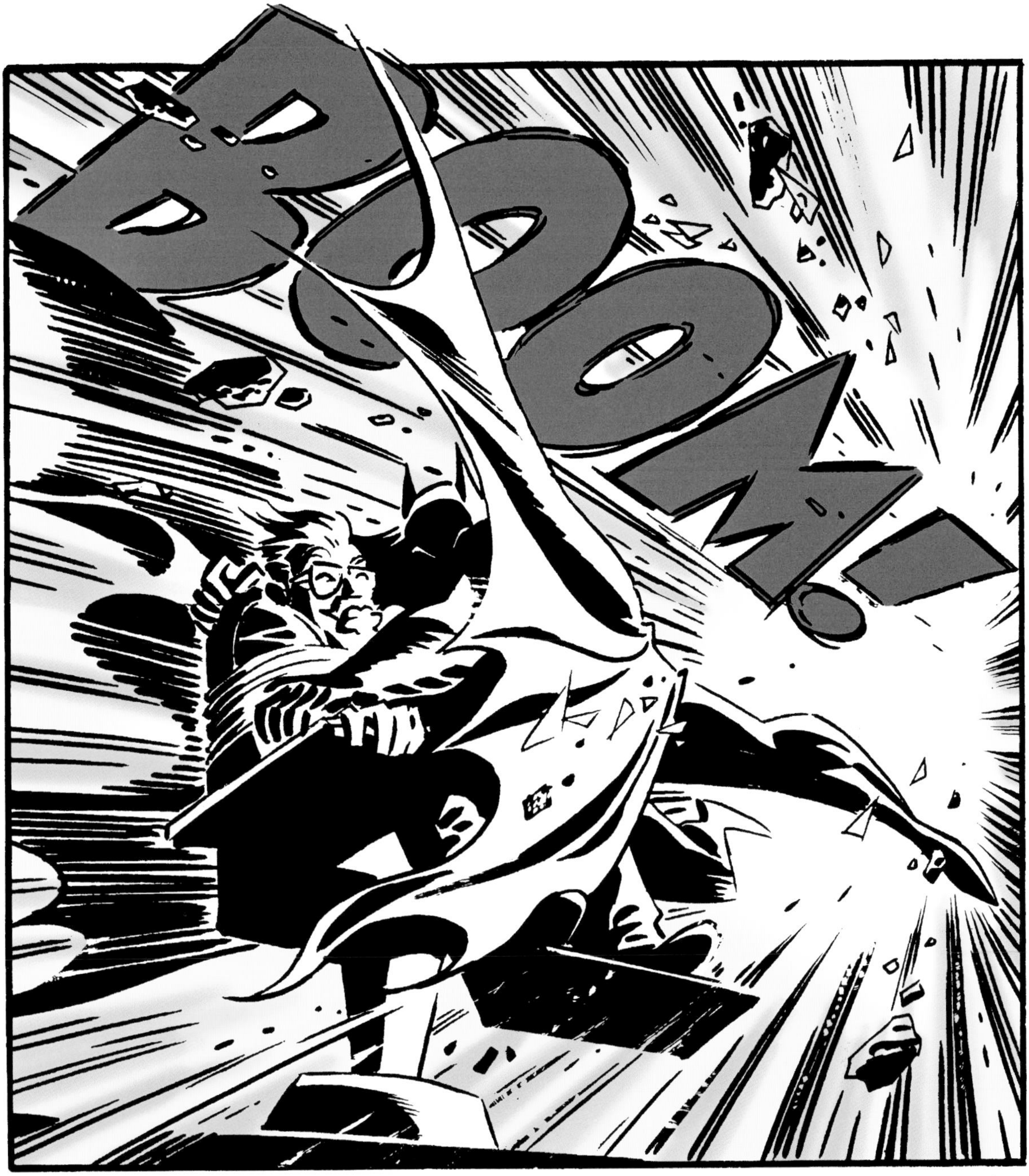
BOOOM!

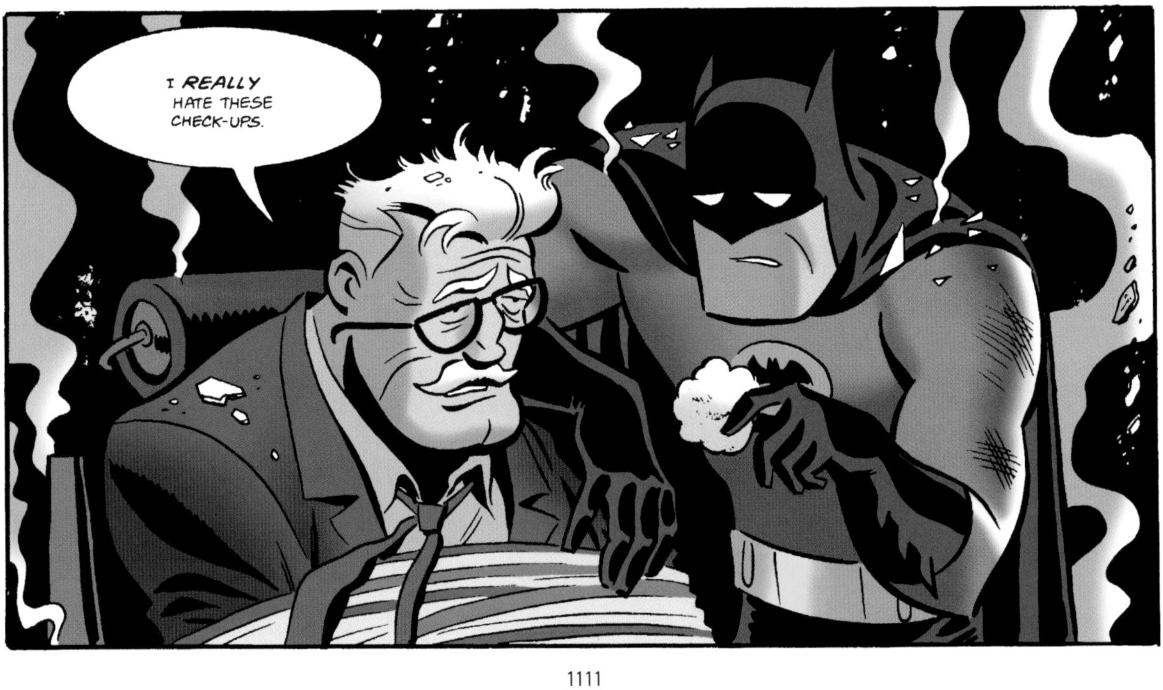
I REALLY HATE THESE CHECK-UPS.

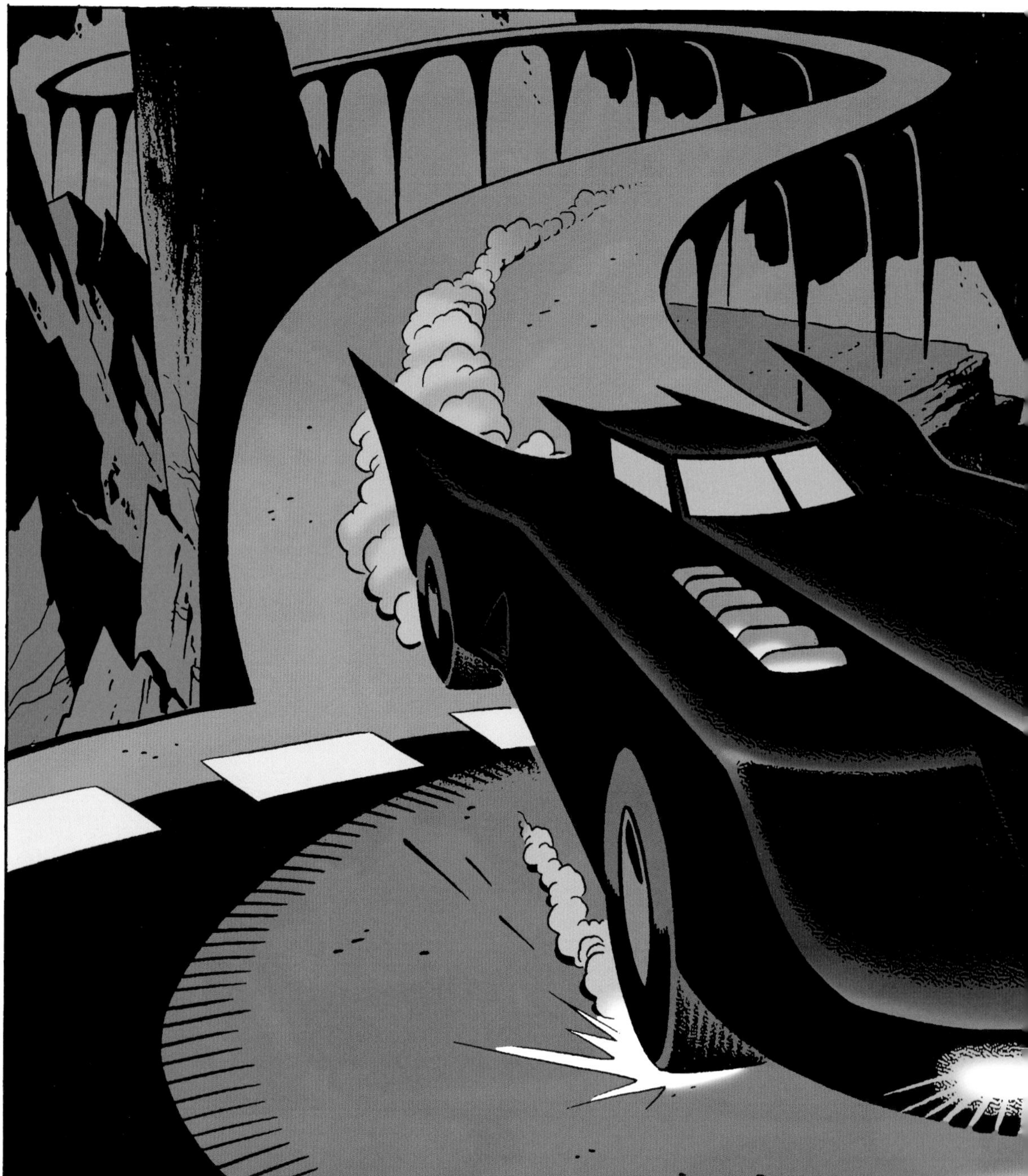

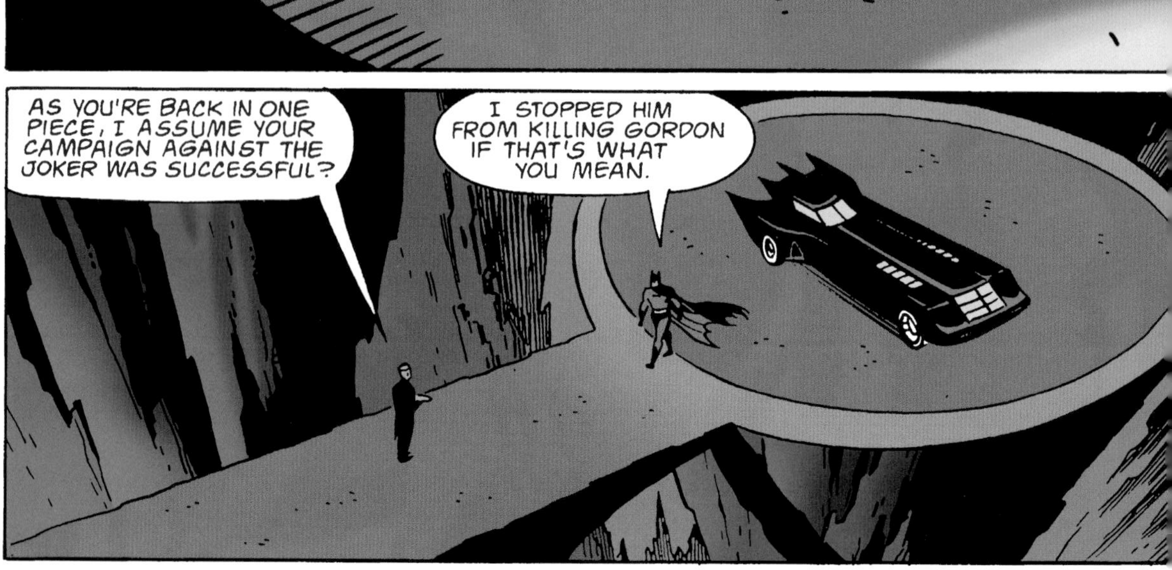
AS YOU'RE BACK IN ONE PIECE, I ASSUME YOUR CAMPAIGN AGAINST THE JOKER WAS SUCCESSFUL?
I STOPPED HIM FROM KILLING GORDON IF THAT'S WHAT YOU MEAN.

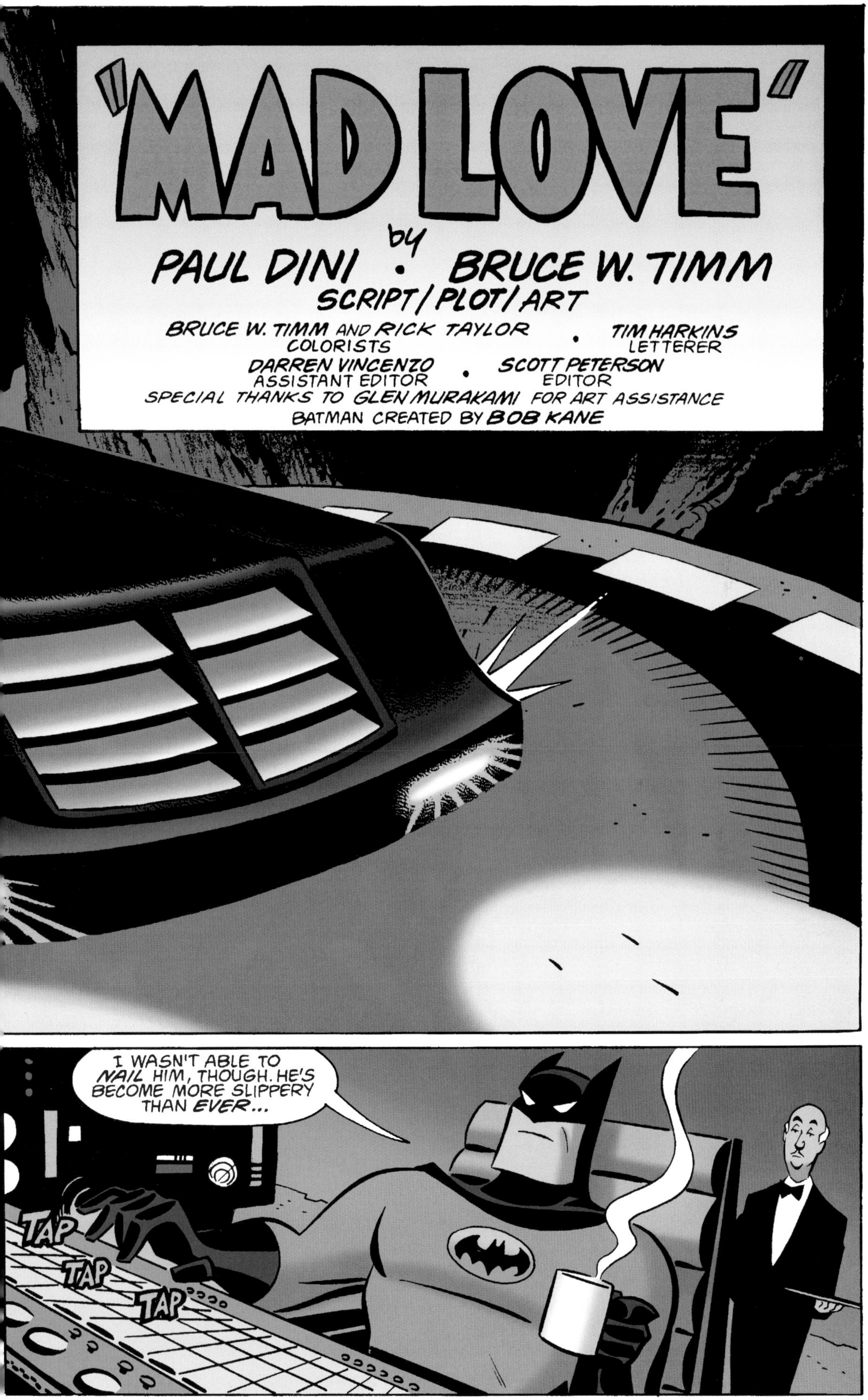
"MAD LOVE"
by
PAUL DINI · BRUCE W. TIMM
SCRIPT/PLOT/ART
BRUCE W. TIMM AND RICK TAYLOR COLORISTS
TIM HARKINS LETTERER
DARREN VINCENZO ASSISTANT EDITOR
SCOTT PETERSON EDITOR
SPECIAL THANKS TO GLEN MURAKAMI FOR ART ASSISTANCE
BATMAN CREATED BY BOB KANE
I WASN'T ABLE TO NAIL HIM, THOUGH. HE'S BECOME MORE SLIPPERY THAN EVER...
TAP
TAP
TAP

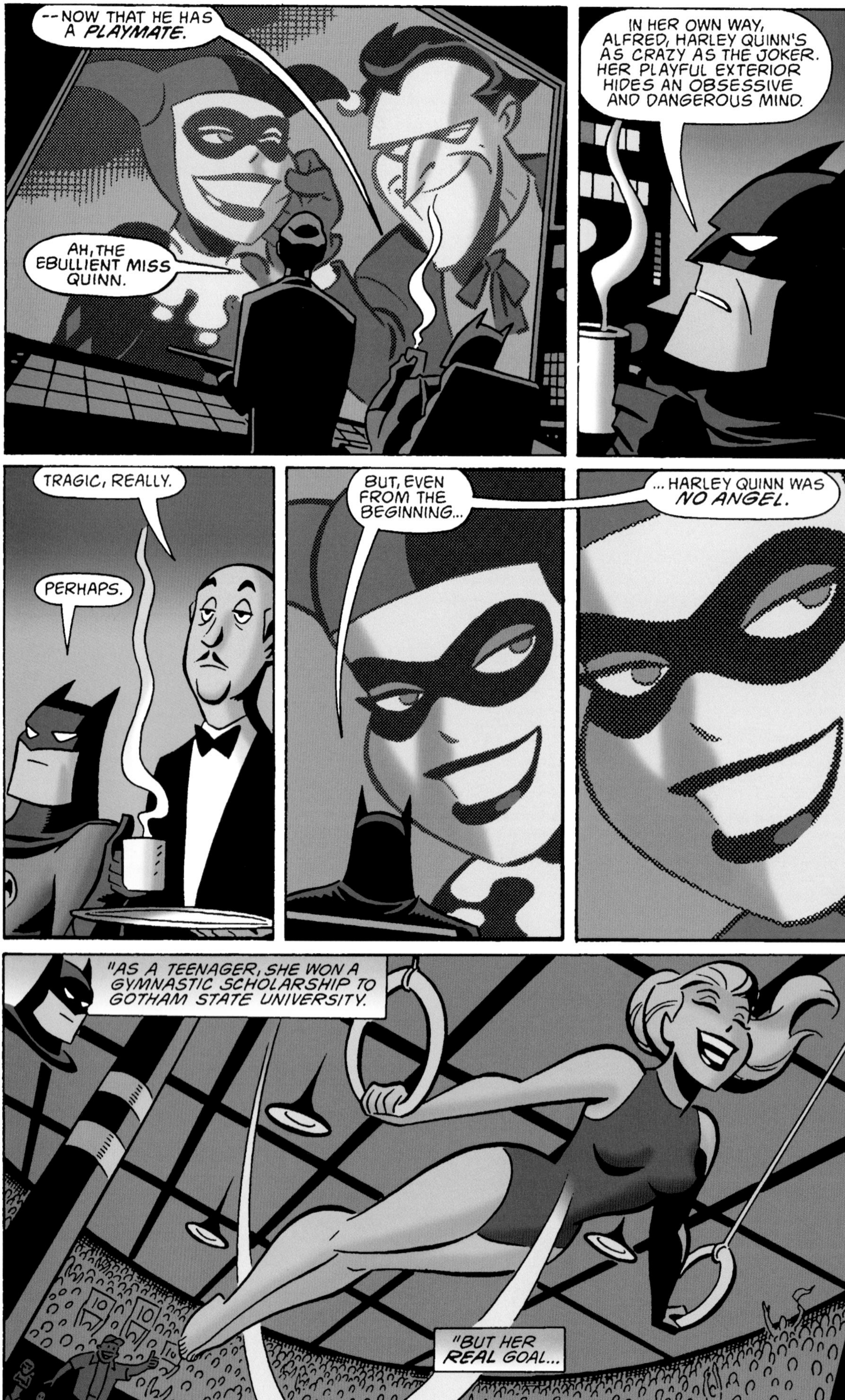

--NOW THAT HE HAS A PLAYMATE.
AH, THE EBULLIENT MISS QUINN.
IN HER OWN WAY, ALFRED, HARLEY QUINN'S AS CRAZY AS THE JOKER. HER PLAYFUL EXTERIOR HIDES AN OBSESSIVE AND DANGEROUS MIND.
TRAGIC, REALLY.
PERHAPS.
BUT, EVEN FROM THE BEGINNING...
... HARLEY QUINN WAS NO ANGEL.
"AS A TEENAGER, SHE WON A GYMNASTIC SCHOLARSHIP TO GOTHAM STATE UNIVERSITY.
"BUT HER REAL GOAL...

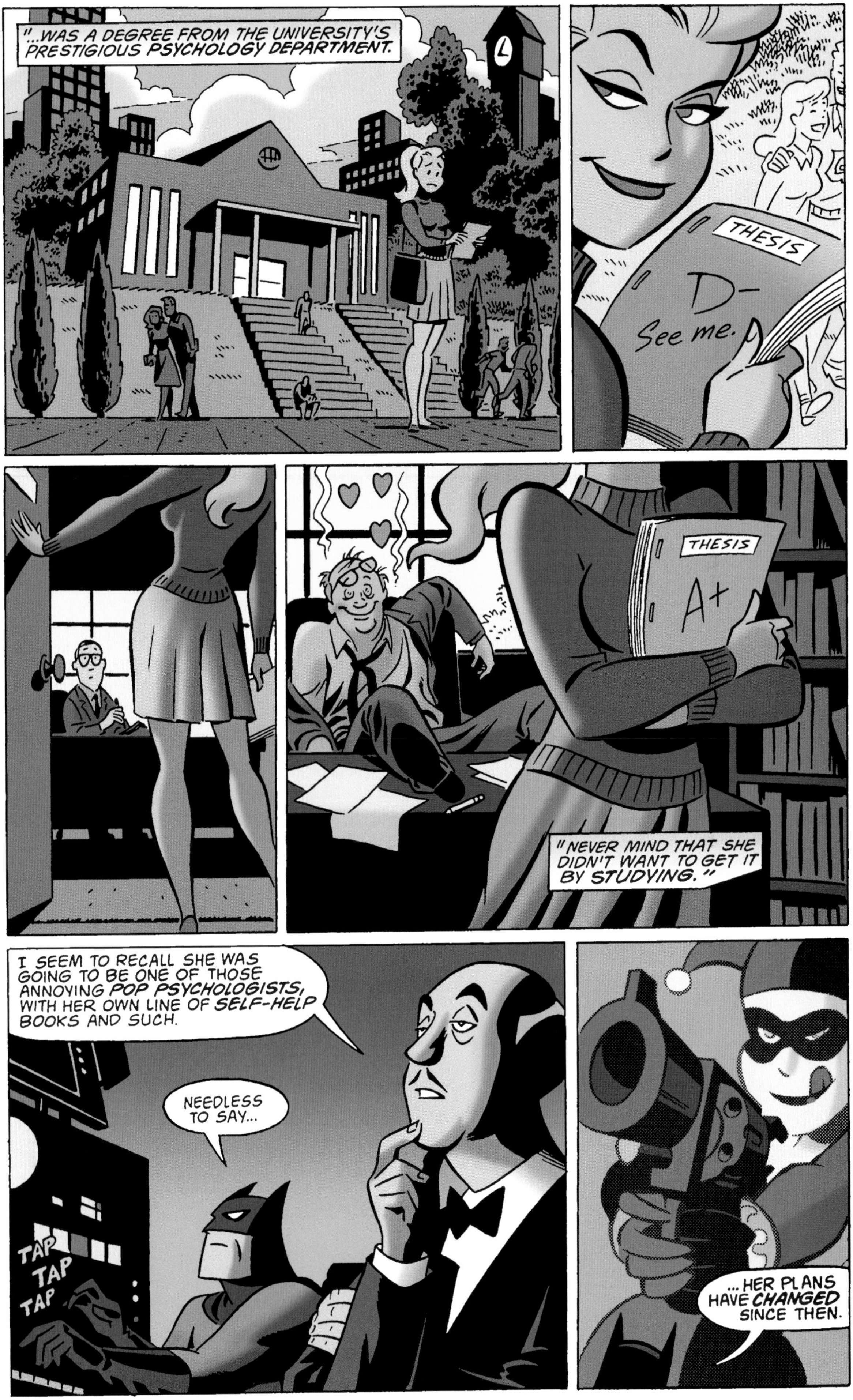
"...WAS A DEGREE FROM THE UNIVERSITY'S PRESTIGIOUS PSYCHOLOGY DEPARTMENT.
THESIS
D-
See me.
THESIS
A+
"NEVER MIND THAT SHE DIDN'T WANT TO GET IT BY STUDYING."
I SEEM TO RECALL SHE WAS GOING TO BE ONE OF THOSE ANNOYING POP PSYCHOLOGISTS, WITH HER OWN LINE OF SELF-HELP BOOKS AND SUCH.
NEEDLESS TO SAY...
TAP TAP TAP
...HER PLANS HAVE CHANGED SINCE THEN.

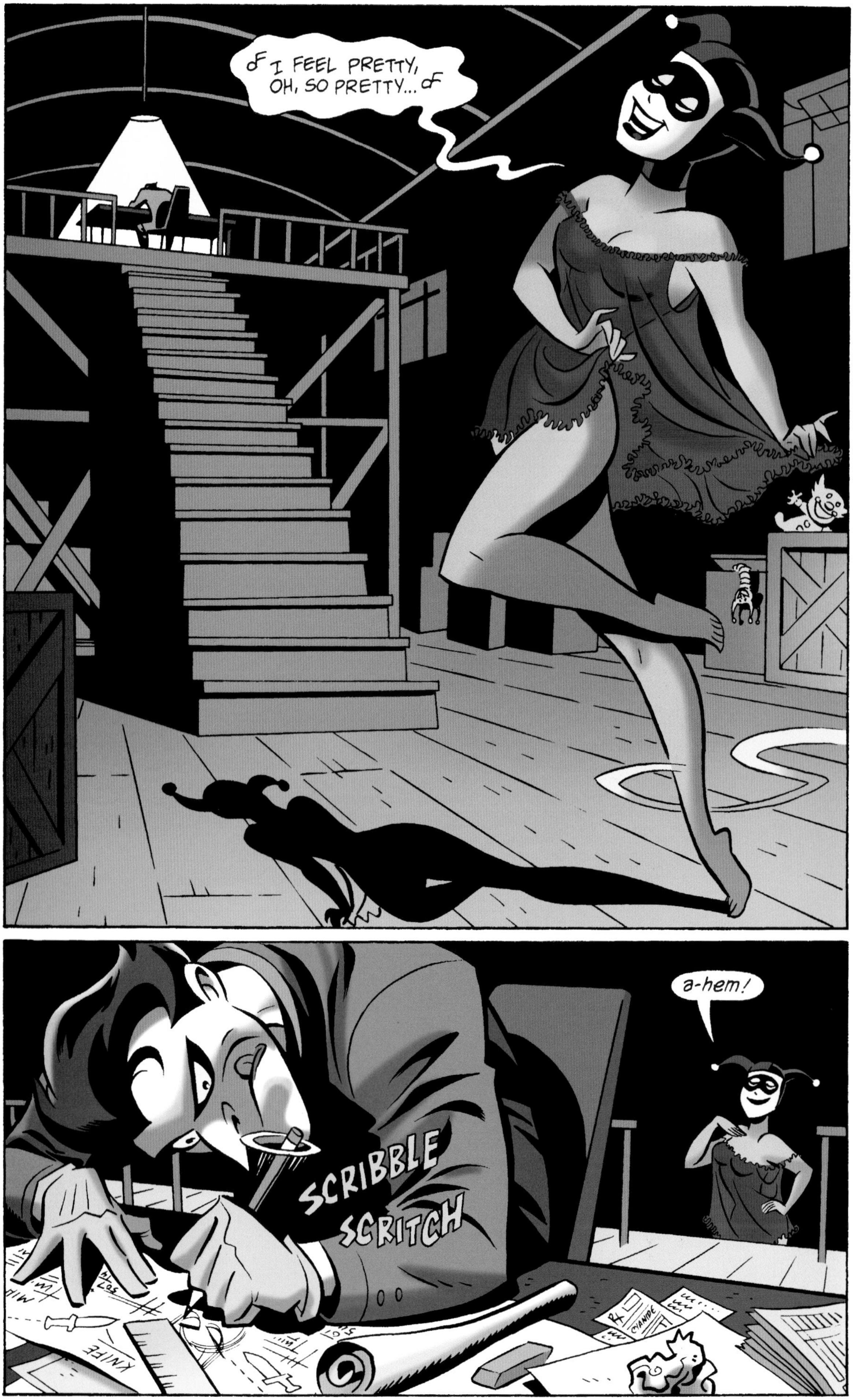
I FEEL PRETTY, OH, SO PRETTY...
SCRIBBLE
SCRITCH
a-hem!

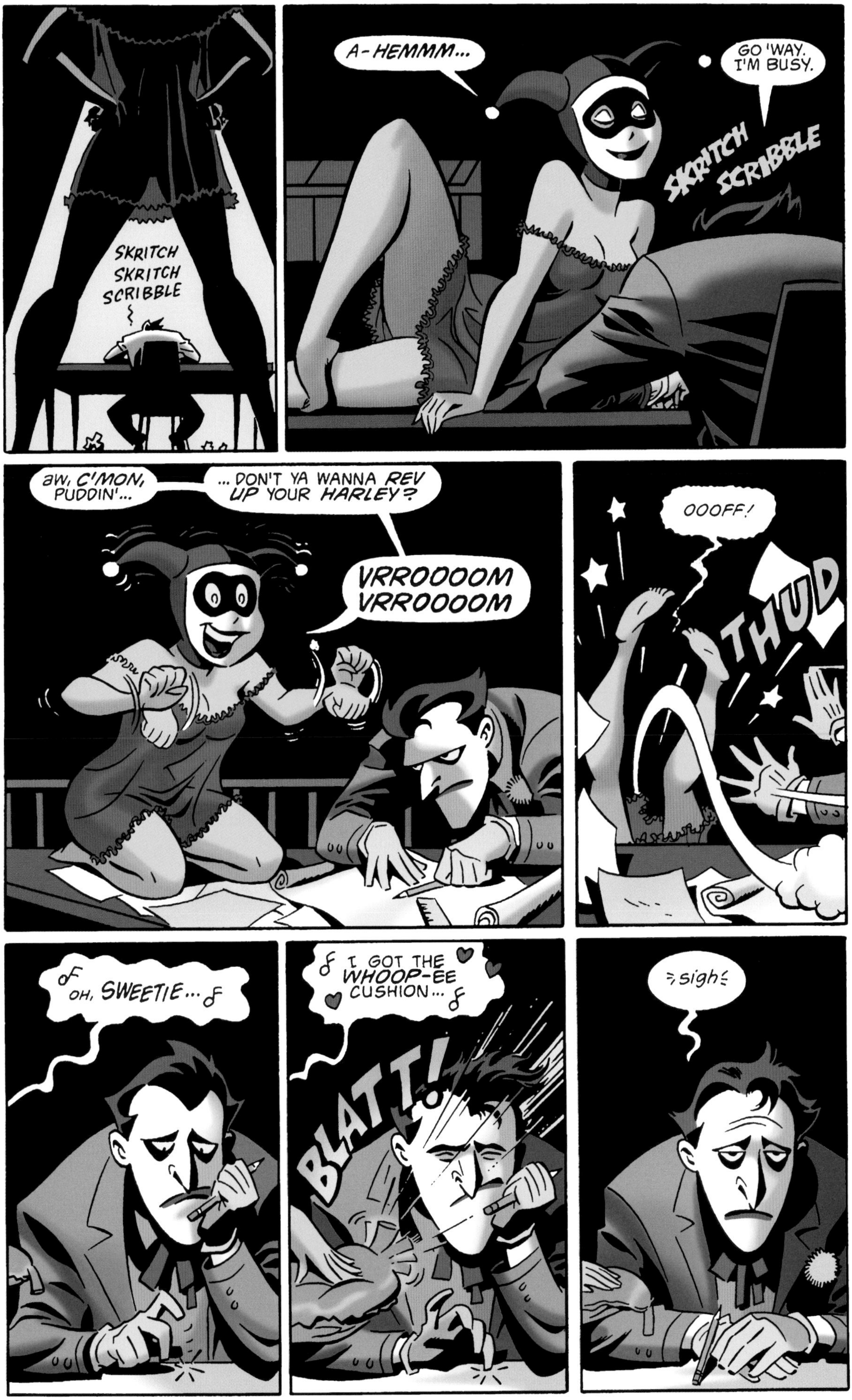
SKRITCH
SKRITCH
SCRIBBLE
A-HEMMM...
GO 'WAY. I'M BUSY.
SKRITCH
SCRIBBLE
AW, C'MON, PUDDIN'...
...DON'T YA WANNA REV UP YOUR HARLEY?
VRROOOOM VRROOOOM
OOOFF!
THUD
OH, SWEETIE...
I GOT THE WHOOP-EE CUSHION...
BLATT!
sigh

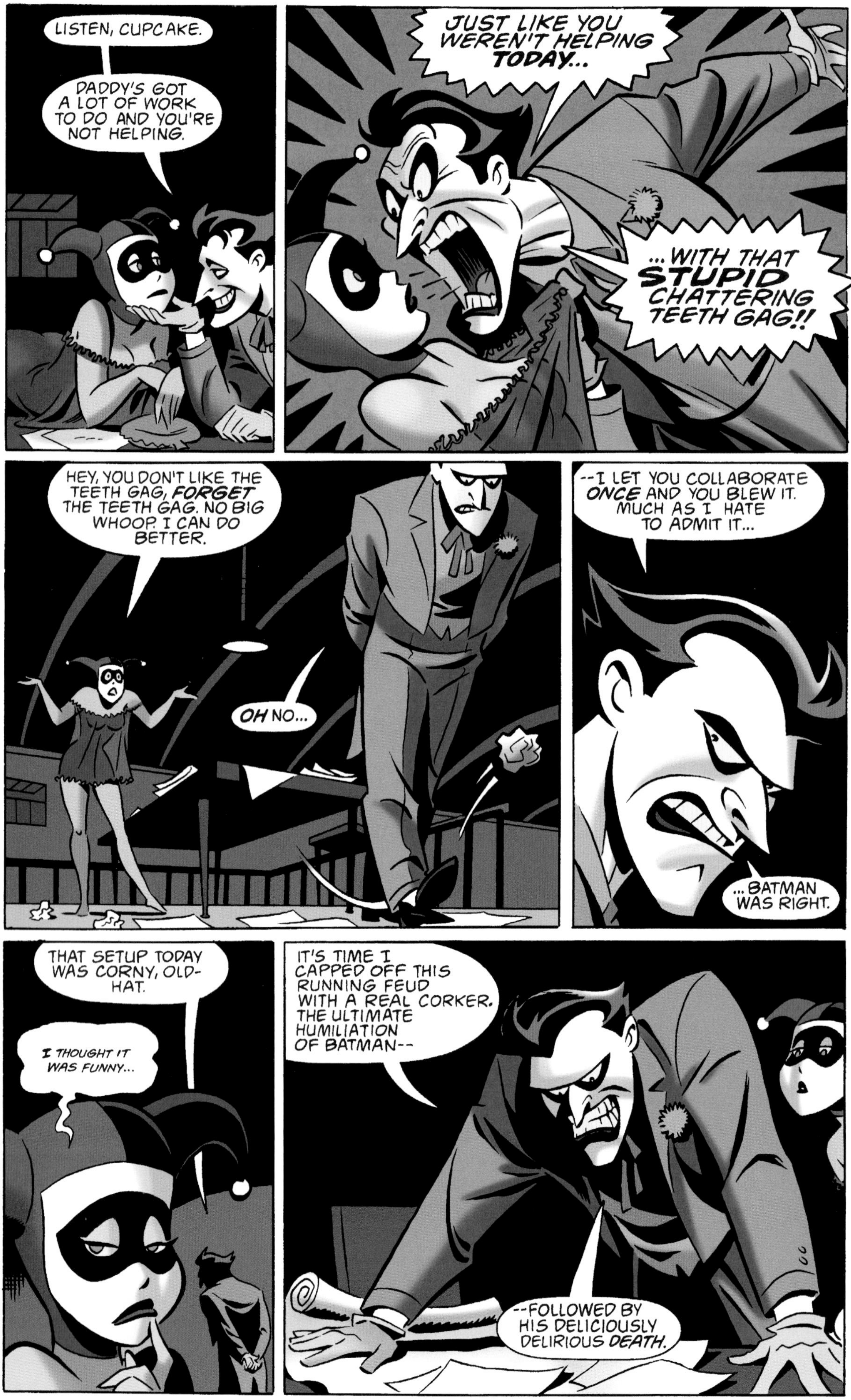

LISTEN, CUPCAKE.
DADDY'S GOT A LOT OF WORK TO DO AND YOU'RE NOT HELPING.
JUST LIKE YOU WEREN'T HELPING TODAY...
...WITH THAT STUPID CHATTERING TEETH GAG!!
HEY, YOU DON'T LIKE THE TEETH GAG, FORGET THE TEETH GAG. NO BIG WHOOP. I CAN DO BETTER.
OH NO...
--I LET YOU COLLABORATE ONCE AND YOU BLEW IT. MUCH AS I HATE TO ADMIT IT...
...BATMAN WAS RIGHT.
THAT SETUP TODAY WAS CORNY, OLD-HAT.
I THOUGHT IT WAS FUNNY...
IT'S TIME I CAPPED OFF THIS RUNNING FEUD WITH A REAL CORKER. THE ULTIMATE HUMILIATION OF BATMAN--
--FOLLOWED BY HIS DELICIOUSLY DELIRIOUS DEATH.

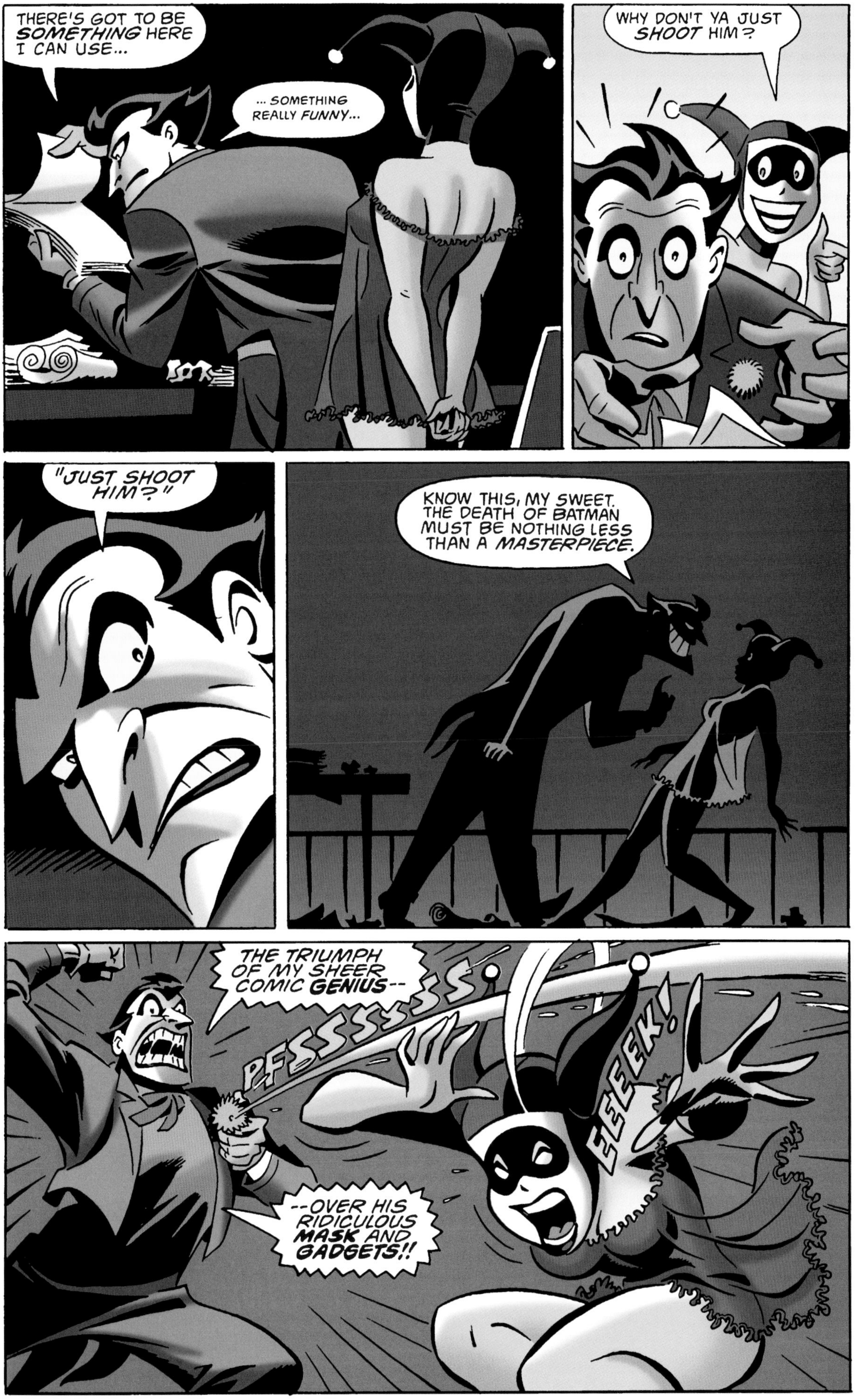
THERE'S GOT TO BE SOMETHING HERE I CAN USE...
... SOMETHING REALLY FUNNY...
WHY DON'T YA JUST SHOOT HIM?
"JUST SHOOT HIM?"
KNOW THIS, MY SWEET. THE DEATH OF BATMAN MUST BE NOTHING LESS THAN A MASTERPIECE.
THE TRIUMPH OF MY SHEER COMIC GENIUS--
PFSSSSSSS
EEEEK!
--OVER HIS RIDICULOUS MASK AND GADGETS!!

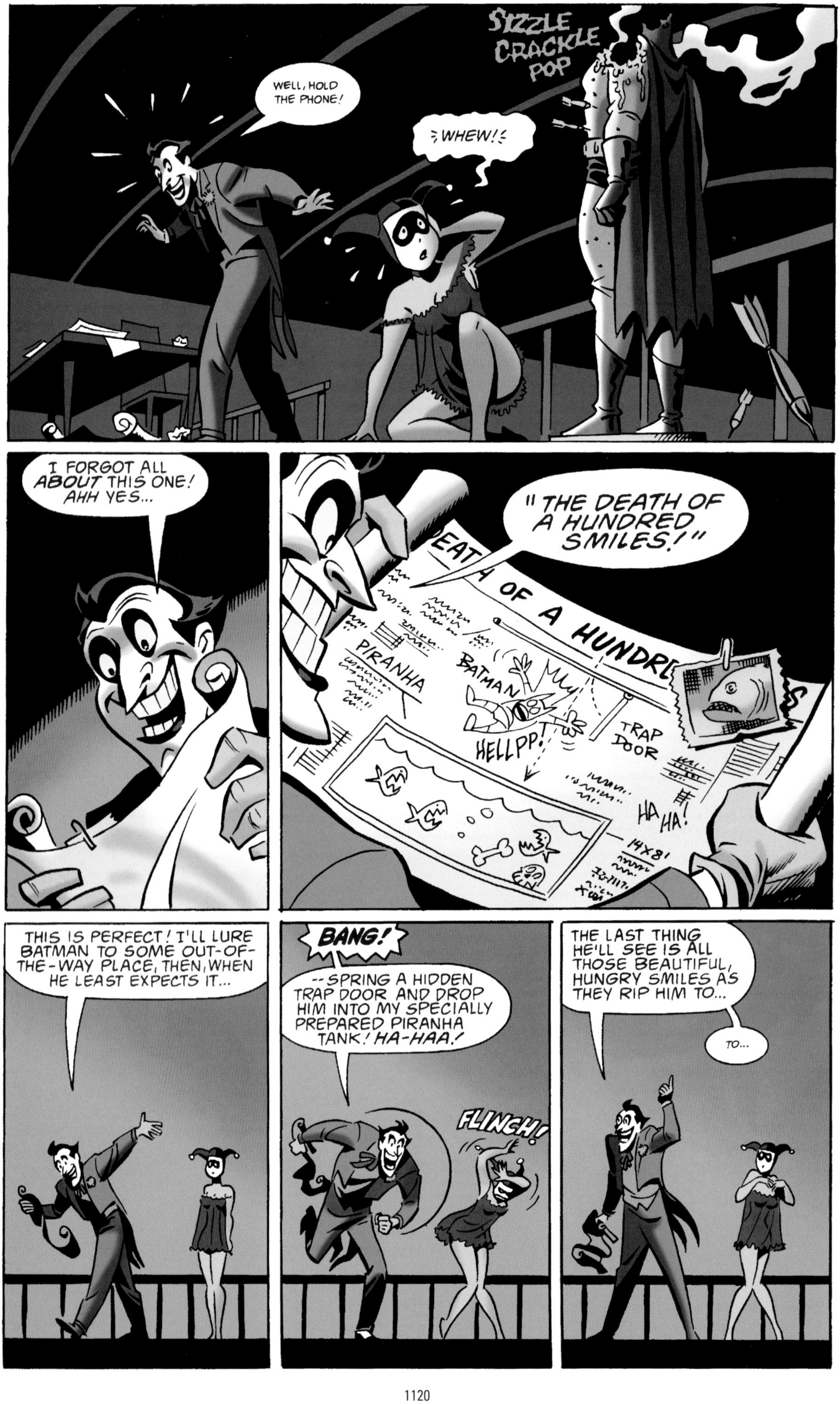
SIZZLE CRACKLE POP
WELL, HOLD THE PHONE!
WHEW!
I FORGOT ALL ABOUT THIS ONE! AHH YES...
"THE DEATH OF A HUNDRED SMILES!"
EATH OF A HUNDRE
PIRANHA
BATMAN
HELLPP!
TRAP DOOR
HA HA!
14X8'
THIS IS PERFECT! I'LL LURE BATMAN TO SOME OUT-OF-THE-WAY PLACE, THEN, WHEN HE LEAST EXPECTS IT...
BANG!
--SPRING A HIDDEN TRAP DOOR AND DROP HIM INTO MY SPECIALLY PREPARED PIRANHA TANK! HA-HAA!
FLINCH!
THE LAST THING HE'LL SEE IS ALL THOSE BEAUTIFUL, HUNGRY SMILES AS THEY RIP HIM TO...
TO...

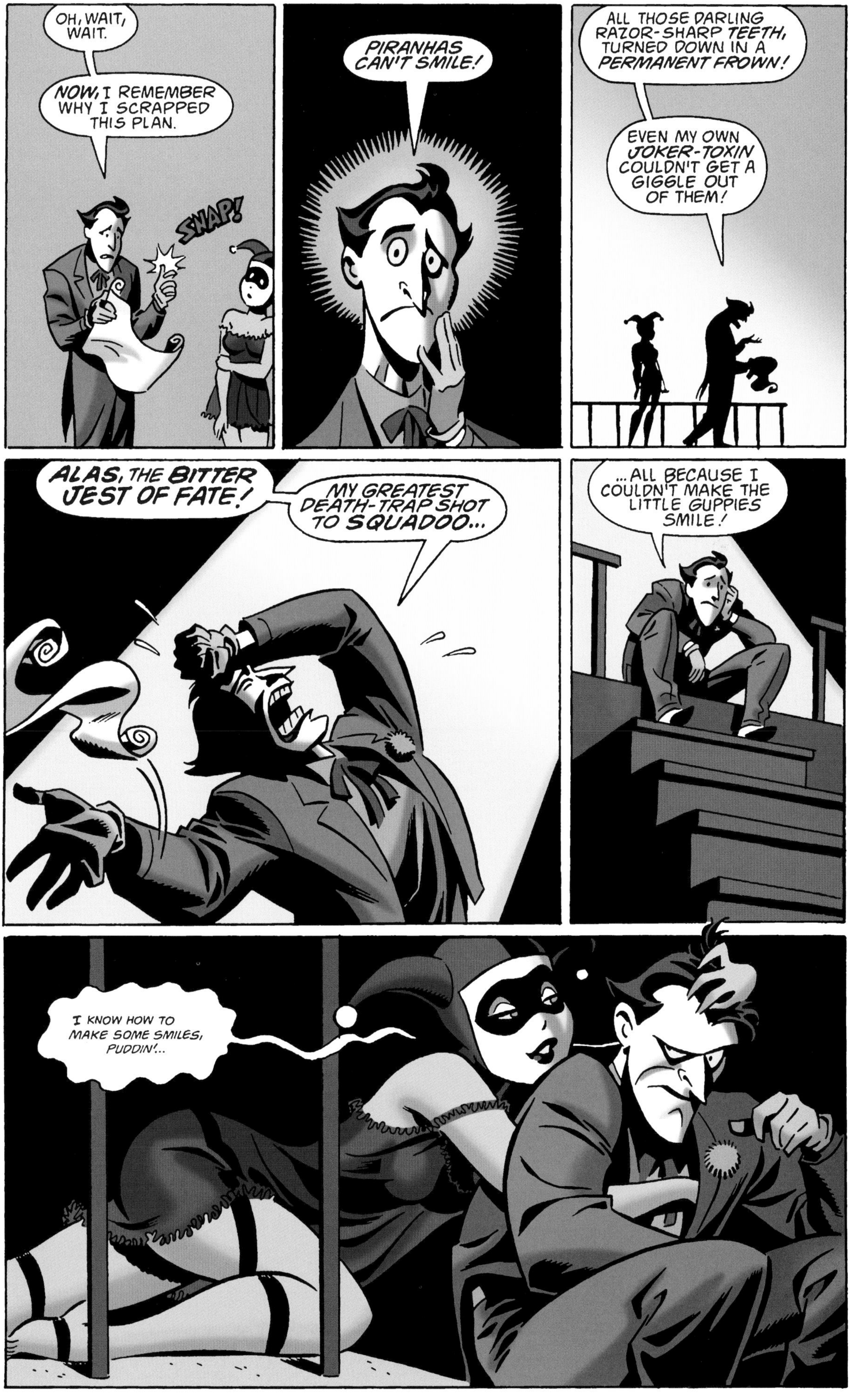
OH, WAIT, WAIT.
NOW, I REMEMBER WHY I SCRAPPED THIS PLAN.
SNAP!
PIRANHAS CAN'T SMILE!
ALL THOSE DARLING RAZOR-SHARP TEETH, TURNED DOWN IN A PERMANENT FROWN!
EVEN MY OWN JOKER-TOXIN COULDN'T GET A GIGGLE OUT OF THEM!
ALAS, THE BITTER JEST OF FATE!
MY GREATEST DEATH-TRAP SHOT TO SQUADOO...
...ALL BECAUSE I COULDN'T MAKE THE LITTLE GUPPIES SMILE!
I KNOW HOW TO MAKE SOME SMILES, PUDDIN'...

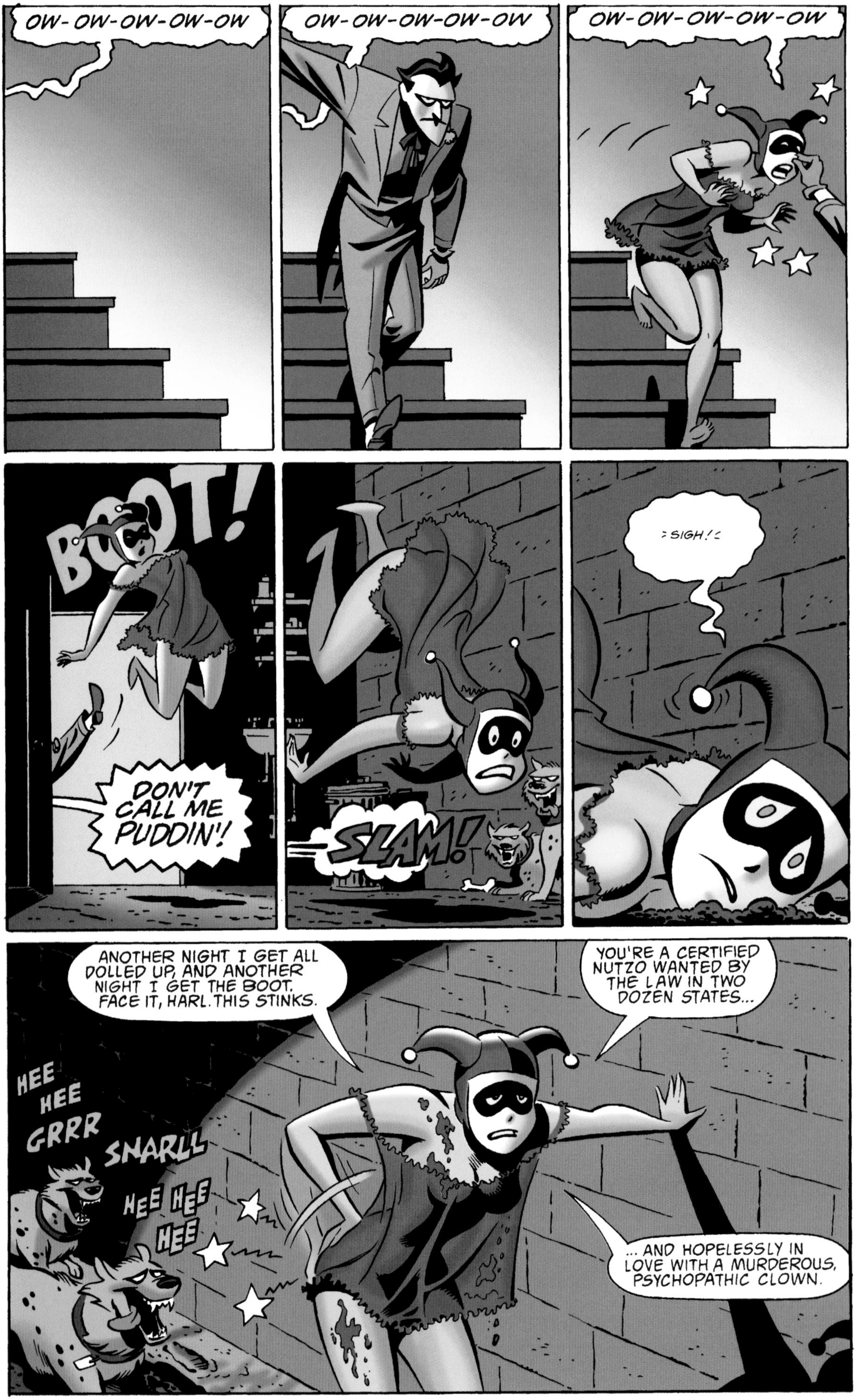
OW-OW-OW-OW-OW
OW-OW-OW-OW-OW
OW-OW-OW-OW-OW
BOOT!
DON'T CALL ME PUDDIN'!
SLAM!
SIGH!
ANOTHER NIGHT I GET ALL DOLLED UP, AND ANOTHER NIGHT I GET THE BOOT. FACE IT, HARL. THIS STINKS.
YOU'RE A CERTIFIED NUTZO WANTED BY THE LAW IN TWO DOZEN STATES...
HEE HEE GRRR
SNARLL
HEE HEE HEE
...AND HOPELESSLY IN LOVE WITH A MURDEROUS, PSYCHOPATHIC CLOWN.

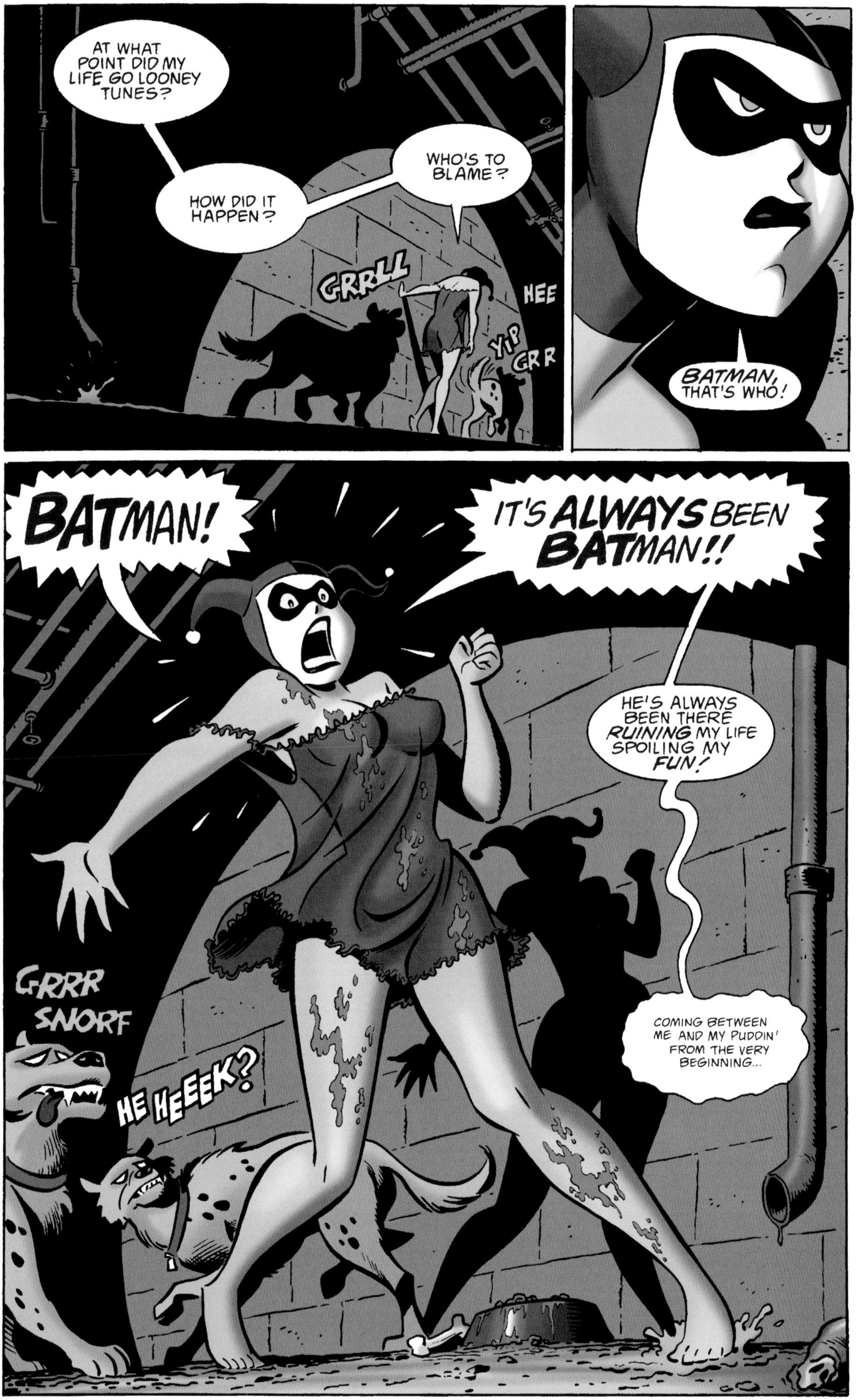
AT WHAT POINT DID MY LIFE GO LOONEY TUNES?
HOW DID IT HAPPEN?
WHO'S TO BLAME?
GRRLL
HEE
YIP
GRR
BATMAN, THAT'S WHO!
BATMAN!
IT'S ALWAYS BEEN BATMAN!!
HE'S ALWAYS BEEN THERE RUINING MY LIFE SPOILING MY FUN!
COMING BETWEEN ME AND MY PUDDIN' FROM THE VERY BEGINNING...
GRRR
SNORF
HE HEEEK?

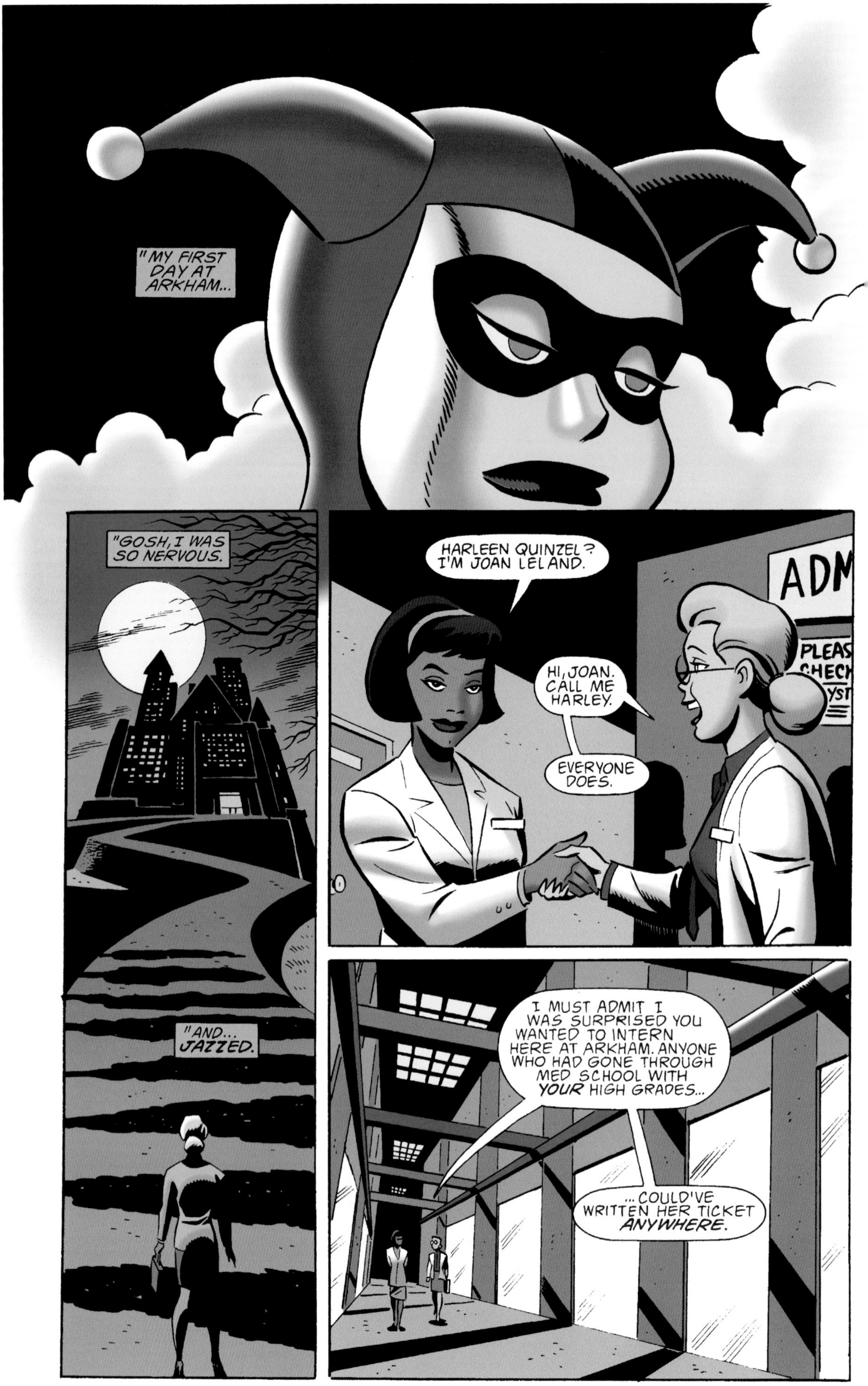
"MY FIRST DAY AT ARKHAM...
"GOSH, I WAS SO NERVOUS.
"AND... JAZZED.
HARLEEN QUINZEL? I'M JOAN LELAND.
HI, JOAN. CALL ME HARLEY.
EVERYONE DOES.
ADM
PLEAS
CHECK
YST
I MUST ADMIT I WAS SURPRISED YOU WANTED TO INTERN HERE AT ARKHAM. ANYONE WHO HAD GONE THROUGH MED SCHOOL WITH *YOUR* HIGH GRADES...
...COULD'VE WRITTEN HER TICKET *ANYWHERE*.

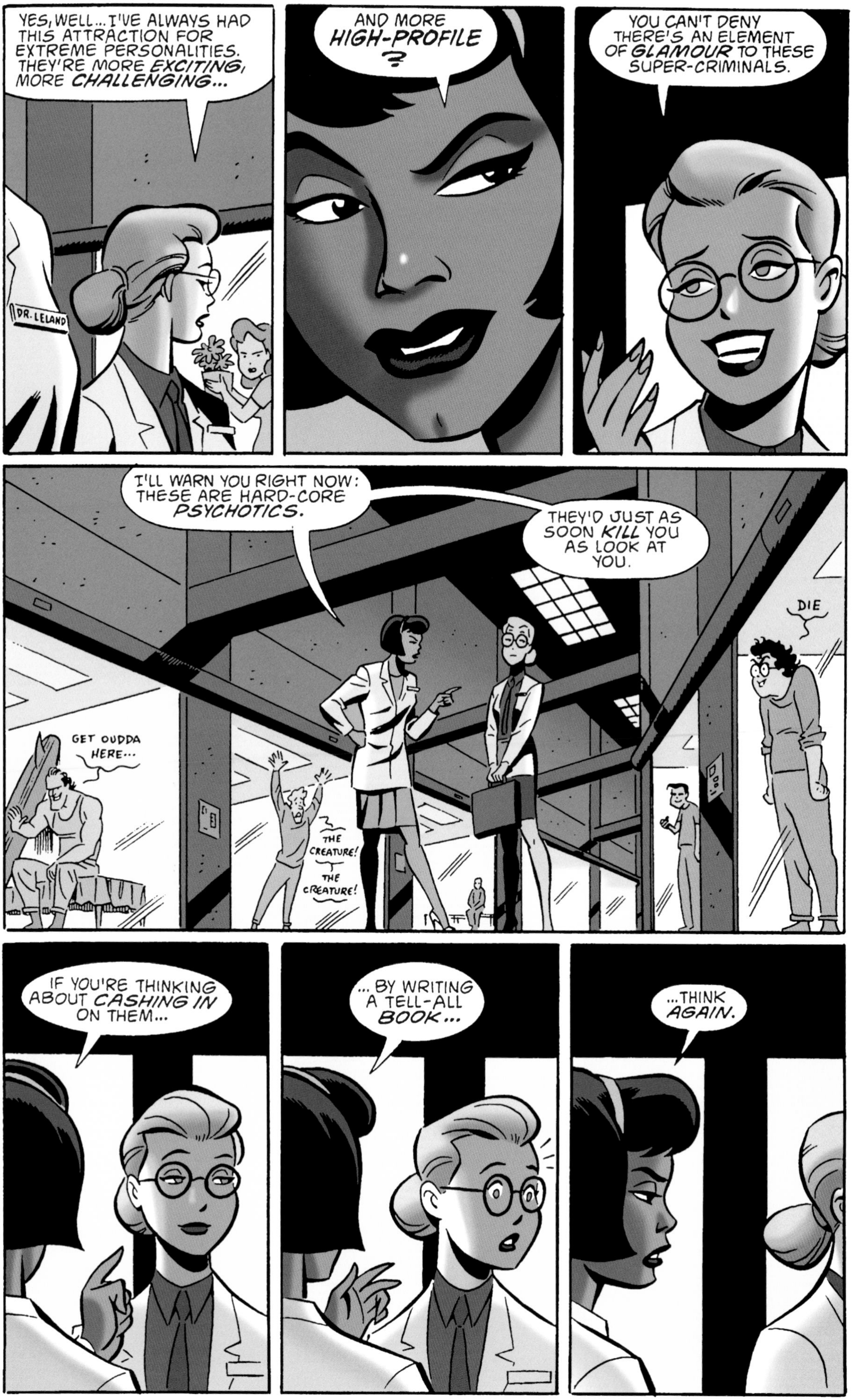
YES, WELL... I'VE ALWAYS HAD THIS ATTRACTION FOR EXTREME PERSONALITIES. THEY'RE MORE EXCITING, MORE CHALLENGING...
DR. LELAND
AND MORE HIGH-PROFILE ?
YOU CAN'T DENY THERE'S AN ELEMENT OF GLAMOUR TO THESE SUPER-CRIMINALS.
I'LL WARN YOU RIGHT NOW: THESE ARE HARD-CORE PSYCHOTICS.
THEY'D JUST AS SOON KILL YOU AS LOOK AT YOU.
GET OUDDA HERE...
THE CREATURE!
THE CREATURE!
DIE
IF YOU'RE THINKING ABOUT CASHING IN ON THEM...
...BY WRITING A TELL-ALL BOOK...
...THINK AGAIN.

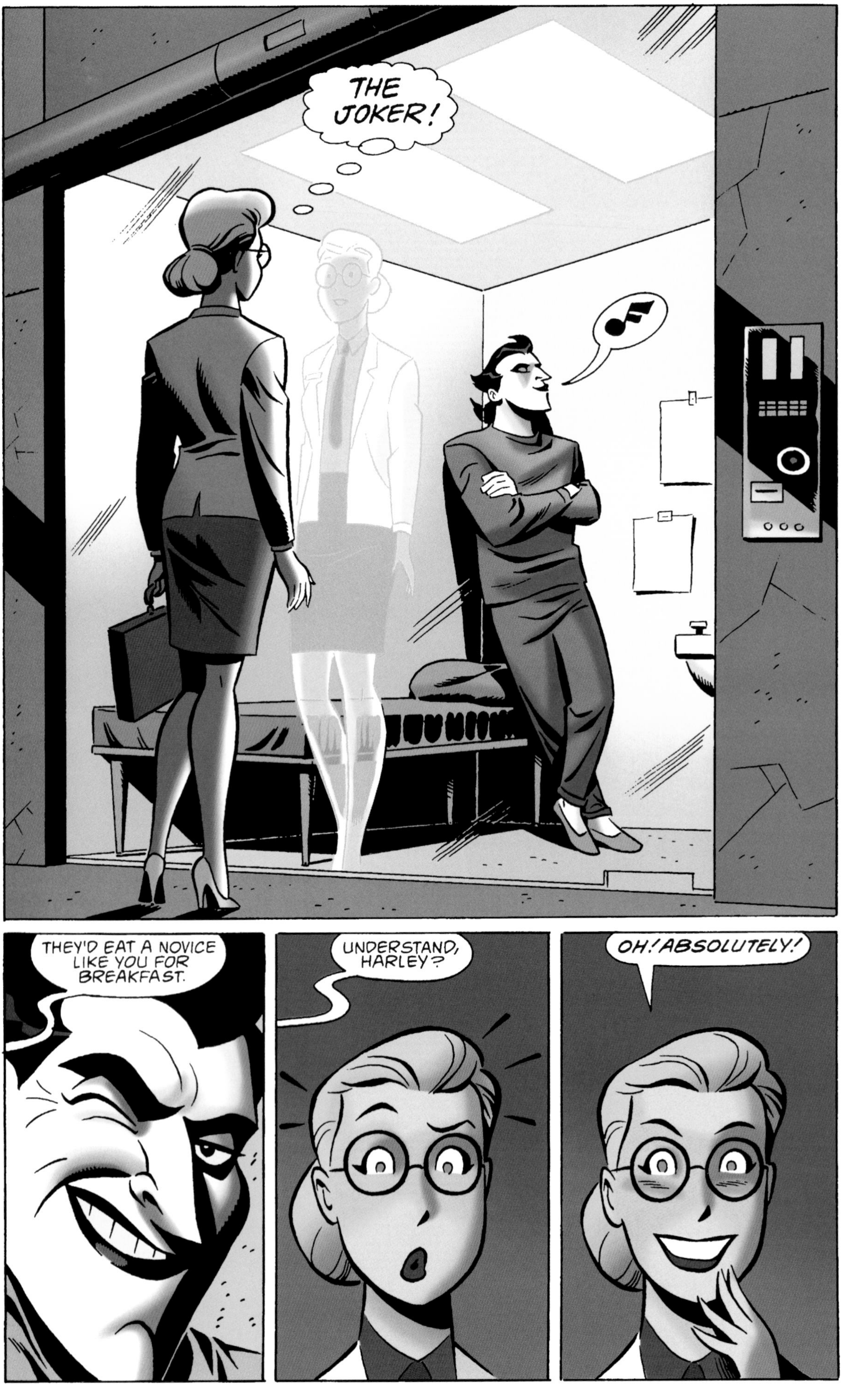
THE JOKER!
THEY'D EAT A NOVICE LIKE YOU FOR BREAKFAST.
UNDERSTAND, HARLEY?
OH! ABSOLUTELY!

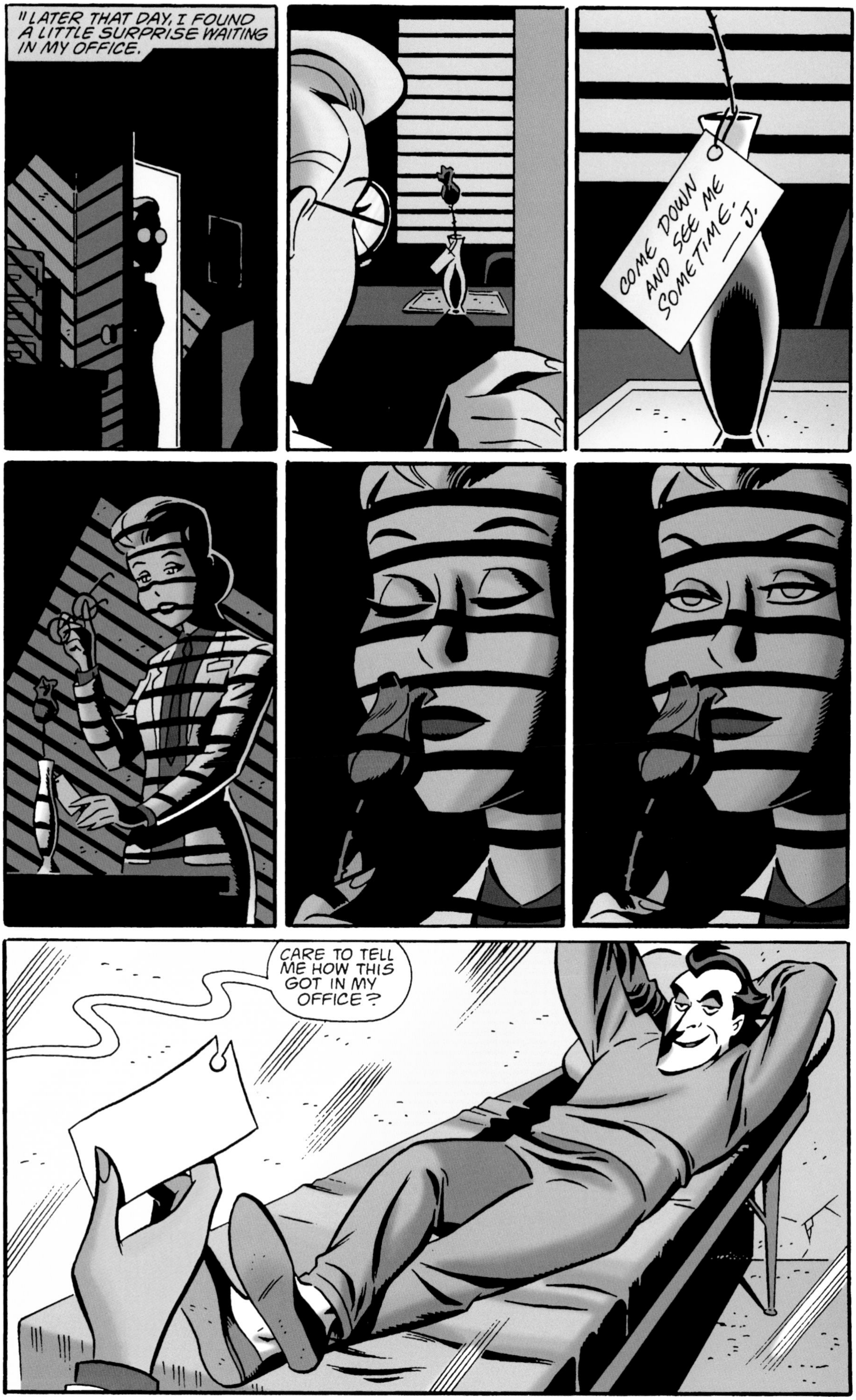
"LATER THAT DAY, I FOUND A LITTLE SURPRISE WAITING IN MY OFFICE.
COME DOWN AND SEE ME SOMETIME. —J.
CARE TO TELL ME HOW THIS GOT IN MY OFFICE?

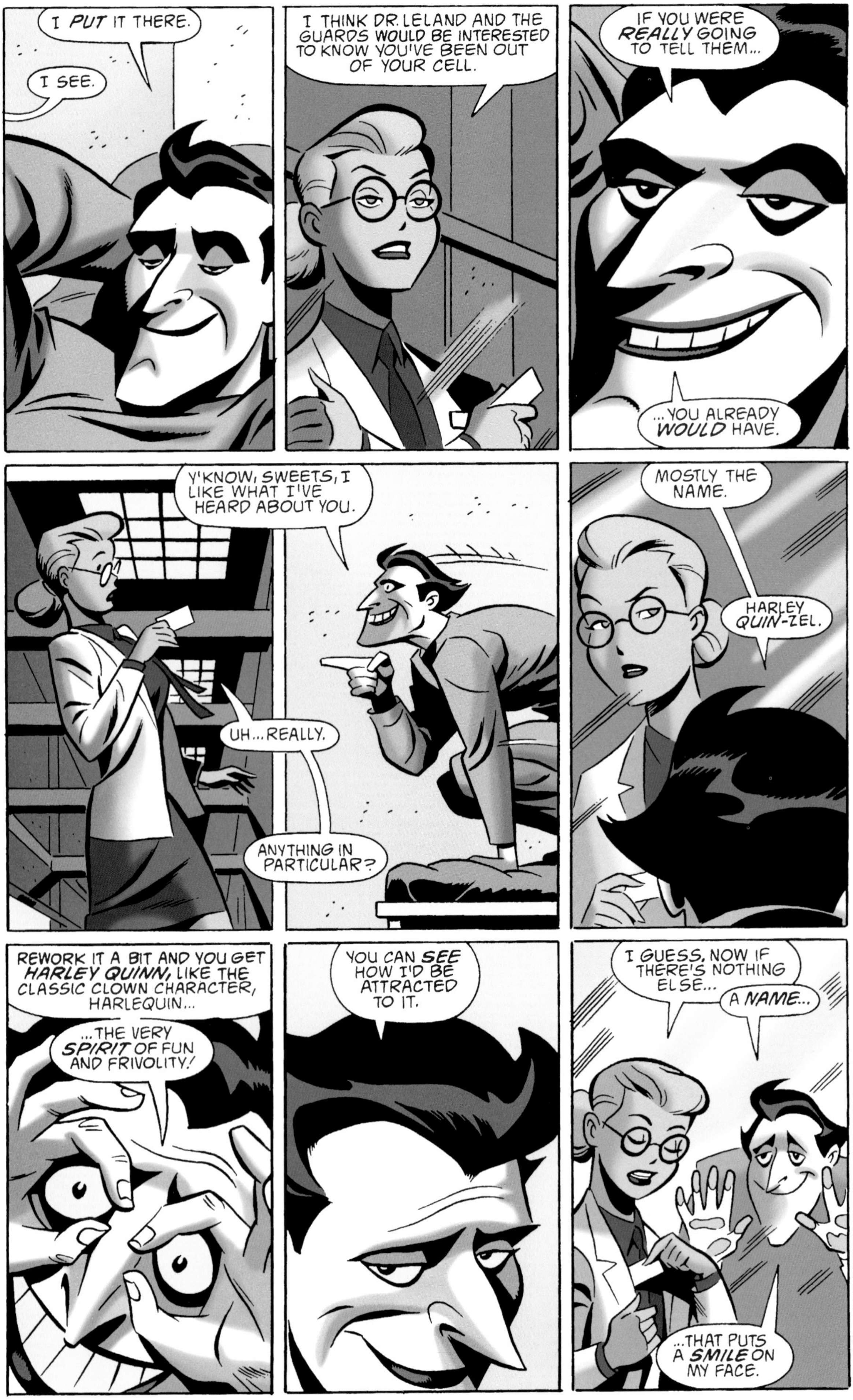
I PUT IT THERE.
I SEE.
I THINK DR. LELAND AND THE GUARDS WOULD BE INTERESTED TO KNOW YOU'VE BEEN OUT OF YOUR CELL.
IF YOU WERE REALLY GOING TO TELL THEM...
...YOU ALREADY WOULD HAVE.
Y'KNOW, SWEETS, I LIKE WHAT I'VE HEARD ABOUT YOU.
UH... REALLY.
ANYTHING IN PARTICULAR?
MOSTLY THE NAME.
HARLEY QUIN-ZEL.
REWORK IT A BIT AND YOU GET HARLEY QUINN, LIKE THE CLASSIC CLOWN CHARACTER, HARLEQUIN...
...THE VERY SPIRIT OF FUN AND FRIVOLITY!
YOU CAN SEE HOW I'D BE ATTRACTED TO IT.
I GUESS. NOW IF THERE'S NOTHING ELSE...
A NAME...
...THAT PUTS A SMILE ON MY FACE.

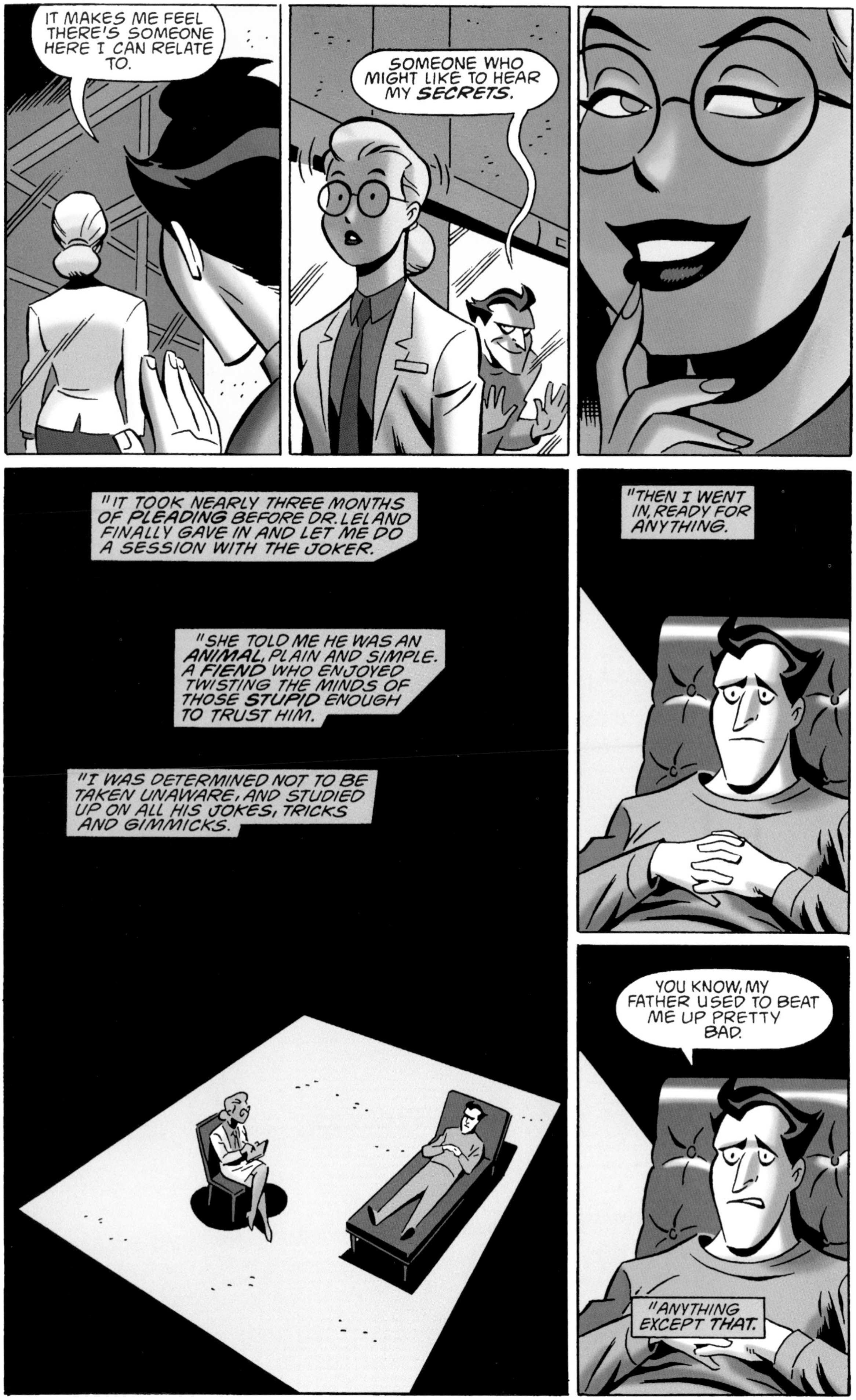

IT MAKES ME FEEL THERE'S SOMEONE HERE I CAN RELATE TO.
SOMEONE WHO MIGHT LIKE TO HEAR MY SECRETS.
"IT TOOK NEARLY THREE MONTHS OF PLEADING BEFORE DR. LELAND FINALLY GAVE IN AND LET ME DO A SESSION WITH THE JOKER.
"SHE TOLD ME HE WAS AN ANIMAL, PLAIN AND SIMPLE. A FIEND WHO ENJOYED TWISTING THE MINDS OF THOSE STUPID ENOUGH TO TRUST HIM.
"I WAS DETERMINED NOT TO BE TAKEN UNAWARE, AND STUDIED UP ON ALL HIS JOKES, TRICKS AND GIMMICKS.
"THEN I WENT IN, READY FOR ANYTHING.
YOU KNOW, MY FATHER USED TO BEAT ME UP PRETTY BAD.
"ANYTHING EXCEPT THAT.

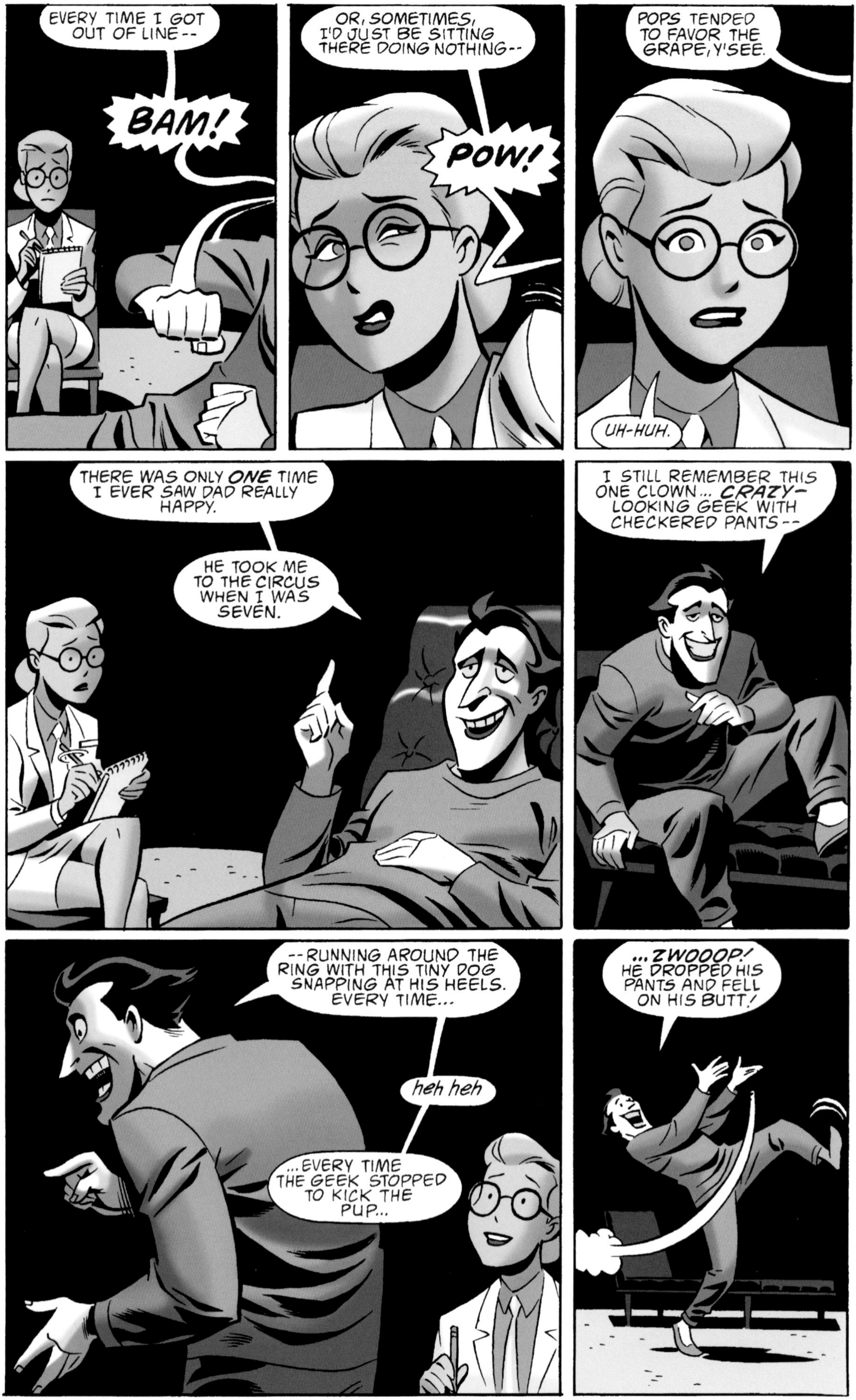
EVERY TIME I GOT OUT OF LINE--
BAM!
OR, SOMETIMES, I'D JUST BE SITTING THERE DOING NOTHING--
POW!
POPS TENDED TO FAVOR THE GRAPE, Y'SEE.
UH-HUH.
THERE WAS ONLY ONE TIME I EVER SAW DAD REALLY HAPPY.
HE TOOK ME TO THE CIRCUS WHEN I WAS SEVEN.
I STILL REMEMBER THIS ONE CLOWN... CRAZY-LOOKING GEEK WITH CHECKERED PANTS--
--RUNNING AROUND THE RING WITH THIS TINY DOG SNAPPING AT HIS HEELS. EVERY TIME...
heh heh
...EVERY TIME THE GEEK STOPPED TO KICK THE PUP...
...ZWOOOP! HE DROPPED HIS PANTS AND FELL ON HIS BUTT!

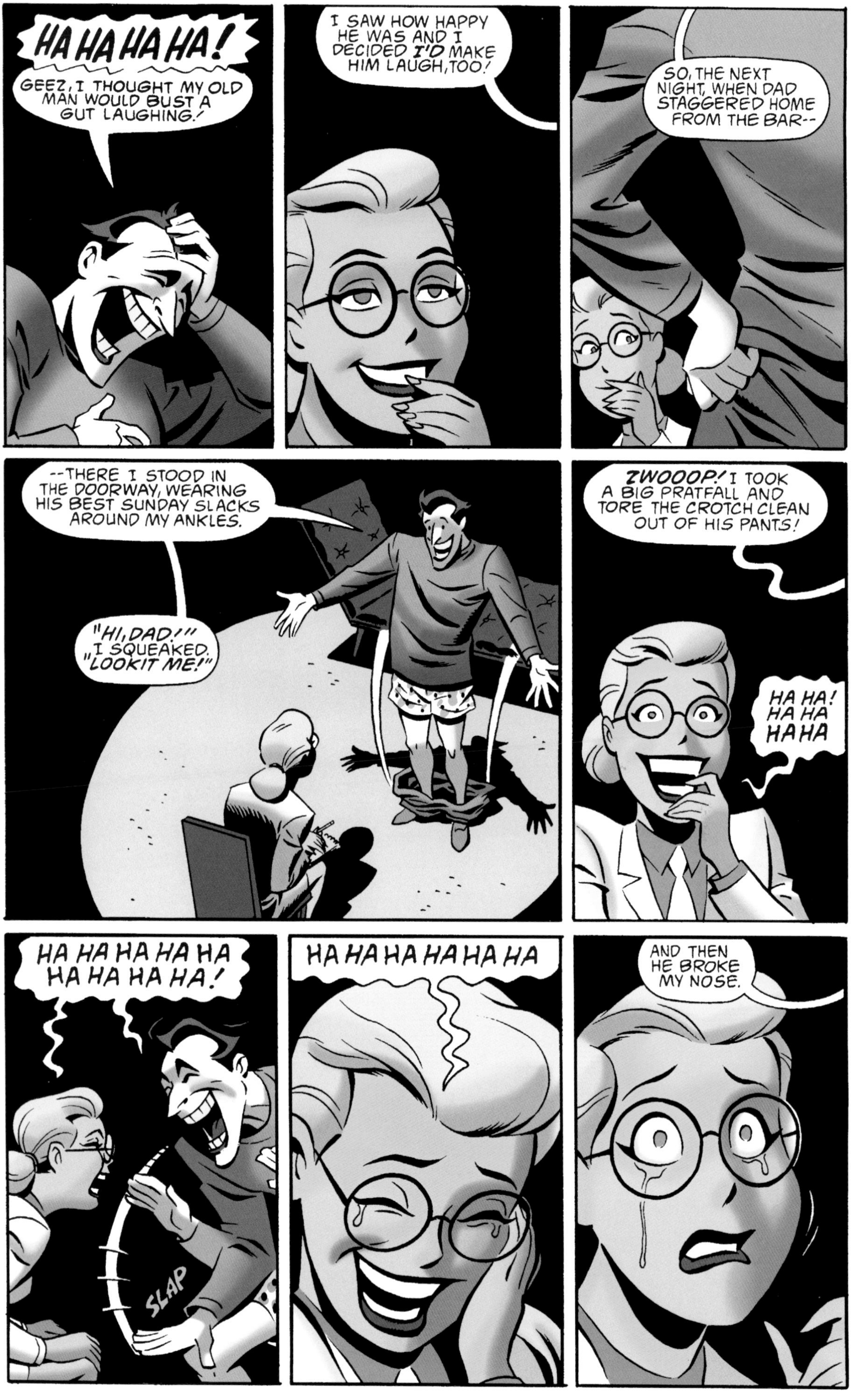
HA HA HA HA HA!
GEEZ, I THOUGHT MY OLD MAN WOULD BUST A GUT LAUGHING!
I SAW HOW HAPPY HE WAS AND I DECIDED I'D MAKE HIM LAUGH, TOO!
SO, THE NEXT NIGHT, WHEN DAD STAGGERED HOME FROM THE BAR--
--THERE I STOOD IN THE DOORWAY, WEARING HIS BEST SUNDAY SLACKS AROUND MY ANKLES.
"HI, DAD!" I SQUEAKED. "LOOKIT ME!"
ZWOOOP! I TOOK A BIG PRATFALL AND TORE THE CROTCH CLEAN OUT OF HIS PANTS!
HA HA! HA HA HA HA
HA HA HA HA HA HA HA HA HA HA!
SLAP
HA HA HA HA HA HA HA
AND THEN HE BROKE MY NOSE.

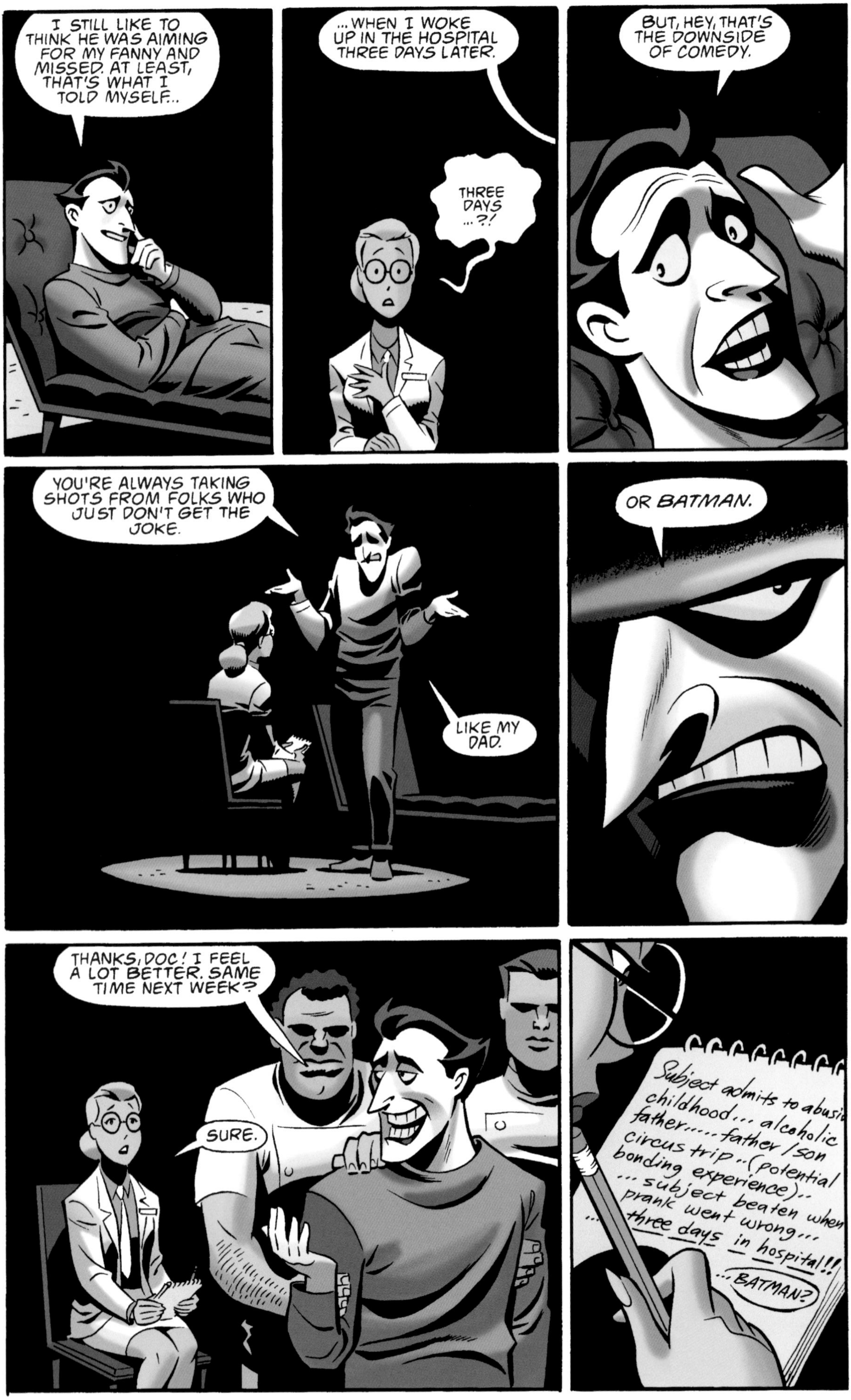

I STILL LIKE TO THINK HE WAS AIMING FOR MY FANNY AND MISSED. AT LEAST, THAT'S WHAT I TOLD MYSELF...
...WHEN I WOKE UP IN THE HOSPITAL THREE DAYS LATER.
THREE DAYS ...?!
BUT, HEY, THAT'S THE DOWNSIDE OF COMEDY.
YOU'RE ALWAYS TAKING SHOTS FROM FOLKS WHO JUST DON'T GET THE JOKE.
LIKE MY DAD.
OR BATMAN.
THANKS, DOC! I FEEL A LOT BETTER. SAME TIME NEXT WEEK?
SURE.
Subject admits to abusi childhood... alcoholic father.....father/son circus trip..(potential bonding experience)... subject beaten when prank went wrong... ...three days in hospital!!
...BATMAN?

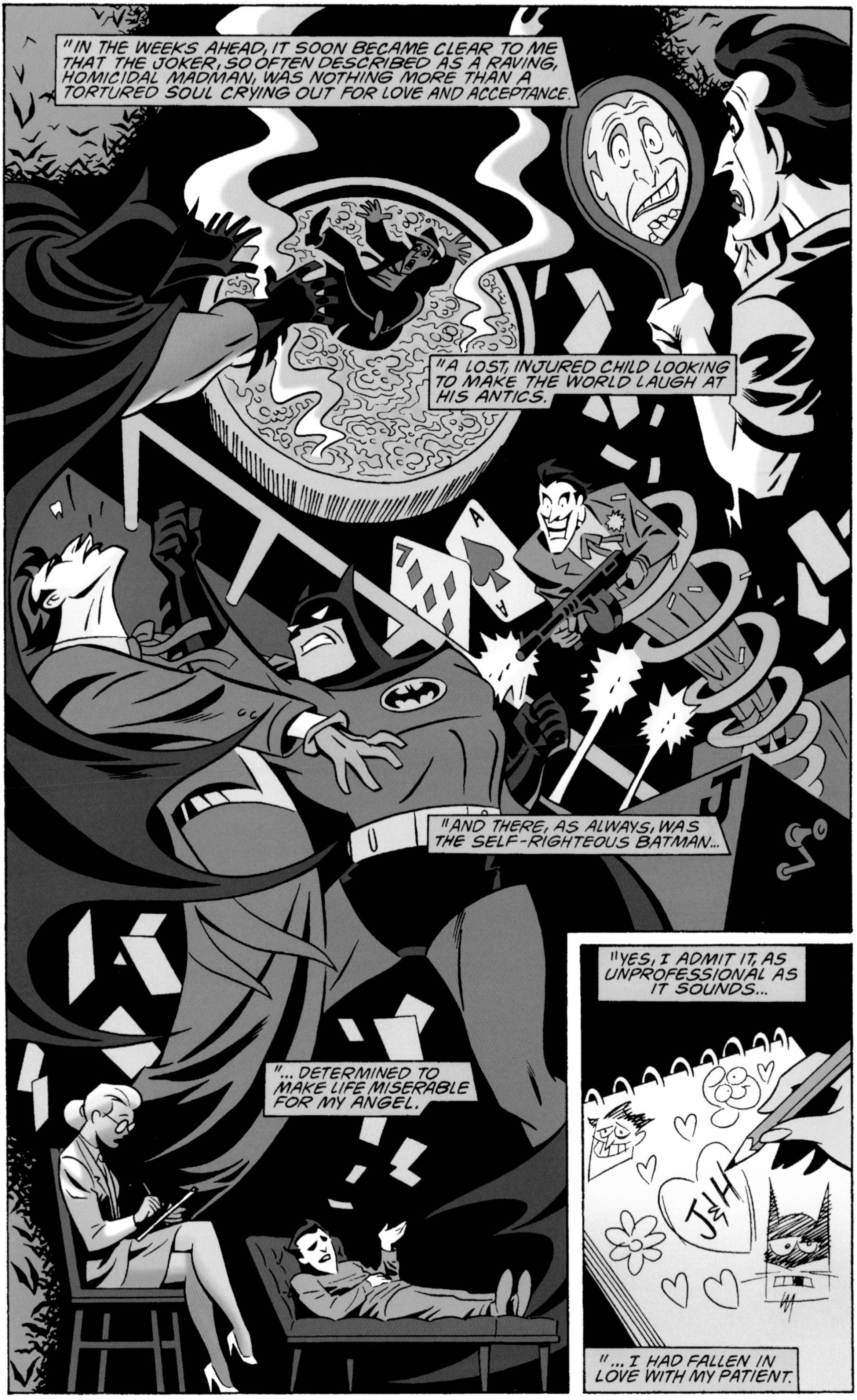
"IN THE WEEKS AHEAD, IT SOON BECAME CLEAR TO ME THAT THE JOKER, SO OFTEN DESCRIBED AS A RAVING, HOMICIDAL MADMAN, WAS NOTHING MORE THAN A TORTURED SOUL CRYING OUT FOR LOVE AND ACCEPTANCE.
"A LOST, INJURED CHILD LOOKING TO MAKE THE WORLD LAUGH AT HIS ANTICS.
"AND THERE, AS ALWAYS, WAS THE SELF-RIGHTEOUS BATMAN...
"... DETERMINED TO MAKE LIFE MISERABLE FOR MY ANGEL.
"YES, I ADMIT IT, AS UNPROFESSIONAL AS IT SOUNDS...
"... I HAD FALLEN IN LOVE WITH MY PATIENT.

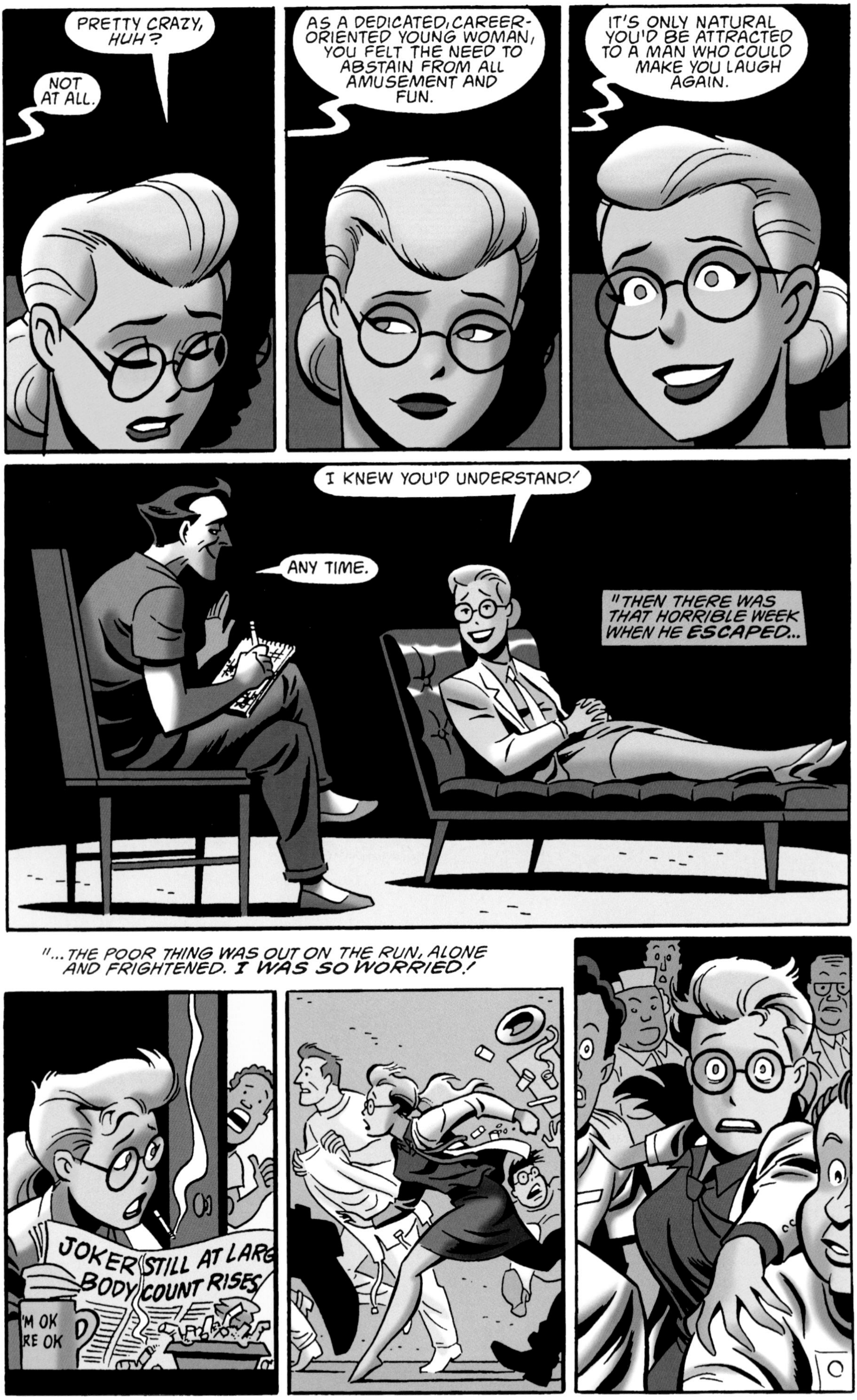

PRETTY CRAZY, HUH?
NOT AT ALL.
AS A DEDICATED, CAREER-ORIENTED YOUNG WOMAN, YOU FELT THE NEED TO ABSTAIN FROM ALL AMUSEMENT AND FUN.
IT'S ONLY NATURAL YOU'D BE ATTRACTED TO A MAN WHO COULD MAKE YOU LAUGH AGAIN.
I KNEW YOU'D UNDERSTAND!
ANY TIME.
"THEN THERE WAS THAT HORRIBLE WEEK WHEN HE ESCAPED...
"...THE POOR THING WAS OUT ON THE RUN, ALONE AND FRIGHTENED. I WAS SO WORRIED!
JOKER STILL AT LARG
BODY COUNT RISES
'M OK
RE OK

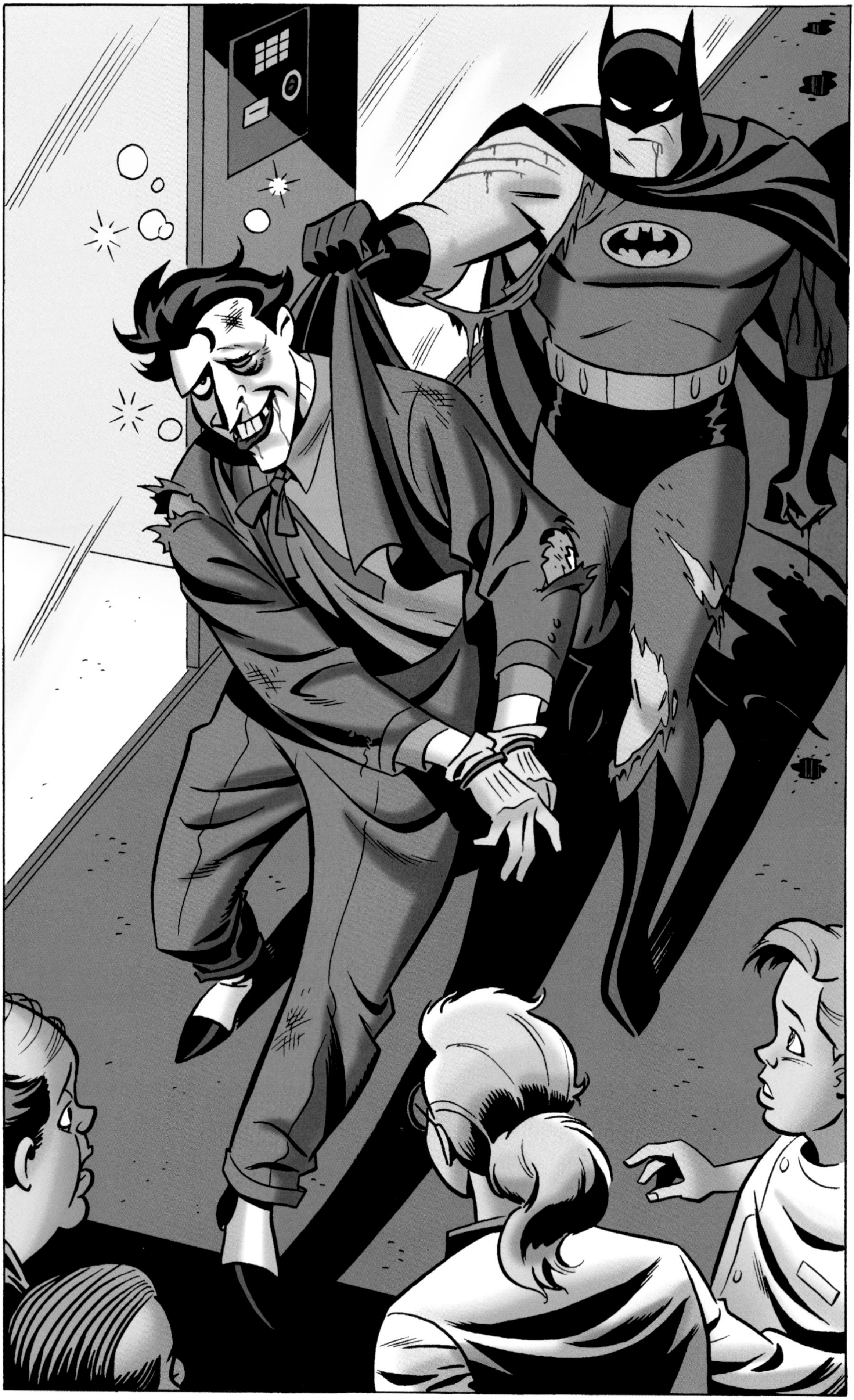

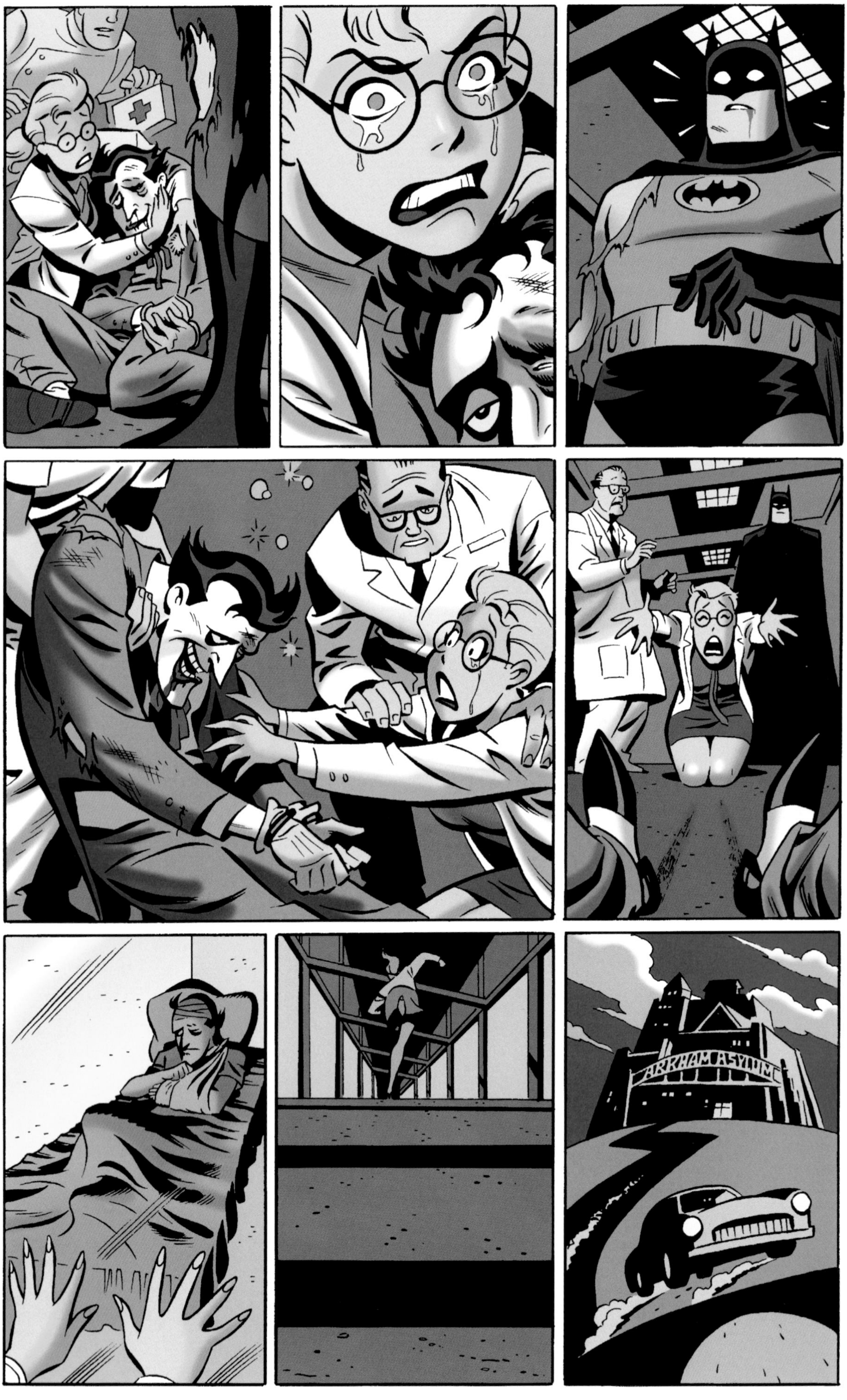
ARKHAM ASYLUM

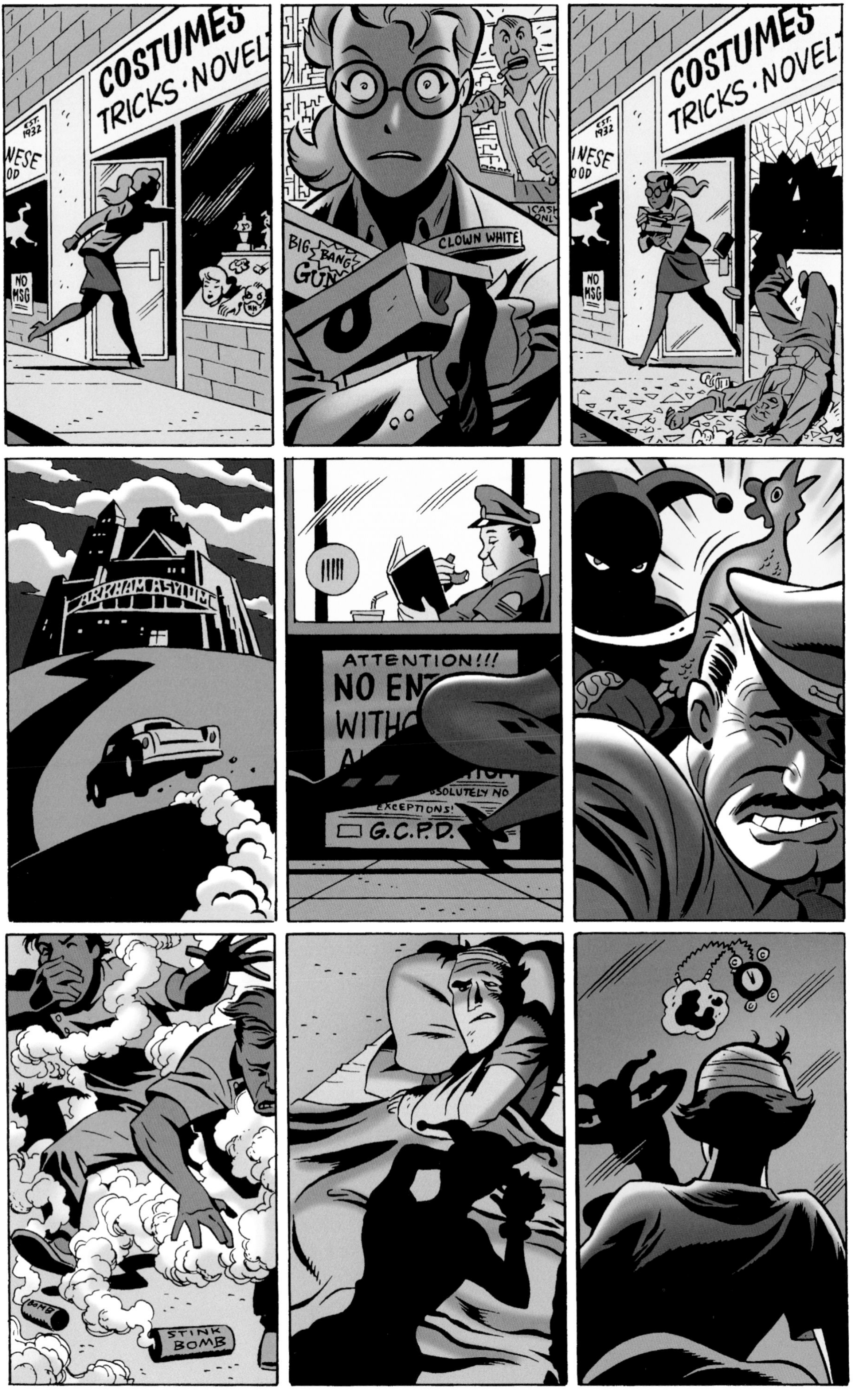
COSTUMES
TRICKS · NOVELT
EST. 1932
NO MSG
BIG BANG GUN
CLOWN WHITE
CASH ONLY
COSTUMES
TRICKS · NOVELT
EST. 1932
NO MSG
ARKHAM ASYLUM
ATTENTION!!!
NO ENT
WITHO
BSOLUTELY NO
EXCEPTIONS!
G.C.P.D.
BOMB
STINK BOMB

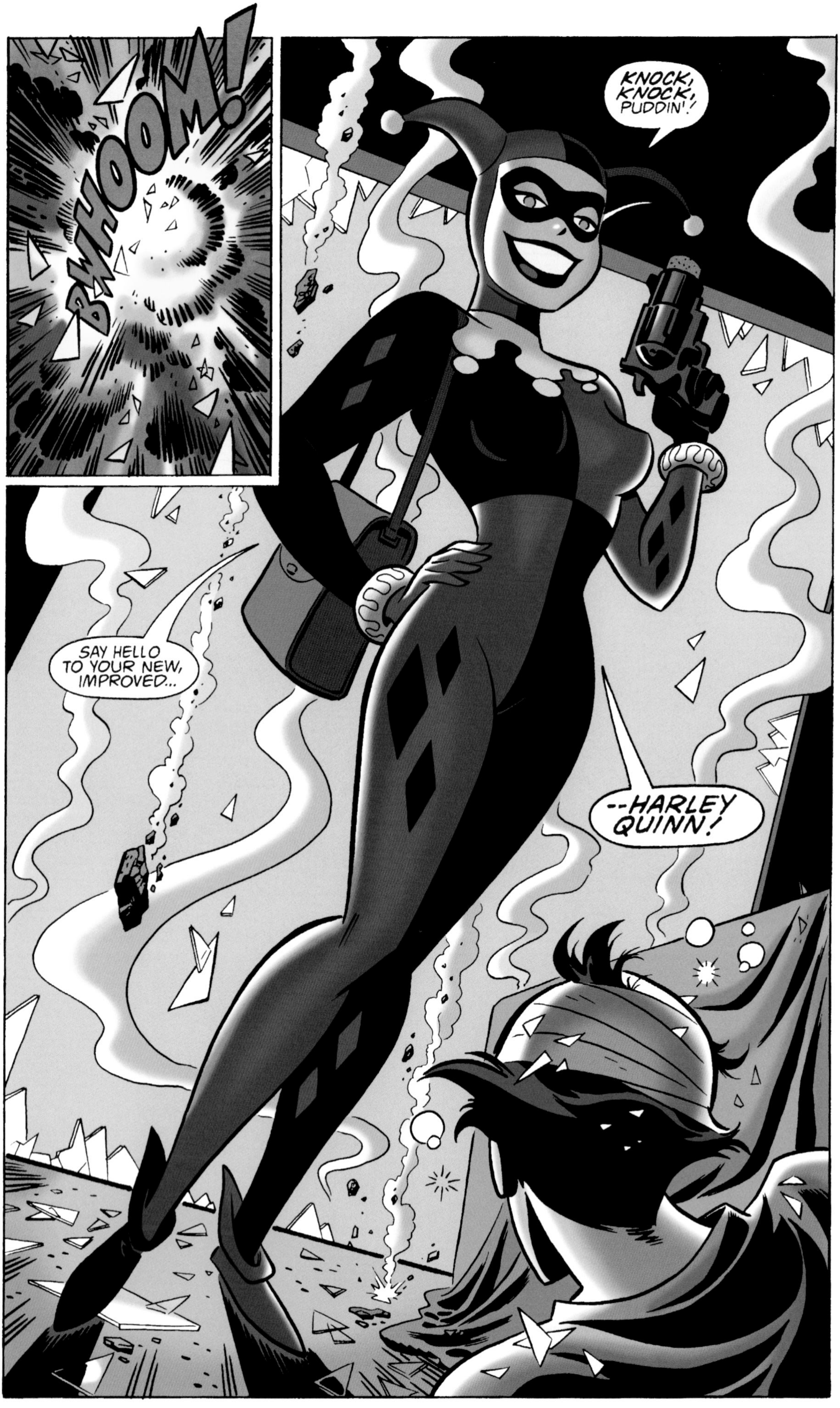
BWHOOM!
KNOCK, KNOCK, PUDDIN'!
SAY HELLO TO YOUR NEW, IMPROVED...
--HARLEY QUINN!

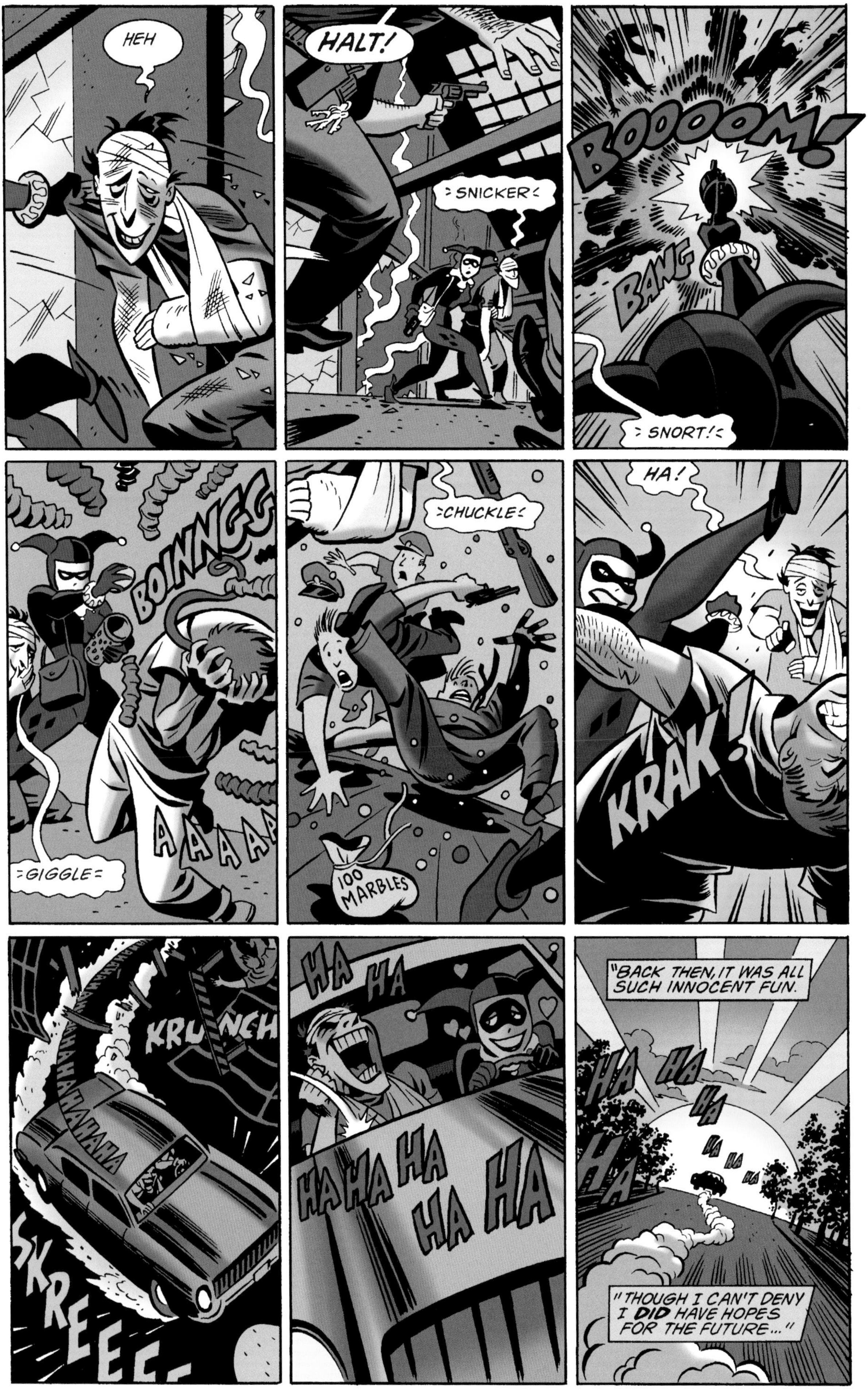
HEH
HALT!
SNICKER
BOOOOM!
BANG
SNORT!
BOINNGG
GIGGLE
AAAAA
CHUCKLE
100 MARBLES
HA!
KRAK!
KRUNCH
SKREEE
HAHAHAHAHA
HA HA
HAHAHA HA HA HA HA
"BACK THEN, IT WAS ALL SUCH INNOCENT FUN.
HA HA HA HA HA HA HA
"THOUGH I CAN'T DENY I DID HAVE HOPES FOR THE FUTURE..."

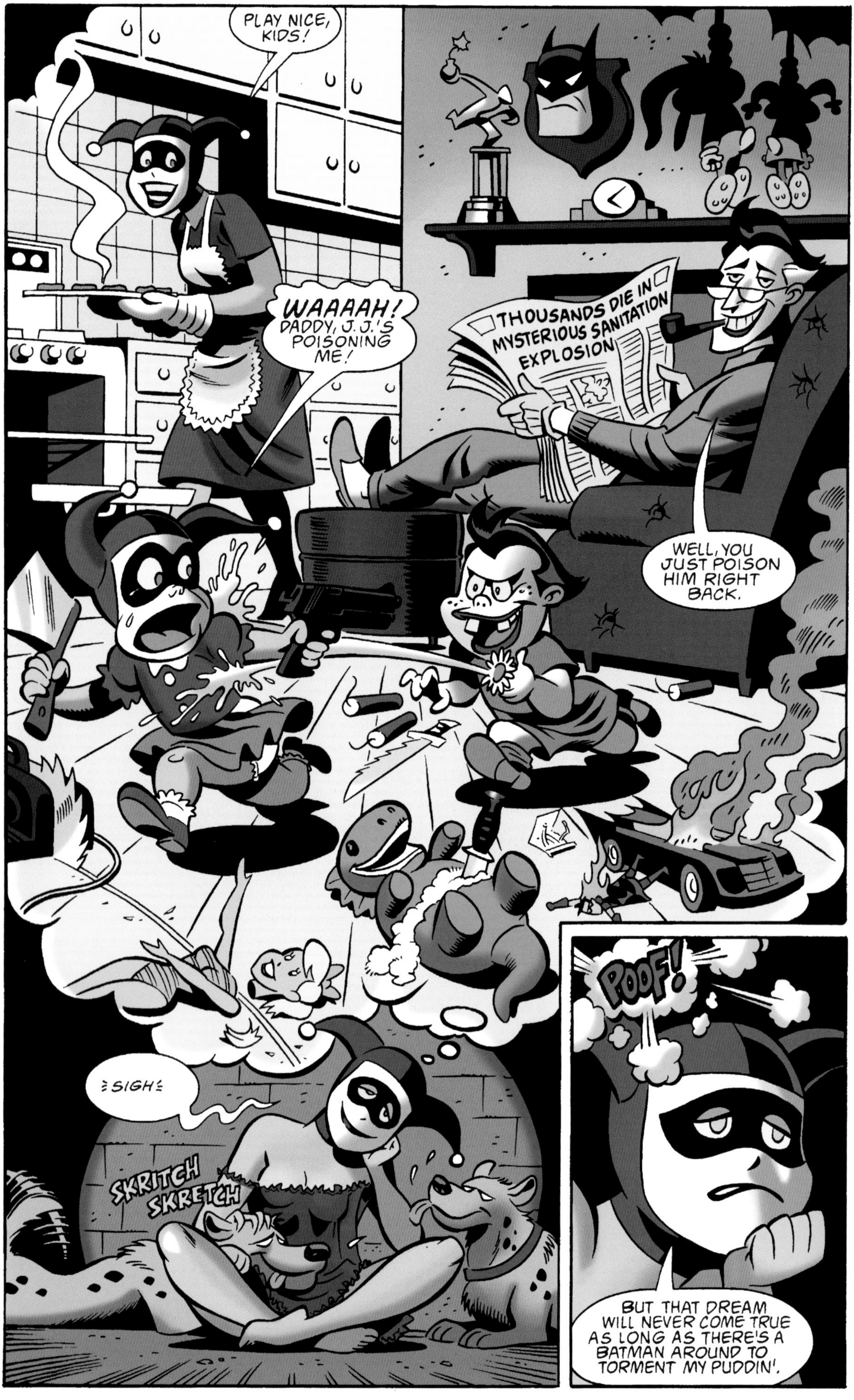
PLAY NICE, KIDS!
WAAAAH! DADDY, J.J.'S POISONING ME!
THOUSANDS DIE IN MYSTERIOUS SANITATION EXPLOSION
WELL, YOU JUST POISON HIM RIGHT BACK.
SIGH
SKRITCH SKRETCH
POOF!
BUT THAT DREAM WILL NEVER COME TRUE AS LONG AS THERE'S A BATMAN AROUND TO TORMENT MY PUDDIN'.

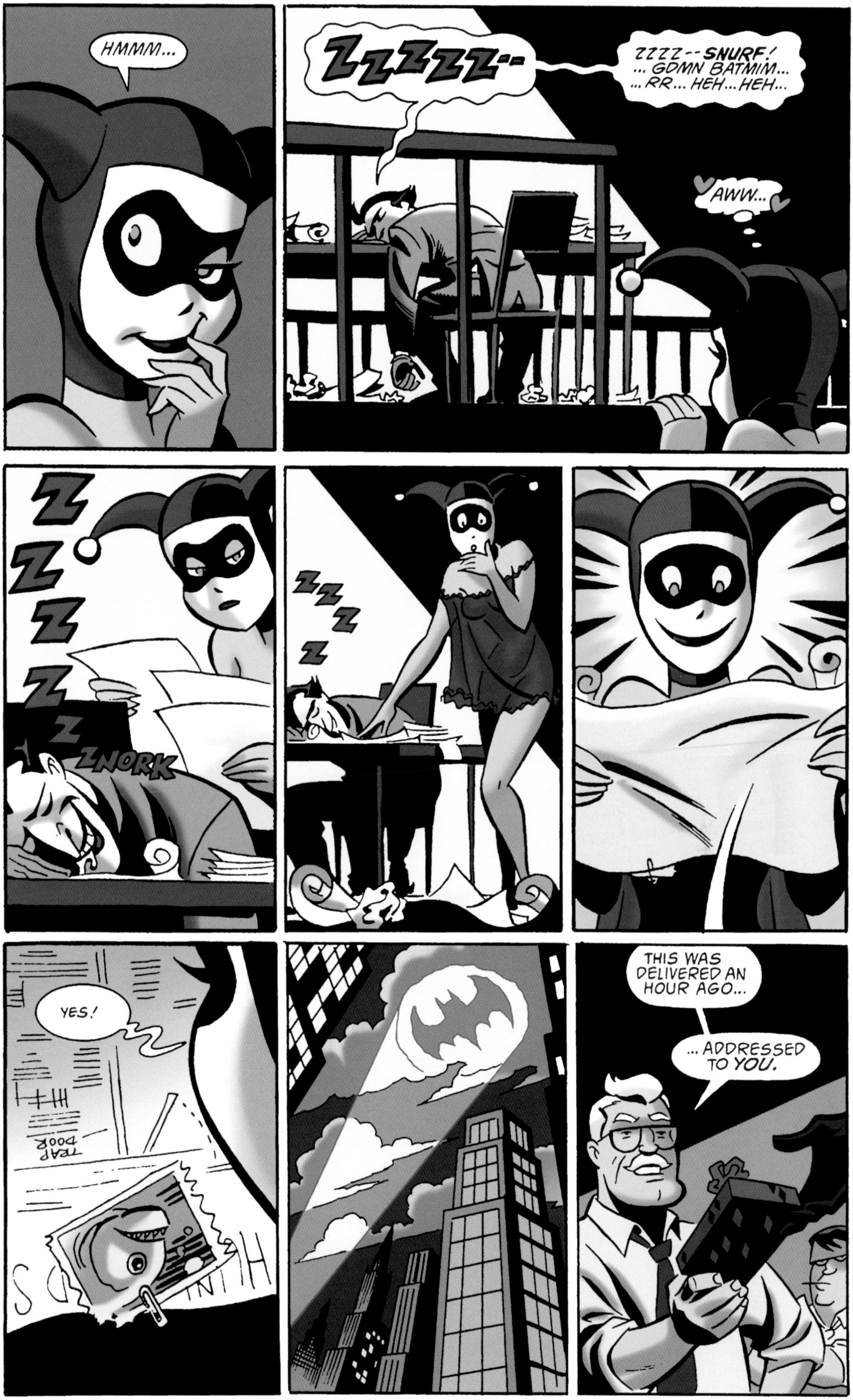
HMMM...
ZZZZZZ--
ZZZZ--SNURF! ...GDMN BATMIM... ...RR...HEH...HEH...
AWW...
ZZZZZZ
ZNORK
ZZZZ
YES!
TRAP DOOR
THIS WAS DELIVERED AN HOUR AGO...
...ADDRESSED TO YOU.

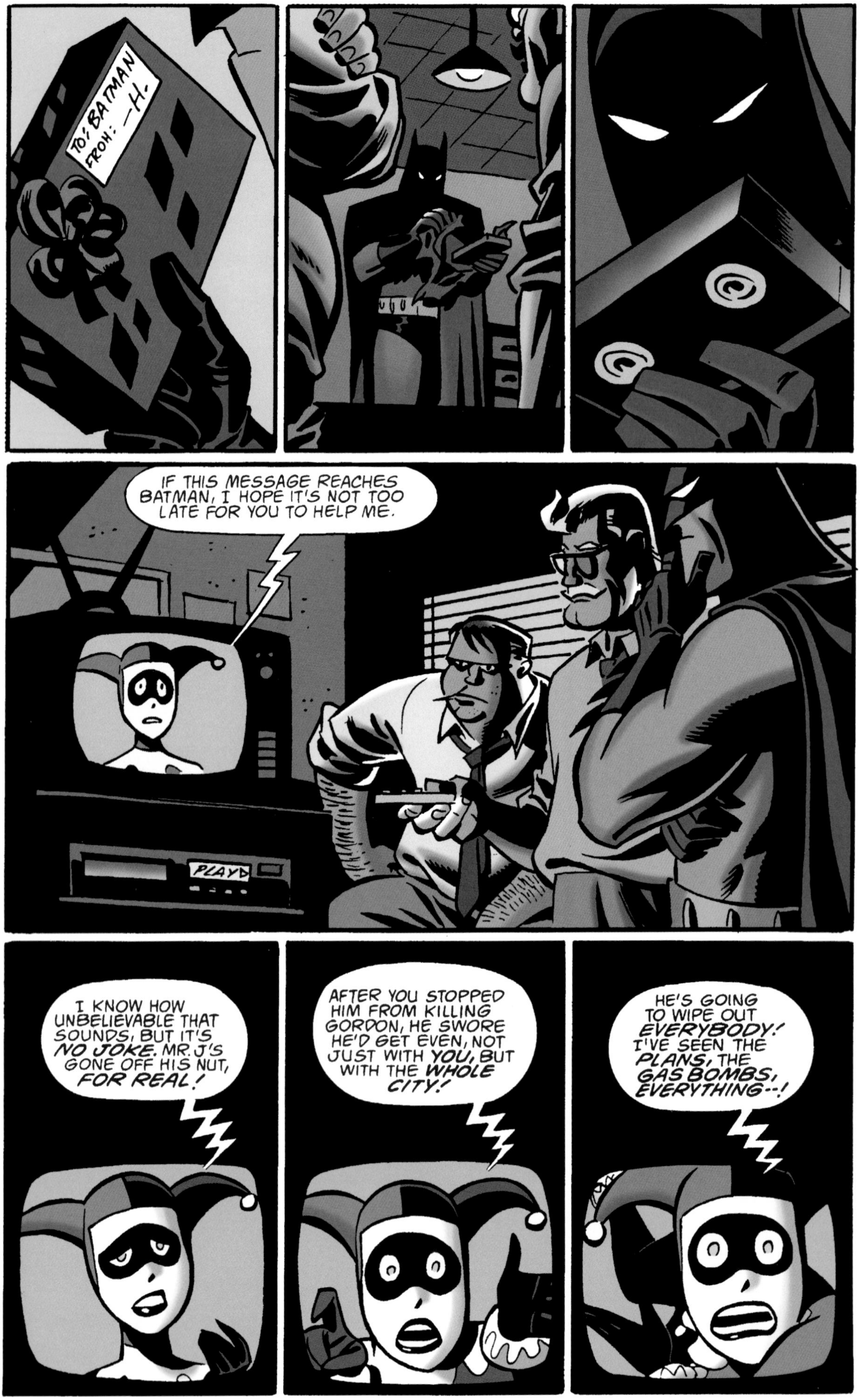
TO: BATMAN
FROM: —H.
IF THIS MESSAGE REACHES BATMAN, I HOPE IT'S NOT TOO LATE FOR YOU TO HELP ME.
PLAY▷
I KNOW HOW UNBELIEVABLE THAT SOUNDS, BUT IT'S NO JOKE. MR. J'S GONE OFF HIS NUT, FOR REAL!
AFTER YOU STOPPED HIM FROM KILLING GORDON, HE SWORE HE'D GET EVEN, NOT JUST WITH YOU, BUT WITH THE WHOLE CITY!
HE'S GOING TO WIPE OUT EVERYBODY! I'VE SEEN THE PLANS, THE GAS BOMBS, EVERYTHING--!

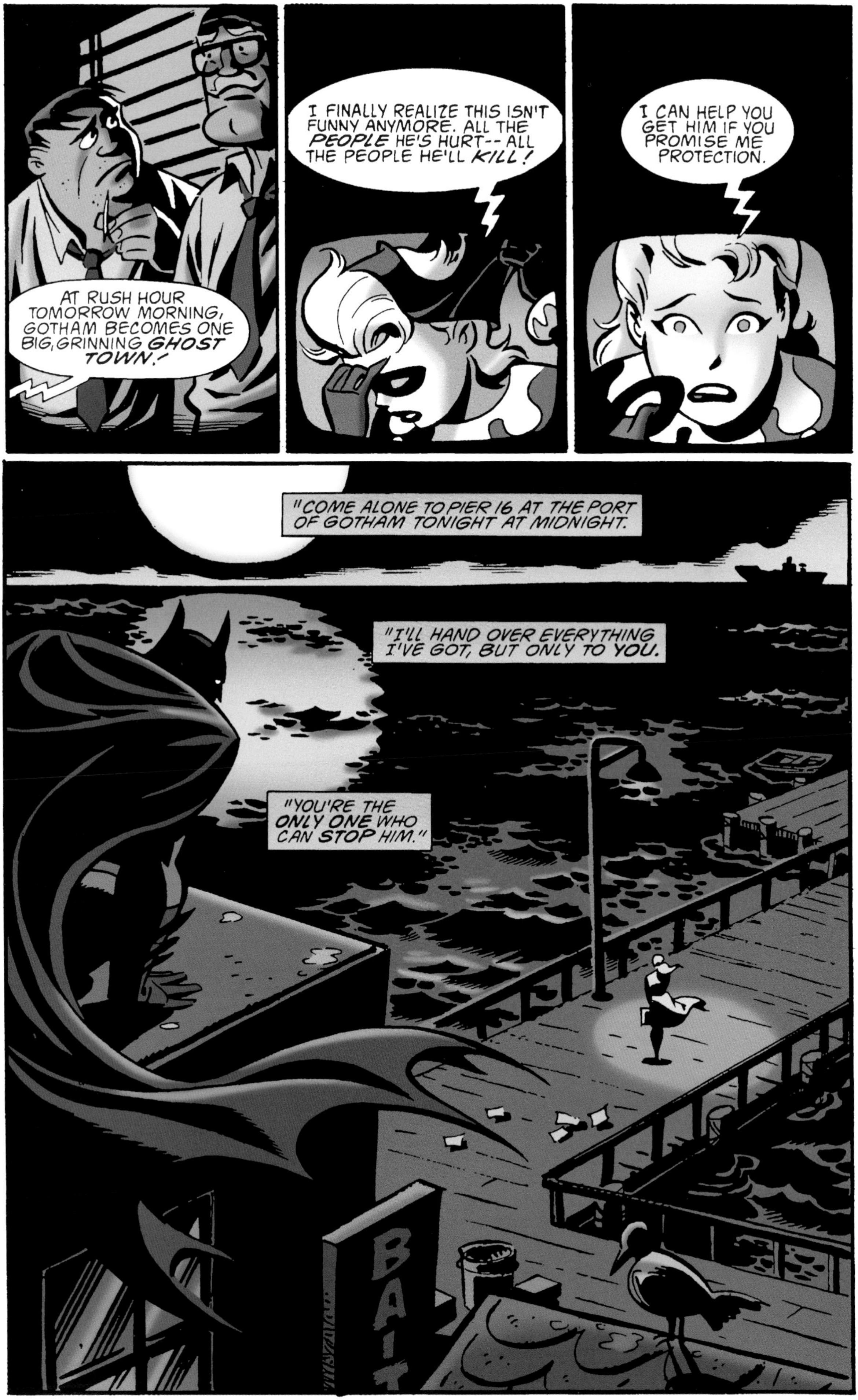
AT RUSH HOUR TOMORROW MORNING, GOTHAM BECOMES ONE BIG, GRINNING GHOST TOWN!
I FINALLY REALIZE THIS ISN'T FUNNY ANYMORE. ALL THE PEOPLE HE'S HURT-- ALL THE PEOPLE HE'LL KILL!
I CAN HELP YOU GET HIM IF YOU PROMISE ME PROTECTION.
"COME ALONE TO PIER 16 AT THE PORT OF GOTHAM TONIGHT AT MIDNIGHT.
"I'LL HAND OVER EVERYTHING I'VE GOT, BUT ONLY TO YOU.
"YOU'RE THE ONLY ONE WHO CAN STOP HIM."
BAIT

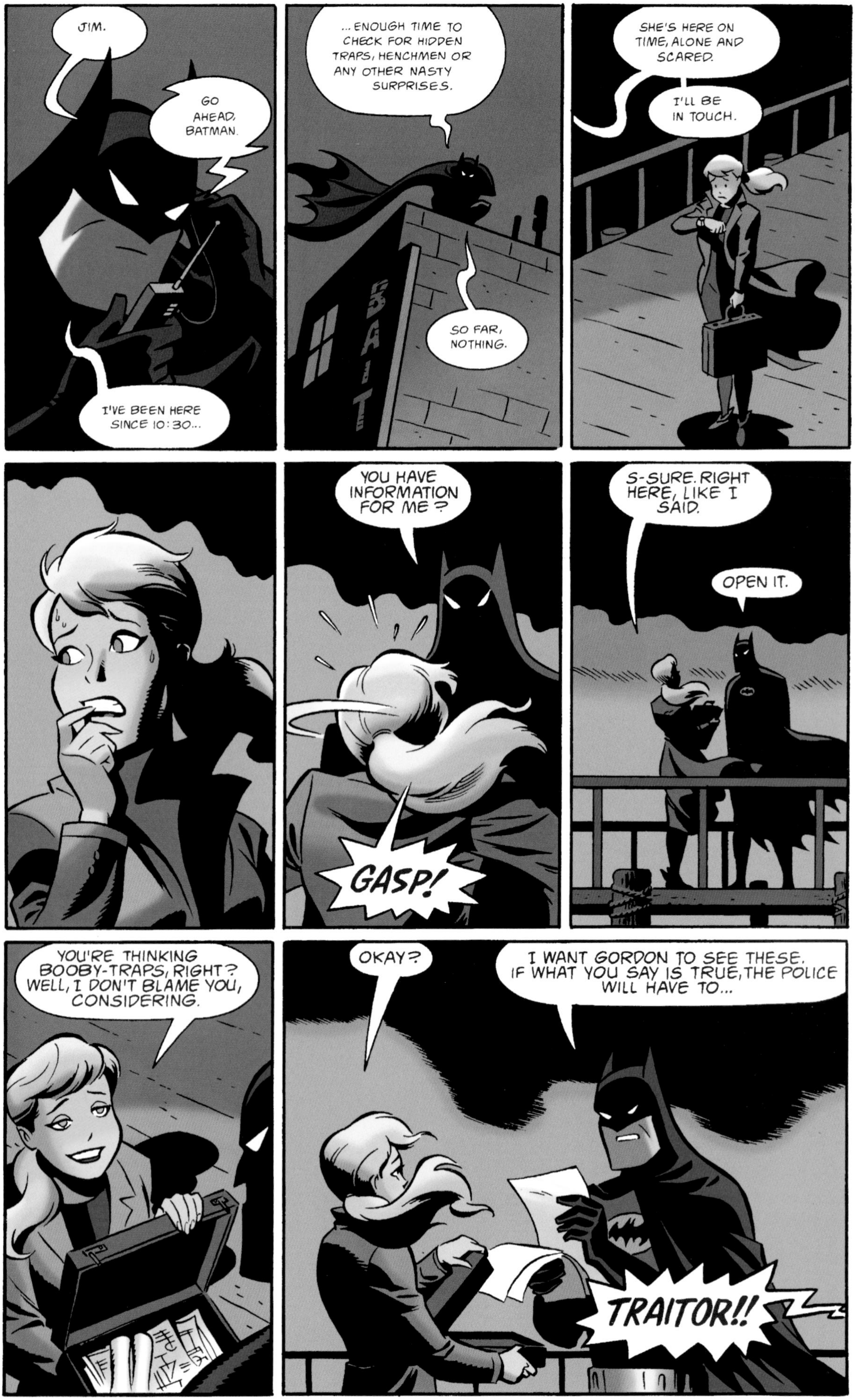
JIM.
GO AHEAD, BATMAN.
I'VE BEEN HERE SINCE 10:30...
...ENOUGH TIME TO CHECK FOR HIDDEN TRAPS, HENCHMEN OR ANY OTHER NASTY SURPRISES.
SO FAR, NOTHING.
BAIT
SHE'S HERE ON TIME, ALONE AND SCARED.
I'LL BE IN TOUCH.
YOU HAVE INFORMATION FOR ME?
GASP!
S-SURE. RIGHT HERE, LIKE I SAID.
OPEN IT.
YOU'RE THINKING BOOBY-TRAPS, RIGHT? WELL, I DON'T BLAME YOU, CONSIDERING.
OKAY?
I WANT GORDON TO SEE THESE. IF WHAT YOU SAY IS TRUE, THE POLICE WILL HAVE TO...
TRAITOR!!

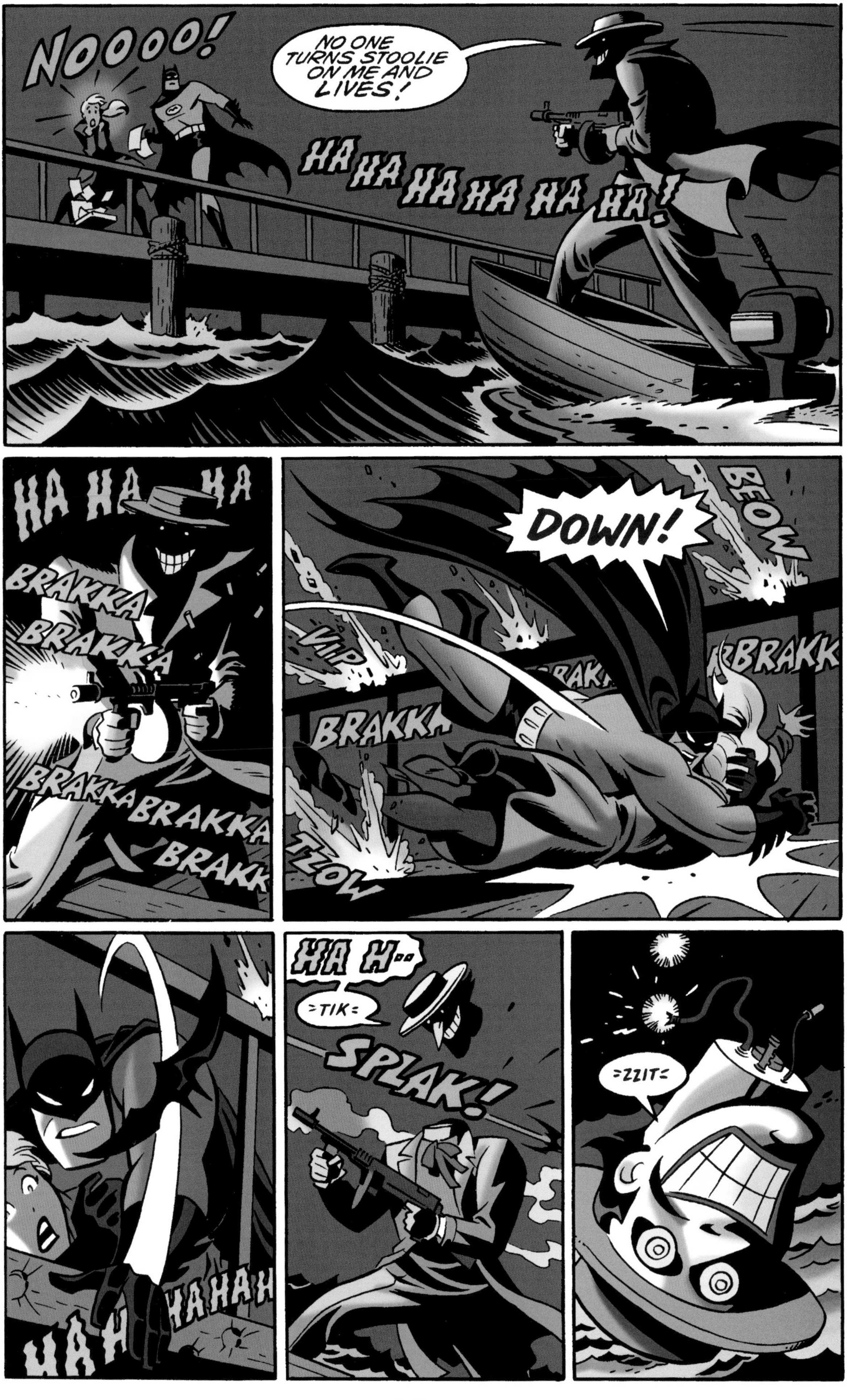
NOOOO!
NO ONE TURNS STOOLIE ON ME AND LIVES!
HA HA HA HA HA HA HA!
HA HA HA
BRAKKA
BRAKKA
BRAKKABRAKKA
BRAKK
DOWN!
BEOW
VIIP
BRAKKA
BRAKK
TZLOW
HAHAHAH
HAH
HA H..
TIK
SPLAK!
ZZIT

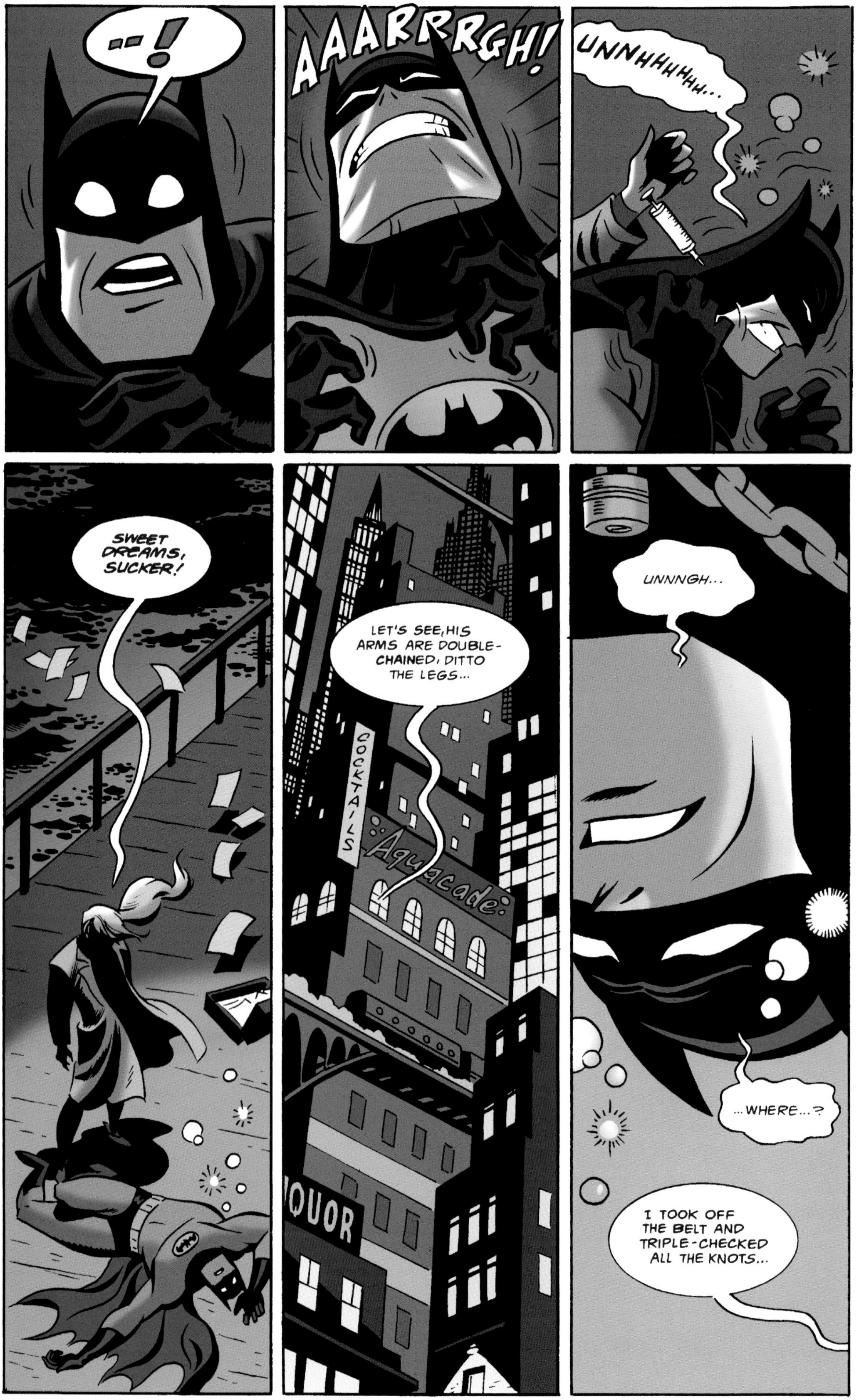
--!
AAARRRGH!
UNNHHHHH...
SWEET DREAMS, SUCKER!
LET'S SEE, HIS ARMS ARE DOUBLE-CHAINED, DITTO THE LEGS...
COCKTAILS
Aquacade
QUOR
UNNNGH...
...WHERE...?
I TOOK OFF THE BELT AND TRIPLE-CHECKED ALL THE KNOTS...

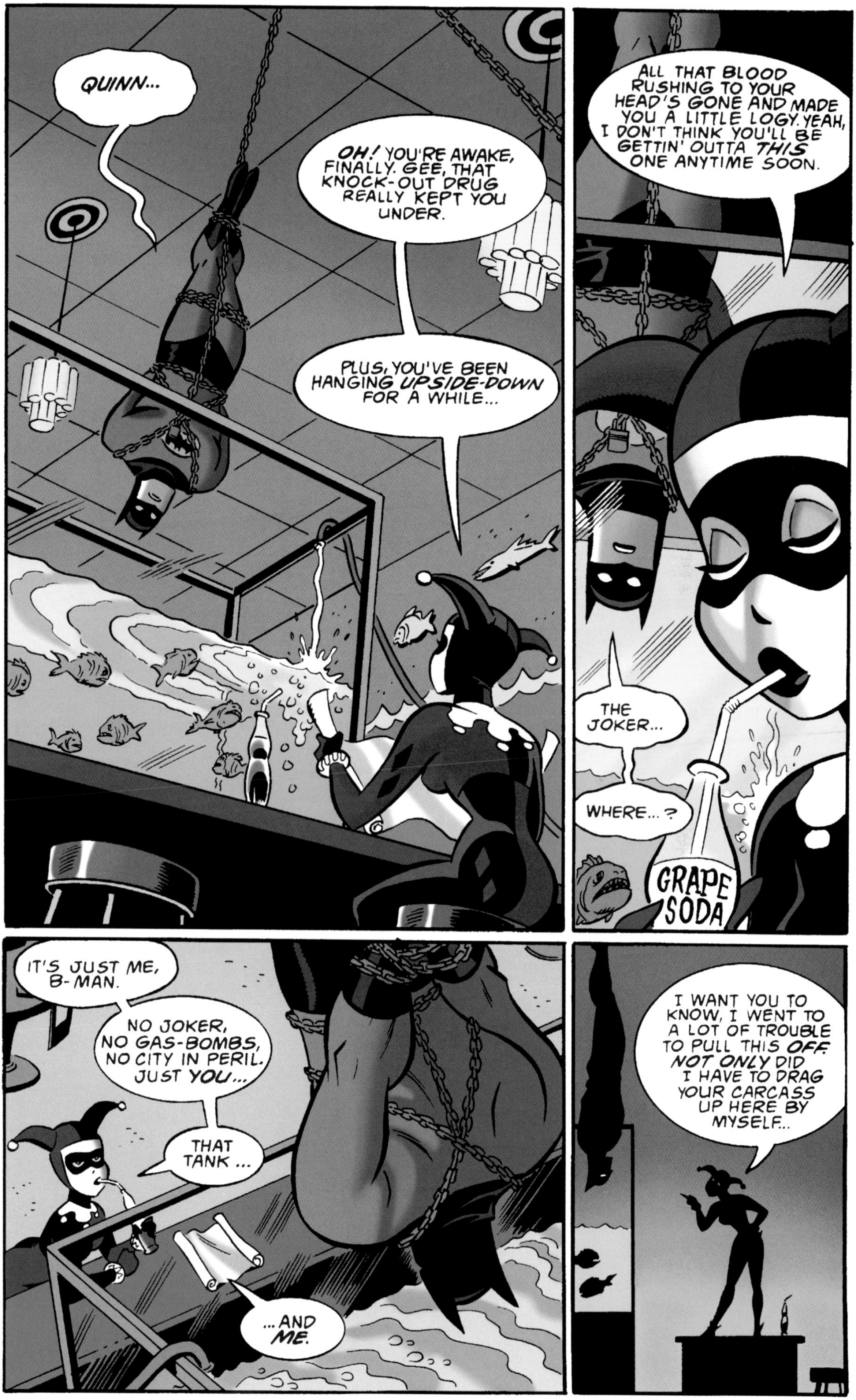
QUINN...
OH! YOU'RE AWAKE, FINALLY. GEE, THAT KNOCK-OUT DRUG REALLY KEPT YOU UNDER.
PLUS, YOU'VE BEEN HANGING UPSIDE-DOWN FOR A WHILE...
ALL THAT BLOOD RUSHING TO YOUR HEAD'S GONE AND MADE YOU A LITTLE LOGY. YEAH, I DON'T THINK YOU'LL BE GETTIN' OUTTA THIS ONE ANYTIME SOON.
THE JOKER...
WHERE...?
GRAPE SODA
IT'S JUST ME, B-MAN.
NO JOKER, NO GAS-BOMBS, NO CITY IN PERIL. JUST YOU...
THAT TANK ...
...AND ME.
I WANT YOU TO KNOW, I WENT TO A LOT OF TROUBLE TO PULL THIS OFF. NOT ONLY DID I HAVE TO DRAG YOUR CARCASS UP HERE BY MYSELF...

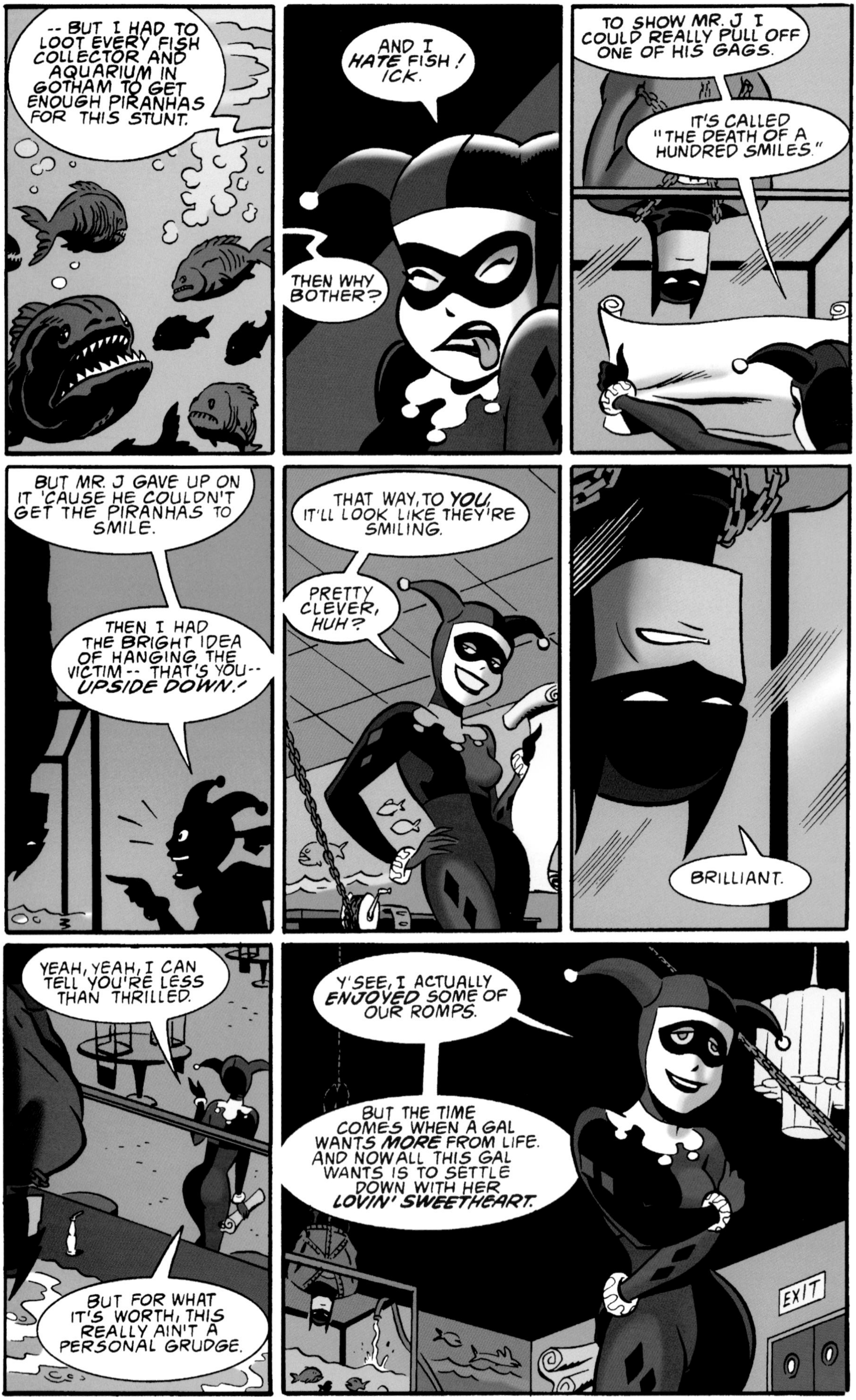
-- BUT I HAD TO LOOT EVERY FISH COLLECTOR AND AQUARIUM IN GOTHAM TO GET ENOUGH PIRANHAS FOR THIS STUNT.
AND I HATE FISH! ICK.
THEN WHY BOTHER?
TO SHOW MR. J I COULD REALLY PULL OFF ONE OF HIS GAGS.
IT'S CALLED "THE DEATH OF A HUNDRED SMILES."
BUT MR. J GAVE UP ON IT 'CAUSE HE COULDN'T GET THE PIRANHAS TO SMILE.
THEN I HAD THE BRIGHT IDEA OF HANGING THE VICTIM -- THAT'S YOU-- UPSIDE DOWN.!
THAT WAY, TO YOU, IT'LL LOOK LIKE THEY'RE SMILING.
PRETTY CLEVER, HUH?
BRILLIANT.
YEAH, YEAH, I CAN TELL YOU'RE LESS THAN THRILLED.
BUT FOR WHAT IT'S WORTH, THIS REALLY AIN'T A PERSONAL GRUDGE.
Y'SEE, I ACTUALLY ENJOYED SOME OF OUR ROMPS.
BUT THE TIME COMES WHEN A GAL WANTS MORE FROM LIFE. AND NOW ALL THIS GAL WANTS IS TO SETTLE DOWN WITH HER LOVIN' SWEETHEART.
EXIT

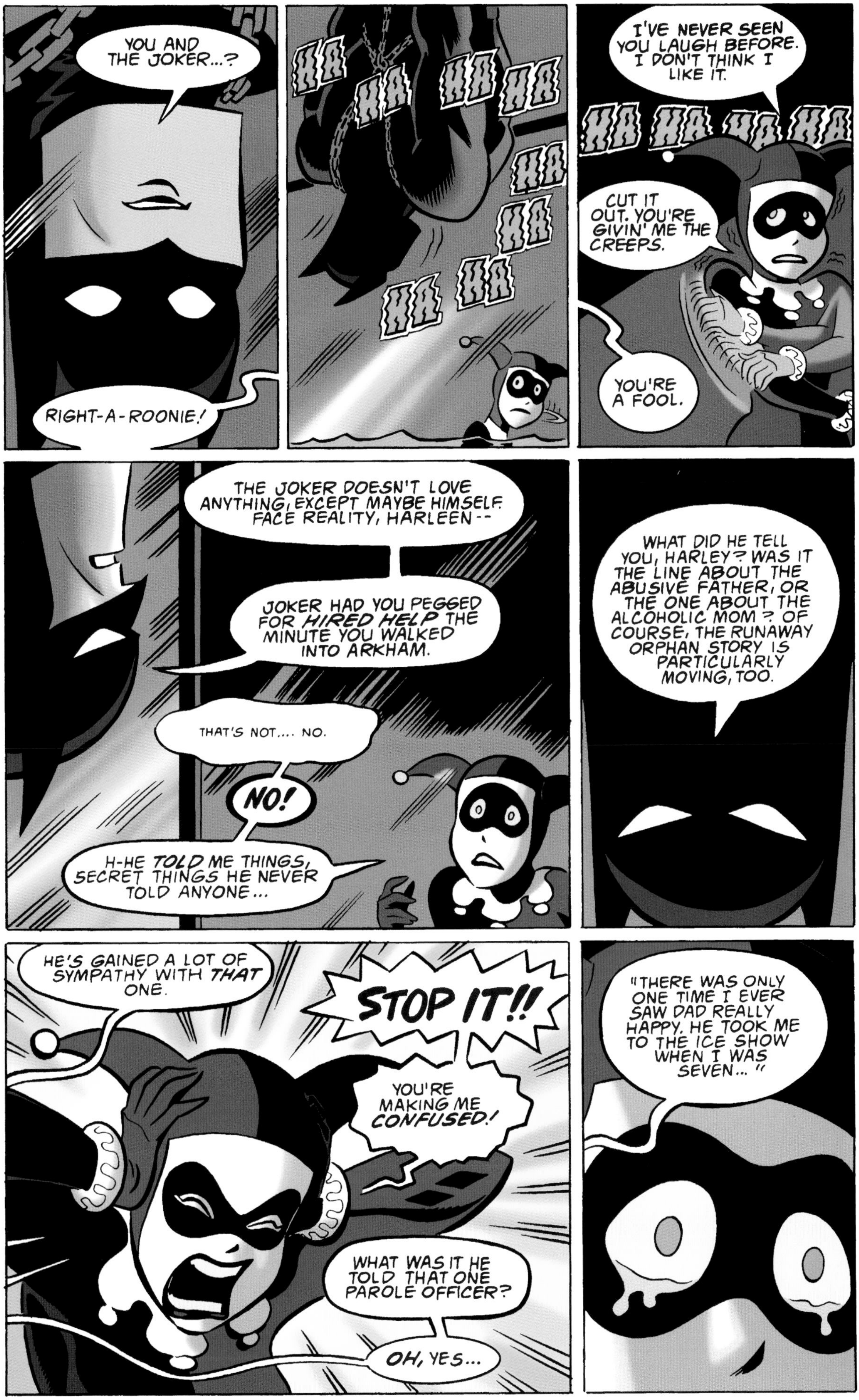

YOU AND THE JOKER...?
RIGHT-A-ROONIE!
HA HA HA HA HA HA HA HA HA
I'VE NEVER SEEN YOU LAUGH BEFORE. I DON'T THINK I LIKE IT.
HA HA HA HA
CUT IT OUT. YOU'RE GIVIN' ME THE CREEPS.
YOU'RE A FOOL.
THE JOKER DOESN'T LOVE ANYTHING, EXCEPT MAYBE HIMSELF. FACE REALITY, HARLEEN--
JOKER HAD YOU PEGGED FOR HIRED HELP THE MINUTE YOU WALKED INTO ARKHAM.
THAT'S NOT.... NO.
NO!
H-HE TOLD ME THINGS, SECRET THINGS HE NEVER TOLD ANYONE...
WHAT DID HE TELL YOU, HARLEY? WAS IT THE LINE ABOUT THE ABUSIVE FATHER, OR THE ONE ABOUT THE ALCOHOLIC MOM? OF COURSE, THE RUNAWAY ORPHAN STORY IS PARTICULARLY MOVING, TOO.
HE'S GAINED A LOT OF SYMPATHY WITH THAT ONE.
STOP IT!!
YOU'RE MAKING ME CONFUSED!
WHAT WAS IT HE TOLD THAT ONE PAROLE OFFICER?
OH, YES...
"THERE WAS ONLY ONE TIME I EVER SAW DAD REALLY HAPPY. HE TOOK ME TO THE ICE SHOW WHEN I WAS SEVEN..."

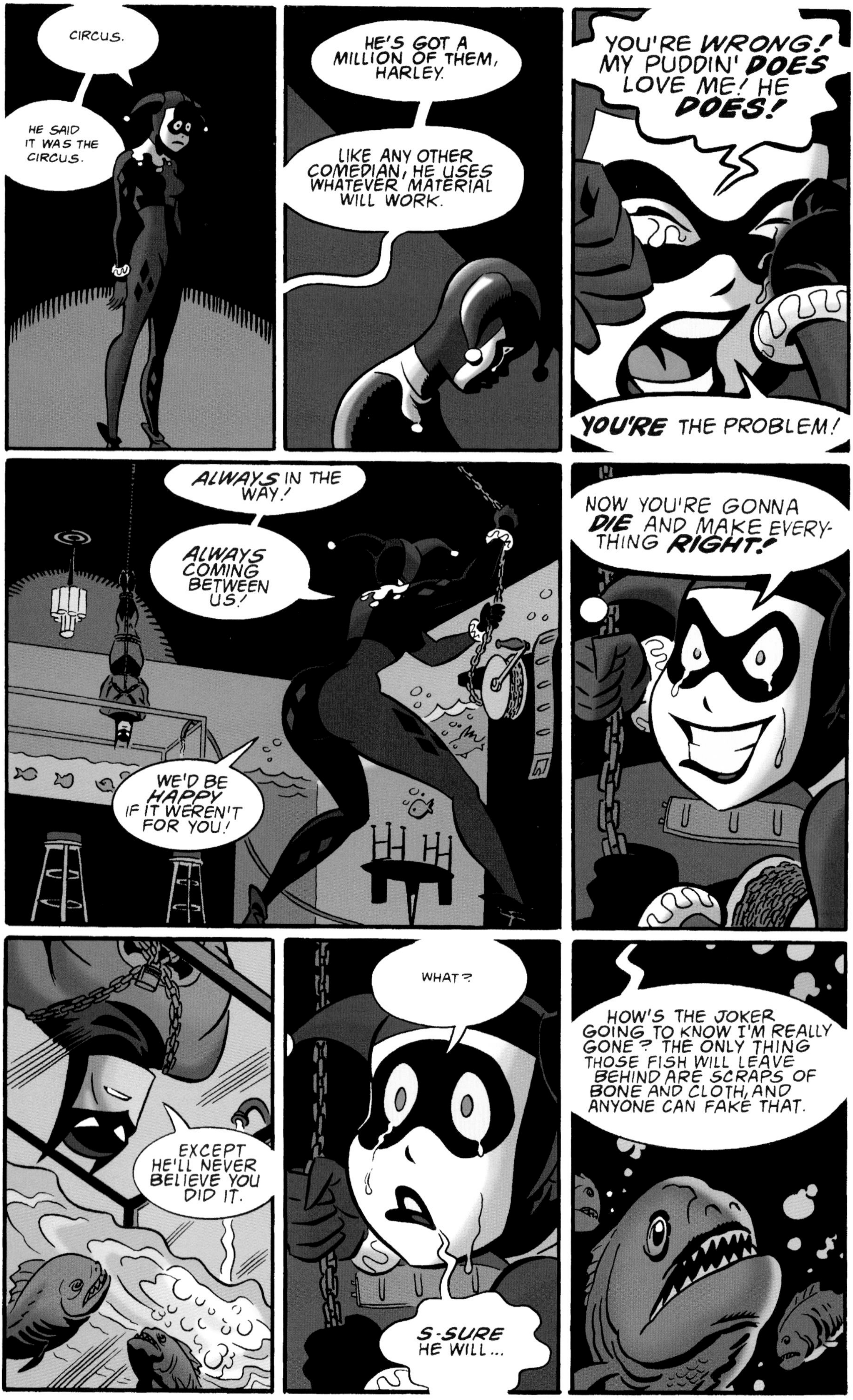
CIRCUS.
HE SAID IT WAS THE CIRCUS.
HE'S GOT A MILLION OF THEM, HARLEY.
LIKE ANY OTHER COMEDIAN, HE USES WHATEVER MATERIAL WILL WORK.
YOU'RE WRONG! MY PUDDIN' DOES LOVE ME! HE DOES!
YOU'RE THE PROBLEM!
ALWAYS IN THE WAY!
ALWAYS COMING BETWEEN US!
WE'D BE HAPPY IF IT WEREN'T FOR YOU!
NOW YOU'RE GONNA DIE AND MAKE EVERY-THING RIGHT!
EXCEPT HE'LL NEVER BELIEVE YOU DID IT.
WHAT?
S-SURE HE WILL...
HOW'S THE JOKER GOING TO KNOW I'M REALLY GONE? THE ONLY THING THOSE FISH WILL LEAVE BEHIND ARE SCRAPS OF BONE AND CLOTH, AND ANYONE CAN FAKE THAT.

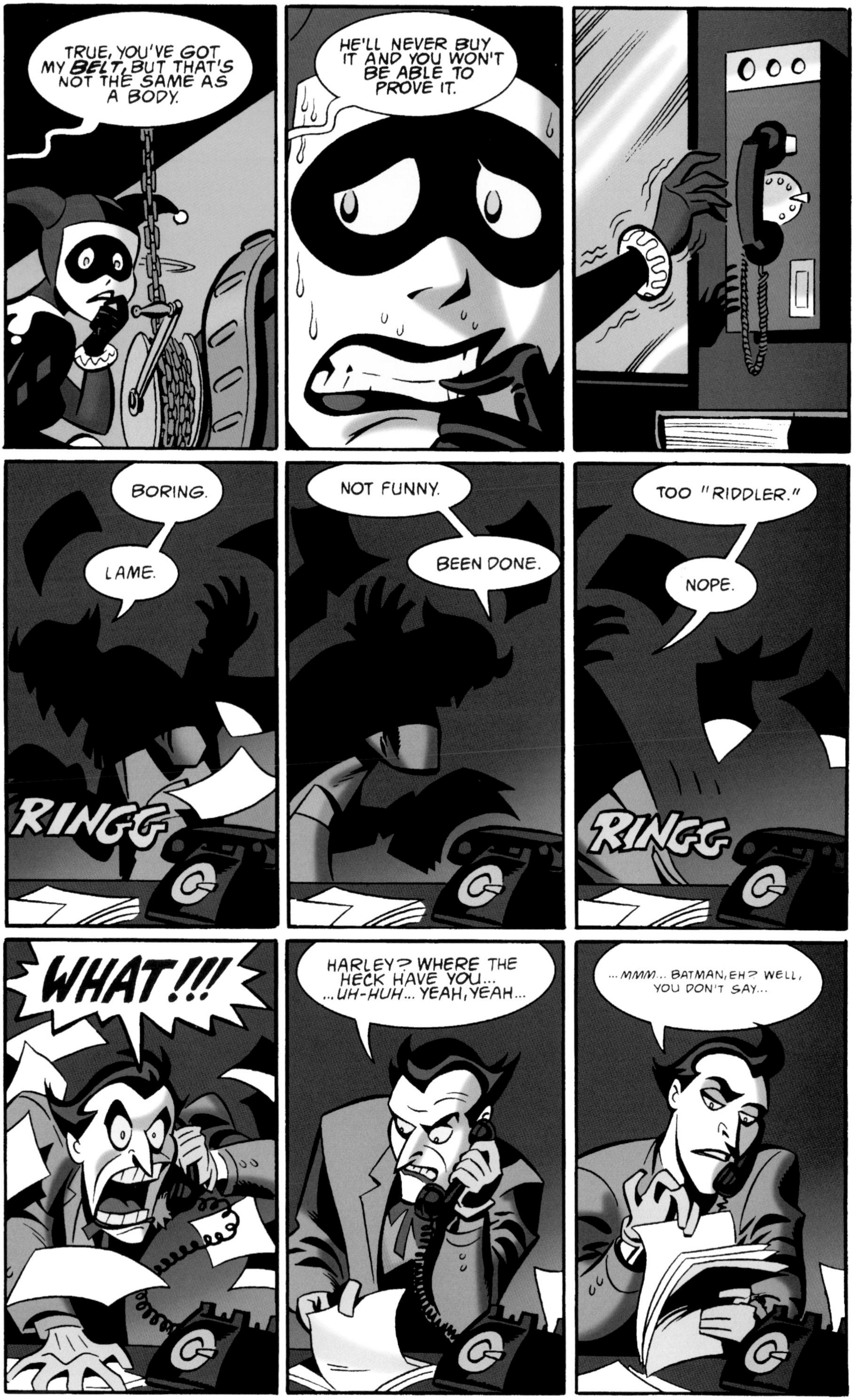
TRUE, YOU'VE GOT MY BELT, BUT THAT'S NOT THE SAME AS A BODY.
HE'LL NEVER BUY IT AND YOU WON'T BE ABLE TO PROVE IT.
BORING.
LAME.
RINGG
NOT FUNNY.
BEEN DONE.
TOO "RIDDLER."
NOPE.
RINGG
WHAT!!!
HARLEY? WHERE THE HECK HAVE YOU... ...UH-HUH... YEAH, YEAH...
...MMM... BATMAN, EH? WELL, YOU DON'T SAY...

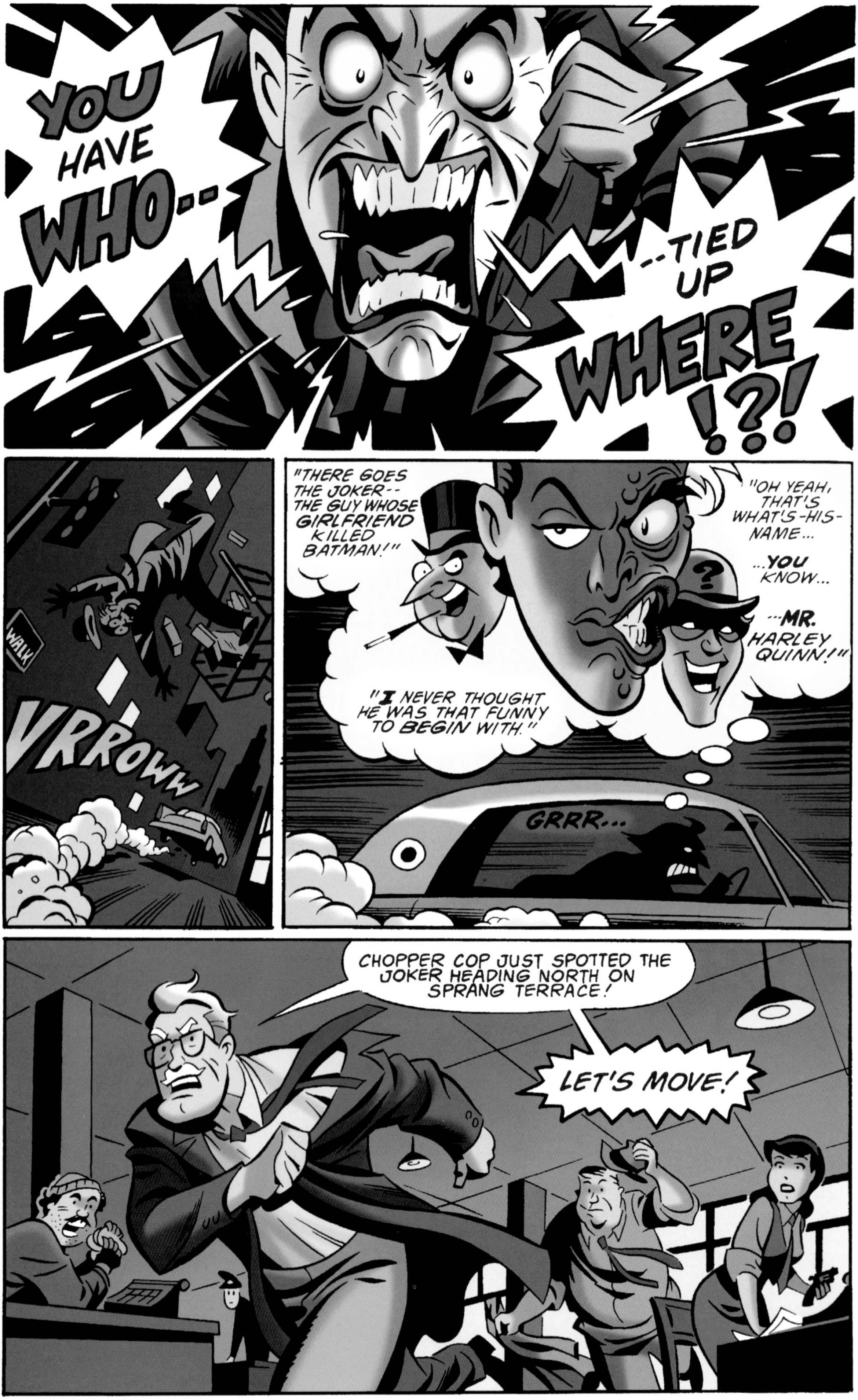

YOU HAVE WHO--
--TIED UP WHERE!?!
VRROWW
"THERE GOES THE JOKER-- THE GUY WHOSE GIRLFRIEND KILLED BATMAN!"
"OH YEAH, THAT'S WHAT'S-HIS-NAME...
...YOU KNOW...
...MR. HARLEY QUINN!"
"I NEVER THOUGHT HE WAS THAT FUNNY TO BEGIN WITH."
GRRR...
CHOPPER COP JUST SPOTTED THE JOKER HEADING NORTH ON SPRANG TERRACE!
LET'S MOVE!

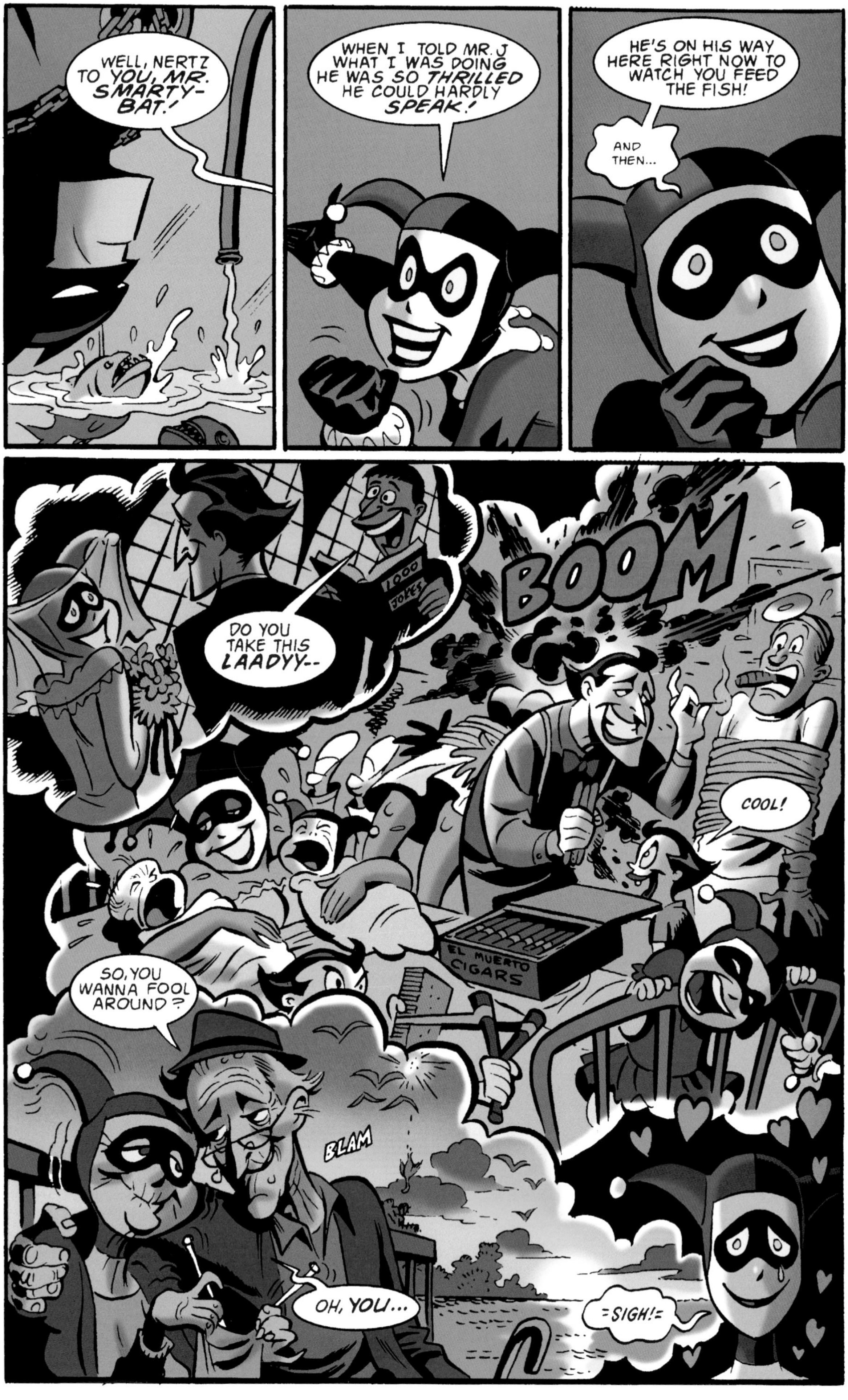

WELL, NERTZ TO YOU, MR. SMARTY-BAT!
WHEN I TOLD MR. J WHAT I WAS DOING HE WAS SO THRILLED HE COULD HARDLY SPEAK!
HE'S ON HIS WAY HERE RIGHT NOW TO WATCH YOU FEED THE FISH!
AND THEN...
1000 JOKES
DO YOU TAKE THIS LAADYY--
BOOM
COOL!
EL MUERTO CIGARS
SO, YOU WANNA FOOL AROUND?
BLAM
OH, YOU...
=SIGH!=

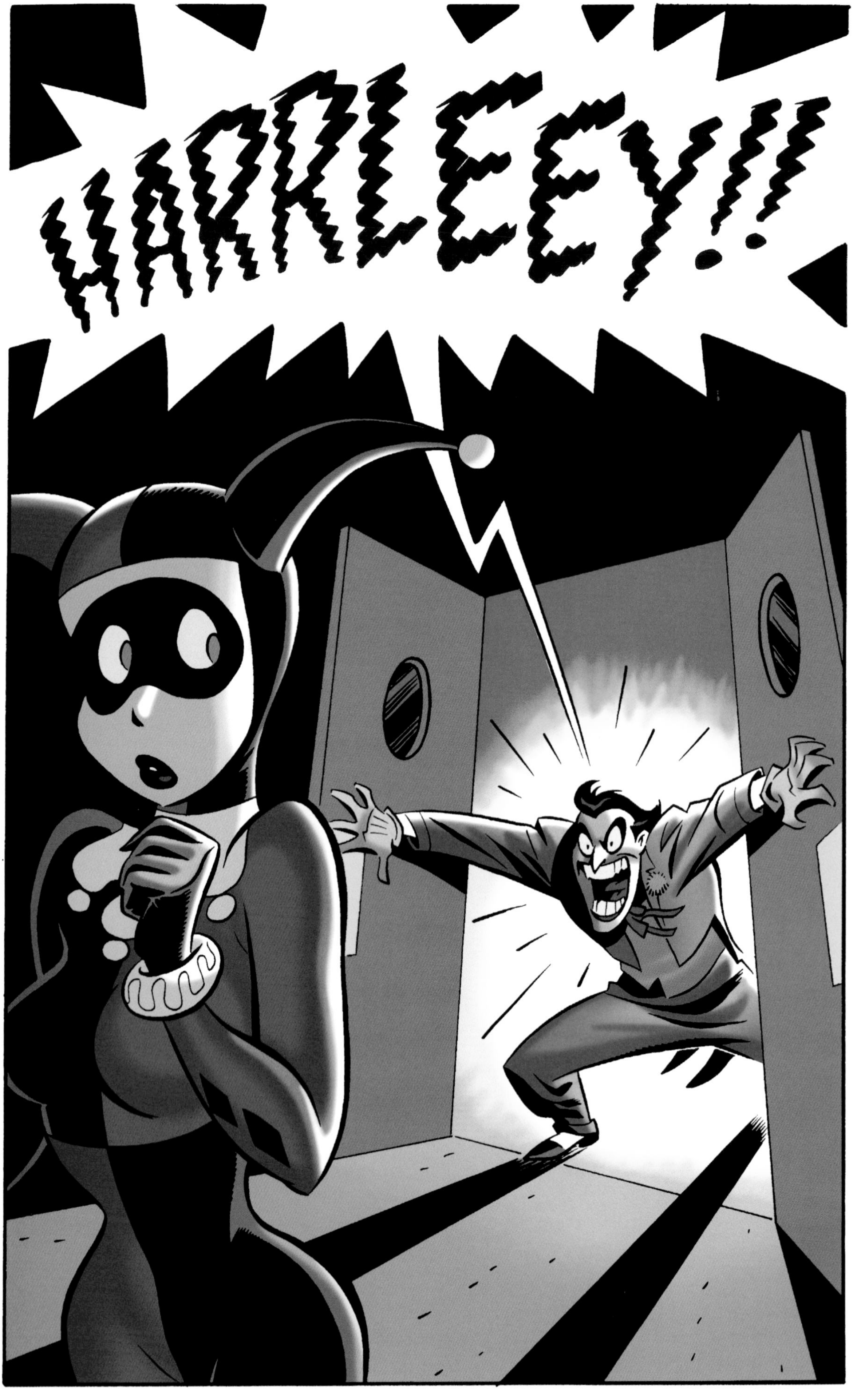
HARRLEEY!!

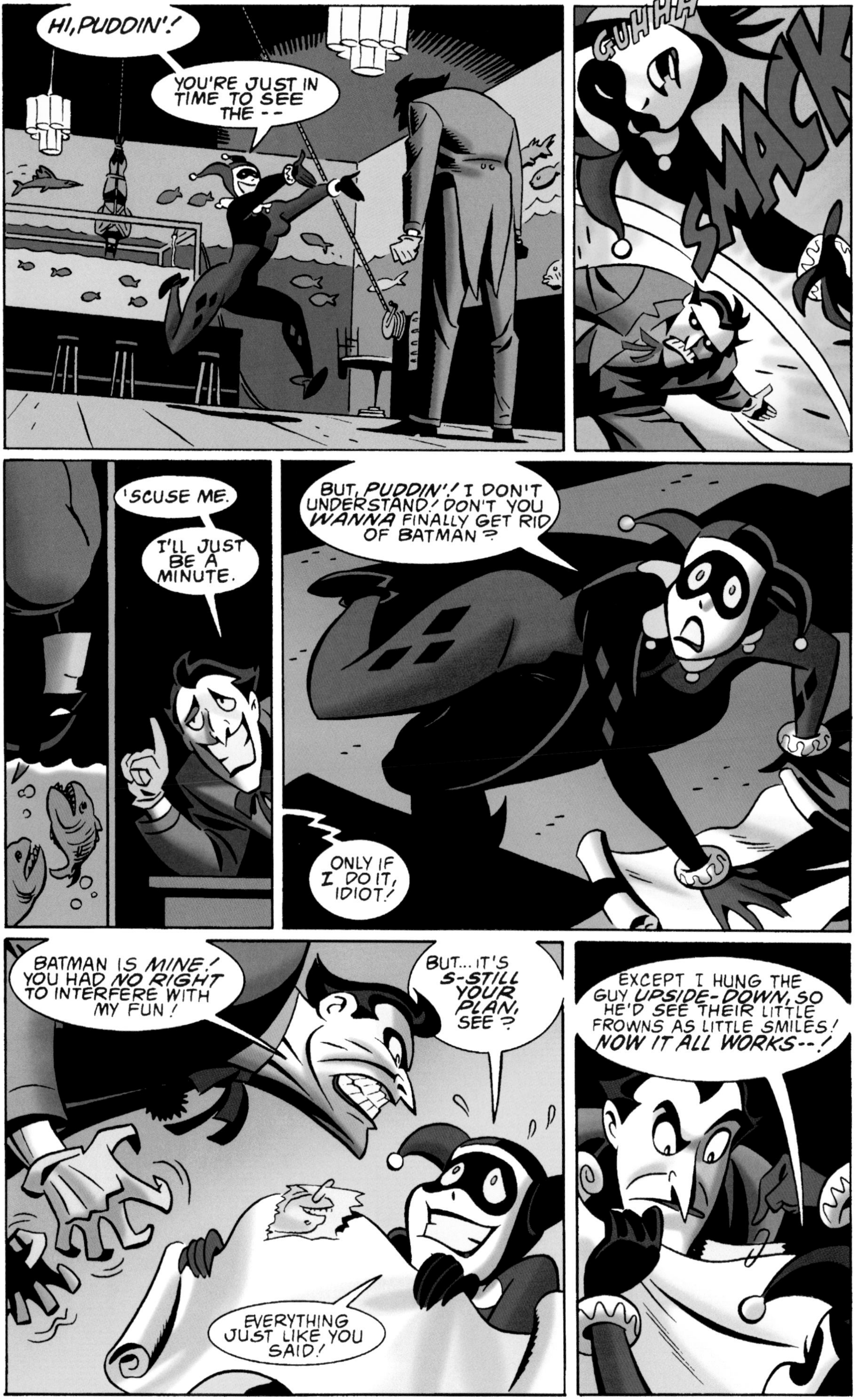
HI, PUDDIN'!
YOU'RE JUST IN TIME TO SEE THE --
GUHHH
SMACK
'SCUSE ME.
I'LL JUST BE A MINUTE.
BUT, PUDDIN'! I DON'T UNDERSTAND! DON'T YOU WANNA FINALLY GET RID OF BATMAN?
ONLY IF I DO IT, IDIOT!
BATMAN IS MINE! YOU HAD NO RIGHT TO INTERFERE WITH MY FUN!
BUT... IT'S S-STILL YOUR PLAN, SEE?
EVERYTHING JUST LIKE YOU SAID!
EXCEPT I HUNG THE GUY UPSIDE-DOWN, SO HE'D SEE THEIR LITTLE FROWNS AS LITTLE SMILES! NOW IT ALL WORKS--!

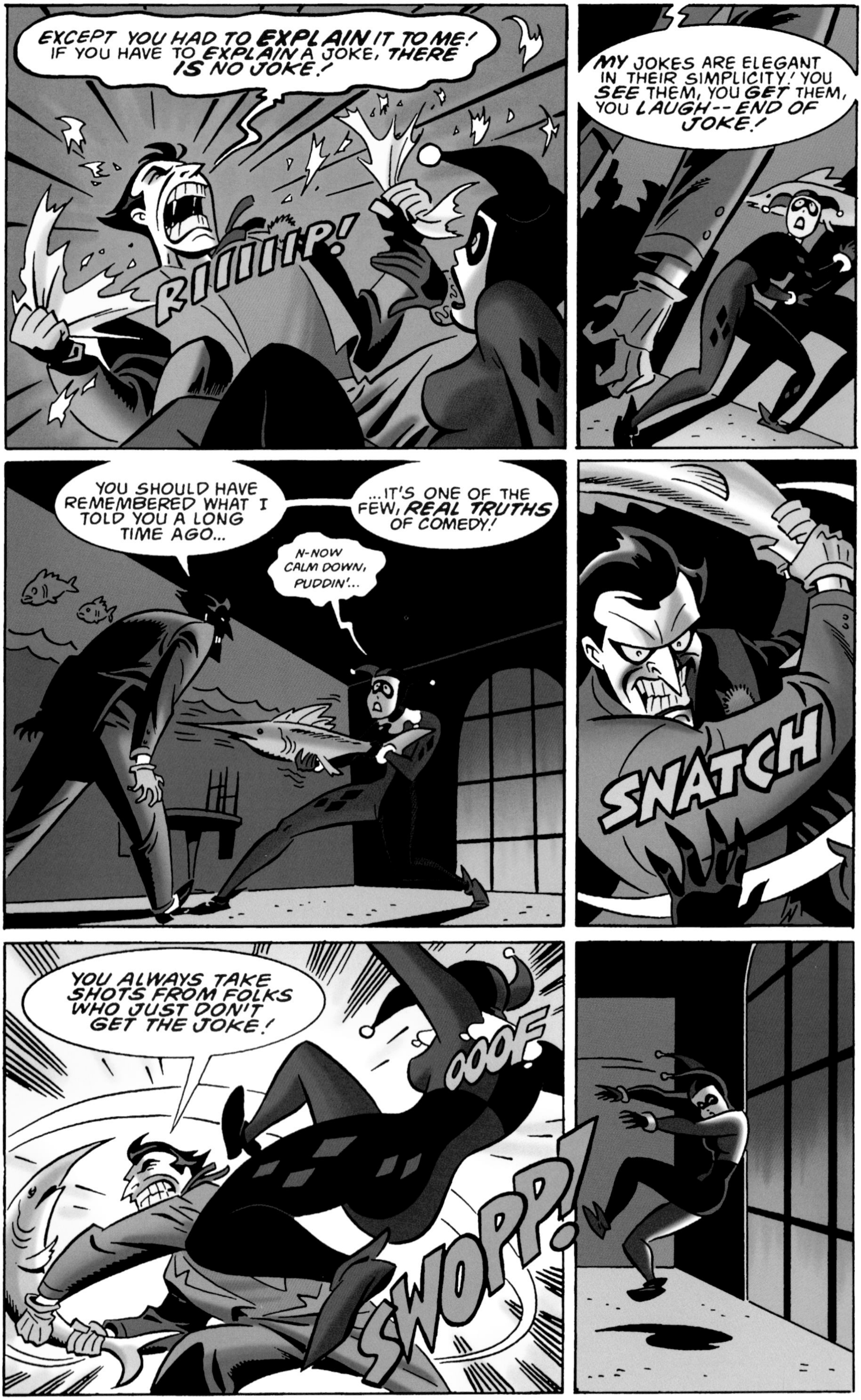
EXCEPT YOU HAD TO EXPLAIN IT TO ME! IF YOU HAVE TO EXPLAIN A JOKE, THERE IS NO JOKE!
RIIIIIIP!
MY JOKES ARE ELEGANT IN THEIR SIMPLICITY! YOU SEE THEM, YOU GET THEM, YOU LAUGH-- END OF JOKE!
YOU SHOULD HAVE REMEMBERED WHAT I TOLD YOU A LONG TIME AGO...
...IT'S ONE OF THE FEW, REAL TRUTHS OF COMEDY!
N-NOW CALM DOWN, PUDDIN'...
SNATCH
YOU ALWAYS TAKE SHOTS FROM FOLKS WHO JUST DON'T GET THE JOKE!
OOOF
SWOPP!

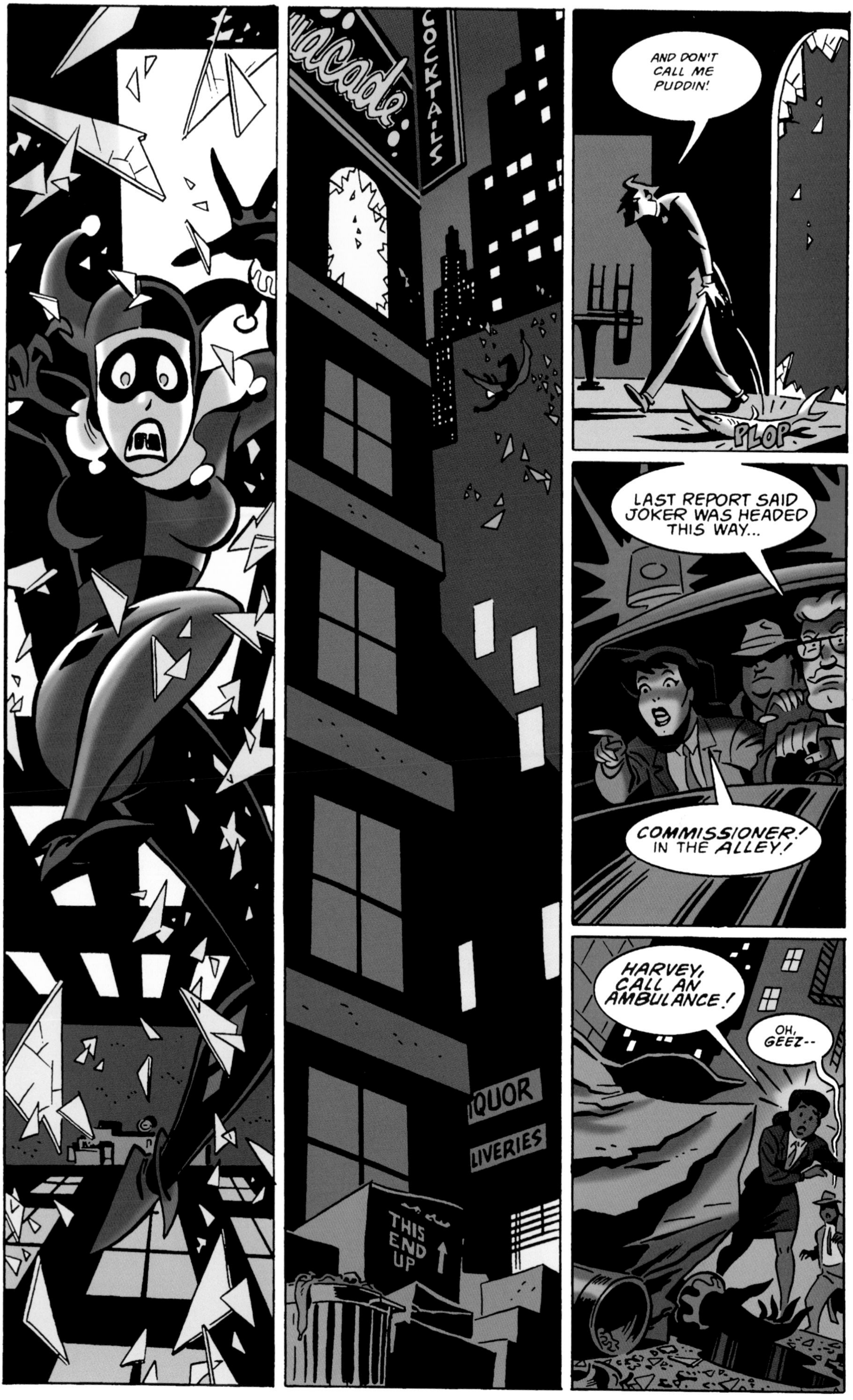
COCKTAILS
AND DON'T CALL ME PUDDIN!
PLOP
LAST REPORT SAID JOKER WAS HEADED THIS WAY...
COMMISSIONER! IN THE ALLEY!
HARVEY, CALL AN AMBULANCE!
OH, GEEZ--
IQUOR
LIVERIES
THIS END UP

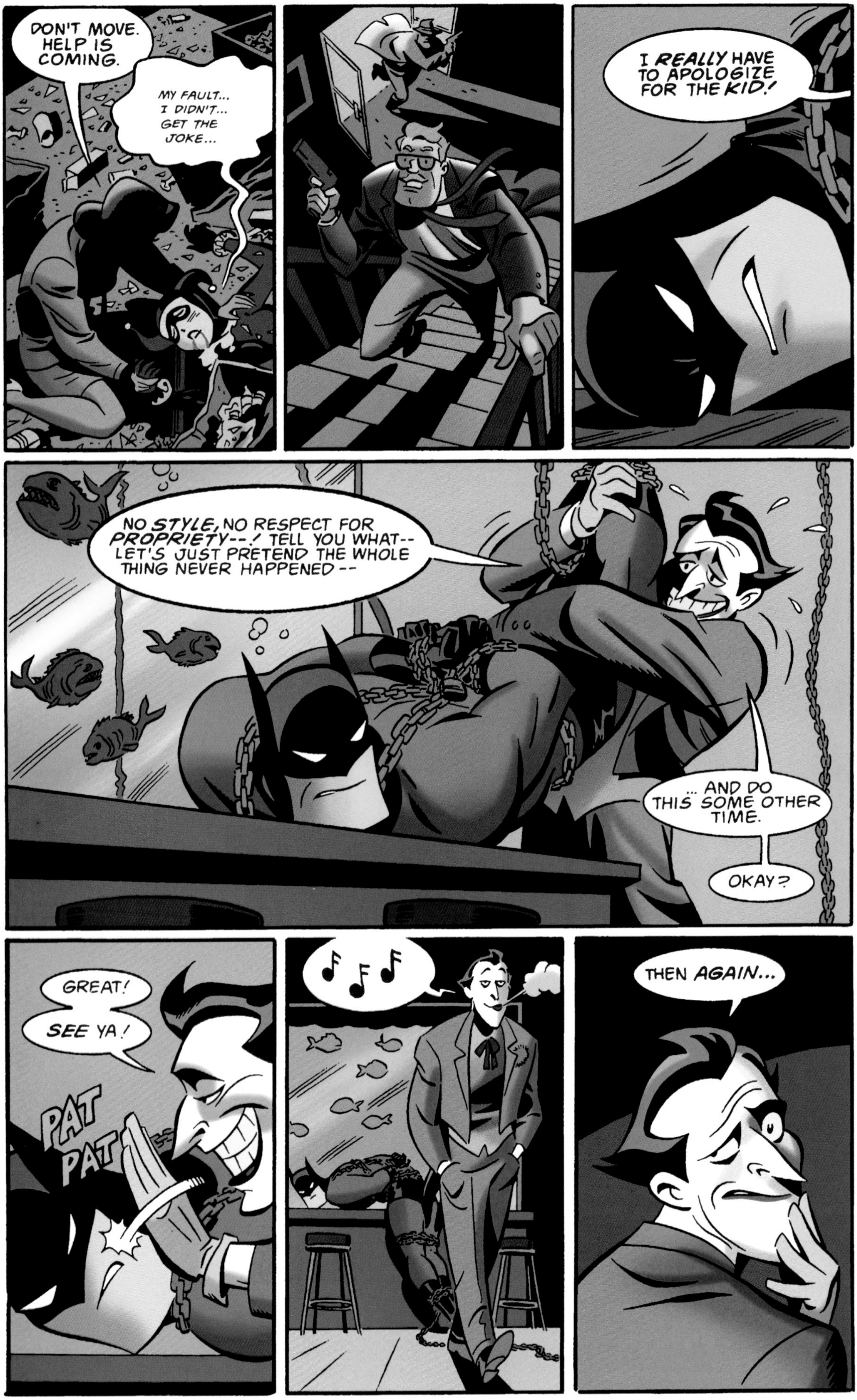

DON'T MOVE. HELP IS COMING.
MY FAULT... I DIDN'T... GET THE JOKE...
I REALLY HAVE TO APOLOGIZE FOR THE KID!
NO STYLE, NO RESPECT FOR PROPRIETY--! TELL YOU WHAT-- LET'S JUST PRETEND THE WHOLE THING NEVER HAPPENED --
... AND DO THIS SOME OTHER TIME.
OKAY?
GREAT!
SEE YA!
PAT PAT
THEN AGAIN...

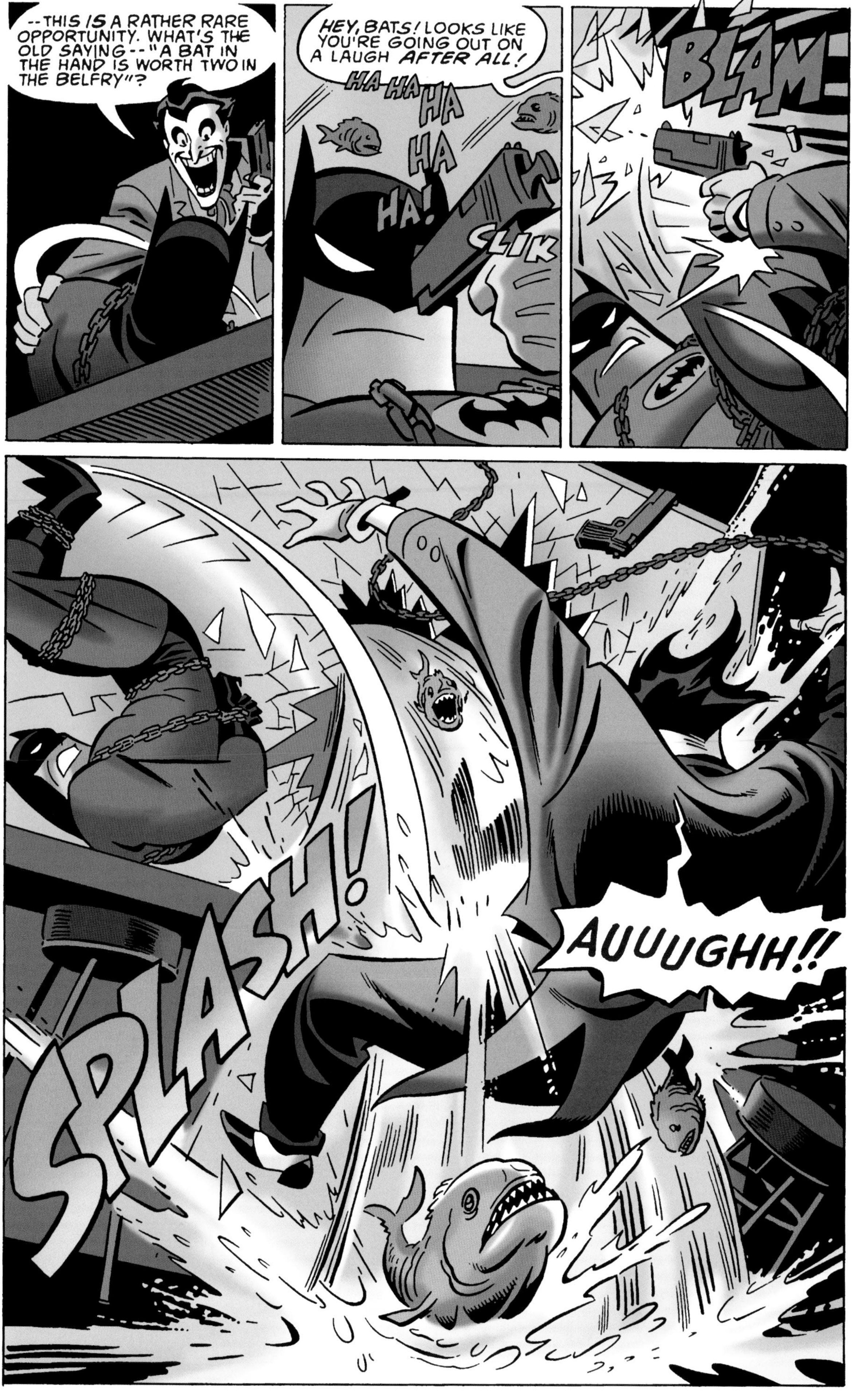
--THIS IS A RATHER RARE OPPORTUNITY. WHAT'S THE OLD SAYING--"A BAT IN THE HAND IS WORTH TWO IN THE BELFRY"?
HEY, BATS! LOOKS LIKE YOU'RE GOING OUT ON A LAUGH AFTER ALL!
HA HA HA HA HA HA!
CLIK
BLAM
SPLASH!
AUUUGHH!!

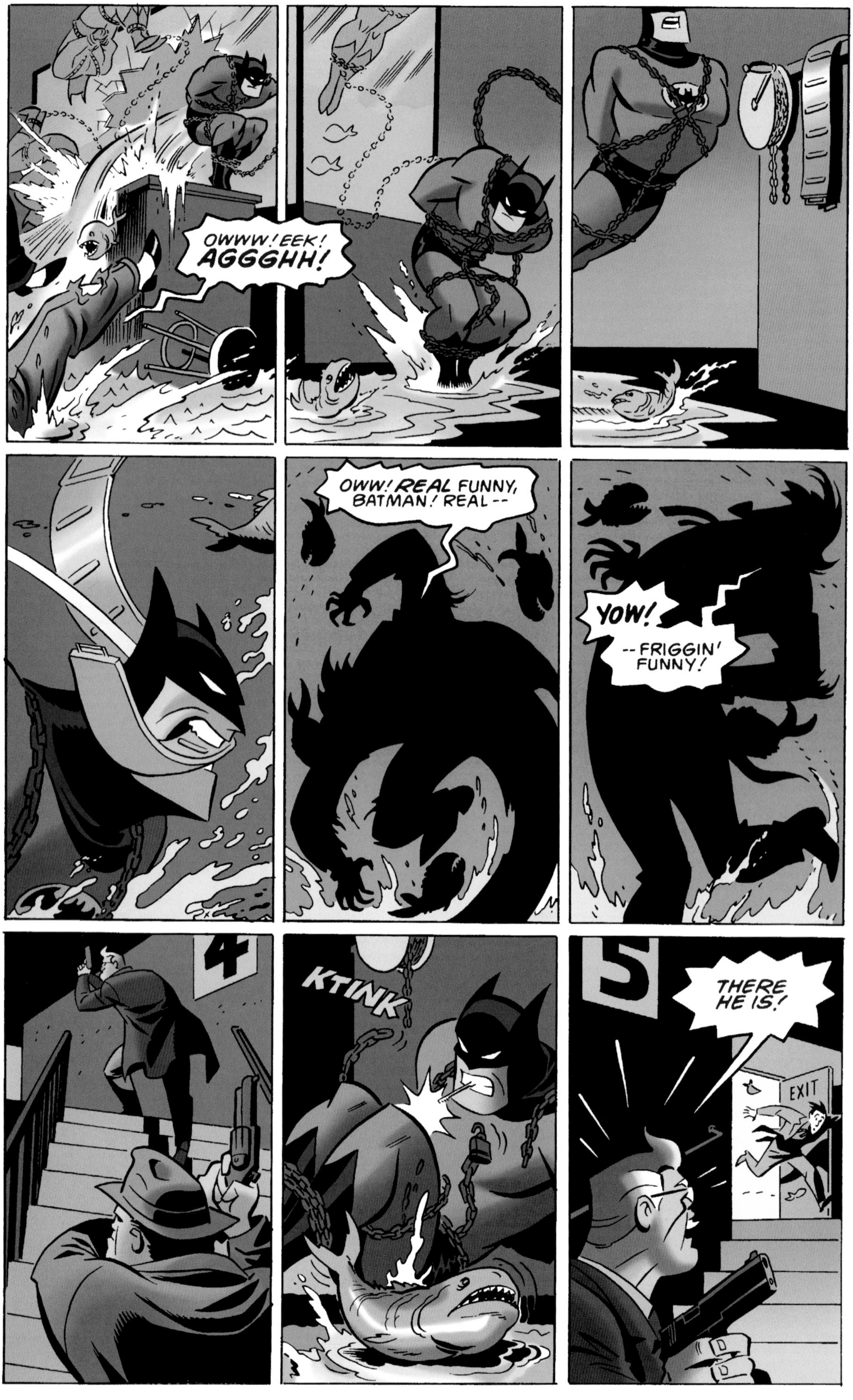

OWWW! EEK! AGGGHH!
OWW! REAL FUNNY, BATMAN! REAL --
YOW!
-- FRIGGIN' FUNNY!
KTINK
THERE HE IS!
EXIT

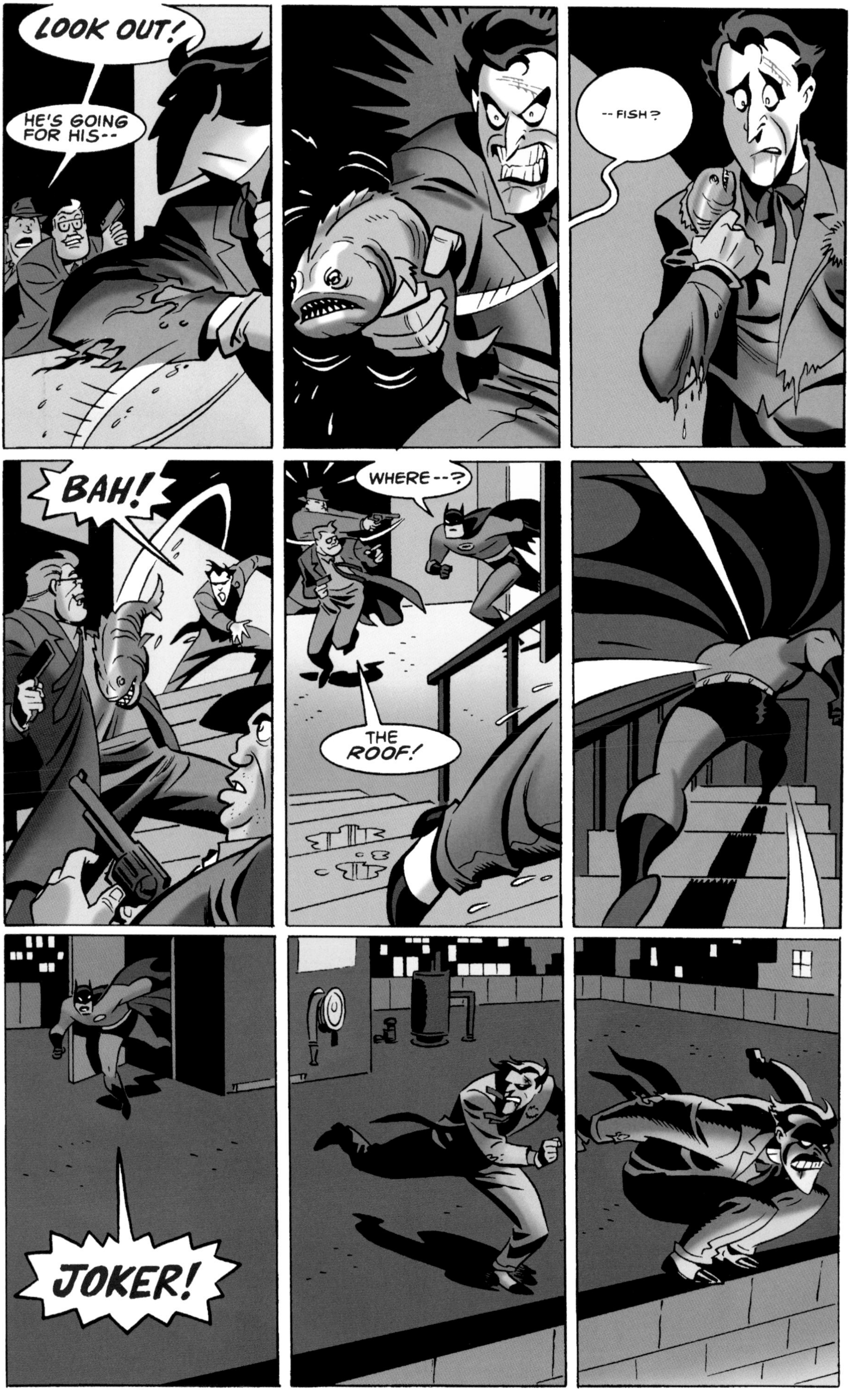
LOOK OUT!
HE'S GOING FOR HIS--
--FISH?
BAH!
WHERE--?
THE ROOF!
JOKER!

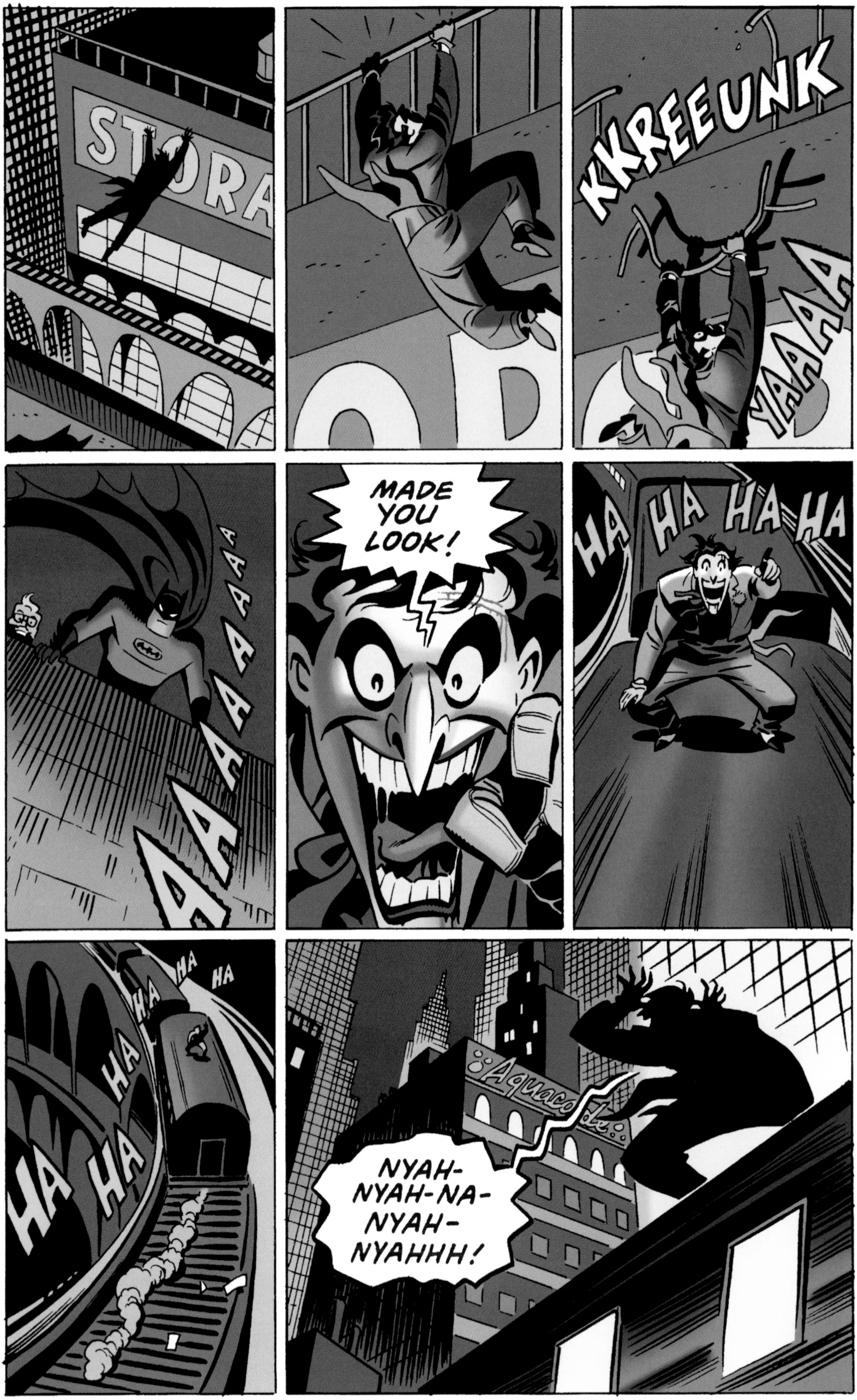
STORA
KKREEUNK
YAAAAA
AAAAAAAAA
MADE YOU LOOK!
HA HA HA HA HA
HA HA HA HA HA HA
NYAH-NYAH-NA-NYAH-NYAHHH!

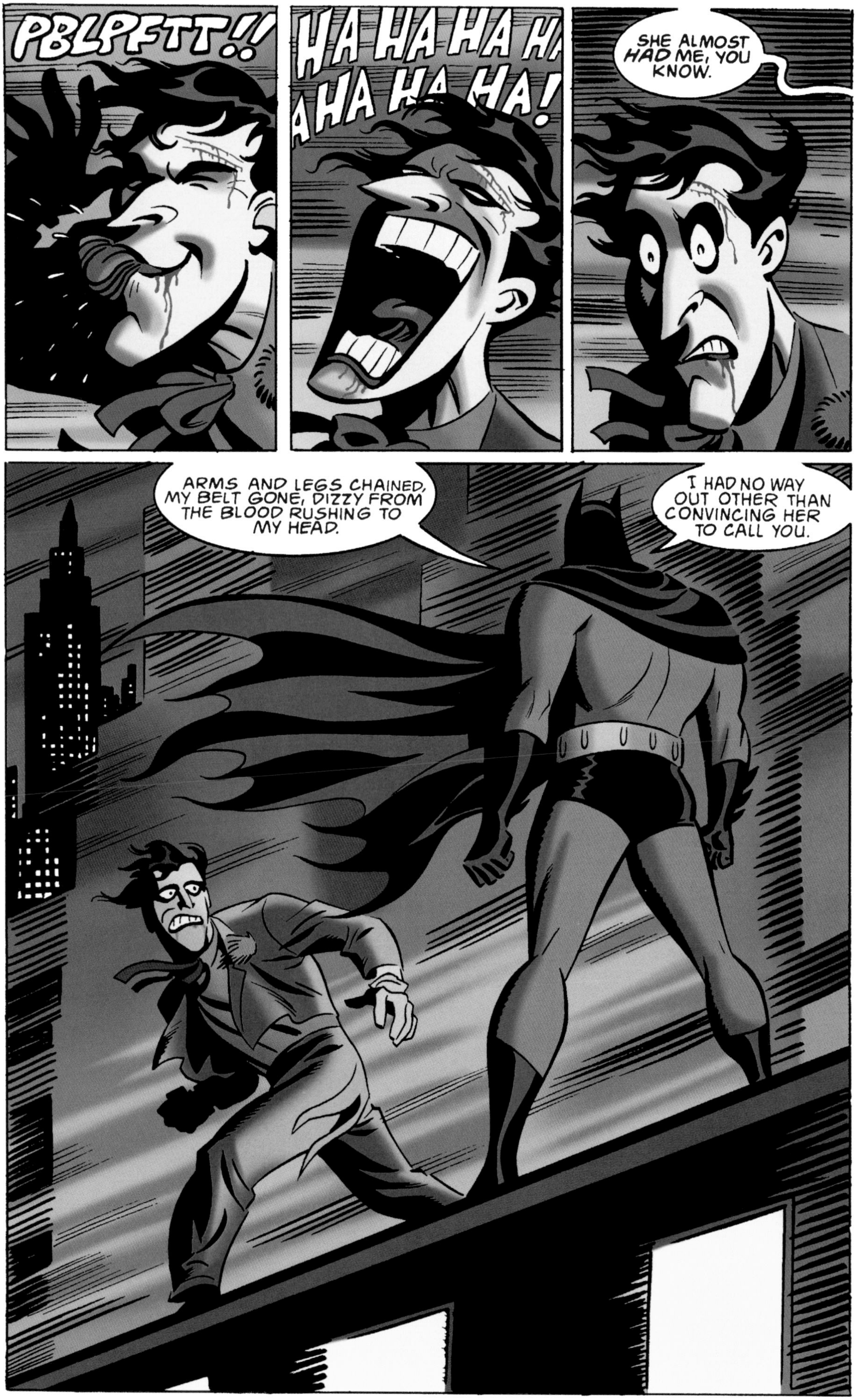
PBLPFTT!!
HA HA HA HA HAHA HA HA HA!
SHE ALMOST HAD ME, YOU KNOW.
ARMS AND LEGS CHAINED, MY BELT GONE, DIZZY FROM THE BLOOD RUSHING TO MY HEAD.
I HAD NO WAY OUT OTHER THAN CONVINCING HER TO CALL YOU.

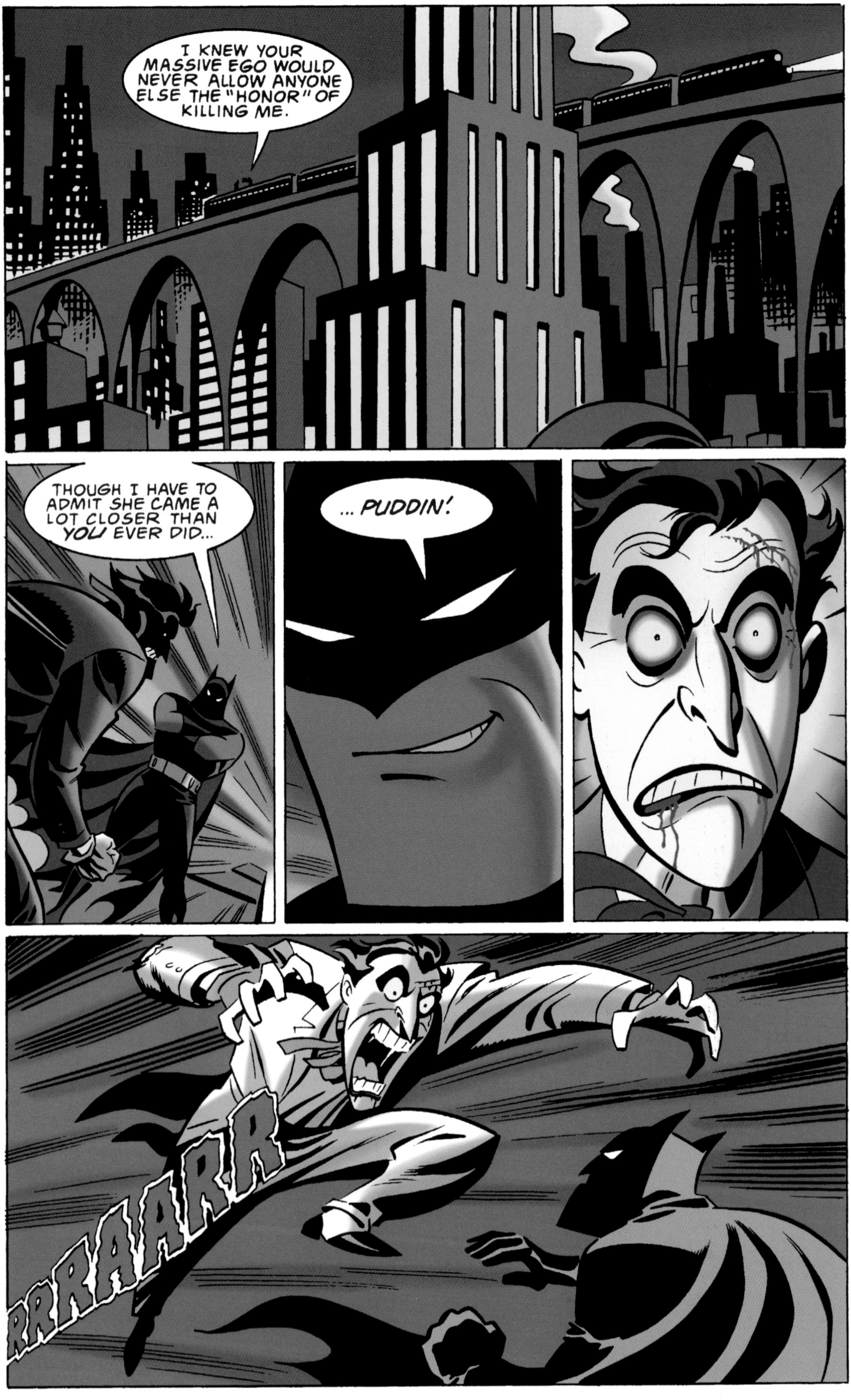
I KNEW YOUR MASSIVE EGO WOULD NEVER ALLOW ANYONE ELSE THE "HONOR" OF KILLING ME.
THOUGH I HAVE TO ADMIT SHE CAME A LOT CLOSER THAN *YOU* EVER DID...
... *PUDDIN'!*
RRRAAARR

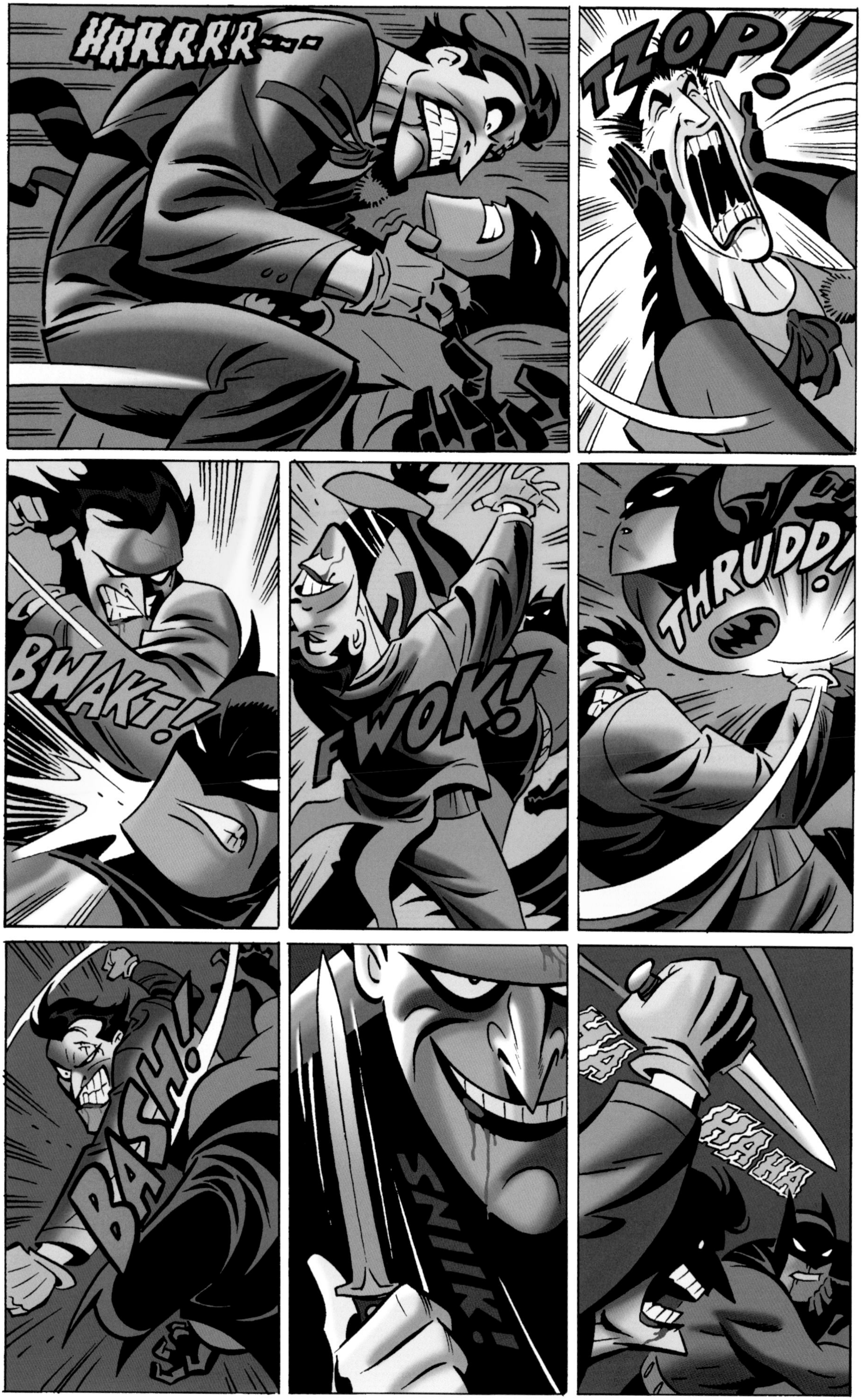
HRRRRR---
TZOP!
BWAKT!
FWOK!
THRUDD!
BASH!
SHIIK!
HA HA
HA HA HA

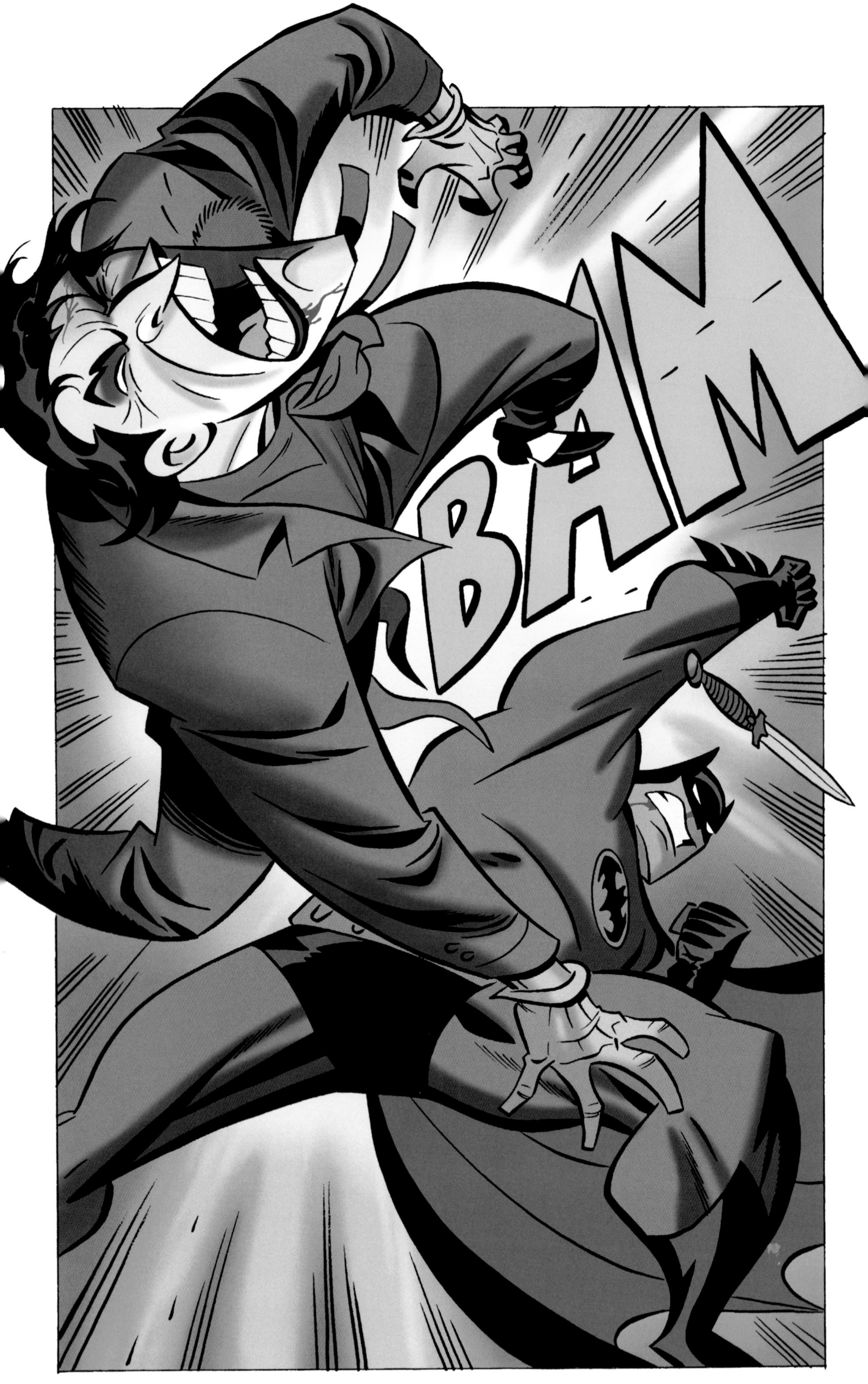
BAM

OH, NO...

NOTT

AGAINN

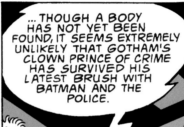

...THOUGH A BODY HAS NOT YET BEEN FOUND, IT SEEMS EXTREMELY UNLIKELY THAT GOTHAM'S CLOWN PRINCE OF CRIME HAS SURVIVED HIS LATEST BRUSH WITH BATMAN AND THE POLICE.

WGBS

RMED UARDS WILL BE PRESENT AT ALL TIMES

ALL REM SEAT

RECREATION THERAPY

STILL, HE *HAS* BEEN NOTORIOUS FOR RESURFACING WHEN LEAST EXPECTED...

NEVER AGAIN.

NO MORE OBSESSION.

NO MORE CRAZINESS.

NO MORE JOKER.

I FINALLY SEE THAT SLIME FOR WHAT HE REALLY IS.

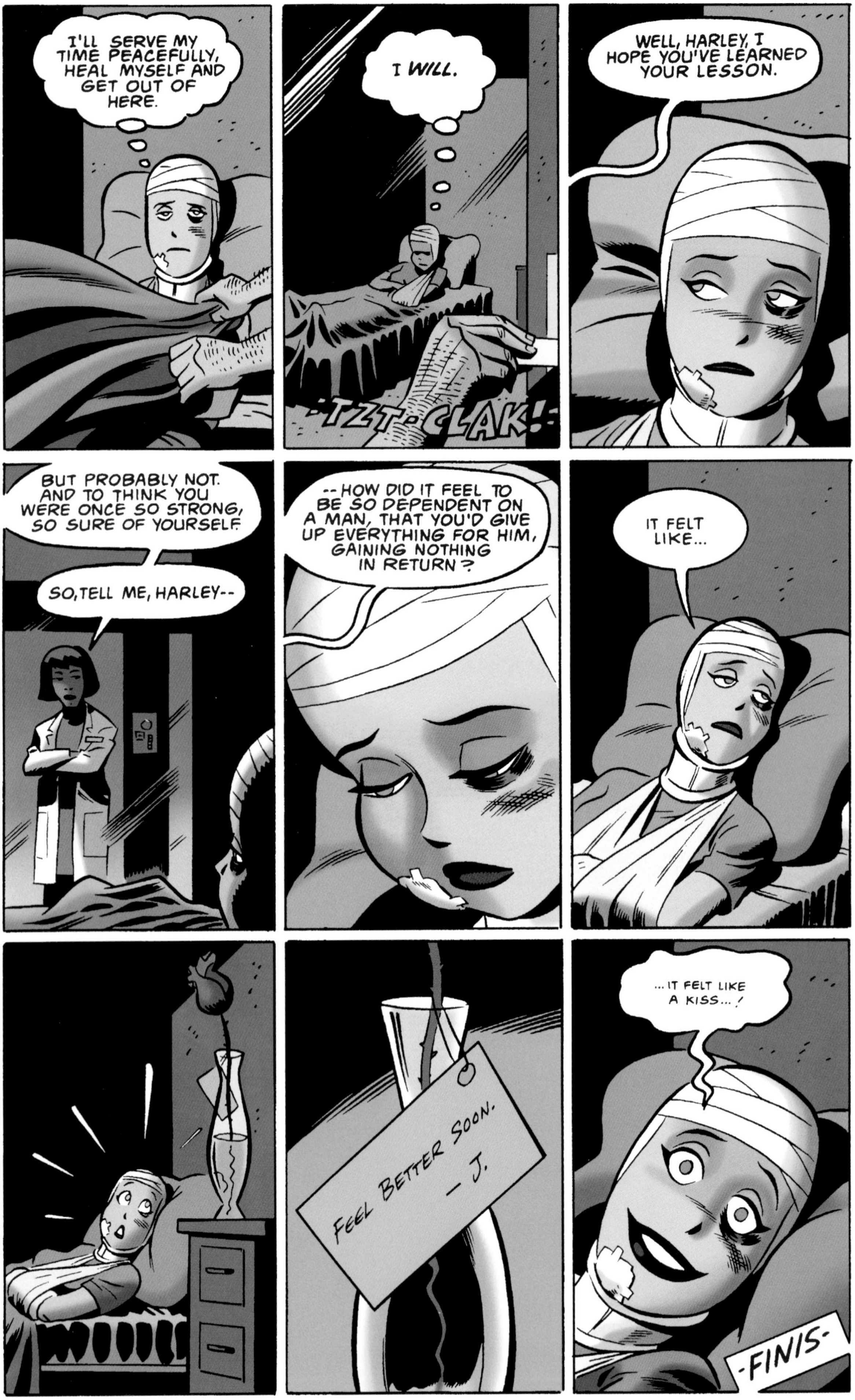
I'LL SERVE MY TIME PEACEFULLY, HEAL MYSELF AND GET OUT OF HERE.
I WILL.
TZT-CLAK!
WELL, HARLEY, I HOPE YOU'VE LEARNED YOUR LESSON.
BUT PROBABLY NOT. AND TO THINK YOU WERE ONCE SO STRONG, SO SURE OF YOURSELF.
SO, TELL ME, HARLEY--
--HOW DID IT FEEL TO BE SO DEPENDENT ON A MAN, THAT YOU'D GIVE UP EVERYTHING FOR HIM, GAINING NOTHING IN RETURN?
IT FELT LIKE...
FEEL BETTER SOON. — J.
...IT FELT LIKE A KISS...!
-FINIS-

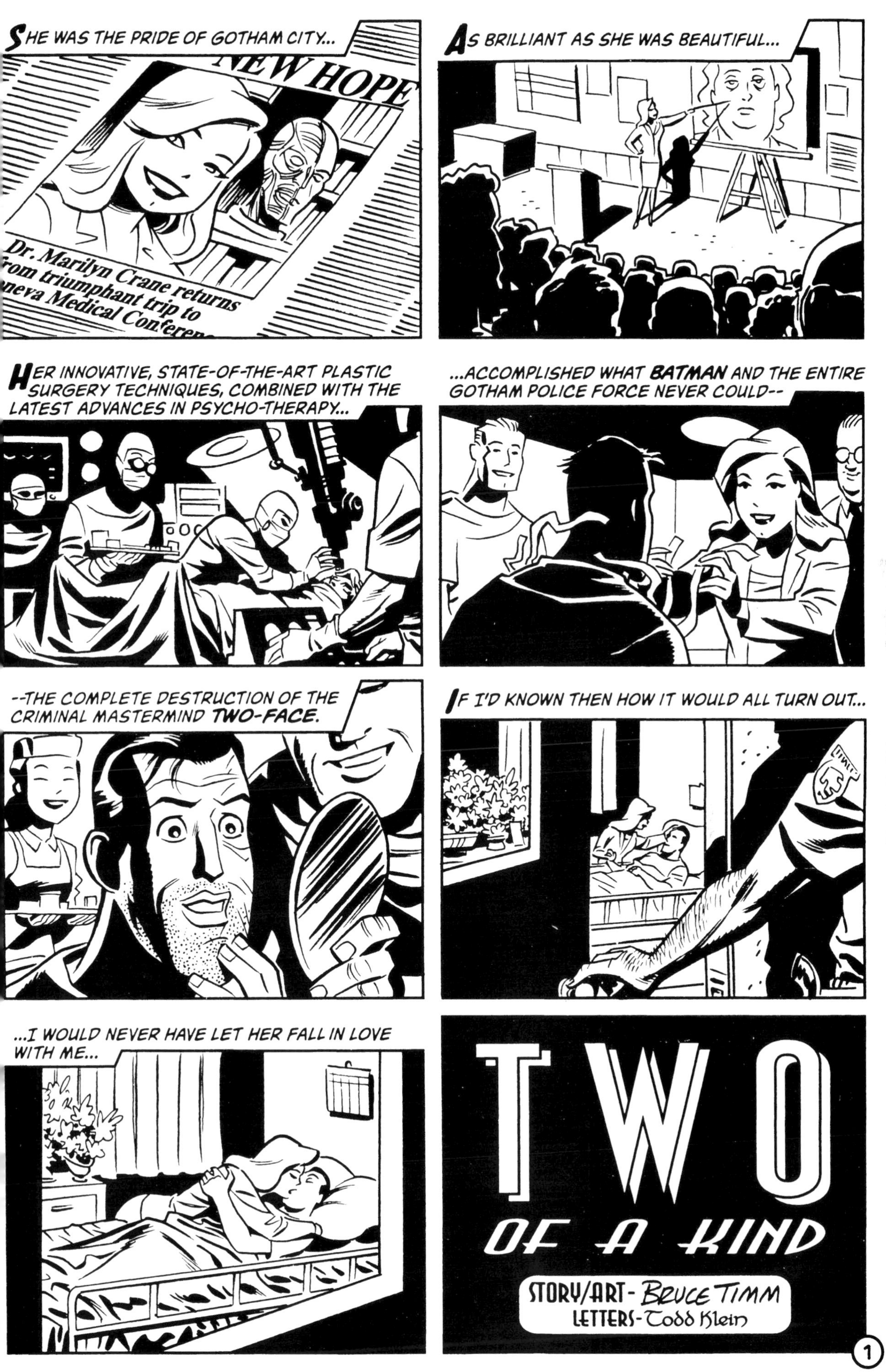
SHE WAS THE PRIDE OF GOTHAM CITY...
NEW HOPE
Dr. Marilyn Crane returns from triumphant trip to neva Medical Conferen
AS BRILLIANT AS SHE WAS BEAUTIFUL...
HER INNOVATIVE, STATE-OF-THE-ART PLASTIC SURGERY TECHNIQUES, COMBINED WITH THE LATEST ADVANCES IN PSYCHO-THERAPY...
...ACCOMPLISHED WHAT BATMAN AND THE ENTIRE GOTHAM POLICE FORCE NEVER COULD--
--THE COMPLETE DESTRUCTION OF THE CRIMINAL MASTERMIND TWO-FACE.
IF I'D KNOWN THEN HOW IT WOULD ALL TURN OUT...
...I WOULD NEVER HAVE LET HER FALL IN LOVE WITH ME...
TWO
OF A KIND
STORY/ART - BRUCE TIMM
LETTERS - Todd Klein
1

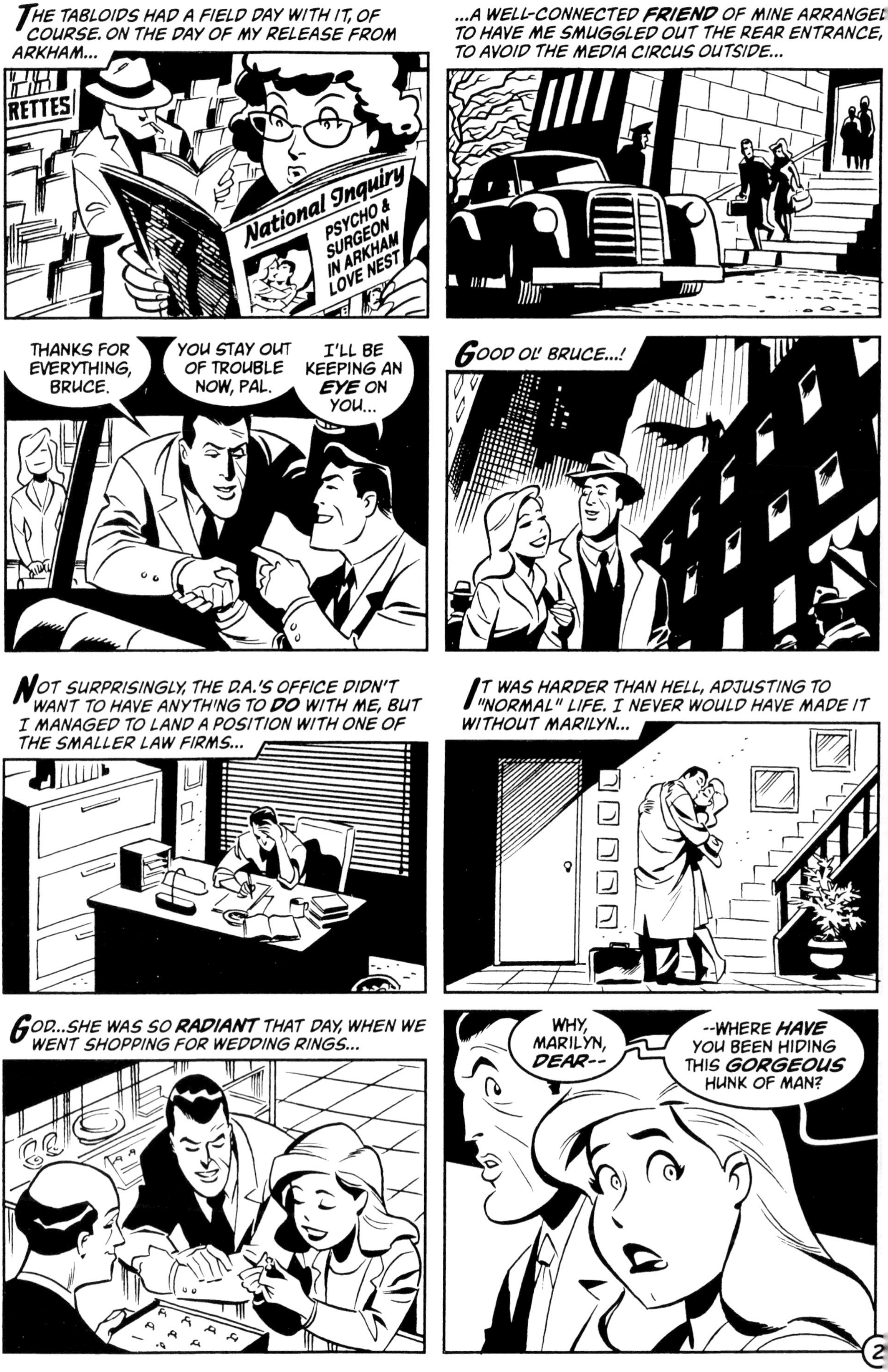
THE TABLOIDS HAD A FIELD DAY WITH IT, OF COURSE. ON THE DAY OF MY RELEASE FROM ARKHAM...
RETTES
National Inquiry
PSYCHO & SURGEON IN ARKHAM LOVE NEST
...A WELL-CONNECTED FRIEND OF MINE ARRANGED TO HAVE ME SMUGGLED OUT THE REAR ENTRANCE, TO AVOID THE MEDIA CIRCUS OUTSIDE...
THANKS FOR EVERYTHING, BRUCE.
YOU STAY OUT OF TROUBLE NOW, PAL.
I'LL BE KEEPING AN EYE ON YOU...
GOOD OL' BRUCE...!
NOT SURPRISINGLY, THE D.A.'S OFFICE DIDN'T WANT TO HAVE ANYTHING TO DO WITH ME, BUT I MANAGED TO LAND A POSITION WITH ONE OF THE SMALLER LAW FIRMS...
IT WAS HARDER THAN HELL, ADJUSTING TO "NORMAL" LIFE. I NEVER WOULD HAVE MADE IT WITHOUT MARILYN...
GOD...SHE WAS SO RADIANT THAT DAY, WHEN WE WENT SHOPPING FOR WEDDING RINGS...
WHY, MARILYN, DEAR--
--WHERE HAVE YOU BEEN HIDING THIS GORGEOUS HUNK OF MAN?
2

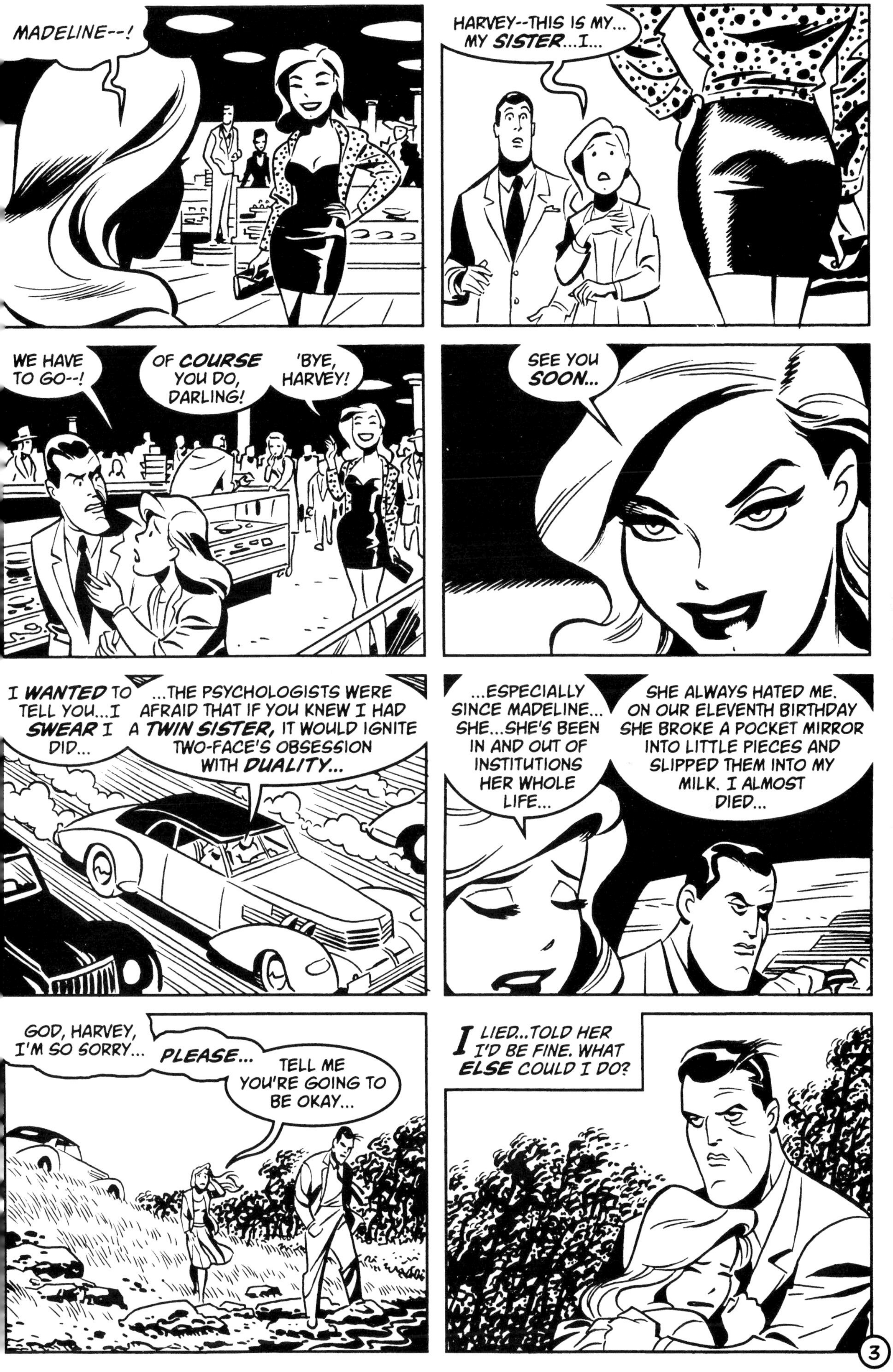
MADELINE--!
HARVEY--THIS IS MY... MY SISTER...I...
WE HAVE TO GO--!
OF COURSE YOU DO, DARLING!
'BYE, HARVEY!
SEE YOU SOON...
I WANTED TO TELL YOU...I SWEAR I DID...
...THE PSYCHOLOGISTS WERE AFRAID THAT IF YOU KNEW I HAD A TWIN SISTER, IT WOULD IGNITE TWO-FACE'S OBSESSION WITH DUALITY...
...ESPECIALLY SINCE MADELINE... SHE...SHE'S BEEN IN AND OUT OF INSTITUTIONS HER WHOLE LIFE...
SHE ALWAYS HATED ME. ON OUR ELEVENTH BIRTHDAY SHE BROKE A POCKET MIRROR INTO LITTLE PIECES AND SLIPPED THEM INTO MY MILK. I ALMOST DIED...
GOD, HARVEY, I'M SO SORRY...
PLEASE...
TELL ME YOU'RE GOING TO BE OKAY...
I LIED...TOLD HER I'D BE FINE. WHAT ELSE COULD I DO?
3

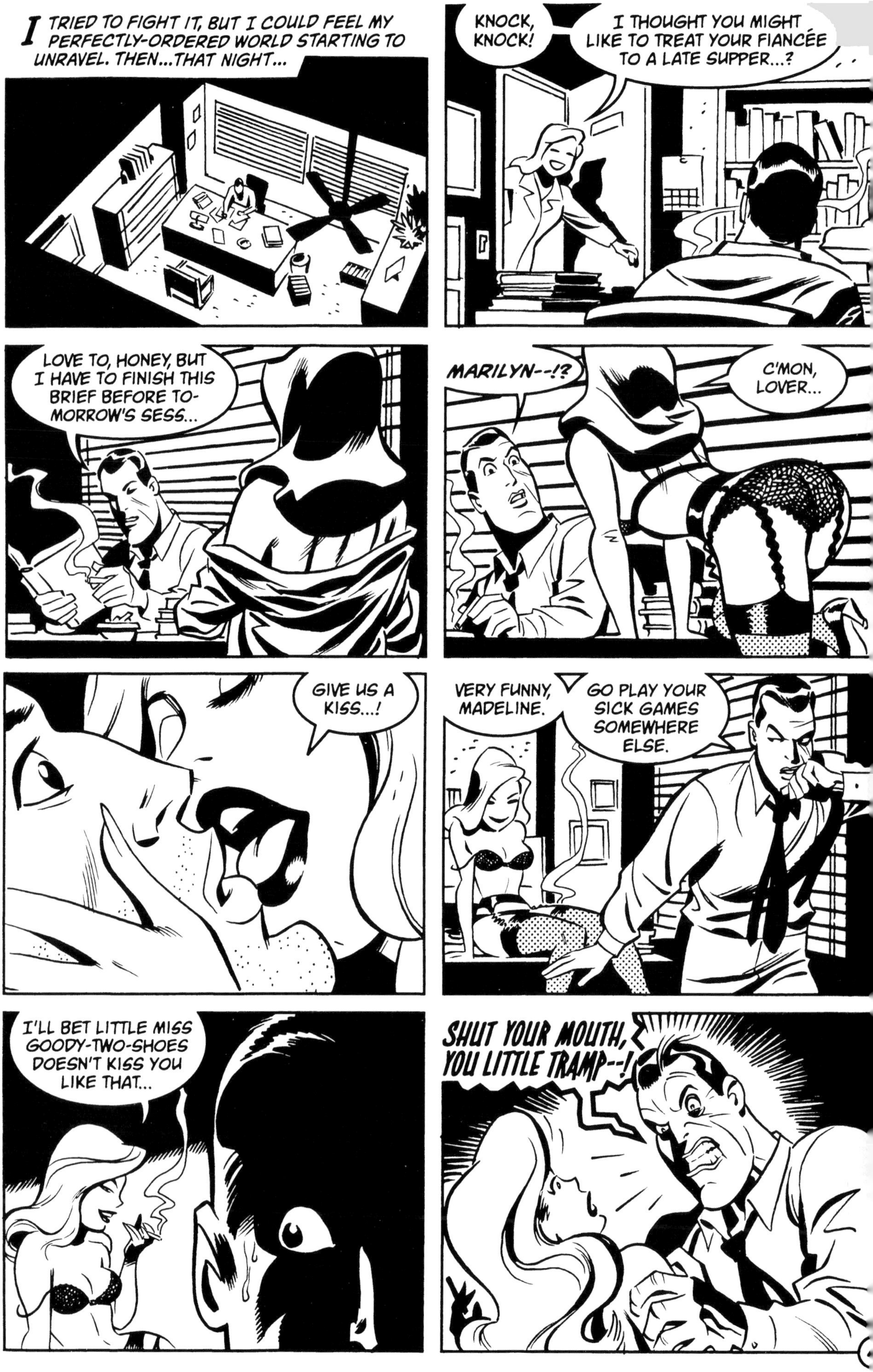
I TRIED TO FIGHT IT, BUT I COULD FEEL MY PERFECTLY-ORDERED WORLD STARTING TO UNRAVEL. THEN...THAT NIGHT...
KNOCK, KNOCK!
I THOUGHT YOU MIGHT LIKE TO TREAT YOUR FIANCÉE TO A LATE SUPPER...?
LOVE TO, HONEY, BUT I HAVE TO FINISH THIS BRIEF BEFORE TO-MORROW'S SESS...
MARILYN--!?
C'MON, LOVER...
GIVE US A KISS...!
VERY FUNNY, MADELINE.
GO PLAY YOUR SICK GAMES SOMEWHERE ELSE.
I'LL BET LITTLE MISS GOODY-TWO-SHOES DOESN'T KISS YOU LIKE THAT...
SHUT YOUR MOUTH, YOU LITTLE TRAMP--!

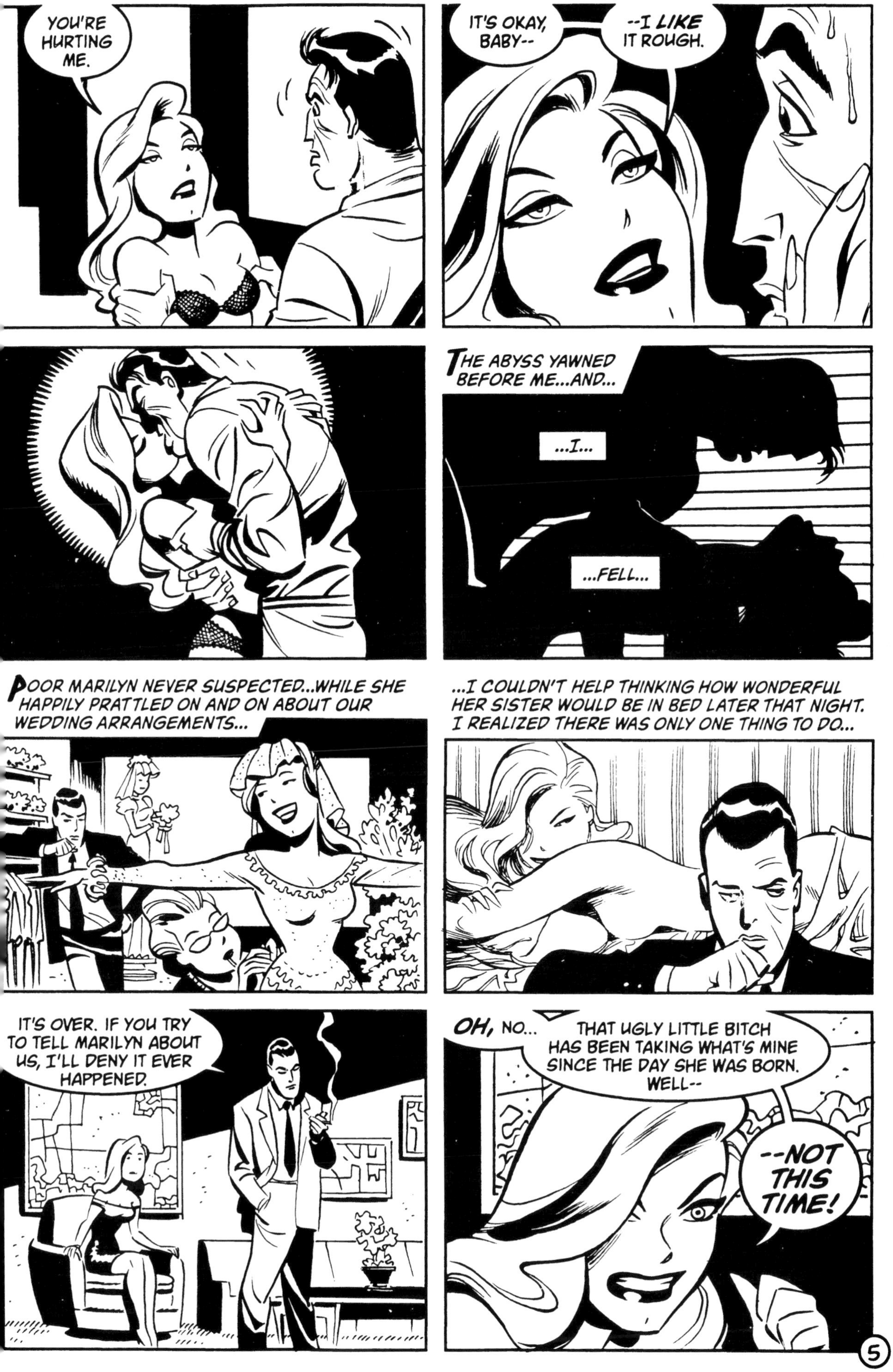

YOU'RE HURTING ME.
IT'S OKAY, BABY--
--I LIKE IT ROUGH.
THE ABYSS YAWNED BEFORE ME...AND...
...I...
...FELL...
POOR MARILYN NEVER SUSPECTED...WHILE SHE HAPPILY PRATTLED ON AND ON ABOUT OUR WEDDING ARRANGEMENTS...
...I COULDN'T HELP THINKING HOW WONDERFUL HER SISTER WOULD BE IN BED LATER THAT NIGHT. I REALIZED THERE WAS ONLY ONE THING TO DO...
IT'S OVER. IF YOU TRY TO TELL MARILYN ABOUT US, I'LL DENY IT EVER HAPPENED.
OH, NO...
THAT UGLY LITTLE BITCH HAS BEEN TAKING WHAT'S MINE SINCE THE DAY SHE WAS BORN. WELL--
--NOT THIS TIME!
5

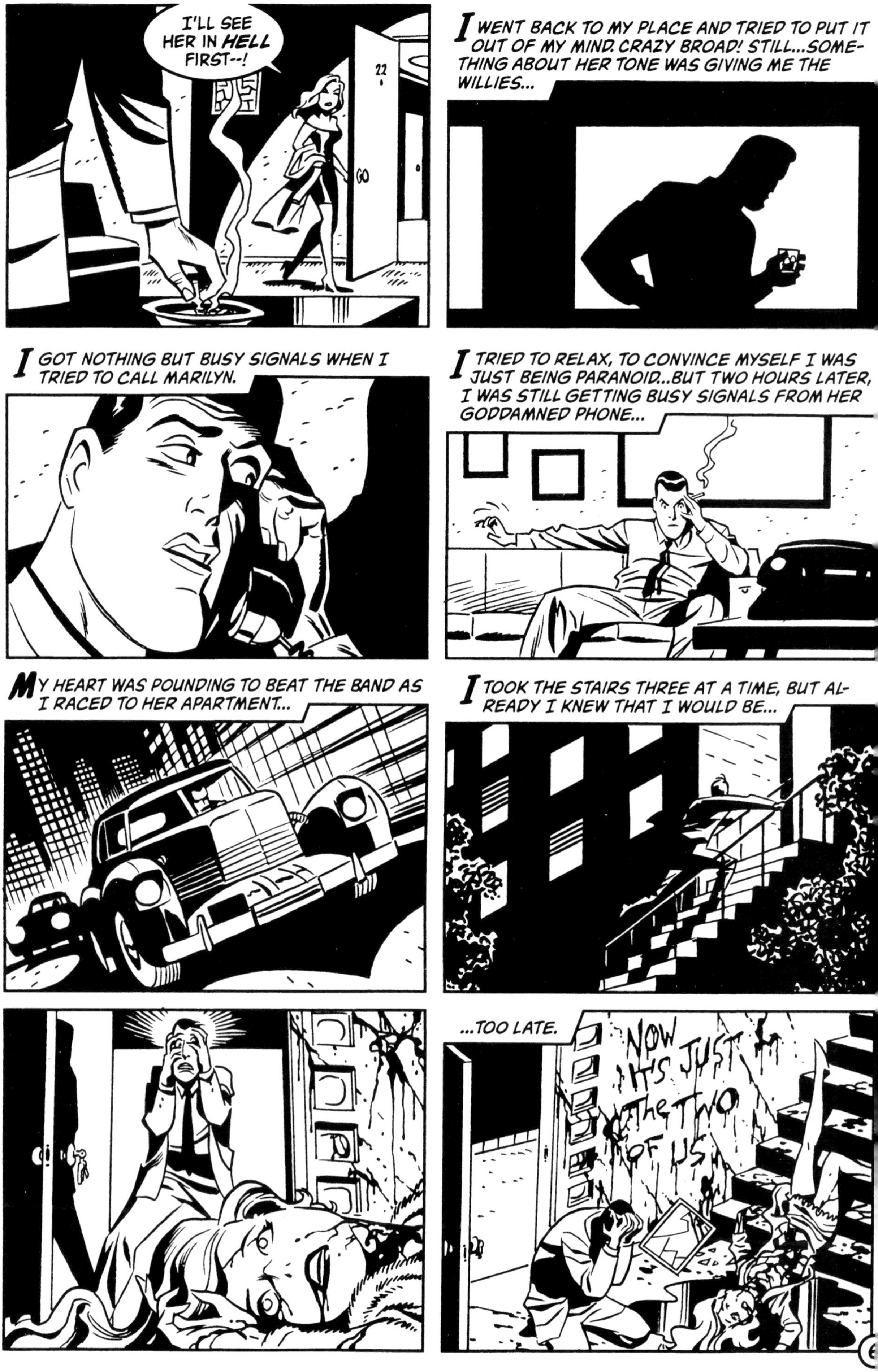

I'LL SEE HER IN HELL FIRST--!
22
GO
I WENT BACK TO MY PLACE AND TRIED TO PUT IT OUT OF MY MIND. CRAZY BROAD! STILL...SOMETHING ABOUT HER TONE WAS GIVING ME THE WILLIES...
I GOT NOTHING BUT BUSY SIGNALS WHEN I TRIED TO CALL MARILYN.
I TRIED TO RELAX, TO CONVINCE MYSELF I WAS JUST BEING PARANOID...BUT TWO HOURS LATER, I WAS STILL GETTING BUSY SIGNALS FROM HER GODDAMNED PHONE...
MY HEART WAS POUNDING TO BEAT THE BAND AS I RACED TO HER APARTMENT...
I TOOK THE STAIRS THREE AT A TIME, BUT ALREADY I KNEW THAT I WOULD BE...
...TOO LATE.
NOW IT'S JUST THE TWO OF US

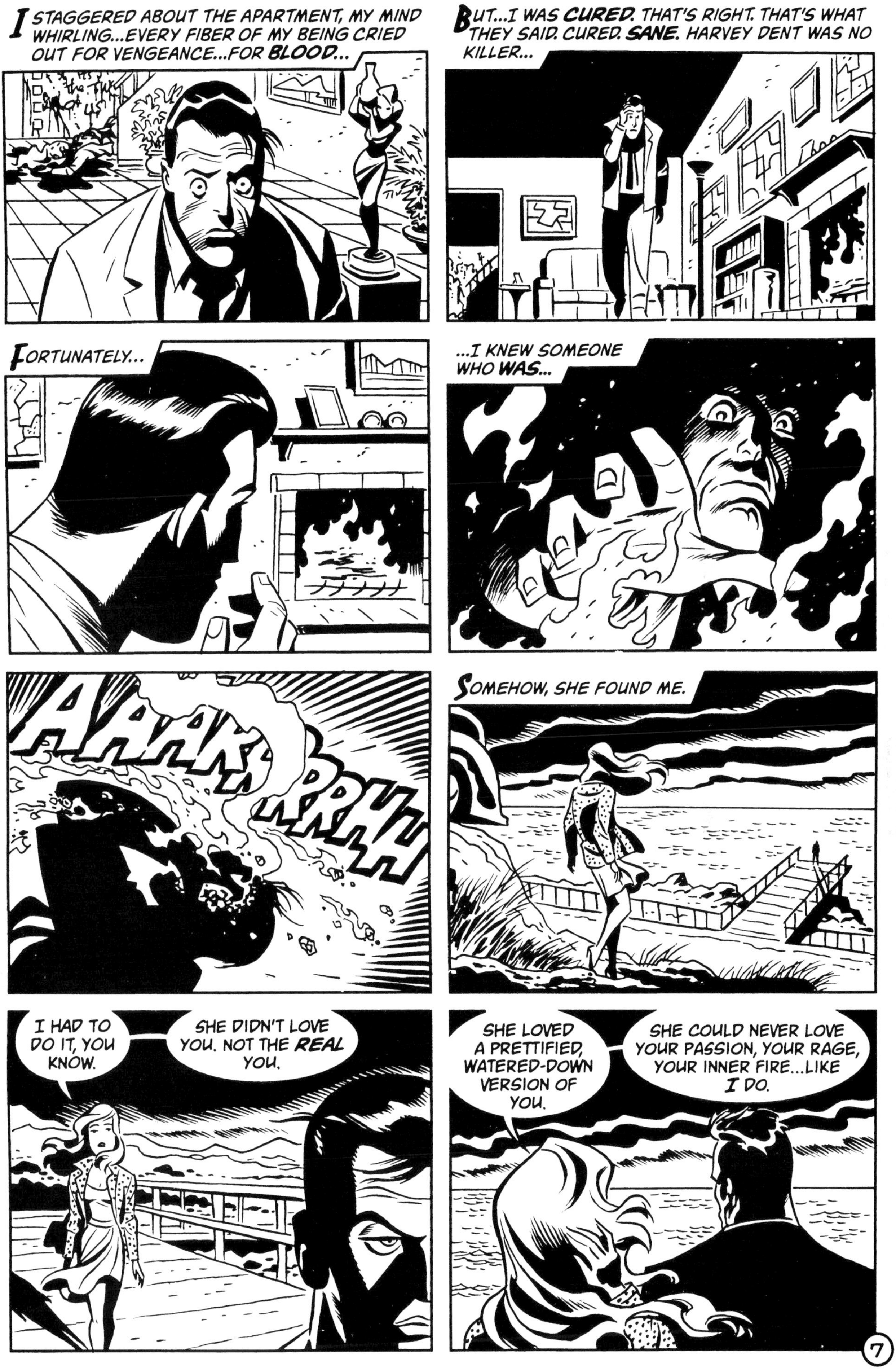
I STAGGERED ABOUT THE APARTMENT, MY MIND WHIRLING...EVERY FIBER OF MY BEING CRIED OUT FOR VENGEANCE...FOR BLOOD...
BUT...I WAS CURED. THAT'S RIGHT. THAT'S WHAT THEY SAID. CURED. SANE. HARVEY DENT WAS NO KILLER...
FORTUNATELY...
...I KNEW SOMEONE WHO WAS...
AAAARRRRHH
SOMEHOW, SHE FOUND ME.
I HAD TO DO IT, YOU KNOW.
SHE DIDN'T LOVE YOU. NOT THE REAL YOU.
SHE LOVED A PRETTIFIED, WATERED-DOWN VERSION OF YOU.
SHE COULD NEVER LOVE YOUR PASSION, YOUR RAGE, YOUR INNER FIRE...LIKE I DO.
7

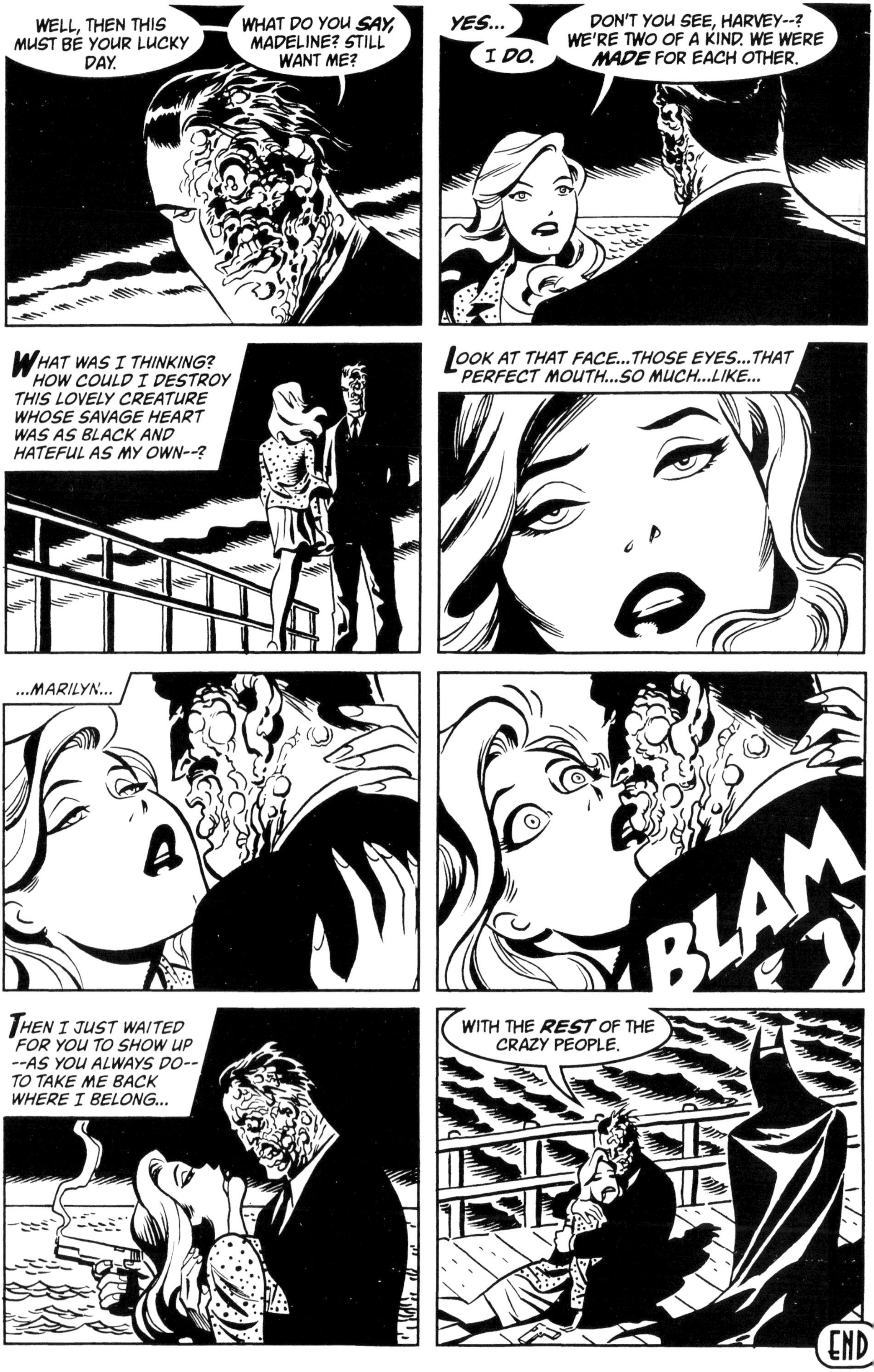
WELL, THEN THIS MUST BE YOUR LUCKY DAY.
WHAT DO YOU SAY, MADELINE? STILL WANT ME?
YES...
I DO.
DON'T YOU SEE, HARVEY--? WE'RE TWO OF A KIND. WE WERE MADE FOR EACH OTHER.
WHAT WAS I THINKING? HOW COULD I DESTROY THIS LOVELY CREATURE WHOSE SAVAGE HEART WAS AS BLACK AND HATEFUL AS MY OWN--?
LOOK AT THAT FACE...THOSE EYES...THAT PERFECT MOUTH...SO MUCH...LIKE...
...MARILYN...
BLAM
THEN I JUST WAITED FOR YOU TO SHOW UP --AS YOU ALWAYS DO-- TO TAKE ME BACK WHERE I BELONG...
WITH THE REST OF THE CRAZY PEOPLE.
END

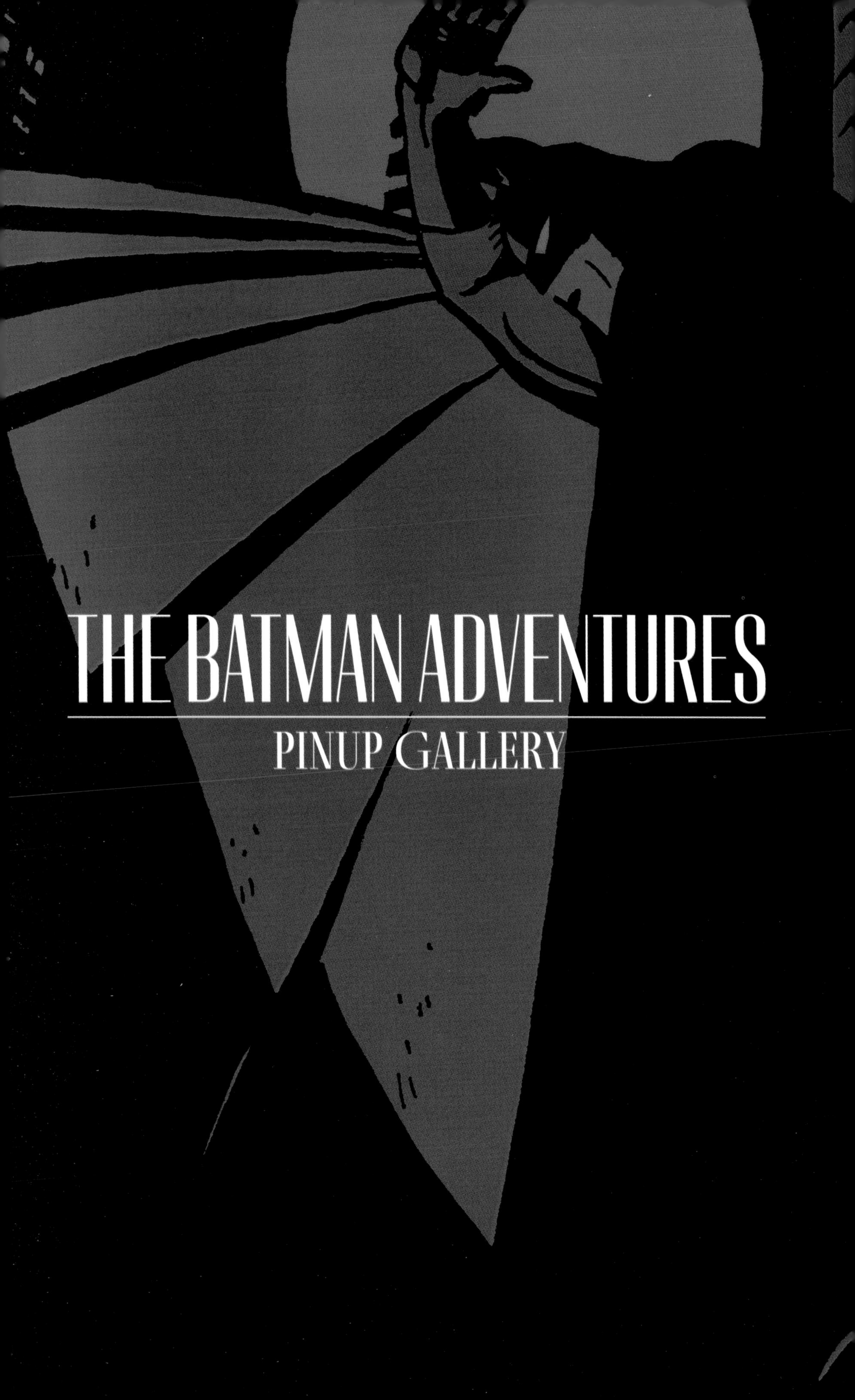
THE BATMAN ADVENTURES
PINUP GALLERY

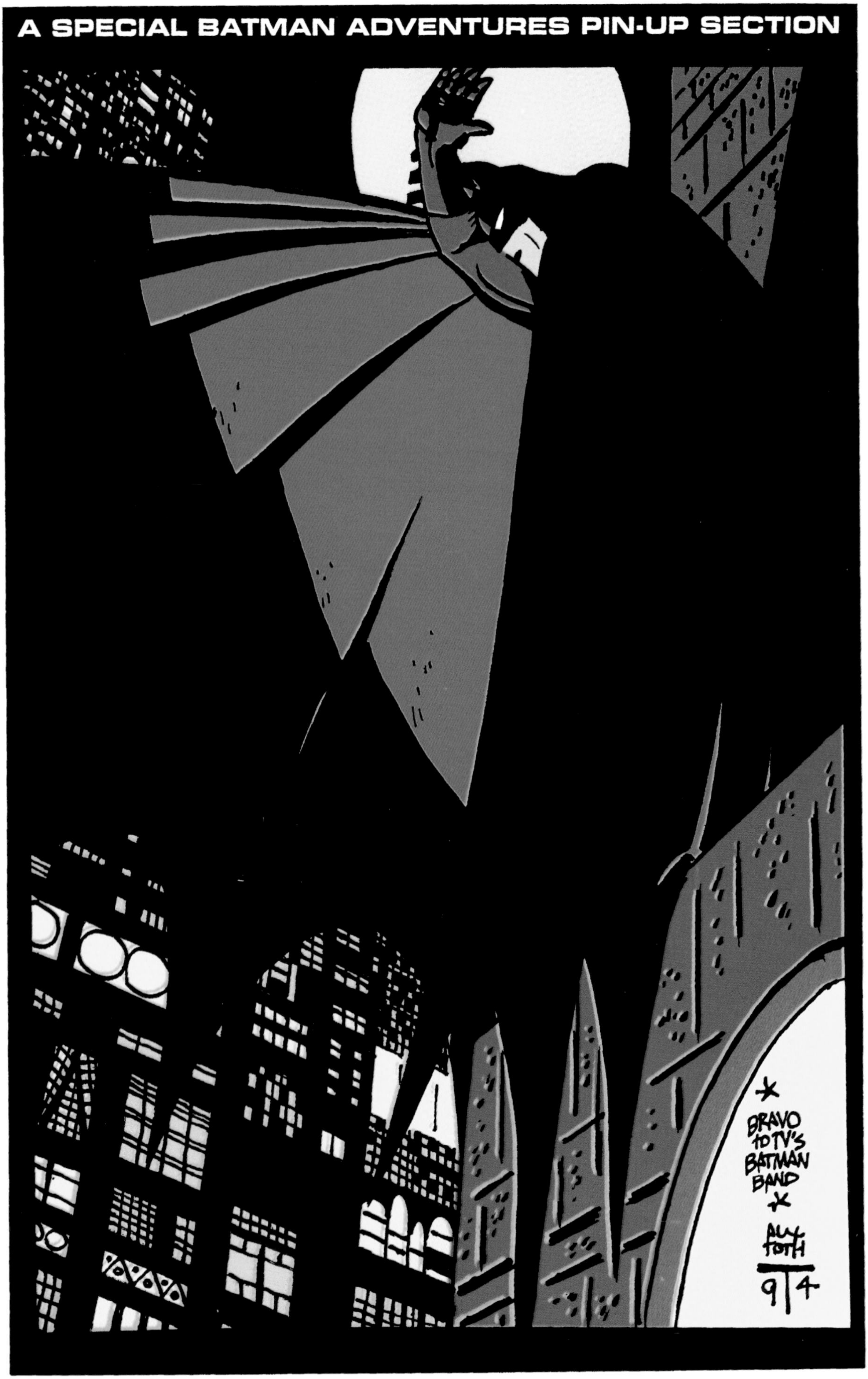
A SPECIAL BATMAN ADVENTURES PIN-UP SECTION
BRAVO TO TV'S BATMAN BAND
ALEX TOTH
9 4

ART **ALEX TOTH** **RICK TAYLOR** COLOR

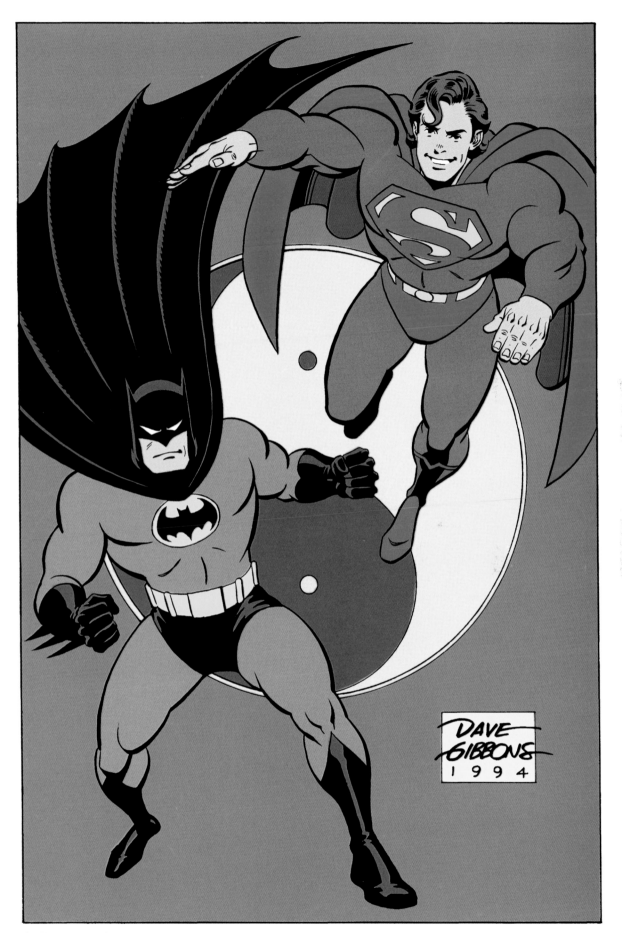

ART **DAVE GIBBONS**

RICK TAYLOR COLOR

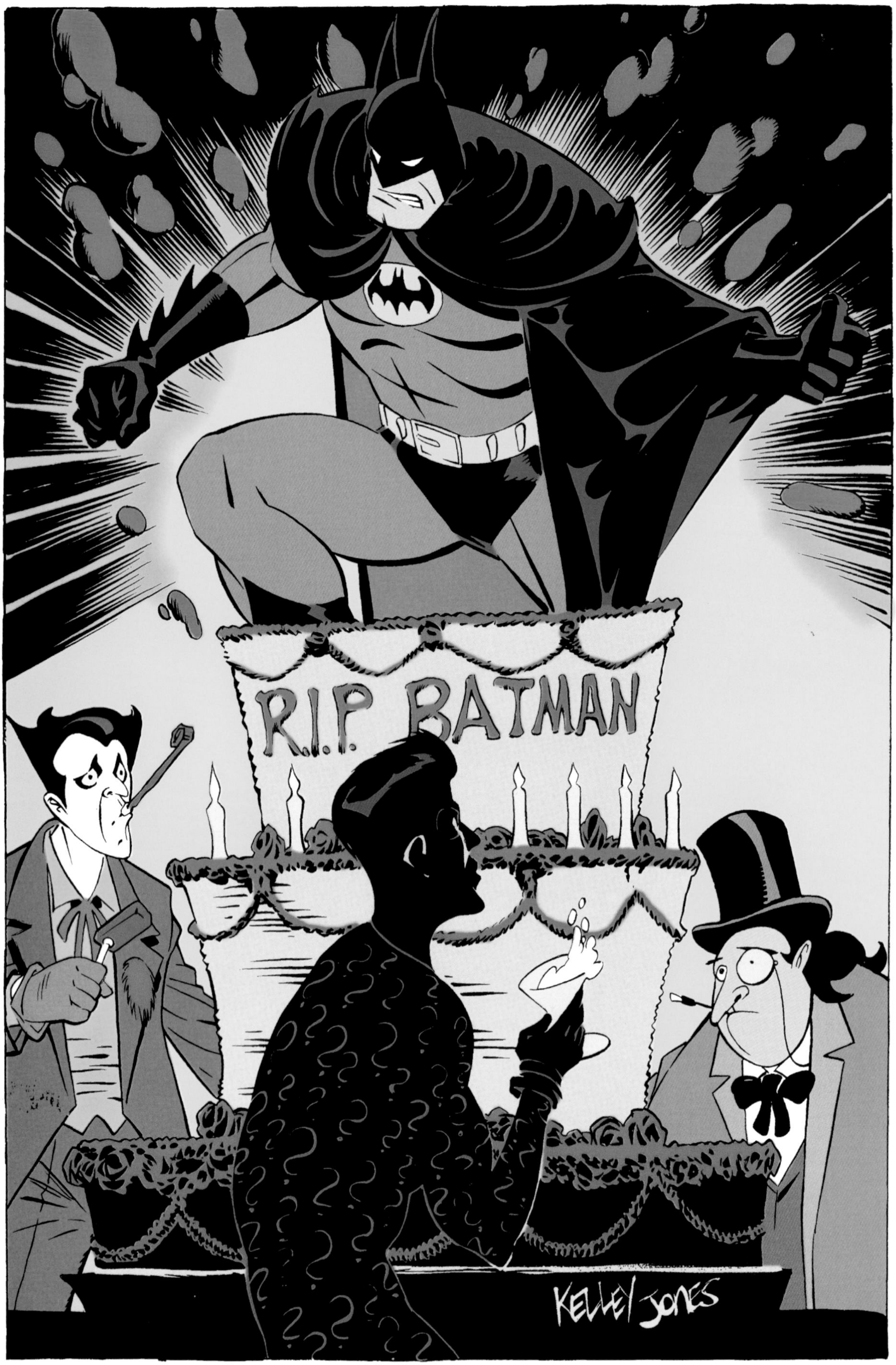
R.I.P. BATMAN
KELLEY JONES

ART **KELLEY JONES** **RICK TAYLOR** COLOR

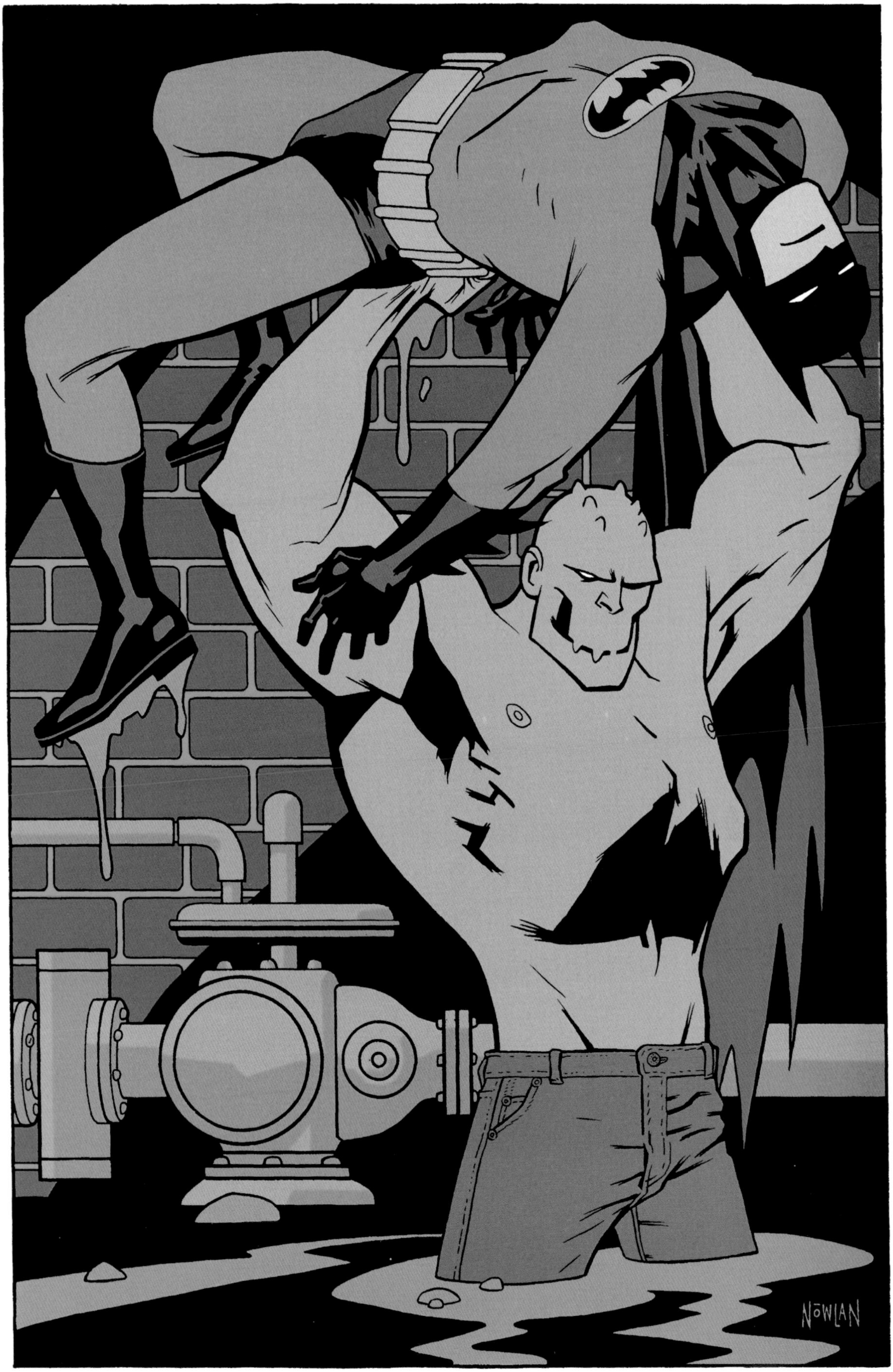
NOWLAN

ART **KEVIN NOWLAN** **RICK TAYLOR** COLOR

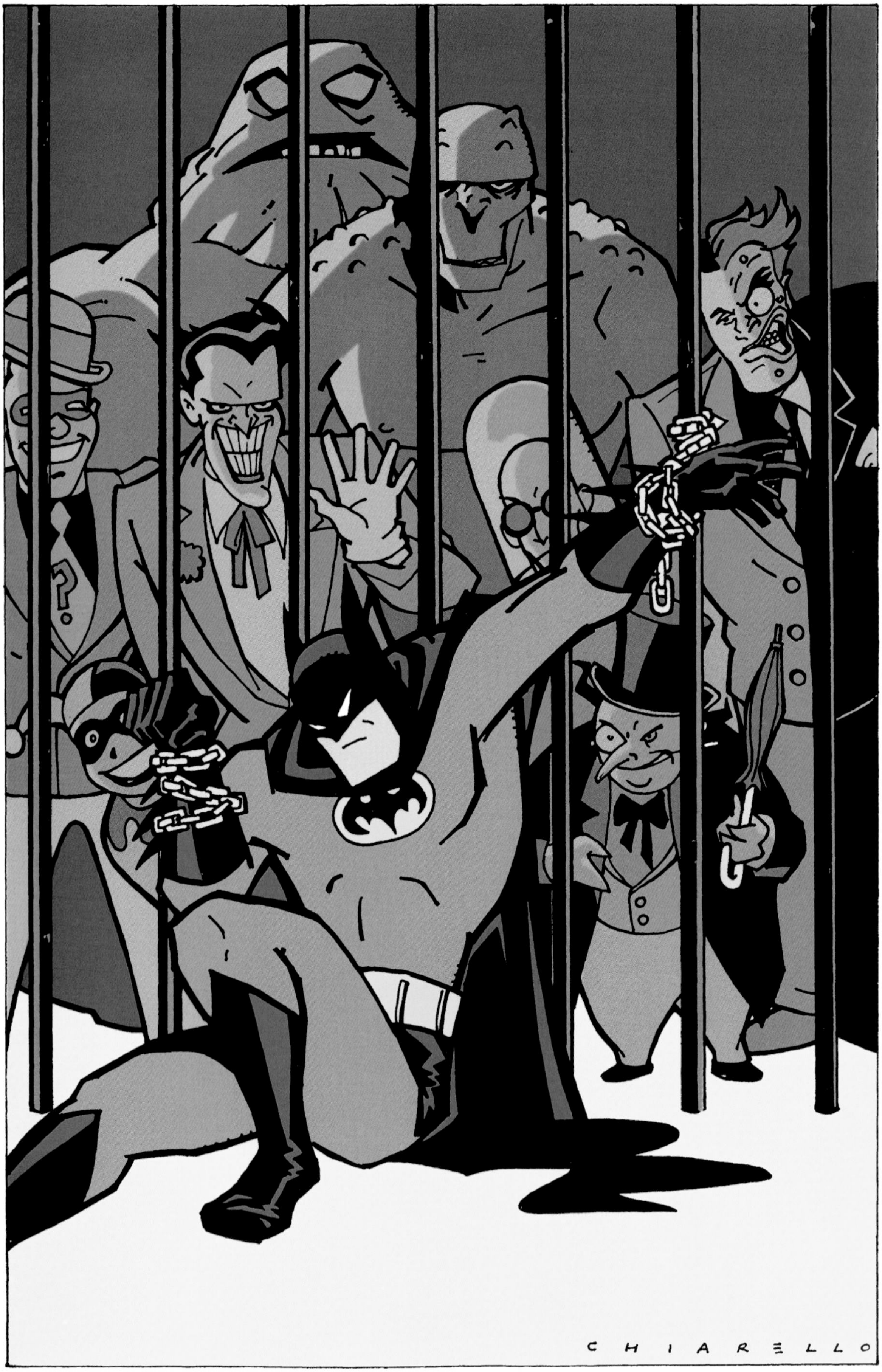
CHIARELLO

ART **MARK CHIARELLO** **RICK TAYLOR** COLOR

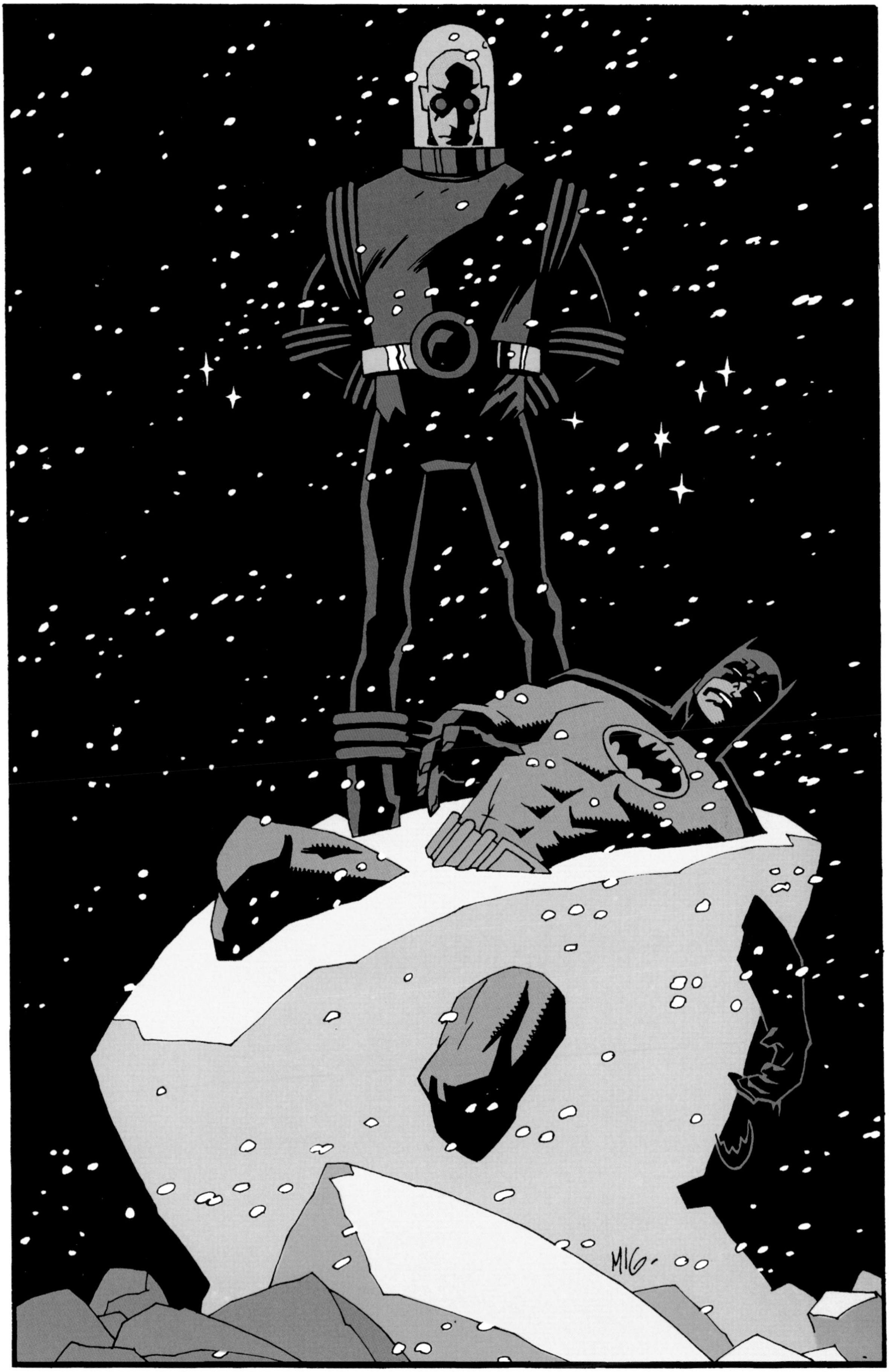
MIG.

ART **MIKE MIGNOLA** **RICK TAYLOR** COLOR

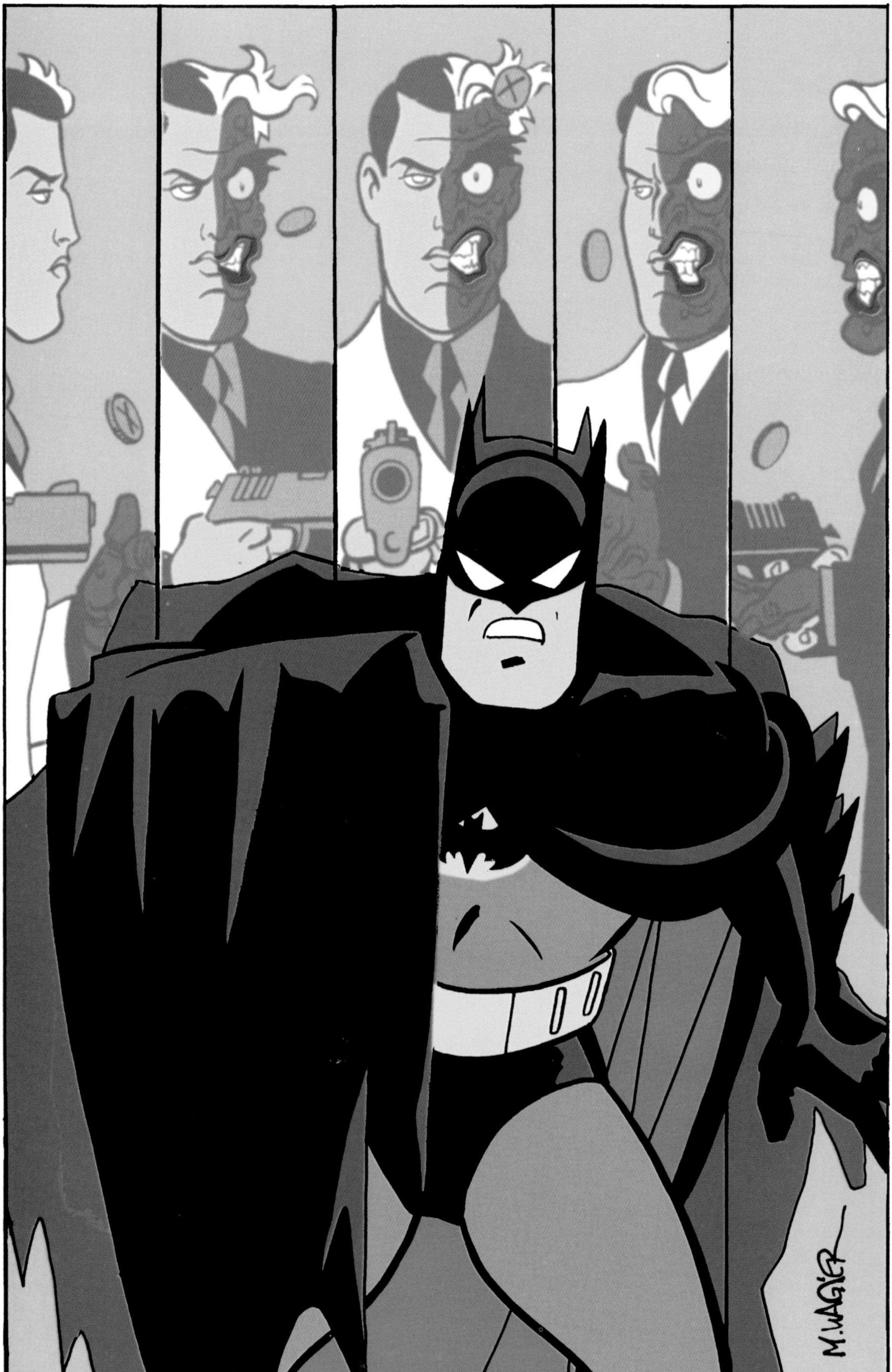

ART **MATT WAGNER** **RICK TAYLOR** COLOR

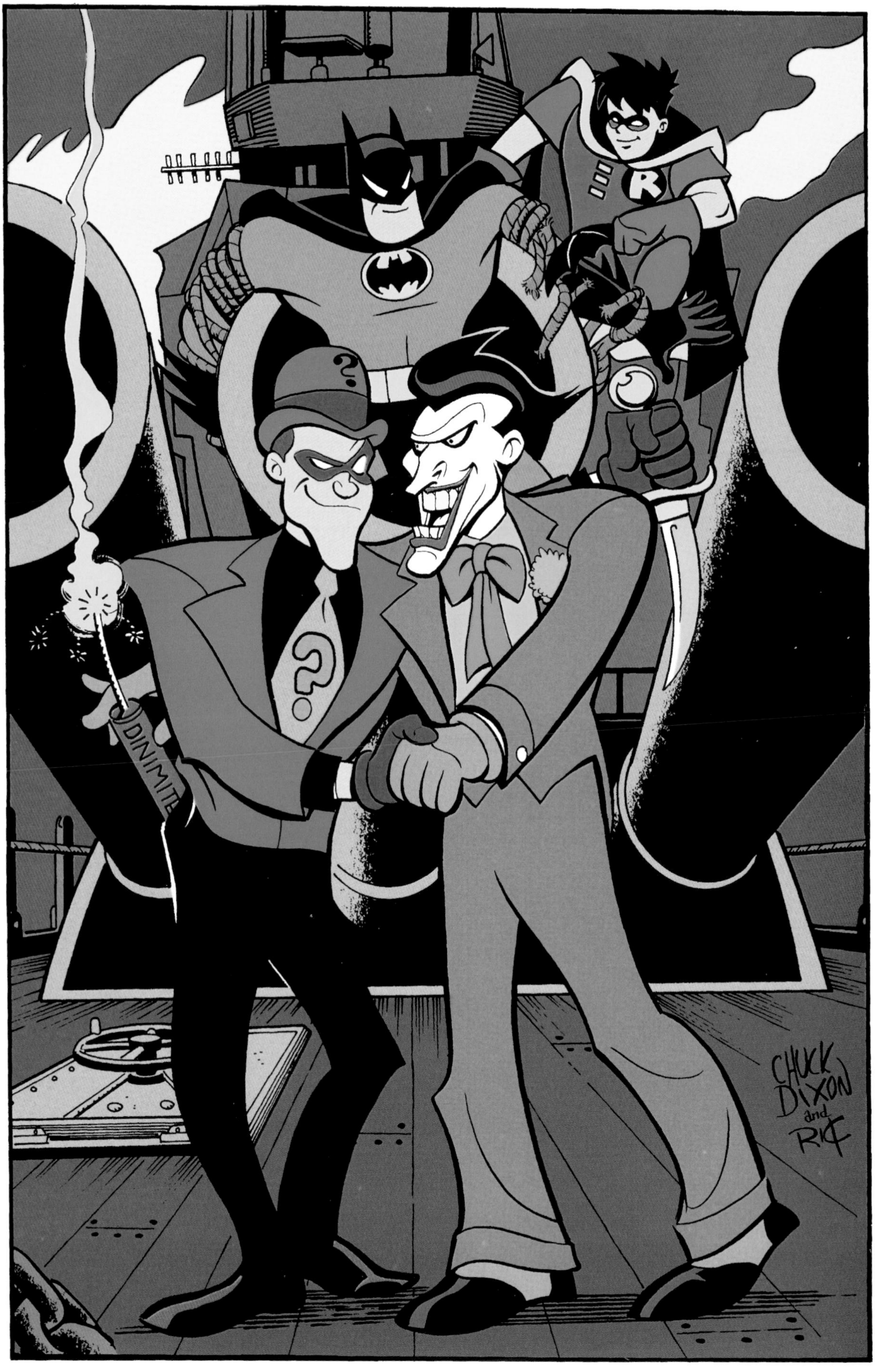
DINIMITE
CHUCK DIXON and RICK

ART **CHUCK DIXON & RICK BURCHETT** **RICK TAYLOR** COLOR

Batman: The Collected Adventures Vol. 1 cover by TY TEMPLETON

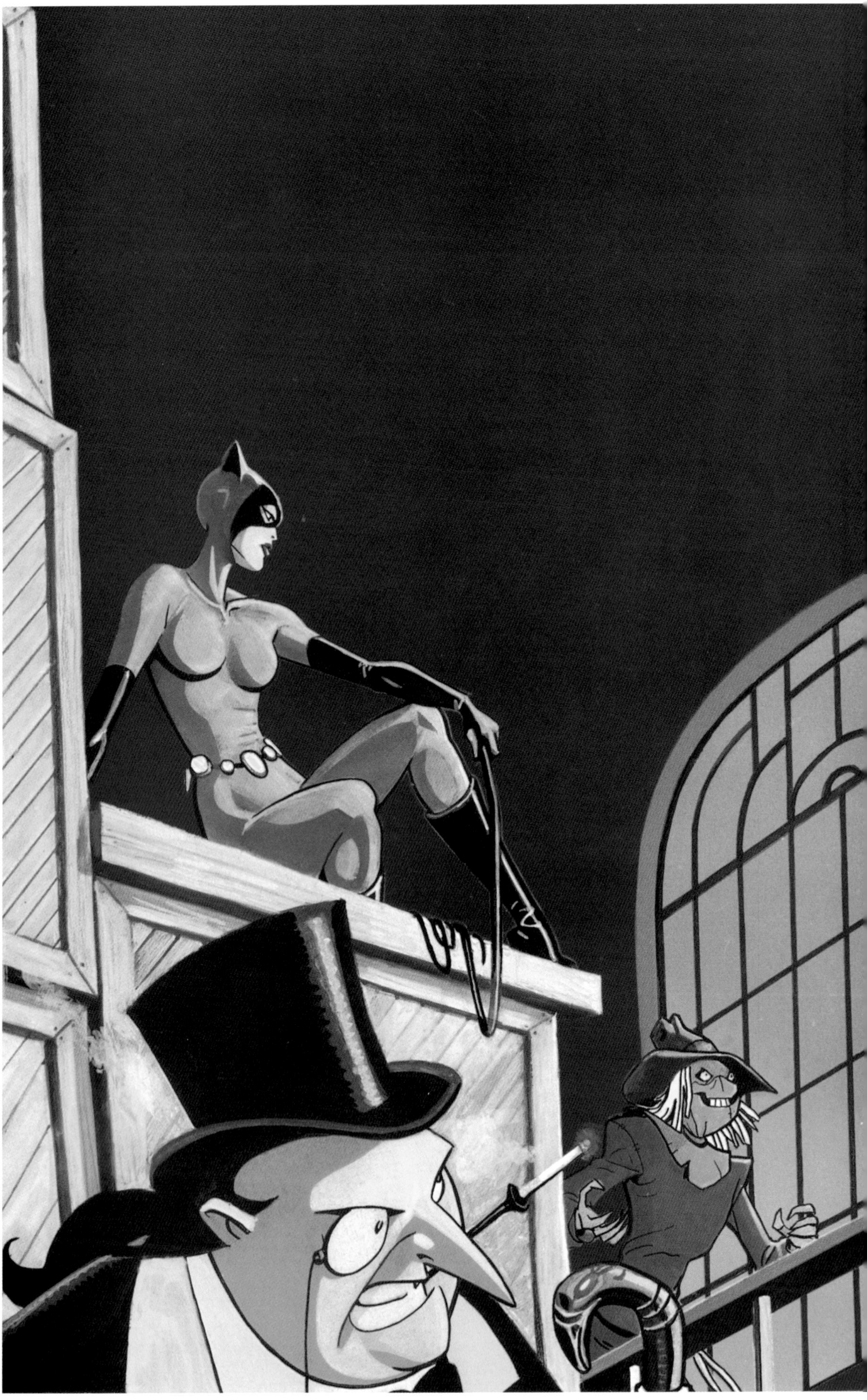

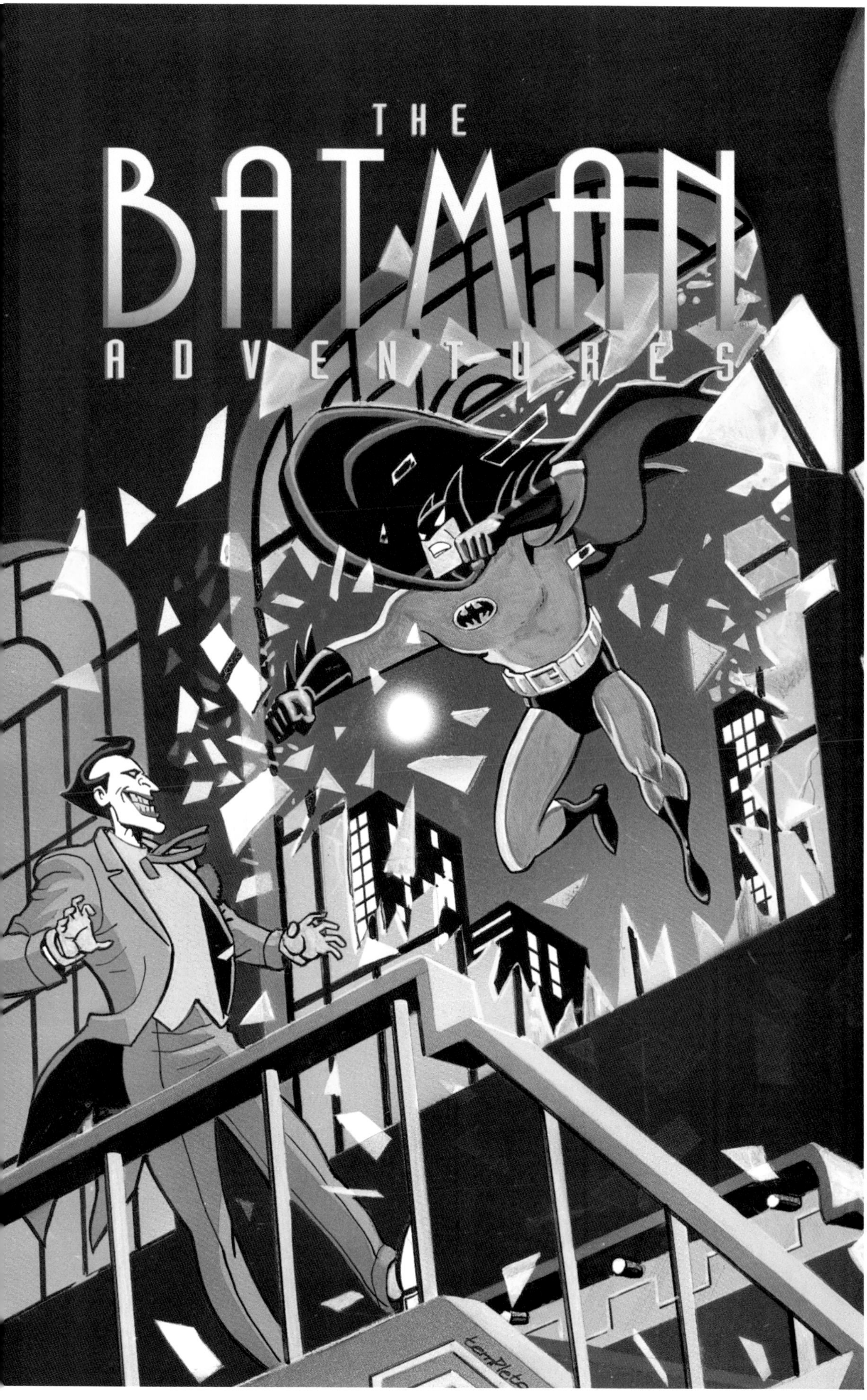
THE
BATMAN
ADVENTURES
templeton

Batman: The Collected Adventures Vol. 2 cover by MIKE PAROBECK and RICK BURCHETT

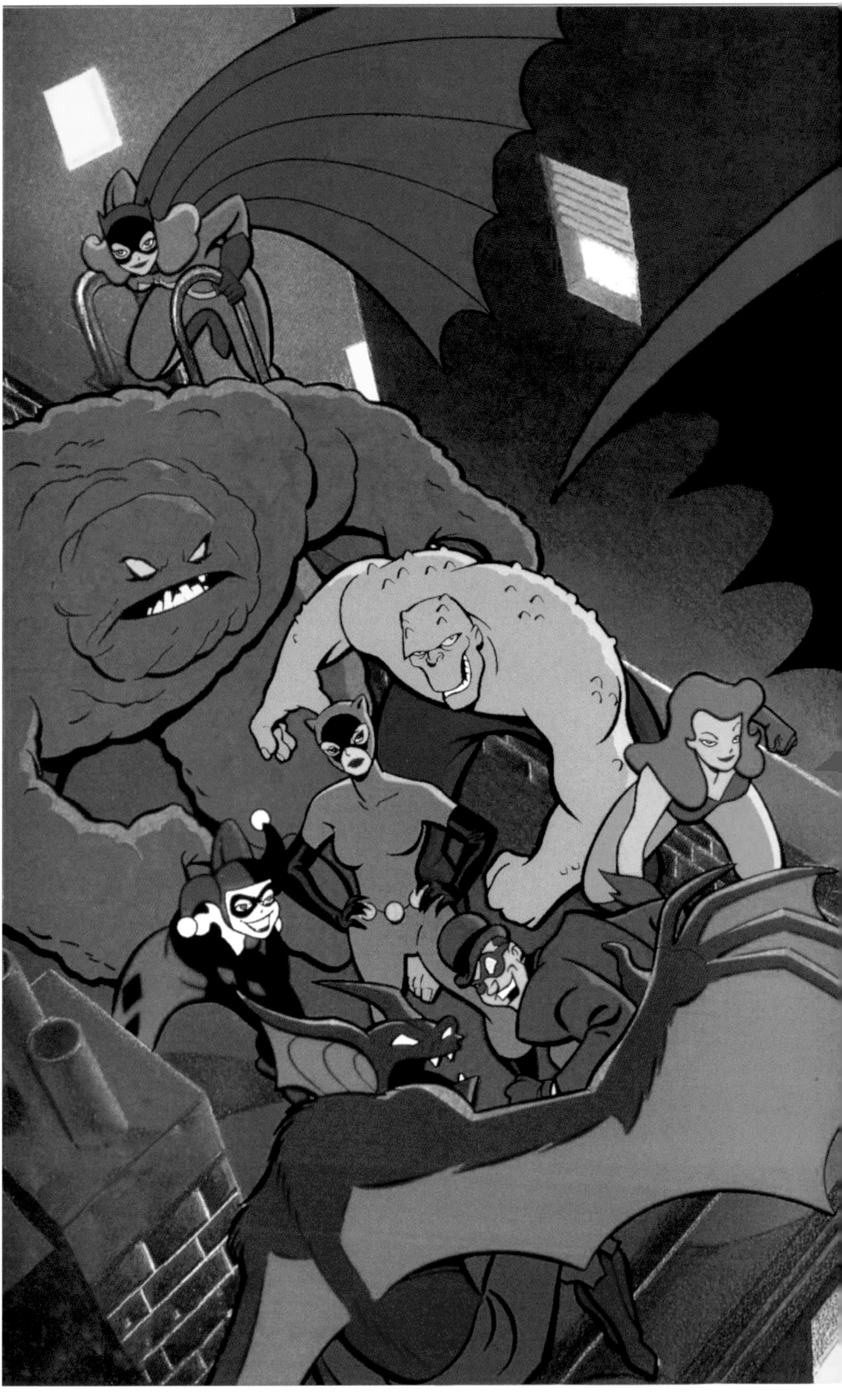

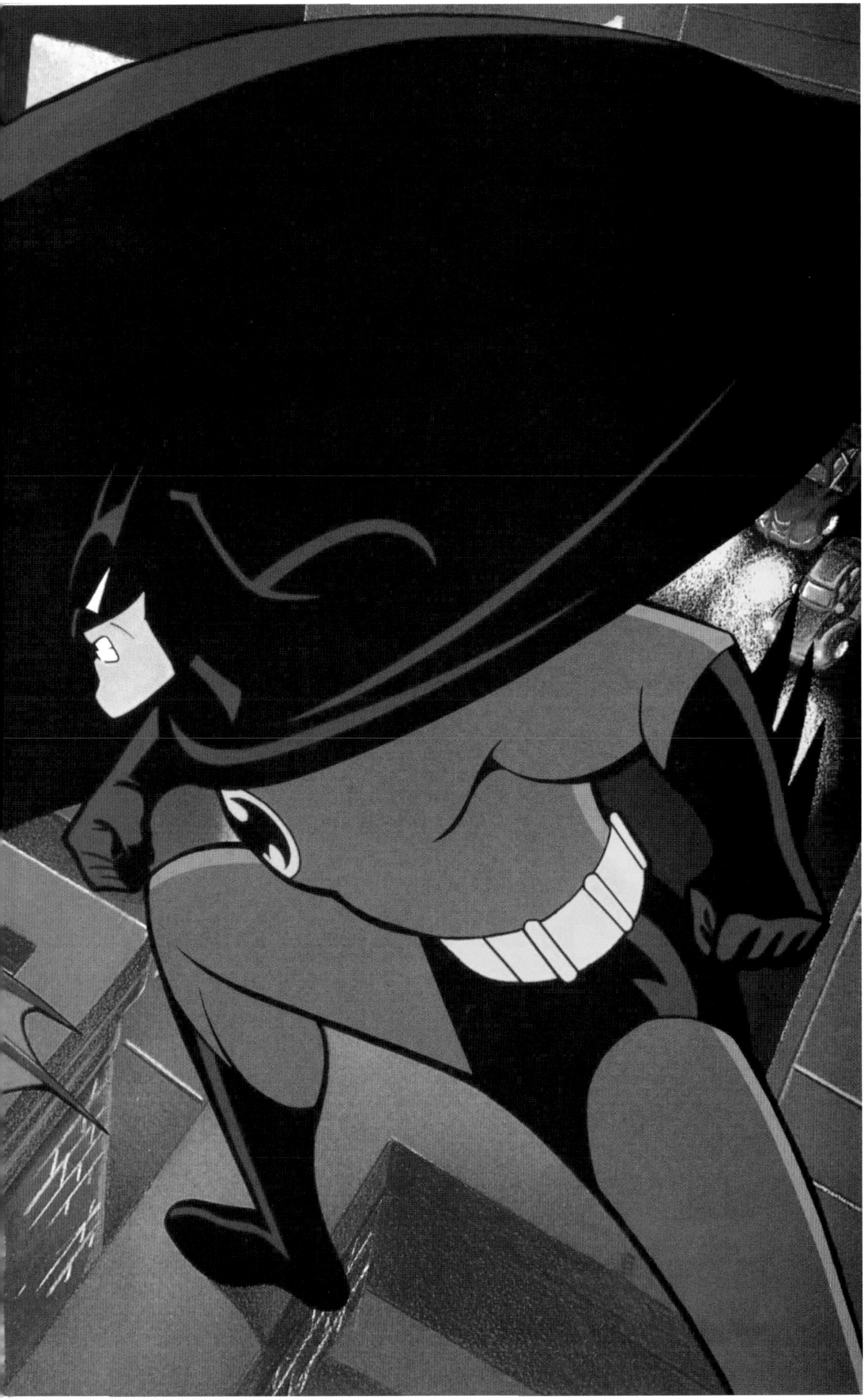

The Batman Adventures #7 polybag art

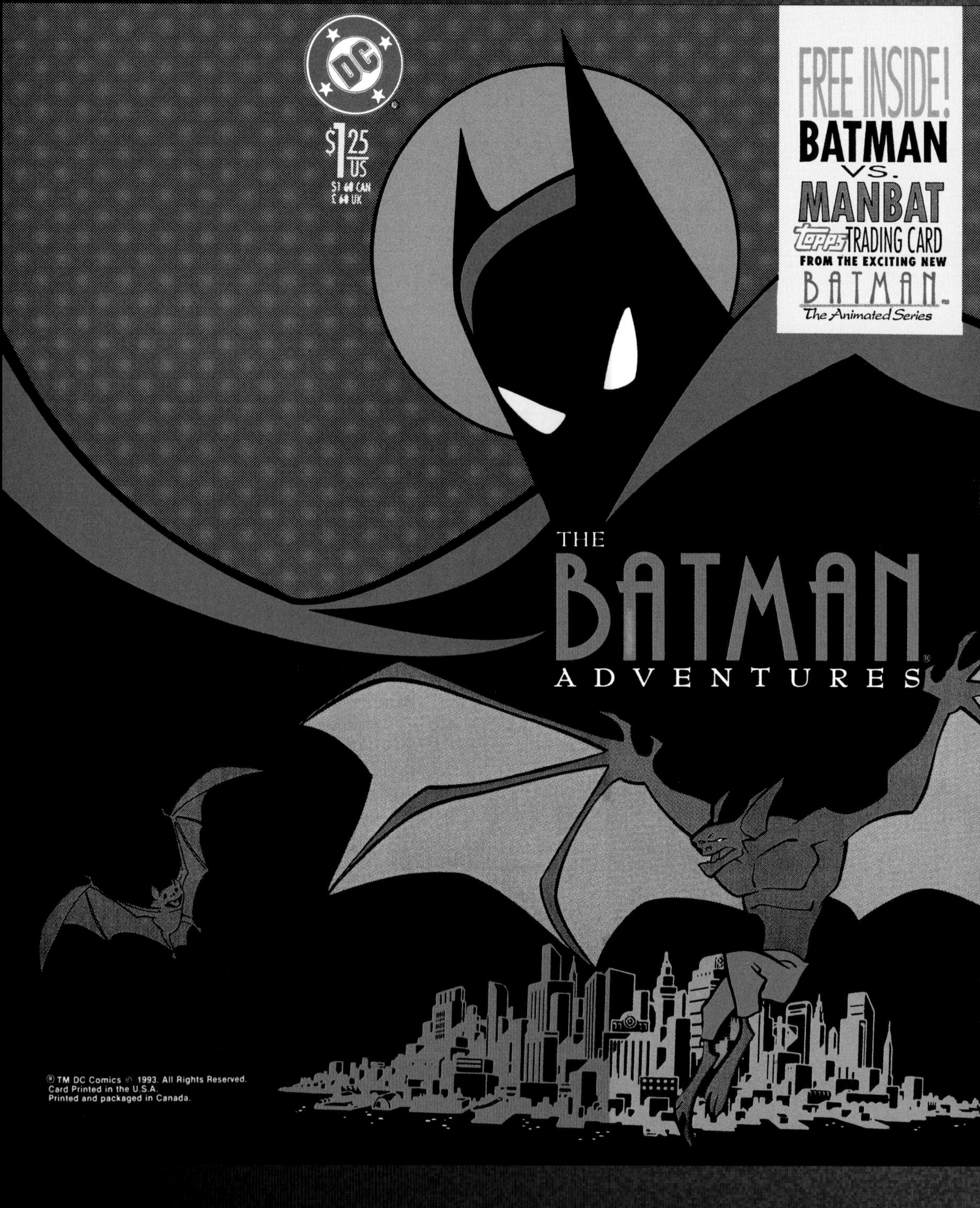
$1.25 US
FREE INSIDE!
BATMAN
VS.
MANBAT
topps TRADING CARD
FROM THE EXCITING NEW
BATMAN
The Animated Series
THE
BATMAN
ADVENTURES
® TM DC Comics © 1993. All Rights Reserved.
Card Printed in the U.S.A.
Printed and packaged in Canada.

An exclusive Topps trading card that came packaged with the polybag edition of *The Batman Adventures* #7

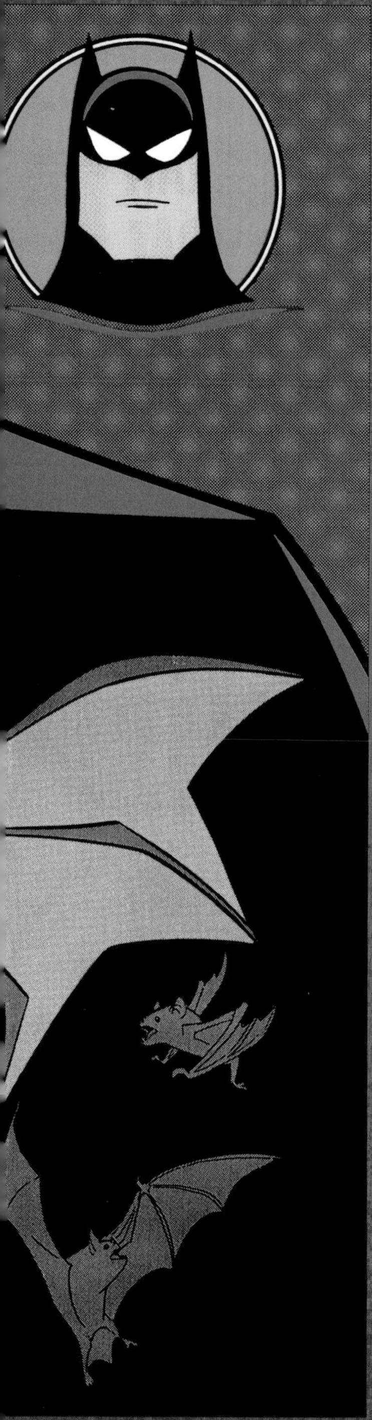

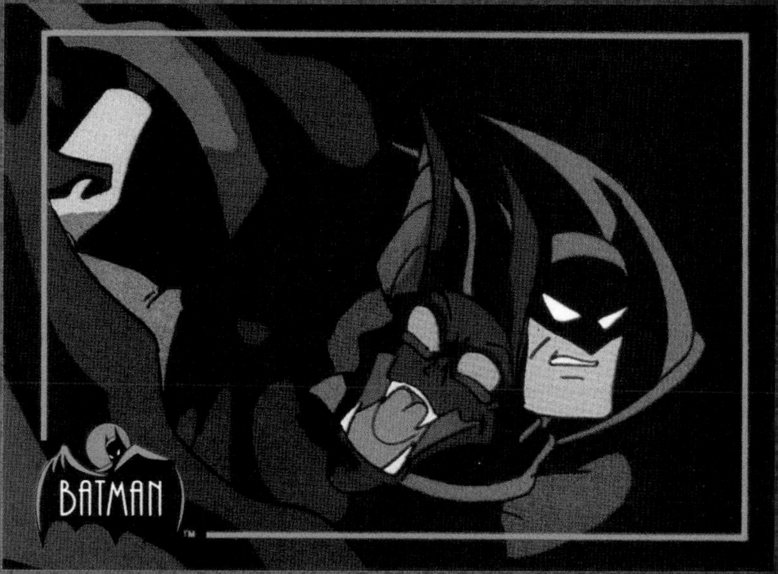
BATMAN
TM

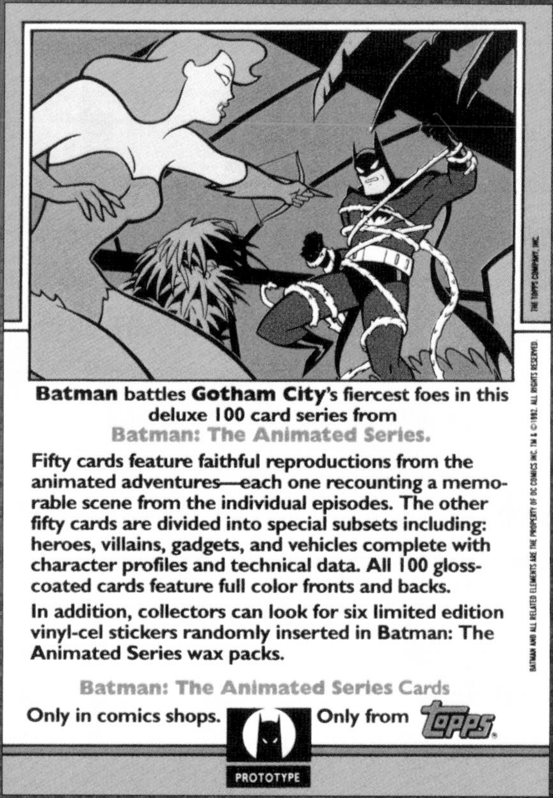
Batman battles Gotham City's fiercest foes in this deluxe 100 card series from
Batman: The Animated Series.
Fifty cards feature faithful reproductions from the animated adventures—each one recounting a memorable scene from the individual episodes. The other fifty cards are divided into special subsets including: heroes, villains, gadgets, and vehicles complete with character profiles and technical data. All 100 gloss-coated cards feature full color fronts and backs.
In addition, collectors can look for six limited edition vinyl-cel stickers randomly inserted in Batman: The Animated Series wax packs.
Batman: The Animated Series Cards
Only in comics shops.
Only from Topps.
PROTOTYPE

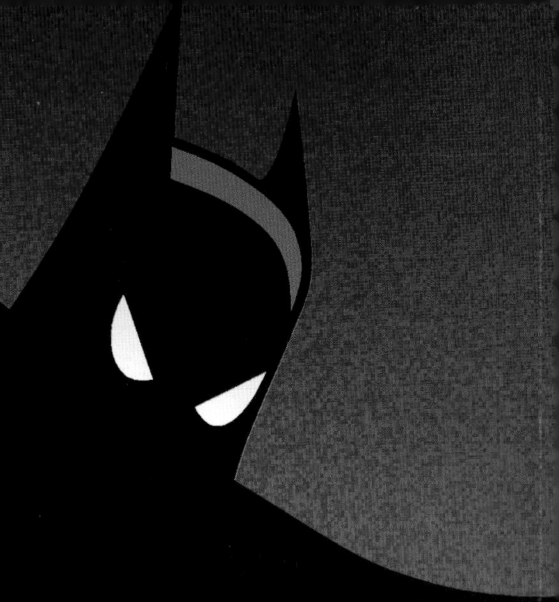

KELLEY PUCKETT

Kelley Puckett has been writing comics for far too long, by general consensus. He has worked on such series as *The Batman Adventures*, *Batgirl*, *Batman: Black & White*, *Kinetic*, and *Supergirl* for DC Comics.

PAUL DINI

Paul Dini authored the *New York Times* best-selling Vertigo graphic novel *Dark Night: A True Batman Story* and co-wrote the Titan Books novel *Harley Quinn: Mad Love*. A five-time Emmy-winning writer and producer, Paul is perhaps best known for his work on such Warner Bros. Animation projects as *Batman: The Animated Series*, *Superman: The Animated Series*, *Batman Beyond*, and various iterations of *Tom and Jerry*, *Looney Tunes*, and *Justice League*. He has scripted numerous comic book series (*Gotham City Sirens*, *Zatanna*, *Detective Comics*), video games (*Batman: Arkham Asylum*, *Batman: Arkham City*), and live-action television series (*Creepshow*, *Lost*, *Tower Prep*). The co-creator of Harley Quinn, Paul continues to write frequent stories about America's screwball sweetheart. Paul lives in Los Angeles with his wife, magician/actress Misty Lee, and their Boston terriers, Pixie and the Tank.

BRUCE TIMM

The driving force behind the wildly successful *Batman: The Animated Series*, BRUCE TIMM both designed the unique look of the show and acted as one of its producers. He went on to co-create and produce *Superman: The Animated Series*, *Batman Beyond*, *Justice League*, and *Justice League Unlimited*. More recently, he has acted as executive producer on a series of direct-to-video films for Warner Bros. Animation, including *Batman: The Killing Joke*, *Justice League vs. the Fatal Five*, and *Superman: Red Son*.

He is currently working on an all-new animated Batman series, executive producing with Ed Brubaker, James Tucker, J.J. Abrams, and Matt Reeves. In addition to his animation work, Timm has written and drawn comics for DC, Marvel, Dark Horse, and Image. He has received several industry awards for his work in the animation and comics fields, including two

MIKE PAROBECK

Mike Parobeck was an artist best known as the regular series penciller on *The Batman Adventures*. He passed away at age 30 on July 2, 1996.

TY TEMPLETON

Ty Templeton was born into a show business family in Canada; his father was a TV personality and novelist, his mother a pop singer. After trying his hand as an actor, a musician, and briefly a stand-up comedian, Ty discovered his true calling in the funny papers, where he has drawn and written comic books for almost 40 years. Chiefly known for his work on various incarnations of *The Batman Adventures*, Ty has written or drawn a wide variety of the industry's usual suspects including Superman, the Justice League, Spider-Man, the Avengers, *The Simpsons*, *MAD Magazine*, *Star Trek*, and many others. He is most proud of his wife and four kids and is only marginally proud of his many cats and singular dog.

MARTIN PASKO

Martin Pasko was one of the most notable contributors to the Bronze Age of comics. After breaking into the comics industry in the early 1970s, he saw his first Superman story, "The Private Life of Clark Kent," published in 1974. While at DC Comics, Pasko penned tales for Superman and other characters such as Wonder Woman, the Flash, and the Justice League of America. Outside of comics, he wrote for television, working on shows such as *Cheers*, *Roseanne*, and *Batman: The Animated Series*, the latter of which earned him a Daytime Emmy Award. Pasko, together with Alan Burnett, Paul Dini, and Michael Reaves, also co-wrote the animated feature film *Batman: Mask of the Phantasm*. He

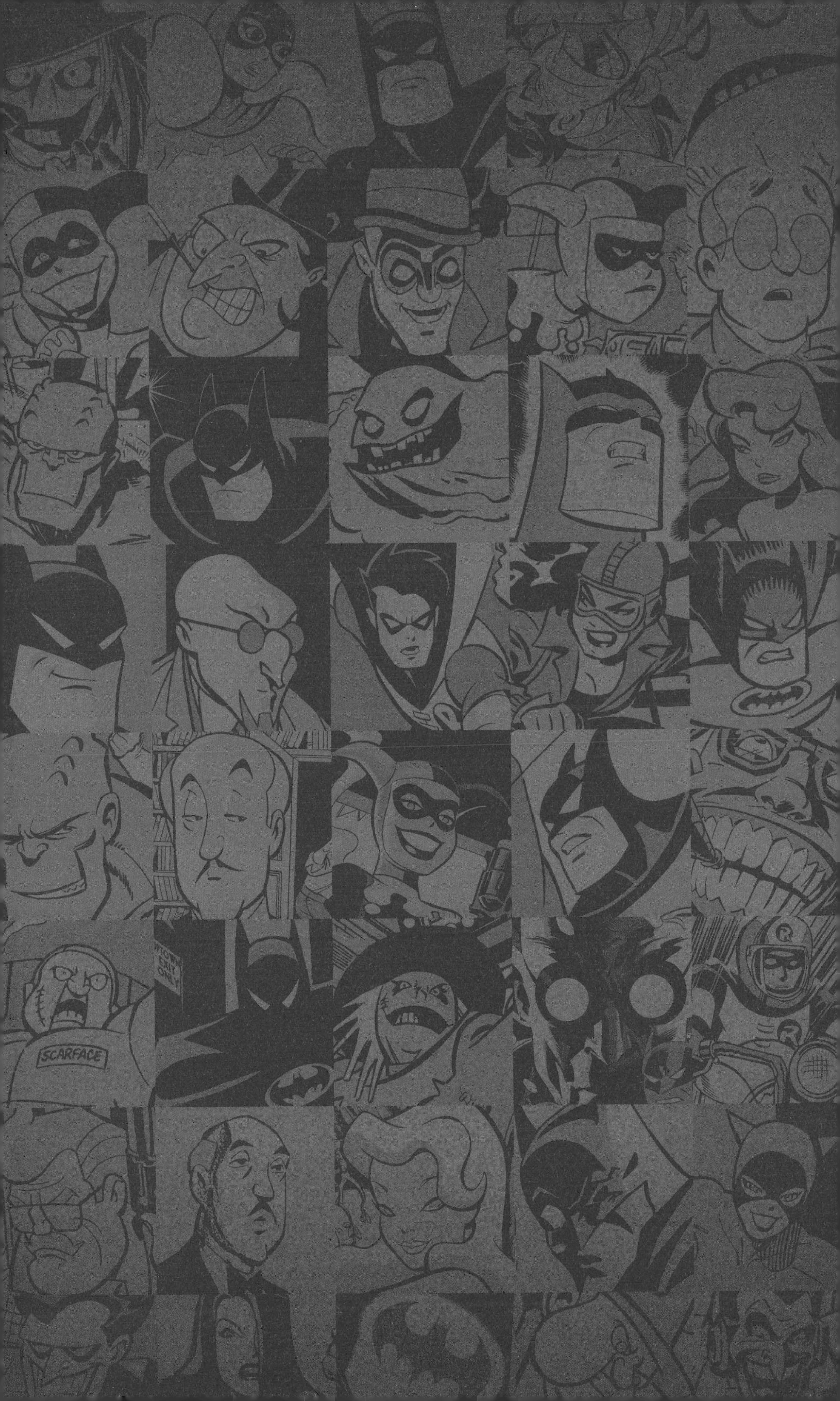
SCARFACE

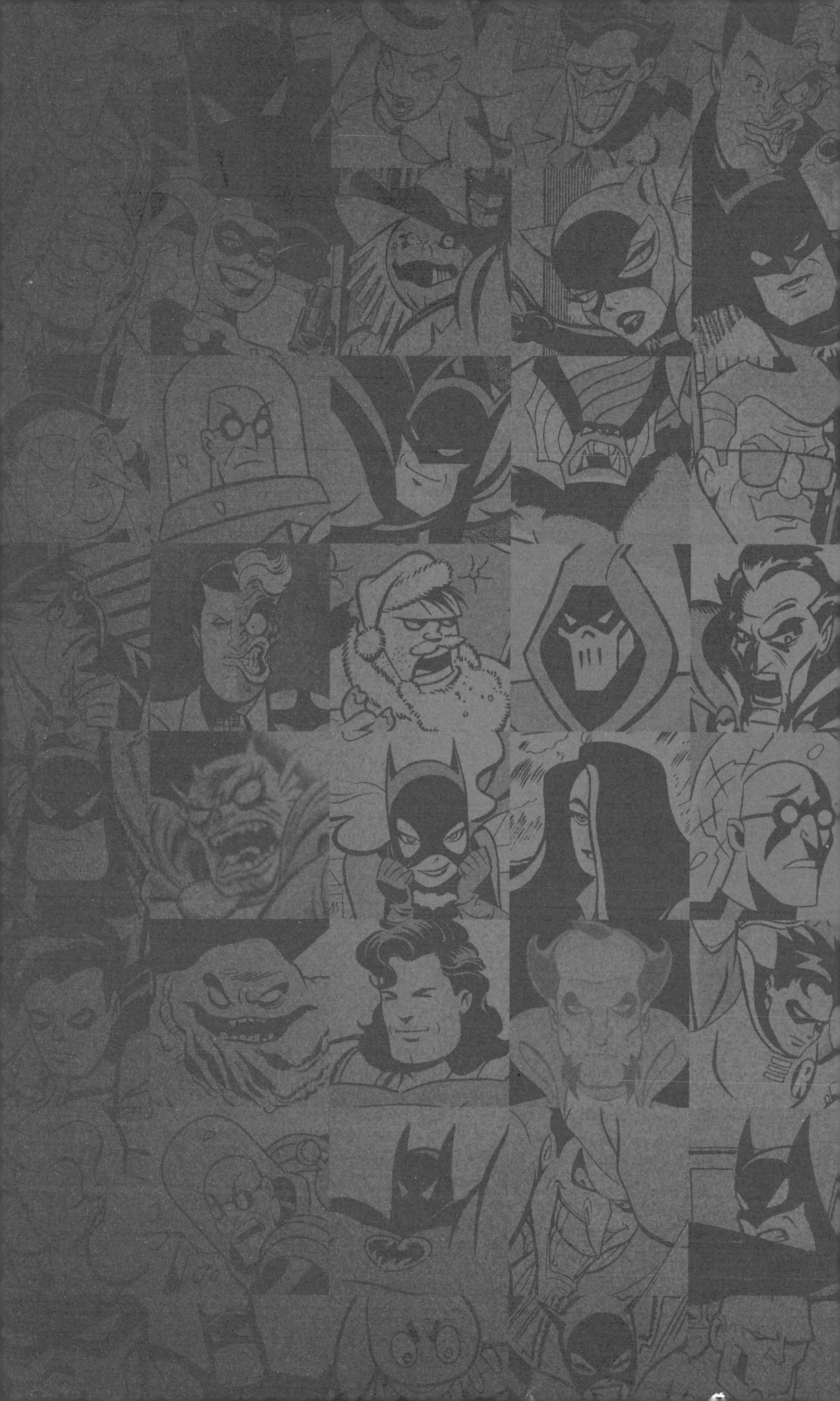